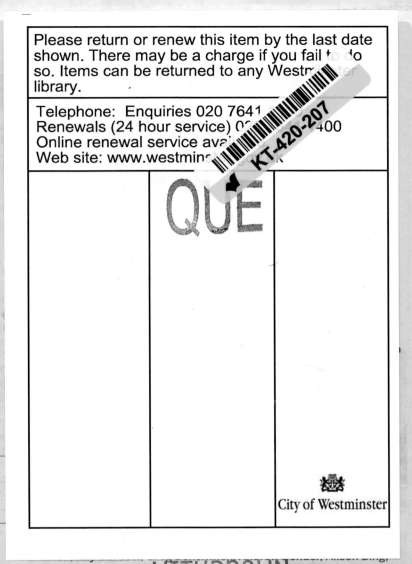

Please return or renew this item by the last date shown. There may be a charge if you fail to do so. Items can be returned to any Westminster library.

Telephone: Enquiries 020 7641
Renewals (24 hour service) 0____400
Online renewal service ava____
Web site: www.westmin____

QUE

City of Westminster

Contents

ON THE ROAD

Contents

Welcome to the USA

The great American experience is about so many things: bluegrass and beaches, snow-covered peaks and redwood forests, restaurant-loving cities and big open skies.

Bright Lights, Big Cities

America is home to LA, Las Vegas, Chicago, Miami, Boston and New York City – each a brimming metropolis whose name alone conjures a million different notions of culture, cuisine and entertainment. Look more closely and the American quilt unfurls in all its surprising variety: the eclectic music scene of Austin, the easygoing charm of Savannah, the eco-consciousness of free-spirited Portland, the magnificent waterfront of San Francisco and the captivating French Quarter of jazz hot spot New Orleans. Each city adds its unique style to the grand patchwork that is America.

On the Road Again

This is a country of road trips and great open skies, where four million miles of highways lead past red-rock deserts, below towering mountain peaks and through fertile wheat fields that roll off toward the horizon. The sun-bleached hillsides of the Great Plains, the lush rainforests of the Pacific Northwest, the sultry swamplands of the South and the scenic country lanes of New England are a few fine starting points for the great American road trip. Veer off the interstate often to discover the bucolic 'blue highways' of lore.

Food-Loving Nation

On one evening in the US, thick barbecue ribs come piping hot at a Texas roadhouse, while chefs blend organic produce with Asian accents at award-winning West Coast restaurants. Locals get their fix of bagels and lox at a century-old deli in Manhattan's Upper West Side and, several states away, plump pancakes and fried eggs disappear under the clatter of cutlery at a 1950s-style diner. Steaming plates of lobster from a Maine pier, oysters and champagne from a California wine bar, Korean tacos out of a Portland food truck – these are just a few ways to dine à la Americana.

Cultural Behemoth

The USA has made tremendous contributions to the arts. Georgia O'Keeffe's wild landscapes, Robert Rauschenberg's surreal collages, Alexander Calder's elegant mobiles and Jackson Pollock's drip paintings have entered the vernacular of 20th-century art. Chicago and New York have become veritable drawing boards for the great architects of the modern era. And from the soulful blues born in the Mississippi Delta to the bluegrass of Appalachia and Detroit's Motown sound – plus jazz, funk, hip-hop, country, and rock and roll – America has invented sounds integral to modern music.

Why I Love the USA

By Trisha Ping, Writer

Even after decades of living and traveling in the USA, I'm still surprised by its natural beauty and vast range of cultures and activities. Moving between regions can feel like going to another country, with unfamiliar menus and new landscapes, not to mention the dialect: a non-English speaker could be forgiven for thinking that a drawling Southerner and a nasal New Yorker were speaking completely different languages. So pick a state, any state – we guarantee you a memorable adventure.

For more about our writers, see p1216.

Above: Navajo people in Monument Valley Navajo Tribal Park (p862), AZ

USA

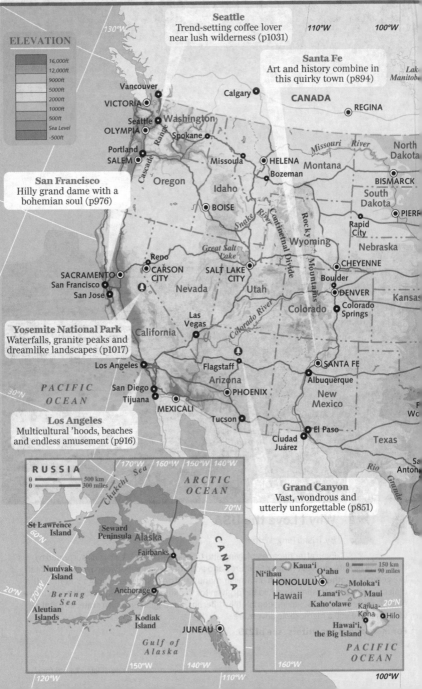

ELEVATION

| 16,000ft |
| 12,000ft |
| 9000ft |
| 5000ft |
| 2000ft |
| 1000ft |
| 500ft |
| Sea Level |
| -500ft |

Seattle
Trend-setting coffee lover
near lush wilderness (p1031)

Santa Fe
Art and history combine in
this quirky town (p894)

San Francisco
Hilly grand dame with a
bohemian soul (p976)

Yosemite National Park
Waterfalls, granite peaks and
dreamlike landscapes (p1017)

Los Angeles
Multicultural 'hoods, beaches
and endless amusement (p916)

Grand Canyon
Vast, wondrous and
utterly unforgettable (p851)

CANADA

Vancouver
VICTORIA
Seattle Washington
OLYMPIA
Portland   Spokane
SALEM
Oregon   Missoula   HELENA
Idaho   Bozeman   Montana
BOISE
Snake River
Great Salt Lake   Wyoming
Reno
CARSON   SALT LAKE
CITY   CITY
SACRAMENTO   Nevada   Utah
San Francisco
San Jose
Las
Vegas
California
Los Angeles
San Diego   Flagstaff
Tijuana   Arizona
MEXICALI   PHOENIX
Tucson
Ciudad
Juárez

Calgary
REGINA

Missouri River
North
Dakota
BISMARCK
South
Dakota
PIERR
Rapid
City
Nebraska
CHEYENNE
Boulder
DENVER
Colorado   Kansas
Colorado
Springs
Colorado River
SANTA FE
Albuquerque
New
Mexico
El Paso   Texas
Sa
Anto

Continental Divide
Rocky Mountains

Cascade Range

PACIFIC
OCEAN

30°N

Lak
Manitob

Rio Grande

F
Wo

130°W   110°W   100°W

Alaska inset

RUSSIA

Chukchi Sea

ARCTIC
OCEAN

70°N

St Lawrence
Island

Seward
Peninsula   Alaska

Nunivak
Island

Fairbanks

CANADA

50°N

Bering
Sea

Aleutian
Islands

Anchorage

Kodiak
Island

JUNEAU

Gulf of
Alaska

20°N

170°W 160°W 150°W 140°W

0 ___ 500 km
0 ___ 300 miles

120°W   150°W   140°W   110°W

Hawaii inset

Kaua'i
Ni'ihau   O'ahu
HONOLULU   Moloka'i
Hawaii   Lana'i   Maui
Kaho'olawe   Kailua-
Kona   Hilo

Hawai'i,
the Big Island

PACIFIC
OCEAN

0 ___ 150 km
0 ___ 90 miles

20°N

160°W   100°W

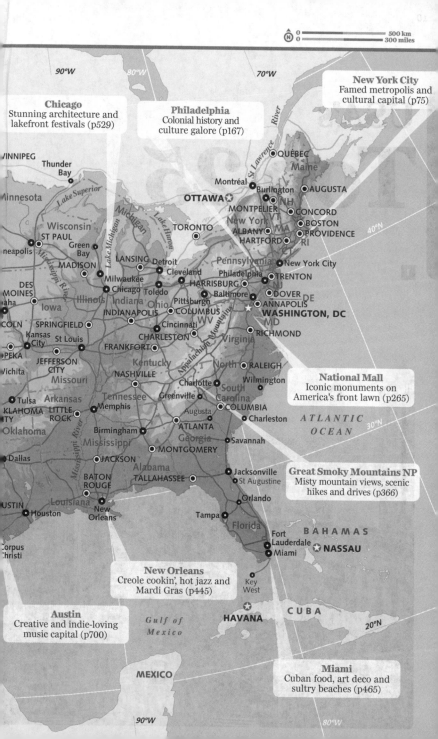

New York City
Famed metropolis and
cultural capital (p75)

Chicago
Stunning architecture and
lakefront festivals (p529)

Philadelphia
Colonial history and
culture galore (p167)

National Mall
Iconic monuments on
America's front lawn (p265)

Great Smoky Mountains NP
Misty mountain views, scenic
hikes and drives (p366)

New Orleans
Creole cookin', hot jazz and
Mardi Gras (p445)

Austin
Creative and indie-loving
music capital (p700)

Miami
Cuban food, art deco and
sultry beaches (p465)

0 500 km
0 300 miles

USA's
Top 25

1

New York City

1 Home to striving artists, hedge-fund moguls and immigrants from every corner of the globe, New York City (p75) is constantly reinventing itself. It remains one of the world centers of fashion, theater, food, music, publishing, advertising and finance. A staggering number of museums, parks and ethnic neighborhoods are scattered through the five boroughs. Do as every New Yorker does: hit the streets. Every block reflects the character and history of this dizzying kaleidoscope, and on even a short walk you can cross continents.

Yellowstone National Park

2 What makes the world's first national park (p792) so enduring? Geological wonders for one thing, from geysers and fluorescent hot springs to fumaroles and bubbling mud pots. Then there's the wildlife: grizzlies, black bears, wolf packs, elk, bison and moose, roaming across some 3500 sq miles of wilderness. Pitch a tent in Yellowstone's own Grand Canyon, watch wildlife in Lamar Valley, admire the Upper and Lower Falls, wait for Old Faithful to blow and hike through the primeval, fuming landscape for a real taste of what is truly the Wild West. Bottom right: Lower Falls (p793)

ALEXANDER SPATARI / GETTY IMAGES ©

KELLY CHENG TRAVEL PHOTOGRAPHY / GETTY IMAGES ©

CANADASTOCK / SHUTTERSTOCK ©

San Francisco

3 Change is afoot in this boom-bust city, currently enjoying a very high-profile boom. Amid the growth, fog and clatter of old-fashioned trams, the diverse neighborhoods of San Francisco (p976) invite long days of wandering, with great indie shops, fabulous restaurants and bohemian nightlife. Highlights include peering into Alcatraz, strolling across the Golden Gate and dining inside the Ferry Building. And you must take at least one ride on the trolley. How cool is San Francisco? Trust us – turn that first corner to a stunning waterfront view and you'll be hooked.

National Mall

4 Nearly 2 miles long and lined with monuments and marble buildings, the National Mall (p265) is the epicenter of Washington, DC's political and cultural life. In the summer, music and food festivals are staged here, while year-round visitors wander the halls of America's finest museums lining the green. For exploring American history, there's no better place to ruminate, whether tracing your hand along the Vietnam Veterans Memorial or ascending the steps of the Lincoln Memorial, where Martin Luther King Jr gave his famous 'I Have a Dream' speech. Top right: Washington Monument (p269)

Acadia National Park

5 Acadia National Park (p261) is where the mountains meet the sea. Miles of rocky coastline and even more miles of hiking and biking trails make this wonderland Maine's most popular destination, and deservedly so. The high point (literally) is Cadillac Mountain, a 1530ft peak that can be accessed by foot, bike or vehicle. Early risers can catch the country's first sunrise from this celebrated summit. Later in the day, cool off with a dip in Echo Lake or take tea and popovers (buttery, hollow muffins) overlooking Jordan Pond.

5

New Orleans

6 Caribbean-colonial architecture, Creole cuisine and a jubilant air of celebration seem more alluring than ever in the Big Easy (p445). Nights are spent catching Dixieland jazz, blues and rock amid bouncing live-music joints, and the city's riotous annual festivals (Mardi Gras, Jazz Fest) are famous the world over. 'Nola', as the city is known, also celebrates its myriad culinary influences. Feast on lip-smacking jambalaya, soft-shelled crab and Louisiana *cochon* (pulled pork) before hitting the bar scene on Frenchman St.

6

ATLANTIDE PHOTOTRAVEL / GETTY IMAGES ©

Grand Canyon National Park

7 The sheer immensity of the canyon (p851) is what grabs you at first – a two-billion-year-old rip across the landscape that reveals the earth's geological secrets with commanding authority. But it's Mother Nature's artistic touches, from sun-dappled ridges and crimson buttes to lush oases and a ribbon-like river, that hold your attention and demand your return. To explore the canyon, take your pick of adventures: hiking, biking, rafting or mule riding. Or simply grab a seat along the Rim Trail and watch the earth change colors before you.

Los Angeles

8 A perpetual influx of dreamers, go-getters and hustlers gives this sprawling coastal city (p916) an energetic buzz. Learn the tricks of movie-making during a studio tour. Bliss out to acoustically perfect symphony sounds in the Walt Disney Concert Hall. Wander gardens and galleries at the hilltop Getty Museum. Interested in stargazing? Take in the big picture at the revamped Griffith Observatory or look for stylish, earthbound 'stars' at the Grove. Ready for your close-up, darling? You will be – an hour on the beach guarantees that sun-kissed LA glow. Above: Hollywood Boulevard

Chicago

9 The Windy City (p529) will blow you away with its architecture, lakefront beaches, top-notch dining scene and world-class museums. But its true mojo is its blend of high culture and earthy pleasures. Is there another metropolis that dresses its Picasso sculpture in local sports-team gear? Where the demand for hot dogs equals the demand for North America's top restaurants? Winters are brutal, but come summer, Chicago fetes the warm days with food and music festivals that make fine use of its waterfront.

Pacific Coast Highways

10 A drive along America's western coastline is road-tripping at its finest. In California, Hwy 1, also called the Pacific Coast Highway (p45), Hwy 101 and I-5 pass sea cliffs, idiosyncratic beach towns and a few major cities: laid-back San Diego, rocker LA and beatnik San Francisco. North of the redwoods, Hwy 101 swoops into Oregon for windswept capes, rocky tide pools and Ecola State Park. Cross the Columbia River into Washington for the wet-and-wild Olympic National Park. Above: Bixby Creek Bridge (p971)

Santa Fe & Taos

11 Santa Fe (p894) is an old city with a young soul. Art lovers have flocked to Canyon Rd and the downtown galleries for years, but openings in the Railyard Arts District and Midtown have added a vibrant edge. Art and history partner up in style within the city's museums, and the food and shopping are first-rate. With that turquoise sky as a backdrop, the experience is darn near sublime. Artists also converge in the adobe city of Taos, where the vibe is quirkier, inhabited by ski bums and sustainable-architecture-loving Earthshippers. Below: Taos (p902)

Everglades

12 The Everglades (p490) unnerve. They don't reach majestically skyward or fill your heart with the aching beauty of a glacier-carved valley. They ooze, flat and watery, a river of grass mottled by islands of trees, cypress domes and mangroves. You can't hike them, not really. To properly explore the Everglades – and to meet the prehistoric residents, like the snaggle-toothed crocodile – you must leave the safety of land. Push a canoe off a muddy bank, tamp down your fear, and explore the waterways on the Everglades' own, unforgettable terms.

GARY SAXE / SHUTTERSTOCK ©

DONALD LAC / SHUTTERSTOCK ©

Philadelphia

13 Philly (p167) is often overlooked in the pantheon of great American cities, and that's a shame. It's a beautiful place, its streets dotted with gracious squares linked by cobbled alleys. As the 'birthplace of American government' – where the founding fathers signed the Declaration of Independence in 1776 – history abounds (the Liberty Bell! Ben Franklin's office!). But it's not all about the past: the dining scene has heated up way beyond the famed cheesesteak sandwich. A democratic selection of restaurants lurks on every corner, and many are reasonably priced.

California Wine Country

14 The Golden State is home to more than 100 wine regions. The rolling vineyards of Napa (p1003), Sonoma and the Russian River Valley lure travelers north from San Francisco. Sample a world-class cabernet in chichi Napa, enjoy a picnic in laid-back Sonoma, or cap off an outdoor adventure with a complex pinot noir near the Russian River. Further south, day-trippers head to the lovely vineyards clustered east of Santa Barbara, a bucolic area made famous by the 2004 wine-centric movie *Sideways*. Top right: Sonoma Valley winery (p1005)

The Catskills

15 Although the original flower children may now have grandkids of their own, their free-spirited ethos lives on in the indie-loving towns of this picturesque region (p146) in upstate New York. In recent years there's been an influx of creative farm-to-table restaurants, bespoke breweries and distilleries, and a growing array of arts collectives and high-profile concert venues. This beautiful region also happens to be prime leaf-peeping territory during the fall, a hiker's paradise in the spring and summer, and an ample playground for winter sports. Above right: Kaaterskill Falls (p148)

Yosemite National Park

16 Meander through wildflower-strewn meadows in valleys carved by rivers and glaciers, whose hard, endless work makes everything look simply colossal here (p1017). Thunderous waterfalls tumble over sheer cliffs, ant-sized climbers scale the enormous granite domes of El Cap and Half Dome, while hikers walk beneath ancient groves of giant sequoias, the planet's biggest trees. Even the subalpine meadows of Tuolumne are magnificently vast. For the most sublime views, perch at Glacier Point on a full-moon night or drive the high country's dizzying Tioga Rd in summer.

Seattle

17 A cutting-edge Pacific Rim city with an uncanny habit of turning locally hatched ideas into global brands, Seattle (p1031) has earned its place among the 'great' US metropolises with a world-renowned music scene, a mercurial coffee culture and a penchant for innovation and political progressiveness. But, while Seattle's trendsetters rush to unearth the next big thing, city traditionalists guard its soul with distinct urban neighborhoods, a homegrown food culture and what is arguably the nation's finest public market, Pike Place (p1032; pictured below).

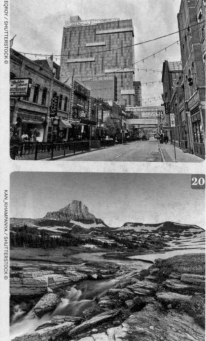

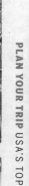

Southwest Nations Tourism

18 The Southwest is home to a fascinating array of Native American sites. To learn about America's earliest inhabitants, climb into the ancient clifftop homes of Ancestral Puebloans at Mesa Verde National Park (p782; pictured) in Colorado. For living cultures, visit the modern-day Pueblo of Taos, or Arizona's Navajo and Hopi Nations. As you'll discover here and in regional museums, many designs have religious significance. The baskets, rugs and jewelry crafted today often put a fresh spin on the ancient traditions – you may even see pottery emblazoned with a Harry Potter theme!

Detroit

19 Forget the 'ruin porn' pictures you may have seen: today's Detroit (p584) has a contagious, freewheeling energy. Downtown, seek out restored art deco skyscrapers, whimsical public parks and edgy street art, as well as sports venues for all of the city's major teams. Motor City's automotive past comes to life at places such as the Packard Plant, the nearby Henry Ford Museum and the River Rouge Plant, the sounds of Motown and jazz ring from historic venues, and restaurants ranging from vegan soul diners to Polish bakeries showcase the city's diverse heritage.

Glacier National Park

20 Yep, the rumors are true. The namesake attractions at Glacier National Park (p807) are melting away. There were 150 glaciers in the area in 1850; today there are 25. But even without the giant ice sheets, Montana's sprawling national park is worthy of an in-depth visit. Road warriors can maneuver the thrilling 50-mile-long Going-to-the-Sun Road; wildlife-watchers can scan for elk, wolves and grizzlies (but don't get too close); and hikers have 700 miles of trails, trees and flora – including mosses, mushrooms and wildflowers – to explore.

GABRIELE MALTINTI / SHUTTERSTOCK ©

Miami

21 How does one city get so lucky? Most content themselves with one or two highlights, but Miami (p465) seems to have it all. Beyond the stunning beaches and Art Deco Historic District, there's culture at every turn. No other US city blends the attitude of North America with the Latin energy of South America and the rhythm of the Caribbean. Throw in African American heritage, a gastronomic edge, pounding nightlife, a skyline plucked from a patrician's dream and miles of gorgeous sand, and you've got yourself the Magic City.

Great Smoky Mountains National Park

22 Named for the heather-colored mist that hangs over the peaks, the Smokies (p366) are part of the most visited national park in the US. The pocket of deep Appalachian woods is split between Tennessee and North Carolina, protecting thickly forested ridges where black bears, white-tailed deer, antlered elk, wild turkeys and more than 1600 kinds of flowers find sanctuary. Nearly 10 million people a year come to hike, camp, ride horses, cycle, raft and fly-fish, though it's easy to lose the crowds if you're willing to walk or paddle.

Las Vegas

23 Just when you think you've got a handle on the West – majestic, sublime, soul-nourishing – here comes Vegas (p820). Beneath the neon lights of the Strip, this city puts on a dazzling show: dancing fountains, a spewing volcano, its Eiffel Tower. Beneath it all is the seductive charm of the casino, where the fresh-pumped air and bright colors share one goal: separating you from your money. Step away if you can for fine restaurants, Cirque du Soleil performances, the Slotzilla zipline and the Mob Museum.

Route 66

24 Launched in 1926 and known as the Mother Road (p43), this fragile ribbon of concrete running clear from Chicago to Los Angeles was the USA's original road trip, and it still offers classic, time-warped touring. Motor along past 2000 miles of vintage Americana, stopping to dig into thick slabs of pie in small-town diners and to snap photos of roadside attractions such as the Snow Cap Drive-In, the Wigwam Motel, the neon signs of Tucumcari, the begging burros of Oatman, AZ, and the Gemini Giant, a sky-high fiberglass spaceman.

Michigan's Gold Coast

25 Michigan's 300-mile western shoreline (p21) is a charming collection of beaches, dunes, wineries, orchards and inn-filled towns, all set against the clear blue waters of Lake Michigan. Dutch-inspired Holland is a kitschy highlight, full of windmills, blue-and-white pottery and spring tulips. Meanwhile, in Harbor Country towns such as Harbert and Sawyer, 'Green Acres' meets Greenwich Village for a bohemian farm-and-arts blend of local antique shops, galleries, boutiques, bakeries and restaurants. Don't miss the sunsets. Bottom: Lake Michigan

Need to Know

For more information, see Survival Guide (p1163)

Currency
US dollar ($)

Language
English, Spanish

Visas
Visitors from the UK, Australia, New Zealand, Japan and many EU countries don't need visas for stays of less than 90 days, though they must get approval from the Electronic System for Travel Authorization (ESTA). Visitors from Canada need neither a visa nor ESTA approval for stays of less than 90 days. Citizens of other nations should check http://travel.state.gov.

Money
ATMs widely available. Credit cards accepted at most hotels, restaurants and shops.

Cell Phones
Foreign phones that operate on tri- or quad-band frequencies will work in the USA. Otherwise, purchase inexpensive cell phones with a pay-as-you-go plan when you arrive.

When to Go

- Tropical climate
- Dry climate
- Warm to hot summers, mild winters
- Mild to hot summers, cold winters
- Polar climate

Seattle
GO May–Sep

New York City
GO May–Sep

Chicago
GO Jun–Sep

Los Angeles
GO Apr–Oct

New Orleans
GO Dec–May

Miami
GO Dec–Apr

High Season
(Jun–Aug)

➡ Warm days across the country, with generally high temperatures.

➡ Busiest season, with big crowds and higher prices.

➡ In ski-resort areas, January to March is high season.

Shoulder (Apr–
May & Sep–Oct)

➡ Milder temperatures, fewer crowds.

➡ Spring flowers (April) and fiery autumn colors (October) in many parts of the country.

Low Season
(Nov–Mar)

➡ Wintry days, with snowfall in the north, and heavier rains in some regions.

➡ Lowest prices for accommodations (aside from ski resorts and warmer getaway destinations).

Useful Websites

Lonely Planet (www.lonely planet.com/usa) Destination information, hotel bookings, traveler forum and more.

National Park Service (www. nps.gov) Gateway to America's greatest natural treasures, its national parks.

Eater (www.eater.com) Foodie insight into two dozen American cities.

Punch (www.punchdrink. com) Quirky guides and helpful insights on how to drink well in America's cities.

New York Times Travel (www. nytimes.com/travel) Travel news, practical advice and engaging features.

Roadside America (www. roadsideamerica.com) For all things weird and wacky.

Important Numbers

Emergency	♪911
USA country code	♪1
Directory assistance	♪411
International directory assistance	♪00
International access code from the USA	♪011

Exchange Rates

Australia	A$1	US$0.67
Canada	C$1	US$0.75
Europe	€1	US$1.09
Japan	¥100	US$0.94
New Zealand	NZ$1	US$0.63
UK	UK£1	US$1.20

For current exchange rates, see www.xe.com

Daily Costs

Budget: Less than $150

➡ Campgrounds and hostel dorms: $10–50

➡ Food from a cafe, farmers market or food truck: $6–15

➡ Local bus, subway or train tickets: $2–4

Midrange: $150–250

➡ Double room in midrange hotel: $75–200

➡ Popular restaurant dinner for two: $30–60

➡ Car rental per day: from $30

Top End: More than $300

➡ Double room in a resort or top-end hotel: from $250

➡ Dinner in a top restaurant: $60–100

➡ Concert or theater tickets: $60–200

Opening Hours

Typical opening times are as follows:

Banks 8:30am to 4:30pm Monday to Thursday, to 5:30pm Friday (and possibly 9am to noon Saturday)

Bars 5pm to midnight Sunday to Thursday, to 2am Friday and Saturday

Nightclubs 10pm to 4am Thursday to Saturday

Post offices 9am to 5pm Monday to Friday

Shopping malls 9am to 9pm

Stores 9am to 6pm Monday to Saturday, noon to 5pm Sunday

Supermarkets 8am to 8pm, some open 24 hours

Arriving in the USA

JFK International Airport (New York) From JFK take the AirTrain to Jamaica Station and then LIRR to Penn Station ($12–16; 45 minutes). A taxi to Manhattan costs around $60, plus toll and tip (45 to 90 minutes).

Los Angeles International Airport LAX Flyaway Bus to Union Station costs $9.75 (30 to 50 minutes); door-to-door Prime Time & SuperShuttle costs $17 to $30 (35 minutes to 1½ hours); and a taxi to Downtown costs $47 (25 to 50 minutes).

Miami International Airport SuperShuttle to South Beach for $22 (50 to 90 minutes); taxi to Miami Beach for $36 (40 to 60 minutes); or take the Metrorail to downtown (Government Center) for $2.25 (15 minutes).

Time Zones in the USA

The continental USA has four time zones:

EST Eastern (GMT/UTC minus five hours): NYC, Boston, Washington, DC, Atlanta

CST Central (GMT/UTC minus six hours): Chicago, New Orleans, Houston

MST Mountain (GMT/UTC minus seven hours): Denver, Santa Fe, Phoenix

PST Pacific (GMT/UTC minus eight hours): Seattle, San Francisco, Las Vegas

Most of Alaska is one hour behind Pacific time (GMT/UTC minus nine hours), while Hawaii is two hours behind Pacific time (GMT/UTC minus 10 hours).

For much more on **getting around**, see p1177

First Time USA

For more information, see Survival Guide (p1163)

Checklist

➡ Check visa requirements for entering the US.

➡ Find out if you can use your phone in the US and ask about roaming charges.

➡ Book at least the first few nights of accommodations for your stay.

➡ Organize travel insurance.

➡ Inform your debit/credit card company of upcoming travel.

What to Pack

➡ Passport and driver's license

➡ Cell phone (and charger)

➡ Good walking shoes

➡ A bathing suit

➡ A rain jacket or umbrella

➡ Electrical adapter, if needed

➡ Pants with a stretchable waistband (to accommodate the generous portions at American restaurants)

Top Tips for Your Trip

➡ Make an effort to meet the locals. Americans are generally quite friendly, and often happy to share insight into their city.

➡ If you're driving, get off the interstates and take the back roads. Some of the best scenery lies on winding country lanes.

➡ Plan carefully to avoid the worst of the crowds. Visit resort areas, popular restaurants and top sights on weekdays.

➡ Take photographic ID out to bars; many venues have a policy to check ID for anyone buying alcohol, even if you're obviously over 21.

➡ US immigration officers can seem intimidating on arrival at border control. For a swift process, answer all questions fully, politely and calmly.

➡ Keep in mind that laws and attitudes vary considerably from state to state. What's legal in Colorado and Washington state, for example (smoking marijuana), is illegal in Texas and South Carolina.

What to Wear

In America just about anything goes, and you'll rarely feel uncomfortable because of what you're wearing. That said, it's worth bringing along dressier attire (smart casual) for dining at nice restaurants, or going to upscale bars or clubs.

Sleeping

There's a wide variety of sleeping options in the USA.

Hotels Options range from boxy and bland chain hotels to beautifully designed boutique and luxury hotels, with an equally varied price range.

B&Bs These small guesthouses offer a more homey stay (but note that many don't cater to kids under a certain age).

Motels Cheaper and simpler than most hotels, these are clustered along interstates and sprinkled across rural America.

Hostels A growing network in the US, though still mostly limited to urban areas.

Camping Options range from primitive backcountry spots to full-facility private campgrounds.

Money

While the US can be a pricey place to visit, there are many ways frugal travelers can save some dollars.

➡ Eat your big meal at lunchtime, when many restaurants offer lunch specials and main courses are much better value for money.

➡ Many museums have one or more free periods in which to visit (Thursday evening or Sunday morning, for instance).

➡ Cheaper rental cars often lie just outside of major city centers (Oakland and Jersey City, we're looking at you).

➡ Booking online and well ahead of time for buses and trains will get you much lower prices than buying tickets on the spot.

For more information, see p1168.

Bargaining

Gentle haggling is common in flea markets; in all other instances you're expected to pay the stated price.

Tipping

Tipping is *not* optional; only withhold tips in cases of outrageously bad service.

Airport & hotel porters $2 per bag, minimum per cart $5

Bartenders 15% to 20% per round, minimum per drink $1

Hotel housekeepers $2 to $5 per night, left under the card provided

Restaurant servers 15% to 20%, unless a gratuity is already charged on the bill

Taxi drivers 10% to 15%, rounded up to the next dollar

Valet parking attendants At least $2 on return of the keys

PLAN YOUR TRIP FIRST TIME USA

CULTURA EXCLUSIVE / HENGLEIN AND STEETS / GETTY IMAGES ©

Brooklyn Bridge Park (p100), New York City, NY

Etiquette

Greeting Don't be overly physical when greeting someone. Some Americans will hug, urbanites may exchange cheek kisses, but most – especially men – shake hands.

Smoking Don't assume you can smoke, even if you're outside. Most Americans have little tolerance for smokers, and smoking has even been banned from many parks, boardwalks and beaches.

Politeness It's common practice to greet the staff when entering and leaving a shop ('hello' and 'have a nice day' will do). Also, Americans smile a lot (often a symbol of politeness, nothing more).

Punctuality Do be on time. Many folks in the US consider it rude to be kept waiting.

What's New

Dense with cities and towns, yet rich in natural beauty, the USA capitalizes on both urban renewal and the rise of experiential travel to provide an ever-expanding roster of destinations and activities for visitors.

Best in Travel

Miami was awarded fourth place in Lonely Planet's list of top 10 cities in 2019. Famed for its beautiful beaches and buzzing nightlife, the city has long captivated travelers seeking a slice of tropical paradise while the rest of North America shivers. Although the Magic City still makes a fine wintertime escape, the past few years have seen Miami transform into a burgeoning center for the arts, a foodie destination and an innovator in urban design. Miami's downtown continues to be rejuvenated with the arrival of a celebrated $305-million science museum, while the Design District has become a cultural magnet with new eye-catching architecture, public art installations and expansive new cultural programming.

CBD Craze

If you see signs for 'CBD' in cafes and bars, it's a reference to cannabidiol – a non-psychotic (completely legal) substance derived from the cannabis plant. Said to reduce anxiety and inflammation, CBD has become a secret ingredient in everyday items such as baked goods, matcha teas, lattes and cocktails.

Presenting Real History

As the USA continues to strive to truly deliver 'liberty and justice for all,' attractions of all kinds are evolving to show history through the eyes of enslaved people, Native Americans and other minority groups, presenting experiences and perspectives not previously seen. A few new or revamped places to get the real story:

LOCAL KNOWLEDGE

WHAT'S HAPPENING IN THE USA

Trisha Ping, Lonely Planet Writer

The adage that anything goes in conversation except politics and religion feels more relevant than ever in today's polarized USA. Luckily, there are plenty of other topics that concern Americans: try the glut of prestige TV, the current sports tournament or the new Marvel film. The sharing economy (home rentals, car-sharing services) and the influx of new residents have turned many midsized cities into exciting places to visit (if occasionally more difficult to live in). From the Rust Belt to the Bible Belt, once overlooked cities like Columbus, OH, and Boise, ID, host enviable food-and-drink scenes and enough sights to easily fill a long weekend, drawing both domestic and international travelers in increasing numbers. Adventure-minded travelers can also find plenty to do in the USA, and activities like ice climbing and kite-surfing are joining the roster of more traditional outdoor fare in the country's state and national parks and recreation areas.

➡ Native Plymouth Tours (p208), Plymouth, MA

➡ Mississippi Civil Rights Museum (p434), Jackson, MS

➡ National Memorial for Peace & Justice (p428), Montgomery, AL

Green Eating

The hunger for vegetarian and vegan dining – which began in California – continues to grow. You'll find meat-free restaurants all across the country, including in places you might not expect: cheesesteak-loving Philly, for example, is emerging as a vegan dining hot spot. A few of the best restaurants for green eating:

➡ Sitka & Spruce (p1040)

➡ Greens (p995)

➡ Ground Control (p552)

➡ Carmo (p455)

Screen Tourism

The early days of TV tourism hit in the late 1990s, when fans of *Sex and the City* flocked to NYC. In the age of 'peak TV,' this trend has never been bigger, and plenty of locations in the USA are cashing in. Some places to take TV- and film-centered tours:

➡ Atlanta, GA (*Black Panther*; *The Hunger Games*)

➡ Senoia, GA (*The Walking Dead*)

➡ Monterey, CA (*Big Little Lies*)

➡ The Ozarks (*Ozark*)

➡ Albuquerque, NM (*Breaking Bad*; *Better Call Saul*)

Hudson Yards

At the northern end of the High Line, a $4.5-billion engineered neighborhood has emerged, transforming a once grotty corner of NYC's Midtown. As well as the highest open-air observatory in the Western Hemisphere and performing arts space the Shed, it houses the Vessel – an astounding Escher-like steel structure of interlocking walkways and staircases for climbing.

Philadelphia Museum of Art

The city's premier gallery (p168), which first opened in 1928, underwent a $196-million renovation program in 2019,

with architect Frank Gehry designing new galleries and common areas, and helping to improve navigation around the museum.

Dallas Holocaust & Human Rights Museum

This museum moved from a small basement to a 55,000-sq-ft building in Dallas' West End neighborhood in September 2019. It takes an in-depth look at the Holocaust, including video testimonies from Dallas-area survivors, along with technology-enriched exhibits on genocide, human rights issues and American ideals.

LISTEN, WATCH & FOLLOW

For inspiration, visit www.lonelyplanet.com/usa/eastern-usa/travel-tips-and-articles.

This American Life Long-running NPR program and podcast featuring in-depth reporting on culture and society.

The Nod Pop-culture podcast with a focus on African American life.

Instagram @usinterior Stunning images from the USA's federal lands.

LatinoUSA US news, culture and media insight from the Latinx community.

Twitter @VisitTheUSA Travel inspiration and articles from across the country.

FAST FACTS

Food trend CBD (cannabidiol) in everything

State with the highest life expectancy Hawaii (81.3 years)

Number of craft breweries 7346

Population 330 million

USA   AUSTRALIA   CANADA

≈ 8 people per sq mile

Accommodations

Find more accommodation reviews throughout the On the Road chapters (from p73)

Accommodation Types

B&Bs and Inns These vary from small, comfy houses with shared baths (least expensive) to romantic, antique-filled historic homes with private baths (most expensive). Reservations are essential. Call ahead to confirm policies (ie minimum stay, kids, pets, smoking) and bathroom arrangements.

Camping Camping is usually limited to 14 days and can be reserved up to six months in advance. Campsites at national and state parks typically come in three types: primitive (free to $10 per night, no facilities); basic ($10 to $20, and include toilets, drinking water, firepits and picnic tables); and developed ($20 to $50, come with more amenities such as showers, barbecue grills, recreational vehicle (RV) sites with hookups etc).

Hostels Most hostels have gender-segregated dorms, a few private rooms, shared baths and a communal kitchen. Overnight fees for dorm beds range from $25 to $45 (though in NYC, a dorm bed can cost upward of $75).

Hotels Hotels in all categories typically include cable TV, in-room wi-fi, private baths and a simple continental breakfast. Many midrange properties provide minibars, microwaves, hair dryers and swimming pools, while top-end hotels add concierge services, fitness and business centers, spas, restaurants and bars.

Motels Distinguishable from hotels by having rooms that open onto a parking lot, motels tend to cluster around interstate exits and along main routes into town. Although most motel rooms won't win any style awards, they can be clean and comfortable and offer good value. Ask to see a room first if you're unsure.

Resorts Found in states like Florida and Arizona, resort facilities can include all manner of fitness and sports options, including pools and spas, as well as other amenities such as restaurants, bars, and so on. Many also have on-site babysitting services. However, some also tack an extra 'resort fee' onto rates, so always ask.

PRICE RANGES

In this book, the following price ranges refer to a double room in high season, excluding taxes (which can add 10% to 15%).

$ less than $150

$$ $150–250

$$$ more than $250

For New York City, San Francisco and Washington, DC, the following price ranges are used:

$ less than $200

$$ $200–350

$$$ more than $350

Best Places to Stay

Best Unique Sleeps

The USA's entrepreneurial spirit is frequently expressed in one-of-a-kind lodging you won't find anywhere else, from lighthouses, houseboats, Airstreams and yurts to lovingly restored retro-kitsch motels and architect-converted factories and firehouses.

➡ Ironworks Hotel (p565), Indianapolis, IN

➡ Many Glacier Hotel (p809), Glacier National Park, MT

➡ Inn at Halona (p894), Zuni Pueblo, NM

Best for Solo Travelers

Solo travel in the USA is only as lonely as you want it to be. From big cities to small towns, locals are usually friendly and curious about visitors. Hostels offer the best chances to meet other travelers and the best prices, but B&Bs are also welcoming to solo travelers, with engaging hosts to give you the lay of the land. Small hotels and pod hotels also have single rooms at typically low rates.

➡ SoBe Hoste (p478), Miami, FL

➡ Mama Shelter (p930), Los Angeles, CA

➡ YMCA of the Rockies (p768), Estes Park, CO

➡ Freehand New York (p107), New York City, NY

➡ Hostel Tahoe (p1026), Lake Tahoe, CA

➡ Apple Hostel (p173), Philadelphia, PA

Best for Families

Family-friendly accommodations are easy to find across the USA, from resorts and dude ranches with a range of activities to places that go out of their way to make children feel welcome. Many standard rooms in US hotels have two double beds, and provide rollaway beds or cribs.

➡ Hotel Beacon (p109), New York City, NY

➡ Vista Verde Guest Ranch (p769), Steamboat Springs, CO

Best on a Budget

Traveling on a budget is easy in the USA, even in – maybe especially in – the largest cities. As in most countries, campsites and hostels remain the best options for those keeping a tight rein on their finances, but hotels and B&Bs can also offer impressive value.

➡ Carlton Arms (p107), New York City, NY

➡ Crash Pad (p395), Chattanooga, TN

➡ Bywater Bed & Breakfast (p453), New Orleans, LA

➡ Yotel San Francisco (p987), San Francisco, CA

➡ Hostel Fish (p756), Denver, CO

NAGEL PHOTOGRAPHY / SHUTTERSTOCK ©

Many Glacier Hotel (p809), Glacier National Park, MT

Booking

It's advisable to book well in advance during the summer months, school holiday weeks and for ski-resort destinations. For popular national parks, it's not unusual to book a year out. Some local and state tourist offices offer hotel reservation services.

Lonely Planet (www.lonelyplanet.com/hotels) Find independent reviews, as well as recommendations on the best places to stay – and then book them online.

BedandBreakfast.com (www.bedandbreakfast.com) Largest B&B booking site in the world featuring thousands of properties in the USA.

Hostelling International USA (www.hiusa.org) National network of hostels; free membership required to get the best rate.

Hotwire (www.hotwire.com) One of the more popular online engines for booking hotels in the US.

National Park Service (www.nps.gov) Information on national parks and monuments, with camping reservations also possible.

Recreation.gov (www.recreation.gov) Camping reservations on federally managed lands.

If You Like...

Beaches

Coastlines on two oceans and the Gulf of Mexico give plenty of choice to beach lovers.

Point Reyes National Seashore The water is cold but the scenery is magical along this beautiful stretch of untamed coastline in Northern California. (p1002)

South Beach This world-famous strand is less about frolicking than taking in the parade of passing people along Miami's favorite playground. (p468)

Big Beach With turquoise waters lapping its long sweep of golden sand, this Maui beauty is one of Hawaii's finest. (p1121)

Cape Cod National Seashore Massive sand dunes, picturesque lighthouses and cool forests invite endless exploration on the Massachusetts cape. (p212)

Outer Banks Runs for 100 miles along North Carolina, with breezy beaches, lighthouses and wild horses at Corolla. (p345)

Theme Parks

America's theme parks come in many varieties – from old-fashioned cotton candy and roller-coaster fun to multiday immersions in make-believe.

Disneyland Trends come and go, but the true classics never die. Now entering its seventh decade, Disney's fairy-tale world still exerts a unique enchantment. (p941)

Dollywood A paean to the much-loved country singer Dolly Parton, with Appalachian-themed rides and attractions in the hills of Tennessee. (p397)

Cedar Point Amusement Park This Ohio favorite is home to several of the globe's tallest and fastest roller coasters, including the 120mph Top Thrill Dragster. (p576)

Universal Orlando Resort Famed home of Universal Studios and the Wizarding World of Harry Potter. (p520)

Santa Cruz Beach Boardwalk Retro thrills await on the 1920s-vintage Giant Dipper roller coaster at the Pacific Coast's oldest beachfront amusement park. (p974)

Wine

Admire the verdant countryside and sample from the enticing farm stands and delectable bistros that often sprout alongside vineyards.

Napa Valley Home to more than 200 vineyards, Napa is synonymous with world-class wine making. You'll find superb varietals, gourmet bites and beautiful scenery. (p1004)

Willamette Valley Outside of Portland, OR, this fertile region produces some of the tastiest pinot noir on the planet. (p1069)

Finger Lakes Upstate New York is a prime growing region – walk it off at nearby state parks. (p149)

Santa Ynez Valley Backed by picturesque oak-clad hills, these sun-drenched vineyards north of Santa Barbara invite laid-back exploration. (p966)

Virginia Wine Country There's much history in this up-and-coming wine district. You can even sample the wines grown on Thomas Jefferson's old estate. (p323)

Dahlonega Plateau This North Georgia region is able to make European-style wines thanks to its high elevation. (p417)

Verde Valley If you think Arizona is all desert, guess again. Take a winery tour in this lush setting near Sedona. (p845)

Yakima Valley Sample velvety reds in Washington state's biggest and oldest wine region. (p1057)

Top: South by Southwest festival (p703), Austin, TX.

Bottom: Neo-Gothic architecture in Savannah, GA (p420)

Great Food

New York City Whatever you crave, the world's great restaurant capital has you covered. (p110)

New England Lobsters, clambakes, oysters and fresh fish galore – the Northeast is seafood paradise. (p184)

San Francisco Real-deal taquerias, a dizzying variety of Asian cuisines, magnificent farmers markets and acclaimed chefs all contribute to SF's culinary mystique. (p993)

Lockhart Texas smokes them all – at least when it comes to barbecue. Carnivores shouldn't miss Lockhart, the legendary capital of mouthwatering brisket. (p707)

Portland Has a cutting-edge food scene; its food trucks serve imaginative dishes from every corner of the globe. (p1065)

New Orleans Flavors of France, Spain, Africa and Vietnam have contributed to the gastro-amalgamation, making Nola one of America's most food-centric cities. (p453)

Offbeat America

When you tire of traipsing through museums and ticking off well-known sights, throw yourself into the strange world of American kitsch.

Carhenge A cheeky homage to Stonehenge made of old cars assembled in a Nebraska field. (p685)

NashTrash Tours Nashville's tall-haired 'Jugg Sisters' take visitors on a deliciously tacky journey through Nashville's spicier side. (p389)

American Visionary Art Museum See outsider art (including eccentric automatons in the Cabaret Mechanical Theater) at this Baltimore gem. (p297)

Loneliest Road Take the empty highway through Nevada, and don't forget to stop at the Shoe Tree. (p834)

Mini Time Machine Museum of Miniatures This whimsical museum in Tucson is entirely devoted to tiny things. (p867)

Marfa Mystery Lights Sit at dusk in West Texas looking for the ghostly lights that many visitors see playing on the horizon. (p743)

Architecture

Chicago Birthplace of the skyscraper, Chicago has magnificent works by many of the great 20th-century architects. (p529)

New York City Much photographed classics include the art deco Chrysler Building, the spiraling Guggenheim and the majestic Brooklyn Bridge. (p75)

Miami Miami's art deco district is a Technicolor dream come to life. (p465)

San Francisco See elegant Victorians and cutting-edge 21st-century masterpieces in what is perhaps America's most architecturally European city. (p976)

Savannah This funky coastal city turns heads with three centuries of striking architecture. (p420)

New Orleans A gorgeous French-colonial center, plus grand antebellum mansions reached via a historic streetcar. (p445)

Native American Culture

Discover the stories of the continent's first peoples.

National Museum of the American Indian Appropriately, the capital holds America's finest museum dedicated to Native American peoples. (p276)

Mesa Verde Carved into the mountains of Southern Colorado, this fascinating site was mysteriously abandoned by Ancestral Puebloans. (p782)

Pine Ridge Indian Reservation Visit the tragic site where Lakotas were massacred by US cavalry. (p672)

Navajo Reservation Take in the stunning scenery and learn more about this proud people in Arizona. (p860)

Zuni Pueblo Purchase beautifully wrought silver jewelry and stay overnight at a tribally licensed inn. (p894)

Historical Sights

Philadelphia The nation's first capital is where the idea of America as an independent nation first coalesced. Excellent museums tell the story. (p167)

Williamsburg Step back into the 1700s in the preserved town of Williamsburg, the largest living-history museum on the planet. (p318)

Mission Santa Barbara The 'Queen of the Missions' witnessed the meeting of California's indigenous Chumash culture and 19th-century Spanish friars. (p963)

Washington, DC Visit the sites where Lincoln was assassinated, Martin Luther King Jr gave his most famous speech and Nixon's presidency was undone. (p265)

Harpers Ferry A fascinating open-air museum of 19th-century village life beautifully framed by mountains and rivers. (p337)

St Augustine Find cobblestone streets, 300-year-old forts and a youthful fountain at this Spanish colonial town founded in the 1500s. (p503)

Beer & Microbreweries

Microbreweries have exploded in popularity – from Alabama to Wyoming, you'll never be far from a finely crafted pint.

Vermont Don't miss the state with the most breweries per capita. (p235)

Denver The Mile High City is dotted with dozens of craft breweries. (p753)

Portland Nirvana for beer lovers, Portland has more than 70 microbreweries within the city limits. (p1066)

Asheville Home to more than 20 microbreweries and brewpubs, Asheville is leading North Carolina's beer renaissance. (p363)

Live Music

Austin Home to more than 200 venues and the country's biggest music fest, Austin proudly wears the music crown. (p700)

New Orleans The Big Easy has a soundtrack as intoxicating as the city itself – from room-filling big-band jazz to indie rock. (p456)

Nashville A showcase for country, bluegrass, blues, folk and plenty of atmospheric honky-tonks. (p385)

Food trucks in Portland, OR (p1059)

Los Angeles LA is a magnet for aspiring stars and draws serious talent. Don't miss the legendary Sunset Strip for A-list artists. (p938)

Memphis Juke joints and dive bars host blazing live bands. (p378)

Kansas City This barbecue-loving Missouri city has a venerable live-music scene, especially when it comes to jazz. (p655)

Museums

From big-city palaces of culture to back-road curiosities, the USA's incomparable collection of museums

celebrates everything from art to rock 'n' roll.

Metropolitan Museum of Art New York City's world-class art collection spans six continents and thousands of years. (p92)

Exploratorium This San Francisco original, which celebrated 50 years in 2019, invites visitors of all ages to discover science 'hands-on.' (p977)

National Museum of African American History and Culture Wins rave reviews for its multifaceted documentation of the African American experience. (p269)

Art Institute of Chicago The nation's second largest art

museum (after the Met) has masterpieces aplenty, especially Impressionist paintings. (p532)

Getty Villa Perched above the Pacific, this faux-Classical villa holds a treasure trove of Etruscan, Greek and Roman antiquities. (p924)

Children's Museum of Indianapolis Interactive exhibits abound at this remarkable five-story children's museum (the world's largest). (p565)

Rock and Roll Hall of Fame & Museum Houses Jimi Hendrix's Stratocaster and John Lennon's Sgt Pepper suit, all in Cleveland. (p573)

Month by Month

January

The New Year starts off with a shiver, as snowfall blankets large swaths of the country. Ski resorts kick into high gear, while sun lovers seek refuge in warmer climes (especially Florida).

✵ Mummer's Parade

Philadelphia's biggest event is this brilliant parade (www.phillymummers.com), where local clubs spend months creating costumes and mobile scenery in order to win top honors on New Year's Day. String bands and clowns add to the general good cheer at this long-running fest.

✵ Chinese New Year

In late January or early February, you'll find colorful celebrations and feasting anywhere there's a Chinatown. NYC throws a festive parade, though San Francisco's is the best, with floats, firecrackers, bands and plenty of merriment.

☆ Sundance Film Festival

The legendary Sundance Film Festival (www.sundance.org) brings Hollywood stars, indie directors and avid filmgoers to Park City, UT, for a 10-day indie extravaganza in late January. Plan well in advance, as passes sell out fast.

February

Unless they're on a mountain getaway, most Americans dread February's long dark nights and frozen days. For foreign visitors, this can be the cheapest time to travel, with discounted rates for flights and hotels.

✵ Mardi Gras

Held in late February or early March on the day before Ash Wednesday, Mardi Gras (Fat Tuesday) is the finale of Carnival. New Orleans' celebrations (www.mardigrasneworleans.com) are legendary as colorful parades, masquerade balls, feasting and plenty of hedonism rule the day.

March

The first blossoms of spring arrive (at least in the south – the north still shivers in the chill). In the mountains, it's still high season for skiing. Meanwhile, drunken spring breakers descend on Florida.

✵ St Patrick's Day

On the 17th, the patron saint of Ireland is honored with brass bands and ever-flowing pints of Guinness; huge parades occur in New York, Boston and Chicago (which goes all-out by dyeing the Chicago River green).

✵ National Cherry Blossom Festival

The brilliant blooms of Japanese cherry blossoms around DC's Tidal Basin are celebrated with more than 100 concerts, parades, *taiko* drumming, kite-flying and other events during the four-week fest (www.nationalcherry

blossomfestival.org). More than 1.5 million go each year, so book ahead.

☆ South by Southwest

Each year Austin, TX, becomes ground zero for one of the biggest music festivals in North America. More than 2000 performers play at nearly 100 venues. SXSW is also a major film festival and interactive fest – a platform for groundbreaking ideas.

April

The weather is warming up, though in the north April can still be unpredictable, bringing chilly weather mixed with a few teasingly warm days. Down south, it's a fine time to travel.

☆ Fiesta San Antonio

Mid-April is the liveliest time to visit this pretty river town in Texas, as you'll find 10 days of fiesta (www.fiesta-sa.org) with carnivals, parades, dancing and lots of great eating options.

☆ Jazz Fest

Beginning the last weekend in April, New Orleans hosts the country's best jazz jam (www.nojazzfest.com), with top-notch acts (local resident Harry Connick Jr sometimes plays) and plenty of good cheer. In addition to world-class jazz, there's also great food and crafts.

☆ Juke Joint Festival

In mid-April, Clarksdale, MS, stages a memorable

blues fest (www.jukejoint festival.com). The feel is very authentic, as you roam among 13 daytime stages and assorted evening venues, with plenty of great food and the odd amusement (pig racing!) to boot.

☆ Patriots' Day

Massachusetts' big day out falls on the third Monday in April and features Revolutionary War reenactments and parades in Lexington and Concord, plus the Boston Marathon and a much-watched Red Sox baseball game enjoyed at home.

☆ Gathering of Nations

For an immersion in indigenous culture, head to Albuquerque in late April for the Gathering of Nations (www.gatheringofnations.com), the largest Native American powwow in the world. You'll find traditional dance, music, food, crafts and the crowning of Miss Indian World.

May

May is true spring and one of the loveliest times to travel, with blooming wildflowers and generally mild sunny weather. Summer crowds and high prices have yet to arrive.

☆ Beale Street Music Festival

Blues lovers descend on Memphis for this venerable music fest held over three days in early May.

☆ Cinco de Mayo

Celebrate Mexico's victory over the French with salsa

music and pitchers of margaritas across the country. LA, San Francisco and Denver throw some of the biggest bashes.

☆ North Charleston Arts Festival

Now in its fourth decade, this five-day South Carolina festival (www.northcharles tonartsfest.com) has grown from humble beginnings to be one of the most comprehensive arts festivals on the eastern seaboard.

June

Summer is here. Americans spend more time at outdoor cafes and restaurants, and head to the shore or to national parks. School is out; vacationers fill the highways and resorts, bringing higher prices.

☆ Bonnaroo Music & Arts Festival

In the heartland of Tennessee, this sprawling music fest (www.bonnaroo.com) showcases big-name rock, soul, country and more over four days in mid-June.

☆ Gay Pride

In some cities, gay-pride celebrations last a week, but in San Francisco, it's a month-long party (www.sfpride.org), where the last weekend in June sees giant parades. You'll find other great pride events in major cities across the country.

☆ Chicago Blues Festival

It's the globe's biggest free blues fest (www.chicago bluesfestival.us), with three days of the music that made Chicago famous. More than 500,000 people unfurl blankets by the multiple stages that take over Grant Park in early June.

✨ Mermaid Parade

In Brooklyn, NYC, Coney Island (www.coneyisland.com) celebrates summer's steamy arrival with a kitsch-loving parade, complete with colorfully attired mermaids and horn-blowing mermen.

☆ CMA Music Festival

Nashville's legendary country-music fest (www.cmaworld.com) has more than 100 artists performing around downtown and in Nissan Stadium.

☆ Telluride Bluegrass Festival

The banjo gets its due at this festive, boot-stomping music jam (www.planet bluegrass.com) in Colorado mountain country. You'll find nonstop performances, excellent regional food stalls and great locally crafted microbrews. It's good all-comers entertainment and many folks even camp.

☆ Tanglewood Music Festival

Open-air concerts run all summer long (from late June to early September) in an enchanting setting in western Massachusetts (www.bso.org).

July

With summer in full swing, Americans break out the backyard barbecues or head for the beach. The prices are high and the crowds can be fierce, but it's one of the liveliest times to visit.

✨ Independence Day

On July 4, the nation celebrates its birthday with a bang, as nearly every town and city stages a massive fireworks show. Washington, DC, New York, Nashville, Philadelphia and Boston are all great spots.

🍷 Oregon Brewers Festival

The beer-loving city of Portland pulls out all the stops to pour a heady array of handcrafted perfection (www.oregonbrewfest. com). With around 100 beers from around the country – and even a few international brews – there are plenty of choices. It's nicely set along the banks of the Willamette River.

☆ Pageant of the Masters

This eight-week arts fest (www.foapom.com) brings a touch of the surreal to Laguna Beach, CA. On stage, meticulously costumed actors create living pictures – imitations of famous works of art – accompanied by narration and an orchestra.

☆ Newport Folk Festival

Newport, RI, a summer haunt of the well-heeled, hosts a world-class music fest (www.newportfolk. org) in late July. Top folk artists take to the stage at this fun, all-welcoming event.

☆ Eastern Music Festival

For half a century, North Carolina's musical treasure (www.easternmusicfestival. org) has been educating and entertaining through its month-long series of workshops and performances.

August

Expect blasting heat in August, with temperatures and humidity less bearable the further south you go. You'll find people-packed beaches, high prices and empty cities on weekends, when residents escape to the nearest waterfront.

☆ Lollapalooza

This mondo rock fest (www. lollapalooza.com) sees more than 170 bands on eight stages in Chicago's Grant Park on the first Thursday-to-Sunday in August.

✨ Iowa State Fair

If you've never been to a state fair, now's your chance. This 11-day event (www.iowastatefair.org) is where you'll find country crooning, wondrous carvings (in butter), livestock shows, sprawling food stalls and a down-home good time in America's heartland.

✨ Maine Lobster Festival

If you love lobster like Maine loves lobster, indulge in this five-day feeding frenzy (www.mainelobsterfestival. com) held in Rockland in early August. King Neptune and the Sea Goddess oversee a week full of events and, of course, as much crustacean as you can eat.

September

With the end of summer, cooler days arrive, making for pleasant outings nationwide. The kids are back in school, and concert halls, gallery spaces and performing-arts venues kick off a new season.

Santa Fe Fiesta

Santa Fe hosts the nation's longest-running festival (www.santafefiesta.org), a spirited two-week-long event with parades, concerts and the burning of Old Man Gloom.

Burning Man Festival

Over one week some 70,000 revelers, artists and assorted free spirits descend on Nevada's Black Rock Desert to create a temporary metropolis of art installations, theme camps and environmental curiosities (www.burningman.com). It culminates in the burning of a giant stick figure.

New Orleans Fried Chicken Festival

The inaugural Fried Chicken Festival (www.friedchickenfestival.com) in 2016 drew crowds of up to 40,000 – come join the hordes for a three-day weekend dedicated to the juicy, golden-fried bird.

October

Temperatures are falling, as autumn brings fiery colors to northern climes. It's high season where the leaves are most brilliant (New England); elsewhere expect lower prices and fewer crowds.

☆ New York Film Festival

Just one of many big film fests in NYC (Tribeca Film Festival in late April is another goodie); this one features world premieres from across the globe (www.filmlinc.com).

Fantasy Fest

Key West's answer to Mardi Gras brings some 75,000 revelers to the subtropical enclave in the 10 days leading up to Halloween. Expect parades, colorful floats, costume parties, the selecting of a conch king and queen, and plenty of alcohol-fueled merriment (www.fantasyfest.com).

Halloween

In NYC, you can don a costume and join the Halloween parade up Sixth Ave. West Hollywood in Los Angeles and San Francisco's Castro district are great places to see outrageous outfits. Salem, MA, also hosts spirited events throughout October.

November

No matter where you go, this is generally low season, with cold winds discouraging visitors despite lower prices (although airfares skyrocket around Thanksgiving). There's much happening culturally in the USA's big cities.

Thanksgiving

On the fourth Thursday of November, Americans gather with family and friends over daylong feasts – roast turkey, sweet potatoes, cranberry sauce, wine, pumpkin pie and loads of other dishes. NYC hosts a huge parade, and there's pro football on TV.

December

Winter arrives as ski season kicks off in the Rockies (out east, conditions aren't usually ideal until January). Aside from winter sports, December means heading inside and curling up by the fire.

Art Basel

This massive arts fest (www.artbaselmiamibeach.com) offers four days of cutting-edge art, film, architecture and design. More than 250 major galleries from across the globe come to the event, with works by some 4000 artists; plus much hobnobbing with a glitterati crowd in Miami Beach.

New Year's Eve

Americans are of two minds when it comes to ringing in the New Year. Some join festive crowds to celebrate, while others plot a getaway to escape the mayhem. Whichever you choose, plan well in advance. Expect high prices (especially in NYC).

Itineraries

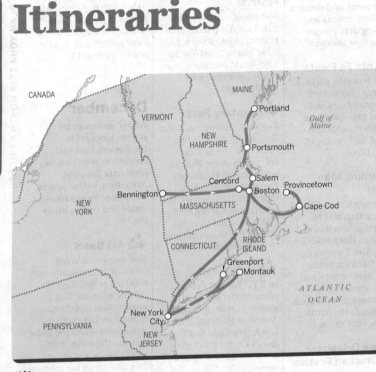

CANADA

MAINE

VERMONT

NEW HAMPSHIRE

Portland

Gulf of Maine

Portsmouth

Concord   Salem

Bennington   Boston   Provincetown

NEW YORK   MASSACHUSETTS   Cape Cod

CONNECTICUT   RHODE ISLAND

Greenport
Montauk

New York City

PENNSYLVANIA   NEW JERSEY

ATLANTIC OCEAN

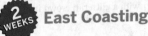

East Coasting

Big cities, historic towns and serene coastlines offer a highlights reel of America's northeastern corner.

The great dynamo of art, fashion and culture, **New York City** is America at its most urbane. Spend four days exploring the metropolis, visiting people-watching 'hoods such as the West and East Villages, Soho and the Upper West Side, with a museum-hop down the Upper East Side. Have a ramble in Central Park, stroll the High Line and take detours to Brooklyn and Queens. After big-city culture, catch your breath at the pretty beaches of **Greenport** and **Montauk** on Long Island. Back in NYC, catch the train to **Boston** for two days of visiting historic sights, dining in the North End and pub-hopping in Cambridge. Strike out for **Cape Cod**, with its idyllic dunes and pretty shores. Leave time for **Provincetown**, the Cape's liveliest settlement. Back in Boston, rent a car and take a three-day jaunt to explore New England's back roads, staying at heritage B&Bs along the way. Highlights include **Salem** and **Concord** in Massachusetts; **Bennington**, VT; and **Portsmouth**, NH. If time allows, head up to Maine for lobster feasts amid beautifully rugged coastline: **Portland** is a great place to start.

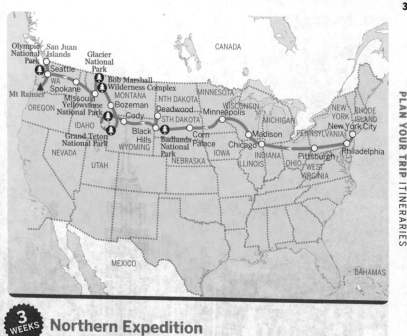

3 WEEKS Northern Expedition

For a different take on the transcontinental journey, plan a route through the north.

From **New York City**, head southwest to historic **Philadelphia**, then continue west to the idyllic back roads of Pennsylvania Dutch Country. Next is **Pittsburgh**, a surprising town of picturesque bridges and green spaces, cutting-edge museums and lively neighborhoods. Enter Ohio by interstate, but quickly step back in time on a drive through old-fashioned Amish Country. Big-hearted **Chicago** is the Midwest's greatest metropolis. Stroll or bike the lakefront, marvel at famous artworks and grand architecture, and check out the celebrated restaurant scene. Head north to **Madison**, a youthful green-loving university town.

Detour north to the land of 10,000 lakes (aka Minnesota) for a stop in friendly, arty **Minneapolis**, followed by a visit to its quieter historic twin, St Paul, across the river. Return to I-90 and activate cruise control, admiring the corn (and the **Corn Palace**) and the flat, flat South Dakota plains. Hit the brakes for the **Badlands National Park** and plunge into the Wild West. In the **Black Hills**, contemplate the nation's complex history at the massive monuments of Mt Rushmore and Crazy Horse, then make a northern detour to watch mythic gunfights in **Deadwood**.

Halfway across Wyoming, cruise into **Cody** to catch a summer rodeo, then take in the wonders of **Yellowstone National Park**. Next, detour south for hikes past jewel-like lakes and soaring peaks in **Grand Teton National Park**. Drive back up north, and continue west through rural Montana. The outdoorsy towns of **Bozeman** and **Missoula** make fun stops between exploring the alpine beauty of **Glacier National Park**.

After a few days out in the wild, surprising **Spokane** is a great place to recharge, with a pleasant riverfront and historic district sprinkled with enticing eating and drinking spots. For more cosmopolitan flavor, keep heading west to **Seattle**, a forward-thinking, eco-minded city with cafe culture, abundant nightlife and speedy island escapes on Puget Sound. If you still have time, the region has some great places to explore, including **Mt Rainier**, **Olympic National Park** and the **San Juan Islands**.

Top: New York City skyline (p75)

Bottom: Snake River, Grand Teton National Park (p797)

LONEROC / SHUTTERSTOCK ©

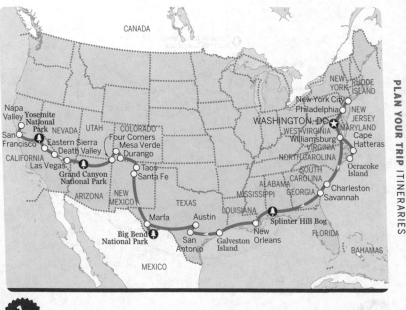

1 MONTH Coast to Coast

The 'Great American Road Trip': it's been mythologized hundreds of ways. Now live the dream, driving from shore to shining shore.

Start in **New York City** (but hire a car in cheaper New Jersey) and hit the road. First stop: **Philadelphia**, a historic city with a burgeoning food, art and music scene. Continue on to **Washington, DC**. The nation's capital has a dizzying array of sights, plus great dining and revelry after the museums close. Continue south through Virginia, taking a detour to visit the fantastic historic settlement of colonial **Williamsburg**. Stick to the coast as you drive south, visiting **Cape Hatteras** with its pristine dunes, marshes and woodlands. Catch the ferry to remote **Ocracoke Island,** where the wild ponies run. Further south, take in the alluring architecture of **Charleston** and **Savannah**. Afterwards stop in Splinter Hill Bog in Alabama, a fantastic site for exploring the biodiversity of the coast, then it's on to jazz hot spot **New Orleans**, with a soundtrack of smokin' hot funk brass bands.

The big open skies of Texas are next. Hit the beach at **Galveston** outside Houston. Follow the Mission Trail and stroll the tree-lined riverwalk in thriving **San Antonio**, then revel in the great music and drinking scene in **Austin**. Afterwards, eat your way through scenic Hill Country, stop for art and star-filled nights at **Marfa**, then hike through jaw-dropping **Big Bend National Park**. Head north to New Mexico, following the Turquoise Trail up to artsy **Santa Fe** and far-out **Taos**. Roll up through Colorado and into mountain beauty **Durango**, continuing to the Native American cliff-top marvel of **Mesa Verde**, and the Four Corners four-state intersection. The awe-inspiring **Grand Canyon** is next. Stay in the area to maximize time near this great wonder. Try your luck amid the bright lights of **Las Vegas**, then take in the stunning desert landscapes at **Death Valley** on your ride into California. From there, head up into the majestic forests of the **Eastern Sierra**, followed by hiking and wildlife-watching in **Yosemite**. The last stop is in hilly **San Francisco**, an enchanting city spread between ocean and bay with beautiful vistas and seemingly endless cultural attractions. If there's time, tack on a grand finale, enjoying the vineyards and gourmet produce of the **Napa Valley**.

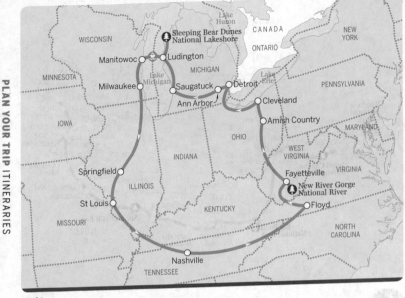

Off the Beaten Path

Underdog cities, lakeside islands and boot-scootin' mountain music are just a few of the things you'll encounter on this off-the-beaten-path ramble around the central US.

Start off in **Detroit**, which has made a remarkable comeback in the past decade. Stroll the riverwalk, explore recent history (Motown, automobiles) and take in the Motor City's nightlife scene. Next head to nearby **Ann Arbor** with its easygoing college-town charm (coffee shops, farmers markets, pubby bars), before continuing west to Lake Michigan. Drive up through waterfront towns – stopping perhaps in **Saugatuck** for gallery-hopping – and continue all the way to **Sleeping Bear Dunes National Lakeshore**, with its dramatic sandscapes, scenic drives and wilderness-covered islands.

From there backtrack to **Ludington** and take the ferry across Lake Michigan to **Manitowoc** in Wisconsin. Continue south to **Milwaukee**, one of the best little cities in America, with great art and architecture, abundant microbreweries, summer festivals and memorable riverfront cycling. From there, it's a 4½-hour drive south to **Springfield**, where you can delve into the fascinating past of hometown hero (and America's favorite president) Abraham Lincoln. Two hours' drive south is **St Louis**, with walkable neighborhoods and green spaces (including a park that dwarfs Central Park), plus blues, barbecue and bumping music joints. Speaking of music, up next is **Nashville**, a place of pilgrimage for lovers of country and blues. Head toward Appalachia – start in **Floyd**, VA – for an authentic music scene (a frenzy of fiddles, banjos and boot-stompin') amid the rolling hills of southeastern Virginia. Continue north to **Fayetteville** in West Virginia, gateway to the breathtaking **New River Gorge**, which has superb hiking, climbing, mountain biking and white-water rafting.

A five-hour drive takes you to the epicenter of America's largest Amish community in **Amish Country** near Kidron in Ohio. Step back in time at antique shops, old-fashioned farms and bakeries, and quaint 19th-century inns. Afterward, fast-forward into **Cleveland**, a city on the cusp of reinvention with up-and-coming gastropubs, newly expanded art museums, green markets and the massive Rock and Roll Hall of Fame. It's less than three hours back to Detroit.

Plan Your Trip

Road Trips & Scenic Drives

Fill up the gas tank and buckle up. Everyone knows road-tripping is the ultimate way to see America. You can drive up, down, across, around or straight through every state in the continental US. Revel in yesteryear along Route 66, marvel at spectacular sunsets on the Pacific Coast Hwy, or take in sublime scenery in the Appalachian Mountains or along the mighty Mississippi.

Route 66

For a classic American road trip, nothing beats good ol' Route 66. Nicknamed the nation's 'Mother Road' by novelist John Steinbeck, this string of small-town main streets and country byways first connected big-shouldered Chicago with the waving palm trees of Los Angeles in 1926.

Why Go?

Whether you seek to explore retro Americana or simply to experience big horizons and captivating scenery far from the madding crowd, Route 66 will take you there. The winding journey passes some of the USA's greatest outdoor attractions – not just the Grand Canyon, but also the Mississippi River, Arizona's Painted Desert and Petrified Forest National Park, and, at road's end, the Pacific beaches of sun-kissed Southern California.

Other highlights along the way: old-fashioned museums stocked with strange and wondrous objects from the past, Norman Rockwell–ish soda fountains, classic mom-and-pop diners, working gas stations that seem to have fallen right out of an old James Dean film clip, and ghost towns (or soon-to-be ghost towns) hunkering on the edge of the desert.

Road-Tripping Tips

Best Experiences

Dazzling coastal scenery on the Pacific Coast Hwy; the charming, rarely visited destinations on Route 66; dramatic sunsets over the Appalachian Mountains on the Blue Ridge Pkwy; listening to Memphis blues at a jumping music joint off the Great River Rd.

Key Starting Points

Chicago or Los Angeles for Route 66; Seattle or San Diego for the Pacific Coast Hwy; Waynesboro, VA, or Cherokee, NC, for Blue Ridge Pkwy; Itasca State Park, MN, or Venice, LA, for Great River Rd.

Major Sights

Grand Canyon on Route 66; Point Reyes National Seashore on the Pacific Coast Hwy; Peaks of Otter on Blue Ridge Pkwy; Shawnee National Forest on Great River Rd.

ROADSIDE ODDITIES: ROUTE 66

Kitschy, time-warped and just plain weird roadside attractions? Route 66 has got 'em in spades. Here are a few beloved Mother Road landmarks to make your own scavenger hunt:

➡ A statue of legendary lumberjack Paul Bunyan clutching a hotdog in Illinois.

➡ The Black Madonna Shrine in Pacific, MO, and Red Oak II outside Carthage, MO.

➡ The 80ft-long Blue Whale in Catoosa, OK.

➡ Devil's Rope Museum, Cadillac Ranch and Slug Bug Ranch in Texas.

➡ Seligman's Snow Cap Drive-In, Holbrook's WigWam Motel and Meteor Crater in Arizona.

➡ Roy's Motel & Cafe in Amboy in the middle of California's Mojave Desert.

Culturally speaking, Route 66 can be an eye-opener. Discard your preconceptions of small-town American life and unearth the joys of what bicoastal types dismissively term 'flyover' states. Mingle with farmers in Illinois and country-and-western stars in Missouri. Visit Native American nations and contemporary pueblos across the Southwest. Then follow the trails of miners and desperadoes deep into the Old West.

When to Go

The best time to travel Route 66 is May to September, when the weather is warm and you can take advantage of open-air activities. Take care if you travel in the height of summer (July and August) as the heat can be unbearable – particularly in desert areas. Avoid traveling in the winter (December to March), when snow can lead to perilous driving conditions or outright road closures.

The Route

The journey starts in Chicago, just west of Michigan Ave, and runs for some 2400 miles across eight states before terminating in Los Angeles near the Santa Monica Pier. The road is a never-ending work in progress, as old sections get resurrected or disappear owing to the rerouting of other major roads.

History of the Mother Road

Route 66 didn't really hit its stride until the Great Depression, when migrant farmers followed it as they fled the Dust Bowl across the Great Plains. Later, during the post-WWII baby boom, newfound prosperity encouraged many Americans to hit the road and 'get their kicks' on Route 66.

Almost as soon as it came of age, though, Route 66 began to lose steam. The shiny blacktop of an ambitious new interstate system started systematically paving over Route 66, bypassing its mom-and-pop diners, drugstore soda fountains and once-stylish motels. Railway towns were forgotten and way stations became dusty. Even entire towns began to disappear.

Preservation associations of Mother Road fans sprung to action to save remaining stretches of the historic highway soon after Route 66 was officially decommissioned in 1985. Upgrades are being planned to line up with the route's 100th anniversary in 2026, which we hope will ensure you can still get your kicks on Route 66 for years to come.

Getting Lost

You need to be an amateur sleuth to follow Route 66 these days. Historical realignments of the route, dead-ends in farm fields and tumbleweed-filled desert patches, and rough, rutted driving conditions are par for the course. Remember that getting lost every now and then is inevitable.

Resources

Before you hit the road, arm yourself with useful maps and key insider tips to help you make the most of your trip.

Lonely Planet's Route 66 Road Trips Itineraries and planning advice to pick the best routes.

Here It Is: Route 66 Maps with directions (traveling both east-to-west and west-to-east) that you'll want to take along for the ride; available from booksellers.

Historic Route 66 (www.historic66.com) Excellent website, with turn-by-turn directions for each state.

Route 66: The Mother Road This book by Michael Wallis is a fascinating look at the history of the great road with old photographs bringing it all to life.

Pacific Coast Highway

The classic West Coast journey through California, Oregon and Washington takes in cosmopolitan cities, surf towns and charming coastal enclaves ripe for exploration. For many travelers, the real appeal of the Pacific Coast Hwy is the magnificent scenery – wild and remote beaches, clifftop views overlooking crashing waves, rolling hills and lush forests (redwoods, eucalyptus trees) – that sometimes lies just beyond a city's outskirts.

Why Go?

The PCH is a road trip for lovers, nomadic ramblers, bohemians, beatniks and curiosity seekers keen to search out every nook and cranny of forgotten beachside hamlets and pastoral farm towns along the way. It's both an epic adventure for water babies, surfers, kayakers, scuba divers and every other kind of outdoor enthusiast, and an insanely scenic route for laid-back road-trippers who dream of cruising alongside the ocean in a cherry-red convertible.

When to Go

There's no very bad time oo drive the PCH, although northern climes will be rainier and snowier during winter. Peak travel season is June through August, which isn't always the best time to see the road, as thick fog blankets many stretches of the coast during early summer (locals call it 'June Gloom'). The shoulder seasons before Memorial Day (ie April and May) and after Labor Day (September and October) can be ideal, with sunny days, crisply cool nights and fewer crowds.

The Route

Technically 'the PCH' is one of several coastal highways, including Hwy 101, stretching nearly 2000 miles from Tijuana, Mexico, to British Columbia, Canada. The route connects the dots between some of the West Coast's most striking cities, starting from surf-style San Diego, through hedonistic Los Angeles and offbeat San Francisco in California, then moving north to equally alternative-minded and arty Seattle, WA.

When the urban streets start to make you feel claustrophobic, just head back out on the open road and hit the coast again, heading north or south. The direction doesn't really matter – the views and hidden places you find along the way make for rewarding exploring.

You could bypass metro areas and just stick to the places in between, like the almost-too-perfect beaches of California's Orange County ('the OC') and Santa Barbara (the 'American Riviera'); wacky Santa Cruz, a university town and surfers' paradise; redwood forests along the Big Sur coast and north of Mendocino; the sand dunes, seaside resorts and fishing villages

---

BEFORE YOU HIT THE ROAD

A few things to remember to ensure your road trip is as happy-go-lucky as possible:

➡ Join an automobile club that provides members with 24-hour emergency roadside assistance and discounts on lodging and attractions; some international clubs have reciprocal agreements with US automobile associations, so check first and bring your member card from home.

➡ Check the spare tire, tool kit (eg jack, jumper cables, ice scraper, tire-pressure gauge) and emergency equipment (eg flashers) in your car; if you're renting a vehicle and these essential safety items are not provided, consider buying them.

➡ Bring good maps, especially if you're touring off-road or away from highways; don't rely on a GPS unit – they can malfunction, and in remote areas such as deep canyons or thick forests they may not even work.

➡ Always carry your driver's license and proof of insurance.

➡ If you're an international traveler, review the USA's road rules and common road hazards.

➡ Fill up the tank often, because gas stations can be few and far between on the USA's scenic byways.

Scenic Drives

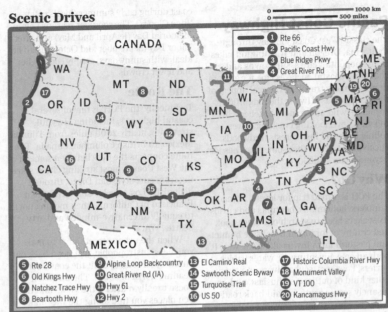

of coastal Oregon; and finally, the wild lands of Washington's Olympic Peninsula, with its primeval rainforest and bucolic San Juan Islands, served by coastal ferries.

Blue Ridge Parkway

Snaking for some 469 miles through the southern Appalachian Mountains, the Blue Ridge Pkwy is the land of great hiking and wildlife-watching, old-fashioned music and captivating mountainous scenery – all of which make for a memorable and easily accessible road trip.

Construction on the parkway began in 1935 under President Franklin D Roosevelt, part of his slate of New Deal projects that helped put people back to work during the Depression. It was a huge effort that took over 52 years to complete, with the final section laid in 1987.

Why Go?

Although it skirts dozens of towns and a few metropolitan areas, the Blue Ridge Pkwy feels far removed from modern-day America. Here, rustic log cabins with rocking chairs on the front porch still dot the rolling hillsides, while signs for folk-art shops and live bluegrass music joints

entice travelers onto side roads. History seems to permeate the air of these rolling backwoods, once home to Cherokee people and later to early colonial homesteads and Civil War battlefields.

There are great places to sleep and eat. Early 20th-century mountain and lakeside resorts still welcome families like old friends, while log-cabin diners dish up heaping piles of buckwheat pancakes with blackberry preserves and a side of country ham.

When you need to work off all that good Southern cooking, over 100 hiking trails can be accessed along the Blue Ridge Pkwy, from gentle nature walks and easily summited peaks to rough-and-ready tramps along the legendary Appalachian Trail. Or clamber on a horse and ride off into the refreshingly shady forests. Then go canoeing, kayaking or inner-tubing along rushing rivers, or dangle a fishing line over the side of a rowboat on petite lakes. And who says you even have to drive? The parkway makes an epic trip for long-distance cyclists, too.

When to Go

Keep in mind that the weather can vary greatly, depending on your elevation. While mountain peaks are snowed in during winter, the valleys can still be invitingly warm.

OTHER GREAT ROAD TRIPS

ROUTE	STATE(S)	START/END	SIGHTS & ACTIVITIES	BEST TIME
Rte 28	NY	Stony Hollow/Arkville	Catskill Mountains, lakes, rivers, hiking, leaf-peeping, tubing	May-Sep
Old Kings Hwy	MA	Sagamore/Provincetown	historic districts, period homes, coastal scenery	Apr-Oct
Natchez Trace Hwy	AL/MS/TN	Nashville/Natchez	history, archaeological sites, scenic waterways, biking, camping, hiking	Mar-Nov
Beartooth Hwy	MT	Red Lodge/Yellowstone	wildflowers, mountains, alpine scenery, camping	Jun-Sep
Alpine Loop Backcountry Byway	CO	Ouray/Lake City	mountains, views, valleys, abandoned mines	Jun-Sep
Great River Rd	IA	Effigy Mounds National Monument/Keokuk	scenic views, riverside beauty, little-visited towns & villages	May-Sep
Hwy 61	MN	Duluth/Canadian border	state parks, waterfalls, quaint towns, hiking	May-Sep
Hwy 2	NE	I-80/Alliance	grass-covered sand dunes, open vistas	May-Sep
El Camino Real	TX	Lajitas/Presidio	desert & mountain landscapes, hot springs, hiking, horseback riding	Feb-Apr & Oct-Nov
Sawtooth Scenic Byway	ID	Ketchum/Stanley	jagged mountains, verdant forests, backpacking, hiking, wildlife-watching	May-Sep
Turquoise Trail	NM	Albuquerque/Santa Fe	mining towns, quirky museums & folk art, cycling, hiking	Mar-May & Sep-Nov
US 50	NV	Fernley/Baker	epic wilderness, biking, hiking, spelunking	May-Sep
Historic Columbia River Hwy	OR	Portland/The Dalles	scenery, waterfalls, wildflowers, cycling, hiking	Apr-Sep
Monument Valley	UT	Monument Valley	iconic buttes, movie-set locations, 4WD tours, horseback riding	year-round
VT 100	VT	Stamford/Newport	rolling pastures, green mountains, hiking, skiing	Jun-Sep
Kancamagus Hwy	NH	Conway/Lincoln	craggy mountains, streams & waterfalls, camping, hiking, swimming	May-Sep
Maui's Road to Hana	HI	Paia/Hana	jungle waterfalls, beaches, hiking, swimming, surfing	year-round

Most visitor services along the parkway are only open from April through October. May is best for wildflowers, although most people come for leaf-peeping during autumn. Spring and autumn are good times for birdwatching, with nearly 160 species having been spotted in the skies over the parkway. Expect big crowds if you go during the summer or early autumn.

The Route

This rolling, scenic byway connects Virginia's Shenandoah National Park with Great Smoky Mountains National Park, winding back and forth across the North Carolina–Tennessee border. Towns include Boone and Asheville in North Carolina, and Galax and Roanoke in Virginia, with

Charlottesville, VA, also within a short drive of the parkway. Major cities within range are Washington, DC (140 miles), and Richmond, VA (95 miles).

Detour: Skyline Drive

If you want to extend your journey through this scenic region, you can do so by hooking up with Skyline Dr. The northern terminus of the Blue Ridge Pkwy meets up with this 105-mile road (which continues northeast) around Rockfish Gap.

Travel along the road is slow (speed limit 35mph), but that forces you to take in the amazing scenery (wildflowers on the hillsides in spring, blazing colors in autumn and gorgeous blue skies in summer). Shenandoah National Park surrounds Skyline Dr and has an excellent range of hikes, some of which scramble up mountain peaks and offer panoramic views. There are campgrounds in the park as well as lodges – nearby attractions include the lively mountain town of Staunton and an elaborate cave system at Luray Caverns.

One caveat: you will have to pay to travel along Skyline Dr ($25 per vehicle for a seven-day pass). This is not a toll, but rather an admission charge for visiting Shenandoah National Park. Expect heavy traffic on weekends.

Resources

Lonely Planet Blue Ridge Parkway Road Trips From three-day escapes to five-day adventures, these road trips are packed full of expert advice and inspirational suggestions.

Blue Ridge Parkway (www.blueridgeparkway. org) Maps, activities and places to stay along the way. You can also download the free *Blue Ridge Parkway Travel Planner.*

Hiking the Blue Ridge Parkway By Randy Johnson; has in-depth trail descriptions, topographic trail maps and other essential info for hikes both short and long (including overnight treks).

Skyline Drive (www.visitskylinedrive.org) Lodging, hiking, wildlife and more: the complete overview of the national park surrounding this picturesque drive.

Great River Road

Established in the late 1930s, the Great River Rd journeys from the Mississippi's headwaters in northern Minnesota all the way to the river's mouth on the Gulf

of Mexico near New Orleans. For a look at America across cultural divides – north-south, urban-rural, Baptist-bohemian – this is the trip to make.

Why Go?

The sweeping scenery alongside North America's second-longest river is astonishing, from the rolling plains of Iowa down to the sunbaked cotton fields of the Mississippi Delta. Limestone cliffs, dense forests, flower-filled meadows and steamy swamps are all part of the backdrop – along with smokestacks, riverboat casinos and urban sprawl. This is the good, the bad and the ugly of life on the Mississippi.

Small towns provide a glimpse into American culture: there's Hibbing, MN, where folk-rocker Bob Dylan grew up; Brainerd, MN, as seen in the Coen Brothers' film *Fargo;* Spring Green, WI, where architect Frank Lloyd Wright cut his teeth; pastoral Hannibal, MO, boyhood home of Mark Twain; and Metropolis, IL, where you'll find Superman's quick-change phone booth.

The southern section of this route traces American musical history, from rock and roll in St Louis to Memphis blues and New Orleans jazz. And you won't go hungry either, with retro Midwestern diners, Southern barbecue joints and smokehouses, and Cajun taverns and dance halls in Louisiana.

When to Go

The best time to travel is from May to October, when the weather is warmest. Skip the trip in the winter (or else stick to the South), to avoid snowstorms.

The Route

The Great River Rd is not a single highway, but a series of linked federal, state and county roads that follow the Mississippi River as it flows through 10 different states. The one constant wherever you are is the green paddle-wheel sign that marks the way. Major urban areas that provide easy access to the road include New Orleans, Memphis, St Louis and Minneapolis.

Resources

The Great River Road (www.experiencemississippi river.com) 'Ten states, one river' is the slogan for this official site, which is a great resource for history, outdoor recreation, live music and more.

Plan Your Trip
Outdoor Activities

Towering redwoods, red-rock canyons, snow-covered peaks and a dramatic coastline of unrivaled beauty: the USA has no shortage of spectacular settings for a bit of adventure. No matter your weakness – hiking, biking, kayaking, rafting, surfing, horseback riding, rock-climbing – you'll find world-class places to commune with the great outdoors.

Hiking & Trekking

Fitness-focused Americans take great pride in their country's formidable network of trails – literally tens of thousands of miles – and there's no better way to experience the countryside up close and at your own pace.

The American wilderness is amazingly accessible, making for easy exploration. National parks are ideal for short and long hikes. If you're hankering for nights beneath star-filled skies, plan on securing a backcountry permit in advance, especially in places like the Grand Canyon – spaces are limited, particularly during summer.

Beyond the parks, you'll find troves of trails in every state. There's no limit to the places you can explore, from sun-blasted hoodoos and red spires in Arizona's Chiricahua Mountains to dripping trees and mossy nooks in Washington's Hoh River Rainforest; from the dogwood-choked Wild Azalea Trail in Louisiana to the tropical paradise of Kaua'i's Na Pali Coast. Almost anywhere you go, great hiking and backpacking is within easy striking distance. All you need to start is a sturdy pair of shoes (sneakers or hiking boots) and a water bottle.

Best Outdoor Adventures

Best Wildlife-Watching

Bears in Glacier National Park, MT; elk, bison and gray wolves in Yellowstone National Park, WY; alligators, manatees and sea turtles in the Florida Everglades; whales and dolphins in Monterey Bay, CA; moose in Baxter State Park, ME.

Top Aquatic Activities

White-water rafting on the New River, WV; surfing perfect waves in Oahu, HI; diving and snorkeling off the Florida Keys; kayaking pristine Penobscot Bay, ME.

Best Multiday Adventures

Hiking the Appalachian Trail; mountain-biking the Kokopelli Trail, UT; climbing 13,770ft Grand Teton in Grand Teton National Park, WY; canoeing, portaging and camping in the vast Boundary Waters, MN.

Best Winter Activities

Downhill skiing in Vail, CO; snowboarding in Stowe, VT; cross-country skiing off Lake Placid, NY.

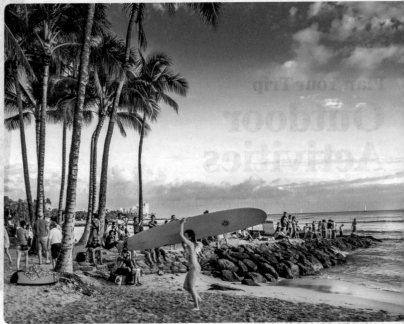

Waikiki beach, HI (p1110)

Hiking Resources

American Hiking Society (www.americanhiking.org) Links to 'volunteer vacations' spent building trails.

Backpacker (www.backpacker.com) Premier national magazine for backpackers, from novices to experts.

Rails-to-Trails Conservancy (www.railstotrails.org) Converts abandoned railroad corridors into hiking and biking trails; publishes free trail reviews at www.traillink.com.

Survive Outdoors (www.surviveoutdoors.com) Dispenses safety and first-aid tips, plus helpful photos of dangerous critters.

Wilderness Survival Gregory Davenport has written what is easily the best book on surviving nearly every contingency.

Cycling

Cycling's popularity increases by the day, with numerous cities (including New York) adding more cycle lanes and becoming more bike-friendly, and a growing number of greenways dotting the countryside.

You'll find diehards in every town, and outfitters offering guided trips for all levels and durations. For the best advice on rides and rentals, stop by a local bike shop.

Many states offer social multiday rides, such as Ride the Rockies (www.ridetherockies.com) in Colorado. For a modest fee, you can join the peloton on a scenic, well-supported route; your gear is ferried ahead to that night's camping spot. Other standout rides include Arizona's Mt Lemmon, a thigh-zinging 28-mile climb from the Sonoran Desert floor to the 9157ft summit, and Tennessee's Cherohala Skyway (www.cherohala.org), 43 glorious miles of undulating road and Great Smoky Mountain views.

For more casual riders, rails-to-trails projects like the Sacramento River Trail; the Swamp Rabbit Trail in Greenville, SC; the BeltLine in Atlanta and the Capital Crescent Trail in Washington, DC, offer fun days out.

Top Cycling Towns

Portland, OR One of America's most bike-friendly cities has a trove of cycling routes.

San Francisco, CA A pedal over the Golden Gate Bridge lands you in the stunningly beautiful, and stunningly hilly, Marin Headlands.

TOP HIKING TRAILS IN THE USA

Ask 10 people for their top trail recommendations and it's possible that no two answers will be alike. The country is varied and distances enormous, so there's little consensus. That said, you can't go wrong with the following all-star sampler.

Appalachian Trail (www.appalachiantrail.org) Completed in 1937, the country's longest footpath is more than 2100 miles, crossing two national parks, traversing eight national forests and hitting 14 states from Georgia to Maine.

Pacific Crest Trail (PCT; www.pcta.org) Follows the spines of the Cascades and Sierra Nevada, traversing 2650 miles from Canada to Mexico, passing through nine of North America's ecoregions.

John Muir Trail in Yosemite National Park, CA (www.johnmuirtrail.org) Find 211 miles of scenic bliss, from Yosemite Valley up to Mt Whitney.

Enchanted Valley Trail, Olympic National Park, WA Magnificent mountain views, roaming wildlife and lush rainforests – all on a 13-mile out-and-back trail.

Great Northern Traverse, Glacier National Park, MT A 58-mile haul that cuts through the heart of grizzly country and crosses the Continental Divide; check out the Lonely Planet *Banff, Jasper & Glacier National Parks* guide for more information.

Kalalau Trail, Na Pali Coast, Kaua'i, HI (www.kalalautrail.com) Wild Hawaii at its finest – 11 miles of lush waterfalls, hidden beaches, verdant valleys and crashing surf.

Mount Katahdin, Baxter State Park, ME A 9.5-mile hike over the 5267ft summit, with panoramic views of the park's 46 peaks.

South Kaibab/North Kaibab Trail, Grand Canyon, AZ A multiday cross-canyon tramp down to the Colorado River and back up to the opposite rim.

South Rim, Big Bend National Park, TX A 13-mile loop through the ruddy 7000ft Chisos Mountains, with views into Mexico.

Tahoe Rim Trail, Lake Tahoe, CA (www.tahoerimtrail.org) This 165-mile all-purpose trail circumnavigates the lake from high above, affording glistening Sierra views.

Minneapolis, MN Miles of green space make for stress-free crosstown connections for the city's abundant cyclists.

Boulder, CO Outdoors-loving town with loads of cycling paths, including the eight-mile Boulder Creek Trail.

Austin, TX Indie-rock town with nearly 200 miles of trails and great year-round weather.

Burlington, VT Northeast bike haven with lovely rides, the best-known along Lake Champlain.

Surfing

Hawaii

Blessed is the state that started it all, where the best swells generally arrive between November and March.

Waikiki (South Shore of Oahu) Hawaii's ancient kings rode waves on wooden boards well before 19th-century missionaries deemed the sport a godless activity. With warm water

and gentle rolling waves, Waikiki is perfect for novices, offering long and sudsy rides.

Pipeline and Sunset Beach (North Shore of Oahu) Home to the classic tubing waves, which form as deepwater swells break over reefs into shallows; these are expert-only spots but well worth an ogle.

West Coast

Huntington Beach, CA (aka Surf City, USA) The quintessential surf capital, with perpetual sun and a 'perfect' break, particularly during winter when the winds are calm.

Black's Beach, San Diego, CA This 2-mile sandy strip at the base of 300ft cliffs in La Jolla is known as one of the most powerful beach breaks in So-Cal, thanks to an underwater canyon just offshore.

Oceanside Beach, Oceanside, CA One of SoCal's prettiest beaches has one of the world's most consistent surf breaks come summer. It's a family-friendly spot.

MAD FOR MOUNTAIN BIKING

Mountain-biking enthusiasts will find trail nirvana in Boulder, CO; Moab, UT; Bend, OR; Ketchum, ID; and Marin, CA, where Gary Fisher and company bunny-hopped the sport forward by careening down the rocky flanks of Mt Tamalpais on home-rigged bikes. There are many other great destinations. For info on trails, tips and gear, check out *Bicycling* magazine (www.bicycling.com) or IMBA (www.imba.com).

Kokopelli Trail, UT One of the premier mountain-biking trails in the Southwest stretches 140 miles on mountainous terrain between Loma, CO, and Moab, UT. Other nearby options include the 206-mile, hut-to-hut ride between Telluride, CO, and Moab, UT, and the shorter but equally stunning 38-mile ride from Aspen to Crested Butte.

Maah Daah Hey Trail, ND A lengthy jaunt over rolling buttes along the Little Missouri River.

Sun Top Loop, WA A 22-mile ride with challenging climbs that rewards with superb views of Mt Rainier and surrounding peaks on the western slopes of Washington's Cascade Mountains.

Flume Trail, CA A moderately challenging trail with stunning views along Lake Tahoe. This 14-mile trail runs one way at 7000ft to 8000ft elevation, with about 4.5 miles of singletrack.

Finger Lakes Trail, Letchworth State Park, NY A little-known treasure 35 miles south of Rochester in upstate New York, featuring more than 20 miles of singletrack along the rim of the 'Grand Canyon of the East.'

McKenzie River Trail, Willamette National Forest, OR (www.mckenzierivertrail.com) Twenty-two miles of blissful singletrack winding through deep forests and volcanic formations. The town of McKenzie is located about 50 miles east of Eugene.

Porcupine Rim, Moab, UT A 30-mile loop from town, this venerable high-desert romp features stunning views and hairy downhills.

Rincon, Santa Barbara, CA Arguably one of the planet's top surfing spots; nearly every major surf champion on the globe has taken Rincon for a ride.

Steamer Lane and Pleasure Point, Santa Cruz, CA There are 11 world-class breaks, including the point breaks over rock bottoms at these two sweet spots.

Swami's, Encinitas, CA Located below Seacliff Roadside Park, this popular surfing beach has multiple breaks guaranteeing you some fantastic waves.

East Coast

The Atlantic seaboard states harbor some terrific and unexpected surfing spots – especially if you're after more moderate swells. You'll find the warmest waters off Florida's Gulf Coast.

Cocoa Beach, Melbourne Beach, FL Small crowds and mellow waves make it a paradise for beginners and longboarders. Just south is the Inlet, known for consistent surf and crowds to match.

Reef Road, Palm Beach, FL This stellar spot has beach and reef breaks with consistent surf, especially at low tide; winter is best.

Cape Hatteras Lighthouse, NC This very popular area has several quality spots and infinitely rideable breaks that gracefully handle swells of all sizes and winds from any direction.

Long Island, Montauk, NY More than a dozen surfing areas dot the length of Long Island, from Montauk's oft-packed Ditch Plains to Nassau County's Long Beach, with its 3 miles of curling waves.

Casino Pier, Seaside Heights, NJ This area is one of the best pier breaks in New Jersey and is always packed with locals.

Point Judith, Narragansett, RI Rhode Island has premier surfing, with 40 miles of coastline and more than 30 surf spots, including this rocky point break offering long rollers as well as hollow barrels. Not for beginners.

Coast Guard Beach, Eastham, MA Part of the Cape Cod National Seashore, this family-friendly beach is known for its consistent shortboard/longboard swell all summer long.

White-Water Rafting

East of the Mississippi, West Virginia has an arsenal of legendary white water. First, there's the New River Gorge National River (p341), which, despite its name, is one of the oldest rivers in the world. Slicing from North Carolina into West Virginia, it cuts a deep gorge known as the Grand Canyon of the East, producing frothy rapids in its wake. Then there's the Gauley, arguably among the world's finest white water. Revered for its ultrasteep and turbulent chutes, this venerable Appalachian river is a watery roller coaster, dropping more than 668ft and churning up 100-plus rapids in a mere 28 miles. Six more rivers, all in the same neighborhood, offer training grounds for less-experienced river rats. North Carolina has two choice places for paddlers: the US National Whitewater Center (p359) outside Charlotte, and the Nantahala Outdoor Center in Bryson City.

Out west there's no shortage of scenic and spectacular rafting, from Utah's Cataract Canyon, a thrilling romp through the red rocks of Canyonlands National Park (p883), to the Rio Grande in Texas, a lazy run through limestone canyons. The North Fork of the Owyhee – which snakes from the high plateau of southwest Oregon to the rangelands of Idaho – is rightfully popular and features towering hoodoos. In California, both the Tuolumne and American Rivers surge with moderate-to-extreme rapids, while in Idaho, the Middle Fork of the Salmon River has it all: abundant wildlife, thrilling rapids, a rich homesteader history, waterfalls and hot springs. If you're organized enough to plan a few years in advance, book a spot on the Colorado River, the quintessential river trip. And if you're not after white-knuckle rapids, fret not – many rivers have sections suitable for peaceful float trips or inner-tube drifts that you can traverse with a cold beer in hand.

Kayaking & Canoeing

For exploring flatwater (no rapids or surf), opt for a kayak or canoe. While kayaks are seaworthy, they are not always suited for carrying bulky gear. For big lakes and the seacoast (including the San Juan Islands), use a sea kayak. For month-long wilderness trips – including the 12,000 miles of watery routes in Minnesota's Boundary Waters (p625), or Alabama's Bartram Canoe Trail, with 300,000 acres of marshy delta bayous, lakes and rivers – use a canoe.

You can kayak or canoe almost anywhere in the USA. Rentals and instruction are yours for the asking, from Wisconsin's Apostle Islands (p612) National Lakeshore and Utah's celebrated Green River to Hawaii's Na Pali Coast). Hire kayaks in Maine's Penobscot Bay to poke around the briny waters and spruce-fringed islets, or join a full-moon paddle in Sausalito's Richardson Bay, CA.

Skiing & Winter Sports

You can hit the slopes in 40 states, making for tremendous variety in terrain and ski-town vibe. Colorado has some of the best skiing in the nation, though California, Vermont and Utah also top-notch destinations. Ski season typically runs from mid-December to April, though some resorts run longer. In summer, many resorts are great for mountain biking and hiking, courtesy of chairlifts. Ski packages (including airfare, hotel and lift tickets) are easy to find through resorts, travel agencies and online travel booking sites, and they can be a good deal.

Wherever you ski, though, it won't come cheap. Find the best deals by going midweek, purchasing multiday tickets, heading to lesser-known 'sibling' resorts (such as Alpine Meadows near Lake Tahoe) or checking out mountains that cater to locals, including Vermont's Mad River Glen, Santa Fe Ski Area and Colorado's Wolf Grade.

Top Ski & Snowboard Resorts

Vermont's first-rate Stowe draws seasoned souls – freeze your tail off on the lifts, but thaw out nicely après-ski in timbered bars with local brews. Find more snow, altitude and attitude out west at Vail, CO, Squaw Valley, CA, and high-glitz Aspen, CO. For an unfussy scene and steep vertical chutes, try Alta, UT, Telluride, CO, Jackson, WY, and Taos, NM. In Alaska, slopes slice through spectacular terrain outside Juneau, Anchorage and Fairbanks. Mt Aurora SkiLand has the most northerly chairlift in North America and, from mid-September to mid-April, the shimmering green-blue aurora borealis.

Rock Climbing

Scads of climbers flock to Joshua Tree National Park, an otherworldly shrine in Southern California's sun-scorched desert. There, amid craggy monoliths and the park's namesake trees, they pay pilgrimage on more than 8000 routes, tackling sheer verticals, sharp edges and bountiful cracks. A top-notch climbing school offers classes for all levels. In Zion National Park, UT, multiday canyoneering classes teach the fine art of going *down:* rappelling off sheer sandstone cliffs into glorious, red-rock canyons filled with trees. Some of the sportier pitches are made in dry suits,

down the flanks of roaring waterfalls into ice-cold pools. Other great spots abound.

Grand Teton National Park, WY A great spot for climbers of all levels: beginners can take basic climbing courses, while the more experienced can join two-day expeditions up to the top of Grand Teton itself: a 13,770ft peak with majestic views.

City of Rocks National Reserve, ID More than 500 routes up wind-scoured granite and pinnacles 60 stories tall.

Yosemite National Park, CA A hallowed shrine for rock climbers with superb climbing courses (p1020) for first-timers as well as for those craving a night in a hammock 1000ft above terra firma.

Bishop, CA Southeast of Yosemite National Park and favored by many top climbers, this sleepy town in the Eastern Sierra is the gateway to excellent climbing in nearby Owens River Gorge and Buttermilk Hills.

Red Rock Canyon, NV Ten miles west of Las Vegas is some of the world's finest sandstone climbing.

HONE YOUR SKILLS (OR LEARN SOME NEW ONES)

Whether you're eager to catch a wave or dangle from a cliff, learn some new outdoor tricks in these high-thrill programs.

Chicks Climbing & Skiing (www.chickswithpicks.net) Based in Ridgway, CO, this group gives women's workshops across the country in mountaineering, climbing, ice climbing and backcountry skiing.

Club Ed Surf Camp (https://club-ed.com) Learn to ride the waves from Manresa Beach to Santa Cruz, CA, with field trips to the surfing museum and surfboard companies included.

Craftsbury Outdoor Center (www.craftsbury.com) Come here for sculling, cross-country skiing and running amid the forests and hills of Vermont.

Joshua Tree Rock Climbing School (www.joshuatreerockclimbing.com) Local guides teach classes and lead beginners to experts on climbs in Joshua Tree National Park, CA.

LL Bean Outdoor Discovery Programs (www.llbean.com) The famous Maine retailer offers instruction in kayaking, snowshoeing, cross-country skiing, wilderness first aid, fly-fishing and more.

Nantahala Outdoor Center (www.noc.com) Learn to paddle like a pro at this North Carolina–based school, which offers world-class instruction in canoeing and kayaking in the Great Smoky Mountains.

Otter Bar Lodge Kayak School (www.otterbar.com) Top-notch white-water kayaking instruction is complemented by saunas, hot tubs, salmon dinners and a woodsy lodge in California's northern wilds.

Steep & Deep Ski Camp (www.jacksonhole.com/steep-ski-camp.html) Finesse skiing extreme terrain (and snagging first tracks), then wind down over dinner parties. You can also ski with Olympian Tommy Moe.

Enchanted Rock State Natural Area, TX Located 70 miles west of Austin, this state park with its huge pink granite dome has hundreds of routes and stellar views of the Texas Hill Country.

Rocky Mountain National Park, CO Offers alpine climbing near Boulder.

Flatirons, CO Near Boulder, with fine multipitch ascents.

Chattanooga, TN A world-class climbing destination with many nearby sites, including the Tennessee Wall, with over 400 established routes.

Red River Gorge, KY With over 100 cliffs and some 2000 different routes, this is a climber's paradise – all the more so given its location inside lush forested parkland.

Shawangunk Ridge, NY Located within a two-hour drive north of NYC, this ridge stretches some 50 miles, and the 'Gunks' are where many East Coast climbers tied their first billets.

Hueco Tanks, TX From October to early April, Hueco Tanks ranks among the world's top rock-climbing destinations, when other prime climbs become inaccessible (although in summer, the desert sun generally makes the rocks too hot to handle).

Hiking in Yosemite National Park (p1017)

Climbing & Canyoneering Resources

American Canyoneering Association (www.canyoneering.net) An online canyons database and links to courses, local climbing groups and more.

Climbing (www.climbing.com) Cutting-edge rock-climbing news and information since 1970.

SuperTopo (www.supertopo.com) One-stop shop for rock-climbing guidebooks, free topo maps and route descriptions.

Scuba Diving & Snorkeling

The most exotic underwater destination in the USA is Hawaii. There, in shimmering aquamarine waters that stay warm year-round, you'll be treated to a psychedelic display of surreal colors and shapes. Swim alongside sea turtles, octopuses and fiesta-colored parrotfish – not to mention lava tubes and black coral. Back on shore, cap off the reverie with *poke* made from just-caught ahi (yellowfin tuna).

The best diving is off the coast or between the islands, so liveaboards are the way to go for scuba buffs. From the green turtles and WWII wrecks off the shores of Oahu to the undersea lava sculptures near little Lana'i, the Aloha State offers endless underwater bliss – but plan ahead, as dive sites change with the seasons.

On the continental USA, Florida has the lion's share of great diving, with more than 1000 miles of coastline subdivided into 20 unique undersea areas. There are hundreds of sites and countless dive shops offering equipment and guided excursions. South of West Palm Beach, you'll find clear waters and fantastic year-round diving with ample reefs. In the Panhandle, or northern part of the state, you can dive in the calm and balmy waters of the Gulf of Mexico; off Pensacola and Destin, there are fabulous wreck dives, and you can dive with manatees near Crystal River.

The Florida Keys, a curving string of 31 islets, are the crown jewel; expect a brilliant mix of marine habitats, North America's only living coral garden and the

CANADASTOCK / SHUTTERSTOCK ©

occasional shipwreck. Key Largo is home to the John Pennekamp Coral Reef State Park and more than 200 miles of underwater idyll.

There's terrific diving and snorkeling (and much warmer water) beyond the mangrove swamps along the Florida Reef, the world's third-largest coral barrier-reef system. Look for manatees off Islamorada or take an expedition to Dry Tortugas, where the expansive reef swarms with barracuda, sea turtles and a couple of hundred sunken ships.

Other Underwater Destinations

For the latest on diving destinations in the US and abroad, visit Scuba Diving (www.scubadiving.com), or check out the USA overview from *DT Mag* (www.dtmag.com/destinations/united-states).

Hanauma Bay Nature Preserve, Oahu, HI
Despite the crowds, this is still one of the world's great spots for snorkeling, with more than 450 resident species of reef fish.

San Diego-La Jolla Underwater Park
Offers excellent shore diving amid four different habitats in a 6000-acre reserve. There are two reefs and seven caves, and with 30ft visibility you have the chance to spot a wide range of sea life, including eels, Garibaldi fish and leopard sharks.

Channel Islands, CA
Lying between Santa Barbara and Los Angeles, these islands harbor spiny lobsters, angel sharks and numerous dive sites best accessed by liveaboard charter.

Jade Cove, CA
About 10 miles south of Lucia on Hwy 1, this aptly named spot has the world's only underwater concentration of jade, making for an unforgettable dive.

Cape Hatteras National Seashore, NC
Along the northern coast of North Carolina, divers can explore historic wrecks from the Civil War (and encounter sand tiger sharks); there are also numerous options for dive charters within the Outer Banks and the Cape Lookout areas.

The Great Lakes The USA's most unexpected dive spot? Lakes Superior and Huron, with thousands of shipwrecks lying strewn on the sandy bottoms – just don't expect to see any angelfish!

Horseback Riding

Cowboy wannabes will be happy to learn that horseback riding of every style, from Western to bareback, is available across the USA. Out west, you'll find truly memorable experiences – everything from weeklong expeditions through the canyons of southern Utah and cattle wrangling in Wyoming, to pony rides along the Oregon coast. Finding horses is easy; rental stables and riding schools are located around and in many of the national parks. Experienced equestrians can explore alone or in the company of guides familiar with local flora, fauna and history. Half- and full-day group trail rides, which usually include lunch in a wildflower-speckled meadow, are popular and plentiful.

California is terrific for riding, with fog-swept trails leading along the cliffs of Point Reyes National Seashore, longer excursions through the high-altitude lakes of the Ansel Adams Wilderness, and multiday pack trips in Yosemite and Kings Canyon. Utah's Capitol Reef and Canyonlands also provide spectacular four-hoofed outings, as do the mountains, arroyos and plains of Colorado, Arizona, New Mexico, Montana and Texas.

Dude ranches come in all varieties, from down-duvet luxurious to barn-duty authentic on working cattle ranches. They're found in most of the western states, and even some eastern ones (such as Tennessee and North Carolina).

Plan Your Trip

Eat & Drink Like a Local

The great variety found in American cuisine can be traced to the local larder of each region, from the seafood of the North Atlantic to the fertile Midwestern farmlands and the vast Western ranchlands. Omaha steaks, Maryland crab cakes and Charleston red rice are but a few of the regional specialties.

Culinary Revolution

Not until the 1960s did food and wine become serious topics for American media, led by a Californian named Julia Child who taught Americans how to cook French food through programs broadcast from Boston's public TV station. By the 1970s, everyday folks had started turning their attention to issues of organic, natural foods and sustainable agriculture. In the 1980s and '90s, the 'foodie revolution' encouraged entrepreneurs to open restaurants featuring regional American cuisine, from the South to the Pacific Northwest, that would rank with Europe's best.

Slow, Local, Organic

The Slow Food movement, along with renewed enthusiasm for eating local organically grown fare, is a leading trend in American restaurants. The movement, which was arguably started in 1971 by chef Alice Waters at Berkeley's Chez Panisse (p1003), continued with First Lady Michelle Obama and her daughters, who even planted an organic garden on the White House lawn. Farmers markets are great places to meet locals and take a big bite out of America's cornucopia of foods, from heritage fruit and vegetables to fresh regional delicacies.

The Year in Food

In a country as large as the US, you'll find food festivals and local specialties all year long.

Spring (March–May)

One of the best times to hit local markets, with bounty from farm and field (ramps, strawberries, rhubarb, spring lamb), plus Easter treats. Across the country are major festivals showcasing crawfish, barbecue, oysters and more.

Summer (June–August)

A great time for seafood feasting by the shore, outdoor barbecues and country fairs. Don't miss fresh berries, peaches, corn on the cob and much more.

Fall (September–November)

Crisp days bring apple picking, pumpkin pies, harvest wine festivals and some major food-focused events, including Thanksgiving.

Winter (December–February)

Hearty stews, roast late-harvest vegetables, plus decadent holiday treats are the order of the day. Get toasty by the fire, with a hot toddy or other warming drink in hand.

Staples & Specialties

Waves of immigrants have added great variety to American gastronomy by adapting foreign ideas to home soil, from Italian pizza and German hamburgers to Eastern European borscht, Mexican huevos rancheros and Japanese sushi.

Pizza

Pizza made its way to New York in the 1900s through Italian immigrants, and the first pizzeria in America – Lombardi's in Manhattan's Little Italy – opened in 1905. Pizza's popularity quickly spread across the country, with different varieties taking root. While Chicago-style pizza is 'deep dish' and Californian tends to be light and doughy, New York prides itself on its thin crust.

Mexican & Tex-Mex

No matter where you roam in the US, you probably won't be far from a restaurant serving up Mexican or Tex-Mex fare (there's much overlap between them). This is not surprising given that people of Mexican descent make up over 11% of the population. Tacos, burritos and other quick foods are favorites, with snack carts and food trucks popular stomping grounds for people of all walks of life. Fast-casual outlets such as Chipotle, which serves up largely organic Tex-Mex in a hurry, are among the fastest-growing chains. Casual sit-down places are also popular, with margaritas and chips and salsa a nearly essential part of every meal.

Barbecue

Barbecue is a big deal in America. Although its popularity is unrivaled in the South, you'll find this smoky, tender meat everywhere from San Francisco to New York City. Barbecue in America dates back to colonial times, and even George Washington (who had a smokehouse at his estate in Mt Vernon) was a fan. The dish is simple enough: meat slow-roasted over firepits until tender. You'll find a wide variety of cooking styles and specialties. Kansas City, MO, serves a range of meats, including lamb, and emphasizes thick, sweet sauces. In the Carolinas, pulled or sliced pork is most popular. Memphis favors ribs, served either 'dry' or 'wet' (ie slathered in sauce). In Texas, beef is the dish of choice – no surprise given this is cattle country. It's also home to some of the nation's best barbecue joints: Lockhart is the epicenter for all things smoked and meaty.

Comfort Foods

While food trends come and go, a simple and hearty meal never goes out of style in the USA. Comfort foods at their roots are warm, traditional dishes that evoke nostalgia for childhood staples. Classics such as mac 'n' cheese, chicken noodle soup, lasagna, pot roast, grilled cheese sandwiches, biscuits and gravy, fried chicken and hamburgers all fall into this category. American diners serve mostly this sort of food, churning out uncomplicated, tried-and-true recipes. Comfort foods can also be found in more creative versions at gastropubs, bistros, and upmarket restaurants

---

TOP VEGETARIAN RESTAURANTS

Most major cities have a wealth of restaurants that cater to vegetarians and vegans. Once you head out into rural areas, the options are slimmer. We note eateries that offer a good selection of vegetarian or vegan options by using the 'V' symbol. To find more vegetarian and vegan restaurants, browse the online directory at www.happy cow.net. Here are a few of our go-tos across the country:

➡ Greens (p995), San Francisco, CA

➡ Moosewood Restaurant (p151), Ithaca, NY

➡ Modern Love (p120), Brooklyn, NY

➡ Sweet Melissa's (p788), Laramie, WY

➡ Sitka & Spruce (p1040), Seattle, WA

➡ Zenith (p182), Pittsburgh, PA

➡ Carmo (p455), New Orleans, LA

and bars. You might find mac 'n' cheese with fresh crabmeat, burgers topped with applewood-smoked bacon and goat cheese and served with duck-fat fries, or spicy Thai chicken noodle soup with coconut milk and curry.

Local Specialties

NYC: Foodie Capital

They say that you could eat at a different restaurant every night of your life in New York City and not exhaust the possibilities. Considering that there are an estimated 24,000 restaurants in Manhattan alone, with scores of new ones opening each year, it's true. Owing to its huge immigrant population and an influx of over 50 million tourists annually, New York captures the title of America's greatest restaurant city, hands down. Its diverse neighborhoods serve up authentic Italian food and thin-crust pizza, all manner of Asian food, French haute cuisine and classic Jewish deli food, from bagels to piled-high pastrami on rye. More uncommon cuisines are found here as well, from Ethiopian to Scandinavian.

Don't let NYC's expensive reputation get to you: you can eat well here without breaking the bank, especially if you limit your cocktail intake. There may be no free lunch in New York, but compared to other world cities, eating here can be a bargain.

New England: Clambakes & Lobster Boils

Seafood is king in New England; the North Atlantic offers up clams, mussels, oysters and huge lobsters, along with shad, bluefish and cod. New Englanders love a good chowder (seafood stew) and a good clambake, an almost ritual meal where the shellfish are buried in a pit fire with corn, chicken, potatoes and sausages. Fried clam fritters and lobster rolls (lobster meat with mayonnaise served in a bread bun) are served throughout the region. There are excellent cheeses made in Vermont, cranberries (a Thanksgiving staple) harvested in Massachusetts and maple syrup tapped from New England's forests. Maine's coast is lined with lobster shacks; baked beans and brown bread are Boston specialties;

and Rhode Islanders embrace traditional cornmeal johnnycakes.

Mid-Atlantic: Crab Cakes & Cheesesteaks

From New York down through Maryland and Virginia, the Mid-Atlantic states share a long coastline and a cornucopia of apple, pear and berry farms. New Jersey and New York's Long Island are famous for their spuds (potatoes). Chesapeake Bay's blue crabs are the finest anywhere, and Virginia salt-cured 'country-style' hams are served with biscuits (a buttery, scone-like baked good). In Philadelphia, you can gorge on 'Philly' cheesesteaks made with thin, sautéed beef and onions and melted cheese on a bun. And in Pennsylvania Dutch Country, stop by a farm restaurant for chicken pot pie, noodles and meatloaf-like scrapple.

Southern USA: BBQ, Biscuits & Gumbo

No region is prouder of its food culture than the South, which has a long history of mingling Anglo, French, African, Spanish and Native American foods in dishes such as slow-cooked barbecue, which has as many meaty and saucy variations as there are towns in the South. Southern fried chicken is crisp outside and moist inside. In Florida, dishes made with alligator, shrimp and conch incorporate hot chili peppers and tropical spices. Breakfasts are big, and treasured dessert recipes tend to produce big layer cakes or pies made with pecans, bananas and citrus. Light, fluffy hot biscuits are served well buttered, and grits (ground corn cooked to a porridge-like consistency) are a passion.

Louisiana's legendary cuisine is influenced by colonial French and Spanish cultures, Afro-Caribbean cooking and Choctaw traditions. Bayou-born Cajun food marries native spices such as sassafras and chili peppers with provincial French cooking. Famous dishes include gumbo, a roux-based stew of chicken and shellfish, or sausage and often okra; jambalaya, a rice-based dish with tomatoes, sausage and shrimp; and blackened catfish. Creole food is more urban and centered on New Orleans, where dishes such as shrimp rémoulade, crabmeat ravigote, crawfish étouffée and beignets are ubiquitous.

Great Plains & Great Lakes: Burgers, Bacon & Beer

Residents of the Great Plains and Great Lakes regions eat big and with plenty of gusto. Portions are huge – this is farm country, where people need sustenance to get their day's work done. So you might start off the day with eggs, bacon and toast; have a double cheeseburger and potato salad for lunch; and fork into steak and baked potatoes for dinner – all washed down with a cold brew, often one of the growing numbers of microbrews. Barbecue is very popular here, especially in Kansas City, St Louis and Chicago. Chicago is also an ethnically diverse culinary center, with some of the country's top restaurants. One of the best places to sample regional foods is at a county fair, which offers everything from bratwurst to fried dough to grilled corn on the cob. Elsewhere at diners and family restaurants, you'll taste the varied influences of Eastern European, Scandinavian, Latinx and Asian immigrants, especially in the cities.

The Southwest: Chili, Steak & Salsa

Two ethnic groups define Southwestern food culture: the Spanish and the Mexicans, who controlled territories from Texas to California until well into the 19th century. While there is little actual Spanish food today, the Spanish brought cattle to Mexico, which the Mexicans adapted to their own corn-and-chili-based gastronomy to make tacos, enchiladas, burritos, chimichangas and other dishes made of corn or flour pancakes filled with everything from chopped meat and poultry to beans. Don't leave New Mexico without trying a bowl of spicy green chili stew. Steaks and barbecue are always favorites on Southwestern menus, and beer is the drink of choice for dinner and a night out.

California: Farm-to-Table & Taquerias

Owing to its vastness and variety of microclimates, California is truly America's cornucopia for fruits and vegetables. The state's natural resources are overwhelming, with wild salmon, Dungeness crab and oysters from the ocean; robust produce year-round; and artisanal products such as cheese, bread, olive oil, wine and chocolate. Starting in the 1970s and '80s, star chefs such as Alice Waters and Wolfgang Puck pioneered 'California cuisine' by incorporating the best local ingredients into simple, yet delectable, preparations. The influx of Asian immigrants, especially after the Vietnam War, enriched the state's urban food cultures with Chinatowns, Koreatowns and Japantowns, along with huge enclaves of Mexican Americans who maintain their own culinary traditions across the state. Global fusion restaurants are another hallmark of California's cuisine. Don't miss the forearm-sized burritos in San Francisco's Mission District and fish tacos in San Diego.

Pacific Northwest: Salmon & Coffee Culture

The cuisine of the Pacific Northwest region draws on the traditions of the local tribes of Native Americans, whose diets traditionally centered on game, seafood – especially salmon – and foraged mushrooms, fruits and berries. Seattle spawned the modern international coffeehouse craze with Starbucks – though these days Portland gets more attention for its excellent coffee scene, with some of the country's best roasters.

Hawaii: Island Style

In the middle of the Pacific Ocean, Hawaii is rooted in a Polynesian food culture that takes full advantage of locally caught fish such as mahimahi, 'opakapaka, ono and ahi. Traditional luau celebrations include cooking kalua pig in an underground pit layered with hot stones and ti leaves. Hawaii's contemporary cuisine incorporates fresh, island-grown produce and borrows liberally from the islands' many Asian and European immigrant groups. This also happens to be the only state to grow coffee commercially; 100% Kona beans from the Big Island have the most gourmet cachet.

Food Experiences

Meals of a Lifetime

Alinea (p550) You'll have to be very lucky to score a ticket to this pillar of molecular gastronomy in Chicago.

Black's Barbecue (p707) Serves up some of America's best brisket, from an atmospheric location in Lockhart, Texas.

Bacchanal (p454) Wine, cheese, bread and a magically lit New Orleans garden are how memories are made.

Faidley's (p299) There are no frills or bay views at this Baltimore institution, just heavenly jumbo-lump crab cakes.

Peche Seafood Grill (☑504-522-1744; www. pecherestaurant.com; 800 Magazine St, Warehouse District; small plates $9-14, mains $14-27; ☺11am-10pm Sun-Thu, to 11pm Fri & Sat) Seafood cooked to perfection over a wood fire in the Warehouse District of New Orleans.

Rolf & Daughters (☑615-866-9897; www. rolfanddaughters.com; 700 Taylor St, Germantown; mains $15-26; ☺5:30-10pm; 🛜) Serves superb new Italian cooking in a buzzing space in Nashville.

French Laundry (p1005) It may cost you a month's wages, but this Northern California icon never fails to dazzle.

Salt (p764) Local, seasonal, organic and delicious dishes in Boulder.

Imperial (☑503-228-7222; www.imperialpdx. com; 410 SW Broadway; mains $11-45; ☺6:30am-10pm Mon-Thu, to 11pm Fri, 8am-11pm Sat, to 10pm Sun) Healthy meals in a warm Portland setting.

Grey Plume (p681) In Omaha; works seasonal magic with the produce and meats of the region.

Cheap Treats

Food trucks The variety of offerings is staggering in towns of all sizes.

Tacos A favorite all across the US. Some of the best are served from street carts and food trucks.

Green chili A Rockies classic, best when served atop a burger.

Doughnuts Look for gourmet varieties (pistachio, hibiscus, lemon ginger).

DANIEL GRILL / GETTY IMAGES ©

Maine lobster meal (p59)

Fried chicken With famed spots in the South, including Nashville's hot chicken culture and Willie Mae's (p454) in New Orleans.

Frozen custard Nothing else quite hits the spot on a hot day, especially if it's from Ted Drewes (p649) in St Louis.

Fried clams A cheap and filling snack available all along the eastern seaboard.

Beignets Fried dough topped with powdered sugar is a must-have when visiting New Orleans.

Half smokes A bigger, spicier version of the hot dog, this is a DC specialty.

Dare to Try

Bison short ribs Sometimes spotted in the Rockies; Yellowstone is a reliable place to find them.

Alligator A roadhouse special in some parts of the South.

Poke A Hawaiian specialty featuring cubed raw fish (often ahi tuna); it's spectacularly good.

Lobster ice cream You'll never go back to strawberry after trying this popular crustacean flavor at **Ben & Bill's Chocolate Emporium** (☑508-548-7878; www.benandbills.com; 209

Main St; cones $6; ☻9am-11pm Jun-Aug, shorter hours rest of year) out on Cape Cod.

Triple bypass burger At the Vortex (p413) in Atlanta you can try a stack of two diner-style patty melts with 18 slices of American cheese, 18 bacon strips and three fried eggs served between grilled cheese sandwiches for buns.

Pig-ear sandwich Served with panache since the 1930s at the **Big Apple Inn** (☎601-354-4549; 509 N Farish St; mains $2; ☻7:30am-9pm Tue-Fri, from 8am Sat) in Jackson, MS.

Dirty water dog It takes a special appetite to crave a hot dog that's been sitting in murky water all day in a NYC food cart.

Opening Hours & Reservations

Some restaurants don't take reservations. For those that do, it's wise to book ahead, especially on weekends. If you don't have reservations (or can't make them), plan to dine early (5pm) or late (9pm) to avoid lengthy waits.

Restaurants Casual places are usually open from about 11am onward; fancier restaurants are often only open from 5pm. Many kitchens close at 10pm.

Cafes and coffee shops Open all day (and sometimes at night).

Informal eateries Look for food trucks, farmers markets and other casual options (some bars also serve great food). A few chains – like Waffle House or Huddle House – are open 24 hours.

Habits & Customs

Outside of major cities, Americans tend to eat early at restaurants and at home, so don't be surprised to find a restaurant half full at noon or 5:30pm. In smaller towns, it may be hard to find anywhere to eat after 8:30pm or 9pm. Dinner parties for adults usually begin around 6:30pm or 7pm with cocktails, followed by a buffet or sit-down meal. If invited to dinner, be prompt: ideally, you should plan to arrive within 15 minutes of the designated time.

Americans are informal in their dining manners, although they will usually wait until everyone is served before eating. Many foods are eaten with the fingers, and an entire piece of bread may be buttered and eaten all at once. To the surprise of some foreign visitors, the sight of beer bottles on the dinner table is not uncommon.

Breakfast

Long billed by American nutritionists as 'the most important meal of the day,' morning meals in America are big business – no matter how many folks insist on skipping them. From a giant stack of buttermilk pancakes at a vintage diner to lavish Sunday brunches, Americans love their eggs and bacon, their waffles and hash browns, and their big glasses of freshly squeezed orange juice. Most of all, they love that seemingly inalienable American right: a steaming cup of morning coffee with unlimited refills.

Lunch

An American worker's lunch is typically a quick sandwich, burger or salad. The formal 'business lunch' is more common in big cities like New York, where food is not necessarily as important as the conversation.

While you may spot diners drinking a beer or a glass of wine with their lunch, long gone are the days when the 'three martini lunch' was socially acceptable. It was a phenomenon common enough in the mid-20th century to become a kind of catchphrase for indulgent business lunches, usually written off as a corporate, tax-deductible expense. The classic noontime

---

DOS & DON'TS

➡ Do tip: 15% to 20% of the total bill (pretax) is standard.

➡ It's customary to place your napkin on your lap, even before the meal is served.

➡ In general, try to avoid putting your elbows on the table.

➡ Wait until everyone is served to begin eating.

➡ In formal situations, diners customarily wait to eat until the host has lifted their fork.

➡ At home, some Americans say a prayer before meals; it's fine to sit quietly if you prefer not to participate.

beverage, in fact, is a far cry from a martini: iced tea or soft drinks (and yes, almost always with unlimited refills).

Dinner

In the evening, Americans settle in to a more substantial weeknight dinner, which, given the workload of so many two-career families, might be takeout (eg pizza or Chinese food) or prepackaged microwave meals. Desserts tend toward ice cream, pies and cakes. Some families still cook a traditional Sunday-night dinner, when relatives and friends gather for a big feast. Traditional dishes might include roast chicken with all the fixings (mashed potatoes, green beans and corn on the cob). In warmer months, many Americans like to fire up the barbecue to grill steaks, burgers and veggies, which are served alongside plenty of cold beer and wine.

Beer, Wine & Beyond

Americans have a staggering range of choices when it comes to beverages. A booming microbrewery industry has brought finely crafted beers to every corner of the country. The US wine industry continues to produce first-rate vintages – and it's not just California vineyards garnering all the awards. Meanwhile, coffee culture continues to prevail, with cafes and roasteries galore.

Beer

Beer is about as American as Chevrolet, football and apple pie. But despite their ubiquity, popular brands of American beer (eg Coors, Budweiser and Miller) have long been the subject of ridicule abroad due to their low alcohol content and 'light' taste. Regardless of what the critics say, sales aren't suffering – and with the meteoric rise of microbreweries and craft beer, even beer snobs admit that American beer has reinvented itself.

Craft & Local Beer

Microbrewery and craft-beer production is quickly rising, generating roughly $28 billion in retail sales in 2018. With around 7300 craft breweries across the USA, it's possible to 'drink local' all over the country – microbreweries are found everywhere from urban centers to small towns. According to the Brewers Association, Chicago, IL, is the current capital of the industry, with 167 craft breweries.

Thanks to this trend, beer aficionados sip and savor beer as they would wine, and some restaurants even have beer 'programs,' 'sommeliers' and cellars. Many brewpubs and restaurants host beer dinners, a chance to experience just how beers pair with different foods.

Wine

Americans are drinking more wine than ever: 2.95 gallons per person in 2018.

The US makes nearly 14% of the world's wine and is the third largest wine producer in the world (behind Italy and France, and just ahead of former #3, Spain). Though most of this wine is grown in California, wineries can now be found in almost every single state, and many American wines are winning prestigious international awards.

Due to higher production costs and taxes, as well as its status as a luxury item, wine isn't especially cheap in the US. But it's possible to procure a perfectly drinkable bottle of American wine at a liquor or wine shop for under $12.

Wine Regions

Today about 80% of US wine comes from California, though other regions are producing wines that have achieved international status. In particular, the wines of New York's Finger Lakes, Hudson Valley and Long Island are well worth sampling, as are the wines from both Washington and Oregon, especially pinot noirs and rieslings.

HAPPY HOURS

Gastropubs, microbreweries that serve meals, and even traditional restaurants with bar seating often host great-value happy hours. Sometime before the dinner rush (usually 3pm to 5pm or 4pm to 6pm), you can score deals on appetizers and other light fare. Add to this drink specials (think half-priced cocktails or $5 glasses of wine), and you have the makings for a great start to the night.

LOW- AND NO-ALCOHOL FUN

After a decade or so of boozy cocktails hogging the drinking spotlight, the pendulum has shifted. Health-conscious millennials are moving toward low- and even no-alcohol options for nights out, and bartenders are responding. Look for 'no-proof,' 'spirit-free' or 'NA' designations on the menu to find flavorful virgin cocktails mixed with local botanicals, cannabidiol (CBD) and/or healthy ingredients like acai or pomegranate juice. So-called 'session cocktails' – with an ABV comparable to beer – are also having a moment. You'll see spritzes and cans of spiked seltzer lining many a bar at happy hour.

Without a doubt, the country's hotbed of wine tourism is in Northern California, just outside of the Bay Area in the Napa and Sonoma Valleys. As other areas, from Oregon's Willamette Valley to Texas' Hill Country, have evolved as wine regions, they have spawned an entire industry of B&B tourism that seems to go hand in hand with the quest to find the perfect pinot noir.

So, what are the best American wines? The most popular white varietals made in the US are chardonnay and sauvignon blanc; best-selling reds include cabernet sauvignon, merlot, pinot noir and zinfandel.

The Hard Stuff

While whiskey and bourbon are the most popular American exports, rye, gin and vodka are also crafted in the USA. Bourbon, made from corn, is the only native spirit and traditionally made in Kentucky – just follow the Bourbon Trail. Good ole Jack Daniels remains the most well-known brand of American whiskey around the world, and its Tennessee distillery is the oldest continually operating US distillery, going strong since 1870.

In the 2010s, America's long history of distilling launched a modern renaissance, much as wine and craft brewing did in preceding decades. By 2018, there were more than 2800 craft distillers in the USA – an increase of 107% since 2013. California and New York lead the charge, with 148 and 123 respectively, but states like North Carolina (57) and Colorado (80) are contributing to the boom. Many of these distillers use local ingredients, from grains to botanicals, to inspire their spirits.

It's a fitting legacy for the country that invented the cocktail. Born in New Orleans, the first cocktail was the Sazerac – a mix of rye whiskey or brandy, simple syrup, bitters and a dash of absinthe (before it was banned in 1912, that is). American cocktails created at bars in the late 19th and early 20th centuries include such long-standing classics as the martini, the Manhattan and the old-fashioned.

Non-Alcoholic Drinks

Tap water in the USA is safe to drink, though its taste varies depending on the region and city. Most nonalcoholic drinks are quite sugary and served over ice, from Southern-style iced 'sweet tea' and lemonade to quintessential American soft drinks such as Coca-Cola, Pepsi and Dr Pepper, along with retro and nouveau soft-drinks, often made with cane sugar instead of corn syrup.

Interestingly, carbonated nonalcoholic beverages have different nicknames depending on where you order them. In many parts of the South, a 'Coke' means any kind of soda, so you may have to specify which kind you mean; for example, if you say 'I'll have a Coke,' the waiter might ask, 'Which kind?'. Around the Great Lakes, northern Great Plains and Pacific Northwest, soda is called 'pop.' On the East Coast and elsewhere, it's called 'soda.' Go figure...

Coffee Addiction

Americans may kick back with beer and unwind with wine, but the country runs on caffeine. The coffee craze has only intensified in the last 30 years, ever since cafe culture exploded in urban centers and spread throughout the country.

Blame it on Starbucks. The world's biggest coffee chain was born amid the Northwest's progressive coffee culture in 1971, when Starbucks opened its first location across from Pike Place Market in Seattle. The idea, to offer a variety of roasted beans from around the world in a comfortable cafe, helped start filling the American coffee mug with relatively more refined, complicated (and expensive) drinks. By the early 1990s, specialty coffeehouses began springing up across the country.

While many coffee chains only have room for a few chairs and a takeout counter, independent shops support a coffeehouse culture that encourages lingering, with free wi-fi, comfortable seating, good snacks and light fare. At the most high-level cafes, experienced baristas will happily banter about the origins of any roast and will share their ideas about bean grinds and more.

Tipping

In the USA, where restaurants and bars often pay the legal minimum wage (or less), servers rely on tips for their livelihood. A good rule: tip at least a dollar per drink (more for pricey cocktails), or roughly 15% to 20% of the total bill.

DUIs

DUI (driving under the influence) is taken very seriously in the USA. Designating a sober driver who doesn't drink has become a widespread practice among groups of friends consuming alcohol at restaurants, bars, nightclubs and parties.

Food Glossary

barbecue – a technique of slow-smoking spice-rubbed and basted meat over a grill

beignet – New Orleans doughnut-like fritter dusted with powdered sugar

biscuit – flaky yeast-free roll served in the South

blintz – Jewish pancake stuffed with various fillings such as jam, cheese or potatoes

BLT – bacon, lettuce and tomato sandwich

blue plate – special of the day in a diner or luncheonette

Boston baked beans – beans cooked with molasses and bacon in a casserole

Buffalo wings – deep-fried chicken wings glazed with a buttery hot sauce and served with blue-cheese dressing; originated in Buffalo, NY

burrito – Mexican American flour tortilla wrapped around beans, meat, salsa and rice

California roll – fusion sushi made with avocado, crabmeat and cucumber wrapped in vinegared rice and *nori* (dried seaweed)

chili – hearty meat stew spiced with ground chilies, vegetables and beans; also called chili con carne

clam chowder – potato-based soup full of clams, vegetables and sometimes bacon, thickened with milk

club sandwich – three-layered sandwich with chicken or turkey, bacon, lettuce and tomato

corned beef – salt-cured or brined beef, traditionally served with cabbage on St Patrick's Day (March 17)

crab cake – crabmeat bound with breadcrumbs and eggs, then fried

eggs Benedict – poached eggs, ham and hollandaise sauce on top of English muffins

French toast – egg-dipped fried bread served with maple syrup

grits – white cornmeal porridge; a Southern breakfast or side dish

guacamole – mashed avocado dip with lime juice, onions, chilies and cilantro, served with tortilla chips

hash browns – shredded pan-fried potatoes

huevos rancheros – Mexican breakfast of corn tortillas topped with fried eggs and salsa

jambalaya – Louisiana stew of rice, ham, sausage, shrimp and seasonings

lobster roll – lobster meat mixed with mayonnaise and seasonings, and served in a toasted frankfurter bun

lox – Jewish version of brine-cured salmon

nachos – Mexican American fried tortilla chips often topped with cheese, ground beef, jalapeño peppers, salsa and sour cream

pastrami – Jewish American brined brisket beef that is smoked and steamed

Reuben sandwich – sandwich of corned beef, Swiss cheese and sauerkraut on rye bread

smoothie – cold, thick drink made with pureed fruit, ice and sometimes yogurt

stone crab – Floribbean crab, the claws of which are eaten with melted butter or mustard-mayonnaise sauce

surf 'n' turf – combination plate of seafood (often lobster) and steak

wrap – tortilla or pita bread stuffed with a variety of fillings

Plan Your Trip
Family Travel

From coast to coast, you'll find superb attractions for all ages: bucket-and-spade fun at the beach, amusement parks, natural history exhibits, camping adventures, hikes in wilderness reserves, leisurely bike rides and plenty of other activities likely to wow young ones.

Keeping Costs Down

Accommodations
In motels and hotels, children under 17 or 18 years old are usually free when sharing a room with their parents. The many campgrounds in the Eastern USA are a fun and affordable way for families to see the country. Homesharing websites are also widely available in the USA and popular with families.

Transport
Most public transportation offers reduced fares for children. Children under the age of two can fly for free. Driving is the cheapest way to travel and often the easiest for families.

Eating
Many restaurants have children's menus with significantly lower prices – always inquire about options. For moderately healthy, affordable meals on the go, hit up the grocery store for some Uncrustables (frozen peanut butter sandwiches) and fruit.

Activities
Most sites and museums offer free admission for children five and under, and reduced admission for children under 12.

Region by Region

New York, New Jersey & Pennsylvania

This region has tons of beaches, bike paths and outdoor activities in stunning natural areas such as Delaware Water Gap (p161) and the Catskills. Kids will love the all-ages fun of the Silverball Museum Arcade (p163), the interactive displays at the Museum of the American Revolution (p168), and the raw energy of New York City.

New England

Roadside stands pepper rural New England, offering kid-friendly fare like fish sticks, burgers and ice cream. Also family-friendly are the many beaches, from the calm waters of Martha's Vineyard (p216) to the superb stretch of shore at Ogunquit Beach (p255). Plus there are museums aplenty for rainy days and Acadia National Park (p261) for rugged adventures.

Washington DC & the Capitol Region

The Mid-Atlantic features fun distractions for all ages: bucket-and-spade adventures on Delaware beaches, the massive National Aquarium (p295) in Baltimore, historic sites like Mount Vernon (p314), and white-water thrills on the New River Gorge National River. The highlight, of course, is DC, with its miles of museums and monuments.

The South

The Great Smoky Mountains (p366) are a wonderful family destination, as are nearby theme parks Anakeesta (p397) and Dollywood (p397). Atlanta holds the child-driven Center for Puppetry Arts (p407), Charlotte has fun simulators at the NASCAR Hall of Fame (p359), Huntsville hosts the US Space & Rocket Center (p427) and vibrant New Orleans is fabulous for music-minded families.

Florida

From Walt Disney World ® (p518) to Everglades National Park (p490), to the calm waters and white beaches of the Panhandle (p523) – the Sunshine State makes it so easy for families to have a good time that many return year after sandy year.

Great Lakes

Chicago has ferocious dinosaurs at the Field Museum (p535), and lively Navy Pier; (p535) Indianapolis features the world's largest kids' museum (p565); and outside of Detroit, Greenfield Village (p591) and the Henry Ford Museum (p591) hold hours of entertainment. Skiing in Minnesota, ice cream in Wisconsin's Door County or biking across Mackinac Island are also good options.

Great Plains

Family-friendly attractions like Mt Rushmore (p676) and the Gateway Arch (p645) spool out along the wide, flat stretch of the Great Plains. Kansas City barbecue and fried treats at the region's myriad state fairs are also sure to please.

Texas

Locals love little cowpokes, so expect a warm welcome here. San Antonio, Austin, Dallas and Houston all have children's museums, public parks and many other attractions. Don't miss the Houston Museum of Natural Science (p717).

Rocky Mountains

The Rocky Mountain states have plenty to offer – plan carefully to conquer the long distances between sites. Hit up museums and water parks in Denver, or family ski resorts just about anywhere. Conquer ziplines and ride horses in the Rockies. Volcano-loving kids will enjoy Craters of the Moon National Monument & Preserve (p814). Go looking for grizzlies, wolves, bison and elk in Yellowstone National Park (p792), and don't miss the cliff houses in Mesa Verde.

Southwest

This region is a goldmine for adventurous families with older kids. Hike into the Grand Canyon (p851), splash in Oak Creek and ponder the saguaro cacti outside Tucson. Water parks, dude ranches and ghost towns should also keep kids entertained. Las Vegas (p820) has a surprising range of child-friendly activities and entertainment.

California

California seems custom-made for kids. See celebrity handprints in Hollywood, ogle the La Brea tar pits (p923), and hit the beach in Santa Monica or San Diego. The Warner Bros Studio Tour (p927) will appeal to lovers of everything from Harry Potter to Batman, while Universal Studios Hollywood (p939) is like a stroll through every movie they've ever watched. And then, of course, there's Disneyland (p941).

Pacific Northwest

From the sun, sand and surf on the coast to the snow-covered slopes further inland, the Pacific Northwest is full of child-oriented museums and amusement parks. National and state parks often organize family-friendly activities, and whale-watching can be a big hit. There are also plenty of playgrounds and skateboard parks in the region. Portland (p1059) and Seattle (p1031) are particular kid-friendly highlights.

Alaska

Alaska has outdoor adventures and attractions to intrigue the entire family – whether you're a kid or a parent. Hike the **Flattop Mountain Trail** in Anchorage or take in one of the city's more than 40 parks.

Hawaii

In Hawaii, kids can play on sandy beaches galore, snorkel amid colorful tropical fish in Hanauma Bay (p1113) and watch lava flow at Hawai'i Volcanoes National Park (p1119). Then get them out of the sun for a spell by visiting museums, aquariums and historical attractions. Don't forget a healthy dose of shave ice.

Good to Know

Look out for the c icon for family-friendly suggestions throughout this guide.

Accommodations Cots and roll-way beds are usually available in hotels and resorts. Children are often not welcome at smaller B&Bs and inns.

Baby items Baby food, formula and disposable diapers (nappies) are available in supermarkets and pharmacies (Walgreens, CVS) across the country.

Breastfeeding All large airports are required to have lactation rooms by 2020. Breastfeeding in public is legal and generally accepted, although many American women use nursing covers.

Changing facilities Many public toilets have a baby-changing table, and gender-neutral 'family' facilities appear in airports.

Driving Seat belts or age-appropriate child safety seats are compulsory. Most rental car companies offer car-seat rentals, but be sure to inquire about availability at the time of booking.

Eating out High chairs or booster seats are usually available, but inquire ahead of time. At upscale restaurants, children are typically tolerated with more grace early in the evening.

Toilets If traveling by car, rest areas are your best bets for bathroom breaks, although a gas station or fast-food restaurant will do in a pinch.

Travel documentation Single parents or guardians traveling with anyone under 18 should carry proof of legal custody or a notarized letter from the non-accompanying parent(s) authorizing the trip. This isn't required, but it can help avoid potential problems entering the USA.

Useful Resources

Family Travel Files (www.thefamilytravelfiles.com) Ready-made vacation ideas, destination profiles and travel tips.

Lonely Planet Kids (www.lonelyplanetkids.com) Loads of activities and great family travel blog content.

My Family Travel Map: North America (shop.lonelyplanet.com) Unfolds into a colorful and detailed poster for kids to personalize with stickers to mark their family's travels. Ages five to eight.

Parents Magazine (www.parents.com) Monthly magazine that includes travel tips and advice.

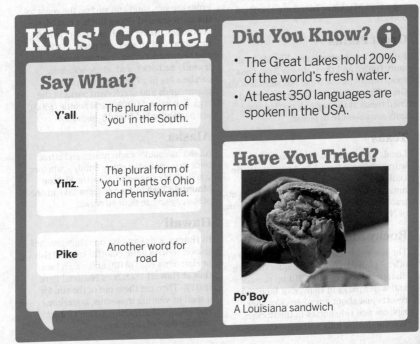

Kids' Corner

Say What?

Y'all.	The plural form of 'you' in the South.
Yinz.	The plural form of 'you' in parts of Ohio and Pennsylvania.
Pike	Another word for road

Did You Know? ℹ

- The Great Lakes hold 20% of the world's fresh water.
- At least 350 languages are spoken in the USA.

Have You Tried?

Po'Boy
A Louisiana sandwich

Regions at a Glance

The USA's crazy quilt of cultures and landscapes creates an enthralling variety of regional identities. Embrace the urban excitement of New York, Chicago or San Francisco; the trendsetting buzz of Austin or Portland; the Southern charm of Charleston; or the picturesque village life of New England. Set your sights on Hawaii's volcanoes, Alaska's glaciated grandeur, the Great Plains' wide-open spaces, the Southwest's red-rock majesty or the Northwest's dazzling greenery. Surf California's legendary beaches, scale the Rockies' soaring peaks or canoe the Great Lakes' birch-lined shores.

Each region offers its own iconic experiences: Maine lobster, Texas barbecue, Memphis blues, California wine. Whichever speaks to you, dive on in; and if you can't manage the multimonth 'Great American Road Trip,' don't despair. Explore a region or two now – and save the rest for next time!

New York, New Jersey & Pennsylvania

Arts
History
Outdoors

Culture Spot
Home to the Met, the Museum of Modern Art and Broadway – and that's just NYC. Buffalo, Philadelphia and Pittsburgh also have a share of world-renowned cultural institutions.

A Living Past
From Gilded Age mansions in the Hudson Valley to Independence National Historic Park in Philadelphia and sites dedicated to formative moments in the nation's founding, the region gives an interactive education.

Wild Outdoors
The outdoors lurks beyond the city's gaze, with hiking in the Adirondack wilderness and Catskills, rafting down the Delaware River, sailing in the Atlantic and frolics along the Jersey Shore and Hamptons.

p74

New England

Seafood
History
Scenery

Land of Lobsters
New England is justifiably famous for its fresh seafood. The coast is peppered with seaside restaurants where you can feast on oysters, lobster and clam chowder as you watch the dayboats haul in their catch.

Legends of the Past
From the Native Americans to the Pilgrims' landing, to Paul Revere's revolutionary ride and Boston's Black Heritage Trail, New England is home to American history.

Fall Foliage
The brilliance of fall in these parts is legendary. Changing leaves put on a fiery display all around New England, from the Litchfield Hills in Connecticut all the way up to the White Mountains in New Hampshire and Maine.

p184

Washington, DC & the Capital Region

Arts
History
Food

Top-Notch Arts

Washington has a superb collection of museums and galleries. You'll also find down-home mountain music on Virginia's Crooked Road, edgy art in Baltimore and memorable museums in Richmond.

Early America

For historical lore, Jamestown, Williamsburg and Yorktown offer windows into Colonial America, while Civil War battlefields litter Virginia. There are fascinating presidential estates such as Mount Vernon and Monticello.

Culinary Feasts

Maryland blue crabs, oysters and seafood platters; international fare in DC; and farm-to-table dining in Baltimore, Charlottesville and Rehoboth.

p264

The South

Food
Music
Charm

Southern Cookin'

Slow-cooked barbecue, fried catfish, butter-smothered biscuits, cornbread, grits and spicy Cajun-Creole dishes – the South knows how to fill up a plate.

Memorable Music

Nowhere on earth has a soundtrack as influential as the South. Head to music hot spots for the authentic experience: country in Nashville, blues in Memphis, hip-hop in Atlanta and big-band jazz in New Orleans.

Pretty Cities

Picture-book towns such as Charleston and Savannah have long captivated visitors with their historic tree-lined streets and antebellum architecture. Other charmers include Chapel Hill, Oxford, Chattanooga and Natchez.

p344

Florida

History
Wildlife
Beaches

Unexpected Historical Bounty

Florida has a complicated soul: the home of Miami's colorful art deco district and Little Havana also holds some of the nation's most underrated historical spots, including St Augustine and the rich island heritage of Key West.

Whales, Birds & Gators

Immerse yourself in aquatic life on a snorkeling or diving trip. For bigger beasts, go on a whale-watching cruise or spy alligators – along with eagles, manatees and more – in the Everglades.

Stretches of Sand

You'll find sandy shores from steamy South Beach to upscale Palm Beach, island allure on Sanibel and Captiva, and Panhandle rowdiness in Pensacola.

p464

Great Lakes

Food
Music
Attractions

Heartland Cuisine

Farms, orchards and breweries satisfy the palate, from James Beard Award–winning restaurants in Chicago and Minneapolis to fresh-from-the-dairy milkshakes.

Rock & Roll

Home to the Rock and Roll Hall of Fame, blowout fests like Lollapalooza and Summerfest, a cacophony of thrashing clubs and the blues bastion of Chicago, the Great Lakes region knows how to turn up the volume.

Quirky Sights

A big ball of twine, a mustard museum, a cow-doo throwing contest: these gems of Americana appear along the region's back roads and in the backyards of passionate folks with imagination to spare.

p528

Great Plains

Scenery
Geology
Nightlife

The Open Road

Beneath big open skies, a two-lane highway passes sun-lit fields, rolling river valleys and dramatic peaks on its journey to the horizon – all par for the course (along with oddball museums and cozy cafes) on the 'Great American Road Trip.'

Nature Unbound

The Badlands are b-a-a-a-d in every good sense. These geologic wonders are matched by the wildlife-filled beauty of the Black Hills and Theodore Roosevelt National Park.

City Soundtracks

In the countryside, streets roll up at sunset, but in St Louis and Kansas City, that's when the fun begins. Legendary jazz, blues and rock play in clubs and bars, big and small.

p641

Texas

Food
Live Music
Outdoors

BBQ Delight

Meat lovers, you've died and gone to heaven (vegetarians, you're somewhere else). Some of the best barbecue on earth is served up in Lockhart near Austin, although you can dig in to brisket, ribs and sausage all across the state.

Tap to the Beat

Austin has proclaimed itself (and no one's arguing) the 'Live Music Capital of the World.' Two-step to live bands on worn wooden floors at honky-tonks and dance halls all around the state.

Big-Sky Scenery

Canyons, mountains and hot springs set the scene for memorable outings in Texas. Go rafting on the Big Bend River or get a beach fix along the pretty southern Gulf Coast.

p697

Rocky Mountains

Outdoors
Culture
Landscapes

Mountain High

Skiing, hiking and boating make the Rockies a playground for adrenaline junkies, with hundreds of races and group rides and an incredible infrastructure of parks, trails and cabins.

Old Meets New

Once a people of Stetsons and prairie dresses, today's Rocky folk are more often spotted in lycra, mountain bike nearby, sipping a microbrew or latte at a cafe. Hard playing and slow living still rule.

Perfect Views

The snow-covered Rocky Mountains are pure majesty. With chiseled peaks, clear rivers and red-rock contours, the Rockies contain some of the world's most famous parks and endless clean mountain air.

p748

Southwest

Scenery
Food
Native Culture

Natural Beauty

The jaw-dropping Grand Canyon, the dramatic Monument Valley, the crimson arches of Moab and the fiery buttes of Sedona – these are just a few of the many geographic wonders here.

Good Eats

Try chile-smothered chicken enchiladas in New Mexico, a messy Sonoran hotdog in Tucson or grilled trout in Utah. In Vegas, stretch your pants and your budget at one of the extravagant buffets, or spring for an epicurean experience on the Strip.

Indigenous Culture

Visiting the Hopi and Navajo Nations, or New Mexico Pueblos, is a fine introduction to America's first inhabitants. This is your best bet for appreciating, and purchasing, crafts made by Native American people.

p816

California

Beaches
Adventure
Food

Sunny Shores

With more than 800 miles of coast, California rules the sands: rugged, pristine beaches in the north and people-packed beauties in the south, with surfing, sea kayaking and beach walking all along the coast.

Get Active

Ride the snow-covered slopes, raft on white-water rivers, kayak beside coastal islands, hike past waterfalls and climb boulders in the desert. The only problem is finding enough time to do it all.

California Cooking

Fertile fields, talented chefs and an appetite for innovation make California a major culinary destination. Browse the local food markets, sample pinot and chardonnay beside lush vineyards and dine on farm-to-table fare.

p913

Pacific Northwest

Food & Wine
Cycling
National Parks

Culinary Bounty

In Portland and Seattle, chefs combine fish caught in local waters with vegetables harvested in the Eden-like valleys surrounding the Columbia River. Washington's wine is second only to California's.

Pedal Power

Bicycle on paved, rolling roads in the tranquil San Juan Islands, cruise the bluff-dotted Oregon coast along Hwy 101 or pedal the streets of Portland, a city that embraces two-wheeled travel.

Vast Nature

The Northwest has four national parks: three Teddy Roosevelt–era classics (Olympic, Mt Rainier and Crater Lake), each bequeathed with historic lodges; and a wilder addition, the North Cascades.

p1027

Alaska

Wildlife
Glaciers
Outdoors

Creatures Great & Small

The sight of breaching whales and foraging bears in Southeast Alaska is unforgettable. Denali National Park is home to caribou, Dall sheep, moose and Alaska's famous grizzly.

Icy Adventures

If you want to explore glaciers in the USA, Alaska is the place. Glacier Bay National Park is the crown jewel for the cruise ships and a favorite for kayakers looking for an icy wilderness.

Hiking

Alaska offers some of the rawest hiking experiences in North America, from following in the footsteps of Klondike stampeders on the Chilkoot Trail, to bushwhacking your way across pathless tundra in Denali National Park.

p1085

Hawaii

Beaches
Adventure
Scenery

Tropical Shores

There's great sunning and people-watching on Waikiki (among dozens of other spots), stunning black-sand beaches on the Kona Coast and world-class surfing all over Hawaii.

Outdoor Highs

Trek through rainforest, kayak the Na Pali Coast, go ziplining on the four biggest islands and float eye-to-eye with aquatic life in marvelous Hanauma Bay.

Unrivaled Landscapes

Hawaii has so many head-turners: volcanoes, ancient rainforests, picturesque waterfalls, cliff-top vistas and jungle-lined valleys – not to mention the sparkling seas surrounding the islands.

p1105

On the Road

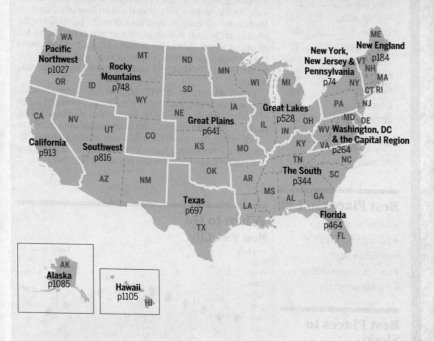

New York, New Jersey & Pennsylvania

Why Go?

Where else could you visit an Amish family's farm, camp on a mountaintop, read the Declaration of Independence and view New York, New York from the 86th floor of an art-deco landmark – all in a few days? Even though this corner of the country is the most densely populated part of the US, it's full of places where jaded city dwellers escape to seek simple lives, where artists retreat for inspiration, and where pretty houses line main streets in small towns set amid stunning scenery.

Urban adventures in NYC, historic and lively Philadelphia and river-rich Pittsburgh are a must. Miles and miles of glorious beaches are within reach, from glamorous Long Island to the Jersey Shore – the latter ranges from stately to kitsch, while the mountain wilderness of the Adirondacks reaches skyward just a day's drive north of NYC, a journey that perfectly encapsulates this region's heady character.

Best Places to Eat

→ Totto Ramen (p116)

→ Smorgasburg (p120)

→ Morimoto (p175)

→ Lobster House (p166)

→ Bar Marco (p182)

Best Places to Sleep

→ Yotel (p107)

→ Scribner's Catskill Lodge (p148)

→ White Pine Camp (p153)

→ Priory Hotel (p181)

→ Asbury Hotel (p162)

When to Go
New York City

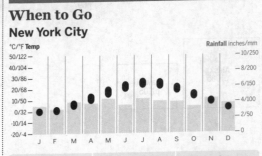

Feb Winter-sports buffs head to the mountains of the Adirondacks, Catskills and Poconos.

Late May–early Sep Memorial Day through Labor Day is for beaches from Montauk to Cape May.

Oct–Nov Autumn in NYC brings cool temps, fruit harvests, the marathon and gearing up for holiday season.

NEW YORK CITY

Epicenter of the arts. Architectural darling. Dining and shopping capital. Trendsetter. New York City wears many crowns, and spreads an irresistible feast for all.

Sights

New York City has a fabled spread of attractions, with dozens of world-class sites sprinkled across the urban landscape. If you want to tick off the marquee attractions, Midtown is a fine place to start. This is where you'll find iconic buildings with panoramic roof decks (Empire State Building, Rockefeller Center), hallowed architecture (Chrysler Building, St Patrick's Cathedral, Grand Central Station) and the city's best modern-art museum (MoMA).

Of course, if it's art you're after, then you could spend days exploring the fabled galleries of the Upper East Side – aka the 'Museum Mile'. The Met, the Met Breuer and the Guggenheim are just the beginning. The UES also makes a fine gateway to Central Park.

Downtown there are plenty of highlights, though with less density. Chelsea and the Meatpacking District have some stars (the Whitney, the High Line, Chelsea Market), as does Lower Manhattan (notably the ferries to the Statue of Liberty and Ellis Island).

Financial District & Lower Manhattan

★Statue of Liberty MONUMENT

(Map p78; ☎212-363-3200, tickets 877-523-9849; www.nps.gov/stli; Liberty Island; adult/child incl Ellis Island $18.50/9, incl crown $21.50/12; 🕒8:30am-5:30pm, hours vary by season; ⛴to Liberty Island, [S]1 to South Ferry, 4/5 to Bowling Green, then ferry) Reserve your tickets online well in advance (up to six months ahead) to access Lady Liberty's crown for breathtaking city and harbor views. If you miss out on crown tickets, you may have better luck with tickets for the pedestal, which also offers commanding views. If you don't score either, don't fret: all ferry tickets to Liberty Island offer basic access to the grounds, including **guided ranger tours** or self-guided audio tours. Book tickets at www.statuecruises.com to avoid long queues.

Conceived as early as 1865 by French intellectual Édouard Laboulaye as a monument to the republican principles shared by France and the USA, the Statue of Liberty is still a symbol of the ideals of opportunity and freedom. French sculptor Frédéric-Auguste Bartholdi traveled to New York in 1871 to select the site, then spent more than 10 years in Paris designing and making the 151ft-tall figure known in full as *Liberty Enlightening the World*. It was then shipped to New York, erected on a small island in the harbor (then known as Bedloe's Island) and unveiled in 1886. Structurally, it consists of an iron skeleton (designed by Gustave Eiffel) with a copper skin attached to it by stiff but flexible metal bars.

The 146-stair slog up to the statue's crown is arduous and should not be undertaken by anyone with significant health conditions that might impair their ability to complete the climb. Access to the torch has been prohibited since 1916.

Liberty Island is usually visited in conjunction with nearby Ellis Island. **Ferries** (Map p80; ☎877-523-9849; www.statuecruises.com; Battery Park, Lower Manhattan; adult/child from $18.50/9; 🕒departures 8:30am-5pm, shorter hours winter; [S]4/5 to Bowling Green, R/W to Whitehall St, 1 to South Ferry) leave from Battery Park; South Ferry and Bowling Green are the closest subway stations. (Ferry tickets include admission to both sights.)

★Ellis Island LANDMARK

(Map p78; ☎212-363-3200, tickets 877-523-9849; www.nps.gov/elis; Ellis Island; ferry incl Liberty Island adult/child $18.50/9; 🕒8:30am-6pm, hours vary by season; ⛴to Ellis Island, [S]1 to South Ferry, 4/5 to Bowling Green, then ferry) Ellis Island is America's most famous and historically important gateway. Between 1892 and 1924 more than 12 million immigrants passed through this processing station; more than 100 million current Americans are their descendants. Today, the island's **Immigration Museum** delivers a poignant tribute to the immigrant experience: narratives from historians, immigrants themselves and other sources animate a fascinating collection of personal objects, official documents, photographs and film footage. Purchase your tickets online in advance (at www.statuecruises.com) to avoid soul-crushingly long queues.

★One World Observatory VIEWPOINT

(Map p80; ☎212-602-4000; www.oneworldobservatory.com; 285 Fulton St, cnr West & Vesey Sts, Lower Manhattan; adult/child $35/29; 🕒9am-9pm Sep-Apr, from 8am May-Aug; [S]E to World Trade Center, 2/3 to Park Pl, A/C, J/Z, 4/5 to Fulton St, R/W to Cortlandt St) Spanning levels 100 to 102 of the tallest building in the Western Hemisphere, One World Observatory offers dazzling panoramic views from its sky-high perch. On a clear day you'll be able to see all

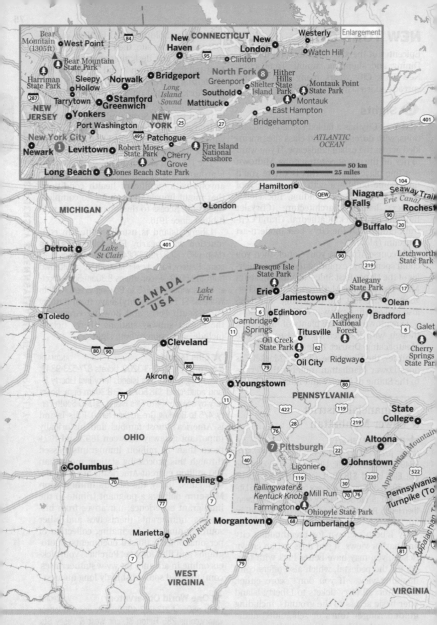

New York, New Jersey & Pennsylvania Highlights

1 **New York City** (p75)
Diving into a kaleidoscope of world-class sights and international cultures in this great cosmopolis.

2 **Jersey Shore** (p162)
Enjoying the kitsch, kettle corn, coastline and calm.

3 **Philadelphia** (p167)
Exploring colonial American history and quirky local flavor.

4 **Catskills** (p146) Hiking the densely forested paths.

5 **Adirondacks** (p151)
Paddling a canoe in the shadow of majestic mountains.

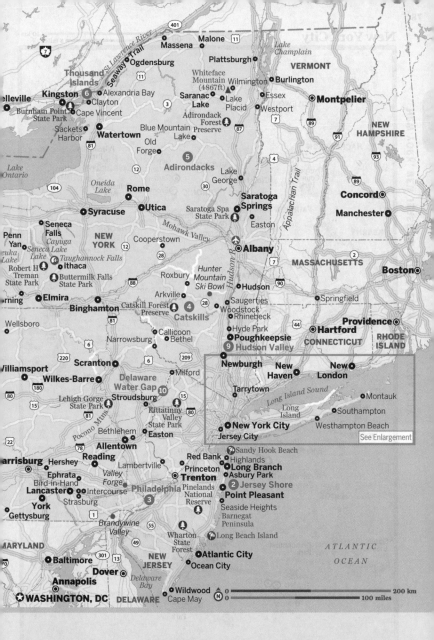

6 Thousand Islands (p155) Camping along the shores of the St Lawrence River.

7 Pittsburgh (p180) Admiring great modern art in an old industry town.

8 North Fork (p141) Tippling the whites and reds of Long Island.

9 Hudson Valley (p143) Savoring local cuisine, contemporary art and historic houses.

10 Delaware Water Gap (p161) Floating gently past bucolic scenery (or whitewater rafting after a wet spring).

New York City

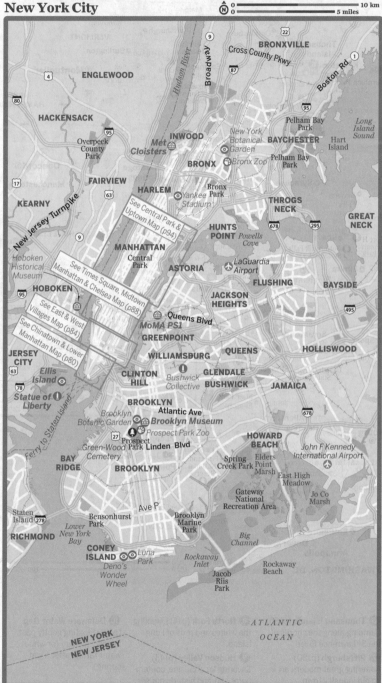

N

0 ——— 10 km
0 ——— 5 miles

BRONXVILLE
Cross County Pkwy
Boston Rd
ENGLEWOOD
Broadway
Hudson River
HACKENSACK
Overpeck County Park
Pelham Bay Park
Long Island Sound
Hart Island
INWOOD
Met Cloisters
New York Botanical Garden
BAYCHESTER
Bronx Zoo
Pelham Bay Park
BRONX
FAIRVIEW
HARLEM
Bronx Park
THROGS NECK
Yankee Stadium
KEARNY
New Jersey Turnpike
HUNTS POINT
Powells Cove
GREAT NECK
MANHATTAN
Central Park
ASTORIA
See Central Park & Uptown Map (p94)
Hoboken Historical Museum
LaGuardia Airport
FLUSHING
BAYSIDE
See Times Square, Midtown Manhattan & Chelsea Map (p88)
HOBOKEN
JACKSON HEIGHTS
Queens Blvd
See East & West Villages Map (p84)
MoMA PS1
GREENPOINT
QUEENS
HOLLISWOOD
JERSEY CITY
See Chinatown & Lower Manhattan Map (p80)
WILLIAMSBURG
GLENDALE
Ellis Island
CLINTON HILL
Bushwick Collective
BUSHWICK
JAMAICA
Statue of Liberty
BROOKLYN
Atlantic Ave
Brooklyn Museum
Ferry to Staten Island
Brooklyn Botanic Garden
Prospect Park Zoo
HOWARD BEACH
John F Kennedy International Airport
Green-Wood Cemetery
Prospect Park
Linden Blvd
BAY RIDGE
Spring Creek Park
Elders Point Marsh
East High Meadow
Staten Island
BROOKLYN
Jo Co Marsh
RICHMOND
Lower New York Bay
Bensonhurst Park
Ave P
Brooklyn Marine Park
Gateway National Recreation Area
Big Channel
CONEY ISLAND
Luna Park
Rockaway Inlet
Deno's Wonder Wheel
Rockaway Beach
Jacob Riis Park
ATLANTIC OCEAN
NEW YORK
NEW JERSEY

five boroughs and some surrounding states, revealed after an introductory video abruptly disappears to allow the dazzling view in through immense picture windows. Not surprisingly, it's a hugely popular attraction. Purchase tickets online in advance, choosing the date and time of your visit.

★National September 11 Memorial MONUMENT

(Map p80; www.911memorial.org; 180 Greenwich St, Lower Manhattan; ⏲7:30am-9pm; [S] E to World Trade Center, 2/3 to Park Pl, R/W to Cortlandt St) [FREE] The focal point of the National September 11 Memorial is **Reflecting Absence**, two imposing reflecting pools that occupy the actual footprints of the ill-fated Twin Towers. From their rim, a steady cascade of water pours 30ft down toward a central void. Bronze panels frame the pools, inscribed with the names of the nearly 3000 people who died in the terrorist attacks of September 11, 2001, and in the World Trade Center car bombing on February 26, 1993.

★National September 11 Memorial Museum MUSEUM

(Map p80; ☎212-312-8800; www.911memorial.org/museum; 180 Greenwich St, Lower Manhattan; memorial free, museum adult/child $26/15, 5-8pm Tue free; ⏲9am-8pm Sun-Thu, to 9pm Fri & Sat, last entry 2hr before close; [S] E to World Trade Center, 2/3 to Park Pl, R/W to Cortlandt St) Just beyond the reflective pools of the September 11 Memorial is the National September 11 Memorial Museum, incorporating part of the site and the few remnants of the towers. Architecturally intriguing and deeply moving, its collection of artifacts, video, photographs and audio create a dignified, reflective exploration of the day of the tragedy, the events that preceded it (including the World Trade Center car bombing of 1993), and the stories of grief, resilience and hope that followed.

Trinity Church CHURCH

(Map p80; ☎212-602-0800; www.trinitywallstreet.org; 75 Broadway, at Wall St, Lower Manhattan; ⏲7am-6pm, churchyard closes 6pm summer, dusk in winter; [S] 1, R/W to Rector St, 2/3, 4/5 to Wall St) New York City's tallest building upon consecration in 1846, Trinity Church features a 280ft-high bell tower and a richly colored stained-glass window over the altar. Famous residents of its serene cemetery include Founding Father and first secretary of the Treasury (and now Broadway superstar) Alexander Hamilton, while its excellent musical program includes organ-recital series Pipes at One (1pm Friday), and evening choral performances including new works co-commissioned by Trinity and an annual December rendition of Handel's *Messiah*.

SoHo & Chinatown

★Chinatown AREA

(Map p80; www.explorechinatown.com; south of Broome St & east of Broadway; [S] N/Q/R/W, J/Z, 6 to Canal St; B/D to Grand St; F to East Broadway) A walk through Manhattan's most colorful, cramped neighborhood is never the same, no matter how many times you hit the pavement. Peek inside temples and exotic storefronts. Catch the whiff of ripe persimmons, hear the clacking of mah-jongg tiles on makeshift tables, eye dangling duck roasts in store windows and shop for anything from rice-paper lanterns and 'faux-lex' watches to tire irons and a pound of pressed nutmeg. America's largest congregation of Chinese immigrants is your oyster.

The area has its own tourist information kiosk with local volunteers giving out free maps, at the intersection of Walker, Baxter and Canal Sts (11am to 5pm).

Little Italy AREA

(Map p84; [S] N/Q/R/W, J/Z, 6 to Canal St; B/D to Grand St) This once-strong Italian neighborhood (film director Martin Scorsese grew up on Elizabeth St) saw an exodus in the mid-20th century when many of its residents moved to more suburban neighborhoods in Brooklyn and beyond. Today, it's mostly concentrated on Mulberry St between Broome and Canal Sts, a stretch packed with checkerboard tablecloths and (mainly mediocre) Italian fare. If you're visiting in late September, be sure to check out the raucous **San Gennaro Festival** (www.sangennaro.nyc; ⏲Sep), which honors the patron saint of Naples. For a more authentic insight into an Italian community in New York, head to Arthur Ave in the Bronx.

West Village, Chelsea & Meatpacking District

★High Line PARK

(Map p84; ☎212-500-6035; www.thehighline.org; Gansevoort St, Meatpacking District; ⏲7am-11pm Jun-Sep, to 10pm Apr, May, Oct & Nov, to 7pm Dec-Mar; 🚌M14 crosstown along 14th St, M23 along 23rd St, [S] A/C/E, L to 8th Ave-14th St, 1, C/E to 23rd St, 7 to 34th St-Hudson Yards) It's hard to believe that the 1½-mile-long High Line – a shining example of brilliant urban renewal – was

Chinatown & Lower Manhattan

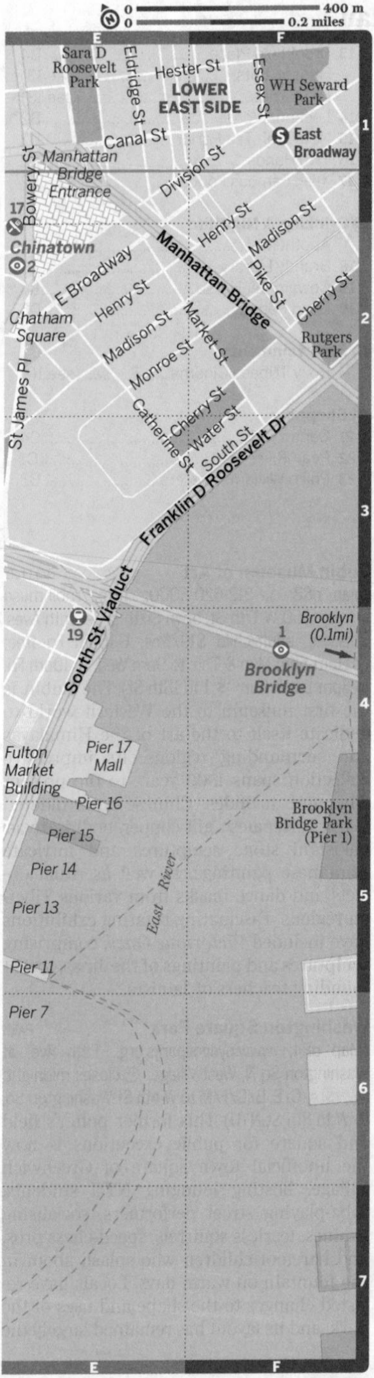

once a dingy freight line that anchored a rather unsavory district of slaughterhouses. Today, this eye-catching attraction is one of New York's best-loved green spaces, drawing visitors who come to stroll, sit and picnic 30ft above the city – while enjoying fabulous views of Manhattan's ever-changing urban landscape. Its final extension, which loops around the Hudson Yards, ends at 34th St.

The attractions are numerous, and include stunning vistas of the Hudson River, public art installations commissioned especially for the park, wide lounge chairs for soaking up some sun, willowy stretches of native-inspired landscaping (including a mini sumac forest), food and drink vendors, and a thoroughly unique perspective on the neighborhood streets below – especially at various overlooks, where bleacher-like seating faces huge panes of glass that frame the traffic, buildings and pedestrians below as living works of art. There's also André Balazs' luxury hotel, the Standard (p106), which straddles the park, as well as the sparkling Whitney Museum, which anchors the southern end.

★Whitney Museum of American Art MUSEUM

(Map p84; ☎212-570-3600; www.whitney.org; 99 Gansevoort St, at Washington St, Meatpacking District; adult/child $25/free, 7-10pm Fri pay-what-you-wish; ⏰10:30am-6pm Mon, Wed, Thu & Sun, to 10pm Fri & Sat; [S] A/C/E, L to 8th Ave-14th St) After years of construction, the Whitney's new downtown location opened to much fanfare in 2015. Anchoring the southern reaches of the High Line, this stunning building – designed by Renzo Piano – provides 63,000 sq ft of space for the museum's unparalleled collection of American art. Inside the light-filled galleries you'll find works by all the greats, including Edward Hopper, Jasper Johns, Georgia O'Keeffe and Mark Rothko. Unlike at many museums, special emphasis is placed on the work of living artists.

★Chelsea Market MARKET

(Map p88; ☎212-652-2110; www.chelseamarket.com; 75 Ninth Ave, btwn W 15th & W 16th Sts, Chelsea; ⏰7am-2am Mon-Sat, 8am-10pm Sun; [S] A/C/E, L to 8th Ave-14th St) In a shining example of redevelopment and preservation, the Chelsea Market has transformed a former factory into a shopping concourse that caters to foodies. More than two-dozen food vendors ply their temptations, including Mokbar (ramen with Korean accents); Takumi (mixing Japanese and Mexican ingredients); Very Fresh Noodles (hand-pulled

Chinatown & Lower Manhattan

northern Chinese noodles); Bar Suzette (crepes); Num Pang (Cambodian sandwiches); Ninth St Espresso (perfect lattes); Doughnuttery (piping-hot mini-doughnuts); and Fat Witch Bakery (brownies and other decadent sugar hits).

Also worth visiting is one of the market's long-time tenants The Lobster Place (over-stuffed lobster rolls and killer sushi). Once you've had your fill make sure to check out Imports from Marrakesh (specializing in Moroccan art and design); Artists and Fleas (a small market chockablock with local artists selling their wares, open 10am to 9pm Monday to Saturday and to 8pm Sunday); and Bowery Kitchen Supply (a dizzying array of cooking odds and ends).

Hudson River Park PARK
(Map p84; ☑9am-5pm Mon-Fri 212-627-2020; www.hudsonriverpark.org; West Village; ☺6am-1am; ⊞; ⧠M23 crosstown bus, ⓢ1 to Christopher St, C/E to 23rd St) The High Line (p79) may be all the rage these days, but one block away from that famous elevated park stretches a 5-mile-long recreational space that has transformed the city over the past decade. Covering 550 acres (400 of which are on the water) and running from Battery Park at Manhattan's southern tip to 59th St in Midtown, Hudson River Park is Manhattan's wondrous backyard. The long riverside path is a great spot for cycling, running and strolling.

Rubin Museum of Art GALLERY
(Map p88; ☑212-620-5000; http://rubinmuseum.org; 150 W 17th St, btwn Sixth & Seventh Aves, Chelsea; adult/child $19/free, 6-10pm Fri free; ☺11am-5pm Mon & Thu, to 9pm Wed, to 10pm Fri, to 6pm Sat & Sun; ⓢ1 to 18th St) The Rubin is the first museum in the Western world to dedicate itself to the art of the Himalayas and surrounding regions. Its impressive collection spans 1500 years to the present day, and includes Chinese embroidered textiles, Nepalese gilt-copper bodhisattvas, Pakistani stone sculptures and intricate Bhutanese paintings, as well as ritual objects and dance masks from various Tibetan regions. Fascinating rotating exhibitions have included *Victorious Ones*, comprising sculptures and paintings of the Jinas, the 24 founding teachers of Jainism.

Washington Square Park PARK
(Map p84; www.nycgovparks.org; Fifth Ave, at Washington Sq N, West Village; ☺closes midnight; ⊞; ⓢA/C/E, B/D/F/M to W 4th St-Washington Sq, R/W to 8th St-NYU) This former potter's field and square for public executions is now the unofficial town square of Greenwich Village, hosting lounging NYU students, tuba-playing street performers, socialising canines, fearless squirrels, speed-chess pros, and barefoot children who splash about in the fountain on warm days. Locals have resisted changes to the shape and uses of the park, and its layout has remained largely the

same since the 1800s. Check out the Washington Square Park Conservancy (www.washingtonsquareparkconservancy.org) for news and events.

Paula Cooper Gallery GALLERY

(Map p88; ☎212-255-1105; www.paulacoopergallery.com; 534 W 21st St, btwn Tenth & Eleventh Aves, Chelsea; ⏰10am-6pm Tue-Sat; [S]1, C/E to 23rd St) An icon of the art world, Paula was one of the first to move from SoHo to Chelsea in 1996 (she was also one of SoHo's pioneers, opening the first gallery south of Houston St back in 1968). She continues to push boundaries, as she did for her exhibition *The Clock,* when the gallery stayed open 24 hours a day on weekends.

Gagosian GALLERY

(Map p88; ☎212-741-1717; www.gagosian.com; 555 W 24th St, at Eleventh Ave, Chelsea; ⏰10am-6pm Mon-Sat; [S]1, C/E to 23rd St) International works dot the walls at the Gagosian. The ever-revolving exhibits feature the work of greats such as Jeff Koons, Andy Warhol and Jean-Michel Basquiat. Gagosian has five New York locations, and 10 more in San Francisco, London, Rome and other cities.

Stonewall National Monument NATIONAL PARK

(Map p84; www.nps.gov/ston; W 4th St, btwn Christopher & Grove Sts, West Village; ⏰9am-dusk; [S]1 to Christopher St-Sheridan Sq, A/C/E, B/D/F/M to W 4th St-Washington Sq) In 2016 President Barack Obama declared Christopher Park, a small fenced-in triangle with benches and some greenery in the heart of the West Village, a national park and on it the first national monument dedicated to LGBTQ history. It's well worth stopping here to reflect on the Stonewall uprising of 1969, when LGBTQ citizens fought back against discriminatory policing of their communities – many consider the event the birth of the modern LGBTQ-rights movement in the US.

👁 East Village & Lower East Side

★Lower East Side Tenement Museum MUSEUM

(Map p84; ☎877-975-3786; www.tenement.org; 103 Orchard St, btwn Broome & Delancey Sts, Lower East Side; tours adult/student & senior $29/24; ⏰visitor center 10am-6:30pm Fri-Wed, to 8:30pm Thu; 👪; [S]B/D to Grand St, F, J/M/Z to Delancey-Essex Sts) This museum allows visitors to briefly inhabit the Lower East Side's heartbreaking, hardscrabble but unexpectedly inspiring heritage. Two remarkably preserved (and minimally restored) 19th-century tenements are the focus of various tours, including the impossibly cramped home and garment shop of the Levines, a family from Poland, and two immigrant dwellings from the Great Depressions of 1873 and 1929. Visits to the tenement building are available only as part of scheduled guided tours, with many departures each day.

In addition to the 'Hard Times' tour that features the homes of two immigrant families, the museum also runs various other tours, including 'Sweatshop Workers,' which illuminates life for garment workers and the balance between work, family life and religion, and 'Irish Outsiders', which visits the restored home of Irish immigrants who dealt with the death of a child in the 1800s. You can have a more interactive experience with 'Meet Victoria Confino,' which gives a firsthand glimpse of life in a tenement as related by a 14-year-old Italian immigrant (played by a costumed interpreter) – it's the only tour recommended for children between five and eight years, but there's really nothing to stop them going on any of the tours.

There are also neighborhood **walking tours**, **food tours** and special **evening tours** exploring the life of the Rogarshevsky family (encountered on the sweatshop tour) on Thursday. New tours are added occasionally, so be sure to check the website.

The visitor center – which has an excellent gift shop – shows a video detailing the difficult life endured by the people who once lived in the surrounding buildings, which initially had no plumbing or electricity. Reserve tickets online – popular tours sell out in advance.

★New Museum of Contemporary Art MUSEUM

(Map p84; ☎212-219-1222; www.newmuseum.org; 235 Bowery, btwn Stanton & Rivington Sts, Lower East Side; adult/child $18/free, 7-9pm Thu by donation; ⏰11am-6pm Tue, Wed & Fri-Sun, to 9pm Thu; [S]F to 2nd Ave, R/W to Prince St, J/Z to Bowery, 6 to Spring St) The New Museum of Contemporary Art is a sight to behold: a seven-story stack of ethereal, off-kilter white boxes (designed by Tokyo-based architects Kazuyo Sejima and Ryue Nishizawa of SANAA and New York firm

East & West Villages

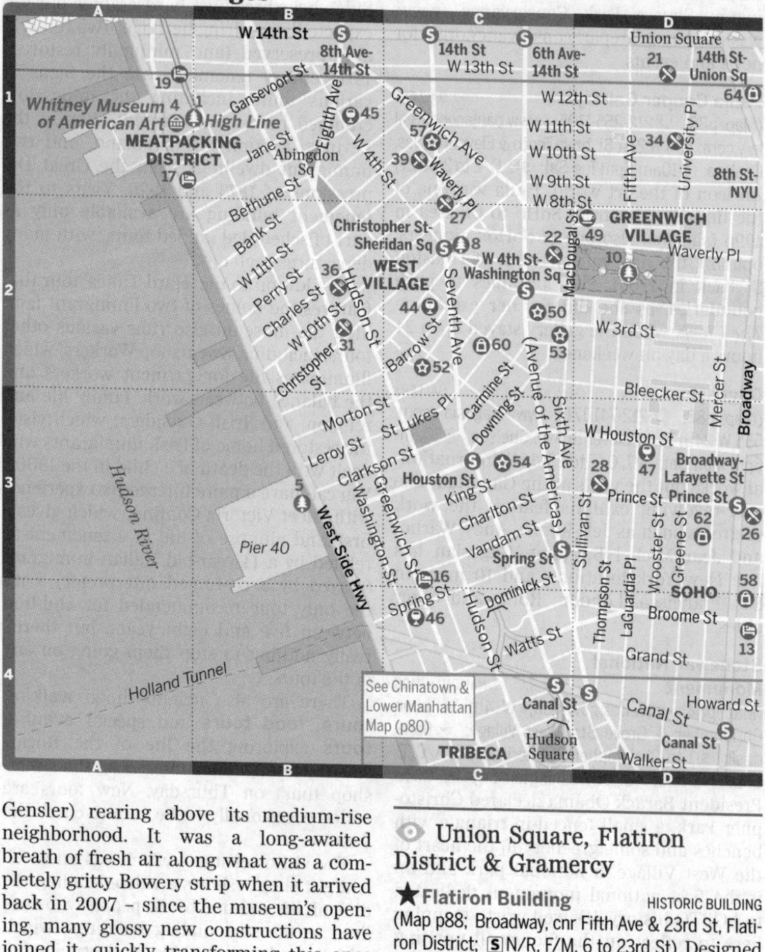

Gensler) rearing above its medium-rise neighborhood. It was a long-awaited breath of fresh air along what was a completely gritty Bowery strip when it arrived back in 2007 – since the museum's opening, many glossy new constructions have joined it, quickly transforming this once down-and-out avenue.

Tompkins Square Park PARK

(Map p84; www.nycgovparks.org; btwn E 7th & E 10th Sts & Aves A & B, East Village; ⏰6am-midnight; [S]6 to Astor Pl) This 10.5-acre park is like a friendly town square for locals, who gather for chess at concrete tables, picnics on the lawn, and spontaneous guitar or drum jams on various grassy knolls. It's also the site of basketball courts, a fun-to-watch dog run (a fenced-in area where humans can unleash their canines), a mini public swimming pool for kids, frequent summer concerts and an always lively playground.

👁 Union Square, Flatiron District & Gramercy

★ **Flatiron Building** HISTORIC BUILDING

(Map p88; Broadway, cnr Fifth Ave & 23rd St, Flatiron District; [S]N/R, F/M, 6 to 23rd St) Designed by Daniel Burnham and built in 1902, the 20-story Flatiron Building has a narrow triangular footprint that resembles the prow of a massive ship. It also features a traditional beaux-arts limestone and terra-cotta facade, built over a steel frame, that gets more complex and beautiful the longer you stare at it. It is best viewed from the traffic island north of 23rd St between Broadway and Fifth Ave, where there's public seating and a beer and wine kiosk that enables admirers to linger.

Madison Square Park PARK

(Map p88; ☎212-520-7600; www.madisonsquarepark.org; E 23rd to 26th Sts, btwn Fifth & Madison Aves, Flatiron District; ⏰6am-11pm; 👪; [S]R/W, F/M, 6 to 23rd St) This park defined

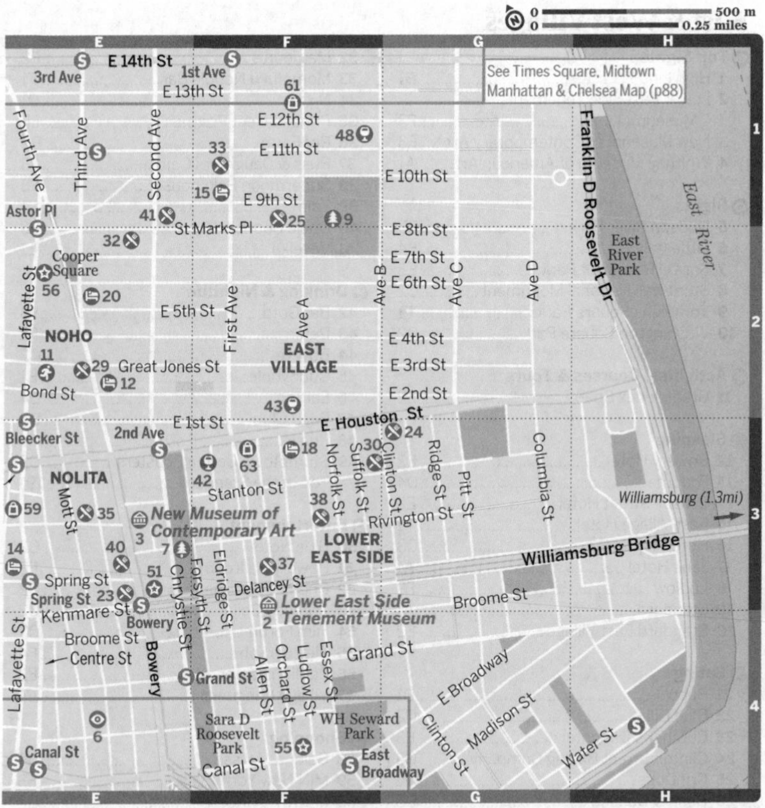

the northern reaches of Manhattan until the island's population exploded after the Civil War. These days it's a much-welcome oasis from Manhattan's relentless pace, with a popular children's playground, dog-run area and the Shake Shack (p115) burger joint. It's also one of the city's most cultured parks, with specially commissioned art installations and (in the warmer months) activities ranging from literary discussions to live-music gigs. See the website for more information.

★ **Union Square** SQUARE

(Map p88; www.unionsquarenyc.org; 17th St, btwn Broadway & Park Ave S, Union Sq; [S] 4/5/6, N/Q/R, L to 14th St-Union Sq) Union Square is like the Noah's Ark of New York, rescuing at least two of every kind from the curling seas of concrete. In fact, one would be hard pressed to find a more eclectic cross-section of locals gathered in one public place: suited businessfolk gulping fresh air during their lunch breaks, dreadlocked musicians tapping beats on their tabla, skateboarders flipping tricks on the southeastern stairs, old-timers pouring over chess boards, and throngs of protesting masses chanting fervently for various causes.

Union Square Greenmarket MARKET

(Map p88; ☎ 212-788-7476; www.grownyc.org/unionsquaregreenmarket; E 17th St, btwn Broadway & Park Ave S, Union Sq; ⏲ 8am-6pm Mon, Wed, Fri & Sat; [S] 4/5/6, N/Q/R/W, L to 14th St-Union Sq) 🍃 Don't be surprised if you spot some of New York's top chefs prodding the produce here: Union Square's greenmarket is arguably the city's most famous. Whet your appetite trawling the stalls, which peddle anything and everything from upstate fruit and vegetables to artisanal breads, cheeses and cider.

👁 Midtown

★ **Empire State Building** HISTORIC BUILDING

(Map p88; www.esbnyc.com; 350 Fifth Ave, at W 34th St; 86th-fl observation deck adult/child $38/32, incl 102nd-fl observation deck $58/52;

East & West Villages

Top Sights
1 High Line B1
2 Lower East Side Tenement Museum F3
3 New Museum of Contemporary Art E3
4 Whitney Museum of American Art A1

Sights
5 Hudson River Park B3
6 Little Italy E4
7 Sara D Roosevelt Park E3
8 Stonewall National Monument C2
9 Tompkins Square Park F1
10 Washington Square Park D2

Activities, Courses & Tours
11 Great Jones Spa E2

Sleeping
12 Bowery Hotel E2
13 Broome D4
14 Crosby Street Hotel E3
15 East Village Hotel F1
16 Hotel Hugo C3
17 Jane Hotel A1
18 Ludlow F3
19 Standard A1
20 Standard East Village E2

Eating
21 Babu Ji D1
22 Blue Hill C2
23 Butcher's Daughter E3
24 Clinton Street Baking Company G3
25 Crif Dogs F1
26 Dean & DeLuca D3
27 Dominique Ansel Kitchen C2
28 Dutch D3
29 Il Buco Alimentari & Vineria E2
30 Ivan Ramen F3
31 JeJu Noodle Bar B2
32 Mamoun's E2
33 Momofuku Noodle Bar F1
34 Nix D1
35 Prince Street Pizza E3
36 RedFarm B2
37 Russ & Daughters Cafe F3
38 Supermoon Bakehouse F3
39 Taïm C1
40 Uncle Boons E3
41 Veselka E1

Drinking & Nightlife
42 Bar Goto F3
43 Berlin F2
44 Buvette C2
45 Cubbyhole B1
46 Ear Inn C4
47 Pegu Club D3
48 Rue B F1
49 Stumptown Coffee Roasters D2
Top of the Standard .... (see 19)

Entertainment
50 Blue Note C2
51 Bowery Ballroom E3
52 Cherry Lane Theatre C2
53 Comedy Cellar C2
54 Film Forum C3
55 Metrograph F4
56 Public Theater E2
57 Village Vanguard C1

Shopping
58 Galeria Melissa D4
59 MiN New York E3
60 Murray's Cheese C2
61 Obscura Antiques F1
62 Rag & Bone D3
63 Russ & Daughters F3
64 Strand Book Store D1

⌚8am-2am, last elevators up 1:15am; [S]6 to 33rd St, B/D/F/M, N/Q/R/W to 34th St-Herald Sq) This limestone classic was built in just 410 days – using seven million hours of labor during the Great Depression – and the views from its 86th-floor outdoor deck and 102nd-floor indoor deck are heavenly. Alas, the queues to the top are notorious. Getting here very early or very late will help you avoid delays – as will buying your tickets online ahead of time (the extra $2 convenience fee is well worth the hassle it will save).

As one would expect, the views from both decks are especially spectacular at sunset. For a little of that 'Arthur's Theme' magic, head to the 86th floor between 9pm and 1am Thursday to Saturday, when the twinkling sea of lights is accompanied by a soundtrack of live saxophone (requests are welcome).

Located on the site of the original Waldorf-Astoria Hotel, the 1454ft-high (to the top of the antenna) behemoth opened in 1931 after the laying of 10 million bricks, installation of 6400 windows and setting of 328,000 sq ft of marble. The construction of the building is now expertly explained in the mezzanine **'Dare to Dream' exhibition** above the W 34th St entrance. The famous **antenna** was originally meant to be a mooring mast for zeppelins, but the Hindenberg disaster slammed the brakes on that plan. Later an aircraft did (accidentally) meet up with the building: a B-25 bomber crashed into the 79th floor on a foggy day in 1945, killing 14 people.

Since 1976, the building's top 30 floors have been floodlit in a spectrum of colors each night, reflecting seasonal and holiday hues. Famous combos include orange, white and green for St Patrick's Day; blue and white for Chanukah; white, red and green for Christmas; and the rainbow colors for Gay Pride week in June. For a full rundown of the color schemes, check the website.

A tour app is available in English, Spanish, French, German, Italian, Mandarin, Portuguese, Japanese and Korean.

New York Public Library HISTORIC BUILDING
(Stephen A Schwarzman Building; Map p88; ☏917-275-6975; www.nypl.org; 476 Fifth Ave, at W 42nd St; ⏱8am-8pm Mon & Thu, to 9pm Tue & Wed, to 6pm Fri, 10am-6pm Sat, 10am-5pm Sun, guided tours 11am & 2pm Mon-Sat, 2pm Sun; ⓈB/D/F/M to 42nd St-Bryant Park, 7 to 5th Ave) FREE Loyally guarded by 'Patience' and 'Fortitude' (the marble lions overlooking Fifth Ave), this beaux-arts show-off is one of NYC's best free attractions. When dedicated in 1911, New York's flagship library ranked as the largest marble structure ever built in the US, and to this day its recently restored **Rose Main Reading Room** steals the breath away with its lavish coffered ceiling. And it's not just for show: anybody who's working can use it, making it surely the most glamorous co-working space in the world.

★**Museum of Modern Art** MUSEUM
(MoMA; Map p88; ☏212-708-9400; www.moma.org; enter at 18 W 54th St, btwn Fifth & Sixth Aves; adult/child under 17yr $25/free, 4-8pm Fri free; ⏱10:30am-5:30pm Sat-Thu, to 8pm Fri; ♿; ⓈE/M to 5th Ave-53rd St; F to 57th St) Superstar of the modern-art scene, MoMA's galleries scintillate with heavyweights: Van Gogh, Matisse, Picasso, Warhol, Lichtenstein, Rothko, Pollock and Bourgeois. Since its founding in 1929, the museum has amassed almost 200,000 artworks, documenting the emerging creative ideas and movements of the late 19th century through to those that dominate today. For art buffs, it's Valhalla. For the uninitiated, it's a thrilling crash course in all that is beautiful and addictive about art.

MoMA's permanent collection spans four levels. Works are on rotation so it's hard to say exactly what you'll find on display, but Van Gogh's phenomenally popular *The Starry Night* is usually a sure bet. Other highlights of the collection include Picasso's *Les Demoiselles d'Avignon* and Henri Rousseau's *The Sleeping Gypsy*, not to mention iconic American works like Warhol's *Campbell's Soup Cans* and *Gold Marilyn Monroe*,

Lichtenstein's equally poptastic *Girl with Ball*, and Hopper's haunting *House by the Railroad*. Audioguides are free, available on a device from the museum or via the app.

A massive redesign in 2019 added another 50,000 sq ft of gallery space, as well as new performance and multimedia spaces and free galleries at street level.

When gallery fatigue sets in, recharge in MoMA's **Abby Aldrich Rockefeller Sculpture Garden**, dotted with works by dexterous greats like Matisse, Miró and Picasso. Or try to catch a film at one of the gallery's theaters; same-day tickets are free with admission (see moma.org/film).

★**Times Square** AREA
(Map p88; www.timessquarenyc.org; Broadway, at Seventh Ave; ⓈN/Q/R/W, S, 1/2/3, 7 to Times Sq-42nd St) Love it or hate it, the intersection of Broadway and Seventh Ave (aka Times Square) pumps out the NYC of the global imagination – yellow cabs, golden arches, soaring skyscrapers and razzle-dazzle Broadway marquees. It's right here that Al Jolson 'made it' in the 1927 film *The Jazz Singer*, photojournalist Alfred Eisenstaedt famously captured a lip-locked sailor and nurse on V-J Day in 1945, and Alicia Keys and Jay-Z waxed lyrically about the concrete jungle.

For several decades, the dream here was a sordid, wet one. The economic crash of the early 1970s led to a mass exodus of corporations from Times Square. Billboard niches went dark, stores shut and once-grand hotels were converted into SRO (single-room occupancy) dives, attracting the poor and the destitute. What was once an area bathed in light and showbiz glitz became a dirty den of drug dealers and crime. While the adjoining **Theater District** survived, its respectable playhouses shared the streets with porn cinemas, strip clubs and adult bookstores.

That all changed with tough-talking mayor Rudolph Giuliani, who in the 1990s forced out the skin flicks, boosted police numbers and lured in a wave of 'respectable' retail chains, restaurants and attractions. By the new millennium, Times Square had gone from X-rated to G-rated, drawing around 50 million visitors annually. On any given night, with the square flooded with light from wall-to-wall LCD screens and the sidewalks packed with people, it can feel like all of them are there at once.

★**Rockefeller Center** HISTORIC BUILDING
(Map p88; ☏212-588-8601; www.rockefellercenter.com; Fifth to Sixth Aves, btwn W 48th & 51st Sts; ⓈB/D/F/M to 47th-50th Sts-Rockefeller

Times Square, Midtown Manhattan & Chelsea

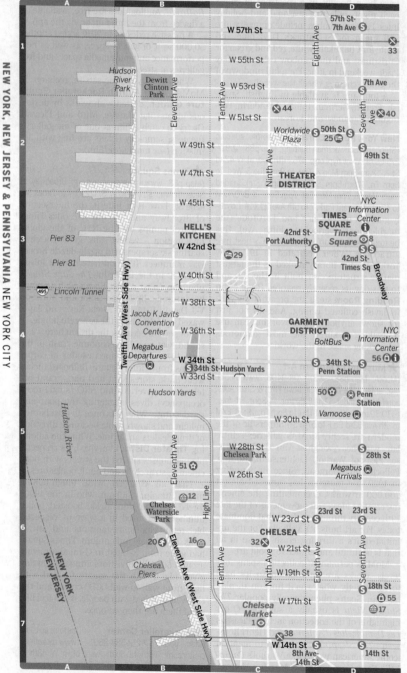

W 57th St

57th St-
7th Ave

Eighth Ave

33

W 55th St

Hudson
River
Park

Dewitt
Clinton
Park

W 53rd St

7th Ave

Tenth Ave

Eleventh Ave

W 51st St

44

Worldwide
Plaza

50th St
25

Seventh Ave

40

49th St

W 49th St

Ninth Ave

W 47th St

THEATER
DISTRICT

W 45th St

NYC
Information
Center

HELL'S
KITCHEN
W 42nd St

42nd St-
Port Authority

TIMES
SQUARE
Times
Square
8

29

42nd St-
Times Sq

Pier 83

Pier 81

W 40th St

Broadway

495 Lincoln Tunnel

W 38th St

Jacob K Javits
Convention
Center

W 36th St

GARMENT
DISTRICT

BoltBus

NYC
Information
Center

Twelfth Ave (West Side Hwy)

Megabus
Departures

W 34th St

W 33rd St

34th St-Hudson Yards

34th St-
Penn Station

56

Hudson River

Hudson Yards

50

Penn
Station

Vamoose

W 30th St

Eleventh Ave

51

W 28th St
Chelsea Park

28th St

W 26th St

Megabus
Arrivals

12

High Line

Chelsea
Waterside
Park

23rd St

23rd St

W 23rd St

CHELSEA

20

16

32

W 21st St

Eighth Ave

Seventh Ave

NEW YORK
NEW JERSEY

Eleventh Ave (West Side Hwy)

Chelsea
Piers

Tenth Ave

Ninth Ave

W 19th St

18th St

55

W 17th St

17

Chelsea
Market

1

38

W 14th St

8th Ave-
14th St

14th St

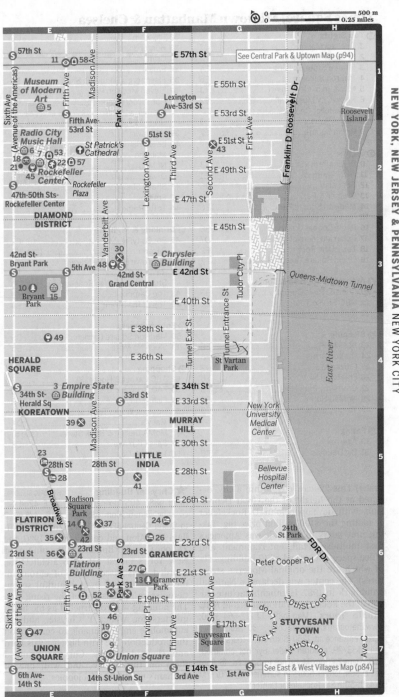

Times Square, Midtown Manhattan & Chelsea

Center) This 22-acre 'city within a city' debuted at the height of the Great Depression, with developer John D Rockefeller Jr footing the $100 million price tag. Taking nine years to build, it was America's first multiuse retail, entertainment and office space – a sprawl of 19 buildings (14 of which are the original Moderne structures). The center was declared a National Landmark in 1987. Highlights include the Top of the Rock observation deck and **NBC Studio Tours** (Map p88; ☏ 212-664-3700; www.thetouratnbcstudios.com; 30 Rockefeller Plaza, entrance at 1250 Sixth Ave; tours adult/child $33/29, children under 6yr not admitted; ⊙ 8:20am-2:20pm Mon-Thu, to 5pm Fri, to 6pm Sat & Sun, longer hours in summer; Ⓢ B/D/F/M to 47th-50th Sts-Rockefeller Center).

★**Chrysler Building**   HISTORIC BUILDING
(Map p88; 405 Lexington Ave, at E 42nd St; ⊙ lobby 7am-6:30pm Mon-Fri; Ⓢ S, 4/5/6, 7 to Grand Central-42nd St) Designed by William Van Alen and completed in 1930, the 77-floor Chrysler Building is the pin-up for New York's purest art deco architecture, guarded by stylised eagles of chromium nickel and topped by a beautiful seven-tiered spire reminiscent of the rising sun. The building was constructed as the headquarters for Walter P Chrysler and his automobile empire; unable to compete on the production line with bigger rivals Ford and General Motors, Chrysler trumped them on the skyline, and with one of Gotham's most beautiful lobbies.

Fifth Avenue   AREA

(Map p88; Fifth Ave, btwn 42nd & 59th Sts; $ E, M to 5th Ave-53rd St, N/R/W to 5th Ave-59th St) Immortalized in film and song, Fifth Ave first developed its high-class reputation in the early 20th century, when it was known for its 'country' air and open spaces. The series of mansions called **Millionaire's Row** extended right up to 130th St, though most of those above 59th St faced subsequent demolition or conversion to the cultural institutions now constituting Museum Mile. Despite a proliferation of ubiquitous chains, the avenue's Midtown stretch still glitters with upmarket establishments, among them **Tiffany & Co** (Map p88; ☎212-755-8000; www. tiffany.com; 727 Fifth Ave, at E 57th St; ⊗10am-7pm Mon-Sat, noon-6pm Sun; $ F to 57th St; N/R/W to 5th Ave-59th St).

New York home of President Donald Trump and family, the **Trump Tower**, at Fifth Ave and 56th St, has become a sight in and of itself and a popular spot for protestors. Security around the building is extremely tight and traffic commensurately slow.

Far more interesting for architecture fans is the succession of lovely beaux-arts and art deco facades, many of them washed in burnished gold, that have been preserved for retail occupants. The section between W 45th and 50th Streets is particularly good: notable facades include the **French Building** at 551 (1926–27), the **Scribner Building** at 597 (1912–13), and the **British Empire Building** at 620 (1932; part of the Rockefeller Center).

★ Radio City Music Hall   HISTORIC BUILDING

(Map p88; www.radiocity.com; 1260 Sixth Ave, at W 51st St; tours adult/child $30/26; ⊗tours 9:30am-5pm; ♿; $ B/D/F/M to 47th-50th Sts-Rockefeller Center) This spectacular Moderne movie palace was the brainchild of vaudeville producer Samuel Lionel 'Roxy' Rothafel. Never one for understatement, Roxy launched his venue on December 23, 1932, with an over-the-top extravaganza that included camp dance troupe the Roxyettes (mercifully renamed the Rockettes). Guided tours (75 minutes) of the sumptuous interiors include the glorious auditorium, Witold Gordon's classically inspired mural *History of Cosmetics* in the Women's Downstairs Lounge, and the VIP Roxy Suite, where luminaries such as Elton John and Alfred Hitchcock have been entertained.

St Patrick's Cathedral   CATHEDRAL

(Map p88; ☎212-753-2261; www.saintpatricks cathedral.org; Fifth Ave, btwn E 50th & 51st Sts; ⊗6:30am-8:45pm; $ B/D/F/M to 47th-50th Sts-Rockefeller Center, E/M to 5th Ave-53rd St) Still shining after a $200 million restoration in 2015, America's largest Catholic cathedral graces Fifth Ave with Gothic Revival splendor. Built at a cost of nearly $2 million during the Civil War, the building did not originally include the two front spires; those were added in 1888. Step inside to appreciate the Louis Tiffany–designed altar, gleaming below a 7000-pipe church organ, and Charles Connick's stunning Rose Window above the Fifth Ave entrance. Occasional walk-in guided tours are available; check the website for details.

A **basement crypt** behind the altar contains the coffins of every New York cardinal and the remains of Pierre Toussaint, a champion of the poor and the first African American up for sainthood.

Bryant Park   PARK

(Map p88; ☎212-768-4242; www.bryantpark.org; 42nd St, btwn Fifth & Sixth Aves; ⊗7am-midnight Mon-Fri, to 11pm Sat & Sun Jun-Sep, shorter hours Oct-May; $ B/D/F/M to 42nd St-Bryant Park, 7 to 5th Ave) European coffee kiosks, alfresco chess games, summer film screenings and winter ice skating: it's hard to believe that this leafy oasis was a crime-ridden hellscape known as 'Needle Park' in the '70s. Nestled behind the beaux-arts New York Public Library building, it's a whimsical spot for a little time-out from the Midtown madness. Fancy taking a beginner Italian language, yoga or juggling class, joining a painting workshop or signing up for a birding tour? There's a daily smorgasbord of quirky activities.

Top of the Rock   VIEWPOINT

(Map p88; ☎212-698-2000, toll free 877-692-7625; www.topoftherocknyc.com; 30 Rockefeller Plaza, entrance on W 50th St, btwn Fifth & Sixth Aves; adult/child $36/30, sunrise/sunset combo $54/43; ⊗8am-midnight, last elevator at 11pm; $ B/D/F/M to 47th-50th Sts-Rockefeller Center) Designed in homage to ocean liners and opened in 1933, this 70th-floor open-air observation deck sits atop the **GE Building**, the tallest skyscraper at the Rockefeller Center. Top of the Rock beats the Empire State Building on several levels: it's less crowded, has wider observation decks (both outdoor and indoor) and offers a view of the Empire State Building itself. Before ascending, a fascinating 2nd-floor exhibition gives an insight into the legendary philanthropist behind the art deco complex.

If you don't have under-21s in tow, note that similar views can be had from the Rockefeller's 65th-floor **Bar SixtyFive** (Map p88;

☎212-632-5000; www.rainbowroom.com/bar-sixty-five; 30 Rockefeller Plaza, entrance on W 49th St; 🕐5pm-midnight Mon-Fri, 4-9pm Sun, closed Sat; [S]B/D/F/M to 47th-50th Sts-Rockefeller Center)...and you don't need a ticket to Top of the Rock to get in.

Upper East Side

★Metropolitan Museum of Art MUSEUM
(Map p94; ☎212-535-7710; www.metmuseum.org; 1000 Fifth Ave, at E 82nd St; 3-day pass adult/senior/child $25/$17/free, pay-as-you-wish for NY State residents; 🕐10am-5:30pm Sun-Thu, to 9pm Fri & Sat; 👪; [S]4/5/6, Q to 86th St; 6 to 77th St) The vast collection of art and antiquities contained within this palatial museum (founded in 1870) is one of the world's largest and most important, with more than two million individual objects in its permanent collection of paintings, sculptures, textiles and artifacts from around the globe – even an ancient Egyptian temple straight from the banks of the Nile. 'The Met' has 17 acres of exhibition space to explore, so plan to spend several hours here. (Wear comfy shoes.)

The 1st-floor ancient Egyptian collection is unrivaled; do not miss the **Temple of Dendur**, built around 10 BC and relocated from Egypt in 1978. On the 2nd floor, numerous **European Paintings galleries** display stunning masterworks from the 13th through 20th centuries, while 15 incredible rooms are devoted to an extensive collection of **Islamic art and artifacts**. The **American Wing** features decorative and fine art from across US history. Other galleries are devoted to classical antiquity (with sculptures dramatically illuminated by natural daylight), Asian art, and modern and contemporary paintings and sculptures – there are simply too many to list.

Kids will most enjoy the artifact-rich Egyptian, African and Oceania galleries, as well as the collection of medieval armor and weaponry (all on the 1st floor). There's a specially designed brochure and map for kids, and events listed on the website.

If visiting from April through October, head up to the excellent **roof garden**, which features rotating sculpture installations by contemporary and 20th-century artists – though the grand city and park views are the real draw. Enjoy a sundowner cocktail from its on-site bar, the Cantor Roof Garden Bar (p124).

Self-guided **audio tours** (adult/child $7/5) are available in 10 languages; download the Met's free smartphone app for excerpts. **Guided tours** of specific galleries are free with admission. Tickets are good for three consecutive days, and also give admission to the Met Breuer and Cloisters (p97).

★Guggenheim Museum MUSEUM
(Map p94; ☎212-423-3500; www.guggenheim.org; 1071 Fifth Ave, at E 89th St; adult/child $25/free, cash-only pay-what-you-wish 5-8pm Sat; 🕐10am-5:30pm Wed-Fri, Sun & Mon, to 8pm Sat & 9pm Tue; 👪; [S]4/5/6, Q to 86th St) A New York icon, architect Frank Lloyd Wright's conical white spiral is probably more famous than the artworks inside, which include works by Kandinsky, Picasso, Pollock, Monet, Van Gogh and Degas; photographs by Mapplethorpe, and important surrealist works. But temporary exhibitions climbing the much-photographed central rotunda are the real draw. Other key works are often exhibited in the more recent adjoining tower (1992). Pick up the free audioguide or download the Guggenheim app for information about the exhibits and architecture.

★Frick Collection GALLERY
(Map p94; www.frick.org; 1 E 70th St, at Fifth Ave; adult/student $22/12, pay-what-you-wish 2-6pm Wed, 6-9pm 1st Fri of month excl Jan & Sep free; 🕐10am-6pm Tue-Sat, 11am-5pm Sun; [S]6 to 68th St-Hunter College) This spectacular art collection sits in a mansion built by steel magnate Henry Clay Frick, one of the many such residences lining the section of Fifth Ave that was once called 'Millionaires' Row.' The museum has more than a dozen splendid rooms displaying masterpieces by Titian, Vermeer, Gilbert Stuart, El Greco, Joshua Reynolds, Van Dyck and Rembrandt. Sculpture, ceramics, antique furniture and clocks are also on display. Fans of classical music will enjoy the piano and violin **concerts** (☎212-547-0715; www.frick.org/programs/concerts; $45) on some Sunday evenings.

Jewish Museum MUSEUM
(Map p94; ☎212-423-3200; www.thejewishmuseum.org; 1109 Fifth Ave, btwn E 92nd & 93rd Sts; adult/child $18/free, Sat free, pay-what-you-wish 5-8pm Thu; 🕐11am-5:45pm Mon-Tue & Fri, 11am-8pm Thu, 10am-5:45pm Sat-Sun; 👪; [S]6, Q to 96th St) This gem occupies a French-Gothic mansion from 1908, housing 30,000 items of Judaica including torah shields and hanukah lamps, as well as sculpture, painting and decorative arts. It does not, however, include any historical exhibitions relating to the Jewish community in New York. Temporary exhibits are often excellent, featuring

CENTRAL PARK

One of the world's most renowned green spaces, **Central Park** (Map p94; www.centralparknyc.org; 59th to 110th Sts, btwn Central Park West & Fifth Ave; ⏰6am-1am; 👪) comprises 843 acres of rolling meadows, boulder-studded outcroppings, elm-lined walkways, manicured European-style gardens, a lake and reservoir — not to mention an outdoor theater, a memorial to John Lennon, an idyllic waterside eatery at the **Loeb Boathouse** (☎212-517-2233; www.thecentralparkboathouse.com; Central Park Lake, near E 74th St; mains lunch $26-38, dinner $29-45; ⏰restaurant noon-4pm Mon-Fri, from 9:30am Sat & Sun year-round, 5:30-9:30pm Mon-Fri, from 6pm Sat & Sun Apr-Nov; [S]B, C to 72nd St; 6 to 77th St), and a famous statue of Alice in Wonderland. Highlights include the 15-acre **Sheep Meadow**, where thousands of people lounge and play on warm days; **Central Park Zoo** (☎212-439-6500; www.centralparkzoo.com; 64th St, at Fifth Ave; adult/child $20/15, without 4-D Theater $14/11; ⏰10am-5pm Mon-Fri, to 5:30 Sat & Sun Apr-Oct, 10am-4:30pm Nov-Mar; 👪; [S]N/R to 5th Ave-59th St); and the forest-like paths of the **Ramble** (btwn 73rd & 78th Sts; [S]B,C to 81st St).

Like the city's subway system, the vast and majestic Central Park, a rectangle of open space in the middle of Manhattan, is a great class leveler – exactly as it was envisioned. Created in the 1860s and '70s by Frederick Law Olmsted and Calvert Vaux on the marshy northern fringe of the city, the immense park was designed as a leisure space for all New Yorkers regardless of color, class or creed. It's also an oasis from the insanity: the lush lawns, cool forests, flowering gardens, glassy bodies of water and meandering, wooded paths provide the dose of serene nature that New Yorkers crave.

Olmsted and Vaux (who also created Prospect Park, p100, in Brooklyn) were determined to keep foot and road traffic separated and cleverly designed the crosstown transverses under elevated roads to do so. That such a large expanse of prime real estate has survived intact for so long is proof that nothing eclipses the heart, soul and pride that forms the foundation of New York City's greatness.

Today, this 'people's park' is still one of the city's most popular attractions, beckoning throngs of New Yorkers with free outdoor concerts on the **Great Lawn** (btwn 79th & 85th Sts; ⏰Apr–mid-Nov; [S]B, C to 86th St) and top-notch drama at the annual Shakespeare in the Park (p105) productions held each summer at the open-air **Delacorte Theater** (www.publictheater.org; enter at W 81st St; [S]B, C to 81st St). Other recommended stops include the ornate **Bethesda Fountain** ([S]B, C to 72nd St), which edges the Lake, and its **Loeb Boathouse** (boating per hr $15; ⏰10am-6:45pm; 👪; [S]B, C to 72nd St), where you can rent rowboats or enjoy lunch; the **Shakespeare Garden**, on the west side between 79th and 80th Sts, with its lush plantings and excellent skyline views; and the Ramble, a wooded thicket that's popular with bird-watchers. While parts of the park swarm with joggers, inline skaters, musicians and tourists on warm weekends, it's quieter on weekday afternoons, especially in the less-trodden spots above 72nd St, such as the **Harlem Meer** and the **North Meadow** (north of 97th St).

Folks flock to the park even in winter, when snowstorms inspire cross-country skiing and sledding or just a simple stroll through the white wonderland, and crowds turn out every New Year's Eve for a midnight run. The **Central Park Conservancy** (☎212-310-6600; www.centralparknyc.org/tours) offers ever-changing guided tours of the park, including ones that focus on public art, wildlife and places of interest to kids (check online for dates and times; most tours are free or $15).

retrospectives on influential figures such as Art Spiegelman or Leonard Cohen, as well as world-class shows on luminaries like Marc Chagall and Modigliani. The landmark Lower East Side deli Russ & Daughters has a restaurant in the basement.

Met Breuer MUSEUM
(Map p94; ☎212-731-1675; www.metmuseum.org/visit/met-breuer; 945 Madison Ave, at E 75th St; 3-day pass adult/senior/child $25/$17/free, pay-as-you-wish for NY State residents; ⏰10am-5:30pm Tue-Thu & Sun, to 9pm Fri & Sat; [S]6 to 77th St, Q to 72nd St) The newest branch of the Metropolitan Museum of Art opened in the landmark former Whitney Museum building (designed by Marcel Breuer; there's an architecture tour you can listen to on the Met's website) in 2016. Exhibits are dedicated to 20th- and 21st-century art, with sculpture, photographs, video, design

Central Park & Uptown

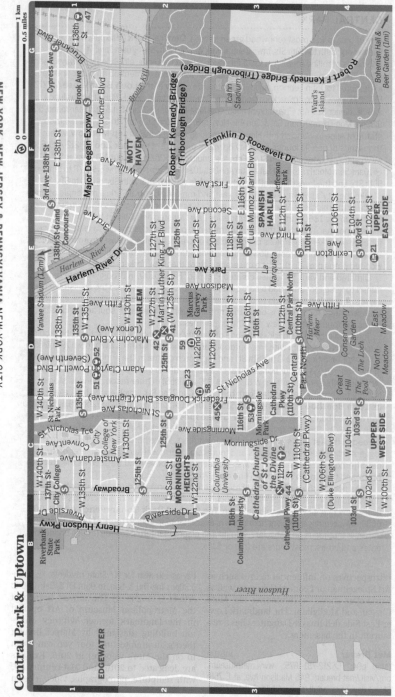

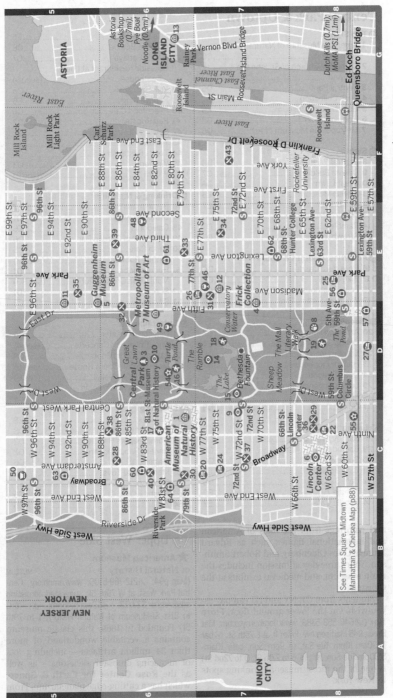

Central Park & Uptown

Top Sights

1 American Museum of Natural History C6
2 Cathedral Church of St John the Divine C3
3 Central Park D6
4 Frick Collection D7
5 Guggenheim Museum E5
6 Lincoln Center C8
7 Metropolitan Museum of Art D6

Sights

8 Central Park Zoo D8
9 Dakota Building C7
10 Great Lawn D6
11 Jewish Museum E5
12 Met Breuer E7
13 Noguchi Museum G6
14 Ramble D7
15 Strawberry Fields D7

Activities, Courses & Tours

16 Belvedere Castle D6
17 Bike & Roll C6
18 Loeb Boathouse D7
19 Wollman Skating Rink D8

Sleeping

20 Arthouse Hotel NYC C7
21 Bubba & Bean Lodges E4
22 Empire Hotel C8
23 Harlem Flophouse D2
24 Hotel Beacon C7
25 Loews Regency Hotel E8
26 Mark E7
27 Quin D8

Eating

28 Barney Greengrass C6
29 Boulud Sud C8
30 Burke & Wills C6
31 Café Boulud E7
32 Café Sabarsky D6
33 Candle 79 .... E6
34 Candle Cafe E7
35 Eli's Essentials E5
36 Épicerie Boulud C8
37 Gray's Papaya C7
Lakeside Restaurant at Loeb Boathouse .... (see 18)
38 Milk Bar C6
39 Papaya King E6
40 Peacefood Cafe C6
41 Red Rooster D2
42 Sylvia's D2
43 Tanoshi F7
44 Tom's Restaurant C3
45 Vinatería C3
Wright .... (see 5)

Drinking & Nightlife

46 Bemelmans Bar E7
47 Bronx Brewery G1
48 Caledonia E6
49 Cantor Roof Garden Bar D6
50 Earth Café C5
Empire Rooftop .... (see 22)
51 Harlem Hops D1
Manhattan Cricket Club .... (see 30)
52 Shrine D1
53 Silvana C3

Entertainment

54 Delacorte Theater D6
Frick Collection Concerts .... (see 4)
55 Jazz at Lincoln Center C8
Metropolitan Opera House .... (see 6)
New York City Ballet .... (see 6)
New York Philharmonic .... (see 6)

Shopping

56 Barneys E8
57 Bergdorf Goodman D8
58 Flamekeepers Hat Club D2
59 Harlem Haberdashery D2
60 Magpie C6
61 Mary Arnold Toys E6
62 Shakespeare & Co E7
63 Shishi C5
64 Zabar's C6

and paintings from the likes of American and international figures such as Edvard Munch, Claes Oldenburg and Robert Smithson. Your three-day admission includes the main museum, and medieval exhibits at the Cloisters.

Students from CT, NY and NJ can pay-as-you-wish. On the lower-ground floor, **Flora Bar** (☎646-558-5383; www.florabarnyc.com; Met Breur, 945 Madison Ave, lower fl, at E 75th St; 🕒bar 11:30am-10pm Tue-Sat, to 9pm Sun, cafe 10am-5:30pm Tue-Sun; 📶; [S]6 to 77th St; Q to 72nd St) is one of the nicest museum drinking spots in New York.

Upper West Side

★American Museum of Natural History MUSEUM

(Map p94; ☎212-769-5100; www.amnh.org; Central Park West, at W 79th St; suggested admission adult/child $23/13; 🕒10am-5:45pm; 👪; [S]C to 81st St-Museum of Natural History; 1 to 79th St) Founded in 1869, this classic museum contains a veritable wonderland of more than 34 million artifacts – including lots of menacing dinosaur skeletons – as well as the **Rose Center for Earth & Space**, which has a cutting-edge planetarium. From

October through May, the museum is home to the **Butterfly Conservatory**, a vivarium featuring 500-plus butterflies from all over the world that will flutter about and land on your outstretched arm.

On the natural history side, the museum is perhaps best known for its light and airy **Fossil Halls** containing nearly 600 specimens, including mammoth crowd pleasers such as an apatosaurus, titanosaurus and fearsome *Tyrannosaurus rex* (they'll all scare the bejesus out of you). There are also plentiful animal exhibits (the stuffed Alaskan brown bears and giant moose are popular), galleries devoted to gems and minerals, and an IMAX theater. The **Milstein Hall of Ocean Life** contains dioramas devoted to marine ecologies, weather and conservation, as well as a beloved 94ft replica of a blue whale suspended from the ceiling. At the 77th St Grand Gallery, there's a 63-foot canoe carved in the 1870s and featuring designs from different Native American peoples of the Northwest Coast.

For the astronomical set, the Rose Center is the star of the show. Every half-hour at the planetarium (check website for specific times) you can drop yourself into a cushy seat to view *Dark Universe* (through 2019), narrated by famed astrophysicist and Frederick P. Rose Center director Neil deGrasse Tyson, which explores the mysteries and wonders of the cosmos. You'll also find an astonishing **Willamette Meteor**, a 15.5-ton hunk of metallic iron that fell to earth in present-day Oregon some 30-40,000-years ago.

Note that while you can pay what you wish for general admission (in person only), in order to see space shows, IMAX films or ticketed exhibits you'll need to pay the posted prices for admission plus one show (adult/child $28/16.50) or admission plus all shows ($33/20).

The museum broke ground in 2019 on a $383-million expansion that is set to be completed by 2022 and will include the Richard Gilder Center for Science, Education, and Innovation.

⭐**Lincoln Center**   ARTS CENTER
(Map p94; 212-875-5456, tours 212-875-5350; www.lincolncenter.org; Columbus Ave, btwn W 62nd & 66th Sts; tours adult/student $25/20; ⏱tours 11:30am & 1:30pm Mon-Sat, 3pm Sun; ♿; S1, 2, 3 to 66th St-Lincoln Center, A/C or B/D to 59th St-Columbus Circle) FREE This stark arrangement of gleaming modernist temples houses some of Manhattan's most important performance companies: the New York Philharmonic (p128), the New York City Ballet (p127) and the Metropolitan Opera

(p127). The lobby of the iconic Opera House is dressed with brightly saturated murals by painter Marc Chagall. Various other venues are tucked in and around the 16-acre campus, including a theater, two film-screening centers and the renowned **Juilliard School** for performing arts.

Strawberry Fields   MEMORIAL
(Map p94; www.centralparknyc.org; Central Park, at 72nd St on west side; SC, B to 72nd St) Standing inside the park across from the famous **Dakota apartment building** (Map p94; 1 W 72nd St, at Central Park West; SB, C to 72nd St), where John Lennon was fatally shot in 1980, is this poignant, tear-shaped garden – a memorial to the slain star. It contains a grove of stately elms and a tiled mosaic that says, simply, 'Imagine.' The spot is officially designated a quiet zone but you wouldn't know it from the multitude of tour guides and buskers who come to vocalize here.

⦿ Harlem & Upper Manhattan

⭐**Met Cloisters**   MUSEUM
(Map p78; 212-923-3700; www.metmuseum.org/cloisters; 99 Margaret Corbin Dr, Fort Tryon Park; 3-day pass adult/senior/child $25/17/free, pay-as-you-wish for residents of NY State & students from CT, NY and NJ; ⏱10am-5:15pm Mar-Oct, to 4:45pm Nov-Feb; SA to 190th St) On a hilltop overlooking the Hudson River, the Cloisters is a curious architectural jigsaw, its many parts made up of various European monasteries and other historic buildings. Built in the 1930s to house the Metropolitan Museum's medieval treasures, its frescoes, tapestries and paintings are set in galleries that sit around a romantic courtyard, connected by grand archways and topped with Moorish terra-cotta roofs. Among its many rare treasures is the beguiling tapestry series *The Hunt of the Unicorn* (1493–1505).

Also worth seeking out is the remarkably well-preserved 15th-century Annunciation Triptych (Merode Altarpiece). Then there's the stunning French 12th-century Saint-Guilhem and Bonnefant cloisters, the latter featuring plants used in medieval medicine, magic, ceremony and the arts, and with views over the Hudson River.

Your ticket gives you three-day admission to the Cloisters as well as the Metropolitan Museum of Art and the Met Breuer. Note that although the Dyckman St subway station looks closest to the museum, there are steep slippery steps between the station and the entrance; use 190th St station instead and walk through the park.

Central Park

THE LUNGS OF NEW YORK

The rectangular patch of green that occupies Manhattan's heart began life in the mid-19th century as a swampy piece of land that was carefully bulldozed into the idyllic naturescape you see today. Since officially becoming Central Park, it has brought New Yorkers of all stripes together in interesting and unexpected ways. The park has served as a place for the rich to show off their fancy carriages (1860s), for the poor to enjoy free Sunday concerts (1880s) and for activists to hold be-ins against the Vietnam War (1960s).

Since then, legions of locals – not to mention travelers from all kinds of faraway places – have poured in to stroll, picnic, sunbathe, play ball and catch free concerts and performances of works by Shakespeare.

Loeb Boathouse
Perched on the shores of the lake, the historic Loeb Boathouse is one of the city's best settings for an idyllic meal. You can also rent rowboats and bicycles and ride on a Venetian gondola.

Duke Ellington Circle

Harlem Meer

The Blockhouse

North Woods

Fifth Ave

97th St Transverse

86th St Transverse

The Great Lawn

Conservatory Garden
The only formal garden in Central Park is perhaps the most tranquil part of the park. On the northern end, chrysanthemums bloom in late October. To the south, the park's largest crab apple tree grows by the Burnett Fountain.

Central Park West

Jacqueline Kennedy Onassis Reservoir
This 106-acre body of water covers roughly an eighth of the park's territory. Its original purpose was to provide clean water for the city. Now it's a good spot to catch a glimpse of water birds.

Belvedere Castle
A so-called 'Victorian folly,' this Gothic-Romanesque castle serves no other purpose than to be a very dramatic lookout point. It was built by Central Park co-designer Calvert Vaux in 1869.

The park's varied terrain offers a wonderland of experiences. There are quiet, woodsy knolls in the north. To the south is the reservoir, crowded with joggers. There are European gardens, a zoo and various bodies of water. For maximum flamboyance, hit the Sheep Meadow on a sunny day, when all of New York shows up to lounge.

Central Park is more than just a green space. It is New York City's backyard.

Conservatory Water

This pond is popular in the warmer months, when children sail their model boats across its surface. Conservatory Water was inspired by 19th-century Parisian model-boat ponds and figured prominently in EB White's classic book, *Stuart Little*.

CHRISTOPHER PENLER/SHUTTERSTOCK ©

KRIDSADA KAMSOMBAT/SHUTTERSTOCK ©

Bethesda Fountain

This neoclassical fountain is one of New York's largest. It's capped by the *Angel of the Waters*, which is supported by four cherubim. The fountain was created by bohemian-feminist sculptor Emma Stebbins in 1868.

Metropolitan Museum of Art

Alice in Wonderland Statue

79th St Transverse

The Ramble

Delacorte Theater

The Lake

Fifth Ave

Central Park Zoo

65th St Transverse

Sheep Meadow

Columbus Circle

Strawberry Fields

A simple mosaic memorial pays tribute to musician John Lennon, who was killed across the street outside the Dakota Building. Funded by Yoko Ono, its name is inspired by the Beatles song 'Strawberry Fields Forever.'

The Mall/ Literary Walk

A Parisian-style promenade – the only straight line in the park – is flanked by statues of literati on the southern end, including Robert Burns and Shakespeare. It is lined with rare North American elms.

★**Cathedral Church
of St John the Divine**　　CATHEDRAL
(Map p94; ☑ tours 212-316-7540; www.stjohndivine.
org; 1047 Amsterdam Ave, at W 112th St, Morningside Heights; adult/student $10/8, highlights tour
$14, vertical tour $20/18; ⊙ 7:30am-6pm Mon-Sat,
12:30-2:30pm Sun; Ⓢ B/C, 1 to 110th St-Cathedral
Pkwy) New York's most impressive house of
worship is a towering monument that looks
like it's straight out of medieval Europe. Built
in a mix of styles – with elements of Romanesque, Gothic and neo-Gothic design – St
John's is packed with treasures, from gorgeous stained-glass windows to 17th-century
tapestries, as well as works by contemporary
artists such as Keith Haring and Tom Otter-
ness. Despite the grandeur, the cathedral has
yet to be completed; some even jokingly refer
to it as 'St John the Unfinished.'

⊙ Brooklyn

★**Brooklyn Bridge**　　BRIDGE
(Map p80; Ⓢ 4/5/6 to Brooklyn Bridge-City Hall,
J/Z to Chambers St, R/W to City Hall, Ⓢ 2/3 to
Clark St, A/F to High St-Brooklyn Bridge Station)
A New York icon, the Brooklyn Bridge was
the world's first steel suspension bridge,
and, at 1596ft, the longest when it opened
in 1883. Although construction was fraught
with disaster, the bridge became a magnificent example of urban design. Its suspended bicycle/pedestrian walkway delivers
soul-stirring views of Manhattan, the East
River and the Brooklyn waterfront. Though
beautiful, the crossing can be challenging –
if walking, stay in the pedestrian portion of
the lane as cyclists move quickly.

Brooklyn Bridge Park　　PARK
(☑ 718-222-9939; www.brooklynbridgepark.org;
East River Waterfront, btwn Atlantic Ave & John St,
Brooklyn Heights/Dumbo; ⊙ 6am-1am, some sections to 11pm, playgrounds to dusk; 🅿 👪; ☐ B63 to
Pier 6/Brooklyn Bridge Park, B25 to Old Fulton St/
Elizabeth Pl, 🚊 East River or South Brooklyn routes
to Dumbo/Pier 1, Ⓢ A/C to High St, 2/3 to Clark St,
F to York St) **FREE** This 85-acre park is one of
Brooklyn's best-loved attractions. Wrapping
itself around a 1.3-mile bend on the East River, it runs from just beyond the far side of the
Manhattan Bridge in Dumbo to the west end
of Atlantic Ave in Brooklyn Heights. It has
revitalized a once-barren stretch of shoreline, turning a series of abandoned piers
into beautifully landscaped parkland with
jaw-dropping views of Manhattan. There's
lots to see and do here, with playgrounds,
walkways and lawns galore.

Brooklyn Heights Promenade　　VIEWPOINT
(www.nycgovparks.org; btwn Orange & Remsen Sts,
Brooklyn Heights; ⊙ 24hr; Ⓢ N/R/W to Court St,
2/3 to Clark St, A/C to High St) Six of of the east–
west streets of well-to-do Brooklyn Heights
(such as Montague and Clark Sts) lead to
the neighborhood's number-one attraction:
a narrow, paved walking strip with breathtaking views of Lower Manhattan and New
York Harbor that is blissfully removed from
the busy Brooklyn–Queens Expwy (BQE)
over which it sits. This little slice of urban
beauty, fiercely defended by locals against
development proposals, is a great spot for a
sunset walk.

★**Prospect Park**　　PARK
(Map p78; ☑ 718-965-8951; www.prospectpark.
org; Grand Army Plaza; ⊙ 5am-1am; Ⓢ 2/3 to
Grand Army Plaza, F, G to 15th St-Prospect Park,
B, Q to Prospect Park, Q to Parkside Ave) Brooklyn is blessed with a number of historic,
view-laden and well-used green spaces, but
its emerald is Prospect Park. The designers
of the 585-acre park – Frederick Law Olmsted and Calvert Vaux – considered it an
improvement on their other New York project, Central Park, and between rambling
its tree-fringed walkways and sighing at ornamental bridges, you might agree. Opened
in 1867, Brooklyn's lovely, faux-natural
greenspace has a long meadow to the west
(filled with dog-walkers, sportspeople or
barbecuers, depending on the season), hilly
woodlands, and a boathouse on the east
side, by its expansive lake. The neoclassical
arches, sculptures and columns at the major entrances were later additions.

Many visitors come to bike, run, stroll,
walk their dogs or just lounge around. The
park has a **zoo** (Map p78; ☑ 718-399-7339; www.
prospectparkzoo.com; 450 Flatbush Ave, Prospect
Park; adult/child $10/7; ⊙ 10am-5pm Mon-Fri, to
5:30pm Sat & Sun Apr-Oct, to 4:30pm Nov-Mar; 👪;
☐ B41 to Flatbush Ave, Ⓢ B, Q to Prospect Park, 2/3
to Grand Army Plaza) and an ice-skating rink
(p103), which becomes a water-play area for
kids in the warm months, when boats are
also available for hire. There are are also
free concerts (☑ 718-683-5600; www.bricarts
media.org; Prospect Park Bandshell, near Prospect
Park W & 11th St, Park Slope; ⊙ Jun-Aug) at the
Prospect Park Bandshell (near the entrance at 9th St and Prospect Park W) and
a year-round **farmers market** (www.grownyc.
org; Grand Army Plaza, cnr Prospect Park W & Flatbush Ave, Prospect Park; ⊙ 8am-4pm Sat; Ⓢ 2, 3 to
Grand Army Plaza) is held on Saturdays at the
Grand Army Plaza entrance.

CONEY ISLAND

Coney Island – a name synonymous in American culture with antique seaside fun and frolicking – achieved worldwide fame as a working-class amusement park and beach-resort area at the turn of the 20th century. After decades of decline, its kitschy charms have experienced a 21st-century revival. Though it's no longer the booming, peninsula-wide attraction it once was, it still draws crowds of tourists and locals alike for legendary roller-coaster rides, hot dogs and beer on the beachside boardwalk.

Luna Park (Map p78; ☑718-373-5862; www.lunaparknyc.com; 1000 Surf Ave, at W 10th St; ☺Apr-Oct; ⓢD/F, N/Q to Coney Island-Stillwell Ave) is one of Coney Island's most popular amusement parks and contains one of its most legendary rides: the Cyclone ($10), a wooden roller-coaster that reaches speeds of 60mph and makes near-vertical drops. In a neighboring park is the 150ft-tall pink-and-mint-green **Deno's Wonder Wheel** (Map p78; ☑718-372-2592; www.denoswonderwheel.com; 1025 Riegelmann Boardwalk, at W 12th St; rides $10; ☺from noon Jul & Aug, from noon Sat & Sun Apr-Jun, Sep & Oct; ☷; ⓢD/F, N/Q to Coney Island-Stillwell Ave), which has been delighting New Yorkers since 1920 as the best place to survey Coney Island from up high.

The hot dog was invented in Coney Island in 1867, and there's no better place to eat one than **Nathan's Famous** (☑718-333-2202; www.nathansfamous.com; 1310 Surf Ave, at Stillwell Ave; hot dogs from $4; ☺10am-11pm Mon-Thu, to midnight Fri, 9am-midnight Sat, to 11pm Sun; ☏; ⓢD/F to Coney Island-Stillwell Ave), established in 1916. When thirst strikes, head to **Ruby's** (☑718-975-7829; www.rubysbar.com; 1213 Riegelmann Boardwalk, btwn Stillwell Ave & W 12th St; ☺11am-10pm Sun-Thu, to 1am Fri & Sat Apr-Sep, weekends only Oct; ⓢD/F, N/Q to Coney Island-Stillwell Ave), a legendary dive bar right on the boardwalk.

★**Brooklyn Museum**   MUSEUM
(Map p78; ☑718-638-5000; www.brooklyn museum.org; 200 Eastern Pkwy, Prospect Park; adult/child $16/free; ☺11am-6pm Wed & Fri-Sun, to 10pm Thu year-round, to 11pm 1st Sat of month Oct-Dec & Feb-Aug; ☷; ⓢ2/3 to Eastern Pkwy-Brooklyn Museum) This encyclopedic museum, imagined as the centrepiece of the 19th-century Brooklyn Institute, occupies a five-story, 560,000-sq-ft beaux-arts building stuffed with more than 1.5 million objects – ancient Egyptian sarcophagi, 19th-century period rooms, and a cornucopia of art. This elegant, airy space is an inspiring place to explore, and a calmer alternative to Manhattan's manic museums.

The collection is augmented by thought-provoking temporary exhibitions on diverse subjects from European art retrospectives to provocative contemporary art, often with a spotlight on feminist thought and LGBTIQ+ artists. Special events run until 11pm on the first Saturday of each month (except September).

Brooklyn Botanic Garden   GARDENS
(Map p78; ☑718-623-7200; www.bbg.org; 150 Eastern Pkwy, Prospect Park; adult/student/child $15/8/free, 8am-noon Fri free, Tue-Fri Dec-Feb free; ☺8am-6pm Tue-Fri, from 10am Sat & Sun Mar-Oct, shorter hours rest of year; ☷; ⓢ2/3 to Eastern Pkwy-Brooklyn Museum, B, Q to Prospect Park) Opened in 1911 and now one of Brooklyn's

most picturesque sights, this 52-acre garden is home to thousands of plants and trees and a **Japanese garden** where river turtles swim alongside a Shinto shrine. The best times to visit are late April or early May, when the blooming cherry trees (a gift from Japan) are celebrated in Sakura Matsuri, the Cherry-Blossom Festival (p105), or fall, when the deciduous trees blaze their colours.

★**Bushwick Collective**   PUBLIC ART
(Map p78; www.instagram.com/thebushwickcollec tive; Bushwick; ⓢL to Jefferson St) **FREE** Further cementing Bushwick's status as Brooklyn's coolest neighborhood is this outdoor gallery of murals by some of the most talented street artists in NYC and beyond. The works change regularly, and can be found mainly along Jefferson and Troutman Sts between Cypress and Knickerbocker Aves, with others along Gardner Ave (north of Flushing Ave). Other street art can be found around the Morgan Ave L stop, particularly on Seigel and Grattan Sts.

The latter two streets are conveniently near Roberta's (p120) and **Pine Box Rock Shop** (☑718-366-6311; www.pineboxrockshop. com; 12 Grattan St, btwn Morgan Ave & Bogart St, East Williamsburg; ☺4pm-2am Mon & Tue, to 4am Wed-Fri, 2pm-4am Sat, noon-2am Sun; ⓢL to Morgan Ave) – great places to stop for a pizza or some drinks.

Though overall safe to visit, Bushwick still has occasional incidents of crime, so pay attention to your surroundings in this area, especially late at night and on weekends.

◉ Queens

★ MoMA PS1
GALLERY

(Map p78; ☑ 718-784-2084; www.momaps1.org; 22-25 Jackson Ave, Long Island City; suggested donation adult/child $10/free, NYC residents or with MoMA ticket free, Warm Up party online/at venue $18/22; ◷ noon-6pm Thu-Mon, Warm Up parties noon-9pm Sat Jul-early Sep; Ⓢ G, 7 to Court Sq, E, M to Court Sq-23rd St) At MoMA's hip contemporary outpost, you'll be peering at videos through floorboards, schmoozing at DJ parties and debating the meaning of nonstatic structures while staring through a hole in the wall. Exhibits include everything from Middle Eastern video art to industrial boilers covered in gold leaf. Many are site-specific installations – *Meeting* (1986), an installation by LA light artist James Turrell, is definitely worth seeking out, especially just before sundown.

Noguchi Museum
MUSEUM

(Map p94; ☑ 718-204-7088; www.noguchi.org; 9-01 33rd Rd, at Vernon Blvd, Long Island City; adult/child $10/free, 1st Fri of month free; ◷ 10am-5pm Wed-Fri, 11am-6pm Sat & Sun; 🚇 Q103, Q104 to Vernon Blvd-33 Rd, Ⓢ N/W to Broadway) Both the art and the context in which it's displayed here are the work of LA-born sculptor, designer and landscape architect Isamu Noguchi, famous for iconic lamps and coffee tables, as well as elegant, abstract stone sculptures. Artifacts are displayed in serene indoor galleries and a minimalist sculpture garden, forming a complete aesthetic vision and an oasis of calm. The 1st floor holds the permanent collection, while the upstairs gallery shows temporary exhibitions.

◉ The Bronx

Bronx Zoo
ZOO

(Map p78; ☑ 718-220-5100; www.bronxzoo.com; 2300 Southern Blvd; full-experience adult/child Apr-Oct $37/27, Nov-Mar $29/21, pay-as-you-wish general admission Wed; ◷ 10am-5pm Mon-Fri, to 5:30pm Sat & Sun Apr-Oct, to 4:30pm Nov-Mar; Ⓢ 2, 5 to West Farms Sq-E Tremont Ave) This 265-acre zoo is the country's biggest and oldest, with more than 6000 animals and re-created habitats from around the world, such as African plains and Asian rainforests. It's deservedly popular, with especially large crowds on discounted Wednesdays and weekends in good weather, and any day in July or August (try to go Monday morning). The southwest Asia Gate (four blocks north of the West Farms Sq–E Tremont Ave stop, up Boston Rd) is your easiest access point by subway.

New York Botanical Garden
GARDENS

(Map p78; ☑ 718-817-8716; www.nybg.org; 2900 Southern Blvd; all-garden pass Mon-Fri adult/child $23/10, Sat & Sun $28/12, grounds only NYC residents $15/4, Wed & 9-10am Sat grounds admission free; ◷ 10am-6pm Tue-Sun; 🚇; Ⓡ Metro-North to Botanical Garden) First opened in 1891 and incorporating 50 acres of old-growth forest, the New York Botanical Garden is home to the restored Enid A Haupt Conservatory, a grand, Victorian iron-and-glass edifice that is now a New York landmark. See the website for a list of regular events, which include themed walking tours, children's book readings and film screenings.

Yankee Stadium
STADIUM

(Map p78; ☑ 212-926-5337; www.mlb.com/yankees; 1 E 161st St, at River Ave; tours $20; Ⓢ B/D, 4 to 161st St-Yankee Stadium) The Boston Red Sox like to talk about their record of nine World Series championships in the last 90 years – well, the Yankees have won a mere 27 in that period. The team's magic appeared to have moved with them across 161st St to the new Yankee Stadium, where they played their first season in 2009 – winning the World Series there in a six-game slugfest against the Phillies. The Yankees play from April to October.

🏃 Activities

Cycling

Central Park Bike Tours
CYCLING

(Map p94; ☑ 212-541-8759; https://centralparkbiketours.com; 203 W 58th, btwn Broadway & 7th Ave; bike rentals per hr/day adult from $10.50/28, child $9/23; ◷ 8am-8pm; 🚇; Ⓢ 1/2/3 to 59th/Columbus Cir) The official bike rental outfitter of NYC Parks has more than 3000 bikes in 12 locations around the city (you can't miss their green-shirted touts around the edge of the park). This outlet is one of two along 58th St just south of the park. Two-hour guided tours of the park ($30) are also offered. Helmut and bike locks are included in the rates. Reserve rentals online to guarantee a bike in summer.

Health & Fitness

Chelsea Piers Complex
HEALTH & FITNESS

(Map p88; ☑ 212-336-6666; www.chelseapiers.com; Pier 62, at W 23rd St, Chelsea; ◷ 5:30am-

11pm Mon-Fri, 8am-9pm Sat & Sun; ♿; 🚇M23 to 12th Ave-W 23 St, 🚇1, C/E to 23rd St) This massive waterfront sports center caters to the athlete in everyone. You can hit endless golf balls at the four-level driving range, skate on an indoor ice rink or rack up strikes in a jazzy bowling alley. There's basketball at Hoop City, a sailing school for kids, batting cages, a huge gym and covered swimming pool, and indoor rock climbing.

Great Jones Spa   SPA

(Map p84; 📞212-505-3185; www.gjspa.com; 29 Great Jones St, btwn Lafayette St & Bowery, NoHo; ⏰9am-10pm; 🚇6 to Bleecker St; B/D/F/M to Broadway-Lafayette St) Don't skimp on the services at this downtown feng shui–designed place, whose offerings include blood-orange salt scrubs and stem-cell facials. If you spend over $100 per person (not difficult: hour-long massages/facials start at $150/135), you get access to the water lounge with thermal hot tub, sauna, steam room and cold plunge pool (swimwear required). There's even a three-story indoor waterfall.

Ice Skating

Wollman Skating Rink   SKATING

(Map p94; 📞212-439-6900; www.wollmanskating rink.com; Central Park, btwn E 62nd & 63rd Sts; adult Mon-Thu $12, Fri-Sun $19, child $6, skate rentals $10; ⏰10am-2:30pm Mon & Tue, to 10pm Wed & Thu, to 11pm Fri & Sat, to 9pm Sun late Oct-early Apr; ♿; 🚇F to 57 St; N/R/W to 5th Ave-59th St) This rink is much larger than the Rockefeller Center skating rink, and not only does it allow all-day skating, its position at the southeastern edge of Central Park offers magical views. There's locker rental for $5 and a spectator fee of $5. Cash only.

Rink at Rockefeller Center   ICE SKATING

(Map p88; 📞212-332-7654; www.therinkatrock center.com; Rockefeller Center, Fifth Ave, btwn W 49th & 50th Sts; adult $25-33, child $15, skate rental $13; ⏰8:30am-midnight mid-Oct–Apr; ♿; 🚇B/D/F/M to 47th-50th Sts-Rockefeller Center) From mid-October to April, Rockefeller Plaza is home to New York's most famous ice-skating rink. Carved out of a recessed oval with the 70-story art deco Rockefeller Center towering above, plus a massive Christmas tree during the holiday season, it's incomparably magical. It's also undeniably small and crowded. Opt for the first skating period of the day (8:30am) to avoid a long wait. Sessions last 90 minutes. Come summer, the rink becomes a cafe.

Outdoor Activities

LeFrak Center at Lakeside   BOATING

(📞718-462-0010; www.lakesideprospectpark.com; 171 East Dr, near Ocean & Parkside Aves, Prospect Park; skating $7.25-10, skate rental $7, boat rental per hour $16-36, bike rental per hour $13-38; ⏰hours vary; ♿; 🚇Q to Parkside Ave) The most significant addition to Prospect Park (p100) since its creation, the LeFrak is a 26-acre ecofriendly playground. In winter there's ice-skating, in summer there's roller-skating and a sprinkler-filled water-play area for kids to splash about in. Pedal boats and kayaks are also available (usually late March to mid-October), and a variety of bikes can be rented to tour the park.

Belvedere Castle   BIRDWATCHING

(Map p94; 📞646-790-4833; www.centralparknyc. org; Central Park, at W 79th St; ⏰9am-7pm mid-Jun–mid-Aug, 10am-5pm mid-Aug–mid-Jun; ♿; 🚇1/2/3, B, C to 72nd St) For a DIY birding expedition with kids, borrow a 'Discovery Kit' at Belvedere Castle in Central Park, which comes with binoculars, a bird book, colored pencils and paper – a perfect way to get the kids excited about birds. Picture ID is required.

🚩 Tours

★ Staten Island Ferry   CRUISE

(Map p80; www.siferry.com; Whitehall Terminal, 4 Whitehall St, at South St, Lower Manhattan; ⏰24hr; 🚇1 to South Ferry, R/W to Whitehall St, 4/5 to Bowling Green) FREE Staten Islanders know these hulking orange ferries as commuter vehicles, while Manhattanites think of them as their secret, romantic vessels for a spring-day escape. Yet many tourists are also wise to the charms of the Staten Island Ferry, whose 25-minute, 5.2-mile journey between Lower Manhattan and the Staten Island neighborhood of St George is one of NYC's finest free adventures.

Museum Hack   WALKING

(📞347-282-5001; www.museumhack.com; 2hr tour from $59) For a fascinating, alternative perspective of the Met, sign up for a tour with Museum Hack. Knowledgeable but delightfully irreverent guides take on topics like 'Badass Bitches' (a look at paradigm-shifting feminist artists) and lead night tours that include wine. Museum Hack also runs tours in the Museum of Natural History, with an 'Un-Highlights Tour' of museum curiosities.

Children under 16 years cannot be accommodated on regular tours but private family-friendly tours can be arranged.

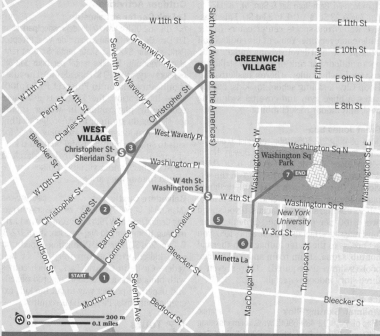

Walking Tour
Greenwich Village

START COMMERCE ST
END WASHINGTON SQUARE PARK
LENGTH 1.2 MILES; ONE HOUR

Greenwich Village's brick-lined byways break Manhattan's signature grid pattern, striking off on intriguing tangents that beg to be explored on foot. Start at ❶ **Cherry Lane Theatre** (www.cherrylanetheater.org; 38 Commerce St), hidden in the crook of handsome, residential Commerce St. Established in 1924, the Cherry is the city's longest continuously running off-Broadway establishment, and has hosted many famous playwrights and thespians.

Make a left on Bedford and turn right into Grove St (number 90, on the corner, may be familiar as the apartment building in *Friends*) to reach your first pit stop, ❷ **Buvette** (p122). Literally 'snack bar,' this dreamy Francophile wine bar is ideal for people-watching over the rim of a flat white or a glass of Côtes du Rhône, depending on the hour.

Continue along Grove St. The next stop is Christopher Park, home to the ❸ **Stonewall National Monument** (p83). On the north side

of the green is the legendary Stonewall Inn, where in 1969 LGBTQ men and women rioted against routine police harassment, sparking what came to be known as the Gay Rights Movement.

Follow Christopher St to Sixth Ave to find the ❹ **Jefferson Market Library** just north. Built as a courthouse in 1885, this gracious red-brick building rises from a tranquil garden of the same name, complete with flowering trees, lawns and a koi pond.

Head south again through Sixth Ave's flurry of foot traffic, then turn left onto West 3rd St, looking for legendary jazz venue ❺ **Blue Note** (www.bluenote.net; 131 W 3rd St) on your left. Sarah Vaughan, Lionel Hampton and other immortals have performed here; try to time your visit for jazz brunch on Sunday (11:30am or 1:30pm).

Turn right onto MacDougal St to reach the ❻ **Comedy Cellar** (www.comedycellar.com; 117 MacDougal St), where the likes of Jerry Seinfeld and Amy Schumer have performed, then double back, heading north on MacDougal to end your stroll in ❼ **Washington Square Park** (p82), the village's unofficial town square.

✨ Festivals & Events

Tribeca Film Festival — FILM
(📞212-941-2400; www.tribecafilm.com; ⏰Apr-May) Founded in 2003 by Robert De Niro and Jane Rosenthal, the Tribeca Film Festival is now a major star of the indie movie circuit. Gaggles of celebs come to walk the red carpets each spring, while New Yorkers snap up tickets to screenings and talks. Vote for the Audience Award by downloading the festival app, which also details the programme lineup and accompanying talks.

Cherry-Blossom Festival — CULTURAL
(📞718-623-7200; www.bbg.org; Brooklyn Botanic Garden, Prospect Park; ⏰late Apr/early May) Known in Japanese as Sakura Matsuri, this tradition celebrates the pink, puffy flowering of myriad varieties of cherry tree in the Brooklyn Botanic Garden (p101), in particular the many-petaled Kwanzan along its famous esplanade. Entry to a full day's program of entertainment, against a photogenic canopy provided by cherry, apricot and almond blooms, costs $30 (under-12s can accompany adults for free).

It's worth booking in advance. If you can't make the festival, check the map on the website for the most florescent times and places anytime from late March through mid-May.

SummerStage — PERFORMING ARTS
(www.cityparksfoundation.org/summerstage; Rumsey Playfield, Central Park, access via Fifth Ave & 69th St; ⏰May-Oct; 🚼; Ⓢ6 to 68th St-Hunter College) Every summer Central Park hosts dozens of outdoor concerts known as SummerStage, showcasing indie rock, jazz, modern dance, rockabilly, African, zydeco and much more. Most performances are free and the festival draws big crowds, so start queuing up early or you may have to listen to the music outside (not always a bad place, especially with a picnic blanket on the grass).

Shakespeare in the Park — THEATER
(www.publictheater.org/Free-Shakespeare-in-the-Park; Central Park; ⏰Jun-Aug; ⓈA/B/C to 81st St) The much-loved Shakespeare in the Park pays tribute to the Bard, with free performances in the open-air Delacorte Theater (p93) in Central Park. It's a magical experience. The catch? You'll have to wait hours in line to score tickets, or win them in the online lottery. It's managed by the Public Theater (p127).

BAM Next Wave Festival — PERFORMING ARTS
(www.bam.org; tickets from $32; ⏰Oct-Dec) Running for around 12 weeks from October to mid-December at the Brooklyn Academy of Music (p129), this arts festival offers the city's edgiest, most comprehensive survey of avant-garde music, theater, opera and dance.

Thanksgiving Day Parade — PARADE
(www.macys.com; ⏰4th Thu Nov) This famous cold-weather event, for hardy viewers only, parades its famous floats and balloons (watch your head) from 77th St to Herald Sq along Central Park W, Central Park S and then Sixth Ave. The parade culminates in live performances, from high-school marching bands to A-list stars.

For a close-up preview, join the throngs who gather at the southwest corner of Central Park to watch the balloons being inflated the night before.

Rockefeller Center
Christmas Tree Lighting — LIGHT SHOW
(www.rockefellercenter.com; Rockefeller Plaza; ⏰Dec; ⓈB/D/F/M to 47th-50th Sts-Rockefeller Center) At this traditional mob-scene event, people flock around the massive spruce tree to watch it come aglow with energy-efficient bulbs before it's taken down and recycled into lumber. It's a green Christmas! The lighting happens in late November or early December and the tree is taken down early in the new year. Expect huge crowds for days around this event.

🛏 Sleeping

Expect high prices and small spaces. Room rates waver by availability, not by any high-season or low-season rules. You'll pay dearly during holidays. Accommodations fill up quickly, especially in summer and December, and range from cookie-cutter chains to stylish boutiques.

You'll find better-value hotels in Brooklyn and Queens; Long Island City has an increasing number of bargain designer hotel options with killer Manhattan views. A few B&Bs and hostels are scattered throughout the city.

🏛 Financial District & Lower Manhattan

★Roxy Hotel — HOTEL $$
(Map p80; 📞212-519-6600; www.roxyhotelnyc.com; 2 Sixth Ave, at White St, Tribeca; standard/superior/deluxe r from $349/359/409; ❄🛜🏊; Ⓢ1 to Franklin St, A/C/E to Canal St) The reimagined Tribeca Grand offers mid-century glamor, luxurious living, cinema, music, drinking and dining in one foxy package. Its

201 rooms, decked out with modern fittings in a retro brown-and-gold palette, surround a spacious central atrium with multiple bars, a boutique **art-house cinema** (☑212-519-6820; www.roxycinematribeca.com; tickets $12) and jazz cellar Django. Regular events such as the annual New Year's Surrealist Ball heighten the fun.

Gild Hall
BOUTIQUE HOTEL $$

(Map p80; ☑212-232-7700; www.thompson hotels.com/hotels/gild-hall; 15 Gold St, at Platt St, Lower Manhattan; superior/deluxe from $249/289; ❄️🛜; Ⓢ2/3 to Fulton St) Boutique and brilliant, Gild Hall's entryway leads to a split-level, book- and sofa-stuffed lobby exuding a style best characterised as 'Wall St meets hunting lodge.' Rooms fuse Euro elegance and American comfort with high tin ceilings, Sferra linens and well-stocked minibars. King-size beds sport leather headboards, which work perfectly in their warmly hued, minimalist surroundings.

★ Greenwich Hotel
BOUTIQUE HOTEL $$$

(Map p80; ☑212-941-8900; www.thegreenwichho tel.com; 377 Greenwich St, btwn N Moore & Franklin Sts, Tribeca; r from $650; ❄️🛜🏊; Ⓢ1 to Franklin St, A/C/E to Canal St) From the plush drawing room (complete with crackling fire and deep armchairs) to the lantern-lit pool inside a reconstructed 18th-century Japanese farmhouse, nothing about Robert De Niro's Greenwich Hotel is generic. Each of the 88 individually designed rooms features aged-wood floors, and bathrooms with opulent Carrara marble or Moroccan tiling. French windows open onto Tuscan-inspired inner courtyards in some rooms.

Extra luxury can be found in-house at the upscale Shibui Spa (treatments from $220) and 'urban Italian' taverna Locanda Verde.

🛏 SoHo & Chinatown

Hotel Hugo
BOUTIQUE HOTEL $$

(Map p84; ☑212-608-4848; www.hotelhugony. com; 525 Greenwich St, btwn Vandam & Spring Sts, SoHo; r from $240; 🛜; Ⓢ1 to Houston St/Canal St, C/E to Spring St) It might not have the bells and whistles of some other SoHo hotels, but Hotel Hugo is a quiet little champion in this pricey 'hood. Rooms subtly channel industrial style, there's a goldmine rooftop terrace bar and suave restaurant-cafe. It's a 10- to 15-minute walk from central SoHo but that's A-OK when prices can be as low as $340 a night even in peak season.

★ Broome
BOUTIQUE HOTEL $$$

(Map p84; ☑212-431-2929; www.thebroomenyc. com; 431 Broome St, at Crosby St, SoHo; r from $399; ❄️🛜; ⓈR/W to Prince St; 6 to Spring St) Occupying a handsomely restored, 19th-century building, the Broome feels far more intimate than most NYC hotels. Its 14 rooms are the epitome of simple, muted elegance, each with locally sourced fittings. There's a hidden surprise here, too: a tranquil open-air internal patio with Parisian-style seating for relaxing with a coffee (which is complimentary, as is the farm-to-table breakfast). Service is personable.

Crosby Street Hotel
BOUTIQUE HOTEL $$$

(Map p84; ☑212-226-6400; www.firmdale hotels.com; 79 Crosby St, btwn Spring & Prince Sts, SoHo; r from $725; ♿❄️🛜; Ⓢ6 to Spring St; N/R to Prince St) The team behind this hotel, converted from a former parking lot, have torn up the rule book in terms of interior design, and the results are sublime. Guest rooms all have oversized headboards with matching mannequins, but that's where the uniformity ends. Some are starkly black and white while others are as floral as an English garden; all are plush, refined and subtly playful.

The lobby is an eccentric, art-filled space that leads to a vibrant public bar, discrete drawing room with honesty bar, and sculpture garden. Downstairs, there's even a film-screening room.

🛏 West Village, Chelsea & Meatpacking District

Jane Hotel
HOTEL $

(Map p84; ☑212-924-6700; www.thejanenyc.com; 113 Jane St, at West St, West Village; r with shared/private bath $135/295; 🅿❄️; ⓈA/C/E, L to 8th Ave-14th St, 1 to Christopher St-Sheridan Sq) The Jane's 50-sq-ft rooms are undeniably snug, but if you have the sea in your blood, check into this renovated red-brick gem, built for mariners in 1908 (*Titanic* survivors stayed here in 1912). The lobby is all pale-green antique tiles, stag's heads, peacocks and liveried bellboys, while the gorgeous ballroom-bar looks like it belongs in a five-star hotel.

The cheaper rooms have bunk beds and shared bathrooms, while the more expensive 'captain's cabins' come with private commodes.

Standard
BOUTIQUE HOTEL $$$

(Map p84; ☑212-645-4646; www.standardhotels. com; 848 Washington St, at W 13th St, Meatpacking District; r from $383; ❄️🛜; ⓈA/C/E, L to 8th Ave-

14th St) Straddling the High Line, this unique hotel welcomes guests with an upside-down sign, a canary-yellow revolving door and a giant gumball machine in the lobby, signalling the offbeat design within. Each of the 338 rooms has sweeping views of Manhattan and the Hudson and is filled with cascading sunlight, making the glossy, wood-framed beds and marbled bathrooms glow.

The amenities are first rate, with a buzzing German beer garden and brasserie at street level, an ice rink in winter, and a plush nightclub on the top floor. The location is also unbeatable, with the best of NYC right outside. There's a hyper-modern **sister hotel** (Map p84; 212-475-5700; 25 Cooper Sq/ Third Ave, btwn E 5th & E 6th Sts; r $400; R/W to 8th St-NYU, 4/6 to Bleecker St, 4/6 to Astor Pl) in the East Village.

East Village & Lower East Side

Ludlow
HOTEL $$

(Map p84; 212-432-1818; www.ludlowhotel.com; 180 Ludlow St, btwn E Houston & Stanton Sts, Lower East Side; d from $325; F to 2nd Ave) This 175-room boutique hotel oozes New York style. Rooms are beautifully designed, with unique features such as huge golden-hued ceiling lights, nightstands made of petrified tree trunks, mosaic-tiled bathrooms and small balconies (although the cheapest rooms are quite small). There's a gorgeous lobby bar and patio, plus an acclaimed French bistro, **Dirty French**, open for breakfast, lunch and dinner.

East Village Hotel
HOTEL $$

(Map p84; 917-635-7757; www.eastvillagehotel.com; 147 First Ave, at E 9th St, East Village; d $250-300; 6 to Astor Pl) In a vibrant location, this place has clean, simple rooms (a little larger than most in NYC) with exposed brick walls, comfy mattresses, wall-mounted flat-screen TVs, irons, hairdryers and small kitchenettes. Street noise is an issue (light sleepers, beware), and it's in an old building, so you'll have to walk your luggage up a few flights.

Bowery Hotel
BOUTIQUE HOTEL $$$

(Map p84; 212-505-9100; www.theboweryhotel.com; 335 Bowery, btwn E 2nd & E 3rd Sts, East Village; r from $435; F to 2nd Ave, 6 to Bleecker St) Pick up your red-tasselled gold room key in the hushed timber-lined lobby, admiring the antique velvet chairs and faded Persian rugs. Walk over mosaic-tiled floors to your room with its huge factory windows and quality bed. Push aside the bowler-hatted 'bowery boy' teddy you'll find there, settle in and watch a movie on your 42in plasma TV.

Union Square, Flatiron District & Gramercy

Carlton Arms
HOTEL $

(Map p88; 212-679-0680; www.carltonarms.com; 160 E 25th St, at Third Ave, Gramercy; s/d with shared bath $90/130, with private bath $130/160; 6 to 23rd St or 28th St) At this divey art hotel, every inch of the interior is a canvas scrawled with artists' musings. Murals crawl up the five flights of stairs and into each of the uniquely decorated guest rooms, ranging from fantastical to downright horrifying (the helpful staff will let you pick your room). Rooms with shared bathrooms still have a small sink.

★ Freehand New York
BOUTIQUE HOTEL $$

(Map p88; 212-475-1920; www.freehandhotels.com/new-york; 23 Lexington Ave, btwn E 23rd & E 24th Sts, Gramercy; d, tr & q from $220; 6 to 23rd St) Budget-conscious style hunters will feel right at home at Freehand, hailed a New York hotel game-changer thanks to its combination of sensible pricing, group-friendly (bunk) and solo room options, and design-led common areas. The aesthetic is mid-century modern, while rooms also feature unobtrusive art murals and frills such as slippers, robes, Argan toiletries and free fruit. Note: prices can double in summer.

Gramercy Park Hotel
BOUTIQUE HOTEL $$$

(Map p88; 212-920-3300; www.gramercyparkhotel.com; 2 Lexington Ave, at 21st St, Gramercy; r from $330, ste from $1000; 6, R/W to 23rd St) More than $50 million in contemporary art decorates the lounge of this stylish hotel, setting a tone of quiet opulence. Dark-wood paneling and sumptuous sofas greet guests in the lobby, with an open fire in winter, and the signature rose-and-jade color scheme is rich and alluring. Some rooms overlook the **park** (E 20th St, btwn Park & Third Aves), and guests have private access.

Midtown

Yotel
HOTEL $$

(Map p88; 646-449-7700; www.yotel.com; 570 Tenth Ave, at 41st St, Midtown West; r from $190; A/C/E to 42nd St-Port Authority Bus Terminal; 1/2/3, N/Q/R, S, 7 to Times Sq-42nd St) Part futuristic spaceport, part *Austin*

Powers set, this uber-cool 713-room hotel bases its rooms on airplane classes: premium cabin (economy), first cabins (business) and suites (first) – some come with terraces and outdoor tubs. Yotel's design trademarks include adjustable beds and color-changing mood walls. Small but cleverly configured, all cabins feature floor-to-ceiling windows with killer views, USB ports and device-streaming tech.

Hidden away on the 1st-floor, the main hotel landing area feels like a city within a city, with an espresso bar, full-service restaurant, covered terrace bar with heaters – even an Off-Broadway entertainment space called the Green Room (ask staff about buying tickets for shows). The highlight is the city's largest outdoor hotel terrace, with stunning skyscraper backdrop (naturally). The only downside is the grungy location, though you're still just a short walk from Times Square and Broadway.

Citizen M
HOTEL $$

(Map p88; ☑ 212-461-3638; www.citizenm.com; 218 W 50th St, btwn Broadway & Eighth Ave, Midtown West; r from $300; ❄ 🛜; 🚇 1, C/E to 50th St) A few steps from Times Square, Citizen M is a true millennial. Communal areas are upbeat, contemporary and buzzing, and rooms are space-agey and compact. A tablet in each controls lighting, blinds and room temperature, and the plush mattresses, free movies and soothing rain showers keep guests purring. On-site perks include gym, a 24-hour canteen and flash rooftop bar with terrace on three sides.

★ NoMad Hotel
BOUTIQUE HOTEL $$$

(Map p88; ☑ 212-796-1500; www.thenomadhotel.com; 1170 Broadway, at 28th St, Midtown West; r/ste from $400/600; ❄ 🛜; 🚇 N/R to 28th St) 🅿 Crowned by a copper cupola and featuring interiors designed by Frenchman Jacques Garcia, this beaux-arts dream is one of the city's hottest addresses. Rooms channel a nostalgic NYC-meets-Paris aesthetic, in which recycled hardwood floors, leather-steam-trunk minibars and clawfoot tubs mix with flat-screen TVs and high-tech LED lighting. The in-house **NoMad** (mains $28-45; ⏱ noon-2pm & 5:30-10:30pm Mon-Thu, to 11pm Fri, 11am-2:30pm & 5:30-11pm Sat, 11am-2:30pm & 5:30-10pm Sun) restaurant is a coveted hangout and its bar is consistently in the World's 50 Best Bars list.

Quin
HOTEL $$$

(Map p94; ☑ 212-245-7846; www.thequinhotel.com; 101 W 57th St, at Sixth Ave, Midtown West; d from $449; ❄ 🛜; 🚇 F to 57th St; N/Q/R/W to 57th St-7th Ave) The Quin is an opulent, modern hotel with the bones of a grand old dame. In the 1920s it was the Buckingham, a storied hotel that hosted artists and musicians like Georgia O'Keefe and Marc Chagall. Today it keeps the artistic connection alive with rotating in-house exhibitions – the hotel lounge has a 15ft video wall showcasing art installations. Rooms are exceedingly comfortable and elegantly restrained.

Highlights include the custom-made, king-sized Duxiana beds and marble bathrooms. Rooms can be linked together for families and those on the 17th floor all benefit from fabulous terraces. Seek out the wall of guitars, hidden on the 2nd floor, painted by artists who have exhibited at the hotel.

Ace Hotel
BOUTIQUE HOTEL $$$

(Map p88; ☑ 212-679-2222; www.acehotel.com/newyork; 20 W 29th St, btwn Broadway & Fifth Ave, Midtown West; r from $399; ❄ 🛜; 🚇 R/W to 28th St) A hit with cashed-up creatives, the Ace's standard and deluxe rooms recall upscale bachelor pads – plaid bedspreads, quirky wall stencils, leather furnishings and fridges. Some even have Gibson guitars and turntables. For cool kids with more 'cred' than 'coins,' there are 'mini' and 'bunk' rooms (with bunk beds), both of which can slip under $200 in winter.

🛏 Upper East Side

Bubba & Bean Lodges
B&B $

(Map p94; ☑ 917-345-7914; www.bblodges.com; 1598 Lexington Ave, btwn E 101st & 102nd Sts; d $110-190, tr $120-230, q $130-260; ❄ 🛜; 🚇 6 to 103rd St) Owners Jonathan and Clement are well known for turning a Manhattan town house into an excellent home-away-from-home, but an unusually high rate of property-initiated last-minute cancellations coupled with their refusal to show us a room means you should tread cautiously here. Five simply furnished guest rooms feature crisp, white walls, hardwood floors and navy linens, providing the place with a modern, youthful feel. All units in this three-floor walk-up have private baths as well as equipped kitchenettes.

★ Mark
DESIGN HOTEL $$$

(Map p94; ☑ 212-744-4300; www.themarkhotel.com; 25 E 77th St, at Madison Ave; r from $895/1275; ❄ 🛜; 🚇 6 to 77th St) French designer Jacques Grange left his artful mark on the Mark, with bold geometric shapes and rich, playful forms that greet visitors in the lobby (the zebra-striped marble floor, which also features in the room bathrooms, is pure eye candy). Upstairs, lavishly renovated rooms and multi-bedroom suites are equally stylish with custom-made furnishings and luxury local linen.

Loews Regency Hotel HOTEL **$$$**
(Map p94; ☎212-759-4100; www.loewshotels.com/regency-hotel; 540 Park Ave, btwn E 61st & 62nd Sts; d $300-600, ste $500-4000; ❄@📶; [S]N/R, 4/5/6 to Lexington Ave/59 St, F, Q to Lexington Ave-63rd St) This fabled hotel is prime territory for Park Ave shoppers. Guests even get 15% off at nearby Bloomingdales (25% during the holidays!). Inside, the hotel is designed to feel like an Upper East Side apartment block. Its 379 rooms – standard clock in huge at 325 to 375 sq ft – come with roomy desks and elegant marble bathrooms that have pro-style hair-dryers – some also have balconies.

Upper West Side

★**Arthouse Hotel NYC** BOUTIQUE HOTEL **$$**
(Map p94; ☎212-362-1100; www.arthousehotelnyc.com; 2178 Broadway, at 77th St; d/ste from $250/350; ❄@📶; [S]1 to 77th St) This art-focused boutique hotel mixes vintage furnishings with contemporary industrial design. The dapper lounge and bar areas on the ground floor are stylish spaces to decamp after a day spent exploring. Above, 291 airy rooms benefit from lots of natural light and restrained decor. Flickers of mid-century design are complemented by contemporary amenities like coffeemakers, flat-screen TVs and marble bathrooms.

Hotel Beacon HOTEL **$$**
(Map p94; ☎212-787-1100, reservations 800-572-4969; www.beaconhotel.com; 2130 Broadway, btwn 74th & 75th Sts; d from $250; 📶; [S]1/2/3 to 72nd St) Adjacent to the Beacon Theatre, this family favorite offers a winning mix of attentive service, comfortable rooms and convenient location. The Beacon has 278 rooms (some are multi-bedroom suites) decorated in muted shades of Pottery Barn green. The units are well-maintained and quite roomy; all come with coffeemakers and kitchenettes. Amenities include a bar, gym, outsourced cycling classes and self-service laundry.

Empire Hotel HOTEL **$$$**
(Map p94; ☎212-265-7400; www.empirehotelnyc.com; 44 W 63rd St, at Broadway; r from $340; ❄📶🏊; [S]1 to 66th St-Lincoln Center) The bones are all that remain of the original Empire, just across the street from Lincoln Center, with wholesale renovations dressing them in earthy tones and contemporary stylings complete with canopied pool deck, huge Empire Rooftop bar (p125) and sexy two-story lobby lounge with sweeping staircase and floor-to-ceiling drapes. Its 420 rooms feature brightly hued walls with plush dark-leather furnishings.

Harlem & Upper Manhattan

Harlem Flophouse GUESTHOUSE **$**
(Map p94; ☎347-632-1960; www.harlemflophouse.com; 242 W 123rd St, btwn Adam Clayton Powell Jr & Frederick Douglass Blvds, Harlem; d with shared bath $99-150; 📶; [S]A/B/C/D, 2/3 to 125th St) Rekindle Harlem's Jazz Age in this atmospheric 1890s town house, its four nostalgic rooms decked out with brass beds and vintage radios (set to a local jazz station). It feels like a delicious step back in time, which also means shared bathrooms, no air-con and no TVs. One of the downstairs lounges doubles as a music room that sometimes hosts intimate concerts.

Last but not least is friendly house-cat Phoebe, who completes the homely, welcoming vibe. For longer stays, the owner also rents out a spacious basement suite (per night $175) with double and single bed plus an ensuite bathroom – contact directly to enquire.

Brooklyn

Wythe Hotel BOUTIQUE HOTEL **$$**
(☎718-460-8000; www.wythehotel.com; 80 Wythe Ave, at N 11th St, Williamsburg; d from $329; ❄📶; [S]L to Bedford Ave, G to Nassau Ave) Set in a converted 1901 factory, the red-brick Wythe (pronounced 'white') Hotel brings a dash of high design to Williamsburg. Exposed brick and 13ft timber ceilings allow the building's history to breathe. Meanwhile beds fashioned from reclaimed wood and a faintly nautical theme conspire with nostalgic paisley, leather and custom-made wallpaper to create a space that feels rough-hewn but elegant.

McCarren Hotel & Pool BOUTIQUE HOTEL **$$**
(☎718-218-7500; www.mccarrenhotel.com; 160 N 12th St, btwn Bedford Ave & Berry St, Williamsburg; d from $286; ❄📶🏊; [S]L to Bedford Ave, G to Nassau Ave) The tropical-style pool area, where patrons armed with cocktails drape themselves across loungers, is the prime draw of this swish, mural-clad hotel. Rooms (most

with balconies) are attired like a hip friend's lounge – velvety sofas, vinyl, the odd guitar – while a rooftop vegan restaurant and jazz bar mean you can kick off your evening on-site. Note: the pool's summer only.

A gym is available for guest use.

NU Hotel
HOTEL $$
(Map p80; ☑718-852-8585; www.nuhotelbrooklyn.com; 85 Smith St, at Atlantic Ave, Boerum Hill; d incl breakfast from $209; P✳@🛜; S F, G to Bergen St) Brooklyn-themed adornments, upcycled teak furnishings and occasionally eyebrow-raising artwork bestow an artful industrial flair on rooms at NU. The location, on the border of Boerum Hill and Downtown, is handy and free bikes are a convenient perk. Groups of four can consider the 'Bunkbed' suite, with a queen and twin bunks, while art-lovers will appreciate the mural-washed 'NU Perspective' rooms.

EVEN Hotel
BOUTIQUE HOTEL $$
(Map p80; ☑718-552-3800; www.evenhotels.com; 46 Nevins St, at Schermerhorn St, Downtown Brooklyn; r from $256; ✳🛜🏊; S 2/3, 4/5 to Nevins St, A/C, G to Hoyt-Schermerhorn) This wellness-concept hotel caters to the fitness-minded, with 'workout zones' (with personal yoga mat, foam roller, yoga block and stability ball) inside the 202 rooms, a 24-hour gym, organic food and fresh-squeezed OJ in the cafe, and free laundry service. Central location in Downtown Brooklyn is super convenient for subway stops.

Williamsburg Hotel
BOUTIQUE HOTEL $$$
(☑718-362-8100; www.thewilliamsburghotel.com; 96 Wythe Ave, at N 10th St, Williamsburg; d from $396; ✳🛜🏊; S L to Bedford Ave) Just two blocks from the water, this eight-story, industrial-chic hotel is blessed with spectacular river and Manhattan views. It's worth paying extra for one of the 'terrace' rooms on the northern side, which give you an unbroken view of the Empire State Building, the Chrysler Building and the Upper East Side from your artificial-grass-carpeted balcony (some have swing chairs).

Floor-to-ceiling windows and glassed-in showers with bright subway tiles make the smallish rooms feel more open. Minibars, leather headboards, safes and essential-oil amenities by local maker Apotheke all come standard. There's a rooftop bar in the shape of a classic NYC water tower (open 6pm to 4am Wednesday to Saturday) and an outdoor rooftop swimming pool, plus free push-bikes for cruising Williamsburg stress-free.

✗ Eating

From inspired iterations of world cuisine to quintessentially local nibbles, New York City's dining scene is infinite, all-consuming and a proud testament to its kaleidoscope of citizens. Even if you're not an obsessive foodie hitting ethnic enclaves or the newest cult-chef openings, an outstanding meal is always only a block away.

✗ Financial District & Lower Manhattan

Arcade Bakery
BAKERY $
(Map p80; ☑212-227-7895; www.arcadebakery.com; 220 Church St, btwn Worth & Thomas Sts, Tribeca; pastries from $3, sandwiches $9, pizzas $10; ☺8am-3pm Mon-Fri; S 1 to Franklin St) It's easy to miss this little treasure in the vaulted lobby of a 1920s office building, with a counter trading in beautiful, just-baked goods. Edibles include artful sandwiches and (between noon and 3pm, or whenever the dough runs out) a small selection of puff-crust pizzas with combos like mushroom, caramelized onion and goat's cheese. Arcade also makes sensational almond croissants.

Hudson Eats
FOOD HALL $
(Map p80; ☑212-978-1698; https://bfplny.com/directory/food; Brookfield Place, 225 Liberty St, at West St, Lower Manhattan; dishes from $7; ☺8am-9pm Mon-Sat, to 7pm Sun; 🛜; S E to World Trade Center, 2/3 to Park Pl, R/W to Cortlandt St, 4/5 to Fulton St, A/C to Chambers St) Sleekly renovated office and retail complex Brookfield Place is home to Hudson Eats, a shiny, upmarket food hall. Decked out with terrazzo floors, marble countertops and floor-to-ceiling windows with expansive views of Jersey City and the Hudson River, it has a string of respected, chef-driven eateries, including Blue Ribbon Sushi, Fuku, Northern Tiger and Dos Toros Taqueria.

Two Hands
AUSTRALIAN $$
(Map p80; www.twohandsnyc.com; 251 Church St, btwn Franklin & Leonard Sts, Tribeca; lunch & brunch mains $14-19; ☺8am-5pm; 🍽; S 1 to Franklin St, N/Q/R/W, 6 to Canal St) An interior of whitewashed brick gives this modern 'Australian-style' cafe-restaurant an airy feel – and the local crowds love it. The menu offers light breakfast and lunch dishes such as a fully loaded açai bowl with berries and granola or a chicken sandwich with feta cream and olive tapenade. The coffee's top-notch, and there's happy hour from 2pm to 5pm.

Brookfield Place FOOD HALL $$
(Map p80; ☎212-978-1673; www.brookfieldplaceny.com; 230 Vesey St, at West St, Lower Manhattan; 📶; [S] E to World Trade Center, 2/3 to Park Pl, R/W to Cortlandt St, 4/5 to Fulton St, A/C to Chambers St) This polished, high-end office and retail complex offers two fabulous food halls. Francophile foodies should hit Le District, a charming and mouthwatering marketplace with several stand-alone restaurants and counters selling everything from stinky cheese to steak-*frites*. One floor above is Hudson Eats, a fashionable enclave of upmarket fast bites, from sushi and tacos to salads and burgers.

Le District FOOD HALL $$$
(Map p80; ☎212-981-8588; www.ledistrict.com; Brookfield Place, 225 Liberty St, at West St, Lower Manhattan; market mains $12-30, Beaubourg dinner mains $19-36; ⏲Beaubourg 8am-10pm Mon, to 11pm Tue & Wed, to midnight Thu & Fri, 10am-midnight Sat, to 10pm Sun, other hours vary; 📶; [S] E to World Trade Center, 2/3 to Park Pl, R/W to Cortlandt St, 4/5 to Fulton St, A/C to Chambers St) Paris on the Hudson reigns at this sprawling French food emporium selling everything from high-gloss pastries and pretty *tartines* to stinky cheese and savory steak-*frites*. Main restaurant Beaubourg does bistro classics such as coq au vin, but for a quick sit-down feed, head to the Market District counter for frites or the Cafe District for a savory crepe. The Garden District offers fresh produce, groceries and a salad bar that's perfect for putting together an impromptu alfresco lunch by the river.

Opening hours vary at each of the restaurants and between the Market, Cafe and Garden District areas; check the website for specific times.

★**Locanda Verde** ITALIAN $$$
(Map p80; ☎212-925-3797; www.locandaverdenyc.com; 377 Greenwich St, at N Moore St, Tribeca; mains lunch $25-32, dinner $38-54; ⏲7am-11pm Mon-Thu, to 11:30pm Fri, 8am-11:30pm Sat, to 11pm Sun; [S] 1 to Franklin St, A/C/E to Canal St) Curbside at the Greenwich Hotel (p106) you'll find this Italian fine diner by Andrew Carmellini, where velvet curtains part onto a scene of loosened button-downs, black dresses and slick bar staff. It's a place to see and be seen, but the food – perhaps Sicilian cod with chickpeas, *orecchiette* with duck sausage and kale, or truffle ravioli – is the main event. Booking ahead is recommended.

Bâtard EUROPEAN $$$
(Map p80; ☎212-219-2777; www.batardtribeca.com; 239 W Broadway, btwn Walker & White Sts, Tribeca; 2/3/4 courses $65/89/99; ⏲5:30-10pm Mon-Wed, to 10:30pm Thu-Sat; [S] 1 to Franklin St, A/C/E to Canal St) Austrian chef Markus Glocker heads this warm, Michelin-starred hot spot, where a pared-back interior puts the focus squarely on the food. Glocker's dishes are precise examples of classical French and Italian cooking: the prix-fixe menus hold rich delights such as striped bass with chanterelle mushrooms, or tagliatelle with roast lamb loin, olives and pecorino.

Service is gracious and the Francophile wine list is particularly strong on the wines of Burgundy. On Monday, bring your own bottle and pay no corkage.

🍴 SoHo & Chinatown

★**Nom Wah Tea Parlor** CHINESE $
(Map p80; ☎212-962-6047; www.nomwah.com; 13 Doyers St, Chinatown; dim sum from $3.75; ⏲10:30am-10pm Sun-Wed, to 11pm Fri & Sat; [S] J/Z to Chambers St; 4/5/6 to Brooklyn Bridge-City Hall) Hidden down a narrow lane, 1920s Nom Wah Tea Parlor might look like an old-school American diner, but it's actually the oldest dim-sum place in town. Grab a table or seat at one of the red banquettes or counter stools and simply tick off what you want on the paper menu provided. Roast pork buns, Shanghainese soup dumplings, shrimp siu mai...it's all finger-licking good.

Prince Street Pizza PIZZA $
(Map p84; ☎212-966-4100; 27 Prince St, btwn Mott & Elizabeth Sts, Nolita; pizza slices from $3.20; ⏲11:45am-11pm Sun-Thu, to 2am Fri & Sat; [S] R/W to Prince St; 6 to Spring St) It's a miracle the oven door hasn't come off its hinges at this classic standing-room-only slice joint, its brick walls hung with shots of celebrity fans like Rebel Wilson, Usher and Kate Hudson. The sauces, mozzarella and ricotta are made in-house and New Yorkers go wild for the pepperoni square variety. The pizza is decent, but not dazzling enough to justify the perpetual queues.

Xi'an Famous Foods CHINESE $
(Map p80; www.xianfoods.com; 45 Bayard St, btwn Elizabeth St & Bowery, Chinatown; dishes $4.70-12; ⏲11:30am-9pm Sun-Thu, to 9:30pm Fri & Sat; [S] N/Q/R/W, J/Z, 6 to Canal St, B/D to Grand St) Food bloggers hyperventilate at the mere mention of this small chain's hand-pulled noodles. The burgers are also menu stars: tender lamb sautéed with ground cumin and toasted chili seeds, or melt-in-the-mouth stewed pork. There are 11 other locations throughout the city.

Butcher's Daughter VEGETARIAN $$
(Map p84; ☎ 212-219-3434; www.thebutchers-daughter.com; 19 Kenmare St, at Elizabeth St, Nolita; salads & sandwiches $13-16, dinner mains $15-18; ⏲ 8am-10pm; 🌱; [S] J to Bowery; 6 to Spring St) The butcher's daughter certainly has rebelled, peddling nothing but fresh herbivorous fare in her whitewashed cafe. While healthy it is, boring it's not: everything from the soaked organic muesli to the spicy kale Caesar salad with almond Parmesan or the dinnertime Butcher's burger (vegetable and black-bean patty with cashew cheddar cheese) is devilishly delish.

★**Uncle Boons** THAI $$
(Map p84; ☎ 646-370-6650; www.uncleboons.com; 7 Spring St, btwn Elizabeth St & Bowery, Nolita; small plates $13-16, large plates $22-32; ⏲ 5:30-11pm Sun-Thu, to midnight Fri & Sat; 📶; [S] J/Z to Bowery; 6 to Spring St) Michelin-star Thai is served up in a fun, tongue-in-cheek combo of retro wood-paneled dining room with Thai film posters and old family snaps. Spanning the old and the new, dishes are tangy, rich and creative. Standouts include the *kob woonsen* (garlic and soy marinated frogs legs), *koong* (grilled baby octopus) and *kaduuk* (roasted bone marrow satay).

★**Dutch** AMERICAN $$$
(Map p84; ☎ 212-677-6200; www.thedutchnyc.com; 131 Sullivan St, at Prince St, SoHo; mains lunch $18-38, dinner $27-68; ⏲ 11:30am-3pm & 5:30-10:30pm Mon-Thu, to 11:30pm Fri, 10am-3pm & 5:30-11:30pm Sat, to 10:30pm Sun; [S] C/E to Spring St; R/W to Prince St; 1 to Houston St) Whether perched at the bar or dining snugly in the back room, you can always expect smart, farm-to-table comfort grub at this see-and-be-seen stalwart. Flavors traverse the globe, from wagyu steak tartare with béarnaise aioli ($22) to grilled lamb chops with jerk sauce and roti pancake ($46). Reservations are recommended, especially for dinner and all day on weekends.

Il Buco Alimentari & Vineria ITALIAN $$$
(Map p84; ☎ 212-837-2622; www.ilbucovineria.com; 53 Great Jones St, btwn Bowery & Lafayette St, NoHo; mains lunch $14-34, dinner $34-70; ⏲ 8am-11pm Mon-Thu, to midnight Fri, 9am-midnight Sat, to 11pm Sun; 📶; [S] 6 to Bleecker St; B/D/F/M to Broadway-Lafayette St) Whether it's espresso at the front bar, cheese from the deli or long-and-lazy Italian feasting in the sunken dining room, Il Buco's trendier spin-off delivers the goods. Brickwork and giant industrial lamps set a hip and rustic tone, echoed in the menu. The lunchtime paninis are huge, decadent and divine: try the porchetta with fried eggs, salsa verde and arugula ($18).

🍴 West Village, Chelsea & Meatpacking District

Dominique Ansel Kitchen BAKERY $
(Map p84; ☎ 212-242-5111; www.dominiqueanselkitchen.com; 137 Seventh Ave, btwn Charles & W 10th Sts, West Village; pastries $6-8, sandwiches $14-15; ⏲ 9am-9m; [S] 1 to Christopher St-Sheridan Sq) The much-garlanded creator of the cronut owns this small, sunlit bakery, where you can nibble on perfectly flaky croissants, brownies finished with smoked sage, lemon-yuzu butter tarts and many other heavenly treats (but no cronuts). There's also light savory fare, such as sausage, kale and lentil soup and an extra-large croque monsieur, served with salad.

Taïm ISRAELI $
(Map p84; ☎ 212-691-1287; www.taimfalafel.com; 222 Waverly Pl, btwn Perry & W 11th Sts, West Village; sandwiches $8.50; ⏲ 11am-10pm; 🌱; [S] 1 to Christopher St-Sheridan Sq, 2/3 to 14th St, A/C/E, L to 8th Ave-14th St) This tiny joint whips up some of the best falafel in the city. You can order it Green (traditional style) or Harissa (with Tunisian spices) – whichever you choose, you'll get it stuffed into pita with tahini, salad and pickles, on a platter with sides such as Moroccan carrots and marinated beets, or over Israeli salad.

Blossom VEGAN $$
(Map p88; ☎ 212-627-1144; www.blossomnyc.com; 187 Ninth Ave, btwn 21st & 22nd Sts, Chelsea; mains lunch $18-19, dinner $22-24; ⏲ noon-2:45pm & 5-9:30pm Mon-Thu, noon-2:45pm & 5-10pm Fri & Sat, noon-2:45pm & 5-9pm Sun; 🌱; [S] 1, C/E to 23rd St) Cozily occupying a historic Chelsea town house, this beacon to hungry vegans is a peaceful, romantic dining spot that offers imaginative, all-kosher tofu, seitan and vegetable creations, some raw. Brunch dishes like tofu Benedict and Florentine impersonate animal proteins deliciously, while superb dinner mains such as risotto with shiitake, cremini and king-trumpet mushrooms and miso-cashew cream need no affectations.

Desserts such as vegan tiramisu and 'cheesecake' are so voluptuous you'll swear they're filled with butter and cream.

JeJu Noodle Bar NOODLES $$
(Map p84; ☎ 646-666-0947; http://jejunoodlebar.com; 679 Greenwich St, at Christopher St, West Village; noodles $18-19; ⏲ 5-10pm Sun-Wed, to 11pm Thu-Sat; 🚌 M8 to Greenwich St-Christopher St,

S 1 to Christopher St-Sheridan Sq) With classic ramen continuing to rampage across the world's tables, perhaps it's time to explore its variations – such as the Korean *ram-yun* served at this welcoming restaurant on Christopher St's quieter western stretch. Start with *toro ssam bap* (fatty tuna, toasted seaweed, *tobiko* rice and scrambled egg) before slurping down a *so ramyun* – brisket and noodles in veal broth.

Babu Ji   INDIAN $$

(Map p84; ✆ 212-951-1082; www.babujinyc.com; 22 E 13th St, btwn University Pl & Fifth Ave, West Village; mains $18-25; ⊙ dinner 5-10:30pm Sun-Thu, to 11:30pm Fri & Sat, brunch 11:30am-3pm Sat & Sun; S 4/5/6, N/Q/R/W, L to 14th St-Union Sq) A playful spirit marks this excellent Australian-run Indian restaurant near Union Sq. Many dishes play fast and loose with tradition, such as 'naan pizza' with sweet-pickled-chili butter, mushroom tikka with lemon-garlic sour cream and herbs, and tandoori-charred dorade with ginger-honey sauce and radish micro-greens. A $62 tasting menu, obligatory for the entire party, can be matched with beers or wines.

★ RedFarm   FUSION $$$

(Map p84; ✆ 212-792-9700; www.redfarmnyc.com; 529 Hudson St, btwn W 10th & Charles Sts, West Village; mains $28-52, dumplings $15-17; ⊙ dinner 5-11:45pm Mon-Sat, to 11pm Sun, brunch 11am-2:30pm Sat & Sun; S 1 to Christopher St-Sheridan Sq, A/C/E, B/D/F/M to W 4th St-Washington Sq) Experience Chinese cooking as unique, delectable artistry in this small, buzzing space. Diced tuna and eggplant bruschetta, juicy rib steak (marinated in papaya, ginger and soy) and pastrami egg rolls are among the many stunning, genre-defying dishes. Other hits include lobster sautéed with egg and chopped pork, cheeseburger spring rolls, and black-truffle chicken-soup dumplings.

★ Blue Hill   AMERICAN $$$

(Map p84; ✆ 212-539-1776; www.bluehillfarm.com; 75 Washington Pl, btwn Sixth Ave & Washington Sq W, West Village; prix-fixe menu $95-108; ⊙ 5-11pm Mon-Sat, to 10pm Sun; S A/C/E, B/D/F/M to W 4th St-Washington Sq) A place for Slow Food junkies with deep pockets, Blue Hill was an early crusader in the farm-to-table movement. Gifted chef-patron Dan Barber, who hails from a farm family in the Berkshires, MA, uses regional harvests to create his widely praised fare.

Expect judiciously seasoned, perfectly ripe vegetables that highlight proteins such as Maine diver scallops or Blue Hill Farm grass-fed beef. The space itself, set just below street level in a former speakeasy on a quaint village block, is sophisticated and serene. Reservations and 'elegant casual' dress are recommended, and cell phones and photography are forbidden in the dining room.

✕ East Village & Lower East Side

Supermoon Bakehouse   BAKERY $

(Map p84; www.supermoonbakehouse.com; 120 Rivington St, at Essex St, Lower East Side; pastries $4-9.5; ⊙ 8am-10pm Mon-Thu, to 11am Fri, 9am-11pm Sat, to 10pm Sun; S F to Delancey St) This super-friendly Aussie-owned bakery, where the bakers can be seen doing their thing behind glass, produces perhaps Manhattan's most imaginative and remarkable baked croissants, both sweet and savory, from the hot apple pie or matcha-blueberry to the ham-and-cheese or the Reuben. Varying flavors of soft-serve ice cream and doughnuts round out the offerings.

Mamoun's   MIDDLE EASTERN $

(Map p84; ✆ 646-870-5785; www.mamouns.com; 30 St Marks Pl, btwn Second & Third Aves, East Village; sandwiches $5-9, plates $9-13; ⊙ 11am-1am Mon-Thu, to 4am Fri & Sat, to midnight Sun; ✎; S 6 to Astor Pl, L to 3rd Ave) This former grab-and-go outpost of the beloved NYC falafel chain has expanded its St Marks storefront with more seating inside and out. Late on weekends a line of inebriated bar-hoppers ends the night with a juicy shawarma covered in Mamoun's famous hot sauce. If you don't do lamb, perhaps a falafel wrap or a sustaining bowl of *fool mudammas* (stewed beans)?

★ Ivan Ramen   RAMEN $$

(Map p84; ✆ 646-678-3859; www.ivanramen.com; 25 Clinton St, btwn Stanton & E Houston Sts, East Village; mains $15-21; ⊙ 12:30-10pm Sun-Thu, to 11pm Fri & Sat; S F, J/M/Z to Delancey-Essex Sts, F to 2nd Ave) After creating two thriving ramen spots in Tokyo, Long Islander Ivan Orkin brought his talents back home. Few can agree about NYC's best ramen, but this intimate shop, where solo ramen heads sit at the bar watching their bowls take shape, is on every short list. The *tsukumen* (dipping-style) ramen with pickled collard greens and shoyu-glazed pork belly is unbeatable.

Russ & Daughters Cafe   JEWISH $$

(Map p84; ✆ 212-475-4880; www.russanddaughterscafe.com; 127 Orchard St, btwn Delancey & Rivington Sts, Lower East Side; mains $18-23; ⊙ 9am-10pm Mon-Fri, from 8am Sat & Sun; S F, J/M/Z

TO MARKET, TO MARKET

Don't let the concrete streets and buildings fool you – New York City has a thriving greens scene that comes in many shapes and sizes. At the top of your list should be the Chelsea Market (p81), which is packed with gourmet goodies of all kinds – both shops (where you can assemble picnics) and food stands (where you can eat on-site). Many other food halls have opened in recent years, including **Gansevoort Market** (Map p88; ☎646-449-8400; www.gansmarket.com; 353 W 14th St, btwn Eighth & Ninth Aves, Meatpacking District; mains $10-15; ⏲7am-9pm; 📶; [S]A/C/E, L to 8th Ave-14th St) in the Meatpacking District and a trio of food halls at Brookfield Place (p110), in Lower Manhattan. Across the river, there's the brand-new DeKalb Market Hall (p119) in downtown Brooklyn, plus the small food hall of **Berg'n** (www.bergn.com; 899 Bergen St, btwn Classon & Franklin Aves, Crown Heights; mains $13-16; ⏲food 9am-10pm Tue-Thu, 10am-11pm Fri & Sat, to 10pm Sun, bar 11am-late Tue-Sun; 📶🥗👪; [S]C, 2/3, 4/5 to Franklin Ave) out in Crown Heights.

Many neighborhoods in NYC have their own Greenmarket. One of the biggest is the Union Square Greenmarket (p85), open four days a week throughout the year. Check Grow NYC (www.grownyc.org/greenmarket) for a list of the other 50-plus markets around the city.

Out in Brooklyn, the best weekend markets for noshers (rather than cook-at-home types) are Smorgasburg (p120), with over 100 craft-food vendors, and the Brooklyn Flea Market (p134), which has several dozen stalls.

Also popular are high-end market-cum-grocers like Eataly (p123) and **Dean & DeLuca** (Map p84; ☎212-226-6800; www.deananddeluca.com; 560 Broadway, at Prince St, SoHo; pastries from $4, sandwiches $12; ⏲7am-9pm Mon-Fri, 8am-9pm Sat & Sun; [S]N/R to Prince St; 6 to Spring St), where fresh produce and ready-made fare are given the five-star treatment. Whole Foods is another big draw, particularly its ecofriendly, locavore-focused **Brooklyn outpost** (☎718-907-3622; www.wholefoodsmarket.com; 214 3rd St, btwn Third Ave & Gowanus Canal, Gowanus; ⏲8am-11pm; 📶🥗👪; [S]R to Union; F, G to 4th Ave-9th St).

to Delancey-Essex Sts) Sit down and feast on shiny boiled bagels and perhaps the best lox in the city in all the comfort of an old-school diner, in this extension of the storied Jewish delicatessen Russ & Daughters (p132), just up Orchard St. Aside from thick, smoky fish, there are potato latkes, borscht, eggs plenty of ways, and even chopped liver, if you must.

★Clinton Street Baking Company — AMERICAN $$

(Map p84; ☎646-602-6263; www.clintonstreetbaking.com; 4 Clinton St, btwn Stanton & E Houston Sts, Lower East Side; mains $12-18; ⏲8am-3:30pm & 5:30-10pm Mon-Fri, 9am-4:30pm Sat & Sun; [S]F, J/M/Z to Delancey-Essex Sts, F to 2nd Ave) Mom-and-pop shop extraordinaire Clinton Street Baking Company takes the cake in so many categories – best pancakes, best muffins, best po'boys (Southern-style sandwiches), best biscuits etc – that you're pretty much guaranteed a stellar meal no matter what time you stop by. In the evening you can opt for 'breakfast for dinner' (pancakes, eggs Benedict), fish tacos or buttermilk fried chicken.

Weekend brunch can see hordes of locals lining up for an hour or more, so do your brunching during the week.

★Veselka — UKRAINIAN $$

(Map p84; ☎212-228-9682; www.veselka.com; 144 Second Ave, at E 9th St, East Village; mains $13-19; ⏲24hr; [S]6 to Astor Pl, L to 3rd Ave) This beloved vestige of the area's Ukrainian past has been serving up handmade *pierogi* (cheese, potato or meat dumplings), borscht and goulash since 1954. The cluttered spread of tables is available to loungers and carb-loaders all night long, though it's a great, warming pit stop any time of day, and a haunt for writers, actors and East Village characters.

Momofuku Noodle Bar — NOODLES $$

(Map p84; ☎212-777-7773; https://momofukunoodlebar.com; 171 First Ave, btwn E 10th & E 11th Sts, East Village; mains $17-27; ⏲lunch noon-4:30pm Mon-Fri, to 4pm Sat & Sun, dinner 5:30-11pm Sun-Thu, to midnight Fri & Sat; 🥗; [S]L to 1st Ave, 6 to Astor Pl) With just a handful of tables and a no-reservations policy, this bustling phenomenon may require you to wait. But you won't regret it: spicy short-rib ramen; ginger noodles with pickled shiitake; cold noodles with Sichuan sausage and Thai basil – it's all amazing. The ever-changing menu includes buns (perhaps brisket and horseradish), snacks (smoked chicken wings) and desserts.

The open kitchen creates quite a bit of steam, but the devoted crowd remains unfazed.

Momofuku is part of David Chang's crazy-popular, now global, restaurant empire (www.momofuku.com). NYC outposts include two-Michelin-starred **Momofuku Ko**, which serves up pricey tasting menus ($225) and has a prohibitive, we-dare-you-to-try reservations scheme; **Momofuku Ssäm Bar**, which features large and small meat-heavy dishes; chicken joint Fuku; and another Noodle Bar in Colombus Circle.

Union Square, Flatiron District & Gramercy

Shake Shack
BURGERS $

(Map p88; ☑646-889-6600; www.shakeshack. com; Madison Square Park, cnr E 23rd St & Madison Ave, Flatiron District; burgers $4.20-9.50; ☺7:30am-11pm Mon-Fri, from 8:30am Sat & Sun; ⑤R/W, F/M, 6 to 23rd St) The flagship of chef Danny Meyer's gourmet burger chain (this is where it all started – in a hot-dog cart), Shake Shack whips up hyper-fresh burgers, hand-cut fries and a rotating lineup of frozen custards. Veg-heads can dip into the crisp portobello burger. Lines are long – but worth it – and you can eat while people-watching at tables and benches in the park. Its breakfast menu is all about egg-based fillings stuffed into its trademark potato buns: a bit like a posh McDonald's, and cheap.

Big Daddy's
DINER $

(Map p88; ☑212-477-1500; www.bigdaddysnyc. com; 239 Park Ave S, btwn E 19th & E 20th Sts, Gramercy; mains $10-16; ☺8am-midnight Mon-Thu, to 5am Fri & Sat, to 11pm Sun; ▮; ⑤6 to 23rd St; 4/5/6, L, N/Q/R/W to 14th St-Union Sq) Giant, fluffy omelettes, hearty burgers and heaps of tater tots (regular or sweet potato) have made Big Daddy's a top choice for both breakfast and late-night treats. The interior is all Americana kitsch, but unlike some theme restaurants the food doesn't break the bank and actually satisfies.

Come later in the afternoon on weekdays for happy-hour deals: its gargantuan shakes are half price 3pm to 5pm, while a rotation of appetizers and other drinks are half price 4pm to 7pm.

Eisenberg's Sandwich Shop
SANDWICHES $

(Map p88; ☑212-675-5096; www.eisenbergs nyc.com; 174 Fifth Ave, btwn W 22nd & 23rd St, Flatiron District; sandwiches $4-14; ☺7:30am-6pm Mon-Fri, 9am-5pm Sat, 10am-3pm Sun; ☎;

⑤R/W to 23rd St) This old-school diner – an anomaly on this mostly upscale stretch of real estate – is a comfy, quiet spot for traditional Jewish-diner fare like chopped liver, pastrami and whitefish salad. Grab a stool at the long bar and rub elbows with an eclectic mix of customers who know meatloaf isn't a joke dish.

★ Eleven Madison Park
AMERICAN $$$

(Map p88; ☑212-889-0905; www.elevenmadison park.com; 11 Madison Ave, btwn 24th & 25th Sts, Flatiron District; tasting menu $315; ☺5:30-10pm Mon-Wed, to 10:30pm Thu, noon-1pm & 5:30-10:30pm Fri-Sun; ⑤R/W, 6 to 23rd St) Eleven Madison Park consistently bags a spot on top restaurant lists. Frankly, we're not surprised: this revamped poster child of modern, sustainable American cooking is also one of only five NYC restaurants sporting three Michelin stars. Insane attention to detail, intense creativity and whimsy are all trademarks of chef Daniel Humm's approach.

After a revamp, it's now more accessible than ever thanks to the addition of dining tables in the bar. Here, an abbreviated tasting menu (five rather than 10 courses, for $175) can be had, or select mains (around $50) from the core tasting menu. Reservations – for both the main dining room and bar tables – open on the first of the month for the following month. Dress to impress.

Maialino
ITALIAN $$$

(Map p88; ☑212-777-2410; www.maialinonyc.com; Gramercy Park Hotel, 2 Lexington Ave, at 21st St, Gramercy; mains $24-58; ☺7:30-10am, noon-2pm & 5:30-10:30pm Mon-Thu, to 11pm Fri, 10am-2pm & 5:30-11pm Sat, to 10:30pm Sun; ⑤6, R/W to 23rd St) Fans reserve tables up to four weeks in advance at this Danny Meyer classic, but the best seats in the house are at the walk-in bar, with sociable, knowledgeable staffers. Wherever you're plonked, take your taste buds on a Roman holiday. Maialino's lip-smacking, rustic Italian fare is created using produce from the nearby Union Square Greenmarket (p85).

A solid wine list and good-value $48 prix-fixe lunch (Monday to Friday) seals the deal.

Gramercy Tavern
AMERICAN $$$

(Map p88; ☑212-477-0777; www.gramercytavern. com; 42 E 20th St, btwn Broadway & Park Ave S, Flatiron District; tavern mains $34-36, dining room 3-course menu $134, tasting menus $164-184; ☺tavern 11:30am-11pm Sun-Thu, to midnight Fri & Sat, lunch 11:30am-2pm, dinner 5-9:45pm Sun-Thu, to 10:30pm Fri & Sat; ☎⁄; ⑤R/W, 6 to 23rd St) ⁄ Seasonal, local ingredients drive this perennial favorite, a vibrant, country-chic institution aglow with copper sconces, murals and dramatic floral arrangements. Choose from two spaces: the walk-in-only tavern and its à la carte menu, or the swankier dining room and its fancier prix-fixe and degustation feasts. Regardless of where you sit, you'll find service is excellent. New Yorkers *love* this place: book ahead.

★ Craft
AMERICAN $$$

(Map p88; 212-780-0880; www.craftrestaurant. com; 43 E 19th St, btwn Broadway & Park Ave S, Union Sq; mains $33-69; 5:30-10pm Mon-Thu, to 11pm Fri, 5-11pm Sat, to 9pm Sun; 4/5/6, N/Q/R/W, L to 14th St-Union Sq) Humming, high-powered Craft flies the flag for small, family-owned farms and food producers, their bounty transformed into pure, polished dishes. Whether nibbling on flawlessly charred braised octopus, juicy roasted quail or pumpkin mezzaluna pasta with sage, brown butter and Parmesan, expect every ingredient to sing with flavor. Book ahead Wednesday to Saturday or head in by 6pm or after 9:30pm.

Midtown

Great Northern Food Hall
FOOD HALL $

(Map p88; www.greatnorthernfood.com; Grand Central Terminal, Vanderbilt Hall, 89 E 42nd St; sandwiches $7-12; 7am-11pm Mon-Fri, 8am-8pm Sat & Sun; S, 4/5/6, 7 to Grand Central-42nd St, Metro North to Grand Central-42nd St) Ensconced in the beautiful beaux-arts Vanderbilt Hall, this airy food hall has upped the ante for food in New York's grandest station terminal. Pull up a stool beneath the glamorous chandelier and enjoy a glass of wine, Danish beer or artisan coffee. Gourmet bites on offer mesh Nordic flair with New York produce. Hours differ for individual kiosks.

The hall is the brainchild of Claus Meyer, the New Nordic rock star who co-founded Noma in Copenhagen. The fare is mostly soups, salads, hot sandwiches and *smorresbord* (Danish open-faced sandwiches) such as curried herring with egg yolk or roast beef with pickled onions. The hall also serves breakfast (8am to 11am weekdays, 10am to 4pm weekends) and brunch.

★ Totto Ramen
JAPANESE $

(Map p88; 212-582-0052; www.tottoramen.com; 366 W 52nd St, btwn Eighth & Ninth Aves; ramen $12-18; noon-4:30pm & 5:30pm-midnight Mon-Sat, 4-11pm Sun; C/E to 50th St) There might be another two branches in Midtown, but purists know that neither beats the tiny 20-seat original. Write your name and number of guests on the clipboard and wait your turn. Your reward: extraordinary ramen. Go for the butter-soft *char siu* (pork), which sings in dishes like miso ramen (with fermented soybean paste, egg, scallion, bean sprouts, onion and homemade chili paste).

Burger Joint
BURGERS $

(Map p88; 212-708-7414; www.burgerjointny. com; Le Parker Meridien, 119 W 56th St, btwn Sixth & Seventh Aves; burgers $9-17; 11am-11:30pm Sun-Thu, to midnight Fri & Sat; F to 57th St) With only a small neon burger as your clue, this speakeasy-style burger hut lurks behind the lobby curtain in the Parker New York hotel. Though it might not be as secret as it once was (you'll see the queues), it still delivers the same winning formula of graffiti-strewn walls, retro booths and attitude-loaded staff slapping up beef 'n' patty brilliance.

★ Smith
AMERICAN $$

(Map p88; 212-644-2700; http://thesmithres taurant.com; 956 Second Ave, at 51st St, Midtown East; mains $22-33; 7:30am-midnight Mon-Thu, to 1am Fri, 9am-1am Sat, to midnight Sun; S 6, E/M to 51st St) This chic, bustling brasserie has an industrial-chic interior, sociable bar and well-executed grub. Much of the food is made from scratch, the seasonal menus a mix of nostalgic American and Italian inspiration (we're talking hot potato chips with blue-cheese fondue, chicken pot pie with cheddar-chive biscuit, and Sicilian baked eggs with artichokes, spinach and spicy tomato sauce).

Hangawi
KOREAN $$

(Map p88; 212-213-0077; www.hangawirestau rant.com; 12 E 32nd St, btwn Fifth & Madison Aves; mains lunch $13-14, dinner $18-30; noon-2:30pm & 5:30-10:15pm Mon-Thu, to 10:30pm Fri, 1-10:30pm Sat, 5-9:30pm Sun; S B/D/F/M, N/Q/R/W to 34th St-Herald Sq) Meat-free Korean is the draw at high-achieving Hangawi. Leave your shoes at the entrance and slip into a soothing, Zen-like space of meditative music, soft low seating and clean, complex dishes. Dishes include pumpkin noodles, spicy kimchi pancakes and a seductively smooth tofu claypot in ginger sauce. At lunch time there's a four-course prix-fixe deal for $25.

★ Agern
NEW NORDIC $$$

(Map p88; 646-568-4018; www.agernrestau rant.com; 89 E 42nd St, Grand Central Terminal; dinner mains $28-44, 2-/3-course prix-fixe lunch $40/48; 11:30am-2:30pm & 5:30-10pm Mon-Fri, 5:30-10pm Sat; S S, 4/5/6, 7 to Grand

Central-42nd St, Metro North to Grand Central-42nd St) Showing off the sleek design principles and seasonal, creative flair you'd expect from an architect of Denmark's New Nordic food revolution, Claus Meyer's restaurant in Grand Central Station features deceptively simple dishes, such as endive with preserved blackberries and pork shoulder with sorrel. Agern is also refreshingly affordable – especially the $40 lunch menu.

The restaurant can be a little tricky to find: it's wedged between the Great Northern Food Hall (Vanderbilt Hall) and the Grand Central Terminal exit ramp to 42nd St.

★ **O-ya** SUSHI $$$
(Map p88; 212-204-0200; https://o-ya.restaurant/o-ya-nyc; 120 E 28th St; nigiri $6-25; 5:30-10pm Mon-Sat; S 4/6 to 28th St) With the cheapest nigiri pairs at close to $15, this is not a spot you'll come to every day. But if you're looking for a special night out and sushi's in the game plan, come here for exquisite flavors, fish so tender it melts like butter on the tongue, and preparations so artful you almost apologize for eating them.

Le Bernardin SEAFOOD $$$
(Map p88; 212-554-1515; www.le-bernardin.com; 155 W 51st St, btwn Sixth & Seventh Aves; prix-fixe lunch/dinner $90/160, tasting menus $170-225; noon-2:30pm & 5:15-10:30pm Mon-Thu, to 11pm Fri, 5:15-11pm Sat; S 1 to 50th St; B/D, E to 7th Ave) The interiors may have been subtly sexed-up for a 'younger clientele' (the stunning storm-themed triptych is by Brooklyn artist Ran Ortner), but triple-Michelin-starred Le Bernardin remains a luxe, fine-dining holy grail. At the helm is French-born celebrity chef Éric Ripert, whose deceptively simple-looking seafood often borders on the transcendental. Life is short, and you only live (er, eat!) once.

The menu works simply: three lunch courses for $90 or four dinner courses for $160, with ample choices per course, and two tastings menus for those with more time and money. The dishes themselves are divided into three categories (Almost Raw, Barely Touched, Lightly Cooked), and most shine with delicious complexity. Book at least three weeks ahead for dinner and two weeks ahead for lunch.

Upper East Side

Eli's Essentials AMERICAN $
(Map p94; 646-755-3999; www.elizabar.com/Elis-Essentials-.aspx; 1270 Madison Ave, at E 91st St; buffet per lb $16.95, sandwiches from $7.50; 7am-11pm; S 6 to 96th St) The youngest son of the founders of Zabar's (p133) delicatessen is building a mini empire on the Upper East Side, and this update on New York's traditional Jewish deli is perfect for a pit stop near Fifth Ave's Museum Mile. As well as lox bagels and Eli's signature egg brioche roll, there's a buffet with fried chicken, mac 'n' cheese and salads.

★ **Papaya King** HOT DOGS $
(Map p94; www.papayaking.com; 179 E 86th St, at Third Ave; hot dogs $3-4.50; 8am-midnight Sun-Thu, to 1am Fri & Sat; S 4/5/6, Q to 86th St) The original hot-dog-and-papaya-juice shop, from 1932, over 40 years before crosstown rival **Gray's Papaya** (Map p94; 212-799-0243; 2090 Broadway, at 72nd St, entrance on Amsterdam Ave; hot dogs $2.50; 24hr; S 1/2/3, B, C to 72nd St) opened, Papaya King has lured many a New Yorker to its neon-lit corner for a cheap and tasty snack of hot dogs and fresh-squeezed papaya juice. (Why papaya? The informative wall signs will explain all.) Try the Homerun, with sauerkraut and New York onion relish.

Wright AMERICAN $$
(Map p94; 212-423-3665; www.guggenheim.org; Guggenheim Museum, 1071 Fifth Ave, at E 89th St; mains $23-28; 11:30am-3:30pm Mon-Fri, from 11am Sat & Sun; S 4/5/6, Q to 86th St) The Wright restaurant at the Guggenheim, serving such dishes as kohlrabi fritters, house-made pasta and seared salmon (the menu changes regularly), is somewhat overshadowed by its gleaming-white, modernist design aesthetic. Four intricately woven canvas collages by Sarah Crowner were installed in early 2017. On weekends it serves brunch.

Café Sabarsky AUSTRIAN $$
(Map p94; www.neuegalerie.org/cafes/sabarsky; 1048 Fifth Ave, at E 86th St; mains $19-32; 9am-6pm Mon & Wed, to 9pm Thu-Sun; S 4/5/6 to 86th St) The lines can get long at this popular cafe evoking an opulent, turn-of-the-century Vienna coffeehouse. The Austrian specialties, courtesy of Michelin-starred chef Kurt Gutenbrunner, include crepes with smoked trout, goulash soup and roasted bratwurst – all beautifully presented. There's also a mouthwatering list of specialty sweets, including a divine Sacher torte (dark chocolate cake with apricot confiture).

If the wait feels too long, you can find the same menu downstairs at Café Fledermaus, which sports a more modern look and is often used when Sabarsky is full.

Candle Cafe VEGAN $$

(Map p94; ☎212-472-0970; www.candlecafe.com; 1307 Third Ave, btwn E 74th & 75th Sts; mains $16-22; ⏲11:30am-10pm Mon-Fri, from 11am Sat, 11am-9:30pm Sun; 🖉; [S]Q to 72nd St-2nd Ave) The moneyed yoga set piles into this minimalist vegan cafe serving a long list of sandwiches, salads, comfort food and market-driven specials. The specialty here is the housemade seitan. There is a juice bar, gluten-free menu and organic cocktails. For a more upscale take on the subject, check out its sister restaurant, **Candle 79** (Map p94; ☎212-537-7179; www.candle79.com; 154 E 79th St, cnr Lexington Ave; mains $22-25; ⏲noon-3:30pm & 5:30-10:30pm Mon-Sat, to 4pm & 10pm Sun; 🖉; [S]6 to 77th St).

★Café Boulud FRENCH $$$

(Map p94; ☎212-772-2600; www.cafeboulud.com/nyc; 20 E 76th St, btwn Fifth & Madison Aves; breakfats $13-29, mains $39-52; ⏲7-10:30am, noon-2:30pm & 5:30-10:30pm Mon-Fri, 8-10:30am, 11:30am-2:30pm & 5:30-10:30pm Sat, 8-10:30am, 11:30am-3pm & 5-10pm Sun; 🖉; [S]6 to 77th St) This long-standing Michelin-starred bistro by Daniel Boulud attracts a rather staid crowd with its globe-trotting French-Vietnamese cuisine. Seasonal menus include classics like bass 'en paupiette', as well as fare such as duck with sour cherry and baby fennel.

Tanoshi SUSHI $$$

(Map p94; www.tanoshisushinyc.com; 1372 York Ave, btwn E 73rd & 74th Sts; chef's sushi selection $95-100; ⏲seatings 6pm, 7:30pm & 9pm Tue-Sat; [S]Q to 72nd St) It's not easy to snag one of the 22 stools at Tanoshi, a wildly popular, pocket-sized sushi spot. The setting may be humble, but the flavors are simply magnificent. Only sushi is on offer and only *omakase* (chef's selection) – which might include Hokkaido scallops, kelp-cured flake or mouthwatering *uni* (sea urchin). BYO beer, sake or whatnot.

Reserve well in advance via website only.

🍴 Upper West Side

Milk Bar BAKERY $

(Map p94; www.milkbarstore.com; 561 Columbus Ave, at 87th St; cookies $2.75; ⏲9am-11pm Sun-Thu, to midnight Fri & Sat; 📶; [S]C, B to 86th St) Conceived by a Momofuku dessert chef with a soft spot for junk food, the big draw at Milk Bar is the delicious, chewy cookies. A popular teeth-rotter is the Compost Cookie: pretzels, potato chips, coffee, oats, graham crackers, butterscotch and chocolate chips. Elsewhere, things are equally inventive, with options like cereal milk soft-serve and pickled strawberry jam and corn cookie milkshakes.

★Épicerie Boulud DELI $

(Map p94; ☎212-595-9606; www.epicerieboulud.com; 1900 Broadway, at W 64th St; sandwiches $8-14.50; ⏲7am-10pm Mon, to 11pm Tue-Sat, 8am-10pm Sun; 📶🖉; [S]1 to 66th St-Lincoln Center) A deli from star chef Daniel Boulud is no ordinary deli. Forget ham on rye – here you can order suckling pig confit, *jambon de Paris* and Gruyère on pressed ciabatta, or paprika-spiced flank steak with caramelized onions and three-grain mustard. Other options at this fast-gourmet spot include salads, soups, pastry, gelato, coffee…even oysters and wine.

Peacefood Cafe VEGAN $

(Map p94; ☎212-362-2266; www.peacefoodcafe.com; 460 Amsterdam Ave, at 82nd St; mains $11-18; ⏲10am-10pm; 📶🖉; [S]1 to 79th St) This bright and airy vegan haven dishes up a popular fried seitan panini (served on homemade focaccia and topped with cashew cheese, arugula, tomatoes and pesto), as well as pizzas, roasted-vegetable plates and an excellent quinoa salad. There are daily raw specials, energy-fueling juices and rich desserts, plus a more substantial dinner menu served 5pm to 10pm.

Barney Greengrass DELI $$

(Map p94; ☎212-724-4707; www.barneygreengrass.com; 541 Amsterdam Ave, at 86th St; mains $5.25-28, fish platters $37-67; ⏲deli 8am-6pm Tue-Sun, cafe 8:30am-4pm Tue-Fri, to 5pm Sat-Sun; [S]1 to 86th St) The self-proclaimed 'King of Sturgeon,' Barney Greengrass serves up the same heaping dishes of eggs and salty lox, luxuriant caviar and melt-in-your-mouth chocolate babkas that first made it famous when it opened over a century ago. Fuel up in the morning at casual tables amid the crowded produce counters, or take lunch at the serviced cafe in an adjoining room.

In addition to an array of Jewish delicacies – seriously, try the smoked sturgeon – you can, of course, get a commendable New York bagel.

Boulud Sud MEDITERRANEAN $$$

(Map p94; ☎212-595-1313; www.bouludsud.com; 20 W 64th St, btwn Broadway & Central Park W; 3-course prix fixe 5-7pm Mon-Sat $65, mains lunch $25-35, dinner $31-63; ⏲11:30am-2:30pm & 5-11pm Mon-Fri, 11am-3pm & 5-11pm Sat, to 10pm Sun; 📶; [S]1 to 66th St-Lincoln Center) Pear-wood paneling and a yellow-grey palette lend a 1960s *Mad Men* feel to Daniel

Boulud's restaurant championing cuisines from the Mediterranean and North Africa. Dishes such as Moroccan tagines, spicy green shakshouka and Sardinian lemon saffron linguini emphasize seafood, vegetables and regional spices. Look out for specials, like the express lunch ($26), pre-theater menu ($65) and happy pasta hour (50% off).

★**Burke & Wills** AUSTRALIAN **$$$**
(Map p94; ☎646-823-9251; www.burkeandwillsny.com; 226 W 79th St, btwn Broadway & Amsterdam Ave; mains $21-38; 🕐bar from 4pm, dinner 5:30-11pm, brunch 11am-3pm Sat & Sun; 📶; [S]1 to 79th St) About as far as you could get from an outback watering hole, this sophisticated bistro and bar brings modern Australian cuisine to the Upper West Side. That means platters of oysters ($35 per dozen), barramundi with broccolini and yuzu cream and even a kangaroo burger in brioche (if you're so inclined). Popular and dimly lit: good for couples.

🍴 Harlem & Upper Manhattan

Tom's Restaurant DINER **$**
(Map p94; ☎212-864-6137; www.tomsrestaurant.net; 2880 Broadway, at 112th St; mains $10-15, sandwiches $6-9; 🕐7am-1am Tue-Thu, 24hr Fri-Mon; 📶; [S]1 to 110th St) The exterior of Tom's may look familiar if you're a fan of the TV series *Seinfeld,* but the interiors are all New York Greek diner. As in, *busy.* Reminisce about those Kramer scenes while chomping on classic burgers, gyros, bagels or gut-warming homemade soups. Breakfast is served all day, and Tom's is open 24 hours Friday to Saturday. Cash only.

Sylvia's SOUTHERN US **$$**
(Map p94; ☎212-996-0660; www.sylviasrestaurant.com; 328 Malcolm X Blvd, btwn 126th & 127th Sts, Harlem; mains $14-27; 🕐8am-10:30pm Mon-Sat, 11am-8pm Sun; [S]2/3 to 125th St) Founded by Sylvia Woods back in 1962, this Harlem icon has been dazzling Harlemites and visitors (including a few presidents) with its lip-smackingly good down-home Southern cooking – succulent fried chicken, baked mac 'n' cheese and cornmeal-dusted catfish, plus requisite sides like collard greens. Come on Sundays for the gospel brunch, and book ahead to avoid the overwhelming scrum for a table.

Vinatería EUROPEAN **$$**
(Map p94; ☎212-662-8462; www.vinaterianyc.com; 2211 Frederick Douglass Blvd, btwn 119th & 120th Sts; mains $19-29; 🕐5-10pm Mon, to 11pm Tue-Thu, to midnight Fri, 10:30am-midnight Sat, to 10pm Sun; [S]A/C, B to 116th St) This classy Michelin-recommended neighborhood restaurant shows a new side to Harlem, taking inspiration from Italy and Spain with flavor-packed dishes such as spicy veal meatballs bedded in parmigiano polenta and grilled octopus with roasted poblano peppers and fennel pollen. Pasta is made in-house, and the black seafood spaghetti is a signature dish.

★**Red Rooster** AMERICAN **$$$**
(Map p94; ☎212-792-9001; www.redroosterharlem.com; 310 Malcolm X Blvd, btwn W 125th & 126th Sts, Harlem; mains lunch $20-25, dinner $25-40; 🕐11:30am-3pm & 4:30-10:30pm Mon-Thu, to 11:30pm Fri, 10am-3pm & 4:30-11:30pm Sat, to 10pm Sun; [S]2/3 to 125th St) Transatlantic superchef Marcus Samuelsson laces upscale comfort food with a world of flavors at his effortlessly cool brasserie. Mac 'n' cheese joins forces with lobster, blackened catfish pairs with pickled mango, and Swedish meatballs salute Samuelsson's home country. The DJ-led bar atmosphere is as good, if not better, than the food: roll in after midnight on weekends and you'll find it's still buzzing.

🍴 Brooklyn

DeKalb Market Hall FOOD HALL **$**
(www.dekalbmarkethall.com; City Point, 445 Albee Sq W, at DeKalb Ave, Downtown Brooklyn; mains $12-15; 🕐7am-10pm; 📶; [S]B, Q/R to DeKalb Ave; 2/3 to Hoyt St; A/C, G to Hoyt-Schermerhorn) One of Downtown Brooklyn's best options for a quick feed is this popular basement food hall in the City Point retail center. Choose from nearly 40 vendors from across the culinary spectrum: pastrami sandwiches, arepas, tacos, Berlin-style doner, hand-pulled noodles, pierogi, rice bowls, sushi, rotisserie chicken, crepes – you name it.

Crif Dogs HOT DOGS **$**
(☎718-302-3200; www.crifdogs.com; 555 Driggs Ave, at N 7th St, Williamsburg; hot dogs $4.50-6.50; 🕐noon-2am Sun-Thu, to 4am Fri & Sat; 🍸; [S]L to Bedford Ave) Many a late-night Billyburg excursion ends up at this laid-back hot-dog joint, with no-nonsense beef-and-pork and veggie weiners done how you like, with two-dozen toppings to choose from. Get a draft beer and a side of tater tots, order your dog with pineapple, sauerkraut or Swiss cheese, and keep the party going. The **original** (Map p84; ☎212-614-2728; 113 St Marks Pl, btwn Ave A & First Ave, East Village; hot dogs from

$4; ⏲ noon-2am Sun-Thu, to 4am Fri & Sat; [S] L to 1st Ave) is in the East Village.

Dough BAKERY $

(☎ 347-533-7544; www.doughdoughnuts.com; 448 Lafayette Ave, cnr Franklin Ave, Bedford-Stuyvesant; doughnuts around $3; ⏲ 6am-9pm; 📶; [S] G to Classon Ave) Situated on the border of Clinton Hill and Bed-Stuy, this tiny, out-of-the-way bakery takes the business of doughnuts seriously – making light, chewy 'nuts in frequent small batches to ensure peak freshness. The brioche-style dough is twice-proved, fried, then rolled in a changing array of glazes and toppings, including salted chocolate caramel, passionfruit, dulche de leche and even hibiscus.

Ample Hills Creamery ICE CREAM $

(☎ 347-240-3926; www.amplehills.com; 623 Vanderbilt Ave, at St Marks Ave, Prospect Heights; ice cream from $4.50; ⏲ noon-10pm Sun-Thu, to 11pm Fri & Sat; [S] B, Q to 7th Ave, 2/3 to Grand Army Plaza) Taking its name from Walt Whitman's 'Crossing Brooklyn Ferry,' Ample Hills makes superb ice cream from organic ingredients. Each Ample Hills outlet has one location-specific flavor; in Prospect Heights it's the salty-sweet 'Commodore', studded with homemade honeycomb and potato chips coated in chocolate. Everything is made from scratch with fresh, hormone-free milk and cream at their factory in Red Hook.

★Smorgasburg MARKET $

(www.smorgasburg.com; mains from $10; ⏲ Williamsburg 11am-6pm Sat, Prospect Park 11am-6pm Sun; 👪) The largest foodie event in Brooklyn (perhaps the US) brings together more than 100 vendors selling an incredible array of goodness. Seize stuffed calamari or Afghan comfort food; queue for hipster inventions like ramen burgers and pizza cupcakes; or wash down Colombian *arepas* (cornbread sandwiches) with lavender lemonade. Note that sites are exposed (bring sunblock in summer, rain-proof gear in poor weather). Locations can change, so check the website. Most vendors accept cards.

★Fette Sau BARBECUE $$

(☎ 718-963-3404; www.fettesaubbq.com; 354 Metropolitan Ave, btwn Havemeyer & Roebling Sts, Williamsburg; meats per half-pound $12-15, sides $4-8; ⏲ 5-11pm Mon, from noon Tue-Sun; [S] L to Bedford Ave) The atmosphere is unfussy, but the reverence for smoky meat is indubitable at the 'Fat Pig,' Brooklyn's best house of barbecue. The cement floor and inside-outside feel echo the garage that once operated from this space, while shared trestles and an 'order by the pound' system put lovers of brisket, pulled pork, smoked chicken and ancho-chili-spiced sausage further at ease.

Completing the package are sides of German-style potato salad, pickles and garlic broccoli, and a stout wooden bar serving craft beers and a great range of bourbon, whiskey and cocktails.

Roberta's PIZZA $$

(☎ 718-417-1118; www.robertaspizza.com; 261 Moore St, near Bogart St, East Williamsburg; pizzas $17-21; ⏲ 11am-midnight Mon-Fri, from 10am Sat & Sun; 🌱; [S] L to Morgan Ave) This hiply renovated warehouse restaurant in one of Brooklyn's booming food enclaves makes some of the best pizza in NYC. Service is relaxed, but the brick-oven pies are serious: chewy, fresh and topped with knowing combinations of outstanding ingredients. The classic margherita is sublime; more adventurous palates can opt for near-legendary options like 'beastmaster' (gorgonzola, pork sausage and jalapeño).

Juliana's PIZZA $$

(☎ 718-596-6700; www.julianaspizza.com; 19 Old Fulton St, btwn Water & Front Sts, Brooklyn Heights; pizzas $26-29; ⏲ 11:30am-10pm, closed 3:15-4pm; 🌱; [S] A/C to High St) Legendary pizza maestro Patsy Grimaldi has returned to Brooklyn, offering delicious, thin-crust perfection in both classic and creative combos – like the No 1, with mozzarella, *scamorza affumicata* (an Italian smoked cow's cheese), pancetta, scallions and white truffles in olive oil. Note that Juliana's closes for 45 minutes every afternoon to stoke the coal-fired pizza oven.

Modern Love VEGAN $$

(☎ 929-298-0626; www.modernlovebrooklyn.com; 317 Union Ave, at S 1st St, East Williamsburg; mains brunch $16-18, dinner $18-24; ⏲ 5:30-10pm Tue-Thu, to 11pm Fri, 10am-2:30pm & 5-11pm Sat, 10am-2:30pm & 5-10pm Sun; 🌱; [S] G to Metropolitan Ave, L to Lorimer St) Celebrated chef Isa Chandra Moskowitz's 'swanky vegan comfort food' has been received with open, watering mouths in Williamsburg. The restaurant is a lovely date spot with sultry lighting and immaculate service, while dishes include 'mac 'n' shews' (with creamy cashew cheese), truffled poutine and a lip-smacking Korean BBQ bowl with glazed tofu and kimchi. It's always buzzing, so consider booking.

Buttermilk Channel AMERICAN $$
(☎718-852-8490; www.buttermilkchannelnyc.com; 524 Court St, at Huntington St, Carroll Gardens; mains brunch $13-18, lunch $14-22, dinner $24-30; ⏰11:30am-3pm & 5-10pm Mon-Thu, 11:30am-3pm & 5-11:30pm Fri, 10am-3pm & 5-11:30pm Sat, 10am-3pm & 5-10pm Sun; [S] F, G to Smith-9th Sts) Taking comfort food to rare heights, Buttermilk Channel is a bustling, friendly place beloved of locals. Brunch is dominated by French toast and syrup-drowned pancakes, while buttermilk-fried chicken and duck meatloaf feature on the dinner menu, always complemented by a head-lightening array of cocktails. Named for the tidal strait between Brooklyn and Governors Island, its weekend brunch draws large crowds.

Reservations aren't taken, so leave a number and the host will text you when a table opens up. Monday nights feature a three-course dinner ($40) that's great value.

★Finch AMERICAN $$$
(☎718-218-4444; www.thefinchnyc.com; 212 Greene Ave, btwn Cambridge Pl & Grand Ave, Clinton Hill; mains $28-40; ⏰6-10pm Mon & Wed-Fri, 5:30-10pm Sat, 5:30-9pm Sun; 🚌B52 to Greene Ave/Grand Ave, [S] G to Classon Ave, G or C to Clinton-Washington) This quiet, residential brownstone block seems an unlikely setting for a Michelin-starred restaurant, but the Finch is the real deal, serving modern American cuisine in a stylishly unadorned setting. The menu is perfect for sharing, with cooked-to-perfection mains like bluefish with tomato panzanella and pork belly with peaches. The ample wine list and sophisticated cocktails induce dilemmas, but it's hard to go wrong.

★Olmsted AMERICAN $$$
(☎718-552-2610; www.olmstednyc.com; 659 Vanderbilt Ave, btwn Prospect Pl & Park Pl, Prospect Heights; small plates $14-17, large plates $23-24; ⏰dinner 5:30-10pm Mon-Thu, 5-10:30pm Fri & Sat, 5-9:30pm Sun, brunch 11:30am-2:30pm Fri, 11am-3pm Sat & Sun; [S] B, Q to 7th Ave) 🌿 Chef-owner Greg Baxtrom, alumnus of a string of hot kitchens, cooks such outstanding, seasonally inspired food that even Manhattanites cross the river to eat here. Much of the menu comes from the restaurant's backyard garden – which doubles as a lovely spot for cocktails or dessert. Whether it's pork belly with dandelion, carrot crepe or scallops with chanterelles, a sensational meal is almost guaranteed. Reservations recommended; Mondays are for walk-ins only.

Miss Ada MEDITERRANEAN $$$
(☎917-909-1023; www.missadanyc.com; 184 DeKalb Ave, at Carlton Ave, Fort Greene; mains $18-27; ⏰5:30-10:30pm Tue-Thu, to 11:30pm Fri & Sat, 11am-2:30pm & 5:30-10:30pm Sun; 📝; [S] G to Fulton St or Clinton/Washington Aves, B, Q/R to DeKalb Ave) Chef-owner Tomer Blechman presents dishes inspired by Mediterranean flavors and recipes from his native Israel: octopus with eggplant, za'atar-seasoned salmon, and shakshuka (eggs baked in spicy tomato with goat's cheese). Many are flavored with herbs grown in the backyard, which features canopied dining in warmer months. And Miss Ada? A misdirection: *misada* is Hebrew for restaurant. Reserve far in advance.

Zenkichi JAPANESE $$$
(☎718-388-8985; www.zenkichi.com; 77 N 6th St, at Wythe Ave, Williamsburg; tasting menus vegetarian/regular $65/75; ⏰5:30pm-midnight Sun-Thu, to midnight Fri & Sat; 📝; [S] L to Bedford Ave) Created by a homesick Tokyo chef, this hushed restaurant promises peace and pleasure in equal proportions. Sink into one of the secluded booths, order the *omakase* (regularly changing tasting menu, for a minimum of two guests) and abandon yourself to a precise succession of delights: silky tofu, miso-marinated cod, and seasonal sashimi.

🍷 Drinking & Nightlife

You'll find all species of thirst-quenching venues here, from terminally hip cocktail lounges and historic dive bars to specialty taprooms and Third Wave coffee shops. Then there's the legendary club scene, spanning everything from celebrity staples to gritty, indie hangouts. Head downtown or to Brooklyn for the parts of the city that, as they say, truly never sleep.

🍷 Financial District & Lower Manhattan

Dead Rabbit BAR
(Map p80; ☎646-422-7906; www.deadrabbitnyc.com; 30 Water St, btwn Broad St & Coenties Slip, Financial District; ⏰Taproom 11am-4am Mon-Fri, 10am-3am Sat & Sun, Parlor 11am-3pm & 5pm-2am Mon-Sat, noon-midnight Sun; [S] R/W to Whitehall St, 1 to South Ferry) Named for a feared 19th-century Irish American gang, this three-story drinking den is regularly voted one of the world's best bars. Hit the sawdust-sprinkled Taproom for specialty beers, historic punches and pop-inns (lightly soured ale spiked with different flavors). On the next floor there's the cozy Parlor, serving

meticulously researched cocktails, and above that the reservation-only Occasional Room, 'for whiskey explorers.'

Be warned: the Wall St crowd packs the place after work.

Brandy Library
COCKTAIL BAR

(Map p80; ✆212-226-5545; www.brandylibrary.com; 25 N Moore St, btwn Varick & Hudson Sts, Tribeca; ⊗5pm-1am Sun-Wed, 4pm-2am Thu, 4pm-4am Fri & Sat; ⓢ1 to Franklin St) This brandy-hued bastion of brown spirits is the place to go for top-shelf cognac, whiskey and brandy. Settle into handsome club chairs facing floor-to-ceiling, bottle-lined shelves and sip your tipple of choice, paired with nibbles such as Gruyère-cheese puffs, hand-cut steak tartare and foie gras. Saturday nights are generally quieter than weeknights, making it a civilized spot for a weekend tête-à-tête.

Cowgirl SeaHorse
BAR

(Map p80; ✆212-608-7873; www.cowgirlseahorse.com; 259 Front St, at Dover St, Lower Manhattan; ⊗11am-2am Mon-Fri, 10am-1am Sat & Sun; ⓢA/C, J/Z, 2/3, 4/5 to Fulton St) In an ocean of more serious bars and restaurants, Cowgirl Sea-Horse is a party ship. Its ranch-meets-sea theme (wagon wheels and seahorses on the walls) and southern home cooking (blackened fish, oyster po'boy sliders, shrimp and grits etc) make it irresistibly fun. Live music on Monday, happy hour every day except Saturday and great frozen margaritas don't hurt, either.

⊖ SoHo & Chinatown

★ Apothéke
COCKTAIL BAR

(Map p80; ✆212-406-0400; www.apothekenyc.com; 9 Doyers St, Chinatown; ⊗6:30pm-2am Mon-Sat, from 8pm Sun; ⓢJ/Z to Chambers St; 4/5/6 to Brooklyn Bridge-City Hall) It takes a little effort to track down this former opium-den-turned-apothecary bar on Doyers St (look for the illustration of a beaker hanging above the doorway). Inside, skilled barkeeps work like careful chemists, using local, seasonal produce from Greenmarkets to produce intense, flavorful 'prescriptions.' The pineapple-cilantro spiced Sitting Buddha is one of the best drinks on the menu.

The menu is just as much fun as sipping the drinks, divided into sections including 'aphrodisiacs', 'pain killers' and 'stress relievers.' On Wednesdays there is a special Prohibition-based theme, and on Sundays it's Belle Époque, with a focus on absinthe.

Ear Inn
PUB

(Map p84; ✆212-226-9060; www.earinn.com; 326 Spring St, btwn Washington & Greenwich Sts, SoHo; ⊗bar 11:30am-4am, kitchen to 2am; 🕾; ⓢC/E to Spring St) Want to see what SoHo was like before the trendsetters and fashionistas? Come to the creaking old Ear Inn, proudly billed as one of the oldest drinking establishments in NYC. The house it occupies was built in the late 18th century for James Brown, an African aide to George Washington. Drinks are cheap and the crowd's eclectic.

Regulars come for late-night dinners at barebones wooden tables with paper table cloths, crammed between walls drowning in old ad signs and Americana. Every Sunday, a corner of the bar is cleared for popular jazz ensembles (8pm to around 11:30pm).

Pegu Club
COCKTAIL BAR

(Map p84; ✆212-473-7348; www.peguclub.com; 2nd fl, 77 W Houston St, btwn W Broadway & Wooster St, SoHo; ⊗5pm-2am Sun-Wed, to 4am Thu-Sat; ⓢB/D/F/M to Broadway-Lafayette St; C/E to Spring St, 1 to Houston St) Dark, elegant Pegu Club (named after a gentleman's club in colonial-era Rangoon) is an obligatory stop for cocktail connoisseurs. Sink into a lounge chair and savor seamless libations such as the silky-smooth Earl Grey MarTE-Ani (tea-infused gin, lemon juice and raw egg white). Grazing options include chicken satay and crispy squid.

⊖ West Village, Chelsea & Meatpacking District

Buvette
WINE BAR

(Map p84; ✆212-255-3590; www.ilovebuvette.com; 42 Grove St, btwn Bedford & Bleecker Sts, West Village; small plates $12-18; ⊗7am-2am; ⓢ1 to Christopher St-Sheridan Sq, A/C/E, B/D/F/M to W 4th St-Washington Sq) Buzzing with the animated conversation of locals, courting couples and theater types, this devotedly Francophile wine bar and restaurant makes a great rest stop amid a West Village backstreet wander. Enjoy a cocktail or a glass of wine, or settle in for a meal. Brunch dishes such as croque monsieurs are replaced by tartines and small plates at dinner.

Buvette also has outposts in Tokyo and Paris.

Cubbyhole
LGBTIQ+

(Map p84; ✆212-243-9041; www.cubbyholebar.com; 281 W 12th St, at W 4th St, West Village; ⊗4pm-4am Mon-Fri, from 2pm Sat & Sun; ⓢA/C/E, L to 8th Ave-14th St) This West Village dive bills itself as 'lesbian, gay and straight friendly since 1994.' While the crowd's mostly ladies, it welcomes anyone looking for a drink in good company beneath a ceiling festooned with lanterns, toys and other ephemera. It's got a great jukebox, friendly bartenders and plenty of regulars who prefer to hang and chat rather than hook up and leave.

Happy hour is 4pm to 7pm Monday to Saturday. There are also daily drink specials, so be sure to check the website.

Top of the Standard

BAR

(Map p84; ✆212-645-7600; www.standardhotels. com; Standard, 848 Washington St, at W 13th St, Meatpacking District; ☺4pm-midnight Sun-Tue, to 9pm Wed-Sat; ⬛A/C/E, L to 8th Ave-14th St) Afternoon tea and drinks morph into evening cocktails in this splendid perch atop the ever-so stylish Standard hotel (p106). Small plates ($16 to $18), such as English-pea risotto or Moroccan shrimp with pickled raisins and Greek yogurt, are on hand to address any pangs of hunger, while live jazz and fabulous views complete the picture of sophistication.

⬤ East Village & Lower East Side

Bar Goto

COCKTAIL BAR

(Map p84; ✆212-475-4411; www.bargoto.com; 245 Eldridge St, btwn E Houston & Stanton Sts, Lower East Side; ☺5pm-midnight Tue-Thu & Sun, to 2am Fri & Sat; ⬛F to 2nd Ave) Maverick mixologist Kenta Goto has cocktail connoisseurs spellbound at his eponymous, intimate hot spot. Expect meticulous, elegant drinks that draw on Goto's Japanese heritage (the Umami Mary, with vodka, shiitake, dashi, miso, lemon, tomato and Clamato, is inspired), paired with authentic Japanese comfort bites, such as *okonomiyaki* (savory cabbage pancakes).

Berlin

CLUB

(Map p84; ✆reservations 347-586-7247; www. berlinundera.com; 25 Ave A, btwn E 1st & E 2nd Sts, East Village; occasional cover $5; ☺8pm-2am Sun-Thu, to 4am Fri & Sat; ⬛F to 2nd Ave) This brick-vaulted cavern beneath Ave A does its best to hide – access is through an unmarked door around the corner on the side of bar that seems to occupy its (Berlin's) address, then steep stairs lead down into a dim, riotous indie lair. Once you're in, enjoy a night of rock, funk, disco, house and other party tunes in close proximity to your fellow revelers. The fun, bohemian crowd mixes with little pretension, and you might

see a vestige of the East Village as it was in its days of full-blown hedonism.

Rue B

BAR

(Map p84; ✆212-358-1700; www.rueb-nyc.com; 188 Ave B, btwn E 11th & E 12th Sts, East Village; ☺6pm-4am; ⬛L to 1st Ave) There's live jazz (and the odd rockabilly group) nightly from 9pm to midnight ($10 cover) at this tiny, amber-lit drinking den on a bar-dappled stretch of Ave B. A celebratory crowd packs the small space – so mind the tight corners, lest the trombonist end up in your lap. Photos and posters of jazz greats and NYC icons enhance the ambience.

If you fancy getting a head start, draft beer, wine and cocktails are half price from opening until 8pm every night. If you overdo it, basic bar snacks may be the answer.

⬤ Union Square, Flatiron District & Gramercy

Old Town Bar & Restaurant

BAR

(Map p88; ✆212-529-6732; www.oldtownbar.com; 45 E 18th St, btwn Broadway & Park Ave S, Union Sq; ☺11:30am-1am Mon-Fri, noon-1am Sat, 3pm-midnight Sun; ☏; ⬛4/5/6, N/Q/R/W, L to 14th St- Union Sq) It still looks like 1892 in here, with the mahogany bar, original tile floors and tin ceilings – the Old Town is an old-world drinking-man's classic. It's frequently used as an old-school shooting location for movies and TV (and even Madonna's 'Bad Girl' video). Most people settle into one of the snug wooden booths for beers and a burger (from $12.50).

Raines Law Room

COCKTAIL BAR

(Map p88; www.raineslawroom.com; 48 W 17th St, btwn Fifth & Sixth Aves, Flatiron District; ☺5pm-2am Mon-Thu, to 3am Fri & Sat, to 1am Sun; ⬛F/M to 14th St, L to 6th Ave, 1 to 18th St) A sea of velvet drapes and overstuffed leather lounge chairs, the perfect amount of exposed brick, expertly crafted cocktails using hard-to-find spirits – these folks are as serious as a mortgage payment when it comes to amplified atmosphere. There's no sign from the street; look for the '48' above the door and ring the bell to gain entry. Reservations (recommended) are only accepted Sunday to Tuesday. Whatever the night, style up for a taste of a far more sumptuous era.

Birreria

ROOFTOP BAR

(Map p88; ✆212-937-8910; www.eataly.com; 200 Fifth Ave, at W 23rd St, Flatiron District; ☺11:30am-11pm; ⬛F/M, R/W, 6 to 23rd St) The crown jewel of Italian food emporium **Eataly** (Map p88;

212-229-2560; www.eataly.com; 200 Fifth Ave, at W 23rd St, Flatiron District; ⊙7am-11pm; ⊘; S R/W, F/M, 6 to 23rd St) is this covered rooftop garden tucked betwixt the Flatiron's corporate towers. The theme is refreshed each season, meaning you might find a Mediterranean beach escape one month and an alpine country retreat the next, but the setting is unfailingly impressive and food and drink always matches up to the gourmet goodies below. The sneaky access elevator is near the checkouts on the 23rd St side of the store.

Midtown

★ **The Campbell**   COCKTAIL BAR
(Map p88; 212-297-1781; www.thecampbellnyc. com; D Hall, Grand Central Terminal; ⊙noon-2am; S S, 4/5/6, 7 to Grand Central-42nd St) In 1923 this hidden-away hall was the office of American financier John W Campbell. It later became a signalman's office, a jail and a gun storage before falling into obscurity. In 2017 it was restored to its original grandeur, complete with the stunning hand-painted ceiling and Campbell's original safe in the fireplace. Come for cocktails and you'll feel like you're waiting for Rockefeller or Carnegie to join you.

Try to book ahead Thursday to Sunday. It's a little tricky to find: take the elevator in the corridor next to the oyster bar.

Top of the Strand   COCKTAIL BAR
(Map p88; 646-368-6426; www.topofthe strand.com; Marriott Vacation Club Pulse, 33 W 37th St, btwn Fifth & Sixth Aves, Midtown East; ⊙5pm-midnight Sun & Mon, to 1am Tue-Sat; ⊚; S B/D/F/M, N/Q/R to 34th St) For that 'Oh my God, I'm in New York' feeling, head to the Marriott Vacation Club Pulse (formerly the Strand) hotel's rooftop bar, order a martini (extra dirty) and drop your jaw (discreetly). Sporting comfy cabana-style seating, a refreshingly mixed-age crowd and a retractable glass roof, its view of the Empire State Building is simply unforgettable.

Stumptown Coffee Roasters   COFFEE
(Map p88; 855-711-3385; www.stumptowncof fee.com; 18 W 29th St, btwn Broadway & Fifth Ave; ⊙6am-8pm Mon-Fri, from 7am Sat & Sun; S R/W to 28th St) Hipster baristas in fedora hats brewing killer coffee? No, you're not in Williamsburg, you're at the Manhattan outpost of Portland's cult-status coffee roaster. The queue is a small price to pay for proper espresso, so count your blessings. It's standing-room only, though weary punters might find a seat in the adjacent Ace Hotel lobby. There's a second branch in **Greenwich Village** (Map p84; 855-711-3385; 30 W 8th St, at MacDougal St, West Village; ⊙7am-8pm; S A/C/E, B/D/F/M to W 4th St-Washington Sq).

Upper East Side

★ **Bemelmans Bar**   LOUNGE
(Map p94; 212-744-1600; www.thecarlyle. com; Carlyle Hotel, 35 E 76th St, at Madison Ave; ⊙noon-1:30am; ⊚; S 6 to 77th St) Sink into a chocolate-leather banquette and take in the glorious, old-school elegance at this atmospheric bar – the sort of place where the waiters wear white jackets and serve martinis, a pianist tinkles on a baby grand and the ceiling is 24-carat gold leaf. The walls are covered in charming murals by the bar's namesake Ludwig Bemelmans, famed creator of the *Madeline* books.

Cantor Roof Garden Bar   ROOFTOP BAR
(Map p94; www.metmuseum.org/visit/dining; Metropolitan Museum, 1000 Fifth Ave, 5th fl, at E 82nd St; ⊙11am-4:30pm Sun-Thu, to 8:15pm Fri & Sat mid-Apr–Oct; ⊚; S 4/5/6 to 86th St) The sort of setting you can't get enough of (even if you are a jaded local). Located atop the Met, this rooftop bar sits right above Central Park's tree canopy, allowing for splendid views of the park and the city skyline all around. Sunset is when you'll find fools in love...then again, it could all be those martinis. Access is via the elevator in the European sculpture and decorative arts galleries.

Caledonia   BAR
(Map p94; www.caledoniabar.com; 1609 Second Ave, btwn E 83rd & 84th Sts; ⊙5pm-2am Mon-Thu, 4pm-4am Fri-Sat 4pm-1am Sun, happy hour to 7pm Mon-Fri; S Q, 4/5/6 to 86th St) The name of this unpretentious, dimly lit bar is a dead giveaway: it's devoted to Scotch whisky, with more than 100 single malts to choose from (be they Highlands, Islands, Islay, Lowlands or Speyside), as well as some blends and even a few from the US, Ireland and Japan. The bartenders know their stuff and will be happy to make recommendations.

Upper West Side

★ **Manhattan Cricket Club**   LOUNGE
(Map p94; 646-823-9252; 226 W 79th St, btwn Amsterdam Ave & Broadway; ⊙4pm-late Mon-Sat, from 11am Sat-Sun; ⊚; S 1 to 79th St) Above Australian bistro Burke & Wills (p119) – ask its host for access – this elegant drinking lounge is modeled on the

classy Anglo-Aussie cricket clubs of the early 1900s. Sepia-toned photos of batsmen adorn the gold-brocaded walls, while mahogany bookshelves and Chesterfield sofas create a fine setting for quaffing well-made and inventive, painstakingly mixed cocktails ($15 to $19).

Martini connoisseurs will find the full service setup and purveyors of the Old Fashioned can jazz them up with smoked Vietnamese cinnamon, Chinese five-spice and the like.

Empire Rooftop   ROOFTOP BAR
(Map p94; ✆212-265-2600; www.empirehotel nyc.com; 44 W 63 St, at Broadway; ⏰3pm-1am Mon-Wed, to 2am Thu & Fri, 11am-2am Sat, to 1am Sun; ☎; Ⓢ1 to 66th St-Lincoln Center) Sprawled across the top of the Empire Hotel, this stylish rooftop bar is one of New York's most expansive drinking spaces in the sky at 8000 sq ft. A bright, glass-roofed wing strewn with palms and sofas is perfect for winter and has a retractable roof for summer, and there's a handful of outdoor terraces.

Earth Café   CAFE
(Map p94; 2578 Broadway, at 97th St; ⏰7am-10:30pm Mon-Fri, from 8am Sat & Sun; ☎; Ⓢ1/2/3 to 96th St) This charming neighborhood cafe-bar beckons you inside with its cheery, sunny interior of whitewashed brick walls and the scent of fresh-roasted coffee beans. Order an expertly poured latte, take a seat at the street-facing counter behind large French windows and watch the city glide past.

Vegetarians are spoilt for choice with the food menu (mains $10.50 to $22); come 3pm to 6pm for happy hour.

🍸 Harlem & Upper Manhattan

★Shrine   BAR
(Map p94; www.shrinenyc.com; 2271 Adam Clayton Powell Jr Blvd, btwn 133rd & 134th Sts, Harlem; ⏰4pm-4am; Ⓢ2/3 to 135th St) Don't fret that it looks like a dive from outside: friendly, unpretentious Shrine is one of the best places in Harlem (if not New York) to hear live bands without a cover charge. Musicians take to its small stage every day of the week with blues, reggae, Afro-beat, funk, and indie rock. Beer is cheap and the crowd is as eclectic as the music.

Silvana   BAR
(Map p94; www.silvana-nyc.com; 300 W 116th St, Harlem; ⏰upstairs 7am-4am, downstairs from 4pm; Ⓢ2/3 to 116th St) This appealing Middle Eastern cafe and shop whips up tasty

hummus and falafel plates; the real draw, though, is the hidden downstairs club, which draws a friendly, easygoing local crowd with good cocktails and live bands (kicking off around 6pm) followed by DJs. The lineup is anything-goes, with jazz, Cuban *son*, reggae and Balkan gypsy punk all in the rotation.

Harlem Hops   CRAFT BEER
(Map p94; ✆646-998-3444; www.harlemhops. com; 2268 Adam Clayton Powell Jr Blvd, btwn 133th & 134th Sts, Harlem; ⏰4pm-midnight Sun-Thu, to 2am Fri & Sat; ☎; Ⓢ2/3 to 135th St) Harlem's only 100% African American–owned beer bar has its home 'hood emblazoned on the ceiling in neon lights, and bratwurst and meat pies on the menu. Order a $15 beer paddle of four 5oz pours, pair with a habanero beef pie with African spices, and settle in.

🍸 Brooklyn

★Maison Premiere   COCKTAIL BAR
(✆347-335-0446; www.maisonpremiere.com; 298 Bedford Ave, btwn S 1st & Grand Sts, Williamsburg; ⏰2pm-2am Sun-Wed, to 4am Thu-Sat; ⓈL to Bedford Ave) Perched on a stool in Maison Premiere, it's hard not to be seduced by this New Orleans–style oyster and cocktail bar, from antique pictures and soft lighting to suspender-wearing staff. Contemplate a small plate ($13 to $19) – perhaps shrimp cocktail or littleneck clams – and enjoy the maracas sound of cocktail shakers preparing another round of Spring Pimm's and gimlets.

June   WINE BAR
(✆917-909-0434; www.junebk.com; 231 Court St, btwn Warren & Baltic Sts, Cobble Hill; happy hour 5-7pm Mon-Fri, brunch 11am-4pm Sat & Sun, dinner 5:30pm-midnight Sun-Thu, to 1am Fri & Sat; ⒮F, G to Bergen St) Seductive use of curved, polished wood, leadlighting and inviting niches make June a delightful place to linger over interesting natural wines from Europe, America and Australia. Dishes such as chicken with fennel and pea leaves, littleneck clams with celery root, and carrot and olive-oil cake prove that the food's no afterthought (snacks from $11). The doors to a lovely terrace are flung open when it's warm.

★Montero Bar & Grill   BAR
(✆646-729-4129; 73 Atlantic Ave, at Hicks St, Brooklyn Heights; ⏰noon-4am; Ⓢ4/5 to Borough Hall) Montero's is the real deal: an anachronistic, neon-fronted, Pabst-peddling longshoreman's bar that's weathered every

change thrown at this corner of Brooklyn since WWII. Its eclectic decor recalls the maritime types who once drank here.

Lavender Lake PUB

(☎ 347-799-2154; www.lavenderlake.com; 383 Carroll St, btwn Bond St & Gowanus Canal, Gowanus; ⏰ 4pm-midnight Mon-Thu, 2pm-1am Fri, noon-2am Sat, to 10pm Sun; [S] F, G to Carroll St, R to Union St) Named after the colorfully polluted Gowanus Canal, this popular local haunt is set in a former stable. Lavender Lake serves carefully selected craft beers and deceptively named cocktails with unorthodox ingredients like hibiscus mezcal and strawberry-infused tequila. The lumber-decked garden is a brilliant spot in summer. Weekday happy hour runs from 4pm to 7pm (and all day on Mondays). Bar food staples like nachos, burgers and a couple of plant-based options are on the menu (mains $12 to $17).

★ **House of Yes** CLUB

(www.houseofyes.org; 2 Wyckoff Ave, at Jefferson St, Bushwick; tickets free-$60; ⏰ usually 7pm-4am Wed-Sat; [S] L to Jefferson St) 🍃 Anything goes at this hedonistic warehouse venue, with two stages, three bars and a covered outdoor area that offers some of the most creative themed performance and dance nights in Brooklyn. You might see aerial-silk acrobats, punk bands, burlesque shows, drag shows or performance artists, or DJs as revered as Jellybean Benítez spinning disco, soul, house and other delights.

Leave the baseball caps and sneakers at home – costumes or other funky outfits will get you priority admission most nights, and on Friday and Saturday they're required for entry. (An on-site pop-up costume shop will let you throw something together – ecofriendly glitter included – if you've arrived unprepared.) This is an inclusive, open-minded and joyous crowd.

Amplifying the feel-good factor, the venue has gone green with water refill stations, biodegradable straws on request and more.

Spuyten Duyvil BAR

(☎ 718-963-4140; www.spuytenduyvilnyc.com; 359 Metropolitan Ave, btwn Havemeyer & Roebling Sts, Williamsburg; ⏰ 5pm-2am Mon-Fri, noon-3am Sat, to 2am Sun; [S] L to Lorimer St, G to Metropolitan Ave) This low-key, beer-centric Williamsburg bar looks as though it was pieced together from a rummage sale, with crimson-painted pressed-tin ceilings, book shelves and a vintage bike mounted on the walls, and mismatched thrift-store furniture. The selection of beer (Belgian especially) is staggering, with knowledgeable bar staff primed to steer you to Danish beers or Normandy ciders.

If you get peckish working through the blackboard of 'rare and obscure' beers, plates of imported cheese and charcuterie (from $8) can provide ballast. There's a large, leafy backyard that's open in good weather.

Partners COFFEE

(☎ 347-586-0063; www.partnerscoffee.com; 125 N 6th St, btwn Bedford Ave & Berry St, Williamsburg; ⏰ 6:30am-7pm; 📶; [S] L to Bedford Ave) The flagship of a small chain roaster bringing aromatic pour-overs, smooth flat whites and punchy *cortados* (espresso with a dash of milk) to the streets of Billyburg. Even if it does follow all the unspoken rules of Williamsburg cafe design (bare brick and wood, retro miscellany on display...) it's an enjoyable place to hang.

Queens

Bohemian Hall & Beer Garden BEER GARDEN

(☎ 718-274-4925; www.bohemianhall.com; 29-19 24th Ave, btwn 29th & 31st Sts, Astoria; ⏰ 5pm-1am Mon-Thu, to 3am Fri, noon-3am Sat, to midnight Sun; [S] N/W to Astoria Blvd) This Czech community center kicked off NYC's beer-garden craze, and nothing quite matches it for space and heaving drinking crowds, which pack every picnic table under the towering trees in summer. There's Czech food such as schnitzels and goulash (mains $10 to $20), but the focus is on cold and foamy Czech beers, augmented by local craft brews.

★ **Dutch Kills** COCKTAIL BAR

(www.dutchkillsbar.com; 27-24 Jackson Ave, btwn Queens & Dutch Kills Sts, Long Island City; ⏰ 5pm-2am Sun-Thu, to 3am Fri & Sat; [S] E/M/R to Queens Plaza, G to Court Sq) Named for the area where Dutch settlers first established themselves around Newtown Creek, this moodily lit bar is all about atmosphere and amazing craft cocktails. Enter through the nondescript door beneath a blinking neon 'bar' sign on an old industrial building, and whistle up an expertly mixed Headless Horseman, or another of the house classic cocktails ($15).

The Bronx

★ **Bronx Brewery** BREWERY

(Map p94; ☎ 718-402-1000; www.thebronxbrewery.com; 856 E 136th St, btwn Willow & Walnut Aves; ⏰ 3-7pm Mon-Wed, to 8pm Thu & Fri, noon-8pm Sat, noon-7pm Sun; [S] 6 to Cypress Ave) This buzzing South Bronx microbrewery comes with a small, graffiti-scrawled taproom, where you can pony up to the bar and choose from a changing lineup of eight or so quality brews on draft. There's also a backyard (open weekends in the summer) and creative events, including Brewers Dinners – local chefs preparing multi-course feasts paired with beers – and open mic nights.

☆ Entertainment

Actors, musicians, dancers and artists flock to the bright lights of the Big Apple, hoping to finally get that big break. The result? Audiences are spoiled by the continual influx of supremely talented, dedicated, boundary-pushing performers. Like the song goes: if you can make it here, you can make it anywhere.

Opera & Ballet

Metropolitan Opera House OPERA
(Map p94; ☎ tickets 212-362-6000, tours 212-769-7028; www.metopera.org; Lincoln Center, Columbus Ave at W 64th St; tickets $25-480; 🕐 box office 10am-10pm Mon-Sat, noon-6pm Sun; [S] 1 to 66th St-Lincoln Center) New York's premier opera company is the place to see classics such as *La Boheme, Madame Butterfly* and *Macbeth*. It also hosts premieres and revivals of more contemporary works, such as John Adams' *The Death of Klinghoffer*. The season runs from September to May. Tickets start at $25 and can get close to $500.

Note that the box seats can be a bargain, but unless you're in boxes right over the stage, the views are dreadful: seeing the stage requires sitting with your head cocked over a handrail – a literal pain in the neck.

For last-minute ticket-buyers there are other deals. You can get bargain-priced standing-room tickets (from $20 to $30) from 10am on the day of the performance. (You won't see much, but you'll hear everything.) Monday through Friday at noon and Saturdays at 2pm, a number of rush tickets are put on sale for starving-artist types – just $25 for a seat; these are available online only. Matinee tickets go on sale four hours before curtain.

Don't miss the gift shop, which is full of operatic knickknacks (like binoculars), and an extensive collection of classical music – many from past Met performances.

For a behind-the-scenes look, the **Met Opera Guild** (www.metguild.org) runs guided tours ($30) weekdays at 3pm and Sundays at 10:30am and 1:30pm during the performance season.

New York City Ballet DANCE
(Map p94; ☎ 212-496-0600; www.nycballet.com; Lincoln Center, Columbus Ave at W 63rd St; tickets $39 to $204; 🕐 box office 10am-7:30pm Mon, to 8:30pm Tue-Sat, 4:30am-7:30pm Sun; 👪; [S] 1 to 66th St-Lincoln Center) This prestigious company was first directed by renowned Russian-born choreographer George Balanchine in the 1940s. Today, it's the largest ballet organization in the US, performing 23 weeks a year at Lincoln Center's David H Koch Theater. Rush tickets for those under 30 years are $30. During the holidays the troupe is best known for its annual production of *The Nutcracker* (tickets go on sale in September: book early).

There are also select one-hour Family Saturday performances, appropriate for young audiences ($22 per ticket, on sale first week of August).

Film & Theater

Public Theater LIVE PERFORMANCE
(Map p84; ☎ 212-539-8500, tickets 212-967-7555; www.publictheater.org; 425 Lafayette St, btwn Astor Pl & 4th St, NoHo; [S] 6 to Astor Pl; R/W to 8th St-NYU) This legendary theater was founded as the Shakespeare Workshop back in 1954 and has launched some of New York's big hits, including *Hamilton* back in 2015. Today, you'll find a lineup of innovative programming as well as reimagined classics from the past, with Shakespeare in heavy rotation. Speaking of the bard, the Public also stages star-studded Shakespeare in the Park (p105) performances during the summer.

★ St Ann's Warehouse THEATER
(☎ 718-254-8779; www.stannswarehouse.org; 45 Water St, at Old Dock St, Dumbo; 🚌 B25 to Water/Main Sts, [S] A/C to High St, F to York St) This handsome red-brick building, a Civil War–era tobacco warehouse, is the first permanent home of avant-garde performance company St Ann's. The 'warehouse' – a high-tech, flexible 320-seat theater – is ideal for staging genre-bending theater, music, dance and puppet performances.

Past shows and screenings of note include Lou Reed and John Cale's *Songs for Drella*, Charlie Kaufman and the Coen Brothers' *Theater of the New Ear*, and the Donmar Warehouse and Phyllida Lloyd's all-female Shakespeare Trilogy.

★ Sleep No More THEATER
(Map p88; ☎ box office 212-904-1880; www.sleepnomorenyc.com; 530 W 27th St, btwn Tenth & Eleventh Aves, Chelsea; tickets from $100; 🕐 sessions begin 4-7pm; [S] 1, C/E to 23rd St) One of the

ⓘ DISCOUNT BROADWAY TICKETS

The dozens of Broadway and off-Broadway theaters near Times Square run everything from blockbuster musicals to new and classic drama. Unless there's a specific show you're after, the best – and cheapest – way to score tickets in the area is at the **TKTS Booth** (www.tdf.org/tkts; Broadway, at W 47th St; ◷ 3-8pm Mon & Fri, 2-8pm Tue, 10am-2pm & 3-8pm Wed, Thu & Sat, 11am-7pm Sun; ⓢ N/Q/R/W, S, 1/2/3, 7 to Times Sq-42nd St), where you can line up and get same-day discounted tickets for top Broadway and off-Broadway shows. Smartphone users can download the free TKTS app, which offers rundowns of both Broadway and off-Broadway shows, as well as real-time updates of what's available on that day. Always have a back-up choice in case your first preference sells out, and never buy from scalpers on the street.

The TKTS Booth is an attraction in its own right, with its illuminated roof of 27 ruby-red steps rising a panoramic 16ft 1in above the 47th St sidewalk.

most immersive theater experiences ever conceived, *Sleep No More* is a loose, noir re-telling of *Macbeth* set inside a series of Chelsea warehouses that have been redesigned to look like the 1930s-era 'McKittrick Hotel' (a nod to Hitchcock's *Vertigo*); the hopping jazz bar, Manderley, is another Hitchcock reference, this time to his adaptation of Daphne du Maurier's *Rebecca*.

First staged in London, it's a choose-your-own-adventure kind of experience, where audience members are free to wander the elaborate rooms (ballroom, graveyard, taxi-dermy shop, lunatic asylum) and follow or interact with the actors, who perform a variety of scenes that can run from the bizarre to the risqué. Be prepared: you must check in everything when you arrive (jackets, bag, cell phone), and you must wear a mask, à la *Eyes Wide Shut*.

★ Metrograph CINEMA

(Map p84; ☏ 212-660-0312; www.metrograph. com; 7 Ludlow St, btwn Canal & Hester Sts, Lower East Side; tickets $15; ◷ 11am-midnight Sun-Wed, to 2am Fri & Sat; ☏; ⓢ F to East Broadway, B/D to Grand St) The Lower East Side hasn't gentrified this far yet, giving the owners of this true movie mecca the chance to acquire a building adequate for their vision. It has two screens, both a state-of-the-art digital projector and an old 35mm reel-to-reel. The expertly curated films often form series on subjects such as Japanese animation studio Ghibli or provocateur Gasper Noé.

Film Forum CINEMA

(Map p84; ☏ 212-727-8110; www.filmforum.com; 209 W Houston St, btwn Varick St & Sixth Ave, SoHo; adult/child $15/9; ◷ noon-midnight; ⓢ 1 to Houston St) This nonprofit cinema shows an astounding array of independent films, revivals and career retrospectives from greats such as Orson Welles. Showings often include director talks or other film-themed discussions for hardcore cinephiles. In 2018, the cinema upgraded its theaters to improve the seating, leg room and sight lines, and expanded to add a fourth screen.

Live Music

New York Philharmonic CLASSICAL MUSIC

(Map p94; ☏ 212-875-5656; www.nyphil.org; Lincoln Center, Columbus Ave at W 65th St; tickets $29-125; ☏; ⓢ 1 to 66 St-Lincoln Center) The oldest professional orchestra in the US (dating to 1842) holds its season every year at David Geffen Hall; music director Jaap van Zweden took over from Alan Gilbert in 2017. The orchestra plays a mix of classics (Tchaikovsky, Mahler, Haydn) and contemporary works, as well as concerts geared toward children.

If you're on a budget, check out the open rehearsals held several times a month (starting at 9:45am) on the day of the concert for only $22. In addition, students with a valid school ID can pick up rush tickets for $21.50 to $23.50 online before some events; check the website for options.

★ Jazz at Lincoln Center JAZZ

(Map p94; ☏ Dizzy's Club Coca-Cola reservations 212-258-9595, Rose Theater & Appel Room tickets 212-721-6500; www.jazz.org; Time Warner Center, 10 Columbus Circle, Broadway at W 59th St; ⓢ A/C, B/D, 1 to 59th St-Columbus Circle) Perched atop the Time Warner Center, Jazz at Lincoln Center consists of three state-of-the-art venues: the midsized Rose Theater; the panoramic, glass-backed Appel Room; and the intimate, atmospheric Dizzy's Club Coca-Cola. It's the last of these that you're most likely to visit, given its nightly shows (cover charge $5 to $45). The talent is often exceptional, as are the dazzling Central Park views.

★Brooklyn Academy of Music PERFORMING ARTS
(BAM; ☎718-636-4100; www.bam.org; 30 Lafayette Ave, at Ashland Pl, Fort Greene; 📶; [S] B/D, N/Q/R, 2/3, 4/5 to Atlantic Ave-Barclays Center) Founded in 1861 (the year the Civil War erupted), BAM is the country's oldest performing-arts center. Spanning several venues in the Fort Greene area, the complex hosts innovative works of opera, modern dance, music, cinema and theater – everything from 'retro-modern' Mark Morris Group ballets and Laurie Anderson multimedia shows to avant-garde Shakespeare productions, comedy and kids' shows.

The 1908 Italian Renaissance–style Peter J Sharp Building houses the **Howard Gilman Opera House**, showing opera, dance, music and more, and the four-screen **Rose Cinemas** (tickets $15-18), showing first-run, indie and foreign films in gorgeously vintage-feel theaters; the on-site bar and restaurant, **BAM Café**, stages free jazz, R&B and pop performances on Friday and Saturday. A block away on Fulton St is the **Harvey Lichtenstein Theater** (651 Fulton St, at Rockwell Pl; [S] B, Q/R to DeKalb Ave, 2/3, 4/5 to Nevins St), aka 'the Harvey,' which stages cutting-edge, contemporary plays and sometimes radical interpretations of classics. Around the corner from the Sharp building is the **Fisher Building** (www.bam.org/fisher; 321 Ashland Pl, at Lafayette Ave; [S] B/D, N/Q/R, 2/3, 4/5 to Atlantic Ave-Barclays Center), with its more intimate 250-seat theater.

From October through December, BAM hosts its acclaimed Next Wave Festival (p105), which presents an array of international avant-garde theater and dance and artist talks. Buy tickets early.

National Sawdust LIVE PERFORMANCE
(☎646-779-8455; www.nationalsawdust.org; 80 N 6th St, at Wythe Ave, Williamsburg; ⏰10am-1am Mon-Fri, noon-11pm Sat & Sun; 👪; 🚌B32 to Wythe Ave-N 6th St, [S] L to Bedford Ave) Covered in wildly hued murals, this cutting-edge space for classical and new music has come a long way since its days as a sawdust factory, with artists as diverse as Pussy Riot and Yo La Tengo performing within. The angular, high-tech interior stages contemporary opera with multimedia projections, electro-acoustic big-band jazz and concerts by experimental composers, alongside less common genres.

National Sawdust's *raison d'être* is shining a light on emerging artists and helping offbeat genres and performers find their audience. Browse their events calendar to decide between Indian classical, ambient 'sound baths' or light-shows with a soundscape of synth.

Village Vanguard JAZZ
(Map p84; ☎212-255-4037; www.villagevanguard.com; 178 Seventh Ave S, btwn W 11th & Perry Sts, West Village; cover around $35; ⏰7:30pm-12:30am; [S] 1/2/3 to 14th St, A/C/E, L to 8th Ave-14th St) Possibly NYC's most prestigious jazz club, the Vanguard has hosted literally every major star of the past 50 years. Starting out in 1935 as a venue for beat poetry and folk music, it occasionally returns to its roots, but most of the time it's just big, bold jazz all night long. The Vanguard Jazz Orchestra has been a Monday-night mainstay since 1966.

Mind your step on the steep stairs, and close your eyes to the signs of wear and tear – acoustically, you're in one of the greatest venues in the world. There's a one-drink minimum.

★Barbès LIVE MUSIC
(☎347-422-0248; www.barbesbrooklyn.com; 376 9th St, at Sixth Ave, Park Slope; requested donation for live music $10; ⏰5pm-2am Mon-Thu, 2pm-4am Fri & Sat, to 2am Sun; [S] F, G to 7th Ave, R to 4th Ave-9th St) This compact bar and performance space, named after a neighborhood in Paris with a strong North African flavor, is owned by French musicians (and longtime Brooklyn residents). There's live music all night, every night: an impressively eclectic lineup including Balkan brass, contemporary opera, Afro-Peruvian grooves, West African funk and other diverse sounds.

Don't miss the brassy nine-piece Slavic Soul Party, which plays here most Tuesdays (from 9pm). There are also DJ nights, book readings and film screenings.

Bowery Ballroom LIVE MUSIC
(Map p84; ☎800-745-3000, 212-533-2111; www.boweryballroom.com; 6 Delancey St, at Bowery, Lower East Side; [S] J/Z to Bowery, B/D to Grand St) This terrific medium-size venue has the perfect sound and feel for well-known indie-rock acts such as The Shins, Jonathan Richman, Stephen Malkmus and Patti Smith.

Sports

Madison Square Garden LIVE PERFORMANCE
(MSG, 'the Garden'; Map p88; www.thegarden.com; 4 Pennsylvania Plaza, Seventh Ave, btwn 31st & 33rd Sts; [S] A/C/E, 1/2/3 to 34th St-Penn Station) NYC's major performance venue – part of the massive complex housing Penn Station –

hosts big-arena performers, from Kanye West to Madonna. It's also a sports arena, with **New York Knicks** (www.nba.com/knicks) and **New York Liberty** (https://liberty.wnba.com) basketball games and **New York Rangers** (www.nhl.com/rangers) hockey games, as well as boxing and events like the Annual Westminster Kennel Club Dog Show.

Dubbed the 'Mecca of basketball' and 'the worlds most famous arena', good basketball has been hard to come by in recent years as the Knicks have endured years of woeful play. The arena has been part of the decades-old redevelopment plans for the claustrophobic underground Penn Station.

Barclays Center STADIUM
(☎917-618-6100; www.barclayscenter.com; cnr Flatbush & Atlantic Aves, Prospect Heights; [S] B/D, N/Q/R, 2/3, 4/5 to Atlantic Ave-Barclays Center) The **Brooklyn Nets** in the NBA (formerly the New Jersey Nets) hold court at this high-tech stadium. Basketball aside, Barclays also stages boxing, professional wrestling, major concerts and shows by big names; Ariana Grande, Justin Bieber, KISS and Cirque de Soleil have all rocked the stadium.

The stadium, with its futuristic design – which looks like a rusting spaceship, topped by a well-kept grassy lawn, rearing above Atlantic Ave – has transformed the neighborhood, though there are regular murmurs about whether the venue has lived up to its own hype.

MCU Park BASEBALL
(☎718-372-5596; www.brooklyncyclones.com; 1904 Surf Ave, at W 17th St, Coney Island; tickets $10-19, all tickets Wed $10; [S] D/F, N/Q to Coney Island-Stillwell Ave) The minor-league baseball team **Brooklyn Cyclones**, part of the New York–Penn League and inter-borough rivals of the **Staten Island Yankees**, plays at this beachside park just off Coney Island boardwalk.

Shopping

Not surprisingly for a capital of commercialism, creativity and fashion, New York City is quite simply one of the best shopping destinations on the planet. Every niche is filled. From indie designer-driven boutiques to landmark department stores, thrift shops to haute couture, record stores to the Apple store, street-eats to gourmet groceries, it's quite easy to blow one's budget.

Financial District & Lower Manhattan

★**Century 21** FASHION & ACCESSORIES
(Map p80; ☎212-227-9092; www.c21stores.com; 22 Cortlandt St, btwn Church St & Broadway, Financial District; ⏰7:45am-9pm Mon-Wed, to 9:30pm Thu & Fri, 10am-9pm Sat, 11am-8pm Sun; [S] A/C, J/Z, 2/3, 4/5 to Fulton St, R/W to Cortlandt St) For penny-pinching fashionistas, this giant cut-price department store is dangerously addictive. It's physically dangerous as well, considering the elbows you might have to throw to ward off the competition beelining for the same rack. Not everything is a knockout or a bargain, but persistence pays off. You'll also find bespoke tailoring, accessories, shoes, cosmetics, homewares and toys.

This Financial District location is the mothership; there are six other stores across Manhattan and the boroughs, and others in New Jersey, Long Island, Philadelphia and Florida.

Pearl River Mart DEPARTMENT STORE
(Map p80; ☎212-431-4770; www.pearlriver.com; 395 Broadway, at Walker St, Tribeca; ⏰10am-7:20pm; [S] N/Q/R/W, J/M/Z, 6 to Canal St) A local institution since 1971, Pearl River offers a dizzying array of Asian gifts, housewares, clothing and accessories: silk men's pajamas, cheongsam dresses, blue-and-white Japanese ceramic tableware, clever kitchen gadgets, paper lanterns, origami and calligraphy kits, bamboo plants and an abundance of lucky-cat figurines. The mezzanine art gallery features free rotating shows with work from Asian American artists and photographers.

There's also a branch at Chelsea Market (p81).

★**Philip Williams Posters** VINTAGE
(Map p80; ☎212-513-0313; www.postermuseum.com; 122 Chambers St, btwn Church St & W Broadway, Lower Manhattan; ⏰10am-7pm Mon-Sat; [S] A/C, 1/2/3 to Chambers St) You'll find more than 100,000 posters dating back to 1870 in this cavernous treasure trove, from oversized French advertisements for perfume and cognac to Eastern European film posters and decorative Chinese *Nianhua* posters. Prices range from $15 for small reproductions to thousands of dollars for rare, showpiece originals like an AM Cassandre. There's a second entrance at 52 Warren St.

Owner Philip Williams, looking for a way out of construction jobs, bought his first trunk of random goods – which included original letters from the Wright brothers – for $50 in 1972. He's since accumulated one of the largest inventories for sale in the world. His passion still alive, he also collects and sells poster books, advertising ephemera and art from the South.

🏠 SoHo & Chinatown

Rag & Bone FASHION & ACCESSORIES
(Map p84; ☎212-219-2204; www.rag-bone. com; 117-119 Mercer St, btwn Prince & Spring Sts, SoHo; ⊙11am-8pm Mon-Sat, to 7pm Sun; ⓢR/W to Prince St) Downtown label Rag & Bone is a hit with many of New York's coolest, sharpest dressers – both men and women. Detail-oriented pieces range from clean-cut shirts and blazers and graphic tees to monochromatic sweaters, feather-light strappy dresses, leather goods and Rag & Bone's highly prized jeans (from $200). Accessories include shoes, hats, bags and wallets. See the website for all its New York locations.

★**Galeria Melissa** SHOES
(Map p84; ☎212-775-1950; www.melissa.com. br/us/galerias/ny; 500 Broadway, btwn Broome & Spring Sts, SoHo; ⊙10am-7pm Mon-Fri, to 8pm Sat, 11am-7pm Sun; 🐾; ⓢ6 to Spring St, R/W to Prince St) This Brazilian designer specializes in downpour-friendly plastic footwear. Recyclable, sustainable, stylish – women's and kids' shoes run the gamut from mod sandals to brogues, runners and, of course, boots.

Melissa's SoHo boutique is the only one in the USA and it's a lesson in the future of retail, with an Instagram room, a vertical rainforest plant wall, shoes displayed on plinths and prismatic mirror walls.

MiN New York COSMETICS
(Map p84; ☎212-206-6366; www.min.com; 117 Crosby St, btwn Jersey & Prince Sts, SoHo; ⊙11am-7pm Tue-Sat, noon-6pm Sun & Mon; ⓢB/D/F/M to Broadway-Lafayette St; N/R to Prince St) This chic, library-like fragrance apothecary has exclusive perfumes, bath and grooming products, and scented candles. Look out for artisanal fragrance 'stories' from MiN's own line. Prices span affordable to astronomical (from $70), and the scents are divine. Unlike many places, here there's no pressure to buy.

🏠 West Village, Chelsea & Meatpacking District

★**Strand Book Store** BOOKS
(Map p84; ☎212-473-1452; www.strandbooks.com; 828 Broadway, at E 12th St, West Village; ⊙9:30am-10:30pm Mon-Sat, from 11am Sun; ⓢL, N/Q/R/W,

4/5/6 to 14th St-Union Sq) Beloved and legendary, the iconic Strand embodies downtown NYC's intellectual bona fides – a bibliophile's Oz, where generations of book lovers carrying the store's trademark tote bags happily lose themselves for hours. In operation since 1927, the Strand sells new, used and rare titles, spreading an incredible 18 miles of books (over 2.5 million of them) among three labyrinthine floors.

★**Murray's Cheese** FOOD & DRINKS
(Map p84; ☎212-243-3289; www.murrayscheese. com; 254 Bleecker St, btwn Morton & Leroy Sts, West Village; sandwiches $7-8; ⊙8am-9pm Mon-Sat, 9am-8pm Sun; ⓢA/C/E, B/D/F/M to W 4th St-Washington Sq, 1 to Christopher St-Sheridan Sq) Founded in 1940 by Spanish Civil War veteran Murray Greenberg, this is one of New York's best cheese shops. Former owner (now 'advisor') Rob Kaufelt is known for his talent for sniffing out the best curds from around the world: you'll find (and be able to taste) all manner of *fromage*, all aged in cheese caves on site and in Queens.

Housing Works Thrift Shop VINTAGE
(Map p88; ☎718-838-5050; www.housingworks. org; 143 W 17th St, btwn Sixth & Seventh Aves, Chelsea; ⊙10am-7pm Mon-Sat, noon-6pm Sun; ⓢ1 to 18th St) The flagship for 13 other branches around town, this shop with its swank window displays looks more boutique than thrift, but its selections of clothes, accessories, furniture, books and records are great value. It's the place to go to find discarded designer clothes for a bargain, and all proceeds benefit the charity serving the city's HIV-positive and AIDS-affected homeless communities.

🏠 East Village & Lower East Side

Obscura Antiques ANTIQUES
(Map p84; ☎212-505-9251; www.obscuraantiques. com; 207 Ave A, btwn E 12th & E 13th Sts, East Village; ⊙1-7:30pm; ⓢL to 1st Ave) This eclectic trove pleases both curio-lovers and inveterate antique hunters. Here you'll find taxidermied animal heads, tiny rodent skulls and skeletons, butterfly displays in glass boxes, Victorian-era postmortem photography, disturbing little (dental?) instruments, German land-mine flags, old poison bottles and glass eyes. A Science Channel TV show, *Oddities*, focuses on the shop, bizarre things, and those who seek them.

★Russ & Daughters FOOD
(Map p84; ☎212-475-4800; www.russanddaughters.com; 179 E Houston St, btwn Orchard & Allen Sts, Lower East Side; ⏲8am-6pm Fri-Wed, to 7pm Thu; [S]F to 2nd Ave) Since 1914 this much-loved deli, has served up Eastern European Jewish delicacies, such as caviar, herring, sturgeon and, of course, lox. Proudly owned by four generations of the Russ family, it's a great place to load up for a picnic or stock your fridge with breakfast goodies. Foodies, history buffs and interior designers will love it.

A Russ & Daughters Cafe (p113) with sit-down service is close by on Orchard St, but it's just as pleasant to order your 'Shtetl' (or other choice of bagel or bialy sandwich) and eat in nearby **Sara D Roosevelt Park** (Map p84; E Houston St, at Chrystie St, Lower East Side; [S]F to Delancey-Essex Sts).

Polish immigrant Joel Russ started out selling herring from a barrel on the street, but with energy and determination built his way up to a storefront deli in 1914. In 1935 he made his daughters Hattie, Ida and Anne full partners, renaming the business and becoming the first-ever American company with '& Daughters' in the name.

Union Square, Flatiron District & Gramercy

ABC Carpet & Home HOMEWARES
(Map p88; ☎212-473-3000; www.abchome.com; 888 Broadway, at E 19th St; ⏲10am-7pm Mon-Sat, noon-6pm Sun; [S]4/5/6, N/Q/R/W, L to 14th St-Union Sq) A mecca for home designers and decorators brainstorming ideas, this beautifully curated, seven-level temple to good taste heaves with all sorts of furnishings, small and large. Shop for easy-to-pack knickknacks, boho textiles and jewelry, as well as statement furniture, designer lighting, ceramics and antique carpets. Come Christmas the shop is a joy to behold and it's a great place to buy decorations.

Fishs Eddy HOMEWARES
(Map p88; ☎212-420-9020; www.fishseddy.com; 889 Broadway, at E 19th St, Union Sq; ⏲10am-9pm Mon-Fri, to 8pm Sat & Sun; [S]R/W, 6 to 23rd St) High-quality and irreverent design has made Fishs Eddy a staple in the homes of hip New Yorkers for years. Its store is a veritable landslide of mugs, plates, dish towels, carafes and anything else that belongs in a cupboard. Styles range from tasteful color blocking to delightfully outrageous patterns. The 'Brooklynese' line (Cawfee, Shuguh, Sawlt etc) makes for great souvenirs.

If you live in the US, you don't have to worry about hauling your new flatware home: staff can arrange affordable shipping for you at the store.

Midtown

★MoMA Design & Book Store GIFTS & SOUVENIRS
(Map p88; ☎212-708-9700; www.momastore.org; 11 W 53rd St, btwn Fifth & Sixth Aves; ⏲9:30am-6:30pm Sat-Thu, to 8pm Fri; [S]E, M to 5th Ave-53rd St) The flagship store at the Museum of Modern Art (p87) is a fab spot for souvenir shopping. Besides gorgeous books (from art and architecture tomes to pop-culture readers and kids' picture books), you'll find art prints and posters and one-of-a-kind knickknacks. For furniture, lighting, homewares, jewelry, bags and arty gifts, head to the MoMA Design Store across the street.

Barneys DEPARTMENT STORE
(Map p94; ☎212-826-8900; www.barneys.com; 660 Madison Ave, at E 61st St; ⏲10am-8pm Mon-Wed & Sat, to 9pm Thu & Fri, 11am-7pm Sun; 📶; [S]N/R/W to 5th Ave) Serious fashionistas swipe their plastic at Barneys, respected for its collections of top-tier labels like Isabel Marant Étoile, Mr & Mrs Italy and Lanvin – all spaced out adequately enough to show just how precious each collection is. If you're not armed with the big bucks, expect to find it a little intimidating.

Highlights include the basement cosmetics department, the chic Freds restaurant and Genes, a futuristic cafe with touch-screen communal tables for online shopping. You'll find other branches on Seventh Ave in downtown Manhattan and on Atlantic Ave in Brooklyn.

Bergdorf Goodman DEPARTMENT STORE
(Map p94; ☎212-753-7300; www.bergdorfgoodman.com; 754 Fifth Ave, btwn W 57th & 58th Sts; ⏲10am-9pm Mon-Fri, to 8pm Sat, 11am-8pm Sun; [S]N/R/W to 5th Ave-59th St, F to 57th St) Not merely loved for its Christmas windows (the city's best), plush BG, at this location since 1928, leads the fashion race, led by its industry-leading fashion director Linda Fargo. A mainstay of ladies who lunch, its draws include exclusive collections and a coveted women's shoe department. The men's store is across the street.

Macy's DEPARTMENT STORE
(Map p88; ☎212-695-4400; www.macys.com; 151 W 34th St, at Broadway; ⏲10am-10pm Mon-Sat, 11am-9pm Sun; [S]B/D/F/M, N/Q/R/W to

34th St-Herald Sq; A/C/E to Penn Station) Occupying most of an entire city block, the country's largest department store covers most bases, with fashion, furnishings, kitchenware, sheets, cafes and hair salons. It's more 'mid-priced' than 'exclusive,' stocking mainstream labels and big-name cosmetics. The store also houses an **NYC Information Center** (📞 212-484-1222; www.nycgo.com) with information desk, free city maps and 10% store discount vouchers for tourists (bring valid ID).

FAO Schwarz   TOYS
(Map p88; 📞 800-326-8638; www.faoschwarz. com; 30 Rockefeller Plaza; ⊘ 9am-10pm Mon-Sat, from 11am Sun; Ⓢ B/D/F/M 47-50 Sts-Rockefeller Center) New Yorkers mourned the loss of this landmark toy store (c 1862) when it closed its famed flagship on Fifth Ave in 2015 (you might remember Tom Hanks playing a giant floor keyboard here in the movie *Big*). It was resurrected in this new Rockefeller location in 2018, looking jazzier than ever. Even the keyboard has made a comeback.

It really is retail nirvana for kids, with giant spaceships to clamber over, magic show demonstrations, a colorful candy bar and loads of different zones stuffed with toys. Highlights include the 'pit crew' area where car fans can customize their racers, the clockwork stairwell and the neon-lit top-floor piano lounge. Expect to feel like a kid in a candy store, whether you're nine or 90.

Saks Fifth Ave   DEPARTMENT STORE
(Map p88; 📞 212-753-4000; www.saksfifthavenue. com; 611 Fifth Ave, at E 50th St; ⊘ 10am-8:30pm Mon-Sat, 11am-7pm Sun; Ⓢ B/D/F/M to 47th-50th Sts-Rockefeller Center, E, M to 5th Ave-53rd St) Graced with vintage escalators, Saks' 10-floor flagship store is home to the 'Shoe Salon,' NYC's biggest women's shoe department (complete with express elevator and zip code). Other fortes include the revamped beauty floor and men's departments, the latter home to destination grooming salon John Allan's and a sharply edited offering of fashion-forward labels. The store's January sale is legendary.

🏛 Upper East Side

Shakespeare & Co   BOOKS
(Map p94; 📞 212-772-3400; www.shakeandco. com; 939 Lexington Ave, at E 69th St; ⊘ 7:30am-8pm Mon-Fri, 8am-7pm Sat, 9am-6pm Sun; 📷; Ⓢ 6 to 68th St) No relation to the Paris seller, this popular bookstore is one of NYC's great indie options. There's a wide array of

contemporary fiction and nonfiction, art and local history books, plus a small but unique collection of periodicals, while an Espresso book machine churns out print-on-demand titles. A small cafe serves coffee, tea and light meals.

Mary Arnold Toys   TOYS
(Map p94; 📞 212-744-8510; www.maryarnoldtoys. com; 1178 Lexington Ave, btwn E 80th & 81st Sts; ⊘ 9am-6pm Mon-Fri, 10am-6pm Sat, to 5pm Sun; ♿; Ⓢ 4/5/6 to 86th St) Several generations of Upper East Siders have spent large chunks of their childhood browsing the stuffed shelves of this personable local toy store, opened in 1931. Its range is extensive – stuffed animals, action figures, science kits, board games, arts and crafts, educational toys – even Lomo cameras for budding retro photographers.

🏛 Upper West Side

Shishi   FASHION & ACCESSORIES
(Map p94; www.shishiboutique.com; 2488 Broadway, btwn 92nd & 93rd Sts; ⊘ 11am-8pm Mon-Sat, to 7pm Sun; Ⓢ 1/2/3 to 96th St) Shishi is a delightful Israeli-owned boutique stocking an ever-changing selection of stylish, affordable apparel: elegant sweaters, sleeveless shift dresses and eye-catching jewelry from Brazilian designers, among others. (All its clothes are wash-and-dry friendly too.) It's fun for browsing, and with the enthusiastic staff kitting you out in the glamorous changing area, you'll feel like you have your own personal stylist.

★Zabar's   FOOD
(Map p94; 📞 212-787-2000; www.zabars.com; 2245 Broadway, at W 80th St; ⊘ 8am-7:30pm Mon-Fri, to 8pm Sat, 9am-6pm Sun; Ⓢ 1 to 79th St) A bastion of gourmet kosher foodie-ism, this sprawling local market has been a neighborhood fixture since the 1930s. And what a fixture it is! It features a heavenly array of cheeses, meats, olives, caviar, smoked fish, pickles, dried fruits, nuts and baked goods, including pillowy, fresh-out-of-the-oven *knishes* (Eastern European–style potato dumplings wrapped in dough; $3).

With cramped and crowded aisles, the shopping experience can feel like a bit of a scrum. Grab a number at the specialty counters upon entering – the wait can be long. Upstairs is an entire floor of oft-overlooked houseware products and next door is a sit-down cafe with frozen yoghurt, paninis and Zabar's own-blend coffee.

Magpie ARTS & CRAFTS
(Map p94; www.magpienewyork.com; 488 Amsterdam Ave, btwn 83rd & 84th Sts; ⏰11am-7pm Mon-Sat, to 6pm Sun; [S]1 to 86th St) 🍃 This charming little shop carries a wide range of ecofriendly objects: elegant stationery, beeswax candles, hand-painted mugs, organic-cotton scarves, recycled-resin necklaces, hand-dyed felt journals and wooden earth puzzles are a few things that may catch your eye. Most products are fair-trade, made of sustainable materials or locally designed and made.

Harlem & Upper Manhattan

Harlem Haberdashery FASHION & ACCESSORIES
(Map p94; ☎646-707-0070; www.harlemhaberdashery.com; 245 Malcolm X Blvd, btwn 122nd & 123rd Sts, Harlem; ⏰noon-8pm Mon-Sat; [S]2/3 to 125th St) Keep your wardrobe fresh at this uberhip uptown boutique, which has covetable apparel in all shapes and sizes. Lovely T-shirts, high-end sneakers, dapper woven hats, bespoke denim jackets and jazzy sunglasses are among the ever-changing collections on display.

Flamekeepers Hat Club FASHION & ACCESSORIES
(Map p94; ☎212-531-3542; 273 W 121st St, at St Nicholas Ave, Harlem; ⏰noon-7pm Tue & Wed, to 8pm Thu-Sat, to 6pm Sun; [S]A/C, B/D to 125th St) Polish your look at this sassy little hat shop owned by affable Harlem local Marc Williamson. His carefully curated stock is a hat-lover's dream: soft Barbisio fedoras from Italy, Selentino top hats from the Czech Republic, and woolen patchwork caps from Ireland's Hanna Hats of Donegal. Prices range from $55 to $1000; ask about hats that Marc has customized himself.

Brooklyn

★ **Artists & Fleas** MARKET
(☎917-488-4203; www.artistsandfleas.com; 70 N 7th St, btwn Wythe & Kent Aves, Williamsburg; ⏰10am-7pm Sat & Sun; [S]L to Bedford Ave) This exuberant flea market provides stripped-back vending space for more than 75 purveyors of vintage and craft wares. Clothing, records, paintings, photographs, hats, handmade jewelry, unique T-shirts and canvas bags, plus an in-store cafe and DJ – it's all here. Two locations in Manhattan are smaller but open daily, one in SoHo, the other inside the Chelsea Market (p81).

Brooklyn Flea MARKET
(www.brooklynflea.com; 80 Pearl St, Manhattan Bridge Archway, Anchorage Pl, at Water St, Dumbo; ⏰10am-6pm Sun Apr-Oct; 👪; 🚌B67 to York/Jay Sts, [S]F to York St) Every Sunday from spring through early fall, numerous vendors sell their wares inside a giant archway under the Manhattan Bridge. There's everything from antiques to records, vintage clothes, homemade foods, quirky handicrafts, housewares and furniture. Locations can change, so check the website before you head out.

A slightly smaller indoor version runs Saturday and Sunday from 10am to 6pm in the Atlantic Center, together with the winter version of superlative food market Smorgasburg.

★ **Dellapietras** FOOD
(☎718-618-9575; 193 Atlantic Ave, btwn Court & Clinton Sts, Downtown Brooklyn; sandwiches $12; ⏰10am-7pm Mon-Sat, to 5pm Sun; [S]4/5 to Borough Hall) Meet the meat – dry-aged prominently in the front window of this outstanding deli-butcher. Great cuts of meat and sausages are augmented by charcuterie and a huge range of lovingly prepared food. Fried chicken, salads, stews and amazing carvery sandwiches make this an ideal lunch stop. The porchetta, broccoli rabe and pecorino sandwich is a thing of immense pleasure.

Twisted Lily PERFUME
(☎347-529-4681; www.twistedlily.com; 360 Atlantic Ave, btwn Bond & Hoyt Sts, Boerum Hill; ⏰noon-7pm Tue-Sun; [S]F, G to Hoyt-Schermerhorn) Come out smelling like a rose (or, if you'd prefer, almond, clary sage or orange blossom) from this 'fragrance boutique and apothecary' specializing in unusual scents from around the world. The attentive staff will help you shop by fragrance for personalized perfumes, scented candles, and skincare and grooming products.

Beacon's Closet VINTAGE
(☎718-486-0816; www.beaconscloset.com; 74 Guernsey St, btwn Nassau & Norman Aves, Greenpoint; ⏰11am-8pm; [S]G to Nassau Ave) This vast warehouse of vintage clothing is both a gold mine and a gauntlet. Arranged by color, its circular racks of coats, dresses, polyester tops and '90s-era T-shirts take time and determination to conquer. The committed will also find shoes of all sorts, flannels, hats, handbags, chunky jewelry and sunglasses. There are other branches in **Bushwick** (☎718-417-5683; 23 Bogart St, btwn

Varet & Cook Sts; ⌚11am-8pm; [S]L to Morgan Ave), **Park Slope** (☎718-230-1630; 92 Fifth Ave, cnr Warren St; ⌚noon-9pm Mon-Fri, 11am-8pm Sat & Sun; [S]2/3 to Bergen St, B, Q to 7th Ave) and Manhattan.

Industry City DESIGN
(☎718-736-2516; www.industrycity.com; 220 36th St, btwn Second & Third Aves, Sunset Park; ⌚9am-9pm; 📶; [S]D, N, R to 36th St) These six towering warehouses by the Brooklyn waterfront have been repurposed as a 35-acre hub for shops, design studios, start-ups and nonprofits. The slick design lacks Brooklyn's characteristic grungy spirit, but it's worth stopping by for lunch at the very good food court or summer performances, held in the outdoor courtyard.

Japan Village stands out for its well-stocked supermarket, complete with takeaway mochi (rice flour dumplings stuffed with sweet fillings like red bean paste) and various other Japanese groceries, plus a cafe-bakery and nearby sake shop. Another worthwhile stop is the outlet of venerable Manhattan chocolatier Li-Lac.

Queens

Astoria Bookshop BOOKS
(☎718-278-2665; www.astoriabookshop.com; 31-29 31st St, btwn 31st Ave & Broadway, Astoria; ⌚11am-7pm; [S]N/W to Broadway) A much-loved indie bookshop with ample shelf space dedicated to local authors, Astoria is a good spot to pick up a title about the Queens dining scene or the borough's wide-ranging ethnic diversity. A stalwart of the community, Astoria also hosts author readings, discussion groups, writing workshops and kids' storytelling (every Thursday at 11am).

The Bronx

Hit the old-school shops and market stalls around Arthur Ave for Italian larder essentials, from truffle oil and anchovies to ripe, sweet *sugo* (tomato sauce).

Information

New York City is one of the USA's safest cities – in 2018 homicides fell to 289, a record low not seen since the early 1950s. Overall violent-crime statistics have also declined for the 28th straight year. Still, it's best to take a common-sense approach when exploring.

- Don't walk around alone at night in unfamiliar, sparsely populated areas.
- Be aware of pickpockets, particularly in mobbed areas like Times Square or Penn Station at rush hour.
- While it's generally safe to ride the subway after midnight, you may want to skip going underground and take a taxi instead, especially if traveling alone.

TIPPING

Tipping is *not* optional; only withhold tips in cases of outrageously bad service.

Restaurant servers 18–20%, unless a gratuity is already charged on the bill (usually only for groups of five or more)

Bartenders 15–20% per round, minimum per drink $1 for standard drinks, and $2 per specialty cocktail

Taxi drivers 10–15%, rounded up to the next dollar

Airport & hotel porters $2 per bag, minimum per cart $5

Hotel maids $2–4 per night, left in envelope or under the card provided

NYC Information Center (Map p88; ☎212-484-1222; www.nycgo.com; Broadway Plaza, btwn W 43rd & 44th Sts; ⌚8am-8pm; [S]N/Q/R/W, S, 1/2/3, 7, A/C/E to Times Sq-42nd St) is the official NYC tourist information booth, with maps, brochures and bilingual staff.

Getting There & Away

AIR

Fifteen miles from Midtown in southeastern Queens, **John F Kennedy International Airport** (JFK; ☎718-244-4444; www.jfkairport.com; [S]A to Howard Beach, E, J/Z to Sutphin Boulevard-Archer Ave then AirTrain) has six working terminals, serves more than 59 million passengers annually and hosts flights coming and going from all corners of the globe. You can use the AirTrain (free within the airport) to move from one terminal to another.

The timeline is uncertain, but a massive $10 billion overhaul of the airport was approved in early 2017. Architectural and structural changes are the focus, but plans also call for a substantial upgrade of amenities and access routes via public transportation.

Used mainly for domestic flights, **LaGuardia** (LGA; ☎718-533-3400; www.laguardiaairport.com; 🚌M60, Q70) is smaller than JFK but only 8 miles from midtown Manhattan; it sees nearly 30 million passengers per year.

ACCESSIBLE TRAVEL IN NYC

Much of the city is accessible with curb cuts for wheelchair users. All the major sites (like the Met museum, the Guggenheim, the National September 11 Memorial and Museum, and the Lincoln Center) are also accessible. Some, but not all, Broadway venues have provisions for theater-goers with disabilities, from listening devices to wheelchair seating; consult http://theatreaccess.nyc.

Unfortunately, only about 100 of New York's 468 subway stations are fully wheelchair accessible. In general, the bigger stations have access, such as 14th St-Union Sq, 34th St-Penn Station, 42nd St-Port Authority Terminal, 59th St-Columbus Circle, and 66th St-Lincoln Center. For a complete list of accessible subway stations, visit http://web.mta.info/accessibility/stations.htm. Also visit www.nycgo.com/accessibility.

On the plus side, all of NYC's MTA buses are wheelchair accessible, and are often a better option than negotiating cramped subway stations. Taxis suitable to travelers with mobility aids are available through Accessible Dispatch (646-599-9999; http://accessibledispatch.org); there's also an app that allows you to request the nearest available service.

Another excellent resource is the **Big Apple Greeter** (☎212-669-8159; www.bigapplegreeter.org) [FREE] program, which has more than 50 volunteers on staff who have various disabilities and are happy to show off their corner of the city.

Restrooms can be found in most department stores and the NYC parks website (www.nycgovparks.org/facilities/bathrooms) is a good source of info regarding bathrooms – some of them wheelchair-accessible – across the city's green spaces.

The city also provides paratransit buses for getting around town for the same price as a subway fare, though this service – called Access-a-Ride (https://access.nyc.gov/programs/access-a-ride) – isn't very practical for tourists as you'll need to attend an assessment appointment and fill in mailed paperwork before eligibility for the service can be confirmed (which can take up to 21 days). Visit the website for more info.

Download Lonely Planet's free Accessible Travel guides from http://lptravel.to/AccessibleTravel.

Much maligned by politicians and ordinary travelers alike, the airport is set to receive a much-needed $4 billion overhaul of its terminal facilities. Scheduled in phases from 2018 to 2021, plans call for a single, unified terminal to replace the four existing stand-alone ones, as well as an upgrade in amenities and access via public transportation.

BUS

A number of budget bus lines operate from locations on the west side of Midtown:

BoltBus (Map p88; ☎877-265-8287; www.boltbus.com; W 36th St, btwn Seventh & Eighth Aves; 📶) Services from New York to Philadelphia, Boston, Baltimore and Washington, DC. The earlier you purchase tickets, the better the deal. Notable for its free wi-fi, which occasionally actually works.

Megabus (Map p88; ☎877-462-6342; https://us.megabus.com; 34th St, btwn 11th & 12th Aves; 📶; [S]7 to 34th St-Hudson Yards) Travels from New York to Boston, Washington, DC, and Toronto, among other destinations. Free (sometimes functioning) wi-fi. Departures leave from 34th St near the Jacob K Javits Convention Center and **arrivals** (Map p88; cnr Seventh Ave & 27th St; [S]1 to 28th St) drop off at 27th and 7th.

Vamoose (Map p88; ☎212-695-6766; www.vamoosebus.com; cnr Seventh Ave & 30th St; from $20; [S]1 to 28th St; A/C/E, 1/2/3 to 34th St-Penn Station) Buses head to Arlington, Virginia, and Bethesda, Maryland.

TRAIN

Penn Station (W 33rd St, btwn Seventh & Eighth Aves; [S]1/2/3, A/C/E to 34th St-Penn Station) The oft-maligned departure point for all Amtrak (www.amtrak.com) trains, including the Acela Express services to Boston and Washington, DC (note that this express service costs twice as much as a normal fare). Fares vary, based on the day of the week and the time you want to travel. There's no baggage-storage facility at Penn Station. A new Amtrak hub is due to open in 2020 as part of long-term renewal plans for the station, but be aware that some services are being compromised as work progresses.

Long Island Rail Road (www.mta.info/lirr) Serves more than 300,000 commuters each day, with services from Penn Station to points in Brooklyn and Queens, and on Long Island. Prices are broken down by zones. A peak-hour ride from Penn Station to Jamaica Station (en route to JFK via AirTrain) costs $10.25 if you buy it at the station (or a whopping $16 on board!).

NJ Transit (www.njtransit.com) Also operates trains from Penn Station, with services to the New Jersey suburbs and the Jersey Shore.

New Jersey PATH (www.panynj.gov/path) An option for getting into NJ's northern points, such as Hoboken and Newark. Trains ($2.75) run from Penn Station along the length of Sixth Ave, with stops at 33rd, 23rd, 14th, 9th and Christopher Sts, as well as at the reopened World Trade Center site. Note that PATH's World Trade Center station will be closed weekends from January 2019 through December 2020.

Metro-North Railroad (www.mta.info/mnr) The last line departing from the magnificent Grand Central Terminal, it serves Connecticut, Westchester County and the Hudson Valley.

Getting Around

Check the Metropolitan Transportation Authority website (www.mta.info) for public transportation information (buses and subway). Delays have increased as ridership has expanded.

Subway Inexpensive, somewhat efficient and operates around the clock, though navigating lines can be confusing. A single ride is $2.75 with a MetroCard.

Buses Convenient during off hours – especially when transferring between the city's eastern and western sides (most subway lines run north to south). Uses the MetroCard; same price as the subway.

Taxi Meters start at $2.50 and increase roughly $5 for every 20 blocks. See www.nyc.gov/taxi.

Bicycle The city's popular bike-share program Citi Bike (www.citibikenyc.com) provides excellent access to most parts of Manhattan.

Inter-borough ferries The New York City Ferry (www.ferry.nyc) provides handy transport between waterside stops in Manhattan, Brooklyn and Queens.

NEW YORK STATE

For most, any trip to the Empire State starts or finishes in its iconic metropolis: New York City. However, if you confine your travels only to the five boroughs there's a considerable amount you're missing out on.

Long Island and upstate New York – generally accepted as anywhere north of the NYC metro area – shouldn't be missed. Long Island has cozy beach towns, while upstate is a dream destination for those who cherish the great outdoors. The Hudson River

valley acts as an escape route from the city, leading eager sojourners north. From Albany, the 524-mile Erie Canal cuts due west to Lake Erie, passing spectacular Niagara Falls, Buffalo and Rochester. In the east you'll find the St Lawrence River and its thousands of islands, as well as the magnificent Adirondack and Catskills mountains. Head to the middle of the state and you'll be ensconced in the serene Finger Lakes.

Resources

511 NY (www.511ny.org) Statewide traffic and transit info.

I Love NY (www.iloveny.com) Comprehensive state tourism bureau, with the iconic heart logo.

New York State Parks, Recreation & Historic Preservation (www.parks.ny.gov) Camping, lodging and general info on all state parks.

And North (www.andnorth.com) A curated online guide to upstate New York.

Escape Brooklyn (www.escapebrooklyn.com) Respected blog by clued-up Brooklynites on upstate getaways.

Lonely Planet (www.lonelyplanet.com/usa/new-york-state) Destination information, hotel bookings, traveler forum and more.

Long Island

Technically, the 118 miles of Long Island includes the boroughs of Brooklyn and Queens on the western edge, but in the popular imagination, 'Long Island' begins only where the city ends, in a mass of traffic-clogged expressways and suburbs that every teenager aspires to leave. (Levittown, the first planned 1950s subdivision, is in central Nassau County.) But there's plenty more out on 'Lawn-guy-land' (per the local accent). Push past the central belt of 'burbs to wind-swept dunes, proud stands of pine, glitzy summer resorts, fresh farms and wineries, a wealth of perfect Pleasantvilles and Mayberry-esque Main Streets and whaling and fishing ports established in the 17th century. Then you'll see why loyalists prefer the nickname 'Strong Island.'

Getting There & Around

Thanks to **Long Island Rail Road** (LIRR; ☎718-217-5477; www.mta.info/lirr), which runs three lines from New York Penn Station to the furthest eastern ends of the island, it's possible to visit without a car. Additionally, the Hampton Jitney (p140) and **Hampton Luxury Liner** (☎631-537-5800; www.hamptonluxuryliner.com)

buses connect Manhattan to various Hamptons villages and Montauk; the former also picks up in Brooklyn, and runs to the North Fork. With a car, however, it is easier to visit several spots on the island in one go. I-495, aka the Long Island Expwy (LIE), runs down the middle of the island – but avoid rush hour, when it's commuter hell.

The **Cross Sound Ferry** (☑ 631-323-2525, 860-443-5281; www.longislandferry.com; 41270 Main Rd, Orient; vehicle/bike/foot from $57/5/16.25) connects Long Island with New London, Connecticut.

South Shore

Easily accessible by public transit, South Shore beaches can get crowded, but they're a fun day out. Not nearly as much of a schlep as the Hamptons, and far more egalitarian, the beach towns along these barrier islands each have their own vibe and audience – you can get lost in the crowds or go solo on the dunes. **Long Beach** is just over the border from Queens, and its main town strip is busy with ice-cream shops, bars and eateries.

⊙ Sights

Fire Island National Seashore   ISLAND
(☑ 631-687-4750; www.nps.gov/fiis) FREE Federally protected, this island offers sand dunes, forests, clean beaches, camping (wilderness permits $25 obtained throughwww.recreation.gov), hiking trails, inns, restaurants, 15 hamlets and two villages. The scenery ranges from car-free areas of summer mansions and packed nightclubs to stretches of sand where you'll find nothing but pitched tents and deer.

Most of the island is accessible only by ferry (☑ 631-665-3600; www.fireislandferries.com; 99 Maple Ave, Bay Shore; one-way adult/child $11/6) and is free of cars – regulars haul their belongings on little wagons instead. You can drive to either end of the island (the lighthouse or the Wilderness Visitor Center) but there is no road in between. The island is edged with a dozen or so tiny hamlets, mostly residential. Party-center **Ocean Beach Village** and quieter **Ocean Bay Park** (take ferries from the Bayshore LIRR stop) have a few hotels; **Cherry Grove** and the **Pines**, via ferries from Sayville, are gay enclaves, also with hotels.

Robert Moses State Park   STATE PARK
(☑ 631-669-0449; www.parks.ny.gov; 600 Robert Moses State Pkwy, Babylon, Fire Island; per car $10, golf adult/senior $11/8; ⊙ dawn-dusk) Robert Moses State Park, one small part of Fire Island accessible by car, lies at the west-

ernmost end and features wide, soft-sand beaches with mellower crowds than those at Jones Beach. It's also adjacent to the **Fire Island Lighthouse** (Fire Island National Seashore; ☑ 631-661-4876; www.fireislandlighthouse.com; Robert Moses Causeway; adult/child $8/4; ⊙ 9:30am-6pm Jul & Aug, shorter hours rest of year), which you can walk to from here.

Sunken Forest   FOREST
(☑ 631-597-6183; www.nps.gov/fiis; Fire Island; ⊙ visitor center mid-May–mid-Oct) FREE This 300-year-old forest, a surprisingly dense stretch of trees behind the dunes, is easily accessible via a 1.5-mile boardwalk trail looping through it. It's pleasantly shady in summer, and vividly colored when the leaves change in fall. It's accessible by its own ferry stop, Sailors Haven, where there's also a visitor center, or a long walk in the winter season, after the ferry shuts down. Ranger-guided tours available.

🍴 Sleeping & Eating

Seashore Condo Motel   HOTEL $$
(☑ 631-583-5860; www.seashorecondomotel.com; Bayview Ave, Ocean Bay Park, Fire Island; week/weekend d from $200/300; ❄️ 🛜) Small, wood-paneled rooms without many frills (but new beds!), despite the price. Take the Ocean Bay Park ferry from Bayside.

Madison Fire Island Pines   BOUTIQUE HOTEL $$$
(☑ 631-597-6061; www.themadisonfi.com; 22 Atlantic Walk, Fire Island Pines, Fire Island; d from $300; ❄️ 🛜 🏊) Fire Island's first 'boutique' hotel, which rivals anything Manhattan has to offer in terms of amenities, but also has killer views from its rooftop deck and a gorgeous pool. The hotel is reached by **Sayville Ferry Service** (☑ 631-589-0810; www.sayvilleferry.com; 41 River Rd, Sayville) to Pines.

Sand Castle   SEAFOOD $$$
(☑ 631-597-4174; www.fireislandsandcastle.com; 106 Lewis Walk, Cherry Grove, Fire Island; mains $24-33; ⊙ 11am-11pm Mon, Tue & Thu-Sat, 9:30am-11pm Sun May-Sep; 🌿) One of Fire Island's only oceanfront (rather than bayfront) options, Sand Castle serves up satisfying appetizers (fried calamari, seafood chowder) and lots of seafood temptations (mussels, octopus carpaccio, grilled King Salmon).

Nice cocktails and people-watching, too.

❶ Getting There & Away

You can drive to Fire Island by taking the Long Island Expwy to Exit 53 (Bayshore), 59 (Sayville) or 63 (Patchogue).

Using public transportation, take the LIRR to one of three stations with connections to the ferries: **Patchogue** (②631-475-1665; www.davisparkferry.com; 80 Brightwood St, Patchogue), Bayshore or Sayville. Patchogue is walking distance from the train to the boat. You can also purchase a train-taxi combination ticket from the railroad for excursions to Sunken Forest and a train-bus combo for Jones Beach.

The LIRR (www.mtainfo.com/lirr) runs directly to Long Beach (55 minutes) from New York Penn Station. You can buy special beach combination excursion tickets from the railroad.

The Hamptons

This string of villages is a summer escape for Manhattan's wealthiest, who zip to mansions by helicopter. Mere mortals take the Hampton Jitney bus and chip in on rowdy rental houses. Behind the glitz is a long cultural history, as noted artists and writers have lived here. Beneath the glamour, the gritty and life-risking tradition of fishing continues. The area is small, and connected by often traffic-clogged Montauk Hwy.

◉ Sights

EAST HAMPTON

East Hampton Town
Marine Museum   MUSEUM
(②631-324-6850; www.easthamptonhistory.org; 301 Bluff Rd, Amagansett; $8; ⊙10am-4pm Fri & Sat Jul & Aug) One of your last outposts before you drive on to Montauk, this small museum dedicated to the fishing and whaling industries is as interesting as its counterpart in Sag Harbor, full of old harpoons, boats half the size of their prey, and a beautiful B&W photographic tribute to the local fishers and their families.

Osborn-Jackson House   MUSEUM
(②631-324-6850; www.easthamptonhistory.org; 101 Main St; donation $5; ⊙10am-4pm Mon-Fri) Check out East Hampton's colonial past with a visit to the Historical Society, including this historic home. The Society tends to five attractions around East Hampton, including several colonial farms, mansions and the marine museum.

Pollock-Krasner House   ARTS CENTER
(②631-324-4929; www.pkhouse.org; 830 Springs Fireplace Rd; Sat $10, guided tours Thu & Fri $15; ⊙noon-5pm Sat, guided tours noon, 2pm & 4pm Thu & Fri May-Oct) Tour the home of husband-and-wife art stars Jackson Pollock and Lee

Krasner – worth it just to see the paint-spattered floor of Pollock's studio. You can simply show up on a Saturday, but reservations are required for the guided tours on Thursday and Friday.

SAG HARBOR

Sag Harbor Whaling
& Historical Museum   MUSEUM
(②631-725-0770; www.sagharborwhalingmuseum. org; 200 Main St; adult/child $8/3; ⊙10am-5pm May-Oct) The cool collection here includes actual artifacts from 19th-century whaling ships: sharp flensing knives, battered pots for rendering blubber, delicate scrimshaw and more. It's a bit surreal to see photos of the giant mammals in a village that's now a cute resort town. It occupies a striking 19th-century residential home that doubles as a Masonic Temple.

SOUTHAMPTON

★Parrish Art Museum   MUSEUM
(②631-283-2118; www.parrishart.org; 279 Montauk Hwy, Water Mill; adult/child $12/free; ⊙10am-5pm Wed-Mon, to 8pm Fri) In a sleek, long barn designed by Herzog & de Meuron, this institution spotlights local artists such as Jackson Pollock, Willem de Kooning, Chuck Close and William Merritt Chase. Special temporary exhibitions change over five times throughout the year; seven of the galleries are dedicated to permanent works that are curated from a 3000-strong collection. For more Pollock, make reservations to see his nearby studio and home.

Southampton History Museum   MUSEUM
(②631-283-2494; www.southamptonhistory.org; 17 Meeting House Lane; adult/child $5/free; ⊙11am-4pm Wed-Sat Mar-Dec) Before the Hamptons was the Hamptons, there was this clutch of buildings, now nicely maintained and spread around Southampton. The main museum is Rogers Mansion, once owned by a whaling captain. You can also visit a former dry-goods store, now occupied by a local jeweler, around the corner at 80 Main St; and a 17th-century homestead, the Halsey House (adult/child $5/free, Saturday only, July to September).

Additional buildings include an 1830 one-room schoolhouse, an 1825 barn and a 19th-century paint store, among others.

St Andrew's Dune Church   CHURCH
(②631-283-0549; www.standrewsdunechurch.com; 12 Gin Lane; ⊙service 11am Sun Jun-Sep) The triple spires of this 19th-century red wooden

church glow beautifully in the afternoon light. You can come to Sunday service if so inclined, admiring the stained glass and quaint wooden pews, or simply enjoy a stroll along the placid waterway across the street from the curious iron pot donated by an early congregant. The building was the earliest life-saving station in New York, and is well worth the short drive or walk from downtown.

🛏 Sleeping

1708 House
B&B $$$

(📞 631-287-1708; www.1708house.com; 126 Main St; d from $300, cottages from $625; ❄🅿) History buffs might gravitate towards this local standout, run by supreme storyteller Skip and his daughters. The deed on the house (and the old world European-style wine cellar in the basement) date to 1651. It's in central Southampton and prides itself on its turn-of-the-century charm and traditional furnishings in the 13 rooms and three cottages.

★ Topping Rose House
BOUTIQUE HOTEL $$$

(📞 631-537-0870; www.toppingrosehouse.com; 1 Bridgehampton-Sag Harbor Turnpike, Bridgehampton; d from $985; 🅿❄🅿🛋) In an 1842 home, this exclusive boutique hotel boasts 22 rooms, including six suites decorated with local artists' work. A Manhattan gallery curates the rotating (for sale) art collection, and there's a spa and heated pool in addition to Jean-Georges Vongerichten's farm-to-table restaurant (mains $28 to $49), some produce for which is sourced from the one-acre garden adjoining the property.

🍴 Eating

Candy Kitchen
DINER $

(2391 Montauk Hwy; mains $4.25-19; ⏰7am-8pm) An antidote to glitz, this old school corner diner has been serving good soups, homemade ice cream and other staples since 1925. Its policy is similarly old school – cash only, please. As far as ice cream goes, give mint chip or coffee chip a go; for lunch, the souvlaki and other Greek staples are popular.

Fellingham's
PUB FOOD $$

(Restaurant Sports Bar; 📞 631-283-9417; www.fellinghamsrestaurant.com; 17 Cameron St; burgers $11-24; ⏰11am-11pm; 🛋) This favored sports bar, rich with historical photos and memorabilia, boasts a hearty menu featuring a bacon-cheeseburger named for baseball legend Babe Ruth and a Sharapova burger with – naturally – Russian dressing. Mains are heavy on the steaks and chops. With

so much local flavor, this qualifies as the 'Cheers' of Southampton.

★ Dockside Bar & Grill
SEAFOOD $$$

(📞 631-725-7100; www.docksidesagharbor.com; 26 Bay St; mains $24-43; ⏰noon-4pm & 5:30-10pm Mon-Thu, noon-4pm & 5:30-10:30pm Fri, 11am-2pm & 5:30-10:30pm Sat, 11am-2pm & 5:30-10pm Sun) A local favorite inside the American Legion Hall (the original bar's still there). The seafood-heavy menu features a prize-winning, stick-to-the-spoon chowder and luscious avocado-lobster spring rolls, among other mouthwatering delights. The outdoor patio can be nice in the summer.

ⓘ Getting There & Away

Driving the Montauk Hwy (Rte 27) to and from New York involves careful planning to avoid major congestion, and it's often at a standstill within the Hamptons itself on busy weekends. Better to take the ever-popular **Hampton Jitney** (📞 631-283-4600; www.hamptonjitney.com) out here from Manhattan or Brooklyn – it serves the entire Hamptons with frequent comfortable buses. The LIRR (p137) is a second but often more time-consuming option.

ⓘ Getting Around

The app-driven, converted turquoise **Hampton Hopper** (📞 631-259-7076; www.hamptonhopper.com; ⏰10am-10pm Jun-Labor Day) school buses are an economical, hassle-free way to get around the towns and operate into the bar hours. Download the app to buy daily passes from $20 (the Montauk Loop is free) and see where the buses are.

Montauk

Towards the east-pointing tip of Long Island's South Fork, you'll find the mellow town of Montauk, aka 'The End,' and the famous surfing beach **Ditch Plains**. With the surfers have come affluent hipsters and boho-chic hotels, but the area is still far less of a scene than the Hamptons, with proudly blue-collar residents and casual seafood restaurants.

Route 27, the Montauk Hwy, divides east of **Napeague State Park**, with the Montauk Hwy continuing down the center of the peninsula while Old Montauk Hwy hugs the water. The roads converge at the edge of central Montauk and Fort Pond, a small lake. Two miles east is a large inlet called **Lake Montauk**, with marinas strung along its shore.

◉ Sights

Montauk Point State Park   STATE PARK
(📞631-668-3781; www.parks.ny.gov; 2000 Montauk Hwy/Rte 27; per car $8; ⊙dawn-dusk) Covering the eastern tip of the South Fork is Montauk Point State Park, with its impressive **lighthouse** (📞631-668-2544; www.montauklighthouse.com; 2000 Montauk Hwy; adult/child $12/5; ⊙10:30am-5:30pm Sun-Fri, to 7pm Sat mid-Jun–Aug, shorter hours mid-Apr–mid-Jun & Sep-Nov). A good place for windswept walks, surfing, surf fishing (with permit) and seal-spotting – call the park for the schedule; rangers will set up spotting scopes to better view the frisky pinnipeds.

Lost at Sea Memorial   MEMORIAL
(2000 Montauk Hwy, Montauk Lighthouse; Montauk State Park parking fee $8; ⊙10:30am-5:30pm Sun-Fri, to 7pm Sat mid-Jun–Aug, shorter hours mid-Apr–mid-Jun & Sep-Nov) Visitors to the Montauk Lighthouse may not immediately notice a smaller 15ft structure at the eastern end of the park, where the 60ft cliffs fall off into the sea, but for local fishers it's a daily reminder of their struggle against the power of the sea. The 8ft, 2600lb bronze statue set on a 7ft slab of granite is inscribed with the names of those lost to the waves, from the colonial days of New York to the present.

⛺ Sleeping

Hither Hills State Park   CAMPGROUND $
(📞631-668-2554; www.parks.ny.gov; 164 Old Montauk Hwy; campsites state residents/nonresidents $35/70) These wooded dunes form a natural barrier between Montauk and the Hamptons. The 189-site campground caters for tents and RVs, and there are spots for fishing (permit required) and hiking through the dunes; online reservations ($9 fee) are a must. The park's western border is the stunning **Walking Dunes** (Napeague Harbor Rd, Hither Hills State Park) **FREE**.

★**Sunrise Guesthouse**   GUESTHOUSE $$$
(📞631-668-7286; www.sunrisebnb.com; 681 Old Montauk Hwy; r/ste $295/425; 🅿❄🛜) A tasteful yet homey four-room B&B a mile from town, and just across the road from the beach. The breakfast is ample and delicious, served in a comfy dining area with a million-dollar view. Summer weekends require a two-night minimum stay.

✗ Eating & Drinking

Lobster Roll   SEAFOOD $$
(📞631-267-3740; www.lobsterroll.com; 1980 Montauk Hwy, Amagansett; mains $14-28; ⊙11:45am-9:30pm Mon-Sat, to 9pm Sun Jun-Sep, shorter hours May & Oct) 'Lunch' is the sign to look for on the roadside west of Montauk, marking this clam-and-lobster shack that has been in operation since 1965. It's now infamous as the liaison site in the Showtime television series *The Affair*.

★**Clam Bar at Napeague**   SEAFOOD $$
(📞631-267-6348; www.clambarhamptons.com; 2025 Montauk Hwy, Amagansett; mains $13-29; ⊙11:30am-8pm Apr-Oct, to 6pm Nov & Dec) You won't get fresher seafood or a saltier waitstaff, and holy mackerel, those lobster rolls are good, even if you choke a bit on the price. Three decades in business – the public has spoken – with cash only, of course. Locals favor this one. Find it on the road between Amagansett and Montauk. Winter hours are weather permitting.

Montauk Brewing Company   MICROBREWERY
(📞631-668-8471; www.montaukbrewingco.com; 62 S Erie Ave; ⊙2-7pm Mon-Fri, noon-7pm Sat & Sun) 'Come as you are,' preaches the small tasting room, and Cobain's family hasn't asked for their lyrics back yet. There's a more-than-palatable rotating range of cervezas, from lagers to stouts, and an outdoor patio on which to enjoy them in the right weather. Take a mixed six-pack to go.

Montauket   BAR
(📞631-668-5992; 88 Firestone Rd; ⊙noon-10pm) Experts agree: this is the best place to watch the sun go down on Long Island. An unassuming slate-blue-shingled building, full of local flavor (and people).

ℹ Getting There & Away

Montauk is the last stop on the eastbound Hampton Jitney bus ($30 to $38), as well as the Long Island Rail Road (p137). Suffolk County bus 10C ($2.25) runs to the Montauk (and the lighthouse) from East Hampton five times per day from July to September.

North Fork & Shelter Island
The North Fork is known for its bucolic farmland and vineyards (though weekends can draw rowdy limo-loads on winery crawls). Rte 25, the main road through **Jamesport**, **Cutchogue** and **Southold**, is pretty and edged with farm stands; the less-traveled Rte 48 also has many wineries.

The largest town on the North Fork is laid-back **Greenport**, with working fishing boats, a history in whaling and a **vintage**

carousel (www.villageofgreenport.org; Mitchell Park; $2; ⊙10am-9pm Jun-Aug, shorter hours rest of yr) in Mitchell Park. It's compact and easily walkable from the LIRR station.

Like a pearl in Long Island's claw, Shelter Island rests between the North and South Forks. The island is a smaller, more low-key version of the Hamptons, with a touch of maritime New England. Parking is limited; long **Crescent Beach**, for instance, has spots only by permit. If you don't mind a few hills, it's a nice place to visit by bike, and Mashomack Nature Preserve is a wildlife lover's dream.

◉ Sights

Mashomack
Nature Preserve
NATURE RESERVE

(☏631-749-1001; www.nature.org/Mashomack; Rte 114, Shelter Island; suggested donation adult/child $3/2; ⊙9am-5pm Jul & Aug, closed Tue Apr-Jun, Sep & Oct, shorter hours rest of year) The 2000 acres of this Shelter Island reserve, shot through with creeks and marshes, are great for kayaking, birding and hiking (no cycling allowed). Take precautions against ticks, an ever-present problem on the island.

Orient Beach State Park
BEACH

(☏631-323-2440; www.parks.ny.gov/parks/106; 40000 Main Rd, Orient; per car $10, kayaks per hour $25; ⊙8am-4pm) A sandy slip of land at the end of the North Fork, where you can swim in the calm ocean water (July and August only; 10:30am to 6pm) or rent kayaks to paddle in the small bay. True believers can view four different lighthouses, including the Orient Point Lighthouse, known as 'the coffee pot' for its stout bearing. To best see the lighthouse, go up the road to Orient Point County Park, which has a half-mile trail to a white-rock beach.

Horton Point Lighthouse
LIGHTHOUSE

(☏631-765-5500; www.southoldhistoricalsociety. org/lighthouse; 3575 Lighthouse Rd, Southold; suggested donation $5; ⊙Memorial Day-mid-Sep 11:30am-4pm Sat-Sun, shorter hours rest of year) Perhaps a poorer sister to the famous Montauk lighthouse, Horton Point was also commissioned by President Washington, but finally built 60 years later by William Sinclair, a Scotsman, who was an engineer in Brooklyn's Navy Yard. There's a nice nature trail in the adjacent park that leads to two Long Island Sound overlooks and steps to the beach.

🛏 Sleeping & Eating

Greenporter Hotel
BOUTIQUE HOTEL $$$

(☏631-477-0066; www.greenporterhotel.com; 326 Front St, Greenport; d incl breakfast $239-309; P❋🐾🛜🌊) An older motel redone with white walls and Ikea furniture but a few steps from the downtown Greenport action. The 30 rooms – big bathrooms, all with bathtubs – wrap around the pool and it all adds up to decent value for the area.

Love Lane Kitchen
AMERICAN $$

(☏631-298-8989; www.lovelanekitchen.com; 240 Love Lane, Mattituck; mains lunch $14-17, dinner $17-34; ⊙7am-4pm Tue & Wed, 7am-4pm & 5-9:30pm Mon, Thu & Fri, 8am-4pm & 5-9:30pm Sat & Sun; 🛜) At this popular place on a cute street, local meat and vegetables drive the global diner menu: burgers, of course, plus portobello panini, fish tacos and duck tagine.

★ North Fork Table & Inn
AMERICAN $$$

(☏631-765-0177; www.nofoti.com; 57225 Main Rd, Southold; mains $33-45, 5-course tasting menu $125; ⊙5:30-9pm Mon-Thu, to 9:30pm Fri, 5-9pm, 11:30am-2pm & Sat-Sun; 🛜) A favorite foodies' escape, this four-room inn (rooms from $250) has an excellent farm-to-table restaurant, run by alums of the esteemed Manhattan restaurant Gramercy Tavern. Dinner is served nightly (along with weekend brunch), but if you're hankering for a gourmand-to-go lunch ($5.50 to $21), the inn's food truck is parked outside Friday to Monday from 11:30am to 3:30pm (daily July and August).

❶ Getting There & Away

The Hampton Jitney (p140) bus picks up passengers on Manhattan's East Side on 96th, 83rd, 77th, 69th, 59th and 40th Sts, and makes stops in 10 North Fork villages (from $21). The Hampton Luxury Liner (p137) also runs to the North Fork. The ride from Manhattan to Greenport takes about 3½ hours.

If you're driving, take the Midtown Tunnel out of Manhattan, which will take you onto I-495/Long Island Expwy. Take this until it ends at Riverhead and follow signs onto Rte 25. You can stay on Rte 25 for all points east, but note that the North Rd (Rte 48) is faster as it does not go through the town centers.

The Long Island Rail Road's (p137) line is the Ronkonkoma Branch, with trips leaving from Penn Station and Brooklyn and running all the way out to Greenport.

To get from the North Fork to the South Fork (or vice versa), take the **North Ferry** (☏631-749-0139; www.northferry.com; NY 114 South, Greenport; one-way car/bike/foot $12/4/2) and the **South Ferry** (☑ 631-749-1200; www. southferry.com; 135 South Ferry Rd, Shelter Island; ⊙ one way car/bike/foot $15/4/2) services, crossing Shelter Island in between. There is no direct ferry – you must take one and then the other.

Hudson Valley

Winding roads along either side of the Hudson River take you by picturesque farms, Victorian cottages, apple orchards and old-money mansions built by New York's elite. Painters of the Hudson River School romanticized these landscapes, especially the region's famous fall foliage.

The eastern side of the river is more populated thanks to the commuter train line between NYC and Albany. Several magnificent homes can be found near Tarrytown and Sleepy Hollow. The formerly industrial town of Beacon has become an outpost of contemporary art, while the galleries and antique shops of historic Hudson attract a wealthier set of weekenders.

The Hudson's west bank is experiencing a boom thanks to its cheaper real estate. Head across the river to explore several state parks, West Point military academy, and New Paltz, which offers access to superb rock climbing in the Minnewaska State Park Preserve and Mohonk Preserve.

❶ Getting There & Away

Metro-North Railroad (www.mta.info/mnr) runs as far north as Poughkeepsie (p146) from NYC's Grand Central; NJ Transit (www.njtransit.com) runs another line through New Jersey that gives access to Harriman. Amtrak (www.amtrak.com) also stops in Rhinecliff (for Rhinebeck), Poughkeepsie and Hudson. For New Paltz, Kingston and other destinations east of the Hudson, you'll need the bus; Trailways (www.trailwaysny.com) runs to these towns.

Lower Hudson Valley

Made famous by 19th-century author Washington Irving as the location of his headless horseman tale, *The Legend of Sleepy Hollow,* Sleepy Hollow and its larger neighbor, Tarrytown, are the jumping-off points for a trio of historic estates, as well as the gourmet and farm-activity destination of Stone Barn Center for Food & Agriculture.

The blue-collar town of Beacon, beside the Hudson River, has steadily evolved into a magnet for creatives, commuters and second-homers. It's backed by Mt Beacon,

the tallest summit in the Hudson Valley and one of the more rewarding hikes in the region. While the town has embraced its status as a retreat for the hip, it still proudly displays its working-class roots and is all the more attractive for it.

⊙ Sights

★ **Dia:Beacon** GALLERY
(☑ 845-440-0100; www.diaart.org; 3 Beekman St, Beacon; adult/child $15/free; ⊙ 11am-6pm Thu-Mon Apr-Oct, to 4pm Thu-Mon Nov & Dec, to 4pm Fri-Mon Jan-Mar) The 300,000-sq-ft former Nabisco box printing factory beside the Hudson River is now a storehouse for a series of stunning monumental works by the likes of Richard Serra, Dan Flavin, Louise Bourgeois and Gerhard Richter. The permanent collection is complemented by temporary shows of large-scale sculptures and installations, making this a must-see for contemporary art fans. Guided tours (free with admission) are offered on weekends at 12:30pm and 2pm.

Boscobel House
& Gardens HISTORIC BUILDING
(☑ 845-265-3638; www.boscobel.org; 1601 Rte 9D, Garrison; house & gardens adult/child $18/9, gardens only $12/6; ⊙ guided tours 10am-4pm Wed-Mon mid-Apr–Oct, to 3pm Nov & Dec) The elegant backdrop for the summer season **Hudson Valley Shakespeare Festival** (☑ 845-265-9575; www.hvshakespeare.org; 1601 Rte 9D, Garrison; tickets $10-100; ⊙ Jun-Sep), Boscobel dates from 1808 and is considered to be one of the finest examples of Federal-style architecture in the state. Entry to the house, which is 8 miles south of Beacon, is by guided tour (45 minutes), running regularly throughout the day.

Stone Barns Center
for Food & Agriculture FARM
(☑ 914-366-6200; www.stonebarnscenter.org; 630 Bedford Rd, Pocantico Hills; ⊙ 10am-4pm Wed-Sun) ✐ Stop by this massive, ecofriendly farm for a peek into the modern agriculture movement. On warm-weather weekends (April to November; adult/child $22/free) you'll find the place teeming with visitors partaking in activities such as egg collecting, lettuce planting and meeting a flock of sheep. Other tours and workshops are available Wednesday through Friday; check their calendar online. Book in advance as they tend to fill up quickly. There's a good shop and a small takeout cafe. For a banquet meal, book ahead for the gourmet Blue Hill at Stone Barns also located here.

Washington Irving's
Sunnyside   HISTORIC BUILDING
(☑914-591-8763, Mon-Fri 914-631-8200; www.
hudsonvalley.org; 3 W Sunnyside Lane, Tarrytown;
adult/child $14/8; ☺tours 10:30am-4pm Wed-Sun
May–mid-Nov) Washington Irving, famous for
tales such as *The Legend of Sleepy Hollow*,
built this imaginative home, which he said
had more nooks and crannies than a cocked
hat. Tour guides in 19th-century costume tell
good stories, and the wisteria Irving planted
a century ago still climbs the walls. Tickets
are $2 cheaper if bought online.

The closest train station to Sunnyside is
Irvington, one stop before Tarrytown.

🛏 Sleeping & Eating

★Roundhouse   BOUTIQUE HOTEL $$
(☑845-765-8369; www.roundhousebeacon.com; 2
E Main St; r from $230; P❂❄🛜) Occupying a
former blacksmiths and hat factory spread
out over both sides of the town's Fishkill
Creek, Roundhouse is a model of Beacon's
renaissance as a tourist destination. Elements of the buildings' industrial past blend
seamlessly with contemporary comforts in
the spacious rooms, which feature designer lighting, timber headboards and alpaca-
wool blankets.

Homespun Foods   CAFE $
(☑845-831-5096; www.homespunfoods.com; 232
Main St, Beacon; mains $10-15; ☺8am-5pm Sun-
Tue, to 8pm Wed-Sat; 🖋) A low-key gourmet
legend in these parts, Homespun offers fresh
everything, including creative salads, sandwiches and a veggie meatloaf made from
nuts and cheese.

★Blue Hill at Stone Barns   AMERICAN $$$
(☑914-366-9600; www.bluehillfarm.com; 630
Bedford Rd, Pocantico Hills; set menu $278; ☺5-
10pm Wed-Sat, 1-7:30pm Sun) 🖋 Go maximum
locavore at chef Dan Barber's farm (which
also supplies his Manhattan restaurant).
Settle in for an eye-popping multicourse
feast based on the day's harvest (allow three
hours), where the service is as theatrical as
the presentation. Be sure to book at least a
month in advance. The dress code prefers
jackets and ties for gentlemen; shorts not
permitted.

❶ Getting There & Away

Metro-North Railroad (www.mta.info/mnr) commuter trains connect NYC with Beacon (one-way
off-peak/peak $24/29, 1½ hours).

Tarrytown Station (www.mta.info/mnr; 1
Depot Plaza, Tarrytown) has regular train con-

nections with NYC (one-way off-peak/peak from
$11.25/14.75, 40 to 50 minutes). Irvington, one
stop before Tarrytown, is the closest station to
Sunnyside, while Philipse Manor, one stop after,
is walkable to Philipsburg Manor.

For the most flexibility in getting around the
area, hire a car.

New Paltz

New Paltz, a short drive from the west bank
of the Hudson, is a college town known for
its charming 'village' downtown and hippie
vibe. New Paltz is also home to a campus
of the State University of New York, great
dining and drinking opportunities, and is
the gateway to Shawangunk Ridge (aka
'The Gunks'), beloved for its hiking and
rock-climbing opportunities.

⦿ Sights & Activities

Historic Huguenot Street   HISTORIC SITE
(☑845-255-1660; www.huguenotstreet.org; 86
Huguenot St; guided tours adult/child $12/free;
☺10am-5pm Thu-Tue May-Oct, 10am-5pm Sat &
Sun Nov–mid-Dec) Step back in time on a stroll
around this picturesque enclave of buildings
remaining from a Huguenot settlement dating back to 1678. Guided tours (which depart
the visitor center every half-hour starting at
10:30am; the last one is at 3:30pm) relate the
history of the various people who have inhabited this site over the centuries: the native Esopus Munsee people, Dutch settlers, Hugenot
families who fled religious persecution in
France, and enslaved African laborers.

As well as a visitor center, the 10-acre National Historic Landmark District includes
seven historic stone houses, a replica Munsee wigwam, a reconstructed 1717 Huguenot
church and a 17th-century burial ground.

Mohonk Preserve   PARK
(☑845-255-0919; www.mohonkpreserve.org; 3197
Rte 55, Gardiner; day pass hikers/climbers & cyclists
$15/20; ☺visitor center 9am-5pm) Some 8000
acres of land held in private trust, with trails
and other services maintained with visitor
fees. This is home to some of the best rock
climbing on the East Coast. The grounds are
open from sunrise to one hour after sunset.

Rock & Snow   ADVENTURE SPORTS
(☑845-255-1311; www.rockandsnow.com; 44 Main
St; ☺9am-6pm Mon-Thu, to 8pm Fri, 8am-8pm
Sat, to 7pm Sun) This long-running outfitters
rents tents, and rock-climbing, ice-climbing
and other equipment. It can also team you
up with guides for climbing and other outdoor adventures in the Gunks.

🛏 Sleeping & Eating

New Paltz Hostel HOSTEL $
(📞845-255-6676; www.newpaltzhostel.com; 145 Main St; dm/r from $40/60; ❄🐾) Aligned with New Paltz's hippie vibe, this hostel in a big old house next to the bus station is popular with visiting rock climbers and hikers. There's one mixed dorm room and several private rooms (both with private and shared bathrooms), as well as a good communal kitchen.

A full-time home to some students, it has a strict no-drugs-or-alcohol policy, as well as a 10pm curfew for the dorms.

Mohonk Mountain House RESORT $$$
(📞855-436-0832; www.mohonk.com; 1000 Mountain Rest Rd; r from $710; ❄@🐾🏊) This giant faux 'Victorian castle' perches over a dark lake, offering guests all the luxuries, from lavish meals to golf to spa services, plus a full roster of outdoor excursions, including hiking and trail rides. Rates include all meals and most activities and you can choose from rooms in the main building, cottages or the luxury Grove Lodge.

★Huckleberry AMERICAN $$
(📞845-633-8443; www.huckleberrynewpaltz.com; 21 Church St; mains $14-18; ⊙noon-2am Mon-Thu, to 4am Fri & Sat, 10am-2am Sun; 🐾) This cute sea-green house set back from the road offers an appealing menu of gourmet items, including grass-fed-beef burgers, fish tacos and IPA mac 'n' cheese. There are also creative cocktails, craft beers and a lovely outdoor dining and drinking area in which to enjoy it all. The kitchen stays open to midnight most nights (to 1am Friday and Saturday).

ℹ Getting There & Away

Trailways (📞800-776-7548; www.trailwaysny.com; 139 Main St) bus services connect New Paltz with NYC ($23, 1½ hours) and Saugerties ($8, one hour).

Poughkeepsie

Six miles south of Hyde Park, where you'll find US President Franklin Roosevelt's family home, is Poughkeepsie (puh-*kip*-see), the largest town in the Hudson Valley. The city is home to the prestigious Vassar College, which was women-only until 1969, as well as an IBM office – once the 'Main Plant' where notable early computers were built.

The main attraction here is the chance to walk across the Hudson River on the world's longest pedestrian bridge, although Vassar's **Frances Lehman Loeb Art Center** (📞845-437-5237; www.fllac.vassar.edu; 124 Raymond Ave; ⊙10am-5pm Tue, Wed, Fri & Sat, to 9pm Thu, 1-5pm Sun) FREE, housed in a building designed by César Pelli, is also worth a visit. While you're here, stop in for a taste of the local distilleries and brew pubs – full details can be found at **Dutchess Tourism** (📞800-445-3131; www.dutchesstourism.com; 3 Neptune Rd, Poughkeepsie; ⊙9am-5pm Tue-Fri).

⊙ Sights

Franklin D Roosevelt Home HISTORIC BUILDING
(📞845-229-5320; www.nps.gov/hofr; 4097 Albany Post Rd; adult/child $20/free, museum or house only adult/child $10/free; ⊙tours every 30min 9am-4pm) Rangers lead interesting hour-long tours around Springwood, the home of Franklin D Roosevelt (FDR) who won a record four presidential elections and led America from the Great Depression through WWII. Considering his family wealth, it's a modest abode, but can be unpleasantly crowded in summer. Intimate details have been preserved, including his desk – left as it was the day before he died – and the hand-pulled elevator he used to hoist his polio-stricken body to the 2nd floor.

The home is part of a 1520-acre estate, formerly a working farm, which also includes the simple marble tomb where FDR and Eleanor (and their dog Fala) were interred, various walking trails and the **FDR Presidential Library & Museum** (📞845-486-7770; www.fdrlibrary.org; ⊙9am-6pm Apr-Oct, to 5pm Nov-Mar), which details important achievements in FDR's presidency. Admission tickets last two days and include the Springwood tour.

Note that Springwood will be closed for several months, from April through October 2020, for a series of repair projects.

Walkway Over the Hudson VIEWPOINT, PARK
(📞845-834-2867; www.walkway.org; 61 Parker Ave, Poughkeepsie; ⊙7am-sunset) This is the main eastern entrance (with parking) to what was once a railroad bridge (built in 1889) crossing the Hudson. Today it's the world's longest pedestrian bridge – 1.28 miles – and a state park. The 212ft-high span provides breathtaking views along the river.

🛏 Sleeping & Eating

Roosevelt Inn MOTEL $
(📞845-229-2443; www.rooseveltinnofhydepark.com; 4360 Albany Post Rd; r $90-210; ⊙Mar-Dec; ❄🐾) Family owned and run since 1971, this

roadside motel offers a great deal, especially for its pine-paneled 'rustic' rooms. The attention paid to the property by the owners – they make yearly improvements to the rooms – elevate the Roosevelt Inn above other motels in the area. Book one of the upper-level deluxe rooms for more space.

A continental breakfast is served at the on-site coffee shop, which can be used as a common space by guests.

Eveready Diner AMERICAN $
(☑ 845-229-8100; www.theevereadydiner.com; 4184 Albany Post Rd/Rte 9; mains $9-21.50; ☺ 6am-midnight Sun-Thu, 24hr Fri & Sat) It's difficult to resist turning off the highway to visit this giant sparkling chrome diner. There's been a diner here since the 1950s, and even though this building is from 1995 it's a classic, with an authentic interior and extensive menu of slightly elevated diner fare to match.

ⓘ Getting There & Away

Metro-North runs trains from NYC's Grand Central (from $19.25, 1¾ hours) to **Poughkeepsie Station** (☑ 800-872-7245; www.amtrak.com; 41 Main St).

Rhinebeck

Midway up the eastern side of the Hudson, Rhinebeck has a charming main street and an affluent air. In town you'll find a plethora of fine dining options and charming boutiques. Further afield is the holistic Omega Institute, as well as the super-liberal Bard College, 8 miles north, worth dropping by for its Frank Gehry–designed performing arts center.

⊙ Sights

**Staatsburgh State
Historic Site** HISTORIC BUILDING
(☑ 845-889-8851; www.parks.ny.gov; Old Post Rd, Staatsburg; adult/child $8/free; ☺ tours 11am-4pm Thu-Sun mid-Apr–Oct, noon-3pm Thu-Sun late Nov–Dec) Take a tour around this beaux-arts mansion, the home of Ogden Mills and his wife Ruth. The Mills family made its fortune by investing in banks, railroads and mines during the Gilded Age; the house boasts 79 luxurious rooms filled with brocaded Flemish tapestries, gilded plasterwork, period paintings and Oriental art. Find it 6 miles south of Rhinebeck, just off Rte 9.

Old Rhinebeck Aerodrome MUSEUM
(☑ 845-752-3200; www.oldrhinebeck.org; 9 Norton Rd, Red Hook; museum adult/child $12/8, air shows adult/child $25/12, flights $100; ☺ 10am-5pm May-Oct, air shows 2pm Sat & Sun) This museum, a short drive north of the center of Rhinebeck, has vintage planes and other related vehicles and artifacts that date back to 1900. On weekends you can watch an air show or take a ride in an old biplane.

🛏 Sleeping & Eating

★**Olde Rhinebeck Inn** B&B $$$
(☑ 845-871-1745; www.rhinebeckinn.com; 340 Wurtemberg Rd; r $225-325; 🕸🖜) Built by German settlers between 1738 and 1745, this expertly restored oak-beamed inn oozes comfort and authenticity. It's run by a charming woman who has decorated the four cozy rooms beautifully and serves a lush breakfast made from local produce.

Bread Alone Bakery & Cafe BAKERY $
(☑ 845-876-3108; www.breadalone.com/rhinebeck; 45 E Market St; sandwiches $8-10.50; ☺ cafe 7am-5pm, dining room 8am-3pm Mon-Fri, 7am-4pm Sat & Sun; 🖜🍴) Superior-quality baked goods, sandwiches and salads (including vegan options) are served up at the Rhinebeck location of this popular bakery and cafe. There's also a full-service dining room with the same menu. Those looking for small-town charm will probably find the uninspired chain restaurant decor lacking, though.

☆ Entertainment

**Fisher Center for the
Performing Arts** ARTS CENTER
(☑ 845-758-7900; www.fishercenter.bard.edu; Robbins Rd, Bard College, Annandale-on-Hudson; ☺ tours 10am-4:30pm Mon-Fri) Architecture buffs will want to drop by to view this Frank Gehry–designed building, whose spectacularly modern metal waves make for a great contrast to Bard College's Gothic buildings and manicured lawns. It contains two theaters and studio spaces and hosts a program of musical concerts, dance performances and theatrical events.

ⓘ Getting There & Away

Amtrak runs trains to/from NYC (from $29, 1¾ hours). **Rhinecliff Station** (☑ 800-872-7245; 455 Rhinecliff Rd, Rhinecliff) is 3 miles west of the center of Rhinebeck. Local taxis wait at the station to ferry people up to town (about $10).

Catskills

This beautiful mountainous region west of the Hudson Valley has been a popular getaway since the 19th century. The romantic image of mossy gorges and rounded peaks, as popularized by Hudson Valley School painters, encouraged a preservation movement: in 1894 the state constitution was amended so that thousands of acres are 'forever kept as wild forest lands.'

In the early 20th century, the Catskills became synonymous with so-called 'borscht belt' hotels, summer escapes for middle-class NYC Jews. The vast majority of these hotels have closed, although orthodox Jewish communities still thrive in many towns – as does a back-to-the-land, hippie ethos on numerous small farms. In the fall, this is the closest place to NYC with really dramatic colors in the trees.

ℹ️ Getting There & Around

There is some bus service, the most useful being Trailways (www.trailwaysny.com) from NYC to Woodstock (from $30, 2½ to three hours) and Phoenicia (from $32, three hours). However, if you really want to tour the area, having a car is essential.

Phoenicia & Mt Tremper

This quirky pair of hamlets (just down the highway from one another) are the perfect jumping-off point to explore the Catskills. Phoenicia is the bigger of the two, while Mt Tremper boasts a few impressive hotels. Outdoor activities are easily arranged and include hiking, cycling, floating down the creek on an inner tube or swimming in mountain pools in summer and skiing at nearby **Belleayre Mountain** (☑ 845-254-5600; www.belleayre.com; 181 Galli Curci Rd, Highmount; 1-day lift pass weekday/weekend $56/68; ⏰ 9am-4pm Dec-Mar) in winter. Fall is prime time to visit and also the best season for a jaunt in an open-air carriage on the Delaware & Ulster Railroad between nearby Arkville and Roxbury.

◎ Sights & Activities

Empire State Railway Museum MUSEUM
(☑ 845-688-7501; www.esrm.com; 70 Lower High St, Phoenicia; donations accepted; ⏰ 11am-4pm Sat & Sun Jun-Oct) **FREE** Maintained by enthusiasts since 1960, this small museum occupies an old railway station on the largely decommissioned Delaware & Ulster line.

Delaware & Ulster Railroad RAIL
(☑ 845-586-3877; www.durr.org; 43510 Rte 28, Arkville; adult/child $18/12; ⏰ Sat & Sun May-Oct) It takes around 2½ hours to travel the 24 miles between Arkville and Roxbury in

open-air carriages on this touristy rail journey; views are at their best during fall.

Belleayre Beach SWIMMING
(☑ 845-254-5202; www.belleayre.com/summer/belleayre-beach; 33 Friendship Manor Rd, Pine Hill; per person/car $5/15; ⏰ 10am-6pm Mon-Fri, to 7pm Sat & Sun mid-Jun–Aug) Near the base of Belleayre Mountain ski resort, this lake is a popular and refreshing swimming spot. Boats, kayaks and paddleboards can be rented, and there's also volleyball and basketball courts and a climbing wall.

🛏️ Sleeping & Eating

⭐ **Graham & Co** MOTEL $$
(☑ 845-688-7871; www.thegrahamandco.com; 80 Rte 214, Phoenicia; r $125-250; ❄️🅿️📶🐾) There's a lot going for this hipster motel an easy walk from the center of town. Rooms are whitewashed and minimalist with the cheapest ones in a 'bunkhouse' where bathrooms are shared. Other pluses include a comfy den with a fireplace, a provisions store, an outdoor pool in summer, a wigwam and lawn games!

Foxfire Mountain House BOUTIQUE HOTEL $$
(☑ 845-688-2500; www.foxfiremountainhouse.com; 72 Andrew Lane, Mt Tremper; r from $200; 🅿️🐾📶🐾) Hidden in the forest, this chic hotel channels modern '70s rugged cool in its 11 individually decorated rooms (the cheapest of which share a bathroom) and one three-bedroom cottage. The cozy restaurant (offering dinner Friday to Sunday) and bar, open to nonguests, serves French-inspired cuisine such as *steak au poivre* (peppercorn steak) and *coq au cidre* (chicken cooked in cider).

⭐ **Phoenicia Diner** AMERICAN $
(☑ 845-688-9957; www.phoeniciadiner.com; 5681 Rte 28, Phoenicia; mains $11-15; ⏰ 7am-5pm late May–Sep, 7am-5pm Mon, Thu & Fri, to 8pm Sat & Sun Oct–mid-May; 🐾) New York hipsters and local families rub shoulders at this elevated roadside diner. The appealing menu offers all-day breakfast, skillets, sandwiches and burgers – all farm-fresh and fabulous.

Peekamoose AMERICAN $$$
(☑ 845-254-6500; www.peekamooserestaurant.com; 8373 Rte 28, Big Indian; mains $24-33; ⏰ 4-10pm Thu-Mon, lounge to midnight Fri & Sat) One of the finest restaurant in the Catskills, this renovated farmhouse approximately 9 miles from Phoenicia has been promoting local farm-to-table dining for more than a decade. The menu changes daily, although the braised beef short ribs are a permanent fixture.

ⓘ Getting There & Away

Trailways (www.trailwaysny.com) runs buses to Phoenicia from NYC (from $32, three hours). Mt Tremper is a short drive once you're there.

Tannersville

The small town of Tannersville, which primarily services the nearby ski resort of Hunter Mountain, also offers access to the gorgeous Kaaterskill Falls. There are superb hikes and drives in the area, as well as rustically charming hotels in which to stay and enjoy the beautiful mountain scenery. Tannersville itself sports a main street lined with brightly painted shops and houses.

◉ Sights & Activities

Kaaterskill Falls   WATERFALL

For the best view of New York State's highest falls – 260ft, compared to Niagara's 167ft – without a strenuous hike, head to the **viewing platform** (Laurel House Rd, Palenville). Popular paintings by the Hudson River Valley School of painters in the mid-1800s elevated this two-tier cascade to iconic status, making it a major draw for hikers, artists and nature lovers.

There's parking just above on Rte 23A; be sure to stick to the shoulder and keep your eyes on cars coming around the bend on your walk down to the trailhead.

Hunter Mountain   SKIING

(☑ 518-263-4223; www.huntermtn.com; 64 Klein Ave, Hunter; day lift pass weekday/weekend $79/89; ⊙ 9am-4pm Dec-Mar) Spectacular views from the 56 trails (including some challenging black runs that are a minefield of moguls) draw crowds of snowhounds to Hunter; avoid weekends and holidays if you don't relish lines at the lifts. Snowmaking ensures that skiing continues through the season, whatever the weather.

Zipline New York   ADVENTURE SPORTS

(☑ 518-263-4388; www.ziplinenewyork.com; Hunter Mountain, Rte 23A; zipline tours $89-129; ⊙ Mon-Sun Jun-Aug, Thu-Sun May, Sep & Oct, Fri-Sun Nov-Apr) Throughout the year Hunter Mountain is the location of this zipline course that's not for the faint hearted. The longest of the six ziplines is 650ft and 60ft above the ground. It's best to book in advance.

ⓒ Sleeping & Eating

★ Scribner's Catskill Lodge   LODGE $$

(☑ 518-628-5130; www.scribnerslodge.com; 13 Scribner Hollow Rd; r $180-375; P❋❄🅿🐾🎵) Run by a super-cool staff, this 1960s motor lodge has been given a stylish contemporary makeover. Snow-white painted rooms, some of which feature gas-fired stoves, contrast with the warm tones of the long library lounge with pool table and comfy nooks.

Deer Mountain Inn   BOUTIQUE HOTEL $$$

(☑ 518-589-6268; www.deermountaininn.com; 790 Rte 25; r/cottages from $250/800; ⊙ restaurant 5-10pm Thu-Sun, 11:30am-2:30pm Sun; P❄❋🌐) There are only six rooms and two cottages (sleeping up to nine guests) at this gorgeous arts-and-crafts-style property hidden within a vast mountainside estate. It's all been interior designed to the max.

Last Chance
Cheese Antiques Cafe   AMERICAN $$

(☑ 518-589-6424; www.lastchanceonline.com; 6009 Main St; mains $11-27; ⊙ 11am-8pm Jun-Aug & Dec-Mar, to 9pm Fri-Sun only Apr, May & Sep-Nov; ☑) A fixture on Main St since 1970, this is part roadhouse with live bands, part candy store and cheese shop, and part restaurant, serving hearty meals. Many of the antiques and whatnots that decorate the place are for sale, too.

ⓘ Getting There & Away

The drive along Rte 23A to and from Tannersville is one of the most scenic in the Catskills, but take it slowly as there are several hairpin bends. It's possible to reach Tannersville from NYC (from $37, three hours) by bus with Trailways (www.trailwaysny.com), but you'll have to change services in Kingston.

Woodstock

A minor technicality: the 1969 music festival was actually held in Bethel, an hour's drive west. Nonetheless, the town of Woodstock still attracts an arty, music-loving crowd and cultivates the free spirit of that era, with rainbow tie-dye style and local grassroots everything, from radio to a respected indie film festival and a farmers market (fittingly billed as a farm festival).

◉ Sights

Center for Photography
at Woodstock   ARTS CENTER

(☑ 845-679-9957; www.cpw.org; 59 Tinker St; ⊙ noon-5pm) FREE Founded in 1977, this creative space gives classes, hosts lectures and mounts exhibitions that expand the strict definition of the art form, thanks to a lively artist-in-residence program.

This was formerly the Café Espresso, and Bob Dylan once had a writing studio above

WORTH A TRIP

SAUGERTIES

Around 10 miles northeast of Woodstock, the town of Saugerties (www.discoversauger ties.com) dates back to the Dutch settling here in the mid-17th century. Today it's well worth making a day trip to a couple of local attractions. **Opus 40 Sculpture Park & Museum** (845-246-3400; www.opus40.org; 50 Fite Rd; adult/child $10/3; 11am-5:30pm Thu-Sun May-Oct) is where artist Harvey Fite worked for nearly four decades to coax an abandoned quarry into an immense work of land art, all sinuous walls, canyons and pools. The picturesque 1869 **Saugerties Lighthouse** (845-247-0656; www.saugerties lighthouse.com; 168 Lighthouse Dr; tour suggested donation adult/child $5/3; trail dawn-dusk), on the point where Esopus Creek joins the Hudson, can be reached by a half-mile nature trail. Classic-rock lovers may also want to search out **Big Pink** (www.bigpinkbase ment.com; Parnassus Lane, West Saugerties; house $580;), the house made famous by Bob Dylan and the Band, although note it's on a private road. It's possible to stay at both the lighthouse and Big Pink, but you'll need to book well ahead.

it – that's where he typed up the liner notes for *Another Side of Bob Dylan* in 1964 – and Janis Joplin was a regular performer.

Karma Triyana Dharmachakra BUDDHIST MONASTERY
(845-679-5906; www.kagyu.org; 335 Meads Mountain Rd; 8:30am-5:30pm) Join stressed-out New Yorkers and others needing a spiritual break at this blissful Buddhist monastery about 3 miles north from Woodstock. Soak up the serenity in the carefully tended grounds. Inside the shrine room is a giant golden Buddha statue; as long as you take off your shoes, you're welcome to sit down and meditate. Free guided tours are given at 12:45pm on Saturday and Sunday.

🛏️ Sleeping & Eating

Woodstock Inn on the Millstream INN $$
(845-679-8211; www.woodstock-inn-ny.com; 48 Tannery Brook Rd; r/cottages from $170/375;) Pleasantly decorated in quiet pastels, some of the rooms at this inn surrounded by serene, flower-filled grounds, come with kitchenettes, electric fireplaces and large tubs.

Village Green B&B B&B $$
(845-679-0313; www.villagegreenbb.com; 12 Tinker St; r $150;) Overlooking Woodstock's 'village green,' this B&B occupies part of a three-story 1847 mansard-roof Victorian. The decor is a bit mumsy, but the rooms are comfortable and the owner is well liked by guests.

⭐ **Garden Cafe** VEGAN $
(845-679-3600; www.thegardencafewoodstock. com; 6 Old Forge Rd; mains $9-22; 11:30am-9pm Mon & Wed-Fri, 10am-9pm Sat & Sun;) All the ingredients used at this relaxed, charm-

ing cafe are organic. The food served is appealing, tasty and fresh, and includes salads, sandwiches, rice bowls and veggie lasagna. It also serves freshly made juices, smoothies, organic wines, craft beers and coffee made with a variety of nondairy milks. In nice weather you can sit outside in their large garden.

Finger Lakes

In west-central New York, the rolling hills are cut through by 11 long narrow bodies of water appropriately named the Finger Lakes. The region is an outdoor paradise, as well as the state's premier wine-growing region, with more than 120 vineyards.

At the south of Cayuga Lake, Ithaca, home to Ivy League Cornell University, is the region's gateway. At the northern tip of Seneca Lake, Geneva is a pretty and lively town, thanks to the student population at Hobart and William Smith Colleges. Here the restored 1894 Smith Opera House is a vibrant center for performing arts.

To the west, Y-shaped Keuka Lake is edged by two small state parks that keep it relatively pristine; it's a favorite for trout fishing. Base yourself at sweet little Hammondsport, on the southwestern end. Arts and crafts lovers should also schedule a stop in Corning to see the brilliant glass museum there.

ℹ️ Getting There & Around

Ithaca is the region's major hub with several daily bus connections to NYC (from $36, five hours). Ithaca Tompkins Regional Airport (p151) has direct flights to Detroit, Newark and Philadelphia.

Ithaca

An idyllic home for college students and first-wave hippies, Ithaca, on the southern tip of Cayuga Lake, is the largest town around the Finger Lakes. With an art-house cinema, good eats and great hiking ('Ithaca is gorges' goes the slogan, for all the surrounding canyons and waterfalls), it's both a destination in itself and a convenient halfway point between NYC and Niagara Falls.

The center of Ithaca is a pedestrian street called the Commons. On a steep hill above is Ivy League Cornell University, founded in 1865, with a small business strip at the campus' front gates, called Collegetown. The drive from Ithaca up scenic Rte 89 (west side) or Rte 90 (east side) to Seneca Falls, at the northern end of Cayuga Lake, takes about an hour.

Sights

★Herbert F Johnson Museum of Art MUSEUM
(☎607-255-6464; www.museum.cornell.edu; 114 Central Ave; ⏰10am-5pm Tue-Sun year-round, to 7:30pm Thu Sep-May) **FREE** IM Pei's brutalist building looms like a giant concrete robot above the ornate neo-Gothic surrounds of Cornell University's campus. Inside you'll find an eclectic collection ranging from medieval wood carvings to modern masters and an extensive collection of Asian art. It's worth a visit if only for the panoramic views of Ithaca and Cayuga Lake from the top floor galleries.

WORTH A TRIP

AURORA

Around 28 miles north of Ithaca on the eastern side of Cayuga Lake is the picturesque village of Aurora. Established in 1795, the village has over 50 buildings on the National Register of Historic Places, including parts of the campus of Wells College, founded in 1868 for the higher education of women (it's now co-ed). The **Inns of Aurora** (☎315-364-8888; www.innsofaurora.com; 391 Main St; r $200-400; P ❄ 📶), which is composed of four grand properties – the Aurora Inn (1833), EB Morgan House (1858), Rowland House (1903) and Wallcourt Hall (1909) – is a wonderful place to stay. Alternatively, stop by the Aurora Inn's lovely dining room for a meal with lakeside views and pick up a copy of the self-guided walking tour of the village.

Cornell Botanic Gardens GARDENS
(☎607-255-2400; www.cornellbotanicgardens.org; 124 Comstock Knoll Dr; ⏰9am-5pm Sun-Thu, to 6pm Fri & Sat) **FREE** The verdant spaces in and around campus includes a 100-acre arboretum, a botanical garden and numerous trails. Stop at the Nevin Welcome Center for maps and to find out about tours.

A great way to reach the campus is by hiking up the dramatic **Cascadilla Gorge** (College Ave Bridge), which starts near the center of town.

Robert H Treman State Park STATE PARK
(☎607-273-3440; www.parks.ny.gov; 105 Enfield Falls Rd; per car mid-Apr–mid-Oct $8, mid-Oct–mid-Apr free) Five-and-a-half miles southwest of Ithaca, the biggest state park in the area offers extensive trails and a very popular **swimming hole** (late June to early September). Treman's gorge trail passes a stunning 12 waterfalls: don't miss Devil's Kitchen and Lucifer Falls, a multi-tiered wonder that spills Enfield Creek over rocks for about 100ft.

Sleeping

★William Henry Miller Inn B&B $$
(☎877-256-4553; www.millerinn.com; 303 N Aurora St; r $215-270; ❄ @ 📶) Gracious and grand, and only a few steps from the Commons pedestrian street, this historic home offers luxurious rooms (two with whirlpool tubs and two in a separate carriage house), gourmet breakfast and a dessert buffet.

Firelight Camps TENTED CAMP $$$
(☎607-229-1644; www.firelightcamps.com; 1150 Danby Rd; tents $190-330; ⏰mid-May–Oct; 📶) Glamping comes to Ithaca at this attractive site attached to the La Tourelle Hotel and with quick access to the trails of nearby Buttermilk Falls State Park. The safari-style canvas tents rise over hardwood platforms and comfy beds. The bathhouse is separate. There's a campfire in the evenings and yoga on Saturday mornings.

Eating & Drinking

Ithaca Bakery CAFE $
(☎607-273-7110; www.ithacabakery.com; 400 N Meadow St; sandwiches $5-11; ⏰6am-8pm Sun-Thu, to 9pm Fri & Sat; 🌱) An epic selection of pastries, smoothies, sandwiches and

prepared food, serving Ithacans of every stripe. Ideal for picnic goods and for vegetarians and vegans.

★ Moosewood Restaurant
VEGETARIAN $$

(☑607-273-9610; www.moosewoodcooks.com; 215 N Cayuga St; mains $17-28; ⊙11:30am-8:30pm Sun-Thu, to 9pm Fri & Sat; ⎘) Established in 1973, this near-legendary veggie restaurant is run by a collective. It has a slightly upscale feel, with a full bar and global menu. It is very popular so reservations are recommended, especially during Cornell events.

Sacred Root Kava Lounge & Tea Bar
TEAHOUSE

(☑607-272-5282; www.sacredrootkava.com; 103 S Geneva St; ⊙3pm-midnight) Pretty much as alternative as it gets for Ithaca is this chilled basement space serving the Polynesian nonalcoholic, psychoactive beverage kava. If that's not your bag, then there's a nice range of teas. Check online for events.

The entrance is on S Geneva St, beneath the Cornell Daily Sun building.

❶ Getting There & Away

Ithaca Tompkins Regional Airport (ITH; ☑607-257-0456; www.flyithaca.com; 1 Culligan Dr) receives flights from Delta and United.

Greyhound (www.greyhound.com) and Shortline buses from NYC (one-way $38, five hours, daily) pull into **Ithaca Bus Station** (710 W State St).

Seneca Falls

The quiet, postindustrial town of Seneca Falls is said to have inspired visiting director Frank Capra to create Bedford Falls, the fictional small American town in his classic movie *It's a Wonderful Life*. Indeed, you can stand on a bridge crossing the town's river and just picture Jimmy Stewart doing the same. The town also has a special place in history as the location of the first American women's rights convention, where the fight for female suffrage was launched.

⦿ Sights

Women's Rights National Historical Park
MUSEUM

(☑315-568-0024; www.nps.gov/wori; 136 Fall St; ⊙9am-5pm Mar-Nov, 9am-5pm Wed-Sun Dec-Feb) FREE Visit the chapel where Elizabeth Cady Stanton and friends declared in 1848 that 'all men and women are created equal,' the first step towards women's suffrage. The adjacent museum tells the story, including the complicated relationship with abolition.

National Women's Hall of Fame
MUSEUM

(☑315-568-8060; www.womenofthehall.org; 76 Fall St; adult/child $5/free; ⊙10am-4pm Mar-Oct, 10am-4pm Wed-Sun Nov-Feb) The tiny National Women's Hall of Fame honors inspiring American women. Learn about some of the 256 inductees, including first lady Abigail Adams, American Red Cross founder Clara Barton and civil-rights activist Rosa Parks.

⛏ Sleeping & Eating

Gould Hotel
BOUTIQUE HOTEL $$

(☑877-788-4010; www.thegouldhotel.com; 108 Fall St; r $210-600; ❄❖) Originally a 1920s-era hotel, the downtown building has undergone a stylish renovation with a nod to the past – the mahogany bar comes from an old Seneca Falls saloon. The standard rooms are small, but the decor, in metallic purple and gray, is quite flash. The hotel's upscale restaurant and tavern serves local food, wine and beer.

Mac's Drive In
BURGERS $

(☑315-539-3064; www.macsdrivein.net; 1166 US-20/Rte 5, Waterloo; mains $4-8; ⊙10:30am-10pm Tue-Sun Jun-Aug, Fri-Sun only Apr & May) Midway between Seneca Falls and Geneva, this classic drive-in restaurant established in 1961 (and little changed since) serves up burgers, fried chicken and fish dinners at bargain prices.

❶ Getting There & Away

The best way to get to Seneca Falls is by car.

The Adirondacks

The Adirondack Mountains (www.visitadirondacks.com) may not compare in drama and height with mountains in the western US, but they more than make up for it in area: the range covers 9375 sq miles, from the center of New York just north of the state capital Albany, up to the Canadian border. And with 46 peaks over 4000ft high, the Adirondacks provide some of the most wild-feeling terrain in the east. Like the Catskills to the south, much of the Adirondacks' dense forest and lake lands are protected by the state constitution, and it's a fabulous location to see the color show of autumn leaves. Hiking, canoeing and backcountry camping are the most popular activities, and there's good fishing, along with powerboating on the bigger lakes.

❶ Getting There & Around

The area's main airport is in Albany, although **Adirondack Regional Airport** (☑518-891-4600; www.adirondackairport.com; 96 Airport Rd) in Saranac Lake has connections via Cape Air (www.capeair.com) to Boston.

Both Greyhound (www.greyhound.com) and Trailways (www.trailwaysny.com) buses serve Albany and various towns in the Adirondacks, though a car is essential for exploring widely.

Amtrak runs from NYC to Albany (from $45, 2½ hours) and on to Ticonderoga ($70, five hours) and Westport ($70, six hours), both on Lake Champlain, with a bus connection to Lake Placid ($90.50, 9½ hours).

Albany

Built between 1965 and 1976, the architectural ensemble of government buildings in Albany's central Empire State Plaza is a sight to behold and includes the excellent New York State Museum, as well as a fine collection of modern public art. In downtown and leafy Washington Park, stately buildings and gracious brownstones speak to the state capital's wealthy past.

Albany became state capital in 1797 because of its geographic centrality to local colonies and its strategic importance in the fur trade. These days it's as much synonymous with legislative dysfunction as with political power. Its struggling economy is reflected in the number of derelict and abandoned buildings (the ones with white cross signs on a red background). Even so, the locals' friendliness and the city's usefulness as a gateway to the Adirondacks and Hudson Valley make it worth more than a casual look.

◉ Sights

★ Empire State Plaza   PUBLIC ART
(☑518-473-7521; www.empirestateplaza.org) FREE
While the plaza's ensemble of architecture surrounding a central pool is hugely impressive, it's the splendid collection of modern American art liberally sprinkled outside, inside and underground the complex that is the true highlight here. The collection includes sculptures and massive paintings by Mark Rothko, Jackson Pollock, Alexander Calder and many other star artists.

★ New York State Museum   MUSEUM
(☑518-474-5877; www.nysm.nysed.gov; 222 Madison Ave; 9:30am-5pm Tue-Sun) FREE There are exhibits on everything from New York's original Native Amerian residents, the state's

history of activism, its architectural and engineering marvels and more in this top-class museum. A large chunk is dedicated to the history and development of New York City. The section on 9/11, including a damaged fire truck and debris from the site, is very moving. Don't miss a ride on the gorgeous antique carousel on the 4th floor.

New York State Capitol   HISTORIC BUILDING
(☑518-474-2418; www.hallofgovernors.ny.gov; Washington Ave; ⊘ guided tours 10am, noon, 2pm & 3pm Mon-Fri, 11am & 1pm Sat) FREE Completed in 1899, this grand building is the heart of the state government. The interior features detailed stone carving, carpentry, and tile and mosaic work, with highlights being the Great Western Staircase, the Governor's Reception Room and the HH Richardson–designed Senate Chamber. Saturday tours require online reservations.

🛏 Sleeping & Eating

Washington Park Inn   BOUTIQUE HOTEL $
(☑518-225-4567; www.washingtonparkinn.com; 643 Madison Ave; r $130-140; P ❋ @ 🛜) Rocking chairs on the covered porch and tennis rackets for guests to use on the courts in the park across the road set the relaxed tone for this appealing hotel in one of Albany's heritage buildings. Big rooms have simple and clean decoration, and food and drink is available on a serve-yourself basis around the clock from the well-stocked kitchen.

Cafe Madison   BREAKFAST $
(☑518-935-1094; www.cafemadisonalbany.com; 1108 Madison Ave; mains $8-14; ⊘7:30am-2pm Mon-Thu, to 3pm Fri-Sun; 🍴) Highly popular breakfast spot, especially on the weekend, when 30-minute waits for one of the cozy booths or tables is not uncommon (you might have more luck sitting at the bar). The staff know all the regulars and the menu includes inventive omelets, crepes, vegan options and a wide variety of specialty cocktails, such as cajun Bloody Marys.

❶ Getting There & Away

As state capital, Albany has the full range of transport connections. **Albany International Airport** (☑518-242-2200; www.albanyairport.com; Albany Shaker Rd, Colonie) is 10 miles north of downtown.

The Amtrak **Albany-Rensselaer Station** (☑800-872 7245; www.amtrak.com; 525 East St, Rensselaer), on the east bank of the Hudson River, has connections with NYC (from

GREAT CAMPS

Far from big fields of canvas tents, the Adirondacks' 'great camps' were typically lake and mountainside compounds of grandiose log cabins built in the latter half of the 19th century, as rustic retreats for the very wealthy. A prime example is **Great Camp Sagamore** (Sagamore Institute; ☑315-354-5311; www.greatcampsagamore.org; Sagamore Rd, Raquette Lake; tours adult/student $18/10; ☉hours vary May–mid-Oct), a former Vanderbilt vacation estate on the western side of the Adirondacks, which is now open to the public for tours, workshops and overnight stays on occasional history-oriented weekends.

Less ostentatious is **White Pine Camp** (☑518-327-3030; www.whitepinecamp.com; 432 White Pine Rd, Paul Smiths; r/cabin from $165/315; ☎), 12 miles northwest of Saranac Lake. This collection of rustically cozy cabins is set amid pine forests, wetlands and scenic Osgood Pond – a boardwalk leads out to an island on which sits a Japanese-style teahouse and an antique all-wood bowling alley. The fact that President Calvin Coolidge spent a few summer months here in 1926 is an interesting historical footnote, but the camp's charm comes through in its modest luxuries such as claw-foot tubs and wood-burning fireplaces. Naturalist walking tours are open to nonguests on select days from mid-June to September.

$45, 2½ hours), upstate New York and beyond. Greyhound and Trailways bus services use the centrally located **bus terminal** (☑518-427-7060; 34 Hamilton St).

Lake George

Lake George covers 45 square miles of the Adirondacks and attracts thousands of visitors to its shores every summer for swimming, boating, and just sitting and staring at its shimmering waters in admiration. The town of Lake George is a major tourist center with arcades, fireworks every Thursday in July and August, and paddleboat rides. It's a chaotic good time for those looking to dive headfirst into summer-by-the-lake culture. Anyone looking for a more mellow experience will find many nearby towns that offer a less hectic atmosphere, such as upscale Bolton Landing, cozy Glens Falls and bucolic Warrensburg.

In the winter, Lake George freezes over and most of the towns surrounding it go into hibernation. Other than skiing up in North Creek you won't find many winter activities and most restaurants and hotels stay closed until early summer.

◉ Sights & Activities

Fort William Henry Museum   MUSEUM
(☑518-668-5471; www.fwhmuseum.com; 48 Canada St, Lake George; adult/child $19.50/8, ghost tours $18/8; ☉9:30am-6pm May-Oct; ☑) Guides dressed as 18th-century British soldiers muster visitors along, with stops for battle reenactments that include firing period muskets and cannons, at this replica of the 1755 wooden fort. Check online for details of the evening ghost tours.

Hyde Collection Art Museum   MUSEUM
(☑518-792-1761; www.hydecollection.org; 161 Warren St, Glens Falls; adult/child $12/free; ☉10am-5pm Tue-Sat, noon-5pm Sun, plus 10am-5pm Mon mid-Jul–Aug) This remarkable gathering of art was amassed by local newspaper heiress Charlotte Pruyn Hyde. In her rambling Florentine renaissance mansion in Glens Falls, you'll stumble across Rembrandts, Rubens, Matisses and Eakins, as well as tapestries, sculptures and turn-of-the-century furnishings.

Lake George Steamboat Cruises   CRUISE
(☑518-668-5777; www.lakegeorgesteamboat.com; 57 Beach Rd, Lake George; adult/child from $17/8; ☉May-Oct) This company has been running cruise boats on Lake George since 1917. In season take your pick from a variety of cruise options on its three vessels: the authentic steamboat *Minne Ha Ha,* the 1907-vintage *Mohican* and the flagship *Lac du Saint Sacrement.*

🛏 Sleeping & Eating

Cornerstone Victorian   B&B $$
(☑518-623-3308; www.cornerstonevictorian.com; 3921 Main St, Warrensburg; r $120-200; 🅿✳☎) There are many Victorian-themed B&Bs in New York state, but few offer a gourmet, five-course breakfast each morning. The menu changes daily and alone is worth the price of a stay, although you'll also find that the rooms are comfortable and the hospitality of the hosts, Doug and Louise, extends well beyond the breakfast table.

SARANAC LAKE

Saranac Lake is not as tourist-oriented as its neighbor Lake Placid and gives a better idea of regular Adirondacks life. The town, built up in the early 20th century as a retreat for tuberculosis patients, has a lively old-fashioned main street leading towards the titular lake. Many other stretches of water pepper the surrounding forested hills, making this another great base for hiking, kayaking and canoeing.

Morgan & Co
AMERICAN $$$

(☑ 518-409-8060; www.morganrestaurant.com; 65 Ridge St, Glens Falls; mains $20-38; ⊘ 4-10pm Tue & Wed, to 11pm Thu-Sat, 10am-8pm Sun) Morgan & Co is the offspring of husband and wife Steve Butters and Rebecca Newell-Butters (who is a *Chopped* winner) and specializes in modern American cuisine with more than a few hints of international flair. Many of the dishes have a twist – swordfish Milanese, beef brisket lasagne – but the real draw here is that everything is exquisitely prepared.

The three-course prix-fixe dinner ($44) is a great deal.

❶ Getting There & Away

Albany International Airport (p152) is 50 miles south of Lake George. Amtrak stops in Fort Edwards, about 20 minutes by car from Lake George. Greyhound and Trailways also have long-distance buses to the region. A rental car is the best way of getting around the lake area.

Lake Placid

The resort town of Lake Placid is synonymous with snow sports – it hosted the Winter Olympics in 1932 and 1980. Elite athletes continue to train here; the rest of us can ride real bobsleds, speed-skate and more. Mirror Lake, which is right downtown, freezes thick enough for ice-skating, tobogganing and dogsledding. The town is also pleasant in summer, as the unofficial center of the High Peaks region of the Adirondacks and a great base for striking out on a hike or going canoeing or kayaking on one of the area's many lakes.

◉ Sights & Activities

A major draw at Lake Placid is the opportunity to play like an Olympian (or just watch athletes train). Most activities are managed by **Whiteface Mountain** (☑ 518-946-2223; www.whiteface.com; 5021 Rte 86, Wilmington; full-day lift ticket adult/child from $68/44, gondola only $24/18; ⊘ 8:30am-4pm Dec-Apr), the ski area where the Olympic ski races were held, but located in other spots around the area. Among other activities, you can do a half-mile on the bobsled track ($75) or a modified biathlon (cross-country skiing and shooting; $55). Lake Placid Speed Skating (www.lakeplacidspeedskating.wildapricot. org) organizes speed-skating rental and tutorials ($25) at the Olympic Center. Many sports are modified for summer – bobsledding on wheels, for instance.

The **Olympic Sites Passport** ($35), available at all Whiteface-managed venues, can be a good deal, covering admission at sites (such as the tower at the ski-jump complex and the gondola ride at Whiteface Mountain) and offering discounts on some activities.

Olympic Center
STADIUM

(☑ 518-523-3330; www.whiteface.com; 2634 Main St; tours $10, adult/child skating $10/8; ⊘ 10am-5pm daily, skating shows 4:30pm Fri; ♿) This is the location of the 1980 'Miracle on Ice,' when the upstart US hockey team trumped the unstoppable Soviets. In winter you can skate on the outside oval rink and year-round take a one-hour tour of the stadium. There are usually free figure-skating shows on Friday, with an additional ticketed show Saturday at 7:30pm in July and August (adult/child $11/9).

There is also a small **museum** (☑ 518-523-3330; www.lpom.org; 2634 Main St; adult/child $8/6; ⊘ 10am-5pm) here.

Whiteface Veteran's Memorial Highway
SCENIC DRIVE

(www.whiteface.com; Rte 431; driver & vehicle $16, additional passengers $9; ⊘ 8:45am-5:30pm late May–mid-Oct) Whiteface, the state's 5th highest peak at 4867ft, is the only summit in the Adirondacks accessible by car, with a neat castle-style lookout and cafe at the top. It can be socked in with clouds, making for an unnerving drive up, but when the fog clears, the 360-degree view is awe-inspiring. Tolls are paid at Lake Steven.

🛏 Sleeping & Eating

★ Adirondack Loj
LODGE $

(☑ 518-523-3441; www.adk.org; 1002 Adirondack Loj Rd; dm/r from $60/170, lean-tos winter/summer from $25/45; 🅿 🛜) The Adirondack Mountain Club runs this rustic retreat on the shore of pretty Heart Lake. All rooms in the lodge share communal bathrooms. Rates for rooms in the lodge include breakfast, and since it's 8 miles south of Lake Placid, you'll want to arrange a trail lunch and dinner here, too.

Lake Placid Lodge HERITAGE HOTEL **$$$**
(☑518-523-2700; www.lakeplacidlodge.com; 144 Lodge Way; r $600-1600; ⊗May-Mar; P⊖❄ @) Overlooking Lake Placid and channeling the rustic glamor of classic Gilded Age Adirondack lodges, this luxury hotel offers 13 gorgeously decorated rooms and cabins. The cabins are 19th-century originals, but the main hotel is a remarkable reconstruction following a devastating 2008 fire.

**Liquids & Solids
at the Handlebar** AMERICAN **$$**
(☑518-837-5012; www.liquidsandsolids.com; 6115 Sentinel Rd; mains $15-24; ⊗4-9pm Tue-Sat, 5-9pm Sun) It's all about craft beers, creative cocktails and fresh, inventive dishes at this rustic bar and restaurant where the kielbasa sausages and other charcuterie are made in-house. Mains may include dishes such as cauliflower stroganoff or crispy confit pork.

❶ Getting There & Away

Trailways buses serve Lake Placid. Amtrak runs once a day to Westport, with a bus connection to Lake Placid ($90.50, 9½ hours).

Adirondack Regional Airport (p152), 17 miles northwest near Saranac Lake, has connections via Cape Air (www.capeair.com) to Boston.

Thousand Islands

To downstate New Yorkers, this region is the source of the Thousand Islands salad dressing made of ketchup, mayonnaise and relish. In fact, it's a scenic wonderland along Lake Ontario and the St Lawrence River speckled with 1864 islands of all shapes and sizes either side of the US–Canada maritime border. The area was a Gilded Age playground for the rich; now it's more populist. Pros: beautiful sunsets, good-value lodging and Canada across the water. Cons: dead in winter and large mosquitoes in summer (bring repellent).

The historic port of Oswego is the region's southern gateway and makes a good base for exploring places like Sackets Harbor, where reenactors stage an annual War of 1812 Weekend. On the northern side, Clayton and Alexandria Bay both offer boat tours to the islands in the St Lawrence River, or you could camp amid glorious nature in the Wellesley Island State Park.

❶ Getting There & Around

The main airport for the region is **Syracuse Hancock International Airport** (☑315-454-4330; www.syrairport.org; 1000 Colonel Eileen Collins Blvd, Syracuse); connections here include NYC on JetBlue and Delta; Newark, Washington, DC, and Chicago on United; and Toronto on Air Canada. Cars can be rented at the airport or in downtown Syracuse, which is connected to other parts of the state by bus and train.

Alexandria Bay

Summer on the western shores of the Lawrence River, which separate New York state from Canada, sees thousands flock to the smattering of small waterfront towns that cater to all kinds of fun in the water. Alexandria Bay (A-Bay or Alex Bay), Clayton and Cape Vincent are the best places to hunker down to experience some of the sunny frivolity. They are all a bit rundown and tacky, but fun, nonetheless, and if you need a break you can always explore the region's wineries and distilleries, or some of the many islands from which the region gets its name. There is incredible nature and unique sights like a castle to discover. Be aware, though, that in winter things more or less close down.

◉ Sights & Activities

★**Boldt Castle** CASTLE
(☑800-847-5263; www.boldtcastle.com; Heart Island; adult/child $10/7; ⊗10am-6:30pm May, Jun & Sep, to 7:30pm Jul & Aug, 11am-5pm Oct) This Gothic gem, a replica of a German castle, was (partly) built by tycoon hotelier George C Boldt in the late 19th century. In 1904, however, midway through construction, Boldt's wife died suddenly, and the project was abandoned. Since 1977 the Thousand Islands Bridge Authority has spent millions restoring the place to something of its planned grandeur.

Singer Castle CASTLE
(☑877-327-5475; www.singercastle.com; Dark Island; adult/child $14.50/7.50; ⊗10am-4pm mid-May–mid-Oct) This stone castle, on Dark Island in the middle of the St Lawrence River, was built in 1905 by American entrepreneur Frederick Bourne. It's full of secret passages and hidden doors and has a dungeon – all of which you'll see on a tour. Uncle Sam (p156) runs boats from Alex Bay; **Schermerhorn Harbor** (☑315-324-5966; www.schermerhornharbor.com; 71 Schermerhorn Landing, Hammond; shuttle to Singer Castle $31.25; ⊗10:30am-2:30pm late May-Aug) also visits.

Uncle Sam Boat Tour

BOATING

(☎ 315-482-2611; www.usboattours.com; 45 James St, Alexandria Bay; adult/child $23/11.75) The main offering from the largest boat-tour operator in the area is a two-hour ride that visits both the US and Canada sides of the river (no passport required) and stops at Boldt Castle. Trips to Singer Castle, too.

🛏 Sleeping & Eating

Bonnie Castle

RESORT $$

(☎ 800-955-4511; www.bonniecastle.com; 31 Holland St, Alexandria Bay; r/apt from $160/242; ❄ 🅿 ≋) This somewhat run-down resort, one of Alex Bay's largest and open year-round, offers a variety of rooms, some with nice views across the St Lawrence River towards Boldt Castle.

Dockside Pub

AMERICAN $

(☎ 315-482-9849; www.thedocksidepub.com; 17 Market St, Alexandria Bay; mains $8-18; ⊙ 11am-midnight Mon-Thu, to 2am Fri & Sat, noon-midnight Sun; ▮) Unpretentious pub fare – burgers, fries, pizza and some specials. Despite the name its location is inland, with no dock view.

❶ Getting There & Away

The region is best reached by car.

Western New York

Tourism in this region revolves around Buffalo, New York State's second-largest city. After being the largest and most prosperous metropolis along the Great Lakes at the turn of the 19th century, Buffalo fell on hard times in the 20th, but is bouncing back in the 21st. Its amazing stock of heritage architecture is being restored and reinvented into hotels, museums and other businesses.

The area first developed thanks to the hydroelectric power of Niagara Falls and the Erie Canal, which linked the Great Lakes to the Atlantic Ocean. The falls are now better known as a tourist destination, with millions of visitors flocking here annually.

Rochester, about an hour northeast, shares a similar economic trajectory but has long been buoyed by its rich history of activism. The city was home to the famed suffragette Susan B Anthony and civil rights pioneer Frederick Douglass, among other 19th- and 20th-century iconoclasts.

❶ Getting There & Around

Buffalo Niagara International Airport (p158) is a regional hub with the widest range of flights, but you can also fly into and out of Niagara Falls International Airport (p159) and the **Greater Rochester International Airport** (☎ 585-753-7000; www2.monroecounty.gov; 1200 Brooks Ave). Amtrak runs trains to Buffalo, Rochester and Niagra, with connections to and from NYC, Albany, Toronto, and from Buffalo to/from Chicago. Greyhound (www.greyhound.com) has bus services to all three locations. For other places in the region you are best getting there by rental car.

Buffalo

The winters may be long and cold, but Buffalo stays warm with a vibrant creative community and strong local pride. Settled by the French in 1758, the city is believed to derive its name from *beau fleuve* (beautiful river). With power from nearby Niagara Falls, it boomed in the early 1900s; Pierce-Arrow cars were made here, and it was the first American city to have electric streetlights. One of its nicknames – Queen City – was because it was the largest city along the Great Lakes.

Those rosy economic times are long over, leaving many abandoned buildings in their wake. But revival is in Buffalo's air. Masterpieces of late 19th- and early-20th-century architecture, including designs by Frank Lloyd Wright and HH Richardson, have been magnificently restored. There's a park system laid out by Frederick Law Olmsted, of NYC's Central Park fame, great museums, and a positive vibe that's impossible to ignore.

◉ Sights & Activities

★ Buffalo City Hall

ARCHITECTURE

(☎ 716-852-3300; www.preservationbuffaloniagara.org; 65 Niagara Sq; ⊙ tours noon Mon-Fri) **FREE** This 32-story art deco masterpiece, opened in 1931 and beautifully detailed inside and out, towers over downtown. It's worth joining the free tour at noon that includes access to the mayor's office, the council chamber and the open-air observation deck.

★ Martin House Complex

ARCHITECTURE

(☎ 716-856-3858; www.darwinmartinhouse.org; 125 Jewett Pkwy; tour basic/extended $22/45; ⊙ tours hourly 10am-3pm Wed-Mon) This 15,000-sq-ft house, completed in 1905, was designed by Frank Lloyd Wright for his friend and patron Darwin D Martin. Representing Wright's Prairie House ideal, it consists of six interconnected buildings, each meticulously restored inside and out. Two tour options (book online) offer different levels of detail on this elaborate project.

⭐ **Albright-Knox Art Gallery** MUSEUM
(☑ 716-882-8700; www.albrightknox.org; 1285 Elmwood Ave; adult/child $16/9; ⊙ 10am-5pm Tue-Sun) The gallery's superb collection, which ranges from Degas and Picasso to Ruscha, Rauschenberg and other abstract expressionists, occupies a neoclassical building planned for Buffalo's 1905 Pan American Expo. Its temporary exhibits are particularly creative and compelling.

Graycliff Estate ARCHITECTURE
(☑ 716-947-9217; www.graycliffestate.org; 6472 Old Lake Shore Rd, Derby; 1/2hr tours $19/35) Occupying a dramatic clifftop location on Lake Erie, 16 miles south of downtown Buffalo, this 1920s vacation home was designed by Frank Lloyd Wright for the wealthy Martin family; a lengthy interior restoration was completed in 2018. You can learn a lot about Wright's overall plan on interesting tours (book in advance).

Guaranty Building ARCHITECTURE
(Prudential Building; www.hodgsonruss.com/Louis-Sullivans-Guaranty-Building.html; 140 Pearl St; ⊙ interpretive center 7:15am-9pm) FREE Completed in 1896 for the Guaranty Construction company, this gorgeous piece of architecture has a facade covered in detailed terra-cotta tiles and a superb stained-glass ceiling in its lobby. The interpretative center provides details of how groundbreaking this Adler & Sullivan–designed building was when it was built, when it was the tallest building in Buffalo.

Explore Buffalo TOURS
(☑ 716-245-3032; www.explorebuffalo.org; 1 Symphony Circle) Architectural and history tours around the Buffalo area by bus, on foot and by bicycle and kayak.

🛏 Sleeping

Hostel Buffalo Niagara HOSTEL $
(☑ 716-852-5222; www.hostelbuffalo.com; 667 Main St; dm/r $31/85; ❄@🛜) Conveniently located in Buffalo's downtown Theater District, this hostel occupies three floors of a former school, with a basement rec room, plenty of kitchen and lounge space, a small art gallery, and spotless if institutional bath-

rooms. Services include laundry facilities, free bikes and lots of info on local music, food and arts happenings.

⭐ **InnBuffalo off Elmwood** GUESTHOUSE $$
(☑ 716-867-7777; www.innbuffalo.com; 619 Lafayette Ave; ste $200-350; ❄🛜) Ellen and Joe Lettieri have done a splendid job restoring this 1898 mansion, originally built for local brass and rubber magnate HH Hewitt. The owners are happy to share how much of the building's original grandeur was uncovered in their restorations, which is evident in the nine superbly decorated suites, some with original features such as Victorian needle-spray showers.

Hotel Henry HERITAGE HOTEL $$
(☑ 716-882-1970; www.hotelhenry.com; cnr Rockwell Rd & Cleveland Circle; r $165-277; 🅿❄🛜) Occupying a grand late-19th-century 'lunatic asylum,' Hotel Henry preserves much of the stately architecture of Henry Richardson's original building. Its 88 rooms, reached off super-broad corridors, have tall ceilings and contemporary decor.

🍴 Eating

⭐ **Cole's** AMERICAN $
(☑ 716-886-1449; www.colesonelmwood.com; 1104 Elmwood Ave; mains $12-15; ⊙ 11am-10pm Mon-Thu, to 11pm Fri & Sat, to 9pm Sun; 🛜) Since 1934 this atmospheric restaurant and bar has been dishing up local favorites such as beef on weck (roast beef on a caraway-seed roll) – try it with a side of spicy Buffalo chicken wings, or go for one of the juicy burgers. It's handy for lunch if you are visiting the Delaware Park area and its museums.

The spacious bar, decorated with all kinds of vintage stuff, offers scores of beers on tap.

Betty's AMERICAN $$
(☑ 716-362-0633; www.bettysbuffalo.com; 370 Virginia St; mains $13-26; ⊙ 8am-9pm Tue-Fri, 9am-9pm Sat, to 2pm Sun; 🍴) On a quiet Allentown corner, bohemian Betty's does flavorful, fresh interpretations of American comfort food such as meatloaf. Brunch is deservedly popular and there's a pleasant bar.

Plenty of vegetarian and vegan, as well as gluten- and dairy-free, options are on the menu.

Black Sheep INTERNATIONAL $$
(☑ 716-884-1100; www.blacksheepbuffalo.com; 367 Connecticut St; mains $17-30; ⊙ 5-10pm Wed-Sat, 11am-2pm Sun) Black Sheep likes to describe its style of western New York farm-to-table

cuisine as 'global nomad,' which means you might find exciting, unique takes on chimichangas, pierogies and vegetable lasagna on the menu. You can also eat at the bar, which serves creative cocktails and local craft ales.

🍷 Drinking & Entertainment

★ Resurgence Brewing Company
MICROBREWERY
(☎716-381-9868; www.resurgencebrewing.com; 1250 Niagara St; ⊙4-10pm Tue-Thu, to 11:30pm Fri, noon-11:30pm Sat, to 5pm Sun) Housed in a former engine factory that was later to become the city's dog pound, Resurgence typifies Buffalo's skill at adaptive reuse of its infrastructure. The beers ($8 for a tasting flight) are excellent, with some 20 different ales on tap from fruity sweet Loganberry Wit to a porter with an amazing peanut-butter flavor.

Kleinhans Music Hall
CLASSICAL MUSIC
(☎716-885-5000; www.kleinhansbuffalo.org; 3 Symphony Circle) This fine concert hall, home to the Buffalo Philharmonic Orchestra, has wonderful acoustics. The building is a National Historic Landmark and was partly designed by the famous Finnish father-and-son architecture team of Eliel and Eero Saarinen.

❶ Getting There & Away

Buffalo Niagara International Airport (BUF; ☎716-630-6000; www.buffaloairport.com; 4200 Genesee St), about 10 miles east of downtown, is a regional hub. JetBlue Airways offers affordable round-trip fares from NYC.

NFTA (www.nfta.com), the local transit service, runs express bus 204 to the **Buffalo Metropolitan Transportation Center** (☎716-855-7300; www.nfta.com; 181 Ellicott St) downtown; Greyhound buses also pull in here. NFTA local bus 40 goes to the American side of Niagara Falls ($2, one hour); express bus 60 also goes to the area, but requires a transfer.

From Amtrak's downtown **Exchange Street Station** (☎716-856-2075; www.amtrak.com; 75 Exchange St), you can catch trains to NYC (from $67, 8½ hours), Niagara Falls (from $14, one hour), Albany (from $53, five hours) and Toronto (from $47, 4½ hours). All services also stop at **Buffalo-Depew Station** (55 Dick Rd), 8 miles east, where you can board trains to Chicago (from $61, 10½ hours).

Niagara Falls

It's a tale of two cities: Niagara Falls, New York (USA), and Niagara Falls, Ontario (Canada). Both overlook a natural wonder – 150,000 gallons of water per second, plunging more than 1000ft – and both provide a load of tourist kitsch around it. The Canadian side offers somewhat better views and a much larger town. However, the view from the New York side is still impressive and the falls surroundings are far more pleasant as they are preserved within a beautifully landscaped state park.

The town itself is also largely devoid of the commercial razzmatazz you'll find on the Canadian side; if that's what you want, it's easy to walk across the Rainbow Bridge between the two – just be sure to bring your passport.

DON'T MISS

NIAGARA FALLS, CANADA

The Canadian side of the falls is naturally blessed with superior views. **Horseshoe Falls**, on the western half of the river, are wider than Bridal Veil Falls on the eastern, American side, and they're especially photogenic from Queen Victoria Park. The **Journey Behind the Falls** (☎905-354-1551; www.niagaraparks.com; 6650 Niagara Pkwy; adult/child $22/14; ⊙9am-10pm, hours vary by season) gives access to a spray-soaked viewing area – similar to Cave of the Winds.

The Canadian town is also livelier, in an over-the-top touristy way. Chain hotels and restaurants dominate, but there is an HI hostel, and some older motels have the classic honeymooners' heart-shaped tubs. For more local info, visit the **Niagara Falls Tourism office** (☎905-356-6061; www.niagarafallstourism.com; 6815 Stanley Ave; ⊙9am-5pm Mon-Fri), near the base of the Skylon Tower observation deck.

Crossing the Rainbow Bridge and returning costs US$3.75/1 per car/pedestrian. Walking takes about 10 minutes; car traffic can grind to a standstill in summer or if there's a major event on in Toronto. US citizens and overseas visitors must show a passport or an enhanced driver's license at immigration at either end. Driving a rental car from the US over the border should not be a problem, but check with your rental company.

⊙ Sights & Activities

★ Cave of the Winds
VIEWPOINT

(☑716-278-1730; www.niagarafallsstatepark.com; Goat Island Rd; adult/child $19/16; ⊙from 9am May-Oct, closing times vary) On the northern corner of Goat Island, don a souvenir rain poncho and sandals (provided) and take an elevator down to walkways just 25ft from the crashing water at the base of Bridal Veil Falls. (Despite the name, the platforms run in front of the falls, not into a cave.)

Old Fort Niagara
MUSEUM

(☑716-745-7611; www.oldfortniagara.org; Youngstown; adult/child $13/9; ⊙9am-7pm Jul & Aug, to 5pm Sep-Jun) This 1726 French-built fortress, restored in the 1930s, defends the once very strategic point where the Niagara River flows into Lake Ontario. It has engaging displays of Native American artifacts, small weapons, furniture and clothing, as well as breathtaking views from its wind-blown ramparts. In summer months there are tours and demonstrations by costumed guides of what life was like here in the past. Surrounding the fort are hiking trails in Fort Niagara State Park.

Whirlpool State Park
PARK

(☑716-284-4691; www.parks.ny.gov; Robert Moses State Pkwy) This park, 3 miles north of the falls, sits just above a sharp bend in the Niagara River – a bend that creates a giant whirlpool easily visible from your vantage point. Steps take you 300ft to the gorge below and mind you don't tumble into the vortex.

Rainbow Bridge
BRIDGE

(www.niagarafallsbridges.com; ⊙cars/pedestrians/cyclists US$3.75/1/1) Bring your passport for the walk or drive across this bridge linking the US and Canadian sides of the falls – there are good views along the way.

★ Maid of the Mist
BOATING

(☑716-284-8897; www.maidofthemist.com; 1 Prospect St; adult/child $19.25/11.20; ⊙hours vary) The traditional way to see Niagara Falls is on this boat cruise, which has ferried visitors into the rapids right below the falls since 1846. Make sure you wear the blue poncho they give you, as the torrential spray from the falls will soak you.

🛏 Sleeping & Eating

Seneca Niagara
Resort & Casino
RESORT $$$

(☑877-873-6322; www.senecaniagaracasino.com; 310 4th St; r $255-405; P ⊖ ❄ @ 🤖 🐕) With some 600 spacious rooms and suites, and a lively casino, this purple-and-glass-covered tower is the American town's answer to the tourist glitz across on the Canadian side of the falls. A variety of music and comedy shows are staged here, too, headlined by relatively big names.

Giacomo
BOUTIQUE HOTEL $$$

(☑716-299-0200; www.thegiacomo.com; 222 1st St; r from $247; P ❄ @ 🤖) A rare bit of style among the bland chain hotels and motels of Niagara, the luxe Giacomo occupies part of a gorgeous art-deco office tower, with spacious, ornately decorated rooms. Even if you're not staying here, grab a drink at the lobby bar (open from 5pm) and take it up to the 19th-floor lounge for spectacular views.

Third Street
Retreat Eatery & Pub
AMERICAN $

(☑716-371-0760; www.thirdstreetretreat.com; 250 Rainbow Blvd; mains $8-13; ⊙9am-3pm Wed-Sat, hours vary) The walls are decorated with old LP covers at this popular local spot serving all-day breakfasts and other comforting pub-grub dishes. There's a good selection of beers on tap or in bottles, plus a pool table and darts in an upstairs section.

❶ Getting There & Away

NFTA (www.nfta.com) bus 40 connects downtown Buffalo and Niagara Falls ($2, one hour); the stop in Niagara Falls is at 1st St and Rainbow Blvd. Express bus 60 goes to a terminal east of the town center; you'll have to transfer to bus 55 to reach the river. The **Amtrak train station** (☑716-285-4224; www.amtrak.com; 825 Depot Ave) is about 2 miles north of downtown; the station on the Canadian side is more central, but coming from NYC, you have to wait for Canadian customs. From Niagara Falls, daily trains go to Buffalo ($14, 50 minutes), Toronto (from $36, three hours) and NYC (from $67, nine hours). **Greyhound** (www.greyhound.com; 240 1st St) buses stop at the Quality Inn.

Flights from Florida and South Carolina are offered by Allegiant Air and Spirit Airlines to **Niagara Falls International Airport** (☑716-297-4494; www.niagarafallsairport.com; 2035 Niagara Falls Blvd).

NEW JERSEY

Everything you've seen on TV, from the Mc-Mansions of *Real Housewives of New Jersey* to the thick accents of *The Sopranos,* is at least partially true. But Jersey (natives lose the 'New') is at least as well defined by its high-tech and banking headquarters, and a quarter of it is lush farmland (hence the Garden State nickname) and pine forests. And on the 127 miles of beautiful beaches, you'll find, yes, the guidos and guidettes of *Jersey Shore*, but also many other oceanfront towns, each with a distinct character.

Stay east and you'll experience the Jersey (sub)urban jungle. Go west to find its opposite: the peaceful, refreshing landscape of the Delaware Water Gap.

❶ Getting There & Around

Though many NJ folks love their cars, there are other transportation options.

PATH (www.panynj.gov/path) train services connect lower Manhattan to Hoboken, Jersey City and Newark. **NJ Transit** (www.njtransit. com) operates buses and trains around the state, including bus service to NYC's Port Authority and downtown Philadelphia, and trains to Penn Station, NYC. Train service has declined severely in the past decade – fair warning.

New York Waterway (www.nywaterway.com) ferries run up the Hudson River, and from the NJ Transit train station in Hoboken to the World Financial Center in Lower Manhattan.

Hoboken

The Square Mile City is among the trendiest of zip codes, with real-estate prices to match. On weekends the bars come alive, and loads of restaurants line Washington St. If you can step over the designer dogs, and navigate the mega-strollers, trolling black Uber cars with NY plates, and lines for Carlo the Cake Boss, it's a good walking town with amazing views of NYC. Get here before the chain stores do.

◉ Sights

Hoboken Historical Museum MUSEUM
(Map p78; 📞 201-656-2240; www.hobokenmu seum.org; 1301 Hudson St; adult/child $5/free; ⏰ 2-7pm Tue-Thu, 1-5pm Fri, noon-5pm Sat & Sun) This small museum conveys a sense of Hoboken that's hard to imagine today – a city of blue-collar Irish and Italian Catholic immigrants, toiling in the shipyards and docks. It also offers self-guided walking tours of Frank Sinatra's Hoboken haunts, and *On the Waterfront* film locales.

✗ Eating

La Isla CUBAN $
(📞 201-659-8197; www.laislarestaurant.com; 104 Washington St; breakfast $8-17, sandwiches $8-16, mains $16-28; ⏰ 7am-10pm Mon-Sat, 10am-9pm

Sun) The most authentic Cuban choice in town since 1970, the Formica counters ring with plates spilling over with grilled Cuban sandwiches, *maduros* (fried plantains) and rice with pigeon peas – all to the soundtrack of staccato Spanish chatter and salsa, under the watchful eye of Celia Cruz portraits. Forget the fancier 'uptown' branch – this is the real thing.

Amanda's GASTRONOMY $$
(📞 201-798-0101; www.amandasrestaurant.com; 908 Washington St; mains $17-31; ⏰ dinner 5-10pm Mon-Thu, to 11pm Fri & Sat, to 9pm Sun, brunch 11am-3pm Sat & Sun) For three decades the Flynn family has served first-rate fare in these conjoined, converted brownstones, each room with a different theme. An extensive wine list and monthly wine evenings make this a classy option. The early dinner special is great value.

❶ Getting There & Away

NY Waterway (www.nywaterway.com) ferries run between 39th St on Manhattan's West Side and Hoboken ($9, eight minutes). There is frequent, if crowded, NJ PATH train service from lower Manhattan to Hoboken terminal. Parking is atrocious – don't even think about driving here.

Princeton

Settled by an English Quaker missionary, this tiny town is filled with lovely architecture and several noteworthy sites, number one of which is its Ivy League university. Princeton is more upper-crust than collegiate, with preppie boutiques edging central Palmer Sq. Just over a mile from campus and town, however, you can escape to the idyllic Institute Woods, a 600-acre forested retreat.

Like any good seat of learning, Princeton has a bookstore, record store, brew pub and indie cinema, all within blocks of the rabbit's warren of streets and alleys that crisscross Palmer Sq, as well as innumerable sweet shops, cafes and ice-cream specialty stores.

◉ Sights

★**Institute Woods** FOREST
(www.ias.edu; 1 Einstein Dr; ⏰ dawn-dusk) Walk 1½ miles down Mercer St to a bucolic slice of countryside seemingly completely removed from the jammed-up campus-area thoroughfares. Nearly 600 acres have been set aside here, and birders, joggers and dog-walkers luxuriate on the soft, loamy

DELAWARE WATER GAP

With one foot in Pennsylvania and the other in New Jersey, the place where the Delaware River makes a tight S-curve through the ridge of the Kittatinny Mountains was, in the days before air-conditioning, a popular resort destination. In the modern era it remains an area of surpassing dramatic beauty, a slice of rugged wilderness within a day's trip of the largest urban conurbations on the North American Eastern Seaboard. The current preserved areas dates to 1965, when the **Delaware Water Gap National Recreation Area** (📞570-426-2452; www.nps.gov/dewa; 1978 River Rd, Bushkill) was established, covering land in both NJ and Pennsylvania.

Note that entrance to most of the park is free, but for some areas there is a $10 amenities fee for cars and a $2 fee for bicycles.

The Delaware Water Gap is about 70 miles west of New York City, accessible by I-80, or 100 miles north of Philadelphia via I-476. A car is by far the easiest way out here.

It's about a two-hour bus ride from NYC to the area. Coach USA (www.coachusa.com) provides bus service from the Port Authority to Milford, PA ($25.75), running seven times a day on weekdays, and at 10am, 2:30pm and 5:35pm daily.

Martz Trailways (www.martztrailways.com) runs from NYC Port Authority to Stroudsburg, PA ($39, 1½ hours, more than 12 daily).

pathways. It's an avian paradise during the spring warbler migration.

Princeton University   UNIVERSITY
(📞609-258-3000; www.princeton.edu) Built in the mid-1700s, this institution soon became one of the largest structures in the early colonies. Now it's in the top-tier Ivy League. You can stroll around on your own, or take a student-led tour.

Morven Museum & Garden   MUSEUM
(📞609-924-8144; www.morven.org; 55 Stockton St; adult/child $10/8; ⏱10am-4pm Wed-Sun) Stop by for fine displays of decorative arts and fully furnished period rooms; other galleries change their exhibitions periodically. The gardens, and the house itself – a perfectly coiffed colonial revival mansion originally built by Richard Stockton, a prominent lawyer in the mid-18th century and signer of the Declaration of Independence – are worth a visit in and of themselves.

🛏 Sleeping & Eating

Inn at Glencairn   B&B $$
(📞609-497-1737; www.innatglencairn.com; 3301 Lawrenceville Rd/Rte 206; r from $220; 🅿) The best value in the Princeton area: five serene rooms in a renovated Georgian manor, a 10-minute drive from campus. The property is visited by flocks of goldfinches (the state bird) and also, legend has it, by the unquiet spirit of a British soldier from the Revolutionary War era: listen for Lord Ralston's footsteps at night.

⭐**Mistral**   MEDITERRANEAN $$
(📞609-688-8808; www.mistralprinceton.com; 66 Witherspoon St; sharing plates $12-18, mains $17-32; ⏱5-9pm Mon, to 9:30pm Tue, 11:30am-3pm & 5-9:30pm Wed & Thu, 11:30am-3pm & 5-10:30pm Fri & Sat, 10:30am-3pm & 4-9pm Sun) Princeton's most creative restaurant offers plates made to share, with flavors ranging from the Caribbean to Scandinavia. Sit at the chef's counter for a bird's-eye view of the controlled chaos in the open-plan kitchen.

**Mediterra
Restaurant & Taverna**   MEDITERRANEAN $$$
(📞609-252-9680; www.mediterrarestaurant.com; 29 Hulfish St; mains $22-36; ⏱11:30am-10pm Mon-Thu, to 11pm Fri & Sat, 11am-9pm Sun) Centrally located in Palmer Sq, Mediterra is the sort of upscale, contemporary place designed for a college town. Visiting parents, flush students and locals all crave the dishes here, which highlight locally sourced and organic ingredients, and reflect the owners' Chilean and Italian heritage. The fish and small plates are particularly good. The daily happy hour (4pm to 6:30pm) features half-price tapas and, sometimes, live music.

ⓘ Getting There & Away

Coach USA (www.coachusa.com) express buses 100 and 600 run frequently between Manhattan and Princeton ($15.70, 1½ hours). NJ Transit (www.njtransit.com) trains run frequently from New York Penn Station to Princeton Junction train station ($16, one to 1½ hours). The 'Dinky' shuttle will then run you to Princeton campus ($3, five minutes).

Jersey Shore

Perhaps the most famous and revered feature of New Jersey is its sparkling shore – and heading 'down the shore' (local parlance – never 'to the beach') is an essential summer ritual. Stretching from Sandy Hook to Cape May, the coastline is dotted with resort towns both tacky and tony. It's mobbed on summer weekends (traffic is especially bad on the bridges to the barrier islands), and finding good-value accommodations is nearly as difficult as locating untattooed skin; campgrounds can be low-cost alternatives. By early fall, however, you could find yourself blissfully alone on the sand.

❶ Getting There & Around

Sitting in bumper-to-bumper traffic on the Garden State Pkwy may turn you lobster red, so driving early in the day to summer destinations is a must.

NJ Transit (www.njtransit.com) runs special Shore Express trains (twice daily June to September), stopping in Asbury Park, Bradley Beach, Belmar, Spring Lake, Manasquan, Point Pleasant Beach and Bay Head. You can buy a beach tag along with your train ticket, and there are two northbound express trains returning in the evening.

NJ Transit buses from New York's Port Authority service Seaside Heights/Seaside Park, Island Beach State Park, Atlantic City, Wildwood and Cape May.

Greyhound (www.greyhound.com) runs special buses to Atlantic City.

Asbury Park & Ocean Grove

During decades of economic stagnation, the town of Asbury Park had nothing more to its name than the fact that state troubadour Bruce Springsteen got his start at the Stone Pony nightclub here in the mid-1970s. But since 2000, blocks of previously abandoned Victorian homes have seen such a revival that Asbury is sometimes called 'Brooklyn on the Beach.' Thousands more units are projected over the next few years, and a 17-story luxury condo complex called the Asbury Ocean Club looms over the boardwalk as of 2019, with one floor comprising a 54-room boutique hotel.

The downtown area, several blocks of Cookman and Bangs Aves, has antiques shops, hip restaurants (from vegan to French bistro) and an art-house cinema. Thirty-nine bars and counting lure trains full of young NY-based revelers to the convenient NJ transit depot, like moths to the vodka.

Immediately south of Asbury Park, Ocean Grove is a kind of time and culture warp. 'God's Square Mile at the Jersey Shore,' as it's known, was founded by Methodists in the 19th century as a revival camp, and it's still a dry town (no liquor) and the beach is closed on Sunday mornings. The Victorian architecture is so covered in gingerbread trim that you may want to eat it. At the center, around a 6500-seat wooden auditorium with a huge pipe organ, the former revival camp is now Tent City – a historic site with more than a hundred quaint canvas tents used as summer homes.

◉ Sights & Activities

Historic Village at Allaire MUSEUM
(☏ 732-919-3500; www.allairevillage.org; 4263 Atlantic Ave, Farmingdale; parking Sat & Sun May-Sep $5; ⊙village 11am-4pm Wed-Sun Jun-Aug, Sat & Sun only Apr, May & Sep-Nov, shorter hours Dec-Mar) **FREE** Just a 15-minute-drive from the 21st century and Asbury Park, this quirky museum is what remains of what was once a thriving 19th-century village called Howell Works, which produced bog iron for James Allaire's New York City steam engine works. Visit shops and historic gardens, all run by folks in period costume, and bake your own bread at the 1835 bakery (11am to 4pm Wednesday to Friday, to 5pm Saturday and Sunday in summer).

🛌 Sleeping

Quaker Inn INN $$
(☏ 732-775-7525; www.quakerinn.com; 39 Main Ave; tw $97-155, d $123-177, f $172-214; ❅⛭) A great old creaky Victorian with 28 rooms, some of which open onto wraparound porches or balconies. There's a nice common area and library to linger over your coffee, and the managers, Liz and Mark, reflect the town's charm and hospitality. Light sleepers take note: the walls are a bit thin.

★ Asbury Hotel BOUTIQUE HOTEL $$$
(☏ 732-774-7100; www.theasburyhotel.com; 210 5th Ave; d $185-425; ℗❅⛭⚊) Wow. From the performance space and lobby stocked with LP records, old books and a solarium to the rooftop bar, this hotel oozes style. Two blocks from Convention Hall and the boardwalk, you could stay inside all day, playing pool or lounging by the heated one. Weeknights are a better deal.

On the flip side: you'll get charged for coffee in a paper cup. Not cool. But it does have an ice-skating rink in winter: very cool.

✖ Eating & Drinking

Moonstruck
ITALIAN $$$

(☑ 732-988-0123; www.moonstrucknj.com; 517 Lake Ave; mains $28-44; ⊙5-10pm Wed-Fri, to 11pm Sat, 4:30-10pm Sun mid-Jun–Aug, shorter hours Sep–mid-Jun) With views of Wesley Lake dividing Asbury and Ocean Grove and an extensive martini menu, it's hard to find fault here. The menu is eclectic, though it leans towards Italian with a good selection of pastas; the meat and fish dishes have varied ethnic influences.

Asbury Festhalle & Biergarten
BEER GARDEN

(☑ 732-997-8767; www.asburybiergarten.com; 527 Lake Ave; ⊙4pm-1am Mon-Fri, noon-1am Sat & Sun) Deutschland by the Sea: quaff from 38 draft ales on the rooftop beer garden or check out live music in a space as big as two barns, with classic long beer-hall tables. Snack on pretzels bigger than your face, fill up on plates of wurst (mains $15 to $28) or tipple some of the different schnapps on offer.

☆ Entertainment

Stone Pony
LIVE MUSIC

(☑ 732-502-0600; www.stoneponyonline.com; 913 Ocean Ave; ⊙box office noon-5pm Wed-Mon & during shows) Best known as the bar where Bruce Springsteen launched his career, the Pony has continued to be a respectable rock venue – a genuine, sweaty, feet-stick-to-the-floor club – and hosts a big outdoor festival at the beginning of summer.

Silverball Museum Arcade
ARCADE

(Pinball Hall of Fame; ☑ 732-774-4994; www.silver ballmuseum.com; 1000 Ocean Ave; per hour/half-day/day $12.50/15/25; ⊙11am-9pm Mon-Thu, to 1am Fri, 10am-1am Sat, 10am-10pm Sun) Dozens of pinball machines in mint condition, from mechanical 1950s games to modern classics such as Addams Family. Play all you like, for a single price.

❶ Getting There & Away

NJ Transit's Asbury Park Station is at the intersection of Cookman and Main Sts and is about 45 minutes from NYC. Some late-night trains run during the summer.

Driving along the S Main St (Rte 71) from the north or south, you'll see the impressive gates that mark the entranceway to Ocean Grove's Main Ave. If you're taking the NJ Transit's Shore Express, disembark at neighboring Asbury Park

---

❶ BEACH FEES

Many communities on the Jersey Shore charge $7 to $15 for access, issuing a badge (also called a tag) for the day. From Long Beach Island north to near Sandy Hook, all beaches have a fee; the southern Shore is mostly, but not entirely, free. If you're staying a few days, it's worthwhile investing in a weekly badge, although some hotels provide them.

---

and walk or taxi over to Ocean Grove. Academy buses from New York's Port Authority (www.academybus.com) go directly to Ocean Grove ($19, 1¾ hours).

Barnegat Peninsula

Locals call this 22-mile stretch 'the barrier island,' though it's technically a peninsula, connected to the mainland at **Point Pleasant Beach**. Surfers should seek out **Inlet Beach** in Manasquan, immediately north (not on the peninsula), for the Shore's most reliable year-round waves.

South of **Mantoloking** and **Lavallette**, midway down the island, a bridge from the mainland (at Toms River) deposits the hordes in **Seaside Heights**, location of the MTV reality show *Jersey Shore,* and epitome of the deliciously tacky Shore culture. It's still a sticky pleasure to lick a Kohr's orange-vanilla twist cone and stroll through the boardwalk's raucous, deeply tanned, scantily clad crowds, refueling at an above-average number of bars. Look out for the 1910 Dentzel-Looff carousel, and the 310ft Ferris wheel and German-built roller coaster added in 2017.

For a bit of quiet, escape south to residential **Seaside Park** and the wilderness of Island Beach State Park beyond.

◎ Sights

Island Beach State Park
PARK

(☑ 732-793-0506; www.islandbeachnj.org; Seaside Park; per car weekday/weekend Jun-Aug $12/20, Sep-May $10; ⊙8am-8pm Mon-Fri, 7am-8pm Sat & Sun Jun-Aug, 8am-dusk Sep-May) This beautiful tidal island offers fishing, wildlife (from foxes to ospreys and other shorebirds), more than 40 trees and shrubs, including pepper-bush and prickly pear cactus, and a killer view of Barnegat Lighthouse, seemingly only an arm's length across the water. Of the 10 miles of relatively untouched beach,

OFF THE BEATEN TRACK

SANDY HOOK

The northernmost tip of the Jersey Shore is the **Sandy Hook Gateway National Recreation Area** (☑718-354-4606; www.nps.gov/gate; 128 S Hartshorne Dr, Highlands; parking late May-Aug $15; ⊙5am-9pm Apr-Oct) **FREE**, a 7-mile barrier island at the entrance to New York Harbor. From your beach blanket, you can see the NYC skyline. The wide beaches, including NJ's only legal nude beach (Gunnison), are edged by a system of bike trails, while the bay side is great for fishing, kayaking and bird-watching.

Historic Fort Hancock and the nation's oldest operational **lighthouse** (☑732-872-5970; www.nps.gov/gate; 85 Mercer Rd, Highlands; ⊙visitor center 9am-5pm, tours half-hourly 1-4:30pm) **FREE** give a glimpse of Sandy Hook's prior importance as a military and navigational site.

one is open for swimming; the rest makes a nice bike ride. On the bay side, the lush tidal marshes are good for kayaking.

Casino Pier AMUSEMENT PARK
(☑732-793-6488; www.casinopiernj.com; 800 Ocean Tce, Seaside Heights; rides $4-30, water park adult/child $35/29; ⊙noon-late Jun-Aug, hours vary Sep-May) The amusement pier at the northern end of the Seaside boardwalk has a few kiddie rides and more extreme thrills for the 48in-and-taller set, plus a chairlift that runs above the boardwalk. Nearby is Breakwater Beach, a water park with tall slides; hours can vary but it generally opens at 9:30am in July and August.

🛏 Sleeping & Eating

Luna-Mar Motel MOTEL **$$**
(☑732-793-7955; www.lunamarmotel.com; 1201 N Ocean Ave, Seaside Park; r from $160; ❉🐾❄) Directly across the road from the beach, this tidy motel has tile floors (no sandy carpets) and a heated pool. Rates include beach badges.

Klee's PUB FOOD **$$**
(☑732-830-1996; www.kleesbarandgrill.com; 101 Boulevard, Seaside Heights; pizza from $8, mains $13-28; ⊙11am-10pm Sun-Thu, to 11pm Fri & Sat) Around for 40 years, this solid sports bar (with 12 screens) plates up big servings of sandwiches, burgers and other pub grub. Klee's is famous for its pizza, and its best recommendation is that it comes at family prices on Monday.

ℹ Getting There & Away

NJ Transit has a special Shore Express train (no transfer required) to Shore towns between Asbury Park and Bay Head; in the summer months it includes a beach pass. It also offers direct bus service to Seaside Heights from New York's Port Authority (bus 137; $27, 1½ hours) and Newark's Penn Station (bus 67; $17, one hour) from the end of June to Labor Day.

Atlantic City

Atlantic City (AC) may be the largest city on the Shore, but the vision of 'Vegas on the East Coast' has foundered and casinos have gone bankrupt. But the hotels can be a bargain and the lovely beach is free and often empty because most visitors are indoors playing the slots. And in contrast with many homogeneous beach enclaves, the population here is more diverse.

As for the Prohibition-era glamour depicted in the HBO series *Boardwalk Empire,* there's little trace – though you can still ride along the boardwalk on a nifty wicker rolling chair. As you do, consider that the first boardwalk was built here, and if Baltic Ave rings a bell, it's because the game Monopoly uses AC's street names. A later contribution: the Miss America pageant, though it's now held in Vegas; the Miss'd America drag pageant fills the gap.

👁 Sights

Steel Pier AMUSEMENT PARK
(☑866-386-6659; www.steelpier.com; 1000 Boardwalk; ⊙1pm-midnight Mon-Fri, noon-1am Sat & Sun mid-Jun–Aug, shorter hours May–mid-Jun, Sep & Oct) The Steel Pier, directly in front of the Taj Mahal casino, was the site of the famous high-diving horses that plunged into the Atlantic before crowds of spectators from the 1920s to the '70s. Today it's a collection of amusement rides, games of chance, candy stands and a go-kart track.

Ripley's Believe it or Not! MUSEUM
(Odditorium; ☑609-347-2001; www.ripleys.com/atlanticcity; 1441 Boardwalk; adult/child $19/12; ⊙11am-8pm Mon-Fri, 10am-9pm Sat, to 8pm Sun) Robert Ripley spent a lifetime collecting bizarre stuff, and a lot of it's here. Two-headed goat fetuses, a baling-wire Jimi Hendrix head, the world's smallest

car and a roulette wheel made of 14,000 jellybeans – you'll have fun for about the cost of a movie.

Historic Pipe Organ THEATRE
(Boardwalk Hall; www.boardwalkorgans.org; 2301 Boardwalk; ⊙ organ recital 12:30pm Wed May-Jul, plus 12:30pm Tue Jun-Sep, tours 10am Wed May-Jul) **FREE** A nonprofit institute runs tours, recitals and silent films to maintain the Boardwalk Hall's two historic – and impressive – pipe organs: the 'sonic Mount Rushmore.' The 2½-hour Curator's Tour (suggestion donation $10) relates the history of both instruments and the hall itself.

🍴 Sleeping & Eating

Tropicana Casino & Resort HOTEL $
(☑609-340-4000; www.tropicana.net; 2831 Boardwalk; r from $70; P ❄ 🖥 🏊) The Trop is a sprawling city-within-a-city, including a casino, the Boogie Nights disco, a spa and high-end restaurants. We recommend the newer 'Havana' wing; try to get up above the 40th floor for spectacular views. Weekday rates can be incredibly cheap.

★ **Kelsey & Kim's Café** SOUTHERN US $$
(Kelsey's Soul Food; ☑609-350-6800; www. kelseysac.com; 201 Melrose Ave; mains $14-20; ⊙8am-9pm Mon-Thu, to 10pm Fri-Sun) In the pretty residential Uptown area, this friendly cafe does excellent Southern comfort food, from morning grits and waffles to fried whiting and barbecue brisket. BYOB makes it a deal.

ℹ️ Getting There & Away

The small **Atlantic City International Airport** (ACY; ☑609-573-4700; www.acairport.com; 101 Atlantic City International Airport, Egg Harbor Township) is a 20-minute drive from the town center. If you happen to be coming from Florida (where most of the flights come from), it's a great option for South Jersey or Philadelphia.

The only train service is NJ Transit from Philadelphia (one way $10.75, 1½ hours), arriving at the **train station** (☑973-491-9400; www. njtransit.com; 1 Atlantic City Expwy) next to the convention center. AC's **bus station** (☑609-345-5403; 1901 Atlantic Ave) receives NJ Transit and Greyhound services from NYC ($39, 2½ hours) and Philadelphia ($18, 1½ hours). A casino will often refund much of the fare (in chips, coins or coupons) if you get a bus, such as Greyhound's Lucky Streak service, directly to its door. When leaving AC, buses first stop at various casinos and only stop at the bus station if not already full.

Wildwood

Wildwood, and its neighboring towns of North Wildwood and Wildwood Crest, is a virtual outdoor museum of 1950s motel architecture and neon signs. The community has a relaxed atmosphere, somewhere between clean-cut fun and wild party. The beach is the widest in NJ (a proposal to ferry beach-goers across the sands on camel was once floated but voted down) and there's no admission fee. Along the 2-mile boardwalk, several massive piers have roller coasters and rides best suited to aspiring astronauts.

◉ Sights

Doo Wop Experience MUSEUM
(☑609-523-1958; www.doowopusa.org; 4500 Ocean Ave; ⊙10am-5pm Mon, to 8pm Tue-Thu, to 9pm Fri-Sun Jun-Aug, shorter hours Apr, May, Sep & Oct) **FREE** The Doo Wop Preservation League runs this small museum that tells the story of Wildwood's 1950s heyday. Its 'neon-sign garden' shows off relics from no-longer-standing buildings. On Tuesday, Wednesday and Thursday nights in summer, a trolley tour (adult/child $13/7) departs from here, passing the most colorful landmarks.

🍴 Sleeping & Eating

Heart of Wildwood HOTEL $$
(☑609-522-4090; www.heartofwildwood.com; cnr Ocean & E Spencer Aves; r $70-250; P ❄ 🖥 🏊) If you're here for waterslides and roller coasters, book a room at Heart of Wildwood, facing the amusement piers. It's not fancy, but gets high marks for cleanliness (the tile floors help), and from the heated rooftop pool you can watch the big wheel go round and round. Smallish suites are handy for families, with stoves, sinks and fridges.

Starlux BOUTIQUE HOTEL $$$
(☑609-522-7412; www.thestarlux.com; 305 E Rio Grande Ave; r/ste from $270/345; P 🖥 🏊) The sea-green-and-white Starlux has the soaring profile, the lava lamps, the boomerang-decorated bedspreads and the sailboat-shaped mirrors, plus it's as clean as a whistle. Even more authentically retro are its two chrome-sided Airstream trailers (sleeping three comfortably).

Key West Cafe BREAKFAST $
(☑609-522-5006; www.keywestcafe.us; 4701 Pacific Ave; mains $7-15; ⊙7am-2pm) Basically every permutation of pancakes and eggs imaginable, all freshly prepared – oh, and lunch too. Bonus: it's open year-round. The eggs Benedict is a fave among frequent diners.

❶ Getting There & Away

NJ Transit runs bus service to Wildwood from NYC ($46, 4½ hours) with a possible transfer in Atlantic City, and express bus service from Philadelphia's 30th St Station ($23, three hours) during summer. Driving from the Garden State Pkwy, take Rte 47 into Wildwood; from the south a more scenic route from Cape May is Rte 109, then Ocean Dr.

Cape May

Established in 1620, Cape May is a town with deep history and some 600 gorgeous Victorian buildings. Its sweeping beaches are a draw in summer, but its year-round population of about 3500 makes it a lively off-season destination, unlike most of the Jersey Shore. Whales can be spotted off the coast May to December, and migratory birds are plentiful in spring and fall: just check in at the Cape May Bird Observatory.

The state's booming wine industry is represented by six different sites here, among them trendy Willow Creek Winery. And thanks to the location on New Jersey's southern tip (it's Exit 0 from the turnpike), you can watch the sun rise or set over the water.

◉ Sights

Cape May Point State Park　　　STATE PARK
(☑ 609-884-2159; www.state.nj.us; ⊙ dawn-dusk, office 8am-4pm) The 190-acre Cape May Point State Park, just off Lighthouse Ave, has 2 miles of trails, plus the famous 1859 **Cape May Lighthouse** (☑ 609-884-5404; www.capemaymac.org; 215 Lighthouse Ave; adult/child $10/5; ⊙ 10am-5pm May-Aug, shorter hours rest of year). You can climb the 199 stairs to the top for the view. Short, easy trails (0.5 to 2 miles) are great for birding and a breath of salty ocean air.

Cape May Bird Observatory　　　BIRD SANCTUARY
(☑ 609-884-2736; www.njaudubon.org; ⊙ 9:30am-4:30pm Apr-Oct, closed Tue Nov-Mar) FREE Cape May is one of the country's top birding spots, with more than 400 species during the spring and fall migration seasons, when neotropical birds are heading south for the winter or north to breed for the summer. The mile-long loop trail here is a good introduction, and there are plenty of books, binoculars and birding bric-a-brac in the bookstore.

⏸ Sleeping

Congress Hall　　　HOTEL $$$
(☑ 609-884-8421; www.caperesorts.com; 200 Congress Pl; r from $240-580; ❋ ❂ ❀) Opened in 1816, the enormous Congress Hall is a local landmark, now suitably modernized without wringing out all the history. It's got everything you could ask for, including a spa and bicycle rentals, but can come off as a bit highfalutin.

✕ Eating & Drinking

Mad Batter　　　AMERICAN $
(☑ 609-884-5970; www.madbatter.com; 19 Jackson St, Carroll Villa Hotel; dinner mains $30, brunch $8-13; ⊙ 8am-10pm; ☑) Tucked away in a white Victorian B&B, this restaurant is locally beloved for brunch – including fluffy oat pancakes and rich clam chowder. The Chesapeake Bay Benedict, stuffed with crab, is to die for. Dinner is fine but pricier.

Lobster House　　　SEAFOOD $$
(☑ 609-884-8296; www.thelobsterhouse.com; 906 Schellengers Landing Rd; mains $15-30; ⊙ 11:30am-3pm & 4:30-10pm Mon-Sat, 11:30am-10pm Sun Apr-Dec, to 9pm Jan-Mar; ℗) This clubby-feeling classic on the wharf serves local oysters and scallops. No reservations means very long waits – go early or late, or have a drink on the boat-bar, the *Schooner American*, which is docked next to the restaurant.

★ **Willow Creek Winery**　　　WINERY
(☑ 609-770-8782; www.willowcreekwinerycapemay.com; 168 Stevens St; tastings $10-20; ⊙ 11am-5pm Mon-Thu, to 9:30pm Fri, to 8pm Sat, to 6pm Sun) The 'baby' of Cape May's six wineries, this former lima bean and dairy farm christened its first bottles in 2011, and produces a solid combo of reds and whites. The weekend tapas menu and sangria bar is pretty mind-blowing, and a tour around the 50 acres on an electric tram ($15) is a kick. The 'educational tasting' will smarten up your palate.

You can pick up fresh Jersey produce like sweet corn and peaches at their nearby Legates Farm.

❶ Getting There & Away

NJ Transit buses serve Cape May from NYC ($48.50, three to five hours), with a possible transfer at Atlantic City, and a discounted round-trip express bus from Philadelphia ($25, 3½ to four hours) during the summer. For onward car travel, the **Cape May-Lewes Ferry** (☑ 800-643-

3779; www.cmlf.com; 1200 Lincoln Blvd; car/passenger $35/10; ⏰7am-7:45pm Apr-Oct) crosses the bay in 1½ hours to Lewes, Delaware, near Rehoboth Beach.

PENNSYLVANIA

A horse and buggy trundles through the Lancaster fog before it is overtaken by a Philadelphia-bound sports car driven by a young tech entrepreneur. In Pittsburgh, children of immigrants who work as nurses in the city's burgeoning hospitals make experimental contemporary art. In Gettysburg, descendants of Union soldiers proudly fly Confederate flags. This is Pennsylvania, which contains within its 46,000 sq miles some of the Eastern seaboard's most striking landscapes, culture clashes and contradictions.

Here you'll find massive elk herds loping across forested ravines in the Pennsylvania Wilds; former steel towns embracing wine-fueled arts walks; cities populated by the descendants of America's founders living side-by-side with immigrants; Mennonites who eschew modern tech but run agribusiness empires. This is a state that never fails to fascinate, and while it's wowing you with its culture, it's feeding you great food and awesome landscapes at the same time.

[i] Getting There & Around

Pennsylvania is home to a number of airports, several of them with international connections; the eastern end is near the giant hub of New Jersey's Newark International, with connections around the world. Trains serve many of its major cities, while buses service most towns. That said, with so much of this state's beauty lying off the beaten path, renting a car and driving around on your own is highly recommended.

The main air access points are Philadelphia International Airport (p177) and Pittsburgh International Airport (p183). Both of these cities are also major hubs for Amtrak trains and Greyhound buses.

Philadelphia

Blessed with the glamour and culture of a big city, 'Philly' as it's affectionately known, also delights visitors with its rich history and small-town charm.

Sights & Activities

★Barnes Foundation MUSEUM

(Map p170; ☎215-278-7200; www.barnesfoundation.org; 2025 Benjamin Franklin Pkwy, Spring Garden; adult/student/child $25/5/free; ⏰11am-5pm Wed-Mon; 🚌7, 32, 33, 38, 48, 49) In the first half of the 20th century, collector and educator Albert C Barnes amassed a remarkable trove of artwork by Cézanne, Degas, Matisse, Renoir, Van Gogh and other European stars. Alongside, he set beautiful pieces of folk art from Africa and the Americas – an artistic desegregation that was shocking at the time. Today's Barnes Foundation is a contemporary shell, inside which is a faithful reproduction of the galleries of Barnes' original mansion (still in the Philadelphia suburbs).

The art is hung according to Barnes' vision, a careful juxtaposition of colors, themes and materials. In one room, all the portraits appear to be staring at a central point. Even more remarkable: you've likely never seen any of these works before, because Barnes' will limits reproduction and lending.

The first Sunday of the month admission is free. Tickets are limited to four per person and there's a focus on family activities.

★Independence Hall HISTORIC BUILDING

(Map p174; ☎877-444-6777; www.nps.gov/inde; 520 Chestnut St, Old City; ⏰8:30am-6pm, to 7pm late May-early Sep; [S]5th St) [FREE] The 'birthplace of American government,' this modest early 18th-century Georgian building is where delegates from the 13 colonies met to approve the Declaration of Independence on July 4, 1776. Expect a line out the door and around the block for this one – it's the prime attraction in a city packed with history.

The entrance is via the security screening area in the east wing on the corner of Chestnut and 5th Sts. Get free advance tickets and times for the next available tour at the nearby Independence Visitor Center (p177) or reserve online (fee $1). Budget for at least an hour-long wait in peak summer months.

Independence National Historical Park PARK

(Map p174; ☎215-965-2305; www.nps.gov/inde; Old City; ⏰visitor center & most sites 9am-5pm; [S]5th St) This L-shaped park, between 6th, 2nd, Walnut and Arch Sts, protects and honors the history and institutions that formed the foundation of the US government. Stroll around and you'll see storied buildings in which the seeds for the Revolutionary War

NEW YORK, NEW JERSEY & PENNSYLVANIA IN…

One Week

Start off in Philadelphia (p167), birthplace of American independence. Visit Independence Hall (p167) and the new Museum of the American Revolution, then spend an evening investigating the great restaurants and nightlife in up-and-coming neighborhoods like Fishtown.

Next, head to New Jersey for a bucolic night in Cape May (p166), a sleepy beach town full of Victorian charm. After a quick, scenic cruise along Ocean Dr, stop off overnight further up the Shore in Wildwood (p165), a treasure trove of iconic '50s kitsch. Land in New York City (p75) the following day and spend at least a couple of days blending touristy must-dos – such as the Top of the Rock (p91) and Central Park (p93) – with vibrant nightlife and eclectic dining.

Two Weeks

With NYC in your rearview mirror, head north along the majestic Hudson and its palisades for a night or two in Beacon (p143) or Hudson (p143), before reaching the Catskills (p146). After touring this beautiful region, head further north to the Adirondacks (p151) and its outdoor wonders, then loop back south through the Finger Lakes (p149) region with stops in wineries and waterfall-laden parks along the way. Spend a night in gorgeous college-town Ithaca (p150).

From here you can head towards the Canadian border to Buffalo (p156) and Niagara Falls (p158), or southwest to Pittsburgh (p180).

were planted and the US government came into bloom. You'll also find beautiful, shaded urban lawns dotted with plenty of squirrels, pigeons and, in warmer months, costumed actors. Rangers can provide information about it all at the Independence Visitor Center (p177).

★Museum of the American Revolution MUSEUM
(Map p174; ☎215-253-6731; www.amrevmuseum.org; 101 S 3rd St; adult/student/child $21/18/13; ⏰10am-5pm Sep-late May, 9:30am-6pm late May-Aug; [S]2nd St) This impressive, multimedia-rich museum will have you virtually participating in the American Revolution; interactive dioramas and 3-D experiences take you all the way from contentment with British rule to the eventual rejection of it. Learn about the events, people, cultures and religions that participated in one of the world's most important revolutions. Lots of hands-on displays and video stories mean kids will have as much fun as adults. Note that all tickets are timed: reserve them early online.

★Philadelphia Museum of Art MUSEUM
(Map p170; ☎215-763-8100; www.philamuseum.org; 2600 Benjamin Franklin Pkwy, East Fairmount Park; adult/student/child $20/14/free; ⏰10am-5pm Tue, Thu, Sat & Sun, to 8:45pm Wed & Fri; 🚌32, 38, 43) The city's premier cultural institution occupies a Grecian temple-like building housing a superb collection of Asian art, Renaissance masterpieces, postimpressionist works and modern pieces by Picasso, Duchamp and Matisse among others. Especially notable are galleries filled with complete architectural ensembles, including a medieval cloister, Chinese and Indian temples and a Japanese teahouse.

There's so much to see that a ticket covers admission for two days, here and at the separate **Perelman Building** (Map p170; ☎215-763-8100; www.philamuseum.org; 2525 Pennsylvania Ave, Fairmount; incl in admission to Philadelphia Museum of Art adult/student/child $20/14/free; ⏰10am-5pm Tue-Sun; 🚌32, 38, 43), Rodin Museum and two historic houses **Mount Pleasant** (www.philamuseum.org; 3800 Mt Pleasant Dr, East Fairmount Park; ⏰closed to public; 🚋W Girard Ave & 33rd St) and **Cedar Grove** (☎215-763-8100; www.philamuseum.org/historichouses; 1 Cedar Grove Dr, West Fairmount Park; adult/child $8/free; ⏰tours at 11am, 1pm & 2pm Thu-Sun, also 10am & 4pm 1st Sun of month Apr-Dec; 🚌38).

Mütter Museum MUSEUM
(Map p170; ☎215-560-8564; www.muttermuseum.org; 19 S 22nd St, Rittenhouse; adult/child $18/13; ⏰10am-5pm; 🚋22nd St) Maintained by the College of Physicians, this unique, only-in-Philadelphia attraction is a museum dedicated to rare, odd or disturbing medical conditions. Not for the squeamish, its nonetheless fascinating exhibits include a saponified body, a conjoined female fetus,

incredibly realistic wax models of medical conditions and skulls by the dozen.

The College of Physicians also hosts many events in the building, including classical music concerts and lectures – check the website for details. Note there's $2 off admission on Monday and Tuesday.

★ **Benjamin Franklin Museum** MUSEUM (Map p174; ☑ 215-965-2305; www.nps.gov/inde; Market St, btwn 3rd & 4th Sts, Old City; adult/child $5/2; ⊙ 9am-5pm; Ⓢ 2nd St) This underground museum is dedicated to Franklin's storied life as a printer (he started the nation's first newspaper), inventor (Bifocals! Lightning rods!) and political figure who signed the Declaration of Independence. The exhibition, divided into five areas, with each focusing on a particular trait of the man, is inventively laid out with interactive elements and plenty of famous Franklin quotations.

In the same courtyard, don't miss the **printing office** (Map p174; ☑ 215-965-2305; www.nps.gov/inde; Franklin Court, Market St btwn 3rd & 4th Sts, Old City; ⊙ 10am-5pm; Ⓢ 2nd St) **FREE**, where park rangers demonstrate an 18th-century printing press similar to that used by Franklin.

Rodin Museum MUSEUM (Map p170; ☑ 215-763-8100; www.rodinmuseum. org; 2151 Benjamin Franklin Pkwy, Spring Garden; suggested donation adult/student/child $10/7/ free; ⊙ 10am-5pm Wed-Mon; ☐ 7, 32, 33, 38, 48) This is the only institution outside of Paris dedicated to the French sculptor Auguste Rodin. The superb collection is based on works amassed by Jules E Mastbaum in the 1920s. There are versions of *The Thinker* and *Burghers of Calais* among its 140 sculptures from every part of Rodin's spectacular career.

Administered by the Philadelphia Museum of Art, the small museum's garden is always open and free.

Liberty Bell Center HISTORIC SITE (Map p174; ☑ 215-965-2305; www.nps.gov/inde; 526 Market St, Old City; ⊙ 9am-5pm, to 7pm late May-early Sep; Ⓢ 5th St) **FREE** A glass-walled building protects this icon of Philadelphia history from the elements. You can peek from outside, or join the line to file past, reading about the history and significance of the 2080lb object along the way. The line – and it can be a long one in peak summer months – starts on the building's northern end.

The gist of the story: originally called the State House Bell, it was made in 1751,

to commemorate the 50th anniversary of Pennsylvania's constitution. Mounted in Independence Hall (p167), it tolled on the first public reading of the Declaration of Independence. The crack developed in the 19th century, and the bell was retired in 1846.

One Liberty Observation Deck OBSERVATORY (Philly From the Top; Map p170; ☑ 215-561-3325; www.phillyfromthetop.com; 1650 Market St, Center City; adult/child $15/10; ⊙ 10am-8pm Sep-Apr, to 9pm May-Aug) One way to get a bird's-eye view of the city, especially pretty after dark, is to ride the ear-popping elevator up to this 883ft-high observation deck on the 57th floor of One Liberty Place. There are tickets allowing two visits within 48 hours, family deals and online discounts.

Shofuso Japanese House & Garden GARDENS (☑ 215-878-5097; www.japanesehouse.org; Horticultural Dr, West Fairmount Park; adult/child $12/8; ⊙ 10am-4pm Wed-Fri, 11am-5pm Sat & Sun Apr-Oct; ☐ 38) This picturesque house, built in Nagoya in 1953 to a 17th-century design, has been set in 1.2 acres of traditional Japanese gardens in Fairmount Park since 1958. Check online for various events, including tea ceremonies, that are held here (bookings and extra payment required).

The cherry trees blooming in spring are not to be missed

★ **City Hall** NOTABLE BUILDING (Map p170; ☑ 215-686-2840; www.phlvisitor center.com; cnr Broad & Market Sts; tower adult/student $8/4, interior & tower $15/8; ⊙ tower tours every 15min 9:30am-4:15pm, interior tour 12:30pm Mon-Fri; Ⓢ City Hall & 15th St) Completed in 1901 following 30 years of construction, City Hall takes up a whole block, and at 548ft is the world's tallest structure without a steel frame. The view from the observation area immediately beneath the 27-ton bronze statue of William Penn that crowns the tower takes in most of the city; reserve tickets as space is limited. The daily interior tour is a treat, too, and will give you a greater appreciation of this grand building. In winter, the **Rothman Ice Rink** (Map p170; www.centercityphila.org/parks/dilworth-park/roth man-rink; 1 S 15th St, Center City; adult/child $5/3, skate rental $10; ⊙ noon-9pm Mon-Thu, to 11pm Fri, 11am-11pm Sat, 11am-8pm Sun mid-Nov–Feb; Ⓜ City Hall & 15th St) sets up in Dilworth Park on the western side of the plaza.

NEW YORK, NEW JERSEY & PENNSYLVANIA PHILADELPHIA

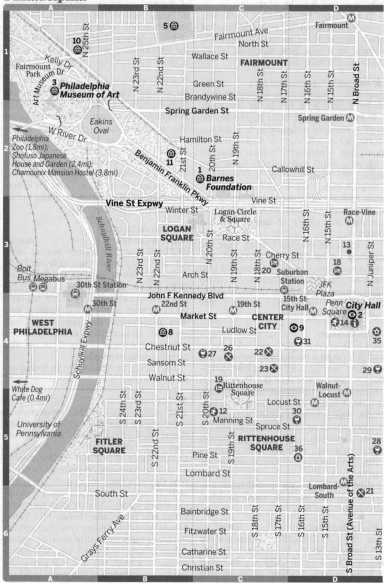

Eastern State Penitentiary   MUSEUM
(Map p170; ☎215-236-3300; www.easternstate.
org; 2027 Fairmount Ave, Fairmount; adult/child
$14/10; ☉10am-5pm; ☐7, 32, 33, 43, 48) The
modern prison didn't just happen – it was
invented, and Eastern State Penitentiary
was the first one, opened in 1829 and finally closed in 1971. A self-guided audio tour
leads you through the eerie, echoing halls;
one stop is Al Capone's famously luxurious
cell. There's also info on America's current
prison system, and art installations throughout. It's a popular stop, so expect crowds at
peak times; tickets are cheaper online. From

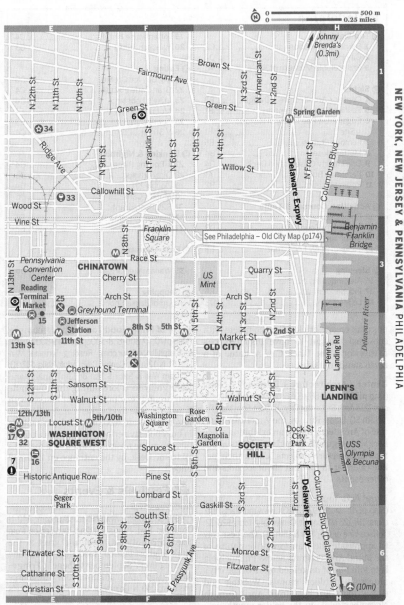

mid-September through Halloween, the prison hosts a terrifying haunted house.

Edgar Allan Poe National Historic Site

HISTORIC SITE

(Map p170; 215-597-8780; www.nps.gov/edal; 532 N 7th St, Poplar; 9am-5pm Fri-Sun; S Spring Garden: Market-Frankford Line) FREE Often called the creator of the horror story, Edgar Allan Poe lived for six years in Philadelphia, in five different houses. This historic site, his only Philly home still remaining, is now a small but interesting museum, with a lot of original items and restored rooms. Don't

Philadelphia

miss the creepy brick cellar (complete with cobwebs) thought to have inspired Poe's masterwork 'The Black Cat.' A statue of a raven stands outside.

Center / Architecture + Design CENTER
(Map p170; ☎215-569-3186; www.philadelphiacfa. org; 1218 Arch St, Center City; ⊗9am-5pm Mon-Fri; ⬛13th St) FREE Run by the American Institute of Architects, there's an exhibition space here with regularly changing exhibits about local architecture projects. Check their online calendar to find out about lectures and other events.

Mural Arts Tours TOURS
(Map p170; ☎215-925-3633; www.muralarts.org/ tours; 118-128 N Broad St, Center City; tours $23-32; ⬛Race-Vine or City Hall & 15th St) The best way to appreciate the transformative nature of the Mural Arts Program across Philadelphia is to join one of its guided tours of the city's numerous outdoor murals. Walking and trolley tours are held from April through November, while in the colder months you can join the excellent Love Letters tour, which uses the subway.

The Mural Finder Mobile, a free self-guided tour with smartphone-optimized map, is available on the website.

Taste of Philly Food Tour FOOD & DRINK
(Map p170; ☎800-838-3006, 215-545-8007; www. tasteofphillyfoodtour.com; Reading Terminal Market, 51 N 12th St, Center City; adult/child $17/10; ⊗10am Wed & Sat; ⬛11th or 13th) Snack and learn Philly food lore during this 75-minute tour around Reading Terminal Market with knowledgeable food writer Carolyn Wyman. Reservations are recommended, particularly in busy holiday periods, but you can also just turn up at the meeting point at the market's Welcome Desk, by the entrance on 12th and Filbert.

🎊 Festivals & Events

Audi Feastival FOOD & DRINK
(☎610-585-7038; www.phillyfeastival.com; 140 N Columbus Blvd, Penn's Landing; per person from $300; ⬛2nd St) Eat, meet and greet at the city's highest-lauded food fest, held one evening every September to benefit **Fringe-Arts** (Map p174; ☎215-413-1318; www.fringe arts.com; 140 N Columbus Blvd, Old City; tickets from $5; ⬛2nd St), the city's cultural organization that puts on the Fringe Festival.

★Mummers Parade CARNIVAL
(www.phillymummers.com; ⊗Jan 1) Uniquely Philly: a cross between Mardi Gras and a marching band competition, the elaborate costumes, music and deep lore of the various

mummer divisions and brigades make this a must-see in the bracing cold of winter. The parade starts by City Hall and moves down Broad St to finish at Washington Ave.

Fringe Festival PERFORMING ARTS
(www.fringearts.com) Running since 1996, the Fringe Festival sees 17 days in mid-September packed with performance art, events, productions and creative craziness.

🛏 Sleeping

★ **Apple Hostels** HOSTEL $
(Map p174; ☑215-922-0222; www.applehostels. com; 33 Bank St, Old St; dm/d with shared bath from $33/106; ❈@ 📶; Ⓢ2nd St) The Old City's best hostel is hidden down an alley and spans both sides of the street. The apple-green color scheme fits the name, but this Hosteling International–affiliated place is also strong on details: two spotless kitchens, lounges and a library, plus power outlets in lockers, USB ports and reading lights at every bed, free coffee and earplugs.

There are male, female and coed dorms, plus eight private rooms. The friendly staff run nightly activities such as walking tours, pasta nights and a Thursday bar crawl.

Chamounix Mansion Hostel HOSTEL $
(☑215-878-3676; www.philahostel.org; 3250 Chamounix Dr, West Fairmount Park; dm $22; ☉closed Dec 15-Jan 15; 🅿@ 📶; 🚌38 & 40) In a lovely wooded area of Fairmount Park, this handsome Hosteling International hostel is best for guests with their own transport. In its public areas, set with antiques, harp, oriental rugs and paintings, the place feels more like a B&B than a hostel; the dorms themselves are basic. There's also a great communal kitchen and free bicycles for getting around. A downside is that the building is closed (and all guests have to leave) between 11am and 4:30pm and there's a 2am curfew, not that you'd want to be wandering around this isolated part of the park at that hour.

From the bus stop on the corner of Ford and Cranston Rds it's around a 1-mile walk to the hostel, which is at the end of Chamounix Dr.

★ **Alexander Inn** BOUTIQUE HOTEL $$
(Map p170; ☑215-923-3535; www.alexanderinn. com; 301 S 12th St, Midtown Village; s/d from $135/150; ❈@ 📶; 🚌23, 40) Online photos undersell this place. The impeccably kept rooms have a subdued, slightly vintage style; some have old-fashioned half-size tubs. Original architectural details – including

stained-glass windows, oak moldings, marble-tiled floors – add to the atmosphere.

The included continental breakfast is convenient, and free snacks are available throughout the day.

Independent BOUTIQUE HOTEL $$
(Map p170; ☑215-772-1440; www.theindepend enthotel.com; 1234 Locust St, Midtown Village; r from $160; ❈@ 📶; Ⓢ Walnut-Locust) At the heart of the 'Gayborhood' and a block from the Avenue of the Arts, the Independent is housed in a handsome brick Georgian Revival building with a four-story atrium decorated with a 30ft watercolor. The 24 wood-floored rooms are uncluttered and sunny, and the complimentary off-site gym pass, and wine and cheese served Monday through Thursday, sweeten the deal.

Le Méridien HOTEL $$
(Map p170; ☑215-422-8200; www.starwood hotels.com; 1421 Arch St, Center City; d from $230; ⊖❈@ 📶; Ⓢ City Hall & 15th St, 🚈Suburban) Though part of a luxury chain, the central location and tasteful appropriation of an old building to make a contemporary hotel sets Le Méridien apart. Entirely smoke-free, the rooms sport monochrome design with red accents. It's also pet-friendly and has a wide range of facilities, including a fitness and business center.

Windsor Suites HOTEL $$
(Map p170; ☑215-981-5678; www.thewindsor suites.com; 1700 Benjamin Franklin Pkwy, Center City; ste from $150; 🅿⊖❈@ 📶; Ⓢ City Hall & 15th St, 🚈Suburban) The comfortable and roomy suites here come with full kitchens; some also have balconies. There are options for extended stays or monthly rentals, as well as good facilities, including a rooftop pool (May to mid-September).

Staff are friendly and the hotel allows pets to stay free (they even get their own amenities).

★ **Rittenhouse Hotel** HOTEL $$$
(Map p170; ☑215-546-9000; www.rittenhouse hotel.com; 210 W Rittenhouse Sq, Rittenhouse; d from $490; 🅿⊖❈@ 📶; 🚌9, 12, 17, 21, 42) Rooms at this five-star – excuse us, make that five-*diamond* – hotel on Rittenhouse Sq have marble baths. Of the downtown options with a half-Olympic-sized pool, this is one of the nicest. It serves a top-notch brunch and a soothing afternoon tea service with music. On Friday and Saturday a live jazz band plays in the library bar.

Philadelphia – Old City

N 0   200 m
0   0.1 miles

Philadelphia – Old City

✕ Eating

Big Gay Ice Cream
ICE CREAM $

(Map p170; ☑ 267-886-8024; www.biggayicecream.com; 1351 South St, Center City; ice cream from $4; ⊙ 11:30am-10pm Sun-Thu, to midnight Fri & Sat; Ⓢ Lombard-South Station) Ranked one of the best ice creams in the world, Big Gay Ice Cream is not a Philly original (it's NYC-based), but who can resist the lure of its signature 'Salty Pimp' cone: vanilla, *dulce de leche* and a chocolate shell. The descriptions are as double-entendre-filled as the cones are good, so prepare for chuckles as you peruse the menu.

Tom's Dim Sum
CHINESE $

(Map p170; ☑ 215-923-8880; www.tomsdimsumpa.com; 59 N 11th St, Chinatown; dim sum $2-7, mains $7-14; ⊙ 11am-9pm Mon-Fri, to 10pm Sat & Sun; Ⓢ 11th St, Ⓡ Jefferson) Dim sum are served throughout the day at this casual spot. Dig into tasty buns and soup dumplings, as well as rice plates and noodles.

★ Zahav
MIDDLE EASTERN $

(Map p174; ☑ 215-625-8800; www.zahavrestaurant.com; 237 St James Pl, Old City; mains $10-14, tasting menus $48; ⊙ 5-10pm Sun-Thu, to 11pm Fri & Sat; Ⓢ 2nd St) Zahav means 'gold' in Hebrew and that's what you'll find here in terms of gastronomy. The menu at this sophisticated modern Israeli restaurant sees chef Michael Solomonov, winner of a James Beard Foundation Award, drawing primarily from North African, Persian and Levantine kitchens for inspiration.

Pick your own meze and grills, or go for the tasting menu, but under no circumstances bypass their luscious hummus served with a chef's selection of toppings. Book well ahead or turn up early (as soon as they open is recommended) for a spot at the bar.

Luke's Lobster
SEAFOOD $$

(Map p170; ☑ 215-564-1415; www.lukeslobster.com; 130 S 17th St, Rittenhouse; lobster roll $17; ⊙ 11am-9pm Sun-Thu, to 10pm Fri & Sat; 🚌 9, 21, 42, Ⓢ City Hall & 15th St) As one diner put it: 'Lobster roll. Drop mic.' Part of a casual East Coast chain serving authentic tastes of Maine using sustainably sourced seafood. Wash down your buttered-bun lobster roll with a wild-blueberry soda.

★ White Dog Cafe
AMERICAN $$

(☑ 215-386-9224; www.whitedog.com; 3420 Sansom St, University City; dinner mains $19-42; ⊙ 11:30am-9:30pm Mon-Thu, to 10pm Fri, 9:30am-10pm Sat, 9:30am-9pm Sun; 🖋; 🚌 30, 42, Ⓢ 34th St) If the dozen Boston terriers on the wall seem incongruous with the food, don't worry: this place has been serving farm-to-table since 1983. Come here for your truffles and artisan cheeses, peak summer tomatoes and plenty more. Yes, the Greyhound is the signature drink. Need you have asked?

Cuba Libre
CUBAN $$

(Map p174; ☑ 215-627-0666; www.cubalibrerestaurant.com; 10 S 2nd St, Old City; mains $20-32; ⊙ 11:30am-10pm Mon-Wed, to 11pm Thu & Fri, 10:30am-11pm Sat, 10:30am-10pm Sun; 🖋; Ⓢ 2nd St) Colonial America couldn't feel further away at this festive, multistory Cuban eatery and rum bar, part of a small chain found in several East Coast cities. The creative menu, featuring Cuba's *criollo* (home-style) cuisine, includes shrimp ceviche, Cuban sandwiches, guava-spiced BBQ and excellent mojitos. A $45 tasting menu lets you get a variety of the specialties.

★ Gran Caffè L'Aquila
ITALIAN $$

(Map p170; ☑ 215-568-5600; www.grancaffelaquila.com; 1716 Chestnut St, Rittenhouse; mains $16-35; ⊙ 7am-10pm Mon-Thu, to 11pm Fri, 8am-11pm Sat, to 10pm Sun, bar open 1hr later; 🚌 9, 21, 42, Ⓡ 19th St) Mamma mia, this is impressive Italian food. Not only are the flavors everything you could ask for, one of the owners is an award-winning gelato maker and the 2nd floor has its own gelato factory. Some of the main courses even have savory gelato as a garnish. Coffee is house-roasted and the dapper waitstaff are eager to please.

The three co-owners came here after their village in Italy was destroyed by a 2014 earthquake. Reservations are recommended.

Morimoto
JAPANESE $$$

(Map p170; ☑ 215-413-9070; www.morimotorestaurant.com; 723 Chestnut St, Washington Sq West; mains $26-58; ⊙ 11:30am-2pm & 5-10pm Mon-Thu, to midnight Fri, 5pm-midnight Sat, 5-10pm Sun; 🖋; Ⓢ 8th St) Morimoto is high concept and heavily stylized, from a dining room that looks like a futuristic aquarium to a menu of globe-spanning influences and eclectic combinations. A meal at this *Iron Chef* regular's restaurant is a theatrical experience.

If price isn't a problem, opt for the *omakase* ($125) – the chef's special choice of dishes.

🍷 Drinking & Nightlife

1 Tippling Place
BAR

(Map p170; ☑ 215-665-0456; www.1tpl.com; 2006 Chestnut St, Rittenhouse; ⊙ 5pm-2am Tue-Sun; 🚌 9, 17, 21, 42, Ⓡ 19th St) Whether you pull up

LOCAL KNOWLEDGE

CLASSIC PHILLY FLAVOUR

If there's one thing you *must* eat while in town its a cheesesteak. Philadelphians argue over the nuances of these hot sandwiches comprised of thin-sliced, griddle-cooked beef on a chewy roll: there are pork, chicken and even vegan versions available, but die-hard fans will tell you that only the classic beef really qualifies. And don't get people started on where the best one is to be found – there's as many opinions on this as there are areas of the city.

What a visitor most needs to know is how to order. First say the kind of cheese you want – prov (provolone), American (melty yellow) or whiz (molten orange Cheez Whiz). Then 'wit' (with) or 'widdout' (without), referring to fried onions: 'Prov wit,' for example, or 'whiz widdout. And if it's a take-out place, have your money ready – cheesesteak vendors are famously in a hurry.

a seat at the bar or find a cozy couch to relax on, this spot has everything you could want in a craft cocktail bar. Extra points if you can spot more than four typos on the menu. Note: this place looks closed even when it isn't, with minimal (read: zero) outdoor signage.

★ Monk's Cafe BAR

(Map p170; ☎215-545-7005; www.monkscafe.com; 264 S 16th St, Rittenhouse; 🕒11:30am-2am, kitchen to 1am; [S]Walnut-Locust) Hop fans crowd this mellow wood-paneled place for Belgian and American craft beers on tap – it has one of the best selections in the city. For those needing assistance, a 'Beer Bible' is available.

There's also a reasonably priced food menu, with typical mussels-and-fries as well as a daily vegan special.

R2L Restaurant LOUNGE

(Map p170; ☎215-564-5337; www.r2lrestaurant.com; 50 S 16th St, Center City; 🕒lounge 4pm-1am Mon-Thu, to 2am Fri & Sat, to 11pm Sun; [S]City Hall & 15th St, [R]Suburban) The view, the view, the view. And did we mention the view? This upscale spot serves up the nightscape of Philly along with whatever is on the menu. Craft cocktails are smooth and balanced, but even tap water would seem ritzy when you're looking out at the cosmos of lights below you.

Happy hour (4:30pm to 6:30pm Monday to Friday) offers $4 beers, $7 wines, $8 cocktails and snacks from $2.

★ Trestle Inn BAR

(Map p170; ☎267-239-0290; www.thetrestleinn.com; 339 N 11th St, Callowhill; 🕒5pm-2am Wed-Sat; [S]Spring Garden: Broad Street Line) On a dark corner this classed-up old dive is notable for its friendliness and craft cocktails, which can be enjoyed in a happy hour that lasts from 5pm until 8pm. From 9pm on Thursday and 10pm on Friday and Saturday go-go dancers get their groove on under the disco ball as DJs play hits from the 1960s onward.

There's a cover charge of $5 after 10pm at the weekends.

Double Knot BAR

(Map p170; ☎215-631-3868; www.doubleknotphilly.com; 120 S 13th St, Midtown Village; 🕒8am-midnight Sun-Tue, to 1am Wed & Thu, to 2am Fri & Sat; [S]13th St or Walnut-Locust) This is one of the few places in Philly that serves sake properly (poured into an overflowing cup inside a wooden *masu* container). They also make great craft cocktails and have a delicious food menu. It can get crowded, but the stylish decor and friendly service make it a fun spot to grab a bite and late-night drink.

From 5pm they open up the basement, which hides an impressive Japanese restaurant with a sushi bar and *robatayaki* (flame-grilled cooked items).

Tavern on Camac GAY & LESBIAN

(TOC; Map p170; ☎215-545-0900; www.tavernoncamac.com; 243 S Camac St, Midtown Village; 🕒piano bar 4pm-2am, restaurant 5pm-midnight Sun, Mon, Wed & Thu, to 1am Fri & Sat, club 9pm-2am; [S]Walnut-Locust) One of the longest-established gay bars in Philly has a piano bar and restaurant downstairs. Upstairs is Ascend, a small club with a dance floor; Tuesday is karaoke night, Friday and Saturday have DJs. And don't overlook Showtune Sunday.

★ Dirty Franks BAR

(Map p170; ☎215-732-5010; www.dirtyfranksbar.com; 347 S 13th St, Washington Sq West; 🕒11am-2am; 🚌23, 40) In business since 1933, Franks' regulars call this bar an 'institution' with some irony, but it does have grunge style as well as housing the Off The Wall gallery. Like many Philly dives, it offers the 'city-wide special': a shot of Jim Beam and a can of PBR for $2.50. Need cheaper? Try the 'DF Shelf of Shame' beer for just two bucks!

The bar's exterior is decorated with the mural **Famous Franks** (Map p170; www. muralarts.org/artworks/famous-franks; 347 S 13th St, Midtown Village; 🚌23, 40).

☆ Entertainment

PhilaMOCA   PERFORMING ARTS
(Philadelphia Mausoleum of Contemporary Art; Map p170; 🗷267-519-9651; www.philamoca.org; 531 N 12th St, Poplar; 🚇Spring Garden: Broad Street Line) A former tombstone store, then producer Diplo's studios, this eclectic space now has an equally eclectic program of cult movie nights, live-music shows, art, comedy and more.

Wanamaker Organ   LIVE MUSIC
(Map p170; 🗷484-684-7250; www.wanamaker organ.com; 1300 Market St, Macy's, Center City; ⊗concerts noon Mon-Sat, plus 5:30pm Mon, Tue, Thu & Sat, 7pm Wed & Fri; 🚇13th St) Back in 1909 when Macy's was Wanamaker's, owner John Wanamaker installed this enormous pipe organ hosting free concerts to delight shoppers and make them linger. The tradition lives on, with classical and pop tunes filling the department store's central atrium a couple of times a day.

It's a treat for visitors who are welcome to tour the console area (2nd floor) and meet the organist following the daily concerts.

Johnny Brenda's   LIVE MUSIC
(🗷215-739-9684; www.johnnybrendas.com; 1201 N Frankford Ave, Fishtown; tickets $5-20; ⊗kitchen 11am-1am, showtimes vary; 🚇Girard, Market-Frankford Line) One of the hubs of Philly's indie-rock scene, this is a great small venue with a balcony, plus a solid restaurant and bar with equally indie-minded beers.

🛍 Shopping

Omoi Zakka Shop   STATIONERY
(Map p170; 🗷215-545-0963; www.omoionline.com; 1608 Pine St, Rittenhouse; ⊗11am-7pm Mon-Sat, noon-5pm Sun; 🚇Lombard-South St) Get your inner Japanophile on with this shop that embraces the concept of *zakka* – stocking all things that might make life a little better. Fashion items, books, housewares, stationery and more, all with a Japan-inspired eye for cuteness or good design.

★Shane Confectionery   FOOD & DRINKS
(Map p174; 🗷215-922-1048; www.shanecandies. com; 110 Market St, Old City; ⊗11am-8pm Sun-Thu, to 10pm Fri & Sat; 🚇2nd St) Since 1863 this wonderfully old-school candy shop has been making sweet treats, including buttercreams and slabs, from antique molds. With the shop assistants dressed in Victorian garb it's like stepping back in time. Settle down in the historic hot-chocolate kitchen in the back where you can indulge in a flight of luscious drinks for $15.

Tours ($10) of the operation are held on Friday at 6:30pm.

ℹ Information

City Hall Visitor Center (Map p170; 🗷267-514-4757; www.phlvisitorcenter.com/attraction/city-hall-visitor-center; City Hall, Center City; ⊗9am-5pm Mon-Fri, 11am-4pm every 3rd Sat; 🚇City Hall & 15th St) Come here to buy tickets for tours of City Hall and its tower. Information on many other city tourist attractions also available.

Independence Visitor Center (Map p174; 🗷800-537-7676; www.phlvisitorcenter.com; 599 Market St, Old City; ⊗8:30am-7pm, longer hours in summer; 🚇5th St) This large center covers the national park and provides tourist information on Philadelphia. You can purchase tickets to many museums, book a slot for a visit to Independence Hall (necessary in peak summer months), watch a historical documentary, grab refreshments and – crucially – take a toilet break.

ℹ Getting There & Away

AIR
Philadelphia International Airport (PHL; 🗷215-937-6937; www.phl.org; 8000 Essington Ave, Southwest Philadelphia; 🚆Airport Line), 10 miles southwest of Center City, is a hub for American Airlines, and is served by direct international flights. There are five terminals so check which one you are arriving at and departing from before you set off.

BUS
Greyhound, Peter Pan Bus Lines (www.peter panbus.com), NJ Transit (www.njtransit.com) and the no-frills Chinatown Bus (www.china town-bus.org) all depart from the **Greyhound Terminal** (Map p170; 🗷215-931-4075; www. greyhound.com; 1001 Filbert St, Chinatown; 🚇11th St, 🚆Jefferson) downtown, near the convention center; Greyhound goes nationwide, Peter Pan focuses on the northeast, NJ Transit gets you to New Jersey and the Chinatown bus connects to NYC.

From just west of 30th St Station, **Megabus** (Map p170; http://us.megabus.com; JFK Blvd & N 30th St, University City; S 30th St, R 30th St) serves major US cities in the northeast and Toronto. For NYC and Boston, **Bolt Bus** (Map p170; ✆ 877-265-8287; www.boltbus.com; JFK Blvd & N 30th St, University City; S 30th St, R 30th St) has the roomiest buses.

Fares to NYC (2½ hours) can be as low as $9 when booked online.

CAR & MOTORCYCLE

From the north and south, I-95 (Delaware Expwy) follows the eastern edge of the city along the Delaware River, with several exits for Center City. In the north of the city, I-276 (Pennsylvania Turnpike) runs east over the river to connect with the New Jersey Turnpike.

TRAIN

Just west of downtown across the Schuylkill, beautiful neoclassical **30th St Station** (✆ 1-800-872-7245; www.amtrak.com; 2955 Market St, University City; S 30th St) is a major hub. From here, Amtrak provides service on its Northeast Corridor line to New York City ($60 to $152, 1½ hours), Boston ($104 to $204, 5½ to 6½ hours) and Washington, DC ($59 to $128, two hours), as well as to Lancaster ($20, 1¼ hours) and Pittsburgh ($87, nine to 10 hours).

A slower but cheaper way to get to NYC is on regional SEPTA (www.septa.org) to Trenton ($9, 50 minutes), then NJ Transit (www.njtransit. com) to NYC's Penn Station ($16.75, 1½ hours). NJ Transit's Atlantic City Rail Line also connects 30th St Station with the seaside resort ($10.75, 1½ hours).

❶ Getting Around

For timetables and further information check with **SEPTA** (✆ 215-580-7800; www.septa.org), which operates Philadelphia's transit system.

Bicycle Walk-up rates for Philly's bike-share system Indego (www.rideindego.com) is $12 for an all-day unlimited-ride pass.

Buses Convenient for quick hops across Center City and further afield.

Ferries From late May to early September the RiverLink ferry connects Penn's Landing and Camden's waterfront.

Subway & Trolley Philly has two subways and a trolley line (fare $2.50, exact change). Purchase the stored-value key card for discounted fares.

Taxi Easy to hail Downtown. Flag fall is $2.70, then $2.70 per mile or portion thereof. All licensed taxis have GPS and most accept credit cards. Rideshares are also commonly used.

Walking Downtown, it's barely 2 miles between the Delaware and Schuylkill Rivers, so you can walk most places.

Pennsylvania Dutch Country

Lancaster County and the broader space between Reading and the Susquehanna River is the center of the so-called Pennsylvania Dutch community. The term refers to myriad religious orders and cultures of Germanic roots (*Deutsch* – mistakenly anglicized to Dutch) who have lived here since the 18th century; Amish, Mennonites and German Baptist (Brethren) are the best known. One common cultural thread: all are devoted to various degrees of low-tech plain living.

This simple life, with its picturesque horse-drawn buggies, ironically attracts busloads of visitors and has spawned an astoundingly kitschy tourist industry. Get onto the back roads and you can appreciate the quiet pastoral serenity these religious orders have preserved.

Small settlements in the area include train-mad Strasburg and pretty, red-brick Lititz. Ephrata is headquarters of Ten Thousand Villages, a massive Mennonite-run fair-trade imports store with branches all over the country.

◉ Sights

★ Railroad Museum of Pennsylvania   MUSEUM

(✆ 717-687-8628; www.rrmuseumpa.org; 300 Gap Rd, Ronks; adult/child $10/8; ⏱ 9am-5pm Tue-Sat, noon-5pm Sun year-round, plus 9am-5pm Mon Apr-Oct) Set over nearly 18 acres, the Railroad Museum of Pennsylvania has 100 gigantic mechanical marvels to climb around and admire. Combo tickets are available for the **Strasburg Railroad** (✆ 866-725-9666; www. strasburgrailroad.com; 301 Gap Rd, Ronks; coach class adult/child $15.50/8.50; ♿) across the road. This place is packed with kids of all ages.

National Toy Train Museum   MUSEUM

(✆ 717-687-8976; www.nttmuseum.org; 300 Paradise Lane, Ronks; adult/child $7.50/4.50; ⏱ 10am-5pm May-Oct, hours vary Nov-Apr; ♿) Let's be clear: you can have never touched a toy train in your life and still love this odd little museum. The push-button interactive dioramas are so up to date and clever (such as a 'drive-in movie' that's a live video of kids working the trains), and the walls packed with so many gleaming railcars, that you can't help but feel a bit of that childlike Christmas-morning wonder.

The **Red Caboose Motel** (✆ 717-687-5000; www.redcaboosemotel.com; 312 Paradise Lane,

Ronks; d from $95; P❋☎) next door to the museum allows even nonguests to climb the silo in back for wonderful views (50¢), and kids can enjoy a small petting zoo.

Landis Valley Museum   MUSEUM
(📞717-569-0401; www.landisvalleymuseum.org; 2451 Kissel Hill Rd, Lancaster; adult/child $12/8; ⊙9am-5pm Wed-Sat, noon-5pm Sun year-round, plus 9am-5pm Tue Mar-Dec; P) Based on an 18th-century village, this open-air museum is the best way to get an overview of early Pennsylvania Dutch culture, and Mennonite culture in particular. Costumed staff are on hand to demonstrate tin-smithing, among other things, and there's a tavern, a gun shop and several beautiful crafts exhibits.

🛏 Sleeping & Eating

🛏 Lancaster

Cork Factory   BOUTIQUE HOTEL $$
(📞717-735-2075; www.corkfactoryhotel.com; 480 New Holland Ave, Suite 3000; r from $160; P❋❋☎) An abandoned brick behemoth of a factory now houses this hotel, one of the more stylish properties in the area. The posh rooms are outfitted with exposed brick, understated decor and a general sense of casual cool. It's a short drive from downtown.

Lancaster Brewing Co   PUB FOOD $$
(📞717-391-6258; www.lancasterbrewing.com; 302 N Plum St; mains $10-29; ⊙11:30am-10pm; ♿) This brewery, established in 1995, is a local favorite. The restaurant serves hearty but sophisticated food – lamb burger with tzatziki, hummus tacos or pretzel-crusted chicken, say – and housemade sausages at tables with copper-clad tops and great views of the brewing tanks.

★Maison   EUROPEAN $$$
(📞717-293-5060; www.maisonlancaster.com; 230 N Prince St; mains $26-32; ⊙5-10pm Wed-Sat; 🍴) A husband-and-wife team run this homey but meticulous place downtown, giving local farm products a rustic Italian-French treatment: pork braised in milk, housemade rabbit sausage, fried squash blossoms or handmade gnocchi, depending on the season.

❶ Getting There & Away

Lancaster lies at the heart of a squished 'H' shape made by Rte 30, Rte 283 and Rte 222. Buses head to Philly and Pittsburgh, but driving your own vehicle is the best option for sightseeing here.

Lancaster town is also served by Amtrak trains, which run frequently to Philadelphia ($20 to $29, 1¼ hours) and twice a day to Pittsburgh ($65, eight to nine hours).

Head 9 miles east from Lancaster on Rte 30 to reach Strasburg. The area is most easily accessible by car, but can also be reached via **RRTA** (Red Rose Transit Authority; 📞717-393-3315; www.redrosetransit.com) bus services.

Pennsylvania Wilds

North-central Pennsylvania, known as 'the Wilds,' is largely deep forest with an occasional regal building or grand mansion – remnants of the late 19th century, when lumber, coal and oil brought wealth to this now little-visited patch of the state. The cash cow of resource extraction was eventually milked dry by the turn of the 20th century, and the land fell on hard times. Since the bust, this swath of 12 counties has reverted to its wild state; much of the area is national forest or state park land.

⊙ Sights

★Cherry Springs State Park   STATE PARK
(📞814-435-1037; www.visitpaparks.com; 4639 Cherry Springs Rd, Coudersport; ⊙24hr) Considered one of the best places for stargazing east of the Mississippi, this mountaintop state park seems to have plenty of space, but be sure to book well ahead in July and August, when the Milky Way is almost directly overhead. There's a $6.50 transaction fee for making overnight reservations.

Leonard Harrison State Park   STATE PARK
(📞570-724-3061; www.visitpaparks.com; 4797 Rte 660, Wellsboro; ⊙park dawn-dusk, visitor center 10am-4:30pm Mon-Thu, to 6:30pm Fri-Sun; P) **FREE** This park has full views of the **Pine Creek Gorge**, aka the Grand Canyon of PA, with trails that descend 800ft down to the creek below. A visitor center has toilets and a modest display of local fauna, and a viewing deck makes this side more accessible for people not planning to hike. For the undeveloped side go to Colton Point State Park instead.

★Kinzua Bridge Skywalk   BRIDGE
(📞814-778-5467; www.visitpaparks.com; 1721 Lindholm Rd, Mt Jewett; ⊙skywalk 8am-dusk, visitor center to 6pm) **FREE** The world's tallest railroad structure when it was built in 1882, this 301ft-high bridge was rebuilt in steel in 1900 – but then partially collapsed in 2003, when it was hit by an F1-grade tornado. The

remaining piece, jutting out into the air, is now an observation deck, with an impressive and perhaps unnerving view over the ruined steel piers and the valley below.

🛏 Sleeping & Eating

Mansfield Inn   MOTEL **$**
(☎570-662-2136; www.mansfieldinn.com; 26 S Main St, Mansfield; d from $60; 🅿😑❄🛜) There may be more charming B&Bs deeper in the PA Wilds, but this motel is hard to beat for straight-ahead value. The walls are thin, the rooms are clean and our wallets are happy.

Night & Day Coffee Cafe   CAFE **$**
(☎570-662-1143; http://nightanddaycoffee.wix site.com/cafe; 2 N Main St, Mansfield; sandwiches $5.50-8.50; ⏰7am-7pm Mon-Fri, to 5pm Sat, 8am-5pm Sun; 🍴) Well worth detouring for, the Night & Day Coffee Cafe proudly claims to be enriching the neighborhood one latte at a time, and it's doing a good job of it. Boutique coffees, great chai and a wide selection of specialty salads and sandwiches make for a perfect breakfast or a great lunch.

ⓘ Getting There & Away

Driving is your only option to reach the Pennsylvania Wilds. Allegheny National Forest is about 100 miles northwest of Pittsburgh and 90 miles southwest of Erie, NY. Route 6 makes for a scenic route that traverses much of the region, with the tiny college town of Mansfield acting as an eastern gateway.

Pittsburgh

There may be more beautiful cities than Pittsburgh, but few mix the seemingly contradictory aesthetics of filigreed beaux-arts elegance with muscular art-deco swagger. This is a city of stone and steel, with old public libraries and brick row houses beside wide bridges and towering skyscrapers. There's an old-school class to Pittsburgh's good looks, underlined by an attitude towards dining, drinking and the arts that is genuinely innovative.

Pittsburgh's surroundings also set the city apart. Situated between the Monongahela and Allegheny Rivers and the upland ridge of Mt Washington, this city has a distinctive geography; physically, it is very much defined by its mountains and rivers. While this is the main urban center for western Pennsylvania, it has avoided the economic depression of the surrounding region by

investing in 'meds and eds' – hospitals and universities – buttressing its economy with expansive intellectual energy.

⊙ Sights & Activities

Points of interest in Pittsburgh are scattered in every neighborhood, but because of the hills it's difficult to walk between them. Bike, taxi or bus (or light rail in some areas) are the best ways to span suburbs. The usual ridesharing services are well represented in Pittsburgh.

★**Andy Warhol Museum**   MUSEUM
(☎412-237-8300; www.warhol.org; 117 Sandusky St; adult/child $20/10, 5-10pm Fri $10/5; ⏰10am-5pm Tue-Thu, Sat & Sun, to 10pm Fri) This six-story museum celebrates Pittsburgh's coolest native son, Andy Warhol, who moved to NYC, got a nose job and made himself famous with pop art. The exhibits start with Warhol's earliest drawings and commercial illustrations and include a simulated Velvet Underground happening, a DIY 'screen test' and pieces of Warhol's extensive knickknack collection. Cans of inflatable Campbell's soup are for sale.

★**Duquesne Incline**   FUNICULAR
(☎412-381-1665; www.duquesneincline.org; 1197 W Carson St; one-way adult/child $2.50/1.25; ⏰5:30am-12:30am Mon-Sat, 7am-12:30am Sun) This nifty funicular and its **Monongahela Incline** (☎412-381-1665; www.duquesneincline.org; 5 Grandview Ave; one-way adult/child $2.50/1.25; ⏰5:30am-12:30am Mon-Sat, 7am-12:30am Sun) twin down the road, both built in the late 19th century, are Pittsburgh icons, zipping up the steep slope of Mt Washington every five to 10 minutes. They provide commuters with a quick connection, and give visitors great city views, especially at night. You can make a loop, going up one, walking along aptly named Grandview Ave (about 1 mile, or take bus 40) and coming down the other.

If you ride just one, make it the Duquesne (du-*kane*). At the top, you can pay 50¢ to see the gears and cables at work.

Frick Art & Historical Center   MUSEUM
(☎412-371-0600; www.thefrickpittsburgh.org; 7227 Reynolds St; ⏰10am-5pm Tue-Thu, Sat & Sun, to 9pm Fri) **FREE** Henry Clay Frick, of New York City's Frick Collection (p92) fame, built his steel fortune in Pittsburgh. This Frick shows a small art collection (including beautiful medieval icons), plus his cars. For more art and general splendor, join a tour (adult/child $15/8) of **Clayton**, the family mansion.

Carnegie Museums
MUSEUM

(☑ 412-622-3131; www.carnegiemuseums.org; 4400 Forbes Ave; adult/child both museums $20/12; ⊙10am-5pm Mon, Wed & Fri-Sun, to 8pm Thu year-round, plus 10am-5pm Tue Jun-Aug; ⊕) Founded in 1895, these neighboring institutions are both tremendous troves of knowledge. The **Carnegie Museum of Art** has European treasures and an excellent architectural collection, while the **Carnegie Museum of Natural History** features a complete *Tyrannosaurus rex* skeleton and beautiful old dioramas. The art museum is open until 11pm on the third Thursday of the month.

Cathedral of Learning
TOWER

(☑ 412-624-6001; www.tour.pitt.edu; 4200 Fifth Ave; ⊙9am-2:30pm Mon-Sat, 11am-2:30pm Sun) **FREE** Soaring 42 stories, this Gothic tower at the center of the University of Pittsburgh is a city landmark. Visit to see the delightful **Nationality Rooms**, 31 classrooms themed to localities ranging from Russia to Syria to Africa to the Philippines. Self-guided audio tours (adult/child $4/2) are available daily in summer, or weekends during school term. New rooms may be added in the future.

Center for PostNatural History
MUSEUM

(☑ 412-223-7698; www.postnatural.org; 4913 Penn Ave; by donation; ⊙noon-4pm Sun) **FREE** 'Postnatural history,' according to the artist-founder of this quirky museum, is the field of plants and animals designed by humankind. Learn all about spider-silk-making goats, selective breeding and more. Probably not your best first-date spot, but definitely a fun and unconventional place to learn about all things *human*-ipulated.

Wigle Whiskey
DISTILLERY

(☑ 412-224-2827; www.wiglewhiskey.com; 2401 Smallman St; tours $20-25; ⊙11am-6pm Mon, to 8pm Tue-Thu, to 10pm Fri, 10am-10pm Sat, 1-5pm Sun) This family-owned craft distillery in a brick warehouse in the Strip gives tours on Saturdays and has inexpensive sample flights ($10) of the many libations. Whiskey is a top choice, but there's also gin, vodka, bitters and even a housemade absinthe and more.

Pittsburgh Glass Center
ART

(☑ 412-365-2145; www.pittsburghglasscenter.org; 5472 Penn Ave; ⊙10am-7pm Mon-Thu, to 4pm Fri-Sun) See a variety of glass-making techniques, and even try your hand at making something yourself in a demo. Or take an actual class; the PGC offers everything from newbie level to advanced (prices vary).

'Burgh Bits & Bites
FOOD & DRINK

(☑ 412-901-7150; www.burghfoodtour.com; tours $43) These two-hour food tours through various neighborhoods are a fun way to discover the city's unique ethnic eats. The Strip District tour is the most popular, but Bits & Bites also visits Bloomfield, Brookline, Lawrenceville, the South Side and more.

Pittsburgh History & Landmarks Foundation
WALKING

(☑ 412-471-5808; www.phlf.org; tours free-$20) This group runs a free walking tour from Market Sq on Wednesday at 10am, among other excursions. Some paid, docent-led tours are also available.

🛏 Sleeping

Residence Inn by Marriott North Shore
HOTEL **$$**

(☑ 412-321-2099; www.marriott.com; 574 W General Robinson St; d from $140, ste $170-320; ⓟ⊕✳@⊛⊜) This renovated chain-hotel option has a pool, a fitness center, free breakfasts and rooms that feel like mansions. It's also well located: a quick zip over the bridges to the downtown area, or within walking distance of some of the North Side attractions. Note: it can be a zoo if the Steelers or the Pirates are playing.

★ Priory Hotel
INN **$$**

(☑ 412-231-3338; www.thepriory.com; 614 Pressley St; s $100-130, d $155-230, ste $180-295; ⓟ✳⊜) The monks had it good when this was still a Catholic monastery: spacious rooms, high ceilings, a fireplace in the parlor. Breakfast, with its pastries and cold cuts, is reminiscent of a European hostel. It's on the North Side, in the historic-but-scruffy Deutschtown area. The tiny Monk's Bar just off the lobby is open 5pm to 11pm daily – perfect for an evening tipple.

Omni William Penn Hotel
HOTEL **$$**

(☑ 412-281-7100; www.omnihotels.com; 530 William Penn Pl; r $180-290; ⓟ⊕✳⊜) Pittsburgh's stateliest old hotel, built by Henry Frick, has a cavernous lobby, with luxury suites that were remodeled in 2016. The great public spaces give it a sense of grandeur that some luxury hotels lack. Worth booking if you have the money...or can find it at a discount, which is often the case in the off-season.

🍴 Eating

E Carson St on the South Side has the highest concentration of restaurants, but the Strip District comes a close second. The North Side, Lawrenceville and the East

Liberties have the most up-and-coming activity. Catering to a large Catholic population, many Pittsburgh restaurants serve fish on Friday, and fried-fish sandwiches are especially popular – despite the city's lack of coastline, they're pretty tasty, too!

Primanti Bros
SANDWICHES $

(☏412-263-2142; www.primantibros.com; 46 18th St; sandwiches $6-10; ⏰24hr) The original location serves up the signature sandwiches Pittsburghers miss when they move away: hot, greasy delights stuffed with grilled meat, french fries and coleslaw. With branches all around Pittsburgh, you're never too far away from a Primanti Bros fix.

La Prima
CAFE $

(☏412-281-1922; www.laprima.com; 205 21st St; pastries $2-4; ⏰6am-4pm Mon-Wed, to 5pm Thu-Sat, 7am-4pm Sun) Great Italian coffee and pastries have people lined up out the door at peak times. The cranberry scone is their most popular sweet, but it has a range of other yummy treats (*sfogliatelle*, tarts, cookies etc). If you speak Italian you can enjoy the weekly quote written on the green chalkboard.

Zenith
VEGAN $

(☏412-481-4833; www.zenithpgh.com; 86 S 26th St; mains $7-11; ⏰11:30am-8:30pm Thu-Sat, 11am-2:30pm Sun; ✐) All meals are vegan here, though cheese is optional. A visit is like eating in an antique shop, as everything, including the Formica tables, is for sale. The Sunday buffet brunch ($11.50) draws a great community of regulars.

Bar Marco
ITALIAN $$

(☏412-471-1900; www.barmarcopgh.com; 2216 Penn Ave; mains $8-20; ⏰dinner 5-11pm Tue-Sat, brunch 10am-3pm Sat & Sun) A Strip District favorite, this is one of the city's more sophisticated kitchens, with an excellent brunch too. Cocktails are creative; you can also try the bartender's suggestion based on what types of drinks you enjoy. The refreshing no-tipping policy means the staff are appropriately compensated in a fair and equitable way.

★ Legume
FUSION $$$

(☏412-621-2700; www.legumebistro.com; 214 N Craig St; mains $23-42; ⏰5-9pm Mon-Thu, to 9:30pm Fri & Sat) Excellent meats and fish here, with a farm-to-table mindset and a menu that changes daily. If it's available, try the stinging-nettle soup – partly because where else can you try stinging nettles, but mostly because it's out of this world.

★ Paris 66
FRENCH $$$

(☏412-404-8166; www.paris66bistro.com; 6018 Centre Ave; dinner mains $20-35; ⏰11am-10pm Mon-Thu, to 11pm Fri & Sat, 10am-3pm Sun) This is top-end French at its best, in a cozy, bistro-style setting. Blink and you'll think you're in France. That said, this isn't *haute* cuisine, but rather solid food of rural France: *coq au vin*, rabbit in mustard sauce, *steak frites* and the rest.

🍷 Drinking & Entertainment

Church Brew Works
MICROBREWERY

(☏412-688-8200; www.churchbrew.com; 3525 Liberty Ave; ⏰11:30am-11:15pm Mon-Thu, to 12:15am Fri & Sat, to 9:15pm Sun) There are some who put drunkenness next to godliness, and they probably invented Church Brew Works. Gleaming and shining, giant brewery vats sit in what was once the pulpit. If you think this is sacrilegious, you'll want to skip this place – although of course many a great Belgian beer was proudly brewed by highly religious monks.

Spice Island Tea House
TEAHOUSE

(☏412-687-8821; www.spiceislandteahouse.com; 253 Atwood St; ⏰11:30am-8:45pm Mon-Thu, to 9:45pm Fri & Sat) If you fancy sipping a quiet cuppa (tea infusions $3.50 to $5.50) while your friend has a cocktail, this is the spot to visit. Alongside a number of delectable teas it also serves Southeast Asian fusion food.

★ Allegheny Wine Mixer
WINE BAR

(☏412-252-2337; www.alleghenywinemixer.com; 5326 Butler St; ⏰5pm-midnight Tue-Thu, to 1am Fri-Sun) All the perks of a high-end wine bar – great list, smart staff, tasty nibbles – in the comfort of a neighborhood dive.

Rex Theater
LIVE MUSIC

(☏412-381-6811; www.rextheatre.com; 1602 E Carson St) A converted movie theater, this South Side favorite hosts touring jazz, rock and indie bands.

★ Elks Lodge
LIVE MUSIC

(☏412-321-1834; www.elks.org; 400 Cedar Ave) Find out why Pittsburgh is known as the Paris of Appalachia at the Elks' Banjo Night (Wednesdays at 7pm; free): the stage is packed with players and the audience sings along to all the banjo classics. Also hosts a big-band night on the first, third and fifth Thursdays of the month (7:15pm; $5 cover). Located on the North Side in Deutschtown.

ⓘ Information

VisitPITTSBURGH Main Branch (☎ 412-281-7711; www.visitpittsburgh.com; 120 Fifth Ave, Ste 2800; ⊗10am-6pm Mon-Fri, to 5pm Sat, hours vary Sun) Publishes the *Official Visitors Guide* and provides maps and tourist advice.

ⓘ Getting There & Away

AIR

Pittsburgh International Airport (PIT; ☎ 412-472-3525; www.flypittsburgh.com; 1000 Airport Blvd), 18 miles west of downtown, has direct connections to Europe, Canada and major US cities via a slew of airlines.

BUS

The **Greyhound bus station** (Grant Street Transportation Center; ☎ 412-392-6514; www.greyhound.com; 55 11th St), at the far edge of the Strip District, has frequent buses to Philadelphia (from $31, six to seven hours), NYC (from $34, 8½ to 11 hours) and Chicago, IL (from $72, 11 to 14 hours).

CAR & MOTORCYCLE

Pittsburgh is accessible via I-76 or I-79 from the west and I-70 from the east. It's about a six-hour drive from NYC and about three hours from Buffalo.

TRAIN

Pittsburgh has a magnificent old train station – and **Amtrak** (☎ 800-872-7245; www.amtrak.com; 1100 Liberty Ave) drops you off in a dismal modern building behind it. Services run daily to Philadelphia (from $68, 7½ hours), NYC (from $81, 9½ hours), Chicago (from $72, 10 hours) and Washington, DC (from $53, eight hours).

ⓘ Getting Around

PortAuthority (www.portauthority.org) provides public transport around Pittsburgh, including the 28X Airport Flyer ($2.75, 40 minutes, every 30 minutes 5:10am to 12:10am) from the airport to downtown and Oakland. A taxi from the airport costs about $43 (not including tip) to downtown. Various shuttles also make downtown runs for around $25 per person.

Driving in Pittsburgh can be frustrating – roads end with no warning or deposit you suddenly on bridges. Parking is scarce downtown. Where possible, use the extensive bus network, which includes a fast express busway (routes beginning with P).

There is also a limited light-rail system, the T, useful for the South Side. Rides on the T downtown are free; other in-city fares are $2.50, plus $1 for a transfer.

New England

Best Places to Eat

➡ Saltie Girl (p202)

➡ Nudel (p221)

➡ Pantry (p234)

➡ Fore Street (p258)

➡ birch (p224)

Best Places to Sleep

➡ The Dean Hotel (p224)

➡ Liberty Hotel (p200)

➡ Inn at Shelburne Farms (p244)

➡ Notch Hostel (p251)

➡ Guest House at Field Farm (p221)

Why Go?

The history of New England is the history of America. It's the Pilgrims who came ashore at Plymouth Rock, the minutemen who fought for independence from Britain, and the abolitionists who challenged America's legacy of slavery. It's the ponderings of Ralph Waldo Emerson and the protests of Harriet Beecher Stowe. It's hundreds of years of poets and philosophers: progressive thinkers who dared to dream and dared to do. It's liberty-loving citizens not afraid to challenge the status quo, as well as generations of immigrants, who have shaped New England into the dynamic region that it is today.

For outdoor adventure, the region undulates with the rolling hills and rocky peaks of the Appalachian Mountains. Nearly 5000 miles of coastline make for unlimited opportunities for fishing, swimming, surfing and sailing. New England also boasts a bounty of epicurean delights: pancakes drenched in maple syrup, just-picked fruit and sharp cheddar cheese, and sublimely fresh seafood that is the hallmark of this region.

When to Go

Boston

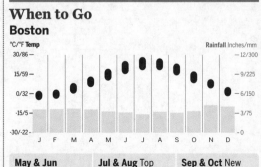

May & Jun Uncrowded sights and lightly trodden trails. Whale-watching begins.

Jul & Aug Top tourist season with summer festivals and warmer ocean weather.

Sep & Oct New England's blazing foliage peaks from mid-September to mid-October.

History

When the first European settlers arrived in the New World, they found about 100,000 Native American inhabitants, mostly Algonquians, organized into small regional tribes. The northern tribes were solely hunter-gatherers, while the southern tribes hunted and practiced slash-and-burn agriculture, growing corn, squash and beans.

In 1602 English Captain Bartholomew Gosnold landed at Cape Cod and sailed north to Maine; but it wasn't until 1614 that Captain John Smith, who charted the region's coastline for King James I, christened the land 'New England.' With the arrival of the Pilgrims at Plymouth in 1620, European settlement began in earnest. Over the next century the colonies expanded, often at the expense of the indigenous people.

Although subjects of the British Crown, New Englanders governed themselves with legislative councils and they came to view their affairs as separate from those of England. In the 1770s King George III imposed a series of taxes to pay for England's involvement in costly wars. The colonists, unrepresented in the British parliament, protested under the slogan, 'No taxation without representation.' Attempts to quash the protests eventually led to battles at Lexington and Concord, MA, setting off the War for Independence. The historic result was the birth of the USA in 1776.

Following independence, New England became an economic powerhouse, its harbors booming centers for shipbuilding and trade. New England's famed Yankee Clippers plied ports from China to South America. A thriving whaling industry brought unprecedented wealth to Nantucket and New Bedford. The USA's first water-powered cotton-spinning mill was established in Rhode Island in 1793.

No boom lasts forever. By the early 20th century many of the mills had moved south. Today, education, finance, biotechnology and tourism are linchpins of the regional economy.

🛈 Resources

Appalachian Mountain Club (www.outdoors. org) Fantastic resource for hiking, biking, camping, climbing and paddling in New England's great outdoors.

Boston.com (www.boston.com/tags/new -england-travel) Travel news, tips and itineraries from the *Boston Globe*.

Lonely Planet (www.lonelyplanet.com/usa/ new-england) Destination information, hotel bookings, traveler forum and more.

New England Network (www.newengland.com) New England travel resources from *Yankee Magazine*.

MASSACHUSETTS

New England's most populous state, Massachusetts packs in appealing variety, from the sandy beaches of Cape Cod to college towns of the Pioneer Valley to the woodsy hills of the Berkshires. The state's rich history oozes from almost every quarter: discover the shoreline in Plymouth, where the Pilgrims first settled in the New World; explore the battlefields in Lexington and Concord, where the first shots of the American Revolution rang out; and wander the cobbled streets and old ports of Salem, Nantucket and New Bedford, where whaling and merchant boats once docked.

Modern-day Massachusetts is also diverse and dynamic. Boston is the state's undisputed cultural (and political) capital, but smaller towns such as Provincetown and Northampton also offer lively art and music scenes, out and active queer populations and plenty of opportunities to enjoy the great outdoors.

History

Massachusetts has played a leading role in American politics since the arrival of the first colonists – the Pilgrims – who landed in Plymouth in 1620.

In the 18th century, spurred by a booming maritime trade, Massachusetts colonists revolted against trade restrictions and taxes imposed by Great Britain. The independence movement grew up in Boston, where the Sons of Liberty instigated uprisings and spread propaganda about their cause. These rebellions against the crown set the stage for battles in nearby Lexington and Concord, which kicked off the War for Independence in 1775.

In the 18th and 19th centuries, the North Shore of Massachusetts was a shipbuilding center, and Salem in particular grew rich on the returns of merchant ships that sailed around the world. In the southern part of the state, the whaling industry brought unprecedented wealth to Nantucket and New Bedford, whose ports are still lined with

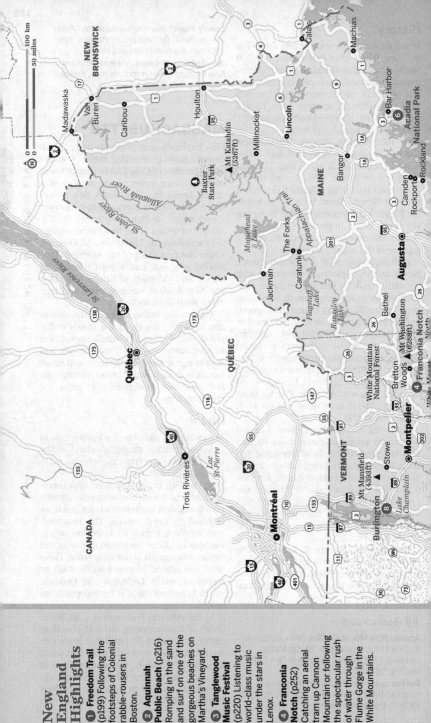

New England Highlights

1 Freedom Trail (p199) Following the footsteps of Colonial rabble-rousers in Boston.

2 Aquinnah Public Beach (p216) Romping in the sand and surf on one of the gorgeous beaches on Martha's Vineyard.

3 Tanglewood Music Festival (p220) Listening to world-class music under the stars in Lenox.

4 Franconia Notch (p252) Catching an aerial tram up Cannon Mountain or following the spectacular rush of water through Flume Gorge in the White Mountains.

100 km
50 miles

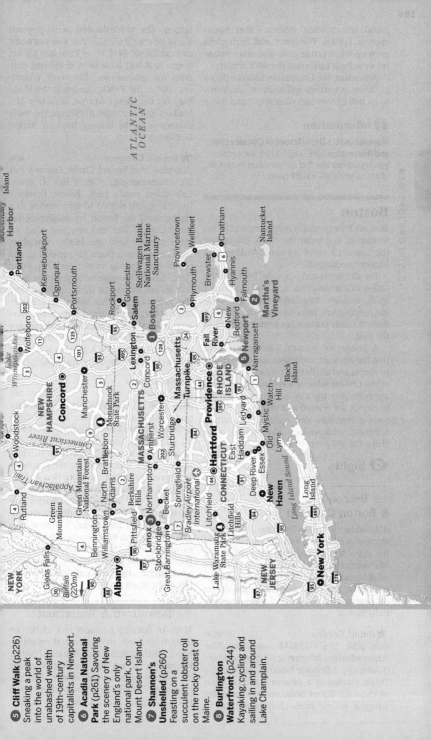

5 Cliff Walk (p226) Sneaking a peak into the world of unabashed wealth of 19th-century capitalists in Newport.

6 Acadia National Park (p261) Savoring the scenery of New England's only national park, on Mount Desert Island.

7 Shannon's Unshelled (p260) Feasting on a succulent lobster roll on the rocky coast of Maine.

8 Burlington Waterfront (p244) Kayaking, cycling and sailing in and around Lake Champlain.

grand sea captains' homes. Other towns such as Lowell, Worcester and Springfield grew up when textile mills and other industry were built up during the 20th century.

Nowadays, the Commonwealth continues to thrive, as tourists and students are drawn to its rich history and vibrant cultural life.

❶ Information

Massachusetts Department of Conservation and Recreation (☑ 617-626-1250; www.mass.gov/orgs/department-of-conservation-recreation) offers camping in 29 state parks.

Boston

Boston's history recalls revolution and transformation, and today the city is still among the country's most forward-thinking and barrier-breaking cities.

For all intents and purposes, Boston is the oldest city in America. And you can hardly walk a step over its cobblestone streets without running into some historic site. But that doesn't mean Boston has been relegated to the past.

A history of cultural patronage means that the city's art and music scenes continue to charm and challenge contemporary audiences. Cutting-edge urban planning projects are reshaping the city even now, as neighborhoods are revived and rediscovered. Historic universities and colleges still attract scientists, philosophers and writers, who shape the city's evolving culture.

❷ Sights

❸ Beacon Hill & Boston Common

Abutted by the Boston Common – the nation's original public park and the centerpiece of the city – and topped with the gold-domed Massachusetts State House, Beacon Hill is the neighborhood most often featured on Boston postcards. The retail and residential streets on Beacon Hill are delightfully, quintessentially Boston.

★**Public Garden**   GARDENS
(Map p194; ☑ 617-723-8144; www.friendsofthe-publicgarden.org; Arlington St; ☉ dawn-dusk; ▣; ⊤ Arlington) Adjoining Boston Common, the Public Garden is a 24-acre botanical oasis of Victorian flower beds, verdant grass and weeping willow trees shading a tranquil

lagoon. The old-fashioned pedal-powered **Swan Boats** (☑ 617-522-1966; www.swanboats.com; adult/child $4/2.50; ☉ 10am-4pm Apr-Jun, to 5pm Jul & Aug) have been delighting children for generations. The most endearing spot in the Public Garden is the **Make Way for Ducklings Statue,** depicting Mrs Mallard and her eight ducklings, the main characters in the beloved book by Robert McCloskey.

★**Boston Common**   PARK
(Map p194; btwn Tremont, Charles, Beacon & Park Sts; ☉ 6am-midnight; ▣ ▣; ⊤ Park St) America's oldest public park, Boston Common has a long and storied history, serving as a campground for British troops during the Revolutionary War and as green grass for cattle grazing until the 1830s. Nowadays, the Common is a place for picnicking and people-watching. In winter, the **Frog Pond** (☑ 617-635-2120; www.bostonfrogpond.com; adult/child $6/free, skate rental $12/6; ☉ 10am-3:45pm Mon, to 9pm Tue-Thu & Sun, to 10pm Fri & Sat mid-Nov–mid-Mar) attracts ice-skaters, while summer draws theater lovers for **Shakespeare on the Common** (☑ 617-426-0863; www.commshakes.org; ☉ Jul & Aug). This is also the starting point for the Freedom Trail.

**Massachusetts
State House**   NOTABLE BUILDING
(Map p194; ☑ 617-727-7030; www.sec.state.ma.us; cnr Beacon & Bowdoin Sts; ☉ 8:45am-5pm Mon-Fri, tours 10am-3:30pm Mon-Fri; ⊤ Park St) FREE High atop Beacon Hill, Massachusetts' leaders and legislators attempt to turn their ideas into concrete policies and practices within the State House. John Hancock provided the land (previously part of his cow pasture) and Charles Bulfinch designed the commanding state capitol, but it was Oliver Wendell Holmes who called it 'the hub of the solar system' (thus earning Boston the nickname 'the Hub'). Free 40-minute tours cover the history, artwork, architecture and political personalities of the State House.

❷ Downtown & Waterfront

Much of Boston's business and tourist activity takes place in this central neighborhood, which includes the Financial District. Downtown is not the thriving shopping area that it once was, especially since the closure of Filene's Department Store. But it is a bustling district crammed with modern

BOSTON IN TWO DAYS...

Day One

Spend your first day in Boston following the Freedom Trail (p198), which starts on the Boston Common and continues through downtown. There isn't time to go inside every museum, but you can admire the architecture and learn the history. Highlights include the Old South Meeting House , the Old State House and Faneuil Hall.

In the afternoon, the Freedom Trail continues into the North End, where you can visit the historic Paul Revere House, Old North Church and Copp's Hill Burying Ground. Move on to the exquisite Liberty Hotel (p200), former site of the Charles St Jail.

Day Two

Spend the morning admiring Boston's most architecturally significant collection of buildings, clustered around Copley Sq (p196). Admire the art and books at the Boston Public Library (p197), and then ogle the magnificent stained-glass windows at Trinity Church (p196).

Your afternoon is reserved for one of Boston's art museums. Unfortunately you'll have to choose between the excellent, encyclopedic collection at the Museum of Fine Arts (p197) or the smaller but no less extraordinary exhibits at the Isabella Stewart Gardner Museum (p197). Either way, you won't be disappointed.

In the evening, catch the Boston Symphony Orchestra at the acoustically magnificent Symphony Hall (p204), or for lower-brow entertainment, catch a baseball game at Fenway Park (p197) or go bar-hopping on Lansdowne St.

NEW ENGLAND BOSTON

complexes and colonial buildings, including Faneuil Hall and Quincy Market. The Waterfront is home to the Harbor Islands ferries and the New England Aquarium.

★**Old State House**   HISTORIC BUILDING
(Map p194; ☑617-720-1713; www.bostonhistory.org; 206 Washington St; adult/child $10/free; ☺9am-6pm Jun-Aug, to 5pm Sep-May; ☐State) Dating from 1713, the Old State House is Boston's oldest surviving public building, where the Massachusetts Assembly used to debate the issues of the day before the Revolution. The building is best known for its balcony, where the Declaration of Independence was first read to Bostonians in 1776. Inside, the Old State House contains a small museum of revolutionary memorabilia, with videos and multimedia presentations about the Boston Massacre, which took place out the front.

Old South Meeting House   HISTORIC BUILDING
(Map p194; ☑617-482-6439; www.osmh.org; 310 Washington St; adult/child $6/1; ☺9:30am-5pm Apr-Oct, 10am-4pm Nov-Mar; ☑; ☐Downtown Crossing, State) 'No tax on tea!' That was the decision on December 16, 1773, when 5000 angry colonists gathered here to protest British taxes, leading to the Boston Tea Party. Download an audio of the historic pre-Tea Party meeting from the museum website, then visit the graceful meeting house to check out the exhibit on the history of the building and the protest.

Rose Kennedy Greenway   PARK
(Map p194; ☑617-292-0020; www.rosekennedy greenway.org; ☑; ☐Aquarium, Haymarket) Where once there was a hulking overhead highway, now winds a 27-acre strip of landscaped gardens, fountain-lined greens and public art installations. The park has something for everyone: the artist-driven Greenway Open Market (p205) for weekend shoppers, food trucks for weekday lunchers, summertime block parties for music lovers and **Trillium Garden** (☑857-449-0083; www.trilliumbrewing.com; cnr Atlantic Ave & High St; ☺2-10pm Wed-Fri, from 11am Sat, 1-8pm Sun May-Oct; ☎; ☐South Station, Aquarium) for beer drinkers. Cool off in the whimsical **Rings Fountain**, walk the calming **labyrinth**, or take a ride on the custom-designed **Greenway Carousel** (per ride $3; ☺11am-7pm Apr-Dec).

Faneuil Hall   HISTORIC BUILDING
(Map p194; ☑617-242-5642; www.nps.gov/bost; Congress St; ☺9am-5pm; ☐State, Haymarket, Government Center) **FREE** 'Those who cannot bear free speech had best go home,' said Wendell Phillips. 'Faneuil Hall is no place for slavish hearts.' Indeed, this public meeting place was the site of so much rabble-rousing that it earned the nickname the 'Cradle of Liberty.' After the revolution, Faneuil Hall

Boston

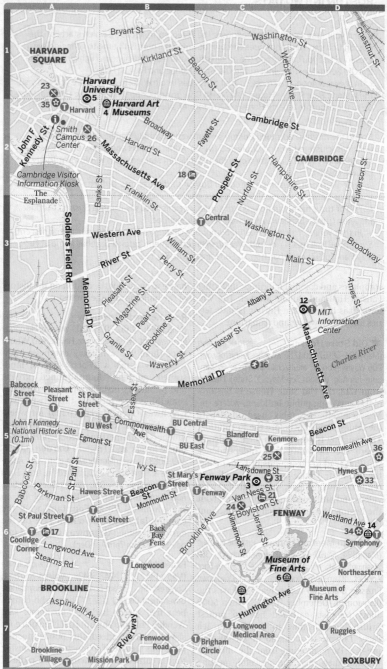

HARVARD SQUARE

Bryant St
Kirkland St
Washington St
Chestnut St

Harvard University 5
Harvard Art Museums 4

23
35
Harvard
Smith Campus Center 26

Cambridge Visitor Information Kiosk
The Esplanade

John F Kennedy St
Soldiers Field Rd
Memorial Dr

Beacon St
Webster Ave
Cambridge St
CAMBRIDGE
Fulkerson St

Broadway
Harvard St
Fayette St
Hampshire St
Prospect St
Norfolk St

Massachusetts Ave
Franklin St
18
Central
Washington St
Main St
Broadway

Western Ave
River St
William St
Perry St
Pleasant St
Magazine St
Pearl St
Brookline St
Granite St
Waverly St
Albany St
Vassar St

MIT Information Center 12

Ames St
Charles River

Memorial Dr
16
Massachusetts Ave

Babcock Street
Pleasant Street
St Paul Street
Essex St
BU West
Commonwealth Ave
BU Central
Blandford
Kenmore
Beacon St
Commonwealth Ave
36

John F Kennedy National Historic Site (0.1mi)
Egmont St
BU East
25
Hynes
33

Ivy St
Lansdowne St
31
Babcock St
St Paul St
St Mary's Street
Fenway Park 3
Van Ness St
21
Boylston St
FENWAY

Parkman St
Hawes Street
Beacon St
Monmouth St
24
Kimarnock St
Jersey St
Westland Ave 14
34
Symphony

St Paul Street
Kent Street
Fenway
Back Bay Fens
Brookline Ave

Coolidge Corner
17
Longwood Ave
Stearns Rd
Longwood
Museum of Fine Arts 6
11
Museum of Fine Arts
Northeastern

BROOKLINE
Aspinwall Ave
Riverway
Fenwood Road
Longwood
Huntington Ave
Longwood Medical Area
Ruggles

Brookline Village
Mission Park
Brigham Circle
ROXBURY

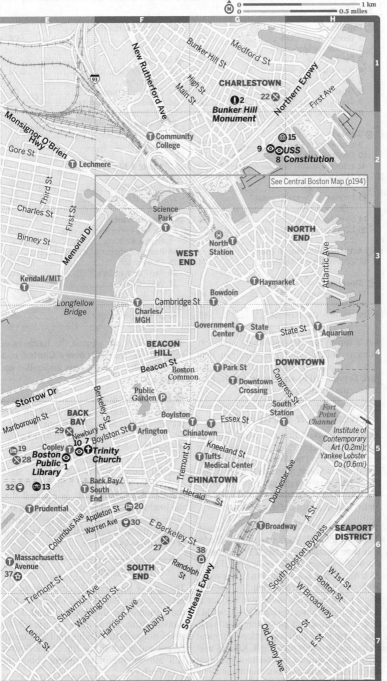

0   1 km
0   0.5 miles

CHARLESTOWN

❶2
**Bunker Hill
Monument**

22 ✕

Northern Expwy

Medford St

Bunker Hill St

High St

Main St

First Ave

Community
College

Monsignor O'Brien Hwy

Gore St

Lechmere

Third St

First St

Charles St

Binney St

Memorial Dr

New Rutherford Ave

🏛15

9 ◎◎◎**USS**
8 **Constitution**

See Central Boston Map (p194)

Science
Park

North
Station

**NORTH
END**

**WEST
END**

Atlantic Ave

Kendall/MIT

Longfellow
Bridge

Cambridge St

Charles/
MGH

Bowdoin

Haymarket

Government
Center

State

State St

Aquarium

**BEACON
HILL**

Beacon St

Park St

DOWNTOWN

Boston
Common

Downtown
Crossing

Storrow Dr

Public
Garden

Boylston

Congress St

South
Station

Fort
Point
Channel

**BACK
BAY**

Marlborough St

29 ✕
Newbury St
10 7
Boylston St
Berkeley St

Arlington

Essex St

Chinatown

Kneeland St

Institute of
Contemporary
Art (0.2mi);
Yankee Lobster
Co (0.6mi)

19
28 ✕

Copley
❶
1 ❶**Trinity
Church**

**Boston
Public
Library**

Tufts
Medical Center

Tremont St

CHINATOWN

32 🔲 13

Back Bay/
South
End

Herald St

Prudential

Columbus Ave

Appleton St 20

Warren Ave 30

Broadway

A St

**SEAPORT
DISTRICT**

South Boston Bypass

W 1st St

27 ✕

E Berkeley St

38

**SOUTH
END**

Randolph
St

Southeast Expwy

Bolton St

W Broadway

Massachusetts
Avenue
37

Tremont St

Shawmut Ave

Washington Ave

Harrison Ave

Albany St

D St

E St

Lenox St

Old Colony Ave

Boston

was a forum for meetings about abolition, women's suffrage and war. You can hear about the building's history from National Park Service (NPS) rangers in the historic hall on the 2nd floor.

⊙ West End & North End

Although the West End and North End are physically adjacent, they are worlds apart atmospherically. The West End is an institutional area without much zest. By contrast, the North End is delightfully spicy, thanks to the many Italian *ristoranti* and *salumerie* (delis) that line the streets.

★ Museum of Science   MUSEUM
(Map p194; ☑ 617-723-2500; www.mos.org; Charles River Dam; museum adult/child $28/23, planetarium $10/8, theater $10/8; ⊙ 9am-7pm Sat-Thu Jul & Aug, to 5pm Sep-Jun, to 9pm Fri year-round; ⓟ⧉; ⓣ Science Park/West End) This educational playground has more than 600 interactive exhibits. Favorites include the world's largest lightning-bolt generator, a full-scale space capsule, a world population meter and an impressive dinosaur exhibit. Kids go wild exploring computers and technology, maps and models, birds and bees, and human evolution. Don't miss the Hall of Human Life,

where visitors can witness the hatching of baby chicks. The Discovery Center is a hands-on play area for kids under the age of eight.

★ Old North Church   CHURCH
(Christ Church; Map p194; ☑ 617-858-8231; www. oldnorth.com; 193 Salem St; adult/child $8/4, tour $2; ⊙ 10am-4pm Nov-March, 9am-6pm Apr-Oct; ⓣ Haymarket, North Station) Longfellow's poem 'Paul Revere's Ride' has immortalized this graceful church. It was here, on the night of April 18, 1775, that the sexton hung two lanterns from the steeple as a signal that the British would advance on Lexington and Concord via the sea route. Also called Christ Church, this 1723 Anglican place of worship is Boston's oldest church.

⊙ Charlestown

The site of the original settlement of the Massachusetts Bay Colony, Charlestown is the terminus for the Freedom Trail. Many tourists tramp across these historic cobblestone sidewalks to admire the USS *Constitution* and climb to the top of the Bunker Hill Monument, which towers above the neighborhood.

★ **Bunker Hill Monument** MONUMENT
(Map p190; ☑ 617-242-7275; www.nps.gov/bost; Monument Sq; ⊙ 9am-5pm Oct-May, to 6pm Jun-Sep; ◻ 93 from Haymarket, Ⓣ Community College) **FREE** This 220ft granite obelisk monument commemorates the turning-point battle that was fought on the surrounding hillside on June 17, 1775. Ultimately, the Redcoats prevailed, but the victory was bittersweet, as they lost more than one-third of their deployed forces, while the colonists suffered relatively few casualties. Climb the 294 steps to the top of the monument to enjoy the panorama of the city, the harbor and the North Shore.

★ **USS Constitution** SHIP
(Map p190; ☑ 617-242-2543; www.navy.mil/local/ constitution; Charlestown Navy Yard; ⊙ 10am-4pm Wed-Sun Jan-Mar, to 6pm Apr, 10am-6pm Tue-Sun May-Sep, to 6pm Oct-Dec; ⚑; ◻ 93 from Haymarket, ⛴ Inner Harbor Ferry from Long Wharf, Ⓣ North Station) **FREE** 'Her sides are made of iron!' cried a crewman upon watching a shot bounce off the thick oak hull of the USS *Constitution* during the War of 1812. This bit of irony earned the legendary ship its nickname. Indeed, it has never gone down in a battle. The USS *Constitution* remains the oldest commissioned US Navy ship, dating from 1797, and it is normally taken out onto Boston Harbor every July 4 in order to maintain its commissioned status.

Make sure you bring a photo ID to go aboard. You'll learn lots, such as how the captain's son died on the ship's maiden voyage (an inauspicious start).

USS Constitution Museum MUSEUM
(Map p190; ☑ 617-426-1812; www.ussconstitution museum.org; First Ave, Charlestown Navy Yard; suggested donation adult $10-15, child $5-10; ⊙ 9am-6pm Apr-Oct, 10am-5pm Nov-Mar; ⚑; ◻ 93 from Haymarket, ⛴ Inner Harbor Ferry from Long Wharf, Ⓣ North Station) Head indoors to this museum for a play-by-play of the various battles of the USS *Constitution*, as well as its current role as the flagship of the US Navy. The exhibits on the War of 1812 and the Barbary War are especially interesting, and trace the birth of the US Navy during these relatively unknown conflicts. Upstairs, kids can experience what it was like to be a sailor on the USS *Constitution* in 1812.

⊙ Seaport District

The Seaport District is a section of South Boston that is fast developing as an attractive waterside destination, thanks to the dynamic contemporary-art museum and the explosion of new dining and entertainment options.

★ **Institute of Contemporary Art** MUSEUM
(ICA; ☑ 617-478-3100; www.icaboston.org; 25 Harbor Shore Dr; adult/child $15/free, 5-9pm Thu free; ⊙ 10am-5pm Tue, Wed, Sat & Sun, to 9pm Thu & Fri; ⚑; ◻ SL1, SL2, Ⓣ South Station) Boston has become a focal point for contemporary art in the 21st century, with the Institute of Contemporary Art leading the way. The building is a work of art in itself: a glass structure cantilevered over a waterside plaza. The vast light-filled interior allows for multimedia presentations, educational

---

BOSTON FOR CHILDREN

Boston is one giant history museum, and the setting for many lively and informative field trips. Cobblestone streets and costume-clad tour guides can bring to life the events that kids read about in history books, while hands-on experimentation and interactive exhibits fuse education and entertainment.

Great tours for kids:

Boston by Foot (p199) Runs 'Boston by Little Feet,' the only Freedom Trail walking tour designed especially for children aged six to 12.

Boston Duck Tours (☑ 617-267-3825; www.bostonducktours.com; adult/child $42/28; ⚑; Ⓣ Aquarium, Science Park, Prudential) Kids of all ages are invited to drive the duck on the raging waters of the Charles River. Bonus: quacking loudly is encouraged.

Freedom Trail Foundation (Map p194; ☑ 617-357-8300; www.thefreedomtrail.org; adult/ child $14/8; Ⓣ Park St) Tours are run by guides in period costume. Download a kid-friendly podcast or reading list for your child before setting out.

Urban AdvenTours (p199) This bike tour is great for all ages. Kids' bikes and helmets are available for rent, as are bike trailers for toddlers.

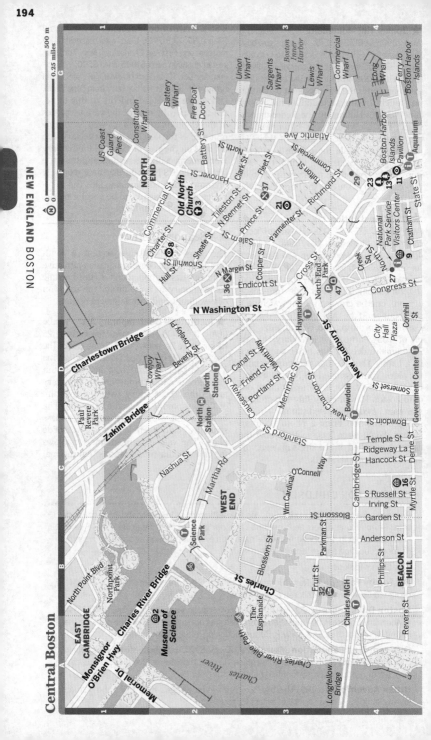

Central Boston

0.25 miles
500 m

Charles River

EAST
CAMBRIDGE

Monsignor O'Brien Hwy

Memorial Dr

North Point Blvd

Northpoint Park

Charles River Bridge

Museum of Science

2

Science Park

WEST END

Nashua St

Martha Rd

Wm Cardinal O'Connell Way

Blossom St

Parkman St

Fruit St

32

Charles/MGH

BEACON HILL

The Esplanade

Charles River Bike Path

Longfellow Bridge

Revere St

Phillips St

Anderson St

Garden St

Irving St

S Russell St

16

Myrtle St

Hancock St

Ridgeway La

Temple St

Cambridge St

Blossom St

Bowdoin St

Bowdoin

New Chardon St

Merrimac St

Stanford St

Portland St

Friend St

Canal St

ValentiWay

Causeway St

North Station

North Station

Beverly St

Lovejoy Wharf

Zakim Bridge

Charlestown Bridge

Paul Revere Park

US Coast Guard Piers

Constitution Wharf

Battery Wharf

Fire Boat Dock

NORTH END

Commercial St

Charter St

Hull St

Snowhill St

8

Old North Church

3

Tileston St

N Bennet St

Prince St

Sheafe St

Salem St

N Margin St

36

Endicott St

N Washington St

N Washington St

Lovejoy St

Hanover St

Battery St

North St

Clark St

Fleet St

37

21

Parmenter St

Cooper St

Cross St

North End Park

Haymarket

New Sudbury St

Creek Sq

North Sq

27

47

Richmond St

Fulton St

Commercial St

Atlantic Ave

Union Wharf

Sargents Wharf

Lewis Wharf

Commercial Wharf

Boston Inner Harbor

Long Wharf

Ferry to Boston Harbor Islands

Aquarium

State St

Chatham St

9

National Park Service Visitors Center

11

13

Boston Harbor Islands Pavilion

23

29

Congress St

City Hall Plaza

Cornhill St

Somerset St

Government Center

Derne St

Hancock St

Phillips St

Charles St

BEACON HILL

N

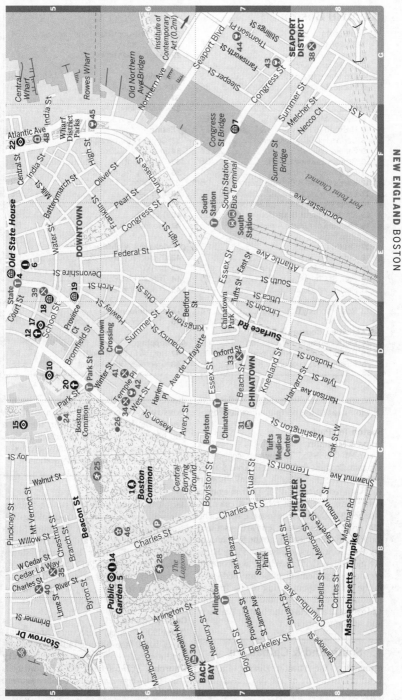

Central Boston

programs and studio space, as well as the development of the permanent collection.

Boston Tea Party
Ships & Museum   MUSEUM
(Map p194; ☑ 866-955-0667; www.bostonteaparty ship.com; Congress St Bridge; adult/child $30/18; ☺10am-5pm; ␁; Ⓣ South Station) 'Boston Harbor a teapot tonight!' To protest against unfair taxes, a gang of rebellious colonists dumped 342 chests of tea into the water. The 1773 protest – the Boston Tea Party – set into motion the events leading to the Revolutionary War. Nowadays, replica Tea Party Ships are moored at Griffin's Wharf, alongside an excellent experiential museum dedicated to the catalytic event. Using re-enactments, multimedia and fun exhibits, the museum addresses all aspects of the Boston Tea Party and subsequent events.

◉ South End & Chinatown

Chinatown, the Theater District and the Leather District are overlapping areas, filled with glitzy theaters, Chinese restaurants and

the remnants of Boston's shoe and leather industry (now converted lofts and clubs). Nearby, the Victorian manses in the South End have been reclaimed by artists and the LGBTIQ+ community, who have created a vibrant restaurant and gallery scene.

◉ Back Bay

Back Bay includes the city's most fashionable window-shopping, latte-drinking and people-watching area, on Newbury St, as well as its most elegant architecture, around Copley Sq. Its streets lined with stately brownstones and shaded by magnolia trees, it is among Boston's most prestigious addresses. For fresh air and riverside strolling, head to the Charles River Esplanade.

Copley Square   PLAZA
(Map p190; Ⓣ Copley) Here you'll find a cluster of handsome historic buildings, including the ornate French-Romanesque **Trinity Church** (☑ 617-536-0944, ext 206; www.trinity churchboston.org; 206 Clarendon St; adult/child $10/free; ☺10am-4:30pm Tue-Sat, 12:15-4:30pm

Sun Easter-Oct, reduced hours rest of year), the masterwork of architect HH Richardson. Across the street, the classic **Boston Public Library** (☑617-536-5400; www.bpl.org; 700 Boylston St; ⊙9am-9pm Mon-Thu, to 5pm Fri & Sat year-round, plus 1-5pm Sun Oct-May) was America's first municipal library. Pick up a self-guided tour brochure and wander around, noting gems such as the murals by John Singer Sargent and sculpture by Augustus Saint-Gaudens.

Prudential Center
Skywalk Observatory   VIEWPOINT
(Map p190; www.skywalkboston.com; 800 Boylston St; adult/child $20/14; ⊙10am-10pm Mar-Oct, to 8pm Nov-Feb; P 🚹; T Prudential) Technically called the Shops at Prudential Center, this landmark Boston building is not much more than a fancy shopping mall. But it does provide a bird's-eye view of Boston from its 50th-floor Skywalk. Completely enclosed by glass, the Skywalk offers spectacular 360-degree views of Boston and Cambridge, accompanied by an entertaining audio tour (with a special version catering to kids). Alternatively, you can enjoy the same view from **Top of the Hub** (☑617-536-1775; www. topofthehub.net; ⊙11:30am-1am; 🐾) for the price of a drink.

◉ Kenmore Square & Fenway

Kenmore Sq and Fenway attract club-goers and baseball fans to the streets surrounding Fenway Park. At the other end of the neighborhood, art-lovers and culture-vultures flock to the artistic institutions along the Avenue of the Arts (Huntington Ave), including the Museum of Fine Arts and Symphony Hall.

★Fenway Park   STADIUM
(Map p190; ☑617-226-6666; www.redsox.com; 4 Jersey St; tours adult/child $20/14, pre-game $35-45; ⊙9am-5pm Apr-Oct, special schedule game days, 10am-5pm Nov-Mar; T Kenmore) Home of the Boston Red Sox since 1912, Fenway Park is the oldest operating baseball park in the country. As such, the park has many quirks that make for a unique experience. See them all on a ballpark tour, or come see the Sox playing in their natural habitat.

★Museum of Fine Arts   MUSEUM
(MFA; Map p190; ☑617-267-9300; www.mfa.org; 465 Huntington Ave; adult/child $25/free; ⊙10am-5pm Sat-Tue, to 10pm Wed-Fri; T Museum of Fine Arts, Ruggles) Founded in 1876, the Museum of Fine Arts is Boston's foremost art museum. The museum covers all parts of the globe and all eras, from the ancient world to contemporary times. The collections are strong in Asian and European art, but the uncontested highlight is the gorgeous Art of the Americas wing.

Isabella Stewart
Gardner Museum   MUSEUM
(Map p190; ☑617-566-1401; www.gardnermuseum. org; 25 Evans Way; adult/child $15/free; ⊙11am-5pm Wed-Mon, to 9pm Thu; T Museum of Fine Arts) Once home to Isabella Stewart Gardner, this splendid palazzo now houses her exquisite collection of art. The museum includes thousands of artistic objects, especially Italian Renaissance and Dutch Golden Age paintings. The interior courtyard, lush with seasonal plants and flowers, is an oasis of tranquility and beauty.

◉ Cambridge

Stretched out along the north shore of the Charles River, Cambridge is a separate city with two distinguished universities, a host of historic sites, and artistic and cultural attractions galore. The streets around Harvard Square are home to restaurants, bars and clubs that rival their counterparts across the river.

★Harvard University   UNIVERSITY
(Map p190; ☑617-495-1000; www.harvard.edu; Massachusetts Ave; T Harvard) America's oldest college, Harvard University was founded in 1636 and remains one of the country's most prestigious universities. Alumni of the original Ivy League school include eight US presidents, and dozens of Nobel Laureates and Pulitzer Prize winners. For visitors, the university campus contains some historic buildings clustered around Harvard Yard, as well as impressive architecture and excellent museums. Free historical tours depart from the **Smith Campus Center** (☑617-495-6916; www.commonspaces.harvard.edu/smith-campus -center/about; 30 Dunster St; ⊙7am-midnight Sun-Fri, to 1am Sat); self-guided tours are also available.

★Harvard Art Museums   MUSEUM
(Map p190; ☑617-495-9400; www.harvardart museums.org; 32 Quincy St; adult/child/student $15/free/free; ⊙10am-5pm; T Harvard) The 2014 renovation and expansion of Harvard's art museums allowed the university's

City Walk Freedom Trail

START BOSTON COMMON
END BUNKER HILL MONUMENT
LENGTH 2.5 MILES; THREE HOURS

Start at [1] **Boston Common** (p188), the USA's oldest public park. On the northern side, you can't miss the gold-domed [2] **Massachusetts State House** (p188) sitting atop Beacon Hill and open for tours. Walk north on Tremont St, passing the soaring steeple of [3] **Park St Church** and the Egyptian Revival gates of the [4] **Granary Burying Ground**, final resting place of many patriots.

At School St, the columned [5] **King's Chapel** overlooks the adjacent burying ground. Turn east on School St, and take note of the plaque outside the [6] **Old City Hall** commemorating this spot as the site of the first public school. Continue down School St past the [7] **Old Corner Bookstore**. Diagonally opposite, the [8] **Old South Meeting House** (p189) saw the beginnings of the Boston Tea Party.

Further north on Washington St, the [9] **Old State House** (p189) was the seat of the colonial government. Later, it was the scene of the city's first public reading of the Declaration of Independence. Outside the Old State House a ring of cobblestones marks the [10] **Boston Massacre site**, where yet another uprising fueled the revolution. Across the intersection, historic [11] **Faneuil Hall** (p189) has served as a public meeting place and marketplace for more than 250 years. National Park Service rangers give free presentations about the site's significance.

From Faneuil Hall, follow Hanover St across the Rose Kennedy Greenway. One block east, charming North Sq is the site of the [12] **Paul Revere House**, the city's oldest wooden house. Back on Hanover St, the Paul Revere Mall offers a lovely vantage point to view the [13] **Old North Church** (p192), where two lanterns were hung to signal the British soldiers' route. From the church, head west on Hull St to [14] **Copp's Hill Burying Ground**, with grand views across the river to Charlestown.

Across the Charlestown Bridge, Constitution Rd brings you to the Charlestown Navy Yard, home of the world's oldest commissioned warship, the [15] **USS Constitution** (p193). Finally, wind your way through the historic streets of Charlestown center to the [16] **Bunker Hill Monument** (p193), site of the turning-point battle of the American Revolution.

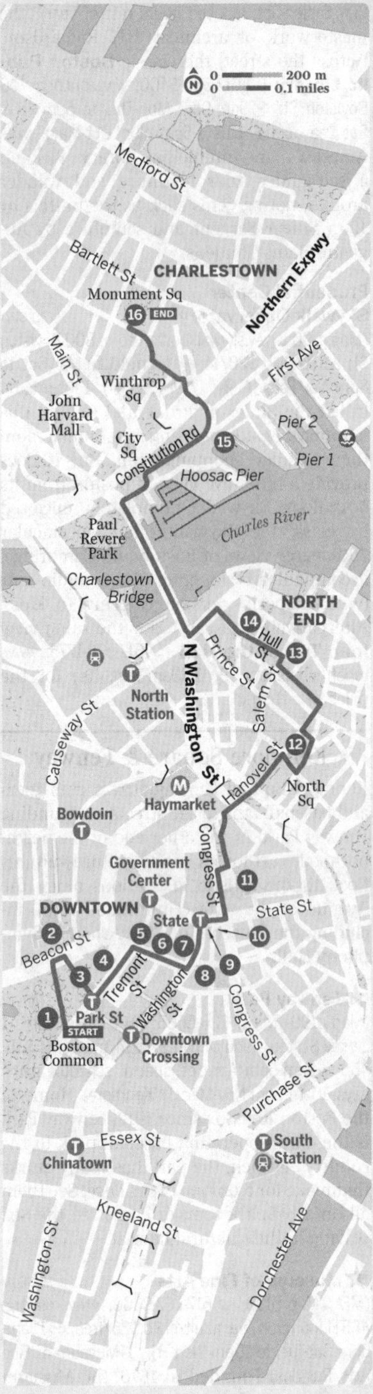

massive 250,000-piece collection to come together under one very stylish roof, designed by architect extraordinaire Renzo Piano. The artwork spans the globe, with separate collections devoted to Asian and Islamic cultures, northern European and Germanic cultures and other Western art, especially European modernism.

Massachusetts Institute of Technology
UNIVERSITY

(MIT; Map p190; ☑617-253-1000; www.mit.edu; 77 Massachusetts Ave; ☺info session incl campus tour 10am & 2:30pm Mon-Fri; ⓣKendall/MIT) The Massachusetts Institute of Technology offers a different perspective on academia. MIT has a proud history of pushing the boundaries, from its innovative architecture and oddball art to its cutting-edge technology and playful pranks. Campus tours depart from the **MIT Information Center** (☑617-253-3400; www.web.mit.edu/visitmit; 77 Massachusetts Ave, No 7-121, Rogers Bldg; ☺9am-5pm Mon-Fri).

🏃 Activities

Considering Boston's large student population and extensive green spaces, it's no surprise to see urban outdoorsy people running along the Esplanade and cycling the Emerald Necklace. For water bugs, the Charles River and the Boston Harbor offer opportunities for kayaking, sailing and even swimming, if you don't mind the frigid temperatures.

★Freedom Trail
WALKING

(☑617-357-8300; www.thefreedomtrail.org; ⓣPark St) **FREE** For a sampler of Boston's revolutionary sights, follow the red-brick road. It leads 2.5 miles through the center of Boston, from Boston Common (p188) to the Bunker Hill Monument (p193), and traces the events leading up to and following the War of Independence. The Freedom Trail is well marked and easy to follow on your own.

Charles River Bike Path
CYCLING

(Map p190; Storrow Dr & Memorial Dr; ♿; ⓣHarvard, Kendall/MIT, Charles/MGH, Science Park) A popular cycling circuit runs along both sides of the Charles River between the Museum of Science and the Mt Auburn St Bridge in Watertown center (5 miles west of Cambridge). The round trip is 17 miles, but 10 bridges in between offer ample opportunities to shorten the trip. Rent a bike at **Cambridge Bicycle** (☑617-876-6555; www.cambridgebicycle.com; 259 Massachusetts Ave;

per 24hr $35; ☺10am-7pm Mon-Sat, noon-6pm Sun; ⓣCentral) or **Back Bay Bicycles** (☑617-247-2336; www.papa-wheelies.com; 362 Commonwealth Ave; rental per day $55-65; ☺10am-7pm Mon-Fri, to 6pm Sat, noon-5pm Sun; ⓣHynes).

🚩 Tours

★Urban AdvenTours
CYCLING

(Map p194; ☑617-670-0637; www.urbanadventours.com; 103 Atlantic Ave; tours from $55, rentals per 24hr $40-75; ☺9am-8pm Apr-Oct, reduced hours rest of year; ⓣAquarium) This outfit was founded by avid cyclists who believe the best views of Boston are from a bicycle. And they're right! The City View Ride tour provides a great overview of how to get around by bike, including ride-bys of some of Boston's best sites. Other specialty tours include Bikes at Night and the Emerald Necklace tour. Bicycles, helmets and water are all provided.

Boston by Foot
WALKING

(☑617-367-2345; www.bostonbyfoot.com; adult/child $15/10; ♿) This fantastic nonprofit organization offers 90-minute walking tours, with neighborhood-specific walks and specialty theme tours such as the Hub of Literary America, the Dark Side of Boston and Boston by Little Feet – a kid-friendly version of the Freedom Trail.

Black Heritage Trail
WALKING

(Map p194; ☑617-742-5415; www.nps.gov/boaf; ☺tours 1pm Mon-Sat, more frequently in summer; ⓣPark St) The NPS conducts excellent, informative 90-minute guided tours exploring the history of the abolitionist movement and African American settlement on Beacon Hill. Tours depart from the Robert Gould Shaw memorial on Boston Common. Alternatively, take a self-guided tour with the NPS Freedom Trail app (www.nps.gov/bost/planyourvisit/app.htm) or grab a route map from the **Museum of African American History** (Map p194; ☑617-725-0022; www.maah.org; 46 Joy St; adult/child $10/free; ☺10am-4pm Mon-Sat; ⓣPark St, Bowdoin).

Free Tours By Foot
WALKING

(☑617-299-0764; www.freetoursbyfoot.com/boston-tours) Take the tour then decide how much you think it's worth. Popular 90-minute walking tours cover the Freedom Trail, Harvard University, the North End and the Beacon Hill 'crime tour.' Tour guides are passionate and entertaining. Best of all, you'll never pay more than you think you should.

✨ Festivals & Events

★ Boston Marathon
SPORTS

(www.baa.org; ⊙ 3rd Mon Apr) One of the country's most prestigious marathons takes runners on a 26.2-mile course ending at Copley Sq on Patriots' Day, a Massachusetts holiday on the third Monday in April.

Independence Day
CULTURAL

(www.bostonpopsjuly4th.org; ⊙ Jul 4) Boston hosts one of the biggest Independence Day bashes in the USA, with a free Boston Pops concert on the Esplanade and a fireworks display that's televised nationally.

Boston Tea Party Reenactment
CULTURAL

(www.oldsouthmeetinghouse.org; $30; ⊙ Dec) On the Sunday prior to December 16, costumed actors march from Old South Meeting House to the waterfront and toss crates of tea into the harbor. Nowadays, the ticketed event takes place on the newly rebuilt Griffin's Wharf, where the Tea Party ships are docked.

🛏 Sleeping

Boston offers a wide range of accommodations, from inviting guesthouses in historic quarters to swanky hotels with all the amenities. There is no shortage of stately homes that have been converted into B&Bs, offering an intimate atmosphere and personal service. Considering that this city is filled with students, there are surprisingly few accommodations targeting budget travelers and backpackers.

★ HI-Boston
HOSTEL $

(Map p194; ☏ 617-536-9455; www.bostonhostel. org; 19 Stuart St; dm from $47, d with bath from $230; ❄@🛜; Ⓣ Chinatown, Boylston) HI-Boston sets the standard for urban hostels, with its modern, ecofriendly facility in the historic Dill Building. Purpose-built rooms are functional and clean, as are the shared bathrooms. Community spaces are numerous, from fully equipped kitchen to ground-floor cafe, and there's a whole calendar of activities on offer. The place is large, but it books out, so reserve in advance.

Revolution Hotel
HOTEL $

(Map p190; ☏ 617-848-9200; www.therevolution hotel.com; 40 Berkeley St; d/tr/q without bath $100/125/150, d/ste from $150/250; ❄🛜; Ⓣ Back Bay) A beacon for budget travelers, the Revolution Hotel is a concept hotel with a cool, creative atmosphere. Rooms are compact, comfortable and affordable. The cheapest share bathrooms are spacious, private and well stocked with plush towels and high-end products. The place exudes innovation, especially thanks to the fantastic mural that adorns the lobby.

★ Newbury Guest House
GUESTHOUSE $$

(Map p190; ☏ 617-670-6000, 800-437-7668; www. newburyguesthouse.com; 261 Newbury St; d from $249; ❄🅿🛜; Ⓣ Hynes, Copley) Dating from 1882, these three interconnected brick and brownstone buildings offer a prime location in the heart of Newbury St. The place has preserved charming features like ceiling medallions and in-room fireplaces, but the rooms also feature clean lines, luxurious linens and modern amenities. Each morning a complimentary buffet breakfast is laid out in the attached restaurant.

Harding House
B&B $$

(Map p190; ☏ 617-876-2888; www.harding-house. com; 288 Harvard St; d without bath $140, d $240-260; 🅿❄🛜; Ⓣ Central) This treasure blends refinement and comfort, artistry and efficiency. Old wooden floors spread with throw rugs furnish a warm glow, and antique decor completes the inviting atmosphere. Noise does travel in this old house, but the place is quite comfortable. Other perks: free parking (a rarity), a thoughtfully designed continental breakfast and complimentary museum passes.

College Club
B&B $$

(Map p194; ☏ 617-536-9510; www.thecollege clubofboston.com; 44 Commonwealth Ave; s without bath from $179, d $269-289; ❄🛜; Ⓣ Arlington) Originally a private club for female college graduates, the College Club has 11 spacious rooms with high ceilings, now open to all genders. Period details – typical of the area's Victorian brownstones – include claw-foot tubs, ornamental fireplaces and bay windows. Local designers have lent their skills to decorate the various rooms, with delightful results. Prices include a continental breakfast.

★ Liberty Hotel
HOTEL $$$

(Map p194; ☏ 866-961-3778, 617-224-4000; www. libertyhotel.com; 215 Charles St; r from $375; 🅿❄🛜; Ⓣ Charles/MGH) It is with intended irony that the notorious Charles St Jail has been converted into the classy Liberty Hotel. Today, the 90ft ceiling soars above a spectacular lobby. All 298 guest rooms come with luxurious linens and high-tech amenities, while the 18 in the original jail wing boast floor-to-ceiling windows with amazing views of the Charles River and Beacon Hill.

Verb Hotel BOUTIQUE HOTEL **$$$**
(Map p190; ☑617-566-4500; www.theverbhotel.com; 1271 Boylston St; r $349-399; P❄🐾🏊📷; ⊤Kenmore, Fenway) The Verb Hotel took a down-and-out HoJo property and turned it into Boston's most radical, retro, rock-and-roll hotel. The style is mid-century modern; the theme is music. Memorabilia is on display throughout the joint, with turntables in the guest rooms and a jukebox cranking out tunes in the lobby. Classy, clean-lined rooms face the swimming pool or Fenway Park.

✖ Eating

✖ Beacon Hill & Boston Common

★Tatte BAKERY **$**
(Map p194; ☑617-723-5555; www.tattebakery.com; 70 Charles St; mains $10-14; ⊙7am-8pm Mon-Fri, from 8am Sat, 8am-7pm Sun; ⊤Charles/MGH) The aroma of buttery goodness – and the lines stretching out the door – signal your arrival at this fabulous bakery on the lower floor of the historic Charles St Meeting House. Swoon-worthy pastries (divinely cinnamon-y buns, chocolate-hazelnut twists, avocado and mushroom tartines) from $3 taste even more amazing if you're lucky enough to score a table on the sunny front patio.

Paramount CAFETERIA **$$**
(Map p194; ☑617-720-1152; www.paramountboston.com; 44 Charles St; mains $17-24; ⊙7am-10pm Mon-Fri, from 8am Sat & Sun; ☑♿; ⊤Charles/MGH) This old-fashioned cafeteria is a neighborhood favorite. A-plus diner fare includes pancakes, home fries, burgers and sandwiches, and big, hearty salads. Banana and caramel French toast is an obvious go-to for the brunch crowd. Don't sit down until you get your food! The wait may seem endless, but patrons swear it is worth it.

✖ Downtown & Waterfront

Spyce INTERNATIONAL **$**
(Map p194; www.spyce.com; 241 Washington St; bowls $7.50; ⊙10:30am-10pm; ☑♿; ⊤State) A new concept in dining, Spyce is the brainchild of four hungry MIT grads, who teamed up with a Michelin-starred chef. The food is

all prepared in a robotic kitchen – that is, self-rotating woks that are programmed for the optimal temperature and time to create consistently perfect 'bowls' of goodness. It's fast, fresh, healthy and pretty darn delicious.

★jm Curley PUB FOOD **$$**
(Map p194; ☑617-338-5333; www.jmcurleyboston.com; 21 Temple Pl; mains $10-20; ⊙11:30am-1am Mon-Sat, to 10pm Sun; ☑; ⊤Downtown Crossing) This dim, inviting bar is a perfect place to settle in for a Dark & Stormy on a dark and stormy night. The fare is bar food like you've never had before: Curley's cracka jack (caramel corn with bacon); mac 'n' cheese (served in a cast-iron skillet); and fried pickles (yes, you read that right). That's why they call it a gastropub.

Yvonne's MODERN AMERICAN **$$$**
(Map p194; ☑617-267-0047; www.yvonnesboston.com; 2 Winter Pl; ⊙5-11pm, bar to 2am; ☑; ⊤Park) Upon arrival at Yvonne's, staff will usher you discreetly through closed doors into a hidden 'modern supper club.' The spectacular space artfully blends old-school luxury with contemporary eclecticism. The menu of mostly small plates does the same, with items from tuna crudo to baked oysters to chicken and quinoa meatballs.

✖ West End & North End

Pizzeria Regina PIZZA **$**
(Map p194; ☑617-227-0765; www.pizzeriaregina.com; 11½ Thacher St; pizzas $13-24; ⊙11am-11:30pm Sun-Thu, to 12:30am Fri & Sat; ☑; ⊤Haymarket) The queen of North End pizzerias is the legendary Pizzeria Regina, famous for brusque but endearing waitstaff and crispy, thin-crust pizza. Thanks to the slightly spicy sauce (flavored with aged Romano cheese), Regina repeatedly wins accolades for its pies, including recognition by a certain unmentionable travel website as the best pizza *in the country*. Worth the wait.

★Pomodoro ITALIAN **$$**
(Map p194; ☑617-367-4348; 351 Hanover St; mains $22-26; ⊙5:30-11pm; ⊤Haymarket) Seductive Pomodoro offers a super-intimate, romantic setting (reservations are essential). The food is simple but perfectly prepared: fresh pasta, spicy tomato sauce, grilled fish and meats, and wine by the glass. If you're lucky, you might be on the receiving end of a complimentary tiramisu for dessert. Cash only.

✕ Charlestown

★ Brewer's Fork
PIZZA $$

(Map p190; ☑617-337-5703; www.brewersfork.com; 7 Moulton St; small plates $8-14, pizzas $14-18; ◷11:30am-10:30pm, to 11pm Thu-Sat, from 10:30am Sat & Sun; ◻93 from Haymarket, ◻Inner Harbor Ferry from Long Wharf, ◔North Station) This casual hipster hangout is a local favorite thanks to its enticing menu of small plates and pizzas, not to mention the excellent, oft-changing selection of about 30 craft beers. The wood-fired oven is the star of the show, but this place also does amazing things with its cheese and charcuterie boards.

✕ Seaport District

Yankee Lobster Co
SEAFOOD $

(☑617-345-9799; www.yankeelobstercompany.com; 300 Northern Ave; mains $11-26; ◷10am-9pm Mon-Sat, 11am-6pm Sun; ◻SL1, SL2, ◔South Station) The Zanti family has been fishing for three generations, so they definitely know their stuff. A relatively recent addition is this retail fish market, scattered with a few tables in case you want to dine in. And you do. Order something simple such as clam chowder or a lobster roll, accompany it with a cold beer, and you won't be disappointed.

★ Row 34
SEAFOOD $$

(Map p194; ☑617-553-5900; www.row34.com; 383 Congress St; oysters $2-3, mains $14-32; ◷11:30am-10pm Sun-Thu, to 11pm Fri & Sat; ◔South Station) In the heart of the new Seaport District, set in a sharp, postindustrial space, this place offers a dozen types of raw oysters and clams, alongside an amazing selection of craft beers. There's also a full menu of cooked seafood, ranging from the traditional to the trendy.

✕ South End & Chinatown

Gourmet Dumpling House
CHINESE $

(Map p194; ☑617-338-6223; www.gourmetdumplinghouse.com; 52 Beach St; dumplings $5-8, mains $9-17; ◷11am-1am; ◻; ◔Chinatown) *Xiao long bao.* That's all the Chinese you need to know to take advantage of the specialty at the Gourmet Dumpling House (or GDH, as it is fondly called). They are Shanghai soup dumplings, and they are fresh, doughy and delicious. The menu offers plenty of other options, including scrumptious crispy scallion pancakes. Come early or be prepared to wait.

★ Myers + Chang
ASIAN $$

(Map p190; ☑617-542-5200; www.myersandchang.com; 1145 Washington St; small plates $7-17, mains $16-25; ◷5-10pm Sun-Thu, to 11pm Fri & Sat; ◻; ◻SL4, SL5, ◔Tufts Medical Center) This super-hip Asian spot blends Thai, Chinese and Vietnamese cuisines, which means delicious dumplings, spicy stir-fries and oodles of noodles. The kitchen staff do amazing things with a wok, and the menu of small plates allows you to sample a wide selection of dishes. Dim sum for dinner? This is your place.

✕ Back Bay

★ Puro Ceviche Bar
LATIN AMERICAN $$

(Map p190; ☑617-266-0707; www.purocevichebar.com; 264 Newbury St; small plates $10-16; ◷4-11pm Mon-Thu, 11am-11pm Fri-Sun; ◔Hynes) This bar serves up delightfully modern yet still authentic Latin American fare in its funky downstairs digs, where exposed brick walls are covered with bold murals. Choose between six types of ceviche, six kinds of tacos and a slew of Latin-inspired small plates. Also on offer are classic cocktails and a nicely curated wine list. Attention, budget-minded travelers: there are $2 tacos on Tuesdays.

Saltie Girl
SEAFOOD $$$

(Map p190; ☑617-267-0691; www.saltiegirl.com; 281 Dartmouth St; small plates $12-18, mains $18-40; ◷11:30am-10pm; ◔Copley) Here's a new concept in dining: the seafood bar. It's a delightfully intimate place to feast on tantalizing dishes that blow away all preconceived notions about seafood. From your traditional Gloucester lobster roll to tinned fish on toast to the irresistible torched salmon belly, this place is full of delightful surprises.

✕ Kenmore Square & Fenway

★ Eventide Fenway
SEAFOOD $

(Map p190; ☑617-545-1060; www.eventideoysterco.com; 1321 Boylston St; mains $9-16; ◷11am-11pm; ◻; ◔Fenway) James Beard–award winners Mike Wiley and Andrew Taylor opened this counter-service version of their beloved Maine seafood restaurant. Fast, fresh and fabulous, the menu features just-shucked oysters and brown-butter lobster rolls, along with some pretty sophisticated seafood specials. Wash it down with a craft beer or a glass of rosé and the whole experience feels (and tastes) gourmet.

LGBTIQ+ BOSTON

Out and active gay communities are visible all around Boston, especially in the South End and Jamaica Plain. There is no shortage of entertainment options catering to LGBTIQ+ travelers. From drag shows to dyke nights, this sexually diverse community has something for everybody.

The biggest event of the year for the Boston gay and lesbian community is **Boston Pride** (www.bostonpride.org; ☺ Jun), a week of parades, parties, festivals and flag-raisings. There are excellent sources of information for the gay and lesbian community.

Bay Windows (www.baywindows.com) is a weekly newspaper for LGBTIQ+ readers. The print edition is distributed throughout New England, but the website is also an excellent source of news and information.

Edge Boston (www.edgeboston.com) is the Boston branch of the nationwide network of publications offering news and entertainment for LGBTIQ+ readers. Includes a nightlife section with culture and club reviews.

Island Creek Oyster Bar SEAFOOD $$$
(Map p190; ☑617-532-5300; www.islandcreek oysterbar.com; 500 Commonwealth Ave; oysters $3, mains lunch $13-21, dinner $24-36; ☺4-11pm Mon-Fri, 11:30am-11:30pm Sat, 10:30am-11pm Sun; ☂Kenmore) Island Creek claims to unite farmer, chef and diner in one space – and what a space it is. It serves up the region's finest oysters, along with other local seafood, in an ethereal new-age setting. The specialty – lobster-roe noodles topped with braised short ribs and grilled lobster – lives up to the hype.

✕ Cambridge

Mr Bartley's Burger Cottage BURGERS $
(Map p190; ☑617-354-6559; www.mrbartley.com; 1246 Massachusetts Ave; burgers $14-21; ☺11am-9pm Tue-Sat; ☂Harvard) Packed with small tables and hungry college students, this burger joint has been a Harvard Square institution for more than 50 years. Bartley's offers two dozen different burgers, including topical newcomers with names such as Trump Tower and Tom Brady Triumphant; sweet-potato fries, onion rings, thick frappés and raspberry-lime rickeys complete the classic American meal.

Cambridge, 1 PIZZA $$
(Map p190; ☑617-576-1111; www.cambridge1.us; 27 Church St; pizzas $22-30; ☺11:30am-11pm; ☑; ☂Harvard) This pizzeria is located in an old fire station – its name comes from the sign chiseled into the stonework out front. The interior is sleek, sparse and industrial, with big windows at the back overlooking the Old Burying Ground. The menu is equally simple: pizza, soup, salad, dessert.

The oddly shaped pizzas are delectable, with crispy crusts and creative toppings.

🍷 Drinking & Nightlife

★**Bleacher Bar** SPORTS BAR
(Map p190; ☑617-262-2424; www.bleacherbarbos ton.com; 82a Lansdowne St; ☺11am-1am Sun-Wed, to 2am Thu-Sat; ☂Kenmore) Tucked under the bleachers at Fenway Park, this classy bar offers a view onto center field. It's not the best place to watch the game as it gets packed, but it's a fun way to experience America's oldest ballpark, even when the Sox are not playing.

★**Drink** COCKTAIL BAR
(Map p194; ☑617-695-1806; www.drinkfortpoint. com; 348 Congress St; ☺4pm-1am; ☒SL1, SL2, ☂South Station) There is no cocktail menu at Drink. Instead you have a chat with the bartender, and he or she will whip something up according to your mood and taste. It takes seriously the art of mixology – and you will too, after you sample one of its concoctions. The subterranean space, with its low-lit, sexy ambience, makes a great date destination.

Trillium Fort Point MICROBREWERY
(Map p194; ☑857-449-0083; www.trilliumbrew ing.com; 50 Thompson Pl; ☺11am-11pm; ☂South Station) Trillium has been brewing beer in the Fort Point area for years. But it was only in 2018 that they opened this fantastic new taproom, complete with bar, dining room and rooftop deck. Enjoy the full range of Trillium favorites – not only India pale ales, but also American pale ales, gose ales, wild ales and stouts.

Democracy Brewing
BREWERY

(Map p194; ☎857-263-8604; www.democracy
brewing.com; 35 Temple Pl; ⏰11:30am-11pm Sun-
Thu, to 1am Fri & Sat; ⓣDowntown Crossing) The
beer is fresh, the fries are crispy perfection
and the politics are 'woke'. Not only do
they brew exceptional beer at Democracy
Brewing, they also foment revolution – by
supporting democratic businesses, organ-
izing community events, and showcasing
the revolutionaries and rabble-rousers from
Boston's past and present.

Beehive
COCKTAIL BAR

(Map p190; ☎617-423-0069; www.beehivebos
ton.com; 541 Tremont St; ⏰5pm-midnight Mon-
Wed, to 1am Thu, to 2am Fri, 9:30am-2am Sat, to
midnight Sun; ⓣBack Bay) The Beehive has
transformed the basement of the Boston
Center for the Arts into a 1920s Paris jazz
club. This place is more about the scene
than the music, which is often provided
by students from Berklee College of Music.
But the food is good and the vibe is definitely hip. Reservations required if you
want a table.

☆ Entertainment

★ Boston Red Sox
BASEBALL

(Map p190; ☎617-226-6666; www.redsox.com; 4
Jersey St; bleachers $10-45, grandstand $23-87,
box $38-189; ⓣKenmore) From April to Sep-
tember you can watch the Red Sox play at
Fenway Park, the nation's oldest and most
storied ballpark. Unfortunately it is also the
most expensive – not that this stops the Fenway faithful from scooping up the tickets.
There are sometimes game-day tickets on
sale, starting 90 minutes before the opening
pitch.

★ Boston
Symphony Orchestra
CLASSICAL MUSIC

(BSO; ☎617-266-1200, 617-266-1492; www.bso.org;
tickets $30-145) Flawless acoustics match the
ambitious programs of the world-renowned
Boston Symphony Orchestra. From Sep-

tember to April, the BSO performs in the
beauteous **Symphony Hall** (Map p190; 301
Massachusetts Ave; ⏰hours vary; ⓣSymphony),
featuring an ornamental high-relief ceiling
and attracting a well-dressed crowd. In summer months the BSO retreats to Tanglewood
in Western Massachusetts.

Red Room @ Cafe 939
LIVE MUSIC

(Map p190; ☎617-747-2261; www.berklee.edu/
cafe939; 939 Boylston St; tickets free-$20; ⏰box
office 10am-6pm Mon-Sat; ⓣHynes) Run by
Berklee students, the Red Room @ Cafe 939
has emerged as one of Boston's least predictable and most enjoyable music venues. It
has an excellent sound system and a baby
grand piano; most importantly, it books interesting, eclectic up-and-coming musicians.
Buy tickets in advance at the **Berklee Performance Center** (Map p190; ☎617-747-2261;
www.berklee.edu/bpc; 136 Massachusetts Ave;
tickets $10-65; ⏰box office 10am-6pm Mon-Sat;
ⓣHynes).

Club Passim
LIVE MUSIC

(Map p190; ☎617-492-7679; www.clubpassim.
org; 47 Palmer St; tickets $10-32; ⓣHarvard)
The legendary Club Passim is a holdout
from the days when folk music was a staple
in Cambridge (and around the country).
The club continues to book top-notch acts,
single-handedly sustaining the city's folk
scene. The colorful, intimate room is hidden
off a side street in Harvard Square, just as it
has been since 1969.

Wally's Café
JAZZ

(Map p190; ☎617-424-1408; www.wallyscafe.com;
427 Massachusetts Ave; ⏰5pm-2am; ⓣMassachu
setts Ave) When Wally's opened in 1947, Bar-
badian immigrant Joseph Walcott became
the first African American to own a nightclub in New England. Old-school, gritty and
small, it still attracts a racially diverse crowd
to hear jammin' jazz music 365 days a year.
Berklee students love this place, especially
the nightly jam sessions (6pm to 9pm).

🛍 Shopping

★ SoWa Open Market
MARKET

(Map p190; ☎857-362-7692; www.sowaboston.
com; 460 Harrison Ave; ⏰10am-4pm Sun May-
Oct; 🚌SL4, SL5, ⓣTufts Medical Center) Boston's
original art market, this outdoor event is a
fabulous opportunity for strolling, shopping and people-watching. More than 100
vendors set up shop under white tents. It's
never the same two weeks in a row, but

ⓘ CHEAP SEATS

ArtsBoston (www.artsboston.org)
offers discounted tickets to theater
productions through BosTix Deals (up
to 25% for advance purchases online;
up to 50% for same-day purchase at
ArtsBoston kiosks at Quincy Market and
Prudential Center).

there's always plenty of arts and crafts, as well as edgier art, jewelry, homewares, and homemade food and body products.

Boston Public Market   MARKET
(BPM; Map p194; ☑617-973-4909; www.boston publicmarket.org; 136 Blackstone St; ◷8am-8pm Mon-Sat, 10am-6pm Sun; ☎; Ⓣ Haymarket) A locavore's longtime dream come true, this daily farmers market – housed in a brick-and-mortar building – gives shoppers access to fresh foodstuffs, grown, harvested and produced right here in New England. Come for seasonal produce, fresh seafood, meats and poultry from local farms, artisanal cheeses and dairy products, maple syrup and other sweets. Don't miss the local brews found in Hopsters' Alley.

Greenway Open Market   ARTS & CRAFTS
(Map p194; ☑800-401-6557; www.newengland openmarkets.com; Rose Kennedy Greenway; ◷11am-5pm Sat, plus 1st & 3rd Sun May-Oct; ☎; Ⓣ Aquarium) This weekend artist market brings out dozens of vendors to display their wares in the open air. Look for unique, handmade gifts, jewelry, bags, paintings, ceramics and other arts and crafts – most of which are locally and ethically made. Food trucks are always on hand to cater to the hungry.

❶ Information

Boston Harbor Islands Pavilion (Map p194; ☑617-223-8666; www.bostonharborislands. org; cnr State St & Atlantic Ave; ◷9am-4:30pm mid-May–Jun & Sep-early Oct, to 6pm Jul & Aug; ☎; Ⓣ Aquarium) Ideally located on the Rose Kennedy Greenway. This information center will tell you everything you need to know to plan your visit to the Boston Harbor Islands. Don't miss the nearby *Harbor Fog* sculpture, which immerses passersby in the sounds and sensations of the harbor.

Cambridge Visitor Information Kiosk (Map p190; ☑617-441-2884; www.cambridge-usa. org; Harvard Sq; ◷9am-5pm Mon-Fri, to 1pm Sat & Sun; Ⓣ Harvard) Has detailed information on current Cambridge happenings and self-guided walking tours.

Greater Boston Convention & Visitors Bureau (www.bostonusa.com) Has a website packed with information on hotels, restaurants and special events, as well as LGBTIQ+, family travel and more.

Massachusetts Office of Travel & Tourism (www.massvacation.com) Information about events and activities throughout the state, including an excellent guide to green tourism.

National Park Service Visitors Center (NPS; Map p194; ☑617-242-5642; www.nps.gov/ bost/planyourvisit/index.htm; Faneuil Hall; ◷9am-6pm; Ⓣ State) Has loads of information about the Freedom Trail sights and is the starting point for the free **NPS Freedom Trail Tour** (◷10am, 11am, 2pm & 3pm Jun-Sep). There is an additional NPS Visitors Center at the **Charlestown Navy Yard** (Map p190; ☑617-242-5601; www.nps.gov/bost; ◷visitor center 10am-5pm Wed-Sun Jan-Apr, 9am-5pm May-Sep, 10am-5pm Oct-Dec; ☒93 from Haymarket, 🚢 Inner Harbor Ferry from Long Wharf, Ⓣ North Station).

❶ Getting There & Away

Most travelers arrive in Boston by plane, with many national and international flights in and out of **Logan International Airport** (BOS; ☑800-235-6426; www.massport.com/ logan-airport). Two smaller regional airports – Manchester Airport in New Hampshire and Green Airport near Providence, RI – offer alternatives that are also accessible to Boston and are sometimes less expensive.

Most trains operated by Amtrak (www.amtrak. com) go in and out of **South Station** (Map p194; ☑617-523-1300; www.south-station.net; 700 Atlantic Ave). Boston is the northern terminus of the Northeast Corridor, which sends frequent trains to New York City, NY (3½ to 4½ hours), Philadelphia, PA (five to six hours) and Washington, DC (6¾ to eight hours). *Lake Shore Limited* goes daily to Buffalo, NY (11 hours) and Chicago, IL (22 hours), while the *Downeaster* goes from North Station to Portland, ME (2½ hours).

Buses are most useful for regional destinations, although Greyhound (www.greyhound. com) operates services around the country. In recent years, there has been a spate of new companies offering cheap and efficient service to New York City (four to five hours).

Flights, cars and tours can be booked online at lonelyplanet.com/bookings.

❶ Getting Around

TO/FROM THE AIRPORT
Boston Logan International Airport Take the silver line bus (free) or blue line subway ($2.25 to $2.75) to central Boston from 5:30am to 12:30am, or catch a taxi for $25 to $30.

Green Airport Take the commuter rail to South Station ($12).

Manchester Airport Book in advance for the hourly Flight Line Inc shuttle bus to Logan International Airport, or catch the infrequent Greyhound bus to South Station.

South Station Located in central Boston on the red line.

PUBLIC TRANSPORTATION

Blue Bikes Boston's bike-share program, with 1800 bikes available to borrow at 200 stations.

MBTA bus Supplements the subway system.

T (Subway) The quickest and easiest way to get to most destinations. Runs from 5:30am or 6am until 1:30am.

Around Boston

Lexington

This upscale suburb, about 18 miles from Boston's center, is a bustling village of white churches and historic taverns, with tour buses surrounding the village green. A skirmish kicked off the War of Independence. Each year on April 19, historians and patriots don their 18th-century costumes and grab their rifles for an elaborate re-enactment of the events of 1775.

While this history is celebrated and preserved, it is in stark contrast to the peaceful, even staid, community that is Lexington today. If you stray more than a few blocks from the green, you could be in Anywhere, USA, with few reminders that this is where it all started. Nonetheless, it is a pleasant enough Anywhere, USA, with restaurants and shops lining the main drag, and impressive Georgian architecture anchoring either end.

★ Minute Man
National Historic Park   PARK

(www.nps.gov/mima; 3113 Marrett Rd; ⊙9am-5pm Apr-Oct; 🔁) **FREE** The route that British troops followed to Concord has been designated the Minute Man National Historic Park. The visitor center at the eastern end of the park shows an informative multimedia presentation depicting Paul Revere's ride and the ensuing battles. Within the park, Battle Rd is a 5-mile wooded trail that connects the historic sites related to the battles – from Meriam's Corner, where gunfire erupted while British soldiers were retreating, to the Paul Revere capture site.

Battle Green   HISTORIC SITE

(Lexington Common; Massachusetts Ave) The historic Battle Green is where the skirmish between patriots and British troops jump-started the War of Independence. The **Lexington Minuteman Statue** (crafted by Henry Hudson Kitson in 1900) stands guard at the southeastern end of Battle Green,

honoring the bravery of the 77 minutemen who met the British here in 1775, and the eight who died.

★ Minuteman
Commuter Bikeway   CYCLING

The Minuteman Commuter Bikeway follows an old railroad right of way from near the Alewife red-line subway terminus in Cambridge through Arlington to Lexington and Bedford, a total distance of about 14 miles. From Lexington center, you can also ride along Massachusetts Ave to Rte 2A, which parallels the Battle Rd trail, and eventually leads into Concord center.

🛈 Getting There & Away

MBTA (www.mbta.com) buses 62 (Bedford VA Hospital) and 76 (Hanscom Field) run from the red-line Alewife subway terminus through Lexington center at least hourly on weekdays and less frequently on Saturday; there are no buses on Sunday.

Concord

On April 18, 1775, British troops marched out of Boston, searching for arms that colonists had hidden west of the city. The following morning, they skirmished with Colonial minutemen in Lexington, then continued on to Concord, where the rivals faced off at North Bridge, in the first battle of the War of Independence.

Today, tall white church steeples rise above ancient oaks, elms and maples, giving Concord a stateliness that belies the revolutionary drama that occurred centuries ago. Indeed, it's easy to see how writers such as Ralph Waldo Emerson, Nathaniel Hawthorne, Henry David Thoreau and Louisa May Alcott found their inspiration here. Concord was also the home of famed sculptor Daniel Chester French (who went on to create the Lincoln Memorial in Washington, DC).

These days travelers can relive history in Concord. **Patriots' Day** (www.lexingtonma.gov/patriotsday) is celebrated with gusto, and many significant literary sites are open for visitors.

★ Old North Bridge   HISTORIC SITE

(www.nps.gov/mima; Monument St; ⊙dawn-dusk) A half-mile north of Monument Sq in Concord center, the wooden span of Old North Bridge is the site of the 'shot heard around the world' (as Emerson wrote in his poem *Concord Hymn*). This is where enraged minutemen fired on British troops, forcing them to retreat to Boston. Daniel Chester French's first statue, *Minute Man*, presides over the park from the opposite side of the bridge.

Concord Museum MUSEUM
(www.concordmuseum.org; 200 Lexington Rd; adult/child $10/5; ⊞) Southeast of Monument Sq, Concord Museum brings the town's diverse history under one roof. The museum's prized possession is one of the 'two if by sea' lanterns that hung in the steeple of the Old North Church in Boston as a signal to Paul Revere. It also has the world's largest collection of Henry David Thoreau artifacts, including his writing desk from Walden Pond.

❶ Getting There & Away

MBTA commuter rail trains run between Boston's North Station and Concord ('the Depot'; $9.25, 40 minutes, 12 daily) on the Fitchburg/South Acton line.

Salem

This town's very name conjures up images of diabolical witchcraft and people being burned at the stake. The famous Salem witch trials of 1692 are ingrained in the national memory. Indeed, Salem goes all out at Halloween, when the town dresses up for parades and parties, and shops sell all manner of Wiccan accessories.

These incidents obscure Salem's true claim to fame: its glory days as a center for clipper-ship trade with the Far East. Elias Hasket Derby, America's first millionaire, built Derby Wharf, which is now the center of the Salem Maritime National Historic Site. The marvelous Peabody Essex Museum displays some of the treasures that were brought home from these merchant expeditions.

Today, Salem is a middle-class commuter suburb of Boston with an enviable location on the sea. Its rich history and culture, from witches to ships to art, continue to cast a spell on visitors.

★ Peabody Essex Museum MUSEUM
(☑ 978-745-9500; www.pem.org; 161 Essex St; adult/child $20/free; ⊙ 10am-5pm Tue-Sun; ⊞) All of the art, artifacts and curiosities that Salem merchants brought back from the Far East were the foundation for this museum. Founded in 1799, it is the country's oldest museum in continuous operation. The building itself is impressive, with a light-filled atrium, and it's a wonderful setting for the vast collections, which focus on New England decorative arts and maritime history.

Salem Maritime
National Historic Site HISTORIC SITE
(www.nps.gov/sama; 160 Derby St; ⊙ 9am-5pm May-Oct, 10am-4pm Wed-Sun Nov-Apr) **FREE** This National Historic Site comprises the Custom House, the wharves and other buildings along Derby St that are remnants of the shipping industry that once thrived along this stretch of Salem. Of the 50 wharves that once lined Salem Harbor, only three remain, the longest of which is Derby Wharf. Check the website for a schedule of guided tours of the various buildings, or download an audio walking tour of the whole area.

❶ Getting There & Away

The Rockport/Newburyport line of the MBTA commuter rail runs from Boston's North Station to Salem Depot ($7.50, 30 minutes). Trains run every 30 minutes during the morning and evening rush hours, hourly during the rest of day, and less frequently at weekends.

Plymouth

Plymouth calls itself 'America's Home Town.' It was here that the Pilgrims first settled in the winter of 1620, seeking a place where they could practice their religion as they wished, without interference from government. An innocuous, weathered ball of granite – the famous Plymouth Rock – marks the spot where they supposedly first stepped ashore in this foreign land, but Plimoth Plantation provides a more informative and accurate account of their experiences. Many other museums and historic houses in the surrounding streets recall their struggles, sacrifices and triumphs.

★ Plimoth Plantation MUSEUM
(☑ 508-746-1622; www.plimoth.org; 137 Warren Ave; adult/child $28/16; ⊙ 9am-5pm Apr-Nov; ⊞) Three miles south of Plymouth center, Plimoth Plantation authentically re-creates the Pilgrims' settlement in its primary exhibit, entitled **1627 English Village**. Everything in the village – costumes, implements, vocabulary, artistry, recipes and crops – has been painstakingly researched and remade. Costumed interpreters, acting in character, explain the details of daily life and answer your questions as you watch them work and play.

★**Mayflower II**   SHIP
(www.plimoth.org/what-see-do/mayflower-ii; State
Pier, Water St; 🚻) If Plymouth Rock tells
us little about the Pilgrims, *Mayflower II*
speaks volumes. Climb aboard this replica of the small ship in which the Pilgrims
made the fateful voyage, where 102 people
lived together for 66 days as the ship passed
through stormy North Atlantic waters. Actors in period costume are on board, re-
counting harrowing tales from the journey.

Native Plymouth Tours   WALKING
(📞774-454-7792; www.facebook.com/nativeply
mouthtours; adult/child $15/10) A two-hour
walking tour with a Native American guide.
You'll see many typical sights, but your
guide Timothy Turner will debunk myths,
give unusual insights and share a completely different perspective on Plymouth (and
American) history. Four-person minimum.

❶ Getting There & Away

You can reach Plymouth from Boston by MBTA
commuter rail trains, which depart from South
Station three or four times a day ($11.50, 90
minutes). From the station at Cordage Park,
GATRA buses connect to Plymouth center.

Cape Cod

Quaint fishing villages, kitschy tourist traps
and genteel towns – the Cape has many
faces. Each attracts a different crowd. Families seeking calm waters perfect for little
tykes favor Cape Cod Bay on the peninsula's
quieter north side. College students looking
to play hard in the day and let loose after
the sun goes down set out for Falmouth or
Wellfleet. Provincetown is a paradise for art
lovers, whale-watchers, LGBTIQ+ travelers
and...well, just about everyone.

❶ Getting There & Around

Your own wheels (two or four) make getting
around easy, but there are also bus links; see
the website of the **Cape Cod Regional Transit
Authority** (📞800-352-7155; www.capecodrta.
org; single ride/day pass $2/6) for routes and
schedules, including summertime shuttles in
Falmouth, Hyannis and Provincetown.

Sandwich

The Cape's oldest town (founded in 1637)
makes a perfect first impression as you
cross over the canal from the mainland.
Head straight to the village center, where

white-steepled churches, period homes and
a working grist mill surround a picturesque
swan pond.

**Heritage
Museums & Gardens**   MUSEUM, GARDENS
(📞508-888-3300; www.heritagemuseumsand
gardens.org; 67 Grove St; adult/child $18/7;
🕙10am-5pm mid-Apr–mid-Oct; 🚻) Fun for
kids and adults alike, the 100-acre Heritage
Museums & Gardens sports a superb vintage automobile collection in a Shaker-style
round barn, an authentic 1908 carousel
(rides free with admission) and unusual folk
art collections. The grounds also contain
one of the finest rhododendron gardens in
America; from mid-May to mid-June thousands of 'rhodies' blaze with color. You'll also
find ways to get your heart racing, via the
Adventure Park (📞508-866-0199; www.herit
ageadventurepark.org; 2hr ticket $38-49; 🕙8am-
8pm Jun & Jul, to 7:30pm mid-Aug, to 7pm late Aug,
shorter hours mid-Apr–May & Sep–mid-Nov; 🚻).

❶ Information

Sandwich Visitor Center (📞508-833-9755;
www.sandwichchamber.com; 520 MA 130;
🕙10am-5pm Mon-Sat, to 4pm Sun mid-May–
mid-Oct, to 4pm Mon-Fri mid-Oct–mid-May)
Stop in for local tips and maps.

Falmouth

Crowd-pleasing beaches, a terrific bike trail
and one of the busiest downtowns outside of
Provincetown make this charmer of a town
worth checking out. There's also plenty for
history buffs to be found here: Falmouth
puffs with pride over its most cherished
daughter, Katharine Lee Bates, who wrote
the words to the nation's favorite patriotic
hymn, *America the Beautiful*.

★**Shining Sea Bikeway**   CYCLING
(🚻) A bright star among the Cape's stellar
bike trails, this 10.7-mile beaut runs along
the entire west coast of Falmouth, from
County Rd in North Falmouth to Woods
Hole ferry terminal, offering unspoiled
views of salt ponds, marsh and seascapes.
Completed in 2009, the bikeway follows an
abandoned railroad bed, taking you places
you'd never get a glimpse of otherwise.

Maison Villatte   CAFE $
(📞774-255-1855; 267 Main St; snacks $4-12;
🕙7am-5pm Tue-Sun) A pair of French bakers
crowned in toques work the ovens at this
buzzing bakery-cafe, creating crusty artisan

DON'T MISS

CAPE COD RAIL TRAIL

The mother of all Cape bicycle trails, the **Cape Cod Rail Trail** (CCRT; www.mass.gov/locations/cape-cod-rail-trail) runs 22 glorious paved miles through forest, past cranberry bogs and along sandy ponds ideal for a dip. This rural route, formerly used as a railroad line, is one of the finest bike trails in all of New England.

The path begins in Dennis on MA 134 and continues through **Nickerson State Park** (☑ 508-896-3491; www.mass.gov/dcr; 3488 MA 6A; parking $15; ☺ dawn-dusk; ♦) in Brewster, into Orleans and across the Cape Cod National Seashore (p212), all the way to South Wellfleet.

There's a hefty dose of Ye Olde Cape Cod scenery en route and you'll have opportunities to detour into villages for lunch or sightseeing. If you have only enough time to do part of the trail, begin at Nickerson State Park and head for the National Seashore – the landscape is unbeatable.

Bicycle rentals are available at the trailheads in Dennis and Wellfleet and opposite the National Seashore's visitor center in Eastham. There's car parking at all four sites (free except for Nickerson).

breads, flaky croissants and sinful pastries. Hearty sandwiches and robust coffee make it an ideal lunch spot.

★ Añejo
MEXICAN $$

(☑ 508-388-7631; www.anejomexicanbistro.com; 188 Main St; mains $13-26; ☺ 11:30am-late Mon-Sat, from 10:30am Sun) This buzzing bistro and tequila bar brings a little year-round heat to the Main St scene, with a big selection of margaritas and tequilas, and a menu of fab street food – enchiladas, tacos, tostadas – that spins fresh Mexican flavors Cape Cod–style, with lots of fish and local seafood.

❶ Information

Falmouth Chamber of Commerce (☑ 508-548-8500; www.falmouthchamber.com; 20 Academy Lane; ☺ 8:30am-4:30pm Mon-Fri, plus 10am-2pm Sat late May-Aug) In the town center, just off Main St.

❶ Getting There & Away

Sitting at the southwest corner of the Cape, Falmouth is reached via MA 28, which becomes Main St in the town center. Buses connect the town with Boston and other Cape destinations.

Ferries to Martha's Vineyard (p217) leave from Falmouth Harbor in summer, and year-round from Woods Hole, 4.5 miles southwest of downtown.

Hyannis

Ferries, buses and planes all converge on Hyannis, the Cape's commercial hub (and part of the larger Barnstable township). So there's a good chance you will, too. Al-

though the downtown area lacks the charm of others on Cape, the village center and harborfront have been rejuvenated, making them a pleasant place to break a journey.

In addition to being a jumping-off point for boats to Nantucket and Martha's Vineyard, Hyannis attracts Kennedy fans – JFK made his summer home here, and it was at the Kennedy compound that Teddy passed away in 2009. Hyannis Harbor, with its waterfront eateries and ferries, is a few minutes' walk from Main St.

◉ Sights

★ John F Kennedy Hyannis Museum
MUSEUM

(☑ 508-790-3077; www.jfkhyannismuseum.org; 397 Main St; adult/child $12/6; ☺ 9am-5pm Mon-Sat, from noon Sun Jun-Oct, 10am-4pm Mon-Sat, from noon Sun Nov, 10am-4pm Thu-Sat Dec-Apr, 10am-5pm Mon-Sat, noon-5pm Sun May) Hyannis has been the summer home of the Kennedy clan for generations. Back in the day, JFK spent the warmer months here – times that are beautifully documented at this museum with photographs and video from JFK's childhood to the Camelot years of his presidency. The exhibits are poignantly done, and present a theme that changes annually (previous years have covered matriarch Rose and explored the brotherly bond between Jack and Bobby).

⌂ Sleeping

HI Hyannis
HOSTEL $

(☑ 508-775-7990; www.hiusa.org; 111 Ocean St; dm/d from $40/119; ☺ mid-May–mid-Oct; P @ ☎) For a million-dollar view on a backpacker's budget, book yourself a bed at this hostel overlooking the harbor. It was built in 2010 by adding new wings to a period home and is within walking distance of the Main St scene, beaches and ferries. Now the caveat: there are only 42 beds, so book well in advance.

★ **Anchor-In**　　　　　　　　HOTEL $$$
(☑508-775-0357; www.anchorin.com; 1 South St; r $206-316; 🌸@🛜🐕) This family-run boutique hotel puts the chains to shame. The harbor-front location offers a fine sense of place, and the heated outdoor pool is a perfect perch from which to watch fishing boats unload their catch. The rooms are bright and smart, with water-view balconies. If you're planning a day trip to Nantucket, the ferry is just a stroll away.

✕ Eating & Drinking

Pain D'Avignon　　　　　BAKERY, BISTRO $$
(☑508-778-8588; www.paindavignon.com; 15 Hinckley Rd; lunch $8-17, dinner mains $19-32; ⊙7am-4pm daily, plus 5-10pm Tue-Thu & Sun, to 11pm Fri & Sat Jun-Sep, also 5-9pm Tue-Thu, to 10pm Fri & Sat Oct-May) It's not in the likeliest of locations (out by the airport, off MA 132), but seek this place out for a delectable slice of Paris. Patisserie favorites beckon in the morning, but more leisurely options like omelets and galettes (savory crepes) can be ordered. At lunch and dinner, classic French bistro fare shines: croque monsieur, quiche Lorraine, steak *frites*.

★ **Naked Oyster**　　　　　SEAFOOD $$$
(☑508-778-6500; www.nakedoyster.com; 410 Main St; lunch $11-20, dinner mains $22-38; ⊙noon-10pm Mon-Sat) 🍴 Limited ingredient travel times are preferred at this upmarket joint, where the eponymous bivalves come from the restaurant's oyster farm in Barnstable Harbor. They keep fine company in the raw

---

OFF THE BEATEN TRACK

SCENIC DRIVE: MA 6A

When exploring the Cape, eschew the speedy Mid-Cape Hwy (MA 6) and follow instead the Old King's Hwy (MA 6A), which snakes along Cape Cod Bay. The longest continuous stretch of historic district in the USA, it's lined with gracious period homes, antique shops and art galleries, all of which make for good browsing en route.

---

bar: shrimp, littlenecks, lobster. The menu borrows global flavors to dress up fresh seafood – Thai shrimp, *moules frites,* fish tacos, curried scallops – with fine results.

Cape Cod Beer　　　　　　　　BREWERY
(☑508-790-4200; www.capecodbeer.com; 1336 Phinneys Lane; ⊙10am-6pm Mon-Fri, 11am-4pm Sat) Not just a place for beer connoisseurs (although they'll be pretty happy), this brewery is a fun spot to while away some time. Free brewery tours happen daily (except Sunday) at 11am, but you can stop in for tastings ($6) any time. Check the website for events, from bring-your-pet 'yappy hour' to painting classes, live music and comedy nights.

❶ Getting There & Away

Hyannis is the Cape's transportation hub. Flights go to/from Boston and Nantucket year-round, as well as Martha's Vineyard and New York in summer. Ferries go to Nantucket. And buses run to Boston and to Provincetown (calling at Cape towns en route).

The **Cape Flyer** (☑508-775-8504; www.capeflyer.com; one-way tickets $5-22; ⊙late May-Aug) is a weekend train service operating from Memorial Day to Labor Day (late May to mid-October), connecting Boston's South Station with Hyannis.

Chatham

The patriarch of Cape Cod towns, Chatham has a genteel reserve that is evident along its shady Main St: the shops are upscale and the lodgings tastefully swank. That said, there's something for everyone here – families flock to town for seal-watching and birders migrate to the wildlife refuge. And then there are all those beaches. Sitting at the 'elbow' of the Cape, Chatham has an amazing 60 miles of shoreline along the ocean, the sound and countless coves and inlets.

MA 28 leads right to Main St, where the lion's share of shops and restaurants are lined up. Chatham is a town made for strolling. You'll find free parking along Main St and in the parking lot behind the Chatham Squire restaurant (but you'll have to fight for a space in summer).

Chatham Shark Center　　　　　MUSEUM
(☑508-348-5901; www.atlanticwhiteshark.org; 235 Orleans Rd, North Chatham; $5; ⊙10am-4pm Fri, Sat & Mon, from 11am Sun Jun, 10am-4pm Mon-Sat, from 11am Sun Jul & Aug, 10am-4pm Sat, from 11am Sun Sep-early Oct) Stop here for the low-

Cape Cod, Martha's Vineyard & Nantucket

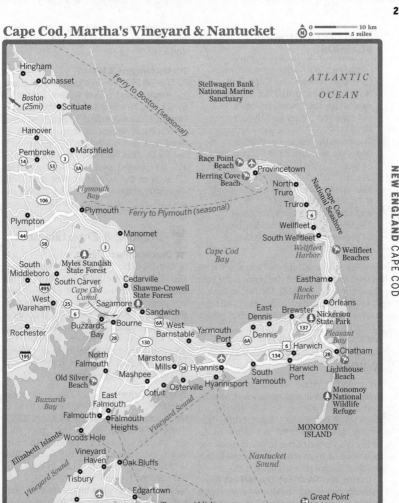

down on one of the Cape's most intriguing summer residents: the great white shark. Interactive exhibits and videos aimed at kids and adults attempt to demystify the animal given a good deal of bad PR in the Cape Cod–set movie, *Jaws*. It's under the auspic-

es of the Atlantic White Shark Conservancy (motto: 'Awareness inspires conservation').

★**Chatham Pier Fish Market** SEAFOOD **$$**
(☑508-945-3474; www.chathampierfishmarket.
com; 45 Barcliff Ave; mains $12-24; ☺10am-7pm
mid-May–mid-Nov) If you like it fresh and

CAPE COD NATIONAL SEASHORE

Extending some 40 miles around the curve of the Outer Cape, **Cape Cod National Seashore** (☑508-255-3421; www.nps.gov/caco; pedestrian/cyclist/motorcycle/car per day $3/3/10/20) encompasses the Atlantic shoreline from Orleans all the way to Provincetown. Under the auspices of the National Park Service, it's a treasure trove of unspoiled beaches, dunes, salt marshes, nature trails and forests. Thanks to the backing of President John F Kennedy, this vast area was set aside for preservation in the 1960s, just before a building boom hit the rest of his native Cape Cod.

hyper-local, this salt-sprayed fish shack with its own sushi chef and day-boats is for you. The chowder's incredible, the fish so fresh it was swimming earlier in the day. It's all takeout, but there are shady picnic tables where you can watch fishers unloading their catch and seals frolicking as you savor dinner.

Wellfleet

Art galleries, primo surfing beaches and those famous Wellfleet oysters lure visitors to this seaside village. Actually, there's not much Wellfleet doesn't have, other than crowds. It's a delightful throwback to an earlier era, from its drive-in movie theater to its unspoiled town center, which has barely changed in appearance since the 1950s.

During the **Wellfleet OysterFest** (www.wellfleetoysterfest.org), held on a weekend in mid-October, the entire town center becomes a food fair, with a beer garden, an oyster-shucking contest and, of course, belly-busters of the blessed bivalves. It's a wildly popular event and a great time to see Wellfleet at its most spirited.

🛏 Sleeping & Eating

★**Wagner at Duck Creek** INN $$$
(☑508-942-8185; www.thewagneratduckcreek.com; 70 Main St; r $217-373; ❋🤖) Energetic owners have breathed new life into this iconic inn – no small undertaking, given it encompasses 27 rooms housed in three antique timber buildings spread over lovely grounds. The result is a boutique feel, with pretty, well-equipped rooms plus an on-site

tavern, open year-round. Future plans think big: bike rental, kayaks for guest use, a pool and a spa.

PB Boulangerie & Bistro BAKERY $
(☑508-349-1600; www.pbboulangeriebistro.com; 15 Lecount Hollow Rd, South Wellfleet; pastries $3-5; ⊙bakery 7am-6pm Wed-Sun, bistro 5-9:30pm Wed-Sat, 10:30am-2pm Sun) A Michelin-starred French baker setting up shop in tiny Wellfleet? You might think he'd gone crazy, if not for the line out the door. You can't miss PB: it's painted pink and set back from US 6. Scan the cabinets full of fruit tarts, chocolate-almond croissants and filled baguettes and you'll think you've died and gone to Paris.

🍷 Drinking & Entertainment

★**Beachcomber** BAR
(☑508-349-6055; www.thebeachcomber.com; 1120 Cahoon Hollow Rd; ⊙11:30am-1am late May-early Sep) If you're ready for some serious partying, 'Da Coma' is *the* place to rock the night away. It's a bar. It's a restaurant. It's a dance club. It's the coolest summertime hangout on the entire Cape. It's set in a former lifeguard station right on Cahoon Hollow Beach, and you can watch the surf action till the sun goes down.

Wellfleet Drive-In CINEMA
(☑508-349-7176; www.wellfleetcinemas.com; 51 US 6, South Wellfleet; tickets adult/child $12/9; ⊙late May–mid-Sep; 🚗) By night, park your car at the 1950s-era Wellfleet Drive-In, where everything except the feature flick is true to the era. Grab a bite to eat at the old-fashioned snack bar, hook the mono speaker over the car window (or tune your car's stereo to the dedicated frequency) and settle in for a double feature. Cash only.

❶ Getting There & Away

Most of Wellfleet east of US 6 is part of the Cape Cod National Seashore. To get to the town center, turn west off US 6 at either Main or School Sts.

Provincetown

This is it: Provincetown is as far as you can go on the Cape, and more than just geographically. The draw is irresistible. Fringe writers and artists began making a summer haven in Provincetown a century ago. Today this sandy outpost has morphed into the hottest LGBTIQ+ destination in the Northeast. Flamboyant street scenes, brilliant art galleries and unbridled nightlife paint the town center. But that's only half the show. Provincetown's untamed coastline and vast beaches also beg to be explored. Sail off on a whale-watching tour, cruise the night away, get lost in the dunes – it's all easy to do in Provincetown.

Summers, specifically between June and August, are when the town shines brightest, but you'll still find plenty of nature adventure opportunities and cute guys in the spring and fall. Whenever you decide to come, make sure you don't miss this unique, welcoming corner of New England.

◉ Sights

★ Provincetown Art Association & Museum   MUSEUM

(PAAM; ☑ 508-487-1750; www.paam.org; 460 Commercial St; adult/child $10/free; ⊙ 11am-5pm Sat-Thu, to 10pm Fri Jun & Sep, to 8pm Mon-Thu, to 10pm Fri, to 5pm Sat & Sun Jul & Aug, noon-5pm Thu-Sun Oct-May) Founded in 1914 to celebrate the town's thriving art community, this vibrant museum showcases the works of hundreds of artists who have found their inspiration on the Lower Cape. Chief among them are Charles Hawthorne, who led the early Provincetown art movement, and Edward Hopper, who had a home and gallery in the Truro dunes.

Pilgrim Monument & Provincetown Museum   MUSEUM

(☑ 508-487-1310; www.pilgrim-monument.org; 1 High Pole Hill Rd; adult/child $12/4; ⊙ 9am-5pm Apr, May & Sep-Jan, to 7pm Jun-Aug) Climb to the top of the country's tallest all-granite structure (253ft) for a sweeping view of town, the beaches and the spine of the Lower Cape. The climb is 116 steps plus 60 ramps and takes about 10 minutes at a leisurely pace. At the base of the c 1910 tower is an evocative, but quite Eurocentric, museum depicting the landing of the *Mayflower* Pilgrims and other Provincetown history.

🏃 Activities

Province Lands Bike Trail (www.nps.gov/caco), an exhilarating 7.5 miles of paved bike trails, crisscrosses the forest and undulating dunes of the Cape Cod National Seashore. As a bonus, you can cool off with a swim: the main 5.5-mile loop trail has spur trails leading to **Herring Cove Beach** (Province Lands Rd) and **Race Point Beach**

(Race Point Rd). There are plenty of bike-rental places in central P-town.

Dolphin Fleet Whale Watch   WILDLIFE

(☑ 508-240-3636, 800-826-9300; www.whale watch.com; 307 Commercial St; adult/child $52/31; ⊙ mid-Apr–Oct; 🚤) 🐟 Dolphin Fleet offers as many as 10 whale-watching tours daily in peak season, each lasting three to four hours. You can expect a lot of splashy fun. Humpback whales have a flair for acrobatic breaching and come surprisingly close to the boats. The naturalists on board are informative and play a vital role in monitoring whale populations.

🛏 Sleeping

★ AWOL   BOUTIQUE HOTEL $$$

(☑ 508-413-9820; www.awolhotel.com; 59 Province Lands Rd; r $397-639; ⊙ May-Oct; 🅿 ❄ 🛜 🏊) Overlooking the salt marsh and away from the bustle of Provincetown's main drag is AWOL, a new boutique hotel with a tropical 1960s vibe. Wood and wicker furniture is featured both in the rooms and on the large front lawn, which is set up with lounge chairs and fire pits, perfect for sipping a tiki cocktail under the moonlight.

Carpe Diem   BOUTIQUE HOTEL $$$

(☑ 508-487-4242; www.carpediemguesthouse. com; 12-14 Johnson St; r $349-599; 🅿 ❄ 🛜) Sophisticated yet relaxed, this boutique inn blends a soothing mix of smiling Buddhas, orchid sprays and artistic decor. Each guest room is inspired by a different LGBTIQ+ literary genius; the room themed on poet Raj Rao, for example, has sumptuous embroidered fabrics draped over the modern furniture. The on-site spa includes a Finnish sauna, a hot tub and massage therapy.

EAST END GALLERY DISTRICT

With the many artists who have worked here, it's no surprise that Provincetown hosts some of the finest art galleries in the region. For the best browsing, begin at PAAM and start walking southwest along Commercial St. Over the next few blocks every second storefront harbors a gallery worth a peek.

Pick up a copy of the *Provincetown Gallery Guide* (www.provincetown galleryguide.com), or check out its website for gallery info, a map and details of events.

✕ Eating

★ Canteen MODERN AMERICAN $
(☎508-487-3800; www.thecanteenptown.com; 225 Commercial St; mains $10-16; ☺11am-9pm Sun-Thu, to 10pm Fri & Sat; ☑🖶) Cool and casual, but unmistakably gourmet – this is your optimal P-town lunch stop. Choose from classics such as lobster rolls and barbecued pulled-pork sandwiches, or innovations like cod *banh mi* and shrimp sliders. We strongly recommend you add crispy Brussels sprouts and a cold beer to your order and then take a seat at the communal picnic table on the sand.

Mews
Restaurant & Cafe MODERN AMERICAN $$$
(☎508-487-1500; www.mews.com; 429 Commercial St; mains $19-44; ☺5-10pm Mon-Sat year-round, plus 10am-2pm Sun mid-May–Sep) A fantastic water view, the hottest martini bar in town and scrumptious food add up to Provincetown's finest dining scene. There are two sections: opt to dine gourmet on lobster risotto and filet mignon downstairs, where you're right on the sand, or go casual with a juicy Angus burger from the bistro menu upstairs. Reservations recommended.

🍷 Drinking & Nightlife

Aqua Bar BAR
(☎774-593-5106; www.facebook.com/aquabar ptown; 207 Commercial St; ☺10:30am-10pm Sun-Thu, to midnight Fri & Sat May-Oct) Imagine a food court where the options include a raw bar, sushi, gelato and other international delights. Add a fully stocked bar with generous bartenders pouring the drinks. Now put the whole place in a gorgeous seaside setting, overlooking a little beach and a beautiful harbor. Now imagine this whole scene at sunset. That's Aqua Bar.

Boatslip Beach Club GAY
(☎508-487-1669; www.boatslipresort.com; 161 Commercial St; ☺tea dances daily from 4pm Jun-early Sep, Fri-Sun mid-Sep–May) Hosts wildly popular afternoon tea dances (4pm to 7pm), often packed with gorgeous guys. DJs fire things up: visit on Thursdays for dance classics from the 1970s and '80s. There's accommodations too.

Crown & Anchor GAY & LESBIAN
(☎508-487-1430; www.onlyatthecrown.com; 247 Commercial St; ☺hours vary) The queen of the scene, this multiwing complex has a nightclub, a video bar and a leather bar and a fun, steamy cabaret that takes it to the limit, plus loads of shows and events – from Broadway concerts to drag revues and burlesque troupes. Check the calendar (and buy tickets) online. Accommodations and restaurant on-site too.

ℹ Information

Provincetown Chamber of Commerce
(☎508-487-3424; www.ptownchamber.com; 307 Commercial St; ☺9am-5pm) The town's helpful tourist office is right at MacMillan Pier.

ℹ Getting There & Away

From the Cape Cod Canal via US 6, it takes about 1½ hours to reach Provincetown (65 miles), depending on traffic.

BOAT

From around May to October, boats connect Provincetown's MacMillan Pier with Boston and Plymouth. Schedules are geared to day-trippers, with morning arrivals into Provincetown and late-afternoon departures. No ferries carry cars, but bikes can be transported for a fee (around $16 round trip in addition to your regular ticket). Advance reservations are recommended, especially on weekends and in peak summer.

Bay State Cruise Co (☎617-748-1428; www. boston-ptown.com; round trip adult/child $95/72) Fast ferry (1½ hours) operates three times daily from Boston's World Trade Center Pier.

Boston Harbor Cruises (☎617-227-4321; www.bostonharborcruises.com; round trip adult/child $93/65) Fast-ferry service (1½ hours) from Long Wharf in Boston up to three times daily.

Plymouth-to-Provincetown Express Ferry
(☎508-927-5587; www.captjohn.com; round trip adult/child $53/32) Ferry from Plymouth (1½ hours, once daily) to Provincetown's MacMillan Pier.

BUS

Plymouth & Brockton (☎508-746-0378; www.p-b.com) Bus service from Boston that runs several times daily (one way $38, three to 3½ hours) and services other Cape towns. To get all the way to Provincetown you must switch buses in Hyannis.

The Islands

Nantucket

One need not be a millionaire to visit Nantucket, but it couldn't hurt. This compact island, 30 miles south of Cape Cod, grew rich from whaling in the 19th century. In recent decades it's experienced a rebirth as a summer getaway for CEOs, society types and other well-heeled visitors from Boston and New York.

It's easy to see why. Nantucket is New England at its most rose-covered, cobblestoned, picture-postcard perfect. Nantucket town is the biggest draw for its fine dining, lively bars and one-of-a-kind history you can experience on just about every street. Elsewhere on the island outdoor activities abound. Even in summer you'll be able to find uncrowded stretches of sandy beach. All on an island that is close enough to reach without much hassle, but still feels deliciously remote.

The town of Nantucket (called 'Town' by locals) is the island's only real population center. Once home port to the world's largest whaling fleet, the town's storied past is reflected in the gracious period buildings lining its leafy streets. It boasts the nation's largest concentration of houses built prior to 1850 and is the only place in the US where the entire town is a National Historic Landmark. It's a thoroughly enjoyable place to amble about the cobblestone streets and soak up the atmosphere.

◉ Sights

★ Nantucket Whaling Museum   MUSEUM
(☑ 508-228-1894; www.nha.org; 13 Broad St; museum & sites/all access $20/25; ☺ 9am-5pm late May–mid-Oct, 10am-4pm mid-Oct–Dec & Apr–mid-May, 10am-4pm Thu-Sun early Feb-Mar, closed Jan) One of the island's highlights, this evocative museum occupies an 1847 spermaceti (whale oil) candle factory and the excellent exhibits relive Nantucket's 19th-century heyday as the whaling center of the world. There's a worthwhile, albeit long (54 minutes), documentary on the island, incredible scrimshaw exhibits (engravings and carvings done by sailors on ivory, whalebone or baleen) and a 46ft sperm-whale skeleton rising above it all. Be sure to head to the rooftop deck for lovely views.

⌂ Sleeping

Unless you've got island friends with a spare room, a summer stay on Nantucket won't be cheap. Don't even look for a motel or a campground – tony Nantucket is all about inns, and many of those are receiving dramatic makeovers to bring them to design-magazine standard.

★ HI Nantucket   HOSTEL $
(Star of the Sea; ☑ 508-228-0433; www.hiusa.org; 31 Western Ave; dm/5-person r $42/210; ☺ mid-May–mid-Oct; @ 🖳) Known locally as Star of the Sea, this cool hostel has a million-dollar setting just minutes from Surfside Beach. It's housed in a former lifesaving station that dates from 1873 and is listed on the National Register of Historic Places. As Nantucket's sole budget option, its 49 beds are in high demand, so book as far in advance as possible.

Barnacle Inn   B&B $$$
(☑ 508-228-0332; www.thebarnacleinn.com; 11 Fair St; r $450, without bath $330; ☺ late Apr-early Nov; ❄ 🖳) This is what old Nantucket is all about: folksy owners and simple, quaint accommodations that hearken back to earlier times. Rooms in this turn-of-the-19th-century inn don't have phones or TVs, but they do have good rates for Nantucket town, particularly if you opt for a shared bathroom.

✕ Eating & Drinking

Corner Table   CAFE $
(☑ 508-228-2665; www.nantucketculinary.com; 22 Federal St; mains $11-19; ☺ 7am-9pm) 🌱 A real local gathering place, this sweet cafe has great coffee, a cabinet full of high-quality eats to have here or take away (black bean and sweet potato salad, Bolognese, mascarpone raspberry cheesecake), daily soups and sandwiches, a sofa or two, and a sustainable, community-minded ethos.

★ Proprietors   MODERN AMERICAN $$
(☑ 508-228-7747; www.proprietorsnantucket.com; 9 India St; plates $17-35; ☺ 5:30pm-late Mon-Sat, 10:30am-2pm Sun Apr-Oct) 🌱 Creative, globally inspired cooking and fine cocktails go down a treat at this bar-restaurant that proudly flaunts local farm-to-table fare. Your eyes may be bigger than your belly when reading the small-plates-focused menu: the housemade charcuterie is a worthy choice, as are kimchi pancakes, roasted bone marrow and tuna crudo. Return on Sundays for the lauded brunch.

Cisco Brewers   BREWERY
(☑ 508-325-5929; www.ciscobrewers.com; 5 Bartlett Farm Rd; tours $20; ☺ noon-7pm Mon-Thu, from 11am Fri & Sat, noon-6pm Sun year-round) Enjoy a hoppy pint of Whale's Tale pale ale at the friendliest brewery you'll likely ever see. Cisco Brewers is the 'other' Nantucket, a laid-back place where fun banter loosens

those stiff upper lips found in primmer quarters. In addition to the brewery, there's a small **distillery**, casual indoor and outdoor bars, regular food trucks and live music.

ⓘ Information

Visitor Services & Information Bureau
(☑ 508-228-0925; www.nantucket-ma.gov; 25 Federal St; ⊘ 9am-5pm daily mid-Apr–mid-Oct, Mon-Sat rest of year) Has everything you'll need, including public restrooms and a list of available accommodations. The folks here also maintain a summertime kiosk (⊘ 9am-5pm late May-early Sep) on Straight Wharf.

ⓘ Getting There & Away

AIR
Nantucket Memorial Airport (☑ 508-325-5300; www.nantucketairport.com; 14 Airport Rd) is 3 miles southeast of Nantucket town. Cape Air (www.capeair.com) offers year-round service to Boston, Hyannis, New Bedford and Martha's Vineyard, and seasonal service to New York. Delta, American, United and JetBlue also offer seasonal services to/from New York, Newark and Washington, DC.

The airport is connected by local bus to town ($2) from mid-June to early September.

BOAT
The most common way to reach Nantucket is by the **Steamship Authority** (☑ 508-548-5011; www.steamshipauthority.com) and **Hy-Line Cruises** (☑ 508-778-2600; www.hylinecruises.com) ferries from Hyannis. The traditional ferry takes 2¼ hours, while the high-speed ferry (passengers only) takes one hour. Additional summertime ferries run to Oak Bluffs on Martha's Vineyard, New Bedford, New Jersey and New York.

Martha's Vineyard

Bathed in unique beauty, Martha's Vineyard attracts wide-eyed day-trippers, celebrity second-home owners, and urbanites seeking a restful getaway; its 15,000 year-round residents include many artists, musicians and back-to-nature types. The Vineyard remains untouched by the kind of rampant commercialism found on the mainland – there's not a single chain restaurant or cookie-cutter motel in sight. Instead you'll find cozy inns, chef-driven restaurants and a bounty of green farms and grand beaches. And there's something for every mood here – fine dining in gentrified Edgartown one day and hitting the cotton candy and carousel scene in Oak Bluffs the next.

Martha's Vineyard is the largest island in New England, extending some 23 miles at its widest. Although it sits just 7 miles off the coast of Cape Cod, Vineyarders feel themselves such a world apart that they often refer to the mainland as 'America.'

⊙ Sights & Activities

★ Campgrounds
& Tabernacle   HISTORIC SITE
(☑ 508-693-0525; www.mvcma.org) Oak Bluffs started out in the mid-19th century as a summer retreat by a revivalist church, whose members enjoyed a day at the beach as much as a gospel service. They first camped out in tents, then built some 300 wooden cottages, each adorned with whimsical filigree trim.

Flying Horses Carousel   HISTORIC SITE
(☑ 508-693-9481; www.mvpreservation.org; Oak Bluffs Ave; 1/10 rides $3/25; ⊘ 11am-4:30pm Sat & Sun May–mid-Jun, 10am-10pm daily mid-Jun–Aug, 11am-4:30pm Sep-early Oct; ♿) Take a nostalgic ride on this National Historic Landmark, which has been captivating kids of all ages since 1876. It's the USA's oldest continuously operating merry-go-round, and these antique horses have manes of real horse hair.

Aquinnah Public Beach   BEACH
(Moshup Trail) Aquinnah Public Beach (also known as Moshup Beach) is an impressive 5 miles long. Access is free, although parking ($10 to $20) is not. From the parking lot, it's a 10-minute walk to the beach.

🛏 Sleeping

HI Martha's Vineyard   HOSTEL $
(☑ 508-693-2665; www.hiusa.org; 525 Edgartown-West Tisbury Rd; dm/d/tr $41/119/159; ⊘ mid-May–early Oct; ℗@ⓢ) Reserve early for a bed at this popular, purpose-built hostel in the center of the island. It has everything you'd expect: a solid kitchen, a games room, bike delivery, no curfew and friendly staff. The public bus stops out front and it's right on the bike path. Dorms and private rooms are available.

Nashua House   INN $$
(☑ 508-693-0043; www.nashuahouse.com; 9 Healy Way; r $129-239; ❋ⓢ) The Vineyard the way it used to be...but with a few concessions to modernity (some rooms have TV, some have private bathroom). You'll find simple, spotless, characterful accommodations at this quaint 1873 inn with restaurants and pubs

just beyond the front door. It's good value in summer; in the off-season, when rates drop by nearly half, it's a steal.

★ Summercamp
HOTEL $$$

(☑ 508-693-6611; www.summercamphotel.com; 70 Lake Ave; r $389-579; ☺ May-Oct; ❄ ☎) We dare you not to smile in response to the detail of this fun place, the 2016 incarnation of an iconic 1879 hotel that borders the Tabernacle area. The nostalgic summer-camp theme extends from the Astroturfed games room to the canteen selling retro snacks. And there's even a twin room with bunks. Decor is fresh and inspired, location is ace.

✗ Eating & Drinking

★ ArtCliff Diner
CAFE $

(☑ 508-693-1224; 39 Beach Rd, Vineyard Haven; mains $9-14; ☺ 7am-2pm Thu-Tue) ⌇ Hands down the best place in town for breakfast and lunch. Chef-owner Gina Stanley, a grad of the prestigious Culinary Institute of America, adds flair to everything she touches, from the almond-encrusted French toast to the fresh fish tacos. The eclectic menu utilizes farm-fresh island ingredients. Expect a line, but it's worth the wait.

Sweet Life Café
MODERN AMERICAN $$$

(☑ 508-696-0200; www.sweetlifemv.com; 63 Circuit Ave; mains $32-38; ☺ 5:30-10pm Wed-Sun mid-May–Oct) New American cuisine with a French accent is offered by this stylish bistro, which provides the town's finest dining. Tuna tartare, fried softshell crab and miso-glazed local cod are joined on the menu by other innovative dishes using local produce (not just seafood). Reservations advised.

★ Offshore Ale Co
MICROBREWERY

(☑ 508-693-2626; www.offshoreale.com; 30 Kennebec Ave; ☺ 11:30am-8:30pm Sun-Thu, to 9:30pm Fri & Sat) Join the throngs of locals and visitors at this popular microbrewery – enjoy a pint of Hop Goddess ale, some superior pub grub (including a knockout lobster roll) and the kind of laid-back atmosphere where boats are suspended from the ceiling and peanut shells are thrown on the floor.

❶ Information

Visitor Information Booth (☑ 508-693-4266; cnr Circuit & Lake Aves; ☺ 9am-5pm late May–mid-Oct) The town hall staffs this convenient summertime info booth near the carousel.

❶ Getting There & Away

AIR

Martha's Vineyard Airport (MVY; ☑ 508-693-7022; www.mvyairport.com; 71 Airport Rd, Vineyard Haven) is in the center of the island, about 6 miles south of Vineyard Haven, and is served by buses. It has year-round service to Boston and Nantucket and seasonal services to Hyannis, New Bedford, MA, and New York. Check Cape Air (www.capeair.com) for schedules. Delta and JetBlue also offer seasonal services from New York's JFK Airport.

BOAT

Steamship Authority (www.steamshipauthority.com) operates a frequent, year-round ferry service connecting Vineyard Haven with Woods Hole, south of Falmouth on the Cape (a 45-minute voyage). This is the only ferry that carries vehicles.

Oak Bluffs is a busy summertime port from mid-May to mid-October, when ferries from Hyannis, Falmouth, Woods Hole and New Bedford bring day-trippers across.

Pioneer Valley

With the exception of gritty Springfield, the Pioneer Valley offers a gentle landscape of college towns, picturesque farms and old mills that have been charmingly converted into modern use. The uber-cool burg of Northampton provides the region's top dining, nightlife and street scenes, while the other destinations offer unique museums, geological marvels and a few unexpected roadside gems.

❶ Getting There & Away

Pioneer Valley Transit Authority (www.pvta.com) provides bus services (with bike racks) throughout the Five College area; the Northampton–Amherst route has the most frequent service.

Northampton

In a region famous for its charming college towns, you'd be hard-pressed to find anything more appealing than the crooked streets of downtown Northampton. Old red-brick buildings and lots of pedestrian traffic provide a lively backdrop for your wanderings, which will likely include cafes, rock clubs and bookstores (which explains why locals call their town 'NoHo'). Move a few steps outside of the picturesque commercial center and you'll stumble onto the bucolic grounds of Smith College. Northampton is

DR SEUSS IN SPRINGFIELD

The innovative **Amazing World of Dr Seuss** (☑413-263-6800; www.seussin springfield.org; 21 Edwards St; adult/child $25/13; ☺10am-5pm Mon-Sat, from 11am Sun; ♿) is dedicated to the life and work of Springfield native Theodore Geisel, aka Dr Seuss. On the 1st floor, interactive exhibits use the stories of Dr Seuss to engage children with rhyming games and storytelling. Upstairs, galleries display original artwork, a moving collection of letters from the author to his great nephew, and a reproduction of Geisel's studio. Your ticket includes admission to four other museums in Springfield.

a well-known liberal enclave in these parts. The lesbian community is famously outspoken, and rainbow flags wave wildly all over town.

◉ Sights & Activities

Northampton is at the center of a series of interconnected, accessible walking and cycling paths. The **Norwottuck Rail Trail** (☑413-586-8706; www.mass.gov/locations/nor wottuck-rail-trail) extends 11 miles to Hadley and Amherst, while the **Manhan Rail Trail** (www.manhanrailtrail.org) connects Northampton and Easthampton. You can rent bikes from **Northampton Bicycle** (☑413-586-3810; www.nohobike.com; 319 Pleasant St; per day from $25; ☺9:30am-6pm Mon-Fri, 9:30am-5pm Sat, noon-5pm Sun).

Smith College　　　　　　　COLLEGE
(☑413-584-2700; www.smith.edu; Elm St) Founded 'for the education of the intelligent gentlewoman' in 1875, Smith College is one of the largest women's colleges in the country, with 2600 students. The verdant 125-acre campus holds an eclectic architectural mix of nearly 100 buildings, set on a pretty pond. Notable alums of the college include Sylvia Plath, Julia Child and Gloria Steinem. After exploring the campus, take a stroll around Paradise Pond and snap a photo at the Japanese tea hut.

Smith College Museum of Art　　MUSEUM
(☑413-585-2760; www.smith.edu/artmuseum; 20 Elm St; adult/child $5/free; ☺10am-4pm Tue, Wed, Fri & Sat, to 8pm Thu, noon-4pm Sun)

This impressive campus museum boasts a 25,000-piece collection. It's particularly strong in 19th- and 20th-century European and North American paintings, including works by Degas, Winslow Homer, Picasso and James Abbott McNeill Whistler. Another highlight is the so-called 'functional art': the remarkable restrooms and the eclectic collection of benches (that you can actually sit on) – all designed and created by contemporary American artists.

✗ Eating

Woodstar Cafe　　　　　　　CAFE $
(www.woodstarcafe.com; 60 Masonic St; mains $5.50-9.30; ☺7am-6pm Mon, to 7pm Tue-Fri, 8am-7pm Sat, 8am-6pm Sun; 🛜🅿) Students flock to this family-run bakery-cafe, just a stone's throw from campus, for tasty sandwiches made on the freshest of bread and named after local towns and landmarks. Save room for dessert, as the pastries – made on-site – are divine.

Local Burger　　　　　　　BURGERS $
(www.localnorthampton.com; 16 Main St; mains $6.50-14; ☺11:30am-10pm Sun-Thu, to 3am Fri & Sat; ♿) Locavores rave about this burger joint on Main St, where every effort is made to use locally sourced beef and produce. Burger-masters turn out eight tasty custom burgers (especially good for satisfying the late-night munchies), while the sweet-potato fries are an irresistible accompaniment. Alcoholic drinks – including spiked milkshakes – are served until midnight.

❶ Information

Greater Northampton Chamber of Commerce (☑413-584-1900; www.explorenorthampton. com; 99 Pleasant St; ☺9am-5pm Mon-Fri, plus 10am-2pm Sat & Sun May-Oct) Get all your questions answered at the local chamber.

Amherst

This quintessential college town is home to the prestigious Amherst College, a pretty 'junior ivy' that borders the town green, as well as the hulking University of Massachusetts and the cozy liberal-arts Hampshire College. Start your explorations at the town green, at the intersection of MA 116 and MA 9. In the surrounding streets, you'll find a few small galleries, a bookstore or two, countless coffeehouses and a few small but worthwhile museums (several of which are associated with the colleges).

Emily Dickinson Museum
MUSEUM

(☑413-542-8161; www.emilydickinsonmuseum.org; 280 Main St; guided tour adult/child $15/free; ☺10am-5pm Wed-Mon Jun-Aug, 11am-4pm Wed-Sun Mar-May & Sep-Dec) During her lifetime, Emily Dickinson (1830–86) published only seven poems, but more than 1000 were discovered and published posthumously, and her verses on love, nature and immortality have made her one of the USA's most important poets. Dickinson spent most of her life in near seclusion in this stately home near the center of Amherst. Worthwhile guided tours (one hour) focus on the poet and her works, visiting both the Dickinson Homestead and the adjacent Evergreens.

Eric Carle Museum of Picture Book Art
MUSEUM

(☑413-559-6300; www.carlemuseum.org; 125 W Bay Rd; adult/child $9/6; ☺10am-4pm Tue-Fri, to 5pm Sat, noon-5pm Sun; ☝) Co-founded by the author and illustrator of *The Very Hungry Caterpillar,* this superb museum celebrates book illustrations from around the world with rotating exhibits in three galleries, as well as a permanent collection. All visitors (grown-ups included) are encouraged to express their own artistic sentiments in the hands-on art studio.

The Berkshires

Few places in America combine culture and country living as deftly as the Berkshire hills, home to world-class music, dance and theater festivals – the likes of Tanglewood and Jacob's Pillow – as well as miles of hiking trails and acres of farmland.

Extending from the highest point in the state – Mt Greylock – southward to the Connecticut state line, the Berkshires have been a summer refuge for more than a century, when the rich and famous arrived to build summer 'cottages' of grand proportions. Many of these mansions survive as inns or performance venues. And still today, on summer weekends when the sidewalks are scorching in Boston and New York, crowds of city dwellers jump in their cars and head for the Berkshire breezes.

❶ Getting There & Around

Most travelers are likely to reach this region by driving from Boston, Hartford or New York. It is possible to arrive by bus or train, but you'll want your own vehicle if you intend to visit the more rural areas. If not, the Berkshire Regional Transit Authority (www.berkshirerta.com) runs buses between major Berkshire towns. A ride costs $1.75 for short trips and $4 for longer journeys.

Great Barrington

Great Barrington's Main St used to consist of Woolworth's, hardware stores, thrift shops and a run-down diner. These have given way to artsy boutiques, antique shops, coffeehouses and restaurants. Nowadays, the town boasts the best dining scene in the region, with easy access to hiking trails and magnificent scenery in the surrounding hills.

The Housatonic River flows through the center of town just east of Main St/US 7, the central thoroughfare.

★ Monument Mountain
HIKING

(www.thetrustees.org; US 7; parking $5; ☺sunrise-sunset) Less than 5 miles north of Great Barrington center on US 7 is Monument Mountain, which has hiking trails to the 1642ft summit of Squaw Peak. Turning right from the parking lot, the 3-mile circular route ascends steeply via the **Hickey trail** and runs along the cliff edge to Squaw Peak and the Devil's Pulpit lookout. From the top you'll get fabulous views all the way to Mt Greylock to the northwest and to the Catskills in New York.

Wainwright Inn
B&B $$

(☑413-528-2062; www.wainwrightinn.com; 518 S Main St; r $140-230; ✳🛜) Great Barrington's finest place to lay your head, this inn (c 1766) exudes historical appeal from its wraparound porches and spacious parlors to the period room decor in the nine guest rooms. Breakfast is a decadent experience. The inn is a short walk from the center of town on a busy road.

★ Allium
MODERN AMERICAN $$

(☑413-528-2118; www.alliumberkshires.com; 42 Railroad St; small plates $9-16, mains $16-34; ☺5-9:30pm Sun-Thu, to 10pm Fri & Sat) 🍴 Allium subscribes to the slow-food movement, with a seasonal menu that relies on fresh organic produce, cheeses and meats. Go for cocktails and small plates in the lounge area, with a window facing the street, or a more formal meal in the dining room, with a view into the kitchen.

❶ Information

Southern Berkshire Chamber of Commerce
(☑ 413-528-1510; www.southernberkshire
chamber.com; 362 Main St; ⊙ 10am-6pm
Thu-Mon) Maintains a kiosk at the corner of St
James Pl that's well stocked with maps, restaurant menus and accommodations lists.

Stockbridge

Take a good look down Stockbridge's wide
Main St. Notice anything? More specifically,
notice anything missing? Not one stoplight
interrupts the view; not one telephone pole
blights the picture-perfect scene – it looks
very much the way Norman Rockwell might
have seen it.

In fact, Rockwell did see it – he lived
and worked in Stockbridge during the last
25 years of his life. Nowadays, Stockbridge
attracts summer and fall visitors en masse,
who come to stroll the streets, inspect the
shops and sit in the rockers on the porch of
the historic Red Lion Inn. And they come by
the busload to visit the Norman Rockwell
Museum on the town's outskirts.

All that fossilized picturesqueness comes
at a price. Noticeably absent from the village
center is the kind of vitality that you find in
the neighboring towns.

★ **Norman Rockwell Museum**   MUSEUM
(☑ 413-298-4100; www.nrm.org; 9 Glendale Rd/MA
183; adult/child $20/free; ⊙ 10am-5pm May-Oct, to
4pm Nov-Apr) Born in New York City, Norman
Rockwell (1894–1978) sold his first magazine
cover illustration to the *Saturday Evening
Post* in 1916. In the following half-century he
did another 321 covers for the *Post,* as well
as illustrations for books, posters and many
other magazines on his way to becoming the
most popular illustrator in US history. This
excellent museum has the largest collection
of Rockwell's original art, as well as Rockwell's studio, which was moved here from
nearby Stockbridge.

Lenox

This appealing, wealthy town is a historical anomaly: firstly, its charm was not
destroyed by the industrial revolution;
and then, prized for its bucolic peace, the
town became a summer retreat for wealthy
families with surnames such as Carnegie,
Vanderbilt and Westinghouse, who had
made their fortunes by building factories
in other towns.

As the cultural heart of the Berkshires,
Lenox's illustrious past remains tangibly
present today. The superstar among its attractions is the Tanglewood Music Festival,
an incredibly popular summer event drawing scores of visitors from New York City,
Boston and beyond.

★ Festivals

Tanglewood Music Festival   MUSIC
(☑ 888-266-1200; www.tanglewood.org; 297 West
St/MA 183, Lenox; lawn tickets from $21; ⊙ late
Jun-early Sep) Dating from 1934, the Tanglewood Music Festival is among the most
esteemed summertime music events in the
world. Symphony, pops, chamber music,
jazz and blues are performed from late June
through early September. You can count on
renowned cellist Yo-Yo Ma, violinist Joshua
Bell and singer James Taylor to perform
each summer, along with a run of world-class guest artists and famed conductors.

🛏 Sleeping

Birchwood Inn   INN $$$
(☑ 413-637-2600; www.birchwood-inn.com; 7 Hubbard St; r $208-399; ❋ 🛜 🐾) A pretty hilltop
inn a couple of blocks from the town center,
Birchwood occupies the oldest (1767) home
in Lenox. The 11 spacious rooms vary in
decor: some swing with a vintage floral design, others are more country classic, but all
are romantic and luxurious. Deluxe rooms
feature king-size beds and wood-burning
fireplaces.

🍴 Eating

Haven Cafe & Bakery   CAFE $
(☑ 413-637-8948; www.havencafebakery.com; 8
Franklin St; mains $7.50-15.50; ⊙ 7:30am-3pm
Mon-Fri, 8am-3pm Sat & Sun; 🛜 🍽) It looks
like a casual cafe, but the sophisticated
food evokes a more upscale experience. For
breakfast, try croissant French toast or inventive egg dishes such as salmon scramble;
for lunch there are fancy salads and sandwiches – all highlighting local organic ingredients. Definitely save room for something
sweet from the bakery counter.

Bagel & Brew   BAGELS $
(www.facebook.com/BagelandBrew; 18 Franklin St;
bagels $5-9; ⊙ bagels 7am-1pm, bar 5-11pm Sat
& Sun) Bagels by day, brews by night. Tasty
bagel sandwiches are served for breakfast
and lunch; then there's a dozen different
beers on tap – most of them regional –

served in the beer garden, starting around the dinner hour. The food that accompanies the brew is not bagels, but truly delicious pub grub. This place has a great vibe.

★Nudel

AMERICAN $$

(☑ 413-551-7183; www.nudelrestaurant.com; 37 Church St; mains $18-26; ⊗ 5-9:15pm) Nudel is a driving force in the area's sustainable food movement, with just about everything on the menu seasonally inspired and locally sourced. The back-to-basics approach rings through in inventive dishes, which change daily but never disappoint. Incredible flavors. Nudel has a loyal following, so reservations are recommended. The last seating is at 9:15pm.

ℹ Information

Visit Lenox (☑ 413-637-3646; www.lenox. org; 4 Housatonic St; ⊗10am-4pm Wed-Sat Sep-Jun, to 6pm daily Jul & Aug) This office is a clearinghouse of information on everything from inns to what's going on.

Williamstown

Small but pretty Williamstown is nestled within the heart of the Purple Valley, so named because the surrounding mountains often seem shrouded in a lavender veil at dusk. Folks congregate in the friendly town center, which is only two blocks long, while dogs and kids frolic in the ample green spaces.

Williamstown is a quintessential New England college town, its charming streets and greens dotted with the stately brick and marble buildings of Williams College. Cultural life is rich, with a pair of exceptional art museums and one of the region's most respected summer theater festivals.

⊙ Sights

★Clark Art Institute

MUSEUM

(☑ 413-458-2303; www.clarkart.edu; 225 South St; adult/child $20/free; ⊗10am-5pm Tue-Sun Sep-Jun, daily Jul & Aug) Even if you're not an avid art lover, don't miss this gem, set on 140 gorgeous acres of expansive lawns, flower-filled meadows and rolling hills. The building – with its triple-tiered reflecting pool – is a stunner. The collections are particularly strong in the impressionists, with significant works by Monet, Pissarro and Renoir. Mary Cassatt, Winslow Homer and John Singer Sargent represent contemporaneous American painting.

MASS MoCA IN NORTH ADAMS

Sprawling over 13 acres of downtown North Adams, **MASS MoCA** (Massachusetts Museum of Contemporary Art; ☑ 413-662-2111; www.massmoca.org; 1040 Mass MoCA Way; adult/child $20/8; ⊗10am-6pm Sun-Wed, to 7pm Thu-Sat Jul & Aug, 11am-5pm Wed-Mon Sep-Jun) makes up one-third of the entire business district. After the Sprague Electric Company closed in 1985, some $31 million was spent to modernize the property into 'the largest gallery in the United States.' The museum encompasses 222,000 sq ft in 25 buildings, including art construction areas, performance centers and 19 galleries. Long-term exhibitions include a gallery of wall paintings by Sol LeWitt. Thought-provoking guided tours run daily at 1pm and 3pm.

Williams College Museum of Art

MUSEUM

(☑ 413-597-2429; https://wcma.williams.edu; 15 Lawrence Hall Dr; ⊗10am-5pm, to 8pm Thu, closed Wed Sep-May) FREE In the center of town is this worthwhile – and free! – art museum. It has a collection of some 15,000 pieces, with substantial works by notables such as Edward Hopper *(Morning in a City)*, Winslow Homer and Grant Wood, to name only a few. The photography collection is also noteworthy. Temporary exhibitions are accompanied by academic talks. To find the museum, look for the huge bronze eyes by Louise Bourgeois, embedded in the front lawn on Main St.

🛏 Sleeping & Eating

River Bend Farm B&B

B&B $$

(☑ 413-458-3121; www.riverbendfarmbb.com; 643 Simonds Rd/US 7; r $120; ⊗Apr-Oct; ✳🕸) Step back in time to 1770, when this Georgian Colonial was a local tavern owned by Benjamin Simonds. The house owes its painstaking restoration to hosts Judy and Dave Loomis. Four simple, comfortable doubles share two bathrooms with claw-foot tubs. Breakfast is served in the wood-paneled taproom, next to the wide stone fireplace. A truly atmospheric place to stay.

★Guest House at Field Farm

INN $$$

(☑ 413-458-3135; www.thetrustees.org/field-farm; 554 Sloan Rd; r $250-350; @🕸🅿) Located about 6 miles south of Williamstown, this

NEW ENGLAND THE BERKSHIRES

one-of-a-kind inn offers an artful blend of mid-20th-century modernity and timeless mountain scenery. The six rooms are spacious and fitted with handcrafted furnishings that reflect the modernist style of the house. The sculpture-laden grounds feature miles of lightly trodden walking trails and a pair of Adirondack chairs set perfectly for unobstructed stargazing.

Pappa Charlie's Deli DELI $

(☑ 413-458-5969; 28 Spring St; sandwiches $5-7; ⊙ 8am-8pm Mon-Sat, to 7pm Sun) Here's a welcoming breakfast spot where locals really do ask for 'the usual.' The stars themselves created the lunch sandwiches that bear their names. The Mary Tyler Moore is a favorite (bacon, lettuce, tomato and avocado); the actress later went vegetarian, so you can also get a version with soy bacon. Order a Politician and get anything you want.

★ Mezze Bistro & Bar FUSION $$

(☑ 413-458-0123; www.mezzerestaurant.com; 777 Cold Spring Rd/US 7; mains $16-28; ⊙ 5-9pm Sun-Thu, to 9:30pm Fri & Sat) You don't know exactly what you're going to get at this contemporary restaurant – the menu changes frequently – but you know it's going to be good. Situated on 3 spectacular acres, Mezze's farm-to-table approach begins with an edible garden right on-site. Much of the rest of the seasonal menu, from small-batch microbrews to organic meats, is locally sourced as well.

RHODE ISLAND

Rhode Island, the smallest of the US states, isn't actually an island. Although it only takes about an hour to traverse, this little wonder packs in more than 400 miles of coastline with wonderful, white-sand swimming beaches and some of the country's finest historic architecture, galleries and museums. What's more, Rhode Islanders are about as friendly as folks come.

Hugging the rugged shoreline before heading inland, seaside resorts, quaint Colonial villages and extravagant country homes give way to lush fields of berry farms, vineyards and horse studs. Rhode Island's main cities – Providence, with working-class roots, and Newport, born of old money the likes of which most cannot conceive – are among New England's finest.

With year-round cultural attractions, festivals, events, top-notch restaurants and seriously cool bars, it's no wonder the nouveau riche continue to flock here for summer shenanigans. While visiting Rhode Island ain't cheap, it's worth every penny.

History

Ever since it was founded in 1636 by Roger Williams, a religious outcast from Boston, Providence has enjoyed an independent frame of mind. Williams' guiding principle, the one that got him ostracized from Massachusetts, was that all people should have freedom of conscience. He put his liberal beliefs into practice when settling Providence, remaining on friendly terms with the local Narragansett Native Americans after purchasing from them the land for a bold experiment in tolerance and peaceful coexistence.

Williams' principles would not last long. As Providence and Newport grew and merged into a single colony, competition and conflict with area tribes sparked several wars, leading to the decimation of the Wampanoag, Pequot, Narragansett and Nipmuck peoples. Rhode Island was also a prolific slave trader and its merchants would control much of that industry in the years after the Revolutionary War.

The city of Pawtucket birthed the American industrial revolution, with the establishment of the water-powered Slater Mill in 1790. Industrialism impacted the character of Providence and surrounds, particularly along the Blackstone River, creating urban density. As with many small East Coast cities, these urban areas went into a precipitous decline in the 1940s and '50s as manufacturing industries (textiles and costume jewelry) faltered. In the 1960s, preservation efforts salvaged the historic architectural framework of Providence and Newport. Today, Newport has flourished into one of the nation's most attractive historical centers.

Providence also rerouted its destiny to emerge as a lively and stylish city with a dynamic economy and vibrant downtown core, largely due to the work of Buddy Cianci, twice-convicted felon and twice-elected mayor (1975–84, 1991–2002). The spectacle of today's wildly popular WaterFire festival is a powerful symbol of the city's phoenixlike rebirth along the confluence of the three rivers that gave it life. Cianci died in 2016, aged 74.

ℹ️ Information

Rhode Island Division of Parks & Recreation
(www.riparks.com) For a listing of all of Rhode Island's state beaches.

Rhode Island Tourism Division (www.visit rhodeisland.com) The official state provider of tourist information on Rhode Island.

Providence

Atop the confluence of the Providence, Moshassuck and Woonasquatucket Rivers, Rhode Island's capital city offers some of the finest urban strolling in New England: around Brown University's historic campus on 18th-century College Hill, along the land-scaped Riverwalk trail, and through down-town's handsome streets and lanes with their hip cafes, art-house theaters, fusion restaurants and trendsetting bars.

Once destined to become an industri-al relic, Providence's fate was spared when Buddy Cianci, its then controversial two-time mayor, rolled out a plan to revitalize the downtown core by rerouting subterranean rivers, reclaiming land and restoring historic facades. It created a city where history's treas-ures are not simply memorialized but rather integrated into a creative present; three cen-turies of architectural styles are unified in colorful urban streetscapes that are at once bold, beautiful and cooler than cool.

Providence's large student population helps keep the city's social and arts scenes cutting edge. Play it cool.

⊙ Sights

★ **Rhode Island**
State House NOTABLE BUILDING
(☑ 401-222-3983; www.sos.ri.gov; 82 Smith St; ⊙ self-guided tours 8:30am-4:30pm Mon-Fri, guid-ed tours 9am, 10am, 11am, 1pm & 2pm Mon-Fri; P) FREE Designed by McKim, Mead and White in 1904, the Rhode Island State House rises above the Providence skyline, easily visible from miles around. Modeled in part on St Peter's Basilica in Vatican City, it has the world's fourth-largest self-supporting mar-ble dome and houses one of Gilbert Stuart's portraits of George Washington, which you might want to compare to a dollar bill from your wallet.

Providence Athenaeum LIBRARY
(☑ 401-421-6970; www.providenceathenaeum.org; 251 Benefit St; ⊙ 10am-7pm Mon-Thu, to 6pm Fri & Sat, 1-5pm Sun) FREE One of the most prom-inent buildings on Benefit St, the Greek Revival Providence Athenaeum was de-signed by William Strickland and completed in 1838. This is a library of the old school with plaster busts and oil paintings filling in spaces not occupied by books. Edgar Al-len Poe used to court ladies here. Pick up a brochure for a self-guided Raven Tour of the building's artwork and architecture.

Brown University UNIVERSITY
(☑ 401-863-1000; www.brown.edu; 1 Prospect St) FREE Dominating the crest of the College Hill neighborhood on the East Side, Brown University's campus exudes Ivy League charm. **University Hall**, a 1770 brick edifice used as a barracks during the Revolutionary War, sits at its center. To explore the cam-pus, start at the wrought-iron gates at the intersection of College St and Prospect St and make your way across the green toward Thayer St.

Benefit Street STREET
(Benefit St) Immediately east of Providence's downtown, you'll find College Hill, where you can see the city's Colonial history re-flected in the 18th-century houses that line Benefit St on the East Side. These are mostly private homes, but many are open for tours one weekend in June during the annual **Fes-tival of Historic Houses** (www.ppsri.org/pro grams-events/signature-events/festival-of-houses/; ⊙ Jun) FREE. Benefit St is a fitting symbol of the Providence renaissance, rescued by local preservationists in the 1960s from misguid-ed urban-renewal efforts that would have destroyed it.

★ **RISD Museum of Art** MUSEUM
(☑ 401-454-6500; www.risdmuseum.org; 20 N Main St; adult/under 18yr $15/free; ⊙ 10am-5pm Tue-Sun, to 9pm 3rd Thu of month; P ♿) Wonderfully eclectic, the Rhode Island School of Design's art museum showcases everything from an-cient Greek art to 20th-century American paintings and decorative arts from its own collection, and always has visiting exhibi-tions and events. Pop in before 1pm on a Sunday and admission is free. Check out the excellent website before you go.

🎆 Festivals

★ **WaterFire** STREET CARNIVAL
(☑ 401-273-1155; www.waterfire.org; ⊙ dates vary) FREE During summer and on a hand-ful of dates in the cooler months, much of downtown Providence transforms into a

NEW ENGLAND PROVIDENCE

carnivalesque festival during the popular WaterFire art installation created by Barnaby Evans in 1994. Marking the convergence of the Providence, Moshassuck and Woonasquatucket rivers, 100 flaming braziers illuminate the water, overlooked by crowds strolling over the bridges and along the riverside.

🛏 Sleeping

★ The Dean Hotel
BOUTIQUE HOTEL $

(☑ 401-455-3326; http://thedeanhotel.com; 122 Fountain St; d from $109) The Dean epitomizes all that is design in Providence. It features a beer hall, a karaoke bar, a cocktail den and a beer hall downstairs; upstairs has eight quirky, design-themed rooms that provide a stylish urban oasis from the fun and frivolity downstairs. If you're a cool kid and you know it, you belong here.

Providence Biltmore
HISTORIC HOTEL $$

(☑ 401-421-0700; www.providencebiltmore.com; 11 Dorrance St; d from $189; ℙ🕏) The granddaddy of Providence's hotels, the Biltmore dates from the 1920s, although its 292 oversized guest rooms and suites have been thoroughly refurbished to a high standard, stretching many stories above the old city: ask for a room on a high floor. The lobby, both intimate and regal, nicely combines dark wood, twisting staircases and chandeliers, harking back to a lost age.

🍴 Eating

Haven Brothers Diner
DINER $

(☑ 401-603-8124; www.havenbrothersmobile.com; cnr Dorrance & Fulton Sts; meals $5-12; ⊙5pm-3am) Parked next to City Hall, this Providence institution is basically a diner on the back of a truck that has rolled into the same spot every evening for decades. Climb up a rickety ladder to get basic diner fare alongside everyone from drunks to prominent politicians and college kids pulling an all-nighter. The murder burger comes highly recommended.

★ Loie Fullers
MODERN AMERICAN $$

(☑ 401-273-4375; https://loiefullersprovidence.com/; 1455 Westminster St; mains $15-24; ⊙5-11pm Mon-Sat, 10am-2pm & 5-11pm Sun) This wonderfully original, atmospheric little bistro on the outskirts of the Federal Hill neighborhood is an oasis of fun and deliciousness on an otherwise drab trunk road. Inside, candles, ornate polished woods, frescoes and art-nouveau elements transport you to another time and place. On the French-inspired Modern American menu, comfort is king.

birch
MODERN AMERICAN $$$

(☑ 401-272-3105; www.birchrestaurant.com; 200 Washington St; 4-course dinner $60, beverage pairings $40; ⊙5-10pm Thu-Mon) With a background at Noma in Copenhagen and the Dorrance at the Biltmore, chef Benjamin Sukle and his wife, Heidi, now have their own place: the understated but fabulously good birch. Its intimate size and style (seating surrounds a U-shaped bar) means attention to detail is exacting in both the decor and the food, which focuses on underutilized, hyper-seasonal produce.

🍷 Drinking

★ Ogie's Trailer Park
BAR

(☑ 401-383-8200; www.ogiestrailerpark.com; 1155 Westminster St; ⊙4pm-1am Mon-Thu, 3pm-2am Fri & Sat, noon-1am Sun) This place is just so awesome and unexpected that we almost want to keep it to ourselves. Let's just say that in terms of thematics and design, if you crossed the *Brady Bunch* with *Mad Men* with *Breaking Bad,* you'd be somewhere in the vicinity. Eat, drink and love.

The Eddy
COCKTAIL BAR

(☑ 401-831-3339; www.eddybar.com; 95 Eddy St; ⊙4pm-1am) Providence's classiest cocktail concoctions are served at the Eddy alongside a healthy selection of on-tap and bottled beers and an impressive wine list. Dress to impress.

ℹ Information

Providence Visitor Information Center
(☑ 401-751-1177; www.goprovidence.com; 1 Sabin St, Rhode Island Convention Center; ⊙9am-5pm Mon-Sat)

Satellite Visitor Information Center
(☑ 401-456-0200; www.goprovidence.com; 10 Memorial Blvd, IGT Center; ⊙9am-5pm)

ℹ Getting There & Away

BUS

All long-distance buses and most local routes stop at the central **Intermodal Transportation Center** (Kennedy Plaza; ⊙6am-7pm). Greyhound and Peter Pan Bus Lines have ticket counters inside and there are maps outlining local services.

Peter Pan connects Providence and Green Airport with Boston's South Station (from $9, one hour, 12 daily) and Boston's Logan International Airport (from $18, 70 minutes, 10 daily).

Greyhound buses depart for Boston (from $9, 65 minutes), New York City (from $15, 5½ to six hours) and elsewhere.

TRAIN

Amtrak trains, including high-speed Acela trains, connect Providence with Boston (from $12, 50 minutes) and New York (from $54, three to 3½ hours).

MBTA commuter rail has regular scheduled services to Boston ($12, 60 to 75 minutes).

❶ Getting Around

Providence is small, pretty and walkable, so once you arrive it makes sense to get around on foot.

RIPTA operates two 'trolley' routes. The Green Line runs from the East Side through downtown to Federal Hill. The Gold Line runs from the Providence Marriott Downtown hotel, south to the hospital via Kennedy Plaza, and stops at the Point St Ferry Dock. Fares are $2 per ride.

Newport

Established by religious moderates, 'new port' flourished in the independent colony of Rhode Island, which declared itself a state here in 1776. Downtown, shutterbugs snap excitedly at immaculately preserved Colonial-era architecture and landmarks at seemingly every turn.

Fascinating as Newport's early history is, the real intrigue began in the late 1850s, when wealthy industrialists began building opulent summer residences along cliff-top Bellevue Ave. Impeccably styled on Italianate palazzi, French châteaux and Elizabethan manor houses, these gloriously restored mansions filled with priceless antiques and their breathtaking location must be seen to be believed. The curiosity, variety and extravagance of this spectacle is unrivaled.

Honoring its maritime roots, Newport remains a global center for yachting. Put simply, summers here sparkle: locals have excellent taste and know how to throw a shindig. There's always something going on, including a series of cross-genre festivals that are among the best in the USA.

⊙ Sights & Activities

★ The Breakers
HISTORIC BUILDING

(☑ 401-847-1000; www.newportmansions.org; 44 Ochre Point Ave; adult/child $24/8; ⊙ 9am-5pm Apr–mid-Oct, hours vary mid-Oct–Mar; ℗) A 70-room Italian Renaissance megapalace inspired by 16th-century Genoese palazzi, the Breakers is the most magnificent of Newport's grandiose mansions. At the behest of Cornelius Vanderbilt II, Richard Morris Hunt did most of the design (though craftspeople from around the world perfected the decorative program). The building was completed in 1895 and sits at Ochre Point, on a grand oceanside site. The furnishings, most made expressly for the Breakers, are all original. Don't miss the **Children's Cottage** on the grounds.

★ The Elms
HISTORIC BUILDING

(☑ 401-847-1000; www.newportmansions.org/explore/the-elms; 367 Bellevue Ave; adult/child $17.50/8, servant life tours adult/child $18/7.50; ⊙ 10am-5pm Apr–mid-Oct, hours vary mid-Oct–Mar; ℗ ♿) Designed by Horace Trumbauer in 1901, the Elms is a replica of Château d'Asnières, built near Paris in 1750. Here you can take a 'behind-the-scenes' tour that will have you snaking through the servants' quarters and up onto the roof. Along the way you'll learn about the activities of the army of servants and the architectural devices that kept them hidden from the view of those drinking port in the formal rooms.

Rough Point
HISTORIC BUILDING

(☑ 401-849-7300; www.newportrestoration.org/roughpoint/; 680 Bellevue Ave; adult/child $25/free; ⊙ 9:30am-2pm Thu-Sun Apr-early May, 9:30am-3:30pm Tue-Sun early May-early Nov; ℗) While the peerless position and splendor of the grounds alone are worth the price of admission, this faux-English manor house also contains heiress and philanthropist Doris Duke's impressive art holdings, including medieval tapestries, furniture owned by French emperors, Ming dynasty ceramics, and paintings by Renoir and Van Dyck.

Fort Adams State Park
STATE PARK

(☑ 401-847-2400; www.riparks.com/Locations/LocationFortAdams.html; Harrison Ave; overnight parking $6; ⊙ dawn-dusk) America's largest coastal fortification and the centerpiece of this gorgeous state park is **Fort Adams** (☑ 401-841-0707; www.fortadams.org; 90 Fort Adams Dr; tours adult/child $12/6; ⊙ 10am-4pm late May-Oct, reduced hours Nov & Dec), which juts out into Narragansett Bay. It's the venue for the Newport jazz and folk festivals and numerous special events. A beach, picnic and fishing areas, and a boat ramp are open daily.

BLOCK ISLAND

From the deck of the ferry, a cluster of mansard roofs and gingerbread houses rises picturesquely from the commercial village of Old Harbor, where little has changed since 1895, short of adding electricity and flushing toilets! If you remain after the departure of the masses on the last ferry, the scale and pace of the island will delight or derange you: some find it blissfully quiet, but others get island fever fast.

Block Island's simple pleasures center on strolling the beach, which stretches for miles to the north of Old Harbor, biking around the island's rolling farmland and getting to know the calls of the many bird species that make the island home. During off-season, when the population dwindles to a few hundred, the landscape has the spare, haunted feeling of an Andrew Wyeth painting, with stone walls demarcating centuries-old property lines and few trees interrupting the spectacular ocean vistas.

Sleeping

Many places have a two- or three-day minimum stay in summer and close between November and April. Advance reservations are essential. Peak season runs roughly from mid-June to Labor Day. Off-season prices can be far cheaper than those listed here. Camping is not allowed on the island.

The **Block Island Hospitality Center** (✆ 401-466-2982; www.blockislandchamber. com; 1 Water St, Old Harbor Ferry Landing; ⊗ 9am-5pm late May-early Sep, 10am-4pm rest of year) near the ferry dock keeps track of vacancies, and will try to help should you arrive *sans réservation*.

Getting There & Away

The island can only be reached by sea or air.

Block Island Ferry (✆ 401-783-7996; www.blockislandferry.com) Runs a year-round traditional car ferry and a high-speed ferry from Point Judith in Narragansett from Memorial Day to mid-October. There are additional high-speed, passenger-only ferries from Newport and Fall River, MA.

Block Island Express (✆ 860-444-4624; www.goblockisland.com) Operates services from New London, CT, to Old Harbor, Block Island, between May and September.

New England Airlines (www.blockislandsairline.com) Flies between Westerly State Airport, on Airport Rd off RI 78, and Block Island State Airport (12 minutes).

Cliff Walk WALKING
(www.cliffwalk.com; Memorial Blvd) For a glorious hike take the 3.5-mile Cliff Walk, which hugs the coast along the back side of Newport's mansions from Memorial Blvd to Bailey's Beach. You will not only enjoy the same dramatic ocean views that were once reserved for the Newport elite, but you'll also get to gawk at their mansions along the way.

★ Festivals

★ **Newport Music Festival** MUSIC
(✆ 401-849-0700; www.newportmusic.org; tickets $25-50; ⊗ mid-Jul) This internationally regarded festival offers a wide program of classical music concerts performed in the spectacular settings of some of the Newport Mansions, as well as other visually delicious and acoustically satisfying venues around town.

Newport Folk Festival MUSIC
(www.newportfolk.org; Fort Adams State Park; check website for current pricing; ⊗ late Jul) Big-name stars and up-and-coming groups perform at Fort Adams State Park and other venues around town during one of the top folk festivals in the USA. Not just limited to music, this popular festival has a family-friendly, carnival-like atmosphere and features workshops, exhibitions and pop-up shops.

Newport Jazz Festival MUSIC
(www.newportjazz.org; Fort Adams State Park; tickets adult/child from $65/15; ⊗ Aug) This classic festival usually takes place on an August weekend, with concerts at Fort Adams State Park and smaller gigs in venues around town. Popular shows can sell out a year in advance.

🛏 Sleeping

Newport International Hostel
HOSTEL $

(William Gyles Guesthouse; 🖵 401-369-0243; www.newporthostel.com; 16 Howard St; dm/d from $29/79; ☉ May-Nov; 🛜) Book as early as you can to get into Rhode Island's only hostel, run by an informal and knowledgeable host. The tiny guesthouse contains the fixings for a simple breakfast, plus a laundry machine and clean digs in a dormitory room.

Francis Malbone House
B&B $$

(🖵 401-846-0392; www.malbone.com; 392 Thames St; d/ste from $149/289; 🅿🛜) This grand brick mansion was designed by Peter Harrison and was built in 1760 for a shipping merchant. Now beautifully decorated and immaculately kept with a lush garden, it is one of Newport's finest inns. Some guest rooms have working fireplaces, as do the public areas. Gourmet breakfast and afternoon tea are included in the tariff.

★ Attwater
BOUTIQUE HOTEL $$$

(🖵 401-846-7444; www.theattwater.com; 22 Liberty St; r $139-659; 🅿❄🛜) Newport's newest hotel has the bold attire of a midsummer beach party with turquoise, lime green and coral prints, ikat headboards and snazzily patterned geometric rugs. Picture windows and porches capture the summer light and rooms come furnished with thoughtful luxuries such as iPads, Apple TVs and beach bags.

🍴 Eating

Rosemary & Thyme Cafe
CAFE $

(🖵 401-619-3338; www.rosemaryandthymecafe.com; 382 Spring St; baked goods $3-6, sandwiches $8-11; ☉ 7am-2pm Tue-Sat, to 11:30am Sun May-Oct, 8am-1pm Fri-Sun Nov-Apr; 🖉🎬) The counter at Rosemary & Thyme is piled high with buttery croissants, apple and cherry tarts, and plump muffins. At lunchtime gourmet sandwiches feature herbed goat's cheese and Tuscan dried tomatoes, Havana Cuban pork loin and an Alsatian cheese mix. A children's menu is also thoughtfully provided.

★ Anthony's Seafood
SEAFOOD $$

(🖵 401-846-9620; www.anthonysseafood.net; 963 Aquidneck Ave; mains $12-32; ☉ 11am-8pm Mon-Sat, from noon Sun) Lauded by locals and featured on TV's *Diners, Drive-ins and Dives*, this wholesale, takeout and dine-in seafood joint tucked away from the main drag in Middletown is always hopping, testament to the quality and freshness of the seafood. It's a great place to try a quahog (also known as 'stuffies' or stuffed clams). Portions are enormous!

Fluke Wine Bar
SEAFOOD $$$

(🖵 401-849-7778; www.flukenewport.com; 41 Bowens Wharf; mains $24-36; ☉ 5-11pm May-Oct, 5-10pm Wed-Sat Nov-Apr) Fluke's Scandinavian-inspired dining room, with blond wood and picture windows, offers an accomplished seafood menu featuring roasted monkfish, seasonal striped sea bass and plump scallops. Upstairs, the Harbor View Bar overlooking the docks and the bay, serves beer and rock-and-roll cocktails, and pours from an extensive wine list. Reservations are recommended.

ℹ Information

Newport Visitor's Center
(🖵 401-845-9131; www.discovernewport.org; 23 America's Cup Ave; ☉ 9am-5pm) Offers maps, brochures, local bus information, tickets to major attractions, public restrooms and an ATM. There's free parking for 30 minutes adjacent to the center.

ℹ Getting There & Away

Peter Pan Bus Lines operates buses to Boston (from $22, 1¾ to two hours, four to five daily) from the Newport Visitor Center.

RIPTA bus 60 serves Providence ($2, one hour) almost every hour. For the West Kingston Amtrak station, take bus 64 ($2, one hour, five buses Monday to Friday, three on Saturday). Bus 14 serves TF Green airport ($2, one hour) in Warwick. Most RIPTA buses arrive and depart from the Newport Visitor Center.

East Bay

Rhode Island's jagged East Bay captures the early American story in microcosm, from the graves of early settlers in Little Compton to the farmsteads and merchant homes of whalers and farmers in Warren and Barrington, and the mansions of slave traders in Bristol.

Aside from Barrington's historic and picturesque **Tyler Point Cemetery**, set between the Warren and Barrington Rivers, and Warren's clutch of early stone and clapboard churches (built in the 18th and 19th centuries), the most interesting of the three communities is Bristol. Further south is Sakonnet, the Wampanoag's 'Place of Black Geese,' a rural landscape of pastures and woods centered on the two tiny communities of Tiverton and Little Compton.

The East Bay is proudly protected by its residents and represents a fascinating, largely unpromoted region for the discerning independent traveler interested in American history and New England's natural delights.

★ **Colt State Park** STATE PARK
(☎ 401-253-7482; www.riparks.com/Locations/LocationColt.html; Rte 114; ⊙ dawn-dusk; P)
FREE Bristol's Colt State Park is Rhode Island's most scenic park, with its entire western border fronting Narragansett Bay. The parks is fringed by 4 miles of cycling trails and has more than 400 shaded picnic tables (you read that correctly!) set among 464 acres of groomed fruit trees, flower beds and lush greenery.

CONNECTICUT

Known for its commuter cities, New York's neighbor is synonymous with the affluent lanes and mansions of *The Stepford Wives* and TV's *Gilmore Girls*. In old-moneyed Greenwich, the Litchfield Hills and the Quiet Corner, these representations ring true.

Many regard the state as a mere stepping stone to the 'real' New England, from whose tourist boom Connecticut has been spared. The upside is that Connecticut retains a more 'authentic' feel. The downside is a slow decaying of former heavyweights like Hartford and New London, where visitors can ponder the price of progress and get enthused about urban renewal. New Haven, home of Yale University, is one such place rewiring itself as a vibrant cultural hub.

Rich in maritime, literary and national history, as well as the farm-to-table food movement, celebrity chefs and enough waterfalls and state parks for the most avid outdoors folk, the Nutmeg State unfolds in incredible layers the longer you stick around.

History

A number of Native American tribes (notably the Pequot and the Mohegan, whose name for the river became the name of the state) were here when the first European explorers, primarily Dutch, appeared in the early 17th century. The first English settlement was at Old Saybrook in 1635, followed a year later by the Connecticut Colony, built by Massachusetts Puritans under Thomas Hooker. A third colony was founded in 1638 in New Haven. After the Pequot War (1637), the Native Americans were no longer able to check Colonial expansion in New England, and Connecticut's English population grew. In 1686 Connecticut was brought into the Dominion of New England.

The American Revolution swept through Connecticut, leaving scars with major battles at Stonington (1775), Danbury (1777), New Haven (1779) and Groton (1781). Connecticut became the fifth state in 1788. It embarked on a period of prosperity, propelled by its whaling, shipbuilding, farming and manufacturing (firearms from bicycles to household tools) industries, which lasted well into the 19th century.

The 20th century brought world wars and the Depression but, thanks in no small part to Connecticut's munitions industries, the state was able to fight back. Everything from planes to submarines were made in the state, and when the defense industry began to decline in the 1990s, the growth of other businesses (such as insurance) helped pick up the slack. Today, two booming casinos are a key source of income for the state – $7 billion since 1997 – so much so that a third casino has been approved by legislators.

ℹ Information

Connecticut Office of Tourism (www.ctvisit.com) The official site for tourism in Connecticut.

Connecticut River Valley and Shoreline Travel Information (www.ctrivervalley.com) A privately maintained resource of tourist information relating to the Connecticut River Valley.

CTNow (www.ctnow.com) Regularly updated listings and information on what's hot, where and when.

Edible Nutmeg: Celebrating the Local Food Community of Fairfield, Litchfield, and New Haven Counties (www.ediblenutmeg.com) Quarterly gourmand's guide to the great cuisine of this part of the state.

Lonely Planet (www.lonelyplanet.com/usa/new-england/connecticut) Destination information, hotel bookings, traveler forum and more.

Hartford

Connecticut's capital, one of America's oldest cities, is famed for the 1794 birth of the lucrative insurance industry, conceived when a local landowner sought fire insurance. Policy documents necessitated printing presses, which spurred a boom in publishing that lured the likes of Mark Twain, Harriet

Beecher Stowe and Wallace Stevens. In 1855 Samuel Colt made the mass production of the revolver commercially viable. Big business boomed in Hartford.

It's ironic that the industries responsible for the city's wealth (insurance and guns) have contributed to its slow decline: Hartford has a gritty track record for crime. Although things are improving, keep this in mind. Old money has left a truly impressive legacy of fine historic attractions worthy of any New England itinerary. Visit during spring when the darling buds burst to life or in summer when trees are green and skies are blue, and you're likely to be pleasantly surprised.

⊙ Sights

★ **Wadsworth Atheneum**　　　MUSEUM
(☏ 860-278-2670; https://thewadsworth.org; 600 Main St; adult/child $15/free; ⊙ 11am-5pm Wed-Fri, 10am-5pm Sat & Sun) In 2015 the nation's oldest public art museum completed a five-year, $33-million renovation, renewing 32 galleries and 15 public spaces. The Wadsworth houses nearly 50,000 pieces of art in a castle-like Gothic Revival building. On display are paintings by members of the Hudson River School, including some by Hartford native Frederic Church; 19th-century impressionist works; 18th-century New England furniture; sculptures by Connecticut artist Alexander Calder; and an outstanding array of surrealist, postwar and contemporary works.

★ **Mark Twain House & Museum**　　MUSEUM
(☏ 860-247-0998; www.marktwainhouse.org; 351 Farmington Ave, parking at 385 Farmington Ave; guided house tours adult/child $20/11, Living History/Ghost tours $25/12, museum only $6; ⊙ 9:30am-5:30pm, closed Tue Jan & Feb; ℗) For 17 years, encompassing the most productive period of his life, Samuel Langhorne Clemens (1835–1910) and his family lived in this striking orange-and-black brick Victorian house, which then stood in the pastoral area of the city called Nook Farm. Architect Edward Tuckerman Potter lavishly embellished it with turrets, gables and verandas, and some of the interiors were done by Louis Comfort Tiffany. Admission to the house is by guided tour only; advance ticket purchase is recommended.

Connecticut Science Center　　MUSEUM
(☏ 860-520-2160; www.ctsciencecenter.org; 250 Columbus Blvd; adult/child $24/17, movies $7/6; ⊙ 10am-5pm Tue-Sun; ℗♿) Designed by Argentinian architect Cesar Pelli, the Connecticut Science Center is both an exciting architectural space and an absorbing museum for adults and kids alike. Innovative, interactive exhibits and programs abound; there's a dedicated KidsZone on the 1st floor; films, stage shows and special events are on offer; and there's always a fascinating world-class visiting themed exhibition. You could easily spend a whole day here, but it's best to arrive after 2pm when the school groups clear out. Check the website for what's on.

Harriet Beecher Stowe Center　　MUSEUM
(☏ 860-522-9258; www.harrietbeecherstowecenter. org/; 77 Forest St; adult/child $16/10; ⊙ 9:30am-5pm Mon-Sat, noon-5pm Sun; ℗) Hartford was home to Harriet Beecher Stowe, author of the antislavery book *Uncle Tom's Cabin*. Upon meeting Stowe, Abraham Lincoln reputedly said, 'So this is the little lady who made this big war.' The facility centers on Stowe House, built in 1871 and restored in 2017, which reflects the author's strong ideas about decorating and domestic efficiency, as expressed in her bestseller *American Woman's Home* (nearly as popular as her famous novel).

🛏 Sleeping

Sadly it's slim pickings for decent hotels in Hartford's downtown core and prices can be steep for what you get. Better value may be found in chain offerings outside the city center, and you'll find contentment in B&Bs just a short drive away.

★ **Goodwin**　　BOUTIQUE HOTEL $$$
(☏ 860-246-1881; www.goodwinhartford.com; 1 Haynes St; r from $359) This historic building reopened with a bang in 2017, redone in modern New York chic. The Queen Anne terracotta facade exudes the building's 19th-century origins while the inside oozes 21st-century cool. Convenient to the downtown scene, the Goodwin gives you no reason to leave the premises; it has its own charming bar-restaurant Porrón and Piña, managed by chef Tyler Anderson.

Silas W. Robbins House　　B&B $$$
(☏ 860-571-8733; www.silaswrobbins.com; 185 Broad St, Wethersfield; d $195-325; ℗🐾🛜) About 6 miles south of downtown Hartford in the charming historic village of Wethersfield, you'll find this beautiful and opulent 1873 French Second Empire home. Its common areas and five plush rooms, with their

soaring ceilings and light-filled windows overlooking the manicured grounds, have been refurbished in the style of the period.

✖ Eating

★ Trumbull Kitchen
MODERN AMERICAN $$

(www.maxrestaurantgroup.com/trumbull; 150 Trumbull St; mains $13-30; ☺noon-11pm Mon-Sat, 4-10pm Sun) TK's smart-yet-casual fine-dining atmosphere awaits, with excellent service and a wonderfully executed, diverse menu, making it a great alternative to some of Hartford's upscale joints. Drop in for a cocktail and some fabulous appetizers, or save that appetite for fish, chicken, burgers and steak, freshly prepared and presented like works of art: dressed-up comfort food. The interior is flash, too.

Bear's Smokehouse
BARBECUE $$

(☑860-724-3100; www.bearsbbq.com; 89 Arch St; mains $10-20; ☺11am-9pm) Locals love this wood-smoked Kansas-style barbecue famed for brisket, baby back ribs and pulled pork. Vegetarians might want to head elsewhere, although there are some kick-ass sides: collard greens, broccoli salad and mac 'n' cheese. Carnivores will dig the Moink balls (a little bit of 'moo' crossed with a little bit of 'oink'): bacon-wrapped meatballs with your choice of sauce.

ℹ Information

Greater Hartford Welcome Center (Greater Hartford Arts Council; ☑860-244-0253; www. letsgoarts.org; 100 Pearl St; ☺9am-5pm Mon-Fri) The bulk of tourist services can be found at this centrally located office.

ℹ Getting There & Away

Central **Union Station** (1 Union Pl) is the city's transportation hub. Catch trains, airport shuttles, intercity buses and taxis from here.

Litchfield Hills

The rolling hills in the northwestern corner of Connecticut are sprinkled with lakes and dotted with forests and state parks. Historic Litchfield is the hub of the region, but lesser-known Bethlehem, Kent and Norfolk boast similarly illustrious lineages and are just as photogenic.

An intentional curb on development continues to preserve the area's rural character. Accommodations are limited. Volunteers staff a useful information booth on Litchfield's town green from June to November.

If you have your own car, there's no shortage of postcard-perfect country roads to explore in the Litchfield Hills. One particularly delightful stretch is from Cornwall Bridge taking CT 4 west and then CT 41 north to Salisbury. Gourmands will also find this area surprisingly rich in good food.

Among the plentiful lakes and ponds in the Litchfield Hills, Lake Waramaug, north of New Preston, stands out. Gracious inns dot its shoreline, parts of which are a state park.

Haight-Brown Vineyards
WINERY

(☑860-567-4045; www.haightvineyards.com; 29 Chestnut Hill Rd; tastings from $12; ☺noon-5pm Fri-Sun) The veranda overlooking the state's first wine-producing vineyard (established 1975) sets the mood, while chocolate and cheese pairings make it even more palatable. Chocolate Decadence rail excursions ($79, April to June) with the nearby Railroad Museum of New England up the ante. There are dog biscuits at the entrance if you care to bring a four-legged friend (they even distribute a canine-themed calendar).

★ Hopkins Inn
INN $$

(☑860-868-7295; www.thehopkinsinn.com; 22 Hopkins Rd, Warren; r $140-150, without bath $130, apt $160-250; P ❀ ☻) The 19th-century Hopkins Inn boasts a well-regarded restaurant with Austrian-influenced country fare (the second-generation chef whips up a mean schnitzel and mouthwatering pastries) and a variety of lodging options, from simple rooms with shared bathrooms to lake-view apartments. Whatever the season, there's something magical about sitting on the porch gazing upon Lake Waramaug and the hills beyond.

★ Community Table
MODERN AMERICAN $$$

(Ct; ☑860-868-9354; http://communitytablect. com; 223 Litchfield Turnpike/US 202, Washington; brunch $22-28, mains $26-42; ☺5-9:30pm Sat, 10am-2pm & 3:30-9pm Sun; P) The name of this Scandinavian-inspired restaurant comes from the 300-year-old black-walnut table, where you can sit down to Sunday brunch. The modern American menu is locally sourced.

ℹ Getting There & Around

The Litchfield Hills run north from Danbury and cover the northwest portion of the state, as far as the Massachusetts and New York borders, to the north and west, respectively. Highways US 7 and CT 8 are the main north–south trunk roads. You'll need a car.

Connecticut Coast

The southeastern corner of Connecticut is home to the state's number-one tourist attraction and the country's largest maritime museum, Mystic Seaport. Built on the site of a former shipbuilding yard in 1929, the museum celebrates the area's seafaring heritage, when fisherers, whalers and clipper-ship engineers broke world speed records and manufactured gunboats and warships for the Civil War.

To the west of Mystic, you'll find the submarine capital of the USA, Groton, where General Dynamics built WWII subs, and, across the Thames River, New London. To the east is the historic fishing village of Stonington, extending along a narrow mile-long peninsula into the sea. It's one of the most charming seaside villages in New England, where Connecticut's only remaining commercial fleet operates and yachties come ashore in summer to enjoy the restaurants on Water St.

❶ Getting There & Around

Car The area is served well by road, with the I-95 plowing through the middle of New London and around the outskirts of Mystic. I-395 runs northeast to Norwich and beyond.

Ferry Services run from New London to Block Island, Fisher's Island and Long Island.

Train Many Amtrak trains from New York City stop in New London (from $39, three hours) and Mystic (from $41, 3¼ hours). The return run from Boston also stops in Mystic (from $26, 80 minutes), then New London (from $29, 1½ hours).

Mystic

A skyline of masts greets you as you arrive in town on US 1. They belong to the vessels bobbing ever so slightly in the postcard-perfect harbor. There's a sense of self-satisfied calm and composure in the air – until suddenly a heart-stopping steamer whistle blows, followed by the cheerful cling of a drawbridge bell. You know you've arrived in Mystic.

From simple beginnings in the 17th century, the village of Mystic grew to become a prosperous whaling center and one of the great shipbuilding ports of the East Coast. In the mid-19th century, Mystic's shipyards launched clipper ships, gunboats and naval transport vessels, many from the George Greenman & Co Shipyard, now the site of Mystic Seaport Museum, Connecticut's largest tourist attraction. Some great food and drink spots have grown up around the tourism, including the state's hottest bakery (p232).

◉ Sights

★**Mystic Seaport Museum** MUSEUM
(☑ 860-572-0711; www.mysticseaport.org; 75 Greenmanville Ave; adult/child $29/19; ◷ 9am-5pm Apr-Oct, 10am-4pm Thu-Sun Nov-Mar; ℗ 🖈) More than a museum, this is a re-creation of an entire New England whaling village spread over 17 acres of the former George Greenman & Co Shipyard. To re-create the past, 60 historic buildings, four tall ships and almost 500 smaller vessels are gathered along the Mystic River. Interpreters staff the site and are glad to discuss traditional crafts and trades. Most illuminating are the demonstrations on such topics as ship rescue, oystering and whaleboat launching.

⌑ Sleeping

Whaler's Inn INN $$
(☑ 860-536-1506; www.whalersinnmystic.com; 20 E Main St; d $159-299; ℗ @ 🛜) Beside Mystic's historic drawbridge, this hotel combines an 1865 Victorian with a reconstructed adults-only luxury hotel from the same era (the landmark 'Hoxie House' burned down in the 1970s) and a modern motel known as Stonington House. Seasonal packages include dinners and area attractions. Rates include continental breakfast at respected Bravo Bravo next door, a small gym and complimentary bicycles.

★**Steamboat Inn** INN $$$
(☑ 860-536-8300; www.steamboatinnmystic.com; 73 Steamboat Wharf; d $220-350; ℗ ❄ 🛜) Located in the heart of downtown Mystic, the 11 rooms and suites of this historic inn have wraparound water views and luxurious amenities, (some) hot tubs, cable TV and fireplaces. Some have stunning floor-to-ceiling windows overlooking the river. Antiques lend the interior a romantic, period feel, and service is top-notch with baked goods for breakfast, complimentary bikes and boat docks.

✗ Eating

Sift Bake Shop   BAKERY **$**

(☑ 860-245-0541; www.siftbakeshopmystic.com; 5 Water St; desserts $4-7, sandwiches $8-10; ⊗ 7am-7pm) When pastry chef Adam Young won the Food Network's Best Baker award in 2018, things blew up at this Water St location. Baguettes, ciabattas, chocolate croissants, brioche and specialties such as pumpkin cheesecake are all so good, it may be worth the (long) line. *So* good.

★ Oyster Club   SEAFOOD **$$$**

(☑ 860-415-9266; www.oysterclubct.com; 13 Water St; oysters $2-2.50, lunch mains $13-20, dinner mains $18-40; ⊗ noon-3pm & 5-10pm Fri & Sat, 10am-3pm & 5-9pm Sun, 5-9pm Mon-Thu; P ✿) Offering casual fine dining at its best, this is the place locals come to knock down oysters on the deck out back. Grilled lobster and pan-roasted monkfish or flounder feature alongside veal, steak and a drool-worthy burger. If oysters are an aphrodisiac, anything could happen at the bar after the daily happy hour (4pm to 6pm), when shucked oysters are a buck each.

Captain Daniel Packer Inne   AMERICAN **$$$**

(☑ 860-536-3555; www.danielpacker.com; 32 Water St; mains $19-34; ⊗ 11am-4pm & 5-10pm) This 1754 historic house has a low-beam ceiling and creaky floorboards. On the lower pub level, you'll find bar denizens, live music, a good selection of tap beer and excellent pub grub: try the fish and chips. Upstairs, the dining room has river views and an imaginative American menu, including petite filet mignon with Gorgonzola sauce and walnut demi-glace. Reservations recommended.

ⓘ Information

Stop in at the **Greater Mystic Chamber of Commerce** (☑ 860-572-9578; www.mysticchamber. org; 62 Greenmanville Ave; ⊗ 9am-6pm Jun-Sep, reduced hours Oct-May) or its kiosk in the train depot, or head to the **Mystic & Shoreline Tourist Information Center** (☑ 860-536-1641; www.mysticinfocenter.com; 27 Coogan Blvd, Olde Mistick Village; ⊗ 10am-5pm Mon-Sat, 11am-4pm Sun).

New London

During its golden age in the mid-19th century, New London, then home to some 200 whaling vessels, was one of the largest whaling centers in the USA and one of the wealthiest port cities. In 1858 the discovery of crude oil in Pennsylvania sent the value of whale oil plummeting and began a long period of decline for the city, from which it has never fully recovered. Even so, New London retains strong links with its seafaring past (the US Coast Guard Academy and US Naval Submarine Base are here) and its downtown is listed on the National Register of Historic Places.

Despite lacking the sanitized tourism push of nearby Mystic and Stonington, remnants of New London's glorious and opulent times are still evident throughout the city, making it one of Connecticut's most surprising destinations for those interested in history, architecture and urban sociology. Hip Bank St is a hopeful sign of rejuvenation.

★ Captain Scott's Lobster Dock   SEAFOOD **$$**

(☑ 860-439-1741; www.captscotts.com; 80 Hamilton St; mains $7-21; ⊗ 11am-9pm May-Oct; ⊛) The Coast Guard knows a bit about the sea, and you'd be remiss if you didn't follow its cadets to *the* place for summer seafood. The setting's just picnic tables by the water (BYOB), but you can feast on succulent (hot or cold) lobster rolls, followed by steamers, fried whole-belly clams, scallops or lobsters, and two kinds of chowder.

On the Waterfront   SEAFOOD **$$**

(☑ 860-444-2800; www.onthewaterfrontnl.com; 250 Pequot Ave; mains $15-28; ⊗ noon-9pm Tue-Thu & Sun, to 10pm Fri & Sat; ⊛) A spectacular lobster bisque and other delights from the deep, such as pistachio-crusted salmon and Montauk-jumbo-stuffed shrimp, are served up with water views from a multitude of windows. The bar is a popular spot with locals who don't like it rowdy. A diverse menu and friendly staff help to accommodate die-hard landlubbers and those with food intolerances.

Essex

Tree-lined Essex, established in 1635, stands as the chief town of the Connecticut River Valley region. It's worth a visit if only to gawk at the beautiful, well-preserved Federal-period houses, legacies of rum and tobacco fortunes made in the 19th century. The town has a strong following with steam train and riverboat enthusiasts, and also has lovely St John's church, a picturesque riverside park, and a handful of galleries and antique dealers.

★ Essex Steam Train & Riverboat Ride

TOURS

(☏ 860-767-0103; www.essexsteamtrain.com; 1 Railroad Ave; adult/child $20/10, incl cruise $30/20; ☉ daily May-Oct, seasonal events year-round; ♿) This wildly popular attraction features a steam locomotive and antique carriages. The journey travels 6 scenic miles to Deep River, where you can cruise to the **Goodspeed Opera House** (☏ 860-873-8668; www.goodspeed. org; 6 Main St; tickets $29-85, tours adult/child $5/1; ☉ performances Wed-Sun Apr-Dec) in East Haddam, before returning to Essex via train. The round-trip train ride takes about an hour; with the riverboat ride it's 2½ hours. This train also connects with Connecticut Audubon for special bird-watching trips in the fall.

Griswold Inn

INN $$

(☏ 860-767-1776; www.griswoldinn.com; 36 Main St; d/ste from $195/240; ℗☏) The 'Gris' is one of the country's oldest continually operating inns, Essex' physical and social centerpiece since 1776. The buffet-style Hunt Breakfast (11am to 1pm Sunday) is a tradition dating from the War of 1812, when British soldiers occupying Essex demanded to be fed. Two main buildings were refurbished and connected in 2017, eliminating walks between in inclement weather.

At other times, the expansive dining room remains a favorite place to enjoy traditional New England cuisine in a historic setting. In kinder weather, the new 2200-sq-ft bluestone patio is a nice place to wine and unwind. The historic taproom has free popcorn and live music.

New Haven

Connecticut's second-largest city radiates out from pretty New Haven Green, laid by Puritan settlers in the 1600s. Around it, Yale University's over-300-year-old accessible campus offers visitors a wealth of world-class attractions, from museums and galleries to a lively concert program and walking-tour tales of secret societies.

As you admire Yale's gorgeous faux-Gothic and Victorian architecture, it's hard to fathom New Haven's struggle to shake its reputation as a dangerous, decaying seaport – but the city is successfully repositioning itself as a thriving home for the arts, architecture and the human mind.

While Yale may have put New Haven on the map, there's much to savor beyond campus. Well-aged dive bars, ethnic restaurants,

HAMMONASSET BEACH

Though not off the beaten path by any means, the two full miles of flat, sandy beach at **Hammonasset Beach State Park** (☏ 203-245-2785; www.ct.gov; 1288 Boston Post Rd, Madison; weekdays/weekends $15/22; ☉ 8am-sunset; ℗), 3 miles southwest of Essex, handily accommodate summer crowds. This is the ideal beach (the state's largest) at which to set up an umbrella chair, crack open a book and forget about the world. The surf is tame, making swimming superb. Restrooms and showering facilities are clean and ample, and a wooden boardwalk runs the length of the park.

barbecue shacks and cocktail lounges make the area almost as lively as Cambridge's Harvard Sq, but with better pizza and less ego.

⊙ Sights

★ Yale University

UNIVERSITY

(☏ 203-432-2300; www.yale.edu/visitor; 149 Elm St) FREE Each year, thousands of highschool students make pilgrimages to Yale, nursing dreams of attending the country's third-oldest university, which boasts such notable alums as Noah Webster, Naomi Wolf and Hillary Clinton, and presidents William H Taft and George W Bush. You don't need to share the students' ambitions in order to take a stroll around the campus – just pick up a map at the visitor center or join a free, one-hour guided tour.

★ Yale Center for British Art

MUSEUM

(☏ 203-432-2800; www.ycba.yale.edu; 1080 Chapel St; ☉ 10am-5pm Tue-Sat, noon-5pm Sun) FREE Reopened in 2016 after extensive restoration, this fabulous gallery was architect Louis Kahn's last commission and is the setting for the largest collection of British art outside the UK. Spanning three centuries from the Elizabethan era to the 19th century, and arranged thematically as well as chronologically, the collection gives an unparalleled insight into British art, life and culture. A visit is an absolute must for anyone interested in beautiful things. And yes, it's free.

Yale University Art Gallery

MUSEUM

(☏ 203-432-0600; http://artgallery.yale.edu; 1111 Chapel St; ☉ 10am-5pm Tue, Wed & Fri, to 8pm Thu, 11am-5pm Sat & Sun) FREE This outstanding museum was architect Louis Kahn's first commission and houses the oldest university art collection in the country; it includes Vincent van Gogh's *The Night Café* and European masterpieces by Frans Hals, Peter Paul Rubens, Manet and Picasso. In addition there are displays of American masterworks by Winslow Homer, Edward Hopper and Jackson Pollock, silver from the 18th century, and art from Africa, Asia, and the pre- and post-Columbian Americas.

Shore Line Trolley Museum
MUSEUM

(☑ 203-467-6927; www.shorelinetrolley.org; 17 River St, East Haven; adult/child $10/7; ⊙ 10:30am-4:30pm daily Jul & Aug, Sat & Sun May, Jun, Sep & Oct; ⏹) For a unique take on East Haven's shoreline, take a ride on this open-sided antique trolley – the oldest continuously running suburban trolley line in the country – along 3 miles of track that takes you from River St in East Haven to Short Beach in Branford. Enjoy the museum and its beautifully maintained carriages when you're done. Bring a picnic lunch.

🛏 Sleeping

★ New Haven Hotel
BOUTIQUE HOTEL $$

(☑ 800-644-6835; www.newhavenhotel.com; 229 George St; d from $169) This robust downtown hotel is both simply stylish and affordable. It's nice to see a private operator raising the bar. The hotel occupies a handsome mid-20th-century brick building with bright, modern common areas, while guest rooms are airy with large windows, clean lines, dark woods and sink-into-me bedding. Reasonable rates mean it's understandably popular. Book in advance.

Study at Yale
HOTEL $$$

(☑ 203-503-3900; www.thestudyatyale.com; 1157 Chapel St; r $250-389; 🅿 🛜) The Study at Yale manages to evoke a mid-century modern sense of sophistication (call it 'Mad Men chic') without being over the top or intimidating. Ultra-contemporary touches include in-room iPod docking stations and cardio machines with built-in TV. Furniture in the rooms and lobby was replaced in 2018. There's also an in-house restaurant and cafe, to which you can stumble for snacks.

🍴 Eating

★ Pantry
AMERICAN $

(☑ 203-787-0392; 2 Mechanic St; breakfast $11-24; ⊙ 7am-2pm Mon-Sat, 8am-3pm Sun) The secret is already out about New Haven's ah-mazing

little breakfast-lunch joint. You'll most likely have to line up then rub shoulders with a bunch of hungry students (who'd probably rather we kept this one to ourselves), but persevere if you can: you won't find a better-value, more drool-worthy breakfast for miles. Take your pick: it's *all* good.

Atticus Bookstore Café
CAFE $

(☑ 203-776-4040; www.atticusbookstorecafe.com; 1082 Chapel St; salads & sandwiches $6-12; ⊙ 7am-9pm Tue-Sat, 8am-8pm Sun-Mon) On the fringe of the Yale campus, come here to get your bearings and mingle with the alumni over great coffee, artisanal sandwiches, stellar breads, soup and salad, surrounded by an immaculately presented selection of books.

Frank Pepe
PIZZA $

(☑ 203-865-5762; www.pepespizzeria.com; 157 Wooster St; pizzas $8-29; ⊙ 11am-10pm; 🍴 ⏹) Pepe's lays claim to baking the 'best pizza in America,' a title it's won three times running. We'll let you be the judge, but can confirm this joint cranks out tasty pies fired in a coal oven, just as it has since 1925; only now it has locations across Connecticut (and New York), making consistency harder to master. Cash only.

★ ZINC
AMERICAN $$$

(☑ 203-624-0507; www.zincfood.com; 964 Chapel St; mains $12-28; ⊙ noon-2:30pm & 5-9pm Tue-Fri, 5-10pm Sat & Mon) Whenever possible, this trendy bistro's ingredients hail from local organic sources, but the chef draws inspiration from all over, notably Asia and the Southwest. There's a constantly changing 'market menu,' but for the most rewarding experience, share several small plates, such as smoked duck nachos or *prosciutto Americano crostini*. Reservations are advised.

🍷 Drinking & Nightlife

★ Ordinary
COCKTAIL BAR

(☑ 203-907-0238; www.ordinarynewhaven.com; 990 Chapel St; ⊙ 4pm-midnight Mon-Thu, to 1am Fri & Sat) Ordinary is anything but. It's tall, dark and handsome, ineffably stylish and a treat for the senses. Its patrons often also fall into at least one of these categories. They come for cheese boards, charcuterie and cocktails. Put on your fancy pants and join them.

116 Crown
BAR

(☑ 203-777-3116; www.116crown.com; 116 Crown St; ⊙ 5pm-1am Tue-Sun) Upscale contemporary design, DJ sets, expertly mixed cocktails and an international wine list draw the style crowd to this Ninth Sq bar. Small plates and a raw bar keep you from toppling off your stool, but style this chic doesn't come cheap.

Toad's Place LIVE MUSIC

(☑ 203-624-8623; www.toadsplace.com; 300 York St) Toad's is arguably New England's premier music hall, having earned its rep hosting the likes of the Rolling Stones, U2 and Bob Dylan. These days, an eclectic range of performers works the intimate stage, including They Might Be Giants and Martin & Wood.

ℹ Information

INFO New Haven (☑ 203-773-9494; www. infonewhaven.com; 1000 Chapel St; ⊙10am-9pm Mon-Sat, noon-5pm Sun) This downtown bureau offers maps and helpful advice.

New Haven Magazine (www.newhavenmagazine.com) Keeps its finger on the urban pulse.

Yale University Visitor Center (☑ 203-432-2300; http://visitorcenter.yale.edu; 149 Elm St; ⊙9am-4:30pm Mon-Fri, 11am-4pm Sat & Sun) Take a free tour or pick up a map of campus here.

ℹ Getting There & Away

BUS

Peter Pan Bus Lines (www.peterpanbus.com) connects New Haven with New York City (from $12, two hours, eight daily), Hartford (from $12, one hour, six daily) and Boston (from $11, four to five hours, seven daily), as does Greyhound (www.greyhound.com). Buses depart from inside New Haven's Union Station.

Connecticut Limousine (www.ctlimo.com) is an airport shuttle servicing Hartford's Bradley airport, New York's JFK and LaGuardia airports, and New Jersey's Newark airport. Pick-up and drop-off are at Union Station and select downtown New Haven hotels. Services to Newark attract a higher rate.

TRAIN

Metro-North (www.mta.info/mnr) trains make the run between **Union Station** (50 Union Ave) and New York City's Grand Central Terminal (peak/off-peak $23.25/17.50, two hours) almost every hour from 7am to midnight.

Shore Line East (www.shorelineeast.com) runs regional trains up the shore of Long Island Sound to Old Saybrook (45 minutes) and New London (70 minutes), and Commuter Connection buses that shuttle passengers from Union Station (in the evenings) and from State St Station (in the mornings) to New Haven Green.

Amtrak trains run express from New York City's Penn Station to New Haven (from $32, 1¾ hours).

VERMONT

Whether seen under blankets of snow, patchworks of blazing fall leaves or the exuberant greens of spring and summer, Vermont's blend of bucolic farmland, mountains and picturesque small villages make it one of America's most appealing states. Hikers, bikers, skiers and kayakers will find four-season bliss on the expansive waters of Lake Champlain, the award-winning Kingdom Trails Network, the 300-mile Long and Catamount Trails, and the fabled slopes of Killington, Stowe and Mad River Glen.

Foodies will love it: small farmers have made Vermont a locavore paradise, complemented by America's densest collection of craft brewers. But most of all, what sets Vermont apart is its independent spirit: the only state with a socialist senator and the only one without a McDonald's in its capital city, Vermont remains a haven for quirky creativity, a champion of grassroots government and a bastion of 'small is beautiful' thinking, unlike anywhere else in America.

History

Frenchman Samuel de Champlain explored Vermont in 1609, becoming the first European to visit these lands long inhabited by the native Abenaki.

Vermont played a key role in the American Revolution in 1775 when Ethan Allen led a local militia, the Green Mountain Boys, to Fort Ticonderoga, capturing it from the British. In 1777 Vermont declared independence as the Vermont Republic, adopting the first New World constitution to abolish slavery and establish a public school system. In 1791 Vermont was admitted to the USA as the 14th state.

The state's independent streak is as long and deep as a vein of Vermont marble. Long a land of dairy farmers, Vermont is still largely agricultural and has the lowest population of any New England state.

ℹ Information

Vermont Chamber of Commerce (www.visitvt. com) Distributes a wealth of information about the state.

Vermont Division of Tourism (www.vermont vacation.com) Maintains a fabulous Welcome Center on I-91 near the Massachusetts state line, one on VT 4A near the New York state line, and three others along I-89 between White River Junction and the Canadian border. Produces a free, detailed road map and camping guide.

NEW ENGLAND VERMONT

Vermont Public Radio (www.vpr.net) Vermont's statewide public radio station features superb local programming, including *Vermont Edition* (weekdays at noon) for coverage of Vermont current events, and the quirky, information-packed *Eye on the Sky* weather forecast.

Vermont Ski Areas Association (www.skivermont.com) Helpful information for planning ski trips, as well as summer adventures at Vermont ski resorts.

Southern Vermont

White churches and inns surround village greens throughout historic southern Vermont, a region that's home to several towns that predate the American Revolution. In summer the roads between the three 'cities' of Brattleboro, Bennington and Manchester roll over green hills; in winter, they wind their way toward the ski slopes of Mt Snow, southern Vermont's cold-weather playground. For hikers, the Appalachian and Long Trails pass through the Green Mountain National Forest here, offering a colorful hiking experience during the fall foliage season.

Brattleboro

Perched at the confluence of the Connecticut and West Rivers, Brattleboro is a little gem that reveals its facets to those who stroll the streets and prowl its dozens of independent shops and eateries. An energetic mix of aging hippies and the latest crop of pierced and tattooed hipsters fuels the town's sophisticated eclecticism, keeping the downtown scene percolating and skewing its politics decidedly leftward.

Whetstone Brook runs through the south end of town, where a wooden stockade dubbed Fort Dummer was built in 1724, becoming the first European settlement in Vermont (theretofore largely a wilderness populated exclusively by the native Abenaki people).

At Brattleboro's old Town Hall, celebrated thinkers and entertainers, including Oliver Wendell Holmes, Horace Greeley and Mark Twain, held forth on civic and political matters. Rudyard Kipling married a Brattleboro woman in 1892, and while living here he wrote *The Jungle Book*.

While most of Brattleboro's action is found in the downtown commercial district, the surrounding hillsides are speckled with farms, cheese makers and artisans, all awaiting discovery on a pleasant back-road ramble.

🛏 Sleeping & Eating

Latchis Hotel
HOTEL $$

(☑802-254-6300; www.latchishotel.com; 50 Main St; r $100-210, ste $190-240; 🔊) You can't beat the location of these 30 reasonably priced rooms and suites, in the center of downtown and adjacent to the historic theater of the same name. The hotel's art-deco overtones are refreshing, and wonderfully surprising for New England.

★ Inn on Putney Road
B&B $$$

(☑802-536-4780; www.vermontbandbinn.com; 192 Putney Rd; r $169-309; @🔊) Designed to resemble a miniature château, this sweet 1930s-vintage B&B north of town has a glorious landscaped yard, five cozy, beautifully appointed rooms and one luxurious suite with fireplace. Overlooking the West River estuary, it offers opportunities for walking, biking and boating right on its doorstep, and plenty of rainy-day activities, including billiards, board games, DVDs and a guest library.

Whetstone Station
PUB FOOD $$

(☑802-490-2354; www.whetstonestation.com; 36 Bridge St; beer garden mains $4-13, restaurant mains $12-22; ⊙11:30am-10pm Sun-Wed, to 11pm Thu-Sat) This place is beloved for its dozen-plus craft brews on tap and excellent pub fare, but the real showstopper is its outstanding roof deck Bier Garten, with bird's-eye views of the Connecticut River and occasional live music. It's the ideal spot for a beer and a bite at sundown.

★ TJ Buckley's
AMERICAN $$$

(☑802-257-4922; www.tjbuckleysuptowndining.com; 132 Elliot St; mains incl salad $45; ⊙5:30-9pm Thu-Sun year-round, plus Wed mid-Jun–early Oct) 🌿 Chef-owner Michael Fuller founded this exceptional, upscale little eatery in an authentic 1925 Worcester dining car more than 30 years ago. Ever since, he's been offering a verbal menu of four seasonally changing items, sourced largely from local farms. Locals rave that the food here is Brattleboro's best. The diner seats just 18 souls, so reserve ahead. No credit cards.

ℹ Information

Brattleboro Chamber of Commerce (☑802-254-4565; www.brattleborochamber.org; 180 Main St; ⊙9am-5pm Mon-Fri) Dependable year-round source of tourist info, with a seasonal info booth (80 Putney Rd; ⊙Sat & Sun late May–mid-Oct) on the green north of downtown.

Vermont & New Hampshire

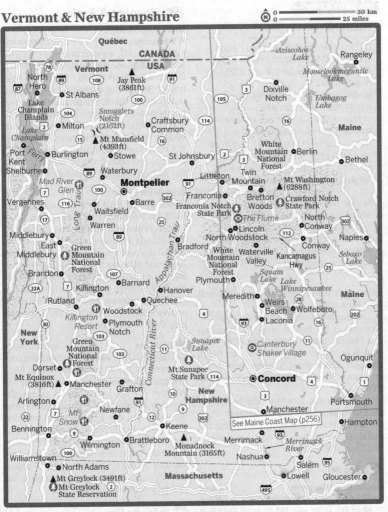

Getting There & Away

Greyhound (www.greyhound.com) runs one bus daily to New York City (from $32, 5¾ hours) via Northampton, MA ($12, one hour) and Hartford, CT ($21, three hours). For the best fares, buy tickets in advance on Greyhound's website.

Amtrak's scenic daily *Vermonter* train (www.amtrak.com/vermonter-train) connects Brattleboro with points north and south, including Montpelier ($30, 2¾ hours), Burlington/Essex Junction ($34, 3½ hours), New York City ($67, 5½ hours) and Washington, DC ($99, nine hours). See Amtrak's website for details.

Bennington

Bennington is a mix of historic Vermont village (Old Bennington), workaday town (Bennington proper) and college town (North Bennington). It is also home to the **Bennington Battle Monument** (802-447-0550; www.benningtonbattlemonument.com; 15 Monument Circle, Old Bennington; adult/child $5/1; 9am-5pm late Apr-Oct), which commemorates the crucial Battle of Bennington during the American Revolution. Had Colonel Seth Warner and the local 'Green Mountain Boys' not helped weaken British defenses

HILDENE

Outside Manchester, **Hildene** (☑ general info 800-578-1788, tour reservations 802-367-7968; www.hildene.org; 1005 Hildene Rd/VT 7A; adult/child $23/6, guided tour $7.50; ⊙ 9:30am-4:30pm), the 24-room Georgian Revival mansion of Robert Todd Lincoln, son of Abraham and Mary Lincoln, is a national treasure. Lincoln family members lived here until 1975, when it was converted into a museum and filled with the family's personal effects and furnishings. These include a vintage 1908 Aeolian pipe organ (still functioning), one of Abraham Lincoln's famous top hats, and remarkable brass casts of his hands, the right one swollen from greeting well-wishers while campaigning for the presidency.

during this battle, the colonies might well have been split.

The charming hilltop site of Colonial Old Bennington is studded with 80 Georgian and Federal houses (dating from 1761 – the year Bennington was founded – to 1830). The poet Robert Frost is buried here and a museum in his old homestead pays eloquent tribute.

As Bennington is within the bounds of the Green Mountain National Forest, there are many hiking trails nearby, including the grandparents of them all: the Appalachian and Long Trails.

⊙ Sights

Bennington Museum　　　　MUSEUM

(☑ 802-447-1571; www.benningtonmuseum.org; 75 Main St; adult/child $10/free; ⊙ 10am-5pm daily Jun-Oct, Thu-Tue Nov-May) Bennington's standout attraction, this museum features the world's largest public collections of Grandma Moses paintings and Bennington pottery, along with a rich array of Vermont paintings, decorative arts and folk art from the 18th century to the present, encompassing everything from Vermont's Gilded Age to Bennington modernism to outsider art. The Works on Paper Gallery displays prints, lithographs, photography and more by nationally recognized regional artists. Don't miss the vintage Martin Wasp, a 1925 luxury car manufactured here in Bennington.

🛏 Sleeping & Eating

Greenwood Lodge & Campsites　　HOSTEL, CAMPGROUND $

(☑ 802-442-2547; www.campvermont.com/greenwood; 311 Greenwood Dr, Woodford; 2-person tent/RV sites $30/39, dm $35-38, r $79; ⊙ mid-May-late Oct; 🐾) Nestled in the Green Mountains in Woodford, this 120-acre space with three ponds is home to one of Vermont's best-sited hostels. Accommodations include 17 budget beds and 40 campsites. You'll find it 8 miles east of Bennington, just off VT 9 near the Prospect Mountain ski area. Facilities include hot showers and a games room.

Blue Benn Diner　　　　DINER $

(☑ 802-442-5140; 314 North St; mains breakfast $4-10, lunch & dinner $6-11; ⊙ 6am-5pm Mon & Tue, to 8pm Wed-Fri, to 4pm Sat, from 7am Sun; ☑) This classic 1950s-era diner serves breakfast all day and a healthy mix of American, Asian and Mexican fare, including vegetarian options. Enhancing the retro experience are little tabletop jukeboxes where you can play Willie Nelson's 'Moonlight in Vermont' or José Feliciano's 'Feliz Navidad' until your neighbors scream for mercy.

★Pangaea　　　　INTERNATIONAL $$

(☑ 802-442-7171; www.vermontfinedining.com; 1 Prospect St, North Bennington; mains $9-31; ⊙ lounge 5-10pm daily, restaurant to 9pm Tue-Sat) Whether you opt for the casual lounge, the riverside terrace or the more upscale dining room, you can expect exceptional food at this cozy North Bennington favorite. The varied menu ranges from burgers, salads, crab cakes, eggplant parmigiana and Thai stir-fries on the lounge side to herb-crusted halibut, roast duck and rack of lamb in the tastefully decorated restaurant.

ⓘ Information

Bennington Welcome Center (☑ 802-447-2456; www.informationcenter.vermont.gov; 100 VT 279; ⊙ 7am-9pm) Bennington's spiffy tourist office has loads of information, long hours, and free coffee and tea for motorists; it's at the highway interchange where VT 279 and US 7 meet.

ⓘ Getting There & Away

Bennington is 40 miles west of Brattleboro via VT 9, or 25 miles south of Manchester via US 7. Vermont Translines (www.vttranslines.com) offers once-daily bus service north to Manchester ($6, 35 minutes), Middlebury ($22.50, 2½ hours) and Burlington ($32, four hours), and west to Albany, NY ($10, one hour).

Central Vermont

Vermont's heart features some of New England's most bucolic countryside. Cows begin to outnumber people just north of Rutland (Vermont's second-largest city, with a whopping 15,500 residents). Lovers of the outdoors make frequent pilgrimages to central Vermont, especially to the resort areas of Killington, Sugarbush and Mad River Glen, which attract countless skiers and summer hikers. For those interested in indoor pleasures, antique shops and art galleries dot the back roads.

Woodstock & Quechee

Chartered in 1761, Woodstock has been the highly dignified seat of scenic Windsor County since 1766. Many grand houses surround the oval village green, and four of Woodstock's churches can claim bells cast by Paul Revere. Senator Jacob Collamer, a friend of Abraham Lincoln's, once observed, 'The good people of Woodstock have less incentive than others to yearn for heaven.'

Today Woodstock is still very beautiful and very wealthy. Spend some time walking around the green, surrounded by Federal and Greek Revival homes and public buildings, or along the Ottauquechee River, spanned by three covered bridges. The Rockefellers and the Rothschilds own estates in the surrounding countryside, and the well-to-do come to stay at the grand Woodstock Inn & Resort.

About a five-minute drive east of Woodstock, small, twee Quechee Village is home to Quechee Gorge – Vermont's diminutive answer to the Grand Canyon – as well as some outstanding restaurants.

◉ Sights

★**Quechee Gorge** CANYON
(US 4, Quechee) FREE Lurking beneath US 4, less than a mile east of Quechee Village, the gorge is a 163ft-deep scar that cuts about 3000ft along a stream that you can view from a bridge or easily access by footpaths from the road. A series of well-marked, undemanding trails, none of which should take more than an hour to cover, lead down into the gorge.

Billings Farm & Museum FARM
(☑802-457-2355; www.billingsfarm.org; 69 Old River Rd, Woodstock; adult/child $16/8; ◐10am-5pm daily Apr-Oct, to 4pm Sat, Sun & holidays Nov-Feb; ⌘) A mile north of Woodstock's village green, this historic farm founded by 19th-century railroad-magnate Frederick Billings delights children with hands-on activities related to old-fashioned farm life. Farm animals, including pretty cows descended from Britain's island of Jersey, are abundant. Family-friendly seasonal events include wagon and sleigh rides, pumpkin and apple festivals, and old-fashioned Halloween, Thanksgiving and Christmas celebrations.

Marsh-Billings-Rockefeller National Historical Park PARK
(☑802-457-3368; www.nps.gov/mabi; 54 Elm St, Woodstock; mansion tours adult/child $8/free, trails & carriage roads free; ◐visitor center & tours 10am-5pm late May-Oct, trails & carriage roads year-round) Built around the historic home of early American conservationist George Perkins Marsh, Vermont's only national park examines the relationship between land stewardship and environmental conservation. The estate's 20 miles of trails and carriage roads are free for exploring on foot, horseback, cross-country skis or snowshoes. There's an admission fee to the mansion itself, where tours are offered every 30 minutes.

⬛ Sleeping & Eating

Shire HOTEL $$
(☑802-457-2211; www.shirewoodstock.com; 46 Pleasant St/US 4, Woodstock; r $119-259; ❄🛜🐾) Within walking distance of Woodstock's town center on US 4, this recently expanded hotel has 50 comfortable rooms, the best of which come with fireplaces, Jacuzzis and/or decks with rockers looking out over the Ottauquechee River. New beds and linens offer a comfy night's sleep, and most units have river views (the ones from room 405 are especially dreamy).

★**Blue Horse Inn** INN $$$
(☑802-457-9999; www.thebluehorseinn.com; 3 Church St, Woodstock; d $179-359, ste $299-389; 🛜🐾) In 2018, Jill and Tony Amato completely renovated and reopened this grand Federal Greek Revival inn in the heart of Woodstock. Set on 2 acres of grassy lawns sloping down to riverside Adirondack chairs, the red-brick and white-clapboard 19th-century home conceals a sprawling collection of fireplace-equipped common areas and carpeted guest rooms gazing out over the yard or downtown Woodstock.

BEST VERMONT SKIING

Mad River Glen (☑ 802-496-3551; www.madriverglen.com; VT 17, Waitsfield; lift tickets adult/child $89/72) The most rugged lift-served ski area in the East, Mad River is also one of the quirkiest. Managed by an owner cooperative, not a major ski corporation, it largely eschews artificial snowmaking, prohibits snowboarding and proudly continues to use America's last operating single chairlift, a vintage 1948 model. It's 6 miles west of Waitsfield.

Killington Resort (☑ info 800-734-9435, reservations 800-621-6867; www.killington.com; 4763 Killington Rd; lift tickets adult/child/senior $124/95/105) Known as the 'Beast of the East,' Vermont's prime ski resort is enormous, yet runs efficiently enough to avoid overcrowding. It has five separate lodges, each with a different emphasis, as well as 29 lifts and 92 miles of trails. The ski season runs from November through early May, enhanced by America's largest snowmaking system.

Stowe Mountain Resort (☑ 802-253-3000; www.stowe.com; 5781 Mountain Rd; lift ticket adult $85-115, child $72-98) Purchased by Colorado's Vail Resorts in 2017, this venerable resort encompasses two mountains: Mt Mansfield (which has a vertical drop of 2360ft) and Spruce Peak (1550ft). It offers 116 beautiful trails, two-thirds for beginners and intermediates, and the remainder for hard-core backcountry skiers – many of whom get their adrenaline rushes from the 'front four' runs: Starr, Goat, National and Liftline.

Mon Vert Cafe   CAFE **$**
(☑ 802-457-7143; www.monvertcafe.com; 28 Central St, Woodstock; breakfast $7-13, lunch $9-11; ☺ 7:30am-5:30pm Mon-Thu, to 6:30pm Fri & Sat, 8am-5:30pm Sun) Pop into this cheerful two-level cafe for croissants, scones, egg sandwiches and maple lattes in the morning, or settle in on the front patio for salads and panini at lunchtime. A large map of Vermont and New Hampshire highlights the multitude of farms and food purveyors that provide the restaurant's locally sourced ingredients.

★ Simon Pearce Restaurant   MODERN AMERICAN **$$$**
(☑ 802-295-1470; www.simonpearce.com; 1760 Quechee Main St, Quechee; mains lunch $14-19, dinner $23-33; ☺ 11:30am-2:45pm & 5:30-9pm) Few views in Vermont compare with those from the window tables overlooking spectacular Ottauquechee Falls in Simon Pearce's dining room, suspended over the river in a converted brick mill. Local ingredients are used to fine effect in salads, cheese plates and dishes such as braised lamb shoulder or cider-brined chicken. The restaurant's stemware is hand-blown in the adjacent glass workshop.

Mangalitsa   BISTRO **$$$**
(☑ 802-457-7467; www.mangalitsavt.com; 61 Central St; mains $26-32; ☺ 5-9pm) Launched in late 2017 to universal acclaim, this sweet, chef-owned bistro is a welcome addition to Woodstock's dining scene. The ever-

changing menu of small and large plates draws on seasonal ingredients such as fiddlehead ferns, house-butchered meats, whole fish and produce from local purveyors such as Fat Sheep Farm. With only 22 seats it fills up fast; book ahead.

❶ Information

Woodstock Welcome Center (☑ 802-457-3555; www.woodstockvt.com; 3 Mechanic St, Woodstock; ☺ 9am-5pm) Woodstock's welcome center is housed in a lovely red building on a riverside backstreet, two blocks from the village green. There's also a small information booth on the village green itself. Both places can help with accommodations.

❶ Getting There & Away

Greyhound buses (www.greyhound.com) from Boston and Amtrak trains (www.amtrak.com/vermonter-train) from New York stop at nearby White River Junction. From either station, it's a 15-mile trip to Woodstock. Vermont Translines (www.vttranslines.com) runs once-daily buses from Woodstock to Quechee ($1.50, 15 minutes), White River Junction ($3.50, 30 minutes) and Killington ($5, 40 minutes).

Mad River Valley

North of Killington, VT 100 is one of the finest stretches of road in the country: a bucolic mix of rolling hills, covered bridges, white steeples and fertile farmland. Here you'll find the Mad River Valley, where the pretty villages of Waitsfield and Warren nestle in the shadow of two major ski areas, Sugarbush and Mad River Glen.

For tantalizing valley perspectives, explore the glorious back roads on either side of VT 100. Leave the pavement behind and meander up the valley's eastern side, following Brook, E Warren, Common, North and Pony Farm Rds from Warren north to Moretown; or head west from Warren over Lincoln Gap Rd, the highest, steepest and perhaps prettiest of all the 'gap roads' that run east to west over the Green Mountains. Stop at Lincoln Gap (2424ft) for the scenic 3-mile hike up the **Long Trail** to Mt Abraham (4017ft), Vermont's fifth-highest peak.

⌂ Sleeping

★**Tevere Hostel** HOSTEL $
(☑ 802-496-9222; www.hosteltevere.com; 203 Powderhound Rd, Warren; dm $35-40; ☎) One of New England's coolest hostels, Tevere spreads across two floors of an artfully renovated old farmhouse in Warren, just downhill from Sugarbush resort. Four-to seven-bed dorms with comfy mattresses and colorful walls are complemented by a lounge with a blazing woodstove and an animated bar-restaurant that hosts live music on Saturdays throughout the ski season.

Inn at Round Barn Farm INN $$$
(☑ 802-496-2276; www.theroundbarn.com; 1661 E Warren Rd, Waitsfield; r $179-359; ☎✈) This place gets its name from the adjacent 1910 round barn – among the few authentic examples remaining in Vermont. The decidedly upscale inn has antique-furnished rooms with mountain views, gas fireplaces and canopy beds. All overlook the meadows and mountains. In winter guests leave their shoes at the door to preserve the hardwood floors. The country-style breakfast is huge.

✗ Eating & Drinking

★**Warren Store** SANDWICHES $
(☑ 802-496-3864; www.warrenstore.com; 284 Main St, Warren; sandwiches & light meals $5-9; ☉7:45am-7pm) This atmospheric country store serves the area's best sandwiches along with delicious pastries and breakfasts. In summer, linger over coffee and the *New York Times* on the front porch, or eat on the deck overlooking the waterfall, then descend for a cool dip among river-sculpted rocks. Browsers will love the store's eclectic upstairs collection of clothing, toys and jewelry.

American Flatbread PIZZA $$
(☑ 802-496-8856; www.americanflatbread.com/restaurants/waitsfield-vt; 46 Lareau Rd, Waitsfield; flatbread $14-22; ☉5-9:30pm Thu-Sun; ⊕) For two decades, this valley mainstay on pretty Lareau Farm has been baking delicious thin-crust pizza in the wood-fired oven, topped with fresh-from-the-farm meats, cheeses and veggies and homemade tomato sauce. Stay cozy by the fireside in winter, or play Frisbee on the lawn against a gorgeous Green Mountain backdrop while waiting to eat alfresco on picnic tables in summer.

★**Lawson's Finest Liquids** MICROBREWERY
(☑ 802-496-4677; www.lawsonsfinest.com; 155 Carroll Rd, Waitsfield; ☉noon-7pm) For years, Mad River locals would line up for special releases of Sean and Karen Lawson's homebrew, dispensed from a converted maple-sugar shack at their home in Warren. In late 2018, the Lawsons opened this cavernous timber-framed brewery, taproom and store in Waitsfield, with 16 beers on tap, a convivial bar and fireside seating indoors and out. Beer lovers, rejoice!

ⓘ Information

Mad River Valley Visitor Information (☑ 802-496-3409; www.madrivervalley.com; cnr Main & Bridge Sts, Waitsfield; ☉10am-5pm Wed-Sat, to 3pm Sun) The valley's info center in downtown Waitsfield can assist with lodging and the latest skiing info.

Northern Vermont

Northern Vermont is home to the state's largest city, Burlington, and the state capital, Montpelier. Even so, this area still has all the rural charms found elsewhere in the Green Mountain State. Even within Burlington, cafe-lined streets coexist with scenic paths along Lake Champlain and the Winooski River. Further north, the pastoral Northeast Kingdom offers a full range of outdoor activities, from skiing to biking, in the heart of the mountains.

Montpelier

Montpelier (mont-*peel*-yer) would qualify as nothing more than a large village in most places. But in sparsely populated Vermont it's the state capital – the smallest in the country (and the only one without a McDonald's, in case you were wondering). Remarkably cosmopolitan for a town of 7500 residents, its two main thoroughfares – State St and Main St – make for a pleasant wander, with some nice bookstores, boutiques and eateries.

Montpelier's smaller, distinctly working-class neighbor Barre (*bear*-ee), which touts itself as the 'granite capital of the world,' is a 15-minute drive southeast of the capital.

ℹ Information

Capitol Region Visitors Center (☑ 802-828-5981; www.informationcenter.vermont.gov; 134 State St; ⊙ 6am-5pm Mon-Fri, from 9am Sat & Sun) Opposite the Vermont state capitol building. Free wi-fi and comfy seating.

ℹ Getting There & Away

On weekdays, you can reach Burlington via the Montpelier LINK Express bus ($4, 1¼ hours) operated by Green Mountain Transit (www.ridegmt.com).

The daily *Vermonter* train (www.amtrak.com/vermonter-train) runs from Montpelier to points northwest and southeast, including Brattleboro ($30, 2½ hours) and Burlington ($12, 45 minutes).

Stowe

In a cozy valley where the West Branch River flows into Little River and mountains rise in all directions, the quintessential Vermont village of Stowe (settled in 1794) bustles quietly. The town's long-standing reputation as one of the east's classiest mountain resorts draws well-heeled urbanites from Boston, New York and beyond. A bounty of inns and eateries lines the thoroughfares leading up to Smugglers Notch, an enchantingly narrow rock-walled pass through the Green Mountains just below Mt Mansfield (4393ft), the highest point in Vermont. More than 200 miles of cross-country ski trails, some of the finest mountain biking and downhill skiing in the east, and world-class rock- and ice-climbing lure adrenaline junkies and active families.

Waterbury, on the interstate highway 10 miles south, is Stowe's gateway. Its attractions include some standout restaurants and the world-famous **Ben & Jerry's Ice Cream Factory** (☑ 802-882-2047; www.benjerry.com/about-us/factory-tours; 1281 VT 100, Waterbury; adult/child under 13yr $4/free; ⊙ 9am-9pm Jul–mid-Aug, to 7pm mid-Aug–mid-Oct, 10am-6pm mid-Oct–late May, to 7pm late May–Jun; ♿).

◉ Sights & Activities

★ Alchemist Brewery   BREWERY
(www.alchemistbeer.com; 100 Cottage Club Rd; ⊙ 11am-7pm Tue-Sat) One of Vermont's most legendary beers, Heady Topper, was born at this microbrewery, which recently expanded operations into a spiffy new Stowe Visitors Center. Visitors to the state-of-the-art, solar-powered building with its silo-like tower can enjoy free tastes, observe the beer production process and purchase four-packs of Heady Topper, Focal Banger and other outstanding brews to bring home.

★ Stowe Recreation Path   OUTDOORS
(www.stowerec.org/parks-facilities/rec-paths/stowe-recreation-path; ♿ 🚲) The flat to gently rolling 5.3-mile Stowe Recreation Path, which starts from the steepled Stowe Community Church in the village center, offers a fabulous four-season escape for all ages. It rambles through woods, meadows and outdoor sculpture gardens along the West Branch of Little River, with sweeping views of Mt Mansfield unfolding in the distance.

Smugglers Notch Boardwalk   OUTDOORS
Opened in 2018, this boardwalk represents a revolutionary improvement in accessibility to the Smugglers Notch area, allowing visitors in strollers or wheelchairs to follow a section of the Long Trail out through a montane wetland to a viewpoint with lovely perspectives on the notch. Pull-offs along the way feature informational displays about the wetlands' ecology, flora, fauna and natural history.

🛏 Sleeping & Eating

Stowe Motel
& Snowdrift   MOTEL, APARTMENT $$
(☑ 802-253-7629; www.stowemotel.com; 2043 Mountain Rd; r $109-215, ste $195-265, apt $179-280; @ 🛜 🏊) In addition to motel-like rooms and suites - some with kitchenette and wood-burning fireplace - this sprawling 16-acre property midway between Stowe village and the slopes offers multibedroom houses and an apartment. Clinching the deal are countless amenities: a tennis court, two swimming pools, a hot tub, badminton, lawn games and free bicycles or snowshoes to use on the nearby recreation path.

Trapp Family Lodge   LODGE $$$
(☑ 802-253-8511; www.trappfamily.com; 700 Trapp Hill Rd; r $175-425, ste $275-750; @ 🛜 🏊 🐾) This hilltop lodge 3km above town boasts

Stowe's most dramatic setting. The Austrian-style chalet, built by Maria von Trapp of *Sound of Music* fame (note the family photos lining the walls), houses 96 traditional lodge rooms, many newly renovated and most with balconies affording lovely mountain vistas. Alternatively, rent one of the cozy villas or guesthouses scattered across the property.

The 2700-acre spread offers stupendous hiking, mountain biking, snowshoeing and cross-country skiing, while the family's Kaffehaus and **Bierhall** (☑802-253-5750; www.vontrappbrewing.com/bierhall.htm; 1333 Luce Hill Rd; mains $13-31; ⊙11:30am-9pm), both located nearby, add another delightful dose of Austria-in-Vermont flavor.

Doc Ponds AMERICAN $$
(☑802-760-6066; www.docponds.com; 294 Mountain Rd; mains $8-22; ⊙4pm-midnight Tue-Thu, from 11:30am Fri-Mon) Casual fare, from tacos to burgers to mac 'n' cheese and milkshakes, dominates the menu at this popular spot near the heart of Stowe village. Walls festooned with skateboards enhance the festive mood, as do the twin turntables spinning vintage vinyl at the entrance. Craft beer and cider specials go for $4 a pint every day.

★**Hen of the Wood** MODERN AMERICAN $$$
(☑802-244-7300; www.henofthewood.com; 92 Stowe St, Waterbury; small plates $12-15, mains $22-35; ⊙5-9pm Tue-Sat) ✒ Arguably the finest dining in Northern Vermont, this chef-driven restaurant, set in a historic grist mill in Waterbury, gets rave reviews for its innovative farm-to-table cuisine. The ambience is as fine as the food, which features seasonal ingredients such as wild mushrooms and densely flavored dishes such as smoked duck breast and sheep's-milk gnocchi.

❶ Information

Barnes Camp Visitor Center (www.green mountainclub.org; VT 108, 2 miles east of Smugglers Notch; ⊙9am-5pm Fri-Sun mid-Jun–mid-Oct) Get hiking info at this seasonal visitor center near the Long Trail's intersection with Smugglers Notch.

Green Mountain Club Visitors Center (☑802-244-7037; www.greenmountainclub.org; 4711 Waterbury-Stowe Rd/VT 100, Waterbury Center; ⊙9am-5pm daily mid-May–mid-Oct, 10am-4pm Mon-Fri rest of year) Stop by this office (5 miles south of Stowe) or check the website for details about the Long Trail and shorter day hikes in the region.

Stowe Area Association (☑802-253-7321; www.gostowe.com; 51 Main St; ⊙9am-6pm Mon-Sat, 11am-5pm Sun; ☎) This well-organized association can help you plan your trip, including making reservations for rental cars and local accommodations.

❶ Getting There & Away

The Amtrak *Vermonter* train stops daily at Waterbury (mornings southbound to Brattleboro and New York City, evenings northbound to Burlington). Some hotels and inns will arrange to pick up guests at the station. Otherwise, get a taxi from **Stowe Taxi** (☑802-253-9490; www.stowetaxi.com).

Burlington

Perched on the shores of Lake Champlain, Vermont's largest city would be considered tiny in most other states, but its relatively diminutive size is one of Burlington's charms. With the University of Vermont (UVM) swelling the city by 13,000 students and contributing to its vibrant cultural and social life, Burlington has a spirited, youthful vibe and more ethnic diversity than anywhere else in Vermont.

Burlington's walkable downtown, bike paths, farmers market, fabulous food co-op, and proximity to nature earn it accolades as one of America's greenest and most livable cities. The city's ongoing Great Streets Initiative (www.greatstreetsbtv.com) aims to sustain that momentum, with wider sidewalks, enhanced green spaces and reduced pollution.

Burlington makes an attractive base for exploring the rest of northwestern Vermont. Two of Vermont's crown jewels, **Shelburne Farms** (☑802-985-8686; www.shelburnefarms.org; 1611 Harbor Rd, Shelburne; adult/child mid-May–mid-Oct $8/5, rest of year free; ⊙9am-5:30pm mid-May–mid-Oct, 10am-5pm rest of year; 🚗) ✒ and the Shelburne Museum (p244), lie just 15 minutes south, while Stowe and the Green Mountains are within an hour's drive.

◉ Sights & Activities

★**Church Street Marketplace** MARKET
(www.churchstmarketplace.com; 🚗) Burlington's pulse can often be taken along this four-block pedestrian zone running from Pearl to Main Sts. When the weather's good, buskers (licensed by the town), food and craft vendors, soapbox demagogues, restless students, curious tourists and kids climbing on rocks mingle in a vibrant human parade.

★ **Shelburne Museum**　　　MUSEUM

(☎802-985-3346; www.shelburnemuseum.org; 6000 Shelburne Rd/US 7, Shelburne; adult/child $25/14 May-Oct, $10/5 Nov-Apr; ◑10am-5pm daily May-Dec, Wed-Sun Jan-Apr; ⊕) This extraordinary 45-acre museum, 9 miles south of Burlington, showcases the priceless Americana collections of Electra Havemeyer Webb (1888–1960) and her parents – 150,000 objects in all. The mix of folk art, decorative arts and more is housed in 39 historic buildings, most of them moved here from other parts of New England to ensure their preservation.

Intervale Center　　　FARM

(☎802-660-0440; www.intervale.org; 180 Intervale Rd) FREE You'd never guess it standing on a busy Burlington street corner, but one of Vermont's most idyllic green spaces is less than 2 miles from downtown. Tucked among the lazy curves of the Winooski River, Burlington's Intervale encompasses half a dozen organic farms and a delightful trail network, open 365 days a year for hiking, biking, skiing, bird-watching, paddling and more.

Waterfront　　　WATERFRONT

A five-minute walk from downtown, Burlington's delightfully uncommercialized waterfront features a scenic, low-key promenade, a 7.5-mile bike path, a pier for Lake Champlain **boat trips** and the family-friendly **Echo aquarium** (☎802-864-1848; www.echovermont.org; 1 College St; adult/child $14.50/11.50; ◑10am-5pm; ⊕).

🛏 Sleeping

Burlington Hostel　　　HOSTEL $

(☎802-540-3043; www.theburlingtonhostel.com; 53 Main St, 2nd fl; dm midweek/weekend $39/49; ◑mid-Feb–Nov; ❊@⚟) Hidden behind an unassuming facade just minutes from the action centers of Church St and Lake Champlain, Burlington's hostel accommodates up to 48 guests in four- to eight-bed mixed and women-only dorms. There's an invitingly open kitchen and lounge area where breakfast (coffee and waffles) is served each morning.

★ **Willard Street Inn**　　　INN $$

(☎802-651-8710; www.willardstreetinn.com; 349 S Willard St; r $155-305; ⚟) Perched on a hill within easy walking distance of UVM and the Church Street Marketplace, this mansion, fusing Queen Anne and Georgian Revival styles, was built in the late 1880s. It

has a fine-wood and cut-glass elegance, yet radiates a welcoming warmth. Many of the guest rooms overlook Lake Champlain.

★ **Inn at Shelburne Farms**　　　INN $$$

(☎802-985-8498; www.shelburnefarms.org/stay dine; 1611 Harbor Rd, Shelburne; r $270-530, without bath $160-230, cottages & houses $270-850; ◑early May-late Oct; ⚟) One of New England's top 10 places to stay, this inn, 7 miles south of Burlington off US 7, was once the summer mansion of the wealthy Webb family. It now welcomes guests, with rooms in the gracious, welcoming country manor house by the lakefront, as well as four independent, kitchen-equipped cottages and guesthouses scattered across the property.

Hotel Vermont　　　HOTEL $$$

(☎802-651-0080; www.hotelvt.com; 41 Cherry St; r/ste from $259/439) Burlington's newest downtown hotel, in a LEED-certified energy-efficient building halfway between Church St and Lake Champlain, pampers guests with 125 bright modern rooms filled with high-end amenities. There's a pair of excellent on-site restaurants and regular live jazz in the lobby.

🍴 Eating

Penny Cluse Cafe　　　CAFE $

(☎802-651-8834; www.pennycluse.com; 169 Cherry St; mains $6-14; ◑6:45am-3pm Mon-Fri, from 8am Sat & Sun) This ever-popular downtown eatery serves pancakes, biscuits and gravy, omelets and tofu scrambles, along with sandwiches, tacos, salads and delightful drinks ranging from smoothies to Bloody Marys. Don't miss its decadent Bucket-o-Spuds (home-fried potatoes with cheddar, salsa, sour cream and scallions) and *chiles rellenos* – among the best you'll find anywhere east of the Mississippi. Expect an hour's wait on weekends.

★ **Revolution Kitchen**　　　VEGAN, VEGETARIAN $$

(☎802-448-3657; www.revolutionkitchen.com; 9 Center St; mains $14-18; ◑5-9pm Tue-Thu, to 10pm Fri & Sat; ⊘) Vegetarian fine dining? And romantic atmosphere to boot? Yep, they all come together at this cozy brick-walled restaurant that makes creative use of Vermont's abundant organic produce. Asian, Mediterranean and Latin American influences abound in house favorites such as Revolution tacos, crispy seitan piccata and the laksa noodle pot. Most items are (or can be adapted to be) vegan.

American Flatbread
PIZZA $$

([☎] 802-861-2999; www.americanflatbread.com; 115 St Paul St; flatbreads $14-23; ⊙ 11:30am-3pm & 5-11:30pm Mon-Fri, 11:30am-11:30pm Sat & Sun) ✦ Central location, great beers on tap from the in-house Zero Gravity microbrewery and superb flatbread (thin-crust pizza) are reason enough to visit this bustling downtown eatery. Throw in an outdoor summer terrace in the back alleyway, and you have one of Burlington's most appealing restaurants.

🍷 Drinking & Entertainment

★ Citizen Cider
MICROBREWERY

([☎] 802-497-1987; www.citizencider.com; 316 Pine St; ⊙ 11am-10pm Mon-Sat, to 7pm Sun) Tucked into an industrial-chic building with painted concrete floors and long wooden tables, this homegrown success story uses tankfuls of apples trucked in from Vermont orchards to make its ever-growing line of hard ciders. Taste test a flight of five for $7, including perennial favorites such as the ginger-and-lemon-peel-infused Dirty Mayor, or go for one of the inventive cider-based cocktails.

Foam Brewers
MICROBREWERY

([☎] 802-399-2511; www.foambrewers.com; 112 Lake St; ⊙ noon-9pm Mon-Thu, 11am-11pm Fri & Sat, to 7pm Sun) Housed in an attractive brick building with exposed post-and-beam woodwork and a dreamy terrace looking out toward Lake Champlain, Foam was founded by a group of local beer aficionados looking to unleash their improvisational spirit. The result: one of Burlington's liveliest new brewpubs, with a rotating selection of inventive craft beers and live music six nights a week.

Radio Bean
BAR

([☎] 802-660-9346; www.facebook.com/radiobean; 8 N Winooski Ave; ⊙ 8am-2am Mon-Fri, from 10am Sat & Sun; 🛜) This is Burlington's social hub for arts and music. Espressos, beer and wine keep things jumping at the all-day cafe, while nightly live performances (jazz, acoustic, Afro-Cuban and more) animate two stages, here and at the semi-attached **Light Club Lamp Shop** ([☎] 802-660-9346; www.radiobean.com/light-club-info; 12 N Winooski Ave; ⊙ 7pm-late Sun-Thu, 6pm-2am Fri & Sat). Radio Bean is also noteworthy for having co-founded the Radiator, Burlington's fabled low-power indie radio station (105.9 FM, www.bigheavyworld.com/live-stream-intro).

ArtsRiot
LIVE MUSIC

([☎] 802-540-0406; www.artsriot.com; 400 Pine St; ⊙ 4:30pm-late Tue-Sat) This brick-walled, exuberantly frescoed former timber warehouse in Burlington's South End is the venue for myriad events, from live music to storytelling. In the late afternoons it's a convivial bar-restaurant with early-bird specials till 5:30pm; come nightfall the door opens onto the performance space and dance floor. On Fridays in summer a host of food trucks parks out back.

❶ Information

BTV Information Center ([☎] 802-863-1889; www.vermont.org; Burlington International Airport; ⊙ 4pm-midnight) This helpful office in Burlington's airport is staffed by the Lake Champlain Regional Chamber of Commerce.

Lake Champlain Regional Chamber of Commerce ([☎] 877-686-5253, 802-863-3489; www.vermont.org; 60 Main St; ⊙ 8:30am-4:30pm Mon-Thu, to 3pm Fri) Staffed tourist office in the heart of downtown.

Waterfront Tourism Center (off Lake St; ⊙ 10am-8pm daily late May–Aug, to 6pm Sep–mid-Oct) Opens seasonally down near the lakefront.

❶ Getting There & Away

AIR

A number of national carriers serve **Burlington International Airport** (BTV; [☎] 802-863-2874; www.btv.aero; 1200 Airport Dr, South Burlington), 3 miles east of the city center. You'll find all the major car-rental companies at the airport.

BUS

Green Mountain Transit (www.ridegmt.com) Operates a few long-distance buses to other cities in northwestern Vermont. See its website for fares and schedules.

Greyhound (www.greyhound.com) Runs multiple buses daily from Burlington International Airport to Montréal, Canada (from $18, 2½ hours) and Boston (from $28, 4½ to 5½ hours).

Megabus ([☎] 877-462-6342; www.megabus.com; 119 Pearl St) Offers a once-daily bus service to Boston (from $25, four hours). Buses stop just around the corner from Burlington's **GMT Downtown Transit Center** (Green Mountain Transit; [☎] 802-864-2282; www.ridegmt.com; cnr St Paul & Cherry Sts; ⊙ 6am-11pm Mon-Fri, 7am-5pm Sat).

Middlebury Routes 46 and 76
Montpelier Route 86

TRAIN

Amtrak's daily *Vermonter* train (www.amtrak.com/vermonter-train), which provides service as far south as New York City and Washington, DC, stops in Essex Junction, 5 miles from Burlington.

NEW HAMPSHIRE

Jagged mountains, serene valleys and island-dotted lakes lurk in every corner of New Hampshire. The whole rugged state begs for exploration, whether kayaking the hidden coves of the Lakes Region or trekking the upper peaks surrounding Mt Washington. Each season yields a bounty of adrenaline and activity: skiing and snowshoeing in winter, with many slopes open into spring; magnificent walks and drives through fall's fiery colors; and swimming in crisp mountain streams and berry-picking in summer.

Jewel-box colonial settlements such as Portsmouth set a sophisticated tone, while historical allure and small-town culture live on in pristine villages like Keene and Peterborough. Manchester and Concord are two urban strongholds sprucing up their main drags with indie shops and innovative eats. There's a relaxing whiff in the air, too – you're encouraged to gaze out at a loon-filled lake, recline on a scenic railway trip or chug across a waterway on a sunset cruise.

History

Named in 1629 after the English county of Hampshire, New Hampshire was one of the first American colonies to declare its independence from England in 1776. During the 19th-century industrialization boom, the state's leading city, Manchester, became such a powerhouse that its textile mills were the world's largest.

New Hampshire played a high-profile role in 1944 when President Franklin D Roosevelt gathered leaders from 44 Allied nations at remote Bretton Woods for a conference to rebuild global capitalism. It was from the Bretton Woods Conference that the World Bank and the International Monetary Fund emerged.

In 1963 New Hampshire, long famed for its anti-tax sentiments, found another way to raise revenue – by becoming the first state in the USA to have a legal lottery.

ℹ Information

New Hampshire Division of Parks & Recreation (www.nhstateparks.org) Offers information on a statewide bicycle route system and a very complete camping guide.

New Hampshire Division of Travel & Tourism Development (www.visitnh.gov) Ski conditions and fall foliage reports, among other things.

Southern New Hampshire

Manchester

Once home to the world's largest textile mill – at its peak, the Amoskeag Manufacturing Company employed 17,000 people (out of a city population of 70,000) – this riverside town retains, both historically and culturally, a bit of its blue-collar roots. Exploiting the abundant water power of the Merrimack River, and stretching along its east bank for more than a mile, the mill made the city into a manufacturing and commercial powerhouse from 1838 until its bankruptcy in the 1930s.

Nowadays, attracted by low taxes and a diverse workforce, the high-tech and financial industries have moved in, bringing city culture with them. The former mill is a prime symbol of successful redevelopment: the redbrick swath of structures houses a museum, an arts center, a college, restaurants and a growing array of local businesses. Manchester has opera, several orchestras, a growing gallery and dining scene, and the state's most important art museum.

Millyard Museum MUSEUM
(☑ 603-622-7531; www.manchesterhistory.org; 200 Bedford St; adult/child 12-18yr $8/4; ⊙ 10am-4pm Tue-Sat) A highlight in the Amoskeag Millyard Historic District, this well-executed museum spotlights the various communities that have lived and worked near Amoskeag Falls from prehistoric times forward, with a focus on the city's years as a textile manufacturing center. Stories about the different immigrant enclaves during this time are particularly fascinating.

Currier Museum of Art MUSEUM
(☑ 603-669-6144; www.currier.org; 150 Ash St; adult/child $15/5, incl Zimmerman House tour $25/10; ⊙ 11am-5pm Sun, Mon & Wed-Fri, 10am-5pm Sat; ℙ) Housing works by John Singer Sargent, Georgia O'Keeffe, Monet, Matisse and Picasso (among many others), this fine-

arts museum is Manchester's greatest cultural gem. With advance reservation, museum guides also offer tours of the nearby **Zimmerman House**, the only Frank Lloyd Wright–designed house in New England that's open to the public.

❶ Getting There & Away

Fast growing but still not too large, **Manchester-Boston Regional Airport** (☑ 603-624-6556; www.flymanchester.com; 1 Airport Rd; ☏), off US 3 south of Manchester, is a civilized alternative to Boston's Logan International Airport.

Concord Coach Lines (www.concordcoach lines.com) runs frequent daily buses to Logan International Airport ($19, 1¾ hours) and South Station ($15, 1½ hours) in Boston, as well as north to Concord ($6, 30 minutes). Buses depart from the Manchester Transportation Center.

Portsmouth

Perched on the edge of the Piscataqua River, Portsmouth is one of New Hampshire's most elegant towns, with a historical center set with tree-lined streets and 18th-century Colonial buildings. Despite its venerable history as an early hub of America's maritime industry, the town exudes a youthful energy, with tourists and locals filling its many restaurants and cafes. Numerous museums and historic houses allow visitors a glimpse into the town's multilayered past, while its proximity to the coast brings both lobster feasts and periodic days of fog that blanket the waterfront.

Still true to its name, Portsmouth remains a working port town, and its economic vitality has been boosted by the naval shipyard (actually located across the river in Maine) and by the influx of high-tech companies.

◎ Sights & Activities

★ **Strawbery Banke Museum**   MUSEUM
(☑ 603-433-1100; www.strawberybanke.org; 14 Hancock St; adult/child 5-17yr $19.50/9; ⊘10am-5pm May-Oct, special events only Nov-Apr; ℗🚼) Spread across a 10-acre site, the Strawbery Banke Museum is an eclectic blend of period homes that date back to the 1690s. Costumed guides recount tales that took place among the 40 buildings (10 furnished). Strawbery Banke includes **Pitt Tavern** (1766), a hotbed of American revolutionary sentiment, **Goodwin Mansion** (a grand 19th-century house from Portsmouth's most prosperous

WORTH A TRIP

MONADNOCK STATE PARK

Visible from 50 miles in any direction, the commanding 3165ft peak of Mt Monadnock is southwestern New Hampshire's spiritual vortex. The surrounding **Mt Monadnock State Park** (☑ 603-532-8862; www.nhstateparks.org; 169 Poole Rd, Jaffrey; day use adult/child 6-11yr $5/2; ℗) is an outdoor wonderland, complete with a visitor center, a camp store, 12 miles of ungroomed cross-country ski trails and more than 40 miles of hiking trails, about 10 miles of which reach the summit. The 3.9-mile White Dot & White Cross loop is a popular hiking route to the top.

time) and **Abbott's Little Corner Store** (1943). The admission ticket is good for two consecutive days.

Isles of Shoals Steamship Co   CRUISE
(☑ 603-431-5500; www.islesofshoals.com; 315 Market St; adult/child from $28/18; 🚼) From mid-June to early October this company runs an excellent tour of the harbor and the historic Isles of Shoals aboard a replica 1900s ferry. It also offers walking tours of Star Island and party cruises featuring DJs or live bands.

🛏 Sleeping & Eating

Port Inn   MOTEL $$$
(☑ 603-436-4378; www.portinnportsmouth.com; 505 US 1 Bypass; r $249-499, ste $499; ℗❋@ ☏❋🐾) Wrapped neatly around a small courtyard, this welcoming and inviting motel is conveniently located off I-95, about 1.5 miles southwest of downtown. In the rooms, monochromatic pillows and throws add a dash of pizzazz to classic furnishings. Breakfast included. Pets are $25 per night.

Ale House Inn   INN $$$
(☑ 603-431-7760; www.alehouseinn.com; 121 Bow St; r $234-304; ℗❋☏) This former brick warehouse for the Portsmouth Brewing Company is Portsmouth's snazziest boutique inn, fusing contemporary design with comfort. Rooms are modern, with clean white lines, flat-screen TVs, and, in the suites, plush tan sofas. All rooms feature an in-room iPad. Rates include use of Trek cruising bikes, but sadly, free beer is no longer included.

Colby's
BREAKFAST $

(☑ 603-436-3033; 105 Daniel St; mains $4-11; ☺ 7am-2pm) If you get to this 28-seat eatery after 8am on the weekend, there's going to be a wait, so give 'em your name and enjoy a cup of free coffee on the patio. Once in, egg lovers can choose from a multitude of Benedicts and omelets, along with French toast, pancakes, huevos rancheros and daily chalkboard specials.

★ Black Trumpet Bistro
INTERNATIONAL $$

(☑ 603-431-0887; www.blacktrumpetbistro.com; 29 Ceres St; mains $19-32; ☺ 5-9pm Sun-Thu, to 10pm Fri & Sat) This bistro, with brick walls and a sophisticated ambience, serves unique combinations – anything from housemade sausages infused with cocoa beans to seared haddock with yuzu (an Asian citrus fruit) and miso. The full menu is also available at its wine bar upstairs, which whips up equally inventive cocktails.

Cure
MODERN AMERICAN $$

(☑ 603-427-8258; www.curerestaurantportsmouth. com; 189 State St; mains $19-35; ☺ 5-9pm Sun-Thu, to 10pm Fri & Sat) Constantly showered with accolades, chef Julie Cutting's refined but cozy brick-walled restaurant makes a romantic dinner spot. The menu revolves around New England cuisine 'revisited': pan-roasted duck breast, maple-glazed salmon, beef ribs slow-braised in red wine, horseradish-sour-cream mashed potatoes, crisp-skinned chicken and lobster bisque, all accompanied by seasonal vegetables and a superb cocktail list.

ⓘ Information

The helpful **Greater Portsmouth Chamber of Commerce** (☑ 603-610-5510; www.ports mouthchamber.org; 500 Market St; ☺ 9am-5pm Mon-Fri year-round, plus 10am-5pm Sat & Sun late May–mid-Oct), which runs a visitor center on the way into Portsmouth just off I-95, also operates a seasonal **information kiosk** (www.goportsmouthnh.com; Market Sq; ☺ 10am-5pm late May–mid-Oct) in the city center.

ⓘ Getting There & Away

Portsmouth is equidistant (about 57 miles) from Boston and Portland, ME. It takes roughly 1¼ hours to reach Portland and 1½ hours to Boston, both via I-95. Rush-hour and high-season traffic can easily double or triple this, however.

Lakes Region

The Lakes Region, with an odd mix of natural beauty and commercial tawdriness, is one of New Hampshire's most popular holiday destinations. Vast Lake Winnipesaukee, the region's centerpiece, has 183 miles of coastline, more than 300 islands and excellent salmon fishing. Catch the early morning mists off the lake and you'll understand why the Native Americans named it 'Smile of the Great Spirit.' The prettiest stretches are in the southwest between Glendale and Alton (on the shoreline Belknap Point Rd), and in the northeast corner between Wolfeboro and Moultonborough (on NH 109). To the north lie the smaller Squam and Little Squam Lakes.

The roads skirting the shores and connecting the lakeside towns pass forested mountains and a riotous spread of small-town Americana: amusement arcades, go-kart tracks, clam shacks, junk-food outlets and boat docks. Even if you're just passing through, stop for a swim, a lakeside picnic or a cruise.

ⓘ Getting There & Around

The fastest way to reach the Lakes Region is via I-93. Coming from Boston and other points south, take exit 15E for Wolfeboro, exit 20 for Weirs Beach, exit 23 for Meredith or exit 24 for Holderness (Squam Lake).

For bus service to or from the Lakes Region, try Concord Coach Lines (www.concordcoach lines.com), which passes through Meredith on its twice-daily run between Boston and North Conway. Buses stop near the Memorial parking lot sign in the public lot near the northeast corner of US 3 and NH 25. This is a flag stop, and you cannot buy tickets here. Destinations include Concord ($13, one hour), Boston's South Station ($25, 2½ hours) and Logan International Airport ($30, 2¾ hours).

Weirs Beach

Called 'Aquedoctan' by its Native American settlers, Weirs Beach takes its English name from the weirs (enclosures for catching fish) that the first European settlers found along the small sand beach. Today Weirs Beach is the honky-tonk heart of Lake Winnipesaukee's childhood amusements, famous for video-game arcades and fried dough. The vacation scene is completed by a lakefront promenade, a public beach and a dock for small cruising ships. A water park and drive-in theater are also in the vicinity. Away from the din on the waterfront, you will notice evocative Victorian-era architecture – somewhat out of place in this capital of kitsch.

South of Weirs Beach lie Laconia, the largest town in the region but devoid of any real sights, and lake-hugging Gilford. Note that this side of the lake gets mobbed with bikers for nine days each June during Laconia Motorcycle Week (www.laconiamcweek.com), the world's oldest motorcycle rally.

★ MV Sophie C   CRUISE
(☑ 603-366-5531; www.cruisenh.com/sophie.php; 211 Lakeside Ave; adult/child 5-12yr $28/14; ☺ 11am & 2pm Mon-Sat mid-Jun–early Sep) The MV *Sophie C* is a veritable floating post office. Passengers are invited to accompany this US mail boat as it delivers packages and letters to quaint ports and otherwise inaccessible island residents across four to five islands. Between mid-June and early September, its two 1½-hour runs depart six days a week from Weirs Beach.

MS Mount Washington   CRUISE
(☑ 603-366-5531; www.cruisenh.com; 211 Lakeside Ave; adult/child 5-12yr regular cruises $32/16, Sun brunch cruises $52/26; ☺ mid-May–late Oct) The classic MS *Mount Washington* steams out of Weirs Beach daily, making a relaxing 2½-hour scenic circuit around Lake Winnipesaukee, with regular stops in Wolfeboro and occasional visits to Alton Bay, Center Harbor and/or Meredith. Special events include Sunday champagne brunch cruises, and themed cruises (sunset dinner-and-dance, an Elvis Tribute, a Lobsterfest cruise) throughout summer and early fall.

NazBar & Grill   BAR
(☑ 603-366-4341; www.naswa.com; 1086 Weirs Blvd, Laconia; ☺ from 11am late May-early Oct) This colorful lakeside bar is recommended because it's a scene. This is Weirs Beach, after all. Watch boats pull up to the dock as you sip your cocktail beside – or in – the lake. Bar fare includes nachos, salads, wraps and burgers.

ⓘ Information

Lakes Region Chamber of Commerce
(☑ 603-524-5531; www.lakesregionchamber.org; 383 S Main St, Laconia; ☺ 9am-3pm Mon-Fri) Supplies information about the greater Laconia/Weirs Beach area.

Wolfeboro

On the eastern shore of Lake Winnipesaukee, Wolfeboro is an idyllic town where children still gather around the ice-cream stand on warm summer nights and a grassy lakeside park draws young and old to weekly concerts. Named for General Wolfe, who died vanquishing Montcalm on the Plains of Abraham in Quebec, Wolfeboro (founded in 1770) claims to be 'the oldest summer resort in America.' Whether that's true or not, it's certainly one of the most charming, with pretty lake beaches, intriguing museums, beautiful New England architecture (from Georgian through Federal, Greek Revival and Second Empire), cozy B&Bs and a worthwhile walking trail that runs along several lakes as it leads out of town.

⊙ Sights & Activities

Wright Museum   MUSEUM
(☑ 603-569-1212; www.wrightmuseum.org; 77 Center St; adult/child 5-17yr $10/6; ☺ 10am-4pm Mon-Sat, noon-4pm Sun May-Oct) For a Rosie-the-riveter and baked-apple-pie look at WWII, visit this museum's interactive exhibitions that feature music, documentary clips, posters and other American paraphernalia. There are also uniforms, equipment and military hardware (including a 42-ton Pershing tank), meticulously restored by the museum. The Tuesday-evening summer lecture series (June to mid-September) is a huge draw – speakers range from authors to war refugees.

Cotton Valley Rail Trail   WALKING
(www.cottonvalleyrailtrail.org; Central Ave) This excellent multiuse rail trail starts at Wolfeboro's information office and runs for 12 miles along an old railway bed. It links the towns of Wolfeboro, Brookfield and Wakefield and passes two lakes, climbs through Cotton Valley, and winds through forests and fields around Brookfield. From Wolfeboro, the trail's first half mile is also known as the Bridge Falls Path.

🛏 Sleeping & Eating

Wolfeboro Inn   INN $$$
(☑ 603-569-3016; www.wolfeboroinn.com; 90 N Main St; r $219-279, ste $319-359; ⓟ@🤖📶❄) The town's best-known lodging is right on the lake with a private beach. One of the region's most prestigious resorts since 1812, it

has 44 rooms across a main inn and a modern annex. Rooms have modern touches like new beds and contemporary furnishings: it feels less historic but oh-so-luxurious. Facilities include a restaurant and pub, **Wolfe's Tavern** (www.wolfestavern.com; dinner mains $12-31; ⊙7am-9pm Sun-Thu, to 10pm Fri & Sat).

Downtown Grille Cafe   CAFE $
(☑603-569-4504; www.downtowngrillecafe.com; 33 S Main St; pastries $2-4, breakfast mains $4-9, lunch mains $8-14; ⊙7am-3pm) Order at the counter then head to the back patio for a great view of Lake Winn with your ham-and-pepper-jack panini, hot-pressed *cubano* or, our favorite, the kickin' buffalo chicken wrap with blue cheese and hot sauce. Stop by in the morning for pastries and breakfast sandwiches. Fancy coffees available, too.

Nolan's Brick Oven Bistro   PIZZA $$
(☑603-515-1028; www.nolansbrickovenbistro.com; 39 N Main St; mains $10-26; ⊙11am-9pm) Delicious pizzas – cooked in the brick oven and laden with ingredients sourced from local farms – are the big draw at this popular spot a block north of the village center. But the kitchen offers a world of alternatives throughout the year, including seafood, soups, salads, wraps and even occasional sushi nights.

ⓘ Information

Wolfeboro Chamber of Commerce Information Booth (☑603-569-2200; www.wolfeboro chamber.com; 32 Central Ave; ⊙10am-3pm Mon-Sat, to noon Sun late May–mid-Oct, reduced hours rest of year) Located inside the old train station, this small office has the scoop on local activities.

White Mountains

Covering one-quarter of New Hampshire (and part of Maine), the vast White Mountains area is a spectacular region of soaring peaks and lush valleys, and contains New England's most rugged mountains. There are numerous activities on offer, including hiking, camping, skiing and canoeing. Much of the area – 786,000 acres – is protected from overdevelopment as part of the White Mountain National Forest (WMNF), which celebrated its centennial in 2018. Note, however, that this wondrous place is popular: six million visitors flock here annually to use its 1200 miles of hiking trails,

23 campgrounds and eight Nordic and alpine ski areas.

Connected by scenic drives and rugged trails, there are four popular areas in the White Mountains for recreation: Mt Washington Valley to the east, Crawford Notch and Bretton Woods along US 302 in the center, the Kancamagus Hwy along the southern fringe and the Franconia Range to the west and northwest.

Kancamagus Highway

One of New Hampshire's prettiest driving routes, the winding 34.5-mile Kancamagus Hwy (NH 112) between Lincoln and Conway runs right through the WMNF and over Kancamagus Pass (2855ft). Paved only in 1964, and still unspoiled by commercial development, the 'Kanc' offers easy access to US Forest Service (USFS) campgrounds, hiking trails and fantastic scenery.

The route is named for Chief Kancamagus (The Fearless One), who assumed the powers of *sagamore* (leader) of the Penacook Native American tribe around 1684. He was the final *sagamore*, succeeding his grandfather, the great Passaconaway, and his uncle Wonalancet. Kancamagus tried to maintain peace between the indigenous peoples and European explorers and settlers, but the newcomers pushed his patience past breaking point. He finally resorted to battle to rid the region of Europeans, but in 1691 he and his followers were forced to escape northward.

Sabbaday Falls   WALKING
(NH 112/Kancamagus Hwy; day use $5) A 0.3-mile one-way stroll on the popular Sabbaday Brook Trail ends at Sabbaday Falls, a gorge waterfall powering through narrow granite walls into lovely pools. Stairs lead to overlooks with mesmerizing views of the flume. The trailhead is about 15 miles west of the Saco Ranger District Office, and the trail is accessible for people with disabilities.

ⓘ Information

Saco Ranger District Office (☑603-447-5448; www.fs.usda.gov/detail/whitemountain/about-forest/offices; 33 Kancamagus Hwy, Conway; ⊙9am-4:30pm Mon, 8am-4:30pm Tue-Sun) You can pick up White Mountain National Forest brochures and hiking maps here, at the eastern end of the Kancamagus Hwy near Conway. Restrooms available.

North Woodstock & Lincoln

North Woodstock and its neighboring settlement Lincoln gather a mix of adventure seekers and drive-by sightseers en route to the Kancamagus Hwy (NH 112). North Woodstock has a busy but small-town feel with weathered motels and diners lining the main street and a gurgling river running parallel to it. Nearby Lincoln has less charm, but serves as the starting point for the entertaining Hobo Railroad and other family-friendly activities such as zipline tours and an aerial adventure park.

★ **Notch Hostel** HOSTEL **$**
(☎603-348-1483; www.notchhostel.com; 324 Lost River Rd, North Woodstock; dm $30, d $75-90; 🅿@🛜🐾) Tibetan prayer flags mark your arrival at this gorgeous hostel, the brainchild of outdoor enthusiasts (and husband-and-wife team) Serena and Justin. A class act all round, it welcomes guests with outdoor decks, a spacious kitchen, a mountain-themed library, a sauna for chilly winter nights and a cozy vibe. Lots of info for Appalachian Trail thru-hikers.

Wilderness Inn B&B **$$**
(☎603-745-3890; www.thewildernessinn.com; 57 S Main St, North Woodstock; r $115-200, cottage $200; 🅿❄🛜) This former lumber-mill-owner's house has seven lovely guest rooms, ranging from small to suite-size, as well as a family-size cottage overlooking Lost River. Each is individually decorated with stenciled walls and cozy furnishings, and all but one have wood floors. Breakfasts (included in room rates) are marvelous and served on the sun porch when it's warm.

Woodstock Inn
Station & Brewery PUB FOOD **$$**
(☎603-745-3951; www.woodstockinnnh.com; 135 Main St/US 3, North Woodstock; mains $9-26; ⊙11:30am-9pm Sun-Thu, to 10pm Fri & Sat, bar open later) Formerly a railroad station, this place tries to be everything to everyone. With more than 150 items, it can probably satisfy just about any food craving, but the pastas, sandwiches and burgers are the most interesting. The beer-sodden rear tavern is one of the most happening places in this neck of the woods. Also a nice front patio.

ℹ️ Information

Start your adventures at the helpful and comprehensive **White Mountains Visitor Center** (☎National Forest info 603-745-3816, visitor info 603-745-8720; www.visitwhitemountains. com; 200 Kancamagus Hwy, off I-93, exit 32, North Woodstock; ⊙visitor center 8:30am-5pm year-round, National Forest desk 9am-3:30pm mid-May–mid-Oct, Fri-Sun rest of year) in Lincoln. It's one of the best resources for information about the region. Here you'll find trail info and be able to purchase National Forest recreation passes. In North Woodstock, stop by the **Western White Mountains Chamber of Commerce** (☎603-745-6621; www.lincolnwood stock.com; 126 Main St/US 3, North Woodstock; ⊙8am-4pm Mon-Fri) for information.

ℹ️ Getting There & Away

Concord Coach Lines (www.concordcoachlines. com) stops in Lincoln at **7-Eleven** (☎800-639-3317; 36 Main St) on its twice-daily run between Boston and Littleton. Destinations include Concord ($17.50, 1½ hours), Boston's South Station ($29, three hours) and Logan International Airport ($34, 3¼ hours).

Franconia Notch State Park

Franconia Notch, a narrow gorge shaped over the eons by a wild stream cutting through craggy granite, is a dramatic mountain pass. This was long the residence of the beloved Old Man of the Mountain, a natural rock formation that became the symbol of the Granite State. Sadly, the Old Man collapsed in 2003, though that does not stop tourists from coming to see the featureless cliff that remains. Despite the Old Man's absence, the attractions of Franconia Notch are many, from the dramatic hike down the Flume Gorge to the fantastic views of the Presidential Range.

The most scenic parts of the notch are protected by the narrow Franconia Notch State Park. Reduced to two lanes, I-93 (renamed the Franconia Notch Pkwy) squeezes through the gorge. Services are available in Lincoln and North Woodstock to the south and in Franconia and Littleton to the north.

⊙ Sights & Activities

Cannon Mountain
Aerial Tramway CABLE CAR
(☎603-823-8800; www.cannonmt.com; 260 Tramway Dr; round trip adult/child 6-12yr $18/16; ⊙8:30am-5pm Jun–mid-Oct; 🅿👣) This tram shoots up the side of Cannon Mountain, offering a breathtaking view of Franconia Notch. You can also hike up the mountain and take the tramway down (adult/child $13/10). At the summit, take the 1500ft walk along the **Rim Trail** to the observatory

deck for gorgeous 360-degree views – on clear days you can see as far as Maine and Canada. There's a snack bar and picnic tables at the tram building. Located off I-93, exit 34B.

★ **Flume Gorge & the Basin** HIKING
(📞 603-745-8391; www.flumegorge.com; I-93, exit 34A; adult/child 6-12yr $16/14; ⊙ 8:30am-5pm early May-Jun & Sep–mid-Oct, to 5:30pm Jul & Aug) To see this natural wonder, take the 2-mile self-guided nature walk, which includes a 800ft boardwalk through the Flume, a natural 12ft- to 20ft-wide cleft in the granite bedrock. The granite walls tower 70ft to 90ft above you, with moss and plants growing from precarious niches and crevices. The Basin is a 15ft-deep granite pothole nearby.

Recreation Trail CYCLING, WALKING
(I-93, exit 34A) For a casual walk or bike ride, you can't do better than head out to this 8-mile paved trail that wends its way along the Pemigewasset River and through the notch. Bikes are available for rental with **Sport Thoma** (www.sportthoma.com; half-/full day $35/50) at Cannon Mountain, with a shuttle drop-off if you're only up for a one-way trip.

❶ Information

Stop by the **Franconia Notch State Park Visitor Center** (📞 603-745-8391; www.nhstateparks. org; I-93, exit 34A; ⊙ 8:30am-5pm mid-May–Jun & Sep-early Oct, to 5:30pm Jul & Aug, to 4:30pm mid-Oct–late Oct) for a wide range of information about the park and the region.

Bretton Woods & Crawford Notch

This beautiful 1773ft mountain pass on the western slopes of Mt Washington is deeply rooted in New Hampshire lore. In 1826 torrential rains here triggered massive mudslides, killing the Willey family in the valley below. The dramatic incident made the newspapers and fired the imaginations of painter Thomas Cole and author Nathaniel Hawthorne. Both men used the incident for inspiration, thus unwittingly putting Crawford Notch on tourist maps.

Even so, the area remained known mainly to locals and wealthy summer visitors who patronized the grand Mt Washington Hotel in Bretton Woods – until 1944, when President Roosevelt chose the hotel as the site of a conference to establish a post-WWII global economic order.

Today the hotel is as grand as ever, while a steady flow of visitors comes to hike the Presidential Range and climb Mt Washington – on foot or aboard a steam-powered locomotive on the dramatic Mt Washington Cog Railway.

⊙ Sights & Activities

★ **Crawford Notch State Park** STATE PARK
(📞 603-374-2272; www.nhstateparks.org; 1464 US 302, Hart's Location; ⊙ visitor center 9:30am-5pm late May–mid-Oct, park year-round unless posted otherwise; Ⓟ) 🆓🆓🆓 This pretty park maintains an extensive system of hiking trails. From the Willey House visitor center, you can walk the easy 0.5-mile **Pond Loop Trail**, the 1-mile **Sam Willey Trail** and the **Ripley Falls Trail**, a 1-mile round-trip hike from US 302 via the **Ethan Pond Trail**. The trailhead for **Arethusa Falls**, a 1.5-mile one-way hike, is 0.5 miles south of the Dry River Campground on US 302. Serious hikers can also tackle the much longer trek up Mt Washington.

★ **Mt Washington Cog Railway** RAIL
(📞 603-278-5404; www.thecog.com; 3168 Base Station Rd; adult $72-78, child 4-12yr $41; ⊙ daily Jun-Oct, Sat & Sun late Apr, May & Nov; ♿) Purists walk and the lazy drive, but the quaintest way to reach Mt Washington's summit is via this cog railway. Since 1869 coal-fired, steam-powered locomotives have climbed a scenic 3.5-mile track up the mountainside (three hours round trip). Two of these old-fashioned trains run daily June to October. The steam trains are supplemented by faster, cleaner, biodiesel-fueled trains. Reservations recommended.

Arethusa Falls Trail HIKING
(US 302, Hart's Location) The highest waterfall in New Hampshire is your goal on this 3-mile round-trip hike in Crawford Notch. The moderately difficult trail ends at the base of the falls, which rise about 200ft. They are most photogenic in spring as snowmelt boosts the water levels. The parking area is 6 miles south of the Crawford Notch Depot.

🛏 Sleeping

★ **AMC Highland Center Lodge** LODGE $$
(📞 front desk 603-278-4453, reservations 603-466-2727; www.outdoors.org; NH 302, Bretton Woods; r incl breakfast & dinner per adult/child/teen $176/54/103, without bath $121/54/103; Ⓟ🛜) This cozy Appalachian Mountain Club (AMC) lodge is set amid the splendor

of Crawford Notch, an ideal base for hiking the trails crisscrossing the Presidential Range. The grounds are beautiful, rooms are basic but comfortable, meals are hearty and guests are outdoor enthusiasts. Discounts for AMC members. The information center, open to the public, has loads of information about regional hiking.

Omni Mt Washington Hotel & Resort HOTEL $$$

(☑ 603-278-1000; www.omnihotels.com; 310 Mt Washington Hotel Rd, Bretton Woods; r/ste from $449/619; P✿@🛜♨) Even if you're not staying here, don't miss the view of Mt Washington from a wicker chair on the veranda of this historic hotel, preferably with a cocktail in hand. Open since 1902, this grand place maintains a sense of fun – note the moose's head overlooking the lobby and the framed local wildflowers in many of the guest rooms.

Pinkham Notch

Pinkham Notch (2032ft) is a mountain-pass area known for its wild beauty, and its useful facilities for campers and hikers make it one of the most popular and crowded activity centers in the White Mountains. Wildcat Mountain and Tuckerman Ravine offer good skiing, and an excellent system of trails provides access to the natural beauties of Mt Washington and the Presidential Range, which stretches north from Crawford Notch to Mt Washington and then on to Mt Madison. For the less athletically inclined, the Mt Washington Auto Road provides easy – if white-knuckled – access to the summit, where you'll find a weather museum, a historic inn and sweeping views on clear days.

🏃 Activities

Tuckerman Ravine Trail HIKING

(361 NH 16, Pinkham Notch Visitor Center) It's not for everyone and you *must* be properly prepared, but this exhilarating hike to Mt Washington's summit, New England's highest mountain, is one for the bucket list. Highlights on the 4.2-mile trail (one way) include climbing a glacial cirque, strolling across an alpine plateau and navigating a half-mile boulder field. On clear days, summit views sweep across five states.

The mountain is renowned for its frighteningly bad weather – the average temperature on the summit is 26.5°F (-3°C). The

mercury has fallen as low as -47°F (-43°C), but only risen as high as 72°F (22°C). About 256in (more than 21ft) of snow falls each year. (One year, it was 47ft.) At times the climate can mimic Antarctica's, and hurricane-force winds blow every three days or so, on average. In fact, the second-highest wind speed ever recorded was here during a storm in 1934, when gusts reached 231mph.

If you attempt to hike to the summit, pack warm, windproof clothes and shoes, even in high summer, and always consult with Appalachian Mountain Club (AMC) hut personnel. Don't be reluctant to turn back if the weather changes for the worse. Dozens of hikers who ignored such warnings and died are commemorated by trail-side monuments and crosses.

Mt Washington Auto Road SCENIC DRIVE

(☑ 603-466-3988; www.mountwashingtonautoroad.com; NH 16; car & driver $31, extra adult/child 5-12yr $9/7, guided tours adult/child $36/16; ⏰8am-6pm mid-Jun–Aug, shorter hours May–mid-Jun & Sep-late Oct) One of New England's top adventures, the serpentine drive up the 7.6-mile Mt Washington Auto Road is not for the faint of heart. The Mt Washington Summit Rd Co operates this narrow, alpine toll road, which soars from the Pinkham Notch area to the parking lot just below the 6288ft summit. The price includes an audio-tour CD and entry to Mt Washington Observatory's **Extreme Weather Museum** (☑ 800-706-0432; www.mountwashington.org/visit-us; Mt Washington summit; $2, with Auto Road ticket free; ⏰hours vary depending on weather; P). 'This car climbed Mt Washington' bumper stickers are sold in the summit gift shop.

🛏 Sleeping

Joe Dodge Lodge LODGE $

(☑ 603-466-2727; www.outdoors.org/lodging/lodges/pinkham; 361 NH 16; r per person adult/child/teen incl breakfast & dinner from $86/39/74; P✿🛜) The AMC complex at Pinkham Notch incorporates this lodge, with dorms holding 100-plus beds. Rooms come in a variety of configurations and the price is per person. With the Tuckerman Ravine trailhead a few steps away, this cozy facility is a great place to overnight before hiking to the summit of Mt Washington. Reservations recommended. Discounts available for AMC members.

Glen House Hotel
HOTEL $$$

(☑603-466-3420; www.glenhousehotel.com; 979 NH 16; r $249-369; P❄☎🛜🐾♿) Opening in late 2018, this classy number will surely go gangbusters due to its fresh rustic style and its location beside the Mt Washington Auto Road. The fifth hotel on the site since 1852, this incarnation embraces its location with big-window views of Mt Washington, clean-line Shaker-style furniture and whimsical touches such as a mounted moosehead made from colorful cloth.

Hanover

Hanover is the quintessential New England college town. On warm days, students toss Frisbees on the wide college green fronting Georgian ivy-covered buildings, while locals and academics mingle at the laid-back cafes, restaurants and shops lining Main St. Dartmouth College has long been the town's focal point, giving the area a vibrant connection to the arts.

Dartmouth was chartered in 1769 primarily 'for the education and instruction of Youth of the Indian Tribes.' Back then, the school was located in the forests where its prospective students lived. Although teaching 'English Youth and others' was its secondary purpose, in fact, Dartmouth College graduated few Native Americans and was soon attended almost exclusively by colonists. The college's most illustrious alumnus is Daniel Webster (1782–1852), who graduated in 1801 and went on to be a prominent lawyer, US senator, secretary of state and perhaps the USA's most esteemed orator.

Dartmouth College
UNIVERSITY

(☑603-646-1110; www.dartmouth.edu) Hanover is all about Dartmouth College, so hit the campus. Join a free student-guided **campus walking tour** (☑603-646-2875; 10 N Main St, 6016 McNutt Hall) or just pick up a map at the admissions office and head off on your own.

Don't miss the **Baker-Berry Library** (☑603-646-2704; 25 N Main St; ⊙8am-2am Mon-Fri, 10am-2am Sat & Sun), splashed with the grand *Epic of American Civilization,* painted by the outspoken Mexican muralist José Clemente Orozco (1883–1949), who taught at Dartmouth in the 1930s.

★ Hood Museum of Art
MUSEUM

(☑603-646-2808; http://hoodmuseum.dartmouth.edu; 6 E Wheelock St; ⊙10am-5pm Tue & Thu-Sat, to 9pm Wed, noon-5pm Sun) **FREE** Shortly after the college's founding in 1769, Dartmouth began to acquire artifacts of artistic or historical interest. Since then the collection has expanded to include nearly 70,000 items, which are housed at the Hood Museum of Art. The collection is particularly strong in American pieces, including Native American art. One of the highlights is a set of Assyrian reliefs from the Palace of Ashurnasirpal that dates to the 9th century BC. Special exhibitions often feature contemporary artists.

Hanover Inn
INN $$$

(☑603-643-4300; www.hanoverinn.com; 2 E Wheelock St; r $319-369, ste $369-569; ❄@🛜♿) Owned by Dartmouth College and situated directly opposite the college green, Hanover's loveliest guesthouse has nicely appointed rooms with elegant wood furnishings. It has a cocktail bar and a farm-to-table restaurant on-site.

🛈 Information

Hanover Area Chamber of Commerce (☑603-643-3115; www.hanoverchamber.org; 53 S Main St, Suite 208; ⊙9am-4pm Mon-Fri) also maintains a seasonal **information booth** (Dartmouth Green; ⊙mid-Jun–mid-Sep) on the village green.

MAINE

Maine offers numerous adventures, from summiting jagged peaks to kayaking cliff-lined shores. With vast forests, seaside villages and island getaways, the state invites seemingly limitless wandering.

Maine seems spoiled when it comes to nature's gifts. It has hundreds of miles of coastline, encompassing sea cliffs, sandy beaches and craggy wave-kissed shores. Offshore, there are countless islands for exploring, with scenic walks amid empty coves and misty forested shorelines, while villages nearby boast year-round populations that don't reach into the triple digits.

Inland, Maine has vast tracts of wilderness, with thick forests, alpine lakes and treeless boulder-strewn peaks. Such a magnificent landscape offers limitless adventures, and you can spend the day cycling along winding shore roads, kayaking beside curious harbor seals or hiking up above falcon nests to wondrous mountaintop overlooks.

History

Maine's past reaches back to the earliest Paleo-Indians, who left traces of a sometimes fascinating culture over the eons. The rugged, glacier-carved wilderness was a serious challenge for early European colonists, and the region has remained sparsely populated up to the present. Other key facets from Maine's history include the involvement of Mainers in the Civil War and the state's transformation from industrial workhouse to a 'Vacationland' for East Coasters.

In 1820 Maine at long last separated from Massachusetts and gained its statehood. Timber brought wealth to the interior. Fishing, shipbuilding, granite quarrying and farming were also boom industries, alongside manufacturing. Unfortunately, the boom days were not to last. By the turn of the 20th century, population growth stagnated and Maine became a backwater.

Maine's rustic, undeveloped landscape later became part of its great appeal to would-be visitors. Maine soon emerged as a summer cottage destination around the time the slogan 'Vacationland' (which still adorns Maine license plates) was coined in the 1890s. Today, tourists spend about $6 billion per year, supporting roughly 16% of the state's work force.

ℹ Information

Maine Bureau of Parks & Lands (☑ 207-287-3821; www.maine.gov/dacf/parks) Oversees 48 state parks and historic sites. Details of each park (including activities and camping) are on the website.

Maine Office of Tourism (www.visitmaine.com) Comprehensive website; can mail out maps and brochures.

Maine Tourism Association (www.mainetourism.com) Runs info centers along the principal routes into Maine: Calais, Fryeburg, Hampden, Houlton, Kittery, West Gardiner and Yarmouth. Each center is generally open 9am to 5:30pm; longer in summer (8am to 6pm).

Ogunquit

The Abenaki came up with the lovely name Ogunquit, which apparently means 'the beautiful place by the sea.' After a few minutes strolling around town, we were inclined to believe it meant, 'Family-friendly resort town with a thriving arts and LGBTIQ+ scene,' but our eastern woodland linguistic skills admittedly aren't up to snuff.

Seriously though, Ogunquit is simply a wonderful little arts colony, LGBTIQ+ vacation escape, and a spot where your kids can experience the American seaside holiday in all its quaint glory. Wide stretches of pounding surf front the Atlantic, while warm backcove waters make an idyllic setting for a swim. In summer, the 3-mile beach draws hordes of visitors from near and far, increasing the town's population exponentially.

Before its resort status, Ogunquit was a shipbuilding center in the 17th century. Later it became an important arts center when the Ogunquit art colony was founded in 1898.

◉ Sights & Activities

Ogunquit Beach BEACH
(access from Beach St) A sublime stretch of family-friendly coastline, Ogunquit Beach is only a five-minute walk along Beach St, east of US 1. Walking to the beach is a good idea in summer as the parking lot fills up early (and it costs $4 per hour to park!). The 3-mile beach fronts Ogunquit Bay to the south; on the west side of the beach are the warmer waters of the tidal Ogunquit River.

★**Marginal Way** WALKING
(access from Shore Rd) Tracing the 'margin' of the sea, Ogunquit's famed mile-long footpath winds above the crashing gray waves, taking in grand sea vistas and rocky coves, and allowing for some excellent real-estate admiring. The neatly paved path, fine for children and slow walkers, is dotted with restful benches. It starts south of Beach St at Shore Rd and ends near **Perkins Cove** (access from Shore Rd).

ℹ Information

Gay Ogunquit (www.gayogunquit.com) Information for LGBTIQ+ visitors.

Ogunquit Chamber of Commerce (☑ 20 7-646-2939; www.ogunquit.org; 36 Main St/US 1; ☺ 9am-5pm Mon-Sat, 10am-4pm Sun late May-early Oct, 10am-4pm Mon-Fri rest of year) Located on US 1, a little way south of the town's center.

Portland

Seagulls scream, the smell of beer and fish fry flows through the streets like the fog off Casco Bay, and everywhere the salt wind licks your skin. Maine's largest city has capitalized on the gifts of its port history – the

Maine Coast

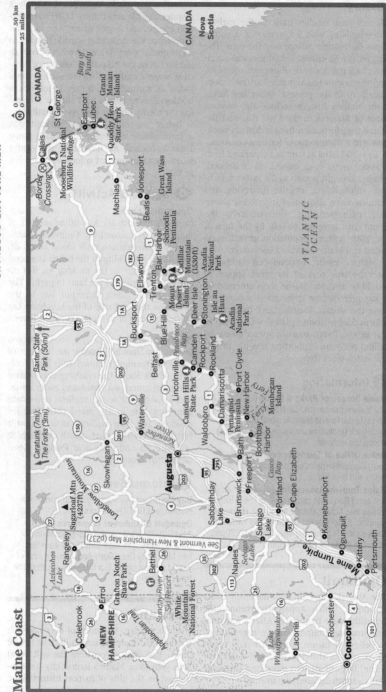

See Vermont & New Hampshire Map (p237)

redbrick warehouse buildings, the narrow cobblestone streets – to become one of the hippest, most vibrant small cities in the Americas. You'll find excellent museums and galleries, abundant green space, and both a food culture and a brewing scene worthy of a town many times its size.

Set on a peninsula, Portland's always been a city of the sea. Today, the Old Port district is the town's historic heart, with handsomely restored brick buildings filled with cafes, shops and bars. There are more hipsters than fishmongers living here these days, but there's also genuine ethnic diversity – Portland boasts a large African population – generally lacking in the rest of Maine.

◉ Sights & Activities

★ Fort Williams Park   PARK
(☏ 207-767-3707; https://fortwilliams.org; 1000 Shore Rd, Cape Elizabeth; ☉ sunrise-sunset) 🅵 FREE Four miles southeast of Portland on Cape Elizabeth, 90-acre Fort Williams Park is worth visiting simply for the panoramas and picnic possibilities. Stroll around the ruins of the fort, a late-19th-century artillery base, checking out the WWII bunkers and gun emplacements that still dot the rolling lawns (a German U-boat was spotted in Casco Bay in 1942). The fort actively guarded the entrance to Casco Bay until 1964.

★ Portland Head Light   LIGHTHOUSE
(☏ 207-799-2661; https://portlandheadlight.com; 1000 Shore Rd, Cape Elizabeth; museum adult/ child $2/1; ☉ museum 10am-4pm Jun-Oct, Sat & Sun only Apr, May & Nov) Within Fort Williams Park stands the beloved, and much-photographed, Portland Head Light, the oldest of Maine's 52 functioning lighthouses. It was commissioned by President George Washington in 1791 and staffed until 1989, when machines took over. The keeper's house is now a museum, which traces the maritime and military history of the region.

Portland Museum of Art   MUSEUM
(☏ 207-775-6148; www.portlandmuseum.org; 7 Congress Sq; adult/child $15/free, 4-8pm Fri free; ☉ 10am-6pm Sat-Wed, to 8pm Thu & Fri, shorter hours Oct-May) Founded in 1882, this well-respected museum houses an outstanding collection of American artists. Maine artists, including Winslow Homer, Edward Hopper, Louise Nevelson and Andrew Wyeth, are particularly well represented. You'll also find a few works by European masters, including Monet, Degas, Picasso and Renoir.

Eastern Promenade   WALKING
(http://trails.org/our-trails/eastern-prom-trail) Don't leave town without having a walk or bicycle ride along this 2.1-mile trail, which offers superb, sweeping views of Casco Bay, all speckled with sailboats and rocky islets. The well-paved path has two small rises, but is otherwise flat and accessible to all levels of physical fitness. The promenade can be easily accessed throughout Portland's East End.

🛏 Sleeping

★ Black Elephant Hostel   HOSTEL $
(☏ 207-712-7062; www.blackelephanthostel.com; 33 Hampshire St; dm $40-60, d $65-150; 🛜) The Black Elephant is Portland's first dedicated hostel, and it's an exceptionally good one, with funky interior art, exterior murals, a central location and a range of clean and comfortable rooms. The lobby and kitchen spaces are super-colorful and inviting, and there's even a 'vampire' themed bathroom.

Press Hotel   HOTEL $$$
(☏ 207-573-2425; www.thepresshotel.com; 119 Exchange St; r $220-413; 🅿🌑🛜) Opened in mid-2015, the Press Hotel, a creative conversion of the building that once housed the offices and printing plant of Maine's largest newspaper, has since become something of a Portland institution. The press theme shines in unique details – a wall of vintage typewriters, and old headlines on hallway wallpapers. Smart, navy-toned rooms are sexy and local art adorns walls.

Danforth Inn   BOUTIQUE HOTEL $$$
(☏ 207-879-8755; www.danforthinn.com; 163 Danforth St; r $199-359, ste $699; 🅿🌑🛜) Staying at this ivy-shrouded West End boutique hotel feels like being a guest at an eccentric millionaire's mansion. Shoot pool in the wood-paneled games room (a former speakeasy) or climb into the rooftop cupola for views across Portland Harbor. The nine rooms are decorated with flair, in a sophisticated mix of antique and modern.

✕ Eating

★ Bayside American Cafe   AMERICAN $
(☏ 207-774-0005; www.baysideamericancafe.com; 98 Portland St; mains $9-17; ☉ 7am-2pm; 🔧) This charming brunch and lunch spot is great for a rib-sticking meal to start your day. It uses steak in its corned beef and one of its eggs Benedict dishes; to go meatless, try the huevos rancheros. Staff are friendly and

ingredients are often locally sourced. Reservations are accepted, otherwise expect a line.

Green Elephant VEGETARIAN, ASIAN $
(☎207-347-3111; http://greenelephantmaine.com; 608 Congress St; mains $12-16; ⊙11:30am-2:30pm & 5-9:30pm Mon-Sat, 5-9pm Sun; ✐) Even carnivores shouldn't miss the vegetarian fare at this Zen-chic, Thai-inspired cafe (with lots of vegan and gluten-free options too). Start with the crispy spinach wontons, then move on to one of the stir-fries, pineapple brown rice, Thai ginger noodles or curry favorites like tofu tikka masala.

Central Provisions MODERN AMERICAN $$
(☎207-805-1085; www.central-provisions.com; 414 Fore St; lunch plates $4-18, dinner plates $5-30; ⊙11am-2pm & 5-10pm Sun-Thu, to 10:30pm Fri & Sat) Snug, redbrick Central Provisions is a consistent winner in the Portland haute cuisine stakes. Angle for a seat at the bar, overlooking the line chefs in action, and choose from a masterful small-plates menu that swings from tuna crudo to suckling pig. Local oysters, fish and cheese are staples.

★ **Fore Street** MODERN AMERICAN $$$
(☎207-775-2717; www.forestreet.biz; 288 Fore St; small plates $12-16, mains $26-42; ⊙5:30-10pm Sun-Thu, to 10:30pm Fri & Sat) ✐ Fore Street is the lauded restaurant many consider to be the originator of today's food obsession in Portland. Chef-owner Sam Hayward has turned roasting into a high art: chickens turn on spits in the open kitchen as chefs slide iron kettles of mussels into the woodburning oven. Local, seasonal eating is taken very seriously and the menu changes daily.

🍷 Drinking & Entertainment

★ **Rising Tide Brewing Company** BREWERY
(☎207-370-2337; www.risingtidebrewing.com; 103 Fox St; ⊙tastings noon-7pm Mon-Sat, to 5pm Sun) In a pocket of town growing in stature (and with a neighboring distillery), Rising Tide is well worth investigating. Locals congregate in the car park, and food trucks visit in summer, from Wednesday to Sunday. Check the website for events (live music etc). Tours are held daily at 3pm and also on Saturday at 1pm and 5pm, and Sunday at 1pm.

Sagamore Hill BAR
(☎207-808-8622; www.sagamorehillmaine.com; 150 Park St; ⊙4pm-1am) Early-20th-century elegance meets a 21st-century cocktail menu, plus lots of Teddy Roosevelt memorabilia and a ton of taxidermy at this excellent bar. The interior has an art-deco appeal that's tough not to love, especially after a Louisiana Purchase (rye, vermouth, bitters, charred thyme). Serves seasonal drinks, plus nonalcoholic mocktails.

🛍 Shopping

Maine Craft ARTS & CRAFTS
(☎207-808-8184; https://mainecrafts.org/center-formaine-craft/portland; 521 Congress St; ⊙10am-6pm Sun-Wed, to 7pm Thu, to 8pm Fri & Sat) Past the clever title of this shop is an excellent retail and arts space, showcasing the best of the state's contemporary crafts and maker movement. You'll find handmade jewelry, objets d'art and general captivating creativity. Even the setting – Mechanic's Hall, a handsome 19th-century gem on the National Register of Historic Places – is superb.

ℹ Information

Ocean Gateway Information Center (☎207-772-5800; www.visitportland.com; 14 Ocean Gateway Pier; ⊙9am-5pm Mon-Fri, to 4pm Sat & Sun Jun-Oct, shorter hours rest of year) Visitor information, down at the waterfront.

ℹ Getting There & Away

AIR

Portland International Jetport (PWM; ☎207-874-8877; www.portlandjetport.org; 1001 Westbrook St) is Maine's largest air terminal. It's served by domestic airlines, with nonstop flights to cities in the Eastern USA. Metro bus 5 takes you to the center of town for $1.50. Taxis are about $20 to downtown.

BUS

Greyhound (☎207-772-6588; www.greyhound.com; 950 Congress St) offers direct daily trips to Bangor and Boston, with connections on to the rest of the USA.

Concord Coach Lines (☎800-639-3317; https://concordcoachlines.com; 100 Thompson's Point Rd) operates daily buses between Boston (including Logan Airport; $30, two hours) and Portland, continuing on to midcoast Maine towns. There are also services connecting Portland and the towns of Augusta ($16, one hour), Waterville ($18, 1¾ hours) and Bangor ($28, 2½ hours). Two services a day link Portland with New York City ($75, six hours).

TRAIN

The *Downeaster*, run by Amtrak, makes five trips daily between Boston and Portland ($29 to \$39, 2½ hours) from **Portland Transportation Center** (100 Thompson's Point Rd).

Services extend up the midcoast all the way to Brunswick.

Midcoast Maine

On a map, rocky 'fingers' claw at Penobscot Bay, each peninsula clad in ancient forests, studded with lonely, windswept fishing villages and fog-wreathed paths through the woods. This is midcoast Maine. But it's also resort towns that cater to wealthy vacationers from the northeast and Canada, offering cheap lobster rolls, organic farm-to-table restaurants, writing retreats and tall masts creaking in harbors icebound in winter, and sun-kissed in summer. Imagine Maine, a hybrid of mountains, ocean, forests and villages, and this, too, is the midcoast.

The English first settled this region in 1607, which coincided with the Jamestown settlement in Virginia. Unlike their southerly compatriots, though, these early settlers returned to England within a year. British colonization resumed in 1620. After suffering through the long years of the French and Indian War, the area became home to a thriving shipbuilding industry, which continues today.

❶ Getting There & Around

US 1 is the key access route for this part of the state, but note that roads along the coast flood with traffic during the summer tourist season.

Concord Coach Lines operates daily buses between Boston (including Logan International Airport) and Portland, continuing on to midcoast Maine towns (Bath, Belfast, Brunswick, Camden, Damariscotta, Lincolnville, Rockland, Searsport and Waldoboro). Greyhound buses stop in Bangor, Portland, Bath, Rockland and various other towns.

Bath

Known as the 'City of Ships,' this quaint Kennebec River town was once home to 20-plus shipyards producing more than a quarter of early America's wooden sailing vessels. In Bath's 19th-century heyday, it was one of Maine's largest cities, with a bustling downtown lined with banks and grand municipal buildings. Bath-built schooners and clipper ships sailed the seven seas and the city's name was known far and wide. Even today, the navy utilizes the shipyards at Bath Iron Works; as you leave town driving east on Rte 1, you may see warships being built along the Kennebec River.

Downtown, redbrick sidewalks and solid 19th-century buildings line quaint Front St. South of Bath stretch two scenic peninsulas well worth a detour: ME 209 takes you to **Phippsburg**, home to excellent beaches and a historic fort, while ME 127 runs south to **Georgetown**, terminating at an island-dotted cove.

★**Maine Maritime Museum**　　　MUSEUM
(☑207-443-1316; www.mainemaritimemuseum. org; 243 Washington St; adult/child \$17.50/10.50; ⊙9:30am-5pm) There's a palpable mix of reflective nostalgia and horizon-scanning adventure at this wonderful museum, which preserves the Kennebec's long shipbuilding tradition with paintings, models and hands-on exhibits that tell the tale of 400 years of seafaring. The on-site 19th-century **Percy & Small Shipyard**, preserved by the museum, is a working wooden-boat shipyard, and there's no shortage of enthusiasts on hand to answer questions on such craft.

Boothbay Harbor

Once a beautiful little seafarers' village on a wide blue harbor, Boothbay Harbor is now an extremely popular tourist resort in the summer, when its narrow and winding streets are packed with visitors. Still, there's good reason to join the holiday masses in this picturesque place. Overlooking a pretty waterfront, large, well-kept Victorian houses crown the town's many knolls, and a wooden footbridge ambles across the harbor. From May to October, whale-watching is a major draw.

After you've strolled the waterfront along Commercial St and the business district along Todd and Townsend Aves, walk along McKown St to the top of **McKown Hill** for a fine view. Then, take the footbridge across the harbor to the town's East Side, where there are several huge dockside seafood restaurants.

Boothbay and **East Boothbay** are separate from Boothbay Harbor, the largest, busiest and prettiest of the three towns.

Topside Inn　　　　　　　　　　B&B \$\$\$
(☑207-633-5404; www.topsideinn.com; 60 McKown St; r \$239-389; ⊙May–mid-Oct; P❄🛜) Atop McKown Hill, this grand gray mansion has Boothbay's best harbor views.

Rooms are elegantly turned out in crisp nautical prints and beachy shades. Main-house rooms have more historic charm, but rooms in the two adjacent modern guesthouses are sunny and lovely too. Enjoy the sunset from an Adirondack chair on the inn's sloping, manicured lawn.

★ **Shannon's Unshelled** SEAFOOD $
(☑ 207-446-4921; www.shannonsunshelled.biz; 11 Granary Way; mains $7-15; ☺ from 10:30am; 🐾) If you like your lobster rolls simple, with no accoutrements but melted butter on the side, Shannon's is ideal. The meat is fresh and there's lots of it, and it comes on thick, nicely toasted bread. Shannon's closes when it runs out of lobster – sometimes late afternoon, sometimes much earlier.

Cabbage Island Clambakes SEAFOOD $$$
(☑ 207-633-7200; www.cabbageislandclambakes. com; 22 Commercial St, Pier 6; clambake incl boat tour $70; ☺ Jul–mid-Sep) A prized Maine tradition: a scenic cruise from Boothbay Harbor to the small, family-owned Cabbage Island, where a traditional clambake provides a fabulously memorable feast for diners, who can explore the island in between courses. Chow down on chowder, steamed clams, lobster and all the fixings, plus delicious blueberry cake. Lunch cruise daily, plus an additional departure on weekends. Book ahead.

❶ Information

Boothbay Harbor Region Chamber of Commerce (☑ 207-633-2353; www.boothbay harbor.com; 192 Townsend Ave; ☺ 8am-5pm Mon-Fri, 9am-4pm Sat Jun-Sep) offers good info on its website; it also operates a downtown **information center** (17 Commercial St; ☺ 9am-6pm late May-early Oct) in summer.

Rockland

This thriving port boasts a large fishing fleet and a proud year-round population that gives Rockland a vibrancy lacking in some other midcoast towns. Main St is a window into the city's sociocultural diversity, with a jumble of working-class diners, bohemian cafes and high-end restaurants alongside galleries, old-fashioned storefronts and one of the state's best art museums, the Center for Maine Contemporary Art (CMCA). Rockland is developing a reputation as an art

center, partly thanks to the CMCA's relocation here in 2016.

Settled in 1769, Rockland was once an important shipbuilding center and a transportation hub for goods moving up and down the coast. Today, tall-masted sailing ships still fill the harbor, as Rockland is a center for Maine's busy windjammer cruises (along with Camden).

Rockland is also the birthplace of poet Edna St Vincent Millay (1892–1950), who grew up in neighboring Camden.

❂ Sights & Activities

★ **Rockland**
Breakwater Lighthouse LIGHTHOUSE
(☑ 207-542-7574; www.rocklandharborlights.org; Samoset Rd; ☺ 10am-5pm Sat & Sun late May–mid-Oct) **FREE** Tackle the rugged stone breakwater that stretches almost 1 mile into Rockland Harbor from Jameson Point at the harbor's northern shore. Made of granite blocks, this 'walkway', which took 18 years to build, ends at the Rockland Breakwater Lighthouse, a sweet light sitting atop a brick house, with a sweeping view of town.

While on the breakwater, watch for slippery rocks and ankle-twisting gaps between stones. Bring a sweater, and don't hike if a storm is on the horizon.

Farnsworth Art Museum MUSEUM
(☑ 207-596-6457; www.farnsworthmuseum.org; 16 Museum St; adult/child $15/free; ☺ 10am-5pm Jun-Oct, to 8pm Wed Jul-Sep, closed Mon Nov, Dec, Apr & May, 10am-4pm Wed-Sun Jan-Mar) One of the country's best small regional museums, the Farnsworth houses a collection spanning 200 years of American art. Artists who have lived or worked in Maine are the museum's definite strength – look for works by the Wyeth family (Andrew, NC and Jamie), Edward Hopper, Louise Nevelson, Rockwell Kent and Robert Indiana. Exhibits on the Wyeth family continue in the **Wyeth Center**, in a renovated church across the garden from the main museum (open in summer).

Maine Windjammer
Association CRUISE
(☑ 800-807-9463; www.sailmainecoast.com; ☺ cruises late May–mid-Oct) Although traveling by schooner largely went out of style at the dawn of the 20th century, adventurers can still explore the rugged Maine coast

the old-fashioned way: aboard fast sailing ships, or windjammers. Nine of these multi-masted vessels anchor at Rockland and Camden and offer trips ranging from over-night to 11 days around Penobscot Bay and further up the coast.

🛏 Sleeping & Eating

Captain
Lindsey Hotel   BOUTIQUE HOTEL $$
(📞 207-596-7950; www.lindseyhotel.com; 5 Lindsey St; r $215; ❄ 🐾) There's a sophisticated seafaring theme at this nine-room boutique hotel on a side street just steps from Main St. The building started as a sea-captain's home, but has had other incarnations; check out the 'snack vault' and the handsome oak-paneled breakfast room, or get cozy by the fire in your guest room or in the hotel library.

★ Fog Bar & Cafe   AMERICAN $$
(📞 207-593-9371; www.facebook.com/Fogbarcafe; 328 Main St; mains $16-23; ⊙ 4:30-10pm Thu-Mon) Industrial-chic aesthetic meets an experimental theater, and everything gets overlaid with maritime Maine ingredients and flourishes. The menu changes according to what's fresh and seasonal – in fall you might try saag pumpkin curry, pork belly and roasted apples or pot pies you'd fight your family for. The cocktails are great too.

ℹ Information

Penobscot Bay Regional Chamber of Commerce (📞 207-596-0376; www.camdenrockland.com; 1 Park Dr; ⊙ 9am-5pm Jun-Oct, to 4pm Mon-Fri Nov-May) Visitor center just off Main St (in the same building as the Maine Lighthouse Museum).

ℹ Getting There & Away

Cape Air (www.capeair.com) connects Rockland's **Knox County Regional Airport** (📞 207-594-4131; www.knoxcountymaine.gov/airport; 19 Airport Rd, Owls Head), 3.5 miles south of town, and Boston's Logan International Airport. Fares are around $80 to $100 one way.

Concord Coach Lines (www.concordcoachlines.com) runs buses to and from Boston ($35, 4½ hours), Portland ($23, two hours) and various other midcoast towns, departing from the **Maine State Ferry Terminal** (517a Main St).

Downeast Maine

Without question, this is quintessential Maine: as you head further up the coast toward Canada, the peninsulas seem to narrow, jutting further into the sea. The fishing villages get smaller; the lobster pounds are closer to the water. If you make time to drive to the edge of the shore, south off US 1, let it be here.

The star of the midcoast is Mount Desert Island, home to the spectacular Acadia National Park, where the mountains meet the sea. It offers some of the best hiking in coastal Maine. Island destinations worth visiting include the vibrant summer resort town of Bar Harbor, the elegant village of Northeast Harbor and heart-of-gold Southwest Harbor.

For quiet walks and traditional coastal villages away from the tourist throngs, continue further up the coast from Bar Harbor all the way to the rugged sea cliffs near Lubec, the last town before the Canadian border.

ℹ Information

Hulls Cove Visitor Center (📞 207-288-3338; www.nps.gov/acad; ME 3; ⊙ 8:30am-4:30pm mid-Apr–Jun, Sep & Oct, 8am-6pm Jul & Aug) anchors the park's main Hulls Cove entrance, 3 miles northwest of Bar Harbor. Buy your park pass and pick up maps and info here. The 27-mile-long Park Loop Road starts near here.

When the visitor center is closed (November to mid-April), head to the **Bar Harbor Chamber of Commerce** (Acadia Welcome Center; 📞 207-288-5103; www.visitbarharbor.com; 2 Cottage St; ⊙ 8am-4pm). National park staff provide information there during winter and spring.

Acadia National Park

The only national park in all of New England, **Acadia** (📞 207-288-3338; www.nps.gov/acad; 7-day admission per car/motorcycle $30/25, walk-ins & cyclists $15) offers unrivaled coastal beauty and activities for both leisurely hikers and adrenaline junkies. Most people spend about three days here, which is just enough to take in the park highlights. But you could easily spend a week, taking in mountaintop hikes, bike rides, scenic drives and shoreline strolls, as well as leaving time to relax on the shores of Echo Lake or Sand Beach.

PARK LOOP ROAD

Looping around the eastern half of Mount Desert Island, this 27-mile road provides a fine overview of Acadia's many natural highlights. In summer, it gets quite crowded. Go early (strike at sunrise!) or consider doing the route by bus. The free **Island Explorer** (www. exploreacadia.com) shuttle (route 4) makes the whole loop during the summer.

Start off at the Hulls Cove Visitor Center (p261), located around 3.5 miles northwest of Bar Harbor. Pick up a map, learn about any trail closures and hit the road. From the visitor center it's about 4 miles southeast to the start of the Park Loop Rd. Once you turn onto this road (one-way until just before Jordan Pond House), slow down and enjoy the view.

After about 2.5 miles, you'll turn off onto the **Wild Gardens of Acadia** (Park Loop Rd & ME 3) FREE. Here you'll see some 400 different plant species representing all of Acadia's unique biospheres. Afterwards, visit the nearby **Abbe Museum at Sieur de Monts Spring** (☑207-288-3519; www.abbemuseum.org; 49 Sweetwater Circel; adult/child $3/1; ⊙10am-5pm late May-Oct), with exhibits on the island's original inhabitants. Continuing south you'll pass a few trailheads, including the start of the challenging **Precipice Trail**.

A little further along, make the turnoff to **Sand Beach**. This lovely stretch of sandy shoreline is one of Acadia's unique finds. But the water is freezing! Down the road is the **Thunder Hole**, worth a stop to see the surf crashing into a cleft in the granite. The effect is most dramatic with a strong incoming tide.

Otter Cliff, not far south of Thunder Hole, is a wall of pink granite rising from the sea. This area is popular with rock climbers. From here, follow the twists and turns for another 5 or so miles to the **Jordan Pond House** (☑207-276-3316; https://jordanpondhouse. com; tea & popovers $11, mains $13-29; ⊙11am-7pm mid-May–mid-Oct). Take a break for tea and the restaurant's famous popovers (buttery, hollow muffins) served with jam. Afterwards, you can stroll around the lake, which intersects with several trails in the north and south. Another 4 miles along, you'll pass the turnoff to **Cadillac Mountain**. Drive up to the top for sublime island views.

The park, which incorporates both coastline and mountains, protects a remarkably diverse landscape. You can spend the morning checking out tidal pools and watching the sea crash against the cliffs down by the waterfront, then head into the interior for a walk through dense forest up past a boulder-filled ridgeline with osprey and the occasional bald eagle soaring overhead. There are scenic lakes and ponds to discover too, plus plenty of fine picnic spots.

Bar Harbor

The agreeable hub for Acadia visits, Bar Harbor is crowded for the warmer months of the year with vacationers and cruise-ship passengers. Downtown is packed with souvenir stores, ice-cream shops, cafes and bars, each advertising bigger and better happy hours, early-bird specials or two-for-one deals. The quieter residential backstreets seem to have almost as many B&Bs as private homes.

Although Bar Harbor's hustle and bustle is not for everybody, it has by far the most amenities of any town around here. Even if you stay elsewhere, you'll probably wind up here to eat dinner, grab a drink or schedule a kayaking, sailing or rock-climbing tour.

Bar Harbor's busiest season is late June through August. There's a short lull just after Labor Day (early September); it gets busy again during foliage season, which lasts through mid-October. The season ends the weekend following Columbus Day with the Mount Desert Island Marathon (www. runmdi.org).

🛏 Sleeping & Eating

Acadia Inn   HOTEL $$
(☑207-288-3500; www.acadiainn.com; 98 Eden St; r $119-229; ⊙mid-Apr–Oct; P⊛🐾🏊) This traditional 95-room hotel with helpful staff sits beside a trail leading into the park. The good-sized rooms are smart and comfortable, there's a laundry and a heated pool, and the park shuttle stops here in summer. It's a good choice if you don't mind being a mile or so out of the town center.

★ Bass Cottage Inn   INN $$$
(☑207-288-1234; www.basscottage.com; 14 The Field; r $280-460; ⊙mid-May–Oct; ⊛🐾) If most Bar Harbor B&Bs rate about a '5' in terms

of stylishness, this Gilded Age mansion deserves an '11.' The 10 light-drenched guest rooms have an elegant summer-cottage chic, all crisp white linens and understated botanical prints. Tinkle the ivories at the parlor's grand piano or read a novel beneath the Tiffany stained-glass ceiling of the wood-paneled sitting room.

Mache Bistro FRENCH $$

(207-288-0447; www.machebistro.com; 321 Main St; mains $21-32; 5:30-9pm Tue-Sat May-Oct;) A strong contender for Bar Harbor's best midrange restaurant, Mache serves contemporary, French-inflected fare in a stylishly renovated cottage. The changing menu highlights the local riches – think sustainably harvested scallops on fennel salad, slow-cooked duck-leg confit and wild blueberry trifle. Specialty cocktails add to the appeal. Reservations are suggested, but the bar is open to walk-ins.

★ Havana LATIN AMERICAN $$$

(207-288-2822; www.havanamaine.com; 318 Main St; mains $30-42; 4:30-9pm Tue-Sat May-Oct, plus 9:30am-2pm Sun Jul & Aug) First things first: order a refreshing mojito or caipirinha. Then you can take your time with the menu and the epic global wine list. Havana puts a Latin spin on dishes that highlight local produce, and the kitchen output is accomplished. Signature dishes include seafood paella, braised lamb shank and a deliciously light lobster *moqueca* (Brazilian-style stew with coconut milk).

Inland Maine

Western Maine receives far fewer visitors than the coast, which thrills the outdoorsy types who love its dense forests and solitary peaks just the way they are. While much of the land is still wilderness, there are some notable settlements. The fine old town of Bethel and the mountain setting of Rangeley are relatively accessible to city dwellers in the northeast, while Bridgton's quirky offerings make it a cool weekend retreat.

In the fall, leaf-peepers make their way inland with cameras and picnic baskets. In winter, skiers and snowmobilers turn the mountains into their playground. In the warmer months, the lakes, rivers, campgrounds and hiking trails draw lovers of the great outdoors.

This is rural America at its most rustic. So bring a map and don't expect to rely on your cell phone – signals can be few and far between in these parts.

Getting Around

A car is necessary to explore this rustic, rural heartland, and there are many scenic routes to choose from. ME 302 from Portland to Bridgton and Fryeburg is a good start; you can then wend your way north to Bethel and Rangeley. Scenic overlooks abound.

Bethel

A 90-minute drive northwest of Portland, Bethel is surprisingly lively and refined for a town surrounded on all sides by deep, dark woods. Summer visitors have been coming here to escape the coastal humidity since the 1800s, and many of its fine old cottages and lodges are still operating. It's a prime spot to be in during Maine's colorful fall-foliage months and during the winter ski season.

If you head west on US 2 toward New Hampshire, be sure to admire the **Shelburne birches**, a high concentration of the white-barked trees that grow between Gilead and Shelburne.

Grafton Notch State Park STATE PARK

(207-824-2912; www.maine.gov/graftonnotch; 1941 Bear River Rd/ME 26; adult/child $4/1; 9am-sunset) Sitting astride the Grafton Notch Scenic Byway within the Mahoosuc Range, this rugged park is a stunner. Carved by a glacier that retreated 12,000 years ago, the Notch is a four-season playground, chock-full of waterfalls, gorges, lofty viewpoints and hiking trails, including over 20 miles of the Appalachian Trail (www.appalachiantrail.org).

Peregrine falcons build nests in the cliffs, helping the park earn its spot on the **Maine Birding Trail** (www.mainebirdingtrail.com); the best viewing is May to October.

Information

Bethel Area Chamber of Commerce (800-442-5826, 207-824-2282; www.bethelmaine.com; 8 Station Pl; 9am-5pm Mon-Fri year-round, weekend hours vary in high season;) This helpful organization maintains an information office in the Bethel Station building, with loads of handouts on various sights, trails and activities.

Washington, DC & the Capital Region

Best Places to Eat

➡ Rose's Luxury (p286)

➡ Woodberry Kitchen (p299)

➡ L'Opossum (p325)

➡ Public Fish & Oyster (p328)

➡ Faidley's (p299)

Best Places to Sleep

➡ Kimpton George Hotel (p283)

➡ Inn at 2920 (p298)

➡ Georges (p332)

➡ HI Richmond (p325)

Why Go?

No matter your politics, it's hard not to fall for the nation's capital. Iconic monuments and vast (and free) museums are just the beginning of the great DC experience. There's much more to discover: leafy, cobblestoned neighborhoods, sprawling markets, heady multicultural nightspots and global cuisine. And, of course, the corridors of power. Beyond the Beltway, the diverse landscapes of Maryland, Virginia, West Virginia and Delaware offer potent enticement to travel beyond the marble city.

Craggy mountains, rushing rivers, rich nature reserves (including islands where wild horses run), sparkling beaches, historic villages and the magnificent Chesapeake Bay form the backdrop to memorable adventures: sailing, hiking, rafting, camping or just sitting on a pretty stretch of shoreline, planning the next seafood feast. It's a place where traditions run deep, from the nation's birthplace to Virginia's bluegrass scene.

When to Go
Washington DC

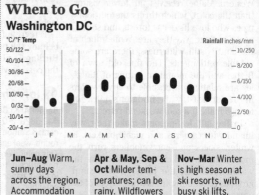

Jun–Aug Warm, sunny days across the region. Accommodation prices peak (up 30% on average).	**Apr & May, Sep & Oct** Milder temperatures; can be rainy. Wildflowers bloom, especially in May.	**Nov–Mar** Winter is high season at ski resorts, with busy ski lifts, accomodations and restaurants.

History

The modern story of America began in 1607 when a determined band of colonists built a fort on the banks of the James River, VA. Named Jamestown, this small community would become the New World's first permanent English settlement. Ever since, residents of the Mid-Atlantic have witnessed – and sparked – transformational moments in American history: wars against the British, the creation of a new nation, slavery and its abolishment, the Civil War and Reconstruction, and the labor and Civil Rights movements.

WASHINGTON, DC

The US capital is home to the corridors of power, where visionaries and demagogues roam. Along with that comes presidential monuments and war memorials, green parks and fantastic museums. Beyond the National Mall, visitors will discover tree-lined neighborhoods, vibrant immigrant populations, and a palpable dynamism percolating just beneath the surface. There's always a buzz here – no surprise, as DC attracts more talent than any city of this size deserves. Plan on jam-packed days sightseeing at museums and monuments, and lively evenings sipping local brews and chowing down in diverse restaurants.

History

Following the Revolutionary War, a balance was struck between Northern and Southern politicians, who wanted to plant a federal city somewhere between their power bases. Potential capitals such as Boston, Philadelphia and Baltimore were rejected by Southern plantation owners, for being too urban-industrial, so it was decided a new city would be carved at the midway point of the 13 colonies, along the banks of the Potomac River. Maryland and Virginia donated the land.

DC was torched by the British during the War of 1812, and ceded the south-bank slave port of Alexandria to Virginia in 1846 (when abolition talk was buzzing in the capital). Over the years, DC evolved along diverging tracks: as a marbled temple to the federal government on one side, and as an urban ghetto for northbound African Americans and overseas immigrants on the other. For decades, the city was governed by the US Congress. The city finally got its own mayor in 1973 (Walter Washington, among the first African American mayors of a major American city). Today DC residents are taxed as other American citizens, yet they lack a voting seat in Congress. DC has undergone extensive gentrification since the late 1990s. A booming economy ensures that the cost of living continues to be among the highest in the nation.

◎ Sights

◎ National Mall

A nation is many things: its people, its history, its politics and its amassed knowledge. Somehow, each one of these is given architectural life on the National Mall, the center of iconography of the most iconic city in America. This is where the nation's ideals are expressed in educational institutions, monuments and memorials. It's also where Americans come to protest, to rally and to watch presidents get inaugurated. A monument-studded park edged by the magnificent Smithsonian museums, this must-visit destination provides days – if not weeks – of enjoyment and edification for visitors.

★ **Lincoln Memorial** MONUMENT
(☏ 202-426-6841; www.nps.gov/linc; 2 Lincoln Memorial Circle NW; ◎ 24hr; ▣ Circulator National Mall, Ⓜ Orange, Silver, Blue Line to Foggy Bottom-GWU) Anchoring the Mall's west end is the hallowed shrine to Abraham Lincoln, who gazes across the **Reflecting Pool** beneath his neoclassical, Doric-columned abode. The words of his Gettysburg Address and Second Inaugural speech flank the huge marble statue on the north and south walls. On the steps, Martin Luther King Jr delivered his famed 'I Have a Dream' speech; look for the engraving that marks the spot (it's on the landing 18 stairs from the top).

★ **National Air & Space Museum** MUSEUM
(☏ 202-633-2214; www.airandspace.si.edu; cnr 6th St & Independence Ave SW; ◎ 10am-5:30pm; ▦; ▣ Circulator National Mall, Ⓜ Orange, Silver, Blue, Green, Yellow Line to L'Enfant Plaza) FREE The legendary exhibits at this hugely popular museum include the Wright brothers' flyer, Chuck Yeager's Bell X-1, Charles Lindbergh's Spirit of St Louis, Howard Hughes'

WASHINGTON, DC & THE CAPITAL REGION WASHINGTON, DC

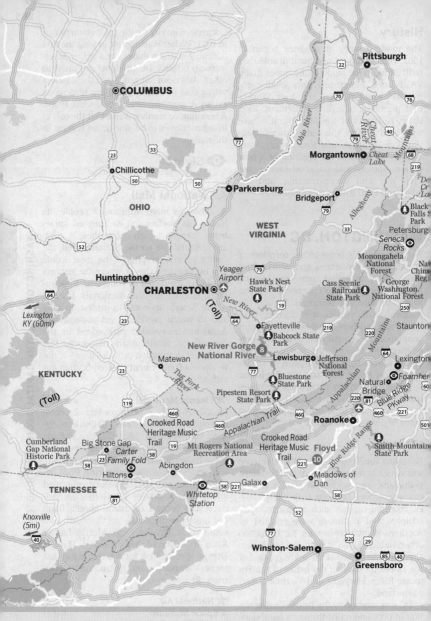

Washington, DC & the Capital Region Highlights

1 **National Air & Space Museum** (p265) Visiting Washington, DC's museums.

2 **Lincoln Memorial** (p265) Watching the sun set over the monument.

3 **Colonial Williamsburg** (p318) Tracing America's roots at this living-history museum.

4 **Annapolis** (p301) Exploring the city's historic and nautical past with a stroll

through the capitol, the Naval Academy and along Main St.

5 **Shenandoah National Park** (p330) Taking a Sunday drive on Skyline Drive, followed

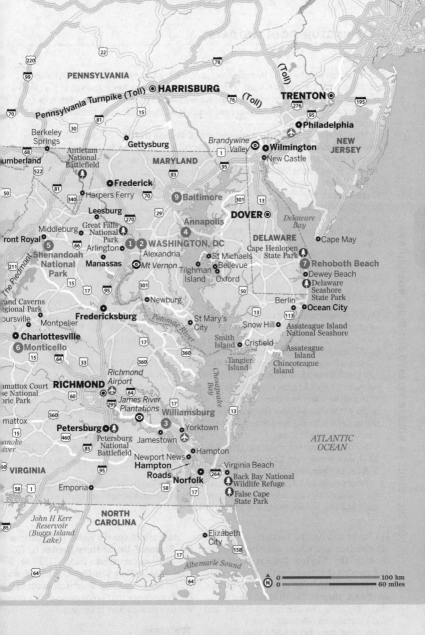

by hiking and camping under the stars.

6 Monticello (p326) Marveling at Thomas Jefferson's masterpiece.

7 Rehoboth Beach (p309) Strolling the boardwalk in this family- and gay-friendly resort.

8 New River Gorge National River (p341) Tackling the Gauley River rapids.

9 Faidley's (p299) Savoring one of the world's best crab cakes in Baltimore.

10 Floyd (p335) Feeling the beat of the old-time music at a jamboree.

WASHINGTON, DC IN TWO DAYS...

Day One

You might as well dive right into the good stuff, and the Lincoln Memorial (p265) is about as iconically DC as it gets. It's also a convenient starting point, since Abe sits at the far end of the Mall. Next up as you walk east is the powerful Vietnam Veterans Memorial. Then comes the Washington Monument, which is pretty hard to miss, being DC's tallest structure and all.

Munch sandwiches by an artsy waterfall at **Cascade Café** (☏ 202-842-6679; www.nga.gov/visit/cafes/cascade-cafe.html; National Gallery of Art, Constitution Ave NW, East Bldg, concourse; sandwiches $7-9.50; ⊙11am-3pm Mon-Sat, to 4pm Sun; ☝; ☐ Circulator National Mall, Ⓜ Green, Yellow Line to Archives-Navy Memorial-Penn Quarter).

After lunch, it's time to explore the National Museum of African American History & Culture (assuming you've procured a ticket) or the National Gallery of Art. Pick a side: East, for modern; or West, for Impressionists and other classics. Afterward, mosey across the lawn to the National Air & Space Museum (p265) and gape at the stuff hanging from the ceiling. The missiles and the Wright Brothers' original plane are incomparably cool.

For dinner, hop the Metro to Bistrot du Coin (p288) in Dupont Circle, then sip cocktails at Bar Charley (p291), hoist brews with locals at Board Room (p291) or hit one of the dance clubs.

Day Two

Do the government thing this morning. Start in the Capitol (p276) and tour the statue-cluttered halls. Then walk across the street and up the grand steps to the Supreme Court (p277); hopefully you'll get to hear a case argument. The Library of Congress (p277) and its 532 miles of books blow minds next door.

Have a burger amid politicos at **Old Ebbitt Grill** (☏ 202-347-4800; www.ebbitt.com; 675 15th St NW, White House Area; mains $18-32; ⊙7:30am-1am Mon-Fri, from 8:30am Sat & Sun, happy hour 3-6pm & 11pm-1am; Ⓜ Red, Orange, Silver, Blue Line to Metro Center).

Hopefully you planned ahead and booked a White House (p278) tour. If not, make do at the White House Visitor Center (p278). Pop into Off the Record (p290) to see if any bigwigs and lobbyists are clinking glasses. Zip over to the Kennedy Center (p292) to watch the free 6pm show.

For dinner, have French fare at Chez Billy Sud (p289) or pizza at **Il Canale** (☏ 202-337-4444; www.ilcanale.com; 1065 31st St NW; mains $23-32; ⊙11:30am-10:30pm Mon-Thu, to 11pm Fri & Sat, to 10pm Sun; ☐ Circulator Georgetown-Union Station).

After dinner, sink a pint in a friendly pub such as the Tombs (p292). On warm nights the outdoor cafes and boating action make Georgetown Waterfront Park (p281) a hot spot. And check if anyone cool is playing at 9:30 Club (p292).

H-1 Racer and Amelia Earhart's natty Vega 5B. Children and adults alike love walking through the **Skylab Orbital Workshop** and viewing the 'Apollo to the Moon' exhibit upstairs. Immersive experiences include an IMAX theater (adult/child two to 12 years $9/7.50), planetarium ($9/7.50) and flight simulators ($8 to $12 each).

On most days from mid-March to early September, the museum extends its hours and stays open until 7:30pm. Exhibits are being overhauled until 2025, with new exhibits such as 'Destination Moon', a comprehensive look at the history of lunar exploration, being added. Other exhibitions will be refreshed.

More avionic pieces reside in Virginia at the **Steven F Udvar-Hazy Center** (☏ 703-572-4118; www.airandspace.si.edu; 14390 Air & Space Museum Pkwy, Chantilly; ⊙10am-5:30pm; ☝; Ⓜ Silver Line to Wiehle-Reston East for bus 983) **FREE**, an annex that holds more of this museum's extraordinary collection.

★**Vietnam Veterans Memorial**　MONUMENT (www.nps.gov/vive; 5 Henry Bacon Dr NW; ⊙24hr; ☐ Circulator National Mall, Ⓜ Orange, Silver, Blue Line to Foggy Bottom-GWU) Maya Lin's design for this hugely evocative memorial takes the form of a black, low-lying 'V' – an expression of the psychic scar wrought by the Vietnam War. The monument descends into the earth, with the names of the war's 58,000-plus American casualties – listed in the order they died – chiseled into the dark, reflective wall. It's a subtle but profound monument – and all the more surprising as Lin was only 21 when she designed it.

★ National Gallery of Art MUSEUM

(📞 202-737-4215; www.nga.gov; Constitution Ave NW, btwn 3rd & 7th Sts; ⊙10am-5pm Mon-Sat, 11am-6pm Sun; 🚻; 🚇Circulator National Mall, Ⓜ Green, Yellow Line to Archives-Navy Memorial-Penn Quarter) FREE Two buildings. Hundreds of masterpieces. Infinite enjoyment. The neoclassical **West Building** showcases European art through to the early 1900s; highlights include works by da Vinci, Manet, Monet and Van Gogh. The IM Pei-designed **East Building** displays modern and contemporary art – don't miss Pollock's *Number 1, 1950 (Lavender Mist),* Picasso's *Family of Saltimbanques* and the massive Calder mobile specially commissioned for the entrance lobby. An underground walkway connects the buildings and is made extraordinary by Leo Villareal's light sculpture, *Multiverse.*

Washington Monument MONUMENT

(www.nps.gov/wamo; 2 15th St NW; 🚇Circulator National Mall, Ⓜ Orange, Silver, Blue Line to Smithsonian) FREE Peaking at 555ft (and 5in) and composed of 36,000 blocks of stone, the Washington Monument is the district's tallest structure. Political shenanigans followed by the Civil War interrupted its construction. When work began anew, a new quarry sourced the marble; note the delineation in color where the old and new marble meet about a third of the way up. The monument is currently closed for repairs; check the website for reopening info.

Martin Luther King Jr Memorial MONUMENT

(www.nps.gov/mlkm; 1964 Independence Ave SW; ⊙24hr; 🚇Circulator National Mall, Ⓜ Orange, Silver, Blue Line to Smithsonian) Opened in 2011, this was the first Mall memorial to honor an African American. Sculptor Lei Yixin carved the piece, which is reminiscent in concept and style to the Mt Rushmore memorial. Besides Dr King's striking, 30ft-tall image, known as the Stone of Hope, there are two blocks of granite behind him that represent the Mountain of Despair. A

wall inscribed with King's powerful quotes about democracy, justice and peace flanks the piece.

★ National Museum of African American History & Culture MUSEUM

(📞 844-750-3012; www.nmaahc.si.edu; 1400 Constitution Ave NW; ⊙10am-5:30pm; 🚻; 🚇Circulator National Mall, Ⓜ Orange, Silver, Blue Line to Smithsonian or Federal Triangle) FREE This sensational museum covers the diverse African American experience and how it helped shape the nation. Start downstairs in the sobering 'Slavery and Freedom' exhibition and work your way up to the community and culture galleries on the 3rd and 4th floors, where African American achievements in sport, music, theater and visual arts are joyfully celebrated. Artifacts, state-of-the-art interactive exhibits, site-specific artworks and fascinating interpretive panels abound in the cleverly designed and dramatically lit exhibition spaces.

National Gallery of Art Sculpture Garden GARDENS

(www.nga.gov; cnr Constitution Ave NW & 7th St NW; ⊙10am-7pm Mon-Thu & Sat, to 9:30pm Fri, 11am-7pm Sun late May-early Oct, 10am-5pm Mon-Sat, 11am-6pm Sun early Oct-late May; 🚻; 🚇Circulator National Mall, Ⓜ Green, Yellow Line to Archives-Navy Memorial-Penn Quarter) FREE This 6-acre garden is studded with whimsical sculptures such as Roy Lichtenstein's *House I* (1998), a giant Claes Oldenburg typewriter eraser (1999) and Roxy Paine's *Graft* (2008–09), a stainless-steel tree. They are scattered around a fountain – a great place to dip your feet in summer.

From mid-November to mid-March the fountain is transformed into an **ice rink** (📞 202-216-9397; www.nga.gov/visit/ice-rink.html; adult/child 12yr & under $9/8, skate rental $4; ⊙10am-9pm Mon-Thu, to 11pm Fri, 11am-11pm Sat, 11am-9pm Sun mid-Nov–mid-Mar), and the garden stays open a bit later.

The garden's **Pavilion Cafe** (📞 202-289-3361; www.pavilioncafe.com; sandwiches $10-12, salads $11-13; ⊙10am-4pm Mon-Sat, 11am-5pm Sun, seasonal late openings) is a popular spot to grab a bite or coffee.

National Museum of Natural History MUSEUM

(📞 202-663-1000; www.naturalhistory.si.edu; cnr 10th St & Constitution Ave NW; ⊙10am-5:30pm, to 7:30pm some days; 🚻; 🚇Circulator National Mall, Ⓜ Orange, Silver, Blue Line to Smithsonian

Washington, DC

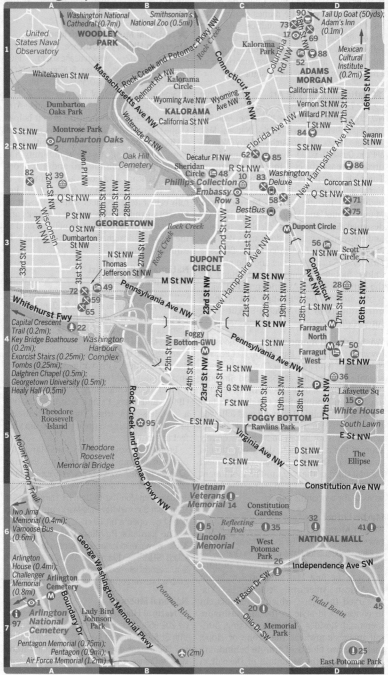

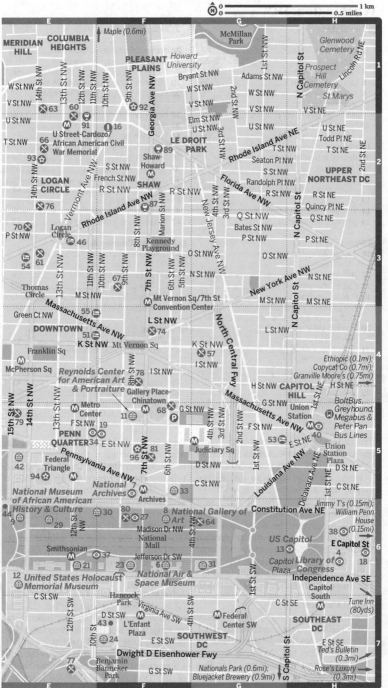

Washington, DC

or Federal Triangle) FREE Arguably the most popular of the Smithsonian museums, so crowds are pretty much guaranteed. Wave to Henry, the elephant who guards the rotunda, then zip to the 2nd floor's Hope Diamond, a 45.52-karat bauble that's said to have cursed its owners, which included Marie Antoinette. The giant squid (1st floor, Ocean Hall), live butterfly pavilion and tarantula feedings provide additional thrills at this kid-packed venue. The beloved dinosaur hall, centered on the Nation's T-Rex, has reopened after being revamped.

National Museum of American History
MUSEUM

(☎202-633-1000; www.americanhistory.si.edu; 1300 Constitution Ave NW, btwn 12th and 14th Sts NW; ◎10am-5:30pm, to 7:30pm some days; ⊞; ⊟ Circulator National Mall, Ⓜ Orange, Silver, Blue Line to Smithsonian or Federal Triangle) FREE

Containing all kinds of artifacts of the American experience, this museum has as its centerpiece the flag that flew over Baltimore's Fort McHenry during the War of 1812 – the same flag that inspired Francis Scott Key to pen 'The Star-Spangled Banner' (it's on the entry level). Other highlights include Julia Child's kitchen (1st floor) and 'The First Ladies' costume exhibit on the 3rd floor. New exhibits include 'American Enterprise' (1st floor) and 'On with the Show' (3rd floor).

Jefferson Memorial
MONUMENT

(☎202-426-6841; www.nps.gov/thje; 13 E Basin Dr SW; ◎24hr; ⊟Circulator National Mall, Ⓜ Orange, Silver, Blue Line to Smithsonian) Set on the south bank of the Tidal Basin amid the cherry trees, this memorial honors the third US president, political philosopher, drafter of the Declaration of Independence and founder of the University of Virginia. Designed by John Russell Pope in the style of the ancient Roman Pantheon, the rounded, open-air monument was initially derided by critics as 'the Jefferson Muffin.' Inside is a 19ft bronze likeness, and excerpts from Jefferson's writings are etched into the walls.

National WWII Memorial MONUMENT
(www.nps.gov/wwii; 17th St SW; ⊙24hr; ☐Circulator National Mall, MOrange, Silver, Blue Line to Smithsonian) Dedicated in 2004, this grandiose memorial honors the 16 million US soldiers who served in WWII. Groups of veterans regularly come here to pay their respects to the 400,000 Americans who died as a result of the conflict. The plaza's dual arches symbolize victory in the Atlantic and Pacific theaters, and the 56 surrounding pillars represent each US state and territory.

Hirshhorn Museum MUSEUM
(☎202-633-1000; www.hirshhorn.si.edu; cnr 7th St & Independence Ave SW; ⊙10am-5:30pm; ☐; ☐Circulator National Mall, MOrange, Silver, Blue, Green, Yellow Line to L'Enfant Plaza) FREE The Smithsonian's cylindrical art museum shows works from modernism's early days to today's most cutting-edge practitioners. Exhibitions of works drawn from the museum's extensive collection are offered alongside curated shows of work by prominent contemporary artists. Visitors can relax in the 3rd-floor sitting area, which has couches, floor-to-ceiling windows and a balcony offering Mall views. A lobby redesign by Japanese artist Hiroshi Sugimoto opened in 2018, and includes **Dolcezza at the Hirshhorn** (www.dolcezzagelato.com; gelato $4, pastries $2-7; ⊙9am-5pm Mon-Fri, from 10am Sat & Sun; ☎), a gelato and coffee bar.

WASHINGTON, DC & THE CAPITAL REGION WASHINGTON, DC

National Mall

A DAY TOUR

Folks often call the Mall 'America's Front Yard,' and that's a pretty good analogy. It is indeed a lawn, unfurling scrubby green grass from the Capitol west to the Lincoln Memorial. It's also America's great public space, where citizens come to protest their government, go for scenic runs and connect with the nation's most cherished ideals writ large in stone, landscaping, monuments and memorials.

You can sample quite a bit in a day, but it'll be a full one that requires roughly 4 miles of walking.

Start at the ❶ **Vietnam Veterans Memorial** then head counterclockwise around the Mall, swooping in on the ❷ **Lincoln Memorial**, ❸ **Martin Luther King Jr Memorial** and ❹ **Washington Monument**. You can also pause for the cause of the Korean War and WWII, among other monuments that dot the Mall's western portion.

Martin Luther King Jr Memorial

Walk all the way around the towering statue of Dr King by Lei Yixin and read the quotes. His likeness, incidentally, is 11ft taller than Lincoln and Jefferson in their memorials.

Smithsonian Castle

Seek out the tomb of James Smithson, the eccentric Englishman whose 1826 financial gift launched the Smithsonian Institution. His crypt is in a room by the Mall entrance.

Tidal Basin

Department of Agriculture

National Air and Space Museum

Simply step inside and look up, and you'll be impressed. Lindbergh's *Spirit of St Louis* and Chuck Yeager's sound barrier–breaking Bell X-1 are among the machines hanging from the ceiling.

West Building

East Building

❺

❻

❼

National Museum of the American Indian

US Capitol

Then it's onward to the museums, all fabulous and all free. Begin at the 5 **Smithsonian Castle** to get your bearings – and to say thanks to the guy making all this awesomeness possible – and commence browsing through the 6 **National Air & Space Museum**, 7 **National Gallery of Art & National Sculpture Garden** and 8 **National Museum of African American History and Culture**.

TOP TIPS

Start early, especially in summer. You'll avoid the crowds, but more importantly you'll avoid the blazing heat. Try to finish with the monuments and be in the air-conditioned museums by 10:30am. Also, consider bringing snacks, since the only food available is from scattered cart vendors and museum cafes.

Lincoln Memorial

Commune with Abe in his chair, then head down the steps to the marker where Martin Luther King Jr gave his 'Dream' speech. The view of the Reflecting Pool and Washington Monument is one of DC's best.

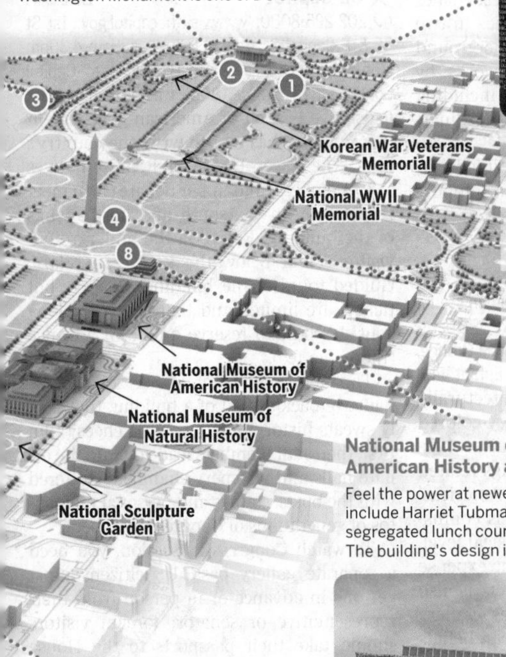
1
2
3
4
8
Korean War Veterans Memorial
National WWII Memorial
National Museum of American History
National Museum of Natural History
National Sculpture Garden

ADAM PARENT / SHUTTERSTOCK ©

Vietnam Veterans Memorial

Check the symbol that's beside each name. A diamond indicates 'killed, body recovered.' A plus sign indicates 'missing and unaccounted for.' There are approximately 1200 of the latter.

Washington Monument

As you approach the obelisk, look a third of the way up. See how it's slightly lighter in color at the bottom? Builders had to use different marble after the first source dried up.

National Museum of African American History and Culture

Feel the power at newest Smithsonian museum, where artifacts include Harriet Tubman's hymnal, Emmett Till's casket, a segregated lunch counter and Michael Jordan's sneakers. The building's design is based on a three-tiered Yoruban crown.

National Gallery of Art & National Sculpture Garden

Beeline to Gallery 6 (West Building) and ogle the Western Hemisphere's only Leonardo da Vinci painting. Outdoors, amble amid whimsical sculptures by Miró, Calder and Lichtenstein. Also check out IM Pei's design of the East Building.

RARRARORRO/SHUTTERSTOCK © ARCHITECT: DAVID ADJAYE

Smithsonian Castle
NOTABLE BUILDING

(☑ 202-633-1000; www.si.edu; 1000 Jefferson Dr SW; ⊙ 8:30am-5:30pm; ☑ Circulator National Mall, Ⓜ Orange, Silver, Blue Line to Smithsonian) James Renwick designed this turreted, red-sandstone fairy-tale in 1855. Today the castle houses the **Smithsonian Visitor Center**, which makes a good first stop on the Mall. Inside you'll find history exhibits, multilingual touch-screen displays, a staffed information desk, free maps, a cafe and the tomb of James Smithson, the institution's founder. His crypt lies inside a little room by the main entrance off the Mall.

Freer | Sackler
MUSEUM

(☑ 202-633-1000; www.asia.si.edu; 1050 Independence Ave SW; ⊙ 10am-5:30pm; ☑ Circulator National Mall, Ⓜ Orange, Silver, Blue Line to Smithsonian) FREE This is a lovely spot in which to while away a Washington afternoon. Japanese silk scrolls, smiling Buddhas, rare Islamic manuscripts and Chinese jades are exhibited in cool, quiet galleries in two museums connected by an underground tunnel. The Freer also houses works by American painter James Whistler, including five *Nocturnes*. Don't miss the extraordinarily beautiful blue-and-gold Peacock Room on its ground floor, designed by Whistler in 1876–77 as an exotic showcase for a shipping magnate's Chinese porcelain collection.

National Museum of the American Indian
MUSEUM

(☑ 202-663-1000; www.americanindian.si.edu; cnr 4th St & Independence Ave SW; ⊙ 10am-5:30pm; ☒; ☑ Circulator National Mall, Ⓜ Orange, Silver, Blue, Green, Yellow Line to L'Enfant Plaza) FREE Ensconced in an architecturally notable building clad in honey-colored limestone, this museum offers cultural artifacts, videos and audio recordings related to the indigenous people of the Americas. Sadly, navigation of the exhibits is confusing on both a curatorial and physical level. The focus on didactic panels at the expense of interpretative labels for artifacts is also problematic. The 'Our Universes' gallery (on Level 4) about Native American beliefs and creation stories is one of the more interesting exhibits.

Franklin Delano Roosevelt Memorial
MONUMENT

(www.nps.gov/frde; 400 W Basin Dr SW; ⊙ 24hr; ☑ Circulator National Mall, Ⓜ Orange, Silver, Blue Line to Smithsonian) The 7.5-acre memorial pays tribute to the longest-serving president in US history. Visitors are taken through four red-granite areas that narrate FDR's time in office, from the Depression to the New Deal to WWII. The story is told through statuary and inscriptions, punctuated with fountains and peaceful alcoves. It's especially pretty at night, when the marble shimmers in the glossy stillness of the Tidal Basin.

◉ Capitol Hill

The city's geographic and legislative heart surprises by being mostly a row-house-lined residential neighborhood. The vast area holds top sights such as the dramatic Capitol, book-stuffed Library of Congress and heartbreaking Holocaust Memorial Museum, but creaky bookshops and cozy pubs also thrive here. The areas around Eastern Market and H St NE are locals' hubs, with good-time restaurants and nightlife.

★ US Capitol
LANDMARK

(☑ 202-226-8000; www.visitthecapitol.gov; 1st St SE & E Capitol St, Capitol Hill; ⊙ 8:30am-4:30pm Mon-Sat; Ⓜ Orange, Silver, Blue Line to Capitol South) FREE Since 1800, this is where the legislative branch of American government (ie Congress) has met to write the country's laws. The lower House of Representatives (435 members) and upper Senate (100) meet respectively in the south and north wings of the building. Enter via the underground visitor center below the East Front Plaza. Guided tours of the building are free, but tickets are limited and there's often a long wait. It's best to reserve online in advance (there's no fee).

The hour-long jaunt showcases the exhaustive background of a building that fairly sweats history. You'll watch a cheesy film first, then staff members lead you into the ornate halls and whispery chambers cluttered with the busts, statues and personal mementos of generations of Congress members.

To watch Congress in session, you need a separate gallery pass. US citizens must get one in advance or in person from their representative or senator; foreign visitors should take their passports to the House and Senate Appointment Desks on the upper level. Congressional committee hearings are more interesting (and substantive) if you care about what's being debated; check for a schedule, locations and to see if they're open to the public (they often are) at www.house. gov and www.senate.gov.

Security measures here are strict, including no food, liquid or bags larger than 18in by 4in.

★ **United States**
Holocaust Memorial Museum MUSEUM
(☎202-488-0400; www.ushmm.org; 100 Raoul Wallenberg Pl SW, South DC; ☉10am-5:20pm, extended hours Apr–mid-Jun; 🚌Circulator, Ⓜ Orange, Silver, Blue Line to Smithsonian) FREE For a deep understanding of the Holocaust – its victims, perpetrators and bystanders – this harrowing museum is a must-see. The main exhibit gives visitors the identity card of a single Holocaust victim, whose story is revealed as you take a winding route into a hellish past marked by ghettos, rail cars and death camps. It also shows the flip side of human nature, documenting the risks many citizens took to help the persecuted.

★ **Library of Congress** LIBRARY
(☎202-707-8000; www.loc.gov; 10 1st St SE, Capitol Hill; ☉8:30am-4:30pm Mon-Sat; Ⓜ Orange, Silver, Blue Line to Capitol South) FREE The world's largest library – with 164 million books, manuscripts, maps, photos, films and other items – awes in both scope and design. The centerpiece is the 1897 **Jefferson Building**. Gawk at the **Great Hall**, done up in stained glass, marble and mosaics of mythical characters, then seek out the **Gutenberg Bible** (c 1455), Thomas Jefferson's round library and the reading room viewing area. Free tours of the building take place between 10:30am and 3:30pm on the half-hour.

Supreme Court LANDMARK
(☎202-479-3000; www.supremecourt.gov; 1 1st St NE, Capitol Hill; ☉9am-4:30pm Mon-Fri; Ⓜ Orange, Silver, Blue Line to Capitol South) FREE The highest court in the USA occupies a pseudo-Greek temple protected by 13,000lb bronze doors. Arrive early to watch arguments (periodic Monday through Wednesday from October to April). You can visit the permanent exhibits and the building's two five-story, marble-and-bronze spiral staircases year-round. On days when court is not in session you can also hear lectures (every hour on the half-hour beginning 9:30am) in the courtroom. Be sure to exit via the doors that lead to the regal front steps.

THE WHARF

The Southwest Waterfront has long been home to the Maine Avenue Fish Market (p285), but the area was otherwise unremarkable – until the Wharf shot up. The huge complex of restaurants, hotels, entertainment venues, parks and piers officially opened in late 2017, and now it buzzes.

The public piers are the niftiest bits. The **Transit Pier** (950 Wharf St SW, Transit Pier; Ⓜ Orange, Silver, Blue, Yellow, Green Lines to L'Enfant Plaza or Green Line to Waterfront) has a winter ice rink, summer mini-golf course and small outdoor stage for free concerts. The Wharf water taxi departs from here, hence the name. The **District Pier** is the longest dock, jutting well out into the Washington Channel and hosting a big stage for festivals. The **Recreation Pier** makes for a fine stroll with its benches, swinging seats and boathouse for kayak and paddleboard rentals.

Loads of eateries sit waterside, including branches of **Shake Shack** (☎202-800-9930; www.shakeshack.com; 800 F St NW, Penn Quarter; mains $5-10; ☉11am-11pm Sun-Thu, to midnight Fri & Sat; Ⓜ Red, Yellow, Green Line to Gallery Pl-Chinatown), Hank's Oyster Bar (p288), Rappahannock Oyster Bar and **Dolcezza** (☎202-299-9116; www.dolcezzagelato.com; 1704 Connecticut Ave NW, Dupont Circle; gelato $6-8; ☉7am-10pm Mon-Thu, 7am-11pm Fri, 8am-11pm Sat, 8am-10pm Sun; 🐾; Ⓜ Red Line to Dupont Circle). Swanky new spots seem to open weekly. The **Anthem** (☎202-888-0020; www.theanthemdc.com; 901 Wharf St SW, South DC; ☉box office noon-7pm, to 9pm show days; Ⓜ Orange, Silver, Blue, Yellow, Green Line to L'Enfant Plaza or Green Line to Waterfront) and **Pearl Street Warehouse** (☎202-380-9620; www.pearlstreetwarehouse.com; 33 Pearl St SW, South DC; ☉4pm-midnight Mon-Wed, 8:30am-2am Thu-Sat, 9am-midnight Sun; Ⓜ Orange, Silver, Blue, Yellow, Green Line to L'Enfant Plaza or Green Line to Waterfront) are fab venues for live music. **Politics & Prose** (☎202-488-3867; www.politics-prose.com/wharf; 70 District Sq SW, South DC; ☉10am-10pm; Ⓜ Orange, Silver, Blue, Yellow, Green Line to L'Enfant Plaza or Green Line to Waterfront) brings the books. And more is on the way, as you'll see from the ongoing construction that will add to the Wharf for the next several years.

Folger Shakespeare Library LIBRARY
(☑ 202-544-4600; www.folger.edu; 201 E Capitol St SE, Capitol Hill; ⊗ 10am-5pm Mon-Sat, noon-5pm Sun; Ⓜ Orange, Silver, Blue Line to Capitol South) **FREE** Bard-o-philes will be all aflutter here, as the library holds the world's largest collection of old Billy's works. Stroll through the Great Hall to see a changing exhibit of Elizabethan artifacts, paintings, etchings and manuscripts. The highlight is the chance to peek at one of the library's First Folios, the first printed collection of Shakespeare's plays, published in 1623. Pop into the on-site Elizabethan-inspired **theater** (www.folger.edu/folger-theatre; tickets from $30); it's worth returning in the evening to catch a show.

⊙ White House & Foggy Bottom

Play image association with the words 'Washington, DC,' and chances are the first thing that comes to mind is the White House. The president's pad is likely to take your breath away the first time you see it, not least because you're standing in front of a building whose image you've seen a thousand times before. The surrounding streets are equally impressive, with handsome building stock and a bustle that comes courtesy of this neighborhood's role as America's center of bureaucratic and political business (or should that be shenanigans?).

★ **White House** LANDMARK
(☑ 202-208-1631, 24hr info 202-456-7041; www.whitehouse.gov; 1600 Pennsylvania Ave NW, White House Area; ⊗ tours 7:30-11:30am Tue-Thu, to 1:30pm Fri & Sat; Ⓜ Orange, Silver, Blue Line to Federal Triangle or McPherson Sq) **FREE** The 'President's House,' built between 1792 and 1800, is an iconic, imposing building that's thrilling to see but difficult to access. Tours must be pre-arranged: Americans must apply via one of their members of Congress; non-Americans must ask their country's embassy in DC for assistance – in reality, there's only a slim chance that the embassy will be able to help source tickets. If you're lucky enough to visit, you'll see several public rooms in the main residence via self-guided tour.

White House Visitor Center MUSEUM
(☑ 202-208-1631; www.nps.gov/whho; 1450 Pennsylvania Ave NW, White House Area; ⊗ 7:30am-4pm; Ⓜ Orange, Silver, Blue Lines to Federal Triangle) **FREE** Getting inside the White House can be difficult, so here is your back-up plan. Housed in the splendiferous 1932 Patent Search Room of the Department of Commerce building, this center has plenty of artifacts, anecdote-packed information panels and informative multimedia exhibits, including a presentation on the history and lives of the presidential families and an interactive touchscreen tour of the White House. It's obviously not the same as seeing the real deal firsthand, but is well worth visiting regardless.

Renwick Gallery MUSEUM
(☑ 202-633-7970; www.renwick.americanart.si.edu; 1661 Pennsylvania Ave NW, White House Area; ⊗ 10am-5:30pm; Ⓜ Orange, Silver, Blue Line to Farragut West) **FREE** Part of the Smithsonian group, the Renwick Gallery is set in a stately 1859 mansion on the same block of Pennsylvania as the White House. It's emerged as a showcase for modern and contemporary artists who use innovative techniques and materials, redefining what 'craft' is and taking contemporary arts and crafts in daring new directions. Recent shows include an interactive homage to Burning Man, and 'WONDER,' with nine artists creating site-specific installations.

⊙ Downtown & Penn Quarter

Penn Quarter forms around Pennsylvania Ave as it runs between the White House and the Capitol. Downtown extends north beyond it. Major sights include the National Archives, a trove of eye-popping documents; the Reynolds Center for American Art & Portraiture, hanging big-name works; and Ford's Theatre, where Abraham Lincoln was assassinated. This is also DC's entertainment district and convention hub, so the place bustles day and night. Heaps of hot bars and restaurants provide sustenance.

★ **National Archives** LANDMARK
(☑ 866-272-6272; www.archives.gov/museum; 701 Constitution Ave NW, Penn Quarter; ⊗ 10am-5:30pm; Ⓜ Green, Yellow Line to Archives-Navy Memorial-Penn Quarter) **FREE** It's hard not to feel a little in awe of the big three documents in the Archives: the Declaration of Independence, the Constitution and the Bill of Rights. Taken together, it becomes clear just how radical the American experiment was. The archival bric-a-brac of the **Public Vaults** makes a flashy rejoinder to the main

exhibit. You can reserve tickets (www.recreation.gov) for $1.50 and use the fast-track entrance on Constitution Ave (especially recommended in spring and summer).

Newseum
MUSEUM

(📞 202-292-6100; www.newseum.org; 555 Pennsylvania Ave NW, Penn Quarter; adult/child $25/15; ⏰ 9am-5pm Mon-Sat, from 10am Sun; 🚇; Ⓜ Green, Yellow Line to Archives-Navy Memorial-Penn Quarter) This six-story, highly interactive news museum is worth the admission price. You can delve into major events (the fall of the Berlin Wall, September 11, Hurricane Katrina), and spend hours watching moving film footage and perusing Pulitzer Prize–winning photographs. If nothing else, stroll up to the museum's entrance, where the front pages of newspapers from around the world – and every US state – are displayed. Tickets are usable for two consecutive days, so you can always return.

Ford's Theatre Center
for Education & Leadership
MUSEUM

(📞 202-347-4833; www.fords.org; 511 10th St NW, Penn Quarter; ⏰ 9am-4:30pm; Ⓜ Red, Orange, Silver, Blue Line to Metro Center) FREE Across the street from the famous theater where Abraham Lincoln was shot, the center holds a gift shop on its 1st floor, as well as a 34ft tower of Lincoln books (it's actually an aluminum sculpture) – a testament to how much has been written about the 16th president. The 2nd, 3rd and 4th floors have excellent exhibits covering the aftermath of his assassination. Tickets, available at Ford's Theatre box office, are free and include the historic theater and Petersen House (516 10th St NW, Penn Quarter; ⏰ 9am-4:30pm; Ⓜ Red, Orange, Silver, Blue Line to Metro Center).

★ Reynolds Center
for American Art & Portraiture
MUSEUM

(📞 202-633-1000; www.americanart.si.edu; cnr 8th & F Sts NW, Penn Quarter; ⏰ 11:30am-7pm; Ⓜ Red, Yellow, Green Line to Gallery Pl-Chinatown) FREE The Reynolds Center is one of DC's finest museums. This Smithsonian venue combines the National Portrait Gallery and the American Art Museum into one whopping collection of American art that's unmatched anywhere in the world. Keep an eye out for famed works by Edward Hopper, Georgia O'Keeffe, Andy Warhol, Winslow Homer and loads more celebrated artists.

International Spy Museum
MUSEUM

(📞 202-393-7798; www.spymuseum.org; 700 L'Enfant Plaza SW, South DC; 🚇; Ⓜ Orange, Silver, Blue, Yellow, Green Line to L'Enfant Plaza) One of DC's most popular museums, the International Spy Museum delivers fun, interactive exhibits portraying the flashy, over-the-top world of intelligence gathering. Highlights include an immersive exhibit exploring communist Berlin, a Situation Room experience of the capture of Osama bin Laden, and an exploration of potential future cyber threats against international security.

◉ Logan Circle, U Street & Columbia Heights

The U St Corridor is the heart of this vast area and a fine spot to begin your explorations. A stroll here rewards with African American historic sights, soul food restaurants, mural-splashed alleys and red-hot music clubs. Spend an afternoon checking it out, or better yet, devote an evening to the nightlife scene.

U St becomes part of the larger Shaw district, which is one of DC's hottest 'hoods. But it's not annoyingly trendy. Instead, the breweries, bars and cafes that seem to pop up weekly are local places, where neighbors come to sip among neighbors. Logan Circle is next door and also booming. Walk down 14th St NW and it's stacked with dapper bars and bistros. An evening spent eating and drinking in the area is a must.

To the north, Columbia Heights is an enclave that mixes Latinx immigrants and hipsters. There are no real sights, but the cheap ethnic food and unassuming punk dive bars can occupy many an evening.

Further on, Northeast DC is a sprawl of leafy streets that hold uncommon sights. Nature lovers have a couple of groovy, free landscapes to explore, while those who like going off the beaten path can play in on-the-rise quarters such as distillery-rich Ivy City and arty, beery Brookland. You won't find many tourists out this way; it takes wheels or a lengthy public-transportation trip to reach most places.

African American
Civil War Memorial
MONUMENT

(www.afroamcivilwar.org; cnr U St NW & Vermont Ave NW, U Street; ⏰ 24hr; Ⓜ Green, Yellow Line to U St/African-American Civil War Memorial/Cardozo) Standing at the center of a granite plaza, this bronze memorial, *Spirit of Freedom*, depicting rifle-bearing troops is DC's first major art piece by black sculptor Ed Hamilton. The statue is surrounded on three sides by the Wall of Honor, listing the names of 209,145 African American troops who fought in the Union Army, as well as the 7000 white soldiers who served alongside them.

To look up individual names and find their location on the memorial, check the website's 'Colored Troops Search.' To reach the plaza, depart the Metro station via the 10th St exit (follow the 'memorial' signs as you leave the train).

Mexican Cultural Institute · CULTURAL CENTER
(☑ 202-728-1628; www.instituteofmexicodc.org; 2829 16th St NW, Columbia Heights; ☺10am-6pm Mon-Fri, noon-4pm Sat; ⓜGreen, Yellow Lines to Columbia Heights) FREE The Mexican Cultural Institute looks locked up and imposing, but don't be deterred. The gilded beaux-arts mansion is open to the public and hosts excellent art and cultural exhibitions related to Mexico. You might see a show on Diego Rivera's art, Mayan religious artifacts or Octavio Paz' writings. Ring the doorbell for entry.

◎ Dupont Circle & Kalorama

Dupont offers flashy new restaurants, hip bars, cafe society and cool bookstores. It's also the heart of the city's LGBTIQ+ community. It used to be where turn-of-the-20th-century millionaires lived. Today those mansions hold DC's greatest concentration of embassies. Kalorama sits in the northwest corner and ups the regal quotient.

★Embassy Row · ARCHITECTURE
(www.embassy.org; Massachusetts Ave NW, btwn Observatory & Dupont Circles NW, Dupont Circle; ⓜRed Line to Dupont Circle) Want to take a trip around the world? Stroll northwest along Massachusetts Ave from Dupont Circle (the actual traffic circle) and you pass more than 40 embassies housed in mansions that range from elegant to imposing to discreet. Tunisia, Chile, Turkmenistan, Togo, Haiti – flags flutter above heavy doors and mark the nations inside, while dark-windowed sedans ease out of driveways ferrying diplomats to and fro. The district has another 130 embassies sprinkled throughout, but this is the main vein.

National Geographic Museum · MUSEUM
(☑ 202-857-7700; www.nationalgeographic.org/dc; 1145 17th St NW, Dupont Circle; adult/child $15/10; ☺10am-6pm; ⓜRed Line to Farragut North) The museum at National Geographic Society headquarters can't compete with the Smithsonian's more extensive offerings, but it can be worth a stop, depending on what's showing. Exhibits are drawn from the society's well-documented expeditions to the far corners of the earth, and they change periodically.

★Phillips Collection · MUSEUM
(☑ 202-387-2151; www.phillipscollection.org; 1600 21st St NW, Dupont Circle; Tue-Fri free, Sat & Sun $10, ticketed exhibitions $12; ☺10am-5pm Tue, Wed, Fri & Sat, to 8:30pm Thu, noon-6:30pm Sun; ⓐCirculator Dupont Circle-Georgetown-Rosslyn, ⓜRed Line to Dupont Circle) The country's first modern-art museum (opened in 1921) houses a small but exquisite collection of European and American works. Renoir's *Luncheon of the Boating Party* is a highlight, along with pieces by Gauguin, Van Gogh, Matisse, Picasso and many other greats. The intimate rooms, set in a restored mansion and adjacent former apartment building, put you unusually close to the artworks. Download the free app or dial 202-595-1839 for audio tours through the works.

◎ Adams Morgan

Adams Morgan has long been Washington's fun, nightlife-driven party zone. It's also a global village of sorts. The result today is a raucous mash-up centered on 18th St NW. Vintage boutiques, record shops and ethnic eats poke up between thumping bars and a growing number of stylish spots for gastronomes.

District of Columbia Arts Center · ARTS CENTER
(DCAC; ☑ 202-462-7833; www.dcartscenter.org; 2438 18th St NW; ☺2-7pm Wed-Sun; ⓜRed Line to Woodley Park-Zoo/Adams Morgan) FREE The grassroots DCAC offers emerging artists a space to showcase their work. The 800-sq-ft gallery features rotating visual-arts exhibits, while plays, improv, avant-garde musicals and other theatrical productions take place in the 42-seat theater. The gallery is free and worth popping into to see what's showing.

Georgetown

Georgetown is DC's most aristocratic neighborhood, home to elite university students, ivory-tower academics and diplomats. Chichi brand-name shops, dark-wood pubs, snug cafes and upscale restaurants line the streets. Lovely parks and gardens color the edges, while sweet cycling trails roll out along the waterways.

★**Dumbarton Oaks**   GARDENS, MUSEUM
(⌨202-339-6400; www.doaks.org; 1703 32nd St NW; museum free, gardens adult/child $10/5; ⏱museum 11:30am-5:30pm Tue-Sun, gardens 2-6pm; ⌷Circulator Georgetown-Union Station) The mansion's 27 acres of enchanting formal gardens are straight out of a storybook. The springtime blooms – including heaps of cherry blossoms – are stunning. The mansion itself is worth a walk-through to see exquisite Byzantine and pre-Columbian art (including El Greco's *The Visitation*) and the fascinating library of rare books that date as far back as 1491. From November to mid-March the gardens are free (and they close at 5pm). Enter them at R and 31st Sts NW.

Georgetown Waterfront Park   PARK
(www.georgetownwaterfrontpark.org; Water St NW/K St, btwn 31st St NW & Key Bridge; ⛳; ⌷Circulator Georgetown-Union Station) This park is a favorite with couples on first dates, families on an evening stroll and power players showing off their yachts. Benches dot the way, where you can sit and watch the rowing teams out on the Potomac River. Alfresco restaurants cluster at nearby Washington Harbour. They ring a terraced plaza filled with fountains (which become an ice rink in winter). The docks are also here for ferries that ply the Potomac to Alexandria, VA, and Capitol Hill's Wharf.

Georgetown University   UNIVERSITY
(⌨202-687-0100; www.georgetown.edu; cnr 37th & O Sts NW; ⌷Circulator Georgetown-Union Station) Georgetown is one of the nation's top universities, with a student body that's equally hard-working and hard-partying. Founded in 1789, it was America's first Roman Catholic university. Notable Hoya (derived from the Latin *hoya saxa*, 'what rocks') alumni include Bill Clinton, as well as many international royals and heads of state. Near the campus' east gate, medieval-looking **Healy Hall** impresses with its tall, Hogwarts-esque clock tower. Pretty **Dalghren Chapel** and its quiet courtyard hide behind it.

Exorcist Stairs   FILM LOCATION
(3600 Prospect St NW; ⌷Circulator Georgetown-Union Station) The steep set of stairs dropping down to M St is a popular track for joggers, but more famously it's the spot where demonically possessed Father Karras tumbles to his death in horror-film classic *The Exorcist* (1973). Come on foggy nights, when the stone steps really are creepy as hell.

Tudor Place   MUSEUM
(⌨202-965-0400; www.tudorplace.org; 1644 31st St NW; 1hr house tour adult/child $10/3, self-guided garden tour $3; ⏱10am-4pm Tue-Sat, from noon Sun, closed Jan; ⌷Circulator Georgetown-Union Station) This 1816 neoclassical mansion was owned by Thomas Peter and Martha Custis Peter, the granddaughter of Martha Washington, and lived in by six generations of her family. Today the manor functions as a small museum, featuring family furnishings and artwork (including some from Mt Vernon), which give a good insight into American decorative arts. The grand, 5-acre gardens bloom with roses, lilies, poplar trees and exotic palms.

Upper Northwest DC

★**Washington National Cathedral**   CHURCH
(⌨202-537-6200; www.cathedral.org; 3101 Wisconsin Ave NW, Cathedral Heights; adult/child 5-17yr $12/8, Sun free; ⏱10am-5pm Mon-Fri, to 4pm Sat, 12:45-4pm Sun; ⌷N2, N3, N4, N6 from Dupont Circle) Constructed between 1907 and 1990, this huge neo-Gothic cathedral blends the spiritual with the profane in its architecture. Most of its richly colored stained-glass windows celebrate religious themes, although the 'Scientists and Technicians' window with its embedded lunar rock is an exception. The famed exterior gargoyles depict everything from Darth Vader to a Missouri bear. Specialty tours are available so check online for details.

The excellent **Open City** (⌨202-965-7670; www.opencitycathedraldc.com; brunch dishes $4-11, sandwiches $8-10; ⏱7am-6pm; 🐾) cafe is in the cathedral's grounds, occupying the historic baptistery building.

Smithsonian's National Zoo   ZOO
(⌨202-633-4888; www.nationalzoo.si.edu; 3001 Connecticut Ave NW, Woodley Park; ⏱9am-6pm mid-Mar–Sep, to 4pm Oct–mid-Mar, grounds 8am-7pm mid-Mar–Sep, to 5pm Oct–mid-Mar; ⓂRed Line to Cleveland Park or Woodley Park) **FREE**

Home to more than 2700 animals and more than 390 species in natural habitats, the National Zoo is famed for its giant pandas, Mei Xiang, Tian Tian and Bei Bei. Other highlights include the African lion pride, Asian elephants, and orangutans swinging 50ft overhead from steel cables and interconnected towers (aka the 'O Line').

🏃 Activities

Hiking & Cycling

Capital Bikeshare   CYCLING
(📞877-430-2453; www.capitalbikeshare.com; per 1/3 days $8/17) It has a network of 4300-plus bicycles scattered at 500-odd stations around the region. Purchase a pass at a kiosk (one day or three days) on the spot. Insert a credit card, get your ride code, then unlock a bike. The first 30 minutes are free; after that, rates rise fast if you don't dock the bike.

Capital Crescent Trail   CYCLING
(www.cctrail.org; Water St; 🚌 Circulator Georgetown-Union Station) Stretching between Georgetown and Bethesda, MD, the constantly evolving Capital Crescent Trail is a fabulous (and very popular) jogging and biking route. Built on an abandoned railroad bed, the 7-mile trail is paved and is a great leisurely day trip. It has beautiful lookouts over the Potomac River, and winds through woodsy areas and upscale neighborhoods.

Boating

Tidal Basin Boathouse   BOATING
(📞202-337-9642; www.boatingindc.com/boathouses/tidal-basin; 1501 Maine Ave SW; 2-/4-person boat per hour $18/30, swan boat per hour $34; ⏰10am-6pm mid-Mar–Sep; 🚌Circulator National Mall, Ⓜ Orange, Silver, Blue Line to Smithsonian) Rents paddleboats to take out on the Tidal Basin. Make sure you bring a camera as there are great views from the water.

Key Bridge Boathouse   WATER SPORTS
(📞202-337-9642; www.boatingindc.com/boathouses/key-bridge-boathouse; 3500 Water St NW; ⏰hours vary mid-Apr–Oct; 🚌Circulator Georgetown-Union Station) Located beneath the Key Bridge, the boathouse rents canoes, kayaks and stand up paddleboards (prices start at $16 per hour). In summer it also offers guided, 90-minute kayak trips ($45 per person) that glide past the Lincoln Memorial as the sun sets. If you have a bike, the boathouse is a mere few steps from the Capital Crescent Trail.

👉 Tours

DC by Foot   WALKING
(📞202-370-1830; www.freetoursbyfoot.com/washington-dc-tours) Guides for this pay-what-you-want walking tour offer engaging stories and historical details on different jaunts covering the National Mall, Lincoln's assassination, Capitol Hill's ghosts and many more. Most takers pay around $10 to $15 per person. Reserve in advance to guarantee a spot.

DC Metro Food Tours   WALKING
(📞202-851-2268; www.dcmetrofoodtours.com; per person $56-67) These walkabouts explore the culinary riches of various neighborhoods, stopping for multiple bites along the way. Offerings include Capitol Hill, U St, Little Ethiopia, Georgetown and Old Town Alexandria, VA. Most last from three to 3½ hours. Departure points vary.

DC Brew Tours   BUS
(📞202-759-8687; www.citybrewtours.com/dc; 801 F St NW, Penn Quarter; tours $70-99; Ⓜ Red, Yellow, Green Line to Gallery Pl-Chinatown) Visit three to four breweries by van. Routes vary but could include DC Brau, Atlas, Hellbender and Port City, among others. Three- to five-hour jaunts feature tastings of 15-plus beers and a light meal. The 3½-hour tour forgoes the meal and pares down the brewery tally. Departure is from outside the Reynolds Center. Tours go daily, at various times.

Bike & Roll   CYCLING
(📞202-842-2453; www.bikeandrolldc.com; 955 L'Enfant Plaza SW, South DC; tours adult/child from $44/34; ⏰9am-8pm, reduced hours spring & fall, closed early Jan–mid-Mar; Ⓜ Orange, Silver, Blue, Yellow, Green Line to L'Enfant Plaza) This branch of the bike-rental company (from $16 per two hours) is the one closest to the Mall. In addition to bike rental, it also provides tours. Three-hour jaunts wheel by the main sights of Capitol Hill and the National Mall. The evening rides to the monuments are particularly good.

Old Town Trolley Tours   BUS
(📞202-832-9800; www.trolleytours.com; 1000 E St NW, Penn Quarter; adult/child $47/30; 🚌Circulator National Mall, Ⓜ Red, Orange, Silver, Blue Line to Metro Center) This open-sided bus offers hop-on, hop-off exploring of some 25 major sights around the Mall, Arlington and Downtown DC. The company also offers a 'monuments by moonlight' tour and the DC

Ducks tour, via an amphibious vehicle that plunges into the Potomac. Buy tickets at the Washington Welcome Center (1000 E St NW), at Union Station or online.

🎊 Festivals & Events

Independence Day CULTURAL
(◎ Jul 4) Huge crowds gather along Constitution Ave to watch marching bands parade and hear the Declaration of Independence read from the National Archives steps. Later the National Symphony Orchestra plays a concert on the Capitol's West Lawn, followed by mega-fireworks over the National Mall.

National Cherry Blossom Festival CULTURAL
(www.nationalcherryblossomfestival.org; ◎ late Mar–mid-Apr) The star of DC's annual calendar celebrates spring's arrival with a kite festival, evening walks by lantern light, cultural fairs and a parade. The three-week event also commemorates Japan's gift of 3000 cherry trees in 1912. It's DC at its prettiest.

Smithsonian Folklife Festival CULTURAL
(www.festival.si.edu; ◎ late Jun–early Jul; 📷; 🚇 Circulator National Mall, Ⓜ Orange, Silver, Blue Line to Smithsonian) This fun family event, held over 10 days in late June and early July, celebrates international and US cultures. The fest features folk music, dance, crafts, storytelling and ethnic fare, and it highlights a diverse mix of countries and regions. It takes place on the National Mall between 12th and 14th Sts.

🛏 Sleeping

🛏 Capitol Hill

William Penn House HOSTEL $
(☎ 202-543-5560; www.williampennhouse.org; 515 E Capitol St SE; dm $50-65; ◉❄🛜; Ⓜ Orange, Silver, Blue Line to Capitol South or Eastern Market) This friendly Quaker-run guesthouse with garden offers clean, well-maintained dorms, though it could use more bathrooms. There are 30 beds in total, including two 10-bed dorms, two four-bed dorms and one two-bed room. The facility doesn't require religious observance, but there is a religious theme throughout, and it prefers guests who are active in progressive causes. Rates include continental breakfast.

★ Kimpton George Hotel HOTEL $$
(☎ 202-347-4200; www.hotelgeorge.com; 15 E St NW; d $210-245; ℗◉❄@🛜🐾; Ⓜ Red Line to Union Station) Nods to namesake George Washington are pervasive at this hotel, which is the hippest lodging on the Hill. Rooms exude a cool, creamy-white Zen and feature large bathrooms, Colonial-inspired work desks, fun presidential pop art and wallpaper adorned with Washington's cursive-written inaugural address. The handy location puts you between Union Station and the Capitol.

🛏 White House & Foggy Bottom

Club Quarters Hotel Washington, DC HOTEL $
(☎ 202-463-6400; www.clubquarters.com/washington-dc; 839 17th St NW, White House Area; d $110-250; ℗◉❄@🛜; Ⓜ Orange, Silver, Blue Line to Farragut West) Club Quarters is a favorite with business travelers on the go. Rooms are small and many don't have views, lacking any semblance of charm or quirk, but the bed is comfortable, the desk workable, the wi-fi fast enough and the coffee maker well stocked. Oh, and the prices are reasonable in an area where they're usually sky-high.

★ Hay-Adams Hotel HERITAGE HOTEL $$$
(☎ 202-638-6600; www.hayadams.com; 800 16th St NW, White House Area; d from $400; ℗❄@🛜🐾; Ⓜ Orange, Silver, Blue Line to McPherson Sq) One of the city's great heritage hotels, the Hay is a beautiful old building where 'nothing is overlooked but the White House.' The property has the best rooms of the old-school luxury genre in the city, sporting elegant decor, top-quality fittings, hugely comfortable beds and luxe bathrooms. Facilities include a gym, restaurant and popular basement bar (p290).

🛏 Downtown & Penn Quarter

★ HI Washington DC Hostel HOSTEL $
(☎ 202-737-2333; www.hiwashingtondc.org; 1009 11th St NW, Downtown; dm $33-55, d $110-130; ◉❄@🛜; Ⓜ Red, Orange, Silver, Blue Line to Metro Center) Top of the budget picks, this large, friendly hostel attracts a laid-back international crowd and has loads of amenities: lounge rooms, a pool table, a 60in TV for movie nights, free tours of various neighborhoods and historic sites, free continental breakfast and free wi-fi.

Morrison-Clark
Historic Inn & Restaurant   HISTORIC HOTEL $$

(☎202-898-1200; www.morrisonclark.com; 1011 L St NW, Downtown; d $180-330; P🐾❄@🛜; Ⓜ Green, Yellow Line to Mt Vernon Sq/7th St-Convention Center) Listed on the Register of Historic Places and helmed by a doting staff, the 114-room Morrison-Clark comprises two 1864 Victorian residences filled with fine antiques, tear-drop chandeliers and gilded mirrors, and a newer wing with Asian-influenced decor set in the repurposed Chinese church next door. It may sound odd, but the overall effect is lovely and dignified.

🛏 Logan Circle, U Street & Columbia Heights

Chester A Arthur House   B&B $

(☎877-893-3233; www.chesterarthurhouse.com; 23 Logan Circle NW, Logan Circle; r $125-165; ❄🐾🛜; Ⓜ Green, Yellow Line to U Street/African-American Civil War Memorial/Cardozo) Snooze in one of four rooms in this beautiful Logan Circle row house, located a stumble from the restaurant boom along P and 14th Sts. The 1883 abode is stuffed with crystal chandeliers, antique oil paintings, oriental rugs and a mahogany paneled staircase, plus ephemera from the hosts' global expeditions.

Kimpton Mason & Rook Hotel   HOTEL $$

(☎202-742-3100; www.masonandrookhotel.com; 1430 Rhode Island Ave NW, Logan Circle; d $189-289; P🐾❄@🛜🐕; Ⓜ Orange, Silver, Blue Line to McPherson Sq) 🐾 Snuggled into a tree-lined neighborhood near trendy 14th St, Mason & Rook feels like your urbane friend's chic apartment. The lobby resembles a handsome living room, with comfy seating, bookshelves and eclectic art. The large guest rooms invite lingering with plush fabrics, rich dark wood and leather decor, and marble bathrooms with walk-in rain showers.

🛏 Dupont Circle & Kalorama

Embassy Circle Guest House   B&B $$

(☎202-232-7744; www.dcinns.com; 2224 R St NW, Dupont Circle; r $200-350; ❄🐾🛜; Ⓜ Red Line to Dupont Circle) Embassies surround this 1902 French-country-style home, which sits a few blocks from Dupont's nightlife hubbub. The 11 big-windowed rooms are decked out with Persian carpets and original art; they don't have TVs, though they do have wi-fi. Staff feed you well throughout the day, with a hot organic breakfast, afternoon cookies and an evening wine-and-beer soirée.

Tabard Inn   BOUTIQUE HOTEL $$

(☎202-785-1277; www.tabardinn.com; 1739 N St NW, Dupont Circle; r $200-270, without bath $125-170; 🐾❄@🛜🐕; Ⓜ Red Line to Dupont Circle) Named for *The Canterbury Tales* inn, the Tabard spreads across three Victorian-era row houses. The 40 rooms are hard to generalize: all come with vintage quirks such as iron bed frames and old armoires, though little accents distinguish them – a Matisse-like painted headboard here, Amish-looking quilts there. There are no TVs, and wi-fi can be dodgy, but the of-yore atmosphere prevails.

🛏 Adams Morgan

Adam's Inn   B&B $

(☎202-745-3600; www.adamsinn.com; 1746 Lanier Pl NW; r $119-199, without bath $99-160; P🐾❄@🛜; Ⓜ Red Line to Woodley Park-Zoo/Adams Morgan) Tucked on a shady residential street, this 27-room inn is known for its personalized service, fluffy linens and handy location just a few blocks from 18th St's global smorgasbord. Inviting, homey rooms sprawl through two adjacent townhouses and a carriage house. The common areas have a nice garden patio, and there's a general sense of sherry-scented chintz.

HighRoad Hostel   HOSTEL $

(☎202-735-3622; www.highroadhostels.com; 1804 Belmont Rd NW; dm $35-60; ❄🛜; Ⓜ Red Line to Woodley Park-Zoo/Adams Morgan) HighRoad's Victorian row-house exterior belies its modern interior. The dorms come in various configurations, from four to 14 beds – some mixed, others gender-specific. There are private rooms too, a couple with en-suite bathrooms. All have stark white walls, gray metal bunks and black lockers. Nighthawks will groove on nearby 18th St's bounty.

There's a fancy (though small) community kitchen and common room with a fireplace, a chandelier and a jumbo, Netflix-wired TV.

Free movie nights, pasta dinners, outings to local bars and other group activities take place several times a week.

🛏 Georgetown

Graham Georgetown   BOUTIQUE HOTEL $$

(☎202-337-0900; www.thegrahamgeorgetown.com; 1075 Thomas Jefferson St NW; r $275-375; P🐾❄@🛜; 🚌 Circulator Georgetown-Union

Station) Set smack in Georgetown's heart, the Graham occupies the intersection between stately tradition and modernist hip. Good-sized rooms have tasteful silver, cream and chocolate decor with pops of ruby and geometric accents. Even the most basic rooms have linens by Liddell Ireland and L'Occitane bath amenities, which means you'll be as fresh, clean and beautiful as the surrounding Georgetown glitterati.

✕ Eating

A homegrown foodie revolution has transformed the once-buttoned-up DC dining scene. Driving it is the bounty of farms at the city's doorstep, along with the booming local economy and influx of worldly younger residents. Small, independent, local-chef-helmed spots now lead the way. And they're doing such a fine job that Michelin deemed the city worthy of its stars.

✕ Capitol Hill

Capitol Hill has long been an outpost for the DC burger bar, the type of unpretentious spot where you roll up your sleeves and knock back a side of beer with your patty. Hip, upscale eateries have colonized the neighborhood, especially along Pennsylvania Ave, Barracks Row (ie 8th St SE, near the Marine Barracks) and around the Navy Yard and Wharf. H St NE, east of Union Station, has seen lots of action. The formerly beat-up area continues to transform with scads of fun, offbeat restaurants and bars stretching from 4th to 14th Sts NE.

Maine Avenue Fish Market　　　SEAFOOD $
(www.wharfdc.com; 1100 Maine Ave SW, South DC; mains $7-13; ⊙8am-9pm; Ⓜ Orange, Silver, Blue, Yellow, Green Line to L'Enfant Plaza) This open-air fish market has long been adored for its no-nonsense vendors selling fish, crabs, oysters and other seafood so fresh it's still flopping. And now it has received a refresh in conjunction with the adjacent District Wharf. You'll find more seating, a plaza and pier for entertainment, and the restoration of its 100-plus-year-old oyster shed into Rappahannock Oyster Bar.

Jimmy T's　　　DINER $
(☎202-546-3646; 501 E Capitol St SE; mains $6-10; ⊙6:30am-3pm Tue, Fri & Sat, to 4pm Wed, to 6pm Thu, 8am-3pm Sun; 🚻👶; Ⓜ Orange, Silver, Blue Line to Eastern Market) Jimmy's is a neighborhood joint of the old school, where folks come in with their dogs, cram in to read the *Post,* have a burger or a coffee or an omelet (breakfast all day, by the way) and basically be themselves. If you're hungover on Sunday and in Cap Hill, come here for a greasy cure. Cash only.

Ted's Bulletin　　　AMERICAN $$
(☎202-544-8337; www.tedsbulletincapitolhill. com; 505 8th St SE; mains $14-24; ⊙7am-10pm Sun-Thu, to 11pm Fri & Sat; 👶; Ⓜ Orange, Silver, Blue Line to Eastern Market) Plop into a booth in the art-deco-meets-diner ambience, and loosen the belt. Nana's biscuits and sausage gravy for breakfast, meatloaf with ketchup glaze for dinner and other hipster spins on comfort foods hit the table. You've got to admire a place that lets you substitute pop tarts for toast. Breakfast is available all day and pulls big crowds on weekends.

Ethiopic　　　ETHIOPIAN $$
(☎202-675-2066; www.ethiopicrestaurant.com; 401 H St NE; mains $14-20; ⊙5-10pm Tue-Thu, from noon Fri-Sun; 🍴; Ⓜ Red Line to Union Station) In a city with no shortage of Ethiopian joints, Ethiopic stands above the rest thanks to its warm, stylish ambience. Top marks go to the various *wats* (stews) and the signature *tibs* (sautéed meat and veg), derived from tender lamb mixed with herbs and hot spices. Vegans get lots of love here too.

EAT STREETS

14th St NW (Logan Circle) DC's most happening road: an explosion of hot-chef bites and bars.

18th St NW (Adams Morgan) Korean, Indian, Thai, Ethiopian, Japanese and Latin mash-up, plus late-night snacks.

8th St SE (Capitol Hill) Known as Barracks Row, it's the locals' favorite for welcoming comfort-food spots.

H St NE (Capitol Hill) Hip strip of pie cafes, noodle shops and gastropubs.

Upshur St (Petworth) Block of cozy, casual *Bon Appetit*–beloved restaurants and cocktail bars.

11th St NW (Columbia Heights) Ever-growing scene of hipster cafes, edgy gastropubs and all-the-rage foodie nooks.

WASHINGTON, DC & THE CAPITAL REGION WASHINGTON, DC

FOOD TRUCKIN'

More than 150 food trucks roll in DC, and the White House neighborhood welcomes the mother lode. They congregate at locations including L St (corner of 20th), Farragut Sq, K St, Franklin Sq, the State Department and George Washington University on weekdays between 11:30am and 1:30pm. Follow the locals' lead, and enjoy a fast and delicious meal for under $15 – maybe a lobster roll poached in butter, a veggie empanada or a bowl of Lao drunken noodles.

★ **Rose's Luxury** AMERICAN $$$

(☎202-580-8889; www.rosesluxury.com; 717 8th St SE; small plates $14-16; family plates $33-36; ⏱5-10pm Mon-Sat; Ⓜ Orange, Silver, Blue Line to Eastern Market) Michelin-starred Rose's is one of DC's most buzzed-about eateries. Crowds fork into worldly Southern comfort food as twinkling lights glow overhead and candles flicker around the industrial-chic, half-finished room. Rose's doesn't take reservations, but ordering your meal at the upstairs bar can save time (and the cocktails are delicious).

✖ Downtown & Penn Quarter

★ **A Baked Joint** CAFE $

(☎202-408-6985; www.abakedjoint.com; 440 K St NW, Downtown; mains $5-11; ⏱7am-6pm Mon-Wed, to 10pm Thu & Fri, 8am-6pm Sat & Sun; Ⓜ Red, Yellow, Green Line to Gallery Pl-Chinatown) Order at the counter then take your luscious, heaped-on-housemade-bread sandwich – perhaps the smoked salmon and scallion cream cheese on an open-faced baguette, or the fried green tomatoes on buttered griddled sourdough – to a bench or table in the big, open room. Natural light streams in the floor-to-ceiling windows. Not hungry? It's also a great place for a well-made latte.

Beer, wine and cocktails are also available. Sweet treats come from sibling Baked & Wired (p289) in Georgetown.

Daikaya JAPANESE $

(☎202-589-1600; www.daikaya.com; 705 6th St NW, Penn Quarter; mains $12-14; ⏱11am-10pm Sun-Tue, to 10:30pm Wed & Thu, to midnight Fri & Sat; Ⓜ Red, Yellow, Green Line to Gallery Pl-Chinatown) Daikaya offers two options. Our favorite is downstairs, which is a casual ramen-noodle shop, where locals swarm in and slurp with friends in the slick wooden booths. Upstairs it's a sake-pouring Japanese *izakaya* (tavern), with rice-bowl lunches and small, fishy plates. Note the upstairs closes between lunch and dinner (ie between 2pm and 5pm).

Matchbox Vintage Pizza Bistro PIZZA $

(☎202-289-4441; www.matchboxrestaurants. com; 713 H St NW, Downtown; 10in pizzas $13-20; ⏱11am-10:30pm Mon-Thu, to 11:30pm Fri, 10am-11:30pm Sat, 10am-10:30pm Sun; Ⓜ Red, Yellow, Green Line to Gallery Pl-Chinatown) The pizza here has a devout following of gastronomes and the restaurant's warm, exposed-brick interior is typically packed. What's so good about it? Fresh ingredients, a thin, blistered crust baked by angels, and more fresh ingredients. Oh, and the beer list rocks, with Belgian ales and hopped-up craft brews flowing from the taps. Reserve ahead to avoid a wait.

Rasika INDIAN $$

(☎202-637-1222; www.rasikarestaurant.com; 633 D St NW, Penn Quarter; mains $19-28; ⏱11:30am-2:30pm Mon-Fri, 5:30-10:30pm Mon-Thu, 5-11pm Fri & Sat; ✐; Ⓜ Green, Yellow Line to Archives-Navy Memorial-Penn Quarter) Rasika is as cutting edge as Indian food gets. The room resembles a Jaipur palace decorated by modernist art-gallery curators. Top marks go to the *murgh mussalam*, a plate of juicy tandoori chicken with cashews and quail eggs; and the deceptively simple *dal* (lentils), which has just the right kiss of sharp fenugreek. Vegetarian diners will feel a lot of love here.

Kinship AMERICAN $$$

(☎202-737-7700; www.kinshipdc.com; 1015 7th St NW, Downtown; mains $16-35; ⏱5:30-10pm; Ⓜ Yellow, Green Line to Mt Vernon Sq/7th St-Convention Center) Round up your friends and enjoy a convivial night at this Michelin-starred restaurant by James Beard Award-winning chef Eric Ziebold. Pick and choose across the menu's five categories echoing the chef's passions: ingredients (crispy Jerusalem artichokes, *yuzukoshō* broth), history (classics), craft (using culinary techniques), indulgence (caviar, white truffles) and 'For the Table.'

The roast chicken from the last category, stuffed with a lemon-garlic-brioche mixture, is to die for. A second restaurant, Métier, also overseen by Ziebold, offers a seven-course tasting menu in an intimate setting in the same building.

★ Dabney
AMERICAN **$$$**

(☑202-450-1015; www.thedabney.com; 122 Blagden Alley NW, Downtown; small plates $14-25; ◎5:30-10pm Tue-Thu, 5-11pm Fri & Sat, 5-10pm Sun; ⓜGreen, Yellow Line to Mt Vernon Sq/7th St-Convention Center) Chef Jeremiah Langhorne studied historic cookbooks, discovering recipes that used local ingredients and lesser-explored flavors in his quest to resuscitate mid-Atlantic cuisine lost to the ages. Most of the dishes are even cooked over a wood-burning hearth, as in George Washington's time. Langhorne gives it all a modern twist – enough to earn him a Michelin star.

You'll need to order two or three small plates to make a meal. The warm, wood-clad spot is tucked away in Blagden Alley. From 9th St NW look for the 'Blagden' street sign and follow the brick lane in past the mural-painted buildings and garages.

✗ Logan Circle, U Street & Columbia Heights

★ Ben's Chili Bowl
AMERICAN **$**

(☑202-667-0058; www.benschilibowl.com; 1213 U St NW, U Street; mains $6-10; ◎6am-2am Mon-Thu, to 4am Fri, 7am-4am Sat, 11am-midnight Sun; ⓜGreen, Yellow Line to U Street/African-American Civil War Memorial/Cardozo) Ben's is a DC institution. The main stock in trade is half-smokes, DC's meatier, smokier version of the hot dog, usually slathered with mustard, onions and the namesake chili. For 60-plus years presidents, rock stars and Supreme Court justices have come to indulge in the humble diner, but despite the hype, Ben's remains a true neighborhood establishment. Cash only.

★ Compass Rose
INTERNATIONAL **$$**

(☑202-506-4765; www.compassrosedc.com; 1346 T St NW, U Street; small plates $8-16; ◎5pm-2am Mon-Thu, to 3am Fri & Sat, 11am-2am Sun; ⓜGreen, Yellow Line to U Street/African-American Civil War Memorial/Cardozo) Compass Rose feels like a secret garden, set in a discreet townhouse a whisker from 14th St's buzz. The exposed brick walls and sky-blue ceiling give it a casually romantic air. The menu is a mash-up of global comfort foods, so dinner might entail dishes such as Jamaican curried lamb, Argentinian asado (rib eye with

chimichurri) and Georgian *khachapuri* (buttery, cheese-filled bread).

Estadio
SPANISH **$$**

(☑202-319-1404; www.estadio-dc.com; 1520 14th St NW, Logan Circle; tapas $7-17; ◎5-10pm Mon-Thu, 11:30am-2pm & 5-11pm Fri, 11am-2pm & 5-11pm Sat, 11am-2pm & 5-9pm Sun; ⓜRed Line to Dupont Circle) Estadio buzzes with a low-lit, date-night vibe. The tapas menu is as deep as an ocean trench. There are four variations of *ibérico* ham and a delicious foie gras, scrambled egg and truffle open-faced sandwich. Wash it down with some traditional *calimocho* (red wine and cola). No reservations after 6pm, which usually means a wait at the bar.

Busboys & Poets
CAFE **$$**

(☑202-387-7638; www.busboysandpoets.com; 2021 14th St NW, U Street; mains $16-22; ◎7am-midnight Mon-Thu, to 1am Fri, 8am-1am Sat, 8am-midnight Sun; ☎🖉; ⓜGreen, Yellow Line to U Street/African-American Civil War Memorial/Cardozo) Busboys & Poets is one of U Street's linchpins. Locals pack the place for coffee, boozy brunches, books and a progressive vibe that makes San Francisco feel conservative. The lengthy, vegetarian-friendly menu spans sandwiches, pizzas and Southern fare such as shrimp and grits. Tuesday night's open-mike poetry reading ($5 admission, from 9pm to 11pm) draws big crowds.

Le Diplomate
FRENCH **$$$**

(☑202-332-3333; www.lediplomatedc.com; 1601 14th St NW, Logan Circle; mains $20-35; ◎5-11pm Mon-Thu, to midnight Fri, 9:30am-midnight Sat, 9:30am-11pm Sun; ⓜGreen, Yellow Line to U Street/African-American Civil War Memorial/Cardozo) This charming French bistro is one of the hottest tables in town. DC celebrities galore cozy up in the leather banquettes and at the sidewalk tables. They come for an authentic slice of Paris, from the coq au vin (wine-braised chicken) and aromatic baguettes to the vintage curios and nudie photos decorating the bathrooms. Make reservations.

✗ Dupont Circle & Kalorama

Zorba's Cafe
GREEK **$**

(☑202-387-8555; www.zorbascafe.com; 1612 20th St NW, Dupont Circle; mains $13-15; ◎11am-11:30pm Mon-Sat, to 10:30pm Sun; 🖈; ⓜRed Line to Dupont Circle) Generous portions of moussaka and souvlaki, as well as pitchers of Rolling Rock beer, make family-run Zorba's

Cafe one of DC's best bargain haunts. On warm days the outdoor patio packs with locals. With the bouzouki music playing in the background, you can almost imagine you're in the Greek islands.

Afterwords Cafe
AMERICAN $$

(☎ 202-387-3825; www.kramers.com; 1517 Connecticut Ave NW, Dupont Circle; mains $18-22; ⊗ 7:30am-1am Sun-Thu, to 3am Fri & Sat; Ⓜ Red Line to Dupont Circle) Attached to Kramerbooks, this buzzing spot is not your average bookstore cafe. The packed indoor tables, wee bar and outdoor patio overflow with good cheer. The menu features tasty bistro fare and an ample beer selection, making it a prime spot for happy hour, brunch and late nights on weekends (open until 3am, baby!).

Browsing the stacks before stuffing the gut is many locals' favorite way to spend a Washington weekend.

★ Bistrot du Coin
FRENCH $$

(☎ 202-234-6969; www.bistrotducoin.com; 1738 Connecticut Ave NW, Dupont Circle; mains $20-30; ⊗ 11:30am-midnight Mon-Wed, 11:30am-1am Thu & Fri, noon-1am Sat, noon-midnight Sun; Ⓜ Red Line to Dupont Circle) The lively and much-loved Bistrot du Coin is a neighborhood favorite for roll-up-your sleeves, working-class French fare. The kitchen sends out consistently good onion soup, classic *steak-frites* (grilled steak and French fries), cassoulet, open-face sandwiches and 11 varieties of its famous *moules* (mussels). Regional wines from around the motherland accompany the food by the glass, carafe and bottle.

★ Little Serow
THAI $$$

(www.littleserow.com; 1511 17th St NW, Dupont Circle; prix-fixe menu $54; ⊗ 5:30-10pm Tue-Thu, to 10:30pm Fri & Sat; Ⓜ Red Line to Dupont Circle) Set in a cavern-like green basement, Little Serow has no phone, no reservations and no sign on the door, and it only seats groups of four or fewer (larger parties will be separated). Despite all this, people line up around the block. What for? Superlative northern Thai cuisine. The single-option menu, consisting of six or so hot-spiced courses, changes weekly.

Komi
FUSION $$$

(☎ 202-332-9200; www.komirestaurant.com; 1509 17th St NW, Dupont Circle; set menu $165; ⊗ 5:30-10pm Tue-Sat; Ⓜ Red Line to Dupont Circle) There is an admirable simplicity to Komi's changing menu, rooted in Greece and influenced by everything – but primarily genius. Its Michelin star proves that. Dinner comprises 12 or so dishes; say suckling pig, scallops and truffles, or roasted baby goat. Komi's cozy space doesn't take groups larger than four. Call a month before your desired dining date for required reservations.

Hank's Oyster Bar
SEAFOOD $$$

(☎ 202-462-4265; www.hanksoysterbar.com; 1624 Q St NW, Dupont Circle; mains $28-36; ⊗ 11:30am-1am Mon-Thu, 11:30am-2am Fri, 11am-2am Sat, 11am-1am Sun; Ⓜ Red Line to Dupont Circle) DC has several oyster bars, but mini-chain Hank's is our favorite, mixing power-player muscle with a casual, beachy ambience. As you'd expect, the oyster menu is extensive and excellent; there are always at least four varieties on hand, along with lobster rolls, fried clams and witty cocktails. It's best to reserve ahead.

Hank's pre-theater menu (three courses for $32, offered between 5:30pm and 6:30pm) earns big praise.

✖ Adams Morgan

Diner
AMERICAN $

(☎ 202-232-8800; www.dinerdc.com; 2453 18th St NW; mains $9-18; ⊗ 24hr; ⚲⚮; Ⓜ Red Line to Woodley Park-Zoo/Adams Morgan) The Diner serves hearty comfort food, any time of the day or night. It's ideal for wee-hour breakfast scarf-downs, weekend Bloody Mary brunches (if you don't mind crowds) or any time you want unfussy, well-prepared American fare. Omelets, fat buttermilk pancakes, mac 'n' cheese, veggie tacos and burgers hit the tables with aplomb. It's a good spot for kids, too.

★ Donburi
JAPANESE $

(☎ 202-629-1047; www.donburidc.com; 2438 18th St NW; mains $11-13; ⊗ 11am-10pm; Ⓜ Red Line to Woodley Park-Zoo/Adams Morgan) Hole-in-the-wall Donburi has 14 seats at a wooden counter where you get a front-row view of the slicing, dicing chefs. *Donburi* means 'bowl' in Japanese, and that's what arrives steaming hot and filled with, say, panko-coated shrimp atop rice, blended with the house's sweet-and-savory sauce. It's a simple, authentic meal. There's often a line, but it moves quickly. No reservations.

Donburi has another venue in Dupont Circle that's larger, but the Adams Morgan location is the atmospheric original.

Julia's Empanadas
LATIN AMERICAN $

(☑202-328-6232; www.juliasempanadas.com; 2452 18th St NW; empanadas from $5; ⏱10am-midnight Mon-Wed, to 4am Thu-Sat, to 8pm Sun; Ⓜ Red Line to Woodley Park-Zoo/Adams Morgan) A frequent winner in DC's 'best late-night eats' polls, Julia's stuffs its dough bombs with chorizo, Jamaican beef curry, spinach and more. Flavors peak if you've been drinking. The little chain has a handful of takeout shops around town.

★ Tail Up Goat
MEDITERRANEAN $$

(☑202-986-9600; www.tailupgoat.com; 1827 Adams Mill Rd NW; mains $18-27; ⏱5:30-10pm Mon-Thu, 5-10pm Fri & Sat, 11am-1pm & 5-10pm Sun; Ⓜ Red Line to Woodley Park-Zoo/Adams Morgan) With its pale-blue walls, light wood decor and lantern-like lights dangling overhead, Tail Up Goat exudes a warm, island-y vibe. The lamb ribs are the specialty – crispy and lusciously fatty, served with date-molasses juice. The housemade breads and spreads star on the menu too – say, flaxseed sourdough with beets. No wonder Michelin gave it a star.

✕ Georgetown

★ Simply Banh Mi
VIETNAMESE $

(☑202-333-5726; www.simplybanhmidc.com; 1624 Wisconsin Ave NW; mains $7-10; ⏱11am-7pm Sun, Tue & Wed, to 9pm Thu-Sat; ✍; ☐ Circulator Georgetown-Union Station) There's nothing fancy about the small, below-street-level space, and the compact menu sticks mostly to sandwiches and bubble tea. But the brother-sister owners know how to take a crusty baguette, stuff it with delicious lemongrass pork or other meat (or tofu), and make your day. They're super-attentive to quality and to customer needs (vegan, gluten-free etc).

Baked & Wired
BAKERY $

(☑703-663-8727; www.bakedandwired.com; 1052 Thomas Jefferson St NW; baked goods $3-8; ⏱7am-8pm Mon-Thu, to 9pm Fri, 8am-9pm Sat, 8am-8pm Sun; ☐ Circulator Georgetown-Union Station) This cheery cafe whips up beautifully made coffees, bacon cheddar buttermilk biscuits and enormous cupcakes (like the banana and peanut-butter-frosted Elvis impersonator). It's a fine spot to join university students and cyclists coming off the nearby trails for a sugar buzz. When the weather permits, patrons take their treats outside to the adjacent grassy area by the C&O Canal. Inside, head to the right for coffee drinks and stay left for the sweet treats.

Chez Billy Sud
FRENCH $$$

(☑202-965-2606; www.chezbillysud.com; 1039 31st St NW; mains $25-38; ⏱5-10pm Mon, 11:30am-2pm & 5-10pm Tue-Thu, 11:30am-2pm & 5-11pm Fri, 11am-2pm & 5-11pm Sat, 11am-2pm & 5-10pm Sun; ☐ Circulator Georgetown-Union Station) An endearing little bistro tucked away on a residential block, Billy's mint-green walls, gilt mirrors and wee marble bar exude laid-back elegance. Mustachioed servers bring baskets of warm bread to the white-linen-clothed tables, along with crispy moulard duck leg, Maine mussels with pastis, and plump cream puffs.

🍷 Drinking & Nightlife

When Andrew Jackson swore the oath of office in 1829, the self-proclaimed populist dispensed with pomp and circumstance and, quite literally, threw a raging kegger. Folks got so gone they started looting art from the White House. The historical lesson: DC loves a drink, and these days it enjoys said tipples in many incarnations besides executive-mansion-trashing throwdowns.

🍸 Capitol Hill

★ Copycat Co
COCKTAIL BAR

(☑202-241-1952; www.copycatcompany.com; 1110 H St NE, Capitol Hill; ⏱5pm-2am Sun-Thu, to 3am Fri & Sat; Ⓜ Red Line to Union Station then streetcar) When you walk into Copycat it feels like a Chinese fast-food restaurant. That's because it is (sort of) on the 1st floor, where Chinese street-food nibbles are available. The fizzy drinks and egg-white-topped cocktails fill glasses upstairs, in the dimly lit, speakeasy-meets-opium-den-vibed bar. Staff are unassuming and gracious in helping newbies figure out what they want from the lengthy menu.

Bluejacket Brewery
BREWERY

(☑202-524-4862; www.bluejacketdc.com; 300 Tingey St SE, South DC; ⏱11am-1am Sun-Thu, to 2am Fri & Sat; 🚲🧆; Ⓜ Green Line to Navy Yard-Ballpark) Beer-lovers' heads will explode in Bluejacket. Pull up a stool at the mod-industrial bar, gaze at the silvery tanks bubbling up the ambitious brews, then make the hard decision about which of the 20 tap beers you want to try. A dry-hopped kolsch? Sweet-spiced stout? A cask-aged farmhouse ale? Four-ounce tasting pours help with decision-making.

BEER

The city is serious about beer. It even brews much of its own delicious stuff. That trend started in 2009, when DC Brau became the District's first brewery to launch in more than 50 years. Several more beer makers followed. As you drink around town, keep an eye out for local concoctions from 3 Stars, Atlas Brew Works, Hellbender and Lost Rhino (from northern Virginia).

Granville Moore's PUB

(☑ 202-399-2546; www.granvillemoores.com; 1238 H St NE, Capitol Hill; ⊙5-10pm Mon-Thu, to 11pm Fri, 11am-11pm Sat, 11am-10pm Sun; Ⓜ Red Line to Union Station then streetcar) Besides being one of DC's best places to grab *frites* and steak au poivre, Granville Moore's has an extensive Belgian-beer menu that should satisfy any fan of low-country boozing. With its raw, wooden fixtures and walls that look like they're made from daub and mud, the interior resembles a medieval barracks. The fireside setting is ideal come winter.

Tune Inn BAR

(☑ 202-543-2725; 331 Pennsylvania Ave SE, Capitol Hill; ⊙8am-2am Sun-Thu, to 3am Fri & Sat; Ⓜ Orange, Silver, Blue Line to Capitol South or Eastern Market) Tune Inn has been helping the thirsty since 1947. Mounted deer heads stare from the wall and watch over old-timers knocking back Budweisers at the bar. Meanwhile, Hill staffers, off-duty cops and other locals scarf greasy-spoon grub and all-day breakfasts in the vinyl-backed booths.

How do you know when you're in a first-rate dive? When your beer-and-shot combo glows under the dim light of an antler chandelier.

White House & Foggy Bottom

★**Off the Record** BAR

(☑ 202-638-6600; www.hayadams.com/dining/off-the-record; 800 16th St NW, Hay-Adams Hotel, White House Area; ⊙11:30am-midnight Sun-Thu, to 12:30am Fri & Sat; Ⓜ Orange, Silver, Blue Line to McPherson Sq) Table seating, an open fire in winter and a discreet basement location in one of the city's most prestigious hotels (p283), right across from the White House – it's no wonder DC's important people submerge to be seen and not heard (as the tagline goes) here. Experienced bartenders swirl martinis and manhattans for the suit-wearing crowd. Enter through the hotel lobby.

Downtown & Penn Quarter

Columbia Room COCKTAIL BAR

(☑ 202-316-9396; www.columbiaroomdc.com; 124 Blagden Alley NW, Downtown; ⊙5pm-12:30am Tue-Thu, to 1:30am Fri & Sat; Ⓜ Green, Yellow Line to Mt Vernon Sq/7th St-Convention Center) Serious mixology goes on at Columbia Room, the kind of place that sources spring water from Scotland, and uses pickled cherry blossom and barley tea among its ingredients. But it's done in a refreshingly nonsnooty environment. Choose from three areas: the festive Punch Garden on the outdoor roof deck, the comfy, leather-chair-dotted Spirits Library, or the 14-seat, prix-fixe Tasting Room.

Logan Circle, U Street & Columbia Heights

★**Right Proper Brewing Co** BREWERY

(☑ 202-607-2337; www.rightproperbrewery.com; 624 T St NW, Logan Circle; ⊙5-11pm Mon-Thu, 11:30am-midnight Fri & Sat, 11:30am-10pm Sun; Ⓜ Green, Yellow Line to Shaw-Howard U) Right Proper Brewing makes sublime ales in a building that shares a wall with the joint where Duke Ellington used to play pool. It's the Shaw district's neighborhood clubhouse, a big, sunny space filled with folks gabbing at reclaimed wood tables. The tap lineup changes regularly as the brewers work their magic, but crisp farmhouse ales are an oft-flowing specialty.

Dacha Beer Garden BEER GARDEN

(☑ 202-350-9888; www.dachadc.com; 1600 7th St NW, Shaw; ⊙4-10:30pm Mon, Tue & Thu, 3pm-midnight Fri, 8am-midnight Sat, noon-10:30pm Sun, reduced hours winter; 🅿🐾; Ⓜ Green, Yellow Line to Shaw-Howard U) Happiness reigns in Dacha's freewheeling beer garden. Kids and dogs bound around the picnic tables, while adults hoist glass boots filled with German brews. When the weather gets nippy, staff bring blankets and stoke the firepit. And it all takes place under the sultry gaze of Elizabeth Taylor (or a mural of her, which sprawls across the back wall).

Churchkey BAR

(☑ 202-567-2576; www.churchkeydc.com; 1337 14th St NW, Logan Circle; ⊙4pm-1am Mon-Thu, to 2am Fri, 11:30am-2am Sat, 11:30am-1am Sun; [M] Orange, Silver, Blue Line to McPherson Sq) Coppery, mod-industrial Churchkey glows with hipness. Fifty beers flow from the taps, plus five brain-walloping, cask-aged ales. If none of those please you, another 500 types of brew are available by bottle (including gluten-free suds). Churchkey is the upstairs counterpart to **Birch & Barley** ([J]202-567-2576; www.birchandbarley.com; mains $17-29; ⊙5:30-10pm Tue-Thu, to 11pm Fri, 11am-3pm & 5:30-11pm Sat, 11am-3pm & 5-9pm Sun), a popular nouveau comfort-food restaurant, and you can order much of its menu at the bar.

U Street Music Hall CLUB
([J]202-588-1889; www.ustreetmusichall.com; 1115 U St NW, U Street; tickets $10-25; ⊙hours vary; [M] Green, Yellow Line to U Street/African-American Civil War Memorial/Cardozo) Two local DJs own and operate the basement club; it looks like a no-frills rock bar, but it has a pro sound system, a cork-cushioned dance floor and other accoutrements of a serious dance club. Alternative bands also thrash a couple of nights per week to keep it fresh. Shows start between 7pm and 10pm.

Dupont Circle & Kalorama

★ **Bar Charley** BAR
([J]202-627-2183; www.barcharley.com; 1825 18th St NW, Dupont Circle; ⊙5pm-12:30am Mon-Thu, 4pm-1:30am Fri, 10am-1:30am Sat, 10am-midnight Sun; [M] Red Line to Dupont Circle) Bar Charley draws a mixed crowd from the neighborhood – young, old, gay and straight. They come for groovy cocktails sloshing in vintage glassware and ceramic tiki mugs, served at very reasonable prices by DC standards. Try the gin and gingery Suffering Bastard. The beer list isn't huge, but it's thoughtfully chosen with some wild ales. Around 60 wines available too.

★ **Board Room** BAR
([J]202-518-7666; www.boardroomdc.com; 1737 Connecticut Ave NW, Dupont Circle; ⊙4pm-2am Mon-Thu, 4pm-3am Fri, noon-3am Sat, noon-2am Sun; [M] Red Line to Dupont Circle) Grab a table, pull up a stool and crush your opponent at Hungry Hungry Hippos. Or cozy up to a serious game of Scrabble. Board Room lets you flash back to childhood via stacks of board games (Battleship, Risk, Operation) – name it, and it's available to rent for $2.

Around 20 beers flow from the taps and are available by pitcher to stoke the festivities.

JR's GAY
([J]202-328-0090; www.jrsbar-dc.com; 1519 17th St NW, Dupont Circle; ⊙4pm-2am Mon-Thu, 4pm-3am Fri, 1pm-3am Sat, 1pm-2am Sun; [M] Red Line to Dupont Circle) Button-down shirts are de rigueur at this gay hangout frequented by the 20- and 30-something, work-hard-and-play-hard set. Some DC residents claim that the crowd here epitomizes the conservative nature of the capital's gay scene, but even if you love to hate it, as many do, JR's knows how to rock a happy hour and is teeming more often than not.

Cobalt GAY
([J]202-232-4416; www.cobaltdc.com; 1639 R St NW, Dupont Circle; ⊙4pm-2am Sun-Thu, to 3am Fri & Sat, to midnight Sun; [M] Red Line to Dupont

WASHINGTON, DC & THE CAPITAL REGION WASHINGTON, DC

LGBTIQ+ DC

DC is one of the most gay-friendly cities in the USA. It has an admirable track record of progressivism and a bit of a scene to boot. The rainbow stereotype here consists of well-dressed professionals and activists working in politics on LGBTIQ+ issues such as gay marriage (legal in DC since 2010). The community concentrates in Dupont Circle, but U Street, Shaw, Capitol Hill and Logan Circle also have lots of gay-friendly businesses.

Capital Area Gay & Lesbian Chamber of Commerce (www.caglcc.org) Sponsors lots of networking events around town.

LGBT DC (https://washington.org/lgbtq) The DC tourism office's portal, with events, neighborhood breakdowns and a travel resource guide.

Metro Weekly (www.metroweekly.com) Free weekly news magazine. Aimed at a younger demographic than its rival, the *Washington Blade*.

Washington Blade (www.washingtonblade.com) Free weekly gay newspaper. Covers politics and has lots of business and nightlife listings.

Circle) Featuring lots of hair product and buff gym bodies, this premier LGBTIQ+ nightspot and bar tends to gather a well-dressed, late-20s to 30-something crowd who come for fun (but loud!) dance parties throughout the week. The time-hallowed dance club is on the 3rd floor; the venue also has a restaurant on the 1st floor and a lounge on the 2nd.

Adams Morgan

★ Dan's Cafe
BAR

(☏ 202-265-0299; 2315 18th St NW; ⊙ 7pm-2am Tue-Thu, to 3am Fri & Sat; Ⓜ Red Line to Woodley Park-Zoo/Adams Morgan) This is one of DC's great dive bars. The interior looks sort of like an evil Elks Club, all unironically old-school 'art', cheap paneling and dim lights barely illuminating the unapologetic slumminess. It's famed for its whopping, mix-it-yourself drinks, where you get a ketchup-type squirt bottle of booze, a can of soda and bucket of ice for $20. Cash only.

Songbyrd Record
Cafe & Music House
CAFE

(☏ 202-450-2917; www.songbyrddc.com; 2475-2477 18th St NW; mains $10-14; ⊙ 8am-2am Sun-Thu, to 3am Fri & Sat, cafe to 10pm; 🛜; Ⓜ Red Line to Woodley Park-Zoo/Adams Morgan) By day hang out in the retro cafe, drinking excellent coffee, munching sandwiches and browsing the soul and indie LPs for sale. You can even cut your own record in the vintage recording booth ($15). By night the party moves to the DJ-spinning bar, where beer and cocktails flow alongside burgers and tacos, and indie bands rock the basement club.

Georgetown

Tombs
PUB

(☏ 202-337-6668; www.tombs.com; 1226 36th St NW; ⊙ 11:30am-1:30am Mon-Thu, to 2:30am Fri, 11am-2:30am Sat, 9:30am-1:30am Sun; 🚃 Circulator Georgetown-Union Station) Every college of a certain pedigree has 'that' bar – the one where faculty and students alike sip pints under athletic regalia of the old school. The Tombs is Georgetown's contribution to the genre. If it looks familiar, think back to the '80s: the subterranean pub was one of the settings for the film St Elmo's Fire. The close-set tables buzz on various Tuesdays for Trivia Night shenanigans; check the website for the schedule.

☆ Entertainment

Live Music

★ Black Cat
LIVE MUSIC

(☏ 202-667-4490; www.blackcatdc.com; 1811 14th St NW, U Street; tickets $10-25; Ⓜ Green, Yellow Line to U Street/African-American Civil War Memorial/Cardozo) The Black Cat is the go-to venue for music that's loud and grungy with a punk edge. The White Stripes, Arcade Fire and Foo Fighters have all thrashed here. The big action takes place on the Mainstage. The legendary Backstage and Red Room bar are being reimagined on the club's 2nd story; check the website for updates.

9:30 Club
LIVE MUSIC

(☏ 202-265-0930; www.930.com; 815 V St NW, U Street; tickets $20-35; Ⓜ Green, Yellow Line to U Street/African-American Civil War Memorial/Cardozo) The 9:30, which can pack 1200 people into a surprisingly compact venue, is the granddaddy of the live-music scene in DC. Pretty much every big name that comes through town ends up on this stage at some point. Headliners usually begin between 10:30pm and 11:30pm.

Performing Arts

★ Kennedy Center
PERFORMING ARTS

(☏ 202-467-4600; www.kennedy-center.org; 2700 F St NW, Foggy Bottom; ⊙ box office 10am-9pm Mon-Sat, noon-9pm Sun; 🛜♿; Ⓜ Orange, Silver, Blue Line to Foggy Bottom-GWU) Overlooking the Potomac River, the magnificent Kennedy Center hosts a staggering array of performances – more than 2000 each year in venues including the Concert Hall, home to the National Symphony (www.kennedy-center.org/nso), and Opera House, home to the National Opera (www.kennedy-center.org/wno). Free performances are staged on the Millennium Stage daily at 6pm as part of the center's 'Performing Arts for Everyone' initiative.

Shakespeare Theatre Company
THEATER

(☏ 202-547-1122; www.shakespearetheatre.org; 450 7th St NW, Lansburgh Theatre, Penn Quarter; average ticket $85; Ⓜ Green, Yellow Line to Archives-Navy Memorial-Penn Quarter) The nation's foremost Shakespeare company presents masterful works by the Bard, as well as plays by George Bernard Shaw, Oscar Wilde, Eugene O'Neill and other greats. The season spans about a half-dozen productions annually, plus a free summer Shakespeare series on-site for two weeks in late August. The company also performs at the nearby Sidney Harman Hall, 610 F St NW.

★ **Woolly Mammoth Theatre Company** THEATER
(☑ 202-393-3939; www.woollymammoth.net; 641 D St NW, Penn Quarter; average ticket $67; Ⓜ Green, Yellow Line to Archives-Navy Memorial-Penn Quarter) Woolly Mammoth is the edgiest of DC's experimental groups. For most shows, $20 'stampede' seats are available at the box office two hours before performances. They're limited in number, and sold first-come, first-served, so get there early.

Capitol Steps COMEDY
(☑ Ticketmaster 202-397-7328; www.capsteps. com; 1300 Pennsylvania Ave NW, Ronald Reagan Bldg, Downtown; tickets from $40; ☺ shows 7:30pm Fri & Sat; Ⓜ Orange, Silver, Blue Line to Federal Triangle) This singing troupe claims to be the only group in America that tries to be funnier than Congress. Many of the performers are former congressional staffers, so they know their political stuff, although sometimes it can be overly corny. The satirical, bipartisan jokes poke fun at both sides of the spectrum.

Sports

★ **Nationals Park** STADIUM
(☑ 202-675-6287; www.mlb.com/nationals; 1500 S Capitol St SE, South DC; ☎; Ⓜ Green Line to Navy Yard-Ballpark) The major-league Washington Nationals play baseball at this spiffy stadium beside the Anacostia River. Don't miss the mid-fourth-inning 'Presidents' Race' – an odd foot race between giant-headed caricatures of George Washington, Abraham Lincoln, Thomas Jefferson and Teddy Roosevelt. Hip bars and eateries and playful green spaces surround the ballpark, and more keep coming as the area gentrifies.

ℹ Information

Cultural Tourism DC (www.culturaltourismdc. org) Neighborhood-oriented events and DIY tours.

Destination DC (www.washington.org) Official tourism site packed with sightseeing and event info.

Lonely Planet (www.lonelyplanet.com/usa/ washington-dc) Destination information, hotel bookings, traveler forum and more.

Washingtonian (www.washingtonian.com) Features on dining, entertainment and local luminaries.

ℹ Getting There & Away

AIR

Dulles International Airport (IAD; ☑ 703-572-2700, 703-572-8296; www.flydulles.com) is in the Virginia suburbs 26 miles west of DC. It has free wi-fi, several currency exchanges and restaurants throughout the terminals. Famed architect Eero Saarinen designed the swooping main building. The Metro Silver Line is slated to reach Dulles in 2020, providing a transfer-free ride at long last.

Ronald Reagan Washington National Airport (DCA; www.flyreagan.com) is 4.5 miles south of downtown in Arlington, VA. It has free wi-fi, several eateries and a currency exchange (National Hall, Concourse Level).

Baltimore/Washington International Thurgood Marshall Airport (BWI; ☑ 410-859-7111; www.bwiairport.com; 7035 Elm Rd; ☎) is 30 miles northeast of DC in Maryland.

BUS

Cheap bus services to and from Washington, DC, abound. Most charge $25 to $30 for a one-way trip to NYC (it takes four to five hours). Many companies use Union Station as their hub; other pickup locations are scattered around town, but are always accessible by Metro. Tickets usually need to be bought online, but can sometimes be purchased on the bus itself if there are still seats available.

BestBus (☑ 202-332-2691; www.bestbus.com; cnr 20th St & Massachusetts Ave NW, Dupont Circle; ☎; Ⓜ Red Line to Dupont Circle) Several trips to/from NYC daily. The main bus stop is by Dupont Circle; there's another at Union Station.

BoltBus (☑ 877-265-8287; www.boltbus.com; 50 Massachusetts Ave NE, Capitol Hill; ☎; Ⓜ Red Line to Union Station) Goes to NYC multiple times each day, and to other East Coast cities. Lateness and spotty wi-fi can be issues. It uses Union Station as its terminal.

Greyhound (☑ 202-589-5141; www.greyhound. com; 50 Massachusetts Ave NE, Capitol Hill; ☎; Ⓜ Red Line to Union Station) Provides nationwide service. The terminal is at Union Station.

Megabus (☑ 877-462-6342; http://us.mega bus.com; 50 Massachusetts Ave NE, Capitol Hill; ☎; Ⓜ Red Line to Union Station) Offers the most trips to NYC (around 15 to 20 per day), as well as other East Coast cities; arrives at/ departs from Union Station. Buses run behind schedule fairly often.

Peter Pan Bus Lines (☑ 800-343-9999; www. peterpanbus.com; 50 Massachusetts Ave NE, Capitol Hill; ☎; Ⓜ Red Line to Union Station) Travels throughout northeastern USA; has its terminal at Union Station.

Vamoose Bus (📞212-695-6766; www.vamoose bus.com; 1801 N Lynn St; $60) Service between NYC and Arlington, VA (the stop is near the Rosslyn Metro station).

Washington Deluxe (📞866-287-6932; www. washny.com; 1610 Connecticut Ave NW, Dupont Circle; 📶; Ⓜ Red Line to Dupont Circle) Good express service to/from NYC. It has stops at both Dupont Circle and Union Station.

TRAIN

Magnificent, beaux-arts **Union Station** (📞20 2-289-1908; www.unionstationdc.com; 50 Massachusetts Ave NE, Capitol Hill; ⊘24hr, ticketed passengers only midnight-5am; Ⓜ Red Line to Union Station) is the city's rail hub. There's a handy Metro station (Red Line) here for transport onward in the city.

Amtrak (www.amtrak.com) arrives at least once per hour from major East Coast cities. Its Northeast Regional trains are cheaper but slower (about 3½ hours between NYC and DC).

Amtrak's Acela Express trains are more expensive but faster (2¾ hours between NYC and DC; 6½ hours between Boston and DC). The express trains also have bigger seats and other business-class amenities.

MARC trains (www.mta.maryland.gov) arrive frequently from downtown Baltimore (one hour) and other Maryland towns, as well as Harpers Ferry, WV.

❶ Getting Around

The Metro is the main way to move around the city. Buy a rechargeable SmarTrip card at any Metro station. You must use the card to enter *and* exit station turnstiles.

Bicycle Capital Bikeshare stations are everywhere; a day pass costs $8.

DC Circulator bus Useful for the Mall, Georgetown, Adams Morgan and other areas with limited Metro service. Fare is $1.

Metro Fast, frequent, ubiquitous (except during weekend track maintenance). It operates between 5am (from 7am weekends) and 11:30pm (1am on Friday and Saturday). Fares are from $2 to $6 depending on distance traveled. A day pass costs $14.75.

Taxi Relatively easy to find (less so at night), but costly. Ridesharing companies are used more in the District.

MARYLAND

The nickname 'America in Miniature' perfectly captures Maryland: this small state possesses all of the best bits of the country, from the Appalachian Mountains in the west to sandy white beaches in the east. A blend of northern street smarts and Southern down-home appeal gives this border state an appealing identity crisis. Its main city, Baltimore, is a sharp, demanding port town; the Eastern Shore jumbles art-and-antique-minded city escapees and working fishermen; and the DC suburbs are packed with government and office workers seeking green space, and those seeking more affordable rents. Yet it all somehow works – scrumptious blue crabs, Natty Boh beer and lovely Chesapeake country being the glue that binds it all. This is also an extremely diverse and progressive state, and was one of the first in the USA to legalize gay marriage.

History

George Calvert established Maryland as a refuge for persecuted English Catholics in 1634 when he purchased St Mary's City from the local Piscataway tribe, with whom he initially tried to coexist. Puritan refugees drove both Piscataway and Catholics from control and shifted power to Annapolis; their harassment of Catholics produced the Tolerance Act, a flawed but progressive law that allowed freedom of any (Christian) worship in Maryland – a North American first.

A commitment to diversity has always characterized this state, despite a mixed record on slavery. Although state loyalties were split during the Civil War, a Confederate invasion was halted here in 1862 at Antietam. Following the war, Maryland harnessed its black, white and immigrant work force, splitting the economy between Baltimore's industry and shipping, and the later need for services in Washington, DC. Today the answer to 'What makes a Marylander?' is 'all of the above': the state mixes rich, poor, foreign-born, urban sophisticates and rural villages like few other states do.

Baltimore

Once among the most important port towns in America, Baltimore – or 'Bawlmer' to locals – is a city of contradictions. It remains a defiant, working-class city tied to its nautical past, but in recent years has earned acclaim for impressive, up-to-the-minute entrepreneurial ventures, from new boutique hotels and edgy exhibits at world-class museums to forgotten neighborhoods now bustling with trendy food courts and farm-to-table restaurants. Traditionalists shouldn't worry,

SCENIC DRIVE: MARITIME MARYLAND

Maryland and the Chesapeake Bay have always been inextricable, but there are some places where the old-fashioned way of life on the bay seems to have changed little over the passing centuries.

About 150 miles south of Baltimore, at the edge of the Eastern Shore, is **Crisfield**, the top working water town in Maryland. Stop by the **chamber of commerce** (☑ 410-968-2500; www.crisfieldchamber.com; 906 W Main St, Crisfield; ⊙ 9am-5pm Mon-Fri, 11am-4pm Sat & Sun Apr-Nov, 10am-4pm Mon-Fri Dec-Mar) for an introduction to regional attractions then delve into the region's history at the **J Millard Tawes Historical Museum** (☑ 410-968-2501; www.crisfieldheritagefoundation.org/museum; 3 9th St, Crisfield; adult/child $3/1; ⊙ 10am-4pm Mon-Sat Jun-Aug, 11am-4pm Sat Sep-late Nov, closed rest of the year; P), nearby. Any seafood you eat will be first-rate, but for a true Shore experience, **Watermen's Inn** (☑ 410-968-2119; www.crisfield.com/watermens; 901 W Main St, Crisfield; sandwiches $8-17, mains $18-28; ⊙ 3-8pm Thu, to 9pm Fri & Sat, noon-8pm Sun) is legendary; you can feast on local catch from an ever-changing menu in an unpretentious setting. You can find local waterfolk at their favorite hangout, **Gordon's Confectionery** (☑ 410-968-0566; www.facebook.com/gordons1924; 831 W Main St, Crisfield; mains $2-9; ⊙ 4am-8:30pm), having 4am coffee before shipping off to check and set traps.

From here you can leave your car and take a boat to **Smith Island** (www.smithisland.org), the only offshore settlement in the state. Settled by fisherfolk from the English West Country some 400 years ago, the island's tiny population still speak with what linguists reckon is the closest thing to a 17th-century Cornish accent.

We'll be frank: this is more of a dying fishing town than a charming tourist attraction, although there are B&Bs and restaurants. But it's also a last link to the state's past, so if you approach Smith Island as such, you may appreciate the limited amenities on offer. These notably include paddling through miles of some of the most pristine marshland on the eastern seaboard. Ferries travel daily between Crisfield and Smith Island year-round but call ahead to confirm departure times. Check the website for details about lodging, restaurants and ferries.

though – local culture and hometown sports, from lacrosse to baseball, remain part of the appeal.

For travelers, a visit to B'more (another nickname) should include one trip to the waterfront, whether it's the Disney-fied Inner Harbor, the cobblestoned streets of portside Fells Point or the shores of Fort McHenry, birthplace of America's national anthem, 'The Star-Spangled Banner.' As you'll discover, there's an intense, sincere friendliness here, which is why Baltimore lives up to its final, most accurate nickname: 'Charm City.'

◉ Sights

◉ Harborplace & Inner Harbor

This is where most tourists start and, unfortunately, end their Baltimore sightseeing. The Inner Harbor is a big, gleaming waterfront-renewal project of shiny glass, air-conditioned malls and flashy bars that manages to capture the maritime heart of this city, albeit in a safe-for-the-whole-family kinda way. The neighborhood is home to an amazing aquarium and several impressive historic ships, but these worthy sights are just the tip of Baltimore's iceberg.

National Aquarium AQUARIUM (☑ 410-576-3800; www.aqua.org; 501 E Pratt St, Piers 3 & 4; adult/child $40/30; ⊙ 9am-5pm Sun-Thu, to 8pm Fri, to 6pm Sat, varies seasonally; ⛴) Standing seven stories high and capped by a glass pyramid, this is widely considered to be America's best aquarium, with almost 20,000 creatures from more than 700 species, a rooftop rainforest, a multistory shark tank and a vast re-creation of an Indo-Pacific reef that is home to blacktip reef sharks, a green sea turtle and stingrays. There's also a reconstruction of the Umbrawarra Gorge in Australia's Northern Territory, complete with 35ft waterfall, rocky cliffs and free-roaming birds and lizards.

The largest exhibit contains seven bottlenose dolphins kept in captivity, though at time of writing the aquarium was planning

BALTIMORE FOR CHILDREN

Most attractions are centered on the Inner Harbor, including the National Aquarium (p295), perfect for pint-size visitors as well as preteens and teenagers. Kids can run wild o'er the ramparts of historic Fort McHenry National Monument & Historic Shrine, too, while older children will appreciate the history.

Maryland Science Center (☑410-685-2370; www.mdsci.org; 601 Light St; adult/child $25/19; ☉10am-5pm Mon-Fri, to 6pm Sat, 11am-5pm Sun, longer hours in summer) is an awesome attraction featuring a three-story atrium, tons of interactive exhibits on dinosaurs, outer space and the human body, and the requisite IMAX theater (adult/child $14/11 for feature films). This one works well for the whole family.

Two blocks north is the converted fish market of **Port Discovery** (☑410-727-8120; www.portdiscovery.org; 35 Market Pl; $16; ☉10am-5pm Tue-Sat, noon-5pm Sun, plus Mon Jun-Aug; ⓘ), which has a tree house, an Egypt-inspired archaeology site and an artist's studio. It's geared to younger kids, so you can wear them out here – especially if they spend time climbing and sliding in the multilevel tree house.

At **Maryland Zoo in Baltimore** (☑410-396-7102; www.marylandzoo.org; 1 Safari Pl, Druid Hill Park; adult/child $22/18; ☉10am-4pm daily Mar-Dec, Fri-Mon only Jan & Feb; ⓟⓘ), lily-pad-hopping adventures with Wade the Bog Turtle and grooming live animals are all in a day's play. Older kids may enjoy the zookeeper chats – and the reptiles!

Many public toilets in Baltimore have a baby-changing table. Items such as baby food, formula and disposable diapers are widely available in supermarkets.

Sidewalks are often crowded downtown during the day, especially north of the Inner Harbor, and you may not feel comfortable pushing a stroller through the busy mix. Sidewalks are wider than normal near Inner Harbor attractions such as the National Aquarium and the **Historic Ships** (☑410-539-1797; www.historicships.org; 301 E Pratt St, Piers 1, 3 & 5; adult/student/child from $15/13/7; ☉10am-5pm, hours vary seasonally; ⓘ) – although strollers won't do well on the claustrophobic submarine, one of the historic ships.

to retire them to an oceanside sanctuary by 2021 (freeing them to the wild is not an option, since they lack survival skills). These dolphins no longer perform in shows. Kids will love the 4-D Immersion Theater (admission costs an additional $5), and there are loads of unique, behind-the-scenes tours, as well as aquarium sleepovers. Go on weekdays (right at opening time) to beat the crowds.

◉ Downtown & Little Italy

You can easily walk from downtown Baltimore to Little Italy, but follow the delineated path: there's a rough housing project along the way.

National Great Blacks in Wax Museum MUSEUM
(☑410-563-3404; www.greatblacksinwax.org; 1601 E North Ave; adult/student/child $15/14/12; ☉9am-5pm Tue-Sat, from noon Sun, longer hours Jul & Aug) This simple but thought-provoking African American history museum has exhibits spotlighting Frederick Douglass, Jackie Robinson, Dr Martin Luther King Jr and Barack Obama, as well as lesser-known figures such as explorer Matthew Henson. It also covers slavery, the Jim Crow era and African leaders – all told in surreal but informative fashion through Madame Tussaud–style wax figures. Unflinching exhibits about the horrors of slave ships and lynchings are graphic and may not be suitable for younger children.

For a compelling first-person introduction to the museum, listen to NPR's *This American Life* Episode 627: 'Suitable for Children,' which aired in October 2017 and is archived online (www.thisamericanlife.org).

◉ Mt Vernon

★**Walters Art Museum** MUSEUM
(☑410-547-9000; www.thewalters.org; 600 N Charles St; ☉10am-5pm Wed & Fri-Sun, to 9pm Thu) FREE The magnificent Chamber of Art & Wonders re-creates the library of an imagined 17th-century scholar, one with a taste for the exotic. The abutting Hall of Arms & Armor displays the most impressive collection of medieval weaponry you'll

see this side of *Game of Thrones*. In sum, don't pass up this excellent, eclectic museum. It spans more than 55 centuries, from ancient to contemporary, with top-notch displays of Asian treasures, rare and ornate manuscripts and books, and a comprehensive French paintings collection.

Washington Monument   MONUMENT

(☑ 410-962-5070; www.mvpconservancy.org; 699 Washington Pl; adult/child $6/4; ⊙10am-5pm Wed-Sun) For the best views of Baltimore, climb the 227 marble steps of the 178ft-tall Doric column dedicated to America's founding father, George Washington. The monument was designed by Robert Mills, who also created DC's Washington Monument, and is looking better than ever following a $6-million restoration project. The ground floor contains a museum about Washington's life. To climb the monument, buy a ticket on-site or reserve online. Spaces are limited. The 1st-floor gallery is free.

Claustrophobes beware – the climb is narrow, steep and surrounded by brick, with only one window before reaching the enclosed viewpoints at the top.

Maryland Historical Society   MUSEUM

(☑ 410-685-3750; www.mdhs.org; 201 W Monument St; adult/child $9/6; ⊙10am-5pm Wed-Sat, from noon Sun) With more than 350,000 objects and seven million books and documents, this is among the world's largest collections of Americana. Highlights include one of two surviving Revolutionary War officer's uniforms, photographs from the Civil Rights movement in Baltimore, and Francis Scott Key's original manuscript of 'The Star-Spangled Banner' (displayed at the top of the hour). The 10ft-tall replica mastodon – the original was preserved by artist and Maryland native Charles Wilson Peale – is impressive. A few original bones are displayed.

There are often excellent temporary exhibits that explore the role of Baltimore residents in historic events.

◉ Federal Hill & Around

On a bluff overlooking the harbor, Federal Hill Park lends its name to the comfortable neighborhood that's set around **Cross St Market** (www.southbaltimore.com; 1065 S Cross St, btwn Light & Charles Sts; ⊙7am-7pm) and comes alive after sundown.

★ American Visionary Art Museum   MUSEUM

(AVAM; ☑ 410-244-1900; www.avam.org; 800 Key Hwy; adult/child $16/10; ⊙10am-6pm Tue-Sun) Housing a jaw-dropping collection of self-taught (or 'outsider' art), AVAM is a celebration of unbridled creativity utterly free of arts-scene pretension. Across two buildings and two sculpture parks, you'll find broken-mirror collages, homemade robots and flying apparatuses, elaborate sculptural works made of needlepoint, and gigantic model ships painstakingly created from matchsticks. The whimsical automatons in the Cabaret Mechanical Theater are worth a closer look. And don't miss the famous Flatulence Post and its, er, 'fart art' in the Basement Gallery.

Fort McHenry National Monument & Historic Shrine   HISTORIC SITE

(☑ 410-962-4290; www.nps.gov/fomc; 2400 E Fort Ave; adult/child $15/free; ⊙9am-5pm; ℗) On September 13 and 14, 1814, this star-shaped fort successfully repelled a British navy attack during the Battle of Baltimore. After a long night of bombs bursting in the air, shipbound prisoner Francis Scott Key saw, 'by dawn's early light,' the tattered flag still waving. Inspired, he penned 'The Star-Spangled Banner,' which was set to the tune of a popular drinking song.

◉ Fell's Point & Canton

Once the center of Baltimore's shipbuilding industry, the historic cobblestoned neighborhood of Fells Point is now a gentrified mix of 18th-century homes and restaurants, bars and shops. The neighborhood has been the setting for several films and TV series, most notably *Homicide: Life on the Street*. Further east, the slightly more sophisticated streets of Canton fan out, with its grassy square surrounded by great restaurants and bars.

◉ North Baltimore

The 'Hon' expression of affection – an often-imitated but never-quite-duplicated 'Bawlmerese' peculiarity – originated in Hampden, an area straddling the line between working class and hipster-creative class. Spend a lazy afternoon browsing kitsch, antiques and vintage clothing along the Avenue (aka W 36th St). To get to Hampden, take I-83 N, merge onto Falls Rd (northbound) and take a right onto the Avenue.

The prestigious **Johns Hopkins University** (☑ 410-516-8000; www.jhu.edu; 3400 N Charles St) is nearby. South of Johns Hopkins, just east of I-83, new restaurants and housing developments mark rapidly gentrifying **Remington**, a walkable neighborhood with a demographic similar to that of Hampden.

★ **Evergreen Museum**   MUSEUM
(☑ 410-516-0341; http://museums.jhu.edu; 4545 N Charles St; adult/child $8/5; ⊘ 11am-4pm Tue-Fri, from noon Sat & Sun; 🅿) Well worth the 7-mile drive north from the Inner Harbor, this grand 19th-century mansion provides a fascinating glimpse into upper-class Baltimore life of the 1800s. The house is packed with fine art and masterpieces of the decorative arts – including paintings by Modigliani, glass by Louis Comfort Tiffany and exquisite Asian porcelain – not to mention the astounding rare book collection, numbering some 32,000 volumes. Visits are by guided tour offered on the hour until 3pm.

Even more impressive than the collection is the compelling story of the Garrett family. Patriarch John W Garrett was president of the B&O Railroad and he purchased the home in 1878 for his son T Harrison. The Garretts were world travelers – T Harrison's son John W, who inherited the house in 1920, was an active diplomat for some years. They were also astute philanthropists, as well as lovers of the arts, if not always successful performers in their own right – though that didn't stop the younger John W's wife, Alice, from taking the stage (her own, which you'll see in the intimate theater below the house).

✿ Festivals & Events

Preakness Stakes   SPORTS
(☑ 410-542-9400; www.preakness.com; 5201 Park Heights Ave; ⊘ May) Held the third Saturday in May at Pimlico, this long-running thoroughbred horse race is the second of three races comprising the Triple Crown, occurring between the Kentucky Derby and Belmont Stakes.

Artscape   ART
(www.artscape.org; 140 W Mt Royal Ave, Patricia & Arthur Modell Performing Arts Center; ⊘ mid-Jul) **FREE** America's largest free arts festival, lasting three days, features art displays, live music and theater and dance performances.

🛏 Sleeping

Stylish, affordable B&Bs are mostly found in the downtown 'burbs of Canton, Fells Point and Federal Hill. New boutique hotels are bringing fresh, hip style to downtown, Mt Vernon and Fells Point.

In Fells Point, you can typically park for free between 8pm and 10am in spots covered by parking kiosks, though read parking signage carefully for variations and remember to move your car or pay ahead in the morning.

HI Baltimore Hostel   HOSTEL $
(☑ 410-576-8880; www.hiusa.org/baltimore; 17 W Mulberry St, Mt Vernon; dm $23-25, d $70; 🅿✳@🛜) Located in a beautifully restored 1857 mansion, the HI Baltimore has dorms with six, eight, 10 and 12 beds, as well as private doubles. Helpful management, a nice location between Mt Vernon and downtown, and a filigreed classical-chic look make this one of the region's best hostels. The front desk is open 24 hours. Breakfast is included. Parking is $8 per night.

Inn at 2920   B&B $$
(☑ 410-342-4450; www.theinnat2920.com; 2920 Elliott St, Canton; d/ste from $160/205; ✳@🛜) Housed in a former bordello, this boutique B&B offers five individual rooms, high-thread-count sheets, sleek and avant-garde decor, and the nightlife-charged neighborhood of Canton right outside your door. The Jacuzzis add a nice touch.

★ **Sagamore Pendry**   BOUTIQUE HOTEL $$$
(☑ 443-552-1400; www.pendryhotels.com; 1715 Thames St, Fells Point; d from $250; 🅿🛜@✳) Hunkered commandingly on the historic Recreation (Rec) Pier, this new luxury property is a game changer, bringing a big dose of charm and panache to Baltimore's favorite party neighborhood. With local art on the walls, nautical and equestrian touches in the common areas, and an 18th-century cannon on display (unearthed during construction), the hotel embraces Charm City's culture and history.

🍴 Eating

Baltimore is an ethnically rich town that sits on top of the greatest seafood repository in the world. The city also straddles the fault line between the down-home South and cutting-edge innovation of the urban North, meaning you'll find Southern comfort-food favorites such as biscuits and gravy at mom-

and-pop diners, and fusion creations such as sushi burritos at glossy food halls.

Handlebar Cafe
AMERICAN $

(📞 443-438-7065; www.handlebarcafe.com; 511 S Caroline St, Fells Point; mains $7-18; ⊙ 11am-2am Tue-Fri, 8am-2am Sat, 8am-2pm Sun) Owned by X-Games champ Marla Streb, this friendly bike shop and bistro – adorned with mountain bikes and gear-themed decor – serves breakfast, burritos and wood-fired pizzas behind its big garage door. Craft beer, live music and an indoor sprint series too. The vibe is so darn cool even the clumsiest goof in town will be considering a career in trick dirt biking.

Artifact Coffee
CAFE $

(📞 410-235-1881; www.artifactcoffee.com; 1500 Union Ave, Woodberry; sandwiches $9-15; ⊙ 7am-7pm Mon-Fri, from 8am Sat & Sun; 🛜📶) From the folks behind Woodberry Kitchen, Artifact serves the city's best coffee, along with tasty light meals, such as egg muffins, spinach salads, vegetarian banh mi and pastrami sandwiches. It's inside a former mill space, handsomely repurposed from its industrial past. It's a two-minute stroll from the Woodberry light-rail station.

Ekiben
FUSION $

(📞 410-558-1914; www.ekibenbaltimore.com; 1622 Eastern Ave, Fells Point; mains $9-12; ⊙ 11am-10pm Mon-Thu, to 11pm Fri & Sat) The 'neighborhood bird' at this Asian fusion box of deliciousness is a sight to behold, and then devour: a giant piece of curry-fried chicken practically leaping from the pillowy embrace of a soft steamed bun. Buns and bowls are the draw at this tiny spot. With just a few tables and stools, it's best for takeout.

Lexington Market
MARKET $

(www.lexingtonmarket.com; 400 W Lexington St, Mt Vernon; ⊙ 6am-6pm Mon-Sat) Around since 1782, Mt Vernon's Lexington Market is one of Baltimore's true old-school food markets. It's a bit shabby on the outside, but the food is great. Don't miss the crab cakes at **Faidley's** (📞 410-727-4898; www.faidleys crabcakes.com; 203 N Paca St; lump crab cakes $15; ⊙ 9:30am-5:30pm Mon-Sat) seafood stall, because my goodness, they are amazing – maybe the best in the city.

★Thames St Oyster House
SEAFOOD $$

(📞 443-449-7726; www.thamesstreetoysterhouse. com; 1728 Thames St, Fells Point; sandwiches $12-28, mains $18-29; ⊙ 5-9:30pm Sun-Thu, to 10:30pm Fri & Sat, plus 11:30am-2:30pm Wed-Sun) A Fells Point icon, this vintage dining and drinking hall serves some of Baltimore's best seafood. Dine in the polished upstairs dining room with waterfront views, take a seat in the backyard, or plunk down at the bar in front (which stays open till midnight) and watch the drink-makers and oyster-shuckers in action. The lobster rolls are recommended too.

★Helmand
AFGHANI $$

(📞 410-752-0311; www.helmand.com; 806 N Charles St, Mt Vernon; mains $14-20; ⊙ 5-10pm Sun-Thu, to 11pm Fri & Sat) The Helmand is a longtime favorite for its *kaddo borawni* (pumpkin in yogurt-garlic sauce), vegetable platters and flavorful beef-and-lamb meatballs, followed by cardamom ice cream. If you've never tried Afghan cuisine, this is a great place to do so.

★Woodberry Kitchen
AMERICAN $$$

(📞 410-464-8000; www.woodberrykitchen.com; 2010 Clipper Park Rd, Woodberry; mains brunch $17-25, dinner $23-33; ⊙ 5-9pm Sun & Tue-Thu, to 10pm Fri & Sat, plus 10am-2pm Sat & Sun) The Woodberry takes everything the Chesapeake region has to offer, plops it into a former flour mill and creates culinary magic. The menu is a playful romp through the best of regional produce, seafood and meats, from Maryland catfish with Heritage grits to Tilghman Island crab cakes, and hearty vegetable dishes made with produce plucked from nearby farms. Reserve ahead.

Food Market
MODERN AMERICAN $$$

(📞 410-366-0606; www.thefoodmarketbaltimore. com; 1017 W 36th St, Hampden; mains dinner $17-40, brunch $14-22; ⊙ 5-10pm Mon-Thu, 9am-11pm Fri & Sat, 9am-10pm Sun) Award-winning local chef Chad Gauss elevates American comfort fare to high art in dishes such as bread-and-butter-crusted sea bass with black-truffle vinaigrette, and spaghetti and crab meatballs in sherry *fra diavolo*. It's located on Hampden's lively restaurant- and shop-lined main drag.

🍸 Drinking & Nightlife

On weekends, Fells Point and Canton turn into temples of alcoholic excess that would make a Roman emperor blush. Mt Vernon and North Baltimore are a little more civilized, but any one of Baltimore's neighborhoods houses a cozy local pub. Closing time is generally 2am.

Brewer's Art
PUB

(📞 410-547-6925; www.thebrewersart.com; 1106 N Charles St, Mt Vernon; ⊙4pm-1:45am Mon-Fri, from noon Sat, from 2pm Sun) In a vintage early-20th-century mansion, Brewer's Art serves well-crafted Belgian-style microbrews to a laid-back Mt Vernon crowd. There's tasty pub fare (mac 'n' cheese, cheeseburgers) in the bar, and upscale American cuisine in the elegant back dining room. Head to the subterranean drinking den for a more raucous crowd. During happy hour (4pm to 7pm) house drafts are just $4.

Cannon Room
COCKTAIL BAR

(📞 443-552-1300; www.pendryhotels.com; 1715 Thames St, Fells Point; ⊙5pm-midnight Sun-Thu, to 1am Fri & Sat) The curved roof of this 20-seat whiskey bar, which is tucked in the deep recesses of the Sagamore Pendry (p298), was designed to resemble an oversized whiskey barrel. Look down to see the namesake cannon, which basks in the spotlight beneath a glass-panel floorboard. The cannon dates from the 1700s and was discovered during construction.

Clavel
BAR

(📞 443-900-8983; www.barclavel.com; 225 W 23rd St, Remington; ⊙5pm-1am Mon-Sat, 10am-3pm Sun) Celebrating agave is the stated mission at this sultry gathering spot, where mescal flights and a mescal library are on the menu. Complement that flight with a few of chef Carlos Raba's traditional Mexican tacos, expertly simmered and seasoned with moles, chiles and salsa. They may be the best in town.

☆ Entertainment

Baltimoreans *love* sports. The town plays hard and parties even harder, with tailgating parties in parking lots and games showing on numerous televisions in bars and restaurants.

★ Oriole Park at Camden Yards
STADIUM

(📞 888-848-2473; www.orioles.com; 333 W Camden St, Downtown; tours adult/child $9/6) The Baltimore Orioles play here, arguably the best ballpark in America, from April through September. Daily tours of the stadium are offered April through November.

M&T Bank Stadium
STADIUM

(📞 410-261-7283; www.baltimoreravens.com; 1101 Russell St, Downtown) The Baltimore Ravens play football here from September to January.

❶ Information

Baltimore Area Visitor Center (📞 877-225-8466; www.baltimore.org; 401 Light St, Inner Harbor; ⊙10am-5pm, closed Mon Jan & Feb; 📶) Located on the Inner Harbor. Sells the Harbor Pass (adult/child $75/57), which gives admission to four major area attractions (select from a total of five options).

University of Maryland Medical Center (📞 ER 410-328-9595, general 410-328-8667; www.umm.edu; 22 S Greene St, University of Maryland-Baltimore) Has a 24-hour emergency room.

❶ Getting There & Away

The Baltimore/Washington International Thurgood Marshall Airport (p293) is 10 miles south of downtown via I-295.

Departing from a terminal 2 miles southwest of Inner Harbor, **Greyhound** (📞 410-752-7682; www.greyhound.com; 2110 Haines St) has numerous buses from Washington, DC ($10 to $23, roughly every 45 minutes, one hour), and from New York ($15 to $54, 15 per day, four hours). **Peter Pan Bus Lines** (📞 800-343-9999; www.peterpanbus.com; 2110 Haines St, Carroll-Camden) also heads to New York ($20, 10 daily, 3½ hours) from the Greyhound station. **BoltBus** (📞 877-265-8287; www.boltbus.com; 1578 Maryland Ave; 📶) services to/from NYC ($14 to $29, five to 10 daily) depart from a streetside location outside Penn Station in north Baltimore.

MARC operates weekday commuter trains between **Penn Station** (https://mta.maryland.gov/marc-train; 1500 N Charles St, Charles North) and Washington's Union Station ($8, about one hour), on the Penn Line. The Brunswick Line runs from Union Station to Frederick and Harpers Ferry, WV. Amtrak trains serve the East Coast and beyond.

Supershuttle (www.supershuttle.com) provides a BWI van service to the Inner Harbor from $17.

❶ Getting Around

The light rail (http://mta.maryland.gov/light-rail) runs from BWI airport to Lexington Market, Mt Vernon and Penn Station, every 10 to 15 minutes. MARC trains run hourly on weekdays (and six to nine times daily on weekends) between Penn Station and BWI for $5. Check Maryland Transit Administration (https://mta.maryland.gov) for all local transportation schedules and fares.

Baltimore Water Taxi (📞 410-563-3900; www.baltimorewatertaxi.com; Inner Harbor; daily pass adult/child $16/9; ⊙11am-10pm Mon-Thu, from 10am Fri-Sun May-Aug, shorter hours Sep-Apr) docks at all harborside attractions and neighborhoods.

The free green-and-purple **Charm City Circulator** (📞 410-545-1956; www.charmcity circulator.com) shuttles travel four routes, three of them to tourist spots in neighborhoods in the downtown area. The Purple Route connects the Inner Harbor, Mt Vernon and Federal Hill. The Green Route runs through Fells Point. The Banner Route runs from the Inner Harbor to Fort McHenry.

Annapolis

Annapolis is as charming as state capitals get. The Colonial architecture, cobblestones, flickering lamps and brick row houses are worthy of Victorian author Charles Dickens, but the effect isn't artificial: this city has preserved, rather than created, its heritage.

Perched on Chesapeake Bay, Annapolis revolves around the city's rich maritime traditions. It's home to the US Naval Academy, whose 'middies' (midshipmen students) stroll through town in their starched white uniforms. Sailing is not just a hobby here but a way of life, and the city docks are crammed with vessels of all shapes and sizes. With its historic sights, water adventures and great dining and shopping, Annapolis is worthy of more than a day trip – try for at least two if you can.

◉ Sights

US Naval Academy UNIVERSITY
(📞 visitor center 410-293-8687; www.usnabsd. com/for-visitors; Randall St, btwn Prince George & King George Sts) The undergraduate college of the US Navy is one of the most selective universities in America. The Armel-Leftwich Visitor Center (p303) is the place to book 75-minute tours and immerse yourself in all things Academy-related. Come for the formation weekdays at 12:05pm sharp, when the 4000 students conduct a 20-minute military marching display in the yard. Photo ID is required for entry. If you've got a thing for American naval history, revel in the well-done **Naval Academy Museum** (📞 410-293-2108; www.usna.edu/museum; 118 Maryland Ave; ⊙9am-5pm Mon-Sat, from 11am Sun) FREE.

The visitor entrance for pedestrians is located at Gate 1 on Prince George St (at Craig St), within easy walking distance of the historic downtown.

Maryland State House HISTORIC BUILDING
(📞 410-260-6445; http://msa.maryland.gov/msa/ mdstatehouse/html/home.html; 99 State Circle; ⊙9am-5pm) FREE The country's oldest state

capitol in continuous legislative use, the grand 1772 State House also served as national capital from 1783 to 1784. Notably, General George Washington returned his commission here as Commander-in-Chief of the Continental Army in 1783 after the Revolutionary War, ensuring that governmental power would be shared with Congress. The exhibits and portraits here are impressive and include Washington's copy of his speech resigning his commission. Pick up a self-guided tour map on the 1st floor.

The upside-down giant acorn atop the building's dome stands for wisdom. The Maryland Senate is in session from January to April.

Photo ID is required at the entrance, where you'll pass through metal detectors.

Hammond Harwood House MUSEUM
(📞 410-263-4683; www.hammondharwoodhouse. org; 19 Maryland Ave; adult/child $10/5; ⊙noon-5pm Wed-Mon Apr-Dec) Of the many historical homes in town, the Hammond Harwood House, dating from 1774, is the one to visit. It has a superb collection of decorative arts, including 18th-century furniture, paintings and ephemera, and is one of the finest existing British Colonial homes in America. Knowledgeable guides help bring the past to life on 50-minute house tours (held at the top of the hour).

Even if you don't have time for a tour, take a moment to stroll past. Thomas Jefferson called the ornate front door the 'most beautiful door in America.' We think it is rather nice too.

Kunta Kinte–Alex Haley Memorial MONUMENT
(City Dock, off Market Space) Beside City Dock, the Kunta Kinte–Alex Haley Memorial marks the spot where Kunta Kinte – ancestor of *Roots* author Alex Haley – was brought in chains from Africa. The statues here depict Haley sharing the story of his ancestor with three children.

🛏 Sleeping

Inns and B&Bs fill the historic downtown. Several hotels line West St, which runs west from Church Circle. National hotel chains cluster near exits 22 and 23 off US 50/301.

ScotLaur Inn GUESTHOUSE $
(📞 410-268-5665; www.scotlaurinn.com; 165 Main St; d $120-150; P❋🐾) The folks from Chick & Ruth's Delly offer 10 rooms above the

MARYLAND BLUE CRABS

Eating at a crab shack, where the dress code stops at shorts and flip-flops, is the quintessential Chesapeake Bay experience. Folks in these parts take their crabs seriously, and can spend hours debating the intricacies of how to crack a crab, the proper way to prepare crabs and where to find the best ones. There is one thing Marylanders can agree on: they must be blue crabs (scientific name: *Callinectes sapidus*, or 'beautiful swimmers'). Sadly, blue crab numbers have suffered with the continuing pollution of the Chesapeake Bay, and many crabs you eat here are imported from elsewhere.

Steamed crabs are prepared very simply, using beer and Old Bay seasoning. One of the best crab shacks in the state is near Annapolis at **Jimmy Cantler's Riverside Inn** (☎ 410-757-1311; www.cantlers.com; 458 Forest Beach Rd; mains $12-29; ⏰ 11am-10pm Sun-Thu, to 11pm Fri & Sat), located 4 miles northeast of the Maryland State House, across the Severn River Bridge; here, eating a steamed crab has been elevated to an art form – a hands-on, messy endeavor, normally accompanied by corn on the cob and ice-cold beer. Another fine spot is across the bay at **Red Roost** (☎ 410-546-5443; www.theredroost.com; 2670 Clara Rd, Whitehaven; mains $18-35; ⏰ 5:30-9pm Mon-Thu, to 10pm Fri, noon-10pm Sat, to 9pm Sun mid-Mar–Oct).

restaurant, each with wrought-iron beds, floral wallpaper and private bath. The quarters are small but have a cozy and familial atmosphere (the guesthouse is named after the owners' children Scott and Lauren, whose photos adorn the hallways). Breakfast included. Two-night minimum stay on weekends.

Historic Inns of Annapolis   HOTEL $$

(☎ 410-263-2641; www.historicinnsofannapolis. com; 58 State Circle; d from $150; P❄🐾) The Historic Inns comprise three different boutique guesthouses, each set in a heritage building in the heart of old Annapolis: the Maryland Inn, the Governor Calvert House and the Robert Johnson House. Common areas are packed with period details, and the best rooms boast antiques, fireplaces and attractive views (the cheapest can be small). Check in at Governor Calvert House.

✗ Eating

With the Chesapeake Bay at its doorstep, Annapolis has superb seafood. The openings of several farm-to-table-minded restaurants have added depth to the dining scene along Main St and near the dock.

Chick & Ruth's Delly   DINER $

(☎ 410-269-6737; www.chickandruths.com; 165 Main St; mains breakfast & lunch $8-15, dinner $10-20; ⏰ 6:30am-11:30pm Sun-Thu, to 12:30am Fri & Sat; 🐾) A cornerstone of Annapolis, the-squeeze-'em-in-tight Delly bursts with affable quirkiness and a big menu, heavy on sandwiches and breakfast fare. Patriots can relive grade-school days reciting the

Pledge of Allegiance at 8:30am weekdays and 9:30am Saturday and Sunday. Breakfast is served all day.

Vida Taco Bar   MEXICAN $

(☎ 443-837-6521; www.vidatacobar.com; 200 Main St; tacos $4-6; ⏰ 5-10pm Tue-Thu, noon-11pm Fri & Sat, noon-9pm Sun) The crowd is stylish – and getting its drink on – at this convivial spot serving fantastic street tacos and strong margaritas.

★ Vin 909   AMERICAN $$

(☎ 410-990-1846; www.vin909.com; 909 Bay Ridge Ave; small plates $12-21; ⏰ 5:30-10pm Wed & Thu, to 11pm Fri, 5-11pm Sat, 5-10pm Sun, plus noon-3pm Wed-Sat, shorter hours in winter) Perched on a little wooded hill and boasting an intimate yet enjoyably casual ambience, Vin is the best thing happening in Annapolis for food. Farm-sourced goodness features in the form of duck confit, dry-aged Angus-beef sliders and homemade pizzas with toppings such as wild-boar meatballs or honey-braised squash with applewood bacon.

There's a great wine selection, including more than three dozen wines by the glass. No reservations are accepted, so arrive early to beat the often lengthy waits.

Boatyard Bar & Grill   SEAFOOD $$

(☎ 410-216-6206; www.boatyardbarandgrill. com; 400 4th St, Eastport; mains $10-27; ⏰ 7:30am-midnight Mon-Fri, from 8am Sat & Sun; 🐾) This bright, nautically themed restaurant with a big central bar is a festive and welcoming spot for crab cakes, fish and chips, oysters, fish tacos and other seafood.

Happy hour (3pm to 7pm Monday to Friday) draws in the crowds with $3 drafts and 99¢ oysters.

Drinking & Entertainment

Fox's Den
PUB

(☑ 443-808-8991; www.foxsden.com; 179 B Main St; ⏱ 5pm-midnight Mon, Wed & Thu, to 1am Fri, 4pm-1am Sat, 4pm-midnight Sun) Head underground for microbrews and craft cocktails, all served in a snug gastropub in the thick of the Main St action. Things are hopping on Monday when the brick-oven pizzas are $10.

Rams Head On Stage
LIVE MUSIC

(☑ 410-268-4545; www.ramsheadonstage.com; 33 West St; tickets $15-115) Settle in at tables to watch performances by well-known bands and musicians, from Dave Davies to Lee Ann Womack to Keller Williams. Small bites ($8 to $16), wine, cocktails and beer are served. The venue is next door to **Rams Head Tavern** (☑ 410-268-4545; www.ramsheadtavern.com; 33 West St; mains lunch & dinner $10-30, brunch $10-16; ⏱ 11am-2am Mon-Sat, from 10am Sun), which has a separate menu.

ℹ Information

There's a **visitor center** (☑ 410-280-0445; www.visitannapolis.org; 26 West St; ⏱ 9am-5pm) in town and a seasonal information booth at City Dock (9am to 5pm March to October). For information about tours and sights at the Naval Academy, stop by the expansive **Armel-Leftwich Visitor Center** (☑ 410-293-8687; www.usnabsd.com/for-visitors; 52 King George St, Gate 1, City Dock entrance; tours adult/child $12/10; ⏱ 9am-5pm Mar-Dec, to 4pm Jan & Feb) on the Yard near the waterfront.

ℹ Getting There & Away

Annapolis is 26 miles from Baltimore and 30 miles from Washington, DC. Check https://mta.maryland.gov for light rail and bus route options connecting Baltimore/Washington International Thurgood Marshall Airport (p293) and Baltimore with Annapolis.

Greyhound (☑ 800-231-2222; www.greyhound.com; 275 Harry S Truman Pkwy) runs buses to Washington, DC ($8 to $10, daily), from a pickup and drop-off stop 5 miles west of the historic downtown.

Eastern Shore

Just across the Chesapeake Bay Bridge, nondescript suburbs give way to unbroken miles of bird-dotted wetlands, serene waterscapes, endless cornfields, sandy beaches and friendly villages. The Eastern Shore retains its charm despite the growing influx of gentrifiers and day-trippers. This area revolves around the water: working waterfront communities still survive off Chesapeake Bay and its tributaries, and boating, fishing, crabbing and hunting are integral to local life. Come here to explore nature by trail, boat or bicycle, to read on the beach, to delve into regional history and, of course, to enjoy the delicious seafood.

🏃 Activities

Rebecca T Ruark
CRUISE

(☑ text 410-829-3976; www.skipjack.org; Dogwood Harbor, off US 33; 2hr cruise adult/child $30/15; ⏱ 11am-1pm & 5-7pm daily May-Oct) For old-fashioned fun, hop aboard this 1886 skipjack, a traditional oyster-dredging boat, for a sunset sail. It's the oldest one on the Chesapeake Bay and is now a historic landmark. Cash or check only.

Lady Patty Classic Yacht Charters
BOATING

(☑ 410-886-1127; www.ladypatty.com; 6176 Tilghman Island Rd, Tilghman Island; cruises adult/child from $47/26; ⏱ tours Wed-Mon May-Oct) Runs two-hour sails on the Chesapeake on a 1935 racing yacht. Think teak, bronze and wind-driven prowess – these trips are for the pure thrill of sailing.

🍴 Eating

★ Blacksmith Bar & Restaurant
AMERICAN $$

(☑ 410-973-2102; www.blacksmithberlin.com; 104 Pitts St, Berlin; mains lunch $11-22, dinner $19-29; ⏱ 11:30am-9:30pm Mon-Sat) Folks across the Eastern Shore recommend this cozy and congenial spot, which began life as a blacksmith shop and now serves hearty portions of delicious farm-to-table comfort food. Servers soon feel like friends – in a non-annoying way – while the low ceiling and thick walls evoke a warm roadside tavern. The jumbo lump crab cakes with herbed potatoes are divine.

Fins Ale House & Raw Bar
SEAFOOD $$

(☑ 410-641-3000; www.facebook.com/finsalehouseberlin; 119 N Main St, Berlin; mains lunch $10-17, dinner $17-29; ⏱ 11:30am-8:30pm Mon-Thu, 11am-9:30pm Fri & Sat, 11am-8:30pm Sun) The lump crab cake is so good you might consider packing up and moving to Berlin. Based on the happy crowds here, others may have had the same idea. It's not on the water, but considerate service, big windows, a cozy patio and enticing seafood dishes make Fins the next best thing to a seafood shack by the ocean.

ℹ Getting There & Around

The region is best explored by car. Baltimore is 70 miles from Easton and 150 miles from Ocean City. Berlin is 23 miles east of Salisbury and 9 miles west of Ocean City, along the route between these two larger towns. Greyhound stops in Easton and Salisbury.

Ocean City

Two words describe 'the OC' from June through August: party central. This is where you'll experience the American seaside resort in its wildest glory. Some might call it tacky. Others might call it, well, fun. Here you can take a spin on nausea-inducing thrill rides, buy a T-shirt with obscene slogans and drink to excess at cheesy theme bars.

The center of action is the 2.5-mile-long boardwalk, which stretches from the inlet to 27th St. The beach is attractive, but you'll have to contend with heavy traffic and noisy crowds; the beaches north of the boardwalk are much quieter. How busy is it? They say Ocean City welcomes eight million visitors annually, with most of them arriving in summer – in a town with a year-round population of just over 7000!

⊙ Sights

Ocean City Life-Saving Station Museum   MUSEUM
(📞 410-289-4991; www.ocmuseum.org; 813 S Atlantic Ave; adult/child $5/3; ⊙ 10am-5pm May-Oct, 10am-4pm Sat & Sun Nov-Apr) This small but engaging museum sits inside an 1891 life-saving station at the southern end of the boardwalk. Here, the station keeper and six to eight 'surfmen' lived and responded to emergency calls from ships in distress. Exhibits include stories about nearby shipwrecks and a display spotlighting rescue gear, including a 26ft-long rescue boat, which would look rather small and fragile in a storm!

Boardwalk history and regional surfing – check out that 1920s pine surfboard – are also covered.

Trimpers Rides   AMUSEMENT PARK
(📞 410-289-8617; www.trimpersrides.com; S 1st St & Boardwalk; unlimited afternoon rides $28; ⊙ 1pm-midnight Mon-Fri, from noon Sat & Sun, hours vary seasonally) If you really want to engage in tacky seaside fun to the fullest possible extent, hit up Trimpers Rides, one of the oldest of old-school amusement parks. Have some fries with vinegar, play the games and enjoy people-watching. Tickets are 75¢ each, with a varying number required per ride.

WORTH A TRIP

ASSATEAGUE ISLAND

The Assateague Island seashore, a perfectly barren landscape of sand dunes and beautiful, secluded beaches, is just 8 miles south but a world away from Ocean City. This undeveloped barrier island is populated by a herd of wild horses, made famous in the book *Misty of Chincoteague*.

The 37-mile-long island is divided into three sections: **Assateague State Park** (📞 410-641-2918; http://dnr.maryland.gov; 6915 Stephen Decatur Hwy; Jun-Aug $6, Sep-May $5; ⊙ day-use areas 7am-sunset, campground late Apr-Oct; 🅿) in Maryland; federally administered **Assateague Island National Seashore** (📞 410-641-1441; www.nps.gov/asis; 7206 National Seashore Lane, Berlin; adult/vehicle access per week $10/20; ⊙ visitor center 9am-5pm daily Mar-Dec, Thu-Mon Jan & Feb; 🅿); and **Chincoteague National Wildlife Refuge** (📞 757-336-6122; www.fws.gov; 8231 Beach Rd, Chincoteague Island; vehicle pass $20; ⊙ 5am-10pm May-Sep, 6am-6pm Nov-Mar, to 8pm Apr & Oct; 🅿🐾) in Virginia. For an overview, check out the Plan your Visit section of the National Park Service website (www.nps.gov/asis) or pick up the *Assateague Island National Seashore* pamphlet, which has a helpful map.

As well as swimming and sunbathing, recreational activities include birding, hiking, kayaking, canoeing, camping, crabbing and fishing. There are no food or drink services on the Maryland side of the island in the off-season. Don't forget insect repellent: the mosquitoes and biting horseflies can be ferocious!

🛏 Sleeping

Hotels and motels line the boardwalk and the streets running parallel to the ocean. These lodgings are a mix of national chains and independently owned accommodations. From June through August they're ready to pack in guests – and prices can skyrocket. For a quieter stay, try a B&B or spend the night in Berlin, 8 miles south. Many smaller properties close in the winter.

King Charles Hotel GUESTHOUSE **$$**
(☑ 410-289-6141; www.kingcharleshotel.com; 1209 N Baltimore Ave, cnr 12th St; d $120-200, q $125-210; ☉ May-Oct; P ❄ ☏) This place could be a quaint summer cottage, except it happens to be a short stroll to the heart of the boardwalk action. It has aging but clean rooms with small porches attached, and it's quiet (ie it's not a party hotel).

🍴 Eating & Drinking

Surf 'n' turf and all-you-can-eat deals are the order of the day.

Liquid Assets MODERN AMERICAN **$$**
(☑ 410-524-7037; https://la94.com; 9301 Coastal Hwy, cnr 94th St; mains $14-38; ☉ 11:30am-11pm Sun-Thu, to midnight Fri & Sat) Like a diamond in the rough, this bistro and wine shop is hidden in a strip mall in north OC. The menu is a refreshing mix of innovative seafood, grilled meats and regional classics. The small bar area is a convivial place to be early in the evening, and the pan-steamed mussels are a hit with the drinking crowd.

Seacrets BAR
(☑ 410-524-4900; www.seacrets.com; 117 49th St; ☉ 11am-2am, hours vary seasonally) This is a Jamaican-themed, rum-soaked bar straight out of MTV's *Spring Break*. You can drift around on a big raft while sipping a drink and people-watching at OC's most famous meat market. When it comes to the wildest beach-party bar, this is the one against which all other claimants must be judged.

ⓘ Getting There & Around

Ocean City is 140 miles southeast of Baltimore via Hwy 10 and US 50. **Greyhound** (☑ 800-231-222; www.greyhound.com; 101 S Division St, S Division St Transit Ctr) stops 30 miles west of Ocean City in Salisbury, where you can transfer to a local shuttle running to the southern end of the boardwalk.

The **Coastal Hwy Beach Bus** (www.ococean.com/explore-oc/getting-around-oc; day pass $3; ☉ 24hr Apr-early Nov, hours vary rest of the year) travels up and down the length of the beach around the clock year-round. There's also a **tram** (☑ 410-289-5311; www.ococean.com/explore-oc/getting-around-oc; per ride $4, day pass $8; ☉ 11am-midnight Jun-Aug, hours vary Sep) that runs along the boardwalk from June through September. For details about off-season transit and schedules, visit www.shoretransit.org.

Western Maryland

The western spine of Maryland is mountain country. The Appalachian peaks soar to 3000ft above sea level, and the surrounding valleys are packed with rugged scenery and Civil War battlefields. This is Maryland's playground, where hiking, cycling, skiing, rock climbing and white-water rafting draw the outdoor-loving crowd. Two long-distance hiking and biking trails are particularly noteworthy: the Great Allegheny Passage and the C&O Canal towpath, both offering an invigorating mix of history, scenery and adventure.

Passionate local chefs are embracing the region's bounty, and you'll find fantastic farm-to-table fare in the larger towns. There are plenty of welcoming microbreweries too.

When trip planning, remember that the narrow Maryland panhandle is bordered by Virginia, West Virginia and Pennsylvania. If you're exploring Civil War battlefields or looking for larger towns for an overnight stay, check for options that may be just a few miles over state lines.

ⓘ Getting There & Around

Towns in western Maryland may look close to each other on a map, but narrow and twisting mountain roads can extend driving times. The main interstates running east–west are I-70 and I-68, with I-81 traveling north–south through the region.

MARC trains (https://mta.maryland.gov) from Union Station in Washington, DC, stop in **Frederick** (☑ 866-743-3682; 100 S East St) and **Brunswick** (100 S Maple St, Brunswick), while Amtrak serves Cumberland (p307) on the Capitol Limited route, which also connects with DC. Greyhound stops in both Cumberland and Frederick.

For flights, consider Washington Dulles International Airport (p312) or Baltimore/Washington International Thurgood Marshall Airport (p293).

Frederick & Mt Airy

Central Frederick is, well, perfect. Its historic, pedestrian-friendly center of red-brick row houses is filled with a diverse array of restaurants and shops. The engaged, cultured arts community is anchored by the excellent Weinberg Center for the Arts. The meandering Carroll Creek runs through it all, flanked by a lovely park with art and gardens. Unlike other communities in the region with historic districts, this is a mid-size city, an important commuter base for thousands of federal government employees and a biotechnology hub in its own right. For travelers, Frederick makes a great central base for exploring Brunswick, Mt Airy and the regional Civil War battlefields.

⊙ Sights

Antietam
National Battlefield   HISTORIC SITE

(☎301-432-5124; www.nps.gov/anti; 5831 Dunker Church Rd, Sharpsburg; 3-day pass per person/vehicle $7/15; ⊙grounds sunrise-sunset, visitor center 9am-5pm) The site of the bloodiest day in American history is now, ironically, supremely peaceful, quiet and haunting – and uncluttered, save for plaques and statues. On September 17, 1862, General Robert E Lee's first invasion of the north was stalled here in a tactical stalemate that left more than 23,000 dead, wounded or missing – more casualties than America had suffered in all its previous wars combined. Check out the exhibits in the visitor center then walk or drive the grounds.

Poignantly, many of the battlefield graves are inscribed with German and Irish names, a roll call of immigrants who died fighting for their new homeland.

The visitor center shows a short film (playing on the hour and half-hour) about the events that transpired here. It also sells books and materials, including self-guided driving and walking tours of the battlefield.

Antietam is 25 miles west of Frederick and just 5 miles northeast of Shepherdstown, WV.

National Museum
of Civil War Medicine   MUSEUM

(☎301-695-1864; www.civilwarmed.org; 48 E Patrick St; adult/student/child $9.50/7/free; ⊙10am-5pm Mon-Sat, from 11am Sun) The National Museum of Civil War Medicine gives a fascinating, and sometimes gruesome, look at the health conditions soldiers and doctors faced during the war, as well as important medical advances that resulted from the conflict.

🛏 Sleeping & Eating

Hollerstown Hill B&B   B&B $

(☎301-228-3630; www.hollerstownhill.com; 4 Clarke Pl; r $130-170; P❈🐾) The elegant, friendly Hollerstown has four pattern-heavy rooms, two resident dogs, a doll collection and a fancy billiards room. This lovely Victorian sits right in the middle of the historic downtown area of Frederick, so you're within easy walking distance of all the goodness. No children under 16.

Brewer's Alley   PUB FOOD $$

(☎301-631-0089; www.brewers-alley.com; 124 N Market St; mains $11-26; ⊙11:30am-11:30pm Sun-Tue, to midnight Wed & Thu, to 2:30am Fri & Sat; 🐾) This bouncy brewpub is one of our favorite places in Frederick for several reasons. First, the beer: house-brewed, plenty of variety, delicious. Second, the burgers: enormous, half-pound monstrosities of staggeringly yummy proportions. Third, the rest of the menu: excellent Chesapeake seafood plus Frederick County farm produce and meats. The small patio is pleasant on sunny days.

Volt   AMERICAN $$

(☎301-696-8658; www.voltrestaurant.com; 228 N Market St; dinner mains $22-29, brunch $16-30; ⊙5:30-9:30pm Tue-Sun, 11:30am-2pm Fri-Sun) Let's class it up a bit, shall we? Step inside an 1800s brownstone mansion in the heart of the historic district for a white-linen dinner of regionally sourced meats, produce and seafood dishes from executive chef and regional restaurateur Bryan Voltaggio. The 15-course tasting menu is $150. Business-casual attire is recommended.

☆ Entertainment

Weinberg Center for the Arts   THEATER

(☎301-600-2828; www.weinbergcenter.org; 20 W Patrick St) Check the calendar for the schedule of classic and silent movies, live music ranging from banjo to funk and an intriguing speaker series – featuring the likes of autism spokesperson and professor Temple Grandin, and actor Mark Ruffalo – supported by an engaged and cultured arts community.

❶ Information

Frederick Visitor Center (☎301-600-4047; www.visitfrederick.org/visit/visitor-center; 151 S East St; ⊙9am-5:30pm)

ℹ Getting There & Away

Frederick is accessible via Greyhound and MARC trains (Monday to Friday only) at the transit center (p305) located one block north of the visitor center. The MARC train Brunswick Line connects Frederick with Harpers Ferry, WV, Silver Spring, MD, and Washington, DC.

Cumberland

At the Potomac River, the frontier outpost of Fort Cumberland (not to be confused with the Cumberland Gap between Virginia and Kentucky) was the pioneer gateway across the Alleghenies to Pittsburgh and the Ohio River. With the completion of the C&O Canal and the arrival of the railroad in the 1800s, the city became a commercial hub, transporting goods and natural resources down the river to Georgetown.

Cumberland today has expanded into the outdoor recreation trade to guide visitors into the region's rivers, forests and mountains. The heart of the outdoor scene is Canal Pl, where two long-distance hike-and-bike paths meet: the C&O Canal towpath and the Great Allegheny Passage. Their junction point is just a few steps from the depot for the popular scenic railroad. Canal Pl is also just a short stroll from the pedestrian-friendly streets of downtown.

◉ Sights & Activities

C&O Canal
National Historic Park　　　NATIONAL PARK
(www.nps.gov/choh; 13 Canal St, Western Maryland Railway Station; ⊙sunrise-sunset) FREE A marvel of engineering, the C&O Canal was designed to stretch alongside the Potomac River from the Chesapeake Bay to the Ohio River. Construction on the canal began in 1828 but was halted here in 1850 by the Appalachian Mountains. The park's protected 184.5-mile corridor includes a 12ft-wide towpath, now a hiking and bicycling trail, which stretches from here to Georgetown in DC. The **Cumberland Visitor Center** (☑301-722-8226; ⊙9am-5pm; ℗), also located here, has displays chronicling the importance of river trade in eastern seaboard history.

Great Allegheny
Passage – Cumberland　　　CYCLING
(www.gaptrail.org; Canal Pl) From its trailhead in Pittsburgh, this biking-and-hiking trail runs 150 scenic miles to its terminus in Cumberland. Here it meets the 184.5-mile C&O Canal towpath. This trail is free of cars.

Cumberland Trail Connection　　　CYCLING
(☑301-777-8724; www.ctcbikes.com; 14 Howard St, Canal Pl; per half-day/day/week from $20/35/175; ⊙8am-7pm Apr-Oct, 10am-5pm Tue-Sun Nov-Mar) Conveniently located near the start of the C&O Canal towpath, this outfit rents bicycles (cruisers, touring bikes and mountain bikes), and also arranges shuttle service anywhere from Pittsburgh to DC. Does bike repair, too. Check the website for a basic map of the towpath.

⊨ Sleeping & Eating

Fairfield Inn & Suites　　　HOTEL $$
(☑301-722-0340; www.marriott.com; 21 N Wineow St; r $154; ℗✳@🛜🏊) This modern and recently renovated property bordering the C&O Canal towpath is a prime spot for cyclists. The included continental buffet breakfast will energize you for your ride. It's also an easy walk to the **Western Maryland Scenic Railroad** (☑800-872-4650; www.wmsr.com; 13 Canal St; adult/child $56/40; ⊙11:30am Thu-Sun, 6pm Sat mid-Apr–Oct, hours & trips vary seasonally) depot as well as downtown. Rooms come with a microwave and mini-fridge.

Queen City Creamery & Deli　　　DINER $
(☑301-777-0011; www.queencitycreamery.com; 108 W Harrison St; sandwiches $8-10, 1 scoop custard $3; ⊙7am-9pm Mon-Thu, to 10pm Fri, 8am-10pm Sat, 8am-9pm Sun, hours vary seasonally) This retro soda fountain is like a 1940s time warp, with creamy shakes and homemade frozen custard, thick sandwiches and belly-filling breakfasts.

ℹ Getting There & Away

The **Amtrak station** (☑800-872-7245; www.amtrak.com; 201 E Harrison St) is close to downtown. Cumberland is on the daily Capitol Limited route that links Washington, DC, and Chicago. Pittsburgh is 100 miles northwest of the city. Greyhound buses also stop at the station. From the eastern part of Maryland, Cumberland can be reached by following I-70 west to I-68 west.

DELAWARE

Tiny Delaware, the nation's second-smallest state (96 miles long and less than 35 miles across at its widest point) is overshadowed by its neighbors – and often overlooked by visitors to the region. And that's too bad, because Delaware has a lot more on offer than just tax-free shopping and chicken farms.

Long, white sandy beaches, cute colonial villages, a cozy countryside and small-town charm characterize the state that happily calls itself the 'Small Wonder.' It's also the home state of former vice president and US senator Joe Biden, a resident of Wilmington.

History

In colonial days, Delaware was the subject of an aggressive land feud between Dutch, Swedish and British settlers. The first two imported classically northern European middle-class concepts, the third a plantation-based aristocracy – which is partly why Delaware remains a typically mid-Atlantic cultural hybrid today.

The little state's big moment came on December 7, 1787, when Delaware became the first colony to ratify the US Constitution, thus becoming the first state in the Union. It remained in that union throughout the Civil War, despite supporting slavery. During this period, as throughout much of the state's history, the economy drew on its chemical industry. DuPont, the world's second-largest chemical company, was founded here in 1802 as a gunpowder factory by French immigrant Eleuthère Irénée du Pont. Low taxes drew other firms (particularly credit-card companies) in the 20th century, boosting the state's prosperity.

ⓘ Getting There & Around

The coastal cities are 120 miles from both Washington, DC, and Baltimore. Wilmington is in the northern reaches of the state, 75 miles northeast of Baltimore via I-95 and 30 miles south of Philadelphia via I-95 – and just a few miles from the Pennsylvania state line. Amtrak runs nine routes through Wilmington. The closest major airport to Wilmington is Philadelphia International Airport (p163).

Delaware Coast

With beach towns for every personality along with gorgeous coastal views, Delaware's 28 miles of sandy Atlantic beaches are the best reason to linger here. They're also quick and easy to reach for city folk from Washington, DC, Baltimore and NYC looking to escape the grind. Head to Lewes for the walkable downtown, filled with history and great restaurants. Gay-friendly Rehoboth also works well for families and those looking for upscale distractions, from pampering spas to fine cocktails. Just south of Rehoboth, wild Dewey is the place to get

your beach party on while Bethany is made for slow days on the sand. Running south all the way to the Maryland border, pretty beaches and state parks stretch between the towns and connect the ocean and the bays. Cycling the parks and kayaking the salt marshes are top outdoor activities.

Most businesses and services are open year-round. Off-season (outside of June to August), price bargains abound.

Lewes

In 1631, the Dutch gave this whaling settlement the pretty name of Zwaanendael (Valley of the Swans), before promptly getting massacred by local Nanticokes. The name was changed to Lewes (loo-iss) when William Penn gained control of the area. Today it's an attractive seaside gem with a mix of English and Dutch architecture – and loads of great restaurants. Pretty Cape Henlopen State Park is only 2.5 miles from downtown.

Cape Henlopen State Park   STATE PARK
(☑ 302-645-8983; www.destateparks.com/beaches/cape-henlopen; 15099 Cape Henlopen Dr; Mar-Nov per vehicle $10, Dec-Feb free; ⊙ 8am-sunset; 🅿️📶) One mile east of Lewes, more than 4000 acres of dune bluffs, pine forests and wetlands are preserved at this lovely state park that's popular with bird-watchers, beachgoers and campers. There's also a 3.5-mile paved loop cycling trail. You can see clear to Cape May from the observation tower. **North Shores beach** draws many gay and lesbian couples. Campsites ($35 to $44) and cabins ($120) are also available. The admission fee is cash only.

Hotel Rodney   HOTEL $$
(☑ 302-645-6466; www.hotelrodneydelaware.com; 142 2nd St; r $150-260, ste $270-330; 🅿️📶@ 📶🔌) This charming boutique hotel features exquisite bedding and restored antique furniture, but it also has plenty of modern touches that keep it all feeling very fresh.

ⓘ Getting There & Away

Cape May–Lewes Ferry (☑ 800-643-3779; www.capemaylewesferry.com; 43 Cape Henlopen Dr; round-trip per car $50, adult/child 6-13yr $18/9) runs daily ferries (1½ hours) across Delaware Bay to New Jersey from the terminal, 1 mile from downtown Lewes. For foot passengers, a seasonal shuttle bus ($5) operates between the ferry terminal and Lewes. Reservations recommended. The town sits on the coast just off the Coastal Hwy/Rte 1.

Rehoboth Beach

As the closest stretch of sand to Washington, DC (121 miles), Rehoboth Beach is often dubbed 'the Nation's Summer Capital.' It is both a family-friendly and gay-friendly destination. To escape the chaos of busy Rehoboth Ave (and the heavily built-up outskirts), wander into the side streets downtown. There you'll find a mix of gingerbread houses, tree-lined streets, posh restaurants and kiddie amusements, plus a wide beach fronted by a mile-long boardwalk.

🛏 Sleeping

★Cottages at
Indian River Marina   COTTAGE $$$
(☑302-227-3071; www.destateparks.com/reservations/cottages; 39415 Inlet Rd; per week peak/shoulder/off-season $1900/1250/850, 2 days off-season $200-300; 🅿❄) These cottages, located in Delaware Seashore State Park 6 miles south of Dewey Beach, are some of our favorite local vacation rentals. Not for the decor per se, but for the patios and unadulterated views across the pristine beach to the water. Each cottage has two bedrooms and a loft.

While they must be rented out by the week during the summer, they're available in two-day increments off-season.

Avenue Inn & Spa   SPA HOTEL $$$
(☑800-433-5870; www.avenueinn.com; 33 Wilmington Ave; d $275-400; 🏠❄) Rooms sport a crisp and unfussy beach style at this relaxing property just one block from the boardwalk. Complimentary perks such as afternoon wine and cheese followed by fresh cookies in the evening contribute to the hospitable vibe. Spa services include deep-tissue massage, organic facials and an Earl Grey 'teatox' body treatment.

🍴 Eating & Drinking

Chesapeake & Maine   GASTROPUB $$
(☑302-226-3600; www.dogfish.com; 316 Rehoboth Ave; mains $18-29; ◷3-10pm) The bar at Chesapeake & Maine sparkles with style and top-notch service. Beer-making powerhouse Dogfish Head owns the place, and the acclaimed cocktails here are mixed with spirits produced by Dogfish Head Distilling Co. The raw bar and the seafood dishes are sourced from Chesapeake Bay and coastal Maine.

Blue Hen   AMERICAN $$
(☑302-278-7842; www.thebluehenrehoboth.com; 33 Wilmington Ave; mains $14-32; ◷noon-late Thu-Mon) From the same team behind the lauded Henlopen City Oyster House, the Blue Hen earned a Best New Restaurant semi-finalist nomination from the James Beard Foundation shortly after it opened in 2017. Inside the eatery's farmhouse-chic digs, chef Julia Robinson whips up gourmet comfort fare, including deviled eggs with chicken cracklins and lobster pot pie.

The cocktail game is strong at the stylish bar, where communal tables keep the vibe festive. There's a firepit out front. The Blue Hen, named after the state bird of Delaware, sits inside Avenue Inn & Spa.

★Henlopen City
Oyster House   SEAFOOD $$$
(☑302-260-9193; www.hcoysterhouse.com; 50 Wilmington Ave; sandwiches $12-24, mains $28-38; ◷dinner from 5pm) Seafood lovers won't want to miss this elegant but inviting spot, where an enticing raw bar and mouthwatering seafood dishes draw crowds (arrive early; no reservations). Good microbrews, cocktails and wine selections round out the appeal. The menu changes every day. Happy hours runs from 3pm to 5pm; lunch is served in the off-season.

★Dogfish Head
Brewings & Eats   PUB
(☑302-226-2739; www.dogfish.com; 320 Rehoboth Ave; mains $12-25; ◷11am-11pm Sun-Thu, to 1am Fri & Sat, to 3pm Sun) There's a long list of beers available at this iconic brewery, which also serves tasty pizzas, burgers, crab cakes and other pub fare. They all go perfectly with the award-winning IPAs. Kids menu available with $6 meals. Dogfish is a regional draw.

ℹ Getting There & Away

BestBus (www.bestbus.com) offers services from DC ($40, 2½ hours) and NYC ($49, 4½ hours) to Rehoboth, running Friday to Sunday in summertime only (late May through early September). Also stops in Dewey Beach.

The Jolly Trolley (www.jollytrolley.com) connects Rehoboth and Dewey beaches, and makes frequent stops along the way. A round-trip costs $5, and the trolley runs from 8am to 2am June through August. Cash only.

Wilmington & Brandywine Valley

A unique cultural milieu (African Americans, Jews and Caribbeans) and an energetic arts scene make this city worth a visit. Wilmington is also a good launchpad for exploring the scenic Brandywine Valley, 6 miles north, and its many historic homes, gardens and mills. Much of the current grandeur traces back to the Du Pont family, whose legacy began with a gunpowder mill on the banks of the Brandywine River.

The 1.3-mile downtown riverfront along the Christina River is a nice place for a patio meal and a stroll. And no description of Wilmington is complete without mentioning hometown politician Joe Biden, former vice-president and US senator, who regularly rode Amtrak between Wilmington and Washington, DC. After his tenure as vice-president ended in 2017, he rode Amtrak home.

◉ Sights

Delaware Art Museum MUSEUM
(☏302-571-9590; www.delart.org; 2301 Kentmere Pkwy; adult/child 7-18yr $12/6, 4-8pm Thu & Sun free; ⊙10am-4pm Wed & Fri-Sun, to 8pm Thu; ℗) Exhibits work of the local Brandywine School, including Edward Hopper, John Sloan and three generations of Wyeths. The museum's fantastic collection of original works by illustrator Howard Pyle, a native of Wilmington, is showcased in six galleries.

Winterthur HISTORIC SITE
(☏302-888-4600; www.winterthur.org; 5105 Kennett Pike/Rte 52; adult/child 2-11yr $20/6; ⊙10am-5pm Tue-Sun Mar-Dec, closed Jan & Feb) Six miles northwest of Wilmington is the 175-room country estate of industrialist Henry Francis du Pont and his collection of antiques and American arts, one of the world's largest. Nice gardens too.

Brandywine Creek State Park STATE PARK
(☏302-577-3534; www.destateparks.com/Brandy wineCreek; 41 Adams Dam Rd; Mar-Nov per vehicle $8, Dec-Feb free; ⊙8am-sunset, nature center 8am-4pm Mon-Fri; ℗) This state park is the gem of the area. A green space this size would be impressive anywhere, but is doubly so considering how close it is to prodigious urban development. Nature trails and shallow streams wend through the park. Come here to watch the annual hawk migrations, flying north in the spring (March to May) and south in the fall (September to November).

🛌 Sleeping & Eating

Holiday Inn Express HOTEL $$
(☏302-479-7900; www.ihg.com; 300 Rocky Run Pkwy; d $150, ste $180-230; ℗✳@🛜) This good-value option sits inside a nondescript hotel building – reminiscent of most midlevel national chains – 5 miles north of downtown Wilmington. Decor is well loved but also well kept, and rooms come with a mini-fridge and microwave. Hot breakfast buffet included. Not far from Brandywine Valley attractions.

★Hotel du Pont HOTEL $$$
(☏302-594-3100; www.hoteldupont.com; 42 W 11th St, cnr Market & 11th Sts; r $440-460, ste $900; ℗✳🛜) Under new ownership in 2017 after 100 years as a Du Pont–owned property, there is only one word to describe this revamped hotel: opulent. The premier hotel in the state, the Du Pont is luxurious and classy enough to satisfy its namesake (one of America's most successful industrialist families). The spot exudes an art-deco majesty that Jay Gatsby would have embraced.

Iron Hill Brewery PUB FOOD $$
(☏302-472-2739; www.ironhillbrewery.com; 620 Justison St; mains $17-27; ⊙11:30am-11pm Mon-Fri, 11am-midnight Sat, 11am-11pm Sun) The spacious and airy multilevel Iron Hill Brewery is set in a converted brick warehouse on the riverfront. Satisfying microbrews pair nicely with the hearty pub fare.

❶ Getting There & Away

Just off I-95, Wilmington is midway between Washington, DC, and New York City, about two hours from either city. **Greyhound** (☏302-655-6111; www.greyhound.com; 101 N French St) stops downtown. Amtrak trains leave from the **Joseph R Biden Jr Railroad Station** (☏800-872-7245; www.amtrak.com; 100 S French St) and connect Wilmington with DC (1½ hours), Baltimore (45 minutes) and New York (two hours).

Dover

Dover's city center is quite attractive; the row-house-lined streets are peppered with restaurants and shops, while broadleaf trees spread their branches over pretty little lanes. Most museums and historic sites are downtown near the capitol, with a couple just south of downtown off Rte 1. Dover Air Force Base is 4 miles south of downtown.

◎ Sights

Old State House
MUSEUM

(☑302-744-5054; http://history.delaware.gov/museums; 25 The Green; ☺9am-4:30pm Mon-Sat, 1:30-4:30pm Sun) FREE Take a moment to enjoy the short docent-led tour of this small but interesting former state capitol building. Built in 1791 and since restored, the Old State House contains art galleries and in-depth exhibits about the First State's history and politics. We learnt here that every state house in the USA has a portrait of George Washington!

First State Heritage Park Welcome Center & Galleries
MUSEUM

(☑302-744-5055; www.destateparks.com/heritagepark; 121 Martin Luther King Blvd N; ☺8am-4:30pm Mon-Fri, 9am-4:30pm Sat; 🅿) FREE Delve into the history of Delaware at First State Heritage Park, which also serves as a welcome center for the city of Dover, the state of Delaware and the adjacent state house. This so-called 'park without boundaries' includes 19 historic sites in a few blocks of one another. Start out at the Welcome Center & Galleries, which has exhibitions exploring Delaware's history. You can pick up more info about other key attractions nearby along with a walking map.

John Dickinson Plantation
MUSEUM

(☑302-739-3277; http://history.delaware.gov/museums; 340 Kitts Hummock Rd; ☺10am-4:30pm Tue-Sat year-round, plus 1:30-4:30pm Sun Apr-Sep; 🅿) FREE A restored 18th-century home of the founding father of the same name, also known as the Penman of the Revolution for his eloquent written arguments for independence. Dickinson is perhaps not as well known as some colonial statesmen because he did not sign the Declaration of Independence. He was a cautious and contemplative man, they say, but he did sign the Constitution. On-site Colonial-era demonstrations – weaving, knitting, fabric dyeing – are held on Saturday.

Air Mobility Command Museum
MUSEUM

(☑302-677-5938; www.amcmuseum.org; 1301 Heritage Rd; ☺9am-4pm Tue-Sun; 🅿) FREE If you're into aviation, you'll enjoy this museum; the nearby airfield holds more than 30 restored vintage cargo and freight planes, including C-130s, a Vietnam War–era C-7 and a WWII-era 'Flying Boxcar.' Guided tours avaliable.

Dover Air Force Base (AFB) is a visible symbol of American military muscle and a poignant reminder of the cost of war. This is the location of the Department of Defense's largest mortuary, and traditionally the first stop on native soil for the remains of American service members killed overseas.

Bombay Hook National Wildlife Refuge
WILDLIFE RESERVE

(☑302-653-9345; www.fws.gov/refuge/Bombay_Hook; 2591 Whitehall Neck Rd, Smyrna; per vehicle/pedestrian or cyclist $4/2; ☺sunrise-sunset, visitor center 8am-4pm Mon-Fri, plus Sat & Sun spring & fall; 🅿) Hundreds of thousands of waterfowl use this protected wetland as a stopping point along their migration routes. A 12-mile wildlife driving trail, running through 16,251 acres of saltwater marsh, cordgrass and tidal mud flats, manages to encapsulate all of the soft beauty of the Del-MarVa peninsula in one perfectly preserved ecosystem. There are also short walking trails and observation towers. On the scenic drive, keep watch for quick-moving red foxes. Admission is cash only.

🛏 Sleeping

Dover may be somewhat small but it's also the state capital and the home of Dover Air Force Base, so there are plenty of lodging options. Nationally known and indie-owned hotels and motels line Dupont Hwy/Rte 13, plus there is one inn downtown near the capitol.

Home2 Suites
HOTEL $$

(☑302-674-3300; http://home2suites3.hilton.com; 222 S Dupont Hwy; ste $152-180; 🅿❄🅰🛑🐾) This all-suites hotel is a short drive – or a half-mile walk – from downtown. Good for multiday stays, the suites are modern, spacious and have full kitchenettes. There's also a combo laundry-fitness area. Hot breakfast included.

🍴 Eating & Drinking

Restaurant 55
BURGERS $

(☑302-535-8102; www.myrestaurant55.com; 2461 S State St; mains $10-15; ☺11am-2pm Tue-Fri, 4-9pm Tue-Thu, 4-10pm Fri, noon-10pm Sat, noon-8pm Sun) An all-ages crowd muscles in for the black-and-bleu burger and other gourmet patties at this hopping restaurant not far from Dover Air Force Base. Regional craft beer from Dogfish Head, Dewey Beer and Evolution keeps the grown-ups happy.

Flavors of India
INDIAN $$

(📞 302-677-0121; www.flavorofindiade.com; 348 N Dupont Hwy; mains $12-19; ⏰ 11am-10pm Mon-Sat, to 9pm Sun; 🅿🚳🍴) To say this place is an unexpected delight would be an understatement. First: it's in a Super 8 Motel off the highway. Second: it's great. The standards – vindaloos and kormas and tikka masalas – are all wonderful. The goat *palakwala* (goat curry with a spinach base)? Amazing. It's also by far the best vegetarian option in the area.

Governor's Cafe
COFFEE

(📞 302-747-7531; www.governorscafe.de; 144 Kings Hwy SW; ⏰ 7:30am-10pm Mon-Fri, 10am-11pm Sat, 10am-6pm Sun) In a rambling 1850s house across the street from the Governor's Mansion, this inviting place is a talented multitasker. Pop in early to grab a coffee and a pastry to go. Come by in the afternoon to nibble cheese and read on the porch. Sip a cocktail in the cozy bar after work. Or tuck in at night for wine and a civilized meal.

❶ Getting There & Away

Dover is 50 miles south of Wilmington via Rte 1. US 301 connects Dover and Baltimore, which is 85 miles west. DART Bus 301 (one-way fare $6) runs between Wilmington and the **Dover Transit Center** (www.dartfirststate.com; S Queen St), which is a half-mile from downtown Dover. **Greyhound** (📞 800-231-2222; www.greyhound.com; 654 N Dupont Hwy) buses stop 2 miles north of downtown.

VIRGINIA

The Commonwealth of Virginia is steeped in history and tradition. It's the birthplace of America, where English settlers established the first permanent colony in the New World in 1607. Since that time, the state has played a lead role in nearly every major American drama, from the Revolutionary and Civil wars to the Civil Rights movement and the attacks of September 11, 2001.

Virginia's natural beauty is as diverse as its history and people. Chesapeake Bay and the wide sandy beaches kiss the Atlantic Ocean. Pine forests, marshes and rolling green hills form the soft curves of the central Piedmont region, while the rolling Blue Ridge mountains and stunning Shenandoah Valley line its back.

There's loads for the visitor to enjoy, including world-class tourist attractions such as Colonial Williamsburg, a wealth of outdoor activities, a foot-tapping mountain-music scene and an ever-growing network of wine, beer and spirit trails to follow.

History

Humans have occupied Virginia for at least 5000 years. Several thousand Native Americans were already here in May 1607 when Captain James Smith and his crew sailed up Chesapeake Bay and founded Jamestown, the first permanent English colony in the New World. Named for Queen Elizabeth I – aka the 'Virgin Queen' – the territory originally occupied most of America's eastern seaboard. By 1610 most of the colonists had died from starvation in their quest for gold, until John Rolfe (husband of Pocahontas) discovered Virginia's real riches: tobacco.

A feudal aristocracy grew out of tobacco farming, and many gentry scions became Founding Fathers, including native son George Washington. In the 19th century, the slave-based plantation system grew both in size and incompatibility with the industrializing North; Virginia seceded in 1861 and became the epicenter of the Civil War. Following its defeat, the state walked a tense cultural tightrope, accruing a layered identity that included older aristocrats, a rural and urban working class, waves of immigrants and, today, the burgeoning tech-heavy suburbs of DC. The state revels in its history, yet still wants to pioneer the American experiment; thus, while Virginia reluctantly desegregated in the 1960s, today it houses one of the most ethnically diverse populations of the New South.

❶ Getting There & Around

The largest regional airports include **Washington Dulles International Airport** (IAD; www.metwashairports.com; 🚏) in Northern Virginia, **Richmond International Airport** (RIC; 📞 804-226-3000; www.flyrichmond.com; 1 Richard E Byrd Terminal Dr; 🚏) in Richmond, **Norfolk International Airport** (NIA; 📞 757-857-3351; www.norfolkairport.com; 2200 Norview Ave; 🚏) in Norfolk, and **Roanoke-Blacksburg Regional Airport** (📞 540-362-1999; www.roanokeairport.com; 5202 Aviation Dr NW) in Southwest Virginia. American, United and Delta serve Charlottesville Albemarle Airport (p328) in the Piedmont region.

Amtrak stops in Richmond at Main St Station (p326) and Staples Mill Rd Station (p326). There are also train stations or platforms in Charlottesville (p328), Staunton (p329), Roanoke (p334), **Williamsburg** (☑ 757-229-8750; http://gowata.org/; 468 N Boundary St, cnr Boundary & Lafayette Sts; ⊙ 7:30am-10pm) and **Newport News**. In and around Northern Virginia, Amtrak stops in Fredericksburg (p318) and near Manassas National Battlefield Park (p315).

Northern Virginia

Arlington

Sitting just across the Potomac River from DC, Arlington is best known as the home of the Arlington National Cemetery and the Pentagon. Other than these two - admittedly major - draws, there's not much to attract the average visitor. The once-vibrant music and club strip on Wilson Blvd has been decimated in recent times as buildings are torn down to make way for sleek new high-rise apartment and office towers.

★**Arlington National Cemetery**   CEMETERY
(☑ 877-907-8585; www.arlingtoncemetery.mil; Memorial Ave; ⊙ 8am-7pm Apr-Sep, to 5pm Oct-Mar; Ⓜ Blue Line to Arlington Cemetery) FREE Arlington is the somber final resting place for more than 400,000 military personnel and their dependents. The 624-acre grounds contain the dead of every war the USA has fought since the Revolution. Highlights include the Tomb of the Unknown Soldier, with its elaborate changing-of-the-guard ceremony (every hour on the hour October through March; every half-hour April through September), and the grave of John F Kennedy and his family, marked by an eternal flame.

Departing from the Welcome Center, hop-on, hop-off **bus tours** (☑ 800-844-7601; www.arlingtontours.com; adult/child $15/7.25; ⊙ 8:30am-6pm Apr-Sep, to 4pm Oct-Mar) are an easy way to visit the cemetery's main sights. Other points of interest include the **Shuttle Challenger Memorial** (off Memorial Dr); the **USS Maine Memorial** (off McPherson Dr), marked by the battleship's huge mast; the controversial **Confederate Memorial** (off McPherson Dr) that honors war dead from the Civil War's breakaway states; and the tomb of DC city planner **Pierre L'Enfant** (off Sherman Dr).

The **Iwo Jima Memorial** (Marine Corps War Memorial; Ord & Weitzel Dr), displaying the famous raising of the flag over Mt Suribachi, is on the cemetery's northern fringes and is included in the bus tour.

Much of the cemetery was built on the grounds of **Arlington House** (☑ 703-235-1530; www.nps.gov/arho; Sherman Dr; ⊙ 10am-4pm) FREE, the former home of Robert E Lee and his wife Mary Anna Custis Lee, a descendant of Martha Washington. When Lee left to lead Virginia's army in the Civil War, Union troops confiscated the property to bury their dead.

★**Pentagon**   NOTABLE BUILDING
(https://pentagontours.osd.mil; Arlington; ⊙ memorial 24hr, tours by appointment 10am-4pm Mon-Thu, noon-4pm Fri; Ⓜ Blue, Yellow Line to Pentagon) South of Arlington Cemetery is the Pentagon, the largest office building in the world and the headquarters of the US Department of Defense, the Army, Navy and Air Force. Outside the building is the **Pentagon Memorial** (https://pentagonmemorial.org; ⊙ 24hr) FREE; 184 illuminated benches honor each person killed in the September 11, 2001, terrorist attack on the Pentagon. To get inside the building, you'll have to book a free guided one-hour tour on the website and provide appropriate photo ID. Make reservations 14 to 90 days in advance.

Nearby, you can spot the three soaring arcs of the **Air Force Memorial** (☑ 703-462-4093; www.airforcememorial.org; 1 Air Force Memorial Dr; ⊙ 9am-9pm Apr-Sep, 8am-8pm Oct-Mar) FREE.

ⓘ Getting There & Away

From DC, use the Arlington Cemetery station (Blue Line) to get to the cemetery and the Pentagon station (Blue and Yellow Lines) to visit Pentagon sites.

Alexandria

The charming town of Alexandria is 5 miles and 250 years away from Washington. Once a salty port, Alexandria - known as 'Old Town' to locals - is today a posh collection of red-brick homes, cobblestone streets, gas lamps and a waterfront promenade near the Potomac River. It's often described as one of the best-preserved historical districts in the nation. Boutiques, outdoor cafes and bars pack the main thoroughfare, making the town a fine afternoon or evening jaunt. Two miles north of Old Town, the residential

Del Ray neighborhood is a pleasant place to stroll, especially along the eatery-lined Mt Vernon Ave. Alexandria is also a jumping-off spot for excursions to Mount Vernon.

◉ Sights

★ **Mount Vernon**   HISTORIC SITE
(☑ 703-780-2000; www.mountvernon.org; 3200 Mount Vernon Memorial Hwy; adult/child 6-11yr $20/12; ⊙ 9am-5pm Apr-Oct, to 4pm Nov-Mar) One of America's most visited historic sites, Mount Vernon was the beloved home of George and Martha Washington, who lived here from the time of their marriage in 1759 until George's death in 1799. Regular guided tours of the furnished main house give a fascinating insight into the Washingtons' daily life, and self-guided tours of the outbuildings and gardens estate offer plenty of opportunities to interact with actors offering first-person narratives of working and living on the 18th-century plantation.

From April to October, the Mount Vernon entrance ticket also includes entry to Washington's nearby **distillery and gristmill** (☑ 703-780-2000; 5514 Mount Vernon Memorial Hwy; $6, with Mount Vernon ticket free; ⊙ 10am-5pm Apr-Oct); a free shuttle travels between these and the estate.

To avoid inevitable queues at the entrance to Mount Vernon, purchase your ticket online ahead of your visit (you'll save money too!). A number of tours and performances are offered daily, including the popular one-hour 'Enslaved People of Mount Vernon' tour ($10). Some tours sell out, so it's best to book these online ahead of your visit. Audio-guide tours of the estate cost $7 and can be shared within a group.

Be sure to allow at least one hour to browse the object-rich exhibits and view the immersive 4D 'Revolutionary War Experience' spectacular in the Donald W Reynolds Museum & Education Center. Kids will love the 'Hands on History' activity room here, too.

Mount Vernon is 16 miles south of DC, off the Mount Vernon Memorial Hwy. By public transportation, take the Metro (Yellow Line) to Huntington, then switch to Fairfax Connector bus 101. **Grayline** (☑ 202-779-9894; www.graylinedc.com; adult/child 3-11yr $105/40; ⊙ 8:30am-5:30pm Tue, Thu & Sat late Jan-Dec), **OnBoard Tours** (☑ 301-839-5261; www.onboardtours.com; adult/child incl incl Mount Vernon Mon-Fri $80/70, Sat & Sun $90/80; ⊙ 10am-4pm) and **USA Guided Tours** (☑ 202-733 7376;

www.usaguidedtours.com; adult/child 3-12yr incl Mount Vernon $79/69; ⊙ 10am) run bus tours from DC.

Several companies offer seasonal boat trips to Mount Vernon; **Potomac Riverboat Company** (☑ 703-684-0580; www.potomacriverboatco.com; return adult/child incl Mount Vernon from $50/30; ⊙ Apr-Oct) has boats that depart from the Alexandria City Marina and **Spirit Cruises** (☑ 866-302-2469; www.spiritcruises.com; return adult/child 6-11yr incl Mount Vernon $51/46; ⊙ Mar-Oct) has the *Spirit of Mount Vernon,* which departs from the SW Waterfront in DC.

Alternatively, it's possible to ride a bike along the Potomac River from DC (18 miles from Roosevelt Island).

★ **Pope-Leighey House**   ARCHITECTURE
(☑ 703-570-6902; www.woodlawnpopeleighey.org; 9000 Richmond Hwy; adult/student $12/7.50, incl Woodlawn $20/11; ⊙ 11am-4pm Fri-Mon Apr-late Nov) Between 1937 and 1959, famed architect Frank Lloyd Wright designed a series of small-scale houses that he called 'Usonian.' Modest in scale but rich in innovation and detail, these site-specific single-story dwellings were constructed using native materials, had flat roofs and clerestory windows, and made the most of natural light, air and the surrounding landscape. This example dates from 1940. Young guides (often architects) conduct tours and impart lots of information about the house and its architect.

The house was originally constructed in Falls Church but was relocated to the Woodlawn estate after the house was threatened with demolition as part of an expansion of Hwy 66. It's now sited in a grassy knoll a short walk from the plantation mansion, which is located near George Washington's Distillery & Gristmill. To get here by public transport, take the Metro to Huntington station and then board Richmond Hwy Express Bus No 171; alight at Jeff Todd Way.

Freedom House Museum   MUSEUM
(☑ 708-746-4702; www.alexandriava.gov/Freedom House; 1315 Duke St; suggested donation $5; ⊙ 1-5pm Fri & Sat; Ⓜ Blue, Yellow Line to King St-Old Town) This demure Federal-style row house holds a tragic story. At a time when Alexandria was the nation's second-largest slave center (after New Orleans), a flourishing slave-trading business occupied this building and adjoining space. A well-presented

MANASSAS NATIONAL BATTLEFIELD SITE

The site of two major Confederate victories early in the Civil War, **Manassas National Battlefield Park** (☎703-361-1339; www.nps.gov/mana; 6511 Sudley Rd, off I-66; ☺park dawn-dusk, visitor center 8:30am-5pm) today is a curving green hillscape, sectioned into fuzzy fields of tall grass and wildflowers by split-rail wood fences. Start your tour at the Henry Hill Visitor Center to watch the orientation film and pick up park and trail maps. Guided tours are offered daily in summer; check the park website for times (which vary seasonally).

The history? On July 21, 1861, Union and Confederate soldiers clashed in the first major land battle of the Civil War. Expecting a quick victory, DC residents flocked here to picnic and watch the First Battle of Bull Run (known in the South as First Manassas). The surprise Southern victory erased any hopes of a quick end to the war. Union and Confederate soldiers again met on the same ground for the larger Second Battle of Manassas in August 1862; again the South was victorious.

Daily Amtrak (www.amtrak.com) and Virginia Railway Express (www.vre.org) trains make the 50- to 70-minute journey between DC's Union Station and the historic Old Town Manassas Railroad Station; from there it's a 6-mile taxi ride to the park. There are several restaurants and bars around the Manassas train station, but the rest of the city is a mess of strip malls and suburban sprawl.

basement museum, developed by the Northern Virginia Urban League, powerfully tells the stories of the thousands of enslaved people who passed through. Personal video narratives and artifacts are on view in a heartbreaking setting.

Up to 150 slaves were kept in the holding pen outside (since torn down). Among those likely held here was Solomon Northup, a free black man who in 1841 was kidnapped from Washington and sold into bondage in the south. His story was portrayed in the film *Twelve Years a Slave*. There's no admission, but donations are encouraged. The museum isn't signed; look for the Franklin and Armfield Slave Office information panel.

George Washington
Masonic National Memorial   MONUMENT
(☎703-683-2007; www.gwmemorial.org; 101 Callahan Dr at King St; adult/child under 13yr $18/ free; ☺9am-5pm; Ⓜ Blue, Yellow Line to King St-Old Town) Alexandria's most prominent landmark features a fine view from the observation deck of its 333ft tower. Modeled after Egypt's Lighthouse of Alexandria, it honors the first president (who was initiated into the Masons in Fredericksburg in 1752 and later became Worshipful Master of Alexandria Lodge No 22). After paying admission, you can explore exhibits on the 1st and 2nd floors, but to visit the tower and see Washington-family artifacts, you must take a 60-minute guided tour.

Tours depart at 9:30am, 11am, 1pm, 2:30pm and 4pm. If you ask one too many questions about masonic symbolism and the *National Treasure* movies, a trapdoor will open and drop you into the parking lot. We jest; it's all quite welcoming and fascinating.

Torpedo Factory Art Center   ARTS CENTER
(☎703-746-4570; www.torpedofactory.org; 105 N Union St; ☺10am-6pm Fri-Wed, to 9pm Thu; Ⓜ Blue, Yellow Line to King St-Old Town) FREE
What do you do with a former munitions dump and arms factory? How about turning it into one of the best art spaces in the region? Three floors of artist studios and galleries are on offer in Old Town Alexandria, as well as the opportunity to buy paintings, sculptures, glass works, textiles and jewelry direct from their creators – all 165 of them. Take the trolley from King St station.

🛏 Sleeping & Eating

Most accommodation options are located on King St, and are on the pricey side. You'll have to travel outside the neighborhood to find cheaper options.

Lorien Hotel & Spa   HOTEL $$
(☎703-894-3434; www.lorienhotelandspa.com; 1600 King St; r $200-400; Ⓟ❄❋📶🐾; Ⓜ Blue, Yellow Line to King St-Old Town) Hidden behind King St shopfronts, this is Alexandria's best accommodation option. Renovated rooms

are comfortable and well sized, but it's the added extras here that matter: a communal wine hour in the early evening, complimentary morning coffee in the foyer, spa treatments (massages $115 to $250), a gym and a steam room. Meals can be enjoyed in the attached Brabo Tasting Room.

Stomping Ground
BREAKFAST $

(☏703-567-6616; www.stompdelray.com; 2309 Mt Vernon Ave; mains $10-12; ☉7am-3pm Tue-Sat, 9am-3pm Sun; Ⓜ Blue, Yellow Line to Braddock Rd/King St-Old Town) Did somebody say biscuit? Oh yes they did. And make that a homemade buttermilk biscuit piled with fillings of your choice (Benton's bacon, eggs, veggie frittata, avocado and many more) and with gouda grits on the side. Or just stop by this stylish Del Ray spot for coffee and to work on your laptop. Order and collect at the counter.

Brabo Tasting Room
INTERNATIONAL $$

(☏703-894-5252; www.braborestaurant.com; 1600 King St; sandwiches & small plates $14-17; ☉7am-11pm Mon-Thu, to midnight Fri, 8am-midnight Sat, 8am-10pm Sun; Ⓜ Blue, Yellow Line to King St-Old Town) The inviting and sunlit Brabo Tasting Room serves its signature mussels, tasty wood-fired tarts and gourmet sandwiches with a good beer and wine selection. In the morning, stop by for brioche French toast and Bloody Marys. Brabo Brasserie, next door, is the high-end counterpart serving seasonal fare (mains $29 to $44).

Take a trolley from King St station.

🍷 Drinking & Entertainment

Head to King St for good bar-hopping with a crowd of folks who seem to be perpetually enrolled in the University of Virginia, Virginia Tech or George Mason University. There is a growing trend here for intimate speakeasies handcrafting cocktails.

★ Captain Gregory's
COCKTAIL BAR

(☏571-659-4934; www.captaingregorys.com; 804 N Henry St; ☉5:30-10:15pm Wed, Thu & Sun, to 11:45pm Fri & Sat; Ⓜ Blue, Yellow Line to Braddock Rd) This nautical-themed speakeasy is hidden inside a Sugar Shack doughnut shop, which explains the decadent gourmet doughnuts on the menu. As for drinks, from Anais Needs a Vacay to Moaning Myrtles Morning Tea, the names are as diverse as the ingredients. Think flavored liqueurs, infused spirits and a range of fruit and spices. The cocktail menu changes frequently. Reservation recommended.

Birchmere
LIVE MUSIC

(☏703-549-7500; www.birchmere.com; 3701 Mt Vernon Ave; tickets $25-100; ☉box office 5-9pm, shows 7:30pm; Ⓜ Blue, Yellow Line to Pentagon City) This 50-year-old place, hailing itself as 'America's Legendary Music Hall', hosts a wide range of fare, from old-time folk musicians to country, blues and R&B stars. The lineup also features the odd burlesque show, indie rock bands and the occasional one-person comedy act.

The talent that graces the stage is reason enough to come, but the venue is pretty great too: it sort of looks like a warehouse that collided with an army of LSD-affected muralists. Located north of Old Town Alexandria, off Glebe Rd. Take bus 10A from Pentagon City station.

ⓘ Getting There & Away

To get to Alexandria from downtown DC, take the Metro (Blue and Yellow Lines) to the King St-Old Town station. A free **trolley** (www.dashbus.com/ride-dash/king-street-trolley; ☉11am-10:30pm Sun-Wed, 10:30am-midnight Thu-Sat, longer hours Jun-Aug; Ⓜ Blue, Yellow Line to King St-Old Town) makes the 1-mile journey from the Metro station to the waterfront and then back again.

Seasonal **water taxis** (☏703-684-0580; www.potomacriverboatco.com; one-way adult/child from $10/7; ☉Mar-Sep) travel between Alexandria's wharf and the Wharf District in DC (25 minutes). There's also a seasonal service between Georgetown and Alexandria. Tour boats travel to/from the Mount Vernon estate during the summer season, too.

Fredericksburg

Fredericksburg is a pretty town with a downtown area that's almost a cliché of small-town Americana. George Washington grew up here, and the Civil War exploded in the streets and surrounding fields. Today the historic district surrounding William St provides opportunities for atmospheric ambles, with Colonial-era architecture to admire, intimate museums to visit and plenty of eating and drinking options to sample.

◉ Sights

Ellwood Manor
HISTORIC SITE

(☏540-786-2880; www.fowb.org; 36380 Constitution Hwy, Rte 20, Locust Grove; ☉10am-5pm early Jun-Aug, Sat & Sun only Apr-early Jun & Aug-Nov) **FREE** This fascinating home sits on the grounds of the Wilderness Battlefield.

SCENIC DRIVE: VIRGINA'S HORSE COUNTRY

About 40 miles west of Washington, DC, suburban sprawl gives way to endless green farms, vineyards, quaint villages and palatial estates and ponies. This is 'Horse Country,' where wealthy Washingtonians pursue their equestrian pastimes.

The following route is the most scenic drive to Shenandoah National Park (p330). From DC, take Rte 50 West to **Middleburg**, a too-cute-for-words town of taverns, antique shops and boutiques. The **National Sporting Museum** (☑540-687-6542; www.nationalsporting.org; 102 The Plains Rd, Middleburg; museum adult/child 13-18yr $10/8, Wed free; ☉10am-5pm Wed-Sun) is a museum and research center devoted to horse and field sports such as foxhunting, dressage, steeplechase and polo. About 20 miles northeast of Middleburg is **Leesburg**, another town with a Colonial feel and historic sites. Stop in **Morven Park** (☑703-777-2414; www.morvenpark.org; 17195 Southern Planter Lane; grounds free, mansion tours adult/child 6-12yr $10/5; ☉grounds 8am-5pm daily, mansion noon-5pm Thu-Mon Mar-Dec) for a tour of a staggering Virginia home on 1000 acres. For more Colonial grandeur, visit **Oatlands Historic House & Gardens** (☑703-777-3174; www.oatlands.org; 20850 Oatlands Plantation Lane, Leesburg; adult/child 6-16yr $15/10, grounds only $10; ☉10am-5pm Apr-Dec, closed Jan-Mar), outside of town.

The area has some wonderful accommodation and dining options. Of these, the historic **Red Fox Tavern** (☑540-687-6301; www.redfox.com/tavern; 2 E Washington St; mains $32-52; ☉8-10am & 5-9pm Mon-Fri, 11am-2pm & 5-9pm Sat, 11am-2pm & 5-8pm Sun) in Middleburg is notable, as is **Goodstone Inn & Restaurant** (☑540-687-3333, 877-219-4663; www.goodstone.com; 36205 Snake Hill Rd; d/ste from $385/435; 🅿☕☎🛜⚡) just outside town.

Further down the road at the foothills of the Blue Ridge Mountains is **Sperryville**. Its many galleries and shops make it a must-stop for antique-lovers. Continue 9 miles west to reach the Thornton Gap entrance of Skyline Dr in Shenandoah National Park.

Perhaps best known as the burial site for Confederate general Stonewall Jackson's amputated arm – there's a marker – the manor (c 1790) here once anchored a 5000-acre estate and has undergone a full interior restoration in recent times. Step inside to learn the interesting history of the house on a docent-led guided tour.

Fredericksburg & Spotsylvania National Military Park
HISTORIC SITE

(☑540-693-3200; www.nps.gov/frsp; 1013 Lafayette Blvd; ☉Fredericksburg & Chancellorsville visitor centers 9am-5pm, hours vary at other exhibit areas) **FREE** More than 13,000 Americans were killed during the Civil War in four battles fought in a 17-mile radius covered by this park: Fredericksburg, Chancellorsville, the Wilderness and Spotsylvania Courthouse. Today the park is maintained by the National Park Service. Check its website for the locations of various visitor centers, and for staffing, which may be seasonal. Orientation films (adult/child under 10 years $2/free) are screened at the Fredericksburg and Chancellorsville visitor centers every 30 minutes, and audioguides can be hired.

James Monroe Museum & Memorial Library
HISTORIC SITE

(☑540-654-1043; http://jamesmonroemuseum. umw.edu; 908 Charles St; adult/child 6-17yr $6/2; ☉10am-5pm Mon-Sat, from 1pm Sun, to 4pm Dec-Feb) The museum's namesake was the nation's fifth president. US history buffs will delight in the small and eclectic collection of Monroe memorabilia, including the desk on which he wrote the famous Monroe Doctrine. His diplomatic court suit, worn at the coronation of Napoleon and dating from 1785 or so, is also on display.

🍴 Sleeping & Eating

There are several inns and B&Bs located in and around the downtown historic district, as well as a good Marriott hotel. Other chains have hotels on the Jefferson David Hwy (US1) on the edge of town.

Richard Johnston Inn
B&B $$

(☑540-899-7606; www.therichardjohnstoninn. com; 711 Caroline St; d $150-225; 🅿❄🛜☎) In an 18th-century brick mansion, this cozy B&B scores points for its downtown location, handsome communal areas and rear garden. Room rates drop midweek. The same friendly team operates the 1890 Caroline House annexe a short distance away, which offers three larger rooms ($225 to $300); its Sawyer Scott Suite is particularly nice. Breakfast (included) can be vegan or gluten-free by arrangement.

Confident Rabbit FRENCH $$
(☑540-371-9999; www.theconfidentrabbit.com; 309 William St; mains lunch $9-14, dinner $14-27; ◷5-9pm Tue & Wed, 11:30am-10pm Thu-Sat, 10:30am-2:30pm & 5-8pm Sun) Classic French bistro cuisine and a raw bar where fresh Chesapeake Bay oysters are shucked are the draws at this modern and extremely stylish eatery in downtown Fredericksburg. Grab a bar stool or banquette and feast on a selection of small plates (rillettes, charcuterie, salads), a succulent steak or seasonal fish. At lunch, the duck burger reigns supreme.

❶ Getting There & Away

Virginia Railway Express (www.vre.org; $12.15, 1½ hours) and Amtrak (www.amtrak.com; from $28, 1½ hours) trains depart from the **Fredericksburg train station** (200 Lafayette Blvd) with service to DC. Greyhound has buses to/from DC ($10 to $24, 1½ hours, four or five per day) and Richmond ($14 to $30, one hour, four per day). The **Greyhound station** (☑540-373-2103; www.greyhound.com; 1400 Jefferson Davis Hwy; ◷ticket office 7am-2pm & 4-7:30pm Mon-Fri, 7am-noon Sat & Sun) is roughly 2 miles west of the historic district. Fredericksburg borders I-95 midway between Washington, DC, and Richmond, VA. It's about 55 miles north to DC and 60 miles south to Richmond.

Historic Triangle

This is America's birthplace. Nowhere else in the country has such a small area played such a pivotal role in the course of the nation's history. The nation's roots were planted in Jamestown, the first permanent English settlement in the New World; the flames of the American Revolution were fanned at the Colonial capital of Williamsburg; and America finally won its independence from Britain at Yorktown. You'll need at least two days to do the Triangle any justice.

❶ Getting There & Around

The Historic Triangle surrounds I-64. The largest regional airport is Norfolk International Airport (p312) followed by **Newport News/Williamsburg International Airport** (PHF; www.flyphf.

com). Williamsburg is serviced by Amtrak (www.amtrak.com), and local WATA buses (www.gowata.org) link it with Jamestown ($1.50).

Williamsburg

If you visit only one historic town in Virginia, make it Williamsburg – home to Colonial Williamsburg, one of the largest, most comprehensive living-history museums in the world. If any place is going to get kids into history, this is it, but it's plenty of fun for adults too. The actual town of Williamsburg, Virginia's capital from 1699 to 1780, is a stately place that can sometimes verge on being twee. Fortunately, the campus of the College of William & Mary adds a decent dash of youth culture.

◉ Sights

★**Colonial Williamsburg** HISTORIC SITE
(☑888-965-7254; www.colonialwilliamsburg.org; adult/child 6-12yr day $41/21, multiday $51/26; ◷8:45am-5pm) The restored capital of England's largest colony in the New World is a must-see attraction for visitors of all ages. This is not some phony, fenced-in theme park: Colonial Williamsburg is a living, breathing, working history museum with a painstakingly researched environment that brilliantly evokes 1700s America. It contains 88 original 18th-century buildings and several hundred faithful reproductions, as well as an impressive museum complex. Townsfolk and 'interpreters' in period dress go about their colonial jobs, emulating daily life.

Laudably, the park doesn't gloss over America's less glorious moments. Today's re-enactors debate and question slavery (52% of the population of 18th-century Williamsburg were slaves), women's suffrage, the rights of indigenous Americans and whether or not it is even moral to engage in revolution.

Walking around the historic district and patronizing the shops and taverns is free, but entry to building tours and most exhibits is restricted to ticket holders. Expect crowds, lines and overtired children, especially in summer. There are a number of taverns and a bakery where visitors can eat, and there's also a bakery in the Art Museums complex.

To park and to purchase tickets, follow signs to the **visitor center** (☑757-220-7645, 888-965-7254; 101 Visitor Center Dr; ◷8:45am-9pm), found north of the historic district between Hwy 132 and Colonial Pkwy. A program detailing the day's events will be given to you with your ticket, which helps when planning your time at the site.

Parking at the visitor center is free; shuttle buses run frequently between it and the historic district, or you can walk along the tree-lined footpath. You can also buy tickets at the **Merchants Square information booth** (W Duke of Gloucester St; ⊘9am-5pm).

★**Art Museums** MUSEUM
(www.colonialwilliamsburg.com/art-museums; Francis St; adult/child 6-12yr $13/6.50, with Colonial Williamsburg admission free; ⊘10am-7pm Mar-Dec, to 5pm Jan & Feb) Entered through Colonial Williamsburg's former public hospital, this complex is home to two equally splendid museums: the **DeWitt Wallace Decorative Arts Museum** and the **Abby Aldrich Rockefeller Folk Art Museum**. The decorative arts museum is home to the world's largest collection of Southern furniture and one of the largest collections of British ceramics outside England. The folk art museum has one of the largest collections of American folk art in the world – portraits, quilts, toys, musical instruments and much more.

College of William & Mary HISTORIC BUILDING
(www.wm.edu; 200 Stadium Dr) Chartered in 1693, the College of William & Mary is the second-oldest college in the country and retains the oldest academic building in continued use in the USA, the **Sir Christopher Wren Building**. The school's alumni include Thomas Jefferson, James Monroe and comedian Jon Stewart. A free campus audio tour and interactive map are available online.

🛏 Sleeping & Eating

Williamsburg White House B&B $$
(☑757-229-8580; www.awilliamsburgwhitehouse.com; 718 Jamestown Rd; r $150-200; P❁❋❂) This romantic, beautifully furnished B&B is located across from the College of William & Mary campus, just a few blocks' walk from Colonial Williamsburg. It's a favorite spot of visiting politicos and bigwigs. Guests love the lavish breakfast and the afternoon drinks and nibbles served in the Diplomatic Reception Room. Book ahead, as there are only six rooms.

Colonial Williamsburg Historic Lodging – Colonial Houses GUESTHOUSE $$
(☑844-280-4578; www.colonialwilliamsburg.com; 136 E Francis St; d from $150, cabin $300-350;

❂❁) For true 18th-century immersion, guests can stay in one of 26 original Colonial houses inside the historic district. Accommodations range in size and style, though the best have period furnishings, canopy beds and wood-burning fireplaces.

Cheese Shop DELI $
(☑757-220-0298; www.cheeseshopwilliamsburg.com; 410 W Duke of Gloucester St, Merchants Square; sandwiches $5.50-8; ⊘10am-8pm Mon-Sat, 11am-6pm Sun) This gourmet deli showcases some flavorful sandwiches and antipasti, plus baguettes, pastries, ready-made meals, wine, beer and wonderful cheeses. Order a sandwich and a glass of wine – at different counters – then enjoy your meal and the people-watching from the patio.

★**Fat Canary** MODERN AMERICAN $$$
(☑757-229-3333; www.fatcanarywilliamsburg.com; 410 W Duke of Gloucester St, Merchants Square; mains $29-42; ⊘5-9:30pm, closed Mon Jan & Feb) The best restaurant in the historic triangle, this friendly and stylish place offers top-notch service, excellent wines and a menu of Modern American cuisine with Asian and Italian accents. We love the fact that local produce is a focus, that orders of half serves are possible and that the list of wine by the glass features interesting choices.

Jamestown

On May 14, 1607, a group of 104 English men and boys settled on this swampy island, bearing a charter from the Virginia Company of London to search for gold and other riches. Instead they found starvation and disease. By January 1608, only about 40 colonists were still alive and had resorted to cannibalism to survive. The colony pulled through the 'Starving Time' with the leadership of Captain James Smith and help from Powhatan, a local Native American leader. In 1619, the elected House of Burgesses convened, forming the first democratic government in the Americas. Today two sites share the story of this early settlement.

★**Historic Jamestowne** HISTORIC SITE
(☑757-856-1250; www.historicjamestowne.org; 1368 Colonial Pkwy; adult/child under 16yr $20/free; ⊘9am-5pm) Run by the NPS, this fascinating place is the original Jamestown site, established in 1607 and home of the first permanent English settlement in North America. The settlement's ruins were

JAMES RIVER PLANTATIONS

The grand homes of Virginia's slaveholding aristocracy were a clear sign of the era's class divisions. A string of them line scenic Hwy 5 on the northern side of the river, though only a few are open to the public.

For cyclists, the new Virginia Capital Trail (p325) linking Richmond and Williamsburg travels beside Rte 5, near the Shirley and Berkeley Plantations.

Berkeley Plantation (☑ 804-829-6018; www.berkeleyplantation.com; 12602 Harrison Landing Rd, Charles City; adult/child 6-16yr $12.50/7; ⏰ 9:30am-4:30pm, shorter hours Jan & Feb) Dating from 1726, this plantation on the James River was the birthplace and home of Benjamin Harrison V, a signatory of the Declaration of Independence, and of his son William Henry Harrison, the ninth US president. It was also the site of the first official Thanksgiving (in 1619) and the first place where bourbon whiskey was distilled (1620). Lively guided tours of its brick Georgian-style house offer plenty of anecdotes.

Shirley Plantation (☑ 800-829-5121; www.shirleyplantation.com; 501 Shirley Plantation Rd, Charles City; grounds adult/child 7-16yr $11/6, guided tour incl admission $20/7.50; ⏰ 9:30am-4pm early Mar-Dec) Built on the banks of the James River, this is Virginia's oldest plantation (1613). It retains an original row of brick service and trade houses – tool barn, ice house, laundry etc – leading up to the big house, which dates from 1738. Established by Edward Hill I, the plantation was subsequently owned by descendants of Robert 'King' Carter and is still home to members of the Hill-Carter family. Guided tours of the downstairs reception rooms are held on the hour.

rediscovered in 1994; visitors can take a free guided tour of the excavations (daily 11am, also 2pm on weekends and between April and September). On arrival, view the orientation film and then head to the Archaearium, an archaeology museum with more than 4000 artifacts and a 'World of Pocahontas, Unearthed' exhibit.

Entry is discounted to $10 for visitors with a ticket receipt for Yorktown Battlefield, and to $5 if you have a National Parks pass. There's a cafe on-site.

Jamestown Settlement   HISTORIC SITE
(☑ 888-593-4682; www.historyisfun.org; 2110 Jamestown Rd; adult/child 6-12yr $17.50/8.25, incl American Revolutionary Museum at Yorktown $26/12.50; ⏰ 9am-5pm, to 6pm mid-Jun–mid-Aug; P) Popular with kids, the state-run Jamestown Settlement reconstructs the 1607 James Fort; a Native American village; and full-scale replicas of the first ships that brought the settlers to Jamestown, along with living-history fun. Multimedia exhibits and costumed interpreters bring the 17th century to life. This one can get uncomfortably busy with elementary-school field trips, so arrive early during the school year.

Yorktown

On October 19, 1781, British General Cornwallis surrendered to George Washington here, effectively ending the American Revolution. Overpowered by massive American guns on land and cut off from the sea by the French, the British were in a hopeless position. Although Washington anticipated a much longer siege, the devastating barrage quickly overwhelmed Cornwallis, who surrendered within days.

The actual town of Yorktown (www.visit yorktown.org) is a pleasant waterfront village overlooking the York River, with a sandy beach, a scattering of shops, and a few restaurants and pubs.

⊙ Sights

American Revolution Museum at Yorktown   MUSEUM
(☑ 757-887-1776; www.historyisfun.org; 200 Water St; adult/child 6-12yr $15/7.50, incl Jamestown Settlement $26/12.50; ⏰ 9am-5pm, to 6pm mid-July–mid-Aug; P) Formerly the Yorktown Victory Center, this expanded exhibition space and living history museum vividly describes the build-up to the Revolutionary War, the war itself and daily life on the home front. The award-winning introductory film *Liberty Fever* sets the stage for the rest of the museum. Lots of significant artifacts are here too, including an early printing of the Declaration of Independence. At the re-created military encampment outside, costumed Continental soldiers share details about life in a Revolutionary War camp.

Yorktown Battlefield HISTORIC SITE

(☑ 757-898-2410; www.nps.gov/york; 1000 Colonial Pkwy; adult/child under 16yr $10/free; ⊙ 9am-5pm; P ♿) Yorktown Battlefield, run by the NPS, is the site of the last major battle of the American Revolution. Start your tour at the visitor center and check out the orientation film and the display of Washington's original tent, then drive the 7-mile Battlefield Rd Tour, which takes you past the major highlights. Don't miss a walk through the last British defensive sites, Redoubts 9 and 10, reached via Ballard St. Entry is free if you have a ticket receipt for Historic Jamestowne (p319).

🛏 Sleeping & Eating

★ Hornsby House Inn B&B $$

(☑ 757-369-0200; www.hornsbyhouseinn.com; 702 Main St; r $160-260; P 🛜) Close to Yorktown's beach and eateries, this house was built by the current owner's grandfather in 1933 and retains its old-fashioned ambience. That's not to say that it's dated or dowdy, because nothing could be further from the truth – we love the elegant ground-floor lounge and the five large, light and elegantly furnished rooms (most accessed by stairs).

Yorktown Pub SEAFOOD $$

(☑ 757-886-9964; www.yorktownpub.com; 540 Water St; sandwiches $6-14, mains $17-27; ⊙ 11am-midnight Sun-Thu, to 2am Fri & Sat) Most of the local action in Yorktown occurs at this pub by the beach. Serving good pub grub (including loads of local seafood) and staging live music on Friday and Saturday nights, it's as popular in winter as it is in the warmer weather due to the open fire and warm welcome offered by the staff.

❶ Getting There & Away

There is no public transportation to Yorktown, so you'll need a car to visit. A free trolley loops between historic sites and the village every 20 to 35 minutes (11am to 5pm mid-March to December; longer hours June to August).

Norfolk

It's home to the world's largest naval base, so it's not surprising that Norfolk has long had a reputation as a rowdy port town filled with drunken sailors. However, in recent years the city has worked hard to clean up its image through development and by

focusing on its burgeoning arts scene, which is spearheaded by the impressive Chrysler Museum of Art. The downtown Ghent District is where most of the town's cultural and entertainment action occurs, and the nearby Waterside District, a dining and entertainment complex on the Elizabeth River, is worth a visit.

◉ Sights

★ Chrysler Museum of Art MUSEUM

(☑ 757-664-6200; www.chrysler.org; 1 Memorial Pl; ⊙ 10am-5pm Tue-Sat, noon-5pm Sun) FREE A glorious setting for an eclectic collection of artifacts from ancient Egypt to the present day, including works by Henri Matisse, Albert Bierstadt, Georgia O'Keeffe, Jackson Pollock and Andy Warhol, and an expansive collection of glass objects spanning 3000 years. Don't miss the collection of Tiffany blown glass.

Naval Station Norfolk MUSEUM

(☑ 757-444-7955; www.cnic.navy.mil/norfolksta; 9079 Hampton Blvd, near Gate 5; adult/child 3-11yr $10/5; ⊙ hours vary) The world's largest navy base, and one of the busiest airfields in the country. Hampton-based company Tidewater Touring works with the base to offer 45-minute bus tours conducted by naval personnel; tours must be booked in advance (hours vary). Photo ID is required for adults.

Nauticus MUSEUM

(☑ 757-664-1000; www.nauticus.org; 1 Waterside Dr; adult/child 4-12yr $16/11.50; ⊙ 10am-5pm Mon-Sat Jun-Aug, 10am-5pm Tue-Sat, noon-5pm Sun Sep-May) This massive, interactive, maritime-themed museum has exhibits on undersea exploration, aquatic life of the Chesapeake Bay and US Naval lore. The museum's highlight is clambering around the decks and inner corridors of the USS *Wisconsin*. Built in 1943, it was the largest (887ft long) and last battleship built by the US Navy.

🛏 Sleeping

For waterfront digs, there are tons of budget to midrange options lining Ocean View Ave (which actually borders the bay).

Main Hotel HOTEL $$$

(☑ 757-763-6200; www.hilton.com; 100 E Main St; d from $230; P ❄ 🛜 ☀) The rooms are swanky at this member of the Hilton family, which is located near the Nauticus Center. Rooms with a river view cost more, but you may not need to book one – just settle in for a drink and river view at the rooftop lounge, Grain, one of the hotel's three dining and drinking establishments. It's popular – book well in advance.

✖ Eating & Drinking

Press 626 Wine Bar MODERN AMERICAN **$$**
(✆757-282-6234; www.press626.com; 626 W Olney Rd; sandwiches $10-14, mains $22-26; ⊘11am-11pm Mon-Fri, 5-11pm Sat, 10:30am-2:30pm Sun; ✍) Embracing the Slow Food movement, this charming place in the Ghent district has a small but well-judged menu, with something to suit most tastes and budgets. The cheese and charcuterie plates are particularly good. Its wine selection is global and interesting, and its popular program of events includes wine seminars.

Smartmouth
Brewing Company BREWERY
(✆757-624-3939; www.smartmouthbrewing.com; 1309 Raleigh Ave; ⊘4:30-9pm Wed & Thu, 4:30-10pm Fri, noon-10pm Sat, noon-6pm Sun; ✦) In the Chelsea arts district, this indoor-outdoor tasting room and brewery has an inviting neighborhood feel, plus there's usually a food truck handy to supply sustenance. If you like *Hefeweizen* (wheat beer), give the seasonal Sommer Fling a try (April to December). There are free brewery tours every hour between 1pm and 4pm on Saturday.

❶ Getting There & Away

The region is served by Norfolk International Airport (p312), 7 miles northeast of downtown Norfolk. **Greyhound** (✆757-625-7500; www.greyhound.com; 701 Monticello Ave) buses serve Virginia Beach (from $6, 40 minutes), Richmond (from $17, two to 2½ hours), and Washington, DC ($20, 5¼ hours).

Virginia Beach

With 35 miles of sandy beaches, a 3-mile concrete oceanfront boardwalk and nearby outdoor activities, it's no surprise that Virginia Beach is a prime tourist destination. The city has worked hard to shed its reputation as a rowdy 'Redneck Riviera,' and hey, the beach *is* wider and cleaner now and there are fewer louts. Beach aside, you'll find some lovely parks and nature sites beyond the crowded high-rises lining the shore. Expect thick crowds, heavy traffic and high prices if visiting in the summer.

◉ Sights

Virginia Aquarium
& Marine Science Center AQUARIUM
(✆757-385-3474; www.virginiaaquarium.com; 717 General Booth Blvd; adult/child 3-11yr $25/20; ⊘9am-5pm) If you want to see an aquarium done right, come here. In various habitats, you can see a great array of aquatic life, including sea turtles, river otters and Komodo dragons.

If you and the kids have extra energy to burn after viewing the aquarium, you can watch a 3-D nature documentary on the largest cinema screen in the state ($8), set off on a 'Whales and Wildlife' boat trip (adult/child three to 11 years $30/25) or try out the ropes course and zipline in the Adventure Park (adult/child seven to 11 years $56/47), tucked in the woods between aquarium buildings.

🛏 Sleeping & Eating

First Landing State Park CAMPGROUND **$**
(✆800-933-7275; www.dcr.virginia.gov; Cape Henry; tent & RV sites $30-46, 2-bedroom cabins $156-173; ⊘early Mar-early Dec; ℗) You couldn't ask for a prettier campground than the one at this bay-front state park, though the cabins have no water view.

Hilton Virginia
Beach Oceanfront HOTEL **$$**
(✆757-213-3000; www.hiltonvb.com; 3001 Atlantic Ave; r from $230; ℗@🅰🛜🏊) One of the premier places to stay on the beach, this 21-story hotel offers spacious and comfortable oceanfront rooms with large balconies that open out to the beach and Neptune Park below. Facilities include a fitness center and two pools: an outdoor rooftop infinity pool and an indoor alternative. In summer, rooms are cheaper midweek than on weekends.

Esoteric AMERICAN **$$**
(✆757-822-6008; www.esotericvb.com; 501 Virginia Beach Blvd; sandwiches & small plates $12-19, mains $22-30; ⊘4-10pm Mon-Thu, to midnight Fri, 3pm-midnight Sat, 10am-3pm Sun) The menu at this joint lives up to its name, including everything from hummus to dolmades, tacos to gnocchi. At lunch, the gourmet sandwiches and craft beer are a winning combination. The husband-and-wife team grow some of their produce in the attached garden, and embrace local food producers as collaborators. Bravo!

VIRGINIA'S VINEYARDS

Home to more than 200 vineyards, Virginia has a rising presence in the wine world. Good places to begin an investigation of the local scene lie just outside of DC in Loudon County, and designated wine trails continue throughout the state. For maps, wine routes and loads of other viticultural info, visit www.virginiawine.org.

It's a hard task to nominate only a few wineries as highlights, but here's our best shot.

Loudoun County

Bluemont Vineyard (☎540-554-8439; www.bluemontvineyard.com; 18755 Foggy Bottom Rd, Bluemont; tastings $15; ⏱11am-7pm; 🖼)

Breaux Vineyards (☎540-668-6299; www.breauxvineyards.com; 36888 Breaux Vineyards Lane, Hillsboro; tastings $15; ⏱11am-6pm mid-Mar–Oct, to 5pm Nov-early Mar; 🖼)

Sunset Hills Vineyard (☎540-882-4560; www.sunsethillsvineyard.com; 38295 Fremont Overlook Lane, Purcellville; tastings $12; ⏱noon-5pm Mon-Thu, to 8pm Fri, 11am-6pm Sat & Sun; ℗) 🌿

Tarara Vineyard (☎703-771-7100; www.tarara.com; 13648 Tarara Lane; tastings $15-20; ⏱11am-5pm Mon-Thu, to 6pm Fri-Sun, closed Tue & Wed Nov-Mar; 🖼)

Also see www.loudounfarms.org/craft-beverages/wine-trail and www.visitloudoun.org/things-to-do/wine-country.

Blue Ridge Parkway

Chateau Morrisette (☎540-593-2865; www.thedogs.com; 287 Winery Rd, Mile 171.5, off Blue Ridge Pkwy; tastings incl glass $10; ⏱10am-5pm Mon-Thu, to 6pm Fri & Sat, 11am-5pm Sun, closed Jan-Mar)

The Piedmont

Barboursville Vineyards (☎540-832-3824; www.bbvwine.com; 17655 Winery Rd; tastings $10; ⏱tasting room 10am-5pm Mon-Sat, from 11am Sun)

Grace Estate (☎434-823-1486; www.graceestatewinery.com; 5273 Mount Juliet Farm, Crozet; tastings $9; ⏱11am-5:30pm Wed, Thu & Sun, to 9pm Fri & Sat)

King Family Vineyards (☎434-823-7800; www.kingfamilyvineyards.com; 6550 Roseland Farm, Crozet; tastings $10, tour $20; ⏱10am-5:30pm Thu-Tue, to 8:30pm Wed; 🖼)

Pippin Hill (☎434-202-8063; www.pippinhillfarm.com; 5022 Plank Rd, North Garden; tastings $10; ⏱11am-5pm Tue-Sun) 🌿

Also see www.americaswinecountry.com and https://monticellowinetrail.com.

ℹ Getting There & Away

Greyhound (☎757-422-2998; www.greyhound.com; 971 Virginia Beach Blvd) runs daily buses to Richmond (from $16, 3½ hours), which also stop in Norfolk and Hampton; transfer in Richmond for services to Washington, DC, Wilmington, NYC and beyond. Buses depart from Circle D Food Mart, 1 mile west of the boardwalk.

Hampton Roads Transit runs the Virginia Beach Wave trolley ($2), which plies Atlantic Ave in summer.

The Piedmont

Nestled between the Blue Ridge Mountains and the coastal plain, this central tract of Virginia is a mix of forest and gently sloping hills with well-drained, mineral-rich soil – perfect conditions in which to cultivate grapes. More than 100 wineries are located here, alongside rural villages, grand colonial estates, microbreweries, cideries and distilleries. The history-rich cities of Charlottesville and Richmond are popular bases for exploring the region.

ℹ Getting There & Around

The Piedmont region is flanked by I-81 and I-64. The area is best explored by car. Charlottesville anchors the region and has an airport (p328), Amtrak station and Greyhound station. On Friday you'll likely join a few UVA students hopping the train to Washington, DC.

Richmond

Richmond has woken up from a very long nap – and we like it. The capital of the commonwealth of Virginia since 1780, and the capital of the Confederacy during the Civil War, it's long been an old-fashioned city clinging too tightly to its Southern roots. But an influx of new and creative young residents is energizing and modernizing the community.

Today the 'River City' shares a buzzing food-and-drink scene and an active arts community. The rough-and-tumble James River has also grabbed more of the spotlight, drawing outdoor adventurers to its rapids and trails. Richmond is also an undeniably handsome town that is easy to stroll, full of redbrick row houses, stately drives and leafy parks.

◎ Sights

★ **Virginia State Capitol**   NOTABLE BUILDING
(☑804-698-1788; www.virginiacapitol.gov; 1000 Bank St, Capitol Sq, Court End; ⊘9am-5pm Mon-Sat, from 1pm Sun) FREE Designed by Thomas Jefferson, the capitol building was completed in 1788 and houses the oldest legislative body in the Western Hemisphere – the Virginia General Assembly, established in 1619. Free one-hour guided tours of the historic building are available between 10am and 4pm Monday to Saturday, and between 1pm and 4pm on Sunday; self-guided tours are also available. Temporary exhibits shown in the underground galleries near the visitor entrance.

★ **Virginia Museum of Fine Arts**   MUSEUM
(VMFA; ☑804-340-1400; www.vmfa.museum; 200 N Blvd, Museum District; ⊘10am-5pm Sat-Wed, to 9pm Thu & Fri) FREE Richmond is a cultured city, and this splendid art museum is the cornerstone of the local arts scene. Highlights of its eclectic, world-class collection include the Sydney and Frances Lewis Art Nouveau and Art Deco Galleries, which include furniture and decorative arts by designers including Eileen Gray, Josef Hoffmann and Charles Rennie Mackintosh. Other galleries house

one of the largest Fabergé egg collections on display outside Russia, and American works by O'Keeffe, Hopper, Henri, Whistler, Sargent and other big names.

★ **Poe Museum**   MUSEUM
(☑804-648-5523; www.poemuseum.org; 1914-16 E Main St, Shockoe Bottom; adult/child 7-17yr $8/6; ⊘10am-5pm Tue-Sat, from 11am Sun) Contains the world's largest collection of manuscripts and memorabilia of poet and horror-writer Edgar Allan Poe, who lived and worked in Richmond. Exhibits include the first printing of 'The Raven,' Poe's vest, his pen knife and a work chair with the back cut off – they say his boss at the *Southern Literary Messenger* wanted Poe to sit up straight. Pesky know-it-all. Stop by on the fourth Thursday of the month for the Poe-themed Unhappy Hour (6pm to 9pm April to October; $8).

Historic Tredegar   MUSEUM
(☑804-649-1861; https://acwm.org; 500 Tredegar St, Gambles Hill; adult/child 6-17yr $15/8; ⊘9am-5pm) Part of the multisite American Civil War Museum, this fascinating exhibit – housed inside an 1861 iron works that at its height employed 800 free and slave laborers – explores the causes and course of the Civil War from the Union, Confederate and African American perspectives.

The new museum building set into the hillside incorporates ruins from the historic Tredegar Iron Works.

St John's Episcopal Church   CHURCH
(☑804-648-5015; www.historicstjohnschurch.org; 2401 E Broad St, Church Hill; tours adult/child 7-18yr $8/6; ⊘10am-4pm Mon-Sat, from 1pm Sun) It was here that firebrand Patrick Henry uttered his famous battle cry – 'Give me Liberty, or give me Death!' – during the rebellious 1775 Second Virginia Convention. The short but informative tour is given by guides dressed in period costume and traces the history of the church and of the famous speech. Above the pulpit, the rare 1741 sounding board and its sunburst are worth a closer look. Henry's speech is re-enacted at 1:15pm on Sunday in summer.

Hollywood Cemetery   CEMETERY
(☑804-648-8501; tour reservations 804-649-0711; www.hollywoodcemetery.org; 412 S Cherry St; ⊘8am-6pm Mar-Oct, to 5pm Nov-Feb) FREE Perched above the James River rapids, this tranquil cemetery contains the gravesites of two US presidents (James Monroe and

John Tyler), the only Confederate president (Jefferson Davis) and 18,000 Confederate soldiers. Guided walking tours are conducted at 10am Monday through Saturday from April to October, plus Saturday (10am) and Sunday (2pm) in November (adult/child under 13 years $15/free). For a self-guided walk, check the virtual tour offered on the website. The entrance is at the corner of Albemarle and Cherry Streets.

🏃 Activities

Virginia Capital Trail   CYCLING
(www.virginiacapitaltrail.org) Open to cyclists and pedestrians, this 52-mile paved trail, completed in 2015, links Richmond with Jamestown and outer Williamsburg, passing several plantations along the way. Check the helpful website for a map showing parking areas, restrooms, bike shops, restaurants and lodging. There are loads of historic sights and markers along the way. Starts at the junction of S 17th and Dock Sts.

🛏 Sleeping

★ HI Richmond   HOSTEL $
(📞 804-729-5410; www.hiusa.org; 7 N 2nd St; dm $29-31, r $85-110, nonmembers add $3; 🚭 ❄ 🛜) 🏊 Inside the 1940s Otis Elevator Co building, this stylish and ecofriendly downtown option is one of the best hostels you'll ever encounter. Rooms and dorms are clean and bright, with lockers and charging stations; linen and towels are supplied. Communal facilities – free washing machines and dryers, lounge with pool table and TV, large and well-equipped kitchen – are excellent.

Quirk Hotel   BOUTIQUE HOTEL $$$
(📞 804-340-6040; www.destinationhotels.com/quirk-hotel; 201 W Broad St, Monroe Ward; d from $180, ste from $430; 🅿 ❄ ❄ 🛜 🐾) From the moment you stroll into the big-windowed lobby, which houses a glam bar and restaurant, this downtown boutique choice impresses. The high ceilings and maple floors in rooms are a direct link to the building's past life as a luxury department store. Beds, bathrooms and amenities are excellent. The hotel's popular rooftop bar is open late April to late October.

🍴 Eating & Drinking

★ Sugar & Twine   CAFE $
(📞 804-204-1755; www.sugartwine.com; 2928 W Cary St, Carytown; pastries $2-3, sandwiches $5-6; ⏰ 7am-8pm Mon-Sat, to 6pm Sun; 🛜 🐾)

Let's face it: contemporary coffee culture hasn't made inroads in Virginia yet. Fortunately, stylish cafes like this one are in the vanguard. We like everything about Sugar & Twine: the excellent espresso coffee, delicious pastries, tasty sandwiches (some vegan and veggie; gluten-free bread available), free wi-fi and friendly staff.

Kuba Kuba   CUBAN $
(📞 804-355-8817; www.kubakuba.info; 1601 Park Ave, Fan District; sandwiches $8-10, mains $13-20; ⏰ 9am-9:30pm Mon-Thu, to 10pm Fri & Sat, to 8pm Sun; 🐾) Kuba Kuba feels like a bodega straight out of Old Havana, with mouthwatering roast pork dishes, Spanish-style omelets and panini offered at rock-bottom prices. Finish with a dessert and good espresso coffee.

Perly's   DELI $
(📞 804-912-1560; www.perlysrichmond.com; 111 E Grace St, Monroe Ward; brunch dishes $7-14, sandwiches $9-13; ⏰ 8am-9pm Mon-Sat, to 3pm Sun) Generations of locals have enjoyed Yiddish specialties at Perly's, which dates from 1962, and we think you should too. Choose from treats including corned-beef hash, cinnamon babka, knish and latkes at brunch (until 3pm daily) and opt for one of the sandwiches at lunch. There's booth and bar seating, and a friendly retro vibe.

Mama J's   AMERICAN $
(📞 804-225-7449; www.mamajskitchen.com; 415 N 1st St, Jackson Ward; sandwiches $5-10, mains $8-16; ⏰ 11am-9pm Sun-Thu, to 10pm Fri & Sat) The fried catfish may not look fancy, but it sure tastes like heaven. Set in the historic African American neighborhood of Jackson Ward, Mama J's serves delicious fried chicken and legendary fried catfish, along with collard greens, mac 'n' cheese, candied yams and other fixings. The service is friendly and the lines are long. Come early to beat the crowds.

★ L'Opossum   AMERICAN, FRENCH $$$
(📞 804-918-6028; www.lopossum.com; 626 China St, Oregon Hill; mains $22-36; ⏰ 5pm-midnight Tue-Sat) We're not exactly sure what's going on at this gastronomic laboratory, but it works. The name of the place is terrible. And dishes come with names that are self-consciously hip and verging on offensive ('Vegan Orgy on Texan Beach'). So what ties it together? The culinary prowess of award-winning chef David Shannon and his attentive and talented staff. Make a reservation or get here early to snag a seat at the bar.

Saison

BAR

(☑804-269-3689; www.saisonrva.com; 23 W Marshall St, Jackson Ward; ☺5pm-2am) This hipster hole-in-the-wall is a peculiar mash-up of wine bar, cafe and restaurant. Creative cocktails, craft beer and local wines are on offer, as is a menu of small plates (many vegetarian), burgers and more gourmet fare. We recommend heading here for drinks rather than meals.

The kitchen closes at 10pm Sunday to Thursday and 11pm Friday and Saturday.

Capital Ale House

BAR

(☑804-780-2537; www.capitalalehouse.com; 623 E Main St, Court End; ☺11am-1:30am Mon-Fri, from 10am Sat & Sun) Popular with political wonks from the nearby state capitol, this downtown pub has a superb beer selection (more than 70 on tap and 100 bottled) and decent pub grub. Regular live gigs are staged in the music hall.

ⓘ Getting There & Away

Amtrak trains stop at the **Staples Mill Rd station** (7519 Staples Mill Rd), 7 miles north of town (accessible to downtown via bus 27). More-convenient but less-frequent trains stop downtown at the **Main St Station** (1500 E Main St). Richmond is serviced by the Northeast Regional, Carolinian, Palmetto, Silver Star and Silver Meteor lines, all of which link the city frequently with Washington, DC (tickets from $38, 2¼ to 2½ hours).

Greyhound and Trailways bus services stop at the **bus station** (☑804-254-5910; 2910 N Arthur Ashe Blvd, The Diamond; ☺24hr).

ⓘ Getting Around

The **RVA Bike Share** (www.rvabikes.com) program has a number of bike stations across the city. A one-way, 45-minute pass costs $1.75 and a day pass costs $6. Download the app from the website for station locations.

Greater Richmond Transit Company (www.ridegrtc.com) runs local buses. Tickets cost $1.50 and exact change is needed. The bus rapid transit line called the GRTC Pulse (often abbreviated as the Pulse) links Willow Lawn with Rockett's Landing via Broad St and Main St.

Street car parking costs $1.25 per hour.

Charlottesville

Set in the shadow of the Blue Ridge Mountains, Charlottesville is regularly ranked as one of the country's best places to live. This culturally rich town is home to the architecturally resplendent University of Virginia (UVA), which attracts Southern aristocracy and artsy lefties in equal proportions. The UVA grounds, Main St and the pedestrian downtown mall area overflow with students, professors and visiting tourists, endowing 'C-ville' with a lively, cultured and diverse atmosphere.

◉ Sights

★Monticello

HISTORIC SITE

(☑434-984-9800; www.monticello.org; 931 Thomas Jefferson Pkwy; adult $23-30, youth 12-18yr $17, child 5-11yr $10; ☺8:30am-6pm Mon-Fri, to 7pm Sat & Sun, hours vary seasonally) The house at Monticello is an architectural masterpiece designed and inhabited by Thomas Jefferson, founding father and third US president, who spent 40 years building his dream home. It was finally completed in 1809. Today it is the only home in America designated a Unesco World Heritage Site. The centerpiece of a plantation that once covered 5000 acres, it can be visited on guided tours (ground floor only), while its grounds and outbuildings can be explored on themed and self-guided tours.

The 45-minute 'Slavery at Monticello' walking tour (included in ticket price) is the highlight of any trip. Guides don't gloss over the complicated past of the man who declared that 'all men are created equal' in the Declaration of Independence, while owning slaves and likely fathering children with slave Sally Hemings. Jefferson and his other family are buried in a small wooded plot near the home.

Two tours per day visit the upstairs rooms of the house ($49 to $65, child under five years free); these are popular so must be booked in advance.

A high-tech exhibition center delves deeper into Jefferson's world – including exhibits on architecture, enlightenment through education, and the complicated idea of liberty. Frequent shuttles run from the visitor center to the hilltop house, or you can walk along a wooded footpath.

Monticello is about 4.5 miles northwest of downtown Charlottesville.

University of Virginia

UNIVERSITY

(☑434-924-0311; www.virginia.edu; University Ave, Charlottesville) Thomas Jefferson founded the University of Virginia, and designed what he called an 'Academical Village' embodying the spirit of communal living and learning. At the heart of this 'village' is the

MONTPELIER

Thomas Jefferson gets all the attention in these parts, but it's well worth branching out and visiting James Madison's **Montpelier** (☑ 540-672-2728; www.montpelier.org; 11350 Constitution Hwy, Montpelier Station; adult/child 6-14yr $22/9; ⊗ 9am-5pm Apr-Oct, 10am-4pm Nov-Mar), a spectacular estate 25 miles northeast of Charlottesville (off Hwy 20). Madison was a brilliant but shy man, who devoted himself to his books; he was almost single-handedly responsible for developing and writing the US Constitution. Guided tours shed a light on the life and times of James as well as his gifted and charismatic wife Dolley, plus other residents of the estate.

Carefully reconstructed cabins show what life was like for Madison's slaves. There's an archeology lab, where on-site archeologists can explain recent findings. Hiking trails lead through the forests beyond the estate – the ambitious can even walk 4 miles to the **Market at Grelen** (☑ 540-672-7268; www.themarketatgrelen.com; 15091 Yager Rd, Somerset; sandwiches $8-9; ⊗ cafe 11:30am-2:30pm Mon-Fri, to 3:30pm Sat & Sun, shop 10am-4pm Wed-Sat, closed late Dec-Feb), a charming lunch spot and garden center, where you can pick your own berries on the rolling, 600-acre grounds.

Lawn, a large gently sloping grassed field fringed by columned pavilions, student rooms, the Standford White–designed Old Cabell Hall (1898) and Jefferson's famous Rotunda (☑ 434-924-7969; www.rotunda.virginia.edu; 1826 University Ave; ⊗ 9am-5pm), modelled on Rome's Pantheon. Together, the original neoclassical and Palladian-style university buildings and Jefferson's Monticello comprise a Unesco World Heritage Site.

Free, student-led **guided tours** (www.uvaguides.org) of the original university and lawn depart daily from the Rotunda at 10am, 11am and 2pm during the school year (September to April).

🛏 Sleeping

Fairhaven   GUESTHOUSE $
(☑ 434-933-2471; www.fairhavencville.com; 413 Fairway Ave; r $55-90; P❋🛜🐾) This friendly and welcoming guesthouse is a great deal if you don't mind sharing facilities (there's just one bathroom for the three rooms). Each room has wood floors, comfy beds and a cheerful color scheme, and guests can use the kitchen, living room and backyard. It's about a 1-mile walk to the pedestrian mall.

⭐ **South Street Inn**   B&B $$
(☑ 434-979-0200; www.southstreetinn.com; 200 W South St; r $193-234, ste $283-291; P❋🛜) Having gone through previous incarnations as a girls' finishing school, a boarding house and a brothel, this elegant 1856 building, with its picture-perfect front porch, now houses a heritage-style B&B with 11 well-sized and beautifully presented rooms. There are ex-

tra rooms in an attached cottage. Breakfast is served in the library, as is complimentary wine and cheese every evening.

Residence Inn by Marriott   HOTEL $$
(☑ 434-220-0075; www.marriott.com; 315 W Main St; studio $175-265, 1-bed apt $205-400, 2-bed apt $298-500; P❋♿🛜🐾🏊) We're not usually chain-hotel fans, but this excellent place deserves serious praise. Its location couldn't be better, and its clean, comfortable and well-equipped studios and apartments make a great base for a Charlottesville stay. Facilities include a pool, bar, gym and coin-operated laundry, and there's even a free shuttle service within a 10-mile radius (including the airport).

🍽 Eating

⭐ **Bodo's Bagels**   BAGELS $
(☑ 434-293-6021; www.bodosbagels.com; 1609 University Ave; bagels $0.80, sandwiches $3-4; ⊗ 7am-8pm Mon-Fri, 8am-4pm Sat & Sun) Students and university staff are regulars at this Charlottesville institution, lured by its wonderful bagels and its location on UVA Corner. Choose from a large array of options (plain, slathered with butter or cream cheese, topped with egg). Also offers sandwiches. Eat in or order to go.

Mudhouse Coffee Roasters   CAFE $
(☑ 434-984-6833; www.mudhouse.com; 213 W Main St; pastry $3; ⊗ 7am-10pm Mon-Sat, to 8pm Sun; 🛜) Its mantra is 'Beautiful coffee. Thoughtfully sourced. Carefully roasted.' and we can attest to the fact that this cafe on the pedestrian mall practices what it

VIRGINIA'S BREW RIDGE TRAIL

A string of craft breweries stretches west from Charlottesville to Crozet and along Hwy 151, which ribbons along the base of the Blue Ridge Mountains below the Blue Ridge Pkwy. Part of the **Brew Ridge Trail** (www.brewridge trail.com), these breweries produce fine craft beer; many also offer mountain views and great food. On pretty days you'll find the patios loaded with beer connoisseurs and outdoor adventurers. **Hop On Virginia** (www. virginiahopontours.com) shuttles between many of the breweries.

WASHINGTON, DC & THE CAPITAL REGION THE PIEDMONT

preaches. Excellent coffee (espresso and drip) and delicious pastries are enjoyed in stylish surrounds or at tables on the mall.

Citizen Burger AMERICAN $
(434-979-9944; www.citizenburgerbar.com; 212 E Main St; burgers $7-21; 11:30am-10:30pm Sun-Thu, to 11:30pm Fri & Sat;) The ethos at this hugely popular burger joint on the pedestrian mall is commendably local and sustainable (organically raised, grass-fed cows, Virginia-made cheeses and beers). Don't miss the truffle fries. The bar stays open after meal service finishes.

★Oakhart Social MODERN AMERICAN $$
(434-995-5449; www.oakhartsocial.com; 511 W Main St; small plates $8-22, pizza $15; 5pm-midnight Tue-Sun, to 2am Fri & Sat) Seasonally inspired small plates and wood-fired pizzas emerge from the kitchen of this hipster haunt at a great rate, keeping its loyal crew of regulars fed and happy. On warm nights, the front patio is a perfect cocktail-sipping spot, and the bar is a great spot for solo diners.

★Public Fish & Oyster SEAFOOD $$$
(434-995-5542; www.publicfo.com; 513 W Main St; mains $19-26; 4-9pm Sun & Mon, to 9:30pm Tue-Thu, to 10pm Fri & Sat) This bright and inviting space will catch your eye, but it's the skillfully seasoned seafood dishes that will keep you inside ordering plate after plate of freshly shucked oysters, mussels and other maritime delights. If you're a raw-oyster virgin, this is the place to change that story. The twice-cooked Belgian fries with sea salt are fantastic. Great service too.

ⓘ Getting There & Away

Amtrak (www.amtrak.com; 810 W Main St; ticket office 6am-9:30pm) trains connect Charlottesville with Washington, DC (from $27, 2¾ hours, two daily). From the **Greyhound/ Trailways Terminal** (434-295-5131; www. greyhound.com; 310 W Main St; ticket office 8am-10pm) buses run to Richmond (from $16, 1¼ hours, four daily), Roanoke (from $27, 2½ hours, four daily) and Washington, DC (from $19, three hours, four daily).

Charlottesville Albemarle Airport (CHO; 434-973-8342; www.gocho.com; 100 Bowen Loop), 10 miles north of downtown, offers nonstop flights along the East Coast and to Chicago.

ⓘ Getting Around

A free trolley (look for a T sign) connects the **Downtown Transit Station** (434-970-3649; www.charlottesville.org; 615 E Water St; 7am-8pm Mon-Sat, 9am-5pm Sun) near Sprint Pavilion with UVA via W Main St. It runs every 15 minutes between 6:30am and 11:30pm Monday to Saturday and from 8am to 5:40pm on Sunday.

Appomattox

The small and somnolent town of Appomattox has one major claim to fame: this is where general Robert E Lee surrendered the Army of Northern Virginia to general Ulysses S Grant, in effect ending the Civil War. These days, Civil War enthusiasts and history buffs head here to visit the Appomattox Court House National Historic Park and American Civil War Museum, and to shop in a scattering of downtown antique shops specializing in Civil War memorabilia. The latter are open on weekends only.

⊙ Sights

★Appomattox Court House National Historic Park PARK
(434-352-8987; www.nps.gov/apco; 111 National Park Dr; 9am-5pm) FREE At the McLean House in the town of Appomattox Court House, General Robert E Lee surrendered to General Ulysses S Grant, effectively ending the Civil War. The park comprises more than two-dozen restored buildings; a number are open to visitors, and set with original and period furnishings from 1865.

Highlights include the parlor of the **McLean House**, where Lee and Grant met; the **Clover Hill Tavern**, used by Union soldiers to print 30,000 parole passes for Confederate soldiers; and the dry goods–filled **Meeks General Store**.

American Civil War
Museum – Appomattox   MUSEUM
(☑434-352 5791; https://acwm.org; 159 Horseshoe Rd; adult/child 6-17yr $12/6; ⊙10am-5pm; ℗) Artifacts, photographs, documents and audiovisual presentations tell the story of the lead-up to the end of the Civil War and the start of America becoming a reunified nation. The museum's pride and joy is the uniform coat and sword that Robert E Lee wore to the surrender.

Shenandoah Valley

Local lore says Shenandoah was named for a Native American word meaning 'Daughter of the Stars.' True or not, there's no question this is God's country, and one of the most beautiful places in America. The 200-mile-long valley and its Blue Ridge Mountains are packed with picturesque small towns, wineries, microbreweries, preserved battlefields and caverns. This was once the western border of Colonial America, settled by Scots-Irish frontiersmen who were Highland Clearance refugees. Outdoor activities such as hiking, cycling, camping, fishing, horseback riding and canoeing abound, and hitting the road on the famed Skyline Drive is an unforgettable experience, particularly in the fall when the palette of the forest canopy ranges from russet red to copper-tinged orange.

❶ Getting There & Around

The best way to explore is by car. The I-81 and I-64 are the primary interstates here. The largest airport is Roanoke-Blacksburg Regional Airport (p312). Amtrak stops at the **train station** (www.amtrak.com; 1 Middlebrook Ave) in Staunton and the **Virginia Breeze** (☑800-827-3490; www.catchthevabreeze.com; tickets $15-50) bus service to/from Washington, DC, stops at Arlington, Front Royal, Staunton and Lexington.

Front Royal & Luray

There's a frontier flavour to this town nestled in the Shenandoah next to the northernmost tip of Skyline Dr. The streets are often deserted, and there aren't many top-drawer tourist attractions. It's a popular destination for outdoor enthusiasts, though, with hiking, horse riding, river rafting and canoeing opportunities aplenty. Stop here for gas and provisions before setting off along Skyline Dr.

◉ Sights

★Luray Caverns   CAVE
(☑540-743-6551; www.luraycaverns.com; 970 US Hwy 211 W, Luray; adult/child 6-12yr $28/15; ⊙9am-7pm daily mid-Jun–Aug, to 6pm Sep-Nov & Apr–mid-Jun, to 4pm Mon-Fri, to 5pm Sat & Sun Dec-Mar) If you can only fit one cavern into your Shenandoah itinerary, head 25 miles south from Front Royal to the world-class Luray Caverns and hear the 'Stalacpipe Organ' – hyped as the largest musical instrument on earth. Tours can feel like a cattle call on busy weekends, but the stunning underground formations make up for all the elbow-bumping. To save time at the entrance, buy your ticket online ahead of time, then join the entry line. Also here is a **Ropes Adventure Park** (adult/child $11/6) and a **Garden Maze** ($10/6).

⌂ Sleeping & Eating

Yogi Bear's Jellystone
Park Camp-Resort   CAMPGROUND $
(☑540-300-1697; www.campluray.com; 2250 Hwy 211 E, Luray; campsite from $40, cabins from $74; ⊙late Mar-late Nov; ℗ 🐾 🎱) Miniature golf courses, a huge splash pad and playground, jumping pillows, four waterslides and paddleboats await at this bizarrely monikered campground. It's a paradise for kids, but could well be nightmarish for those not traveling in family groups. Facilities include a camp store, cafe, dog park, laundry and clean ablutions blocks.

★Hotel Laurance   BOUTIQUE HOTEL $$
(☑540-742-7060; www.hotellaurance.com; 2 S Court St; ste $225-265; 🎱) Owner Melinda Kramer has done a splendid job of transforming this handsome but once-dilapidated 1830s building into Luray's only boutique hotel. Most of the 12 suites have an equipped kitchen; all are stylishly decorated and have comfortable beds. The only disappointment is the lack of staff to greet guests on arrival. Weekend bookings require a two- or three-night stay.

Element   FUSION $$
(☑540-636-1695; www.elementonmain.com; 317 E Main St; mains lunch $8-16, dinner $16-32; ⊙11am-3pm & 5-9pm Tue-Sat) When it comes to local popularity, this friendly Front Royal eatery wins hands down. Serving good-quality bistro fare, it offers sandwiches, soups and salads at lunch, with more substantial dishes including pastas, steaks and fish-and-chips for dinner.

SHENANDOAH NATIONAL PARK

One of the most spectacular national parks in the country, **Shenandoah National Park** (☏540-999-3500; www.nps.gov/shen; Skyline Dr; 1-week pass per car $30; ☺year-round) is a showcase of natural color and beauty: in spring and summer the wildflowers explode, in fall the leaves burn bright red and orange, and in winter a cold, starkly beautiful hibernation period sets in. White-tailed deer are a common sight and, if you're lucky, you might spot a black bear, bobcat or wild turkey. The park lies just 75 miles west of Washington, DC.

Your first stop should be the **Dickey Ridge Visitor Center** (Mile 4.6, Skyline Dr; ☺9am-5pm Apr-Nov), close to the northern end of Skyline Dr, or the **Harry F Byrd Visitor Center** (Mile 51, Skyline Dr; ☺9am-5pm Apr-Nov). Both places have exhibits on flora and fauna, as well as maps and information about hiking trails and activities.

The surrounds are mighty easy on the eyes, set against a backdrop of the dreamy Blue Ridge Mountains, ancient granite and metamorphic formations that are more than one billion years old. The park itself was founded in 1935 as a retreat for East Coast urban populations. It is an accessible day-trip destination from DC, but you should aim to stay longer if you can. The 500 miles of hiking trails, 75 scenic overlooks, 30 fishing streams, seven picnic areas and four campgrounds are sure to keep you entertained.

Skyline Dr is the breathtaking road that follows the main ridge of the Blue Ridge Mountains and winds 105 miles through the center of the park. It begins in Front Royal at the western end of I-66, and ends in the southern part of the range at Rockfish Gap near I-64. Mile markers at the side of the road provide a reference. Miles and miles of blazed trails wander through the park.

The most famous trail in the park is a 101-mile stretch of the **Appalachian Trail** (AT), a 2175-mile route crossing through 14 states. Access the trail from Skyline Dr, which roughly runs parallel. Aside from the AT, Shenandoah has more than 400 miles of hiking trails in the park. Options for shorter hikes include **Compton Peak** (Mile 10.4; 2.4 miles return; easy to moderate), **Traces** (Mile 22.2; 1.7 miles return; easy), **Overall Run** (Mile 22.2; 6 miles return; moderate) and **White Oak Canyon** (Mile 42.6; 4.6 miles return; strenuous). **Hawksbill Mountain Summit** (Mile 46.7; 2.1 miles return; moderate) is the park's highest peak.

Getting There & Around

You'll really need your own wheels if you want to explore the length and breadth of the park, which can be easily accessed from several exits off I-81. The Virginia Breeze (p329) bus service to/from Washington, DC, stops at Front Royal and Staunton near the main park entrances/exits. Amtrak (p328) runs train services between DC and Staunton.

There is a **gas station** (☏540-999-2211; Mile 51.2, Skyline Dr; ☺8am-8pm) at Big Meadows Wayside.

❶ Getting There & Away

Front Royal is 70 miles east of Washington, DC. The Virginia Breeze (p329) bus service from DC stops at Front Royal and continues to Harrisonburg, Staunton, Lexington, Christianburg and Blacksburg before returning along the same route.

Staunton

This small-town beauty has much going for it, including a historic and walkable town center, a fantastic foodie scene, great microbreweries, regular live music downtown and a first-rate theater. Add to this an abundance of outdoor activities nearby and you may find yourself looking into local real estate when you get here.

❂ Sights

The pedestrian-friendly, handsome town center boasts more than 200 buildings designed by noted Victorian architect TJ Collins. There's an artsy yet unpretentious bohemian vibe thanks to the presence of Mary Baldwin, a small liberal arts university.

Woodrow Wilson
Presidential Library
HISTORIC SITE

(☎540-885-0897; www.woodrowwilson.org; 18 N Coalter St; adult/student/child 6-12yr $14/7/5; ☉9am-5pm Mon-Sat, from noon Sun Mar-Oct, to 4pm Nov-Feb) History buffs should check out the Woodrow Wilson Presidential Library near downtown. Stop by and tour the hilltop Greek Revival house where Wilson grew up, which has been faithfully restored to its original 1856 appearance. 'Behind the Scenes' guided tours ($40) at 2pm Tuesday and Thursday; 'Wilson and Slavery' tours ($25) at 11:30am first and third Friday of the month.

🍴 Sleeping & Eating

Frederick House
B&B $$

(☎540-885-4220; www.frederickhouse.com; 28 N New St; d/ste from $156/180; ❈✿❋✿) Genial owners Ross and Brooke Williams work hard to ensure that guests at their downtown guesthouse are happy. Rooms are scattered throughout five historical residences with 23 varied rooms and suites – all with private bathrooms and some with air-con. The nicest rooms are in Patrick House (request room 26). Breakfast is included.

Chicano Boy
MEXICAN $

(☎540-569-2105; www.chicanoboytaco.com; 240 N Central Ave, Suite 6; tacos/burritos $10/12; ☉11am-9pm Tue-Sun; ✐❋) It's hard to beat the value offered by this taquería's $8.50 lunch deal, which delivers a drink, a dip and two tacos. Prices don't rise much at dinner, when tacos – including the Carnitas (pork with pico and cilantro) and vegetarian (sweet potato and black bean) – run out the door. Eat in or take out.

Newtown Bakery
BAKERY, PIZZERIA $

(☎540-885-3799; www.newtownbaking.com; 960 W Beverley St; sandwiches $6-12, pizzas $10-14; ☉7:30am-3pm & 5-9pm Wed-Fri, 8am-2pm & 5-9pm Sat; ❉✐❋) This is the type of place that every small town needs. It bakes its own European-style bread and pastries; serves soup and sandwiches at lunch; and cranks up the wood-fired pizza oven at night to offer piping hot, super-tasty pies. Coffee is from the Staunton Coffee Company, and wine and beer are available, too. Love it.

★ Shack
AMERICAN $$

(☎540-490-1961; www.theshackva.com; 105 S Coalter St; mains brunch $12-15, dinner $13-30; ☉5-9pm Wed-Sat, 10:30am-2pm Sun; ✐) It may be cooked and served in a small and unadorned space (hence the name), but the dishes served here are among the best in the state. Chef Ian Boden, a two-time James Beard semi-finalist, makes the most of seasonal local produce in his menu, which is inspired by his mountain roots and Eastern European Jewish heritage. Good wine list.

🍷 Drinking & Entertainment

Yelping Dog
WINE BAR

(☎540-885-2275; www.yelpingdogwine.com; 9 E Beverly St; ☉11am-9pm Tue-Thu, to 10pm Fri & Sat, noon-6pm Sun) An inviting wine bar in the thick of the downtown action, the Yelping Dog has its priorities right: wine, cheese and charcuterie. It also serves craft beer. If you're on the fence about ordering one of the gourmet grilled cheese sandwiches ($9 to $10), go ahead and fall off. They're delicious. Live music some Saturday nights.

★ Blackfriars Playhouse
THEATER

(☎540-851-1733; www.americanshakespearecenter.com; 10 S Market St; tickets $29-49) Don't leave Staunton without catching a show at the Blackfriars Playhouse, where actors from the American Shakespeare Center perform in a re-creation of Shakespeare's original indoor theater. The acting is up close and engaged, and brave guests can grab a seat on the side of the stage.

ℹ Getting There & Away

Staunton sits beside I-81, not far from the junction with I-64 E. Amtrak trains stop here three times per week on their way to/from Charlottesville and Washington, DC.

Lexington

The fighting spirit of the South is visually encapsulated by the sight of cadets from the Virginia Military Institute (VMI) strutting their stuff at Friday's full dress parade. The institute is one of Lexington's two major historic institutions, the other being Washington & Lee University (W&L). Two Civil War generals, Robert E Lee and Stonewall Jackson, lived here and are buried in town, and Lexington has long been a favorite stop for Civil War enthusiasts. Today you're as likely to see hikers, cyclists and paddlers using Lexington as a launchpad for adventures in the nearby Blue Ridge Mountains, where the Blue Ridge Pkwy and the Appalachian Trail overlook the valley, as well as on the James River. The opening of new hotels, bars and restaurants has re-energized the city in recent years – it's a great Shenandoah base.

◉ Sights & Activities

Virginia Military Institute UNIVERSITY
(VMI; www.vmi.edu; Letcher Ave) You'll either be impressed or put off by the extreme discipline of the cadets at Virginia Military Institute, the only university to have sent its entire graduating class into combat (plaques to student war dead are touching and ubiquitous). The **VMI Museum** (☑540-464-7334; www.vmi.edu/museum; 415 Letcher Ave; $5; ⊙9am-5pm) houses the stuffed carcass of Stonewall Jackson's horse among its 15,000 artifacts and the **George C Marshall Museum** (☑540-463-2083; www.marshallfoundation.org/museum; VMI Parade; adult/student/child under 13yr $5/2/free; ⊙11am-4pm Tue-Sat) honors the creator of the Marshall Plan for post-WWII European reconstruction.

Contact the museum for a free 45-minute cadet-guided tour of the campus, offered at noon during term time. A full-dress parade takes place most Fridays at 4pm during the school year.

Washington & Lee University UNIVERSITY
(☑540-458-8400; www.wlu.edu; 204 West Washington St) Named for George Washington and Robert E Lee, this pretty and preppy liberal arts college was founded in 1749. George Washington saved the young school in 1796 with a gift of $20,000. Confederate general Robert E Lee served as president after the Civil War in the hope of unifying the country through education. Visitors today can stroll along the striking redbrick Colonnade and visit **Lee Chapel & Museum** (☑540-458-8768; www.wlu.edu/lee-chapel-and-museum; donation adult/child $4/2; ⊙9am-4pm Mon-Sat, 1-4pm Sun Nov-Mar, to 5pm Apr-Oct).

Note that doors on the garage stall of the university president's house will likely be open. While president of the school, Lee left the door ajar for his wandering horse Traveller. Today, tradition keeps them open in case Traveller's ghost wanders home.

Natural Bridge State Park BRIDGE
(☑540-291-1326; www.dcr.virginia.gov; 6477 S Lee Hwy; adult/child 6-12yr $8/6; ⊙8am-9pm) We're going to let Thomas Jefferson write the review of the main feature in this state park,

which he described in his book *Notes on Virginia*: 'It is impossible for the emotions arising from the sublime to be felt beyond what they are here: so beautiful an arch, so elevated, so light, and springing as it were up to heaven...' As well as the 215ft-high limestone bridge here described, the park has 6 miles of hiking trails through forests and meadows.

Dinosaur Kingdom II AMUSEMENT PARK
(☑540-464-2253; www.dinosaurkingdomii.com; 5781 S Lee Hwy; adult/child 3-12yr $12/8; ⊙11am-5pm Sat & Sun May & Sep-early Nov, 10am-6pm Jun-Aug; ◉) One of the wackiest attractions yet from artist and creative wunderkind Mark Cline, this kitschy theme park transports visitors to an alternate reality: a forested kingdom where Union soldiers are attempting to use life-size dinosaurs as weapons of mass destruction against Confederate forces during the Civil War. Even President Lincoln is here, trying to lasso a flying pteranodon. The Styrofoam and fiberglass creations are lifelike enough to amaze younger kids, and the offbeat historic juxtapositions will entertain even the grouchiest of adults. The park is about 12 miles south of Lexington on S Lee Hwy/Rte 11.

Upper James River Water Trail CANOEING
(https://upperjamesriverwatertrail.com; Botetourt) This 74-mile paddling trail follows the James River as it flows through the foothills of the Blue Ridge Mountains toward Richmond and the coast. The trail is divided into various sections taking between one and seven hours to traverse by canoe or kayak.

Twin River Outfitters CANOEING; TUBING
(☑540-254-8012; https://canoevirginia.net; 640 Lowe St, Buchanan; paddling trips from $34; ⊙9am-5pm Apr-Oct) Scan for eagles and deer as you paddle or tube down the James River on the Upper James River Water Trail with this popular outfitter, owned by twin brothers. Mileage and travel times vary, as does difficulty. A shuttle ride is included in the price.

🛏 Sleeping & Eating

Georges BOUTIQUE HOTEL $$$
(☑540-463-2500; www.thegeorges.com; 11 N Main St; d $185-240, ste from $335; ℗❄🖭) Set in two historic buildings on opposite sides of Main St, Georges has 18 classy rooms featuring high-end furnishings and luxury linens. The great location, friendly

service and delicious breakfast (included in the room rate) make it Lexington's best accommodation option, and put it in the running for the accolade of best in the Shenandoah, too.

Pure Eats   AMERICAN $
(☏540-462-6000; www.pure-eats.com; 107 N Main St; burgers $7-12, doughnuts $1.25; ☺8am-8pm) In a former filling station, Pure Eats doles out delicious house-made doughnuts and egg-and-cheese biscuits in the morning; later in the day, burgers are the popular choice. Also sells local craft brews, milkshakes made with local milk and ice cream from a local creamery.

★ Red Hen   FRENCH $$$
(☏540-464-4401; www.redhenlex.com; 11 E Washington St; mains $22-28; ☺5-9pm Tue-Sat; 🖉) 🍷 Reserve well ahead for a memorable meal at Red Hen, an intimate restaurant occupying an 1890 building just off Main St. The limited menu features a creative, French-focused menu showcasing fine local produce. Great cocktails too.

🍷 Drinking & Entertainment

Taps   BAR
(☏540-463-2500; www.thegeorges.com; 11 N Main St, Georges; ☺3-11pm Mon-Thu, 11am-11pm Fri & Sat) This cozy place in Georges doubles as Lexington's living room, with students, professors and other locals hanging out on the fancy couches or at the small bar. Come here for craft beer, fine cocktails and local gossip. There's also a short pub-grub menu (sandwiches $12 to $13).

Hull's Drive-in   CINEMA
(☏540-463-2621; www.hullsdrivein.com; 2367 N Lee Hwy/US 11; adult/child 5-11yr $7/3; ☺gates open 6:30pm Fri & Sat Mar-Oct; 🖟) For old-fashioned amusement, catch a movie at this 1950s drive-in movie theater, set 5.5 miles north of Lexington. Movies start 20 minutes after sunset. Concession stand sells burgers, popcorn and sno-cones.

❶ Getting There & Away

Lexington sits at the junction of I-81 and I-64. The closest airport is Roanoke-Blacksburg Regional Airport (p312), which is 55 miles south. The Virginia Breeze (p329) bus service from DC travels here daily via Front Royal, Harrisonburg and Staunton and continues to Christianburg and Blacksburg before returning along the same route.

Blue Ridge Highlands & Southwest Virginia

The Blue Ridge Highlands and the Roanoke Valley are two of the most attractive regions in the state, with farm-dotted valleys unfurling between the Blue Ridge and Allegheny Mountains. The Blue Ridge Pkwy and Appalachian Trail roll across the mountains here, which are home to scenic rivers, streams and lakes. Old-time mountain music can be heard regularly, and wineries and craft breweries offer tastings in small towns and on mountain slopes. The most rugged part of the region – and the state – is the southwestern tip of Virginia, where mountain music was born. Turn onto any side road and you'll plunge into dark strands of dogwood and fir, and see fast streams and white waterfalls. You might even hear banjos twanging and feet stomping in the distance.

❶ Getting There & Around

To explore the byways and country roads, you will need a car. The primary interstate here is I-81, running north–south through the western edge of the state. The Blue Ridge Pkwy runs parallel to I-81, but it is much slower going.

Roanoke is served by Amtrak, with daily services linking it to New York (from $75, 9½ hours) and Washington, DC (from $37, five hours). The major airport in the region is the Roanoke-Blacksburg Regional Airport (p312).

Roanoke

Illuminated by the giant star atop Mill Mountain, Roanoke is the largest city in the Roanoke Valley and is the self-proclaimed 'Capital of the Blue Ridge.' Close to the Blue Ridge Pkwy and the Appalachian Trail, it's a convenient base camp for exploring the great outdoors. An expanding greenway system, a burgeoning arts scene and a slowly growing portfolio of farm-to-table restaurants have energized the city in recent years, flipping Roanoke from sleepy to almost hip.

◉ Sights & Activities

★ O. Winston Link Museum   MUSEUM
(☏540-982-5465; http://roanokehistory.org; 101 Shenandoah Ave NE; adult/child 3-11yr $6/5; ☺10am-5pm Tue-Sat) Trainspotters aren't the only ones who will find this museum fascinating. It is home to a large collection of

BLUE RIDGE PARKWAY

Where Skyline Dr (p330) ends, the Blue Ridge Pkwy (www.nps.gov/blri) picks up. Managed by the national park service, this pretty-as-a-picture drive stretches from the southern Appalachian ridge in Shenandoah National Park (at Mile 0) to North Carolina's Great Smoky Mountains National Park (at Mile 469). Wildflowers bloom in spring, and fall colors are spectacular, but watch out for foggy days; the lack of guardrails can make for hairy driving. There are a dozen visitor centers scattered over the parkway, and any of them make a good kick-off point for your trip. You won't find one stoplight on the entire drive, but we can almost guarantee you'll see deer. A helpful website is www.blueridge parkway.org.

Along the Blue Ridge Pkwy there are trails to the tops of three peaks clustered at the **Peaks of Otter** (Mile 85.6, Blue Ridge Pkwy; 🏠): Sharp Top, Flat Top and Harkening Hill. Seasonal shuttles run within a quarter-mile of Sharp Top, or you can take the challenging 3-mile round-trip hike. The 360-degree view of the Blue Ridge Mountains from the rocky summit is fantastic. A short trail leads to the nearby Johnson Farm, which grew apples for the local inn before the arrival of the parkway.

photographs, sound recordings and film by O Winston Link (1914–2001), a New Yorker who in the 1950s spent nine months recording the last years of steam power on the Norfolk and Western Railway. The gelatin silver prints of Link's B&W photographs are hugely atmospheric – many were shot at night, a rarity at the time – and are very dramatic.

Center in the Square MUSEUM
(☑ 540-342-5700; www.centerinthesquare.org; 1 Market Sq; ⊙ 10am-5pm Mon, to 8pm Tue-Sat, 1-6pm Sun) The city's cultural heartbeat, where you'll find three museums, a butterfly garden, aquariums and a theater. The museums cover African American culture, pinball and science. The atrium aquariums and green rooftop can be visited free of charge; admission fees apply for other attractions.

Taubman Museum of Art MUSEUM
(☑ 540-342-5760; www.taubmanmuseum.org; 110 Salem Ave SE; ⊙ 10am-5pm Wed-Sat, noon-5pm Sun, 10am-9pm 1st Fri of month; ℗) FREE The jewel in Roanoke's cultural crown, this impressive museum is set in a sculptural steel-and-glass edifice. Inside, you'll find a small permanent collection strong in 19th- and 20th-century American works including Norman Rockwell's crowd-pleasing *Framed* (1946) and Winslow Homer's *Woodchopper in the Adirondacks* (c 1870). Four temporary exhibition galleries host everything from craft to video to installation art.

🛏 Sleeping & Eating

Hotel Roanoke HOTEL $$$
(☑ 540-985-5900; www.hotelroanoke.com; 110 Shenandoah Ave NW; r from $120; ℗@🛜🏊) This Tudor-style grand dame has presided over this city at the base of the Blue Ridge Mountains for more than a century. Now part of the Hilton Group, it's in desperate need of refurbishment. Rooms are only adequate; service can be lackadaisical. A covered elevated walkway links the hotel with the downtown precinct.

Lucky MODERN AMERICAN $$
(☑ 540-982-1249; www.eatatlucky.com; 18 Kirk Ave SW; mains $19-40; ⊙ 5-9pm Mon-Wed, to 10pm Thu-Sat) Lucky has excellent cocktails (try 'The Cube') and a seasonally inspired menu of small plates (hickory-smoked porchetta, roasted oysters) and heartier mains (buttermilk fried chicken, morel and asparagus gnocchi). It also operates the equally wonderful Italian restaurant Fortunato (www.fortunatoroanoke.com) a few doors down, where the wood-fired pizzas are the stuff of dreams and poems.

❶ Getting There & Away

Amtrak operates daily services between Roanoke and New York (from $75, 9½ hours) on the Northeast Regional line. These leave from the downtown **train station** (55 Norfolk Avenue SW) and travel via Washington, DC (from $37, five hours).

The airport (p312) is 5 miles north of downtown and serves the Roanoke and Shenandoah Valley regions. Smart Way (www.smartwaybus.com) buses link Roanoke and Blacksburg, with a stop at the airport ($4) along the way; there is no service on Sunday. If you're driving, I-81 and I-581 link to the city. The Blue Ridge Pkwy is just 5 miles from downtown.

Abingdon

One of the most photogenic towns in Virginia, Abingdon retains fine Federal and Victorian architecture in its historic district. The long-running regional theater in the center of town is a statewide draw, as is the magnificent Virginia Creeper Trail. Popular with cyclists and hikers, this leafy path down from the mountains unfurls along an old railroad bed.

Virginia Creeper Trail   CYCLING, HIKING
(www.vacreepertrail.com) This 33.4-mile cycling and hiking trail on an old railroad corridor rolls through the Mount Rogers National Recreation Area, connecting lofty Whitetop with Damascus and eventually Abingdon. Local bike companies rent out bikes and provide shuttle services.

Barter Theatre   THEATER
(☑276-628-3991; www.bartertheatre.com; 127 W Main St; ⊙box office 9am-5pm Tue-Sat, from 1pm Sun) Founded during the Depression, Barter Theatre earned its name from audiences trading food for performances. Actors Gregory Peck and Ernest Borgnine cut their teeth on Barter's stage.

❶ Getting There & Away

Abingdon borders I-81 near the Virginia–Tennessee border. The city is 366 miles southwest of Washington, DC, and about 180 miles northwest of Charlotte, NC. Close regional airports include Asheville Regional Airport in Asheville, NC, and Roanoke-Blacksburg Regional Airport (p312) in Roanoke.

Floyd

Tucked in the foothills of the Blue Ridge Mountains close to the Blue Ridge Pkwy, tiny, cute-as-a-postcard Floyd isn't much more than an intersection between Hwy 8 and Hwy 221. In fact, the whole county only has one stoplight. But life explodes on Friday nights during the Friday Night Jamboree at the Floyd Country Store and the surrounding sidewalks when folks from far and wide converge for a night of live old-time music and communal good cheer.

🍽 Sleeping & Eating

Hotel Floyd   HOTEL $
(☑540-745-6080; www.hotelfloyd.com; 300 Rick Lewis Way; r $100-140, ste $150-180; P❄@🛜🐾) There may not be much style on show at this place, but who cares? Rooms are large, impeccably clean and very comfortable. Service is friendly, breakfast is included in the room rate and Main St is only a short walk away. It's cheap, too. All of this makes it deservedly popular, so book ahead.

Dogtown Roadhouse   PIZZA $
(☑540-745-6836; www.dogtownroadhouse.com; 302 S Locust St; pizzas $10-18; ⊙4-10pm Wed & Thu, noon-midnight Fri & Sat, noon-10pm Sun) You might see a local farmer walk in with produce for the toppings at this lively pizzeria, which serves wood-fired pies including the Appalachian (apple butter base, sausage, caramelized onion, cheddar and goat cheeses). Lagers, stouts, porters and ciders are on tap, and there's live rock on Friday and Saturday nights from 8pm.

DON'T MISS

THE CROOKED ROAD

When Scots–Irish fiddle-and-reel joined with African American banjo-and-percussion, American mountain or 'old-time' music was born, spawning such genres as country and bluegrass. The latter genre still dominates the Blue Ridge, and Virginia's Heritage Music Trail, the 330-mile-long Crooked Road (www.myswva.org/tcr), takes you through nine sites associated with that history, along with some eye-stretching mountain scenery. It's well worth taking a detour and joining the music-loving fans of all ages who kick up their heels (many arrive with tap shoes) at these festive jamborees. During a live show you'll witness elders connecting to deep cultural roots and a new generation of musicians keeping that heritage alive and evolving.

Top venues include the Blue Ridge Music Center (p336) near Galax, the **Floyd Country Store** (☑540-745-4563; www.floydcountrystore.com; 206 S Locust St; ⊙10am-5pm Mon-Thu & Sat, to 10:30pm Fri, 11am-9pm Sun) on Friday nights and the **Carter Family Fold** (☑276-386-6054; www.carterfamilyfold.org; 3449 AP Carter Hwy/SR 614, Hiltons; adult $10-15, child 6-11yr $2; ⊙7:30pm Sat; ♿) in Hiltons on Saturday nights.

Pine Tavern

AMERICAN $

(☎540-745-4482; www.thepinetavern.com; 611 Floyd Hwy N; per person $15-17; ⊗4:30-9pm Fri, from noon Sat, 11am-8pm Sun; P⊞) One taste of the buttermilk biscuits, fried chicken and country ham at this all-you-can-eat family-style restaurant and your mouth won't stop salivating. We thoroughly approve of the way they pile on dumplings, pinto beans, green beans and mashed potatoes. There's occasional live music in the outside pavilion during spring and summer.

❶ Getting There & Away

Floyd is 20 miles southeast of I-81 and is best reached by car. The closest major airport is Roanoke-Blacksburg Regional Airport (p312), about 50 miles north.

Galax

Galax claims to be the world capital of mountain music, although it feels like anywhere-else-ville outside of the immediate downtown area, which is on the National Register of Historic Places. The town is an important stop on the 330-mile-long Crooked Road (p335) music trail, and is close to the Blue Ridge Pkwy.

⌂ Sleeping

Fiddlers Roost CABIN $$

(☎276-236-1212; www.fiddlersroostcabins.com; 485 Fishers Peak Rd; cabins $120-300; P) These eight cabins resemble Lincoln Logs playsets. The interiors are decorated in 'quilt' chic; they may not win a place in *Wallpaper* magazine, but they're cozy and have gas fireplaces, kitchens, TVs and DVD players. Breakfast is included with all but Cabin on the Blue. Two-night minimum stay on weekends.

❡ Drinking & Entertainment

Creek Bottom Brews MICROBREWERY

(☎276-236-2337; www.cbbrews.com; 307 N Meadow St; sandwiches $8-11, pizza $16; ⊗11am-9pm Tue-Thu, to 10pm Fri & Sat) Has a changing lineup of its own craft brews, which go nicely with the brick-oven pizza and smoked chicken wings fired up on-site. Try the Hellgrammite Brown Ale. The brewery is hidden behind a corrugated iron fence next to Pronets.

★ Blue Ridge Music Center LIVE MUSIC

(☎276-236-5309; www.blueridgemusiccenter.net; 700 Foothills Rd/Mile 213, Blue Ridge Pkwy; ⊗10am-5pm late May-late Oct, 10am-5pm Thu-Mon early May-late May) An arts and music hub for the region that offers programming that focuses on local musicians carrying on the traditions of Appalachian music. Headline performances are mostly on weekends, but local musicians give free concerts on the breezeway of the visitor center most days from noon to 4pm. Bring a lawn chair and sit yourself down for an afternoon or evening performance. There's a free 'Roots of American Music' exhibit on-site, too.

Rex Theater LIVE MUSIC

(☎276-236-0329; www.rextheatergalax.com; 113 E Grayson St) A musty, red-curtained belle of yore. Frequent bluegrass acts cross its stage, but the easiest one to catch is the Friday-night live WBRF 98.1 show 'Blue Ridge Backroads' (admission $5), which pulls in crowds from across the mountains.

❶ Getting There & Away

The best way to get to Galax is by car. The town borders US 58 about 10 miles southwest of I-77. Roanoke-Blacksburg Regional Airport (p312) is 90 miles northeast via I-77 north and I-81 N. The city is about 10 miles from the Blue Ridge Pkwy.

WEST VIRGINIA

Ready for rugged East Coast adventuring with a gorgeous mountain backdrop? Then set your car toward wild and wonderful West Virginia, a state often overlooked by both American and foreign travelers. It doesn't help that the state can't seem to shake its negative stereotypes. That's too bad, because West Virginia is one of the prettiest states in the Union. With its line of unbroken green mountains, raging white-water rivers and snowcapped ski resorts, this is an outdoor-lovers' paradise.

In a state created by secessionists, the people here still think of themselves as hard-scrabble sons of miners, and that perception isn't entirely off. But the Mountain State is also gentrifying and, occasionally, that's a good thing: the arts are flourishing in the valleys, where some towns offer a welcome break from the state's constantly evolving outdoor activities. Charleston is the capital and the state's largest city – and its population is under 50,000.

History

Virginia was once the biggest state in America, divided between the plantation aristocracy of the Tidewater and the mountains of what is now West Virginia. The latter were settled by tough farmers who staked out independent freeholds across the Appalachians. Always resentful of their Eastern brethren and their reliance on cheap (ie slave) labor, the mountaineers of West Virginia declared their independence from Virginia when the latter tried to break off from America during the Civil War.

Yet the scrappy, independent-at-all-costs stereotype was challenged in the late-19th and early-20th centuries, when miners here formed into cooperative unions and fought employers in some of the bloodiest battles in American labor history. That mix of chip-on-the-shoulder resentment toward authority and look-out-for-your-neighbor community values continues to characterize West Virginia today.

ⓘ Information

West Virginia Division of Tourism (www.wvtourism.com) operates welcome centers at interstate borders and in **Harpers Ferry** (☏ 866-435-5698, 304-535-2627; www.discoveritallwv.com; 37 Washington Ct; ⊙ 9am-5pm). Check the Division of Tourism website for info on the state's myriad adventure-tourism opportunities.

ⓘ Getting There & Around

West Virginia's Eastern Panhandle begins about 60 miles northwest of Washington, DC, and it's a fairly easy drive from the busy metropolitan area – but expect traffic.

Amtrak and MARC trains stop at the station (p338) in Harpers Ferry. Charleston has a small airport (p342).

For the national forest and the southern reaches of the state, you will need a car to explore and will likely be accessing most mountain towns and parks on two-lane roads. So although the mileage looks short, the distance will take longer to cover than on the interstate. Cell phone coverage can be very spotty on mountain roads, so check your directions – and maybe write them down – before starting your trip.

Eastern Panhandle

The most accessible part of West Virginia has always been a mountain getaway for DC types – the region is just 70 miles west of the capital-area sprawl. Here, Civil War–era history, soothing hot springs, leafy scenery

and outdoor recreation on trails and rivers work together for visitors, offering an easy package of experiences than can be enjoyed on one long weekend.

One tricky part of travel in the panhandle is the practically overlapping proximity of three states – West Virginia, Virginia and Maryland – with Pennsylvania lying in wait just north. When planning, get out your maps to make sure you've spotted all attractions in the multistate region.

Harpers Ferry

History lives on in this attractive town, set with steep cobblestoned streets, and framed by the Shenandoah Mountains and the confluence of the rushing Potomac and Shenandoah Rivers. The lower town functions as an open-air museum, with more than a dozen buildings that you can explore to get a taste of 19th-century, small-town life. Exhibits narrate the town's role at the forefront of westward expansion, American industry and, most famously, the slavery debate – in 1859 old John Brown tried to spark a slave uprising here and was hanged for his efforts; the incident rubbed friction between North and South into the fires of Civil War.

The upper town is dotted with cafes and B&Bs. Harpers Ferry sits beside the Appalachian Trail across the Potomac from the C&O Canal bike path, so there are lots of outdoorsy types filling the coffee houses and hostels. The town is touristy for sure, but it has a fun and energetic vibe.

◎ Sights & Activities

Harpers Ferry
National Historic Park   PARK
(☏ 304-535-6029; www.nps.gov/hafe; 171 Shoreline Dr; per person on foot or bicycle $7, vehicle $15; ⊙ trails sunrise-sunset, visitor center 9am-5pm; 🅿🚻) Historic buildings and museums are accessible to those with passes, which can be found, along with parking and shuttles, north of town at the **Harpers Ferry National Historic Park Visitor Center** off Hwy 340. Parking is incredibly limited in Harpers Ferry proper so plan to park at the visitor center and catch the frequent shuttle. It's a short and scenic ride.

John Brown Museum   MUSEUM
(www.nps.gov/hafe; Shenandoah St; ⊙ 9am-5pm) **FREE** Across from Arsenal Sq and one of the park's museums, this three-room gallery

gives a fine overview (through videos and period relics) of the events surrounding John Brown's famous raid.

African American
History Museum
MUSEUM

(www.nps.gov/hafe; High St; ⊙9am-5pm) FREE Part of the national park, this worthwhile, interactive exhibit has narrated stories of hardships and hard-won victories by African Americans from the times of enslavement through the Civil Rights era. Across the street is the Storer College exhibit, which gives an overview of the groundbreaking educational center and Niagara movement that formed in its wake.

C&O Canal National
Historic Park
CYCLING, HIKING

(☎301-739-4200; www.nps.gov/choh) The 184.5-mile towpath passes along the Potomac River on the Maryland side. From the historic downtown you can reach it via the Appalachian Trail across the Potomac Bridge. Check www.nps.gov/hafe for additional access points to the towpath and a list of bike-rental companies.

River Riders
ADVENTURE SPORTS

(☎304-535-2663; www.riverriders.com; 408 Alstadts Hill Rd; tubing/kayaking/rafting per person from $29/59/79; ⊙8am-6pm Jun-Aug, hours vary rest of year) The go-to place for rafting, canoeing, tubing, kayaking and multiday cycling trips, plus cycle rental (two hours is $34 per person). There's even a 1200ft zipline.

🛏 Sleeping & Eating

HI-Harpers Ferry Hostel
HOSTEL $

(☎301-834-7652; www.hiusa.org; 19123 Sandy Hook Rd, Knoxville; dm $25; ⊙mid-Apr–mid-Nov; P❀@🛜) This friendly hostel has plenty of amenities, including a kitchen, laundry and lounge area with games and books. It's popular with cyclists on the C&O Canal towpath and hikers on the Appalachian Trail, both nearby. Breakfast is included. It's 2 miles from downtown Harpers Ferry, on the Maryland side of the Potomac River.

Jackson Rose
B&B $$

(☎304-535-1528; www.thejacksonrose.com; 1167 W Washington St; r weekday/weekend $135/150, closed Jan & Feb; P❀🛜) This marvelous 18th-century brick residence with stately gardens has three attractive guest rooms, including a room where Stonewall Jackson lodged briefly during the Civil War. Antique furnishings and vintage curios are sprinkled

about the house, and the cooked breakfast is excellent. It's a 600m walk downhill to the historic district. No children under 12.

Beans in the Belfry
AMERICAN $

(☎301-834-7178; www.beansinthebelfry.com; 122 W Potomac St, Brunswick; sandwiches $7; ⊙8am-9pm Mon-Thu, to 10pm Fri & Sat, to 7pm Sun; 🛜❀) This converted redbrick church about 6 miles east of Harpers Ferry, WV, shelters mismatched couches and kitsch-laden walls. The menu features coffee and light fare (chili, sandwiches, quiche), and there's a tiny stage where live folk, blues and bluegrass bands strike up several nights a week. Sunday jazz brunch ($18) is a hit. A cool spot and worth the drive.

ℹ Information

Appalachian Trail Conservancy (ATC; ☎304-535-6331; www.appalachiantrail.org; 799 Washington St, cnr Washington & Jackson Sts; ⊙9am-5pm) The 2160-mile Appalachian Trail is headquartered here at this tremendous resource for hikers, which offers a chance for conversation, information, trail updates and restrooms. Less-ambitious travelers will appreciate the helpful Harpers Ferry map with a summary of several area day hikes, including the 1.5-mile loop around Harpers Ferry that begins here.

ℹ Getting There & Away

Amtrak trains run from the **Harpers Ferry Station** (Potomac St) to Washington's Union Station (from $14, 70 minutes, daily) on the Capitol Limited route. MARC trains (http://mta.maryland.gov) run to Washington's Union Station several times per day (Monday to Friday) on the Brunswick Line.

Berkeley Springs

America's first spa town (George Washington relaxed here) is an odd jumble of spiritualism, artistic expression and pampering spa centers. Farmers in pickups sporting Confederate flags, and acupuncturists in tie-dye smocks regard each other with bemusement on the roads of Bath (still the official name).

Berkeley Springs State Park
SPA

(☎304-258-2711; www.berkeleyspringssp.com; 2 S Washington St; 30min bath $27, 1hr massage $99-129; ⊙9am-6pm) Don't let the locker-room appearance deter you from the Berkeley Springs State Park's Roman Baths – it's the cheapest spa deal in town. Fill your water bottle with some of the magic stuff at the fountain outside the door – it's mineral-filled and it's free! In the summer, kids will enjoy the spring-fed (but chlorinated) outdoor swimming pool (adult/child under 12 years $5/3) in the middle of the green.

Country Inn of Berkeley Springs HOTEL $$
(☑ 304-258-1200; www.thecountryinnwv.com; 110 S Washington St; r/ste from $120/170; P❋🗢) The Country Inn, right next to the park, offers luxurious treatments and comfortable but not overly fancy rooms. You'll also find lodging package deals. There's a good restaurant on hand.

★ Tari's FUSION $$$
(☑ 304-258-1196; www.tariscafe.com; 33 N Washington St; mains lunch $10-15, dinner $21-30; ⊘ 11am-9pm Mon-Sat, to 8pm Sun; 🖉) 🖉 Tari's is a very Berkeley Springs sort of spot, with fresh local food and good vegetarian options served in a laid-back atmosphere with all the right hints of good karma abounding. Dig into the jumbo lake crab cakes with a side of fries at dinner.

❶ Getting There & Away

Berkeley Springs is 40 miles west of I-95. It's about 90 minutes from the Washington, DC, metro area.

Monongahela National Forest

Almost the entire eastern half of West Virginia is marked green parkland on the map, and most of that goodness falls under the auspices of this stunning national forest. Established in 1920 with just 7200 acres, the forest today covers more than 900,000 acres across 10 counties. The region, also known as the Potomac Highlands, is the adventure capital of the state. Within its boundaries are wild rivers, striking rock formations and the highest peak in the state, Spruce Knob. More than 850 miles of trails include the nearly 330-mile **Allegheny Trail** and the 78-mile rails-to-trails **Greenbrier River Trail** (☑ 304-799-4087; www.wvstateparks.com; off WV 66, Cass). The surreal landscapes at Seneca Rocks attract rock climbers.

The towns of Thomas and Davis, in the northern reaches of the region, are good base camps for Canaan Valley and Dolly Sods. Seneca Rocks is centrally located within the forest region. Snowshoe Mountain Resort is a good launchpad in the south.

◉ Sights

★ Seneca Rocks NATURAL FEATURE
(☑ 304-567-2827; www.fs.usda.gov/mnf; Hwy 28/55; ⊘ sunrise-sunset; P) A striking rock formation rising 900ft above a fork of the Potomac River, Seneca Rocks is one of the most recognizable natural features in the state. Rock climbers have scaled the sandstone walls here since the mid-1930s. Today there are more than 370 mapped climbing routes. Hikers can walk 1.5 miles to an observation platform near the top of the formation.

Dolly Sods Wilderness FOREST
(☑ 304-636-1800; www.fs.usda.gov; Fire Road 19, Davis; P) FREE Red spruce trees, windswept boulders, valley views and boggy forests set a striking scene in the northern reaches of this remote but popular wilderness atop the Allegheny Plateau. The alpine landscape evokes the mountain scenery of northern Canada, and with 47 miles of trails crisscrossing its 17,371 acres, Dolly Sods is a prime spot for a day-long or weekend adventure. You can build your own loop hike from the Beaver Dam or Bear Rocks trailheads.

There are 11 primitive first-come first-served sites at the Red Creek Campground (campsites $11 per night).

Blackwater Falls State Park STATE PARK
(☑ 304-259-5216; www.blackwaterfalls.com; 1584 Blackwater Lodge Rd; P) FREE The falls tumble into an 8-mile gorge lined by red spruce, hickory and hemlock trees. With more than 24 miles of trails, there are loads of hiking options; look for the **Pendleton Point Overlook**, which perches over the deepest, widest point of the Canaan Valley. There's an inviting lodge here as well as cabins and campsites ($23 to $26 per night).

🏃 Activities

★ NROCKS Outdoor Adventures CLIMBING
(☑ 877-435-4842; www.nrocks.com; 141 Nelson Gap Rd, Circleville; $125) The thrills begin the moment you clip into your harness for this rugged *via ferrata* adventure, a fixed-anchor guided rock climb that scrambles up and over a double-fin rock formation. One highlight is the crossing of a suspension bridge 150ft above a canyon. Guides are upbeat and fun but professional, and tours last from 3½ to five hours.

Highland Scenic Highway   SCENIC DRIVE
(📳304-846-2695, 304-799-4334; www.fs.usda.
gov/mnf; Hwy 150) This 43-mile National Scenic Byway unfurls across the leafy heights of the Allegheny Highlands and Plateau, passing four overlooks with expansive mountain and valley views. It's an exhilarating drive that soars toward the sky, rising from 2235ft to more than 4500ft. The highway rolls north on Rte 39/55 from Richwood to the **Cranberry Nature Center** (📳304-653-4826; www.fs.usda.gov/mnf; cnr Hwys 150 & 39/55; ⏱9am-4:30pm Thu-Mon mid-Apr–mid-Oct; 🅿♿). From there, hop onto the 22-mile parkway section on Hwy 150.

Picnic tables and restrooms are located at each overlook. Note that the parkway section is not maintained in winter and is typically closed December through March. More than 150 miles of trail can be accessed from the highway.

Snowshoe Mountain Resort   SKIING
(📳877-441-4386; www.snowshoemtn.com; 10 Snowshoe Dr; lift tickets adult/child 13-17yr/child 6-12yr from $79/70/66; ♿) The largest ski resort in the region, Snowshoe attracts skiers and snowboarders from across the country with 59 trails across three ski areas. Twelve trails are open for night skiing. In summer, mountain bikers hurtle down wooded terrain on more than 35 trails. You can visit Snowshoe and enjoy the facilities without staying overnight. Lodging options range from large cabins with expansive mountain views to condos just steps from the slopes. In the central village, the Junction restaurant is open year-round. There's also a play area on the resort lake.

🛏 Sleeping

In the national forest, there are 23 campgrounds across six different districts, so pick your region and go from there. There's also dispersed camping in two districts and cabins in the Greenbrier District. For more creature comforts, you'll find half a dozen or so hotels in Elkins. Ski resorts Snowshoe and Canaan Valley have a range of options, from simple cabins to plush hotel rooms.

Seneca
Shadows Campground   CAMPGROUND $
(📳877-444-6777; www.recreation.gov; US 33/WV 28; campsites $22-35; ⏱Apr-Oct; 🅿) Flanked by mountains and sitting 1 mile east of

rock-climbing spot Seneca Rocks (p339), this leafy campground has picnic tables, firepits and flush toilets. Many sites have a view of the rocks.

Billy Motel   MOTEL $
(📳304-851-6125; www.thebillymotel.com; 1080 William Ave, Davis; r $100; 🅿❄🛜) The 10 rooms pop with bright colors and fresh modern style inside this classic motor court. The cozy lobby has a fireplace and a lounge bar, which serves cocktails from Tuesday to Saturday.

Cooper House Bed & Cocktail   B&B $
(📳304-851-4553; www.cooperhousebandc.com; 114 East Ave, Thomas; r $100-120; ❄🛜) Proprietor Joy Malinowski brings the spark to this creaky but inviting house. There's a fun communal vibe, but don't worry, the four bedrooms each have their own bathroom. Guests can enjoy a cocktail in the common area.

Allegheny Springs   LODGE $$
(📳877-441-4386; http://alleghenyspringssnowshoe.usotels.co; 10 Snowshoe Dr, The Village, Snowshoe Mountain Resort; apt $143-176; 🅿❄🛜🏊) Well hello there, lobby lounge. Comfy chairs, a big stone hearth – we like your rugged style. Studios and condo units in this flagship property are in the thick of the mountaintop action and steps from the slopes and several restaurants. For the glossiest digs, reserve a condo unit in the Brigham Collection.

🍴 Eating & Drinking

Hellbender Burritos   MEXICAN $
(📳304-259-5557; www.hellbenderburritos.com; 457 William Ave, Davis; mains $7-10; ⏱11:30am-9pm Wed, Thu & Sun, to 10pm Fri & Sat) 🍃 They stuff the big burritos here Mountain State style – think blue-cheese dressing, Fritos, homemade pulled pork and other stuff that may not be Mexican but sure tastes good. There's even a PB&J burrito for the kiddies. Lots of vegetarian options too. Grab a table upstairs or head down to the bar.

Mountain State Brewing Co   MICROBREWERY
(📳304-463-4500; www.mountainstatebrewing.com; 1 Nelson Blvd, Thomas; ⏱6pm-midnight Thu & Fri, 3pm-midnight Sat, 1-7pm Sun) The $6 flight of eight beers may be the best deal going in the state. And staff might even throw in a sample of sangria, because heck, why not? On a cold night the Coal Miner's Daughter

Oatmeal Stout hits the spot. The wood-hewn tasting room feels like a camp lodge in the deep woods.

Stumptown Ales MICROBREWERY
(📞 304-259-5570; www.stumptownales.com; 390 William Ave, Davis; ⊗ 5-9pm Mon-Wed, 5-10pm Thu & Fri, noon-10pm Sat, 1-7pm Sun) The saws on the wall and the 21ft-long, red-oak bar give a nod to the region's logging past. And the tasty hop-forward beers give a kick to the taste buds at this welcoming taproom.

❶ Getting There & Away

To explore this remote and rugged region, you will need a car. Thomas is 68 miles southeast of Morgantown. Snowshoe is 230 miles from Washington, DC.

New River & Greenbrier Valley

This part of the state has carved out a viable stake as the adventure-sports capital of the eastern seaboard, with wild white-water rafting, terrific mountain biking, lots of leafy trails, and inviting small towns holding it all together. Home to mineral springs and five golf courses, the swanky Greenbrier resort brings big spenders to the region.

❶ Getting There & Around

Fayetteville is 22 miles north of Beckley off I-64. Amtrak stops along the New River Valley on the Cardinal route, which runs between Washington, DC, and Chicago. Stops include **White Sulphur Springs** (315 W Main St) and the Prince Depot (p342), outside Beckley. The best way to explore the region is by car.

New River Gorge National River

The New River is actually one of the oldest in the world, and the primeval forest gorge it runs through is one of the most breathtaking in the Appalachians. The National Park Service (NPS) protects a stretch of the New River that falls 750ft over 50 miles, with a compact set of rapids up to Class V concentrated at the northernmost end. The region is an adventure mecca, with world-class white-water runs and challenging single-track trails. Rim and gorge hiking trails offer beautiful views.

The graceful New River Gorge Bridge sits 876ft above the river and is the

---

DON'T MISS

GREENBRIER RESORT & BUNKER TOUR
....

Travelers have enjoyed the mineral springs at **Greenbrier** (📞 855-453-4858; www.greenbrier.com; 300 W Main St, White Sulphur Springs; d $280-360; 🅿 ❈ 🛜 ⛱) since the 1770s. The resort itself has impressed presidents and celebrities since the 1830s. Today, this striking white, luxury property holds more than 710 rooms and suites. Common areas pop with the bright designs of famed decorator Dorothy Draper.

Don't miss the **Bunker Tour** (📞 844-223-3173; www.greenbrier.com/activities/activity-collection/bunker-tours; adult/child 10-18yr $39/20; ⊗ 9:30am-3:30pm), which explores a nuclear-war hideaway built for Congress during the Cold War.

---

third-highest bridge in the US. It carries traffic on US 19. One of four NPS visitor centers, the **Canyon Rim Visitor Center** (📞 304-574-2115; www.nps.gov/neri; 162 Visitor Center Rd, Lansing; ⊗ 9am-5pm; 🚻) 🅿 just south of the bridge has information about scenic drives, river outfitters and other outdoor adventures.

There is no lodging in the park. The only camping available is free primitive camping near the river, with no drinking water or hookups. Many outdoor outfitters offer a mix of campsites and cabins near the river that are a convenient choice before an early-morning rafting trip. For more traditional lodging options head to Fayetteville (p342) or the lodge at Hawks Nest State Park.

⊙ Sights

New River Gorge Bridge BRIDGE
(www.nps.gov/neri; Hwy 19; 🅿) FREE Completed in 1977, the New River Gorge Bridge is the third-highest bridge in the US and the longest single-arch bridge in the Western Hemisphere. Made from 22,000 tons of structural steel, it rises 876ft above the New River and stretches 3030ft across the gorge. For the best view of the span, head to the overlooks behind the Canyon Rim Visitor Center or join a Bridgewalk tour.

Hawks Nest State Park   STATE PARK

(☎ 304-658-5212; www.hawksnestsp.com; 49 Hawks Nest Park Rd; tram & jet boat tour adult/child $29/14; P) There are hiking trails, a nature center and an aerial tram, which runs from the lodge down to the river's edge for jet boat tours of the river and views of the New River Gorge Bridge (May to October). The layout of the lodge is a little confusing, but the comfy rooms (double $109 to $134) offer fabulous views over the gorge. Book early for the fall foliage display.

Hawks Nest Overlook   VIEWPOINT

(www.wvstateparks.com; Hwy 60; P) FREE An 80yd paved trail leads to a lofty view of the New River. The photogenic rock wall surrounding the overlook was built by the Civilian Conservation Corps in the 1930s. It's worth the short walk from the parking lot to get there. The viewpoint is a quarter-mile south of the main lodge at Hawks Nest State Park.

Mystery Hole   MUSEUM

(☎ 304-658-9101; www.mysteryhole.com; 16724 Midland Trail, Ansted; adult/child $7/6; ⊙ 10:30am-5:30pm Thu-Mon Jun-Aug, Fri-Sun May, Sat & Sun only Sep & Oct; P ♿) See gravity and the known limits of tackiness defied at the Mystery Hole, one of the great attractions of roadside America. Everything inside this madhouse *tilts at an angle!* It's 1 mile west of Hawks Nest State Park.

🏃 Activities

★ Bridgewalk   WALKING

(☎ 304-574-1300; www.bridgewalk.com; 57 Fayette Mine Rd; $72; ⊙ 9am-4pm) Wow. The bird's-eye view of the New River from the catwalk running below the river's namesake bridge is amazing. And it's eerie to hear traffic rattling by overhead. If you're not afraid of heights – you're 851ft above the river – this is a recommended bucket-list adventure. The tours, which last two to three hours, are guided and very informative. Expect to walk 1.25 miles.

Long Point Trail   HIKING

(www.nps.gov/neri/planyourvisit/fayetteville_trails.htm; Newtown Rd, off Gatewood Rd) At just over 3 miles for the round trip, this trail leads to a rocky outcrop with big views of the New River Gorge and the New River Gorge Bridge. This is a great short hike and the outcrop is perfect for a picnic.

Adventures on the Gorge   ADVENTURE

(☎ 855-379-8738; www.adventuresonthegorge.com; 219 Chestnutburg Rd, Lansing; guided rafting trips per person from $109; ♿) How many experiences does this reputable outfit offer? Well, their catalog is 63 pages long and covers everything from white-water rafting on the New and Gauley Rivers to ziplining, rappelling, rock climbing and more. It has a wide array of cabins (including some with Jacuzzis), plus campsites and several restaurants, including Smokey's Cast Iron Grill (open for breakfast and dinner May to October; mains $14 to $36) near the rim of the gorge.

Cantrell Ultimate Rafting   RAFTING

(☎ 304-877-8235; www.cantrellultimaterafting.com; 49 Cantrell Dr; rafting from $89) Among the many state-licensed rafting outfitters in the area, Cantrell Ultimate Rafting stands out for its white-water rafting trips.

❶ Getting There & Away

The **Yeager Airport** (☎ 304-344-8033; https://yeagerairport.com; 100 Airport Rd) in Charleston is located 70 miles northwest. Amtrak stops at three places in the NPS region on the Cardinal route, which runs between Chicago, Washington, DC, and New York City. One of these stops is the **Prince Depot** (☎ 800-872-7245; 5034 Stanaford Rd, Prince), which is 23 miles south of Fayetteville near Beckley. Greyhound (www.greyhound.com) stops in Beckley at 360 Prince St.

Fayetteville

Packed tight with good restaurants and watering holes, pint-size Fayetteville acts as a jumping-off point for New River thrill-seekers. Definitely plan to stop here for a meal if you're adventuring in the area. It's an artsy mountain enclave as well.

◉ Sights & Activities

Beckley Exhibition Coal Mine   MINE

(☎ 304-256-1747; www.beckley.org/general-information-coal-mine; 513 Ewart Ave, Beckley; adult/child $22/12.50; ⊙ 10am-6pm Apr-Oct) This mine in Beckley, 22 miles south of Fayetteville, is a museum about the region's coal heritage. Visitors can ride a train 1500ft into a former coal mine, check out exhibits about mining life and explore the camp town village. Don't like enclosed places? You can see everything except the mine for $11. If you do go in the mine, bring a jacket; it's cold underground!

New River Bikes CYCLING
(📞 304-574-2453; www.newriverbikes.com; 221 N Court St; bike hire per day $35, tours $79-110; 🕙10am-6pm Mon, Tue, Thu & Fri, to 4pm Sat) Mountain biking is superb on the graded loops of the Arrowhead Trails. You can hire wheels or take a guided trip through this outfit in Fayetteville.

🛏 Sleeping & Eating

River Rock Retreat Hostel HOSTEL $
(📞 304-574-0394; www.riverrockretreatandhostel.com; cnr Lansing-Edmond & Fayette Station Rds; dm $30; 🅿 ❄ 🛜) Less than 1 mile north of the New River Gorge Bridge, this is a well-run hostel with basic, clean rooms and plenty of common space. No host on-site, but owner Joy Marr is a wealth of local information.

★ Secret Sandwich Society AMERICAN $
(📞 304-574-4777; www.secretsandwichsociety.com; 103 Keller Ave; mains $10-15; 🕙11am-10pm) If you're a connoisseur of sandwiches, or just super hungry, this easygoing spot is a must. The eatery has sandwiches slathered in tasty toppings, delicious burgers, hearty salads and a changing lineup of local microbrews. Eat on the pleasant deck for a fine breeze.

Pies & Pints PIZZA $$
(📞 304-574-2200; www.piesandpints.net; 219 W Maple Ave; pizzas $10-25; 🕙11am-10pm Sun-Thu, to 11pm Fri & Sat) Oooh baby. Let's talk about the Gouda Chicken. Topped with gourmet cheese, chipotle crema, apple-smoked bacon and grilled yard bird, this decadent pizza is darn near heaven. The flagship location of the popular West Virginia and Ohio pizza-and-craft-beer mini-chain, this is a place where folks come to celebrate after a good time in the great outdoors.

From ales and IPAs to sours, the craft-beer list is impressive, with selections both local and national.

ℹ Getting There & Away

You will need a car to check out regional attractions.

Amtrak (www.amtrak.com) stops on Wednesday, Friday and Sunday at the Prince Depot, 23 miles south of Fayetteville on the Cardinal route linking NYC, Washington, DC, and Chicago. It's a fairly remote stop and there are no rental-car companies on-site. You will need to arrange for pickup by a friend or a taxi.

The South

Includes ➡

Why Go?

The South falls from the granite, forested fists of Kentucky and Tennessee into craggy hill country and thick woods. This rugged landscape slowly changes as the waters of its rivers – including North America's greatest, the Mississippi – saturate the land into boggy, black-water blankets and sun-seared marsh, all thinning into the salty membrane of the Atlantic Ocean and Gulf of Mexico.

Arguably the first region of the USA to be considered its own distinct place, the South is defined by its cuisine, landscape, accent, literature, music and, undergirding all of the above, history – one that is long and beautiful in places, brutal and bloody in others.

Yet while Southerners consider themselves tied to this land and water, they are also the inhabitants of cities deeply in tune with the American experience, from the sweat-drenched noir of Charleston and New Orleans to the accept-all-comers diversity of Atlanta and Nashville.

Best Places to Eat

➡ Bacchanal (p454)

➡ Hattie B's (p391)

➡ Dish Dive (p413)

➡ Edmund's Oast (p372)

Best Places to Sleep

➡ 21c Museum Hotel Louisville (p401)

➡ Park View Historic Hotel (p453)

➡ Bunn House (p364)

➡ Urban Oasis B&B (p412)

When to Go
New Orleans

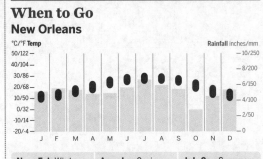

Nov–Feb Winter is generally mild in the South, and Christmas is a capital-E Event.

Apr–Jun Spring is lush and warm, abloom with fragrant jasmine, gardenia and tuberose.

Jul–Sep Summer is steamy, often unpleasantly so, and locals hit the beaches.

NORTH CAROLINA

The rural, conservative Old South and the urban, liberal-leaning New South jostle for precedence in the fast-growing Tar Heel State, home to hipsters, hog farmers and high-tech wunderkinds. From the mighty mountains in the west to the ethereal islands lining the Atlantic coast, all kinds of cultures and communities manage to coexist.

The locals are joined, especially in summer, by visitors from around the world. Many are drawn by the limitless opportunities for adventures, including hiking the woods, rafting the rivers and cruising the Blue Ridge Parkway in a convertible. Others come to savor the dynamic cities of Raleigh, Charlotte and Wilmington, with their top-class museums and restaurants – and astonishing number of craft breweries.

So grab yourself a barbecue platter and a local brew, and watch the Duke Blue Devils battle the North Carolina Tar Heels in the college-basketball league.

History

The tides of history have flowed back and forth across North Carolina. For Native Americans, the fragile coastline fringed the periphery of their world; for European colonizers, it marked the point from which they steadily pushed the original inhabitants westwards. Once it became part of the United States, North Carolina's fortunes became entwined with the plantation South, and it eventually seceded to join the Confederacy. Since then, the state has continued to identify with the South, while industrializing and entering the global economy.

North Carolina Coast

The coastline of North Carolina stretches more than 300 miles. Remarkably, it remains underdeveloped and the beach is often visible from coastal roads. Yes, the wall of cottages stretching south from Corolla to Kitty Hawk can seem endless, but for the most part the state's shores remain free of flashy, highly commercialized resort areas. Instead you'll find rugged, windswept barrier islands, Colonial villages once frequented by pirates, and laid-back beach towns full of locally owned ice-cream shops and mom-and-pop motels. Even the most touristy beaches have a small-town vibe.

For solitude, head to the isolated Outer Banks (OBX), where fishermen and women still make their living hauling in shrimp, and the older locals speak in an archaic British-tinged brogue. Further south, groovy Wilmington is known as a center of film and TV production, and its surrounding beaches are popular with local spring breakers and tourists.

❶ Getting There & Away

The closest commercial airports to the Outer Banks are Norfolk International Airport (p312), 82 miles north of the Outer Banks, in Virginia, and North Carolina's Raleigh-Durham International Airport (p357), 192 miles west. Ferries link more isolated Ocracoke Island in the Outer Banks with Hatteras Island and Cedar Island as well as Swan Quarter on the mainland.

If you are only heading to the Crystal Coast, Coastal Carolina Regional Airport, serviced by commercial flights from Charlotte and Atlanta, is your closest bet.

Wilmington has its own **Wilmington International Airport** (ILM; ☐ 910-341-4125; www.flyilm.com; 1740 Airport Blvd).

Outer Banks

The Outer Banks are fragile ribbons of sand tracing the coastline for more than 100 miles, separated from the mainland by sounds and waterways. From north to south, barrier islands Bodie (pronounced 'body'), Roanoke, Hatteras and Ocracoke, essentially large sandbars, are linked by bridges and ferries. The far-northern communities **Corolla** (kur-all-ah), **Duck** and **Southern Shores** are former duck-hunting grounds for the wealthy, and are quiet and upscale. Nearly contiguous Bodie Island towns **Kitty Hawk**, **Kill Devil Hills** and **Nags Head** are developed and more populated, with fried-fish joints, drive-through beer shops, motels, and sandals and sunblock stores. **Roanoke Island**, west of Bodie, offers Colonial history and the quaint waterfront town **Manteo**. Further south, **Hatteras Island** is a protected national seashore with tiny villages and a wild, windswept beauty. At Outer Banks' southern end, find old salts, shuck oysters and weave hammocks on **Ocracoke Island**, accessible only by ferry.

◉ Sights

Corolla, the northernmost town on Hwy 158, is famed for its wild horses. Descendants of Colonial Spanish mustangs, the horses

The South Highlights

1 New Orleans (p445) Losing yourself in the magic of America's strangest, most celebratory city.

2 Great Smoky Mountains National Park (p366) Hiking and camping amid some of the South's most magnificent scenery.

3 Nashville (p385) Stomping your boots in honky-tonks along Lower Broadway.

4 Outer Banks (p345) Driving windswept NC 12 the length of North Carolina.

5 Charleston (p368) Touring antebellum homes and dining on Lowcountry fare.

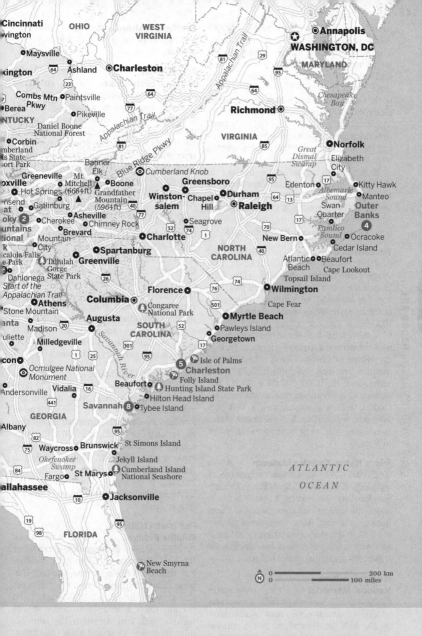

6 **Birmingham Civil Rights Institute** (p426) Learning the story of segregation and the Civil Rights movement.

7 **Ozark Mountains** (p442) Exploring the caverns, mountains, rivers, forests and folk music of Arkansas' Ozarks.

8 **Savannah** (p420) Falling for the hauntings, murderous tales and Southern hospitality of Georgia's living romance novel.

9 **Oxford** (p431) Enjoying great food and a vibrant town square.

10 **Atlanta** (p406) Embracing the energy of the most diverse city in the South.

roam the northern dunes, and numerous commercial outfitters go in search of them. The ribbon of Cape Hatteras National Seashore, broken up by villages, is home to several noteworthy lighthouses. A meandering drive down Hwy 12, which connects much of the Outer Banks and makes up part of the Outer Banks National Scenic Byway (and its 21 coastal villages), is one of the truly great American road trips, whether you come during the stunningly desolate winter months or in the sunny summer.

If you're driving on some beaches in the Outer Banks, or within Cape Hatteras National Seashore, you'll need an off-road-vehicle (ORV) permit ($50 valid for 10 days). See www.outerbanks.org/plan-your-trip/beaches/driving-on-beach for more info.

Whalehead Club HISTORIC BUILDING
(☑ 252-453-9040; www.visitcurrituck.com; 1160 Village Lane, Corolla; adult/child 6-12yr $7/5; ⊙ tours 10am-4pm Mon-Sat year-round, plus 11am-4pm Sun Jun-Nov) The sunflower-yellow, art nouveau–style Whalehead Club, built in the 1920s as a hunting 'cottage' for a Philadelphia industrialist, is the centerpiece of the well-manicured Currituck Heritage Park in the village of Corolla. Tours take about 45 minutes and are self-guided. Visitors can learn about the history of the property and explore its art-nouveau ornamentation – including Tiffany glass sconces, a Victorian safe, and a Steinway & Sons grand piano. Tour times may vary in winter (November to March).

Frisco Native America Museum MUSEUM
(☑ 252-995-4440; www.nativeamericanmuseum.org; 53536 NC 12, Frisco; $5, family $15; ⊙ 10:30am-5pm Tue-Sun) Showcasing historic artifacts about the original inhabitants of the Outer Banks. Collectors' items come from all over the USA and include everything from masks and woven baskets to rare headdresses, instruments and tribal police badges.

Wright Brothers
National Memorial PARK, MUSEUM
(☑ 252-473-2111; www.nps.gov/wrbr; Prospect Ave off 1000 N Croatan Hwy, Kitty Hawk; adult/child under 16yr $10/free; ⊙ 9am-5pm) Self-taught engineers Wilbur and Orville Wright launched the world's first successful airplane flight on December 17, 1903 (it lasted 12 seconds). A boulder marks the take-off spot. Climb a nearby hill, where the brothers conducted earlier glider experiments, for fantastic views of sea and sound. The on-site **Wright**

Brothers Visitor Center has a full-size reproduction of the 1903 flyer and intriguing exhibits.

Fort Raleigh
National Historic Site HISTORIC SITE
(☑ 252-473-2111; www.nps.gov/fora; 1401 National Park Dr; ⊙ grounds dawn-dusk) FREE In the late 1580s, three decades before the Pilgrims landed at Plymouth Rock, a group of 116 British colonists disappeared without a trace from their Roanoke Island settlement. Were they killed off by drought? Did they run away with a Native American tribe? The fate of the 'Lost Colony' remains one of America's greatest mysteries. Explore their story in the visitor center (p350).

Cape Hatteras National Seashore ISLAND
(☑ 252-473-2111; www.nps.gov/caha) Extending some 70 miles from south of Nags Head to the south end of Ocracoke Island, this fragile necklace of islands remains blissfully free from overdevelopment. Natural attractions include local and migratory waterbirds, marshes, woodlands, dunes and miles of empty beaches; historic lighthouses such as those on Cape Hatteras, Bodie Island and Ocracoke are also part of the park.

Bodie Island Lighthouse LIGHTHOUSE
(☑ 252-473-2111; www.nps.gov/caha; 8210 Bodie Island Lighthouse Rd, Nags Head; museum free, tours adult/child under 11yr $10/5; ⊙ visitor center 9am-5pm Jan-Dec, lighthouse climb 9am-4:30pm late Apr-early Oct; ♿) Built in 1872, this photogenic lighthouse opened its doors to visitors in 2013. The 170ft-high structure still has its original Fresnel lens – a rarity. It is 219 steps to the top, with nine landings. The lighthouse keeper's former home is now the visitor center.

Pea Island National
Wildlife Refuge WILDLIFE RESERVE
(☑ 252-987-2394; www.fws.gov/refuge/pea_island; NC Hwy 12, Rodanthe; ⊙ visitor center 9am-4pm, trails dawn-dusk) At the northern end of Hatteras Island, and named after the dune peas that grow in the sand, this 5834-acre (land portion only) reserve is a bird-watcher's heaven, with two nature trails (both are fully accessible to people with disabilities) and 13 miles of unspoiled beach for the 365 recorded species here. Viewer scopes inside the visitor center overlook an adjacent pond. Check the online calendar for details about guided bird walks, turtle talks and canoe tours.

THE SOUTH IN...

One Week

Fly into New Orleans (p445) and stretch your legs with a walking tour in the legendary French Quarter, before devoting your remaining time to celebrating jazz history and partying the night away in a zydeco joint. Then wind your way upward through the languid Delta, stopping in Clarksdale (p433) for a sultry evening of blues at the juke joints before alighting in Memphis (p378) to walk in the footsteps of the King at Graceland (p379). From here, head down the Music Hwy to Nashville (p385) to see Elvis' gold Cadillac at the Country Music Hall of Fame & Museum (p387) and practice your line dancing at the honky-tonks (country-music clubs) of the District.

Two Weeks

From Nashville, head east to hike amid the craggy peaks and waterfalls of Great Smoky Mountains National Park (p366) before a revitalizing overnight in the arty mountain town of Asheville (p363) and a tour of the scandalously opulent Biltmore Estate, America's largest private home. Plow straight through to the Atlantic coast to loll on the sandy barrier islands of the isolated Outer Banks (p345), then head down the coast to finish up in Charleston (p368), with decadent food and postcard-pretty architecture.

Cape Hatteras Lighthouse LIGHTHOUSE
(☑ 252-473-2111; www.nps.gov/caha; 46379 Lighthouse Rd, Buxton; climbing tours adult/child under 12yr $8/4; ⊘ visitor center 9am-5pm, lighthouse to 4:30pm late Apr-early Oct) At 193ft (or 198ft to the lighting rod), this striking black-and-white-striped edifice is one of North Carolina's most iconic images. The first version of the Hatteras Lighthouse was lit in October of 1803, a modest 90ft tall back then, with a lamp powered by whale oil, and a sandstone structure. Climb the 248 steps inside the current structure, then check out the interesting exhibits about local history in the **Museum of the Sea**, located in the lighthouse keeper's former home.

Graveyard of the Atlantic Museum MUSEUM
(☑ 252-986-0720; www.graveyardoftheatlantic.com; 59200 Museum Dr, Hattaras; ⊘ 10am-5pm Mon-Sat Apr-Sep, to 4pm Oct-Mar) FREE Exhibits about shipwrecks, piracy and salvaged cargo are highlights at this maritime museum at the end of the road. There have been more than 2000 shipwrecks off the coast of the Outer Banks. According to one exhibit, in 2006 a container washed ashore near Frisco, releasing thousands of Doritos bags. One local told us that residents were enjoying Doritos casseroles for months! Donations appreciated.

🏃 Activities

Kitty Hawk Kites ADVENTURE SPORTS
(☑ 252-441-6800; www.kittyhawk.com; 3933 S Croatan Hwy, Jockey's Ridge Crossing, Nags Head; bikes per day $15, kayaks per 2hr $39, stand-up paddleboards per hour/day $29/59; ⊘ 9am-6pm) In business more than 30 years, Kitty Hawk Kites has several locations along the OBX coast. It offers beginners' kiteboarding lessons (five hours, $400) in Rodanthe and hang-gliding lessons at Jockey's Ridge State Park (from $109). Also rents out kayaks, sailboats, stand-up paddleboards, bikes and in-line skates (at Kitty Hawk Surf Co in the same shopping complex).

Corolla Outback Adventures TOURS
(☑ 252-453-4484; www.corollaoutback.com; 1150 Ocean Trail, Corolla; 2hr tour adult/child under 13yr $50/25) Tour operator Jay Bender, whose family started Corolla's first guide service, knows his local history and his local horses. Tours bounce you down the beach and through the dunes to see the wild mustangs that roam the northern Outer Banks.

🛏 Sleeping

Cape Hatteras KOA Resort CAMPGROUND $
(☑ 252-987-2307; www.koa.com/campgrounds/cape-hatteras; 25094 NC Hwy 12, Rodanthe; tent sites with hookup & water from $84, RV sites with hookup from $84, 4-person cabins from $112; P 🤖 ☒) Beachfront campground open all year, with lots of facilities (including a hot tub) and sites for RVs and tents, plus cabin accommodation. Kayak and paddleboard rental are available on-site. There's a cafe, a Wednesday outdoor cinema, and Monday-night bingo during high season (May to September). Tent and RV sites accommodate up to six people.

Shutters on the Banks HOTEL $$

(☑ 252-441-5581; www.shuttersonthebanks.com;
405 S Virginia Dare Trail, Kill Devil Hills; r with/
without ocean view from $225/185, honeymoon
ste from $499; [P][❄][🔊][☕]) Centrally located
in Kill Devil Hills, this welcoming 88-room
beachfront hotel exudes a snappy, colorful
style with pastel tones and beach art on the
walls. The inviting rooms come with plantation windows and colorful art as well as
flat-screen TV, refrigerator and microwave.
Some rooms come with a full kitchen.

Sanderling Resort & Spa RESORT $$$

(☑ 855-412-7866; www.sanderling-resort.com; 1461
Duck Rd, Duck; r $320-710; [P][❄][🔊][☕]) Remod-
eled rooms have given this posh place a stylish feel. Decor is impeccably tasteful, and
the attached balconies are an inviting place
to enjoy the ocean sounds and breezes. Plus,
the resort offers sunrise yoga on the beach.
Open year-round. Standard-room deals
from $179 in low season.

✕ Eating & Drinking

John's Drive-In SEAFOOD, ICE CREAM $

(www.johnsdrivein.com; 3716 N Virginia Dare Trail, Kitty Hawk; mains $6-12, ice cream from $3.25; ⊗ 11am-
5pm Thu-Sun, to 3pm Mon & Tue May-Oct) A Kitty
Hawk institution for perfectly fried boats
(trays) of shrimp or crab cakes, to be eaten
at outdoor picnic tables and washed down
with one of many possible milkshake combinations – like M&M, peanut butter, Oreo,
mint chocolate chip, pineapple and cherry, to
name but a few. Some folks just come for a
burger and some soft-serve ice cream.

★ Kill Devil Grill SEAFOOD, AMERICAN $$

(☑ 252-449-8181; www.thekilldevilgrill.com; 2008 S
Virginia Dare Trail, Kill Devil Hills; lunch $9-14, dinner
$11-24; ⊗ 11:30am-10pm Tue-Sat) Yowza, this
place is good. It's also historic – the entrance
is a 1939 dining car that's listed in the National Register of Historic Places. Pub grub
and seafood arrive with tasty flair, and portions are generous. Check out the specials,
and things like prime ribs or sea scallops,
where the kitchen can really shine. Often
closed between December and January.

★ Blue Moon

Beach Grill SEAFOOD, SANDWICHES $$

(☑ 252-261-2583; www.bluemoonbeachgrill.com;
4104 S Virginia Dare Trail, Nags Head; mains $12-
29; ⊗ 11:30am-9pm) Would it be wrong to
write an ode to a side of french fries? Because Lord Almighty, the lightly spiced fries

at this casual hot spot are the stuff of son-
nets and monologues. And we haven't even
mentioned the BLT with seared mahi-mahi,
applewood bacon, local Currituck tomatoes
and a jalapeño rémoulade for slathering.

❶ Information

The best sources of information are at the main
visitor centers, and there are plenty of them.
Many smaller centers open seasonally. Also
useful is www.outerbanks.org.

Aycock Brown Welcome Center (Outer Banks
Visitor Bureau; ☑ 877-629-4386; www.outer
banks.org; 5230 N Croatian Hwy, Kitty Hawk;
⊗ 8am-5pm Mon-Fri) On the bypass in Kitty
Hawk; has maps and information.

**Fort Raleigh National Historic Site Visitor
Center** (Lindsay Warren Vistor Center; ☑ 252-
475-9001; www.nps.gov/fora; 1401 National
Park Dr; ⊗ 9am-5pm)

Hatteras Island Visitor Center (☑ 252-475-
9000; www.nps.gov/caha; 46368 Lighthouse
Rd, Buxton; ⊗ 9am-5pm) Beside Cape Hatteras
Lighthouse.

Ocracoke Island Visitor Center (☑ 252-475-
9701; www.nps.gov/caha; 38 Irvin Garrish Hwy;
⊗ 9am-5pm) Near the southern ferry dock.

Sarah Owen Welcome Center (☑ 877-629-
4386; www.outerbanks.org; 1 Visitors Center
Circle; ⊗ 9am-5pm) Just east of Virginia Dare
Memorial Bridge on the Hwy 64 Bypass on
Roanoke Island.

Whalebone Welcome Center (☑ 877-629-
4386; www.outerbanks.org; 2 NC Hwy 12, Nags
Head; ⊗ 8:30am-5pm Mar-Dec) At the intersection of Hwy 64 and Hwy 12 in Nags Head.

❶ Getting There & Away

No public transportation exists to or on the
Outer Banks.

If driving, try to avoid arriving or departing
on weekends in summer, when traffic can be
maddening. The **Outer Banks Visitors Bureau**
(www.outerbanks.org) offers a comprehensive
guide to driving to OBX, including tips and al-
ternate routes to avoid spending your vacation
stuck in your vehicle. In winter, the roads are
empty.

FERRY

The **North Carolina Ferry System** (www.ferry.
ncdot.gov) operates several routes, including
the free one-hour Hatteras–Ocracoke car ferry,
which fluctuates between hourly and half-hourly,
with 36 departures from 5am to midnight from
Hatteras in high season; reservations aren't
accepted. North Carolina ferries also run between Ocracoke and Cedar Islands (one way
car/motorcycle $15/10, 2¼ hours) and between
Ocracoke Island and Swan Quarter on the main-

land ($15/10, 2¾ hours) every three hours or so; reservations are recommended in summer for these two routes. Pedestrians may use the ferries for $1 per one-way trip. Cyclists can use the ferries for $3 per one-way trip. There's also a high-speed passenger-only ferry between Hatteras and Ocracoke Village (one way $2, 70 minutes).

Ocracoke Island

Ocracoke Village is a funky little community that moves at a slower pace. With the exception of the village, the National Park Service owns the island. The older residents still speak in the 17th-century British dialect known as 'Hoi Toide' (their pronunciation of 'high tide') and refer to non-islanders as 'dingbatters'. Edward Teach, aka Blackbeard the pirate, used to hide out in the area and was killed here in 1718. You can camp by Pony Pen, filled with the descendants of wild ponies abandoned by explorers hundreds of years ago, have a fish sandwich in a local pub, cycle around the village's narrow streets or nestle into holes in the sand dunes along 16 miles of coastline and catch some rays.

Many people come to Ocracoke on a day trip from Hatteras, but with its preserved culture and laid-back vibe, it's a nice place to spend a night or two. There are a handful of B&Bs, several motels, a park-service campground near the beach and rental cottages.

◉ Sights & Activities

Ocracoke Beach BEACH
(Irvin Garrish Hwy; P🚻) Dolphins are commonly spotted on Ocracoke's gorgeous, undeveloped 16-mile stretch of sandy beach. Swimmers should be aware of rip currents. Find parking and toilet facilities at this access point on the right-hand side of Irvin Garrish Hwy when traveling north out of town.

Ocracoke Lighthouse LIGHTHOUSE
(www.nps.gov/caha; Lighthouse Rd) Built in 1823, this is the oldest lighthouse still operating in North Carolina, though it cannot be climbed. The walls are 5ft thick and the non-rotating light at the top sits only 75ft above sea level. It can be seen as far as 14 miles away.

Portsmouth Island ATV Tours HISTORY
(☑252-928-4484; www.portsmouthislandatv.com; 396 Irvin Garrish Hwy; tours $90, max 6 people; ⊙2 trips per day 8am-noon & 1-5pm Apr-Oct) Runs two fascinating daily tours to the nearby island of Portsmouth, a 20-minute boat ride from Ocracoke, where you'll find an Outer Banks ghost town that was abandoned in the 1970s. Guided ATV tours focus on shelling, bird-watching and swimming, in addition to the historic village.

Ride the Wind KAYAKING
(☑252-928-6311; www.surfocracoke.com; 486 Irvin Garrish Hwy; 2-2½hr kayaking tours adult/child under 13yr $45/18, group surf lessons from $75; ⊙10am-7pm Mon-Sat, to 6pm Sun) Want to get on the water? Take a kayaking tour with Ride the Wind. The sunset tours are easy on the arms, and it also offers sunrise, midday yoga and tai chi tours, and surf lessons, and rents surfboards ($22 per day), bodyboards ($12 per day), skimboards ($19 per day), SUPs ($19 per hour) and kayaks ($14 per hour).

🛏 Sleeping & Eating

Ocracoke Campgrounds CAMPGROUND $
(☑877-444-6777, 252-928-6671; www.recreation.gov; 4352 Irvin Garrish Hwy; tent sites $28; ⊙Apr-late Nov; P🐾) Good value for money for

---

OCRACOKE'S PENNED PONIES

Legend has it the Ocracoke Island 'wild' ponies are descended from feral Spanish mustangs abandoned by shipwrecked explorers in the 16th or 17th century, when it was common to unload livestock to lighten the load and get back out to sea after running aground. Known as 'banker' ponies, these horses are unique in the equine world – they harbor a different number of vertebrae and ribs as well as a distinct shape, posture, color, size and weight compared with those of other horses. But what's more fascinating about Ocracoke's ponies is they were eventually broken and tamed by a troop of Boy Scouts in the 1950s – you can see photos at the **Pony Island Restaurant** (☑252-928-5701; 51 Ocean View Rd; breakfast dishes $5-14; ⊙7:30-11:30am Apr-Oct). They were eventually pastured in a 'pony pen' in 1959 to prevent overgrazing and protect them from the dangers of NC Hwy 12, which was under construction. They're cared for by the National Park Service at the **Ocracoke Pony Pen** (www.nps.gov/caha; Irvin Garrish Hwy) at Pony Pen Beach. You can view them from an observation deck.

small groups, Ocracoke Campgrounds offers more than 100 sites on sand on the island. Flush toilets, drinking water, showers and grills are available. Electric hookups are not available. There's a maximum of six people per site.

Pam's Pelican B&B
B&B $$

(☑ 252-928-1661; www.pamspelican.com; 1021 Irvin Garrish Hwy; r $175-220; P ❋ @ 🛜 🐾) This wildly popular B&B has just four rooms, reached via a series of colorful corridors, in a typical island home loaded with artsy knick-knacks. Rates include use of bikes (and rides to the beach if you're so inclined) and there is sometimes live music streamed from the front-yard gazebo in high season. Guests have access to the 2nd-floor patio.

★ Eduardo's Taco Stand
MEXICAN $

(☑ 252-928-0234; www.facebook.com/amadowoch; 950 Irvin Garrish Hwy; mains $4-13; ☺ 8am-3pm & 5-8pm Mon-Sat, 8am-3pm Sun; P 🍽) There's a long list of tacos, burritos and fresh and spicy salsas at this sensational taco stand. If you're over fried clams and crab cakes, dishes such as prime rib-eye tacos with salsa *de xoconostle* (sour prickly pears) hit the spot, as do the fish with creamy chipotle apple slaw or poblano chowder with shrimp or clams. Full veggie menu, too.

Gaffer's
PUB FOOD $$

(☑ 252-928-3456; www.gafferssportspubocracoke. com; 1050 Irvin Garrish Hwy; mains $11-23; ☺ 8am-2am; P) Casual pub decorated with fishing memorabilia, and bright blue booths. Good place to stop for a bite when traveling north on the way to the ferry. Classic NC dishes include shrimp and grits, grilled tuna plates, burgers and fish sarnies. Free poker nights on Tuesdays (from 7pm).

❶ Getting There & Away

The village is at the southern end of 16-mile-long Ocracoke Island and is accessed from Hatteras via the free **Hatteras–Ocracoke ferry** (www. ncdot.gov/ferry; first come, first served). The ferry lands at the northeastern end of the island. Other options are via the $15 Cedar Island–Ocracoke or Swan Quarter–Ocracoke ferries (which land at the southern dock; reservations accepted). Pedestrians/cyclists can board the ferries for $1/3.

Crystal Coast

The southern Outer Banks are collectively called the 'Crystal Coast.' Less rugged than the northern beaches, they include several historic coastal towns, sparsely populated islands and vacation-friendly beaches.

An industrial and commercial stretch of Hwy 70 goes through **Morehead City**, with plenty of chain hotels and restaurants. The **Bogue Banks**, across the Sound from Morehead City via the Atlantic Beach Causeway, have several well-trafficked beach communities – try Atlantic Beach if you like the smell of coconut suntan oil and doughnuts.

Just north, postcard-pretty **Beaufort** (bow-fort), the third-oldest town in the state, has a charming boardwalk and lots of B&Bs. Blackbeard himself is said to have lived in the Hammock House off Front St. You can't go inside, but some claim you can still hear the screams of the pirate's murdered wife at night.

◉ Sights & Activities

Fort Macon State Park
FORT

(☑ 252-726-3775; www.ncparks.gov/fort-macon-state-park; 2303 E Fort Macon Rd, Atlantic Beach; ☺ 9am-5:30pm; P) FREE This remarkable five-sided fort, with 26 vaulted rooms, is one of North Carolina's most visited attractions. Completed in 1834, it was the site of the Battle of Fort Macon fought in 1862. Exhibits inside the fort's walls and tunnels document the daily lives of soldiers stationed there. Constructed from brick and stone, the fort changed hands twice during the Civil War. Visitors can walk around the exterior and climb the stairs of the grassy structure for 360-degree views.

North Carolina Maritime Museum
MUSEUM

(☑ 252-504-7740; www.ncmaritimemuseumbeaufort.com; 315 Front St, Beaufort; ☺ 9am-5pm Mon-Fri, 10am-5pm Sat, 1-5pm Sun) FREE The pirate Blackbeard was a frequent visitor to the Beaufort area in the early 1700s. In 1996, the wreckage of his flagship, the *Queen Anne's Revenge,* was discovered at the bottom of Beaufort Inlet. You'll see plates, bottles and other artifacts from the ship in this small but engaging museum, which also spotlights the seafood industry as well as maritime rescue operations.

Olympus Dive Center
DIVING

(☑ 252-726-9432; www.olympusdiving.com; 713 Shepard St, Morehead City; half-day dives from $70; ☺ 6am-8pm) Not only are North Carolina's warm, clear waters home to a variety of marine life, they also contain more than 2000 sunken ships, which date back as far as 1526. This excellent dive outfit takes qualified divers to see them at depths of 60ft to 140ft (18m to 42m). Divers in this area make new discoveries every day.

🛏 Sleeping & Eating

Hampton Inn Morehead City HOTEL $$
(☑ 252-240-2300; www.hamptoninn3.hilton.com; 4035 Arendell St, Morehead City; r from $175; ✱@🛜≋) Yep, it's part of a national chain, but the helpful staff and the views of Bogue Sound make this Hampton Inn a nice choice – plus it's in a convenient location near to Hwy 70, helpful for those driving the coast. Rates drop significantly on weeknights in summer.

★ Inn on Turner B&B $$
(☑ 919-271-6144; www.innonturner.com; 217 Turner St; r $200-250; P✱🛜) ⌁ Impeccably tasteful aqua-toned coastal contemporary decor – no gaudy antiques here – dominates this four-room B&B occupying a historic 1866 wooden cream-colored home two blocks back from the water. Innkeepers Kim and Jon are pillars of small-town Southern hospitality, despite not being from the South, and never having slept in a B&B before they opened this one in 2015.

El's Drive-In SEAFOOD $
(☑ 252-726-3002; www.elsdrivein.com; 3706 Arendell St, Morehead City; mains $2-15; ⊙10:30am-10pm Sun-Thu, to 11pm Fri & Sat) The food is brought right to your car at this old-school drive-in and legendary seafood spot, open since 1959. It serves fish fillets, po'boys and hot dogs. Our recommendation? The fried shrimp burger with ketchup and slaw plus a side of fries. Cash only.

Beaufort Grocery MODERN AMERICAN $$$
(☑ 252-728-3903; www.beaufortgrocery.com; 117 Queen St; mains $25-42; ⊙11:30am-2:30pm & 5:30-9:30pm Wed-Mon; 🛜) You'd never guess by the simple, unassuming nature of the decor, but chef Charles Park is a James Beard winner, and the food shines, whether that be smoked sea-salt tuna with chili yogurt, duck two ways with sweet-potato caramel or sage-wrapped chicken saltimbocca over tagliatelle. We didn't hear a bad thing about the place – and weren't disappointed.

Wilmington

Wilmington is pretty darn fun, and it's worth carving out a day or two for a visit if you're driving the coast. This seaside charmer may not have the name recognition of Charleston and Savannah, but eastern North Carolina's largest city has historic neighborhoods, azalea-choked gardens and cute cafes aplenty. All that, plus reasonable hotel prices. At night the historic riverfront downtown becomes the playground for local college students, craft-beer enthusiasts, tourists and the occasional Hollywood type – there are so many movie studios here the town has earned the nickname 'Wilmywood.' You saw *Dawson's Creek*, right?

◉ Sights & Activities

Battleship North Carolina HISTORIC SITE
(☑ 910-399-9100; www.battleshipnc.com; 1 Battleship Rd; self-guided tours adult/child 6-11yr/under 5yr $14/6/free, full-guided tours adult/child under 5yr $17.50/free; ⊙8am-5pm Sep-May, to 8pm Jun-Aug; P🚻) Self-guided tours take you through the decks of this 45,000-ton megaship, which earned 15 battle stars in the Pacific theater in WWII before it was decommissioned in 1947. Sights include the bake shop and galley, the print shop, the engine room, the powder magazine and the communications center. Note that there are several steep stairways leading to lower decks. Take the Cape Fear Bridge from downtown to get here. Full guided tours run on Saturdays and Sundays at 9am.

Airlie Gardens GARDENS
(☑ 910-798-7700; www.airliegardens.org; 300 Airlie Rd; adult/child 4-12yr $9/3; ⊙9am-5pm Apr-Dec, 9am-5pm Tue-Sun Jan-Mar) In spring, wander past thousands of bright azaleas at this 67-acre wonderland, also home to bewitching formal flowerbeds, seasonal gardens, pine trees, lakes and trails. The Airlie Oak dates from 1545.

Museum of the Bizarre MUSEUM
(☑ 910-399-2641; www.museumbizarre.com; 201 S Water St; adult/child under 3yr $3/free; ⊙11am-8pm; 🚻) Pickled specimens, occult memorabilia, a taxidermied two-headed lamb, a bigfoot imprint and plenty of other oddities are on show at this truly peculiar place. It came about after a Wilmington-based collector of strange artifacts was convinced by his wife to move all the weird stuff out of the house and into a museum. We're glad he did.

🛏 Sleeping & Eating

Best Western Plus Coastline Inn HOTEL $$
(☑ 910-763-2800; www.bestwestern.com; 503 Nutt St; r $89-199, ste $129-279; ✱@🛜≋) We're not sure what we like best: the gorgeous views of the Cape Fear River, the wooden boardwalk or the short walk to downtown fun.

THE SOUTH NORTH CAROLINA COAST

Standard rooms aren't huge or too fancy, but every room has a river view. Pet fee is $30 per day.

★ CW Worth House
B&B $$

(☎910-762-8562; www.worthhouse.com; 412 S 3rd St; r $160-200; ❋@🐾) One of our favorite B&Bs in North Carolina, this turreted 1893 Queen Anne home is dotted with antiques and Victorian touches, but still manages to feel laid-back and cozy. Breakfasts are top-notch. The B&B is within a few blocks of downtown.

Dixie Grill
DINER $

(☎910-762-7280; www.thedixiegrillwilmington.word press.com; 116 Market St; breakfast mains $5-9, lunch mains $9-10; ⏱8am-3pm Mon-Sat, to 2pm Sun; ☑🖐) A top breakfast spot in central Wilmington. This retro setting, with lime-green booths and a bar area for solo diners, serves apple-sage sausage patties, eggs all ways, and Southern classics including baked biscuits with onion gravy and all the trimmings. For lunch the menu is filled with burgers, sandwiches and salads.

★ PinPoint
SOUTHERN US $$$

(☎910-769-2972; www.pinpointrestaurant.com; 114 Market St; mains $24-38; ⏱5:30-9:30pm Mon-Thu, to 10pm Fri & Sat, 10:30am-2pm & 5:30-9pm Sun; 🐾) PinPoint was declared by *Southern Living* magazine as one of the South's best new restaurants – and they weren't lyin'! Chef Dean Neff was Hugh Acheson's kitchen compadre in Athens, Georgia's excellent Five & Ten, and he's sailing solo and shining in Wilmington, where he has a personal relationship with his farmers and fishers.

🍸 Drinking & Entertainment

★ Satellite Lounge
BAR

(☎910-399-2796; www.facebook.com/satellitebar andlounge; 120 Greenfield St; ⏱4pm-2am Mon-Sat, from 2pm Sun; 🐾) If you want to belly up to North Carolina's most stunning bar, you'll need to head in the opposite direction of Wilmington's historic downtown and into its up-and-coming South Front district. A gorgeously restored tavern highlights the space, which includes near-professional-level cornhole lanes, a fire pit and an outdoor cinema. It's also a bikers' favorite.

Dead Crow Comedy Room
COMEDY

(☎910-399-1492; www.deadcrowcomedy.com; 265 N Front St; $15-18; ⏱from 7pm Tue-Thu, from 6pm Fri & Sat) Dark, cramped, underground and in the heart of downtown, just like a comedy club should be. Stop in for improv, open-mic nights and touring comedians, plus comedy bingo. Bar service and full menu available.

ℹ Information

Visitor information center (☎877-406-2356, 910-341-4030; www.wilmingtonandbeaches. com; 505 Nutt St; ⏱8:30am-5pm Mon-Fri, 9am-4pm Sat, 1-4pm Sun) In an 1800s freight warehouse; has a walking-tour map of downtown.

ℹ Getting There & Around

American Airlines and Delta Airlines serve Wilmington International Airport (p345) from Atlanta, Charlotte, New York and Philadelphia. It's 5 miles northeast of downtown. The **Greyhound** (☎910-791-8040; www.greyhound.com; 505 Cando St) station is an inconvenient 5 miles east of downtown.

The downtown area is easy to cover on foot, but a **free trolley** (www.wavetransit.com/ free-downtown-trolley-schedule; ⏱7:10am-8:50pm Mon-Fri, 10:30am-8:50pm Sat, 10:30am-5:30pm Sun) runs through the historic district from morning through evening.

The Triangle

The cities of Raleigh, Durham and Chapel Hill form a rough triangle in the central Piedmont region. Three top research universities – Duke, University of North Carolina and North Carolina State – are located here, as is the 7000-acre computer and biotech-office campus known as Research Triangle Park. Swarming with egghead computer programmers, bearded peace activists and hip young families, each town has its own unique personality, despite being only a few miles apart. In March, everyone – we mean *everyone* – goes crazy for college basketball.

ℹ Getting There & Around

Raleigh-Durham International Airport (p357), a 15-mile ride northwest of downtown Raleigh, receives nonstop flights from 49 locations, including London, Paris and Cancun.

Raleigh's **Greyhound station** (☎919-834-8275; 2210 Capital Blvd) is inconveniently located 3 miles northeast of downtown. For a better downtown stop, try Durham's **Greyhound station** (☎919-687-4800; 515 W Pettigrew St) in the Durham Station Transportation Center (p357), across the street from the **Amtrak station** (601 W Main St).

GoTriangle (www.gotriangle.org) operates a regional bus system that connects Raleigh, Durham and Chapel Hill. Bus 100 runs from downtown Raleigh to the airport, and continues to the Regional Transit Center near Research Triangle Park, from where connecting buses run to Durham and Chapel Hill. The adult single fare is $2.25.

Raleigh

Founded in 1792 as a new capital for North Carolina, and named for Sir Walter Raleigh – whose image crops up in all sorts of unlikely places around the city – Raleigh remains a somewhat staid government town with major sprawl issues. Downtown is undeniably handsome, though, and is home to some top-notch (and free!) museums and galleries, while the food and music scenes are on a definite upswing.

⊙ Sights

★North Carolina Museum of Art   MUSEUM
(☑919-839-6262; www.ncartmuseum.org; 2110 Blue Ridge Rd; ☺10am-5pm Tue-Thu, Sat & Sun, to 9pm Fri, park dawn-dusk; P) FREE Expanded in 2010 with the completion of the stunning, glass-and-steel West Building, this superb museum stands 6 miles west of downtown. Ranging far and wide, from ancient Egypt to modern Africa, its permanent collection includes works credited to Giotto and Botticelli – albeit with 'assistance' – and even a 17th-century 'Golf Player' etched by Rembrandt. The museum also holds around 20 jet-black Rodin bronzes, and a gallery celebrating alumni of the pioneering Black Mountain College near Asheville, including Robert Rauschenberg.

North Carolina Museum of History   MUSEUM
(☑919-814-7000; www.ncmuseumofhistory.org; 5 E Edenton St; ☺9am-5pm Mon-Sat, from noon Sun) FREE For a comprehensive, evenhanded and engaging look at the story of North Carolina, immerse yourself in the state history museum. Starting with a 3000-year-old dugout canoe, it continues through to the Civil Rights era by way of the European arrival and the Revolutionary and Civil wars. Look out for the cannon retrieved from the 1718 wreck of Blackbeard's ship, *Queen Anne's Revenge,* and the Woolworth's lunch counter that witnessed a sit-in in 1960.

North Carolina Museum of Natural Sciences   MUSEUM
(☑919-707-9800; www.naturalsciences.org; 11 W Jones St; ☺9am-5pm Mon-Sat, from noon Sun) FREE Whale skeletons hang from the ceiling. Butterflies flutter past your shoulder. Emerald tree boas make you shiver. And be warned: if you arrive after 10am on a school day, swarms of elementary-school children rampage all over the place. Skywalks lead to a glossy extension, the Nature Research Center, where you can watch scientists at work on their projects (and displays make it clear they're in no doubt as to the reality of climate change).

🛏 Sleeping & Eating

Umstead Hotel & Spa   SPA HOTEL $$$
(☑919-447-4000; www.theumstead.com; 100 Woodland Pond Dr; r/ste from $329/455; P✴@ 🛜🏊🐾) Set in a wooded suburban office park, 10 miles west of downtown, and backing onto a small lake, the Umstead is targeted squarely at visiting biotech CEOs. As well as simple but sumptuous rooms – deep-soak bathtubs, twin vanities – it has a Zen-like spa complete with meditation courtyard. There's a dog playground, and a pet fee of $200 per stay.

★La Farm Bakery   BAKERY $
(☑919-657-0657; www.lafarmbakery.com; 4248 NW Cary Pkwy, Cary; dishes $8-11; ☺7am-8pm; 🛜) This much-loved French bakery is hard to find, halfway to Chapel Hill and inconspicuous even once you spot the right strip mall. Its breads and pastries are truly out of this world, though – whether you grab a classic baguette or apple challah, or linger over a miso pork and kimchi brioche or a fig and prosciutto tartine.

Beasley's Chicken & Honey   SOUTHERN US $
(☑919-322-0127; www.ac-restaurants.com/beasleys; 237 S Wilmington St; mains $8-13; ☺11:30am-10pm Sun-Wed, to midnight Thu-Sat) You'll need to loosen your belt after a meal at this crispy venture from James Beard Award–winning chef Ashley Christensen. Inside her airy downtown canteen, fried chicken is the star – on a biscuit, with waffles, in a potpie. The sides are decadent too – the creamed collard greens make a perfect introduction for nervous neophytes.

Bida Manda   LAOTIAN $$
(☑919-829-9999; www.bidamanda.com; 222 S Blount St; lunch mains $11-22, dinner mains $18-30;

⊙ 11:30am-2pm & 5-10pm Mon-Thu, 11:30am-2pm & 5pm-midnight Fri, 5pm-midnight Sat; 🎧) The food at this artfully decorated establishment – one of very few Laotian restaurants in the US – looks as gorgeous as the space itself. Enhanced with Thai, Vietnamese and Chinese flavors, it tastes wonderful too.

From pumpkin curry to lemongrass sausage or crispy pork-belly soup, everything's bold and very satisfying. The little shot of Laos-style coffee is a nice touch, too.

ℹ Information

Really just a small counter adjoining the Convention Center, the **Raleigh Visitor Information Center** (☑ 919-834-5900; www.visitraleigh.com; 500 Fayetteville St; ⊙ 9am-5pm Mon-Sat) is stocked with maps and local information that you can pick up even when it's closed.

Durham

Home a century ago to the world's largest tobacco company – American Tobacco – Durham remains at heart a working-class Southern city. Its fortunes collapsed in the 1960s, however, along with the cigarette industry, and Durham's recent revival owes much to the presence of the prestigious Duke University. The city's downtown has been comprehensively rebuilt, and transformed into a hot spot for gourmands and artists, gays and lesbians. The changing winds were epitomized in 2017, when protesters toppled the Confederate monument that had stood outside the former county courthouse since 1924.

◉ Sights

★Historic
Stagville Plantation PLANTATION
(☑ 919-620-0120; www.stagville.org; 5828 Old Oxford Hwy; ⊙ 9am-5pm Tue-Sat, tours 11am, 1pm & 3pm; P) FREE Exceptional in prioritizing the 1000 or so 'enslaved persons' who worked here above the families that claimed their ownership, Stagville Plantation ranks among North Carolina's most important historic sites. What survives today, 10 miles north of downtown, is just a fragment of the huge plantation where the state's largest enslaved population lived in scattered groups. The fascinating guided tours drive in convoy to an emotive cluster of slave homes, along with a massive barn, a mile from the main house.

★Duke Lemur Center ZOO
(☑ 919-401-7240; www.lemur.duke.edu; 3705 Erwin Rd; adult/child under 8yr $12/9; ⊙ 9am-4pm, by appointment; 🚗) The secret is out – Durham's coolest attraction has to be this research and conservation center, home to the largest collection of lemurs outside their native Madagascar. No one could fail to melt at the sight of these big-eyed fuzzy creatures. Visits are by guided tour only, and must be reserved well in advance.

Duke University UNIVERSITY
(www.duke.edu; Chapel Dr) Although it can trace its history back to 1838, Duke University became a university, and took its current name, in 1926, thanks to a major endowment from the Duke cigarette family. Spreading across the Georgian-style East Campus and the neo-Gothic West Campus, 1 and 2 miles respectively west of downtown, it has just over 15,000 students.

American Tobacco Campus HISTORIC SITE
(www.americantobaccocampus.com; 300 Blackwell St) The massive former American Tobacco factory has been transformed into a million-square-foot cavalcade of restaurants, bars and entertainment venues. Still dominated by the towering 'Lucky Strike' chimney, but now centering on gardens traversed by artificial cascades, it's a lively combination of thriving mall and urban park. On the south side of downtown, it's just steps across the tracks from Main St.

🛏 Sleeping & Eating

★The Durham BOUTIQUE HOTEL $$
(☑ 919-768-8830; www.thedurham.com; 315 E Chapel Hill St; r from $180; P🅿❄@🎧) When the suave, 53-room Durham turned a former bank building – a marvel of midcentury modernist might – into a supremely retro, fiercely local haven in 2015, it marked the moment when the city's revitalized downtown finally got an independent hipster sleep. Raleigh Denim bedspreads, music programming by Durham-based Merge Records – it's go local or go home.

Arrowhead Inn B&B $$
(☑ 919-477-8430; www.arrowheadinn.com; 106 Mason Rd; r $159, cottages/cabins $279/309; ❄🎧) Set in an imposing white clapboard home dating back to 1775, this plush B&B is 9 miles north of downtown. Every antique-furnished room in the main house has its own fireplace, and several have private spa

baths; there's a separate cottage and cabin in the grounds. Rates include a sumptuous breakfast.

Dame's Chicken & Waffles   CHICKEN $

(📞919-682-9235; www.dameschickenwaffles.com; 530 Foster St; mains $10-16; ⊙10am-4pm Mon & Sun, to 9pm Tue-Thu, to 10pm Fri & Sat) While it can't claim to have invented chicken and waffles – it's been a 'thing' for a couple of centuries – Dame's has raised the ultimate comfort food to a fine art. Its relocation to these larger premises should mean customers won't have to wait before enjoying crispy Southern fried chicken atop, yes, fluffy, syrup-drenched, breakfast-style waffles.

★Mateo   TAPAS $$

(📞919-530-8700; www.mateotapas.com; 109 W Chapel Hill St; small plates $8-15; ⊙11:30am-2:30pm & 5-10:30pm Tue-Thu, 11:30am-2:30pm & 5pm-midnight Fri, 5pm-midnight Sat, 5-9:30pm Sun) A poster child for Durham's remarkable comeback, this James Beard–nominated 'bar de tapas' is downtown's culinary anchor. Many dishes come with a Southern bent, and particular revelations include the *pan com tomate* with Manchego cheese; the brussels sprouts with pine nuts, raisins and saffron yogurt; and the fried egg and cheese (in which the 'whites' are fried farmer's cheese!).

🍷 Drinking & Entertainment

★Cocoa Cinnamon   COFFEE

(www.cocoacinnamon.com; 420 W Geer St; ⊙7am-10pm Mon-Fri, from 8am Sat & Sun; 🛜) If a local says you *must* order a hot chocolate at Cocoa Cinnamon, ask them to be more specific. This former service station, on downtown's northern fringes, offers so many cocoas (along with teas and single-source coffee) that newbies may be paralyzed by the sheer chocolaty awesomeness.

Fullsteam Brewery   BREWERY

(📞919-682-2377; www.fullsteam.ag; 726 Rigsbee Ave; ⊙4pm-midnight Mon-Thu, 11am-1am Fri & Sat, noon-10pm Sun; 🛜) Calling itself a 'plow-to-pint' brewery, Fullsteam has gained national attention for pushing the boundaries of beer with wild, Southernized concoctions. Going out of its way to support local farmers, neighborhood foragers and agricultural entrepreneurs, it uses Carolinian ingredients wherever possible. The excellent taproom features ping-pong, arcade games, cafeteria-style seating and killer T-shirts, and there's live music Sunday evenings.

Durham Bulls Athletic Park   STADIUM

(📞box office 919-956-2855; www.dbulls.com; 409 Blackwell St; tickets $9-26) While away a quintessentially American afternoon of beer and watching the Durham Bulls minor-league baseball team, as seen in the 1988 Kevin Costner movie *Bull Durham*. They play between April and early September.

ℹ Information

Set in a former bank building downtown, the **Durham Visitor Info Center** (📞919-687-0288; www.durham-nc.com; 212 W Main St; ⊙9am-5pm Mon, to 6pm Tue-Fri, 11am-7pm Sat, noon-4pm Sun, closed Sun Nov-Mar) offers information, maps and interactive displays.

ℹ Getting There & Away

Raleigh-Durham International Airport (RDU; 📞919-840-2123; www.rdu.com; 1000 Trade Dr, Morrisville) is 13 miles southeast of downtown Durham – a ride that costs around $20 in an off-peak Uber. Greyhound (p354) sits across the street from Amtrak (p354), in the **Durham Station Transportation Center** (📞919-485-7433; www.godurhamtransit.org; 515 W Pettigrew St; ⊙8am-midnight Mon-Sat, 7am-9pm Sun), which is also the main downtown interchange for Durham's local bus network.

Chapel Hill & Carrboro

While smaller and homier than Raleigh and Durham, its Triangle cohorts, Chapel Hill is a pretty college town that bubbles with life and energy. That's largely due to the 30,000 students – and Tar Heels basketball team – of its University of North Carolina, founded in 1789 as the nation's first state university. While commercialization has increasingly cost Chapel Hill's short downtown strip some of its former charm, its near-neighbor Carrboro remains as appealing as ever. Between the two, they boast some great restaurants and bars, and continue to nurture a dynamic indie rock scene.

⊙ Sights

University of North Carolina   UNIVERSITY

(www.unc.edu) The imposing buildings of America's oldest public university center on a quad lined with flowering pear trees. Pick up a map either at the university's **visitor center** (📞919-962-1630; www.unc.edu/visitors; 250 E Franklin St; ⊙9am-5pm Mon-Fri) or the **Chapel Hill Visitor Center** (📞919-245-4320; www.visitchapelhill.org; 501 W Franklin St; ⊙8:30am-5pm Mon-Fri, 10am-3pm Sat).

Carolina Basketball Museum

MUSEUM

(☎919-962-6000; www.goheels.com; 450 Skipper Bowles Dr, Ernie Williamson Athletics Center; ⏰10am-4pm Mon-Fri, 9am-1pm Sat, hours vary on game days; ℙ) FREE Regardless of allegiances, any basketball fan will appreciate this small but well-done temple to Tar Heel hoops. The numbers say it all – six national championships, 20 final-four appearances, 31 Atlantic Coast Conference (ACC) regular-season championships and 47 NBA first-round draft picks. Memorabilia, trophies and video footage abound, including Michael Jordan's original signed national letter of intent and other recruiting documents.

🛏 Sleeping & Eating

Carolina Inn

HOTEL $$$

(☎919-933-2001; www.carolinainn.com; 211 Pittsboro St; r from $250; ℙ❄🛜) Even if you're not a Tar Heel, this lovely on-campus inn will win you over with its hospitality and historic touches. The charm starts in the snappy lobby and continues through hallways lined with photos of alumni and championship teams. Classic decor – inspired by Southern antiques – feels fresh in the 185 bright rooms.

Neal's Deli

DELI $

(☎919-967-2185; www.nealsdeli.com; 100 E Main St, Carrboro; breakfast dishes $3.50-7, lunch dishes $6-9.50; ⏰8am-4pm Tue-Sun; 🛜) Start your day by digging into a delicious buttermilk breakfast biscuit at this tiny deli in downtown Carrboro. The egg, cheese and bacon is some kind of good. For lunch, Neal's serves sandwiches and subs, including chicken salad, pastrami and a three-cheese pimento with a splash of bourbon.

★Lantern

ASIAN $$$

(☎919-969-8846; www.lanternrestaurant.com; 423 W Franklin St; mains $25-32; ⏰5:30-10pm Mon-Sat) A strong contender for best dining spot in the entire Triangle, this modern, dinner-only, Asian-fusion spot is very much a farm-to-table affair, with all ingredients sourced from North Carolina. Thank chef Andrea Reusing, a James Beard Award winner, for triumphs such as crispy whole black bass with hot chili, fresh turmeric, dill, fried shallots and roasted peanuts.

🍷 Drinking & Entertainment

★Glasshalfull

WINE BAR

(☎919-967-9784; www.glasshalfull.net; 106 S Greensboro St, Carrboro; ⏰11:30am-2:30pm & 5-9:30pm Mon-Fri, 5-10pm Sat) OK, so the name doesn't quite roll off the tongue, but everything else about this Carrboro wine bar – sorry, 'wine-centric restaurant' – oozes sleek sophistication. The food is exquisite, with pan-seared scallops or duck confit for dinner, but it's the majestic array of international wines in the adjoining shop, also sold at the bar, that really draws in the crowds.

Beer Study

CRAFT BEER

(☎919-240-5423; www.facebook.com/BeerStudyNC; 106 N Graham St; ⏰noon-midnight; 🛜) Half bar, half bottle shop, and a refreshingly grungy alternative to Chapel Hill's smattering of breweries, this place offers 18 taps of local and regional craft beer and more than 500 bottles. City ordinances impose plastic cups on dog-friendly establishments, but that's a small price to pay for pup. Pints cost $4, and you can buy burgers next door.

Dean Smith Center

STADIUM

(☎919-962-2296; www.goheels.com; 300 Skipper Bowles Dr; ⏰box office 8am-4:30pm Mon-Fri) There are no tours of the Tar Heels' home, but basketball fans can visit the 2nd and 3rd floors during business hours. It's named for legendary coach Dean Smith, who retired with 879 career wins and two national titles. Current coach Roy Williams won his third title in 2017, which put him ahead.

Cat's Cradle

LIVE MUSIC

(☎919-967-9053; www.catscradle.com; 300 E Main St, Carrboro) Everyone from Nirvana to Arcade Fire has played the Cradle, which has been hosting the cream of the indie-music world for four decades. Most shows are all-ages.

ℹ Getting There & Away

Raleigh-Durham International Airport (p357) is 18 miles east of Chapel Hill, a journey that costs around $25 in an off-peak Uber.

Charlotte

North Carolina's largest city, Charlotte sprawls 15 miles in every direction from its compact, high-rise core. Futuristic skyscrapers pepper downtown Charlotte, which is officially known as 'Uptown,' supposedly because it sits on a barely visible ridge, but really because the council decided that sounds cooler. Uptown holds several fine museums plus the high-octane NASCAR Hall of Fame, while more museums and historic sites are scattered further afield. Hotels and restaurants are also concentrated Uptown, though funkier neighborhoods within easy reach include Plaza Midwood, just east, with its boutiques and restaurants, and hip NoDa, along North Davidson St, where former textile mills hold breweries and cafes.

Named after the wife of George III – hence its nickname, the Queen City – Charlotte boomed when gold was discovered nearby, and later prospered from cotton and textiles. Having pioneered interstate banking in the 1980s, it's now the third-largest banking center in the US.

◉ Sights & Activities

NASCAR Hall of Fame   MUSEUM
(☑704-654-4400; www.nascarhall.com; 400 E Martin Luther King Jr Blvd; adult/child 4-12yr $25/18; ⊙10am-6pm) The race-car simulator ($5) at this rip-roaring Uptown museum hurtles you onto the track and into a 15-car race that feels surprisingly real. Elsewhere, learn the history of an American-born sport whose roots lie in moonshine running, check out six generations of race cars on 'Glory Road,' and test your pit-crew skills.

Levine Museum of
the New South   MUSEUM
(www.museumofthenewsouth.org; 200 E 7th St; adult/child 6-18yr $10/6; ⊙10am-5pm Mon-Fri, to 4pm Sat, noon-5pm Sun; ℙ) Tracing the story of the 'New South' that emerged from the ashes of the Civil War, this committed museum explores the years of Reconstruction, Jim Crow and the Civil Rights movement. Haunting Dorothea Lange photos illuminate the Depression era on North Carolina's plantations, while changing exhibits highlight current issues such as the 2016 shooting of Keith Lamont Scott by police.

Mint Museum Randolph   MUSEUM
(☑704-337-2000; www.mintmuseum.org; 2730 Randolph Rd; adult/child 5-17yr $15/6, 5-9pm Wed free; ⊙11am-6pm Tue & Thu-Sat, to 9pm Wed, 1-5pm Sun; ℙ) The US Mint opened its first-ever outpost in Uptown Charlotte in 1837, using gold mined from the mountains nearby. Transported 3 miles southeast a century later, the building now holds treasures ranging from ceramic masterpieces from Britain and North Carolina to stunning modern American decorative glasswork. Best of all are the wonderful pre-Columbian artifacts created by the Aztecs and Maya.

SOUTHERN FAVORITES
....
Fundamentally, in food as in so much else, North Carolina's heart lies in the South. Classic Southern favorites such as fried chicken, fried green tomatoes, shrimp and grits, biscuits (including extra-large 'catheads') and gravy, collard greens and okra, and mac and cheese, feature on menus across the state, and that's what the locals are eating at home.

★US National
Whitewater Center   ADVENTURE SPORTS
(☑704-391-3900; www.usnwc.org; 5000 Whitewater Center Pkwy; all-sport day pass adult/child under 10yr $59/49, individual activities $25, 3hr canopy tour $89; ⊙dawn-dusk) A beyond-awesome hybrid of nature center and water park, this 1300-acre facility is home to the largest artificial white-water river in the world. You can paddle its rapids – which serve as training grounds for Olympic canoeists and kayakers – as part of a guided trip, or enjoy a range of other adventure activities.

🛏 Sleeping & Eating

Duke Mansion   INN $$
(☑704-714-4400; www.dukemansion.com; 400 Hermitage Rd; r $140-360; ℙ❀🕾) The century-old former home of the Duke family, including legendary heiress Doris Duke, is now a delightful B&B inn. Set in wooded gardens in the attractive Myers Park neighborhood, a couple of miles south of Uptown, it holds 20 light-filled rooms. Many still have their original tiled bathrooms, and some upstairs open onto their own screened sections of porch.

★Ivey's Hotel   BOUTIQUE HOTEL $$$
(☑704-228-1111; www.theiveyshotel.com; 127 N Tryon St; r $299-499; ℙ@🕾🐾) The Ivey's 42 Parisian-inspired rooms – all on the 2nd floor of a 1924 department-store building – are steeped in history (the 400-year-old oak-wood floors were sourced from a French winery) but have modern flair (55in Sony TVs, Bose soundbars). The balcony executive corner suites, awash in natural-light-sucking windows and exposed brick, are divine.

Optimist Hall   FOOD HALL $
(www.optimisthall.com; 1115 N Brevard St; dishes $5-15; ⊙7am-9pm Mon-Fri, 8am-10pm Sat,

8am-9pm Sun) This sprawling new food hall and retail space, in a former textile mill, is set to revitalize the neighborhood of Optimist Park. Look for beloved local vendors such as The Dumpling Lady (Asian dumplings) and Fonta Flora Brewery.

★ Soul
Gastrolounge Tapas
SUSHI, SANDWICHES $$

(☑704-348-1848; www.soulgastrolounge.com; 1500 Central Ave; small plates $7-20, sushi $4-14, sandwiches $9-15; ☉5pm-2am) This sultry but welcoming Plaza Midwood speakeasy serves a globally inspired selection of small plates. Choices are wide-ranging, from skewers and sushi rolls to Cuban and Vietnamese sandwiches, but the kitchen takes care to infuse each little gem with unique, satisfying flavors. The dancing tuna rolls, with jalapeños and two spicy mayos, are highly recommended if you like heat.

Asbury
SOUTHERN US $$$

(☑704-342-1193; www.theasbury.com; 235 N Tryon St; sandwiches $8-14, mains $20-38; ☉5-10pm Mon, from 11am Tue-Fri, from 9am Sat & Sun) Uptown's finest dining is to be had in the Dunhill Hotel's restaurant, opening straight onto Tryon St. Rooted in Carolinian classics, but given a contemporary makeover, chef Matthew Krenz' cuisine ranges from sorghum-glazed duck with walnut and garlic gremolata to simpler staples, served anytime, such as mac, cheese and country ham.

🍷 Drinking & Nightlife
NoDa Brewing Company
MICROBREWERY

(☑704-900-6851; www.nodabrewing.com; 2921 N Tryon St; ☉4-9pm Mon-Thu, 2-10pm Fri, noon-10pm Sat, noon-7pm Sun; 🛜) Charlotte's best craft-beer playground is hidden behind NoDa's new and easy-to-overlook North End brewery. We went up on a Friday night and it looked abandoned. At the back, however, we found a packed playhouse of brews (pints $4 to $7) and boccie ball, plus cornhole, Frisbee golf, a fire pit, a massive patio and Charlotte's top food truck, Tin Kitchen.

ℹ️ Information
Visitor Info Center (☑800-231-4636; www.charlottesgotalot.com; 501 S College St, Charlotte Convention Center; ☉9am-5pm Mon-Sat) Charlotte's main visitor center is in Uptown. As well as offering maps and a visitors' guide, it sells regional gifts and souvenirs.

ℹ️ Getting There & Around
Charlotte Douglas International Airport (CLT; ☑704-359-4013; www.cltairport.com; 5501 Josh Birmingham Pkwy), 7 miles west of Uptown, is an American Airlines hub that welcomes nonstop flights from continental Europe and the UK. Both the **Greyhound** (☑704-372-0456; www.greyhound.com; 601 W Trade St) and **Amtrak** (www.amtrak.com; 1914 N Tryon St) stations are handy to Uptown.

Charlotte's public transport system, known as CATS (Charlotte Area Transit System), encompasses city buses; a streetcar line known as the CityLYNX Gold Line; and the LYNX Blue Line light-rail line, extended in 2018 to reach the UNC campus, 9 miles northeast of Uptown. One-way fares range $2.20 to $4.40. The **Charlotte Transportation Center** (☑704-336-7433; www.ridetransit.org; 310 E Trade St), the system's Uptown interchange, can be accessed from Brevard St between 4th and Trade St.

Charlotte also operates a shared-bike network called Charlotte B-cycle (https://charlotte.bcycle.com).

North Carolina Mountains

Towering along the skyline of western North Carolina, the mighty Appalachian Mountains hold several distinct subranges, among which the Great Smoky, Blue Ridge, Pisgah and Black Mountain ranges are especially dramatic. Carpeted in blue-green hemlock, pine and oak trees – logged a century ago but now preserved and protected – these cool hills are home to cougars, deer, black bears, wild turkeys and great horned owls. For adventurous travelers, the potential for hiking, camping, climbing and rafting expeditions is all but endless, while yet another photo opportunity lies around every bend.

The Cherokee who hunted on these forested slopes were later joined by 18th-century Scots-Irish immigrants looking for a better life. Lofty towns such as Blowing Rock enticed the sickly, lured by the fresh mountain air. Today, scenic drives, leafy trails and roaring rivers draw visitors from around the world.

ℹ️ Getting There & Around
Asheville Regional Airport (p365) is the gateway to the North Carolina mountains, with nonstop flights to/from Atlanta, Charlotte, Chicago and Newark, among others. Asheville also has a Greyhound (p366) station.

SCENIC DRIVE: BLUE RIDGE PARKWAY

You won't find a single stoplight or billboard along the entire Blue Ridge Pkwy, which traverses the southern Appalachians from Virginia's Shenandoah National Park at Mile 0 to North Carolina's Great Smoky Mountains National Park at Mile 469.

Commissioned by President Franklin D Roosevelt as a Great Depression–era public-works project, it's one of America's classic drives. North Carolina's piece of the parkway sweeps and swoops for 262 sinuous miles of sublime mountain vistas. The fall colors, at their finest in October, are out of this world.

The **National Park Service** (☑ 828-348-3400; www.nps.gov/blri; Mile 384; ☉ 9am-5pm) runs campgrounds and visitor centers. Note that restrooms and gas stations are few and far between, and the speed limit never rises above 45mph. For more details about stops, visit www.blueridgeparkway.org.

Parkway highlights and campgrounds include the following, from the Virginia border south:

Cumberland Knob (Mile 217.5) NPS visitor center; easy walk to the knob.

Doughton Park (Mile 241.1) Trails and camping.

Blowing Rock (Mile 291.8) Small town named for a craggy, commercialized cliff that offers great views, occasional updrafts and a Native American love story.

Moses H Cone Memorial Park (Mile 294.1) A lovely old estate with carriage trails and a craft shop.

Julian Price Memorial Park (Mile 296.9) Camping.

Grandfather Mountain (Mile 305.1) Hugely popular for its mile-high pedestrian 'swinging bridge.' Also has a nature center and a small wildlife reserve.

Linville Falls (Mile 316.4) Short hiking trails to stunning falls; campsites.

Little Switzerland (Mile 334) Old-style mountain resort.

Mt Mitchell State Park (Mile 355.5) Highest peak east of the Mississippi (6684ft); hiking and camping.

Craggy Gardens (Mile 364) Hiking trails explode with rhododendron blossoms in summer.

Folk Art Center (Mile 382) High-end Appalachian crafts for sale.

Blue Ridge Parkway Visitor Center (Mile 384) Inspiring film, interactive map, trail information.

Mt Pisgah (Mile 408.8) Hiking, camping, restaurant, inn.

Graveyard Fields (Mile 418) Short hiking trails to waterfalls.

High Country

The northwestern corner of North Carolina, flanking the Blue Ridge Pkwy as it sets off across the state from Virginia, is known as the High Country. Of the main towns, Boone is a lively college community that's home to Appalachian State University (ASU), while Blowing Rock and Banner Elk are quaint tourist centers near the winter ski areas.

BLOWING ROCK

A stately and idyllic mountain village, tiny Blowing Rock beckons from its perch at 4000ft above sea level, the only full-service town directly on the Blue Ridge Pkwy. It's easy to be seduced by its postcard-perfect Main St, lined with antique shops, kitschy boutiques, potters, silversmiths, sweet shops, lively taverns and excellent restaurants. There are even a couple of bucolic, duck-filled lakes to drive home the storybook nature of it all. The only thing that spoils the illusion is the sheer difficulty of finding a place to park in high season.

◉ Sights & Activities

Grandfather Mountain MOUNTAIN
(☑ 800-468-7325; www.grandfather.com; 2050 Blowing Rock Hwy, Linville; adult/child 4-12yr $22/9; ☉ 8am-7pm Jun-Aug, 9am-6pm Apr, May, Sep & Oct, 9am-5pm Nov-Mar; ℗ ⓐ) The highest of the

Blue Ridge Mountains, Grandfather Mountain looms north of the parkway 20 miles southwest of Blowing Rock. As a visitor destination, it's famous for the Mile High Swinging Bridge, the centerpiece of a private attraction that also includes hiking trails plus a small museum and wildlife reserve. Don't let a fear of heights scare you away; though the bridge is a mile above sea level, it spans a less fearsome chasm that's just 80ft deep.

River & Earth Adventures
ADVENTURE

(☑ 828-355-9797; www.raftcavehike.com; 6201 Castle Ford Rd, Todd; half-/full-day rafting $60/100; ⊞) Eco-conscious operators offering everything from family-friendly caving trips to rafting class V rapids at Watauga Gorge – plus organic lunches! Canoe ($65), kayak ($35 to $65) and tube ($20) rentals are offered too.

🛏 Sleeping & Eating

Cliff Dwellers Inn
MOTEL $

(☑ 828-414-9596; www.cliffdwellers.com; 116 Lakeview Terrace; r/apt from $124/144; ❄🗑🌐) From its perch above town, this aptly named motel entices guests with good service, reasonable prices, stylish rooms and balconies with sweeping vistas.

Green Park Inn
HISTORIC HOTEL $$

(☑ 828-414-9230; www.greenparkinn.com; 9239 Valley Blvd; r $94-299; P ❄🗑🌐) This grand white clapboard hotel, 1 mile south of downtown, opened its doors in 1891, and was renovated in 2010 to hold 88 plush rooms and a grill restaurant. The eastern continental divide runs straight through the bar, and Margaret Mitchell stayed here while writing *Gone with the Wind*.

★ Bistro Roca
AMERICAN $$

(☑ 828-295-4008; www.bistroroca.com; 143 Wonderland Trail; lunch mains $9-16, dinner mains $10-32; ⏰11am-3pm & 5-10pm Wed-Mon; 🌐) This cozy, lodge-like bistro, in a Prohibition-era building just off Main St, serves upscale New American cuisine – lobster or pork-belly mac and cheese, kicked-up habanero burgers, mountain-trout *banh mi* sandwiches – with an emphasis on local everything. Check out the walls of the atmospheric Antlers Bar, North Carolina's longest continually operating bar, plastered with fantastic B&W pet photos.

❶ Getting There & Away

Blowing Rock is 8 miles south of Boone via Hwy 321, or more like 25 miles if you detour along the Blue Ridge Pkwy. The nearest commercial airport is Charlotte Douglas International Airport (p360), 87 miles southeast.

BOONE

Boone is a fun and lively mountain town where the predominantly youthful inhabitants – many of them students at bustling Appalachian State University – share a hankering for the outdoors. Renowned for its bluegrass musicians and Appalachian storytellers, the town is named after pioneer and explorer Daniel Boone, who often camped in the area. Downtown Boone features a fine assortment of low-rise brick-broad, Colonial Revival, art-deco and streamline-modern buildings. Those that line King St in particular now tend to house charming boutiques, cafes, and crafts galleries.

Every summer since 1952, local history has been presented in a dramatization called *Horn in the West,* performed in an outdoor amphitheater above town.

Accommodations in Boone traditionally consisted of standard chain hotels, but the **Horton** (☑ 828-832-8060; www.thehorton.com; 611 W King St; r from $189; ❄🌐), downtown's first boutique hotel, opened in 2018. You can also find the occasional historic B&B, rental farmhouse or cozy log cabin around town and in the surrounding countryside.

Folk Art Center
CULTURAL CENTER

(☑ 828-298-7928; www.southernhighlandguild.org; Mile 382, Blue Ridge Pkwy; ⏰9am-6pm Apr-Dec, to 5pm Jan-Mar; P) 𝐅𝐑𝐄𝐄 Part gallery, part store, and wholly dedicated to Southern craftsmanship, the superb Folk Art Center stands directly off the Blue Ridge Pkwy, 6 miles east of downtown Asheville. Handcrafted Appalachian chairs hanging above its lobby make an impressive appetizer for the Southern Highland Craft Guild's permanent collection, a treasury of pottery, baskets, quilts and woodcarvings that's displayed on the 2nd floor.

Lovill House Inn
B&B $$

(☑ 828-264-4204; www.lovillhouseinn.com; 404 Old Bristol Rd; r from $179; 🌐) Boone's finest B&B is a splendid 19th-century farmhouse, a mile west of downtown and surrounded by woods. With its snug rooms, white clapboard walls, and wraparound porch decked out with rocking chairs, it's all wonderfully restful; the breakfast is worth getting up for, though.

Wild Craft Eatery   LATIN AMERICAN $
(☑ 828-262-5000; www.facebook.com/wildcraft
eatery; 506 W King St; mains lunch $7-12, dinner
$10-15; ⊙ 11am-10pm Wed-Mon; ☑) Colorful,
quirky downtown cafe, with an outdoor
deck on King St, and an emphasis on local
ingredients. There's a definite Latin flavor to
the menu, with tacos and tamales aplenty,
but it also offers Thai noodles and shepherd's pie. Not everything's vegetarian, but
most of the standout dishes are, including
the Cuzco Cakes, made with smoked quinoa,
Gouda and yams.

❶ Getting There & Away

The closest commercial airport to Boone is
Charlotte Douglas International Airport (p360),
94 miles southeast.

Asheville

The undisputed 'capital' of the North Carolina mountains, Asheville is both a major
tourist destination and one of the coolest small cities in the South. Cradled in a
sweeping curve of the Blue Ridge Pkwy, it
offers easy access to outdoor adventures
of all kinds, while downtown's historic art-
deco buildings hold stylish New Southern
restaurants, decadent chocolate shops, and
the homegrown microbreweries that explain
the nickname 'Beer City.'

Despite rapid gentrification, Asheville
remains recognizably an overgrown mountain town that holds tight to its traditional
roots. It's also a rare liberal enclave in the
conservative countryside, home to a sizable
population of artists and hard-core hippies.
Alternative Asheville life is largely lived in
neighborhoods such as the waterfront River
Arts District and, across the French Broad
River, West Asheville. Remarkably enough,
the French Broad River is the world's
third-oldest river, its course laid before life
on Earth even began.

◉ Sights & Activities

Biltmore Estate   HOUSE
(☑ 800-411-3812; www.biltmore.com; 1 Approach
Rd; adult/child 10-16yr $75/37.50; ⊙ house 9am-
4:30pm, with seasonal variations; ☑) The largest
privately owned home in the US, Biltmore
House was completed in 1895 for shipping
and railroad heir George Washington Vanderbilt II, and modeled after three châteaux
that he'd seen in France's Loire Valley. It's extraordinarily expensive to visit, but there's a

lot to see; allow several hours to explore the
entire 8000-acre estate. Self-guided tours of
the house itself take in 39 points of interest,
including our favorite, the two-lane bowling
alley.

Chimney Rock Park   PARK
(☑ 828-625-9611; www.chimneyrockpark.com;
Hwy 74A; adult/child 5-15yr $17/8; ⊙ 8:30am-7pm
mid-Mar–Oct, 8:30am-6pm Nov & Dec, 10am-6pm
Jan-mid-Mar; ☑) The stupendous 315ft mon-
olith known as Chimney Rock towers above
the slender, forested valley of the Rocky
Broad River, a gorgeous 28-mile drive southeast of Asheville. Protruding in naked splendor from soaring granite walls, its flat top
bears the fluttering American flag. Climb
there via the 499 steps of the Outcropping
Trail, or simply ride the elevator deep inside
the rock.

BREW-ed   BREWERY
(☑ 828-278-9255; www.brew-ed.com; adults $37-
50, nondrinkers $20) Beer-focused historical
walking tours, led by Cicerone-certified
beer geeks and sampling at two or three
different downtown breweries, on Thursdays (5:30pm), Fridays (2pm), Saturdays
(11:30am and 2pm) and Sundays (1pm).

Smoky Mountain
Adventure Center   OUTDOORS
(☑ 828-505-4446; www.smacasheville.com; 173
Amboy Rd; ⊙ 8am-8pm Mon, to 10pm Tue-Sat,
10am-8pm Sun) One-stop adventure shopping, across the French Broad River 3 miles
southwest of downtown. On-site there's an
indoor climbing wall, as well as yoga and
tai chi classes. They can also arrange bikes
for the Blue Ridge Pkwy, inner-tubes and
paddleboards for the river, plus guided
rock climbing, backpacking, day hiking, ice
climbing and mountaineering trips.

🛏 Sleeping

★ **Sweet Peas Hostel**   HOSTEL $
(☑ 828-285-8488; www.sweetpeashostel.com;
23 Rankin Ave; dm/pod $32/40, r with/without
bath $105/75; ❈ @ 🛜) This spick-and-span,
well-run, contemporary hostel occupies an
unbeatable downtown location. The loft-
like open-plan space, with its exposed brick
walls, steel bunks and blond-wood sleeping
'pods', can get noisy, but at least there's a
10% discount at the Lexington Ave Brewery
downstairs. They also warn you if an event
coincides with your planned dates.

Campfire Lodgings CAMPGROUND $$
(☑ 828-658-8012; www.campfirelodgings.com; 116 Appalachian Village Rd; tent sites $35-40, RV sites $50-70, yurts $115-135, cabins $160; ℗❀☎) All yurts should have flat-screen TVs, don't you think? Sleep like the world's most stylish Mongolian nomad in a furnished multiroom tent, half a mile up a wooded hillside on an unpaved but passable road, 6 miles north of town. Cabins and tent sites are also available. RV sites, higher up, enjoy stunning valley views and the only wi-fi access.

Omni Grove Park Inn HISTORIC HOTEL $$$
(☑ 828-252-2711; www.omnihotels.com; 290 Macon Ave; r $189-434; ℗❀@☎❊❂) Commanding sweeping Blue Ridge views, this titanic Arts and Crafts–style stone lodge harks back to a bygone era of mountain glamor. Each of the 36ft-wide lobby fireplaces can hold a standing grown man, and has its own elevator to the chimney. Beyond the spectacular public spaces, though, the guest rooms can seem small by modern standards.

Aloft Asheville Downtown HOTEL $$$
(☑ 828-232-2838; www.aloftashevilledowntown. com; 51 Biltmore Ave; r from $289; ℗❀@☎❊❂) With a giant chalkboard in the lobby, groovy young staff and an outdoor clothing store on the 1st floor, this place looks like the inner circle of hipster. The only thing missing is a wool-cap-wearing bearded guy drinking a hoppy microbrew – oh wait, over there. We jest. Once settled, you'll find the staff knowledgeable and the rooms colorful and spacious.

★Bunn House BOUTIQUE HOTEL $$$
(☑ 828-333-8700; www.bunnhouse.com; 15 Clayton St; d $249-424; ℗❀☎) The six rooms and suites in this meticulously restored 1905 home, in a residential neighborhood half a mile north of downtown, are awash with exposed brick and dark hardwoods. The small rooftop terrace boasts Blue Ridge vistas, while the heated bathroom floors and subway-tiled steam showers are glorious on chilly mountain mornings.

✖ Eating

Asheville is a true foodie haven. Downtown and South Slope are bursting with enticing options, including simple (but oh-so-hip!) Southern-fried cafes, ethnic diners and elaborate Modern American and Appalachian kitchens. Farm-to-table is the rule; local, organic and sustainable are mantras.

With more alternatives down in the River Arts District and over in West Asheville, you won't starve in these mountains.

★12 Bones BARBECUE $
(☑ 828-253-4499; www.12bones.com; 5 Foundy St; dishes $5.50-22.50; ☉11am-4pm Mon-Fri) How good is the barbecue at 12 Bones? Good enough to lure the vacationing Barack and Michelle Obama back to the River Arts District, a few years back. Expect a long wait, though, before you get to enjoy the slow-cooked, smoky and tender meats, or succulent sides from jalapeño-cheese grits to smoked potato salad.

Chai Pani INDIAN $
(☑ 828-254-4003; www.chaipaniasheville.com; 22 Battery Park Ave; snacks $8-10, meals $10-13; ☉11:30am-3:30pm & 5:30-9:30pm; ☝) Literally 'tea and water,' *chai pani* refers more generally to inexpensive snacks. Hence the ever-changing array of irresistible street food at this popular, no-reservations downtown restaurant. Fill up on crunchy *bhel puri* (chickpea noodles and puffed rice) or live it larger with a lamb burger, fish roll or chicken or vegetarian *thali* (a full meal on a metal tray).

White Duck Taco Shop MEXICAN $
(☑ 828-232-9191; www.whiteducktacoshop.com; 12 Biltmore Ave; tacos $3.45-5.25; ☉11:30am-9pm) The chalkboard menu at this downtown taco shop will give you fits. Every single one of these hefty soft tacos sounds like a must-have flavor bomb: spicy buffalo chicken with blue-cheese sauce, crispy pork belly, mole-roasted duck – even shrimp and grits! The margaritas are mighty fine too.

★Cúrate TAPAS $$
(☑ 828-239-2946; www.curatetapasbar.com; 13 Biltmore Ave; small plates $6-18; ☉11:30am-10:30pm Tue-Fri, 10am-11pm Sat, 10am-10:30pm Sun) ☝ Owned by hip Ashevillian chef Katie Button and her Catalan husband Félix, this convivial downtown hangout celebrates the simple charms and sensual flavors of Spanish tapas, while adding an occasional Southern twist. Standout dishes run long and wide: *pan con tomate* (grilled bread with tomato), lightly fried eggplant drizzled with honey and rosemary, and a knockout squid-ink 'paella' with vermicelli.

Smoky Park Supper Club AMERICAN $$
(☑ 828-350-0315; www.smokypark.com; 350 Riverside Dr; mains $13-36; ☉5-9pm Tue-Thu, 4-10pm

BEER CITY USA

If ever a city was transformed by the craft-beer movement, it's Asheville. A sleepy mountain city when its first brewery, Highland Brewing, opened in 1994, Asheville has become a true destination city for booze-bent hopheads. It now holds almost 30 breweries, catering to a population of around 90,000 locals; were it not for the half-million tourists who join them each year, that would be a lot of beer per person!

Inevitably, big-name national breweries have been flocking to Asheville too. Both New Belgium and Sierra Nevada, respectively from California and Colorado, have opened major brewing and taproom facilities here. Strolling from brewery to beerhouse in the pub-packed South Slope district – which, yes, slopes south from downtown – it's easy to see why Asheville has been nicknamed Beer City.

If you're ready to tackle the taps in Asheville, be sure to try a few of our favorite taprooms:

Burial (www.burialbeer.com; 40 Collier Ave; ⊘2-10pm Mon-Thu, from noon Fri-Sun; 🕿) Never mind its menacing logo; this friendly joint whips up some of Asheville's finest and most experimental Belgian-leaning styles (farmhouse saisons, strong dubbels and tripels).

Funkatorium (🗷828-552-3203; www.wickedweedbrewing.com/locations/funkatorium; 147 Coxe Ave; ⊘2-10pm Mon-Thu, noon-midnight Fri & Sat, 11am-10pm Sun; 🕿) Wicked Weed's all-sour taproom is a temple of tart and funk.

Wedge Brewing (🗷828-505-2792; www.wedgebrewing.com; 37 Paynes Way; ⊘noon-10pm; 🕿) Our favorite microbrewery ambience – a festive, come-one, come-all outdoor space, rife with dogs, kids on tricycles, swooning couples and outdoorsy types.

Wicked Weed (🗷828-575-9599; www.wickedweedbrewing.com; 91 Biltmore Ave; ⊘11:30am-11pm Mon-Thu, to 1am Fri & Sat, noon-11pm Sun; 🕿) A former gas station turned craft-brew wonderland – with 58 taps!

Fri & Sat, 10:30am-9pm Sun; 🕿) An anchor of cool in the River Arts District, the largest container-constructed restaurant in the USA is more than the sum of its parts – 19 shipping containers to be exact. Choose between such wood-fired delights as garlic- and lemon-roasted half chicken, cast-iron-seared Carolina fish, or, for vegetarians, roasted local apples stuffed with kale, walnuts and smoked cheddar.

🍷 Drinking & Entertainment

★**Battery Park Book Exchange & Champagne Bar**   WINE BAR
(🗷828-252-0020; www.batteryparkbookexchange.com; 1 Page Ave; ⊘11am-9pm Mon-Thu, to 10pm Fri & Sat, noon-7pm Sun) A charming champagne bar, sprawling through several opulent vintage-furnished rooms of a glorious old downtown shopping arcade, with every nook and cranny lined with shelves of neatly cataloged secondhand books covering every imaginable topic. Seriously, who could resist that as a combination? Other wines are also available, along with coffee, cakes, cheese and charcuterie.

Orange Peel   LIVE MUSIC
(🗷828-398-1837; www.theorangepeel.net; 101 Biltmore Ave; tickets $10-35; ⊘shows from 8pm) Asheville's premier live-music venue, downtown's Orange Peel Social Aid & Pleasure Club has been a showcase for big-name indie and punk bands since 2002. A warehouse-sized place, it seats – well, stands – a thousand-strong crowd.

ℹ Information

Asheville's main **visitor center** (🗷828-258-6129; www.exploreasheville.com; 36 Montford Ave; ⊘8:30am-5:30pm Mon-Fri, 9am-5pm Sat & Sun), alongside I-240 exit 4C, sells Biltmore Estate admission tickets at a $10 discount. Downtown holds a satellite **visitor pavilion** (🗷828-258-6129; www.exploreasheville.com; 80 Court Pl; ⊘9am-5pm), with restrooms, beside Pack Sq Park.

ℹ Getting There & Around

Asheville Regional Airport (AVL; 🗷828-684-2226; www.flyavl.com; 61 Terminal Dr, Fletcher), 16 miles south of Asheville, is served by a handful of nonstop flights, with destinations including Atlanta, Charlotte, Chicago and

New York. **Greyhound** (☏ 828-253-8451; 2 Tunnel Rd) is 1 mile northeast of downtown.

Although there's very little free parking downtown, public garages are free for the first hour and only cost $1 per hour thereafter. The handy Passport app (https://passportinc.com) facilitates paying for Asheville's parking meters and paid lots.

The 18 local bus routes run by Asheville Transit (ART) typically operate between 5:30am and 10:30pm Monday through Saturday, and shorter hours Sunday. Tickets cost $1, and there are free bike racks. Route S3 connects the **downtown ART station** (☏ 828-253-5691; www.asheville transit.com; 49 Coxe Ave; ⊙ 6am-9:30pm Mon-Fri, from 7am Sat, 8:30am-5.30pm Sun) with Asheville Regional Airport 10 times daily.

Great Smoky Mountains National Park

Get back to nature among mist-shrouded peaks, shimmering waterfalls and lush forests in the great American wilderness.

⊙ Sights

★ **Great Smoky Mountains National Park**   NATIONAL PARK
(www.nps.gov/grsm) FREE The 816-sq-mile Great Smoky Mountains National Park is the country's most visited park and, while the main arteries and attractions can get crowded, it's easy to leave the masses behind. There are scores of memorable hikes along 850 miles of trails, with thundering waterfalls and cliff-top views among the highlights. Unlike most national parks, Great Smoky charges no admission fee.

Stop by a visitor center to pick up a park map and the free *Smokies Guide*. The remains of the 19th-century settlement at **Cades Cove** (www.nps.gov/grsm/planyourvisit/cadescove.htm; Cades Cove Loop Rd; P) are one of the park's most popular sights, as evidenced by the teeth-grinding summer traffic jams on the 11-mile loop road (it closes to vehicles on Wednesday and Saturday morning from late May through late September, making it perfect for a bike ride). **Mt LeConte** offers terrific hiking, as well as the park's only non-camping accommodations, LeConte Lodge. Although the only way to get to the lodge's rustic, electricity-free cabins is via five uphill hiking trails varying in length from 5.5 miles (Alum Cave Bluffs trail, off Newfound Gap Rd) to 8.9 miles (Trillium Gap Trail), it's so popular you need to reserve up to a year in advance.

You can drive right up to the dizzying heights of **Clingmans Dome** (off Clingmans Dome Rd), the third-highest mountain east of the Mississippi, with its futuristic observation tower.

Other popular hikes include trails to **Laurel Falls** (off Fighting Creek Gap Rd), **Rainbow Falls** (off Cherokee Orchard Rd) and **Gregorys Bald**. For something less trafficked, check out the Lakeshore Trail in the southwest part of the park, Mt Sterling in the east, or **Baskins Creek** near Gatlinburg. There are also ample opportunities for multiday backpacking adventures, with dozens of backcountry campsites (reserve online through the park website). Some 71 miles of the Appalachian Trail also traverse the park.

🏃 Activities

Whether you have an irrepressible urge to climb a mountain or just want to get some fresh air, hiking in Great Smoky Mountains National Park is the single best way to experience the sublime beauty of this area. Even if you're only here for a short visit, be sure to include at least one hike in your itinerary. Trails range from flat, easy and short paths to longer, more strenuous endeavors. Many are excellent for families and there's even one wheelchair-accessible trail. No matter what your physical ability or endurance level, there's a hike out there for you.

Foothills Parkway   SCENIC DRIVE
This scenic drive runs along the western edge of the park between Chilhowee and – thanks to the completion of the 'missing link' in November 2018 – Wears Valley. There are numerous spots to pull off and admire the view, as well as a lookout tower (and weather monitoring station) you can climb at the aptly named **Look Rock** (Foothills Pkwy).

🛏 Sleeping & Eating

You'll have to book on October 1 to reserve a spot for the following season in the **LeConte Lodge** (☏ 865-429-5704; www.lecontelodge.com; cabins incl breakfast & dinner adult/ child 4-12yr $152/88; ⊙ mid-Mar–mid-Nov); the hilltop inn, reachable only by a long uphill hike, books solid within a few days. Outside the park, Gatlinburg has the most sleeping options of any gateway town.

The National Park Service maintains developed campgrounds at nine locations in the park. Each campground has restrooms with cold running water and flush toilets, but there are no showers or electrical or water hookups in the park. Each individual campsite has a fire grate and picnic table. Many sites can be reserved in advance, and several campgrounds (Cataloochee, Abrams Creek, Big Creek and Balsam Mountain) require advance reservations. Reserve through www.recreation.gov.

Campgrounds book up in the busy summer season, so plan ahead. Cades Cove and Smokemont campgrounds are open year-round; others are open March to October.

Backcountry camping is an excellent option, which is only chargeable up to five nights ($4 per night; after that, it's free). A permit is required. You can make reservations online at http://smokiespermits.nps.gov, and get permits at the ranger stations or visitor centers.

Nuts and berries notwithstanding, there's nothing to eat in Great Smoky Mountains National Park, save for items from vending machines at Sugarlands Visitor Center and the meager offerings sold at the **Cades Cove Campground store** ([☑] 865-448-9034; www.cadescovetrading.com; 10035 Campground Dr; ☺9am-9pm late May-Oct, to 5pm Mar-May, Nov & late Dec). If you make the hike up to LeConte Lodge, you can purchase cookies, drinks and sack lunches (which means a bagel with cream cheese, beef summer sausage, trail mix and fruit leather). Dinner is included for those staying overnight.

Luckily, there are lots of restaurant options in the surrounding towns.

❶ Tourist Information

Cades Cove Visitor Center ([☑] 865-436-7318; www.nps.gov/grsm; Cades Cove Loop Rd; ☺9am-7pm Apr-Aug, closes earlier Sep-Mar) Halfway up Cades Cove Loop Rd, 24 miles off Hwy 441 from the Gatlinburg entrance.

Clingmans Dome Visitor Station ([☑] 865-436-1200; Clingmans Dome Rd; ☺10am-6pm Apr-Oct, 9:30am-5pm Nov) Small, very busy center at the start of the paved path up to the Clingmans Dome lookout.

Oconaluftee Visitor Center ([☑] 828-497-1904; www.nps.gov/grsm; 1194 Newfound Gap Rd, North Cherokee; ☺8am-7pm Jun-Aug, to 6pm Apr, May, Sep & Oct, to 5pm Mar & Nov, to 4:30pm Dec-Feb; ☎) At the park's southern entrance near Cherokee.

Sugarlands Visitor Center ([☑] 865-436-1291; www.nps.gov/grsm; 107 Park Headquarters Rd; ☺8am-7:30pm Jun-Aug, hours vary Sep-May; ☎) At the park's northern entrance near Gatlinburg.

❶ Getting There & Away

The closest airports to the national park are McGhee Tyson Airport (p397) near Knoxville (40 miles northwest of Sugarlands Visitor Center) and Asheville Regional Airport (p365), 58 miles east of the Oconaluftee Visitor Center. Further afield you'll find Chattanooga Metropolitan Airport (p396), 140 miles southwest of the park, Charlotte Douglas International Airport (p360), 170 miles east, and Hartsfield-Jackson International Airport (p416) in Atlanta, 175 miles south of the park.

After you fly in, you'll need a car as there's no public transportation to the park. There's a wide variety of car-rental outfits at each of the airports.

SOUTH CAROLINA

Moss-draped oaks. Stately mansions. Wide beaches. Rolling mountains. And an ornery streak as old as the state itself. Ah yes, South Carolina, where the accents are thicker and the traditions more dear. From its Revolutionary War patriots to its 1860s secessionist government to its outspoken legislators, the Palmetto State has never shied away from a fight.

Most travelers stick to the coast, with its splendid antebellum cities and palm-tree-studded beaches. But the interior has a wealth of sleepy old towns, wild and undeveloped state parks and spooky black-water swamps. Along the sea islands you hear the sweet songs of the Gullah, a culture and language created by former slaves who held on to many West African traditions through the ravages of time.

From well-bred, gardenia-scented Charleston to up-and-coming Greenville to bright, tacky Myrtle Beach, South Carolina is always a fascinating destination.

History

South Carolina is one fiery state, as its contentious and bloody history rarely fails to demonstrate. Over the last 350 years, its settlers have squared off against natural disasters, Native American residents, the British, and – when the state became the first to secede from the Union in 1860 – countrymen to the north. Race relations may have improved since the days of slavery, but poverty, inequality and discrimination have proven difficult to eradicate. Occasionally these issues still flare up, with devastating consequences.

THE SOUTH SOUTH CAROLINA

ℹ Information

South Carolina Department of Parks, Recreation & Tourism (☏803-734-0124; www.discoversouthcarolina.com) Can mail you the state's official vacation guide on request. The state's nine highway welcome centers offer free wi-fi (ask inside for the passwords).

Charleston

The zenith of old-world charm, Charleston whisks you into the nation's tumultuous past and nourishes your mind, heart and stomach in roughly equal measure.

History

In strolling the tidy, peaceful streets of Charleston today, it's sometimes difficult to imagine the terrors that came before: the earthquakes, the fires, the hurricanes, slavery, the Revolutionary War and the Civil War, just to name a few. The city has managed to survive it all, and to rebuild stronger each time. Today Charleston is a living museum, and its battle scars teach important lessons. Perhaps that is exactly the reason so many people feel compelled to visit.

◉ Sights

The quarter south of Beaufain and Hasell Sts has the bulk of the antebellum mansions, shops, bars and cafes. At the southernmost tip of the peninsula are the antebellum mansions of the Battery. A loose path, the **Gateway Walk**, winds through several church grounds and graveyards between St John's Lutheran Church and **St Philip's Church** (www.stphilipschurchsc.org; 146 Church St).

◉ Historic District

Old Exchange
& Provost Dungeon   HISTORIC BUILDING
(☏843-727-2165; www.oldexchange.org; 122 E Bay St; adult/child 7-12yr $10/5; ☉9am-5pm; 🚼) Kids love the creepy dungeon, used as a prison for American patriots held by the British during the Revolutionary War. The cramped space sits beneath a stately Georgian Palladian customs house completed in 1771. Costumed guides lead the dungeon tours. Exhibits about the city are displayed on the upper floors.

★Old Slave Mart Museum   MUSEUM
(☏843-958-6467; www.oldslavemart.org; 6 Chalmers St; adult/child 5-17yr $8/5; ☉9am-5pm

Mon-Sat) Formerly called Ryan's Mart, this building once housed an open-air market that auctioned African American men, women and children in the mid-1800s, the largest of 40 or so similar auction houses. South Carolina's shameful past is unraveled in text-heavy exhibits illuminating the slave experience; the few artifacts, such as leg shackles, are especially chilling.

Gibbes Museum of Art   GALLERY
(☏843-722-2706; www.gibbesmuseum.org; 135 Meeting St; adult/child $12/6; ☉10am-5pm Tue & Thu-Sat, to 8pm Wed, 1-5pm Sun) Houses a decent collection of American and Southern works. The contemporary collection includes works by local artists, with Lowcountry life as a highlight. A 2016 renovation added a new museum store and cafe as well as 30% more gallery space.

Battery & White Point Garden   GARDENS
(cnr East Battery & Murray Blvd; ☉9am-sunset) The Battery is the southern tip of the Charleston Peninsula, buffered by a seawall. Stroll past cannons and statues of military heroes in the gardens, then walk the promenade and look for Fort Sumter.

Rainbow Row   AREA
(83 E Bay St) With its 13 candy-colored houses, this stretch of Georgian row houses is one of the most photographed areas in Charleston. The structures date back to 1730, when they served as merchant stores on the wharf, a sketchy part of town at the time. Starting in the 1920s the buildings were restored and painted over in pastels. People dug it, and soon much of the rest of Charleston was getting a similar makeover.

Historic Homes
★Aiken-Rhett House   HISTORIC BUILDING
(☏843-723-1159; www.historiccharleston.org; 48 Elizabeth St; adult/child 6-16yr $12/5; ☉10am-5pm, last tour 4:15pm) The only surviving urban town-house complex, this 1820 abode gives a fascinating glimpse into antebellum life on a 45-minute self-guided audio tour. The role of slaves is emphasized, and visitors wander into their dorm-style quarters behind the house before moving on to the lifestyle of the rich and famous.

The Historic Charleston Foundation manages the property 'preserved as found,' conserving but not restoring it. There have been few alterations and you get it as is, peeling Parisian wallpaper and all.

Joseph Manigault House   HISTORIC BUILDING
(🖉843-722-2996; www.charlestonmuseum.org;
350 Meeting St; adult/child 13-17yr/child 3-12yr
$12/10/5; ⏱10am-5pm Mon-Sat, noon-5pm Sun,
last tour 4:30pm) This three-story Federal-style
house from 1803 was once the showpiece of
a French Huguenot rice planter. There's a
tiny neoclassical gate temple in the garden
and the house is full of 19th-century furnishings from the collection of the Charleston
Museum, which runs the site.

Nathaniel Russell House   HISTORIC BUILDING
(🖉843-724-8481; www.historiccharleston.org; 51
Meeting St; adult/child 6-16yr $12/5; ⏱10am-5pm,
last tour 4pm) A spectacular, self-supporting
spiral staircase is the highlight at this 1808
Federal-style house, built by a Rhode Islander, known in Charleston as 'King of the
Yankees.' A meticulous ongoing restoration
honors the home to the finest details, such
as the 1000 sheets of 22-karat gold leaf in
the withdrawing room. Twenty layers of wall
paint were peeled back to uncover the original colors, and handmade, fitted, contoured
rugs were imported from the UK, as originally done by the Russells.

◉ Marion Square

Marion Sq (🖉843-724-7327; www.nps.gov/nr/
travel/charleston/mar.htm; 329 Meeting St; ⏱24hr)
was formerly home to the state weapons arsenal. This 10-acre park is Charleston's living
room, with various monuments and an excellent **farmers market** (www.charlestonfarm
ersmarket.com; ⏱8am-2pm Sat mid-Apr–Nov) on
Saturdays.

Charleston Museum   MUSEUM
(🖉843-722-2996; www.charlestonmuseum.org;
360 Meeting St; adult/child 3-17yr/child 3-12yr
$12/10/5; ⏱9am-5pm Mon-Sat, from noon Sun)
Founded in 1773, this is the country's oldest museum. It's helpful and informative
if you're looking for historical background
before strolling through the Historic District. Exhibits spotlight various periods of
Charleston's long and storied history.

◉ Aquarium Wharf

Aquarium Wharf surrounds pretty Liberty Sq and is a great place to stroll and
watch the tugboats guiding ships into the
fourth-largest container port in the USA.
The wharf is home to the **South Carolina
Aquarium** (🖉843-577-3474; www.scaquarium.
org; 100 Aquarium Wharf; adult/child $30/23;

⏱9am-5pm; ♿) and is one of two embar-
kation points for tours to Fort Sumter; the
other is at Patriot's Point.

★Fort Sumter
National Monument   HISTORIC SITE
(🖉843-883-3123; www.nps.gov/fosu) The first
shots of the Civil War rang out at Fort
Sumter, on a pentagon-shaped island in the
harbor. A Confederate stronghold, this fort
was shelled to bits by Union forces from
1863 to 1865. A few original guns and fortifications give a feel for the momentous
history here.

The only way to get here is by **boat tour**
(🖉boat tour 843-722-2628, park 843-883-3123;
www.fortsumtertours.com; 340 Concord St; adult/
child 4-11yr $23/15), which departs from 340
Concord St and from Patriot's Point in Mt
Pleasant at varying times depending on the
season (check the website). The monument
also includes **Fort Moultrie** (🖉843-883-3123;
www.nps.gov/fosu; 1214 Middle St, Sullivan's Island;
adult/child $7/free; ⏱9am-5pm).

◉ Ashley River Plantations

Three significant plantations line the Ashley
River about a 20-minute drive from downtown Charleston. All offer talks and tours
concerning the role of slavery (though another, McLeod Plantation (p373), located on
the northern shores of James Island, is the
best for an eye-opening and highly important experience on that topic).

Of the three on the Ashley River, **Drayton
Hall** (🖉843-769-2600; www.draytonhall.org; 3380
Ashley River Rd; adult/child $32/25, grounds only
$12; ⏱9am-3:30pm Mon-Sat, from 10:30am Sun,
last tour 3pm) is the best for history buffs, as
it features the oldest plantation house open
to the public in America. **Magnolia Plantation** (🖉843-571-1266; www.magnoliaplanta
tion.com; 3550 Ashley River Rd; adult/child 6-10yr
$20/10, tours $8; ⏱8am-5:30pm Mar-Oct, to
4:30pm Nov-Feb) has great tours and wild gardens, with a Disney vibe. **Middleton Place**
(🖉843-556-6020; www.middletonplace.org; 4300
Ashley River Rd; gardens adult/child 6-13yr $28/10,
house-museum tour extra $15, carriage tour $18;
⏱9am-5pm) has the country's oldest, most
elegant gardens and a fancy restaurant and
hotel. You'll be hard-pressed to find the time
to visit all three of these in one day, but you
could squeeze in two (allow at least a couple
of hours for each). Ashley River Rd is also
known as SC 61, which can be reached from
downtown Charleston via Hwy 17.

THE SOUTH CHARLESTON

GULLAH CULTURE

Starting in the 16th century, African slaves were transported from the region known as the Rice Coast (Sierra Leone, Senegal, Gambia and Angola) to a landscape of remote islands that was shockingly similar – swampy coastlines and tropical vegetation, plus hot, humid summers. These new African Americans were able to retain many of their homeland traditions after the fall of slavery and well into the 20th century. The resulting culture of Gullah (also known as Geechee in Georgia) has its own language, an English-based Creole with many African words and sentence structures, and many traditions, including fantastic storytelling, art, music and crafts. The Gullah culture is celebrated annually with the energetic **Gullah Festival** (www.theoriginalgullahfestival.org; ☺late May) in Beaufort.

St Helena Island, to the east of Beaufort, has the highest concentration of Gullah people in the state, and is the best place for a traveler to obtain an education on the culture – the Penn Center (p375) has a museum that's a great starting place. You'll also notice plenty of Gullah restaurants around the island, and their menus are heavy with shrimp, fish, okra, rice, tomatoes and cabbage. Basically, Gullah cuisine consists of whatever the state's early African American residents could find, catch or grow. There's also a distinctly African influence in the cooking style.

Gullah art, too, has stood the test of time. In Beaufort and St Helena there are several folk art galleries with many brightly colored paintings influenced by the vibrance of similar works in West Africa. Sweetgrass baskets are another mainstay; these charming, coiled baskets are prevalent in Africa and are most easily procured on the streets and in the markets of Charleston.

Also popular, **Boone Hall Plantation** (☑843-884-4371; www.boonehallplantation.com; 1235 Long Point Rd; adult/child 6-12yr $24/12; ☺8:30am-6:30pm Mon-Sat, noon-5pm Sun early Mar-Aug, shorter hours Sep-Jan) in Mt Pleasant is where many celebrities get married, and is a very pretty spot for tourists and families. It's 11 miles from downtown Charleston on Hwy 17N.

☞ Tours

Charleston is chock-full of worthwhile walking, horse-carriage, bus and boat tours, and you can ask at the visitor center for the gamut. If you don't feel like wading through giant stacks of brochures, though, our top recs include: Charleston Footprints for a historical walking tour in South of Broad, Culinary Tours of Charleston for food tours, **Charleston Brews Cruise** (☑843-860-9847; www.charlestonbrewscruise.com; 375 Meeting St; drinker/nondrinker $75/25; ☺tours 1:30pm Sun & Tue-Thu, 12:30pm Fri & Sat) for brewery tours and **Bulldog Tours** (☑843-722-8687; www.bulldogtours.com; 18 Anson St; ghost tour adult/child $29/19) for anything.

Charleston Footprints　　　WALKING
(☑843-478-4718; www.charlestonfootprints.com; 2hr tour $20) An excellent walking tour of historical Charleston sights led by a knowledgeable and theatrical local. Tours begin at the Shops of Historic Charleston Foundation.

Culinary Tours of Charleston　　　FOOD & DRINK
(☑843-727-1100; www.culinarytoursofcharleston.com; 18 Anson St; 2½-hr tour from $65) Sample grits, pralines and barbecue on food-centric walking tours of restaurants and markets. Also available: dessert tours and a celebrity-chef experience.

Adventure Harbor Tours　　　BOATING
(☑843-442-9455; www.adventureharbortours.com; 56 Ashley Point Dr, Charleston; adult/child 3-12yr $55/30) Runs harbor cruises, sunset cruises and fun trips to uninhabited Morris Island – great for shelling.

☆ Festivals & Events

Spoleto USA　　　PERFORMING ARTS
(☑843-722-2764; www.spoletousa.org; ☺late May-early Jun) This 17-day performing-arts festival is South Carolina's biggest event, with operas, dramas and concerts staged across the city.

Lowcountry Oyster Festival　　　FOOD & DRINK
(www.lowcountryhospitalityassociation.com/oyster-fest/; 1235 Longpoint Rd, Boone Hall Plantation, Mt Pleasant; ☺Jan) Oyster lovers in Mt Pleasant feast on 80,000lb of the salty bivalves at this festival (oyster buckets are $12 to $16). There's also oyster shucking and eating contests, live music, local food and a whole lotta beer.

MOJA Arts Festival PERFORMING ARTS
(☑ 843-724-7305; www.mojafestival.com; ☺ late Sep-early Oct) Spirited poetry readings and gospel concerts mark this two-week celebration of African American and Caribbean culture.

🛏 Sleeping

Not So Hostel HOSTEL **$**
(☑ 843-722-8383; www.notsohostel.com; 156 Spring St; dm $30, r $72-106; 🅿❄🛜🐕) 🍽
Housed mainly in a wonderful 1840 dwelling complete with atmospheric blue porches and an odd, twin-matching architecture setup, Charleston's one hostel is creaky and inviting. A couple of eight-bed co-ed dorms, various four-bed male and female dorms, and nice but cramped private rooms (some with private baths) are spread over three buildings, with guest kitchens throughout. Green initiatives abound.

1837 Bed & Breakfast B&B **$$**
(☑ 843-723-7166; www.1837bb.com; 126 Wentworth St; r $139-295; 🅿❄🛜) Close to the College of Charleston, this B&B may bring to mind the home of your eccentric, antique-loving aunt. The 1837 has nine charmingly overdecorated rooms, including three in the old brick carriage house. And, no, you're not drunk – those warped porches are lopsided as hell and full of history.

Indigo Inn BOUTIQUE HOTEL **$$**
(☑ 843-577-5900; www.indigoinn.com; 1 Maiden Lane; r $209-359; 🅿❄🛜) This snazzy 40-room inn enjoys a prime location in the middle of the Historic District and has an oasis-like private courtyard, where guests can enjoy free wine and cheese by the fountain. Decor gives a nod to the 18th century and is a tad frilly, but the beds are comfy and renovated bathrooms have been modernized. Pets are $40 per night.

★ Ansonborough Inn HOTEL **$$**
(☑ 800-723-1655; www.ansonboroughinn.com; 21 Hasell St; r from $180-340; 🅿❄@🛜) Droll neo-Victorian touches such as the closet-sized British pub and the formal portraits of dogs add a sense of fun to this intimate Historic District hotel, which also manages to feel like an antique sailing ship. Huge guest rooms mix old and new, with worn leather couches, high ceilings and flat-screen TVs.

★ Wentworth Mansion HISTORIC HOTEL **$$$**
(☑ 843-853-1886; www.wentworthmansion.com; 149 Wentworth St; r $400-755; 🅿❄🛜) Routinely named a top stay in the country, this Gilded Age mansion would be the ideal setting for an elaborate Clue dinner party – and who wouldn't die for a glimpse of these Tiffany stained-glass windows, Italian crystal chandeliers and hand-carved mahogany moldings? An enclosed cupola on the roof offers breathtaking cityscapes, and the service here redefines Southern hospitality.

🍴 Eating

Charleston is one of America's finest eating cities, and there are enough fabulous restaurants here for a town three times its size. The 'classic' Charleston establishments stick to fancy seafood with a French flair, while many of the trendy up-and-comers are reinventing Southern cuisine with a focus on the area's copious local bounty, from oysters to heirloom rice to heritage pork.

★ Gaulart & Maliclet FRENCH **$**
(☑ 843-577-9797; www.fastandfrenchcharleston. com; 98 Broad St; breakfast $5-13, lunch & dinner mains $13-22; ☺ 8am-8pm Mon-Wed, to 10pm Thu-Sat) Ooh la la. Locals crowd around the shared tables at this tiny spot, known as 'Fast & French,' to nibble on Gallic cheeses and sausages, fondues or nightly specials ($21 to $24) that include bread, soup, a main dish and wine.

Xiao Bao Biscuit ASIAN **$**
(www.xiaobaobiscuit.com; 224 Rutledge Ave; lunch mains $13, dinner mains $14-18; ☺ 11:30am-2pm & 5:30-10pm Mon-Sat) Housed in a former gas station, with exposed brick walls and concrete floor, this casual but stylish eatery hits the hipster high marks. But the food? Now we're talking. The short but palate-kicking menu spotlights simple pan-Asian fare enhanced by local ingredients and spicy flavors. For something different and memorable, try the *okonomiyaki* – a Japanese cabbage pancake – with egg and bacon.

★ Tu FUSION **$$**
(www.tu-charleston.com; 430 Meeting St; small plates $12-16; ☺ 5:30-10pm Thu-Sun) From the food geniuses who brought us Xiao Bao Biscuit comes this fusion place where there are no phones, no spoons and seemingly no rules. The playful, strange menu includes items like guava, habanero and cheese ice, which arrives and simply blows your mind. It's the kind of place you don't even want to explain to people, because you can't.

★ **Edmund's Oast** PUB FOOD $$
(☎843-727-1145; www.edmundsoast.com; 1081 Morrison Dr; mains $14-29; ⊙4:30-10pm Mon-Thu, to 11pm Fri & Sat, 10am-10pm Sun; 🖘) Occupying a gutted former hardware store in gentrifying NoMo, Charleston's highest-brow brewpub got a fancy new executive chef, Bob Cook, in 2017. The new grub: Southern faves such as salt chicken skins, hanger steaks and hot-and-sour tilefish. The drink pairings: 64 taps (eight devoted to cocktails, meads and sherries, and a dozen proprietary craft beers, among other craft offerings). Pints are $6 to $9.

167 Raw SEAFOOD $$
(☎843-579-4997; www.167raw.com/charleston; 289 E Bay St; oysters each $2.75, mains $14-27; ⊙11am-10pm Mon-Sat) There are no reservations at this tiny hole-in-the-wall that unassumingly serves up the city's best seafood. People wait in lines down the block for the delicious lobster roll, and the tuna burger and sea-scallop po'boy are also off-the-charts toothsome. Oysters arrive fresh daily from Nantucket (where the restaurant runs its very own oyster farm), and the service is truly on point.

Fleet Landing SEAFOOD $$
(☎843-722-8100; www.fleetlanding.net; 186 Concord St; lunch mains $9-24, dinner $13-26; ⊙11am-3:30pm daily, 5-10pm Sun-Thu, 5-11pm Fri & Sat; 🖘) Come here for the perfect Charleston lunch: a river view, a cup of she-crab soup with a splash of sherry, and a big bowl of shrimp and grits. Housed in a former naval degaussing building on a pier, it's a convenient and scenic spot to enjoy fresh fish, a fried seafood platter or a burger after a morning of downtown exploring.

Ordinary SEAFOOD $$
(☎843-414-7060; www.eattheordinary.com; 544 King St; dishes $10-33; ⊙5-10:30pm Tue-Sun) Inside a cavernous 1927 bank building, this buzzy seafood hall and oyster bar feels like the best party in town. The menu is short, but the savory fare is prepared with finesse – from the oyster sliders to the lobster rolls to the nightly fish dishes.

★ **FIG** SOUTHERN US $$$
(☎843-805-5900; www.eatatfig.com; 232 Meeting St; mains $30-46; ⊙5-10:30pm Mon-Thu, to 11pm Fri & Sat; 🖘) 🖊 FIG is a longtime foodie favorite, and it's easy to see why: welcoming staff, efficient but unrushed service and top-notch, sustainably sourced nouvelle Southern fare from James Beard Award–winner Mike Lata. The six nightly changing dishes embrace what's fresh from the sea and local farms and mills. FIG stands for Food is Good. And the gourmets agree.

🍷 Drinking & Nightlife

Proof COCKTAIL BAR
(☎843-793-1422; www.charlestonproof.com; 437 King St; ⊙4pm-2am Mon-Fri, from 6pm Sat & Sun) It may be snug in here, but the cocktails ($10 to $13) sure are first class – the mixologist is some kind of visionary. Case in point: the 'knuckleball' has Old Grand-Dad, a spicy cola reduction, orange bitters and pickled boiled peanuts.

Edmund's Oast Brewing Co BREWERY
(☎843-718-3224; www.edmundsoast.com/brewing-co; 1505 King St Ext; ⊙11am-10pm) Edmund's Oast in NoMo has this new baby brewing cousin just down the street, set in a 20,000-sq-ft facility with 26 boozy beverages on tap and two hangover-prevention chambers (a wood-fired brick oven and a Polish smokehouse). Brews are ambitious and, at times, downright medieval: Domesday is brewed with yarrow, mugwort, lavender and marshmallow flower.

Revelry Brewery MICROBREWERY
(www.revelrybrewingco.com; 10 Conroy St; ⊙4-10pm Mon-Thu, noon-midnight Fri & Sat, noon-10pm Sun) Probably the hippest of the Northern Peninsula breweries. It's hard to beat knocking back a few artfully crafted cold ones on Revelry's fairy-lit and fire-pit-heated rooftop, which affords expansive views all the way to the cable-stayed Ravenel Bridge. The downstairs bar, seemingly owned by the brewery's black Lab, is a mere 5ft from the tanks.

🛍 Shopping

Shops of Historic Charleston Foundation GIFTS & SOUVENIRS
(☎843-724-8484; www.historiccharleston.org; 108 Meeting St; ⊙9am-6pm Mon-Sat, noon-5pm Sun) This place showcases jewelry, home furnishings and furniture inspired by the city's historic homes, much of which is based on Blue Canton porcelain.

Blue Bicycle Books BOOKS
(☎843-722-2666; www.bluebicyclebooks.com; 420 King St; ⊙10am-7:30pm Mon-Sat, 1-6pm Sun) Excellent new-and-used bookstore with a great selection on Southern history and culture.

ℹ Information

Charleston Visitor Center (☏843-724-7174; www.charlestoncvb.com; 375 Meeting St; ⊙8:30am-5:30pm Apr-Oct, to 5pm Nov-Mar) Find help with accommodations and tours or watch a half-hour video on Charleston history in this spacious renovated warehouse.

North Charleston Visitor Center (☏800-774-0006; www.charlestoncvb.com; 4975b Centre Point Dr; ⊙10am-5pm Mon-Sat, from 1pm Sun) Has brochures, maps and staff who can help you plan your trip.

ℹ Getting There & Around

The vast majority of travelers arrive in Charleston in their own vehicles, but other visitors get here via planes, trains and buses. Flights, cars and tours can be booked online at lonelyplanet.com/bookings.

Bicycle A great way to get around, with plenty of city bike-share stations, rental shops and racks.

Boat A ferry service makes four stops around Charleston Harbor.

Bus City buses cost $2 a ride, and there's also a free streetcar that makes loops from the visitor center.

Car & Motorcycle There are car-rental companies at the airport. Note that parking can be difficult downtown.

Taxi Ridesharing apps are usually cheaper and easier than calling or finding taxis.

Lowcountry

The southern half of the South Carolina coast is a tangle of islands cut off from the mainland by inlets and tidal marshes. Here, descendants of West African slaves known as the Gullah maintain small communities in the face of resort and golf-course development. The landscape ranges from tidy stretches of shimmery, oyster-gray sand to wild, moss-shrouded maritime forests.

The southernmost stretch of South Carolina's coast is popular with a mostly upscale set of golfers and B&B aficionados, but the area has quirky charms aplenty for everyone.

Charleston County Sea Islands

A dozen islands within an hour's drive of Charleston make up the Charleston County Sea Islands. Around 10 miles by road southeast of Charleston on the Mt Pleasant side, **Sullivan's Island** and **Isle of Palms** beckon day-trippers for sand-lounging and reveling

---

WORTH A TRIP

MCLEOD PLANTATION

Part of a visit to Charleston is reckoning with the large role that slavery played in the development of the city. A tour at the **McLeod Plantation** (☏843-795-4386; www.ccprc.com/1447/McLeod-Plantation-Historic-Site; 325 Country Club Dr; adult/child $15/6; ⊙9am-4pm Tue-Sun) on James Island lends keen insight into what the lives of enslaved people were like on an upper-middle-class plantation, where the planters were constantly trying to keep up with the Middletons, the Draytons and the Pinckneys. It's a crucial sight for understanding antebellum and Reconstruction Era South Carolina.

---

on blue-sky days. Around 4 miles in the other direction brings you to **James Island**, one of the most urban of Charleston's barrier sea islands. A further 9 miles south of Charleston, **Folly Beach** is good for a day of sun and sand. The other end of the island is popular with surfers.

Upscale rental homes, golf courses and the swanky Sanctuary resort mark **Kiawah Island**, 26 miles southwest of Charleston, where you'll find those lucky enough to stay here cruising on their bikes along one of the most gorgeous beaches in the South. Nearby **Edisto Island** (ed-is-tow) is a homespun family vacation spot without a single traffic light.

⊙ Sights

Kiawah Beachwater Park   BEACH
(www.ccprc.com; 8 Beachwalker Dr, Kiawah Island; parking $5-15; ⊙9am-8pm May-Sep, shorter hours rest of year) This idyllic stretch of sun-toasted sand at the southern end of Kiawah Island has been called one of the top 10 beaches in the USA and is the only publicly accessible beach on Kiawah. Take a bike – the compact sand is perfect for a ride along the 10-mile barrier island.

🛏 Sleeping & Eating

James Island County Park   CAMPGROUND $
(☏843-795-4386; www.ccprc.com; 871 Riverland Dr, James Island; tent sites from $33, 8-person cottages from $169; 🐾) A great budget option, this 643-acre park southwest of downtown Charleston has meadows, a marsh and a

THE SOUTH LOWCOUNTRY

DON'T MISS

FIREFLY DISTILLERY

The world's first hand-crafted sweet-tea-flavored vodka came from **Firefly Distillery** (☎843-557-1405; www.fireflyspirits.com; 6775 Bears Bluff Rd; ⊙11am-5pm Tue-Sat), tucked into the forest on Wadmalaw Island. Sampling this classic, which is made with tea grown on the nearby **Charleston Tea Plantation** (☎843-559-0383; www.charlestonteaplantation.com; 6617 Maybank Hwy; trolley tour adult/child under 13yr $14/6; ⊙10am-4pm Mon-Sat, from noon Sun), distilled four times and blended with sugarcane from Louisiana, is what brings most people to the door. Tastings are $6.

dog park. You can rent bikes ($10 per day) and kayaks ($5.50 per hour), go for a run or frolic with your pup. The park offers shuttle services to downtown and Folly Beach ($10). Reservations are highly recommended. There are 124 campsites and 10 marsh-adjacent rental cottages.

★**Bowens Island
Restaurant**   SEAFOOD $
(www.bowensisland.biz; 1870 Bowens Island Rd, Folly Island; mains $10-35; ⊙5-9:30pm Tue-Sat) Down a long dirt road through Lowcountry marshland near Folly Beach, this unpainted wooden shack is one of the South's most venerable seafood dives – grab an oyster knife and start shucking! Cool beer and friendly locals give the place its soul.

Obstinate Daughter   AMERICAN $$
(☎843-416-5020; www.theobstinatedaughter.com; 2063 Middle St, Sullivan's Island; pizzas $15-19, mains $20-31; ⊙11am-10pm Mon-Fri, from 10am Sat & Sun; ☑) Sullivan's Island wasn't on the region's culinary map till this place showed up and made serious waves. The chef-owner, who also received high praise for **Wild Olive** (☎843-737-4177; www.wildoliverestaurant.com; 2867 Maybank Hwy, Johns Island; pastas $13-22, mains $20-37; ⊙5:30-10pm Sun-Thu, to 11:30pm Fri & Sat, bar from 4pm; P), has demonstrated considerable range here, refocusing on light and playful plates of fresh veggies, pasta, seafood and unusual ingredients. Raw oysters are flown in from top locales, and vegetarians will leave exuberant.

ℹ Information

Kiawah Island Visitor Center (☎800-774-0006; www.charlestoncvb.com; 4475 Betsy Kerrison Pkwy; ⊙9am-3pm) Has maps, tourist info and helps with accommodations and tours in the Charleston area.

ℹ Getting There & Away

Charleston's barrier sea islands are all accessed via a series of byways and bridges from the city, though not always with a connection from one to another. You'll need to take the long way round if you want to go from Sullivan's Island to Kiawah or Edisto Islands, for example. Coming from the south, Edisto (via SC 174), Kiawah and Johns (via SC 17) can be accessed without going through Charleston. From the north coast, SC 17 also reaches Sullivan's and Isle of Palms without going through the city.

Beaufort & Hilton Head

On Port Royal Island, darling colonial Beaufort (byoo-furt) is the second-oldest city in South Carolina, and perhaps the nation's greatest educator on the turbulent post–Civil War period. In 2017 President Obama established four Reconstruction Era National Monuments within the county, and in pockets of the city and neighboring islands Gullah culture still thrives.

The streets of this fair city are lined with gorgeous antebellum homes, restored 18th-century mansions and twisting magnolias that drip with Spanish moss. Unsurprisingly, Beaufort is often used as a backdrop for Hollywood films, and is best explored either on foot or from the perch of a horse and buggy.

The riverfront downtown has plenty of linger-worthy cafes and galleries, and the Southern hospitality here is at its finest. Expect to be invited by perfect strangers to hop on a boat and drink beer at everybody's favorite sandbar in the middle of Port Royal Sound.

Across Port Royal Sound, tiny Hilton Head Island is South Carolina's largest barrier island and one of America's top golf spots. There are dozens of courses, many enclosed in posh private residential communities. The island was the first eco-planned destination in the USA. Founder Charles Fraser believed a resort should blend with nature, so subdued colors, strict zoning laws (no building over five stories high, signage must be low and lit from below) and a distinct lack of streetlights all characterize the environment here. But while summer traffic and miles of stoplights can stifle an appreciation of the beauty of the island, you can find some lush nature preserves, wide, white beaches hard-packed enough for bike riding, and a whole lot of dolphins.

◉ Sights

Parris Island Museum
MUSEUM

(☑843-228-2951; www.parrisislandmuseum.com; 111 Panama St; ⊙10am-4:30pm) FREE This fascinating museum covering Marine Corps history contains antique uniforms and weaponry, but is most engaging for its exhibits chronicling the grueling, intense and scary (that CS gas-chamber exercise!) 13-week Marine basic training, which takes place here and at a second facility in San Diego, California. It's far worse than in *An Officer and a Gentleman!*

Penn Center
MUSEUM

(☑843-838-2432; www.penncenter.com; 16 Penn Center Circle W, St Helena Island; $7; ⊙9am-4pm Tue-Sat) Once the home of one of the nation's first schools for freed slaves, the Penn Center has a small museum that covers Gullah culture and traces the history of Penn School. Two sites on the property became part of the National Reconstruction Era Site in 2017: Darrah Hall, the school building, and Brick Baptist Church, which was originally constructed by slaves who were not allowed to worship inside. Freed slaves took control of it in 1861.

Hunting Island State Park
STATE PARK

(☑843-838-2011; www.southcarolinaparks.com/huntingisland; 2555 Sea Island Pkwy; adult/child 6-15yr $5/3; ⊙park 6am-6pm, to 9pm Mar-Sep, visitor center 9am-5pm Mon-Fri, from 11am Sat & Sun, nature center 9am-5pm Tue-Sat, daily Jun-Aug) Lush and inviting Hunting Island State Park impresses visitors with acres of spooky maritime forest, tidal lagoons and a bone-white beach littered with seashells and the occasional shark tooth. The Vietnam War scenes from *Forrest Gump* were filmed in the marsh, a nature-lover's dream. **Campgrounds** (☑office 843-838-2011, reservations 866-345-7275; RV sites $24-45, cabins from $249; ⊙6am-9pm early Mar-early Nov, to 6pm rest of year) fill quickly in summer. Climb the **lighthouse** ($2) for sweeping coastal views. Much of the park was affected by Hurricanes Matthew and Irma, but has largely recovered.

🍽 Sleeping & Eating

City Loft Hotel
BOUTIQUE HOTEL **$$**

(☑843-379-5638; www.citylofthotel.com; 301 Carteret St; r/ste $169/209; P❋☎❋) The chic City Loft Hotel adds a refreshing dash of modern style to a town heavy on historic homes and stately oak trees. Enjoy flat-screen TVs in the bedroom and bathroom, artisan-tile showers and memory-foam beds. Other perks include a gym, complimentary bicycle use and an on-site coffee shop ($5 voucher included in rates).

Cuthbert House Inn
B&B **$$$**

(☑843-521-1315; www.cuthberthouseinn.com; 1203 Bay St; r $190-325; P❋☎) The most romantic of Beaufort's B&Bs, this sumptuously grand white-columned mansion is straight out of *Gone with the Wind*. Antique furnishings are found throughout, but monochromatic walls add a fresh, modern feel. Some rooms have a river view (three have fireplaces). On his march through the South in 1865, General William T Sherman slept at the house.

Lowcountry Produce
SOUTHERN US **$**

(☑843-322-1900; www.lowcountryproduce.com; 302 Carteret St; breakfast $9-15, sandwiches $10-18; ⊙8am-3pm; ☎) A fantastic cafe and market for picnic rations such as pies, housemade relishes, local cheeses and all kinds of Lowcountry-spun awesomeness (including a bizarre but wildly popular cream-cheese lasagna). Or eat in and indulge in an Oooey Gooey, a grilled pimento-cheese sandwich with bacon and garlic-pepper jelly (one hot mess!), or a tasty crab-cake sandwich with brussels-sprout slaw.

ℹ Information

Beaufort Tourist Information Center (☑843-525-8500; www.beaufortsc.org; 713 Craven St; ⊙9am-5pm Mon-Sat) Inside the Beaufort History Museum, offering maps, brochures and advice.

Myrtle Beach

The towering SkyWheel spins fantastically beside the sea in downtown Myrtle Beach, anchoring a 60-mile swath of sun-bleached excess known as the Grand Strand. This stretch of coastline is now infamously overdeveloped and littered with innumerable mini-golf courses, pancake houses, beach resorts and T-shirt shops – an alarming

FIREFLIES & SPANISH MOSS: CONGAREE NATIONAL PARK

Inky-black water, dyed with tannic acid leached from decaying plant matter. Bone-white cypress stumps like the femurs of long-dead giants. Spanish moss as dry and gray as witches' hair. **Congaree National Park** (☏803-776-4396; www.nps.gov/cong; 100 National Park Rd, Hopkins) protects the largest contiguous, old-growth bottomland forest in the eastern US, and there's nothing like canoeing through its unearthly swamp to make you feel like you've stepped into a Southern Gothic novel.

The park stretches over nearly 27,000 acres, offering excellent camping and ranger-led canoe trips and hikes.

Casual day-trippers can wander the 2.4-mile elevated boardwalk. Look carefully at the Blue Sky mural in the visitor center – the scene seems to change as you move. From mid-May through mid-June, the *Photinus carolinus*, a rare species of firefly, blink in unison, turning the forest floor into a twinkling light show. The phenomenon only occurs in a handful of spots around the world. Columbia-based **River Runner Outdoor Center** (☏803-771-0353; www.shopriverrunner.com; 905 Gervais St) can get you on the water.

The park is just a 30-minute drive from downtown Columbia.

departure from its beginnings as a laid-back summer retreat for working-class Southerners.

Love it or hate it, Myrtle Beach offers one all-American vacation. Enormous outlet malls, water parks and daiquiri bars compete for attention, bikini-clad teenagers play video games and eat hot dogs in smoky arcades, and Midwestern families roast like chickens on the white sand. North Myrtle Beach, actually a separate town, is slightly lower-key, with a thriving culture based on the 'shag' – a jitterbug-like dance invented here in the 1940s.

It isn't for nature lovers, but it's a rowdy good time and certainly a hit with the kiddos.

◉ Sights & Activities

SkyWheel AMUSEMENT PARK
(☏843-839-9200; www.myrtlebeachskywheel.com; 1110 N Ocean Blvd; adult/child 3-11yr $14/9; ⊙11am-midnight, varying shorter hours in low season) The 187ft-high SkyWheel overlooks the 1.2-mile coastal boardwalk. One ticket includes four revolutions in an enclosed glass gondola; the whole thing lasts about 10 to 15 minutes. At night the wheel is bewitching, with more than a million dazzling colored lights.

★ **Brookgreen Gardens** GARDENS
(☏843-235-6000; www.brookgreen.org; 1931 Brookgreen Garden Dr, Murrells Inlet; adult/child 4-12yr $18/10; ⊙9:30am-5pm) These magical gardens, 16 miles south of Myrtle Beach on Hwy 17S, are home to the largest collection of American sculpture in the country, set amid

more than 9000 acres of rice-plantation-turned-subtropical-garden paradise. Seasonal blooms are listed on the website.

🛏 Sleeping & Eating

Myrtle Beach State Park CAMPGROUND $
(☏843-238-5325; www.southcarolinaparks.com/myrtle-beach; 4401 S Kings Hwy; tent & RV sites from $32, cabins $156-250; P🐾) Sleep beneath the pines or rent a cabin, all just steps from the shore. During summer, cabins must be rented on a weekly basis, and there's a two-night minimum the rest of the year. Reserve months in advance.

The state park is 3 miles south of central Myrtle Beach and includes a nice beach, a fishing pier and swaths of protected maritime forest.

**Hampton Inn
Broadway at the Beach** HOTEL $$$
(☏843-916-0600; www.myrtlebroadway.hamptoninn.com; 1140 Celebrity Circle; r/ste from $249/389; ❄@🛜🏊) The bright, renovated rooms overlooking the lake and Broadway at the Beach are a great choice at this hotel. If you're traveling with preteens, you may feel more comfortable letting them roam the adjacent shops and attractions rather than the boardwalk, particularly at night.

Prosser's BBQ SOUTHERN US $$
(☏843-357-6146; www.prossersbbq.com; 3750 Hwy 17 Business, Murrells Inlet; buffet breakfast $8, lunch $11-12, dinner $14-16; ⊙6:30-10:30am & 11am-2pm daily, plus 4-8pm Tue-Sat) It's weird to come to Murrells Inlet's 'restaurant row' and not spring for seafood, but who are we

to judge? The gut-busting lunch buffet here is down-home delicious. It includes fried fish and chicken, sweet-potato souffle, mac 'n' cheese, green beans and vinegary pulled pork.

★ **Wicked Tuna**   SEAFOOD $$$
(☏843-651-9987; www.thewickedtuna.com; 4123 Hwy 17 Business, Murrells Inlet; mains $26-48, sandwiches $14-24; ⊙11am-10pm; 🛜) Murrells Inlet is full of kitschy seafooders and, at first glance, the Wicked Tuna looks no different. Guess again! You are in for a real treat at this trip-worthy spot overlooking the beautiful inlet – it employs six fishing boats that go out for three- to six-day stints and bring back upward of 600lb of fresh fish each.

🍷 **Drinking & Entertainment**

American Tap House   CRAFT BEER
(☏843-712-2301; www.americantaphouse.com; 1320 Celebrity Circle; ⊙11am-2am; 🛜) If you prefer your craft-beer experience to come supersized, you'll find 53 taps of national options (pints $5.50 to $9) at this chef-driven gastropub at Broadway at the Beach.

★ **Fat Harold's Beach Club**   DANCE
(☏843-249-5779; www.fatharolds.com; 212 Main St; ⊙4pm-2am Mon & Tue, from 11am Wed-Sun) Folks groove to doo-wop, old-time R&B and beach music at this North Myrtle institution, which calls itself 'Home of the Shag.' The dance, that is. Free shag lessons are offered at 7pm every Tuesday. On Monday they're $10 per person.

ℹ️ **Information**

Myrtle Beach Visitor Information (☏843-626-7444; www.visitmyrtlebeach.com; 1200 N Oak St; ⊙8:30am-5pm) Has maps and brochures.

ℹ️ **Getting There & Around**

The traffic coming and going on Hwy 17 Business/Kings Hwy can be infuriating. To avoid 'the Strand' altogether, stay on the Hwy 17 bypass, or take Hwy 31/Carolina Bays Pkwy, which parallels Hwy 17 between Hwy 501 and Hwy 9.

Myrtle Beach International Airport (☏843-448-1580; www.flymyrtlebeach.com; 1100 Jetport Rd) is located within the city limits, as is the **Greyhound station** (☏843-448-2472; www.greyhound.com; 511 7th Ave N) – the airport receives direct flights from more than 30 domestic destinations.

Greenville & the Upcountry

Cherokee Indians once roamed the state's mountain foothills, which they called the 'Great Blue Hills of God.' The region today is known as the Upcountry. Geographically, it's the spot where the Blue Ridge Mountains drop dramatically to meet the Piedmont.

The region is anchored by Greenville, home to one of the most photogenic downtowns in the South. The Reedy River twists through the city center, and its dramatic falls tumble beneath Main St at Falls Park (www.fallspark.com).

Falls Park's fabulous **Liberty Bridge** (www.fallspark.com/175/The-Liberty-Bridge; Falls Park on the Reedy) is a must-cross.

◉ **Sights & Activities**

★ **Table Rock State Park**   STATE PARK
(☏864-878-9813; www.southcarolinaparks.com; 158 Ellison Lane, Pickens; adult/child 6-15yr $5/3; ⊙7am-7pm Sun-Thu, to 9pm Fri & Sat, extended hours mid-May–early Nov) The Upcountry's marquee natural attraction is Table Rock Mountain, a 3124ft-high mountain with a striking granite face. The 7.2-mile round-trip hike to its summit is a popular local challenge. For overnight stays, there is the **Table Rock State Park Campground & Cabins** (campsites $16-21, cabins $155-181; ❄).

BMW Performance Center   SPORTS
(☏864-968-3000; www.bmwperformancecenter.com; 1155 Hwy 101 S, Greer; 1-/2-day school from $849/1699; ⊙8:30am-8pm Mon-Fri) Your need for speed is quenched at America's only BMW performance-driving academy. Delve into fast and furious behind-the-wheel experiences over the course of one- or two-day classes with various vehicles, including the high-performance M series, or drive a Mini in stunt-driving school – *The Italian Job* will have nothing on you.

🛏️ **Sleeping**

★ **Swamp Rabbit Inn**   B&B $$
(☏864-345-7990; www.swamprabbitinn.com; 1 Logan St; r $135-200; 🅿❄🛜) This fun six-room inn occupies a '50s-era former boarding house downtown. It feels like a hostel but features colorfully decked-out private rooms that are as cozy and quirky as any in the South. Wonderful common spaces include a modern guest kitchen and wooden patio with barbecue.

Westin Poinsett HOTEL $$$
(☑ 864-421-9700; www.westinpoinsettgreenville.
com; 120 S Main St; r $210-330; P❄@🐶📶)
This grand hotel, which originally opened
in 1925, is in the heart of downtown Green-
ville, just steps from the Reedy River Falls.
Past guests include Amelia Earhart, Cor-
nelius Vanderbilt and Bobby Kennedy. The
modern, comfortably furnished rooms have
high-end mattresses and recently renovated
bathrooms.

✕ Eating & Drinking

Stax Omega Diner & Bakery DINER $
(☑ 864-297-6639; www.staxs.net; 72 Orchard
Park Dr; breakfast $9-15, lunch & dinner $12-16;
☺ 6:30am-9pm; 🐶) Nobody quite does break-
fast excess like the USA, and this bustling
family-owned diner 4 miles east of down-
town Greenville is everything fantastic
about that. It's massive – capacity 500! – and
it does it all really well: omelets, pancakes,
French toast, eggs Benedict, scrambles – the
list goes on and on...and on...

Soby's SOUTHERN US $$
(☑ 864-232-7007; http://sobys.com; 207 S Main
St; mains $22-32; ☺ 5-9:30pm Mon-Thu, to
10:30pm Fri & Sat, 10am-1:30pm & 5-9pm Sun; 🐶)
Book yourself one of the intimate, brick-
walled banquettes at this downtown Greenville bastion of New Southern cuisine that
also caters to wine lovers (the 5000-bottle
list has been awarded a *Wine Spectator*
Award of Excellence 20 years running). The
oft-changing menu is steeped in the wares
of local farmers, foragers and ranchers.

Dark Corner Distillery DISTILLERY
(☑ 864-631-1144; www.darkcornerdistillery.com;
14 S Main St; ☺ noon-7pm Mon-Fri, from 11am Sat)
The Dark Corner is the nickname given to
the secretive upland corner of Greenville
County, which was famed for its bootlegging
and hardscrabble Scots-Irish residents. Tastings ($10) at this distillery include six spir-
its; don't miss the delectable butterscotch
whiskey or the spiced rum.

❶ Getting There & Away

**Greenville–Spartanburg International
Airport** (☑ 864-877-7426; www.gspairport.
com; 2000 GSP Dr, Greer) is 13 miles east of
the city, nearly halfway between Greenville and
Spartanburg.

The **Greyhound bus station** (☑ 864-235-
4741; www.greyhound.com; 9 Hendrix Dr) is also
out that way, 7 miles southeast of downtown.

The **Amtrak train station** (☑ 800-872-
7245; www.amtrak.com; 1120 W Washington
St) is more conveniently located, just west of
downtown.

TENNESSEE

Most states have one official state song. Tennessee has 10! And there's a reason for that:
Tennessee has music deep within its soul.
Here, the folk music of the Scots-Irish in
the eastern mountains combined with the
bluesy rhythms of the African Americans in
the western Delta to give birth to the modern
country music that makes Nashville famous.

The state's three geographic regions,
East, Middle and West Tennessee, are represented by the three stars on the Tennessee
flag. Each has its own unique beauty: the
heather-colored peaks of the Great Smoky
Mountains; the lush green valleys of the central plateau around Nashville; and the hot,
sultry lowlands near Memphis.

In Tennessee you can hike shady mountain trails in the morning, and by evening
whoop it up in a Nashville honky-tonk or on
the blues-infused sidewalks of Beale St.

❶ Information

Department of Tourist Development (☑ 615-
741-2159; www.tnvacation.com) Has welcome
centers at the state borders.
Tennessee State Parks (https://tnstateparks.
com) Check out this well-organized website for
camping, hiking and fishing info for Tennessee's more than 50 state parks.

Memphis

Memphis doesn't just attract tourists; it
draws pilgrims. Music-lovers lose themselves to the throb of blues guitar on Beale
St. Barbecue connoisseurs descend to stuff
themselves silly on smoky pulled pork and
dry-rubbed ribs. Elvis fanatics fly in to pay
their respects at Graceland. You could spend
days hopping from one museum or historic
site to another, stopping only for barbecue,
and leave happy.

Celebrating its bicentennial in 2019,
Memphis has long been marked by a certain baroque, ruined quality both sad and
beguiling. But the city these days feels re-
energized. Neighborhoods once downtrod-
den and abandoned – South Main, Bing-
hampton, Crosstown and others – are being

reinvented with kitschy boutiques, hipster lofts, daring restaurants, welcoming microbreweries and design-minded revamps of old buildings, all dripping with Memphis' wild river-town spirit. Poverty is still prevalent, and some neighborhoods are considered unsafe at night, but the vibe overall is one of optimism and local pride.

◉ Sights

The pedestrian-only stretch of Beale St is a 24-hour carnival zone, where you'll find deep-fried funnel cakes, to-go beer counters, and music, music, music. Locals don't hang out here much, except after Memphis Grizzlies basketball games at FedEx Forum, but visitors tend to get a kick out of it.

★ **National Civil Rights Museum** MUSEUM
(Map p382; ☑ 901-521-9699; www.civilrightsmuseum.org; 450 Mulberry St; adult/child 5-17yr $16/13; ◎ 9am-5pm Wed-Sun; ☑) Housed partly inside the Lorraine Motel, where Martin Luther King Jr was fatally shot on April 4, 1968, is the gut-wrenching National Civil Rights Museum. Its immersive and compelling exhibits chronicle the struggle for African American freedom and equality from the earliest days of slavery in America. Both Dr King's cultural contribution and his assassination serve as prisms for looking at the Civil Rights movement, its precursors and its continuing impact on American life.

★ **Graceland** HISTORIC BUILDING
(Map p380; ☑ 901-332-3322; www.graceland.com; 3717 Elvis Presley Blvd/US 51; house only adult/13-18yr/7-12yr $41/37/21, with airplanes $46/42/26, with Elvis Presley's Memphis $61/55/31, expanded tours adult/child under 7yr from $99/free; ◎ 9am-5pm Mon-Sat, to 4pm Sun Mar-Oct, shorter hours Nov-Feb; ☑) If you only make one stop in Memphis, it should be here: the sublimely kitschy, gloriously bizarre home of the King of Rock and Roll. Though born in Mississippi, Elvis Presley was a true son of Memphis, raised in the Lauderdale Courts public-housing projects, inspired by blues clubs on Beale St, and discovered at Sun Studio. In the spring of 1957, the already-famous 22-year-old spent $100,000 on a colonial-style mansion, named Graceland by its previous owners.

★ **Sun Studio** HISTORIC SITE
(Map p380; ☑ 901-521-0664; www.sunstudio.com; 706 Union Ave; adult/child 5-11yr $14/free; ◎ 10am-6pm) This dusty storefront is ground

zero for American rock and roll. Starting in the early 1950s, Sun's Sam Phillips recorded blues artists such as Howlin' Wolf, BB King and Ike Turner, followed by the rockabilly dynasty of Jerry Lee Lewis, Johnny Cash, Roy Orbison and, of course, the King himself (who started here in 1953). Tours last 45 minutes.

★ **Stax Museum of American Soul Music** MUSEUM
(Map p380; ☑ 901-942-7685; www.staxmuseum.com; 926 E McLemore Ave; adult/child 9-12yr $13/10; ◎ 10am-5pm Tue-Sun; ☑) Wanna get funky? Head directly to Soulsville, USA, where this 17,000-sq-ft museum sits on the site of the old Stax recording studio. This venerable spot was soul music's epicenter in the 1960s, when Otis Redding, Booker T and the MGs, and Wilson Pickett recorded here.

Memphis Rock 'n' Soul Museum MUSEUM
(Map p382; ☑ 901-205-2526; www.memphisrocknsoul.org; 191 Beale St; adult/child 5-17yr $13/10; ◎ 9:30am-7pm) This Smithsonian museum, next to FedEx Forum, examines how African American and white music mingled in the Mississippi Delta to create the modern rock and soul sound.

Memphis Pyramid LANDMARK
(Map p380; ☑ 901-291-8200; https://stores.basspro.com; 1 Bass Pro Dr; Sky High $10; ◎ store 8am-10pm Mon-Sat, to 7pm Sun, Sky High 9am-10pm Mon-Sat, to 7pm Sun; ☑) Don't laugh, but the most striking building in Memphis, a 32-story pyramid completed in 1991, is now home to an enormous Bass Pro Shop. Even if

Greater Memphis

THE SOUTH MEMPHIS

Greater Memphis

you don't need fishing gear or hiking boots, pop in to see the artificial swamp and the aquariums, or test your skill at the shooting range. Most fun is the Sky High, a central clear-walled elevator rising 28 stories to a glass observation deck with big views of downtown and the river.

Slave Haven Underground Railroad Museum/Burkle Estate   MUSEUM

(Map p380; ☑901-527-3427; www.slavehaven undergroundrailroadmuseum.org; 826 N 2nd St; adult/child 4-17yr $12/11; ☉10am-4pm Mon-Sat, to 5pm Jun-Aug; P) This unimposing clapboard house is thought to have been a way station for runaway slaves on the Underground Railroad, complete with trapdoors, cellar entry and cubbyholes. Guided tours share details about the Railroad and include a chilling stop in the dark cellar, which would have served as a final hideout before a dash to a boat on the Mississippi River.

Full Gospel Tabernacle Church   CHURCH

(787 Hale Rd; ☉services 11am) On Sunday, put on your 'smell goods' and head to services in South Memphis, where soul-music legend turned reverend Al Green presides over a powerful choir. Visitors are welcome; it's a fascinating cultural experience. Services may last several hours, so sit in the back if you're not sure you can stay the entire time.

🏃 Activities

★ Shelby Farms Park   OUTDOORS

(☑901-222-7275; www.shelbyfarmspark.org; 6903 Great View Dr N; ☉dawn-dusk; ♿) With a children's playground, a zipline and fishing, as well as buffalo (yes, really) roaming their own 50-acre range, 4500-acre Shelby Farms is a wonderful multipurpose urban park. It's crisscrossed by 40 miles of hiking and biking trails (two-hour rentals from $28), and the 10.65-mile Shelby Farms green-line path connects the park with midtown Memphis.

Big River Crossing   OUTDOORS

(Map p380; www.bigrivercrossing.com; ☉6am-10pm) FREE In 2016 Memphis turned its historic Mississippi-traversing Harahan Bridge, out of service since 1949, into the country's longest active rail/bicycle/pedestrian bridge. Together with the Delta Regional River Park and Big River Trail, Big River Crossing makes up a 10-mile multi-modal corridor that connects the main streets of Memphis and West Memphis (AR). It's a great spot for a run, walk or cycle.

There's a light show along the span on the hour from sunset until 10pm.

🎊 Festivals & Events

Peabody Ducks   PARADE

(Map p382; www.peabodymemphis.com; 149 Union Ave; ☉11am & 5pm; ♿) FREE A tradition dating from the 1930s begins every day at 11am sharp when five ducks file from the Peabody Hotel's gilded elevator, waddle across the red-carpeted lobby, and ensconce themselves in the marble lobby fountain for a day of happy splashing. The ducks make the reverse march at 5pm, when they retire to their penthouse accompanied by their red-coated Duckmaster.

Elvis Week   CULTURAL

(☑901-332-3322, 800-238-2000; www.graceland. com/elvisweek; Graceland, Elvis Presley Blvd; ☉mid-Aug) The King's passing and his life are celebrated across Memphis during Elvis Week, when tens of thousands of shiny-eyed pilgrims descend for nine days of festivities. *This* is Weird America. Attend a *Viva Las Vegas* or *Aloha From Hawaii* screening, a dance party, Elvis discussion panels, and an Elvis gospel brunch.

Beale Street Music Festival   MUSIC

(www.memphisinmay.org; Tom Lee Park; 1/3-day passes $55/$115; ☉1st weekend May) You've heard of Coachella, New Orleans Jazz Fest and Bonnaroo (p394), but Memphis' Beale Street Music Festival gets very little attention, despite the fact that it offers one of the country's best lineups of old-school blues masters, up-and-coming rockers, and gloriously past-their-prime pop and hip-hop artists.

🛏 Sleeping

Graceland RV Park & Campground   CAMPGROUND $

(Map p380; ☑901-396-7125; www.graceland.com/rv-park-campground; 3691 Elvis Presley Blvd; tent sites/cabins from $25/52; P♿📶) Keep Lisa Marie in business when you camp out or sleep in the no-frills log cabins (with shared bathrooms) next to Graceland. Pool open June through September.

Talbot Heirs   GUESTHOUSE $$

(Map p382; ☑901-527-9772; www.talbotheirs. com; 99 S 2nd St; ste $170-225; P❄@🛜) Inconspicuously located on the 2nd floor of a busy downtown street, this unique, cheerful guesthouse is one of Memphis' best-kept secrets. Spacious suites, all with recently modernized bathrooms, are more like hip studio apartments than hotel rooms, with Asian rugs, funky local artwork and kitchens stocked with (included!) snacks.

Peabody Hotel   HOTEL $$

(Map p382; ☑901-529-4000; www.peabodymem phis.com; 149 Union Ave; r/ste from $225/629; P❄🛜📶♿) Memphis' most storied hotel

Memphis

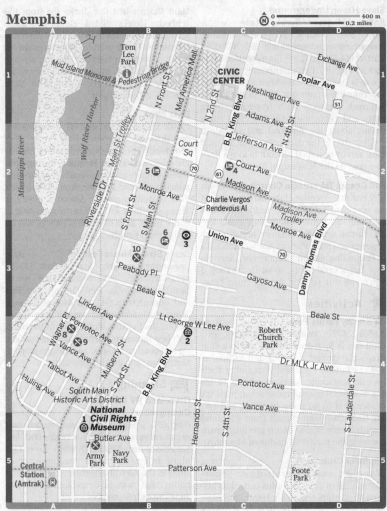

THE SOUTH MEMPHIS

Memphis

◉ Top Sights
1 National Civil Rights Museum............A5

◉ Sights
2 Memphis Rock 'n' Soul Museum.........B4
3 Peabody Ducks...........................B3

🛏 Sleeping
4 Hotel Indigo Memphis Downtown......C2
5 Hu. Hotel...................................B2
  Peabody Hotel............................(see 3)

6 Talbot Heirs...............................B3

✕ Eating
7 Central BBQ................................A5
8 Gray Canary................................A4
9 Gus's World Famous Fried Chicken.....A4
10 Majestic Grille...........................B3

◉ Drinking & Nightlife
  Old Dominick Distillery.................(see 8)

has been catering to a who's who of Southern gentry since the 1860s. The current incarnation, a 13-story Renaissance Revival–style building, dates to the 1920s and remains a social center, with a spa, shops, restaurants, an atmospheric lobby bar and 464 guest rooms in soothing turquoise tones.

Hotel Indigo Memphis Downtown
HOTEL $$
(Map p382; 901-527-2215; www.ihg.com; 22 N BB King Blvd; r $163-180; P@🛜⚡) The brand-new Indigo gives a nod to the Memphis music industry with mid-century style. From the vintage radios in the lobby to the wall-size photos of microphones and musical accoutrements, the hotel exudes an energizing sense of fun. Three floors overlook the hip central pool.

Hu. Hotel
BOUTIQUE HOTEL $$$
(Map p382; 901-333-1200; www.huhotelmemphis.com; 79 Madison Ave; r/ste from $249/349; P❄@🛜⚡⚡) Formerly the Madison, this sleek treat offers swanky but inviting boutique sleeps. Modern, stylish rooms have nice touches like high ceilings and private bars. The rooftop bar is one of the best places in town to watch a sunset. Check in at the lobby coffee shop.

★ James Lee House
B&B $$$
(Map p380; 901-359-6750; www.jamesleehouse.com; 690 Adams Ave; r $250-450; P❄@🛜) Dating in parts to 1848 and 1872, this exquisite Victorian mansion in the city's historic Victorian Village at the edge of downtown is one of Memphis' most refined sleeps. The building sat abandoned for 56 years before it underwent a glorious $2-million renovation guided by the owner's keen eye for detail and design.

Guest House at Graceland
BOUTIQUE HOTEL $$$
(Map p380; 901-443-3000, 800-238-2000; www.guesthousegraceland.com; 3600 Elvis Presley Blvd; r/ste from $229/379; P❄@🛜⚡⚡) Intimate in name only, the Guest House, Graceland's new flagship, is a 450-room hunk of burning hotel. Stylish slate-gray standard rooms are spacious, with Dreamcatcher beds, three-sided display clocks, work-station desks and 55in flat-screen TVs. Suites, whose designs were coordinated by Priscilla Presley, all evoke themes from Elvis' life (one features a red-draped TV on the ceiling above the bed!).

✗ Eating

Locals come to blows over which of the city's chopped-pork sandwiches or dry-rubbed ribs are the best. Barbecue joints are scattered across the city; the ugliest exteriors often yield the tastiest goods. Hip young locals head to the South Main Historic Arts District, Midtown's Cooper-Young or Overton Square neighborhoods, all fashionable dining enclaves.

★ Central BBQ
BARBECUE $
(Map p382; 901-672-7760; www.cbqmemphis.com; 147 E Butler Ave; plates $11-28, sandwiches from $5; 11am-9pm) The downtown location of this iconic Memphis barbecue joint is the perfect side dish to an afternoon at the National Civil Rights Museum (p379). The transcendent pulled pork – almost always voted the city's best – can and should be doused in a number of sauces so good you'll want to drink them by the pint.

Crosstown Concourse
FOOD HALL $
(Map p380; https://crosstownconcourse.com; 1350 Concourse Ave; hours vary) It's not your typical food hall – you won't find rows of kiosks – but there's an international array of casual eateries in the city's newest hot spot. Built in 1927 as a massive retail and distribution center for Sears, and then sitting vacant for two decades, Crosstown Concourse now holds a mix of indie restaurants, shops and businesses, and even a school.

Gus's World Famous Fried Chicken
FAST FOOD $
(Map p382; 901-527-4877; www.gusfriedchicken.com; 310 S Front St; plates $7-12; 11am-9pm Sun-Thu, to 10pm Fri & Sat) Fried-chicken connoisseurs across the globe twitch in their sleep as they dream about the gossamer-light offerings at this downtown concrete bunker, with a fun, neon-lit interior and a vintage jukebox. On busy nights waits can top an hour.

Imagine Vegan Cafe
VEGAN $
(Map p380; 901-654-3455; www.imaginevegancafe.com; 2158 Young Ave; most mains $6-14; 11am-9pm; 🛜♿) Vegans and veggies face an uphill battle in Memphis (hell, all over the South...), but this inventive Cooper-Young cafe swims alone in a sea of pulled pork and fried chicken, pulling off all the iconic Southern staples without even changing their names (don't worry – everything is vegan!).

THE SOUTH MEMPHIS

Bar DKDC

INTERNATIONAL $

(Map p380; ☑901-272-0830; www.bardkdc.com; 964 S Cooper St; dishes $8-14; ☺5pm-3am) Cheap and flavorful – and at times global – street food is the calling at this ever-evolving Cooper-Young staple, which serves up everything from *muffulettas* (classic New Orleans sandwiches) to Vietnamese *banh mi* rolls to Thai chicken dumplings. The space has eclectic decor, a chalkboard wine and beer list, and friendly bartenders.

★ Gray Canary

SEAFOOD $$

(Map p382; ☑901-249-2932; www.thegraycanary. com; 301 S Front St; small plates $6-18, mains $24-56; ☺5-10pm Tue-Thu, to 11pm Fri & Sat, 3-9pm Sun) Served in a simmering hug of chili-garlic butter, spinach and Parmesan, the grilled oysters are an oh-so-delicious introduction to this newcomer, where tip-top service, chic digs and simple but exquisite seafood dishes merge for a perfect evening out. The front bar ensures a festive mood with winning craft cocktails and more than two dozen wines by the glass.

Alchemy

TAPAS $$

(Map p380; ☑901-726-4444; www.alchemymem phis.com; 940 S Cooper St; tapas $7-18, mains $17-21; ☺4pm-2am Mon, Fri & Sat, to 11pm Tue-Thu, 10:30am-2:30pm & 4-10pm Sun) A flash spot in the Cooper-Young district, serving tasty Southern tapas like truffled deviled eggs with smoked salmon, shrimp and grits with smoked Gouda and tasso-ham gravy, and poached-pear salad with candied pecans and blue cheese. The kitchen stays open until midnight on weekends. Good selection of cocktails, bourbons and local beers, too, at the well-run bar.

Hog & Hominy

SOUTHERN, ITALIAN $$

(☑901-207-7396; www.hogandhominy.com; 707 W Brookhaven Circle; pizza $14-17; ☺11am-2pm & 5-10pm Mon-Wed, to midnight Thu-Sat, 11am-11pm Sun; 🐾) The chef-driven, Southern-rooted Italian at this Brookhaven Circle hot spot has grabbed the nation's attention, winning best new this and best new that from publications ranging from *GQ* to *Food & Wine* since it opened in 2011. Small plates and perfect brick-oven pizza are the mainstays, along with seasonal cocktails, craft beers and bocce.

Majestic Grille

EUROPEAN $$$

(Map p382; ☑901-522-8555; www.majesticgrille. com; 145 S Main St; mains lunch $8-36, dinner $12-51; ☺11am-10pm Mon-Thu, to 10pm Fri, 11am-2:30pm & 4-11pm Sat, 10am-2pm & 4-9pm Sun; 🐾) Set in an old silent-movie theater near Beale St, with pre-talkie black-and-whites strobing in the handsome dark-wood dining room, Majestic serves classic continental fare, from roasted half chickens to seared tuna and grilled pork tenderloin, and four varieties of hand-cut filet mignon.

Sweet Grass

SOUTHERN US $$$

(Map p380; ☑901-278-0278; www.sweetgrass memphis.com; 937 S Cooper St; small plates $14-23, mains $25-41; ☺5-9pm Mon-Thu, to 11pm Sat, 10:30am-2pm & 5-11pm Sun; 🐾) Contemporary Lowcountry cuisine (the seafood-heavy cooking of the South Carolina and Georgia coasts) wins rave reviews at this casual Midtown restaurant, split between a more rambunctious bar side called **Next Door** (go for the fried-egg sandwich!) and a more refined bistro side with a more sophisticated menu, a new raw bar and some unforgettable shrimp and grits.

🍷 Drinking & Entertainment

Beale St is party central but caters nearly 100% to tourists. The East Memphis neighborhoods of Cooper-Young and Overton Square are where locals go, and these offer the best concentration of hip bars and restaurants. Both are about 4 miles east of downtown. Last call is 3am. The city's first distillery, **Old Dominick** (Map p382; ☑901-260-1250; www.olddominick.com; 305 S Front St; tours $12; ☺noon-7pm Thu, to 8pm Fri & Sat, to 5pm Sun), opened in 2017.

★ Loflin Yard

BEER GARDEN

(Map p380; ☑901-290-1140; www.loflinyard.com; 7 W Carolina Ave; ☺4-11pm Wed & Thu, to 1am Fri, 11:30am-1am Sat, 11:30am-10pm Sun; 🐾) A massive, countrified adult-play oasis in downtown Memphis, this buzzy spot sits on nearly an acre of junkyard-aesthetic beer garden anchored by the old Loflin Safe & Lock Co and wrapping around the trickling canal remains of Gayoso Bayou. Besides the space itself, the seasonal and oak-barrel-aged cocktails steal the show, though the mostly smoked offerings (chicken wings, brisket) compete.

★ Wiseacre Brewing Co

MICROBREWERY

(Map p380; www.wiseacrebrew.com; 2783 Broad Ave; ☺4-10pm Mon-Thu, 1-10pm Fri & Sat; 🐾) A favorite Memphis taproom, Wiseacre is in the warehouse district of Binghampton, 5 miles east of downtown. Sample year-round and seasonal craft brews on the deck, which features a wraparound porch hugging two enormous, near-100-year-old concrete wheat silos, and swarms with people and pets.

Young Avenue Deli   LIVE MUSIC
(Map p380; ☑901-278-0034; www.youngave-nuedeli.com; 2119 Young Ave; ◎11am-3am; 🛜) This Midtown favorite has food, pool and occasional live music that caters to a laid-back young crowd hyped up on 36 taps of draft craft and another 130 can and bottle options.

⭐ **Wild Bill's**   BLUES
(Map p380; www.wildbillsmemphis.com; 1580 Vollintine Ave; ◎5-11pm Thu, 8pm-3am Fri & Sat, 4pm-midnight Sun) Don't even think of showing up at this gritty, hole-in-the-wall juke joint before midnight. Order a 40oz beer and a basket of wings, then sit back to watch some of the greatest blues acts in Memphis (from 11pm Friday and Saturday only). Expect some stares from the locals; it's worth it for the kick-ass, ultra-authentic jams.

ℹ Information

Memphis Visitor Center (Map p380; ☑888-633-9099; www.memphistravel.com; 3205 Elvis Presley Blvd; ◎9am-6pm Apr-Sep, to 5pm Oct-Mar) City information center near the exit for Graceland.

Tennessee State Visitor Center (Map p382; ☑901-543-6757; www.tnvacation.com; 119 N Riverside Dr; ◎7am-11pm) Brochures for the whole state. Near Mud Island.

ℹ Getting There & Around

Memphis International Airport (MEM; Map p380; ☑901-922-8000; www.flymemphis.com; 2491 Winchester Rd; 🛜) is around 10.5 miles southeast of Beale St via I-55; taxis to downtown cost between $23 and $25. Rideshare options are also available. The **Memphis Area Transit Authority** (MATA; Map p380; www.matatransit.com; 444 N Main St; fares $1.75) operates local buses; buses 2 and 4 go to the Airways Transit Center, where you can pick up the airport shuttle bus. The shuttle-bus stop is near Terminal C.

The station serving **Greyhound** (Map p380; ☑901-395-8770; www.greyhound.com; 3033 Airways Blvd; 🛜) and **Megabus** (Map p380; https://us.megabus.com; 3033 Airways Blvd; 🛜) is located at MATA's Airways Transit Center near Memphis International Airport. The **Amtrak Central Station** (www.amtrak.com; 545 S Main St) is right downtown.

Nashville

Nashville is on a roll that just won't stop. Country-music stars are slapping their names on brand-new honky-tonks. Boutique hotels seem to open monthly. Bachelors and bachelorettes are arriving in hordes to party. And acclaimed chefs are going far beyond the meat-and-three, though biscuits and hot chicken are doing just fine.

But don't fret about all the change. For country fans and wannabe songwriters all over the world, a trip to Nashville is still the ultimate pilgrimage. Since the 1920s the city has been attracting musicians who have taken the country genre from the 'hillbilly music' of the early 20th century to the slick 'Nashville sound' of the 1960s to the punk-tinged alt-country of the 1990s to the heartfelt indie troubadours of today. Nashville's musical attractions range from the Country Music Hall of Fame to the revered Grand Ole Opry to Jack White's niche record label.

◎ Sights

Nashville sits on a rise beside the Cumberland River, with the state capitol situated at the highest point. The city's most engaging museums are downtown, but you'll find cultural attractions aplenty in and around the universities. Further afield, plantations, battlefields and forts draw Civil War enthusiasts and history fans. The city teems with inviting parks. Several are connected by paved greenways. South of downtown, the zoo and science center are nice distractions for the kids.

◎ Downtown & the Gulch

Lower Broadway is downtown's country heart, thumping with shops, restaurants and honky-tonks. South of Lower Broadway is **SoBro**, revitalized by the Music City Center and the Country Music Hall of Fame. **Printers Alley**, just west of 2nd Ave N, is a narrow cobblestoned lane known for its nightlife. Along the Cumberland River, **Riverfront Park** and, across the pedestrian bridge, **Cumberland Park** are landscaped promenades, home to a greenway, a dog park and a new amphitheater. **The Gulch**, once industrial, has gone glossy with hip restaurants and upscale shops, while microbreweries cluster in the **Brewery District**.

Nashville

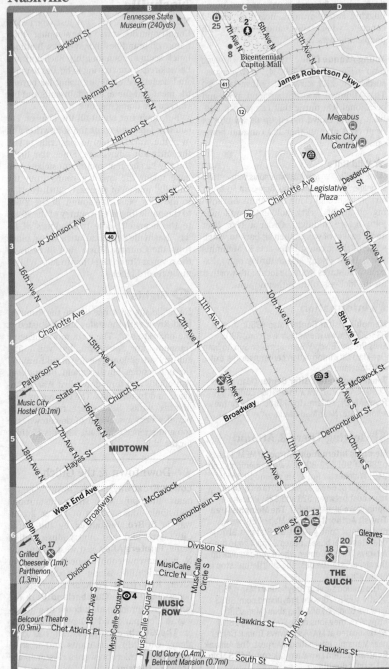

THE SOUTH NASHVILLE

Tennessee State Museum (240yds)

Jackson St

Herman St

10th Ave N

Harrison St

25

7th Ave N

2

6th Ave N

8

Bicentennial Capitol Mall

5th Ave N

James Robertson Pkwy

41

12

Megabus

Music City Central

Gay St

7

Legislative Plaza

Charlotte Ave

Deaderick St

Union St

70

Jo Johnson Ave

40

16th Ave N

Charlotte Ave

15th Ave N

11th Ave N

12th Ave N

10th Ave N

7th Ave N

6th Ave N

8th Ave N

Patterson St

State St

16th Ave N

Church St

12th Ave N

15

Broadway

3

9th Ave S

McGavock St

Music City Hostel (0.1mi)

17th Ave N

Hayes St

18th Ave N

MIDTOWN

12th Ave S

11th Ave S

Demonbreun St

10th Ave S

West End Ave

Broadway

McGavock

Demonbreun St

Pine St

10

13

27

Gleaves St

18

20

THE GULCH

19th Ave S

17

Grilled Cheeserie (1mi); Parthenon (1.3mi)

Division St

Division St

MusiCalle Circle N

MusiCalle Circle S

MusiCalle Square W

MusiCalle Square E

4

MUSIC ROW

Hawkins St

12th Ave S

Belcourt Theatre (0.9mi)

18th Ave S

Chet Atkins Pl

Old Glory (0.4mi); Belmont Mansion (0.7mi)

South St

Hawkins St

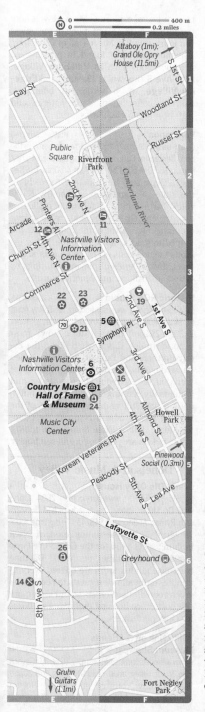

Nashville

◎ Top Sights

1 Country Music Hall of Fame & Museum	E4

◎ Sights

2 Bicentennial Capitol Mall	C1
3 Frist Center for the Visual Arts	D4
4 Historic RCA Studio B	B7
5 Johnny Cash Museum & Store	F4
6 Music City Walk of Fame Park	E4
7 Tennessee State Capitol	D2

⚙ Activities, Courses & Tours

8 NashTrash	C1

⌂ Sleeping

9 21c Museum Hotel	E2
10 404	D6
11 Nashville Downtown Hostel	F2
12 Noelle	E3
13 Thompson Nashville	D6

⊗ Eating

14 Arnold's	E6
15 Chauhan Ale & Masala House	C4
16 Etch	F4
17 Hattie B's	A6
18 Otaku Ramen	D6

⊕ Drinking & Nightlife

19 Acme Feed & Seed	F3
20 Barista Parlor	D6

⊕ Entertainment

21 Robert's Western World	E4
22 Ryman Auditorium	E3
Station Inn	(see 10)
23 Tootsie's Orchid Lounge	E3

ⓐ Shopping

24 Hatch Show Print	E4
25 Nashville Farmers Market	C1
26 Third Man Records	E6
27 Two Old Hippies	D6

★ **Country Music
Hall of Fame & Museum** MUSEUM
(www.countrymusichalloffame.org; 222 5th Ave S; adult/child $26/16, with audio tour $28/19, with Studio B 1hr tour $41/31; ⏱ 9am-5pm) Fresh off its 50th anniversary in 2017, this monumental museum, reflecting the near-biblical importance of country music to Nashville's soul, is a must-see whether you're a country music fan or not. Gaze at Carl Perkins' blue suede shoes, Elvis' gold Cadillac (actually white) and gold piano (actually gold), and Hank Williams' Western-cut suit with musical note appliqués.

Johnny Cash Museum & Store MUSEUM
(www.johnnycashmuseum.com; 119 3rd Ave S; adult/child $22/18; ⏱9am-7pm) Nashville's museum dedicated to 'The Man in Black' is smallish but houses the most comprehensive collection of Johnny Cash artifacts and memorabilia in the world, officially endorsed by the Cash family.

Frist Center for the Visual Arts GALLERY
(www.fristartmuseum.org; 919 Broadway; adult/senior/child $15/10/free, military discounts available; ⏱10am-5:30pm Mon-Wed & Sat, to 9pm Thu & Fri, 1-5:30pm Sun; P♿) A top-notch post office turned art museum and complex, hosting traveling exhibitions of everything from American folk art to Picasso, and as off-the-wall as auto shows and fashion displays.

Tennessee State Museum MUSEUM
(www.tnmuseum.org; 1000 Rosa L Parks Blvd, Bicentennial Mall; ⏱10am-5pm Tue, Wed, Fri & Sat, to 8pm Thu, 1-5pm Sun; ♿) FREE This engaging museum, which moved into spiffy new digs in 2018, offers a worthy, balanced look at the state's past, with Native American handicrafts, interactive exhibits and quirky historical artifacts such as President Andrew Jackson's inaugural hat and a dress worn by First Lady Sarah Childress Polk. There's also a hands-on Children's Gallery and space for changing exhibits.

Tennessee State Capitol HISTORIC BUILDING
(☎615-741-0830; www.capitol.tn.gov; Charlotte Ave; ⏱tours 9am-3pm Mon-Fri) FREE This 1845-59 Greek Revival building was built from local limestone and marble by slaves and prison inmates working alongside European artisans. Around the back, steep stairs lead down to the **Bicentennial Capitol Mall** (☎615-741-5280; 600 James Robertson Parkway) FREE, whose outdoor walls are covered with historical facts about Tennessee's history, and the wonderful daily **Farmers Market** (☎615-880-2001; www.nashvillefarmersmarket. org; 900 Rosa L Parks Blvd; ⏱8am-6pm Sun-Thu, to 8pm Fri & Sat except farm sheds).

◉ Midtown, Music Row & 12South

This area is anchored by Belmont and Vanderbilt Universities. Centennial Park, home to the Parthenon, and the 1853 **Belmont Mansion** (☎615-460-5459; www.belmontmansion.com; 1900 Belmont Blvd, Hillsboro; adult/youth 13-18yr/child 6-12yr $15/7/5; ⏱10am-4pm Mon-Sat, from 11am Sun; P) are top picks for an hour or two of exploring. Music Row is here too, although there's not much to see unless you join a Country Music Hall of Fame tour. The most action is found in pocket-sized neighborhoods such as **Hillsboro Village**, **12th Ave S** (known as 12South) and **Edgehill Village**, which bustle with boutiques, bakeries, coffee shops, indie eateries and craft beer and cocktail bars.

Parthenon HISTORIC BUILDING
(www.nashville.gov/parks-and-recreation/parthenon; Centennial Park, West End; adult/child 4-17yr/senior $6.50/4.50/4.50; ⏱9am-4:30pm Tue-Sat, from 12:30pm Sun) Built in 1897 to celebrate the state of Tennessee's centenary, Nashville's Parthenon is a full-scale replica of the Ancient Greece original, with a jaw-dropping huge statue of the goddess Athena draped in gold as its centerpiece. Other exhibits include casts of the pediments' sculptures, and galleries displaying paintings by 19th- and 20th-century American artists.

Historic RCA Studio B LANDMARK
(☎615-416-2001; www.studiob.org; 1611 Roy Acuff Pl, Music Row; tours adult/child $41/31; ⏱tours 10:30am-2:30pm) One of Music Row's most historic studios, this is where Elvis, the Everly Brothers and Dolly Parton all recorded numerous hits. The latter did a little more than that, once arriving late to a session and accidentally running her car into the building – a scar still visible today. Tours of the Historic RCA Studio B begin at the Country Music Hall of Fame & Museum (p387), where tickets are purchased, and run hourly.

◉ Donelson & Music Valley

Grand Ole Opry House MUSEUM
(☎615-871-6779; www.opry.com; 2804 Opryland Dr, Music Valley; tours adult/child $33/28, with Ryman Auditorium $48/43; ⏱daytime tours 9am-4pm) This unassuming modern brick building seats 4400 for the Grand Ole Opry (p392) multiple times per week. Daytime backstage guided tours are offered every 15 minutes daily, allowing guests to peek in the green rooms, stand on stage and see an onsite post office housing exclusive mailboxes for Opry performers.

Willie Nelson & Friends Museum Showcase MUSEUM
(www.willienelsonmuseum.com; 2613 McGavock Pike, Music Valley; adult/child $10/free; ⏱8:30am-9pm) 'Outlaw country' star Willie Nelson sold all his worldly goods to pay off a $16.7

million tax debt in the early 1990s. You can see them at this quirky museum, not far from the Grand Ole Opry.

🖝 Tours

★ NashTrash
BUS

(☎ 615-226-7300; www.nashtrash.com; 900 Rosa L Parks Blvd; tours $35-38) The big-haired 'Jugg Sisters' lead a campy frolic through the risqué side of Nashville history, while guests sip BYO booze on the big pink bus. Book ahead as tours can sell out weeks in advance. Meet the bus at the southeast end of the Nashville Farmers Market.

Joyride
SHUTTLE

(☎ 615-285-9835; www.joyrideus.com/nashville; complimentary shuttle but tips accepted, tours from $45) Tricked-out golf carts offer complimentary point-to-point shuttle service across Nashville. Rides are free, but drivers make their money on tips. For a fee the service also offers sightseeing tours, brewery tours and a bar golf crawl.

Tommy's Tours
BUS

(☎ 615-335-2863; www.tommystours.com; tours $45) Wisecracking local Tommy Garmon leads highly entertaining three-hour tours of country-music sights. Cash or check only.

✨ Festivals & Events

CMA Music Festival
MUSIC

(www.cmafest.com; ⊘ Jun) This four-day country-music extravaganza draws tens of thousands of fans to town.

Tennessee State Fair
FAIR

(☎ 615-800-3675; www.tnstatefair.org; 500 Wedgewood Ave, Wedgewood-Houston; ⊘ early Sep) Held yearly since 1869, the Tennessee State Fair is a classic American tradition to celebrate the harvest. Kids spend all year raising animals and perfecting their crafting skills to be judged in the many competitions. Spectators can enjoy pig races, mule-pulls, cake bake-offs and fun games – Hula-Hoop competition anyone? There are nightly concerts, carnival rides and plenty of fried food.

🛏 Sleeping

🛏 Downtown & the Gulch

★ Nashville Downtown Hostel
HOSTEL $

(☎ 615-497-1208; www.nashvilledowntownhostel.com; 177 1st Ave N; dm $32-45, r $100-250; P) Well located, only a block from Lower Broad-

---

WORTH A TRIP

FRANKLIN

The town of Franklin, 17 miles south of Nashville, has a charming downtown filled with boutiques, antique stores and lively eateries. Here one of the Civil War's bloodiest battles was fought. On November 30, 1864, during the Battle of Franklin, some 37,000 men (20,000 Confederates and 17,000 Union soldiers) fought over a 2-mile stretch on Franklin's outskirts. Nashville's sprawl has turned much of that battlefield into suburbs, but several historic sites spotlight the turbulent conflict. The rural community of **Arrington**, home to a popular vineyard, is 10 miles southeast of downtown.

---

way, and up to the minute in style and function. The common space in the basement, with its rather regal exposed stone walls and beamed rafters, is your all-hours mingle den. Dorm rooms are on the 3rd and 4th floors, and have lovely wood floors, exposed timber columns, silver-beamed ceilings and four, six or eight bunks.

21c Museum Hotel
BOUTIQUE HOTEL $$$

(☎ 615-610-6400; www.21cMuseumHotels.com; 221 2nd Ave N; r from $299; P❋☏) The South's hippest hotel-museum-hybrid chain has settled into a rehabilitated historic Gray & Dudley Building. In addition to its 124 trademark modern, art-forward rooms – five of which have access to rooftop terraces with Cumberland River views – there's a dedicated spa, six galleries and a hip restaurant that spills out into the adjoining alleyway.

★ Noelle
BOUTIQUE HOTEL $$$

(☎ 615-649-5000; www.noelle-nashville.com; 200 4th Ave N; r from $280) Nashville's best sleep conjures 1930s glamor through a modern lens, and its lobby bar, Trade Room, stuns with original brass detailing and Tennessee pink marble. The rooftop bar, Rare Bird, offers panoramic downtown views from 5pm when the weather cooperates. Rooms are a minimalist take on mid-century modern style in blue, white and gray, with beautiful rustic hardwood floors.

404
BOUTIQUE HOTEL $$$

(☎ 615-242-7404; www.the404nashville.com; 404 12th Ave S; r $309-399; P❋❋@☏) Guests let themselves into Nashville's hippest – and smallest – hotel. Beyond the ebonized cedar frontage, industrial grays under violet lighting lead to four rooms in the minimalist space, most featuring painstakingly hip loft spaces. Local photography by Caroline Allison adds a splash of color. There's a highly regarded restaurant in a shipping container, and parking is included.

Thompson Nashville BOUTIQUE HOTEL **$$$**
(☎615-262-6000; www.thompsonhotels.com; 401 11th Ave S; r from $349; P@🐾🛜) A bastion of finely polished, mid-century modern cool, the Thompson Nashville is the Gulch's see-and-be-seen seat of style, whether that be agonizing over which of the Third Man Records–curated vinyl collection to spin in the lobby, or where to sit at the immensely hip, open-air rooftop bar, **LA Jackson**.

🛏 Midtown, Music Row & 12South

Music City Hostel HOSTEL **$**
(☎615-497-1208; www.musiccityhostel.com; 1809 Patterson St, Midtown; dm $33-46, d $110-126, r $128-156; P🌀@🛜) These squat brick bungalows are humble, but Nashville's West End hostel is lively and welcoming, with a common kitchen, an outdoor grill, a fire pit and some fun touches: the brightly painted doors are covered in artwork by guests passing through. The crowd is young and international, and many hoppin' West End bars are within walking distance.

1501 Linden Manor B&B **$$**
(☎615-298-2701; www.nashville-bed-breakfast. com; 1501 Linden Ave; r from $195; P🌀🛜🐾) The husband-and-wife owners have filled this yellow Victorian cottage with antiques collected on their world travels – Persian rugs, Asian carvings, old Victrolas. Have homemade egg soufflés for breakfast in the sunny dining room, or dip your hand into the 'bottomless cookie jar' anytime. Three rooms are available for booking, and breakfast is included in the room rate.

🛏 Donelson & Music Valley

Gaylord Opryland Resort RESORT **$$**
(☎615-889-1000; www.marriott.com; 2800 Opryland Dr, Music Valley; r from $200; P🌀@🛜🐾) This whopping 2888-room hotel is a universe unto itself, the largest non-casino resort in the USA. Why set foot outdoors when you can ride a flatboat along an artificial river, eat sushi beneath faux water-

falls in an indoor garden, or sip whisky in an antebellum-style mansion, all *inside* the hotel's three massive glass atriums?

🍴 Eating

🍴 Downtown & the Gulch

Arnold's SOUTHERN US **$**
(www.arnoldscountrykitchen.com; 605 8th Ave S, The Gulch; mains from $10.74; ◷10:30am-2:45pm Mon-Fri) Grab a tray and line up with college students, garbage collectors and country-music stars at Arnold's, king of the meat-and-three ($10.74). That line is often out the door. Slabs of drippy roast beef are the house specialty, along with fried chicken on Mondays, fried green tomatoes, cornbread two ways, and big gooey wedges of chocolate meringue pie.

Otaku Ramen RAMEN **$**
(☎615-942-8281; www.otakuramen.com; 1104 Division St, The Gulch; ramen dishes $13-16; ◷11am-2:30pm Mon-Fri, 5-10pm Tue-Thu & Sun, noon-10pm Sat & Sun) Angle for a seat overlooking the open kitchen at this spare but stylish ramen joint. Behind the counter, efficient cooks stuff duck confit into pillowy buns, sizzle tender morsels in hot skillets and load custom noodles and regionally sourced pork into ramen bowls. Slurping is expected. One hour of free parking in the lot across the street and next door.

Chauhan Ale & Masala House INDIAN **$$**
(☎615-242-8426; www.chauhannashville.com; 123 12th Ave N, The Gulch; mains $12-28; ◷11am-2pm & 5-10pm Sun-Thu, to 11pm Fri & Sat; 🛜) Namaste and Nashville collide at celebrity chef Maneet Chauhan's Gulch eatery that showcases inventive Indian fusion on a global scale. Typical Desi fare meets Mexican, Canadian, British and American Southern influences. Dishes such as chili paneer bhurjee relleno, tandoori chicken poutine and a tiffin-inspired meat-and-three pair gorgeously with Indian spice-infused microbrews and creative cocktails.

★Etch MODERN AMERICAN **$$$**
(☎615-522-0685; www.etchrestaurant.com; 303 Demonbreun St; mains $23-39; ◷11am-2pm & 4:30-10pm Mon-Fri, 4:30-10:30pm Sat; 🛜) Well-known Nashville chef Deb Paquette's Etch serves some of the city's most inventive cuisine – comfort food whose flavors and textures have been manipulated into tantalizing

combinations, surpassing expectations at every bite. Octopus and shrimp bruschetta, roasted cauliflower with truffled pea pesto, lamb loin with ginger grits, venison with walnut pomegranate sauce – all masterpieces. Reservations essential.

✕ Midtown, Music Row & 12South

★Hattie B's
CHICKEN $

(☑615-678-4794; www.hattieb.com; 112 19th Ave S, Midtown; quarter/half plates from $8.50/12; ☺11am-10pm Mon-Thu, to midnight Fri & Sat, to 4pm Sun) When it comes to hot chicken supremacy, based on sheer numbers, Hattie B's reigns supreme in Nashville. The ultra-popular fried chicken spot serves up moist, high-quality birds, which come devilishly fried to levels that top out at 'Shut the Cluck Up!' hot, and it means business (nose-runnin', head-itchin' 'Damn Hot' was our limit). Get in line.

Grilled Cheeserie
AMERICAN $

(www.grilledcheeserie.com; 2003 Belcourt Ave, Hillsboro Village; sandwiches $8-9; ☺11am-9pm; 🖥🚻) Hurry up and wait for gussied up, gourmet versions of an American classic: the grilled cheese sandwich. It's done up here in versions so satisfying, you'll forget a simpler sandwich ever existed. Go for pimiento mac 'n' cheese and dip it in the creamy tomato soup, a match made in foodie heaven. Follow with an outrageous gourmet milkshake.

★Epice
LEBANESE $$

(☑615-720-6765; www.epicenashville.com; 2902 12th Ave S, 12South; lunch mains $12-15, dinner mains $23-33; ☺11am-9:30pm Tue-Thu, to 10pm Fri & Sat, to 9pm Sun) For an inviting and delicious respite from exploring the shops of 12South, pop into this bright and sparkling Lebanese bistro. The highlight at lunch? The sandwiches, which are served with a hearty peasant salad and potatoes roasted with cilantro. Sandwich choices include lamb, sirloin and grilled salmon. At dinner, the sandwiches graduate to rack of lamb, tenderloin skewers and fish fillets.

Edley's Bar-B-Que
BARBECUE $$

(☑615-953-2951; www.edleysbbq.com; 2706 12th Ave S, 12South; mains $10-23.50; ☺11am-10pm Sun-Fri, from 8am Sat; 🚻) This barbecue joint, with its simple, down-home decor and some seriously great aromas wafting from the kitchen, is a Nashville staple. The

pork platter is the obvious choice, though the brisket sandwich isn't a bad pick either. The meat will melt in your mouth and the peppery-sweet sauce will satisfy the pickiest of barbecue connoisseurs.

✕ East Nashville

★Wild Cow
VEGETARIAN $

(☑615-262-2717; www.thewildcow.com; 1896 Eastland Ave; mains $8-12; ☺11am-9pm Mon, Wed, Thu & Sun, to 10pm Fri & Sat; 🖉) Looking for a fresh and flavor-packed meal in East Nashville? Then hit up this small but inviting vegetarian eatery, where photos of happy livestock beam down on a mostly organic line-up of sandwiches, wraps, tacos and salads. The peanut tempeh tacos, with kale, avocado and peanut-marinaded tempeh, are superb. Nice staff and significant charitable donations round out the appeal.

Pepperfire Hot Chicken
SOUTHERN US $

(☑615-582-4824; www.pepperfirehotchicken.com; 1000 Gallatin Ave, Suite C; mains $10-13; ☺11am-9pm Mon-Wed, to 10pm Thu-Sat) Since 2010, East Nashville's Pepperfire has been slinging spicy bird to heat seekers who appreciate a creative twist on classic hot chicken. A thin, crispy batter with a distinctive spice blend lends a rich, complex smokiness that sets Pepperfire's chicken apart. Tasty sides include crinkle fries, fried okra and mac and cheese. And there's cold, local beer to ease the heat.

♟ Drinking & Nightlife

★Barista Parlor
COFFEE

(www.baristaparlor.com; 610 Magazine St; ☺7am-6pm; 🖥) Nashville's best artisan coffeehouse (coffee $3-7) has enlisted an old stereo shop in the Gulch for its downtown location, and its retro aesthetic is a great backdrop for socializing or getting some work done. The exquisite espresso – courtesy of an $18,000 hand-built Slayer coffee machine – is every bit as memorable as in its original East Nashville location.

★Old Glory
COCKTAIL BAR

(☑615-679-0509; http://oldglorynashville.com; 1200 Villa Pl, Edgehill Village; ☺5pm-1am Sun-Thu, to 2am Fri, noon-2am Sat) A towering smokestack rises like an altar in a corner of this steampunk speakeasy. Tucked off an alley in Edgehill Village, the space was a laundromat boiler room in the 1930s. Today the exposed brick, industrial piping, lofty ceiling and curved staircase are the backdrop for the city's most stunning cocktail bar – if you can find it!

Attaboy
COCKTAIL BAR

(http://attaboy.us; 8 McFerrin Ave; ⏱5pm-3am) New York City's famed Attaboy is one of the bars credited with the entire modern craft-cocktail movement – its cocktails are accorded near mythological status by connoisseurs. The minimalist speakeasy-style East Nashville iteration of this tipple lab concocts flat-rate ($15), off-the-cuff creations, chilled with block ice. There's no menu – drinks are personalized.

Pinewood Social
BAR

(☑615-751-8111; http://pinewoodsocial.com; 33 Peabody St; ⏱7am-1am Mon-Fri, from 9am Sat & Sun; 🛜) You could spend days at Pinewood Social and never run low on things to do. There are couches to hang at and play board games, a large circular bar with finely crafted cocktails, and coffee from Crema, a Nashville favorite. Lounge by the plunge pool or play bocce on the outdoor patio. Oh, and there's a bowling alley, too.

Acme Feed & Seed
BAR

(www.theacmenashville.com; 101 Broadway; ⏱11am-11pm Mon-Thu, to 2am Fri & Sat, 10am-11pm Sun; 🛜) This ambitious, four-floor takeover of an old 1875 farm supply warehouse has finally given Nashvillians a reason to go downtown even when family is *not* visiting. The 1st floor is devoted to lightning-fast, but elevated, pub grub, with 27 beer taps and live music that's defiantly un-country most nights (Southern rock, indie, roots etc). This place is always buzzing.

☆ Entertainment

Nashville's opportunities for hearing live music are unparalleled. As well as the big venues, many talented country, folk, bluegrass, Southern-rock and blues performers play smoky honky-tonks, college bars, coffee shops and organic cafes for tips. Cover charges are rare. The singer-songwriter is just as respected as the stadium superstar, so look for well-attended songwriter nights at smaller venues.

★ Station Inn
LIVE MUSIC

(☑615-255-3307; www.stationinn.com; 402 12th Ave S; cover $10-20; ⏱open mic 7pm, live bands 9pm) Sit at one of the small cocktail tables, squeezed together on the worn wood floor in this beer-only dive, and behold the lightning fingers of bluegrass savants, illuminated by stage lights and neon signs. We are talking stand-up bass, banjo, mandolin, fiddle and a modicum of yodeling.

Ryman Auditorium
CONCERT VENUE

(☑615-889-3060; www.ryman.com; 116 5th Ave N) The so-called 'Mother Church of Country Music' has hosted a laundry list of performers, from Martha Graham to Elvis, and from Katharine Hepburn to Bob Dylan. The Ryman's excellent acoustics, historic charm and large seating capacity have kept it the premier venue in town, with big names frequently passing through. The *Grand Ole Opry* country music stage show returns here for winter runs.

Bluebird Cafe
LIVE MUSIC

(☑615-383-1461; www.bluebirdcafe.com; 4104 Hillsboro Pike, Green Hills; cover free-$30) It's in a strip mall in suburban South Nashville, but don't let that fool you: some of the best original singer-songwriters in country music have graced this tiny stage. Steve Earle, Emmylou Harris and the Cowboy Junkies have all played the Bluebird, which is the setting for the popular CMT television series, *Nashville*. Try your luck at the Monday open-mic nights.

Grand Ole Opry
LIVE MUSIC

(☑615-871-6779; www.opry.com; 2804 Opryland Dr, Music Valley; tickets $40-110; ⏱Tue, Fri & Sat Feb-Oct, plus Wed Jun-Oct; 🅿) Though you'll find a variety of country shows throughout the week, *the* performance to see is the *Grand Ole Opry,* a lavish tribute to classic Nashville country music, every Tuesday, Friday and Saturday night from February through October, with Wednesday shows added in summer. Performances return to the Ryman Auditorium from November through January.

Tootsie's Orchid Lounge
HONKY-TONK

(☑615-726-7937; www.tootsies.net; 422 Broadway; ⏱10am-2:30am) The most venerated of the downtown honky-tonks, with music on three levels at any given moment, Tootsie's is a blessed dive oozing boot-stomping, hillbilly, beer-soaked grace. In the 1960s, club owner and den mother 'Tootsie' Bess nurtured Willie Nelson, Kris Kristofferson and Waylon Jennings when they were on the rise.

Robert's Western World
LIVE MUSIC

(www.robertswesternworld.com; 416 Broadway; ⏱11am-2am Mon-Sat, from noon Sun) A dozen bars wouldn't get you halfway down Lower

Broadway, and this is a cut above all the other joints. It pulls out all the stops for folks making a country music pilgrimage, and you can even get a burger or a fried bologna sandwich at the grill. Music starts at opening and goes all night.

★ **Belcourt Theatre** CINEMA
(☑ 615-383-9140; www.belcourt.org; 2102 Belcourt Ave, Hillsboro Village) A true Nashville gem, this nonprofit cinema showcases the best of independent, documentary, world, repertory and classic cinema 365 days a year. It's also one of the only movie houses chosen to be part of the Sundance Film Festival USA program. Alongside the usual cola and popcorn offerings, there's full bar service.

🛍 Shopping

★ **Hatch Show Print** ART
(☑ 615-577-7710; www.hatchshowprint.com; 224 5th Ave S; ☉ 9:30am-6pm) One of the oldest letterpress print shops in the USA, Hatch has been using old-school, hand-cut blocks to print its bright, iconic posters since vaudeville. The company has produced graphic ads and posters for almost every country star and now has a permanent place inside the Country Music Hall of Fame.

★ **Third Man Records** MUSIC
(www.thirdmanrecords.com; 623 7th Ave S; ☉ 10am-6pm) In a still-industrial slice of downtown you'll find Jack White's boutique record label, shop and novelty lounge, complete with its own lathe and live venue. It sells mostly Third Man recordings on vinyl and CD, collectible T-shirts, stickers, headphones and Pro-Ject record players. You'll also find White's entire catalog of recordings, and you can record yourself on vinyl ($20).

Two Old Hippies CLOTHING
(www.twooldhippies.com; 401 12th Ave S; ☉ 10am-7pm Mon-Sat, 11am-5pm Sun) Only in Nashville would an upscale retro-inspired clothing shop have a bandstand with regular live shows of high quality. And, yes, just like the threads, countrified hippie rock is the rule. The shop itself has books, fitted T-shirts, excellent belts, made-in-Tennessee jewelry, candles and rocker wear, plus a bounty of stage-worthy shirts, jackets and incredible acoustic guitars.

Gruhn Guitars MUSICAL INSTRUMENTS
(www.guitars.com; 2120 8th Ave S, Melrose; ☉ 10am-6pm Mon-Sat) This renowned vintage

DON'T MISS

BONNAROO MUSIC FESTIVAL

One of America's premier music festivals, **Bonnaroo** (www.bonnaroo.com; Manchester; ☉ mid-Jun) is the only large-scale 24/7 event in the country. Set on a 700-acre farm in Manchester, 60 miles southeast of Nashville, Bonnaroo combines camping, comedy, food, beverage and arts components, which lends it a communal feel. But it's the music that rules, spread over four blissfully raging days.

instrument store has been serving the Nashville community since 1970. The expert staff and amazing inventory attract musicians of all kinds; at any minute, some unassuming virtuoso may just walk in, grab a guitar, mandolin or banjo off the wall and jam.

ℹ Information

Metro Nashville's parks and community centers have free wi-fi, as do many hotels, restaurants and coffee shops.

Nashville Visitors Information Center (☑ 615-259-4747; www.visitmusiccity.com; 501 Broadway, Bridgestone Arena; ☉ 8am-5:30pm Mon-Sat, 10am-5pm Sun) Pick up free city maps here at the glass tower.

Nashville Visitors Information Center (www.visitmusiccity.com; 150 4th Ave N; ☉ 8am-5pm Mon-Thu, to 4pm Fri) In the Regions Bank Building lobby.

INTERNET RESOURCES

Nashville Public Radio (www.nashvillepublicradio.org) News, music and NPR programming on 90.3 WPLN FM.

Nashville Scene (www.nashvillescene.com) Free alternative weekly with entertainment listings.

Tennessean (www.tennessean.com) Nashville's daily newspaper.

ℹ Getting There & Away

Nashville is located in Middle Tennessee at the junction of three interstates: I-40, I-65 and I-24. **Nashville International Airport** (BNA; ☑ 615-275-1675; www.flynashville.com; One Terminal Dr), 8 miles east of downtown, offers direct flights to more than 60 US cities, as well as Calgary, Cancun, the Bahamas and the Dominican Republic. **Greyhound** (☑ 615-255-3556; www.greyhound.com; 709 5th Ave S) and **Megabus** (www.megabus.com; 5th Ave N, btwn Gay St & Charlotte Ave; ☎) are both located downtown and offer interstate bus services.

ℹ️ Getting Around

TO/FROM THE AIRPORT

It takes about 35 to 45 minutes to get downtown on MTA bus 18 ($1.70), which runs from the airport. Express 18 takes about 20 minutes. The airport bus stop is on level 1 in the Ground Transportation area.

Shuttles can be found on the Ground Transportation level (Level 1). The rate to downtown is about $30. A list of shuttle companies is provided on the airport website.

Taxis charge a flat rate of $25 for a ride to downtown or Opryland. A taxi to Vanderbilt/West End costs about $27. A trip to Franklin runs $55 to $60.

BICYCLE

Nashville's public bike-share scheme, **Nashville B-Cycle** (https://nashville.bcycle.com; ⊘ check-out hours 5am-10pm), offers more than 30 stations throughout the city. After purchasing a 24-hour membership for $5, your first hour is free; after that your credit card will be charged $1.50 per half-hour. Weekly, monthly and annual plans are also available. Maps can be found online.

Greenways run through the larger parks and connect a few of them – you can find B-Cycle stations at Shelby Bottoms Nature Center near the **Shelby Bottoms Greenway** (www.nashville.gov/parks-and-recreation; 1900 Davidson St, Main Trailhead parking lot; ⊘ dawn-dusk) and at the **Music City Walk of Fame Park** (📞 866-584-6874; www.visitmusiccity.com/walkoffame; Demonbreun St, btwn 4th Ave S & 5th Ave S). B-Cycles are heavy, however, and may not be comfortable for longer cross-city rides. **Bike the Greenway** (📞 615-920-1388; www.bikethegreenway.net; Two Rivers Park Trailhead, Music Valley; 2/4hr rental $30/45; ⊘ by reservation) offers rentals.

BUS

Now rebranding itself We Go, the MTA (www.nashvillemta.org) operates city bus services, based downtown at **Music City Central** (400 Charlotte Ave), including the free Music City Circuit, whose two routes hit the majority of Nashville attractions.

Eastern Tennessee

Dolly Parton, East Tennessee's most famous native, loves her home region so much that she's made a career out of singing about girls who leave the honeysuckle-scented embrace of the Smoky Mountains for the false glitter of the city. They're always sorry.

Largely a rural region of small towns, rolling hills and river valleys, the eastern third of the state is noteworthy for its friendly folks and pastoral charm. The lush southern Appalachian Mountains are great for hiking, camping and rafting. Pretty waterfalls are a regional specialty. Nearby Great Smoky Mountains National Park lures millions every year, but the crowds are easily ditched in East Tennessee's Cherokee National Forest.

The region's two main urban areas, Knoxville and Chattanooga, are easygoing riverside cities with lively student populations, great restaurants, fun craft breweries and outdoor adventures galore. For a blast of all things tacky and wacky, Gatlinburg and Pigeon Forge await.

Chattanooga

Chattanooga has charisma to spare. With world-class rock climbing, hiking, cycling and water-sports opportunities, it's one of the South's best cities for outdoorsy types. It's gorgeous, too: just check out those views from the Bluff View Art District! It's also remarkably eco-forward, with free electric buses, miles of well-used waterfront trails, and pedestrian bridges crossing the Tennessee River. All this makes it hard to credit its reputation in the 1960s as America's dirtiest city.

The city was a major railway hub throughout the 19th and 20th centuries, hence the 'Chattanooga Choo-Choo,' which was originally a reference to the Cincinnati Southern Railroad's passenger service from Cincinnati to Chattanooga, and later the title of a 1941 Glen Miller tune. The eminently walkable downtown is a maze of historic stone and brick buildings featuring tasty gourmet kitchens, craft breweries and distilleries. Burgeoning neighborhoods keep the vibe compelling. It's easy to love the 'Noog!

⊙ Sights & Activities

⭐ **Songbirds**   MUSEUM
(📞 423-531-2473;   www.songbirdsguitars.com; Chattanooga Choo Choo Hotel, 35 Station St; adult/child under 13yr $16/free, all access $39; ⊘ 10am-6pm Mon-Wed, to 8pm Thu-Sat, noon-6pm Sun) This astonishing guitar collection – the largest assemblage of vintage and rare guitars anywhere – is Chattanooga's newest world-class attraction. More than 500 guitars, many arranged in time-line fashion from the 1950 Fender Broadcasters (the first mass-produced solid-body electric guitar) to the 1970s, grace this small space, including

rock-star axes from Chuck Berry, BB King, Bo Diddley, Roy Orbison and Robby Krieger of the Doors, among others.

Hunter Museum of American Art
GALLERY

(☑423-267-0968; www.huntermuseum.org; 10 Bluff View; adult/child under 18yr $15/free; ☺10am-5pm Mon, Tue, Fri & Sat, to 8pm Thu, noon-5pm Wed & Sun; P) Set high on the river bluffs, this striking edifice of melted steel and glass – fronted by an early-20th-century mansion – is easily the most singular architectural achievement in Tennessee. Oh, and its 19th- and 20th-century art collection is fantastic. Permanent exhibits are free the first Thursday of the month between 4pm and 8pm, but special exhibits will cost $5.

Coolidge Park
PARK

(www.chattanoogafun.com; 150 River St; P🚲) A good place to start a riverfront stroll, Coolidge Park has a play fountain, a carousel ($1 per ride), well-used playing fields, and a 50ft climbing wall attached to one of the columns supporting the **Walnut Street Bridge** (1 Walnut St; P), one of the world's largest pedestrian bridges.

★ Lookout Mountain
NATURAL FEATURE

(☑800-825-8366; www.lookoutmountain.com; 827 East Brow Rd; combo ticket adult/child 3-12yr $57/32; ☺hours vary; P🚲) Some of Chattanooga's oldest and best-loved attractions are 6 miles outside the city at Lookout Mountain. Combination admission includes the **Incline Railway**, which chugs up a steep slope to the mountaintop; the stunning **Ruby Falls** (1720 S Scenic Hwy), the world's longest underground waterfall; and **Rock City** (1400 Patten Rd), a lofty garden marked by dramatic rock formations and a clifftop overlook with views across seven states. You can also purchase a ticket for each of the three attractions individually.

Tennessee Aquarium
AQUARIUM

(☑800-262-0695; www.tnaqua.org; 1 Broad St; adult/child 3-12yr $35/22, incl IMAX $43/30; ☺10am-6pm; P🚲) Occupying two side-by-side but separate buildings, this well-done aquarium is a fun and educational rainy-day destination. The River Journey building spotlights the inhabitants and ecology of the Tennessee River as it flows from the Appalachian Mountains to the Mississippi Delta. Exhibits in the Ocean Journey building showcase saltwater marine life – including piranhas! Crowd-pleasers include river otters, penguins, and leaping lemurs, which swung their way into the aquarium from Madagascar in 2017.

🛏 Sleeping & Eating

★ Crash Pad
HOSTEL $

(☑423-648-8393; www.crashpadchattanooga.com; 29 Johnson St; dm $38, d $89-99, tr $119; P✳@🛜) 🅿 The South's best hostel, run by climbers, is a sustainable den of coolness in Southside, the 'Noog's hippest downtown neighborhood. Co-ed dorms overachieve: built-in lights, power outlets, fans and privacy curtains for each bed. Private rooms feature exposed concrete and bedside tables built into the bed frames. Access throughout is via hi-tech fobs, and linens, padlocks and breakfast supplies are included.

★ Moxy Chattanooga Downtown
HOTEL $$

(☑423-664-1180; www.moxy-hotels.marriott.com; 1220 King St; r $169-179; P✳🛜🏊) Guests check in at the bar at this sharp, sassy new hotel, where a kaleidoscope of bright colors and unique design details make for a compelling stay. Geared to younger travelers (but still appealing to young-at-heart visitors), the Moxy encourages communing, with numerous lounge areas tucked here and there. Rooms are on the small side, and spare, but comfortable.

Flying Squirrel
AMERICAN $

(☑423-602-5980; www.flyingsquirrelbar.com; 55 Johnson St; mains $9-19; ☺5pm-midnight Tue-Thu, to 2am Fri & Sat, 10:30am-3pm Sun; 🛜) A neighbor to Crash Pad (same owners), Flying Squirrel is at its heart a very cool bar (21 and over only, except for Sunday brunch), but its locally sourced small-plate takes on fusion comfort food make for mighty fine pub grub – pork-belly fried rice, fried-chicken *bao* (Chinese steamed buns) and chocolate-hazelnut cheesecake, to name a few.

St John's Meeting Place
AMERICAN $$

(☑423-266-4571; www.stjohnsmeetingplace.com; 1274 Market St; mains $12-35; ☺5-9:30pm Mon-Thu, to 10pm Fri & Sat) The culinary anchor of Chattanooga's Southside is widely considered the city's best night out. It's Johnny Cash black (black-granite floor, black-glass chandeliers, black banquettes), lending it an unorthodox but mod elegance. The farm-to-table cuisine features the likes of duck tacos with jalapeño crema, braised-lamb sliders, and wild Alaskan halibut with wasabi-avocado mousse.

Drinking & Nightlife

Plus Coffee
COFFEE

(☑423-521-2098; www.pluscoffee.co; 3800 St Elmo Ave; ☺7am-6pm Mon-Fri, 8am-6pm Sat & Sun; 🛜) It's easy to drive right by this delightfully minimalist coffeehouse in the up-and-coming neighborhood of St Elmo at the foot of the Incline Railway (p395) – the sign disappears somewhat into the historic brick building on which it sits. Reclaimed-wood tables and vintage furniture dot the loft-like space, and the menu is simple: brew, pour over and espresso.

Hutton & Smith Brewing
MICROBREWERY

(☑423-760-3600; www.huttonandsmithbrewing. com; 431 E ML King Blvd; ☺4-10pm Mon-Thu, noon-midnight Fri & Sat, noon-6pm Sun; 🛜) 🍃 One of the anchors of the newly hip MLK district, this 20-tap microbrewery ironically added a garage door so that it appears that its taproom is housed in a former mechanic's shop (or some such hipster industrial-building flip), but alas it wasn't anything special previously. Nevertheless, the beer – namely the Good Schist APA, coffee IPA and On-Sight Alt – pleases. Welcoming staff.

ℹ Information

Located in an outdoor public breezeway beside **High Point Climbing** (☑423-602-7625; www. highpointclimbing.com; 219 Broad St; day pass adult/child under 11yr $18/16; ☺6am-10pm Mon, Wed & Fri, 10am-10pm Tue, Thu & Sat, 10am-8pm Sun; ♿), the **visitor center** (☑800-322-3344; www.chattanoogafun.com; 215 Broad St; ☺10am-5pm) is easy to miss.

ℹ Getting There & Around

Chattanooga's modest **airport** (CHA; ☑423-855-2202; www.chattairport.com; 1001 Airport Rd) is 9 miles east of the city. The **Greyhound station** (☑423-892-1277; 960 Airport Rd) is just down the road from the airport.

For access to most downtown sites, ride the free **Downtown Electric Shuttle** (☑423-629-1473; www.gocarta.org) that plies the center and the North Shore. The visitor center has a route map.

Bike Chattanooga (www.bikechatta nooga.com; daily pass $8) is Chattanooga's city-sponsored bike-share program. Bikes are lined and locked up at 41 stations throughout the city and riders can purchase access passes (starting at $8 for 24 hours) by credit card at any of the station kiosks. Rides under an hour are free.

Knoxville

Dubbed a 'scruffy little city' by the *Wall Street Journal* before the 1982 World's Fair, Knoxville is strutting its stuff these days as an increasingly prominent and polished destination for outdoor, gastronomy and craft-beer enthusiasts. Knoxville is also home to the University of Tennessee and its rabid college-football fan base.

Knoxville is a handy base for visiting Great Smoky Mountains National Park. Sugarlands Visitor Center is just 29 miles away, and Knoxville is a far more enticing spot to eat and drink than other cities near the park. For hikers and mountain bikers, the city's ever-expanding Urban Wilderness is becoming its own reason to visit.

◉ Sights & Activities

Women's Basketball Hall of Fame
MUSEUM

(☑865-633-9000; www.wbhof.com; 700 Hall of Fame Dr; adult/child 6-15yr $8/6; ☺10am-5pm Mon-Sat May-Aug, 11am-5pm Tue-Fri, 10am-5pm Sat Sep-Apr; 🅿♿) You can't miss the massive orange basketball that marks the Women's Basketball Hall of Fame, a nifty look at the sport from the time when women were forced to play in full-length dresses. Interactive features include a half-time locker-room talk by legendary University of Tennessee coach Pat Summitt and a dribbling course to test your skills.

Ijams Nature Center
OUTDOORS

(☑865-577-4717; www.ijams.org; 2915 Island Home Ave; ☺visitor center 9am-5pm Mon-Sat, from 11am Sun, grounds 8am-sunset; ♿🐾) A one-stop shop for enjoying nature in Knoxville, 300-acre Ijams (pronounced 'eye-ams') is the de facto headquarters for the sprawling Urban Wilderness. Here you can stroll the scenic **River Boardwalk Trail** beside the Tennessee River, enjoy a canopy adventure tour (with a zipline), rent bikes ($20 per half day) and let the kids roam free in the nature-themed playground.

🛏 Sleeping & Eating

★ Oliver Hotel
BOUTIQUE HOTEL $$

(☑865-521-0500; www.theoliverhotel.com; 407 Union Ave; r $175-210, ste $295-330; 🅿❄@🛜) Knoxville's first boutique hotel boasts 28 modern, stylish rooms with fun subway-tiled showers (with rain-style shower heads), luxe linens, plush throwback furniture and carpets, and gorgeous hand-crafted coffee tables. The **Peter Kern Library bar** (⊙4pm-midnight Mon-Fri, 11am-2am Sat & Sun) draws craft-cocktail enthusiasts by night. The restaurant, **Oliver Royale** (mains lunch $10-18, dinner $16-34), is highly recommended.

★**Balter Beerworks**   GASTROPUB $

(☑865-999-5015; www.balterbeerworks.com; 100 S Broadway; mains lunch $10-16, dinner $12-17; ⊙11am-11pm Mon-Thu, to midnight Fri, 10am-midnight Sat, 10am-10pm Sun) From the communal tables on the patio to the standing-room-only bar to the buzzing dining room, this joint – a former gas station – exudes a welcoming vibe. The pub fare is delicious, and options range from the Gouda-topped burger with sriracha sauce to cheesy shrimp and grits with andouille sausage. The easy-drinking house beer is brewed on-site.

★**JC Holdway**   AMERICAN $$

(☑865-312-9050; www.jcholdway.com; 501 Union Ave; most mains $20-26; ⊙5:30-9:30pm Tue-Thu, to 10pm Fri & Sat; 🕿) You'll want to reserve ahead for the privilege of noshing on James Beard Award–winning chef Joseph Lenn's modern Appalachian comfort cuisine. Lenn, who spent nearly a decade as executive chef at famed Blackberry Farm before returning home to Knoxville in 2016, does a ridiculously perfect wood-grilled pork with sweet-potato puree, and anything with smoked meat from Benton's Farm.

❶ Information

Besides providing tourism info, including a free downtown walking-tour brochure, the **visitor center** (Visit Knoxville; ☑800-727-8045; www.visitknoxville.com; 301 S Gay St; ⊙8:30am-5pm Mon-Fri, 9am-5pm Sat, noon-4pm Sun) welcomes bands from across the Americana genre for WDVX's **Blue Plate Special**, a free concert series at noon Monday to Saturday.

❶ Getting There & Around

Knoxville's **McGhee Tyson Airport** (☑865-342-3000; www.flyknoxville.com; 2055 Alcoa Hwy, Alcoa), 15 miles south of town, is served by around 20 nonstop domestic flights. The **Greyhound bus station** (☑865-524-0369; 100 E Magnolia Ave) is only about 1 mile north of downtown, making it a convenient option for ground travelers.

Gatlinburg & Pigeon Forge

Wildly kitschy and family-friendly Gatlinburg hunkers at the entrance to Great Smoky Mountains National Park, waiting to stun hikers with the scent of fudge, cotton candy and pancakes, and various odd museums and campy attractions. Boisterous new tasting rooms are drawing thirsty crowds to a slew of moonshine distilleries along Parkway, the main drag through town that rolls right into the national park. It's a wild ride of all that's good and bad about the USA at the same time, wrapped up in a gaudy explosion of magic shows and whiskey.

With the exception of the Gatlinburg Sky Lift and Anakeesta Mountain, the town emerged from the devastating 2016 wildfires largely unscathed, but reminders of the conflagration linger. If you tire of all the flash and bling, you can find a handful of quality cultural and natural attractions within – or very close to – the busy downtown.

Around eight miles north of Gatlinburg, popular Pigeon Forge offers loads of amusement in a city packed tight with hotels, restaurants and family-friendly attractions.

⊙ Sights & Activities

★**Dollywood**   AMUSEMENT PARK

(☑800-365-5996; www.dollywood.com; 2700 Dollywood Parks Blvd; adult/child 4-9yr $74/61; ⊙mid-Mar–Dec, hours vary seasonally; P♿) Dollywood is a self-created ode to the patron saint of East Tennessee: the big-haired, big-bosomed and big-hearted country singer Dolly Parton. A clean and friendly place, the park features Appalachian-themed rides and attractions, the Splash Country water park, mountain crafts, restaurants serving Southern-fried food, and the **DreamMore Resort** (☑865-365-1900; www.dollywood.com/resort; 2525 DreamMore Way; r/ste from $359/379; P❄🛜🏊). Highlights include nationally acclaimed roller-coasters, live-music shows and the Chasing Rainbows Museum, which traces Dolly's fascinating life – her hometown is nearby Sevierville.

Gatlinburg SkyLift   CABLE CAR

(☑865-436-4307; www.gatlinburgskylift.com; 765 Parkway; adult/child $16/13; ⊙9am-11pm Jun-Aug, hours vary rest of year) This ski-resort chairlift swoops you high into the Smokies, providing stellar views. The lofty SkyDeck and the 680ft-long SkyBridge, the longest suspension bridge in North America, opened at the top of the lift in spring 2019.

Anakeesta   AMUSEMENT PARK

(☑865-325-2400; www.anakeesta.com; 576 Parkway; adult/child under 12yr $22/18; ⊙9am-10pm Jul–mid-Aug, shorter hours rest of year, closed

Tue-Thu Jan & Feb; Ⓟ🐾) A 'chondola' whisks visitors from downtown Gatlinburg to this playground in the sky, where views of the Great Smokies are superb. Once atop Anakeesta Mountain you can bounce across 16 elevated bridges on the tree-canopy walk, hold tight on dueling ziplines (adult/child $30/26), ride the mountain coaster, let the kids explore Treehouse Village, or settle into a rocking chair and appreciate the view. Burgers and beer are available at the new **Clifftop Grill** (mains $10 to $12).

★**Ole Smoky Moonshine** DISTILLERY
(☑865-436-6995; www.olesmoky.com; 903 Parkway; tasting $5; ⊙10am-10pm Sun-Thu, to 11pm Fri & Sat) Nicknamed The Holler, this stone-and-wood moonshine distillery – Tennessee's first licensed moonshine maker – appears at first glance to have a Disney flair, but it's the real deal. Gathering around the hilarious bartenders, sampling eight to 10 flavors of hooch and taking in the colorful commentary is Gatlinburg's best time.

★**Titanic Museum** MUSEUM
(☑417-334-9500; www.titanicpigeonforge.com; 2134 Parkway; adult/child 5-11yr $27/14; ⊙9am-10pm Jul & early Aug, closes earlier rest of year; Ⓟ) On April 15, 1912, the steamship *Titanic* sank on her maiden voyage after colliding with an iceberg. The ship's history and the stories of many of her passengers are shared through artifacts, black-and-white photographs, personal histories and thoughtful interactive displays. Highlights include an actual deck chair from the ship, a replica of the grand staircase, and a haunting musical tribute to the ship's young musicians, who chose to stay onboard and play, possibly to keep passengers calm. All perished.

🛏 **Sleeping & Eating**

Bearskin Lodge LODGE $$
(☑877-795-7546; www.thebearskinlodge.com; 840 River Rd; r/ste from $139/164; Ⓟ❄🐾🌐) Near the entrance to Great Smoky Mountains National Park (p366), this shingled riverside lodge is blessed with timber accents and a bit more panache than other Gatlinburg comers. All of the 96 spacious rooms have flat-screen TVs, and some have gas fireplaces and private balconies jutting over the river. There's an outdoor pool and a lazy river.

Buckhorn Inn INN $$
(☑865-436-4668; www.buckhorninn.com; 2140 Tudor Mountain Rd; r $125-205, cottages $185,

2-bedroom guesthouses from $240; Ⓟ❄@🌐) A few minutes' drive and several light years away from the kitsch and crowds of downtown Gatlinburg, the tranquil Buckhorn has nine elegant rooms, seven private cottages and three guesthouses on a property that's a well-manicured private haven. If the unbroken views of Mt LeConte don't relax you enough, have a wander through the fieldstone meditation labyrinth.

Three Jimmys AMERICAN $
(☑865-325-1210; www.threejimmys.com; 1359 E Parkway; mains $10-26; ⊙11am-1am; 🐾) Escape the tourist hordes on the main drag and grab a bite at this locals' favorite with friendly waitstaff ('Here's your menu, baby...') and a long list of everything: barbecue, turkey Reubens, burgers, champagne chicken, steaks, a great spinach salad and so on. Hours vary seasonally. Good bar as well, with a dozen or so beers on tap.

ℹ **Information**

Pop into the **Gatlinburg Welcome Center** (☑865-277-8947; www.gatlinburg.com; 1011 Banner Rd; ⊙8:30am-7pm Jun-Oct, to 5:30pm Nov-May) for official information and maps – including a handy $1 waterfalls map – for both Gatlinburg and Great Smoky Mountains National Park.

ℹ **Getting There & Around**

The vast majority of visitors arrive in Gatlinburg by car. The nearest airport is Knoxville's McGhee Tyson Airport (p397), 41 miles away, and there's no regular intercity bus service.

Traffic and parking are serious issues in Gatlinburg. The **Gatlinburg Trolley** (www.gatlinburgtrolley.org; ⊙8:30am-midnight May-Oct, hours vary rest of year) serves downtown, and the trolley's tan line ($2 round trip) goes into the national park from June through October, with stops at Sugarlands Visitor Center, Laurel Falls and Elkmont Campground. Parking lots around town generally charge $10 for the day. If you get to Gatlinburg very early, you may snag free on-street parking on River Rd.

KENTUCKY

Horses thunder around racetracks, bourbon pours from distilleries and banjos twang in Kentucky, a geographical and cultural crossroads that's part North, part South, part genteel and part country cousin. Every corner is easy on the eye, but there are few sights more beautiful than the rolling limestone hills around Lexington, where long-legged steeds nibble under poplar trees on multi-million-dollar farms that you can visit. Bourbon distilleries also speckle the countryside, prime for scenic road tripping to swirl and sniff a dram at the source. It's like an off-beat version of California's Napa Valley, but with fewer crowds and headier alcohol. Caving, rock climbing and hiking prevail in the unspoiled parks and forests. And while big cities Louisville and Lexington have farm-to-table restaurants, cocktail bars and all of the other hipster requirements, most of Kentucky is made up of small towns with quiet scenes.

❶ Information

Kentucky State Parks (502-564-2172; www.parks.ky.gov) Offers info on hiking, caving, fishing, camping and more in Kentucky's 52 state parks. So-called 'Resort Parks' have lodges. 'Recreation Parks' are for roughin' it. All are free.

Kentucky Tourism (www.kentuckytourism.com) Go online to request a detailed booklet on the state's attractions.

Louisville

Louisville (or Loo-a-vul, as the locals say) is handsome, underrated and undeniably cool. Think of it as a hipster with good Southern manners. A fun and artsy town built on bourbon and American sport icons (it's home to the Kentucky Derby, and was the birthplace of Muhammad Ali and the Louisville Slugger baseball bat), it has evolved into one of the South's most foodie-centric cities, a lovely spot to eat and museum-hop between rounds of pursuing North America's best bourbon old-fashioned cocktail.

❍ Sights & Activities

Churchill Downs   HORSE RACING
(502-636-4400; www.churchilldowns.com; 700 Central Ave) Churchill Downs is the landmark racetrack that hosts the epic Kentucky Derby (p401) in May. But there's plenty of action besides that: warm-ups and other thoroughbred races take place from late April to late June and again in September and throughout November. Tickets start at $5. You also can go on a guided tour of the grounds year-round via the onsite Kentucky Derby Museum.

Kentucky Derby Museum   MUSEUM
(502-637-1111; www.derbymuseum.org; 704 Central Ave; adult/child $15/8; ⏱8am-5pm Mon-Sat, 11am-5pm Sun mid-Mar–Nov, 9am-5pm Mon-Sat, 11am-5pm Sun Dec–mid-Mar) On the Churchill Downs racetrack grounds, the museum has exhibits on derby history, including a peek into the life of jockeys and a roundup of the most illustrious horses. Highlights include a 360-degree HD film about the race that lets you feel the horses thundering by, the 30-minute walking tour of the grandstands (which includes some engaging yarns), the eye-popping derby hat collection and sipping mint juleps in the museum cafe.

★**Muhammad Ali Center**   MUSEUM
(502-584-9254; www.alicenter.org; 144 N 6th St; adult/child $14/9; ⏱9:30am-5pm Tue-Sat, noon-5pm Sun) This must-see museum tells the tale of the city's most famous native: a local boxer nicknamed the Louisville Lip or, simply, The Greatest. Highlights among the interactive exhibits include a ring where you shadowbox with Ali, and a punching bag to practice your rhythm. Videos of his famous fights and street poetry captivate, but it's the way they're put in context with the Vietnam War and civil rights issues that Ali fought for that give the place its power.

★**Louisville Slugger
Museum & Factory**   MUSEUM
(877-775-8443; www.sluggermuseum.com; 800 W Main St; adult/child $15/8; ⏱9am-5pm Mon-Sat, 11am-5pm Sun) See how baseball's most famous bat is made. Hillerich & Bradsby Co have been manufacturing the Louisville Slugger here since 1884. Admission includes a plant tour and a hall of baseball memorabilia that features Babe Ruth's 1927 record-setting bat and Hank Aaron's 700th home run bat. The displays will blow the minds of diehard fans. A take-home mini-slugger bat is included with the entrance fee.

Speed Art Museum   MUSEUM
(502-634-2700; www.speedmuseum.org; 2035 S 3rd St; adult/child $15/10, free Sun; ⏱10am-5pm Wed, Thu & Sat, 10am-8pm Fri, noon-5pm Sun) Built in 1927 and revamped to the tune of $60 million in recent years, Kentucky's most important art museum – unaffiliated but on the University of Louisville campus – is a beautiful juxtaposition of classic and

THE BOURBON TRAIL

Silky, caramel-colored bourbon whiskey was likely first distilled in Bourbon County, north of Lexington, around 1789. Today 95% of the world's bourbon is made in Kentucky, thanks to the state's pure, limestone-filtered water. Bourbon must contain at least 51% corn, and be stored in charred oak barrels for a minimum of two years. While connoisseurs drink it straight or with water, you must try a mint julep, the archetypal Southern drink made with bourbon, simple syrup and crushed mint.

The **Oscar Getz Museum of Whiskey History** (502-348-2999; www.oscargetzwhiskeymuseum.com; 114 N 5th St; 10am-5pm Mon-Fri, 10am-4pm Sat, noon-4pm Sun May-Oct, 10am-4pm Tue-Sat, noon-4pm Sun Nov-Apr) FREE in Bardstown tells the bourbon story with old moonshine stills and other artifacts.

Most of Kentucky's traditional distilleries, which are centered on Bardstown and Frankfort, offer tours and tastings. Several new craft distilleries also have joined the pack. Plan on taking in about three sites per day. The official Bourbon Trail website (www.kybourbontrail.com) has details. Note that it doesn't include every distillery.

Distilleries near Bardstown include the following:

Maker's Mark (p405) This restored Victorian distillery is like a bourbon theme park, with an old gristmill and a gift shop where you can seal your own bottle in molten red wax. Tours depart on a rolling basis.

Willet (502-348-0899; www.kentuckybourbonwhiskey.com; 1869 Loretto Rd; tours $18-22; 9:30am-5:30pm Mon-Sat) A family-owned distillery making small-batch bourbon in its own patented style. It's a gorgeous 120-acre property and a crowd favorite. Tours go on the hour.

Jim Beam American Stillhouse (502-543-9877; www.jimbeam.com; 526 Happy Hollow Rd, Clermont; 90min tours $14; 9am-5:30pm Mon-Sat, noon-4:30pm Sun) It makes the country's best-selling bourbon. Watch a film about the Beam family, take the 90-minute tour through the factory and warehouses, and then converge on the distillery's high-tech tasting room to sample the wares. Tours depart every half-hour.

Limestone Branch (270-699-9004; www.limestonebranch.com; 1280 Veterans Memorial Hwy, Lebanon; 1hr tours $8; 10am-5:30pm Mon-Thu, 10am-6pm Fri & Sat, 1-5:30pm Sun) Laid-back micro-distillery with a great backstory and venue like a western lodge.

Distilleries near Frankfort include:

Castle & Key (502-395-9070; www.castleandkey.com; 4445 McCracken Pike; tours $20-30; 9:30am-5pm Wed-Sat, 10:30am-5pm Sun, closed Wed Jan & Feb) Craft distillery in a fairy-tale setting, complete with turreted stone castle and lush gardens. The distiller makes gin and vodka; her bourbon is still aging. Intimate, small-group tours; reservations advised.

Woodford Reserve (859-879-1812; www.woodfordreserve.com; 7855 McCracken Pike, Versailles; 1hr tours weekday/weekend $15/20; 9am-5pm Mon-Sat, noon-4:30pm Sun, reduced hrs Jan & Feb) The prettiest of the lot, restored to its 1800s glory. The distillery still uses old-fashioned copper pots. Tours are hourly on the hour.

Buffalo Trace (800-654-8471; www.buffalotracedistillery.com; 1001 Wilkinson Blvd; 9am-5:30pm Mon-Sat, noon-5pm Sun) FREE The nation's oldest continuously operating distillery has free tours and tastings – a rarity these days. Tours go at least hourly.

If you'd rather not drive, sit back with your whiskey snifter on a tour with **Mint Julep Experiences** (502-583-1433; www.mintjuleptours.com; 140 N 4th St, Ste 326; full-day tours $129-159).

contemporary. It's highlighted by Spencer Finch's (of National September 11 Memorial Museum fame) Grand Atrium walled with fretted glass and Thai architect Kulapat Yantrasast's striking stacked concrete exterior. Collection highlights include Chuck Close's Barack Obama tapestry and Rembrandt's *Portrait of a 40-Year-Old Woman*.

✨ Festivals & Events

★ Kentucky Derby
SPORTS

(☏502-636-4400; www.kentuckyderby.com; 700 Central Ave) On the first Saturday in May, a who's who of upper-crust USA puts on their seersucker suits and most flamboyant hats and descends for the 'greatest two minutes in sports': the Kentucky Derby, the longest-running continuous sporting event in North America, when 20 horses thunder around the track at Churchill Downs for the race of a lifetime.

First Friday Hop
ART

(www.firstfridayhop.com; Main & Market Sts; ⊘7am-7pm, 1st Fri of month) More than 50 galleries, boutiques and restaurants participate in this monthly event that takes place downtown and in NuLu along Main and Market Sts. The LouLift bus provides free transportation.

☞ Tours

★ Waverly Hills Sanatorium
TOURS

(☏502-933-2142; www.therealwaverlyhills.com; 4400 Paralee Lane; 2/6hr tours $25/75; ⊘Fri & Sat Mar-Aug) Towering over Louisville like a mad king's castle, the abandoned Waverly Hills Sanatorium once housed victims of an early-20th-century tuberculosis epidemic. When patients died, workers dumped their bodies down a chute into the basement. No wonder the place is said to be one of the USA's most haunted buildings. Search for spooks with a nighttime ghost-hunting tour; the genuinely fearless can even spend the night!

Big Four Bridge
WALKING, CYCLING

(www.louisvillewaterfront.com; East River Rd; ⊘24hr) Built between 1888 and 1895, the Big Four Bridge, which spans the Ohio River and reaches the Indiana shore, has been closed to vehicular traffic since 1969 but was reopened in 2013 as a pedestrian and cycling path offering excellent city and river views.

🛏 Sleeping

Bed and Bike
APARTMENT $

(www.bedandbike.com; 822 E Market St; apt $100-160; ❄🐾) The owners of Parkside Bikes rent out several apartments on the second floor of their building, from studios to two-bedroom units. They're all brightly furnished in urban-cool style, and you have access to two bicycles to ride around town. The heart of NuLu location is superb, with a slew of eating and drinking options on your doorstep.

Rocking Horse B&B
B&B $$

(☏502-583-0408; www.rockinghorse-bb.com; 1022 S 3rd St; r $125-250; P❄🐾) Near the University of Louisville on a stretch of 3rd St once known as Millionaire's Row, this 1888 Richardsonian Romanesque mansion is chock-full of astounding historic detail. The six guest rooms are decorated with Victorian antiques and splendid original stained glass. Guests can eat their two-course breakfast in the English country garden and sip complimentary port in the parlor.

★ 21c Museum Hotel Louisville
DESIGN HOTEL $$$

(☏502-217-6300; www.21cmuseumhotels.com; 700 W Main St; r $209-329; P❄🐾🐾) This contemporary art museum–hotel features edgy design details: video screens project your distorted image and falling language on the wall as you wait for the elevator; water-blurred, see-through glass urinal walls line the men's rooms. Rooms, though not as interesting as the five contemporary art galleries that double as common areas, have high ceilings and lots of natural light.

🍴 Eating

★ Boujie Biscuit
AMERICAN $

(☏502-269-8426; www.facebook.com/boujiebiscuit; 1813 Frankfort Ave; mains $7-12; ⊘8am-3pm Thu & Fri, from 9am Sat, from 10am Sun) Each dish has the chef's signature biscuit as its base – a big, square, butter-brushed beauty – that's then loaded with something comforting and delicious, say chicken pot pie filling or chunky sausage gravy or peaches and brown sugar. The food and wee dining room are so homey you'll want to move in.

Gralehaus
AMERICAN $

(☏502-454-7075; www.gralehaus.com; 1001 Baxter Ave; mains $8-13; ⊘8am-4pm; 🐾) There's breakfast all day at this snug eatery housed in a historic early-20th-century home, and you should indeed indulge in its chef-centric takes on traditional Southern comforts (think locally sourced biscuits and duck gravy, lamb and grits). It's typically crowded, but seats seem to open up when you need them. Gralehaus links to Holy Grale pub across the back courtyard.

Garage Bar
PUB FOOD $

(☏502-749-7100; www.garageonmarket.com; 700 E Market St; mains $13-16; ⊘5-10pm Mon-Thu, 11am-11pm Fri & Sat, 11am-10pm Sun; 🐾) The best thing to do on a warm afternoon in

Louisville is to make your way to this uber-hip converted NuLu service station (accented by two kissing Camaros) and order a round of basil gimlets and the ham and cheese platter (a tasting of three in each category, all locally made, served with fresh bread and preserves; $28).

Silver Dollar　　　　SOUTHERN US **$$**
(☑502-259-9540; www.whiskeybythedrink.com; 1761 Frankfort Ave; mains $15-27; ◷5pm-2am Mon-Fri, from 10am Sat & Sun; ☎) Gastronomically noncommittal – we'll call the cuisine California-inspired New Southern – but unrepentantly bourbon obsessed, the Silver Dollar will dazzle your taste buds. Feast on chicken and waffles, beer can hen (roasted game hen served on an Old Milwaukee beer can) or fantastic *chilaquiles;* chase it with one of a 'poop ton' of bourbons (240 to be exact).

Decca　　　　AMERICAN **$$$**
(☑502-749-8128; www.deccarestaurant.com; 812 E Market St; mains $28-31; ◷5:30-10pm Mon-Sat; ☎) A beautiful space with a cork-and-wood floor, fountain-strewn patio and gorgeous Laguiole cutlery opened by a chef from San Francisco (albeit a Southerner by birth). Kentuckians were skeptical, but Annie Petry wooed and won. The emphasis of the delectable, seasonally changing menu is wood-fired roasts.

★**Proof on Main**　　　　AMERICAN **$$$**
(☑502-217-6360; www.proofonmain.com; 702 W Main St; mains $29-40; ◷7am-2pm & 5:30-10pm Mon-Thu, to 11pm Fri, 7am-2:30pm & 5:30-11pm Sat, to 10pm Sun; ☎) Arguably Louisville's best restaurant. The cocktails are incredible, the wine and bourbon 'library' (they're known to pour from exclusive and rare barrels of Woodford Reserve and Van Winkle) is long and satisfying, and exquisite dishes range from gourmet grilled cheese to a deliciously messy bison burger or a high-minded take on 'hot' fried chicken.

🍷 Drinking & Nightlife

★**Holy Grale**　　　　PUB
(☑502-459-9939; www.holygralelouisville.com; 1034 Bardstown Rd; ◷4pm-midnight Mon-Thu, 4pm-1am Fri, noon-1am Sat, noon-midnight Sun; ☎) One of Louisville's best bars is housed in an old church, with a menu of funked-up pub grub (gourmet Belgian *frites,* green curry mussels, short rib poutine; mains $6 to $14) and a buzzworthy beer list focusing on rare German, Danish, Belgian and Japanese brews (on tap). The most intense beers (up to 13% alcohol) can be found in the choir loft. Hallelujah!

Mr Lee's　　　　COCKTAIL BAR
(☑502-450-5368; www.mrleeslounge.com; 935 Goss Ave; ◷5pm-2am Wed-Sat, 6pm-1am Sun) Germantown's craft cocktail anchor is this satisfyingly retro establishment that serves a small but serious list of tipples. The semi-circular red leather bar gives way to a long mid-century-modern–styled, candlelit line of intimate tables and banquettes that are perfect for settling in for a boozy evening. It's even carpeted!

Monnik Beer Co　　　　MICROBREWERY
(☑502-742-6564; www.monnikbeer.com; 1036 E Burnett Ave; ◷11am-10pm Sun-Tue, to midnight Wed & Thu, to 1am Fri & Sat; ☎) Megapopular Monnik is in up-and-coming Schnitzelburg. There are 20 taps – the IPA stands out – in this restrained hipster environment where the beer isn't the only thing that's fabulous. The beer cheese with spent grain bread is so good you should need a prescription for it; and the seared grass-fed burgers are perfect. Bottoms up!

❶ Information

Visitor Center (☑502-379-6109; www.gotolouisville.com; 301 S 4th St; ◷10am-5pm Mon-Sat, noon-5pm Sun) Stuffed with brochures and has helpful staff. You can also pick up or redeem Bourbon Trail passports here.

❶ Getting There & Around

Louisville Muhammad Ali International Airport (p405) is 5 miles south of town on I-65. Get there by cab, Lyft or Uber ($20 to $25) or local bus 2 ($1.75, exact change required). The **Greyhound** (☑502-561-2807; www.greyhound.com; 720 W Muhammad Ali Blvd) station is just west of downtown.

TARC (www.ridetarc.org) operates the free LouLift buses that cover most of the city's attractions and coolest restaurants. The Silver Line travels on 4th St and goes to Churchill Downs, while the Red Line runs along Main and Market Sts in NuLu and downtown.

Louvelo (www.louvelo.com) is Louisville's bikeshare program, with 321 lime-green bikes at stations around town. Cost is $3.50 for a one-off 30-minute ride, or $7.50 for unlimited hour-long rides for a 24hr period.

Uber and Lyft are both handy for getting around the city.

Bluegrass Country

Drive through Bluegrass Country on a sunny day and you'll spy horses grazing in the brilliant-green hills dotted with ponds, poplar trees and handsome estate houses. These once-wild woodlands and meadows have been a center of horse breeding for more than 250 years. The region's natural limestone deposits – you'll see limestone bluffs rise majestically from out of nowhere – are said to produce especially nutritious grass. In spring the pastures bloom with tiny azure buds, hence the 'Bluegrass' name. Steer your wheels to Old Frankfort Pike (aka KY 1681), a byway between Frankfort and Lexington, and experience the landscape in all its glory.

Lexington

Cities don't get more genteel than Lexington, home of million-dollar houses and multimillion-dollar horses. Once the wealthiest and most cultured city west of the Allegheny Mountains, it was called 'the Athens of the West.' It's home to the University of Kentucky and is the heart of the thoroughbred industry. Pretty Victorian neighborhoods, garden-clad historic properties and small distilleries speckle the compact downtown. Brewery buffs and horse racing fans will find plenty to keep them occupied.

⊙ Sights

Kentucky Horse Park   PARK
(www.kyhorsepark.com; 4089 Iron Works Pkwy; summer adult/child $20/10, winter adult/child $12/6, horseback riding Apr-Oct $25; ⊙9am-5pm Apr-Oct, closed Mon & Tue Nov-Mar; 🅼) This educational theme park and equestrian sports center sits on 1200 acres just north of Lexington. Horses representing 50 different breeds live in the park and participate in special live shows.

Ashland   HISTORIC BUILDING
(🖉859-266-8581; www.henryclay.org; 120 Sycamore Rd; adult/child $15/7; ⊙10am-4pm Tue-Sat, 1-4pm Sun Apr-Nov, closed Sun Mar & Dec, closed Jan & Feb) Part historic home and part public park with storybook gardens, Ashland was the Italianate estate of famed statesman and great compromiser Henry Clay (1777–1852), who was one of Kentucky's favorite sons.

THOROUGHBREDS

For insight into the famed racehorses reared in these parts, sign up for an excursion with **Thoroughbred Heritage Horse Farm Tours** (🖉859-260-8687; www.seethechampions.com; 3hr tours adult/child $38/28; ⊙8:30am & 12:30pm). These narrated tours by van typically take you to Keeneland track for a walkabout, as well as to a thoroughbred farm or two. Destinations vary depending on racing schedules. Pick up is from various hotels around Lexington.

If you prefer to go on your own, you can visit the **Thoroughbred Center** (🖉859-293-1853; www.thorough bred-center.com; 3380 Paris Pike; adult/child $15/8; ⊙tours 9am Mon-Sat Apr-Oct, Mon-Fri 9am Nov-Mar). There you can see working racehorses up close during 90-minute tours of the stables, practice tracks and paddock

---

**Lexington Art League
at Loudoun House**   GALLERY
(🖉859-254-7024; www.lexingtonartleague.org; 209 Castlewood Dr; ⊙10am-4pm Tue-Thu, 10am-8pm Fri, 1-4pm Sat & Sun) **FREE** Art and architecture buffs won't want to miss this edgy, contemporary visual arts gallery housed in a freestanding American Gothic Revival mansion in the NoLi neighborhood, one of only five such structures left in the USA. The cutting-edge exhibitions, around six per year, are quite provocative by Lexington standards. Playful modern sculptures dot the grounds.

🛏 Sleeping

Lyndon House   B&B $$
(🖉859-420-2683; www.lyndonhouse.com; 507 N Broadway; r $199-279; 🅿❉@🛇) A detail-oriented ordained-minister-turned-foodie is your host at this discerning and spacious downtown B&B in a historic mansion dating from 1885. Anton takes hospitality seriously, particularly when it comes to breakfast. The seven rooms feature period furnishings and all the mod-cons, and you're steps from a long list of restaurants and breweries.

**★21c Museum
Hotel Lexington**   DESIGN HOTEL $$$
(🖉859-899-6800; www.21cmuseumhotels.com; 167 W Main St; r $209-329; 🅿❉🛇) This downtown design hotel is marked by twisted

sidewalk lampposts – hand-blown in Venice – outside its entrance. A Louisville transplant that's now in several states, it's more like a museum you can sleep in, with four contemporary art galleries throughout the hotel (as well as permanent local art on each floor).

✖ Eating & Drinking

★ Blue Door Smokehouse BARBECUE $

(☎859-252-4227; www.bluedoorsmokehouse.com; 226 Walton Ave; mains $9-16; ⊗11am-3pm Mon-Thu, to 8pm Fri & Sat) Follow your nose to this small smokehouse marked by a bright blue door where the buttery-tender brisket is the meat to beat. Arrive early to get a juicy plateful, because they run out as the day progresses. Back-up plan: pulled pork, baby.

Stella's Kentucky Deli DELI $

(☎859-255-3354; www.stellaskentuckydeli.com; 143 Jefferson St; sandwiches $6-10; ⊗9am-4pm; 🖥🍴) 🍴 This don't-miss deli has more than 30 years under its apron, but the latest owners have upped the cool quotient and concentrated on delicious provisions from local farmers. Great sandwiches, soups and salads, along with seasonal brews, are served in a colorful historic home with a reclaimed tin roof and sociable bar.

★ Carson's Food & Drink AMERICAN $$$

(☎859-309-3039; www.carsonsfoodanddrink. com; 362 E Main St; brunch $11-17, mains $20-36; ⊗11:30am-10pm Mon-Thu, 11:30am-11pm Fri, 10am-11pm Sat, 10am-10pm Sun; 🖥) Prohibition-era cocktails ($8 to $10) and bloody Marys (garnished with bacon, shrimp, celery, olives, pepper jack cheese and pepperoncini) make for great chasers at this rustic upscale spot that serves a meat-heavy menu of decadent contemporary comfort food. The béarnaise truffle fries with soft-shell crab are divine; and there's a BBQ pork belly and beer-cheese burger.

★ Country Boy Brewing MICROBREWERY

(☎859-554-6200; www.countryboybrewing.com; 436 Chair Ave; ⊗11am-midnight Mon-Sat, to 10pm Sun) True to its name, Country Boy – all trucker hats, taxidermy and camouflage – delivers great beer in an authentically Kentuckian venue. Up to 24 taps are devoted to the brewery's experimental concoctions, brewed with a rural Mikkeller-like approach (oak-aged sours with strawberries, jalapeño smoked porters, barrel-aged DIPAs). Guest beers are frequent, too.

★ Chocolate Holler COFFEE

(☎859-523-3619; www.facebook.com/chocolate hollerky; 400 Old Vine St, Ste 104; ⊗7:30am-10pm Mon-Fri, 10am-10pm Sat, noon-7pm Sun) Why isn't this concept on every street corner? A bar devoted to drinking chocolate! Baristas can help you choose from the seven types on offer, maybe the chili-spiked one from Mexico or the strong dark one from Tanzania. Can't decide? Get a flight of three ($8).

☆ Entertainment

★ Keeneland HORSE RACING

(☎859-254-3412; www.keeneland.com; 4201 Versailles Rd; general admission $5; ⊗races Apr & Oct) Second only to Churchill Downs in terms of quality of competition, Keeneland's races run in April and October, when you can also glimpse champions train from sunrise to 10am. Frequent horse auctions lure sheikhs, sultans, hedge-fund princes and those who love (or serve) them.

The Burl LIVE MUSIC

(www.theburlky.com; 375 Thompson Rd; cover $10-20; ⊗4pm-2:30am Mon & Wed-Sun) Across the railroad tracks from the Distillery District campus inside a finely restored 1928 train depot, the Burl has transformed Lexington's live music scene, which finally has a consistent home for local and regional acts.

ℹ Information

Visitor Center (VisitLEX; ☎859-233-7299; www.visitlex.com; 215 W Main St; ⊗9am-5pm Mon-Fri, from 10am Sat) Pick up maps and area driving tour information. Knowledgeable staff can help with just about anything. Located in the Historic Lexington Courthouse.

ℹ Getting There & Around

Blue Grass Airport (LEX; ☎859-425-3100; www.bluegrassairport.com; 4000 Terminal Dr) is 6 miles west of downtown, offering nonstop flights to 18 domestic destinations. **Greyhound** (☎859-299-0428; 477 NW New Circle Rd) is 2 miles northeast of downtown.

Lextran (☎859-253-4636; www.lextran.com; 150 E Vine St; ⊗6am-6pm Mon-Fri, 8am-4pm Sat & Sun) runs local buses (all fares $1). Bus 6 goes to the Greyhound station, bus 21 goes to the airport and Keeneland.

The city is testing a dockless bikeshare program with Spin (www.spin.pm). Use the app to find and unlock the orange bikes; cost is $1 per 30 minutes. Uber and Lyft both have decent networks in town.

Central Kentucky

Central Kentucky is the state's most celebrated region. The key reason: it's bourbon country! Kentucky's world-renowned homegrown spirit pays the bills, keeps the population buzzed and even flavors the local cuisine. Small and scenic Bardstown is the epicenter of big-name distilleries. More bucolic hooch makers cluster around Frankfort, the picture-postcard capital. Hip Louisville provides your urban fix with buzzy restaurants and exceptional museums (and bourbon, of course). Not to mention it hosts the world's most famous horse race. Lexington likewise knows its ponies. The refined city is the global hub for the horse-breeding industry, plus it brews a mean beer. Add in Berea's arts, Bowling Green's Corvettes and Mammoth Cave's eerie underworld and you've got the best of Kentucky.

Shaker Village of Pleasant Hill　　MUSEUM
(☑800-734-5611; www.shakervillageky.org; 3501 Lexington Rd, Harrodsburg; adult/child $14/7, riverboat rides $10/5; ⊙10am-5pm Mon-Thu & Sun, to 8pm Fri & Sat) This area was home to a community of the Shaker religious sect until the early 1900s. Tour dozens of impeccably restored buildings, set amid buttercup meadows and winding stone paths. There's an inn and restaurant, and a gift shop selling the Shakers' famous handicrafts. Hour-long riverboat rides show off the stunning limestone cliffs that rise up along the Kentucky River.

Shaker Village Inn　　INN $$
(☑859-734-5611; www.shakervillageky.org; 3501 Lexington Rd, Harrodsburg; r $125-195; 🅿🐾🛜) The main building is set in Harrodsburg's old trustee office, with its elaborate double-helix stairwell. Rooms are large, lovely and full of light, with high ceilings, wood furnishings and two rockers to read/snooze in. Rooms in 12 other heritage buildings follow suit. There are 72 rooms in total.

❶ Getting There & Around

Louisville Muhammad Ali International Airport (SDF; ☑502-367-4636; www.flylouisville.com; 600 Terminal Dr) – international in name only – is Kentucky's biggest airport, receiving direct domestic flights from Atlanta, Charlotte, Chicago, Minneapolis, New York and Washington, DC, among others.

The Bluegrass Pkwy runs from I-65 in the west to US 60 in the east, passing through some of the most luscious pasturelands in Kentucky.

MAKER'S MARK

Touring **Maker's Mark** (☑270-865-2099; www.makersmark.com; 3350 Burks Spring Rd, Loretto; 1hr tours $14; ⊙9:30am-5pm Mon-Thu, 9:30am-7pm Fri & Sat, 11:30am-5pm Sun May-Oct, to 5pm daily Nov-Apr) is like visiting a historic theme park, in a good way. You'll see the old gristmill, the 1840s master distiller's house and the old-fashioned firehouse. Watch oatmeal-esque sour mash ferment in huge cypress vats, see whiskey being double-distilled in copper pots and peek at bourbon barrels aging in wooden warehouses. Tours depart on a rolling basis; the last one is 90 minutes before closing time. At the gift shop you can stamp your own bottle with the iconic red-wax seal.

The tasting included with the tour is generous. Longer specialty tours are also available, but require advance booking. Star Hill Provisions, the restaurant on-site, lets you soak up any bourbon overindulgence with tasty Southern fare.

Bardstown and the heart of bourbon country are located 40 miles southeast of Louisville, with Mammoth Cave National Park another 70 miles or so south. Lexington lies about 78 miles east of Louisville. Renting your own ride is undoubtedly the best way to take it all in.

Daniel Boone National Forest

Rugged ravines and gravity-defying sandstone cliffs fill massive Daniel Boone National Forest in the Appalachian foothills of eastern Kentucky. Highlights include the wild crags of Red River Gorge in the northern portion and Cumberland Falls, aka the Niagara of the South, in the southern expanse. Hiking, rock climbing, camping, boating and fishing are the big to-dos.

**Cumberland Falls
State Resort Park**　　STATE PARK
(☑606-528-4121; www.parks.ky.gov; 7351 Hwy 90, Corbin) FREE Cumberland Falls is one of the few places in the world to see a moonbow, a rainbow that forms in the water's mist at night. The park website has dates for when the phenomenon occurs each month. A one-mile round-trip trail takes you to the falls, a 125ft-wide curtain of water that's pretty dramatic anytime.

Natural Bridge
State Resort Park
STATE PARK

(☑606-663-2214; www.parks.ky.gov; 2135 Natural Bridge Rd, Slade) FREE This state park borders Red River Gorge and is notable for its 65ft-high, 78ft-long sandstone arch. The grounds offer 20 miles of mostly short hiking trails; the most popular is the Original Trail to the arch's base (0.75 miles one way). If you don't want to walk, you can ride the sky lift over the bridge (adult/child $15/12 return).

Red River Outdoors
CLIMBING

(☑859-230-3567; www.redriveroutdoors.com; 415 Natural Bridge Rd, Slade; half/full-day climb from $65/90) ✐ Offers guided climbing trips for both beginners and experienced climbers, as well as cabin rentals ($110 to $145) on the ridgeline and occasional yoga retreats.

Mammoth Cave National Park

With the longest cave system on earth, this **national park** (☑270-758-2180; www.nps.gov/maca; 1 Mammoth Cave Pkwy; park entry free, tours adult $8-60, child $6-24; ☺8am-6:30pm mid-Mar–mid-Aug, 8am-6pm mid-Aug–Oct, 8:30am-4:30pm Nov–mid-Mar) has some 400 miles of surveyed passageways. Mammoth is at least three times longer than any other known cave, with vast interior cathedrals, bottomless pits and strange, undulating rock formations. Excellent ranger-guided tours explore the subterranean expanse. Book ahead if possible (at www.recreation.gov). Tours do sell out, especially in summer and on weekends.

In addition to the caves, the park contains 85 miles of trails – all for hiking, 60 miles for horseback riding and 25 miles for mountain biking. There are also three campgrounds (sites from $20). Reservations for camping (www.recreation.gov) and lodging (www.mammothcavelodge.com) can be made online.

GEORGIA

The largest state east of the Mississippi River is a labyrinth of geographic and cultural extremes: right-leaning Republican politics in the countryside rubs against liberal idealism in Atlanta and Savannah; small, conservative towns merge with sprawling, progressive, financially flush cities; northern mountains rise to the clouds and produce roaring rivers; and coastal marshlands teem with fiddler crabs and swaying cordgrass.

Georgia's southern beaches and islands are a treat, and so are its kitchens, bars and yes, its contradictions.

Atlanta, Georgia's culturally rich and multifaceted capital, best illustrates the paradox: on one side it's a bastion of African American enlightenment, a hip-hop hotbed, a film and tech industry upstart and LGBTIQ+ epicenter; on the other, Old South wealth and Fortune 500 investment marry in a city that is an international financial workhorse steeped in conservative Southern values. Together, a sexy metropolis emerges – it's way past *Gone with the Wind*.

❶ Information

Statewide tourism information is available through the Georgia Department of Economic Development (800-847-4842, www.explore georgia.org).

For information on camping and activities in state parks, contact Georgia Department of National Resources (800-864-7275, www. gastateparks.org).

Atlanta

With more than six million residents in the metro and outlying areas, Atlanta continues to experience explosive growth thanks to domestic transplants and international immigrants alike. Beyond the big-ticket Downtown attractions you will find a constellation of superlative restaurants, a palpable Hollywood influence (Atlanta is a hugely popular film-production center) and iconic African American history. That last point can't be overstated: any nationwide African American intellectual, political and artistic movement you can mention either had its genesis in Atlanta, or found a center of gravity here.

◉ Sights & Activities

◉ Downtown

Atlanta's Downtown packs a whole lot of world-class museums and attractions into an unbelievably condensed area, something few US cities can boast.

★Center for Civil
& Human Rights
MUSEUM

(☑678-999-8990; www.civilandhumanrights.org; 100 Ivan Allen Jr Blvd; adult/student & senior/child $20/18/16; ☺10am-5pm Mon-Sat, from noon Sun) This striking 2014 addition to Atlanta's **Centennial Olympic Park** (www.centennialpark.

ATLANTA FOR CHILDREN

Atlanta knows how to keep children entertained, delighted and educated. Many of the city's top attractions are both kid- and adult-friendly (bonus!), such as the World of Coca-Cola and **Georgia Aquarium** (☑404-581-4000; www.georgiaaquarium.com; 225 Baker St; adult/child $40/34; ☺10am-9pm Mon-Fri, from 9am Sat & Sun), while others are some of the Southeast's top child-driven attractions, for example the **Center for Puppetry Arts** (☑tickets 404-873-3391; www.puppet.org; 1401 Spring St NW; museum $12.50, guided tours $16.50; ☺9am-5pm Tue-Fri, from 10am Sat, from noon Sun) and **Fernbank Museum of Natural History** (☑404-929-6300; www.fernbankmuseum.org; 767 Clifton Rd; adult/child $20/18; ☺10am-5pm; ℗).

com; 265 Park Ave NW; ☺7am-11pm) is a sobering $68-million memorial to the American Civil Rights and global human-rights movements. Beautifully designed and thoughtfully executed, the indisputable highlight centers on an absolutely harrowing interactive mock Woolworth's lunch-counter sit-in simulation that will leave you speechless and move some to tears.

College Football Hall of Fame   MUSEUM
(www.cfbhall.com; 250 Marietta St; adult/senior/child $22/19/18; ☺10am-5pm Sun-Fri, 9am-6pm Sat; ℗🖶) It is impossible to overstate the importance of college football to American culture. This museum, relocated from Indiana in 2014 and revamped into this three-story, 94,256-sq-ft gridiron sanctuary, is a supremely cool and suitable shrine.

World of Coca-Cola   MUSEUM
(☑404-676-5151; www.woccatlanta.com; 121 Baker St; adult/senior/child $17/15/13; ☺10am-5pm Mon-Fri, from 9am Sat & Sun) This self-congratulatory museum might prove entertaining to fans of fizzy beverages and rampant commercialization. The climactic moment comes when guests sample Coke products from around the world – a taste-bud-twisting good time. But there are also Andy Warhol pieces on view, a 4-D film, company history and promotional materials aplenty.

Atlanta Movie Tours   TOURS
(☑855-255-3456; www.atlantamovietours.com; 327 Nelson St SW; adult/child from $20/10) Offers several *Walking Dead* filming location tours, including a trip into the fictional Woodbury, narrated by extras from the show who are chomping at the bit (get it?) to reveal all sorts of insider tidbits about cast members and filming. Other themed tours take in sites from *The Hunger Games*, *Taken* and other franchises.

CNN Center   TOURS
(☑404-827-2300; http://tours.cnn.com; 1 CNN Center, cnr Marietta St & Centennial Olympic Park Dr; adult/senior/child $15/14/12, VIP tour $33; ☺9am-5pm, VIP tours 9:30am, 11:30am, 1:30pm & 3:30pm Mon-Sat) The 55-minute behind-the-scenes tour through the headquarters of the international, 24-hour news giant is a good time for fans. Although visitors don't get very close to Wolf Blitzer (or his cronies), the 9am and noon time slots offer the best bets for seeing anchors live on air. A VIP tour gets you access to live newsrooms, control rooms and production studios.

⊙ Midtown

Midtown is like a hipper version of Downtown, with plenty of great bars, restaurants and cultural venues.

★High Museum of Art   MUSEUM
(☑404-733-4400; www.high.org; 1280 Peachtree St NE; adult/child under 5yr $14.50/free; ☺10am-5pm Tue-Thu & Sat, to 9pm Fri, noon-5pm Sun) Atlanta's modern High Museum was the first to exhibit art from Paris' Louvre and is a destination as much for its architecture as its world-class exhibits. The striking whitewashed multilevel building houses a permanent collection of eye-catching late-19th-century furniture, early American modern canvases from the likes of George Morris and Albert Gallatin, and postwar work from Mark Rothko.

Atlanta Botanical Garden   GARDENS
(☑404-876-5859; www.atlantabotanicalgarden.org; 1345 Piedmont Ave NE; adult/child $22/19; ☺9am-7pm Tue-Sun Apr-Oct, to 5pm Nov-Mar; ℗) In the northwest corner of Piedmont Park, this stunning 30-acre botanical garden has a Japanese garden, winding paths and the amazing Fuqua Orchid Center.

Atlanta

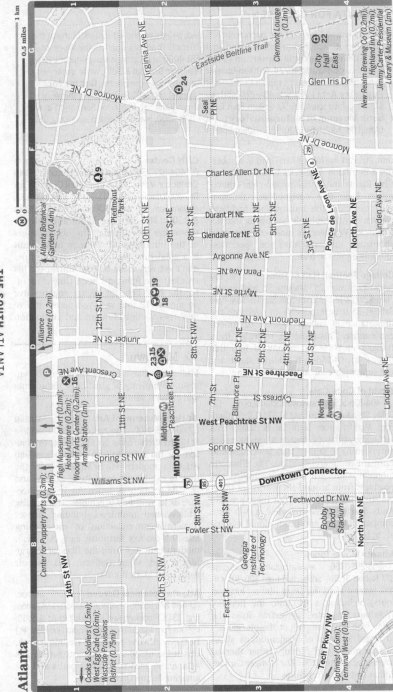

Cooks & Soldiers (0.5mi);
West Egg Cafe (0.6mi);
Westside Provisions
District (0.75mi)

Center for Puppetry Arts (0.3mi);
(14mi)

High Museum of Art (0.1mi);
Hotel Artmore (0.2mi);
Woodruff Arts Center (0.2mi); 16
Amtrak Station (1mi)

Alliance Theatre (0.2mi)

Atlanta Botanical
Garden (0.4mi)

New Realm Brewing Co (0.2mi);
Highland Inn (0.7mi);
Jimmy Carter Presidential
Library & Museum (1mi)

Clermont Lounge
(0.1mi)

City Hall
East

Glen Iris Dr

Seal
Pl NE

Eastside Beltline Trail

Virginia Ave NE

Monroe Dr NE

Monroe Dr NE

Ponce de Leon Ave NE

Charles Allen Dr NE

Durant Pl NE

Glendale Tce NE

Argonne Ave NE

Penn Ave NE

Myrtle St NE

Piedmont Ave NE

North Ave NE

Linden Ave NE

Linden Ave NE

North Ave NE

10th St NE

9th St NE

8th St NE

7th St NE

6th St NE

5th St NE

4th St NE

3rd St NE

12th St NE

11th St NE

Crescent Ave NE

Juniper St NE

Peachtree St NE

Peachtree Pl NE

Biltmore Pl

Cypress St

West Peachtree St NW

Spring St NW

Williams St NW

Downtown Connector

Techwood Dr NW

Bobby
Dodd
Stadium

North Avenue

Midtown

MIDTOWN

Piedmont
Park

8th St NW

6th St NW

10th St NW

Fowler St NW

Georgia Institute
of Technology

Ferst Dr

Tech Pkwy NW

Optimist (0.6mi);
Terminal West (0.9mi)

14th St NW

9

24

22

19
18

23 15
16

7

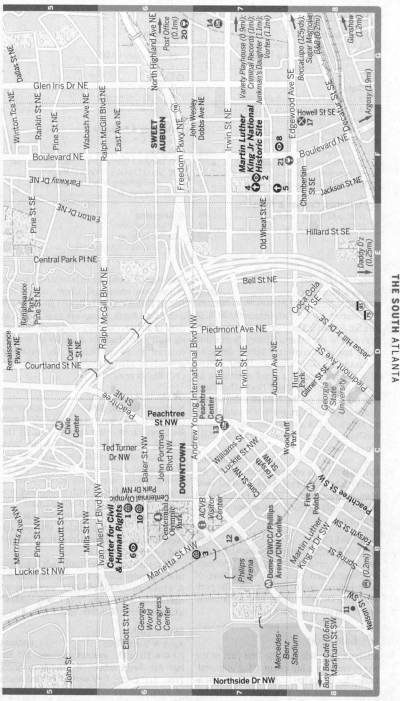

Atlanta

Margaret Mitchell House & Museum MUSEUM
(☑404-249-7015; www.atlantahistorycenter.com; 979 Crescent Ave NE; adult/student/child $13/10/5.50; ⊙10am-5:30pm Mon-Sat, from noon Sun) Operated by the Atlanta History Center, this home has been converted into a shrine to the author of *Gone With the Wind*. Mitchell wrote her epic in a small apartment in the basement of this Tudor Revival building, which is listed on the National Register of Historic Places. There are on-site exhibitions on Mitchell's life and writing career, and a two-hour looping documentary, *The Making of a Legend*.

A combo ticket (adult/student/child $21.50/18/9) also gets you access to the **Atlanta History Center** (☑404-814-4000; www.atlantahistorycenter.com; 130 West Paces Ferry Rd NW; adult/child $16.50/11; ⊙11am-4pm Mon-Sat, 1-4pm Sun).

Piedmont Park PARK
(☑404-875-7275; www.piedmontpark.org; 400 Park Dr NE; ⊙6am-11pm) FREE A glorious, rambling urban park and the setting of many cultural and music festivals. The park has fantastic bike paths and a Saturday Green Market (from 9am to 1pm).

⊙ East Side

Atlanta's East Side was the first part of the city to embrace a hip urban living upheaval: Little Five Points has been a bastion of counterculture since the '80s; quality foodie ha-

vens started sprouting in bohemian Decatur in the '90s; revitalized urban districts like Inman Park, Candler Park, Old Fourth Ward and East Atlanta Village are now reborn as darling districts for deep-pocketed millennials with a penchant for craft. It's all in stark contrast to Sweet Auburn, the stomping grounds of Martin Luther King Jr and the Civil Rights revolution.

★ **Martin Luther King Jr National Historic Site** HISTORIC SITE
(☑404-331-5190; www.nps.gov/malu; 450 Auburn Ave, Sweet Auburn; ⊙9am-5pm; P⊞) FREE The historic site commemorates the life, work and legacy of the Civil Rights leader and one of the great Americans. The site takes up several blocks. Stop by the excellent visitor center to get oriented with a map and brochure of area sites, a 20-minute film, *New Time, New Voice*, and exhibits that elucidate the context – the segregation, systemic oppression and racial violence that inspired and fueled King's work.

A 1.5-mile landscaped trail leads from here to the **Jimmy Carter Presidential Library & Museum** (☑404-865-7100; www.jimmycarterlibrary.org; 441 Freedom Pkwy, Poncey-Highland; adult/senior/child $8/6/free; ⊙8am-5pm; P).

Martin Luther King Jr Birthplace LANDMARK
(☑404-331-5190; www.nps.gov/malu; 501 Auburn Ave, Sweet Auburn; ⊙10am-4pm) FREE Free, first-come, first-served guided tours of King's childhood home take about 30

minutes to complete and require same-day registration, which can be made at the visitor center at the National Historic Site – arrive early, as slots fill fast. The tours can depart anytime between 10am and 4pm, but you are free to visit the rest of the park at your leisure before your designated tour time.

First Ebenezer
Baptist Church
CHURCH

(📞404-331-5190; www.nps.gov/malu; 407 Auburn Ave NE, Sweet Auburn; ⊙9am-5pm) **FREE** Martin Luther King Jr, his father and grandfather were all pastors here, and King Jr's mother was the choir director. Sadly she was murdered here by a deranged gunman while she sat at the organ in 1974. A multimillion-dollar restoration, completed in 2011, brought the church back to the 1960–68 period when King Jr served as co-pastor with his father. Today looped recordings of King's speeches play in the church building.

Sunday services are now held at the new **Ebenezer Church** (📞404-688-7300; www.historicebenezer.org; 101 Jackson St NE, Sweet Auburn; ⊙service 9am & 11:30am Sun) across the street.

⊙ Westside

This largely industrial swath is home to the Westside Provisions District in West Midtown, a booming shopping and dining complex. Here, and along the BeltLine's soon-to-explode Westside Trail, are the focal points of this burgeoning destination entertainment district, which has been prime fodder for breweries and film studios.

✺ Festivals & Events

Atlanta Jazz Festival MUSIC
(📞404-546-7246; www.atlanta.net/events/atlanta-jazz-festival; Piedmont Park; ⊙May) **FREE** One of the largest free jazz festivals in the country has attracted big names such as Miles Davis, Dizzy Gillespie and Nina Simone over its 40-year history. The month-long event culminates in live concerts in Piedmont Park on Memorial Day weekend.

🛏 Sleeping

Atlanta remains short on independent boutique options, long on chains. Rates at Downtown hotels tend to fluctuate wildly depending on whether there is a large convention in town. The least expensive option is to stay in one of the many chain hotels along the MARTA line outside Downtown and take the train into the city for sightseeing.

Highland Inn INN $
(📞404-874-5756; www.thehighlandinn.com; 644 N Highland Ave, Virginia-Highland; s/d from $73/103; 🅿✳🛜) This European-style, 65-room independent inn, built in 1927, has appealed to touring musicians over the years. Rooms aren't huge, but it has a great location in the Virginia-Highland area and is as affordably comfortable as being Downtown. It's one of the few accommodations in town with single rooms.

Ellis Hotel BOUTIQUE HOTEL $$
(📞404-523-5155; www.ellishotel.com; 176 Peachtree St NW; r $159-249; 🅿✳🛜🐾) With business-chic rooms warmly dressed in blue and gray hues and ostrich-skin headboards, the Ellis is contemporary and subtly boutique. You can sleep inside a magnetic field in the Wellness Room; or pick a room on the pet-friendly floor, women-only floor or 'Fresh Air' floor (with private access and special cleaning rules for allergy sufferers).

Hotel Artmore BOUTIQUE HOTEL $$
(📞404-876-6100; www.artmorehotel.com; 1302 W Peachtree St; r $150-320; 🅿✳@🛜) This 1924 Spanish-Mediterranean architectural landmark has been completely revamped into an artistic boutique hotel that's become an urban sanctuary for those who

THE SOUTH ATLANTA

MARTIN LUTHER KING JR: A CIVIL RIGHTS GIANT

Martin Luther King Jr, the quintessential figure of the Civil Rights movement and arguably America's greatest leader, was born and raised in Atlanta, the son of a preacher and choir leader. His lineage was significant not only because he followed his father to the pulpit of Ebenezer Baptist Church, but also because his political speeches rang out with a preacher's inflections. King remains one of the most respected figures of the 20th century and is Atlanta's quintessential African American hero, his legacy emblazoned across the city's historic Sweet Auburn district, home to the Martin Luther King Jr National Historic Site.

appreciate their trendiness with a dollop of discretion. It wins all sorts of accolades: excellent service, a wonderful courtyard with fire pit and a superb location across the street from Arts Center MARTA station.

Sugar Magnolia B&B B&B $$
(☎404-222-0226; www.sugarmagnoliabb.com; 804 Edgewood Ave NE, Inman Park; r $165-205; [P]❄@📶) This lovely four-room inn occupies an impeccable 1892 Queen Anne Victorian mansion in Inman Park. Five original working fireplaces, a supremely relaxing back porch and firepit are highlights, as is Debbie, hostess with the mostest who whips up Belgian waffles and Dutch baby pancakes for breakfast. Our favorite room is the blue-curtained Royal Suite with a massive terrace and a tiled bathroom.

★**Urban Oasis B&B** B&B $$
(☎770-714-8618; www.urbanoasisbandb.com; 130a Krog St NE, Inman Park; r $155-215; [P]❄📶🐾) Hidden inside a gated and repurposed 1950s cotton-sorting warehouse, this retro-modern loft B&B is urban dwelling at its best. Enter into a huge and funky common area with natural light streaming through massive windows and make your way to one of three rooms, all discerningly appointed with Haywood Wakefield mid-century modern furnishings. In 2019, Urban Oasis featured on MTV's *Real World* reality series.

★**Social Goat B&B** B&B $$
(☎404-626-4830; www.thesocialgoatbandb.com; 548 Robinson Ave SE, Grant Park; r $135-240; [P]❄📶) Skirting Grant Park, this wonderfully restored 1900 Queen Anne Victorian mansion has six rooms decorated in country-French-style and is loaded with period antiques. More importantly, however, you'll share the real estate with goats, turkeys, ducks, chickens and cats. A true country escape, plunked into one of the nation's largest urban areas.

🍴 Eating

After New Orleans, Atlanta is the best city in the South to eat, and the food culture here is nothing short of obsessive. The Westside Provisions District, Krog Street Market and Ponce City Market are all newish and hip mixed-use residential and restaurant complexes sprinkled among Atlanta's continually transitioning urban neighborhoods.

🍴 Downtown & Midtown

★**BoccaLupo** ITALIAN $$
(☎404-577-2332; www.boccalupoatl.com; 753 Edgewood Ave NE, Inman Park; mains $17-19; ⏲5:30-10pm Tue-Thu, to 11pm Fri & Sat; 📶) There is so much to love about this candlelit Italian Southern comfort-food haunt led by Mario Batali–trained chef Bruce Logue, but perhaps none more than his Southern-fried-chicken parma with creamy collards and *strano* pasta. It's hands down a top-five Atlanta dish. This Southern soul food with Italian tweak is made with a lotta love and not to be missed.

Daddy D'z BARBECUE $$
(☎404-222-0206; www.daddydz.com; 264 Memorial Dr SE; sandwiches $8-14, plates $14-24; ⏲11am-10pm Mon-Thu, to 11pm Fri & Sat, noon-9pm Sun; [P]) A juke joint of a barbecue shack, consistently voted one of the top in town, with a central location. From the graffiti murals on the red, white and blue exterior, to the all-powerful smoky essence, to the reclaimed booths on the covered patio, there is soul to spare. Order the succulent ribs with corn bread, and you'll leave smiling.

Empire State South SOUTHERN US $$$
(☎404-541-1105; www.empirestatesouth.com; 999 Peachtree St NE; mains lunch $13-22, dinner $28-39; ⏲7am-10pm Mon-Fri, from 4pm Sat; 📶) This rustic-hip Midtown bistro serves imaginative New Southern fare and it does not disappoint, be it at breakfast ($8 to $11) or throughout the day. It makes its own bagels, the attention to coffee detail approaches Pacific Northwest levels, and it mixes fried chicken, bacon marmalade *and* pimento cheese on a biscuit!

South City Kitchen SOUTHERN US $$$
(☎404-873-7358; www.southcitykitchen.com; 1144 Crescent Ave NE; mains lunch $11-25, dinner $18-41; ⏲11am-3:30pm & 5-10pm Mon-Fri, from 10am Sat & Sun; 📶) An upscale, long-standing Southern kitchen featuring tasty updated and elaborated staples like buttermilk-fried chicken served with sautéed collards and red-bliss potatoes, catfish Reubens and shrimp and Geechee Boy grits with tasso ham and smoked tomato-poblano gravy. Start with goat's-cheese-stuffed fried green tomatoes, a Southern specialty *before* the movie.

🍴 East Side

★**Octopus Bar** FUSION $$
(☎404-627-9911; www.octopusbaratl.com; 560 Gresham Ave SE, East Atlanta; dishes $8-22;

⊙10:30pm-2:30am Tue-Sat) Leave your hang-ups at the hotel – this is punk-rock dining – and get to know what's good at this unsigned indoor-outdoor patio dive nuanced with graffitied-up walls and ethereal electronica. No reservations, so line up early, and chow down on a Maine lobster roll (drawn butter, tomalley mayo), shoyu ramen (farm egg) or many other innovative executions of fusion excellence.

★**Dish Dive** AMERICAN $$
(☑404-957-7918; www.dishdivekitchen.com; 2233 College Ave NE; mains $10-18; ⊙5-10pm Tue-Sat) Located in a teeny house near some railroad tracks, Dish Dive is cooler than you and it doesn't care. Anyone is welcome here, and the food – fresh, seasonal cuisine such as turmeric and black-pepper pappardelle, fried spaghetti squash with poblano-chocolate sauce and the never-off-the-menu master-piece, braised pork-belly French toast – is high-value, easy-on-the-wallet eating.

Leon's Full Service FUSION $$
(☑404-687-0500; www.leonsfullservice.com; 131 E Ponce de Leon Ave; mains lunch $10-21, $16-35; ⊙5pm-midnight Mon, from 11:30am Tue-Thu & Sun, to 2am Fri & Sat; 🐾) Leon's can come across as a bit pretentious, but the gorgeous concrete bar and open floor plan spilling out of a former service station and on to a groovy heated deck with floating beams remains cooler than thou and fully packed at all times. You may find prosciutto-wrapped trout and braised short ribs on the changing menu.

Vortex BURGERS $$
(☑404-688-1828; www.thevortexbarandgrill.com; 438 Moreland Ave NE, Little Five Points; burgers $10-15; ⊙11am-midnight Sun-Thu, to 2am Fri & Sat) An age-21-and-up joint cluttered with Americana memorabilia, the godfather of Atlanta burger joints is where alterna-hipsters mingle alongside Texas tourists and Morehouse College steppers. Burgers range from impressive to outlandish but are always some of the most heralded and heart-stopping in Atlanta. The 20ft-tall skull facade is a Little Five Points landmark of pre–Olympic Games outrageousness.

★**Gunshow** MODERN AMERICAN $$$
(☑404-380-1886; www.gunshowatl.com; 924 Garrett St SE, Glenwood Park; small plates $10-18; ⊙6-9pm Tue-Sat; 🐾) Celebrity chef Kevin Gillespie's innovative and unorthodox Gunshow is an explosively good night out. Guests

choose between a dozen or so smallish dishes, dreamed up by chefs in the open kitchen, who then hawk their blood, sweat and culinary tears dim-sum-style tableside.

Staplehouse AMERICAN $$$
(☑404-524-5005; www.staplehouse.com; 541 Edgewood Ave SE; small plates $8-30, tasting menu $105; ⊙5:30-10pm Sun & Tue-Thu, to 11pm Fri & Sat; 🅿🐾) 🍴 The hottest table in Atlanta and the darling du jour of Southern foodies, Staplehouse dishes up innovative, seasonal New American cuisine. Small to medium plates including chicken-liver tart with burnt honey and blood orange are served with such artful precision you kinda feel bad about eating them (except they're delicious, so not *that* bad). The seasonal menu changes often.

✕ Westside

★**Busy Bee Café** SOUTHERN US $
(☑404-525-9212; www.thebusybeecafe.com; 810 Martin Luther King Jr Dr NW; mains $14-19; ⊙11am-7pm Mon-Sat, from noon Sun) Politicians, police officers, urbanites and hungry miscreants, along with celebrities (it's had pop-ins by MLK Jr, Obama and OutKast), all converge over the city's best fried chicken paired with soul-food sides such as collard greens, candied yams, fried okra and mac 'n' cheese. This Westside classic has been steeped in hospitality and honest-to-goodness food since 1947.

West Egg Cafe DINER $
(☑404-872-3973; www.westeggcafe.com; 1100 Howell Mill Rd, Westside Provisions District; mains $8-15; ⊙7am-4pm Mon-Fri, 8am-5pm Sat & Sun; 🅿🐾♿) Belly up to the marble breakfast counter or grab a table and dive into black-bean cakes and eggs, turkey-sausage Benedict, pimento-cheese and bacon omelet, or a fried green tomato BLT. It's all reimagined versions of old-school classics, served in a stylish and spare dining room.

★**Cooks & Soldiers** BASQUE $$
(☑404-996-2623; www.cooksandsoldiers.com; 691 14th St NW; small plates $6-18; ⊙5-10pm Sun-Wed, to 11pm Thu, to midnight Fri & Sat; 🐾) A game-changing Westside choice, this Basque-inspired hot spot specializes in *pintxos* (Basque-style tapas) and wood-fired *asadas* (grills) designed to share. Both the food and cocktails are outstanding. Highlights include the house gin and tonics, coal-roasted mushrooms with goat's cheese,

crème fraîche and black truffle, and an $84 wood-grilled bone-in rib eye that clocks in at an obviously shareable 2.2lbs (1kg)!

★ Optimist
SEAFOOD $$$

([phone] 404-477-6260; www.theoptimistrestaurant. com; 914 Howell Mill Rd; mains $32-50; ⊙ 11:30am-2:30pm & 5-10pm Mon-Fri, 5-11pm Sat, 5-10pm Sun; [wifi]) ∅ In a short space, we could never do this Westside sustainable-seafood mecca justice. In a word, astonishing! Start with crispy calamari with salsa *matcha* and almonds then move on to a duck-fat-poached swordfish or a daring whole grilled octopus with *aji amarillo* and poblano peppers, and finish with a scoop of house-made salted-caramel ice cream.

🍷 Drinking & Nightlife

Atlanta has a busy bar scene, ranging from neighborhood dives to hipster hangouts that want to pass for neighborhood dives to straight-up opulent night haunts for the wealthy and beautiful. Wherever you go, you may notice that this city has one of the most racially integrated social scenes in the country, and that's reason enough to raise a glass.

★ Sister Louisa's Church of the Living Room & Ping Pong Emporium
BAR

([phone] 404-522-8275; www.facebook.com/SisterLoui sasChurch; 466 Edgewood Ave, Edgewood; ⊙ 5pm-3am Mon-Sat, to midnight Sun; [wifi]) This cradle of Edgewood's bar revival fosters a church theme, but it's nothing like Westminster Abbey. Sacrilegious art peppers every patch of free wall space, the kind of offensive stuff that starts wars in some parts. Praise the resistance to fancy craft cocktails and join the congregation, chuckling at the artistry or staring at mesmerizing table-tennis matches.

★ Argosy
PUB

([phone] 404-577-0407; www.argosy-east.com; 470 Flat Shoals Ave SE; ⊙ 5pm-2:30am Mon-Fri, noon-2:30am Sat, to midnight Sun; [wifi]) This East Atlanta gastropub nails it with an extensive list of rare craft beers (35 taps), elevated bar food – house-cut Kennebec potato fries, miso quinoa burger, wood-fired pizzas – and a vibe that invites you to stay for the rest of the evening. The multi-angled bar snakes its way through a rustic-chic space and living-room-style lounge areas.

Ladybird Grove & Mess Hall
BAR

([phone] 404-458-6838; www.ladybirdatlanta.com; 684 John Wesley Dobbs Ave NE; ⊙ 11am-late Tue-Sun) With an enviable location (and enormous patio) overlooking the BeltLine, Ladybird offers its patrons one of the best drinking views in Atlanta. Complement that cocktail or draft beer with some of the classy pub grub on offer from the kitchen. Last call depends on how busy the bar is.

Brick Store Pub
BAR

([phone] 404-687-0990; www.brickstorepub.com; 125 E Court Sq, Decatur; draft beers $5-12; ⊙ 11am-1am Mon-Wed, to 2am Thu-Sat, noon-1am Sun) Beer hounds geek out on Atlanta's best craft-beer selection at this pub in Decatur, with some 30 meticulously chosen drafts (including those in the more intimate Belgian beer bar upstairs). Nearly 300 beers by the bottle are served from a 15,000-bottle vault, drawing a fun, young crowd every night.

Kimball House
COCKTAIL BAR

([phone] 404-378-3502; www.kimball-house.com; 303 E Howard Ave, Decatur; ⊙ 5pm-midnight Sun-Thu, to 1am Fri & Sat; [wifi]) Housed in an atmospheric period dining room in a restored train depot slightly off the grid in Decatur, Kimball House harbors a vaguely saloon-like feel under overhead belt-driven fans. It specializes in craft cocktails (around $13), absinthe and a long list of flown-in-fresh oysters.

★ New Realm Brewing Co
MICROBREWERY

([phone] 404-968-2778; www.newrealmbrewing.com; 550 Somerset Tce NE, No 101; ⊙ 4-10pm Mon-Thu, to midnight Fri & Sat, 11am-10pm Sun; [wifi]) Ex-Stone Brewing Co brewmaster Mitch Steele wrote the book on IPAs. His latest venture, a 20,000-sq-ft restaurant and brewery along the BeltLine's Eastside Trail, is a coup for Southern hopheads. Eight taps (four direct from serving tanks behind the bar) harbor triple IPAs and small-batch brews guzzled by a fun crowd ogling the Atlanta skyline from the upstairs terrace.

☆ Entertainment

Clermont Lounge
DANCE

(www.clermontlounge.net; 789 Ponce de Leon Ave NE, Poncey-Highland; ⊙ 3pm-4am) The Clermont is a strip club, the oldest in Atlanta. But not *just* a strip club. It's a bedrock of the Atlanta scene that welcomes dancers of all ages, races and body types. In short, it's a strip club built for strippers, although

LGBTIQ+ ATLANTA

Atlanta is one of the few places in Georgia with a noticeable and active gay and lesbian population, probably second only to San Francisco in terms of visibility and population nationwide. Midtown is the center of gay life; the epicenter is around Piedmont Park and the intersection of 10th St and Piedmont Ave, where you can check out **Blake's** (☏404-892-5786; www.blakesontheparkatlanta.com; 227 10th St NE; ⊘3pm-3am Mon-Fri, 1pm-3am Sat, 1pm-1am Sun), Atlanta's classic gay bar, or **10th & Piedmont** (www.10thandpiedmont.com; 991 Piedmont Ave NE; ⊘10am-3pm & 5-10pm Mon-Thu, to 11pm Fri, 10am-4pm & 5-11pm Sat, 10am-6pm Sun), good for food and late-night shenanigans. The town of Decatur, east of downtown Atlanta, has a significant lesbian community. For news and information, grab a copy of the weekly *Peach ATL* (www.peachatl.com), monthly *Goliath Atlanta* (www.goliathatlanta.com) or visit www.gayatlanta.com.

Atlanta Pride Festival (www.atlantapride.org) is a massive annual celebration of the city's gay and lesbian community. It's held in October in and around Piedmont Park.

the audience – and *everyone* comes here at some point – has a grand time as well.

Terminal West
LIVE MUSIC
(☏404-876-5566; www.terminalwestatl.com; 887 W Marietta St, Westside; ⊘box office 11am-5pm Tue-Fri) One of Atlanta's best live-music venues, this concert space is located inside a beautifully revamped 100-year-old iron and steel foundry on the Westside.

Woodruff Arts Center
ARTS CENTER
(☏404-733-4200; www.woodruffcenter.org; 1280 Peachtree St NE; ⊘box office noon-6pm Tue-Sat, to 5pm Sun) This arts complex contains within its campus the High Museum (p407), the Atlanta Symphony Orchestra and the **Alliance Theatre** (☏404-733-4650; www.alliancetheatre.org).

Variety Playhouse
LIVE MUSIC
(☏404-524-7354; www.variety-playhouse.com; 1099 Euclid Ave NE, Little Five Points; ⊘box office noon-6pm Mon-Fri) A historic, smartly booked and well-run concert venue built in 1940 and fully renovated in 2015. It hosts a variety of touring artists and is one of the main anchors of the Little Five Points scene.

🔒 Shopping

★ Criminal Records
MUSIC
(☏404-215-9511; www.criminalatl.com; 1154 Euclid Ave, Little Five Points; ⊘11am-9pm Mon-Sat, noon-7pm Sun) This throwback record store is stacked wall to wall with a library's worth of new pop, soul, jazz and metal, on CD or vinyl. It has a fun music-related book section, and a great collection of comic books and graphic novels. Basically, a certain kind of music-lover and genre-loving geek could live here.

Junkman's Daughter
VINTAGE
(☏404-577-3188; www.thejunkmansdaughter.com; 464 Moreland Ave NE, Little Five Points; ⊘11am-7pm Mon-Fri, to 8pm Sat, noon-7pm Sun) A defiant and fiercely independent cradle of counterculture since 1982, this 10,000-sq-ft alternative superstore stocks racks of vintage, ornery bumper stickers, kitschy toys and tchotchkes, *Star Wars* lunch boxes, incense, wigs, offensive coffee mugs and a whole lot more. It put Little Five Points on the map.

Citizen Supply
CLOTHING
(www.citizensupply.com; 675 Ponce de Leon Ave NE, Ponce City Market; ⊘10am-9pm Mon-Sat, noon-8pm Sun) This fiercely curated all-under-one-roof flagship shop stocks a dizzying array of top-quality – some say hipster – brands of products you didn't know you wanted until you saw them: foresty pomades from Mail Room Barber Co, Edison electric bikes, Bradley Mountain canvas and leather bags, **Wander North Georgia** (www.wandernorthgeorgia.com; 33 N Main St; ⊘11am-5pm Mon-Thu, to 6pm Fri & Sat, noon-5pm Sun) T-shirts, Atlanta-centric art, Loyal Stricklin leather-bound Aviator mugs and a whole lot more.

Richards Variety Store
GIFTS & SOUVENIRS
(www.richardsvarietystore.com; 931 Monroe Dr NE; ⊘10am-8pm Mon-Sat, 11am-6pm Sun) There is almost nothing this massive, good-time emporium doesn't have. Hebrew alphabet kits? Ouija boards? Paper pinhole cameras? 3-D White House puzzles? Stuffed penguins? You'll tap into your inner child as you rummage sections devoted to toys, puzzles, housewares, books, art, gadgets – the aisles go on and on. There is *something* in here you didn't know you needed!

THE SOUTH ATLANTA

ATLANTA BELTLINE

With an 8:1 return on investment and a transformative way of moving through the city, Atlanta is wallowing in the afterglow of its best idea in decades: the Atlanta BeltLine, a 22-mile rail corridor encircling the city that's being repurposed as a multiuse trail. In all fairness, it was the idea of former Georgia Tech student Ryan Gravel, but the city's adaptation of his master's thesis – the most comprehensive transportation and economic development effort ever undertaken in Atlanta and among the largest, most wide-ranging urbanredevelopment programs currently under way in the US – has spawned a payout that would send a Las Vegas casino into crisis mode: some $4.1 billion in economic development from an initial city investment of $500 million – and a lot more on the way where that came from.

Eco Denizen GIFTS & SOUVENIRS
(www.ecodenizen.net; 999 Peachtree St NE; ⊙11am-8pm Mon-Sat, noon-6pm Sun) This eco-driven mom-and-pop-run gift shop is full of coveted stuff: vegan wallets from Matt & Nat, Tokens & Icons wine openers fashioned from recycled Major League Baseball bats and professional tennis rackets, and local art such as Houston Llew's glass-oncopper pop-art pieces.

ⓘ Information

EMERGENCY & MEDICAL SERVICES
Atlanta Medical Center (☑404-265-4000; www.atlantamedcenter.com; 303 Parkway Dr NE; ⊙24hr) A tertiary-care hospital considered Atlanta's best since 1901.

Grady Memorial Hospital (☑404-616-1000; www.gradyhealth.org; 80 Jesse Hill Jr Drive SE) Home to the Marcus Trauma Center, Atlanta's only nationally verified Level 1 trauma center.

MEDIA
Atlanta (www.atlantamagazine.com) A monthly general-interest magazine covering local issues, arts and dining.

Atlanta Daily World (www.atlantadailyworld. com) The nation's oldest continuously running African American newspaper (since 1928).

Atlanta Journal-Constitution (www.ajc.com) Atlanta's major daily newspaper, with a good travel section on Sunday.

Creative Loafing (www.creativeloafing. com) For hip tips on music, arts and theater, this free alternative weekly comes out every Wednesday.

TOURIST INFORMATION
Atlanta Convention & Visitors Bureau (www. atlanta.net) Maps, information about attractions, restaurants, outdoor recreation and accommodations; operates visitor centers at Centennial Olympic Park (☑404-577-2148; 65 Upper Alabama St, Underground Atlanta; ⊙10am-6pm Mon-Sat, noon-6pm Sun) and Hartsfield-Jackson Atlanta International Airport (☑404-305-8426; 6000 N Terminal Pkwy, North Terminal; ⊙9am-9pm Mon-Fri, to 6pm Sat, noon-6pm Sun).

ⓘ Getting There & Away

Atlanta straddles the intersection of three interstates: I-20, I-75 and I-85. **Hartsfield-Jackson International Airport** (ATL, Atlanta; ☑800-897-1910; www.atl.com), 9.5 miles south of Downtown, is the world's busiest airport by passenger traffic. The easiest way into the city from the airport is MARTA, the city's rail system. **Greyhound** (☑404-584-1728; www.greyhound. com; 232 Forsyth St) and **Amtrak** (www.amtrak. com/stations/atl; 1688 Peachtree St NW) both serve the city as well.

Flights, cars and tours can be booked online at lonelyplanet.com/bookings.

ⓘ Getting Around

Despite its sprawling layout and debilitating traffic, Atlanta is fairly easy to navigate both with your own set of wheels or on public transportation. The city is well served by the MARTA bus and rail system and a Downtown tram. And once the groundbreaking Atlanta BeltLine completes its loop by 2030, Atlanta's multiuse trail system will be one of the most progressive in North America, if not the world.

North Georgia

Elevation seekers should head to North Georgia, which sits at the southern end of the great Appalachian Range. Those mountains, and their surrounding foothills and upcountry, provide superb mountain scenery, as well as some decent wines and frothing rivers. Fall colors emerge late here, peaking in October. A few days are warranted to see sites such as the 1200ft-deep Tallulah Gorge, and the mountain scenery and hiking trails at Vogel State Park and Unicoi State Park.

Dahlonega

In 1828 Dahlonega was the site of the first gold rush in the USA (locals are known as 'Nuggets'). These days the boom is in tourism, as it's an easy day excursion from Atlanta and a fantastic mountain destination. Not only is Dahlonega a hotbed of outdoor activities, but downtown in Courthouse Sq is an attractive mélange of wine-tasting rooms, gourmet emporiums, great food, countrified shops and foothill charm. Wine tasting in the surrounding vineyards is on the rise too. There's a vaguely artistic vibe permeating throughout town (especially when it comes to music), often fueled by students at the University of North Georgia, located off the square. Tack on Amicalola Falls State Park just 18 miles west and you have a pretty irresistible bundle of mountain fun.

⊙ Sights & Activities

Amicalola Falls WATERFALL
(☑706-344-1500; www.amicalolafallslodge.com/ga-state-park; 418 Amicalola Falls State Park Rd, Dawsonville; per vehicle $5; ⊙7am-10pm, visitor center 9am-5pm Sun-Wed, to 7pm Thu-Sat; 🅿🐾) 🐾 The tallest cascading waterfall in the Southeast is a spectacular sight. It tumbles 729ft through protected North Georgia mountain scenery within Amicalola Falls State Park. You can also watch it fall right underfoot from the viewpoint bridge on the West Ridge Trail.

★ Wolf Mountain Vineyards WINERY
(☑706-867-9862; www.wolfmountainvineyards.com; 180 Wolf Mountain Trail; tastings $20, mains $15, brunch $35; ⊙tastings 11am-5pm Thu-Sat, 12:30-5pm Sun, cafe noon-3pm Thu-Sat, brunch 12:30pm & 2:30pm Sun) Wolf lures a hip and trendy 30-something crowd to its gorgeous, 30-acre winery that frames epic sunsets over Springer Mountain from its tasting-room terrace. Top wines like its *méthode champenoise* 100% chardonnay Blanc de Blanc and crisp and fresh Plentitude (an unoaked chardonnay/Viognier blend) are the way to go. Reservations required for cafe and brunch.

🛏 Sleeping & Eating

Barefoot Hills HOTEL $
(☑770-312-7342; www.barefoothills.com; 7693 Hwy 19 N; dm from $35, r $85-155, cabins $140-195; 🅿❄🐾) On Hwy 19 N, 7 miles or so north of town, this revamped option could be known as the Boutique Hotel Formerly Known as Hiker Hostel. New owners upgraded this former backpackers in 2017, transitioning the converted log cabin to a near boutique-level hotel – but maintaining a hiker focus with bunk beds in another location, a supply store and shuttles to trailheads.

Cedar House Inn & Yurts B&B $$
(☑706-867-9446; www.georgiamountaininn.com; 6463 Hwy 19 N; r $140-160, yurts $160; 🅿❄🐾) 🐾 Prayer flags, a permaculture farm, bottle trees and, as you may guess, a fairly progressive, environmentally conscious approach to life define the vibe at the Cedar House, on Hwy 19 north of town. Staff can most definitely accommodate gluten-free and vegan breakfast requests. Cozy rooms and two colorful yurts (without air-conditioning) are all inviting places to crash out.

★ Spirits Tavern BURGERS $
(☑706-482-0580; www.spirits-tavern.com; 19 E Main St; burgers $12-15; ⊙11am-11pm Sun-Thu, to 1am Fri, to midnight Sat; 🐾) This full bar dishes up surprisingly creative burgers made from Angus beef or free-range, hormone-free turkey and veggies, including gooey mac 'n' cheese, Greek and Cajun versions. With eight taps and a seasonally changing list of serious cocktails, it's also the best 'bar' in town.

Picnic Cafe & Dessertery CAFE $
(☑706-864-1095; www.thepicniccafe.wixsite.com/picniccafe; 30 Public Sq; sandwiches $8.49; ⊙7:30am-7pm Sun-Wed, to 8pm Thu-Sat; 🐾) Owned by Dahlonega mayor Sam Norten and the absolute best spot around to mingle with town characters and university students engrossed in local gossip. Picnic does simple and quick biscuit sandwiches for breakfast, and sandwiches such as honey-ham salad, pimento cheese and sweet Georgia peach chicken salad for lunch.

❶ Information

Dahlonega-Lumpkin County Visitors Center
(☑706-864-3711; www.dahlonega.org; 13 S Park St; ⊙9am-5:30pm Mon-Fri, 10am-5pm Sat & Sun) has plenty of information on area sights and activities, including hiking, canoeing, kayaking, rafting and mountain biking.

❶ Getting There & Away

Dahlonega is about 70 miles north of Atlanta; the quickest way here is via Hwy 19. There is no public bus service, but folks traveling from Atlanta often take a Metropolitan Atlanta Rapid Transit Authority (MARTA) train to North Springs station in Atlanta and catch an Uber from there ($55 to $75). The nearest Amtrak station is in Gainesville, 21 miles south.

Athens

A beery, artsy and laid-back college town, Athens has an extremely popular football team (the University of Georgia Bulldogs, College Football Playoff National Championship runners-up in 2018), a world-famous music scene, a bona fide restaurant culture and surprisingly diverse nightlife. The university – UGA – drives the culture of Athens and ensures an ever-replenishing supply of young bar-hoppers and concert-goers, some of whom stick around long after graduation and become 'townies'. The pleasant, walkable downtown offers a plethora of funky choices for eating, drinking and shopping.

◎ Sights

★ Georgia Museum of Art   MUSEUM
(☑ 706-542-4662; www.georgiamuseum.org; 90 Carlton St; ⊙ 10am-5pm Tue, Wed, Fri & Sat, to 9pm Thu, 1-5pm Sun) FREE A smart, modern gallery where brainy, arty types set up in the wired lobby for personal study, while art hounds gawk at modern sculpture in the courtyard garden as well as the tremendous collection from American realists of the 1930s.

State Botanical
Garden of Georgia   GARDENS
(☑ 706-542-1244; www.botgarden.uga.edu; 2450 S Milledge Ave; ⊙ 8am-7pm) ✿ FREE Truly gorgeous, with winding outdoor paths and a sociohistorical edge, Athens' gardens are a gift for a city of this size. Signs provide smart context for its amazing collection of plants, which includes rare and threatened species. There are nearly 5 miles of top-notch woodland walking trails too.

⌂ Sleeping & Eating

★ Graduate Athens   INN $$
(☑ 706-549-7020; www.graduateathens.com; 295 E Dougherty St; r $155-259, ste $280-500; P @ 🕾 ✕) This wonderfully designed boutique hotel, the first of a college-campus chain, is drowning in sexy retro hipness, from potted plants inside old-school, Dewey decimal card–catalog filing cabinets in the lobby to the sweet Crosley turntables and classic video games in the suites.

Hotel Indigo   BOUTIQUE HOTEL $$
(☑ 706-546-0430; www.indigoathens.com; 500 College Ave; r/ste from $192/313; P @ 🕾 ✕ 🖢) ✿ Rooms are spacious, loftlike pods of cool at this ecochic boutique hotel. Part of the Indigo chain, it's a Leadership in Energy and Environmental Design (LEED) gold-certified sustainable standout. Green elements include regenerative elevators and priority parking for hybrid vehicles; 30% of the building was constructed from recycled content.

Pouch   PIES $
(☑ 706-395-6696; www.pouchpies.com; 151 E Broad St; pies $5.50; ⊙ 11am-9pm Mon-Sat; ✕) In the South, 'pie' usually means something sweet, buttery and served after dinner. For the South African owners of Pouch, 'pie' means savory pastries from around the world: Aussie pies with beef and gravy, Portuguese pies with piripiri white-wine sauce, chorizo and spicy chicken, and even a local offering with pulled pork and peach BBQ sauce!

White Tiger   BARBECUE $
(☑ 706-353-6847; www.whitetigergourmet.com; 217 Hiawassee Ave; mains $7.50-11; ⊙ 11am-3pm Mon-Wed, 11am-3pm & 6-8pm Thu-Sat, 10am-2pm Sun; 🕾 ✕ 🖢) The 100-year-old structure doesn't invite confidence, but this off-the-beaten-path local favorite does killer wood-smoked pulled-pork sandwiches – add pimento cheese (and send us a thank-you note!) – plus burgers and even barbecue-smoked tofu and a whole lot more for vegetarians. Chef Ken Manring honed his skills in much higher-brow kitchens before settling in Athens.

★ Home.made
from Scratch   SOUTHERN US $$
(☑ 706-206-9216; www.homemadeathens.com; 1072 Baxter St; mains lunch $10-13, dinner $18-24; ⊙ 11am-2pm & 5-9pm Tue-Sat, 10am-2pm Sun; 🕾) Home.made is upping the game when it comes to nouveau Southern cuisine. The menu constantly changes based on ingredient availability, but whatever these folks source is always turned into something creative, delicious, rooted in local flavors and often playfully over the top. At lunch, don't miss the fried chicken and pimento-cheese sandwich with a side upgrade to tomato pie.

Five & Ten   AMERICAN $$$
(☑ 706-546-7300; www.fiveandten.com; 1073 S Milledge Ave; mains $22-48; ⊙ 5:30-10pm Sun-Thu, to 11pm Fri & Sat, 10:30am-2:30pm Sun; ✕) ✿ Sustainably driven, James Beard Award-winning Five & Ten ranks among the South's best restaurants. Its menu is earthy and slightly gamey: Georgia quail with pickled

---

NATURE & ADVENTURE IN NORTH GEORGIA

The 1000ft-deep **Tallulah Gorge** (☑706-754-7981; www.gastateparks.org/tallulahgorge; 338 Jane Hurt Yarn Dr, Tallulah Falls; per vehicle $5; ⊙8am-sunset; **P**) carves a dark scar across the wooded hills of North Georgia. Walk over the *Indiana Jones*–worthy suspension bridge, and be on the lookout (literally) for rim trails to overlooks. Or get a first-come, first-served permit to hike to the gorge floor – only 100 are given out each day (arrive early, they're usually gone in the morning) and not offered on water-release dates (check schedule online).

Located at the base of the evocatively named Blood Mountain, **Vogel State Park** (☑706-745-2628; www.gastateparks.org/vogel; 405 Vogel State Park Rd; per vehicle $5; ⊙7am-10pm; **P**) is one of Georgia's oldest parks, and constitutes a quilt of wooded mountains surrounding a 22-acre lake. There's a multitude of trails to pick from, catering to beginners and advanced hikers. Many of the on-site facilities were built by the Civilian Conservation Corp; a seasonal museum tells the story of these work teams, who both built the park and rescued the local economy during the Great Depression.

At adventure-oriented **Unicoi State Park** (☑706-878-2201; www.unicoilodge.com; 1788 Hwy 356; per vehicle $5; ⊙7am-10pm; **P** **⛵**), visitors can rent kayaks ($10 per hour), take paddleboard lessons ($25), hike some 12 miles of trails, mountain bike, or take a zipline safari through the local forest canopy ($59).

---

yacón and white-miso aioli, and Frogmore stew (stewed corn, sausage and potato). Vegetarians should try baked Crescenza cheese with confit parsnips and blue collard greens or pasta ribbons with grilled tomato sauce, jalapeños and Parmesan.

🍷 Drinking & Entertainment

★**Creature**
Comforts Brewing Co MICROBREWERY
(www.creaturecomfortsbeer.com; 271 W Hancock Ave; pints $6-8; ⊙5-10pm Tue-Thu, 3-10pm Fri, 1-10pm Sat, 1-6pm Sun; 🕸) Athens' best craft beer emerges from 33 taps at this cutting-edge, dog-friendly former tire shop which excels at staples – Indian Pale Ales (IPAs), amber ales – but isn't afraid to play around with suds (tart blonde ale aged in wine barrels, mixed fermentation ale aged in bourbon barrels with blackberries). Local ingredients often form the backbone of the memorable brews.

Trapeze Pub CRAFT BEER
(www.trappezepub.com; 269 N Hull St; ⊙11am-midnight; 🕸) Downtown's best craft-beer bar installed itself well before the suds revolution. You'll find dozens of taps spanning regional, national and international brews, and another 100 or so at any given time in bottles. Soak it up with its Belgian-style fries ($4), the best in town.

Old Pal BAR
(www.theoldpal.com; 1320 Prince Ave; ⊙4pm-2am Mon-Sat; 🕸) This is Normaltown's thinking-person's bar, devoted to seasonal craft cocktails ($9) and a thoughtfully curated bourbon list. It's a beautiful, dark space that has been showered with local preservation awards.

40 Watt Club LIVE MUSIC
(☑706-549-7871; www.40watt.com; 285 W Washington St; $5-25; ⊙8pm-2am Thu-Sat) Athens' most storied joint has lounges, a tiki bar and $2.50 PBRs. The venue has welcomed indie rock to its stage since REM, the B-52's and Widespread Panic owned this town and today this is still where the big hitters play when they come to town. It has recently embraced comedy as well.

ℹ Information

Athens Welcome Center (☑706-353-1820; www.athenswelcomecenter.com; 280 E Dougherty St; ⊙10am-5pm Mon-Sat, noon-5pm Sun) This visitor center, in a historic antebellum house at the corner of Thomas St, provides maps and information on local tours.

ℹ Getting There & Away

This college town is about 70 miles east of Atlanta. There's no main highway that leads here, so traffic can be an issue on secondary state and county roads. The local **Greyhound station** (☑706-549-2255; www.greyhound.com; 4020 Atlanta Hwy, Bogart) is actually about 6 miles west of downtown Athens. Buses leave for Atlanta (from $15, 1½ hours, twice daily) and Savannah (from $59, 7 hours, twice daily).

Groome Transportation (☑ 706-612-1155; https://groometransportation.com; 3190 Atlanta Hwy, Suite 22) operates 23 shuttles per day year-round between Athens and Hartsfield–Jackson Atlanta International Airport ($41, 2½ hours). Shuttles leave from the UGA Georgia Center (1197 S Lumpkin St) and its Athens office 35 minutes later between 2:05am and 9:25pm.

Coastal Georgia

Driving through South Georgia's expansive wide-open pastures, cotton fields and fruit farms is a chance to see the 'Peach State' in all its glory. Surprisingly, South Georgia actually produces more blueberries and peanuts than it does peaches, and there's plenty of opportunity to experience local produce grown in these fertile parts.

Come for the region's simple, warm country-style hospitality, excellent barbecue and a number of underrated natural sights. Kayak along the untamed waters of Okefenokee's alligator-ravaged swamp, and trek around Providence Canyon's remarkable orange, red and purple formations. Meanwhile, visitors from around the world flock to Plains, the birthplace of former US President Jimmy Carter, and the sleepy historic town of Senoia, dubbed the 'Hollywood of the South' (it doubles as Woodbury and Alexandria in the wildly popular zombie series *The Walking Dead*).

Savannah

Rife with elegant townhouses, antebellum mansions, green public squares, pristine tidal freshwater marshes and mammoth oak trees bedecked in moss, Savannah is a beautiful and culturally rich city.

⊙ Sights & Activities

★ Wormsloe Historic Site   HISTORIC SITE
(☑ 912-353-3023; www.gastateparks.org/wormsloe; 7601 Skidaway Rd; adult/senior/child 6-17yr/child 1-5yr $10/9/4.50/2; ☉ 9am-5pm; Ⓟ) 🏊 A short drive from downtown, on the beautiful Isle of Hope, this is one of the most photographed sites in town. As soon as you enter, you feel as if you've been roused from the last snatch of an arboreal dream as you gaze at a corridor of mossy, ancient oaks that runs for 1.5 miles, known as the Avenue of the Oaks.

★ Forsyth Park   PARK
FREE The Central Park of Savannah is a sprawling rectangular green space, anchored by a beautiful fountain that forms a quintessential photo op.

Mercer-Williams House   HISTORIC BUILDING
(☑ 912-236-6352; www.mercerhouse.com; 429 Bull St; adult/student $12.50/8; ☉ 10:30am-4pm Mon-Sat, from noon Sun) Although Jim Williams, the Savannah art dealer portrayed by Kevin Spacey in the film version of *Midnight in the Garden of Good and Evil*, died back in 1990, his infamous mansion didn't become a museum until 2004. You're not allowed to visit the upstairs, where Williams' family still lives, but the downstairs is an interior decorator's fantasy.

★ Laurel Grove Cemetery   CEMETERY
(2101 Kollock St; ☉ 8am-5pm) Originally part of a plantation, this segregated cemetery has major historical significance to Savannah. From the mid-19th century, whites – including Confederate veterans of the Civil War – were buried in the north section (which has a separate entrance); the south section contains graves of thousands of African Americans, both once-enslaved and free. Laurel Grove South is one of the largest African American cemeteries in the South and many influential figures from the community, including from during the Civil Rights Movement, are interred here.

Telfair Academy   MUSEUM
(☑ 912-790-8800; www.telfair.org/visit/telfair; 121 Barnard St; adult/student/child $20/15/5; ☉ noon-5pm Sun & Mon, from 10am Tue-Sat) Considered Savannah's top art museum, the historic Telfair family mansion is filled with 19th-century American art and silver and a smattering of European pieces. The home itself is gorgeous and sunrise-hued – an artifact in its own right that wows visitors to this day.

SCAD Museum of Art   MUSEUM
(☑ 912-525-7191; www.scadmoa.org; 601 Turner Blvd; adult/child under 14yr $10/free; ☉ 10am-5pm Tue, Wed, Fri & Sat, to 8pm Thu, noon-5pm Sun) Architecturally striking (but what else would you expect from this school of design?), this brick, steel, concrete and glass longhouse delivers your contemporary-art fix. There are groovy, creative sitting areas inside and out, and a number of rotating and visiting exhibitions that showcase some of the most impressive talents within the contemporary-art world.

Jepson Center for the Arts   GALLERY
(JCA; ☑ 912-790-8800; www.telfair.org/visit/jepson; 207 W York St; adult/student/child $20/15/5; ☉ noon-5pm Sun & Mon, from 10am Tue-Sat; 🚼) Designed by the great Moshe Safdie, and

looking pretty darn space-age by Savannah's standards, the JCA – rather appropriately, given its architecture – focuses on 20th- and 21st-century art. Be on the lookout for wandering scads of SCAD students (ha!) and temporary exhibitions covering topics from race to art in virtual-reality video games.

Savannah Bike Tours
CYCLING

(☑ 912-704-4043; www.savannahbiketours.com; 41 Habersham St; tours $30; ⊙ varies by season) This outfit offers two-hour bike tours over easy flat terrain on its fleet of cruisers. Call ahead or check the website for tour times.

🛏 Sleeping

Thunderbird Inn
MOTEL $

(☑ 912-232-2661; www.thethunderbirdinn.com; 611 W Oglethorpe Ave; r $125-175; P❄@🛜🏊) 'A tad Palm Springs, a touch Vegas' best describes this vintage-chic 1964 motel that wins its own popularity contest – a 'Hippest hotel in Savannah' proclamation greets guests in the '60s-soundtracked lobby. In a land of stuffy B&Bs, this groovy place is an oasis, made all the better by local SCAD student art.

★ Beachview Bed & Breakfast
B&B $$

(☑ 912-786-5500; www.beachviewbbtybee.com; 1701 Butler Ave, Tybee Island; r $180-320; P🛜🏊) The tastefully themed rooms in this stately home feature bright, breezy decor, clawfoot tubs and comfortable beds, all within walking distance of Tybee's south-end beachfront. Breakfast is farm-to-table, and Wendy, the on-site manager and owner's daughter, is as chipper and helpful as they come.

Kimpton Brice
BOUTIQUE HOTEL $$$

(☑ 912-238-1200; www.bricehotel.com; 601 E Bay St; r from $260; ❄🛜🏊) Kimpton is known for its design-conscious hotels, so you'd figure it would bring its A game to one of the country's leading design cities. The Kimpton Brice does not disappoint in this, or any other, regard. Modern rooms have playful swatches of color, while the hotel's entrance and lobby feels like it could accommodate a cool club.

Kehoe House
B&B $$$

(☑ 912-232-1020; www.kehoehouse.com; 123 Habersham St; r $250-400; ❄🛜) This romantic, upscale Renaissance Revival B&B dates from 1892. Twins are said to have died in a chimney here, making it one of America's most haunted hotels (if you're skittish, steer clear of rooms 201 and 203). Ghosts aside, it's a beautifully appointed worthwhile splurge on picturesque Columbia Sq.

Mansion on Forsyth Park
BOUTIQUE HOTEL $$$

(☑ 912-238-5158; www.mansiononforsythpark.com; 700 Drayton St; r weekday/weekend from $220/ 320; P❄@🛜🏊) A choice location and chic design highlight the luxe accommodations on offer at the 18,000-sq-ft Mansion – the sexy bathrooms alone are practically worth the money. The best part of the hotel-spa is the amazing local and international art that crowds its walls and hallways – over 400 pieces in all.

🍴 Eating

★ B's Cracklin' BBQ
BARBECUE $

(☑ 912-330-6921; www.bscracklinbbq.com; 12409 White Bluff Rd; mains $10-22; ⊙ 11am-9pm Tue-Sat, to 6pm Sun; P) This is *very* good barbecue. Pit-master Bryan Furman left his job as a welder to raise his own hogs and source local ingredients for homemade sides. The result is smoky heaven: melting brisket, falling-off-the-bone ribs and perfect Carolina-style pork. The portions are more than generous; prepare to leave as stuffed as one of Bryan's hogs. B's is about 8 miles south of downtown.

Sweet Spice
JAMAICAN $

(☑ 912-335-8146; www.sweetspicesavannah.net; 5515 Waters Ave; mains $10-17; ⊙ 11am-8pm Mon-Thu, to 9pm Fri & Sat) This easygoing Jamaican spot, about 4.5 miles southeast of downtown, is a welcome break from all the American and Southern fare you get around here. A large platter of curry goat or jerk chicken costs just a smidge more than a fast-food meal and it's utterly delicious. It will also keep you filled up for a long time.

★ Wyld
SEAFOOD $$

(Wyld Dock Bar; ☑ 912-692-1219; www.thewyld dockbar.com; 2740 Livingston Ave; mains $13-22; ⊙ noon-9pm Tue-Thu & Sun, to 10pm Fri & Sat) Hidden along an estuary of the Savannah marshlands, this laid-back, local favorite features a seasonal, New American menu with a heavy seafood emphasis. It's also an ace spot to catch live music, chill in a hammock, rally around a firepit, play bocce ball or drop a fishing line off the dock.

★ Husk Savannah
SOUTHERN US $$$

(☑ 912-349-2600; www.husksavannah.com; 12 W Oglethorpe Ave; mains $25-36; ⊙ 11:30am-2pm & 5:30-9pm Mon & Tue, to 10pm Wed-Fri, 10am-2pm & 5:30-11pm Sat, to 9pm Sun) After acclaimed success with Charleston, Nashville and Greenville locations, celebrity-chef Sean Brock brings Husk's hyperlocal, agriculturally driven Southern food sorcery to Savannah. This outpost is the only one boasting a raw seafood bar and is the biggest of all, set in a historic, three-story space that hosts 200 people. Like all locations, the daily menu depends on what's locally available.

Local11Ten MODERN AMERICAN $$$
(☏912-790-9000; www.local11ten.com; 1110 Bull St; mains $27-42; ⊗5:30-10pm; ☞) Upscale, sustainable, local and fresh: these elements help create an elegant, well-run restaurant that's one of Savannah's best. Start with a blue-crab soufflé, then move on to the seared

sea scallops in chive-lemon beurre blanc or the honey and brown-sugar-rubbed pork chop and a salted-caramel pot de crème to finish. Wait. Scratch that. The menu already changed.

🍷 Drinking & Entertainment

River and Congress Sts, with Savannah's plastic-cup, open-container laws, are the bar-hopping nightlife corridors, but the scene is more than spring-break bacchanalia. There are some smart watering holes downtown, from speakeasy-style hidden haunts and upscale cocktail bars to quirky,

Savannah

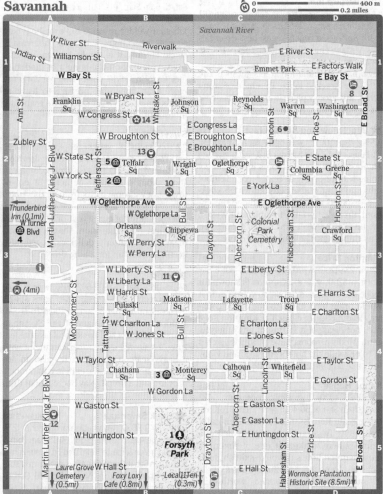

geek-themed hangouts. The club scene is lacking and paltry at best, but solid DJs spin at several bars if you're looking to cut a rug.

Foxy Loxy Cafe
CAFE

(☑912-401-0543; www.foxyloxycafe.com; 1919 Bull St; ☺7am-11pm Mon-Sat, 8am-6pm Sun) Buzzing cafe and art-print gallery full of students and creatives set in an old Victorian house. The courtyard out back is the loveliest in this area. It has tasty tacos for when you get peckish, and freshly baked kolaches (fruit pastries) that are positively addictive. There's Sunday brunch, weekday happy hour, and monthly vinyl nights and poetry slams to boot.

★ El-Rocko Lounge
COCKTAIL BAR

(☑912-495-5808; www.elrockolounge.com; 117 Whitaker St; ☺5pm-3am Mon-Sat) One step in the door and you feel the '70s-inspired swank, but then realize the vibe – in true Savannah fashion – is absolutely chill. Friendly barkeeps mix fancy cocktails while DJs keep the energy high and dance moves steady with diverse jams on vinyl. The crowd is superhip and delightfully unpretentious, and the owner is as rad as they come.

Chromatic Dragon
BAR

(☑912-289-0350; www.chromaticdragon.com; 514 Martin Luther King Jr Blvd; ☺11am-11pm Sun-Thu, to 2am Fri & Sat) If the name of this place made you smile, you'll be right at home in this gamer's pub, which features videogame consoles, board games and drinks named for fantasy references, from *Harry Potter* butterbeer to fantasy role-playing game 'healing potions.' There's a warm, welcoming atmosphere – truly, this is a certain kind of nerd's ultimate neighborhood bar.

Artillery
COCKTAIL BAR

(www.artillerybar.com; 307 Bull St; ☺4pm-midnight Mon-Sat) Talented mixologists craft novel, quality cocktails in this opulent space where elements of 19th-century eclecticism and romanticism meld with modern design touches. To drink here, abide by the house rules: no hats, sandals, tank tops, noisy phones, or shots. The signature Artillery Punch – a concoction of rye whiskey, gin, brandy and rum – packs a powerful punch. Sip slowly.

Jinx
LIVE MUSIC

(☑912-236-2281; www.thejinx912.com; 127 W Congress St; ☺4pm-3am Tue-Sat) A good slice of odd-duck Savannah nightlife, the Jinx is popular with students, townies, musicians, and basically anyone who has a thing for dive-y watering holes with live music – from rock to punk to alt-country to hip-hop – and funky stuff decorating the walls.

ℹ Information

Candler Hospital (☑912-819-4100; www.sjchs.org; 5353 Reynolds St; ☺24hr) About 4 miles south of downtown, the Candler Hospital provides good 24/7 care and service. There's another campus at 11075 Mercy Blvd.

Savannah Visitors Center (☑912-944-0455; www.savannahvisit.com; 301 Martin Luther King Jr Blvd; ☺9am-5:30pm) Excellent resources and services are available in this center, based in a restored 1860s train station. Many privately operated city tours start here. There is also a small, interactive tourist-info kiosk in the visitor center at Forsyth Park.

ℹ Getting There & Around

For a city of its size, Savannah is quite well connected and easy to access by bus or train, and even easier by plane or car. Within the downtown area, Savannah is very foot-friendly. Areas south of Midtown are best accessed by car or bus.

Brunswick & the Golden Isles

With its large shrimp-boat fleet and downtown historic district shaded by lush live oaks, Brunswick has charms you might miss when sailing by on I-95 or the Golden Isle Pkwy (Hwy 17). The town dates from 1733, and it feels very different from its neighbors. There were several plantations nearby, and a large African American population worked on the farms as slaves. Brunswick is not as tourism-oriented as other parts of the coast, and visitors may find multicultural Brunswick, with its West Indian flavors and rich local art scene, a refreshing change of pace.

Hostel in the Forest　　　HOSTEL **$**

(☑ 912-264-9738; www.foresthostel.com; 3901 Hwy 82; d $30, plus lifetime membership for first time visitors $10; P🐾) 🌱 The only budget base in the area is this set of bare-bones octagonal cedar huts and tree houses (sans air or heat) on an ecofriendly, sustainable campus. You must pay a lifetime member fee to stay, and a vegetarian dinner is included. As you might guess, the hostel is in the woods, about 10 miles outside Brunswick. Phone reservations only.

ⓘ Getting There & Around

Brunswick is located off Hwy 17. **Greyhound** (☑ 800-231-2222; 2990 Hwy 17 S) buses stop at the Flying J gas station, 10 miles west of town. Destinations include Savannah (from $12, two hours, twice daily) and Jacksonville ($12, 70 minutes, twice daily). You can catch onward buses from either city.

ST SIMONS ISLAND

St Simons Island is the largest and most developed of the Golden Isles. There are pretty beaches galore, majestic live oaks, and different neighborhoods to explore – spanning retail parks to cute villages. However, the sheer natural beauty of St Simons isn't as easy to access compared to other nearby islands, given the presence of heavy residential and resort development. For example, the island of Little St Simons is an all-natural jewel, but it's only accessible to guests staying at the exclusive Lodge on Little St Simons. That said, golf fans will be in their element – it has some fine courses.

Kingfisher Paddleventures　　ECOTOUR

(☑ 912-230-4323; www.kfpaddle.com; 2hr tours from $65, paddleboards & kayaks per hour $25) Friendly and knowledgeable conservation biologist Norm runs exciting and informative paddleboarding and kayaking tours on and around the different Golden Isles (depending on your island preference). Norm also offers rentals, and will deliver them to your location.

🛌 Sleeping & Eating

St Simons Inn By The Lighthouse　INN **$$**

(☑ 912-638-1101; www.saintsimonsinn.com; 609 Beachview Dr; r $179-290; P🌀🏊🛜) This cute and comfortable good-value inn is accented with white wooden shutters and a general sense of seaside breeziness. It's well located next to the downtown drag and a short pedal from East Beach. Continental breakfast included.

Lodge on Little
St Simons Island　　　　LODGE **$$$**

(☑ 888-733-5774; www.littlestsimonsisland.com; ferry dock 1000 Hampton River Club Marina Dr, hotel Little St Simons Island; d all inclusive $600-750; 🌀🛜) This isolated historic lodge sits on pristine and private Little St Simons. Stays include accommodations, boat transfers to and from the island, three prepared meals daily, beverages (including soft drinks, beer and wine), all activities (including naturalist-led excursions) and use of recreation equipment. Rooms have a rustic, cabin vibe, with modern amenities. It's only accessible by boat. Prebooking is essential.

Southern Soul BBQ　　　BARBECUE **$**

(☑ 912-638-7685; www.southernsoulbbq.com; 2020 Demere Rd; mains $8-17; ⊙11am-9pm Mon-Sat, to 4pm Sun; P🚙) Housed inside a former gas station at the side of a roundabout, Southern Soul BBQ serves succulent slow oak-smoked pulled pork, burnt-tipped brisket, full slab of sticky ribs, and daily specials such as jerk chicken burritos. There's a number of wonderful house-made sauces – sweet and firey BBQ, tangy mustard and big vinegar pepper – which 'cue fans can slather over their meat.

★Halyards　　　　SEAFOOD **$$$**

(☑ 912-638-9100; www.halyardsrestaurant. com; 55 Cinema Lane; mains $20-38; ⊙5-9pm Mon-Thu, to 10pm Fri-Sun; 🛜) 🌱 Chef Dave Snyder's classy, sustainable, seasonal seafood consistently hogs best-of-everything awards on St Simons, and for good reason. The menu changes with the seasons, but may include dishes like sautéed black grouper with broccoli, leek and mascarpone *farrotto*, and roasted tomato butter. Ask for the Chef's Highlights for something extraspecial.

JEKYLL ISLAND

An exclusive refuge for millionaires in the late 19th and early 20th centuries, Jekyll is a 4000-year-old barrier island with 10 miles of beaches. Today it's an unusual clash of wilderness, preserved historic buildings, modern hotels and a massive campground. It's an easily navigable place – you can get around by car, horse or bicycle.

◉ Sights & Activities

Georgia Sea Turtle Center WILDLIFE RESERVE
(☏912-635-4444; www.georgiaseaturtlecenter. org; 214 Stable Rd; adult/child 4-12yr/child under 3yr $10/7.50/free, tours from $27; ⏰9am-5pm; P🚼) This endearing attraction is a conservation center and turtle hospital where patients are on view for the public. Behind the Scenes tours (3pm on Wednesday, Friday and Saturday) and Sunrise Turtle Walks (around 7am on Saturday and Sunday) are also available, among other programs.

★ 4-H Tidelands Nature Center MUSEUM
(☏912-635-5032; www.tidelands4h.org; 100 S Riverview Dr; $5; ⏰9am-4pm Mon-Fri, 10am-2pm Sat & Sun; P🚼) 🗲 Run by a staff of peppy University of Georgia science students, the Tidelands is a kid-friendly nature center with some neat display cases on local ecology and resident wildlife, including a baby alligator, loggerhead turtle and snakes. Your children can lift, look inside and open various interactive exhibits and even feel or hold certain animals in the touch tanks.

The center also conducts highly recommended two- and three-hour **tours** (www. tidelands4h.org/tours.html; single/tandem kayak 2hr tour $60/116, 3hr tour $70/135) of the salt marshes; on any given day, you may paddle past wood storks, great blue herons, pelicans and dolphins. This is by far the best local means of accessing the understated beauty of the barrier-island salt marshes. Canoe rentals (per hour/day $20/40) and aqua bikes are also available.

CUMBERLAND ISLAND NATIONAL SEASHORE

Georgia's largest and southernmost barrier island, **Cumberland Island National Seashore** (☏912-882-4336; www.nps.gov/cuis; $10) is an unspoiled paradise. A campers' fantasy, place for family day trips and secluded retreat for couples – it's no wonder the wealthy Carnegie family used Cumberland as a retreat (the derelict but spectacular mansion of Dungeness Ruins is free with entry to Cumberland Island) in the 1800s. The 36,415 acres consist of marsh, mudflats and tidal creeks. Plus, 17 miles of wide, sandy beach that you'll likely have to yourself. The interior has maritime forest, and mysterious jagged tree-lined pathways that would be at home in a *Game of Thrones* episode.

🛏 Sleeping & Eating

Villas By The Sea VILLA **$$**
(☏912-635-2521; www.villasbythesearesort.com; 1175 N Beachview Dr; r/condos from $140/260; P❄🐾🛜🏊) A nice choice on the north coast, close to the best beaches. Rooms are spacious and the one-, two- and three-bedroom condos, set in a complex of lodge buildings sprinkled over a garden, aren't fancy but they're plenty comfy.

Jekyll Island Club Hotel HISTORIC HOTEL **$$$**
(☏844-201-6871; www.jekyllclub.com; 371 Riverview Dr; d/ste from $185/290, resort fee $20; P❄@🛜🏊) From a distance, with its turrets and balconies, this hotel could be a castle. This posh and storied property is the backbone of the island, featuring a rambling array of rooms spread out over five historic structures. Each building feels plucked from a novel about Jazz Age decadence, although the current vibe is a little more Hilton Head Island country club.

The Wharf SOUTHERN US **$$**
(☏912-635-3612; www.jekyllwharf.com; 371 Riverview Dr; mains $12-28; ⏰11:30am-10pm; P) The prettiest dining setting on the island is this wooden boathouse-style restaurant situated on a pier. There's indoor seating and an airy nautical-themed vibe, plus outdoor seating overlooking the water. Unpretentious seafood and Southern mains include

Southern chicken, cathead biscuits, grilled ahi tuna, broiled sea scallops, and chipotle lobster mac 'n' cheese. Live music takes place weekly.

ALABAMA

History suffuses Alabama, a description that could be true of many states. But there are few places where the perception of said history is so emotionally fraught. The Mississippian Native American culture built great mound cities here, and Mobile is dotted with Franco-Caribbean architecture. But for many, the word Alabama is synonymous with the American Civil Rights movement.

Perhaps such a struggle, and all of the nobility and desperation it entailed, was bound for a state like this, with its Gothic plantations, hardscrabble farmland and fiercely local sense of place. From the smallest hunting town to river-bound cities, Alabama is a place all its own, and its character is hard to forget. Some visitors have a hard time looking beyond the state's past, but the troubling elements of that narrative are tied up in a passion that constantly manifests in Alabama's arts, food and culture.

🛈 Getting There & Away

While there are mid-sized domestic airports in Mobile and Montgomery, the most common air entry to Alabama is via Birmingham-Shuttlesworth International Airport (p428).

You can find Greyhound stations in major towns. Amtrak has service to Birmingham, and there is talk of reestablishing an Amtrak line across the Gulf Coast.

Birmingham

Birmingham is a confluence of leafy green space, fantastic bars and restaurants, and innovative public space projects. It's also a far more liberal town than you may expect given the political proclivities of its home state. This town may lack the name-brand recognition of musical powerhouses like New Orleans and Nashville, or business centers like Atlanta and Houston, but as mid-sized cities go, Birmingham is hard to beat.

This hilly, shady city, founded as an iron mine, is still a center for manufacturing – many Birmingham residents work at Mercedes Benz USA in Tuscaloosa. In addition, universities and colleges pepper the town, and all of this comes together to create a city with an unreservedly excellent dining and drinking scene. The past also lurks in Birmingham, once named 'Bombingham,' and the history of the Civil Rights movement is very much at your fingers.

◉ Sights & Activities

Art-deco buildings abound in trendy **Five Points South**, where you'll find shops, restaurants and nightspots. Once-industrial **Avondale** is where the hipsters are congregating. Equally noteworthy is the upscale **Homewood** community's quaint commercial drag on 18th St S, close to the Vulcan, which looms illuminated above the city and is visible from nearly all angles, day and night.

★**Birmingham Civil Rights Institute** MUSEUM
(☑866-328-9696; www.bcri.org; 520 16th St N; adult/student/child $15/6/5, Sun by donation; ⊙10am-5pm Tue-Sat, 1-5pm Sun) A maze of moving audio, video and photography exhibits tell the story of racial segregation and the Civil Rights movement, with a focus on activities in and around Birmingham. There's an extensive exhibit on the **16th Street Baptist Church** (☑205-251-9402; www.16thstreetbaptist.org; cnr 16th St & 6th Ave N; $5; ⊙ministry tours 10am-3pm Tue-Fri, by appt only 10am-1pm Sat), located across the street, which was bombed in 1963; it's the beginning of the city's Civil Rights Memorial Trail.

★**Sloss Furnaces** FACTORY
(☑205-254-2025; www.slossfurnaces.com; 20 32nd St N; ⊙10am-4pm Tue-Sat, noon-4pm Sun; 🅿) 🌿FREE This is one of Birmingham's can't-miss sites. From 1882 to 1971, it was a pig iron–producing blast furnace and a cornerstone of Birmingham's economy. Today, instead of a wasteland it's a National Historic Landmark, a red mass of steel and girders rusted into a Gothic monument to American industry. Quiet pathways pass cobwebbed workshops and production lines that form a photographer's dream playground. A small museum on-site explores the furnaces' history.

Vulcan Park PARK
(☑205-933-1409; www.visitvulcan.com; 1701 Valley View Dr; observation tower & museum adult/child $6/4, 6-10pm adult/child $5/4; ⊙observation

ROCKET CITY

The city of **Huntsville** stretches over the green North Alabama hills like a prosperous afterthought to all of the area's surrounding natural beauty. It's home to the world renowned **US Space & Rocket Center** (☎256-837-3400; www.rocketcenter.com; 1 Tranquility Base; adult/child $25/17; ⊙9am-5pm; ℗♿), a Smithsonian-affiliated museum with a jaw-dropping collection of space artifacts, from rockets and lunar landers to space capsules and shuttle components. There's also a working, walk-through replica of the International Space Station, plus simulator rides for kids and adults (try the G Force simulator!).

When hunger strikes, head to **Betty Mae's Restaurant** (☎256-533-2188; http://bettymaes.restaurantsnapshot.com; 1222 Grace St NW; mains $6-10; ⊙11am-3pm Mon-Fri, to 6pm Sun; ℗), a bustling eatery that does fabulous soul food (African American Southern food) and whips up some decadent red velvet cake.

Huntsville is a handy stop while road-tripping through the south: it's roughly halfway between Birmingham and Nashville.

tower 10am-10pm, museum 10am-6pm; ♿☀) Imagine Christ the Redeemer in Rio, but made of iron and depicting a beefcake Roman god of metalworking. *Vulcan* is visible from all over the city – this is the world's largest cast-iron statue – and the park he resides in offers fantastic views, along with an **observation tower**. A small on-site museum explores Birmingham history.

Birmingham Museum of Art
GALLERY
(☎205-254-2565; www.artsbma.org; 2000 Rev Abraham Woods Jr Blvd; ⊙10am-5pm Tue-Sat, noon-5pm Sun) **FREE** This fine museum boasts an impressive collection, especially given Birmingham's status as a mid-sized city. Inside, you'll find works from Asia, Africa, Europe and the Americas. Don't miss pieces by Rodin, Botero and Dalí in the sculpture garden.

Birmingham Civil Rights Memorial Trail
WALKING
(www.bcri.org; 520 16th St N) Installed in 2013 for the Civil Rights campaign's 50th anniversary, this poignant walk, stretching over seven blocks, depicts 22 scenes with plaques, statues and photography, some of it quite conceptual and moving – to wit, a gauntlet of snapping, sculpted dog statues that pedestrians must traverse. The experience peels back yet another layer of the sweat and blood behind a campaign that changed America.

🛏 Sleeping

★Elyton Hotel
BOUTIQUE HOTEL $$
(☎205-731-3600; www.elytonhotel.com; 1928 1st Ave N; r $149-199, ste $349-369; ℗🖥☀) 🌿 The Elyton holds an admirable middle ground between boutique design and business-class amenities and dimensions. Over 100 rooms, decked out in a crisp white aesthetic accented with pops of color and modern art, occupy the Empire building, an early 20th-century architectural landmark.

Redmont Hotel
HISTORIC HOTEL $$
(☎205-957-6828; www.redmontbirmingham.com; 2101 5th Ave N; r $150-170, ste $220; ✳@🛜) The piano and chandelier in the lobby of this 1925 hotel lend a certain historical, old-world feel, and all deluxe rooms were renovated in 2016, giving it a modern edge. The spacious rooftop bar doesn't hurt, either. It's walking distance to the Civil Rights sights.

🍴 Eating

★Saw's Soul Kitchen
BARBECUE $
(☎205-591-1409; www.sawsbbq.com; 215 41st St S; mains $9-16; ⊙11am-8pm Mon-Sat, to 4pm Sun; ♿) Saw's offers some of the most mouthwatering smoked meat in the city, served in a family-friendly atmosphere. Stuffed potatoes make a nice addition to your meal, and the smoked chicken with a tangy local white sauce is divine – although with that said, bring on the ribs!

Blue Pacific at Hoover Food Mart
THAI $
(☎205-978-0754; 3219 Lorna Rd, Hoover Food Mart; mains from $8; ⊙11am-2:30pm, 5-8:30pm Tue-Sat) It may look like a convenience store but this tiny building serves up some of the best Thai food in Birmingham. As you'd expect, the place ain't fancy but the value can't be beat. Try the spicy Pad Kee Mao.

★ **Highlands Bar & Grill** AMERICAN $$$
(☑ 205-939-1400; www.highlandsbarandgrill.com; 2011 11th Ave S; mains $33-44; ⏱5:30-10pm Tue-Sat, bar from 4pm) Frank Stitt's most acclaimed restaurant, Highlands has been serving up modern Southern cuisine using French cooking techniques since 1982 in this elegant, 1920s-inspired dining room. The service is as outstanding as the food. Come dressed to impress – suit jackets are not required but you'll probably feel out of place without one.

🍷 Drinking & Nightlife

★ **Atomic Lounge** BAR
(☑ 205-983-7887; www.theatomiclounge.com; 2113 1st Avenue N; ⏱4pm-midnight Tue-Thu, to 2am Fri & Sat) This is the sort of bar Birmingham boasts would be the envy of New York or Los Angeles. Atomic Lounge is just funky and fun – a cross between a 1950s rec room, a Warhol painting, a mid-century design showcase and, hey, a craft cocktail bar.

Marty's PM BAR
(1813 10th Ct S; ⏱8pm-6am daily, plus 10am-3pm Sat) Marty's plays to hipsters, cool kids and an unapologetically geeky crowd, who are all attracted to a friendly bar packed with comic book art, *Star Wars* memorabilia, role-playing-game references, DJ nights, pop-up dining events and the occasional live-music gig.

ℹ️ Getting There & Around

The **Birmingham-Shuttlesworth International Airport** (BHM; ☑ 205-599-0500; www.flybirmingham.com) is about 5 miles northeast of downtown.

Greyhound (☑ 205-252-7190; www.greyhound.com; 1801 Morris Ave) serves cities including Huntsville (1½ to 2 hours, from $19, four daily), Montgomery (1½ hours, from $20, three daily), Atlanta, GA (2½ hours, from $22, six daily), Jackson, MS (4½ hours, from $23, six daily), and New Orleans, LA (nine hours, from $67, one daily).

Amtrak (www.amtrak.com; 1801 Morris Avenue), downtown, has trains daily to New York (22 hours, from $124) and New Orleans (eight hours, from $38).

Birmingham Transit Authority (www.bjcta.org) runs local MAX buses. Adult fare is $1.25. You can also get around via the Zyp BikeShare program (www.zypbikeshare.com), which offers 24h, 3-day or 1-month passes.

Montgomery

Alabama's capital is a skein of forested streets, redbrick architecture and lonely railways, attached to a few government buildings and a cobblestoned downtown that accrues much of the area's new investment.

With a few exceptions, most of the main points of interest here are tied to the Civil Rights movement, which the city played a key role in. In 1955 Rosa Parks refused to give up her seat to a white man on a city bus, launching a bus boycott led by Martin Luther King Jr, then pastor of Montgomery's Dexter Avenue Baptist Church. This action ultimately desegregated city buses and galvanized the Civil Rights movement nationwide, helping to lay the foundation for the Selma to Montgomery protest marches of 1965.

Modern Montgomery has thoughtfully acknowledged its past while attracting a slew of young entrepreneurs, many of them African American.

◉ Sights

★ **Dexter Avenue Parsonage** HISTORIC SITE
(☑ 334-263-3970; www.dexterkingmemorial.org/tours/parsonage-museum; 309 S Jackson St; adult/child $7.50/5.50; ⏱10am-3pm Tue-Fri, to 1pm Sat; P) The home of Martin Luther King Jr and Coretta Scott King has been frozen in time, a snapshot of a mid-century home complete with *Mad Men*–era furniture, appliances and indoor ashtrays (King was a regular smoker). The most fascinating part of the tour is King's old office, which still contains some of the books that influenced his theology, philosophy and activism. In the back, there's a garden filled with stones inscribed with Christian virtues.

★ **National Memorial for Peace & Justice** MEMORIAL
(National Lynching Memorial; ☑ 334-386-9100; www.eji.org/national-lynching-memorial; 417 Caroline St; memorial/combination with Legacy Museum ticket $5/10; ⏱9am-5pm Wed-Mon, last entrance 4:30pm) Stark and harrowing in its simplicity, this memorial stands in honor of 4400 African American victims of lynching. Great rectangular steel slabs, each the size and shape of a coffin, are inscribed with the name of a county, the dates of every documented lynching incident within that county and the name of the victim. The

immensity of the space and the mute testimony of the slabs underlines the ubiquity of racial violence in American history.

Civil Rights Memorial Center MEMORIAL

(📞334-956-8200; www.splcenter.org/civil-rights-memorial; 400 Washington Ave; memorial free, museum adult/child $2/free; ⊙memorial 24hr, museum 9am-4:30pm Mon-Fri, 10am-4pm Sat) With its circular design crafted by Maya Lin, this haunting memorial focuses on 40 martyrs of the Civil Rights movement. Some cases remain unsolved. Martin Luther King Jr was the most famous, but there were many 'faceless' deaths along the way, both white and African American. The memorial is part of the Southern Poverty Law Center, a legal foundation committed to racial equality and equal opportunity for justice under the law.

Scott & Zelda Fitzgerald Museum MUSEUM

(📞334-264-4222; www.thefitzgeraldmuseum.org; 919 Felder Ave; adult/child donation $10/free; ⊙10am-5pm Tue-Sat, noon-5pm Sun) The writers' home from 1931 to 1932 now houses first editions, translations and original artwork by Zelda from her sad last days when she was committed to a mental health facility. Unlike many 'homes of famous people,' there's a ramshackle charm to this museum – while the space is curated, you also feel as if you've stumbled into the Fitzgeralds' attic, exemplified by loving handwritten letters from Zelda to Scott.

🛏 Sleeping & Eating

⭐Lattice Inn B&B $$

(📞334-263-1414; www.thelatticeinn.com; 1414 South Hull St; r from $115; 🅿🖥) This well-run B&B is a long-standing favorite with Montgomery travelers. The owners are warm and accommodating, the lodgings drip with thoughtful vintage chic, and the grounds are surrounded by lovely, enormous gardens. A winner all around.

Mrs B's SOUTHERN US $

(📞334-264-5495; www.facebook.com/Mrsbscooking; 17 Cullman St; plates $8-13; ⊙6am-5pm Mon-Fri, 11am-4:30pm Sun) Locals pack in at this culinary institution, where they serve true soul classics, including oxtail and liver or onions and neck bones (there's fried chicken and pork chops and the like for the less adventurous). The dining room is well-worn in a good way, and the food is cooked and served with a lot of love.

Vintage Year SOUTHERN US $$$

(📞334-819-7215; www.vymgm.com; 405 Cloverdale Rd; mains $15-42; ⊙5-10pm Tue-Sat, 10:30am-2pm Sun) Fine Southern cuisine served in an elegantly romantic dining room? We're in. Dine on pistachio-crusted salmon, or Gulf shrimp pasta, or tempura fried chicken with charred asparagus. Tuesday night is burger night, with some eight variations of meat (and vegetables for the garden burger!) on a bun.

ℹ Information

Montgomery Area Visitor Center (📞334-262-0013; www.visitingmontgomery.com; 300 Water St; ⊙8:30am-5pm Mon-Sat) Has tourist information and a helpful website.

ℹ Getting There & Around

Montgomery Regional Airport (MGM; 📞334-281-5040; www.flymgm.com; 4445 Selma Hwy) is about 15 miles from downtown and is served by daily flights from Atlanta, Charlotte and Dallas. **Greyhound** (📞334-286-0658; 950 W South Blvd) also serves the city, with routes to Birmingham (2½ hours, from $24) and New Orleans (6½ hours, from $41). Montgomery is about 100 miles south of Birmingham via I-65.

The **Montgomery Area Transit System** (www.montgomerytransit.com) operates city bus lines. Tickets are $2.

Selma

Selma is a quiet town located in the heart of the Alabama 'Black Belt,' a moniker once used to describe the area's dark, high-quality soil, then later the large population of African Americans enslaved to work the fruits of that same soil. It's most well known for Bloody Sunday: March 7, 1965. The media captured state troopers and deputies beating and gassing African Americans and white sympathizers near the Edmund Pettus Bridge.

Selma is a must-visit for those interested in the history of the Civil Rights movement, and is an attractive spot to linger in its own right.

◉ Sights

Edmund Pettus Bridge LANDMARK

(Broad St & Water Ave) Few sites are as iconic to the American Civil Rights movement as the Pettus Bridge. On March 7, 1965, a crowd prepared to march to Montgomery

WORTH A TRIP

OLD CAHAWBA ARCHAEOLOGICAL PARK

Around 14 miles southwest of Selma, this eerie **ghost town** (☑334-872-8058.; https://ahc.alabama.gov/properties/cahawba/cahawba.aspx; 9518 Cahaba Rd, Orrville; adult/child $2/1; ⊙9am-5pm; ℗), faded by time and jungly overgrowth, was once the capital of Alabama. By the 20th century, Cahawba was abandoned, and today its remains constitute an important archaeological site. It's best to explore the area on a guided tour (call and reserve at least two weeks in advance) or by bicycle – the site is flat and crossed by paved trails, and a limited number of bicycles are freely available on a first-come basis.

Within the grounds of the ghost town are ruins, a nature trail, a visitor center (noon-5pm Thu-Mon) with self-guided tour maps, and a general sense of decay. Historical re-enactments and activities like haunted history tours are pretty common; check the website for updated information.

to demonstrate against the murder of a local black activist by police during a demonstration for voting rights. As those activists gathered into a crowd, the news cameras of the media were trained on the bridge and a line of state troopers and their dogs, who proceeded to lay into the nonviolent marchers.

Selma Interpretive Center   MUSEUM
(☑334-877-1983; www.nps.gov/semo; 2 Broad St; ⊙9am-4:30pm Mon-Sat) FREE This museum, near the north side of the Pettus Bridge, has a small interpretive center that fleshes out the history and narrative of the Jim Crow South, and the subsequent struggle against legalized segregation.

Lowndes County Interpretive Center   MUSEUM
(☑334-877-1983; www.nps.gov/semo; 7002 US Hwy 80; ⊙9am-4:30pm Mon-Sat; ℗) FREE Marking the rough halfway point on the marching route between Selma and Montgomery, this center presents small, solid exhibitions that delve into the history of Jim Crow and the Civil Rights movement.

🛏 Sleeping & Eating

At the time of writing, the historic **St James Hotel** was under renovation. The town is otherwise served by the usual midrange American hotel chains.

Lannie's BBQ (☑334-874-4478; 2115 Minter Ave; mains $5-12; ⊙9am-9pm Mon-Sat; ℗) is a little shack that cranks out some of the finest smoked meat around.

ℹ Getting There & Away

There's a **Greyhound** (☑800-231-2222) station at 434 Broad St (US 80). But you really need a car to get around. Tuscaloosa is about 75 miles to the north on US 80, and Montgomery is 50 miles to the east.

Mobile

Wedged between Mississippi and Florida, the only real Alabama coastal city is Mobile (mo-*beel*), a busy industrial seaport with a smattering of green space, shady boulevards and four historic districts. It's ablaze with azaleas in early spring, and festivities are held throughout February for **Mardi Gras** (www.mobilemardigras.com; ⊙late Feb/early Mar), which has been celebrated here for nearly 200 years (longer than in New Orleans).

Mobile's sights can be covered in a day; otherwise the town makes for an interesting diversion between Pensacola and New Orleans.

◉ Sights

USS Alabama   MUSEUM
(☑251-433-2703; www.ussalabama.com; 2703 Battleship Pkwy; adult/child $15/6; ⊙8am-6pm Apr-Sep, to 5pm Oct-Mar; ℗) The battleship *Alabama* is a 690ft behemoth famous for escaping nine major WWII battles unscathed – the 'Lucky A' never lost any of its sailors while they served aboard ship. It's a worthwhile self-guided tour just to experience its awesome size and might; at the end of the day, this ship is an engineering marvel.

Gulf Coast Exploreum   MUSEUM
(☑251-208-6893; www.exploreum.com; 65 Government St; adult/student/child $13/11/6, with IMAX $17/15/10; ⊙9am-4pm Tue-Thu, to 5pm Fri & Sat, noon-5pm Sun Sep-May, 10am-5pm Mon-Sat, noon-5pm Sun Jun-Aug; 👶) This science center contains some 150 interactive exhibits and displays in three galleries, an IMAX theater

and live demonstrations in its chemistry and biology labs. The exhibits are mainly aimed at kids, and make a good time killer for those with children.

🛏 Sleeping & Eating

Malaga Inn   BOUTIQUE HOTEL **$$**
(☑800-235-1586, 251-438-4701; www.malagainn. com; 359 Church St; r $79-165, ste $235; 🅿🛜🐾) Graced with a pretty courtyard and general historic vibe, the Malaga, which occupies a 19th-century building, is a good deal for central Mobile. Courtyard rooms have classy hardwood floors and understated sheets, while the historic rooms have a tasteful, Victorian-era vibe. Wrought-iron balconies make you feel like you're in a New Orleans–style production of *Romeo & Juliet*.

★ Meat Boss   BARBECUE **$**
(☑251-591-4842; http://meatboss.com; 5401 Cottage Hill Rd; mains $7-11) If the name hasn't done it, we'll explain the appeal of Meat Boss: fresh barbecue, and lots of it, served slow-smoked and glistening. Order meat, add sides from banana pudding to potato salad – and have a great meal.

Mary's Southern Cooking   AMERICAN **$**
(☑251-476-2232; 3011 SpringHill Ave; mains $6-12; ⊙11am-6pm; 🖐) Mary's serves up soul food with a smile. Daily specials run the gamut from beef tips to pig's feet to chicken pot pie, served alongside groaning portions of sides, including collard greens, rice and gravy and mashed potatoes. Simple food, done simply very well.

❶ Getting There & Away

There has been talk for years of reestablishing rail service through Mobile. Until then, you can arrive via **Greyhound** (☑251-478-6089; 2545 Government Blvd) or drive; the city sits at the intersection of I-10 and I-65, about 60 miles west of Pensacola, and 150 miles east of New Orleans.

MISSISSIPPI

Flanked by the mighty Mississippi River along its entire western border, the Magnolia State encompasses many identities. You'll find palatial mansions and rural poverty; haunting cotton flats and verdant hill country; honey-dipped sand on the coast and serene farmland in the north. Often mythologized and misunderstood, this is the womb of some of the rawest history

in the country. And that's why the state is worth an extended visit. The novels, music and art birthed here tell deeply personal stories. They're not always easy to hear. But there's a compelling sense of connection – even joy – in the sharing. See for yourself in a late-night blues club in the Delta. Or on a wander through the homes of the state's great novelists. Or during a quiet moment inside an artist's cabin where bright murals depict the wonders of nature here. Immersion sparks conversations and will challenge your assumptions.

❶ Information

Mississippi Division of Tourism Development (601-359-3297; www.visitmississippi.org) Has a directory of visitor bureaus and thematic travel itineraries. Most are well thought-out and run quite deep.
Mississippi Wildlife, Fisheries, & Parks (800-467-2757; www.mississippistateparks. reserveamerica.com) Manages camping reservations in state parks.

❶ Getting There & Away

There are three routes most folks take when traveling through Mississippi. I-55 and US 61 both run north–south from the state's northern to southern borders. US 61 goes through the Delta, and I-55 flows in and out of Jackson. The gorgeous Natchez Trace Pkwy runs diagonally across the state from Tupelo to Natchez. Amtrak's daily **City of New Orleans** train links Chicago and New Orleans, with stops in Memphis, TN, Greenwood and Jackson.

Oxford

Oxford both confirms and explodes any preconceptions you may have of Mississippi's most famous college town. Frat boys in Ford pickup trucks and debutante sorority sisters? Sure. But they're alongside doctoral candidates debating critical theory, and a lively arts scene. Local culture revolves around the Square (aka Courthouse Sq), where you'll find bars, restaurants, decent shopping and the regal University of Mississippi, aka Ole Miss. All around are quiet residential streets, sprinkled with antebellum homes and shaded by majestic oaks.

◎ Sights & Activities

The gorgeous, 0.6-mile-long and rather painless **Bailey's Woods Trail** (www.muse um.olemiss.edu/baileys-woods-trail;   Old Taylor

Rd) connects two of the town's popular sights: Rowan Oak and the **University of Mississippi Museum** ([J]662-915-7073; www.museum.olemiss.edu; University Ave at 5th St; ⊙10am-6pm Tue-Sat) FREE. The Grove, the shady heart of Ole Miss, is generally peaceful, except on football Saturdays, when it buzzes with one of the most unforgettable tailgating (pre-game) parties in American university sports.

Rowan Oak HISTORIC BUILDING
([J]662-234-3284; www.rowanoak.com; Old Taylor Rd; adult/child $5/free; ⊙house 10am-4pm Tue-Sat, from 1pm Sun Sep-May, 10am-6pm Tue-Sat, from 1pm Sun Jun-Aug; grounds open dawn-dusk) Literary pilgrims head here to the graceful 1840s home of William Faulkner. He authored many brilliant and dense novels set in Mississippi, and his work is celebrated in Oxford with an annual conference in July. Tours of Rowan Oak – where Faulkner lived from 1930 until his death in 1962, and which may reasonably be dubbed, to use the author's own elegant words, his 'postage stamp of native soil' – are self-guided. Admission is cash only.

🛏 Sleeping & Eating

Inn at Ole Miss HOTEL $
([J]662-234-2331; www.theinnatolemiss.com; 120 Alumni Dr; r from $119; P❄@🛜🏊) Unless it's a football weekend, in which case you'd be wise to book well ahead, you can usually find a nice room at this 180-room hotel and conference center right on the Ole Miss Grove. Although it's not super-personal, it's comfortable, well located and walkable to downtown.

⭐**Big Bad Breakfast** BREAKFAST $
([J]662-236-2666; www.bigbadbreakfast.com; 719 N Lamar; mains $5-15; ⊙7am-1:30pm Mon-Fri, 8am-3pm Sat & Sun) Any place with an Elvis tapestry is gonna be good. This busy spot is no exception, serving hearty gourmet Southern breakfasts to appreciative hordes. From the egg scramble with fried Gulf oysters to the Redneck benny with country ham and sausage gravy to the brandy-spiked French toast with berries, there's something big and bad (in a good way) for everyone.

City Grocery AMERICAN $$$
([J]662-232-8080; www.citygroceryonline.com; 152 Courthouse Sq; lunch mains $11-24, dinner mains $26-32; ⊙11:30am-2:30pm Mon-Sat, 6-10pm Mon-Wed, to 10:30pm Thu-Sat, 11am-2:30pm Sun) Chef John Currence won a James Beard award and quickly set about dominating the Ox-ford culinary scene. City Grocery is one of his finest restaurants, offering a menu of haute Southern goodness such as blackened catfish with ham hock, stewed black-eyed peas and lard-braised hangar steak. The upstairs bar, decked out with local folk art, is a treat. Reservations recommended.

Nightlife & Entertainment

Rafter's Music & Food BAR
([J]662-234-5757; www.facebook.com/RaftersOxford; 1000 Jackson Ave E; ⊙5pm-midnight Mon-Wed, to 1am Thu, 11am-1am Fri, to midnight Sat, 10:45am-3pm Sun) Climb the stairs for the spicy bloody Marys and live bluegrass music on Sunday mornings. Gets busy on weekend nights.

Proud Larry's LIVE MUSIC
([J]662-236-0050; www.proudlarrys.com; 211 S Lamar Blvd; ⊙shows 9pm) On the Square, this iconic music venue hosts consistently good bands. It also does a nice pub-grub business at lunch and dinner before the stage lights dim.

🛍 Shopping

⭐**Square Books** BOOKS
([J]662-236-2262; www.squarebooks.com; 160 Courthouse Sq; ⊙9am-9pm Mon-Sat, to 6pm Sun) Square Books, one of the South's great independent bookstores, is the epicenter of Oxford's lively literary scene and a frequent stop for traveling authors. There's a cafe and balcony upstairs, along with an immense section devoted to Faulkner.

❶ Getting There & Away

The closest interstates to Oxford are I-55 and I-22. You can get here via US 278 or MS 7; the latter is a slightly more scenic route.

Mississippi Delta

A long, low land of silent cotton plots bending under a severe sky, the Delta is a place of surreal, Gothic extremes. Here, in a feudal society of great manors and enslaved servitude, songs of labor and love eventually became American pop music. Those songs traveled from Africa via sharecropping fields, where they unfolded into the blues and ultimately into rock and roll. Tourism in this area, which still suffers some of the worst rural poverty rates in the country, largely revolves around discovering the sweat-soaked roots of this original American art form. Hwy 61 is the Delta's legendary road, traversing endless, eerie miles of flat fields, imposing agricultural and industrial facilities, one-room churches and moldering cemeteries.

Clarksdale

The scrappy epicenter of the Delta blues scene, Clarksdale is also the region's most useful base. It's within a couple of hours of all the blues sights, and big-name blues acts are regular weekend visitors. But this is still a poor Delta town, with crumbling edges and washed-out storefronts evident in ways that go beyond romantic dilapidation. It's jarring to see how many businesses find private security details a necessity after dark. On the other hand, there is a genuine warmth to the place, and most tourists in the region end up lingering for longer than they expected.

◉ Sights

Delta Blues Museum MUSEUM
(☑ 662-627-6820; www.deltabluesmuseum.org; 1 Blues Alley; adult/child 6-12yr $10/8; ⊘ 9am-5pm Mon-Sat Mar-Oct, from 10am Nov-Feb; ℗) A small but well-presented collection of memorabilia is on display here. The shrine to Delta legend Muddy Waters includes the actual cabin where he grew up. Local art exhibits and a gift shop round out the display. May host live music during special events.

Quapaw Canoe Co CANOEING
(☑ 662-627-4070; www.island63.com; 291 Sunflower Ave; per person per day $175-400) John Ruskey and his team run trip-of-a-lifetime canoe excursions on the Lower Mississippi River and its tributaries for groups of almost every size, from solo paddlers to Boy Scout troops. Tell him where you'd like to go or let Quapaw choose your adventure. The five-day Muddy Waters Wilderness paddle is a favorite. One-day outings to multiday camping trips are available.

⬛ Sleeping & Eating

Shack Up Inn INN $
(☑ 662-624-8329; www.shackupinn.com; 001 Commissary Circle, off US 49; r/shack $95/100; ℗✳☞) Located on the Hopson Plantation, these unique accommodations allow you to stay in refurbished sharecropper cabins or the creatively renovated cotton gin. The cabins have covered porches and are filled with old furniture and musical instruments.

THE SOUL OF THE DELTA

Stopping in the tiny Delta town of Indianola is worthwhile to visit the **BB King Museum and Delta Interpretive Center** (☑ 662-887-9539; https://bbkingmuseum.org; 400 2nd St; adult/child 7-17yr $15/10; ⊘ 10am-5pm Tue-Sat, from noon Sun & Mon, closed Mon Nov-Mar; ℗). While it's ostensibly dedicated to the legendary bluesman, in many ways it tackles life in the Delta as a whole. The museum is filled with interactive displays, video exhibits and an amazing array of artifacts, effectively communicating the history and legacy of the blues while shedding light on the soul of the Delta.

Sunsets from the porches can be gorgeous, but historical context gets a bit lost, despite all the 'authenticity.' Bar and stage inside the Gin.

Bluesberry Cafe SOUTHERN US $
(☑ 662-627-7008; 235 Yazoo Ave; mains $5-12; ⊘ 7:30am-1pm Sat & Sun, 6:30pm-midnight Mon) This isn't just a greasy spoon – there's grease on the forks, knives and napkins too. But who cares? The food – eggs, bacon, housemade sausages and big sandwiches – is made to order and delicious. Live blues starts at 10am on weekends and 8pm on Monday. Some blues legends may stop in and play an impromptu set. Pass the hot sauce.

Yazoo Pass CAFE $$
(☑ 662-627-8686; www.yazoopass.com; 207 Yazoo Ave; lunch mains $8-10, dinner $12-36; ⊘ 7am-9pm Mon-Sat; ☞) A contemporary space where you can enjoy fresh scones and croissants in the mornings, a salad bar, sandwiches and soups at lunch, and pan-seared ahi, filet mignon, burgers and pastas at dinner. Espresso bar too.

☆ Entertainment

★Red's BLUES
(☑ 662-627-3166; 395 Sunflower Ave; cover $7-10; ⊘ live music 9pm Fri & Sat) Clarksdale's best juke joint, with its neon-red mood lighting, plastic-bag ceiling and general soulful disintegration, is the place to see bluesmen howl. Red runs the bar, knows the acts and slings a cold beer whenever you need one.

THE SOUTH MISSISSIPPI DELTA

ℹ Getting There & Away

Clarksdale sits off US 49 and 61, 80 miles south of Memphis, and 70 miles west of Oxford. The **Greyhound** (🚌 662-627-7893; www.greyhound. com; 1604 N State St) station is on State St.

Vicksburg

Lovely Vicksburg sits atop a high bluff overlooking the Mississippi River. During the Civil War, Gen Ulysses S Grant besieged the city for 47 days until its surrender on July 4, 1863, at which point the North gained dominance over North America's greatest river. Although Vicksburg is most famous for a siege and a battle, many of its historic homes have survived the centuries, and today the town's historic core is considered one of the most attractive in the state.

◉ Sights

Vicksburg National Military Park

HISTORIC SITE

(🚌 601-636-0583; www.nps.gov/vick; 3201 Clay St; per bicycle/car $10/20; ⊙ grounds dawn-dusk, visitor center 8am-5pm Apr-Oct, 8:30-4:30pm Nov-Mar; 🅿 ♿) Vicksburg controlled access to the Mississippi River, and its seizure was one of the turning points of the Civil War. A 16-mile driving tour passes historic markers explaining battle scenarios and key events from the city's long siege, when residents lived in caverns to avoid Union shells. Plan on staying for at least 90 minutes. The USS Cairo Museum, which spotlights the ironclad gunboats used by Union forces, is worth a stop, and the salvaged USS *Cairo* is on view.

Lower Mississippi River Museum

MUSEUM

(🚌 601-638-9900; www.lmrm.org; 910 Washington St; ⊙ 9am-4pm Mon-Sat, from 1pm Sun; ♿) **FREE** Downtown Vicksburg's pride and joy is this low-key museum, which delves into such topics as the famed 1927 flood and the Army Corps of Engineers, who have managed the river since the 18th century. Kids will enjoy climbing around the dry-docked research vessel, the MV *Mississippi IV*.

✕ Eating & Drinking

★ Walnut Hills

SOUTHERN US $$

(🚌 601-638-4910; www.walnuthillsms.com; 1214 Adams St; mains $8-32; ⊙ 11am-9pm Mon & Wed-Sat, to 2pm Sun) For a dining experience that takes you back in time, head to this eatery where you can enjoy rib-sticking, down-home Southern food elbow to elbow, family-style – but there's plenty of seating for solo diners and introverts too. The corn and crab bisque is loaded with crab, and the shrimp and grits, with tasso ham, is wonderful.

Highway 61 Coffeehouse

COFFEE

(🚌 601-638-9221; 1101 Washington St; ⊙ 7am-5pm Mon-Fri, from 9am Sat; 🛜) ☕ This awesome coffee shop has occasional live music on Saturday afternoons, serves Fair Trade coffee and is an energetic epicenter of artsiness, poetry readings and the like.

ℹ Getting There & Away

There's a **Greyhound** (🚌 601-638-8389; 1295 S Frontage Rd) station a little way south of town. Vicksburg sits off I-20 and US 61, about 50 miles west of Jackson.

Jackson

Mississippi's capital and largest city mixes stately residential areas with large swaths of blight, peppered throughout with a surprisingly funky arts-cum-hipster scene in the Fondren District. The recent opening of the Museum of Mississippi History and the adjacent Mississippi Civil Rights Museum has boosted the appeal of downtown and drawn national acclaim – now if city officials would just do something about the terrible condition of its streets. Trust us, they're bad, especially the potholes. On the bright side, there's a slew of decent bars, good restaurants and a lot of love for live music; it's easy to have a good time in Jackson.

◉ Sights

★ Mississippi Civil Rights Museum

MUSEUM

(🚌 601-576-6800; www.mcrm.mdah.ms.gov; 222 North St; adult/child 4-18yr $10/6; ⊙ 9am-5pm Tue-Sat, from 1pm Sun; 🅿) Whether it's a voice from overhead yelling at you to 'keep on moving,' graphic photos of lynchings hitting you with a gut punch, or the towering wall of mugshots of Freedom Riders stopping you in your tracks, the exhibits at this compelling new museum keep you on high alert. The national Civil Rights movement is explored through the lens of the fight for racial equality in Mississippi, with eight exhibit halls tackling the key eras. Plan to spend a half-day.

Museum of Mississippi History
MUSEUM
(☎601-576-6800; www.mmh.mdah.ms.gov; 222 North St; adult/child 4-18yr $10/6; ⊙9am-5pm Tue-Sat, from 1pm Sun; 🅿) In the 10-minute introductory film, the voice of God himself, Mississippian Morgan Freeman, introduces visitors to this compelling new museum. Exhibits tell the story of Mississippi and its residents, beginning in 13,000 BC and continuing to the present. Noteworthy displays, which are often supplemented by informative videos, cover prehistoric mound builders, the Chickasaw and Choctaw tribes and their legends, the cotton industry, the Civil War and Mississippi's rich cultural heritage – don't miss Lucille's Place, a recreated juke joint.

Eudora Welty House
HISTORIC BUILDING
(☎601-353-7762; www.eudorawelty.org; 1119 Pinehurst St; adult/student/child $5/3/free; ⊙tours 9am, 11am, 1pm & 3pm Tue-Fri) Literature buffs should plan to tour the Pulitzer Prize–winning author's Tudor Revival house, where she lived for more than 75 years. It's now a true historical preservation, down to the most minute details. It's free on the 13th day of any month, assuming that's a normal operating day. Reservations recommended but not required.

🛌 Sleeping & Eating

Old Capitol Inn
BOUTIQUE HOTEL $
(☎601-359-9000; www.oldcapitolinn.com; 226 N State St; r/ste from $99/145; 🅿🐾@🛜🏊) This 24-room boutique hotel, located near museums and restaurants, is terrific. Rooms are comfortable and uniquely furnished, and a delicious full Southern breakfast is included. The rooftop garden offers views of downtown.

Fairview Inn
INN $$$
(☎888-948-1908, 601-948-3429; www.fairview-inn.com; 734 Fairview St; r/ste from $199/219; 🅿🐾@🛜) For a Colonial-estate experience, the 18-room Fairview Inn, set in a converted historic mansion, will not let you down. The antique decor is stunning rather than stuffy and tastefully deployed across each individually appointed room. It also has a full spa and a cozy cocktail bar, the Library Lounge (11am-midnight Mon-Fri, 4pm-1am Sat).

Bully's
SOUTHERN US $
(☎601-362-0484; 3118 Livingston Rd; mains $7-10; ⊙11am-6pm Mon-Sat) With its golden crispiness and tender meat, Bully's fried chicken is a culinary home run and worth a detour from downtown. Or pick up some chicken to go for a picnic along the Natchez Trace, five miles northwest. How good is the soul food at this low-key spot? The James Beard Foundation honored Bully's as an American Classic in 2016.

Iron Horse Grill
SOUTHERN US; MEXICAN $$
(☎601-398-0151; www.theironhorsegrill.com; 320 W Pearl St; mains $11-32; ⊙11am-midnight) During Friday lunch, you'd swear that all of downtown Jackson is happily digging into the delicious burgers, po'boys, tacos and seafood dishes served here. Though the space is cavernous and busy, the conscientious staff and a friendly vibe keep it feeling intimate. Free chips and salsa and live music (Thu-Sat night) round out the appeal. Get yourself here!

🍷 Drinking & Entertainment

Apothecary at Brent's Drugs
COCKTAIL BAR
(www.apothecaryjackson.com; 655 Duling Ave; ⊙5pm-1am Tue-Thu, to 2am Fri & Sat) Tucked into the back of a '50s-style soda fountain shop is a distinctly early-21st-century craft cocktail bar, complete with bartenders sporting thick-framed glasses, customers with sleeve tattoos and a fine menu of expertly mixed libations.

F Jones Corner
BLUES
(☎601-983-1148; www.fjonescorner.com; 303 N Farish St; ⊙10am-4am Thu-Sat) All shapes and sizes, colors and creeds descend on this down-home Farish St club when everywhere else closes. It hosts authentic Delta musicians, who have been known to play until sunrise.

ℹ Information

Convention & Visitors Bureau (☎601-960-1891; www.visitjackson.com; 111 E Capitol St, Suite 102; ⊙8:30am-5pm Mon-Fri) Free information.

ℹ Getting There & Away

Since downtown sits at the junction of I-20 and I-55, it's easy to get in and out. The city's international **airport** (JAN; ☎601-939-5631; www.jmaa.com; 100 International Dr) is 10 miles east of downtown. **Greyhound** (☎601-353-6342; 300 W Capitol St) buses serve Birmingham, Memphis and New Orleans (with transfers). Amtrak's *City of New Orleans* stops at the **station** (Union Station; 300 W Capitol St).

Natchez

Sprawled across a bluff overlooking the Mississippi River, this old city is packed tight with historic buildings. But there's a sense of devil-may-care mischief these days that keeps the history from becoming oppressive. In fact, Natchez is one of the more inclusive and diverse cities in the state, despite its 668 or so antebellum homes. Historically, Natchez is the oldest post-European contact settlement on the Mississippi (beating New Orleans by two years). It is also at one end of the scenic 444-mile Natchez Trace Parkway, a popular travel corridor in the 1800s and now the state's cycling and recreational jewel. Today, the city has a boisterous party vibe on weekends, with cars parked every which way on the sidewalks and well-sauced revelers filling the watering holes, dancing to live music and gambling at the casino. During the 'pilgrimage' seasons in spring and fall, local mansions are opened to visitors.

◉ Sights & Activities

Emerald Mound   ARCHAEOLOGICAL SITE
(www.nps.gov/natr; Mile 10.3 Natchez Trace Pkwy; ☉ dawn-dusk; P 🐾) FREE Just outside town, along the Trace, you'll find Emerald Mound, the grassy ruins of a Native American city that includes the second-largest pre-Columbian earthworks in the US. Using stone tools, pre-Columbian ancestors to the Natchez people graded this eight-acre mountain into a flat-topped pyramid. It is now the second-largest mound site in America. There are shady, creekside picnic spots here, and you can and should climb to the top, where you'll find a vast lawn.

Melrose   HISTORIC BUILDING
(☎ 601-446-5790; www.nps.gov/natc; 1 Melrose-Montebello Pkwy; adult/child 6-17yr $10/5; ☉ tours 10am, 11am, 1pm, 2pm, 3pm, 4pm; P) Tours of this Greek Revival home take a fascinating, multi-perspective look at life on the city estate of a slave-owning cotton magnate. A lawyer, state legislator and businessman, John McMurran moved into the home – fronted by four Doric columns – in 1849 with his family. Today, the property is run by the National Park Service. Rangers share stories about the McMurran family inside the home; visitors can then explore the slave cabins and related exhibits out back. Cash or check only.

🛌 Sleeping & Eating

⭐ **Historic Oak Hill Inn**   INN $$
(☎ 601-446-2500; www.historicoakhill.com; 409 S Rankin St; r $140-170, ste $250; P ❊ 🛰) At this B&B you can sleep in an original 1835 bed and dine on pre–Civil War porcelain under 1850 Waterford Crystal gasoliers. It's all about purist antebellum aristocratic living. Co-owner Doug Mauro defines Southern hospitality, and his Natchez knowledge runs deep. Prepared by fellow owner Donald McGlynn, an alum of Brennan's restaurant in New Orleans, breakfasts are a highlight.

Magnolia Grill   SOUTHERN US $$
(☎ 601-446-7670; www.magnoliagrill.com; 49 Silver St; mains $10-35; ☉ 11am-9pm Sun, Tue & Wed, to 10pm Fri & Sat; 🍴) Down by the riverside, this attractive wooden storefront grill with exposed rafters and outdoor patio is a good place for a pork tenderloin po'boy or a fried crawfish and spinach salad.

WORTH A TRIP

NATCHEZ TRACE PARKWAY

If you're driving through Mississippi, we highly recommend planning at least part of your trip around one of the oldest roads in North America: the Natchez Trace. This 444-mile trail follows a natural ridge line that was widely used by prehistoric animals as a grazing route; later, the area those animals trampled became a footpath and trading route utilized by Native American tribes. That route would go on to become the Natchez Trace, a major roadway into the early western interior of the young USA, that was often plagued by roving bandits.

In 1938, 444 miles of the Trace, stretching from Pasquo, TN, southwest to Natchez, MS, was designated the federally protected Natchez Trace Parkway (www.nps.gov/natr), administered by the National Park Service. It's a lovely, scenic drive that traverses a wide panoply of Southern landscapes: thick, dark forests, soggy wetlands, gentle hill country and long swaths of farmland. There are more than 50 access points to the parkway and a helpful **visitor center** (☎ 662-680-4027; www.nps.gov/natr; Mile 266 Natchez Trace Pkwy; ☉ 9am-4:30pm; 🍴❊) 🖋 outside Tupelo. There are no stoplights or stop signs to ruin your ride.

Drinking & Entertainment

Under the Hill Saloon BAR
(☑ 601-446-8023; 25 Silver St; ⊙ 10am-late) A tremendously fun and historic bar that was once a favorite haunt of Samuel Clemens, a riverboat pilot who would go on to be known by his pen name, Mark Twain. The bar closes whenever everyone has emptied out. You might catch live music on the weekend.

Smoot's Grocery LIVE MUSIC
(☑ 601-653-0731; www.smootsgrocery.com; 319 N Broadway St; ⊙ 4pm-midnight Thu & Fri, from noon Sat, noon-8pm Sun) Smoot's Grocery, we like how you sing the blues. Housed in a well-worn former grocery close to the Mississippi, this beer hall loves live music. It's mostly blues bands, but you might catch swamp rock, roots music, soul or zydeco. Tuxedoed wedding guests, dance-floor divas and pool-playing good ole boys – it seems everyone's here at some point.

ⓘ Information

The **Visitor and Welcome Center** (☑ 800-647-6724; www.visitnatchez.org; 640 S Canal St; ⊙ 8:30am-5pm Mon-Sat, 9am-4pm Sun) is a large, well-done tourist resource with exhibits of area history and a ton of information on local sites. You'll find information centers for several entities – Natchez National Historical Park, Natchez Pilgrimage Tours, the City of Natchez Visitor Information, and Mississippi Tourism – clustered here.

ⓘ Getting There & Away

Natchez is located off US 61, and also forms the terminus (or beginning, depending on which way you're heading) of the Natchez Trace Pkwy. The **Greyhound** (☑ 601-445-5291; 127 Wood Ave) station is about 3.5 miles east of town.

Gulf Coast

The Mississippi Gulf Coast comprises a long, low series of breeze-swept dunes, patches of sea oats, lonely barrier islands, bayside art galleries and clusters of Vegas-style casinos. This is a popular retreat for families and military personnel; several important bases pepper the coast from Florida to Texas.

Charming Bay St Louis attracts federal employees, including many scientists based out at Stennis Space Center near the Louisiana border; their presence gives the town a slightly more progressive cast than you might expect from Mississippi. Yoga studios, antique stores and galleries cluster on Main St.

Ocean Springs is a peaceful getaway, with a lineup of shrimp boats in the harbor alongside recreational sailing yachts, a historic downtown core and a powdery fringe of white sand on the Gulf.

Cheap chain accommodations can be found at the I-10 exits that lead to various Gulf Coast towns. Within said towns, you may find nice B&Bs and small hotels. You'll often find the lowest-priced options at the casino hotels in Biloxi.

ⓘ Getting There & Away

Biloxi is tucked between neighbor Gulfport to the west and Ocean Springs to the east. The city is 90 miles east of New Orleans and 30 miles east of Bay St Louis. Ocean Springs is 33 miles east of Bay St Louis and 60 miles west of Mobile, off I-10.

ARKANSAS

Forming the mountainous joint between the Midwest and the Deep South, Arkansas (*ar-kan-saw*) is an often-overlooked treasure of swift rushing rivers, dark leafy hollows, crenelated granite outcrops and the rugged spine of the Ozark and the Ouachita (wash-ee-tah) mountains. The entire state is blessed with exceptionally well-presented state parks and tiny, empty roads crisscrossing dense forests that let out onto breathtaking vistas and gentle pastures dotted with grazing horses. Mountain towns juke between Christian fundamentalism, hippie communes and biker bars, yet all of these divergent cultures share a love of their home state's stunning natural beauty.

ⓘ Information

Arkansas State Parks (☑ 888-287-2757; www.arkansasstateparks.com), Arkansas' well-reputed park system, has 52 state parks. Thirty offer camping and some offer lodge and cabin accommodations. Due to popularity, reservations on weekends and holidays often require multiday stays.

Little Rock

Little Rock lives up to its name: as state capitals go, this one feels pretty petite. But this is also the center of urban life in Arkansas, and amid the leafy residential neighborhoods are friendly bars, fresh restaurants, plenty of bike trails and a tolerant vibe. Little Rock's small demographics are complemented by a wide sense of geographic space; the town is situated on the Arkansas River, and as befits this state of natural wonders, you always feel as if you're within arm's reach of lush, wooded river valleys.

◉ Sights

William J Clinton Presidential Center MUSEUM
(☑ 501-374-4242; www.clintonlibrary.gov; 1200 President Clinton Ave; adult/child $10/6; ⊙ 9am-5pm Mon-Sat, 1-5pm Sun; Ⓟ 🚼) 🅿 This library houses the largest archival collection in presidential history, including 80 million pages of documents and two million photographs (although there's not a lot related to a certain intern scandal). The entire experience feels like a time travel journey to the 1990s. Peruse the full-scale replica of the Oval Office, the exhibits on all stages of Clinton's life, or gifts from visiting dignitaries. The complex is built to environmentally friendly standards.

Riverfront Park PARK
(☑ 501-371-4770; www.littlerock.com/little-rock-destinations/riverfront-park; Ottenheimer Plaza; ⊙ sunrise-sunset) **FREE** This park rolls pleasantly along the Arkansas River, and both pedestrians and cyclists take advantage of it. It's a truly fine integration of the river into its urban setting. The most noticeable landmark is the Clinton Presidential Park Bridge, a gorgeous pedestrian path that spans the river.

Little Rock Central High School HISTORIC SITE
(☑ 501-374-1957; www.nps.gov/chsc; 2125 Daisy L Gatson Bates Dr; ⊙ 9am-4:30pm; Ⓟ) **FREE** Little Rock's most riveting historic attraction is the site of the 1957 desegregation crisis that changed the country forever. This was where a group of African American students known as the Little Rock Nine were first denied entry to the then all-white high school despite a unanimous 1954 Supreme Court ruling forcing the integration of public schools. Images of the students being escorted to class by national guard soldiers remain some of the most iconic records of the Civil Rights movement.

🏃 Activities

Rocktown River Outfitters KAYAKING
(☑ 501-831-0548; www.rocktownriveroutfitters. com; 400 President Clinton Ave; 2hr bicycle/kayak rental from $20/35; ⊙ 10am-5pm Wed & Thu, 9am-6pm Fri & Sat, 11am-6pm Sun) This outfitter can help you explore local waterways, including the **Arkansas River and Fourche Creek** (http://ar.audubon.org/fourche-creek), a major regional urban wetland. You can either opt for guided paddling tours ($45 to $65), or you can rent a kayak and get out on the water yourself. It's best to call ahead instead of just dropping in. Also rents bicycles and conducts a bicycle and brunch tour ($65).

🛏 Sleeping & Eating

Little Rock Firehouse Hostel & Museum HOSTEL $
(☑ 501-476-0294; www.firehousehostel.org; 1201 Commerce St; dm $31; Ⓟ 🛜) As the name not so subtly implies, this was once a fire station. Now it's a spiffy hostel located in a gorgeous 1917 Craftsman-style building that includes a small on-site museum on early-20th-century firefighting. Dorms are clean, if very basic, and there's a good, social backpacker vibe.

★ Capital Hotel BOUTIQUE HOTEL $$
(☑ 501-374-7474; www.capitalhotel.com; 111 W Markham St; r $195-265, ste $315-515; Ⓟ ❄ @ 🛜) This 1872 former bank building with a cast-iron facade – a near-extinct architectural feature – is the top digs in Little Rock. There is a wonderful outdoor mezzanine for cocktails, and a sense of suited, cigar-chomping posh throughout. If you want to feel like a wining, dining lobbyist, you've found your spot.

★ The Root Cafe SOUTHERN US $
(☑ 501-414-0423; www.therootcafe.com; 1500 S Main St; mains $9-15; ⊙ 7am-2:30pm Tue-Fri, 5-9pm Wed-Sat, 8am-3:30pm Sat, 9am-2pm Sun; 🎋) 🅿 Little Rock boasts a genuinely innovative dining scene, and even then, the Root is where local diners look for boundary breakers. The menu is exhaustively sourced from local providers whenever possible, and the food is upscaled Arkansas cuisine: purple-hull peas and cornbread, pork carnitas, and country fried tofu with vegan gravy. The setting is rustic funky, airy and friendly.

South on Main AMERICAN $$
(☑ 501-244-9660; www.southonmain.com; 1304 S Main St; mains $16-24; ⊙ 11am-2:30pm Mon-Fri, 5-10pm Tue-Sat, 10am-2pm Sun) This wonderful spot is a gastronomic pet project of *The Oxford American*, the South's seminal quarterly literary magazine. It embraces the foodways of the region with a verve and dynamism

that is creative and delicious: catfish comes with cornmeal pancakes, while rabbit leg is wrapped in country ham. A great bar and frequent live music round out the awesome.

♚ Drinking & Entertainment

★**White Water Tavern**   LIVE MUSIC
(☑ 501-375-8400; www.whitewatertavern.com; 2500 W 7th St; ☉ noon-2am Mon-Fri, 6pm-1am Sat) The White Water manages to line up some excellent acts for its small stage, with bands ranging from straight-up rockers to alt-country heroes to indie poppers to hip-hop MCs. When the music isn't playing, this is an excellent, friendly corner pub – a night out here is a quintessential Little Rock experience.

❶ Information

Little Rock Convention Center & Tourism Bureau (☑ 501-376-4781; www.littlerock.com; 101 S Spring St; ☉ 8:30am-5pm Mon-Fri) is a good gateway into the city.

❶ Getting There & Around

Bill & Hillary Clinton National Airport (LIT; Little Rock National Airport; ☑ 501-372-3439; www.fly-lit.com; 1 Airport Dr) lies just east of downtown. The **Greyhound station** (☑ 501-372-3007; 118 E Washington St, North Little Rock) serves Memphis, TN (from $12, 2½ hours) and New Orleans (from $80, 18 hours), among many other cities. **Union Station** (☑ 800-872-7245; 1400 W Markham St) is a stop on Amtrak's *Texas Eagle* line, which runs from Chicago ($100, 14 hours) to Los Angeles ($154, 19 hours), stopping at dozens of cities in between.

Little Rock is connected to the US highway system via I-30 and I-40. The closest large city is Memphis, about 140 miles to the east.

Central Arkansas Transit (www.cat.org) runs local buses and the **METRO Streetcar** (☑ 501-375-6717; https://rrmetro.org/services/streetcar), a free trolley that has two lines. The green makes a loop on W Markham and 3rd Sts, while the blue crosses the Main St Bridge into North Little Rock.

Taxis and ride shares serve the airport; fares should run around $10 to $15 to downtown Little Rock.

Hot Springs

Hot Springs is a gem of a mountain town, and we're not the first to notice. The healing waters the town is named for have been attracting everyone from Native Americans – for centuries – and early-20th-century health nuts, to a good chunk of the nation's organized-crime leadership. When Hot Springs was at full throttle in the 1930s, it was a hotbed of gambling, bootlegging, prostitution and opulence.

Today the appeal of Hot Springs is less the actual springs than the tourism infrastructure that commemorates them. That said, a few elaborate, restored bathhouses offering old-school spa treatments line Bathhouse Row, which sits behind shady magnolias on the east side of Central Ave. Hot Springs is an attractive town that has managed to preserve its historic center, which is always a cause for celebration.

◎ Sights & Activities

Hot Springs National Park   MUSEUM
(Fordyce Bathhouse; ☑ 501-620-6715; www.nps.gov/hosp; 369 Central Ave; ☉ Fordyce Bathhouse Visitor Center 9am-5pm) **FREE** On Bathhouse Row in the 1915 Fordyce bathhouse, the NPS visitor center and museum has exhibits about the park's history, first as a Native American free-trade zone, and later as a turn-of-the-20th-century European spa. Most fascinating are the amenities and standards set forth by an early-20th-century spa: the stained-glass work and Greek statues are opulent, but we could pass on the bare white walls, grout and electroshock therapy.

Hot Springs Mountain Tower   VIEWPOINT
(☑ 501-881-4020; https://hotspringstower.com; 401 Hot Springs Mountain Rd; adult/child $8/4.50; ☉ 9am-9pm Jun-Aug, to 5pm Nov-Mar, hrs vary other months; ℗) On top of Hot Springs Mountain, the 216ft tower has spectacular views of the surrounding mountains covered with dogwood, hickory, oak and pine – lovely in the spring and fall.

**Adventureworks
Hot Springs**   ADVENTURE SPORTS
(☑ 501-262-9182; www.adventureworks.com; 1700 Shady Grove Rd; adult/child 8-17 from $65/49; ☉ 10am-4pm Mon-Sat, from 1pm Sun) This popular outfitter organizes zipline tours across the local forest canopy, where a dozen lines stretch for a mile through the treetops. Zipline options include a once-a-month full-moon zipline and a 'haunted forest' zipline. You can also attempt an aerial obstacle course that includes swinging rope bridges, Tarzan vines and other fun (from $19).

DON'T MISS

ARCHITECTURE & GARDENS

Some 8 miles south of Hot Springs, the **Anthony Chapel** (550 Arkridge Rd S; ⊙9am-6pm; [P]) [FREE] is an architectural masterpiece. This soaring, wood-and-glass complex, built in 2006, synchronizes with and underlines the beauty of the surrounding forest. Inside, the structure is both tellingly modern and man-made, and deeply connected to its surrounding environment. The chapel is, not for nothing, one of the most popular wedding venues in the state.

The chapel lays outside of the ticketed area for **Garvan Woodland Gardens** ([✆]501-262-9300; www.garvangardens.org; 550 Arkridge Rd; adult/child $15/5; ⊙9am-6pm; [P][♿]), which feels like a forest grove caught between the mountains and an alpine lake. The grounds include the Garden of the Pine Wind (a local ravine refashioned into a Japanese rock garden), a wildflower overlook, a children's garden, bridges, pergolas, and a general surfeit of landscaped loveliness.

Sleeping & Eating

★ Gold-Inn   INN $
([✆]501-624-9164; https://gold-inn.webflow.io; 741 Park Ave; r $88-100; [P][※][❄][⛱]) With friendly, welcoming owners, this inn, less than a mile from Bathhouse Row, is an old road motel that has been upgraded into a mid-century boutique hotel. The rooms are impeccable, comfortable and include flat-screen TVs and comfy beds.

Lake Catherine State Park   CABIN $
(https://arkansasstateparks.reserveamerica.com; 1200 Catherine Park Rd; tent camping $13-35, cabins $97-190, yurt $55; [P][⛱]) The lodging at this state park is excellent. The real gems are 20 lovely Civilian Conservation Corps–built rustic cabins overlooking the lake; some come with wood fireplaces or spa tubs. You can also opt for tent camping (most sites have water and electric hookups, but some are rated as primitive), or even rent a yurt (sleeps eight).

McClard's   BARBECUE $
([✆]501-623-9665; www.mcclards.com; 505 Albert Pike; mains $4-15; ⊙11am-7pm Tue-Thu, to 8pm Fri & Sat) Southwest of the center, Bill Clinton's favorite boyhood barbecue is still popular for ribs, slow-cooked beans, chili and tamales. It's on the outskirts of downtown Hot Springs.

Rolando's   LATIN AMERICAN $$
([✆]501-318-6054; https://rolandosrestaurant.com; 210 Central Ave; mains $9-23; ⊙11am-9pm Sun-Thu, to 10pm Fri & Sat; [♿]) An Ecuadoran is behind the concept of this *nuevo latino* joint, where customers enjoy a colorful dining space and solid mains like shrimp sauteed in a lime and tequila sauce, or fish tacos. Start your meal with a flaming bowl of chorizo and queso (cheese). There's a kids' menu and dishes can be ordered as small plates to share.

Drinking & Nightlife

Maxine's   BAR
([✆]501-321-0909; www.maxineslive.com; 700 Central Ave; ⊙5pm-3am Mon-Fri, 2pm-2am Sat, noon-midnight Sun) If you're looking for some (loud) night music, head to this infamous cathouse turned live-music venue. It hosts bands out of Austin regularly.

Superior Bathhouse
Brewery and Distillery   BREWERY
([✆]501-624-2337; www.superiorbathhouse.com; 329 Central Ave; ⊙11am-9pm Mon-Thu, to 10pm Fri, to 11pm Sat, to 8pm Sun) It's surprising that an outdoorsy town with this many hikers and hipsters lacked a craft brewery for so long, but as the sun rises in the east, so too does Hot Springs have an indie brewery. The local suds are delicious and perfect for washing away any healthy effects of Hot Springs.

❶ Getting There & Away

Hot Springs is located off I-30, about 60 miles southwest of Little Rock. There is no public transportation out here.

Tri-Peaks Region

The Tri-Peaks Region is the crown jewel in the gem that is the great green Arkansas River Valley, which forms one of the state's major geographic zones. In the shadow of the Tri-Peaks, you'll find four state parks and fantastic hiking, trekking and boating activities.

The area, which comprises multiple Arkansas counties, is named for the triumvirate of Mt Magazine, Mt Nebo and Petit Jean Mountain. While there is no real central base for exploring the area, you can stock up on supplies in numerous small towns, the largest of which is Russellville. We have named the closest supply town in each park's individual entry.

◎ Sights & Activities

Each of the parks we list in the Tri-Peaks Region, with the exception of water-oriented Lake Dardanelle, contain multiple **hikes** ranging from flat, easy nature loops to difficult ascents along mountain peaks. Check with each park website for a full list of the many trails, and be sure to ask rangers about current conditions.

Mt Magazine State Park   STATE PARK
(☑479-963-8502; www.arkansasstateparks.com/ parks/mount-magazine-state-park; 577 Lodge Dr, Paris, GPS: N 35°09'52.4 W 93°38'49.7; ⊙visitor center 8am-5pm; Ⓟ⛟) FREE This stellar state park features some 14 miles of trails that wind around Arkansas' highest point. The surrounding vistas are spectacular, taking in all of the forested montane beauty of the Arkansas River Valley. If you don't have time to stop, the **Mt Magazine Scenic Byway** traverses the park and includes some drop-dead gorgeous views. If you need food or gas, the closest town is **Paris**, about 17 miles away.

Mt Nebo State Park   STATE PARK
(☑479-229-3655; www.arkansasstateparks.com/ mountnebo; 16728 W State Hwy 155, Dardanelle, GPS: N 35°13'41.0; ⊙visitor center 8am-5pm daily, to 7pm Fri & Sat Jun-Aug; Ⓟ⛟🎿) FREE Mt Nebo and surrounds are crisscrossed by 14 miles of trails that plunge into the woodsy mountainscape. The strenuous **Nebo Springs** trail makes a loop that heads to a mossy, watery slice of outdoors loveliness. The closest town, **Dardanelle**, is 8 miles to the east.

Petit Jean State Park   STATE PARK
(☑501-727-5441; www.petitjeanstatepark.com; 1285 Petit Jean Mountain Rd, Morrilton, GPS: N 35°07'04.3; ⊙visitor center 8am-8pm Jun & Jul, to 7pm Sep & Oct, to 5pm Nov-May & Aug; Ⓟ⛟🎿) FREE The excellently maintained trails of this state park, the oldest in Arkansas, wind past a lush 95ft waterfall, romantic grottoes, expansive vistas and dense forests. Be on the lookout for a natural bridge spanning the

Arcadian wilderness, as well as overlooks that take in huge swaths of the Arkansas River Valley. The closest town is **Morrilton** (18 miles away), although Little Rock is only about 70 miles southeast of here if you fancy a long day trip from the capital.

Lake Dardanelle State Park   STATE PARK
(☑479-967-5516; www.arkansasstateparks.com/ lakedardanelle; 100 State Park Dr (Breakwater Rd), Russellville; ⊙visitor center 8am-8pm May-Aug, to 5pm rest of year; Ⓟ⛟) FREE Miles of icy-blue water mark this 34,300-acre reservoir, which is surrounded by boat-launch ramps and flat-out pretty views. There's a big visitor center in **Russellville** that includes kid-friendly interpretive exhibits, aquariums and kayak-rental facilities.

Buffalo National River   RAFTING
(☑870-439-2502; www.nps.gov/buff; ⛟) 🌿 An under-acknowledged Arkansas gem, and perhaps the best of them all, this 135-mile river flows beneath dramatic bluffs through unspoiled Ozark forest. The upriver section tends to have most of the white water, while the lower reaches ease lazily along – perfect for an easy paddle.

The Buffalo National River has multiple **campgrounds** and three designated wilderness areas; the most accessible is through the Tyler Bend visitor center (p442), 11 miles north of Marshall on Hwy 65, where you can also pick up a list of approved outfitters for self-guided rafting or canoe trips (the best way to tour the park and see the gargantuan limestone bluffs). Or seek out Buffalo Outdoor Center (p444), which will point you in the right direction and rents out attractive cabins in the woods too.

Kayaking   BOATING
(☑479-967-5516; www.arkansasstateparks.com; 100 State Park Dr (Breakwater Rd), Russellville; per hr/half-day/full day from $7.50/10/18) 🌿 You can rent solo or tandem kayaks to explore the waters of Lake Dardanelle, or opt for a 90-minute kayak tour for an extra $12/6 per adult/child.

🛏 Sleeping & Eating

Accommodations in the four state parks range from primitive campsites to lodges. The dozens of campsites (www.arkansasstateparks.com/camping-cabins-lodging) range from those with no hookups to sites with full electricity, running water and toilets. Contact each park for details, and book

THE SOUTH TRI-PEAKS REGION

through the state park website. Rates run from $12 for primitive sites to $30 or more for fully serviced areas.

There are uninspiring motels and hotels in the nearby towns.

You'll want to stock up on groceries before exploring any of the Tri-Peaks parks in-depth, with the exception of Lake Dardanelle, which is located in Russellville proper.

ⓘ Information

The **Tyler Bend Visitor Center** (☎870-439-2502; www.nps.gov/buff; 170 Ranger Rd, St Joe; ⓧ8:30am-4:30pm) is a must visit for those who want to explore the Buffalo National River.

ⓘ Getting There & Away

The Tri-Peaks Region occupies an oddly Arkansas-shaped chunk of north-central Arkansas. The four parks can only be accessed via your own vehicle. None is more than two hours from Little Rock.

The spectacular Highway 23/Pig Trail Byway, which runs from Eureka Springs to Mt Magazine State Park, runs through mountain ranges and Ozark National Forest – it's well worth your time to take this scenic drive.

Ozark Mountains

Stretching from northwest and central Arkansas into Missouri, the Ozark Mountains are an ancient range, once surrounded by sea and now well worn by time. Verdant peaks give way to misty fields and hard-dirt farms, while dramatic karst formations line sparkling lakes, rivers and capillary-thin back roads. The region derives a lot of pride from its independence and sense of place, a zeitgeist at least partially informed by multiple generations of familial roots and a long history of regional poverty. For literary company, pick up Daniel Woodrell's novel *Winter's Bone,* which was adapted into a critically acclaimed film of the same name.

ⓘ Getting There & Away

The Ozarks encompass a large area, riven by numerous mountain roads, some of which are big enough to count as highways. Major roads include Hwy 62, AR 21, AR 43 and AR 66. The closest regional airport is **Northwest Arkansas Regional Airport** (XNA; ☎479-205-1000; www.flyxna.com; 1 Airport Blvd), near Bentonville. Eureka Springs is also served by **Greyhound** (☎800-451-5333; 131 E Van Buren).

Mountain View

Mountain View is a low-key tourism magnet where the main attraction is a daily showcasing of Ozark folkways, particularly regional music. It's a village filled with both culture creators and seekers. Folk-music enthusiasts rub shoulders with a local populace grounded in deeply spiritual Christianity. Folks tend to wear their religion on their sleeve, which may feel jarring to visitors from more secular backgrounds, but that faith considerably animates Mountain View's embrace of music and the arts.

The **Visitor Information Center** (☎870-269-8068; www.yourplaceinthemountains.com; 122 W Main St; ⓧ9am-4:30pm Mon-Sat) promotes Mountain View as the 'Folk Music Capital of the World,' and while that may be ambitious, you can catch live music here every night of the week. This pleasant vibe stands out amidst many surrounding towns that have fallen on hard times. Mountain View, in contrast, has survived and thrived by marrying its traditions to a tourism economy, all without sacrificing its soul.

⦿ Sights & Activities

Blanchard Springs Caverns CAVE
(☎870-757-2211, tours 877-444-6777; www.fs.usda.gov; NF 54, Forest Rd, off Hwy 14; Dripstone tour adult/child$12/7, Wild Cave tour $85; ⓧvaries; ♿) ⦿ The spectacular Blanchard Springs Caverns, 15 miles northwest of Mountain View, were carved by an underground river. It's a little-known, mind-blowing spot in Arkansas. Guided tours range from accessible-travel to adventurous three- to four-hour spelunking sessions. The caverns maintain seasonal hours, but usually open at 9:30am and close around sunset.

Ozark Folk Center State Park STATE PARK
(☎870-269-3851; www.ozarkfolkcenter.com; 1032 Park Ave; auditorium adult/child $12/7; ⓧ10am-5pm Tue-Sat Apr-Nov, evening shows 7pm; ⓟ) The town's top cultural attraction, just north of Mountain View, hosts ongoing craft demonstrations, a traditional herb garden and nightly live music that brings in an avid crowd. Beyond those shows, the center maintains a busy concert schedule that ropes in some of the nation's best folk and bluegrass acts.

LocoRopes OUTDOORS
(☎870-269-6566, 888-669-6717; www.locoropes.com; 1025 Park Ave; zipline from $15; ⓧ10am-5pm Mar 1-Nov 30) This popular outdoors outfitter

offers a ropes course, slack lining, a freefall, a climbing wall and three ziplines. Its 'loco lines' adventures ($15 to $60) pretty much combine all of the above into an absolutely thrilling aerial obstacle course and zipline experience.

🛏 Sleeping & Eating

The Inn at Mountain View B&B $
(☑870-269-4200, 800-535-1301; www.innatmountainview.com; 307 W Washington St; r $94-120, ste $145; P🐾) It's the rare property we review that hosts banjo and fiddle workshops, but then along comes the Inn at Mountain View. Besides being an active participant in the Mountain View folk-music world, the Inn boasts 10 rooms, all appointed in a cozy-quilt grandma-chic style. Feel free to relax on the big porch and soak up the music come evening.

Tommy's Famous
Pizza and BBQ PIZZA, BARBECUE $
(☑870-269-3278; www.tommysfamous.com; cnr Carpenter & W Main Sts; pizza $7-26, mains $7-13; ◷from 3pm) The barbecue pizza here marries Tommy's stated specialties indulgently. The affable owner, a former rocker from Memphis, plays great music, has a fun vibe, and just two conditions: no attitude and no loud kids.

PJ's Rainbow Cafe AMERICAN $
(☑870-269-8633; www.facebook.com/Pjsrainbowcafe; 216 W Main St; mains $5.50-13; ◷7am-8pm Tue-Sat, to 2pm Sun; 🖉🚻) This country-fried cafe serves up some truly tasty diner food done with flair: think spinach-stuffed pork loin and fresh-grilled rainbow trout caught in local rivers. Cash only.

Eureka Springs

Eureka Springs, near Arkansas' northwestern corner, perches in a steep valley and is filled with Victorian buildings, crooked streets and a crunchy, New Age–aligned local population that welcomes all. This is one of the most explicitly gay-friendly towns in the Ozarks, and mixes up an odd mash of liberal politics and rainbow flags with biker-friendly Harley bars. Hiking, cycling and horseback-riding opportunities abound.

The **visitor center** (☑479- 253-8737; www.eurekaspringschamber.com; 516 Village Circle, Hwy 62 E; ◷10am-4pm Tue-Sat) has information about lodging, activities, tours and local attractions.

⊙ Sights & Activities

Historic Loop HISTORIC SITE
(www.eurekasprings.org) 🖉 FREE This 3.5-mile walking tour winds through downtown Eureka Springs and neighboring residential areas. The route is dotted with more than 300 Victorian homes, all built before 1910, each a jaw-dropper and on par with any preserved historic district in the USA. You can access the loop via the **Eureka Trolley** (☑479-253-9572; www.eurekatrolley.org; 137 W Van Buren St; day pass adult/child $6/2; ◷10am-6pm Sun-Fri, 9am-8pm Sat May-Oct, reduced hrs other times; 🚻), or just walk it – recommended if you're fit (the streets are steep!); pick up a map or buy trolley tickets at the Visitor Center.

Thorncrown Chapel CHURCH
(☑479-253-7401; www.thorncrown.com; 12968 Hwy 62 W; ◷9am-5pm Apr-Nov, 11am-4pm Mar & Dec; P) FREE Thorncrown Chapel is a magnificent sanctuary made of glass, with its 48ft-tall wooden skeleton holding 425 windows. There's not much between your prayers and God's green earth here. It's just outside of Eureka Springs in the woods. Donation suggested.

Lake Leatherwood City Park PARK
(☑479-253-7921; http://eurekaparks.com; 1303 Co Rd 204; ◷24hr; P🚻) 🖉 This expansive park includes 21 miles of hiking and biking trails that crisscross the forested mountains and surround an 85-acre lake. Located about 3.5 miles from downtown Eureka Springs, this is the closest managed wild space to Eureka Springs.

🛏 Sleeping & Eating

⭐ **Treehouse Cottages** COTTAGE $$
(☑479-253-9493; www.estreehouses.com; 3018 E Van Buren; cottage $106-189; P❄🐾) Sprinkled amid 33 acres of pine forest, these cute, kitschy and spacious stilted wooden cottages are worth finding. Some rooms boast a Jacuzzi tub, a private balcony with grill at the ready, a flat-screen TV, a fireplace, or all of the above. You can also opt for an underground 'Hobbit cave,' if that's your preference, Bilbo. Two-night minimum stay.

1886 Crescent Hotel HISTORIC HOTEL $$
(☑855-725-5720; www.crescent-hotel.com; 75 Prospect Ave; r $145-220, ste $270-300; P🐾) Of all the pretty historic buildings in Eureka Springs, the Crescent stands out: it's like *Downton Abbey* meets the Jazz Age (which happened in season 4, right?). Rooms are a

well-executed synthesis of historic accents and modern comforts, and the whole vibe of the place is both elegant and fun. Rates go up on weekends.

★ Oscar's Cafe SANDWICHES $

(☑479-981-1436; www.facebook.com/oscarson whitestreet; 17 White St; mains $4-9; ☉9am-3pm Wed-Sun, to 5pm Tue; ☑♿) This little cafe has a small menu, but what a menu: chicken, walnut and cranberry salad, prosciutto sandwiches and fresh quiche. This is bright, breezy cuisine, the sort of food that fills you up without weighing you down (rare in the South), and served in the heart of Eureka Springs' cute historic district.

Stone House AMERICAN $$$

(☑479-363-6411; 89 S Main St; cheese plates $25-47; ☉1-10pm Thu-Sun) The Stone House has all the ingredients for a pretty perfect evening: lots of wine; a menu that focuses on cheese, bread, olives, honey and charcuterie; live music; a cute courtyard; and did we mention lots of wine? It's open until 10pm, which constitutes late-night dining in Eureka Springs.

🍷 Drinking & Entertainment

Chelsea's Corner Cafe & Bar BAR

(☑479-253-6723; www.chelseascafeeureka.com; 10 Mountain St; ☉11am-midnight) Live-music acts frequently take to the stage at this bar, which attracts a typically Eureka Springs blend of hippies and bikers. The kitchen is one of the few places in town open past 9pm, and even does pizza delivery.

Opera in the Ozarks OPERA

(☑479-253-8595; www.opera.org; 16311 Hwy 62 W; tickets from $20) This much-acclaimed fine-arts program has kept opera alive and loud in the mountains. A packed performance schedule and a playhouse located just outside of town is the pride of Eureka Springs.

Buffalo National River

The USA's first national river rolls for 135 glorious miles through the heart of northern Arkansas. Along the way, the rushing waters pass by ochre cliffs and granite outcroppings, while lapping at small sandy beaches that fringe deep tracts of Ozark forest.

Ponca is the best base for adventures, with a fair few outdoor outfitters here to help you set up a wilderness excursion.

🏃 Activities

Buffalo Outdoor Center ADVENTURE

(BOC; ☑870-861-5514; www.buffaloriver.com; 4699 AR 43; kayak/canoe per day $55/62, zipline tour $89; ☉8am-6pm Mar-Oct, to 5pm Nov-Feb; ♿🐾) Arranges paddling trips, hiking tours, fishing trips, horseback rides and a zipline tour. Reserve in advance.

Big Bluff via Centerpoint & Goat Trail HIKING

(AR 43 & Fire Tower Rd, GPS: N 36°03'50.7) 🚶 Standing a dramatic 550ft tall, Big Bluff is the highest sheer rock face between the Rocky Mountains and the Appalachians. To get out here, take the Centerpoint Trail, three miles north of Ponca on AR 43 (look for the trailhead near the junction of Fire Tower Rd). Take the narrow spur route – the Goat Trail – that leads to the bluff.

This is a 2.5 mile round-trip trail, and it's pretty much uphill all the way – fair warning.

Lost Valley Canoe CANOEING

(☑870-861-5522; www.lostvalleycanoe.com; AR 43; kayaks per day from $55, shuttle service from $20) 🚶 This knowledgeable outfitter can arrange canoe and kayak rentals, as well as shuttle pick-up services. It also rents comfortable cabins (with hot tubs!) that can sleep two for $150 ($20 for each extra guest).

🛈 Getting There & Away

Ponca sits far off any beaten tracks. You need to come by road, and it's located about 50 miles south of Eureka Springs and 80 miles east of Bentonville.

LOUISIANA

Louisiana runs deep: a French colony turned Spanish protectorate turned reluctant American purchase; a southern fringe of swampland, bayou and alligators dissolving into the Gulf of Mexico; a northern patchwork prairie of heartland farm country; and everywhere, a population tied together by a deep, unshakable appreciation for the good things in life: food and music.

New Orleans, its first city, lives and dies by these qualities, and its restaurants and music halls are second to none. But everywhere, the state shares a love for this joie de vivre. We're not dropping French for fun, by the way; while the language is not

CAJUNS, CREOLES &...CREOLES

Tourists in Louisiana often use the terms 'Cajun' and 'Creole' interchangeably, but the two cultures are quite distinct. 'Creole' refers to descendants of the original European settlers of Louisiana, a blended mix of mainly French and Spanish ancestry. The Creoles tend to have urban connections to New Orleans and consider their own culture refined and urbanized.

The Cajuns can trace their lineage to the Acadians, colonists from rural France who settled Nova Scotia, New Brunswick, Prince Edward Island and parts of Quebec. After the British conquered Canada, the proud Acadians refused to kneel to the new crown and were exiled in the mid-18th century – an act known as the Grand Dérangement. Many exiles settled in South Louisiana; they knew the area was French, but the Acadians ('Cajun' is an English bastardization of the word) were often treated as country bumpkins by the Creoles. The Acadians-cum-Cajuns settled in the bayous and prairies, and to this day see themselves as a more rural, frontier-style culture.

Adding confusion to this is the practice, standard in many post-colonial French societies, of referring to mixed-race individuals as 'Creoles.' This happens in Louisiana, but there is a cultural difference between Franco-Spanish Creoles and mixed-race Creoles, even though these two communities very likely share actual blood ancestry.

a cultural component of North Louisiana, near I-10 and below, the French language – or Louisiana's particular version of it – is a cultural touchstone.

History

The lower Mississippi River area was dominated by the Mississippian mound-building culture until around 1592 when Europeans arrived and decimated the Native Americans with the usual combination of disease, unfavorable treaties and outright hostility.

The land was then passed back and forth between France, Spain and England. Under the French 'Code Noir,' slaves were kept but retained a somewhat greater degree of freedom – and thus native culture – than their counterparts in British North America.

After the American Revolution the whole area passed to the USA in the 1803 Louisiana Purchase, and Louisiana became a state in 1812. The resulting blend of American and Franco-Spanish traditions, plus the influence of Afro-Caribbean communities, gave Louisiana the unique culture it retains to this day.

Following the Civil War, Louisiana was readmitted to the Union in 1868 and the next 30 years saw political wrangling, economic stagnation and renewed discrimination against African Americans.

Hurricane Katrina (2005) and the BP Gulf Coast Oil Spill (2010) significantly damaged the local economy and infrastructure. Louisiana remains a bottom-rung state in terms of per capita income and education levels, yet it ranks high in national happiness scales.

ℹ Information

Louisiana Office of Tourism (800-677-4082; www.louisianatravel.com) Ten welcome centers dot freeways throughout the state, or contact the office directly.

Louisiana State Parks (888-677-1400; www.crt.state.la.us/louisiana-state-parks) Louisiana has 20 state parks that offer camping. Some parks also offer lodge accommodations and cabins. Reservations can be made online, by phone or on a drop-in basis if there's availability. Camping fees increase slightly from April to September.

New Orleans

New Orleans is very much of America, but extraordinarily removed from it as well. Founded by the French and administered by the Spanish (and then the French again), New Orleans is the most European city in America. But, with the *vodoun* (voodoo), weekly second-line parades, Mardi Gras Indians, jazz, brass and gumbo, it's also the most African and Caribbean city in America.

New Orleans celebrates life; while America is on deadline, this city is sipping a cocktail after a long lunch. But if you saw how people here rebuilt their homes after floods and tempests, you'd be foolish to call the locals lazy.

Tolerating everything and learning from it is the soul of this city. When New Orleans' citizens aspire to that overarching Creole ideal, where the whole is greater than the sum of its parts, we get: jazz; Nouveau

Louisiana cuisine; storytellers from African *griots* (West African bards) to Seventh Ward rappers to Tennessee Williams; French townhouses a few blocks from Foghorn Leghorn mansions groaning under sweet myrtle and bougainvillea; and Mardi Gras celebrations that mix pagan mysticism with Catholic pageantry.

Just don't forget the indulgence and immersion, because that Creolization gets watered down when folks don't live life to its intellectual and epicurean hilt.

⊙ Sights

◎ French Quarter

Also known as Vieux Carré ('voo car-*ray*'; Old Quarter) and 'the Quarter,' the French Quarter is the original city as planned by the French in the 1800s. Here lies the infamous Bourbon St, but of more interest is an elegantly aged grid of shopfronts, iron lamps and courtyard gardens. Most visitors begin exploring the city here and some never leave the area. That's not to say the Quarter isn't lovely, but it's a bit like a theme park: heavy on tourist traffic and light on locals (apart from your bartender or waiter).

★ Jackson Square　　SQUARE
(Decatur & St Peter Sts) Sprinkled with lazing loungers, surrounded by sketch artists, fortune tellers and traveling performers, and watched over by cathedrals, offices and shops plucked from a Parisian fantasy, Jackson Sq is one of America's great town greens and the heart of the Quarter. The identical, block-long Pontalba Buildings overlook the scene, and the nearly identical Cabildo and **Presbytère** (☑504-568-6968; https://louisianastatemuseum.org/museum/presbytere; 751 Chartres St; adult/student/child $6/5/free; ⊗10am-4:30pm Tue-Sun) ⏉ structures flank the impressive St Louis Cathedral, which fronts the square.

★ St Louis Cathedral　　CATHEDRAL
(☑504-525-9585; www.stlouiscathedral.org; Jackson Sq; donations accepted, audio guide $8; ⊗8:30am-4pm, Mass 12:05pm Mon-Fri, 5pm Sat, 9am & 11am Sun) One of the best examples of French architecture in the country, this triple-spired 18th-century cathedral is dedicated to Louis IX, the French king sainted in 1297. It's an attractive bit of Gallic heritage in the heart of an American city. In addition to hosting black, white and Creole Catho-

lic congregants, St Louis has also attracted those who, in the best New Orleanian tradition, mix their influences, such as voodoo queen Marie Laveau.

★ Cabildo　　MUSEUM
(☑504-568-6968; https://louisianastatemuseum.org/museum/cabildo; 701 Chartres St; adult/student/child under 6yr $9/7/free; ⊗10am-4:30pm Tue-Sun) The former seat of government in colonial Louisiana now serves as the gateway to exploring the history of the state in general, and New Orleans in particular. It's also a magnificent building in its own right; the elegant Cabildo marries elements of Spanish Colonial architecture and French urban design better than most buildings in the city. The diverse exhibits include Native American tools, 'Wanted' posters for escaped slaves, and a gallery's worth of paintings of stone-faced old New Orleanians.

Historic New Orleans Collection　　MUSEUM
(THNOC; ☑504-523-4662; www.hnoc.org; 533 Royal St; admission free, tours $5; ⊗9:30am-4:30pm Tue-Sat, from 10:30am Sun, tours 10am, 11am, 2pm & 3pm Tue-Sat, 11am, 2pm & 3pm Sun) A combination of preserved buildings, museums and research centers all rolled into one, the Historic New Orleans Collection is a good introduction to the history of the city. The complex is anchored by its Royal St campus, which presents a series of regularly rotating exhibits and occasional temporary exhibits. Artifacts on display include an original Jazz Fest poster, transfer documents of the Louisiana Purchase and utterly disturbing slave advertisements.

◎ Mid-City & The Tremé

Back in the day, this was the back of beyond: the bottom of the depression that is the New Orleans geographic bowl, an area of swampy lowlands and hidden gambler dens. Today? Mid-City and its adjacent neighborhoods form one of the loveliest residential areas in the city. This semiamorphous district includes long lanes of shotgun houses, bike lanes, the gorgeous green spaces of City Park, the elegant mansions of Esplanade Ave and the slow, lovely laze of Bayou St John.

★ Backstreet Cultural Museum　　MUSEUM
(☑504-657-6700; www.backstreetmuseum.org; 1116 Henriette Delille St; $10; ⊗11am-5pm Mon-Fri, 10am-3pm Sat) Mardi Gras Indian suits grab the spotlight with dazzling flair – and finely crafted detail – in this informative museum

NEW ORLEANS FOR CHILDREN

New Orleans is a fairy-tale city, with its colorful beads, weekly costume parties and daily music wafting through the air. The same flights of fancy and whimsy that give this city such appeal for poets and artists also make it an imaginative wonderland for children, especially creative ones.

The **Louisiana Children's Museum** (☑504-523-1357; www.lcm.org; 420 Julia St, Warehouse District; $10; ⊗9:30am-4:30pm Tue-Sat, noon-4:30pm Sun; ◉) is a good intro to the region for toddlers, while older children and teenagers may appreciate the Ogden Museum (p451), Cabildo and Presbytère. Little ones often take a shine to the candy-colored houses in the French Quarter, Faubourg Marigny and Uptown.

The **Latter Library** (☑504-596-2625; www.nolalibrary.org; 5120 St Charles Ave, Uptown; ⊗10am-8pm Mon-Thu, to 5pm Fri & Sat, 1-5pm Sun) on St Charles Ave has a good selection of children's literature and is located in a pretty historical mansion. The city's cemeteries, especially Lafayette Cemetery No 1 (p451) in the Garden District, are authentic slices of the past and enjoyably spooky to boot.

The many **street parties** and **outdoor festivals** of New Orleans bring food stalls and, of course, great music. Children will love dancing to the beat. Seek out festivals held during the day, such as Bayou Boogaloo (www.thebayouboogaloo.com).

Mardi Gras and the **Carnival Season** are surprisingly family-friendly affairs outside of the well-known boozy debauch in the French Quarter. St Charles Ave hosts many day parades where lots of krewes roll and families set up grilling posts and tents – drinking revelers aren't welcome. Kids are set up on 'ladder seats' (www.momsminivan.com/extras/ladderseat.html) so they can get an adult-height view of the proceedings and catch throws from the floats. The crazy costumes add to the child-friendly feel of the whole affair. See www.neworleansonline.com/neworleans/mardigras/mgfamilies.html.

examining the distinctive elements of African American culture in New Orleans. The museum isn't terribly big (it's the former Blandin's Funeral Home), but if you have any interest in the suits and rituals of Mardi Gras Indians, as well as second-line parades and Social Aid and Pleasure Clubs (the local African American community version of civic associations), you should stop by.

★**City Park**   PARK
(☑504-482-4888; www.neworleanscitypark.com; Esplanade Ave & City Park Ave; ⊗dawn-dusk; ℗◉▣) FREE Live oaks, Spanish moss and lazy bayous frame this masterpiece of urban planning. Three miles long and 1 mile wide, dotted with gardens, waterways and bridges and home to a captivating art museum, City Park is bigger than Central Park in NYC and it's New Orleans' prettiest green space.

Art- and nature-lovers could easily spend a day exploring the park. Anchoring the action is the stately New Orleans Museum of Art, which spotlights regional and American artists. From there, stroll past the whimsical creations in the **Sydney & Walda Besthoff Sculpture Garden** (www.noma.org/sculpture-garden; 1 Collins Diboll Circle; ⊗10am-6pm Apr-Sep, to 5pm Oct-Mar) FREE,

then check out the lush **Botanical Gardens** (☑504-483-9488; www.neworleanscitypark.com/botanical-garden; adult/child/under 3 $8/4/free; ⊗10am-5pm; ℗). Kids in tow? Hop the rides at the **Carousel Gardens Amusement Park** (☑504-483-9402; www.neworleanscitypark.com/in-the-park/carousel-gardens; 7 Victory Ave; adult/child 36in & under $4/free, each ride $4; ⊗11am-6pm Sat & Sun Mar-May & Aug-Oct, 11am-5pm Tue-Fri, to 6pm Sat & Sun Jun & Jul) or climb the fantastical statuary inside **Storyland** (http://neworleanscitypark.com/in-the-park/storyland; 5 Victory Ave; adult/child 36in & under $4/free; ⊗10am-5pm; ◉).

Louis Armstrong Park   PARK
(701 N Rampart St; ⊗sunrise-sunset) The entrance to this massive park has got to be one of the greatest gateways in the US, a picturesque arch that ought rightfully to be the final set piece in a period drama about Jazz Age New Orleans. The original Congo Sq is here, as well as a Louis Armstrong Statue and a bust of Sidney Bechet. The **Mahalia Jackson Theater** (☑504-287-0350; www.mahaliajacksontheater.com; 1419 Basin St) hosts opera and Broadway productions. The park often hosts live-music festivals throughout the year.

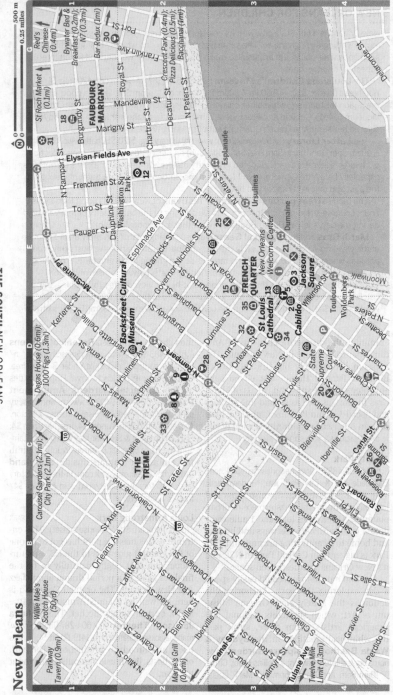

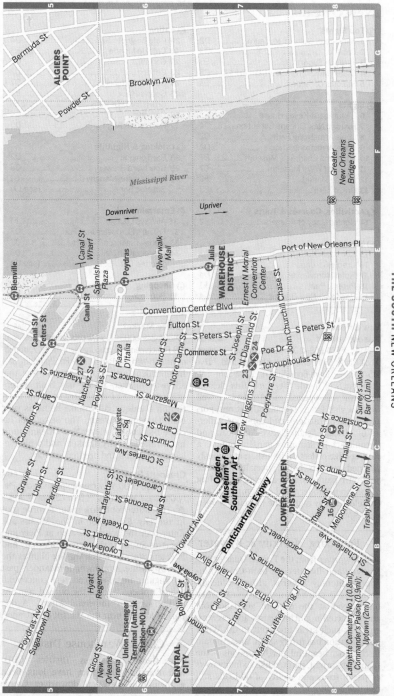

New Orleans

New Orleans Museum of Art MUSEUM
(NOMA; ☎504-658-4100; www.noma.org; 1 Collins Diboll Circle, City Park; adult/student/child 7-17yr $15/8/6; ⊙10am-6pm Tue-Fri, 10am-5pm Sat, 11am-5pm Sun) Inside City Park, this elegant museum was opened in 1911 and is well worth a visit for its special exhibitions, gorgeous marble atrium and top-floor galleries of African, Asian, Native American and Oceanic art. Its sculpture garden contains a cutting-edge collection in lush, meticulously planned grounds. Other specialties include Southern painters and an ever-expanding collection of modern and contemporary art. On select Friday nights, the museum is open until 9pm.

⦿ Faubourg Marigny & Bywater

Just downriver from the French Quarter, the Marigny and Bywater are both Creole *faubourgs* (literally 'suburbs,' although 'neighborhoods' is more accurate in spirit). They once stood at the edge of gentrification, and attracted a glut of artists and creative types, as such areas are wont to do. While gentrification has firmly set in, these remain fascinating, beautiful neighborhoods – the homes are bright, painted like so many rows of pastel fruit, and plenty of oddballs still call this home.

Palace Market MARKET
(☎504-249-9003; www.palacemarketnola.com; 619 Frenchmen St, Faubourg Marigny; ⊙7pm-midnight Sun-Wed, to 1am Thu & Fri, 2pm-1am Sat) Independent artists and artisans line this alleyway market, which has built a reputation as one of the better spots in town to find a unique gift to take home as your New Orleans souvenir. The selections include T-shirts with clever New Orleans puns, handcrafted jewelry, trinkets and a nice selection of prints and original artwork.

Crescent Park PARK
(☎504-636-6400; www.crescentparknola.org; Piety, Chartres & Mazant Sts; ⊙6am-7:30pm; P ♿ 🎨) This waterfront park is our favorite spot in the city for taking in the Mississippi. Enter over the enormous arch at Piety and Chartres Sts, or at the steps at Marigny and N Peters Sts, and watch the fog blanket the nearby skyline. A promenade meanders past an angular metal-and-concrete conceptual 'wharf' (placed next to the burned remains of the former commercial wharf). A dog park is located near the Mazant St entrance.

⦿ CBD & Warehouse District

The Central Business District (CBD) and Warehouse District have long been a membrane between downriver Creole *faubourgs* like the French Quarter and the large leafy lots of the Garden District and Uptown. This is an area that has always been in search of an identity, in a city with a distinct sense of place. These days it asserts itself via cultural institutions and convention-center infrastructure. Between offices and forgettable municipal buildings lie some of the city's best museums, as well as posh restaurants, art galleries and converted condos.

★Ogden Museum
of Southern Art   MUSEUM
(☑504-539-9650; www.ogdenmuseum.org; 925 Camp St, Warehouse District; adult/child 5-17yr $13.50/6.75; ☺10am-5pm Fri-Wed, to 8pm Thu) The South has one of the most distinctive aesthetic cultures in the US artistic universe, a creative vision indelibly influenced by the region's complicated history and deep links to the land. Few museums explore the throughlines of Southern art like the Ogden, which boasts lovely gallery spaces, an awesome gift shop and kicking after-hours performances.

National WWII Museum   MUSEUM
(☑504-528-1944; www.nationalww2museum.org; 945 Magazine St; adult/senior/child $28/24/18, films $7; ☺9am-5pm) This extensive museum presents a fairly thorough analysis of the largest war in history. The exhibits, which are displayed across multiple grand pavilions, are enormous and immersive. The experience is designed to be both personal and awe-inducing, but with that said, the museum focuses so intently on providing the American perspective, it sometimes underplays the narrative of other Allied nations.

◉ Garden, Lower
Garden & Central City

As one proceeds south along the curve of the Mississippi River, the streets become tree-lined and the houses considerably grander. When you tire of craning back to take in multiwing mansions, you're in the Garden and Lower Garden Districts, the beginning of New Orleans' 'American Sector' (so named because it was settled after the Louisiana Purchase). This is a place of leafy, bucolic splendor and considerable wealth – and wealth disparities. Nearby Central City's main thoroughfare, Oretha Castle Haley Blvd, is undergoing a fitful but steady renaissance following years of neglect.

★Lafayette Cemetery No 1   CEMETERY
(☑504-658-3781; Washington Ave, at Prytania St, Garden District; ☺7am-3pm) **FREE** Of all the cemeteries in New Orleans, Lafayette exudes the strongest sense of subtropical Southern Gothic. The stark contrast of moldering crypts and gentle decay with the forceful fertility of the fecund greenery is incredibly jarring. It's a place filled with stories – of German and Irish immigrants, deaths by yellow fever, social societies doing right by their dead – that pulls the living into New Orleans' long, troubled past.

C Tours

Confederacy of Cruisers   CYCLING
(☑504-400-5468; www.confederacyofcruisers.com; 634 Elysian Fields Ave, Faubourg Marigny; tours $49-89) This company sets you up on cruiser bikes that come with fat tires and padded seats for Nola's flat, potholed roads. The 'Creole New Orleans' tour takes in the best architecture of Marigny, Bywater, Esplanade Ave and the Tremé. Confederacy also does a 'History of Drinking' tour (for those 21 and over) and a tasty culinary tour.

★ Festivals & Events

Mardi Gras   CULTURAL
(www.mardigrasneworleans.com; ☺Feb/early Mar) Fat Tuesday marks the orgasmic finale of the Carnival season. Expect parades, floats, insane costumes, and a day of absolute madcap revelry as the entire city throws down for an all-day party.

Jazz Fest   MUSIC
(www.nojazzfest.com; entrances at Fortin St, Fair Grounds Race Course; adult/child $85/5; ☺last weekend in Apr & first weekend in May) This world-renowned extravaganza of music, food, crafts and good living is a mainstay of the New Orleans festival calendar, attracting both international headliners and local artists. Tickets are cheaper if you order in advance.

St Joseph's Day
– Super Sunday   CULTURAL
(2600 Lasalle St, AL Davis Park) March 19 and its nearest Sunday bring 'gangs' of Mardi Gras Indians out into the streets in all their feathered, drumming glory. The Super Sunday parade usually begins around noon at AL Davis Park in Central City.

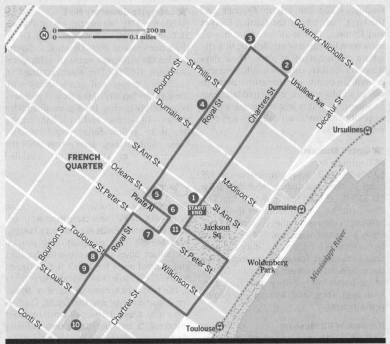

🏃 City Walk
French Quarter

START JACKSON SQ
END JACKSON SQ
LENGTH 1.1 MILES; 1½ HOURS

Begin your walk at the **1 Presbytère** (p446) on Jackson Sq and head down Chartres St to the corner of Ursulines Ave. Directly across Chartres St, at No 1113, the 1826 **2 Beauregard-Keyes House** (www.bkhouse.org) combines Creole and American styles of design. Walk along Ursulines Ave to Royal St – the soda fountain at the **3 Royal Pharmacy** is a preserved relic from halcyon malt-shop days.

When it comes to quintessential New Orleans postcard images, Royal St takes the prize. Cast-iron galleries grace the buildings and a profusion of flowers garland the facades, while buoyant buskers blare their tunes from practically every street corner, often to wild acclaim. At No 915 Royal, the **4 Cornstalk Hotel** (www.cornstalkhotel.com) stands behind one of the most frequently photographed fences anywhere. At Orleans St, stately magnolia trees and lush tropical plants fill **5 St Anthony's Garden** (tough to see beyond the rows of street art) behind **6 St Louis Cathedral** (p446).

Alongside the garden, take the inviting Pirate Alley and turn right down Cabildo Alley and then right up St Peter St toward Royal St. Tennessee Williams shacked up at No 632 St Peter, the **7 Avart-Peretti House**, in 1946–47 while he wrote *A Streetcar Named Desire*.

Turn left on Royal St. At the corner of Royal and Toulouse Sts stands a pair of houses built by Jean François Merieult in the 1790s. The building known as the **8 Court of Two Lions** (now a gallery), at 541 Royal St, opens onto Toulouse St and next door is the **9 Historic New Orleans Collection** (p446) museum.

On the next block, the massive 1909 **10 State Supreme Court Building** was the setting for many scenes in director Oliver Stone's movie *JFK*.

Turn around and head right on Toulouse St to Decatur St and turn left. Cut across the road and walk the last stretch of this tour along the river. As Jackson Sq comes into view, cross back over to the Presbytère's near-identical twin, the **11 Cabildo** (p446).

French Quarter Festival   MUSIC
(☑504-522-5730; https://frenchquarterfest.org)
During the second weekend of April, the
largest free music festival in the country
takes over the French Quarter.

🛌 Sleeping

★ Bywater Bed & Breakfast   B&B $
(☑504-944-8438; www.bywaterbnb.com; 1026
Clouet St, Bywater; r without bath $100-150; 🛜)
This is what happens when you fall through
the rabbit hole and Wonderland is a B&B.
This spot is homey and laid-back, but it's also
bursting with wild New Orleans aesthetic
touches. Expect to stay in what amounts to a
folk-art gallery with a bit of historical heritage and a hallucinogenic vibe.

Creole Gardens   B&B $
(☑504-569-8700; http://creolegardens.com; 1415
Prytania St, Lower Garden District; r $89-159;
😊❄🛜🖼) Friendly, knowledgeable hosts, a
rainbow-hued property with individualized
rooms and plenty of New Orleans bordello-
esque vibe, and they're cool with pets? Of
any size? Hey, sign us up. This is a winning
B&B that's dripping with character and out-
of-the-box charm (one room is called Coun-
tess Willie Piazza's Hall of Splendors).

★ Peter & Paul   BOUTIQUE HOTEL $$
(☑504-356-5200; https://hotelpeterandpaul.com;
2317 Burgundy St, Faubourg Marigny; r $110-249,
ste $499; P🛜) This lovely hotel has taken
over the grounds of the former Sts Peter and
Paul Catholic church and school. The rooms
are a study in elegant historical understatement, with muted linens, hand-painted tiles,
canopied beds and highly individualized
touches. The on-site church has become a
performance venue – praise the higher power of your choice.

Degas House   HISTORIC HOTEL $$
(☑504-821-5009; www.degashouse.com; 2306 Esplanade Ave; r $189-250, ste from $300; P😊❄🛜)
Edgar Degas, the famed French Impressionist, lived in this 1852 Italianate house when
visiting his mother's family in the early
1870s. Rooms recall his time here through
period furnishings and reproductions of his
work. The suites have balconies and fireplaces, while the less expensive garret rooms are
cramped top-floor quarters that once housed
the Degas family's servants.

★ Park View Historic Hotel   HOTEL $$
(☑504-861-7564; http://parkviewguesthouse.com;
7004 St Charles Ave, Uptown; r $169-219; 😊@🛜)

The breakfasts are amazing (oh, those cheese
grits) at this well-appointed three-story inn,
where everyone seems glad to see you. Beside Audubon Park, this ornate wooden masterpiece was built in 1884 to impress people
attending the World Cotton Exchange Exposition. The rooms and guest lounge are heavy
with antiques, and the veranda overlooking
the park and St Charles Ave is lovely.

★ Roosevelt New Orleans   HOTEL $$$
(☑504-648-1200; www.therooseveltneworleans.
com; 123 Baronne St, CBD; r $200-309, ste $329-
2000; P😊❄@🛜🖼) The majestic, block-
long lobby harks back to the early 20th
century, a golden age of opulent hotels and
grand retreats. Swish rooms have classical
details, but the spa, restaurant **Domeni-
ca** (☑504-648-6020; www.domenicarestaurant.
com; mains $15-34; ⊘11am-11pm; 🖊), storied
Sazerac Bar (☑504-648-1200; ⊘11am-
midnight daily) and swanky jazz lounge are
at least half the reason to stay. The rooftop
pool is pretty swell too. It's an easy walk to
the French Quarter.

Hotel Monteleone   HOTEL $$$
(☑504-523-3341; www.hotelmonteleone.com; 214
Royal St; r $220-400; 😊❄🛜🖼) Perhaps the
city's most venerable hotel, the Monteleone
is also the Quarter's largest. Not long after
it was built, preservationists put a stop to
building on this scale below Iberville St.
Since its inception in 1866, the hotel has
lodged literary luminaries including William Faulkner, Truman Capote and Rebecca
Wells. Rooms exude an old-world appeal
with French toile and chandeliers.

🍴 Eating

🍴 French Quarter

Café Beignet   CAFE $
(☑504-525-2611; www.cafebeignet.com; 311 Bourbon St, Musical Legends Park; breakfast $3.50-7;
⊘8am-midnight) Serves omelets, Belgian waffles, quiche and beignets. There's a low-level
war among foodies over who does the better beignet – this place or **Café du Monde**
(☑504-525-4544; www.cafedumonde.com; 800 Decatur St; beignets $3; ⊘24hr) – with the general
consensus being that this spot uses less powdered sugar. This location has live jazz daily.

Croissant D'Or Patisserie   BAKERY $
(☑504-524-4663; www.croissantdornola.com;
615-617 Ursulines Ave; mains $3-7; ⊘6am-3pm
Wed-Mon) Bring a paper, order coffee and

a croissant – or a tart, quiche or sandwich topped with béchamel sauce – and bliss out. Check out the tiled sign on the threshold that says 'ladies entrance' – a holdover from earlier days. While the coffee is bland, the pastries are perfect, and the shop is well-lit, friendly and clean.

★ Coop's Place
CAJUN $$

(☑504-525-9053; www.coopsplace.net; 1109 Decatur St; mains $10-20; ☺11am-midnight Sun-Thu, to 1am Fri & Sat) Coop's is an authentic Cajun dive, but more rocked out. Make no mistake: it can be grotty and chaotic, the servers have attitude and the layout is annoying. But it's worth it for the food: rabbit jambalaya or chicken with shrimp and tasso (smoked ham) in a cream sauce – there's no such thing as 'too heavy' here. No patrons under 21.

✖ Mid-City & The Tremé

★ Parkway Tavern
SANDWICHES $

(☑504-482-3047; www.parkwaypoorboys.com; 538 Hagan Ave, Bayou St John; po'boys $8-14; ☺11am-10pm Wed-Mon; P ⊞) Who makes the best po'boy in New Orleans? Honestly, who can say? But tell a local you think the top sandwich comes from Parkway and you will get, at the least, a nod of respect. The roast beef in particular – a craft some would say is dying among the great po'boy makers – is messy as hell and twice as good.

★ 1000 Figs
MIDDLE EASTERN $$

(☑504-301-0848; www.1000figs.com; 3141 Ponce de Leon St, Bayou St John; small plates $5-16; ☺11am-9pm Mon-Sat; ☑) Although the menu isn't exclusively vegetarian, 1000 Figs serves our favorite vegetarian fare in town. The falafel, hummus, baba ghanoush and lentil soup are just *good* – freshly prepared and expertly executed. The dining space is well lit and the seating makes you feel as if you're eating in a best friend's stylish dining room.

Marjie's Grill
ASIAN $$

(☑504-603-2234; www.marjiesgrill.com; 320 S Broad St, Mid-City; mains $8-26; ☺11am-2:30pm & 5-10pm Mon-Fri, 4-10pm Sat) In one word: brilliant. Marjie's is run by chefs who were inspired by Southeast Asian street food, but rather than coming home and doing pale imitations of the real thing, they've turned an old house on Broad St into a corner in Hanoi, Luang Prabang or Chiang Mai. With that said, there's a hint of New Orleans at work.

Willie Mae's Scotch House
SOUTHERN US $$

(☑504-822-9503; www.williemaesnola.com; 2401 St Ann St; fried chicken $15; ☺10am-5pm Mon-Sat) Willie Mae's has been dubbed the best fried chicken in the world by the James Beard Foundation, the Food Network and other media, and in this case, the hype isn't far off – this is superlative fried bird. The white beans are also amazing. The drawback is everyone knows about it, so expect long lines, sometimes around the block.

✖ Faubourg Marigny & Bywater

★ Pizza Delicious
ITALIAN $

(☑504-676-8482; www.pizzadelicious.com; 617 Piety St, Bywater; pizza slice from $2.25, whole pie from $15; ☺11am-11pm Tue-Sun; ☑⊞▣) The thin-crust pies here are done New York–style and taste great. The preparation is simple, but the ingredients are fresh and consistently top-notch. An easy, family-friendly ambience makes for a lovely spot for a casual dinner, and it serves good beer too if you're in the mood. Vegan pizzas are available. The outdoor area is pet-friendly.

St Roch Market
MARKET $

(☑504-609-3813; www.strochmarket.com; 2381 St Claude Ave, St Roch; prices vary by vendor; ☺7am-10pm Sun-Thu, to 11pm Fri & Sat; ☑⊞) The St Roch Market was once the seafood and produce market for a working-class neighborhood. But after it was nearly destroyed by Hurricane Katrina, it was renovated into a shiny food court. The airy interior space now hosts 13 restaurants serving a broad range of food, including crepes, burritos, Haitian cuisine and coffee.

Red's Chinese
CHINESE $

(☑504-304-6030; www.redschinese.com; 3048 St Claude Ave, Bywater; mains $5-18; ☺noon-11pm; ☑) Red's has upped the Chinese cuisine game in New Orleans in a big way. The chefs aren't afraid to add lashings of Louisiana flavor, yet this isn't what we'd call 'fusion' cuisine. The food is grounded deeply in spicy Szechuan flavors, which pair well with the occasional dash of cayenne.

★ Bacchanal
AMERICAN $$

(☑504-948-9111; www.bacchanalwine.com; 600 Poland Ave, Bywater; mains $8-21, cheese from $6; ☺11am-midnight Sun-Thu, to 1am Fri & Sat) From the outside, Bacchanal looks like a leaning Bywater shack; inside are racks of wine and stinky-but-sexy cheese. Musicians play in the garden, while cooks dispense delicious meals on paper plates from the kitchen in the back; on any given day you may try chorizo-stuffed dates or seared diver scallops that will blow your gastronomic mind.

N7
TAPAS $$

(www.n7nola.com; 1117 Montegut St, St Roch; small plates $8-23; ⊙6-10pm Mon-Thu, to 11pm Fri & Sat) Dining at N7 is deeply memorable, right down to the dining space. You walk down a potholed road to a garden littered with a vintage French junkyard theme. The food? 'Can to table' – smoked mackerel, habanero oysters etc, along with French and Japanese tapas: escargot tempura, chicken cooked in wine and pork *katsu* (breaded and fried).

CBD & Warehouse District

Cochon Butcher
SANDWICHES $

(☑504-588-7675; www.cochonbutcher.com; 930 Tchoupitoulas St, Warehouse District; mains $10-14; ⊙10am-10pm Mon-Thu, to 11pm Fri & Sat, to 4pm Sun) Tucked behind the slightly more formal Cochon (☑504-588-2123; www.cochonrestaurant.com; 930 Tchoupitoulas St; small plates $8-14, mains $19-32; ⊙11am-10pm Mon-Thu, to 11pm Fri & Sat), this sandwich and meat shop calls itself a 'swine bar and deli.' We call it one of our favorite sandwich shops in the city, if not the South. From the convivial lunch crowds to the savory sandwiches to the fun-loving cocktails, this welcoming place encapsulates the best of New Orleans.

★ Carmo
VEGETARIAN $

(☑504-875-4132; www.cafecarmo.com; 527 Julia St, Warehouse District; lunch $9-12, dinner $9-16; ⊙9am-10pm Mon-Sat; ☑) ⌀ Carmo isn't just an alternative to the fatty, carnivorous New Orleans menu – it's an excellent restaurant by any gastronomic measuring stick. Both the aesthetic and the food speak to deep tropical influences, from Southeast Asia to South America. Dishes range from pescatarian to full vegan; try Peruvian-style sashimi or Burmese tea-leaf salad and walk away happy.

★ Restaurant August
CREOLE $$$

(☑504-299-9777; www.restaurantaugust.com; 301 Tchoupitoulas St, CBD; lunch fixed menu $29, dinner mains $34-50; ⊙5-10pm daily, 11am-2pm Mon-Fri; ☑) For a little romance, reserve a table at Restaurant August. This converted 19th-century tobacco warehouse, with its flickering candles and warm, soft shades, earns a nod for most aristocratic dining room in New Orleans, but somehow manages to be both intimate and lively. Delicious meals take you to another level of gastronomic perception.

Garden, Lower Garden & Central City

★ Surrey's Juice Bar
AMERICAN $

(☑504-524-3828; www.surreysnola.com; 1418 Magazine St, Garden District; mains $6.50-13; ⊙8am-3pm; ☑) Surrey's makes a simple bacon-and-egg sandwich taste – and look – like the most delicious breakfast you've ever been served. And you know what? It probably *is* the best. Boudin biscuits; eggs scrambled with salmon; biscuits swimming in salty sausage gravy; and a shrimp, grits and bacon dish that should be illegal. And the juice, as you might guess, is blessedly fresh.

Commander's Palace
CREOLE $$$

(☑504-899-8221; www.commanderspalace.com; 1403 Washington Ave, Garden District; dinner mains $28-46; ⊙11:30am-1pm & 6:30-10:30pm Mon-Fri, from 11am Sat, from 10am Sun) Commander's Palace is a dapper host who wows with white-linen dining rooms, decadent dishes and attentive Southern hospitality. The nouveau Creole menu shifts, running from crispy oysters with brie-cauliflower fondue to pecan-crusted gulf fish. The dress code adds to the charm: no shorts or T-shirts; jackets preferred at dinner. It's a *very* nice place – and lots of fun.

Drinking & Nightlife

★ Bar Tonique
COCKTAIL BAR

(☑504-324-6045; www.bartonique.com; 820 N Rampart St; ⊙noon-2am) 'Providing shelter from sobriety since 08/08/08', Tonique is a bartender's bar. Seriously, on a Sunday night, when the weekend rush is over, we've seen no fewer than three of the city's top bartenders arrive here to unwind. This gem mixes some of the best drinks in the city, offering a spirits menu as long as a Tolstoy novel.

★ Twelve Mile Limit
BAR

(☑504-488-8114; www.facebook.com/twelve.mile.limit; 500 S Telemachus St, Mid-City; ⊙5pm-2am Mon-Fri, 10am-2am Sat, 10am-midnight Sun) Twelve Mile is simply a great bar. It's staffed by people who have the skill, both behind the bar and in the kitchen, to work in four-star spots, but who chose to set up shop in

LGBTIQ+ NEW ORLEANS

Louisiana is a culturally conservative state, but its largest city bucks that trend. New Orleans has always had a reputation for tolerance and remains one of the oldest gay-friendly cities in the Western hemisphere. While local gay history is not without its tragedies – in particular, the arson of the UpStairs Lounge in the French Quarter in the 1970s – there have been pioneering moments as well; the New Orleans city council passed an antidiscrimination ordinance covering the sexual orientation of city workers back in 1991.

Neighborhoods such as the French Quarter and Marigny are major destinations on the LGBTIQ+ travel circuit.

a neighborhood, for a neighborhood. The mixed drinks are excellent, the match of any mixologist's cocktail in Manhattan, and the vibe is super-accepting.

Mimi's in the Marigny BAR
(☏ 504-872-9868; www.mimismarigny.com; 2601 Royal St, Faubourg Marigny; ⏲ 11am-late) The name of this bar could justifiably change to 'Mimi's *is* the Marigny' – it's impossible to imagine the neighborhood without this institution. It's an attractively disheveled place, with comfy furniture, pool tables, an upstairs dance hall decorated like a Creole mansion gone punk, and dim lighting like a fantasy in sepia. The bar closes when the bartenders want it to.

Bar Redux BAR
(☏ 504-592-7083; www.facebook.com/BarRedux; 801 Poland Ave, Bywater; ⏲ 4pm-2am Sun-Thu, to 3am Fri & Sat) A friendly little bar with an outdoor courtyard that's full of offbeat local art, the sound of the nearby train tracks and lots of live performances, ranging from cabaret to theater and from comedy to music. There's a kitchen on-site slinging decent bar food and a warm, idiosyncratic vibe that's very Bywater.

Courtyard Brewery MICROBREWERY
(www.courtyardbrewing.com; 1020 Erato St, Lower Garden District; ⏲ 4:30-9:30pm Mon-Wed, 11am-10:30pm Thu-Sat, 11am-9:30pm Sun; ⏹⏹) Beyond its home-brewed products, Courtyard also carries a few dozen beers from around the world, and hosts a regular, rotating slate of food trucks. Pets and kids are welcome and have a great time running around; their parents and owners have an even better time.

☆ Entertainment

★ Preservation Hall JAZZ
(☏ 504-522-2841; www.preservationhall.com; 726 St Peter St; cover Sun-Thu $15, Fri & Sat $20, reserved

seats $40-50; ⏲ showtimes 5pm, 6pm, 8pm, 9pm & 10pm; ⏹) Preservation Hall, housed in a former art gallery dating from 1803, is one of New Orleans' most storied live-music venues. The resident performers, the Preservation Hall Jazz Band, are ludicrously talented, and regularly tour the world. 'The Hall' dates from 1961, when Barbara Reid and Grayson 'Ken' Mills formed the Society for the Preservation of New Orleans Jazz.

Spotted Cat LIVE MUSIC
(www.spottedcatmusicclub.com; 623 Frenchmen St, Faubourg Marigny; cover $5-10; ⏲ 2pm-2am Mon-Fri, noon-2am Sat & Sun) The Cat might just be your sexy dream of a New Orleans jazz club, a thumping sweatbox where drinks are served in plastic cups, impromptu dances break out at the drop of a feathered hat and the music is always exceptional. Fair warning, though, it can get crowded.

★ AllWays Lounge THEATER, LIVE MUSIC
(☏ 504-218-5778; www.theallwayslounge.net; 2240 St Claude Ave; cover $5-10; ⏲ 6pm-2am Sun-Thu, to 4am Fri & Sat) In a city full of funky music venues, AllWays stands out as one of the funkiest. On any given night of the week you may see experimental guitar, local theater, thrash-y rock, live comedy, burlesque or a '60s-inspired shagadelic dance party. Also, the drinks are super-cheap. A cover fee applies only during shows.

★ Tipitina's LIVE MUSIC
(☏ 504-895-8477; www.tipitinas.com; 501 Napoleon Ave, Uptown; cover $5-20; ⏲ 8pm-2am) 'Tips,' as locals call it, is one of New Orleans' great musical icons. The legendary Uptown nightclub, which takes its name from Professor Longhair's 1953 hit single, is the site of some of the city's most memorable shows, particularly when big names such as Dr John come home to perform. Outstanding music from local talent packs 'em in year-round.

Fritzel's European Jazz Pub JAZZ

(☑ 504-586-4800; www.fritzelsjazz.net; 733 Bourbon St; ☺ noon-2am) There's no cover charge at this awesome venue for live jazz, which is so small that you really can't have a bad seat. The seating is kind of rustic: benches and chairs so tightly packed that you'll be apologizing for disturbing people each time you go to the bathroom. But the music is great, so come in for a set.

🛍 Shopping

Boutique du Vampyre GIFTS & SOUVENIRS

(☑ 504-561-8267; www.feelthebite.com; 709 St Ann St; ☺ 10am-9pm) This dungeon-esque store stocks all kinds of vampire-themed gifts. Come here for books, curses, spells, souvenirs and witty banter with the awesome clerks who oversee this curious crypt. Among the items is a deck of tarot cards with truly surreal, somewhat disturbing artwork. If your fangs have chipped, their on-call fangsmith can even shape you a new custom pair.

★ Trashy Diva CLOTHING

(☑ 504-299-8777; www.trashydiva.com; 2048 Magazine St, Lower Garden District; ☺ noon-6pm Mon-Fri, from 11am Sat, 1-5pm Sun) It isn't really as scandalous as the name suggests, except by Victorian standards. Diva's specialty is sassy 1940s- and '50s-style cinched, hourglass dresses and belle-epoque undergarments – lots of corsets, lace and such. The shop also features Kabuki-inspired dresses with embroidered dragons, and retro tops, skirts and shawls reflecting styles plucked from just about every era.

ℹ Information

DANGERS AND ANNOYANCES

New Orleans has a high crime rate, but the majority of violent crime occurs between parties that already know each other.

➟ Muggings do occur. Solo travelers are targeted more often; avoid entering secluded areas alone.

➟ The French Quarter has a high police presence, but there are still lonely blocks near Rampart St and Esplanade Ave. Also, drunken misbehavior can happen anywhere in the Quarter.

➟ The CBD and Warehouse District are busy on weekdays, and some blocks are relatively deserted at night and on weekends.

➟ Some areas of Central City can feel lonely after dark. At night, park close to your destination on a well-traveled street.

➟ Be wary before entering an intersection: local drivers are notorious for running yellow and even red lights.

➟ Drink spikings do occur. Do not leave your drink unattended.

➟ If you're staying in an area and want to know what surrounding crime is like, check out www.crimemapping.com/map/la/neworleans.

MEDIA

The Advocate (www.nola.com) Broadsheet news and arts coverage.

Gambit (www.theadvocate.com/gambit) Weekly publication that covers arts, culture and music.

The Lens (http://thelensnola.org) Investigative journalism and culture coverage; online only.

New Orleans Magazine (www.myneworleans.com/new-orleans-magazine) Monthly focus on city society.

TOURIST INFORMATION

New Orleans Welcome Center (☑ 504-568-5661; www.crt.state.la.us/tourism; 529 St Ann St; ☺ 8:30am-5pm) In the heart of the French Quarter; offers maps, events listings and a variety of brochures for sights, restaurants and hotels.

ℹ Getting There & Away

The majority of travelers to New Orleans will arrive by air, landing in **Louis Armstrong New Orleans International Airport** (MSY; ☑ 504-303-7500; www.flymsy.com; 900 Airline Hwy, Kenner; 🛜). The airport was originally named for aviator John Moisant and was known as Moisant Stock Yards, hence the airport code (MSY).

Another option is to fly into Baton Rouge (BTR), 89 miles north of the city, or Gulfport-Biloxi (GPT; ☑ 228-863-5951; www.flygpt.com; 14035-L Airport Rd, Gulfport), Mississippi, 77 miles east. Neither of these options is as convenient as a direct flight to New Orleans, but they may be cheaper during big events such as Mardi Gras or Jazz Fest.

Many travelers drive or bus to New Orleans, which is located at the crossroads of several major highways. Train travel to New Orleans is easy; the city is served by major Amtrak lines.

Flights, cars and tours can be booked online at lonelyplanet.com/bookings.

ℹ Getting Around

Bicycle Flat New Orleans is easy to cycle – you can cross the entirety of town in 45 minutes.

Bus Services are OK, but try not to time your trip around them. Fares won't run more than $2.

Car This is the easiest way to access outer neighborhoods such as Mid-City. Parking is problematic in the French Quarter and CBD.

Streetcar Service on the charming streetcars is limited. One-way fares cost $1.25, and multi-trip passes are available.

Walk If you're just exploring the French Quarter, your feet will serve just fine.

TO/FROM THE AIRPORT

Louis Armstrong New Orleans International Airport (MSY) Located 13 miles west of New Orleans. A taxi to the CBD costs $36, or $15 per passenger for three or more passengers. Shuttles to the CBD cost $24/44 per person one way/return. The E2 bus takes you to Carrollton and Tulane Ave in Mid-City for $2. It's about a five-minute walk to the airport rental car facility from the main terminal.

Amtrak & Greyhound Located adjacent to each other downtown on Loyola Ave. You can walk to the CBD or French Quarter, but don't do so at night, or with heavy luggage. A taxi from here to the French Quarter should cost around $10; further afield you'll be pressed to spend more than $20.

Around New Orleans

Leaving colorful New Orleans behind quickly catapults you into a world of swamps, bayous, antebellum plantation homes, laid-back small communities and miles of bedroom suburbs and strip malls.

Barataria Preserve

★ **Barataria Preserve**   PARK

(⊙ parking lot for trails 9am-5pm) 🗲 **FREE** This section of the Jean Lafitte National Historical Park and Preserve, south of New Orleans near the town of Marrero (and Crown Point), provides the easiest access to the dense swamplands that ring New Orleans. The 8 miles of boardwalk trails are a stunning way to tread lightly through the swamp, but sadly, the area's wildlife – which does include plenty of alligators – can be tough to spot due to the proliferation of invasive water hyacinth.

Start at the **National Park Service Visitor Center** (NPS; ☎ 504-689-3690; www.nps. gov/jela; 6588 Barataria Blvd, Marrero; ⊙ 9:30am-4:30pm Wed-Sun), 1 mile west of Hwy 45 off the Barataria Blvd exit, where you can pick up a map or join a guided wetland walk or canoe trip (call for more information). To rent canoes or kayaks for a tour or an independent paddle, go to **Bayou Barn** (☎ 504-689-2663; www.bayoubarn.com; 7145 Barataria Blvd, Marrero; canoe/kayak hire per person $20/25; ⊙ 10am-6pm Thu-Sun) about 3 miles from the park entrance.

The North Shore

The north shore of Lake Pontchartrain is a collection of middle-to-upper-class New Orleans bedroom suburbs. Nearby, the bucolic village of Abita Springs was popular in the late 19th century for its curative waters. Today spring water still flows from a fountain in the center of the village, but more importantly for many residents, beer still bubbles from the Abita Brewery, the largest regional beer producer in Louisiana. The entirety of this region is separated from New Orleans by Lake Pontchartrain, which is spanned by the Lake Pontchartrain Causeway – at almost 24 miles long, the enormous bridge is a sight in itself.

River Road

Elaborate plantation homes dot the east and west banks of the Mississippi River between New Orleans and Baton Rouge. First indigo, then cotton and sugarcane brought great wealth to the plantation owners; today, many plantations are open to the public. Most tours focus on the lives of the owners, the restored architecture and the ornate gardens of antebellum Louisiana.

💿 Sights

★ **Whitney Plantation**   HISTORIC SITE

(☎ 225-265-3300; www.whitneyplantation.com; 5099 Hwy 18, Wallace; adult/student/child under 6yr $23/10/free; ⊙ museum 9:30am-4:30pm Wed-Mon, tours hourly 10am-3pm; **P**) The Whitney is the first plantation in the state to focus on slavery, and in doing so they've flipped the script on plantation tours. Whereas before the story told was that of the 'big house,' here the emphasis is given to the hundreds who died to keep the residents of the big house comfortable. There's a museum on-site that you can self-tour, but admission to the plantation is by 1½-hour guided tour only.

Laura Plantation   HISTORIC SITE

(☎ 225-265-7690; www.lauraplantation.com; 2247 Hwy 18, Vacherie; adult/student 13-17yr/child $25/15/10; ⊙ 10am-4pm; **P**) This ever-evolving and popular plantation tour teases out the distinctions between Creole, Anglo, free and enslaved African Americans via meticulous research and the written records of the Creole women who ran the place for generations. Laura is also fascinating because it was a *Creole* mansion, founded and maintained by a continental

European–descended elite, as opposed to Anglo Americans; the cultural and architectural distinctions between this and other plantations is obvious and striking. Tours are offered in English or French.

River Road African American Museum
MUSEUM

(📞 225-474-5553; http://africanamericanmuseum.org; 406 Charles St, Donaldsonville; $10; ⏰ 10am-5pm Wed-Sat; 🅿) Learn about the region's African American history, including the truth about slave ships, the vicious toils of slavery, slave revolts, the Underground Railroad, reconstruction and Jim Crow laws. Exhibits include antiques, artifacts, photographs and video interviews.

St Francisville

Lush St Francisville is the quintessential Southern artsy small town, a blend of historical homes, bohemian shops and outdoor activities courtesy of the nearby Tunica Hills (you read that right – hills in Louisiana). During the antebellum years (pre–Civil War) this was home to plantation millionaires, and much of the architecture these aristocrats built is still intact, forming a historic core that has magnetized tourists for over a century.

◉ Sights & Activities

Myrtles Plantation
HISTORIC BUILDING

(📞 225-635-6277; www.myrtlesplantation.com; 7747 Hwy 61 N; tours adult/child $15/12, night tours $15; ⏰ 9am-4:30pm, evening tours 6pm, 7pm & 8pm Fri & Sat; 🅿) Owners and docents alike perpetuate the idea that Myrtles is one of the most haunted houses in America. And hey, this place is certifiably creepy. Tours paint a vivid picture of life during the plantation era, with a hybrid focus on the history of the building on the one hand, and the spookier intrigue and ghost stories that have become synonymous with the Myrtles brand on the other.

Oakley Plantation & Audubon State Historic Site
HISTORIC SITE

(📞 225-635-3739; www.crt.state.la.us; 11788 Hwy 965; adult/student $10/5; ⏰ 9am-5pm Wed-Sun; 🅿) Outside of St Francisville, this is where naturalist John James Audubon spent his tenure, arriving in 1821 to tutor the owner's daughter. Though his assignment lasted only four months (and his room was pretty spartan), he and his assistant finished 32 paintings of birds found in the plantation's surrounding forest. The small West Indies–influenced house (1806) includes several original Audubon prints.

Mary Ann Brown Preserve
NATURE RESERVE

(📞 225-338-1040; www.nature.org; 13515 Hwy 965; ⏰ sunrise-sunset; 🅿) 🎫 FREE Operated by the Nature Conservancy, the 110-acre Mary Ann Brown Preserve takes in some of the beech woodlands, dark wetlands and low, clay-soil hill country of the Tunica uplands. A 2-mile series of trails and boardwalks crosses the woods – the same trees that John James Audubon tramped around when he began work on *Birds of America*.

🛏 Sleeping

3-V Tourist Court
INN $

(📞 225-721-7003; www.themagnoliacafe.net; 5687 Commerce St; 1-/2-bedroom cabin $75/140; 🅿🛜) One of the oldest motor inns in the USA – started in the 1930s and now on the National Register of Historic Places. The five units here take you back to simpler times. Rooms have period decorations and fixtures, though renovations have upgraded the beds, hardwood floors and flat-screen TVs into trendy territory.

Shadetree Inn
B&B $$

(📞 225-635-6116; www.shadetreeinn.com; 9704 Royal St; r $165-215; 🅿🛜) Edging the historic district and a bird sanctuary, this supercozy B&B has a gorgeous flower-strewn, hammock-hung courtyard and spacious but rustic upscale rooms. A deluxe continental breakfast can be served in your room, and is included along with a bottle of wine or champagne. Rates drop if you cut out breakfast and stay midweek.

🍴 Eating & Drinking

Magnolia Café
CAFE $

(📞 225-635-6528; www.themagnoliacafe.net; 5687 Commerce St; mains $8-16; ⏰ 10am-4pm daily, to 9pm Thu & Sat, to 10pm Fri) The Magnolia Café was once a health-food store and VW-bus repair shop. Today it's the nucleus of what's happening in St Francisville – it's where people go to eat, socialize and, on Friday night, dance to live music. Try the cheesy shrimp po'boy.

Birdman Coffee & Books
CAFE

(📞 225-635-3665; 5695 Commerce St; mains $5-8; ⏰ 7am-5pm Tue-Fri, 8am-2pm Sat, 8am-noon Sun; 🛜) Birdman is *the* spot for strong coffee, acoustic live music several times a month, delicious baked goods and local art – both via paintings and exposure to the local arts community that makes said paintings.

ℹ Getting There & Away

St Francisville lies about 35 miles north of Baton Rouge on Hwy 61, which winds right through town.

Cajun Country

When people think of Louisiana, this – and New Orleans – is the image that comes to mind: miles of bayou, sawdust-strewn shacks, a unique take on French and lots of good food. Welcome to Cajun Country, also called Acadiana for the French settlers exiled from L'Acadie (now Nova Scotia, Canada) by the British in 1755. Cajuns are the largest French-speaking minority in the USA, and while you may not hear French spoken at the grocery store, it's still present in radio shows, church services and the singsong lilt of local English accents.

It's largely a socially conservative region, but the Cajuns also have a well-deserved reputation for hedonism. It's hard to find a bad meal here; jambalaya (a rice-based dish with tomatoes, sausage and shrimp) and crawfish étouffée are prepared slowly with pride, and if folks aren't fishing, they're probably dancing. Don't expect to sit on the sidelines...*allons danson* (let's dance).

Lafayette

The term 'undiscovered gem' gets thrown around too much in travel writing, but Lafayette really fits the bill. On Sunday this town is deader than a cemetery, but for the rest of the week there's an entirely fantastic amount of good eating to be done and lots of music venues – this is a university town so bands are rocking almost any night. One of the best free music festivals in the country is also held here. Heck, even those quiet Sundays have a saving grace: some famously delicious brunch options.

◉ Sights

Vermilionville   MUSEUM
(☏ 337-233-4077; www.vermilionville.org; 300 Fisher Rd; adult/student $10/6, 90min boat tour $12/8; ⊙10am-4pm Tue-Sun; P♿) This tranquil, recreated 19th-century Cajun village wends along the bayou near the airport. Friendly,

enthusiastic costumed docents explain Cajun, Creole and Native American history, and local bands or dance-hall-esque events go off on Sunday (1pm to 4pm). Guided boat tours of Bayou Vermilion are also offered at 10:30am Tuesday to Saturday in spring and fall; you can combine a boat tour with a buffet lunch and a visit to Vermilionville for $31.50/27.50 per adult/child.

Acadian Village   MUSEUM
(☏ 337-981-2364; www.acadianvillage.org; 200 Greenleaf Dr; adult/student $9/7; ⊙10am-4pm Mon-Sat Jan-Oct, 5:30-9pm Dec, closed Nov; P♿) At the understated, educational Acadian Village, you follow a brick path around a rippling bayou to restored houses, craftsman barns and a church. Old-timers sometimes still hang out here, regaling visitors with Cajun songs and stories from days gone by. The village becomes a Christmas light extravaganza in December, when it is open every evening, weather permitting.

✸ Festivals & Events

★**Festival International de Louisiane**   MUSIC
(www.festivalinternational.org) At the fabulous Festival International de Louisiane, hundreds of local and international artists rock out for five days over the last weekend in April, in the largest free music festival of its caliber in the USA. Although 'Festival' avowedly celebrates Francophone music and culture, the event's remit has grown to accommodate world music in all its iterations and languages.

🛏 Sleeping & Eating

★**Blue Moon Guest House**   GUESTHOUSE $
(☏ 337-234-2422; www.bluemoonpresents.com; 215 E Convent St; dm $23-45, r $75-95; P♿◉🐾) This tidy home is one of Louisiana's best travel finds: an upscale hostel-like hangout within walking distance from downtown. Snag a bed and you're on the guest list for Lafayette's most popular down-home music venue, located in the backyard. The friendly owners, full kitchen and camaraderie create a unique music-meets-migration environment catering to backpackers, flashpackers and those in transition (flashbackpackers?).

Buchanan Lofts   APARTMENT $$
(☏ 337-534-4922; www.buchananlofts.com; 403 S Buchanan St; r per night $190-220, per week $1000-1200; P♿◉🐾) These uberhip lofts have a Manhattan vibe, or would if they weren't

so big. Doused in contemporary-cool art and design – all fruits of the friendly owner's globetrotting – the extra-spacious units come with kitchenettes and are awash with exposed brick and hardwoods.

★ **French Press** BREAKFAST $
(☑337-233-9449; www.facebook.com/french-presslaf; 214 E Vermillion St; mains $9-15; ⊗7am-2pm Mon-Fri, from 9am Sat & Sun; 🐾) This French Cajun hybrid is one of the best culinary things going in Lafayette. Breakfast is mind-blowing, with a sinful Cajun Benedict (boudin instead of ham), cheddar grits (that will kill you dead) and organic granola (to offset the grits). Lunch ain't half bad either; the 'Buffalo Bill,' with fried seafood, blue cheese and hot sauce, is gorgeously decadent.

★ **Johnson's Boucanière** CAJUN $
(☑337-269-8878; www.johnsonsboucaniere.com; 1111 St John St; mains $4.25-10; ⊗7am-3pm Tue-Fri, to 5:30pm Sat; 🐾) This 70-year-old smoker business turns out detour-worthy boudin (Cajun-style pork-and-rice sausage), an unstoppable smoked-pork-brisket sandwich topped with smoked sausage, smoked garlic sausage that will set your mouth to watering, pulled pork stuffed into grilled cheese biscuits (!), and dozens of other delicious variations on the theme of meat, meat and by God, more meat.

Social Southern Table SOUTHERN US $$
(☑337-456-3274; www.socialsouthern.com; 3901 Johnston St; mains $12-36; ⊗11am-10pm Tue-Sat, 10:30am-2pm Sun) The hip culinary crowd out in Acadiana pack into Social to feast on fried chicken 'n' biscuits, wild mushroom flatbreads, and local vegetables drenched in curry, among other delights. This isn't the first restaurant to elevate Southern staples, but it's doing so at a level beyond most of the competition.

☆ Entertainment

★ **Blue Moon Saloon** LIVE MUSIC
(☑337-234-2422; www.bluemoonpresents.com; 215 E Convent St; cover $5-15; ⊗showtimes vary) This intimate venue on the back porch of the accompanying guesthouse is what Louisiana is all about: good music, good people and good beer. Everyone dances, eats well and gets pleasantly buzzed. What's not to love? Music tends to go off Wednesday to Saturday, usually around 8pm or 9pm.

Artmosphere LIVE MUSIC
(☑337-233-3331; www.artmosphere.vpweb.com; 902 Johnston St; ⊗11am-2am Mon-Sat, to midnight Sun) There's a deep counterculture vein running within Lafayette, a sort of bohemian backlash to the area's prevailing Christian conservatism, and this radical community finds a home (and performance venue) in Artmosphere. With walls of graffiti, hookahs, hipsters and an edgy lineup of acts, this spot feels more CBGBs than Cajun dance hall, although really, it blends both concepts.

❶ Information

Visitors Center (☑337-232-3737; www.lafayettetravel.com; 1400 NW Evangeline Thruway; ⊗8:30am-5pm Mon-Fri, from 9am Sat & Sun) Helpful staff with French speakers.

❶ Getting There & Away

From I-10, exit 103A, the Evangeline Thruway (Hwy 167) goes to the center of town. **Greyhound** (☑337-235-1541; www.greyhound.com; 100 Lee Ave) operates from a hub beside the central commercial district, making several runs daily to New Orleans (from $23, 3½ hours) and Baton Rouge (from $11, one hour). The **Amtrak** (www.amtrak.com; 100 Lee Ave) *Sunset Limited* service, which runs between New Orleans and Los Angeles, stops in Lafayette.

Cajun Wetlands

In 1755, the Grand Dérangement, the British expulsion of rural French settlers from Acadiana (now Nova Scotia, New Brunswick, Prince Edward Island and parts of Quebec, Canada), created a homeless population of Acadians who searched for decades for a place to settle. Some went to other British colonies, where the Catholic exiles were often rejected on religious grounds. Some returned to France, where they were denied the rights to land ownership and autonomy they had obtained in the New World.

In 1785 seven boatloads of Acadian exiles arrived in New Orleans, seeking a better life in a corner of the Western Hemisphere that was still culturally, if not politically, French (at the time Louisiana was ruled by the Spanish). By the early 19th century, 3000 to 4000 Acadians occupied the swamplands southwest of New Orleans. Native American tribes such as the Atakapas helped them learn to eke out a living based on fishing and trapping, and those practices are still near

THE SOUTH CAJUN WETLANDS

THE TAO OF FRED'S

Deep in the heart of Cajun country, Mamou is a typical South Louisiana small town six days of the week, worth a peek and a short stop before rolling on to nearby Eunice. But on Saturday morning, Mamou's hometown hangout, little **Fred's Lounge** (📞337-468-5411; 420 6th St, Mamou; ⏰8am-2pm Sat), becomes the apotheosis of a Cajun dance hall.

This small place gets more than a little crowded on Saturdays, when the staff host a Francophone-friendly music morning, with bands, beer and dancing. Doors open around 8am and the place is usually packed by the time the music starts around 9am. Back in the day, owner Tante Sue herself would take to the stage to dispense wisdom and songs in Cajun French, all while taking pulls from a bottle of brown liquor she kept in a pistol holster. She has since passed, but something of her amazing, anarchic energy has been imbued into the very bricks of this place.

and dear to the hearts of many descendants of the Acadians, now known as the Cajuns.

For decades this was one of the poorest parts of Louisiana, an area where French-language education was repressed and infrastructure was dire. This situation largely changed thanks to an increase in Cajun political influence within Louisiana state government in the 1970s, and the presence of the oil and gas industry. While canal and pipeline dredging has been deemed a culprit in the continuing saga of Louisiana land loss, the jobs and economic revitalization that came with oil-industry jobs is undeniable. This goes some way toward explaining the enduring popularity of the oil and gas sectors in the state, culminating in events such as – no kidding – Morgan City's annual Shrimp & Petroleum Festival.

◉ Sights

Lake Martin　　　　　　BIRD SANCTUARY
(Lake Martin Rd; ⏰24hr) FREE This lake – a mossy green dollop surrounded by thin trees and cypress trunks – serves as a wonderful, easily accessible introduction to bayou landscapes. A few walking paths, as well as a boardwalk, take visitors over the mirror-reflection sheen of the swamp, while over-

head thousands of great and cattle egrets and blue herons perch in haughty indifference.

It's about 5 miles south of Breaux Bridge.

**Louisiana Universities
Marine Consortium**　　　　　NATURE CENTER
(LUMCON; 📞985-851-2800; www.lumcon.edu; 8124 Hwy 56, Chauvin; ⏰8am-4pm; 🚻) 🅿FREE LUMCON? Sounds like something out of a science fiction novel, right? Well, there is science here, but it's all fact, and still fascinating. LUMCON is one of the premier research facilities dedicated to the Gulf of Mexico. At the consortium's DeFelice Marine Center, there are nature trails running through hairy tufts of grassy marsh, several small aquariums, and an observation tower offering unbeatable views of the great swaths of flat, fuzzy wetlands that make up the south Louisiana coast.

❶ Getting There & Away

Greyhound buses stop in Thibodaux and Lafayette. Otherwise, the region is easily accessed via I-10, which cuts across Louisiana like a belt.

Cajun Prairie

Dancing cowboys? Works for us. Cajun and African American settlers in the higher, drier terrain north of Lafayette developed a culture based around animal husbandry and farming, and the 10-gallon hat still rules. In many ways, this region is a blend of both South Louisiana and East Texas.

Physically, this truly is prairie: wide expanses of green flatlands, broken up by rice and crawfish ponds. This is the heartland of zydeco music; come evening, keep your ears peeled for the accordion, fiddle and distinctive 'zzzzzzzzip' sound of the *frottoir,* a corrugated metal vest that is played as its own percussion instrument.

Eunice and **Opelousas** are the major towns in the prairie, but you'll also find interesting diversions in **Mamou** and **Ville Platte**.

◉ Sights

Chicot State Park　　　　　STATE PARK
(📞337-363-2403; www.crt.louisiana.gov; 3469 Chicot Park Rd, Ville Platte; $3; ⏰6am-9pm Sun-Thu, to 10pm Fri & Sat; 🅿🚻) 🅿 A wonderful place to access the natural beauty of Cajun country. The excellent arboretum is fun for kids and informative for adults, and deserves enormous accolades for its open, airy design. Miles of trails extend into the nearby

forests, cypress swamps and wetlands. If you can, stay for early evening – the sunsets over the Spanish-moss-draped trees that fringe Lake Chicot are superb.

Prairie Acadian Cultural Center MUSEUM
(📞337-457-8499; www.nps.gov/jela; 250 Park Ave, Eunice; ⊙9:30am-4:30pm Wed-Fri, to 6pm Sat) ✏️**FREE** This NPS-run museum has exhibits on rural life and Cajun culture, and shows a variety of documentaries explaining the history of the area. It's the perfect place to begin your exploration of the Cajun Prairie. There's a full slate of events and activities on offer, including music and food demonstrations and Cajun French–language lessons – call ahead or check online for a schedule.

🛏️ Sleeping & Eating

⭐ **Le Village** B&B $$
(📞337-457-3573; www.levillagehouse.com; 121 Seale Lane, Eunice; r $125-185; 🅿️🛜) This cute spot is a typically pretty rural B&B, but where many places opt for wedding-cake frilly decor, Le Village is stocked with a tasteful collection of rustic, often Cajun-derived folk art. If you need space, there's an entire cottage available for rent. Prices drop significantly over the weekend. A two-night minimum stay is required.

Billy's Boudin & Cracklins CAJUN $
(📞337-942-9150; http://billysboudin.com; 904 Short Vine St, Opelousas; boudin per lb $9; ⊙7:30am-6pm Mon-Fri, 8am-5pm Sat, 8am-2pm Sun) Folks will literally drive for hours, sometimes crossing state lines, to grab some of Billy's goods. Most folks treat this as a takeout counter, but there's a seating area and some coolers where you can snag a cold drink. There's cracklin', which is amazing, and some other pork products as well.

🛈 Getting There & Away

Lafayette makes a good base for exploring the Cajun Prairie. There's a **Greyhound stop** (📞337-942-2702; 1312 Creswell Lane) in Opelousas that has buses to Lafayette (from $14, 30 minutes), Baton Rouge (from $18, one hour 40 minutes) and New Orleans (from $35, three hours 40 minutes). The heart of the Cajun Prairie can best be accessed via I-49 or LA 13.

THE SOUTH CAJUN WETLANDS

Florida

Best Places to Eat

➔ Ulele (p510)

➔ Rok:Brgr (p485)

➔ La Luce (p518)

➔ Kyu (p480)

➔ Cress (p523)

Best Places to Sleep

➔ 1 Hotel (p478)

➔ Hotel Palms (p506)

➔ Biltmore Hotel (p479)

➔ W Fort Lauderdale (p484)

➔ Hoosville Hostel (p492)

Why Go?

For countless visitors Florida is a place of promises: of eternal youth, sun, relaxation, clear skies, space, success, escape, prosperity and, for the kids, a chance to meet much-loved Disney characters in person.

No other state in America is as built on tourism, and tourism here comes in a thousand facets: cartoon mice, *Miami Vice*, country fried oysters, Spanish villas, gators kicking footballs, gators prowling golf courses, and of course, the beach. So. Much. Beach.

Don't think Florida is all marketing, though. This is one of the most genuinely fascinating states in the country. It's as if someone shook the nation and tipped it over, filling this sun-bleached peninsula with immigrants, country boys, Jews, Cubans, military bases, shopping malls and a subtropical wilderness laced with crystal ponds and sugary sand.

Florida means almost anything: amusement kingdoms, Latin and Caribbean capitals, wild wetlands, artist colonies, and wild surf beaches. This vast, flat peninsula has it all.

When to Go
Miami

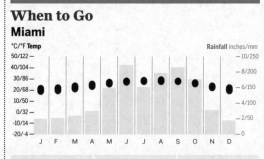

Mar–Aug Hot, humid high season sees busy theme parks; beaches peak in summer.

Oct–Dec Beach towns are quiet until winter snow-birds arrive.

Feb & Sep Shoulder season sees the region less crowded but still hot.

SOUTH FLORIDA

Once you head far enough south in Florida, you're no longer in 'the South' as a regional entity – you've slipped those bonds into South Florida, which is truly a hybrid of the USA, the Caribbean and Latin America. Miami is the area's beating urban heart and one of the few truly international cities in the country. Wealthy oceanfront communities stretch from the Palm Beaches to Fort Lauderdale, while inland, the dreamscape of the Everglades, the state's most unique, dynamic wilderness, await. And when the state's peninsula ends, it doesn't truly end, but rather stretches into the Overseas Hwy which leads across hundreds of mangrove islands to colorful Key West.

Miami

Even if there was no beach, Miami would still have undeniable allure. The gorgeous 1930s hotels lining Ocean Dr are part of the world's greatest collection of art deco buildings. Tropical motifs, whimsical nautical elements and those iconic pastel shades create a cinematic backdrop for exploring the streets of Miami Beach. Of course, you don't have to see these architectural beauties at arm's length. Lavishly restored, Miami's art deco and mid-century-modern hotels are also the playground for locals and out-of-towners alike, with sunny poolside terraces, artfully designed dining rooms and plush nightclubs.

Chalk it up to Miami's diverse population, or perhaps its love of always being on the cutting edge. Whatever the reason, creativity is one of the great hallmarks of this city. From art and design to global cuisine, Miami remains ever on the search for bold new ideas, which manifest themselves in surprising ways. You'll find brilliantly inventive chefs blending Eastern and Western cooking styles, sustainably designed buildings inspired by South Florida ecosystems and open-air galleries where museum-quality artwork covers once-derelict warehouses. The one constant in Miami is its uncanny ability to astonish.

History

It's always been the weather that's attracted Miami's two most prominent species: developers and tourists. But it wasn't the sun per se that got people moving here – it was an ice storm. The great Florida freeze of 1895 wiped out the state's citrus industry; at the same time, widowed Julia Tuttle bought out parcels of land that would become modern Miami, and Henry Flagler was building his Florida East Coast Railroad. Tuttle offered to split her land with Flagler if he extended the railway to Miami, but the train man didn't pay her any heed until north Florida froze over and Tuttle sent him an 'I told you so' message: an orange blossom clipped from her Miami garden.

The rest is a history of boom, bust, dreamers and opportunists. Generally, Miami has grown in leaps and bounds following major world events and natural disasters. Hurricanes (particularly the deadly Great Miami Hurricane of 1926) have wiped away the town, but it just keeps bouncing and building back better than before. In the late 19th and early 20th centuries, Miami earned a reputation for attracting design and city-planning mavericks such as George Merrick, who fashioned the artful Mediterranean village of Coral Gables, and James Deering, designer of the fairy-tale Vizcaya mansion.

◉ Sights

Miami's major sights aren't concentrated in one neighborhood. The most frequently visited area is South Beach, home to hot nightlife, beautiful beaches and art deco hotels, but you'll find historic sites and museums in the Downtown area, street art in Wynwood and galleries in the Design District, old-fashioned hotels and eateries in Mid-Beach (in Miami Beach), more beaches on Key Biscayne, and peaceful neighborhood attractions in Coral Gables and Coconut Grove.

Water and income – canals, bays and bank accounts – are the geographic and social boundaries that divide Miami. Of course, the great water that divides here is Biscayne Bay, holding the city of Miami apart from its preening sibling Miami Beach (along with the fine feathers of South Beach). Don't forget, as many do, that Miami Beach is not Miami's beach, but its own distinct town.

◉ South Beach

South Beach (SoBe) is everything Miami is known for – the sparkling beach, beautiful art-deco architecture, top-end boutiques and buzzing bars and restaurants. South Beach has its glamour, but there's more to this district than just velvet ropes and high-priced

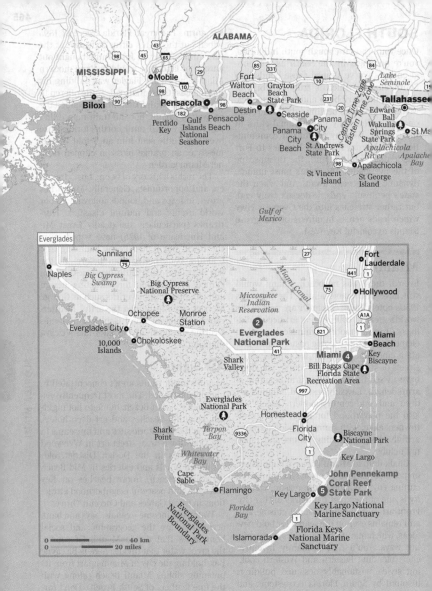

Florida Highlights

1 **Mallory Square** (p498) Joining the sunset bacchanal in Key West.

2 **Everglades National Park** (p490) Paddling among

alligators and sawgrass in the Everglades.

3 **Walt Disney World® Resort** (p518) Being swept up in nostalgia and thrill rides in Orlando.

4 **Wynwood Walls** (p473) Marvelling at mural after mural in Miami.

5 **John Pennekamp Coral Reef State Park** (p495) Snorkelling the

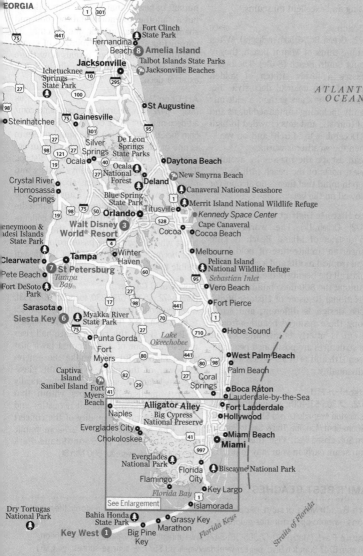

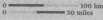
GEORGIA

ATLANTIC
OCEAN

Fort Clinch
State Park
Fernandina
Beach ❽ **Amelia Island**
Talbot Islands State Parks
Jacksonville Beaches

Jacksonville

Ichetucknee
Springs
State Park

●St Augustine

●Steinhatchee

Gainesville

Silver
Springs
Ocala

De Leon
Springs
State Parks

Ocala
National
Forest

●Daytona Beach

●New Smyrna Beach

Deland

Crystal River
Homosassa
Springs

Blue Spring
State Park

❷Canaveral National Seashore

Titusville●
●Merritt Island National Wildlife Refuge

Orlando

● *Kennedy Space Center*

eneymoon &
adesi Islands
State Park

**Walt Disney
World® Resort** ❸

Cape Canaveral
Cocoa ● ● Cocoa Beach

Clearwater●

Winter
Haven

●Melbourne

Tampa

Pelican Island
National Wildlife Refuge

te Beach●
St Petersburg ❼

*Tampa
Bay*

Sebastian Inlet
●Vero Beach

Fort DeSoto
Park

Sarasota●
Siesta Key ❻ ❹Myakka River
State Park

●Fort Pierce

●Punta Gorda

*Lake
Okeechobee*

●Hobe Sound

Fort
Myers

Captiva
Island
Sanibel Island Fort
Myers
Beach ❼

Coral
Springs

●West Palm Beach
Palm Beach

●Boca Raton
●Lauderdale-by-the-Sea
❹**Fort Lauderdale**
❹**Hollywood**

Alligator Alley

Naples

Big Cypress
National Preserve

Everglades City●
Chokoloskee●

●Miami Beach
❹**Miami**

Everglades
National Park

Florida
City
❷Biscayne National Park

Flamingo

Florida Bay

Key Largo

See Enlargement

●Islamorada

Dry Tortugas
National Park
❹

Bahia Honda
State Park ❹

Grassy Key
Marathon

Florida Keys

Key West ❶

Big Pine
Key

Straits of Florida

---

continental USA's most
extensive coral reef.

❻ **Siesta Key** (p512)
Relaxing on these sugar sand
beaches, in Sarasota.

❼ **Salvador Dali
Museum** (p511) Pondering
the symbolism of the
Hallucinogenic Toreador
in St Petersburg.

❽ **Amelia Island** (p507)
Taking a breather among the
greenery of this historic island
near the Georgia border.

lodging (though there's a lot of this too). You'll find some great down-to-earth bars, good eating and excellent museums.

South Beach
BEACH

(Map p472; Ocean Dr; ⏰5am-midnight) When most people think of Miami Beach, they're envisioning South Beach (SoBe). The beach encompasses a lovely stretch of golden sands, dotted with colorful deco-style lifeguard stations. The shore gathers a wide mix of humanity, including suntanned locals and plenty of tourists, and gets crowded in high season (December to March) and on weekends when the weather is warm.

You can escape the masses by avoiding the densest parts of the beach (5th to 15th Sts). Keep in mind that there's no alcohol (or pets) allowed on the beach.

Art Deco Historic District
AREA

(Map p472; Ocean Dr) The world-famous art-deco district of Miami Beach is pure exuberance: an architecture of bold lines, whimsical tropical motifs and a color palette that evokes all the beauty of the Miami landscape. Among the 800 deco buildings listed on the National Register of Historic Buildings, each design is different, and strolling among these restored beauties from a bygone era is utterly enthralling. Classic art-deco structures are positioned beautifully between 11th and 14th Sts – each bursting with individuality.

★ Wolfsonian-FIU
MUSEUM

(Map p472; ☎305-531-1001; www.wolfsonian.org; 1001 Washington Ave; adult/child $12/8, 6-9pm Fri free; ⏰10am-6pm Mon, Tue, Thu & Sat, to 9pm Fri, noon-6pm Sun, closed Wed) Visit this excellent design museum early in your stay to put the aesthetics of Miami Beach into context. It's one thing to see how wealth, leisure and the pursuit of beauty manifest in Miami Beach, but it's another to understand the roots and shadings of local artistic movements. By chronicling the interior evolution of everyday life, the Wolfsonian reveals how these trends manifested architecturally in SoBe's exterior deco.

Art Deco Museum
MUSEUM

(Map p472; www.artdecowelcomecenter.com/art-deco-museum; 1001 Ocean Dr; $5; ⏰9am-5pm Tue-Sun, to 7pm Thu) This small museum is one of the best places in town for an enlightening overview of the art-deco district. Through videos, photography, models and other displays, you'll learn about the pioneering work of Barbara Capitman, who helped save these buildings from certain destruction back in the 1970s, and her collaboration with Leonard Horowitz, the talented artist who designed the pastel color palette that become an integral part of the design visible today.

New World Center
NOTABLE BUILDING

(Map p472; ☎305-673-3330, tours 305-673-3331; www.newworldcenter.com; 500 17th St; tours $5; ⏰tours 4pm Tue & Thu, 1pm Fri & Sat) Designed by Frank Gehry, this performance hall rises majestically out of a manicured lawn just above Lincoln Rd. Not unlike the ethereal power of the music within, the glass-and-steel facade encases characteristically Gehry-esque sail-like shapes within that help create the magnificent acoustics and add to the futuristic quality of the concert hall. The grounds form a 2.5-acre public park aptly known as **SoundScape Park** (Map p472; www.nws.edu; 500 17th St).

MIAMI'S BEST BEACHES

South Beach Miles of sand, people watching, art deco buildings and iconic lifeguard stations – photo opportunities galore!

Crandon Park (Map p470; ☎305-361-5421; www.miamidade.gov/parks/parks/crandon_beach.asp; 6747 Crandon Blvd; per car weekday/weekend $5/7; ⏰sunrise-sunset; P 🚻🎨) Nature and quiet times on this beautiful Key Biscayne beach.

Haulover Beach Park (Map p470; ☎305-947-3525; www.miamidade.gov/parks/haulover.asp; 10800 Collins Ave; per car Mon-Fri $5, Sat-Sun $7; ⏰sunrise-sunset; P) In North Beach, Haulover provides privacy and tranquility for nudists and clothed bathers alike.

Bill Baggs Cape Florida State Park (p475) A picture-perfect lighthouse and miles of sand on Key Biscayne's southern end.

Boardwalk North Beach's stretch of gorgeous beach with a laid-back, real-world vibe.

MIAMI IN...

Two Days

Focus your first day on South Beach. Bookend an afternoon of sunning and swimming with a walking tour through the Art Deco Historic District and a visit to Wolfsonian-FIU, which explains it all. When the sun fades, head to Yardbird (p479) where southern comfort cooking gets a Miami foodie makeover.

Next morning, shop for Cuban music at Exquisito Restaurant (p480). Go for a stroll at Vizcaya Museum & Gardens (p474), then enjoy the tropical ambience and exceptional food at 27 Restaurant (p479) before sipping cocktails at Broken Shaker (p481).

Four Days

Follow the two-day itinerary, then head to the Everglades (p490) on day three and jump in a kayak. For your last day, immerse yourself in art and design in Wynwood (p473) and the Design District (p473), followed by a visit to the Museum of Contemporary Art North Miami (p475). In the evening, join the party at Sweet Liberty (p481).

👁 North Beach

If you're after fewer people along a gorgeous strip of sand that more than matches South Beach, then North Beach is for you. Instead of art deco, you'll find the so-called MiMo (Miami Modern) style, of grand buildings constructed in the post-WWII boom days. Although it has fewer restaurants, bars and shops, there's good quality eating and drinking here, and a colourful and strong local community.

Boardwalk   BEACH
(Map p470; www.miamibeachboardwalk.com; 21st St–46th St) Posing is what many people do best in Miami, and there are plenty of skimpily dressed hotties on the Mid-Beach boardwalk, but there are also middle-class Latinos and Jews, who walk their dogs and play with their kids here, giving the entire place a laid-back, real-world vibe that contrasts with the nonstop glamour of South Beach.

Eden Roc Renaissance   HISTORIC BUILDING
(Map p470; www.nobuedenroc.com; 4525 Collins Ave) The Eden Roc was the second ground-breaking resort from Morris Lapidus, and it's a fine example of the architecture known as MiMo. It was the hangout for the 1960s Rat Pack – Sammy Davis Jr, Dean Martin, Frank Sinatra and crew. Extensive renovation has eclipsed some of Lapidus' style, but with that said, the building is still an iconic piece of Miami Beach architecture, and an exemplar of the brash beauty of Millionaire's Row.

Fontainebleau   HISTORIC BUILDING
(Map p470; www.fontainebleau.com; 4441 Collins Ave) As you proceed north on Collins, the condos and apartment buildings grow in grandeur and embellishment until you enter an area nicknamed Millionaire's Row. The most fantastic jewel in this glittering crown is the Fontainebleau hotel. The pool here, which has since been renovated, features in Brian de Palma's classic *Scarface*.

👁 Downtown Miami

Most of the sights in Downtown are on the north side of the river. While you can walk between a few highlights, it's handy to use Metromover, the free trolley, or a Citi Bike when you really need to cover some ground.

★ HistoryMiami   MUSEUM
(Map p470; ☎ 305-375-1492; www.historymiami.org; 101 W Flagler St; adult/child $10/5; ⊙10am-5pm Tue-Sat, from noon Sun; 🖈) South Florida – a land of escaped slaves, guerrilla Native Americans, gangsters, land grabbers, pirates, tourists, drug dealers and alligators – has a special history, and it takes a special kind of museum to capture that narrative. This highly recommended place, located in the Miami-Dade Cultural Center, does just that, weaving together the stories of the region's successive waves of population, from Native Americans to Nicaraguans.

Pérez Art Museum Miami   MUSEUM
(PAMM; Map p470; ☎ 305-375-3000; www.pamm.org; 1103 Biscayne Blvd; adult/senior & student $16/12, 1st Thu & 2nd Sat of month free;

Greater Miami

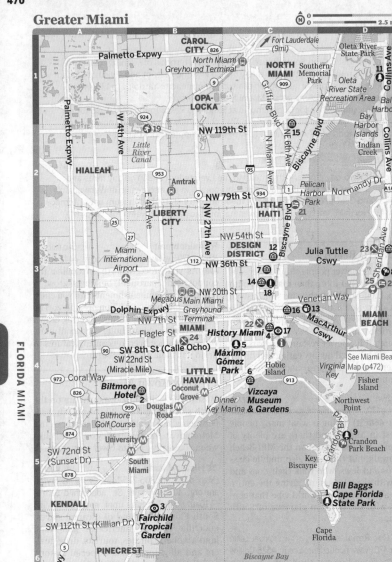

0 ___ 5 km
0 ___ 2.5 miles

CAROL CITY
826
Palmetto Expwy
North Miami
Greyhound Terminal
Fort Lauderdale
(9mi)
Oleta River
State Park
NORTH
MIAMI
Southern
Memorial
Park
909
11
Collins Ave
Griffing Blvd
NE 6th Ave
Oleta
River State
Recreation Area
9
Bal
Harbour
OPA-
LOCKA
NW 119th St
15
Biscayne Blvd
Bay
Harbor
Islands
924
19
Indian Creek
W 4th Ave
Little
River
Canal
HIALEAH
953
Amtrak
95
N Miami Ave
Normandy Dr
Collins Ave
A1A
E 4th Ave
9
NW 79th St
934
Pelican
Harbor
Park
LIBERTY
CITY
LITTLE
HAITI
21
NW 27th Ave
25
NW 54th St
Biscayne Blvd
27
DESIGN
DISTRICT
12
Julia Tuttle
Cswy
23
10
Miami
International
Airport
112
NW 36th St
7
14
18
Sheridan Ave
8
25
20
NW 20th St
Megabus
Main Miami
Greyhound
Terminal
Dolphin Expwy
NW 7th St
Flagler St
MIAMI
24
Venetian Way
16
13
MacArthur
Cswy
MIAMI
BEACH
22
History Miami
4
17
90
SW 8th St (Calle Ocho)
SW 22nd St
(Miracle Mile)
Máximo
Gómez
Park
5
6
See Miami Beach
Map (p472)
972
Coral Way
LITTLE
HAVANA
Coconut
Grove
Hobie
Island
Virginia
Key
Biltmore
Hotel
2
826
959
Douglas
Road
Dinner
Key Marina
Vizcaya
Museum
& Gardens
913
Fisher
Island
Biltmore
Golf Course
874
University
SW 72nd St
(Sunset Dr)
South
Miami
Northwest
Point
Crandon Blvd
9
Crandon
Park Beach
878
KENDALL
Key
Biscayne
Bill Baggs
Cape Florida
State Park
1
5
SW 112th St (Killian Dr)
3
Fairchild
Tropical
Garden
Cape
Florida
Dixie Hwy
5
PINECREST
SW 152nd St
Biscayne Bay
ATLANTIC
OCEAN

Greater Miami

FLORIDA MIAMI

⊙10am-6pm Fri-Tue, to 9pm Thu, closed Wed; ℗) One of Miami's most impressive spaces, designed by Swiss architects Herzog & de Meuron, integrates tropical foliage, glass, concrete and wood – a melding of tropical vitality and fresh modernism that fits perfectly in Miami. PAMM stages some of the best contemporary exhibitions in the city, with established artists and impressive newcomers. The permanent collection rotates through unique pieces every few months – drawing from a treasure trove of work spanning the last 80 years. Don't miss.

**Patricia & Phillip
Frost Museum of Science** MUSEUM
(Map p470; ☏305-434-9600; www.frostscience. org; 1101 Biscayne Blvd; adult/child $30/21; ⊙9am-6pm; ℗♿) This sprawling new Downtown museum spreads across 250,000 sq ft that includes a three-level aquarium, a 250-seat, state-of-the-art planetarium and two distinct wings that delve into the wonders of science and nature. Exhibitions range from weather phenomena to creepy crawlies,

feathered dinosaurs and vital-microbe displays, while Florida's fascinating Everglades and biologically rich coral reefs play starring roles. The building you now see, which cost a staggering $305 million to complete, was built with sustainability in mind and opened in 2017.

Void Projects ARTS CENTER
(Map p470; www.voidprojects.org; 60 SE 1st St; ⊙11am-6pm) FREE If you'd like to meet local artists and see how life is lived on a smaller, more modest scale in Miami's creative pockets, visit this arts collective – run by artist Axel Void – where resident artists paint and hold exhibitions (by visiting artists) and organise free life drawing classes for the public (Thursdays from 6.30pm) and movie screenings.

◎ Little Havana

The Cubaness of Little Havana is slightly exaggerated for visitors, though it's still an atmospheric area to explore for an afternoon, with the crack of dominoes, the scent of

Miami Beach

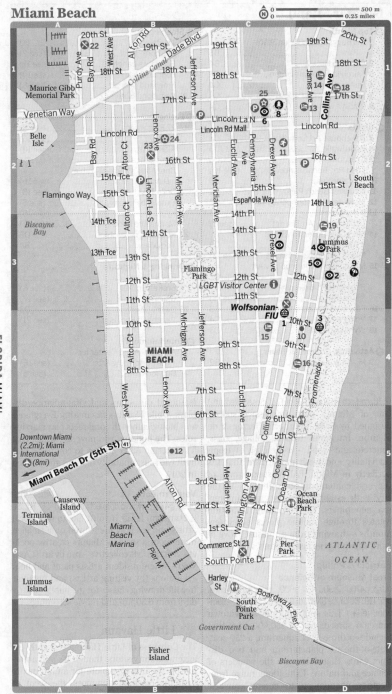

Miami Beach

wafting cigars and salsa spilling out of store-fronts. Little Havana's main thoroughfare, Calle Ocho (SW 8th St), is the heart of the neighborhood. In many ways, this is every immigrant enclave in the USA – full of restaurants, mom-and-pop convenience shops and phonecard kiosks, except here you get intermittent tourists posing and taking selfies.

★ **Máximo Gómez Park** PARK
(Map p470; cnr SW 8th St & SW 15th Ave; ⊙9am-6pm) Little Havana's most evocative reminder of Cuba is Máximo Gómez Park ('Domino Park'), where the sound of elderly men trash-talking over games of dominoes is harmonized with the quick clack-clack of slapping tiles – though the tourists taking photos all the while does take away from the authenticity of the place somewhat. The heavy cigar smell and a sunrise-bright mural of the 1994 Summit of the Americas add to the atmosphere.

Little Havana Art District AREA
(Map p470; Calle Ocho, btwn SW 15th & 17th Aves) This particular stretch of Little Havana is the epicenter of the **Viernes Culturales** (Cultural Fridays; www.viernesculturales.org; ⊙7-11pm last Fri of month) celebration and has a handful of galleries and studios still in business that are worth a browse.

⊙ **Wynwood &
the Design District**

Wynwood and the Design District are two of Miami's arts neighborhoods (though it's fair to say the edge has worn off a bit) –

Wynwood is packed with galleries and lots of street art and has a lively night life, and there are some good music festivals held here every year. It's very popular with tourists who are looking for an alternative to South Beach. The Design District is a high-end shopping area, with a couple of great little art museums and a mixed bag of restaurants.

Institute of Contemporary Art MUSEUM
(Map p470; www.icamiami.org; 61 NE 41st St; ⊙11am-7pm Tue-Sun) **FREE** An excellent contemporary arts museum, the ICA sits in the midst of the Design District, and hosts a fantastic range of contemporary exhibitions alongside its permanent collection pieces. The building, designed in 2017 by Aranguren & Gallegos architects, is especially beautiful, with its sharp geometric lines and large windows overlooking the back garden. The metallic grey facade is simultaneously industrial and elegant

Wynwood Walls PUBLIC ART
(Map p470; www.thewynwoodwalls.com; NW 2nd Ave, btwn 25th & 26th Sts) **FREE** In the midst of rusted warehouses and concrete blah, there's a pastel-and-graffiti explosion of urban art. Wynwood Walls is a collection of murals and paintings laid out over an open courtyard that invariably bowls people over with its sheer color profile and unexpected location. What's on offer tends to change with the coming and going of major arts events, such as Art Basel (p477), but it's always interesting stuff.

FLORIDA MIAMI

Margulies Collection at the Warehouse GALLERY

(Map p470; ☑305-576-1051; www.marguliesware house.com; 591 NW 27th St; adult/student $10/5; ⏱11am-4pm Tue-Sat mid-Oct–Apr) Encompassing 45,000 sq ft, this vast not-for-profit exhibition space houses one of the best art collections in Wynwood – Martin Margulies' awe-inspiring 4000-piece collection includes sculptures by Isamu Noguchi, George Segal, Richard Serra and Olafur Eliasson, among many others, plus sound installations by Susan Philipsz and jaw-dropping room-sized works by Anselm Kiefer. Thought-provoking, large-format installations are the focus at the Warehouse, and you'll see works by some leading 21st-century artists here.

Bakehouse Art Complex GALLERY

(BAC; Map p470; ☑305-576-2828; www.bacfl.org; 561 NW 32nd St; ⏱noon-5pm; ℗) **FREE** One of the pivotal art destinations in Wynwood, the Bakehouse has been an arts incubator since well before the creation of the Wynwood Walls. Today this former bakery houses galleries and some 60 studios, and the range of works is quite impressive. Check the schedule for upcoming artist talks and other events.

◉ Coral Gables

The lovely city of Coral Gables, filled with Mediterranean-style buildings, feels like a world removed from other parts of Miami. Here you'll find pretty banyan-lined streets, and a walkable village-like center, dotted with shops, cafes and restaurants. The big draws are the striking Biltmore Hotel, a lush tropical garden and one of America's loveliest swimming pools.

★Fairchild Tropical Garden GARDENS

(Map p470; ☑305-667-1651; www.fairchildgarden. org; 10901 Old Cutler Rd; adult/child/senior $25/12/18; ⏱9:30am-4:30pm; ℗⛟) If you need to escape Miami's madness, consider a green day in one of the country's largest tropical botanical gardens. A butterfly grove, tropical plant conservatory and gentle vistas of marsh and keys habitats, plus frequent art installations from artists like Roy Lichtenstein, are all stunning. In addition to easy-to-follow, self-guided walking tours, a free 45-minute tram tours the entire park on the hour from 10am to 3pm (till 4pm weekends).

★Biltmore Hotel HISTORIC BUILDING

(Map p470; ☑855-311-6903; www.biltmorehotel. com; 1200 Anastasia Ave; ⏱tours 1:30pm & 2:30pm Sun; ℗) In the most opulent neighborhood of one of the showiest cities in the world, the Biltmore is the greatest of the grand hotels of the American Jazz Age. If this joint were a fictional character from a novel, it'd be, without question, Jay Gatsby. Al Capone had a speakeasy on-site, and the Capone Suite is said to be haunted by the spirit of Fats Walsh, who was murdered here.

◉ Coconut Grove

Coconut Grove was once a hippie colony, but these days its demographic is middle-class, mall-going Miamians and college students – so much so that at the time of research, CocoWalk, the main street, was undergoing massive renovations that will bring it up to the new standards.

It's a pleasant place to explore, with intriguing shops and cafes, and a walkable village-like vibe. It's particularly appealing in the evenings, when residents fill the outdoor tables of its bars and restaurants. Coconut Grove backs onto the waterfront, with a pretty marina and some pleasant green spaces.

★Vizcaya Museum & Gardens HISTORIC BUILDING

(Map p470; ☑305-250-9133; www.vizcayamuse um.org; 3251 S Miami Ave; adult/6-12yr/student & senior $22/10/16; ⏱9.30am-4.30pm Wed-Mon; ℗) If you want to see something that is 'very Miami', this is it – lush, big, over the top, a patchwork of all that a rich US businessman might want to show off to his friends. Which is essentially what industrialist James Deering did in 1916, starting a Miami tradition of making a ton of money and building ridiculously grandiose digs. He employed 1000 people (then 10% of the local population) and stuffed his home with Renaissance furniture, tapestries, paintings and decorative arts.

◉ Key Biscayne

Key Biscayne and neighboring Virginia Key are a quick and easy getaway from Downtown Miami. Once you pass those scenic causeways you'll feel like you've been transported to a far-off tropical realm, with magnificent beaches, lush nature trails in state parks and aquatic adventures aplenty. The

MIAMI FOR CHILDREN

The best beaches for kids are in Miami Beach north of 21st St, especially at 53rd St, which has a playground and public toilets, and the dune-packed beach around 73rd St. Also head south to Matheson Hammock Park, which has calm artificial lagoons.

Miami Children's Museum (Map p470; ☑ 305-373-5437; www.miamichildrensmuseum.org; 980 MacArthur Causeway; $20; ☻10am-6pm; 🚼) On Watson Island, between Downtown Miami and Miami Beach, this hands-on museum has fun music and art studios, as well as some branded 'work' experiences that make it feel a tad corporate.

Jungle Island (Map p470; ☑ 305-400-7000; www.jungleisland.com; 1111 Parrot Jungle Trail, off MacArthur Causeway; adult/child $50/38; ☻10am-5pm; 🅿🚼) Jungle Island is packed with tropical birds, alligators, orangutans, chimps and (to the delight of Napoleon Dynamite fans) a liger – a cross between a lion and a tiger.

Zoo Miami (Metrozoo; ☑ 305-251-0400; www.zoomiami.org; 12400 SW 152nd St; adult/child $23/19; ☻10am-5pm; 🅿🚼) Miami's tropical weather makes strolling around Zoo Miami almost feel like a day in the wild. For a quick overview (and because the zoo is so big and the sun is broiling), hop on the Safari Monorail; it departs every 20 minutes.

Monkey Jungle (☑ 305-235-1611; www.monkeyjungle.com; 14805 SW 216th St; adult/child/senior $30/24/28; ☻9:30am-5pm, last entry 4pm; 🅿🚼) The tagline, 'Where humans are caged and monkeys run free,' tells you all you need to know – except for the fact that it's in far south Miami.

stunning skyline views of Miami alone are worth the trip out.

★ **Bill Baggs Cape Florida State Park**　　　STATE PARK
(Map p470; ☑ 305-361-5811; www.florida stateparks.org/capeflorida; 1200 S Crandon Blvd; per car/person $8/2; ☻8am-sunset, lighthouse 9am-5pm; 🅿🚼🐾) 🍴 If you don't make it to the Florida Keys, come to this park for a taste of their unique island ecosystems. The 494-acre space is a tangled clot of tropical fauna and dark mangroves – look for the 'snorkel' roots that provide air for half-submerged mangrove trees – all interconnected by sandy trails and wooden boardwalks, and surrounded by miles of pale ocean. A concession shack rents out kayaks, bikes, in-line skates, beach chairs and umbrellas.

◉ **Greater Miami**

Museum of Contemporary Art North Miami　　MUSEUM
(MoCA; Map p470; ☑ 305-893-6211; www.moca nomi.org; 770 NE 125th St; adult/student/child under 12yr $10/3/free; ☻11am-5pm Tue-Fri & Sun, 1-9pm Sat; 🅿) The Museum of Contemporary Art has long been a reason to hike up to North Miami – its galleries feature excellent rotating exhibitions of contemporary art by local, national and international artists, usually themed along socially engaged lines of interest. There is a pay what you wish gallery policy during Jazz@MOCA from 7pm to 10pm on the last Friday of every month, when live outdoor jazz concerts are held.

Gold Coast Railroad Museum　　MUSEUM
(☑ 305-253-0063; www.gcrm.org; 12450 SW 152nd St; adult/child 2-12yr $8/6; ☻10am-4pm Mon-Fri, from 11am Sat & Sun; 🅿) Primarily of interest to train buffs, this museum displays more than 30 antique railway cars, including the Ferdinand Magellan presidential car, where President Harry Truman famously brandished a newspaper with the erroneous headline 'Dewey Defeats Truman.'

🏃 **Activities**

Miami doesn't lack for ways to keep yourself busy. From sailing the teal waters to hiking through tropical undergrowth, yoga in the parks and (why not?) trapeze artistry above the city's head, the Magic City rewards those who want an active holiday.

Citi Bike　　CYCLING
(☑ 305-532-9494; www.citibikemiami.com; rental per 30min $4.50, 1/2/4hr $6.50/10/18, day $24) This bike-sharing program, modeled after similar initiatives in New York, London and Paris, makes getting on a bike a relative breeze. Just rock up to a solar-powered Citi Bike station (a handy map can be found on the website), insert a credit card and ride away. You can return your bike at any Citi Bike location.

FLORIDA MIAMI

🏃 City Walk
Art Deco Magic

START ART DECO MUSEUM
END OCEAN'S TEN
LENGTH 1.2 MILES; TWO TO THREE HOURS

Start at the **1 Art Deco Museum** (p468), at the corner of Ocean Dr and 10th St (named Barbara Capitman Way here, after the Miami Design Preservation League's founder). Step in for an exhibit on art-deco style, then head out and north along Ocean Dr; between 12th and 14th Sts you'll see three examples of deco hotels: the **2 Leslie**, a boxy shape with eyebrows (cantilevered sunshades) wrapped around the side of the building; the **3 Carlyle**, featured in the film *The Birdcage* and boasting modernistic styling; and the graceful **4 Cardozo Hotel**, built by Henry Hohauser, owned by Gloria Estefan and featuring sleek, rounded edges.

At 14th St peek inside the sun-drenched **5 Winter Haven Hotel** to see its fabulous terrazzo floors, made of stone chips set in mortar that's polished when dry. Turn left and down 14th St to Washington Ave and the **6 US Post Office**, at 13th St. It's a curvy block of white deco in the stripped classical style. Step inside to admire the wall mural, domed ceiling and marble stamp tables.

Lunch at the **7 11th St Diner** (p479), a gleaming aluminum Pullman car that was imported in 1992 from Wilkes-Barre, PA. Get a window seat and gaze across the avenue to the corner of 10th St and the stunningly restored **8 Hotel Astor**, designed in 1936 by T Hunter Henderson. After your meal, walk half a block east from there to the imposing **9 Wolfsonian-FIU** (p468), an excellent design museum, formerly the Washington Storage Company. Wealthy snowbirds of the '30s stashed their pricey belongings here before heading back up north.

Continue walking on Washington Ave, turn left on 8th St and then continue north along Collins Ave to the **10 Hotel of South Beach**, featuring an interior and roof deck by Todd Oldham. Walk for two more blocks to Ocean Dr, where you'll spy nonstop deco beauties; at 960 Ocean Dr (the **11 Ocean's Ten** restaurant) you'll see an exterior designed in 1935 by deco legend Henry Hohauser.

Bike & Roll

CYCLING

(Map p472; ☑ 305-604-0001; www.bikemiami. com; 210 10th St; hire per 2/4hr from $10/18, day from $24, tours $40; ⊘ 9am-7pm) This well-run outfit offers a good selection of bikes, including single-speed cruisers, geared hybrids and speedy road bikes; all rentals include helmets, lights, locks and maps. Staff move things along quickly, so you won't have to waste time waiting to get out and riding. Bike tours are also available (daily at 10am).

Fritz's Skate, Bike & Surf

SKATING

(Map p472; ☑ 305-532-1954; www.fritzsmiami beach.com; 1620 Washington Ave; bike & skate rental per hour/day/5 days $10/24/69; ⊘ 10am-9pm Mon-Sat, to 8pm Sun) Rent your wheels from Fritz's, which offers skateboards, longboards, in-line skates, roller skates, scooters and bicycles (cruisers, mountain bikes, kids' bikes). Protective gear is included with skate rentals, and bikes come with locks. Be mindful that there's a deposit for each rental – skates $100, longboards $150 and bicycles $200.

SoBe Surf

SURFING

(☑ 786-216-7703; www.sobesurf.com; group/ private lessons from $70/100) Offers surf lessons both in Miami Beach and in Cocoa Beach, where there tends to be better waves. Instruction on Miami Beach usually happens around South Point. All bookings are done by phone or email.

Miami Watersports Complex

WATER SPORTS

(MWCC; Map p470; ☑ 305-476-9253; www.ak tionparks.com; Amelia Earhart Park, 401 E 65th St, Hialeah; ⊘ 11am-6pm Mar-Oct, to dusk Nov-Feb) Offers lessons in cableboarding, where the rider is pulled along by an overhead cable system. That means no boat, less pollution and less noise. A 20-minute/one-hour lesson costs $25/90, or opt for a $59 package that includes a beginner lesson, rental gear and four-hour cable pass. Call ahead to reserve a spot.

⌂ Tours

History Miami Tours

TOURS

(www.historymiami.org/city-tour; tours $30-60) Historian extraordinaire Dr Paul George leads fascinating walking tours, including culturally rich strolls through Little Haiti, Little Havana, Downtown and Coral Gables at twilight, plus the occasional boat trip to Stiltsville and Key Biscayne. Tours happen once a week or so. Get the full menu and sign up online.

Miami Food Tours

FOOD & DRINK

(Map p472; ☑ 786-361-0991; www.miamifood tours.com; 429 Lenox Ave; South Beach tour adult/ child $58/35, Wynwood tour $75/55, Swooped with Forks $129/109; ⊘ tours South Beach 11am & 4:30pm daily, Wynwood 10:30am Mon-Sat) This highly rated tour explores various facets of the city – culture, history, art and of course cuisine – while making stops at restaurants and cafes along the way. It's a walking tour, though distances aren't great, and happens in South Beach and Wynwood. There is also the Swooped with Forks food tour that takes you places in a golf cart.

Miami Design Preservation League

WALKING

(MDPL; Map p472; ☑ 305-672-2014; www.mdpl.org; 1001 Ocean Dr; guided tours adult/student $25/20; ⊘ 10:30am daily & 6:30pm Thu) Tells the stories and history behind the art-deco buildings in South Beach, with a lively guide from the Miami Design Preservation League. Tours last 90 minutes. Also offers tours of Jewish Miami Beach, Gay & Lesbian Miami Beach and a once-monthly tour (first Saturday at 9:30am) of the MiMo district in the North Beach area. Check website for details.

🎉 Festivals & Events

Winter Music Conference

MUSIC

(www.wintermusicconference.com; ⊘ Mar) Party promoters, DJs, producers and revelers come from around the globe to hear new electronic-music artists, catch up on technology and party the nights away.

Miami Spice Restaurant Month

FOOD & DRINK

(www.miamiandbeaches.com/offers/temptations/ miami-spice-months; ⊘ Aug-Sep) Top restaurants around Miami offer three-course lunches and dinners to try to lure folks out during the heat wave. Prices hover around $25 for lunch and $40 for dinner. Reservations essential.

White Party

MUSIC

(www.whiteparty.org; ⊘ Nov) If you're gay and not here, there's a problem. This weeklong extravaganza draws more than 15,000 gay men and women for nonstop partying at clubs and venues all over town.

Art Basel Miami Beach

ART

(www.artbasel.com/miami-beach; ⊘ early Dec) One of the most important international art shows in the world, with works from more than 250 galleries and a slew of trendy parties. Even if you're not a billion-aire collector, there's much to enjoy at this four-day fest, with open-air art installations around town, special exhibitions at many Miami galleries and outdoor film screenings, among other goings-on.

🛏 Sleeping

Miami has some alluring lodging options, but beware that high-season prices can be sky-high. South Beach has all the name recognition with boutique hotels set in lovely art deco buildings, but there are plenty of other options in Miami – from Downtown high-rises with sweeping views and endless amenities to historic charmers in Coral Gables and Coconut Grove and some modern – MiMo – beauties along Biscayne Boulevard.

🛏 South Beach

Bed & Drinks HOSTEL $
(Map p472; ☑ 786-230-1234; www.bedsndrinks. com; 1676 James Ave; dm/d from $29/154) This hostel pretty shamelessly plays to the sexy, party, beautiful-people crowd – check the name – so know this before booking. The beach is a few blocks away. The rooms range from average to slightly below average. Friendly staff, a lively on-site bar and nightlife outings to clubs around town make up for the minuses.

SoBe Hostel HOSTEL $
(Map p472; ☑ 305-534-6669; www.sobe-hostel. com; 235 Washington Ave; dm $22-52; ✴@🖥) On a quiet end of SoFi (the area south of 5th St, South Beach), this massive multilingual hostel has a happening common area and spartan rooms. The staff are friendly and the on-site bar (open to 5am) is a great spot to meet other travelers. Free breakfasts and dinners are included in the rates.

There are loads of activities on offer – from volleyball games to mojito-making nights, screenings of big games and bar crawls.

Catalina Hotel BOUTIQUE HOTEL $$
(Map p472; ☑ 305-674-1160; www.catalinahotel. com; 1732 Collins Ave; r from $220; P✴🖥🏊) The Catalina is a lovely example of mid-range deco style. Most appealing, besides the playfully minimalist rooms, is the vibe – the Catalina doesn't take itself too seriously, and staff and guests all seem to be having fun as a result. The back pool, concealed behind the main building's crisp white facade,

is particularly attractive and fringed by a whispery grove of bamboo trees.

It was renovated to incorporate the Dorset, next door, which means that it now has two pools, a roof terrace and a reasonable Mexican restaurant.

★ 1 Hotel HOTEL $$$
(Map p470; ☑ 866-615-1111; www.1hotels.com; 2341 Collins Ave; r from $400; ✴🖥🏊) 🏊 One of the top hotels in the USA, the 1 Hotel has 400-plus gorgeous rooms that embrace both luxurious and ecofriendly features – including tree-trunk coffee tables/desks, custom hemp-blend mattresses and salvaged driftwood feature walls, plus in-room water filtration (no need for plastic bottles). The common areas are impressive, with four pools, including an adults-only rooftop infinity pool.

★ Surfcomber HOTEL $$$
(Map p472; ☑ 305-532-7715; www.surfcomber.com; 1717 Collins Ave; r $250-480; P✴🖥🏊🍸) The Surfcomber has a classic art-deco exterior with strong lines and shade-providing 'eyebrows' that zigzag across the facade. But the interior is the really impressive part – rooms have undeniable appeal, with elegant lines in keeping with the art-deco aesthetic, while bursts of color keep things contemporary.

🛏 North Beach

★ Freehand Miami BOUTIQUE HOTEL $$
(Map p470; ☑ 305-531-2727; www.thefreehand. com; 2727 Indian Creek Dr; dm $28-55, r $160-250; ✴🖥🏊) The Freehand is the brilliant reimagining of the old Indian Creek Hotel, a classic of the Miami Beach scene. Rooms are sunny and attractively designed, with local artwork and wooden details. The vintage-filled common areas are the reason to stay here though – especially the lovely pool area and backyard that transforms into one of the best bars in town.

Dorms serve the hostel crowd, while private rooms are quite appealing. There are also bungalows for self-catering groups.

🛏 Downtown Miami

Eurostars Langford HERITAGE HOTEL $$
(Map p470; ☑ 305-250-0782; http://the-langford. miamiallhotels.com; 121 SE 1st St; r from $180; ✴🖥) Set in a beautifully restored 1925 beaux-arts high-rise, the Langford's 126 rooms blend comfort and nostalgia, with el-

egant fixtures and vintage details, including oak flooring and lush furniture. Thoughtful design touches abound, and there's a rooftop bar and an excellent ground-floor restaurant on-site.

Coral Gables

★Biltmore Hotel HISTORIC HOTEL $$$
(Map p470; ☑855-311-6903; www.biltmorehotel. com; 1200 Anastasia Ave; r/ste from $699/730; P❋⌁≋) Though the Biltmore's standard rooms can be small, a stay here is a chance to sleep in one of the great laps of US luxury. The grounds are so palatial it would take a week to explore everything the Biltmore has to offer – sunbathe underneath enormous columns and take a dip in the largest hotel pool in continental USA.

✗ Eating

Miami has tons of immigrants – mainly from Latin America, the Caribbean and Russia – and it's a sucker for food trends. Thus you get a good mix of cheap ethnic eateries and high-quality top-end cuisine, alongside some poor-value dross in touristy zones like Miami Beach. Downtown, Wynwood and Upper East Side have excellent offerings; for great classics, head to Coral Gables.

✗ South Beach

11th Street Diner DINER $
(Map p472; ☑305-534-6373; www.eleventh streetdiner.com; 1065 Washington Ave; mains $10-20; ⊙7am-midnight Sun-Wed, 24hr Thu-Sat) A gorgeous slice of Americana, this Pullman-car diner trucked down from Wilkes-Barre, PA, is where you can replicate Edward Hopper's *Nighthawks* – if that's something you've always wanted to do. The food is as classic as the architecture, with oven-roasted turkey, baby back ribs and mac 'n' cheese among the hits – plus breakfast at all hours.

★Yardbird SOUTHERN US $$
(Map p472; ☑305-538-5220; www.runchickenrun. com; 1600 Lenox Ave; mains $18-38; ⊙11am-midnight Mon-Fri, from 8:30am Sat & Sun; ☑) Yardbird has earned a die-hard following for its delicious haute Southern comfort food. The kitchen churns out some nice shrimp and grits, St Louis–style pork ribs, charred okra, and biscuits with smoked brisket, but it's most famous for its supremely good plate of fried chicken, spiced watermelon and waffles with bourbon maple syrup.

★Pubbelly FUSION $$
(Map p472; ☑305-532-7555; http://pubbellyglobal. com; 1424 20th St; plates $7-18; ⊙6pm-midnight Tue-Thu & Sun, to 1am Fri & Sat; ☑) A mix of Asian and Latin flavors, Pubbelly serves delicacies such as grilled miso black cod with spring onions, beef tartare rolls with mustard and truffle poached egg, and Japanese fried chicken with kimchi. Super popular and decently priced, it's a real treat on South Beach.

Joe's Stone Crab Restaurant AMERICAN $$$
(Map p472; ☑305-673-0365; www.joesstonecrab. com; 11 Washington Ave; mains lunch $14-30, dinner $19-60; ⊙11:30am-2:30pm Tue-Sat, 5-10pm daily) The wait is long and the prices for iconic dishes can be high. But if those aren't deal breakers, queue to don a bib in Miami's most famous restaurant (around years 1913!) and enjoy deliciously fresh stone-crab claws. Aside from tender stone crab (which can top $60 for half-a-dozen jumbo claws), you'll find excellent blackened codfish sandwiches and creamy lobster mac 'n' cheese.

✗ North Beach

Roasters 'n Toasters DELI $
(Map p470; ☑305-531-7691; www.roastersntoast ers.com; 525 Arthur Godfrey Rd; mains $10-18; ⊙6:30am-3:30pm) Given the crowds and the satisfied smiles of customers, Roasters 'n Toasters meets the demanding standards of Miami Beach's large Jewish demographic, thanks to juicy deli meat, fresh bread, crispy bagels and warm latkes. Sliders (mini-sandwiches) are served on challah bread, an innovation that's as charming as it is tasty.

★27 Restaurant FUSION $$
(Map p470; ☑786-476-7020; www.freehandho tels.com; 2727 Indian Creek Dr, Freehand Miami Hotel; mains $17-28; ⊙6:30pm-2am Mon-Sat, 11am-4pm & 6:30pm-2am Sun; ☑) Part of Freehand Miami and the very popular Broken Shaker (p481), 27 has a lovely setting – akin to dining in an old tropical cottage, with worn floorboards, candlelit tables, and various rooms slung with artwork and curious knickknacks, plus a lovely terrace. Try the braised octopus, crispy pork shoulder, kimchi fried rice and yogurt-tahini-massaged kale. Book ahead. Brunch is also quite popular.

Downtown Miami

★ All Day   CAFE $

(Map p470; www.alldaymia.com; 1035 N Miami
Ave; coffee from $3.50, breakfast $10-14; ⊙7am-
7pm Mon-Fri, from 9am Sat & Sun; 🕿) All Day
is positively Miami's best cafe – with locally sourced ingredients forming the basis of
its simple menu, as well as excellent cof-
fees, teas, beer and wine, and an airy, light
Scandinavian-style decor, this is a winner
all-around. Stylish chairs, wood-and-marble
tables, friendly staff and an always enticing
soundtrack lend it an easygoing vibe.

★ Casablanca   SEAFOOD $$

(Map p470; www.casablancaseafood.com; 400 N
River Dr; mains $15-34; ⊙11am-10pm Sun-Thu, to
11pm Fri & Sat) Perched over the Miami River,
Casablanca serves some of the best seafood
in town. The setting is a big draw – with tables on a long wooden deck just above the
water, and the odd seagull winging past. But
the fresh fish is the real star here.

Chef Allen's
Farm-to-Table Dinner   VEGETARIAN $$$

(Map p470; 📞786-405-1745; 1300 Biscayne Blvd;
dinner $40, with wine pairing $60; ⊙6:30pm
Mon; 🍷) A great way to get to know some
locals, this Monday-night feast is served
family-style at outdoor tables in front of the
Arsht Center, with live music and plenty of
chatting between the diners. The vegetarian
menu is inspired by the farmers market held
on the same day. Call ahead to reserve a spot
or book online.

Little Havana

★ Versailles   CUBAN $

(Map p470; 📞305-444-0240; www.versailles-
restaurant.com; 3555 SW 8th St; mains $6-21;
⊙8am-1am Mon-Thu, to 2:30am Fri & Sat, 9am-
1am Sun) Versailles (ver-*sigh*-yay) is an institution – one of the mainstays of Miami's
Cuban gastronomic scene. Try the excellent
black-bean soup or the fried yucca before
moving onto heartier meat and seafood
plates. Older Cubans and Miami's Latin political elite still love coming here, so you've
got a real chance to rub elbows with Miami's most prominent Latin citizens.

Exquisito Restaurant   CUBAN $

(Map p470; 📞305-643-0227; www.elexquisito
miami.com; 1510 SW 8th St; mains $9-13; ⊙7am-
11pm) Great Cuban cuisine in the heart of
Little Havana – the roast pork has a tangy
citrus kick and the *ropa vieja* (spiced shredded beef and rice) is wonderfully rich. Even
standard sides like beans and rice and
roasted plantains are executed with a little
more care and are extra tasty. Prices are a
steal, too.

Wynwood &
the Design District

Della Test Kitchen   VEGAN $

(Map p470; 📞305-351-2961; www.dellabowls.
com; 56 NW 29th St, Wynwood Yard; mains $11-14;
⊙noon-10pm Tue-Sun; 🍷) From a food truck
parked in Wynwood Yard, this place offers
delicious 'bowls' – build-your-own culinary
works of art featuring ingredients such as
black coconut rice, ginger tempeh, chick-
peas, sweet potato and marinated kale. It's
heavenly good and quite healthy. Not surprisingly, DTK has quite a following.

★ Kyu   FUSION $$

(Map p470; 📞786-577-0150; www.kyumiami.com;
251 NW 25th St; sharing plates $17-38; ⊙noon-
11:30pm Mon-Sat, 11am-10:30pm Sun, bar till 1am
Fri & Sat; 🍷) 🌿 Kyu has been dazzling locals and food critics alike with its creative
Asian-inspired dishes, most of which are
cooked over the open flames of a wood-
fired grill. Try the Florida red snapper, beef
tenderloin and a magnificent head of cauliflower. There's also grilled octopus, soft-
shell-crab steamed buns and smoked beef
brisket. Book well ahead, or turn up and
wait (one-hour average).

Alter   MODERN AMERICAN $$$

(Map p470; 📞305-573-5996; www.alter
miami.com; 223 NW 23rd St; set menu 5/7 courses
$79/99; ⊙7-11pm Tue-Sun) Alter brings crea-
tive high-end cooking via its award-winning
young chef Brad Kilgore. The changing
menu showcases Florida's high-quality ingredients from sea and land in seasonally
inspired dishes with Asian and European-
flavoured haute cuisine. Expect dishes such
as eggs with sea scallop foam, truffle pearls
and Siberian caviar, or lamb neck, forest
consommé, toasted apple miso and shaved
kombu. Reserve well ahead.

🍷 Drinking & Nightlife

Miami has an intense variety of bars,
ranging from grotty jazz and punk dives
(with excellent music) to beautiful – and
laid-back – lounges and nightclubs. There

is a great live-music scene across the city. Miami's nightlife reputation for being all about wealth, good looks and phoniness is thankfully mostly isolated to the South Beach scene.

★ Broken Shaker
BAR

(Map p470; ☑ 305-531-2727; www.freehandhotels. com; 2727 Indian Creek Dr, Freehand Miami Hotel; ☺ 6pm-3am Mon-Fri, 2pm-3am Sat & Sun) A single small room with a well-equipped bar produces expert cocktails, which are mostly consumed in the beautiful, softly lit garden – all of it part of the Freehand Miami hotel (p478). There's a great soundtrack at all times, and the drinks are excellent. The clientele is a mix of hotel guests (young and into partying) and hip locals.

★ Sweet Liberty
BAR

(Map p470; www.mysweetliberty.com; 237 20th St; ☺ 4pm-5am Mon-Sat, from noon Sun) A much-loved local haunt near Collins Park, Sweet Liberty has all the right ingredients for a fun night out: friendly, easygoing bartenders who whip up excellent cocktails (try a mint julep), great happy-hour specials (including 75¢ oysters) and a relaxed, pretension-free crowd. The space is huge, with flickering candles, a long wooden bar and the odd band adding to the cheer.

Ball & Chain
BAR

(Map p470; www.ballandchainmiami.com; 1513 SW 8th St; ☺ noon-midnight Mon-Wed, to 3am Thu-Sat, 2-10pm Sun) The Ball & Chain has survived several incarnations over the years. Back in 1935, when 8th St was more Jewish than Latino, it was the sort of jazz joint Billie Holiday would croon in. That iteration closed in 1957, but today's Ball & Chain is still dedicated to music and good times – specifically, Latin music and tropical cocktails.

Vagabond Pool Bar
BAR

(Map p470; ☑ 305-400-8420; www.thevagabond-hotelmiami.com; 7301 Biscayne Blvd; ☺ 5-11pm Sun-Thu, to midnight Fri & Sat) Tucked behind the Vagabond Hotel, this is a great spot to start the evening, with perfectly mixed cocktails, courtesy of pro bartenders (the kind who will shake your hand and introduce themselves). The outdoor setting overlooking the palm-fringed pool and eclectic crowd pairs nicely with elixirs like the Lost in Smoke (mezcal, amaro, amaretto and orange bitters).

★ Galleria
CAFE

(Map p470; http://galleriadowntown.com; 69 SE 1st St; ☺ 11am-4pm) Galleria is a tiny spot of beauty, with its tiled benches and coral walls. The owner, Jeremy Sapienza, makes all his own nut milks, and everything here, including the pastries, is vegan. There are also vintage ceramics on sale – if you'd like an alternative Miami souvenir.

☆ Entertainment

Miami's artistic merits are obvious, even from a distance. Could there be a better creative base? There's Southern homegrown talent, migratory snowbirds bringing the funding and attention of northeastern galleries, and immigrants from across the Americas. All that adds up to some great live music, theater and dance – with plenty of room for experimentation.

★ Adrienne Arsht Center
for the Performing Arts
PERFORMING ARTS

(Map p470; ☑ 305-949-6722; www.arshtcenter. org; 1300 Biscayne Blvd; ☺ box office 10am-6pm Mon-Fri, plus 2hr before performances) This magnificent venue manages to both humble and enthrall visitors. Today the Arsht is where the biggest cultural acts in Miami come to perform; a show here is a must-see on any Miami trip. There's an Adrienne Arsht Center stop on the Metromover.

★ Cubaocho
LIVE PERFORMANCE

(Map p470; ☑ 305-285-5880; www.cubaocho. com; 1465 SW 8th St; ☺ 11am-10pm Tue-Thu, to 3am Fri & Sat) Jewel of the Little Havana Art District, Cubaocho is renowned for its concerts, with excellent bands from across the Spanish-speaking world. It's also a community center, art gallery and research outpost for all things Cuban. The interior resembles an old Havana cigar bar, yet the walls are decked out in artwork that references both the classical past of Cuban art and its avant-garde future.

Colony Theater PERFORMING ARTS
(Map p472; 305-674-1040, box office 800-211-1414; www.colonymb.org; 1040 Lincoln Rd) The Colony was built in 1935 and was the main cinema in upper South Beach before it fell into disrepair in the mid-20th century. It was renovated and revived in 1976 and now boasts 465 seats and great acoustics. It's an absolute art-deco gem, with a classic marquee and Inca-style crenellations, and now serves as a major venue for performing arts.

New World Symphony CLASSICAL MUSIC
(NWS; Map p472; 305-673-3330; www.nws.edu; 500 17th St) Housed in the New World Center (p468) – a funky explosion of cubist lines and geometric curves, fresh white against the blue Miami sky – the acclaimed New World Symphony holds performances from October to May. The deservedly heralded NWS serves as a three- to four-year preparatory program for talented musicians from prestigious music schools.

ℹ Information

DANGERS & ANNOYANCES
Miami is a fairly safe city, but there are a few areas considered by locals to be dangerous:
➡ Liberty City, in northwest Miami; Overtown, from 14th to 20th Sts; Little Haiti and stretches of the Miami riverfront.
➡ South Beach, particularly along the carnival-like mayhem of Ocean Dr between 8th and 11th Sts, and deserted areas below 5th St are also dangerous at night.
➡ Use caution around causeways, bridges and overpasses where homeless people have set up shantytowns.

In these and other reputedly 'bad' areas you should avoid walking around alone late at night. It's best to take a taxi.

TOURIST INFORMATION
Greater Miami & the Beaches Convention & Visitors Bureau (Map p470; 305-539-3000; www.miamiandbeaches.com; 701 Brickell Ave, 27th fl; 8:30am-6pm Mon-Fri) Offers loads of info on Miami and keeps up-to-date with the latest events and cultural offerings.

ℹ Getting There & Away

Located 6 miles west of Downtown, the busy **Miami International Airport** (MIA; Map p470; 305-876-7000; www.miami-airport.com; 2100 NW 42nd Ave) has three terminals and serves more than 40 million passengers each year. Around 60 airlines fly into Miami. The airport is open 24 hours and is laid out in a horse-

shoe design. There are left-luggage facilities on two concourses at MIA, between B and C, and on G; prices vary according to bag size.

For bus trips, **Greyhound** (www.greyhound.com) is the main long-distance operator. **Megabus** (Map p470; https://us.megabus.com; Miami International Center, 3801 NW 21st St) offers service to Tampa and Orlando.

Greyhound's **main bus terminal** (Map p470; 305-871-1810; 3801 NW 21st) is near the airport, though additional services also depart from the company's **Cutler Bay terminal** (Cutler Bay; 305-296-9072; 10801 Caribbean Blvd) and **North Miami terminal** (Map p470; 305-688-7277; 16000 NW 7th Ave).

If you are traveling very long distances (say, across several states), bargain airfares can sometimes undercut buses. On shorter routes, renting a car can sometimes be cheaper. Nonetheless, discounted (even half-price) long-distance bus trips are often available by purchasing tickets online seven to 14 days in advance.

The main Miami terminal of **Amtrak** (305-835-1222; www.amtrak.com; 8303 NW 37th Ave, West Little River), about 9 miles northwest of Downtown, connects the city with several other points in Florida (including Orlando and Jacksonville) on the Silver Service line that runs up to New York City. Travel time between New York and Miami is 27 to 31 hours. The Miami Amtrak station is connected by Tri-rail to Downtown Miami and has a left-luggage facility.

ℹ Getting Around

Bus Extensive system, though slow for long journeys.
Citi Bike Bike-sharing network in both Miami and Miami Beach. With heavy traffic, however, take care riding long distances – it can be hazardous.
Rental Car Convenient for zipping around town, but parking can be expensive.
Taxi & Ride-Sharing Services Best for getting between destinations if you don't want to drive, but can be pricey for long distances. Difficult to hail on the street; call or use an app (Lyft or Uber are the most popular) for a pick-up.
Trolley Free service with various routes in Miami Beach, Downtown, Wynwood, Coconut Grove, Coral Gables, Little Havana and other neighborhoods.

Fort Lauderdale

After years of building a reputation as *the* destination for beer-swilling college students on raucous spring breaks, Fort Lauderdale now angles for a slightly more mature and sophisticated crowd. Think martinis rather than tequila shots; jazz concerts instead of wet T-shirt contests. But don't worry, there's still plenty of carrying-on within the confines of area bars and nightclubs.

Few visitors venture far inland – except maybe to dine and shop along Las Olas Blvd; most spend the bulk of their time on the coast. It's understandable. Truly, it's hard to compete with beautiful beaches, a system of Venice-like waterways, an international yachting scene, spiffy new hotels and top-notch restaurants.

The city's Port Everglades is one of the busiest cruise-ship ports in the world, with megaships departing daily for the Caribbean, Mexico and beyond.

◉ Sights

Fort Lauderdale
Beach & Promenade   BEACH
(N Atlantic Blvd; P🚻🐾) Fort Lauderdale's promenade – a wide, brick, palm-tree-dotted pathway swooping along the beach and the A1A – is a magnet for runners, in-line skaters, walkers and cyclists. The white-sand beach, meanwhile, is one of the nation's cleanest and best. Stretching 7 miles to Lauderdale-by-the-Sea, it has dedicated family-, gay- and dog-friendly sections. Boating, diving, snorkeling and fishing are all extremely popular.

NSU Art Museum
Fort Lauderdale   MUSEUM
(☑954-525-5500; www.nsuartmuseum.org; 1 E Las Olas Blvd; adult/student/child $12/free; ⊙11am-5pm Tue-Sat, from noon Sun) A curvaceous Florida standout with an interesting spilled rainbow design outside, the museum is known for its William Glackens collection (among Glackens fans) and its exhibitions on wide-ranging themes from northern European art to contemporary Cuban art, American pop art and contemporary photography. On first Thursdays, the museum stays open to 8pm and hosts lectures, films and performances, as well as a happy hour in the museum cafe. Day courses and workshops are also available. Check the website for details.

★ Bonnet House   HISTORIC BUILDING
(☑954-563-5393; www.bonnethouse.org; 900 N Birch Rd; adult/child $20/16, grounds only $10; ⊙9am-4pm Tue-Sun) This pretty plantation-style property was once the home of artists and collectors Frederic and Evelyn Bartlett. It is now open to guided tours that swing

through its art-filled rooms and studios. Beyond the house, 35 acres of lush, subtropical gardens protect a pristine barrier-island ecosystem, including one of the finest orchid collections in the country.

Riverwalk   LANDMARK
(www.goriverwalk.com) Curving along the New River, the meandering Riverwalk runs from Stranahan House to the Broward Center for the Performing Arts. Host to culinary tastings and other events, the walk connects a number of sights, restaurants and shops.

Museum of
Discovery & Science   MUSEUM
(☑954-467-6637; www.mods.org; 401 SW 2nd St; adult/child $17/14; ⊙10am-5pm Mon-Sat, noon-6pm Sun; 🐾) A 52ft kinetic-energy sculpture greets you here, and fun exhibits include Gizmo City and Runways to Rockets – where it actually *is* rocket science. Plus there's an Everglades exhibit and IMAX theater. You can even have an 'Otter Encounter' for $50 per person (reservations only), where you can feed otters, participate in a training, and learn about their habits and diet.

🏃 Activities

Fort Lauderdale lies on the same reef system as the Keys. Snorkeling is a popular pastime but the real action in the water lies within a 50-minute boat ride at the site of some two-dozen wrecks. Here divers can nose around the Mercedes freighter and the Tenneco Towers artificial reef made up from an old oil platform. Soft corals bloom prolifically, and barracuda, jacks and parrotfish duck and dive between the wreckage.

Besides the underwater scenery, everything from jet-skis to parasailing to deep-sea fishing charters is available at the beach.

★ Sea Experience   BOATING, SNORKELING
(☑954-770-3483; www.seaxp.com; 801 Seabreeze Blvd; snorkeling adult/child $40/25, 2-tank dive $85 (not incl gear); ⊙10:15am & 2:15pm; 🐾) Sea Experience takes guests in a 40ft glass-bottom boat along the Intracoastal and into the ocean to snorkel on a natural reef, thriving with marine life, in 10ft to 20ft of water. Tours last 2½ hours. Also offers scuba trips to multiple wreck sites.

Carrie B   BOATING
(☑954-642-1601; www.carriebcruises.com; 440 N New River Dr E; tours adult/child $29/15; ⊙tours 11am, 1pm & 3pm, closed Tue & Wed May-Sep) Hop aboard this replica 19th-century riverboat

for a narrated 90-minute 'lifestyles of the rich and famous' tour of the ginormous mansions along the Intracoastal and New River. Tours leave from Las Olas at SE 5th Ave.

★ Bar-B-Ranch
HORSEBACK RIDING

(☑954-424-1060; www.bar-b-ranch.com; 3500 Peaceful Ridge Rd, Davie; 60/90 min trail rides $50/60; ⊙9am-5pm Mon-Fri, to 4:30pm Sat) With the glitter of Ft Lauderdale so close, it's hard to feel like any 'old' Florida is left, but Davie is just 15 minutes away and at Bar-B-Ranch, a family-owned riding stable since 1969, you can truly get away from it all: on top of a horse. It offers trail and rental options, including a day and summer kids' camp.

The real magic though is just being in the saddle and seeing some of the nearby preserved woodlands and fields that once comprised most of this part of Florida. Davie has done a good job of preserving these spaces, so if the 23 acres of ranchland are too wimpy for you, there's 160-plus acres of additional countryside to explore, including live oak hammocks, wetlands, and a citrus grove.

Blue Moon Outdoor Adventures
BOATING

(☑954-781-0073; www.bluemoonoutdoor.com; 1101 Bayview Dr, George English Park & Boat ramp; 1st hour kayak 1/2 person $15/25, SUP $35, then $10 per hour after; ⊙10am-sunset Thu-Sun or by appointment) Paddle the Island City Loop or go south through 'Venice of America,' Fort Lauderdale. Day, sunset, and moonlight tours are available by appointment. Tours include light refreshments.

🛏 Sleeping

The splashiest hotels are found along the beach. Of course, those places are also the priciest. Meander inland and you'll discover some wonderful inns with Old Florida charm. For more budget-friendly accommodations, check out Lauderdale-by-the-Sea.

Tranquilo
MOTEL $$

(☑954-565-5790; www.tranquilofortlauderdale. com; 2909 Vistamar St; r $149-194; P❄❄🐾🏊) This white-on-white retro 1950s motel offers fantastic value for families. Rooms range over five buildings, each with its own pool, and some include newly refurbished kitchens along with access to outdoor grills and laundry services. No shuttle, but the beach is three blocks away. The main pool even has an accessible entry for those with mobility needs.

B Ocean Resort
HOTEL $$

(☑954-524-5551; www.bhotelsandresorts.com; 1140 Seabreeze Blvd; r from $144; P❄❄🐾🏊) Defining the southern end of Seabreeze Blvd, this hotel straddles the uberpopular South Beach and offers breezy ocean views from the majority of its airy rooms. Built by M Tony Sherman in 1956, it looks like a giant cruise ship tethered to the sidewalk.

★ W Fort Lauderdale
HOTEL $$$

(☑954-414-8200; www.wfortlauderdalehotel.com; 401 N Fort Lauderdale Beach Blvd; r $289-699; P❄@🐾🏊) With an exterior resembling two giant sails and an interior that looks like the backdrop for a J Lo video, this is where the glitterati stay – bust out your stiletto heels/skinny ties and join them. The massive lobby is built for leisure, with a silver-and-aqua lounge area, a moodily lit bar, and a deck lined with wicker chaises.

★ Lago Mar Resort
RESORT $$$

(☑954-523-6511; www.lagomar.com; 1700 S Ocean Lane; r $300-700; P❄❄@🐾🏊) On the south end of South Beach, this wonderfully noncorporate resort has it all: a private beach, grand lobby, massive island-style rooms, a full-service spa, on-site restaurants, a lagoon-style pool set amid tropical plantings and the personal touch of family ownership. (And no, not to be confused with President Trump's Mar-a-Lago.) A lovely fish mosaic graces the lobby floor.

🍴 Eating

Fort Lauderdale's food scene is heavily influenced by the area's large Italian American population but increasingly it's becoming known for its casual chic, farm-to-table options. Las Olas Blvd has a number of eating places, especially the stretch between 5th and 16th Aves, though these can be more touristy.

Lester's Diner
DINER $

(☑954-525-5641; www.lestersdiner.com; 250 W State Rd 84; mains $6-19; ⊙24hr) Hailed endearingly as a greasy spoon, retro-since-it-was-new Lester's Diner has been keeping folks happy since the late 1960s. Everyone makes their way here at some point, from business types on cell phones to clubbers to travel writers needing pancakes at 4am.

Green Bar & Kitchen
VEGAN $

(☑954-533-7507; www.greenbarkitchen.com; 1075 SE 17th St; mains $8-16; ⊙10am-9pm Mon-Sat, to 4pm Sun; P🍽) Discover bright flavors and

LGBTIQ+ FORT LAUDERDALE

Sure, South Beach is a hot location for gay travelers, but Fort Lauderdale nips at the high heels of its southern neighbor. Compared to South Beach, Lauderdale is a little more rainbow-flag-oriented and a little less exclusive. And for the hordes of gay men who flock here, either to party or to settle down, therein lies the charm.

Fort Lauderdale is home to several-dozen gay bars and clubs, as many gay guesthouses, and a couple of way-gay residential areas. **Victoria Park** is the established gay hub just northeast of downtown Fort Lauderdale. A bit further north, **Wilton Manors** is a more recently gay-gentrified area boasting endless nightlife options. Look for **Rosie's** (☑ 954-563-0123; www.rosiesbng.com; 2449 Wilton Dr; ⊘ 11am-11pm), a low-key neighborhood watering hole; **The Manor** (☑ 954-626-0082; www.themanorcomplex.com; 2345 Wilton Dr; cover $10-20; ⊘ varies), for nationally recognized performers and an epic dance floor; and **Georgie's Alibi** (☑ 954-565-2526; www.alibiwiltonmanors.com; 2266 Wilton Dr; ⊘ 11am-2am), best for its Wednesday comedy night with Cashetta, a fabulous female impersonator. Spots like Stache offer non-binary nights. There's even a leather/bear/cowboy club, **Ramrod** (☑ 954-763-8219; www.ramrodbar.com; 1508 NE 4th Ave; ⊘ 3pm-2am).

Gay guesthouses are plentiful; visit www.gayftlauderdale.com. Consult the glossy weekly rag *Hot Spots* (www.hotspotsmagazine.com) to keep updated on gay nightlife. For the most insanely comprehensive list of everything gay, log on to www.jumpon markslist.com.

innovative dishes at this modern, plant-based shop located in a strip mall. Get your fresh celery-juice fix, veggie voodoo shots, or non-dairy gelato. Almond milk replaces dairy in cold-pressed fruit smoothies, and the delectable cashew cup gives Reese's a run for its money.

★ **Burlock Coast** INTERNATIONAL $$$
(☑ 954-302-6460; www.burlockcoast.com; Ritz Carlton, 1 N Fort Lauderdale Beach Blvd; mains $19-46; ⊘ 7am-10pm) Situated in the lovely Ritz Carlton Hotel, this chic, casual spot somehow manages to be all things to all people: a cafe, bar, market and upmarket restaurant. The menu has been crafted to the mantra: local farmers and vendors. The menu changes seasonally but errs towards modern international, like pulled pork or simple fish-and-chips. The deck outside is prime for people watching.

15th Street Fisheries SEAFOOD $$$
(☑ 954-763-2777; www.15streetfisheries.com; 1900 SE 15th St; bar mains $7-16, restaurant mains $38-55; Ⓟ) Tucked away in Lauderdale Marina with an open-fronted deck offering a front-row view of yachts, this place is hard to beat for waterfront dining. The wooden interior is kitted out like an Old Florida boathouse. The fine-dining restaurant is upstairs and a more informal dockside bar serves shrimp, crab and grilled mahi-mahi. You can feed the tarpon, too, which is popular with kids.

🍷 Drinking & Entertainment

Fort Lauderdale bars can stay open until 4am on weekends and 2am during the week. A handful of great bars and pubs are found in the Himmarshee Village area on SW 2nd St, while the beach offers plenty of open-air boozing.

★ **Rok:Brgr** PUB
(☑ 954-525-7656; www.rokbrgr.com; 208 SW 2nd St; ⊘ 11:30am-midnight Mon-Thu, to 1am Fri & Sat, 10am-11pm Sun) One of several dining spots in this strip of hip bars and restaurants, Rok:Brgr shoots for a 1920s Chicago-era 'American kitchen' and pulls it off. Edison light bulbs and contemporary industrial decor creates the ambience, while the cuisine is contemporary – gourmet burgers using locally sourced ingredients, plus Prohibition-style cocktails.

★ **Stache** COCKTAIL BAR
(☑ 954-449-1044; www.stacheftl.com; 109 SW 2nd Ave; ⊘ 7am-5pm Mon & Thu, to 4am Fri, 8pm-4am Sat) A tall, sleek and sexy 1920s-themed drinking den serving crafted cocktails and rocking a crossover classic rock/funk/soul/R&B blend. At weekends there's live music, dancing and burlesque. Dress up; this is where the cool cats come to play. Serves coffee during the day; open late on weekends only. 'Non-binary night' is one of their themed evenings.

FLORIDA FORT LAUDERDALE

Revolutions Live

CONCERT VENUE

(☑954-449-1025; www.jointherevolution.net; 100 SW 3rd Ave; varies, usually per person from $25; ⊙varies) Great event space with concerts that range from local up-and-comings to legends and household names. It's a multilevel space where up to 1300 people can rock on, and you actually have to try hard to not get a good view of the performers. No smoking is allowed.

Blue Jean Blues

JAZZ

(☑954-306-6330; www.bjblive.com; 3320 NE 33rd St; snacks $9-17; ⊙11am-2am Sun-Thu, to 3am Fri & Sat) Get away from the beach for a low-key evening of jazz and blues at this cool little neighborhood bar, often packed. There's live music seven nights and four afternoons a week, featuring a who's who of the southern Florida music scene. From East Sunrise Blvd head north for 2.3 miles and then turn left onto NE 33rd Street.

ℹ Information

Greater Fort Lauderdale Convention & Visitors Bureau (☑954-765-4466; www.sunny.org; 101 NE 3rd Ave, Suite 100; ⊙8:30am-5pm Mon-Fri) Has an excellent array of visitor information about the greater Fort Lauderdale region.

ℹ Getting There & Around

Fort Lauderdale is served by its own international **airport** (FLL; ☑866-435-9355; www.broward.org/airport; 100 Terminal Dr).

If you're driving here, I-95 and Florida's Turnpike run north–south and provide good access to Fort Lauderdale. I-595, the major east–west artery, intersects I-95, Florida's Turnpike and the Sawgrass Expwy. It also feeds into I-75, which runs to Florida's west coast.

Sun Trolley (☑954-876-5539; www.suntrolley.com; per ride/day $1/3; ⊙10:30am-5pm) runs between Las Olas and the beaches between 9:30am and 6:30pm Friday to Monday. **Broward County Transit** (BCT; www.broward.org/bct; single fare/day pass $2/5) operates between downtown, the beach and Port Everglades. From **Broward Central Terminal** (101 NW 1st Ave), take bus 11 to upper Fort Lauderdale Beach and Lauderdale-by-the-Sea; bus 4 to Port Everglades; and bus 40 to 17th St and the beaches.

The fun, yellow **water taxi** (☑954-467-6677; www.watertaxi.com; day pass adult/child $28/14) travels the canals and waterways between 17th St to the south, Atlantic Blvd/Pompano Beach to the north, the Riverwalk to the west and the Atlantic Ocean to the east. There are also services to Hollywood ($15 per person).

Palm Beach

The third-wealthiest city in America, Palm Beach, a barrier island connected by bridges to the mainland, is home to dozens of billionaires and looks every inch the playground for the rich and famous. Palatial Greco-Roman mansions line the shore; Bentleys and Porsches cruise the wide avenues of downtown; you may even see an entirely chrome Rolls Royce or two. Life here revolves around charity balls, designer shopping and cocktail-soaked lunches. Though all the bling may make you nauseated, fear not – much of Palm Beach is within the reach of all travelers. Stroll along the truly gold Gold Coast beach, ogle the massive gated compounds on A1A or window-shop in uber-ritzy Worth Ave – all for free.

These days, Palm Beach is frequently in the news because of US president Donald Trump, whose mansion-cum-private-club, Mar-a-Lago, is here.

Despite all the glitz, the architecture and history is nothing but fascinating, and offers some insight into how it might have been to live during the Gilded Age of late-19th-century USA.

◉ Sights & Activities

Worth Avenue

AREA

(www.worth-avenue.com) This quarter-mile, palm-tree-lined strip of more than 200 high-end brand shops is like the Rodeo Dr of the East. You can trace its history back to the 1920s when the now-gone Everglades Club staged weekly fashion shows and launched the careers of designers such as Elizabeth Arden. Even if you don't have the slightest urge to sling a swag of glossy bags over your arm, the people-watching is priceless, as is the Spanish Revival architecture.

★ Flagler Museum

MUSEUM

(☑561-655-2833; www.flaglermuseum.us; 1 Whitehall Way; adult/child $18/10; ⊙10am-5pm Tue-Sat, from noon Sun) This museum is housed in the spectacular 1902 mansion built by Henry Flagler as a gift for his bride, Mary Lily Kenan. The beaux arts–styled Whitehall was one of the most modern houses of its era and quickly became the focus of the winter season. It was designed by John Carrère and Thomas Hastings, both students of the Ecole des Beaux-Arts in Paris and collaborators on other Gilded Age landmarks such as the New York Public Library.

★ Palm Beach Lake Trail   CYCLING

(Royal Palm Way, at the Intracoastal Waterway) Running along the Intracoastal Waterway, this 5-mile paved path stretches from Worth Ave (in the south) to Indian Rd (in the north). Nicknamed 'The Trail of Conspicuous Consumption,' it is sandwiched between two amazing views: Lake Worth lagoon to the west, and an unending series of mansions to the east, and it originally allowed Flagler hotel guests to check out the social scene.

Palm Beach Bicycle Trail Shop   CYCLING

(☑ 561-659-4583; http://palmbeachbicycle.com; 50 Cocoanut Row, Suite 117, In the Slat House; bikes/electric bikes per day $49/89; ☺ 9am-5:30pm Mon-Sat, 10am-5pm Sun) This shop rents out bikes and electric bikes at a convenient spot for cycling. Helmets cost $5 extra.

🍽 Sleeping & Eating

Bradley Park Hotel   HOTEL $$

(☑ 561-832-7050; www.bradleyparkhotel.com; 2080 Sunset Ave; r $229, ste $329-359; ⓟ❄🤖) Though undergoing restoration at the time of research, the midrange Bradley (built in 1921) offers large rooms and will likely retain much of its previous charm. Some rooms included original features from the era and characterful furniture. It's located just a short walk from the shops and restaurants of Royal Poinciana Way. Expect that the decor may change but the grandeur will remain.

★ Breakers   RESORT $$$

(☑ 855-801-7057; www.thebreakers.com; 1 S County Rd; r/ste from $699/2000; ⓟ❄❄@🤖🏊) 🏌 Originally built by Henry Flagler (in 1904, rooms cost $4 per night, including meals), today this 538-room resort sprawls across 140 acres and boasts a staff of 2000 plus, fluent in 56 languages. Just feet from the county's best snorkeling, this palace has two 18-hole golf courses, a mile of semiprivate beach, four pools and the best brunch around.

Surfside Diner   DINER, BREAKFAST $

(☑ 561-659-7495; 314 S County Rd; mains $8-13; ☺ 8am-3pm) This classy remake of a classic diner serves decent breakfasts and brunch. Pancakes, chicken breakfast burritos and French toast are all tasty. For lunch there's a healthy offering of grilled cheese and tomato soup, BLTs, PB&Js and sliders.

★ Būccan   AMERICAN $$$

(☑ 561-833-3450; www.buccanpalmbeach.com; 350 S County Rd; mains $18-40; ☺ 5pm-10pm Sun-Thu, to 11pm Fri & Sat) With its modern American menu and James Beard–nominated chef, Clay Conley, at the helm, Būccan is the 'it' place to eat in Palm Beach. Flavor-hop with a selection of small plates, including smoked chicken sliders, and move on to snapper ceviche. Reservations recommended.

The bar will stay open later if it's busy, to midnight Sunday to Thursday and to 1am on Friday and Saturday.

★ Café Boulud   FRENCH $$$

(☑ 561-655-6060; www.cafeboulud.com/palmbeach; 301 Australian Ave; mains $16-49, fixed-price menu $48; ☺ cafe 7am-11pm, bar to midnight) Created by renowned New York chef Daniel Boulud, the restaurant at the Brazilian Court hotel is one of the few places in Palm Beach that truly justifies the sky-high prices. The warm dining room, beautiful lit-marble bar, and terrace complements a rich menu of classic French and fusion dishes, all displaying Boulud's signature sophistication and subtlety.

🍸 Drinking & Entertainment

Leopard Lounge   LOUNGE

(www.chesterfieldpb.com; 363 Cocoanut Row; ☺ 7am-2:30pm & 5:30-11pm Mon-Fri, to midnight or later Sat & Sun) This gold, black and red lounge attracts a mature crowd and the occasional celeb (neither photos nor autograph hounds are allowed). The piano player and the waitstaff give off a there's-a-place-they'd-rather-be vibe, but if you want to relax with a drink or strike up a chat with someone next to you, this is the spot.

Society of the Four Arts   PERFORMING ARTS

(☑ 561-655-7226; www.fourarts.org; 2 Four Arts Plaza) The concert series here includes cabaret, the Palm Beach Symphony, chamber orchestras, string quartets and piano performances.

ℹ Information

Chamber of Commerce (☑ 561-655-3282;

www.palmbeachchamber.com; 400 Royal Palm Way, Suite 106; ☺ 9am-5pm Mon-Fri) Excellent maps and racks of pamphlets, plus a dog to pat.

ℹ Getting There & Around

Palm Tran (http://discover.pbcgov.org/palmtran; per ride $2, day pass $5) bus 41 covers the bulk of the island, from Lantana Rd to Sunrise Ave; transfer to bus 1 at Publix to go north or south along Hwy 1. To get to Palm Beach International Airport (p489) in West

FLORIDA PALM BEACH

Palm Beach, take bus 41 to the downtown transfer and hop on bus 44.

Though it's a fairly compact city, the two major downtown neighborhoods, centered on Royal Poinciana Way and Worth Ave, are a fair hike apart.

West Palm Beach

When Henry Flagler decided to develop what is now West Palm Beach, he knew precisely what it would become: a working-class community for the labor force that would support his glittering resort town across the causeway. And so the fraternal twins were born – Palm Beach, considered the fairer of the two, and West Palm Beach, a cooler work-hard-play-hard community. West Palm has a surprisingly diverse collection of restaurants, friendly inhabitants (including a strong gay community) and a gorgeous waterway that always seems to reflect the perfect amount of starlight.

⊙ Sights & Activities

★ Norton Museum of Art   MUSEUM
(☑ 561-832-5196; www.norton.org; 1451 S Olive Ave; adult/child $18/5, free on Sat; ⊙ 10am-5pm Mon, Tue, Thu & Sat, to 10pm Fri, from 11am Sun) This is the largest art museum in Florida and arguably the most impressive. It opened in 1941 to display the enormous art collection of industrialist Ralph Hubbard Norton and his wife Elizabeth. The Nortons' permanent collection of more than 5000 pieces (including works by Matisse, Warhol and O'Keeffe) is displayed alongside important Chinese, pre-Columbian Mexican and Southwestern USA artifacts, plus some wonderful contemporary photography and regular traveling exhibitions.

South Florida Science Center & Aquarium   MUSEUM
(☑ 561-832-1988; www.sfsciencecenter.org; 4801 Dreher Trail North; adult/child $18/14; ⊙ 9am-5pm Mon-Fri, 10am-6pm Sat & Sun) A great little hands-on science center, aquarium and planetarium with weekend programs, traveling exhibits, a science trail, mini-golf and butterfly garden. On the last Friday of the month the museum stays open from 6pm to 9pm so you can view the night sky from the county's only public observatory (weather permitting). Prices change according to the exhibition.

Peanut Island   ISLAND
(http://discover.pbcgov.org; $12 round-trip; ⊙ 11am-4pm Thu-Sun) Plopped right off the north-

eastern corner of West Palm, Peanut Island was created in 1918 by dredging projects. Originally named Inlet Island, the spit was renamed for a peanut-oil-shipping operation that failed in 1946. There is even a disused nuclear fallout bunker that was constructed for John F Kennedy during the days of the Cuban missile crisis (although it was closed at the time of research).

Rapids Water Park   WATER PARK
(☑ 561-848-6272; www.rapidswaterpark.com; 6566 North Military Trail, Riviera Beach; weekday/weekend $46/52; ⊙ 10am-5pm mid-Mar-Dec, to 7pm or 9pm Jun-Aug) South Florida's largest water park features 30 action-packed acres of wet and wild rides. Don't let the squeals of fear and delight from the Big Thunder funnel put you off. Awesome fun. Parking costs an extra $15.

⌂ Sleeping

Hotel Biba   MOTEL $
(☑ 561-832-0094; www.hotelbiba.com; 320 Belvedere Rd; r $149-179; 🅿❄🛜☒) With plain, white, slightly missing-a-small-something rooms, this place lacks a bit of color, but is one of the better (if only) budget options around. It's well located – only a block from the Intracoastal, and perched on the edge of the El Cid district. Suffice to say it's clean and fine if you just want a bed. Includes a simple Continental breakfast.

★ Grandview Gardens   B&B $$
(☑ 561-833-9023; www.grandview-gardens.com; 1608 Lake Ave; r $139-249; 🅿❄🛜☒) Book a room at this intimate resort and you'll feel like a local in no time. Hidden in a tropical garden on Howard Park, the enormous suites with their wrought-iron and four-poster beds access the pool patio through French doors. They're decorated to reflect the Spanish Mediterranean style that is so popular in these parts.

✕ Eating

★ Grandview Public Market   MARKET $
(www.grandviewpublic.com; 1401 Clare Ave; ⊙ 7am-10:30pm) Recently opened, the Grandview Public Market is an expansive array of small shops, stalls and foodcarts with all kinds of offerings. This is by far the best option for budget travelers or a group who may want individual items. The selection ranges from Cuban sandwiches to Thai rolled ice cream and everything in between. Plenty of public seating, too!

Restoration Hardware
BRASSERIE **$$**

(☑ 561-804-6826; www.restorationhardware.com; 560 Okeechobee Blvd; mains $19-27; ⊙10am-8pm Mon-Sat, 11am-7pm Sun) Both the name and the location (atop a furniture store) belie the exquisite experience that awaits those who seek out Restoration Hardware, an as-ritzy-as-it-gets rooftop dining experience with a full bar and spectacular wine room. Presentation is as lovely as the food is tasty, with beautiful salads, artfully presented burgers and snazzy lobster rolls.

Darbster
VEGAN **$$**

(☑ 561-586-2622; www.darbster.com; 8020 S Dixie Hwy; mains $12-18; ⊙5-10pm Tue-Fri, 10:30am-3pm & 5-10pm Sat, to 9pm Sun) This place is out on a limb in many respects: it's 5 miles south of town in an incongruous location by the S Dixie Hwy on the Palm Beach canal; the menu is 100% vegan; all profits go to a foundation for animal care; and it attracts everyone from Birkenstock-wearing hippies to diamond-wearing Palm Beachers.

★ Table 26 Degrees
AMERICAN **$$$**

(☑ 561-855-2660; www.table26palmbeach.com; 1700 S Dixie Hwy; mains $20-49; ⊙11:30am-2pm Mon-Sat, from 10:30am Sun, plus 4:30-10pm Sun-Thu, to 11pm Fri & Sat) Don't be put off by the price of this sophisticated restaurant. It is filled with locals, conversation and the clinking of glasses for good reason. They flock here for the bar (great happy hour 4:30pm to 6:30pm daily) plus the share plates and mains that are divided by water, land, field, and hands (the latter covers fried chicken and burgers).

🍷 Drinking & Entertainment

Roosters
GAY

(☑ 561-832-9119; www.roosterswpb.com; 823 Belvedere Rd; ⊙3pm-3am Sun-Thu, to 4am Fri & Sat) A mainstay of West Palm's thriving gay community, this bar has been offering popcorn, hot dogs, bingo and hot male dancers since 1984.

★ Voltaire
CLUB

(☑ 561-408-5603; www.voltairewpb.com; 526 Clematis St; ⊙8pm-2am Sun-Wed, to 3am Thu, to 4am Fri-Sat) Part of the Subculture umbrella and next door to Respectable Street, Voltaire is the wildebeest of clubs: fresh sushi, craft cocktails and live music don't always go together, but this quirky spot is fantastic, offering great drinks, excellent maki and nigiri, and some fun, interesting bands. Spoken word, live-mic nights, and other events happen here too. Don't miss it!

Respectable Street
LIVE MUSIC

(☑ 561-832-9999; www.respectablestreet.com; 518 Clematis St; ⊙9pm-3am Wed-Thu, to 4am Fri & Sat) Respectables has kept South Florida jamming to great bands for two decades; it also organizes October's MoonFest, the city's best block party. Great DJs, strong drinks and a breezy chill-out patio are added bonuses. See if you can find the hole that the Red Hot Chili Peppers' Anthony Kiedis punched in the wall when they played here.

International Polo Club
SPECTATOR SPORT

(☑ 561-204-5687; www.internationalpoloclub.com; 3667 120th Ave S, Wellington; general admission $10, lawn seating from $30; ⊙Sun Jan-Apr) Between January and April the International Polo Club hosts 16 weeks of polo and glamour. As one of the finest polo facilities in the world, it not only attracts the most elite players but also the local and international glitterati who whoop it up in head-turning fashion over champagne brunches ($125, with bottle of Veuve Cliquot, $325). Why not?

ℹ Information

The *Palm Beach Post* (www.palmbeachpost.com) is the largest paper.

Discover The Palm Beaches Visitor Center (☑ 561-233-3000; www.thepalmbeaches.com; 2195 Southern Blvd, Suite 400; ⊙8:30am-5:30pm Mon-Fri) is a good for area information, maps and online guides.

Music lovers will want to pick up a free copy of Pure Honey (www.purehoneymagazine.com) for details of great music, live shows and other entertainment going on.

ℹ Getting There & Around

Palm Beach International Airport (PBI; ☑ 561-471-7420; www.pbia.org; 1000 James L Turnage Blvd) is served by most major airlines and car-rental companies. It's about a mile west of I-95 on Belvedere Rd. Palm Tran (p487) bus 44 runs between the airport, the train station and downtown ($2).

Greyhound (☑ 561-833-8534; www.greyhound.com; 205 S Tamarind Ave; ⊙6am-10:45pm), **Tri-Rail** (☑ 800-875-7245; www.tri-rail.com; 203 S Tamarind Ave) and **Amtrak** (☑ 800-872-7245; www.amtrak.com; 209 S Tamarind Ave) share the same building: the historic Seaboard Train Station. Palm Tran serves the station with bus 44 (from the airport).

A cute and convenient (and free!) trolley runs between Clematis St and CityPlace starting at 11am.

FLORIDA PALM BEACH

The Everglades

There is no wilderness in America quite like the Everglades. Called the 'River of Grass' by Native American inhabitants, this is not just a wetland, or a swamp, or a lake, or a river, or a prairie, or a grassland – it is all of those, twisted together into a series of soft horizons, long vistas, sunsets that stretch across your entire field of vision and the toothy grins of a healthy population of dinosaur-era reptiles.

The park's quiet majesty is evident when you see anhinga flexing their wings before breaking into a corkscrew dive, or the slow, rhythmic flap of a great blue heron gliding over its domain, or the shimmer of light on miles of untrammeled saw grass as the sun sets behind hunkering cypress domes. In a nation where natural beauty is measured by its capacity for drama, the Everglades subtly, contentedly flows on.

Everglades National Park

This vast **wilderness** (☎305-242-7700; www.nps.gov/ever; 40001 SR-9336, Homestead; ☺visitor center 9am-5pm), encompassing 1.5 million acres, is one of America's great natural treasures. There's much to see and do – from spying alligators basking in the noonday sun as herons stalk patiently through nearby waters in search of prey, to going kayaking in mangrove canals and on peaceful lakes. You can also wade into murky knee-high waters among cypress domes on a rough-and-ready 'slough slog.'

There are sunrise strolls on boardwalks amid the awakening glimmers of birdsong, and moonlit glimpses of gators swimming gracefully along narrow channels in search of dinner. Backcountry camping, bicycle tours and ranger-led activities help bring the magic of this place to life. The biggest challenge is really just deciding where to begin.

There are three main entrances and three main areas of the park: one along the southeast edge near Homestead and Florida City (Ernest Coe section); at the central-north side on the Tamiami Trail (Shark Valley section); and a third at the northwest shore (Gulf Coast section), past Everglades City. The Shark Valley and Gulf Coast sections of the park come one after the other in geographic succession, but the Ernest Coe area is entirely separate.

The admission fee – $30 per vehicle, $15 per hiker and cyclist – covers the whole park, and is good for seven consecutive days. Because the Tamiami Trail is a public road, there's no admission to access national park sights along this highway, aside from Shark Valley. In the southern half of the park, one staffed checkpoint oversees access to all sights on the road between Ernest Coe down to Flamingo.

Three types of **backcountry campsites** (☎239-695-3311, 239-695-2945; www.nps.gov/ever/planyourvisit/backcamp.htm; ☺Flamingo & Gulf Coast Visitor Centers 8am-4.30pm) are available: beach sites, on coastal shell beaches and in the 10,000 Islands; ground sites, which are basically mounds of dirt built up above the mangroves; and *chickees,* wooden platforms built above the waterline where you can pitch a freestanding (no spikes) tent. *Chickees,* which have toilets, are the most civilized – there's a serenity found in sleeping on what feels like a raft levitating above the water. Ground sites tend to be the most bug infested.

From November to April, backcountry camping permits cost $15, plus $2 per person per night; from May to October sites are free, but you must still self-register at Flamingo and Gulf Coast Visitor Centers or call ☎239-695-2945.

Warning: if you're paddling around and see an island that looks pleasant for camping but isn't a designated campsite, beware – you may end up submerged when the tides change.

Some backcountry tips:

➡ Store food in a hand-sized, raccoon-proof container (available at gear stores).

➡ Bury your waste at least 10in below ground, but keep in mind some ground sites have hard turf.

➡ Use a backcountry stove to cook. Ground fires are only permitted at beach sites, and you can only burn dead or downed wood.

Load up on provisions before you enter the park. Homestead or Florida City are your best options if going into the Southern Everglades. If heading to the Tamiami Trail, plan to stock up in Miami – or the western suburbs.

❶ Getting There & Around

The largest subtropical wilderness in the continental USA is easily accessible from Miami. The Glades, which comprise the 80 southernmost miles of Florida, are bound by the Atlantic Ocean to the east and the Gulf of Mexico to the west. The Tamiami Trail (Hwy 41) goes east–west, parallel to the more northern (and less interesting) Alligator Alley (I-75).

You need a car to properly enter the Everglades and once you're in, wearing a good pair of walking boots is essential to penetrate the interior. Having a canoe or a kayak helps as well; these can be rented from outfits inside and outside the park, or else you can seek out guided canoe and kayak tours. Bicycles are well suited to the flat roads of Everglades National Park, particularly in the area between Ernest Coe and Flamingo Point. Road shoulders in the park tend to be dangerously small.

Around the Everglades

Biscayne National Park

Just to the east of the Everglades is **Biscayne National Park** (📞305-230-1144, boat tours 786-335-3644; www.nps.gov/bisc; 9700 SW 328th St; boat tours adult/child $35/25; ⏱7am-5:30pm), or the 5% of it that isn't underwater. In fact, a portion of the world's third-largest reef sits here off the coast of Florida, along with mangrove forests and the northernmost Florida Keys. This is some of the best reef viewing and snorkeling you'll find in the USA, outside Hawaii and nearby Key Largo.

Biscayne requires a little extra planning, but you'll be rewarded for your effort. This unique 300-sq-mile park is easy to explore independently with a canoe, or via a boat tour. Generally summer and fall are the best times to visit the park; you'll want to snorkel when the water is calm. The offshore Keys, accessible only by boat, offer pristine opportunities for camping.

Primitive camping (www.nps.gov/bisc/planyourvisit/camping.htm; tent sites per night $25, May-Sep free) is available on Elliott and Boca Chita Keys, though you'll need a boat to get there. No-see-ums (tiny flies) are invasive, and their bites are devastating. Make sure your tent is devoid of minuscule entry points.

❶ Information

Dante Fascell Visitor Center (📞305-230-1144; www.nps.gov/bisc; 9700 SW 328th St; ⏱9am-5pm) Located at Convoy Point, this center shows a great introductory film for an overview of the park, and has maps, information and excellent ranger activities. The grounds around the center are a popular picnic spot on weekends and holidays, especially for families from Homestead. Also showcases local artwork.

❶ Getting There & Away

To get here, you'll have to drive about 9 miles east of Homestead (the way is pretty well signposted) on SW 328th St (North Canal Dr) into a long series of green-and-gold flat fields and marsh.

Homestead & Florida City

Homestead and neighboring Florida City, 2 miles to the south, aren't of obvious appeal upon arrival. Part of the ever-expanding subdivisions of South Miami, this bustling corridor can feel like an endless strip of big-box shopping centers, fast-food joints, car dealerships and gas stations. However, look beneath the veneer and you'll find much more than meets the eye: strange curiosities like a 'castle' built single-handedly by one lovestruck immigrant, an animal rescue center for exotic species, a winery showcasing Florida's produce (hint: it's not grapes), an up-and-coming microbrewery, and one of the best farm stands in America.

This area makes a great base for forays into the stunning Everglades National Park.

◎ Sights & Activities

★**Coral Castle**   CASTLE
(📞305-248-6345; www.coralcastle.com; 28655 S Dixie Hwy; adult/senior/child $18/15/8; ⏱8am-6pm Sun-Thu, to 8pm Fri & Sat) 'You will be seeing unusual accomplishment,' reads the inscription on the rough-hewn quarried wall. That's an understatement. There is no greater temple to all that is weird and wacky about South Florida. The legend goes that a Latvian man got snubbed at the altar, came to the USA and settled in Florida, and hand-carved, unseen, in the dead of night, a monument to unrequited love.

Everglades Outpost   WILDLIFE RESERVE
(📞305-562-8000; www.evergladesoutpost.org; 35601 SW 192nd Ave, Homestead; adult/child $15/10; ⏱10am-5:30pm Mon, Tue & Fri-Sun, by appointment Wed & Thu) The Everglades Outpost houses, feeds and cares for wild animals that have been seized from illegal traders, abused, neglected or donated by people who could not care for them. Residents of the outpost include a lemur, wolves, a black bear, a zebra, cobras, alligators and a pair of majestic tigers (one of whom was bought by

an exotic dancer who thought she could incorporate it into her act). Your money goes toward helping the outpost's mission.

Garls Coastal
Kayaking Everglades
KAYAKING

(www.garlscoastalkayaking.com; 19200 SW 344th St, Homestead; single/double kayak per day $40/55, half-/full-day tour $125/150) On the property of the **Robert Is Here** (☑ 305-246-1592; www.robertishere.com; juices $7-9; ☺ 8am-7pm) 🍴 fruit stand, this outfitter leads highly recommended excursions into the Everglades. A full-day outing includes hiking (more of a wet walk or slog into the lush landscape of cypress domes), followed by kayaking in both the mangroves and in Florida Bay, and, time permitting, a night walk.

🛏 Sleeping & Eating

⭐ Hoosville Hostel
HOSTEL $

(☑ 305-248-1122; www.hoosvillehostel.com; 20 SW 2nd Ave, Florida City; tent sites per person $18, dm $35, d $65-80, ste $149-190; 🅿 ❄ 🛜 🏊) Formerly the Everglades International Hostel, the Hoosville has kept the good-value dorms, private rooms and 'semi-privates' (you have an enclosed room within the dorms and share a bathroom with dorm residents). The creatively configured backyard is the best feature. There's a small rock-cut pool with a waterfall and a gazebo.

Gator Grill
AMERICAN $

(☑ 786-243-0620; 36650 SW 192nd Ave, Homestead; mains $9-16; ☺ 11am-6:30pm) A handy pit stop before or after visiting the Everglades National Park, the Gator Grill is a white shack with picnic tables, where you can munch on all manner of alligator dishes. There are gator tacos, gator stir-fry, gator kebabs and straight-up fried alligator served in a basket.

ℹ Information

There are several info centers where you can get tips on attractions, lodging and dining.

Chamber of Commerce (☑ 305-247-2332; www.southdadechamber.org; 455 N Flagler Ave, Homestead; ☺ 9am-5pm Mon-Fri)

Tropical Everglades Visitor Association (www.tropicaleverglades.com; 160 N 1st St, Florida City; ☺ 8am-5pm Mon-Sat, 10am-2pm Sun)

ℹ Getting There & Away

Homestead runs a free weekend **trolley bus service** (☑ 305-224-4457; www.cityofhomestead.com; ☺ Sat & Sun Dec-Apr), which takes

visitors from Losner Park (downtown Homestead) out to the **Royal Palm Visitor Center** (☑ 305-242-7700; www.nps.gov/ever; State Rd 9336; ☺ 9am-4:15pm) in Everglades National Park. It also runs between Losner Park and Biscayne National Park (p491). Call for the latest departure times.

Tamiami Trail

Calle Ocho, in Miami's Little Havana, is the eastern end of the Tamiami Trail/Hwy 41, which cuts through the Everglades to the Gulf of Mexico. So going west along Hwy 41, you may only cross a few dozen miles but you'll feel several different worlds away – this trip leads you into the northern edges of the Everglades, past long landscapes of flooded forest, pine woods, gambling halls, swamp-buggy tours and roadside food shacks.

Airboat tours are an old-school way of seeing the Everglades (and there is something to be said for getting a tour from a raging Skynyrd fan with killer tats and better camo), but there are other ways of exploring the park as well.

◉ Sights & Activities

⭐ Fakahatchee Strand Preserve
PARK

(☑ 239-695-4593; www.floridastateparks.org/parks-and-trails/fakahatchee-strand-preserve-state-park; 137 Coastline Dr, Copeland; vehicle/pedestrian/bicycle $3/2/2; ☺ 8am-sunset; 🅿 🚻) 🍴 The Fakahatchee Strand, besides having a fantastic name, also houses a 20-mile by 5-mile estuarine wetland that looks like something from the beginning of time. A 2000ft boardwalk traverses this wet and wild wonderland, where panthers still stalk their prey amid the black waters. While it's unlikely you'll spot any panthers, there's a great chance you'll see a large variety of blooming orchids, bird life and reptiles ranging in size from tiny skinks to grinning alligators.

Shark Valley Tram Tour
TOURS

(☑ 305-221-8455; www.sharkvalleytramtours.com; adult/child under 12yr/senior $25/19/12.75; ☺ departures 9:30am, 11am, 2pm & 4pm May-Dec, 9am-4pm Jan-Apr hourly on the hour) This excellent two-hour tour runs along a 15-mile asphalt trail allowing you to see copious amounts of alligators in the winter months. Tours are narrated by knowledgeable park rangers who give a fascinating overview of the Everglades.

DETOUR: LOOP ROAD

The 24-mile-long Loop Rd, off Tamiami Trail (Hwy 41), offers some unique sites. One: the homes of the **Miccosukee**, some of which have been considerably expanded by gambling revenue. You'll see some traditional *chickee*-style huts and some trailers with massive add-on wings that are bigger than the original trailer – all seem to have shiny new pickup trucks parked out front. Two: great pull-offs for viewing flooded forests, where egrets that look like pterodactyls perch in the trees, and alligators lurk in the depths below. Three: houses with large Confederate flags and 'Stay off my property' signs; these homes are as much a part of the landscape as the swamp. And four: the short, pleasantly jungly **Tree Snail Hammock Nature Trail**. Though unpaved, the graded road is in good shape and fine for 2WD vehicles. True to its name, the road loops right back onto the Tamiami; expect a leisurely jaunt on the Loop to add an hour or two to your trip.

🛈 Information

Shark Valley Visitor Center (☑ 305-221-8776; www.nps.gov/ever/planyourvisit/svdirections. htm; national park entry per vehicle/bicycle/pedestrian $25/8/8; ⊙ 9am-5pm) A good place to pick up information about the Everglades, including trails, wildlife watching and free ranger-led activities.

Everglades City

On the edge of Chokoloskee Bay, you'll find an Old Florida fishing village of raised houses, turquoise water and scattershot emerald-green mangrove islands. 'City' is stretching it for Everglades City – this is really a friendly fishing town where you can easily lose yourself for a day or three. You'll find some intriguing vestiges of the past here, including an excellent regional museum, as well as delicious seafood.

Hwy 29 runs south through town onto the small, peaceful residential island of Chokoloskee, which has some pretty views over the watery wilderness of the 10,000 Islands. You can arrange boating excursions from either Everglades City or Chokoloskee to explore this pristine environment.

◉ Sights & Activities

★ **Museum of the Everglades** MUSEUM (☑ 239-695-0008; www.evergladesmuseum.org; 105 W Broadway, Everglades City; ⊙ 9am-4pm Mon-Sat; ℗) **FREE** For a break from the outdoors, don't miss this small museum run by volunteers who have a wealth of knowledge on the region's history. Located in the town's former laundry house, the collection delves into human settlement in the area from the early pioneers of the 1800s to the boom days of the 1920s and its tragic moments (Hurricane Donna devastated the town in 1960), and subsequent transformation into the quiet backwater of today.

10,000 Islands ISLAND

One of the best ways to experience the serenity of the Everglades – somehow desolate yet lush, tropical and forbidding – is by paddling the network of waterways that skirt the northwest portion of the park. The 10,000 Islands consist of many (but not really 10,000) tiny islands and a mangrove swamp that hugs the southwestern-most border of Florida.

Everglades Adventures CANOEING (☑ 877-567-0679; www.evergladesadventures.com; 107 Camellia St, Everglades City; 3-4hr tours from $99, canoe/kayak rental per day from $30/50) 🛶 For a real taste of the Everglades, nothing beats getting out on the water. This highly recommended outfitter offers a range of half-day kayak tours, from sunrise paddles to twilight trips through mangroves that return under a sky full of stars. Tours shuttle you to places like Chokoloskee Island, Collier-Seminole State Park, Rabbit Key or Tiger Key for excursions.

🛏 Sleeping & Eating

Outdoor Resorts of Chokoloskee MOTEL $ (☑ 239-695-2881; www.outdoorresortsofchokolo skee.com; 150 Smallwood Dr, Chokoloskee; r $119; ❄ 🏊) At the northern end of Chokoloskee Island, this good-value place is a big draw for its extensive facilities, including several swimming pools, hot tubs, tennis and shuffleboard courts, a fitness center and boat rentals. The fairly basic motel-style rooms have kitchenettes and a back deck overlooking the marina.

Everglades City Motel
MOTEL **$$**

(☑239-695-4224; www.evergladescitymotel.com; 310 Collier Ave, Everglades City; r $150-250; P❄🖥) With large rooms that have all the mod cons (flat-screen TVs, fridge, coffeemaker) and friendly staff who can hook you up with boat tours, this motel provides good value for those looking to spend some time near the 10,000 Islands.

★ Havana Cafe
LATIN AMERICAN **$$**

(☑239-695-2214; www.havanacafeoftheevergla des.com; 191 Smallwood Dr, Chokoloskee; mains lunch $10-19, dinner $22-30; ⏱7am-3pm Mon-Thu, to 8pm Fri & Sat, closed mid-Apr–mid-Oct) This cafe is famed far and wide for its deliciously prepared seafood served with Latin accents. Lunch favorites include stone-crab enchiladas, blackened grouper with rice and beans, and a decadent Cuban sandwich. The outdoor dining amid palm trees and vibrant bougainvillea – not to mention the incredibly friendly service – adds to the appeal.

Oyster House
SEAFOOD **$$**

(☑239-695-2073; www.oysterhouserestaurant. com; 901 Copeland Ave, Everglades City; mains lunch $12-18, dinner $19-30; ⏱11am-9pm Sun-Thu, to 10pm Fri & Sat; 🅿♿) Besides serving the Everglades staples of excellent seafood (oysters, crab, grouper, cobia, lobster), this buzzing, family-run spot serves alligator dishes (tacos, jambalaya, fried platters) and simpler baskets (burgers, fried seafood), plus not-to-be-missed desserts. The cabin-like interior is decorated with vintage knickknacks and taxidermy, which might make you feel like you're in the deep woods.

❶ Information

Everglades Area Chamber of Commerce
(☑239-695-3941; cnr Hwys 41 & 29; ⏱9am-4pm) General information about the region is available here.

❶ Getting There & Away

There is no public transportation out this way. If driving, it's a fairly straight 85-mile drive west from Miami. The trip takes about 1¾ hours in good traffic.

Florida Keys

If Florida is a state apart from the USA, the Keys are islands apart from Florida – in other words, it's different down here. This is a place for those escaping everyday life on the mainland. You'll find about 113 mangrove-and-sandbar islands where the white sun melts over deep green mangroves; long, soft mudflats and tidal bars; teal waters and a bunch of charming polite society castaways. Key West is still defined by its motto – One Human Family – an ideal that equals a tolerant, accepting ethos where anything goes and life is always a party (or at least a hungover day after). The color scheme: watercolor pastels cooled by breezes on a sunset-kissed Bahamian porch. Welcome to the End of the USA.

❶ Information

The Monroe County Tourist Development Council's Florida Keys & Key West Visitors Bureau runs an excellent website (www.fla-keys.com), which is packed with information on everything the Keys has to offer.

Check www.keysnews.com for good daily online news and information about the islands.

❶ Getting There & Away

Getting here can be half the fun – or, if you're unlucky, a whopping dose of frustration. Imagine a tropical-island hop, from one bar-studded mangrove islet to the next, via one of the most remarkable roads in the world: the Overseas Hwy (Hwy 1). On a good day, driving along the Overseas with the windows down – the wind in your face and the twin sisters of Florida Bay and the Atlantic stretching on either side – is the US road trip in tropical perfection. On a bad day, you end up sitting in gridlock behind some guy who is riding a midlife-crisis Harley.

Greyhound (www.greyhound.com) buses serve all Keys destinations along Hwy 1 and depart from Downtown Miami and Key West; you can pick up a bus along the way by standing on the Overseas Hwy and flagging one down. If you fly into Fort Lauderdale or Miami, the **Keys Shuttle** (☑888-765-9997; www.keysshuttle. com) provides door-to-door service to most of the Keys ($70/80/90 to the Upper and Middle Keys/Lower Keys/Key West). Reserve at least a day in advance.

Key Largo

We're not going to lie: Key Largo (both the name of the town and the island it's on) is slightly underwhelming at a glance. 'Under' is the key word, as its main sights are under the water – including a hotel. As you drive onto the islands, Key Largo resembles a long line of low-lying hammock and strip development. But head down a side road and duck into this warm little bar, or that converted Keys plantation house, and the island idiosyncrasies become more pronounced.

The 33-mile-long Largo, which starts at Mile Marker 106, is the longest island in the Keys, and those 33 miles have attracted a lot of marine life, all accessible from the biggest concentration of dive sites in the islands. The town of Tavernier (Mile Marker 93) is just south of the town of Key Largo.

◉ Sights & Activities

John Pennekamp
Coral Reef State Park   STATE PARK
(☎305-451-6300; www.pennekamppark.com; Mile 102.6 oceanside; car with 1/2 people $4.50/9, cyclist or pedestrian $2.50; ⊗8am-sunset, aquarium to 5pm; P⋒) ✦ John Pennekamp has the singular distinction of being the first underwater park in the USA. There's 170 acres of dry parkland here and over 48,000 acres (75 sq miles) of wet: the vast majority of the protected area is the ocean. Before you get out in that water, be sure to take in some pleasant beaches and stroll over the nature trails.

Laura Quinn Wild
Bird Sanctuary   WILDLIFE RESERVE
(☎305-852-4486; www.keepthemflying.org; 93600 Overseas Hwy, Mile 93.6; donations accepted; ⊗sunrise-sunset; P⋒) ✦ This 7-acre sanctuary serves as a protected refuge for a wide variety of injured birds. A boardwalk leads through various enclosures where you can learn a bit about some of the permanent residents – those unable to be released back in the wild. The species here include masked boobies, great horned owls, green herons, brown pelicans, double-crested cormorants and others. Keep walking along the path to reach a nice vista of Florida Bay and a wading bird pond.

African Queen   BOATING
(☎305-451-8080; www.africanqueenflkeys.com; Key Largo Holiday Inn, 99701 Overseas Hwy; canal/dinner cruises $49/89) The steamboat used in the 1951 movie starring Humphrey Bogart and Katharine Hepburn has been restored to its former splendor. It was built in England, in 1912, and used in Africa to transport goods, missionaries and hunters, before becoming a movie star. The boat was brought to the US in 1968 and registered as a National Historic Site.

Garl's Coastal Kayaking   ECOTOUR
(☎305-393-3223; www.garlscoastalkayaking.com; 4hr tours adult/child $75/50, single/double kayak hire per day $40/55) ✦ Garl's is an excellent ecotour operator that gets customers into the Everglades backcountry and mangrove islets of Florida Bay via kayak and canoe. It also provides reasonable equipment rentals.

🛏 Sleeping & Eating

Hilton Key Largo Resort   HOTEL $$
(☎305-852-5553; www.keylargoresort.com; Mile 102 bayside; r/ste from $200/280; P⋒❄) This Hilton has a ton of character. Folks just seem to get all laid-back when lounging in clean, designer rooms outfitted in blues and greens with balconies overlooking the water. The grounds are enormous and include an artificial waterfall-fed pool and frontage to a rather large stretch of private white-sand beach. Book online for the best rates.

Jules' Undersea Lodge   HOTEL $$$
(☎305-451-2353; www.jul.com; 51 Shoreland Dr, Mile 103.2 oceanside; s/d/tr $675/800/1050) If you fancy diving to your hotel, this place is for you. Once a research station, this module has been converted into a delightfully cheesy Keys motel, but wetter. In addition to two private guest rooms, there are common rooms, a kitchen-dining room and a wet room with hot showers and gear storage. Telephones and an intercom connect guests with the surface.

DJ's Diner   AMERICAN $
(☎305-451-2999; 99411 Overseas Hwy; mains $8-15; ⊗7am-3pm; P⋒) You're greeted by a mural of Humphrey Bogart, James Dean and Marilyn Monroe – that's a lot of Americana. It's all served with a heapin' helpin' of diner faves amid vinyl-boothed ambience. Breakfast is a big draw with fluffy omelets, eggs Benedict and waffles (including a key lime pie version). Stop in later for sandwiches, burgers and seafood (fish tacos, crab cakes, conch fritters).

Fish House   SEAFOOD $$
(☎305-451-4665; www.fishhouse.com; Mile 102.4 oceanside; mains lunch $12-21, dinner $21-30; ⊗11:30am-10pm; P⋒) The Fish House delivers on the promise of its title – very good fish, bought from local fishers and prepared fried, broiled, jerked, blackened or chargrilled. Because the Fish House only uses fresh fish, the menu changes daily based on what is available.

Islamorada

Islamorada (is-luh-murr-*ah*-da) is also known as 'The Village of Islands.' A beautiful string of pearls, or rather, six keys – Plantation, Upper and Lower Matecumbe, Shell and Lignumvitae (lignum-*vite*-ee) – shimmers as one of the prettiest stretches of the islands. The scrubby mangrove is replaced by unbroken horizons of ocean and sky, one perfect shade of blue mirroring the other. Islamorada stretches across some 20 miles, from Mile Marker 90 to Mile Marker 74.

⊙ Sights & Activities

★ Florida Keys
History of Diving Museum   MUSEUM
(✆305-664-9737; www.divingmuseum.org; Mile 83; adult/child $12/6; ⊙10am-5pm, 10am-6:45pm 3rd Wed of month; P🚻) You can't miss the diving museum – it's the building with the enormous mural of whale sharks on the side. The journey into the undersea covers 4000 years, with fascinating pieces like the 1797 Klingert's copper kettle, a whimsical room devoted to Jules Verne's Captain Nemo, massive deep-diving suits and an exquisite display of diving helmets from around the world. These imaginative galleries reflect the charming quirks of the Keys.

Windley Key Fossil
Reef Geological State Site   STATE PARK
(✆305-664-2540; www.floridastateparks.org/parks-and-trails/windley-key-fossil-reef-geological-state-park; Mile 85.5 oceanside; admission $2.50, tour $2; ⊙8am-5pm Thu-Mon) To get his railroad built across the islands, Henry Flagler had to quarry out some sizable chunks of the Keys. The best evidence of those efforts can be found at this former quarry-turned-state park. Windley has leftover quarry machinery scattered along an 8ft former quarry wall, with fossilized evidence of brain and staghorn coral embedded right in the rock. The wall offers a cool (and rare) public peek into the stratum of coral that forms the substrate of the Keys.

★ Robbie's Marina   BOATING
(✆305-664-8070; https://robbies.com; Mile 77.5 bayside; kayak & stand-up paddleboard rentals $45-80; ⊙9am-8pm; 🚻) Robbie's covers all bases – it's a local flea market, tacky tourist shop, sea pen for tarpons (massive fish) and jumping-off point for fishing expeditions, all wrapped into one driftwood-laced compound. Boat-rental and tour options are also available. The best reason to visit is to escape the mayhem and hire a kayak for a peaceful paddle through nearby mangroves, hammocks and lagoons.

🛏 Sleeping & Eating

Conch On Inn   MOTEL $
(✆305-852-9309; 103 Caloosa St, Mile 89.5; r $100-180; P🛜) A motel popular with yearly snowbirds, Conch On Inn has simple but cheerfully painted rooms that are clean, comfortable and well equipped. The waterfront deck is a fine spot to unwind – and look for manatees; up to 14 have been spotted off the dock here!

Lime Tree Bay Resort Motel   MOTEL $$
(✆305-664-4740; www.limetreebayresort.com; Mile 68.5 bayside; r $180-360; 🅿🛜🌊) Hammocks and lawn chairs provide front-row seats for the spectacular sunsets at this 2.5-acre waterfront hideaway. The rooms are comfortable, airy and elegant, with wood floors and decorative rope details – the best have balconies overlooking the water. The extensive facilities include use of tennis courts, bikes, kayaks and stand-up paddleboards.

Bad Boy Burrito   MEXICAN $
(✆305-509-7782; 103 Mastic St, Mile 81.8 bayside; mains $8-15; ⊙10am-6pm Mon-Sat; ✔) Tucked away in a tiny plaza among a gurgling fountain, orchids and swaying palms, Bad Boy Burrito whips up superb fish tacos and its namesake burritos – with quality ingredients (skirt steak, duck confit, zucchini and squash) and all the fixings (shaved cabbage, chipotle mayo, housemade salsa). Top it off with a hibiscus tea and some chips and guacamole.

★ Lazy Days   SEAFOOD $$
(✆305-664-5256; www.lazydaysislamorada.com; 79867 Overseas Hwy, oceanside; mains $18-34; ⊙11am-11pm Mon-Sat, to 10pm Sun; 🅿🚻) One of Islamorada's culinary icons, Lazy Days has a stellar reputation for its fresh seafood plates. Start off with a conch chowder topped with a little sherry (provided), before moving on to a decadent hogfish Poseidon (fish topped with shrimp, scallops and key lime butter) or a straight-up boiled seafood platter (half lobster, shrimp, catch of the day and other delicacies).

Marathon

Marathon sits right on the halfway point between Key Largo and Key West, and it's a good place to stop on a road trip across the islands. Outside Key West, it's perhaps the most 'developed' key (though that might be pushing the definition of the word 'developed') – it has large shopping centers and a population of more than 8000. It's still a place where exiles from the mainland fish, booze it up and have a good time though, so while Marathon is more family-friendly than Key West, it's maintained its wild side.

Sleeping & Eating

Seascape Motel & Marina MOTEL $$$
(305-743-6212; www.seascapemotelandmarina.com; 1075 75th St Ocean E, btwn Mile 51 & 52; r $250-550; P ❄ 📶 🏊) The understated luxury in this B&B manifests in its 12 rooms, with their minimalist and sleek decor. There is a waterfront pool, kayaks and stand-up paddleboards for guests to use, and its secluded setting will make you feel like you've gotten away from it all. Seascape also hosts afternoon wine and snacks (included).

Tranquility Bay RESORT $$$
(305-289-0667; www.tranquilitybay.com; Mile 48.5 bayside; r $340-700; P ❄ 📶 🏊) If you're serious about going upscale, you should book in here. Tranquility Bay is a massive condo-hotel resort with plush townhouses, high-thread-count sheets and all-in-white chic – the beach is just steps away from your bed. The grounds are enormous and activity-filled; they really don't want you to leave.

★ **Keys Fisheries** SEAFOOD $$
(866-743-4353; www.keysfisheries.com; 3502 Louisa St; mains $12-27; 11am-9pm; P 👪) The lobster Reuben is the stuff of legend. Sweet, chunky, creamy – so good you'll be daydreaming about it afterward. But you can't go wrong with any of the excellent seafood here, all served with sass. Expect some seagull harassment as you dine on a working waterfront.

Lower Keys

The people of the Lower Keys vary between winter escapees and native Conchs. Some local families have been Keys castaways for generations, and there is somewhat of a more insular feel than other parts of the Overseas Hwy. The islands get at their most isolated, rural and quintessentially 'Keez-y' before opening onto (relatively) cosmopolitan, heterogeneous and free-spirited Key West.

People aside, the big draw in the lower Keys is nature. You'll find the loveliest state park in the Keys here, and one of its rarest species. For paddlers, there is a great mangrove wilderness to explore in a photogenic and pristine environment.

★ **Bahia Honda State Park** STATE PARK
(305-872-3210; www.bahiahondapark.com; Mile 37; car $4-8, cyclist & pedestrian $2.50; 8am-sunset; 👪) 🌿 This park, with its long, white-sand (and at times seaweed-strewn) beach, named Sandspur Beach by locals, is the big attraction in these parts. As Keys beaches go, this one is probably the best natural stretch of sand in the island chain. There's also the novel experience of walking on the **old Bahia Honda Rail Bridge**, which offers nice views of the surrounding islands. Heading out on kayaking adventures (from $12/36 per hour/half day) is another great way to spend a sun-drenched afternoon.

Key West

Key West is the far frontier, edgier and more eccentric than the other Keys, and also far more captivating. At its heart, this 7-sq-mile island feels like a beautiful tropical oasis, where the moonflowers bloom at night and the classical Caribbean homes are so sad and romantic it's hard not to sigh at them.

While Key West has obvious allure, it's not without its contradictions. On one side of the road, there are literary festivals, Caribbean villas, tropical dining rooms and expensive art galleries. On the other, an S&M fetishist parade, frat boys passing out on the sidewalk and grizzly bars filled with bearded burnouts. With all that in mind, it's easy to find your groove in this setting, no matter where your interests lie.

As in other parts of the Keys, nature plays a starring role here, with some breathtaking sunsets – cause for nightly celebration down on Mallory Sq.

Sights

★ **Museum of Art & History at the Custom House** MUSEUM
(305-295-6616; www.kwahs.com; 281 Front St; adult/child $10/5; 9:30am-4:30pm) This excellent museum, set in a grand 1891 red-brick building that once served as the Customs House, covers Key West's history. Highlights are the archival footage from the building of the ambitious Overseas Hwy (and the hurricane that killed 400 people), a model of the ill-fated USS *Maine* (sunk during the Spanish-American War) and the Navy's role in Key West (once the largest employer), and the 'wreckers' of Key West, who scavenged sunken treasure ships.

★ Mallory Square
SQUARE

(www.mallorysquare.com; 🚐) Take all those energies, subcultures and oddities of Keys life and focus them into one torchlit, family-friendly (but playfully edgy), sunset-enriched street party. The result of all these raucous forces is Mallory Sq, one of the greatest shows on earth that starts in the hours leading up to dusk, the sinking sun a signal to bring on the madness. Watch a dog walk a tightrope, a man swallow fire, and British acrobats tumble and sass each other.

Duval Street
AREA

Key West locals have a love-hate relationship with the most famous road in Key West (if not the Keys). Duval, Old Town Key West's main strip, is a miracle mile of booze, tacky everything and awful behavior – but it's a lot of fun. The 'Duval Crawl' is one of the wildest pub crawls in the country. The mix of neon drink, drag shows, T-shirt kitsch, local theaters, art studios and boutiques is more charming and entertaining than jarring.

Hemingway House
NOTABLE BUILDING

(☎ 305-294-1136; www.hemingwayhome.com; 907 Whitehead St; adult/child $14/6; ⏰ 9am-5pm) Key West's biggest darling, Ernest Hemingway, lived in this gorgeous Spanish Colonial house from 1931 to 1940. Papa moved here in his early 1930s with his second wife, a *Vogue* fashion editor and (former) friend of his first wife (he left the house when he ran off with his third wife). *The Short Happy Life of Francis Macomber* and *The Green Hills of Africa* were produced here, as well as many cats, whose descendants basically run the grounds.

🏃 Activities

Dive Key West
DIVING

(☎ 305-296-3823; www.divekeywest.com; 3128 N Roosevelt Blvd; snorkel/scuba from $69/95) Largest dive facility on the island, offering morning, afternoon and night dives. Wreck-diving trips cost $145 with all equipment and air provided (it's $160 with a wetsuit). The rate for snorkelers is $69.

☞ Tours

Old Town Trolley Tours
TOURS

(☎ 855-623-8289; www.trolleytours.com; adult/child $37/14; ⏰ tours 9am-4:30pm; 🚐) These tours are a great introduction to the city, providing a good overview of Key West history. The 90-minute, hop-on, hop-off narrated tram tour starts at Mallory Sq and makes a loop around the whole city, with 12 stops along the way. Trolleys depart every 15 to 30 minutes.

★☆ Festivals & Events

Womenfest
LGBTIQ+

(http://gaykeywestfl.com/womenfest; ⏰ Sep) One of North America's biggest lesbian celebrations, Womenfest is four days of merrymaking, with pool parties, art shows, roller derby, drag brunches, sunset sails, flag football, and a tattoo and moustache bicycle ride. It's great fun, with thousands descending on Key West from all corners of the USA and beyond.

★ Fantasy Fest
CULTURAL

(https://fantasyfest.com; ⏰ late Oct) Akin to New Orleans' riotous Mardi Gras revelry, Fantasy Fest is 10 days of burlesque parties, parades, street fairs, concerts and loads of costumed events. Bars and inns get competitive about decorating their properties, and everyone gets decked out in the most outrageous costumes they can cobble together (or get mostly naked with daring body paint).

🛏 Sleeping

Key West Youth Hostel & Seashell Motel
HOSTEL $$

(☎ 305-296-5719; www.keywesthostel.com; 718 South St; dm from $55, d $120-325; 🅿 ❄ 🛜) This place isn't winning any design awards, but the staff are kind, and it's one of the only lower-priced choices on the island. The dorms and rooms have white tile floors, with the cheery paint job (yellow in dorms and blue and white in doubles) somewhat breaking up the monotony. The back patio is a fine place to meet other travelers.

Casablanca Key West
GUESTHOUSE $$

(☎ 305-296-0815; www.keywestcasablanca.com; 900 Duval St; r $145-725; ❄ 🛜 🌊) On the quieter end of Duval St, the Casablanca is a friendly guesthouse with eight bright rooms, all with polished wood floors and comfy beds; some have small balconies. This lush, tropical and elegant inn, once a private house, was built in 1898. It has hosted a few luminaries, including Humphrey Bogart, who stayed here in 1937.

The open-sided terrace just above the street is perfect for afternoon drinks and snacks.

Saint Hotel BOUTIQUE HOTEL **$$$**
(☏305-294-3200; www.sainthotels.com/key-west; 417 Eaton St; r $360-700; ❄☎☂) Despite its proximity to Duval St, the Saint feels like a world removed with its plush rooms – that play with the ideas of 'Saint' and 'Sinner' – chic minimalist lobby, photogenic pool with small cascading waterfall, and artfully designed bar. The best rooms have balconies overlooking the pool. Book well in advance.

🍴 Eating

Pierogi Polish Market EASTERN EUROPEAN **$**
(☏305-292-0464; www.facebook.com/Pierogi PolishMarket; 1008 White St; mains $5-11; ☺pierogi counter 11am-7pm Mon-Sat, shop 10am-8pm Mon-Sat, noon-6pm Sun; P♿) The Keys have an enormous seasonal population of temporary workers largely drawn from Central and Eastern Europe. This is where those workers can revisit the motherland, via pierogies, dumplings, blinis and a great sandwich selection. Although it's called a Polish market, there's food here that caters to Hungarians, Czechs and Russians (among others). They do takeout and delivery, too.

Garbo's Grill FUSION **$**
(www.garbosgrillkw.com; 409 Caroline St; mains $10-14; ☺11am-10pm Mon-Sat, noon-6pm Sun) Just off the beaten path, Garbo's whips up delicious tacos with creative toppings like mango ginger habanero-glazed shrimp, Korean barbecue, and fresh mahimahi with all the fixings, as well as gourmet burgers and hot dogs. It's served out of a sleek Airstream trailer, which faces onto a shaded brick patio dotted with outdoor tables.

The Café VEGETARIAN **$$**
(☏305-296-5515; www.thecafekw.com; 509 Southard St; mains $12-22; ☺9am-10pm; ♿) The oldest vegetarian spot in Key West is a sunny luncheonette by day that morphs into a buzzing, low-lit eating and drinking spot by night. The cooking is outstanding, with an eclectic range of dishes: Thai curry stir-fries, Italian veggie meatball subs, pizza with shaved Brussels sprouts, and a famous veggie burger.

★Thirsty Mermaid SEAFOOD **$$**
(☏305-204-4828; www.thirstymermaidkeywest. com; 521 Fleming St; mains $12-28; ☺11am-11:30pm; ♿) The lovely Thirsty Mermaid serves outstanding seafood in an elegant, easygoing space. The menu is a collection of sea-life culinary treasures such as an oyster bar, ceviche, middleneck clams and caviar. Among the main courses, seared diver scallops or togarashi-spiced tuna with jasmine rice are outstanding. There are also luxurious sandwiches with lobster, fried oysters or local snapper fillings.

★Blue Heaven AMERICAN **$$$**
(☏305-296-8666; www.blueheavenkw.com; 729 Thomas St; mains breakfast & lunch $10-19, dinner $22-35; ☺8am-10:30pm; ♿) This is one of the quirkiest venues on an island of oddities – customers, together with free-ranging fowl, flock to dine in the ramshackle, tropical plant-filled garden where Hemingway once officiated boxing matches. This place gets packed with customers who come for the delectable breakfasts (blueberry pancakes) and Keys cuisine with French touches (like yellowtail snapper with citrus *beurre blanc*).

🍸 Drinking & Entertainment

★Green Parrot BAR
(☏305-294-6133; www.greenparrot.com; 601 Whitehead St; ☺10am-4am) The oldest bar on an island of bars – 'A sunny place for shady people' being one of its mottos – this rogues' cantina opened in the late 19th century and keeps going. Its ramshackle interior, with local artwork on the walls and a parachute stretched across the ceiling, only adds to the atmosphere, as does the fun-loving, colorful crowd.

Captain Tony's Saloon BAR
(☏305-294-1838; www.capttonyssaloon.com; 428 Greene St; ☺10am-2am) Propagandists would have you believe the nearby megabar complex of Sloppy Joe's was Hemingway's original bar, but the physical place where the old man famously drank was right here, the original Sloppy Joe's location (before it was moved onto Duval St and into frat-boy hell). Hemingway's third wife (a journalist sent to profile Papa) seduced him in this very bar.

Irish Kevin's BAR
(☏305-292-1262; www.irishkevins.com; 211 Duval St; ☺10am-3:30am) One of the most popular megabars on Duval, Kevin's has a pretty good entertainment formula pinned down: nightly live acts that are a cross between a folk singer, radio shock jock and peprally cheerleader. The crowd consistently goes wild for acoustic covers of favorites from 1980 onward mixed with boozy, Lee Greenwoodesque patriotic exhortations.

La Te Da CABARET

(☎ 305-296-6706; www.lateda.com; 1125 Duval St; tickets $33; ⊙ shows 8:30pm) While the outside bar is where locals gather for mellow chats over beer, you can catch high-quality drag acts – big names come here from around the country – upstairs at the fabulous Crystal Room on weekends. More low-key cabaret acts grace the downstairs lounge. The Sunday tea dance – an afternoon dance party (4pm to 7pm) by the pool – is great fun.

ℹ️ Information

Citizen (www.keysnews.com) A well-written, oft-amusing daily.

Key West Chamber of Commerce (☎ 305-294-2587; www.keywestchamber.org; 510 Greene St; ⊙ 9am-6pm) An excellent source of information.

Key Wester (http://thekeywester.com) Restaurant reviews and upcoming events.

ℹ️ Getting Around

Once you're in Key West, the best way to get around is by bicycle (rentals from the Duval St area, hotels and hostels cost from $10 a day). For transportation within the Duval St area, the free Duval Loop shuttle (www.carfreekeywest.com/duval-loop) runs from 6pm to midnight.

Other options include **Key West Transit** (☎ 305-600-1455; www.kwtransit.com; day pass $4-8) with color-coded buses running about every 15 minutes; mopeds, which generally cost from $35 per day ($60 for a two-seater); or the open-sided electric tourist cars, aka 'Conch cruisers,' which travel at 35mph and cost about $140/200 for a four-/six-seater per day.

A&M Scooter Rentals (☎ 305-896-1921; www.amscooterskeywest.com; 523 Truman Ave; bicycle/scooter/electric car per day from $10/35/140; ⊙ 9am-7pm) rents out scooters and bicycles, as well as open-sided electric cars that can seat two to six people, and offers free delivery.

Parking can be tricky in town. There's a free parking lot on Fort St off Truman Ave.

ATLANTIC COAST

Florida's northern Atlantic Coast – known as the 'First Coast' thanks to its early colonization – is a land of long beaches shadowed by tall condo complexes and seaside mansions, serving as an exurb riviera for the Southern USA. Heading from south to north, you'll pass the exhaust pipes and biker bars of Daytona Beach, continue through mellow Flagler Beach, and on to historic St Augustine, where a one- or two-night sojourn is highly recommended.

An affluent series of beaches can be found just south of spread-out Jacksonville, which forms an urban break in the coastal living; many continue north from here to charming Amelia Island and the Florida–Georgia border. Along the way you'll discover a jumbled necklace of grassy barrier islands, interlaced with tidal inlets, salt marsh flats and dark clumps of maritime forest.

Space Coast

More than 40 miles of barrier-island Atlantic Coast stretch from Canaveral National Seashore south to Melbourne Beach, encompassing undeveloped stretches of endless white sand, an entrenched surf culture and pockets of Old Florida.

The Kennedy Space Center and several small museums dedicated to the history, heroes and science of the United States' space program give the Space Coast its name, and the region's tourist hub of Cocoa Beach is just south of Cape Canaveral's launching point for massive cruise ships. But beyond the 3D space movies, tiki-hut bars and surf shops, the Space Coast offers quintessential Florida wildlife for everyone from toddlers to seniors. Kayak with manatees, camp on a private island or simply stroll along miles and miles of sandy white beaches – it's easy to find a quiet spot.

◉ Sights & Activities

★**Kennedy Space Center** MUSEUM
(☎ 866-737-5235; www.kennedyspacecenter.com; NASA Pkwy, State Rd 405, Merritt Island; adult/child 3-11yr $61/50; ⊙ 9am-6pm, to 8pm for special events) Whether you're mildly interested in space or a die-hard sci-fi fan, a visit to the Kennedy Space Center is awe inspiring. To get a good overview, start at the Early Space Exploration exhibit, progress to the 90-minute bus tour to the Apollo/Saturn V Center (where you'll find the best on-site cafe) and finish at the awesome *Atlantis* exhibit, where you can walk beneath the heat-scorched fuselage of a shuttle that traveled more than 126,000,000 miles through space on 33 missions.

★**Merritt Island**
National Wildlife Refuge WILDLIFE RESERVE
(☎ 321-861-5601; www.fws.gov/merrittisland; Black Point Wildlife Dr, off FL 406; vehicle $10; ⊙ dawn-dusk) **FREE** This unspoiled 140,000-acre refuge is one of the country's best birding

spots, especially from October to May (early morning and after 4pm). More endangered and threatened species of wildlife inhabit the swamps, marshes and hardwood hammocks here than at any other site in the continental US. The best viewing is on **Black Point Wildlife Drive** (off FL-406; per vehicle $10; ⏱ sunrise-sunset).

Canaveral National Seashore NATIONAL PARK
(🖉 headquarters 321-267-1110, visitors center 386-428-3384; www.nps.gov/cana; car/bike/pedestrian $15/5/5; ⏱ 6am-8pm Mar-Nov, to 6pm Dec-Feb) The 24 miles of pristine, windswept beaches here comprise the longest stretch of undeveloped beach on Florida's east coast. They include family-friendly **Apollo Beach** on the north end with its gentle surf, untrammeled **Klondike Beach** in the middle – a favorite of nature lovers – and **Playalinda Beach** to the south, which is surfer central and includes a nudist section near lot 13.

Sea-Turtle Nesting Tours ECOTOUR
(🖉 386-428-3384; adult/child 8-16yr $15/free; ⏱ 8pm-midnight Jun & Jul) In the summer, rangers lead groups of up to 30 people on these nightly tours, with about a 75% chance of spotting the little guys. Reservations are required (beginning May 15 for June trips, June 15 for July trips); children under eight years are not allowed.

🛏 Sleeping

★ Beach Place Guesthouses APARTMENT $$
(🖉 321-783-4045; www.beachplaceguesthouses.com; 1445 S Atlantic Ave; ste $199-399; P⊖❋🛜) A slice of heavenly relaxation in Cocoa Beach's partying beach scene, this laid-back two-story guesthouse has roomy suites with hammocks and a lovely deck, all just steps from the dunes and beach. Colorful art and greenery abound on the property. No pets.

Fawlty Towers MOTEL $$
(🖉 321-784-3870; 100 E Cocoa Beach Causeway; r $99-250; P⊖❋🛜🏊) It's all about location, location, location. This motel is gloriously garish and extremely pink: unmissable. It has clean, non-fancy rooms with an unbeatable beachside location, a quiet pool and a BYOB tiki hut. Sometimes a decent room is what you need.

Residence Inn Cape Canaveral HOTEL $$$
(🖉 321-323-1100; www.marriott.com; 8959 Astronaut Blvd; r $240-300; P❋🛜🏊) If you want to get away from the Cocoa Beach party scene, book into this comfortable Marriott

hotel. Rooms may be corporate, but they offer acres of space, comfortable beds and kitchenettes. Staff are also extremely accommodating and there's a pretty pool area. Park-n-cruise packages are popular. The big astronaut in the lobby makes it fun for kids.

🍴 Eating

Melbourne Beach Market MARKET $
(🖉 321-676-5225; 302 Ocean Ave; ⏱ 8am-8pm Mon-Sat, to 7pm Sun) Pick up picnic essentials here, including ready-to-eat Greek and Italian meals.

★ Green Room Cafe VEGETARIAN $
(🖉 321-868-0203; www.greenroomcafecocoa beach.com; 222 N 1st St; mains $7-13; ⏱ 10:30am-9pm Mon-Sat; 🖉) Focusing all its energies on the 'goodness within,' this super cafe delights the health-conscious with fruit-combo acai bowls, wheat- and gluten-free sandwiches, real fruit smoothies, and homemade soups and wraps. If the 'Tower of Power' smoothie (acai, peach, strawberry, honey and apple juice) fails to lift you, the vibrant decor and friendly company will.

Those who don't surf might wonder at the name, which comes from the chamber of green water one finds when inside the barrel of a wave. Eco-minded folk will appreciate their no straws policy.

Seafood Atlantic SEAFOOD $$
(🖉 321-784-1963; www.seafoodatlantic.org; 520 Glen Cheek Dr, Port Canaveral; mains $8-19; ⏱ 11am-7pm Wed-Sun, seafood market from 10am) With deep roots in Canaveral's fishing industry, this restaurant (with outdoor deck) is one of the few places to serve locally sourced shrimp, crabs, mussels, clams, oysters and fish. If they're in, order a bucket of Florida's deep-sea golden crab, which has a deliciously moist and creamy texture. Also, bring a bag and stock up at the market next door.

If you've been missing the swampy taste of Florida gator, they have that too. Plus, you can take home recipe cards for popular items.

ℹ Information

Canaveral National Seashore Visitor Information Center (🖉 386-428-3384; www.nps.gov/cana; 7611 S Atlantic Ave, New Smyrna; ⏱ 8am-6pm Oct-Mar, to 8pm Apr-Sep) is located just south of the North District entrance gate. Alternatively, the visitor center at Merritt Island National Wildlife Refuge can also provide information.

FLORIDA SPACE COAST

There is a fee station at both the North and South District entrances. There is a toilet at most beach parking areas.

Note that the park can experience temporary closures around launch time. For information on launch closures, call ☑ 321-867-4077.

❶ Getting There & Away

Orlando Melbourne International Airport (☑ 321-723-6227; www.mlbair.com; 1 Air Terminal Pkwy) is the closest airport to most destinations on the Space Coast. It is a growing airport served by Delta, American Airlines, Elite Airways, Porter Airlines and Baer, as well as all the major rental-car companies and SCAT bus 21.

Alternatively, Orlando International Airport is about 50 minutes west of Cocoa Beach, and Orlando Sanford International Airport is a little over an hour to the northwest of Cocoa Beach.

There are two ways to arrive in Cape Canaveral: traveling north on A1A from Cocoa Beach, or west on A1A across the Banana River via Merritt Island.

Cape Canaveral is served by **SCAT** (SCAT; ☑ 321-633-1878; www.321transit.com; per ride $1.50, 10-ride/30-day pass $12/42; ⊙ schedule varies) buses. Rte 9 connects it with Cocoa Beach and Rte 4 connects it with Cocoa Village.

Daytona Beach

Long the vacation destination of choice for leather-clad bikers, rev heads and spring breakers, Daytona Beach is most famous as the birthplace of NASCAR racing and the home of the Daytona 500.

The area's population quintuples during Speedweeks; as many as half a million bikers roar into town for **Bike Week** in March and **Biketoberfest** in October. If Confederate flags, loud motorcycles, jacked-up pickup trucks and the folks who love all of the above are your thing, you might have found your heaven on earth. If not, move on.

If you can see past the garish beachside barricade of '70s high-rise blocks, nightclubs and tourist traps (if not quite literally), you might witness the phenomena of nesting sea turtles (in season) or explore a handful of interesting and worthwhile cultural attractions.

◉ Sights & Activities

★ Daytona International Speedway

STADIUM

(☑ 800-748-7467; www.daytonainternationalspeedway.com; 1801 W International Speedway Blvd; tours from $23; ⊙ tours 9:30am-3:30pm) The Holy Grail of raceways has a diverse race schedule. Ticket prices skyrocket for good seats at big races, headlined by the **Daytona 500** in February. It's worth wandering the massive stands for free on non-race days. First-come, first-served tram tours take in the track, pits and behind-the-scenes areas, while all-access tours give you a glimpse of media rooms and pit stalls.

Southeast Museum of Photography

MUSEUM

(☑ 386-506-3894; www.smponline.org; 1200 W International Speedway Blvd, Bldg 1200; ⊙ 11am-5pm Tue, Thu & Fri, to 6pm Wed, from 1pm Sat & Sun) **FREE** We love this hidden treasure in Daytona, a service of the Daytona State College: it's the only museum in Florida dedicated solely to photography. This vibrant modern gallery with excellent lighting and facilities doesn't shy away from provocative subjects in its rotating exhibitions. Best of all, it's free (though donations are welcome)!

NASCAR Racing Experience

DRIVING

(☑ 740-886-2400; www.nascarracingexperience.com; 1801 W International Speedway Blvd; from $149, discounts online; ⊙ dates vary) If merely watching NASCAR drivers streak around the track isn't adrenaline-pumping enough for you, get in the car yourself via the NASCAR Racing Experience. Choose from several levels of death-defying action, from the three-lap passenger-seat Race Ride (from $149) to the intensive Advanced Experience ($4000), with multiple laps, celeb meetings, and even a certificate on completion. Dates vary; check online.

🛏 Sleeping & Eating

Hyatt Place Daytona Beach Oceanfront

HOTEL $

(☑ 386-944-2010; www.daytonabeach.place.hyatt.com; 3161 S Atlantic Ave, Daytona Beach Shores; r from $114; 🅿 @ 🛜 🏊) Some of Daytona's freshest, funkiest and most functional rooms can be found here. All rooms feature balconies, plush bedding, separate living and sleeping areas and a nifty panel to easily connect your laptop or phone to the 42in panel TV.

Plaza Resort & Spa

RESORT $

(☑ 855-327-5292, 844-284-2685; www.plazaresortandspa.com; 600 N Atlantic Ave; r $109-149; 🅿 ❄ 🛜 🏊) Built in 1888, Daytona's most historic resort has undergone extensive renovations in its time, but still maintains its old-world charm. If only the walls could talk... From the miles of honey-colored marble lining the lobby to the 42in plasma TVs and cloud-soft beds in the rooms, to the 15,000-sq-ft spa, this resort coos luxury.

★ **House of Donuts** BAKERY $
(☑ 386-441-4066; 1350 Ocean Shore Blvd, Ormond Beach; 1/6 donuts $1.25/6; ⊙6am-2pm) Just north of Daytona in Ormond Beach is this great little donut stop, with all the flavors you'd expect plus some totally over-the-top creations, like Key Lime or Fruity Pebbles. Smores, with graham cracker cereal, chocolate and mini marshmallows, is over-the-top caloric decadence, and why not? You're in Florida, live a little!

Cracked Egg Diner BREAKFAST $
(☑ 386-788-6772; www.thecrackedeggdiner.com; 3280D S Atlantic Ave, Daytona Beach Shores; breakfast items $5-13; ⊙7am-3pm; ℗🖶) Best for breakfast, this cheery joint in Daytona Beach Shores became so popular they annexed the building next door. Brainchild of brothers Chris and Kevin, one of whom will usually greet you at the door with a smile, their mission is to deliver breakfast egg-cellence. (Sorry. It had to happen.) We think they do a fine job. Kids will have a grand time with the various meal names: the Chunky Monkey Pancakes, for instance, or the Fruity Pebble French Toast.

Aunt Catfish's on the River SOUTHERN US $$
(☑ 386-767-4768; www.auntcatfishontheriver.com; 4009 Halifax Dr, Port Orange; mains $9-31, brunch $18; ⊙11:30am-9pm Mon-Sat, from 9am Sun; ℗🖶) Fresh-from-the-boat grouper and mahi-mahi lolling in butter or deeply and deliciously fried, as well as Southern-style Cajun-spiced catfish, make this riverside seafood establishment insanely popular with tourists: table waits can be expected. It's just outside Daytona Beach in Port Orange. A kiddie play area gives the little ones something to do while you wait.

ℹ Information

Daytona Beach Area Convention & Visitors Bureau (☑ 386-255-0415; www.daytonabeach.com; 126 E Orange Ave; ⊙8:30am-5pm Mon-Fri) In person or online, these guys are *the* authority on all things Daytona Beach.

ℹ Getting There & Away

Daytona Beach is close to the intersection of two major interstates, I-95 and I-4. The I-95 is the

quickest way to Jacksonville (about 90 miles) and Miami (260 miles), though Hwy A1A and Hwy 1 are more scenic. Beville Rd, an east–west thoroughfare south of Daytona proper, becomes I-4 after crossing I-95; it's the fastest route to Orlando (55 miles).

A cab journey from the airport to South Atlantic Ave costs $20. Ride-sharing services are also available.

Daytona Beach International Airport (☑ 386-248-8030; www.flydaytonafirst.com; 700 Catalina Dr) is just east of the Speedway; it's served by Delta and US Airways, and all major car-rental companies.

Greyhound (☑ 386-255-7076; www.greyhound.com; 138 S Ridgewood Ave) has connections to most major cities in Florida, and beyond.

St Augustine

The oldest continuously occupied European settlement in the US, St Augustine was founded by the Spanish in 1565. Today, its 144-block National Historic Landmark District is a major tourist destination. For the most part, St Augustine exudes charm and maintains its integrity, although there's no denying the presence of some tacky tourist traps: miniature theme parks, tour operators at almost every turn and horse-drawn carriages clip-clopping past townsfolk dressed in period costume.

What makes St Augustine so genuinely endearing is the accessibility of its rich history via countless top-notch museums and the authenticity of its centuries-old architecture, monuments and narrow cobbled lanes. Unlike Florida's numerous historical theme parks, St Augustine is the real deal.

You'll find a diverse array of wonderful B&Bs, cozy cafes and lamp-lit pubs, and while fine dining might not be the first thing that comes to mind at Florida's mention, it is certainly synonymous with St Augustine.

History

Timucuans settled what is now St Augustine about 1000 BC, hunting alligators and cultivating corn and tobacco. In 1513, Spanish explorer Juan Ponce de León sighted land, came ashore and claimed La Florida (Land of Flowers) for Spain. In 1565 his compatriot Don Pedro Menéndez de Avilés arrived on the feast day of Augustine of Hippo, and accordingly christened the town San Augustín: 42 years prior to the founding of Jamestown (Virginia) and 55 years before that of Plymouth (Massachusetts).

Menéndez quickly established a military base against the French, who had established Fort Caroline near present-day Jacksonville. The French fleet did him the favor of getting stuck in a hurricane; Menéndez' men butchered the survivors. By the time Spain ceded Florida to the US in 1821, St Augustine had been sacked, looted, burned and occupied by pirates and Spanish, British, Georgian and South Carolinian forces.

Today the city's buildings, made of coquina – a DIY concrete made of sedimentary rock mixed with crushed shells – lend an enchanting quality to the slender streets. The city's long and colorful history is palpable, narrated vividly by what seems like innumerable museums, monuments and galleries.

◉ Sights

All of St Augustine's historic district feels like a museum; there are literally dozens of attractions to choose from. Narrow little **Aviles St**, the oldest European-settled street in the country, and long, pedestrian-only **St George St** are both lined with galleries, cafes, museums and pubs, and are attractions in themselves.

★ Lightner Museum MUSEUM
(☏ 904-824-2874; www.lightnermuseum.org; 75 King St; adult/child $15/8; ⊙ 9am-5pm) Henry Flagler's former Hotel Alcazar is home to this wonderful museum with a little bit of everything, from ornate Gilded Age furnishings to collections of marbles and cigar-box labels. The dramatic and imposing building itself is a must-see, dating back to 1887 and designed in the Spanish Renaissance Revival style by New York City architects Carrère & Hastings.

Castillo de San Marcos National Monument FORT
(☏ 904-829-6506; www.nps.gov/casa; 1 S Castillo Dr; adult/child under 15yr $15/free; ⊙ 9am-5pm; P⛟) ✐ This photogenic fort is an atmospheric monument to longevity: it's the country's oldest masonry fort, completed by the Spanish in 1695. In its time, the fort has been besieged twice and changed hands between nations six times – from Spain to Britain to Spain Part II to the USA to the Confederate States of America to the USA again. Park rangers lead programs hourly and shoot off cannons most weekends.

Villa Zorayda Museum MUSEUM
(☏ 904-829-9887; www.villazorayda.com; 83 King St; adult/child $10/5; ⊙ 10am-5pm Mon-Sat, 11am-4pm Sun; P) Looking like a faux Spanish castle from a medieval theme park, this gray edifice was built out of a mix of concrete and local coquina shells in 1883. The structure was the fantasy (and maybe fever dream) of an eccentric millionaire who was obsessed with Spain's 12th-century Alhambra Palace. Today, it's an odd but engaging museum. The Moorish-style atrium and rooms contain quirky antiques, archaeological pieces and other artifacts: highlights being a 2400-year-old mummy's foot and an Egyptian 'Sacred Cat Rug.'

Hotel Ponce de León HISTORIC BUILDING
(☏ 904-823-3378; http://legacy.flagler.edu/pages/tours; 74 King St; tours adult/child $12/free; ⊙ tours hourly 10am-3pm mid-May–mid-Aug, 10am & 2pm during school year) This striking former luxury hotel, built in the 1880s, is now the world's most gorgeous dormitory, belonging to Flagler College, who purchased and saved it in 1967. Guided tours are recommended to get a sense of the detail and history of this magnificent Spanish Renaissance building. At the very least, take a peek inside the lobby for free.

Colonial Quarter MUSEUM
(☏ 904-342-2857; www.colonialquarter.com; 43 St George St; adult/child $13/7; ⊙ 10am-5pm) See how they did things back in the 18th century at this re-creation of Spanish Colonial St Augustine, complete with craftspeople demonstrating blacksmithing, leather working, musket shooting and all sorts of historical stuff. A replica Spanish *caravel* (ship) is among the items. They also do canon and musket firing.

St Augustine Beach BEACH
(350 A1A Beach Blvd) This white-sand beach almost gets lost in the historical mix, but hey, it's Florida, so a visit wouldn't be complete without a little bit of sun and surf. There's a visitor information booth at the foot of St Johns Pier, where you can rent a rod and reel (two hours for $15). About three blocks south of the pier, the end of A St has – as Florida goes – some fine waves.

🛏 Sleeping

Jaybird's Inn MOTEL $
(☏ 904-342-7938; www.jaybirdsinn.com; 2700 N Ponce de Leon Blvd; r $139-159; ☎☀) This motel

has fresh and funky decor in an aquamarine color scheme that works. Beds are big and comfy, Continental breakfast is included and free bikes will get you whizzing around in no time. There's an on-site restaurant as well.

★ At Journey's End

B&B $$

(☑ 904-829-0076; www.atjourneysend.com; 89 Cedar St; r $169-329; P🐾🛜🐶) Free from the granny-ish decor that haunts many St Augustine B&Bs, this pet-friendly, kids-welcome and gay-friendly spot is outfitted in a chic mix of antiques and modern furniture and is run by kind, knowledgeable hosts. Mouthwatering breakfasts and complimentary wi-fi, concierge services, and beer, wine and soda throughout your stay are some of the inclusions that set At Journey's End apart.

✕ Eating & Drinking

Collage

INTERNATIONAL $$$

(☑ 904-829-0055; www.collagestaug.com; 60 Hypolita St; mains $29-56; ⊙5-9pm) This upscale restaurant is renowned for its impeccable service, intimate atmosphere and the consistency of its cuisine: the menu makes the most of St Augustine's seaside locale and nearby local farms. It's all here: artisan salads, chicken, lamb, veal and pork, lobster, scallops and grouper. A subtle mélange of global flavors enhance the natural goodness of the freshest produce.

★ Odd Birds Bar

COCKTAIL BAR

(☑ 904-679-4933; www.oddbirdsbar.com; 33 Charlotte St; ⊙5pm-2am Mon-Fri, from 1pm Sat-Sun) Odd Birds embodies just about everything one could want in a quirky, totally unique craft cocktail bar: innovative, imaginative, often playful drinks; bartenders that are serious about their art (they even invite bartender 'diplomats' from other bars to spend an evening sharing their tricks of the trade); and a casual setting that's unpretentious (even though it could be).

If you're a fan of the cocktail you'll make sure this is in your itinerary.

ℹ Information

Visitor Information Center (☑ 904-825-1000; www.floridashistoriccoast.com; 10 W Castillo Dr; ⊙8:30am-5:30pm) Helpful, period-dressed staff sell tour tickets and can advise you on everything St Augustinian.

The daily *St Augustine Record* (www.staugustine.com) has good visitor information on its website.

ℹ Getting There & Around

Driving from the north, take I-95 exit 318 and head east past Hwy 1 to San Marcos Ave; turn right and you'll end up at the Old City Gate, just past the fort. Alternatively, you can take Hwy A1A along the beach, which intersects with San Marco Ave, or Hwy 1 south from Jacksonville. From the south, take exit 298, merge onto Hwy 1 and follow it into town.

Cars are a nightmare downtown, with one-way and pedestrian-only streets and severely limited parking; outside the city center, you'll need wheels. There's a big parking lot at the Visitor Information Center. Use it.

Northeast Florida Regional Airport (☑ 904-209-0090; www.flynf.com; 4900 US Hwy 1), 5 miles north of town, receives limited commercial flights. **Airport Express** (☑ 904-824-9400; www.airportexpresspickup.com; ⊙24hr) charges $65 to drop you downtown in a shuttle. For an additional fee, it'll take you to your hotel. Reservations required. Private services are also available.

The **Greyhound bus station** (☑ 904-829-6401; www.greyhound.com; 3 Cordova St) is just a few blocks north of the visitor center.

Jacksonville

At a whopping 840 sq miles, Jacksonville is the largest city by area in the contiguous United States and the most populous in Florida. The city sprawls along three meandering rivers, with sweeping bridges and twinkling city lights reflected in the water. A glut of high-rises, corporate HQs and chain hotels can make 'Jax' feel a little soulless, but patient exploration yields some interesting streets, curious characters and a Southern-fried, friendly heart.

The city's museums and restored historic districts are worth a wander if you have the time, and the Five Points and San Marco neighborhoods are charming, walkable areas lined with bistros, boutiques and bars.

The Jacksonville area beaches – a world unto themselves – are 30 to 50 minutes' drive from the city, depending on traffic and where you're coming from.

◉ Sights

★ Cummer Museum of Art & Gardens

MUSEUM

(www.cummermuseum.org; 829 Riverside Ave; adult/student $10/6; ⊙10am-9pm Tue, to 4pm Wed-Sat, noon-4pm Sun) This handsome museum, Jacksonville's premier cultural space, has an excellent collection of American and

European paintings, Asian decorative art and antiquities. An outdoor area showcases classical English and Italian gardens, and is one of the loveliest alfresco spaces in the city.

★ Museum of Contemporary Art Jacksonville
MUSEUM

(MOCA; ☑ 904-366-6911; https://mocajacksonville.unf.edu; 333 N Laura St; adult/child $8/5; ⊙11am-5pm Tue-Sat, to 9pm Thu, from noon Sun) The focus of this ultramodern space extends beyond painting: get lost among contemporary sculpture, prints, photography and film.

Check out www.jacksonvilleartwalk.com for details of the free MOCA-run Art Walk, held on the first Wednesday of every month from 5pm to 9pm: it has more than 56 stops and is a great way to see the city.

Southbank Riverwalk
WATERFRONT

This 1.2-mile boardwalk, on the south side of the St Johns River, opposite downtown and Jacksonville Landing, has excellent views of the city's expansive skyline. Most nights yield scenes that'll up your likes on social media, but the firework displays on 4 July and New Years' Eve are a real blast. The Southbank Riverwalk connects the museums flanking Museum Circle and makes a pleasant promenade.

Treaty Oak
LANDMARK

(1123 Prudential Dr, Jesse Ball duPont Park) At first glance, it looks like a small forest is growing in the middle of the concrete on Jacksonville's south side. But upon closer inspection you'll see that the 'forest' is really one single enormous tree, with a trunk circumference of 25ft and a shade diameter of nearly 200ft. According to local lore, the live oak tree is the oldest thing in Jacksonville – its age is estimated to be 250 years.

🛏 Sleeping & Eating

Hotel Indigo Jacksonville
HOTEL $$

(☑ 904-996-7199; www.hoteldeerwoodpark.com; 9840 Tapestry Park Circle; r from $150; P❄❄ ❄❄❄) Lush blue color accents and airy, design-conscious rooms with hardwood floors, fluffy king beds, flat-screen TVs and a general sense of stylish yet accessible luxury define the experience at this excellent branch of the Indigo chain. The pool makes for a relaxing spot to get some sun if you're not heading for the beaches. Located about 11 miles south of downtown Jacksonville.

★ Hotel Palms
HOTEL $$

(☑ 904-241-7776; www.thehotelpalms.com; 28 Sherry Dr, Atlantic Beach; r $140-180, ste from $200; ❄) An old-school courtyard motel turned into a chic little property with reclaimed headboards, concrete floors and open, airy design. Treat yourself to an outdoor shower, free beach-cruiser bicycles, an outdoor fireplace and some gorgeous rooms looking like they've been pulled straight off some fancy interior decorator's Instagram.

Beach Road Chicken Dinners
SOUTHERN US $

(☑ 904-398-7980; www.facebook.com/BRCD1939; 4132 Atlantic Blvd; items $8-18; ⊙11am-8:30pm Tue-Sat, to 6pm Sun) You know a place does it right if its signature meal pre-dates the Cold War, and this deliciously retro joint has been frying chicken since 1939. Tear off a chunk of tender thigh meat and wrap it up in a fluffy biscuit, and you'll understand why people line up every day at this much-loved shack.

Note the hefty sharing charge of $7!

★ Black Sheep Restaurant
AMERICAN $$

(☑ 904-380-3091; www.blacksheep5points.com; 1534 Oak St; mains from $14-27; ⊙10:30am-10pm Tue-Thu, to midnight Fri, 9:30am-midnight Sat, 9:30am-10pm Sun; ❄) 🌿 A commitment to good, local ingredients, delicious food, plus a bar with a retractable rooftop and a craft cocktail menu? Sign us up! Try miso-glazed duck confit, citrus-marinated tofu, pastrami sandwiches made from in-house deli meat, or crispy skinned steelhead fish cooked in brown butter; it's all good. The cardamom pancakes and salmon on bagels served for weekend brunch are pretty fine, too.

🍺 Drinking & Entertainment

★ De Real Ting Cafe
CLUB

(☑ 904-633-9738; www.facebook.com/derealtingcafe; 125 W Adams; ⊙11am-3pm Tue-Fri, 4-11pm Wed, 4pm-3am Fri, 8:30pm-3am Sat) This Jamaican-themed spot has decent eats, but it's the music and the vibe that people come here for: great Caribbean music, dancing, and hanging out. Hosts open-mic nights and other performers and events, too.

Birdies
BAR

(☑ 904-356-4444; www.birdiesfivepoints.com; 1044 Park St; ⊙4pm-2am Mon-Fri, from 1pm Sat & Sun) There's a lot to see at this funky spot. Local art graces the walls, there's a photo booth, and old-timers and 20-somethings will be sharing the pool tables while indie rock fills the place. It has DJs on the weekends, making for even more good vibes.

★**Florida Theatre**   THEATER
(🖉administrative office 904-355-5661, box office 904-355-2787; www.floridatheatre.com; 128 E Forsyth St) Home to Elvis' first indoor concert in 1956, which a local judge endured to ensure Presley was not overly suggestive, this opulent 1927 venue is an intimate place to catch big-name musicians, musicals and movies.

❶ Information

There are a bunch of sources of information for Jacksonville and the surrounding areas.

Florida Times-Union (www.jacksonville.com) Conservative daily paper, in print and online; Friday's *Weekend* magazine features family-oriented events listings.

Folio Weekly (www.folioweekly.com) Free; with club, restaurant and events listings. Found all over town.

Visit Jacksonville Tourist Information Center (🖉800-733-2668; www.visitjacksonville.com; 208 N Laura St, Suite 102; ⊙9am-5:30pm Mon-Fri, 11am-4pm Sat & Sun) Has all there is to know about Jax and surrounds.

❶ Getting There & Around

Jacksonville International Airport (JAX; 🖉904-741-3044; www.flyjax.com; 2400 Yankee Clipper Dr; 🛜), about 18 miles north of downtown on I-95, is served by major and regional airlines and car-rental companies. A cab downtown costs around $40. Otherwise, follow the signs for shuttle services: there are numerous licensed providers and reservations aren't necessary.

The **Greyhound bus station** (🖉904-356-9976; www.greyhound.com; 1111 W Forsyth St) is at the west end of downtown. The **Amtrak station** (🖉904-766-5110, reservations 800-872-7245; www.amtrak.com; 3570 Clifford Lane) is 5 miles northwest of downtown.

The Jacksonville Transportation Authority (www.jtafla.com) runs buses and trolleys around town and the beaches (fare $1.50), as well as a free, scenic (and underused) river-crossing Skyway (monorail).

Amelia Island

Located just 13 miles from the Georgia border, Amelia Island is a moss-draped, sun- and sand-soaked blend of the Deep South and Florida coast. It is believed the island's original inhabitants, the Timucuan tribespeople, arrived as early as 4000 years ago. Since that time, eight flags have flown here,

starting with the French in 1562, followed by the Spanish, the English, the Spanish again, the Patriots, the Green Cross of Florida, the Mexican Rebels, the US, the Confederates, then the US again.

Vacationers have flocked to Amelia since the 1890s, when Henry Flagler converted a coast of salt marsh and unspoiled beaches into a vacation spot for the wealthy. The legacy of that era is evident in the central town of Fernandina Beach, 50 blocks of historic buildings, Victorian B&Bs and restaurants housed in converted fishing cottages. Dotting the rest of the island are lush parks, green fairways and miles of shoreline.

◉ Sights & Activties

Amelia Island Museum of History   MUSEUM
(🖉904-261-7378; www.ameliamuseum.org; 233 S 3rd St, Fernandina Beach; adult/student $8/5; ⊙10am-4pm Mon-Sat, from 1pm Sun) Housed in the former county jail (1879–1975), this oral-history museum is tiny but has informative exhibits exploring Native American history, the Spanish Mission period, the Civil War and historic preservation. A variety of tours are available, including the eight-flags tour (11am and 2pm Monday to Saturday, and 2pm Sunday), providing lively interpretations of the island's fascinating history, as well as architecture tours, and pub crawls.

Fort Clinch State Park   STATE PARK
(🖉904-277-7274; www.floridastateparks.org/fort clinch; 2601 Atlantic Ave, Fernandina Beach; car/pedestrian $6/2; ⊙park 8am-sunset, fort 9am-5pm; Ⓟ) 🧭 Although construction commenced in 1847, rapid technological advancements rendered Fort Clinch's masonry walls obsolete by as early as 1861, when the fort was taken easily by Confederate militia in the Civil War and later evacuated. Federal troops again occupied the fort during WWII. Today, the park offers a variety of activities, serene beaches for shelling (of the non-military kind) and 6 miles of peaceful, unpaved trails for hiking and cycling.

★**Kayak Amelia**   KAYAKING
(🖉904-251-0016, 904-261-5702; www.kayakame lia.com; 4 N 2nd St, Fernandina Beach; tours adult/child from $65/55, kayak rental half-day single/double from $40/55) The charms of Amelia Island are best appreciated through a quiet day on the water, with the sun glinting off the estuaries and cordgrass. That's the experience offered by Kayak Amelia, which leads paddling excursions into the watery ecosystem

that ensconces the Atlantic barrier island. They also offer stand-up paddleboarding (SUP) classes and SUP yoga (both $30).

🛏 Sleeping

★ Addison
B&B $$

(☎904-277-1604; www.addisononamelia.com; 614 Ash St, Fernandina Beach; r $220-330; 🅿🛜) Built in 1876, the Addison has modern upgrades (Jacuzzi tubs, deluge showers, Turkish-cotton towels and wi-fi) that'll trick you into thinking it was finished last week. Its white, aqua and sage color scheme is bright and totally unstuffy. Enjoy daily happy hours overlooking a delightful courtyard with some of the most accommodating innkeepers on Amelia.

Ritz Carlton
HOTEL $$$

(☎904-277-1100; www.ritzcarlton.com; 4750 Amelia Island Pkwy, Fernandina Beach; r from $313; 🅿⊜✳@🛜🐾) The height of luxury, decadence and impeccable service awaits at this unexpectedly located Ritz Carlton. Set on 13 miles of pristine beaches, with its own private 18-hole golf course, and lavish rooms and suites furnished with casual elegance, this is a property for those with fat wallets, accustomed to the best in life, or for that very special vacation experience.

🍴 Eating & Drinking

★ Patio Place
BISTRO $

(☎904-410-3717; http://patioplacebistro.com; 416 Ash St; mains $7-14; ⊙11am-8pm Wed-Thu, 8:30am-9:30pm Fri & Sat, to 2pm Sun; 🅿🍴) Tables named by country not numbers, international music, distressed wood, lots of outdoor seating, and pleasant service make this a joy to dine at. Known for its crepes, there are also bowls, soups, bruschettas, and daily specials. House-made sangria goes down awfully smoothly on a hot Florida day.

T-Ray's Burger Station
BURGERS $

(☎904-261-6310; www.traysburgerstation.com; 202 S 8th St, Fernandina Beach; mains $4-14; ⊙7am-2:15pm Mon-Fri, 8am-1pm Sat) Inside an Exxon gas station, this high-carb, high-fat, low-pretense diner and takeout joint is worth the cholesterol spike. Revered by locals, the big breakfasts are just that, and daily specials sell out fast. Juicy burgers, chunky fries, fried shrimp and tender crab cakes all make the mouth water. Believe the hype: the line's there for a reason.

29 South
SOUTHERN US $$

(☎904-277-7919; www.29southrestaurant.com; 29 S 3rd St, Fernandina Beach; mains $16-28; ⊙5:30-9:30pm daily, plus 10am-2pm Sat & Sun; 🅿) Lobster corn dogs, sweet-tea-brined pork chops, homemade doughnut-bread pudding and mocha ice cream – we're in business. Tucked into a pale-purple cottage, this neo-Southern bistro takes culinary risks and executes them well. It's casual yet classy and full of flavor.

★ Palace Saloon
BAR

(www.thepalacesaloon.com; 113-117 Centre St, Fernandina Beach; ⊙noon-2am) Push through the swinging doors at the oldest continuously operated bar in Florida (since 1878), and the first thing you'll notice is the 40ft gas-lamp-lit bar. Knock back the saloon's rum-laced Pirate's Punch in dark, velvet-draped surroundings, curiously appealing to both bikers and Shakespeare buffs.

❶ Information

Historic Downtown Visitor Center (☎904-277-0717; www.ameliaisland.com; 102 Centre St, Fernandina Beach; ⊙10am-4pm) Reams of useful information and maps in the old railroad depot. A fun stop in itself.

Shrimping Museum & Welcome Center (☎904-261-7378; 17 S Front St, Fernandina Beach; ⊙10am-4pm Mon-Sat, from 1pm Sun) This small museum on the harborfront has local maps and pamphlets.

❶ Getting There & Away

Hwy A1A splits in two directions on Amelia Island, one heading west toward I-95 and the other following the coast; both are well marked.

To get to Amelia, the fastest route from the mainland is to take I-95 north to exit 373 and head east about 15 miles straight to the island.

Want a prettier route? Heading from Jacksonville Beach to the town of Mayport, catch the **St Johns River Ferry** (☎904-630-3100; www.jtafla.com; per pedestrian/car $1/6; ⊙from Mayport every 30min 6am-7pm Mon-Fri, 7am-8:30pm Sat & Sun; from George Island every 30min 6:15am-7:15pm Mon-Fri, 7:15am-8:45pm Sat & Sun), which runs around every 30 minutes.

SOUTHWEST FLORIDA

To drive southwest Florida's Gulf Coast is to enter an impressionistic watercolor painting: first, there is the dazzling white quartz sand of its barrier-island beaches, whose turquoise waters darken to silver-mantled indigo as the fiery sun lowers to the horizon. Later, seen from the causeways, those same islands become a phosphorescent smear beneath the inky black night sky.

The Gulf Coast's beauty is its main attraction, but variety is a close second: from Tampa to St Petersburg to Sarasota to Naples, there is urban sophistication and exquisite cuisine. There are secluded islands, family-friendly resorts and spring-break-style parties.

Here Salvador Dalí's melting canvases, Ringling's Venetian Gothic palace and Chihuly's tentacled glass sculptures fit perfectly – all are bright, bold, surreal entertainments to match wintering manatees, roseate spoonbills, open-mouthed alligators and the peacock-colored, sequined costumes of twirling trapeze artists.

Tampa

Tampa, or 'Trampa' as some locals say, is gritty in spots, but also home to a bunch of museums, parks and ambitious restaurants, many of which have popped up recently and brought the city dangerously close to becoming stylish. In the heart of downtown, the revitalized Riverwalk along the Hillsborough River glitters with contemporary architecture and scenic spaces. Plus, between the zoo, the aquarium, the children's museums and the theme parks, families have enough top-shelf entertainment to last a week. By evening Ybor City's streets transform into southwest Florida's hottest bar and nightclub scene.

◉ Sights

Ybor (ee-bore) City is a short car or trolley ride northeast of downtown. Like the illicit love child of Key West and Miami's Little Havana, this 19th-century district is a multiethnic neighborhood that hosts the Tampa Bay area's hippest party scene. It also preserves a strong Cuban, Spanish and Italian heritage from its days as the epicenter of Tampa's cigar industry. You'll quickly find out why the rooster is Ybor's symbol: the birds are wild and proudly strutting everywhere.

★ Florida Aquarium   AQUARIUM
(☑813-273-4000; www.flaquarium.org; 701 Channelside Dr; adult/child from $28/24; ◉9:30am-5pm; ⊕) Tampa's excellent aquarium is among the state's best. Cleverly designed, the re-created swamp lets you walk among herons and ibis as they prowl the mangroves. Programs let you swim with the fishes (and the sharks) or take a catamaran ecotour in Tampa Bay. For better control of the crowds, tickets are priced by entry time.

Busch Gardens   AMUSEMENT PARK
(☑813-884-4386; www.buschgardenstampabay.com; 10165 McKinley Dr; 3yr & older $105; ◉10am-6pm, hours vary) This theme park has 10 loosely named African zones, which flow together without much fuss. The entire park is walkable. Admission includes three types of fun: epic roller coasters and rides, animal encounters, and various shows, performances and entertainment. All are spread throughout the park, so successful days require some planning: check show schedules before arriving and plan what rides and animals to visit around the shows. Coaster lines only get longer as the day goes on. Parking costs $25.

Ybor City Museum State Park   MUSEUM
(☑813-247-6323; www.ybormuseum.org; 1818 E 9th Ave; adult/child $4/free; ◉9am-5pm Wed-Sun) This dusty, old-school history museum preserves a bygone era, with cigar-worker houses (open 10am to 3pm) and wonderful photos. The museum has information on a free, self-guided, multimedia **tour** (☑813-505-6779; www.yborwalkingtours.com; adult/child $20/10) of Ybor City, accessible with any internet-connected device. The tour includes 21 stops and narration from prominent characters within the community.

Florida Museum of Photographic Arts   MUSEUM
(FMoPA; ☑813-221-2222; www.fmopa.org; The Cube, 400 N Ashley Dr; adult/student $10/8; ◉11am-6pm Mon-Thu, to 7pm Fri, noon-5pm Sat & Sun) This small, intimate photography museum is housed on the 2nd and 3rd stories of the Cube, a five-story atrium in downtown Tampa. In addition to a permanent collection from Harold Edgerton and Len Prince, temporary exhibits have included the work of Ansel Adams, Andy Warhol and contemporary photographers such as Jerry Uelsmann. Photography courses are also offered.

Manatee Viewing Center   WILDLIFE RESERVE
(☑813-228-4289; www.tampaelectric.com/manatee; 6990 Dickman Rd, Apollo Beach; ◉10am-5pm Nov–mid-Apr) **FREE** One of Florida's more surreal wildlife encounters is spotting manatees in the warm-water discharge canals of coal-fired power plants. Yet these placid mammals show up here so reliably from

November through April that this is now a protected sanctuary. Tarpon and sharks can be spotted as well, and a new interactive stingray exhibit in a 10,000-gallon tank allows up-close interaction. The latter can be touched (two fingers only!).

🛏 Sleeping

Gram's Place Hostel   HOSTEL $
(✆813-221-0596; www.grams-inn-tampa.com; 3109 N Ola Ave, Seminole Heights; dm $32, r $63-74; ❄@🛜) As charismatic as an aging rock star, Gram's is a small, welcoming hostel for international travelers who prefer personality over perfect linens. Dig the in-ground hot tub. Simple breakfast is included, but there are two fully serviced kitchens. Gram's Place is in Tampa Heights, 2 miles north of the Museum of Art.

Tahitian Inn   HOTEL $
(✆813-877-6721; www.tahitianinn.com; 601 S Dale Mabry Hwy, South Tampa; r $89-155; P❄@🛜🏊🐾) The name is reminiscent of a tiki-themed motel, but this family-owned, full-service hotel offers fresh, boutique stylings on the cheap. Nice pool, and the quaint cafe offers outdoor seating by a waterfall and pond. Also, pets are welcome and airport/cruise terminal transportation is included (guests only).

★Epicurean Hotel   BOUTIQUE HOTEL $$$
(✆813-999-8700; www.epicureanhotel.com; 1207 S Howard Ave, South Tampa; r $220-450; P❄@🛜🏊) Foodies rejoice! Tampa's coolest hotel, which opened in 2014, is a food-and-drink-themed boutique Eden steeped in detailed design: a zinc bar, reclaimed woods from an 1820s railway station, oversize kitchen tools as door handles – everywhere you look, a story, usually involving **Bern's Steak House** (✆813-251-2421; www.bernssteakhouse. com; 1208 S Howard Ave; steaks for 1-2 people $37-105; ⏱5-10pm Sun-Thu, to 11pm Fri & Sat), which is a partner. The bathrooms even have rugs. Opulent to the extreme.

🍴 Eating

Tre Amici @ the Bunker   CAFE $
(✆813-247-6964; www.bunkerybor.com; 1907 19th St N, Ybor City; items $4-9; ⏱7am-8pm Mon-Sat, 9am-4pm Sun) Ybor City's youth contingent wake up at this relaxed community coffeehouse, which offers a range of breakfast burritos, soups and sandwiches all day. Come evening, it hosts open mics, poetry

slams and 'noise nights,' which are exactly what they sound like.

Ichicoro   RAMEN $
(✆813-517-9989; www.ichicoro.com; 5229 N Florida Ave, Seminole Heights; ramen $12-16; ⏱11am-4pm daily, plus 5pm-11pm Sun-Wed, to 1am Thu-Sat) This trendy, chic ramen shop in Seminole Heights has unique options that you'd never see in Japan (like oh-so-umami mushroom broth). Also not in Japan: undercooked noodles, which waitstaff insist are *al dente* but to which we toss a well-deserved penalty card. Still, the *chāshū* (pork slabs), nearly as thick as the wooden table tops, are superb.

★Columbia Restaurant   SPANISH $$
(✆813-248-4961; www.columbiarestaurant.com; 2117 E 7th Ave, Ybor City; mains lunch $12-25, dinner $23-39; ⏱11am-10pm Mon-Thu, to 11pm Fri & Sat, noon-9pm Sun) Celebrating its centennial in 2015, this Spanish Cuban restaurant is the oldest in Florida. Occupying an entire block, it consists of 15 elegant dining rooms and romantic, fountain-centered courtyards. Many of the gloved waiters have been here a lifetime, and owner Richard Gonzmart is zealous about authentic Spanish and Cuban cuisine.

★Ulele   AMERICAN $$$
(✆813-999-4952; www.ulele.com; 1810 N Highland Ave; mains $19-42; ⏱11am-10pm Sun-Thu, to 11pm Fri & Sat; 🛜🍴) In a pleasant Riverwalk setting, this former water-pumping station has been transformed into an enchanting restaurant and brewery whose menu harkens back to native Floridan staples made over for modern times. That means liberal use of datil peppers, sides like alligator beans and okra 'fries' (amazing!), mains like local pompano fish and desserts like guava pie.

With green lawns, walking paths, Jack & the Beanstalk statues, and goldfish ponds, this spot could involve most of the day. There's even free fish food for kids to use while the adults sip a beverage of choice outside.

🍷 Drinking & Entertainment

Independent Bar   BAR
(✆813-341-4883; www.independentbartampa.com; 5016 N Florida Ave, Seminole Heights; ⏱11am-midnight Mon-Thu, 10:30am to 1am Fri-Sun) If you appreciate craft brews, roll into this converted gas station, now a low-key, hip bar in Seminole Heights. You can count on one or more local Cigar City Brews, and it serves some good pub grub.

★**Skipper's Smokehouse** LIVE MUSIC
(☑813-971-0666; www.skipperssmokehouse.com;
910 Skipper Rd, Village of Tampa; cover $5-25;
☺11am-11pm Tue, to midnight Wed-Fri, noon-midnight Sat, 1-9pm Sun) Like it blew in from the
Keys, Skipper's is a beloved, unpretentious
open-air venue for blues, folk, reggae and
gator-swamp rockabilly, beneath beautiful
live oaks. It's 9 miles directly north of downtown, on a side street off N Nebraska Ave.

★**Tampa Theatre** CINEMA
(☑813-274-8981, box office 813-274-8286; www.
tampatheatre.org; 711 N Franklin St; tickets adult/
child 2-12yr $11/9) This historic 1926 theater in
downtown is a gorgeous venue in which to
see an independent film. The mighty Wur-
litzer organ plays before most movies. Too
bad showtimes are so limited, with only one
or two films playing on any given day. Look
for special events.

❶ Information

Unlock Tampa Bay Visitors Center (☑813-
223-2752; www.visittampabay.com; 201 N
Franklin St, Ste 102; ☺10am-5:30pm Mon-Sat,
noon-5pm Sun) Good free maps and lots of
information.
Ybor City Visitor Center (☑813-241-8838;
www.ybor.org; 1600 E 8th Ave; ☺10am-5pm
Mon-Sat, noon-5pm Sun) Provides an excellent
introduction with walking-tour maps and info.

❶ Getting There & Around

Tampa International Airport (TPA; ☑813-
870-8700; www.tampaairport.com; 4100
George J Bean Pkwy) is the region's third-
busiest hub. It's 6 miles west of downtown,
off Hwy 589.

HART bus 30 ($2, 25 minutes, every 30 min-
utes) picks up and drops off at the Red Arrival
Desk on the lower level of the airport; exact
change is required.

All major car agencies have desks at the airport. By car, take I-275 to N Ashley Dr, turn right
and you're in downtown.

St Petersburg

Long known as little more than a bawdy
spring-break party town and a retirement
capital, St Petersburg is now forging a new
name for itself as a culturally savvy southern
city. Spurred on by awe-inspiring downtown
murals, a revitalized historic district and the
stunning Dalí Museum, the downtown energy is creeping up Central Ave, spawning
sophisticated restaurants, craft breweries,

farmers markets and artsy galleries, all of
which are attracting a younger professional
crowd and a new wave of culturally curious
travelers.

◉ Sights & Activities

★**Salvador Dalí Museum** MUSEUM
(☑727-823-3767; www.thedali.org; 1 Dali Blvd;
adult/child 13-17yr/child 6-12yr $24/17/10, after 5pm
Thu $10; ☺10am-5:30pm Fri-Wed, to 8pm Thu) The
theatrical exterior of the Salvador Dalí Museum speaks of great things: out of a wound in
the towering white shoe box oozes a 75ft geodesic glass atrium. Even better, what unfolds
inside is like a blueprint of what a modern
art museum, or at least one devoted to the
life, art and impact of Salvador Dalí, should
be. Even those who dismiss his dripping
clocks and curlicue mustache will be awed
by the museum and its grand works, especially the *Hallucinogenic Toreador*.

★**Weedon Island Preserve** NATURE RESERVE
(☑727-453-6500; www.weedonislandpreserve.
org; 1800 Weedon Dr NE; ☺7am-sunset) Like a
patchwork quilt of variegated greens tossed
out over Tampa Bay, this 3700-acre preserve
protects a diverse aquatic and wetland
ecosystem. At the heart of the preserve is
the excellent Cultural and Natural History
Center (open from 11am to 4pm Thursday
to Saturday) where you can browse exhibits
about the natural environment and the early
Weedon Island people. Sign-up also for interpretive hikes over miles of boardwalk or
go it alone with the online map.

St Petersburg
Museum of Fine Arts MUSEUM
(☑727-896-2667; www.mfastpete.org; 255 Beach
Dr NE; adult/child 7-18yr $20/10; ☺10am-5pm
Mon-Sat, to 8pm Thu, from noon Sun) The Museum of Fine Arts' collection is as broad as
the Dalí Museum's is deep, traversing the
world's antiquities and following art's pro-
gression through nearly every era.

Walking Mural Tours CULTURAL
(☑727-821-7391; www.stpetemuraltour.com; adult/
child $19/11; ☺10-11:30am Sat) This excellent
walking tour introduces visitors to St Pete's
vibrant mural scene, which got its start
when artists were given cheap gallery space
downtown after the economy crashed in
2008. Now upward of 30 highly creative and
one-of-a-kind murals, many with nods to the
city's history and culture, grace its buildings
and rival Miami's Wynwood Walls.

🛏 Sleeping

★ Hollander Hotel
BOUTIQUE HOTEL **$**

(☎727-873-7900; www.hollanderhotel.com; 421 4th Ave N; r $110-179; P🅿😊❄🛜🏊) The Hollander can do no wrong with its art-deco flavor, 130ft porch, convivial Tap Room, full-service spa and Common Grounds coffee shop. Shared spaces feature gorgeous period detailing and rooms retain a hint of 1930s romance with their polished wooden floors, lazy ceiling fans and cane furniture. The new pool and bar out back becomes a party scene on weekends.

Dickens House
B&B **$$**

(☎727-822-8622; www.dickenshouse.com; 335 8th Ave NE; r $160-275; P😊❄🛜) Five lushly designed rooms await in this passionately restored 1912 Arts and Crafts–style home. The gay-friendly owners whip up a gourmet breakfast often involving egg-white frittata. There's a lovely fern and bamboo garden as well.

🍴 Eating & Drinking

Meze 119
VEGETARIAN **$**

(☎727-498-8627; www.meze119.com; 119 2nd St N; mains $7-15; ⊙11am-9pm Sun-Thu, to 10pm Fri & Sat; 🍴) Using Middle Eastern spices to create rich, complex flavors, this vegetarian restaurant satisfies even demanding omnivores with its Scotch egg and falafel or couscous and raisin-stuffed acorn squash. Other popular standards include the multi-flavor hummus plate and sautéed eggplant on open-faced pita bread. Wash it all down with the delightful house 'meze-naide.'

★ Brick & Mortar
AMERICAN **$$$**

(☎727-822-6540; www.facebook.com/brickandmortarkitchen; 539 Central Ave; mains $16-43; ⊙5-9pm Tue, to 10pm Wed & Thu, 4:30-11pm Fri & Sat) A husband-and-wife catering team launched this, well, brick-and-mortar establishment in 2015, and despite the fact that St Pete has been overrun with great restaurants, this New American experiment dominated. Best thing in the menu? A divine house carpaccio with leek, some goat's cheese mousse, a touch of truffle oil and a single ravioli stuffed with deliciously runny egg yolk ($17).

Cycle Brewing
BREWERY

(534 Central Ave; ⊙3pm-midnight Mon-Thu, noon-1am Fri & Sat, noon-10pm Sun) Unique brewhouse with sidewalk seating and up to 24 rotating taps of world-class beer. The Crank IPA is a great choice.

ℹ Getting There & Around

Downtown Looper (www.loopertrolley.com; free; ⊙7am-10pm Mon-Thu, to midnight Fri, 8am-midnight Sat, 8am-10pm Sun) Old-fashioned trolley cars run a downtown circuit every 15 to 20 minutes; great for sightseeing.

Greyhound (☎727-898-1496; www.greyhound.com; 180 Dr Martin Luther King Jr St N) Buses connect to Miami, Orlando and Tampa.

Pinellas Suncoast Transit Authority (PSTA; www.psta.net; adult/student $2.25/1.10) St Petersburg buses serve the barrier-island beaches and Clearwater; unlimited-ride Go Cards cost $5 per day.

Sarasota

Vacations today can be spent soaking up the sights and beaches of sophisticated Sarasota, but this city took its time becoming the culturally rich place it is today. After marauding Spanish explorers expelled the Calusa people in the 15th century, this land lay virtually empty until the Seminole Wars inspired the Armed Occupation Act (1842), which deeded 160 acres and six months' provisions to anyone who would settle here and protect their farms.

Sailing boats and steamships were the only connection to the outside world, until the Tampa railroad came in 1902. Sarasota then grew popular as a winter resort for the affluent, and the city's arts institutions followed. Finally, circus magnate John Ringling decided to relocate his circus here, building a winter residence, art museum and college, and setting the struggling town on course to become the welcoming, well-to-do bastion of the arts it is today.

👁 Sights & Activities

★ Ringling Museum Complex
MUSEUM

(☎941-359-5700; www.ringling.org; 5401 Bay Shore Rd; adult/child 6-17yr $25/5; ⊙10am-5pm Fri-Wed, to 8pm Thu; ♿) The 66-acre winter estate of railroad, real-estate and circus baron John Ringling and his wife, Mable, is one of the Gulf Coast's premier attractions and incorporates their personal collection of artworks in what is now Florida's state art museum. Nearby, Ringling's Circus Museum documents his theatrical successes, while their lavish Venetian Gothic home, Cà d'Zan, reveals the impresario's extravagant tastes. Don't miss the PBS-produced film on Ringling's life, which is screened in the Circus Museum.

Island Park   PARK

Sarasota's marina is notable for Island Park, an attractive green space poking into the harbor: it has a great playground and play fountain, restrooms, tree-shaded benches, a restaurant and tiki bar; and kayak, jet-ski and boat rentals.

★ Siesta Key Rum   DISTILLERY

(Drum Circle Distilling; ☑941-702-8143; www. drumcircledistilling.com; 2212 Industrial Blvd; ⊙10am-5pm Mon-Sat, from noon Sun) FREE The oldest rum distillery in Florida offers an educational and intoxicating tour in its facility within an industrial park a bit outside of town. You'll learn the entire process of rum-making from the company founder Troy, who is a gifted and hilarious public speaker. Delicious free samples at the end will likely result in purchases.

🛏 Sleeping & Eating

Hotel Ranola   BOUTIQUE HOTEL $$

(☑941-951-0111; www.hotelranola.com; 118 Indian Pl, No 6; r $129-199, ste $209-259; P❋❄🐾) This small hotel has been under new management since January 2019, so previous guests can expect changes, but it's clean, rates are a decent value, and it is convenient to the downtown area.

Mattison's City Grille   GRILL $$

(☑941-330-0440; https://mattisons.com; 1 N Lemon Ave; mains $19-36; ⊙11am-10pm Sun-Mon, to 11pm Tue-Thu, to midnight Fri, 9:30am-midnight Sat; 🐾🛴) Dinners won't wow you, but healthy salads and hearty sandwiches are fine at Sarasota's central Mattison's. The outdoor dining area doubles as a bar that gets going with music, giving the place its 'party on the corner' nickname.

★ Owen's Fish Camp   SOUTHERN US $$

(☑941-951-6936; www.owensfishcamp.com; 516 Burns Ct; mains $14-25; ⊙4-9:30pm Sun-Thu, to 10:30pm Fri & Sat) The wait rarely dips below an hour at this hip, Old Florida swamp shack downtown. The menu consists of upscale Southern cuisine with an emphasis on seafood, including whatever's fresh, and solid regular dishes like scallops with braised pork, succotash and grits. Those willing to eat in the courtyard order at the bar, which also serves wine and craft beer.

❶ Information

Arts & Cultural Alliance (www.sarasotaarts. org) All-encompassing event info.

Sarasota Herald-Tribune (www.heraldtribune. com) The main daily newspaper.

Sarasota Visitor Information Center (☑941-706-1253; www.visitsarasota.org; 1945 Fruitville Rd; ⊙10am-5pm Mon-Fri, to 2pm Sat; 🐾) Very friendly office with tons of info; sells good maps.

❶ Getting There & Away

Sarasota is roughly 60 miles south of Tampa and about 75 miles north of Fort Myers. The main roads into town are Tamiami Trail/Hwy 41 and I-75.

Greyhound (☑941-342-1720; www.greyhound. com; 5951 Porter Way; ⊙8:30-10am & 1:30-6pm) Connects Sarasota with Miami, Fort Myers and Tampa.

Sarasota-Bradenton International Airport (SRQ; ☑941-359-2770; www.srq-airport.com; 6000 Airport Circle) Served by many major airlines. Go north on Hwy 41, and right on University Ave.

Sanibel & Captiva Islands

By preference and by design, island life on Sanibel is informal and egalitarian, and riches are rarely flaunted. Development on Sanibel has been carefully managed: the northern half is almost entirely protected within the JN 'Ding' Darling National Wildlife Refuge. While there are hotels aplenty, the beachfront is free of commercial-and-condo blight. Plus, public beach access is limited to a handful of spread-out parking lots, so there is no crush of day-trippers in one place.

The pirate José Gaspar, who called himself Gasparilla, once roamed the Gulf Coast plundering treasure and seizing beautiful women, whom he held captive on the aptly named Captiva Island. Today the tiny village is confined to a single street, Andy Rosse Lane, and there are still no traffic lights. The preferred mode of transportation is the family-friendly bike, and life here is informal and egalitarian, with island riches rarely being flaunted. Captiva's mansions are hidden behind thick foliage and sport playful names such as 'Seas the Day.'

⊙ Sights & Activities

Captiva Beach   BEACH

(14790 Captiva Dr) Besides looking directly out onto heart-melting Gulf sunsets, Captiva Beach has lovely sand and is close to several romantic restaurants. Arrive early if you want to park in the small lot, or come by bike.

FLORIDA SANIBEL & CAPTIVA ISLANDS

JN 'Ding' Darling
National Wildlife Refuge WILDLIFE RESERVE
(☑239-472-1100; www.fws.gov/dingdarling; 1 Wildlife Dr; car/cyclist/pedestrian $5/1/1; ☉7am-sun-
set) Named for cartoonist Jay Norwood 'Ding'
Darling, an environmentalist who helped
establish more than 300 sanctuaries across
the USA, this 6300-acre refuge is home to an
abundance of seabirds and wildlife, including alligators, night herons, red-shouldered
hawks, spotted sandpipers, roseate spoon-
bills, pelicans and anhingas. The refuge's
5-mile Wildlife Drive provides easy access,
but bring binoculars; flocks sometimes sit
at expansive distances. Only a few very short
walks lead into the mangroves.

Captiva Cruises CRUISE
(☑239-472-5300; www.captivacruises.com; 11401
Andy Rosse Lane; adult/child from $30/20) De-
parting from McCarthy's Marina (☑239-
472-5200; www.mccarthysmarina.com; 11401 Andy
Rosse Lane), Captiva Cruises offers everything
from dolphin and sunset cruises to various
island excursions, such as Cayo Costa (adult/
child $50/35), Cabbage Key ($40/25), and
Boca Grande ($50/35) on Gasparilla Island.

Tarpon Bay Explorers KAYAKING
(☑239-472-8900; www.tarponbayexplorers.com;
900 Tarpon Bay Rd; canoe & kayak rental 2hr $25;
☉8am-6pm) Within the Darling refuge, this
outfitter rents canoes and kayaks for easy,
self-guided paddles in Tarpon Bay, a perfect
place for young paddlers. Guided kayak trips
(adult from $30 to $40, child from $20 to
$25) are also excellent, and there's a range of
other trips and deck talks. Reserve ahead or
come early, as trips book up.

🛏 Sleeping & Eating

Sandpiper Inn INN $$
(☑239-472-1606; www.palmviewsanibel.com;
720 Donax St; r $149-229; P❄🐾) Set a block
back from the water and in close proximity
to the shops and restaurants on Periwinkle
Way, this cheery, yellow-and-teal Old Florida inn offers good value for Sanibel. Each of
the one-bedroom units has a functional (if
dated) kitchen and a spacious sitting area
decked out in tropical colors.

★'Tween Waters Inn RESORT $$$
(☑239-472-5161; www.tween-waters.com; 15951
Captiva Dr; r $200-300, ste $285-425, cottages
$265-460; P❄🐾@🐾🐾) For great resort
value on Captiva, choose 'Tween Waters Inn.
Rooms are attractive roosts with granite

counters, rainfall showerheads and bright,
garish decor. All have balconies and those
directly facing the Gulf are splendid. The
tidy little cottages are romantic. Families
make good use of the big pool, tennis courts,
full-service marina, children's pool, and spa.
Multi-night discounts are attractive.

★Sweet Melissa's Cafe AMERICAN $$$
(☑239-472-1956; www.sweetmelissascafe.com;
1625 Periwinkle Way; tapas $9-18, mains $30-49;
☉11:30am-2:30pm & 5pm-close Mon-Fri, 5pm-
close Sat) From menu to mood, Sweet Melissa's offers well-balanced, relaxed refinement.
Dishes are ever-changing, but may include
things like farro fettuccine, escargot with
marrow and whole crispy fish. Creative
without trying too hard. Lots of small-plate
options encourage experimentation. Service
is attentive and the atmosphere upbeat.

ℹ Information
Sanibel & Captiva Islands Chamber of Commerce (☑239-472-1080; www.sanibel-captiva.
org; 1159 Causeway Rd; ☉9am-5pm; 🐾) One
of the more helpful visitor centers around;
keeps an updated hotel-vacancy list with
dedicated hotel hotline, and they even put
out buckets of brochures to help after-hours
visitors.

ℹ Getting There & Away
Driving is the only way to come and go. The Sanibel Causeway (Hwy 867) charges an entrance
toll (cars/motorcycles $6/2). Sanibel is 12 miles
long, but low speed limits and traffic makes it
seem longer. The main drag is Periwinkle Way,
which becomes Sanibel-Captiva Rd.

Naples
For upscale romance and the prettiest, most
serene city beach in southwest Florida, come
to Naples, the Gulf Coast's answer to Palm
Beach. Development along the shoreline has
been kept residential. The soft white sand
is backed only by narrow dunes and half-
hidden mansions. More than that, though,
Naples is a cultured, sophisticated town,
unabashedly stylish and privileged but also
welcoming and fun loving. Families, teens,
couture-wearing matrons, middle-aged ex-
ecutives and smartly dressed young couples
all mix and mingle as they stroll downtown's
5th Ave on a balmy evening. Travelers sometimes complain that Naples is expensive, but
you can spend just as much elsewhere on a
less impressive vacation.

⊙ Sights & Activities

★ Naples Botanical Gardens GARDENS
(☑ 239-643-7275; www.naplesgarden.org; 4820 Bayshore Dr; adult/4-14yr $20/10; ☺ 9am-5pm Wed-Mon, from 8am Tue) This outstanding botanical garden styles itself as 'a place of bliss, a region of supreme delight.' And after spending some time wandering its 2½-mile trail through nine cultivated gardens you'll rapidly find your inner Zen. Children will dig the thatched-roof tree house, butterfly house and interactive fountain, while adults get dreamy-eyed contemplating landscape architect Raymond Jungles' Scott Florida garden, filled with cascades, 12ft-tall oolite rocks and legacy tree species like date palms, sycamore leaf figs and lemon ficus.

★ Baker Museum MUSEUM
(☑ 239-597-1900; www.artisnaples.org; 5833 Pelican Bay Blvd; adult/child $10/free; ☺ 10am-4pm Tue-Sat, from noon Sun) The pride of Naples, this engaging, sophisticated art museum is part of the Artis–Naples campus, which includes the fabulous Philharmonic Center next door. Devoted to 20th-century modern art, the museum's 15 galleries and glass dome conservatory host exciting temporary and permanent shows, ranging from postmodern works to photography and paper craft to glass sculpture, including a stunning Chihuly exhibition. Note that due to damage from Hurricane Irma, the museum was under repair at the time of research, scheduled to reopen in November 2019.

Naples Municipal Beach BEACH
(12th Ave S & Gulf Shore Blvd) Naples' city beach is a long, dreamy white strand that succeeds in feeling lively but rarely overcrowded. At the end of 12th Ave S, the 1000ft pier is a symbol of civic pride, having been constructed in 1888, destroyed a few times by fire and hurricane, and reconstructed each time. Parking is spread out in small lots between 7th Ave N and 17th Ave S, each with 10 to 15 spots of mixed resident and metered parking ($1.50 per hour).

🛏 Sleeping & Eating

Inn on 5th HOTEL $$$
(☑ 239-403-8777; www.innonfifth.com; 699 5th Ave S; r $399, ste $599-999; P ❋ @ 🛜 ⛱) This well-polished, Mediterranean-style luxury hotel provides an unbeatable location on either side of 5th Ave. Giant red vases grace the entryway. Stylish rooms are more corporate than romantic, but who complains about pillow-top mattresses and glass-walled showers? Full-service amenities include a 2nd-floor heated pool, business and fitness centers, and an indulgent spa. Free valet parking.

★ Escalante BOUTIQUE HOTEL $$$
(☑ 239-659-3466; www.hotelescalante.com; 290 5th Ave S; r $505-1285) Hidden in plain sight at 5th Ave and 3rd St, the wonderful Escalante is a boutique hotel crafted in the fashion of a Tuscan villa. Rooms and suites are nestled behind luxuriant foliage and flowering pergolas, and feature plantation-style furniture, European linens and designer bath products.

The Local AMERICAN $$
(☑ 239-596-3276; www.thelocalnaples.com; 5323 Airport Pulling Rd N; mains $12-29; ☺ 11am-9pm; 🛜) ⌀ Aside from the irony of driving 6 miles from downtown to eat local, this strip-mall farm-to-table bistro is worth the carbon footprint for fab sustainable fare, from the Mediterranean watermelon salad to the grass-fed beef. Try the 'Not Too Effin Hot Sauce,' if you're feeling feisty. Escape tourists. Eat local.

★ Bha! Bha! Persian Bistro IRANIAN $$$
(☑ 239-594-5557; www.bhabhabistro.com; 865 5th Ave S; mains $27-49; ☺ 5-9pm Sun-Thu, to 10pm Fri & Sat) This experimental, high-end establishment takes its name from the Farsi phrase for 'yum, yum,' and that turns out to be a serious understatement. Wash down the pistachio lamb meatballs ($18) with a saffron lemongrass martini, then continue on to a kebab marinated in exotic spices or the duck *fesenjune* ($38), slow braised with pomegranate and walnut sauce.

ⓘ Information

Third St Concierge Kiosk
(☑ 239-434-6533; www.thirdstreetsouth.com; Camargo Park, 3rd St S; ☺ 10am-6pm Mon-Wed, to 9pm Thu & Fri, from 9am Sat, noon-5pm Sun) What's in Old Naples? This friendly outdoor kiosk attendant is glad you asked.

Visitor Information Center
(☑ 239-262-6376; www.napleschamber.org; 2390 Tamiami Trail N; ☺ 9am-5pm Mon-Fri) Will help with accommodations; good maps, internet access and acres of brochures.

ⓘ Getting There & Away

A car is essential; ample and free downtown parking makes things easy. Naples is about 40 miles southwest of Fort Myers via I-75.

Greyhound (☎239-774-5660; www.greyhound. com; 3825 Tollgate Blvd) Connects Naples to Miami, Orlando and Tampa.

Southwest Florida International Airport (RSW; ☎239-590-4800; www.flylcpa.com; 11000 Terminal Access Rd) This is the main airport for Naples. It's about a 45-minute drive north, along I-75.

CENTRAL FLORIDA

Central Florida is like a *matryoshka*, the Russian doll that encases similar dolls of diminishing size. The region features pretty state parks, gardens and rivers, all ideal for leisurely exploration. One layer down, Central Florida then embraces Kissimmee, Celebration and the vast, sprawling area of Greater Orlando. Greater Orlando's network of multi-lane highways and overpasses leads to a huge number of theme parks, including Walt Disney World®, Universal Orlando Resort, SeaWorld and Legoland. Judging from the crowds, these parks are the reason most people visit.

But at Central Florida's core is a city: pretty, leafy downtown Orlando, whose great field-to-fork eating scene and world-class museums get overlooked by the hype, sparkle and colors of the theme parks. Many visitors never reach this kernel, the final 'doll,' and the city of Orlando tends to lie in the shadow of Cinderella and Hogwarts School of Witchcraft & Wizardry.

Orlando

It's so easy to get caught up in Greater Orlando – in the isolated, fabricated worlds of Disney or Universal Orlando (for which, let's face it, you're probably here) – that you forget all about the downtown city of Orlando itself. It has a lot to offer: lovely tree-lined neighborhoods; a rich performing arts and museum scene; several fantastic gardens and nature preserves; fabulous cuisine; great craft cocktails; and a delightfully slower pace devoid of manic crowds. So, sure, enjoy the theme parks and the sparkles, nostalgia and adrenaline-pumped fantasy there, but also take time to 'Find Orlando.' Come down off the coasters for one day to explore the quieter, gentler side of the city. You may be surprised to find that you enjoy the theme parks all that much more as a result.

◉ Sights

★**Mennello Museum of American Art** MUSEUM (☎407-246-4278; www.mennellomuseum.org; 900 E Princeton St, Loch Haven Park, Downtown; adult/child 6-18yr $5/1; ◷10:30am-4:30pm Tue-Sat, from noon Sun; ☒Lynx 125, ☒Florida Hospital Health Village) Tiny but excellent lakeside art museum featuring the work of Earl Cunningham, whose brightly colored images, a fusion of pop and folk art, leap off the canvas. Visiting exhibits often feature American folk art. Every four months there's a new exhibition, everything from a Smithsonian collection to a local artist. The mystical live oak in front makes even parking beautiful.

★**Orlando Museum of Art** MUSEUM (☎407-896-4231; www.omart.org; 2416 N Mills Ave, Loch Haven Park, Downtown; adult/child $15/5; ◷10am-4pm Tue-Fri, from noon Sat & Sun; ☒; ☒Lynx 125, ☒Florida Hospital Health Village) Founded in 1924, Orlando's grand center for the arts boasts a fantastic collection – both permanent and temporary – and hosts an array of adult and family-friendly art events and classes. The popular First Thursday ($15), from 6pm to 9pm on the first Thursday of the month, celebrates local artists with regional work, live music and food from Orlando restaurants.

ICON Orlando AMUSEMENT PARK (www.iconorlando.com; I-Drive 360, 8401 International Dr, International Drive; from $24; ◷10am-10pm Sun-Thu, to midnight Fri & Sat) Orlando has got everything else that goes up and down, so why not round and around? Opened in 2017, ICON Orlando is one of International Drive's latest landmarks. Orlando is flat, but a trip in this, especially at night, affords views of the theme parks and the greater area. Check ahead as it sometimes closes for private events.

SeaWorld AMUSEMENT PARK (☎407-545-5550; www.seaworldparks.com; 7007 Sea World Dr; $99, discounts online, prices vary daily; ◷9am-8pm; ☒; ☒Lynx 8, 38, 50, 111, ☒I-Ride Trolley Red Line Stop 28) One of Orlando's largest theme parks, SeaWorld is an aquatic-themed park filled with marine animal shows, roller coasters and up-close sea-life encounters. However, the park's biggest draw is controversial: live shows featuring trained dolphins, sea lions and killer whales. Since the release of the 2013 documentary *Blackfish*, SeaWorld's treatment of its captive orcas has come under intense scrutiny and the company has been hit by falling visitor numbers and negative PR.

Titanic: the Artifact Exhibition MUSEUM
(☑ 407-248-1166; www.premierexhibitions.com; 7324 International Dr, International Drive; adult/child 6-11yr $24/17; ⊙ Fri-Sat 10am-6pm, to 8pm Sun-Thu; 🚹; 🚌 Lynx 8, 38, 42, 🚋 I-Ride Trolley Red Line Stop 9) Full-scale replicas of the doomed ship's interior and artifacts found at the bottom of the sea, 170 in all, including one of only two pieces of the actual ship's hull. Kids especially love the dramatic and realistic interpretation of history – each passenger receives a boarding pass, with the name of a real passenger, and at the end of the experience (once the ship has sunk) you learn your fate.

🛏 Sleeping

⭐ **Floridian Hotel & Suites** HOTEL $
(☑ 407-212-3021; www.floridianhotelorlando.com; 7531 Canada Ave, International Drive; r from $75; P ✱ ❄ 🏨 🛜 🏊) A wonderful, privately owned budget hotel with similarities to a chain brand, but oh so much better in other respects: delightful front office staff, spotless rooms with fridges, and even a complimentary (if basic) breakfast, plus shuttles to various parks. It's near Restaurant Row and handy to International Dr.

Hyatt Regency
Grand Cypress Resort RESORT $$
(☑ 407-239-1234; www.hyattregencygrandcypress.com; 1 Grand Cypress Blvd, Lake Buena Vista; r $189-300, resort fee per day $35, self-/valet parking $22/31; P @ ❄ 🛜 🏊 🏨) Considering the proximity to Disney's Magic Kingdom (7 miles) and Universal Resort Orlando (8 miles), plus the quality of the rooms, service, grounds and amenities, this atrium-style resort is one of the best-value options in Orlando, though it's certainly not a unique nor boutique experience.

⭐ **Bay Hill Club and Lodge** HOTEL $$$
(☑ 407-876-2429; www.bayhill.com; 9000 Bay Hill Blvd; r $250-700; P ✱ ❄ @ 🛜 🏊) Quiet and genteel Bay Hill feels like a time warp; as though you're walking into a TV set or your grandmother's photo album. It is reassuringly calm and simple. Handsome rooms are spread among a series of two-story buildings bordering the Arnold Palmer–designed golf course. Internet deals are frequent.

Aloft Orlando
Downtown BUSINESS HOTEL $$$
(☑ 407-380-3500; www.aloftorlandododowntown.com; 500 S Orange Ave, Downtown; r from $250; P ⊜ @ 🛜 🏊) Open, streamlined and decidedly modern, although the carefully constructed minimalist decor might render the rooms oddly empty for some. The sleek little pool sits unpleasantly on the main road. But it is one of the few hotels within an easy walk to downtown Orlando's bars and restaurants.

🍴 Eating

⭐ **P Is for Pie** BAKERY $
(☑ 407-745-4743; www.crazyforpies.com; 2806 Corrine Dr, Audubon Park; from $2; ⊙ 7:30am-4:30pm Mon-Sat) Clean-lined with an artisan twist to classic pies (as in sweet tarts with a biscuit base), offering mini and specialty options. Flavors include a sublime key lime and tiramisu. Sublime.

⭐ **Dandelion**
Communitea Café VEGETARIAN $
(☑ 407-362-1864; www.dandelioncommunity.com; 618 N Thornton Ave, Thornton Park; mains $9-12; ⊙ 11am-10pm Mon-Sat, to 5pm Sun; 🅿 🚹) 🌱 Unabashedly crunchy and definitively organic, this pillar of the sprouts and tempeh and green-tea dining scene serves up creative and excellent plant-based fare in a refurbished old house that invites folks to sit down and hang out.

Graffiti Junktion
American Burger Bar BURGERS $
(☑ 321-424-5800; www.graffitijunktion.com; 700 E Washington St, Thornton Park; mains $9-15; ⊙ 11am-2am) This little neon, happenin' hangout, with courtyard dining and regular drink specials, is all about massive burgers with attitude. Go with a Brotherly Love (Angus beef; $11) or veggie option ($9). Happy hour is all day on Monday and from 4pm to 7pm Tuesday to Sunday.

Pho 88 VIETNAMESE $
(☑ 407-897-3488; www.pho88orlando.com; 730 N Mills Ave, Mills 50; mains $9-17; ⊙ 10am-10pm; 🅿) A flagship in Orlando's thriving Vietnamese district (known as Little Saigon), just northeast of downtown in an area informally referred to as Mills 50, this authentic, no frills, *pho* (noodle soup) specialist is always packed. Big bowls of noodles are cheap and tasty, as are the popular potstickers. Many of the items are, or can be done, vegetarian.

Melting Pot   EUROPEAN $$
(☎ 407-903-1100; www.meltingpot.com; 7549
W Sand Lake Rd, Restaurant Row; mains $11-48;
⏱ 5-10pm Mon-Thu, to 11pm Fri, noon-11pm Sat,
noon-10pm Sun; 🚸) Kids in particular love
the novelty of a fondue dinner (cheese, beef,
chicken, seafood and, of course, chocolate).
Having said that, it's an elegant spot and a
popular date-night place.

★**La Luce**   ITALIAN $$$
(☎ 407-597-3675; www.laluceorlando.com; 14100
Bonnet Creek Resort Ln; mains $26-44; ⏱ 6-11pm;
🅿) La Luce is a gem – whether it's a quiet corner table with a special someone or
a friendly chat with folks at the bar – and
feels like that place you've been going to for
years even if it's your first time here. Meals
are fantastic, sometimes quirky, always
tasty. Duck *ragu* (meat sauce), crisp salads,
melt-in-your-mouth desserts. Just a world
of yum. The butterscotch pudding is so
good it even has its own Facebook fan page.

🍷 Drinking & Nightlife

★**Icebar**   BAR
(☎ 407-426-7555; www.icebarorlando.com; 8967
International Dr; entry at door/advance online
$20/15; ⏱ 5pm-midnight Sun-Wed, to 1am Thu, to
2am Fri & Sat; 🚊 I-Trolley Red Line Stop 18 or Green
Line Stop 10) More classic Orlando gimmicky
fun. Step into the 22ºF (-5ºC) ice house, sit
on the ice seat, admire the ice carvings and
sip the icy drinks. Coat and gloves are provided at the door (or upgrade to the photogenic faux fur for $10), and the fire room,
bathrooms and other areas of the bar are
kept at normal temperature.

Independent Bar   CLUB
(☎ 407-839-0457; 70 N Orange Ave, Downtown;
varies, often $10; ⏱ 10pm-2:30am Sat-Thu, from
9:30pm Fri) Known to locals as simply the
'I-Bar,' it's hip, crowded and loud, with DJs
spinning underground dance and alternative rock into the wee hours.

ℹ Information

Official Visitor Center (☎ 407-363-5872;
www.visitorlando.com; 8102 International Dr;
⏱ 8am-8pm; 🚊 I-Ride Trolley Red Line 11)

ℹ Getting There & Around

Amtrak (www.amtrak.com; 1400 Sligh Blvd)
offers daily trains south to Miami (from $47)
and north to New York City (from $150).

Greyhound (☎ 407-292-3424; www.grey
hound.com; 555 N John Young Pkwy) serves
numerous cities from Orlando.

LYMMO (www.golynx.com; free; ⏱ 6am-
10:45pm Mon-Fri, from 10am Sat, 10am-10pm
Sun) circles downtown Orlando for free with
stops near Lynx Central Station, near SunRail's
Church St Station, at Central and Magnolia,
Jefferson and Magnolia and outside the Westin
Grand Bohemian.

SunRail (www.sunrail.com), Orlando's commuter rail train, runs north–south. It doesn't
stop at or near any theme parks.

In addition to the downtown station, Amtrak
serves Winter Park, Kissimmee and Winter
Haven (home to Legoland).

Walt Disney World® Resort

This mega-scale **resort** (☎ 407-939-5277; www.
disneyworld.disney.go.com; Lake Buena Vista, outside Orlando; daily rates vary, from around $109, see
website for discount packages & tickets up to 10 days;
🚸), with its own monorail, sections of eight-
lane highway, and thousands of acres of rides,
amusements, parks, and hotels, is larger than
a good sized international airport...and about
as easy to navigate. Disney World is in fact
an unfenced 40-sq-mile area. But within this,
although several miles apart from each other,
are four contained, spotlessly sanitized theme
parks: **Magic Kingdom, Epcot, Hollywood
Studios** and **Animal Kingdom**.

Also within the Walt Disney World® pa-
rameters are two water parks, two shopping
districts, golf courses, more than 20 Disney-
owned-and-run hotels, countless places to
eat, a police force, transport systems (did
someone say monorail?), and kennels for
the pooch.

And let's clarify something else: Walt Disney World® offers a lot more than rides. The
huge number of attractions include interactive meet 'n' greets with well-known characters, including Mickey Mouse and Donald
Duck, as well as more contemporary casts
such as Gaston, Elsa, Anna and so on. Then
there are parades, musical productions,
interactive facilities, Disney promotions
of the latest projects and plenty of stunt
shows. And (here's the surprising part), it's
not just for kids. Disney World has cleverly maintained its loyal following, resulting
in hundreds of thousands of more mature
visitors who just can't get enough, through
programs, cuisine, cruises and behind-the-
scenes tours.

Each of the four parks has its own theme, although when most people think of Walt Disney World®, they're often thinking of one of the four parks – **the Magic Kingdom**, with Cinderella Castle at its core. This is the Disney of commercials, of princesses and pirates, Tinkerbell and dreams come true; this is quintessential, old-school Disney with classic rides such as It's a Small World and Space Mountain.

Epcot is a wonderful sensory experience. The park is divided into two sections that are situated around a lake: Future World and World Showcase. **Future World** has Epcot's only two thrill rides plus several pavilions with attractions, restaurants, and character-greeting spots. **World Showcase** comprises 11 re-created nations featuring country-specific food, shopping and entertainment. This is the place to slow down a little and enjoy, where you can smell the incense in Morocco, listen to the Beatles in the UK and sip miso in Japan.

Hollywood Studios conjures the heydays of Hollywood, with a replica of Graumann's Chinese Theatre (the main focal icon), but most of the activities reflect unabashed 21st-century energy with attractions focusing on everything from *Star Wars* Jedi training to *Indiana Jones* stunt shows, from Muppet extravaganzas to the latest craze, the Frozen Sing-Along Celebration.

Set apart from the rest of Disney both in miles and in tone, **Animal Kingdom** attempts to blend theme park with zoo, carnival and African safari, all stirred together with a healthy dose of Disney characters, storytelling and transformative magic. Like the other parts, it's also divided into different sections, with wildlife experiences, rides, and musical shows at every corner, including the *The Lion King* and *Nemo*. At the time of research, Animal Kingdom was about to open another area: the much-awaited **Pandora – The World of Avatar**.

To round off the Disney experience, Walt Disney World® runs a number of accommodations, including family options and couples' luxury experiences. The advantage of staying at one of these is that most things, including meals and transportation, are arranged or easily accessible to you (but, although you make things run smoothly, especially if you have children, they're not the be all and end all; other hotels nearby also offer similar services). But they do serve up further fun and yes, even more entertainment including opportunities to dine with Disney characters. It is well designed for travelers with disabilities, with wheelchair rental, easy access and excellent arrangements for line access and the like.

In short, an experience at Walt Disney World® is extraordinary. It's an unabashed stimulation overload of music, light, sound, color, thrills and spills. It offers an other worldliness that is fully, inexplicably intoxicating, no matter your age. And that's despite the long lines, the occasional jostling and the over-priced meals. For most of the time, this is indeed the Happiest Place on Earth.

And, just when the sun has set and you think you're done for the day, there's more; each park has a nighttime fireworks show (the names of which change according to the annual program).

Daily ticket prices vary, but a ticketing system introduced in February 2017 provides for multiday tickets (one park per day over a set number of days) and Park Hopper options, which allow you to 'park hop' (note: logistically, this is time consuming and, with the exception of, say, Epcot and Hollywood Studios, not very feasible).

🛏 Sleeping & Eating

Disney resort hotels are divided according to location (Magic Kingdom, Epcot, Animal Kingdom and Disney Boardwalk). Prices vary drastically according to season, week and day.

While deluxe resorts are the best Disney has to offer, note that you're paying for Disney theming and location convenience, not luxury. Most offer multiroom suites and villas, upscale restaurants, children's programs and easy access to theme parks.

With the exception of Epcot, expect mediocre fast food, bad coffee and cafeteria cuisine at premium prices. Table-service restaurants accept 'priority seating' reservations up to 180 days in advance. Reserve through **Disney Dining** (☑ 407-939-3463; www.disneyworld.disney.go.com) or through the My Disney Experience app. Remember: while restaurants in the theme parks require theme-park admission, resort hotel restaurants do not.

Disney also offers character meals, dinner shows and specialty dining.

❶ Getting There & Around

Disney lies 25 minutes' drive south of downtown Orlando. Take I-4 to well-signed exits 64, 65 or 67. Alamos and National car rental is available inside the Walt Disney World® Dolphin Resort.

If you're staying at a Walt Disney World® hotel and are arriving at Orlando International Airport (as opposed to Sanford), arrange in advance for complimentary luggage handling and deluxe bus transportation with **Disney's Magical Express** (☎ 866-599-0951; www.disneyworld.disney. go.com). They will send you baggage labels in advance, collect your luggage at the airport and, if during your stay you transfer from one Disney hotel to another, the resort will transfer your luggage while you're off for the day.

The Disney transportation system utilizes boats, buses, and even a monorail to shuttle visitors to hotels, theme parks and other attractions within Walt Disney World®. The Transportation & Ticket Center operates as the main hub of this system. Note that it can take an hour to get from point A to point B using the Disney transportation system, and there is not always a direct route.

Universal Orlando Resort

Pedestrian-friendly **Universal Orlando Resort** (☎ 407-363-8000; www.universalorlando. com; 1000 Universal Studios Plaza; single park 1/2 days adult $105/185, child $100/175, both parks adult/child $155/150; ☉ daily, hours vary; ☐ Lynx 21, 37 & 40, ☐ Universal) has got spunk, spirit and attitude. With fantastic rides, excellent children's attractions and entertain-

Greater Orlando & Theme Parks

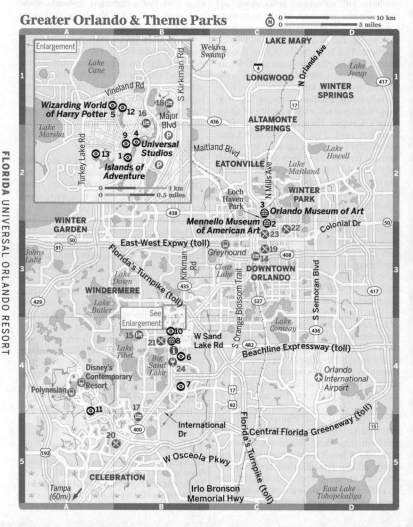

ing shows, it's comparable to Walt Disney World®. But Universal does everything just a bit smarter, funnier, and more smoothly, as well as being smaller and easier to navigate. Universal offers pure, unabashed, adrenaline-pumped, full-speed-ahead fun for the entire family.

The Universal Orlando Resort consists of three theme parks – Islands of Adventure, with the bulk of the thrill rides, and Universal Studios, with movie-based attractions and shows (including the Wizarding World of Harry Potter). Volcano Bay is a water park of thrills and splashes and state-of-the-art rides through a 200ft volcano.

Universal's dining and entertainment district is CityWalk and it has six resort hotels. Water taxis and pleasant walking paths connect the entire resort.

Multiday and multipark tickets are available, so check online for the latest combinations and offers.

◉ Sights

★Universal Studios AREA
(☑ 407-363-8000; www.universalorlando.com; 1000 Universal Studios Plaza, Universal Orlando Resort; 1 day adult $115, child $110; ⊙ from 9am, closing hours vary; ⬚ Lynx 21, 37 or 40, 🚢 Universal) Divided geographically by region-specific architecture and ambience and fabulously themed as a Hollywood backlot, Universal Studios' simulation-heavy rides and shows are dedicated to silver screen and TV icons. Drink Duff beer, a Homer favorite, in Spring-

ville; ride the Hogwarts Express into Diagon Alley; and sidle up to Lucille Ball on Hollywood Blvd. And if you're looking for thrills, you'll find two of Orlando's best roller coasters: Revenge of the Mummy and Hollywood Rip Ride Rockit.

For some downtime, a fenced-in grassy area with shade trees, flowers and views across the lagoon sits just across from the entrance to Woody Woodpecker's Kidzone.

★Wizarding World of Harry Potter AREA
(☑ 407-363-8000; www.universalorlando.com; Islands of Adventure & Universal Studios; theme park admission required; ⊙ from 9am (closing hours vary); ⬚ Lynx 21, 37 or 40) Alan Gilmore and Stuart Craig, art director and production designer for the films, collaborated closely with the Universal Orlando Resort engineers to create what is without exception the most fantastically realized themed experience in Florida. The detail and authenticity tickle the fancy at every turn, from the screeches of the mandrakes in the shop windows to the groans of Moaning Myrtle in the bathroom.

Poke along the cobbled streets and impossibly crooked buildings of Hogsmeade, sip frothy Butterbeer, munch on Cauldron Cakes and mail a card via Owl Post, all in the shadow of Hogwarts Castle, and keep your eyes peeled for magical happenings. The Wizarding World of Harry Potter is divided into two sections, each with rides and shows: **Hogsmeade** (☑ 407-363-8000;

(side tab) **FLORIDA** UNIVERSAL ORLANDO RESORT

Greater Orlando & Theme Parks

www.universalorlando.com; Islands of Adventure; theme-park admission required; ⊗9am-6pm, hours vary; 🚃Lynx 21, 37 or 40) sits in Islands of Adventure and **Diagon Alley** (www.universalorlando.com; Universal Studios; theme-park admission required; ⊗from 9am; 🚃Lynx 21, 37 or 40), completed in 2014, is in Universal Studios. If you have a park-to-park ticket, hop on the Hogwarts Express from one section to the other. New to Hogsmeade is Hagrid's Magical Creatures Motorbike Adventure, where visitors buckle in and 'fly' through the Forbidden Forest.

One hour early admission is available for guests at Universal Orlando Resort hotels.

★ **Islands of Adventure**   AREA
(☑407-363-8000; www.universalorlando.com; 6000 Universal Blvd, Universal Orlando Resort; 1 day adult $115, child $110; ⊗from 9am, closing hours vary; 🚃Lynx 21, 37 or 40, 🚢Universal) Good ol' scream-it-from-the-rooftops, no-holds-barred, laugh-out-loud fun, packed with adrenaline rides and marvelous theming. Superheroes zoom by on motorcycles, roller coasters whiz overhead and plenty of rides will get you soaked. Highlights include Marvel Super Hero Island, with the Amazing Adventures of Spiderman and the Hulk Coaster; kid-friendly Seuss Landing; and, most famously of all, Hogwarts in the Wizarding World of Harry Potter – Hogsmeade. Multiday and multipark tickets available.

Volcano Bay   AREA
(www.universalorlando.com; 6000 Universal Blvd, Universal Resort; 1 day adult $70, child $65; ⊗from 9am, closing hours vary) Universal Resort's third theme park – a water park – launched in 2017. Modeled on a Pacific island, the tropical oasis' main feature is a colossal volcano through and down which, you guessed it, run watery thrills and spills. Among the 18 attractions are winding rivers with family raft rides, pools and two intertwining slides, but the main attraction is the Ko'okiri Body Plunge. At a hair-raising 125ft, it's the tallest trap-door body plunge ride in North America.

It's located alongside Islands of Adventure and Universal. Hold your spot in line with a TapuTapu wristband.

🛏 Sleeping & Eating

Universal Orlando Resort is home to a number of excellent resort hotels. Staying at a resort hotel eliminates many logistical hassles: it's a pleasant gardened walk or a quiet boat ride to the parks; most offer Unlimited Express Pass access to park attractions and priority dining; several popular rides open one hour earlier for all guests. Each Universal Resort has high-quality bars and restaurants that can be enjoyed even if you're not a guest.

★ **Loews Portofino Bay Hotel**   RESORT $$$
(☑407-503-1000; www.loewshotels.com/portofino-bay-hotel; 5601 Universal Blvd, Universal Orlando Resort; r & ste $325-$390, self/valet parking per day $22/30; 🅿❄@🛜🏊🐾; 🚢Universal) Sumptuous and elegant, with beautiful rooms, cobblestone streets and sidewalk cafes around a central lagoon, this resort evokes the relaxing charm of seaside Italy. There's a sandy zero-entrance family pool, the secluded Hillside pool and the elegant Villa pool, as well as the Mandara Spa, evening waterside minstrel music and the excellent Mama Della's Ristorante. Rates include one-hour early entrance to the Wizarding World of Harry Potter and an Unlimited Express Pass.

Hard Rock Hotel   RESORT $$$
(☑407-503-2000; www.hardrockhotels.com/orlando; 5800 Universal Blvd, Universal Orlando Resort; r & ste $329 to $393, self-/valet parking per day $22/30; 🅿❄@🛜🏊🐾; 🚢Universal) From the grand lawn with the massive guitar fountain at its entrance to the pumped-in, underwater music at the pool, the modern and stylized Hard Rock embodies the pure essence and energy of rock 'n' roll cool. Rates include one-hour early entrance to the Wizarding World of Harry Potter and an Unlimited Express Pass.

There's a huge zero-entry pool with a waterslide, and families mingle harmoniously alongside a young party crowd, but the loud live band that sometimes plays in the lobby and the rockin' vibe may be overkill for folk looking for a peaceful getaway. If you're looking for something more subdued, head to Portofino Bay.

★ **Mama Della's Ristorante**   ITALIAN $$
(☑407-503-3463; www.universalorlando.com; 5601 Universal Blvd, Loews Portofino Bay Hotel; mains $10-22; ⊗5:30-11pm; 🚗👶; 🚢Universal) Charming, cozy and friendly, with vintage wallpaper, dark wood and several rooms with romantic nooks. You really do feel like you're a welcomed guest at a private home nestled in Italy. Strolling musicians entertain tableside and the simple Italian fare is both fresh and excellent; the service is efficient but relaxed.

Good wine, old-fashioned soda in a bottle and a bowl of pasta at Mama Della's makes a very nice ending to a day at the parks, for both kids and adults.

ℹ️ Getting There & Around

From I-4, take exit 74B or 75A and follow the signs. From International Dr, follow the signs west onto Universal Blvd.

Lynx buses 21, 37 and 40 service the Universal Orlando Resort parking garage (40 runs directly from the downtown Orlando Amtrak station). International Dr's **I-Ride Trolley** (☑ 407-354-5656; www.iridetrolley.com; rides adult/child 3-9yr $2/1, passes 1/3/5/7/14 days $5/7/9/12/18; ☺ 8am-10:30pm) stops at Universal Blvd, a 0.6-mile walk away.

Universal Orlando Resort – that is, Universal Orlando's resort hotels, Islands of Adventure and Universal Studios theme parks and CityWalk – are linked by pedestrian walkways. It's a 10- to 15-minute walk from the theme parks and CityWalk to the deluxe resort hotels. Cabana Bay Beach Resort is about a 25-minute walk. Several hotels outside the park are within a 20-minute walk, but it's not a very pleasant journey.

Rent strollers, wheelchairs and Electric Convenience Vehicles (ECVs) at the entrance to each park and manual wheelchairs at the Rotunda section of the parking lot. To reserve an ECV in advance, call ☑ 407-224-4233.

FLORIDA PANHANDLE

The most geographically northern end of Florida is by far its most culturally Southern side. The Panhandle – that spit of land embedded in the left shoulder of the Florida peninsula – is hemmed in by Alabama and Georgia, and in many ways the region's beaches are effectively coastal extensions of those states.

This is a coast of primal, wind-blown beauty in many places, particularly the undeveloped stretches of salt marsh and slash pine that spill east and west of Apalachee Bay. In other areas, the seashore is given to rental houses and high-rise condos.

Inland, you'll find a tangle of palmetto fans and thin pine woods interspersed with crystal springs, lazy rivers and military testing ranges – this area has one of the highest concentrations of defense facilities in the country.

In October, 2018, the area was hit by devastating Hurricane Michael, which decimated many parts of the region. Recovery was ongoing at the time of research.

WORTH A TRIP

DELAND: CRESS

Citified foodies have been known to trek to sleepy DeLand just to eat at cutting-edge **Cress** (☑ 386-734-3740; www.cressrestaurant.com; 103 W Indiana Ave; events $65-95; ☺ ticketed reservations only), whose menu might offer such delights as local seafood *mofongo* (a classic Caribbean dish), Indonesian shrimp curry, and a salad of delicate pea tendrils with passion-fruit emulsion. It has recently switched to a ticket-only reservation system, so you must call ahead and check the website for events.

Tallahassee

Florida's capital, cradled between gently rising hills and nestled beneath tree-canopied roadways, is geographically closer to Atlanta than it is to Miami. Culturally, it's far closer to the Deep South than the majority of the state it governs.

Despite its status as a government center, and the presence of two major universities (Florida State and Florida Agricultural & Mechanical University), the pace here is slower than syrup. That said, there are interesting museums and outlying attractions that will appeal to history and nature buffs and could easily detain a visitor for a day or two.

👁️ Sights & Activities

⭐ **Tallahassee Museum**   MUSEUM
(☑ 850-575-8684; www.tallahasseemuseum.org; 3945 Museum Rd; adult/child $12/9; ☺ 9am-5pm Mon-Sat, from 11am Sun; 🅿️ 🚹) 🌿 Occupying 52 acres of pristine manicured gardens and wilderness on the outskirts of Tallahassee, near the airport, this wonderful natural-history museum features living exhibits of Floridian flora and fauna – including the incredibly rare Floridan panther and red wolf – and has delighted visitors for more than 50 years. Be sure to check out the otters in their new home, or try ziplining above the canopy in the Tree to Tree Adventures – a variety of scenarios are available, costing $17 to $45 depending on the options.

Tallahassee Automobile & Collectibles Museum   MUSEUM
(☑ 850-942-0137; www.tacm.com; 6800 Mahan Dr; adult/student/child under 10yr $18/12/8; ☺ 8am-5pm Mon-Fri, from 10am Sat, from noon

APALACHICOLA NATIONAL FOREST

The largest of Florida's three national forests, the **Apalachicola National Forest** (☎850-523-8500, 850-643-2282; www.fs.usda.gov/main/apalachicola; entrance off FL 13, FL 67, & other locations; day-use fee $3; ⏰8am-sunset; 🅿) 🏊 occupies almost 938 sq miles – more than half a million acres – of the Panhandle from just west of Tallahassee to the Apalachicola River. It's made up of lowlands, pines, cypress hammocks and oaks, and dozens of species call the area home, including mink, gray and red foxes, coyotes, six bat species, beavers, woodpeckers, alligators, Florida black bears and the elusive Florida panther. Numerous lakes and miles of trails make this one of the most diverse outdoor recreation areas in the state. Though the region was hit hard by Hurricane Michael in 2018, the natural beauty still shines through – if with a lot more broken trees.

You'll need wheels to explore the forest, either a bicycle for the exceedingly fit, or a car for the rest of us. Given that the woods cover such an enormous area, there are multiple entry points, including along SR 65 (easier if you're coming from Apalachicola) and SR 20 (good for those coming from Tallahassee).

The western half of the forest is controlled by the **Apalachicola Ranger Station** (☎850-643-2282; www.fs.usda.gov/apalachicola; 11152 NW SR-20, Bristol), northwest of the forest near the intersection of Hwys 12 and 20, just south of Bristol.

The eastern half of the forest is managed by the **Wakulla Ranger Station** (☎850-926-3561; www.fs.usda.gov/apalachicola; 57 Taff Dr, Crawfordville), just off Hwy 319 in Crawfordville.

Sun; 🅿) If you like motor vehicles, welcome to heaven! This museum houses a pristine collection of more than 165 unique and historical automobiles from around the world, including an Elvismobile. Top that with collections of boats, motorcycles, books, pianos and sports memorabilia and you've got a full day on your hands. There's even a Tie-Fighter. It is about 8 miles northeast of downtown, off I-10.

Florida State Capitol NOTABLE BUILDING
(www.floridacapitol.myflorida.com; 400 South Monroe St; ⏰8am-5pm Mon-Fri) FREE The stark and imposing 22-story Florida State Capitol's top-floor observation deck affords 360-degree views of the city. In session the capitol is a hive of activity, with politicians, staffers and lobby groups buzzing in and around its honeycombed corridors. There are few states that have as diverse a legislature as Florida's – in one hall, you may hear Cuban Americans from Miami brokering deals with good old boys from the Panhandle. America! Locals and tourists alike have noted that the new building, a lone shaft with rounded domes on either side, bears striking resemblance to a, um, er...well, go look for yourself.

Tallahassee-St Marks Historic Railroad State Trail CYCLING
(☎850-487-7989; www.floridastateparks.org/tallahasseestmarks; 1358 Old Woodville Rd, Craw-fordville; ⏰8am-sunset) 🚲 FREE The ultimate treat for runners, skaters and cyclists, this trail has 16 miles of smooth pavement shooting due south to the gulf-port town of St Marks and not a car or traffic light in sight. It's easy and flat for all riders, sitting on a coastal plain and shaded at many points by canopies of gracious live oaks.

🛏 Sleeping & Eating

aloft Tallahassee Downtown HOTEL $$
(☎850-513-0313; www.alofttallahassee.com; 200 N Monroe St; r $119-230; 🅿⊛❄@🛜🐾) This branch of the popular aloft chain boasts a prime downtown location and funky, functional rooms. Bathrooms feature counter-to-ceiling mirrors and lots of space for all the makeup in the world. Beds are uber-comfy, and free high-speed internet is included.

★ Canopy Road Cafe CAFE $
(☎850-668-6600; www.canopyroadcafe.com; 1913 N Munroe; mains $8-11; ⏰6:30am-2:15pm) Canopy Road, named for Tallahassee's beautiful canopy byways, is a modest chain (a new location has just opened in Jacksonville!), but they do everything right: great plates of good food, prices are reasonable, and service comes with a smile. Try the croissant French toast, their popular breakfast combos, or an avocado smash. Light eaters can get a half order. Wow!

Kool Beanz Café FUSION $$
(📞850-224-2466; www.koolbeanz-cafe.com; 921
Thomasville Rd; dinner mains $19-27; ⏱11am-
2:30pm & 5:30-10pm Mon-Fri, 5:30-10pm Sat,
10:30am-2pm Sun; 🅿🍴) It's got a corny name
but a wonderfully eclectic and homey vibe –
plus great, creative fare. The menu changes
daily, but you can count on finding some-
thing tasty. That can be almost anything:
from hummus plates to monkfish or jerk-
spiced scallops to duck in blueberry-ginger
sauce. Meyer-lemon pudding was a dessert
option at the time of research.

🍷 Drinking & Entertainment

Madison Social PUB
(📞850-894-6276; www.madisonsocial.com; 705
South Woodward Ave; mains $9-20; ⏱11:30am-
2am Sun-Thu, from 10am Fri & Sat; 🛜) Never
mind the trend of flipping former transmis-
sion shops into hip, retro locales, this trendy
hot spot was built to look that way from the
get go. It swarms with a bold and beautiful
mix of locals and FSU students, downing
drinks at the stellar bar or aluminum picnic
tables as the sun sets over Doak Campbell
football stadium, the largest continuous
brick structure in the USA.

Bradfordville Blues Club LIVE MUSIC
(📞850-906-0766; www.bradfordvilleblues.com;
7152 Moses Lane, off Bradfordville Rd; tickets $15-
35; ⏱shows start 8-10pm) Down the end of
a dirt road lit by tiki torches, you'll find a
bonfire raging under the live oaks at this
hidden-away juke joint that hosts excellent
national blues acts. Event times and days
vary; check online.

ℹ Information

Florida Welcome Center (📞850-488-6167;
www.visitflorida.com; 400 S Munroe St;
⏱8am-5pm Mon-Fri) In the Florida State
Capitol, this is a fantastic resource.
Leon County Welcome Center (📞850-606-
2305; www.visittallahassee.com; 106 E Jeffer-
son St; ⏱8am-5pm Mon-Fri) Runs the excellent
visitor information center, with brochures on
walking and driving tours.

ℹ Getting There & Around

Tallahassee is 98 miles from Panama City
Beach, 135 miles from Jacksonville, 192 miles
from Pensacola, 120 miles from Gainesville and
470 miles from Miami. The main access road
is I-10; to reach the Gulf Coast, follow Hwy 319
south to Hwy 98.

Tiny **Tallahassee International Airport**
(📞850-891-7800; www.talgov.com/airport;
3300 Capital Circle SW) is served by American
and Delta for US domestic and international
connections, and Silver Airways for direct flights
to Tampa and Orlando. It's about 5 miles south-
west of downtown, off Hwy 263. There's no pub-
lic transportation. Some hotels have shuttles,
but otherwise a taxi to downtown costs around
$25: try **Yellow Cab** (📞850-999-9999; www.
tallahasseeyellowcab.com).

The **Greyhound bus station** (📞850-222-
4249; www.greyhound.com; 112 W Tennessee
St; ⏱24hr) is at the corner of Duval, opposite
the downtown **StarMetro** (📞850-891-5200;
www.talgov.com/starmetro; per trip/day
$1.25/3) transfer center.

Pensacola

The Alabama border is just a few miles
down the road, which helps explain the vibe
of Pensacola, a city that jumbles laid-back
Southern syrup with Florida brashness.
With lively beaches, a Spanish-style down-
town, and a thrumming military culture,
this is by far the most interesting city in the
Panhandle.

While urban-chic trends (locavore food,
craft cocktails etc) are taking root, visitors
still primarily come to Pensacola for an all-
American, blue-collar vacation experience:
white-sand beaches, fried seafood and bars
serving cheap domestic drinks. During March
and April, things reach fever pitch when
droves of students descend for the weeklong
bacchanalia of spring break. Beware.

Downtown, centered on Palafox St, lies
north of the waterfront. Across the Pensaco-
la Bay Bridge from here is the mostly resi-
dential peninsula of Gulf Breeze. Cross one
more bridge, the Bob Sikes (toll $1), to reach
pretty Pensacola Beach, the ultimate desti-
nation for most visitors.

Distinctly separate from Pensacola it-
self, Pensacola Beach is a pretty stretch of
powdery white sand, gentle, warm waters
and a string of mellow beachfront hotels.
The beach occupies nearly 8 miles of the
40-mile-long Santa Rosa barrier island, sur-
rounded by the Santa Rosa Sound and the
Gulf of Mexico to the north and south, and
by the federally protected Gulf Islands Na-
tional Seashore on either side. Though de-
termined residents have protected much of
the barrier island from development, several
high-rise condos have created a bit of a Gulf
Coast skyline.

PENSACOLA SCENIC BLUFFS HIGHWAY

This 11-mile stretch of road, which winds around the precipice of the highest point along the Gulf Coast, makes for a peaceful drive or slightly challenging bike ride. You'll see stunning views of Escambia Bay and pass a notable crumbling brick chimney – part of the steam-power plant for the Hyer-Knowles lumber mill in the 1850s – the only remnant of what was the first major industrial belt in the area.

The area is a major hub for local entertainment and special events, including Mardi Gras celebrations, a triathlon, wine tastings, a summer music series and parades.

⊙ Sights

★National Naval
Aviation Museum   MUSEUM
(☑800-327-5002; www.navalaviationmuseum. org; 1750 Radford Blvd; ⊙9am-5pm; 🚻) **FREE**
A visit to Pensacola is not complete without a trip to this enormous collection of military aircraft muscle and artifacts. Adults and children alike will be fascinated by the range of planes on display: more than 150! That's before we even get to the high-tech stuff like flight simulators and an IMAX theater. You can watch the **Blue Angels** (☑850-452-3806; www.naspensacolaairshow. com; 390 San Carlos Rd, Suite A; ⊙8:30am Tue & Wed Mar-Nov) **FREE** practice their death-defying air show at 8:30am most Tuesdays and Wednesdays between March and November.

Note that the entry for non–Department of Defense identification holders is via the NAS Pensacola West Gate located at 1878 South Blue Angel Parkway.

Historic Pensacola Village   MUSEUM
(☑850-595-5985; www.historicpensacola.org; Tarragona & Church St; adult/child $8/4; ⊙10am-4pm Tue-Sat; 🅿🚻) 🖉 Pensacola's rich colonial history spans more than 450 years. This fascinating and attractive village is a self-contained enclave of photogenic historic homes turned into museums: it's the perfect starting point for familiarizing yourself with the city. Admission is good for one week and includes a guided tour and entrance to each building.

★**Gulf Islands National Seashore**   PARK
(☑850-934-2600; www.nps.gov/guis; vehicle $20; ⊙sunrise-sunset; 🚻) 🖉 The highlight of the Florida Panhandle, this 150-mile stretch of mostly undeveloped white-sand beach is a prime example of what the Gulf Coast looked like before human settlement (which, to be fair, can often be seen in the form of high-rises in the distance). The National Seashore is not contiguous, but you'll find portions all along the coast: long swaths of sugar-white dunes crowned with sea oats, a perfect example of pristine flatland beach.

🛏 Sleeping & Eating

Solé Inn   MOTEL $
(☑850-470-9298; www.soleinnandsuites.com; 200 N Palafox St; r $79-199; 🅿⊜❄@🤖🌊)
Just north of downtown, this motel goes for a 1960s mod look, with a black-and-white color scheme, animal-print accents and acrylic bubble lamps. The dandelion fountain in the patio is a unique touch. Rooms aren't huge, but price, location and originality make up for the lack of space. And who can complain about the self-serve happy hour between 5pm and 7pm?

Holiday Inn Resort   HOTEL $$
(☑850-932-5331; www.holidayinnresortpensaco labeach.com; 14 Via de Luna Dr; r from $210; 🅿⊜❄@🤖🌊) This beachfront hotel has cool, inviting rooms with ultra-comfy beds, flat-screen TVs and great showers. Oceanfront rooms have spacious balconies overhanging the soft, white sands and the cool turquoise waters below. Suites and kids' suites are available, and the 'Lazy River' pool is killer. Friendly, obliging staff help seal the deal. Excellent value.

Peg Leg Pete's   SEAFOOD $$
(☑850-932-4139; www.peglegpetes.com; 1010 Fort Pickens Rd; mains $10-22; ⊙11am-10pm; 🚻) Ah-har, me hearties, walk ye olde plank... you get the idea, this place has a theme going. Anyways, pop into Pete's for almost-beachfront oysters, fat grouper sandwiches, crab legs and jumbo sea scallops. There's nothing fancy about the woodsy, somewhat grungy sea-shanty decor with license plates covering the walls, but the service is swift, despite how busy it gets.

★**Iron**   AMERICAN $$$
(☑850-476-7776; www.restaurantiron.com; 22 N Palafox St; mains $26-46; ⊙4:30-10pm Sun-Thu, to 1am Fri & Sat; 🍸) Armed with New Orleans

experience, chef Alex McPhail works his ever-changing menu magic at downtown's Iron, the best of Pensacola's line of vibrant, locally sourced, high-end culinary hotbeds. Extremely friendly mixologists know their craft; and McPhail's food – from beer-braised pork belly to Creole-seasoned catch of the day – punches above the Emerald Coast's weight class.

Drinking & Entertainment

McGuire's Irish Pub PUB
(☑ 850-433-6789; www.mcguiresirishpub.com; 600 E Gregory St; ☺11am-2am) This ginor-mous Irish theme park of a pub gets rowdy around 9pm and is super popular at din-ner time: the pub grub is top-notch. Don't try to pay for your drinks with one of the thousands of dollar bills hanging from the ceiling – a local once found himself in the slammer that way!

Roundup GAY
(☑850-433-8482; www.theroundup.net; 560 E Heinberg St; ☺2pm-3am) For those who like their men manly, check out this niche-y, neighborhood hangout with a killer furry-friendly patio. Ladies are welcome, but cowboys, tradies and bikers are always fla-vor of the month. There's a Facebook page (www.facebook.com/theroundupbar) that lists events.

Saenger Theatre THEATER
(☑850-595-3880; www.pensacolasaenger.com; 118 S Palafox Pl; ☺box office 10am-4:30pm Mon-Fri) This Spanish baroque beauty was recon-structed in 1925 using bricks from the Pen-sacola Opera House, which was destroyed in a 1916 hurricane. It now hosts popular musi-cals and top-billing music acts and is home

to the Pensacola Symphony Orchestra and the Pensacola Opera.

ℹ Information

Pensacola Beach Visitors Information Center (☑850-932-1500; www.visitpensacola beach.com; 7 Casino Beach Blvd; ☺9am-5pm Mon-Sat, 10am-3pm Sun) This is a small place with some useful maps and brochures about goings-on, road closures (due to storms) and anything else beach oriented.

Pensacola Visitors Information Center (☑800-874-1234; www.visitpensacola.com; 1401 E Gregory St; ☺8am-5pm Mon-Fri, 9am-4pm Sat, 10am-4pm Sun) Come to the foot of the Pensacola Bay Bridge for a bounty of tourist information, knowledgeable staff and a free internet kiosk.

ℹ Getting There & Around

Pensacola Regional Airport (☑850-436-5000; www.flypensacola.com; 2430 Airport Blvd) is served by most major US airlines. Primary direct connections outside Florida include Atlanta, Charlotte, Dallas and Houston. The airport is 4 miles northeast of downtown, off 9th Ave on Airport Blvd. A taxi costs about $20 to downtown and around $35 to the beach. Try **zTrip** (☑850-433-3333; www.ztrip.com/ pensacola), previously known as Yellow Cab, a convenient hybrid of the rideshare and tradi-tional cab experiences.

The **Greyhound station** (☑850-476-4800; www.greyhound.com; 505 W Burgess Rd) is located north of the downtown area. **Escambia County Transit** (ECAT; ☑850-595-3228; www. goecat.com; rides $1.75) has a free trolley ser-vice (ECAT) connecting downtown Pensacola and the beach between Memorial Day weekend and the end of September.

I-10 is the major east–west thoroughfare used by buses, and many pass down Palafox St.

Great Lakes

Best Places to Eat

➡ Sister Pie (p589)

➡ Story Inn (p569)

➡ Hopleaf (p551)

➡ Tucker's (p582)

➡ Birch + Butcher (p605)

Best Places to Sleep

➡ Shinola Hotel (p588)

➡ Ironworks Hotel (p565)

➡ Fieldhouse Jones (p547)

➡ Kimpton Schofield Hotel (p573)

➡ Lora (p621)

Why Go?

Don't be fooled by all the corn. Behind it lurks surfing beaches and Tibetan temples, car-free islands and the green-draped night lights of the aurora borealis. The Great Lakes takes its knocks for being middle-of-nowhere boring, so consider the moose-filled national parks and Hemingway, Dylan and Vonnegut sites to be its little secret.

Roll call for the region's cities starts with Chicago, which unfurls what is arguably the country's mightiest skyline. Milwaukee keeps the beer-and-Harley flame burning, while Minneapolis shines a hipster beacon out over the fields. Detroit rocks, plain and simple. The Great Lakes themselves are huge, and offer beaches, dunes, resort towns and lighthouse-dotted scenery. Dairy farms and fruit orchards blanket the region, meaning fresh pie and ice cream aplenty. And when the scenery does flatten out? There's always a goofball roadside attraction, such as the Spam Museum or the world's biggest ball of twine, to revive imaginations.

When to Go

Chicago

| Jan & Feb Skiers and snowmobilers hit the trails. | Jul & Aug Finally, it's warm! Beer gardens hop, beaches splash, and festivals rock most weekends. | Sep & Oct Fair weather, bountiful farm and orchard harvests, and shoulder-season bargains. |

History

The region's first residents included the Hopewell (around 200 BC) and Mississippi River mound builders (around AD 700). Both left behind mysterious piles of earth that were tombs for their leaders and possibly tributes to their deities. You can see remnants at Cahokia in southern Illinois, and Mound City in southeastern Ohio.

French voyagers (fur traders) arrived in the early 17th century and established missions and forts. The British turned up soon after that, with the rivalry spilling over into the French and Indian Wars (Seven Years' War; 1754–61), after which Britain took control of all the land east of the Mississippi. Following the Revolutionary War, the Great Lakes area became the new USA's Northwest Territory, which soon was divided into states and locked to the region after it developed its impressive canal and railroad network. But conflicts erupted between the newcomers and the Native Americans, including the 1811 Battle of Tippecanoe in Indiana; the bloody 1832 Black Hawk War in Wisconsin, Illinois and around, which forced indigenous people to move west of the Mississippi; and the 1862 Sioux uprising in Minnesota.

Throughout the late 19th and early 20th centuries, industries sprang up and grew quickly, fueled by resources of coal and iron, and cheap transportation on the lakes. The availability of work brought huge influxes of immigrants from Ireland, Germany, Scandinavia and southern and eastern Europe. For decades after the Civil War, a great number of African Americans also migrated to the region's urban centers from the South.

The area prospered during WWII and throughout the 1950s, but this was followed by 20 years of social turmoil and economic stagnation. Manufacturing industries declined, which walloped Rust Belt cities such as Detroit and Cleveland with high unemployment and 'white flight' (white middle-class families who fled to the suburbs).

The 1980s and '90s brought urban revitalization. The region's population increased, notably with newcomers from Asia and Mexico. Growth in the service and high-tech sectors resulted in economic balance, although manufacturing industries such as car making and steel still played a big role, meaning that when the economic crisis hit in 2008, Great Lakes towns felt the pinch first.

Some 10 years later, many of the big cities have rallied. Detroit, Cleveland, Cincinnati and Milwaukee are among those that have experienced reinvigorated cores, where businesses and residents are moving back to the downtown areas and making them shine again.

ILLINOIS

Chicago dominates the state with its sky-high architecture and superlative museums, restaurants and music clubs. But venturing further afield reveals Oak Park, Hemingway's mannerly hometown, scattered shrines to local hero Abe Lincoln, and a trail of corn dogs, pies and drive-in movie theaters down Route 66. A cypress swamp and a prehistoric World Heritage Site make appearances in Illinois too.

ⓘ Information

Illinois Highway Conditions (www.getting aroundillinois.com)

Illinois Office of Tourism (www.enjoyillinois.com)

Illinois State Park Information (www.dnr. illinois.gov) State parks are free to visit. Campsites cost $6 to $35; some accept reservations (www.reserveamerica.com; fee $5).

Chicago

Steely skyscrapers, top chefs, rocking festivals – the Windy City will blow you away with its low-key cultured awesomeness.

It's hard to know what to gawk at first. High-flying architecture is everywhere, from the stratospheric, glass-floored Willis Tower to Frank Gehry's swooping silver Pritzker Pavilion to Frank Lloyd Wright's stained-glass Robie House. Whimsical public art studs the streets; you might be walking along and wham, there's an abstract Picasso statue that's not only cool to look at, but you're allowed to go right up and climb on it. For art museums, take your pick: impressionist masterpieces at the massive Art Institute, psychedelic paintings at the midsized Museum of Mexican Art or outsider drawings at the small Intuit gallery.

History

Much of Chicago's past is downright legendary. You've probably heard about Mrs O'Leary's cow that kicked over a lantern that started the Great Fire that torched the city. And about a man named Al Capone who wielded a mean machine gun during an unsavory era of booze-fueled vice. And about

Great Lakes Highlights

1 Chicago
(p529) Absorbing the skyscrapers, museums, festivals and foodie bounty.

2 Detroit (p584) Embracing the city's can-do spirit and partaking of its art, eateries and neighborhood bicycle rides.

3 Boundary Waters (p625) Paddling deep into the piney woods and sleeping under a blanket of stars.

4 Ohio's Amish Country (p577) Slowing down for clip-clopping horses and buggies.

5 Michigan's Western Shore (p595) Beach lounging, dune climbing, berry eating and surfing.

6 Milwaukee (p603) Polka dancing at a Friday-night fish fry and drinking lots o' beer.

7 Route 66 (p563) Taking the slowpoke route through Illinois, past pie-filled diners and oddball roadside attractions.

8 Southern Indiana (p568) Being surprised by the Tibetan temples, phenomenal architecture and green hills.

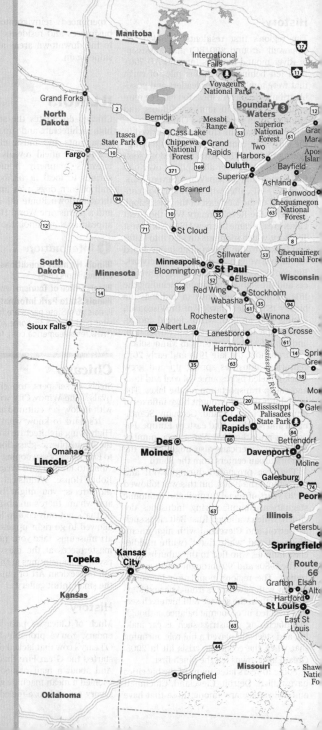

CANADA

Isle Royale
National Park

nder
Bay

nd
tage

Copper
Harbor

cupine
untains
derness
e Park

Keweenaw
Peninsula

Houghton

Ottawa
National
Forest

Marquette

Iron
Mountain

Nicolet
National
Forest

ausau

Green Bay

Manitowoc

nkosh

Milwaukee

adison

Racine

East Chicago

Lexington

Bloomington
tlanta

Champaign

Terre
Haute

Vincennes

New
Harmony

Cypress Creek
National Wildlife
Refuge

iro

Paducah

Lake
Superior

Pictured Rocks
National
Lakeshore

Tahquamenon Falls

Sault Ste Marie

Ontario

Lake
Nipissing

Naubinway

Lake
Michigan

Washington
Island

Leelanau
Peninsula

Mackinaw
City

St Ignace

Mackinac
Island

Manitoulin
Island

Georgian
Bay

Lake
Simcoe

Manitou
Islands

Petoskey
Boyne City

Charlevoix

Empire

Leland

Frankfort

Traverse City

Sleeping Bear
Dunes National
Lakeshore

Huron
National
Forest

Lake
Huron

Saginaw
Bay

Toronto

Hamilton

Ludington

Michigan

Muskegon

Grand
Rapids

Lansing

Flint

Port
Huron

London

Michigan's
Western
Shore

Holland

Saugatuck/
Douglas

Kalamazoo

Detroit

Dearborn

Lake Erie

New
York

Erie

Ann Arbor

Chicago

Gary

South
Bend

Middlebury

Auburn

Bass
Islands

Pelee Island

Kelleys
Island

Cleveland

Cuyahoga Valley
National Park

Madison

Akron

Indiana Dunes
National Park

Toledo

Canton

Indiana

Fairmount

Marion

Ohio

Millersburg

Ohio's Amish
Country

COLUMBUS

Indianapolis

Dayton

Yellow
Springs

Lancaster

Logan

Marietta

Athens

Bloomington

Nashville

Columbus

Southern
Indiana

Madison

Cincinnati

Covington

Chillicothe

West Virginia

Louisville

Frankfort

Ohio River

Huntington

Charleston

Lexington

Kentucky

Virginia

Harmonie
State Park

200 km
100 miles

Central Time Zone

Eastern Time Zone

Door Peninsula

the 'machine' that has controlled local politics for decades. Throw in the invention of the skyscraper and Ferris wheel, and you've got a whopper of a tale.

⊙ Sights

Big-ticket draws such as Millennium Park, Willis Tower and the Art Institute are downtown right in the Loop. Next door is the lakefront Museum Campus, with three popular sights including the Field Museum (p535). To the Loop's north are Navy Pier (p535) and the 360° Chicago (p539) observatory. A short distance onward Lincoln Park (p540) and Wrigley Field (p540) do their thing. All of these places are within a 6-mile span, and all are easy to reach on public transportation. Hyde Park is the one neighborhood with top sights that is further flung and requires some planning to reach.

All of the major attractions are open daily. Smaller museums are often closed on Monday and/or Tuesday.

⊙ The Loop

★ **Art Institute of Chicago**   MUSEUM
(Map p536; ☑312-443-3600; www.artic.edu; 111 S Michigan Ave; adult/child $25/free; ⊙10:30am-5pm Fri-Wed, to 8pm Thu; ⓐ; ⓜBrown, Orange,

Green, Purple, Pink Line to Adams) The Art Institute is the second-largest art museum in the USA. Its collection of impressionist and post-impressionist paintings rivals those in France, and the number of surrealist works is tremendous. Download the free app for DIY audio tours; it offers several quick-hit jaunts, from highlights (including Georges Seurat's *A Sunday Afternoon on the Island of La Grande Jatte* and Edward Hopper's *Nighthawks*) to architecture and pop-art tours. Allow two hours to browse the must-sees; art buffs should allocate much longer.

More comprehensive audio guides ($7) are also available in English, Spanish, French and Mandarin. You can buy a ticket in advance online (for a $2 surcharge) but unless there's a huge exhibit on, the entrance lines move pretty quickly. Or you can skip the lines altogether with the Fast Pass ticket, available online for $10 more.

The main entrance is on Michigan Ave, but you can also enter via the dazzling Modern Wing on Monroe St. Ask at the front desk about free talks and tours once you're inside. Note that the 3rd-floor contemporary sculpture terrace is always free. It has great city views and connects to Millennium Park via the mod, pedestrian-only Nichols Bridgeway.

CHICAGO IN TWO DAYS...

Day One

You might as well dive right in with the big stuff. Take a boat or walking tour with the Chicago Architecture Foundation (p544) and ogle the most sky-scraping collection of buildings the US has to offer. Saunter over to Millennium Park to see the 'Bean' reflect the skyline and to splash under Crown Fountain's human gargoyles.

Explore the Art Institute of Chicago, the nation's second-largest art museum. It holds masterpieces aplenty, especially impressionist and post-impressionist paintings (and paperweights). Next, head over to Willis Tower, zip up to the 103rd floor and step out onto the glass-floored ledge. Yes, it is a long way down.

The West Loop parties in the evening. Sit on the glittery patio sipping a glass of bubbly at RM Champagne Salon (p555). Haymarket Pub & Brewery (p555) pours great beers. Or down a cocktail made with the house vodka at CH Distillery (p555).

Day Two

Take a stroll on Michigan Ave – aka the Magnificent Mile (p539) – where big-name department stores ka-ching in a glittering row. Mosey over to Navy Pier (p535). Wander the half-mile promenade and take a spin on the high-in-the-sky Ferris wheel.

Spend the afternoon at the Museum Campus (p535) (the water taxi from Navy Pier is a fine way to get there). Miles of aisles of dinosaurs and gemstones stuff the Field Museum of Natural History (p535). Sharks and other fish swim in the kiddie-mobbed Shedd Aquarium (p535). Meteorites and supernovas are on view at the Adler Planetarium (p535).

Wander along Milwaukee Ave and take your pick of booming bars, indie-rock clubs and hipster shops. Quimby's (p559) shows the local spirit: the bookstore stocks zines and graphic novels, and is a linchpin of Chicago's underground culture The Hideout (p556) and Empty Bottle (p556) are sweet spots to catch a bad-ass band.

★ **Millennium Park** PARK

(Map p536; ☑ 312-742-1168; www.millenniumpark.
org; 201 E Randolph St; ☺ 6am-11pm; ⓐ; Ⓜ Brown,
Orange, Green, Purple, Pink Line to Washington/
Wabash) The city's showpiece is a trove of
free and arty sights. It includes **Pritzker Pavilion**, Frank Gehry's swooping silver band
shell, which hosts free weekly concerts in
summer (6:30pm; bring a picnic and bottle of wine); Anish Kapoor's beloved silvery
sculpture **Cloud Gate**, aka the 'Bean'; and
Jaume Plensa's **Crown Fountain**, a de facto
water park that projects video images of locals spitting water, gargoyle-style.

★ **Willis Tower** TOWER

(Map p536; ☑ 312-875-9696; www.theskydeck.
com; 233 S Wacker Dr; adult/child $24/16; ☺ 9am-
10pm Mar-Sep, 10am-8pm Oct-Feb, last entry 30min
prior; Ⓜ Brown, Orange, Purple, Pink Line to Quincy)
It's Chicago's tallest building, and the 103rd-
floor Skydeck puts you high into the heavens. Take the ear-popping, 70-second elevator ride to the top and then step onto one of
the glass-floored ledges jutting out into midair for a knee-buckling perspective straight
down. On clear days the view sweeps over
four states. The entrance is on Jackson Blvd.
Queues can take up to an hour on busy days
(peak times are in summer, between 11am
and 4pm Friday through Sunday).

Chicago Cultural Center NOTABLE BUILDING

(Map p536; ☑ 312-744-6630; www.chicagocul
turalcenter.org; 78 E Washington St; ☺ 10am-7pm
Mon-Fri, to 5pm Sat & Sun; Ⓜ Brown, Orange, Green,
Purple, Pink Line to Washington/Wabash) **FREE**
This exquisite, beaux-arts building began
its life as the Chicago Public Library in 1897.
Today the block-long structure houses terrific art exhibitions (especially the 4th-floor
Yates Gallery), as well as classical concerts
at lunchtime every Wednesday (12:15pm).
It also contains the world's largest Tiffany
stained-glass dome, on the 3rd floor where
the library circulation desk used to be. **Insta-Greeter** (Map p536; www.chicagogreeter.com/ins
tagreeter; 77 E Randolph St; ☺ 10am-3pm Fri & Sat,
11am-2pm Sun) **FREE** tours of the Loop depart
from the Randolph St lobby, as do Millennium Park tours. And it's all free!

Chicago Architecture Center GALLERY

(CAC; Map p536; ☑ 312-922-3432; www.archi
tecture.org; 111 E Wacker Dr; adult/student/child
$12/8/free; ☺ 9:30am-5pm; ☐ 151, Ⓜ Brown, Or-
ange, Green, Purple, Pink Line to Clark/Lake) The
CAC is the premier keeper of Chicago's archi-

ⓘ DISCOUNT CARDS
....

The following options let you skip the
regular queues at sights.

The **Go Chicago Card** (www.smart
destinations.com/chicago) allows you
to visit an unlimited number of attractions for a flat fee. It's good for one,
two, three or five consecutive days. The
company also offers a three-, four- or
five-choice **Explorer Pass** where you
pick among 29 options for sights. It's
valid for 30 days. Architecture cruises,
the Navy Pier Ferris wheel and all major
museums are among the choices.

CityPass (www.citypass.com/
chicago) gives access to five of the city's
top draws, including the Art Institute,
Shedd Aquarium and Willis Tower, over
nine consecutive days. It's less flexible
than Go Chicago's pass, but cheaper for
those wanting a more leisurely pace.

---

tectural flame. Pop in to explore its excellent
galleries, which feature an interactive 3-D
model of Chicago and displays on the city's
architectural history, as well as giant models
of and exhibits on skyscrapers around the
world and the amazing technologies needed
to build them, from construction to security
to sustainability. You can also check out the
CAC's extensive roster of boat and walking
tours (p544) and make bookings here.

Buckingham Fountain FOUNTAIN

(Map p536; 301 S Columbus Dr; Ⓜ Red Line to
Harrison) Grant Park's centerpiece is one
of the world's largest fountains, with a
1.5-million-gallon capacity and a 15-story-high
spray. It lets loose on the hour from 9am to
11pm early May to mid-October, accompanied
at night by multicolored lights and music.

Route 66 Sign HISTORIC SITE

(Map p536; E Adams St, btwn S Michigan & Wabash
Aves; Ⓜ Brown, Orange, Green, Purple, Pink Line to
Adams) Attention Route 66 buffs: the Mother Road begins in downtown Chicago. Look
for the 'Historic 66 Begin' sign at the northwestern corner of Adams St and Michigan
Ave, across from the Art Institute. (There's
another sign at the end of the block, but
this one is a replica of the original.) From
Chicago the route traverses 2400 miles to
Los Angeles, past neon signs, mom-and-pop
motels and pie-and-coffee diners...but it all
starts here.

Metro Chicago Area

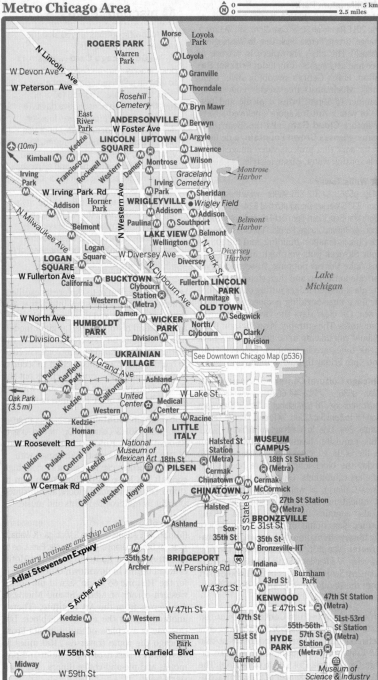

GREAT LAKES CHICAGO

0 — 5 km
0 — 2.5 miles

ROGERS PARK

Morse
Loyola
Park
Loyola

Warren
Park

W Devon Ave

Granville

W Peterson Ave

Thorndale

Rosehill
Cemetery

Bryn Mawr

East
River
Park

ANDERSONVILLE
W Foster Ave

Berwyn

LINCOLN
SQUARE

UPTOWN

Argyle

Kedzie

Lawrence

Kimball

Wilson

Francisco

Montrose

Rockwell

Western

Damen

Irving
Park

Graceland
Cemetery

Montrose
Harbor

Irving
Park

Sheridan

W Irving Park Rd

WRIGLEYVILLE

Wrigley Field

Addison

Horner
Park

Addison

Addison

Belmont

Paulina

Southport

Belmont
Harbor

LAKE VIEW

Belmont

N Western Ave

Wellington

LOGAN
SQUARE

Logan
Square

W Diversey Ave

Diversey
Harbor

N Clark St

Diversey

W Fullerton Ave

Fullerton

LINCOLN
PARK

Lake
Michigan

California

BUCKTOWN

N Clybourn Ave

Armitage

Clybourn
Station
(Metra)

Western

OLD TOWN

Damen

WICKER
PARK

North/
Clybourn

Sedgwick

W North Ave

HUMBOLDT
PARK

Clark/
Division

W Division St

Division

UKRAINIAN
VILLAGE

W Grand Ave

See Downtown Chicago Map (p536)

Ashland

Pulaski

Garfield
Park

California

W Lake St

Oak Park
(3.5 mi)

Kedzie

Western

United
Center

Medical
Center

Racine

Kedzie-
Homan

Polk

LITTLE
ITALY

Halsted St
Station
(Metra)

MUSEUM
CAMPUS

W Roosevelt Rd

Pulaski

Kildare

Central Park

Kedzie

National
Museum of
Mexican Art

18th St
(Metra)

PILSEN

18th St Station
(Metra)

Cermak-
Chinatown

Cermak-
McCormick

W Cermak Rd

California

Western

Hoyne

CHINATOWN

27th St Station
(Metra)

Halsted

BRONZEVILLE

Sox-
35th St

E 31st St

35th St-
Bronzeville-IIT

Ashland

35th St/
Archer

BRIDGEPORT

90

Indiana

Sanitary Drainage and Ship Canal

Adlai Stevenson Expwy

W Pershing Rd

43rd St

Burnham
Park

S Archer Ave

W 43rd St

KENWOOD

47th St Station
(Metra)

W 47th St

E 47th St

Kedzie

Western

47th St

51st-53rd
St Station
(Metra)

Pulaski

Sherman
Park

51st St

55th-56th-
57th St
Station
(Metra)

HYDE
PARK

Midway

W 55th St

W Garfield Blvd

Garfield

Museum of
Science & Industry

W 59th St

(10mi)

Kedzie

Logan
Square

Museum of Contemporary Photography

MUSEUM

(Map p536; ☑ 312-663-5554; www.mocp.org; 600 S Michigan Ave, Columbia College; ⊙ 10am-5pm Mon-Wed, Fri & Sat, to 8pm Thu, noon-5pm Sun; Ⓜ Red Line to Harrison) FREE This small museum focuses on American and international photography from the early 20th century onward, and is the only institution of its kind between the coasts. The permanent collection includes the works of Henri Cartier-Bresson, Harry Callahan, Sally Mann, Victor Skrebneski, Catherine Wagner and 500 more of the best photographers working today. Special exhibitions (also free) augment the rotating permanent collection.

◉ Pilsen & Near South Side

★ Field Museum of Natural History

MUSEUM

(Map p536; ☑ 312-922-9410; www.fieldmuseum.org; 1400 S Lake Shore Dr, Near South Side; adult/child $24/17; ⊙ 9am-5pm; ♿; ☐ 146, 130) The Field Museum houses some 30 million artifacts and includes everything but the kitchen sink – beetles, mummies, gemstones, Bushman the stuffed ape – all tended by a slew of PhD-wielding scientists, as the Field remains an active research institution. The collection's rock star is Sue, the largest *Tyrannosaurus rex* yet discovered. She even gets her own gift shop. Special exhibits, such as the 3-D movie, cost extra. Other highlights include 'Inside Ancient Egypt,' a burial chamber reproduction that contains 23 real mummies; the Hall of Gems; and the Northwest Coast and Arctic Peoples' totem pole collection. The museum is vast, so get a map at the desk and make a plan of attack.

Northerly Island

PARK

(1521 S Linn White Dr, Near South Side; ☐ 146, 130) This prairie-grassed park has a walking and cycling trail, bird-watching, fishing and an outdoor venue for concerts. It's actually a peninsula, not an island, but the Chicago skyline views are tremendous no matter what you call it. Stop in at the field house, if it's open, for tour information. Bicycles are available at the Divvy bike-share station by the Adler Planetarium. Note that parts of the trail are closed at times due to weather damage.

★ National Museum of Mexican Art

MUSEUM

(Map p534; ☑ 312-738-1503; www.nationalmuseumofmexicanart.org; 1852 W 19th St, Pilsen; ⊙ 10am-5pm Tue-Sun; Ⓜ Pink Line to 18th St) FREE Found-ed in 1982, this vibrant museum – the largest Latinx arts institution in the US – has become one of the city's best. The vivid permanent collection sums up 1000 years of Mexican art and culture through classical paintings, shining gold altars, skeleton-rich folk art, beadwork and much more.

Adler Planetarium

MUSEUM

(Map p536; ☑ 312-922-7827; www.adlerplanetarium.org; 1300 S Lake Shore Dr, Near South Side; adult/child $12/8; ⊙ 9:30am-4pm; ♿; ☐ 146, 130) Space enthusiasts will get a big bang (pun!) out of the Adler. There are public telescopes to view the stars (10am to 1pm daily, by the Galileo Cafe), 3-D lectures to learn about supernovas (in the Space Visualization Lab), and the Planet Explorers exhibit where kids can 'launch' a rocket. The immersive digital films cost extra (from $13 per ticket). The Adler's front steps offer Chicago's best skyline view, so get your camera ready.

Shedd Aquarium

AQUARIUM

(Map p536; ☑ 312-939-2438; www.sheddaquarium.org; 1200 S Lake Shore Dr, Near South Side; adult/child $40/30; ⊙ 9am-6pm Jun-Aug, 9am-5pm Mon-Fri, to 6pm Sat & Sun Sep-May; ☐ 146, 130) Top draws at the kiddie-mobbed Shedd Aquarium include the Wild Reef exhibit, where there's just 5in of Plexiglas between you and two-dozen fierce-looking sharks, and the Oceanarium, with its rescued sea otters. Note the Oceanarium also keeps beluga whales and Pacific white-sided dolphins, a practice that's increasingly frowned upon as captivity is stressful for these sensitive creatures.

◉ Near North & Navy Pier

★ Navy Pier

WATERFRONT

(Map p536; ☑ 312-595-7437; www.navypier.com; 600 E Grand Ave; ⊙ 10am-10pm Sun-Thu, to midnight Fri & Sat Jun-Aug, 10am-8pm Sun-Thu, to 10pm Fri & Sat Sep-May; ♿; ☐ 65) FREE Half-mile-long Navy Pier is one of Chicago's most-visited attractions, sporting a 196ft Ferris wheel (adult/child $18/15) and other carnival rides ($9 to $18 each), an IMAX theater (☑ 312-595-5629; www.amctheatres.com; 700 E Grand Ave; tickets $15-22), a beer garden and lots of chain restaurants. A renovation added public plazas, performance spaces and free cultural programming. Locals still groan over its commercialization, but its lakefront view and cool breezes can't be beat. The fireworks displays on summer Wednesdays (9:30pm) and Saturdays (10:15pm) are a treat too.

Downtown Chicago

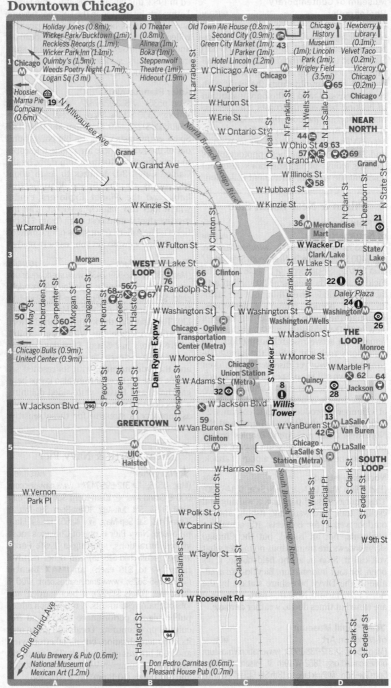

Holiday Jones (0.8mi);
Wicker Park/Bucktown (1mi);
Reckless Records (1.1mi);
Wicker Park Inn (1.1mi);
Quimby's (1.5mi);
Weeds Poetry Night (1.7mi);
Logan Sq (3 mi)

iO Theater
(0.8mi);
Boka (1mi);
Alinea (1mi);
Steppenwolf
Theatre (1mi);
Hideout (1.9mi)

Old Town Ale House (0.8mi);
Second City (0.9mi);
Green City Market (1mi);
J Parker (1mi);
Hotel Lincoln (1.2mi)

Chicago
History
Museum
(1mi); Lincoln
Park (1mi);
Wrigley Field
(3.5mi)

Newberry
Library
(0.1mi);
Velvet Taco
(0.2mi);
Viceroy
Chicago
(0.2mi)

Hoosier
Mama Pie
Company
(0.6mi)

NEAR
NORTH

Chicago Bulls (0.9mi);
United Center (0.9mi)

WEST
LOOP

GREEKTOWN

Daley Plaza

THE
LOOP

Willis
Tower

SOUTH
LOOP

Alulu Brewery & Pub (0.6mi);
National Museum of
Mexican Art (1.2mi)

Don Pedro Carnitas (0.6mi);
Pleasant House Pub (0.7mi)

N 0 ____ 1 km
0 ____ 0.5 miles

Waldorf
Astoria
Chicago
(0.04mi);
Le Colonial
(0.07mi)

16 ⊙ 1 360° Chicago

Drake Hotel
(0.08mi)

Oak St Beach (0.3mi);
North Ave Beach (1.3mi)

E Pearson St   Lake Shore Park

E Chicago Ave   6 ⌂ Museum of
Contemporary Art

⊗ 55   ⊗ 54
E Superior St

3 ⌂   20 ⊙
Driehaus
Museum

45 ⊟

53 ⊗

33 ⊙   31 ⊙
E Kinzie St   Chicago
Architecture
27 ⊙   Foundation Boat
Tour Dock

46 ⊟
12 ⌂ 75
E Wacker Pl   39
ILLINOIS   E Wacker Dr
CENTER

52 ⊟
E Lake St
72 ⊗

48 ⊟
Randolph ⊟
37 ⊙   34 ⊙   E Randolph St
15   25 ⊙
Madison Ⓜ
38 ⊙ 17 ⓘ
⊙ 18   🎭 Millennium Park
51 ⊟ 61 ⊗   5
E Monroe St

29 Ⓜ ⌂ 2   Millennium Park
Adams/   Art   Garage
Wabash 71   Institute   Butler
of Chicago   Field

H W Library
47 ⊟

Harrison Ⓜ
23 ⌂
41 ⌂

70   Grant
PRINTER'S   Park
ROW   Tennis
E 9th St   Courts   Hutchinson
Field
E 11th St

Roosevelt Ⓜ
E Roosevelt Rd

E 13th St   CENTRAL
STATION

Qing Xiang   E 14th St
Yuan
Dumplings   Willie Dixon's Blues
(0.7mi)   (0.6mi)

Ohio
Street
Beach

Olive
Park

Water
Filtration Plant

E Ontario St
STREETERVILLE
E Grand Ave   35 ⊙

E Illinois St
7 ⊙ 74 ⊙   11 ⊙ P
Navy Pier
14 ⌂

E North Water St

River
Esplanade

N Lake Shore Dr

Lakefront Trail

N Michigan Ave (Magnificent Mile)
N Rush St
N Wabash Ave

⊙ 10

Grant
Park

Van Buren
St (Metra)

S Holden Ct
S Michigan Ave
S State St
S Wabash Ave

Grant
Park

Museum
Campus/11th
St (Metra)

MUSEUM
CAMPUS
30 ⊙

⌂ Field Museum
4 of Natural   E Solidarity Dr   9 ⌂
History   Burnham
Harbor

Burnham
Park
Northerly Island
(0.7mi)

S Linn
White Dr

Hyde Park &
South Side (5mi)

LAKE
MICHIGAN

Downtown Chicago

★ **Driehaus Museum** MUSEUM
(Map p536; ☎312-482-8933; www.driehausmuse um.org; 40 E Erie St, River North; adult/child $20/ free; ⊙10am-5pm Tue-Sun; Ⓜ Red Line to Chicago) Set in the exquisite Nickerson Mansion, the Driehaus immerses visitors in Gilded Age decorative arts and architecture. You'll feel like a *Great Gatsby* character as you wander three floors stuffed with sumptuous objets d'art and heaps of Tiffany stained glass.

Recommended guided tours ($5 extra) are available four times daily. The price seems steep, but the museum is a prize for those intrigued by opulent interiors.

Tribune Tower ARCHITECTURE
(Map p536; 435 N Michigan Ave, Streeterville; Ⓜ Red Line to Grand) Take a close look when passing by this 1925 neo-Gothic edifice. Colonel Robert McCormick, eccentric owner

of the *Chicago Tribune* in the early 1900s, collected – and asked his reporters to send – rocks from famous buildings and monuments around the world. He stockpiled pieces of the Taj Mahal, Westminster Abbey, the Great Pyramid and more than 140 others, which are now embedded around the tower's base.

Marina City ARCHITECTURE

(Map p536; 300 N State St, River North; M Brown, Orange, Green, Purple, Pink Line to State/Lake) The twin corncob towers of Marina City are an Instagram favorite for their futuristic, cartoony look. Bertrand Goldberg designed the 1964 high-rise, and it has become an iconic part of the Chicago skyline (check out the cover of the Wilco CD *Yankee Hotel Foxtrot*). And yes, there is a marina at the towers' base.

Magnificent Mile AREA

(Map p536; www.themagnificentmile.com; N Michigan Ave, Streeterville; M Red Line to Grand) Spanning N Michigan Ave between the river and Oak St, the 'Mag Mile' is Chicago's much-touted upscale shopping strip, where Bloomingdale's, Apple, Burberry and many more will lighten your wallet. The retailers are mostly high-end chains that have stores nationwide.

⊙ Gold Coast

★ 360° Chicago OBSERVATORY

(Map p536; 📞888-875-8439; www.360chicago.com; 875 N Michigan Ave, 94th fl; adult/child $22/15; ⊙9am-11pm, last tickets 10:30pm; M Red Line to Chicago) The views from the 94th-floor observatory of this iconic building (formerly known as the John Hancock Center) in many ways surpass those at the Willis Tower (p533); there are informative displays and the 'Tilt' feature (floor-to-ceiling windows you stand in as they tip out over the ground), which costs $7.20 extra and is less exciting than it sounds. Or just shoot straight up to the 96th-floor **Signature Lounge** (www.signatureroom.com; ⊙11am-12:30am Sun-Thu, to 1:30am Fri & Sat), where the view is free if you buy a drink ($10 to $18).

★ Museum of Contemporary Art MUSEUM

(MCA; Map p536; 📞312-280-2660; www.mcachicago.org; 220 E Chicago Ave; adult/child $15/free; ⊙10am-9pm Tue & Fri, to 5pm Wed, Thu, Sat & Sun; M Red Line to Chicago) Consider it the Art Institute's brash, rebellious sibling, with especially strong minimalist, surrealist and conceptual photography collections, and permanent works by René Magritte, Cindy Sherman and Andy Warhol. Covering art from the 1920s onward, the MCA's collection spans the gamut, with displays arranged to blur the boundaries between painting, sculpture, video and other media. Exhibits change regularly so you never know what you'll see, but count on it being offbeat and provocative. Illinois residents get free admission on Tuesday.

Newberry Library LIBRARY

(📞312-943-9090; www.newberry.org; 60 W Walton St; ⊙galleries 8:15am-5pm Mon, Fri & Sat, to 7:30pm Tue-Thu; M Red Line to Chicago) FREE The Newberry's public galleries are a treat for bibliophiles: those who swoon over original Thomas Paine pamphlets about the French Revolution, or get weak-kneed seeing Thomas Jefferson's copy of the *History of the Expedition under Captains Lewis and Clark* (with margin notes!). Intriguing exhibits rotate yellowed manuscripts and tattered 1st editions from the library's extensive collection. The on-site bookstore is tops for Chicago-themed titles. Free tours of the impressive building take place at 3pm Thursday and 10:30am Saturday.

Chicago Sports Museum MUSEUM

(Map p536; 📞312-202-0500; www.chicagosportsmuseum.com; 835 N Michigan Ave, 7th fl, Water Tower Place; adult/child $10/6; ⊙11:30am-8:30pm Mon-Thu, to 9pm Fri, 11am-9pm Sat, 11am-6pm Sun; M Red Line to Chicago) To understand Chicago's sports psyche, peruse

---

BLUES FANS' PILGRIMAGE

From 1957 to 1967, Chess Records was the seminal electric blues label. The building it occupied is now known as **Willie Dixon's Blues Heaven** (📞312-808-1286; www.bluesheaven.com; 2120 S Michigan Ave, Near South Side; adult/child $15/10; ⊙noon-4pm Tue-Sat; M Green Line to Cermak-McCormick Pl), for the bassist who wrote most of Chess' hits. Staff give hour-long tours of the premises. It's pretty ramshackle, with few original artifacts on display. Still, hard-core fans will get a thrill out of hearing stories from the heady era and walking into the studio where their musical heroes recorded. Free blues concerts rock the side garden on summer Thursdays at 6pm.

the memorabilia-filled cases at this gallery attached to Harry Caray's 7th Inning Stretch restaurant. See the cleats Cubs infielder Kris Bryant wore on the winning final play of the 2016 World Series, which ended the team's 108-year championship drought. Examine Sammy Sosa's corked bat and the infamous 'Bartman ball.' The museum also enshrines relics for Da Bears, Bulls, Blackhawks and White Sox. (Admission is free if you eat or drink at the restaurant.)

⊙ Lincoln Park & Old Town

★**Lincoln Park** PARK
(www.chicagoparkdistrict.com; Lincoln Park; ⊙6am-11pm; ♿; ☐22, 151, 156) The park that gave the neighborhood its name is Chicago's largest. Its 1200 acres stretch for 6 miles from North Ave north to Diversey Pkwy, where it narrows along the lake and continues on until the end of Lake Shore Dr. On sunny days locals come out to play in droves, taking advantage of the ponds, paths and playing fields or visiting the zoo and beaches. It's a fine spot to while away a morning or afternoon (or both).

Green City Market MARKET
(☑773-880-1266; www.greencitymarket.org; 1790 N Clark St, Lincoln Park; ⊙7am-1pm Wed & Sat May-Oct; ☐22) Stands of purple cabbages, red radishes, green asparagus and other bright-hued produce sprawl through Lincoln Park at Chicago's biggest farmers market. Follow your nose to the demonstration tent, where local cooks such as *Top Chef* winner Stephanie Izard prepare dishes – say rice crepes with a mushroom *gastrique* (reduction) – using market ingredients.

Chicago History Museum MUSEUM
(☑312-642-4600; www.chicagohistory.org; 1601 N Clark St, Lincoln Park; adult/child $19/free; ⊙9:30am-4:30pm Mon & Wed-Sat, to 9pm Tue, noon-5pm Sun; ♿; ☐22) Curious about Chicago's storied past? Multimedia displays at this museum cover it all, from the Great Fire to the 1968 Democratic Convention. President Lincoln's deathbed is here, as is the bell worn by Mrs O'Leary's cow. So is the chance to 'become' a Chicago hot dog covered in condiments (in the kids' area, but adults are welcome for the photo op).

⊙ Lake View & Wrigleyville

★**Wrigley Field** STADIUM
(Map p534; ☑800-843-2827; www.cubs.com; 1060 W Addison St, Wrigleyville; Ⓜ Red Line to Addison)

Built in 1914 and named for the chewing-gum guy, Wrigley Field is the second-oldest baseball park in the major leagues. It's known for its hand-turned scoreboard, ivy-covered outfield walls and neon sign over the front entrance. The Cubs are the home team. Games are always packed. Ticket prices vary, but in general you'll be hard-pressed to get in for under $45. The area around the stadium is like a big street festival on game days.

The ballpark is filled with legendary traditions and curses, including a team that didn't win a championship for 108 years. But a 2016 World Series victory coupled with heaps of new family-friendly and foodie hot spots around the stadium have given it new life. The grassy plaza just north of the main entrance – aka **Gallagher Way** (www.gallagherway.com; 3637 N Clark St) – hosts free events including concerts, alfresco fitness classes and movie nights on the jumbo video screen.

Ninety-minute Wrigley Field tours (per person $25) are available April through September.

⊙ Wicker Park, Bucktown & Ukrainian Village

Intuit: The Center for Intuitive & Outsider Art GALLERY
(Map p536; ☑312-243-9088; www.art.org; 756 N Milwaukee Ave, River West; $5; ⊙11am-6pm Tue, Wed, Fri & Sat, to 7pm Thu, noon-5pm Sun; Ⓜ Blue Line to Chicago) Behold this small museum's collection of naive and outsider art from Chicago artists, including rotating mixed-media exhibits and watercolors by famed local Henry Darger. In a back room the museum has re-created Darger's awesomely cluttered studio apartment, complete with balls of twine, teetering stacks of old magazines, an ancient typewriter and a Victrola phonograph. The gift shop carries groovy jewelry (such as pencil-eraser necklaces), bags and wallets made from recycled material, and art books.

⊙ Logan Square & Humboldt Park

★**Galerie F** GALLERY
(☑872-817-7067; www.galeriefchicago.com; 2415 N Milwaukee Ave, Logan Square; ⊙11am-6pm Mon & Thu-Sun; Ⓜ Blue Line to California) Galerie F is exactly the type of laid-back, ubercool gallery you'd expect to find in Logan Square. It specializes in rock-and-roll gig posters, printmaking and street art. Walk into the

bright, open space and browse – the vibe here is totally welcoming. Dip into the basement to listen to records, play chess or just linger in the sitting area.

★**Busy Beaver Button Museum** MUSEUM
(☑ 773-645-3359; www.buttonmuseum.org; 3407 W Armitage Ave, Logan Square; ⊙ 10am-4pm Mon-Fri; 🚌 73) **FREE** Even George Washington gave out campaign buttons, though in his era they were the sew-on kind. Pin-back buttons came along in 1896. Badge-making company Busy Beaver chronicles its history in displays holding thousands of the little round mementos. They tout everything from Dale Bozzio to Bozo the clown, Cabbage Patch Kids to Big Rock Point Nuclear Plant.

⊙ Hyde Park & South Side

★**Museum of Science & Industry** MUSEUM
(Map p534; MSI; ☑ 773-684-1414; www.msichicago.org; 5700 S Lake Shore Dr, Hyde Park; adult/child $22/13; ⊙ 9:30am-5:30pm Jun-Aug, shorter hours Sep-May; 🖼; 🚌 6 or 10, Ⓜ Metra Electric Line to 55th-56th-57th St) Geek out at the largest science museum in the Western Hemisphere. Highlights include a **WWII German U-boat** nestled in an underground display (adult/child $18/14 extra to tour it) and the **Science Storms** exhibit with a mock tornado and tsunami. Other popular exhibits include the baby chick hatchery, the minuscule furnishings in Colleen Moore's fairy castle and the life-size shaft of a coal mine (adult/child $12/9 extra to descend and tour its workings).

The museum's main building served as the Palace of Fine Arts at the landmark 1893 World's Expo, which was set in the surrounding **Jackson Park** (6401 S Stony Island Ave, Woodlawn; 🚌 6, Ⓜ Metra Electric Line to 59th or 63rd St). When you've had your fill of the sensory-overload sights inside, the park makes an excellent setting to recuperate.

★**Robie House** ARCHITECTURE
(☑ 312-994-4000; www.flwright.org; 5757 S Woodlawn Ave, Hyde Park; adult/child $18/15; ⊙ 10:30am-3pm Thu-Mon; 🚌 6, Ⓜ Metra Electric Line to 59th St) Of the numerous buildings that Frank Lloyd Wright designed around Chicago, none is more famous or influential than Robie House. Because its horizontal lines resembled the flat landscape of the Midwestern prairie, the style became known as the Prairie style. Inside are 174 stained-glass windows and doors, which you'll see on the hour-long tours (frequency varies by season, but there's usually at least one tour per hour). Advance tickets are highly recommended.

DuSable Museum of African American History MUSEUM
(☑ 773-947-0600; www.dusablemuseum.org; 740 E 56th Pl, Washington Park; adult/child $10/3, Tue free; ⊙ 10am-5pm Tue-Sat, noon-5pm Sun; 🚌 6, Ⓜ Metra Electric Line to 55th-56th-57th St) This was the first independent museum in the country dedicated to African American art, history and culture. The collection features African American artworks and photography, permanent exhibits that illustrate African Americans' experiences from slavery through the Civil Rights movement, and rotating exhibits that cover topics such as Chicago blues music or the Black Panther movement. It's affiliated with the Smithsonian Institution.

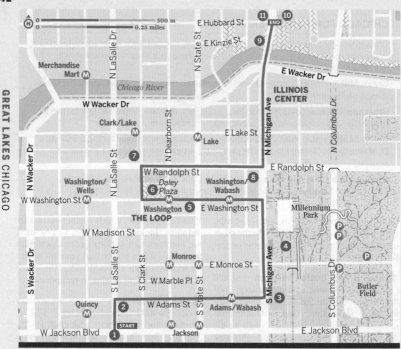

City Walk
The Loop

START CHICAGO BOARD OF TRADE
FINISH BILLY GOAT TAVERN
LENGTH 3 MILES; ABOUT TWO HOURS

This tour winds through the Loop and across the Chicago River, passing some of the city's finest old buildings and notable public art.

Start at the ❶ **Chicago Board of Trade** (141 W Jackson Blvd), a 1930 art-deco temple of commerce. The nearby ❷ **Rookery** (www.flwright.org; 209 S LaSalle St) was built in 1888 by Daniel Burnham – a monumental brick building maximizing light and air with a central atrium. Frank Lloyd Wright redesigned the lobby 19 years later.

Head east on Adams to the ❸ **Art Institute** (p532), one of the world's finest art museums. The lion statues out front make a classic keepsake photo. Just north is ❹ **Millennium Park** (p533), filled with avant-garde works from world-famous names such as Frank Gehry and Anish Kapoor.

Two blocks west on Washington is the 1895 ❺ **Reliance Building**. Another Burn-

ham design, it's a posh hotel today (it originally housed medical offices – Al Capone's dentist practiced in room 809).

Another block west is Pablo Picasso's ❻ **untitled sculpture** (50 W Washington St). He never revealed what it portrayed – popular guesses include a woman, a dog or a baboon – so interpret it however you like. Just northwest is another inscrutable sculpture, Jean Dubuffet's ❼ **Monument with Standing Beast** (100 W Randolph St).

Walk east on Randolph to beaux-arts beauty the ❽ **Chicago Cultural Center** (p533). Further famous edifices are north of the Chicago River: the gleaming-white terra-cotta ❾ **Wrigley Building** (400 N Michigan Ave) and the neo-Gothic, eye-popping ❿ **Tribune Tower** (p538).

Finish up at the ⓫ **Billy Goat Tavern** (p550), a classic dive bar whose owner invoked the Cubs' famous curse in 1945 after being ejected from Wrigley Field because of his pet goat. Raise a glass to the Cubs, who broke it – and their 108-year-long World Series drought – in 2016.

Obama's House
HOUSE

(5046 S Greenwood Ave, Kenwood; 🚃 6, Ⓜ Metra Electric Line to 51st-53rd St) Among the handsome manors lining S Greenwood Ave is the redbrick Georgian-style home at number 5046, where Barack Obama and his family lived from 2005 until he became president in 2008. The Obamas still own the house, though they chose to stay in Washington, DC, after his time in office. You can't go inside, and fences block the sidewalk, but you can get close enough for a photo.

🏃 Activities

Chicago offers plenty of places to get active via its city-spanning shoreline, 26 beaches and 580 parks. After a long, cold winter, everyone dashes outside to play. Top marks go to the 18-mile Lakefront Trail, prime for cycling and running. Meanwhile, Lake Michigan and the Chicago River provide loads of paddling possibilities.

On The Land

The flat, 18-mile **Lakefront Trail** is a beautiful ride along the water, though on nice days it's jam-packed. It starts at Ardmore Ave and rolls all the way south to 71st St. The path is split so cyclists and runners have separate lanes; look for signposts and markers painted on the ground to tell you what's what. The trail is most congested between Lincoln Park and the Museum Campus; it's least congested heading south from the museums. The Active Transportation Alliance (www.activetrans.org) publishes a bike trail map. Check @activetransLFT on Twitter for updates on trail conditions; some parts close in bad weather.

⭐ Bobby's Bike Hike
CYCLING

(Map p536; ☎ 312-245-9300; www.bobbysbikehike. com; 540 N Lake Shore Dr, Streeterville; per hr/day from $8/27, tours $38-70; ⊙ 8:30am-8pm Mon-Fri, 8am-8pm Sat & Sun Jun-Aug, 9am-7pm Mar-May & Sep-Nov; Ⓜ Red Line to Grand) Locally based Bobby's earns rave reviews from riders. It rents bikes and has easy access to the Lakefront Trail. It also offers cool tours of gangster sites, the lakefront, nighttime vistas, and venues to indulge in pizza and beer. The Tike Hike caters to kids. Enter through the covered driveway to reach the shop. Call for winter hours.

Bike & Roll
CYCLING

(Map p536; ☎ 312-729-1000; www.bikechicago. com; 239 E Randolph St; tours adult/child from $45/35; ⊙ 9am-7pm; Ⓜ Brown, Orange, Green,

DON'T MISS

THE 606

Like NYC's High Line, Chicago's **606** (www.the606.org; Wicker Park/Bucktown; ⊙ 6am-11pm; Ⓜ Blue Line to Damen) is a similar urban-cool elevated path along an old train track. Bike or stroll past factories, smokestacks, clattering L trains and locals' backyard affairs for 2.7 miles between Wicker Park and Logan Square. It's a fascinating trek through Chicago's socioeconomic strata: moneyed at the east, becoming more industrial and immigrant to the west.

Purple, Pink Line to Washington/Wabash) Summer guided tours (adult/child from $45/35) cover themes such as lakefront parks, breweries and historic neighborhoods, or downtown's sights and fireworks at night (highly recommended). Prices include lock, helmet and map. Operates out of the McDonald's Cycle Center in Millennium Park; there's another branch on Navy Pier. It also rents out bikes for DIY explorations (per hour/day from $12.50/35).

McCormick Tribune Ice Rink
ICE SKATING

(Map p536; www.millenniumpark.org; 55 N Michigan Ave; ⊙ noon-8pm Mon-Thu, to 10pm Fri, 10am-9pm Sat & Sun mid-Nov–mid-Mar; Ⓜ Brown, Orange, Green, Purple, Pink Line to Washington/Wabash) Millennium Park's busy rink is the city's most scenic, tucked between the reflecting Bean sculpture and the twinkling lights of Michigan Ave. Admission to the ice is free; skate rental costs $13 (Monday through Thursday) or $15 (Friday through Sunday). Free ice-skating lessons are offered an hour before the rink opens.

On The Water

Visitors often don't realize Chicago is a beach town, thanks to mammoth Lake Michigan lapping its side. There are 26 official strands of sand patrolled by lifeguards in summer. Swimming is popular, though the water is pretty freaking cold. Beaches at Montrose and North Ave have rental places offering kayaks and stand-up paddleboards. Other kayak companies have set up shop along the Chicago River.

⭐ Montrose Beach
BEACH

(www.cpdbeaches.com; 4400 N Lake Shore Dr, Uptown; 🚃 146) One of the city's best beaches. You can rent kayaks, stand-up paddleboards

CHICAGO FOR CHILDREN

Ferocious dinosaurs, an ark's worth of beasts, lakefront boat rides and sandy beaches are among the top choices for toddlin' times. Add in magical playgrounds, family cycling tours and lots of pizza, and it's clear Chicago is a kid's kind of town.

Chicago Children's Museum (Map p536; ☑ 312-527-1000; www.chicagochildrens museum.org; 700 E Grand Ave, Navy Pier; $15; ☺ 10am-5pm, to 8pm Thu; ☑; ☑ 65) is the reigning favorite, geared to kids aged 10 and under, with a slew of hands-on building, climbing and inventing exhibits. Bonus: it's located on Navy Pier.

Bring on the dinosaurs at Field Museum of Natural History (p535). The Crown Family PlayLab, on the ground floor, lets kids excavate bones and make loads of other discoveries. It's open Thursday to Monday from 10am to 3:30pm.

Families could spend a week the Museum of Science & Industry (p541) and not see it all. Staff conduct 'experiments' in various galleries throughout the day, such as dropping things off the balcony and creating mini explosions. The Idea Factory lets scientists aged 10 and under 'research' properties of light, balance and water pressure.

The **Peggy Notebaert Nature Museum** (☑ 773-755-5100; www.naturemuseum.org; 2430 N Cannon Dr, Lincoln Park; adult/child $9/6; ☺ 9am-5pm Mon-Fri, from 10am Sat & Sun; ☑; ☑ 76, 151) is somewhat overlooked, but its butterfly haven and marsh full of frogs provide gentle thrills. Bonus: it's located in Lincoln Park by the zoo.

At the Art Institute of Chicago (p532), the Ryan Learning Center provides interactive games (such as puzzles of famous works) and art-making activities.

---

and Jet Skis; sometimes you'll see surfers and kitesurfers, and anglers frequently cast here. Watch sailboats glide in the harbor over some waterside snacks or a drink at the **Dock Bar and Grill**. A wide, dog-friendly beach with a curving breakwater abuts the main beach to the north.

North Avenue Beach BEACH
(www.cpdbeaches.com; 1600 N Lake Shore Dr, Lincoln Park; ☺ 6am-11pm; ☑; ☑ 151) Chicago's most popular strand of sand gives off a bit of a Southern California vibe in summer. Buff teams spike volleyballs, kids build sandcastles and everyone jumps in for a swim when the weather heats up. Bands and DJs rock the steamboat-shaped beach house, which serves ice cream and margaritas in equal measure. Kayaks, Jet Skis, stand-up paddleboards, bicycles and lounge chairs are available to rent, and there are daily beach yoga classes.

Urban Kayaks KAYAKING
(Map p536; ☑ 312-965-0035; www.urbankayaks. com; 435 E Riverwalk S; rental per hour per person $30, tours $55; ☺ 9am-6pm Mon-Fri, to 7pm Sat & Sun May-early Oct; ☑ Brown, Orange, Green, Purple, Pink Line to State/Lake) On the River-walk (www.chicagoriverwalk.us; Chicago River waterfront, btwn N Lake Shore Dr & W Lake St; ☺ 6am-11pm), this outfitter rents out kayaks for DIY explorations and offers guided tours

that glide past downtown's skyscrapers and historic sites; beginners are welcome, with a 20-minute training session starting off each tour. For extra help, try the hour-long 'intro to paddling' class ($35). Nighttime tours on Wednesdays and Saturdays take in the Navy Pier summer fireworks show.

⛵ Tours

★**Chicago**
Architecture Center Tours BOAT TOURS
(CAC; ☑ 312-922-3432; www.architecture.org; 111 E Wacker Dr; tours $20-55) Gold-standard boat tours ($47) sail from the **river dock** (Map p536; ☑ Brown, Orange, Green, Purple, Pink Line to State/Lake) on the southeast side of the Michigan Ave Bridge. Also popular are the Historic Skyscrapers walking tours ($26) and tours exploring individual landmark buildings ($20). CAC sponsors bus, bike and L train tours, too. Buy tickets online or at the CAC's front desk; boat tickets can also be purchased at the dock.

Chicago by Foot WALKING
(☑ 312-612-0826; www.freetoursbyfoot.com/chica go-tours) Guides for this pay-what-you-want walking tour offer engaging stories and historical details on different jaunts covering Loop architecture, West Loop history, Lincoln Park's gangster sites and much more. It's recommended to pay about $20 per

person. Reserve in advance to guarantee a spot; walk-up guests are welcome if space is available (chancy). Tours usually last around two hours.

Chicago Detours
WALKING

(☑312-350-1131; www.chicagodetours.com; tours from $28) Chicago Detours offers engrossing, detail-rich tours (mostly walking, but also some by bus) that take in Chicago's architecture, history and culture. The 2½-hour Historic Bar Tour is a popular one.

Chicago Beer Experience
WALKING

(☑312-818-2172; www.chicagobeerexperience. com; 3hr tours $67) These walking tours visit a neighborhood in order to discover its beer history along with general Chicago history. Expect to hit four bars over the course of a mile or so. Beer and a snack (such as a stuffed pizza slice or hot dog) are included. Departure points vary.

🎭 Festivals & Events

St Patrick's Day Parade
CULTURAL

(www.chicagostpatricksdayparade.org; ⊘mid-Mar) The local plumbers union dyes the Chicago River shamrock-green; a big parade follows downtown in Grant Park. Held the Saturday before March 17.

Chicago Blues Festival
MUSIC

(www.chicagobluesfestival.us; ⊘Jun) The biggest free blues fest in the world, with three days of the music that made Chicago famous. Held in Millennium Park.

★Taste of Chicago
FOOD & DRINK

(www.tasteofchicago.us; ⊘Jul) This five-day food festival in Grant Park draws hordes for a smorgasbord of ethnic, meaty, sweet and local edibles – much of it served on a stick. Several stages host free live music, including big-name bands.

Pride Parade
LGBTIQ+

(http://chicagopride.gopride.com; Boystown; ⊘late Jun; Ⓜ Red Line to Addison) On the last Sunday in June, colorful floats and risqué revelers pack Halsted St in Boystown. It's the LGBTIQ+ community's main event, and more than 800,000 people come to the party.

Pitchfork Music Festival
MUSIC

(http://pitchforkmusicfestival.com; Union Park, Near West Side; day pass $75; ⊘mid-Jul; Ⓜ Green, Pink Line to Ashland) Taste-making alternative and emerging bands strum for three days in Union Park in mid-July.

Lollapalooza
MUSIC

(www.lollapalooza.com; ⊘Aug) Up to 170 bands spill off eight stages at Grant Park's four-day mega-gig.

Jazz Festival
MUSIC

(www.chicagojazzfestival.us; ⊘Aug/Sep) Top names on the national jazz scene play for free over Labor Day weekend. Performances are held in Millennium Park and the Chicago Cultural Center.

Open House Chicago
CULTURAL

(☑312-922-3432; www.openhousechicago.org; ⊘Oct) FREE Design geeks, take note: for one weekend in mid-October the Chicago Architecture Center (p533) coordinates free tours of more than 200 architectural gems around the city, many of them normally off-limits to the public.

Chicago Marathon
SPORTS

(www.chicagomarathon.com; ⊘Oct) More than 45,000 runners compete on the 26-mile course through the city's heart, cheered on by a million spectators. Held on a Sunday in October (when the weather can be pleasant or freezing), it's considered one of the world's top five marathons.

🛏 Sleeping

Chicago's lodgings rise high in the sky, many in architectural landmarks. Snooze in the building that gave birth to the skyscraper, in one of Mies van der Rohe's boxy structures, or in a century-old art deco masterpiece. Huge business hotels, trendy boutique hotels and snazzy hostels blanket the cityscape too. But nothing comes cheap...

🛏 The Loop

HI-Chicago
HOSTEL $

(Map p536; ☑312-360-0300; www.hichicago. org; 24 E Congress Pkwy; dm $35-55; ✳@🛜; Ⓜ Brown, Orange, Purple, Pink Line to Library) Chicago's most stalwart hostel is immaculate, conveniently placed in the Loop, and offers bonuses such as a staffed information desk, free volunteer-led tours and discount passes to some sights. The simple dorm rooms have eight or 10 beds, and most have attached baths; others share hallway bathrooms. Dorms are segregated by gender.

★Hampton Inn
Chicago Downtown/N Loop
HOTEL $$

(Map p536; ☑312-419-9014; www.hamptonchi-cago.com; 68 E Wacker Pl; r $200-290; Ⓟ✳🛜;

Ⓜ Brown, Orange, Green, Purple, Pink Line to State/ Lake) This unique property with a central location makes you feel like a road-tripper of yore. Set in the 1928 art deco Chicago Motor Club Building, the lobby sports a vintage Ford and a cool USA mural map from the era. The dark-wood-paneled rooms strike the right balance of retro vibe and modern amenities. Free wi-fi.

★ **Virgin Hotel** HOTEL $$

(Map p536; ☏ 312-940-4400; www.virgin hotels.com; 203 N Wabash Ave; r $240-380; P ❄ ⊛ 🤖 🐾; Ⓜ Brown, Orange, Green, Purple, Pink Line to State/Lake) Billionaire Richard Branson transformed the 27-story, art deco Dearborn Bank Building into the first outpost of his cheeky new hotel chain. The airy, suite-like rooms have speedy free wi-fi, low-cost minibar items and a bed that doubles as a work desk. An app controls electronics including thermostat and TV. Guests receive earplugs, handy for dulling noise from nearby L trains.

★ **Hotel Julian** HOTEL $$

(Map p536; ☏ 312-346-1200; www.hoteljulianchi cago.com; 168 N Michigan Ave; r $200-400; P ❄ ⊛ 🤖; Ⓜ Brown, Orange, Green, Purple, Pink Line to Washington/Wabash) Twelve stories in a 1912 office building now comprise one of the Loop's newest mod-luxe hotels. Large rooms are elegantly decorated with a slightly masculine retro-1930s vibe and feature king-sized captain's beds with Frette linens and leather headboards, espresso makers and 55in TVs – not to mention stunning views of Millennium Park through some of the city-view rooms.

Buckingham Athletic Club Hotel BOUTIQUE HOTEL $$

(Map p536; ☏ 312-663-8910; www.thebucking hamclub.com; 440 S LaSalle St; r $200-280; P ❄ 🤖 🐾; Ⓜ Brown, Orange, Purple, Pink Line to LaSalle) On the 40th floor of the Chicago Stock Exchange building, this 21-room hotel isn't easy to find. The benefit if you do? It's quiet (on weekends and evenings especially) and has expansive views. Elegant rooms are so spacious they'd be considered suites elsewhere. Lots of freebies add to the excellence, including access to the namesake gym with lap pool.

Silversmith HISTORIC HOTEL $$

(Map p536; ☏ 312-372-7696; www.silversmith chicagohotel.com; 10 S Wabash Ave; r $200-350; P ❄ @ 🤖; Ⓜ Red, Blue Line to Monroe) De-signed by renowned architect Daniel Burnham's firm as a place for jewelers and silversmiths to ply their trade, this 1897 building's gem-inspired theme carries over to the current, vintage-cool design. Rooms are good-sized, with pearl-colored decor and ruby and gold accents. A cushioned seat nestles in each floor-to-ceiling window, prime for city-watching.

🏨 Near North & Navy Pier

★ **Found Hotel Chicago** HOSTEL, HOTEL $

(Map p536; ☏ 224-243-6863; www.foundhotels. com; 613 N Wells St, River North; dm $25-55, r $120-330; P ❄ 🤖; Ⓜ Brown, Purple Line to Merchandise Mart) Breezy Found Hotel joins the elevated hostel/casual-hotel brigade. The 60 rooms come in several configurations, including four-bed dorms with sturdy (and quite comfy) bunk beds, and private rooms with twin or queen beds – all with en-suite bathrooms. Rooms are small and plain, but who cares? The price is often right, and the common areas are where the fun is.

Freehand Chicago HOSTEL, HOTEL $

(Map p536; ☏ 312-940-3699; www.freehandhotels. com/chicago; 19 E Ohio St, River North; dm $35-55, r $220-310; ❄ 🤖; Ⓜ Red Line to Grand) 🍃 At this super-hip hostel-hotel hybrid, travelers split evenly between the four-person, bunk-bed dorms and private rooms. All feature warm woods, bright tiles and Central American–tinged fabrics. Everyone mingles in the totem-pole-filled common area and groovy Broken Shaker bar. The Freehand works best as a hostel, its dorms spiffier than most, with en-suite bathrooms and privacy curtains around each bed.

★ **Acme Hotel** BOUTIQUE HOTEL $$

(Map p536; ☏ 312-894-0800; www.acmehotelcom pany.com; 15 E Ohio St, River North; r $170-310; P ❄ @ 🤖; Ⓜ Red Line to Grand) Urban bohemians love the Acme for its indie-cool style at (usually) affordable rates. The 130 rooms mix industrial fixtures with retro lamps, mid-century furniture and funky modern art. They're wired up with free wi-fi, good speakers, smart TVs and easy connections to stream your own music and movies. Graffiti, neon and a rock-and-roll elevator embellish the common areas.

Moxy Chicago Downtown HOTEL $$

(Map p536; ☏ 312-527-7200; http://moxy-hotels. marriott.com; 530 N LaSalle Dr, River North; r $224-299; P ❄ 🤖 🐾; Ⓜ Red Line to Grand) When a hotel's front desk doubles as a bar, you know you're in for a good time. So it goes at Moxy, where the lobby is a communal area with a 24-hour taco joint and novelty-size Jenga and Connect Four games. The wee rooms feel bigger than they are thanks to floor-to-ceiling windows and a pegboard wall to hang items.

Gold Coast

★ Fieldhouse Jones   HOSTEL, HOTEL $

(Map p536; ☎ 312-291-9922; www.fieldhousejones. com; 312 W Chestnut St; r/apt from $125/180; P ✴ ☎; M Brown, Purple Line to Chicago) This hip hotel occupies a vintage, redbrick dairy warehouse. It's great value for the Gold Coast, drawing a wide range of travelers – global backpackers, families – for its quality rooms and sociable common areas. There are standard hotel rooms, studios and one- and two-bedroom apartments, all with en-suite bathrooms, wi-fi and fun, sporty decor (dartboard wall art, old trophies etc).

Drake Hotel   HISTORIC HOTEL $$

(☎ 312-787-2200; www.thedrakehotel.com; 140 E Walton St; r $230-360; P ✴ @ ☎; M Red Line to Chicago) Queen Elizabeth, Princess Di, the Reagans, the Bushes, the Clintons, the late, great Aretha Franklin... Who *hasn't* stayed at the Drake since its 1920 opening? The elegant, chandelier-strewn grande dame anchors the northern end of Michigan Ave, near Oak Street Beach. While the public spaces are gilded eye-poppers, the 535 rooms are more everyday but well-sized and comfy.

★ Viceroy Chicago   LUXURY HOTEL $$$

(☎ 312-586-2000; www.viceroyhotelsandresorts. com; 1118 N State St; d $275-450, ste from $550; P ☐ ✴ ☎ ☒; M Red Line to Clark/Division) The Gold Coast's newest luxury hotel, the Viceroy has 198 rooms and suites with art deco–inspired design elements with warm woods, gold accents and luxe furnishings. Blue-velvet curtains float across floor-to-ceiling windows with lake and skyline views; the restaurant, helmed by a Michelin-starred chef, features nautical yacht-club motifs. In summer you can use the rooftop dipping pool. Free wi-fi.

★ Waldorf
Astoria Chicago   LUXURY HOTEL $$$

(☎ 312-646-1300; www.waldorfastoriachicagohotel. com; 11 E Walton St; r from $400; P ✴ @ ☎ ☒ ☒; M Red Line to Chicago) The Waldorf routinely tops the list for Chicago's best uber-luxury hotel. It models itself on 1920s Parisian glamour and, we have to admit, it delivers it in spades. Rooms are large – they have to be, to hold the fireplaces, the bars, the marble soaking tubs, the beds with 460-thread-count sheets and the fully wired work spaces and other techno gadgets.

Lincoln Park & Old Town

Hotel Lincoln   BOUTIQUE HOTEL $$

(☎ 312-254-4700; www.jdvhotels.com; 1816 N Clark St, Lincoln Park; r $150-399; P ✴ @ ☎; ☐22) The boutique Lincoln is all about kitschy fun, as the lobby's 'wall of bad art' and front desk patched together from flea-market dresser drawers attest. Standard rooms are small, but vintage-cool and colorful; many have sweet views. Leafy Lincoln Park and the city's largest farmers market (p540) sprawl across the street. The hotel's **rooftop bar** (☑312-254-4747; www.jparkerchicago.com; ⏱5pm-1am Mon-Thu, from 3pm Fri, from 11:30am Sat & Sun) offers spectacular lake views.

Lake View & Wrigleyville

★ Majestic Hotel   BOUTIQUE HOTEL $$
(☑773-404-3499; www.majestic-chicago.com; 528 W Brompton Ave, Lake View; r $159-275; [P][❄][🛜]; 🚇151) Nestled into a row of residential housing, the Majestic is walking distance to Wrigley Field and Boystown and mere steps from the lakefront. From the lobby fireplace and dark-wood furnishings to the handsome, paisley-swirled decor, the interior has the cozy feel of an English manor. Free wi-fi and continental breakfast are included.

★ Wheelhouse Hotel   BOUTIQUE HOTEL $$
(☑773-248-9001; www.wheelhousehotel.com; 3475 N Clark St, Wrigleyville; r $250-350; [P][❄][🛜]; [M]Red Line to Addison) A 2018 newbie, the Wheelhouse features 21 rooms in a restored greystone building not far from Wrigley Field. The smallish rooms have an earthy, urban loft feel, with exposed brick walls, cool vintage decor and bold shades of peach, yellow and blue; some even have bunk beds. The playful, baseball-tinged vibe extends to the lobby's wood-bat ceiling and scoreboard wall.

Hotel Zachary   HOTEL $$
(☑773-302-2300; www.hotelzachary.com; 3630 N Clark St, Wrigleyville; r $250-425; [P][❄][🛜][🐾]; [M]Red Line to Addison) Gleaming Hotel Zachary – named after Zachary Taylor Davis, the architect of Wrigley Field – opened in 2018 right across the street from the celebrated ballpark. Nods to baseball are subtle in the 173 stylish, natural-light-filled rooms: ivy-green headboards, baseball-glove-colored leather chairs, gray pinstripe carpet. On game days it's a high-energy scene, and it can be noisy into the wee hours.

Wicker Park, Bucktown & Ukrainian Village

Holiday Jones   HOSTEL $
(☑312-804-3335; www.holidayjones.com; 1659 W Division St, East Village; dm/r from $28/76; ⊛❄@🛜; [M]Blue Line to Division) Holiday Jones has an irreverent personality, with old steamer trunks turned stereo speakers comprising the front desk and cartoony posters lining the stairwell. Rooms are compact but tidy, with splashes of comforting plaid. Gender-segregated dorms have four to six bunk beds; private rooms are available too. The large common room has couches and a flat-screen TV, plus free wi-fi and lockers.

Urban Holiday Lofts   HOSTEL $
(☑312-532-6949; www.urbanholidaylofts.com; 2014 W Wabansia Ave, Wicker Park; dm $25-40, r $79-115; ⊛@🛜; [M]Blue Line to Damen) An international crowd fills the gender-segregated dorms (with four to eight beds) and private rooms of these converted loft condos; some rooms have private bathrooms. Exposed-brick walls, hardwood floors and bunks with plump bedding feature in all 21 rooms. It's close to the L station and in the thick of Wicker Park's nightlife. Continental breakfast is included. No elevator.

Wicker Park Inn   B&B $
(☑773-486-2743; www.wickerparkinn.com; 1331 N Wicker Park Ave, Wicker Park; r $180-200, apt $200-250; ⊛🛜; [M]Blue Line to Damen) This classic brick row house is steps away from great restaurants and nightlife. The sunny rooms aren't huge, but all have hardwood floors, small desk spaces and soothing color schemes with bright splashes of floral wallpaper. Breakfast is rich in baked goods and fruit. Across the street, three apartments with kitchens provide a self-contained experience.

Logan Square & Humboldt Park

Longman & Eagle   INN $
(☑773-276-7110; www.longmanandeagle.com; 2657 N Kedzie Ave, Logan Square; r $95-250; ⊛🛜; [M]Blue Line to Logan Square) Check in at the tavern downstairs and then head to your wood-floored, vintage-stylish accommodations on the floor above. The six rooms aren't particularly soundproof, but after using your whiskey tokens in the bar, you probably won't care.

West Loop & Near West Side

★ Ace Hotel   HOTEL $$
(Map p536; ☑312-548-1177; www.acehotel.com/chicago; 311 N Morgan St, West Loop; r $250-400; [P][❄][🛜]; [M]Green, Pink Line to Morgan) Chicago's branch of the super-hip Ace chain rises up

across the street from Google's shiny office. Hints of Frank Lloyd Wright, Ludwig Mies van der Rohe and other famed local architects show up in the mod, earthy design. The 159 minimalist rooms are on the small side but have cool decor, including a turntable or Martin guitar in most.

Publishing House Bed & Breakfast

B&B **$$**

(Map p536; ☑312-554-5857; https://publishinghousebnb.com; 108 N May St, West Loop; r $179-379; Ⓜ Green, Pink Line to Morgan) The building was indeed a publishing house more than a century ago, and it's now transformed so it looks like the stylish home of your coolest city friend. The 11 warm-toned rooms, each named for a Chicago writer, have hardwood floors, mid-century modern decor and original art on the walls. A fireplace and reading nooks fill the cozy common areas.

🛏 Hyde Park & South Side

Sophy Hyde Park

BOUTIQUE HOTEL **$$**

(☑773-289-1003; www.sophyhotel.com; 1411 E 53rd St, Hyde Park; r $229-329; P❋🐾; 🚲6, Ⓜ Metra Electric Line to 51st-53rd St) Hyde Park got its first boutique hotel in 2018, and it's a design winner. The 98 rooms have an artsy-hip look that feels truly fresh. Each is a good size, with hardwood floors, a record player and albums by local blues and rock musicians, plus an 8ft, bright-hued, abstract painting (by a local artist) that anchors the space. Free wi-fi, to boot.

✕ Eating

Chicago has become a chowhound's hot spot. For the most part, restaurants here are reasonably priced and pretension-free, serving masterful food in come-as-you-are environs. You can also fork into a superb range of international eats, especially if you break out of downtown and head for neighborhoods such as Pilsen or Uptown.

✕ The Loop

⭐ Revival Food Hall

AMERICAN **$**

(Map p536; ☑773-999-9411; www.revivalfoodhall.com; 125 S Clark St; mains $7-12; ☺7am-7pm Mon-Fri; 🐾; Ⓜ Blue Line to Monroe) The Loop needed a forward-thinking food court, and Revival Food Hall delivered. Come lunchtime, hip office workers pack the blond-wood tables of this ground-floor modern marketplace in the historic National building. The all-local dining concept brings 15 of Chicago's best fast-casual food outlets to the masses, from Antique Taco and Smoque BBQ to Furious Spoon ramen and HotChocolate Bakery.

Mercat a la Planxa

SPANISH **$$$**

(Map p536; ☑312-765-0524; www.mercatchicago.com; 638 S Michigan Ave; tapas $10-18, tasting menus from $65; ☺dinner 5-10pm Sun-Thu, to 11pm Fri & Sat, brunch 7am-3pm Sat & Sun; Ⓜ Red Line to Harrison) This Barcelona-style tapas and seafood restaurant buzzes in an enormous, convivial room where light streams in through the floor-to-ceiling windows. It cooks all the specialties of Catalonia and stokes a festive atmosphere, enhanced by copious quantities of *cava* (sparkling wine) and sangria. It's located in the beaux-arts Blackstone Hotel.

✕ Pilsen & Near South Side

⭐ Don Pedro Carnitas

MEXICAN **$**

(1113 W 18th St, Pilsen; tacos $2.50; ☺6am-6pm Mon-Thu, 5am-5pm Fri-Sun; Ⓜ Pink Line to 18th St) At this no-frills meat den, a man with a machete salutes you at the front counter. He awaits your command to hack off pork pieces and then wraps the thick chunks with onion and cilantro in a warm tortilla. You then devour the tacos at the tables in back. Goat stew and tripe add to the carnivorous menu. Cash only.

Qing Xiang Yuan Dumplings

DUMPLINGS **$**

(☑312-799-1118; www.qxydumplings.com; 2002 S Wentworth Ave, Suite 103, Chinatown; mains $9-14; ☺11:30am-9pm; Ⓜ Red Line to Cermak-Chinatown) The name doesn't lie: it's all about dumplings in this bright room under bamboo lanterns. The dough pockets come steamed or pan-fried, in serves of 12 or 18, with fillings such as lamb and coriander, ground pork and cabbage, sea whelk and leek, and some 30 other types. Bite into one and a hot shot of flavor erupts in your mouth.

Pleasant House Pub

PUB FOOD **$**

(☑773-523-7437; www.pleasanthousepub.com; 2119 S Halsted St, Pilsen; mains $10.50-15; ☺10am-10pm Tue-Thu, to midnight Fri & Sat, to 10pm Sun; 🐾; 🚲8) Follow your nose to Pleasant House, which bakes tall, fluffy, savory pies. Daily flavors include chicken and chutney, steak and ale, or kale and mushroom, made with produce the chefs grow themselves. The pub also serves excellent UK and local beers to accompany the food. Friday is a good day to visit, when there's a fish fry.

Near North & Navy Pier

★ **Billy Goat Tavern** BURGERS $
(Map p536; 312-222-1525; www.billygoattavern.
com; 430 N Michigan Ave, lower level, Streeterville;
burgers $4-8; 6am-1am Mon-Thu, to 2am Fri,
to 3am Sat, 9am-2am Sun; Red Line to Grand)
Tribune and *Sun Times* reporters have
guzzled in the subterranean Billy Goat for
decades. Order a 'cheezborger' and Schlitz
beer, then look around at the newspapered
walls to get the scoop on infamous local stories, such as the Cubs' Curse. This is a tourist magnet, but a deserving one. Follow the
tavern signs leading below Michigan Ave to
get here.

GT Fish & Oyster SEAFOOD $$
(Map p536; 312-929-3501; www.gtoyster.com;
531 N Wells St, River North; mains $17-30; 5-
10pm Mon-Thu, to 11pm Fri, 10am-2:30pm & 5-11pm
Sat, 10am-2:30pm & 5-10pm Sun; Red Line to
Grand) Seafood restaurants can be fusty. Not
so GT Fish & Oyster. The clean-lined room
bustles with date-night couples and groups
of friends drinking fizzy wines and slurping
mollusks. Many of the dishes are shareable,
which adds to the convivial, plate-clattering
ambience. The sublime clam chowder ar-
rives in a glass jar with housemade oyster
crackers and bacon.

Gold Coast

Velvet Taco TACOS $
(312-763-2654; www.velvettaco.com; 1110 N
State St; tacos $3.50-7; 11am-midnight Mon, to
2am Tue & Wed, to 3am Thu, to 5am Fri, 10am-5am
Sat, 10am-midnight Sun; 36, Red Line to
Clark/Division) An excellent late-night option
for this area, Velvet Taco features hip new
takes on the eminently adaptable taco: spicy
chicken tikka; Nashville hot tofu with Napa
slaw; shredded pork with avocado crema
and grilled pineapple; Kobe bacon-burger
with smoked cheddar; even shrimp and
grits. Down a few accompanied by a marga-
rita or a beer.

★ **Le Colonial** FRENCH, VIETNAMESE $$$
(312-255-0088; www.lecolonialchicago.com;
937 N Rush St; mains $20-34; 11:30am-3pm &
5-10pm Sun-Thu, to 11pm Fri & Sat; Red Line
to Chicago) Step into the dark-wood, candlelit
room, where ceiling fans swirl lazily and big-
leafed palms sway in the breeze, and you'd
swear you were in 1920s Saigon. Staff can
arrange vegetarian and gluten-free substi-
tutions among the curries and banana-leaf-
wrapped fish dishes. If you want spicy, be
specific; everything typically comes out mild.

Lincoln Park & Old Town

★ **Sultan's Market** MIDDLE EASTERN $
(872-253-1489; 2521 N Clark St, Lincoln Park;
mains $4-10; 10am-10pm Mon-Sat, to 9pm
Sun; Brown, Purple, Red Line to Fullerton)
Neighborhood folks dig into plates heaped
with falafel sandwiches, creamy hummus,
lamb shawarma, spinach pies and other
quality Middle Eastern fare at family-run
Sultan's Market. There's a large salad bar,
too. The small, homey space doesn't have
many tables, but Lincoln Park is nearby for
picnicking.

★ **Alinea** GASTRONOMY $$$
(312-867-0110; www.alinearestaurant.com; 1723
N Halsted St, Lincoln Park; 10-/16-course menus
from $205/290; 5-10pm; Red Line to North/
Clybourn) One of the world's best restaurants,
the triple-Michelin-starred Alinea purveys
multiple courses of molecular gastronomy.
Dishes may emanate from a centrifuge or
be pressed into a capsule, à la duck served
with a 'pillow of lavender air.' There are no
reservations; instead Alinea sells tickets two
to three months in advance via its website.
Check Twitter (@Alinea) for last-minute
seats.

Boka MODERN AMERICAN $$$
(312-337-6070; www.bokachicago.com; 1729 N
Halsted St, Lincoln Park; mains $21-42, small plates
$14-20, 8-course menus $125; 5-10pm Sun-Thu,
to 11pm Fri & Sat; Red Line to North/Clybourn) A
Michelin-starred restaurant-lounge hybrid,
Boka is a pre- and post-theater stomping
ground for younger Steppenwolf patrons.
Order a cocktail at the bar or slip into one
of the booths for small-plate dishes such as
striped-jack crudo or veal sweetbreads with
charred cabbage.

Lake View & Wrigleyville

★ **Jennivee's** BAKERY $
(773-697-3341; www.facebook.com/jennivees;
3301 N Sheffield Ave, Lake View; items $3.25-7.50;
noon-midnight Tue-Thu, to 2am Fri, 10am-2am
Sat, 10am-midnight Sun; Red, Brown, Purple
Line to Belmont) This LGBTIQ-friendly bakery
mixes Filipino and American flavors. The
teeny room couldn't be any cuter. Chandeliers dangle from the ceiling, and a handful

DEEP-DISH CHICAGO

Deep-dish pizza is Chicago's most famous concoction. These behemoths are nothing like the flat circular disks known as pizza in the rest of the world. Chicago's thick-crusted pie stacks up like this: a fat and crumbly crust baked in a cast-iron pan (kind of like a skillet without a handle), capped by mozzarella, then toppings and sauce. **Gino's East** (Map p536; 312-266-3337; www.ginoseast.com; 162 E Superior St, Streeterville; small pizzas from $18; 11am-9pm Sun-Thu, to 10pm Fri & Sat; Red Line to Chicago), **Pizano's** (Map p536; 312-236-1777; www.pizanoschicago.com; 61 E Madison St; small pizzas from $16; 11am-2am Sun-Fri, to 3am Sat; Red, Blue Line to Monroe) and **Lou Malnati's** (Map p536; 312-828-9800; www.loumalnatis.com; 439 N Wells St, River North; small pizzas from $13; 11am-11pm Sun-Thu, to midnight Fri & Sat; Brown, Purple Line to Merchandise Mart) offer classic deep-dish.

An adjunct to the genre is stuffed pizza. It's like deep dish on steroids, bigger and more decadent. Basically it's dough, with cheese on top, then another layer of dough atop that, plus toppings. **Giordano's** (Map p536; 312-951-0747; www.giordanos.com; 730 N Rush St, River North; small pizzas from $18; 11am-11pm Sun-Thu, to midnight Fri & Sat; Red Line to Chicago) bakes a mighty one.

Pan pizza is the third contender. It's similar to deep dish, but the crust is baked differently so it's breadier, and it has a ring of caramelized cheese that crisps in the pan. **Pequod's** (773-327-1512; www.pequodspizza.com; 2207 N Clybourn Ave, Lincoln Park; small pizzas from $12; 11am-2am Mon-Sat, to midnight Sun; 9 to Webster) sets the standard for pan deliciousness.

of French-inspired tables and chairs let you sit in dainty comfort as you dig into Jennivee's moist, creamy-frosted layer cakes and cupcakes. Specialties include purple velvet (made with purple yam) and mango cream cakes.

Gundis Kurdish Kitchen KURDISH $$
(773-904-8120; www.thegundis.com; 2909 N Clark St, Lake View; mains $17-26; 9am-9pm Mon, Wed & Thu, to 10pm Fri & Sat, to 8pm Sun; Brown, Purple Line to Wellington) The owners, who hail from southern Turkey, prepare meals from their Kurdish homeland. Dishes include *sac tawa*, a traditional stir-fry of meat, peppers and tomatoes on a sizzling plate, and *tirsik*, a stew of eggplant, carrots and other veggies in a spicy sauce. Sunshine streams into the airy, exposed-brick room by day, while pendant lights create a romantic vibe at night.

Andersonville & Uptown

★Hopleaf EUROPEAN $$
(773-334-9851; www.hopleaf.com; 5148 N Clark St, Uptown; mains $9-32; noon-10pm Sun-Thu, to 11pm Fri & Sat; 22, Red Line to Berwyn) A cozy, European-like tavern, Hopleaf draws crowds for its Montreal-style smoked brisket, cashew-butter-and-fig-jam sandwich, ubercreamy macaroni and Stilton cheese, and the house-specialty *frites* (fries) and beer-broth-soaked mussels. It also pours 200

types of brew (with around 60 on tap), emphasizing craft and Belgian suds. (The bar stays open several hours after the kitchen closes.)

Passerotto KOREAN $$
(708-607-2102; www.passerottochicago.com; 5420 N Clark St, Andersonville; small plates $9-16; 5-10pm Tue-Thu, to 11pm Fri & Sat; 22, Red Line to Berwyn) Korean American chef Jennifer Kim showcases the food of her childhood through the influences of Italian cooking at Andersonville's hottest new restaurant. The regularly changing menu features sharing plates of varying sizes, from raw Atlantic fluke or bay scallops to *ddukbokki* lamb ragu or *kalbi* short ribs for two ($38). Finish with Tuscan biscotti dipped in Italian raisin wine. Bookings advised.

Lincoln Square & Ravenswood

Goosefoot AMERICAN $$$
(773-942-7547; www.goosefoot.net; 2656 W Lawrence Ave, Lincoln Square; tasting menu $145; 6-8:30pm Wed-Sat; Brown Line to Rockwell) Michelin-starred Goosefoot serves a cutting-edge, modern American tasting menu that never fails to surprise. For instance, your dessert – a vanilla-truffle-cherry-pink-peppercorn ice-cream cone – will arrive in a toy goose-foot-shaped holder

surrounded by moss. Prepare for around six courses of richly textured, amazing-looking food. It's BYOB, with most people buying a bottle at Goosefoot's wine shop next door. Reservations required.

Wicker Park, Bucktown & Ukrainian Village

★ Hoosier Mama Pie Company PIES $

(☎312-243-4846; www.hoosiermamapie.com; 1618 W Chicago Ave, East Village; slices $5-6; ⊗8am-7pm Tue-Fri, 9am-5pm Sat, 10am-4pm Sun; ◻66, Ⓜ Blue Line to Chicago) Soothing 1950s pastels and antique pie tins set the Americana vibe at Paula Haney's celebrated pie shop, where hand-rolled, buttery-flaky crust is plumped full with fruit or creamy fillings. Favorites include sour-cream Dutch cranberry, banana cream, chocolate chess (aka 'brownie pie') and apple-blueberry-walnut. A handful of savory pies tempt, but let's not kid ourselves – we're here for the sweet stuff.

Irazu LATIN AMERICAN $

(☎773-252-5687; www.irazuchicago.com; 1865 N Milwaukee Ave, Bucktown; mains $7-16; ⊗11:30am-9:30pm Mon-Sat; ✐; Ⓜ Blue Line to Western) Chicago's lone Costa Rican eatery turns out burritos bursting with chicken, black beans and fresh avocado, and sandwiches dressed in a heavenly, spicy-sweet vegetable sauce. Wash them down with an *avena* (a slurpable milkshake in tropical-fruit flavors). For breakfast, the *arroz con huevos* (peppery eggs scrambled into rice) relieves hangovers. Irazu is BYOB with no corkage fee. Cash only.

Dove's Luncheonette TEX-MEX $$

(☎773-645-4060; www.doveschicago.com; 1545 N Damen Ave, Wicker Park; mains $13-22; ⊗9am-10pm Mon-Thu, to 11pm Fri, 8am-11pm Sat, 8am-10pm Sun; Ⓜ Blue Line to Damen) Sit at the retro counter for Tex-Mex plates of pork-shoulder posole and buttermilk fried chicken with chorizo-verde gravy. Dessert? It's pie, of course – maybe horchata, lemon cream or peach jalapeño, baked by Hoosier Mama. Soul music spins on a record player, tequila flows from the 70 bottles rattling behind the bar, and presto: all is right in the world.

Logan Square & Humboldt Park

★ Spinning J BAKERY $

(☎872-829-2793; www.spinningj.com; 1000 N California Ave, Humboldt Park; mains $9-12; ⊗7am-9pm Tue-Fri, 8am-9pm Sat & Sun; ◻52) Retro-cute as can be, little Spinning J harks back to a 1950s soda fountain, with a line of counter stools and a smattering of booths where you can sip egg creams and malts made with housemade syrups in flavors such as Thai tea and bay rum cola. Classic sandwiches, hearty soups and sweet and savory pies also please the artsy-crafty patrons.

Ground Control VEGETARIAN $

(☎773-772-9446; www.groundcontrolchicago.com; 3315 W Armitage Ave, Logan Square; mains $10-12; ⊗5-10pm Tue-Thu, 5-11pm Fri, 11am-11pm Sat, 11am-9pm Sun; ✐; ◻73) Ground Control is an industrial, trippy mural-clad restaurant with pinball machines and craft beer on tap. That it's meat-free is incidental. The dishes play off Asian, Latin and Southern flavors, like the Nashville hot tofu, sweet-potato tacos and wasabi portobello sandwich. It's super delicious, and there's always a cool-cat crowd.

Giant AMERICAN $$$

(☎773-252-0997; www.giantrestaurant.com; 3209 W Armitage Ave, Logan Square; small plates $14-19; ⊗5-10:30pm Tue-Sat; ◻73) This wee storefront eatery produces huge flavors in its heady comfort food. Dishes like the king-crab tagliatelle, biscuits with jalapeño butter and sweet-and-sour eggplant have wowed the foodie masses, and rightfully so. The small plate portions mean you'll need to order a few dishes to make a meal. Well-matched cocktails and wine add luster to the spread. Reserve ahead.

West Loop & Near West Side

★ Lou Mitchell's BREAKFAST $

(Map p536; ☎312-939-3111; www.loumitchells.com; 565 W Jackson Blvd, West Loop; mains $9-14; ⊗5:30am-3pm Mon-Fri, 7am-4pm Sat, to 3pm Sun; ⋒; Ⓜ Blue Line to Clinton) A relic of Route 66, Lou's brings in elbow-to-elbow locals and tourists for breakfast. The old-school waitstaff deliver big fluffy omelets and thick-cut French toast with a jug of syrup. They call you 'honey' and fill your coffee cup endlessly. There's often a queue to get in, but free doughnut holes and Milk Duds help ease the wait.

Monteverde ITALIAN $$

(Map p536; ☎312-888-3041; www.monteverde chicago.com; 1020 W Madison St, West Loop; mains $18-24; ⊗5-10:30pm Tue-Fri, 11:30am-10:30pm Sat, 11:30am-9pm Sun; Ⓜ Green, Pink

Line to Morgan) Housemade pastas are the specialty here. They seem simple in concept, such as the *cacio whey pepe* (small tube pasta with pecorino Romano, ricotta whey and four-peppercorn blend), but the flavors are lusciously complex. That's why the light-wood tables in the lively room are always packed. Reserve ahead, especially for weekends, or try the bar or patio for walk-in seats.

★ **Girl & the Goat**   AMERICAN $$$
(Map p536; ☑ 312-492-6262; www.girlandthegoat.com; 809 W Randolph St, West Loop; small plates $12-19; ⊘4:30-11pm Sun-Thu, to midnight Fri & Sat; ☑; Ⓜ Green, Pink Line to Morgan) 🍴 Stephanie Izard's flagship restaurant rocks. The soaring ceilings, polished wood tables and cartoon-y art on the walls offer a convivial atmosphere where local beer and housemade wine hit the tables, along with unique small plates such as catfish with pickled persimmons. Reservations are difficult; try for walk-in seats before 5pm or see if anything opens up at the bar.

Hyde Park & South Side

Gorée Cuisine   SENEGALESE $$
(☑ 773-855-8120; www.goreecuisine.com; 1126 E 47th St, Kenwood; mains $11-19; ⊘9am-10pm Mon-Wed, 8am-11pm Thu-Sun; Ⓜ Metra Electric Line to 47th St) You'll feel transported to Dakar upon entering this tidy, white-curtained cafe where spicy *yassa* chicken (marinated in lemon and onion), *bissap* (hibiscus flower drink) and a slew of other Senegalese dishes hit the tables. If you're new to the cuisine, the friendly staff will help you order. Gorée offers a terrific, authentic, reasonably priced experience that's rare to find.

🍷 Drinking & Nightlife

Chicagoans love to hang out in drinking establishments. Blame it on the long winter, when folks need to huddle together somewhere warm. Blame it on summer, when sunny days make beer gardens and sidewalk patios so splendid. Whatever the reason, drinking in the city is a widely cherished civic pastime.

🍸 The Loop

Berghoff   BAR
(Map p536; ☑ 312-427-3170; www.theberghoff.com; 17 W Adams St; ⊘11am-9pm Mon-Fri, from 11:30am Sat; Ⓜ Blue, Red Line to Jackson) The Berghoff dates from 1898 and was the first Chicago bar to serve a legal drink after Prohibition (ask to see the liquor license stamped '#1'). Little has changed around the antique wood bar since. Belly up for mugs of local and imported beers and order sauerbraten, schnitzel and pretzels the size of your head from the adjoining German restaurant.

🍷 Pilsen & Near South Side

★ **Alulu Brewery & Pub**   MICROBREWERY
(☑ 312-600-9865; www.alulubrew.com; 2011 S Laflin St, Pilsen; ⊘5pm-2am Mon, Wed & Thu, 3pm-2am Fri & Sun, 3pm-3am Sat; Ⓜ Pink Line to 18th St) Pilsen's bohemians love this intimate brewpub and no wonder. Join them at the reclaimed wood tables for a flight and fancy pub grub such as poutine with *merguez*-sausage gravy. The brewers play around with styles, so anything from a watermelon sour to coffee blond, wheat beer or Mexican lager may be pouring from the 20 taps when you visit.

🍷 Near North & Navy Pier

★ **Arbella**   COCKTAIL BAR
(Map p536; ☑ 312-846-6654; www.arbellachicago.com; 112 W Grand Ave, River North; ⊘5pm-midnight Mon, to 2am Tue-Fri, to 3am Sat; Ⓜ Red Line to Grand) Named for a 17th-century ship full of wine-guzzling passengers, Arbella is an adventuresome cocktail bar. Booze from around the globe makes its way into the drinks, from rye to rum, pisco to mezcal. Park yourself at a dark leather banquette, under sparkly globe lights, and taste-trip the night away in one of the city's warmest, coziest rooms.

Centennial Crafted Beer & Eatery   CRAFT BEER
(Map p536; ☑ 312-284-5353; www.centennialchicago.com; 733 N LaSalle Dr, Near North; ⊘4pm-midnight Mon-Wed, 11:30am-midnight Thu, to 2am Fri, 10:30am-3am Sat, 10:30am-midnight Sun; Ⓜ Brown, Purple Line to Chicago) Centennial hides in plain sight. It's rarely mobbed, like many of its neighborhood competitors, yet its 50 taps of carefully chosen craft beer and its cozy, candelabra-and-weathered-wood vibe are exactly what you want in a bar. Beer lovers will never want to leave. Four-beer flights are available that let you expand your hops horizon.

Lincoln Park & Old Town

★ Delilah's   BAR

(☎773-472-2771; www.delilahschicago.com; 2771 N Lincoln Ave, Lincoln Park; ⊙4pm-2am Sun-Fri, to 3am Sat; ⓂBrown Line to Diversey) A bartender rightfully referred to this hard-edged black sheep of the neighborhood as the 'pride of Lincoln Ave': a title earned for the heavy pours and the best whiskey selection in the city – more than 860 different labels! The no-nonsense staff know their way around a beer list, too, tapping unusual domestic and international suds. Cheap Pabst longnecks are always available.

Old Town Ale House   BAR

(☎312-944-2020; www.theoldtownalehouse.com; 219 W North Ave, Old Town; ⊙3pm-4am Mon-Fri, noon-5am Sat, noon-4am Sun; ⓂBrown, Purple Line to Sedgwick) Located near the Second City (p557) comedy club and the scene of late-night musings since the 1960s, this unpretentious neighborhood favorite lets you mingle with beautiful people and grizzled regulars, seated pint by pint under the paintings of nude politicians (just go with it). Classic jazz on the jukebox provides the soundtrack for the jovial goings-on. Cash only.

Lake View & Wrigleyville

★ Hungry Brain   BAR

(☎773-935-2118; www.hungrybrainchicago.com; 2319 W Belmont Ave, Roscoe Village; ⊙7pm-2am, closed Tue; ☐77) The owner of nearby music club Constellation (p556) also owns this off-the-beaten-path little bar. It charms with its kind bartenders and well-worn, thrift-store decor. It's a hub of the underground jazz scene; Sunday nights are the mainstay (suggested donation $10), though there are shows and literary readings other nights of the week, too. Cash only.

Ten Cat Tavern   PUB

(☎773-935-5377; 3931 N Ashland Ave, Lake View; ⊙3pm-2am; ⓂBrown Line to Irving Park) Pool is serious business on the two vintage tables that the pub refelts regularly with Belgian material. The ever-changing, eye-catching art comes courtesy of neighborhood artists and the furniture is a garage saler's dream. Regulars (most in their 30s) down leisurely drinks at the bar or, in warm weather, in the beer garden. The back room has a toasty fireplace.

Lincoln Square & Ravenswood

★ Spiteful Brewing   MICROBREWERY

(☎773-293-6600; www.spitefulbrewing.com; 2024 W Balmoral Ave, Ravenswood; ⊙4-10pm Mon-Wed, to 11pm Thu, noon-midnight Fri & Sat, 11am-10pm Sun; 🛜🍽; ☐50) Spiteful's taproom has a rock-and-roll, DIY vibe. Two home brewers launched the brand, and they now operate out of a renovated garage. The concrete floored, exposed-ductwork place has a long bar where you can belly up for hard-hitting pale ales, IPAs and double IPAs.

Begyle Brewing   MICROBREWERY

(☎773-661-6963; www.begylebrewing.com; 1800 W Cuyler Ave, Ravenswood; ⊙noon-9pm Mon-Thu, to 10pm Fri, 11am-10pm Sat, noon-8pm Sun; 🛜🍽; ⓂBrown Line to Irving Park) Tucked in a warehouse by the train tracks, Begyle's little taproom is a community hub. Friends play cards at one table, an old guy chills with his dog next to them, while work mates discuss business nearby. The blond and wheat ales are mainstays of the 15 beers on tap, but there are also some monster stouts and triple IPAs. They come in 5oz pours and pints, and you can bring in your own food to eat alongside them. Brewery tours ($10) take place at noon on Saturday and include generous samples.

Northman   BAR

(☎773-935-2255; www.thenorthman.com; 4337 N Lincoln Ave, Lincoln Square; ⊙5pm-midnight Mon, to 2am Tue-Fri, noon-3am Sat, noon-2am Sun; ⓂBrown Line to Montrose) The Northman gives the neighborhood beer scene a twist by focusing on cider. Around 20 taps flow with tart, fermented creations from the US, England, France and Spain, and there's a long list of calvados (apple or pear brandies), as well. The low-lit, dark-wood pub feels like it has been plucked from the English countryside.

Wicker Park, Bucktown & Ukrainian Village

Violet Hour   COCKTAIL BAR

(☎773-252-1500; www.theviolethour.com; 1520 N Damen Ave, Wicker Park; ⊙6pm-2am Sun-Fri, to 3am Sat; ⓂBlue Line to Damen) This nouveau speakeasy isn't marked, so look for the wood-paneled building with a full mural and a yellow light over the door. Inside, high-backed booths, chandeliers and long velvet drapes provide the backdrop to elaborately engineered, award-winning seasonal cocktails with droll names. As highbrow as it sounds, friendly staff make Violet Hour welcoming and accessible.

Logan Square & Humboldt Park

Metropolitan Brewing MICROBREWERY
(☑ 773-754-0494; www.metrobrewing.com; 3057 N Rockwell St, Avondale; ⊙ 4-10pm Mon, to 11pm Tue-Thu, to midnight Fri, noon-midnight Sat, noon-10pm Sun; ☐ 77) An elder of the local beer scene, Metropolitan has expanded into a striking, retrofitted old tannery overlooking the Chicago River. The floor-to-ceiling windows provide water views, while the tables made of salvaged wood provide a place to put your slew of German-style lagers.

West Loop & Near West Side

CH Distillery DISTILLERY
(Map p536; ☑ 312-707-8780; www.chdistillery.com; 564 W Randolph St, West Loop; ⊙ 4-10pm Mon-Thu, to midnight Fri & Sat; Ⓜ Green, Pink Line to Clinton) This slick tasting room has a cool, naturalistic look with exposed concrete posts and knotty wood beams across the ceiling. Slip into a seat at the bar and watch the silver tanks behind the big glass window distilling the organic vodka and gin that go into your creative cocktail.

★**RM Champagne Salon** WINE BAR
(Map p536; ☑ 312-243-1199; www.rmchampagne salon.com; 116 N Green St, West Loop; ⊙ 5pm-midnight Mon-Wed & Sun, 5pm-2am Thu-Sat, plus 11am-2pm Sat & Sun; Ⓜ Green, Pink Line to Morgan) This West Loop spot is a twinkling-light charmer for bubbles. Score a table in the cobblestoned courtyard and you'll feel transported to Paris. In winter, the indoor fireplace and plush seats provide a toasty refuge.

Haymarket Pub & Brewery BREWERY
(Map p536; ☑ 312-638-0700; www.haymarket beer.com; 737 W Randolph St, West Loop; ⊙ 11am-2am Sun-Fri, to 3am Sat; Ⓜ Green, Pink Line to Clinton) An early arrival on the West Loop scene, Haymarket remains nicely low-key. It doesn't try to win you over with uberhipness like many of its neighbors. Locals hang out in the cavernous, barrel-strewn space drinking fresh-from-the-tank recipes. The focus is on classic Belgian and German styles, but saisons, IPAs and barrel-aged barley wines fill glasses, too.

Hyde Park & South Side

Marz Community Brewing MICROBREWERY
(☑ 773-579-1935; www.marzbrewing.com; 3630 S Iron St, McKinley Park; ⊙ noon-11pm Tue-Thu, to midnight Fri & Sat, to 10pm Sun; ☐ 9) Marz started as a group of home brewers whose friends demanded more. The small brewery is known for its peculiar creations, such as Potion #1 (aged in absinthe barrels), Diliner Weisse (with fresh dill) and Churros Y Chocolate (milk stout brewed with cocoa nibs and cinnamon). The taproom is a gathering spot for local artists and beer buffs.

☆ Entertainment

From the evening-wear elegance of the Lyric Opera to pay-what-you-can storefront theaters and quirky magic lounges, Chicago puts on an impressive slate of performances. Improv laughs and live music spill out of muggy clubs and DIY dive bars nightly. Chicago's spectator sports might just have the most rabid fans of all.

Jazz, Blues & Folk

★**Green Mill** JAZZ
(☑ 773-878-5552; www.greenmilljazz.com; 4802 N Broadway, Uptown; ⊙ noon-4am Mon-Fri, to 5am Sat, 11am-4am Sun; Ⓜ Red Line to Lawrence) The timeless – and notorious – Green Mill was Al Capone's favorite speakeasy (a trap door behind the bar accessed tunnels for running booze and escaping the feds). Sit in one of the curved booths and feel his ghost urging you on to another martini. Local and national jazz artists perform nightly; on Sunday is the nationally acclaimed **poetry slam** (cover charge $7; ⊙ 7-10pm Sun). Cash only.

★**Buddy Guy's Legends** BLUES
(Map p536; ☑ 312-427-1190; www.buddyguy.com; 700 S Wabash Ave; cover charge Sun-Thu $10, Fri & Sat $20; ⊙ 5pm-2am Mon & Tue, from 11am Wed-Fri, noon-3am Sat, noon-2am Sun; Ⓜ Red Line to Harrison) Top local and national acts wail on the stage of local icon Buddy Guy. The man himself usually plays a series of shows in January; tickets go on sale in October. Free, all-ages acoustic shows are staged at lunch and dinner (the place doubles as a Cajun restaurant); note that you must pay to stay on for late-evening shows.

Rosa's Lounge BLUES
(☑ 773-342-0452; www.rosaslounge.com; 3420 W Armitage Ave, Logan Square; tickets $10-20; ⊙ 8pm-2am Tue-Sat; ☐ 73) Rosa's is an

unadorned, real-deal blues club that brings in top local talent and dedicated fans to a somewhat derelict Logan Square block. Get ready to dance. At night a taxi or rideshare is probably the best way to get here.

★ Constellation
LIVE MUSIC

(www.constellation-chicago.com; 3111 N Western Ave, Roscoe Village; ☉6pm-midnight Mon & Tue, 7pm-2am Wed, Thu & Sun, 6pm-2am Fri & Sat; 📵77) The producer of Pitchfork Music Festival (p545) opened this intimate club, which actually breaks down into two small venues inside. The city's hepcats come out of the woodwork for the progressive jazz and improvisational music. Many acts are free, most cost $10 to $15, and none costs more than $25.

Old Town School of Folk Music
LIVE MUSIC

(📞773-728-6000; www.oldtownschool.org; 4544 N Lincoln Ave, Lincoln Square; 🚼; Ⓜ Brown Line to Western) You can hear the call of the banjos from the street outside this venerable institution, where major national and international acts such as Richard Thompson and Joan Baez play when they come to town. Old Town also hosts superb world-music shows, including every Wednesday at 8:30pm when they're free (or a $10 donation).

Blue Chicago
BLUES

(Map p536; 📞312-661-0100; www.bluechicago. com; 536 N Clark St, River North; tickets $10-12; ☉8pm-1:30am Sun-Fri, to 2:30am Sat; Ⓜ Red Line to Grand) Commanding local acts wither the mikes nightly at this mainstream blues club. It's a pretty spartan setup, with a small, narrow room that gets packed. Arrive early to get a seat. While the crowd and River North environs are touristy, the bands are the real deal.

Rock & World Music

★ Hideout
LIVE MUSIC

(📞773-227-4433; www.hideoutchicago.com; 1354 W Wabansia Ave, West Town; tickets $5-15; ☉4pm-midnight Mon-Thu, to 2am Fri, 6pm-3am Sat, hours vary Sun; 📵72) Hidden behind a factory past the edge of Bucktown, this two-room lodge of indie rock and alt-country is well worth seeking out. The owners have nursed an outsider, underground vibe, and the place feels like your grandma's rumpus room. Music and other events (talk shows, literary readings, comedy etc) take place nightly. On Mondays there's a great open-mike **poetry night** (www.facebook.com/Weeds Poetry; by donation; ☉9:30pm Mon).

★ Whistler
LIVE MUSIC

(📞773-227-3530; www.whistlerchicago.com; 2421 N Milwaukee Ave, Logan Square; ☉6pm-2am Mon-Thu, 5pm-2am Fri-Sun; Ⓜ Blue Line to California) Hometown indie bands, jazz combos and DJs rock this wee, arty bar most nights. There's never a cover charge, but you'd be a schmuck if you didn't order at least one of the swanky cocktails or craft beers to keep the scene going.

Whistler is also a gallery: the front window showcases local artists' work. The venue is easy to miss, as the sign on the door is discreet.

Metro
LIVE MUSIC

(📞773-549-4140; www.metrochicago.com; 3730 N Clark St, Wrigleyville; ☉box office noon-6pm Mon, to 8pm Tue-Sat; Ⓜ Red Line to Addison) For more than three decades, the Metro has been synonymous with loud rock. Sonic Youth and the Ramones in the '80s. Nirvana and Jane's Addiction in the '90s. White Stripes and the Killers in the new millennium. Each night prepare to hear noise by three or four bands who may well be teetering on the verge of stardom.

Empty Bottle
LIVE MUSIC

(📞773-276-3600; www.emptybottle.com; 1035 N Western Ave, Ukrainian Village; ☉5pm-2am Mon-Wed, from 3pm Thu & Fri, from 11am Sat & Sun; 📵49) Chicago's music insiders fawn over the Empty Bottle, the city's scruffy, go-to club for edgy indie rock, jazz and other beats that's been a west-side institution for almost three decades. Monday's show is often a freebie by a couple of up-and-coming bands. Cheap beer, a photo booth and good graffiti-reading in the bathrooms add to the dive-bar fun.

Theater

★ Steppenwolf Theatre
THEATER

(📞312-335-1650; www.steppenwolf.org; 1650 N Halsted St, Lincoln Park; ☉box office 11am-6:30pm Tue-Sat, from 1pm Sun; Ⓜ Red Line to North/Clybourn) Steppenwolf is Chicago's top stage for quality, provocative theater productions. The Hollywood-heavy ensemble includes Gary Sinise, John Malkovich, Martha Plimpton, Gary Cole, Joan Allen and Tracy Letts. A money-saving tip: the box office releases 20 tickets for $20 for each day's shows; they go on sale at 11am Tuesday to Saturday and at 1pm Sunday, and are available by phone.

LGBTIQ+ CHICAGO

Exploring kinky artifacts in the Leather Archives & Museum, or playing a game of naughty Twister at a rollicking street fair? Shopping for gay literature, or clubbing alongside male go-go dancers? Chicago's flourishing gay and lesbian scene in party-hearty Boystown and easygoing Andersonville offers plenty of choices.

The main event on the calendar is the Pride Parade (p545), held the last Sunday in June. It winds through Boystown and attracts more than 800,000 risqué revelers. **Northalsted Market Days** (www.northalsted.com; Boystown; ☉mid-Aug; Ⓜ Red Line to Addison), held in Boystown, is a steamy two-day street fair in mid-August. Crafty, incense-wafting vendors line Halsted St, but most folks come for the drag queens in feather boas, Twister games played in the street and disco divas (Gloria Gaynor!) on the main stage. The **International Mr Leather** (www.imrl.com; ☉May) contest brings out lots of men in, well, leather in late May. Workshops and parties take place around town, with the main event happening at a downtown hotel or theater.

The following resources will assist with your explorations:

Chicago Pride (www.chicagopride.org) Events and happenings in the community.

Purple Roofs (www.purpleroofs.com) Listings for queer accommodations, travel agencies and tours.

Windy City Times (www.windycitymediagroup.com) LGBTIQ+ newspaper, published weekly. The website is the main source for events and entertainment.

Goodman Theatre THEATER
(Map p536; ☎312-443-3800; www.goodmantheatre.org; 170 N Dearborn St; Ⓜ Brown, Orange, Green, Purple, Pink, Blue Line to Clark/Lake) One of Chicago's premier drama houses, with a gorgeous Theater District facility. It specializes in new and classic American productions and has been cited several times as one of the USA's best regional theaters. Unsold tickets for the current day's performance go on sale at 10am for half-price online; they're also available at the box office from noon.

Chicago Theatre THEATER
(Map p536; ☎312-462-6300; www.thechicagotheatre.com; 175 N State St; Ⓜ Brown, Orange, Green, Purple, Pink Line to State/Lake) Take a gander at the illuminated six-story sign – it's an official landmark and an excellent photo op. Everyone from Duke Ellington to Dolly Parton to Prince has played here over the years (and left their signature on the famous backstage walls). The real showstopper, though, is the opulent French baroque architecture, including a lobby modeled on the Palace of Versailles.

★**Neo-Futurist Theater** THEATER
(☎773-878-4557; www.neofuturists.org; 5153 N Ashland Ave, Uptown; ☉11:30pm Fri & Sat, 7pm Sun; ☐50, Ⓜ Red Line to Berwyn) The Neo-Futurists are best known for their show *The Infinite Wrench*, in which the hyper troupe makes a manic attempt to perform 30 original plays

in 60 minutes. Admission costs $10 to $15 – you pay $9 plus the roll of a six-sided die.

Comedy

★**iO Theater** COMEDY
(☎312-929-2401; www.ioimprov.com; 1501 N Kingsbury St, Old Town; tickets $5-16; Ⓜ Red Line to North/Clybourn) One of Chicago's top-tier (and original) improv houses, iO is a bit edgier (and cheaper) than its competition, with four stages hosting bawdy shows of regular and musical improv nightly. Two bars and a beer garden add to the fun. The Improvised Shakespeare Company is awesome; catch them if you can.

Second City COMEDY
(☎312-337-3992; www.secondcity.com; 1616 N Wells St, Lincoln Park; tickets $35-55; Ⓜ Brown, Purple Line to Sedgwick) Bill Murray, Stephen Colbert, Tina Fey and more honed their wit at this slick venue with nightly shows. The Mainstage and ETC stage host sketch revues (with an improv scene thrown in); they're similar in price and quality. If you turn up around 10pm Monday through Thursday (or 1am Saturday or 9pm Sunday) you can watch a free improv set.

Cinema

Music Box Theatre CINEMA
(☎773-871-6604; www.musicboxtheatre.com; 3733 N Southport Ave, Lake View; Ⓜ Brown Line to Southport) It hardly matters what's playing

here; the Music Box itself is worth the visit. The restored theater dates from 1929 and looks like a Moorish palace, with clouds floating across the ceiling under twinkling stars. The art-house films are always first-rate and there's a midnight roster of cult hits such as *The Big Lebowski*. A second, smaller theater shows held-over films.

Davis Theater CINEMA
(☎ 773-769-3999; www.davistheater.com; 4614 N Lincoln Ave, Lincoln Square; ⏱ 4:30pm-1am Mon-Fri, 11am-2am Sat, 11am-1am Sun; Ⓜ Brown Line to Western) Thanks to a renovation, the century-old Davis has burnished its deco charm while adding modern amenities such as stadium seating and state-of-the-art sound. The first-run theater also attached a bar-restaurant called Carbon Arc, named after the carbon arc lamps in old film projectors, serving fancy snacks (Thai mussels, duck-and-bean stew) and craft beers that you can take into the movie.

Performing Arts

★ **Grant Park Orchestra** CLASSICAL MUSIC
(Map p536; ☎ 312-742-7638; www.grantparkmusicfestival.com; Pritzker Pavilion, Millennium Park; ⏱ 6:30pm Wed & Fri, 7:30pm Sat mid-Jun–mid-Aug; Ⓜ Brown, Orange, Green, Purple, Pink Line to Washington/Wabash) It's a summertime must-do. The Grant Park Orchestra – composed of top-notch musicians from symphonies worldwide – puts on free classical concerts at Millennium Park's Pritzker Pavilion (p533). Patrons bring lawn chairs, blankets, wine and picnic fixings to set the scene as the sun dips, the skyscraper lights flicker on and glorious music fills the night air.

Chicago Symphony Orchestra CLASSICAL MUSIC
(CSO; Map p536; ☎ 312-294-3000; www.cso.org; 220 S Michigan Ave; Ⓜ Brown, Orange, Green, Purple, Pink Line to Adams) Riccardo Muti leads the CSO, one of America's best symphonies, known for its fervent subscribers and an untouchable brass section. Cellist Yo-Yo Ma is the creative consultant and a frequent soloist. The season runs from September to June at Symphony Center; Daniel Burnham designed the Orchestra Hall.

🔒 Shopping

From the glossy stores of the Magnificent Mile to the indie designers of Wicker Park to the brainy booksellers of Hyde Park, Chicago is a shopper's destination. It has been that way from the get-go. After all, this is the city that birthed the department store and traditions such as the money-back guarantee, bridal registry and bargain basement.

★ **Chicago Architecture Center Shop** GIFTS & SOUVENIRS
(Map p536; ☎ 312-922-3432; http://shop.architecture.org; 111 E Wacker Dr; ⏱ 9am-5pm Mon, Wed & Fri-Sun, to 8pm Tue & Thu; 🚌 151, Ⓜ Brown, Orange, Green, Purple, Pink Line to State/Lake) Browse through skyline T-shirts and posters, Frank Lloyd Wright note cards, skyscraper models and heaps of books that celebrate local architecture at this haven for anyone with an edifice complex; a children's section has books to pique the interest of budding builders. The items make excellent 'only in Chicago' souvenirs.

★ **Reckless Records** MUSIC
(☎ 773-235-3727; www.reckless.com; 1379 N Milwaukee Ave, Wicker Park; ⏱ 10am-10pm Mon-Sat, to 8pm Sun; Ⓜ Blue Line to Damen) Chicago's best indie-rock record and CD emporium lets you listen to everything before you buy. There's plenty of elbow room in the big, sunny space, which makes for happy hunting through the new and used bins. DVDs and cassette tapes, too. Stop by for flyers and listing calendars of the local live-music and theater scene.

★ **Open Books** BOOKS
(Map p536; ☎ 312-475-1355; www.open-books.org; 651 W Lake St, West Loop; ⏱ 9am-7pm Mon-Sat, noon-6pm Sun; 🚹; Ⓜ Green, Pink Line to Clinton) Buy a used book here and you're helping to fund this volunteer-based literacy group's programs, which range from in-school reading help for grade-schoolers to book-publishing courses for teens. The jam-packed store has good-quality tomes and plenty of cushy sofas where you can sit and peruse your finds. Kids will find lots of imaginative wares. Books average around $5.

Gene's Sausage Shop FOOD & DRINKS
(☎ 773-728-7243; www.genessausage.com; 4750 N Lincoln Ave, Lincoln Square; ⏱ 9am-8pm Mon-Sat, to 4pm Sun; Ⓜ Brown Line to Western) As if the hanging sausages, ripe cheeses and flaky pastries lining the shelves at this European market weren't enough, Gene's also rocks a rooftop summer beer garden. Sit at communal picnic tables and munch hot-off-the-grill bratwursts while sipping worldly brews from the tap.

Quimby's
BOOKS

(📞 773-342-0910; www.quimbys.com; 1854 W North Ave, Wicker Park; ⊗ noon-9pm Mon-Thu, to 10pm Fri, 11am-10pm Sat, noon-7pm Sun; Ⓜ Blue Line to Damen) The epicenter of Chicago's comic and zine worlds, Quimby's is one of the linchpins of underground literary culture in the city. Here you can find everything from crayon-powered punk-rock manifestos to slickly produced graphic novels. It's a groovy place for cheeky literary souvenirs and bizarro readings.

Koval Distillery
DRINKS

(📞 312-878-7988; www.koval-distillery.com; 5121 N Ravenswood Ave, Ravenswood; ⊗ 2-7pm Mon-Fri, 1-6:30pm Sat, 2-5pm Sun; Ⓜ Brown Line to Damen) Koval distills organic, small-batch whiskey and gin in the shiny copper tanks that you see inside. It also makes ginger, jasmine, walnut and other unique liqueurs. The shop in front sells them; you can sample the wares before buying.

The distillery also offers hour-long tours ($10) on Wednesday, Saturday and Sunday, and weekly cocktail classes. The website has the schedule.

ⓘ Information

Chicago Reader (www.chicagoreader.com) Great listings for music, arts, restaurants and film, plus news and politics.

Choose Chicago (www.choosechicago.com) Official tourism site with sightseeing and event info.

Lonely Planet (www.lonelyplanet.com/chicago) Destination information, hotel bookings, traveler forum and more.

ⓘ Getting There & Away

AIR

Seventeen miles northwest of the Loop, **O'Hare International Airport** (ORD; 📞 800-832-6352; www.flychicago.com/ohare; 10000 W O'Hare Ave) is the headquarters for United Airlines and a hub for American Airlines. Most non-US airlines and international flights use Terminal 5. The domestic terminals are 1, 2 and 3. ATMs and currency exchanges are available throughout. Wi-fi is free, but slow.

Eleven miles southwest of the Loop, **Midway International Airport** (MDW; 📞 773-838-0600; www.flychicago.com/midway; 5700 S Cicero Ave, Clearing) has three concourses: A, B and C. Southwest Airlines uses B; most other airlines go out of A. There's a currency exchange in A and ATMs throughout. Wi-fi is free, but slow.

TRAIN

Grand, Doric-columned **Union Station** (www.chicagounionstation.com; 225 S Canal St; Ⓜ Blue Line to Clinton) is the city's rail hub, located at the Loop's western edge. **Amtrak** (www.amtrak.com) has more connections here than anywhere else in the country.

ⓘ Getting Around

TO/FROM THE AIRPORT

O'Hare International Airport The Blue Line L train ($5) runs 24/7 and departs every 10 minutes or so. The journey to the city center takes 40 minutes. Shuttle vans cost $35, taxis around $50.

Midway International Airport The Orange Line L train ($3) runs between 4am and 1am, departing every 10 minutes or so. The journey takes 30 minutes to downtown. Shuttle vans cost $28, taxis $35 to $40.

Union Station All trains arrive here. For transportation onward, the Blue Line Clinton stop is a few blocks south (thought it's not a great option at night). The Brown, Orange, Purple and Pink Line station at Quincy is about a half-mile east. Taxis queue along Canal St outside the station entrance.

PUBLIC TRANSPORTATION

Elevated/subway trains are part of the city's public transportation system. Metra commuter trains venture out into the suburbs.

The L (a system of elevated and subway trains) is fast, frequent and will get you to most sights and neighborhoods.

Two of the eight color-coded lines – the Red Line, and the Blue Line to O'Hare airport – operate 24 hours a day. The other lines run from roughly 4am to 1am daily, departing every 10 minutes or so.

The standard fare is $3 (except from O'Hare airport, where it costs $5) and includes two transfers. Enter the turnstile using a Ventra Ticket, which is sold from vending machines at train stations.

You can also buy a Ventra Card, aka a rechargeable fare card, at stations. It has a one-time $5 fee that gets refunded once you register the card. It knocks around 75¢ off the cost of each ride.

Unlimited ride passes (one/three/seven days $10/20/28) are another handy option. Get them at train stations and drugstores.

For maps and route planning, check the website of the Chicago Transit Authority (www.transitchicago.com). The 'Trackers' section tells you when the next train or bus is due to arrive at your station.

Metra (www.metrarail.com) commuter trains traverse 12 routes serving the suburbs from four terminals ringing the Loop: LaSalle St

Station, **Millennium Station** (151 N Michigan Ave; Ⓜ Brown, Orange, Green, Purple, Pink Line to Washington/Wabash), which is below street level (look for the stairs down), Union Station (p559) and **Richard B Ogilvie Transportation Center** (OTC, Ogilvie Station; 500 W Madison St; Ⓜ Green, Pink Line to Clinton), a few blocks north of Union Station. Some train lines run daily, while others operate only during weekday rush hours. Buy tickets from agents and machines at major stations.

City buses operate from early morning until late evening. The fare is $2.25 ($2.50 if you want a transfer). You can use a Ventra Card or pay the driver with exact change. Buses are particularly useful for reaching the Museum Campus, Hyde Park and Lincoln Park's zoo.

TAXI

Taxis are plentiful in the Loop, north to Andersonville and northwest to Wicker Park/Bucktown. Hail them with a wave of the hand. Fares are meter-based and start at $3.25 when you get into the cab, then it's $2.25 per mile. The first extra passenger costs $1; extra passengers after that are 50¢ apiece. Add 10% to 15% for a tip. All major companies accept credit cards.

Reliable companies:

Checker Taxi (☎312-243-2537; www.checker taxichicago.com)

Flash Cab (☎773-561-4444; www.flash cab.com)

The ridesharing companies **Uber** (www.uber. com), **Lyft** (www.lyft.com) and **Via** (www.ride-withvia.com) are also popular in Chicago. They can be a bit cheaper than taxis.

Around Chicago

Oak Park

This suburb next door to Chicago spawned two famous sons: novelist Ernest Hemingway was born here, and architect Frank Lloyd Wright lived and worked here for 20 years. The town's main sights revolve around the two men. For Hemingway, a low-key museum and his birthplace provide an intriguing peek at his formative years. For Wright, the studio where he developed the Prairie style is the big draw, as is a slew of surrounding houses he designed for his neighbors. Ten of them cluster within a mile along Forest and Chicago Aves (though gawking must occur from the sidewalk since they're privately owned).

◉ Sights

★ Frank Lloyd Wright Home & Studio   ARCHITECTURE

(☎312-994-4000; www.flwright.org; 951 Chicago Ave; adult/child $18/15; ☉10am-4pm) This is where Wright lived and worked from 1889 to 1909 and it's the first home he ever designed. Tour frequency varies, from every 20 minutes on summer weekends to every hour or so in winter. The hour-long walk-through reveals a fascinating place, filled with the details that made Wright's style distinctive. The studio also offers guided neighborhood walking tours ($15) on Sundays; a self-guided audio version ($15) is available on other days.

ⓘ Information

Visit Oak Park (www.visitoakpark.com) A wealth of online info, but their physical visitors center has closed.

ⓘ Getting There & Away

I-290 edges the town; exit on Harlem Ave. Take Harlem north to Lake St and turn right. There's a parking garage within a few blocks.

Metra commuter trains on the Union Pacific West Line stop at Oak Park on their Chicago–western suburbs route. Green Line trains also run to/from Chicago as part of the city's public transit system. The sights are walkable from the stations.

North Shore Suburbs

Mansion-strewn real estate fringes Lake Michigan in the suburbs north of Chicago. The area became popular with the wealthy in the late 19th century.

◉ Sights

★ Illinois Holocaust Museum   MUSEUM

(www.ilholocaustmuseum.org; 9603 Woods Dr, Skokie; adult/child $12/6; ☉10am-5pm, to 8pm Thu) This is the third-largest holocaust museum in the world, after those in Jerusalem and Washington, DC. Besides its haunting Nazi-era rail car and its videos of survivors' stories from WWII, the venue contains thought-provoking art about genocides in Armenia, Rwanda, Cambodia and other countries. The special exhibitions are particularly impressive.

ⓘ Getting There & Away

I-94 slices by the suburbs to the west. Sheridan Rd rambles through the towns along the lakefront to the east. Metra commuter trains on the Union Pacific North Line stop at each North Shore community as they zip between downtown Chicago and Kenosha, WI. In Evanston, Purple Line trains also run to/from downtown Chicago as part of the Windy City's public transit system.

Galena

Wee Galena spreads across wooded hillsides near the Mississippi River, amid rolling, barn-dotted farmland. Redbrick mansions in Greek Revival, Gothic Revival and Queen Anne styles line the streets, left over from the town's heyday in the mid-1800s, when local lead mines made it rich. Even with all the touristy B&Bs, fudge and antique shops, there's no denying Galena's beauty – 85% of its structures make up the Galena Historic District, which is on the National Register of Historic Places, and its Main St is about as Pleasantville-perfect as one gets. Throw in cool kayak trips and back-road drives, and you've got a lovely, slow-paced getaway. More than a million visitors come to the town each year; summer and fall weekends see the most action.

Sights & Activities

Ulysses S Grant Home HISTORIC SITE
(www.granthome.com; 500 Bouthillier St; adult/child $5/3; ⏱9am-4:45pm Wed-Sun Apr-Oct, reduced hours Nov-Mar) The 1860 abode was a gift from local Republicans to the victorious general at the Civil War's end. Grant lived here until he became the country's 18th president. Docents take you through the house. Around 90% of the furnishings are original.

Fever River Outfitters OUTDOORS
(☎815-776-9425; www.feverriveroutfitters.com; 525 S Main St; canoe rental 2/4hr $40/50, bike rental 2hr/day from $23/40; ⏱9am-5pm Mon & Fri-Sun, Tue-Thu by appointment) Fever River rents canoes, kayaks, bicycles, paddleboards and snowshoes. It also offers guided tours, such as 12-mile bike trips ($45 per person, gear included) to a local winery and various paddling excursions.

Sleeping & Eating

★ Jail Hill Inn B&B $$$
(☎815-777-3000; www.jailhillgalena.com; 319 Meeker St; d $345-445; P ✳ 🛜) Convicts and town drunks were locked away here until 1977, but this former jail has been lavishly converted into one of the country's best B&Bs and now you'll definitely want to spend the night in this 140-year-old Second Empire building. Six rooms with exposed-brick ceilings clock in at a huge 800 sq ft; luxurious accoutrements include soaking tubs and fireplaces.

★ Otto's Place BREAKFAST $
(www.ottosplace.com; 100 Bouthillier St; mains $3.50-13; ⏱7am-2pm Wed-Mon) Just off Main St (read: lures in more locals), Otto constructed this historic building in 1899 and turned it into a restaurant. He and his restaurant are long gone, but new proprietors pay homage to history at this excellent breakfast stop, which serves up killer sautéed potatoes and recommended breakfast tacos, plus wildly popular sweet-potato hash and banana bread.

ⓘ Information

Galena Country Welcome Center (☎815-776-9200; www.visitgalena.org; 123 N Commerce St; ⊙10am-4pm) Brochures and local info.

ⓘ Getting There & Away

Hwy 20 rolls into Galena. Driving is the only way to get here. The closest transportation hubs are Chicago (165 miles southeast), Madison, WI (95 miles northeast), and Dubuque, IA (16 miles northwest). There is a free **parking lot** (Bouthillier St) beside the old train depot (street parking in town is also free but limited to three hours). Most sights, shops and restaurants are walkable from here.

Central Illinois

Abraham Lincoln and Route 66 sights are sprinkled liberally throughout central Illinois, which is otherwise farmland plain, though the state capital of Springfield offers worthwhile Lincoln-themed history, a bit of architecture and a burgeoning craft-beer scene. East of Decatur, Arthur and Arcola are Amish centers.

Springfield

The small state capital has a serious obsession with Abraham Lincoln, who practiced law here from 1837 to 1861. Many of the attractions, such as the Lincoln Home National Historic Site and the Lincoln Presidential Library & Museum, are walkable downtown.

⊙ Sights

★**Dana Thomas House**   ARCHITECTURE (☎217-782-6776; www.dana-thomas.org; 300 E Lawrence Ave; adult/child $10/5; ⊙10am-2pm Mon & Tue, 9am-5pm Wed-Sun) The third-largest home Frank Lloyd Wright ever designed, this remarkably preserved Prairie School icon dating to 1902-04 is - dare we say it - more interesting than Wright's own home in Oak Park. The 16-level abode, considered experimental from a Wright perspective, includes a duckpin bowling alley and two of the three barrel-vaulted ceilings he ever designed (the other is in Oak Park). An astounding 90% of the furniture is original and there's exquisite, color-shifting art glass.

Lincoln Home
National Historic Site   HISTORIC SITE (☎217-492-4150; www.nps.gov/liho; 426 S 7th St; ⊙8:30am-5pm) `FREE` An entire four-block neighborhood has been preserved as part of the Lincoln Home National Historic Site. Visits begin at the National Park Service visitor center, where you must pick up a ticket to enter Lincoln's 12-room abode, located one block east. Rangers then lead you through the house (the only home Lincoln ever owned) where Abe and Mary Lincoln lived from 1844 until they moved to the White House in 1861. A remarkable 80% of the home is original.

Lincoln Presidential
Library & Museum   MUSEUM (☎217-558-8844; www.illinois.gov/alplm; 212 N 6th St; adult/child $15/6; ⊙9am-5pm; ⓓ) This museum contains the most complete Lincoln collection in the world. Real-deal artifacts such as Abe's shaving mirror and presidential seal join whiz-bang exhibits and Disneyesque holograms that keep the kids agog.

🛏 Sleeping

★**Inn at 835**   B&B $$ (☎217-523-4466; www.innat835.com; 835 S 2nd St; r $135-205; P🅿🅰) This historic arts-and-crafts-style luxury apartment building from 1908 offers 11 rooms of the four-poster bed, claw-foot bathtub variety (along with two additional abodes in the adjacent Bell House). You're spoiled with nightly wine and cheese, and fresh-baked cookies delivered to your room.

🍷 Drinking & Nightlife

★**Obed & Isaac's**   MICROBREWERY (☎217-670-0627; www.obedandisaacs.com; 500 S 6th St; ⊙11am-11:30pm) Occupying a rambling, 150-year-old mansion by Abe Lincoln's home, Obed & Isaac's offers a maze of sunny rooms to drink its wildly changing menu of ales and stouts brewed on-site. Flights let you sample freely, while the menu of elevated bar food helps soak up the alcohol. An outdoor bar, patio and bocce courts await in summer.

ⓘ Information

Springfield Visitors Center (☎217-789-2360; www.visitspringfieldillinois.com; 1 S Old State Capitol Plaza; ⊙9am-5pm Mon-Fri) Produces a useful visitors' guide. The location - inside the Lincoln-Herndon Law Offices - is where Abraham Lincoln practiced law.

ⓘ Getting There & Away

The downtown **Amtrak station** (☎800-872-7245; www.amtrak.com; 100 N 3rd St) has daily

ROUTE 66: GET YOUR KICKS IN ILLINOIS

America's 'Mother Road' kicks off in Chicago on Adams St, just west of Michigan Ave. Before embarking, fuel up at Lou Mitchell's (p552) near Union Station. After all, it's 300 miles from here to the Missouri state line.

Sadly, most of the original Route 66 has been superseded by I-55 in Illinois, though the old road still exists in scattered sections often paralleling the interstate. Keep an eye out for brown 'Historic Route 66' signs, which pop up at crucial junctions to mark the way. Top stops include the following:

Gemini Giant (810 E Baltimore St, Wilmington) The first must-see rises from the corn-fields 60 miles south of Chicago in Wilmington. Here the Gemini Giant – a 28ft fiberglass spaceman holding a rocket – stands guard outside the Launching Pad Drive In and makes a terrific photo op. To reach it, leave I-55 at exit 241, and follow Hwy 44 south a short distance to Hwy 53, which rolls into town.

Funks Grove (✆309-874-3360; www.funksmaplesirup.com; 5257 Old Rte 66, Shirley; ⊙9am-5pm Mon-Sat, from 1pm Sun) FREE Drive 90 miles onward to see Funk's pretty, 19th-century maple-sirup farm (yes, that's sirup with an 'i'). It's in Shirley (exit 154 off I-55). Afterward, get on Old Route 66 – a frontage road that parallels the interstate here – and in 10 miles you'll reach...

Palms Grill Cafe (✆217-648-2233; www.thepalmsgrillcafe.com; 110 SW Arch St, Atlanta; mains $5-11; ⊙10am-2pm Wed-Fri, to 3pm Sat & Sun) Pull up a chair at this diner in the throwback hamlet of Atlanta, where thick slabs of gooseberry, chocolate cream and other retro pies tempt from the glass case. Then walk across the street to snap a photo with Tall Paul, a sky-high statue of Paul Bunyan clutching a hot dog.

Cozy Dog Drive In (✆217-525-1992; www.cozydogdrivein.com; 2935 S 6th St; mains $2-6; ⊙8am-8pm Mon-Sat) It's in Springfield, 50 miles down the road from Palms Grill, and it's where the cornmeal-battered, fried hot dog on a stick was born.

Ariston Cafe (✆217-324-2023; www.ariston-cafe.com; 413 N Old Route 66, Litchfield; mains $6-29; ⊙11am-8pm Tue-Thu, to 9pm Fri & Sat, to 8pm Sun) Further south, a good section of Old Route 66 parallels I-55 through Litchfield, where you can fork into chicken fried steak and red velvet cake while chatting up locals at this 1924 restaurant.

Old Chain of Rocks Bridge (10820 Riverview Dr; ⊙9am-sunset) Before driving into Missouri, detour off I-270 at exit 3. Follow Hwy 3 (aka Lewis and Clark Blvd) south, turn right at the first stoplight and drive west to the 1929 bridge. Open only to pedestrians and cyclists these days, the mile-long span over the Mississippi River has a 22-degree angled bend (the cause of many a crash, hence the ban on cars).

For more information, visit the Route 66 Association of Illinois (www.il66assoc.org) or Illinois Route 66 Scenic Byway (www.illinoisroute66.org). Detailed driving directions are at www.historic66.com/illinois.

---

trains to/from St Louis (two hours) and Chicago (3½ hours). I-55 is the busy interstate route to Springfield. Route 66 also dawdles into town.

Southern Illinois

Southern Illinois looks wildly different from the rest of the state, with rivers and rugged green hills dominating the landscape. The Mississippi River forms the western boundary, and alongside it the Great River Road unfolds. The water-hugging byway (actually a series of roads) curls by bluff-strewn scenery and forgotten towns with real-deal Main Streets. One of the knockout stretches is Hwy 100 between Grafton and Alton (near St Louis). As you slip under wind-beaten cliffs, keep an eye out for the turnoff to El-sah, a hidden hamlet of 19th-century stone cottages, wood buggy shops and farmhous-es. To the south, Lewis and Clark's launch site, a prehistoric World Heritage Site and a lonely hilltop fort appear.

Inland and south, the population thins and the forested Shawnee Hills rise up, looking a lot like mini mountains. Some sur-prises hide around here, including an eerie swamp and a fantastic destination brewery.

◉ Sights & Activities

Union County, near the state's southern tip, has wineries and orchards. Sample the wares on the 35-mile **Shawnee Hills Wine Trail** (www.shawneewinetrail.com), which connects 11 vineyards.

Cahokia Mounds
State Historic Site   HISTORIC SITE
(☑618-346-5160; www.cahokiamounds.org; Collinsville Rd, Collinsville; suggested donation adult/child $7/2; ⊘grounds 8am-dusk, visitor center 9am-5pm Wed-Sun) A surprise awaits near Collinsville, 8 miles east of East St Louis: classified as a Unesco World Heritage Site, with the likes of Stonehenge and the Egyptian pyramids, is Cahokia Mounds State Historic Site. Cahokia protects the remnants of North America's largest prehistoric city (20,000 people, with suburbs), dating from AD 1200.

Cypress Creek
National Wildlife Refuge   WILDLIFE RESERVE
(☑618-634-2231; www.fws.gov/refuge/cypress_creek; Ullin) **FREE** You certainly don't expect to find a Southern-style swampland, complete with moss-draped cypress trees and croaking bullfrogs in Illinois. But it's here, at Cypress Creek National Wildlife Refuge. Check it out from the **Bellrose Viewing Platform** off Cache Chapel Rd. Or head to Section 8 Woods and take a short stroll on the boardwalk for a taste of the waterlogged, primeval landscape; it's near the **Cache River Wetlands Center** (☑618-657-2064; www.friendsofthecache.org; 8885 Hwy 37, Cypress; ⊘9am-4pm Wed-Sun), which also has hiking and canoeing information.

✖ Eating & Drinking

★ **Firefly Grill**   AMERICAN $$
(☑217-342-2002; www.ffgrill.com; 1810 Ave of Mid-America, Effingham; mains $10-55; ⊘11am-9pm Mon-Thu, to 10pm Fri & Sat, 10am-8pm Sun; 🖥) 🖉 This fiercely sustainable, farm-to-fork destination restaurant in Effingham (of all places!) is arguably Illinois' top gastronomic haven outside of Chicago. Inside a beautiful reclaimed wooded barn, chef Niall Campbell II cooks up his proudly local creations sourced from artisan farmers, foragers and fisherman, with stunning results.

Scratch Brewing   MICROBREWERY
(☑618-426-1415; www.scratchbeer.com; 264 Thompson Rd, Ava; ⊘4-10pm Fri, from noon Sat, noon-8pm Sun; 🖥) You'll find this farmhouse brewery hidden away amid horse- and sheep-grazing pastures just 5 miles outside Shawnee National Forest in Ava. Twigs, bark, berries and herbs from the farm are thrown into their foraged wild ales and sours (goblets and snifters from $5), often aged in their own split-out oak trees from the property. File under: travel-worthy beer nirvana.

❶ Getting There & Away

You'll need to drive to reach the area's far-flung sights. I-57 is the main interstate through the heart of the region. The Great River Road dawdles along the water to the west. St Louis is the nearest transportation hub.

INDIANA

The state revs up around the Indy 500 race, but otherwise it's about slow-paced pleasures in corn-stubbled Indiana: pie-eating in Amish Country, meditating in Bloomington's Tibetan temples and admiring the big architecture in small Columbus. The northwest has moody sand dunes to climb, while the south has caves to explore and rivers to canoe. Spooky labyrinths, bluegrass music shrines and a famed, lipstick-kissed gravestone also make appearances in the state.

For the record, folks have called Indianans 'Hoosiers' since the 1830s, but the word's origin is unknown. One theory is that early settlers knocking on a door were met with 'Who's here?' which soon became 'Hoosier.' It's certainly something to discuss with locals, perhaps over a traditional pork tenderloin sandwich.

Fun fact: Indiana is called 'the mother of vice presidents' for the six veeps it has spawned.

❶ Information

Indiana Highway Conditions (https://indot.carsprogram.org)

Indiana State Park Information (☑866-622-6746; www.indianastateparks.reserveamerica.com) Park entry costs $2 per day by foot or bicycle, $7 to $12 by vehicle. Campsites cost $12 to $44; reservations accepted.

Indiana Tourism (www.visitindiana.com)

Indianapolis

Clean-cut Indy is the state capital and a perfectly pleasant place to ogle **race cars** (www.indycarfactory.com; 1201 W Main St; adult/child $10/5; ⊘10am-5pm Wed-Sat) and take a spin around the renowned speedway. The art museum and **White River State Park** (☎317-233-2434; www.whiteriverstatepark.org; 801 W Washington St; ⊙park 5am-11pm, vistors center 10am-5pm Mon-Sat, from noon Sun) have their merits, as do the Mass Ave and Broad Ripple hoods for eating and drinking. And fans of author Kurt Vonnegut are in for a treat. A swell walking and biking trail connects it all.

◉ Sights & Activities

★Children's Museum of Indianapolis
MUSEUM

(☎317-334-4000; www.childrensmuseum.org; 3000 N Meridian St; $5-35; ⊙10am-5pm, closed Mon mid-Sep–Feb; 🚼🚹) It's the world's largest kids' museum, sprawled over five floors holding incredible exhibitions on dinosaurs, space stations and so much more. The museum is centered around a stunning 43ft sculpture by Dale Chihuly that teaches tykes to blow glass (virtually!); and the fantastic new 7.5-acre Sports Legends Experience is the outdoor playground of your dreams, with numerous fields and courts dedicated to all major sports. Within the context of children's museums, it's world-class.

★Indianapolis Motor Speedway
MUSEUM

(☎317-492-6784; www.indianapolismotorspeedway.com; 4790 W 16th St; adult/child $10/8; ⊙9am-5pm Mar-Oct, 10am-4pm Nov-Feb) The Speedway, home of the Indianapolis 500 motor race, is Indy's super-sight. The Speedway Museum features some 75 racing cars (including former winners) and a 500lb Tiffany trophy. Limited availability golfcart tours of the grounds and track ($50) are available from March to October (OK, you're not exactly burning rubber in a golf cart, but it's still fun to pretend while you take a lap!).

Newfields
MUSEUM, GARDENS

(☎317-920-2660; www.discovernewfields.org; 4000 Michigan Rd; adult/child $18/10; ⊙11am-5pm Tue-Sat, to 9pm Thu, noon-5pm Sun) The 152-acre Newfields campus houses the **Indianapolis Museum of Art**, home to a terrific collection of European art (especially Turner and post-Impressionists), African tribal art, South Pacific art, Chinese works, Robert Indiana's original pop-art Love sculpture and the largest gallery dedicated to contemporary and modern design in the US.

Kurt Vonnegut Museum & Library
MUSEUM

(☎317-423-0391; www.vonnegutlibrary.org; 543 Indiana Ave; ⊙11am-6pm Mon, Tue, Thu & Fri, noon-5pm Sat & Sun) **FREE** Author Kurt Vonnegut was born and raised in Indy, and this humble museum pays homage with displays including his Pall Mall cigarettes, droll drawings and rejection letters from publishers. The museum also replicates his office, complete with a blue Coronamatic typewriter. You're welcome to sit at the desk and type Kurt a note; the museum tweets the musings.

Monon Trail
OUTDOORS

(www.bikethemonon.com; ⊙24hr) This cycling and walking trail (no motorized vehicles allowed) plies through some of Indy's coolest districts along a 26-mile former rail path that stretches from downtown (connecting with the **Cultural Trail** (www.indyculturaltrail.org; 132 W Walnut St) at 10th and Lewis Sts) through hip Broad Ripple; Carmel, a tony North Indy suburb; and eventually on to Sheridan in central Indiana, passing bars, breweries, restaurants and attractions.

🛏 Sleeping

Indy Hostel
HOSTEL $

(☎317-727-1696; www.indyhostel.us; 4903 Winthrop Ave; dm/d from $32/85, d without bath $65; 🅿✳@🤖) This fun hostel was completely revamped in 2019 after a drunk driver plowed through the living room. A hip and friendly couple manage the two houses, offering a six-bed female dorm, a 12-bed mixed dorm and five private rooms, as well as a new dining room, a design-forward lounge and a kitchen island. A summer concert series draws eclectic crowds.

★Hotel Broad Ripple
BOUTIQUE HOTEL $$

(☎317-787-2665; www.hotelbroadripple.com; 6520 E Westfield Blvd; d $165-250; 🅿@🤖) This Scandinavian-accented boutique hotel (the owner has Norwegian roots) is a cozy getaway in hip Broad Ripple, offering 13 spacious rooms right along the Monon Trail. A woodsy patio leads to a small bar and lounge, and modern rooms (most with outdoor decks): our favorites are numbers 3, 4, 7 and 8 facing the trail.

★Ironworks Hotel
BOUTIQUE HOTEL $$

(☎463-221-2200; www.ironworkshotel.com; 2721 E 86th St; d from $189; 🅿✳🤖) With design touches forged from industrial parts from an abandoned Wisconsin iron foundry, this

GRAY BROTHERS CAFETERIA

Cafeterias are an Indiana tradition, but most have disappeared – except for **Gray Brothers Cafeteria** (www.gray-broscafe.com; 555 S Indiana St, Mooresville; meals $7-10; ⏰11am-8:30pm). Enter the time-warped dining room, grab a blue tray and behold a corridor of food that seems to stretch the length of a football field. Stack on plates of pan-fried chicken, meatloaf, mac 'n' cheese and sugar cream pie, then fork in with abandon.

2017 newcomer to Indy is a boutique game-changer. The lobby is an Industrial Age–chic jawdropper highlighted by a massive American flag of interconnecting machinery parts by artist Jim Spelman. Steel girders, reclaimed barnwood and worn leather feature throughout, including in the 120 rooms.

✖ Eating

Sinking Ship VEGAN $
(www.sinkingshipindy.com; 4923 N College Ave; mains $9-13; ⏰2pm-3am Mon-Thu, from 11am Fri-Sun; 🛜🍴) This rock 'n' roll craft-beer pub has Indy's heart, serving up innovative vegan and vegetarian fare until 2am, when most (drunk!) vegans are relegated to French fries! But worry not, carnivores, there are great burgers, smoked brisket and Amish chicken as well. It's dark and divey, harking back to a bygone, pre-craft era.

★**Milktooth** BREAKFAST $$
(www.milktoothindy.com; 534 Virginia Ave; mains $4-17; ⏰7am-3pm; 🛜) Breakfast lovers of the world unite at artsy Milktooth, a can't-miss morning hot spot set in a tchotchke-peppered garage. In 2015, Jonathan Brooks was *Food & Wine* magazine's first ever chef to win Best New Chef without serving dinner. Wondrous farm-to-fork stunners include the sourdough pearl sugar waffle with burnt honeycomb candy, parmesan, whipped citrus honey butter and raw honey.

★**Tinker Street** AMERICAN $$
(☎317-925-5000; www.tinkerstreetindy.com; 402 E 16th St; small plates $8-20, mains $14-28; ⏰5-10pm Tue-Sat; 🍴) Fork into seasonal dishes such as Indiana mushroom stroganoff with pappardelle, sherry, crème fraîche and parsley pistou or an incredible pork belly with housemade kimchi and sorghum-tamari glaze. Vegetarian and gluten-free options are plentiful. The industrial-meets-rustic-wood decor is just right for romantics, while the year-round patio is more casual. Tinker Street is located in leafy Old Northside just north of downtown.

★**St Elmo's** STEAK $$$
(☎317-635-0636; www.stelmos.com; 127 S Illinois St; steaks $43-81; ⏰4-11pm Mon-Fri, from 3pm Sat, 4-10pm Sun; 🛜) This nearly 120-year-old carnivore haunt is Indy's best – and one of its only – independent steakhouses. It receives consistent accolades for service, romance and fine dining, but it's really about woofing down the legendary shrimp cocktail ($16) and top-quality slabs of perfectly grilled beef, rubbing elbows with Colt and Pacer elite in the classic American dining room as you do.

🍷 Drinking & Nightlife

★**Central State Brewing – The Koelschip** CRAFT BEER
(www.thekoelschip.com; 2505 N Delaware St; ⏰2-10pm Mon-Thu, from noon Fri & Sat, noon-8pm Sun; 🛜) Until it opens its proprietary taproom near the old Central State psychiatric hospital grounds (from which it takes its name), the Koelschip bar is where you'll find Central State Brewing's barrel-aged farmhouse ales and exotically hopped IPAs as well as its mixed cultured sours and other funk. This is the bar of craft connoisseurs.

★**Sun King Brewery** BREWERY
(www.sunkingbrewing.com; 135 N College Ave; ⏰10am-9pm Mon-Wed, to 10pm Thu & Fri, 11am-10pm Sat, 11am-8pm Sun, reduced hours winter; 🛜) You never know what'll be flowing at Sun King's unvarnished downtown taproom. Indy's young and hip pile in to find out, swilling brews from a cocoa-y Baltic porter to juice IPAs and imperial stouts. Flights (six 3oz samples) cost $8. Fridays are packed for cheap growler fills. The outdoor patio hops in summer. All tips given to a monthly changing charity.

Slippery Noodle Inn BAR
(www.slipperynoodle.com; 372 S Meridian St; ⏰11am-3am Mon-Fri, from noon Sat, 4pm-1am Sun) Downtown's Slippery Noodle Inn is the oldest bar in the state (slinging drinks since 1850), and has seen action as a brothel, a slaughterhouse, a gangster hangout and an Underground Railroad station; currently, it's one of the best blues clubs in the country. There's live music nightly; and it's cheap.

⭐ Entertainment

Chatterbox Jazz Club LIVE MUSIC
(https://chatterboxjazz.com; 435 Massachusetts
Ave; ⊙ 4pm-midnight Mon-Thu, to 1:30am Fri-Sun)
This historic bar and its grungy interior is
one of Indy's best for live jazz and was one of
the anchors of Mass Ave's rejuvenation.

Bankers Life Fieldhouse BASKETBALL
(📞 317-917-2727; www.bankerslifefieldhouse.com;
125 S Pennsylvania St) Basketball is huge in
Indiana, and Bankers Life Fieldhouse is
ground zero, where the NBA's Pacers make
it happen.

Lucas Oil Stadium FOOTBALL
(📞 317-262-8600; www.lucasoilstadium.com; 500
S Capitol Ave) Where the NFL's Colts play football under a huge retractable roof. Tours of
the stadium are available at 11am, 1pm and
3pm Monday through Friday ($10 to $15).

ℹ️ Information

Indianapolis has no official visitors center, but
there is a a welcome center at White River State
Park (p565) and a welcome desk with visitor
information inside the **Artsgarden** (the glass
structure over West Washington St downtown).

Indianapolis Convention & Visitors Bureau
(www.visitindy.com) Download a free city guide
and print out coupons for attractions and tours
from the website.

Indianapolis Star (www.indystar.com) The
city's daily newspaper.

Indy Rainbow Chamber (www.gayindynow.
com) Provides info for gay and lesbian visitors.

Nuvo (www.nuvo.net) Free, weekly alternative
paper with the arts and music lowdown.

ℹ️ Getting There & Around

The fancy **Indianapolis International Airport**
(IND; 📞 317-487-7243; www.indianapolisairport.
com; 7800 Col H Weir Cook Memorial Dr) is 16
miles southwest of town. The Washington bus
(8) runs between the airport and downtown
($1.75, 50 minutes); the **Go Green Airport
Shuttle** (www.goexpresstravel.com/indy_ex-
press) does it quicker ($12, 20 minutes). An
off-peak UberX is around $20 to $22.

Greyhound shares **Union Station** (📞 800-872-
7245; 350 S Illinois St) with Amtrak. Buses go
frequently to Cincinnati (2½ hours) and Chicago
(3½ hours). **Megabus** (www.megabus.com/us;
cnr N Delaware & E Market Sts) is often cheaper.
Amtrak travels these routes but takes almost
twice as long.

IndyGo (www.indygo.net) runs the local buses. The fare is $1.75 (a one-day pass is $4). Bus
17 goes to Broad Ripple. Service is minimal dur-

ing weekends. It's also in charge of Indy's forth-
coming $140-million light-rail Red Line, which
will connect Broad Ripple with the University
of Indianapolis, traversing the entire city from
north to south. It is scheduled to be operational
in 2020. A Blue Line will follow by 2023.

Pacers Bikeshare (www.pacersbikeshare.org)
has 250 bikes at 26 stations along the Cultural
Trail downtown. A 24-hour pass costs $8, and
additional charges apply for trips longer than 30
minutes.

Central Indiana

Indy Car racing is the world-recognizable
draw to Indiana's Midwestern heartland,
but a wealth of museums, craft breweries
and James Dean remembrances all fur-
row into the farmland around here, where
countryside basketball hoops are as as common as corn stalks.

Fairmount

Pocket-sized Fairmount is but a few streets
surrounded by farmland, but it's on the international map as the hometown of 1950s actor
James Dean, one of the original icons of cool
(he was born 10.5 miles north in Marion), as
well as *Garfield* creator Jim Davis. You may
also recognize it from Morrissey's video for
his 1988 debut solo single, 'Suedehead.'

⦿ Sights

Fairmount Historical Museum MUSEUM
(www.jamesdeanartifacts.com; 203 E Washington
St; by donation; ⊙ 11am-5pm Mon, Wed & Fri-Sun
May-Oct) FREE Fans of actor James Dean
should head directly here to see the Hollywood icon's bongo drums and 1955 Triumph
Trophy 500, among other artifacts.

James Dean Gallery MUSEUM
(📞 765-948-3326; www.jamesdeangallery.com;
425 N Main St; ⊙ 9am-6pm) FREE The privately owned James Dean Gallery has several
rooms of memorabilia (bronze busts, photos, clocks, Dean's high-school yearbooks) in
an old Victorian home downtown. The owners are a font of local information and are
more focused on post-death international
collector's items and knickknacks.

ℹ️ Getting There & Away

Fairmount is 70 miles northeast from Indianapolis, the closest transportation hub. I-69 passes
the town to the east.

GREAT LAKES CENTRAL INDIANA

Southern Indiana

The pretty hills, caves, bluegrass, Tibetan temples, architectural hot spots and utopian history of Southern Indiana mark it as a completely different region from the rest of the state. The farmland of the north begins to yield here to rolling hills and winding rivers that cultivate a more diverse ethos found in places from hip and liberal Bloomington to artist-driven Nashville and architecturally magnificent Columbus.

Bloomington

Lively and lovely, limestone-clad and cycling-mad, Bloomington is the home of Indiana University. The town centers on Courthouse Sq, surrounded by restaurants, bars and bookshops. Nearly everything is walkable. Also, perhaps surprisingly, there's a significant Tibetan community here too. The Dalai Lama's brother came to teach at IU in the 1960s, and Tibetan temples, monasteries and culture followed.

◉ Sights

★ **Indiana University** UNIVERSITY
(☏ 812-856-4648; www.iu.edu; 107 S Indiana Ave) Indiana University (*not* University of Indiana!) routinely ranks with the cream of the crop of America's most beautiful college campuses. Founded in 1820 and forged from locally quarried Indiana Limestone, the grounds feature cycling and walking trails, alongside numerous sculptures and historic buildings, including Old Crescent, which is listed on the National Register of Historic Places.

Tibetan Mongolian
Buddhist Cultural Center BUDDHIST SITE
(☏ 812-336-6807; www.tmbcc.org; 3655 Snoddy Rd; ⊙ sunrise-sunset) FREE Founded by the Dalai Lama's brother, this colorful, prayer-flag-covered cultural building and its traditional stupas are worth a look. A gift shop sells traditional Tibetan items, and meditation sessions open to the public take place Wednesdays and Thursday at 6pm. Check the website for other activities.

✕ Eating & Drinking

★ **Cardinal Spirits** AMERICAN $$
(☏ 812-202-6789; www.cardinalspirits.com; 922 S Morton St; mains $17-20; ⊙ 4-10pm Mon-Thu, noon-midnight Fri, 10am-midnight Sat, 10am-9pm Sun; 🛜) Bloomington's only craft distillery

makes fantastic spirits with local botanicals, but their equally interesting, seasonally changing food menu is one of the town's most innovative. Chef Dean Wirkerman sowed his culinary oats in Japan and Italy, and his menu is designed to instill feelings as well as flavors. Think porchetta benedicts for brunch, maitake mushroom and fontina cheeseburgers for dinner.

Wood Shop MICROBREWERY
(www.uplandbeer.com/locations/woodshop; 350 W 11th St; ⊙ 4-9pm Thu & Fri, 1-9pm Sat & Sun; 🛜) Leave the more mainstream Upland Brewing Co next door to casual hopheads – it's here at Upland's all-sours brewery that the dank and funk flows among near-3000-gallon oak aging barrels. Ten taps are devoted to sours and wild ales (collaborations with Denmark's Mikkeller and Tennessee's Blackberry Farm are not uncommon) and another 10 from Upland next door.

ⓘ Information

Bloomington Visitors Center (☏ 812-334-8900; www.visitbloomington.com; 2855 N Walnut St; ⊙ 8:30am-5pm Mon-Fri, 10am-3pm Sat)

ⓘ Getting There & Away

Indianapolis, 50 miles northeast, has the closest airport. Go Express Travel (www.goexpresstravel.com) runs a shuttle bus to/from the airport several times daily; it costs $23 one way. I-69 and Hwy 46 are the main roads to Bloomington.

Nashville

Nashville is the jumping-off point for **Brown County State Park** (☏ 812-988-6406; www.in.gov/dnr; 1801 Hwy 46 E; per car $7-9), known as the Little Smoky Mountains for its steep wooded hills and fog-cloaked ravines. Gentrified and antique-filled, the 19th-century town founded in 1872 as a pioneer artists colony is now a bustling tourist center. Nashville's bucolic landscapes – all rolling hills, pastures and picket fences, log cabins and country corrals – are busiest in fall when visitors pour in to see the area's leafy oak, hickory and birch trees burst into color.

🛏 Sleeping & Eating

Robinwood Inn CABIN $$
(☏ 812-988-7094; www.robinwoodinn.com; 914 Highland Ave; cabins $175-250; 🅿 ❄ 🛜 🐾) Idyllically set in the woods just far enough outside Nashville to feel isolated, these wonderful one- and two-bedroom cabins feel like

they're half a world away: woodsy and rustic on one hand, but wonderfully appointed and modern on another. You'll want for nothin', with various configurations boasting fireplaces, kitchens and/or vintage waterfall showers. Did we mention outdoor hot tubs?

★ **Story Inn** GASTRONOMY $$$
(☑ 812-988-2273; www.storyinn.com; 6404 S State Rd 135, Story; mains $26-32; ⊙ 9am-2:30pm & 5-8pm Wed & Thu, to 9pm Fri, 8am-2:30pm & 5-9pm Sat, 8am-2:30pm & 5-8pm Sun; 🐾) This former general store dating to 1851 (tin roof and metal facade still intact!) drips with countrified rustic charm, beckoning foodies for culinary getaways in the one-horse, once-abandoned town of Story 12 miles south of Nashville. Pair vintages from the *Wine Spectator*–awarded wine list with elevated Midwestern staples such as corned beef and cabbage with Smoking Goose wagyu brisket.

ℹ️ Information

Brown County Visitors Center (☑ 812-988-7303; www.browncounty.com; 211 S Van Buren St; ⊙ 9am-5pm Mon-Fri, from 10am Sat; 🐾) Staffed facility with maps and coupons.

ℹ️ Getting There & Away

Nashville lies midway between Bloomington and Columbus on Hwy 46. Indianapolis, 60 miles north, is the closest big city and transportation center. Free parking is scarce in town – lots charge $5.

Columbus

When you think of the USA's great architectural cities – Chicago, New York, Washington, DC – Columbus, IN, doesn't quite leap to mind, but it should. The city is a remarkable gallery of physical design. Since the 1940s, Columbus and its leading corporation, Fortune 500 engineering company Cummins, have commissioned some of the world's best architects, including Eero Saarinen, Richard Meier and IM Pei, to create both public and private buildings. And with the 2017 critically acclaimed film *Columbus* (a love letter to the town), folks outside of the architectural scope are now taking notice.

◎ Sights

Architecture-gaping is the big attraction. More than 70 notable buildings and pieces of public art are spread over a wide area (car required), but about 15 diverse architectural standouts can be seen on foot downtown.

The visitors center provides self-guided tour maps online and on-site. **Bus tours** (☑ 812-378-2622; www.columbus.in.us; 506 5th St; adult/student $25/20; ⊙ 10am Tue-Fri, 10am & 2pm Sat, 2:30pm Sun Apr-Nov, 10pm Fri & Sat Dec-Mar) also depart from the city center.

Miller House & Garden ARCHITECTURE
(www.discovernewfields.org/do-and-see/places-to-go/miller-house-and-garden; 2860 Washington St; $25; ⊙ 12:45pm & 2:45pm Tue-Sat Apr-Nov, 12:45pm & 2:45pm Fri & Sat Dec & Mar, closed Jan & Feb) A dream team is responsible for the design of the former private home of hero industrialist, architectural visionary and former Cummins President/Chairman J Irwin Miller: architect Eero Saarinen, landscape architect Dan Kiley and interior designer Alexander Girard combined their keen eyes for modernism in 1953 and churned out one of the most important – and stunning – mid-century modern residences in the US.

🛏️ Sleeping & Eating

Inn at Irwin Gardens B&B $$
(☑ 812-376-3663; www.irwingardens.com; 608 5th St; d $205-260; 🅿️❄️🐾) A mighty antidote to Columbus' modernist flare, this 1864 Victorian monolith with Edwardian furnishings and Italianate gardens (inspired by Pompeii) sits steps from the architectural soul of town, but in stark contrast to its mid-century modern ethos. Chock-full of vintage furniture (some items favor form over function, but that hardly matters) and drowning in extraordinary detail, these are historic sleeps.

★ **Henry Social Club** AMERICAN $$
(☑ 812-799-1371; www.henrysocialclub.com; 423 Washington St; mains $16-44; ⊙ 5-9pm Tue-Sat; 🐾) Punching above its culinary class by Columbus standards, HSC's seasonally changing menu satiates local foodies (and visiting architects) and is the best bar in town for a proper cocktail (from $11). The filet and roasted cod are surefire choices, but don't discount the barley-and-wild-rice bowl with butternut-squash puree – it's a vegetarian stunner!

ℹ️ Information

Columbus Visitors Center (☑ 812-378-2622; www.columbus.in.us; 506 5th St; ⊙ 9am-5pm Mon-Sat, closed Sun Dec-Apr) is the place to pick up a self-guided tour map ($3) or join a two-hour bus tour to see the city's renowned architecture.

❶ Getting There & Away

I-65 is the main highway that skirts the city. The closest airports are in Indianapolis (46 miles north) and Louisville (73 miles south). Alas, no shuttle buses connect Columbus to these cities.

Ohio River

The Ohio River marks the state's southern border. Hwys 56, 156, 62 and 66, known collectively as the Ohio River Scenic Byway, wind through a lush and hilly landscape covering 300 miles along the churning waterway. Sweet stops en route include Madison, a beautifully preserved river settlement from the mid-19th century whose genteel architecture counts as the largest contiguous National Historic Landmark District in the United States; food-focused New Albany and artsy Jeffersonville, which both hug the river across from Louisville; **Marengo Cave** (☑812-365-2705; www.marengocave.com; 400 E State Rd 64, Marengo; tours adult/child from $18/10; ⊙9am-6pm Jun-Aug, to 5pm Sep-May), with its eye-popping underground formations; and former US president Abraham Lincoln's **childhood home** (☑812-937-4541; www.nps.gov/libo; 3027 E South St, Lincoln City; ⊙8am-3pm) **FREE** near Dale. Canoeing, farm stays and worthwhile breweries pop up in between.

🛏 Sleeping & Eating

★Pepin Mansion   B&B $$
(☑812-725-9186; www.thepepinmansion.com; 1003 E Main St, New Albany; d from $145; P❋❖⊛) Standing supremely along New Albany's historical Mansion Row, this easy-on-the-eyes 1851 Italianate abode features ornate hand-painted ceilings, original hardwood flooring and gas chandeliers among other period details. The four antique-filled but modern rooms (TVs by Roku, for example) are wildly different but equally spectacular. Our favorite, the Culbertson Suite, has a claw-foot bathtub.

Exchange   AMERICAN $$
(☑812-948-6501; www.exchangeforfood.com; 118 W Main St, New Albany; mains $11-27; ⊙11am-10pm Mon-Thu, to 11pm Fri & Sat, 4-8pm Sun; ⊛) All things considered, New Albany's best restaurant is a one-stop evening out. Sky-high exposed-brick walls and and true-to-their-name Big Ass Fans dominate the industrial-hip ambience. Foodwise, goat's-cheese fritters with bacon and date aioli and smoked honey woo diners to start, then

spring for blueberry-brie grilled cheese, an awesome black-bean burger or far more elevated pub grub.

❶ Information

Check out **Ohio River Scenic Byway** (www.ohioriverbyway.com) for Byway-specific info; you'll find visitors centers in **Jeffersonville** (☑812-280-5566; www.gosoin.com; 305 Southern Indiana Ave; ⊙10am-5pm Mon-Sat, from noon Sun) and **Madison** (☑812-265-2956; www.visitmadison.org; 601 W First St; ⊙9am-5pm Mon-Fri, to 4pm Sat, 11am-4pm Sun Apr–mid-Dec, 9am-5pm Mon-Fri, 10am-3pm Sat, 11am-3pm Sun mid-Dec–Mar).

❶ Getting There & Away

Louisville and Cincinnati are the closest big-city transportation hubs. Louisville International Airport (p405) sits 8 and 13 miles south of Jeffersonville and New Albany, respectively.

In addition to the Ohio River Scenic Byway's gaggle of roads, I-64 cuts across the region. For distance reference, Madison is about 75 miles east of Marengo Cave, which is about 55 miles east of the Lincoln Boyhood National Memorial.

Northern Indiana

While much of Northern Indiana is industrial, unexpected treats rise from the flatland, too. Wild sand dunes (at America's newest national park), classic cars, Amish pies and the infamous Dark Lord brewer are all within range.

Indiana Dunes

In addition to being home to America's newest national park, sunny beaches, rustling grasses and woodsy campgrounds are the Indiana Dunes' claim to fame. The area is hugely popular on summer days with sunbathers from Chicago and towns throughout Northern Indiana. In addition to its beaches, the area is noted for its plant variety (more than 1100 species, including everything from cacti to pine trees, sprout here) and birds (370 species). Sweet hiking trails meander up the dunes and through the woodlands.

The Dunes can be visited on a day trip from Chicago. If you're looking to spend the night, Chesterton (the closest; popular for trainspotting) and Valparaiso (the most charming; food and drink hotbed) are both worthwhile small-town options.

INDIANA AMISH COUNTRY

The area around Shipshewana and Middlebury is the USA's third-largest Amish community. Horses and buggies clip-clop by, and long-bearded men hand-plow the tidy fields. It's not far off the interstate, but it's a whole different world.

Pick a back road between the two towns and head down it. Often you'll see families selling beeswax candles, quilts and fresh produce on their porch, which beats the often-touristy shops and restaurants on the main roads. Note that most places close on Sunday.

The Indiana Toll Rd (I-80/90) passes the region to the north. Hwy 20 comes through the area to the south, and connects Middlebury and Shipshewana (which are about 7 miles apart).

◉ Sights & Activities

Indiana Dunes National Park NATIONAL PARK
(☑219-926-7561; www.nps.gov/indu; 1100 N Mineral Springs Rd, Porter; ☺6am-11pm) FREE The Dunes, which became the USA's 61st national park in 2019, stretch along 15 miles of Lake Michigan shoreline. Swimming is allowed anywhere along the shore. A short walk away from the beaches, several hiking paths crisscross the dunes and woodlands. The best are the Bailly-Chellberg Trail (2.5 miles) that winds by a still-operating 1870s farm, and the Heron Rookery Trail (2 miles), where blue herons flock (though there's no actual rookery) and native wildflowers bloom.

Pedal Power CYCLING
(☑219-921-3085; www.pedalpowerrentals.com; 1215 Hwy 49; per hr/day $9/36; ☺9am-7pm Sat & Sun late May-early Oct) This outfitter rents bicycles (including a helmet, a lock and a map) from the cul-de-sac next to the Indiana Dunes Visitor Center. From here, the 2-mile Dunes-Kankakee Trail runs to **Indiana Dunes State Park** (☑219-926-1952; www.in.gov/dnr/parklake; Chesterton; ☺7am-11pm). Pedal Power also offers tours, such as the Beach Sunset Tour ($15 per person; Saturdays); check the website for times.

🛏 Sleeping & Eating

Riley's Railhouse B&B $
(☑219-395-9999; www.rileysrailhouse.com; 123 N 4th St, Chesterton; d $120-160; ❄ ☎) Occupying a decommissioned 1914 freight station in Chesterton, this railway-themed boutique B&B offers a beautiful, fireplace-warmed lounge with discerning recycled design touches, a bar and a massive open kitchen from which Richard's awesome breakfast emerges. Modern rooms – inside both the depot and the parked antique rail cars – are comfortably appointed with locomotive-themed art. Two big Labradoodles hold down the fort.

Octave Grill BURGERS $
(www.octavegrill.com; 105 S Calumet Rd, Chesterton; burgers $8.50-11.75; ☺3-10pm Mon-Fri, noon-11pm Sat, noon-9pm Sun; ☎) Octave Grill's burgers made with grass-fed beef and piled high with gourmet goodness were voted best in Porter County. Indeed, they are cooked to perfection, just juicy and greasy enough, and are chased with a wonderful selection of five rotating craft beers.

ℹ Information

Indiana Dunes Visitor Center (☑219-395-1882; www.indianadunes.com; 1215 Hwy 49; ☺8am-6pm Jun-Aug, 8:30am-4:30pm Sep-May) The best place to start a visit to the Dunes. Staff can provide beach details; a schedule of ranger-guided walks and activities; hiking, biking and birding maps; and general information on the area.

ℹ Getting There & Away

The Indiana Toll Rd (I-80/90), I-94, Hwy 12, Hwy 20 and Hwy 49 all skirt the lakeshore. Look for large brown signs on the roads that point the way in to the Dunes.

The **South Shore Line** (www.mysouthshoreline.com) commuter train also services the area on its Chicago–South Bend route. The stops at Dune Park and Beverly Shores put you about a 1½-mile walk from the beaches.

South Bend

You know how people in certain towns say, 'Football is a religion here'? They mean it in South Bend, home to the University of Notre Dame. Here 'Touchdown Jesus' lords over the 80,000-capacity stadium (it's a mural of the resurrected Christ with arms raised, though the pose bears a striking resemblance to a referee signaling a touchdown). The renowned campus – Indiana's second biggest tourist attraction after the Indianapolis Motor Speedway – is worth

OFF THE BEATEN TRACK

AUBURN

Classic-car connoisseurs should stop in Auburn, where the Cord Company produced the USA's favorite autos in the 1920s and '30s. Two remarkable car museums – **Auburn Cord Duesenberg Museum** (www.automobilemuseum.org; 1600 S Wayne St; adult/child $12.50/7.50; ⏱ 9am-5pm) and the **National Automotive and Truck Museum** (www.natmus.org; 1000 Gordon Buehrig Pl; adult/child $10/5; ⏱ 9am-5pm) – are conveniently lined up next door to one another. Round out your day with a trip to **Mad Anthony's Auburn Tap Room** (☏ 260-927-0500; www.madbrew.com/auburn; 114 N Main St, Auburn; ⏱ 11am-11pm Mon-Thu, to midnight Fri & Sat, to 10pm Sun) for local brews and serviceable pub grub.

Auburn is about 50 miles southeast of Amish Country and about 25 miles north of Fort Wayne.

a pit stop, but South Bend is more than pigskin (football is only 12 days per year, after all).

⊙ Sights & Activities

Studebaker National Museum   MUSEUM
(www.studebakermuseum.org; 201 S Chapin St; adult/child $10/6; ⏱ 10am-5pm Mon-Sat, from noon Sun) Gaze at a gorgeous 1956 Packard and other classic beauties that used to be built in South Bend, where the Studebaker car company was based. The shiny vehicles, including vintage carriages and military tanks, spread over three floors. A local history museum shares the building. The entrance is on Thomas St.

Notre Dame Tours   WALKING
(☏ 574-631-5726; www.nd.edu/visitors; 111 Eck Center) FREE Two-mile, 75-minute walking tours of the pretty university campus, with its two lakes, Gothic-style architecture and iconic Golden Dome atop the main building, start at the Eck Visitors Center. Tour times vary, but there's usually at least a 10am and 3pm jaunt Monday through Friday.

🛏 Sleeping & Eating

★ **Oliver Inn**   B&B $$
(☏ 574-232-4545; www.oliverinn.com; 630 W Washington St; d $140-220, carriage house $330; ❄ 🙝 🐾) This elegant salmon- and green-trimmed B&B occupies a gorgeous, Queen Anne–style home dating to 1886. Corner turrets, curved-glass bay windows, spindles and balustrades abound while the nine rooms ooze dignity and romance (we dig the Clem Studebaker for its spaciousness, hardwood floors and fireplace). Chicago escapees Alice and Tom couldn't be more gracious hosts and your breakfast is candlelit.

Oh Mamma's on the Avenue   DELI $
(www.facebook.com/OhMamma; 1202 Mishawaka Ave; sandwiches $6-10; ⏱ 10am-6pm Tue-Fri, 9am-4pm Sat) This cute grocery store and deli features toasted sandwiches, heaps of cheeses from the region (including awesome house-made goat's-milk cheese), fresh-baked bread, cannoli and gelato. Staff are super-friendly and generous with samples. Eat in at the smattering of tables, or take away.

❶ Information

Eck Visitors Center (www.tour.nd.edu/locations/eck-visitors-center; 100 Eck Center, Notre Dame; ⏱ 8am-5pm Mon-Fri, noon-4pm Sat & Sun)

❶ Getting There & Away

South Bend has a surprisingly large **airport** (☏ 574-282-4590; www.flysbn.com; 4477 Progress Dr) with flights to Chicago and Detroit among other destinations. The airport is also a station on the **South Shore Line** (www.mysouthshoreline.com) commuter train that goes to/from Chicago ($14.25 one way to Millennium Station). By car, the Indiana Toll Rd (I-80/90) and Hwy 20 are the primary routes to the city.

OHIO

Ohio has a split personality. The nation's seventh most populous state has big cities Cleveland, Cincinnati and Columbus that lead its urban charge, rolling out a spread of kicky eateries, IPA-loving breweries and one-of-a-kind museums. Northern Cleveland exudes a feisty, rock-and-roll vibe, while southern Cincinnati feels more languorous and European. Columbus is the polished art and tech hub that rises up in the middle. Meanwhile, Ohio's rural side is way off the grid, from the horse-and-buggy-filled roads of its enormous Amish community to the moonshine makers in its southeastern hills. It makes for an intriguing mash-up, with just a short drive between wildly different lifestyles. In between, the roadways lead to the world's fastest roller coasters, rocking party islands, beatnik towns, pie shops and a mist-draped national park.

❶ Information

Ohio Highway Conditions (www.ohgo.com)

Ohio State Park Information Reservations to camp accepted; tent and RV sites cost $17 to $43, plus $8 booking fee. State parks are free to visit; some have free wi-fi.

Tourism Ohio (www.ohio.org)

Cleveland

Cleveland wears its Rust Belt badge with honor. While smoke-belching steel mills no longer rule the scene, the city still wafts an evocative industrial look. Railroad tracks, vertical lift bridges and stark warehouses pepper its shores on Lake Erie and the Cuyahoga River, only now stylish eateries, breweries and galleries fill the old factories, and bike trails have emerged along the waterways. Star attractions include the Rock and Roll Hall of Fame and Museum of Art, but the best action is in Cleveland's walkable neighborhoods. Meander around Ohio City, Tremont, Collinwood or Asiatown and you'll be among locals in the markets and corner taverns. Sit for a pint and hear about generations-deep businesses started by Slovenian grandparents, about epic sports team grudges and about how the city clawed its way back from financial and environmental ruin. Rust Belt realness is Cleveland's calling card.

◉ Sights

★ Rock and Roll Hall of Fame & Museum · MUSEUM

(☏ 216-781-7625; www.rockhall.com; 1100 E 9th St; adult/child $24/16; ◷ 10am-5:30pm daily, to 9pm Wed & Sat Jun-Aug) Cleveland's top attraction is like an overstuffed attic bursting with groovy finds: Jimi Hendrix's Stratocaster, Keith Moon's platform shoes, John Lennon's Sgt Pepper suit and a 1966 piece of hate mail to the Rolling Stones from a cursive-writing Fijian. It's more than memorabilia, though. Multimedia exhibits trace the history and social context of rock music and the performers who created it.

★ Cleveland Museum of Art · MUSEUM

(☏ 216-421-7340; www.clevelandart.org; 11150 East Blvd; ◷ 10am-5pm Tue, Thu, Sat & Sun, to 9pm Wed & Fri) FREE Cleveland's whopping art museum houses an excellent collection of European paintings, as well as African, Asian and American art. Head to the 2nd floor for rock-star works from Impressionists, Picasso and surrealists. Interactive touchscreens are stationed throughout the galleries and provide fun ways to learn more. Download the free ArtLens app for additional content, including self-guided jaunts by theme. Free guided tours through the museum's highlights depart from the dazzling, light-drenched atrium at 1pm each day.

Great Lakes Science Center · MUSEUM

(☏ 216-694-2000; www.greatscience.com; 601 Erieside Ave; adult/child $17/14; ◷ 10am-5pm Mon-Sat, from noon Sun, closed Mon Sep-May; ♿) One of 10 museums in the country with a NASA affiliation, Great Lakes goes deep in space with rockets, moon stones and the 1973 Apollo capsule, as well as exhibits on the lakes' environmental problems.

The Flats · WATERFRONT

The Flats, an old industrial zone turned nightlife hub on the Cuyahoga River, has had a checkered life. After years of neglect, it's on the upswing once again. The East Bank has a waterfront boardwalk, stylish restaurants, bars and outdoor concert pavilion. The West Bank is a bit edgier and further flung, with an old garage turned brewery-winery, a skateboard park and some vintage dive bars among its assets.

🛏 Sleeping

★ Cleveland Hostel · HOSTEL $

(☏ 216-394-0616; www.theclevelandhostel.com; 2090 W 25th St; dm/r from $26/68; ❀♫) This hostel in Ohio City, steps from an RTA stop and the West Side Market, is fantastic. There are 15 rooms, a mix of dorms and private chambers. All have fluffy beds, fresh paint in soothing hues and nifty antique decor. Add in the sociable rooftop deck, coffee-roasting lobby cafe and free parking lot, and no wonder it's packed.

★ Kimpton Schofield Hotel · HOTEL $$

(☏ 216-357-3250; www.theschofieldhotel.com; 2000 E 9th St; r $180-270; ❇❀♫❀) Set in a rehabbed 1902 building downtown, the Schofield is for the cool cats in the crowd. Rooms are spacious and have funky artwork (such as prints of toy cars), colorful clocks and art deco–inspired lamps and chairs. Amenities include free loaner bicycles, a free wine social hour each evening and free acoustic guitar loans for in-room jam sessions. Parking costs $36.

Metropolitan at the 9 HOTEL $$$
(☑ 216-239-1200; www.metropolitancleveland. com; 2017 E 9th St; r $199-319; P ✶ @ 🛜 🐾) Check in at the Metropolitan, an upscale Marriott-branded property, and perks include a seasonal rooftop lounge, indoor dog park, on-site theater for live performances and a subterranean cocktail lounge set in the building's old bank vaults. The 156 rooms are good-sized, each with a sitting area, 55in flat-screen TV and contemporary decor. Parking costs $36.

🍴 Eating

Top spots for hot-chef eats are E 4th St, Ohio City and Tremont. For global fare, Little Italy and Asiatown prevail. Goulash, stuffed cabbage and other Eastern European dishes are common around town, as Cleveland has the nation's largest concentration of Hungarians, Slovenes and Slovaks; **West Side Market** (www.westsidemarket.org; 1979 W 25th St; ⊙ 7am-4pm Mon & Wed, 7am-6pm Fri & Sat, 10am-4pm Sun) is a good place to explore the scene.

★ Larder Delicatessen & Bakery DELI $
(☑ 216-912-8203; https://larderdb.com; 1455 W 29th St; sandwiches $9-12; ⊙ 10am-7pm Tue-Sat, to 2pm Sun) 🌿 Set in a historic firehouse, Larder has an old-time vibe. Jars of pickled veggies line the wall, and the pantry sells everything from hickory nuts to dried beans and barley. The Beard Award–nominated chef stacks a mighty sandwich, maybe juicy fried chicken or schnitzel and apple slaw on thick-sliced bread. Housemade root beer and chocolate sodas add to the goodness.

Nate's Deli MIDDLE EASTERN $
(☑ 216-696-7529; www.natesohiocity.com; 1923 W 25th St; mains $8-16; ⊙ 10am-5pm Mon-Fri, to 4pm Sat) Nate's small, unfussy dining room offers an unusual mix of Middle Eastern dishes and deli sandwiches, with choices from stuffed grape-leaf platters to reubens (corned beef, Swiss cheese and sauerkraut on rye), and crunchy falafel to chicken noodle soup made from scratch. It has been cooking in Ohio City for more than 30 years.

★ Citizen Pie PIZZA $$
(☑ 216-860-1388; www.citizenpie.com; 2144 W 25th St; mains $14-17; ⊙ 11:30am-9pm Tue-Thu, to 10pm Fri & Sat, to 8pm Sun) Citizen Pie fires up Neapolitan-style pizzas using an oven straight from the motherland. Watch the pizza maker slide your meal into the fiery dome, and then skim it out 90 seconds later, cheese perfectly melted and crust perfectly browned. The smoked pepperoni is the meat to beat. The wee establishment has just a few counter seats and a smattering of tables.

Black Pig AMERICAN $$
(☑ 216-862-7551; www.blackpigcle.com; 2801 Bridge Ave; mains $18-26; ⊙ 4-10pm Tue-Thu, 4-11pm Fri, 11am-2pm & 5-11pm Sat, 11am-3pm Sun) Pork takes pride of place at the Pig, where rosy brick walls and chunky wood tables create a warm atmosphere. Indulge in pork rinds (pickle dusted), pork meatballs (with kale pesto), pork tenderloin (with yucca dumplings) – you get the gist. A fair number of vegetable-focused small plates make it doable for vegetarians. Three-course tasting menus are also available (prices vary).

Lola AMERICAN $$$
(☑ 216-621-5652; www.lolabistro.com; 2058 E 4th St; mains $30-45; ⊙ 5-10pm Sun-Thu, to 11pm Fri & Sat) Famous for his tattoos, Food Network TV appearances and multiple national awards, local boy Michael Symon put Cleveland on the foodie map with Lola. While the menu changes based on what's seasonal, expect dishes such as beef hanger steak with pickle sauce or braised lamb shank with mint and root vegetables. The glowy bar and open kitchen add a swanky vibe.

🍷 Drinking & Nightlife

Tremont is chockablock with chic bars, Ohio City with breweries. Downtown has the young, testosterone-fueled Warehouse District (around W 6th St) and the resurgent Flats. Most places stay open until 2am.

★ Platform Beer Co BREWERY
(☑ 216-202-1386; www.platformbeer.co; 4125 Lorain Ave; ⊙ 3pm-midnight Mon-Thu, 3pm-1am Fri, 10am-2am Sat, 10am-10pm Sun) An all-ages, cool-cat crowd gathers around the silvery tanks in Platform's tasting room for $5 to $6 pints of innovative saisons, pale ales and more flowing from the 30 taps. When the weather warms, everyone heads out to the picnic table–dotted patio. The location at Ohio City's southern edge is a bit out of the way, but starting to see development.

Noble Beast Brewing Co   MICROBREWERY
(☑216-417-8588; www.noblebeastbeer.com; 1470 Lakeside Ave; ⊘11am-11pm Sun & Tue-Thu, to 1am Fri & Sat) No wonder so many locals hang out at Noble Beast: it feels like home. Plants dangle from the ceiling. A skylight lets the sun shine in. The garage doors open in warm weather so a breeze blows through. From afternoon to evening, office workers and young urbanites hobnob at the tables here over glasses of German-style ales and fruit beers.

★**Millard Fillmore Presidential Library**   BAR
(☑216-481-9444; 15617 Waterloo Rd; ⊘4pm-2:30am Mon-Sat, to 12:30am Sun) Mention to pals that you're going to the Millard Fillmore Presidential Library, and you can tell they're impressed by your intellectual curiosity. Then they figure out it's a dive bar with craft beer in burgeoning Collinwood, and they're even more impressed. Fillmore was the USA's 13th president, and from New York incidentally. But that shouldn't hinder a great bar name.

Jerman's Cafe   BAR
(☑216-361-8771; 3840 St Clair Ave NE; ⊘11am-midnight Mon-Sat) Jerman's is Cleveland's second-oldest bar. Slovenian immigrant John Jerman opened it in 1908, and

his family still runs it. It's a terrific, old-school dive, with a pressed zinc ceiling, Indians baseball games flickering on the TVs and just a few beers on tap (usually a German lager). Friendly barkeeps and regulars are happy to share stories of the old days.

☆ Entertainment

Check *Scene* (www.clevescene.com) and the Friday section of the local newspaper, *Plain Dealer* (www.cleveland.com), for listings.

★**Happy Dog**   LIVE MUSIC
(☑216-651-9474; www.happydogcleveland.com; 5801 Detroit Ave; ⊘4pm-12:30am Mon-Wed, 11am-12:30am Thu & Sun, 11am-2:30am Fri & Sat) Listen to scrappy bands, DJs, storytellers or science lectures while munching on a weenie, for which you can choose from among 50 toppings, from gourmet (black truffle) to, er, less gourmet (chunky peanut butter). It's in the Gordon Sq district.

Severance Hall   CLASSICAL MUSIC
(☑216-231-1111; www.clevelandorchestra.com; 11001 Euclid Ave) The acclaimed Cleveland Symphony Orchestra holds its season (August to May) at Severance Hall, a gorgeous art-deco-meets-classic building located by the University Circle museums.

WORTH A TRIP

CUYAHOGA VALLEY NATIONAL PARK

Like a great, cold snake, the Cuyahoga River worms over a forested valley, earning its Native American name of 'crooked river' (or possibly 'place of the jawbone'). Either name is evocative, and hints at the mystical beauty that Ohio's only national park engenders on a cool morning, when the mists thread the woods and all you hear is the honk of Canadian geese and the *fwup-fwup-whoosh* of a great blue heron flapping over its hunting grounds.

There was a time, early in United States history, when this was the frontier for those settlers huddled in the Eastern colonies; at the same time it was home for vast confederations of Native Americans. Today, a mere 20 miles from Cleveland and 18 miles from Akron, you can walk trails that sneak past white waterfalls and dark hollows to find the frontier still, and the traces of a great indigenous nation.

Boston Store Visitor Center (☑330-657-2752; www.nps.gov/cuva; 1550 Boston Mills Rd, Boston Village; ⊘9:30am-5pm Sep-May, 9am-6pm Jun-Aug) is the main visitor center here – originally a 19th-century warehouse and boarding house. Inside you'll find helpful park rangers, interpretive displays, trail maps and info on trail closures. By the time you read this the new Boston Mill Visitor Center should have taken its place, located in a much larger facility across the river.

The park is easily accessible by car from Cleveland (20 miles) or Akron (18 miles), and lies just off of I-77.

If you'd rather go on a relaxing train ride, consider riding the rails with the **Cuyahoga Valley Scenic Railroad** (CVSR; ☑800-468-4070; www.cvsr.org; 27 Ridge St, Akron; adult $15-28, child $10-23).

Progressive Field BASEBALL
(☎216-420-4487; www.mlb.com/indians; 2401 Ontario St) The Indians (aka 'the Tribe') hit here; great sight lines make it a good park to see a game. The cheapest tickets cost $15 for standing room – and include a beer – in the rowdy District.

Rocket Mortgage Fieldhouse BASKETBALL
(☎216-420-2000; www.nba.com/cavaliers; 1 Center Ct) The Cavaliers play basketball at the Fieldhouse, which reopened in 2019 after a $185 million renovation. The revamp added a spiffy glass atrium and new public spaces. The Fieldhouse doubles as an entertainment venue for big touring acts.

❶ Information

Cleveland Visitors Center (☎216-875-6680; 334 Euclid Ave; ⊙9am-6pm Mon-Sat) Super-friendly staff provide maps, brewery guide booklets and reservation assistance.

Cool Cleveland (www.coolcleveland.com) Arts and cultural happenings.

Destination Cleveland (www.thisiscleveland. com) Official website, chock-full for planning.

Ohio City (www.ohiocity.org) Eats and drinks in the neighborhood.

Tremont (www.experiencetremont.com) Eats, drinks and gallery hops.

❶ Getting There & Around

Eleven miles southwest of downtown, **Cleveland Hopkins International Airport** (CLE; ☎216-265-6000; www.clevelandairport.com; 5300

DON'T MISS

CEDAR POINT'S RAGING ROLLER COASTERS

One of the world's top amusement parks, **Cedar Point Amusement Park** (☎419-627-2350; www.cedarpoint. com; 1 Cedar Point Dr; adult/child $73/45; ⊙10am-10pm Jun-Aug, reduced hours May, Sep & Oct) is known for its 18 adrenaline-pumping roller coasters. Stomach-droppers include the Top Thrill Dragster, among the globe's tallest and fastest rides. It climbs 420ft into the air before plunging and whipping around at 120mph. Steel Vengeance provides 27 seconds of weightlessness, the most 'airtime' of any coaster on the planet. Meanwhile, the wing-like GateKeeper loops, corkscrews and dangles riders from the world's highest inversion.

Riverside Dr) is linked by the Red Line train ($2.50) that reaches the center in less than 30 minutes. A cab to downtown costs about $40. Uber and Lyft are usually a bit less.

From downtown, **Greyhound** (☎216-781-0520; www.greyhound.com; 1465 Chester Ave) offers frequent departures to Chicago ($29 to $76, 7½ hours) and New York City ($60 to $113, nine to 13 hours). **Megabus** (www.megabus. com; 2115 E 22nd St) also goes to Chicago, often for lower fares.

Amtrak (☎216-696-5115; www.amtrak.com; 200 Cleveland Memorial Shoreway) runs once daily to Chicago ($59 to $113, seven hours) and New York City ($84 to $162, 13 hours). The station has no ATM, wi-fi or lounge.

The Regional Transit Authority (www.riderta. com) operates the Red Line train that goes to both the airport and Ohio City. It also runs the HealthLine bus that motors along Euclid Ave from downtown to University Circle's museums. The fare is $2.50, or day passes are $5.50. Free trolleys also loop around downtown's core business and entertainment zones.

UH Bikes (www.uhbikes.com) is Cleveland's bike-share program, with 29 stations and 250 bikes mostly in downtown and University Circle. A 30-minute ride costs $3.50. The system is easiest to use if you download the app.

For cab service, call **Americab** (☎216-881-1111).

Erie Lakeshore & Islands

In summer this good-time resort area is one of the busiest places in Ohio. Boaters come to party, daredevils come to ride roller coasters, and outdoorsy types come to bike and kayak. The season lasts from mid-May to mid-September – and then just about everything shuts down.

Kelleys Island

Peaceful and green, Kelleys Island is a popular weekend escape, especially for families. It has pretty 19th-century buildings, Native American pictographs, a good beach and glacial grooves raked through its landscape. Even its old limestone quarries are scenic.

◉ Sights & Activities

Kelleys Islands State Park STATE PARK
(☎419-746-2546; http://parks.ohiodnr.gov/kelleysisland; Division St, Kelleys Island) FREE The park features a popular campground with 126 tent and RV sites ($17 to $39), 6 miles of hiking trails with birds flitting by and a

secluded, sandy beach on the island's north side. It's a favorite of families, especially the beach and its shallow water.

Glacial Grooves
NATURAL FEATURE

(Division St, Kelleys Island; ☺ sunrise-sunset) **FREE** The deep scars in the limestone here – which a glacier rubbed in some 18,000 years ago – are the largest and most easily accessible grooves in the world. Look down from the walkway and stairs and behold gouges that are 400ft long, 35ft wide and up to 10ft deep.

❶ Information

Kelleys Island Chamber of Commerce (www. kelleysislandchamber.com) Useful info on lodgings, restaurants and activities.

❶ Getting There & Away

Kelleys Island Ferry (☑ 419-798-9763; www. kelleysislandferry.com; off W Main St, Marblehead) departs from the teeny village of Marblehead (one way adult/child $10/6.25, car $16). The crossing takes about 20 minutes and leaves hourly (every half-hour in summer).

Jet Express (☑ 800-245-1538; www.jet-express.com; 101 W Shoreline Dr) departs from Sandusky (one way adult/child $20/3, no cars); the trip takes 25 minutes. It also goes onward to Put-in-Bay on South Bass Island (one way adult/child $15/3, no cars), which takes 20 minutes. Both ferries arrive on Kelleys Island downtown (Jet Express at the foot of Division St; Kelleys Island Ferry about a half-mile east at the Seaway Marina).

Ohio Amish Country

Rural Wayne and Holmes Counties are home to the USA's largest Amish community. Visiting here is like entering a pre-industrial time warp.

Descendants of conservative Dutch-Swiss religious factions who migrated to the USA during the 18th century, the Amish continue to follow the *ordnung* (way of life), in varying degrees. Many adhere to rules prohibiting the use of electricity, telephones and motorized vehicles. They wear traditional clothing, farm the land with plow and mule, and go to church in horse-drawn buggies. Others are not so strict.

A sojourn in the region provides pleasures of a slow kind. Eat pie, buy a goat at auction, ride a horse. While parts of the bucolic area are blatantly touristy, there's always a back road to veer onto that'll take you past

WORTH A TRIP

PELEE ISLAND

Pelee, the largest Erie island, is a ridiculously green, quiet wine-producing and bird-watching destination that belongs to Canada. The **Pelee Island Ferry** (☑ 800-661-2220; www.ontarioferries.com; 109 W Shoreline Dr; adult/child $13.75/6.75, per car $30) makes the 1¾-hour trip from Sandusky to Pelee, and then onward to Ontario's mainland. One-way. Check www.pelee.com for lodging and trip-planning information.

cow-dotted pastures and farms selling eggs, beekeeping supplies or windmill parts from their front porches. Most places are closed on Sunday.

◉ Sights

Kidron, on Rte 52, makes a good starting point. A short distance south, **Berlin** is the area's tchotchke shop–filled core, while **Millersburg** is the region's largest town, more antique-y than Amish; US 62 connects these two 'busy' spots. To get further off the beaten path, take Rte 557 or County Rd 70, both of which twist through the countryside to little **Charm**, about 5 miles south of Berlin. **Sugarcreek**, 10 miles west, channels a slice of Switzerland with alpine-style architecture and giant cuckoo clocks.

Keep in mind the Amish typically view photographs as taboo, so don't take photos of people without permission.

Lehman's
HOMEWARES

(☑ 800-438-5346; www.lehmans.com; 4779 Kidron Rd, Kidron; ☺ 9am-6pm Mon-Sat, to 5pm Jan-May) Lehman's is an absolute must-see. It is the Amish community's main purveyor of modern-looking products that use no electricity, housed in a 32,000-sq-ft barn. Stroll through to ogle wind-up flashlights, wood-burning stoves and hand-cranked meat grinders.

🛏 Sleeping & Eating

Inn at Honey Run
INN $$$

(☑ 330-674-0011; www.innathoneyrun.com; 6920 County Rd 203, Millersburg; r $199-329; ❄ ☎) Any stress you carry eases within minutes of arriving at the inn's forested grounds. Twenty-five rooms occupy the lodge-like main building complex, while 12 'honeycomb' rooms are built right into the hillside

Frank Lloyd Wright–style. All are spacious, earth-toned chambers with a cool bird feeder outside the window. Hiking trails, outdoor art installations and well-tended beehives add to the nature-loving ambience.

★Boyd &
Wurthmann Restaurant   AMERICAN $
(☑330-893-4000; www.boydandwurthmann.com; 4819 E Main St, Berlin; mains $7-13; ◷5:30am-7:30pm Mon-Sat) Hubcap-sized pancakes, 20 pie flavors each day, fat sandwiches and Amish specialties such as country-fried steak draw locals and tourists alike. Cash only.

ℹ Information

Holmes County Chamber of Commerce (www.visitamishcountry.com)

ℹ Getting There & Around

Amish Country lies between Cleveland (80 miles north) and Columbus (100 miles southwest). I-71 and I-77 flank the area to the west and east, respectively, but you'll have to exit and drive along a series of narrow, winding back roads to reach the little towns.

Columbus

Ohio's capital city (and largest city) isn't going to wow you with a bunch of razzle-dazzle. It doesn't flaunt mega-sights, scenic splendor or wild quirks. But Columbus makes up for it with unexpected food and arts scenes. Better yet, Columbus is easy on the wallet, an influence from Ohio State University's 59,000-plus students (the campus is the nation's second largest). Entrepreneurs, tech types and artists have flocked in, drawn by low costs and a 'go ahead and try it' atmosphere. It's not in your face, but this place quietly buzzes with creativity.

◉ Sights & Activities

Just north of downtown, the browse-worthy Short North is a redeveloped strip of High St that holds contemporary art galleries, stylish boutiques, and bars and restaurants galore.

★COSI   MUSEUM
(☑614-228-2674; www.cosi.org; 333 W Broad St; adult/child $25/20; ◷10am-5pm, closed Mon & Tue in winter; ⊛) The acronym stands for Center of Science and Industry, and it ranks high in the pantheon of children's museums

around the country. Of the 300-plus hands-on exhibits jammed into the building, the dinosaur gallery (with a mechanical T-rex), space gallery (with a replica space station to explore) and high-wire unicycle ride are highlights. Live science shows, Ohio's largest planetarium ($5 extra) and a 3D theater ($5 extra) are also part of the whopping spread.

Pizzuti Collection   MUSEUM
(☑614-221-6801; www.pizzuti.columbusmuseum. org; 632 N Park St; $10; ◷10am-5pm Wed-Sat, from noon Sun) Curators show off the amazing collection of contemporary paintings, sculpture, film, photography and prints via exhibitions that change every three months or so. You never know what you'll see, but count on it being provocative with a focus on underrepresented voices from around the world. The lovely classical building holds three floors of works; a sculpture garden adorns the grounds. It's affiliated with the Columbus Museum of Art.

Columbus Food Tours   FOOD & DRINK
(☑614-440-3177; www.columbusfoodadventures. com; tours $58-72) Foodie guides lead tours by neighborhood or theme (taco trucks, desserts, coffee), some by foot and others by van. Most jaunts take three to four hours. Departure points vary.

🛏 Sleeping & Eating

BrewDog DogHouse   BOUTIQUE HOTEL $$
(☑614-908-3051; www.brewdog.com; 96 Gender Rd, Canal Winchester; r $175-200; ⊛ 🕸 😺) Brew-Dog – the Scottish beer maker known for its audacious, come-what-may attitude – has a huge brewing facility in Canal Winchester, about 15 miles southeast of downtown Columbus. And that facility now includes a 32-room hotel. That's right: a hotel inside the brewery, where the modern-industrial rooms each have a tap, plus a beer fridge in the shower.

Katalina's   BREAKFAST $
(☑614-294-2233; www.katalinascafe.com; 1105 Pennsylvania Ave; mains $10-13; ◷8am-3pm) 🍴 It seems all of Columbus gets in line at Katalina's for breakfast. Tucked in a vintage gas station where you're welcome to add to the graffitied walls and tables, the colorful cafe is famed for its pancake balls (filled with Nutella or pumpkin-apple butter), sweet and spicy bacon, breakfast tacos and pork-and-egg sandwiches.

★ Momo Ghar
NEPALI $

(☑ 614-749-2901; www.facebook.com/momogharo-hio; 1265 Morse Rd; mains $10; ⊙ 11am-8pm Mon, Tue & Thu-Sat, 9am-5pm Sun) It's hard not to fall for this Nepalese dumpling counter hiding inside a global foods supermarket. Look for the bright-hued prayer flags fluttering over the little enclave, and then bowl up to order a plate of steamed beauties stuffed with chopped chicken, pork, potatoes or veggies. The *jhol momos* (dumplings in a fragrant tomato broth) are awesome.

★ Skillet
BREAKFAST $$

(☑ 614-443-2266; www.skilletruf.com; 410 E Whittier St; mains $14-21; ⊙ 8am-2pm Wed-Sun) 🍴 This teeny restaurant in German Village serves rustic, locally sourced brunch fare. The menu changes, but you might fill a plate with griddled cinnamon rolls or braised pork cheeks with gravy and grits. It's almost always crowded, and you can't make reservations. On weekends you can call ahead (30 minutes before you arrive) and put your name on the wait list.

🍷 Drinking & Nightlife

Land-Grant Brewing Company
MICROBREWERY

(☑ 614-427-3946; www.landgrantbrewing.com; 424 W Town St; ⊙ 3:30-10pm Mon-Wed, 11:30am-10pm Thu, 11:30am-midnight Fri & Sat, 11:30am-8pm Sun) Beer gurus gather around Land-Grant's communal picnic tables to discuss the finer points of hazy brut IPAs versus Baltic porters and Mexican lagers. They're all here among the 24 taps, with flights available for heady sampling. Food trucks provide the noshes, with Ray Ray's Hog Pit doing the honors barbecue-style Thursday through Sunday.

🛍 Shopping

Book Loft
BOOKS

(☑ 614-464-1774; www.bookloft.com; 631 S 3rd St; ⊙ 10am-11pm) Bibliophiles go gaga in this sprawling German Village bookshop occupying a block of pre–Civil War era buildings. You're guaranteed to get lost in the labyrinth of 32 rooms stacked to the rafters with best sellers, children's books, manga, memoirs and more – all new, with many at bargain rates.

❶ Information

Columbus Convention & Visitors Bureau
(☑ 866-397-2657; www.experiencecolumbus. com; 277 W Nationwide Blvd; ⊙ 8am-5pm Mon-

> **GERMAN VILLAGE: COLUMBUS, OHIO**
>
> The remarkably large, all-brick German Village, a half-mile south of downtown, is a restored 19th-century neighborhood with beer halls, cobbled streets, arts-filled parks, and Italianate and Queen Anne architecture.

Fri, 10am-4pm Sat, noon-5pm Sun) This visitor center in the Arena District is staffed and has a gift shop of local goods.

❶ Getting There & Away

John Glenn Columbus International Airport (CMH; ☑ 614-239-4000; www.flycolumbus. com; 4600 International Gateway) is 10 miles east of town. A cab or rideshare to downtown costs about $30.

Greyhound (☑ 614-221-4642; www.grey hound.com; 111 E Town St) buses run at least six times daily to Cincinnati ($11 to $21, two hours) and Cleveland ($13 to $23, 2½ hours).

Yellow Springs

Artsy, beatnik little Yellow Springs was a counterculture hot spot in the 1960s and '70s, thanks to Antioch University. You can still buy a bong at the local head shop, but now galleries, craft shops and sustainable eateries cluster downtown. It's a sweet spot to hang out for a day or two. Visit the local dairy farm to milk a cow or lick an ice cream made on-site. Limestone gorges, waterfalls and canoe-able rivers fill the surrounding parkland.

◉ Sights

★ Young's Jersey Dairy
FARM

(☑ 937-325-0629; www.youngsdairy.com; 6880 Springfield-Xenia Rd; ⊙ 9am-11pm Jun-Aug, reduced hours Sep-May; 🚗) **FREE** Young's is a working dairy farm with a famous ice-cream shop, the Dairy Store, which many say whips up Ohio's best milkshakes. There are also lots of fun family activities, including mini-golf, batting cages and opportunities to feed goats and watch the cows get milked (the latter happens from 4:30pm to 5:30pm). The golf and batting cages have a fee, the animal viewings do not. The Golden Jersey Inn restaurant is also on-site.

🛏 Sleeping & Eating

Morgan House   B&B $$

(☎937-767-1761; www.arthurmorganhouse.com; 120 W Limestone St; r $145-180; ⌗🅿) The six comfy rooms have super-soft linens and private baths. Breakfasts are organic. It's walking distance to the main business district.

Winds Cafe   AMERICAN $$$

(☎937-767-1144; www.windscafe.com; 215 Xenia Ave; mains $24-30; ⏰11:30am-2pm & 5-10pm Tue-Sat, 10am-3pm Sun) A hippie co-op 40-plus years ago, the Winds has grown up to become a sophisticated foodie favorite plating seasonal dishes such as fig-sauced asparagus crepes and rhubarb halibut. Choose from small plates, large plates, cocktails and wine. Reservations are a good idea for the snug dining room.

ℹ Getting There & Away

Yellow Springs is about 18 miles northeast of Dayton and linked by – wait for it – Dayton–Yellow Springs Rd.

Dayton

Dayton leans hard on its 'Birthplace of Aviation' tagline, and the Wright sights deliver. It's surprisingly moving to see the cluttered workshop where Orville and Wilbur conjured their ideas and the lonely field where they tested their plane. Then there's the Air Force museum, a mind-blowing expanse for aviation buffs. The vast complex of hangars holds just about every aircraft you can think of through the ages.

👁 Sights

★National Museum
of the US Air Force   MUSEUM

(☎937-255-3286; www.nationalmuseum.af.mil; 1100 Spaatz St; ⏰9am-5pm) FREE Located at Wright-Patterson Air Force Base, 6 miles northeast of Dayton, this huuuuge museum has everything from a Wright Brothers 1909 Flyer to a Sopwith Camel (WWI biplane) and the 'Little Boy' type atomic bomb (decommissioned and rendered safe for display) dropped on Hiroshima. The hangars hold miles of planes, rockets and aviation machines. Be sure to visit Building 4 for spacecraft and presidential planes (including the first Air Force One). Plan on three hours overall; aviation buffs should allocate longer.

Carillon Historical Park   HISTORIC SITE

(☎937-293-2841; www.daytonhistory.org; 1000 Carillon Blvd; adult/child $10/7; ⏰9:30am-5pm Mon-Sat, from noon Sun) Highlights in this open-air heritage park include the Wright Brothers National Museum, where you'll see the 1905 Wright Flyer III biplane and a replica of the Wright workshop, and the Carillon Brewing Company, an 1850s-style brewery where you can drink the wares.

🍴 Eating & Drinking

Corner Kitchen   AMERICAN $$

(☎937-719-0999; www.afinerdiner.com; 613 E 5th St; mains $15-26; ⏰4:30-10pm Tue-Thu, to 11pm Fri & Sat) Simple wood tables, white panel walls and mismatched china plates set the mod-rustic tone at Corner Kitchen, a bustling diner-meets-French-cafe. Enjoy zingy cocktails alongside meals such as wine-steeped mussels, eggplant stew and gravy-laden poutine (though the menu changes often). The four-course tasting menu ($34; with wine pairings $60) is a fine way to go. It's located in the bohemian Oregon District.

Warped Wing
Brewing Company   MICROBREWERY

(☎937-222-7003; www.warpedwing.com; 26 Wyandot St; ⏰5-10pm Tue-Thu, 3pm-midnight Fri, noon-midnight Sat, noon-8pm Sun) The brewery takes its name from the Wright brothers' concept of wing-warping, which was their breakthrough idea that enabled flight. The taproom's inventions are equally awesome. Many beer fanatics have dubbed the IPAs, stouts, lagers and cucumber sour ales as the best beers in town. The housemade root beer and ginger beer are excellent, too.

ℹ Getting There & Away

Dayton has a good-sized airport north of town. Greyhound buses also serve the city, which is equidistant from Cincinnati ($13 to $25, 1½ hours, four daily) and Columbus ($13 to $25, 1½ hours, six daily).

Cincinnati

Cincinnati splashes up the Ohio River's banks. Its prettiness surprises, as do its neon troves, its European-style neighborhoods and the locals' unashamed ardor for a five-way (c'mon, that's a term for the city's famed chili). Amid all that action, don't forget to catch a soccer game, stroll the bridge-striped riverfront and visit the dummy museum.

◐ Sights & Activities

National Underground Railroad Freedom Center　MUSEUM

(☑513-333-7500; www.freedomcenter.org; 50 E Freedom Way; adult/child $15/10.50; ⊙noon-5pm Sun & Mon, 10am-5pm Tue-Sat, closed Mon Oct-Feb) Cincinnati was a prominent stop on the Underground Railroad and a hub for abolitionist activities. The center displays artifacts from the era, such as an eerie shackle-filled pen that once held slaves bound for auction. The museum also covers modern struggles for civil rights. The Rosa Parks virtual-reality exhibit ($5 extra) shows how it's done: visitors don a headset and goggles, then sit on a 'bus' to stand in Parks' shoes when she refused to give up her seat.

Cincinnati Museum Center　MUSEUM

(☑513-287-7000; www.cincymuseum.org; 1301 Western Ave; adult/child $14.50/10.50; ⊙10am-5pm; ⋒) This museum complex occupies the 1933 Union Terminal, an art deco jewel still used by Amtrak. The interior has fantastic murals made of local Rookwood tiles. The complex includes a nifty Museum of Natural History (with a cave and real bats inside), a children's museum, a history museum, an Omnimax theater and a special hall for traveling exhibitions. Admission includes the three museums; the theater and special exhibits cost extra. Parking costs $6.

American Sign Museum　MUSEUM

(☑513-541-6366; www.americansignmuseum.org; 1330 Monmouth Ave; adult/child $15/free; ⊙10am-4pm Wed-Sat, from noon Sun) This museum stocks an awesome cache of flashing, light-bulb-studded beacons in an old parachute factory. You'll burn your retinas staring at vintage neon drive-in signs, hulking genies and the Frisch's Big Boy, among other nostalgic novelties. Guides lead hour-long tours at 11am and 2pm that also visit the on-site neon sign-making shop.

Contemporary Arts Center　MUSEUM

(CAC; ☑513-345-8400; www.contemporaryartscenter.org; 44 E 6th St; ⊙10am-4pm Sat-Mon, to 9pm Wed-Fri; ⋒) FREE The center displays modern art in an avant-garde building designed by star architect Zaha Hadid. The free exhibitions – say, a retrospective of fanciful paper cutouts by street artist Swoon, or the surreal multimedia sculptures of Chris Larson – change every three months or so. Kids go gaga in the interactive UnMuseum gallery on the 6th floor.

Roebling Suspension Bridge　BRIDGE

(www.roeblingbridge.org) The elegant 1867 spanner was a forerunner of John Roebling's famous Brooklyn Bridge in New York. The Romanesque arches and draped cables have made it an Instagram star. It's cool to walk across while passing cars make it 'sing' around you (the sound as they drive over the grates). It links to Covington, KY.

Fifty West Canoe & Kayak　KAYAKING

(☑513-479-0337; www.fiftywestcanoe.com; 7605 Wooster Pike; tube/canoe/kayak trips from $20/26/32; ⊙10am-6pm Mon-Fri, 9am-7pm Sat & Sun late May-early Sep) On a hot Cincy day it's hard to beat a relaxing 2-mile, inner-tube float or 6-mile kayak trip that ends at a festive brewpub. Local brewery Fifty West shuttles you to a put-in on the Little Miami River, and then you glide back to where the wheat beers, IPAs and sand volleyball courts await.

☞ Tours

American Legacy Tours　WALKING

(www.americanlegacytours.com; 1332 Vine St; 90min tours $25) Offers a variety of historical jaunts. The best is the Queen City Underground Tour that submerges into old lagering cellars deep beneath the Over-the-Rhine district and ends at a modern brewery taproom.

✺ Festivals & Events

Oktoberfest　FOOD & DRINK

(www.oktoberfestzinzinnati.com; ⊙mid-Sep) German beer, bratwursts and mania. It's the USA's largest Oktoberfest celebration, with well over half a million revelers. It takes place on W 2nd and 3rd Sts downtown between Walnut and Elm Sts.

⊨ Sleeping

Symphony Hotel　B&B $$

(☑513-721-3353; www.symphonyhotel.com; 210 W 14th St; ⊙r $139-249) Around the corner from Music Hall, the Symphony Hotel offers nine rooms in a traditional Italianate building. Each is named after a classical composer, and each is chock-full of period antique decor, such as a four-post bed or cherrywood armoire (they vary in style). Breakfast and parking are included in the rates.

★ 21c Museum Hotel Cincinnati　HOTEL $$$

(☑513-578-6600; www.21cmuseumhotels.com; 609 Walnut St; r $189-379; P ❉ @ ⧴ ⧲) An outpost of Louisville's popular art hotel, the

21c sits next door to the Contemporary Arts Center. The modern rooms have a Nespresso machine, free wi-fi, plush bedding and, of course, original art. The lobby is a public gallery, so feel free to ogle the trippy videos and nude sculptures. The on-site restaurant and rooftop bar draw crowds. Parking costs $38.

✗ Eating

★ Tucker's
DINER $

(☑ 513-954-8920; www.facebook.com/TuckersRestaurantOTR; 1637 Vine St; mains $5-9; ☺8am-2pm Tue-Sun; ☑) Located in a tough zone a few blocks from Findlay Market, family-run Tucker's has been feeding locals – African American, white, foodies, penniless, friars, drug dealers – since 1946. It's an archetypal diner, serving six-cheese omelets, shrimp and grits, biscuits and gravy, potatoes with bacon jam and other hulking breakfast dishes, along with several vegetarian dishes using ingredients sourced from the market.

Eli's BBQ
BARBECUE $

(☑ 513-533-1957; www.elisbarbeque.com; 3313 Riverside Dr; mains $7-16; ☺11am-9pm) Eli's is a wee spot that makes awesome barbecue, which is why there's always a line snaking out the door. Order at the counter, find a seat, then wait for staff to bring out your hickory-smoked ribs on a red plastic tray. The meat is tender, the sauce sweet with a smoky kick, and the jalapeño cheddar grits beyond addictive.

★ Bauer Farm Kitchen
EUROPEAN $$$

(☑ 513-621-8555; www.bauercincinnati.com; 435 Elm St; mains $22-32; ☺5-9:30pm Tue-Thu, to 10pm Fri & Sat) It's odd that for all its German heritage, Cincinnati doesn't have many German restaurants. Enter downtown's Bauer Farm Kitchen, which specializes in rustic Franco-German cuisine served in a wood-paneled, farmhouse-chic dining room. If you can tear yourself away from the seasonal sausage, wild mushroom goulash and other small plates, main dishes like the sauerbraten brisket with foraged spiceberries await. Book ahead.

☐ Drinking & Nightlife

★ Rhinegeist Brewery
BREWERY

(☑ 513-381-1367; www.rhinegeist.com; 1910 Elm St, 2nd fl; ☺3pm-midnight Mon-Thu, 3pm-2am Fri, noon-2am Sat, noon-9pm Sun) Beer buffs pile in to Rhinegeist's hoppy clubhouse to knock back Truth IPA and around 20 other brews

on tap. Swig at picnic tables while watching bottles roll off the production line, or play table tennis and bean-bag toss in the sprawling open warehouse. The brewery is one of Ohio's biggest. The rooftop bar offers sweet skyline views.

★ Longfellow
COCKTAIL BAR

(☑ 513-549-0744; www.longfellowbar.com; 1233 Clay St; ☺4pm-2am Tue-Fri, 2pm-2am Sat & Sun) Longfellow looks like a cafe you'd find in Amsterdam, all cozy and candlelit in a vintage building with creaking hardwood floors and exposed brick walls. Punk music drifts from the speakers while stylish locals hobnob over wine, craft beers and cocktails like the Spruce Goose, a deceptively strong refresher made with gin, tonic, lime and honey.

☆ Entertainment

Nippert Stadium
SOCCER

(☑ 513-977-5425; www.fccincinnati.com; 2700 Bearcats Way; tickets $15-50) Nippert Stadium is home to FC Cincinnati, the city's new Major League Soccer team. It's known for its rabid fans cloaked in orange and blue (the team colors) and their pre-game rituals that include a march with drums and flares to the venue.

Great American Ballpark
BASEBALL

(☑ 513-765-7000; www.reds.com; 100 Main St) Home to the Reds – pro baseball's first team – Cincy is a great place to catch a game thanks to its bells-and-whistles riverside ballpark. Many of the beer stands pour top-notch local brews.

❶ Information

Cincinnati Visitor Center (☑ 513-534-5877; www.cincinnatiusa.com; 511 Walnut St; ☺11am-5pm Sep-May, 9am-6pm Jun-Aug) The visitor center on Fountain Sq has maps and info.

❶ Getting There & Around

The **Cincinnati/Northern Kentucky International Airport** (CVG; www.cvgairport.com; 3087 Terminal Dr, Hebron) is in Kentucky, 13 miles south. To get downtown, take the TANK bus ($2), which departs from the baggage claim area's east end. A cab costs $35; Uber and Lyft are typically a bit less.

Greyhound (☑ 513-352-6012; www.greyhound.com; 1005 Gilbert Ave) buses travel daily to Columbus (two hours), Indianapolis (2½ hours) and Chicago (seven hours). Megabus (www.megabus.com) travels the same routes from downtown and the University of Cincinnati; check the website for curbside locations.

Amtrak choo-choos into **Union Terminal** (☑ 800-872-7245; 1301 Western Ave) thrice weekly en route to Chicago (9½ hours) and Washington, DC (14½ hours), departing in the middle of the night. There is no ticket window; buy tickets in advance online.

Metro (www.go-metro.com; fare $1.75) runs the local buses and links with the Transit Authority of Northern Kentucky (www.tankbus.org). Bus 1 between downtown and Mt Adams can be useful.

Red Bike (www.cincyredbike.org) has 442 bicycles at 57 stations, mostly in downtown and Over-the-Rhine. A day pass costs $8 for unlimited 60-minute rides in a 24-hour period; bikes must be docked every hour or additional charges apply. Several electric bikes are mixed in at the stations.

Cincy's **streetcar** (www.cincinnatibellconnector.com) runs on a handy, 3½-mile loop connecting the Banks, downtown and Over-the-Rhine (including Findlay Market). A day pass costs $2.

Southeastern Ohio

Ohio's southeastern corner cradles most of its forested areas, as well as the rolling foothills of the Appalachian Mountains and scattered farms. Parts are far prettier than you'd expect. The Hocking Hills region, near Logan, impresses with streams and waterfalls, sandstone cliffs and cave-like formations. Further on is Athens, a university town and the area's free-spirited hot spot. To the east, around Chillicothe, mysterious Native American mounds rise from the fields.

Athens

Athens makes a lovely base for exploring southeastern Ohio. Situated where US 50 crosses US 33, it's set among wooded hills and built around the Ohio University campus (which comprises half the town). Vintage brick buildings edge the main streets, while young, bohemian types pop in and out of the cafes and groovy shops inside.

🛏 Sleeping

Bodhi Tree Guesthouse   B&B **$$**
(☑ 740-707-2050; www.bodhitreeguesthouse.com; 8950 Lavelle Rd; r $150-200) The four rooms at this serene, hippy-esque farmhouse have tasteful modern (if minimal) decor. There are no TVs, but there is wi-fi, as well as a wholesome breakfast of local cheeses, eggs,

fruit and yogurt. A 4-acre organic farm surrounds the abode. The on-site studio offers yoga classes and massage. It's about a 3-mile drive from downtown Athens.

🍷 Drinking

Little Fish Brewing Co   MICROBREWERY
(☑ 740-204-6187; www.littlefishbrewing.com; 8675 Armitage Rd; ⏲ 3-10pm Mon-Thu, 11am-11pm Fri & Sat, 11am-10pm Sun) Little Fish specializes in saisons and barrel-aged sour beers, though pale ales, porters and smoked lagers mix in among the taps. The brewers source the majority of their grain and some of their hops in Ohio, and their flagship beer – Saison du Poisson – is made entirely with Ohio ingredients.

ℹ Getting There & Away

The closest big city is Columbus, 75 miles northwest via US 33. **GoBus** (☑ 888-954-6287; www.ridegobus.com; Ohio University Baker Center, Oxbow Trail entrance) runs a few times a day to/from downtown Columbus (one way $10, two hours).

Logan

Logan is a handy headquarters for checking out the Hocking Hills area, where hiking, canoeing, camping and other activities amid dramatic gorges and grottoes are de rigueur. Hocking Hills State Park lets you immerse in the green scene by day and stargaze by night, while Logan offers local cultural quirks including a washboard museum and moonshine distillery.

⊙ Sights & Activities

Hocking Hills State Park   STATE PARK
(☑ 740-385-6842; http://parks.ohiodnr.gov/hockinghills; 19852 Hwy 664) **FREE** Ohio's most popular park is splendid to explore in any season, but it's especially lovely in autumn. Thirty miles of hiking trails meander through the forest past waterfalls and gorges. Old Man's Cave is the park's hot spot, with several short paths (less than a half-mile) that deliver a scenic payoff. Nearby Cedar Falls offers a half-mile trail edged by steep rock walls that leads to a peaceful waterfall and pool. The park is 12 miles southwest of Logan.

Hocking Hills Adventures   CANOEING
(☑ 740-385-8685; www.hockinghillscanoeing.com; 31251 Chieftain Dr; kayak/canoe trips from $23/39; ⏲ Apr-Oct) Offers a variety of self-guided

WORTH A TRIP

ANCIENT MOUNDS OF OHIO

The area south of Columbus was a center for the ancient Hopewell people, who left behind huge geometric earthworks and burial mounds from around 200 BC to AD 500. The **Hopewell Culture National Historical Park** (☏ 740-774-1126; www.nps.gov/hocu; 16062 Hwy 104, Chillicothe; ☉ sunrise-sunset) tells their story. The visitor center (8:30am to 5pm) provides intriguing background information, but the highlight is wandering about the variously shaped ceremonial mounds spread over 13-acre Mound City, a mysterious town of the dead. It's 3 miles north of Chillicothe, next to one of Ohio's largest prisons.

Serpent Mound (☏ 937-587-2796; www.ohiohistory.org; 3850 Hwy 73, Peebles; per car $8; ☉ 9am-sunset) is perhaps the most captivating of all of the native mounds that dot southeastern Ohio. The giant, uncoiling snake stretches over a quarter of a mile and is the largest effigy mound in the world. You can walk around it or go up the observation tower for a sweeping view. The site is far flung, but cool enough to be worth the effort. It's 50 miles southwest of Chillicothe.

trips on the Hocking River, from two-hour jaunts to full-day expeditions. The monthly nighttime trip that lets you paddle by moonlight and tiki torch is festive. The outfitter also has tent and RV sites ($26 to $35) and rustic cabins ($65 to $95) on-site. Note the latter do not have bathrooms, and you must provide your own linens.

❶ Getting There & Away

US 33 is the main road to Logan. GoBus (p583) makes a stop in town a few times a day on its route between downtown Columbus ($10, 80 minutes) and Athens ($10, 40 minutes).

MICHIGAN

More, more, more – Michigan is the Midwest state that cranks it up. It sports more beaches than the Atlantic seaboard. More than half the state is covered by forests. And more cherries and berries get shoveled into pies here than anywhere else in the USA. Plus Detroit is the Midwest's most exciting city of all, reinventing itself daily with street art and fresh architecture.

Michigan occupies prime real estate, surrounded by four of the five Great Lakes – Superior, Michigan, Huron and Erie. Islands – Mackinac, Manitou and Isle Royale – freckle its coast and make top touring destinations. Surf beaches, colored sandstone cliffs and trekkable sand dunes also woo visitors.

The state consists of two parts split by water: the larger Lower Peninsula, shaped like a mitten, and the smaller, lightly populated Upper Peninsula, shaped like a slipper. They are linked by the gasp-worthy Mackinac Bridge, which spans the Straits of Mackinac.

❶ Information

Michigan Highway Conditions (www.michigan.gov/mdot)

Michigan State Park Information Park entry requires a vehicle permit (per day/year $9/33). Tent and RV sites cost $15 to $45; reservations accepted (www.midnrreservations.com; fee $8). Some parks have wi-fi.

Travel Michigan (www.michigan.org)

Detroit

After decades of neglect, Detroit is rolling again. It's like the whole place is caffeine-buzzed, freewheeling in ideas. Young creative types have moved to the city and transformed the glut of abandoned buildings into distilleries, cafes, galleries and chocolate shops. Downtown will pop your eyeballs, from the extraordinary art deco skyscrapers to the whimsical public parks and edgy street art. By day, intriguing sights bring Detroit's car-making history to life. By night, timeless jazz clubs show off its musical chops. Sweet bike rides and sprawling markets add to the energy.

History

French explorer Antoine de La Mothe Cadillac founded Detroit in 1701. Sweet fortune arrived in the 1920s, when Henry Ford began churning out cars. He didn't invent the automobile, as so many mistakenly believe, but he did perfect assembly-line manufacturing and mass-production techniques. The result was the Model T, the first car the USA's middle class could afford to own.

Detroit quickly became the motor capital of the world. General Motors (GM), Chrysler and Ford were all headquartered in or near Detroit (and still are). The 1950s were the city's heyday, when the population exceeded two million and Motown music hit the airwaves. But racial tensions in 1967 and Japanese car competitors in the 1970s shook the city and its industry. Detroit entered an era of deep decline, losing about two-thirds of its population.

In July 2013, Detroit filed the largest municipal bankruptcy claim in US history: $18 billion. After extreme belt-tightening, it emerged from bankruptcy in December 2014. Since then, the fortunes of downtown have been on the rise, thanks to a real-estate boom, but the tide has yet to turn for many long-term residents outside the city's core.

◉ Sights

★ Detroit Institute of Arts   MUSEUM
(DIA; ☑ 313-833-7900; www.dia.org; 5200 Woodward Ave; adult/child $14/6; ⊙ 9am-4pm Tue-Thu, 9am-10pm Fri, 10am-5pm Sat & Sun) The DIA holds one of the world's finest art collections. The centerpiece is Diego Rivera's mural *Detroit Industry,* which fills an entire room and reflects the city's blue-collar labor history. Beyond it are Picassos, Caravaggios, suits of armor, modern African American paintings, puppets and troves more spread through 100-plus galleries.

★ Fisher Building   ARCHITECTURE
(☑ 313-872-1000; www.thefisherbuilding.com; 3011 W Grand Boulevard) This 1928 masterpiece from the man who built Detroit, Albert Kahn, has an imposing art deco exterior made from Minnesota granite and Maryland marble, and an interior to rival any Italian cathedral. From the soaring vaulted ceilings, featuring an array of intricate, hand-painted patterns, to the sparkling mosaics by Hungarian artist Géza Maróti and gleaming marble on the walls, the visual inspiration here is endless.

★ Eastern Market   MARKET
(www.easternmarket.org; Adelaide & Russell Sts) Produce, cheese, spice and flower vendors fill the large halls on Saturday, but you also can turn up Monday through Friday to browse the specialty shops (props to the peanut roaster) and cafes that flank the halls on Russell and Market Sts. In addition, from June through September there's a scaled-down market on Tuesdays and a Sunday craft market with food trucks. Or arrive any day for mural gaping. Eastern Market has become an internationally renowned hot spot for street art.

Campus Martius Park   PARK
(www.downtowndetroitparks.com; 800 Woodward Ave; 🖼) This public space in the heart of Detroit's downtown is the perfect spot to while away a sunny afternoon. A fountain dots the middle, surrounded by umbrella-shaded tables. Beside it, a sandy beach with lounge chairs appears in warmer months; in winter, the space becomes the city's most popular ice rink. There's a stage for concerts and, in summer, a pop-up restaurant and bar. At the foot of the park is the Michigan Soldiers & Sailors Monument.

Guardian Building   ARCHITECTURE
(☑ 313-963-4567; www.guardianbuilding.com; 500 Griswold St; ⊙ 8:30am-6pm Mon-Sat, 11am-5pm Sun) Commissioned as a 'cathedral of finance,' this distinctive, 40-story, redbrick building with green and white accents was the world's tallest masonry structure when it opened in 1929. The interior is a colorful explosion of marble, mosaic and murals that draw from Aztec, art deco and local influences. It's certainly the prettiest Bank of America you'll ever see. **Pure Detroit** (☑ 313-963-1440; www.puredetroit.com; ⊙ 9:30am-6pm Mon-Sat, 11am-5pm Sun), whose flagship store is in the building, leads tours most Saturdays and Sundays.

Museum of Contemporary Art Detroit   MUSEUM
(MOCAD; ☑ 313-832-6622; www.mocadetroit.org; 4454 Woodward Ave; suggested donation $5; ⊙ 11am-5pm Wed, Sat & Sun, to 8pm Thu & Fri) MOCAD is set in an abandoned, graffiti-slathered auto dealership. Heat lamps hang from the ceiling over peculiar exhibits that

WORTH A TRIP

BELLE ISLE PARK

Pretty **Belle Isle Park** (www.belleisle conservancy.org; per car/bike $9/free; ⊙ 5am-10pm) floats in the Detroit River. The entire expanse is parkland where kayaking, walking trails and a glass-domed conservatory await. There's a beach, zoo, aquarium and maritime museum, too. Once you pay the entry fee, the individual sights are free. The cycling here is terrific.

GREAT LAKES DETROIT

Detroit

0 500 m
0 0.25 miles

Fisher Building
(0.8mi)

Motown Historical
Museum (0.7mi)

Amtrak (0.3mi)

Ford Piquette
Avenue Plant (0.2mi)

E Edsel Ford Fwy

NEW
CENTER

Palmer Ave

Ferry St

Chrysler Fwy

Russell St

I-94

Merrick Ave

Wayne State
University

Cass Ave

3rd Ave

2nd Ave

Kirby St

Frederick

Douglass Ave

Farnsworth
St

Detroit
Institute
of Arts

Warren Ave

Hancock Ave

Hancock Ave

St Antoine St

Chrysler Dr

Warren Ave

Russell St

Trumbull Ave

4th Ave

Forest Ave

Forest Ave

Prentis
Ave

John R St

Brush St

Lincoln Ave

Gibson St

Carfield Ave

Canfield St

Woodward Ave

Cass Ave

Willis St

Canfield Ave

Lodge Fwy

Selden St

Alexandrine St

Selden St

Selden St

Parsens
St

MIDTOWN

Chrysler Dr

Rivard St

Brainard St

Mack Ave

Martin Luther King Jr Blvd

Tolan
Park

I-75

Ash St

Elm St

Peterboro St

Erskine St

3rd Ave

Charlotte Ave

Watson
St

Wilkins St

Chrysler Fwy

Wilkins St

Temple St

Perry St

Temple Ave

Cass
Park

Park Ave

Edmund
Pl

Alfred St

Alfred St

Spruce St

Ledyard St

Adelaide St

Eastern
Market

Hostel Detroit
(0.3mi)

Grand River Ave

Henry St

Winder St

Winder St

Fisher Fwy

Montcalm St

I-75

Gratiot Ave

Michigan Central
Station (0.7mi)

Plum St

Clifford St

Cass Ave

Woodward Ave

Brush St

St Antoine St

Elizabeth St

Adams Ave

Beacon
St

Beech St

Plaza Dr

Madison St

5th Ave

4th Ave

Park Pl

Library
Ave

Broadway
Ave

Lafayette
Plaisance

CORKTOWN

Labrosse St

Michigan Ave

Abbott St

Clinton St

Macomb St

Porter St

1st St

State St

Farmer St

Monroe St

Rivard St

Abbott St

Lafayette Blvd

Howard St

Greyhound Station

Fort St

GREEKTOWN

Lafayette Blvd

6th Ave

2nd Ave

3rd Ave

Washington Blvd

Shelby St

Griswold St

Bates St

Randolph St

Congress St

I-375

Navarre Ple

Fort St

3rd Ave

Jefferson Ave

Fort St

Larned St

Riopelle St

Jefferson Ave

Cobo
Center

Hart
Plaza

Transit
Windsor

Woodbridge St

Franklin St

Detroit River

Riverwalk

Atwater St

change every few months. Music and literary events take place regularly. The on-site cafe–cocktail bar is popular.

Motown Historical Museum MUSEUM
(☑ 313-875-2264; www.motownmuseum.org; 2648 W Grand Blvd; adult/child $15/10; ⊙10am-6pm Tue-Fri & Sun, to 8pm Sat Jun-Aug, to 6pm Tue-Sat Sep-May) In this row of modest houses Berry Gordy launched Motown Records – and the careers of Stevie Wonder, Diana Ross, Marvin Gaye and Michael Jackson – with an $800 loan in 1959. Gordy and Motown split for Los Angeles in 1972, but you can still step into humble Studio A and see where the famed names recorded their first hits.

Ford Piquette Avenue Plant MUSEUM
(☑ 313-872-8759; www.fordpiquetteplant.org; 461 Piquette Ave; adult/child $12/free; ⊙10am-4pm Wed-Sun Apr-Oct) Henry Ford cranked out the first Model T in this landmark factory. Admission includes a detailed tour by enthusiastic docents, plus loads of shiny vehicles from 1904 onward. It's about 1 mile northeast of the Detroit Institute of Arts.

Activities

★ Slow Roll CYCLING
(www.slowroll.bike; ⊙Mon late May-Oct) Up to 6000 cyclists come out for this leisurely 8-to-12-mile pedal through a different neighborhood each Monday. It's a great way to meet locals. Detroiters of all ages and fitness levels partake. Check the website for the week's location. Start time is at 6pm

through early September, and then moves up to 5:30pm through October.

Riverwalk & Dequindre Cut WALKING
(www.detroitriverfront.org) The city's swell riverfront path runs for 3 miles along the churning Detroit River from Hart Plaza east to Mt Elliott St, passing several parks, outdoor theaters, riverboats and fishing spots en route. Eventually it will extend all the way to beachy Belle Isle (detour onto Jefferson Ave to get there now). About halfway along the Riverwalk, near Orleans St, the 1.5-mile Dequindre Cut Greenway path juts north, offering a convenient passageway to Eastern Market.

Tours

★ Pure Detroit Tours WALKING
(☑ 855-874-7873; www.puredetroit.com; ⊙Sat & Sun) **FREE** Purveyors of locally inspired gifts, Pure Detroit also offers guided tours of some of the city's best sights, including the Fisher Building, the Guardian Building and the Packard Plant. Guides – typically local historians – are knowledgeable and friendly. Stop in at one of Pure Detroit's five locations or check the website for details.

Wheelhouse Bikes CYCLING
(☑ 313-656-2453; www.wheelhousedetroit.com; 1340 E Atwater St; per 2hr $17; ⊙11am-7pm Mon-Thu, 10am-8pm Fri & Sat, 10am-5pm Sun, reduced hours in winter) Cycling is a great way to explore the city. Wheelhouse rents sturdy two-wheelers (helmet and lock included) on the Riverwalk at Rivard Plaza. Themed

GREAT LAKES DETROIT

Detroit

DETROIT'S RUINS

The derelict buildings that represent Detroit in the popular imagination aren't as prevalent as they once were – at least, not downtown, where many architectural gems have been restored and buffed to a shine, thanks to dedicated locals and private investors. National chains have also jumped on the bandwagon as the city's fortunes turn for the better, with retailers such as Madewell and Nike and hotel brands such as Element and Aloft moving in to formerly vacant commercial buildings.

You'll see construction going on everywhere in the city center. Even iconic ruins – buildings such as **Michigan Central Station** (2405 W Vernor Hwy) and the **Packard Plant** (E Grand Blvd at Concord St), thought to be entirely beyond redemption – are feeling the love. The former is getting a $350 million makeover to become Ford Motor Company's new innovation campus, while the latter is being (slowly) redeveloped into an office and entertainment complex.

Still, with 139 sq miles of city, there are plenty of vacant buildings that remain, especially outside the downtown core. But Detroit's days as the capital of 'ruin porn' (as in, people getting excited by urban decay) are dissipating as the ruins continue to vanish. Note it is illegal to enter any abandoned building.

tours ($45 including bike rental) roll by various neighborhoods, architectural sites and urban farms.

✦ Festivals & Events

North American International Auto Show
CULTURAL
(www.naias.com; 1 Washington Blvd; $14; ⊙mid-Jan) It's autos galore for two weeks at the Cobo Center.

Movement Electronic Music Festival
MUSIC
(www.movement.us; cnr Jefferson & Woodward Aves; day pass $85; ⊙late May) The world's largest electronic music festival congregates in Hart Plaza over Memorial Day weekend.

🛏 Sleeping

Detroit is having a hotel boom: several design-savvy properties have opened in downtown and Midtown over the past few years, with more on the way. Myriad Airbnb rentals in these areas can be a cheaper alternative. Taxes add 9% to 15% to rates (it varies by lodging size and location).

Hostel Detroit
HOSTEL $
(☑313-451-0333; www.hosteldetroit.com; 2700 Vermont St; dm $30-39, r $64-74; P✳@🕏) Volunteers rehabbed this old building using recycled materials and donations for the patchwork furnishings, and painted it in vivid colors inside and out. There are two 10-bed dorms, two four-bed dorms and a handful of private rooms; everyone shares the four bathrooms and three kitchens.

Bookings are taken online only (and must be done at least 24 hours in advance).

★ Inn on Ferry Street
INN $$
(☑313-871-6000; www.innonferrystreet.com; 84 E Ferry St; r $179-279; P✳@🕏) Forty guest rooms fill a row of Victorian mansions right by the art museum. The lower-cost rooms are small but have deliciously soft bedding; the larger rooms feature plenty of antique wood furnishings. The healthy, hot breakfast and shuttle to downtown are nice touches.

El Moore Lodge
BOUTIQUE HOTEL $$
(☑313-924-4374; www.elmoore.com; 624 W Alexandrine St; r $75-170, cabins from $200; P✳🕏) 🍃 A unique option in Midtown with a great friendly vibe, El Moore occupies a turreted 1898 building that has been renovated with solar panels and a geothermal heating and cooling system. Reclaimed wood and tiles feature in the interior. The 11 rooms vary widely, from basement digs with two bunk beds to chic rooftop 'cabins' with a private balcony.

★ Shinola Hotel
DESIGN HOTEL $$$
(☑313-356-1400; www.shinolahotel.com; 1400 Woodward Ave; r $215-325; P✳🕏❄) Shinola, Detroit's homegrown company known for its luxury crafted watches, extended the brand to this superbly stylish hotel. The 129 earth-toned rooms have hardwood floors, mid-century modern furniture, big windows letting in natural light and local beers in the minibar; some have turntables and records. The downtown location is super-convenient near the sports arenas, QLine and shops.

✗ Eating

Detroit's food scene is buzzing, with edgy restaurants clustered in downtown, Midtown and Corktown in particular. Two nearby suburbs also have caches of stylish eats: walkable, gay-oriented Ferndale at 9 Mile Rd and Woodward Ave, and Royal Oak just north of Ferndale between 12 and 13 Mile Rds.

★ Sister Pie
PIES $

(☑313-447-5550; www.sisterpie.com; 8066 Kercheval Ave; baked goods $1-5, pie slice $4; ⊗8am-4pm Mon-Fri, 9am-sold out Sat & Sun) ∅ Owner Lisa Ludwinski (a 2019 James Beard Award finalist) and her army of female bakers create amazing treats at this corner storefront. The milk chocolate chess, salted maple, marshmallow butterscotch and other flaky-crust pies are fabulous, and the perfectly soft peanut-butter paprika cookies will spoil your taste buds forevermore. Everything is made with seasonal ingredients and produce purchased from local farmers.

Parks & Rec Diner
DINER $

(☑313-446-8370; www.parksandrecdiner.com; 1942 Grand River Ave; mains $10-14; ⊗8am-2pm Mon-Thu, to 3pm Fri-Sun) This homey diner, located in the imposing GAR building, takes its name from the government department that was once housed here. There are no wrong choices from the seasonal menu of sandwiches and brunch dishes such as pistachio French toast and panzanella with charred bacon. The fries, seasoned with a BBQ spice, are excellent.

Dime Store
AMERICAN $

(☑313-962-9106; www.eatdimestore.com; 719 Griswold St; mains $9-14; ⊗8am-3pm) Take a seat in a chunky wood swivel chair in this cozy, diner-esque eatery and chow down on a duck Reuben and truffle mayo–dipped fries, alongside a cold beer. Eggy brunch dishes are a big hit and are served all day.

★ Detroit Vegan Soul
VEGAN $$

(☑313-649-2759; www.detroitvegansoul.com; 8029 Agnes St; mains $13-17; ⊗noon-8pm Tue-Sat; ☑) Step inside this light-wood cafe staffed by hippies and fork into splendid soul food dishes that just happen to be vegan. The soul platter, with black-eyed peas, maple-glazed yams, mac and cheese, smoked collard greens and a cornbread muffin, is the way to go. The menu also features catfish and barbecue (both tofu-based).

Selden Standard
AMERICAN $$$

(☑313-438-5055; www.seldenstandard.com; 3921 2nd Ave; small plates $12-18; ⊗11am-2:30pm & 5-10pm Mon-Fri, 10am-2pm & 5-10pm Sat & Sun) ∅ Farm-to-table Selden Standard is the kind of place that cares enough to churn its own butter and hand-make its own pasta. The menu changes, but you'll see dishes such as fresh-caught trout and celery-root ravioli, plus creative cocktails.

☕ Drinking & Nightlife

★ Standby
COCKTAIL BAR

(☑313-241-5719; www.standbydetroit.com; 225 Gratiot Ave; ⊗5pm-2am) Standby hides in the alleyway known as the Belt. Find it, and crazy-creative cocktails like Snake in the Grass (gin, lime, celery bitters and nitro-muddled mustard greens) are your reward. The boisterous, space fills up fast on weekends; reservations are a good idea.

Batch Brewing Company
MICROBREWERY

(☑313-338-8008; www.batchbrewingcompany. com; 1400 Porter St; ⊗11am-10pm Mon-Thu, 11am-midnight Fri & Sat, 10am-8pm Sun) Batch's little taproom bustles most nights of the week. Friends play board games at one table, a young couple on a date sits next to them, while workmates discuss business nearby. German-style lagers and pale ales are mainstays of the 18 beers on tap, but there are also some monster doppelbocks and double IPAs.

Grand Trunk Pub
BAR

(☑313-961-3043; www.grandtrunk.pub; 612 Woodward Ave; ⊗11am-2am Mon-Fri, from 10am Sat & Sun) Once the ticket hall for the Grand Trunk Railroad, this high-ceilinged space still buzzes, but this time patrons are content to sit and stop a while. With good reason: there's a vast beer selection and a full bar menu. The patio is an excellent spot to people-watch, thanks to the pedestrian esplanade down Woodward Ave.

★ Entertainment

Cliff Bell's
JAZZ

(☑313-961-2543; www.cliffbells.com; 2030 Park Ave; ⊗5pm-midnight Tue-Fri, 5pm-12:30am Sat, 11am-10pm Sun) The candlelit, art deco ambience at Cliff Bell's attracts a diverse young crowd to hear local jazz bands. The elegant club, decked out in mahogany and brass, has been around since 1935. Weeknight shows typically are free, while weekend shows cost $10 to $15.

FROM MOTOWN TO ROCK CITY

Motown Records and soul music put Detroit on the map in the 1960s, while the thrashing punk rock of the Stooges and MC5 was the 1970s response to that smooth sound. By 1976, Detroit was dubbed 'Rock City' by a Kiss song (though – just Detroit's luck – the tune was eclipsed by its B-side, 'Beth'). In the early 2000s hard-edged garage rock pushed the city to the music-scene forefront, thanks to homegrown stars such as the White Stripes, Von Bondies and Dirtbombs, while Eminem gave Detroit its rap bona fides. And then there's techno, the electronic dance music that DJs in the city created in the mid-1980s. It went heavy on synthesizer melodies and complex machine rhythms, and became a global sensation. The world's largest electronic music festival (p588) still takes place in the city annually in honor of the style. Scope free publications such as the *Metro Times* for current show and club listings.

Magic Stick   LIVE MUSIC
(☑ 313-833-9700; www.majesticdetroit.com; 4120-4140 Woodward Ave; ⏰ 11am-2am) The grungy Magic Stick is the place to go for rappers and rock bands on the rise. The attached Majestic Theater hosts larger shows. While the venues have lost some luster in recent years, you're still likely to see cool bands here most nights. The complex also holds a bowling alley, rooftop deck and pizza joint.

Fox Theatre   PERFORMING ARTS
(☑ 313-471-6611; www.olympiaentertainment.com; 2211 Woodward Ave) This opulent 1928 theater, built in the Oriental style, is one of the icons of Detroit – and one of the few venues that has consistently offered entertainment during the city's ups and downs. First used to show silent films (it still has two organs), today the Fox hosts comedians, top music acts and Broadway shows.

Comerica Park   BASEBALL
(☑ 313-962-4000; www.detroittigers.com; 2100 Woodward Ave; 🎟) The Detroit Tigers play pro baseball at Comerica, one of the league's most decked-out stadiums. The park is particularly kid friendly, with a small Ferris wheel and carousel inside ($2 per ride each).

Little Caesars Arena   STADIUM
(☑ 313-471-6606; www.olympiaentertainment.com; 2645 Woodward Ave) Opened in 2017, this is Detroit's spiffy arena for big-name concerts and sporting events. Detroit's rough-and-tumble pro hockey team the Red Wings (www.nhl.com/redwings) and pro basketball team the Pistons (www.nba.com/pistons) both play here from October through April.

Ford Field   FOOTBALL
(☑ 877-212-8898; www.detroitlions.com; 2000 Brush St) The Lions pro football team tosses the pigskin at this indoor stadium next to Comerica Park.

🛍 Shopping

★ **John K. King**
Used & Rare Books   BOOKS
(☑ 313-961-0622; www.johnkingbooksdetroit.com; 901 W Lafayette Blvd; ⏰ 9:30am-5:30pm Mon-Sat) This cluttered, multistory bookstore is a Detroit landmark sure to delight any bibliophile. Treasures await in the dusty stacks, and exploring the building is an adventure in itself.

★ **Third Man Records**   MUSIC
(☑ 313-209-5205; www.thirdmanrecords.com; 441 W Canfield St; ⏰ 10am-7pm Mon-Sat, 11am-5pm Sun) Local boy Jack White opened Third Man, and it's a super-fun browse. The store sells records (of course), turntables, T-shirts and other gear, but the coolest bits are the recording booth (where you can make your own record for $20) and the record pressing plant that you can peek into for free (or tour for $15 on select Saturdays).

ℹ Information

Detroit Convention & Visitors Bureau
(☑ 800-338-7648; www.visitdetroit.com)

ℹ Getting There & Around

Detroit Metro Airport (DTW; ☑ 734-247-7678; www.metroairport.com; 11050 Rogell Dr), a Delta Airlines hub, is about 20 miles southwest of Detroit. Transportation options to the city are few. Taxis cost $50 or so; Lyft and Uber typically are a bit less. The 261 Fast Michigan SMART bus (fare $2) runs along Michigan Ave and takes an hour to get downtown.

Greyhound (☑ 313-961-8011; 1001 Howard St) runs to various cities in Michigan and beyond, including Grand Rapids ($21 to $40, 4½ hours) and Traverse City ($45 to $55, 7½ hours). Megabus (www.megabus.com/us) runs to/from Chicago ($25 to $45, 5½ hours) daily; departures are from downtown and Wayne State University. Check the website for exact locations.

Amtrak trains go three times daily to Chicago ($39 to $93, 5½ hours) from **Detroit Station** (☑ 313-873-3442; 11 W Baltimore Ave), located right by the QLine stop at Baltimore St. You can also head east – to New York ($95 to $223, 16½ hours) or destinations en route – but you'll first be bused to Toledo.

The **QLine streetcar** (www.qlinedetroit.com; single fare $1.50, day pass $3) provides handy transport along Woodward Ave from Congress St downtown, past the sports venues and museums of Midtown, to the Amtrak station and W Grand Blvd at the route's northern end.

MoGo (www.mogodetroit.org) is Detroit's bike-share program, with 44 stations scattered around downtown and Midtown. A 24-hour pass costs $8 for an unlimited number of 30-minute trips; additional charges apply for trips longer than 30 minutes.

Transit Windsor (☑ 519-944-4111; www.citywindsor.ca/transitwindsor) operates the Tunnel Bus to Windsor, Canada. It costs $5 (American or Canadian) and departs by Mariner's Church (corner of Randolph St and Jefferson Ave) near the Detroit-Windsor Tunnel entrance, as well as other spots downtown. Bring your passport.

Uber and Lyft are very popular in Detroit. For taxi service, call Checker Cab at ☑ 313-963-7000.

Dearborn

A stone's throw from Detroit, Dearborn is home to the Henry Ford Museum, one of the USA's finest museum complexes. It's also home to the nation's largest Arab American community, and a visit here offers a fascinating immersion into the local culture.

⊙ Sights

★**Henry Ford Museum**   MUSEUM
(☑ 313-982-6001; www.thehenryford.org; 20900 Oakwood Blvd; adult/child $24/18; ⊙ 9:30am-5pm) The indoor Henry Ford Museum contains a fascinating wealth of American culture, such as the chair Lincoln was sitting in when he was assassinated, the presidential limo in which Kennedy was killed, the hot dog–shaped Oscar Mayer Wienermobile (photo op!) and the bus on which Rosa Parks refused to give up her seat. Don't worry: you'll get your vintage car fix here, too. Parking costs $6.

Greenfield Village   MUSEUM
(☑ 313-982-6001; www.thehenryford.org; 20900 Oakwood Blvd; adult/child $28/21; ⊙ 9:30am-5pm daily mid-Apr–Oct, Fri-Sun Nov & Dec; ▣) Adjacent to the Henry Ford Museum (and part of its complex), outdoor Greenfield Village spreads across 80 acres and features historic buildings shipped in from all over the country, reconstructed and restored, such as Thomas Edison's laboratory from Menlo Park and the Wright Brothers' airplane workshop.

Ford Rouge Factory Tour   FACTORY
(☑ 312-982-6001; www.thehenryford.org; adult/child $18/13.50; ⊙ 9:30am-3pm Mon-Sat) See F-150 trucks roll off the assembly line where

---

CLASSIC CARS IN MICHIGAN

More than sand dunes, beaches and Mackinac Island fudge, Michigan is synonymous with cars. While the connection hasn't been so positive in recent years, the state commemorates its glory days via several auto museums. The following fleets are within a few hours' drive of the Motor City.

Henry Ford Museum This Dearborn museum is loaded with vintage cars, including the first one Henry Ford ever built. In adjacent Greenfield Village, you can ride in a Model T that rolled off the assembly line in 1923.

Automotive Hall of Fame (☑ 313-240-4000; www.automotivehalloffame.org; 21400 Oakwood Blvd; adult/child $10/4; ⊙ 9am-5pm Wed-Sun May-Sep, Fri-Sun only Oct-Apr) Next door to the Henry Ford Museum, the interactive Auto Hall focuses on the people behind famed cars, such as Mr Ferdinand Porsche and Mr Soichiro Honda.

Gilmore Car Museum (☑ 269-671-5089; www.gilmorecarmuseum.org; 6865 Hickory Rd, Hickory Corners; adult/child $15/10; ⊙ 9am-5pm Mon-Fri, to 6pm Sat & Sun) North of Kalamazoo along Hwy 43, this museum complex offers some 20 buildings filled with nearly 400 vintage autos, including 15 Rolls-Royces dating back to a 1910 Silver Ghost.

RE Olds Transportation Museum (☑ 517-372-0529; www.reoldsmuseum.org; 240 Museum Dr, Lansing; adult/child $7/5; ⊙ 10am-5pm Tue-Sat year-round, noon-5pm Sun Apr-Oct) It's a whopping garage full of shiny vintage cars that date back more than 130 years.

Henry Ford first perfected his self-sufficient, mass-production techniques. The self-guided tours start at the Henry Ford Museum, from which a bus takes you over to the factory. Allow a couple of hours for the overall visit.

❶ Getting There & Away

Dearborn is 10 miles west of downtown Detroit and about the same distance east of Detroit Metro Airport; a rideshare to either place costs about $20. I-94 is the primary road to town. Amtrak has a station by the Henry Ford Museum with service to Detroit ($6.50 to $17, 25 minutes, three daily).

Ann Arbor

Liberal and bookish Ann Arbor is home to the University of Michigan. The walkable downtown, which abuts the campus, is loaded with free-trade coffee shops, bookstores and brewpubs. It's also a mecca for chowhounds. Zingerman's Delicatessen led the way decades ago, but now all sorts of inventive farm-to-table and butcher-your-own-meat type places pop up in cozy spaces.

⊙ Sights

Ann Arbor Farmers Market　　MARKET
(☏734-794-6255; www.a2farmersmarket.org; 315 Detroit St; ⊙7am-3pm Wed & Sat May-Dec, 8am-3pm Sat Jan-Apr) Given the surrounding bounty of orchards and farms, it's no surprise this place is stuffed to the rafters with everything from spicy pickles to cider to mushroom-growing kits; located downtown near Zingerman's Delicatessen. On Sunday, an **artisan market** with jewelry, ceramics and textiles takes over from 11am to 4pm.

🛏 Sleeping & Eating

Burnt Toast Inn　　B&B $$
(☏734-395-4114; www.burnttoastinn.com; 415 W William St; r $135-225; ❋ 🛜) The colorful house has five rooms that mix sturdy antiques with funky art. Two rooms share a bathroom; the rest have private facilities. It's an excellent location, on a leafy street walkable to downtown and the university campus. The lovely garden and big porch add to the homey vibe. Breakfast, featuring locally made bread, milk, granola and other fare, is included.

★Lunch Room　　VEGAN $
(☏734-224-8859; www.thelunchrooma2.com; 407 N 5th Ave; mains $9-14; ⊙11am-9pm Mon-Sat, from 3pm Sun; 🍴) Order at the spice jar–lined

counter, and then grab one of the close-set tables to await your beet burger with tofu bacon, Korean sweet-potato noodle stir-fry, raspberry and basil grilled cheese or other wildly flavorful vegan dishes. The bar serves beer, wine and cocktails. It's located in the Kerrytown Market & Shops complex.

★Zingerman's Delicatessen　　DELI $$
(☏734-663-3354; www.zingermansdeli.com; 422 Detroit St; sandwiches $14-19; ⊙7am-9pm) The shop that launched the area's foodie frenzy, Zingerman's piles local, organic and specialty ingredients onto towering sandwiches in a sprawling downtown complex that also includes a coffee shop and bakery.

❶ Tourist Information

Destination Ann Arbor (www.visitannarbor. org) Accommodation information and more.

❶ Getting There & Away

Detroit's airport is 30 miles east; shuttle buses (one way $12 to $15) make the trip. Amtrak trains come through Ann Arbor three times daily to/from Detroit ($12 to $15). The train station is downtown and shared by Greyhound. Megabus serves the city, but it stops inconveniently far from its center.

Central Michigan

Michigan's heartland, plunked in the center of the Lower Peninsula, alternates between fertile farms and highway-crossed urban areas. The larger cities excel in cool art, while the entire regions shine in stellar beer making.

Lansing & East Lansing

Smallish Lansing is the state capital. A few miles east lies East Lansing, home of Michigan State University. They're worth a stop to peek into a couple of impressive museums and enjoy the simple pleasures of beer, baseball and fresh-from-the-dairy ice cream.

⊙ Sights & Activities

Broad Art Museum　　MUSEUM
(☏517-884-4800; www.broadmuseum.msu.edu; 547 E Circle Dr, East Lansing; ⊙noon-7pm Tue-Sun) [FREE] Renowned architect Zaha Hadid designed this wild-looking parallelogram of stainless steel and glass. It holds everything from Greek ceramics to Salvador Dalí

paintings. Much of the space is devoted to avant-garde exhibitions.

Lansing River Trail WALKING
(www.lansingrivertrail.org) The paved, 20-mile river trail runs alongside the Grand River from the city's north edge to downtown, and then meanders east along the Red Cedar River to the university. It's popular with runners and cyclists, and the downtown portion links a number of attractions, including the RE Olds Transportation Museum, a children's museum, zoo and fish ladder.

🛏 Sleeping & Eating

Wild Goose Inn B&B $$
(☑517-333-3334; www.wildgooseinn.com; 512 Albert St, East Lansing; r $159-179; 🛜) The Wild Goose Inn is a six-room B&B one block from Michigan State's campus in East Lansing. All rooms have fireplaces and most have Jacuzzis. Decor is fairly low-key – except for the Arbor room and its wild faux branches!

Golden Harvest BREAKFAST $
(☑517-485-3663; 1625 Turner St, Lansing; mains $8-13; ⊙8am-2:30pm) Golden Harvest is a loud, punk-rock-meets-hippie diner serving the sausage-and-French-toast Bubba Sandwich and hearty omelets; cash only.

🍸 Drinking & Nightlife

Ellison Brewery and Spirits MICROBREWERY
(☑517-203-5498; www.ellisonbrewing.com; 4903 Dawn Ave, East Lansing; ⊙3-10pm Mon & Tue, 3-11pm Wed & Thu, noon-midnight Fri & Sat, noon-8pm Sun) Ellison hides in a no-frills warehouse in an East Lansing industrial park. Bowl up to the corrugated metal bar and order a Tiramisu coffee stout, 3 Stacks boysenberry sour ale, Relativity double IPA or any of the other 14 beers on tap, fresh from the tanks behind the bartender. Lots of locals unwind over a pint here.

ℹ Information

Greater Lansing CVB (www.lansing.org)

ℹ Getting There & Away

Amtrak stops in East Lansing on its Blue Water route; the train goes once daily to/from Chicago ($30 to $53, four hours). Greyhound has stations in both Lansing and East Lansing with service to Detroit ($10 to $28, two to three hours, four to five daily) and Grand Rapids ($14 to $23, 70 to 95 minutes, five to six daily). I-96, I-69 and Hwy 127 are the main roadways to the city.

Lansing does have a teeny airport, but Detroit (87 miles southeast) is the nearest airport for international flights.

Grand Rapids

The second-largest city in Michigan, Grand Rapids has gotten its groove on thanks to beer. Around 25 craft breweries operate in town, and suds connoisseurs have been piling in, drawn to their high quality, density, proximity to each other and low prices. A foodie scene has built up around the beer makers, and new farm-to-table eateries seem to pop up weekly. Grand Rapids' big-name sculpture park and elegant manors in Heritage Hill intrigue, as well.

🔾 Sights

Frederik Meijer Gardens & Sculpture Park GARDENS
(☑616-957-1580; www.meijergardens.org; 1000 E Beltline NE; adult/child $14.50/7; ⊙9am-5pm Mon & Wed-Sat, 9am-9pm Tue, 11am-5pm Sun) The 158-acre gardens feature impressive blooms and hulking works by Auguste Rodin, Henry Moore and others. The sculpture park is star of the show, offering paths and lawns bejeweled with 50 works by artists such as Ai Weiwei, Claes Oldenburg and Anish Kapoor. The five-story glass conservatory impresses, bursting with tropical plants. The children's garden provides lots to smell, touch and dig into. The tranquil Japanese Garden is another highlight. It is 5 miles east of downtown via I-196.

Gerald R Ford Museum MUSEUM
(☑616-254-0400; www.fordlibrarymuseum.gov; 303 Pearl St NW; adult/child $10/4; ⊙9am-5pm Mon-Sat, from noon Sun) The downtown museum is dedicated to Michigan's only president. Ford stepped into the Oval Office after Richard Nixon and his vice president, Spiro Agnew, resigned in disgrace. It's a bizarre period in US history, and the museum does an excellent job of covering it, down to displaying the burglary tools used in the Watergate break-in. Ford and wife Betty are buried on the museum's grounds.

☞ Tours

Grand Rapids Beer Tours FOOD & DRINK
(☑616-901-9719; www.grbeertours.com; 250 Grandville Ave SW; 4/6hr tours $55/75) These van tours stop at three or four breweries (depending on tour length). A guide leads you through production facilities and tastings

that include four good-sized samples per venue. Pickup is in front of Grand Rapids' bus station. Tours are limited to 14 people, and they do sell out, so book ahead if possible.

🛏 Sleeping & Eating

CityFlats Hotel HOTEL $$

(📞616-608-1720; www.cityflatshotel.com; 83 Monroe Center St NW; r $175-275; ❄🛜) 🅿 Rooms at this ecofriendly hotel have big windows for lots of natural light, bamboo linens, cork floors and locally made, reclaimed wood furniture. The building is gold-certified by the Leadership in Energy and Environmental Design (LEED) program. The downtown location puts you near museums, breweries and restaurants.

⭐**Downtown**
Market Grand Rapids MARKET $

(📞616-805-5308; www.downtownmarketgr.com; 435 Ionia Ave SW; baked goods $2-5, mains $10-16; ⊙10am-7pm Sun-Thu, 10am-8pm Fri, 9am-8pm Sat; 🛜) Chowhounds hobnob at this stylish food hall, perusing top picks such as Slows

Bar BQ, Fish Lads (stellar fish and chips), Love's Ice Cream and Madcap Coffee. The main floor has tables and benches lit by floor-to-ceiling windows, or head upstairs where more tables await, along with a large, veggie-growing greenhouse.

⭐**Green Well** AMERICAN $$

(📞616-808-3566; www.thegreenwell.com; 924 Cherry St SE; mains $15-20; ⊙11am-10pm Sun-Tue, to 11pm Wed & Thu, to midnight Fri & Sat) 🅿 Burgers, green curry, and barbecue pork and polenta feature on the menu, where everything is made with sustainably farmed ingredients. Beer plays a role in many dishes, such as the beer-steamed mussels and beer cheese. The bar taps hard-to-find Michigan brews and pours Michigan wines (flights available). Plus, you can buy awesome art by local artists right off the walls.

❶ Information

Grand Rapids CVB (www.experiencegr.com) Has maps and self-guided brewery tour information online.

GRAND RAPIDS BEER CITY

How did Grand Rapids – a town known for ho-hum office-furniture manufacturing – become hot Beer City? Well, as the manufacturing companies closed up shop over the years, they left behind abandoned industrial buildings – ie cheap space perfect for brewers. There was also a young, thirsty population from the dozen colleges and universities in town.

So people starting cooking up suds. It was pretty under the radar until 2012, when Grand Rapids was voted best beer city in the USA by the national Beer Examiner blog. It happened again in 2013. Then the scene boomed.

Grand Rapids now has around 25 craft breweries in the city proper, and about 20 more in nearby towns. The **Ale Trail** takes you there (download a map at www.experiencegr.com/beer). What makes the scene so popular is the breweries' density – you can walk between many makers – and the relatively low cost of drinking.

The breweries also cater to beer tourists and make it easy to taste the wares. Every taproom offers flights, where you choose the 5oz samples you want to try. Ask at any establishment for the **Brewsader Passport**, a handy little booklet that lists all the beer makers. Collect eight stamps as you make the rounds, and a free Brewsader T-shirt comes your way. You can also download the **Brewsader app** and check in at each brewery you visit.

Top picks in town include **Brewery Vivant** (📞616-719-1604; www.breweryvivant.com; 925 Cherry St SE; ⊙3-11pm Mon-Thu, 3pm-midnight Fri, 11am-midnight Sat, noon-10pm Sun) 🅿 for Belgian-style beers in an old chapel, the huge rock-and-roll–style **Founders Brewing Co** (📞616-776-1195; www.foundersbrewing.com; 235 Grandville Ave SW; ⊙11am-2am Mon-Sat, to midnight Sun; 🛜), **Mitten Brewing Company** (📞616-608-5612; www.mittenbrewing.com; 527 Leonard St NW; ⊙11:30am-10pm Sun & Mon, to midnight Tue-Sat) and its wide-ranging brews in a cool old firehouse, and inventive neighborhood gem **Harmony Brewing Company** (📞616-233-0063; www.harmonybeer.com; 1551 Lake Dr SE; ⊙11am-10pm Mon, 11am-midnight Tue-Sat, noon-10pm Sun). These breweries also serve terrific food, which you'll need to stay upright through the evening.

❶ Getting There & Away

Grand Rapids has a decent-sized airport with flights to many US cities. Amtrak trains chug to/from Chicago three times daily (once directly, and twice via bus transfers in Kalamazoo; $35 to $70, four hours); the station is downtown near Founders Brewing Co.

The **bus station** (☑616-456-1700; 250 Grandville Ave SW) is directly across from Founders; coaches go to Lansing ($14 to $23, 70 to 95 minutes, five to six daily) and Traverse City ($25 to $30, 4¾ hours, daily), among other destinations. I-96, I-196 and US 131 are the main roadways to the city.

Gold Coast

They don't call it the Gold Coast for nothing. Michigan's 300-mile western shoreline features seemingly endless stretches of beaches, dunes, wineries, orchards and inn-filled towns that boom during the summer – and shiver during the snow-packed winter.

Grand Haven

Grand Haven rocks the classic, old-fashioned beach-town attributes. You know the kind: a waterfront boardwalk, ice-cream shops, sand so clean it squeaks and ooh-and-aah sunsets. The bars and restaurants buzz each evening, and everyone congregates for the eye-popping show by the musical fountain once night falls. Add in the surfing, cycling and inventive breweries, and it's easy to see why Grand Haven blows up each summer.

❷ Sights & Activities

Chinook Pier   PIER
(301 N Harbor Dr) Chinook Pier has a lot going on. There's a seasonal mini-golf course (adult/child $3/2) and farmers market (8am to 1pm Wednesday and Saturday). **Wet Mitten Surf Shop** (☑616-844-3388; www.wetmittensurfshop.com; ⊙10am-8pm Mon-Sat, 12:30-7pm Sun) and other water-sports outfitters are here. But its biggest claim to fame is its charter fishing fleet. Boats head out to land king salmon and lake trout that occasionally exceed 20 pounds. It's fascinating to be here at the end of the day when the charters return and display their catch.

Musical Fountain   FOUNTAIN
(www.ghfountain.com; 101 N Harbor Dr, Waterfront Stadium; ⊙sunset May-Sep) Everyone gathers for the musical fountain performance each evening in summer. It's a trippy tradition to watch water spray high in the sky while synchronized to glowy lights and music. The 25-minute show lets loose nightly in June, July and August, and on Fridays and Saturdays in May and September. The fountain actually is on the west side of the Grand River, but spectators watch it from Waterfront Stadium's outdoor seats on the east side of the river.

🛏 Sleeping

Boyden House   B&B $$
(☑616-846-3538; www.boydenhouse.com; 301 S 5th St; r $120-255; ❊⬛) This rambling Victorian home with gorgeous interior woodwork offers eight rooms that mix antique and modern decor. Some have a private balcony, others have a clawfoot tub or fireplace. All have a comfy featherbed, private bathroom, flat-screen TV and wi-fi. Breakfast is a full cooked extravaganza. It's about a mile walk to the beach.

🍴 Eating & Drinking

Morning Star Café   BREAKFAST $
(☑616-844-1131; 711 Washington Ave; mains $6-12; ⊙6:30am-2:30pm) This bright-hued, whimsically decorated cafe cooks the best breakfast in town. The blueberry oatmeal pancakes, pumpkin and cream-cheese crepes, and egg, bacon and cornbread scramble top the list, but there are loads of dishes to choose from, many with a Southwestern bent.

Odd Side Ales   MICROBREWERY
(☑616-935-7326; www.oddsideales.com; 41 Washington Ave; ⊙11:30am-11pm Mon-Thu, to midnight Fri & Sat, to 10pm Sun) Odd Side brews some peculiar experimental suds, like the Mayan Mocha stout (with coffee, cinnamon, nutmeg and habenero chilies) and Aestas sour ale (aged in oak with sea salt, coriander, strawberry and cucumber). The convivial brewpub recently underwent a hefty expansion and now has more than 40 taps delivering the goods.

❶ Information

Grand Haven CVB (www.visitgrandhaven.com) Provides lodging, activities and events info.

❶ Getting There & Away

You'll need a car to get to Grand Haven. US 31 is the most direct route to town and its main street, Washington Ave. The nearest cities with bus, train and plane connections are Grand Rapids (34 miles east) and Holland (23 miles south).

WORTH A TRIP

MUSKEGON

The western shore's largest city, Muskegon (population 37,290) features nifty architecture in its downtown district thanks to lumber barons trying to outbuild each other in the late 1800s. Hip taverns, juice bars, bistros and galleries now occupy the structures along Western Ave and its neighboring blocks. **Pigeon Hill Brewing Company** (☎231-375-5184; www.pigeonhillbrew.com; 500 W Western Ave; ⏰noon-10pm Mon-Thu, to midnight Fri & Sat, to 8pm Sun) shows how it's done. Locals hoist pints of eclectic stouts and IPAs in the former garage whose doors slide up to let in fresh air.

Adventure-sports enthusiasts will find action here. The **Muskegon Winter Sports Complex** (☎877-879-5843; www.msports.org; 462 Scenic Dr) has one of the nation's only public luge tracks. **Pere Marquette Beach** (Beach Street Rd; ⏰6am-11pm) is a hot spot for kiteboarding and paddleboarding, and it hosts the **Great Lakes Surf Festival** (www.greatlakessurffestival.com) in mid-July.

Muskegon is also the departure point for the **Lake Express** (☎866-914-1010; www.lake-express.com; 1918 Lakeshore Dr; one way adult/child/car $96/39/105; ⏰May-Oct) ferry that glides to Milwaukee, WI. **Shoreline Inn** (☎231-727-8483; www.shorelineinn.com; 750 Terrace Point Rd; r $120-190; ❄@📶🏊) provides waterfront lodging if you need a place to crash before or after your boat ride.

The city is 15 miles north of Grand Haven on US 31. See www.visitmuskegon.org for more information.

Saugatuck & Douglas

Saugatuck is one of the Gold Coast's most popular resort areas, known for its strong arts community, numerous B&Bs and gay-friendly vibe. Douglas is its twin city a mile or so to the south, and they've pretty much sprawled into one. It's a touristy but funky place, with ice cream–licking families, yuppie boaters and martini-drinking gay couples sharing the waterfront. Galleries and shops fill the compact downtown core. Weekends attract the masses.

Sights & Activities

Oval Beach BEACH
(Oval Beach Dr, Saugatuck; ⏰8am-10pm) Life guards patrol the long expanse of fine sand. There are bathrooms and concession stands, though not enough to spoil the peaceful, dune-laden scene. It costs $10 to park. Or arrive the adventurous way, via chain ferry and a trek over Mt Baldhead.

Mt Baldhead WALKING
(Saugatuck) Huff up the stairs of this 200ft-high dune for a stellar view. Then race down the other side to Oval Beach. Get here via the chain ferry; walk right (north) from the dock.

Sleeping & Eating

★**Pines Motorlodge** MOTEL $$
(☎269-857-5211; www.thepinesmotorlodge.com; 56 Blue Star Hwy, Douglas; r $139-249; 📶) Retro-cool tiki lamps, pinewood furniture and communal lawn chairs add up to a fun, social ambience amid the firs in Douglas.

★**Farmhouse Deli** DELI $
(☎269-455-5274; www.thefarmhousedeli.com; 100 Blue Star Hwy, Douglas; mains $8-12; ⏰9am-7pm; 🖉) 🌿 While it could coast on its looks – the shabby-chic farmhouse decor is cute as a button – the deli ups the ante with seriously top-notch food. The Cubano sandwich (pulled pork, porchetta and Gruyère), tarragon-tinged chicken salad, tangy goat cheeses, cleansing juices and house-baked croissants, cakes and cookies (try the triple ginger molasses one) dazzle.

Drinking

Virtue Cider WINERY
(☎269-722-3232; www.virtuecider.com; 2170 62nd St, Fennville; ⏰noon-7pm Mon-Wed, to 8pm Thu-Sun) Head to Virtue's farm in Fennville and sip a pint while sheep bleat, pigs oink and chickens cluck around you. The taproom is in a barrel-strewn barn, where the Brut (crisp and dry) and Percheron (slightly sweet) star among the 13 taps. Flights are available.

Information

Saugatuck/Douglas CVB (www.saugatuck.com) Provides foodie, family and LGBTIQ-focused trip-planning info.

ⓘ Getting There & Away

Most visitors drive to Saugatuck/Douglas. The I-196/US 31 whizzes by to the east, while the Blue Star Hwy goes into both towns. The closest Amtrak station is in Holland, about 12 miles north.

Sleeping Bear Dunes National Lakeshore

Eye-popping lake views from atop colossal sand dunes? Water blue enough to be in the Caribbean? Miles of unspoiled beaches? Secluded islands with mystical trees? All here at Sleeping Bear Dunes, along with lush forests, terrific day hikes and glass-clear waterways for paddling. The national park stretches from north of Frankfort to just before Leland, on the Leelanau Peninsula. Several cute little towns fringe the area.

◉ Sights & Activities

Manitou Islands   ISLAND
(per family $25) The forest-cloaked Manitou Islands provide an off-the-beaten-path adventure. They're part of Sleeping Bear Dunes National Lakeshore, hence the entrance fee. North Manitou is known for star-speckled backcountry camping, while South Manitou is terrific for wilderness-rich day trips. Kayaking and hiking are the big to-dos, especially the 7-mile trek to the Valley of the Giants, an otherworldly stand of cedar trees on South Manitou. **Manitou Island Transit** (☑ 231-256-9061; www.manitoutransit.com; 207 W River St, Leland; return adult/child $42/21) runs ferries from Leland; the trip takes 1½ hours.

Dune Climb   HIKING
(Hwy 109, Glen Arbor; ⊙ 24hr) The Dune Climb is the park's most popular attraction, where you trudge up a 200ft-high dune and then run or roll down. Gluttons for leg-muscle punishment can keep slogging all the way to Lake Michigan, a strenuous 1½-hour trek one way; bring water. The site, with a parking lot and bathrooms, is on Hwy 109, 5 miles north of Empire.

Sleeping Bear Heritage Trail   CYCLING
(www.sleepingbeartrail.org; Empire) The 22-mile paved path goes from Empire to Bohemian Rd (aka County Rd 669), passing dreamy forested areas, quaint towns and the Dune Climb along the way. For the most part it rolls gently up and down, though there are some larger hills at the southern end. Trailheads

with parking lots are located roughly every 3 miles; the one at Bar Lake Rd, near Empire, is a good place to embark.

🛌 Sleeping & Eating

Glen Arbor B&B   B&B $$
(☑ 231-334-6789; www.glenarborlodging.com; 6548 Western Ave, Glen Arbor; r $155-290, without bath $115-160; ⊙ closed mid-Nov–Apr) The owners renovated this century-old farmhouse into a sunny, French country inn with six themed rooms.

Empire Village Inn   AMERICAN $
(☑ 231-326-5101; www.empirevillageinn.com; 11601 S Lacore Rd, Empire; mains $10-17; ⊙ noon-10pm) Enter the low A-frame building, grab a seat at a scuffed wood table and order one of the local beers on tap while waiting for your excellent, doughy-crust pizza to arrive. Burgers and sandwiches satisfy too, along with the housemade root beer. It's a swell place to refuel after a day of hiking or biking, if you don't mind the noisy hubbub.

🍷 Drinking

Stormcloud Brewing Company   MICROBREWERY
(☑ 231-352-0118; www.stormcloudbrewing.com; 303 Main St, Frankfort; ⊙ 11:30am-10pm Sun-Thu, to 11pm Fri & Sat) Belgian-style beers are

---

HARBOR COUNTRY

Harbor Country refers to a group of eight small, lake-hugging towns that roll out beaches, wineries, cool shops and all-round rustic charm.

New Buffalo is the largest community, home to a surf school, a busy public beach, ice-cream shops and a beer church. Three Oaks is the only Harbor community that's inland (6 miles in, via Hwy 12). Here Green Acres meets Greenwich Village in a bohemian farm-and-arts blend. Cycle backroads and browse antique stores by day, then visit the cocktail-swirling distillery and folksy theater by night. Union Pier, Lakeside, Harbert and Sawyer are some of the other cutesy towns, chock-full of historic inns, breweries and galleries. Several wineries surround the communities and offer tastings.

For information, see Harbor Country Chamber of Commerce (www.harborcountry.org).

Stormcloud's gift to the universe. Rainmaker Ale is its medal winner (bronze at the Great American Beer Festival), and there are 15 other taps of unusual and sometimes fruity brews. They're terrific paired with the flat-bread pizzas and sharable plates such as smoked whitefish spread on toast. Gluten-free and vegan options are available.

❶ Information

Sleeping Bear Dunes National Lakeshore Visitor Center (☑ 231-326-4700; www.nps. gov; 9922 W Front St, Empire; ⊙ 8am-6pm Jun-Aug, 8:30am-4pm Sep-May) The park's visitor center in Empire has information, trail maps and vehicle entry permits (week/annual $25/45).

❶ Getting There & Away

The park is only accessible by car. US 31 is the main highway to the area. From there make your way onto Hwy 22, which is the road that goes through the park. The nearest airport is in Traverse City, about 50 miles east.

Traverse City

Michigan's 'cherry capital' is the largest city in the northern half of the Lower Peninsula. It's got a bit of urban sprawl, but it's still a happenin' base from which to see the Sleeping Bear Dunes, Mission Peninsula wineries, U-pick orchards and other area attractions. The food and arts scenes are superb, comparable to those of a much larger urban area.

◉ Sights & Activities

Road-tripping out to the wineries is a must. Head north from Traverse City on Hwy 37 for 20 miles to the end of the grape- and cherry-planted Old Mission Peninsula. You'll be spoiled for choice. The wineries stay open all year round, with reduced hours in winter.

Brys Estate Vineyard & Winery   WINERY
(☑ 231-223-9303; www.brysestate.com; 3309 Blue Water Rd; ⊙ 11am-7pm Mon-Sat, to 6pm Sun late May-early Sep, reduced hours rest of year) Michigan's excellent wines taste even better on Brys Estate's sprawling deck, which provides stunning vineyard and bay views. Tastings from $8; cheese and charcuterie plates available.

Paddle TC   WATER SPORTS
(☑ 231-492-0223; www.paddletc.com; 111 E Grandview Pkwy, Clinch Park; kayaks per hr from $30, tours from $45; ⊙ 9am-9pm May-Oct) Offers bike, kayak and stand-up-paddleboard rentals, starting at $30 per hour. Tours and lessons are available; the KaBrew tour ($69), a kayak and bike crawl of local craft breweries, is highly recommended. Call for times.

🛏 Sleeping & Eating

Sugar Beach Resort   HOTEL $$
(☑ 231-938-0100; www.tcbeaches.com; 1773 US 31 N; r $150-250; ❈ 🐾 🛜 🗷) Sugar Beach has decent prices and it's right on the water. Rooms are nothing fancy, but they're well maintained and have small refrigerators, coffee makers and microwave ovens. Pricier rooms have a balcony and view. Continental breakfast is included. A 4% resort fee gets added to your final bill.

★ **Filling Station**   PIZZA $
(☑ 231-946-8168; www.thefillingstationmicrobrew ery.com; 642 Railroad Pl; mains $10-16; ⊙ 11:30am-11pm Mon-Thu, 11:30am-midnight Fri & Sat, noon-10pm Sun) This family-owned business in a former railway terminal has been serving up wood-fired pizzas, fresh green salads and craft beer since 2012. Check out the specials board for seasonal items such as the Oktoberfest pizza, with brats, sauerkraut and a mustard crème fraîche. A s'mores dessert pizza is a sweet ending.

🍷 Drinking

★ **Short's Production Facility Pull Barn**   BREWERY
(☑ 231-498-2300; www.shortsbrewing.com; 211 Industrial Park Dr; ⊙ noon-8pm Mon-Fri, 11am-9pm Sat & Sun late May-early Sep) Beer buffs adore Short's for its Huma Lupa Licious IPA and Juicy Brut ale, and they come en masse to this sprawling outdoor drinking yard in Elk Rapids (18 miles northeast of Traverse City) to get their fill. Folks settle in at shaded picnic tables, play bean-bag toss games and while away the afternoon gulping brews from the 15 on tap.

❶ Information

Traverse City Tourism (www.traversecity.com)

❶ Getting There & Away

Traverse City's small airport has several daily flights to Chicago, Detroit and Minneapolis. US 31 is the main highway to town. Indian Trails (www.indiantrails.com) runs a bus once daily to/from Grand Rapids (one way $25 to $30, 4¾ hours).

HEMINGWAY'S HAUNTS

A number of writers have ties to northwest Michigan, but none are as famous as Ernest Hemingway, who spent the summers of his youth at his family's cottage on Walloon Lake. Hemingway buffs often tour the area to view the places that made their way into his writing.

Horton Bay General Store (☏231-582-7827; www.hortonbaygeneralstore.com; 5115 Boyne City Rd, Boyne City; ◷8am-2pm Wed & Thu, 8am-2pm & 6-9pm Fri-Sun, closed mid-Oct–mid-May) A short distance north of Charlevoix, Boyne City Rd veers off to the east. It skirts Lake Charlevoix and eventually arrives at Horton Bay. Hemingway fans will recognize the store, with its 'high false front,' from his short story 'Up in Michigan.' The old-time shop now sells groceries, souvenirs, sandwiches and ice cream, plus wine and tapas on weekend nights (reservations required for the latter).

Little Traverse History Museum (☏231-347-2620; www.petoskeymuseum.org; 100 Depot Ct, Petoskey; $3; ◷10am-4pm Mon-Sat, closed mid-Oct–late May) Further north on US 31, stop in Petoskey to see the museum's Hemingway collection, including rare first-edition books that the author autographed for a friend when he visited in 1947.

City Park Grill (☏231-347-0101; www.cityparkgrill.com; 432 E Lake St, Petoskey; ◷11:30am-10pm Sun-Thu, to 1:30am Fri & Sat) A few blocks from the museum, toss back a drink at this bar where Hemingway was a regular.

Tour Hemingway's Michigan (www.mihemingwaytour.com) provides further information for self-guided jaunts.

Charlevoix & Petoskey

These two towns, among the most affluent along Michigan's western shore, brim with yacht-filled marinas and fancy summer homes. They're not snooty though, and they provide a fair bit of offbeat adventure. Beachcombing, island trekking and following in the footsteps of Ernest Hemingway await those who make the trip.

🛏 Sleeping

★ Stafford's Perry Hotel HOTEL $$
(☏231-347-4000; www.staffords.com; 100 Lewis St, Petoskey; r $169-279; ❄@❡) The Perry Hotel is a grand historic place. Hemingway once stayed here (in 1916 after a hiking and camping trip in the region). Count on comfy beds, vintage furniture and a cozy on-site pub. Pricier rooms have bay views.

🍷 Drinking

★ Beards Brewery MICROBREWERY
(☏231-753-2221; www.beardsbrewery.com; 215 E Lake St, Petoskey; ◷11:30am-10pm Tue-Thu, 11:30am-11pm Fri, 10am-11pm Sat, 11:30am-9pm Sun) A couple of hairy-faced home brewers got together to open Beards, and they know their stuff, as the hoppy IPAs, tart saisons and nutty brown ales flowing from the 20

taps attest. It's a community gathering spot hosting trivia nights and local musicians. The awesome outdoor patio overlooks the bay, and a fire pit keeps you toasty on cool nights.

ℹ Getting There & Away

US 31 is the main highway to the area. It also connects Charlevoix and Petoskey, which are about 17 mile apart. The closest airport is in Traverse City.

To reach Beaver Island, hop aboard the **ferry** (☏231-547-2311; www.bibco.com; 103 Bridge Park Dr, Charlevoix; one way adult/child/car $32.50/20/105; ◷mid-Apr–late Dec) in downtown Charlevoix. The journey takes two hours. Reserve ahead if bringing a car.

Straits of Mackinac

This region, between the Upper and Lower Peninsulas, features a long history of forts and fudge shops. Car-free Mackinac Island is Michigan's premier tourist draw.

One of the most spectacular sights in the area is the 5-mile-long Mackinac Bridge (known locally as 'Big Mac'), which spans the Straits of Mackinac. The $4 toll is worth every penny as the views from the bridge, which include two Great Lakes, two peninsulas and hundreds of islands, are second to none in Michigan. And remember: despite the spelling, it's pronounced *mac*-in-aw.

Mackinaw City

At the south end of Mackinac Bridge, bordering I-75, is touristy Mackinaw City. It serves mainly as a jumping-off point to Mackinac Island, but it does have a couple of intriguing historic sights.

◉ Sights

Colonial Michilimackinac   HISTORIC SITE
(☑231-436-5564; www.mackinacparks.com; 102 W Straits Ave; adult/child $12.50/7.25; ◷9am-7pm Jun-Aug, to 5pm May & Sep-early Oct; 🖈) Next to the Big Mac bridge (its visitor center is actually beneath the bridge) is Colonial Michilimackinac, a National Historic Landmark that features a reconstructed stockade first built in 1715 by the French. Costumed interpreters cook and craft here.

ℹ Getting There & Away

The main road to Mackinaw City is I-75. The docks for **Star Line** (☑800-638-9892; www.mackinacferry.com; 801 S Huron Ave; return adult/child/bicycle $27/15/12) and **Shepler's** (☑800-828-6157; www.sheplersferry.com; 556 E Central Ave; return adult/child/bicycle $27/15/11; ◷late Apr-Oct) are a short distance off the interstate. Both send ferries to Mackinac Island. The trip takes 20 minutes; boats go at least hourly during daylight hours in spring and fall, and up to four times per hour in June, July and August. Both companies having free parking lots in which to leave your car for the day ($5 to park overnight).

Mackinac Island

From either Mackinaw City or St Ignace, you can catch a ferry to Mackinac Island. The island's location in the straits between Lake Michigan and Lake Huron made it a prized port in the North American fur trade, and a site the British and Americans battled over many times.

The most important date on this 3.8-sq-mile island was 1898 – the year cars were banned in order to encourage tourism. Today all travel is by horse or bicycle; even the police use bikes to patrol the town. The crowds of tourists – called Fudgies by the islanders – can be crushing at times, particularly during summer weekends. But when the last ferry leaves in the evening and clears

out the day-trippers, Mackinac's real charm emerges and you drift back into another, slower era.

Eighty percent of the island is state parkland. Not much stays open between November and April.

Arch Rock   NATURAL FEATURE
FREE This huge limestone arch curves 150ft above Lake Huron and provides dramatic photo opportunities. You can get here two ways: from stairs that lead up from the lakeshore road, or from the island's interior via Arch Rock Rd. The site crowds with tour groups around midday, so try visiting early in the morning.

Fort Mackinac   HISTORIC SITE
(☑906-847-3328; www.mackinacparks.com; 7127 Huron Rd; adult/child $13.50/7.75; ◷9:30am-7pm Jun-Aug, reduced hours May & Sep–mid-Oct, closed mid-Oct–Apr; 🖈) Fort Mackinac sits atop limestone cliffs near downtown. Built by the British in 1780, it's one of the best-preserved military forts in the country. Costumed interpreters and cannon and rifle firings (every half-hour) entertain the kids. Stop into the tearoom for a bite and a million-dollar view of downtown and the Straits of Mackinac from the outdoor tables.

ℹ Information

Mackinac Island Visitor Center (☑906-847-3783; www.mackinacisland.org; 7274 Main St; ◷9am-5pm May-Oct) Downtown booth with maps for hiking and cycling.

ℹ Getting There & Away

Two ferry companies – **Shepler's** (☑800-828-6157; www.sheplersferry.com; Main St; return adult/child/bicycle $27/15/11; ◷late Apr-Oct) and **Star Line** (☑800-638-9892; www.mackinacferry.com; Main St; return adult/child/bicycle $27/15/12) – operate out of Mackinaw City and St Ignace, and charge roughly the same rates. Book online and you'll save a few bucks. The ferries go at least hourly during daylight hours in spring and fall, and up to four times per hour in summer. The trip takes about 20 minutes. Both companies have parking lots to leave your car (free for the day, $5 for overnight).

Upper Peninsula

Rugged and isolated, with hardwood forests blanketing 90% of its land, the Upper Peninsula (UP) is a Midwest highlight. Only 45 miles of interstate highway slice through the trees, punctuated by a handful of cities, of which Marquette is the largest. Between the small towns lie miles of undeveloped shoreline on Lakes Huron, Michigan and Superior; scenic two-lane roads; and pasties, the local meat-and-vegetable pot pies brought over by Cornish miners 150 years ago.

You'll find it's a different world up north. Residents of the UP, aka 'Yoopers,' consider themselves distinct from the rest of the state – they've even threatened to secede in the past.

Pictured Rocks National Lakeshore

Stretching along prime Lake Superior real estate, Pictured Rocks National Lakeshore is a series of wild cliffs and caves, where blue and green minerals have streaked the red and yellow sandstone into a kaleidoscope of color. County Rd H-58 spans the park for 52 slow miles from Grand Marais in the east to Munising in the west. Either town makes a good base for exploring the area. In between you'll find lakeside hikes, kayak trips and boat tours that offer brilliant ways to take in the area's shipwrecks, waterfalls and artist's-palette geology.

Sights & Activities

Top sights (from east to west) include **Au Sable Point Lighthouse** (County Rd H-58, Grand Marais) and its shipwrecks, agate-strewn **Twelvemile Beach** (County Rd H-58, Grand Marais), hike-rich **Chapel Falls** (Chapel Rd, Munising) and view-worthy **Miners Castle** (Miners Castle Rd, Munising). Boat rides and kayak trips along the shore are an excellent way to absorb the dramatic scenery.

Pictured Rock Cruises   BOATING
(☑ 906-387-2379; www.picturedrocks.com; 100 City Park Dr, Munising; 2½hr tours adult/child $38/10; ⊙ mid-May–mid-Oct) Boats with both deck and enclosed seating hug the shore for 16 miles. They depart from Munising's city dock and glide along the shore to Miners Castle. The sunset cruises are particularly lovely. Advance reservations are wise.

Pictured Rocks Kayaking   KAYAKING
(☑ 906-387-5500; www.paddlepicturedrocks.com; 1348 Commercial St, Munising; 4½hr tours adult/child $149/110; ⊙ late May-Sep) This company takes you out on a 56ft passenger boat and drops you off close to the key caves and arches. A guide leads the way from there. It's good for beginners since you're only paddling for two hours or so. Tours depart at 9am and 2:30pm daily.

❶ Getting There & Away

You'll need your own wheels to get here. Marquette, 42 miles west, offers the closest airport. Hwy 28 and Hwy 94 are the primary roads to the area. County Rd H-58 runs through Pictured Rocks; it closes in parts during winter due to snow.

The **Grand Island Ferry** (☑ 906-387-2600; www.grandislandup.com; N8016 Grand Island Landing Rd, Munising; return adult/child $20/15; ⊙ late May–mid-Oct) makes the 15-minute trip to the island three to 10 times daily.

WORTH A TRIP

SAULT STE MARIE

Founded in 1668, Sault Ste Marie (population 13,550) is Michigan's oldest city and the third oldest in the USA. Today it's a busy port and border crossing to Canada, where twin city Sault Ste Marie, Ontario, winks across the bridge. While that's all dandy, the best reason for a visit here is to see the Soo Locks raise and lower hulking freighters.

Catch the action at the **Soo Locks Visitor Center** (☑ 906-253-9290; Portage Ave; ⊙ 9am-9pm mid-May–mid-Oct) **FREE**. It features displays, videos and observation decks from which you can watch 1000ft-long boats leap 21ft from Lake Superior to Lake Huron. It's weirdly awesome. Afterwards head down the block to **Karl's Cuisine, Winery & Brewery** (☑ 906-0253-1900; www.karlscuisine.com; 447 W Portage Ave; mains $13-24; ⊙ 11am-9pm Wed-Sat) 🍴 for pasties, Lake Superior whitefish and pasta dishes along with housemade booze.

I-75 is the main road to town, which is 59 miles north of Mackinaw City. To reach the locks, take exit 394 off the interstate and go left. To continue onward into Canada, make for the International Bridge. The border crossing is open 24/7. See www.saultstemarie.com for more information.

GREAT LAKES UPPER PENINSULA

KEWEENAW PENINSULA & ISLE ROYALE NATIONAL PARK

The Keweenaw Peninsula is the UP's northernmost bit, a wild timberland that juts by its lonesome into Lake Superior. Energetic small towns, jam-making monks and view-tastic mountain drives await adventurers who make the journey.

US 41 is the main highway on the peninsula. Take it to Houghton (population 8000), the Keweenaw's largest town. It bustles with students – Michigan Tech University is here – and it's the jump-off to **Isle Royale National Park**, with ferries and seaplanes departing in summer. **Keweenaw Brewing Company** (☑ 906-482-5596; www.kbc.beer; 408 Shelden Ave, Houghton; ⊙ 3-10pm Mon-Wed, 11am-11pm Thu-Sat, noon-8pm Sun) gives a good feel for the local scene. Grab a $3 pint and enjoy it by the fireplace.

Totally free of vehicles and roads, Isle Royale National Park – a 210-sq-mile island in Lake Superior – is certainly the place to go for peace and quiet. It gets fewer visitors in a year than Yellowstone National Park gets in a day, which means the 165 miles of hiking trails and 2000 moose roaming through the forest are all yours.

Continue north for 25 miles, veer onto Hwy 26 north, and a short distance past Eagle River you'll come to the **Jampot** (www.poorrockabbey.com; 6500 Hwy 26, Eagle Harbor; baked goods $1-3; ⊙ 10am-5pm Tue-Sat May–mid-Oct). Bearded, black-robed monks work in the little bakery selling jams they make from foraged berries, coffee from their house-roasted beans, and pound cake muffins that they bake.

Stay on Hwy 26 another 9 miles. Just past Lake Bailey you'll see the turnoff for the **Brockway Mountain Drive** (Eagle Harbor). The 10-mile jaunt along the spine of the eponymous crag shows off terrific views of Lake Superior. It deposits you in tiny Copper Harbor, where yet another ferry sets sail for Isle Royale. For more information, see www.copperharbor.org.

Marquette

Lakeside Marquette is the perfect place to stay put for a few days to explore the region. It's the Upper Peninsula's largest (and snowiest) town, known as a hot spot for outdoors enthusiasts. Forests, beaches and cliffs provide a playground spitting distance from downtown. Locals ski in winter and hit the trails with their fat-tire bikes in summer. Northern Michigan University is here, so the population skews young. Beer and good food await in the historic town center.

◉ Sights & Activities

Da Yoopers Tourist Trap and Museum MUSEUM
(☑ 906-485-5595; www.dayoopers.com; 490 N Steel St; ⊙ 10am-6pm Mon-Fri, to 5pm Sat & Sun) FREE Behold Big Gus, the world's largest chainsaw. And Big Ernie, the world's largest rifle. Kitsch runs rampant at Da Yoopers Tourist Trap and Museum, 15 miles west of Marquette on Hwy 28/41, past Ishpeming. Browse the store for only-in-the-UP gifts such as a polyester moose tie or beer-can wind chimes.

Down Wind Sports KAYAKING
(☑ 906-226-7112; www.downwindsports.com; 514 N 3rd St; ⊙ 10am-7pm Mon-Fri, 10am-5pm Sat, 11am-3pm Sun) Rents all kinds of gear and has the lowdown on kayaking, fly fishing, surfing, ice climbing and other adventures.

⊨ Sleeping

Landmark Inn HISTORIC HOTEL $$
(☑ 906-228-2580; www.thelandmarkinn.com; 230 N Front St; r $179-249; 🅿 ❖) The elegant, six-story Landmark Inn fills a historic lakefront building and has a couple of resident ghosts.

❶ Information

Visitor Center (2201 US 41; ⊙ 9am-5:30pm) Stop at the log-lodge visitors center at the town's edge for brochures on local hiking trails and waterfalls.

❶ Getting There & Away

The main roadways to town are US 41 and Hwy 28. Marquette has a small airport with flights to Detroit, Chicago and Minneapolis. Indian Trails buses (www.indiantrails.com) go daily to Milwaukee ($60 to $80, eight hours) and Hancock ($18 to $25, three hours).

Porcupine Mountains Wilderness State Park

Michigan's largest state park, with 90 miles of trails, is a wilderness winner. 'The Porkies,' as they're called, are so rugged that loggers bypassed most of the range in the early 19th century, leaving the park with the largest tract of virgin forest between the Rocky Mountains and Adirondacks. Along with 300-year-old hemlock trees, the Porkies are known for waterfalls, 20 miles of undeveloped Lake Superior shoreline, black bears lumbering about, and the view of the park's stunning Lake of the Clouds.

⊙ Sights & Activities

Lake of the Clouds   LAKE
(Hwy 107, Ontonagon; per car $9) This lake is the area's most photographed sight. After stopping at the visitor center to pay the park entrance fee, continue to the end of Hwy 107 and climb 300ft via a short path for the stunning view of the shimmering water. Lengthier trails depart from the parking lot.

Porcupine Mountain Ski Area   SKIING
(☑ 906-885-5209; www.porkiesfun.com; Hwy 107, Ontonagon; half-/full day $33/43; ⊙ Dec–early Apr) Winter is a busy time here, with downhill skiing (a 787ft vertical drop) and 26 miles of cross-country trails on offer. Rentals are available for skis and snowboards ($27 each per day) and snowshoes (per day $15).

ⓘ Information

Friends of the Porkies (www.porkies.org) Lowdown on local arts and events.
Porcupine Mountains and Ontonagon Area CVB (www.porcupineup.com) List of waterfalls and activities.
Porcupine Mountains Visitor Center (☑ 906-885-5275; www.michigan.gov/porkies; S Boundary Rd, Ontonagon; ⊙ 8am–6pm mid-May–mid-Oct) Where you buy vehicle entry permits ($9/33 per day/year) and pick up backcountry camping permits.

ⓘ Getting There & Away

You'll need a car to get here. US 45 is the main highway to the area.

WISCONSIN

Wisconsin is cheesy and proud of it. The state pumps out 2.5 billion pounds of cheddar, Gouda and other smelly goodness – a quarter of America's hunks – from its cow-speckled farmland per year. Local license plates read 'The Dairy State' with udder dignity. Folks here even refer to themselves as 'cheeseheads' and emphasize it by wearing novelty foam rubber cheese-wedge hats for special occasions (most notably during Green Bay Packers football games).

So embrace the cheese thing, because there's a good chance you'll be here for a while. Wisconsin has a ton to offer: exploring the craggy cliffs and lighthouses of Door County, kayaking through sea caves at Apostle Islands National Lakeshore, touring Green Bay's football shrine of Lambeau Field, cow chip–throwing along Hwy 12, or simply soaking up the beer, art and festivals in Milwaukee and Madison.

ⓘ Information

Wisconsin B&B Association (www.wbba.org) Convenient listing of the state's B&Bs by city and region.
Wisconsin Department of Tourism (www.travelwisconsin.com) Produces tons of free guides on subjects such as biking, golf and rustic roads; also has a free app.
Wisconsin Highway Conditions (www.511wi.gov) Handy for checking winter driving conditions.
Wisconsin Milk Marketing Board (www.wisconsincheese.com) Provides a free statewide map of cheesemakers titled *A Traveler's Guide to America's Dairyland*.
Wisconsin State Park Information (☑ 608-266-2181; www.dnr.wi.gov/topic/parks) Entry requires a vehicle permit ($11/38 per day/year). Campsites cost $21 to $35; reservations accepted.

Milwaukee

Here's the thing about Milwaukee: it's cool, but for some reason it slips under the radar. The city's reputation as a working man's town of brewskis, bowling alleys and polka halls persists. But attractions such as the Calatrava-designed art museum, the badass Harley-Davidson Museum and stylish eating and shopping enclaves have turned Wisconsin's largest city into an unassumingly groovy place.

Milwaukee's enduring relationship with beer is no accident. The city was settled by Germans in the 1840s and many started breweries. A few decades later, the introduction of bulk-brewing technology turned beer production into a major industry.

Milwaukee earned its 'Brew City' nickname in the 1880s when Pabst, Schlitz, Blatz, Miller and 80 other breweries made suds here. Today, only Miller remains of the national brands, though smaller brewers have made a big comeback and bars around town feature the best microbrews from Wisconsin and the region.

⊙ Sights & Activities

Lake Michigan sits to the east of the city, and is rimmed by parkland. The scenic Riverwalk path cuts through downtown along both sides of the Milwaukee River.

★ **Harley-Davidson Museum**   MUSEUM
(☑ 414-287-2789; www.harley-davidson.com; 400 W Canal St; adult/child $20/10; ⊙ 9am-6pm Fri-Wed, 9am-8pm Thu May-Sep, 10am-6pm Fri-Wed, 10am-8pm Thu Oct-Apr) Hundreds of motorcycles show the styles through the decades, including the flashy rides of Elvis and Evel Knievel. You can sit in the saddle of various bikes (on the bottom floor, in the Experience Gallery) and take badass photos. Even nonbikers will enjoy the interactive exhibits and tough, leather-clad crowds.

★ **Milwaukee Art Museum**   MUSEUM
(☑ 414-224-3200; www.mam.org; 700 N Art Museum Dr; adult/child $19/free; ⊙ 10am-5pm Tue, Wed & Fri-Sun, to 8pm Thu) You have to see this lakeside institution, which features a stunning winglike addition by Santiago Calatrava. It soars open and closed every day at 10am, noon and 5pm (8pm on Thursday), which is wild to watch; head to the suspension bridge outside for the best view. There are fabulous folk and outsider art galleries, and a sizeable collection of Georgia O'Keeffe paintings. A 2015 renovation added photography and new media galleries to the trove.

DON'T MISS

THE BRONZE FONZ

Rumor has it the **Bronze Fonz** (east side of Riverwalk), just south of Wells St downtown, is the most photographed sight in Milwaukee. The Fonz, aka Arthur Fonzarelli, was a character from the 1970s TV show *Happy Days*, which was set in the city. What do you think – do the blue pants get an 'Aaay' or 'Whoa!'?

American Black Holocaust Museum   MUSEUM
(ABHM; www.abhmuseum.org; 411 W North Ave) This museum aims to tell the story of what it calls the 'Black Holocaust' – which includes the slave trade from Africa, slavery in the American South, the aftermath of the Civil War and the Civil Rights movement – through pictures and stories. It was founded in 1984 as a virtual museum by James Cameron, who survived a lynching as a 16-year-old boy. Check the website to see if the museum has reopened after a 2019 redevelopment.

Miller Brewing Company   BREWERY
(☑ 414-931-2337; www.millercoors.com; 4251 W State St; tours $10; ⊙ 10:30am-4:30pm Mon-Sat Jun-Aug, to 3:30pm Mon-Sat Sep-May) FREE Founded in 1855, the historic Miller facility preserves Milwaukee's beer legacy. Join the legions lined up for the free, hour-long tours. Though the mass-produced beer may not be your favorite, the factory impresses with its sheer scale: you'll visit the packaging plant where 2000 cans are filled each minute, and the warehouse where a half-million cases await shipment. And then there's the generous tasting session at the tour's end, where you can down three full-size samples. Don't forget your ID.

✦ Festivals & Events

★ **Summerfest**   MUSIC
(www.summerfest.com; 639 E Summerfest Pl; day pass $23; ⊙ late Jun-early Jul) It's dubbed 'the world's largest music festival,' and indeed hundreds of rock, blues, jazz, country and alternative bands swarm its 11 stages over 11 days. The scene totally rocks; it is held at downtown's lakefront festival grounds (aka Henry Maier Festival Park). The headline concerts cost extra.

⊨ Sleeping

★ **Ambassador**   HOTEL $
(☑ 877-935-2189; www.ambassadormilwaukee.com; 2308 W Wisconsin Ave; r $119-139; P ❄ @ 🖤) This renovated art deco gem, on the city's western side, near Marquette University, is an affordable central option. Architecture buffs will love all of those 'jazz age' period details, such as the polished marbled flooring in the lobby and the bronze elevator doors. The in-house restaurant exudes a 'supper club' vibe and the adjacent bar pours the perfect Wisconsin-style old-fashioned.

LOCAL KNOWLEDGE

FISH FRIES & SUPPER CLUBS

Wisconsin has a couple of unique dining traditions that you'll likely encounter when visiting the state:

Fish Fry Friday is the hallowed day of the 'fish fry.' This communal meal of beer-battered cod, French fries and coleslaw came about years ago, providing locals with a cheap meal to socialize around and celebrate the end of the working week. The convention is still going strong at many bars and restaurants, including **Lakefront Brewery** (☑414-372-8800; www.lakefrontbrewery.com; 1872 N Commerce St; 45min tours $11; ⊙11am-8pm Mon-Thu, 11am-9pm Fri, 9am-9pm Sat, 10am-5pm Sun) in Milwaukee.

Supper Club This is a type of time-warped restaurant common in the upper Midwest. Supper clubs started in the 1930s, and most retain a retro vibe. Hallmarks include a woodsy location, a radish-and-carrot-laden relish tray on the table, a surf-and-turf menu and a mile-long, unironic cocktail list. See www.wisconsinsupperclubs.net for more information. Old Fashioned (p609) in Madison is a modern take on the venue (it's named after the quintessential, brandy-laced supper-club drink).

Brewhouse Inn & Suites HOTEL $$
(☑414-810-3350; www.brewhousesuites.com; 1215 N 10th St; r $199-249; P❋@☎) This 90-room hotel sits in the exquisitely renovated old Pabst Brewery complex. Each of the large chambers has steampunk decor, a kitchenette and free wi-fi. It's at downtown's far west edge, about a half-mile walk from sausagey Old World 3rd St and a good 2 miles from the festival grounds. Parking costs $28.

Iron Horse Hotel HOTEL $$$
(☑888-543-4766; www.theironhorsehotel.com; 500 W Florida St; r $250-360; P❋☎) The property's location, in Milwaukee's up-and-coming but still a little rough around the edges Fifth Ward, doesn't quite fit the upmarket price tag. That said, the rooms are big, and we do love the industrial post-and-beam, exposed-brick interiors. The Iron Horse is within walking distance of the Harley-Davidson Museum and some great restaurants and bars. Parking costs $30.

✕ Eating

Good places to scope for eats include Germanic Old World 3rd St downtown; multi-ethnic E Brady St by its intersection with N Farwell Ave; and the gastro pub–filled Third Ward, anchored along N Milwaukee St south of I-94.

★**Birch + Butcher** AMERICAN $$
(☑414-323-7372; www.birchandbutcher.com; 459 E Pleasant St; mains $22-34; ⊙7:30am-2pm Mon-Thu, to 10pm Fri & Sat, to 2pm Sun; ☎⚑) Birch + Butcher claims to have the city's only open-fire hearth for serious searing and grilling. However it does it, we love the results.

Choose from a tempting menu of grilled fish, steaks and veggies. Weekend brunches draw big crowds for unusual offerings like whitefish bagels and pulled-pork shoulder, served with polenta. The space is airy and casual.

Pitch's Lounge & Restaurant STEAK $$
(☑414-272-9313; www.pitchsribs.com; 1801 N Humboldt Ave; mains $18-26; ⊙5-10pm Sun-Thu, 3-11pm Fri & Sat; ☎) Steaks, chops, seafood, and the house ribs are on the menu here at this Milwaukee supper club that's been going strong since the 1940s. Walk into the hushed dining room to step back in time a few decades when an evening out always started with a brandy old-fashioned. Enjoy the traditional beer-battered cod at the Friday-night fish fry.

Ardent AMERICAN $$$
(☑414-897-7022; www.ardentmke.com; 1751 N Farwell St; tasting menu $95; ⊙6-10pm Wed-Sat; ☎) Milwaukee's foodies get weak in the knees when they sniff the Beard-nominated chef's ever-changing, farm-to-table dishes. Dinner is a lingering affair in the tiny glowing room, with two seatings each night for the 10-course tasting menu. Reserve well in advance. Or head next door to Ardent's sibling restaurant, open 6pm to 1am Wednesday to Saturday, for slurpable bowls of ramen noodles.

🍷 Drinking & Entertainment

★**Champion's** BAR
(☑414-332-2440; www.championspub.com; 2417 N Bartlett Ave; ⊙3pm-2am Mon-Fri, from 1pm Sat, from 11:30am Sun; ☎) Champion's is the

RACING SAUSAGES

It's common to see strange things after too many stadium beers. But a group of giant sausages sprinting around Miller Park's perimeter – is that for *real*? It is if it's the middle of the 6th inning. That's when the famous 'Racing Sausages' (actually five people in costumes) waddle onto the field to give the fans a thrill. If you don't know your encased meats, that's Brat, Polish, Italian, Hot Dog and Chorizo vying for supremacy.

perfect choice if you're looking for something quiet, friendly and authentic. It has been a neighborhood fixture since the 1950s and not much has changed since. You'll find friendly locals, New Glarus' own Spotted Cow on tap and a low-key beer garden out back for relaxing summer nights.

Hi Hat COCKTAIL BAR
(☑414-225-9330; www.hihatlounge.com; 1701 N Arlington Place, cnr E Brady St; ⊙4pm-2am Mon-Fri, 10am-2am Sat & Sun; ☎) One of the city's best watering holes, Hi Hat sits along a strip of legendary bars on E Brady St on the near-north side. There's drinking on two levels, with an adjacent sports bar. The cocktails and decor have a retro vibe, and you'll occasionally catch live bands here in the evening.

★ Rave LIVE MUSIC
(Eagles Club; ☑414-342-7283; www.therave.com; 2401 West Wisconsin Ave; concerts from $25; ⊙shows from 8pm; ☎; ▣) The former Eagles Club was built in 1926 and has hosted a 'who's who' of legendary music acts, including Guy Lombardo, Glenn Miller, Buddy Holly, Bob Dylan, the Sex Pistols, all the way up to Ed Sheeran. It's still going strong, with nightly shows in one of half a dozen venues. See the website for a program and ticket info.

★ Miller Park BASEBALL
(☑414-902-4400; www.brewers.com; 1 Brewers Way; ⊙box office 9am-7pm Mon-Fri, 9am-5pm Sat, 11am-5pm Sun) From April through September, the National League Milwaukee Brewers play baseball at fab Miller Park, which has a retractable roof and real grass. Buy tickets online or at the stadium box office. The stadium is about 5 miles west of downtown. The Brewers Line bus runs there on game days; pick it up along Wisconsin Ave.

❶ Information

Milwaukee Convention & Visitors Bureau
(☑800-554-1448; www.visitmilwaukee.org; 648 N Plankinton Ave; ⊙8am-5pm Mon-Fri)

❶ Getting There & Around

General Mitchell International Airport (MKE; ☑414-747-5245; www.mitchellairport.com; 5300 S Howell Ave) is 8 miles south of downtown. Take public bus 80 ($2.25) or a cab ($35).

The **Lake Express ferry** (☑866-914-1010; www.lake-express.com; 2330 S Lincoln Memorial Dr; one way adult/child/car from $96/39/105; ⊙May-Oct) sails from downtown (the terminal is located a few miles south of the city center) to Muskegon, MI, providing easy access to Michigan's beach-lined Gold Coast.

Several bus companies use the **Milwaukee Intermodal Station** (433 St Paul Ave). Badger Bus (www.badgerbus.com) goes to Madison ($20, two hours) eight times per day. Greyhound (www.greyhound.com) and Megabus (www.megabus.com) run frequent buses to Chicago (two hours) and Minneapolis (6½ to seven hours).

Amtrak (www.amtrakhiawatha.com) runs the *Hiawatha* train seven times a day to/from Chicago ($25 to $35, 1½ hours). It also uses the Milwaukee Intermodal Station.

Central Milwaukee, including the downtown area, riverwalk and neighbouring districts such as the North Side and Third Ward, is spread out, but reasonably walkable with comfortable shoes.

South Central Wisconsin

The south-central portion of Wisconsin is often overlooked, but has some unique and surprising charms. Besides being green and largely unspoiled, the area is linked with architect Frank Lloyd Wright. Wright spent the better part of his life living and working near Spring Green and maintained a school at Taliesin. Wright's students designed several distinctive buildings in and around Spring Green.

Moving south into Green County, visitors might wonder if they need to bring along their passports, so visible are the region's connections to Switzerland. Dairies around here cut a lot of cheese. New Glarus is the place to tuck into some locally made raclette and cheese fondue, while the county seat at Monroe has its own share of limburger-loving taverns. Madison is the area's cultural jewel. A livable, walkable, cyclable state capital with a boisterous student scene and some excellent places to eat, drink and party.

Green County

This pastoral area holds the nation's greatest concentration of cheesemakers. As you're road-tripping through, you can stop at local dairy farms and shops and learn your artisanal from farmstead, Gruyere from Gouda, curd from whey. Why so cheesy here? It has to do with the limestone-rich soil. It grows distinctive grass, which makes distinctive food for cows, and that results in distinctive milk that creates distinctive cheese. Got it? Old World Europeans did, particularly the Swiss. They flocked to the region in the 1800s, bringing their cheesemaking skills with them.

Pretty New Glarus, all bedecked in Swiss flags, owing to the town's cultural and commercial roots, makes for a fun stroll. It's got plenty of cowbells and cuckoo clocks (as well as atmospheric restaurants and bars for sampling the region's wares). Monroe, the biggest town and the seat of Green County, is also stuffed with cheese history and limburger taverns.

✖ Eating & Drinking

Cow & Quince　　　　　　　　AMERICAN $
(www.cowandquince.com; 407 2nd St, New Glarus; mains $12-15; ⊙9am-3pm Thu-Mon; 🐦🖋) 🅿
Excellent farm-to-table breakfast and lunch spot in central New Glarus. The owners pride themselves in sourcing nearly all the menu items within a 50-mile radius, and this dedication to detail shows up in the 'biscuits and gravy,' French toast, cheese boards and BLTs.

New Glarus Brewery　　　　　　　BREWERY
(🖉608-527-5850; www.newglarusbrewing.com; 2400 Hwy 69, New Glarus; guided tours $30; ⊙tasting room 10am-5pm Mon-Sat, from noon Sun, tours 1pm Fri; 🐦) This hilltop brewery, about a mile south of New Glarus, has won kudos around the state for its excellent Spotted Cow ale and Belgian Red (with Door County cherries). A visit here entails wandering around the brewery and then hitting the tasting room for a pint ($8 to $9.50) or three-beer sampler ($8). On Fridays, budding brewmasters are offered the possibility of a three-hour 'hard hat' guided tour ($30).

ℹ Information

Green County Tourism (www.greencounty. org) Comprehensive, well-organized website.

Traveler's Guide to America's Dairyland (www.eatwisconsincheese.com) Good map showing local dairy producers and plant tours.

ℹ Getting There & Away

Madison is the closet urban area and transportation hub. From there you'll need a car to access Green County. Hwy 69 is a main artery connecting Madison, New Glarus and Monroe. Most roads in the region are slowpoke, two-lane byways.

WORTH A TRIP

FRANK LLOYD WRIGHT'S RACINE

By most accounts, the southeastern city of Racine is an unremarkable industrial town, but it does have some key Frank Lloyd Wright sights that architecture fans won't want to miss. What's more, it's a prime place to sample the mega-sized state pastry known as the 'kringle.'

Wright devotees will want to start their exploration at the **SC Johnson Administration Building & Research Tower** (🖉262-260-2154; www.scjohnson.com/visit; 1525 Howe St; ⊙tours 10am & 2pm Thu-Sun Mar-Dec) FREE, where the architect designed several striking buildings. Free 90-minute tours take in the 1939 Admin Building, a magnificent space with tall, flared columns in its vast Great Workroom and 43 miles worth of Pyrex glass-tube windows letting in soft, natural light. You'll also see the 1950 Research Tower – where Raid, Off and other famous products were developed – which features 15 floors of curved brick bands and more Pyrex windows.

About 5 miles north of downtown, **Wingspread** (🖉262-681-3353; www.scjohnson.com/ visit; 33 E Four Mile Rd; ⊙9:30am-3:30pm Wed-Fri, 11:30am-3:30pm Sat, noon-2:30pm Sun Mar-Dec) FREE is the house Frank Lloyd Wright designed for HF Johnson Jr, one of the company's leaders. It's the last and largest of Wright's Prairie-style abodes, completed in 1939. It's enormous, with 500 windows and a 30ft-high chimney. Free tours through the building take one hour, and must be booked in advance.

I-94 runs to Racine, which is 30 miles south of Milwaukee and 75 miles north of Chicago.

Madison

Madison reaps a lot of kudos – most walkable city, best road-biking city, most vegetarian-friendly, gay-friendly, environmentally friendly and just plain all-round friendliest city in the USA. Ensconced on a narrow isthmus between Mendota and Monona Lakes, it's a pretty combination of small, grassy state capital and liberal, bookish college town.

Start your exploration around Capitol Sq, where several museums are clustered. The capitol building itself and most of the attractions around town, including the museums, are free. From here, expand your horizons outward toward the lakes, where more natural sights, including an arboretum and botanical gardens, are located. This being Wisconsin, the botanical gardens are located not far from a beer garden. Madison excels at nightlife. Find the usual cluster of student bars and clubs along State St. There's an emerging dining and drinking scene northeast of the capitol along Williamson St, which the locals simply call 'Willy.'

⊙ Sights

★ Dane County Farmers Market
FOOD & DRINKS

(www.dcfm.org; Capitol Sq; ⊙6:15am-1:45pm Sat mid-Apr–early Nov) On Saturdays, a food bazaar takes over Capitol Sq. It's one of the nation's most expansive markets, famed for its artisan cheeses and breads. Craft vendors and street musicians add to the festivities. In winter, the market moves indoors to varying locations on Wednesdays.

Olbrich Botanical Gardens
GARDENS

(☑608-246-4550; www.olbrich.org; 3330 Atwood Ave; conservatory $2, garden free; ⊙conservatory 10am-4pm, garden 9am-8pm Apr-Aug, to 6pm Sep & Oct, to 4pm Nov-Mar) Roam the 16 acres of lush outdoor gardens, including an unusual gilded Thai pavilion. The Bolz Conservatory houses rare tropical plants, free-flying birds and, from mid-July to mid-August, 'blooming' butterflies.

Chazen Museum of Art
MUSEUM

(☑608-263-2246; www.chazen.wisc.edu; 750 University Ave; ⊙9am-5pm Tue, Wed & Fri, 9am-9pm Thu, 11am-5pm Sat & Sun) FREE The universi-

---

WORTH A TRIP

ODDBALL HIGHWAY 12

Unusual sights huddle around Hwy 12 in south-central Wisconsin, all within a 55-mile span:

National Mustard Museum (☑800-438-6878; www.mustardmuseum.com; 7477 Hubbard Ave, Middleton; ⊙10am-5pm, closed Tue Jan-Mar) FREE Born of one man's ridiculously intense passion, the museum houses around 6000 mustards and kooky condiment memorabilia. Tongue-in-cheek humor abounds, especially if CMO (chief mustard officer) Barry Levenson is there to give you the shtick. It's located in Middleton, a short distance northwest of Madison.

Cow Chip Throw (www.wiscowchip.com; Grand Ave & First St, Prairie du Sac; ⊙1st weekend Sep) Prairie du Sac hosts the annual Cow Chip Throw, where 800 competitors fling dried manure patties as far as the eye can see; the record is 248ft.

Dr Evermor's Sculpture Park (☑608-219-7830; www.worldofdrevermor.com; S7703 Hwy 12, Bluffview; ⊙11am-5pm Mon & Thu-Sat, from noon Sun) FREE The doc has welded old pipes, carburetors and other salvaged metal into a hallucinatory world of futuristic birds, dragons and other bizarre structures. The crowning glory is the giant, egg-domed Forevertron, once cited by Guinness World Records as the globe's largest scrap-metal sculpture. Finding the park entrance is tricky. It is behind Delaney's Surplus on Hwy 12; look for a small road just south of Delaney's leading in. Hours can be erratic, so call to confirm it's open.

Wisconsin Dells (☑800-223-3557; www.wisdells.com; Hwy 12; ♿) The Dells is a megacenter of kitschy diversions, including 20-plus water parks, water-skiing thrill shows and epic mini-golf courses. It's a jolting contrast to the natural appeal of the area, with its scenic limestone formations carved by the Wisconsin River. To appreciate the original attraction, take a boat tour or walk the trails at nearby Mirror Lake or Devil's Lake state parks.

ty's art museum is huge and fabulous, and way beyond the norm for a campus collection. The 3rd floor holds most of the genre-spanning trove: everything from the Old Dutch Masters to Qing Dynasty porcelain vases, Picasso sculptures and Andy Warhol pop art. Free chamber-music concerts and art-house film showings take place on Sundays from September to mid-May.

🛏 Sleeping

Hotel Ruby Marie   BOUTIQUE HOTEL $$
(📞608-327-7829; www.rubymarie.com; 524 E Wilson St; r $159-179; P @ 🛜) This quirky central boutique began life in the 19th century as a modest railroad hotel. These days it's been retrofitted with all modern conveniences while retaining atmospheric period touches, like fireplaces and four-poster beds. Some rooms come with Jacuzzis. The included breakfast buffet might just rate as the best in Madison.

Graduate Madison   BOUTIQUE HOTEL $$
(📞608-257-4391; www.graduatehotels.com/madison; 601 Langdon St; r $139-219; P 🛜 🛜 🛜) A block from campus and right off State St's action, this 72-room hotel wafts a hip academic vibe with its mod-meets-plaid decor and book-themed artwork. Rooms are on the small side and can be a bit noisy, but the location rocks.

🍴 Eating & Drinking

★Old Fashioned   AMERICAN $$
(📞608-310-4545; www.theoldfashioned.com; 23 N Pinckney St; mains $12-25; ⏱7am-2am Mon-Fri, 9am-2am Sat, 9am-10pm Sun; 🛜🍴) With its dark, woodsy decor, the Old Fashioned evokes a supper club, a type of retro eatery common in Wisconsin. The menu is all local specialties, including walleye, cheese soup and sausages. It's hard to choose from among the 150 types of state-brewed suds in bottles, so opt for a sampler (four or eight little glasses) from the 50 Wisconsin tap beers.

L'Etoile   AMERICAN $$$
(📞608-251-0500; www.letoile-restaurant.com; 1 S Pinckney St; mains $44-52, multicourse tasting menu from $150; ⏱5:30-9:30pm Tue-Thu, from 5pm Fri & Sat; 🛜) 🍴 L'Etoile started doing the farm-to-table thing more than three decades ago. It's still the best in the biz, offering creative meat, fish and vegetable dishes, all sourced locally and served in a casually elegant room. Reserve in advance.

WORTH A TRIP

SPRING GREEN

Spring Green is a tiny town with big culture. **Taliesin** (📞608-588-7900; www.taliesinpreservation.org; 5607 County Rd C; ⏱9am-5:30pm May-Oct) is here, Frank Lloyd Wright's ballyhooed home and architectural school. The respected **American Players Theatre** (📞608-588-2361; www.americanplayers.org; 5950 Golf Course Rd) is also here, staging classics outdoors amid the trees (bring a picnic). And the **House on the Rock** (📞608-935-3639; www.thehouseontherock.com; 5754 Hwy 23; adult/child $15/9; ⏱9am-5pm May–mid-Oct, Thu-Mon only mid-Oct–Nov & mid-Mar–Apr, closed mid-Nov–mid-Mar) offers enough whimsy for a lifetime. Round out your art-filled day with a stay at the Prairie-style **Usonian Inn** (📞608-588-2323; www.usonianinn.com; E 5116 US 14; r $100-135; 🅿 🛜 🛜).

Spring Green is about 40 miles west of Madison on US 14.

★Memorial Union   PUB
(📞608-265-3000; www.union.wisc.edu/visit/memorial-union; 800 Langdon St; ⏱7am-midnight Mon-Fri, from 8am Sat & Sun; 🛜) The campus Union is Madison's gathering spot. The festive terrace, overlooking Lake Mendota, pours microbrews and hosts free live music and free Monday-night films, while the indoor ice-cream shop scoops hulking cones from the university dairy.

ℹ Information

Madison Convention & Visitors Bureau (www.visitmadison.com)

ℹ Getting There & Away

Badger Bus (www.badgerbus.com) has a streetside stop on campus at 700 Langdon St (next to the Memorial Union) for trips to/from Milwaukee ($20, two hours). Megabus (www.megabus.com) uses the same stop for trips to Chicago ($30, four hours) and Minneapolis ($50 to $60, five hours).

Western Wisconsin

Western Wisconsin brings on swooping green hills and button-cute towns with tree-shaded streets. Two-lane byways dip and curve through the region, revealing eating hot spots around many a bend.

EAU CLAIRE

Eau Claire (population 68,590) is basking in the glow of some favorable national publication comparisons to Austin and Portland for its aspiring hipster vibe, and city hall has begun referring to itself as the 'Indie Capital of the Midwest.' You'll still have to squint pretty hard to find a resemblance to those other cities but Eau Claire does have some great bars and restaurants, a decent live-music scene and some inspired choices for an overnight stay.

The city got its start in the middle of the 19th century and was able to leverage its position at the confluence of two important rivers, the Eau Claire and the Chippewa, to dominate the local logging industry for decades. These days, much of that industry is gone, though the riverside location continues to offer some pretty views and fun waterborne activities, such as rafting and tubing, in nice weather.

Downtown Eau Claire offers a couple of funky overnight options: the hipster-inspired **Oxbow** (☎715-839-0601; www.theoxbowhotel.com; 516 Galloway St; r/ste $145/185; P❄🛜) boutique hotel and a renovated historic **Lismore** (☎715-835-8888; www.doubletree3.hilton.com; 333 Gibson St; r/ste $130/220; P❄@🛜), plus some very good restaurants and a bustling bar and pub scene.

For an up-to-date list of events and festivals and a nice overview of things to do, check out www.visiteauclaire.com.

Eau Claire lies astride I-94, a major east–west interstate highway. US Hwy 12, a historic motorway that crisscrosses the country, passes through downtown.

The Mississippi River forms the southwest's border, and alongside it run some of the prettiest sections of the Great River Rd – the designated route that follows Old Man River throughout its 2300-mile flow. Top stops along the water include Stockholm (pie), Pepin (for Laura Ingalls Wilder fans), Nelson (cheese and ice cream), La Crosse (history, culture and bars) and Potosi (beer).

Road-tripping inland turns up bike trails in Sparta, organic farms and round barns in Viroqua, and a Frank Lloyd Wright sight in Richland Center. The old logging and industrial city of Eau Claire has a very good live-music scene and is busy trying to refashion itself as a miniature version of Austin or Portland.

Eastern Wisconsin

The eastern part of the state is a vacation favorite thanks to its miles of craggy shoreline for boating, swimming and fishing, its beaming lighthouses and its atmospheric maritime communities. Lonely islands, meals of fiery fish and football shrines all await, and there's always a lake or forest nearby for a nature fix.

Door County, a long, slender appendage that stretches out into Lake Michigan just beyond Green Bay, is a popular summer retreat for people throughout the Midwest.

People come for the coastline, camping and cycling, but mainly for that timeless summertime feel that lives on in July and August at the coastal resorts. True hermits make a beeline north to remote Washington Island, and to even more remote Rock Island. Green Bay is an unexpected treat. Fans of the NFL's Green Bay Packers will enjoy the stadium tours and football lore, while everyone else will appreciate the relaxed small-city vibe.

Green Bay

To football fans, Green Bay is synonymous with the Green Bay Packers, a legendary team in the National Football League's smallest (by far) market that's won 13 league championships, including four Super Bowls, over the past 100 years. The franchise is unique as the only community-owned nonprofit team in the NFL; perhaps pride in ownership is what makes the fans so die-hard (and also makes them wear foam-rubber cheese wedges on their heads). Indeed, football aficionados will think they died and went to heaven, with stadium tours, 'hall of fame' visits and even the chance to catch a game on the agenda.

The good news for everyone else is that Green Bay is not just football. The city has a rapidly reviving downtown, with lots of decent restaurants and authentic bars and taverns. The charming riverside port of De Pere, with its whiff of edgy chic, is just a couple of miles away.

◉ Sights & Activities

Green Bay Packers Hall of Fame   MUSEUM
(☑920-569-7512; www.lambeaufield.com; 1265 Lombardi Ave; adult/child $15/12; ◉9am-6pm Mon-Sat, 10am-5pm Sun) The two-floor Hall of Fame, located inside the atrium adjacent to Lambeau Field, is filled with Green Bay Packer memorabilia, shiny trophies and movies about the storied NFL team that'll intrigue any football fan. Buy tickets at the corner where stadium tours are offered; package deals are available for reduced rates. See the website for options and prices.

National Railroad Museum   MUSEUM
(☑920-437-7623; www.nationalrrmuseum.org; 2285 S Broadway; adult/child $10/7.50; ◉9am-5pm Mon-Sat, 11am-5pm Sun, closed Mon Jan-Mar; 👪) Forget the Packers (for just a moment), this is a must for train lovers: an enormous museum featuring some of the biggest locomotives ever to haul freight into Green Bay's vast yards. Train rides ($2) are offered in summer.

Lambeau Stadium Tours   TOURS
(☑920-569-7512; www.lambeaufield.com; 1265 Lombardi Ave; classic tour adult/child $15/9; ◉tours daily 10am, 11am, noon, 1pm, 2:30pm, 3:30pm & 4:30pm) A must for football fans of any age or stripe, Lambeau offers three tours of varying length, but most visitors will be satisfied with the hour-long 'classic' tour that takes in the luxury boxes upstairs and (the highlight) a chance to walk out onto the field. The guides are full of great stories of Packer lore.

🛏 Sleeping & Eating

Hotel Northland   HOTEL $$
(☑920-393-7499; www.thehotelnorthland.com; 304 N Adams St; r from $149; P🅿️❄@🛜) The landmark Northland, located in downtown Green Bay, opened in the 1920s as the biggest hotel in the state. After some lean years, it's re-emerged as part of Marriott's luxurious 'Autograph' collection. The spacious, dark-panelled lobby and public areas retain period charm, while the rooms are lighter and more contemporary. There's a good in-house restaurant on the ground floor.

Cannery Public Market   AMERICAN $$
(☑920-432-3300; www.thecannerymarket.com; 320 N Broadway; mains $15-30; ◉11am-9pm Tue-Fri, from 9am Sat & Sun; 🛜☑) 🍃 Every town should have a 'Cannery,' a farm-to-table restaurant serving popular regional foods with locally sourced ingredients. Green Bay's is situated in an actual cannery from the early 20th century that's been refitted with a central bar and open kitchen (though many factory details remain intact). There's a small grocery selling local meats, cheeses and beer.

❶ Getting There & Away

Green Bay has a small airport with flights to Chicago, Minneapolis, Detroit and Atlanta.

Greyhound has a station in town. It runs regularly to Milwaukee ($20, three hours) and Chicago ($25, five hours).

For motorists, I-43 comes into Green Bay from the east. I-41 comes in from the west.

Door County

With its rocky coastline, picturesque lighthouses, cherry orchards and small 19th-century villages, you have to admit Door County is pretty darn lovely. Honeymooners, families and outdoorsy types all flock in to take advantage of the parkland that blankets the area and the clapboard hamlets packed with winsome cafes, galleries and inns.

The county spreads across a narrow peninsula jutting 75 miles into Lake Michigan. Sturgeon Bay, at the southern end, is the county seat and its only real city; it's home to some decent museums. Running north, the side of the peninsula that borders the lake proper is the more scenic 'quiet side', and home to the communities of Jacksonport and Baileys Harbor. The side that borders Green Bay is more action-oriented, where hamlets such as Egg Harbor, Fish Creek, Ephraim and Sister Bay welcome travelers. Summer is prime time. Only about half the businesses stay open from November to April.

◉ Sights & Activities

Cave Point County Park   PARK
(☑920-746-9959; www.co.door.wi.gov; 5360 Schauer Rd; ◉6am-11pm) FREE As you watch waves explode into the caves beneath the shoreline cliffs here, you're likely to agree, nature is pretty amazing. There are great photo opportunities for shutterbugs and

hiking and biking paths take you to gorgeous vistas. The bonus? Cave Point is off the beaten path and is less visited than its state-park siblings. It's also free.

Newport State Park STATE PARK

(✐ campground 888-947-2757; www.dnr.wi.gov; 475 County Rd NP; per vehicle $11; ⊙ 6am-11pm) Newport is one of Door County's quietest parks, tucked away at the peninsula's northern fringe. It has a beautiful beach, 30 miles of hiking trails (about half of which double as off-road bike trails) and limited year-round camping in forested seclusion (reserve in advance). It's also an excellent spot for bird-watching and star-gazing.

Bay Shore Outfitters OUTDOORS

(✐ 920-854-7598; www.kayakdoorcounty.com; 2457 S Bay Shore Dr, Sister Bay; ⊙ 10am-5pm Mon-Sat, to 4pm Sun May-Oct) Rents kayaks, stand-up paddleboards and winter gear in season, and offers a variety of kayaking tours (from $55 per two-hour trip).

🍴 Sleeping & Eating

⭐ **White Gull Inn** HOTEL $$$

(✐ 920-868-3517; www.whitegullinn.com; 4225 Main St, Fish Creek; r $270-330; P ✹ @ ⊙) This gleaming, white-boarded inn, a short walk from the bay and central Fish Creek, looks as if it stepped from the pages of *Town & Country* magazine. The rooms are all floral-print wallpaper and four-poster beds. The inn is open year-round; rates drop out of season.

Bluefront Cafe AMERICAN $

(✐ 920-743-9218; www.thebluefrontcafe.com; 86 W Maple St, Sturgeon Bay; mains $10-13; ⊙ 11am-3pm Tue-Sun) Hands-down, this tiny cafe-restaurant is the best lunch option in Sturgeon Bay. Choose from an eclectic mix of well-done dishes such as walleye sandwiches, fish tacos and homemade meatloaf as well as more far-flung choices like curried chicken, Vietnamese-style banh mi and Asian chicken wraps. The only downside? Limited opening hours.

❶ Information

Door County Visitor Bureau (✐ 920-743-4456; www.doorcounty.com; 1015 Green Bay Rd; ⊙ 8am-5pm Mon-Fri, from 10am Sat Apr, 8am-6pm Mon-Fri, from 9am Sat & Sun May-Oct, 8am-5pm Mon-Fri, 10am-4pm Sat & Sun

Nov-Mar; ☏) The main tourist information office for the county is located just south of Sturgeon Bay. It's a good source of local information and activity maps; has brochures on art galleries, biking and lighthouses.

Egg Harbor Visitor Bureau (✐ 920-868-3717; www.doorcounty.com; 4666 Orchard Rd, Egg Harbor; ⊙ 10am-5pm Mon-Sat, 10am-3pm Sun May-Sep, noon-5pm Fri, 10am-5pm Sat, 11am-2pm Sun Oct-Apr; ☏)

Fish Creek Visitor Bureau (✐ 920-868-2316; www.doorcounty.com; 4097 Main St, Fish Creek; ⊙ 10am-5pm Mon-Sat, 10am-3pm Sun May-Oct, noon-5pm Fri, 10am-5pm Sat, 11am-2pm Sun Nov-Apr; ☏)

Sister Bay Visitor Bureau (✐ 920-854-2812; www.doorcounty.com; 2380 Gateway Dr, Sister Bay; ⊙ 10am-5pm Mon-Sat, 10am-3pm Sun May-Oct; ☏)

Sturgeon Bay Visitor Bureau (✐ 920-743-6246; www.doorcounty.com; 36 S 3rd Ave, Sturgeon Bay; ⊙ 9am-5pm Mon-Fri, 9am-3pm Sat May-Oct; ☏)

❶ Getting There & Away

You'll need a car to get to Door County. Two small highways serve the peninsula. Hwy 57 runs beside Lake Michigan, while Hwy 42 moseys beside Green Bay (the body of water, not the city). Be prepared for heavy traffic on weekends.

Northern Wisconsin

The north is a thinly populated region of forests and lakes, where folks paddle and fish in summer, and ski and snowmobile in winter. Mountain-biking trails continue to expand and draw fat tires. Nicolet National Forest and Chequamegon National Forest protect much of the area and provide the playground for these activities. But it's the windswept Apostle Islands that really steal the show.

Apostle Islands

The National Park Service's Apostle Islands, 21 rugged pieces of rock and turf floating in Lake Superior and freckling Wisconsin's northern tip, are a state highlight. Forested and windblown, trimmed with cliffs and caves, the national park gems have no facilities. Various companies offer seasonal boat trips around the islands, and kayaking is very popular. Jump off from Bayfield, a humming resort with hilly streets, Victorian-era buildings, apple orchards and nary a fast-food restaurant in sight. Outside of the kayaking opportunities, people come for the leisurely hikes or bike rides, or to poke around Bayfield's sleepy shops and enjoy some good food.

Madeline Island, an Apostle Island though not part of the national park, is a popular day trip by ferry and home to a beautiful state park and campground. Beyond Bayfield, shore towns to the north and west, such as Cornucopia, feel like a slice of heaven on a sunny July afternoon.

◉ Sights & Activities

Kayaking in the Apostles pays off big in scenery, with stacks of dusty red-rock arches and pillars rising from the water. Caves along the mainland near Meyers Beach and the craggy shores of Devils Island and Sand Island are stars of the show. Note that much of the kayaking here is for experienced paddlers only; novices should go with a guide, as conditions can be rough and windy. The national park publishes a *Paddling in the Apostles* brochure with information on kayak launch points and tips on how to prepare.

Popular outfitters, offering half- and full-day outings include **Lost Creek Outfitters** (☏715-953-2223; www.lostcreekadventures.org; 22475 Hwy 13, Cornucopia; half-/full-day tour $60/119; ☉Jun-Sep) and **Trek & Trail** (☏715-779-3595; www.trek-trail.com; 7 Washington Ave, Bayfield; half-/full-day tour $60/119; ☉Jun-Sep).

🛌 Sleeping & Eating

Camping permits (per night $15) are required for the national park islands. You must get them in advance online (www.recreation.gov; reservation fee $10).

Bayfield loads up on tidy motels, B&Bs and swanky inns. Madeline Island has a handful of inns and cottages. Book well in advance for July and August, particularly if your travels take you over a summer holiday.

★ Old Rittenhouse Inn   B&B $$
(☏715-779-5111; www.rittenhouseinn.com; 301 Rittenhouse Ave, Bayfield; r $160-230; P❋@🖥) This beautiful Victorian on a high hill, with a commanding view of the water, is a worthy splurge if you're looking for lace, creaky floorboards and a romantic escape. The location is ideal, within an easy walk of the port and downtown restaurants. Even if

WORTH A TRIP

SCENIC DRIVE: HIGHWAY 13

Hwy 13 moseys through a pretty landscape between Bayfield and Superior. Toward the east it routes around the Lake Superior shore, past the Chippewa community of **Red Cliff** and the Apostle Islands' mainland segment, which has a beach.

Tiny **Cornucopia**, looking every bit like a seaside village, has great sunsets. Toward the west, the road runs through a timeless countryside of forest and farm. See www.lakesuperiorbyway.org for more.

you're not staying here, get a table for breakfast, served in the stunning, period-piece dining room.

★ Fat Radish   AMERICAN $$
(☏715-779-9700; www.thefatradish.weebly.com; 200 Rittenhouse Ave, Bayfield; sandwiches $7-10, mains $16-24; ☉9am-3pm & 5-9pm Mon-Sat, 9am-2pm Sun, closed Mon winter; 🖥) ✐ The Radish uses quality, sustainable ingredients in its deli wares. It's located by the docks and handy for amassing snacks to take on boat tours. At night, the chef serves a scrumptious mix of beef and fish dishes, including to-die-for fish tacos, as well as plenty of vegan and vegetarian entrees. Book in advance.

❶ Information

Apostle Islands National Lakeshore Visitors Center (☏715-779-3397; www.nps.gov/apis; 410 Washington Ave, Bayfield; ☉8am-4:30pm late May-Sep, closed Sat & Sun rest of year) Has camping, paddling and hiking information.

Bayfield Chamber of Commerce (☏715-779-3335; www.bayfield.org; 42 S Broad St, Bayfield; ☉6am-8pm) Good listings of lodgings and things to do in Bayfield and the surrounding towns.

Madeline Island Information Station (☏715-747-2051; www.madferry.com; Washington Ave, Bayfield; ☉9am-6pm May-Oct) Adjacent to the Madeline Island Ferry terminal in Bayfield, the first port of call for what to see and do on Madeline Island.

❶ Getting There & Away

The **Madeline Island Ferry** (☏715-747-2051; www.madferry.com; Washington Ave, Bayfield; return adult/child/bicycle/car $15/7/7.50/27;

⏱ 7:30am-5:30pm Oct-May, to around 10pm Jun-Sep) makes the 25-minute trip from Bayfield to Madeline Island. It goes year-round, except when the water freezes (usually between January and March, when there is an ice bridge).

Apostle Islands Cruises (☑ 715-779-3925; www.apostleisland.com; 2 N Front St, Bayfield; grand tour adult/child $46/27; ⏱ mid-May–mid-Oct) drops off kayakers at various islands. Experienced paddlers kayak out to some of the closer islands.

Hwy 13 is the main road into Bayfield.

MINNESOTA

Is Minnesota really the land of 10,000 lakes, as it's so often advertised? You betcha! Actually, in typically modest style, the state has undermarketed itself – there are 11,842 lakes. Which is great news for travelers. Intrepid outdoors folk can wet their paddles in the Boundary Waters, where nighttime brings a blanket of stars and the lullaby of wolf howls.

Those wanting to get further off the beaten path can journey to Voyageurs National Park, where there's more water than roadway. If that all seems too far-flung, stick to the Twin Cities of Minneapolis and St Paul, where you can't swing a moose without hitting something cool or cultural. And for those looking for middle ground – a cross between the big city and big woods – the dramatic, freighter-filled port of Duluth beckons.

ⓘ Information

Minnesota Highway Conditions (www.511mn. org) Handy for checking winter road conditions before heading out.

Minnesota Office of Tourism (www.exploreminnesota.com) Official Minnesota travel portal.

Minnesota State Park Information (☑ reservations 866-857-2757; www.state.mn.us) Park entry requires a vehicle permit (per day/year $7/35). Tent and RV sites cost $15 to $31; reservations accepted for a $7 fee online, $10 by phone.

Minneapolis

Minneapolis is the biggest and artsiest town on the prairie, with all the trimmings of progressive prosperity – swank art museums, rowdy rock clubs, organic and ethnic eateries, and edgy theaters. It's always happenin', even in winter. And here's the bonus: folks are attitude-free and the embodiment of 'Minnesota Nice.' Count how many times they tell you to 'Have a great day,' come rain, shine or snow.

The city owes its existence to the Mississippi. Water-powered sawmills along the river fueled a boom in timber in the mid-1800s. Wheat from the prairies also needed to be processed, so flour mills churned into the next big business. The population grew rapidly in the late 19th century with mass immigration, especially from Scandinavia and Germany. There has been a more recent wave of immigration in the past few decades, from places such as Vietnam and Somalia.

MINNEAPOLIS FOR CHILDREN

Note that there are many other top sights for little ones in St Paul, at the Mall of America and Fort Snelling.

Minnesota Zoo (☑ 952-431-9500; www.mnzoo.org; 13000 Zoo Blvd; adult/child $18/12; ⏱ 9am-6pm May-Sep, to 4pm Oct-Apr; 🚼) You'll have to travel a way to get to the respected zoo in suburban Apple Valley, which is 20 miles south of town. It has naturalistic habitats for its 400-plus species, with an emphasis on cold-climate creatures. Parking is $7.

Valleyfair (☑ 952-445-7600; www.valleyfair.com; 1 Valleyfair Dr, Shakopee; adult/child $55/37; ⏱ from 10am Jun-Aug, reduced hours May, Sep & Oct; 🚼) If the rides at the Mall of America aren't enough, drive out to this full-scale amusement park 22 miles southwest in Shakopee. The animatronic dinosaur park ($5 extra) is a big hit. Save money by booking tickets online. Parking costs $12.

Children's Theatre Company (☑ 612-874-0400; www.childrenstheatre.org; 2400 3rd Ave S; shows $15-70; ⏱ box office 11am-5pm Tue-Fri; 🚼) This local troupe is so good it won a Tony award for 'outstanding regional theater.'

◉ Sights & Activities

★ **Walker Art Center**   MUSEUM
(☑612-375-7600; www.walkerart.org; 1750 Hennepin Ave; adult/child $15/free; ⊙11am-5pm Tue, Wed & Sun, to 9pm Thu, to 6pm Fri & Sat) The first-class art center has a strong permanent collection of 20th-century art and photography, including big-name US painters and great US pop art. On Monday evenings from late July to late August, the museum hosts free movies and music across the pedestrian bridge in Loring Park that are quite the to-do.

**Minneapolis
Sculpture Garden**   GARDENS
(www.walkerart.org/visit/garden; 725 Vineland Pl; ⊙6am-midnight) **FREE** This 19-acre green space, studded with contemporary works such as the oft-photographed *Spoonbridge & Cherry* by Claes Oldenburg, sits beside the Walker Art Center. The Cowles Conservatory, abloom with exotic hothouse flowers, is also on the grounds. In summer (May to September) a trippy mini-golf course (adult/child $10/8) amid the sculptures adds to the fun.

★ **Endless Bridge**   OBSERVATORY
(Guthrie Theater; 818 2nd St S; ⊙8am-8pm, to 11pm performance days) **FREE** Head inside the cobalt-blue Guthrie Theater and make your way up the escalator to the Endless Bridge, a far-out cantilevered walkway overlooking the Mississippi River. You don't need a theater ticket, as it's intended as a public space. The theater's 9th-floor Amber Box provides another knockout view.

★ **Weisman Art Museum**   MUSEUM
(☑612-625-9494; www.wam.umn.edu; 333 E River Parkway; ⊙10am-5pm Tue, Thu & Fri, 10am-8pm Wed, 11am-5pm Sat & Sun) **FREE** The Weisman, which occupies a swooping silver structure by architect Frank Gehry, is a university (and city) highlight. The airy main galleries hold cool collections of 20th-century American art, ceramics, Korean furniture and works on paper.

Minneapolis Institute of Art   MUSEUM
(☑612-870-3000; https://new.artsmia.org; 2400 3rd Ave S; ⊙10am-5pm Tue, Wed & Sat, 10am-9pm Thu & Fri, 11am-5pm Sun) **FREE** This museum is a huge trove housing a veritable history of art. The modern and contemporary collections will astonish, while the Asian galleries (2nd floor) and Decorative Arts rooms (3rd floor) are also highlights. Allot at least a few hours to visit. The museum is a mile south of downtown via 3rd Ave S.

**St Anthony Falls
Heritage Trail**   WALKING
The 1.8-mile path provides both interesting history (placards dot the route) and the city's best access to the banks of the Mississippi River. It starts at the foot of Portland Ave and goes over the car-free **Stone Arch Bridge**, from which you can view cascading St Anthony Falls.

★ Festivals & Events

Art-A-Whirl   ART
(www.nemaa.org; ⊙mid-May) The weekend-long, rock-and-roll art-gallery crawl throughout northeastern Minneapolis heralds the arrival of spring. Held at studios across the neighborhood.

Twin Cities Pride   LGBTIQ+
(www.tcpride.org; 1382 Willow St, Loring Park; ⊙mid-Jun) One of the USA's largest, the Twin Cities Pride Festival draws more than 300,000 revelers to Loring Park.

🛏 Sleeping

★ **Wales House**   GUESTHOUSE $
(☑612-331-3931; www.waleshouse.com; 1115 5th St SE; r $95, without bath $90; P❄🔊) This historic 10-bedroom B&B, in a house dating from 1910, serves as a home away from home for scholars from nearby University of Minnesota. The hosts, Kelly and Julie, go out of their way to ensure a comfortable stay. Rooms are clean and cosy, and the house has plenty of nooks and crannies for relaxing or curling up with a book.

PRINCE SIGHTS
....
Minneapolis' most famous former resident is the late music star Prince. Even before his untimely death in 2016, visitors flocked to town to follow his trail. The city's tourism bureau has a map of Prince hot spots, including his childhood home, the house from *Purple Rain* and **Paisley Park** (www.officialpaisleypark.com; 7801 Audubon Rd, Chanhassen; tours from $38.50, service fee $7.50; ⊙Thu-Mon), his famed home and recording studio. For more, check out www.minneapolis.org/princes-minneapolis.

Minneapolis

Minneapolis

Aloft   HOTEL **$$**
(☏ 612-455-8400; www.marriott.com; 900 Washington Ave S; r $159-265; P ✳ @ 🛜 ☲) Aloft's efficiently designed, industrial-toned rooms draw a younger clientele. The clubby lobby has board games, a cocktail lounge and 24-hour snacks. There's a tiny pool, a decent fitness room and a bike-share station outside the front door. Parking costs $25.

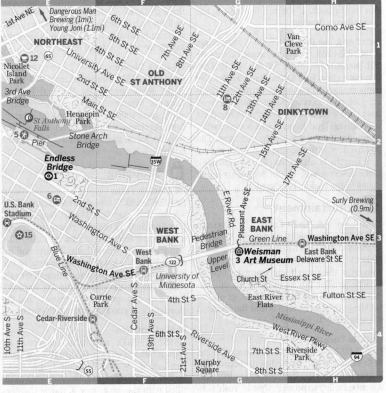

Hewing Hotel

HOTEL **$$**

(☑ 651-468-0400; www.hewinghotel.com; 300 Washington Ave N; r $140-260; P✱❄☎✉☎) This North Loop stunner offers 124 rooms spread through a century-old farm-machine warehouse. The vibe is rustic and cozy. The handsome chambers feature wood-beam ceilings, exposed brick walls and distinctive outdoorsy decor, such as deer-print wallpaper and plaid wool blankets. It's within walking distance of downtown's action (plus there's a bar-restaurant on-site). Parking costs $46.

✕ Eating

My Huong

VIETNAMESE **$**

(☑ 612-702-2922; www.myhuongkitchen.com; 2718 Nicollet Ave S; mains $10-14; ☉ 11am-9pm Tue-Sat, to 6pm Sun; ☑) A modest Vietnamese restaurant turning out authentic versions of banh mi, pho, rolls and lemongrass dishes to an appreciative 'Eat Street' public. The dining room is tiny, but don't let that dissuade you from arguably the best Vietnamese food in the area.

Safari

SOMALI **$**

(☑ 612-353-5341; www.safarirestaurant.net; 3010 4th Avenue S; mains $12-15; ☉ 11am-midnight) Widely considered the city's best Somali restaurant, Safari is the place to dabble in chicken *suqaar*, marinated slices of meat served in a heap of spiced Somali rice, or 'Chicken Fantastic,' grilled chicken breast placed over rice and covered in a mild cream sauce.

★ Young Joni

PIZZA **$$**

(☑ 612-345-5719; www.youngjoni.com; 165 13th Ave NE; mains $14-19; ☉ 4-11pm Tue-Thu, 4pm-midnight Fri, noon-midnight Sat, noon-10pm Sun) Young Joni fuses two seemingly unrelated types: pizza and Korean food. Here, you can order a wood-fired, crisp-crusted prosciutto, gruyere and ricotta pie with a side of spicy clams, kimchi and tofu. It sounds odd, but the dishes are terrific. Bonus: the hip, industrial space has a hidden bar in back. If the red light is on, the cocktails are flowing.

Butcher & the Boar
AMERICAN $$$

(☑612-238-8888; www.butcherandtheboar.com; 1121 Hennepin Ave; mains $35-60; ⊗5-10:30pm Mon-Thu, to 11pm Fri & Sat, to 10pm Sun; 🔊) The coppery, candlelit room is carnivore nirvana. Get your carving knife ready for wild boar ham with country butter, chicken-fried veal sausage and many more house-crafted meats. Sampler plates are the way to go. The 30 taps flow with regional brews, backed up by a lengthy bourbon list (flights available). Make reservations, or opt for meaty small plates in the rockin' beer garden.

☆ Entertainment

First Avenue & 7th St Entry
LIVE MUSIC

(☑612-332-1775; www.first-avenue.com; 701 1st Ave N; shows from $20) This is the long-standing bedrock of Minneapolis' music scene. First Avenue is the main room featuring national acts; smaller 7th St Entry is for up-and-comers. Check out the exterior stars on the building: they're all bands that have graced the stage. Buy tickets via the website.

Guthrie Theater
THEATER

(☑612-377-2224; www.guthrietheater.org; 818 2nd St S; shows $30-90; ⊗box office 11am-5pm) This is Minneapolis's top-gun theater troupe, with a jumbo facility to prove it. Unsold 'rush' tickets go on sale 30 minutes before showtime for $15 to $35 (cash only). Download free audio tours from the website for self-guided jaunts around the funky building.

Target Field
BASEBALL

(☑800-338-9467; www.mlb.com/twins; 353 N 5th St; 🅁blue, green) This downtown stadium is home field for Major League Baseball's Minnesota Twins. The season runs from April through October (that is, if the Twins play well enough to make it into October). The stadium is notable for its beyond-the-norm, locally focused food and drink.

US Bank Stadium
SPECTATOR SPORT

(☑612-338-4537; www.vikings.com; 900 5th St S; 🔊; 🅁blue, green) The National Football League's Minnesota Vikings play at this spiffy, glass-walled indoor arena on Sundays from September through December. See the website for a game schedule. Buy tickets online.

🛍 Shopping

★ Electric Fetus
MUSIC

(☑612-870-9300; www.electricfetus.com; 2000 4th Ave S; ⊗9am-9pm Mon-Fri, 9am-8pm Sat, 11am-6pm Sun) This indie record store sells a whopping selection of new and used CDs and vinyl, plus groovy hats, T-shirts and incense. It has the lowdown on the local music scene, complete with concert tickets for sale (check the whiteboard behind the counter). Prince used to come here to browse, and the store stocks a good selection of his tunes.

Mall of America
MALL

(☑952-883-8800; www.mallofamerica.com; off I-494 at 24th Ave; ⊗10am-9:30pm Mon-Sat, 11am-7pm Sun; 🚼; 🅁blue) Welcome to the USA's largest shopping center. Yes, it's just a mall, filled with the usual stores, movie theaters and eateries. But there's also a wedding chapel inside. And an 18-hole **mini-golf course** (☑952-883-8777; 3rd fl; per person $12; ⊗10am-9:30pm Mon-Sat, 11am-7pm Sun). And a zipline. And an amusement park, aka **Nickelodeon Universe** (☑952-883-8800; www.nickelodeonuniverse.com; ⊗10am-9:30pm Mon-

---

LGBTIQ+ MINNEAPOLIS

Minneapolis has one of the country's highest percentages of lesbian, gay, bisexual and transgender residents, and the city enjoys strong LGBTIQ+ rights. Pick up the free, bi-weekly magazine *Lavender* (www.lavendermagazine.com) at coffee shops around town for info on the scene. Pride Festival (p615) is one of the USA's largest, drawing more than 300,000 revelers. Top picks:

Wilde Cafe (☑612-331-4544; www.wildecafe.com; 65 Main St SE; ⊗7am-9pm Sun-Thu, to 11pm Fri & Sat; 🔊) It features amazing baked goods, riverfront digs and a Victorian ambience worthy of its namesake, Oscar Wilde; *Lavender* once ranked it 'best cafe.'

Gay Nineties (☑612-333-7755; www.gay90s.com; 408 Hennepin Ave; cover $5-10; ⊗8am-2am Mon-Sat, from 10am Sun; 🔊) This long-standing club has dancing, dining and drag shows that attract both a gay and straight clientele.

TAP ROOM BOOM

Minneapolis is all in on the local brewing trend, and most makers have taprooms. Excellent ones to try for beer fresh from the tank:

LynLake Brewery (☎612-224-9682; www.lynlakebrewery.com; 2934 Lyndale Ave S; ☺5-10pm Mon-Thu, 5pm-1am Fri, noon-1am Sat, noon-10pm Sun; ☎) The setting is ideal: an atmospheric, rehabbed former theater with a fun rooftop terrace.

Fulton Beer (☎612-333-3208; www.fultonbeer.com; 414 6th Ave N; ☺3-10pm Tue-Thu, to 3-11pm Fri, 11am-11pm Sat, 11am-6pm Sun) There's usually a fab pale ale and blonde ale among the selection that you sip at communal picnic tables in the warehouse. It's a few blocks from the baseball stadium and fills up on game days.

Dangerous Man Brewing (☎612-236-4087; www.dangerousmanbrewing.com; 1304 2nd St NE; ☺4-10pm Tue-Thu, 3pm-midnight Fri, noon-midnight Sat, noon-8pm Sun) Pours strong, European-style beers in the happenin' Northeast. You're welcome to bring in your own food (there's a choice fish-and-chips place a block east).

Surly Brewing (☎763-999-4040; www.surlybrewing.com; 520 Malcolm Ave SE; ☺11am-11pm Sun-Thu, to midnight Fri & Sat; ☎; ♻green) Surly's sprawling, mod-industrial, family-friendly beer hall is mobbed by locals who come for the rotating taps and abundant meaty snacks. It's in the Prospect Park neighborhood, next to the university and a short walk from the Prospect Park Green Line rail station.

Sat, 11am-7pm Sun), with 28 rides, including a couple of scream-inducing roller coasters. To walk through will cost you nothing; a one-day, unlimited-ride wristband is $37; or you can pay for rides individually ($3.60 to $7.20).

❶ Information

Minneapolis Visitor Information (☎612-397-9278; www.minneapolis.org; 505 Nicollet Mall, Suite 100; ☺9am-6pm Mon-Fri, to 5pm Sat, to 3pm Sun; ☎) The staff at this downtown tourist office will bend over backwards to help you set up an itinerary, sort out transportation or find a place to eat or drink. In addition to the copious brochures and maps, there's also an on-site souvenir and gift shop.

❶ Getting There & Away

The Minneapolis–St Paul International Airport (p621), 10 miles south of central Minneapolis, is a major regional hub, with direct connections to cities around the United States. Delta Airlines operates direct flights to/from Europe. The airport has two terminals, Lindbergh and Humphrey, with most airlines operating from the former. Always double-check the correct terminal when purchasing tickets.

Both terminals have ATMs and car-rental agencies. The Blue Line light-rail service (regular/rush-hour $2/2.50, 25 minutes) is the cheapest way to get to downtown Minneapolis. Taxis cost around $45.

Greyhound (☎612-371-3325; www.greyhound.com; 950 Hawthorne Ave; ☎) runs frequent buses to Milwaukee ($30 to $40, seven hours), Chicago ($35 to $45, nine hours) and Duluth ($25 to $30, three hours).

Megabus (www.megabus.com) runs express to Milwaukee ($40 to $45, 6½ hours) and Chicago ($45, 8½ hours). It departs from both downtown and the university; check the website for exact locations.

Amtrak chugs in to the gleaming Union Depot (p621) in nearby St Paul. Trains go daily to Chicago ($35, eight hours) and Milwaukee ($30, seven hours).

❶ Getting Around

Minneapolis hovers near the top of rankings for best bike city in the US. **Nice Ride** (www.niceridemn.org) is the local bike-share program, with 1800 lime-green bikes in 200 self-serve kiosks around the Twin Cities. A 30-minute ride costs $3. Insert a credit card, get your ride code, then unlock a bike. See the **Minneapolis Bicycle Program** (www.ci.minneapolis.mn.us/bicycles) for cycling information and trail maps.

Traditional rentals work better for longer recreational rides. Several companies offer rentals around town.

Wheel Fun Rentals (Kiosk at Bde Maka Ska; ☎612-823-5765; www.wheelfunrentals.com; 3000 Calhoun Parkway E, base of W Lake St; bike per hr/day $12/40; ☺9am-8:30pm late May–mid-Aug, reduced hours mid-Aug–late Oct) rents mountain bikes and tandems by the hour or day from a convenient location near Uptown.

Metro Transit (☑612-373-3333; www.metro-transit.org; ☺peak/off-peak $2.50/$2) runs the handy Blue Line light rail between downtown and the Mall of America (stopping at the airport en route). The Green Line light rail connects downtown Minneapolis with Union Depot in downtown St Paul.

Machines at each station sell fare cards, including all-day passes ($6.50) that also can be used on public buses.

St Paul

St Paul, Minnesota's capital city, is smaller and quieter than its twin to the west, Minneapolis. While Minneapolis is all glitz and bustle, St Paul is more prim and proper and has managed to retain more of its historic character. St Paul's amenities are more modest as well, though the capital does excel when it comes to breweries and brew pubs.

The city is well worth a day's diversion from Minneapolis to stroll through the historic residential areas southwest of downtown, particularly along Summit Ave, or closer to the Mississippi River around Irvine Park, to gawk at the late-19th- and early-20th-century mansions. This is also F Scott Fitzgerald's old stomping grounds, and the house he was born in as well as the house where he lived when he published *This Side of Paradise* are still standing.

◉ Sights & Activities

Landmark Center MUSEUM
(☑651-292-3225; www.landmarkcenter.org; 75 W 5th St; ☺8am-5pm Mon-Fri, 8am-8pm Thu, 10am-5pm Sat, noon-5pm Sun) Downtown's turreted 1902 Landmark Center used to be the federal courthouse, where gangsters such as Alvin 'Creepy' Karpis were tried; plaques next to the various rooms show who was brought to justice here. In addition to the city's visitor center, the building also contains a couple of small museums (one focusing on wood art, another on music).

Down In History Tours WALKING
(☑651-292-1220; www.wabashastreetcaves.com; 215 S Wabasha St; tours $9-10; ☺4pm Mon, 5pm Thu, 11am Sat & Sun May-Sep) These 45-minute tours explore St Paul's underground caves, which gangsters once used as a speakeasy. The fun ramps up on Thursday nights, when a swing band plays in the caverns (additional $8).

🎊 Festivals & Events

St Paul Winter Carnival CULTURAL
(www.winter-carnival.com; ☺late Jan-early Feb) Ten days of ice sculptures, ice-skating and ice fishing. Events take place at Rice Park and other venues around the city.

🛏 Sleeping & Eating

★**Hotel 340** BOUTIQUE HOTEL $$
(☑651-280-4120; www.hotel340.com; 340 Cedar St; r $109-199; P❄@☂) Hotel 340 delivers old-world ambience aplenty, and it's usually a great deal to boot. The 56 rooms in the stately old building have hardwood floors and plush linens. The two-story lobby stokes a grand fireplace and a nifty little bar (the desk staff double as bartenders). Parking costs $17 per night.

Covington Inn B&B $$
(☑651-292-1411; www.covingtoninn.com; 100 Harriet Island Rd; r $165-250; P❄☂) This four-room, Harriet Island B&B is on a tugboat floating in the Mississippi River; watch the river traffic glide by while sipping your morning coffee. The stately rooms have bright splashes of color, and each has a gas fireplace to keep you toasty in winter.

★**Keg & Case** FOOD HALL $
(☑651-443-6060; www.kegandcase.com; 928 7th St W; sandwiches $12-15; ☺6:30am-10pm Sun-Fri, to midnight Sat; ☂🅿) 🌱 A scrumptious food hall, with stalls serving locally sourced sandwiches, pizza, ice cream and other food items in a spiffy, remodeled brewery space. In addition to food vendors, there are stalls where you can purchase mushrooms, condiments, jellies and gifts. It's well worth the trip south of downtown. There are plenty of vegetarian options.

Cook AMERICAN $
(☑651-756-1787; www.cookstp.com; 1124 Payne Ave; mains $10-15; ☺7am-2pm Mon, Thu & Fri, 7am-3pm Sat & Sun) This cute, sunny spot serves creative diner dishes (gingery French toast, curried veggie burgers, braised short-rib sandwiches), including some with a spicy Korean twist. Cook also hosts Korean dinners on Friday nights. It's located in the burgeoning East Side neighborhood, where several other foodie hot spots are sprouting on Payne Ave.

🍷 Drinking & Entertainment

Summit Brewing Company BREWERY
(☑651-265-7800; www.summitbrewing.com; 910
Montreal Circle; ⊙2-9pm Thu & Fri, noon-9pm
Sat, noon-6pm Sun) While Summit is one of
the state's largest brewers, its beer hall is
welcomingly low-key. Inside it's a big open
space with communal tables, large windows
and around 14 beers on tap. Outside there's a
patio that overlooks the river bluffs. Try the
Keller pils, oatmeal stout or anything in the
experimental Unchained series. Everything
is really reasonably priced.

Allianz Field SPECTATOR SPORT
(www.mnufc.com; 400 Snelling Ave N) The gleaming home field of Minnesota United FC of
the North American Soccer League opened
its doors in 2019. See the website for a current schedule. Buy tickets online.

Fitzgerald Theater THEATER
(☑651-290-1200; www.thefitzgeraldtheater.com;
10 E Exchange St) This atmospheric theater
hosts big-name musicians, comedians and
authors in association with Minnesota Public Radio. See the website for a list of events
and ticket information.

ℹ️ Information

Mississippi River Visitor Center (☑651-
293-0200; www.nps.gov; 120 W Kellogg Blvd;
⊙9:30am-5pm Sun & Tue-Thu, to 9pm Fri &
Sat) Operated by the National Park Service,
it occupies an alcove in the science museum
lobby. Stop by to pick up trail maps and see
what sort of free ranger-guided activities are
going on. In summer these include short hikes
to the river and bicycle rides. In winter, there
are ice-fishing and snowshoeing jaunts.

St Paul Visitor Center (☑651-292-3225; www.
visitsaintpaul.com; 75 W 5th St; ⊙10am-4pm
Mon-Sat, from noon Sun) In the Landmark
Center, it makes a good first stop for maps and
DIY walking-tour info.

ℹ️ Getting There & Around

Union Depot (☑651-202-2700; www.union
depot.org; 214 E 4th St; 🛜), St Paul's grand
train station, is the hub for everything: Greyhound buses, city buses, the Green Line light
rail and Amtrak trains.

Minneapolis–St Paul International Airport
(MSP; ☑612-726-5555; www.mspairport.com;
4300 Glumack Dr, St Paul; 🛜; 🚇 blue) is 15
miles southwest. Bus 54 (regular/rush-hour
$2/2.50, 25 minutes) goes downtown. A taxi
costs around $35.

WORTH A TRIP

STILLWATER

Hilly Stillwater (population 19,400)
on the lower St Croix River, is an old
logging town with beautifully restored
19th-century buildings, paddle-wheel
steamboats churning by and antique
shops galore. It's touristy, but it's hard to
deny its time-warped charm. Stillwater
proudly declaims itself as the birthplace
of Minnesota. It was here in 1848 where
settlers from then-Wisconsin's vast
northwestern territories met to petition
the US Congress for statehood. They
agreed on the name 'Minnesota', with the
state eventually joining the union in 1858.

For a terrific boutique overnighter, try
Lora (☑651-571-3500; www.lorahotel.com;
402 Main St S; r $160-260; 🅿️✳️@🛜).

Discover Stillwater (www.discover
stillwater.com) has good online listings
of what to see and do.

To get here from Minneapolis-St Paul,
follow I-694, turning off onto Hwy 36.

Metro Transit (www.metrotransit.org) op-
erates bus service in both Minneapolis and
St Paul and runs the handy Green Line light
rail (regular/rush hour $2/2.50) between St
Paul, starting at Union Depot, and downtown
Minneapolis.

Southern Minnesota

Southern Minnesota keeps it fresh with a
mix of historic river towns, Bluff Country's
pastoral hamlets and oddball attractions, including the **Spam Museum** (☑507-437-5100;
www.spam.com; 101 3rd Ave NE, Austin; ⊙10am-
6pm Mon-Sat, 11am-5pm Sun May-Sep, 10am-5pm
Mon-Sat, 11am-4pm Sun Oct-Apr) **FREE** and the
world's largest ball of twine (1st St, Darwin;
⊙24hr) **FREE**.

Atmospheric towns on the water include
Stillwater (antique laden), Red Wing (known
for its Red Wing Shoes – actually more like
sturdy boots – and salt glaze pottery) and
Wabasha (where eagles flock). More intriguing little burgs also pop up along this stretch
of the Great River Rd, the scenic thoroughfare that clasps the Mississippi River. Pull
over for a slice of pie or kitschy garden-
gnome shop whenever the mood strikes.

Inland and south, Bluff Country is dotted
with pretty limestone cliffs and teeny villages. Lanesboro is a gem for rails-to-trails

cycling. Harmony, south of Lanesboro, is the center of an Amish community and another welcoming spot.

The river towns feature inns and B&Bs in vintage, restored buildings; Stillwater has them in abundance. Bluff Country towns are also big on B&Bs, as well as campgrounds.

Old-school diners and coffee shops are common, especially along the Great River Rd. But surprisingly polished cafes also appear in what seems like the middle of nowhere.

The Great River Rd, aka Hwy 61, rolls along the Mississippi River. If you cross a bridge to the Wisconsin side, it becomes Hwy 35. Minneapolis is an hour or two by car from most hot spots in the region.

Northern Minnesota

Northern Minnesota is a veritable outdoor playground. The immense Boundary Waters wilderness is the main draw, and from May through September, kayaks and canoes ply the state's many fabled lakes, though the area is big enough to still feel as if you have the place to yourself. The red-cliffed Lake Superior shoreline and watery Voyageurs National Park are also popular seasonal destinations.

The north has a compelling heritage story to tell as well. For decades the region's biggest city and port, Duluth, shipped the iron ore that fueled mills throughout the Midwest. You can see the old ships and catch some of the city's revivalist spirit, this time centered around craft beer. The old mining town of Hibbing, at the heart of the Iron Range District, is home to an iron-ore mine so vast, it's referred to as Minnesota's 'Grand Canyon.'

Duluth

Duluth is a brawny shot-and-a-beer port town that offers visitors a glimpse into its storied history as a major shipping center, as well as some citified cultural, dining and drinking amenities. Duluth grew wealthy throughout most of the 20th century as a major exporter of high-quality iron ore, which was carted away on vast ships over the Great Lakes to factories and mills in Michigan, Indiana and Ohio. The port suffered in the 1970s and '80s, though, as the mills shut and the ore reserves dried up. Shipping is still a major industry, but offi-cials have now turned to tourism to supplement the local economy. You'll find a smattering of interesting sights near the port centered on Duluth's industrial past as well as a burgeoning adventure-sports scene. The downtown is rejuvenating rapidly and there's a fun craft-beer and cider subculture developing on the formerly seedy streets, west of the downtown.

⊙ Sights & Activities

Aerial Lift Bridge   BRIDGE
Duluth's main landmark raises its mighty arm to let horn-bellowing ships into port. About 1000 vessels per year glide through.

Maritime Visitor Center   MUSEUM
(☑ 218-720-5260; www.lsmma.com; 600 S Lake Ave; ⊙ 10am-9pm Jun-Aug, reduced hours Sep-May) FREE Located next to the Aerial Lift Bridge, the center has computer screens inside that tell what time the big ships will be sailing through. Cool model boats and exhibits on Great Lakes shipwrecks also make it a top stop in town.

Duluth Traverse   BICYCLING
(www.coggs.com) A 40-mile mountain-bike trail that spans the city and surrounding area? Riders are stoked for the Duluth Traverse, a single-track path that's opening bit by bit and linking several existing trails. When it's finished, no Duluth resident will be more than a few minutes from the route. Runners, hikers and snowshoers can also commune with the pines along the way.

Duluth Experience   ADVENTURE
(☑ 218-464-6337; www.theduluthexperience.com; tours from $79) This outfit offers a range of kayaking, cycling and brewery tours; gear and transportation are provided. Most jaunts depart from Fitger's.

🛏 Sleeping

Park Point Marina Inn   HOTEL $$
(☑ 218-491-7111; www.parkpointmarinainn.com; 1033 Minnesota Ave; r $110-170; P ✳ @ 🤖 🐾) This immaculate property is located south of the Aerial Lift Bridge on the point that juts out into Lake Superior. Don't expect luxury, but rather tidy, well-maintained rooms and public areas, and a clean pool for the kids. The attractions around Canal Park are 10 minutes' walk away, but you'll need your own wheels to get much further than that.

Fitger's Inn
HOTEL $$$

(☑218-722-8826; www.fitgers.com; 600 E Superior St; r $185-290; P@🛜) Fitger's created its 62 large rooms, each with slightly varied decor, from an old brewery. Located on the Lakewalk, the pricier rooms have great water views. The free shuttle to local sights is handy.

✕ Eating

Corktown Deli & Brews
DELI $

(☑218-606-1607; www.corktowndeli.com; 1906 W Superior St; mains $10-13; ⊗7:45am-9pm Sun-Thu, to 10pm Fri & Sat) This lively, informal deli in the Lincoln Park Craft District is hands-down the best lunch option around. Grab a table or sit at the bar, and choose from a tantalizing list of excellent sandwiches and salads, including our new fave, the 'Lake Superior' (wild rice and smoked whitefish). There's a daily mix of craft beers on the board.

★OMC Smokehouse
BARBECUE $$

(☑218-606-1611; www.omcsmokehouse.com; 1909 W Superior St; mains $15-30; ⊗11am-9pm Sun-Thu, to 10pm Fri & Sat) The 'OMC' stands for 'Oink, Moo, Cluck,' but we'll give them a pass because of the outstanding quality of the smoked meats, as well as inventive menu items such as catfish tacos and pork 'n' grits. For drinks, there's a strong lineup of local craft brews from Bent Paddle and Castle Danger. Find it in the Lincoln Park Craft District

New Scenic Cafe
AMERICAN $$$

(☑218-525-6274; www.newsceniccafe.com; 5461 North Shore Dr; sandwiches $15-17, mains $26-32; ⊗11am-9pm Sun-Thu, to 10pm Fri & Sat) 🍴 Foodies travel from far and near to New Scenic Cafe, 8 miles beyond Duluth on Old Hwy 61. There, in a humble wood-paneled room, they fork into rustic salmon with creamed leeks or a slice of triple berry pie, all served with a generous helping of lake views. Make reservations.

🍷 Drinking & Entertainment

Duluth Cider
BAR

(☑218-464-1111; www.duluthcider.com; 2307 W Superior St; ⊗noon-10pm Mon-Thu, to 11pm Fri & Sat, to 8pm Sun; 🛜) This cider-maker and taproom, in the Lincoln Park Craft District, was hived from an old livery for the Duluth post office. You'll find a creative menu of apple-based hard ciders, including varieties infused with tequila-oak, orange and strawberry.

DYLAN IN DULUTH

While the town of Hibbing and the Iron Range are most often associated with Bob Dylan, he was born in Duluth in 1941. You'll see brown-and-white signs on Superior St and London Rd for **Bob Dylan Way** (www.bobdylanway.com), pointing out places associated with the legend (like the armory where he saw Buddy Holly in concert, and decided to become a musician). But you're on your own to find **Dylan's birthplace** (519 N 3rd Ave E), up a hill a few blocks northeast of downtown. Dylan lived on the top floor until age six, when his family moved inland to Hibbing. It's a private residence (and unmarked), so all you can do is stare from the street.

Norshor Theatre
THEATER

(☑218-733-7555; www.norshortheatre.com; 211 E Superior St) Standing at the center of the city's efforts to revitalize the central business district, this landmark's offerings vary from standard theater to concert performances and screenings of classic films. Check the website.

ℹ Information

Duluth Visitors Center (☑800-438-5884; www.visitduluth.com; 21 W Superior St; ⊗8:30am-5pm Mon-Fri) Pick up a visitor guide; the website has deals and coupons.

ℹ Getting There & Away

Greyhound (☑218-722-5591; www.greyhound. com; 228 W Michigan St) has several buses daily to Minneapolis ($25 to $30, three hours).

North Shore

A trip here is dominated by water – mainly enormous, tempestuous Lake Superior – where ore-toting freighters ply the ports, little fishing fleets haul in the day's catch and wave-bashed cliffs offer awesome views if you're willing to trek. Numerous river valleys, waterfalls, hiking trails and little towns speckle the landscape as it unfurls to the Canadian border.

The highlights along the shoreline highway that leads north from Duluth include a series of state parks that offer their own unique delights. You'll find twisting gorges and dramatic waterfalls at Gooseberry Falls,

Judge CR Magney and Temperance River state parks. A lonely lighthouse beckons at Split Rock, not far from Two Harbors. The picturesque artistic retreat at Grand Marais, with its relatively 'big city' amenities such as good food and drink, caps off the drive. The town's tranquil harbor and seaside locale have been luring painters and other romantic types here for more than 70 years.

◉ Sights & Activities

The 300-mile **Superior Hiking Trail** (www. shta.org) follows the lake-hugging ridgeline between Duluth and the Canadian border. Along the way it passes dramatic red-rock overlooks and the occasional moose and black bear. Trailheads with parking lots pop up every 5 to 10 miles, making it ideal for day hikes. The **Superior Shuttle** (☑218-834-5511; www.superiorhikingshuttle.com; from $20; ⊙Fri-Sun mid-May–mid-Oct) makes life even easier, picking up trekkers from 17 stops along the route. Overnight hikers will find 86 backcountry campsites and several lodges to cushion the body come nightfall; the trail website has details. The whole footpath is free, with no reservations or permits required. The **trail office** (☑218-834-2700; www.superiorhiking.org; 731 7th Ave, Suite 2; ⊙10am-4:30pm Mon, Thu & Fri) in Two Harbors provides maps and planning assistance.

Split Rock Lighthouse
State Park   STATE PARK
(☑218-595-7625; www.dnr.state.mn.us; 3755 Split Rock Lighthouse Rd, Two Harbors; per car $7, lighthouse adult/child $10/8; ⊙10am-6pm mid-May–mid-Oct, 11am-4pm Thu-Mon mid-Oct–mid-May) This is the most visited spot on the entire North Shore. The shiner itself is a state historic site with a separate admission fee. Guided tours are available (they depart

hourly), or you can explore on your own. If you don't mind stairs, say 170 or so each way, tramp down the cliff to the beach for incredible views of the lighthouse and surrounding shore.

Sawtooth Outfitters   KAYAKING
(☑218-663-7643; www.sawtoothoutfitters.com; 7216 Hwy 61, Tofte; ⊙8am-6pm daily May-late Oct & mid-late Dec, 8am-6pm Thu-Mon Jan-early Apr) Offers guided kayaking tours (half-/full day $60/120) for all levels of paddling on the Temperance River and out on Lake Superior, as well as easier jaunts on wildlife-rich inland lakes. Sawtooth also rents mountain bikes (from $22 per day) to pedal over the many trails in the area, including the popular **Gitchi Gami State Bike Trail** (www. ggta.org).

🛏 Sleeping & Eating

★Hungry Hippie
Farm & Hostel   HOSTEL $
(☑218-387-2256; www.hungryhippiehostel.com/the-farm; 410 County Rd 14; dm/r $35/60; ᴘ🅿❄🛜) If you've ever dreamt of escaping and just getting away from it all, this remote farmhouse-hostel, 8 miles east of Grand Marais, is the place to indulge those fantasies. The rooms are farmhouse chic, straight out of a design magazine. The welcome is warm. Choose from a bunk in a six-bed dorm or your own private room.

★Northern Rail Traincar Inn   HOTEL $$
(☑218-834-0955; www.northernrail.net; 1730 Hwy 3; r/ste $139/199; ❄🛜) It doesn't get much cooler than 17 rooms built into renovated train boxcars. Rooms are on the small side, but quaintly furnished by theme (Victorian, golf, moose, safari). They have private bathrooms and TVs with DVD players.

SCENIC DRIVE: HIGHWAY 61

Hwy 61 conjures a headful of images. Local boy Bob Dylan mythologized it in his angry 1965 album *Highway 61 Revisited*. It's the fabled 'Blues Highway' clasping the Mississippi River en route to New Orleans. And in northern Minnesota, it evokes red-tinged cliffs and forested beaches as it follows Lake Superior's shoreline.

But let's back up and get a few things straight. The Blues Highway is actually US 61, and it starts just north of the Twin Cities. Hwy 61 is a state scenic road, and it starts in Duluth. To confuse matters more, there are two 61s between Duluth and Two Harbors: a four-lane expressway and a two-lane 'Old Hwy 61' (also called North Shore Scenic Drive). Take the latter; it morphs from London Rd in Duluth and veers off to the right just past the entrance to Brighton Beach. After Two Harbors, Hwy 61 returns to one strip of pavement – a gorgeous drive that goes all the way to the Canadian border. For more information, check the North Shore Scenic Drive at www.superiorbyways.com.

Wi-fi is hit or miss in the steel cars, but it's available in the lobby. Continental breakfast is included.

Naniboujou Lodge LODGE $$
(☑ 218-387-2688; www.naniboujou.com; 20 Naniboujou Trail; r $130-180; ☺ late May-late Oct; P✳︎🐾) Built in the 1920s, the property was once a private club for Babe Ruth and his contemporaries, who smoked cigars in the Great Hall, warmed by the 20ft-high stone fireplace. The pièce de résistance is the hall's massive domed ceiling painted with mind-blowing, psychedelic-colored Cree Indian designs. Rooms vary in decor, but each offers an away-from-it-all experience. It's 14 miles northeast of Grand Marais.

★**Gun Flint Tavern** AMERICAN $$
(☑ 218-387-1563; www.gunflinttavern.com; 111 W Wisconsin St; mains $18-25; ☺ 11am-10pm; 🐾) You'll find excellent soups and sandwiches, the town's best burgers, and an array of heartier evening meals, such as steaks and walleye, at this central restaurant and tavern. A good range of seasonal and popular microbrews pour from the taps, and the adjacent Raven lounge carries on after the restaurant closes. Book in advance for dinner.

❶ Getting There & Away

Hwy 61 is the main vein through the North Shore. The state scenic route moseys all the way to Canada. Duluth is the closest urban area with an airport. Public transport is scarce in these parts and you'll mostly need your own wheels to get around.

Boundary Waters

Legendarily remote and pristine, the Boundary Waters Canoe Area Wilderness (BWCAW) is one of the world's premier paddling regions. More than 1000 lakes and streams speckle the piney, 1.1-million-acre expanse. Nature lovers make the pilgrimage for the 1500 miles of canoe routes, rich wildlife and sweeping solitude. If you're willing to dig in and canoe for a while, it'll just be you and the moose, bears, wolves and loons that roam the landscape.

It's possible to glide in for the day, but most people opt for at least a night of camping. Experienced paddlers flock here, but beginners are welcome, too, and everyone can get set up with gear from local lodges and outfitters. The engaging town of Ely (pronounced *ee*-lee), northeast of the Iron Range, is the best place to start, as it has scores of accommodations, restaurants and outfitters. You can also access the Boundary Waters from coastal Grand Marais by following the Gunflint Trail (www.gunflint-trail.com), aka Hwy 12.

Canoeing is what everyone is here for May through September. In winter, Ely gets mushy – it's a renowned dogsledding town. **Ely Bike & Kicksled** (☑ 218-365-2453; www.elybikeandkicksled.com; 125 N Central Ave, Ely; mountain bikes per hr/day $8/40; ☺ 9:30am-5pm Thu-Sat) rents bikes from May to September, and kicksleds during the winter.

You need to be prepared for a real wilderness adventure when canoeing in the Boundary Waters. The **Superior National Forest Office** (☑ 218-626-4395; www.fs.usda.gov/attmain/superior/specialplaces) publishes a handy BWCAW trip planning guide. It has information on what to bring and how to get the required entry permits. For camping, an overnight permit from the **National Park Service** (☑ camping permits 877-444-6777; www.recreation.gov; overnight permits adult/child $16/8, plus reservation fee $6) is necessary. Day-visit permits, though free, are also required; get them at BWCAW entry-point kiosks or ranger stations. Plan ahead, as permits are quota restricted and often run out. Outfitters can help plan the logistics.

Besides remote camping, the area has loads of lodges, though these often have a minimum-stay requirement (usually three days). Downtown Ely has several midrange inns and small hotels. July and August are busy, so book ahead.

❶ Information

Kawishiwi Ranger Station (☑ 218-365-7600; www.fs.usda.gov; 1393 Hwy 169, Ely; ☺ 8am-4:30pm May-Sep, closed Sat & Sun Oct-Apr) Provides expert BWCAW camping and canoeing details, trip suggestions and required permits.

❶ Getting There & Away

Hwy 169 (which becomes Sheridan St in Ely) connects the Boundary Waters to the Iron Range and its towns. Hwy 1 links the Boundary Waters to the Lake Superior shore.

Voyageurs National Park

Northern Voyageurs National Park (www.nps.gov/voya), which marks the border between the USA and Canada, is a wet wilderness of some 218,000 acres. It's almost 40% water and only accessible by hiking or motorboat – the waters are mostly too wide and too rough for canoeing. In summer, people come to boat, swim and fish in the park's five main lakes: Kabetogama, Namakan, Sand Point, Crane and Rainy Lake. In winter, people come to cross-country ski or snowmobile on specially marked trails. In addition to offering waterborne fun, the park is filled with wildlife, including large populations of deer, moose, black bears and white pelicans.

The park traces its roots to the 17th century, when French-Canadian fur traders, called voyageurs, began exploring the Great Lakes and northern rivers by canoe. Though the idea of establishing a national park here began in the early 20th century, the park was only formally founded in the 1970s.

When the boats get put away for the winter, the snowmobiles come out. Voyageurs is a hot spot for the sport, with 110 miles of staked and groomed trails slicing through the pines. Rainy Lake Visitor Center provides maps and advice. It also lends out free snowshoes and cross-country skis for local trails, including a couple that depart from outside the center. To the south, an ice road for cars spans the boat launches of the Ash River and Kabetogama Lake visitor centers. There's also a fun sledding hill near the Kabetogama center.

ℹ️ Information

The park's visitor centers are accessible by car and good places to begin your visit.

Ash River (☑ 218-374-3221; Mead Wood Rd; ⊙ 9am-5pm late May-late Sep) Seasonal center; staff offer occasional guided hikes around the bays and bluffs.

Destination Voyageurs National Park (www.dvnpmn.com) Has lodging and activity details for the park's gateway communities.

Kabetogama Lake (☑ 218-875-2111; off Hwy 53; ⊙ 9am-5pm late May-late Sep) Seasonal center with ranger-led programs.

Rainy Lake Visitor Center (☑ 218-286-5258; off Hwy 11; ⊙ 9am-5pm Jun-Sep, 10am-4:30pm Thu-Sun Oct-May) Eleven miles east of International Falls, just off of Hwy 11, is the main park office. Ranger-guided walks and boat tours are available here in summer, with snowshoe and ski rentals in winter.

ℹ️ Getting There & Away

Hwy 53 is the main highway to the region. It's about a five-hour drive from the Twin Cities (or a three-hour drive from Duluth) to Crane Lake, Ash River or Lake Kabetogama. International Falls, near the park's northwest edge, has the closest airport. It also has a busy border crossing with Canada.

MANUELA BIGLER / EYEEM / GETTY IMAGES ©

USA's National Parks

National parks are America's big backyards. No cross-country road trip would be complete without a visit to at least one of these remarkable natural treasures, rich in unspoiled wilderness, rare wildlife and history. The National Park Service (NPS), which celebrated its centennial in 2016, is responsible for the country's 60 glorious national parks, which are complemented by a slew of federally protected areas numbering in their thousands.

Above Grand Canyon National Park (p851)

Contents

Evolution of the Parks

Many parks look much the same as they did centuries ago. From craggy islands off the Atlantic Coast, to prairie grasslands and buffalo herds across the Great Plains, to the Rocky Mountains raising their jagged teeth along the Continental Divide, and onward to the tallest trees on earth – coast redwoods – standing sentinel on Pacific shores, you'll be amazed by the USA's natural bounty.

Go West!

Historically speaking, the nation's voracious appetite for land and material riches drove not only the false doctrine of Manifest Destiny, but also a bonanza of building: pioneer homesteads, farms, livestock fences, great dams, roadways and train tracks from sea to shining sea. This artificial infrastructure quickly swallowed up vast wilderness tracts from the Appalachian Mountains to the mighty Mississippi River and far into the West. In response to this, the National Parks Service was founded to form a web of federally protected public lands.

Voices in the Wilderness

During a trip to the Dakotas in 1831, artist George Catlin had a dream. As he watched the USA's rapid westward expansion harm both the wilderness and Native American tribes, Catlin penned a call to action for 'a nation's park, containing man and beast, in all the wild and freshness of their nature's beauty!' Four decades later, Congress created Yellowstone National Park, the nation's first.

The late 19th century saw a rush of new parks – including Yosemite, Sequoia and Mount Rainier – as a nascent conservation

1. Zion National Park (p888) 2. Coyote in Yellowstone National Park (p792)

movement fired up public enthusiasm. The poetic herald of the Sierra Nevada, naturalist John Muir, galvanized the public while campaigning for a national park system, delivering open-air lectures and writing about the spiritual value of wilderness above its economic opportunities.

Growing the Parks

Inspired by a visit to Yosemite with Muir in 1903, President Theodore Roosevelt, a big-game hunter and one-time rancher, worked to establish more wildlife preserves, national forests and national parks and monuments. The Antiquities Act of 1906, signed by the president, preserved a priceless trove of archaeological sites from Native American cultures, including Mesa Verde, and two years later the Grand Canyon itself.

The National Park Service (NPS) was created in 1916, with self-made millionaire and tireless parks promoter Stephen Mather as its first director. In the 1930s, President Franklin D Roosevelt added 50 more historic sites and monuments to the NPS portfolio and hired Depression-era Civilian Conservation Corps (CCC) workers to build scenic byways and create recreational opportunities in the parks.

After WWII the NPS kept growing. First lady during the 1960s, 'Lady Bird' Johnson contributed to the groundbreaking report *With Heritage So Rich,* which led to the National Historic Preservation Act of 1966 expanding the NPS system. Her parks advocacy also influenced her husband, President Lyndon Johnson, who enacted more environmental-protection legislation than any administration since FDR.

The Parks Today

In 2017, following a wide-ranging Interior Department review of more recent monument designations, the Trump administration committed to reducing several of the protected areas significantly. Utah's Bears Ears National Monument shrank by around 85% from 1.35 million acres to 160,000 acres, and 1996-designated Grand Staircase Escalante National Monument was cut by 1,345 square miles.

Though Congress stipulated that the land not be sold, millions of formerly protected acres are now available for commercial use, generating billions of dollars of revenue through extraction leases of natural resources, including copper, oil and gas. Though the projected revenues are considerable, the cost is likewise significant: the activity is likely to cause irreversible damage to these pristine, culturally significant lands, and has prompted large-scale protests from Native American and environmental advocacy groups.

In January 2019, the longest government shutdown in US history took a toll on the NPS. With workers on furlough, many of the parks were completely unprotected and unsupervised. In Joshua Tree National Park, vandals drove off-road through miles of previously untouched desert and destroyed several Joshua trees. Other parks saw everything from an increase in human waste to the interruption of scientific studies, including the longest continuous water quality study, which had been ongoing in Shenandoah National Park since 1979.

Though more than 300,000 people visit the parks system each year, the 2019 federal budget proposed a 14% cut to

1. A Camping in Arches National Park (p883)
2. Black bear cubs, Great Smoky Mountains National Park (p366)
3. Rafting the Colorado River, Grand Canyon National Park (p851)

existing park funding, which is already struggling to keep up with maintenance to aging infrastructure. In 2019, Indiana Dunes became the 61st National Park. For the lowdown on the NPS and the most up-to-date information about the changes afoot, visit www.nps.org.

Practical Tips for Park Visitors

Park entrance fees vary from nothing at all to $30 per vehicle; those these may increase in the coming years.

The 'America the Beautiful' annual pass ($80; www.nps.gov/planyourvisit/passes. htm), which admits four adults and all children under 16 years old free to all federal recreational lands for 12 calendar months, is sold at park entrances and visitor centers. Lifetime senior-citizen passes ($80) and access passes for those with disabilities (free) are also available.

Because ATMs are scarce in parks, bring cash to pay for campsites, wilderness permits, and guided tours and activities.

Park lodges and campgrounds book up far in advance; for summer vacations, reserve six months to one year ahead. Some parks offer first-come, first-served campgrounds – if so, try to arrive between 10am and noon, when other campers may be checking out. For overnight backpacking and some day hikes, you'll need a wilderness permit; the number of permits is often subject to quotas, so apply far in advance (up to six months before your trip, depending on park regulations). Some park stores sell (or occasionally rent) basic camping and outdoor supplies, but prices are usually inflated and some items may be out of stock – try to bring your own gear if you can.

1. Great Smoky Mountains National Park (p366) 2. Shenandoah National Park (p330) 3. Alligator, Everglades National Park (p490) 4. Acadia National Park (p261)

KENCANNING / GETTY IMAGES ©

ORHAN CAM / SHUTTERSTOCK ©

Eastern USA

Roam from New England's rocky, wild and weather-beaten shores to Florida's sugar-sand beaches shaded by palm trees. Or immerse yourself in the USA's wealth of historic sites, starting in the nation's capital, Washington, DC, then roll through the pastoral hills of old-timey Appalachia on the scenic Blue Ridge Pkwy.

Great Smoky Mountains National Park

Receiving more visitors than any other US national park, this southern Appalachian woodland pocket protects thickly forested ridges where black bears, white-tailed deer, antlered elk, wild turkeys and more than 1500 kinds of flowering plants find sanctuary.

Acadia National Park

Catch the first sunrise of the new year atop Cadillac Mountain, the highest point on the USA's eastern seaboard. Or come in summer to play on end-of-the-world islands tossed along this craggy, wind-whipped North Atlantic coastline.

Shenandoah National Park

Drive from the Great Smoky Mountains north along the historic Blue Ridge Pkwy past Appalachian hillside hamlets to Shenandoah, a pastoral preserve where waterfall and woodland paths await, just 75 miles from the nation's capital.

Everglades National Park

Home to snaggle-toothed crocodiles, stealthy panthers, pink flamingos and mellow manatees, South Florida's Caribbean bays and 'rivers of grass' attract wildlife-watchers, especially to unique, isolated flood-plain stands of trees called hammocks.

Mammoth Cave National Park

With hidden underground rivers and more than 400 miles of explored terrain, the world's longest cave system shows off sci-fi-looking stalactites and stalagmites up close.

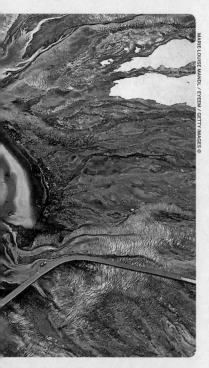

Grand Prismatic Spring (p793), Yellowstone National Park
Puebloan cliffside dwellings, Mesa Verde National Park (p782)
Elk, Rocky Mountain National Park (p766)

Great Plains & Rocky Mountains

Wildflower-strewn meadows, saw-toothed peaks and placid lakes along the spine of the Continental Divide are among America's most prized national parks. Equally rich in wildlife, Native American culture and Old West history, the Rocky Mountains and Great Plains embody the American frontier.

Yellowstone National Park

The country's oldest national park is full of geysers, hot springs and a wealth of megafauna – grizzly bears, bison, elk and more – that range across North America's largest intact natural ecosystem.

Rocky Mountain National Park

Atop the Continental Divide, jagged mountain peaks are only the start of adventures at this park, speckled with more than 150 lakes and 450 miles of streams running through aromatic pine forests.

Glacier National Park

Fly along the high-altitude Going-to-the-Sun Road, which appears to defy gravity as it winds for 50 miles through the mountainous landscape that some Native Americans call 'The Backbone of the World.'

Badlands National Park

Amid native prairie grasslands, where bison and bighorn sheep roam, this alarmingly named park is a captivating outdoor museum of geology, with fossil beds revealing traces of North America's prehistoric past.

Mesa Verde National Park

Clamber onto the edge of the Colorado Plateau to visit the well-preserved Native American cliff dwellings of Ancestral Puebloans who inhabited the remote Four Corners area for many generations.

Southwest USA

It takes time to explore the Southwest's meandering canyon country, arid deserts and Native American archaeological ruins. An immense, colorful chasm carved by one of the USA's most powerful rivers is just the beginning. Meander down backcountry byways to discover ancient sand dunes, twisting slot canyons and giant cacti.

Grand Canyon National Park

Arguably the USA's best-known natural attraction, the Grand Canyon is an incredible spectacle of colored rock strata, carved by the irresistible flow of the Colorado River. Its buttes and peaks spire into a landscape that's always changing with the weather.

Zion National Park

Pioneers almost believed they'd reached the promised land at this desert oasis, run through by a life-giving river. Get a thrill by rappelling down a slot canyon or pulling yourself up the cables to aerial Angels Landing viewpoint.

Bryce Canyon National Park

On the same geological 'Grand Staircase' as the Grand Canyon, Bryce Canyon shows off a whimsical landscape of totem-shaped hoodoo rock formations, some rising as tall as a 10-story building.

Arches National Park

Just outside the four-seasons base camp of Moab, UT, this iconic landscape of more than 2000 naturally formed sandstone arches is most mesmerizing at sunrise and sunset, when the gorgeously eroded desert rocks seem to glow.

Saguaro National Park

An icon of the American West, spiky saguaro cacti stretch toward the sky in this Arizona desert park, where coyotes howl, spotted owls hoot and desert tortoises slowly crawl through the sere landscape.

1. Havasupai Canyon, Grand Canyon National Park (p859)
2. Arches National Park (p883) 3. Path to Angels Landing, Zion National Park (p888) 4. Saguaro National Park (p866)

FRANK BACH / SHUTTERSTOCK ©

CHARLES HARKER / GETTY IMAGES ©

1. Kayaking on Lake Crescent, Olympic National Park (p1046) 2. Yosemite National Park (p1017) 3. Redwood National Park (p1011) 4. Death Valley National Park (p962)

West Coast

Thunderous waterfalls, the sirens' call of glacier-carved peaks and the world's tallest, biggest *and* oldest trees are just some of the natural wonders that California offers. Meet smoking volcanic mountains, misty rainforests and untamed beaches in the Pacific Northwest.

Yosemite National Park

Visit glaciated valleys, alpine wildflower meadows, groves of giant sequoia trees and earth-shaking waterfalls that tumble over sheer granite cliffs in the USA's second-oldest national park.

Olympic National Park

Lose yourself in the primeval rainforests, mist-clouded mountains carved by glaciers, and lonely, wild Pacific Coast beaches. Watch salmon swim free in the restored Elwha River, site of the world's largest dam-removal project.

Death Valley & Joshua Tree National Parks

Slide down sand dunes and stroll across salt flats at Badwater, the USA's lowest-elevation spot, in hellishly hot Death Valley. Or hop between boulders, native fan-palm oases and forests of crooked Joshua trees, all in Southern California's deserts.

Mt Rainier National Park

Meet a glacier-covered, rumbling giant that may have last erupted only 120 years ago and still reigns over the Pacific Northwest's volcanic Cascades Range. Day-hike among wildflower meadows or tramp across snow fields even in midsummer.

Redwood National Park

Be awed by towering ancient stands of coast redwoods, the tallest trees on earth, along the often-foggy Northern California coast. Spot shaggy Roosevelt elk foraging in woodland prairies, then go tide-pooling along rugged beaches.

Waimoku Falls, Haleakalā National Park (p11...

Final Frontiers

Far-flung Alaska and Hawaii offer some unforgettable wilderness experiences you just can't get in the 'Lower 48' or on 'da mainland.' Active volcanoes, icy glaciers, rare and endangered wildlife and a rich vein of historic sites make these parks worth a detour.

Alaska

In 1980 the Alaska National Interest Lands Conservation Act turned more than 47 million acres of wilderness over to the NPS, more than doubling the federal agency's holdings with a single stroke of President Jimmy Carter's pen.

Today Alaska's national parks give visitors a chance to see glacial icebergs calve at Kenai Fjords and Glacier Bay, watch brown bears catch salmon at Katmai, or summit the USA's highest peak, Denali (Mt McKinley). Along the aquatic Inside Passage, admire Native Alaskan totem poles in Sitka and retrace the hardy steps of 19th-century Klondike gold-rush pioneers at Skagway.

Hawaii

The USA's most remote archipelago is tailor-made for tropical escapades. On Hawai'i, the Big Island, witness the world's longest continuous volcanic eruption or possibly see lava flow at Hawai'i Volcanoes National Park, then snorkel with sea turtles beside an ancient Hawaiian place of refuge on the Kona coast. On Maui, trek deep inside a volcano and swim in stream-fed pools at mind-bogglingly diverse Haleakalā National Park. Last, pay your respects to O'ahu's WWII–era USS Arizona Memorial.

Great Plains

Best Places to Eat

➡ MB Haskett Delicatessen (p669)

➡ Cheever's Cafe (p690)

➡ Shaved Duck (p649)

➡ Bluestem (p657)

➡ Grey Plume (p681)

➡ Indigo Bridge (p682)

Best Places to Stay

➡ Hotel Alex Johnson (p673)

➡ Barn Anew (p685)

➡ Hotel Donaldson (p667)

➡ Millstream Resort Motel (p689)

➡ Hotel Deco (p680)

➡ Hotel Campbell (p693)

Why Go?

To best comprehend this vast and underappreciated region in the heart of the US, you need to split up the name. The first word, 'great,' is easy. Great scenery, great food, great people: all apply. The problem is with 'plains.' 'Humdrum' and 'flat' come to mind. Neither word applies. Amid the endless horizons are cosmopolitan oases like Kansas City, alpine wonders in the Black Hills, and soaring bluffs along the Mississippi and Missouri Rivers. There are also illuminating tales of comings and goings, from Okies fleeing the Dust Bowl along Route 66 to Lewis and Clark navigating the American frontier and the Five Civilized Tribes marching westward on a Trail of Tears.

Great distances across the beguiling wide-open spaces are the biggest impediment to enjoying this enormous region. Many sights lie near the interstates, but many more are found along the ever-intriguing small roads – the 'blue highways' of lore.

When to Go
St Louis

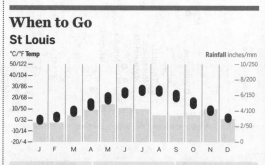

Apr, May, Sep & Oct Average highs of 55°F (13°C) in the north, warmer in the south; uncrowded months.

Jun–Aug Thunderstorms and even tornadoes; sultry days with blooming wildflowers.

Nov–Mar Attractions cut back hours, or close. Blizzards shut down roads for days.

The Great Plains Highlights

1 St Louis (p645) Immersing yourself in the blues rhythms of one of America's great old cities.

2 Black Hills (p672) Finding mountain highs within this green island rising above the golden plains.

3 Theodore Roosevelt National Park (p668) Gaping at the wildly striated, otherworldly landscapes of America's lesser-known Badlands.

4 Kansas City (p655) Eating yourself silly on amazing barbecue while grooving to Kansas City jazz.

5 Great River Road (p667) Driving atop Iowa bluffs for soaring Mississippi River vistas.

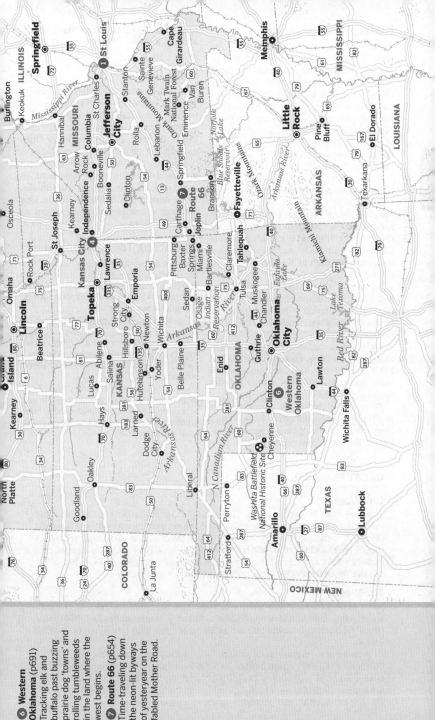

6 Western Oklahoma (p691)
Tracking elk and buffalo past buzzing prairie dog 'towns' and rolling tumbleweeds in the land where the west begins.

7 Route 66 (p654)
Time-traveling down the neon-lit byways of yesteryear on the fabled Mother Road.

History

Spear-toting nomads hunted mammoths here 11,000 years ago, long before cannon-toting Spaniards introduced the horse (accidentally) around 1630. Fur-frenzied French explorers, following the Mississippi and Missouri Rivers, claimed most of the land between the Mississippi and the Rocky Mountains for France. The territory passed to Spain in 1763, the French got it back in 1800 and then sold it to the USA in the 1803 Louisiana Purchase.

Settlers' hunger for land pushed resident Native American tribes westward, often forcibly, as in the notorious relocation of the Five Civilized Tribes – Cherokee, Chickasaw, Choctaw, Creek and Seminole – along the 1838–39 Trail of Tears, which led to Oklahoma from back east. Pioneers blazed west on trails such as the Santa Fe across Kansas.

Earlier occupants, including the Osage and Sioux, had different, but often tragic, fates. Many resettled in pockets across the region, while others fought for lands once promised.

Railroads, barbed wire and oil all brought change as the 20th century hovered. The 1930s Dust Bowl ruined farms and spurred many fed-up residents to head west. Even today, many regions remain eerily empty.

Farm consolidation in recent decades and the lure of economically vibrant cities have left hundreds of small towns withering on the vine. Frustrated residents have responded by voting increasingly conservative in a region once known for its populism.

Local Culture

The people who attempted to settle the Great Plains after the Native Americans usually faced difficult lives, marked by scarcity, uncertainty and isolation – and it literally drove many of them crazy. Others gave up and got out (failed homesteads dot the region). Only fiercely independent people could thrive in those conditions and that born-and-bred rugged individualism is the core of Plains culture today. Quiet restraint is considered an important and polite trait here.

ℹ Getting There & Around

The main airports are in St Louis, Kansas City and Omaha. Each has service from major American cities. Dozens more airports in the region have services from major hub airports such as Chicago, Denver and Dallas.

Greyhound (www.greyhound.com) buses cover some interstates, while Jefferson Lines (www.jeffersonlines.com) and Burlington Trailways (www.burlingtontrailways.com) take up some of the slack. Many smaller towns have no bus service at all.

Amtrak (www.amtrak.com) runs four major routes across the Plains, making it easy to get here by train. However, getting around by train is impractical with the exception of between St Louis and Kansas City.

GREAT PLAINS IN...

One Week

Spend your first two or three days in St Louis (p645) before snaking up the Mississippi River to Iowa along the Great River Road (p667). Skirt past the folksy Amana Colonies (p663) en route to the bucolic countrysides (and famous bridges) of Madison County (p661). Head west to link up with Nebraska's Hwy 2 (p683) for a drive through the remote Sandhills. Then cut north to South Dakota where the gorgeous Black Hills (p672) and Badlands National Park (p671) will vie for your remaining time.

Two Weeks

With two weeks behind the wheel, you can take a big bite out of the Plains. Do the trip as above, then head south from South Dakota into the Nebraska Panhandle (p684), stopping at fascinating, isolated sites such as the Agate Fossil Beds (p684) and Scotts Bluff (p684).

Meander down to Kansas and pick up US 50 heading east. Stop at the astonishing Cosmosphere (p687) in Hutchinson. Continue south to Oklahoma where you can join historic Route 66 in Oklahoma City (p689) heading northeast to Tulsa (p693). Follow the Mother Road into Missouri where you can dip into the lush Ozark Mountains (p652) and zip up to Kansas City (p655) before finishing your trip back in St Louis.

MISSOURI

The most populated state in the Plains, Missouri likes to mix things up, serving visitors ample portions of both sophisticated city life and down-home country sights. St Louis and Kansas City are the region's most interesting cities, and each is a destination in its own right. But, with more forest and less farm field than neighboring states, Missouri also cradles plenty of wild places and wide-open spaces, most notably the rolling Ozark Mountains, where the winding valleys invite adventurous exploration or just some laid-back meandering behind the steering wheel. Maybe you'll find an adventure worthy of Hannibal native Mark Twain as you wander the state.

ℹ Information

Missouri Division of Tourism (www.visitmo.com)
Bed & Breakfast Inns of Missouri (www.bbim.org)
Missouri State Parks (www.mostateparks.com) State parks are free to visit.

St Louis

POP 318,100

Slide into St Louis and revel in the unique vibe of the largest city in the Great Plains. Beer, bowling and baseball are some of the top attractions, but history and culture, much of it linked to the Mississippi River, are a vital part of the fabric. And, of course, there's the iconic Gateway Arch that you have seen in a million pictures; it's even more impressive in reality. Many music legends, including Scott Joplin, Chuck Berry, Tina Turner and Miles Davis, got their start here and jammin' live-music venues keep the flame burning.

This old city by the river is a sensational place for food and nightlife. Plan on adding an extra day or more to your trip, for time to explore.

◉ Sights

★ Gateway Arch
National Park   NATIONAL PARK

(Map p648; ☎877-982-1410; www.gatewayarch.com; 11 N 4th St; tram ride adult/child from $12/8; ⊙grounds 5am-11pm, Arch 8am-10pm Jun-Aug, 9am-6pm Sep-May, last tram 1hr before closing; ♿) As a symbol for St Louis, the Gateway Arch has soared above any expectations its backers could have had in 1965 when it opened. Now the centerpiece of its own recently

christened national park, the silvery, shimmering Arch is the Great Plains' own Eiffel Tower. It stands 630ft high and symbolizes St Louis' historical role as 'Gateway to the West.' It's the design of the legendary Finnish American architect Eero Saarinen (1910–1961).

The tram ride takes you to the tight confines at the top. Book tickets in advance online or by phone. At busy times, same-day tickets may be sold out. At the base, there is the interesting **Museum at the Gateway Arch** (Map p648; www.nps.gov/jeff; Gateway Arch; adult/child $3/free; ⊙8am-10pm Jun-Aug, 9am-6pm Sep-May; ♿). You can also buy tickets for a documentary *Monument to the Dream* (adult/child $7/3). Various money-saving combo tickets are available; some include rides on the Gateway Arch Riverboats (p647).

A massive project transformed the area around the Arch in time for its 50th birthday. The large **Luther Ely Smith Square** (Map p648; www.archpark.org; 20 N 4th St) FREE now covers noxious I-44 and connects the Arch and its park to the **Old Courthouse** (Map p648; ☎314-655-1700; www.gatewayarch.com; ⊙8am-4:30pm) FREE and the rest of Downtown. It's a huge and welcome improvement.

A pro tip: the parkland around the Arch is a great place to escape the crowds and relax with a view of the Mississippi River.

★ City Museum   MUSEUM

(Map p648; www.citymuseum.org; 701 N 15th St; $16, with rooftop $21; ⊙9am-5pm Mon-Thu, to midnight Fri & Sat, 11am-5pm Sun; ♿) Possibly the wildest highlight of any visit to St Louis is this frivolous, frilly fun house in a vast old shoe factory. The Museum of Mirth, Mystery & Mayhem sets the tone. Run, jump and explore all manner of exhibits, including a seven-story slide. The summer-only rooftop offers all manner of weird and wonderful fun, including a flamboyant Ferris wheel and a wild slide.

★ Forest Park   PARK

(Map p646; ☎314-367-7275; www.forestparkforever.org; bounded by Lindell Blvd, Kingshighway Blvd & I-64; ⊙6am-10pm; ♿) FREE New York City may have Central Park, but St Louis has the bigger (by 528 acres) Forest Park. The superb, 1371-acre spread was the setting of the 1904 World's Fair. It's a beautiful place to escape to and is dotted with attractions, many free. Two walkable neighborhoods, the Loop and Central West End, are close.

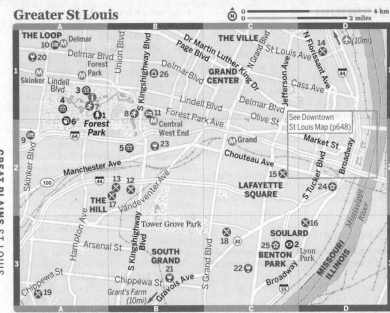

Greater St Louis

The Visitor & Education Center (p650) is in an old streetcar pavilion and has a cafe. Free walking tours leave from here, or you can borrow an audio tour.

National Blues Museum MUSEUM
(Map p648; ☎314-925-0016; www.national bluesmuseum.org; 615 Washington Ave; adult/ child $15/10; ⊙10am-5pm Tue-Thu & Sat, to 9pm Fri, noon-5pm Sun & Mon) This flashy museum explores blues legends like hometown hero Chuck Berry, while making a strong case for the genre's myriad influences on modern rock, folk, R&B and more. There are interactive exhibits from the likes of Jack White, and stories about the early years of blues and its (almost exclusively female) pioneers.

St Louis Art Museum   MUSEUM

(Map p646; www.slam.org; 1 Fine Arts Dr, Forest Park; ⊙10am-5pm Tue-Thu, Sat & Sun, to 9pm Fri) FREE This grand beaux-arts palace (with a striking modern wing) was originally built for the World's Fair. Now housing this storied institution, its collection spans time and styles, and includes a variety of household names from Picasso to Van Gogh and Warhol. The beguiling Grace Taylor Broughton Sculpture Garden opened in 2015.

St Louis Zoo   ZOO

(Map p646; ☏314-781-0900; www.stlzoo.org; 1 Government Dr, Forest Park; fee for some exhibits; ⊙9am-5pm daily, to 7pm Fri-Sun May-Sep; P⊕) FREE Divided into themed zones, this vast park includes a fascinating River's Edge area with African critters. Don't leave without saying hello to the zoo's superstar: Kali the polar bear. Note that some exhibits such as the Sea Lion Show have admission charges averaging $4 per person.

St Louis Science Center   MUSEUM

(Map p646; ☏314-289-4400; www.slsc.org; 5050 Oakland Ave, Forest Park; ⊙9:30am-5:30pm Mon-Sat, from 11am Sun; P⊕) FREE The interactive exhibits at this three-story museum are geared toward kids (and the young at heart). Expect live demonstrations, dinosaurs, a planetarium and an IMAX theater (additional fee). The museum is connected to Forest Park by a dramatic pedestrian bridge.

Missouri History Museum   MUSEUM

(Map p646; ☏314-746-4599; www.mohistory.org; 5700 Lindell Blvd, Forest Park; ⊙10am-5pm Wed-Mon, to 8pm Tue; P) FREE Presents the story of St Louis, starring such worthies as the World's Fair; a replica of Charles Lindbergh's plane, *Spirit of St Louis;* and a host of bluesmen. Oral histories from those who fought segregation are moving.

🏃 Activities

Boathouse   BOATING

(Map p646; ☏314-722-6872; www.boathousestl. com; 6101 Government Dr, Forest Park; boat rental per hour from $15; ⊙11am-approx 1hr before sunset, weather permitting) In warm weather, rent a rowboat to paddle over Forest Park's Post-Dispatch Lake. Traveling couples should inquire about Moonlight Paddleboat Picnics, which run Thursday nights from May to October. Other rentals include canoes and kayaks. There's also a good **restaurant** (Map

p646; ☏314-366-1555; mains $11-24; ⊙11am-8pm Mon-Thu, to 9pm Fri & Sat, 10am-7pm Sun) here.

Steinberg Skating Rink   ICE SKATING

(Map p646; ☏314-367-7465; www.steinbergskating rink.com; 400 Jefferson Dr, Forest Park; admission $8, skate rental $7; ⊙10am-9pm Sun-Thu, to midnight Fri & Sat mid-Nov–Feb) The balm for cold weather: fun on the ice.

🎭 Festivals & Events

Big Muddy Blues Festival   MUSIC

(www.bigmuddybluesfestival.com; Laclede's Landing; ⊙early Sep) Three stages of riverfront blues at Laclede's Landing on the Labor Day weekend.

🧭 Tours

Gateway Arch Riverboats   BOATING

(Map p648; ☏877-982-1410; www.gatewayarch. com; 50 S Leonor K Sullivan Blvd; 1hr tour adult/child from $19/8; ⊙Mar-Nov) Churn up the Big Muddy on replica 19th-century steamboats. A park ranger narrates the midday cruises in season, and those after 3pm sail subject to availability. There are also numerous dinner and drinking cruises. Various combo tickets are available with attractions at the Gateway Arch National Park (p645).

Downtown St Louis

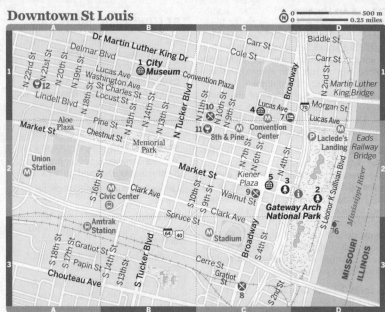

Downtown St Louis

🛏 Sleeping

★ Cheshire
HOTEL **$$**

(Map p646; ☑ 314-647-7300; www.cheshirestl.com; 6300 Clayton Rd; r $145-250; P❋🐾🛜🏊) This upscale inn near Forest Park (p645) oozes character, from its stained-glass windows to the all-encompassing British literary theme. The hodgepodge of artworks, antique furnishings and (occasionally frightening) taxidermy are sure to delight.

Parkway Hotel
HOTEL **$$**

(Map p646; ☑ 314-256-7777; www.thepark wayhotel.com; 4550 Forest Park Ave; r $160-250; P❋@🛜) Right in the midst of Central West End's upscale fun, this indie eight-story hotel contains 217 remodeled rooms (with refrigerators and microwaves) inside a grand limestone building. A hot buffet breakfast is included, and you can't beat the location right across from Forest Park (p645). The decor is sleek and contemporary.

Missouri Athletic Club
HOTEL **$$**

(Map p648; ☑ 314-231-7220; www.mac-stl.org; 405 Washington Ave; r $115-160; P❋🛜) Stay in style Downtown close to the Arch (p645). The Missouri Athletic Club is a grand old facility with 73 nice, traditional hotel rooms.

Moonrise Hotel
BOUTIQUE HOTEL **$$**

(Map p646; ☑ 314-721-1111; www.moonrisehotel. com; 6177 Delmar Blvd; r $155-450; P❋🛜🏊) The stylish eight-story Moonrise has a high profile amid the high energy of the Loop neighborhood. Its 125 rooms sport a lunar motif, but are grounded enough to slow things down to comfy.

✕ Eating

★ Adriana's
ITALIAN $

(Map p646; ☏ 314-773-3833; www.adrianason thehill.com; 5101 Shaw Ave, The Hill; mains $5-10; ⏲ 10:30am-3pm Mon-Sat) Redolent of herbs, this family-owned Italian deli serves up fresh salads and sandwiches (get the meaty Hill Boy) to ravenous lunching crowds. The thin-crust pizza is also a treat; ask about the off-the-menu specials. Expect lines.

★ Crown Candy Kitchen
CAFE $

(Map p646; ☏ 314-621-9650; www.crowncandy kitchen.net; 1401 St Louis Ave; mains $5-10; ⏲ 10:30am-8pm Mon-Thu, to 9pm Fri & Sat; ⊛) An authentic family-run soda fountain that's been making families smile since 1913. Malts (hot fudge, yum!) come with spoons, the floats, well, float, and you can try the famous BLT. Homemade candies top it off.

Park Avenue Coffee
CAFE $

(Map p648; ☏ 314-231-5282; www.parkavenue coffee.com; 417 N 10th St; ⏲ 7am-6pm) A treat unique to St Louis is the butter cake, a buttery treat that reminds one of a heavenly cross between cake and fudge. This small chain of local coffee shops sells much-loved examples that come in dozens of flavors. Have a dark coffee with a red velvet or a lemon raspberry version.

★ Broadway Oyster Bar
CAJUN $$

(Map p648; ☏ 314-621-8811; www.broadway oysterbar.com; 736 S Broadway; mains $10-20; ⏲ 11am-3am) Part bar, part live-music venue, but all restaurant, this joint jumps year-round. When the sun shines, people flock outside where they suck down crawfish and other Cajun treats. It's nuts before and after Cardinals games.

★ Shaved Duck
AMERICAN $$

(Map p646; ☏ 314-776-1407; www.theshavedduck. com; 2900 Virginia Ave; mains $10-23; ⏲ 11am-9pm Mon, to 10pm Tue-Sat, noon-8pm Sun) A South Grand stalwart, the Shaved Duck fires up its grills early in the day and turns out excellent BBQ, such as the signature smoked duck. Options include fab sandwiches and veggie sides. Live music weeknights.

★ Eleven Eleven Mississippi
TUSCAN $$

(Map p646; ☏ 314-241-9999; www.1111-m.com; 1111 Mississippi Ave; mains $9-25; ⏲ 11am-10pm Mon-Thu, to midnight Fri, 5pm-midnight Sat; ♠) This popular bistro and wine bar fills an old shoe factory. Dinner mains have a Tuscan flair and farm-to-table vibe. Other options on the seasonal menu include sandwiches, pizzas, steaks and veggie dishes. Excellent wine selection.

☕ Drinking & Nightlife

Laclede's Landing, Soulard and the Loop are loaded with pubs and bars, many with live music. Most bars close at 1:30am, though some have 3am licenses.

ST LOUIS LOCAL SPECIALTIES

Toasted ravioli They're filled with meat, coated in breadcrumbs, then deep-fried. Practically every restaurant on The Hill serves them, most notably **Mama Toscano's** (Map p646; ☏ 314-776-2926; www.mamatoscano.com; 2201 Macklind Ave; mains $6-15; ⏲ 8am-5:30pm Tue-Fri, to 5pm Sat). Another good source is **Charlie Gitto's** (Map p646; ☏ 314-772-8898; www. charliegittos.com; 5226 Shaw Ave; mains $16-30; ⏲ 5-10pm Mon-Thu, to 11pm Fri & Sat, 4-9pm Sun; Ⓟ).

St Louis pizza Its thin-crusted, square-cut pizzas are really addictive. They're made with Provel cheese, a locally beloved gooey concoction of processed cheddar, Swiss and provolone. Local chain **Imo's** (Map p648; ☏ 314-641-8899; www.imospizza.com; 1 S Broadway; mains from $10; ⏲ 11am-7pm Mon-Sat), with over 70 locations across the metro area, bakes 'the square beyond compare,' or get your pizza with Provel at the popular **Joanie's Pizzeria** (Map p646; ☏ 314-865-1994; www.joanies.com; 2101 Menard St; mains $10-15; ⏲ 11am-11pm Sun-Wed, to midnight Thu-Sat, bar 11am-2am).

Frozen custard Generations have found joy delighting in the local version of ice cream at historic **Ted Drewes** (Map p646; ☏ 314-481-2652; www.teddrewes.com; 6726 Chippewa St; cones $2-6; ⏲ 11am-11pm Feb-Dec), southwest of the city center on old Route 66. There's a smaller summer-only branch south of the city center at 4224 S Grand Blvd. Frozen custard differs from regular ice cream because – like its namesake – it contains egg yolks, which make the treat creamier and richer.

The Grove, a strip of Manchester Ave between Kingshighway Blvd and S Vandeventer Ave, is the hub of St Louis' LGBT+ community. Peruse *Vital Voice* (www.the vitalvoice.com) for info.

★ **Blueberry Hill**   BAR
(Map p646; ☑ 314-727-4444; www.blueberryhill. com; 6504 Delmar Blvd; ⊙ 11am-late) St Louis native Chuck Berry rocked the small basement bar here until the day he died in 2017. The venue hosts bands big and small and has good pub food (mains $7 to $15), arcade games, darts and walls covered in pop-culture memorabilia.

Bridge Tap House & Wine Bar   BAR
(Map p648; ☑ 314-241-8141; www.thebridgestl. com; 1004 Locust St; ⊙ 11am-1am Mon-Sat, to midnight Sun) Slip onto a sofa or rest your elbows on a table at this romantic bar where you can savor fine wine or the best local beer (over 50 on tap) and nibble a variety of exquisite little bites from a seasonal menu.

☆ Entertainment

★ **Venice Cafe**   BLUES, JAZZ
(Map p646; ☑ 314-772-5994; www.thevenicecafe. com; 1903 Pestalozzi St; ⊙ 4pm-1am Mon-Sat) A true cabinet of curiosities. The interior of this two-level club is a master class in mosaics, while the rambling outdoor garden is chock-full of folk art and twinkling lights.

DRINK LOCAL
....

Schlafly (Map p648; ☑ 314-241-2337; www.schlafly.com; 2100 Locust St; ⊙ 11am-10pm Mon-Thu, to midnight Fri & Sat, noon-9pm Sun), **Civil Life** (Map p646; www. thecivillife.com; 3714 Holt Ave; ⊙ 4-11pm Tue-Thu, noon-11pm Fri & Sat, 11am-9pm Sun), **Earthbound Brewing** (Map p646; ☑ 314-769-9576; www.earthboundbeer.com; 2724 Cherokee St; ⊙ 4pm-midnight Tue-Fri, from noon Sat, noon-10pm Sun) and **Urban Chestnut** (Map p646; ☑ 314-222-0143; www.urbanchestnut.com; 4465 Manchester Ave; ⊙ 11am-11pm Mon-Thu, to 1am Fri & Sat, to 9pm Sun) are excellent local microbrews that will let you forget that you're in the home of Bud. The website STL Hops (www.stlhops.com) is an excellent guide to local beers and where to drink them.

Best of all, the drinks are cheap and there's live blues, rock and jazz seven days a week.

Old Rock House   LIVE MUSIC
(Map p646; ☑ 314-534-1111; www.oldrockhouse. com; 1200 S 7th St) A great, sweaty club that draws big regional acts. Look for rock (new *and* old), blues, country, punk, metal and more.

🛍 Shopping

★ **Left Bank Books**   BOOKS
(Map p646; ☑ 314-367-6731; www.left-bank.com; 399 N Euclid Ave; ⊙ 10am-10pm Mon-Sat, 11am-6pm Sun) A great indie bookstore stocking new and used titles. There are recommendations of books by local authors and frequent author readings.

ℹ Information

Explore St Louis (Map p648; ☑ 314-421-1023; www.explorestlouis.com; Gateway Arch Visitor Center, Luther Ely Smith Square, West entrance; ⊙ 9am-5pm; 🖥) An excellent resource, with another branch at the airport.

Forest Park Visitor & Education Center (Map p646; ☑ 314-367-7275; www.forestparkforever. org; 5595 Grand Dr; ⊙ 6am-8pm Mon-Fri, to 7pm Sat & Sun; 🖥) Located in an old streetcar pavilion and has a cafe. Free walking tours leave from here, or you can borrow an audio tour.

Missouri Welcome Center (☑ 314-869-7100; www.visitmo.com; Riverview Dr, I-270 exit 34; ⊙ 8am-5pm Mon-Sat)

ℹ Getting There & Away

St Louis Lambert International Airport (STL; www.flystl.com; I-70 exit 238A), a primary Great Plains airport, is 12 miles northwest of Downtown and is connected by the light-rail MetroLink ($2.50) and taxi (about $45).

Amtrak's (www.amtrak.com) *Lincoln Service* travels five times daily to Chicago (from $25, 5½ hours). Two daily *Missouri River Runner* trains serve Kansas City (from $34, 5½ hours). The daily *Texas Eagle* goes to Dallas (16 hours). Trains leave from the **Gateway Transportation Center** (Map p648; 430 S 15th St).

Greyhound (www.greyhound.com) buses depart several times daily to Chicago ($18, five to seven hours), Memphis ($26, six hours), Kansas City ($24, 4½ hours) and many more cities from Gateway Transportation Center.

Megabus (www.megabus.com) runs services to Chicago for as little as $10 one way from the same station.

ℹ Getting Around

Metro (www.metrostlouis.org) runs local buses and the MetroLink light-rail system (which connects the airport, the Loop, Central West End, the Gateway Transportation Center (p650)/ Union Station and Downtown). Buses 30 and 40 serve Soulard from Downtown. A single bus/ light rail ticket is $2/2.50. A day pass is $7.50.

St Louis County Cabs (☏ 314-991-5300; www.countycab.com) Call, book online or use the app.

St Charles

POP 70,300

This Missouri River town, founded by the French in 1769, is just 20 miles northwest of St Louis. The cobblestoned Main St anchors a well-preserved downtown with artisan shops, cafes and gourmet grocers. The **visitor center** (☏ 800-366-2427; www.historic stcharles.com; 230 S Main St; ⊙ 8am-5pm Mon-Fri, from 10am Sat, from noon Sun) has an excellent audio walking tour available online, which covers some rare French-colonial architecture in the Frenchtown neighborhood just north of downtown.

The 240-mile-long Katy Trail (p653), which spans the state, passes through St Charles.

Lewis & Clark Boat House & Museum
MUSEUM

(☏ 636-947-3199; www.lewisandclarkcenter.org; 1050 S Riverside Dr; adult/child $5/2; ⊙ 10am-5pm Mon-Sat, from noon Sun) Lewis and Clark began their journey in St Charles on May 21, 1804, and their time here is reenacted annually on that date. This museum has displays about the journey and replicas of the boats.

★ Boone's Colonial Inn
B&B $$$

(☏ 636-493-1077; www.boonescolonialinn.com; 322 S Main St; r $190-300; P ※ 🛜) The four suites in these 1820 stone row houses are posh escapes. If all are booked out, try the sister property, Boone's Lick Trail Inn, five blocks down the road. The innkeeper of both, Venetia, is extraordinarily knowledgeable about the town and its history.

ℹ Getting There & Away

St Charles is just 20 miles northwest of St Louis. The St Charles Area Transit system, SCAT, has an I-70 commuter service that provides bus transportation to the St Louis MetroLink at North Hanley Station.

YOUR BELGIAN BUD

One of the world's largest beer plants, the historic **Anheuser-Busch Brewery** (Map p646; ☏ 314-577-2626; www. budweisertours.com; cnr 12th & Lynch Sts; ⊙ 10am-5pm Mar-Oct, 11am-4:30pm Nov-Feb)gives marketing-driven tours. View the bottling plant and Clydesdale horses. One thing to note: the purchase of this St Louis (and American) icon by Belgium's InBev in 2008 is still a sore spot locally. And don't ask: 'How do you remove all the flavor?'

Hannibal

POP 17,600

When the air is sultry in this old river town, you almost expect to hear the whistle of a paddle steamer. Mark Twain's boyhood home, 115 miles northwest of St Louis, has some authentically vintage sections and plenty of sites (including caves) where you can get a sense of the author and his creations Tom Sawyer and Huck Finn.

★ Mark Twain Boyhood Home & Museum
MUSEUM

(☏ 573-221-9010; www.marktwainmuseum.org; 120 N Main St; adult/child $12/6; ⊙ 9am-5pm mid-Mar–Dec, 10am-4pm Jan–mid-Mar; 👪) This museum presents eight buildings, including two homes Twain lived in and that of Laura Hawkins, the real-life inspiration for Becky Thatcher in *The Adventures of Tom Sawyer*. Be sure to check out the Twain-inspired Norman Rockwell paintings at the Museum Gallery before you leave. In summer, an actor gives readings from Twain's writing.

ℹ Information

Hannibal Convention and Visitors Bureau (☏ 573-221-2477; www.visithannibal.com; 505 N 3rd St; ⊙ 9am-5pm Mon-Fri, to 4pm Sat & Sun) The visitor center can hook you up with all things Twain.

ℹ Getting There & Away

Hannibal is 115 miles northwest of St Louis on either Hwy 61 or the longer and more scenic MO 79. Burlington Trailways (www.burlington trailways.com) links the two cities with a daily bus ($40, 2¼ hours).

Springfield

POP 167,400

Whether you're tooling along Route 66 or transiting to or from Branson to the south, Springfield makes an excellent stop. The compact downtown is an attractive collection of historic brick buildings while the Commercial St district to the north is also appealing, historic and boasts a good range of places to eat and drink.

◉ Sights

Fantastic Caverns   CAVE
(☑417-833-2010; www.fantasticcaverns.com; 4872 N Farm Rd 125; adult/child $26/17; ☺8am-8pm Apr-Aug, shorter hours other times) All manner of geologic wonders are on display at these caverns, which wend through the eroded limestone beneath the Ozarks, 8 miles northwest of downtown Springfield. As the countless billboards and other hype never tire of reminding, visitors are hauled around the stalactites in trailers pulled by jeeps and never need do any walking at all. Besides all the natural wonders, there's good info on how mere drops of water create this geologic beauty.

Wilson's Creek
National Battlefield   HISTORIC SITE
(☑417-732-2662; www.nps.gov/wicr; 6424 W Farm Road 182, Republic; adult/child $10/free) The sight of the first major Civil War battle fought west of the Mississippi River, this large rolling open space is a fascinating place to visit. The land looks much as it did in 1861 when a large Union force tried to surprise a Confederate force here. After a day's intense fighting leading to 2500 total casualties, the Union troops retreated. Visitors can drive, walk or bike a 4.9-mile loop through the battlefield. Signs explain what happened where.

🛏 Sleeping & Eating

★**Best Western**
Route 66 Rail Haven   MOTEL **$**
(☑417-866-1963; www.bestwestern.com; 203 S Glenstone Ave; r $70-120; ❉🅿🛜❄) Perfectly maintained and right up-to-date where it counts, this 1956 motor court is a Route 66 classic. Lovingly restored by its owners, the motel has stylish midcentury decor inside and a huge pool outside. Rooms have microwaves and fridges.

★**Artisan's Oven**   CAFE **$**
(☑417-885-5030; www.theartisansoven.com; 206 E Commercial St; mains $5-12; ☺7am-4pm Mon-Fri, to 2pm Sat; 🛜) This exceptional bakery and cafe makes some of the best sandwiches in southwest Missouri. Eat in or takeaway, the breads on offer are all housemade. Other treats include cinnamon rolls, blueberry muffins and house-made granola. Save room for a slice of pie.

❶ Information

Route 66 Springfield Visitor Center (☑800-678-8767; www.springfieldmo.org; 815 E St Louis St; ☺8am-5pm; 🛜) An excellent resource, this super-friendly tourist office will provide you with a refreshing drink and answer any question. It has extensive Route 66 material.

❶ Getting There & Away

Greyhound runs buses along I-44 northeast to St Louis ($40, four hours, four daily) and southwest to Tulsa ($38, 3½ hours, four daily). Jefferson Lines (www.jeffersonlines.com) has buses north to Kansas City ($29, four hours, one daily).

The Ozarks

Ozark hill country spreads across southern Missouri and extends into northern Arkansas and eastern Oklahoma. Flashy Branson receives the lion's share of tourists, though the region's true charms lie further afield in the rolling hills and deep clefts, where wild

---

WORTH A TRIP

SAINTE GENEVIEVE

Sixty-five miles south of St Louis, this petite, French-founded Mississippi River town is home to plenty of history. Many of the restored 18th- and 19th-century buildings are now B&Bs or gift shops. Follow the **Route du Vin** (www.rdvwine trail.com) out of town to explore one of Missouri's finest wine trails and the five vineyards along it.

Yes, the town's **Cave Vineyard** (☑573-543-5284; www.cavevineyard.com; 21124 Cave Rd; ☺10am-6pm Apr-Oct, to 5pm Nov-Mar) is a vineyard with a cave (and yes, you can drink in the cave). If you'd like to stay the night, the **Inn St Gemme Beauvais** (☑573-883-5744; www.innstgemme.com; 78 N Main St; r $100-190; ❉🛜) is the oldest continuously operated B&B in Missouri.

spring-fed rivers carry legions of happy people floating downstream.

North of US 60, the Ozark National Scenic Riverways (p653) – the Current and Jacks Fork Rivers – boast 134 miles of splendid canoeing and inner-tubing (rental agencies abound). Weekends often get busy and boisterous. The park headquarters, outfitters and motels are in Van Buren. Eminence also makes a good base. There are many campgrounds along the rivers. Sinuous Hwy E and Hwy 19 are scenic gems.

Amid it all are forgotten small towns, and both popular and remote beautiful state parks.

Sights & Activities

Echo Bluff State Park   STATE PARK
(☎844-322-3246; www.echobluffstatepark.com; 34489 Echo Bluff Dr, Eminence; ⊙dawn-10pm; ⊕) FREE With lush forests and facilities befitting a top-tier national park, Echo Bluff is a true Ozarks highlight. Opened in 2016, this state park has a soaring stone lodge, spacious cabins and ample camping options. Use it as a base for hiking, fishing and mountain biking. It is a great place for river floats.

Taum Sauk Mountain State Park   STATE PARK
(☎573-546-2450; www.mostateparks.com/park/taum-sauk-mountain-state-park; Hwy. CC, Middle Brook) FREE Many Missouri state parks cater to fun and games like fishing and tubing. Not this one. You can scale the state's highest peak, Taum Sauk Mountain (1772ft) and cool off under one of the state's tallest waterfalls, 132ft Mina Sauk Falls. Both are reached by trails through rocky, raw forest that are just challenging enough to make it interesting. The view of the Ozarks from the summit – especially in fall – is sublime.

Ozark National Scenic Riverways   NATIONAL PARK
(☎573-323-4236; www.nps.gov/ozar; 404 Watercress Dr, Van Buren; ⊙park 24hr, visitor center 8am-4:30pm daily Jun-Aug, Mon-Fri Sep-May) FREE Two wild rivers, the Current and the Jacks Fork, wind through 80,000 acres of raw Ozark beauty in this area managed by the National Park Service. There are myriad natural pursuits here, with canoeing being a top activity along with river floating. Numerous natural springs feed the river, the most famous being **Big Spring** (www.nps.gov/ozar/planyourvisit/big-spring.htm; Pea Vine Rd, Van Buren). Hiking is popular, especially

CATCHIN' THE KATY
Katy Trail State Park (☎573-449-7402; www.katytrailstatepark.com; ⊙dawn-dusk; ⊕), America's longest rail-to-trail walking and biking route, starts in Machens near St Louis and St Charles and ends in Clinton, 70 miles southwest of Kansas City. Its 240 miles span the state from east to west and pass through some bucolic, sylvan countryside and atmospheric small towns. Built on an abandoned line of the Missouri-Kansas-Texas Railroad (known as the Katy), the trail has very gentle slopes, wide curves and a smooth gravel surface, making it suitable for almost everyone.

along the **Ozark Trail** (☎573-436-0540; www.ozarktrail.com), which runs for more than 350 miles in 13 sections.

Harvey's Alley Spring Canoe Rental   CANOEING
(☎573-226-3386; www.harveysalleyspring.com; 13863 Hwy 106, Alley Spring Campground, Eminence; canoe rental per day from $45; ⊙8am-8pm Jun-Aug, shorter hours other times) One of several outfitters on the Current River, Harvey's wins plaudits for its welcoming attitude, especially to river novices. Besides renting canoes and kayaks, it offers transport services so you can leave your car at one spot, float away and get a ride back later. It also organizes guided trips.

Sleeping & Eating

The small towns of Van Buren and Eminence have scenic campgrounds, basic motels, rustic cabins and picturesque riverside resorts. You'll also find top-notch lodgings in Echo Bluff State Park. Campgrounds are found everywhere. In Branson and the surrounds your lodging options are near limitless.

Landing Current River   HOTEL $$
(☎573-323-8156; www.eatsleepfloat.com; 106 Olive St, Van Buren; r $95-160) Perched along the banks of the Current River near Van Buren, this scenic hotel is the perfect base for exploring the Ozark National Scenic Riverways. All the rooms have balconies overlooking the river. You can also book overnight camping trips by canoe or raft, ranging from one to five nights out.

ROUTE 66: GET YOUR KICKS IN MISSOURI

The Show-Me State will show you a long swath of the Mother Road. Meet the route in **St Louis**, where Ted Drewes (p649) has been serving frozen custard to generations of roadies from its Route 66 location on Chippewa St. There are a couple of well-signed historic routes through the city.

Follow I-44 (the interstate is built over most of Route 66 in Missouri) on a westbound journey down the Mother Road to **Route 66 State Park** (☑636-938-7198; www.mo stateparks.com; N Outer Rd, I-44 exit 266; ☉7am-30min after sunset, museum 9am-4:30pm Mar-Nov) FREE, with its visitor center and museum inside a 1935 roadhouse. Although the displays show vintage scenes from around St Louis, the real intrigue here concerns the town of Times Beach, which once stood on this very site. It was contaminated with dioxin and in the 1980s the government had to raze the entire area.

Head southwest on I-44 to **Stanton**, then follow the signs to family-mobbed **Meramec Caverns** (☑573-468-3166; www.americascave.com; I-44 exit 230, Stanton; adult/child $22/12; ☉8:30am-7:30pm Jul & Aug, 9am-7pm May & Jun, reduced hours Sep-Apr; 🅟), as interesting for the Civil War history and hokey charm as for the stalactites; and the conspiracy-crazy **Jesse James Wax Museum** (☑573-927-5233; www.jessejameswax museum.com; I-44 exit 230, Stanton; adult/child $10/5; ☉9am-6pm daily Jun-Aug, 9am-5pm Sat & Sun Apr-May & Sep-Oct), which posits that James faked his death and lived until 1951.

The **Route 66 Museum & Research Center** (☑417-532-2148; www.lebanon-laclede. lib.mo.us; 915 S Jefferson Ave; ☉8am-8pm Mon-Thu, to 5pm Fri & Sat) FREE at the library in **Lebanon** has memorabilia past and present. Ready for a snooze? Head to the 1940s **Munger Moss Motel** (☑417-532-3111; www.mungermoss.com; 1336 E Seminole Ave (Rte 66), near I-44 exit 130; r from $60; 🅟🅰🅿🅣). It's got a monster of a neon sign and Mother Road–xloving owners.

Or continue on to **Springfield** where you can stay at the iconic Best Western Route 66 Rail Haven (p652). Then take Hwy 96 to Civil War-era **Carthage** with its historic town square and **66 Drive-In Theatre** (☑417-359-5959; www.66drivein.com; 17231 Old 66 Blvd, Carthage; adult/child $8/4; ☉after dusk Thu-Sun Apr-Sep; 🅟). In **Joplin** get on State Hwy 66, turning onto old Route 66 (the pre-1940s route), before the Kansas state line.

The Route 66 Association of Missouri (www.missouri66.org) is a great resource. And don't miss the **Conway Welcome Center** (☑417-589-0023; I-44 Mile 110, near Conway; ☉8am-5pm), which has an over-the-top Route 66 theme and scads of info on this most historic of roads.

Slice of Pie BAKERY $

(☑573-364-6203; www.asliceofpierolla.com; 601 Kingshighway St, Rolla; snacks from $4; ☉10am-10pm) Pie! Who doesn't say they love it, but when was the last time you had a really good slice? Amid pervasive mediocrity, this family-run pie shop is a winner. Every day there are different flavors and the most popular sell out early. Order yourself a 'pie sampler' – a selection of eight different slices in a pie tin – to go with you on your Ozarks adventure.

❶ Getting There & Around

Part of the Ozarks' charm is its remote location. Accessing the region beyond Branson will likely require a curvaceous drive on scenic two-lane byways. Public transportation is nonexistent in the Ozarks.

Branson

POP 11,500

Hokey Branson is a cheerfully shameless tourist resort. The main attractions are the more than 50 theaters hosting 100-plus country music, magic and comedy shows. The neon-lit '76 Strip' (Hwy 76) packs in miles of motels, restaurants, wax museums, fudgeries, fun parks and theaters. Drive just a few minutes out of town, however, and you'll find yourself in pristine Ozark wilderness.

◉ Sights

Silver Dollar City AMUSEMENT PARK

(☑800-831-4386; www.silverdollarcity.com; 399 Silver Dollar City Pkwy; 1-day adult/child $68/58; ☉hours vary) A Branson original, this huge amusement park west of town has thrilling roller-coasters, water rides, a firefighter-themed area and musical shows.

Table Rock Lake   LAKE
(www.visittablerocklake.com) Snaking through the hills 2 miles southwest of Branson, large Table Rock Lake is a deservedly popular destination for boating, fishing, camping and other outdoor activities.

🛏 Sleeping & Eating

★ Branson Hotel   B&B $$
(☑417-544-9814; www.thebransonhotel.com; 214 W Main St; r $130-180; ☀☎) Dating to 1903, this plush nine-room B&B is right in the old town. It's away from the frenetic commercialism of the Strip, and has a great on-site wine bar. No children.

★ Dobyns Dining Room   AMERICAN $$
(☑417-239-1900; www.keetercenter.edu; 1 Opportunity Ave, Keeter Center; mains $8-20; ⊙10:30am-8pm Mon-Sat, 10am-2pm Sun) Located by College of the Ozarks (and staffed by its students, who also make the ice cream), this is as close to fine dining as Branson gets. The setting is grand (think country chic), the prices are reasonable (particularly at lunch) and the service is impeccable (we'd give the staff an A+).

Gettin' Basted   BARBECUE $$
(☑417-320-6357; www.gettinbasted.com; 2845 W Hwy 76; mains $9-25; ⊙11am-10pm) Brisket, pulled pork and that holy grail of barbecue, burnt ends, are the stars at one of the very best places to eat on the Strip. The pitmasters here have the awards to prove it.

☆ Entertainment

Branson's Famous Baldknobbers   LIVE PERFORMANCE
(☑417-231-4999; www./baldknobbers.com; 645 Hwy 165, Branson Famous Theatre; adult/child $39/19; ⊙usually Apr-Dec) If you're going Branson, go all in with the musical comedy show that started it all in 1959. Three generations of the Mabe family – and a lot of 'friends' – cover country and gospel tunes, dance and offer up cornball comedy that thinks fake buck teeth are a hoot. The entire enterprise was chronicled in the reality TV series *Branson Famous*.

❶ Information

Branson/Lakes Area Convention and Visitors Bureau (☑417-334-4084; www.explorebranson.com; 4100 Gretna Rd, Shoppes at Branson Meadows; ⊙8am-5pm Mon-Fri) The CVB has oodles of information; the website is an excellent resource.

❶ Getting There & Around

Tucked into the scenic southern corner of the state, Branson is surprisingly hard to reach, although this means you may end up driving some rural and lovely two-lane Ozark roads to get here.

Branson Airport (BKG; www.flybranson.com; 4000 Branson Airport Blvd), 10 miles south of the Hwy 76 Strip, is a small airport with Frontier Airlines services from Chicago, Denver and Dallas.

Jefferson Lines (www.jeffersonlines.com) has buses to Kansas City ($35, five hours, one daily).

During the summer, the SUV-laden roads often crawl with traffic and it can be faster to walk than drive, although few visitors consider doing this.

Kansas City
POP 489,000
With its fiery barbecues (100-plus joints smoke it up), bubbling fountains (more than 200; on par with Rome) and blaring jazz, Kansas City is one of America's most appealing cities. It's certainly a don't-miss Great Plains highlight with world-class museums and quirky art-filled neighborhoods that jostle for your attention. You can easily run aground for several days as you tune into the local vibe.

◉ Sights

State Line Rd divides KCMO (Kansas City, MO) and KCK (Kansas City, KS). The latter is a bland swath of suburban sprawl with little to offer travelers. KCMO has some distinct areas, including the art-deco-filled downtown area.

★ Negro Leagues Baseball Museum   MUSEUM
(☑816-221-1920; www.nlbm.com; 1616 E 18th St; adult/child $10/6; ⊙9am-6pm Tue-Sat, from noon Sun) This comprehensive museum covers the lesser-known history of African American teams, such as the KC Monarchs and New York Black Yankees, that flourished until baseball became fully integrated. It's part of the Museums at 18th & Vine complex.

★ National WWI Museum   MUSEUM
(☑816-888-8100; www.theworldwar.org; 2 Memorial Dr; adult/child $18/10; ⊙10am-5pm daily Jun-Aug, Tue-Sun Sep-May; ℗) Enter this impressive modern museum on a glass walkway over a

field of red poppies, the symbol of remembrance of WWI. Through detailed and engaging displays, learn about a war that is almost forgotten by many Americans. The only quibble is that military hardware and uniforms take precedence over the horrible toll of the trench fighting. The museum is crowned by the historic Liberty Memorial, which has sweeping views over the city.

★ **Nelson-Atkins Museum of Art** MUSEUM
(☑ 816-751-1278; www.nelson-atkins.org; 4525 Oak St; ⊙ 10am-5pm Mon, Wed, Sat & Sun, to 9pm Thu & Fri; P) FREE Giant badminton shuttlecocks (the building represents the net) surround this encyclopedic museum, which has standout European painting, photography and Asian art collections. With free entry, a gorgeous sculpture garden and an expansive collection from top-tier artists, what's not to like? Blockbuster special exhibits carry admission fees.

Union Station HISTORIC BUILDING
(☑ 816-460-2020; www.unionstation.org; 30 W Pershing Rd; station free, Science City $13.25; ⊙ hours vary; ⊞) Opened in 1914, KC's Union Station is a sublime example of the magnificent architecture that once was the hallmark of American train stations. Today it has been beautifully renovated and houses an array of attractions as well as the station where four Amtrak trains stop daily. There's Science City, an interactive museum devoted to just that, plus a planetarium, shops, a performance venue, a train museum and a huge, free model train exhibit that draws mobs at Christmas.

☞ Tours

Kansas City Walking Tours WALKING
(☑ 816-725-0794; www.kcwalkingtours.com; 200 Main St; tours from $48) Walking tours of River

Market, including a themed food tour that takes two hours and does a deep dive at City Market and the surrounding blocks. Other tours utilize the excellent KC Streetcar to explore the city.

☆ Festivals & Events

American Royal World Series of Barbecue FOOD & DRINK
(www.americanroyal.com; 400 Speedway Blvd, Kansas Speedway; tickets $6-55; ⊙ Sep) For over 40 years, the world's largest barbecue contest has taken over Kansas City for one weekend, with more than 500 international teams in competition.

⊨ Sleeping

★ **Jefferson House B&B** B&B $$
(☑ 816-673-6291; www.jeffersonhousekc.com; 1728 Jefferson St; r $155-195; P ❈ 🛇) Jefferson House is funkier than most Missouri mansion-cum-B&Bs, with a mix of modern and classic touches. There are just three rooms and one has sweeping city views. It's the kind of home you'd live in if you had exquisite taste. Stylish touches abound; breakfasts are excellent.

Aladdin BOUTIQUE HOTEL $$
(☑ 816-421-8888; www.hialaddin.com; 1215 Wyandotte St; r $120-220; ❈ 🛇) Affiliated with Holiday Inn, this 16-story hotel dates from 1925. It has been restored to its Italian Romanesque splendor and has 193 compact yet stylish rooms. It was a legendary haunt of mobsters and Greta Garbo. Not your ordinary chain hotel.

Southmoreland on the Plaza B&B $$
(☑ 816-531-7979; www.southmoreland.com; 116 E 46th St, Country Club Plaza; r $130-250; P ❈ 🛇) The 12 rooms at this posh B&B are furnished like the home of your rich country-club friends. It's a big old mansion between the art museums and the **Plaza** (☑ 816-753-0100; www.countryclubplaza.com). Extras include Jacuzzis, sherry, a fireplace and more. Some rooms have outside sitting areas, others are snug.

✗ Eating

★ **Betty Rae's Ice Cream** ICE CREAM $
(☑ 816-214-8753; www.bettyraes.com; 412 Delaware St; from $4; ⊙ 11am-10pm Sun-Thu, to 11pm Fri & Sat; ⊞) The best ice cream in the Great Plains? Could be. Choose from 25 flavors of sensationally creamy ice cream, including the remarkable lavender honey. After surviving the queue, relax on the tree-shaded patio.

Winstead's Steakburger
BURGERS $

(☑816-753-2244; www.winsteadssteakburger.com; 101 Emmanuel Cleaver II Blvd; mains $4-6; ⊘6:30am-midnight Sun-Thu, to 1am Fri & Sat; ☻) Cheery servers sling plates of top-notch burgers to families, hungover hipsters and more at this Country Club Plaza institution, which dates to 1940. Don't miss the onion rings and chili, or breakfasts.

★Golden Ox
STEAK $$

(☑816-842-2866; www.goldenoxkc.com; 1600 Genessee St; mains $12-60; ⊘5-10pm Tue-Sat, 4-9pm Sun) In 1949, when this riverfront strip was the site of the KC stockyards, the Golden Ox served its first steak. Over the years it became a legend for serving the very best cuts of beef. Even after the stockyards were demolished, the Ox soldiered on. Recently it's had a makeover and once again serves KC's best steak.

★Bluestem
MODERN AMERICAN $$$

(☑816-561-1101; www.bluestemkc.com; 900 Westport Rd; 3-/5-/10-course meal $80/90/115, bar snacks $5-20; ⊘kitchen 5-10pm Tue-Sat, bar 4-11pm; ℗☻) Multiple-award-winning Bluestem has a casual elegance that extends from the bar to the dining room. Many stop into this Westport star just for a fine cocktail and some of the small plates of exquisite snacks (the cheeses, oh!). Dinner features an array of seasonal small courses (go for the wine pairings).

🍷 Drinking & Nightlife

Up-Down
BAR

(☑816-982-9455; www.updownkc.com; 101 Southwest Blvd; ⊘3pm-1am Mon-Fri, 11am-1am Sat, 11am-midnight Sun) A popular bar-cum-playground south of downtown, Up-Down caters to the inner child with an array of games from pinball to video. There are huge decks and great music. The superb tap-beer lineup includes all the beers from **Boulevard Brewery** (☑816-474-7095; www.boulevard.com; 2501 Southwest Blvd; tours from $5; ⊘11am-8pm Mon-Thu, 10am-9pm Fri & Sat, to 6pm Sun), which are brewed just up the hill.

Border Brewing Co
BREWERY

(☑816-315-6807; www.borderbrewco.com; 406 E 18 St; ⊘4-9pm Wed & Thu, noon-11pm Fri & Sat, noon-8pm Sun) Border brews its beers with an edge of extra hops and other flavors like citrus berries. The line-up changes with the seasons. Its tap room in the Crossroads district is compact and welcoming. In summer the front opens up and there is a commodious deck.

Tom's Town
DISTILLERY

(☑816-541-2400; www.toms-town.com; 1701 Main St; tours $10; ⊘4pm-midnight Tue-Fri, 2pm-midnight Sat, 2-10pm Sun) Tom's Town, downtown KC's first legal distillery since Prohibition, pays homage to the city's Prohibition-flouting political boss Tom Pendergast. Try the housemade vodka, gin or bourbon and let the art deco furnishings take you back to the days when Kansas City was known as the 'Paris of the Plains.' Creative small bites are on the menu.

☆ Entertainment

The free weekly *Pitch* (www.thepitchkc.com) has the best cultural calendar.

★Mutual Musicians Foundation
JAZZ

(☑816-471-5212; www.mutualmusicianslive.com; 1823 Highland Ave; ⊘midnight-5am Sat & Sun) Near 18th and Vine in the Historic Jazz

---

GREAT BARBECUE IN KANSAS CITY

Savoring hickory-smoked brisket, pork, chicken or ribs at one of the barbecue joints around town is a must for any visitor. The local style is pit-smoked and slathered with heavily seasoned vinegar-based sauces. You may well swoon for 'burnt ends,' the crispy ends of smoked pork or beef brisket. Amazing.

Q39 (☑816-255-3753; www.q39kc.com; 1000 W 39th St; mains $9-30; ⊘11am-10pm Mon-Thu, to 11pm Fri & Sat, to 9pm Sun; ℗) BBQ cooking goes upmarket without losing its soul.

Arthur Bryant's (☑816-231-1123; www.arthurbryantsbbq.com; 1727 Brooklyn Ave; mains $9-16; ⊘10am-9pm Mon-Sat, 11am-8pm Sun; ℗) The silky, fiery sauce is reason enough for a visit.

Joe's Kansas City Bar-B-Que (☑913-722-3366; www.joeskc.com; 3002 W 47th Ave; mains $8-26; ⊘11am-9pm Mon-Thu, to 10pm Fri & Sat; ℗) The lines outside attest to the pull of Joe's juicy pulled-pork sandwiches.

LC's Bar-B-Q (☑816-923-4484; www.lcsbarbq.com; 5800 Blue Pkwy; mains $9-22; ⊘11am-9pm Mon-Sat; ℗) For those who like their BBQ sauce sweet and thick.

District, this former union hall for African American musicians has hosted after-hours jam sessions since 1930. Famous veteran musicians gig with young hotshots. It's friendly and pretension-free. A little bar serves cheap drinks in plastic cups. No cover charge (though a $10 donation is suggested). It only opens late on Friday and Saturday nights.

Blue Room Jazz Club   LIVE MUSIC
(www.americanjazzmuseum.org; 1600 E 18th St; Mon & Thu free, cover varies Fri & Sat; ⊙ 5-11pm Mon & Thu, to 1am Fri & Sat) This slick club, known for its jazz, blues and instrumentals, is part of the **American Jazz Museum** (☑ 816-474-8463; 1616 E 18th St; adult/child $10/6; ⊙ 9am-6pm Tue-Sat, noon-6pm Sun, plus 9am-6pm Mon Jun-Aug). It hosts local talent for free performances on Monday and Thursday. Touring acts perform weekends. Major shows are held at the adjoining Gem Theater.

Truman Sports Complex   STADIUM
(I-70 exit 9) Locals are passionate about major-league baseball's Royals (who won the World Series in 2015) and the NFL's close-but-no-cigar Chiefs. Both play at gleaming side-by-side stadiums east of the city near Independence.

ⓘ Information

Greater Kansas City Visitor Center (☑ 816-691-3800; www.visitkc.com; 1321 Baltimore Ave; ⊙ 9am-5pm Mon-Fri, 10am-3pm Sat) Other locations include the National WWI Museum (p655) and Union Station.

Missouri Welcome Center (☑ 816-889-3330; www.visitmo.com; 4010 Blue Ridge Cutoff, Truman Sports Complex; ⊙ 8:30am-4:30pm Mon-Fri) Statewide maps and information at I-70 exit 9.

ⓘ Getting There & Away

Kansas City International Airport (MCI; www.flykci.com; off I-29 exit 13) is a confusing array of circular terminals 15 miles northwest of downtown. It has good domestic service. A taxi to downtown/Plaza costs about $40 to $45. Or take the cheaper **Super Shuttle** (☑ 800-258-3826; www.supershuttle.com; from $25).

Amtrak (www.amtrak.com) trains stop in majestic **Union Station** (www.unionstation.org; 30 W Pershing Rd; ⊙ 6am-midnight). Two daily *Missouri River Runner* trains go to St Louis (from $34, 5½ hours). The *Southwest Chief* stops here on its daily runs between Chicago and LA via Omaha.

Greyhound (☑ 816-221-2835; www.greyhound.com; 1101 Troost St) runs buses daily to St Louis ($24, 4½ hours) from the station poorly located east of downtown.

Jefferson Lines (☑ 816-221-2885; www.jeffersonlines.com; 1101 Troost St, Greyhound Terminal) travels along I-29 north to Omaha ($49, three hours), I-35 to Des Moines ($32, 3½ hours) and southwest to Tulsa ($50, five hours).

ⓘ Getting Around

Ride KC (www.ridekc.org) fares are $1.50. A one-day pass costs $3 and you can buy it on the bus. Bus 47 runs regularly between downtown, Westport and Country Club Plaza.

KC Streetcar (www.kcstreetcar.org; ⊙ 6am-midnight Mon-Thu, to 2am Fri, 7am-2am Sat, 7am-11pm Sun) is very handy and free. It travels for 2 miles downtown largely on Main St from River Market to Union Station and Crown Center, running every 10 to 15 minutes.

Independence
POP 117,300

Picture-perfect Independence is the ideal stereotype of an old Midwestern small town. It was the home of Harry S Truman for 64 years, including when he was US president from 1945 to 1953. It has some unmissable museums as well as Truman's actual home – which today astounds for its simplicity and accessibility.

⊙ Sights

★**Truman Home**   HISTORIC BUILDING
(☑ ticket info 816-254-9929; www.nps.gov/hstr; 219 N Delaware St; ⊙ 9am-4:30pm, closed Mon Nov-May) **FREE** See the simple life Harry (1884–1972) and Bess (1885–1982) lived in this basic but charming wood house. It's furnished with their original belongings and you fully expect the couple to wander out and say hello. The former president lived here from 1919 to 1972 and in retirement entertained visiting dignitaries in his strictly pedestrian front room. He's said to have hoped none of the callers would linger more than 30 minutes. Tour tickets are distributed at the visitor center (p659).

🛏 Sleeping & Eating

Higher Ground Hotel   HOTEL **$$**
(☑ 816-836-0292; www.highergroundhotel.com; 200 N Delaware St; r $90-130; ❈ 🅢) Across the street from the Truman Home, this 30-room hotel looks basic from the outside. Enter

its cheery halls, however, and you'll find well-appointed (and individually designed) digs, some of which look out over a serene garden. It's close to Independence's modest nightlife.

Englewood Cafe AMERICAN $
(☑816-461-9588; 10904 E Winner Rd; mains $6-12; ☺6am-8pm Mon, Wed & Fri, noon-3pm Tue & Thu, 6am-2pm Sat & Sun) Follow the glow of the red neon sign in the window to this great diner a short drive from the Truman Home. The pot roast special draws diners from miles around while the many homemade pies keep them coming back for more.

❶ Information

Truman Home Visitor Center (☑816-254-9929; www.nps.gov/hstr; 223 N Main St; ☺8:30am-5pm) Truman Home (p658) tour tickets are distributed here on a first-come, first-served basis. There's a good bookstore.

❶ Getting There & Away

Independence is a quick 20-minute drive east of Kansas City. For public transportation, grab bus 24 on Grand Blvd in downtown KC for the 50-minute journey to Independence.

St Joseph

POP 76,400

A major departure point for pioneers, this scruffy riverside town is a tad unkempt around the edges but has a revitalized downtown district with quirky shops and dining options filling once-abandoned storefronts. There are several compelling museums. Get details at the visitor center near I-29.

◉ Sights

Glore Psychiatric Museum MUSEUM
(☑816-232-8471; www.stjosephmuseum.org; 3406 Frederick Ave; adult/child $6/4; ☺10am-5pm Mon-Sat, from 1pm Sun) Housed in the former 'State Lunatic Asylum No 2,' this museum gives a frightening and fascinating look at lobotomies, the 'bath of surprise' and other discredited treatments. Price includes admission to three other museums on-site, covering Native American art, local African American history and toy dolls.

⊨ Sleeping

★Shakespeare Chateau B&B $$
(☑816-232-2667; www.shakespearechateau. com; 809 Hall St; r $135-200; ❈❀❈) This elegant 1885 mansion houses five spacious guest rooms upstairs and a handful of common parlors from which to soak in the opulence of yesteryear. Spread throughout are 47 stained-glass windows (look for the masterpiece in the stairwell), as well as swooping chandeliers, cherry-wood carvings and a fine art collection. Prepare to be dazzled.

✕ Eating & Drinking

Ben Magoon's
Famous Delicatessen PUB FOOD $
(☑816-232-3611; www.magoonsdeli.com; 632 S 8th St; mains $7-8; ☺11am-1:30am Mon-Sat, food until 3pm Mon-Thu, until 9pm Fri & Sat) This downtown tavern dates back to the 1920s, when the real Ben Magoon started serving what became much-loved sandwiches. The current owners carry on this tradition, including Magoon's original Reuben. Drinks are creative and include fresh ingredients; the beer list is good. On many nights there's live music.

★Tiger's Den BAR
(☑816-617-2108; 519 Felix St; ☺3-11pm Mon-Wed, from 11am Thu-Sat) Part used bookstore, part cocktail bar, Tiger's Den is the stuff of Hemingway dreams. Sit on one of the plush sofas and order a drink inspired by the contents of the all-surrounding bookshelves, including Agatha Christie's *Sparkling Cyanide* or a *Tequila Mockingbird*.

❶ Information

St Joseph Visitor Center (☑816-232-1839; www.stjomo.com; 502 N Woodbine Rd, near I-29 exit 47; ☺9am-3pm Mon-Fri, plus Sat Jun-Aug) Get details on the town's many museums at the visitor center near I-29.

❶ Getting There & Away

St Joseph is about an hour north of Kansas City along I-29. Greyhound buses ply I-29, serving Kansas City ($12, one hour, two daily).

IOWA

The towering bluffs on the Mississippi River and the soaring Loess Hills lining the Missouri River bookend the rolling farmland of this bucolic state. In the middle you'll find the writers' town of Iowa City, the commune dwellers of the Amana Colonies, and plenty of picture-perfect rural towns, including those amid the covered bridges of Madison County.

Iowa emerges from slumber every four years as the make-or-break state for presidential hopefuls. The Iowa Caucus opens the national election battle, and wins by George W Bush in 2000 and Barack Obama in 2008 stunned many pundits and launched their victorious campaigns.

ℹ Information

Iowa Tourism Office (www.traveliowa.com)
Iowa State Parks (www.iowadnr.gov) State parks are free to visit.

Des Moines

POP 217,500

Des Moines, meaning 'of the monks' not 'in the corn' as the surrounding fields might suggest, is Iowa's fast-growing capital. The city has an amazing state capitol building, buzzing enclaves like the East Village and one of the nation's best state fairs. Pause for a night, then get out and see the rest of Iowa.

◉ Sights

★**State Capitol**   HISTORIC BUILDING
(📞515-281-5591; www.legis.iowa.gov/resources/tourCapitol; cnr E 9th St & Grand Ave; ⊙8am-5pm Mon-Fri, 9am-4pm Sat) FREE From the sparkling gold dome to the spiral staircases and stained glass in the law library, every detail at this bling-heavy capitol (1886) seems to try to outdo the next. Join a free tour and you can climb halfway up the dome. The gift shop is filled with Iowa goodies.

Valley Junction   AREA
(www.valleyjunction.com; cnr 5th St & Maple St) This historic old village is now part of West Des Moines. The five-block-long commercial strip on Fifth St is the most interesting in the region. Over 60 locally owned shops, bars, bakeries, cafes and more line the strip in attractive old brick buildings. It's ungentrified and there's not a franchise or chain in sight. Great strolling.

Des Moines Art Center   MUSEUM
(📞515-277-4405; www.desmoinesartcenter.org; 4700 Grand Ave; ⊙11am-4pm Tue-Wed, Fri-Sun, to 9pm Thu) FREE This art museum's complex is an all-star monument to some of the greatest architects of the modern era; Eliel Saarinen, IM Pei and Richard Meier all designed portions. Inside there's a solid collection of art from the 19th century onwards. Matisse, O'Keefe, Rodin and Warhol are some of the names represented. Don't miss the museum's

Pappajohn Sculpture Park (📞515-277-4405; www.desmoinesartcenter.org; 1330 Grand Ave; ⊙6am-midnight) FREE closer to downtown.

🎊 Festivals & Events

★**Iowa State Fair**   FAIR
(📞800-545-3247; www.iowastatefair.org; cnr E 30th St & E University Ave; adult/child $12/6; ⊙7am-1am mid-Aug; 🖐) Much more than just country music and butter sculpture, this festival draws a million visitors over its 11-day run. They enjoy the award-winning farm critters and just about every food imaginable that can be shoved on a stick. It's the setting for the Rodgers and Hammerstein musical *State Fair* and the 1945 film version.

🛌 Sleeping

Des Lux Hotel   BOUTIQUE HOTEL $$$
(📞515-288-5800; www.desluxhotel.com; 800 Locust St; r $180-350; 🅿🕸) An elegant five-story commercial building downtown has been transformed into a luxurious hotel with only 51 rooms. It's got more character than the chains and lots of extras, like a lavish breakfast.

Renaissance Savery Hotel   HISTORIC HOTEL $$$
(📞515-244-2151; www.marriott.com; 401 Locust St; r $160-400; 🅿🕸) Dating to 1919, this 11-story hotel presents a dignified appearance, thanks to its stolid colonial revival style. The 233 rooms are comfortable and have a safe corporate style.

🍴 Eating

Machine Shed   AMERICAN $
(📞515-270-6818; www.machineshed.com/urbandale; 11151 Hickman Rd, Urbandale; mains $6-15; 🖐) This excellent restaurant serving hearty fare is out west near I-35/80 exit 125 and the Living History Farms. It's a bustling place that emphasizes top quality, with phenomenal breakfasts and favorites like chicken-fried steak and pork tenderloin. The biggest challenge is saving room for the banana cream pie. The Machine Shed is a great stop if you're just zipping by on the interstate.

★**Roca**   AMERICAN $$
(📞515-282-3663; www.rocadsm.com; 208 Court Ave; mains $14-30; ⊙3-10pm Mon-Thu, to midnight Fri & Sat, 4-9pm Sun) Inventive, fresh seasonal fare is the hallmark of this industrial chic eatery downtown. Always crowded, diners share large and small plates of the familiar and the unfamiliar, all prepared with flair from local sources. A tater tot appetizer

shares the menu with shrimp and polenta. The wine and cocktail list is superb; happy hour is a local phenomenon.

Tumea & Sons ITALIAN $$
(☑515-282-7976; www.tumeaandsons.net; 1501 SE 1st St; mains $9-30; ☺11am-2pm & 4:30-9pm Mon-Thu, 11am-2pm & 4:30-10pm Fri, 4:30-10pm Sat) Generations of locals have feasted on homestyle Italian classics at this proudly family-run restaurant. Have an amazingly cheap mixed drink at the bar while you wait for your table. Then navigate the long menu for a plethora of pasta and sauce combinations. The steaks are good, as are the meatballs. Out back is a grapevine-shaded bocce ball court.

🍷 Drinking

★Iowa Taproom CRAFT BEER
(☑515-243-0827; www.iowataproom.com; 215 E 3rd St; ☺11am-midnight Mon-Sat, to 10pm Sun) The best beers from over 30 Iowa breweries feature at this fiercely local pub in East Village. It's got the expected industrial vibe (the building was a series of factories starting in 1882) and it also has a great menu of burgers and other beer-friendly comfort fare.

Black Sheep BAR
(www.facebook.com/blacksheepdsm; 223 E Walnut St; ☺7pm-2am Wed-Sat) Tequila and vampires: those are two of the main themes at East Village's edgiest bar. Let the red neon glow lure you down to this small basement space where DJs spin vinyl that usually results in a lot of uninhibited dancing. Beach goth is a common theme.

🛍 Shopping

★Des Moines
Downtown Farmers Market MARKET
(☑515-286-4928; www.dsmpartnership.com/desmoinesfarmersmarket; cnr Court Ave & 4th St; ☺7am-noon Sat May-Oct) Around 95% of Iowa's land is considered very fertile – the highest percentage of any state in the US – and you'll see the best of the bounty the state produces at this hugely popular farmers market. Hundreds of stalls selling produce, prepared foods, baked goods, meals, snacks, handicrafts and much more draw in crowds every week.

ⓘ Getting There & Away
Located 3 miles southwest of town, **Des Moines International Airport** (DSM; ☑515-256-5050;

www.dsmairport.com; 5800 Fleur Dr) has services from major US cities and hubs.

Burlington Trailways (www.burlingtontrailways.com) has daily buses on I-80 to Omaha ($43, 2¼ hours) and Chicago ($52, six hours) while Jefferson Lines (www.jeffersonlines.com) follows I-35 to Kansas City ($32, 3¼ hours).

Sioux City
POP 82,600
Right on the Missouri River, Sioux City makes for a fine stop when traveling to or from South Dakota. There's an excellent museum dedicated to explorers Lewis and Clark, and some classic places to eat that date back decades, to a time when the city was still a major industrial center known for its huge stockyards (now mostly closed).

Lewis & Clark Interpretive Center MUSEUM
(☑712-224-5242; www.siouxcitylcic.com; 900 Larsen Park Rd, near I-29 exit 149; ☺9am-5pm Tue-Fri, from noon Sat & Sun; 🅿) FREE On August 20, 1804, Sergeant Charles Floyd became the only person to die on the Lewis and Clark expedition team, probably from appendicitis. You can learn much more about this and other aspects of the journey at the beautiful Lewis & Clark Interpretive Center, which is right on the Missouri River.

Tastee Inn & Out FAST FOOD $
(☑712-255-0857; www.tasteeinnandout.com; 2610 Gordon Dr; mains $4-7; ☺11am-11pm Sun-Thu, to

---

MADISON COUNTY

This scenic county, about 30 miles southwest of Des Moines, slumbered for half a century until Robert James Waller's blockbuster, tear-jerking novel *The Bridges of Madison County*. That and its 1995 Clint Eastwood/Meryl Streep movie version brought in scores of fans to check out the covered bridges where Robert and Francesca fueled their affair.

The farms and open land in this area are pleasantly bucolic, and the towns postcard-perfect. **St Charles** is home to the oldest of the six surviving covered bridges, while tourism-hub **Winterset** has the rest, as well as a gorgeous silver-domed **courthouse** (☑515-462-4451; www.madisoncoia.us; 112 John Wayne Dr; ☺8am-4:30pm) FREE. In between the two you'll find a few vineyards, breweries and cideries.

midnight Fri & Sat) Run by the Calligan family since 1955, this Sioux City institution is a true drive-in (the only interior seating is the seats in your car). There are two specials here. One is the Tastee, an Iowa loosemeat sandwich (a much-loved regional specialty that combines loose ground beef, onions and orange cheese). The other is onion chips, which are battered and fried.

ⓘ Getting There & Away

Jefferson Lines (www.jeffersonlines.com) runs two buses daily along I-29 south to Omaha ($39, 95 minutes) and north to Sioux Falls ($28, 80 minutes).

Davenport

POP 102,300

Davenport is the largest and most appealing of the Quad Cities that cluster around this region of the Mississippi riverfront (the other three are Bettendorf in Iowa and Moline and Rock Island in Illinois). It boasts a grand setting with a vast network of walking and biking trails.

⊙ Sights

Figge Art Museum   MUSEUM
(☑ 563-326-7804; www.figgeartmuseum.org; 225 W 2nd St; adult/child $10/4; ⊙ 10am-5pm Tue, Wed, Fri & Sat, to 9pm Thu, noon-5pm Sun) The glass-walled Figge Art Museum sparkles above the River Road. The museum's Midwest Regionalist Collection includes many works by Iowa native (and *American Gothic* painter) Grant Wood; you can also stroll through the world-class Haitian and Mexican Colonial collections.

🛏 Sleeping & Eating

★**Beiderbecke Bed & Breakfast**   B&B $
(☑ 563-323-0047; www.beiderbeckeinn.com; 532 W 7th St; r $95-110; ▣▣) This is the Stick-style Victorian home of jazz legend Bix Beiderbecke's grandparents. Now a four-room B&B, it's got some incredible period wallpaper and wild rugs with competing patterns. The rooms are spacious and two have river views.

Freight House Farmers Market   MARKET $
(☑ 563-322-6009; www.freighthousefarmers market.com; 421 W River Dr; ⊙ 4-8pm Wed, 8am-1pm Sat, 10am-2pm Sun) Your one-stop year-round source for organic goods, local craft beers and deli sandwiches in an old rail freight house on the waterfront. The two-story brick complex also has a fantastic seasonal outdoor market with heaps of regional produce.

ⓘ Information

The **visitor center** (☑ 563-322-3911; www. visitquadcities.com; 136 E 3rd St, RiverCenter; ⊙ 8:30am-5pm Mon-Fri year-round, 9am-4pm Sat May-Oct) is downtown in the RiverCenter development. It has info for the entire Quad Cities region.

ⓘ Getting There & Away

Davenport lies on the border with Illinois. Greyhound (www.greyhound.com) has several buses a day to Chicago ($30, three hours), while Burlington Trailways (www.burlingtontrailways.com) serves major Iowa cities.

Iowa City

POP 75,800

The youthful, artsy vibe here is courtesy of the University of Iowa campus. It spills across both sides of the Iowa River (which has good walks on the banks); to the east it mingles with the charming downtown. In summer, when the student-to-townie ratio evens out, the city mellows somewhat.

The school's writing programs are renowned, and Iowa City was named a Unesco City of Literature in 2008. For a sharp parody of the town and school, read Jane Smiley's *Moo*. If you have time, the University of Iowa has good art and natural-history museums.

Note that neighboring Coralville is everything that Iowa City is not: overrun with chains and strip malls.

⊙ Sights

Herbert Hoover
National Historic Site   MUSEUM
(☑ 319-643-2541; www.nps.gov/heho; 110 Parkside Dr, West Branch, near I-80 exit 254; site free, museum adult/child $10/3; ⊙ 9am-5pm) Herbert Hoover, the president of the United States from 1929 to 1933, will forever be remembered for the Great Depression, the economic cataclysm that wiped out the livelihoods of millions. However, he lived a long life (1874–1964) and devoted much of it to public service. This complex preserves the house and some of the nearby structures from the time of his birth until age nine, when he was orphaned and left the area. The museum places his life into context.

📖 Sleeping & Eating

★ Brown Street Inn
B&B **$$**

(☑319-338-0435; www.brownstreetinn.com; 430 Brown St; r $110-170; ❋@🅿️) Four-poster beds and other antiques adorn this six-room 1913 Dutch Colonial place that's an easy walk from downtown. Ask the amiable owner about the house next door, where Kurt Vonnegut wrote early chapters of *Slaughterhouse-Five*.

Clinton Street Social Club
GASTROPUB **$$**

(☑319-351-1690; www.clintonstreetsocial.com; 18½ S Clinton St; mains $11-28; ⊘kitchen 4-10pm, bar to 1am) This swanky 2nd-floor gastropub boasts locally sourced meals and killer libations at the long cocktail bar. Classic movies play on Monday nights and there's live jazz at least twice a month on Thursdays. Professors often come here for half-priced cocktails and bar food during 'social hour' (weekdays 4pm to 6pm).

ℹ️ Getting There & Away

Iowa City is right off I-80. Burlington Trailways (www.burlingtontrailways.com) buses link Iowa City with Des Moines ($18, two hours), Davenport ($12, one hour) and other Iowa cities.

Amana Colonies

These seven villages, just north of I-80, are stretched along a 17-mile loop. All were first established as German religious communes between 1855 and 1861 by Inspirationists who, until the Great Depression, lived a utopian life with no wages paid and all assets communally owned. Unlike the Amish and Mennonite religions, Inspirationists embrace modern technology (and tourism).

Today the well-preserved (and discreetly tasteful) villages offer a glimpse of this unique religious culture, and there are lots of arts, crafts, cheeses, baked goods and wines to buy.

👁 Sights

Amana Heritage Museum
MUSEUM

(☑319-622-3567; www.amanaheritage.org; 705 44th Ave, Amana; adult/child $8/4; ⊘10am-5pm Mon-Sat, noon-4pm Sun Apr-Oct, 10am-5pm Sat Mar, Nov & Dec) Offers a good overview of the colonies. Ask about the self-guided walking and driving routes that can be accessed via your phone.

ELDON

Grab a 'tool' out of your trunk and make your very own parody of Grant Wood's iconic *American Gothic* (1930) – the pitchfork painting – in tiny Eldon, about 100 miles southeast of Des Moines. The original house depicted in the artwork is across from the **American Gothic House Center** (☑641-652-3352; www.americangothichouse.net; American Gothic St; ⊘10am-5pm Tue-Sat, 1-4pm Sun & Mon) **FREE**, which interprets the painting that sparked a million parodies (it even has loaner costumes so you can make your own parody selfie). The actual painting is in the Art Institute of Chicago.

📖 Sleeping & Eating

Zuber's Homestead Hotel
INN **$**

(☑319-622-3911; www.zubershomesteadhotel. com; 2206 44th Ave, Homestead; r $100-140; ❋🅿️) Each of the 15 rooms in this 1860s brick building has an individual Iowa theme, as well as a note from the owner detailing a day trip to the area where you can further explore that theme. Rates include a hot breakfast buffet.

Amana Meat Shop & Smokehouse
DELI **$**

(☑800-373-6328; www.amanameatshop.com; 4513 F St, Amana; snacks from $3; ⊘9am-5pm Mon-Sat, 10am-4pm Sun) A kingdom of locally produced cheeses and smoked meats. Get your picnic supplies here.

ℹ️ Information

Amana Colonies Visitors Center (☑319-622-7622; www.amanacolonies.com; 622 46th Ave, Amana; ⊘9am-5pm Mon-Sat, 10am-5pm Sun May-Oct, 10am-4pm daily Nov-Apr) Stop at the visitor center in an old corn crib for the essential guide-map. Ask about the bus and walking tours.

ℹ️ Getting There & Away

There is no public transportation in the colonies.

Cedar Valley

Cedar Valley is a regional hub for outdoor recreation with numerous trails for biking, hiking and paddling. At its heart are the towns of Waterloo and Cedar Falls. The latter is home to five John Deere tractor factories and is the place to get one of those prized green-and-yellow caps you've seen across middle America. There are also some regal old buildings in its otherwise gritty downtown. Nearby Cedar Falls is Waterloo's posh little sister city, with a crooked Main St brimming with boutique shops and cafes.

Tours

John Deere Tractor Cab
Assembly Tours   TOURS
(☎800-765-9588; www.deere.com; 3500 E Donald St, Waterloo; ☉tours 8am, 10am & 1pm Mon-Fri) FREE Fun 90-minute tractor-driven tours show how parts of tractors are made. The minimum age is 13 and reservations are required at least 48 hours in advance. Afterwards visit the **John Deere Tractor & Engine Museum** (☎319-292-6126; www.deere. com; 500 Westfield Ave, Waterloo; ☉9am-5pm Mon-Sat, noon-4pm Sun) FREE.

Sleeping & Eating

★**Black Hawk Hotel**   HISTORIC HOTEL $$
(☎319-277-1161; www.theblackhawkhotel.com; 115 Main St, Cedar Falls; r $100-200; P❋🐾) This is the longest continuously operating hotel west of the Mississippi and a true treasure of downtown Cedar Falls. Open since 1853, it's been kept in fine fettle ever since. There are 28 rooms in the historic hotel and 15 cheaper ones in a modern building behind it. The restaurant and bar serve innovative and farm-fresh food and drinks.

DON'T MISS

SILOS & SMOKESTACKS NATIONAL HERITAGE AREA

Comprising 37 counties in northeast Iowa, this National Park Service–designated region includes more than 100 sites and attractions that honor the region's industrial past and storybook farm beauty. Highlights include the scenic bluffs of Effigy Mounds National Monument (p667), the rustic villages of the Amana Colonies (p663) and the informative exhibits of the National Mississippi River Museum & Aquarium (p665). Back-road drives abound. Look for the useful *Silos & Smokestacks* annual guide at hotels and visitor centers or learn more at www.silosandsmokestacks.org.

★**Galleria De Paco**   ITALIAN $$
(☎319-833-7226;https://galleria-de-paco.business. site; 622 Commercial St, Waterloo; mains $15-35; ☉4:30-10pm Tue-Sat) It took Michelangelo four years to paint the ceiling of the Sistine Chapel, but it took Evelin 'Paco' Rosic just four months to make a half-sized reproduction of it in spray paint on the ceiling of his Italian restaurant in downtown Waterloo. This over-the-top place lures visitors in with its lavish theatrics, but the gourmet meals have yet to disappoint.

ⓘ Getting There & Away

Burlington Trailways (www.burlingtontrailways. com) runs daily local service buses east to Dubuque ($34, two hours) and west to Des Moines ($37, five hours).

Mt Vernon

POP 4440

In a state blessed with pretty places, Mt Vernon is one of the loveliest. It's located along the historic Lincoln Hwy – one of the first transcontinental routes across America – and boasts tree-lined streets brimming with antique dealers, art galleries and eclectic little stores.

Big Grove Brewery   MODERN AMERICAN $$
(☎319-624-2337; www.biggrovebrewery.com; 101 W Main St, Solon; mains $9-28; ☉kitchen 11am-9pm Tue-Thu & Sun, to 10pm Fri & Sat) Hits a home run with cliché-busting takes on Iowa comfort food; it's seasonal, locally sourced and great alongside its home-brewed beers. Located 10 miles south of Mt Vernon in neighboring Solon.

ⓘ Information

Mt Vernon Visitors Center (☎319-210-9935; www.visitmvl.com; 311 1st St NW; ☉9am-4pm Mon-Fri) Grab a map here and set off on a self-guided audio tour of historic Mt Vernon.

ⓘ Getting There & Away

Mt Vernon is 20 miles north of Iowa City on IA-1. There is no public transportation.

Dubuque

POP 58,300

This historic city, with its 19th-century Victorian homes lining narrow streets between the Mississippi River and seven steep limestone hills, makes a fine base for Great River Road (p667) explorations. Take a stroll down the 9-mile path along the waterfront and explore neighborhoods in the midst of urban revitalization, thanks to tax money from gaudy new riverfront casinos.

Don't miss the gentrified Millwork District immediately north of downtown past 6th St. Its old wood-working factories are now home to great restaurants and nightlife.

◉ Sights

★National Mississippi River Museum & Aquarium
MUSEUM

(☑563-557-9545; www.rivermuseum.com; 350 E 3rd St; adult/child $18/13; ⊙9am-6pm Jun-Aug, 10am-5pm Sep-May, closed Mon Nov-Feb; ⊕) Learn about life (of all sorts) along the length of the Mississippi at this impressive museum, part of a vast riverfront development. Exhibits span steamboating, aquatic life and indigenous Mississippi River dwellers. Interactive exhibits include touch ponds where you can feel a jellyfish, among other critters.

⌂ Sleeping & Eating

Hotel Julien
HISTORIC HOTEL $$

(☑563-556-4200; www.hoteljuliendubuque.com; 200 Main St; r $110-250; ❋🕸) The historic eight-story Hotel Julien was built in 1915 and was once a refuge for Al Capone. It's quite spiffy after a lavish renovation and is a real antidote to chains.

Brazen Open Kitchen
AMERICAN $$

(☑563-587-8899; www.brazenopenkitchen.com; 955 Washington St; mains $16-37; ⊙4:30-9pm Tue-Thu, to 10pm Fri & Sat, 10am-2pm Sun) The poetic menus at this stylish amber-lit restaurant in the Millwork District are organized like so: roots + soil, flour + water, farm + fish. The resulting seasonal New American cuisine is heavenly. There's a sizable wine list and inventive cocktails at the long wooden bar.

❶ Information

Dubuque Visitor Center (☑800-798-8844; www.traveldubuque.com; 280 Main St; ⊙9am-5pm Mon-Sat, 10am-3pm Sun) Downtown, Dubuque's visitor center has information for the entire region and state.

❶ Getting There & Away

Dubuque is just over three hours west of Chicago via US 20 and I-90. Burlington Trailways (www.burlingtontrailways.com) runs one bus a day west on a meandering route (Waterloo, Cedar Rapids, Ames etc) to Des Moines ($50, seven hours). Another bus goes east to Chicago ($45, 4½ hours).

CEDAR RAPIDS

A small old industrial city built on meat-packing and eastern European immigration, Cedar Rapids is worth the detour north from I-80. Of course, US 30 is the much more interesting road and it passes right through.

See the **studio** (☑319-366-7503; www.crma.org; 810 2nd Avenue SE; ⊙noon-4pm Sat & Sun Apr-Dec) FREE where Grant Wood painted his most famous work, American Gothic, then stroll the revitalized NewBo neighborhood along the Cedar River and enjoy a traditional Czech treat at **Sykora Bakery** (☑319-364-5271; www.facebook.com/sykora bakery; 73 16th Ave SW; snacks from $2; ⊙7am-7pm Mon-Sat, 10am-5pm Sun).

Iowa's Great Lakes

Iowa's Great Lakes consist of three big, clear blue lakes and a dozen smaller ones. They've catered to family holidays for over a century and long balmy nights sitting by the water are a cherished childhood memory for many an Iowan.

Swimming, boating and fishing are the big activities and there's a sensational amusement park in the town of **Arnolds Park,** the hub of the action. Travelling across northern Iowa, the lakes come as a surprise as there's no hint these vast water-filled depressions exist in the corn-covered countryside until you're almost upon them.

On the downside, the area's spine, US 71, is a charmless road lined with strip malls, fast food and even some light industry. Get to a bucolic lakeshore and don't look back.

◉ Sights

The three main bodies of water that comprise Iowa's Great Lakes each have different personalities.

Big Spirit Lake is the largest lake (some 5700 acres) and the most genteel. Small parks around its shoreline are popular with young families and those who appreciate time to contemplate the big, placid waters. The village is relaxed and good for strolling, with a handful of appealing cafes, pubs and services. It had various traditional names, which translated roughly as 'lake of the spirits.'

East Lake Okoboji is long, narrow and unfortunately colon-shaped. This 6-mile-long lake in every way connects the two worlds of the Great Lakes region. In the north it's the backdrop for the mannered streets of the Spirit Lake community. In the south it joins with its west counterpart in a raucous hub of bars and boats.

West Lake Okoboji is the original holiday lake here. Home to Arnolds Park and a plethora of other amusements, diversions, holiday camps, resorts etc. It's the most popular lake in Iowa and was originally known as Minnetonka by the Sioux people, which meant 'great waters.'

★**Arnolds Park
Amusement Park**   AMUSEMENT PARK

(☏712-332-2183; www.arnoldspark.com; 37 Lake St, Arnolds Park; day-pass from $35; ☺hours vary, mid-May–early Sep; ♠) Dating back to the 1880s, this old-fashioned lakeside amusement park is pure fun. The Legend is the seventh-oldest wooden roller coaster in the world and dates to 1930. Other rides cater to every age and temperament. It's a carefree place of simple delights. Interestingly, the park is owned by a nonprofit foundation which has embarked on an ambitious restoration program. Already completed are the Wild Mouse metal roller coaster and the Funhouse Slide, among others.

★**Gull Point State Park**   STATE PARK

(☏712-337-3211; www.iowadnr.gov; 1500 Harpen St, Milford; ♠) **FREE** The best state park locally is on the west side of West Okoboji Lake. It has a beach, lovely lakeside picnic areas and an excellent 1.3-mile long nature trail.

ℹ **Information**

Visitor Center (☏712-322-6550; www.vacation okoboji.com; 243 W Broadway, Arnolds Park; ☺9am-5pm Mon-Fri) volunteers in Arnolds Park can answer any question about the Great Lakes and offer info for the region and the entire state. The center is in the same complex as the **Maritime Museum** (☏712-332-2183; www.arnoldspark.com; ☺hours vary, mid-May–early Sep).

ℹ **Getting There & Away**

There is no public transportation in the Great Lake region.

NORTH DAKOTA

Fields of grain – green in spring and summer, bronze in fall and white in winter – stretch beyond every horizon in much of desolate North Dakota. Except for the rugged 'badlands' of the far west, geographic relief is subtle; often it's the collapsing remains of a failed homestead that break up the vista.

This is one of the least-visited states in the US. However the lack of holiday-makers doesn't mean the state is a sleepy backwater. The Bakken oil boom (named for geologic formations beneath the surface) has transformed the northwest quadrant into one vast drilling site. At night, fires burning off waste gas give the landscape hellish vistas. Once sleepy towns like Williston and Watford City have been transformed into industrial warrens.

Near the Montana border you'll find natural beauty that justifies a trip while the Missouri River is dotted with sights tied to the Lewis and Clark Expedition.

ℹ **Information**

North Dakota Tourism (www.ndtourism.com)
North Dakota Bed & Breakfast Association (www.ndbba.com)
North Dakota State Parks (www.parkrec. nd.gov) Vehicle entrance fees cost $7/35 per day/year.

Fargo

POP 122,000

Named for the Fargo of Wells Fargo Bank, North Dakota's biggest city has been a fur-trading post, a frontier town, a quick-divorce capital and a haven for folks in the Federal Witness Protection Program; not to mention the namesake of the Coen Brothers' film *Fargo* (and more recently, the movie-inspired TV series) – though the movie was both filmed and set across the Red River in Minnesota. Still, expect to hear a lot of accents similar to Frances McDormand's unforgettable version in the movie.

Like much of North Dakota, the city is thin on actual sights. But it has a spunk to its character that's infectious and a bevy of attractive brick establishments downtown that make it a worthy of a one-night stopover.

IOWA'S GREAT RIVER ROAD

Iowa's Great River Road mostly hugs the Mississippi along the state's eastern edge. It combines numerous country byways and passes through some beautifully isolated riverfront towns. Meet the route in Iowa's far northeastern corner at **Lansing**, an attractive resort town with a grand panorama of three states from the top of **Mt Hosmer Park**.

Continue south to **Effigy Mounds National Monument** (☑563-873-3491; www.nps. gov/efmo; Hwy 76, Marquette; ☺9am-5pm Jun-Aug, to 4pm Sep-May) FREE, where hundreds of mysterious Native American burial mounds lie in bluffs above the Mississippi River. Listen to songbirds as you hike the lush trails.

Neighboring **Marquette** and **McGregor** are next up. Both are delightful historic villages whose main drags are worthy of a quick stroll. The latter is the gateway to **Pikes Peak State Park** (☑563-873-2341; www.iowadnr.gov/Places-to-Go/State-Parks; 32264 Pikes Peak Rd, McGregor; campsites from $11-19 May-Sep, $6-14 Oct-Apr) FREE, a nature reserve at the confluence of the Wisconsin and Mississippi Rivers with 10 intertwined hiking trails and sweeping views from the hilltop campground.

Dip down into **Guttenberg**, a modern town with a strip of shops and eateries along the riverfront, before entering the regional hub of **Dubuque** where you can learn about life on the Mississippi at the impressive National Mississippi River Museum & Aquarium (p665). Part of a vast riverfront development, its exhibits span steamboating, aquatic life and the history of the indigenous peoples of the Mississippi River.

Along an especially scenic stretch of the road south of Dubuque you'll find **Bellevue**, which lives up to its name with good river views and some verdant, rural scenery. Stop at **Potter's Mill** (☑563-872-3838; www.pottersmill.net; 300 Potter Dr, Bellevue; mains $10-23; ☺11am-8pm Sun-Thu, to 9pm Fri & Sat, closed Mon Oct-Apr), an old grain mill where you can chow down on hearty Southern cooking while listening to live jazz and blues music. Further south, **Clinton** embraces the river with waterfront walkways and **Eagle Point Park** (☑563-243-1260; 3923 N 3rd St, Clinton; ☺dawn-dusk) FREE, which has sweeping river views from a 100-foot bluff (and a castle!).

The landscape flattens out from here with wide-open vistas as you enter the bustling streets of **Davenport**, the largest of the so-called Quad Cities. Further south, **Burlington** has an excellent welcome center and is good for a quick break before you finish up the journey past **Old Fort Madison**, a reconstruction of the Midwest's oldest American military garrison on the upper Mississippi, in **Keokuk.**

Get more info on the route at www.iowagreatriverroad.com.

◉ Sights

Plains Art Museum MUSEUM
(☑701-551-6100; www.plainsart.org; 704 1st Ave N; ☺11am-5pm Tue-Wed & Fri-Sat, to 9pm Thu) FREE This ambitious and free museum features sophisticated programs in a renovated warehouse. The permanent collection includes contemporary work by Native American artists.

Fargo Woodchipper VISITOR CENTER
(☑701-282-3653; www.fargomoorhead.org; 2001 44th St, I-94 exit 348; ☺8am-8pm Mon-Fri, 9am-6pm Sat & Sun Jun-Sep, 8am-5pm Mon-Fri, 10am-4pm Sat Sep-May) FREE Fargo's embrace of its namesake film is on display at the town's engaging visitor center, which houses the actual woodchipper used for the scene where Gaear feeds the last of Carl's body into its maw and is discovered by Marge. You can reenact the scene – although not the results – while wearing Fargo-style hats and jamming in a fake leg (both provided).

🛏 Sleeping & Eating

★**Hotel Donaldson** HOTEL **$$**
(☑701-478-1000; www.hoteldonaldson.com; 101 Broadway; r from $185; ❄@🛜) A stylish and swank revamp of a flophouse, the 17 well-appointed rooms here are each decorated by a local artist. Fargo's most chic restaurant, HoDo, and rooftop bar (and hot tub!) await. There's also free wine and cheese each evening at 5pm.

Wurst Bier Hall GERMAN **$**
(☑701-478-2437; www.wurstfargo.com; 630 1st Ave N; mains $6-12; ☺11am-11pm; 🍴) This always-hopping German-style beer hall ups the stakes with inventive sausage

ℹ MOUNTAIN TIME IN NORTH DAKOTA

The southwest quarter of North Dakota, including Medora, uses Mountain Time, which is one hour earlier than the rest of the state's Central Time.

sandwiches, exotic meats and a creative list of over 40 beers on tap. There's even a number of veggie options.

ℹ Getting There & Away

Hector International Airport (FAR; ☑701-241-8168; www.fargoairport.com; 2801 32nd Ave N) is the busiest in the state and has services from regional hubs such as Chicago, Minneapolis and Denver. Jefferson Lines (www.jeffersonlines.com) has daily buses to Bismarck ($40, three hours), Minneapolis ($45, four hours) and Sioux Falls ($40, four hours) from downtown Fargo. Amtrak's *Empire Builder* links Fargo with St Paul ($47, 5½ hours, one daily).

Bismarck

POP 72,900

Like the surrounding plains of wheat, Bismarck, North Dakota's capital, has a quick and bountiful summer. Otherwise, it's a place that hunkers down for the long winters, where temperature averages drop to -4°F (-20°C). The compact downtown has a modest collection of shops and restaurants; the sprawl that radiates out from it is rather uninspiring. The industrial adjoining city of Mandan is just west across the Missouri River.

The city was named for the 19th-century German statesman in hopes of attracting German immigrants. Ultimately Bismarck was settled by scores of German immigrants, but there's no proof that the name played a role in this.

★**North Dakota Heritage Center** MUSEUM (☑701-328-2666; www.history.nd.gov; 612 East Boulevard Ave, Capitol Hill; ⊗8am-5pm Mon-Fri, from 10am Sat & Sun) **FREE** Behind a statue of Sacagawea, the Shoshone woman who guided Lewis and Clark on their expedition in 1804, the state's history museum has details on everything from Norwegian bachelor farmers to the scores of nuclear bombs perched on missiles in silos across the state.

Fort Abraham Lincoln State Park HISTORIC SITE (☑701-667-6340; www.parkrec.nd.gov/fort-abraham-lincoln-state-park; off Hwy 1806; per vehicle $7, tours adult/child $8/5; ⊗park 9am-5pm) The highlight at this attractive rural park on the west bank of the Missouri is On-a-Slant Indian Village, which has five re-created Mandan earth lodges. The fort, with several replica buildings, was Custer's last stop before the Battle of Little Bighorn. It's 7 miles south of Mandan (or about 13 miles from downtown Bismarck). It has extensive hiking trails and summertime tours.

ℹ Information

Bismarck-Mandan Visitor Center (☑701-222-4308; www.noboundariesnd.com; 1600 Burnt Boat Dr, I-94 exit 157; ⊗7.30am-5pm Mon-Fri) Has oodles of North Dakota souvenirs.

ℹ Getting There & Away

Bismarck Airport (BIS; ☑701-355-1800; www.bismarckairport.com; 2301 University Dr) is 3 miles southeast of the city and receives flights from regional hubs such as Denver, Minneapolis and Chicago. Jefferson Lines (www.jeffersonlines.com) has daily buses to Fargo ($40, three hours).

Theodore Roosevelt National Park

Future president Theodore Roosevelt retreated from New York to this remote spot in his early 20s after losing both his wife and mother in a matter of hours. It's said that his time in the Dakota badlands inspired him to become an avid conservationist, and he set aside 230 million acres of federal land while in office, a quantity of land larger than Texas. His North Dakota legacy is this 110-sq-mile **national park** (☑701-623-4466; www.nps.gov/thro; 7-day pass per vehicle $30; ⊗park 24hr), one of the most underappreciated stars of the park system.

Wildlife abounds in these surreal mounds of striated earth, from mule deer to wild horses, bison, bighorn sheep and elk. There are also around 200 bird species, and innumerable prairie dogs in sprawling subterranean towns. Sunrise is your best time for animal encounters, while sunset is particularly evocative as shadows dance across the lonely buttes, painting them in an array of earth tones before they fade to black.

🛏 Sleeping

The resort town of Medora makes a great base with comfortable lodgings across all budgets. The park itself has two campgrounds; the most popular is **Cottonwood Campground** (☎ 701-623-4466; www.recreation.gov; E River Rd; tent sites $7-14; ☺ year-round). Wild camping is permitted in the backcountry for up to 14 consecutive nights; get a free permit at the visitor centers.

ℹ Information

The park has three visitor centers, the most substantial being **South Unit Visitor Center** (off I-94 exits 24 & 27, Medora; ☺ 8am-6pm Mountain Time Jun-Sep, to 4:30pm Oct-May), with Theodore Roosevelt's old cabin out back.

ℹ Getting There & Away

The park is divided into North and South Units, which are located 70 miles apart. The South Unit is in Medora, 135 miles west of Bismarck along I-94. It houses the park's main visitor center and receives more traffic due to its proximity to I-94. The more remote North Unit is to the north, 15 miles south of Watford City, accessed via US 85. You'll need your own wheels to get here.

The nearest airports are Theodore Roosevelt Regional Airport in Dickinson (42 miles east of the South Unit), with direct flights to Denver, and Sloulin Field International Airport in Williston (61 miles north of the North Unit), with services to Minneapolis and Denver.

Medora is a four-hour drive north from Rapid City, SD.

SOUTH DAKOTA

Gently rolling prairies through shallow fertile valleys mark much of this endlessly attractive state. But head southwest and all hell breaks loose – in the best possible way. The Badlands National Park is the geologic equivalent of fireworks. The Black Hills are like opera: majestic, challenging, intriguing and even frustrating. Mt Rushmore matches the Statue of Liberty for five-star icon status.

ℹ Information

South Dakota Department of Tourism (www.travelsd.com)
Bed & Breakfast Innkeepers of South Dakota (www.southdakotabb.com)
South Dakota State Parks (www.gfp.sd.gov) Vehicle permits cost $6/30 per day/year.

Sioux Falls

POP 176,900
South Dakota's largest city lives up to its name at Falls Park, where the Big Sioux River plunges through a long series of rock faces. Just south of here lies a buzzing downtown district graced with a burgeoning foodie scene and some of the best eats in the region.

⭐**Falls Park**   PARK
(131 E Falls Park Dr; ☺ 5am-midnight) Stroll along the grass-lined paths to Sioux Falls' star attraction – its rambling namesake waterfall – at this picturesque park. Popular with amorous couples, it has a perfectly placed cafe and plenty of scenic overlooks and picnic tables. Visit between mid-November and mid-January and it becomes a winter wonderland with 355,000 twinkling lights.

⭐**MB Haskett Delicatessen**   MODERN AMERICAN **$$**
(☎ 605-367-1100; www.mbhaskett.com; 324 S Phillips Ave; mains $8-24; ☺ 7am-4pm Mon, to 9pm Tue-Thu, to 10pm Fri, 8am-10pm Sat, 8am-3pm Sun) Michael Haskett's retro cafe serves brilliant food throughout the day, from breakfast through dinner. The ever-changing menu draws inspiration from the seasons and from around the globe.

ℹ Information

Sioux Falls Visitor Information Center (☎ 605-367-7430; www.visitsiouxfalls.com; 900 N Phillips Ave; ☺ 9am-9pm May-Sep, reduced hours Oct-Apr) This visitor center in Falls Park has city-wide information and an observation tower.

THE ENCHANTED HIGHWAY

Boasting huge whimsical metal sculptures of local folks and critters by artist Gary Greff, the Enchanted Hwy runs for 32 miles straight south to Regent from I-94 exit 72. Once there, you can stay in a themed motel, the **Enchanted Castle** (☎ 701-563-4858; www.enchantedcastlend.com; 607 Main St, Regent; r $100-135; ❄@🐾), which is an elementary school remodeled with crenelations.

The roadside artworks include the world's largest scrap metal sculpture, the 110ft-tall 'Geese in Flight'.

❶ Getting There & Away

Sioux Falls Regional Airport (FSD; ☑605-336-0762; www.sfairport.com; 2801 N Jaycee Lane) has services from major regional hubs such as Chicago, Denver and Minneapolis. Jefferson Lines (www.jeffersonlines.com) buses travel along I-90 to Rapid City ($74, six hours, one daily) and along I-29 twice daily to Fargo ($50, 4 hours) and Omaha ($50, 3½ hours).

Chamberlain

POP 2400

In a picturesque site where I-90 crosses the muddy Missouri River, Chamberlain (exit 263) is home to some worthwhile spots to learn about both local tribes and the historic Lewis and Clark expedition that passed through the area.

The best reason to detour off I-90 immerses you in large swaths of South Dakota that haven't changed since the 19th century, when the Native Americans and US Army clashed. The **Native American Scenic Byway** (www.scenicbyways.info) begins in Chamberlain on Hwy 50 and meanders 100 miles northwest to Pierre along Hwy 1806, following the Missouri River through rolling, rugged countryside.

★ Akta Lakota

Museum & Cultural Center　　　MUSEUM
(☑800-798-3452; www.aktalakota.org; 1301 N Main St, St Joseph's Indian School; suggested donation $5; ⊙8am-6pm Mon-Sat, 9am-5pm Sun May-Oct, 8am-4:30pm Mon-Fri Nov-Apr) This engaging museum and cultural center at St Joseph's Indian School has Lakota cultural displays and contemporary art from numerous tribes. Check the gift shop for locally made jewelry, quilts and dream catchers.

Lewis & Clark Information Center　MUSEUM
(☑605-734-4562; I-90 exit 264; ⊙8:30am-4:30pm mid-May–Sep) FREE Get out of your car – instead of your canoe – at this hilltop rest stop, south of town, for exhibits on the intrepid duo and their voyages past here on the Missouri below in 1804 and 1806.

❶ Getting There & Away

Chamberlain is about 100 miles southeast of Pierre along the Native American Scenic Byway. Jefferson Lines (www.jeffersonlines.com) runs a daily bus along I-90.

Pierre

POP 14,000

Pierre (pronounced 'peer') boasts a scenic location on the Missouri River and makes a decent stopover in the middle of South Dakota. It's the capital of South Dakota, but it's just too small to feel like the seat of power.

Getting here is more than half the fun: the **Native American Scenic Byway** (www.scenicbyways.info) begins in Chamberlain on Hwy 50 and meanders 100 crooked miles following the Missouri River through rolling, rugged countryside northwest to Pierre. It mostly follows Hwy 1806.

❍ Sights

South Dakota

Cultural Heritage Center　　　MUSEUM
(☑605-773-3458; www.history.sd.gov; 900 Governors Dr; adult/child $4/free; ⊙9am-6:30pm Mon-Sat, 1-4:30pm Sun Jun-Aug, to 4:30pm Sep-May) Exhibits at this ecologically groundbreaking museum (it's completely underground) include a bloody Ghost Dance shirt from Wounded Knee. Exhibits trace the state's history from before European contact through to its role as a base for nuclear missiles and bombs during the Cold War.

🛏 Sleeping & Eating

Hitching Horse Inn　　　　　B&B $
(☑605-494-0550; 635 N Euclid Ave; r $60-100; ❄🏠) This welcoming four-room inn has an understated charm and is free of the suffocating twee doodads common in other B&Bs. Two of the rooms have Jacuzzi tubs and there's a tiny equestrian-themed beer and wine bar on the 1st floor that's popular with locals.

Cattleman's Club　　　　　STEAK $$
(☑605-224-9774; www.cattlemansclubsteakhouse.com; 29608 Hwy 34; mains $8-35; ⊙5-10pm Mon-Sat) Offering a gorgeous view over the Missouri River, this famed steakhouse 6 miles east of Pierre hopes you won't order your hunk of beef well done (enjoy it pink and juicy!).

❶ Getting There & Away

Smack in the middle of South Dakota, Pierre is about 3½ hours from Sioux Falls and three hours from Rapid City by car, mostly along I-90. Jefferson Lines (www.jeffersonlines.com) runs daily from Pierre to Rapid City ($46, 3¾ hours) and Sioux Falls ($55, 4½ hours).

Wall

POP 870

This is the town that a thousand billboards built. Hyped for hundreds of miles thanks to the tourist magnet of Wall Drug, a sprawling faux frontier complex, there's no reason not to succumb.

◉ Sights

★**Wall Drug**   LANDMARK
(🗹605-279-2175; www.walldrug.com; 510 Main St; ⊙7am-9pm; 🖶) Wall Drug is a surprisingly enjoyable tourist attraction of the old school. It really does have 5¢ coffee, free ice water, good donuts and enough diversions and come-ons to warm the heart of schlock-lovers everywhere. But amid the fudge is a superb bookstore with a great selection of regional titles. Out back, ride the mythical jackalope and check out the historical photos.

Story of Wounded Knee   MUSEUM
(🗹605-279-2573; www.woundedkneemuseum.org; 207 10th Ave; adult/child $6/free; ⊙10am-5pm late May–Sep) This important small museum tells the story of the Wounded Knee massacre from the Lakota perspective using photos and narratives. It's more insightful than anything at the actual site.

Delta-09 Missile Silo   HISTORIC SITE
(195th Ave, I-90 exit 116; ⊙9am-3pm) `FREE` This Cold War–era missile silo, located down a dirt road in a desolate area 5 miles southeast of Wall, gives you a glimpse into the enormous network of similar sites scattered across the American heartland during a time when the US hoped to secure itself against a Soviet nuclear attack. The silo can be viewed without a ticket through a glass cover. It's part of the **Minuteman Missile National Historic Site** (🗹tour reservations 866-601-5129; www.nps.gov/mimi; I-90 exit 131; visitor center free, tours adult/child $12/8; ⊙visitor center 8am-4pm, missile silo tours 9am-3pm) – the visitor center is 15 miles southeast.

ℹ Information

National Grasslands Visitors Center (🗹605-279-2125; www.blackhillsparks.org; 798 Main St; ⊙8am-4:30pm Mon-Fri) The National Grasslands Visitors Center in Wall has good displays on this underappreciated and complex ecosystem, which comprises much of the land between Wall and the Badlands.

ℹ Getting There & Away

Wall is just under an hour east of Rapid City via I-90. Jefferson Lines (www.jeffersonlines.com) stops here on its trips along I-90.

Badlands National Park

The otherworldly landscape of **Badlands National Park** (🗹605-433-5361; www.nps.gov/badl; Hwy 240; 7-day park pass bicycle/car $12/25), oddly softened by its fantastic rainbow hues, is a spectacle of sheer walls and spikes stabbing the dry air. It was understandably named *mako sica* (badland) by Native Americans. Looking over the bizarre formations from the corrugated walls surrounding the park is like seeing an ocean someone boiled dry.

The North Unit of the park is easily viewed on a half-day drive for those in a rush, though there are a number of short hiking trails that can get you right out into this earthen wonderland, including the surreal **Door Trail** near the Ben Reifel Visitor Center (p672). The less-accessible Stronghold Unit is in the Pine Ridge Indian Reservation and sees few visitors. Bisecting the two is Hwy 44, which makes a scenic alternative between the Badlands and Rapid City.

◉ Sights

★**Hwy 240 Badlands Loop Rd**   AREA
Badlands National Park's North Unit gets the most visitors; this stunning road is easily reached from I-90 (exits 110 and 131) and you can drive it in an hour if you're in a hurry (and not stuck behind an RV). It is the main thoroughfare through the park,

---

`OFF THE BEATEN TRACK`

MITCHELL: THE CORN PALACE

The **Corn Palace** (🗹605-995-8430; www.cornpalace.com; 604 N Main St; ⊙8am-9pm Jun-Aug, reduced hours Sep-May) is the king of roadside attractions, enticing more than half a million people to pull off I-90 each year. Close to 300,000 ears of corn are used annually to create a new tableaux of murals on the outside of the building. Ponder the scenes and you may find a kernel of truth or just say, 'aw, shucks.' Head inside to see photos of how the facade has evolved over the years.

GREAT PLAINS WALL

with lookouts, vistas and animal sightings aplenty.

Sage Creek Rim Rd AREA
The portion of the Badlands west of Hwy 240 along this gravel road is much less visited than the sights of the Badlands Loop Rd (p671). There are scenic overlooks and stops at prairie-dog towns; this is where most backcountry hikers and campers go to escape the crowds. As there is almost no water or shade here, don't strike out into the wilderness unprepared.

🛏 Sleeping

The park has two campgrounds and a seasonal lodge. Hotels can be found on I-90 in Kadoka and Wall. There are also campgrounds and inns near the southern entrance at Interior.

ℹ Information

Ben Reifel Visitor Center (☎605-433-5361; www.nps.gov/badl; Hwy 240; 7-day park pass bicycle/car $12/25; ⏰7am-7pm Jun-Aug, 8am-5pm Apr-May & Sep-Oct, 8am-4pm Nov-Mar) The main visitor center for the park; has good exhibits and advice for ways to ditch your car to appreciate the geologic wonders.

White River Visitor Center (☎605-455-2878; Hwy 27; ⏰9am-5pm Jun-Aug) Small information outlet in the little-visited Stronghold Unit.

ℹ Getting There & Around

Badlands National Park is about 70 miles east of Rapid City. You can access the park at several points north and south. There is no public transportation to (or within) the park.

Pine Ridge Indian Reservation

Home to the Oglala Lakota Sioux, the Pine Ridge Reservation south of Badlands National Park is one of the nation's poorest counties, with more than half the population living below the poverty line. Despite being at times a jarring dose of reality, it is also a place welcoming to visitors. Tune in to KILI (90.1FM), which often plays traditional music.

History

In 1890 the new Ghost Dance religion became popular and Lakota followers believed it would both bring back their ancestors and eliminate the white man. This struck fear into the area's soldiers and settlers, and the frenetic circle dances were outlawed. The 7th US Cavalry rounded up a band of Lakota people under Chief Big Foot and brought them to the small village of Wounded Knee.

On December 29, as the soldiers began to search for weapons, a shot was fired (nobody knows by who), leading to the massacre of more than 250 men, women and children, most of them unarmed. It's one of the most infamous atrocities in US history. Twenty-five soldiers also died.

⊙ Sights

Wounded Knee Massacre Site HISTORIC SITE
(Hwy 27) The massacre site, 16 miles northeast of Pine Ridge town, is marked by a faded sign. It helps to read up on the events before you arrive. The mass grave sits atop the hill near a church. Small memorials appear daily amid the stones listing dozens of names. It's a desolate place, with sweeping views. You may encounter locals looking for donations. An ad hoc timeline lists acts of genocide against Native Americans.

Red Cloud Heritage Center MUSEUM
(☎605-867-8257; www.redcloudschool.org; 100 Mission Dr, Pine Ridge; ⏰8am-6pm Mon-Sat, 10am-5pm Sun Jun-Aug, 9am-5pm Tue-Sat Sep-May) FREE This well-curated art museum has traditional and contemporary works and a craft shop with locally made artisan goods. Haunting photos taken after the Wounded Knee massacre show the frozen bodies of the dead with their expressions of shock locked in place. It's 4 miles north of Pine Ridge on Hwy 18 at the Red Cloud Indian School.

ℹ Getting There & Away

The town of Pine Ridge is near the Nebraska border about two hours south of Rapid City via Hwy 27. There are no public buses in the region.

Black Hills

They call the Black Hills an evergreen island in a sea of high-prairie grassland. This stunning region on the Wyoming–South Dakota border lures scores of visitors with its winding canyons and wildly eroded 7000ft peaks. The region's name – the 'Black' comes from the dark ponderosa-pine-covered slopes – was conferred by the Lakota Sioux. In the 1868 Fort Laramie Treaty, they were assured that the hills would be theirs for eternity, but the discovery of gold changed that and the Sioux were shoved out to low-value flatlands only six years later. The 1990 film *Dances with Wolves* covers some of this period.

You'll need several days to explore the bucolic back-road drives, caves, bison herds, forests, Deadwood, and Mt Rushmore and Crazy Horse monuments, and to experience the abundant outdoor activities (cycling, rock climbing, boating, hiking, downhill skiing, gold-panning etc). Like fool's gold, gaudy tourist traps lurk in corners.

ℹ️ Information

Avoid visiting during the **Sturgis Motorcycle Rally** (📱605-720-0800; www.sturgismotorcyclerally.com; 🕑 early Aug) in early August, when hogs rule the roads and fill the rooms. Much is closed October to April.

Black Hills Visitor Center (📱605-355-3700; www.blackhillsbadlands.com; I-90 exit 61, Rapid City, 1851 Discovery Circle; 🕑8am-7pm Jun-Aug, to 5pm Sep-May; 🛜) has tons of info. Ask about various informative and useful apps on offer.

ℹ️ Getting There & Around

Rapid City Regional Airport (RAP; 📱605-394-4195; www.rapairport.com; 4550 Terminal Rd) is 9 miles southeast of Rapid City. It's the main gateway for trips into the Badlands and Black Hills, and has services from major American hubs. Jefferson Lines (www.jeffersonlines.com) buses travel along I-90, east to Sioux Falls ($74, six hours, one daily) and west into Wyoming.

There is no public transportation to (or within) the Black Hills so it's best to visit the region with your own wheels.

Rapid City

POP 74,500

An appealing capital to the region, 'Rapid' has a cosmopolitan air best appreciated in the intriguing, lively and walkable downtown. Well-preserved brick buildings, filled with quality shopping and dining, make it a good urban base for Black Hills exploration, particularly for those who enjoy their creature comforts.

👁 Sights

Get a walking-tour brochure of Rapid's historic buildings and public art from the Black Hills Visitor Center or the city's visitor center (p675). Check out the watery fun and regular events downtown on **Main St Square**. Nearby, visit **Art Alley** (north of Main St between 6th and 7th Sts), where urban-style graffiti and pop art has turned a mundane alley into a kaleidoscope of color. And besides presidents, look for **statues of dinosaurs** around town.

Family-friendly and proudly hokey tourist attractions vie for dollars along Hwy 16 on the way to Mt Rushmore.

⭐**Statues of Presidents** STATUE (www.presidentsrc.com; 631 Main St; 🕑 info center noon-9pm Mon-Sat, to 5pm Sun May-Sep, shorter hours other times) **FREE** From a shifty-eyed Nixon in repose to a triumphant Harry Truman, lifelike statues dot corners throughout the center of Rapid City. Collect all 42. Maps are available online and at the friendly info center on Main St (which also sells ice cream). A much-anticipated 43rd statue, for Barack Obama, was due to debut at the corner of St Joseph and Fourth Sts in late 2019.

Journey Museum & Learning Center MUSEUM (📱605-394-6923; www.journeymuseum.org; 222 New York St; adult/child $12/7; 🕑9am-6pm Mon-Sat, 11am-5pm Sun May-Sep, 10am-5pm Mon-Sat, 1-5pm Sun Oct-Apr; 👶) This impressive downtown facility is four museums in one, looking at the history of the region from prehistoric times until today. Collections come from the vaunted **Museum of Geology** (📱605-394-2467; http://museum.sdsmt.edu; 501 E St Joseph St, O'Harra Bldg; 🕑9am-6pm Mon-Sat Jun-Aug, 8:30am-4pm Mon-Sat Sep-May) **FREE**, the Sioux Indian Museum, the Minnilusa Pioneer Museum and the South Dakota Archaeological Research Center.

🛏 Sleeping

Rushmore Hotel & Suites HOTEL $$ (📱605-348-8300; www.therushmorehotel.com; 445 Mt Rushmore Rd; r $100-200; 🅿🌀@🛜🐕) This high-rise hotel has been transformed into a high-concept downtown gem with eco-friendly accents. A lot of the furniture is made from recycled materials, yet there's no skimping on comfort. The marble floor in the lobby is a stunner.

⭐**Hotel Alex Johnson** HISTORIC HOTEL $$$ (📱605-342-1210; www.alexjohnson.com; 523 6th St; r $150-300; 🌀@🛜) The design of this 1927 classic magically blends Germanic Tudor architecture with traditional Lakota Sioux symbols – note the lobby's painted ceiling and the chandelier made of war lances. The rooftop bar is a delight, while the 143 rooms are modernized retro (some have fabulous views). Ask at reception about the hotel's role in Hitchcock's *North by Northwest*.

Black Hills & Badlands National Park

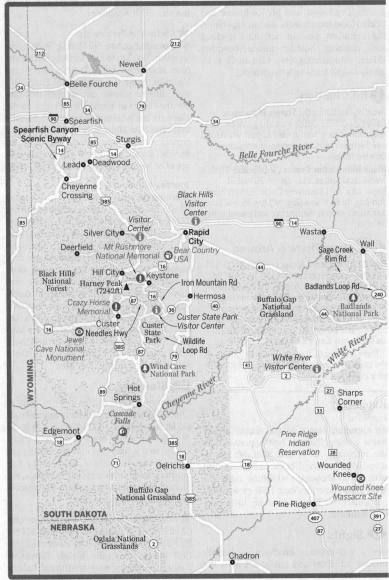

✕ Eating

★ **Harriet & Oak** CAFE $

(☎605-791-0396; www.facebook.com/harrietand
oak; 329 Main St; mains $5-12; ⊘7am-6pm Mon-
Fri, 8am-4pm Sat & Sun; 🛜) This top-notch
bakery, cafe and coffee bar has a fun boho
vibe. The food is tasty and healthy, especially the banana bread and the breakfast burrito on a whole-wheat tortilla. Lunchtime
sandwiches are creative, and there are good
microbrews on tap.

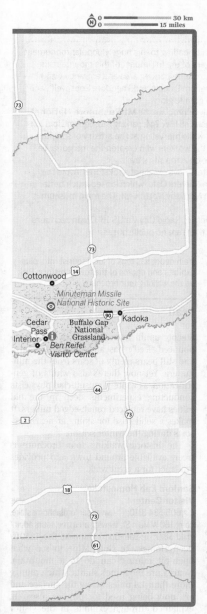

Breakfasts are always good; more creative regional fare is on offer at night. Nab a sidewalk table; on weekends there's live music. Great service.

🛍 Shopping

⭐ Prairie Edge   ARTS & CRAFTS
(☎ 605-342-3408; www.prairieedge.com; 606 Main St; ⊗ 9am-7pm Mon-Sat, 11am-5pm Sun May-Sep, shorter hours other times) This labyrinthine three-story shop has a truly mesmerizing collection of art, furniture and home goods made by members of the Northern Plains tribes. You'll also find out-of-print books and supplies to make your own Native American–inspired works. The upstairs galleries have better items on display than you'll find in many regional museums.

ℹ️ Information

Rapid City Visitor Information Center (www.visitrapidcity.com; 512 Main St, Main Street Square; ⊗ 8am-5pm Mon-Fri) A helpful resource located on Main Street Square.

Deadwood

POP 1300

Once the very definition of lawless, this town built on gold attracts a different kind of fortune seeker these days, with dozens of gambling halls big and small that would no doubt put a sly grin on the faces of the hard characters who once stomped these grounds. Then again, loser's largesse is paying for Deadwood's restoration, which makes it a fascinating place to explore, especially if you can ignore the, er, gamier aspects of mass tourism.

Settled illegally by eager gold rushers in the 1870s, Deadwood is now a National Historic Landmark. Its atmospheric streets are lined with gold-rush-era buildings lavishly restored with gambling dollars. Its storied past – made famous by the namesake HBO TV series and 2019 movie – is easy to find, and there's eternal devotion to Wild Bill Hickok, who was shot in the back of the head here in 1876 while gambling.

⊙ Sights

⭐ Mt Moriah Cemetery   CEMETERY
(☎ 605-578-2600; 2 Mt Moriah Dr; adult/child $2/free, tours $10/5; ⊗ 8am-6pm Jun-Aug, dawn-dusk Sep-May) Calamity Jane (born Martha Jane Burke; 1852–1903) and Wild Bill Hickok (1837–76) rest side by side up on Boot Hill

Tally's Silver Spoon   AMERICAN $$
(☎ 605-342-7621; www.tallyssilverspoon.com; 530 6th St; mains $6-30; ⊗ 7am-9pm Sun-Thu, to 10pm Fri & Sat) Carter or Reagan? Both statues are visible out front and you can ponder your preference while you savor the upscale diner fare at this slick downtown cafe and bar.

DON'T MISS

MT RUSHMORE

Glimpses of Washington's nose from the roads leading to this hugely popular monument never cease to surprise and are but harbingers of the full impact of this mountainside sculpture once you're up close (and past the dreary parking area and entrance walk). George Washington, Thomas Jefferson, Abraham Lincoln and Theodore Roosevelt each iconically stare into the distance in 60ft-tall granite glory.

You can easily escape the crowds and fully appreciate the **Mt Rushmore National Memorial** (☑605-574-2523; www.nps.gov/moru; off Hwy 244; parking $10; ⊙5am-11pm Jun-Aug, to 9pm Sep, much shorter hrs other times) while marveling at the artistry of sculptor Gutzon Borglum and the immense labor of the workers who created the memorial between 1927 and 1941, as few visitors venture onto the site's trails.

The official Park Service information centers have excellent bookstores. Avoid the schlocky Xanterra gift shop and the ho-hum Carvers Cafe, which looked much better in the scene where Cary Grant gets plugged in *North by Northwest*. The main museum is underwhelming.

Mt Rushmore is a half-hour drive southwest of Rapid City via US 16. Organized tours travel to Mt Rushmore from Rapid City, but there are no public buses.

at this very steep cemetery. Pick up the map and explore. Bus tours stop here.

Adams Museum　　　　　　MUSEUM
(☑605-578-1714; www.deadwoodhistory.com; 54 Sherman St; by donation adult/child $5/2; ⊙9am-5pm May-Sep, 10am-4pm Tue-Sun Oct-Apr) Recently revitalized, this museum does an excellent job of capturing the town's colorful past. There's also a small store with books on the region.

🛏 Sleeping & Eating

Bullock Hotel　　　　HISTORIC HOTEL $$
(☑605-578-1745; www.historicbullock.com; 633 Main St; r $70-200; ❋🐾) Fans of the *Deadwood* TV show will recall the conflicted but upstanding sheriff Seth Bullock. This hotel was opened by the real Bullock in 1895. The 28 rooms are modern while retaining the building's period charm. Like most hotels here, it has a casino.

Deadwood Social Club　　　ITALIAN $$
(☑800-952-9398; www.saloon10.com; 657 Main St; mains $20-30; ⊙4-9pm Sun-Thu, to 10pm Fri & Sat) Housed with the historic **Saloon No 10** (⊙kitchen 11am-9pm, bar 8am-2am), this busy restaurant offers crowd-pleasing Italian fare plus steaks. The wine list is long and you can enjoy a drink or a meal under the stars on the rooftop deck.

ℹ Information

Deadwood History & Information Center
(☑800-999-1876; www.deadwood.com; 3 Siever St; ⊙8am-7pm Jun-Aug, 9am-5pm Sep-May) This splendid center in the restored train depot has tons of local tourist info, plus exhibits and photos of the town's history. Pick up the walking tour brochure.

Lead
POP 3000

Steeply uphill from Deadwood, Lead (pronounced 'leed') has an unpolished charm and still bears plenty of scars from the mining era. Yet now there's also whiffs of gentrification, as white-jumpsuit-clad physicists conducting experiments deep in the old mines have replaced rough-edged miners. It makes a solid base for skiing at nearby resorts during the winter season.

The historic walking tour brochure is freely available around town and provides guidance for a great walk.

Sanford Lab Homestake
Visitor Center　　　　　MINE
(☑605-584-3110; www.sanfordlabhomestake. com; 160 W Main St; viewing area free, tours adult/child $8/7; ⊙9am-5pm) Gape at the 1250ft-deep Homestake Gold Mine to see what open-pit mining can do to a mountain. Nearby are the mine's shafts, which plunge more than 1.5 miles below the surface and are now being used for physics research, explained through exhibits in the visitor center. For $10 you can whack golf balls into the seemingly bottomless pit from the observation deck.

★ Town Hall Inn　　　HISTORIC HOTEL $
(☑605-584-1112; www.townhallinn.com; 215 W Main St; r $50-120; 🐾) This 12-room inn oc-

cupies the 1912 Town Hall and has spacious suites named and themed in honor of their former purpose, from the municipal judges chamber to the jury room and mayor's office.

Black Hills National Forest

The majority of the Black Hills lie within this 1.2-million-acre mixture of protected and logged forest, perforated by pockets of private land on most roads. The scenery is fantastic, whether you get deep into it on the 450 miles of hiking trails or drive the byways and gravel fire roads.

⊙ Sights & Activities

Spearfish Canyon Scenic Byway (www.by ways.org) is a waterfall-lined, curvaceous 20-mile road (US 14A) that cleaves into the heart of the hills from Spearfish. There's a sight worth stopping for around every bend; pause for longer than a minute and you'll hear beavers hard at work. It's an excellent alternative to I-90 if you're traveling to Lead and Deadwood.

★ **George S Mickelson Trail**   HIKING
(☑605-584-3896; www.mickelsontrail.com; day/annual pass $4/15) The 109-mile George S Mickelson Trail cuts through much of the Black Hills forest, running from Deadwood through Hill City and Custer to Edgemont on an abandoned railway line. There are bike rentals at various trailside towns and 15 trailheads along the way. Download a useful trail guide from the website.

🛏 Sleeping

Good camping abounds in the forest. There are 30 basic campgrounds (sites $14 to $25; no showers or electricity) and cabins ($35); reserve in summer (877-444-6777, www.rec reation.gov). Free backcountry camping is allowed just about anywhere; no open fires.

Spearfish Canyon Lodge   LODGE $$
(☑605-584-3435; www.spfcanyon.com; 10619 Roughlock Falls Rd, off US 14A, Lead; r $90-260; ❋🐾🐕) This rural retreat is 13 miles south of Spearfish near trails and streams. The lodge's massive lobby fireplace adds charm and the 54 modern piney rooms are cozy. There's a hot tub on a deck.

ℹ Information

Pactola Visitor Center (☑605-343-8755; www.fs.usda.gov/blackhills; US 385, near Hwy 44; ⊙9am-5pm mid-May–Aug) A modern visitor center overlooking the Pactola Reservoir between Hill City and Rapid City. It's a scenic spot for a picnic.

Hill City

POP 1000

One of the more appealing towns up in the hills, Hill City is less frenzied than places such as Keystone, though it virtually shuts down outside of the summer season. Its main drag has cafes, many galleries, cutesy candy shops and Western outfitters.

★ **1880 Train**   TOURS
(☑605-574-2222; www.1880train.com; 222 Railroad Ave, Hill City; adult/child round-trip $29/14; ⊙mid-May–Dec) This classic steam train runs 10 miles through rugged country to Hill City from Keystone. There are one to five departures each way daily. A train museum is next door.

★ **Alpine Inn**   HISTORIC HOTEL $$
(☑605-574-2749; www.alpineinnhillcity.com; 133 Main St; r $80-180; ⊙restaurant 11am-2:30pm & 5-9pm; 🐾) Right in the center of town, the Alpine Inn dates to 1884 and has comfy rooms in regal red. The restaurant serves filling German-accented fare (mains from $8 to $15).

Custer State Park

The only reason 111-sq-mile **Custer State Park** (☑605-255-4515; www.custerstatepark. com; 7-day pass per car $20; ⊙24hr) isn't a national park is that the state grabbed it first. It boasts one of the largest free-roaming bison herds in the world (about 1500), the famous 'begging burros' (donkeys seeking handouts) and more than 200 bird species. Other wildlife include elk, pronghorns, mountain goats, bighorn sheep, coyotes, prairie dogs, mountain lions and bobcats.

The park has five impressive resorts (www.custerresorts.com) – book well ahead – and nine campgrounds (tent sites $19 to $35). At four of the campgrounds, you can rent a well-equipped camping cabin ($50). Sylvan Lake is the most scenic (and popular) campground so reserve well ahead (via www.campsd.com). Reservations are vital for all sites in summer. Backcountry camping ($7 per person per night) is allowed only in the French Creek Natural Area.

ℹ Information

Located on the east side of Custer State Park, the **Custer State Park Visitor Center** (☑ 605-255-4020; www.custerstatepark.com; junction US 16A & Wildlife Loop Rd; ⊙ 8am-8pm Jun-Aug, to 4pm Sep-May) has good exhibits and offers activities such as guided nature walks.

Custer City

POP 1900

Custer City (or just Custer) is a major Black Hills hub, at the junction of US 16 and US 385. On the downside, its main drag is busy with traffic. On the upside, it has a good selection of places to eat and stay plus one of the region's best visitor centers. It's close to Custer State Park and Mt Rushmore.

◉ Sights

Crazy Horse Memorial   MONUMENT
(☑ 605-673-4681; www.crazyhorsememorial.org; 12151 Ave of the Chiefs, off US 385; per person/car $12/30; ⊙ 7am-10pm Jun-Sep, reduced hours Oct-May) The world's largest monument is this 563ft-tall work-in-progress (with a lot of work to go). When finished it will depict the Sioux leader astride his horse, pointing to the horizon saying, 'My lands are where my dead lie buried.' No one is predicting when the sculpture will be complete (the face was dedicated in 1998). Although you can see the mountain in the distance, you need to pay another $4 for a van ride to get close.

Jewel Cave National Monument   CAVE
(☑ 605-673-8300; www.nps.gov/jeca; off US 16; tours adult $4-31, child free-$8; ⊙ visitor center

---

WORTH A TRIP

WIND CAVE NATIONAL PARK

This **park** (☑ 605-745-4600; www.nps. gov/wica; off US 385; admission free, cave tours $10-30; ⊙ visitor center 8am-7pm Jun–mid-Aug, reduced hours mid-Aug–May), protecting 44 sq miles of grassland and forest, sits just south of Custer State Park (p677). The central draw is, of course, the cave, which contains 148 miles of mapped passages. The strong wind gusts, which are felt at the entrance, but not inside, give the cave its name. The visitor center has details on the variety of tours that are offered, from one-hour candlelit walks to four-hour crawls.

8am-6pm Jun-Sep, 8:30am-4:30pm Oct-May) If you visit only one Black Hills cave, this would be a good choice. It's 13 miles west of Custer and is so named because calcite crystals line much of its walls. Some 187 miles have been surveyed so far (3% of the estimated total), making it the third-longest known cave in the world. Tours vary in length and difficulty and can be reserved three to 90 days in advance (605-717-7629, www.blackhillsvacations.com). The visitor center has useful exhibits.

⌸ Sleeping

Rocket Motel   MOTEL $
(☑ 605-673-4401; www.rocketmotel.com; 211 Mt Rushmore Rd; r $60-160; ✳ ⛶) The jaunty neon sign out front alone makes this old-style motor court a good option. However, it's also well located in the center, is well maintained and has great prices. As they say, 'It's a blast from the past!'

ℹ Information

Visitor Center (☑ 605-673-2244; www. custersd.com; 615 Washington St; ⊙ 8am-5pm Mon-Fri, 9am-5pm Sat, 10am-4pm Sun) The best tourist office in the Black Hills can help with any question. Reams of brochures and reading material.

Hot Springs

POP 3500

This attractive and unhurried town, south of the main Black Hills circuit, boasts ornate 1890s red sandstone buildings that glow at sunset. The big attraction, though, is the warm mineral springs feeding the Fall River.

You can fill your water bottles at **Kidney Springs**, just south of the visitor center, or swim at **Cascade Falls**, which is 71°F (22°C) all year, 11 miles south on US 71.

Mammoth Site   HISTORIC SITE
(☑ 605-745-6017; www.mammothsite.com; 1800 US 18 bypass; adult/child $11/8; ⊙ 8am-8pm mid-May–mid-Aug, reduced hrs mid-Aug–mid-May) Right near the center, this is the country's largest left-as-found mammoth fossil display. Hundreds of animals perished in a sinkhole here about 26,000 years ago, and you can walk around the active archaeological dig.

Red Rock River Resort   HOTEL $
(☑ 605-745-4400;   www.redrockriverresort.com; 603 N River St; r $85-150; ✳ ⛶) This resort has cozy and stylish rooms in a beautiful 1891

red sandstone building downtown, plus spa facilities (day passes for nonguests $25) that include optional therapies and massages.

ℹ Information

Hot Springs Visitor Center (📞 605-745-4140; www.hotsprings-sd.com; 630 N River St; ⏰ 9am-5:30pm Mon-Sat, noon-4pm Sun May-Oct) Located in a train station dating to 1891.

NEBRASKA

The Cornhusker State (they do grow a lot of ears) has beautiful river valleys and an often stark bleakness that is entrancing. Its links to the past – from vast fields of dinosaur remains to Native American culture to the toils of hardy settlers – provide a dramatic story line. Alongside the state's sprinkling of cute little towns, Nebraska's two main cities, Omaha and Lincoln, are vibrant and artful.

The key to enjoying this long, stoic stretch of country is to take the smaller roads, whether it's US 30 instead of I-80, US 20 to the Black Hills, or the lonely and magnificent US 2.

ℹ Information

Nebraska Tourism Commission (www.visit nebraska.com)
Nebraska Association of Bed & Breakfasts (www.nebraskabb.com)
Nebraska State Parks (www.outdoornebraska. gov) Vehicle permits cost on average $8/46 per day/year.

Omaha

POP 466,900

Don't plan a quick pit stop in Omaha. Home to the brick-and-cobblestoned Old Market neighborhood, a booming riverfront, a lively food and music scene and several good museums, a few hours can turn into a few days in this town.

Omaha grew to prominence as a transport hub. Its location on the Missouri River and proximity to the Platte River made it an important stop on the Oregon, California and Mormon Trails, and later the Union Pacific Railroad stretched west from here. These days Omaha is in the nation's top 10 for billionaires and Fortune 500 companies per capita. Money pours back into the city in spectacular ways thanks to several wealthy benefactors (including famed investor Warren Buffett).

◉ Sights

★ Riverfront   WATERFRONT

(8th St & Riverfront Dr) The riverfront along the Missouri River celebrates the waterway's past and present. Highlights include the architecturally stunning **Bob Kerrey Pedestrian Bridge** (705 Riverfront Dr), which soars over to Iowa; the **Heartland of America Park** (800 Douglas St), with fountains and lush gardens; and **Lewis & Clark Landing** (345 Riverfront Dr), where the explorers did just that in 1804. The riverfront is also home to the **Lewis & Clark National Historic Trail Visitor Center** (📞 402-661-1804; www. nps.gov/lecl; 601 Riverfront Dr; ⏰ 8am-5pm Mon-Fri, from 9:30am Sat & Sun May-Oct, 8am-4:30pm Mon-Fri Nov-Apr), which has exhibits and a bookstore.

★ Union Pacific
Railroad Museum   MUSEUM

(📞 712-329-8307; www.uprrmuseum.org; 200 Pearl St, Council Bluffs; ⏰ 10am-4pm Thu-Sat; 🚻) **FREE** Just across the river from Omaha in the cute little downtown area of Council Bluffs, IA, this highly interactive museum tells the story of the world's most profitable railroad (it's headquartered in Omaha) and the company that rammed the transcontinental line west from here in the 1860s. The three levels of exhibits offer a nostalgia-filled ode to train travel and how it forever changed America.

Omaha's Henry Doorly
Zoo & Aquarium   ZOO

(📞 402-733-8401; www.omahazoo.com; 3701 S 10th St; adult/child $22/16 May-Sep, reduced admission other times; ⏰ 9am-6pm Apr-Oct, 10am-5pm Nov-Mar; 🚻) The world's largest indoor desert? Check. The world's largest nocturnal exhibit? Check. America's largest indoor rainforest? Check. An aquarium showing habitats from the Arctic to coral reefs? Check, yet again. The superlatives say it all. You could easily spend an entire day wandering through this massive and well-crafted complex, which is frequently named the best zoo in America. Optional animal encounters can be arranged if you pay extra.

Durham Museum   MUSEUM

(📞 402-444-5071; www.durhammuseum.org; 801 S 10th St; adult/child $11/7; ⏰ 10am-8pm Tue, to 5pm Wed-Sat, 1-5pm Sun year-round, plus 10am-5pm Mon Jun-Aug & Dec) The soaring art deco Union Station train depot is a sight to behold with its cathedral windows, geometric chandeliers, ornate ceilings and reliefs of railroad workers carved into the facade. It houses a fine museum covering local history from the Lewis and Clark expedition to the Omaha stockyards and the trains that once called here. The soda fountain still serves hot dogs and phosphate sodas.

Hot Shops Art Center ARTS CENTER
(📞 402-342-6452; www.hotshopsartcenter.com; 1301 Nicholas St; ⏱ 9am-6pm Mon-Fri, 11am-5pm Sat & Sun) Entering into this three-story arts center (a former mattress warehouse) is like diving down the rabbit hole into an alternative universe ruled by eccentric artists. The namesake 'hot shops' are the glassblowing, pottery, bronze-casting and blacksmithing studios that anchor the building. Above them are 55 studios where artists create and display their works for all to see. Peruse the labyrinthine studios, sign up for art classes or attend an event.

Tours

Nebraska Tour Company TOURS
(📞 402-881-3548; www.nebraskatourcompany.com; tours from $30) Walking tours, brewery or winery-hopping trips and off-the-beaten-path excursions to Omaha's hidden treasures are among the tours offered by this excellent operator. History and art tours are led by local experts. A jaunt around Old Market is one of its most popular walking tours.

AIR FORCE IN OMAHA

If you see large military planes drifting slowly across the sky, they're likely headed for one of the Omaha region's large air-force bases.

After WWII Omaha's Offutt Air Force Base was home to the US Air Force Strategic Air Command, the nuclear force detailed in *Dr Strangelove*. This legacy is documented at the cavernous **Strategic Air Command & Aerospace Museum** (📞 402-944-3100; www.sacmuseum.org; 28210 West Park Hwy, I-80 exit 426; adult/child $12/6; ⏱ 9am-5pm), which bulges with bombers, from the B-17 to the B-52 to the B-1. Don't expect exhibits looking at the wider implications of bombing. It's 30 miles southwest of Omaha, well within the kill radius of a 1-megaton bomb.

Sleeping

Hotel Deco HISTORIC HOTEL $$
(📞 402-991-4981; www.hoteldecoomaha.com; 1504 Harney St; r from $140; ✳ 🐾 🖥) This soaring hotel is in a repurposed 1930 commercial building that, as the name implies, was designed in sleek art deco style. Rooms are very comfortable and decorated in a period palette of silver, grey, black and white. The public spaces are grand and the house steakhouse Monarch is well-regarded.

Magnolia Hotel HISTORIC HOTEL $$
(📞 402-341-2500; www.magnoliahotelomaha.com; 1615 Howard St; r $140-250; ✳ @ 🐾 🖥) Not far from Old Market, the Magnolia is a boutique hotel housed in a restored 1923 Italianate high-rise. The 145 rooms have a vibrant, modern style. Get ready for bedtime milk and cookies.

Eating

Johnny's Cafe STEAK $$
(📞 402-731-4774; 4702 S 27th St; mains $15-35; ⏱ 11am-2pm Mon-Fri, 5-9pm Mon-Thu, to 10pm Fri & Sat) The same family has been running this local legend of a steakhouse since 1922. The restaurant itself is a living museum of decor, with custom artwork spread throughout the lavish 1950s interior (they'll give you a tour, just ask). Settle into one of the plush chairs on casters and select from a superb line-up of steaks and other meaty mains.

A perfect meal: the trademark onion rings, the house salad with blue cheese and the Omaha strip steak. Portions are vast.

Upstream Brewing Company AMERICAN $$
(📞 402-344-0200; www.upstreambrewing.com; 514 S 11th St; mains $10-30; ⏱ 11am-1am Mon-Thu, to 2am Fri & Sat, 10am-midnight Sun) In a big old firehouse in Old Market, the beer here is equally big on flavor. The Caesar salads have enough garlic to propel you over the Missouri to Iowa. Steaks are thick and up to local standards. There are sidewalk tables, a rooftop deck and a huge bar.

Au Courant Restaurant BISTRO $$
(📞 402-505-9917; www.aucourantrestaurant.com; 6064 Maple St; mains $13-27; ⏱ 5pm-late Tue-Sat) Farm-fresh fare with a French accent is served in this artful restaurant. The bar is a real draw; after the last meal is served, people linger, enjoying the creative cocktails. Au Courant is a star among many in the Benson neighborhood.

★ Grey Plume
MODERN AMERICAN $$$

(☎402-763-4447; www.thegreyplume.com; 220 S 31st Ave; mains bar $9-18, restaurant $25-42; ☺5-10pm Mon, Thu-Sat) West of downtown in Midtown, chef Clayton Chapman has challenged perceptions of Great Plains cuisine with his fiercely local and seasonal dishes. Winners: the bar burger, the duck-fat fries, the steaks and anything with trout. Polished service.

Drinking & Nightlife

★ Mister Toad's
PUB

(☎402-345-4488; www.mrtoadspub.com; 1002 Howard St; ☺2pm-2am Sun-Fri, noon-2am Sat) Sit out front on benches under big trees or nab a corner table inside. It's woodsy, worn and flirting with dive-bar status. There's live jazz Sunday nights and Ray Williams on the piano Wednesday nights.

Brothers Lounge
BAR

(☎402-558-4096; www.facebook.com/brothersloungeomaha; 3812 Farnam St; ☺4pm-2am Mon-Sat) The best jukebox in Omaha draws crowds into this Blackstone District bar. It's warmly divey with a punk soul and a great beer selection. There's live music some nights.

Shopping

Omaha Farmers Market
MARKET

(www.omahafarmersmarket.com; cnr 11th & Jackson Sts; ☺8am-12:30pm Sat May–mid-Oct;) Dozens of vendors celebrate the best of Nebraska's farms and food producers at this huge and popular market fittingly located in Old Market. Besides exquisite produce, look for baked goods and prepared foods plus crafts by artisans.

ⓘ Information

Omaha Visitor Center (☎866-937-6624; www.visitomaha.com; 1001 Farnam St; ☺9am-4:30pm Mon-Fri, 10am-4pm Sat, 10am-2pm Sun;) Close to Old Market, has info for the entire region.

ⓘ Getting There & Away

Eppley Airfield (OMA; www.flyoma.com; 4501 Abbott Dr) is only 3 miles northeast of downtown and has services from across the region and major American cities.

Amtrak's *California Zephyr* stops in Omaha on its run between Chicago ($62, 9½ hours, one daily) and Northern California via Denver ($66, 9½ hours, one daily).

Jefferson Lines (www.jeffersonlines.com) travels along I-29 north to Sioux Falls ($50, 3½ hours, one daily) and south to Kansas City ($49, three hours, two daily). Greyhound runs buses along I-80. Megabus (www.megabus.com) links Omaha with Des Moines ($20, four hours, one daily) and beyond.

Lincoln
POP 284,700

Lincoln reminds visitors that Nebraska isn't all cornfields and prairies. With its lively nightlife thanks to the huge central campus of the University of Nebraska, it makes a good overnight stop. But it's the friendly Midwest attitude that might encourage you to stay longer. Looming over it all is the political vibe emanating from the state capitol.

⊙ Sights

Nebraska History Museum
MUSEUM

(☎402-471-4782; www.nebraskahistory.org; 131 Centennial Mall N; ☺10am-5:30pm Mon-Fri, 1-5:30pm Sat) FREE Follows the Cornhusker State's story, starting with the large First Nebraskans room. Compare the pioneer sod house to the Pawnee earth lodge.

Lincoln Children's Museum
MUSEUM

(☎402-477-4000; www.lincolnchildrensmuseum.org; 1420 P St; adult/child $10/11; ☺9:30am-5pm Mon-Wed, Fri & Sat, to 8pm Thu, 1-5pm Sun;) Three floors of excitement keep kids of all ages breathing fast with anticipation at this downtown museum. Fire engines, a moon lander, a prairie dog town, crazy water experiments and a whole lot more mix learning with heaps of fun.

State Capitol
LANDMARK

(☎402-471-0448; www.capitol.org; 1445 K St; ☺8am-5pm Mon-Fri, from 10am Sat, from 1pm Sun, tours hourly) FREE From the outside, Nebraska's remarkable 1932 400ft-high state capitol represents the apex of phallic architecture (like many tall buildings in the Plains, it's often called 'the penis on the prairie'), while the symbolically rich interior curiously combines classical and art deco motifs. Enjoy views from the 14th-floor observation decks.

Sleeping & Eating

Rogers House
B&B $$

(☎402-476-6961; www.rogershouseinn.com; 2145 B St; r $100-170;) Close to downtown, the seven spacious rooms here occupy a 100-year-old brick home. Refreshingly, the decor eschews the froufrou silliness of many B&Bs. Expect a hearty two-course breakfast.

★ **Indigo Bridge** CAFE $
(✆ 402-477-7770; www.indigobridgebooks.com; 701 P St; mains $4-10; ⊗ 8am-9pm Mon-Sat, 10am-8pm Sun; 🛜) This fine Haymarket cafe in a fantastic bookstore serves excellent coffee, snacks and sandwiches throughout the day. Best of all, 100% of all coffee purchases go directly to a local cause.

Hub Cafe CAFE $
(✆ 402-474-2453; www.hubcafelincoln.com; 250 N 21st St; mains $5-11; ⊗ 7:30am-2:30pm Tue-Sun) Right in the amphitheater building on Lincoln's main square, Union Plaza, this creative cafe serves locally sourced breakfasts all day. Try the *huevos rancheros* or grilled cheese sandwich, which drips with pesto. The coffee is excellent; there are sunny tables outside.

★ **UNL Dairy Store** ICE CREAM $
(✆ 402-472-2828; www.dairystore.unl.edu; 114 Food Industry Complex, near cnr Holdrege St & N 33rd St; snacks from $3; ⊗ 10am-9pm) Agriculture majors make the ice cream with milk from the university's own herd at this store on the East Campus. The results are amazingly creamy and come in over a dozen flavors. Also on offer are several varieties of homemade cheese. Chat with the student

WORTH A TRIP

KEARNEY

Kearney (pronounced *carny*) makes a worthwhile stopover on the otherwise monotonous trip along I-80. It has an appealing brick-built downtown district by the Union Pacific tracks and a collection of notable attractions, including the over-the-top **Great Platte River Road Archway Monument** (✆ 308-237-1000; www.archway.org; 3060 E 1st St, near I-80 exit 275; adult/child $13/6; ⊗ 9am-6pm Mon-Sat, noon-6pm Sun May-Sep, to 5pm Oct-Apr; 🅿). And there's some stellar food and drink.

Long an important stop for travelers, in the 1800s the major pioneer routes – the California and Oregon Trails – converged here heading west.

Kearney is 180 miles west of Omaha on I-80. Express Arrow (www.express arrow.com) runs buses along I-80.

workers about animal husbandry while you wait for your sundae.

🍷 Drinking & Nightlife

Zoo Bar BAR
(✆ 402-435-8754; www.zoobar.com; 136 N 14th St; ⊗ 3pm-2am) Generations of Huskers have guzzled and gulped at this sweaty, divey bar that has live blues, jazz and rock most nights. It's an institution, no matter how you define the word.

Other Room COCKTAIL BAR
(✆ 402-261-4608; www.facebook.com/theother roomlincoln; 824 P St; ⊗ 5pm-1am) Look for an unmarked black door with a lion door knocker next to it. If the light above the door is green, give the lion a knock. If it's red, you'll have to wait outside for the chance to enter into this compact speakeasy, which has a 25-person capacity and offers up some spectacular cocktails described as 'pre-Prohibition-style.'

ℹ Information

Lincoln Visitor Center (✆ 402-434-5348; www.lincoln.org; 201 N 7th St; ⊗ 9am-6pm Mon-Fri, 8am-2pm Sat, from 10am Sun Jun-Aug, reduced hours Sep-May) Inside Haymarket's historic former train station.

ℹ Getting There & Away

Lincoln is 55 miles southwest of Omaha on I-80. Megabus (www.megabus.com) connects the two cities once daily ($10, one hour). Amtrak's *California Zephyr* train stops here on its run between Chicago and Northern California.

Grand Island

POP 51,400

A classic midsized Nebraska town along the lush Platte River Valley, Grand Island bursts to life each spring when hundreds of thousands of sandhill cranes converge on a critical sliver of threatened habitat just south of the city limits. Birders and biologists from around the world flock to see this massive migration, dubbed one of North America's greatest wildlife phenomena.

Throughout the year, don't miss the Stuhr Museum of the Prairie Pioneer.

★ **Crane Trust**
Nature & Visitor Center NATURE RESERVE
(✆ 308-382-1820; www.cranetrust.org; 9325 S Alda Rd, I-80 exit 305; ⊗ 9am-5pm Mon-Sat) FREE Upstream of Grand Island, the Platte River hosts

500,000 sandhill cranes (80% of the world population) and millions more waterfowl during the spring migration (mid-February to early April). Expert guides lead seasonal Sandhill Crane Migration Tours ($35, 2½ hours, reserve in advance) to prime viewing blinds on the river. This nature center is a good place for viewing and has worthwhile hikes year-round.

★ **Stuhr Museum**
of the Prairie Pioneer MUSEUM
(✆ 308-385-5316; www.stuhrmuseum.org; 3133 W Hwy 34, near I-80 exit 312; adult/child $8/6; ⊙ 9am-5pm Mon-Sat, from noon Sun, closed Mon Jan-Mar; ♿) A remarkable combination of indoor exhibits and a vast outdoor living museum. Note how conditions dramatically improved in the homes in 1860 to 1890 thanks to riches made possible by the railroad.

❶ Getting There & Away

Grand Island is 145 miles west of Omaha along I-80. Express Arrow (www.expressarrow.com) runs buses along I-80.

North Platte

POP 23,900

The name North Platte may not ring a bell with the average traveler, but hard-core railroad fans know it as the home of Union Pacific's Bailey Yard, the world's largest railroad classification yard. Meanwhile, American-history buffs come here to see the place where Bill Cody launched his famed rodeo show, Buffalo Bill's Wild West. Cody's frontier spirit lives on, even as hundreds of trains thunder in and out of town each day.

◎ Sights

Golden Spike Tower TOWER
(✆ 308-532-9920; www.goldenspiketower.com; 1249 N Homestead Rd; adult/child $7/5; ⊙ 9am-7pm May-Sep, 10am-5pm Oct-Apr; ♿) Enjoy sweeping views of Union Pacific's Bailey Yard, the world's largest railroad classification yard, from this eight-story observation tower with indoor and outdoor decks. Bailey Yard spans 2850 acres and handles 10,000 railroad cars every 24 hours.

Buffalo Bill Ranch
State Historical Park HISTORIC SITE
(✆ 308-535-8035; www.outdoornebraska.gov/buffalobillranch; 2921 Scouts Rest Ranch Rd; museum adult/child $2/1, grounds vehicle permit $8; ⊙ 8am-5pm Jun-Aug, 10am-4pm Sat, noon-4pm

SCENIC DRIVE: NEBRASKA'S SANDHILLS

Nebraska's **Hwy 2** branches northwest from I-80 and Grand Island through Broken Bow 272 miles to Alliance in the panhandle. It crosses the lonely and lovely Sandhills – 19,000 sq miles of sand dunes covered in grass – one of the country's most isolated areas. With the wind whistling in your ears, the distant call of a hawk and the biggest skies imaginable, this is pure Great Plains travel.

Sun late Apr-May & Sep-early Oct; ♿) Once the home of Bill Cody (the father of rodeo and the famed Wild West show), this park includes a fun museum in Cody's house that reflects his colorful life.

🛏 Sleeping

Husker Inn MOTEL $
(✆ 308-534-6960; www.huskerinn.com; 721 E 4th St; r $50-60; ❃ 🛜) This basic 21-room vintage motel exceeds expectations with well-manicured grounds, immaculately clean (if small) rooms and yummy home-baked goodies on arrival.

❶ Getting There & Away

North Platte is 275 miles west of Omaha along I-80. Express Arrow (www.expressarrow.com) runs buses along I-80.

Valentine

POP 2800

Fortunately, 'America's Heart City' doesn't milk the shtick. It sits on the edge of the Sandhills and is a great base for canoeing, kayaking and inner-tubing the winding canyons of the federally protected Niobrara National Scenic River.

🏃 Activities

Valentine lies at the heart of what will one day be the longest rail-to-trail conversion in the US: the **Cowboy Trail** (www.bikecowboytrail.com), popular with cyclists.

Floating down the Niobrara River draws scores of people through the summer. Sheer limestone bluffs, lush forests and more than 200 spring-fed waterfalls along the banks shatter any 'flat Nebraska' stereotypes. Most float tours are based here.

AVOID I-80: DISCOVERING NEBRASKA'S SOUL

Few travelers wax poetic about their time driving across Nebraska on I-80. It's one long procession of exits, where the only real sightseeing on offer is a forest of fast-food signs. But just a couple miles off I-80 is another Nebraska entirely. A series of characterful small towns, diners, roadside attractions, historic artifacts, train tracks busy with mile-long trains, verdant roadside parks on the Platte River and much, much more.

The key to this bounty of diversions and interests is US 30, the old, mostly two-lane highway that parallels I-80. It dates back to 1913 when the first segments of America's first transcontinental road, the Lincoln Hwy, were completed. A classic example of what lies off I-80 is the pretty little town of **Gothenburg** (1 mile north of I-80 exit 211). Its tidy downtown of brick buildings holds several pleasures, including non-chain donut shops. Nearby is the restored 1860 **Pony Express Station** (☑ 308-537-9876; www.ponyexpressstation.org; 1500 Lake Ave, Gothenburg; ☺ 9am-7pm May-Sep, to 3pm Apr & Oct, by appointment Nov-Mar) FREE .

The beauty of going local on US 30 is that you can dip in and out from I-80 as your schedule and spirit allows. Look for the free booklet *Nebraska Lincoln Highway Historic Byway Guide* at tourist offices. It lists hundreds of things to see and do along US 30.

Brewers Canoers & Tubers CANOEING
(☑ 402-376-2046; www.brewerscanoers.com; 433 E US 20/83; guided tubing trips $20-50; ☺ daily trips Jun-Aug, rentals year-round) Brewers is one of the original outfitters in the area and was the first to introduce tubing on the Niobrara River. You can rent canoes, kayaks or tubes with them and arrange shuttles to and from their launch and landing sites. Guided trips come in a variety of flavors.

🛏 Sleeping & Eating

Trade Winds Motel MOTEL $
(☑ 402-376-1600; www.tradewindslodge.com; 1009 E US 20/83; r $70-140; ❄🛜🐕) The classic red-brick Trade Winds Motel has 32 comfy and clean rooms with fridges and microwaves. It's a great indie choice with a hot continental breakfast.

Peppermill STEAK $$
(☑ 402-376-2800; www.peppermillvalentine.com; 502 E Hwy 20; mains $12-30; ☺ 11am-10pm Mon-Fri, 3-10pm Sat & Sun) This low-lit Valentine institution, which specializes in hand-cut Nebraska beef, is one of the state's most storied steakhouses. What it serves are thick, juicy chunks of perfection. You'll forgive the uninspiring decor when you try the Mulligan, Peppermill's signature center-cut sirloin. It also serves burgers and salads.

❶ Getting There & Away

Remote Valentine is one hour north of Hwy 2, the scenic drive (p683) through the Sand Hills. There is no public transportation in the region.

Nebraska Panhandle

The remote and little-visited Nebraska Panhandle is for many the most evocative part of the state. Stark vistas stretch to the horizon in lands little changed in a millennia. **Scottsbluff** makes a good base. Heading north, **Hwy 29** (aka the 'Fossil Freeway') is a great drive and it segues right onto equally scenic US 20.

◉ Sights

★**Scotts Bluff National Monument** PARK
(☑ 308-436-9700; www.nps.gov/scbl; 190276 Old Oregon Trail, Gering; ☺ visitor center 8am-6pm Jun-Aug, to 4:30pm Sep-May) Scotts Bluff has been a beacon to travelers for centuries. Rising 800ft above the flat plains of western Nebraska, it was an important waypoint on the Oregon Trail in the mid-19th century. You can still see wagon ruts today. The visitor center has displays and its staff can guide you to walks and drives up the bluff. It's 5 miles south of Scottsbluff town. There is good hiking all around the park.

★**Agate Fossil Beds National Monument** MONUMENT
(☑ 308-436-9760; www.nps.gov/agfo; 301 River Rd, off Hwy 29, Harrison; ☺ 9am-5pm May-Sep, 8am-4pm Oct-Apr) FREE Some 20 million years ago, this part of Nebraska was like the Serengeti in Africa today: a gathering place for a rich variety of creatures. Today the bones of thousands of these ancient mammals are found at this isolated site. Displays and walks detail the amazing –

and ongoing – finds. Don't miss the **Bone Cabin** and the burrowing beaver, plus the Native American exhibits.

Chimney Rock
National Historic Site   NATURAL FEATURE

(✆308-586-2581; Chimney Rock Rd, off US 26, Bayard; visitors center adult/child $3/free; ◯9am-5pm) Eons-old bluff formations rise up from the horizon, their striking presence a dramatic sentinel connecting modern-day travelers with their pioneer forebears. One of these links is Chimney Rock, located inside the Chimney Rock National Historic Site. Chimney Rock's fragile 120ft spire was an inspiring landmark for pioneers, and it was mentioned in hundreds of journals. It also marked the end of the first leg of the journey and the beginning of the tough – but final – push to the coast.

🛏 Sleeping

⭐ **Barn Anew**   B&B $$

(✆308-632-8647; www.barnanew.com; 170549 County Rd L, Mitchell; r $140-160; ❇🐾) This charming B&B lies within a restored barn on an old sugar-beet farm. The walls are adorned with the owners' museum-quality collection of Native American artifacts, while the views of Scotts Bluff 3 miles distant are mesmerizing. Up for an adventure? Stay in one of the two frontier wagons that have been converted into cozy rooms.

🍴 Eating & Drinking

Tangled Tumbleweed   CAFE $

(✆308-633-3867; 1823 Ave A, Scottsbluff; mains $8-15; ◯10am-10pm Wed-Sat) Part home-goods store (with products made by the owner) and part top-notch restaurant, this Scottsbluff establishment has an eclectic menu of fresh, seasonal fare with global influences. Small-plate dishes are complemented by rotating wine and craft-beer selections. Linger on the outdoor patio on a warm evening.

Flyover Brewing Company   BREWERY

(✆308-575-0335; www.flyoverbrewingcompany.com; 1824 Broadway, Scottsbluff; ◯3-11pm Wed-Fri, from 11am Sat & Sun) Everyone drinking in this attractive brewery with eight house-made beers is enjoying a better brew than anyone flying far overhead. On balmy nights, sit on the terrace and enjoy a personal pizza ($10).

❶ Getting There & Away

The remote Panhandle is closer to Denver and Rapid City than Omaha. Both cities are three hours away by vehicle from Scottsbluff in opposite directions. There is no public transportation in the region.

KANSAS

Wicked witches and yellow-brick roads, pitched battles over slavery and tornadoes powerful enough to pulverize entire towns are some of the more vivid images of Kansas. But the common image – amber waves of grain from north to south and east to west – is closer to modern reality.

There's a simple beauty to the green rolling hills and limitless horizons. Places such as Chase County beguile those who value understatement. Gems abound, from the superb space museum in Hutchinson to the indie music clubs of Lawrence. Most importantly, follow the Great Plains credo of ditching the interstate for the two-laners and make your own discoveries.

❶ Information

Kansas Travel & Tourism (www.travelks.com)
Kansas Bed & Breakfast Association (www.kbba.com)
Kansas State Parks (www.ksoutdoors.com) Per vehicle per day/year $5/25.

Wichita
POP 390,600

From its early cow town days at the head of the Chisholm Trail in the 1870s to its current claim as Air Capital of the World (thanks to over half the world's general aviation aircraft being built here by the likes of Cessna and others, plus large chunks of Boeing airliners by subcontractors), Kansas' largest city is a worthwhile stopover.

Check out sights related to the Old West such as the Old Cowtown Museum (p686).

WORTH A TRIP

CARHENGE

Pay homage to the auto at **Carhenge** (✆308-762-3569; www.carhenge.com; Hwy 87, Alliance; ◯24hr), assembled from 39 discarded cars. The faithful reproduction of Stonehenge, along with other car-part art, rises out of a field 3 miles north of Alliance and the junction with US 385, the road to the Black Hills of South Dakota.

You can have a fine evening sampling the nightlife in Old Town.

Sights

★ Old Cowtown Museum
MUSEUM

(☑316-350-3323; www.oldcowtown.org; 1865 Museum Blvd; adult/child $9/6; ◷10am-5pm Tue-Sat, from noon Sun; ☒) An open-air museum that re-creates the Wild West (as seen on TV...). Over 50 pioneer-era buildings, staged gunfights (April to October) and guides in cowboy costumes thrill kids. Enjoy the river walks.

Exploration Place
MUSEUM

(☑316-660-0600; www.exploration.org; 300 N McLean Blvd; adult/child from $13.50/8; ◷10am-5pm Mon-Sat, noon-5pm Sun; ☒) Right on the river confluence, this architecturally striking children's museum has no end of cool exhibits, including a tornado chamber where you can feel 75mph winds, and a sublime erosion model that shows water creating a new little Kansas. One gallery details the ups and downs of the local aviation industry.

Sleeping

Hotel at Old Town
HOTEL $$

(☑316-267-4800; www.hotelatoldtown.com; 830 E 1st St; r $105-200; ☏☒☒☒☒) In the midst of Old Town nightlife, this restored hotel is housed in the 1906 factory of the Keen Kutter Corp, a maker of household goods. The 115 rooms have high ceilings and kitchen facilities.

Eating & Drinking

★ Doo-Dah Diner
DINER $

(☑316-265-7011; www.doodahdiner.com; 206 E Kellogg Dr; mains $8-15; ◷7am-2pm Tue-Fri, from 8am Sat & Sun) The model for diners everywhere. This bustling local downtown fave has fabulous chow, including corned-beef hash, banana-bread French toast and eggs Benedict. Recently remodeled, it's regularly named Wichita's favorite restaurant.

Anchor
CRAFT BEER

(☑316-260-8989; www.anchorwichita.com; 1109 E Douglas Ave; mains $9-20; ◷11am-late) On the edge of Old Town, this vintage pub has high ceilings, a tiled floor, a superb beer selection (best in the state) and tasty food. The good burgers and specials totally outclass the nearby chain and theme bars.

Getting There & Away

Wichita Dwight D Eisenhower National Airport (ICT; ☑316-946-4700; www.flywichita. com; 2277 Eisenhower Airport Pkwy) is 7 miles west of town and has services from major hubs. Greyhound has buses south to Oklahoma City ($50, three hours) and northeast to Kansas City ($45, three hours).

CHASING TORNADOES

Much of the Great Plains is prone to severe weather, including violent thunderstorms, hail the size of softballs, spectacular lightning storms and more. Tornadoes, however, are the real stars of these meteorological nightmares. Far less benign than the cyclones that carried Dorothy off to Oz, every year tornadoes cause death and destruction from the Great Plains east across the central US.

With winds of 300mph or more, tornadoes are both awesome and terrifying. Still, each year many people visit the region hoping to spot a funnel cloud, drawn by the sheer spectacle and elemental drama.

Tour companies use gadget-filled vans to chase storms across multiple states, with no guarantee that you'll actually see a storm. Costs average $200 to $400 a day for multiday trips; April to June offer the best spotting, with May being the prime month. Operators include the following:

Cloud 9 Tours (☑405-323-1145; www.cloud9tours.com; 2-week tour $3100)

Silver Lining Tours (☑720-273-3948; www.silverliningtours.com; multiday tours from $1550)

Tempest Tours (☑817-274-9313; www.tempesttours.com; multiday tours from $2400)

The book *Storm Kings: The Untold History of America's First Tornado Chasers*, by Lee Sandlin, is an excellent and surprise-filled account of early tornado research. Read the recollections of veteran tornado chaser Roger Hill in *Hunting Nature's Fury*. And Brantley Hargrove's *The Man Who Caught the Storm: The Life of Legendary Tornado Chaser Tim Samaras* chronicles the passion of a storm chaser who died while on the hunt.

Lawrence

POP 96,900

Lawrence has been an island of progressive politics since the start. Founded by abolitionists in 1854 and an important stop on the Underground Railroad, it became a battlefield in the clash between pro- and antislavery factions. The city's free-thinking spirit continues, fueled in no small part by the University of Kansas, its faculty and legions of students. It's one of America's most vibrant college towns.

Sights

The appealing downtown, where townies and students merge, centers on Massachusetts St, one of the most pleasant streets in this part of the country for a stroll. The Kansas River adds to the appeal.

Sleeping

Eldridge Hotel   HISTORIC HOTEL **$$**
(785-749-5011; www.eldridgehotel.com; 701 Massachusetts St; r $120-180;) The 48 modern two-room suites at this historic 1926 downtown hotel have antique-style furnishings. The bar and restaurant are stylish, the ghost misunderstood (rumors abound). Great location for nightlife.

Halcyon House B&B   B&B **$**
(785-841-0314; www.thehalcyonhouse.com; 1000 Ohio St; r $70-130;) The nine colorful bedrooms here (two share a bathroom) have lots of natural light. There's a landscaped garden and homemade baked goods for breakfast. Downtown and university campus are just short walks away.

Eating & Drinking

★**Free State Brewing**   PUB FOOD **$**
(785-843-4555; www.freestatebrewing.com; 636 Massachusetts St; mains $8-20; 11am-midnight Mon-Sat, noon-11pm Sun) One of many good places on Massachusetts St downtown, this is the first brewery in Kansas since temperance campaigner Carrie Nation got one closed in 1880. The beers are excellent and the food creative, with daily specials. There's always at least 12 choices on tap.

Wheatfields Bakery Cafe   CAFE **$**
(785-841-5553; http://wheatfieldsbakery.com; 904 Vermont St; mains $5-14; 6:30am-8pm Mon-Fri, to 6:30pm Sat, 7:30am-4pm Sun;) This renowned bakery uses a huge wood-fired oven to bake loaves that bring devotees from as

COSMOSPHERE

Possibly the most surprising sight in Kansas, this amazing **museum** (800-397-0330; www.cosmo.org; 1100 N Plum St, Hutchinson; all-attraction pass adult/child $26/17, museum only $13.50/10; 9am-7pm Mon-Sat, from noon Sun;) captures the race to the moon better than any museum on the planet. Absorbing displays and artifacts such as the Apollo 13 command module and entire rockets will enthrall you for hours. You'll come to realize why the museum is regularly called in to build props for Hollywood movies portraying the space race, including *Apollo 13*. It's an easy day trip from Wichita or diversion off I-70 or US 50.

The all-attraction pass includes access to the planetarium and space simulator.

far away as Kansas City. It has a full breakfast menu and a range of hot and cold dishes at lunch and dinner. Much is sourced locally, and there are tables outside.

Henry's   BAR
(785-331-3511; www.facebook.com/henryson8th; 11 E 8th St; 7am-2am;) Downstairs is a moody low-lit coffeehouse with underground tunes and for-sale artwork on the walls. Upstairs is a boho bar popular with Lawrence's edgier crowd. It's a college town classic.

Information

Lawrence Visitor Center (785-865-5282; www.unmistakablylawrence.com; 402 N 2nd St; 9am-5pm Mon-Sat, 1-5pm Sun) In the restored old Union Pacific depot across the river from the center.

Getting There & Away

Lawrence is a quick half-hour drive east of Topeka or 45 minutes west of Kansas City along I-70. Amtrak's *Southwest Chief*, which runs from Chicago to Los Angeles, stops daily in Lawrence. Greyhound runs bus services west along I-70, south to Wichita and east to Kansas City and beyond.

Topeka

POP 126,600

Kansas and its vital role in America's race relations is documented in the otherwise humdrum state capital of Topeka. The emerging arts district in historic North Topeka (predictably called Noto) is a bright spot with eclectic shops, galleries and restaurants, many on or near N Kansas Ave.

◉ Sights

★ Brown v Board of Education National Historic Site   MUSEUM

(📞785-354-4273; www.nps.gov/brvb; 1515 SE Monroe St; ⊙9am-5pm Mon-Sat, & Sun April-Oct) **FREE** It took real guts to challenge the segregationist laws common in the US in the 1950s and the stories of these courageous men and women are here. This National Historic Site is set in Monroe Elementary School, one of Topeka's African American schools at the time of the landmark 1954 Supreme Court decision that banned segregation in US schools. The displays cover the entire Civil Rights movement.

🛏 Sleeping & Eating

Senate Luxury Suites   HOTEL $$

(📞785-233-5050; www.senatesuites.com; 900 SW Tyler St; r $80-160; 🅿❄📶) Not quite as luxurious as the name might have you believe, this 51-room hotel near the capitol is nevertheless one of the better bets in Topeka. The building once housed apartments, so the rooms are spacious (some have balconies and kitchenettes). There's a small gym with a hot tub in the basement.

Bobo's Drive In   FAST FOOD $

(📞785-234-4511; 2300 SW 10th Ave; mains $4-7; ⊙11am-8pm Mon-Sat) Follow the pink neon to this classic drive-in, beloved for its cheeseburgers, homemade onion rings, malts and more. Save room for the famous apple pie.

❶ Getting There & Away

Topeka is about an hour west of Kansas City on I-70. Greyhound has bus service west along I-70, southwest to Wichita and east to Kansas City and beyond.

Chase County

Nearly a perfect square, this is the county William Least Heat-Moon examined mile by mile in his best-selling book *PrairyErth*. The beautiful Flint Hills roll through here and are home to two-thirds of the nation's remaining tallgrass prairie. Give yourself a day to explore the lush countryside and the two adjoining small towns of Strong City and Cottonwood Falls.

◉ Sights

★ Tallgrass Prairie National Preserve   NATURE RESERVE

(📞620-273-8494; www.nps.gov/tapr; Hwy 177; ⊙buildings 9am-4:30pm, trails 24hr) **FREE** This 11,000-acre national preserve, 2 miles northwest of Strong City, is a perfect place to hike the prairie, with its 40 miles of scenic trails.

ROUTE 66: GET YOUR KICKS IN KANSAS

The sunflower state holds a mere 13 miles of Mother Road (less than 1% of the total) but there's still a lot to see. Entering from Missouri on Hwy 66, you'll first pass through mine-scarred **Galena**, which had a turbulent labor history during the Depression. It's also where a rusty old tow truck inspired Pixar animators to create the character Mater in *Cars* (look for the original on display outside a restored gas station along Route 66 in town at the corner of Front and S Main Sts).

Four miles west, stop at the red-brick **Nelson's Old Riverton Store** (📞620-848-3330; www.eislerbros.com; 7109 SE Hwy 66, Riverton; ⊙7:30am-8pm Mon-Sat, noon-7pm Sun) and stock up on top-notch sandwiches and Route 66 memorabilia. The 1925 property looks much like it did when it was first built – note the pressed-tin ceiling and the outhouse. You might consider a detour 20 miles north to **Crawford County**, where legendary fried chicken is a hallmark of several famous restaurants around Pittsburg. Try **Chicken Mary's** (📞620-231-9510; http://chicken-marys.com; 1133 E 600th Ave, Pittsburg; meals from $8; ⊙4-8:30pm Tue-Sat, 11am-8pm Sun), one of the best.

Otherwise, cross Hwy 400 and continue on Hwy 69/old Route 66 to the iconic 1923 **Marsh Arch Bridge**. From here, it's less than 3 miles south to **Baxter Springs**, the site of a Civil War massacre and numerous bank robberies. A restored 1939 Phillips 66 gas station is the **Kansas Route 66 Visitor Center** (📞620-856-2385; www.baxterspringsmuseum.org; cnr 10th St & Military Ave, Baxter Springs; ⊙visitor center hours vary Mar-Oct, museum 10am-4:30pm Tue-Sat, 1-4pm Sun) **FREE**. Military Ave (US 69A) takes you into Oklahoma.

Bison were reintroduced here in 2009 and now number about 100, sharing the space with prairie chickens (whose mating rituals are legendary!). Rangers give tours of a preserved ranch and offer bus tours from the visitor center, explaining just how rare this ecosystem is (less than 4% of North America's original tallgrass prairie remains).

🛏 Sleeping & Eating

★**Millstream Resort Motel**　　　MOTEL **$**
(☑620-273-8114; 401 Mill St, Cottonwood Falls; r $65-110; 🅿🖥📶) There is so much to love about this charming motel overlooking Cottonwood River and the falls, not least of which is the bargain price. Stone walls, wood floors and individually decorated rooms with riverside balconies make this an ideal Flint Hills retreat. Owners Richard and Sharon will go out of their way to welcome you.

Ad Astra Food & Drink　　　AMERICAN **$$**
(☑620-273-8440; www.adastrafoodanddrink.com; 318 Cottonwood St, Strong City; mains $10-18; ⊙5-9pm Thu, 11am-10pm Fri-Sun) American classics done right make the seasonal menus of this stylish Strong City restaurant very appealing. Enjoy great folk tunes, works of local artists on the walls and craft beer flowing from the taps. It's close to the town's historic train station.

❶ Getting There & Away

Chase County is bisected by historic US 50. There is no public transportation in the region.

OKLAHOMA

Oklahoma gets its name from the Choctaw name for 'Red People.' One look at the state's red earth and you'll wonder if the name is more of a literal than an ethnic comment. Still, with 39 tribes located here, it is a place with deep Native American heritage. Museums, cultural displays and more abound.

The other side of the Old West coin, cowboys also figure prominently in the Sooner State. Although pickups have replaced horses, there's still a great sense of the open range here, interrupted only by urban Oklahoma City and Tulsa. Oklahoma's share of Route 66 (the largest of any state) links some of the Mother Road's iconic highlights and there are myriad atmospheric old towns.

❶ Information

Oklahoma Tourism & Recreation Department
(www.travelok.com)
Oklahoma Bed & Breakfast Association
(www.okbba.com)
Oklahoma State Parks (www.travelok.com/state_parks) Most parks are free for day use.

Oklahoma City

POP 643,600
Often abbreviated to OKC, Oklahoma City is nearly dead center in the state and is the cultural and political capital. It has worked hard over the years to become more than just a cow town, all without turning its back on its cowboy heritage. It makes a good pause on your Route 66 travels.

The city is forever linked to the 1995 bombing of the Alfred P Murrah Federal Building; the memorials to this tragedy are moving. Away from the center, you'll find interesting neighborhoods like the Paseo Arts District.

◉ Sights

★**National Cowboy &**
Western Heritage Museum　　　MUSEUM
(☑405-478-2250; www.nationalcowboymuseum.org; 1700 NE 63rd St; adult/child $12.50/6; ⊙10am-5pm Mon-Sat, from noon Sun) Only the smells are missing. Vibrant historic displays are complemented by a mock frontier village and an excellent collection of Western painting and sculpture, featuring many works by Charles M Russell and Frederic Remington.

★**Oklahoma City**
National Memorial & Museum　　　MUSEUM
(☑405-235-3313; www.oklahomacitynationalmemorial.org; 620 N Harvey Ave; adult/student $15/12; ⊙9am-6pm Mon-Sat, from noon Sun, last ticket sold 1hr before close) The story of America's worst incident of domestic terrorism is told at this poignant museum, which avoids becoming mawkish and lets the horrible events of April 19, 1995, speak for themselves. The outdoor Symbolic Memorial has 168 empty chair sculptures for each of the people killed in the attack (the 19 small ones are for the children who perished in the daycare center).

Paseo Arts District　　　AREA
(www.thepaseo.org; NW 30th St & Paseo) With its Spanish Revival architecture, lively bars and over 20 funky art galleries, this is Oklahoma City's most bohemian corner.

Centennial Land Run Monument SCULPTURE
(www.visitokc.com/listings/oklahoma-land-run-monument/467/; 200 Centennial Ave; ⊘24hr) FREE Four dozen huge bronze sculptures, spread across several hundred feet of open land near Bricktown, capture the chaos and drama of the 1889 land rush that settled a large part of the future state – and dispossessed Native Americans from their lands. Despite the enduring controversy, the land rushes remain etched in Oklahoma's soul.

Stockyards City AREA
(www.stockyardscity.org; Agnew Ave & Exchange Ave) You'll brush up against real cowboys in Stockyards City, southwest of downtown, either in the shops and restaurants that cater to them or at the Oklahoma National Stockyards – the world's largest stocker and feeder cattle market. It dates back to 1910.

Oklahoma History Center MUSEUM
(☏405-521-2491; www.okhistory.org/historycenter; 800 Nazih Zuhdi Dr; adult/child $7/4; ⊘10am-5pm Mon-Sat) Near the **capitol building** (☏405-521-3356; www.okhouse.gov; 2300 N Lincoln Blvd; ⊘7am-7pm Mon-Fri, 9am-4pm Sat & Sun, tours 9am-3pm Mon-Fri) FREE, this museum makes people the focus as it tells the story of the Sooner State through interactive exhibits. There are good Native American galleries.

🛏 Sleeping

Lincoln Inn MOTEL $
(☏405-528-7563; www.lincolninnokc.com; 5405 N Lincoln Blvd; r from $50; P✳🐾🍳) The best of Oklahoma City's budget options, located off I-44 not far from the State Capitol building. There's a big pool, a small gym and interior-access rooms.

★Colcord Hotel BOUTIQUE HOTEL $$
(☏405-601-4300; www.colcordhotel.com; 15 N Robinson Ave; r from $180; P✳🐾) Oklahoma City's first skyscraper, built in 1911, is now a luxurious 12-story hotel. Many original flourishes, such as the marble-clad lobby, survive while the 108 rooms have a stylish, contemporary touch. It's near Bricktown.

Grandison Inn at Maney Park B&B $$
(☏405-232-8778; www.grandisoninn.com; 1200 N Shartel Ave; r $110-190; P✳🐾) In a genteel quarter of the city just northwest of downtown, this gracious 1904-vintage B&B welcomes guests to eight rooms with period charm, plenty of doodads and modern amenities. The house has amazing woodwork, including a showstopping staircase.

✗ Eating

★Nic's Grill BURGERS $
(☏405-524-0999; www.nicsokc.com; 1201 N Pennsylvania Ave; mains $10; ⊘10:30am-2pm Mon-Fri, 11am-3pm Sat) The hamburgers at this outlet are lauded nationwide. The limited hours mean that crowds form to get a chance at one of the juicy masterpieces. Be sure to get yours with jalapeños.

Pho Lien Hoa VIETNAMESE $
(☏405-521-8087; 901 NW 23rd St; mains from $8; ⊘8:30am-9pm) Many Vietnamese refugees settled in Oklahoma after the Vietnam War in the mid-1970s and many opened restaurants. One of the very best is this otherwise nondescript, no-frills, cash-only outlet in a humdrum strip mall. The food could not be fresher or more authentic.

Sunnyside Diner DINER $
(☏405-778-8861; www.eatatsunnyside.com; 916 NW 6th St; mains $5-12; ⊘6am-3pm; ♿) Enjoy the best breakfasts in town at this seemingly traditional diner. But take one bite of the fresh blueberry pancakes or the eggs Benedict and you'll know you've found morning nirvana. It has an excellent kids menu.

★Cheever's Cafe MODERN AMERICAN $$
(☏405-525-7007; www.cheeverscafe.com; 2409 N Hudson Ave; mains $10-40; ⊘11am-9pm Sun-Thu, to 10:30pm Fri & Sat) This former art deco flower shop is now an upscale cafe with excellent Southern- and Mexican-influenced fare. The menu changes seasonally and is locally sourced. The ice-cream-ball dessert is the stuff of dreams. The chicken fried steak is considered the best in the state.

★Cattlemen's Steakhouse STEAK $$
(☏405-236-0416; www.cattlemensrestaurant.com; 1309 S Agnew Ave; mains $7-30; ⊘6am-10pm Sun-Thu, to midnight Fri & Sat) Oklahoma City's most storied restaurant, this Stockyards City institution has been feeding cowpokes and city slickers slabs of beef since 1910. Deals are still cut at the counter (where you can jump the wait for tables) and back in the comfy booths. Get the side salad drenched in the house garlic dressings and be sure to have some onion rings. Breakfasts are an insider's secret.

🍷 Drinking & Entertainment

Pump Bar BAR
(☏405-702-8898; www.pumpbar.net; 2425 N Walker Ave; ⊘4pm-2am Mon-Fri, from 11am Sat & Sun)

WORTH A TRIP

DODGE CITY

Dodge City – where famous lawmen Bat Masterson and Wyatt Earp tried, sometimes successfully, to keep law and order – had a notorious reputation during the 1870s and 1880s. The long-running TV series *Gunsmoke* (1955–75) spurred further interest in the city's storied past, though historical authenticity has always played a distant third fiddle to fun and frolic here.

Today Dodge City milks its heritage while it slaughters more than 10,000 head of cattle every 24 hours at huge factories. You may be inspired to get the hell out of Dodge, but it can make a good pause if you're out touring historic US 50.

The historic downtown, away from the attractions, is good for a wander. The visitor center has historic walking and driving route maps and audioguides.

View surviving **Santa Fe Trail wagon-wheel ruts** about 9 miles west of town off US 50. The site is well marked. For a visual taste – and smell – of Dodge City's economic engine today, head 3 miles east of the visitor center on US 283 to an **overlook** with a sweeping view of two vast stockyards and meat processing plants.

The **visitor center** (☑ 800-653-9378; www.visitdodgecity.org; 400 W Wyatt Earp Blvd; ☺ 8am-6:30pm daily Jun-Aug, 8am-5pm Mon-Fri Sep-May) has information for all of Kansas.

Dodge City is about 150 miles west of Wichita along US 400. Amtrak's *Southwest Chief*, which runs from Chicago to Los Angeles, stops daily in Dodge City.

This bar is, er, a real gas! A former filling station has been transformed into a whimsical bar. The large patio (which is where the gas pumps were once installed) is decorated with pink flamingos and stuffed cacti. Drinks are served in oddball containers that include several tiki numbers. The crowd is a cheery bunch of neighborhood locals.

Oklahoma City Thunder　　　BASKETBALL
(www.nba.com/thunder; 100 W Reno Ave; tickets from $40) The NBA's Thunder play downtown at Chesapeake Energy Arena. The team has made the playoffs every season since 2009.

🛍 Shopping

Langston's　　　CLOTHING
(☑ 405-235-9536; www.langstons.com; 2224 Exchange Ave; ☺ 10am-8pm Mon-Sat, noon-5pm Sun) You can buy all forms of Western wear and gear at Langston's. The boot selection alone is mind-blowing.

ℹ Information

Oklahoma City Visitor Information Center
(☑ 405-602-5141; www.visitokc.com; 58 W Sheridan Ave; ☺ 9am-6pm Mon-Fri) Located in the northeast corner of the Cox Convention Center, it has info on area attractions, restaurants, events and more.

ℹ Getting There & Away

Will Rogers World Airport (OKC; ☑ 405-316-3271; www.flyokc.com; 7100 Terminal Dr) is 5 miles southwest of downtown; a taxi ride costs about $25 to the center. There's services from major American hubs.

Amtrak's (www.amtrak.com) *Heartland Flyer* goes from **Santa Fe Depot** (100 S EK Gaylord Blvd) to Fort Worth ($31, four hours, one daily).

Greyhound (☑ 405-606-4382; www.greyhound.com; 1948 E Reno Ave) has daily buses to Dallas ($35, five hours), Wichita ($30, three hours) and Tulsa ($20, two hours, five daily), among other destinations including west on I-40.

Western Oklahoma

West of Oklahoma City toward Texas, the land opens into expansive prairies, nowhere as beautifully as in the Wichita Mountains. These hills, along with some Route 66 attractions and Native American sites, make Western Oklahoma prime road-tripping country.

**Washita Battlefield
National Historic Site**　　　HISTORIC SITE
(☑ 580-497-2742; www.nps.gov/waba; Hwy 47A, Cheyenne; ☺ site dawn-dusk, visitor center 8am-4:30pm) FREE On November 27, 1868, George Custer's troops launched a dawn attack on the peaceful village of Chief Black Kettle. It was a slaughter of men, women, children and domestic animals, an act some would say led to karmic revenge on Custer eight years later. Trails traverse the site of the killings, which is remarkably unchanged. An excellent visitor center 0.7 miles away contains a good museum; seasonal tours and talks are worthwhile.

ROUTE 66: GET YOUR KICKS IN OKLAHOMA

Oklahoma's connection with America's Main Street runs deep: the road's chief proponent, Cyrus Avery, was a Sooner; John Steinbeck's *Grapes of Wrath* told of the plight of Depression-era Okie farmers fleeing west on Route 66; and Oklahoma has more miles of the original alignment than any other state. The Oklahoma Route 66 Association (www.oklahomaroute66.com) publishes an excellent booklet – look for it at visitor centers.

Shortly after you enter the state from Kansas on US 69A, you'll come to **Miami**. Across the Neosho River south of town is the first of two original and very rough 9ft-wide alignments. The second, E 140 Rd (turn west), comes soon after the first, just before I-44. You'll cross I-44 twice before rolling into **Vinita**. **Clanton's** (☑ 918-256-9053; www.clantonscafe.com; 319 E Illinois Ave, Vinita; mains $4-12; ⏰ 6am-8pm Mon-Fri, to 2pm Sat) dates back to 1927 and is the place for chicken fried steak and calf fries (don't ask).

Thirty miles further on, **Foyil** is worth a 4-mile detour on Hwy 28A to see the 'world's largest totem pole.' Another 10 miles brings you to **Claremore**, the home of the **Will Rogers Memorial Museum** (☑ 918-341-0719; www.willrogers.com; 1720 W Will Rogers Blvd; adult/child $7/3; ⏰ 10am-5pm Mar-Oct, Wed-Sun Nov-Feb).

Next up at the city of **Catoosa**, just before Tulsa, is one of the most photographed Route 66 landmarks: the 80ft-long **Blue Whale** (2680 N Hwy 66, Catoosa; ⏰ 8am-6pm), centerpiece of a long-gone water park. East 11th St takes you into and right through art-deco-rich **Tulsa**; be sure to look for the iconic neon wonder of the restored 1930s **Meadow Gold Sign** (www.meadowgolddistrict.com; 1324 E 11th St) at S Quaker Ave. Southwest Blvd takes you across the river and out of town.

State Hwy 66 from Tulsa to Oklahoma City is one of the longest continuous stretches of Mother Road remaining (110 miles). At **Chandler**, 60 miles southwest of Tulsa, the **Route 66 Interpretive Center** (☑ 405-258-1300; www.route66interpretivecenter.org; 400 E 1st St, Chandler; adult/child $5/4; ⏰ 10am-5pm Mon-Sat Jun-Aug, closed Mon Sep-May) re-creates the experience of driving the road through the decades.

Route 66 follows US 77 into **Oklahoma City**. You'll leave Oklahoma City by turning north on May Ave and west on NW 39th St past **Ann's Chicken Fry House** (☑ 405-943-8915; 4106 NW 39th St; mains $5-12; ⏰ 11am-8:30pm Tue-Sat). Beyond this, the route follows Business I-40 west.

El Reno, 20 miles west of Oklahoma City, is home to the fried-onion burger (average $3), a road-food classic. Among several historic drive-ins and dives, try **Sid's Diner** (☑ 405-262-7757; www.sidsdinerelreno.com; 300 S Choctaw Ave, El Reno; mains from $4; ⏰ 7am-8pm Mon-Sat), which has tables outside.

Some 17 miles west of El Reno, take a stretch of US 281 that runs on the north side of I-40 between exits 108 and 101. Where it crosses the Canadian River on the 38-truss-long **Pony Bridge** (US 281, near Bridgeport), stop at the west end. It's the spot they had to bury grampa in the 1939 movie version of *The Grapes of Wrath.*

Just west of **Hydro** and Hwy 58, **Lucille's** is the atmospheric moldering remains of a legendary roadhouse. Some 4 miles further on as you approach **Weatherford**, the modern **Lucille's Roadhouse** (☑ 580-772-8808; www.lucillesroadhouse.com; 1301 N Airport Rd, I-40 exit 84, Weatherford; mains $6-25; ⏰ 6am-10pm Mon-Sat, 11am-9pm Sun) carries on the legacy.

In **Clinton**, walk through six decades of history, memorabilia and music at the mid-sized **Route 66 Museum** (☑ 580-323-7866; www.route66.org; 2229 W Gary Blvd, Clinton; adult/child $7/4; ⏰ 9am-7pm Mon-Sat, 1-6pm Sun May-Aug, reduced hours Sep-Apr).

Thirty miles further west in **Elk City**, home of the **National Route 66 Museum** (☑ 580-225-3234; 320 W 3rd St/Hwy 66, Elk City; adult/child $5/4; ⏰ 9am-5pm Mon-Sat, & 2-5pm Sun Apr-Oct). Route 66 spills into Texas at **Texola**, which is just a dust devil away from being a ghost town.

❶ Getting There & Away

Route 66 road-trippers will pass through Western Oklahoma mostly along I-40 (take exit 32 for Cheyenne and the Washita Battlefield; p691). Use I-44 out of Oklahoma City instead to dip down toward **Fort Sill** (☑ 580-442-5123; http://sill-www.army.mil/museum/; 6701 Sheridan Rd, Visitors Control Center; ⏰ 9am-5pm Tue-Sat) and the Wichita Mountains. Greyhound runs along I-40 to Amarillo, TX.

Tulsa

POP 401,800

Self-billed as the 'Oil Capital of the World,' Tulsa has never dirtied its hands much on the black gold that oozes out elsewhere in the state. Rather, it is home to scores of energy companies that make their living drilling for oil, selling it or supplying those who do. The steady wealth this provides once helped create Tulsa's richly detailed art deco downtown.

Today Tulsa suffers from suburban sprawl, although the Brady Arts District downtown is a bright spot. It also has a clutch of Route 66 sights and businesses, plus a lively music scene.

◉ Sights

Downtown Tulsa has so much art deco architecture it was once known as the 'Terra-Cotta City' for the building material typically used to create the distinctive architectural detailing. The **Philcade Building** (www.tulsaartdecomuseum.com; 511 S Boston Ave; ⊙ lobby exhibits 8am-9pm Mon-Sat, to 3pm Sun), with its glorious T-shaped lobby, the nearby **Philtower Building** (427 S Boston Ave) and the **Boston Avenue United Methodist Church** (☑ 918-583-5181; www.bostonavenue. org; 1301 S Boston Ave; ⊙ 8:30am-5pm Mon-Fri, 8am-5pm Sun, guided tours noon Sun), rising at the end of downtown, are three exceptional examples.

Be sure to visit the essential **Decopolis** (☑ 918-382-7388; www.decopolis.net; 502 S Boston Ave; ⊙ 10am-6pm Mon & Tue, to 9pm Wed-Sat, 11am-3pm Sun) for info and download a walking guide at www.visittulsa.com (search for 'self-guided art deco walking tour.')

The nascent **Brady Arts District** is centered on Brady and Main Sts immediately north of downtown. It has galleries, venues, good restaurants and plenty of parking.

★ Woody Guthrie Center   MUSEUM
(☑ 918-574-2710; www.woodyguthriecenter.org; 102 E Brady St; adult/child $12/free; ⊙ 10am-6pm Tue-Sun) Woody Guthrie gained fame for his 1930s folk ballads that told stories of the Dust Bowl and the Great Depression. His life and music are recalled in this impressive museum, where you can listen to his music and explore his legacy via the works of Bob Dylan and more. Evening concerts are held at the on-site theater (check the website for dates and times).

★ Oklahoma Jazz Hall of Fame   MUSEUM
(☑ 918-928-5299; www.okjazz.org; 5 S Boston Ave; Sun jazz concerts adult/child $15/5; ⊙ 9am-5pm Mon-Fri, live music 6-10pm Tue & 4-7:30pm Sun) **FREE** Tulsa's beautiful Union Station is filled with sound again, but now it's melodious as opposed to cacophonous. During the first half of the 20th century, Tulsa was literally at the crossroads of American music with performers both homegrown and from afar. Learn about greats like Charlie Christian, Ernie Fields Senior and Wallace Willis in detailed exhibits. Sunday jazz concerts are played in the once-segregated grand concourse. On Tuesday nights there are free jam sessions.

★ Gilcrease Museum   MUSEUM
(☑ 918-596-2700; www.gilcrease.org; 1400 Gilcrease Museum Rd; adult/child $8/free; ⊙ museum 10am-5pm Tue-Sun, gardens 6am-11pm) Northwest of downtown, off Hwy 64, this superb museum sits on the manicured estate of Thomas Gilcrease of the Muscogee Creek Nation, who discovered oil on his allotment. Exhibits explore Native American art, textiles, pottery and more, while the surrounding free gardens make for a great stroll.

Philbrook Museum of Art   MUSEUM
(☑ 918-749-7941; www.philbrook.org; 2727 S Rockford Rd; adult/child $9/free; ⊙ 9am-5pm Wed, Thu, Sat & Sun, to 8pm Fri) South of town, this oil magnate's converted Italianate villa, ringed by fabulous foliage, houses fine Native American works and classic international art. There is a second location, **Philbrook Downtown** (116 E Brady St; adult/child $7/free; ⊙ 11am-5pm Wed-Sun, to 9pm Fri), in the Brady Arts District. It shows contemporary art.

⌁ Sleeping

Desert Hills Motel   MOTEL $
(☑ 918-834-3311; 5220 E 11th St; r from $60; P ❋ 🛜) The glowing neon cactus out front beckons you in to this restored 1950s motel, which has 50 rooms (with refrigerators and microwaves) arranged diagonally around the parking lot. It's 5 miles east of downtown, on 11th St, which is part of historic Route 66.

★ Hotel Campbell   HOTEL $$
(☑ 918-744-5500; www.thecampbellhotel.com; 2636 E 11th St; r $140-210; P ❋ @ 🛜) Restored to its 1927-era Route 66 splendor, this historic hotel east of downtown has 26 luxurious rooms with hardwood floors and plush period furniture. Ask for a tour.

Hotel Ambassador
HOTEL $$$

(☑918-587-8200; www.ambassadortulsa.com; 1324 S Main St; r $200-400; P❄@☎) Look in the hallway for the photos of this 1929 10-story hotel before its opulent renovation. Public spaces are suitably grand; the 55 rooms are newly revamped and have a contemporary feel that helps the somewhat close quarters seem a tad larger.

✖ Eating

★ Elmer's
BARBECUE $

(☑918-742-6524; www.elmersbbqtulsa.com; 4130 S Peoria Ave; mains $7-26; ⊙11am-7pm Tue & Wed, to 8pm Thu-Sat) A legendary barbecue joint where the star of the menu is the potentially deadly 'Badwich,' a bun-crushing combo of superbly smoked sausages, ham, beef, pork and more. There's also smoked salmon and a showstopping side: green beans with chunks of succulent rib meat. The dining room is bright and has a house piano for the blues.

Freddie's Hamburgers
BURGERS $

(☑918-585-3544; 802 S Lewis Ave; mains from $4; ⊙10am-7pm Mon-Fri, to 3pm Sat) You'll never be satisfied with a burger from a fast-food chain again after you wipe the juices from these beauties off your chin. Burgers come with an array of toppings, including thick tomato slices and grilled onions. They're served from a bare-bones stand, with a table back behind the counter.

Ike's Chili House
DINER $

(☑918-838-9410; www.ikeschilius.com; 1503 E 11th St; mains $5-9; ⊙10am-7pm Mon-Fri, to 3pm Sat)

THE 1921 TULSA RACE RIOTS

On Memorial Day, May 30, 1921, an African American man and a white woman were alone in an elevator in downtown Tulsa and the woman screamed. The how and why have never been answered, but the incident sparked three days of race riots in which 35 blocks of Tulsa's main African American neighborhood, Greenwood, were destroyed by roving gangs and even bombs that were lobbed from airplanes. Thousands were left homeless, hundreds injured and scores killed.

Learn more about the riot at the **John Hope Franklin Reconciliation Park** (www.jhfcenter.org; 290 N Elgin Ave; ⊙8am-8pm).

Ike's has been serving chili for more than 110 years and its classic version is much loved. You can get it straight or over Fritos (a local sensation), a hot dog, fries or spaghetti. Top with red peppers, onions, jalapeños, saltines and cheddar cheese for pure joy. A Route 66 classic.

♟ Drinking & Entertainment

American Solera
BREWERY

(☑918-779-7763; www.americansolera.com; 108 E 18th St; ⊙4-9pm Mon-Thu, noon-11pm Fri & Sat, noon-9pm Sun) A prime destination in the SoBo nightlife district, this pub is the perfect venue for American Solera's award-winning brews. Try the Norton Fellowship, a sour ale made with the native Norton grape. Also notable are the sour IPAs and the fruity ales.

Mercury Lounge
BAR

(www.mercurylounge918.com; 1747 S Boston Ave; ⊙2pm-2am) A former gas station is now a classic dive bar with a pool table and two patios perfect for Tulsa's many balmy evenings. On some nights there's live rock performed hard by top local bands.

★ Cain's Ballroom
LIVE MUSIC

(☑918-584-2306; www.cainsballroom.com; 423 N Main St) Rising rockers grace the boards where Bob Wills played Western swing in the '30s and the Sex Pistols caused confusion in 1978 (check out the hole Sid Vicious punched in a wall).

ⓘ Getting There & Around

Tulsa International Airport (☑918-838-5000; www.tulsaairports.com; 7777 Airport Dr) is northeast of the center and has services from major hubs across the US.

Greyhound (www.greyhound.com; 317 S Detroit Ave) destinations include Oklahoma City ($20, two hours, five daily) and Muskogee ($26, one hour, one daily). Jefferson Lines (www.jeffersonlines.com) buses ply the route to Bartlesville ($22, one hour, one daily).

Tulsa Transit (☑918-582-2100; www.tulsa transit.org; 319 S Denver Ave; 2hr/1-day pass $1.75/3.75) operates buses from the downtown bus hub to the airport and other points around greater Tulsa.

Guthrie

POP 11,350

Guthrie likes to call itself 'Offbeat Oklahoma,' a moniker it wears well. The arts-driven community here prides itself on the town's bluegrass music scenes; look out

MEDICINE PARK
....

This charming creekside resort town woos travelers with its scenic setting and unique cobblestone architecture (with buildings made of rounded red rocks). It's the kind of place where artists rub shoulders with trout fishers as landscaped parks give way to a unique prairie paradise. The town is just a mile down the road from **Wichita Mountains Wildlife Refuge** (☑ 580-429-3222; www.fws.gov/refuge/wichita_mountains; 20539 State Hwy 115, Cache; ⊙ visitor center 9am-5pm; 🅿 🐾) **FREE**, where herds of elk, buffalo and longhorn cattle roam free.

Medicine Park is about 1½ hours southwest of Oklahoma City by car, mostly on I-44. There is no public transportation.

for performances by the local Byron Berline Band. Galleries and antique shops fill the brick-and-stone Victorian buildings that line its historic core. Some 30 miles north of Oklahoma City, this was the state's first capital.

Frontier Drugstore Museum MUSEUM
(☑ 405-282-1895; www.drugmuseum.org; 214 W Oklahoma Ave; suggested donation $3; ⊙ 10am-5pm Tue-Sat) A kooky little museum that shows you the intriguing remedies (like jars of leeches) offered at a frontier pharmacy at the turn of the century.

Pollard Inn HISTORIC HOTEL $$
(☑ 405-517-9266; www.pollardbb.com; 124 W Harrison Ave; r from $135; 🅿 🐾) Look up at the tin ceilings to check out the bullet holes at this bank-cum-inn, the site of many a frontier times robbery. The 12 rooms are spacious and hark back to Guthrie's heyday. Happily, the decor – while authentic – avoids the twee overload of some B&Bs.

ⓘ Getting There & Away

Guthrie is 30 miles north of Oklahoma City via I-35. There is no public transportation.

Anadarko
POP 6600

Eight tribal lands are located in this area, and students from many different tribes are enrolled in Anadarko schools. The town regularly hosts powwows and events, and is a good place to steep yourself in Native American culture.

National Hall of Fame for Famous American Indians MONUMENT
(☑ 405-247-5555; www.americanindianhof.com; 901 E Central Blvd, Hwy 62; ⊙ site 24hr, visitor center 9am-5pm Mon-Sat, from 2pm Sun) **FREE** A short outdoor walk leads past 41 bronze busts of well-known Native Americans including Pocahontas, Geronimo and Sitting Bull. The nearby visitor center has a good selection of books on Native Americans from Oklahoma.

Southern Plains Indian Museum MUSEUM
(☑ 405-247-6221; www.doi.gov/iacb/southern-plains-indian-museum; 801 E Central Blvd; ⊙ 10am-4:30pm Tue-Fri; 🅿) **FREE** This museum houses a small but diverse collection of Plains Indian clothing, weaponry and musical instruments. There's also a collection of Native American art.

ⓘ Getting There & Away

Anadarko is a little over an hour southwest of Oklahoma City by car. There is no public transportation in the region.

Muskogee
POP 37,900

Namesake of Merle Haggard's 1969 hit 'Okie from Muskogee,' this town on the Arkansas River was, and to some degree still is, Creek and Cherokee land. It's an excellent place to learn about Native American culture, especially before the 1800s.

◉ Sights

Fort Gibson Historic Site HISTORIC SITE
(☑ 918-478-4088; www.okhistory.org/sites/fortgibson; 907 N Garrison Rd, Fort Gibson; adult/child $7/4; ⊙ 10am-5pm Tue-Sat) Built as a frontier fort in 1824, Fort Gibson came to play an integral – and notorious – role in the Trail of Tears. It was home to the removal commission in the 1830s and is where surviving Creek and Seminole people were brought after the forced march. From here they were dispatched around the Indian Territory. You can get a good sense of military life 180 years ago at the restored grounds and buildings. It's seven miles northeast of the center of Muskogee.

FRANK LLOYD WRIGHT IN BARTLESVILLE

This town still shows the riches that flowed from the ground during the first oil boom in 1905. The Phillips petroleum empire has left behind well-funded museums and a huge mansion. Soaring over it all is the 1956 221ft-tall **Price Tower** (☑918-336-1000; www.pricetower.org; 510 Dewey Ave; gallery adult/child $6/free, tours adult/child $15/10; ◷gallery 10am-8pm Tue-Sat, noon-5pm Sun, tours 11am & 2pm Tue-Sat, 2pm Sun), the only Frank Lloyd Wright–designed skyscraper ever built.

Inside and out, the tower is like an edition of *Architectural Digest* meets *The Jetsons*. All but abandoned in the 1990s, the building now houses a ground-floor art gallery and the **Inn at Price Tower** (www.pricetower.org/stay; r from $135; P❉☎), located within the building's top floors. You can ride the rickety elevators to the 15th-floor bar.

Bartlesville is 45 miles north of Tulsa on US 75. Jefferson Lines (www.jeffersonlines.com) plies the route once a day ($22, one hour).

Five Civilized Tribes Museum   MUSEUM

(☑918-683-1701; www.fivetribes.org; 1101 Honor Heights Dr, Agency Hill; adult/student $3/1.50; ◷10am-5pm Mon-Fri, to 2pm Sat) This museum is inside an 1875 Union Indian Agency house. It recalls the cultures of the Native Americans – the Cherokee, Chickasaw, Choctaw, Creek (Muscogee) and Seminole tribes – forcibly moved here from America's southeast on what became known as the Trail of Tears.

🛏 Sleeping & Eating

Graham-Carroll House   B&B $$

(☑918-683-0100; www.grahamcarrollhouse.com; 501 N 16th St; r $130-160; ❉☎) This grand four-room B&B lies within a genteel English Tudor manor house in the Founder's Place Historic District. Some rooms have jet tubs and all stays include a gourmet three-course breakfast. Don't miss the rooftop balcony and lavish gardens.

Harmony House   BAKERY $

(☑918-687-8653; www.harmonyhouse4lunch.com; 208 S 7th St; mains $8-10; ◷cafe 11am-2:30pm Mon-Sat, bakery 9am-5pm Mon-Fri, to 3pm Sat) With fresh-baked cookies waiting for you at the table, pitchers of apricot iced tea and knickknacks aplenty, you may feel as though you've just arrived at your long-lost Oklahoma grandma's house. There are soups, salads and sandwiches, but the main reason to come here is for the bakery's desserts, like the Toll House pie (made with much of the deliciousness of the iconic chocolate chip cookie).

❶ Getting There & Away

Muskogee is 50 miles southeast of Tulsa. Greyhound links the two cities with a daily bus ($26, one hour).

Tahlequah

POP 16,700

Tahlequah (tal-*ah*-quaw) has been the Cherokee capital since 1839. The excellent **Cherokee Heritage Center** (☑918-456-6007; www.cherokeeheritage.org; 21192 S Keeler Dr; adult/child $12/7; ◷9am-5pm Mon-Sat May-Oct, Tue-Sat Nov-Apr) lies at Park Hill, once known as 'The Athens of Indian Territory.' Meanwhile, the compact downtown area has a youthful energy and vibrant shopping and dining options thanks to Northeastern State University.

Blue Fern B&B   B&B $

(☑918-316-6973; www.bluefernbedandbreakfast.net; 224 W Chickasaw St; r $110-140; ❉☎) This 1904 Victorian house – built before Oklahoma was a state – has been lovingly restored into a colorful B&B. Each of the three rooms has its own gas fireplace and two of them have kitchenettes. Relax on the wide porches.

❶ Getting There & Away

Tahlequah is 65 miles southeast of Tulsa. There is no public transportation to the town.

Texas

Why Go?

Cue the theme music, and make it something epic: Texas is as big and sweeping a state as can be imagined. If it were a country, it would be the world's 40th largest. And as big as it is geographically, it is equally as large in people's imaginations.

Cattle ranches, pickup trucks, cowboy boots and thick Texas drawls – all of those are part of the culture, to be sure. But an Old West theme park it is not. With a state this big there's room for Texas to be whatever you want it to be.

You can find beaches, sprawling national parks, historic towns, citified shopping and nightlife, and a vibrant music scene. And the nearly year-round warm weather makes it ideal for outdoor activities such as hiking, cycling, rock climbing and kayaking. So saddle up for whatever adventure suits you best: the Lone Star State is ready to ride.

Best Places to Eat

➜ Franklin Barbecue (p704)

➜ Javier's (p734)

➜ Pieous (p714)

➜ Killen's Barbecue (p723)

➜ L&J Cafe (p746)

Best Places to Sleep

➜ Hotel Emma (p710)

➜ Indian Lodge (p742)

➜ Hotel Van Zandt (p704)

➜ Hotel ZaZa Houston (p720)

➜ El Cosmico (p743)

When to Go
Austin

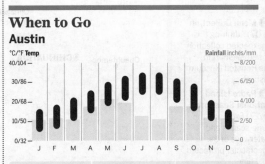

Mar Warm weather during spring break attracts college students and families with kids.

Apr & May Wildflowers line roadsides, festivals are in full swing and summer is yet to swelter.

Oct Crowds have thinned, the heat has broken, but it's still warm enough for shorts.

Texas Highlights

❶ Gruene Hall (p712) Scooting across the well-worn wooden floor of Texas' oldest dance hall.

❷ River Walk (p708) Strolling by cafes and riverside restaurants along the promenade in San Antonio.

❸ Austin (p700) Getting your fill of live music, backyard bars and wildly creative food trucks.

❹ Sixth Floor Museum (p731) Pondering JFK conspiracy theories at this one-of-a-kind museum in Dallas.

❺ Fort Worth (p736) Watching longhorn cattle being driven through the dusty streets of this cowboy city.

❻ Big Bend National Park (p739) Discovering a different kind of rugged Texan beauty.

❼ Galveston (p724) Getting to know this historic Gulf Coast survivor.

❽ Menil Collection (p717) Admiring this unexpected collection of surrealist art in the Houston Museum District.

❾ Padre Island National Seashore (p727) Exploring the dune-scapes and waterways of this spectacular protected coastline.

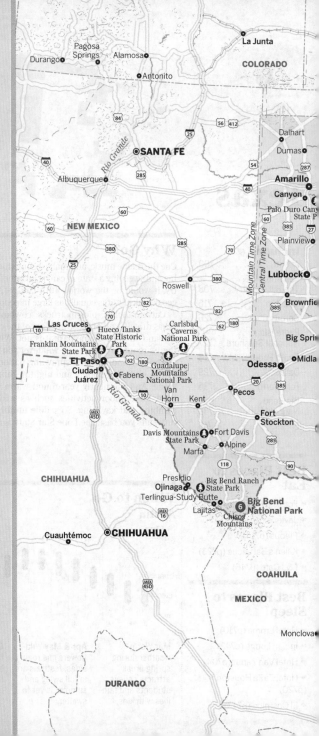

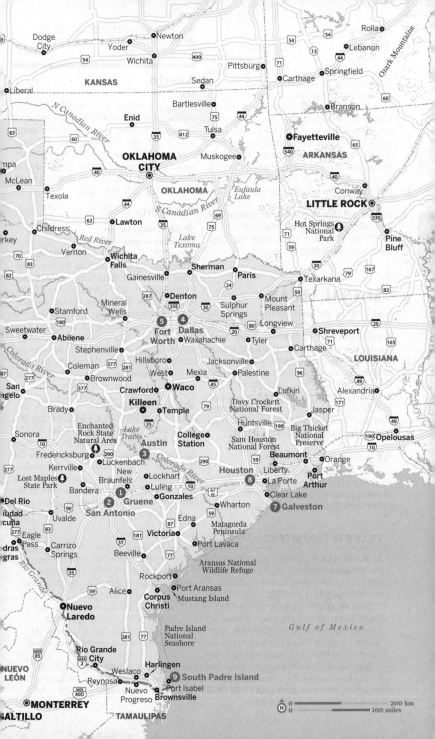

History

Texas hasn't always been Texas. Or Mexico, for that matter. Or the United States, or Spain, or France, or any of the six flags that flew over this epic state during its eight changes of sovereignty (and that doesn't even include the little Republic of the Rio Grande). The earliest evidence of humans in what is now Texas exists in the *llano estacado* ('staked plain') section of Texas and New Mexico. Little is known about the various indigenous peoples, but by the time the first Europeans arrived in the 16th century, several distinct Native American groups were settled in the region. One such, the Caddo people, still figures strongly as a namesake and cultural influence in east Texas, where the Caddo Mounds State Historic Site commemorates their unique history.

CENTRAL TEXAS

Lakes, rivers and hills distinguish Central Texas from most of the rest of the state. The major urban hubs of Austin and San Antonio, each with a busy international airport and diverse lodging options, stand just 80 miles apart, while the Hill Country rolls west from both. Within this diverse region you can enjoy big-city nightlife, nation-building history, scenic vineyards, delicious Tex-Mex food and loads of outdoor activities, from hiking to tubing to wildflower viewing.

Getting There & Away

Austin is home to Austin-Bergstrom International Airport (p706), which serves more than 15 million passengers annually, while over 10 million passengers come through San Antonio

International Airport (p713) each year. Both airports have rental car centers with a broad choice of companies.

Austin

POP 932,000

With a population that's rapidly approaching a million, and an annual influx of almost 30 million visitors, Austin is by any standards a big city. Somehow, though, Texas' state capital has kept its small-town heart, earning the love with great music, culinary prowess, whip-smart locals and a sociable streak impossible to resist.

⊙ Sights

★**Bat Colony Under Congress Avenue Bridge** BRIDGE
(Map p702; Congress Ave; ⊙sunset Apr-Nov) Every year up to 1.5 million Mexican free-tailed bats make their home upon a platform beneath the Congress Ave Bridge, which crosses the Colorado at the southern end of downtown. It's an Austin tradition to sit on the grassy banks of Lady Bird Lake and watch the bats swarm out as dusk approaches each evening, like a fast-moving, black, chittering river. Each night, they feed on an estimated 30,000lb (13,500kg) of insects. The best viewing is in August.

★**Texas State Capitol** HISTORIC BUILDING
(Map p702; ☑tours 512-305-8402; cnr 11th St & Congress Ave; ⊙7am-10pm Mon-Fri, 9am-8pm Sat & Sun; ☀) FREE Completed in 1888 using sunset-red granite, Texas' state capitol is the largest in the US, backing up the familiar claim that everything's bigger hereabouts. Drop in even if only to take a peek at the lovely rotunda – look up at the dome – and

---

TEXAS IN TWO WEEKS

So you want to do it all but are short on time? Start with three days in Dallas (p729). See the JFK assassination sites downtown and eat in trendy Uptown, then the next day take a trip out to the historic Fort Worth Stockyards. After heading out of town on day three, spend two nights in Austin listening to live music and watching the bats fly.

Stop for a night in the Old West settlement of Gruene (p712) to two-step at one of Texas' oldest dance halls, then continue on to San Antonio (p708). In two days there you can explore the Alamo and River Walk. From there Corpus Christi (p726) is just a three-hour drive south; it's a good base to kick back for a couple of nights and hit the beach at Padre Island National Seashore or Port Aransas.

Afterwards it's time to turn north for three nights in Houston (p716). NASA's Space Center Houston is a don't-miss attraction, as is the museum district. For a third day's excursion, hikers could trek out to Big Thicket National Preserve, while history and sunshine lovers should see Galveston.

try out the whispering gallery created by its curved ceiling.

Mexic-Arte Museum   MUSEUM
(Map p702; ☑512-480-9373; www.mexic-arte museum.org; 419 Congress Ave; adult/child under 12yr/student $7/1/4, free Sun; ⊙10am-6pm Mon-Thu, to 5pm Fri & Sat, noon-5pm Sun, closed during SXSW) This wonderful, eclectic downtown museum features works from Mexican and Mexican American artists in exhibitions that change every two months. Many are drawn from the permanent collection, which includes carved wooden masks, modern Latin American paintings, historic photographs and contemporary art. Don't miss the new and experimental talent on show in the back gallery.

Bob Bullock Texas
State History Museum   MUSEUM
(☑512-936-8746; www.thestoryoftexas.com; 1800 Congress Ave; adult/child $13/9; ⊙9am-5pm Mon-Sat, noon-5pm Sun) Big, glitzy and bursting with high-tech interactive exhibits, this showcase museum celebrates the story of the Lone Star State, from its earliest inhabitants, via the era when it formed part of Mexico, up to the present day. The highlight is on the 1st floor, where you can see the hull of La Belle, a French ship that sank off the Gulf Coast in 1686, along with artifacts recovered from the wreck. Allow a few hours for your visit.

Lyndon Baines Johnson (LBJ)
Library & Museum   MUSEUM
(☑512-721-0200; www.lbjlibrary.org; 2313 Red River St; adult/child 13-17yr $10/3; ⊙9am-5pm) Devoted to the 36th US president, who launched his political career in Austin, this museum is still attracting the crowds more than 50 years since he left office. Beyond the hokey, animatronic LBJ that regales visitors with the president's favourite anecdotes, the displays are fascinating and comprehensive, covering such major 1960s events as the assassination of President Kennedy, Johnson's subsequent role in pushing through Civil Rights legislation, and the role played by the Vietnam War in his eventual downfall.

Thinkery   MUSEUM
(☑512-469-6200; www.thinkeryaustin.org; 1830 Simond Ave; adult/child under 2yr $12/free; ⊙10am-5pm Tue, Thu & Fri, to 8pm Wed, to 6pm Sat & Sun; ▣) This huge, red, box-like building north of downtown inspires young minds with hands-on activities in the realms of science, technology and the arts. Kids can get wet learning about fluid dynamics, build LED light structures and explore chemical reactions in the Kitchen Lab, among other attractions. A spectacular outdoor play area holds nets and climbing toys. Closed Monday except for Baby Bloomers and other special events.

Museum of the Weird   MUSEUM
(Map p702; ☑512-476-5493; www.museumofthe weird.com; 412 E 6th St; adult/child $12/8; ⊙10am-midnight) Pay the entrance fee in the gift shop, then step inside Austin's version of a cabinet of curiosities. It's more of a hallway of curiosities, really, lined with shrunken heads, malformed mammals and other unusual artifacts. The show stealer? The legendary Minnesota Ice Man – is that a frozen prehistoric man under all that ice? See for yourself, then grab a seat for a live show of amazing physical derring-do.

🏃 Activities

Barton Springs Pool   SWIMMING
(☑512-974-6300; 2201 Barton Springs Rd; adult/child $9/5; ⊙5am-10pm) Hot? Not for long. Even when the temperature hits 100, you'll be shivering in a jiff after you jump into this icy-cold natural-spring pool. Draped with century-old pecan trees, the area around the pool is a social scene in itself, and the place gets packed on hot summer days.

Deep Eddy Pool   SWIMMING
(☑512-472-8546; www.deepeddy.org; 401 Deep Eddy Ave; adult/child under 11yr/12-17yr $9/5/4; ⊙8am-10pm Mon-Fri, to 9pm Sat & Sun) Complete with vintage 1930s bathhouse, built by the Works Progress Administration, Texas' oldest swimming pool is fed by cold springs and surrounded by cottonwood trees. Separate areas accommodate waders and lap swimmers.

Lady Bird Lake   CANOEING
(☑512-459-0999; www.rowingdock.com; 2418 Stratford Dr; ⊙9am-8pm) Named after former first lady 'Lady Bird' Johnson, Lady Bird Lake looks like a river. And no wonder: it's actually a dammed-off section of the Colorado River. Get on the water at the rowing dock, which rents kayaks, stand-up paddleboards and canoes from $10 to $20 per hour Monday to Thursday, and slightly higher prices on weekends.

Austin

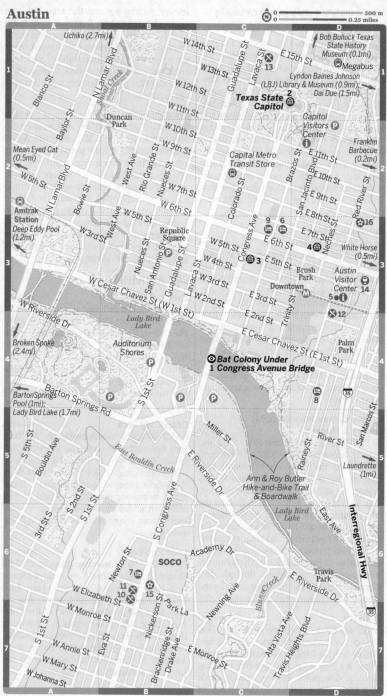

Uchiko (2.7mi)

N Lamar Blvd

Shoal Creek

Blanco St

Baylor St

W 14th St

W 13th St

W 12th St

W 11th St

W 10th St

W 9th St

Duncan Park

Guadalupe St

Lavaca St

E 15th St

13

Bob Bullock Texas State History Museum (0.1mi)

Megabus

Lyndon Baines Johnson (LBJ) Library & Museum (0.9mi); Dai Due (1.5mi)

Texas State Capitol

2

Capitol Visitors Center

Franklin Barbecue (0.2mi)

Mean Eyed Cat (0.5mi)

W 5th St

N Lamar Blvd

West Ave

Rio Grande St

Nueces St

W 7th St

W 6th St

Capital Metro Transit Store

Colorado St

Brazos St

San Jacinto Blvd

E 11th St

E 10th St

E 9th St

E 8th St

E 7th St

Neches St

Red River St

16

Amtrak Station

Deep Eddy Pool (1.2mi)

Bowie St

West Ave

W 3rd St

Nueces St

San Antonio St

Republic Square

W 5th St

W 4th St

Guadalupe St

Lavaca St

Colorado St

Congress Ave

E 6th St

9 **6**

E 5th St

3

4

White Horse (0.5mi)

Brush Park

Austin Visitor Center

14

W Cesar Chavez St (W 1st St)

W 3rd St

W 2nd St

E 3rd St

E 2nd St

Trinity St

Downtown

5

12

Lady Bird Lake

E Cesar Chavez St (E 1st St)

Palm Park

W Riverside Dr

Broken Spoke (2.4mi)

Auditorium Shores

S 1st St

Bat Colony Under Congress Avenue Bridge
1

35

Barton Springs Pool (1mi); Lady Bird Lake (1.7mi)

Barton Springs Rd

8

S 5th St

Bouldin Ave

3rd St St

S 2nd St

S 1st St

East Bouldin Creek

Miller St

E Riverside Dr

Rainey St

River St

San Marcos St

Laundrette (1mi)

Ann & Roy Butler Hike-and-Bike Trail & Boardwalk

Lady Bird Lake

East Ave

Interregional Hwy

S Congress Ave

Newton St

SOCO

Academy Dr

Blunn Creek

Travis Park

E Riverside Dr

35

7

11

10 **15**

W Elizabeth St

Nickerson St

Park La

Newning Ave

Alta Vista Ave

Travis Heights Blvd

W Monroe St

S 1st St

W Annie St

Eva St

Brackenridge St

Drake Ave

E Monroe St

W Mary St

W Johanna St

Austin

👉 Tours

Texpert Tours TOURS
(☑512-383-8989; www.texperttours.com; per hour from $100, minimum 3hr) For an interesting alternative to your stereotypical, run-of-the-mill bus and van tour, contact public-radio host Howie Richey (aka the 'Texas Back Roads Scholar'). Historical anecdotes, natural history and environmental tips are all part of the educational experience. A three-hour tour of central Austin takes visitors to the state capitol, the Governor's Mansion and the top of Mt Bonnell.

Downtown Walking Tours WALKING
(Map p702; ☑512-478-0098; www.austintexas. org; 602 E 4th St; $10; ⊙schedules vary) The Austin Visitor Center (p706) runs a program of three different downtown walking tours. Each lasts 1½ hours, costs $10, and starts either from the capitol steps or the visitor center itself, nearby. Check schedules online, and reserve 48 hours in advance if possible.

✦✦ Festivals & Events

★ **South by Southwest** MUSIC, FILM
(SXSW; www.sxsw.com; single festival $825-1325, combo pass $1150-1650; ⊙mid-Mar) The American music industry's major annual gathering has expanded to include film, interactive media and comedy. Austin is absolutely besieged with visitors during this two-week window; many a new resident first came to the city to hear a little live music. Admission to festival events is by badge only, but many bands also play free shows.

Austin City Limits Music Festival MUSIC
(www.aclfestival.com; Zilker Park; 1-/3-day pass $100/255; ⊙Oct) What do music lovers do in the fall? They head to the Austin City Limits Festival, which, though not as big as SXSW (what is?), seems to grow larger every year. Spreading through the first two weekends in October, in Zilker Park, it books more than 100 impressive acts – Paul McCartney, say – and sells out months in advance.

🛏 Sleeping

Firehouse Hostel HOSTEL $
(Map p702; ☑512-201-2522; www.firehouse hostel.com; 605 Brazos St; dm $33-35, d $109-139; ❄✳🛜) Set in a former firehouse, right across from the historic Driskill hotel in downtown Austin, this spiffy hostel has been open since 2013 but feels as fresh as ever. As well as 'economy' and 'deluxe' dorms, it offers private rooms with and without en-suite bathrooms. And the downtown location is as perfect as you can get.

**Emma Long
Metropolitan Park** CAMPGROUND $
(☑512-974-1831; www.austintexas.gov; 1600 City Park Rd; tent sites $10, tent sites with hookups $10-20, RV sites with hookups $20-25, entrance fee per vehicle Mon-Thu/Fri-Sun $5/10; ⊙gates open 7am-10pm; 🅿✳) The only Austin city park to offer overnight camping, 1000-acre Emma Long Metropolitan Park (aka 'City Park') on Lake Austin, 16 miles northwest of downtown, has good swimming, sunbathing, fishing and boating. It often attracts a partying crowd, especially at weekends. Advance online reservations required.

★ **Hotel San José** BOUTIQUE HOTEL $$
(Map p702; ☑512-852-2350; www.sanjosehotel. com; 1316 S Congress Ave; d/ste from $189/257; 🅿❄✳🛜✳) This 1930s-vintage motel has been revamped by celebrated local hotelier Liz Lambert to create a chic SoCo retreat.

Stucco bungalows hold minimalist, uncluttered rooms, and there's a lovely (if tiny) bamboo-fringed pool plus a very Austin-esque courtyard bar, renowned for celebrity-spotting. South Congress is quite the scene these days, and this location puts you right in the thick of it.

★ **The Driskill** HISTORIC HOTEL **$$**
(Map p702; ☑512-439-1234; www.driskillhotel.com; 604 Brazos St; d/ste from $190/280; P ◉ ❋ @ 🛜 ❄) Every city needs a beautiful historic hotel, ideally made from native stone and built by a 19th-century cattle baron. Although this one is now owned by the Hyatt, you'll find no generic hotel decor here; everything is pure Texas, especially the bar with wall-mounted longhorns, leather couches and a stained-glass dome. The elegant rooms are taxidermy free.

Lone Star Court HOTEL **$$**
(☑512-814-2625; www.lonestarcourt.com; 10901 Domain Dr; r/ste from $220/330; P ❋ 🛜 ❄ ❄) This stylish hotel, 9 miles north of downtown, exudes cowboy cool. Spacious rooms feature barn-style doors and retro refrigerators stocked with local brews. In the courtyard, firepits await your cowboy beans and trail coffee...oh wait, we meant your modern-day s'mores fixin's. The on-site Water Trough restaurant offers live music regularly, plus a tasty hot breakfast.

★ **Hotel Van Zandt** HOTEL **$$$**
(Map p702; ☑512-542-5300; www.hotelvanzandt.com; 605 Davis St; d/ste from $250/450; P 🛜 ❄ ❄) Named for Texas singer-songwriter Townes Van Zandt, this Kimpton-run property impresses with the details. Touches like the French horn chandelier above the lobby and leather chairs with low-key

buckles give a stylish nod to Austin's cowboy and musical sensibilities. The big-windowed rooms come in various configurations, but whatever you do, angle for a view of Lady Bird Lake.

🍴 Eating

★ **Franklin Barbecue** BARBECUE **$**
(☑512-653-1187; www.franklinbbq.com; 900 E 11th St; sandwiches $7-12.50, ribs/brisket per lb $19/25; ◐11am-2pm Tue-Sun) This famous BBQ joint only serves lunch, and only until it runs out – usually well before 2pm. To avoid missing out, join the line – and there will be a line – by 10am (9am on weekends). Treat it as a tailgating party: bring beer or mimosas to share and make friends. And yes, you do want the fatty brisket.

Hopdoddy Burger Bar BURGERS **$**
(Map p702; ☑512-243-7505; www.hopdoddy.com; 1400 S Congress Ave; burgers $7-13; ◐5pm-3am Sun-Thu, to 4am Fri & Sat; 🛜) Folks line up around the block for burgers, fries and shakes – and it's not because they're hard to come by in Austin. It's because the Hopdoddy chain's flagship outlet slathers love into everything it makes, from the humanely raised beef to the locally sourced ingredients to the fresh-baked buns. The sleek, modern building is pretty sweet, too.

Texas Chili Parlor TEX-MEX **$**
(Map p702; ☑512-472-2828; 1409 Lavaca St; mains $4-10; ◐11am-2am Mon-Sat, to 1am Sun) Ready for an X-rated meal? Venture into the large dining room that lurks behind the frankly unenticing facade of this Austin institution. When ordering your chili, keep in mind that 'X' is mild, 'XX' is spicy and 'XXX' is melt-your-face-off hot. Of course there's

TEXAS FOR KIDS

The regions best suited for travel with children are the following:

San Antonio & Hill Country Historic sites with activity books, plus theme parks, make San Antonio especially family-friendly. In Hill Country, Kerrville and New Braunfels serve as launch points for river inner-tubing.

Gulf Coast & South Texas Beaches line the southern Gulf Coast: some have diversions, some simply star nature herself. Galveston Island, with its organized beaches, pleasure pier, water park and amusements, is a whole lot of fun. Corpus Christi is home to the USS *Lexington* Museum, the huge Texas State Aquarium and a lovely bayfront promenade.

Houston The Houston Museum of Natural Science holds popular hands-on exhibits on chemistry, energy and other science disciplines.

Dallas & the Panhandle Plains Arlington boasts a theme park and water park.

more than just chili here; there's Frito pie, which is chili over Fritos.

★ Güero's Taco Bar
TEX-MEX $$

(Map p702; ☑ 512-447-7688; www.gueros.com; 1412 S Congress Ave; breakfast $5-7, lunch & dinner $9-38; ⊗ 11am-10pm Mon-Wed, to 11pm Thu & Fri, 8am-11pm Sat, to 10pm Sun; 🛜) Set in a sprawling former feed-and-seed store from the late 1800s, this Austin classic always draws a crowd. Güero's may not serve the best Tex-Mex in town, but with its free chips and salsa, refreshing margaritas and convivial vibe, we can almost guarantee a fantastic time. And the food? Try the homemade corn tortillas and chicken tortilla soup.

Launderette
MODERN AMERICAN $$

(☑ 512-382-1599; www.launderetteaustin.com; 2115 Holly St; mains $18-42; ⊗ 11am-2:30pm daily, 5-10pm Sun-Thu, to 11pm Fri & Sat) A brilliant repurposing of a former washeteria, Launderette has a stylish, streamlined design that provides a fine backdrop to the delicious Mediterranean-inspired cooking. Among the many hits: crab toast, wood-grilled octopus, brussels sprouts with apple-bacon marmalade, a perfectly rendered brick chicken and whole grilled branzino.

Moonshine Patio Bar & Grill
AMERICAN $$

(Map p702; ☑ 512-236-9599; www.moonshinegrill.com; 303 Red River St; dinner mains $14-25; ⊗ 11am-10pm Mon-Thu, to 11pm Fri & Sat, 9am-2pm & 5-10pm Sun) A remarkable relic from Austin's early days, this historic mid-1850s building now houses a large and deservedly popular restaurant, serving upscale Southern-flavored comfort food like shrimp and grits or chicken-fried steak. Happy hour sees half-price appetizers, and there's a lavish Sunday brunch buffet ($20). Dine indoors or beneath the pecan trees on the patio.

★ Uchiko
JAPANESE $$$

(☑ 512-916-4808; www.uchikoaustin.com; 4200 N Lamar Blvd; small plates $4-28, sushi rolls $10-16; ⊗ 5-10pm Sun-Thu, to 11pm Fri & Sat) Not content to rest on his Uchi laurels, chef Tyson Cole opened this bustling North Lamar restaurant, which describes itself as 'Japanese farmhouse dining.' All we can say is, if these fantastic and unique delicacies are anything to go by, you'll soon be yearning to visit a few Japanese farmhouses. Reservations are highly recommended.

★ Dai Due
AMERICAN $$$

(☑ 512-719-3332; www.daidue.com; 2406 Manor Rd; breakfast & lunch $13-22, dinner $21-69; ⊗ 11am-3pm & 5-10pm Tue-Fri, from 10am Sat & Sun) Even an eggs-and-sausage breakfast is a meal to remember at this lauded East Austin favorite. All ingredients come from Texas farms, rivers and hunting grounds, as well as the Gulf of Mexico. Supper Club dinners spotlight items like wild game and foraged treats. Like your cut of meat? See if the attached butcher shop has a few pounds to go.

🍷 Drinking & Nightlife

There are bejillions of bars in Austin. The legendary 6th St bar scene has spilled onto nearby thoroughfares, especially Red River St. Many of the 6th St places are shot bars aimed at college students and tourists, while the Red River establishments retain a harder local edge. A few blocks south, Rainey St is also jumping, with old bungalows now home to watering holes.

★ Little Longhorn Saloon
BAR

(www.thelittlelonghornsaloon.com; 5434 Burnet Rd; ⊗ 5pm-midnight Tue & Wed, to 1am Thu-Sat, 2-10pm Sun) This little cinder-block building, 5 miles north of downtown, is one of those dive bars that Austinites love so very much. They did even before it became nationally famous for Chicken Shit Bingo on Sunday night, when it's so crowded you can barely see the darn chicken – but, hey, it's still fun. There's live music most other nights.

Easy Tiger
BEER GARDEN

(Map p702; ☑ 512-614-4972; www.easytigeraustin.com; 709 E 6th St; ⊗ 11am-midnight Sun-Wed, to 2am Thu-Sat) The one bar on Dirty 6th that all locals love? Easy Tiger, an inside-outside beer garden overlooking Waller Creek, which welcomes all comers with an upbeat communal vibe. Craft beers like local favorite Electric Jellyfish are listed on the chalkboard, while the artisanal sandwiches use tasty bread from the bakery upstairs (7am to 2am). The meat is cooked in-house.

Mean Eyed Cat
BAR

(☑ 512-920-6645; www.themeaneyedcat.com; 1621 W 5th St; ⊗ 11am-2am) We're not sure if this watering hole is a legit dive bar or a calculated dive bar (it opened in 2004). Either way, a bar dedicated to Johnny Cash has our utmost respect. Inside this former chainsaw repair shop, Man in Black album covers, show posters and other knickknackery adorn the walls. A 300-year-old live oak anchors the lively patio.

☆ Entertainment

Austin calls itself the 'Live Music Capital of the World,' and you won't hear any argument from us. Music is not just the city's leading nighttime attraction, it's a major industry, with bands and performers from all over the world clamoring for attention in countless clubs and bars. Most bars stay open until 2am, while some clubs stay hoppin' till 4am.

★ Continental Club   LIVE MUSIC

(Map p702; 512-441-2444; www.continental club.com; 1315 S Congress Ave; 4pm-2am Mon-Fri, from 1pm Sat, from 3pm Sun) No passive toe-tapping here; the dance floor at this 1950s-era lounge is always swinging with some of the city's best local acts. On most Monday nights you can catch local legend Dale Watson and his Lone Stars (10:15pm).

White Horse   LIVE MUSIC

(www.thewhitehorseaustin.com; 500 Comal St; 3pm-2am) Ladies, you will be asked to dance at this East Austin honky-tonk, where two-steppers and hipsters mingle like siblings in a diverse but happy family. Play pool, take a dance lesson or step outside to sip a microbrew on the patio. Live music nightly – only on weekends is a (small) cover charged – and whiskey on tap. We like this place.

DON'T MISS

BROKEN SPOKE

When you're feeling ready for a little Texas two-steppin', there's only one place you should dream of going: the **Broken Spoke** (512-442-6189; www.broken spokeaustintx.net; 3201 S Lamar Blvd; 4-11:30pm Tue, to midnight Wed & Thu, 11am-1:30am Fri & Sat). This is honky-tonk heaven – a totally authentic Texas dance hall that's been in business since 1964. Here you'll find dudes in boots and Wranglers two-stepping around a crowded dance floor alongside hipsters, college students and slackers; it's one of the great, essential Austin experiences. (You'll know you've arrived when you spot a big old oak tree propping up an old wagon wheel out front.)

Stubb's Bar-B-Q   LIVE MUSIC

(Map p702; 512-480-8341; www.stubbsaustin. com; 801 Red River St; 11am-10pm Mon-Thu, to 11pm Fri & Sat, 10:30am-9pm Sun) Stubb's puts on live music almost every night, with a great mix of premier local and touring acts from across the musical spectrum. Many warm-weather shows are held out back along Waller Creek. It has two stages, a smaller stage indoors and a larger backyard venue. Every Sunday, there's a gospel brunch at 10:30am and 12:30pm.

ℹ Information

Austin Visitor Center (Map p702; 512-478-0098; www.austintexas.org; 602 E 4th St; 9am-5pm Mon-Sat, from 10am Sun) Maps, brochures and gift shop downtown.

Capitol Visitors Center (CVC; Map p702; 512-305-8400; www.tspb.texas.gov/prop/tcvc/cvc/cvc.html; 112 E 11th St; 9am-5pm Mon-Sat, noon-5pm Sun) Self-guided-tour booklets for the capitol itself, plus information and maps for Austin and the entire state.

ℹ Getting There & Away

Austin-Bergstrom International Airport (AUS; 512-530-2242; www.austintexas.gov/airport; 3600 Presidential Blvd) is about 10 miles southeast of downtown. A taxi to or from downtown costs around $30, while Capital Metro bus 20 connects the airport with downtown for just $1.25, with departures every 15 minutes.

Austin's Greyhound **bus station** (512-458-4463; 916 E Koenig Lane) is 4 miles north of downtown, off I-35. Buses leave from here for other major Texas cities frequently, while CapMetro bus 7 (Duval; $1.25) connects with downtown. **Megabus** (Map p702; www.megabus. com; 1500 San Jacinto Blvd) has a pick-up and drop-off stop on San Jacinto Blvd, at the northeast corner of the state capitol grounds.

The **Amtrak station** (www.amtrak.com; 250 N Lamar Blvd), less than a mile west of downtown, is served by the *Texas Eagle*, en route between Chicago and Los Angeles, with stops in Texas in Dallas, Fort Worth, San Antonio, Alpine and El Paso. There's free parking and an enclosed waiting area, but no staff.

ℹ Getting Around

Austin's handy public-transit system is run by **Capital Metro** (CapMetro; 512-474-1200, transit store 512-389-7454; www.capmetro. org; transit store 7:30am-5:30pm Mon-Fri). Call for directions to anywhere or stop in at the downtown **Capital Metro Transit Store** (Map p702; 512-389-7454; www.capmetro.org;

209 W 9th St; ⏱7:30am-5:30pm Mon-Fri) for information. Regular city buses – not including the more expensive express routes – cost $1.25. Children under six years of age are free. Almost all CapMetro buses, including more than a dozen UT shuttle routes, have bicycle racks on front, to which you can hitch your bike for free.

Around Austin

Northwest of Austin, a series of dams along the Colorado River has blessed the area with the six Highland Lakes, along with a handsome network of lakeside greenbelts and parks to help you enjoy them. Recent years have seen serious droughts, but when there's water, one of the most popular lakes for recreation is the 19,000-sq-acre **Lake Travis**.

You can rent boats and Jet Skis at the associated marina, let it all hang out – literally – at the nude beach at the county-run **Hippie Hollow park** (☎512-854-7275; https://parks.traviscountytx.gov; 7000 Comanche Trail, Austin; day pass car/bicycle $15/8; ⏱9am-dusk), or stay overnight at the **Lakeway Resort & Spa** (☎512-261-6600; www.lakewayresortandspa.com; 101 Lakeway Dr, Austin; d from $159; P❋@⏰☲). Feel like splurging? Head for **Lake Austin Spa Resort** (☎512-372-7300; www.lakeaustin.com; 1705 S Quinlan Park Rd, off FM 2222, Austin; 2-night packages from $1530; P❋⏰☲☲), one of the premier places to be pampered in the state.

Lockhart

POP 13,800

There's only one reason you might visit tiny Lockhart, but it's a good one: the Texas Legislature has officially named it the 'Barbecue Capital of Texas.' Of course, in real terms that makes Lockhart the barbecue capital of the *world*. You can eat very well for around $15 or less at any of its big-name restaurants, each of which has been ranked among

the top 10 barbecue places in the state by *Texas Monthly* magazine.

🍴 Eating

★**Black's Barbecue** BARBECUE $
(☎512-398-2712; www.blacksbbq.com; 215 N Main St; sandwiches $6.50-12, brisket per lb $18; ⏱10am-8pm Sun-Thu, to 8:30pm Fri & Sat) Lined with animal heads and photos of long-gone high-school football teams, this Lockhart favorite has been owned by the same family since 1932. Lyndon Johnson liked the sausage so much he had Black's cater a party in Washington, DC. It also serves good salads, veggies and desserts. It's nothing fancy inside, but we found it Lockhart's most welcoming BBQ joint.

Smitty's Market BARBECUE $
(☎512-398-9344; www.smittysmarket.com; 208 S Commerce St; brisket per lb $14.90; ⏱7am-6pm Mon-Fri, to 6:30pm Sat, 9am-6:30pm Sun) The blackened pit room and homely dining room are all original (they used to have knives chained to the tables). Choose from a succulent array of barbecued meats – and ask them to trim the fat off the brisket if you're particular about that.

Kreuz Market BARBECUE $
(☎512-398-2361; www.kreuzmarket.com; 619 N Colorado St; brisket per lb $18.50; ⏱10:30am-8pm Mon-Sat, to 6pm Sun) Serving Lockhart since 1900, the barn-like Kreuz Market uses a dry rub. Don't insult them by asking for barbecue sauce: Kreuz doesn't serve it, and the meat doesn't need it. Don't ask for a fork, either. But do grab a lot of napkins.

ℹ Getting There & Away

Lockhart is 30 miles south of Austin. The quickest route from Austin is I-35 S and TX 130 S. (The latter charges tolls, ranging up to around $2, depending on where you enter.)

BASTROP

The quintessential little settlement of Bastrop, just 30 miles southeast of Austin, has earned the title of 'Most Historic Small Town in Texas'. More than 130 of its buildings are listed on the National Register of Historic Places, but it's the redevelopment of the cute **historic center** (www.bastropdowntown.com) that makes Bastrop a fun place to spend a day or two. This happening little burg also has first-Friday **art walks** from 5:30pm to 8:30pm.

Bastrop is also near several family-friendly parks, with attractions ranging from prehistoric replicas at **Dinosaur Park** (☑512-321-6262; www.thedinopark.com; 893 Union Chapel Rd, Cedar Creek; adult/child $9/8; ⊙10am-4pm daily late-May to mid-Aug, Thu-Sun mid-Aug to late-May; ⊛) to hiking trails and ziplines at **McKinney Roughs Nature Park** (☑512-303-5073; www.lcra.org; 1884 TX 71, Cedar Creek; adult/child $5/free; ⊙visitor center 8am-5pm, trails 8am-dusk). A 12-mile scenic drive leads through **Bastrop State Park** (☑512-321-2101; www.tpwd.texas.gov; Hwy 21, Bastrop; adult/under 13yr $5/free), home to a collection of cabins built by the Civilian Conservation Corps (CCC) in the 1930s.

The most interesting accommodations are B&Bs and cabins. It's all about pecans at the **Pecan Street Inn** (☑512-321-3315; www.pecanstreetinn.com; 1010 Pecan St, Bastrop; d $109-119, ste $129-139), which sits under, you guessed it, pecan trees. (The hosts might just mix them into your breakfast pancakes.) Chain hotels and a couple of indie motels line Hwy 21 west of the Colorado River.

Stroll Main St downtown for a mix of bakeries, coffee shops and cafes, plus Mexican food, steaks and pub grub. Meals get charmingly southern at **Maxine's** (☑512-303-0919; www.maxinescafe.com; 905 Main St, Bastrop; mains breakfast $6-25, lunch & dinner $9-22.50; ⊙7am-3pm Sun-Thu, to 9pm Fri & Sat), with fried-green tomato BLTs served at lunch.

Contact the **Bastrop Museum & Visitor Center** (☑512-303-0904; www.bastrop-countyhistoricalsociety.com; 904 Main St, Bastrop; adult/child under 12yr $5/free; ⊙10am-5pm Mon-Sat, 1-4pm Sun) for more information.

San Antonio & The Hill Country

Tourism has been good to San Antonio, and the sprawling city reciprocates with enough attractions to keep everyone entertained. In addition to its colorful, European-style River Walk, away from the traffic and lined with cafes and bars, it rewards visitors with a well-rounded array of museums, historic sites, theme parks and outdoor activities. The Alamo, the scene of the most famous battle in the fight for Texas' independence from Mexico, is a stalwart tourist favorite, while four other beautifully preserved Spanish missions lie within the city limits.

San Antonio also puts you in close proximity to the Hill Country, a beautiful region known for its wildflower-lined roadways, charming small towns, gorgeous wineries and, yes, hills. Fredericksburg is the most visited of the Hill Country towns, but the area is more about winding roads and stopping along the way than any particular destination.

San Antonio

POP 1.5 MILLION

Much the most attractive of Texas' major cities – and much the oldest, too, having celebrated its 300th birthday in 2018 – San Antonio continues to delight visitors. The legendary Alamo, symbol of Texan independence, stands at the very heart of the city, while the River Walk, a glorious network of waterside pathways that's tucked below street level and lined with bars and restaurants, offers leisurely strolling through downtown and beyond.

Add historic buildings ranging from tumbledown mission churches to repurposed industrial landmarks, some fabulous parks and museums, and a truly cosmopolitan mix of peoples and cultures, and you can see why San Antonio is currently the fastest-growing city in the US.

◉ Sights

★ **River Walk**   WATERFRONT
(Map p710; www.thesanantonioriverwalk.com) A little slice of Europe in the heart of downtown, the 15-mile River Walk is an essential

part of the San Antonio experience. Wandering this charming network of canals and pedestrian walkways, set just below the downtown streets, you can pass landscaped gardens and riverfront cafes, and linger on stone footbridges that arch across the water.

★ The Alamo
HISTORIC BUILDING

(Map p710; ☑ 210-225-1391; www.thealamo.org; 300 Alamo Plaza; ☺ 9am-5:30pm Sep-May, to 9pm Jun-Aug) FREE For proud Texans, the much-fabled Alamo, entered freely off San Antonio's central plaza, is not so much a tourist attraction as a place of pilgrimage. Many visitors get downright dewy-eyed as they explore the site of the 1836 siege, in which a few hundred revolutionaries, including Davy Crockett, William Travis and James Bowie, died defending the fort against thousands of Mexican troops.

★ McNay Art Museum
MUSEUM

(☑ 210-824-5368; www.mcnayart.org; 6000 N New Braunfels Ave; adult/child under 20yr $20/free, special exhibits extra; ☺ 10am-6pm Wed & Fri, to 9pm Thu, to 5pm Sat, noon-5pm Sun, grounds 7am-7pm Mar-Oct, to 6pm Nov-Feb) This Spanish Colonial revival-style mansion, situated 5 miles north of downtown and originally owned by Marion Koogler McNay, is spectacular. McNay's collection of European and American art, which she graciously left to the city after her death in 1950, is even more stunning. Wandering from room to room, you encounter treasure after treasure, with Picasso's *Woman With a Plumed Hat* and Van Gogh's *Women Crossing the Fields* standing out amid works by Matisse, Cézanne, Munch, Rodin and more besides.

San Fernando Cathedral
HISTORIC BUILDING

(Map p710; ☑ 210-227-1297; www.sfcathedral.org; 115 W Main Plaza; ☺ gift shop 9am-1pm & 2-5pm Mon-Sat, 8:30am-3:30pm Sun) Founded in 1731, San Antonio's cathedral ranks as the oldest church in Texas. Its prime interest for modern visitors is as the screen – literally – for *San Antonio: The Saga*. This after-dark sound-and-light show, telling the story of the city with dazzling colorful effects, is projected onto the facade on four nights weekly (9pm, 9:30pm and 10pm, Tuesday and Friday to Sunday; free; www.mainplaza.org).

Brackenridge Park
PARK

(www.brackenridgepark.org; 3700 N St Marys St; ☺ 5am-11pm; ☝) North of downtown near Trinity University, this 343-acre park is a great place to spend a family day. As well as the **San Antonio Zoo** (☑ 210-734-7184; www.sazoo.org; 3903 N St Marys St; adult/child $16.90/13.35; ☺ 9am-5pm Mon-Fri, to 6pm Sat & Sun, to 8pm Sat & Sun Jun-Aug; ☝), you'll find the **Kiddie Park** (☑ 210-824-4351; www.kiddiepark.com; 3015 Broadway; 1 ticket $2.50, 6 tickets $11.25, day pass $13; ☺ 10am-7pm Wed-Sun Mar-Aug, 10am-7pm Fri-Sun Sep-Feb; ☝), the *San Antonio Zoo Eagle* **miniature train** ($4), an old-fashioned **carousel** ($2.50) and the **Japanese Tea Garden** (☑ 210-212-4814; www.saparksfoundation.org/japanese-tea-garden; 3853 N St Marys St; ☺ dawn-dusk) FREE.

Witte Museum
MUSEUM

(☑ 210-357-1900; www.wittemuseum.org; 3801 Broadway St; adult/child 4-11yr $14/10, 3-8pm Tue free; ☺ 10am-5pm Mon & Wed-Sat, to 8pm Tue, noon-5pm Sun; ☝) Set on the eastern edge of Brackenridge Park, the Witte is an engaging museum of natural history, science and Texas history. Pronounced 'witty', it's targeted especially at local schoolkids, with hands-on exhibitions covering topics like dinosaurs, the Peoples of the Pecos, and regional wildlife. A model of the winged *Quetzalcoatlus*, the largest flying creature ever to exist, hangs above the foyer.

🏃 Activities

SWell Cycle
CYCLING

(B-Cycle; ☑ 210-281-0101; www.sanantonio.bcycle.com; day/monthly pass $12/18) Cycle racks all around downtown, now branded as SWell Cycle but widely known by the former name of B-Cycle, make hopping on a bike convenient and tempting. It's great for sightseeing beyond downtown; dock your bike at a station when you're done using it, and the meter stops. Come back when you're ready, hop on any bike and go.

Go Rio
CRUISE

(Map p710; ☑ 210-227-4746; www.goriocruises.com; 706 River Walk; tour $12, river taxi one way $10, 24hr pass from $12; ☺ 9am-10pm) These 35-minute narrated cruises leave every 15 to 20 minutes, and give a good visual overview of the river plus a light history lesson. No reservations are necessary; buy tickets online, at the ticket booth at 706 River Walk, or at any of the other boarding points listed on the website.

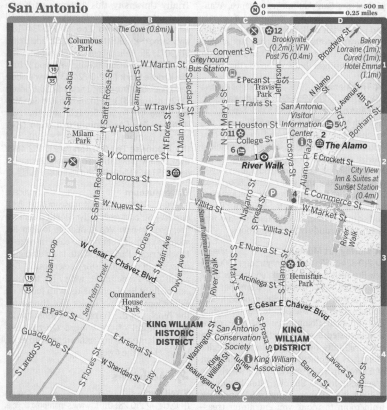

Sleeping

★ City View Inn & Suites at Sunset Station

MOTEL **$**

(☎210-222-2220; www.cityviewinns.com; 1306 E Commerce St; d from $84; P❀❁❄☎) Just beyond I-37, a mile east of the Alamo and just two blocks from the Amtrak station, this skinny little three-story building is full of clean, modern and reasonably spacious rooms. Shared amenities are minimal, but the welcome is friendly, and if you just want a decent sleep, somewhere to park your bags, and free parking, it's a great option.

Emily Morgan Hotel

BOUTIQUE HOTEL **$$**

(Map p710; ☎210-225-5100; www.emilymorganhotel.com; 705 E Houston St; d $189-229, ste from $239; P☎❄❁❀) The name may sound as though this historic hotel, right behind the Alamo and now run by Hilton, will be awash in floral prints and lace runners, but it's actually pretty stylish. The boutique-style rooms are clean, large and enjoy luxurious amenities.

★ Hotel Emma

BOUTIQUE HOTEL **$$$**

(☎210-448-8300; www.thehotelemma.com; 136 E Grayson St; r/ste from $276/596; P❄❁☎❀) Is steampunk-glam a thing? Going by this showcase hotel, originally a 19th-century brewhouse and now the centerpiece of the Pearl District, it most certainly is. Common areas impress with a striking mix of Victorian-era decor and post-industrial fixtures like the colossal pipes that snake through the lobby, while guest rooms evoke the charms of a stylish but understated Texas ranch.

Omni La Mansion del Rio

HISTORIC HOTEL **$$$**

(Map p710; ☎210-518-1000; www.lamansion.com; 112 College St; r/ste from $238/809; P❀❄@❁❀) This fabulous downtown property was born out of 19th-century religious school buildings in the Spanish-Mexican hacienda style. Set beside the River Walk,

San Antonio

its discreet oasis attracts stars and other notables. Enjoy in-room spa services, swim in the outdoor heated pool or unwind at the on-site Las Canarias restaurant.

✗ Eating

Bakery Lorraine
CAFE $

(☏ 210-862-5582; www.bakerylorraine.com; 306 Pearl Pkwy; pastries $3-6, salads & sandwiches $7-10; ☺ 7am-8pm) There's a reason why everyone you see in the Pearl District seems to be carrying a box from Bakery Lorraine – the pastries are delicious. Macaroons. Tarts. Cookies. You won't walk away empty-handed. And with plentiful seating in the bright interior, and patio tables perfect for a spring day, it's also a great spot for a gourmet lunchtime sandwich or salad.

Green Vegetarian Cuisine
VEGETARIAN $

(☏ 210-320-5865; www.eatatgreen.com; 200 E Grayson St; mains breakfast $4-8, lunch & dinner $8-12; ☺ 8am-9pm Mon-Thu, to 8pm Fri, 9am-9pm Sun, closed Sat; ☏) ⊘ San Antonio's pioneer vegetarian restaurant has an appealing location in the Pearl Brewery complex, with lots of outdoor seating. Not only are dishes like the portabella burger, the 'Big Nasty' chickpea burger, the 'fishless' fish and chips, and

the enchiladas all 100% vegetarian, they're also 100% kosher, and any meal can be made vegan.

Ocho at Hotel Havana
CUBAN $$

(Map p710; ☏ 210-222-2008; www.havanasanantonio.com; 1015 Navarro St; mains breakfast $12-16, lunch & dinner $12-28; ☺ 7am-10pm Sun-Thu, to midnight Fri & Sat; ☏) Set in a tall, narrow glassed-in conservatory, perched above the quiet northern stretch of the River Walk, this hotel restaurant makes a pleasant 20-minute stroll from downtown on a warm evening. Its Cuban-inspired menu is relatively short, but mains like the bone-in pork chop with chorizo Brussels sprouts are excellent, and you can get everything from breakfast to late-night cocktails.

Mi Tierra Cafe & Bakery
TEX-MEX $$

(Map p710; ☏ 210-225-1262; www.mitierracafe.com; Market Sq, 218 Produce Row; mains $9-29; ☺ 24hr) Part restaurant, part bakery, and total explosion of light and colour, decorated for Christmas year-round, this Market Sq behemoth has been dishing out Mexican staples since 1941. Its interlinked dining rooms are busy with scuttling waitstaff and strolling mariachis, and there's always a long line for take-out pastries and pies. Open 24 hours, it's ideal for 3am enchilada cravings.

★ Cured
AMERICAN $$$

(☏ 210-314-3929; www.curedatpearl.com; 306 Pearl Pkwy; lunch $12-28, dinner $20-42; ☺ 11am-3pm & 5-11pm Mon-Fri, 10am-3pm & 5-11pm Sat) Mighty slabs of meat hang smack-dab in the center of the dining room at this Pearl District crowd-pleaser, where charcuterie platters ($20 to $36) are loaded with meats, spreads, pickles and crackers. At lunch, look for daily gourmet po'boys and a few salads and sandwiches. Dinner is a carnivore's delight, with pork cheeks, roasted bone marrow, spiced quail and more.

Las Canarias
NEW AMERICAN $$$

(Map p710; ☏ 210-518-1063; www.omnihotels.com; 112 College St; mains breakfast $11-19, lunch $12-21, dinner $27-49; ☺ 6:30am-10pm Mon-Thu, to 11pm Fri & Sat, 10am-10pm Sun) American standards are classed up with a dash of global flair at the signature restaurant in the upscale Omni La Mansion del Rio (p710). Shrimp and grits with chorizo, anyone? The River Walk patio makes a more romantic setting than the indoor room.

🍸 Drinking & Nightlife

★ Friendly Spot Ice House
BAR

(Map p710; 📞 210-224-2337; www.thefriendlyspot.com; 943 S Alamo St; ⊗ noon-midnight; 🖶🐾) This place feels like a big neighborhood party where everyone is getting along. What could be more inviting than a pecan tree-shaded yard filled with colorful lawn chairs? Friends (and their dogs) gather to knock back long-necks – as well as 300 bottled beers, there are 76 on tap – while the kids amuse themselves in the playground area.

Brooklynite
COCKTAIL BAR

(📞 212-444-0707; www.thebrooklynitesa.com; 516 Brooklyn Ave; ⊗ 4pm-2am Mon-Sat, from 8pm Sun) It's not exactly hard to find beer or wine in San Antonio, but head here for a creative, handcrafted cocktail. Vintage wallpaper and wingback chairs give the place a dark, Victorian-esque vibe. Sip away your cares with a gin-based 'Photo Booth Kisses,' with hints of raspberry and rose petals, or a classic old-fashioned – all in a fittingly dignified atmosphere.

VFW Post 76
BAR

(📞 210-223-4581; www.vfwpost76ontheriverwalk.org; 10 10th St; ⊗ noon-midnight Mon-Thu, to 2am Fri-Sun) We're giving this hidden-away joint, on the River Walk near the Pearl development, a medal for outstanding service as a dive bar. But don't get us wrong – it's one of the classiest dives you'll ever visit, where hipsters and old-timers chug longnecks side by side in a two-story Victorian house that's the oldest Veterans of Foreign Wars post in Texas.

The Cove
BEER HALL

(📞 210-227-2683; www.thecove.us; 606 W Cypress St; ⊗ 11am-11pm Tue-Thu & Sun, to midnight Fri & Sat; 🖶) Live music is just part of the reason to hang out at this chill beer hall, which has more than 50 Texas beers on tap. The Cove is a unique combo of food-stand/cafe/laundromat/car-wash – it even has a kiddie playground. The **restaurant** (📞 210-227-2683; www.thecove.us; 606 W Cypress St; tacos $4-5, burgers $9-13; ⊗ 11am-10pm Tue-Thu & Sun, to 11pm Fri & Sat; 🖶) closes one hour earlier than the bar Tuesday through Saturday.

☆ Entertainment

Magik Children's Theatre
THEATER

(Map p710; 📞 210-227-2751; www.magiktheatre.org; 420 S Alamo St; $15; ⊗ box office 9am-5pm Mon-Fri, noon-4pm Sat & Sun; 🖶) This merry troupe stages adaptations of favorite children's books, hilarious original musicals and retellings of Texas legends and classic fairy tales, such as the witty, bilingual *La Cinderella*. Check the website for details of contemporary plays for adults, plus summertime Shakespeare performances along the River Walk.

Majestic Theatre
THEATER

(Map p710; 📞 210-226-5700, box office 210-226-3333; www.majesticempire.com; 224 E Houston St; ⊗ box office 10am-5pm Mon-Fri, hours vary Sat) Head to historic, city-owned Majestic Theatre, downtown, for concerts, touring Broadway shows and other live events year-round.

Tobin Center for the Performing Arts
THEATER

(Map p710; 📞 210-223-8624; www.tobincenter.org; 100 Auditorium Circle; ⊗ box office 10am-6pm Mon-

---

EXPLORING THE HILL COUNTRY

With so many day-trip destinations so close to San Antonio, it's hard to choose between them, but if you have some time to spare, the following route lets you cover a lot of ground. The entire loop can be driven in 4½ hours, but how long you decide to linger is up to you.

From San Antonio, head northwest on I-10, stopping for a little antique shopping in **Boerne** and **Comfort**. Continue on to **Kerrville** and enjoy cowboy art or swimming in the Guadalupe River. From Kerrville, take Hwy 16 to Fredericksburg (p713), the unofficial capital of the Hill Country, and listen to live music under the trees in tiny Luckenbach (p713).

Continue east to the **LBJ Ranch** (📞 national park visitor center 830-868-7128, state park visitor center 830-644-2252; www.nps.gov/lyjo; Hwy 290, Stonewall; ⊗ 9am-5:30pm, last admission 4pm) **FREE**, then see his childhood home in **Johnson City**. Grab a bite and a beer in **Dripping Springs**, then continue south, passing through **Wimberley** and its giant boots. Next, stop in San Marcos, land of the outlet mall. Don't miss **Texas' oldest dance hall** (📞 830-606-1281; www.gruenehall.com; 1280 Gruene Rd; ⊗ 11am-midnight Mon-Fri, 10am-1am Sat, to 9pm Sun) in **Gruene** – a short detour. Just south, **New Braunfels** invites you to float the Guadalupe River, then it's just 32 miles back to San Antonio.

LUCKENBACH

Come to tiny Luckenbach prepared to relax, get to know some folks, and bask in the small-town atmosphere. Actually, 'small town' doesn't describe it right: Luckenbach holds just a handful of Old-West structures, to which access is normally free, though there's an entry fee for events. The heart of the, er, action is the old trading post established back in 1849 – now the **Luckenbach General Store** (☑830-997-3224; www.luckenbachtexas.com; 412 Luckenbach Town Loop; ⊘9am-11pm Sun-Thu, to midnight Fri, to 1am Sat), which also serves as the local post office, saloon and community center.

Despite the dearth of amenities, there's a busy music schedule, which is posted on the store's website. Sometimes the picking circle starts at 1pm and sometimes it's 5pm, and there are usually live-music events on the weekends in the old **dance hall** (☑830-997-3224; www.luckenbachtexas.com; Luckenbach Town Loop) – a Texas classic. The 4th of July and Labor Day weekends see a deluge of visitors for concerts.

We'd be remiss not to mention that Luckenbach was made famous by a smash 1976 country song by Waylon Jennings – but we figured you already knew that.

To get here from nearby Fredericksburg, drive 5 miles southeast on US 290, then take FM 1376 south for another 4.5 miles.

Fri, to 2pm Sat, plus 1hr before showtime) On the River Walk, and sparkling after a seven-year renovation project, San Antonio's performance hall hosts performances by **Ballet San Antonio** (www.balletsanantonio.org) and the **San Antonio Symphony** (Map p710; ☑210-223-8624; www.sasymphony.org; 100 Auditorium Circle; tickets from $15). The innovative in-house theater company **Attic Rep** (www.atticrep.org) produces shows that are edgy, compelling and current.

A fun way to arrive? On a river taxi (p709).

ⓘ Information

San Antonio Visitor Information Center (Map p710; ☑210-244-2000; www.visitsanantonio.com; 317 Alamo Plaza; ⊘9am-5pm) Staff in the city's official visitor center, opposite the Alamo, hand out maps and brochures, answer questions, plus distribute tour and VIA bus/streetcar passes. The website holds loads of useful information.

King William Association (Map p710; ☑210-227-8786; www.ourkwa.org; 122 Madison St; ⊘9am-3pm Mon-Fri) Stop by to pick up walking-tour maps for the King William District, which you can also download from the website.

ⓘ Getting There & Away

San Antonio International Airport (SAT; ☑210-207-3433; www.sanantonio.gov/sat; 9800 Airport Blvd) is 8 miles north of downtown, just north of the intersection of Loop 410 and US 281. Frequent flights connect it with destinations in Texas, the rest of the USA, and Mexico. Terminal A is used by AeroMexico, Alaska Airlines, Delta, Frontier, Interjet, Southwest, US Airways and Volaris,

while Terminal B houses American and United Airlines.

The airport is served by taxis, public transportation, shuttles and Uber, Lyft and GetMe.

Greyhound (Map p710; ☑210-270-5868; www.greyhound.com; 500 N St Marys St) has a terminal downtown, while **Megabus** (☑877-462-6342; www.usmegabus.com; 840 Probandt St), which picks up and drops off 3 miles south of downtown, connects to Houston, Austin and Dallas–Fort Worth.

Fredericksburg

POP 11,400

While we highly recommend meandering through the entire Hill Country, if you're only going to see one town, make it Fredericksburg. This 19th-century German settlement packs plenty of charm into a relatively small area. Its street signs proclaim 'Willkommen,' and you'll be welcome indeed along its main street, lined with historic buildings that house German restaurants, beer gardens, antique stores and wine-tasting rooms, and in its cheerful inns and B&Bs. The downtown museums are interesting too.

Many of the shops are typical tourist-town offerings, packed with T-shirts, fudge and faux-quaint painted signs, but there are enough unique stores to make it fun to wander. Plus, Fredericksburg is a great base for checking out the surrounding peach orchards, vineyards and getaways, such as Enchanted Rock and Johnson City, as well as little Luckenbach, just 10 miles southeast.

GOOD PIZZA IN DRIPPING SPRINGS

Pieous (☑512-394-7041; www.facebook.com/pieous; 166 Hargraves Dr, Belterra Village; pizzas $10-16; ☺11am-2pm & 4-9pm Mon-Fri, 11am-9pm Sat, to 8pm Sun; P) Holy moly, this wood-fired pizza joint, in a strip mall 7 miles east of Dripping Springs – almost in Austin – serves good pie. Its motto, 'food is our religion,' gives a nod to its name, and to its focus on using fresh and homemade ingredients. The beloved pastrami is cooked in a BBQ smoker.

⊙ Sights & Activities

National Museum of the Pacific War
MUSEUM

(☑830-997-8600; www.pacificwarmuseum.org; 340 E Main St; adult/child $15/7; ☺9am-5pm) The only US museum devoted exclusively to the Pacific War, in which over 100,000 American military personnel lost their lives, spreads through three sites in downtown Fredericksburg. The huge **George HW Bush Gallery**, complementing gripping footage of the conflict with actual planes and submarines, is the place to learn the full story. The **Admiral Nimitz Museum** chronicles the career of Fredericksburg's most famous son, while the 2-acre indoor/outdoor **Pacific Combat Zone** spotlights PT (Patrol Torpedo) boats and military vehicles.

Pioneer Museum
HISTORIC SITE

(☑830-990-8441; www.pioneermuseum.net; 325 W Main St; adult/child 6-17yr $7.50/3; ☺10am-5pm Mon-Sat) For an exhaustive insight into what life was like for Fredericksburg's first settlers, take a fascinating self-guided stroll through this grassy downtown precinct. Visitors are surprisingly free to inspect the artifacts displayed in its 10 restored historic buildings, ranging from log cabins and sturdy stone homes to barns and a blacksmith's forge. Costumed docents demonstrate skills such as rope-making, while displays tell the stories of local notables.

Old Tunnel Wildlife Management Area
WILDLIFE WATCHING

(☑866-978-2287; http://tpwd.texas.gov/stateparks/old-tunnel; 10619 Old San Antonio Rd; ☺sunrise-5pm, bat viewing after 5pm May-Oct) Around dusk between May and October, visitors gather in two viewing areas to watch three million Mexican free-tailed bats emerge from an abandoned railroad tunnel in search of their nightly meal. The **lower** area, which has closer-up views, opens Thursday to Sunday, and charges $5 for bench seating, for up to 70 spectators. The **upper-deck** area, open daily, is free.

⊨ Sleeping & Eating

Sunset Inn & Suites
MOTEL $

(☑830-997-9581; www.sunset-inn.com; 900 S Adams St; d $56, ste $119; P✳︎❖) This old-fashioned and rather charming family-run motor court, a mile south of downtown on the highway toward Kerrville, offers unbeatable value. The simple rooms have homey touches like attractive quilted bed linen, and there are chairs outside each room where guests gather and chat at sunset.

Cotton Gin Village
CABIN $$

(☑830-990-8381; www.cottonginlodging.com; 2805 S Hwy 16; cabins $199; P❖) Rustic on the outside, posh on the inside. Oh yes, we like it here. Just south of town, this cluster of stone-and-timber cabins offers vacationers a supremely private stay away from both the crowds and their fellow guests. Cabins come with a stone wood-burning fireplace. Romantic getaway? Start packing.

Fredericksburg Inn & Suites
MOTEL $$

(☑830-997-0202; www.fredericksburg-inn.com; 201 S Washington St; d $199-219, ste $249; P✳︎❖≋❖) Tops in the midpriced-motel category, this two-story place, within walking distance of Main St, was cleverly built to resemble the historic house that it sits behind. Features include a fabulously inviting pool with a water slide, and a spacious hot tub; the rooms themselves are unremarkable, but clean and reasonably well equipped. Pets are $50 per stay.

★ Vaudeville
BISTRO $$

(☑830-992-3234; www.vaudeville-living.com; 230 E Main St; lunch mains $15-20, dinner mains $16-38, prix fixe $48; ☺10am-4pm Mon-Thu, to 9pm Fri & Sat, to 5pm Sun) This dapper basement bistro, tucked beneath a swish design and furnishings store, looks like a soda fountain gone posh. The folks who lunch here are as stylish as the decor, but don't worry, there's Hill Country hospitality to match the gourmet salads and sandwiches. Dinner, served weekends only, features sumptuous entrees like grilled lamb rack, duck confit or seared tuna.

ℹ Information

Fredericksburg Visitor Information Center
(☑ 888-997-3600, 830-997-6523; www.
visitfredericksburgtx.com; 302 E Austin St;
⊙ 8:30am-5pm Mon-Fri, 9am-5pm Sat, 11am-
3pm Sun; ⊛) Friendly staff in this attractive
building, a block off Main St near the Pacific
War museum, can advise on local attractions.
Lots of parking, too, if you can't find anything
on Main St.

ℹ Getting There & Around

It's not easy to get to Fredericksburg without
driving, and in any case half the fun of coming
here is to explore the Hill Country by car. US 290,
which heads west from Austin to Fredericksburg,
becomes Main St as it enters town, while Hwy
16, between Fredericksburg and Kerrville, is S
Adams St here.

The closest bus station is at Kerrville, but
Greyhound drops and picks up passengers at the
Stripes Shell Station (2204 Hwy 16 S, Stripes
Shell Station), 2½ miles southwest of downtown.
Stagecoach Taxi and Shuttle (☑ 830-385-
7722; www.stagecoachtaxiandshuttle.com)
offers local tours and shuttle service, and con-
nections with the airports in San Antonio and
Austin.

In town, you can rent bicycles at **Hill Country
Bicycle Works** (☑ 830-990-2609; www.hill-
countrybicycle.com; 702 E Main St; rental per
day $30-70; ⊙ 10am-6pm Mon, Tue, Thu & Fri,
to 4pm Sat).

Bandera

POP 900

It's not always easy to find real, live cowboys
in Texas, but the pickin's are ripe in Bandera, which brands itself the Cowboy Capital of
the World. There are certainly lots of dude
ranches around, and rodeos and horseback
riding are everywhere you look. Another
great reason to come to Bandera? Drinking
beer and dancing in one of its many hole-in-
the-wall cowboy bars and honky-tonk clubs,
where you'll find friendly locals, good live
music and a rich atmosphere. Giddy up!

⦿ Sights & Activities

Frontier Times Museum   MUSEUM
(☑ 830-796-3864;   www.frontiertimesmuseum.
org; 510 13th St; adult/child 6-17yr/senior $6/2/4;
⊙ 10am-4:30pm Mon-Sat) For a little perspective on bygone days in Bandera, stop
by these displays of Western art, cowboy
tchotchkes such as guns and branding irons,
and 'curiosities' including a celebrated two-
faced goat, collected by the museum's founder J Marvin Hunter.

Silver Spur Guest Ranch   HORSEBACK RIDING
(☑ 830-796-3037;   www.silverspur-ranch.com;
9266 Bandera Creek Rd; horseback riding nonguests
1hr $50) Day visitors can enjoy one-hour
rides for $50, and throw in lunch or dinner
for another $15. Accommodation costs from
$125 for a two-person cabin; guests pay $40

TEXAS SAN ANTONIO & THE HILL COUNTRY

NEW BRAUNFELS: GUADALUPE RIVER TUBING

Floating down the Guadalupe River in an inner tube is a Texas summer tradition. For the
most part, the river is calm, with a few good rapids to make things exciting.

Dozens of local outfitters rent tubes, rafts, kayaks and canoes, then bus you upstream
so you can float the three to four hours back to base. Put a plastic cooler full of snacks
and beverages (no bottles) in a bottom-fortified tube beside you, and make a day of it.
Don't forget to bring sunscreen, a hat and drinking water, and also be sure to wear shoes
or sandals that you don't mind getting wet. Double-check drinking regulations before
you buy supplies, to make sure what types of containers and coolers are permitted.

Many operators let you choose between a bottom-fortified tube and a regular old
inner tube; there's not always a price difference. Opting for a bottom-fortified tube will
keep your backside from scraping on the rocks that line the riverbed – and it gets rockier
the longer the region goes without rain, which can be months during summer. On the
outfitters' websites, look for discounts on online bookings, and look too for links to current river conditions, so you'll know what to expect.

New Braunfels' outfitters who rent tubes include **Gruene River Company** (☑ 830-
625-2800; www.gruenerivercompany.com; 1404 Gruene Rd; tube rental $20; ⊙ 10am-2pm
Sep-May, 9am-4pm Jun-Aug) and **Rockin' 'R' River Rides** (☑ 830-629-9999; www.rockinr.
com; 1405 Gruene Rd; tube rental $23, rafts from $40; ⊙ 9am-5pm Sun-Fri, from 8am Sat). Their
prices include shuttle service, and for an additional fee they'll hook you up with an ice
chest for your beverages plus a tube to float it on.

DUDE RANCHES

Bandera is renowned for its dozen or so dude ranches, which tend to center on enormous houses set amid hundreds of acres, and are geared primarily toward tourism. At a typical ranch, you can ride horses for around $35 to $50 an hour, and pay a little extra for a meal as well. Many take advantage of the **Hill Country State Natural Area**, a park 10 miles southwest of town that holds over 5000 acres. Texas law dictates that riders must not weigh more than 240lb.

If you'd like to stay longer, ranches also offer all-inclusive experiences that take in horseback riding, meals and a place to hang your hat for the night. Some also offer such amenities as hayrides, campfires and barbecues.

for a one-hour ride, plus $45 for breakfast, lunch and dinner. For overnight guests, after a long day on the dusty trails, the junior Olympic pool is a great way to cool off.

🛏 Sleeping & Eating

River Front Motel   CABIN $
(☎830-328-5110; www.theriverfrontmotel.com; 1103 Maple St; cabins $99; 🅿❄🛜🐾) This friendly, family-run motel on the south side of downtown offers 11 very simple standalone cabins by the river, each with a fridge, a coffeemaker and cable TV. It's your best bet for the money. Pet fee is $15 per night.

Chikin Coop   SANDWICHES $
(☎830-796-4496; www.facebook.com/chikincoop; 402 Main St; mains $8-10; ⊙11am-2am Tue-Sun) With plentiful parking out front, for motorbikes and horses alike, Chikin Coop always seems to be packed with lively diners, chomping on burgers and sandwiches of all kinds, including BBQ pork as well as chicken (of course) and chicken-fried steak.

ℹ Information

Bandera Visitor Center (CVB; ☎830-796-3045; www.banderacowboycapital.com; 126 Hwy 16; ⊙9am-5pm Mon-Fri, 10am-3pm Sat) Get friendly advice at this helpful office, a half block off Main St.

ℹ Getting There & Away

The quickest route from Kerrville to Bandera is Hwy 173 (Bandera Hwy). For a more scenic drive, take Hwy 16 south, over hill and dale and past Medina. The 50-mile trip from San Antonio to Bandera follows I-10 west and then Hwy 16 north.

After Hwy 16 enters Bandera from the east, it follows Cypress St beside the river along the southern edge of town. It then turns north onto Main St, which runs roughly north–south through downtown, and leaves town via its northwest end.

EAST TEXAS

More down-home than Dallas, more buttoned-up than Austin, Houston has money and culture, but wears them like a good ol' country boy come to town. What's that mean? Award-winning, chef-run restaurants where ties are rarely required. Attending world-class museum exhibits followed by cheap beer at patio bars. Enclaves of attractions spread all across the state's largest – and widest – city.

When you get sick of the concrete maze of interstates, it's easy to escape. Within daytrip distance you can visit NASA and the place where Texas won its independence. Washington County entices antique hunters, history buffs and anyone who just loves beautiful, rural countryside. Further afield, northeast Texas *is* the Piney Woods, with towering forests, winding roads, natural attractions and Southern belle historic towns like Jefferson and Nacogdoches.

As you wander the back roads, keep your nose at the ready to follow the scent of superb barbecue and chicken-fried steak.

Houston

POP 2.3 MILLION

Laid-back, pickup truck and boot-scooting town meets high-powered, high-cultured and high-heeled metropolis, Texas' largest city – the fourth largest in the entire US – encompasses everything you'd expect to find in the Lone Star State, and plenty more besides. The energy capital of the world, it's said to enjoy the nation's highest standard of living, and all that oil wealth has brought plenty of dividends. Its museums – especially the Menil Collection and the associated Rothko Chapel – are extraordinary, while the dining and entertainment scenes are renowned across the region.

Diverse residential neighborhoods and enclaves of restaurants and luxurious shops spread far and wide, but you can also enjoy down-home fun in abundant pubs, patios and parks. Just be sure you don't underestimate Houston's sauna-like summers. And don't forget that one of its main attractions, NASA's Space Center Houston, lies outside the city limits, a 30-minute drive down I-45.

◉ Sights & Activities

★ Houston Museum of Natural Science   MUSEUM
(Map p718; ☑ 713-639-4629; www.hmns.org; 5555 Hermann Park Dr; adult/child $25/15, free Thu 2-5pm; ☺ 9am-5pm; ♠; ☐ Hermann Park/Rice U) Don't even dream you'll see the whole of this colossal and absolutely stellar museum – the most popular in Texas – in a single visit. The permanent collection alone is extraordinary, with colorful models and massive skeletons of dinosaurs as the headline attraction, complemented by real mummies from ancient Egypt, mockups of Aztec temples, rare gems including a 2000-carat blue topaz, and interactive exhibits on the earth's biosphere.

★ Menil Collection   MUSEUM
(Map p718; ☑ 713-525-9400; www.menil.org; 1533 Sul Ross St; ☺ 11am-7pm Wed-Sun) FREE As the name suggests, the Menil Collection is rooted in the extraordinary array of art and archaeological artifacts amassed by Houstonians John and Dominique de Menil. Housed in a modernist building designed by Renzo Piano, it only displays a careful selection of highlights at any one time. Representative pieces span the ages, from Ice Age carvings, via Cycladic figures from 2800 BC and Benin bronzes, to more recent works by Pablo Picasso, Francis Bacon, Andy Warhol and Kara Walker.

★ Rothko Chapel   MUSEUM
(Map p718; ☑ 713-524-9839; www.rothkochapel.org; 3900 Yupon St at Sul Ross St; ☺ 10am-6pm) FREE Commissioned by the Menils in 1964 to create a nondenominational chapel, American abstract expressionist Mark Rothko (1903–70) devoted the final years of his life to the project. The octagonal brick structure now holds 14 large Rothko canvases. At first glance they seem to be an almost uniform black. The longer you spend in this supremely meditative space, however, the more the subtleties appear, and just as Rothko intended, many visitors experience a profoundly emotional, even spiritual reaction.

Note that the Chapel was closed for restoration at the time of research, scheduled to reopen in early 2020.

★ Buffalo Bayou Park   PARK
(☑ 713-752-0314; http://buffalobayou.org; Shepherd Dr to Sabine St, btwn Allen Pkwy & Memorial Dr; ☺ dawn-dusk most areas; ♠ ☺) This sinuous 160-acre city park follows Buffalo Bayou west from downtown, with easy pedestrian access and plentiful parking en route. Sweeping views stretch back to the downtown skyline, while assorted areas are devoted to exercise, contemplation, art exhibits and more besides. Potential activities range from kayak tours with **Bayou City Adventures** (☑ 713-538-7433; http://bayoucityadventures.org; Lost Lake Visitor Center, 3324 Allen Pkwy; kayak tours from $60; ☺ 9am-5pm) to bike rentals with **Buffalo Bayou Rentals** (☑ 713-955-4455; www.bayoubikerental.com; 105 Sabine St, Buffalo Bayou Park, Water Works; rentals per hour from $12; ☺ 10am-dusk daily summer, weekends only other times).

Museum of Fine Arts, Houston   MUSEUM
(Map p718; ☑ 713-639-7300; www.mfah.org; 1001 Bissonnet St; adult/child $17/10, free Thu; ☺ 10am-5pm Tue & Wed, to 9pm Thu, to 7pm Fri & Sat, 12:15-7pm Sun; ☐ Museum District) This nationally renowned palace of art starts its displays with 'Splendors of the Ancient World', and has a fine collection of pre-Columbian golden treasures from South America. Its chief emphasis, though, lies in tracing art history from the Renaissance, via the Impressionists, to post-1945 European and American painting. Along the way you'll encounter major works by Tintoretto, Rembrandt and Picasso.

Lone Star Flight Museum   MUSEUM
(☑ 346-708-2517; http://lsfm.org; Ellington Airport, 11551 Aerospace Ave; adult/child $15/13; ☺ 9am-5pm Tue-Sat, from noon Sun) Rehoused in a superb new facility 17 miles southeast of Houston, after its previous Galveston home was battered by Hurricane Ike in 2008, the Lone Star Flight Museum celebrates Texas aviation history. Its two hangars hold restored WWII warplanes like the ground-attack specialist Thunderbolt, alongside visiting aircraft that may include Russian MiG jet fighters. Would-be pilots can try their hands at flight simulators.

Central Houston

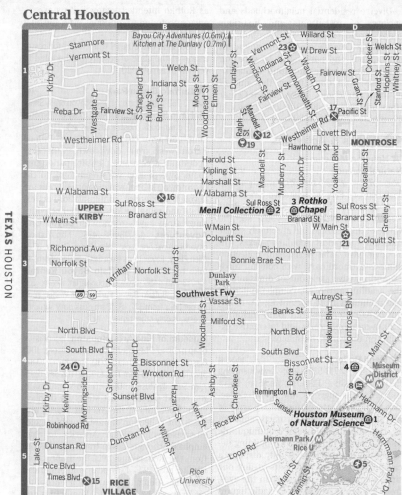

Many visitors combine the museum with a trip to the Space Center (p722), 8 miles southeast.

Hermann Park Railroad OUTDOORS
(Map p718; ☑ 713-526-2183; www.hermann park.org; 6102 Hermann Park Dr, Kinder Station, Lake Plaza; per ride $3.75; ⊙ 10am-6pm; ⊕; ⊕ Hermann Park/Rice U) This kid-pleasing miniature train takes an 18-minute loop around Hermann Park, with three stops along the way for passengers to hop on and off.

☞ Tours

Texana Tours TOURS
(☑ 281-772-9526; www.texanatours.com; rates vary) To get to grips with Houston in just three hours, take this fascinating tour with a born-and-bred Houstonite that takes in most significant neighborhoods and offers a mine of intriguing city facts. Other themed tours venture further afield, to NASA and beyond. Rates depend on group size.

Houston Culinary Tours FOOD & DRINK
(☑ 713-554-1735; www.visithoustontexas.com; tours from $65) Local chefs and food celebri-

Central Houston

◎ Top Sights
1 Houston Museum of Natural
  Science D5
2 Menil Collection C2
3 Rothko Chapel.. C2

◎ Sights
4 Museum of Fine Arts, Houston............. D4

○ Activities, Courses & Tours
5 Hermann Park Railroad........................... D5

⊜ Sleeping
6 Aloft Houston Downtown E5
7 Hotel Icon F4
8 Hotel ZaZa Houston D4
9 La Maison in Midtown.............................. E1
10 Sam Houston Hotel F5

⊗ Eating
11 Brennan's of Houston............................. E2
12 Hugo's C2
13 Lankford Grocery..................................... E1
14 Local Foods F4
15 Oh My Gogi! A5
16 Tacos Tierra Caliente B2
17 The Hay Merchant D1

⊝ Drinking & Nightlife
18 La Carafe F4
19 Poison Girl Cocktail Lounge C2

✪ Entertainment
20 AvantGarden E2
21 Cézanne D3
22 Match E2
23 Rudyard's Pub C1

ⓐ Shopping
24 Brazos Bookstore A4

festivities, including concerts and a legendary ball (buy tickets well in advance).

Juneteenth Emancipation Celebration CULTURAL
(http://juneteenthfest.com; Emancipation Park, 3018 Dowling St; ⊘mid-Jun) This celebration of African American culture, with plenty of gospel, jazz and blues, takes place at Emancipation Park around June 19 – the day in 1865 when word reached Texas that slaves had been emancipated.

⊨ Sleeping

Those few Houston hotels that stand out for their historic charms or design flair tend to be downtown, and charge not only high room rates but also valet parking fees of $25 to $40 per night. Otherwise the vast majority

ties lead monthly foodie adventures; prices vary according to how much actual eating is involved. Book well in advance.

✪ Festivals & Events

★ **Houston Art Car Parade** PARADE
(www.thehoustonartcarparade.com; along Smith St, downtown; ⊘2nd Sat Apr) Wacky, arted-out vehicles – *Mad Max*, dinosaurs, giant gerbils and more – hit the streets en masse at the city's top alt event. The parade, which centers on Smith St downtown then continues along Allen Pkwy on the south side of Buffalo Bayou Park, is complemented by weekend-long

of sleeping spots are generic chains, which get cheaper the further out you go. Choose Midtown, Montrose or the Museum District, and you're well located for museums, shops and restaurants.

★ **La Maison in Midtown** INN $$

(Map p718; ☑ 713-529-3600; www.lamaisonmidtown.com; 2800 Brazos St; d $170-230; P ❋ ☎; ☐ McGowen Station) Relaxing on the wrap-around porch at this purpose-built, urban inn, whether enjoying a breakfast feast or admiring the skyline views, you'll feel the Southern hospitality. All seven rooms are individually decorated, and have elevator access. Rates include breakfast.

★ **Hotel ZaZa Houston** DESIGN HOTEL $$

(Map p718; ☑ 713-526-1991; www.hotelzaza.com; 5701 Main St; d from $199; P ❋ @ ☎ ☒; ☐ Museum District) Hip, flamboyant and fabulous. From the bordello-esque colors to the zebra-accent chairs, everything about Hotel ZaZa is good fun. The standard rooms are large but not that extraordinary; our favorites are the concept suites like the eccentric Geisha House, or the space-age 'Houston We Have a Problem.' And you can't beat the location overlooking the Museum District's Hermann Park.

Aloft Houston Downtown HOTEL $$

(Map p718; ☑ 713-225-0200; www.alofthoustondowntown.com; 820 Fannin St; d from $155; P ❋ ☎ ☒; ☐ Central Station) Housed in a historic commercial building downtown, the Aloft (a Marriott brand) offers modishly decorated rooms across 10 floors. It's been much remodelled over the years, so don't expect period charm; rather, look for trendy design details like the hipster motif on the delightful rooftop pool.

Sam Houston Hotel HISTORIC HOTEL $$

(Map p718; ☑ 832-200-8800; www.thesamhoustonhotel.com; 1117 Prairie St; d from $193; P ❋ @ ☎ ☒; ☐ Preston) Sleek yet low-key, the smallish rooms at this historic, 10-story 1924 property have a contemporary all-gray decor, plus luxe features like plush towels, gourmet coffeemakers and more. Its current Hilton branding is a far cry from its roots as a budget hotel for traveling salesmen.

Hotel Icon HOTEL $$

(Map p718; ☑ 713-224-4266; www.hotelicon.com; 220 Main St; d from $199; P ❋ @ ☎; ☐ Preston) You can feel the history in the ornate red-and-gold lobby of this hotel, now part of the Marriott empire. A landmark bank building from 1911, it features a bank-vault reception area, soaring marble columns and coffered ceilings. Take the antique elevator up to modern-chic rooms.

✖ Eating

Houston's restaurant scene is the city's most vibrant feature. Locals love to eat out and you'll find everything from comforting Tex-Mex to smokin' barbecue to inventive bistros run by top chefs. Most neighborhoods hold appealing options.

To keep track of the latest, check out the features and listings at *Texas Monthly*, as well as www.thrillist.com/Houston or www.houston.eater.com.

★ **Lankford Grocery** BURGERS $

(Map p718; ☑ 713-522-9555; 88 Dennis St; mains $7-13; ☺ 7am-3pm Mon-Sat) This vintage neighborhood grocery store is now dedicated to serving some of Houston's finest burgers. Thick, juicy and loaded condiments, what more could you want? The interior is shambolic but there's plenty of outdoor seating too. Regulars cheerfully razz each other while busy waiters recite the day's specials. Come early to beat the lunchtime rush.

Crawfish & Noodles VIETNAMESE $

(☑ 281-988-8098; www.crawfishandnoodles.com; 11360 Bellaire Blvd; mains $10-18; ☺ 3-10pm Mon, Wed & Thu, 5-10pm Tue, 3-11pm Fri, noon-11pm Sat, noon-10pm Sun) Pairing Vietnamese seafood with Cajun flavors was inevitable once Vietnamese immigrants entered the Gulf Coast fishing economy. This shiny, hugely successful place stands out from the endless strip of Asian supermarkets and restaurants west of central Houston. It doesn't literally serve its namesake pairing; just order a mass of boiled crawfish (or crabs) plus a bowl of tangy rice noodles. Delish!

Local Foods AMERICAN $

(Map p718; ☑ 713-227-0531; www.houstonlocalfoods.com; 420 Main St; mains $12-17; ☺ 10am-8pm) A striking art deco edifice houses the busy downtown location of this ever-growing Houston cafe chain. It's won local hearts with fresh and flavorful faves such as a spicy falafel sandwich with sweet pea hummus. Other healthy menu staples include kale and quinoa.

Kitchen at The Dunlavy AMERICAN $

(☑ 713-360-6477; www.thedunlavy.com; 3422 Allen Pkwy; mains $7-14; ☺ 7am-2pm) Though essentially a park cafe, adjoining the Lost Lake Visitor Center at Buffalo Bayou Park, this flamboyant place is festooned with chandeliers and even offers (optional) valet parking. The food is creative and imaginative, too. Order at the counter, then enjoy views of the Lost Lake itself – in truth just steps from the highway – from the high-ceilinged dining room.

★**Original Ninfas** MEXICAN $$
(☑713-228-1175; www.ninfas.com; 2704 Navigation Blvd; mains $13-29; ☺11am-10pm Mon-Fri, from 10am Sat & Sun) Formal but friendly, this large Mexican restaurant, just east of downtown, is a true local institution. Houstonians have flocked here since the 1970s to savor the legendary shrimp diablo, tacos al carbon (beef cooked over charcoal), and handmade tamales crafted with pride. Great service, very fine salsas, and a spacious, well-shaded patio.

The Hay Merchant MODERN AMERICAN $$
(Map p718; ☑713-528-9800; www.haymerchant.com; 1100 Westheimer Rd; mains $10-45; ☺11am-midnight Sun-Wed, to 2am Thu-Sat; ☒Ensemble) Renowned for fusing Houston's multicultural influences, chef Chris Shepherd offers a combination of top-quality restaurant food served in a pub setting. The changing array of beers, draft and/or craft, is truly impressive, while standout dishes range from the signature Korean braised goat and dumplings to sharing plates like half a pig's head, a crispy feast for four people.

★**Brennan's of Houston** CREOLE $$$
(Map p718; ☑713-522-9711; www.brennanshouston.com; 3300 Smith St; mains $19-42; ☺11am-2pm Mon-Sat, from 10am Sun, 5:45-10pm daily) The most famous name in New Orleans cooking runs this refined restaurant in Midtown. No mere offshoot, it's a culinary temple all of its own, blending New Orleans flavors with Texas. Ingredients are uber fresh and the menu changes with the seasons. Service is excellent and the dining room elegant. Reserve in advance for a table in the beautiful courtyard.

Hugo's MEXICAN $$$
(Map p718; ☑713-524-7744; www.hugosrestaurant.net; 1600 Westheimer Rd; mains $15-37; ☺11am-10pm Mon-Thu, to 11pm Fri & Sat, 10am-9pm Sun) Chef Hugo Ortega elevates regional Mexican cooking and street food to high art in this much-celebrated Montrose bodega. Many menu items may seem familiar, but these well-spiced meats and Oaxacan-style dishes

are much closer to Mexico than Tex-Mex. Book ahead.

🍷 **Drinking & Nightlife**

★**La Carafe** BAR
(Map p718; ☑713-229-9399; 813 Congress St; ☺1pm-2am) Set in Houston's oldest building (1848 or thereabouts), La Carafe has to be the city's most atmospheric bar. It's a warmly lit drinking den, with exposed brick, sepia photos on the walls and flickering candles. You'll also find a great jukebox and a friendly, eclectic crowd. On weekends, the upstairs bar room opens, with a 2nd-floor balcony overlooking Market Sq.

Moon Tower Inn BEER GARDEN
(www.damngoodfoodcoldassbeer.com; 3004 Canal St; ☺noon-2am Mon-Thu, to 3am Fri & Sat, to midnight Sun) A simple shack with an edgy Warehouse District vibe, Moon Tower Inn draws a lively crowd of young and old. They hunker down at picnic tables in its huge yard, strung with lights, over frothy housemade microbrews plus burgers, weenies and more.

Poison Girl Cocktail Lounge BAR
(Map p718; ☑713-527-9929; 1641 Westheimer Rd; ☺3pm-2am) Take an arty interior with vintage pinball games, add a festive back patio with a baby-boomer-friendly Kool Aid man statue, and you get one very cool, dive-y bar that attracts an eclectic crowd. Lounge outside or find a dark make-out corner inside.

☆ **Entertainment**

★**Match** LIVE PERFORMANCE
(Midtown Arts and Theater Center Houston; Map p718; ☑713-521-4533; https://matchouston.org; 3400 Main St; ☒Ensemble/HCC) Opened in 2017, this impressive performance venue is used by over 500 Houston cultural groups and organizations that aren't part of the big money Theater District downtown. Its four venues seat from 70 to 350 people each, for theater, dance, music and more. Be sure to check the ever-stimulating calendar.

Rudyard's Pub LIVE PERFORMANCE
(Map p718; ☑713-521-0521; www.rudyardspub.com; 2010 Waugh Dr; ☺4pm-2am Mon-Thu, from 11:30am Fri-Sun) Rudyard's puts on live events most nights, typically including edgy and indie bands at weekends, comedy on Mondays and karaoke on Tuesdays. A fine selection of microbrews and good grub (especially the burgers) – and a streetfront terrace – make

this 'British pub' a great place to hang out even when there's nothing else on.

AvantGarden
LIVE PERFORMANCE

(Map p718; ☎832-287-5577; www.avantgarden houston.com; 411 Westheimer Rd; ☉6pm-2am Mon-Sat) The center for alt-anything in Houston, this old house has a great garden patio and hosts an eclectic mix of performances, from strange theater to poetry readings to live music. Some days you can try your hand at figure modeling. A good bar provides creative lubricants.

Cézanne
JAZZ

(Map p718; ☎832-592-7464; www.cezannejazz. com; 4100 Montrose Blvd; ☉9pm-midnight Fri & Sat) Quite simply, Houston's best place to hear jazz – just be sure to come during the six hours it's open each week. Set above the Black Labrador, this classy, intimate venue mixes the finest Texas and international jazz with a very cool piano bar.

🛍 Shopping

★ Brazos Bookstore
BOOKS

(Map p718; ☎713-523-0701; www.brazosbookstore. com; 2421 Bissonnet St; ☉10am-8pm Mon-Sat, noon-6pm Sun) Houston's top independent bookseller since 1974. Carefully curated, with a strong literary bent, it's a wonderful spot to browse local titles or meet authors at its many monthly events.

Casa Ramirez Folkart Gallery
ART

(☎713-880-2420; 241 W 19th St; ☉10am-5pm Tue-Fri, to 6pm Sat, noon-5pm Sun) A beautiful shop filled with vintage art and handicrafts from Mexico, plus unique items from top artisans south of the border.

ℹ Information

Houston Visitors Center (☎713-853-8100; www.visithoustontexas.com; 701 Avenida de las Americas; ☉10am-6pm Mon-Sat), near the convention center downtown, doubles as a shop selling local gits and souvenirs.

ℹ Getting There & Away

Houston has two airports.

George Bush Intercontinental Airport (IAH; ☎281-230-3100; www.fly2houston.com/iah; 2800 N Terminal Rd, off I-59, Beltway 8 or I-45; ☎) Houston's principal airport, located 22 miles north of downtown, is a major center for national and international services, especially with United Airlines. It's a bit of a labyrinth, though; allow plenty of time to make your way through its confusing layout.

William P Hobby Airport (HOU; ☎713-640-3000; www.fly2houston.com/hobby; 7800 Airport Blvd; ☎) Used mostly by domestic services, with Southwest Airlines in particular, the small Hobby Airport is 10 miles southeast of town.

The downtown **Greyhound Bus Terminal** (Map p718; ☎713-759-6565; www.greyhound.com; 2121 Main St; ☐ Downtown) has links with cities across Texas.

Houston's **Amtrak Station** (☎800-872-7245; www.amtrak.com; 902 Washington Ave) is served by the *Sunset Limited*, which connects New Orleans and Los Angeles three times weekly in each direction, and also calls at San Antonio and El Paso.

ℹ Getting Around

While Houston's Metrorail system provides a convenient link between downtown and the Museum District, the sprawling metropolitan expanse is poorly served by public transportation. If you're without a car, you can expect to take a lot of taxis or shared rides.

Clear Lake & Around

Less than 30 miles southeast of downtown Houston, the greater Clear Lake area is home to the immensely popular Space Center Houston as well as aquatic diversions of all kinds, including a fun amusement park, and some important historic sites.

To the north, where Buffalo Bayou empties into the estuary that flows into the bay, you'll find the industrial town of La Porte with its vital attractions. At Clear Lake's outlet, look out for the communities of Seabrook and Kemah; the latter is an entertaining waterfront village with amusements and restaurant. You could definitely visit the area as a day trip or en route to Galveston, but the number of things to do – and the traffic to and from Houston – makes an overnight stop worthwhile.

No matter what your itinerary, don't miss Killen's, the best barbecue in the Houston region.

◉ Sights

★ Space Center Houston
MUSEUM

(☎281-244-2100; http://spacecenter.org; 1601 NASA Pkwy; adult/child $30/25; ☉10am-5pm, 9am-6pm or later during some summer & holiday periods; last tour departs 2hr before close) Dream of landing on the moon? You can't get closer than the visitor center/museum alongside NASA's Johnson Space Center, where interactive displays explain past, present

ON THE GO: HOUSTON FOOD TRUCKS

Unlike in some other cities, food trucks in Houston really move. You might see the same one in two or three places on the same day. Check online for their latest locations, but they're often near bars and cafes in Montrose. Thanks to restrictive parking regulations, you'll rarely see them downtown, but other frequent stopovers include the parking lots at the Menil Collection (p717) and Museum of Fine Arts (p717).

Oh My Gogi! (Map p718; ☑281-694-4644; www.ohmygogi.com; 5555 Morningside Dr; mains $3-8; ◑9pm-midnight Tue, to 1am Wed, to 2am Thu, to 3am Fri & Sat, 8pm-midnight Sun; ⊕Dryden/TMC) Perfectly situated for the Rice U bars, this student favorite fuses two local cultures: try Korean barbecue tacos or kimchi quesadillas.

Tacos Tierra Caliente (Map p718; ☑713-584-9359; 2003 W Alabama St; mains $2-5; ◑7:30am-11pm Mon-Sat, to 10pm Sun) Customers are always clustered around this battered food truck, seeking Houston's finest tacos – try the pastor (spicy roast pork). There's nowhere to sit, but tables outside the neighboring West Alabama Ice House make a fine spot for a taco feast while nursing a few cold ones. Earlier in the day, it serves Mexican breakfasts.

Waffle Bus (☑713-391-6301; www.thewafflebus.com; mains $3-7) Waffles and waffle sandwiches, with toppings from sweet to savory (cheeseburger, smoked salmon etc). Usually open for lunch, often around the University of Houston.

and future missions, with lots of eager anticipation of prospective Mars expeditions. Stages offer short audience-participation presentations, perfect for excited kids. Frequent 90-minute tram tours set off to see the center itself, where highlights include Mission Control (the 'Houston' in 'Houston, we have a problem'), the Astronaut Training Facility and Rocket Park.

Rocket Park　　　　　　　　HISTORIC SITE
(☑281-244-2100; http://spacecenter.org; 1601 NASA Pkwy, Johnson Space Center; ◑9am-6pm) **FREE** It's as impressive as it is sad: this never-used Saturn V rocket, a specimen of the most powerful rocket ever used by the US, which took astronauts to the moon, lies on its side in a hangar, just inside the Johnson Space Center. You can only see it on one of the Space Center's tram tours. The close confines of the building make it hard to comprehend its full 363ft height, but you can still sense its incredible power.

✖ Eating

★**Killen's Barbecue**　　　　　BARBECUE $$
(☑281-485-2272; www.killensbarbecue.com; 3613 E Broadway St, Pearland; mains $9-32; ◑11am-8pm Tue-Thu & Sun, to 9pm Fri & Sat) This tidy wooden restaurant, with its grassy site and outdoor patio, is a pilgrimage spot for barbecue fans. Ronnie Killen has achieved meaty nirvana with his brisket, ribs, sausages, pulled pork and more. Everything is superb: in addition to the meat, even often-hum-

drum sides like coleslaw and creamed corn (always made with fresh corn) shine.

❶ Information

The Bay Area Houston Convention & Visitors Bureau (www.visitbayareahouston.com) has information on the welter of areas south of Houston.

❶ Getting There & Away

This is car country; I-45 slices right through the heart of the region.

GULF COAST & SOUTH TEXAS

America's 'Third Coast,' as it calls itself, varies enormously from place to place. Thus the beach-town scene of Port Aransas is a sea of calm compared with the frenetic hedonism of South Padre Island. There are reminders of Texas' dramatic history, too, from the Palo Alto Battlefield, site of the first shots of the Mexican–American War, to the long and bumpy history of the port city of Galveston.

Along the Rio Grande, border politics affect all aspects of life. In many ways the area has a different cultural identity to both Mexico and Texas, a unique multicultural and bilingual region that for a short time was even an independent state. The Republic of the Rio Grande may not have survived as a political entity, but its unique history still accents the towns and remote stretches from Brownsville to Laredo and beyond.

Galveston

POP 50,500

Part historic Southern town, part sunburned beach resort: Galveston Island is Houston's favorite seaside bolthole, now more or less back to normal after taking a severe beating from Hurricane Ike in 2008. Sitting on a barrier island near the northern end of Texas' long coastline, Galveston may not have the state's favorite beaches, but nowhere else can boast such a fine-looking combination of sun-drenched historic charms.

History

History and Mother Nature have not always been kind to Galveston Island.

Europeans first arrived in 1528, when some shipwrecked Spanish explorers spent months alternately living with and fleeing from the local Karankawa people as they attempted to find their way to what's now Mexico. Jean Laffite, the notorious pirate, founded the first European settlement here in 1817 (albeit a lawless and bacchanalian one). The party ended when Laffite was chased off and the town of nearly 1000 burned behind him. Needless to say, stories of buried treasure still abound...

After developers arrived in the mid-1830s, and incorporation in 1839, Galveston quickly became the nation's third-busiest port, a jumping-off point for settlers heading west. By the start of the 20th century, it was the largest city in Texas, with a long list of state firsts, including first opera house (1870) and first electric lights (1883).

All that changed when a string of misfortunes toppled the city's dominance of the Texas Coast. In 1885 a massive fire spread through the Strand district, consuming 42 city blocks and destroying more than 500 buildings and residences. Then on September 8, 1900, a hurricane still known as 'The Great Storm' devastated the island. Galveston never regained its status, ceding port traffic and population to nearby Houston. The island lost even more when the construction of the Houston Ship Channel in 1914 allowed oceangoing ships to bypass the Port of Galveston and head further inland. It took until the 1970s for the beaches' potential to bring back large-scale investment, but the local economy was humming along by the 2000s. Then Hurricane Ike hit in 2008. It has been a slow journey to rebuild – and fortunately 2017's Hurricane Harvey caused little lasting damage – but the island's industries have once more hit their stride.

◉ Sights & Activities

★ Bishop's Palace   HISTORIC BUILDING

(☑ 409-762-2475; www.galvestonhistory.org; 1402 Broadway (Ave J); adult/child $14/9; ◷ 10am-5pm Sun-Fri, to 6pm Sat) This sumptuous Gothic mansion, built in the 1880s for the Gresham family, became home to the Catholic bishop of neighboring Sacred Heart Church in 1923. Venture past its forbidding exterior, and inside it's quite glorious, centering on a huge rotunda, and complete with hidden back stairs, false-lit stained glass and other fun features. Self-guided tours explain its history; discount coupons are widely available.

Bryan Museum   MUSEUM

(☑ 409-632-7685; www.thebryanmuseum.org; 1315 21st St; adult/child $14/5; ◷ 10am-5pm Tue-Sun) Housed in the 1895 Galveston Orphans' Home, this excellent museum displays documents and artifacts from the Bryan family's collection, covering state and local history. Look out for a Confederate soldier's violin-shaped shotgun, complete with velvet case; western paintings by Frank Reaugh; and a diorama of miniature soldiers fighting the 1836 Battle of San Jacinto.

East Beach   BEACH

(☑ 409-797-5111; www.galveston.com/eastbeach; 1923 Boddecker Dr, off Seawall Blvd; per vehicle Mon-Thu $12, Fri-Sun $15; ◷ dawn-dusk) Also called Apffel Park, this vast expanse of hard-packed sand is at the very far northeastern end of the island. On summer weekends, it hosts live concerts and becomes one huge outdoor party (large signs proclaim 'drinking permitted').

Strand Historical District   AREA

(www.galveston.com/downtowntour; btwn 25th & 20th Sts, Strand & Church Sts) Strolling the historic Strand District will give you an appreciation of Galveston's glory days in the late-19th century. Commercial horse-drawn carriages clip-clop over historic trolley tracks, and past elaborate brick facades fronting Victorian-era buildings that now contain shops and restaurants. Informative markers identify various structures; look for the Grand 1894 Opera House (p725), still in operation.

Moody Mansion & Museum   HISTORIC BUILDING

(☑ 409-762-7668; www.moodymansion.org; 2618 Broadway (Ave J); adult/child $12/6; ◷ 10-6pm; last ticket sold 5pm) One of the grandest mansions on the island, dating from 1895, this 28,000-sq-ft home still shines with the splendor of Galveston's heyday as an American boomtown. Self-guided audio tours take in 20 rooms of original family furnishings, and last about an hour.

★ **Artist Boat Kayak Adventures** KAYAKING
(☑ 409-770-0722; www.artistboat.org; 1021 61st Street Suite 200-A; per person 2/4hr tours $50/75; 🚹) This nonprofit eco-art organization runs educational programs that meld nature and culture. Guides combine science and art during creative and fascinating kayak tours of the wetlands around Galveston Island, ideal for families traveling with kids; reservations required. Ask about discounted tours that support the Coastal Heritage Preserve area off the West Bay, and see the website for the current schedule.

🛏️ Sleeping & Eating

Hotel Galvez HERITAGE HOTEL $$
(☑ 409-515-2154; www.hotelgalvez.com; 2024 Seawall Blvd; r $199-399; 🅿️🚻🛜🏊) Bask in palm-fringed Spanish Colonial luxury at this 1911 historic hotel, managed by the Wyndham corporation. A full-service spa offers treatments like muscle-soaking milk baths or seaweed contour wraps – ask about spa package deals – and the pool deck has a lovely gulf view. The cheapest, city-view rooms are surprisingly small.

★ **Maceo Spice & Import** CAJUN $
(☑ 409-763-3331; www.maceospice.com; 2706 Market St; mains $10-16; ⏱ 11am-3pm Mon-Sat, 10am-2pm Sun) This excellent importer and spice market also happens to serve the best muffulettas and Cajun food in town, at tables crammed between the shelves. On Sunday, the shop itself is closed; otherwise, it stays open till 5pm, but lunch service ends at 3pm.

Nick's Kitchen & Beach Bar SEAFOOD $$
(☑ 409-761-5502; http://nicksgalveston.com; 3828 Seawall Blvd; mains $13-26; ⏱ 11am-10pm Mon-Fri, to 10:30pm Sat & Sun) This casual branch of Gaido's, in the self-same seafront building, is also more fun. It basically serves much the same fresh fishy ingredients, but fries everything up rather than following fancy-pants recipes. Sit outside overlooking the gulf and ponder the stupefying selection of seafood combos. It's all tasty.

Gaido's SEAFOOD $$$
(☑ 409-761-5500; www.gaidos.com; 3802 Seawall Blvd; mains $17-42; ⏱ 11am-9pm Sun-Thu, to 10pm Fri & Sat; 🚻) Run by the same family since 1911, Gaido's is a Galveston favorite. Expect vast platters of no-compromise seafood (oh, the oysters, raw or cooked...) served on white tablecloths amid hushed tones. It's not so very posh, but if you like things more casual, wander through to its adjoining sister restaurant, Nick's Kitchen & Beach Bar.

🍷 Drinking & Entertainment

Galveston Island Brewing MICROBREWERY
(☑ 409-740-7000; www.galvestonislandbrewing. com; 8423 Stewart Rd; ⏱ 3-10pm Mon-Thu, to midnight Fri, noon-midnight Sat, to 9pm Sun; 🚹) This local icon brews up some excellent quaffs, including a refreshing half-wheat, half-barley beer (the Tiki Wheat), all served out of 11 taps on-site. There's a grassy yard where you can relax (while kids clamber about on the playground), watch the sunset and mingle with a friendly Galveston crowd.

Spot BAR
(☑ 409-621-5237; http://thespot.islandfamous. com; 3204 Seawall Blvd; ⏱ 11am-10pm Sun-Thu, to 11pm Fri & Sat) This boisterous bar complex overlooking the gulf is the best of many competitors. The huge complex holds all sorts of rooms, including a bamboo-filled tiki bar. Head upstairs to the Sideyard for ocean breezes and lawn furniture over Astroturf. Good burgers and tacos help absorb the vast array of fancy cocktails. There's live music on weekends.

Grand 1894 Opera House THEATER
(☑ 409-765-1894; www.thegrand.com; 2020 Postoffice St; ⏱ box office 9am-5pm Mon-Sat) The beautifully restored 1894 Opera House well illustrates Galveston's turn-of-the-20th-century culture and wealth, and still puts on popular concerts, Broadway shows and theatrical entertainments. On days when there are no shows or set-up activities underway, self-guided tours are allowed. Check the website for schedules.

ℹ️ Information

The **Galveston Island Visitors Center** (☑ 409-797-5144; www.galveston.com; Ashton Villa, 2328 Broadway (Ave J); ⏱ 9am-5pm) is full of suggestions for things to do (and places to eat) in Galveston, and sells discount passes (www. galvestonislandpass.com) for travelers who plan to hit the big tourist sites.

On the south side of the small harbor on Wharf Rd a string of **Fishing Boat Information Booths** (Wharf Rd; ⏱ 6am-7pm) organize fishing trips and party boats, while the head office of the Galveston **Yacht Basin** (☑ 409-765-3000; http://galvestonyachtbasin.com; 715 N Holiday Dr; ☺ 9am-5pm) can provide contact details for others boating options.

ⓘ Getting There & Around

From Houston, follow I-45 southeast for 51 miles. Once on the island, the highway morphs into Broadway Ave and travels toward the historic districts. Turn off onto 61st St to reach Seawall Blvd.

From points east, including Beaumont and Port Arthur, the **Galveston–Port Bolivar Ferry** (☑ 409-795-2230; http://traffic.houston-transtar.org/ferrytimes; 1 Ferry Rd; ☺ 24hr) connects the long, lonely Bolivar Peninsula to the island around the clock, via TX 87. Trust us, cruising the peninsula with the waves about 300ft beyond is much more enjoyable than battling Houston traffic.

South of the Moody Gardens area, Seawall Blvd continues down the length of the island as Sun Luis Pass Rd and then Bluewater Hwy before turning back onto the mainland in the Brazosport area. When the interstate isn't busy, this interesting route adds about half an hour to the journey to Rockport or Corpus Christi, but given the reality of Houston traffic, it's actually faster most of the time.

Within town, the **Galveston Island Trolley** (www.galvestontrolley.com), run by **Island Transit** (☑ 409-797-3900; www.galvestontx. gov; adult/child $1/50¢), provides an excellent link between the Strand and Seawall, and also follows a separate route along the Seawall between Stewart Reach and Moody Gardens. The two routes intersect at 21st St and Seawall. Otherwise, with the island's bus service catering to commuters and students more than tourists, you really need a car to get around.

Corpus Christi

POP 326,500

Nicknamed the 'Sparkling City by the Sea,' but more generally known as 'Corpus,' this city by the placid bay of the same name is a growing and vibrant place. Plenty of its attractions make a visit worthwhile, and its perpetually sunny location is beguiling.

Spaniards named the bay after the Roman Catholic holy day of Corpus Christi in 1519, when Alonso Álvarez de Piñeda discovered its calm waters. The town established here in the early 1800s later took the name as well. Growth was slow, however, due to yellow fever in the 19th century and a hurricane in 1919. Construction of Shoreline Blvd and the deepwater port between 1933 and 1941, combined with a boom brought on by migration during WWII, triggered rapid growth. Although downtown is sleepy away from the water, Corpus does good business attracting large conventions and meetings at the vast American Bank Center.

◉ Sights

Texas State Aquarium　　AQUARIUM
(☑ 361-881-1230; www.texasstateaquarium.org; 2710 N Shoreline Blvd, North Beach; adult/child $36/26; ☺ 10am-6pm; ℗) Learn about Gulf Coast marine life, just across from downtown at the southern end of North Beach. Three large handling tanks let you get close to sharks, jellyfish, stingrays and the like, while further exhibits explore ocean creatures of all kinds. Frequent 30-minute presentations cover everything from stingray feeding and raptor flights to turtles and diving shows.

Art Museum of South Texas　　MUSEUM
(☑ 361-825-3500; www.artmuseumofsouthtexas. org; 1902 N Shoreline Blvd; adult/child $8/free; ☺ 10am-5pm Tue-Sat, 1-5pm Sun; ℗) Enjoying a spectacular seafront setting, across from the Museum of Science & History, this modern museum focuses on changing exhibitions of contemporary American art. In its Spanish Colonial section, interesting works are juxtaposed with pre-Columbian artifacts. On the first Friday of each month, admission is $1.

USS Lexington Museum　　MUSEUM
(☑ 316-888-4873; www.usslexington.com; 2914 N Shoreline Blvd, North Beach; adult/child $17/12; ☺ 9am-5pm, to 6pm Jun-Aug) Moored just north of the ship channel and aquarium, this 900ft-long aircraft carrier dominates Corpus Christi bay. The *Lexington* served in the Pacific during WWII and was finally retired in 1991. High-tech exhibits enable visitors to relive wartime experiences on five self-guided tours. Each evening, in keeping with its WWII nickname 'the Blue Ghost,' the ship is eerily lit with blue lights. Admission includes a 3-D movie in the on-board Mega Theater, and there's even an escape room (extra charge).

Museum of Science & History　　MUSEUM
(☑ 361-826-4667; www.ccmuseum.com; 1900 N Chaparral St; adult/child $11/9; ☺ 10am-5pm Mon-Sat, noon-5pm Sun; closed Mon Sep–mid-Jun; ⓐ) This fun museum explores Texas' natural history, and displays gold bars and huge

disks of silver recovered from three Spanish ships wrecked nearby in 1534. Follow the doomed expedition of French explorer La Salle, and gawp at the peculiar 'Guns & Ammo' gallery, devoted to historic and modern firearms. There's also a huge two-story science center, targeted at kids.

🛏 Sleeping

Best Western Corpus Christi
HOTEL $

(📞 361-883-5111; www.bestwestern.com; 300 N Shoreline Blvd; r $125-150; 🅿 ❄ 🛜 ☕ 🏊) There's nothing very remarkable about this chain hotel, but it's right by the seafront, conveniently close to downtown, and offers 11 floors of decent, reasonably sized rooms with balconies. A bar alongside the rooftop pool enjoys fine gulf views.

Hotel DeVille
HOTEL $

(📞 361-882-3500; www.hoteldevillecc.com; 3500 E Surfside Blvd, North Beach; r $142, ste $450; ❄ 🛜) With its playfully colorful exterior, not to mention its own Ferris wheel, it's easy to spot this bright modern hotel, 500ft back from the shoreline at North Beach. The actual rooms within are spacious and relatively sober; one three-bedroom suite can sleep eight guests.

🍴 Eating & Drinking

El Mexicano
MEXICAN $

(📞 361-885-0117; 2110 Laredo St; meals $6-10; ⏱ 5:30am-10pm Mon-Sat, 7am-3pm Sun) This very welcoming, no-nonsense Mexican diner serves high-class food at great prices. Breakfast starts early, with orders from $2.15, but even if you can't make it by 11am everything is fantastic value.

Blackbeard's on the Beach
TEX-MEX $

(📞 361-884-1030; http://blackbeards.restaurant; 3117 E Surfside Blvd, North Beach; mains $8-24; ⏱ 11am-9pm Sun-Thu, to 10pm Fri & Sat; 🛜) This rollicking North Beach place serves up tasty Mexican and American cuisine, with a strong focus on seafood, from fish tacos to seared tuna. Wash it down with cheap margaritas while sitting back for the live music. It's your birthday? Yours is on the house.

★ Brewster Street Icehouse
BAR

(📞 361-884-2739; www.brewsterstreet.net; 1724 N Tancahua St; ⏱ 11am-11pm Sun-Wed, 11am-2am Thu-Sat; 🛜) The epitome of the Texas icehouse. Bring the kids for a burger, friends for a beer, or wander over after a game at Whataburger Field for live music (cover $10). Thursday nights are Texas Country, Friday to Sunday other genres. The food is pretty good, too, including the $9 lunch special.

House of Rock
BAR

(📞 361-882-7625; www.texashouseofrock.com; 511 Starr St; ⏱ 11am-2am Mon-Fri, from noon Sat & Sun; 🛜) Sort of like an extension of your living room...if only you were cooler and had better taste in music. The bar (21+) and restaurant (all ages) are open daily and there's no cover, while the much-larger event space only opens for concerts – of which there are many. Check the website for upcoming shows.

ℹ Information

The friendly staff at the **Corpus Christi Visitor Information Center** (📞 361-561-2000; www. visitcorpuschristitx.org; 1521 N Chaparral St; ⏱ 9am-5pm), a couple of blocks south of the Harbor Bridge, proffer tips on dining, attractions, places to stay and more.

ℹ Getting There & Away

Corpus Christi International Airport (CRP; 📞 361-289-0171; www.corpuschristiairport.com; 1000 International Dr) is 9 miles west of downtown at International Dr and TX 44. American serves Dallas–Fort Worth, United serves Houston IAH and Southwest serves Houston Hobby.

Greyhound (📞 361-226-4393; www.greyhound. com; 602 N Staples St; ⏱ 6:30am-11:30pm) has regular services to Houston ($29, four hours), Brownsville ($17, 3½ hours), San Antonio ($26, 2½ hours) and beyond.

Padre Island National Seashore

The longest stretch of undeveloped barrier island in the world, the southern part of **Padre Island** (📞 361-949-8068; www.nps.gov/ pais; Park Rd 22; per car 1-day pass $10, 7-day pass $20; ⏱ park 24hr) is administered by the National Park Service (NPS). Its main feature is 65 miles of white sand and shell beaches, backed by grassy dunes and the very salty Laguna Madre.

The island is home to all the coastal wildlife found elsewhere along the coast, and then some. There's excellent birding, of course, plus numerous coyotes, white-tailed deer, sea turtles and more. It offers a delightful day's outing for anyone who wants to savor a little natural beauty, or a major adventure for anyone who wants to escape civilization.

The **Malaquite Beach Visitor Center** (📞 361-949-8068; www.nps.gov/pais; North Padre

Island; ⊙9am-5pm), on the beach just before the end of the paved road, offers excellent information, plus showers, restrooms and picnic facilities, plus a small store selling convenience foods and souvenirs. Check the schedule for interpretive walks; one usually sets off along the beach at 11am.

As it enters Padre Island, Corpus Christi's TX 358 becomes PR 22/South Padre Island Dr (known as SPID). It then heads south for 13 miles to the National Seashore entrance gate and another 3½ miles to the Malaquite Beach Visitor Center (p727). From there on, it's just beaches and dunes for the next 60 miles.

Note that Padre Island National Seashore is separated from South Padre Island by the Mansfield Channel. No transport crosses this gap, and the resort town of South Padre Island is only accessible from the far south of Texas.

South Padre Island

POP 2850

Covering the southernmost 5 miles of South Padre Island, the resort town of South Padre Island (SPI) works hard to exploit its sunny climate. The water is warm for much of the year, the beaches are clean and the laid-back locals are ready to welcome every tourist who crosses the 2.5-mile Queen Isabella Causeway from the mainland. (The permanent population is augmented by 10,000 or more visitors at any given time, more in peak periods.)

January and February, when the weather can be either balmy or a bit chilly, are the quietest months to visit (though still popular with winter Texans). The busiest and most expensive periods are spring break (all of March except the first week) and summer, when the moderating gulf breezes make the shore more tolerable than the sweltering inland areas, and the normally chill vibe turns into hedonistic party central for weeks at a time.

⊙ Sights & Activities

★ Sea Turtle, Inc   WILDLIFE RESERVE
(☑956-761-4511; www.seaturtleinc.org; 6617 Padre Blvd; adult/child $10/4 Jun–mid-Aug, $6/4 mid-Aug–May; ⊙10am-5pm Tue-Sun Jun–mid-Aug, to 4pm mid-Aug–May) No, you can't handle the sea turtles. But you can see rescued turtles and learn firsthand about the slow regrowth of critically endangered Kemp's ridley turtle populations. The center serves as a hospital for injured animals, runs public educational programs and releases young turtles once

they're old enough to face the world on their own. On several summer mornings, hatchling releases take place at sunrise; check the website for the latest details.

South Padre Island
Birding & Nature Center   NATURE RESERVE
(☑956-761-6801; www.southpadreislandbirding. com; 6801 Padre Blvd; adult/child $6/3; ⊙9am-5pm) This 50-acre nature preserve features boardwalks through the dunes, bird blinds, spotting towers and more besides. Look for butterflies, egrets, alligators, turtles and crabs, and learn the differences between a dune meadow, a salt marsh and an intertidal flat in its sumptuous exhibit hall. A blackboard out front lists recent sightings. The visitor center only opens office hours, but ticketed guests can access the boardwalks from dawn to dusk.

North End   BEACH
(Padre Blvd (Park Rd 100), North End; ⊙24hr) FREE Padre Blvd ends 12 miles north of Isla Blanca. North of here, another 20 miles of empty sand and dunes stretch all the way to Port Mansfield Pass. Nude sunbathers, anglers, bird-watchers and other outdoorsy types can find a sandy acre to call their own; vehicles can drive on the beach, but be wary of soft sand.

Sandy Feet   SAND CASTLES
(☑956-459-2928; www.sandyfeet.com; 117 E Saturn Lane; group lessons from $50; ⊙by appt; ⚑) Everything your inner child – or actual child – ever wanted to know about building sandcastles, from 30-minute crash courses ($50) up to multihour master classes (from $180). Check online for its Sand Camp program of free summer-afternoon castle-building sessions (5pm Monday to Thursday).

⛏ Sleeping

★ Palms Resort   MOTEL $$
(☑800-466-1316; www.palmsresortcafe.com; 3616 Gulf Blvd; r $184-250; ❋ ☞ ☲) This friendly two-story motel has a great location beside the grass-covered dunes on the gulf. While the rooms themselves don't have waterfront views, the excellent alfresco beachfront restaurant/bar has nothing but. Units are large and tidy with ceramic-tile floors, fridges and microwaves.

Tiki Condominium Hotel   RESORT $$
(☑956-761-2694; https://thetikispi.com; 6608 Padre Blvd; r $135-290; ❋ ☞ ☲ ☲) This Polynesian-themed veteran turns up the tiki clichés toward SPI's northern end. Units have one

to three bedrooms, with full kitchens. Even on the furthest block you're not far from the beach, let alone the two swimming pools. Two-night minimum, plus a one-off $75 housekeeping fee, and another $75 for pets.

✗ Eating & Drinking

Sea Ranch   SEAFOOD $$
(☑ 956-761-1314; www.searanchrestaurant.com; 1 Padre Blvd; mains $15-27; ⊙5-9pm Sun-Thu, to 10pm Fri & Sat) A little classier than the beach-bum norm on SPI, this dinner-only option offers an impressive menu of wild-caught seafood and Angus steaks. It overlooks the harbor and has an elegant vibe. No reservations, but it's worth the wait.

Pier 19   SEAFOOD $$
(☑ 956-761-7437; www.pier19.us; 1 Padre Blvd; mains $9.50-25; ⊙7am-11pm; 🕸) On a pier jutting far into the water near SPI's southern end, this rambling restaurant has a huge menu of fried seafood, burgers, ceviche, fish tacos, po'boys and plenty more. If you just fancy a sundowner, head right out to the bar at the end for postcard views.

★Padre Island Brewing Company   MICROBREWERY
(☑ 956-761-9585; www.pibrewingcompany.com; 3400 Padre Blvd; ⊙11:30am-10pm, to 11pm Fri & Sat) Although it's not on the beach, it's well worth visiting this microbrewery for its changing lineup of local brews. The sampler ($7) is 6oz pours of all five on tap, or if you've already picked a favorite the pitchers cost $12.75. Burgers, pizzas and other bar food are popular, and there's a full seafood menu, too (mains $10 to $28).

Wanna Wanna Beach Bar & Grill   BAR
(☑ 956-761-7677; www.wannawanna.com; 5100 Gulf Blvd, Beach Access 19; ⊙11am-10:30pm) A picture-perfect cliché of the laid-back beach bar and restaurant, on the sand behind the **Wanna Wanna Inn** (☑956-761-7677; www.wannawanna.com; 5100 Gulf Blvd; r $169-199; 🕸🕸). Lounge barefoot beneath the palm-leaf parasols on the shaded deck and take in the surf and sights, plus live music at weekends. Burgers and other basics ($7 to $15) go down easy, but nothing competes with a large cold drink.

❶ Information

The **South Padre Island Convention & Visitors Bureau** (☑ 956-761-4412; www.sopadre.com; 610 Padre Blvd; ⊙9am-5pm) stocks brochures detailing tourist services, and hosts displays on island and regional history.

❶ Getting There & Around

No long-range public transit serves the island. The nearest option is the **Greyhound** (☑956-546-2264; www.greyhound.com; 755 International Blvd, Suite H; ⊙4am-midnight) station in Brownsville.

If you can get out to SPI, you won't necessarily need a car. The developed area is fairly compact, easy for walking or cycling, and there's a shuttle around the island and across the causeway to Port Isabel and onward to Brownsville airport.

DALLAS–FORT WORTH

Dallas and Fort Worth may be next-door neighbors, but they're hardly twins. Long regarded as being as divergent as an Escalade-driving sophisticate and a rancher in a dusty pickup truck, these two cities have starkly different facades. Beyond appearances, however, they share a love of high (and low) culture and good old-fashioned Texan fun. A plethora of fabulous small towns, like Waxahachie and McKinney, makes the surrounding area worthy of a road trip.

Leave the big smoke behind and you'll find that the Panhandle and Central Plains may be the part of Texas that most typifies the state to outsiders. This is a land of sprawling cattle ranches, where people can still make a living on horseback. The landscape appears endlessly flat, punctuated only by utility poles and windmills, until a vast canyon materializes and seems to plunge into another world.

Dallas

POP 1.35 MILLION

Dallas, the 'Big D', is Texas' most mythologized city, rich in the stuff of which American legends are woven. For a time, the eponymous TV series *Dallas* served to define the USA to the world, while the Cowboys and their cheerleaders remain iconic. Unlike many Texan cities, Dallas has avoided the boom-and-bust cycle of the oil industry, to the point where this is the country's fastest-growing metropolitan area. There's money here aplenty, and conspicuous consumption is very much the norm.

Excellent museums in the massive, recently developed Arts District downtown offer world-class displays of art, while unmissable sites commemorate the city's rendezvous with

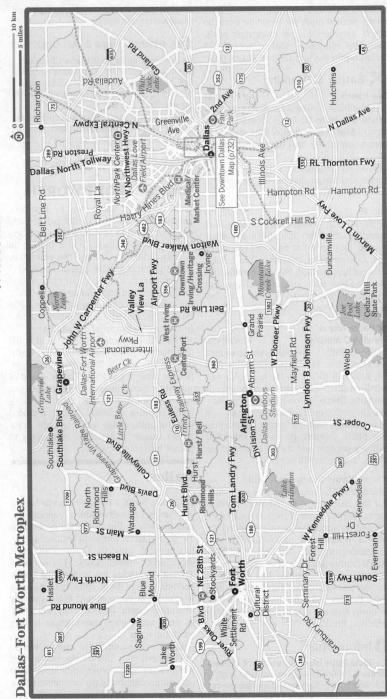

TEXAS DALLAS

Dallas–Fort Worth Metroplex

history in 1963, as the site of President John F Kennedy's assassination.

For the quintessential Dallas experience, explore its distinctive neighborhoods, like down-and-dirty Deep Ellum, pivotal in the stories of blues and jazz, or contemporary hipster hangouts like Lower Greenville or the Bishop Arts District.

Sights & Activities

★ Sixth Floor Museum   MUSEUM
(Map p732; ☎214-747-6660; www.jfk.org; Book Depository, 411 Elm St; adult/child $18/14; ⊗10am-6pm Tue-Sun, noon-6pm Mon; light-rail West End) No city would want the notoriety that comes with being the site of an assassination, let alone when the victim happens to be President John F Kennedy. Dallas visitors can, however, delve into the world-shaking events of 1963 by exploring the very room in the former Texas School Book Depository where Lee Harvey Oswald – then an employee – lay in wait.

★ Pioneer Plaza   SQUARE
(Map p732; cnr S Griffin & Young Sts) For a Tex-as-sized photo op, or simply a sight of what claims to be the largest bronze monument on earth, head to Pioneer Plaza. Its show-piece – 40 larger-than-life bronze longhorns, amassed as though on a cattle drive – has an unmistakable and compelling power.

★ Dallas Arboretum & Botanical Gardens   GARDENS
(☎214-515-6615; www.dallasarboretum.org; 8525 Garland Rd; adult/child $15/10; ⊗9am-5pm) Spreading along the shores of White Rock Lake, 6 miles northeast of downtown, this gorgeous 66-acre arboretum showcases plants and flowers in themed areas such as the Sunken Garden and the Woman's Gar-den. Expect to see plenty of wedding parties posing for pictures amid the posies. Dur-ing the spring wildflower season it gets so mobbed that nearby streets are closed.

Dallas Museum of Art   MUSEUM
(Map p732; www.dallasmuseumofart.org; 1717 N Harwood St; ⊗11am-5pm Tue, Wed, Fri-Sun, to 9pm Thu; 🖬; light rail St Paul) FREE This major museum offers a high-caliber world tour of ancient and contemporary art. Archaeologi-cal treasures range from Greek, Roman and Etruscan masterpieces to wonderful bowls from the Mimbres pueblos of New Mexico and a pre-Columbian Peruvian gold mask. Alongside paintings by Picasso, Monet and Van Gogh, American works include Edward

Hopper's enigmatic *Lighthouse Hill* and Frederic Church's sublime *The Icebergs*. A re-created villa modeled on Coco Chanel's Mediterranean mansion holds canvases by statesman Winston Churchill.

Dealey Plaza & the Grassy Knoll   HISTORIC SITE
(Map p732; light rail West End) Infamous for its location alongside the road where John F Kennedy's motorcade was ambushed in No-vember 1963, the tiny park known as Dea-ley Plaza is now a haunting, eerily familiar National Historic Landmark. It was created in 1935, however, to mark the center of the original settlement of Dallas.

Perot Museum of Nature & Science   MUSEUM
(Map p732; ☎214-428-5555; www.perotmuseum. org; 2201 N Field St; adult/child from $20/13; ⊗10am-5pm Mon-Sat, 11am-5pm Sun; 🖬; light rail St Paul) A soaring star of the Arts District, this state-of-the-art museum wows both inside and out. Several floors of interactive exhib-its, geared especially toward school groups, allow visitors to design their own birds, journey through the solar system, command robots, and commune with dinosaurs in-cluding the eel-like Dallasaurus. As befits the Texas location, there's lots about energy extraction, including a 10-minute simulation of hydraulic fracturing or 'fracking'.

Nasher Sculpture Center   MUSEUM
(Map p732; ☎214-242-5100; www.nashersculp turecenter.org; 2001 Flora St; adult/child $10/free; ⊗11am-5pm Tue-Sun; light rail St Paul) The fabu-lous glass-and-steel Nasher Sculpture Center stands across from the Dallas Museum of Art downtown. Partnered by a divine sculp-ture garden, its main Renzo Piano-designed building is a work of art in its own right. Ray-mond and Patsy Nasher accumulated one of the greatest private sculpture collections in the world, including works by Calder, de Kooning, Rodin, Serra and Miró.

Dallas Heritage Village   HISTORIC SITE
(Map p732; ☎214-421-5141; www.dallasheritage village.org; 1515 S Harwood St; adult/child $10/6; ⊗10am-4pm Tue-Sat, noon-4pm Sun; light rail Cedars) Laid out in wooded parklands less than a mile south of downtown, the Dallas Heritage Village is a living-history museum comprising 38 historic structures, relocated from their original sites. Ranging from a tipi to a Civil War–era farmhouse, they serve to illuminate life in North Texas between around 1840 and 1910.

TEXAS DALLAS

Downtown Dallas

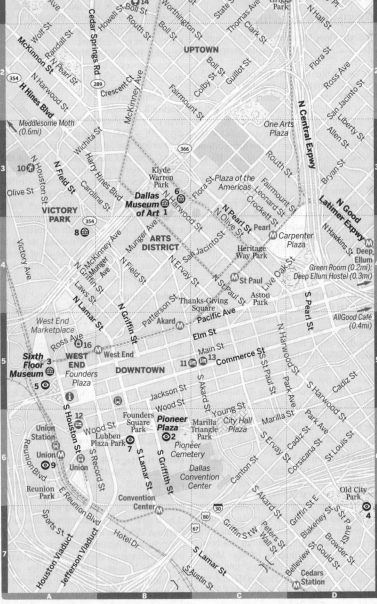

N 0 ———— 500 m
0 ———— 0.25 miles

William B Dean Park

Greenwood Cemetery

The Quadrangle

UPTOWN

Meddlesome Moth (0.6mi)

Klyde Warren Park

Plaza of the Americas

Dallas Museum of Art

One Arts Plaza

VICTORY PARK

ARTS DISTRICT

Heritage Way Park

Carpenter Plaza

Green Room (0.2mi); Deep Ellum Hostel (0.3mi)

Deep. Ellum

St Paul

Aston Park

AllGood Café (0.4mi)

Thanks-Giving Square

West End Marketplace

Pacific Ave

Elm St

Sixth Floor Museum

WEST END

Founders Plaza

West End

DOWNTOWN

Commerce St

Founders Square Park

Pioneer Plaza

Marilla Triangle Park

City Hall Plaza

Union Station

Lubben Plaza Park

Pioneer Cemetery

Dallas Convention Center

Union

Reunion Park

Convention Center

Old City Park

Hotel Dr

Cedars Station

Downtown Dallas

Reunion Tower   LANDMARK
(Map p732; ☑214-712-7040; www.reuniontower.
com; 300 Reunion Blvd E; adult/child from $17/8;
⊙hours vary by season; light rail Union Station)
What's 50 stories high and has a three-level
spherical dome with 260 flashing lights? Reunion Tower of course, the unofficial symbol
of Dallas. Take the 68-second elevator ride
up for a pricey sky-high panorama. Or enjoy
the view from the celebrity-chef restaurant
and lounge **Five Sixty by Wolfgang Puck**
(Map p732; ☑214-571-5784; www.wolfgangpuck.
com; Reunion Tower, 300 E Reunion Blvd; mains
from $37; ⊙restaurant 5-10pm Sun-Thu, to 11pm Fri
& Sat). A pedestrian tunnel connects Reunion Tower with Union Station and the Hyatt
Regency Dallas.

Katy Trail   WALKING
(Map p732; ☑214-303-1180; www.katytraildallas.
org; ⊙5am-midnight) To enjoy some see-and-
be-seen walking, running or cycling, hit the
tree-lined Katy Trail. Following a former
railroad line for 3.5 miles from the American Airlines Center downtown almost all
the way to Southern Methodist University
(SMU), it passes through interesting neigh-

borhoods. At times it has a true rural feel. A
program of extensions is progressively linking it to other walking routes.

⚑ Festivals & Events

★ State Fair of Texas   FAIR
(www.bigtex.com; Fair Park, 3921 Martin Luther
King Jr Blvd; adult/child $18/14; ⊙late-Sep–
mid-Oct) This massive fair is the fall highlight for many a Texan. Come ride one of
the tallest Ferris wheels in North America, eat corn dogs (it's claimed that this is
where they were invented), and browse the
prize-winning cows, sheep and quilts.

Martin Luther King Jr Parade   PARADE
(⊙Jan) For approaching 40 years Dallas has
hosted one of the largest events in the country commemorating Dr King's life. On the
third Monday in January, the parade, a festive mix of floats and marching bands, goes
from MLK Blvd and Lamar to Fair Park.

🛏 Sleeping

★ Belmont Hotel   BOUTIQUE HOTEL $
(☑866-870-8010; www.belmontdallas.com; 901
Fort Worth Ave; d from $87; ℗❄@🛜🏊) Just
2 miles west of downtown, this stylish bungalow hotel makes a fabulously low-key
antidote to Dallas' flashier digs. The whole
structure is imbued with art moderne design – the 1940s' take on art deco – and has
plenty of soul. The garden rooms – with
soaking tubs, Moroccan-blue tile work, kilim
rugs and some city views – are tops.

Deep Ellum Hostel   HOSTEL $
(☑214-712-8118; www.deepellumhostel.com; 2801
Elm St; dm $33-41, r $109, ste $129; ❄🛜) Assum-
ing you're in Deep Ellum for the nightlife –
you'll hear it whether you want to or not –
this hostel couldn't be more ideal. Opened
in 2018, with polished dark-wood fittings
and spacious communal kitchen, it holds
nine dorms, plus en-suite rooms that sleep
up to four. The same owners run Izkina, the
adjoining Spanish cocktail bar, and Austin's
Firehouse Hostel.

The Lumen   HOTEL $$
(☑214-219-2400; www.thelumendallas.com; 6101
Hillcrest Ave; r $190-243; ℗😊@🛜🏊) Yes, it
would be hard for this ultramodern con-
crete reimagining of what was originally a
1960s motel, across from SMU, to live up to
the local hype. But you have to love the pa-
rade of poodles and shih tzus through the
lobby, the video library and the strong coffee

in the morning. There's also a breezy rooftop lounge.

Magnolia Hotel
HISTORIC HOTEL **$$**

(Map p732; ☑214-915-6500; www.magnolia hotels.com; 1401 Commerce St; r from $216; ❖✺❀@✿❄) Housed in the 29-story Magnolia Petroleum Company Building, dating from 1922, this elegant hotel offers a sumptuous stay. Period details in the sizable rooms include wooden blinds and retro furniture, while the 100-plus suites have kitchenettes.

La Quinta Inns & Suites Downtown
HOTEL **$$**

(Map p732; ☑214-761-9090; www.laquintadallas downtown.com; 302 S Houston St; r from $169; ✺@✿) One of the better deals downtown, across from Union Station, this chain hotel beats the generic blues with a unique design in a 1925 building. Rates include a small breakfast.

★Adolphus
HISTORIC HOTEL **$$$**

(Map p732; ☑214-742-8200; www.adolphus.com; 1321 Commerce St; d $260-305; ❖✺@✿❄; light rail Akard) Feel like royalty (yes, Queen Elizabeth has stayed here) the old-fashioned way. The 422-room Adolphus takes us back to the days when gentlemen wore ties and hotels were truly grand, not bastions of ascetic minimalism. Just exploring the 22 floors of this 1912 labyrinth, now part of the Marriott empire, is an adventure. Note that room sizes vary widely.

✗ Eating

Downtown Dallas, other than the touristed West End area, is short of interesting dining options. Deep Ellum, 'deep' up Elm St just east, holds all sorts of eclectic offerings. Prime eating neighborhoods away from the city center include Lower Greenfield, with its walkable blocks; the Arts District and uptown to the west; and the funky Bishop Arts District further southwest.

★Sonny Bryan's Smokehouse
BARBECUE **$**

(☑214-357-7120; www.sonnybryans.com; 2202 Inwood Rd; mains $6-19; ⊙24hr) Dallas' favorite barbecue joint also has a handy downtown location, but for the full authentic experience you can't beat a visit to the place it all began, 4 miles northwest. You can even drop in for breakfast; it stays open to sate your smoky fantasies around the clock.

AllGood Café
TEX-MEX **$**

(☑214-742-5362; www.allgoodcafe.com; 2934 Main St; mains $9-17; ⊙8am-9pm Tue-Sat, to 7pm Sun, to 2pm Mon; ✐) Self-styled as a 'Bohemian Bistro,' this funky street-corner Deep Ellum diner is a true home from home. Families and rocker types alike chow down on Tex-Mex breakfasts, $9 blue-plate lunch specials like smothered pork chops, or a huge range of veggie options. A small stage hosts live music Friday to Sunday.

★Meddlesome Moth
MODERN AMERICAN **$$**

(☑214-628-7900; www.mothinthe.net; 1621 Oak Lawn Ave; mains $10-20; ⊙11am-midnight Mon-Thu, to 1am Fri & Sat, 10am-10pm Sun) Small groups of friends flock to this buzzing Design District gastropub, 2 miles northwest of downtown, to linger over Belgian-style mussels, shrimp and homestead grits, great burgers and beautifully turned out sharing plates. You'll find good cocktails and a superb rotating selection of craft brews (including 40 on draft).

Kalachandji's
VEGETARIAN **$$**

(☑214-821-1048; www.kalachandjis.com; 5430 Gurley Ave; buffet lunch/dinner $12/15; ⊙11:30am-2pm & 5:30-9pm Tue-Fri, noon-3pm & 5:30-9pm Sat & Sun; ✐) A lavishly decorated Hare Krishna temple, 3 miles east of downtown, holds a fine counterpoint to Texas' many meaty temptations. The small but varying buffet features basmati rice, curries, mustard greens, popadams and chutneys, pakoras, tamarind tea and other daily specials. You can dine in the peaceful, plant-filled courtyard.

★Javier's
MEXICAN **$$$**

(☑214-521-4211; www.javiers.net; 4912 Cole Ave; mains $22-35; ⊙5:30-10pm Sun-Wed, to 10:30pm Thu, to 11pm Fri & Sat) This deeply cultured restaurant takes the gentrified cuisine of old Mexico City to new levels; forget whatever ideas you may have previously held about Tex-Mex. The setting is dark, leathery and quiet, while the food is meaty and piquant. Steaks come with Mexican flavors that bring out the best in beef. Ask for a table under the stars.

Abacus
AMERICAN **$$$**

(☑214-559-3111; www.abacus-restaurant.com; 4511 McKinney Ave; mains $23-49, tasting menus from $80; ⊙5-10pm Tue-Thu, to 11pm Fri & Sat; ✿) For meat eaters wanting something more than a chain steakhouse, or anyone with a taste for inventive contemporary cuisine, Abacus, 3 miles north of downtown, delivers the beef. Start with sushi or the wildly popular lobster shooters ($22), then choose from a selection of small, seasonal plates or feast on superb steaks and substantial fish mains. The bar is excellent.

🍷 Drinking & Nightlife

★ Two Corks & a Bottle   LOUNGE

(Map p732; ☑ 214-871-9463; www.twocorksandabottle.com; 2800 Routh St; ⊙ noon-7pm Sun & Tue, to 10pm Wed & Thu, to 11pm Fri & Sat) Creative owners make all the difference, as the pair behind this cork-sized little uptown wine bar certainly prove. Besides a fine selection of vino, with wine flights to help you sample from the list, it offers regular entertainment, especially live jazz at weekends. That it's romantic is a bonus.

Ginger Man   PUB

(Map p732; ☑ 214-754-8771; www.thegingerman.com; 2718 Boll St; ⊙ 1pm-2am) This always-busy neighborhood pub occupies an appropriately spice-colored house, with multilevel patios, and porches out front and back. One of the city's best beer menus features around 50 on draft at any one time. The bartenders are great, and there's live music every Saturday night.

Green Room   BAR

(☑ 214-748-7666; www.dallasgreenroom.com; 2715 Elm St; ⊙ 4pm-2am Tue-Sun) In bar-lined Deep Ellum, the Green Room is a go-to spot for rooftop cocktails, a fun crowd and excellent food, from snacks to meals (tacos, burgers, poutine). Pick from three bar areas.

☆ Entertainment

★ Kessler Theater   LIVE MUSIC

(☑ 214-272-8346; www.thekessler.org; 1230 W Davis St; ⊙ 6pm-midnight) Let the aqua neon outside catch your eye and draw you in to Oak Cliff's art deco landmark. The one-time neighborhood movie house has been transformed into an intimate live music venue. Drink prices are friendly, the bands and acts are good (drag shows!) and the vibe is down-home fun.

★ Sons of Hermann Hall   LIVE MUSIC

(☑ 214-747-4422; www.sonsofhermann.com; 3414 Elm St; ⊙ 7pm-midnight Wed & Thu, to 2am Fri & Sat) For over 100 years, this classic Texas dance hall has been a Deep Ellum fixture, and a chameleon, too: equal parts pick-up bar, live-music venue, honky-tonk and swing-dancing club. Come here and plunge deep into the heart of full-on Big D. Opening hours vary; check ahead to find out what's on.

Granada Theater   LIVE MUSIC

(☑ 214-824-9933; www.granadatheater.com; 3524 Greenville Ave) Long the anchor of Lower Greenwood, this former movie theater is widely regarded as the best live-music venue in town. Check the website for upcoming gigs, largely featuring rock and country bands.

Balcony Club   LIVE MUSIC

(☑ 214-826-8104; www.balconyclub.com; 1825 Abrams Rd; ⊙ bar 5pm-2am) This mysterious upstairs hideaway may feel like a secret, but it's a pilgrimage spot for local jazz fans. With emerald walls, a tiny stage and a cozy patio nook above the Landmark Theater, it draws all ages for nightly live music – not exclusively jazz – and sassy drinks such as moonlight martinis and three-way tropical punch.

🛍 Shopping

★ Wild Bill's Western Store   CLOTHING

(Map p732; ☑ 214-954-1050; www.wildbillswestern.com; 311 N Market St; ⊙ 10am-7pm Mon & Tue, to 9pm Wed-Sat, noon-6pm Sun; light rail West End) Wild Bill's is a West End treasure chest of Western wear. You'll find Stetsons, snakeskin boots, oilskin jackets, oversize belt buckles, rhinestone-covered T-shirts, fun kitschy souvenirs, popguns and other toys, country-music CDs and much more. Enjoy a cold beer while you shop.

Highland Park Village   MALL

(☑ 214-443-9898; www.hpvillage.com; Preston Rd & Mockingbird Lane; ⊙ hours vary by store) For an eye-rolling, gasp-inducing and credit-card-maxing experience, head to Spanish Mission–style Highland Park Village in upper-crust Highland Park, which claims to be the oldest suburban shopping center in the world. If Jimmy Choo and Carolina Herrera are among your intimate acquaintances, you'll feel at home.

ℹ Information

Dallas Visitors Center (Map p732; ☑ 214-571-1316; www.visitdallas.com; Old Red Courthouse, 100 S Houston St; ⊙ 9am-5pm; 🛜) This useful downtown office, across from Dealey Plaza, answers questions and hands out local guides.

ℹ Getting There & Away

Dallas-Fort Worth International Airport (DFW; ☑ 972-973-3112; www.dfwairport.com; 2400 Aviation Dr), 19 miles northwest of the city via I-35 E, is a hub for American Airlines. Major airlines provide extensive domestic and international service.

Dallas Love Field Airport (DAL; ☑ 214-670-5683; www.dallas-lovefield.com; 8008 Herb Kelleher Way), 6 miles northwest of downtown, is a hub for Southwest Airlines and has extensive domestic service.

Greyhound buses (www.greyhound.com) make runs to major cities in the region from the **Dallas Bus Station** (Map p732; ☑ 214-849-6831; 205 S Lamar St).

The **Amtrak** (www.amtrak.com) San Antonio–Chicago *Texas Eagle* train stops at downtown's **Union Station** (☑ 800-872-7245; www.unionstationdallas.com; 400 S Houston St; light rail Union Station), which is also a hub for local transit.

❶ Getting Around

DART (Dallas Area Rapid Transit; ☑ 214-979-1111; www.dart.org; single ride $2.50, daypass $6) operates buses and an extensive light-rail system that connects downtown with outlying areas. Buy tickets on board buses or from vending machines at rail stops. DART also runs the Trinity Railway Express, which links Dallas Union Station with Fort Worth (one hour), and the Dallas Streetcar between Union Station and the Bishop Arts District.

Travel from downtown to uptown on the historic, free **M-Line Trolley** (☑ 214-855-0006; www.mata.org; ⏲ 7am-10pm Mon-Thu, to midnight Fri, 10am-midnight Sat, to 10pm Sun), which runs from the St Paul DART station via the Arts District and up McKinney Ave to City Place/Uptown Station.

Trinity Railway Express (TRE; ☑ info 214-979-1111; www.trinityrailwayexpress.org; 221 W Lancaster Ave; single ride 1/2 zones $2.50/5, daypass 1/2 zones $5/12; ⏲ half-hourly 5am-1am Mon-Sat) trains connect Dallas Union Station with Fort Worth (one hour). Free shuttles link the CenterPort/DFW Airport stop with the airport.

Fort Worth

POP 874,000

Famous as being 'Where the West Begins,' Fort Worth still has the cowboy feel. It first rose to prominence during the great open-range cattle drives of the late 19th century, when more than 10 million head of cattle tramped here along the Chisholm Trail. These days, the legendary Stockyards are the prime visitor destination, hosting twice-daily mini-cattle drives, rodeos every weekend, and Billy Bob's, the world's biggest honky-tonk.

Downtown Fort Worth, 3 miles south, is bursting with restaurants and bars – especially around Sundance Sq – while the Cultural District not far west has three amazing art museums.

Whatever you do, don't mistake Fort Worth for being some sort of sidekick to Dallas. This city's got a headstrong spirit of its own, and it's a lot more user-friendly than its near-neighbor (not to mention greener and cleaner). Bottom line? There's a lot to do here – without a whole lot of pretense.

◉ Sights

★**Stockyards** HISTORIC SITE
(☑ 817-624-4741; www.fortworthstockyards.org; 130 E Exchange Ave) Western-wear stores and knickknack shops, saloons and steakhouses now occupy the Old West–era buildings of the Stockyards. Although it can seem touristy at times, there's still a genuine authenticity here. Don't miss the twice-daily cattle drive along E Exchange Ave, featuring the longhorn of the small Fort Worth Herd. Start by picking info at the Fort Worth Stockyards Visitor Center (p738).

★**Fort Worth Herd** HISTORIC SITE
(☑ 817-336-4373; www.fortworth.com/the-herd; 131 E Exchange Ave; ⏲ cattle drive 11:30am & 4pm) Each morning and afternoon, spectators line the street to watch cowboys wearing authentic 19th-century garb drive the 16 longhorn cattle of the Fort Worth Herd along E Exchange Ave. For the rest of the day, you can inspect them in their corral behind the Livestock Exchange Building; each critter comes complete with its own name-tagged picture-portrait.

★**Kimbell Art Museum** MUSEUM
(☑ 817-332-8451; www.kimbellart.org; 3333 Camp Bowie Blvd; ⏲ 10am-5pm Tue-Thu & Sat, noon-8pm Fri, to 5pm Sun) FREE While the small Kimbell Art Museum holds treasures from Greece, Egypt, China, Japan and the ancient Americas, it's the astonishing array of big European names that makes it truly extraordinary. As well as Michelangelo's first known painting, *The Torment of St Anthony*, the permanent collection includes masterpieces by everyone from Rembrandt and Van Gogh to Matisse, Cézanne and Gauguin.

Modern Art Museum of Fort Worth MUSEUM
(☑ 817-738-9215; www.themodern.org; 3200 Darnell St; adult/child $16/free; ⏲ 10am-5pm Tue-Thu, Sat & Sun, to 8pm Fri) In a stunning building across from the Kimbell Art Museum, this stimulating museum displays paintings by the likes of Picasso, Mark Rothko and Francis Bacon, as well as sculptures including Anselm Kiefer's lead-wrought *Book with*

Wings and Martin Puryear's soaring wooden *Ladder for Booker T Washington*.

Amon Carter
Museum of American Art   MUSEUM
(☑ 817-738-1933; www.cartermuseum.org; 3501 Camp Bowie Blvd; ◷ 10am-5pm Tue, Wed, Fri & Sat, to 8pm Thu, noon-5pm Sun) **FREE** Texas oilman Amon Carter starting collecting the art of the American West in the 1930s. Since his death, his impressive array of paintings and sculpture by Frederic Remington and Charles M Russell has been supplemented with works by John Singer Sargent, Georgia O'Keeffe, Winslow Homer and Alexander Calder.

Bureau of Engraving & Printing   MUSEUM
(☑ 817-231-4000; www.moneyfactory.gov; 9000 Blue Mound Rd; ◷ 8:30am-5:30pm Tue-Fri) **FREE** Fort Worth is one of two US locations where the nation prints its paper currency. This US Treasury facility 8 miles north of the Stockyards produces the green stuff with which engagement rings are purchased, narcotics snorted, bets wagered, waiters tipped and babysitters paid, and over which wars are fought. You don't need a reservation to watch the presses roll on a self-guided tour, but the bureau suggests allowing 30 minutes to clear security.

National Cowgirl Museum   MUSEUM
(☑ 817-336-4475; www.cowgirl.net; 1720 Gendy St; adult/child $12/6; ◷ 10am-5pm Tue-Sat, noon-5pm Sun) This airy, impressive museum explores the myth and reality of cowgirls in American culture. Graced by a 2019 expansion that focuses especially on the relationship between horse and woman, and ranging from rhinestone costumes to rare film footage, it's a fun and educational ride. By the time you walk out, you'll have a whole new appreciation for these tough workers.

☞ Tours

★ Stockyards
Guided Walking Tour   WALKING
(☑ 817-625-9715; www.fortworthstockyards.com/tours; Stockyards Station, 140 E Exchange Ave; adult/child from $8/5; ◷ daily) Three or four walking tours explore the history of the Stockyards each day; longer options include Billy Bob's honky-tonk.

🛏 Sleeping

Hotel Texas   INN $
(☑ 817-624-2224; www.magnusonhotels.com/hotel/hotel-texas-fort-worth; 2415 Ellis Ave; r from $76; ⊛ ✳ ☎) Built as a 'cattleman's home away from home' in 1939, this simple hotel stands just one block from the Stockyards action. The rooms are small and basic, but nicely furnished and decorated with Western art. They're much cheaper than other Stockyards options, so you can spend the savings on a steak dinner!

★ Stockyards Hotel   HISTORIC HOTEL $$
(☑ 817-625-6427; www.stockyardshotel.com; 109 E Exchange Ave; d $199-349; ✳ ☎) Opened in 1907, this fine old hotel celebrates its cowboy heritage with Western-themed art, 50-plus comfortable cowboy-inspired rooms and a grand Old West lobby with lots of leather. Hide out in the Bonnie and Clyde room, where the true-life outlaws stayed while on the lam in 1933 (the faux bullet holes and Bonnie's .38 revolver only add to the mystique).

Hilton Fort Worth   HISTORIC HOTEL $$
(☑ 817-870-2100; www.hilton.com; 815 Main St; d from $165; ✳ @ ☎) Built in 1921 as the Hotel Texas, this landmark hotel, in the heart of downtown, holds 294 rooms spread across 15 floors. Guest rooms are tastefully furnished with dark woods, framed historic photos and plush upholstery, and have modern bathrooms. Parking is valet only.

John F Kennedy spent the night here before he went to Dallas on November 22, 1963; hence the statue outside.

✖ Eating

★ Heim Barbecue   BARBECUE $
(☑ 817-882-6970; www.heimbbq.com; 1109 W Magnolia Ave; mains $9-18; ◷ 11am-10pm Wed-Mon) The family behind this joint brings knowledge and passion to the cause of creating barbecue for a new age. Sausage, brisket (of course!), turkey, pulled pork and more are smoky and delectable. Meats sell out daily, so don't delay too long. Try to save room for the banana pudding – not that that's going to happen.

Kincaid's   BURGERS $
(☑ 817-732-2881; www.kincaidshamburgers.com; 4901 Camp Bowie Blvd; mains $5-9; ◷ 11am-8pm Mon-Sat, to 3pm Sun) A local institution, complete with the sickly green walls, this former grocery is stuffed with picnic tables, and serves some of the best burgers in the region – thick, juicy and covered in condiments.

Casablanca Coffee   BREAKFAST $
(☑ 817-862-7149; 215 W 8th St; mains $5-10; ◷ 6.30am-3pm Mon-Thu, to 1pm Fri) Thanks to friendly Moroccan owner Driss, this tiny

downtown hole-in-the-wall exudes charm. Breakfast and lunch choices include spinach omelets and pita pockets as well as pastries, while the coffee comes 'traditional' or (superstrong) 'Moroccan'.

Woodshed Smokehouse
BARBECUE $$

(☑ 817-877-4545; www.woodshedsmokehouse. com; 3201 Riverfront Dr; mains $9-28; ☺ 11am-10pm Mon-Thu, 8am-11pm Fri & Sat, 8am-10pm Sun; 🔄) 🖉 In this hugely successful Trinity River joint, Texas celebrity chef Tim Love serves up gourmet barbecue and more besides, including deep dark bowls of ramen broth. Thanks to the breezy riverside setting and eco-friendly design, there's no need for air-conditioning. Enjoy live bluegrass on the vast terrace Wednesday to Sunday.

H3 Ranch
STEAK $$$

(☑ 817-624-1246; www.h3ranch.com; 1059 E Exchange Ave; mains $19-50; ☺ 11am-10pm Mon-Thu, to 11pm Fri, 9am-11pm Sat, to 10pm Sun) If you've come to the Stockyards to eat steak – and that's a damn good reason – then this is the steakhouse to choose. Take your pick from hickory-grilled slabs of beef, served beneath the gaze of a mounted longhorn head.

🍷 Drinking & Nightlife

★ Lola's Saloon
BAR

(☑ 817-877-0666; www.lolassaloon.com; 2736 W 6th St; ☺ 2pm-2am Mon-Fri, noon-2am Sat & Sun) If you're looking for an intimate music experience, simply dive into this dive bar, a perennial favorite with local fans. Bands – indie, honky-tonk, bluegrass, experimental, you name it – play most nights to a fun, eclectic crowd. Catch your breath on the small outside patio. When no show is on, the jukebox is addictive.

★ Usual Bar
COCKTAIL BAR

(☑ 817-810-0114; www.facebook.com/theusual bar; 1408 W Magnolia Ave; ☺ 4pm-2am Mon-Fri, from 5pm Sat & Sun) Craft-cocktail lust packs hipsters in nightly at this bar that serves up debonair drinks such as the 'Maximillian-aire' and 'the Parlor.' Of course you can be ironic and just have a well-poured Sidecar. Great terrace.

Fort Brewery
BREWERY

(☑ 817-923-8000; www.fortbrewery.com; 1001 W Magnolia Ave; ☺ 11am-midnight Mon-Sat, to 10pm Sun; 🔄) Fort Worth's top brewery keeps six beers of its own on tap, plus a rotating array of guest brews. Enjoy in the exposed brick dining area or outside on the patio,

alongside a menu of thin-crust pizza, which comes in a dozen inventive varieties.

☆ Entertainment

Billy Bob's Texas
LIVE MUSIC

(☑ 817-624-7117; www.billybobstexas.com; 2520 Rodeo Plaza; cover Sun-Thu $2-5, Fri & Sat varies; ☺ 11am-10pm Mon & Tue, to 11pm Wed, to 2am Thu-Sat, noon-10pm Sun) Previously a cattle barn, an airplane factory and a department store, the world's largest honky-tonk now caters to over 6000 customers with 40 bars. Top country stars, DJs and house bands perform on two stages. Friday and Saturday nights see live bull-riding in the indoor arena, and mechanical bull-riding competitions in the main building.

Texas Motor Speedway
SPECTATOR SPORT

(☑ 817-215-8500; www.texasmotorspeedway.com; cnr Hwy 114 & I-35, exit 72; tours adult/child $10/8; ☺ 9am-5pm Mon-Fri, 10am-5pm Sat, noon-5pm Sun) Have yourself a full-on Nascar experience. November's Texas 500 is the biggest annual event, but other races take place throughout the year. You can even go for a ride with a racer (from $125). The speedway is 20 miles north of downtown, on I-35 W.

ℹ Information

Fort Worth Stockyards Visitor Center (☑ 817-624-4741; www.fortworthstockyards. org; 2501 Rodeo Plaza; ☺ 9am-5pm) The place to pick up details on the Stockyards National Historic District.

Main Street Visitor Center (☑ 817-698-3300; 508 Main St;) Fort Worth's helpful downtown tourist office provides info on the whole region.

ℹ Getting There & Away

Dallas–Fort Worth International Airport (p735) is 22 miles northeast of Fort Worth.

Buses and trains in Fort Worth share the **Intermodal Transportation Center** (☑ 817-215-8654; 1001 Jones St), easing transfers.

The **Amtrak** (☑ 800-872-7245; www.amtrak. com; 1001 Jones St) Texas Eagle stops in Fort Worth en route west to San Antonio and east to Chicago. The Heartland Flyer serves Oklahoma City.

Trinity Railway Express (p736) trains run between Fort Worth and Dallas Union Station (one hour). Free shuttles link the CenterPort/DFW Airport stop en route with the airport.

Several **Greyhound** (www.greyhound.com; 1001 Jones St) buses each day connect downtown Fort Worth with Dallas ($13 to $15; 40 to 45 minutes). There's also service to other major Texas cities.

WEST TEXAS

Welcome to the land of wide-open spaces. Along I-10 there's not much to look at – just scrub brush and lots of sky – but dip below the interstate and you'll encounter vistas every bit as captivating as they are endless. Sometimes the rugged terrain looks like the backdrop in an old Western movie; then it suddenly turns into an alien landscape, with huge rock formations erupting out of the desert.

But what is there to do? Plenty. Exploring an enormous national park that's nearly the size of Rhode Island. Stopping in small towns that will surprise you with minimalist art, planet-watching parties or fascinating ghost-town ruins. Checking out the latest microbreweries in a reenergized El Paso. Chatting with friendly locals whenever the mood strikes you. And letting the delicious slowness of West Texas get thoroughly under your skin.

Big Bend National Park

Everyone knows Texas is huge. But you can't really appreciate just how big it is until you visit this **national park** (☑ 432-477-2251; www.nps.gov/bibe; US Hwy 385, Panther Junction; 7-day pass per vehicle $30). When you're traversing Big Bend's 1252 sq miles, you come to appreciate what 'big' really means. It's a land of incredible diversity, vast enough to allow a lifetime of discovery, yet laced with well-placed roads and trails that enable short-term visitors to see a lot in two to three days.

One area of Big Bend – the Chisos Basin – absorbs the vast majority of traffic. Yes, the **Chisos Mountains** are beautiful, and no trip here would be complete without an excursion into the high country. But any visit should also include time in the **Chihuahuan Desert**, home to curious creatures and adaptable plants, and down along the **Rio Grande**, the watery dividing line between the US and Mexico.

Park headquarters and the main visitor center (p740) are at Panther Junction, which is on the main road 29 miles south of the Persimmon Gap entrance and 22 miles east of the Maverick entrance (near Study Butte). A **gas station** (☑ 432-477-2294; Panther Junction; ⊙ convenience store 7am-6:30pm May-Sep, 8am-5:30pm Jun-Aug, pumps 24hr) here offers fuel, repairs and a small stock of snacks and beverages.

From Panther Junction, it's a (relatively) short 10-mile drive to the Chisos Basin. Sharp curves and steep grades make Chisos Basin Rd unsuitable for recreational vehicles longer than 24ft and trailers longer than 20ft.

Another major road leads 20 miles southeast to Rio Grande Village, where you can find the only other **fuel pumps** (☑ 432-477-2293; Rio Grande Village; ⊙ 8am-7pm Oct-May, to 5pm Jun-Sep) within the park (good to know because you're a long way from anywhere).

The other principal road, the 30-mile Ross Maxwell Scenic Dr, takes off from the main park road west of Panther Junction.

🏃 Activities

With more than 200 miles of trails to explore, it's no wonder hiking is big in Big Bend. There are countless trails and many popular hikes; get specifics from any of the visitor centers.

★ Lost Mine Trail   HIKING
(www.nps.gov/bibe; Chisos Basin Rd) This Chisos Mountains hike is all about the views – as you climb over 1000ft in elevation, they get better and better. You'll be right up there with **Casa Grande**, **Lost Mine Peak** and, from the highest point, the **Sierra del Carmen**. When you think you've reached the summit, keep going – the trail's end, reached via a long bare ridge, is a big-whoa drop.

The whole hike is 4.8 miles round trip, and takes at least two hours. The one drawback is that there's very little parking at the trailhead, 1.2 miles by road from the visitor center (p740). If time is limited, you can get a partial payoff by catching the views from the first crest, 1 mile up from the trailhead.

Santa Elena Canyon Trail   HIKING
(www.nps.gov/bibe) If you don't have time to float the Rio Grande, hike into narrow, sheer-walled Santa Elena Canyon. From the end of Ross Maxwell Scenic Dr, at the canyon's eastern end, this magnificent 1.7-mile round-trip trek switchbacks over jumbled rocks then drops back down to the riverside bosk. The trail crosses Terlingua Creek early on, which you may have to wade.

🛏 Sleeping

Tent campers or smaller RVs that don't require hookups can use the three main campgrounds; some take reservations, others are first-come, first-served. Sites typically fill during spring break, Thanksgiving and

Christmas. There are also primitive roadside campsites in the backcountry.

Chisos Basin Campground CAMPGROUND $
(☎877-444-6777; www.nps.gov/bibe; tent & RV sites $14) The most central of the main campgrounds – right near the **Chisos Lodge Restaurant** (Lodge Dining Room; www.chisosmountainslodge.com; Chisos Mountain Lodge; lunch $8-13, dinner $10-22; ⏲7-10am, 11am-4pm & 5-9pm), the **Basin store** (☎432-477-2291; Chisos Basin; ⏲7am-9pm), and several popular trails – this 60-site place has stone shelters and picnic tables, with bathroom facilities nearby. Most sites are first-come, first-served, but from November 15 through May, 26 can be reserved in advance at www.recreation.gov.

Chisos Mountain Lodge MOTEL $
(☎877-386-4383, 432-477-2291; www.chisosmountainslodge.com; lodge & motel r $143-147, cottages $162; P ❄ 🛜 🐾) Collectively known as Chisos Mountain Lodge, and run by Forever Resorts, the four lodging options in Chisos Basin get good, if not great, marks. You can do better outside the park, but the scenery here is much better, and it's nice not to have to drive 45 minutes after your hike. Reservations are a must, but check for (frequent) cancellations.

ℹ Information

In addition to the park headquarters and visitor center at **Panther Junction** (Main Visitor Center; ☎432-477-1158; www.nps.gov/bibe; ⏲8:30am-5pm), there's another year-round visitor center in **Chisos Basin** (☎432-477-2264; www.nps.gov/bibe; ⏲8:30am-noon & 1-4pm), while the visitor centers at **Persimmon Gap** (☎432-477-2393; www.nps.gov/bibe; ⏲10am-noon & 1-4pm Nov-Apr), **Castolon** (☎432-477-2666; www.nps.gov/bibe; ⏲10am-noon & 1-4pm Nov-Apr) and the **Rio Grande Village** (☎432-477-2271; www.nps.gov/bibe; ⏲9am-noon & 1-4:30pm Nov-Apr) open November through April only.

Ask park rangers how to make the most of your visit and check bulletin boards for upcoming interpretive activities. You'll also find free leaflets on special-interest topics including biological diversity, hiking and backpacking, geology, archaeology and dinosaurs.

ℹ Getting There & Around

There is no public transportation to, from or within the park. The closest buses and trains run through Alpine, 100 miles northwest of Panther Junction. The nearest major airports are 220 miles northeast in Midland and 314 miles northwest in El Paso (p742).

You'll find gas at the service stations at Panther Junction (p739) and Rio Grande Village (p739).

Please note that the border patrol operates checkpoints for vehicles coming from Big Bend. If you're not a US citizen, you'll be required to present your passport.

Big Bend Ranch State Park

The 486-sq-mile **Big Bend Ranch State Park** (☎432-358-4444; http://tpwd.texas.gov; off Rte 170; adult Oct-Apr/May-Sep $5/3, child under 13yr free) sprawls across the desert between Lajitas and Presidio, reaching north from the Rio Grande into some of North America's wildest country. This massive former ranch is filled with notable features, most prominently the **Solitario**, a dome-shaped formation thrust upwards by a volcanic explosion 36 million years ago. The resulting caldera measures 8 miles east to west and 9 miles north to south.

The scenic River Road (p741) ribbons across the park beside the Rio Grande on FM 170; you don't have to pay the admission fee if you simply drive through. Roadside pull-outs enable you to admire and/or approach the river itself – boats can enter or leave the water at various points – while short hiking trails allow day-trippers to stretch their legs and explore some of the remarkable scenery. More rugged and extensive hiking and mountain-biking trails crisscross the backcountry.

🛏 Sleeping

There are vehicle-accessible sites ($12), equipped with picnic tables, firepits and pit toilets, in four campgrounds along FM 170, and also in the interior of the park. No-frills camping ($10) is available in the backcountry, where there are no designated campsites. All camping requires reservations (512-389-8919) and a permit.

ℹ Information

Pick up or download a copy of *El Solitario*, the park newspaper, for helpful information.

Barton Warnock Visitor Center (☎432-424-3327; http://tpwd.texas.gov; FM 170; park entry adult Oct-Apr/May-Sep $5/3, child under 13yr free; ⏲8am-4:30pm)

Fort Leaton State Historic Site (☎432-229-3613; http://tpwd.texas.gov; FM 170 E, Presidio;

RIVER ROAD

West of Lajitas, **Route 170** (also known as the River Road, or El Camino del Rio in Spanish) hugs the Rio Grande through some of the most spectacular and remote scenery in Big Bend country. Relatively few Big Bend visitors experience this driving adventure, even though it can be navigated in any vehicle with good brakes. Strap in and hold on: you have the Rio Grande on one side and fanciful geological formations all around, and at one point there's a 15% grade – the maximum allowable. Stop for easy and scenic short hikes and overlooks along the way.

When you reach Presidio, head north on US 67 to get to Marfa. If you plan to go back the way you came, travel at least as far as **Colorado Canyon** (20 miles from Lajitas) for the best scenery.

adult Nov-Apr/May-Oct $5/3, child under 13yr free; ⊘ 8am-4:30pm Thu-Mon)

Sauceda Ranger Station (🖪 432-358-4444; http://tpwd.texas.gov; 1900 Sauceda Ranch Rd; ⊘ 8am-6pm) In the park interior, this outpost requires a 27-mile drive up a dirt road and may not be easy to access. Check the park website for GPS coordinates and maps.

❶ Getting There & Away

The Barton Warnock Visitor Center (p740), at the east end of the park, is 95 miles south of Alpine. The western entrance, at Fort Leaton State Historic Park, 47 miles west along the River Road, is 63 miles south of Marfa.

A scenic and highly recommended **loop drive** takes in Alpine, Terlingua, River Road/FM 170 through the park, and Marfa.

Central West Texas

The small towns of west Texas have become more than just the gateway to Big Bend National Park (p739). Fort Davis, Marfa, Alpine and Marathon have a sprawling, easygoing charm and plenty of ways to keep a road-tripper entertained. Art enthusiasts will enjoy the galleries and museums in Marfa, while outdoor adventurers can hike and camp in the Davis Mountains, where stargazing at McDonald Observatory is highly recommended. And if you're fond of quirky sights, bars and lodging, well, this region has got you covered. From mystery lights to a white-buffalo bar to tipis, it's all just a bit offbeat.

Fort Davis & Davis Mountains

Standing more than 5000ft above sea level, Fort Davis has an altitudinal advantage over the rest of Texas, both in terms of elevation and of the cooler weather it brings. That makes it a popular oasis during the summer,

when West Texans head to the mountains to escape the searing heat. Belonging to the Chihuahuan Desert as well as the Davis Mountains, this area has some staggering scenery, with its wide-open spaces suddenly pierced by rock formations springing from the earth.

As for the town itself, it sprang up alongside the eponymous fort, built in 1854 to protect westward pioneers and goldrushers from Comanche and Apache warriors. It still retains an Old West feel to match its history.

◉ Sights & Activities

★ **McDonald Observatory**   OBSERVATORY
(🖪 432-426-3640; www.mcdonaldobservatory.org; 3640 Dark Sky Dr; day pass adult/child 6-12yr/under 6yr $8/7/free; ⊘ visitor center 10am-5:30pm; 🖝) Far from the light pollution of big cities, West Texas boasts some of North America's clearest and darkest skies, making it the perfect spot for an observatory. Some of the world's largest telescopes are perched on the peak of Mt Locke (6791ft), so enormous you'll spot them long before you arrive. A real thrill for science-minded kids, the popular Star Party programs (Tuesday, Friday and Saturday; timings vary seasonally) help visitors see the night sky in a whole new way.

Davis Mountains State Park   STATE PARK
(🖪 432-426-3337; http://tpwd.texas.gov; Hwy 118; adult/child under 13yr $6/free) For majestic sunrises and sunsets, this remote park rivals any we've seen – and we've seen plenty. This wonderful place is just 3 miles northwest of Fort Davis on Hwy 118, set amid the most extensive mountain range in Texas. Hiking, mountain biking, horseback riding (BYO horse) and stargazing are all big attractions, as is bird-watching (pick up a bird checklist from park headquarters). Overnighters can use the campground, or bunk down at Indian Lodge (p742); both are just inside the park.

Fort Davis
National Historic Site
HISTORIC SITE

(📞 432-426-3224; www.nps.gov/foda; Hwy 17; adult/child under 16yr $10/free; ⊙ 8am-5pm; 🚗) Established in 1854, this well-preserved, beautifully sited frontier fort was named for then–Secretary of War Jefferson Davis. Staffed exclusively by black soldiers between 1867 and 1881, it was abandoned in 1891, but more than 20 buildings remain amid the 100-plus ruins, and five now hold period furnishings. Bugle calls echo at regular intervals, and in summer costumed interpreters tell tales of military life. In the refurbished barracks, each bed bears the name of its actual 1884 occupant.

Balmorhea State Park
SWIMMING

(📞 432-375-2370; http://tpwd.texas.gov; Hwy 17; adult/child under 13yr $7/free; ⊙ 8am-7:30pm or sunset (if earlier)) Swimming, scuba diving and snorkeling are the attractions at this 46-acre park, a true oasis in the West Texas desert. It's home to the largest spring-fed swimming pool in the US, constructed by the Civilian Conservation Corps in the 1930s, which is 25ft deep, covers 1.3 acres, and stays at about 75°F year-round.

🛏 Sleeping & Eating

Stone Village Tourist Camp
MOTEL $

(📞 432-426-3941; www.stonevillagetouristcamp.com; 509 N State St; camp r $44, motel r $81-98, ste $111; 🅿️🛜🏊) A fun little bargain, this charming and very central old motel offers two kinds of lodging. The regular rooms are cheery and comfortable, while the much more basic Camp Rooms have concrete floors, stone walls, electricity and wi-fi, plus sinks that only have water between Easter and October. They share bathrooms – one male, one female – divided by screens and privacy curtains.

Indian Lodge
INN $$

(📞 lodge 432-426-3254, reservations 512-389-8982; http://tpwd.texas.gov; Hwy 118, Davis Mountains State Park; r $105-125, ste $150; 🅿️❄️🛜🏊) Located just inside Davis Mountains State Park (p741), this historic 39-room inn is actually a state park in its own right. Built by the Civilian Conservation Corps in the 1930s, its 18in-thick adobe walls, hand-carved cedar furniture and pine-slatted ceilings give it the look of a Southwestern pueblo – albeit one with a swimming pool and gift shop. Reserve early.

Stone Village Market
MARKET, SANDWICHES $

(📞 432-426-2226; www.stonevillagetouristcamp.com; 509 N State St; sandwiches $5-7; ⊙ 7am-7pm; 🛜) Looking for the perfect sandwich for your sunset picnic? Then step up to the deli counter at this welcoming market for the touted cranberry-almond chicken salad. There are plenty of snacks and drinks in the surrounding market to round out your meal.

ℹ Information

Fort Davis Chamber of Commerce (📞 432-426-3015; www.fortdavis.com; 100 Memorial Sq; ⊙ 9am-4pm Mon-Fri) Fort Davis' visitor center is at the junction of Hwys 118 and 17.

ℹ Getting There & Away

No regularly scheduled public transportation serves Fort Davis or the Davis Mountains. From El Paso and San Antonio you can get to nearby Alpine (24 miles away) by train or bus, then rent a car.

The closest airports are **Midland International Airport**, 60 miles northeast, and **El Paso International Airport** (ELP; 📞 915-212-0330; www.elpasointernationalairport.com; 6701 Convair Rd; 🛜), 200 miles northwest.

Marfa
POP 1800

The New York art scene collides with West Texas cowboy culture and Border Patrol formality in tiny, dusty Marfa, where the factions somehow seem to lead their separate lives without conflict. Maybe it's the baffling Marfa Mystery Lights (p743) that keep the vibe more quirky than antagonistic.

Founded in the 1880s, Marfa's major cultural hallmarks date from the latter part of the 20th century. Since Rock Hudson, Elizabeth Taylor and James Dean came to town to film the 1956 movie *Giant,* it's served as a location for *There Will Be Blood* and *No Country for Old Men.*

As for those New Yorkers: Marfa is a pilgrimage destination for art lovers, thanks to one of the world's largest installations of minimalist art, which has attracted galleries, quirky lodging options and interesting restaurants. The US Border Patrol has a headquarters here and has conspicuously amplified its presence in recent years.

◉ Sights

★ Chinati Foundation Museum
MUSEUM

(📞 432-729-4362; www.chinati.org; 1 Calvary Row; adult/student Full Collection Tour $25/10, Selections Tour $20/10; ⊙ 9am-5pm Wed-Sun, Full Collection Tour 10am or 10:30am, Selections Tour 11am or 11:30am) As you step inside the historic artillery shed, with its enormous windows,

WHAT THE...? PRADA & TARGET

So you're driving along a two-lane highway in dusty west Texas – out in the middle of *nowhere* – when suddenly a small, solitary building looms like a mirage on the horizon. As you zip past you glance over and see...a Prada store? Labelled the **Prada Marfa** (although in fact it's 1.5 miles north of Valentine), this art installation from the Ballroom Marfa folks really is a tiny store, given permission by Prada to use its logo, and stocked with the 2005 collection. The only snag is, you can't get in, but it does get your attention as a tongue-in-cheek comment on consumerism. The original idea was that it would naturally deteriorate, but in fact it's still looking spick-and-span.

To the east, on Hwy 90 halfway between Alpine and Marathon, the **Target Marathon** (Hwy 90), a guerrilla-art installation that appeared in 2016, seems to be taking a jab at Prada Marfa. What's next? Let us know if you spot anything.

sweeping desert views and sun-dappled aluminum boxes, the Marfa hoopla suddenly makes sense. Artist Donald Judd put Marfa on the art-world map when he created this museum on the site of a former army post. The grounds and abandoned buildings now house one of the world's largest permanent installations of minimalist art. The whole place is an immersive, breathtaking blend of art, architecture and landscape.

Marfa Mystery
Lights Viewing Area VIEWPOINT
(Hwy 90) Ghost lights, mystery lights...call them what you want, but the Marfa Lights, flickering beneath the Chinati Mountains, have been capturing travelers' imaginations for over a century. On many nights, the mystery seems to be whether you're merely seeing car headlights in the distance, though convincing-enough descriptions of mysterious lights on the horizon date back long before there were cars. Try your luck at this viewing area, equipped with benches, binoculars and restrooms, 9 miles east of Marfa on Hwy 90/67.

Ballroom Marfa GALLERY
(☑ 432-729-3600; www.ballroommarfa.org; 108 E San Antonio St; suggested donation $5; ☉10am-6pm Wed-Sat, to 3pm Sun) FREE Be sure to find out what's happening at Ballroom Marfa, a nonprofit art space located in a former dance hall. The focus is on offbeat, interesting projects, including film installations and excellent monthly concerts.

🛏 Sleeping

★ **El Cosmico** CAMPGROUND $
(☑ 432-729-1950; www.elcosmico.com; 802 S Highland Ave; tent sites per person $20, safari tents $95, tipis & yurts $165, trailers $165-210; P 🛜 🐾) Marfa's 'glampground' has to be one of the

funkiest choices in all Texas; you can sleep in a stylishly converted travel trailer, tipi, safari tent or even a yurt. It's not for everyone: the grounds are dry and dusty, you might have to shower outdoors, and there's no air-conditioning (luckily, it's cool at night).

★ **Hotel St George** BOUTIQUE HOTEL $$
(☑ 432-729-3700; www.marfasaintgeorge.com; 105 S Highland Ave; r from $225; 🌐 @ 🛜) In a town with a thing for minimalist cubes, this has to be our favorite. The design-minded digs, which opened in 2016, are the brainchild of local resident and Chinati Foundation board member Tim Crowley. Details and decor reflect fine artisanship, regional history and Marfa-sourced creativity, from the eye-catching art to the spare but inviting **Marfa Book Company** (☑ 432-729-3700; www.marfabookco.com; Hotel St George, 105 S Highland Ave; ☉9am-8pm) bookstore.

🍴 Eating & Drinking

Food Shark FOOD TRUCK $
(www.facebook.com/foodsharkmarfa; 909 W San Antonio St; mains $8-12; ☉noon-3pm Wed-Sat; 🚗) It's easy to miss this battered old trailer, beside the main road, but if you're lucky enough to pass through during Food Shark's limited opening hours, seize the chance to try its ultra-fresh Greek salad and the specialty, the Marfalafel. You can eat in the nice little desert garden in front. Excellent daily specials sell out early.

Cochineal AMERICAN $$$
(☑ 432-729-3300; www.cochinealmarfa.com; 107 W San Antonio St; small plates $10-18, mains $18-28; ☉5:30-10pm Thu-Mon; 🌐 🛜) Foodies flock to this stylish but minimalist restaurant (with outdoor courtyard) for a changing menu that showcases high-quality organic ingredients. For the full experience, share a few small

plates – maybe along the lines of brisket tacos, oyster-mushroom risotto or housemade ramen with duck breast – in lieu of a full dinner. Reservations are recommended.

Planet Marfa BAR
(☑ 432-386-5099; 200 S Abbott St; ☺ 2pm-midnight Fri & Sun, to 1am Sun mid-Mar–Nov) Marfa-style nightlife is epitomized by this wonderfully funky beer garden on the main drag. Complete with live music most nights, ping-pong, scattered shelters to protect you from the elements, and kids' games, it's officially open on weekends from spring break to Thanksgiving. If you're lucky, someone will save you a spot inside the basement-area tipi.

❶ Information

Marfa Visitor Center (☑ 432-729-4772; www.visitmarfa.com; 302 S Highland Ave; ☺ 8am-5pm Mon-Fri, 10am-1pm Sat) Lots of great information on galleries, restaurants and local attractions. The restaurant handout, with opening hours for everywhere in town, is superhelpful.

❶ Getting There & Away

There's an airport in Marfa, but you can't catch a flight there unless you actually charter one. The closest commercial airports are 180 miles northeast at **Midland** and 190 miles northwest at El Paso (p742).

You can, however, catch a Greyhound. The **bus station** (☑ 432-729-1992; www.greyhound.com; 1412 Berlin St) is just west of downtown. For train service, Amtrak serves nearby Alpine (26 miles away).

Alpine

POP 6100

Poised between Fort Davis, Marfa and Marathon, about a half-hour's drive from each one, and packed with hotels and restaurants, Alpine makes a great base for regional exploring. As the only city hereabouts with more than 5000 people, and the seat of Brewster County, it offers services and amenities its neighbors can't much, including the area's sole four-year college and only modern hospital. And it's a transportation hub, with an Amtrak station right in the heart of downtown.

More important than all that, though, is that it's a nice place just to hang out, with a charming vintage-flavored center and residents who are pretty darn friendly.

Hwy 90 through downtown splits into two one-way thoroughfares. Avenue E rolls west while traffic on Holland Ave runs east.

◉ Sights

Museum of the Big Bend MUSEUM
(☑ 432-837-8143; www.museumofthebigbend.com; 400 N Harrison St, Entrance 4, Sul Ross State University; ☺ 9am-5pm Tue-Sat, 1-5pm Sun; ⓟ) FREE On the campus of Sul Ross State University, this great little museum holds exhibits on locally found marine fossils, Native American pictographs, Spanish explorers, and – of course – cowboys, including a full-scale chuck wagon. It's a multimedia experience, relying on impressive re-creations rather than cases full of relics.

🛏 Sleeping & Eating

Maverick Inn MOTEL $
(☑ 432-837-0628; www.themaverickinn.com; 1200 E Holland Ave; r $105-145; ⓟ❄🐾🐕) Maverick road-trippers will feel right at home at this retro motel, smartly renovated with luxury bedding and flat-screen TVs. The mock-adobe casitas have Texas-style furnishings and terracotta floors, and the pool looks mighty nice after a hot, dusty day. You can also borrow a guitar or peruse Texas coffee-table books in the lobby. We like your attitude, Maverick Inn.

★ Holland Hotel HISTORIC HOTEL $$
(☑ 432-837-2800; www.thehollandhoteltexas.com; 209 W Holland Ave; s $75, d $135-185, ste $155-250; ⓟ❄🐕) This beautiful 1928 Spanish Colonial building has elegant rooms with carved wood furniture, Western-style artwork and sleek bathrooms. The lobby, with its leather chairs and wood-beamed ceiling, is a classy place to unwind, with the good **Century restaurant** attached. The fanciest room is the 4th-floor 'Crow's Nest' ($250), while the tiny 'Nina's Room' is ideal for solo travelers ($75).

Alicia's Burrito Place MEXICAN $
(☑ 432-837-2802; 708 E Gallego Ave; mains $5-12; ☺ 9am-3pm Mon & Wed, 8am-3pm Tue & Thu-Sun) Alicia's is known for its quick-and-hot breakfast burritos. Eggs, bacon and the like get rolled up in a portable meal you can eat with your hands – known to cure a hangover or two in their time. The Mexican cheeseburger is also a favorite. Drive-through service is available. Cash only.

Reata STEAK $$
(☑ 432-837-9232; www.reata.net; 203 N 5th St; lunch $10-15, dinner $13-40; ☺ 11:30am-2pm & 5-10pm Mon-Sat; ⓟ) Named after the ranch in the 1956 movie *Giant*, this yellow, tin-roofed ranch house turns on the upscale charm – at

least in the front dining room, where serious diners go. Step back into the lively bar area or the shady patio for a completely different vibe, where you can nibble your way around the steak-and-Mexican menu and enjoy a margarita.

Drinking & Entertainment

Big Bend Brewing Co MICROBREWERY
(☑432-837-3700; www.bigbendbrewing.com; 3401 W Hwy 90; ⊗taproom 4-8pm Mon, Thu & Fri, 1-8pm Sat & Sun) The taproom is bare bones at this microbrewery 2.5 miles west of town, but with picnic tables inside and out, chatty beer drinkers all around and wide-open views of the western landscape, you'll hardly notice the lack of frills. Its flagship Tejas lager makes an easy-drinking end to your epic afternoon.

Railroad Blues LIVE MUSIC
(☑432-837-3103; www.railroadblues.com; 504 W Holland Ave; ⊗4pm-2am Mon-Sat) This is the place to go in Alpine for live music and the biggest beer selection in Big Bend country. The club has hosted an impressive list of musicians, and sometimes draws Austin-based bands heading west on tour. If you'd rather just enjoy some friendly conversation, hit up happy hour (4pm to 7pm).

Information

Alpine Chamber of Commerce (☑432-837-2326; www.visitalpinetx.com; 106 N 3rd St; ⊗9am-5pm Mon-Fri, to 2pm Sat) Offers a *Historic Walking Tour* brochure featuring 44 stops in the downtown area.

Getting There & Away

There are no scheduled flights around these parts, but Alpine's **airport**, north of town along Hwy 118, can accommodate charter flights.

Greyhound (☑432-837-5497; www.greyhound. com; KCS Quick Stop, 2305 E Hwy 90; ⊗6am-10pm) offers bus service to and from El Paso and San Antonio, with a transfer in Fort Stockton. Buy tickets online or at the convenience store where the bus stops.

Amtrak's *Texas Eagle* and *Sunset Limited* routes stop at the **train station** (☑800-872-7245; www.amtrak.com; 102 W Holland Ave). Service frequently runs late, so check for updates with Amtrak before you set out.

El Paso

POP 684,000

Long considered a sleepy western backwater, El Paso used to just mosey along, keeping its head low while its notorious Mexican neighbour Ciudad Juárez grabbed the headlines. But no more; El Paso has been making its own headlines. Successive runs for the US Senate and Presidency by former local Congressman Beto O'Rourke, and repeated visits by President Trump promoting his border policies, have brought national attention. A construction boom – and we don't just mean the Wall – has given downtown El Paso a facelift, and it can now boast a fist-full of new high-rise hotels, a restored streetcar line, the Chihuahuas baseball team and even its very own crop of microbreweries.

Outdoorsy types have it made, thanks to wonderful cycling and hiking in Franklin Mountains State Park. Prefer the indoors? El Paso's top museums are free. Best of all is the local hospitality, which gives the city a welcoming small-town feel.

Sights & Activities

★**El Paso Museum of Art** MUSEUM
(☑915-212-0300; www.epma.art; 1 Arts Festival Plaza; ⊗9am-5pm Tue, Wed, Fri & Sat, to 9pm Thu, noon-5pm Sun; P) FREE This thoroughly enjoyable small-scale museum is housed in a former Greyhound station. Its pride and joy is a 13th-century Byzantine *Madonna and Child*, but the Southwestern art is terrific, too, and the engaging modern pieces round out the collection nicely. All this and it's free? Well done, El Paso, well done.

El Paso Holocaust Museum MUSEUM
(☑915-351-0048; www.elpasoholocaustmuseum. org; 715 N Oregon St; ⊗9am-5pm Tue-Fri, 1-5pm Sat & Sun; P) FREE El Paso might not seem an obvious location for a Holocaust museum. Created by local survivors, though, this excellent little memorial holds thoughtful and moving exhibits, imaginatively presented for maximum impact.

Franklin Mountains State Park PARK
(☑915-566-6441; www.tpwd.texas.gov; 1331 McKelligon Canyon Rd; adult/child under 13yr $5/ free; ⊗Tom Mays Unit 8am-5pm May–mid-Sep, 8am-5pm Mon-Fri, 6:30am-8pm Sat & Sun Apr–mid-Sep) The largest urban park in the US, at over 24,000 acres, offers a quick escape from the city to the home of ringtail cats, coyotes and countless other smaller animals and reptiles, with North Franklin Peak (7192ft) looming overhead. Most of the excellent mountain-biking and hiking trails are in the **Tom Mays Unit**, east of I-10 off Transmountain Rd.

Ysleta Mission
HISTORIC BUILDING

(La Misión de San Antonio de Ysleta del Sur; Our Lady of Mount Carmel; ☑ 915-859-9848; www.ysletamission.org; 131 S Zaragoza Rd; ⊙ 9am-1pm & 2-5pm Mon & Wed-Fri, 10am-1pm & 2-5pm Tue; P) FREE Home to Texas' oldest continually active congregation, tracing back to 1680, Ysleta Mission was established for Spanish refugees and Tigua people fleeing New Mexico after the Pueblo Indian revolt. The original building, erected by the Tigua in 1682, was replaced in the mid-1800s by the adobe-brick structure you see today. The silver-domed **bell tower** was added a few decades later.

Border Patrol Museum
MUSEUM

(☑ 915-759-6060; www.borderpatrolmuseum.com; 4315 Woodrow Bean Transmountain Rd; ⊙ 9am-5pm Tue-Sat; P) FREE This small but informative museum spotlights the history of the US Border Patrol, which was founded in 1924. This happened three days after Congress passed the National Origins Act, severely restricting immigration via country-of-origin quotas. The displays of tools and vehicles used to cross the border and elude capture, from ladders to boats to motorized hanggliders, are fascinating.

🛏 Sleeping & Eating

Gardner Hotel
HISTORIC HOTEL $

(☑ 915-532-3661; www.gardnerhotel.com; 311 E Franklin Ave; dm $26, r $44-62; 🕾) To appreciate El Paso's longest-running hotel, little changed since outlaw John Dillinger slept in room 221 in the 1930s, you'll need a sense of history. Some of its fan-cooled, period-furnished rooms share bathrooms, some are en suite, while four hostel-style dorm rooms hold four beds each. There are only two free parking spaces, and at weekends the noise can be horrendous.

Hotel Indigo
HOTEL $$

(☑ 915-532-5200; www.hotelindigo.com; 325 N Kansas St; r from $157; P🗗@🛜🌊🐕) From young business travelers passing through to locals sipping cocktails in the glossy bar, the Indigo has become a downtown destination in itself. Its inviting modern rooms start above the 5th floor – where a roof terrace holds the lobby, the bar and the pool – so views are big. The poolside bar hosts loud parties on Friday and Saturday nights.

L&J Cafe
MEXICAN $

(☑ 915-566-8418; www.landjcafe.com; 3622 E Missouri Ave; mains $9-14; ⊙ 9am-9pm Sun-Wed, 9am-10pm Thu & Fri, 8am-10pm Sat, 8am-9pm Sun; P) One of El Paso's best-loved Mexican joints, L&J serves up delicious tacos, fajitas and famous green-chile chicken enchiladas – plus a legendary menudo (tripe stew) on weekends. Next to the historic Concordia cemetery, it looks a bit divey at first glance. Don't be deterred: it's been open since 1927, and the inside is much more inviting.

★ Crave Kitchen & Bar
AMERICAN $$

(☑ 915-351-3677; www.cravekitchenandbar.com; 300 Cincinnati Ave, Kern Place; breakfast mains $8-19.50, lunch & dinner $11.50-29; ⊙ 7am-11pm Mon-Sat, to 6pm Sun) Winning extra points for style – from the cool sign to the cutlery hanging from the ceiling – this hip little restaurant serves up creative comfort food: green-chile mac 'n' cheese, juicy burgers with sweet-potato waffle fries, and decadent breakfasts. Lots of craft-beer choices on the menu, too.

Cattleman's Steakhouse
STEAK $$$

(☑ 915-544-3200; www.cattlemansranch.com; Indian Cliffs Ranch, Fabens; mains $30-50; ⊙ 5-10pm Mon-Fri, 12:30-10pm Sat, 12:30-9pm Sun; 🚸) This working cattle ranch is 35 miles southeast of downtown – follow signs 4.7 miles northeast from I-10 exit 49 – but locals would probably drive 200 miles to eat here. The food is good and the scenery is even better. Portions are huge, and for just $6 you can share a main and gain full access to the family-style sides.

🍷 Drinking & Entertainment

★ Hillside Coffee & Donut Co.
COFFEE

(☑ 915-474-3453; www.facebook.com/Hillside Coffee; 4935 N Mesa St; ⊙ 6am-10pm Sun-Wed, to midnight Thu-Sat) We don't know whether to recommend this place for the iced coffee, the gourmet doughnuts or the welcoming service. How about all three? If you're in west El Paso and need a jolt – from caffeine, sugar or a bright, buzzing locale – stop by. The barista's helpful friendliness almost made us cry, as if we'd encountered a unicorn or something.

Ode Brewing Co
MICROBREWERY

(☑ 915-351-4377; www.odebrewingco.com; 3233 N Mesa St; ⊙ 11am-11pm Sun-Thu, to midnight Fri & Sat) 'Beer Here – Made Fresh' says the sign, and the founding member of El Paso's ever-growing crop of microbreweries is still drawing imbibers with easy-drinking ales and lagers. Set back from the highway, it has a great open patio facing the mountain. The gourmet pub grub has a decadently global spin: the poutine duck-fat fries are smothered with green-chile sausage gravy.

Abraham Chavez Theatre THEATER
(☑ 915-534-0609; www.elpasolive.com; 1 Civic Center Plaza) The sombrero-shaped Abraham Chavez Theatre hosts most of El Paso's major performing organizations – including **El Paso Symphony Orchestra** (☑ 915-532-3776; www.epso.org), **Showtime! El Paso** (☑ 915-247-2726; www.showtimeelpaso.com) and **El Paso Opera** (☑ 915-581-5534; www.epopera.org) – as well as touring concerts and plays.

McKelligon Canyon Amphitheater LIVE PERFORMANCE
(☑ 915-534-0600; www.vivaelpaso.org; McKelligon Canyon Rd) The **Viva! El Paso musical** (☑ 915-231-1100; www.vivaelpaso.org; adult/child under 13yr $20/12; ☺ mid-Jun–Jul) plays in this scenic outdoor amphitheater on Friday and Saturday nights in June and July. It's located in Franklin Mountains State Park, 7 miles north of downtown.

❶ Information

El Paso Visitor Center (☑ 915-534-0661; www.visitelpaso.com; 400 W San Antonio Ave, Union Depot; ☺ 9am-4pm Mon-Fri, to 2pm Sat)
Franklin Mountains State Park Visitor Center (☑ 915-566-6441; www.tpwd.texas.gov; 1331 McKelligon Canyon Rd; ☺ 8am-4pm Mon-Fri)
Mission Valley Visitors Information Center (☑ 915-851-9997; http://visitelpasomissiontrail.com; 9065 Alameda Ave; ☺ 9am-4pm Mon-Fri, to 3pm Sat & Sun; 🛜) The website offers the history of the Mission Trail and a self-guided walking tour of San Elizario.

❶ Getting There & Away

El Paso International Airport (p742), 8 miles northeast of downtown, is accessible by bus (33 and 50), taxi and shuttles. Southwest Airlines is the biggest carrier, with other airlines including American, Delta, United and Alaska.

El Paso's **Greyhound** (☑ 915-532-5095; www.greyhound.com; 200 W San Antonio Ave) terminal is on the southwestern edge of downtown.

Two Amtrak routes serve El Paso's **Union Depot** (☑ 800-872-7245; www.amtrak.com; 700 W San Francisco Ave), half a mile southwest of central downtown. The *Texas Eagle* connects Los Angeles with Chicago via San Antonio, Austin, Fort Worth and Dallas, while the *Sunset Limited* connects Los Angeles with New Orleans via San Antonio and Houston. Check online for fares and schedules.

Guadalupe Mountains National Park

Few Texans seem to know about Guadalupe Mountains, but **Guadalupe Mountains National Park** (☑ 915-828-3251; www.nps.gov/gumo; US Hwy 62/180; 7-day pass adult/child under 16yr $7/free; ☺ visitor center 8am-4:30pm) is a true Texas high spot, literally as well as figuratively. At 8749ft, **Guadalupe Peak** is the highest point in the state. Just south of New Mexico, 110 miles east of El Paso, this remote desert enclave is a long way from anywhere. For the best day-use, drive 12 miles northeast from Pine Springs Visitor Center to reach **McKittrick Canyon**, which sees the finest fall foliage in West Texas.

More than half the park is a designated wilderness area, and the park service has curbed development to keep it wild. There are no restaurants or indoor accommodations and only a smattering of services and programs (keep your gas tank full and your cooler stocked). And with no paved roads within the park proper, you're going to have to hike to see its high-country splendor.

Interpretive programs are held on summer evenings in the Pine Springs campground amphitheater, as well as several times a week during the spring. Topics depend on the rangers' interests, but they have included everything from stargazing to geology.

❶ Information

Both the **Pine Springs Visitor Center** (☑ 915-828-3251; www.nps.gov/gumo; US Hwy 62/180; ☺ 8am-4:30pm) and the **Dog Canyon Ranger Station** provide information, restrooms and drinking water, while **McKittrick Canyon** holds water, restrooms and outdoor exhibits.

You can also find downloadable maps on the park website.

❶ Getting There & Away

Guadalupe Mountains National Park is on Hwy 62/180, 110 miles east of El Paso and 55 miles southwest of Carlsbad, NM. The closest gas stations are 35 miles in either direction on Hwy 62/180, while the closest services are in Whites City, NM, 45 minutes northeast toward Carlsbad on Hwy 62/180.

TEXAS GUADALUPE MOUNTAINS NATIONAL PARK

Rocky Mountains

Best Places to Eat

➔ Frasca (p764)

➔ Follow Yer' Nose BBQ (p802)

➔ Snake River Grill (p791)

➔ Sweet Melissa's (p788)

Best Places to Sleep

➔ Broadmoor (p776)

➔ Nagle Warren Mansion Bed & Breakfast (p786)

➔ Mill House (p788)

➔ Wort Hotel (p790)

Why Go?

Welcome to where the US takes on truly epic proportions. Here in Colorado, Wyoming, Montana and Idaho, the Great Plains of the American West collide with the drama-filled Rockies, one of the most beautiful mountain ranges on Earth. You'll lose count of how often you look up and have the beauty of what you see bid you silent.

The region's Native American story brings to life landscapes where tribes lived and hunted for thousands of years in a land littered with poignant battlefield memorials. Elsewhere, the Rockies specialises in cool urban centres where culinary excellence meets microbreweries, from Boise to Jackson, Missoula to Denver.

But it's the call of the wild that reigns out here in the realm of grizzlies and wolves, elk and bison. Yellowstone, Rocky Mountain, Grand Teton and Glacier national parks are simply extraordinary, and there are few limits on possible ways to get out and explore them.

When to Go

Denver

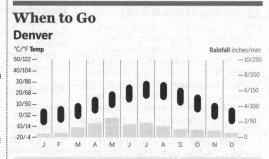

Jun–Aug Long days of sunshine for cycling, hiking, farmers markets and summer festivals.

Sep & Oct Fall foliage coincides with terrific lodging deals and far fewer crowds.

Jan–Mar Snowdusted peaks, powdery slopes and deluxe après-ski parties.

History

When French trappers and Spaniards 'discovered' the Rocky Mountains in the late 18th century, they found the area was already home to several tribes of Native Americans, including the Nez Percé, the Shoshone, the Crow, the Lakota and the Ute. This fact merely slowed the European conquest, and countries began claiming, defending, buying and selling what they called 'unclaimed' territory.

A young US government purchased all lands east of the Continental Divide from France in the 1803 Louisiana Purchase. Shortly thereafter it dispatched Meriwether Lewis and William Clark to survey the area and see exactly what they had bought. Their epic survey covered nearly 8000 miles in two-and-a-half years, and tales of what they found urged on other adventurers, setting migration in motion.

Wagon trains voyaged to the Rockies and beyond right into the 20th century, and the process accelerated with the completion of the Transcontinental Railroad across southern Wyoming in the late 1860s.

To accommodate settlers, the US purged the western frontier of the Spanish, British and, in a truly shameful era, most of the Native American population. The government signed endless treaties to defuse Native American objections to increasing settlement, but always reneged and shunted tribes onto smaller reservations. Gold-miners' incursions into Native American territory in Montana and the building of US Army forts along the Bozeman Trail ignited a series of wars with the Lakota, Cheyenne, Arapaho and others.

ROCKY MOUNTAINS IN...

Two Weeks

Start your Rocky Mountain odyssey in the Denver area. Go tubing, vintage-clothes shopping or biking in outdoor-mad, boho Boulder (p762), then soak up the liberal rays while eavesdropping at a sidewalk cafe. Enjoy the vistas of Rocky Mountain National Park (p766) before heading west on I-70 to play in the mountains around Breckenridge (p770), which also has some of the best beginner slopes in Colorado. Go to ski and mountain-bike hot spot Steamboat Springs (p768) before crossing the border into Wyoming.

Get a taste of prairie-town life in Cheyenne (p785), then stop in Lander (p788) – rock-climbing destination extraordinaire. Continue northwest to chic Jackson (p789) and majestic Grand Teton National Park (p797) before hitting iconic Yellowstone National Park (p792). Save at least three days for exploring this geyser-packed natural wonderland.

Cross the state line into 'big sky country' and slowly make your way northwest through Montana, stopping in funky Bozeman (p801) and lively Missoula (p805) Wrap up your trip in Idaho, exploring Basque culture in up-and-coming Boise (p810).

One Month

With a month on your hands, you can really delve into the region's off-the-beaten-path treasures. Follow the two-week itinerary, but dip southwest into Colorado – a developing wine region – before visiting Wyoming. Ride the 4WD trails around Ouray (p778). Be sure to visit Mesa Verde National Park (p782) and its ancient cliff dwellings.

In Montana, you'll want to visit Glacier National Park (p807) before the glaciers disappear altogether. In Idaho, spend more time playing in Sun Valley (p812) and be sure to explore the shops, pubs and yummy organic restaurants in delightful little Ketchum (p812). You also have time to drive along a few of Idaho's fantastically remote scenic byways. Make sure you cruise Hwy 75 from Sun Valley north to Stanley (p814). Situated on the wide banks of the Salmon River, this stunning mountain hamlet is completely surrounded by national forestland and wilderness areas. Stanley is also blessed with world-class trout fishing and mild to wild rafting.

Take Hwy 21 (the Ponderosa Pine Scenic Byway) from Stanley to Boise. This scenic drive takes you through miles of dense ponderosa forests and past some excellent, solitary riverside camping spots – some of which come with their own natural hot-springs pools.

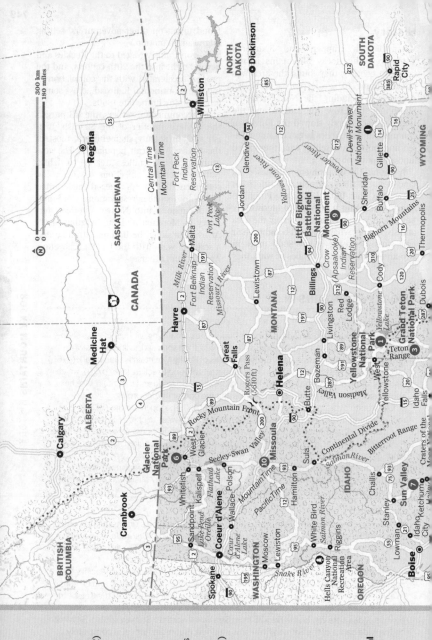

Rocky Mountain Highlights

1 Yellowstone National Park (p792) Spotting bears, wolves and bison between hot springs and geysers.

2 Aspen (p773) Reveling in Hollywood-gone-cowboy at Colorado's premier party resort.

3 Grand Teton National Park (p797) Hiking and climbing the craggiest of mountains.

4 Boulder (p762) Getting high on altitude in an urban outdoor paradise.

5 Southern Colorado (p777) Roaming the living Wild West towns of the San Juans.

6 Glacier National Park (p807) Photographing untamed natural

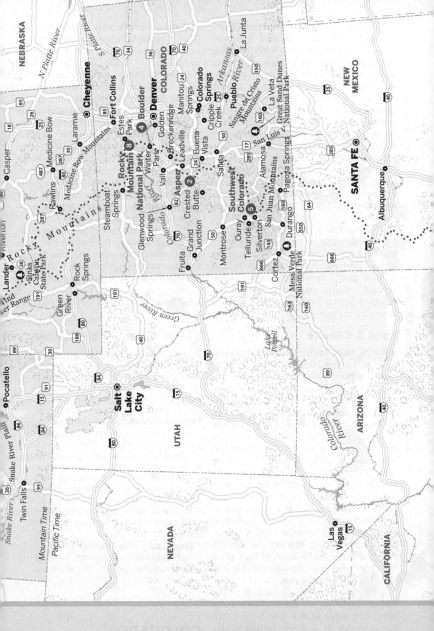

splendor on Going-to-the-Sun Road.

7 Sun Valley
(p812) Powder skiing with the stars in Idaho's winter playground resort.

8 Rocky Mountain National Park (p766)
Scaling to majestic heights by road or trail.

9 Little Bighorn Battlefield National Monument (p804)
Following the trail of an epic battle for the American West.

10 Missoula (p805)
Wandering along the riverbank and soaking up Montana's small-town urban cool.

Gold and silver mania preceded Colorado's entry to statehood in 1876. Statehood soon followed for Montana (1889), Wyoming (1890) and Idaho (1890). Mining, grazing and timber played major roles in regional economic development, sparking growth in financial and industrial support. The miners, white farmers and ranchers controlled power in the late 19th century, but the boom-and-bust cycles of their industries coupled with unsustainable resource management took their toll on the landscape.

When the economy thrived post-WWII, national parks started attracting vacationers, and a heightened conservation movement flourished. Tourism became a leading industry in all four states, with the military a close second (particularly in Colorado).

Political shifts in recent years have placed many of the Rocky Mountain region's protected areas in jeopardy. Special interest groups continually lobby for increased resource extraction and development on federal lands, which may cut off access for the public.

Land & Climate

Running from British Columbia (Canada) to northern New Mexico, the Rocky Mountains are North America's longest chain of mountains. More than 100 separate ranges make up the Rockies. Most were uplifted during the Laramide orogeny, which began around 80 million years ago when a chunk of oceanic crust took a shallow dive under the continental plate, bumping along just under the surface of the Earth. This movement forced the Rockies upwards, sideways and in some cases on top of themselves – such as at the Lewis Overthrust Fault in Glacier National Park, where older rock, miles thick, was pushed some 50 miles (80km) across the top of younger rock. Over time, glaciers and erosion have worn the peaks down to their present form, revealing rock layers that betray their long and chaotic past.

With the retreat of the glaciers at the end of the last ice age, the Rockies became more hospitable to life, though they still see extremes of weather. During winter months much of the Rockies is covered under several feet of snow. Although this is a burden on large mammals who have to migrate to lower areas to find food – or instead choose to hibernate through the winter, as bears do – it's a boon for skiers

and snowboarders, who revel in the light, fluffy continental snow pack. Words such as 'champagne powder' and 'cold smoke' are the envy of Pacific Coast skiers.

Spring is largely a muddy time as the snow melts and deciduous trees begin to bud. It generally doesn't feel 'summery' in many regions of the mountains until late June. During the brief summer months (typically July through September) all of the plants must get on with the business of reproduction at once, and high alpine meadows glow with the colors of the rainbow. Humans must get on with the business of recreating during this time, too, and trails are flooded with cyclists and backpackers – particularly in much of Colorado.

It can snow any time of year in the Rockies, though typically the first flurries fly in early October while aspen leaves blanket the hillsides with shimmering gold. The days are warm, nights are cool and most of the crowds have gone back to school. This is possibly the best time to visit (but don't tell anyone).

🛈 Getting There & Around

Denver has the only major international airport (p761) in the Rocky Mountains area. Both Denver and Colorado Springs offer flights on smaller planes to Jackson, WY; Boise, ID; Bozeman, MT; Aspen, CO; and other destinations. Salt Lake City, UT, may be more convenient to destinations in the west and northern regions.

Two **Amtrak** (www.amtrak.com) train routes pass through the region. *California Zephyr*, traveling daily between Emeryville, CA, and Chicago, IL, has six stops in Colorado, including Denver, Fraser-Winter Park, Glenwood Springs and Grand Junction. *Empire Builder* runs daily from Seattle, WA, or Portland, OR, to Chicago, IL, with 12 stops in Montana (including Whitefish, East Glacier and West Glacier) and one stop in Idaho at Sandpoint.

Greyhound (☑ 214-849-8100; www.greyhound.com) travels some parts of the Rocky Mountains, but to really get out and explore you'll need a car.

COLORADO

Remarkable in its diversity, beauty and grandeur, Colorado delivers endless powder runs, outdoors adventures, surprisingly cosmopolitan arts and dining scenes, and 300 days of sunshine.

ℹ Information

Bureau of Land Management Colorado (BLM; ☎303-239-3600, 800-877-8339; www.co.blm. gov; 2850 Youngfield St, Lakewood; ⊙8:30am-4pm Mon-Fri; ☒28) Provides information on historic sites, trails and more.

Camping USA (www.camping-usa.com) A great resource, with more than 12,000 campgrounds in its database.

Colorado Parks & Wildlife (CPW; Map p754; ☎303-297-1192; https://cpw.state.co.us; 1313 Sherman St, Denver; ⊙8am-5pm Mon-Fri) Manages more than 40 state parks and 300 wildlife areas; handles reservations for camp-grounds.

Colorado Road & Traffic Conditions (☎511; www.codot.gov; ⊙24hr) Provides up-to-date information on Colorado highway and traffic conditions, including cycling maps.

Colorado Travel & Tourism Authority (☎800-265-6723; www.colorado.com) Offers detailed information on sights, activities and more throughout the state.

Denver

Denver is rising. It's one of the fastest growing cities in the US. It's got beautiful weather and beautiful people. It's got good restaurants, even better bars, and a pretty lively arts and music scene.

Like other cities that are all grown up, each of Denver's neighborhoods has a flavor of its own.

For art, warehouses and street art, hit up River North (RiNo). Highlands and Lower Highlands (LoHi) have shopping and restaurant districts and a slightly less edgy attitude, while South Broadway is all leather and edge. At the core, you have the fun bars of Lower Downtown (LoDo), historic Five Points, the Santa Fe Arts District and the upscale Cherry Creek area. The entire city is connected through a beautiful series of bike paths and parks.

Best of all, within a couple hours' drive you have access to vast areas of wilderness, world-class skiing and hiking, and much, much more.

◉ Sights & Activities

★Denver Art Museum   MUSEUM
(DAM; Map p754; ☎ticket sales 720-865-5000; www.denverartmuseum.org; 100 W 14th Ave; adult/child $13/free, 1st Sat of month free; ⊙10am-5pm Tue-Thu, Sat & Sun, to 8pm Fri; ℗☻; ☒0, 52) ☀ The Denver Art Museum (DAM) is home to one of the largest Native American art

---

COLORADO FACTS

Nickname Centennial State

Population 5,700,000

Area 104,185 sq miles

Capital city Denver (population 693,100)

Other cities Boulder (population 97,385), Colorado Springs (population 445,830)

Sales tax 2.9% state tax, plus individual city taxes

Birthplace of Ute tribal leader Chief Ouray (1833–80); South Park creator Trey Parker (b 1969); actor Amy Adams (b 1974); climber Tommy Caldwell (b 1978)

Peaks higher than 14,000ft 53, 54 or 58 (depending on who's counting)

Politics Swing state

Famous for Sunny days (300 per year), the highest-altitude vineyards and longest ski run in the continental USA

Kitschiest souvenir Deer-hoof bottle-opener

Driving distances Denver to Vail 100 miles, Boulder to Rocky Mountain National Park 38 miles

---

collections in the USA, and puts on special multimedia exhibits that vary from treasures of British art to *Star Wars* costumes. The Western American Art section of the permanent collection is justifiably famous. This isn't an old, stodgy art museum, and the best part is diving into the interactive exhibits, which kids love.

★Confluence Park   PARK
(Map p754; 2200 15th St; ☻; ☒10, 28, 32, 44) ☀ Where Cherry Creek and South Platte River meet is the nexus and plexus of Denver's sunshine-loving culture. It's a good place for an afternoon picnic and there's a short white-water park for kayakers and tubers. Families also enjoy a small beach and shallow water areas for playing.

Children's Museum
Denver Marisco Campus   MUSEUM
(Map p754; ☎303-433-7444; www.mychilds museum.org; 2121 Children's Museum Dr; $14; ⊙9am-4pm Mon, Tue, Thu & Fri, to 7:30pm Wed, 10am-5pm Sat & Sun; ☻; ☒10) This is one of the hottest tickets in town...well, at least

Denver

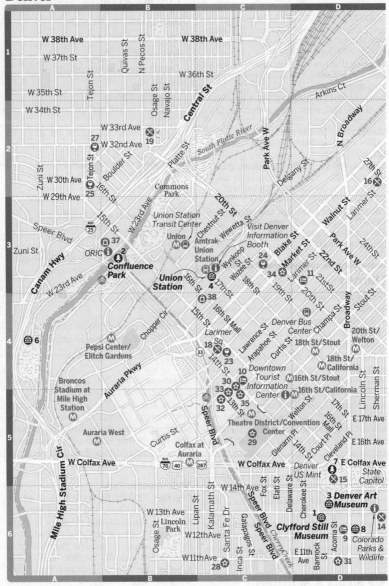

for kids. Highlights include an enclosed three-story climbing structure (helmets provided), a kids' kitchen with hands-on cooking classes, a 2300-sq-ft art studio, a maker space, a life-size marble run and a huge outdoor playground with lots of climbing, digging and splashing areas. Tod-

dlers also enjoy a section with fun areas designed for crawlers and new walkers.

⭐**Clyfford Still Museum**   MUSEUM
(Map p754; ☏ 720-354-4880; www.clyffordstill museum.org; 1250 Bannock St; adult/child $10/ free; ⏱10am-5pm Tue-Thu, Sat & Sun, to 8pm

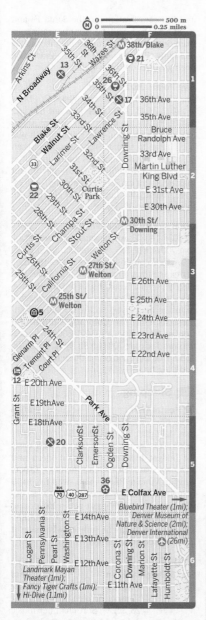

Denver

◉ Top Sights
1 Clyfford Still Museum	D6
2 Confluence Park	B3
3 Denver Art Museum	D6
4 Union Station	C3

◉ Sights
5 Blair-Caldwell African American Museum	E3
6 Children's Museum Denver Marisco Campus	A4
7 Civic Center Park	D5
8 History Colorado Center	D6

🛏 Sleeping
9 Art – a Hotel	D6
Crawford Hotel	(see 4)
10 Curtis	C4
11 Hostel Fish	D3
12 Queen Anne Bed & Breakfast Inn	E4

✖ Eating
13 Acorn	E1
14 City O' City	D6
15 Civic Center Eats	D5
16 Denver Central Market	D2
17 Hop Alley	F1
18 Rioja	C4
19 Root Down	B2
20 Steuben's Food Service	E5

🍷 Drinking & Nightlife
21 Black Shirt Brewing Co.	F1
22 Crema Coffee House	E2
23 Crú	C4
24 Falling Rock Tap House	C3
25 Linger	A2
26 Tracks	F1
27 Williams & Graham	A2

🎭 Entertainment
28 Colorado Ballet	C6
29 Colorado Convention Center	C5
30 Colorado Symphony Orchestra	C4
31 Curious Theatre	D6
32 Denver Center for the Performing Arts	C5
33 Denver Performing Arts Complex	C5
34 El Chapultepec	C3
35 Ellie Caulkins Opera House	C5
36 Ogden Theatre	F5
Opera Colorado	(see 35)

🛍 Shopping
37 REI	B3
38 Tattered Cover Bookstore	C4

Fri; 👤; 🚊 0, 52) Dedicated exclusively to the work and legacy of 20th-century American abstract expressionist Clyfford Still, this fascinating museum's collection includes more than 2400 pieces – 95% of his work – by the powerful and narcissistic master of bold. In his will, Still insisted that his body of work only be exhibited in a singular space, so Denver built him a museum. Free tours are offered throughout the week; check the website for dates and times.

History Colorado Center   MUSEUM
(Map p754; ☑303-447-8679; www.historycolorado center.org; 1200 Broadway; adult/child $14/8; ⏰10am-5pm; P♿; ☐0, 10) Discover Colorado's frontier roots and high-tech modern triumphs at this sharp, smart and charming museum. There are plenty of interactive exhibits, including a Jules Verne–esque 'Time Machine' that you push across a giant map of Colorado to explore seminal moments in the Centennial State's history. Periodically, story times for toddlers and low-sensory morning sessions are offered before the museum opens.

Blair-Caldwell
African American Museum   MUSEUM
(Map p754; ☑720-865-2401; https://history. denverlibrary.org/blair; 2401 Welton St, 3rd fl; ⏰noon-8pm Mon & Wed, 10am-6pm Tue, Thu & Fri, 9am-5pm Sat; P♿; ☐43, ☐D) FREE Tucked into the 3rd floor of a public library, this multimedia museum provides an excellent overview of the history of African Americans in the Rocky Mountain region – from migration and settlement to discrimination and achievements. Exhibits on Wellington Webb, Denver's first African American mayor, as well as Five Points, Denver's historically African American neighborhood, are particularly interesting.

Denver Museum of
Nature & Science   MUSEUM
(DMNS; ☑303-370-6000; www.dmns.org; 2001 Colorado Blvd; museum adult/child $19/14, IMAX $7/6, Planetarium $5/4; ⏰9am-5pm; P♿; ☐20, 32, 40) A classic natural-science museum with excellent temporary exhibits on topics such as the biomechanics of bugs, Pompeii and mythical creatures. Permanent exhibits are equally engaging and include those cool panoramas we all loved as kids. The IMAX Theatre and Gates Planetarium are especially fun. The museum is located on the eastern edge of City Park, allowing for fun picnics or connected visits with the nearby zoo.

🎪 Festivals & Events

First Friday   CULTURAL
(www.rivernorthart.com) FREE On the first Friday of every month, Denverites come out for an art stroll, cruising galleries for free wine and fun conversations in the Santa Fe and RiNo Arts Districts. The event typically runs from 6pm to 10pm. Smaller neighborhoods including Berkeley and South Pearl also open galleries on these nights.

Five Points Jazz Festival   MUSIC
(www.artsandvenuesdenver.com; Welton St; ⏰May; ♿; ☐12, 28, 43, ☐D) FREE This one-day jazz fest celebrates the historically African American neighborhood of Five Points, which was once home to several jazz clubs. More than 50 bands perform on stages set up on Welton St. Several kid-friendly activities – instrument making, drum circles, face painting – are offered, making it a fun event for all. Held the third Saturday of May.

Great American Beer Festival   BEER
(☑303-447-0816; www.greatamericanbeerfestival. com; 700 14th St; $85; ⏰Sep or Oct; ☐1, 8, 19, 48, ☐D, F, H) Colorado has more microbreweries per capita than any other US state, and this hugely popular festival sells out in advance. More than 500 breweries are represented, from the big players to the home-brew enthusiasts. Only the **Colorado Convention Center** (Map p754; ☑303-228-8000; www.denverconvention.com; 700 14th St; 🚇; ☐1, 8, 19, 48, ☐D, F, H) is big enough for these big brewers and their fat brews.

🛏 Sleeping

★Hostel Fish   HOSTEL $
(Map p754; ☑303-954-0962; www.hostelfish. com; 1217 20th St; dm/r from $40/190; ✳🛜; ☐38) This swanked-out hostel is an oasis for budget travelers. Stylish, modern and squeaky clean, dorms have themes – Aspen, Graffiti, Vintage Biker – and sleep five to 10 people in bunks. Mattresses are thick, duvets plush and each guest gets a locker and individual charging station. The common kitchen and frequent pub crawls make it easy to make new friends.

★Queen Anne
Bed & Breakfast Inn   B&B $$
(Map p754; ☑303-296-6666; www.queenanne bnb.com; 2147 Tremont Pl; r/ste from $165/230; P♿✳🛜; ☐28, 32) 🌿 Soft chamber music wafting through public areas, fresh flowers, manicured gardens and evening wine tastings create a romantic ambience at this eco-conscious B&B in two late-1800s Victorian homes. Featuring period antiques, private hot tubs and exquisite hand-painted murals, each room has its own personality.

BEST DAY HIKES & RIDES FROM DENVER

There are literally hundreds of day hikes within an hour of Denver.

Golden Gate Canyon State Park (☑ 303-582-3707; www.cpw.state.co.us; 92 Crawford Gulch Rd; entrance $7, camping $20-26; ⊙ 5am-10pm; 🚻 🎫) Located halfway between Golden and Nederland, this massive 12,000-acre state park has plenty of hiking trails and climbing opportunities.

Staunton State Park (☑ 303-816-0912; www.parks.state.co.us/parks; 12102 S Elk Creek Rd; individual pass/vehicle $4/8; ⊙ 7am-9pm; 🚻 🎫) Colorado's newest state park sits on a historic ranch site 40 miles west of Denver. Ranging in elevation from 8100ft to 10,000ft, it has a rich variety of landscapes – from grassy meadows to dramatic granite cliffs.

Waterton Canyon (☑ 303-634-3745; www.denverwater.org/recreation/waterton-canyon-strontia-springs-resevoir; 11300 Waterton Rd; ⊙ 30min before dawn-30min after dusk; 🚻) South of Denver, just west of Chatfield Reservoir, this pretty canyon has an easy 6.5-mile trail to the Strontia Springs Dam.

Buffalo Creek Mountain Bike Area (www.frmbp.org; 18268 S Buffalo Creek Rd, Pine; ⊙ 7am-7pm; 🚻) If you're into singletrack mountain biking, this area has about 40 miles of bike trails, including the sections of the Colorado Trail that permit bikes.

★ **Crawford Hotel** HOTEL $$$

(Map p754; ☑ 855-362-5098; www.thecrawford hotel.com; 1701 Wynkoop St, Union Station; r from 290, ste from $529; 🅿🛜🎫; 🚇55L, 72L,120L, FF2, 🚌A, B, C, E, W) Set in the historic Union Station (p761), the Crawford Hotel is an example of Denver's amazing transformation. Rooms are luxurious and artful, with high ceilings and throwbacks such as the art-deco headboards and claw-foot tubs. Service is impeccable and the station's bar, the Terminal, is a fun hangout. Steps away, there's light-rail service to Denver International Airport (p761).

Curtis HOTEL $$$

(Map p754; ☑ 303-571-0300; www.thecurtis.com; 1405 Curtis St; r $309-449; 🚇🅿@🛜; 🚌9, 10, 15, 20, 28, 32, 38, 43, 44) The Curtis is like stepping into a doo-bop Warhol wonderworld: 13 themed floors, each devoted to a different genre of American pop culture. Rooms are spacious and very mod. Attention to detail – either through the service or the decor – is paramount at the Curtis. While it's managed by the Doubletree, this is a one-of-a-kind hotel in the heart of downtown.

★ **Art – a Hotel** BOUTIQUE HOTEL $$$

(Map p754; ☑ 303-572-8000; www.thearthotel. com; 1201 Broadway; r from $400; 🅿🚇@🛜🎫; 🚌0, 6, 10, 52) As the name suggests, this hotel has intriguing artwork in the guest rooms and common areas, befitting its location, just around the corner from the Denver Art Museum (p753). Rooms are sizable and

modern, and the large patio (open to the general public) with firepits and great views is perfect for happy-hour cocktails.

✖ Eating

Denver's food scene is booming, with new restaurants, cafes and food trucks seemingly opening every month. Downtown offers the greatest variety in Denver, though strollable neighborhoods like LoHi, RiNo, South Broadway, Uptown and Five Points hold some of Denver's best eateries. Out in the burbs, the city of Aurora has Denver's best ethnic food. Check out www.5280.com for new eats.

★ **Denver Central Market** FOOD HALL $

(Map p754; www.denvercentralmarket.com; 2669 Larimer St; ⊙ 8am-9pm Sun-Thu, to 10pm Fri & Sat; 🚌44, 48) Set in a repurposed warehouse, this gourmet marketplace wows with its style and breadth of options. Eat a bowl of handmade pasta or an artisanal sandwich; consider a wood-fired pizza or street tacos. Or just grab a cocktail at the bar and wander between the fruit stand and chocolatier. Patrons eat at communal tables or on the street-side patio.

Civic Center Eats FOOD TRUCK $

(Map p754; ☑ 303-861-4633; www.civiccenter conservancy.org; cnr Broadway & Colfax Ave, Civic Center Park; mains $5-10; ⊙ 11am-2pm Tue-Thu May-Oct; 🚻🎫; 🚌0, 9, 10, 52) When the weather gets warm, head to **Civic Center Park** for lunch. There, a huge number of food trucks – everything from BBQ and pizza to sushi and Indian – roll into the park and serve up hearty meals. Tables are set up, live bands play, office workers picnic on the grass. It's Denver at its best.

★ **Hop Alley** CHINESE $$

(Map p754; ☑720-379-8340; www.hopalleydenver. com; 3500 Larimer St; mains $10-25; ⊙5:30-10:30pm Mon-Sat; ☑; ☐12, 44) Hop Alley was a slur used for Denver's hardscrabble Chinatown in the 1880s, until a race riot and anti-Chinese legislation scattered the community. The moniker was reclaimed for this small bustling restaurant located in (what else?) a former soy-sauce plant. Come for authentic yet inventive Chinese dishes and equally creative cocktails, named after the signs of the Chinese zodiac.

★ **Acorn** AMERICAN $$$

(Map p754; ☑720-542-3721; www.denveracorn. com; 3350 Brighton Blvd, Source; dishes $14-30; ⊙11:30am-10pm Mon-Sat, from 5:30pm Sun; ☑☑☑; ☐12, 20, 48) The oak-fired oven and grill are the shining stars of this superb restaurant, where small plates of innovative and shareable eats make up meals. The menu changes seasonally but dishes like crispy fried pickles, oak-grilled broccolini and smoked-pork posole are hits. If dinner is too pricey, consider a midday meal (2:30pm to 5:30pm) – the menu is limited but more affordable.

Rioja MODERN AMERICAN $$$

(Map p754; ☑303-820-2282; www.riojadenver. com; 1431 Larimer St; mains $20-40; ⊙11:30am-2:30pm Wed-Fri, from 10am Sat & Sun, 5-10pm daily; ☑; ☐10, 28, 32, 38, 44) This is one of Denver's most innovative restaurants. Smart, busy and upscale, yet relaxed and casual – just like Colorado – Rioja features modern cuisine inspired by Italian and Spanish traditions and powered by modern culinary flavors.

Root Down MODERN AMERICAN $$$

(Map p754; ☑303-993-4200; www.rootdowndenver.com; 1600 W 33rd Ave; small plates $8-19, mains $14-35; ⊙5-10pm Sun-Thu, 5-11pm Fri & Sat, 11am-2pm Fri, 10am-2:30pm Sat & Sun; ☑; ☐19, 52) 🍴 In a converted gas station, this is one of the city's most ambitious culinary concepts, marrying sustainable 'field-to-fork' practices, high-concept culinary fusions and a low-impact, energy-efficient ethos. The menu changes seasonally, but consider yourself lucky if it includes the sweet-potato falafel or Colorado lamb sliders. Vegetarian, vegan, raw and gluten-free diets very welcome.

🍷 Drinking & Nightlife

Denver's top nightlife districts include Uptown for gay bars and a young professional crowd, LoDo for loud sports bars and heavy drinking, RiNo for hipsters, LoHi for an eclectic mix, and South Broadway and Colfax for Old School wannabes.

★ **Black Shirt Brewing Co** BREWERY

(Map p754; ☑303-993-2799; www.blackshirtbrewingco.com; 3719 Walnut St; ⊙11am-10pm Sun-Thu, to midnight Fri & Sat; ☑; ☐12, 44, ☒A) Artisanal brewers create the all-red-ale menu at the popular BSB; ales take anywhere from two months to three years to brew. So careful are they with the handcrafted beers, the brewers developed lopsided glasses to showcase the aromas. Live music is part of the culture here, as is good food. A kitchen offers brick-oven pizzas and gourmet salads.

★ **Crema Coffee House** CAFE

(Map p754; ☑720-284-9648; www.cremacoffeehouse.net; 2862 Larimer St; ⊙7am-5pm; ☎; ☐44) Noah Price, a clothing designer turned coffee impresario, takes his job seriously, selecting, brewing and pouring Denver's absolute-best coffee. The espresso and French-pressed are complete perfection, but it's the oatmeal latte, delicately infused iced teas and spectacularly eclectic menu – Moroccan meatballs to peanut-butter and jelly sandwiches with goat's cheese – that put this place over the top.

Williams & Graham COCKTAIL BAR

(Map p754; ☑303-997-8886; www.williamsandgraham.com; 3160 Tejon St; ⊙5pm-1am; ☐32, 44) Denver's top speakeasy looks like an old Western bookstore, but ask for a seat and the cashier pushes a wall of books and leads you deeper into the era. Polished wood, gleaming brass features, antique lamps, tin ceilings and mixologists in aprons await. Cocktails are creative and artfully prepared – almost too beautiful to drink. Almost.

Linger LOUNGE

(Map p754; ☑303-993-3120; www.lingerdenver.com; 2030 W 30th Ave; ⊙11:30am-2:30pm & 4-10pm Tue-Thu, to 11pm Fri, 10am-2:30pm & 4-11pm Sat, 10am-2:30pm Sun; ☐28, 32, 44) This rambling LoHi complex sits in the former Olinger mortuary. Come nighttime, they black out the 'O' and it just becomes Linger. There's an interesting international menu, but most people come for the tony feel and light-up-the-night rooftop bar, which even has a replica of the RV made famous by the Bill Murray smash *Stripes*.

Tracks
GAY

(Map p754; ☑303-863-7326; www.tracksdenver. com; 3500 Walnut St; ⊙9pm-2am Fri & Sat, hours vary Sun-Thu; ⬚44, ⬚A) Denver's best gay dance club has an 18+ night on Thursday, and Friday drag shows. There's a definite pretty-boy focus, with good music and a scene to match. Saturday is the biggest dance night. No cover before 10pm, after 10pm it's $10.

Falling Rock Tap House
BAR

(Map p754; ☑303-293-8338; www.fallingrock taphouse.com; 1919 Blake St; ⊙11am-2am; ⬚0, 15, 20) High fives and hollers punctuate the scene when the Rockies triumph and beer drinkers file in to forget an afternoon of drinking Coors at the ball park. There are – count 'em – 80-plus beers on tap and the bottle list has almost 150. With all the local favorites, this is *the* place to drink beer downtown.

Crú
WINE BAR

(Map p754; ☑303-893-9463; www.cruawinebar. com; 1442 Larimer St; ⊙2pm-midnight Mon-Thu, noon-2am Fri & Sat, 10:30am-3pm Sun; ⬚10, 28, 32, 38, 44) This classy Larimer Sq wine bar is decked out in wine labels and glassware, with dim lighting and gentle music. It looks so bespoke it's surprising to learn it's a chain (Dallas, Austin). Come for happy hour (4pm to 6:30pm Monday to Friday) when flights of wine are $3 off and light fare includes mussels and goat's cheese beignets.

☆ Entertainment

Denver is bursting with entertainment options. There's live music and theater practically everywhere, from intimate jazz clubs to the amazing Denver Center for the Performing Arts (p759). Denver is a four-sport town (one of few in the country) and also has professional soccer and lacrosse. Add to that comedy, movies, dance, up-and-coming all-ages shows, and yearly festivals and there's something for everyone.

☆ Denver Performing Arts Complex
PERFORMING ARTS

(Map p754; ☑720-865-4220; www.artscomplex. com; cnr 14th & Champa Sts; ⬚9, 15, 28, 32, 38, 43, 44) This massive complex – one of the largest of its kind – occupies four city blocks and houses 10 major venues, including the historic **Ellie Caulkins Opera House** and the Boettcher Concert Hall. It's also home to the **Colorado Ballet** (Map p754; ☑303-837-8888; www.coloradoballet.org; 1075 Santa Fe Dr; ⊙box office 9am-5pm Mon-Fri; ⬥; ⬚1, 9), **Denver Center for the Performing Arts** (Map p754; ☑303-893-4100; www.denvercenter. org; 1101 13th St; ⊙box office 10am-6pm Mon-Sat & 1hr before each show; ⬥; ⬚9, 15, 28, 32, 38, 43, 44), **Opera Colorado** (Map p754; ☑303-468-2030; www.operacolorado.org; ⊙box office 10am-5pm Mon-Fri; ⬥; ⬚9, 15, 28, 32, 38, 43, 44) and the Colorado Symphony Orchestra (p760). Not sure what you want to do tonight? Come here.

☆ Curious Theatre
THEATER

(Map p754; ☑303-623-0524; www.curious theatre.org; 1080 Acoma St; ⊙box office 2-6pm Tue-Sat; ⬚0, 6, 52) 'No guts, no story' is the tagline of this award-winning theater company, set in a converted church. Plays pack a punch with thought-provoking stories that take on social justice issues. Think race, immigration, sexuality. Stay for talks at the end of each show, when actors engage with the audience about everything from the plot to the set. Tickets from $18.

El Chapultepec
JAZZ

(Map p754; ☑303-295-9126; www.thepeclodo. com; 1962 Market St; ⊙7am-1am, music from 9pm; ⬚38) This smoky, old-school jazz joint attracts a diverse mix of people. Since it opened in 1951, Frank Sinatra, Tony Bennett and Ella Fitzgerald have played here, as have Jagger and Richards. Local jazz bands take the tiny stage nightly, but you never know who might drop by.

Hi-Dive
LIVE MUSIC

(☑303-733-0230; www.hi-dive.com; 7 S Broadway; ⬚0) Local rock heroes and touring indie bands light up the stage at the Hi-Dive, a venue at the heart of Denver's local live-music scene. During big shows it gets deafeningly loud, cheek-to-jowl with hipsters and humid as an armpit. In other words, perfection.

Ogden Theatre
LIVE MUSIC

(Map p754; ☑303-832-1874; www.ogdentheatre. com; 935 E Colfax Ave; ⊙box office 10am-2pm Sat, 1hr before doors open show days; ⬚15) One of Denver's best live-music venues, the Ogden Theatre has a checkered past. Built in 1917, it was derelict for many years and might have been bulldozed in the early 1990s, but it's now listed on the National Register

LIVE AT RED ROCKS!

Red Rocks Amphitheatre (⌀720-865-2494; www.redrocksonline.com; 18300 W Alameda Pkwy, Morrison; ⊗5am-11pm; 🚻) is set between 400ft-high red sandstone rocks 15 miles southwest of Denver. Acoustics are so good many artists record live albums here. The 9000-seat theater offers stunning views and draws big-name bands all summer. To see your favorite singer go to work on the stage is to witness a performance in one of the most exceptional music venues in the world. For many, it's reason enough for a trip to Colorado.

of Historic Places. Bands such as Edward Sharpe & the Magnetic Zeros and Lady Gaga have played here.

Colorado Symphony Orchestra　CLASSICAL MUSIC
(CSO; Map p754; ⌀303-623-7876; www.colorado symphony.org; 1000 14th St, Boettcher Concert Hall; ⊗box office 10am-6pm Mon-Fri, from noon Sat; 🚻; 🚌9, 15, 28, 32, 38, 43, 44) The Boettcher Concert Hall in the Denver Performing Arts Complex (p759) is home to this renowned symphony orchestra. The orchestra performs an annual 21-week Masterworks season, as well as concerts aimed at a broader audience – think live performances of movie scores during the screening of films such as *La La Land* or *Harry Potter and the Prisoner of Azkaban*.

Bluebird Theater　LIVE MUSIC
(⌀303-377-1666; www.bluebirdtheater.net; 3317 E Colfax Ave; 🚻; 🚌15) This medium-sized theater is general admission standing room and has terrific sound and clear sight lines from the balcony. The venue often offers the last chance to catch bands – Denver faves the Lumineers and DeVotchKa both headlined here – on their way up to the big time.

Landmark Mayan Theatre　CINEMA
(⌀303-744-6799; www.landmarktheatres.com; 110 Broadway; 🚻; 🚌0) Even without the fancy sound system and enormous screen, this is the best place in Denver to take in a film. The 1930s movie palace is a romantic, historic gem and – bonus! – it serves beer.

🛍 Shopping

★ Tattered Cover Bookstore　BOOKS
(Map p754; ⌀303-436-1070; www.tatteredcover. com; 1628 16th St; ⊗6:30am-9pm Mon-Fri, 9am-9pm Sat, 10am-6pm Sun; 🖥🚻; 🚌10, 19, 28, 32, 44, MallRide) There are plenty of places to curl up with a book in Denver's beloved independent bookstore. Bursting with new and used books, it has a good stock of regional travel guides and nonfiction titles dedicated to the Western states and Western folklore. There's a second smaller location on Colfax near City Park.

REI　SPORTS & OUTDOORS
(Recreational Equipment Incorporated; Map p754; ⌀303-756-3100; www.rei.com; 1416 Platte St; ⊗9am-9pm Mon-Sat, to 7pm Sun; 🚻; 🚌10, 28, 32, 44) The flagship store of this outdoor-equipment super-supplier is an essential stop if you are heading to the mountains or just cruising through Confluence. In addition to top gear for camping, cycling, climbing and skiing, it has a rental department, maps and the Pinnacle, a 47ft-high indoor structure of simulated red sandstone for climbing and rappelling.

Fancy Tiger Crafts　ARTS & CRAFTS
(⌀303-733-3855; www.fancytigercrafts.com; 59 Broadway; ⊗10am-7pm Mon & Wed-Sat, to 9pm Tue, 11am-6pm Sun; 🚻; 🚌0) So you dig crochet and quilting? You knit a mean sweater and have a few too many tattoos? Welcome to Fancy Tiger Crafts, a sophisticated remodel of granny's yarn barn that's ground zero for Denver's crafty hipsters. There are classes in the back (including some by Jessica, 'mistress of patchwork') and a rad selection of fabric, yarn and books.

ⓘ Information

The Tourist Information Center website (www. denver.org) has great information about events.

Downtown Tourist Information Center (Map p754; ⌀303-892-1505; www.denver.org; 1575 California St; ⊗9am-6pm Mon-Fri, 9am-5pm Sat, 10am-2pm Sun May-Oct, 9am-5pm Mon-Fri, 9am-2pm Sat, 10am-2pm Sun Nov-Apr; 🚌9, 15, 20, MallRide, 🚇D, F, H) When you get to town, make for the largest and most central information center, located just off the 16th St Mall. You can load up on brochures, browse online travel pages and get solid information from knowledgeable staffers. A small gift shop sells high-quality souvenirs too.

ORIC (Outdoor Recreation Information Center; Map p754; ⌀REI main line 303-756-3100; www.

oriconline.org; 1416 Platte St; ⏰ hours vary; ☎; 📶 10, 28, 32, 44) Inside REI, this information desk is a must for those looking to get out of town for outdoor adventure. It has maps and expert information on trip planning and safety. The desk is staffed by volunteers, so hours vary wildly, but arriving on a weekend afternoon is a good bet.

Visit Denver Information Booth (Map p754; ☎ 303-317-0629; www.visitdenver.com; Union Station; ⏰ 9am-5:30pm Mon-Sat, 10am-2pm Sun; ☎ 📶; 🚆 A) This Union Station desk is regularly staffed with knowledgeable folks who can help you curate an afternoon or a week.

ⓘ Getting There & Away

AIR

Denver International Airport (DIA; ☎ 303-342-2000; www.flydenver.com; 8500 Peña Blvd; ⏰ 24hr; ☎ 📶; 🚆 A) is a major air hub and one of the country's busiest facilities. DIA has an automated subway that links the terminal to three concourses (Concourse C is almost 1 mile from the terminal).

DIA is 24 miles from downtown. Take the I-70 and exit 238 (Peña Blvd). From there, it's 12 miles to the main terminal. You'll see the Teflon-coated fiberglass roof that peaks out to mirror the mountains in the distance. A RTD Train (p761) will get you from the airport to Union Station as well.

BUS

Greyhound offers frequent buses on routes along the Front Range and on transcontinental routes. All buses stop at the **Denver Bus Center** (Map p754; ☎ 303-293-6555; 1055 19th St; ⏰ 6am-midnight; ☎; 📶 8, 48).

The **Epic Mountain Express** (☎ 800-525-6363; www.epicmountainexpress.com; 8500 Peña Blvd, Denver International Airport; ☎ 📶; 🚆 A) has shuttle services from Denver International Airport (DIA), downtown Denver or Morrison to Summit County, including Breckenridge and Keystone (adult/child $66/35, 2½ hours) and Vail (adult/child $84/44, three hours).

The **Colorado Springs Shuttle** (☎ 877-587-3456; www.coloradoshuttle.com; 8500 Peña Blvd, Denver International Airport; ☎ 📶; 🚆 A) offers trips from DIA to Colorado Springs (adult/child $50/25, two hours).

Regional Transportation District (RTD; Map p754; ☎ 303-299-6000; 1600 Blake St; 📶 10, 19, 28, 32, 44, MallRide) buses to Boulder (Rte FF1, $4.50) carry bicycles in the cargo compartment and offer frequent service from Union Station (p761). To reach Golden, take the 16L bus ($4.50) that stops at the corner of Colfax and Broadway.

TRAIN

Amtrak's (☎ 800-872-7245; www.amtrak.com) *California Zephyr* train runs daily between Chicago ($121 to $325, 19 hours) and San Francisco ($144 to $446, 33 hours) stopping in Denver's gorgeous **Union Station** (Map p754; ☎ 303-592-6712; www.unionstationindenver.com; 1701 Wynkoop St; 🅿; 📶 55L, 72L,120L, FF2, 🚆 A, B, C, E, W).

ⓘ Getting Around

TO/FROM THE AIRPORT

A complete Ground Transportation Center is centrally located on the 5th level of DIA's terminal, near the baggage claim. All transportation companies have their booths here and passengers can catch vans, shuttles and taxis outside the doors.

Complimentary hotel shuttles represent the cheapest means of getting to or from the airport. Courtesy phones for hotel shuttles are available in the Ground Transportation Center.

An RTD (p761) light-rail (Line A; $10.50, 45 minutes) transports people from DIA to downtown Denver, servicing Denver suburbs along the way.

Taxi service to downtown Denver costs around $60, excluding tip. Lyft and Uber are both popular.

There are a number of airport shuttle vans, such as **SuperShuttle** (☎ 800-258-3826; www.supershuttle.com; ⏰ 24hr; 🚆 A) and limousine services. Airport shuttles to the Front Range and mountain/ski areas are also not hard to come by.

BICYCLE

Denver has lots of bike lanes on the city streets and an excellent network of trails to get out of town. These include routes along the Platte River Pkwy, the Cherry Creek Bike Path and a network that heads all the way out to Golden (about a two-hour ride). You can get all the information you need from a pair of excellent websites: Bike Denver (www.bikedenver.org) and City of Denver (www.denvergov.org), both of which have downloadable bike maps for the city. Lyft and Jump both have bike shares here that are accessible with the app.

B-Cycle (☎ 303-825-3325; www.denverbcycle.com; 1-day membership $9; ⏰ 5am-midnight; 📶) is a bike-share company with more than 80 stations throughout Denver. The daily rate includes unlimited rides as long as they're under 30 minutes.

PUBLIC TRANSPORTATION

Regional Transportation District provides public transportation throughout the Denver and Boulder area (local/regional fares $3/5.25). The website has schedules, routes, fares and a trip planner.

ROCKY MOUNTAINS DENVER

TAXI

Two major taxi companies offer door-to-door service in Denver. Ridesharing services are huge.

Metro Taxi (☎303-333-3333; www.metrotaxi denver.com; ⊙24hr)

Yellow Cab (☎303-777-7777; www.denveryel lowcab.com; ⊙24hr)

Boulder

Boulder comes with plenty of stereotypes. It's a hippie town. It's a yuppie town. It's pretentious. It's the most beautiful place on earth. Like many preconceived notions, many of these have at least a grain of truth. But the real Boulder, the one behind the layers of perception, is simply a wonderful place to be.

At the center of it all is the University of Colorado campus with its manicured quads and towering stone buildings. The college-town atmosphere also means Boulder has plenty of arts, culture, live music, hippie drum circles, and sharp-nosed intellectual debates.

Beyond the campus, the town is a lovely grouping of small retail enclaves, like the pedestrian Pearl Street Mall, walking paths, parks and Victorian houses dating back 100 years.

On the edge of town you have one of the best open-space park systems in the US, with amazing outdoor adventures right at your door.

⊙ Sights & Activities

★**Chautauqua Park** PARK

(☎303-442-3282; www.chautauqua.com; 900 Baseline Rd; ☐HOP 2) This historic landmark park is the gateway to Boulder's most magnificent slab of open space adjoining the iconic Flatirons; its wide, lush lawn attracts picnicking families, sunbathers, Frisbee folk and students from nearby CU. It also gets lots of hikers, climbers and trail runners. It's a popular site so parking can be a hassle. During the summer the city of Boulder runs a free shuttle on the weekends from downtown and satellite parking lots (http://parktopark.org).

Dairy Arts Center ARTS CENTER

(☎303-440-7826; www.thedairy.org; 2590 Walnut St; prices vary; ℗⊕; ☐HOP) A historic milk-processing factory turned arts center, the Dairy is one of Boulder's top cultural hubs. It's a state-of-the-art facility with three stages, four gallery spaces and a 60-seat cinema. There's always something going on – from lectures and plays to modern dance and art exhibits. There's a small cafe and bar on-site, too.

★**Boulder Creek** WATER SPORTS

(⊕) An all-time favorite Boulder summer ritual is to tube down Boulder Creek. Most people put in at **Eben G Fine Park** (Boulder Canyon Dr; ℗⊕⊕; ☐205, N) and float as far as 30th St, or even 55th St. Be sure to check the water volume, especially early in the season; anything over 200 cu ft per second can be a real rodeo.

Eldorado Canyon State Park OUTDOORS

(☎303-494-3943; https://cpw.state.co.us/places-togo/parks/EldoradoCanyon; 9 Kneale Rd, Eldorado Springs; $9; ⊙dawn-dusk, visitor center 9am-5pm) Among the country's best rock-climbing areas, Eldorado has class 5.5 to 5.14 climbs focusing mostly on traditional crack climbing. Suitable for all visitors, a dozen miles of hiking trails also link up to Chautauqua Park. A public pool offers chilly swims in the canyon's famous spring water. Located 5 miles southwest of town.

Local Table Tours FOOD & DRINK

(☎303-909-5747; www.localtabletours.com; tours $49-79; ⊙hours vary; ⊛) ∅ Go behind the scenes with one of these fun downtown walking tours presenting a smattering of great local cuisine and inside knowledge on food and wine. There are specialty tours for brews, cocktails, coffee and chocolate. The tours also highlight locally owned businesses with regional or sustainable food sources.

★★ Festivals & Events

Bolder Boulder SPORTS

(☎303-444-7223; www.bolderboulder.com; adult/child from $73/58; ⊙Memorial Day; ⊕; ☐209, STAMPEDE) With more than 50,000 runners and pros mingling with costumed racers, live bands and sideline merrymakers, this may be the most fun 10km run in the US. To make it even better, it ends at Folsom Field, CU's football stadium.

Boulder Creek Festival MUSIC, FOOD

(☎303-777-6887; www.bouldercreekfest.com; Canyon Blvd, Central Park; ⊙May; ⊕; ☐203, 204, 225, AB, B, DASH, DD, DM, GS, SKIP) FREE Billed as the kick-off to summer and capped with the Bolder Boulder (p762), this summer festival is massive. At least 10 event areas feature more than 30 live entertainers and 500 vendors, plus a whole carnival ride zone. There's food and drink, entertainment and sunshine. What's not to love?

🛏 Sleeping

★Chautauqua
Lodge & Cottages   HISTORIC HOTEL $$
(☑303-952-1611; www.chautauqua.com; 900 Baseline Rd; r from $129, cottages from $200; P🐾❄🛜🏊; 🚌HOP 2) Adjoining beautiful hiking trails to the Flatirons and in a leafy neighborhood inside Chautauqua Park, this is our top Boulder pick. It has contemporary rooms and one- to three-bedroom cottages with porches and patchwork-quilt beds. It's perfect for families and pets. All have full kitchens, though the wraparound porch of the Chautauqua Dining Hall is a local favorite for breakfast.

Boulder Adventure Lodge   HOTEL $
(A-Lodge; ☑303-444-0882; www.a-lodge.com; 91 Fourmile Canyon Dr; campsite/dm/r $45/65/189; P🐾❄🛜🏊; 🚌N) You've come to Boulder to get outdoors, so why not stay nearer the action? Located a short distance from town, the A-Lodge has hiking, biking, climbing and fishing right from the property. Rooms are simple but well appointed, ranging from dorms to suites. There's a pool and firepit, generating a warm esprit de corps among guests and staff alike.

Briar Rose B&B   B&B $$
(☑303-442-3007; www.briarrosebb.com; 2151 Arapahoe Ave; r from $184; ❄🛜; 🚌JUMP) 🌿 Gorgeous and comfy, this tranquil home is a stone's throw from Naropa University. A tall fence and landscaped garden insulate it from busy Arapahoe Ave. Inside there are cozy rooms with a Buddhist influence, reflecting the Zen monk practice of one of the owners. The organic vegetarian breakfast features a wide tea selection and there's one loaner bike.

★St Julien Hotel & Spa   HOTEL $$$
(☑720-406-9696, reservations 877-303-0900; www.stjulien.com; 900 Walnut St; r/ste from $400/495; P❄@❄🏊; 🚌205, HOP, SKIP) In the heart of downtown, Boulder's finest four-star option is modern and refined, with photographs of local scenery and cork walls that warm the ambience. With fabulous views of the Flatirons, the back patio hosts live world music, jazz concerts and popular Latin dance parties. Rooms are spacious and plush. The on-site spa is considered one of the best around.

🍴 Eating

★Rayback Collective   FOOD TRUCK $
(☑303-214-2127; www.therayback.com; 2775 Valmont Rd; mains $6-12; ⏰11am-10pm Mon-Fri, to 11pm Sat, to 9pm Sun; 🍴🐾🏊; 🚌205, BOLT) A plumbing-supplies warehouse turned urban oasis, Rayback is a snapshot of Boulder. A place to feel community. A huge outdoor space with firepit and lawn games. A lounge with cozy chairs and live music. A bar serving up Colorado brews and kombucha. A food-truck park with loads of good eats. Young, old and even furry friends are welcome here.

Rincón Argentino   ARGENTINE $
(☑303-442-4133; www.rinconargentinoboulder.com; 2525 Arapahoe Ave; mains $4-13; ⏰11am-8pm Mon-Thu, to 9pm Fri & Sat; 🍴🐾; 🚌JUMP) Don't be turned off by the shopping plaza setting: Rincón packs a wallop of authentic Argentinean flavors. It bakes fresh empanadas – savory, small turnovers filled with spiced meat, or mozzarella and basil – which are perfect with a glass of Malbec. It also offers *milanesas* (breaded-beef-cutlet sandwiches); and gourds of yerba maté, a high-octane coffee alternative.

Oak at Fourteenth   MODERN AMERICAN $$
(☑303-444-3622; www.oakatfourteenth.com; 1400 Pearl St; mains $13-30; ⏰11:30am-10pm Mon-Sat, from 5:30pm Sun; 🚌205, 206) Zesty and innovative, locally owned Oak manufactures

ROCKY MOUNTAINS BOULDER

BOULDER COUNTY FARMERS MARKET

Boulder County Farmers Market (☑303-910-2236; www.boulderfarmers.org; 13th St, btwn Canyon Blvd & Arapahoe Ave; ⏰8am-2pm Sat Apr-Nov plus 4-8pm Wed May-Oct; 🍴🐾🏊; 🚌203, 204, 205, 206, 208, 225, DASH, JUMP, SKIP) is a massive spring and summer sprawl of colorful, mostly organic local food. Find flowers and herbs, as well as brain-sized mushrooms, delicate squash blossoms, crusty pretzels, vegan dips, grass-fed beef, raw granola and yogurt. Booths selling prepared food offer all sorts of international tasty treats. Live music is as standard as the family picnics in the park along Boulder Creek.

top-notch cocktails and tasty small plates for stylish diners. Standouts include the grilled bacon-wrapped pork tenderloin and cucumber sashimi drizzled with passion fruit. Portions at this farm-to-table eatery are minimal – when it's this scrumptious, you notice. Waiters advise well. The only downside: it tends to be noisy, so save your intimate confessions.

★ Brasserie Ten Ten
BISTRO $$

(☑ 303-998-1010; www.brasserietenten.com; 1011 Walnut St; mains $15-27; ☺ 11am-10pm Mon-Thu, 11am-11pm Fri, 9am-11pm Sat, 9am-9pm Sun; ☐ 203, 204, 225, AB, B) A go-to place for both students and professors, this sunny French bistro has a refined menu and an elegant atmosphere – think fresh flowers, marble high tops and polished brass. Sure, it's fancy, but not too uppity to offer killer happy-hour deals on crepes, sliders, mussels and beer. Don't miss the truffle fries.

★ Salt
MODERN AMERICAN $$

(☑ 303-444-7258; www.saltthebistro.com; 1047 Pearl St; mains $15-30; ☺ 11am-9pm Mon-Thu, 11am-11pm Fri & Sat, 10am-9pm Sun; ☒; ☐ 208, HOP, SKIP) While farm-to-table is ubiquitous in Boulder, this is one spot that delivers and surpasses expectations. The handmade fettuccine with snap peas, radicchio and herb cream is a feverish delight. But Salt also knows meat: local and grass-fed, basted, braised and slow roasted to utter perfection. When in doubt, ask – the waiters really know their stuff.

★ Frasca
ITALIAN $$$

(☑ 303-442-6966; www.frascafoodandwine.com; 1738 Pearl St; mains $35, tasting menus $65-130; ☺ 5:30-9:30pm Mon-Thu, to 10:30pm Fri, 5-10:30pm Sat; ☒; ☐ HOP, 204) Deemed Boulder's finest by many (the wine service earned a James Beard award), Frasca has an impeccable kitchen and only the freshest farm-to-table ingredients. Rotating dishes range from earthy braised pork to housemade gnocchi and grilled quail served with leeks and wilted pea shoots. Reserve days, even weeks, in advance. Mondays offer 'bargain' $65 tasting menus with suggested wine pairings.

🍷 Drinking & Entertainment

★ Mountain Sun
BREWERY

(☑ 303-546-0886; www.mountainsunpub.com; 1535 Pearl St; ☺ 11am-1am; ☒; ☐ HOP, 205, 206) As Boulder as it gets, this is the town's favorite brewery. It cheerfully serves a smorgasbord of fine brews and packs in everyone from yuppies to hippies. Best of all is its community atmosphere. The pub grub, especially the burgers and chili, is delicious and it's fully family-ly-friendly, with board games and kids' meals.

Avery Brewing Company
BREWERY

(☑ 303-440-4324; www.averybrewing.com; 4910 Nautilus Ct; ☺ 11am-11pm Tue-Sun, from 3pm Mon; ☐ 205) For craft breweries, how big is too big? Avery pushes the limit, with its imposing two-story building, complete with gift shop selling hats and tees. But the 1st-floor patio and tap room are lively and fun, while upstairs has a quieter restaurant feel. One thing's for sure: the beer's outstanding, from Apricot Sour to a devilish Mephistopheles Stout.

Bitter Bar
COCKTAIL BAR

(☑ 303-442-3050; www.thebitterbar.com; 835 Walnut St; ☺ 5pm-midnight Mon-Thu, to 2am Fri & Sat; ☐ HOP) A chic Boulder bar where killer cocktails – such as the lavender-infused Kiss the Sky or the elderflower tonic Guns n' Roses – make the evening slip happily out of focus. Happy hours that run till 8pm don't hurt either. The patio is great for conversation.

Boulder Dushanbe Teahouse
TEAHOUSE

(☑ 303-442-4993; www.boulderteahouse.com; 1770 13th St; mains $8-24; ☺ 8am-9pm; ☒; ☐ 203, 204, 205, 206, 208, 225, DASH, JUMP, SKIP) It's impossible to find better ambience than at this incredible Tajik teahouse, a gift from Dushanbe, Boulder's sister city. The elaborate carvings and paintings were reassembled over an eight-year period on the edge of **Central Park** (Canyon Blvd; ☐☒; ☐ 206, JUMP).

eTown Hall
LIVE MUSIC

(☑ 303-443-8696; www.etown.org; 1535 Spruce St; from $25; ☺ hours vary; ☐ HOP) Beautiful, brand-new and solar-powered, this repurposed church is the home of the eTown radio show (heard on National Public Radio). The show features rising and well-known artists and you can get in on it by attending a live taping in its 200-seat theater. Tapings run for two hours starting at 7pm, and are typically held on weeknights.

🛍 Shopping

★ Pearl Street Mall
AREA

(www.boulderdowntown.com; Pearl St, btwn 9th & 15th Sts; ☒☎; ☐ 205, 206, 208, HOP, SKIP) The highlight of downtown Boulder is the Pearl

Street Mall, a vibrant pedestrian zone filled with kids' climbing boulders and splash fountains, bars, galleries and restaurants. Street performers often come out in force on weekends, and there are featured concerts and events throughout the year (especially in the summer months).

★ **Boulder Book Store** BOOKS
(☑ 303-447-2074; www.boulderbookstore.net; 1107 Pearl St; ☉ 10am-10pm Mon-Sat, to 9pm Sun; 🛜🍴; 🚌 208, HOP, SKIP) Boulder's favorite indie bookstore has a huge travel section downstairs, along with all the hottest new fiction and nonfiction. Check the visiting-authors lineup posted at the entry and on its website, or simply grab a corner to read for a while.

★ **Common Threads** CLOTHING
(☑ 303-449-5431; www.shopcommonthreads.com; 2707 Spruce St; ☉ 10am-6pm Mon, Tue & Thu-Sat, to 7pm Wed; 🚌 205, BOLT, HOP) Vintage shopping at its most haute couture: this fun place is where to go for secondhand Choos and Prada purses. Prices are higher than at your run-of-the-mill vintage shop, but clothes, shoes and bags are always in good condition, and the designer clothing is guaranteed authentic. Offers fun classes on altering and creating clothes.

❶ Information

Boulder Ranger District (☑ 303-541-2500; www.fs.usda.gov; 2140 Yarmouth Ave; ☉ 8:30am-4:30pm Mon-Fri; 🚌 204) This US Forest Service outpost provides information on the national forests that surround the Rocky Mountain National Park, including campgrounds and trails that cross between the two.

Boulder Visitor Center (☑ 303-442-2911; www.bouldercoloradousa.com; 2440 Pearl St; ☉ 8:30am-5pm Mon-Fri; 🚌 HOP) Set in the Boulder Chamber of Commerce, this visitor center offers basic information, maps and tips on nearby hiking trails and other activities. There's a more accessible **tourist information kiosk** (☑ 303-417-1365; cnr Pearl & 13th Sts; ☉ 10am-8pm; 🚌 208, HOP, SKIP) on the Pearl Street Mall in front of the courthouse.

Downtown Boulder (www.boulderdowntown.com) This alliance of downtown businesses offers comprehensive dining and event listings in the downtown area, including the Pearl Street Mall.

Get Boulder (www.getboulder.com) A local print and online magazine with helpful information on things to do in Boulder.

❶ Getting There & Around

AIR

Denver International Airport (p761) Located just 45 miles from Boulder, this is the main entry point for travelers arriving by air.

Green Ride (☑ 303-997-0238; www.greenride-boulder.com; 4800 Baseline Rd, D110; one way $30-40) Serving Boulder and its satellite suburbs, this Denver International Airport shuttle is cheap and convenient, working on an hourly schedule (3:25am to 11:25pm). The cheapest service leaves from the depot. Additional travelers in groups are discounted.

SuperShuttle (☑ 303-444-0808; www.supershuttle.com; one way from $84) This shuttle provides a private van service to the airport. The base fare includes up to three people. Unless you have loads of luggage, parties of four or more are better served by a taxi.

BICYCLE

Owning a bicycle is almost a Boulder prerequisite. Most streets have dedicated bike lanes and the Boulder Creek Bike Path is a must-ride commuter corridor. There are plenty of places to get your hands on a rental.

Boulder B-Cycle (☑ 303-532-4412; https://boulder.bcycle.com; 24hr rental $8; ☉ office 9am-5pm Mon-Fri, 10am-3pm Sat) With rental cruisers stationed all over the city, this is a popular citywide program of hourly or daily bike rentals, but riders must sign up online first.

Full Cycle (☑ 303-440-7771; www.full-cyclebikes.com; 1211 13th St; daily rental $25-95; ☉ 10am-7pm Mon-Fri, to 6pm Sat, to 5pm Sun; 🍴; 🚌 203, 204, 225, AB, B, DASH, DD, GS, SKIP) This terrific bike shop rents cruisers on the cheap, and higher-end road and full-suspension mountain bikes. Ask staff about the best cycling routes (from easy Boulder Creek Trail to the searing pain of the 4-mile ride up Flagstaff). There's another branch on E Pearl.

University Bicycles (☑ 303-444-4196; www.ubikes.com; 839 Pearl St; per day rental from $25; ☉ 10am-7pm Mon-Fri, to 6pm Sat, to 5pm Sun; 🍴; 🚌 HOP) There are plenty of rental shops in this town, but this cavernous place has the widest range of rides and the most helpful staff.

CAR & MOTORCYCLE

RTD buses (p761) travel to Denver, Denver International Airport, Nederland and within Boulder. Dedicated bike lanes and paths make the city ideal for two-wheel traffic, and the downtown area is pleasantly walkable.

Northern Mountains

With one foot on either side of the continental divide and behemoths of granite in every direction, Colorado's Northern Mountains offer out-of-this-world alpine adventures, laid-back skiing, kick-butt hiking and biking, and plenty of rivers to raft, fish and float.

Rocky Mountain National Park

The crown jewel of Colorado's national parks, **Rocky Mountain National Park** (www.nps. gov/romo; vehicle 1/7 days $25/35, motorcycle $25/30, foot & bicycle $15/20, annual passes $80) encompasses some 415 sq miles of granite mountain top, alpine lake, wildflower-filled meadow, hiking trails, star-filled nights and adventures large and small for everyone in your group.

Like many national parks, it can be a zoo in the height of the summer season. But leave the main trails behind and you will find beautiful quiet and solitude in the area that protects moose, elk, bighorn sheep, black bear and more. Climbers will be challenged on the area's high peaks, while families and sightseers will love driving over the rooftop of the Rockies on Trail Ridge Road, taking part in ranger-led activities and taking on short forays into the glorious wilderness.

Winter in the park is different. Expect stillness and a landscape blanketed in sweet snow.

⊙ Sights & Activities

With more than 300 miles of trails, traversing all aspects of its diverse terrain, the park is suited to every hiking ability. Those with kids in tow might consider the easy hikes in the **Wild Basin** to Calypso Falls, or to Gem Lake in the **Lumpy Ridge** area, while those with unlimited ambition, strong legs and enough trail mix will be lured by the challenge of summiting **Longs Peak**. Regardless, it's best to spend at least one night at 7000ft to 8000ft prior to setting out to allow your body to adjust to the elevation. Before July many trails are snowbound and high water runoff makes passage difficult. In winter avalanches are a hazard, and you should only enter if you know what you are doing and are well equipped. Dogs and other pets are not allowed on the trails. All overnight stays in the backcountry require **permits**

(🕿 970-586-1242; www.nps.gov/romo; 1000 W Hwy 36, Estes Park, CO 80517).

The golden rule in Colorado mountaineering: if you haven't made the summit by noon, return (no matter how close you are). It's the best way to avoid getting hit by lightning.

⭐**Moraine Park Discovery Center** MUSEUM (🕿 970-586-1206; Bear Lake Rd; ⊙ 9am-4:30pm Jun-Oct; 🅿) 🆓 Built by the Civilian Conservation Corps in 1923 and once the park's proud visitors lodge, this building has been renovated in recent years to host exhibits on geology, glaciers and wildlife. Kids will like the interactive exhibits and half-mile nature trail out the door.

🛏 Sleeping

Glacier Basin Campground CAMPGROUND $ (🕿 877-444-6777; www.recreation.gov; off Bear Lake Rd; RV & tent sites summer $26) This developed campground is surrounded by evergreens, offering plenty of sun and shade. It also sports a large area for group camping and accommodates RVs – though there are no electric hookups. It is served by the shuttle buses on Bear Lake Rd throughout the summer. Make reservations through the website.

Aspenglen Campground CAMPGROUND $ (🕿 877-444-6777; www.recreation.gov; State Hwy 34; tent & RV sites $26; ⊙ summer only) With only 54 sites, this is the smallest of the park's reservable camping grounds. There are many tent-only sites, including some walkins; a limited number of trailers are allowed. This is the quietest campground in the park while still being highly accessible (5 miles west of Estes Park on US 34). Make reservations through the website.

Moraine Park Campground CAMPGROUND $ (🕿 877-444-6777; www.recreation.gov; off Bear Lake Rd; tent & RV sites summer $26, winter $18) In the middle of a stand of ponderosa pine forest off Bear Lake Rd, this is the biggest of the park's campgrounds, approximately 2.5 miles south of the Beaver Meadows Visitor Center (p767) and with 244 sites. The walkin, tent-only sites in the D Loop are recommended if you want some quiet. Make reservations through the website.

Olive Ridge Campground CAMPGROUND $ (🕿 303-541-2500; www.recreation.gov; State Hwy 7; tent/RV site $15.75/31.50; ⊙ mid-May–Nov) This well-kept USFS campground has access to four trailheads: St Vrain Mountain,

Wild Basin, Longs Peak and Twin Sisters. In the summer it can get full, though sites are mostly first-come, first-served.

ℹ Information

For private vehicles, the park entrance fee is $25 for one day and $35 for seven. Annual passes are $70. Individuals entering the park on foot, bicycle or bus pay $15 each for one day and $20 for seven. Motorcycles pay $25 for one day and $30 for seven.

Backcounty permits ($30 for a group of up to seven people for seven days) are required for overnight stays in the 260 designated backcountry camping sites in the park. A bear box to store your food in is required if you are staying overnight in the backcountry between May and October (established campsites already have them).

Alpine Visitor Center (www.nps.gov/romo; Fall River Pass; ⊙10:30am-4:30pm late May–mid-Jun & early Sep–mid-Oct, 9am-5pm late Jun-early Sep; 🚻)

Beaver Meadows Visitor Center (☑970-586-1206; www.nps.gov/romo; US Hwy 36; ⊙8am-9pm late Jun-late Aug, to 4:30pm or 5pm rest of the year; 🚻)

Kawuneeche Visitor Center (☑970-627-3471; 16018 US Hwy 34; ⊙8am-6pm last week May–Labor Day, to 5pm Labor Day–Sep, to 4:30pm Oct-May; 🚻)

ℹ Getting There & Away

Trail Ridge Rd (US 34) is the only east–west route through the park; the US 34 eastern approach from I-25 and Loveland follows the Big Thompson River Canyon. The most direct route from Boulder follows US 36 through Lyons to the east entrances. Another approach from the south, mountainous Hwy 7, passes by **Enos Mills Cabin** (☑970-586-4706; www.enosmills.com; 6760 Hwy 7; adult/child $20/10; ⊙11am-4pm Tue & Wed summer, by appointment only; 🚻) and provides access to campsites and trailheads on the east side of the divide. Winter closure of US 34 through the park makes access to the park's west side dependent on US 40 at Granby.

There are two entrance stations on the east side: **Fall River** (US 34) and **Beaver Meadows** (US 36). The **Grand Lake Entrance Station** (US 34) is the only entry on the west side. Year-round access is available through Kawuneeche Valley along the Colorado River headwaters to **Timber Creek Campground** (Trail Ridge Rd, US Hwy 34; tent & RV sites $26). The main centers of visitor activity on the park's east side are the Alpine Visitor Center (p767), high on Trail Ridge Rd, and Bear Lake Rd, which leads to campgrounds, trailheads and the Moraine Park Museum (p766).

North of Estes Park, Devils Gulch Rd leads to several hiking trails. Further out on Devils Gulch Rd, you pass through the village of Glen Haven to reach the trailhead entry to the park along the North Fork of the Big Thompson River.

ℹ Getting Around

The majority of visitors enter the park in their own cars, using the long and winding Trail Ridge Rd (US 34) to cross the Continental Divide. There are options for those without wheels, however. In summer a free shuttle bus operates from the **Estes Park Visitor Center** (☑970-577-9900; www.visitestespark.com; 500 Big Thompson Ave; ⊙9am-8pm Jun-Aug, 8am-5pm Mon-Fri, 9am-5pm Sat, 10am-4pm Sun Sep-May) multiple times daily, bringing hikers to a park-and-ride location where you can pick up other shuttles. The year-round option leaves the Glacier Basin parking area and heads to Bear Lake, in the park's lower elevations. During the summer peak, a second shuttle operates between Moraine Park campground and the Glacier Basin parking area. The second shuttle runs on weekends only from mid-August through September.

Taking public transit or bikes is without a doubt the best way to get into the overcrowded park.

Estes Park

Estes Park is just seconds from one of the US's most popular national parks. The town itself is a hodgepodge of T-shirt shops and ice-cream parlors, sidewalks crowded with tourists and streets jammed with RVs. But when the sun reflects just right off Lake Estes, or you spend an afternoon with a lazy coffee on the riverwalk, you might just find a little piece of zen.

🏃 Activities

★**Colorado Mountain School**   CLIMBING
(☑720-387-8944; https://coloradomountain school.com; 341 Moraine Ave; half-day guided climbs per person from $300) Simply put, there's no better resource for climbers in Colorado – this outfit is the largest climbing operator in the region, has the most expert guides and is the only organization allowed to operate within Rocky Mountain National Park. It has a clutch of classes taught by world-class instructors.

🛏 Sleeping

Estes Park KOA   CAMPGROUND **$**
(☑800-562-1887, 970-586-2888; www.estespark koa.com; 2051 Big Thompson Ave; tent sites $52-58, RV sites $52-85, cabins from $87; 🛜) With so

much excellent camping just up the road in Rocky Mountain National Park, it's hard to see the allure of this roadside RV-oriented camping spot. But for those in need of a staging day before a big adventure, the proximity to town is appealing.

★ YMCA of the Rockies – Estes Park Center
RESORT $$

(☑888-613-9622; www.ymcarockies.org; 2515 Tunnel Rd; r from $145, cabins from $160; P ⊜ ✳ 🛇 🛈) Estes Park Center is not your typical YMCA boarding house. Instead it's a favorite vacation spot with families, boasting upmarket motel-style accommodations and cabins set on hundreds of acres of high alpine terrain. Choose from roomy cabins that sleep up to 10 or motel-style rooms for singles or doubles. Both are simple and practical.

Stanley Hotel
HOTEL $$

(☑970-577-4000; www.stanleyhotel.com; 333 Wonderview Ave; r from $150; P 🛇 ✳ 🛈) The white Georgian Colonial Revival hotel stands in brilliant contrast to the towering peaks of Rocky Mountain National Park that frame the skyline. A favorite local retreat, this best-in-class hotel served as the inspiration for Stephen King's cult novel *The Shining*. Rooms are decorated to retain some of the Old West feel while still ensuring all the creature comforts.

Black Canyon
LODGE $$

(☑800-897-3730; www.blackcanyoninn.com; 800 MacGregor Ave; 1-/2-/3-bed r from $150/200/400; P ⊜ ✳ 🛈) A fine place to splurge, this lovely, secluded 14-acre property offers luxury suites and a 'rustic' log cabin (which comes with a Jacuzzi). The rooms are dressed out with stone fireplaces, dark wood and woven tapestries in rich dark colors, just like you imagined.

✕ Eating

Ed's Cantina & Grill
MEXICAN $

(☑970-586-2919; www.edscantina.com; 390 E Elkhorn Ave; mains $9-12; ⊙11am-late Mon-Fri, 8am-10pm Sat & Sun; 🛈) With an outdoor patio right on the river, Ed's is a great place to kick back with a margarita. Serving Mexican and American staples, the restaurant is in a retro woodsy space with leather booth seating and bold primary colors.

Smokin' Dave's BBQ & Tap House
BARBECUE $$

(☑866-674-2793; www.smokindavesbbq.com; 820 Moraine Ave; mains $8-20; ⊙11am-9pm Sun-Thu, to

10pm Fri & Sat; 🛈) Half-assed BBQ joints are all too common in Colorado's mountain towns, but Dave's fully delivers. The buffalo ribs and pulled pork come dressed in a slightly sweet, smoky, tangy sauce and the sweet-potato fries are crisply fried. Also excellent? The long, well-selected beer list. Check out its other location at the Golf Course.

🛈 Getting There & Away

The **Estes Park Shuttle** (☑970-586-5151; www.estesparkshuttle.com; one way/return $45/85) connects Denver's airport to Estes Park about four times a day. The trip takes two hours.

Steamboat Springs

Steamboat is Colorado magic. The area delivers big on adventures, family fun and some of the best champagne-powder skiing in the world, and yet the people here are delightfully direct and unassuming.

On the edge of Colorado's Western Slope, Steamboat got its roots a hundred years ago as a railway hub, and in the well-preserved Old Town area you'll have the chance to mix with real-life cowboys, dirt-bag ski bums and millionaires as you cruise past tony bistros and historic bars, and take summer walks along the Yampa River.

🏃 Activities

Steamboat Mountain Resort
SNOW SPORTS

(☑ticket office 970-871-5252; www.steamboat.com; 2305 Mt Werner Circle; lift ticket adult/child $175/110; ⊙ticket office 8am-5pm) The stats of the Steamboat Ski Area speak volumes for the town's claim as 'Ski Town, USA' – 165 trails, 3668ft vertical and nearly 3000 acres. With excellent powder, super-fun tree runs and trails for all levels, this is the main draw for winter visitors and one of the best family skiing resorts in all of the US.

★ Strawberry Park Hot Springs
HOT SPRINGS

(☑970-879-0342; www.strawberryhotsprings.com; 44200 County Rd; per day adult/child $15/8; ⊙10am-10:30pm Sun-Thu, to midnight Fri & Sat; 🛈) ✎ Steamboat's favorite hot springs are actually outside the city limits. Offering great back-to-basics relaxation, the natural pools sit lovingly beside a river. After dark it is adults only and clothing optional (though most people wear swimsuits these days); you'll want a headlamp if you are visiting at this time. On weekends, expect a 15- to 45-minute wait to park.

Orange Peel Bikes
CYCLING

(☑970-879-2957; www.orangepeelbikes.com; 1136 Yampa St; bike rental per day $45-75; ⊙10am-6pm Mon-Fri, to 5pm Sat; ☑) In a cone-shaped building at the end of Yampa (the building looks like a Martian outpost), this is perfectly situated for renting a bike to ride the trails crisscrossing Howelsen Hill. A staff of serious riders and mechanics can offer tons of information about local trails, including maps. This is the coolest bike shop in town, hands down.

Bucking Rainbow Outfitters
RAFTING

(☑970-879-8747; www.buckingrainbow.com; 730 Lincoln Ave; inner tubes $20, rafting $50-100, fishing $150-500) This excellent outfitter has fly-fishing, rafting, outdoor apparel and the area's best fly shop, but it's most renowned for its rafting trips on the Yampa and beyond. Rafting trips run from half-day to full-day excursions. Two-hour in-town fly-fishing trips start at $155 per person. It has a tube shack that runs shuttles (included with rental) from Sunpies Bistro on Yampa St. It's a wonderful way to spend an afternoon.

Old Town Hot Springs
HOT SPRINGS

(☑970-879-1828; www.oldtownhotsprings.org; 136 Lincoln Ave; adult/child $18/12, waterslide $2-7; ⊙5:30am-10pm Mon-Fri, 7am-9pm Sat, 8am-9pm Sun; ☑) Smack dab in the center of town, the water here is warmer than most other springs in the area. Known by the Utes as the 'medicine springs,' the mineral waters here are said to have special healing powers. Because there's a 230ft waterslide, a climbing wall and plenty of shallow areas, this is your best family-friendly hot springs in town.

🛏 Sleeping & Eating

★ Vista Verde Guest Ranch
RANCH $$$

(☑800-526-7433; www.vistaverde.com; 31100 Seedhouse Rd; per week per person summer/winter from $5125/3195; ❄🐾) This is the most luxurious of Colorado's top-end guest ranches. Here you spend the day riding with expert staff, the evening around the fire in an elegantly appointed lodge, and the night in between high-thread-count sheets. If you have the means, this is it.

Rex's American Bar & Grill
AMERICAN $

(☑970-870-0438; www.rexsgrill.com; 3190 S Lincoln Ave; mains $11-15; ⊙7am-11pm; 🅿☑) Grass-fed steaks, elk sausage, bison burgers and other carnivorous delights are the ticket at this place, and they're so good that you'll have to forgive the restaurant's location – attached to the Holiday Inn. Rex's is also one of the most family-friendly spots in town and the latest dinner you'll find (serving until 11pm).

★ Laundry
AMERICAN $$

(☑970-870-0681; www.thelaundryrestaurant.com; 127 11th St; small plates $10-16, large plates $35-38; ⊙4:30pm-2am) This new-generation Steamboat eatery has some of the best food in town. You'll love creative takes on comfort food, charcuterie boards, big steaks, barbecue, creative presentations and pickled everything. Budget-busters will love sharing small plates – which all go a long way.

ℹ Information

Steamboat Springs Visitor Center (☑970-879-0880; www.steamboat-chamber.com; 125 Anglers Dr; ⊙8am-5pm Mon-Fri, 10am-3pm Sat) This visitor center, facing Sundance Plaza, has a wealth of local information. Its website is excellent for planning.

USFS Hahns Peak Ranger Office (☑970-879-1870; www.fs.usda.gov; 925 Weiss Dr; ⊙8am-5pm Mon-Sat) Rangers staff this office offering information about surrounding national forests, including Mount Zirkel Wilderness, plus hiking, mountain biking, fishing and other activities in the area. Permits are also available here.

ℹ Getting There & Away

Most people get into town by car from Denver via Rabbit Ears Pass on Hwy 40. Another option is **Yampa Valley Regional Airport** (YVRA; ☑970-276-5000; 11005 RCR 51A), with direct flights in winter from many US destinations. The airport is in Hayden, 22 miles west of Steamboat.

The **Go Alpine** (☑970-879-2800; www.goalpine.com; 1755 Lincoln Ave) taxi and shuttle service makes several daily runs between Steamboat and Denver International Airport (DIA; $93, four hours one way). It also makes trips to the Yampa Valley Regional Airport ($39 one way) and operates an in-town taxi.

Greyhound's US 40 service between Denver and Salt Lake City stops at the **Greyhound Terminal** (☑800-231-2222; www.greyhound.com; 1505 Lincoln Ave), about half a mile west of town. One-way tickets to Denver run from $35 to $43 (four hours).

The **Storm Mountain Express** (☑877-844-8787; www.stormmountainexpress.com) shuttle service runs to Yampa Valley Regional Airport ($39 one way) and beyond, though trips to DIA and Vail get very pricey.

Central Colorado

At the center of Colorado in the dizzying heights of the Rocky Mountains, you will find a million and one attractions. Much of the adventure centers in iconic ski resorts such as Aspen, Vail and Breckenridge. By summer, these are also great spots for hiking, mountain biking and other adventures into the vast alpine wilderness found here.

In the less-known areas around South Park and Leadville, you can still find world-class rafting, mountain climbing and vistas that go on for miles. There are alpine lakes to be visited, wildlife to be seen, backroads to mining ghost towns to be explored, steam trains to be ridden and much more.

It's also a place of fun-loving irreverence, wild parties and plenty of mountain-town high jinx. Part of the journey is connecting with the sun-kissed, broad-smiled locals.

Winter Park

Located less than two hours from Denver, unpretentious Winter Park Resort is a favorite with Front Rangers, who drive here to ski fresh tracks each weekend. Beginners can frolic on miles of heavily trafficked groomers while experts test their skills on Mary Jane's world-class bumps. For skiers with disabilities, the resort also offers one of the best adaptive skiing programs in the US.

The congenial oh-so-slightly '70s town is a wonderful base for year-round romping. Most services are found either in the ski village, which is actually south of Winter Park proper, or strung along US 40 (the main drag), which is where you'll also find the visitor center. Follow Hwy 40 and you'll get to Fraser – essentially the same town – then Tabernash and eventually the back of Rocky Mountain National Park.

🏃 Activities

In addition to downhill and cross-country skiing, Winter Park has some 600 miles of mountain-biking trails for all levels. The paved 5.5-mile **Fraser River Trail** runs through the valley from the ski resort to Fraser, connecting to different trail systems. Pick up trail maps at the **visitor center** (📞970-726-4118; www.winterpark-info.com; 78841 Hwy 40; ⊗9am-5pm). You can even bike in winter – it's known as fatbiking.

🛏 Sleeping & Eating

There are two first-come, first-served USFS campgrounds off Hwy 40 on the way into Winter Park: **Robber's Roost** (Hwy 40; tent & RV sites $20; ⊗mid-Jun–Aug; 🐾), which has no water, 5 miles from town, and **Idlewild** (Hwy 40; tent & RV sites $20; ⊗late May-Sep; 🐾), 1 mile from town. There's also plenty of free dispersed camping in the surrounding national forest; try heading up **Rollins Pass** (USFS Rd 149; ⊗mid-Jun–mid-Nov). In town, condos reign supreme, but there are also a few hotels and lodging worth checking out.

⭐**Devil's Thumb Ranch**　　　　LODGE $$$
(📞970-726-7000;　www.devilsthumbranch.com; 3530 County Rd 83; lodge from $350, cabins from $450; ❄🛜🏊🐾) ⚓ The classiest digs in the Winter Park area, this high-altitude ranch is a fantastic base for year-round **activities** (trail passes $10, horseback riding $85-175, zipline $55-110; 🛝). Accommodations are plush, but not out of reach. The cowboy-chic lodge is a must for a romantic weekend escape. Cabins are a good bet for groups or for more privacy. Reserve well in advance.

⭐**Pepe Osaka's Fish Taco**　　　JAPANESE $
(📞970-726-7159;　https://pepeosakasfishtaco. com; 78707 US Hwy 40; 2 tacos $13-15; ⊗4-9pm daily, plus noon-3pm Sat & Sun) You like sushi. You like fish tacos. And as it turns out, you love sushi tacos, because...why not? At this almost-but-not-quite Nikkei eatery (that's Japanese-Peruvian cuisine if you haven't been keeping up), dig in to some outstandingly spicy tuna tacos, *ahi poke* ceviche tacos and blackened mahi-mahi tacos *al pastor*. All served with delish fried plantains and margaritas.

Breckenridge & Around

Breckenridge is unique to Summit County in that the town wasn't built as a ski resort. Rather, it was built from the sweat and dreams of miners more than a hundred years ago. The quaint historic center now houses T-shirt shops, high-end restaurants and converted Victorian inns.

👁 Sights & Activities

⭐**Barney Ford Museum**　　　　MUSEUM
(www.breckheritage.com; 111 E Washington Ave; suggested donation $5; ⊗11am-3pm Tue-Sun, hours vary seasonally) FREE Barney Ford was an escaped slave who became a prominent

entrepreneur and Colorado civil-rights pioneer, and made two stops in Breckenridge (where he ran a 24-hour chop stand serving delicacies such as oysters) over the course of his incredibly rich, tragic and triumphant life. He also owned a restaurant and hotel in Denver. The museum is set in his old home, where he lived from 1882 to 1890.

Breckenridge Ski Area SNOW SPORTS
(☑800-789-7669; www.breckenridge.com; lift ticket adult/child $189/123; ⊗8:30am-4pm Nov–mid-Apr; ♠) Breckenridge spans five mountains (Peaks 6 to 10), covering 2900 acres and featuring some of the best beginner and intermediate terrain in the state, as well as plenty of exhilarating high-alpine runs and hike-to bowls. There are also four terrain parks and a superpipe.

🛏 Sleeping

Bivvi Hostel HOSTEL $
(☑970-423-6553; www.thebivvi.com; 9511 Hwy 9; dm winter/summer from $85/29; 🅿🤶) A modern hostel with a log-cabin vibe, the Bivvi wins points for style, friendliness and affordability. The four- to six-person dorm rooms come with private lockers, en suites and complimentary breakfast; chill out in the funky common room or out on the gorgeous deck, equipped with a gas grill and hot tub. Private rooms are also available.

🍴 Eating & Drinking

★Breckenridge Distillery AMERICAN $$
(☑970-547-9759; www.breckenridgedistillery.com; 1925 Airport Rd; small plates $10-18; ⊗4-9pm Tue-Sat) Served in a big-city-cool dining space, the eclectic menu at this **distillery** (☑970-547-9759; www.breckenridgedistillery.com; 1925 Airport Rd; ⊗11am-9pm Tue-Sat, to 6pm Sun & Mon) follows the delightful whims of its high-caliber chefs, jumping from the sublime *cacio e pepe* (Roman spaghetti and cheese) to chicken-liver profiteroles or dates and mascarpone without missing a beat. It's mostly small plates, perfect for sharing over the top-notch cocktails.

Crown CAFE
(☑970-453-6022; www.thecrownbreckenridge.com; 215 S Main St; ⊗7:30am-8pm; 🤶) Breck's living room might as well be at the Crown, a buzzing cafe and social hub. Grab a mug of Silver Canyon coffee and a sandwich or salad, and catch up on all the latest town gossip.

CLIMBING YOUR FIRST FOURTEENER

Known as Colorado's easiest fourteener, **Quandary Peak** (www.14ers.com; County Rd 851) is the state's 15th-highest peak at 14,265ft. Though you'll see plenty of dogs and children, 'easiest' may be misleading – the summit remains 3 grueling miles from the trailhead. Go between June and September.

Broken Compass Brewing BREWERY
(☑970-368-2772; www.brokencompassbrewing.com; 68 Continental Ct; ⊗11:30am-11pm) Set in an industrial complex at the north end of Airport Road, the Broken Compass is generally regarded as the best brewery in Breckenridge. Fill up with a pint of their Coconut Porter or Chili Pepper Pale and sink back with a couple of friends in the old chairlift. They run a shuttle every two hours between the brewery and town.

ℹ Information

Visitor Center (☑877-864-0868; www.gobreck.com; 203 S Main St; ⊗9am-6pm; 🤶) Along with a host of maps and brochures, this center has a pleasant riverside museum that delves into Breck's gold-mining past.

ℹ Getting There & Away

Breckenridge is 80 miles west of Denver via I-70 exit 203, then Hwy 9 south.

Vail

Tucked beneath the Gore Range on I-70, Vail offers up just about everything you could ever ask for from a mountain resort. The village areas at the ski area base have cobblestone walkways and are designed to look and feel like a Tyrolean mountain town. The town has some of Colorado's best restaurants – and a gorgeous crowd of well-heeled spenders that light up the night when slopes close.

◉ Sights & Activities

The draw to Vail is no secret. It's the endless outdoor activities in both winter and summer that make this resort so attractive. Remember, though, that the mud season (mid-April through May, plus November) holds little attraction for visitors – you can't ski, nor can you really get up into the mountains to hike around.

★ Vail Mountain
SNOW SPORTS

(📞 970-754-8245; www.vail.com; lift ticket adult/child $189/130; ⏰ 9am-4pm Nov–mid-Apr; ♿) Vail Mountain is hands-down one of the best ski resorts in the world, with 5289 skiable acres, 195 trails, three terrain parks and, ahem, the highest lift-ticket prices on the continent. If you're a Colorado ski virgin, it's worth experiencing your first time here – especially on a bluebird fresh-powder day. Skiing more than three days? Consider the Epic Pass.

Vail to Breckenridge Bike Path
CYCLING

(www.summitbiking.org) This paved, car-free bike path stretches 8.7 miles from East Vail to the top of Vail Pass (elevation gain 1831ft), before descending 14 miles into Frisco (it's 9 miles more if you go all the way to Breckenridge). If you're only interested in the downhill, hop on a shuttle from Bike Valet (📞 970-476-7770; www.bikevalet.net; 616 W Lionshead Cir; bike rental per day from $51; ⏰ 9am-6pm; ♿) and enjoy the ride back to Vail.

🛏 Sleeping

Gore Creek Campground
CAMPGROUND $

(📞 877-444-6777; www.recreation.gov; Bighorn Rd; tent sites $22-24; ⏰ mid-May–Sep; ♿) This campground at the end of Bighorn Rd has 19 tent sites with picnic tables and fire grates nestled in the woods by Gore Creek. There is excellent fishing near here – try the Slate Creek or Deluge Lake trails; the latter leads to a fish-packed lake. The campground is 6 miles east of Vail Village via exit 180 (East Vail) off I-70.

★ Sebastian Hotel
HOTEL $$$

(📞 800-354-6908; www.thesebastianvail.com; 16 Vail Rd; r winter/summer from $800/300; 🅿❄🛜🏊) Deluxe and modern, this sophisticated hotel showcases tasteful contemporary art and an impressive list of amenities, including a mountainside ski valet, luxury spa and 'adventure concierge.' Room rates dip in the summer, the perfect time to enjoy the tapas bar and spectacular pool area, with hot tubs frothing and spilling over like champagne.

Austria Haus
HOTEL $$$

(📞 866-921-4050; www.austriahaushotel.com; 242 E Meadow Dr; r winter/summer from $500/290; 🅿❄🛜🏊) One of Vail's longest-running properties, the Austria Haus offers both hotel rooms and condos (more information at www.austriahausclub.com), so make sure you're clear on what you're signing up for. In the hotel, charming details such as wood-framed doorways, Berber carpet and marble baths make for a pleasant stay. Fuel up at the generous breakfast spread in the morning.

🍴 Eating & Drinking

★ Westside Cafe
DINER $

(📞 970-476-7890; www.westsidecafe.net; 2211 N Frontage Rd; mains $9-16; ⏰ 7am-3pm Mon-Wed, to 10pm Thu-Sun; 🛜♿) Set in a West Vail strip mall, the Westside is a local institution. It does terrific all-day-breakfast skillets – like the 'My Big Fat Greek Skillet' with scrambled eggs, gyro, red onion, tomato and feta served with warm pita – along with all the usual high-cal offerings you need before or after a day on the slopes.

★ Game Creek Restaurant
AMERICAN $$$

(📞 970-754-4275; www.gamecreekvail.com; Game Creek Bowl; 4-/5-course meal $115/135; ⏰ 5:30-9pm Tue-Sat Dec-Apr, 5:30-8:30pm Thu-Sat, 11am-2pm Sun late Jun-Aug; 🍴♿) This gourmet destination is nestled high in the spectacular Game Creek Bowl. Take the Eagle Bahn Gondola to Eagle's Nest and staff will shuttle you (via snowcat in winter) to their lodge-style restaurant, which serves an American-French menu starring wild boar, elk tenderloin and succulent leg of lamb. Reserve ahead.

Sweet Basil
AMERICAN $$$

(📞 970-476-0125; www.sweetbasilvail.com; 193 Gore Creek Dr; mains lunch $18-22, dinner $27-48; ⏰ 11:30am-2:30pm & 6pm-late) 🌿 In business since 1977, Sweet Basil remains one of Vail's top restaurants. The menu changes seasonally, but the eclectic American fare, which usually includes favorites such as Colorado lamb and seared Rocky Mountain trout, is consistently innovative and excellent. The ambience is also fantastic. Reservations are required – especially in high season.

❶ Information

Vail Visitor Center (📞 970-477-3522; www.vailgov.com; 241 S Frontage Rd; ⏰ 8:30am-5:30pm winter, to 8pm summer; 🛜) Provides maps, last-minute lodging deals and information on the town and activities. It's located next to the Transportation Center. The larger Lionshead welcome center is located at the entrance to the parking garage.

❶ Getting There & Around

The **Eagle County Regional Airport** (EGE; 📞 970-328-2680; www.flyvail.com; 217 Eldon Wilson Dr, Gypsum) is 35 miles west of Vail and has services to destinations across the country (many of which fly through Denver) and rental-car counters.

Aspen

Live the dream. Aspen is one of the world's most famous mountain destinations.

The town's four ski slopes offer up some of Colorado's best champagne powder turns, and there are excellent restaurants at nearly every corner of the historic downtown area. Top it off with an understated chic that permeates nearly everything you do, eat, see and experience here, and you have the makings of the best mountain vacation ever.

Aspen takes on new shades and personalities with the seasons. In fall, the hills are set afire with the quaking of a million golden Aspen leaves; in winter, the slopes come to life and the party hits maximum velocity; come springtime, the flowers start to bud near the mirrored alpine lakes; and finally, in summer – ah, summer in Aspen! – everything unites with music festivals, arts, miles upon miles of trails to explore and perfect days under the bluebird Colorado sky.

◉ Sights & Activities

Aspen Art Museum MUSEUM
(📞 970-925-8050; www.aspenartmuseum.org; 637 E Hyman Ave; ⊙ 10am-6pm Tue-Sun) **FREE** This art museum's striking building features a warm, lattice-like exterior designed by Pritzker Prize–winner Shigeru Ban and contains three floors of gallery space. There's no permanent collection, just edgy, innovative contemporary exhibitions featuring paintings, mixed media, sculpture, video installations and photography by artists such as Mamma Andersson, Mark Manders and Susan Philipsz. Art lovers will not leave disappointed. Head up to the roof for views and a bite to eat at the cool cafe.

★ **Aspen Center for Environmental Studies** OUTDOORS
(ACES; 📞 970-925-5756; www.aspennature.org; 100 Puppy Smith St, Hallam Lake; ⊙ 9am-5pm Mon-Fri; 📷) The Aspen Center for Environmental Studies manages the 25-acre Hallam Lake wildlife sanctuary that hugs the Roaring Fork River and miles of hiking trails in the Hunter Creek Valley. With a mission to advance environmental conservation, the center's naturalists provide free guided hikes and snowshoe tours, raptor demonstrations (eagles and owls are among the residents) and special programs for youngsters.

★ **Snowmass Ski Resort** SNOW SPORTS
(📞 800-525-6200; www.aspensnowmass.com; 4-mountain lift ticket adult/child $174-116; ⊙ 9am-4pm Dec–mid-Apr; 📷) OK, the top winter activity here is pretty much a given: the pursuit of powder, and lots of it. Snowmass is undoubtedly built for families. There's some pretty steep terrain here if you want to get rad, but the overall draw is plenty of options for beginners, intermediates and advanced skiers. The Snowmass Village area has restaurants and hotels.

Maroon Bells HIKING
If you have but one day to enjoy a slice of pristine wilderness, spend it in the shadow of Colorado's most iconic mountains: the pyramid-shaped twins of **North Maroon Peak** (14,014ft) and **South Maroon Peak** (14,156ft). Eleven miles southwest of Aspen, it all starts on the shores of **Maroon Lake**, an absolutely stunning spot backed by the towering, striated summits.

🛌 Sleeping

★ **Difficult Campground** CAMPGROUND $
(📞 877-444-6777; www.recreation.gov; Hwy 82; tent & RV sites $24-26; ⊙ mid-May–Sep; 📷) The largest campground in the Aspen area, Difficult is one of four sites at the foot of Independence Pass and the only one that takes reservations. Located 5 miles west of town, it also has the lowest altitude (8000ft). Higher up are three smaller campgrounds: Weller, Lincoln Gulch and Lost Man. Water is available, but no electrical hookups for RVs.

Annabelle Inn HOTEL $$
(📞 877-266-2466; www.annabelleinn.com; 232 W Main St; r winter/summer from $250/200; 🅿️ ❄️ @ 🛜) Personable and unpretentious, the cute and quirky Annabelle Inn resembles an old-school European-style ski lodge in a central location. Rooms are cozy without being too cute, and come with flat-screen TVs and warm duvets. After a long day of skiing or hiking, the hot tub and firepit await. The breakfast is fantastic.

Limelight Hotel HOTEL $$$
(📞 855-925-3025; www.limelighthotel.com; 355 S Monarch St; r winter/summer from $500/250; 🅿️ ❄️ 🛜 ♨️ 📷) Sleek and trendy, the Lime-

light's brick-and-glass modernism reflects Aspen's new school. Rooms are spacious, with stylish accoutrements: granite wash-basins, leather headboards and mountain views from the balconies and rooftop terraces. Additional perks include shuttles that run to all the slopes and a fab breakfast. This is life on top! A sister Limelight is found in Snowmass (p773) near the Gondola.

✗ Eating & Drinking

★ Pyramid Bistro   CAFE $$
(☑970-925-5338; www.pyramidbistro.com; 221 E Main St; mains lunch $12-18, dinner $19-29; ⊗11:30am-9:30pm; ✐) ✐ Set on the top floor of **Explore Booksellers** (☑970-925-5336; www.explorebooksellers.com; 221 E Main St; ⊗10am-9pm; 🛜), this gourmet veggie cafe serves up some delightful creations, including sweet-potato gnocchi with goat's cheese, red-lentil sliders and quinoa salad with avocado, goji berries and sesame vinaigrette. Definitely Aspen's top choice for health-conscious fare.

Matsuhisa   JAPANESE $$$
(☑970-544-6628; www.matsuhisarestaurants.com; 303 E Main St; mains $29-42, 2 pieces sushi $8-12; ⊗5:30pm-close) The original Colorado link in Matsuhisa Nobu's iconic global chain that now wraps around the world, this converted house is more intimate than its Vail sibling and still turns out spectacular dishes such as miso black cod, Chilean sea bass with truffle and flavorful uni (sea urchin) shooters.

Aspen Brewing Co   BREWERY
(☑970-920-2739; www.aspenbrewingcompany. com; 304 E Hopkins Ave; ⊗noon-late; 🛜) With five signature flavors and a sun-soaked balcony facing the mountain, this is definitely the place to unwind after a hard day's play. Brews range from the flavorful This Year's Blonde and high-altitude Independence Pass Ale (its IPA) to the mellower Conundrum Red Ale and the chocolatey Pyramid Peak Porter.

Woody Creek Tavern   PUB
(☑970-923-4585; www.woodycreektavern.com; 2 Woody Creek Plaza, 2858 Upper River Rd; ⊗11am-10pm) Enjoying a 100% agave tequila and fresh-lime margarita at the late, great gonzo journalist Hunter S Thompson's favorite watering hole is well worth the 8-mile drive – or **Rio Grande Trail** (www.riograndetrail.com; Puppy Smith St) bike ride – from Aspen. The walls at this rustic funky tavern, a local haunt since

1980, are plastered with newspaper clippings, photos of customers and paraphernalia.

ℹ Information

Aspen-Sopris Ranger District (☑970-925-3445; www.fs.usda.gov/whiteriver; 806 W Hallam St; ⊗8am-4:30pm Mon-Fri) The USFS Aspen-Sopris Ranger District operates and 20 campgrounds and covers Roaring Fork Valley and from Independence Pass to Glenwood Springs, including the Maroon Bells Wilderness. Come here for maps and hiking tips.

Aspen Visitor Center (☑970-925-1940; www.aspenchamber.org; 425 Rio Grande Pl; ⊗8:30am-5pm Mon-Fri) Located across from Rio Grande Park, this little visitor center can help you pick a hike, a restaurant or a far-out adventure.

Cooper Street Kiosk (cnr E Cooper Ave & S Galena St; ⊗10am-6pm) Maps, brochures and magazines.

ℹ Getting There & Around

Four miles northwest of Aspen on Hwy 82, the busy **Aspen-Pitkin County Airport** (ASE; ☑970-920-5380; www.aspenairport.com; 233 E Airport Rd; 🛜) has direct year-round flights from Denver, as well as seasonal flights direct to eight US cities, including Los Angeles and Chicago. Several car-rental agencies operate here. A free bus runs to/from the airport, departing every 10 to 15 minutes.

Roaring Fork Transportation Authority (RFTA; ☑970-925-8484; www.rfta.com; 430 E Durant Ave; ⊗6:15am-2:15am; 🛜) buses connect Aspen with the Highlands, Snowmass and Buttermilk via free shuttles, while the VelociR-FTA serves the down-valley towns of Basalt ($4, 25 minutes), Carbondale ($6, 45 minutes) and Glenwood Springs ($7, one hour).

Salida

Under Colorado's sun, life just seems a little better here. You really can't beat the good-time mountain vibes, chart-topping wilderness access and historic charms of Salida. The sprawling, immaculately preserved historic downtown center has top-notch antiques and crafts shopping.

This is also raft-country USA. With the Arkansas running straight through town, you can access everything from class II family runs to big-time class V waters. Salida sits in a valley below a massive mountain range, meaning there is also excellent hiking, mountain biking and skiing to be had. It's really up to you. Adventure awaits on every corner.

When the sun sets, come back to town to cozy up at one of the many microbrews and hatch your plans for the next day's adventure. Most people come here in the summers.

🏃 Activities

Both bikers and hikers should note that some big-time trails – the **Continental Divide** (www.continentaldividetrail.org), the **Colorado Trail** (www.coloradotrail.org) and the **Rainbow Trail** – are within spitting distance of town. If you don't want to sweat it, a **gondola** (📞719-539-4091; www.monarchcrest. net; adult/child $10/5; ⊗8:30am-5:30pm mid-May–mid-Sep) can haul you from Monarch Pass nearly 1000ft up to the top of the ridge. **Monarch ski area** (📞719-530-5000; www.ski-monarch.com; 23715 Hwy 50; adult/child $84/40; ⊗Dec–mid-Apr; 🚻) also has some surprisingly excellent terrain and affordable prices. The biggest draw around is of course the wicked rafting runs on the Arkansas (p776). You can do family-friendly floats, go fishing, or take on bigger challenges on runs such as Numbers, the Royal Gorge and Brown's Canyon from here.

⭐ Absolute Bikes · · · · · · · · · CYCLING
(📞719-539-9295; www.absolutebikes.com; 330 W Sackett Ave; bike rental per day $25-105, tours from $175; ⊗9am-6pm; 🚻) The go-to place for bike enthusiasts, offering maps, gear, advice, rentals (cruisers and mountain bikes) and, most importantly, shuttles to the trailhead. Check out the great selection of guided rides, ranging from St Elmo ghost town to the Monarch Crest.

⭐ Monarch Crest Trail · · · MOUNTAIN BIKING
One of the most famous rides in all of Colorado, the Monarch Crest is an extreme 20- to 35-mile adventure. It starts off at Monarch Pass (11,312ft), follows the exposed ridge 12 miles to Marshall Pass and then either cuts down to Poncha Springs on an old railroad grade or hooks onto the Rainbow Trail. A classic ride with fabulous high-altitude views.

🛏 Sleeping

Salida has a good hostel and hotel in town, along with a smattering of generic motels on the outskirts. The **Arkansas Headwaters Recreation Area** (📞719-539-7289; http://cpw.state.co.us; 307 W Sackett Ave; ⊗8am-5pm, closed noon-1pm Sat & Sun) operates six campgrounds (bring your own water) along the river, including **Hecla Junction** (📞719-539-7289; http://coloradostateparks.reserveamerica.com; Hwy 285, Mile 135; tent & RV sites $18, plus daily pass $7; 🚻). Another top campground is **Monarch Park** (📞877-444-6777; www.recreation.gov; off Hwy 50; tent & RV sites $18; ⊗Jun-Sep; 🚻), up by the pass, near the hiking and biking along the Monarch Crest and Rainbow Trails.

⭐ Simple Lodge & Hostel · · · · · · HOSTEL $
(📞719-650-7381; www.simplelodge.com; 224 E 1st St; dm/d/q $24/65/84; 🅿@🛜🚻) If only Colorado had more spots like this. Run by the super-friendly Mel and Justin, this hostel is simple but stylish, with a fully stocked kitchen and a comfy communal area that feels just like home. It's a popular stopover for touring cyclists following the coast-to-coast Rte 50 – you're likely to meet some interesting folks here.

🍴 Eating

The Fritz · TAPAS $
(📞719-539-0364; https://thefritzsalida.com; 113 E Sackett St; tapas $6-10, mains $11-16; ⊗11am-9pm; 🛜) This fun riverside watering hole serves up clever American-style tapas: think three-cheese mac with bacon, fries and truffle aioli, seared ahi wontons, and brie ciabatta with date jam. It also does a mean grass-fed beef burger and other salads and sandwiches. Good selection of local beers on tap.

⭐ Amícas · · · · · · · · · · · · · · · · · · · PIZZA $$
(📞719-539-5219; www.amicassalida.com; 127 F St; pizzas & paninis $6.90-13; ⊗11am-9pm Mon-Wed, 7am-9pm Thu-Sun; 🚻🚻) Thin-crust wood-fired pizzas, panini, housemade lasagna and microbrews on tap? Amícas can do no wrong. This high-ceilinged, laid-back hangout is the perfect spot to replenish all those calories you burned off during the day. Savor a Michelangelo (pesto, sausage and goat cheese) or Vesuvio (artichoke hearts, sun-dried tomatoes, roasted peppers) alongside a cool glass of Headwaters IPA.

ℹ Information

Salida Chamber of Commerce (📞719-539-2068; www.nowthisiscolorado.com; 406 W Rainbow Blvd; ⊗9am-5pm Mon-Fri) General tourist info.

USFS Ranger Office (📞719-539-3591; www. fs.usda.gov; 5575 Cleora Rd; ⊗8am-4:30pm Mon-Fri) Located east of town off Hwy 50, with camping and trail info for the Sawatch and northern Sangre de Cristo Ranges.

WORTH A TRIP

RAFTING THE ARKANSAS RIVER

Running from Leadville down the eastern flank of Buena Vista, through Browns Canyon National Monument, and then rocketing through the spectacular Royal Gorge at class V speeds, the Arkansas River is the most diverse, the longest and arguably the wildest river in the state. Brace yourself for yet another icy splash as you plunge into a roaring set of big waves, or surrender to the power of the current as your hoot-hollering, thoroughly drenched crew unintentionally spins backwards around a monster boulder. Is this fun? You bet!

❶ Getting There & Away

Located at the 'exit' of the Arkansas River Valley, Salida occupies a prime location at the crossroads of Hwys 285 and 50. Indeed, this used to be a railroad hub, and you'll likely spot an abandoned line or two while exploring the area. Gunnison, Colorado Springs, the Great Sand Dunes and Summit County are all within one to two hours' drive, provided you have your own car.

Colorado Springs

Colorado Springs is an interesting beast. The town has grown by leaps and bounds in recent years, but still retains some of its small-town charms. It's absolutely gorgeous, with Pikes Peak hanging over the city, the vertical sandstone towers of the Garden of the Gods, and cute little neighborhoods that make it feel like a cozy mountain town. It's also home to a big military presence and ultra-right-wing evangelicals. Beyond the politics, taking a day or two to explore everything the town and its environs have to offer should make it onto any Colorado Top Five list.

On the West Side of town, you'll find cute shops and bistros in Manitou Springs and Old Colorado City. As you head into the foothills, there is amazing hiking, mountain biking, outdoor adventures, cliff dwellings, cave tours, and a trip by car to the top of Pikes Peak.

◉ Sights & Activities

★ Pikes Peak   MOUNTAIN
(☎719-385-7325; www.springsgov.com; highway per adult/child $15/5; ⊙7:30am-8pm Jun-Aug,

to 5pm Sep, 9am-3pm Oct-May; ℗) Pikes Peak (14,110ft) may not be the tallest of Colorado's 54 fourteeners, but it's certainly the most famous. The Ute originally called it the Mountain of the Sun, an apt description for this majestic peak, which crowns the southern Front Range. Rising 7400ft straight up from the plains, more than half a million visitors climb it every year.

★ Garden of the Gods   PARK
(www.gardenofgods.com; 1805 N 30th St; ⊙5am-9pm; ℗) FREE This gorgeous vein of red sandstone (about 290 million years old) appears elsewhere along Colorado's Front Range, but the exquisitely thin cathedral spires and mountain backdrop of the Garden of the Gods are particularly striking. Explore the network of paved and unpaved trails, enjoy a picnic and watch climbers test their nerve on the sometimes flaky rock.

⬛ Sleeping

Mining Exchange   HOTEL $$
(☎719-323-2000; www.wyndhamhotels.com; 8 S Nevada Ave; r from $225; ℗❄☎) Opened in 2012 and set in the former turn-of-the-century bank where Cripple Creek prospectors traded in their gold for cash (check out the vault door in the lobby), the Mining Exchange takes the prize for Colorado Springs' most stylish hotel. Twelve-foot-high ceilings, exposed brick walls and leather furnishings make for an inviting, contemporary feel.

★ Broadmoor   RESORT $$$
(☎866-620-7083; www.broadmoor.com; 1 Lake Ave; r from $335; ℗❄☎⛤⛱) One of the top five-star resorts in the US, the 784-room Broadmoor sits in a picture-perfect location against the blue-green slopes of Cheyenne Mountain. Everything here is exquisite: acres of lush grounds and a lake, a glimmering pool, world-class golf, myriad bars and restaurants, an incredible spa and ubercomfortable guest rooms. Check out the wilderness camps for closer proximity to nature.

★ Garden of the Gods Resort   RESORT $$$
(☎719-632-5541; www.gardenofthegodsclub.com; 3320 Mesa Rd; d/ste from $380/465; ℗❄☎⛱) The best views in town are had from this elegant resort that overlooks Garden of the Gods. Elegantly appointed with just the hint of southwest touches, the assortment of rooms, suites, cottages and casitas all have

easy access to the infinity pool and spa area. Stay and play deals are available for golfers.

✕ Eating & Drinking

Shuga's
CAFE $

(☑719-328-1412; www.facebook.com/shugasbar; 702 S Cascade Ave; dishes $8-9; ☺11am-midnight; ☜) If you thought Colorado Springs couldn't be hip, stroll to Shuga's, a Southern-style cafe with a knack for knockout espresso drinks and hot cocktails. Cuter than a button, this little white house is decked out in paper cranes and red vinyl chairs; there's also patio seating. The food – Brie BLT on rosemary toast, Brazilian coconut shrimp soup – comforts and delights.

★ Uchenna
ETHIOPIAN $$

(☑719-634-5070; www.uchennaalive.com; 2501 W Colorado Ave, Suite 105; mains $12-22; ☺noon-2pm & 5-8pm Tue-Sun; ��❊⑆) Chef Maya learned her recipes from her mother before she moved to America, and you'll love the homey cooking and family-friendly vibe at this authentic Ethiopian restaurant. Go for well-spiced meat or veg options and mop everything up with the spongy *injera*.

★ Marigold
FRENCH $$

(☑719-599-4776; www.marigoldcafeandbakery. com; 4605 Centennial Blvd; mains lunch $8-13, dinner $11-24; ☺bistro 11am-2:30pm & 5-9pm, bakery 8am-9pm Mon-Sat) Way out by the Garden of the Gods is this buzzy French bistro and bakery that's easy on both the palate and the wallet. Feast on delicacies such as snapper Marseillaise, garlic-and-rosemary rotisserie chicken, and gourmet salads and pizzas, but be sure to leave room for the double (and triple!) chocolate mousse cake or the lemon tarts.

ⓘ Getting There & Away

A smart alternative to flying into Denver, **Colorado Springs Airport** (COS; ☑719-550-1900; www.fly cos.com; 7770 Milton E Proby Pkwy; ☜) is served principally by United and Delta, with flights to a number of major cities around the country. There is no public transportation into town, however, so you'll have to rent a car or take a cab.

Greyhound (☑800-231-2222; www.greyhound. com) buses ply the route between Colorado Springs and Denver (from $13, 1½ hours, up to six daily), departing from the **Colorado Springs Downtown Transit Terminal** (☑719-385-7433; 127 E Kiowa St; ☺8am-5pm Mon-Fri). Here you can find schedule information and route maps for all local buses.

Southern Colorado

Home to the dramatic San Juan and Sangre de Cristo mountain ranges, Colorado's bottom half is just as pretty as its top.

Crested Butte

Crested Butte is quite simply one of the best mountain towns in the whole world. There's an amazing ski area here, punctuated by some of the steepest lines in Colorado.

This was one of the birthplaces of mountain biking, and you can ride or hike for hundreds of miles on the wondrous trails found in the wilderness areas surrounding town. And the scenery is off-the-charts gorgeous, with Aspen-choked hillsides, scenic alpine lakes, towering snowcapped peaks and more.

⊙ Sights & Activities

★ Crested Butte
Center for the Arts
ARTS CENTER

(☑970-349-7487; www.crestedbuttearts.org; 606 6th St; admission varies; ☺10am-6pm; ⓟ⑆) The arts center hosts shifting exhibitions of local artists and a stellar schedule of live music and performance pieces. There's always something lively and interesting happening here. The classes, workshops and lecture series are especially interesting.

★ Crested Butte Mountain Resort
SKIING

(☑970-349-2222; www.skicb.com; 12 Snowmass Rd; lift ticket adult/child $125/70; ⑆) One of Colorado's best, Crested Butte is known for its extreme lines, deep powder, ripping locals and down-home ski-town fun. This is one of America's last great ski areas, a place where skiing still stands for the renegade spirit, where locals occasionally take runs naked, and where freedom, irreverence and the simple joys of fresh powder on a bluebird day still stand true.

Alpineer
MOUNTAIN BIKING

(☑970-349-5210; www.alpineer.com; 419 6th St; bike rental per day $29-75) This great local shop serves the mountain-biking mecca with maps, information and rentals, plus an excellent selection of men's and women's clothing. Skis and hiking and camping equipment can be rented here. Top tip: go ahead and splurge on a full-suspension bike (it feels like riding on a cloud).

🛏 Sleeping

Inn at Crested Butte
BOUTIQUE HOTEL **$$**

(☑970-349-2111, toll-free 877-343-211; www.innat
crestedbutte.com; 510 Whiterock Ave; d $110-250;
P🌸🐾🐾) This refurbished boutique hotel
offers intimate lodgings in stylish and lux-
urious surrounds. With just a handful of
rooms, some opening onto a balcony with
views over Mt Crested Butte, and all decked
out with antiques, flat-screen TVs, coffee
makers and minibars, this is one of Crested
Butte's nicest vacation addresses.

★ Ruby of Crested Butte
B&B **$$$**

(☑800-390-1338; www.therubyofcrestedbutte.
com; 624 Gothic Ave; d $300-350, ste from $400;
P😊🌸🐾🐾) Thoughtfully outfitted, down
to the bowls of jellybeans and nuts in the
stylish communal lounge. Rooms are brilliant, with heated floors, flat-screen TVs with
DVD players and DVD selections, iPod docks
and deluxe linens. There's also a Jacuzzi, library, ski-gear drying room and use of retro
townie bikes. Hosts help with dinner reservations and other services.

🍴 Eating & Drinking

★ Secret Stash
PIZZA **$$**

(☑970-349-6245; www.secretstash.com; 303
Elk Ave; mains $12-18; ⊙8am-late; 🚸🐾) With
phenomenal food, the funky-casual Stash
is adored by locals, who also dig the origi-
nal cocktails. The sprawling space was once
a general store but is now outfitted with
teahouse seating and tapestries. The house
specialty is pizza; its Notorious Fig (with
prosciutto, fresh figs and truffle oil) won the
World Pizza Championship. Start with the
salt-and-pepper fries.

Soupçon
FRENCH **$$$**

(☑970-349-5448; www.soupconcb.com; 127 Elk
Ave; mains $39-47; ⊙6-10:30pm) 🍃 Specializ-
ing in seduction, this petite French bistro occupies a characterful old mining cabin with
just a few tables. The chefs keep it fresh with
changing menus of local meat and organic
produce. Reserve ahead.

★ Montana
BAR

(www.montanyarum.com; 212 Elk Ave; snacks $3-12;
⊙11am-9pm; 🐾) The Montanya distillery receives wide acclaim for its high-quality rums.
Its basiltini, made with basil-infused rum,
fresh grapefruit and lime, will have you levitating. There are also tours, free tastings and
worthy mocktails. The street-food inspired
menu is pretty good as well. Expect this place

to be packed and occasional live music. In
the afternoon, it's a good family spot.

ℹ Information

Crested Butte Visitor Center (☑970-349-
6438; www.crestedbuttechamber.com; 601 Elk
Ave; ⊙9am-5pm) Just past the entrance to
town on the main road. Stocks loads of brochures and maps.

ℹ Getting There & Away

Crested Butte is about four hours' drive from Denver, and about 3½ hours from Colorado Springs.
Head for Gunnison on US 50 and from there head
north for about 30 minutes to Crested Butte on
Hwy 135. In winter, there are regular flights to
Gunnison Airport (GUC; ☑970-641-2304; www.
gunnisoncounty.org/airport; 519 Rio Grande Ave).

Ouray

With gorgeous icefalls draping the box canyon and soothing hot springs dotting the
valley floor, Ouray (you-ray) is privileged
even for Colorado. For ice climbers it's a
world-class destination, but hikers and
4WD fans can also appreciate its rugged and
sometimes stunning charms. The town is a
well-preserved quarter-mile mining village
sandwiched between imposing peaks. The
sun rarely shines here, and there is a bit of a
Twin Peaks air about town.

🏃 Activities

★ Million Dollar Highway
SCENIC DRIVE

The whole of US Hwy 550 has been called
the Million Dollar Hwy, but more properly it's the amazing stretch south of Ouray
through the Uncompahgre Gorge up to
Red Mountain Pass at 11,018ft. The alpine
scenery is truly awesome and driving south
towards Silverton positions drivers on the
outside edge of the skinny, winding road, a
heartbeat away from free-fall.

Ouray Hot Springs
HOT SPRINGS

(☑970-325-7073; www.ourayhotsprings.com; 1200
Main St; adult/child $18/12; ⊙10am-10pm Jun-
Aug, noon-9pm Mon-Fri, 11am-9pm Sat & Sun Sep-
May; 🐾) For a healing soak or kiddish fun,
try the historic Ouray Hot Springs. The natural spring water is crystal-clear and free of
the sulfur smells plaguing other hot springs.
There's a lap pool, waterslides, a climbing
wall overhanging a splash pool and prime
soaking areas (100°F to 106°F; 37.7°C to
41.1°C). The complex also offers a gym and
massage service.

Ouray Ice Park
CLIMBING

(☑970-325-4061; www.ourayicepark.com; County Rd 361; membership $40-150; ⊙7am-5pm mid-Dec–Mar; ⊞) Enthusiasts from around the globe come to ice climb at the world's first public ice park, spanning a 2-mile stretch of the Uncompahgre Gorge. The sublime (if chilly) experience offers something for all skill levels. Get instruction through a local guide service.

🎉 Festivals & Events

Ouray Ice Festival
CULTURAL

(☑970-325-4288; www.ourayicefestival.com; donation for evening events; ⊙Jan; ⊞) The Ouray Ice Festival features four days of climbing competitions, dinners, slide shows and clinics. There's even a climbing wall set up for kids. You can watch the competitions for free, but various evening events require a donation to the ice park. Once inside, you'll get free brews from popular Colorado microbrewer New Belgium.

🛏 Sleeping & Eating

Amphitheater Forest Service Campground
CAMPGROUND $

(☑877-444-6777; www.recreation.gov; US Hwy 550; tent sites $24; ⊙Jun-Aug) With great tent sites under the trees, this high-altitude campground is a score. Some of the gorgeous trees here are falling down, however, and the Forest Service has closed some of the campsites. On holiday weekends a three-night minimum applies. South of town on Hwy 550, take a signposted left-hand turn.

★Wiesbaden
HOTEL $$

(☑970-325-4347; www.wiesbadenhotsprings.com; 625 5th St; r $133-350; ⊖🐾🎾) Quirky, quaint and new age, Wiesbaden even boasts a natural indoor vapor cave, which, in another era, was frequented by Chief Ouray. Rooms with quilted bedcovers are cozy and romantic, but the sunlit suite with a natural rock wall tops all. In the morning, guests roam in thick robes, drinking the free organic coffee or tea, post-soak or awaiting massages.

Box Canyon Lodge & Hot Springs
LODGE $$

(☑970-325-4981, 800-327-5080; www.boxcanyonouray.com; 45 3rd Ave; r from $200; 🐾) 🌿 It's not every hotel that offers geothermal heating, not to mention pineboard rooms that are spacious and fresh, and spring-fed barrel hot tubs – perfect for a romantic stargazing soak. With good hospitality that includes free apples and bottled water, it's popular, so book ahead.

Bon Ton Restaurant
FRENCH, ITALIAN $$$

(☑970-325-4419; www.bontonrestaurant.com; 426 Main St; mains $16-40; ⊙5:30-11pm Thu-Mon, 9:30am-12:30pm Sat & Sun; 🐾) Bon Ton has been serving supper for a century in a beautiful room under the historic St Elmo Hotel. The French-Italian menu includes roast duck in cherry peppercorn sauce and tortellini with bacon and shallots. The wine list is extensive and the weekend Champagne brunch comes recommended.

ℹ Information

Ouray Visitor Center (☑970-325-4746, 800-228-1876; www.ouraycolorado.com; 1230 Main St; ⊙9am-6pm Mon-Sat, 10am-4pm Sun; 🐾) Located behind the Ouray hot-springs pool.

ℹ Getting There & Away

Ouray is on Hwy 550, 70 miles north of Durango, 24 miles north of Silverton and 37 miles south of Montrose. There are no bus services in the area and private transportation is necessary.

Telluride

Telluride is a unique destination cut off from much of the world by the towering peaks that surround the old mining town on three sides. No other town in Colorado feels this close to a Swiss mountain village.

Walking the downtown strip you have skyrocketing mountain ranges right in front of you. There's also a pretty darned good ski resort here, plenty of hiking and biking opportunities, and Colorado's best summer festivals. While there aren't that many restaurants and nightlife spots, what they do have is always high quality.

🏃 Activities

Telluride Ski Resort
SNOW SPORTS

(☑970-728-7533, 888-288-7360; www.tellurideskiresort.com; 565 Mountain Village Blvd; adult/child full-day lift ticket $139/83) Known for its steep and deep terrain – with plunging runs and deep powder at the best times – Telluride is a real skier's mountain, but dilettantes love the gorgeous San Juan mountain views and the social town atmosphere. Covering three distinct areas, the resort is served by 16 lifts. Much of the terrain is for advanced and intermediate skiers, but there's still ample choice for beginners.

In summer, there is a **mountain bike park** (day lift ticket $36) here.

★ Ashley Boling HISTORY
(☑970-728-6639; per person $20; ☺by appointment) Local Ashley Boling has been giving engaging historical walking tours of Telluride for more than 20 years. They last over an hour and are offered year-round. Rates are for a minimum of three participants, but he'll cut a reasonable deal for two or more. By reservation.

★✩ Festivals & Events

Telluride Bluegrass Festival MUSIC
(☑800-624-2422; www.planetbluegrass.com; 1-/4-day pass $90/255; ☺late Jun) This festival attracts thousands for a weekend of top-notch rollicking alfresco bluegrass. Stalls sell all sorts of food and local microbrews to keep you happy, and acts continue well into the night. Camping out for the four-day festival is very popular. Check out the website for info on sites, shuttle services and combo ticket-and-camping packages – it's all very organized!

⌂ Sleeping

★ Telluride Town Park Campground CAMPGROUND $
(☑970-728-2173; www.telluride-co.gov/181/campground; 500 E Colorado Ave; campsite with/without vehicle space $33/19; ☺mid-May–mid-Oct; ☎⚄) Right in the center of town, this convenient creekside campground has 43 campsites, along with showers, swimming and tennis. Sites are all on a first-come, first-served basis, unless it's festival time (consult ahead with festival organizers). Fancy some nightlife with your camping? Why not.

New Sheridan Hotel HOTEL $$
(☑970-728-4351, 800-200-1891; www.newsheridan.com; 231 W Colorado Ave; d from $220; ☻☎) Elegant and understated, this historic brick hotel (erected in 1895) provides a lovely base camp for exploring Telluride. High-ceilinged rooms feature crisp linens and snug flannel throws. Check out the hot-tub deck with mountain views. In the bull's eye of downtown, the location is perfect, but some rooms are small for the price.

Inn at Lost Creek BOUTIQUE HOTEL $$$
(☑970-728-5678; www.innatlostcreek.com; 119 Lost Creek Lane, Mountain Village; r $275-500; ☻☎) This lush boutique-style hotel in Mountain Village knows cozy. At the bottom of Telluride's main lift, it's also very convenient. Service is personalized, and impeccable rooms have alpine hardwoods, Southwestern designs and molded tin. There are also two rooftop spas. Check the website for packages.

✗ Eating & Drinking
There's more good times to be had in Telluride than the rest of southern Colorado combined. But bring your wallet – those drinks aren't free or even close. Live bands spark it up.

Tacos del Gnar MEXICAN $
(☑970-728-7938; www.gnarlytacos.com; 123 S Oak St; mains $7-14; ☺noon-9pm Tue-Sat; ✐) The second outlet of a no-nonsense taco shop that puts flavor ahead of frills. Its fusion-style tacos, borrowing from Korean BBQ and Asian flavors, will make your taste buds sing. Do it.

Oak BARBECUE $$
(New Fat Alley; ☑970-728-3985; www.oakstelluride.com; 250 San Juan Ave, base of chair 8; mains $11-23; ☺11am-10pm; ✈) You can pick something off the chalkboard or just take what the other guy has his face in – a cheap and messy delight. If in doubt, go for the pulled-pork sandwich with coleslaw on top. Do it right by siding it with a bowl of crispy sweet-potato fries. The beer specials are outrageous. And it's located right next to the free town Gondola.

★ Chop House MODERN AMERICAN $$$
(☑970-728-4531; www.newsheridan.com; 231 W Colorado Ave, New Sheridan Hotel; mains $26-65; ☺5pm-2am) With superb service and a chic decor with embroidered velvet benches, this is an easy pick for an intimate dinner. Start with a cheese plate. From there the menu gets Western with exquisite elk short loin and ravioli with tomato relish and local sheep-milk ricotta. Top it off with a flourless dark chocolate cake in fresh caramel sauce.

New Sheridan Bar BAR
(☑970-728-3911; www.newsheridan.com; 231 W Colorado Ave, New Sheridan Hotel; ☺5pm-2am) It's rush hour for beautiful people, though in low season you'll find real local flavor and opinions. In summertime, beeline for the breezy rooftop. Old bullet holes in the wall testify to the plucky survival of the bar itself, even as the adjoining hotel sold off chandeliers and antiques to pay the heating bills when mining fortunes waned.

☆ Entertainment

Fly Me to the Moon Saloon   LIVE MUSIC
(☑970-728-6666; www.facebook.com/flymetothe
moonsaloon; 132 E Colorado Ave; ⊘3pm-2am) Let
your hair down and kick up your heels to
the tunes of live bands at this saloon, the
best place in Telluride to party hard.

Sheridan Opera House   THEATER
(☑970-728-4539; www.sheridanoperahouse.com;
110 N Oak St; ⊕) This historic venue has a
burlesque charm and is always the center of
Telluride's cultural life. It hosts the Telluride
Repertory Theater, and frequently has special performances for children.

ⓘ Information

Telluride Central Reservations (☑888-355-
8743; 700 W Colorado Ave; ⊘9am-5pm Mon-
Sat, 10am-1pm Sun) Handles accommodations
and sells festival tickets.

Telluride Visitor Center (☑888-353-5473,
970-728-3041; www.telluride.com; 230 W
Colorado Ave; ⊘10am-5pm winter, to 7pm
summer) Well-stocked visitor center with good
resources.

Wilkinson Public Library (☑970-728-4519;
www.telluridelibrary.org; 100 W Pacific Ave;
⊘10am-8pm Mon-Thu, to 6pm Fri & Sat, noon-
5pm Sun; ☎⊕) Good resource for maps and
local information, with some free public events.

ⓘ Getting There & Around

In ski season **Montrose Regional Airport** (MTJ;
☑970-249-3203; www.montroseairport.com;
2100 Airport Rd), 65 miles north, has direct
flights to/from Denver (on United), Houston,
Phoenix and limited cities on the east coast.
Commuter aircraft serve the mesa-top **Telluride
Airport** (TEX; ☑970-778-5051; www.tellu-
rideairport.com; 1500 Last Dollar Rd). At other
times, planes fly into Montrose.

Telluride Express (☑970-728-6000; www.tel-
lurideexpress.com) provides low-cost shuttles
to Telluride from the Montrose and Telluride
Airports.

Silverton

Ringed by snowy peaks and steeped in the
sooty tales of a tawdry mining town, Silverton would seem more at home in Alaska
than in the Lower 48. But here it is. And for
those into snowmobiling, biking, fly-fishing
or just basking in some very high-altitude
sunshine, Silverton delivers. This is also
home to one of America's unique ski mountains: the experts-only, one-chair wonder of
Silverton Mountain.

It's a two-street town, but only one is
paved. Greene St is where you'll find most
businesses (think homemade jerky, fudge
and feather art). Still unpaved, notorious
Blair St – renamed Empire – runs parallel
to Greene. During the silver rush, Blair St
was home to thriving brothels and boozing
establishments.

🏃 Activities

★ Silverton Railroad Depot   RAIL
(☑970-387-5416, toll-free 877-872-4607; www.
durangotrain.com; 12th St; return adult/child 4-11yr
from $114/80; ⊘departures 1:45pm, 2:30pm &
3pm; ⊕) You can buy one-way and round-
trip tickets for the brilliant Durango & Silverton Narrow Gauge Railroad (p783) at
the Silverton depot or via the website. The
Silverton Freight Yard Museum is located at
the Silverton depot; the train ticket provides
admission two days prior to and following
your ride on the train. The train service offers combination train-bus return trips (the
bus route is much quicker).

★ Silverton Mountain Ski Area   SKIING
(☑970-387-5706; www.silvertonmountain.com;
State Hwy 110; guided skiing $179, unguided skiing
$79; ⊘guided skiing Thu-Sun Dec-Mar, unguided
skiing late Mar-Apr) Silverton is an experts-only
ski mountain that's perfect for advanced skiers looking to take it up a notch. The resort
has just one lift to take you to the top. From
there, you hike with your guide to any number of amazing lines with some of the best
untracked powder in the state.

San Juan Backcountry   DRIVING
(☑970-387-5565; www.sanjuanbackcountry.com;
1119 Greene St; tours $40-140; ⊘May-Oct; ⊕)
Offering both 4WD tours and rentals, the
folks at San Juan Backcountry can get you
out and into the brilliant San Juan Mountain wilderness areas around Silverton. The
tours are in modified open-top Chevy Sub-
urbans and ATVs. Rafting trips down the
Lower Animas by Durango are also possible.

🛏 Sleeping & Eating

**Inn of the Rockies at the
Historic Alma House**   B&B $$
(☑970-387-5336; www.innoftherockies.com; 220
E 10th St; r $125-200; P⊕❅) Opened by a
local in 1898, this inn has 10 unique rooms
furnished with Victorian antiques. The hos-
pitality is first-rate and its breakfasts, served
in a chandelier-lit dining room, merit special

mention. There's also a garden hot tub for soaking after a long day.

Wyman Hotel
B&B $$

(☑ 877-504-5272; www.thewyman.com; 1371 Greene St; d from $250-375; ☺ closed Nov; ☻ ☎) A handsome sandstone on the National Register of Historic Places, this revamped 1902 building offers sleek rooms with Scandinavian sensibilities and a fine-tuned minimalist touch. It's a stylish alternative to the usual bric-a-brac approach. Check out the historic caboose alongside a gravel patio out back.

Grand Restaurant & Saloon
AMERICAN $$

(☑ 970-387-5527; www.grandimperialhotel.com; 1219 Greene St; mains $8-26; ☺ 11am-3pm May-Oct, occasional dinners 5-9pm; ⚐) Stick with the burgers and club sandwiches at this atmospheric eatery, where the full bar is well patronised by locals and visitors. The player piano and historic decor are big draws.

❶ Getting There & Away

Silverton is on Hwy 550 midway between Montrose, about 60 miles to the north, and Durango, some 48 miles to the south.

Other than private car, the only way to get to and from Silverton is by using the Durango & Silverton Narrow Gauge Railroad (p783), or the private buses that run its return journeys.

Mesa Verde National Park

More than 700 years after its inhabitants disappeared, Mesa Verde retains an air of mystery. No one knows for sure why the Ancestral Puebloans left their elaborate cliff dwellings in the 1300s. What remains is a wonderland for adventurers of all sizes, who can clamber up ladders to carved-out dwellings, see rock art and delve into the mysteries of ancient America.

Mesa Verde National Park (☑ 970-529-4465; www.nps.gov/meve; 7-day car/motorcycle pass May-Oct $25/20, Nov-Apr $15/10; ⓅⓅ⚐☻) ⚐ occupies 81 sq miles of the northernmost portion of the mesa. Ancestral Puebloan sites are found throughout the park's canyons and mesas, perched on a high plateau south of Cortez and Mancos.

❂ Sights & Activities

If you only have time for a short visit, check out the Chapin Mesa Museum and try to get in on a ranger-guided tour of one of the dwellings (available only with in-person reservations up to two days in advance).

Mesa Verde rewards travelers who set aside a day or more to take ranger-led tours of Cliff Palace and Balcony House, explore Wetherill Mesa (the quieter side of the canyon), linger around the museum or participate in one of the campfire programs run at Morefield Campground.

Chapin Mesa Museum
MUSEUM

(☑ 970-529-4475; www.nps.gov/meve; Chapin Mesa Rd; admission incl with park entry; ☺ 8am-6:30pm Apr–mid-Oct, to 5pm mid-Oct–Apr; Ⓟ⚐) The Chapin Mesa Museum has exhibits pertaining to the park and is a good first stop. Staff at the museum provide information on weekends when the park headquarters is closed.

Chapin Mesa
ARCHAEOLOGICAL SITE

(ranger-led hikes $5; ☺ year-round, ranger-led hikes Apr-Oct) The largest concentration of Ancestral Puebloan sites is at Chapin Mesa, where you'll see the densely clustered **Far View Site** and the large **Spruce Tree House** (Chapin Mesa Rd; admission incl with park entry; Ⓟ⚐) ⚐, the most accessible of sites, with a paved half-mile round-trip path. Spruce Tree House is currently closed to visitors, but you can see it easily from the museum overlook.

Wetherill Mesa
ARCHAEOLOGICAL SITE

(guided tours per person $5) Wetherill Mesa is the second-largest concentration of sites. Visitors may enter stabilized surface sites and two cliff dwellings, including the Long House (ranger-led only), open from late May through August.

Aramark Mesa Verde
HIKING

(☑ 970-529-4421; www.visitmesaverde.com; Mile 15, Far View Lodge; adult $70-75) The park concessionaire offers various guided private and group tours throughout the park daily from May to mid-October. Tours include bus transit and hikes. Book online or at the office at Far View Lodge.

🛏 Sleeping & Eating

Morefield Campground
CAMPGROUND $

(☑ 970-529-4465; www.visitmesaverde.com; Mile 4; tent sites $33, RV sites with/without hookups $33/45; ☺ May-early Oct; ☻) ⚐ The park's camping option, located 4 miles from the entrance gate, has 445 regular tent sites on grassy grounds conveniently located near Morefield Village. The village has a general store, gas station, restaurant, showers and laundry. It's managed by Aramark.

Far View Lodge
LODGE **$$**

(☑toll-free 800-449-2288; www.visitmesaverde. com; Mile 15; r $165-230; ☉mid-Apr–Oct; ℗☺ ❋☎❀) Perched on a mesa top 15 miles inside the park entrance, this tasteful Pueblo-style lodge has 150 Southwestern-style rooms, some with kiva fireplaces. Don't miss sunset over the mesa from your private balcony. Standard rooms don't have air-con (or TV) and summer daytimes can be hot. You can even bring your dog for an extra $10 per night.

Metate Room
MODERN AMERICAN **$$$**

(☑800-449-2288; www.visitmesaverde.com; Mile 15, Far View Lodge; mains $20-36; ☉7-10am & 5:30-9:30pm Apr–mid-Oct, 5-7:30pm mid-Oct–Mar; ☑❀) ❂ With an award in culinary excellence, this upscale restaurant in the Far View Lodge offers an innovative menu inspired by Native American food and flavors. Interesting dishes include stuffed poblano chilies, prickly-pear pork belly and cold smoked trout. Not your average national park dining, and the views are nothing short of spectacular.

❶ Information

Mesa Verde Visitor & Research Center
(☑970-529-4465; www.nps.gov/meve; ☉7:30am-7pm Jun-early Sep, 8am-5pm early Sep–mid-Oct & mid-Apr–May, closed mid-Oct–mid-Apr; ☎❀) This huge visitor center has water, wi-fi and bathrooms, in addition to information desks selling tickets for tours of Cliff Palace, Balcony House and Long House. It also displays museum-quality artifacts.

Durango

Durango is paradise unleashed. The historic mining town offers the perfect combination of easy access to adventures by river, by bike and by ski, super-cool locals, a fun nightlife scene powered by the local college kids, and plenty of great eateries, drinking holes, boutiques and more.

❊ Activities

★Durango & Silverton Narrow Gauge Railroad
RAIL

(☑970-247-2733; www.durangotrain.com; 479 Main Ave; return adult/child 4-11yr from $114/80; ❀) Riding the Durango & Silverton Narrow Gauge Railroad is a Durango must. These vintage steam locomotives have been making the scenic 45-mile trip north to Silverton (3½ hours each way) for more than

125 years. The dazzling journey allows two hours for exploring Silverton. The Skyway Tour to Silverton operates only from May through October.

Mild to Wild Rafting
RAFTING

(☑970-247-4789, toll-free 800-567-6745; www. mild2wildrafting.com; 50 Animas View Dr; trips from $55; ☉9am-5pm; ❀) In spring and summer white-water rafting is one of the most popular sports in Durango. Mild to Wild Rafting is one of numerous companies around town offering rafting trips on the Animas River. Beginners should check out the one-hour introduction to rafting, while the more adventurous (and experienced) can run the upper Animas, which boasts class III to class V rapids.

Purgatory
SKIING

(☑970-247-9000; www.purgatoryresort.com; 1 Skier Pl; lift ticket adult/child from $89/60; ☉mid-Nov–Mar; ❀) Durango's winter highlight is 25 miles north on Hwy 550. The resort offers 1200 skiable acres of varying difficulty, and boasts 260in of snow per year. Two terrain parks offer plenty of opportunities for snowboarders to catch big air. This is really a local's hill that offers up plenty of good groomers for families and a few steeper runs.

⏤ Sleeping

★Rochester House
HOTEL **$$**

(☑970-385-1920, toll-free 800-664-1920; www. rochesterhotel.com; 721 E 2nd Ave; d $190-300; ☺❋☎❀) Influenced by old Westerns (movie posters and marquee lights adorn the hallways), the Rochester is a little bit of old Hollywood in the new West. Rooms are spacious, with high ceilings. Two formal sitting rooms, where you're served cookies, and a breakfast room in an old train car are other perks at this pet-friendly establishment.

Antlers on the Creek
B&B **$$**

(☑970-259-1565; www.antlersonthecreek.com; 999 Lightner Creek Rd; r from $180; ℗☎) Tuck yourself into this peaceful creekside setting surrounded by sprawling lawns and cottonwoods and you may never want to leave. Between the spacious main house and the carriage house there are seven tasteful rooms with jetted tubs, plush bed linens and gas fireplaces. There's also a decadent three-course breakfast and hot tub in the outdoor gazebo. It's open year-round.

General Palmer Hotel HOTEL $$

(☑970-247-4747, toll-free 800-523-3358; www.generalpalmer.com; 567 Main Ave; r from $160; P✳@☎) With turn-of-the century elegance, this 1898 Victorian has a damsel's taste, with pewter four-poster beds, floral prints and teddies on every bed. Rooms are small but elegant, and if you tire of TV, there's a collection of board games at the front desk. Check out the cozy library and the relaxing solarium.

✕ Eating & Drinking

★**James Ranch** MARKET $

(☑970-385-9143; www.jamesranch.net; 33800 US Hwy 550; mains $5-18; ⊙11am-7pm Mon-Sat) 🍴 A must for those road-tripping the San Juan Skyway, the family-run James Ranch, 10 miles out of Durango, features a market and an outstanding farmstand grill featuring the farm's own organic grass-fed beef and fresh produce. Steak sandwiches and fresh cheese melts with caramelized onions rock. Kids dig the goats.

El Moro GASTROPUB $$

(☑970-259-5555; www.elmorotavern.com; 945 Main Ave; mains $12-30; ⊙11am-midnight Mon-Fri, 9am-midnight Sat & Sun) There are two reasons to come here: drinking damned good custom cocktails at the bar and dining on some innovative small plates including Korean fried cauliflower, cheeses, housemade sausages and fresh salads. It's ground zero for Durango hipsters but really aims to please all.

★**Bookcase & the Barber** COCKTAIL BAR

(☑970-764-4123; www.bookcaseandbarber.com; 601 E 2nd Ave, Suite B; ⊙2pm-midnight) This modern speakeasy may be Durango's sexiest nightcap, hidden behind a heavy bookcase, with a dimly lit allure and exquisite cocktails worth the $12 price tag. Enter via the barbershop, but you'll need the password (found somewhere on their Facebook page). Try a spicy *paloma celosa* (jealous dove), a perfect tease of tequila, grapefruit and ancho chili.

Ska Brewing Company BREWERY

(☑970-247-5792; www.skabrewing.com; 225 Girard St; mains $9-15; ⊙9am-9pm Mon-Fri, 11am-9pm Sat, to 7pm Sun) Big on flavor and variety, these are the best handcrafted beers in town. Although the small, friendly tasting-room bar was once mainly a production facility, over the years it's steadily climbed

in popularity. Today it is usually jam-packed with friends meeting for an after-work beer.

ℹ Information

Durango Public Library (☑970-375-3380; www.durangopubliclibrary.org; 1900 E 3rd Ave; ⊙9am-8pm Mon-Wed, 10am-5:30pm Thu, 9am-5:30pm Fri & Sat; ☎) A handy resource for regional information.

Durango Welcome Center (☑970-247-3500, www.durango.org; 802 Main Ave; ⊙9am-7pm Sun-Thu, to 9pm Fri & Sat; ☎) An excellent information center located downtown. There is a second **visitor center** (111 S Camino del Rio) south of town, at the Santa Rita exit from US Hwy 550.

San Juan–Rio Grande National Forest HQ (☑970-247-4874; www.fs.fed.us/r2/sanjuan; 15 Burnett Ct; ⊙9am-5pm Mon-Sat) Located a half-mile west of Durango off US Hwy 160. Offers camping and hiking information and maps.

ℹ Getting There & Around

Durango-La Plata County Airport (DRO; ☑970-247-8143; www.flydurango.com; 1000 Airport Rd) is 18 miles southwest of Durango via US Hwy 160 and Hwy 172. Both United and American Airlines have direct flights to Denver; United offers seasonal flights (summer only) to Chicago, Houston and LA; American flies to Dallas–Fort Worth and Phoenix.

Great Sand Dunes National Park

For all of Colorado's striking natural sights, the surreal **Great Sand Dunes National Park** (☑719-378-6399; www.nps.gov/grsa; 11999 Hwy 150; ⊙8:30am-5pm Jun-Aug, 9am-4:30pm Sep-May; ♿), a veritable sea of sand bounded by jagged peaks and scrubby plains, is a place of stirring optical illusions where nature's magic is on full display.

From the approach up Hwy 150, watch as the angles of sunlight make shifting shadows on the dunes; the most dramatic time is the day's end, when the hills come into high contrast as the sun drops low on the horizon. Hike past the edge of the dune field to see the shifting sand up close; the ceaseless wind works like a disconsolate sculptor, constantly rearranging the sandy landscape.

Most visitors limit their activities to the area where Medano Creek divides the main dune mass from the towering Sangre de Cristo Mountains. The remaining 85% of the park's area is designated wilderness: not for the unfit or fainthearted.

Hiking

There are no trails through this expansive field of sand, but it's the star attraction for hikers. Two informal hikes afford excellent panoramic views of the dunes. The first is a hike to High Dune (strangely, not the highest dune in the park), which departs from a parking area just beyond the visitor center. It's about 2.5 miles out to the peak and back, but be warned: it's not easy. As you trudge along up the hills of sand, it feels like you're taking a half-step back for every one forward. If you're up for it, try pushing on to the second worthy goal: just west of High Dune is Star Dune (750ft), the tallest in the park.

From the Great Sand Dunes National Park Visitor Center (p784), a short trail leads to the Mosca Picnic Area next to ankle-deep Medano Creek, which you must ford (when the creek is running) to reach the dunes. Across the road from the visitor center, Mosca Pass Trail climbs up into the Sangre de Cristo Wilderness.

🛌 Sleeping & Eating

★ **Zapata Falls Campground**   CAMPGROUND **$**
(☑719-852-7074; www.fs.usda.gov; BLM Rd 5415; tent & RV sites $11; 🐾) Seven miles south of the national park, this campground offers glorious panoramas of the San Luis Valley from its 9000ft perch in the Sangre de Cristos. There are 23 first-come, first-served sites, but there is no water and the 3.6-mile access road is steep and fairly washed out, making for slow going. The payoff, however, is worth it, especially if you prefer a secluded location.

Zapata Ranch   RANCH **$$$**
(☑719-378-2356; www.zranch.org; 5303 Hwy 150; 2-nights per person with full board $875) Ideal for horseback-riding enthusiasts, this exclusive preserve is a working cattle and bison ranch set amid groves of cottonwood trees. Owned and operated by the Nature Conservancy, the main inn is a refurbished 19th-century log structure, with distant views of the sand dunes. Stays include meals and horseback-riding excursions; other adventures such as rock climbing and rafting cost extra.

ℹ️ Getting There & Away

Great Sand Dunes National Park is 33 miles northeast of Alamosa. There is no public transit to get here.

WYOMING

Much of Wyoming is the essence of the Great Plains, a vast and empty land of windswept plains and sagebrush hills baking under brooding blue skies. What towns do exist are steeped in history and infused with pioneer grit. This is Oregon Trail and outlaw country, and the current inhabitants are content to keep this chunk of the West wild. Cody or Laramie offer a taste of the living past, while Jackson and Lander serve as the advanced outposts of the New West revolution.

But the country's least populated state is also home to some of its most dramatic mountains, most diverse wildlife and most unique geology. From the unspoiled Snowy Range near Laramie to the granite wilderness of the Wind River Range behind Lander, the peaks only become more impressive as you travel across Wyoming toward the archetypal – and truly grand – Teton Range, to say nothing of Yellowstone, one of the most beautiful places in America's Lower 48.

ℹ️ Information

Travel Wyoming (☑800-225-5996, 307-777-7777; www.travelwyoming.com) The state's excellent tourism portal.
Wapiti Ranger Station (☑307-587-3925) The oldest ranger station in the country.
Wyoming State Parks & Historic Sites (☑307-777-6323; http://wyoparks.state.wy.us) Information on Wyoming's 13 state parks and 26 historic sites. Campsite reservations are taken online or over the phone

Cheyenne

Once known as the 'Magic City' for its seemingly overnight growth on the edge of the plains, windy Cheyenne may not wow you with its looks, but like the rough-skinned cowboys you'll meet here, there's good-natured charm once you scratch the surface. Wander to the depot after hitting up the city's museums and you'll see this town is a solid step above a convenient pit stop on I-80.

👁 Sights

Frontier Days Old West Museum   MUSEUM
(☑307-778-7290; www.oldwestmuseum.org; 4610 Carey Ave; adult/child $10/free; ⊙9am-5pm; 👶) For a deep dive into Cheyenne's pioneer past and rodeo present, visit this museum year-

round on the Frontier Days rodeo grounds. It is chock-full of rodeo memorabilia, from saddles to trophies, displays cowboy art and photography, houses a fine collection of horse-drawn buggies, and dispenses nuggets of history – such as the story of Steamboat, the un-rideable bronco who likely isn't the one depicted on Wyoming's license plates (though many will tell you he is.)

★ Festivals & Events

Cheyenne Frontier Days RODEO
(☑307-778-7222; www.cfdrodeo.com; 4610 Carey Ave; rodeo per day $17-55, concerts $20-75; ⊙2nd half of Jul; ▣) During the last full week in July, the world's largest outdoor rodeo and celebration of all things Wyoming features 10 days of roping, bucking, riding, singing and dancing between air shows, parades, melodramas, carnivals and chili cook-offs. There's also a lively Frontier Town, Indian village and free morning 'slack' rodeos.

🛏 Sleeping & Eating

★ **Nagle Warren Mansion B&B** B&B $$
(☑307-637-3333; www.naglewarrenmansion.com; 222 E 17th St; r from $195; ❋🐾🏠) This historic 1888 mansion is a rare find. The house still has the original carved leather ceiling, and is decked out with late-19th-century regional antiques in 12 spacious and elegant rooms. The property boasts a hot tub, a reading room tucked into a turret and classic 1954 Schwinn bikes for cruising. It's among Wyoming's most atmospheric places to stay.

★ **Historic Plains Hotel** HISTORIC HOTEL $
(☑307-638-3311; 1600 Central Ave; r from $140; 🐾) Around since 1911, this beautiful old belle drips with period atmosphere in the public areas; the antique lift is deliberately small so that cowboys wouldn't try to sneak their horses upstairs and into the rooms. Ask for a street-facing room; those facing onto the internal light well are a little dark.

★ **Bunkhouse Bar & Grill** STEAK $$
(☑307-632-6184; www.bunkhousebar.com; 1064 Happy Jack Rd; mains $10-28; ⊙11am-9pm Sun-Thu, to 11:30pm Fri & Sat) West of Cheyenne on the W-210, this storied steakhouse is worth the trip. Around since 1898, they've learned a thing or two about local tastes – burgers, steaks and similar predilections rule. The house specialty is the remarkable Bunk-Nut Sandwich with fried Rocky Mountain oysters with American cheese on Texas toast...

There's even live music on Friday and Saturday evening.

★ **Restaurant at the Plains** AMERICAN $$
(☑307-638-3311; www.theplainshotel.com; 1600 Central Ave; mains lunch $8-13, dinner $15-24; ⊙noon-3pm & 6-10pm Tue-Sun) Arguably Cheyenne's finest, the restaurant at the Historic Plains Hotel serves up some outstanding dinner dishes, such as crab-stuffed salmon or bourbon-glazed tenderloin, while lunch is a lighter affair with burgers, sandwiches and a soup-and-salad bar.

🍷 Drinking & Nightlife

Accomplice Brewing Company MICROBREWERY
(☑307-632-2337; www.accomplicebeer.com; 115 W 15th, Depot; ⊙11am-10pm Sun-Thu, to midnight Fri & Sat; 🚃🍴) Sample as many beers as you like as often as you like at the crowded pour-it-yourself taproom in Cheyenne's latest brewery to occupy the historic Depot building. The drafts are tasty – we particularly enjoyed the Nue Dogma Pale Ale and the Lincoln Squared IPA – and food options don't disappoint.

★ **Nagle Warren Mansion B&B** TEAHOUSE
(☑307-637-3333; www.naglewarrenmansion.com; 222 E 17th St; per person $12; ⊙2-4pm Fri & Sat) For an old-world taste of the West, come for afternoon tea at this atmospheric mansion where you'll be served tea, scones, cookies, sandwiches and pastries – high tea as it used to be.

ℹ Information

Cheyenne Visitor Center (☑800-426-5009, 307-778-3133; www.cheyenne.org; 1 Depot Sq/121 W 15th St; ⊙9am-5pm Mon-Fri, to 3pm Sat, 11am-3pm Sun; 🚃) Check the website for a comprehensive guide to Cheyenne. Downtown **trolley tours** (☑307-778-3133; www.cheyennetrolley.com; 121 W 15th St, Depot Plaza; adult/child $12/6; ⊙10am, 11:30am, 1pm, 2:30pm & 4pm May-Sep) leave from here.

Wyoming Travel & Tourism (☑800-225-5996; www.wyomingtourism.org; 5611 High Plains Rd; ⊙9am-5pm Mon-Fri) At a rest area just south of Cheyenne on I-25, this info center has tons of information and kid-friendly displays about local wildlife, activities and the environment. Worth a stop.

ℹ Getting There & Around

For a capital city, Cheyenne is hard to reach. Black Hills Stage Lines/Express Arrow stops at the **bus terminal** (☑307-635-1327; www.grey

hound.com; 5401 Walker Rd, Rodeway Inn) at the northern end of town with direct service to Denver ($40, 2¼ hours) and Salt Lake City ($133, 8½ hours) as well as anywhere Greyhound travels. Sleepy **Cheyenne Airport** (CYS; ☑ 307-634-7071; www.cheyenneairport.com; 200 E 8th Ave) will get you to Denver every Thursday.

Laramie

Worth an overnight stop on your way across Wyoming, this prairie town has Wyoming's only four-year university (University of Wyoming), and has a constant flow of hip and lively students who re-energize an otherwise sleepy city. The small historic downtown, with its grid of brick buildings pressed up against the railroad tracks, can occupy an hour of window shopping, and a few museums on the pleasantly green university campus are informative ways to stretch your legs. The real reason to visit, however, is the Wyoming Territorial Prison): a well-preserved piece of frontier past with echoes of Butch Cassidy.

◉ Sights

★**Wyoming Territorial Prison**   MUSEUM
(☑ 307-745-3733; www.wyomingterritorialprison.com; 975 Snowy Range Rd; adult/child $7/3.50; ☺ 8am-7pm May-Sep, 10am-3pm Wed-Sat Oct-Apr; ⓓ) See the only prison ever to hold Butch Cassidy, who was in for grand larceny in 1894–96, only to emerge a well-connected criminal who fast became one of history's greatest robbers. His story is told in thrilling detail in a back room, while the faces of other 'malicious and desperate outlaws' stare hauntingly at you as you explore the main cellblocks. Outside, tour the factory where convicts produced more than 700 brooms a day – one of the prison's short-lived revenue-generating schemes.

Geological Museum   MUSEUM
(☑ 307-766-2646; www.uwyo.edu/geomuseum; SH Knight Geology Bldg, University of Wyoming; ☺ 10am-4pm Mon-Sat) FREE The Morrison Formation – a Jurassic sedimentary rock – stretches from New Mexico to Montana and is centered in Wyoming. This layer has produced many of the world's dinosaurs fossils, an impressive collection of which are on display in this tiny university museum, including a 75ft *Apatosaurus excelsus* (formerly known as the Brontosaurus) and a *Diatryma gigantea* (a 7ft-tall carnivorous bird discovered in Wyoming). Linger at the new 'Prep Lab' and watch researchers liberate brittle fossils from solid rock. Science!

🛏 Sleeping

Gas Lite Motel   MOTEL $
(☑ 307-399-6176; 960 N 3rd St; s/d $55/65; ✸❄🐾🖥) The Gas Lite Motel stands out – more due to the plastic horse and rooster on the roof and the tattered plywood cowboys lounging against the banisters than the modernity of the amenities. However, the rooms are clean if dated, the owners reasonably friendly, and the price is right if variable.

★**Mad Carpenter Inn**   B&B $$
(☑ 307-742-0870; www.madcarpenterinn.net; 353 N 8th St; r $95-125; 🖥) With landscaped gardens, hot breakfast, and comfy, snug wood-trimmed rooms, the Mad Carpenter Inn has warmth and class to spare. A serious game room features billiards and ping-pong while the detached 'Doll House' with its kitchenette and Jacuzzi is an absolute steal for a couple looking for a quiet escape.

WYOMING FACTS

Nickname Equality State

Population 577,740

Area 97,914 sq miles

Capital city Cheyenne (population 63,600)

Other cities Laramie (population 32,300), Jackson (10,500), Cody (9890)

Sales tax 4%

Birthplace of Artist Jackson Pollock (1912–56)

Home of Women's suffrage, coal mining, geysers, wolves, Yellowstone

Politics Conservative to the core (except Teton County)

Famous for Rodeo, ranches, former vice-president Dick Cheney

Random fact Wyoming is the 10th-largest state by area but has the smallest population of any US state.

Tallest mountain Gannett Peak 13,809ft (4209m)

Driving distances Cheyenne to Jackson 432 miles

✕ Eating & Drinking

★ Sweet Melissa's
VEGETARIAN $

(☑307-742-9607; www.facebook.com/sweetmelissacafe; 213 S 1st St; mains $8.50-14; ⊙11am-9pm Mon-Thu, to 10pm Fri & Sat; 🛜☑) Sweet Melissa's makes delicious vegetarian and gluten-free dishes, no doubt the healthiest food for miles, such as gorgonzola-leek mac 'n' cheese. The cauliflower wings are bomber, as is the service.

Wyoming's Rib & Chop House
AMERICAN $$

(☑307-460-9090; www.ribandchophouse.com; 2415 Grand Ave; mains $11-24; ⊙11am-10pm) For a real slice of modern Americana, wait in line at this wildly popular place, order from an extensive menu that ranges from slow-cooked ribs and Black Angus steaks to crab-stuffed mushrooms and lobster potpie, then watch from nearly a dozen TV screens streaming live sports.

Coal Creek Coffee Co
COFFEE

(☑307-745-7737; www.coalcreekcoffee.com; 110 E Grand Ave; mains $5-11; ⊙6am-11pm; 🛜) With superlative brews, Coal Creek Coffee is everything you want in a coffeehouse: modern and stylish, even borderline hipster – but not in a bad way. When the fair-trade beans and expertly prepared lattes start to feel so 10am, roll over to Coal Creek Tap in the west wing where you'll find more than a dozen draft beers.

ⓘ Getting There & Away

Five miles west of town on Hwy 130, **Laramie Regional Airport** (☑307-742-4164; www.laramieairport.com; 555 General Brees Rd) has twice-daily flights to Denver, as well as to a few smaller regional airstrips.

Greyhound (☑307-745-7394; www.greyhound.com; 1952 N Banner Rd) buses stop at the gas station everyone calls the 'Diamond Shamrock,' though it is unclear what brand it operates under these days. Destinations include Denver ($40, three hours).

Lander

Sprawled out near the foothills of the Wind River Range, Lander has always been a frontier town. Originally established as a fort on a spur of the Oregon Trail, it was later the end of the rail line and a frequent haunt of outlaws and horse thieves. It is also the gateway to the Wind River Indian Reservation, where indigenous Eastern Shoshone share 2.2 million acres of land with displaced Northern Arapaho at the base of the state's tallest peak.

Lander has a strong pedigree among climbers, hikers and other adventure seekers. But the town's remoteness means few stay for long, leaving Lander in relative peace, retaining its mellow blend of the Old and New West.

⊙ Sights & Activities

Sinks Canyon State Park
PARK

(☑307-332-3077; www.sinkscanyonstatepark.org; 3079 Sinks Canyon Rd; tent & RV $11-16; ⊙visitor center 9am-6pm Jun-Sep) Beautiful Sinks Canyon State Park, 6 miles southwest of Lander on Hwy 131, centers on a curious feature of the Middle Fork of the Popo Agie River, where the rushing water suddenly turns into a small cave and disappears into the soluble Madison limestone. Although the water bubbles up a quarter-mile downstream, scientists have learned it takes nearly two hours for it to make the subterranean journey before emerging warmer and with more volume.

🛏 Sleeping

Outlaw Cabins
B&B $$

(☑307-332-9655; www.outlawcabins.com; 2411 Squaw Creek Rd; cabins $125) On a working ranch are a pair of real cabins done real nice. The Lawman was built by a county sheriff over 120 years ago, but has been maintained and restored for modern sensibilities. The Outlaw is our favorite, however, on account of its more Wild West vibe. Both are beautifully appointed with quiet porches made for sittin' on.

★ Mill House
BOUTIQUE HOTEL $$

(☑307-349-9254; http://millhouselander.com/; 125 Main St; ste from $190; 🛜) Lander's most stylish address is an artful conversion of the town's old mill house, with exposed brick walls, hardwood floors and muted color schemes that carry a strong sense of contemporary style. You can book individual suites, each of which is different, or the whole house, but however you stay, this is one of Wyoming's best.

✕ Eating

Middle Fork
BREAKFAST $

(☑307-335-5035; www.themiddleforklander.com; 351 Main St; mains $6-11; ⊙7am-2pm Mon-Sat, 9am-2pm Sun; 🛜☑) A large hall with spartan ambience leaves you free to focus on the food – which is excellent. Homemade baked goods hold court with eggs Benedict and in-house corned-beef hash washed down with mimosas.

★Cowfish   GRILL $$
(☎307-332-8227;   www.cowfishlander.com; 148 Main St; brunch $9-16, dinner $17-35; ☺5-10pm Mon-Fri, 9am-2pm & 5-10pm Sat & Sun; ☎) Spring for a candlelit dinner of brussels-sprout carbonara or coffee-rubbed rib eye at Lander's upscale restaurant suitable for date nights. The attached brewery serves the same food in a more casual atmosphere among the mash tuns (steel brewing vessels) that churn out a rotating menu of handcrafted beer experiments – many of which are excellent (sample a few before committing).

❶ Information

Lander Visitor Center (☎307-332-3892; www. landerchamber.org; 160 N 1st St; ☺9am-5pm Mon-Fri)

❶ Getting There & Away

Wind River Transportation Authority (☎307-856-7118; www.wrtabuslines.com; cnr West Main St & Baldwin Creek Rd, Shopko; one way $1) provides scheduled services Monday to Friday between Riverton and Lander, plus reserved service to Casper or Jackson (prices vary based on number of riders). You'll want a car, however, to access trailheads and climbing crags.

Jackson

Welcome to the other side of Wyoming, not to mention one of the state's most appealing towns. Hiding in a verdant valley between some of America's most rugged and wild mountains, Jackson looks similar to other towns in the state – false-front roof lines, covered wooden walkways, saloons on every block – but it ain't quite the same.

Here, hard-core climbers, cyclists and skiers (recognizable as sunburned baristas) outnumber cowboys by a wide margin, and you're just as likely to see a celebrity as a moose wandering the urban trails.

Although Jackson, being posh and popular, does have its downsides for the traveler, it does mean you'll find a lively urban buzz, a refreshing variety of foods and no shortage of things to do – both in and out of town.

◉ Sights & Activities

★**National Museum of Wildlife Art** MUSEUM
(Map p798; ☎307-733-5771; www.wildlifeart.org; 2820 Rungius Rd; adult/child $15/6; ☺9am-5pm May-Oct, 9am-5pm Tue-Sat, 11am-5pm Sun Nov-Apr; ⊕) Major works by Bierstadt, Rungius, Remington and Russell breathe life into their subjects in impressive and inspiring ways. The outdoor sculptures and building itself (inspired, oddly, by a ruined Scottish castle) are worth stopping by to see even if the museum is closed.

National Elk Refuge   WILDLIFE RESERVE
(Map p798; ☎307-733-9212; www.fws.gov/ref uge/national_elk_refuge; Hwy 89; sleigh ride adult/ child $25/15; ☺10am-4pm mid-Dec–mid-Apr) This refuge protects Jackson's herd of several thousand elk, offering them a winter habitat from November to May. During summer, ask at the Jackson visitor center (p791) for the best places to see elk. An hour-long horse-drawn sleigh ride is the highlight of a winter visit; buy tickets at the visitor center.

★**Jackson Hole
Mountain Resort**   SNOW SPORTS
(Map p798; ☎307-733-2292; www.jacksonhole. com; adult/child ski pass $155/94, Grand Adventure pass $75; ☺Nov-Apr & Jun-Sep) This mountain is larger than life. Whether tackling Jackson Hole with skis, board, boots or mountain bike, you will be humbled. With more than 4000ft of vertical rise and some of the world's most infamous slopes, Jackson Hole's 2500 acres and average 400in of snow sit at the top of every serious shredder's bucket list.

★**Continental Divide
Dogsled Adventures**   TOUR
(Map p798; ☎307-455-3052; www.dogsledad ventures.com; half-day tour incl transportation & lunch $305; ☺Dec-Apr) Experience Wyoming's wintry backcountry from a dog's point of view with five-time Iditarod veteran Billy Snodgrass. Half-day trips include transportation from your Jackson hotel to Togwotee Pass, where you'll learn dogsled lore and the sport's history while teams of eight to 14 Alaskan huskies whisk you (and a guide) silently through the wilderness.

Jackson Hole Paragliding   PARAGLIDING
(Map p798; ☎307-739-2626; www.jhparagliding. com; tandem flight $345; ☺May-Oct) The only thing better than being in the Tetons is to be soaring above the Tetons. Tandem rides

with experienced pilots take off from Jackson Hole Mountain Resort (p789) in the mornings or **Snow King** (Map p798; ☑307-201-5464; https://snowkingmountain.com; 400 E Snow King Ave; lift ticket adult/child $58/48) in the afternoons. No experience necessary, but age and weight limits apply.

✦ Festivals & Events

Grand Teton Music Festival
MUSIC

(GTMF; ☎307-733-1128; www.gtmf.org; Walk Festival Hall, Teton Village; ⊙Jul & Aug) A near-continuous celebration of classical music in a fantastic summer venue. The Festival Orchestra plays every Friday at 8pm and Saturday at 6pm showcasing worldwide musicians and directors. The GTMF Presents program highlights and noted talent on most Wednesdays. Free family concerts provide a more informal way to experience things.

🛏 Sleeping

In Jackson, the quality of accommodations is high, but so are the prices. Jackson has plenty of lodging, both in town and at Jackson Hole Mountain Resort (p789), but reservations are still essential in summer and winter high season. There are a few camping options scattered in the forest nearby, but most require a long drive, often down poor roads.

The Hostel
HOSTEL $

(Map p798; ☑307-733-3415; www.thehostel.us; 3315 Village Dr, Teton Village; dm $32-55, r $50-170; @🛜🐾) This skier's favorite has been here so long it doesn't need a name – everybody knows the Hostel. Budget privates and cramped four-person bunk rooms are smack in the middle of everything (meaning you'll only be in them when you're sleeping). The spacious lounge, with fireplace and pool table, foosball and ski waxing station, are all chill places to socialize.

Antler Inn
HOTEL $$

(Map p798; ☑307-733-2535; www.townsquareinns.com/antler-inn; 43 W Pearl Ave; r $85-220, cabin $115-290; ❄🛜🐾) Right in the middle of the Jackson action, this sprawling complex provides clean and comfortable rooms, some with fireplaces and bathtubs. Stepping into the cheaper 'cedar log' rooms feels like you're coming home to a cozy Wyoming cabin, mostly because you are: they were hauled here and attached to the back of the hotel.

Modern Mountain Motel
MOTEL $$$

(Map p798; ☑307-733-4340; https://mountainmodernmotel.com; 380 W Broadway; r $125-330; 🅿🛜🐾) Marrying functionality (there's room to store your snow gear) with style (wall-sized B&W photographs and wall maps), Modern Mountain Motel takes the old motel idea and updates it for the modern age. Despite having 135 rooms, they're often full, and deservedly so.

★ Wort Hotel
HISTORIC HOTEL $$$

(Map p798; ☑307-733-2190; www.worthotel.com; 50 N Glenwood St; r from $450; ❄@🛜) A distinctly Wyoming feel permeates this luxury historic hotel that has only gotten better with age. Knotty pine furniture and hand-crafted bedspreads complement full-size baths and Jacuzzis while the best concierge service in Jackson helps you fill out your itinerary with outdoor adventures. Even if staying here is out of your reach, swing by the antique **Silver Dollar Bar** downstairs.

★ Rusty Parrot Lodge & Spa
LODGE $$$

(Map p798; ☑888-739-1749; www.rustyparrot.com; 175 N Jackson St; r from $475; ❄🛜) With a collection of Remington sculptures and amazing Western art, this elegant lodge oozes luxury. Service is top-notch and rooms pamper with well-tended bedroom fireplaces and a plush teddy bear posed on the bed. Those who don't ski will get distracted at the spa, where the arnica sports massages and herbal lavender wraps are pure hedonism.

The gourmet restaurant prepares innovative international cuisine.

🍴 Eating

Persephone
BAKERY $

(Map p798; ☑307-200-6708; www.persephonebakery.com; 145 E Broadway; mains $8-13; ⊙7am-6pm Mon-Sat, to 5pm Sun; 🛜) With rustic breads, oversized pastries and breakfast masterpieces, this tiny white-washed French bakery is worth waiting in line for (and you will). In summer the spacious patio provides more room for lingering with your coffee – or go for a pitcher of Bloody Mary.

★ Gun Barrel
STEAK $$

(Map p798; ☑307-733-3287; http://jackson.gunbarrel.com; 852 W Broadway; mains $16-56; ⊙5:30pm-late) The line stretches out the door for Jackson's best steakhouse, where the buffalo prime rib and elk chop rival the grilled bone-in rib eye for the title of 'king cut.' For a fun game, try to match the meat with the animal watching you eat it: this place was once the wildlife and taxidermy museum, and many original tenants remain.

Mangy Moose Saloon   PUB FOOD $$
(Map p798; ☑ 307-733-4913; www.mangymoose.com; 3295 Village Dr, Teton Village; mains lunch $8-23, dinner $18-48; ☺ 7am-9pm, saloon 11am-2am; ☎) For more than half a century Mangy Moose has been the rowdy epicenter for après-ski, big-name bands, slopeside dining and general mountain mischief at Jackson Hole Mountain Resort (p789). The cavernous pub offers a decent salad bar and cranks out bowls of chili, buffalo burgers and steaks from local farms, while the Rocky Mountain Oyster Cafe has your breakfast needs covered.

Snake River Grill   AMERICAN $$$
(Map p798; ☑ 307-733-0557; www.snakerivergrill.com; 84 E Broadway; mains $22-62; ☺ 5:30-9pm) With a roaring stone fireplace, an extensive wine list and snappy white linens, this grill creates notable American haute cuisine. Try the pan-roasted Alaskan halibut or the Wagyu short ribs. Or munch on a cast-iron bucket of truffle fries. Splurge on desserts such as roasted strawberry sorbet.

⚲ Drinking & Nightlife

From breweries to bars to concerts to theaters, there's no lack of things to fill your evenings in Jackson, especially during the summer and winter high seasons. Consult the *Jackson Hole News & Guide* (www.jhnewsandguide.com) for the latest happenings, or just head downtown and follow the sound of happy crowds.

★ Snake River Brewing Co   MICROBREWERY
(Map p798; ☑ 307-739-2337; www.snakeriverbrewing.com; 265 S Millward St; ☺ food 11am-11pm, drinks till late; ☎) With an arsenal of microbrews crafted on the spot (some award-winning), it's no wonder this is a favorite among the younger, outdoor-sports-positive crowd. Food (mains $13 to $21) includes wood-fired pizzas, bison burgers and pasta served in a modern-industrial warehouse with two floors and plenty of (but not too many) TVs broadcasting the game.

The Rose   COCKTAIL BAR
(Map p798; ☑ 307-733-1500; www.therosejh.com; 50 W Broadway; ☺ 5:30pm-2am Thu-Sat, 8pm-1:30am Sun, Tue & Wed) Slide into a red-leather booth at this swanky little lounge upstairs at the Pink Garter theater and enjoy the best craft cocktails in Jackson.

ℹ Information

The excellent *Jackson Hole Traveler Visitor Guide*, available from the visitor center, is an excellent resource.

Jackson Hole & Greater Yellowstone Visitor Center (Map p798; ☑ 307-733-3316; www.jacksonholechamber.com; 532 N Cache St; ☺ 8am-7pm Jun-Sep; ☎) Everything you need to know about Jackson, the nearby national parks, wildlife and more. Enjoy a handful of exhibits, pick up hunting or fishing licenses, buy park passes and otherwise plan your visit with expert guidance.

ℹ Getting There & Around

Jackson Hole Airport (JAC; Map p798; ☑ 307-733-7682; www.jacksonholeairport.com; 1250 E Airport Rd) is inside Grand Teton National Park 7 miles north of Jackson. Daily direct flights go to Chicago, Dallas, Denver, Los Angeles, Minneapolis, Phoenix, Salt Lake City, and San Francisco, plus many more seasonal flights.

Alltrans (Mountain States Express; ☑ 800-652-9510, 307-733-1719; www.jacksonholealltrans.com) runs a shuttle to Salt Lake ($82, 5¼ hours) and Grand Targhee ski area (adult/child including lift pass $128/97) in winter.

Greyhound (www.greyhound.com) has long-haul buses to Denver (from $90, 23½ hours).

Cody

You have a few choices when it comes to getting into Yellowstone National Park, and approaching from the Cody side of life should be top on your list. Not just for the mesmerizing drive along the North Fork of the Shoshone – which Theodore Roosevelt once called the '50 most beautiful miles in America' – but also for the town.

Cody revels in its frontier image, a legacy that started with its founder, William 'Buffalo Bill' Cody: Chief of Scouts for the army, notorious buffalo hunter, and showman who spent years touring the world with his Wild West extravaganza. The town rallies around nightly rodeos in summer, rowdy saloons and a world-class museum that was started by Buffalo Bill's estate and is a worthy destination all by itself.

◉ Sights

★ Buffalo Bill Center of the West   MUSEUM
(☑ 307-587-4771; www.centerofthewest.org; 720 Sheridan Ave; adult/child $19.50/13; ☺ 8am-6pm May–mid-Sep, 8am-5pm mid-Sep–Oct, 10am-5pm Nov, Mar & Apr, 10am-5pm Thu-Sun Dec-Feb) Do not miss Wyoming's most impressive

human-made attraction. This sprawling complex of six museums showcases everything Western: from the spectacle of Buffalo Bill's world-famous Wild West shows and galleries featuring powerful frontier-oriented artwork, to the visually absorbing **Plains Indian Museum**. Meanwhile, the **Draper Museum of Natural History** brilliantly explores the Yellowstone region's ecosystem. Look for Teddy Roosevelt's saddle, the busy beaver ball and one of the world's last buffalo tepees. Entry is valid for two consecutive days – and you'll need 'em. Save a couple of bucks by booking online.

Sleeping

Irma Hotel   HISTORIC HOTEL **$$**
(☑307-587-4221; www.irmahotel.com; 1192 Sheridan Ave; r $155-175, ste $230; ❋🖥) Built in 1902 by Buffalo Bill as the cornerstone of his planned city, this creaky hotel has old-fashioned charm with a few modern touches. The original high-ceiling historical suites are named after past guests (Annie Oakley, Calamity Jane), while the slightly more modern annex rooms are very similar but cheaper (and still have classic pull-chain toilets).

The Cody   HOTEL **$$$**
(☑307-587-5915; www.thecody.com; 232 W Yellowstone Ave; d $260-290; ❋🖥🏊) 🅿 One of Cody's most luxurious hotels, the Cody combines New Western chic with green credentials, incorporating paneling made with recycled wood from park facilities and offering free bicycles to guests. Pay $10 extra for a balcony room away from the road, or $30 more for a king Jacuzzi suite. Breakfast included.

Cody Cowboy Village   CABIN **$$**
(☑307-587-7555; www.thecodycowboyvillage.com; 203 W Yellowstone Ave; r & cabins $100-230; ☉May–mid-Oct; 🖥🏊🐾) Popular and well-run, the modern and stylish duplex cabins or stand-alone suites come with small porch. There's a large outdoor plunge pool. Breakfast is included.

✕ Eating

★ **The Local**   MODERN AMERICAN **$$**
(☑307-586-4262; www.thelocalcody.com; 1134 13th St; lunch $11-14, dinner $9-38; ☉9am-2pm & 5-8pm Tue-Sat; 🅟) 🅿 When Cody's cowboy cuisine starts to weigh on your arteries, find the antidote in the Local's fresh, organic and locally sourced dishes. Think a falafel sandwich or grilled trout.

Cassie's Western Saloon   STEAK **$$**
(☑307-527-5500; https://cassies.com; 214 Yellowstone Ave; lunch $12-29, steaks $22-50; ☉food 11am-10pm, drinks to 2am) This classic roadhouse and former house of ill repute hosts heavy swilling, swingin' country-and-western music and the occasional bar fight. Strap on the feedbag at the attached supper club and tackle tender steaks ranging in size from 8oz to 36oz.

☆ Entertainment

Cody Nite Rodeo   SPECTATOR SPORT
(☑307-587-5155; www.codystampederodeo.com; 519 W Yellowstone Ave; adult/child $21/10.50; ☉8pm Jun-Aug) Experience a quintessential small-town rodeo at this summer-night Cody tradition. Note that animal welfare groups often criticize rodeo events as being harmful to animals.

❶ Getting There & Away

Yellowstone Regional Airport (COD; ☑307-587-5096; www.flyyra.com; 2101 Roger Sedam Dr), Cody's small airport on the eastern edge of town, connects this otherwise isolated town with Salt Lake City and Denver in summer, and you can thank Buffalo Bill Cody for the scenic byway that bears his name and connects Cody to Yellowstone – a spectacular approach to the park.

Yellowstone National Park

Teeming with moose, elk, bison, grizzly bears and wolves, America's first **national park** (Map p794; ☑307-344-7381; www.nps.gov/yell; Grand Loop Rd, Mammoth; vehicle $35; ☉North Entrance year-round, South Entrance May-Oct) also contains some of the country's wildest lands, just begging to be explored.

Yellowstone is home to more than 60% of the world's geysers – natural hot springs with unique plumbing that causes them to periodically erupt in towering explosions of boiling water and steam. And while these astounding phenomena and their neighboring Technicolor hot springs and bubbling mud pots draw in the crowds (more than 4 million people each year), the surrounding canyons, mountains and forests are no less impressive.

◉ Sights

◉ Geyser Country

Yellowstone's Geyser Country holds the park's most spectacular geothermal features (more than half the world's total), within the world's densest concentration of geysers (more than 200 spouters in 1.5 sq miles). It is Geyser Country that makes the Yellowstone plateau utterly and globally unique.

Highlights of the area include **Old Faithful** (Map p794) and the **Upper Geyser Basin** (Map p794) and Grand Prismatic Spring. The majority of the geysers line the Firehole River, the aquatic backbone of the basin, whose tributaries feed 21 of the park's 110 waterfalls. Both the Firehole and Madison Rivers offer superb fly-fishing, and the meadows along them support large wildlife populations.

Old Faithful
Visitor Education Center   VISITOR CENTER
(Map p794; ☑ 307-545-2751; Old Faithful; ◷ 8am-8pm Jun-Sep, 9am-5pm Dec-Mar, hours vary spring & fall; 🖫) ✐ This environmentally friendly center is all about the thermal features at Yellowstone, exploring the differences between geysers, hot springs, fumaroles and mud pots, and explaining why there are no geysers in Mammoth. Kids will enjoy the hands-on Young Scientist displays, which include a working laboratory geyser. Predicted eruption times are posted for a handful of the park's most famous gushers.

★ **Grand Prismatic Spring**   HOT SPRINGS
(Map p794; Midway Geyser Basin) At 370ft wide and 121ft deep, Grand Prismatic Spring is the park's largest and deepest hot spring. It's also considered by many to be the most beautiful thermal feature in the park. Boardwalks lead around the multicolored mist of the gorgeous pool and its spectacularly colored rainbow rings of algae. From above, the spring looks like a giant blue eye weeping exquisite multicolored tears.

◉ Mammoth Country

Mammoth Country is renowned for its graceful geothermal terraces and the towering Gallatin Range to the northwest.

For visitors (and most elk) the focal point of the Mammoth region is Mammoth Junction (6239ft), 5 miles south of the North Entrance, on a plateau above Mammoth

WORTH A TRIP

SCENIC DRIVE: THE ROOF OF THE ROCKIES

Depending on who's talking, the **Beartooth Hwy** (www.beartoothhighway.com; Hwy 212; ◷ late May–mid-Oct) is either the best way to get to Yellowstone, the most exciting motorbike ride in the West or the most scenic highway in the USA. We'd say it is all three. The head-spinning tarmac snakes up the mountainside to deposit you in a different world, high above the tree line, onto a rolling plateau of mountain tundra, alpine lakes and Rocky Mountain goats. The views are superb, the fishing awesome and the hiking literally breathtaking.

Campground. Just south of the junction is Mammoth Hot Springs, the area's main thermal attraction. From here roads go south to Norris (21 miles) and east to Tower-Roosevelt Junction (18 miles).

◉ Tower-Roosevelt Country

Fossil forests, the wildlife-rich **Lamar Valley** (Map p794), its tributary trout streams of Slough and Pebble Creeks and the dramatic and craggy peaks of the Absaroka Range are the highlights of this remote, scenic and undeveloped region.

◉ Canyon Country

A series of scenic overlooks linked by hiking trails punctuate the cliffs, precipices and waterfalls of the Grand Canyon of the Yellowstone. Here the river continues to gouge out a fault line through an ancient golden geyser basin, most impressively at **Lower Falls**. South Rim Drive leads to the canyon's most spectacular overlook, at **Artist Point** (Map p794; South Rim Dr, Canyon), while **North Rim Drive** accesses the daring precipices of the Upper and Lower Falls.

Grand Canyon of the Yellowstone   CANYON
(Map p794) Near Canyon Village, this is one of the park's true blockbuster sights. After its placid meanderings north from Yellowstone Lake, the Yellowstone River suddenly plummets over Upper Falls and then the much larger Lower Falls before raging through the 1000ft-deep canyon. Scenic overlooks and a network of trails along the canyon's

Yellowstone National Park

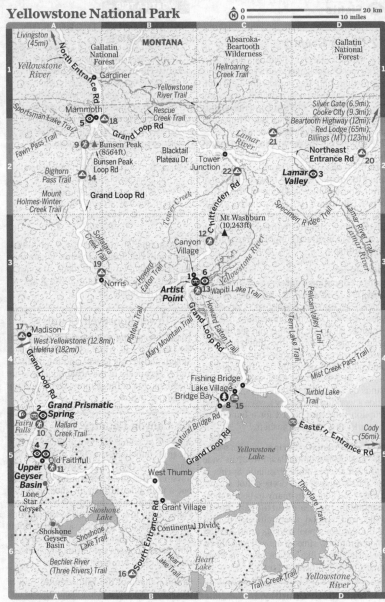

rims highlight its multicolored beauty from a dozen angles.

Lake Country

Yellowstone Lake (7733ft) is Lake Country's shimmering centerpiece – one of the world's largest alpine lakes, with the biggest inland population of cutthroat trout in the US. Yellowstone River emerges from the north end of the lake and flows through Hayden Valley into the Grand Canyon of the Yellowstone. The lake's southern and eastern borders flank the steep Absaroka Range and

Yellowstone National Park

the pristine Thorofare region, some of the wildest and remotest lands in the lower 48. This watery wilderness lined with volcanic beaches is best explored by **boat** (Map p798; ☑ 307-734-9227; www.jennylakeboating.com; round-trip shuttle adult/child 2-11yrs $15/8, scenic cruise US$19/11; ☉ 7am-7pm Jun-late Sep) or sea kayak.

🏃 Activities

★ Bunsen Peak & Osprey Falls   HIKING, MOUNTAIN BIKING
(Map p794) Bunsen Peak (8564ft) is a popular early-season half-day hike that offers superb views in all directions. You can extend it to a more demanding day hike by continuing down the mountain's gentler eastern slope to the Bunsen Peak Rd and then *waaay* down (800ft) to the base of seldom-visited Osprey Falls.

Lone Star Geyser Trail   HIKING, CYCLING
(Map p794) This paved and pine-lined hike is an easy stroll (or family bike ride) along a former service road to one of the park's largest backcountry geysers. Isolated Lone Star erupts every three hours for two to 30 minutes and reaches 30ft to 45ft in height. It is definitely worth hanging around for an eruption if possible.

Mt Washburn   HIKING, MOUNTAIN BIKING
(Map p794; Tower-Roosevelt) This fairly strenuous two-hour uphill hike from Dunraven Pass trailhead to a mountaintop fire tower with 360-degree views over the park and nearby bighorn sheep is Yellowstone's most

popular hike (6.4 miles round-trip, four hours). Alternatively, tackle the climb on a bicycle via the dirt Chittenden Rd from the north. The route's often blocked by snow until the end of June.

Fairy Falls Trail & Twin Buttes   HIKING
(Map p794) Tucked away in the northwestern corner of the Midway Geyser Basin, Fairy Falls (197ft) is a popular hike. Beyond Fairy Falls the trail continues to a hidden thermal area at the base of the Twin Buttes. The geysers are undeveloped, and you're likely to have them to yourself – a stark contrast to the throngs surrounding Grand Prismatic Spring (p793) below.

🛏 Sleeping

NPS and private campgrounds, along with cabins, lodges and hotels are all available in the park. Reservations, where possible, are essential in summer. Plentiful accommodations can also be found in the gateway towns of Cody, Gardiner and West Yellowstone.

The best budget options are the seven NPS-run campgrounds in **Mammoth** (Map p794; Mammoth; campsites $20; ☉ year-round), **Tower Fall** (Map p794; Tower-Roosevelt; campsites $15; ☉ mid-May–late Sep), **Indian Creek** (Map p794; Mammoth; campsites $15; ☉ early Jun–mid-Sep), **Pebble Creek** (Map p794; campsites $15; ☉ mid-Jun–late Sep), **Slough Creek** (Map p794; Tower-Roosevelt; campsites $15; ☉ mid-Jun–early Oct), Norris Campground (p796) and **Lewis Lake** (Map p794; South Entrance; campsites $15; ⊘ mid-Jun–Oct), which are first come, first served.

Xanterra (☑ 307-344-7311; www.yellowstonenationalparklodges.com) runs five more reservable campgrounds, all with cold-water bathrooms, flush toilets and drinking water. RV sites with full hookups are available at Fishing Bridge.

Norris Campground   CAMPGROUND $
(Map p794; Norris; campsites $20; ⊘ mid-May–Sep) Nestled in a scenic, open, lodgepole-pine forest on a sunny hill overlooking the Gibbon River and meadows, this is one of the park's nicest campgrounds. Sites are given on a first-come basis and the few loop-A riverside spots get snapped up quickly. Campfire talks are at 7:30pm and firewood is sold between 7pm and 8:30pm. Generators allowed 8am to 8pm.

Madison Campground   CAMPGROUND $
(Map p794; ☑ 307-344-7311; www.yellowstonenationalparklodges.com; W Entrance Rd, Madison; campsites $26; ⊘ May-Oct) The nearest campground to Old Faithful and the West Entrance occupies a sunny, open forest in a broad meadow above the Madison River. Bison and the park's largest elk herd frequent the meadows to its west, making for great wildlife-watching, and it's a fine base for fly-fishing the Madison. You can (and should) reserve your site in advance.

★**Old Faithful Inn**   HOTEL $$
(Map p794; ☑ 307-344-7311; www.yellowstonenationalparklodges.com; Old Faithful; d with shared/private bath from $167/288, r $368-437; ⊘ early May-early Oct) A stay at this historic log masterpiece is a quintessential Yellowstone experience. The lobby alone is worth a visit, just to sit in front of the impossibly large rhyolite fireplace and listen to the pianist

upstairs. The cheapest 'Old House' rooms provide the most atmosphere, with log walls and original washbasins, but bathrooms are down the hall.

Lake Yellowstone Hotel   HOTEL $$$
(Map p794; ☑ 866-439-7375; www.yellowstonenationalparklodges.com; cottages $209, Sandpiper $305-341, hotel r $277-632; ⊘ mid-May–early Oct; @) ⚲ Commanding the northern lakeshore, this buttercup-yellow colonial behemoth sets romantics aflutter. It harks back to a bygone era, though the rooms that cost $4 in 1895 have appreciated somewhat. Lakeside rooms cost extra, sell out first and don't guarantee lake views. Small cottages have rooms with two double beds. Internet access is wired only, and available in main hotel rooms.

✖ Eating

★**Mammoth Hot Springs Dining Room**   AMERICAN $$
(Map p794; Mammoth; dinner mains $12-26; ⊘ 6:30-10am, 11:30am-2:30pm & 5-10pm May–mid-Sep; 🔊) There are a few surprises in this elegant place, including a delicious dinner starter of Thai-curry mussels. Dinner is a serious affair, with Montana meatloaf, and pistachio-and-parmesan-crusted trout. For dessert, try the 'Yellowstone caldera': a warm chocolate-truffle torte with a suitably molten center. Reservations only necessary in winter. From mid-September through October hours remain the same, except dinner is served until 9pm.

Lake Yellowstone Hotel Dining Room   AMERICAN $$$
(Map p794; ☑ 307-344-7311; www.yellowstonenationalparklodges.com; Lake Village; dinner mains $16-37; ⊘ 6:30-10am, 11:30am-2:30pm & 5-10pm mid-May–early Oct; ✐) Save your one unwrinkled outfit to feast in style in Lake Yellowstone Hotel's dining room. Lunch options include trout, poached-pear salad and sandwiches. Dinner ups the ante with starters of lobster ravioli and mains of beef tenderloin, elk chops, quail and rack of Montana lamb. Dinner reservations are required.

ℹ Information

The park is open year-round, but most roads close in winter. Park entrance permits (hiker/vehicle $15/30) are valid for seven days. For entry into both Yellowstone and Grand Teton the fee is $50.

SOUTH RIM TRAIL

Southeast of the Yellowstone canyon's South Rimx, a network of **trails** Map p794) meanders through meadows and forests and past some small lakes, including **Ribbon Lake**. Linking several of these trails, the South Rim Trail loop hike (6 miles, four hours) combines awesome views of the Grand Canyon of the Yellowstone (p###) with a couple of lakes and even a backcountry thermal area.

ℹ️ BEAT THE CROWDS

Yellowstone's wonderland attracts up to 30,000 visitors daily in July and August and tops four million gatecrashers annually. Avoid the worst of the crowds with the following advice:

Visit in May or October Services may be limited, but there will be far fewer people.

Hit the trail Most (95%) of visitors never set foot on a backcountry trail; only 1% camp at a backcountry site (permit required).

Bike the park Most campgrounds have underutilized hiker/biker sites, and your skinny tires can slip through any traffic jam.

Mimic the wildlife Be active during the golden hours after dawn and before dusk.

Pack a lunch Eat at one of the park's many overlooked and often lovely scenic picnic areas.

Bundle up Enjoy a private Old Faithful eruption during the winter months.

Cell service is limited in the park, and wi-fi can only be found at Mammoth's **Albright Visitor Center** (Map p794; ☑ 307-344-2263; www. nps.gov/yell/planyourvisit/mammothvc.htm; Mammoth; ☺ 8am-6pm mid-Jun–Aug, 9am-5pm Sep–mid-Jun).

ℹ️ Getting There & Away

Most visitors to Yellowstone fly into Jackson, WY, or Bozeman, MT, but it's often more affordable to choose Billings, MT. You will need a car; there is no public transportation to or within Yellowstone National Park.

Grand Teton National Park

Awesome in their grandeur, the Tetons have captivated the imagination from the moment humans laid eyes on them. This **wilderness** (Map p798; ☑ 307-739-3300; www. nps.gov/grte; entrance per vehicle/motorcyclist $35/30, hiker or cyclist $20) is home to bear, moose and elk in number, and played a fundamental role in the history of American alpine climbing.

Some 12 imposing glacier-carved summits frame the singular Grand Teton (13,775ft). And while the view is breathtaking from the valley floor, it only gets more impressive on the trail. It's well worth hiking the dramatic canyons of fragrant forest to sublime alpine lakes surrounded by wildflowers in summer.

👁️ Sights & Activities

With almost 250 miles of **hiking trails**, options are plentiful. Backcountry-use permits are required for overnight trips. **Rock climbing** and **fishing** are also possible.

Cross-country skiing and **snowshoeing** are the best ways to take advantage of park winters. Pick up a brochure detailing routes at Craig Thomas Discovery & Visitor Center.

Craig Thomas Discovery & Visitor Center   TOURIST INFORMATION
(Map p798; ☑ 307-739-3399; www.nps.gov/grte/planyourvisit/ctdvc.htm; Teton Park Rd, Moose; ☺ 8am-7pm Jun-Aug, hours vary Mar-May, Sep & Oct; 🛜♿) Your first stop should be this incredibly well-done visitor center. The raised-relief map helps you focus on where to go, while informative kid-friendly interactive displays show what you'll see. Rangers are on hand to help plan your visit, and you can get backcountry permits here, too.

Mormon Row   GHOST TOWN
(Map p798; Antelope Flats Rd; 🅿) This is possibly the most photographed spot in the park – and for good reason. The aged wooden barns and fence rails make a quintessential pastoral scene, perfectly framed by the imposing bulk of the Tetons. The barns and houses were built in the 1890s by Mormon settlers, who farmed the fertile alluvial soil irrigated by miles of hand-dug ditches.

Oxbow Bend   RIVER
(Map p798; N Park Rd; 🅿) One of the most famous scenic spots in Grand Teton National Park for wildlife-watching is Oxbow Bend, with the reflection of Mt Moran as a stunning backdrop. Dawn and dusk are the best times to spot moose, elk, sandhill cranes, ospreys, bald eagles, trumpeter swans, Canada geese, blue herons and white pelicans. The oxbow was created as the river's faster

ROCKY MOUNTAINS GRAND TETON NATIONAL PARK

Grand Teton National Park

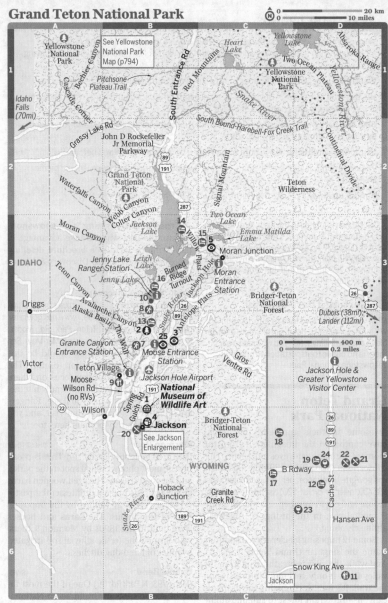

water eroded the outer bank while the slower inner flow deposited sediment.

Death Canyon Trail HIKING

(Map p798) Death Canyon is one of our favorite hikes – both for the challenge and the astounding scenery. The trail ascends a mile

to the Phelps Lake overlook before dropping down into the valley bottom and following Death Canyon.

Garnet Canyon HIKING, CLIMBING

(Map p798) Garnet Canyon is the hard-won gateway to scrambles to Middle and South

Grand Teton National Park

Teton and the technical ascent of Grand Teton – but you need technical climbing skills and an existing familiarity with the routes. However, even non-climbers will find the 4-mile hike to the starting point of the Grand Teton climb a memorable one.

Grand Teton Multiuse Bike Path CYCLING (www.nps.gov/grte/planyourvisit/bike.htm; ☉dawn-dusk May-Oct) Starting in the town of Jackson from Jackson Visitor Center (p791) and continuing 20 miles to the **Jenny Lake Ranger Station** (Map p798; ☑307-739-3343; 407 Jenny Lake Campground Road, Moose, WY; ☉8am-5pm Jun-Aug), this multiuse path is an excellent way to see the park at a slow, intimate pace. For a shorter ride, rent bikes at **Dornan's** (Map p798; ☑307-733-3307; www.dornans.com; ☉9am-6pm) in Moose for the 8-mile ride to Jenny Lake.

🛏 Sleeping

★**Climbers' Ranch** CABIN $ (Map p798; ☑307-733-7271; www.americanalpineclub.org/grand-teton-climbers-ranch; End Highlands Rd; dm $27; ☉Jun-Sep; ℗) Started as a refuge for serious climbers, these rustic log cabins run by the American Alpine Club are now available to hikers, who can take advantage of the spectacular in-park location. There is a bathhouse with showers and a sheltered cook station with locking bins for coolers. Bring your own sleeping bag and pad (bunks are bare, but still a steal).

Colter Bay Village CABIN $$ (Map p798; ☑307-543-3100; www.gtlc.com/lodges/colter-bay-village; Colter Bay; tent cabins $76, cabins with bath $189-267; ☉late May-Sep; ℗) In this busy village, comfortable log cabins, some original, are your best bet, available late May through September. Tent cabins (available June to early September) are very basic log-and-canvas structures sporting Siberian gulag charm. Expect bare bunks, a wood-burning stove, a picnic table and an outdoor grill. Bathrooms are separate and sleeping bags can be rented.

★**Jackson Lake Lodge** LODGE $$$ (Map p798; ☑307-543-3100; www.gtlc.com/lodges/jackson-lake-lodge; Jackson Lake Lodge Rd; r & cottages $339-459, ste $850; ☉mid-May–early Oct; ℗🅿🛜🏊🐾) With soft sheets, meandering trails for long walks and enormous picture windows framing the peaks, the Teton's premier lodge is the perfect place to romance. Nearby, you may find the 348 cinder-block cottages overpriced for their viewless, barracks-like arrangement, though renovations have made them pleasant inside. The secluded Moose Pond View cottages feature amazing porch-side panoramas.

★ Jenny Lake Lodge
LODGE $$$

(Map p798; ☐ 307-543-3100; www.gtlc.com/lodges/jenny-lake-lodge; Jenny Lake Scenic Dr; all-inclusive cabins from $542; ☺ Jun-early Oct; ℙ) Worn timbers, down comforters and colorful quilts imbue these elegant cabins with a cozy atmosphere. It doesn't come cheap, but the Signature Stay package includes breakfast, five-course dinner, bicycle use and guided horseback riding. Rainy days are for hunkering down at the fireplace in the main lodge with a game or book from the stacks.

✗ Eating

Pizza & Pasta Company
PIZZA $

(Map p798; ☐ 307-733-2415; www.dornans.com; Moose; mains $10-13, pizzas $9-17; ☺ 11:30am-9:30pm; ☎) If there is a more compelling place for pizza and beers than **Dornan's** (Map p798; ☐ 307-733-2415; www.dornans.com; Moose; ☺ 8am-8pm) rooftop deck, looking across the Snake River and Menor's Ferry at the towering Tetons, we've yet to find it. Unfortunately service can be slow and the food comes second to the view. One of the only independently owned restaurants in the park, it's open year-round.

Blue Heron Lounge
BARBECUE $$

(Map p798; ☐ 307-543-2811; www.gtlc.com/dining/blue-heron-lounge-jackson-lake-lodge; Jackson Lake Lodge; mains $11-23; ☺ 11am-midnight mid-May–Sep) A must for sunset cocktails, this attractive wraparound bar features knee-to-ceiling windows. Alcohol and tasty small plates consisting of charcuterie and salads are locally sourced. If the weather is good, the outdoor grill offers great barbecue. Occasionally you'll hit on live music.

Dornan's Chuckwagon
BARBECUE $$

(Map p798; ☐ 307-733-2415; www.dornans.com; Moose; breakfast & lunch mains $8-20, dinner $9-35; ☺ 7-11am, noon-3pm & 5-9pm Jun-Aug) At this outdoor family favorite, breakfast means sourdough pancakes and eggs off the griddle, while lunchtime offers light fare and sandwiches. Come dinner, Dutch ovens are steaming. There's beef, ribs or trout, along with a bottomless salad bar. Picnic tables have unparalleled views of the Grand. Kids get special rates. There's live music from 5:30pm to 8:30pm, Tuesday to Thursday.

★ Jenny Lake Lodge Dining Room
AMERICAN $$$

(Map p798; ☐ 307-543-3351; www.gtlc.com/dining/the-dining-room-at-jenny-lake-lodge; Jenny Lake; lunch $12-18, 5-course prix-fixe dinner $98; ☺ 7:30-10am, 11:30am-1:30pm & 6-9pm) ✎ A real splurge, this may be the only five-course wilderness meal of your life, and it's well worth it. For breakfast, crab-cake eggs Benedict is prepared to perfection. Elk tenderloin and daikon watermelon salad satisfy hungry hikers, and you can't beat the warm atmosphere snuggled in the Tetons. Dress up in the evening, when reservations are a must.

ⓘ Information

Park permits (hiker/bicycle/vehicle $20/30/35) are valid for seven days.

ⓘ Getting There & Away

Jackson Hole Airport (p791) lies inside the park's boundaries and sees a steady stream of traffic. Currently there is no regular shuttle service through the park, though several companies in Jackson provide guided tours.

The park begins 4.5 miles north of Jackson. There are three entrance stations. The closest to Jackson is the **South Entrance** (Map p798; Teton Park Rd, Moose Village; ☺ hours vary), west of Moose Junction. From Teton Village, the **Southwest Entrance** (Map p798; Moose-Wilson Rd; ☺ hours vary) is a mile or so north via the Moose–Wilson Rd. If driving south from Yellowstone, take the **North Entrance** (Map p798; Hwy 287; ☺ hours vary), 3 miles inside the park on US 89/191/287 just north of Moran Junction.

MONTANA

Welcome to Big Sky Country, where the Great Plains hit the Rockies and just about anything seems possible. Wilderness areas rule out here, whether it's the pre-Yellowstone valleys of Montana's south to Absaroka Beartooth, Bob Marshall or the American Prairie Reserve and the horizons-without-end in Montana's rural heartland. Not far away, Missoula and Bozeman are hip urban centers rich in brewpubs, great restaurants and scenes of emerging culinary excellence. Montana is also home to Little Bighorn Battlefield and, the state's major drawcard, the sculpted peaks of Glacier National Park, one of the most dramatically beautiful corners of the continent.

ⓘ Information

There are tourist offices in towns across the state. The better ones are in **Bozeman** (☐ 406-586-5421; www.bozemancvb.com; 2000 Commerce Way; ☺ 8am-5pm Mon-Fri), **Billings**

(☑ 800-735-2635, 406-252-4016; www.vis-itbillings.com; 815 S 27th St; ☺ 8:30am-5pm Mon-Fri), Helena (p804), **West Yellowstone** (☑ 406-646-7701; www.destinationyellowstone.com; 30 Yellowstone Ave; ☺ 8am-8pm mid-May–Aug, 8am-4pm Mon-Fri Sep–mid-May; ☎) and Missoula (p806).

Visit Montana (☑ 800-847-4868; www.visitmt.com), the state's informative tourism website, has maps, guides and trip suggestions.

Bozeman & Gallatin Valley

Bozeman is what all those formerly hip, now-overrun Colorado mountain towns used to be like. The laid-back, old-school rancher legacy still dominates over the New West pioneers with their mountain bikes, skis and climbing racks. But that's changing rapidly. It is now one of the fastest-growing towns in America.

The brick buildings downtown, overflowing with brewpubs and boutiques, still retain their dusty historic appeal and you can spend days in the surrounding Bridger and Gallatin Mountains without seeing another human.

And, while Big Sky up the forested Gallatin Valley is besieged with condos and townhomes, Bridger Bowl is so underdeveloped you might question whether the place is still open. In short, get here quick so you can tell your kids about the time you were in Bozeman while it was still one of the coolest unknown towns in the Rockies.

⊙ Sights & Activities

⭐ **Museum of the Rockies** MUSEUM
(☑ 406-994-2251; www.museumoftherockies.org; 600 W Kagy Blvd; adult/child $14.50/9.50; ☺ 8am-6pm Jun-Aug, 9am-5pm Sep-May) The most entertaining museum in Montana should not be missed. It has stellar displays on the geological history of the Rockies, and dinosaur exhibits including an Edmontosaurus jaw with its incredible battery of teeth, the largest T. rex skull in the world, and a full T. rex (with only a slightly smaller skull). Laser planetarium shows are interesting, as is the living-history outdoors section (closed in winter).

⭐ **Bridger Bowl Ski Area** SNOW SPORTS
(☑ 406-587-2111; www.bridgerbowl.com; 15795 Bridger Canyon Rd; lift ticket adult/child $64/25; ☺ mid-Dec–Apr) As the nation's leading nonprofit ski resort, it's all about the 'cold smoke,' not cold, hard cash, at Bridger Bowl.

All you'll find at this small (2000 acres) community-owned hill 16 miles north of Bozeman is passionate skiers, reasonable prices and surprisingly great skiing.

Big Sky Resort SNOW SPORTS
(☑ 800-548-4486; www.bigskyresort.com; 50 Big Sky Resort Rd; ski/bike lift $142/46) The fourth-largest ski hill in North America is actually four mountains covering 5800 acres of skiable terrain (60% advanced/expert) that get more than 400in of powder a year. In short, Big Sky is big skiing. And when the snow melts, you get more than 40 miles of lift-served mountain-bike and hiking trails making it a worthy summer destination as well.

Explore Rentals OUTDOORS
(Phasmid; ☑ 406-922-0179; www.explore-rentals.com; 32 Dollar Dr; ☺ 9am-5pm Mon-Sat, 10am-4pm Sun) Imagine stepping off the plane and there waiting for you is a car complete with luggage box, camping trailer, cook set, sleeping bags, backpacks, tent, bear spray and full fly-fishing setup – all ready to go for your ultimate outdoor adventure. Or maybe you just forgot your stove. Explore has that and (just about) everything else for rent. Reservations highly recommended.

🛏 Sleeping

Most big-box chain motels are north of downtown Bozeman on 7th Ave, near I-90, with a handful of budget options east of downtown. Camping is plentiful in the Gallatin Valley toward Big Sky.

⭐ **Howlers Inn** B&B $$
(☑ 406-587-2050; www.howlersinn.com; 3185 Jackson Creek Rd; r $135-180, cabin $225; ☎) Wolf-watchers will love this beautiful sanctuary 15 minutes outside of Bozeman. Rescued captive-born wolves live in enclosed natural areas on 4 acres, supported by the profits of the B&B. There are three spacious Western-style rooms in the main lodge and a two-bedroom carriage house. Minimum two-night stay from May to mid-October.

The Lark MOTEL $$
(☑ 406-624-3070; www.larkbozeman.com; 122 W Main St; r $130-270; ✳ ☎) With a lively yellow palette and modern graphic design, this hip place is a big step up from its former life as a grungy motel. Rooms are fresh and the fine location puts it in walking distance of downtown's bars and restaurants.

MONTANA FACTS

Nickname Treasure State, Big Sky Country

Population 1,062,000

Area 147,040 sq miles

Capital city Helena (population 31,400)

Other cities Billings (population 109,600), Missoula (73,300), Bozeman (46,600)

Sales tax No state sales tax

Birthplace of Movie star Gary Cooper (1901–61); motorcycle daredevil Evel Knievel (1938–2007); actress Michelle Williams (b 1980)

Home of Crow, Blackfeet, Chippewa, Gros Ventre and Salish Native Americans

Politics Republican ranchers and oil barons generally edge out the Democratic students and progressives of left-leaning Bozeman and Missoula.

Famous for Fly-fishing, cowboys and grizzly bears

Random fact Some Montana highways didn't have a speed limit until the 1990s.

Driving distances Bozeman to Denver 695 miles, Missoula to Whitefish 133 miles

★ **Rainbow Ranch Lodge** RESORT $$
(☎ 406-995-4132; www.rainbowranchbigsky.com; Hwy 191; r $180-420; 🕸🐾) Rustic but ultrachic, Rainbow Ranch offers a select group of pondside or riverside rooms, most with roaring stone fireplaces, balconies and access to the romantic outdoor hot tub. The Pondside Luxury rooms are easily the most stylish. The lodge is 5 miles south of the Big Sky turnoff and 12 miles north of Yellowstone National Park.

✖ Eating & Drinking

With plenty of breweries and an active live music scene, if you're not having fun in Bozeman, you're doing it wrong. Check the Bozone (www.bozone.com) for a good music calendar.

★ **Nova Cafe** CAFE $
(☎ 406-587-3973; www.thenovacafe.com; 312 E Main St; breakfast $7.50-13, mains $10-14; 🕖7am-

2pm; 🕸🐾) 🌿 A helpful map at the entrance shows you where the food you'll be eating comes from at this retro-contemporary locals' favorite. The hollandaise is a bit on the sweet side, but still excessively delicious – as is everything else. The forbidden rice salad with ginger and lemongrass is another highlight. There's a special menu for vegans, too.

★ **Follow Yer' Nose BBQ** BARBECUE $
(☎ 406-599 -7302; www.followyernosebbq.com; 504 N Broadway; mains $10-20; 🕑2-8pm Sun-Tue, noon-8pm Wed-Sat) Lovers of some of Montana's best grills have for years been forced out into the backblocks of Paradise Valley for their fix. No longer. This city outpost does all the usual heavily smoked meats to perfection, alongside the Bozeman Brewing Company (☎406-585-9142; www.bozemanbrewing.com; 504 N Broadway; 🕑2-8pm Mon-Thu, Sat & Sun, noon-8pm Fri), and better still, they do so year-round.

★ **Montana Ale Works** PUB
(☎406-587-7700; www.montanaaleworks.com; 611 E Main St; 🕑4pm-close) Bozeman's former Northern Pacific freight warehouse brings industrial chic to this ever-reliable bar-restaurant, with excellent food (mains $11 to $26), pool tables and people-watching. Staff are happy to let you taste any of the 30 microbrews on tap, including the local Bozones.

★ **Rockford Coffee Roasters** CAFE
(☎406-556-1053; www.rockfordcoffee.com; 18 E Main St; 🕑6:30am-7pm Mon-Fri, 7:30am-7pm Sat & Sun) Bozeman's best and coolest coffee cafe, Rockford's is where local artists and creative types hang out. The coffee is outstanding, and the high ceilings and exposed brick walls make for a classy but casual affair.

Bozeman
Taproom & Fill Station BEER GARDEN
(☎406-577-2337; www.bozemantaproom.com; 101 N Rouse Ave; 🕑11am-midnight Sun-Thu, to 1am Fri & Sat) One of Bozeman's coolest places to grab a pint and fill a growler has an open-air rooftop beer garden. Its 44 draft brews served from 75 taps can be combined in as many ways as you like with the 'build your own flight' program. Hot dogs and sandwiches keep your belly full while you sample them all.

ℹ Getting There & Away

Bozeman Yellowstone International Airport
(BZN; ☎406-388-8321; www.bozemanairport.com; 850 Gallatin Field Rd), 8 miles northwest of downtown, serves most major hubs including

Atlanta, New York, Chicago, Denver, Seattle, Dallas, Salt Lake City, San Francisco and Minneapolis.

Jefferson Lines connects to Greyhound from a nondescript **bus depot** (Jefferson Lines; ☑ 612-499-3468; www.jeffersonlines.com; 1500 North 7th Ave; ☺ noon-5pm) on the southern side of the Super Walmart near the garden center. Between noon and 5pm, a well-marked Jefferson Lines car parked nearby can sell you tickets and check your luggage. Destinations include Missoula (from $55, 3½ hours), Billings (from $42, 2¼ hours) and Denver (from $149, 14¾ hours).

Billings

It's hard to believe laid-back Billings is Montana's largest city. The friendly oil-and-ranching center is not a must-see but makes for a decent overnight pit stop, or a point of departure for Yellowstone National Park via the breathtaking Beartooth Hwy.

Pompey's Pillar and the further away Little Bighorn Battlefield National Monuments are worthwhile stops for history buffs, and downtown has a certain unpolished charm for those who prefer the modern West.

🛏 Sleeping

The main knot of chain motels is outside Billings on I-90, exit 446, but there are a few standout independent options downtown – as well as a few mediocre ones.

Dude Rancher Lodge MOTEL $
(☑ 406-545-6331; www.duderancherlodge.com; 415 N 29th St; d from $75; ✳@🕸🐾) This historic motor lodge looks a little out of place in the downtown area, but has been well maintained, with about half the rooms renovated to good effect. Western touches like tongue-and-groove walls and cattle-brand carpet give it a welcoming rustic feel. The attached diner is a local breakfast favorite.

Northern Hotel HOTEL $$
(☑ 406-867-6767; www.northernhotel.com; 19 N Broadway; r/ste $165/215; ✳🕸) The historic Northern combines its previous elegance with fresh and modern facilities that are a solid step above generic business hotel. Breakfast and lunch are served in the attached 1950s diner.

🍴 Eating & Drinking

McCormick Cafe BREAKFAST $
(☑ 406-255-9555; www.mccormickcafe.com; 2419 Montana Ave; breakfast $6-10, meals $9-12; ☺ 7am-2pm Mon-Fri, 8am-2pm Sat & Sun; 🕸) For espresso, granola breakfasts, French-style crepes, good sandwiches and a lively atmosphere, stop by this downtown favorite that started life as an internet cafe.

★ **Walkers Grill** AMERICAN $$
(☑ 406-245-9291; www.walkersgrill.com; 2700 1st Ave N; tapas $8-14, mains $16-34; ☺ 4-10pm Mon-Thu, to 10:30pm Fri, 5-10:30pm Sat, 5-10pm Sun) Upscale Walkers offers good grill items and fine tapas at the bar accompanied by cocktails crafted by expert mixologists. It's an elegant, large-windowed space that would be right at home in Manhattan, though maybe without the barbed-wire light fixtures – or with. The menu changes with the seasons but is always filled with flavor. Check the website for live jazz.

Überbrew MICROBREWERY
(☑ 406-534-6960; www.facebook.com/uberbrew; 2305 Montana Ave; ☺ 11am-9pm, beer until 8pm) The most polished of Billings' half-dozen downtown brewpubs also happens to create award-winning beers that are a noticeable step above the rest. The food isn't half bad either: wash down a beer-marinated bockwurst with a glass of the White Noise Hefeweizen, which outsells the other drafts three to one.

❶ Getting There & Away

Downtown Billings is just off I-90 occupying a wide valley of the Yellowstone River.

Helena

It's pretty easy to overlook diminutive Helena as you zip by on the interstate, but you'd be doing yourself a grave disservice. Penetrate the drab, utilitarian commerce sprawl toward Last Chance Gulch and old Helena where imposing brick and stone buildings – all arches and angles – portray a resolute commitment to permanence. It's in this historic core, rather than the uninspiring urban sprawl, that Helena's charm resides.

🏃 Activities

★ **Trail Rider** OUTDOORS
(☑ 406-449-2107; www.bikehelena.com/trail-rider; cnr Broadway & Last Chance Gulch; ☺ Wed-Sun late May-Sep) During the summer months a dedicated city bus pulling a bike trailer runs mountain bikers and hikers to one of three

WORTH A TRIP

CUSTER'S LAST STAND

The best detour from Billings is to the **Little Bighorn Battlefield National Monument** (406-638-2621; www.nps.gov/libi; 756 Battlefield Tour Rd; per car $25; 8am-8pm Jun-Sep, to 4:30pm Oct-May), 65 miles outside town in the arid plains of the Crow (Apsaalooke) Indian Reservation. Home to one of the USA's best-known Native American battlefields, this is where General George Custer made his famous 'last stand.' Another way to look at it is that the victory by the Cheyenne and Lakota Sioux was something of a last victory for Native American peoples. Swift retaliation followed and, within a decade, these lands were under the control of government forces.

At Little Bighorn on 25 and 26 June 1876, Custer, and 272 soldiers, messed one too many times with Native Americans (including Crazy Horse and Sitting Bull of the Lakota Sioux), who overwhelmed the force in a frequently painted massacre. A visitor center tells the tale, including in the form of an excellent video.

A 5-mile road runs through the site, with frequent turnouts with information panels (including quotes from both government and Native American sources) that bring the battle alive. All across the fields and valleys, and within sight of the road, white tombstones mark the sites where soldiers fell. Crowning the battlefield is Last Stand Hill, while nearby the Indian Memorial is a fascinating tribute to the Sioux and Cheyenne stories. In summer, you can take one of the five daily tours with a Crow guide through **Apsaalooke Tours** (406-679-2790; www.crow-nsn.gov/apsaalooke-tours.html; adult/child $10/5; 10am, 11am, noon, 2pm & 3pm Memorial Day-Labor Day).

The entrance to the site is a mile east of I-90 on US 212. If you're here for the last weekend of June, the **Custer's Last Stand Re-enactment** (www.littlebighornreenactment.com; Little Bighorn National Monument; adult/child $20/10; Jun) is an annual hoot, 6 miles west of Hardin.

---

trailheads for epic singletrack journeys back to town. Destinations include the Mt Helena Ridge Trail, the Mt Ascension trails, and the Continental Divide Trail at MacDonald pass.

🛏 Sleeping

Sanders B&B $$
(406-442-3309; www.sandersbb.com; 328 N Ewing St; r $150-175; 🎫🛜) Located in the old mansion district, this historic B&B once belonged to Wilbur Sanders, a frontier lawyer and Montana's first senator. It now has seven elegant guest rooms, a wonderful old parlor and a breezy front porch. Each bedroom is unique and thoughtfully decorated, and it's run by a relative of the Ringling Brothers Circus family, with appropriate memorabilia.

🍴 Eating & Drinking

Murry's CAFE $
(406-431-2886; www.murryscafe.com; 438 N Last Chance Gulch; breakfast & brunch $4-8.50, lunch mains $5-16; 8am-3pm Mon-Fri, 9am-2pm Sat & Sun; 🛜🅿) From spanakopita to soufflés, this little cafe on the southern end of downtown offers something a little different from the regular breakfast fare. Things really go off

the hook during their Saturday and Sunday brunch when the name of the game is waffles – regular, stuffed, topped or drenched.

★ **General Mercantile** COFFEE
(406-442-6028; www.generalmerc.com; 413 N Last Chance Gulch; 8am-5:30pm Mon-Fri, 9am-5pm Sat, 11am-4pm Sun; 🛜) You'll have to weave through all sorts of Montana eclectica for sale – hummingbird feeders, postcards and homemade jam – to get what is widely regarded as the best coffee in the universe. Take your espresso to a private nook where you can contemplate what you'd look like with a mermaid fin and an octopus mustache – both also available.

ℹ Information

Helena Visitor Center (406-442-4120; www.helenamt.com; 225 Cruse Ave; 8am-5pm Mon-Fri) Local information.

Montana Fish, Wildlife & Parks (406-444-2535; http://fwp.mt.gov; 1420 E 6th Ave)

Montana Outfitters & Guides Association (406-449-3578; www.montanaoutfitters.org; 5 Microwave Hill Rd, Montana City) Clearinghouse for everything from fishing and dude ranches to hunting.

● Getting There & Away

Helena Regional Airport (HNL; ☑ 406-442-2821; www.helenaairport.com; 2850 Mercer Loop), 2 miles north of downtown Helena, connects to regional hubs including Salt Lake City, Seattle, Denver and Minneapolis. A planned expansion is due to be completed in 2020. The **Salt Lake Express** (www.saltlakeexpress.com; 1415 N Montana Ave) bus heads south to join up with the Greyhound network at Butte ($29.25, 1¼ hours).

Missoula

Missoula regularly turns up near the top of the list for travelers' favorite small cities in America. With a walkable, low-rise city center, plenty of riverside walking trails, the in-town University of Montana and a palpable sense of civic pride, it's not difficult to see why. Missoulians love to get outside, and summer means an almost endless stream of farmers markets, concerts in the park, outdoor cinema and similar celebrations of community life, while students from the University of Montana ensure a real sense of energy coursing through its streets. Patio seating is the rule not the exception, and an afternoon outing will surely involve some human-powered activity on the miles of urban and foothills trails. The wandering Clark Fork River is popular with stand up paddleboarders where it cuts through town, and is a fly-fishing magnet downstream. Put simply, it's one of the most agreeable urban spaces in the West.

● Sights & Activities

★ **Garnet Ghost Town**   GHOST TOWN
(☑ 406-329-3914;   www.garnetghosttown.org; Bear Gulch Rd; adult/child $3/free; ☺ 9:30am-4:30pm Jun-Sep; 👶) More than a dozen buildings preserved in a state of 'arrested decay' transport you back to gold-rush days, when cities were built overnight and vanished almost as quickly. It's an evocative place, having been founded in the late 19th century, but deserted since the 1930s. Located 40 miles east of Missoula on dirt forest roads, accessible (and signposted) off the Missoula–Butte road (90) – check the website for detailed directions. Call in advance to arrange a guided tour.

Smokejumper Visitor Center   MUSEUM
(☑ 406-329-4934;   www.fs.fed.us/science-technology/fire/smokejumpers/missoula/center; 5765 West Broadway; ☺ 8:30am-5pm Jun-Aug, guided tours 10am, 11am, 1pm, 2pm, 3pm & 4pm) **FREE** The visitor center on this active base for the heroic men and women who parachute into forests to combat raging wildfires has thought-provoking displays about an increasingly hazardous job. The real treat is touring the facility where the crew lives, trains and sews their own parachutes; tours last 45 minutes to an hour. For more on the perilous possibilities of the job, pick up a copy of Norman MacLean's *Young Men and Fire* (1992).

A Carousel for Missoula   PLAYGROUND
(☑ 406-549-8382;   www.carouselformissoula. com; 101 Carousel Dr, Caras Park; adult/child $2.25/0.75; ☺ 11am-5:30pm Sep-May, 11am-7pm Jun-Aug; 👶) Hand-carved and individually painted by local artists, every horse that gallops around the classic carousel at Caras Park has a story to tell. But the bigger story is how a community rallied around one man's dream to restore a bit of whimsy to downtown. The carousel shares space with Dragon Hollow, a playground that excites the imagination.

Mount Sentinel   HIKING
(Campus Dr) A steep switchback trail from behind the University of Montana football stadium leads up to a concrete whitewashed 'M' (visible for miles around) on 5158ft Mt Sentinel. Tackle it on a warm summer's evening for glistening views of this much-loved city and its spectacular environs. The trailhead is at Phyllis Washington Park on the eastern edge of campus.

● Sleeping & Eating

★ **Shady Spruce Hostel**   HOSTEL $
(☑ 406-285-1197; www.shadysprucehostel.com; 204 E Spruce St; dm $35-40, s/ste $55/85; ❋ 🛜) We're super-excited to see the resurgence of the hostel in the US, and this clean, bright and spacious new addition to the family nails it in all the right places. Although it's presence here is no longer news, they've maintained standards. Downtown is literally a block away from the converted house, but they have bikes for the walking-averse.

Goldsmith's B&B   B&B $$
(☑ 406-728-1585; www.missoulabedandbreakfast. com; 809 E Front St; r $160-210; ❋ 🛜 👶) Before being moved here in two massive pieces, this inviting riverside B&B was a frat house, and before that, home to the University of

Montana president. The modern-Victorian rooms are all comfortable, but we're partial to the Greenough Suite with its writing table and private river-view deck.

★ **Market on Front** CAFE $
(☑ 406-541-0246; www.marketonfront.com; 201 E Front St; mains $5-10; ⊙ 8am-7pm Mon-Fri, to 8pm Sat, to 7pm Sun; 🛜) 🍴 Order a fresh-made sandwich or overflowing breakfast bowl, or take advantage of the gourmet grab-and-go picnic items such as local teas, organic chocolate and local beer. Or dine in – with all those windows it feels like you're outside anyway. Casual but cool atmosphere, free wi-fi, friendly staff, seriously good sandwiches – what's not to like.

★ **Pearl Cafe** FRENCH $$$
(☑ 406-541-0231; http://pearlcafe.us; 231 E Front St; mains $23-38; ⊙ 5-9pm Mon-Sat) Our pick as Missoula's culinary superstar, Pearl Cafe does French country cooking with a western-US twist – try the walnut and herb prawns, the grilled salmon with mustard butter or, for traditionalists, the classic filet mignon. Service is assured and the atmosphere is refined but not too stuffy; dress nice nonetheless.

🍷 Drinking & Nightlife

Missoula has a surprisingly high-profile music scene for a smaller town. Bars downtown provide choices between laid-back brewpubs and distilleries, or more traditional professional drinking establishments.

★ **Top Hat Lounge** LOUNGE
(☑ 406-830-4640; www.tophatlounge.com; 134 W Front St; ⊙ 11am-10pm Mon-Thu, to 2am Fri & Sat) Where Missoula goes to get its groove on. This dark venue features live music most weekends in a space large enough to cut a rug, but small enough to feel like the band is playing just for you. It's one of Montana's best live-music venues.

★ **Liquid Planet** COFFEE
(☑ 406-541-4541; www.liquidplanet.com; 223 N Higgins; ⊙ 7:30am-9pm; 🛜) 🍴 Considering how much Missoula loves its beverages, it's no surprise Liquid Planet was born here. Opened by a university professor in 2003, it's a sustainable coffeehouse, cafe and bottle shop selling carefully curated wines and craft beers, loose-leaf tea, coffee beans (with handwritten pedigrees) and sports drinks.

ℹ️ Information

Missoula Visitor Center (☑ 800-526-3465; www.destinationmissoula.org; 101 E Main St; ⊙ 8am-5pm Mon-Fri) Destination Missoula has a useful website as well as a small walk-in space downtown.

ℹ️ Getting There & Away

Missoula International Airport (MSO; ☑ 406-728-4381; www.flymissoula.com; 5225 Hwy 10 W), 5 miles west of Missoula, serves Salt Lake City, Denver, Phoenix, LA, San Francisco, Portland, Seattle and Minneapolis, among others. Seasonal service to Atlanta and Chicago.

Greyhound (☑ 406-549-2339; www.greyhound.com; 1660 W Broadway) buses serve most of the state and stop at the depot, 1 mile west of town. Destinations include Bozeman (from $52, 3½ hours), Denver (from $164, 17¼ hours), Portland (from $78, 9½ hours) and Seattle (from $83, around 10 hours).

Whitefish

Tiny Whitefish blends an easygoing outdoorsy mountain town with a fur-lined playground for the glitterati. It's not quite there yet, thankfully, but there's something suspiciously refined about this charismatic and caffeinated New West town. It is home to an attractive stash of restaurants, a historic railway station and an underrated ski resort, as well as excellent biking and hiking on a rapidly growing network of trails. Whitefish is well worth a visit – just get here while it's still affordable. Locals, however, are decidedly unpretentious and measure their wealth not in terms of money, but how many days they get out on the slopes and how many outdoor adventures they have.

🏃 Activities

Whitefish Legacy Partners HIKING
(☑ 406-862-3880; www.whitefishlegacy.org; 525 Railway St; ⊙ hours vary) Whitefish is surrounded by a growing network of trails ideal for hiking and mountain biking. The driving force behind the development, Whitefish Legacy Partners rallies support for the system with offerings such as guided walks focusing on wildflowers, bears and noxious weeds. Its focus is more on residents than tourists, but everyone's welcome.

Whitefish Mountain Resort SKIING
(☑ 406-862-2900; www.skiwhitefish.com; Big Mountain Rd; ski/bike lift $81/41) Big mountain skiing

at Whitefish Mountain Resort (formerly Big Mountain), is a laid-back old-school affair, great for families, as well as expert skiiers and snowboarders willing to hike up in order to rip up off-piste double black diamond glades. The mountain is known for its foggy days, but views from the summit are unsurpassed (when clear). On fresh powder days, locals ditch work and other responsibilities to make fresh tracks.

Sleeping

★ Whitefish Bike Retreat   HOSTEL $
(406-260-0274; www.whitefishbikeretreat.com; 855 Beaver Lake Rd; tent sites/dm/r $40/50/110; ✱ ≈) Celebrating all things bicycle, this forested compound run by passionate outdoorsperson Cricket Butler is a must-stay for two-wheel enthusiasts. The spacious polished-wood house with bunks, private rooms and a communal living area is a great place to hang when you're not hot-lapping the property trails or exploring the excellent Whitefish Trail that runs nearby. Hard-core cyclists can bike all the way here from town.

Firebrand   BOUTIQUE HOTEL $$
(406-863-1900; www.firebrandhotel.com; 650 E 3rd St; r from $140; ✱ @ ≈) Easily downtown Whitefish's nicest hotel, this handsome brick structure shelters large and supremely comfortable rooms, a spa and fitness center, a rooftop hot tub, a bar-restaurant and a genuine touch of class.

Lodge at Whitefish Lake   RESORT $$$
(406-863-4000; www.lodgeatwhitefishlake.com; 1380 Wisconsin Ave; r from $285; ✱ ≈ ☀) Consistently ranked among Montana's top luxury hotels, the Lodge exudes refinement and sophistication. It offers a range of rooms, from standards to fully stocked condos, on the sprawling complex. The unifying theme is a classic, patrician decor and high levels of comfort. The lakefront restaurant and poolside tiki bar are both great places to catch the sunset.

Eating & Drinking

Loula's   CAFE $
(406-862-5614; www.whitefishrestaurant.com; 300 E 2nd St; breakfast $7-12, lunch mains $8-13, dinner mains $10-20; ⊙7am-2pm Mon-Sun, 5-9:30pm Thu-Sun; ≈) Downstairs in the century-old Masonic temple building, this bustling cafe has local art on the wall and culinary artists in the kitchen. The highly recommended lemon crème–filled French toast dripping with raspberry sauce is a sinfully delicious breakfast, or try the truffle eggs Benedict. At other times, it's burgers, salads and dishes such as blackened wild salmon or chicken potpie.

★ Spotted Bear Spirits   DISTILLERY
(406-730-2436; www.spottedbearspirits. com; 503 Railway St, Suite A; ⊙noon-8pm; ≈) Award-winning spirits (vodka, gin, and agave) are paired with secret blends of herbs and spices to create unique, award-winning cocktails you won't find anywhere else. Grab a drink and head to the sofa upstairs for a relaxing break from your day. A Spotted Bear whisky is in the works and will be available in the next year or two.

Montana Coffee Traders   COFFEE
(406-862-7667; www.coffeetraders.com; 110 Central Ave; ⊙7am-6pm Mon-Sat, 8am-4pm Sun; ≈) Whitefish's homegrown microroaster runs this always-busy cafe and gift shop in the old Skyles building in the center of town. The organic, fair-trade beans are roasted in an old farmhouse on Hwy 93 that you can tour (10am Friday by reservation).

ℹ Information

Whitefish Visitor Center (877-862-3548; www.explorewhitefish.com; 307 Spokane Ave; ⊙9am-5pm Mon-Fri) Professional and helpful office; the excellent website has loads of information on news, events, activities, and places to stay and eat.

ℹ Getting There & Away

Glacier Park International Airport (p810), located 11 miles south of Whitefish, has daily service to Denver, Minneapolis, Salt Lake and Seattle. Additional summer-only destinations include Chicago, Dallas and Los Angeles.

The most scenic way to get here is via **Amtrak** (406-862-2268; www.amtrak.com/empire-builder-train; 500 Depot St; ⊙6am-1:30pm, 4:30pm-midnight) on the *Empire Builder* line, which also connects to Glacier National Park via West Glacier ($7.50, 30 minutes) and East Glacier ($16, two hours).

Glacier National Park

Few places on earth are as magnificent and pristine as **Glacier** (www.nps.gov/glac; 7-day pass by car/foot & bicycle/motorcycle $35/20/30). Protected in 1910 during the first flowering of the American

NATIONAL BISON RANGE

National Bison Range (☑406-644-2211; www.fws.gov/refuge/national_bison_range; 58355 Bison Range Rd, Moiese; ☺sunrise-sunset, visitor center 9am-5pm) is home to bison, black bear, a range of deer and antelope species, a handful of predators and more than 200 bird varieties. Located in Montana's northwest, the Range is a fabulous place to tick off wildlife species that you might not see elsewhere.

conservationist movement, Glacier ranks with Yellowstone, Yosemite and the Grand Canyon among the United States' most astounding natural wonders.

The glacially carved remnants of an ancient thrust fault have left us a brilliant landscape of towering snowcapped pinnacles laced with plunging waterfalls and glassy turquoise lakes. The mountains are surrounded by dense forests, which host a virtually intact pre-Columbian ecosystem. Grizzly bears still roam in abundance and smart park management has kept the place accessible and authentically wild.

Glacier is renowned for its historic 'parkitecture' lodges, the spectacular Going-to-the-Sun Rd and 740 miles of hiking trails. These all put visitors within easy reach of some 1489 sq miles of the wild and astonishing landscapes found at the crown of the continent.

◎ Sights & Activities

Visitor centers and ranger stations in Glacier National Park sell field guides and hand out hiking maps. Those at Apgar and St Mary are open daily May to October, and Logan Pass Visitor Center is open when Going-to-the-Sun Rd is open. Many Glacier, Two Medicine and Polebridge Ranger Stations close at the end of September.

Logan Pass Visitor Center VISITOR CENTER
(☑406-888-7800; Going-to-the-Sun Rd; ☺9am-7pm late Jun-late Aug, 9:30am-4pm Sep) Certainly in the most magnificent setting of all the park's visitor centers, the building has park information, interactive exhibits, and a good gift shop. Both the **Hidden Lake Overlook Trail** and the Highline Trail begin here.

Bird Woman Falls WATERFALL
(Going-to-the-Sun Rd) Standing at the artificially created Weeping Wall, look across the valley to this distant natural watery spectacle; the spectacular Bird Woman Falls drops 500ft from one of Glacier's many hanging valleys. There are several pull-outs along the western side of Going-to-the Sun Rd to view the falls.

Sunrift Gorge CANYON
(Going-to-the-Sun Rd) Just off Going-to-the-Sun Rd and adjacent to a shuttle stop lies this narrow canyon carved over millennia by the gushing glacial meltwaters of Baring Creek. Look out for picturesque **Baring Bridge**, a classic example of rustic Going-to-the-Sun Rd architecture, and follow a short trail down to misty **Baring Falls**. Most of the tree cover in this area was thinned out by the 2015 Reynolds Creek fire.

Jackson Glacier Overlook VIEWPOINT
This popular pull-over, located a short walk from the Gunsight Pass trailhead, offers telescopic views of the park's fifth-largest glacier, which sits close to its eponymous 10,052ft peak – one of the park's highest.

★**Going-to-the-Sun Road** SCENIC DRIVE
(www.nps.gov/glac/planyourvisit/goingtothesunroad.htm; ☺late Jun-late Sep) A strong contender for the most spectacular road in America, the 50-mile Going-to-the-Sun Rd was built for the express purpose of giving visitors a way to explore the park's interior without having to hike. This marvel of engineering is a national historic landmark that crosses Logan Pass (6,646ft) and is flanked by hiking trails, waterfalls and endless views. The opening of the road marks the official start of the park's crowded summer season.

★**Highline Trail** HIKING
(Logan Pass) A Glacier classic, the Highline Trail contours across the face of the famous Garden Wall to Granite Park Chalet – one of two historic lodges only accessible by trail. The summer slopes are covered with alpine plants and wildflowers while the views are nothing short of stupendous. With only 800ft elevation gain over 7.6 miles, the treats come with minimal sweat.

Avalanche Lake Trail HIKING
(north of Lake McDonald) This low-commitment introduction to Glacier hiking pays big dividends in the form of a pristine alpine lake,

waterfalls and cascades. The 2.3-mile hike is relatively gentle and easily accessed by the shuttle. It's, therefore, invariably mobbed in peak season with everyone from flip-flop-wearing families to stick-wielding seniors making boldly for the tree line.

Glacier Park Boat Co   BOATING
(☑406-257-2426; www.glacierparkboats.com; adult/child $18.25/9.25) Six historic boats – some dating back to the 1920s – ply five of Glacier's attractive mountain lakes, and some of them combine the float with a short **guided hike** led by interpretive, often witty, ranger guides. For those looking for a bit of a workout, it also rents rowboats ($18 per hour), kayaks ($18 per hour) and paddleboards ($10 per hour) at Lake McDonald, Mary, Many Glacier and Two Medicine.

🛏 Sleeping

There are 13 NPS campgrounds. For comprehensive information about camping in the park, see www.nps.gov.

★ Izaak Walton Inn   HISTORIC HOTEL $$
(☑406-888-5700; www.izaakwaltoninn.com; 290 Izaak Walton Inn Rd, Essex; r $109-179, cabins & cabooses $199-249; ☺year-round; ☏) Perched on a hill within snowball-throwing distance of Glacier National Park's southern boundary, this historic mock-Tudor inn was originally built in 1939 to accommodate local railway personnel. It remains a daily flag-stop (request stop) on Amtrak's *Empire Builder* route – a romantic way to arrive. Caboose cottages with kitchenettes are available, along with a historic GN441 locomotive refurbished as a luxury four-person suite ($329).

★ Many Glacier Hotel   HISTORIC HOTEL $$
(☑303-265-7010; www.glaciernationalparklodges. com; 1 Many Glacier Rd; r $207-322, ste $476; ☺mid-Jun–mid-Sep; ☏) Enjoying the most wondrous setting in the park, this massive, Swiss chalet–inspired lodge (some of the male staff even wear lederhosen) commands the northeastern shore of Swiftcurrent Lake. It was first built by the Great Northern Railway in 1915, and the comfortable, if rustic, rooms have been updated (restoration work continues) over the last 15 years. The deluxe rooms feature boutique-style elements, including high-end, contemporary tiled bathrooms.

🍴 Eating

In summer in Glacier National Park, there are grocery stores with camping supplies in Apgar, Lake McDonald Lodge, Rising Sun and at the Swiftcurrent Motor Inn. Most lodges have on-site restaurants. Dining options in West Glacier and St Mary offer mainly hearty hiking fare.

If cooking at a campground or picnic area, be sure to take appropriate bear safety precautions and do not leave food unattended.

★ Serrano's
Mexican Restaurant   MEXICAN $$
(☑406-226-9392; www.serranosmexican.com; 29 Dawson Ave, East Glacier; mains $14-21; ☺5-10pm May-Sep; ☏) East Glacier Park's most buzzed-about restaurant serves a mean chile relleno. Renowned for its excellent iced margaritas, Serrano's also has economical burritos, enchiladas and quesadillas in the vintage Dawson house log cabin, originally built in 1909. Expect a wait.

Belton Chalet
Grill & Taproom   AMERICAN $$$
(☑406-888-5000; www.beltonchalet.com; 12575 Hwy 2, West Yellowstone; mains $24-35; ☺5-9pm, tap room from 3pm) 🌿 West Glacier's finest dining option, housed in one of its most historic buildings, has evolved with the times, the faux Swiss milkmaid waitress uniforms aside. The head chef, a Whitefish native now in his second season at the helm, has created a sophisticated menu featuring locally sourced ingredients and mains such as bison meatloaf with broccolini and bacon lardons (strips of fatty bacon).

> ### ℹ FREE PARK SHUTTLE
>
> See more with less stress by ditching the car and taking the park's free hop-on, hop-off **shuttle service** (www.nps. gov/glac; ☺7am-7pm Jul & Aug) that hits all major points along Going-to-the-Sun Rd between Apgar and St Mary visitor centers. Buses run every 15 to 30 minutes depending on traffic from Apgar (every 40 minutes from St Mary on the east side), with the last trips down from Logan Pass leaving at 7pm.

ROCKY MOUNTAINS GLACIER NATIONAL PARK

❶ Information

Glacier National Park Headquarters (✆406-888-7800; www.nps.gov/glac; West Glacier; ⏰8am-4:30pm Mon-Fri)

❶ Getting There & Around

Glacier Park International Airport (FCA; ✆406-257-5994; www.iflyglacier.com; 4170 Hwy 2 East, Kalispell; ☎) in Kalispell has year-round service to Salt Lake, Minneapolis, Denver, Seattle and Las Vegas, and seasonal service to Atlanta, Oakland, LA, Chicago and Portland. Alaska, Allegiant, American Airlines, Delta and United have flights to FCA.

The **Great Falls International Airport** (GTF; www.flygtf.com) is 140 miles south of East Glacier.

Amtrak's *Empire Builder* (www.amtrak.com) stops daily at **West Glacier** (⏰year-round) and **East Glacier Park** (⏰Apr-Oct), with a whistle stop in Browning. Xanterra provides a shuttle (adult $6 to $10, child $3 to $5, 10 to 20 minutes) from West Glacier to their lodges on the west end, and Glacier Park Collection by Pursuit offers shuttles (from $15, one hour) connecting East Glacier Park to St Mary and Whitefish.

Glacier National Park runs a free hop-on, hop-off shuttle bus (p809) from **Apgar Transit Center** to St Mary over Going-to-the-Sun Rd during summer months; it stops at all major trailheads. Xanterra concession operates the classic guided **Red Bus Tours** (✆855-733-4522; www.glaciernationalparklodges.com/red-bus-tours; adult $46-100, child $23-50; ⏰mid-May–end Oct).

If driving a personal vehicle, be prepared for narrow, winding roads, traffic jams, and limited parking at most stops along Going-to-the-Sun Rd.

IDAHO

Wedged between Montana and Oregon, and often overlooked as a result, Idaho is truly one of Western USA's most underrated destinations. This rather large chunk of land has 114 mountain ranges and some of the most rugged mountains in the Lower 48. More than 60% of the state is public land, and with 3.9 million acres of wilderness, it's the third-wildest state in the union.

Boise, the state capital, is a pleasant place to linger, Sun Valley is a classic US ski resort, and the wild treasures range from Craters of the Moon National Park and the National Bison Range to Teton

Valley and the dramatic Sawtooth National Recreation Area, one of the West's premier adventure areas.

Boise

One of the US's least-known state capitals, Boise can catch you unawares. Refreshingly modern, urban and trendy, Idaho's largest city has a lively downtown scene – complete with walking streets, bistros and sophisticated wine bars – that wouldn't look out of place on the East Coast. The network of trails that shoots up from town to the forested hills above rivals some of Colorado's best hiking destinations. Floating through the Greenbelt is as good as anything you'll find along Austin, Texas' beloved tubing circuit. Sample a steaming pan of paella in the Basque Block and you might as well be in Bilbao. With so much going on, it can be difficult for newbies to know what to make of Boise. But Boise is well worth the detour if you're anywhere nearby.

◉ Sights & Activities

★**Basque Block**   AREA
(www.thebasqueblock.com; Grove St, 6th St & Capitol Blvd) Boise is home to one of the largest Basque populations outside Spain, with up to 15,000 members of that community residing here. The original émigrés arrived in the 1910s to work as shepherds when sheep outnumbered people seven to one. Few continue that work today, but many extended families have remained, and the rich elements of their distinct culture are still very much alive – glimpses of which can be seen along Grove St between 6th St and Capitol Blvd.

Boise River Greenbelt   PARK
(http://parks.cityofboise.org) ⟋ The glowing emerald of Treasure Valley began as an ambitious plan in the 1960s to prevent development in the Boise River's floodplain and provide open space in a rapidly growing city. Today the growing collection of parks and museums along the tree-lined riverway is connected by more than 30 miles of multiuse paths, and hosts an insanely popular summer floating scene. A white-water park, complete with hydraulically controlled waves, is one of the largest in the country.

World Center for Birds of Prey
BIRD SANCTUARY

(Peregrine Fund; ☑ 208-362-8687; www.per egrinefund.org/visit; 5668 W Flying Hawk Lane; adult/child $10/5; ⊙10am-5pm Tue-Sun Mar-Nov, 10am-4pm Dec-Feb) 🏶 The Peregrine Fund's worldwide raptor conservation programs have brought many species back from the brink of extinction – including the iconic California Condor, successfully bred in captivity here for release in California and the Grand Canyon. A pair of condors reside at the center, along with a dozen other impressive birds including the northern aplomado falcon, whose mating pairs work in tandem to hunt grassland sparrows. The live raptor presentations are excellent.

Idaho State Museum
MUSEUM

(☑208-334-2120; https://history.idaho.gov/ location/museum; 610 N Julia Davis Dr; adult/ child $10/5; ⊙10am-5pm Mon-Sat, noon-5pm Sun) After a multi-year renovation, which brought this museum back to life, traditional exhibits now share space with multimedia installations for a fascinating journey through the state's history. The Origins Gallery, with its Native American voices, is especially rewarding.

Ridge to Rivers Trail System
HIKING

(☑208-493-2531; www.ridgetorivers.org; 🏶) Some 190 miles of hiking and mountain-biking trails meander the foothills northeast of town, crossing grasslands, scrub slopes and tree-lined creeks on their way to the Boise National Forest. The options are literally endless. The most convenient access is via Cottonwood Creek Trailhead east of the capitol building, or **Camel's Back Park** to the north.

Boise River Float
PARK

(www.boiseriverraftandtube.com; 4049 S Eckert Rd, Barber Park; tube/kayak rental $12/35, 4-person raft $45; ⊙noon-5pm Mon-Thu, to 6pm Fri, 10am-6pm Sat & Sun; 🏶) There is no better way to spend a sunny summer day in Boise than floating down the river. Rent watercraft – from tubes to six-person rafts – at Barber Park (parking $5 Monday to Thursday, $6 Friday to Sunday) where you'll put in for a self-guided 6-mile, 1½- to three-hour float downstream to Ann Morrison Park. Open June through August depending on river flows.

🛏 Sleeping

★Boise Guest House
GUESTHOUSE $$

(☑208-761-6798; www.boiseguesthouse.com; 614 N 5th St; ste $180-230; 🏶🏶) A veritable home away from home, this appealing old house has a handful of contemporary-styled suites with kitchenettes and living areas comfortably arranged and tastefully decorated. All rooms have access to the large grill in the relaxing backyard, red-and-white cruiser bikes and laundry.

Inn at 500
HOTEL $$

(☑208-227-0500; www.innat500.com; 500 S Capitol Blvd; r $215-280, ste $290-325; 🏶🏶🏶) Finally, a luxury boutique hotel that doesn't give up at the lobby. Fine art, unique dioramas and blown glass – all from local artists – adorn the hallways and rooms, creating warm and inviting spaces a step above your standard high-quality-bed-in-a-box affair. All within walking distance of Boise's buzzing downtown.

🍴 Eating

Boise's vibrant downtown hosts numerous dining options from casual to formal. The concentration of Basque specialties downtown is a particular highlight, while options abound along 8th St. The hip Hyde Park region on 13th St is even more laid-back, and a great place to grab a snack after hiking.

★Goldy's Breakfast Bistro
BREAKFAST $

(☑208-345-4100; www.goldysbreakfastbistro. com; 108 S Capitol Blvd; mains $6-20; ⊙6:30am-2pm Mon-Fri, 7:30am-2pm Sat & Sun) Assuming an egg is just an egg, Goldy's offers 866,320 'Create Your Own Breakfast Combos.' Check our math – we were already drunk on hollandaise sauce when we put pen to napkin. Or go for the frittatas, bennies or massive breakfast burrito. Pass through the velvet curtain and go for a table on the internal balcony.

Fork
MODERN AMERICAN $$

(☑207-287-1700; https://boisefork.com; 199 N 8th St; mains $10-34; ⊙11:30am-10pm Mon-Thu, to 11pm Fri, 9:30am-11pm Sat, 9:30am-9pm Sun; 🏶) 🏶 This cavernous corner restaurant occupying the old bank building downtown is good anytime, but excels during weekend brunch when things like the Dungeness crab scramble pair unbelievably well with the local favorite: asparagus fries. Try the Fork Lemonade for a refreshing pickup on a sunny summer day.

Drinking & Nightlife

★ **Bodovino** WINE BAR
(☑ 208-336-8466; www.bodovino.com; 404 S 8th St; ☺ 11am-11pm Mon-Thu, to 1am Fri & Sat, 11am-9pm Sun; 🛜) Whether you're a sommelier or a swiller, the variety of vintages on tap here is nothing short of hazardous – especially considering the fact that you're on your own with walls of vending machines that decant tastes or pours from 144 different wines.

Bardenay DISTILLERY
(☑ 208-426-0538; www.bardenay.com; 610 Grove St; cocktails from $8; ☺ 11am-late Mon-Fri, from 10am Sat & Sun) Bardenay was the USA's very first 'distillery-pub,' and remains a one-of-a-kind watering hole. Located on Basque Block, it makes rum in-house and has whiskey aging for imminent release. A dizzying array of cocktails are created from spirits crafted in all three of Bardenay's Idaho locations, including the dizzying Sunday Morning Paper – a lemon-vodka–Bloody Mary experience.

IDAHO FACTS

Nickname Gem State

Population 1,754,000

Area 83,570 sq miles

Capital city Boise (population 226,600)

Other cities Idaho Falls (population 61,100)

Sales tax 6%

Birthplace of Lewis and Clark guide Sacagawea (1788–1812); politician Sarah Palin (b 1964); poet Ezra Pound (1885–1972)

Home of Star garnet, Sun Valley ski resort

Politics Reliably Republican with small pockets of Democrats, eg Sun Valley

Famous for Potatoes, wilderness, the world's first chairlift

North America's deepest river gorge Idaho's Hells Canyon (7900ft deep)

Driving distances Boise to Idaho Falls 280 miles, Lewiston to Coeur d'Alene 116 miles

---

ℹ Information

Visitor Center (☑ 208-810-7324; www.boise.org; 8th & Grove Sts, Grove Plaza; ☺ 9am-6pm Mon-Sat) This office has plenty of printed material on Boise and the wider area, while the website has a useful events calendar.

ℹ Getting There & Around

Small but busy **Boise Municipal Airport** (BOI; ☑ 208-383-3110; www.iflyboise.com; 3201 Airport Way, I-84 exit 53) is well connected, with nonstop flights to a range of locations including Denver, Las Vegas, Phoenix, Portland, Salt Lake City, Seattle, San Francisco, Los Angeles, Dallas and Chicago.

Greyhound services depart from the **bus station** (www.greyhound.com; 1212 W Bannock St; ☺ 6-11am & 4pm-midnight) with routes fanning out to Spokane (from $45, 8½ to 10 hours), Missoula (from $78, 15 hours), Pendleton (from $37, five hours), Portland (from $74, 9½ hours), Twin Falls (from $32, 2¼ hours) and Salt Lake City (from $64, seven hours).

The coolest way to get around downtown is by far the **Green Bike** (☑ 208-345-7433; https://boise.greenbike.com; per hr/month $5/15) system. Book online or download the app to unlock one of more than 100 bicycles locked at over 20 downtown stations, and feel the wind in your hair as you cruise the city in emissions-free style. The program has expanded to include the Boise River Greenbelt (p810) and area parks.

Ketchum & Sun Valley

Occupying one of Idaho's more stunning natural locations, Sun Valley is a living piece of ski history. It was the first purpose-built ski resort in the US (a venture by the Union Pacific Railroad to boost ridership) and opened in 1936 to much fanfare, thanks to both its luxury showcase lodge and the world's first chairlift.

The ski area and town of Ketchum were popularized early on by celebrities including Ernest Hemingway, Clark Gable and Gary Cooper (who received free trips as a marketing ploy by Averell Harriman – politician, railroad heir and Sun Valley's founder). It has maintained its love affair with swanky Hollywood clientele ever since.

For all that, Sun Valley remains a pretty and accessible place flush with hot springs, hiking trails, fishing, hunting and mountain biking, extending from Galena Pass down to the foothills of Hailey.

🏃 Activities

⭐ Galena Lodge   OUTDOORS
(📞208-726-4010; www.galenalodge.com; 15187 Hwy 75; XC ski pass adult/child $17/free; ⊘lodge 9am-4pm, kitchen 11am-3:30pm) Miles of mountain bike and groomed XC ski trails spiderweb out from this cool lodge that rents equipment and serves up lunch to keep you fueled for the day. It's 23 miles north of Ketchum.

Sun Valley Resort   SNOW SPORTS
(📞888-490-5950; www.sunvalley.com; Ketchum; winter ski ticket $90-145) Sun Valley has been synonymous with luxury skiing ever since they invented the chairlift in 1936. But while you can now sit-to-ski elsewhere, people still flock here for the fluffy powder and celebrity spotting. Two mountains – mellow **Dollar Mountain** with its extensive terrain parks to the east of town and black-and-blue **Bald Mountain** to the west – provide plenty of variety.

Wood River Trail System   OUTDOORS
(www.bcrd.org/wood-river-trail-summer.php) Good things happen when a community rallies behind outdoor activities. This paved urban trail system extends over 32 miles, connecting the major hubs of Sun Valley with the towns of Ketchum, Hailey and Bellevue (20 miles to the south) following the old Union Pacific Railroad line. Several shops rent bikes in the valley.

🛏 Sleeping

Ketchum has a small sprinkling of hotels, with at least one decent option in all categories. Rates vary with the seasons, winter being most expensive. For budget travelers, there's an in-town hostel and free camping on Bureau of Land Management (BLM) and Forest Service lands near town.

Tamarack Lodge   HOTEL $$
(📞208-726-3344; www.tamaracksunvalley.com; 291 Walnut Ave; r/ste from $165/215; ❄🗑📶🖥🏊) Rooms are tasteful at this aging but clean downtown lodge that exudes a charming '1970s ski condo' vibe. Some rooms are a bit dark, but many have fireplaces and all have a balcony and use of the Jacuzzi and indoor pool.

⭐ Limelight Hotel   HOTEL $$$
(📞208-726-0888; www.limelighthotels.com/ketchum; 151 Main St; r $260-545; 📶🏊) Downtown Ketchum's coolest hotel, the Limelight has an appealing stone facade, muted earthy tones in the semi-luxurious rooms and some fine views from the floor-to-ceiling windows in rooms on the upper floors. With a bar, restaurants, equipment rental and other services, they have most bases covered.

Sun Valley Lodge   HOTEL $$$
(📞208-622-2001; www.sunvalley.com; 1 Sun Valley Rd; inn/lodge from $355/445; ❄@📶🏊) The celebrities already came in droves before the 2015 renovation that spruced up this swank 1930s-era lodge – Sun Valley's first and finest. Standard rooms have the exact same amenities as the higher end picks – including the spacious bathrooms with tub – just less floor space around the bed. Cheaper accommodation is available beyond the main lodge.

🍴 Eating & Drinking

You'll want to après-ski at **Apple's** (📞208-726-7067; www.facebook.com/applesbarandgrill; 205 Picabo St; ⊘11am-6pm) before checking out the valley's regular live-music scene. The more swanky bars are not averse to turning out the riffraff. If you unexpectedly find yourself in that category, the **Casino Club** (The Casbah; 📞208-726-9901; www.facebook.com/thecasbah36; 220 N Main St; ⊘11am-2am) has a stool for you.

The Kneadery   BREAKFAST $
(📞208-726-9462; www.kneadery.com; 260 N Leadville Ave; mains $10-15; ⊘8am-2pm) A solid bet for breakfast or lunch, the Kneadery is off the main drag in an old split-log cabin outfitted with large fireplace, western art and a birchbark canoe hanging from the ceiling. The ambience is almost as fine as their pancakes.

⭐ Enoteca   INTERNATIONAL $$
(📞208-928-6280; www.ketchum-enoteca.com; 300 N Main St; mains $8-16; ⊘5-9pm) By the people who once presided over Ketchum Grill, Enoteca combines a classy, softly lit space with an enticing selection of large and small tapas-style plates. From wood-fired pizzas and mac and cheese to Idaho trout, from cured meats and cheeses to duck confit, it's all good. It offers a terrific wine list, too.

⭐ Pioneer Saloon   STEAK $$$
(📞208-726-3139; www.pioneersaloon.com; 320 N Main St; mains $15-36; ⊘5-10pm, bar 4pm-late)

CRATERS OF THE MOON

In Idaho's far south, between Sun Valley and Idaho Falls, **Craters of the Moon National Monument & Preserve** (🖉 208-527-1300; www.nps.gov/crmo; 1266 Craters Loop Rd; ⊙ visitor center 8am-6pm late May–mid-Sep, to 4:30pm mid-Sep–late May) is one of Western USA's most unusual landscapes. Described by President Calvin Coolidge at the time of its recognition in 1924 as 'a weird and scenic landscape, peculiar to itself,' Craters of the Moon does indeed resemble a lunar land.

Beginning some 15,000 years ago, a series of volcanic eruptions laid waste to the Snake River Plain, leaving a blistered land of lunar-like craters, lava tubes caves and fissures. The last eruption took place a mere 2000 years ago. The results now cover 750,000 acres.

There's a **visitor center** at the entrance to the national monument, which is accessible along the US 93/26/20 between Arco and Carey. Beyond the center, a series of drives and hiking trails crisscross the reserve. The **North Crater Trail** and the summer-only **Tree Molds Trail** are the hiking highlights, while the **Loop Road**, accessible only from May to September, passes some of the most dramatic formations. These include **Devil's Orchard** (island-like lava fragments surrounded by cinders), **Inferno Cone** (with fabulous views from the summit) and the **Cave Area**.

For the best steak in Ketchum (and, some argue, Idaho) step into the former illicit gambling hall, now an unashamed Western den decorated with deer heads, antique guns (one being Hemingway's) and bullet boards. If red meat isn't your thing, they also have a range of fish options and a tasty mango-chutney and grilled-vegetable chicken kabob.

❶ Information

Sun Valley/Ketchum Visitor Center (🖉 208-726-3423; www.visitsunvalley.com; 491 Sun Valley Rd; ⊙ 6am-7pm; 🛜) Volunteers are a wealth of information when the station is staffed from 9am to 6pm. Maps and brochures available at all hours.

❶ Getting There & Around

Friedman Memorial Airport (SUN; 🖉 208-788-4956; www.iflysun.com; 1616 Airport Circle, Hailey) is located 12 miles south of Ketchum in Hailey. It has daily service to most western-states hubs (LA, San Francisco, Seattle, Salt Lake City and Denver, as well as twice-weekly flights to Portland), though it can sometimes be more economical to fly into Boise and take the three-hour **Sun Valley Express** (Caldwell Transportation; 🖉 208-576-7381; www.sunvalleyexpress.com; adult/child $90/80) from there.

Mountain Rides (🖉 208-788-7433; www.mountainrides.org) offers free transportation throughout Ketchum; trips between Hailey and Ketchum cost $3/2 per adult/child.

Stanley

Barely more than a cluster of rustic log cabins just across from the jagged Sawtooth mountains, Stanley might be the most scenic small town in Idaho. For much of the year, the town is snowed in and very quiet, but it comes to life during the brief summer months as adventurers come to boat the world-class white water of the Middle Fork, fish the blue-ribbon rivers teeming with salmon and trout, or stock up on last-minute supplies before exploring the foreboding peaks and hidden valleys of the Sawtooth range.

➤ Activities

⭐ **Sawtooth**
National Recreation Area OUTDOORS
(🖉 208-423-7500; www.fs.usda.gov/sawtooth) You'll find rivers to boat, mountains to climb, more than 300 lakes to fish, and in excess of 700 miles of trails to hike or mountain bike in the dramatic Sawtooth National Recreation Area. It protects 1170 sq miles of America's public lands stretching between Stanley and Ketchum, offering unparalleled opportunities for exploration and recreation.

Solitude River Trips RAFTING
(🖉 208-806-1218, 800-396-1776; www.rivertrips.com; 6-day trip per person $2690; ⊙ Jun-Aug) Offers top-notch, multiday trips on the famed Middle Fork of the Salmon. Camping is riverside and guides cook excellent food.

White Otter

RAFTING

(☏ 208-788-5005; www.whiteotter.com; 100 Yankee Fork Rd & Hwy 75, Sunbeam; full-day float trips per person $160, half-day river rafting adult/child $80/65) One of few rafting outfits to be locally run, White Otter is recommended for fun class III day trips. It also arranges float trips in inflatable kayaks.

🍽 Sleeping & Eating

Sawtooth Hotel

HOTEL $

(☏ 208-721-2459; www.sawtoothhotel.com; 755 Ace of Diamonds St; d with/without bath $115/80; ⊗ mid-May–mid-Oct; 🛜) Set in a nostalgic 1931 log motel, the Sawtooth updates the slim comforts of yesteryear, but keeps the hospitality effusively Stanley-esque. Six rooms are furnished old-country style, two with private bathrooms. Don't expect TVs or speedy wi-fi, but count on excellent dining (mains $14 to $23) with vegetarian and gluten-free options and a tiny selection of drinkable wines.

★ Stanley Baking Company

BAKERY $

(www.stanleybakingco.com; 250 Wall St; mains $9-13; ⊗ 7am-2pm mid-May–Oct) Something of a legend, this middle-of-nowhere bakery and brunch spot is a must stop. Operating for five months of the year out of a small log cabin, Stanley Baking Co is the only place in town where you're likely to see a queue. The reason: off-the-ratings-scale homemade baked goods, oatmeal pancakes and a fabulous meatloaf sandwich.

Bridge Street Grill

GRILL $$

(☏ 208-774-2208; www.bridgestgrill.com; Hwy 75, Lower Stanley; mains $11-23; ⊗ 11am-10pm) Although the town is literally surrounded by postcard-perfect scenery, somehow it's all the sweeter when viewed from the busy deck of Bridge Street Grill on the banks of the river – especially with a cold beer in hand and the remains of a green-chile-cheese Border Burger or house-smoked brisket on your plate.

Southwest

Best Places to Eat

➡ Kai Restaurant (p841)

➡ Cafe Pasqual's (p898)

➡ Red Iguana (p873)

➡ Kerouac's (p834)

Best Places to Sleep

➡ Washington School House (p877)

➡ NoMad (p826)

➡ La Fonda (p897)

➡ Arizona Biltmore Resort & Spa (p839)

➡ Hotel Luna Mystica (p903)

Why Go?

Rugged. Beautiful. And fun. The Southwest is America's wild backyard, luring adventurous travelers with red-rock canyons, Wild West legends and the kicky delights of green-chile stew. Reminders of the region's Native American heritage and hardscrabble Wild West heyday dot the landscape, from enigmatic pictographs and abandoned cliff dwellings to crumbling Hispanic missions and rusty mining towns. Today, history making continues, with astronomers and rocket builders peering into starry skies, while artists and entrepreneurs flock to urban centers and quirky mountain towns. It's an ideal destination for road-trippers, with a splendid network of scenic drives linking the most beautiful and iconic sites. But remember: it's not just larger-than-life landscapes that make a trip through the Southwest memorable. Study that saguaro up close; ask a Hopi artist about their craft; savor that green-chile stew. You may cherish those smaller moments the most.

When to Go
Las Vegas

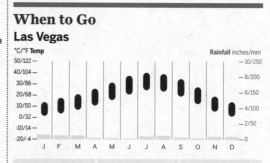

Jan Ski near Taos and Flagstaff. In Park City, hit the slopes and the Sundance Film Festival.

Jun–Aug High season for exploring national parks in New Mexico, Utah and northern Arizona.

Sep–Nov Hike to the bottom of the Grand Canyon or gaze at bright leaves in northern New Mexico.

History

By about AD 100, three dominant cultures were emerging in the Southwest: the Hohokam of the desert, the Mogollon of the central mountains and valleys, and the Ancestral Puebloans. Archaeologists originally called the Ancestral Puebloans the Anasazi, which comes from a Navajo term meaning 'ancient enemy' and has fallen out of favor.

Francisco Vásquez de Coronado led the first major expedition into North America in 1540. It included 300 soldiers, hundreds of Native American guides and herds of livestock. It also marked the first major violence between Spanish explorers and the native people.

In addition to armed conflict, Europeans introduced smallpox, measles and typhus, to which the Native Americans had no resistance. Pueblo populations were decimated by these diseases, shattering cultures and trade routes and proving a destructive force that far outstripped combat.

Development in the Southwest expanded rapidly during the 19th century, mainly due to railroad and geological surveys. As the US pushed west, the army forcibly removed entire tribes of Native Americans in horrifyingly brutal Indian Wars. Gold and silver mines drew fortune seekers, and the lawless mining towns of the Wild West mushroomed practically overnight. Soon the Santa Fe Railroad was luring a flood of tourists to the West.

Modern settlement is closely linked to water use. Following the Reclamation Act of 1902, huge federally funded dams were built to control rivers and irrigate the desert. Rancorous disagreements over water rights are ongoing, especially with the phenomenal boom in residential development and the extensive recent drought. The other major issue in recent years, especially in southern Arizona, has been illegal immigration across the border from Mexico.

Local Culture

Rugged individuality is the cultural idiom of the Southwest. But the reality? It's a bit more complex. The major identities of the region, centered on a trio of tribes – Anglo, Hispanic and Native American – are as vast and varied as the land that has shaped them. Whether their personal religion involves aliens, art, nuclear fission, slot machines, peyote or Joseph Smith, there's plenty of room for you in this beautiful, barely tamed chunk of America.

❶ Getting There & Around

Las Vegas' McCarran International Airport (p831) and Phoenix's Sky Harbor International Airport (p843) are the region's busiest airports, with plenty of domestic and international connections.

Greyhound stops at major cities, but barely serves national parks or off-the-beaten-path towns such as Moab. Amtrak train service is even more limited, although it too links several southwestern cities and offers bus connections to others (including Santa Fe and Phoenix). The *California Zephyr* crosses Utah and Nevada; the *Southwest Chief* stops in Arizona and New Mexico;

SOUTHWEST IN...

One Week
Museums and a burgeoning arts scene set an inspirational tone in **Phoenix**. In the morning, follow Camelback Rd into **Scottsdale** for top-notch shopping and gallery-hopping in Old Town. Drive north to **Sedona** for spiritual recharging before pondering the immensity of the **Grand Canyon**. From here, choose either bling or buttes. For bling, detour onto **Route 66**, cross the bridge beside **Hoover Dam** then indulge your fantasies in **Las Vegas**. For buttes, drive east from the Grand Canyon into Navajo country, cruising beneath the giant rock formations in **Monument Valley Navajo Tribal Park** then stepping back in time at stunning **Canyon de Chelly National Monument**.

Two Weeks
Start in glitzy **Las Vegas** before kicking back in funky **Flagstaff** and peering into the abyss at **Grand Canyon National Park**. Check out collegiate **Tucson** and hike amid cacti at **Saguaro National Park**. Watch the gunslingers in **Tombstone** before settling into offbeat Victorian **Bisbee**. Secure your sunglasses for the blinding dunes of **White Sands National Monument** in New Mexico then sink into **Santa Fe**, a magnet for art-lovers. Explore the pueblo in **Taos** and watch the sunrise at awesome **Monument Valley Navajo Tribal Park**. Head into Utah for the red-rock national parks, **Canyonlands** and **Arches**. Do the hoodoos at **Bryce Canyon** then pay your respects at glorious **Zion**.

Southwest Highlights

1 Grand Canyon National Park (p851) Catching the sunset from a South Rim viewpoint

2 Santa Fe (p894) Exploring the cultural diversions, from Meow Wolf to international folk art.

3 Angels Landing, Zion National Park (p888) Staying brave while hiking this stunning slice of Utah canyonland.

4 Las Vegas (p820) Finding out it's even more brash, synthetic and irresponsible than you'd hoped!

5 Sedona (p844) Rejoicing that even monetised hippy culture can't tarnish this unique red-rock city.

6 Route 66 (p863) Winding along the Mother Road through remote landscapes and time-capsule townships.

7 Moab (p881) Celebrating the great outdoors while mountain biking, hiking, rafting or camping.

8 Monument Valley (p862) Snapping impossibly photogenic brick-red buttes and mesas, the stars of countless Westerns.

9 Acoma Pueblo (p894) Learning about one of the nation's oldest communities on a sky-high mesa.

and the *Sunset Limited* traverses southern Arizona and New Mexico.

Ultimately, this means private vehicles are often the only means to reach out-of-the-way towns, trailheads and swimming spots, and to explore the region in any depth.

NEVADA

Nevada is defined by contrasts and contradictions, juxtaposing arid plains with skyward, snowcapped mountains, while stilettos demand equal suitcase space with ski boots. Many visitors come only for the main event: Las Vegas. Nevada's twinkling desert jewel is a mecca for pleasure-seekers, and where privilege and poverty collide and three-quarters of the state's population resides.

In this libertarian state, rural brothels coexist with Mormon churches, casinos and cowboys. Isolated ghost towns recall a pioneering past and the promise of a better life. But Nevada's rightful drawcard is nature, with Reno's rushing Truckee River, Lake Tahoe's crystal waters and forested peaks, the playas of the Black Rock Desert where Burning Man's utopia was born, and the craggy peaks of the Great Basin and the austere expanses of Hwy 50, the 'Loneliest Road in America.'

❶ Information

Nevada Division of State Parks (☑ 775-684-2770; www.parks.nv.gov; 901 S Stewart St, 5th fl; ☺ 8am-5pm Mon-Fri) Camping in state parks ($10 to $15 per night) is first come, first served.
Nevada Tourism Commission (☑ 775-687-4322; www.travelnevada.com; 401 N Carson St; ☺ 9am-5pm Mon-Fri) Sends free books, maps and information on accommodations, campgrounds and events.

Las Vegas

An oasis of indulgence in the desert, Vegas is hypnotically seductive. Where else can you party in ancient Rome, get hitched at midnight, wake up in Egypt and brunch beneath the Eiffel Tower? Double down with the high rollers, browse couture or tacky souvenirs, sip a neon 3ft-high margarita or a frozen vodka martini from a bar made of ice – it's all here.

It's also a desert dreamscape of boom and bust, where once-famous signs collect dust in a neon boneyard while the clang of construction echoes over the Strip. These days, with hotels and bars opening at a rapid pace and a fresh collection of pop divas kicking off residencies, the city is as hot as ever, attracting well over 40 million visitors per year.

Las Vegas' largest casinos – each one a gigantic and baffling mélange of theme park, gambling den, shopping and dining destination, hotel and theater district – line up along the legendary Strip. Once you've explored those, head to the compact downtown to encounter Vegas' nostalgic beginnings, peppered with indie shops and cocktail bars where local culture thrives. Then detour further afield to find intriguing museums that investigate Vegas' gangster, atomic-fueled past.

◉ Sights

Vegas' sights are primarily concentrated along the 4.2-mile stretch of Las Vegas Blvd anchored by Mandalay Bay to the south (at Russell Rd) and the Stratosphere to the north (at Sahara Ave) and in the Downtown area around the intersection of Las Vegas Blvd (N Las Vegas Blvd at this point) and Fremont St. Note that while the street has the same name, there's an additional 2 miles between Downtown and the northern end of the Strip, with not much of interest

---

NEVADA FACTS

Nickname Silver State

Population 3.03 million

Area 109,800 sq miles

Capital city Carson City (population 54,439)

Other cities Las Vegas (population 641,700), Reno (248,853)

Sales tax 4.6%

Birthplace of Andre Agassi (b 1970), Greg LeMond (b 1961)

Home of The slot machine, Burning Man

Politics Nevada has six electoral votes – the state went for Clinton in the 2016 presidential election

Famous for The 1859 Comstock Lode (the country's richest known silver deposit), legalized gambling and prostitution (outlawed in certain counties), and liberal alcohol laws allowing 24-hour bars

Driving distances Las Vegas to Reno 452 miles, Great Basin National Park to Las Vegas 313 miles

in between. It's not a great idea to walk between the two; this neighborhood can be a little dicey. Rideshares, the Monorail and Deuce bus services are by far the easiest ways to get around this spaced-out (in more ways than one) city.

◉ The Strip

★ Aria
LANDMARK

(CityCenter; Map p822; www.aria.com; 3780 S Las Vegas Blvd; P) We've seen this symbiotic relationship before (think giant hotel anchored by a mall 'concept'), but the way that this futuristic-feeling complex places a small galaxy of hypermodern, chichi hotels in orbit around the glitzy **Shops at Crystals** (Map p822; www.simon.com/mall/the-shops-at-crystals; ⊗ 10am-11pm Mon-Thu, to midnight Fri-Sun) is a first. The upscale spread includes the subdued, stylish **Vdara** (Map p822; ☑ 702-590-2111; www.vdara.com; 2600 W Harmon Ave, Aria; weekday/weekend ste from $103/189; P ❋ ✳ @ 🎧 ➿ 🐾), the hush-hush opulent **Waldorf Astoria** (Map p822; www.waldorfastorialasvegas.com; 3752 S Las Vegas Blvd; r from $200; P ❋ ✳ 🎧 ➿) and the dramatic architectural showpiece **Aria**, whose sophisticated casino provides a fitting backdrop to its many drop-dead-gorgeous restaurants. CityCenter's hotels have in excess of 6700 rooms!

★ Bellagio
CASINO

(Map p822; ☑ 702-693-7111; www.bellagio.com; 3600 S Las Vegas Blvd; ⊗ 24hr; P) The Bellagio experience transcends its decadent casino floor of high-limit gaming tables and in excess of 2300 slot machines; locals say odds here are less than favorable. A stop on the World Poker Tour, Bellagio's tournament-worthy poker room offers kitchen-to-gaming-table delivery around the clock. Most, however, come for the property's stunning architecture, interiors and amenities, including the **Conservatory & Botanical Gardens** (Map p822; ⊗ 24hr; P 🚻) 🆓, **Gallery of Fine Art** (Map p822; ☑ 702-693-7871; adult/child under 12yr $18/free; ⊗ 10am-8pm, last entry 7:30pm; P 🚻), unmissable **Fountains of Bellagio** (Map p822; ⊗ shows every 30min 3-8pm Mon-Fri, noon-8pm Sat, 11am-7pm Sun, every 15min 8pm-midnight Mon-Sat, from 7pm Sun; P 🚻) 🆓 and the 2000-plus hand-blown glass flowers embellishing the hotel (p826) lobby.

★ Caesars Palace
CASINO

(Map p822; ☑ 866-227-5938; www.caesars.com/caesars-palace; 3570 S Las Vegas Blvd; ⊗ 24hr; P)

Caesars Palace claims that its smartly renovated casino floor has more million-dollar slots than anywhere in the world, but its claims to fame are far more numerous than that. Entertainment heavyweights Celine Dion and Elton John 'own' its custom-built **Colosseum** (Map p822; ☑ 866-227-5938; www.thecolosseum.com; tickets $55-500) theater, fashionistas saunter around **The Forum Shops** (Map p822; ☑ 702-893-4800; www.simon.com/mall/the-forum-shops-at-caesars-palace; ⊗ 10am-11pm Sun-Thu, to midnight Fri & Sat), while Caesars' hotel guests quaff cocktails in the Garden of the Gods Pool Oasis. By night, megaclub **Omnia** (Map p822; ☑ 702-785-6200; www.omniaclubs.com/las-vegas; cover female/male from $20/40; ⊗ 10:30pm-4am Tue & Thu-Sun) is one of the best places to get off your face this side of Ibiza.

NoMad
CASINO

(Map p822; ☑ 702-730-7000; www.thenomadhotel.com; 3772 S Las Vegas Blvd; ⊗ 24hr) If a Las Vegas casino can be classy, the NoMad comes in pretty close to the mark. High-limit roulette, blackjack and baccarat are available under a Tiffany-glass ceiling. The NoMad's pool is modeled on the Majorelle Gardens in Morocco, and is quietly relaxing on weekdays (weekend Jemaa parties are another story).

LINQ Casino
CASINO

(Map p822; ☑ 800-634-6441; www.caesars.com/linq; 3535 S Las Vegas Blvd; ⊗ 24hr; P) With a fresh, young and funky vibe, one of Vegas' newest casinos benefits from also being one of its smallest with just over 60 tables and around 750 slot machines. There's an airy, spacious feel to the place, tables feature high-backed, ruby-red, patent-vinyl chairs, and when you need to escape, the fun and frivolity of **LINQ Promenade** (Map p822; ☑ 800-634-6441; www.caesars.com/linq; ⊗ 24hr; P 🚻) are just outside the door.

Venetian
CASINO

(Map p822; ☑ 702-414-1000; www.venetian.com; 3355 S Las Vegas Blvd; ⊗ 24hr; P) The Venetian's regal 120,000-sq-ft casino has marble floors, hand-painted ceiling frescoes and 120 table games, including a high-limit lounge and an elegant nonsmoking poker room, where women are especially welcome (unlike at many other poker rooms in town). When combined with its younger, neighboring sibling **Palazzo** (Map p822; ☑ 702-607-7777; www.palazzo.com; 3325 S Las Vegas Blvd; ⊗ 24hr; P), the properties claim the largest

Las Vegas

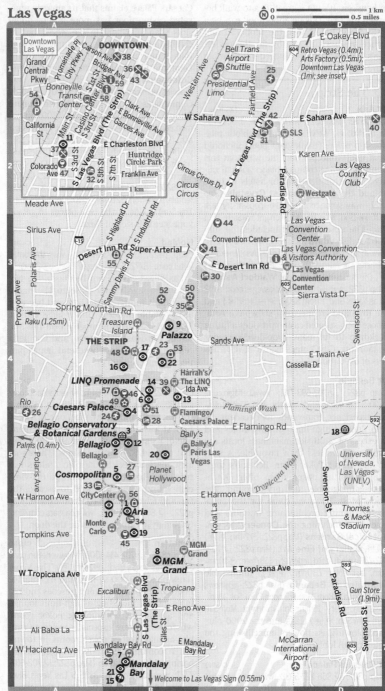

0 — 1 km
0 — 0.5 miles

Downtown Las Vegas

DOWNTOWN

38
36
43
59
58
Grand Central Pkwy
54
California St
11
37
Colorado Ave 47
32

Promenade Pl
City Pkwy
Carson Ave
Bridger Ave
Bonneville Ave
Clark Ave
E Bonneville Ave
Garces Ave
E Charleston Blvd
Huntridge Circle Park
Franklin Ave

Main St
Casino Center Blvd
S 1st St
S 3rd St
S 4th St
S 5th St
S 7th St
S Las Vegas Blvd (The Strip)

1 km

Western Ave

Bell Trans Airport Shuttle
Presidential Limo
W Sahara Ave

Fairfield Ave
25
31
SLS

E Oakey Blvd

604
Retro Vegas (0.4mi);
Arts Factory (0.5mi);
Downtown Las Vegas (1mi; see inset)

42 E Sahara Ave
40
Karen Ave
Las Vegas Country Club
Westgate
Paradise Rd

Meade Ave
Sirius Ave
Procyon Ave

I-15

Desert Inn Rd Super-Arterial
55

S Highland Dr
Sammy Davis Jr Jr Industrial Rd
S Industrial Rd

Circus Circus Dr
Circus Circus
Riviera Blvd

44
Convention Center Dr
41
E Desert Inn Rd
30

Las Vegas Convention Center
Las Vegas Convention & Visitors Authority
605
Las Vegas Convention Center
Sierra Vista Dr
Swenson St

Spring Mountain Rd
THE STRIP
Raku (1.25mi)
Treasure Island
48 17
16
Palms (0.4mi)
Rio
26
Caesars Palace
57 46
49
24 4
3
Bellagio Conservatory & Botanical Gardens
Bellagio
2
Bellagio
Cosmopolitan
33
CityCenter
56
1
10 Aria
Monte Carlo
45
34
19

52
50
35

9 Palazzo
23 53
22
Sands Ave
E Twain Ave
Cassella Dr

14 39
6 Harrah's/ The LINQ
LINQ Promenade
Ida Ave
13
51
28
Flamingo/ Caesars Palace
Flamingo Wash
E Flamingo Rd
18

592
605
University of Nevada, Las Vegas (UNLV)

20
Planet Hollywood
Bally's
Bally's/ Paris Las Vegas
E Harmon Ave
Koval La
Tropicana Wash

W Harmon Ave
Tompkins Ave
W Tropicana Ave

8 MGM Grand
MGM Grand
E Tropicana Ave

Thomas & Mack Stadium
Swenson St
593
Paradise Rd
Gun Store (1.9mi)

Excalibur
Tropicana
E Reno Ave

S Las Vegas Blvd (The Strip)
Giles St

I-15
Ali Baba La
W Hacienda Ave

Mandalay Bay Rd
7
29
21
15 Mandalay Bay

E Mandalay Bay Rd

McCarran International Airport
605

Welcome to Las Vegas Sign (0.55mi)

SOUTHWEST LAS VEGAS

Las Vegas

SOUTHWEST LAS VEGAS

casino space in Las Vegas. Unmissable on the Strip, a highlight of this miniature replica of Venice is a gondola ride (p825) down its Grand Canal.

★ **Cosmopolitan**　　　　　　CASINO
(Map p822; ☎ 702-698-7000; www.cosmopolitan lasvegas.com; 3708 S Las Vegas Blvd; ☺24hr; P)

Hipsters who thought they were too cool for Vegas finally have a place to go where they don't need irony to endure – or enjoy – the aesthetics of the Strip. Like the new Hollywood 'It' girl, the Cosmopolitan casino looks absolutely fabulous at all times. A steady stream of ingenues and entourages parade through the lobby (with some of the coolest design elements we've seen) along with anyone else who adores contemporary art and design.

★ Mandalay Bay
CASINO

(Map p822; ☑702-632-7700; www.mandalaybay. com; 3950 S Las Vegas Blvd; ☉24hr; 🅿️ 🐾) Since opening in 1999, in place of the former '50s-era Hacienda, Mandalay Bay has anchored the southern Strip. Its theme may be tropical, but it sure ain't tacky, nor is its 135,000-sq-ft casino. Well-dressed sports fans find their way to the upscale race and sports book near the high-stakes poker room. Refusing to be pigeonholed, the Bay's standout attractions include the multilevel **Shark Reef Aquarium** (Map p822; ☑702-632-4555; www.sharkreef.com; adult/child $25/19; ☉10am-8pm Sun-Thu, to 10pm Fri & Sat; 🅿️ 🐾), decadent day spas, oodles of signature dining and the unrivaled **Mandalay Bay Beach** (Map p822; ☑702-632-4760; www.mandalaybay.com/en/amen ities/beach.html; ☉pool 8am-7pm, Moorea Beach Club from 10am; 🐾).

Paris Las Vegas
CASINO

(Map p822; ☑877-796-2096; www.caesars.com/ paris-las-vegas; 3655 S Las Vegas Blvd; ☉24hr; 🅿️) This mini version of the French capital might lack the charm of the City of Light, but its efforts to emulate Paris' landmarks, including a 34-story Hotel de Ville and facades from the Opera House and Louvre, make it a fun stop for families and anyone yet to see the real thing. Its vaulted casino ceilings simulate sunny skies above myriad tables and slots, while its high-limit, authentic French roulette wheels, sans 0 and 00, slightly improve your odds.

High Roller
FERRIS WHEEL

(Map p822; ☑702-777-2782; www.caesars.com/ linq/high-roller; LINQ Promenade; adult/child from $22/9, after 5pm $32/19; ☉11:30am-1:30am; 🅿️ 🐾; 🚋Flamingo or Harrah's/Linq) The world's largest observation wheel towers 550ft above LINQ Promenade (p821). Each of the 28 air-conditioned passenger cabins is enclosed by handcrafted Italian glass. Outside, 2000 colorful LED lights glow from dusk until dawn. One revolution takes about 30 minutes and each pod can hold 40 guests. From 4pm to 7pm, select pods host the adults-only (21-plus) 'happy half-hour' ($35, or $47 after 5pm) with an open bar (read all-you-can-drink) shared between your fellow riders. Things can get messy, fast.

Mirage Volcano
LANDMARK

(Map p822; ☑702-791-7111; www.mirage.com; Mirage; ☉shows 8pm, 9pm & 10pm daily) FREE When the Mirage's trademark artificial volcano erupts with a roar out of a 3-acre lagoon, it inevitably brings traffic on the Strip to a screeching halt. Be on the lookout for wisps of smoke escaping from the top, signaling that the fiery Polynesian-style inferno, with a soundtrack by a Grateful Dead drummer and an Indian tabla musician, is about to begin.

◉ Downtown & off the Strip

For tourists, the five-block **Fremont Street Experience** (☑702-678-5600; www.vegasexp erience.com; Fremont St Mall; ☉shows hourly dusk-midnight or 1am; 🚋Deuce, SDX) FREE is the focal point of Downtown, with its wealth of vintage casinos, where today's Vegas was born – and fear not, they're still going strong. Further south, the **Arts District** (www.18b.org) revolves around the **Arts Factory** (Map p822; ☑702-383-9907; www.theartsfactory.com; 107 E Charleston Blvd; ☉9am-6pm; 🚋Deuce, SDX), while heading east on Fremont St will take you to an adorable little hodgepodge of hip bars and happening restaurants.

★ Mob Museum
MUSEUM

(☑702-229-2734; www.themobmuseum.org; 300 Stewart Ave; adult/child $27/17; ☉9am-9pm; 🅿️; 🚋Deuce) It's hard to say what's more impressive: the museum's physical location in a historic federal courthouse where mobsters sat for federal hearings in 1950–51, the fact that the board of directors is headed up by a former FBI special agent, or the thoughtfully curated exhibits telling the story of organized crime in America. The museum features hands-on FBI equipment and mob-related artifacts, as well as interviews with real-life Tony Sopranos.

★ Neon Museum – Neon Boneyard
MUSEUM

(☑702-387-6366; www.neonmuseum.org; 770 N Las Vegas Blvd; 1hr tour adult/child $28/24; ☉tours daily, schedules vary; 🚋113) This nonprofit project is doing what almost no one else does: saving Las Vegas' history. Book ahead for a fascinating guided walking tour of the 'Neon Boneyard,' where irreplaceable vintage neon signs – Las Vegas' original art form – spend their retirement. Start exploring at the visitor center inside the salvaged

La Concha Motel lobby, a mid-century modern icon designed by African American architect Paul Revere Williams. Tours are usually given throughout the day, but are most spectacular at night.

National Atomic Testing Museum MUSEUM
(Map p822; 702-794-5151; www.nationalatomic testingmuseum.org; 755 Flamingo Rd E, Desert Research Institute; adult/child $22/16; 10am-5pm Mon-Sat, noon-5pm Sun; 202) Fascinating multimedia exhibits focus on science, technology and the social history of the 'Atomic Age,' which lasted from WWII until a worldwide ban on nuclear testing was declared in 1992. Experience a (legitimately scary) simulation of witnessing an atomic test, and examine southern Nevada's nuclear past, present and future, from Native American ways of life to the environmental legacy of atomic testing. Don't miss the ticket booth: it's a Nevada Test Site guard-station replica.

Activities

★**Qua Baths & Spa** SPA
(Map p822; 866-782-0655; www.caesars.com/caesars-palace; Caesars Palace; fitness center day pass $25, incl spa facilities $50; 6am-8pm) Qua evokes the ancient Roman rituals of indulgent bathing. Try a signature 'bath liqueur,' a personalized potion of herbs and oils poured into your own private tub. The women's side includes a tea lounge, a herbal steam room and an Arctic ice room where artificial snow

falls. On the men's side, there's a barber spa and big-screen sports TVs.

★**Desert Adventures** KAYAKING
(702-293-5026; www.kayaklasvegas.com; 1647 Nevada Hwy; full-day Colorado River kayak $195; 9am-6pm Apr-Oct, 10am-4pm Nov-Mar) Would-be river rats should check in here for guided kayaking and SUP tours on Lake Mead and the Colorado River. Experienced paddlers can rent canoes and kayaks for DIY trips. Also offers fishing, hiking and boating guided tours – including smooth water floats on the Colorado River through Black Canyon ($199).

Gondola Ride BOATING
(Map p822; 877-691-1997; www.venetian.com/resort/attractions/gondola-rides.html; Venetian; shared ride per person $29, child under 3yr free, private 2-passenger ride $116; indoor rides 10am-11pm Sun-Thu, to midnight Fri & Sat, outdoor rides 11am-10pm, weather permitting;) As in Venice itself, a gondola ride in Vegas is a touristy activity that nonetheless holds allure for visitors from all over the world. Choose between a moonlit outdoor cruise in the resort's miniature lake facing the Strip or float through winding indoor canals past shoppers and diners. Buy tickets inside the **Grand Canal Shoppes at the Venetian** (Map p822; 702-414-4525; www.grandcanalshoppes.com; 3377 S Las Vegas Blvd, Venetian; 10am-11pm Sun-Thu, to midnight Fri & Sat).

SOUTHWEST LAS VEGAS

THRILLS & SPILLS IN LAS VEGAS

Stratosphere (Map p822; 702-380-7777; www.stratospherehotel.com/ThrillRides; Stratosphere; elevator adult $20, incl 3 thrill rides $35, all-day pass $40; 10am-1am Sun-Thu, to 2am Fri & Sat; Sahara) The world's highest thrill rides await, a whopping 110 stories above the Strip.

Sky Combat Ace (888-494-5850; www.skycombatace.com; 1420 Jet Stream Dr #100; from $299) A bona-fide fighter pilot takes you through the paces of air-to-air dogfights and extreme acrobatics!

VooDoo ZipLine (Map p822; 702-388-0477; www.voodoozipline.com; Rio; from $25; 11am-midnight) At last, your chance to zipline between two skyscrapers.

Gravady (702-843-0395; www.gravady.com; 7350 Prairie Falcon Rd #120; 1hr flight adult/child $15/12; 9am-9pm Mon-Wed, from 3:30pm Thu, 9am-11pm Fri & Sat, 11am-7pm Sun;) Get bouncy with the kids at this high-energy trampoline park in Summerlin.

Speedvegas (702-874-8888; www.speedvegas.com; 14200 S Las Vegas Blvd; laps $39-99, experiences $395-1800; 10am-4:30pm) Burn serious rubber at the wheel of a sports car on Vegas' only custom-built track.

Richard Petty Driving Experience (800-237-3889; www.drivepetty.com; 7000 N Las Vegas Blvd, Las Vegas Motor Speedway; ride-alongs from $136, drives from $199; hours vary) This is your chance to ride shotgun during a Nascar-style qualifying run.

🛏 Sleeping

Room rates in Las Vegas rise and fall every day; visiting on weekdays is almost always cheaper than weekends. Note that almost every Strip hotel also charges an additional 'resort fee' of $30 to $45 per day.

🛏 The Strip

★ Cosmopolitan
CASINO HOTEL $

(Map p822; ☎702-698-7000; www.cosmopol itanlasvegas.com; 3708 S Las Vegas Blvd; r from $140; ◻❀@🕏🕏; 🚌Deuce) With at least eight distinctively different and equally stylish room types to choose from, Cosmo's digs are the hippest on the Strip. Ranging from oversized to decadent, about 2200 of its 2900 or so rooms have balconies (all but the entry-level category), many sport sunken Japanese tubs and all feature plush furnishings and design quirks you'll delight in uncovering.

★ Mandalay Bay
CASINO HOTEL $$

(Map p822; ☎702-632-7700; www.mandalaybay. com; 3950 S Las Vegas Blvd; r weekday/weekend from $79/388; ◻❀@🕏🕏) Anchoring the south Strip, upscale Mandalay Bay's (p824) same-named hotel has a cache of classy rooms worthy of your attention in their own right, not to mention the exclusive **Four Seasons Hotel** (Map p822; ☎702-632-5000; www.fourseasons.com/lasvegas; r weekday/weekend from $305/440; ◻❀@🕏🕏) and boutique **Delano** (Map p822; ☎702-632-7888; www.delanolasvegas.com; r weekday/weekend from $143/369; ◻❀@🕏🕏🕏) within its bounds. Plus there's a diverse range of noteworthy attractions and amenities, not least of which is Mandalay Bay Beach (p824).

★ Bellagio
CASINO HOTEL $$

(Map p822; ☎702-693-7111; www.bellagio.com; 3600 S Las Vegas Blvd; r weekday/weekend from $169/399; ◻❀@🕏🕏🕏) When it opened in 1998, Bellagio was the world's most expensive hotel. Aging gracefully, it remains one of America's finest. Its sumptuous oversized guest rooms fuse classic style with modern amenities and feature palettes of platinum, indigo and muted white-gold, or rusty autumnal oranges with subtle splashes of matcha green. Cashmere throws, mood lighting and automatic drapes complete the picture.

Aria Las Vegas Resort
CASINO HOTEL $$

(Map p822; ☎702-590-7111; www.aria.com; 3730 S Las Vegas Blvd, CityCenter; r weekday/weekend from $119/169; ◻❀@🕏🕏) Aria's (p821)

sleek resort hotel has no theme, unlike some of the Strip's other megaproperties. Instead, its 4000-plus deluxe rooms (520 sq ft) and 560 tower suites (920-plus sq ft) are all about soothing design, spaciousness and luxury, and every room has a corner view. If you've cash to burn, **Aria Sky Suites & Villas** (Map p822; ☎702-590-7111; www.aria.com; 3730 S Las Vegas Blvd, Aria; ste $400), a hotel-within-a-hotel, might be for you.

LINQ Hotel
CASINO HOTEL $$

(Map p822; ☎800-634-6441; www.caesars. com/linq; 3535 S Las Vegas Blvd; r from $99; ◻❀🕏🕏🕏) Launching onto the Las Vegas Strip in late 2014, LINQ, formerly the Quad, has cemented its position as a solid all-rounder. Its fresh, white rooms have fun splashes of color and sleek furniture, there's a wealth of available amenities (this being part of the Caesars group) and it has an enviable location at the center of its eponymous promenade (p821).

SLS
HOTEL $$

(Map p822; ☎702-761-7000; www.slslasvegas. com; 2535 S Las Vegas Blvd; d from $102; ◻❀🕏🕏) The SLS replaced the Sahara in 2011, and now the Sahara is replacing the SLS (the $100 million renovation is due to finish in 2020). In the meantime, you can nab a room here on the north Strip at very good rates compared to same-branded properties in other cities. The hotel's quirky style is infectious.

★ Cromwell Las Vegas
BOUTIQUE HOTEL $$$

(Map p822; ☎702-777-3777; www.caesars.com/ cromwell; 3595 S Las Vegas Blvd; r from $288; ◻❀🕏🕏🕏) If you're 20- to 30-something, can hold your own with the cool kids, or you're just effortlessly stylish whatever your demographic, there are a few good reasons to choose Cromwell, the best being its location and frequently excellent rates on sassy, entry-level rooms. The others? You've got your sights set on partying at **Drai's** (Map p822; ☎702-777-3800; www.draisgroup.com/las-vegas/; nightclub cover $20-50; ⏰nightclub 10:30pm-4am Thu-Sun, beach club 11am-6pm Fri-Sun) or dining downstairs at **Giada** (Map p822; ☎855-442-3271; www.caesars.com/cromwell; mains $24-60; ⏰5pm-10:30pm, brunch 9am-3pm Fri-Sun).

NoMad
CASINO HOTEL $$$

(Map p822; www.thenomadhotel.com/las-vegas; 3772 S Las Vegas Blvd, Park MGM; r from $249; ◻❀🕏🕏) The NoMad has taken things to truly a ridiculous level: it's a hotel within a hotel within a hotel. It's a good thing the rooms are exquisite, most with freestanding bath tubs and custom-made furniture. There's a fun party vibe in the restaurant and bar, which spills out onto the classier-than-most casino floor.

Downtown & off the Strip

★ Thunderbird Hotel   BOUTIQUE HOTEL $
(Map p822; ☑ 702-489-7500; www.thunderbird hotellasvegas.com; 1215 S Las Vegas Blvd; d from $39; P ✳ 🛜 ☃) Nestled between the north Strip and Fremont St, this retro renovated job is an instant winner with its great rates, funky fresh rooms with chunky, reclaimed-wood furniture, and fun, youthful vibe. It's not a hostel or a boutique hotel, but lies somewhere in between.

The neighborhood is dicey, especially after dark. Plan to drive or rideshare.

Golden Nugget   CASINO HOTEL $
(☑ 702-385-7111; www.goldennugget.com; 129 Fremont St E; d from $49; P ✳ @ 🛜 ☃) Pretend to relive the fabulous heyday of Vegas in the 1950s at this swank Fremont St address. Rooms in the Rush Tower are the best in the house.

✗ Eating

The Strip has been studded with celebrity chefs for years. All-you-can-eat buffets and $10 steaks still exist, but today's high-rolling visitors demand ever more sophisticated dining experiences, with meals designed – although not personally prepared – by famous taste-makers.

✗ The Strip

★ Umami Burger   BURGERS $
(Map p822; ☑ 702-761-7614; www.umamiburger. com; 2535 S Las Vegas Blvd, SLS; burgers $12-15; ☺ 11am-10pm; P) This SLS (p826) burger offering is one of the best on the Strip, with its outdoor beer garden, extensive craft-beer selection and juicy boutique burgers made by the chain that won *GQ* magazine's 'burger of the year' crown. This is a great place to try the new, vegan 'Impossible' burger everyone keeps banging on about.

★ Tacos El Gordo   MEXICAN $
(Map p822; ☑ 702-982-5420; www.tacoselgordo bc.com; 3049 S Las Vegas Blvd; small plates $3-12; ☺ 10am-2am, to 4am Fri & Sat; P 🅿 🚶; 🚌 Deuce, SDX) This Tijuana-style taco shop from SoCal is just the ticket when it's way late, you've got almost no money left and you're desperately craving *carne asada* (beef) or *adobada* (chili-marinated pork) tacos in hot, handmade tortillas. Adventurous eaters will be lured by the authentic *sesos* (beef brains), *cabeza* (roasted cow's head) or tripe (intestines) variations.

★ Milk Bar   DESSERTS $
(Map p822; ☑ 7020-698-7000; www.cosmopol itanlasvegas.com; Cosmopolitan; soft serve from $6; ☺ 9am-1am, to 2am Fri & Sat) Momofuku dessert program wünderkind Christina Tosi has brought her Milk Bar concept to Las Vegas, inspiring rapture and adoration. Try her cereal-milk soft serve, corn cookies or (and?) cake truffles and feel smug.

Jaburrito   SUSHI $
(Map p822; ☑ 702-901-7375; www.jaburritos.com; LINQ Promenade; items $10-13; ☺ 11am-11pm Sun-Thu, to midnight Fri & Sat) It's simple: hybridize a nori (seaweed) sushi roll with a burrito. What could go wrong? Nothing actually... they're awesome! Mochi ice-cream pops for dessert are extremely fun to eat.

Peppermill   DINER $$
(Map p822; ☑ 702-735-4177; www.peppermill lasvegas.com; 2985 S Las Vegas Blvd; mains $13-31; ☺ 24hr) Slide into a crescent-shaped booth at this retro casino coffee shop and revel in the old-school Vegas atmosphere. You can eavesdrop on Nevada cowboys and downtown politicos digging into a gigantic late-night bite or early breakfast. For tropical tiki drinks, step into a sexy booth at Peppermill's **Fireside Lounge** (Map p822; ☑ 702-735-7635).

★ Joël Robuchon   FRENCH $$$
(Map p822; ☑ 702-891-7925; www.mgmgrand.com; MGM Grand; tasting menus $120-425; ☺ 5:30-10pm) The acclaimed 'Chef of the Century' leads the pack in the French culinary invasion of the Strip. Adjacent to the **MGM Grand's** (Map p822; ☑ 877-880-0880; www. mgmgrand.com; 3799 S Las Vegas Blvd; ☺ 24hr; P 🚶) high-rollers' gaming area, Robuchon's plush dining rooms, done up in leather and velvet, feel like a dinner party at a 1930s Paris mansion. Complex seasonal tasting menus promise the meal of a lifetime – and they often deliver.

★ Morimoto   FUSION $$$
(Map p822; ☑ 702-891-3001; www.mgmgrand.com; MGM Grand; mains $24-75; ☺ 5-10pm, to 10:30pm Fri & Sat) Iron Chef Masaharu Morimoto's latest Vegas incarnation is in his eponymous

BUFFET ALL THE WAY

Extravagant all-you-can-eat buffets are a Sin City tradition. Here are three of the best:

Bacchanal Buffet (3570 Las Vegas Blvd S, Caesars Palace; $40-65 per adult, 7:30am-10pm Mon-Fri, from 8am Sat & Sun)

Wicked Spoon Buffet (3708 Las Vegas Blvd S, Cosmopolitan; $28-49 per adult, 8am-9pm Sun-Thu, to 10pm Fri & Sat)

Buffet at Wynn (3131 Las Vegas Blvd S; Wynn; $32-60 per person, 7:30am-9:30pm)

showcase restaurant, which pays homage to his Japanese roots and the cuisine of this city that has propelled him to legend status around the world. Dining here is an experience in every possible way and, we think, worth every penny.

★**Catch**   SEAFOOD $$$
(Map p822; ☑702-590-5757; https://aria.mgm resorts.com; Aria; mains from $40; ⏲5:30-11:30pm; P ❄) Fresh from a $7 million renovation, this space had better be beautiful – and it does not disappoint. The seafood-centric menu is massive, focusing on Asian preparations including truffled sashimi and whole fish and crustaceans (the whole lobster, steamed in sake, is the thing to order if you're looking to impress your dining companion or someone across the room).

🍴 Downtown & off the Strip

★**VegeNation**   VEGAN $
(Map p822; ☑702-366-8515; https://vegenationlv.com; 616 E Carson Ave; mains $13; ⏲8am-9pm Sun-Thu, to 10pm Fri & Sat; ☎🚲) 🍴 Faced with a health crisis, veteran chef Donald Lemperle adopted a plant-based diet, and used his learnings to open Downtown's most exciting new cafe. His kitchen sends out insanely delicious plant-based tacos, sandwiches, pizzas and desserts made from local products and community gardens to an adoring local fan base. You can even get CBD kombucha. Welcome to the new Vegas.

★**Esther's Kitchen**   ITALIAN $$
(Map p822; ☑702-570-7864; www.estherslv.com; 1130 S Casino Center Blvd; pasta from $15; ⏲11am-3pm & 5-10pm Mon-Fri, from 10am Sat & Sun; ❄☎) Locals are justifiably mad for the housemade

seasonal pasta and heritage sourdough at this little Arts District bistro. Everything is extremely delicious, but we're partial to the anchovy-garlic butter you can order with the sourdough, and a kale-cauliflower salad that has no right to be as delectable as it is.

★**Carson Kitchen**   AMERICAN $$
(Map p822; ☑702-473-9523; www.carsonkitchen.com; 124 S 6th St; tapas & mains $8-22; ⏲11:30am-11pm Thu-Sat, to 10pm Sun-Wed; 🚌Deuce) This tiny eatery with an industrial theme of exposed beams, bare bulbs and chunky share tables hops with downtowners looking to escape the mayhem of Fremont St or the Strip's high prices. Excellent shared plates include rainbow cauliflower, watermelon and feta salad, and decadent mac 'n' cheese. There's also a creative drinks menu.

★**Lotus of Siam**   THAI $$
(Map p822; ☑702-735-3033; www.lotusofsiamlv.com; 953 E Sahara Ave; mains $9-30; ⏲11am-2:30pm Mon-Fri, 5:30-10pm daily; 🅿; 🚌SDX) Saipin Chutima's authentic northern Thai cooking has won almost as many awards as her distinguished, geographically diverse wine cellar. Critics have suggested this might be America's best Thai restaurant and we're sure it's at least very close. Although the strip-mall hole-in-the-wall may not look like much, those in the know flock here. Reservations essential.

Hugo's Cellar   AMERICAN $$$
(Map p822; ☑702-385-4011; www.hugoscellar.com; Fremont St Mall, Fremont Street Experience, Four Queens Casino; mains $34-62; ⏲5-10pm) This is old-school Vegas, in the best way. In a dark and clubby space beneath Four Queens casino, Hugo's Cellar is a return to the days when service was king. Ladies are given a rose, salads are tossed table-side and service is attentive but not intrusive. Party like it's 1959 with veal Oscar, beef Wellington and cherries jubilee. Reservations essential.

🍷 Drinking & Nightlife

🍷 The Strip

★**Hakkasan**   CLUB
(Map p822; ☑702-891-3838; http://hakkasan nightclub.com; MGM Grand; cover $20-75; ⏲10:30pm-4am Thu-Sun) At this lavish Asian-inspired nightclub, international jet-set DJs such as Tiësto and Steve Aoki rule the jam-packed main dance floor bordered by VIP booths and floor-to-ceiling LED

screens. More offbeat sounds spin in the intimate Ling Ling Club, revealing leather sofas and backlit amber glass.

Bouncers enforce the dress code: upscale nightlife attire (no athletic wear, collared shirts required for men).

NoMad Bar
COCKTAIL BAR

(Map p822; ☑702-730-6785; www.mgmresorts.com; NoMad Hotel; cocktails $17; ☺5-11pm Mon-Thu, to 1am Fri & Sat, 11am-5pm Sun) You have to walk across the restaurant to check in with the hostess at this bar – all the better for checking out the gorgeous decor (and people) at this sumptuous new addition to Vegas' craft cocktail scene. This place isn't just beautiful though – the drinks are truly out of this world, and well worth the hefty price tag.

Skyfall Lounge
BAR

(Map p822; ☑702-632-7575; www.delanolasvegas.com; Delano; ☺5pm-midnight Sun-Thu, to 1am Fri & Sat) Enjoy unparalleled views of the southern Strip from this rooftop bar atop Mandalay Bay's Delano (p826) hotel. Sit and sip cocktails as the sun sets over the Spring Mountains to the west, then dance the night away to mellow DJ beats, spun from 9pm.

XS
CLUB

(Map p822; ☑702-770-0097; www.xslasvegas.com; Encore; cover $20-30; ☺10:30pm-4am Fri-Sun) A few years in, XS is hitting its stride. Its extravagantly gold-drenched decor and over-the-top design mean you'll be waiting in line for cocktails at a bar towered over by ultra-curvaceous, larger-than-life golden statues of female torsos. Famous electronica DJs make the dance floor writhe, while high rollers opt for VIP bottle service at private poolside cabanas.

Downtown & off the Strip

Locals and in-the-know tourists make a bee-line for the **Fremont East Entertainment District** (www.fremonteast.com) for the city's best grassroots nightlife. The precinct runs east of Las Vegas Blvd along Fremont St for about four blocks.

★ReBAR
BAR

(Map p822; ☑702-349-2283; www.rebarlv.com; 1225 S Main St; ☺1pm-midnight Sun-Wed, to 1am Thu, to 2am Fri & Sat) Las Vegas definitely revels in kitsch, and it absolutely loves drinking spots. ReBAR unites both. Located in the Arts District, it's a temple of nutty craft items, vintage bar signs, outrageous beer steins and one-of-a-kind doohickeys. Peruse the walls for that perfect retro souvenir, then sit down for a respectable selection of beers and spirits. Bask in the vintage glow.

★ Entertainment

There's always plenty going on in Las Vegas, and Ticketmaster (www.ticketmaster.com) sells tickets for pretty much everything. **Tix 4 Tonight** (Map p822; ☑877-849-4868; www.tix4tonight.com; 3200 S Las Vegas Blvd, Fashion Show Mall; ☺10am-8pm) offers half-price tickets for a limited lineup of same-day shows, plus smaller discounts on 'always sold-out' shows.

☆ Nightclubs & Live Music

Nightclubs are serious businesses in Las Vegas. Admission prices vary wildly, according to the mood of door staff, male-to-female ratio, the acts that night and how crowded the club may be. Avoid waiting in line by booking ahead with the club VIP host. Most bigger clubs have someone working the door in the late afternoon and early evening. Hotel concierges often have free passes for clubs, or can at least make reservations. Bottle service usually waives cover charges and waiting in line, but is hugely expensive.

★House of Blues
Gospel Brunch
LIVE PERFORMANCE

(Map p822; ☑702-632-7600; www.houseofblues.com/lasvegas; Mandalay Bay; adult/child under 11yr $54/27; ☺seatings 10am & 1pm Sun; ♣) Saturday night sinners can find redemption at HOB's Sunday gospel brunch, where your ticket includes unlimited Bloody Marys and Southern and soul-food favorites such as jambalaya, chicken and waffles, jalapeño cornbread and warm banana-bread pudding. Buy tickets in advance, as they often sell out.

Legends in Concert
LIVE MUSIC

(Map p822; ☑702-777-2782; www.legendsinconcert.com; Tropicana; tickets from $50; ☺shows 4pm, 7:30pm & 9:30pm) Vegas' top pop-star impersonator show features real singing and dancing talent mimicking famous performers such as the Beatles, Elvis, Madonna, James Brown, Britney Spears, Shania Twain and many more.

☆ Production Shows

There are hundreds of shows to choose from in Vegas. Any Cirque du Soleil offering tends to be an unforgettable experience.

★ Le Rêve the Dream THEATER

(Map p822; ☑702-770-9966; http://boxoffice.
wynnlasvegas.com; Wynn; tickets $115-175;
⊙shows 7pm & 9:30pm Fri-Tue) Underwater
acrobatic feats by scuba-certified performers are the centerpiece of this intimate
'aqua-in-the-round' theater, which holds a
million-gallon swimming pool. Critics call it
a less-inspiring version of Cirque's O, while
devoted fans find the romantic underwater
tango, thrilling high dives and visually spectacular adventures to be superior. Beware:
the cheapest seats are in the 'splash zone.'

O THEATER

(Map p822; ☑702-693-8866; www.cirquedusoleil.
com/o; Bellagio; tickets $99-212; ⊙7pm & 9:30pm
Wed-Sun) Phonetically speaking, it's the French
word for water (eau). With a lithe international cast performing in, on and above water,
Cirque du Soleil's O tells the tale of theater
through the ages. It's a spectacular feat of
imagination and engineering, and you'll pay
dearly to see it – it's one of the Strip's few
shows that rarely sells discounted tickets.

★ Aces of Comedy COMEDY

(Map p822; ☑702-792-7777; www.mirage.com; 3400
S Las Vegas Blvd, Mirage; tickets $40-100; ⊙sched-
ules vary, box office 10am-10pm Thu-Mon, to 8pm Tue
& Wed) You'd be hard pressed to find a better
A-list collection of famous stand-up comedians than this year-round series of appearances
at the Mirage (Map p822; ☑702-791-7111; www.
mirage.com; ⊙24hr; ℗), which delivers the likes
of Jay Leno, Joe Rogan and George Lopez to
the Strip. Buy tickets in advance online or by

VALLEY OF FIRE STATE PARK

Valley of Fire State Park (Map p854;
☑702-397-2088; www.parks.nv.gov/parks/
valley-of-fire; Valley of Fire Hwy, Overton;
per vehicle $10; ⊙7am-7pm) It's about 50
miles from Downtown Las Vegas to the
Valley of Fire State Park visitor center
(⊙8:30am-4:30pm). Make the center
your first port of call to find out how best
to tackle this masterpiece of Southwest
desert scenery containing 40,000
acres of red Aztec sandstone, petrified
trees and ancient Native American
petroglyphs (at Atlatl Rock). Dedicated
in 1935, the park was Nevada's first
designated state park. Its psychedelic
landscape has been carved by wind and
water over thousands of years.

---

phone, or go in person to the Mirage's Cirque
du Soleil (☑877-924-7783; www.cirquedusoleil.
com/las-vegas; discount tickets from $49, full price
from $69) box office.

🛍 Shopping

★ Las Vegas Premium Outlets North MALL

(Map p822; ☑702-474-7500; www.premiumout
lets.com/vegasnorth; 875 S Grand Central Pkwy;
⊙9am-9pm Mon-Sat, to 8pm Sun; 🚹; 🚌SDX)
Vegas' biggest-ticket outlet mall features
120 brands including high-end names such
as Armani, Brooks Brothers, Diane von
Furstenberg, Kate Spade, Michael Kors and
Theory, alongside casual favorites such as
Banana Republic, Diesel, Nike and Adidas.

Planet 13 DISPENSARY

(Map p822; ☑702-815-1313; www.planet13las
vegas.com; 2548 W Desert Inn Rd; ⊙24hr; 🎧) File
this under only-in-Vegas: this self-described
'cannabis superstore and entertainment
complex' is an emporium the size of several
city blocks devoted to all things weed. Your
personal concierge walks you through the
myriad products, from flower, seeds, edibles,
CBD products and accessories. Even if you're
not partial to a toke, this totally unprecedented shopping experience is worth a visit.

Retro Vegas VINTAGE

(Map p822; ☑702-384-2700; www.retro-vegas.
com; 1131 S Main St; ⊙11am-6pm Mon-Sat, noon-
5pm Sun; 🚌108, Deuce) Near Downtown's
Arts District, this flamingo-pink-painted
antiques shop is a primo place for picking
up mid-20th-century modern and swingin'
1960s and '70s gems, from artwork to home
decor, as well as vintage Vegas souvenirs
such as casino-hotel ashtrays. Red Kat's secondhand clothing, handbags and accessories are also found here.

ℹ Information

EMERGENCY & MEDICAL SERVICES

Police ☑911 (emergencies) or ☑702-828-3111
Sunrise Hospital & Medical Center (☑702-731-
8000; www.sunrisehospital.com; 3186 S Maryland Pkwy; ⊙24hr) Specialized children's trauma
services available at a 24-hour emergency room.
University Medical Center (UMC; ☑702-383-
2000; www.umcsn.com; 1800 W Charleston
Blvd; ⊙24hr) Southern Nevada's most advanced trauma center has a 24-hour ER.

TOURIST INFORMATION

Las Vegas Convention & Visitors Authority
(LVCVA; Map p822; ☑702-892-7575; www.

lasvegas.com; 3150 Paradise Rd; ⊙8am-5pm Mon-Fri; 🖳 Las Vegas Convention Center)

❶ Getting There & Around

Vegas is served by **McCarran International Airport** (LAS; Map p822; ☑702-261-5211; www. mccarran.com; 5757 Wayne Newton Blvd; 🖘), near the south end of the Strip. A free, wheel-chair-accessible tram links outlying gates, while free shuttle buses link Terminals 1 and 3 and serve the **McCarran Rent-a-Car Center** (☑702-261-6001; www.mccarran.com/Transportation/RentalCars; 7135 Gillespie St; ⊙24hr).

Shuttle buses run to Strip hotels from $6 one way, and from $8 to Downtown and off-Strip hotels. You'll pay at least $15 plus tip for a taxi to the Strip – tell your driver to use surface streets, not the I-15 Fwy airport connector tunnel ('long-hauling'). Rideshare service runs from $13.

Greyhound runs long-distance buses connecting Las Vegas with Reno ($81, 9½ hours) and Salt Lake City (from $40, eight hours), as well as regular discounted services to/from Los Angeles (from $20, five to eight hours). You'll disembark at a downtown station just off the Fremont Street Experience. To reach the Strip, catch a south-bound **SDX** bus (two-hour pass $6). **Megabus** (www.megabus.com) runs daily direct routes from the **South Strip Transfer Terminal** (SSTT; ☑702-228-7433; www.rtcsnv.com; 6675 Gillespie St; ⊙24hr) to three destinations in southern California: Los Angeles (from $19, six hours), Anaheim (from $15, 6½ hours) and Riverside (from $10, 4¼ hours). Book in advance for best rates.

Day passes on the 24-hour Deuce and faster (though not 24-hour and not servicing all casinos) SDX buses are an excellent way to get around.

Around Las Vegas

Lake Mead and **Hoover Dam** are the most visited sites within the **Lake Mead National Recreation Area** (☑ info desk 702-293-8906, visitor center 702-293-8990; www.nps.gov/lake; Lakeshore Scenic Dr; 7-day entry per vehicle $10; ⊙24hr; 🖰), which encompasses 110-mile-long Lake Mead, 67-mile-long Lake Mohave and many miles of desert around the lakes. The excellent **Visitor Center** (Alan Bible Visitor Center; ☑702-293-8990; www.nps.gov/lake; Lakeshore Scenic Dr, off US Hwy 93; per vehicle $25; ⊙9am-4:30pm), on Hwy 93 halfway between Boulder City and Hoover Dam, has information on recreation and desert life. From there, North Shore Rd winds around the lake and makes a great scenic drive.

Straddling the Arizona–Nevada border, the graceful curve and art-deco style of the 726ft **Hoover Dam** (☑866-730-9097, 702-494-2517; www.usbr.gov/lc/hooverdam; off Hwy 93; incl parking $10; ⊙9am-5pm; 🖰) contrasts superbly with the stark landscape. Don't miss a stroll over the **Mike O'Callaghan-Pat Tillman Memorial Bridge** (Hwy 93), which features a pedestrian walkway with perfect views upstream of Hoover Dam.

For a relaxing lunch or dinner break, head to nearby downtown Boulder City, where **Milo's** (☑702-293-9540; www.milosbouldercity.com; 534 Nevada Hwy; mains $9-14; ⊙11am-9pm) serves fresh sandwiches, salads and gourmet cheese plates at sidewalk tables outside the wine bar.

Red Rock Canyon National Conservation Area   NATURE RESERVE
(☑702-515-5350; www.redrockcanyonlv.org; 1000 Scenic Loop Dr; car/bicycle $15/5; ⊙scenic loop 6am-8pm Apr-Sep, to 7pm Mar & Oct, to 5pm Nov-Feb; 🖰) Red Rock's dramatic vistas are revered by Las Vegas locals and adored by visitors from around the world. Formed by extreme tectonic forces, it's thought the canyon, whose 3000ft red rock escarpment rises sharply from the valley floor, was formed around 65 million years ago. A 13-mile, one-way scenic loop drive offers mesmerizing vistas of the canyon's most striking features. Hiking trails and rock-climbing routes radiate from roadside parking areas.

The canyon is situated about 13 miles from the central Strip and just three miles from Summerlin.

Western Nevada

The state's western corner, carved by the conifer-clad Sierra Nevada, drops off near Genoa. It's a vast treeless steppe of sagebrush, unfurling itself like a plush green-gray carpet across the undulating plains of the Great Basin. From Lake Tahoe's sandy shores to the historic hamlet of Virginia City, to little Reno, Burning Man, Black Rock and beyond, Western Nevada has plenty to entice you.

Reno

In downtown Reno you can gamble at one of two-dozen casinos in the morning then walk down the street and shoot rapids at the Truckee River Whitewater Park. That's what makes 'The Biggest Little City in the World' so interesting – it's holding tight to its gambling roots but also earning kudos as a top-notch basecamp for outdoor adventure. Stealing a piece of California's tech-pie, the gargantuan

Tesla Gigafactory opened here in 2016, bringing plenty of cashed-up youngsters to town. The Sierra Nevada Mountains and Lake Tahoe are less than an hour's drive away, and the region teems with lakes, trails and ski resorts. Wedged between I-80 and the Truckee River, downtown's N Virginia St is casino central; south of the river it continues as S Virginia St.

◉ Sights

★ National Automobile Museum   MUSEUM
(☏775-333-9300; www.automuseum.org; 10 S Lake St; adult/child $12/6; ◷9:30am-5:30pm Mon-Sat, 10am-4pm Sun) Stylized street scenes illustrate a century's worth of automobile history at this engaging car museum. The collection is enormous and impressive, with one-of-a-kind vehicles – including James Dean's 1949 Mercury from *Rebel Without a Cause,* a 1938 Phantom Corsair and a 24-karat gold-plated DeLorean – and rotating exhibits with all kinds of souped-up and fabulously retro rides.

Discovery   MUSEUM
(Terry Lee Wells Nevada Discovery Museum; ☏775-786-1000; www.nvdm.org; 490 S Center St; $10; ◷10am-5pm Tue, Thu-Sat, to 8pm Wed, from noon Sun; P⛟) Since opening its doors in 2011 as a children's museum, the Discovery rapidly grew in popularity and expanded its focus to become a world-class, hands-on center for 'science, technology, engineering, art and math' (STEAM) learning, with 11 permanent, participatory exhibitions designed to inspire kids and young adults to have fun and develop an interest in these disciplines.

Nevada Museum of Art   MUSEUM
(☏775-329-3333; www.nevadaart.org; 160 W Liberty St; adult/child $10/1; ◷10am-5pm Wed & Fr-Sun, to 8pm Thu) In a sparkling building inspired by the geological formations of the Black Rock Desert north of town, a floating staircase leads to galleries showcasing temporary exhibits and eclectic collections on

---

ⓘ RENO AREA TRAIL INFORMATION

For information about regional hiking and mountain-biking trails, including the Mt Rose summit trail and Tahoe-Pyramid Bikeway, download the *Truckee Meadows Trails Guide* (https://www.washoecounty.us/parks/files/TrailsGuideFinal.pdf).

---

the American West, labor and contemporary landscape photography. In 2016 the museum opened its $6.2-million Sky Room function area. Visitors are free to explore and enjoy the space – essentially a fabulous rooftop penthouse and patio with killer views – providing it's not in use.

Galena Creek Recreation Area   NATURE RESERVE
(☏775-849-4948; www.galenacreekvisitorcenter.org/trail-map.html; 18250 Mt Rose Hwy; ◷24hr) [FREE] Nineteen miles from downtown Reno, a complex network of scenic hiking trails beginning at this recreation area within the Humboldt-Toiyabe National Forest gets you right into the heart of the wilderness. Check in with the **Galena Creek Visitor Center** (◷9am-6pm Tue-Sun) when you arrive for the latest conditions and friendly advice.

🏃 Activities

Reno is a 30- to 60-minute drive from Tahoe ski resorts. Many hotels and casinos offer special stay-and-ski packages.

Mere steps from the casinos, the class II and III rapids at the city-run Truckee River Whitewater Park (www.reno.gov) are gentle enough for kids riding inner tubes, yet sufficiently challenging for professional freestyle kayakers. Two courses wrap around Wingfield Park, a small river island that hosts free concerts in summertime. **Tahoe Whitewater Tours** (☏775-787-5000; www.gowhitewater.com; 400 Island Ave; kayak rental from $48) and **Sierra Adventures** (☏775-323-8928, 866-323-8928; www.wildsierra.com; Truckee River Lane; kayak rental from $22) offer kayak trips and lessons.

🛏 Sleeping

Lodging rates vary widely, day by day. Sunday through Thursday are generally the best; Friday is more expensive and Saturday can be as much as triple the midweek rate.

In summer there's gorgeous high-altitude camping at **Mt Rose** (☏877-444-6777; www.recreation.gov; Mt Rose Hwy/Hwy 431; RV & tent sites $20-50; ◷mid-Jun–Sep; P🐕).

Sands Regency   HOTEL $
(☏775-348-2200; www.sandsregency.com; 345 N Arlington Ave; r from $35; P❄🐕🛜🐕🐕) The Sands Regency has some of the largest standard digs in town, decked out in a cheerful tropical palette of upbeat color. Empress Tower rooms are best. Rates triple on Friday and Saturday nights, but are great

value during the week (especially given the 17th-floor gym and outdoor pool).

★ Whitney Peak
DESIGN HOTEL $$

(☑775-398-5400; www.whitneypeakhotel.com; 255 N Virginia St; d from $129; P❄☎) 🖋 What's not to love about this independent, inventive, funky, friendly, nonsmoking, non-gambling downtown hotel? Spacious guest rooms have a youthful, fun vibe celebrating the great outdoors and don't skimp on designer creature comforts. With an executive-level concierge lounge, an external climbing wall (if you're game), a decent on-site restaurant and friendly, professional staff, Whitney Peak is unbeatable in Reno.

Renaissance Reno Downtown
HOTEL $$

(☑775-682-3900; www.marriott.com/hotels/travel/rnobr-renaissance-reno-downtown-hotel; 1 Lake St; r from $135; P☎🏊) It's part of a hotel group, but you could be forgiven for thinking it's a boutique hotel (in fact, it used to be). Renovated, oversized guest rooms follow a contemporary theme that's reminiscent of a stylish friend's cozy living room. With the best rooftop pool in town, this is a smart alternative to casino hotels.

✗ Eating

★ Great Full Gardens
HEALTH FOOD $

(☑775-324-2013; 555 S Virginia St; bowls from $10; ⊙8am-9pm, to 2pm Sun; P♿) Extensive menu chock-full of salads, smoothies and sandwiches that will make you feel healthy enough to justify another cocktail later on. Delicious grain bowls are categorized by lifestyle choice (vegan, paleo, macrobiotic). Chili fiends should not miss the housemade hot sauce.

Gold 'n Silver Inn
DINER $

(☑775-323-2696; www.goldnsilverreno.com; 790 W 4th St; mains $6-20; ⊙24hr) A Reno institution for more than 50 years, this slightly divey but super-friendly 24-hour diner has a huge menu of home-style American favorites such as meatloaf, plated dinners, all-day breakfasts and burgers, not to mention seriously incredible caramel milkshakes.

Louis' Basque Corner
BASQUE $$

(☑775-323-7203; www.louisbasquecorner.com; 301 E 4th St; dinner menu $12-29; ⊙11am-9:30pm Tue-Sat, from 4pm Sun & Mon) Get ready to dine on lamb, rabbit, sweetbreads and more lamb at a big table full of people you've never met before. After a picon punch you'll be getting along like *vieux amis*.

Wild River Grille
GRILL $$

(☑775-847-455; www.wildrivergrille.com; 17 S Virginia St; mains $21-37; ⊙11am-9pm; ♿) At the Wild River Grille you'll love the smart-casual dining and the varied menu of creative cuisine, from the Gruyère croquettes to the lobster ravioli, but most of all the wonderful patio overlooking the lovely Truckee River: it's also the best spot in town for a drink on a balmy summer's evening.

▼ Drinking & Nightlife

★ Imperial Bar & Lounge
BAR

(☑775-324-6399; www.imperialbarandlounge.com; 150 N Arlington Ave; ⊙11am-10pm, to 2am Fri & Sat) A classy bar inhabiting a relic of the past – this building was once an old bank, and in the middle of the wood floor you can see cement where the vault once stood. Sandwiches and pizzas go with 16 beers on tap and a buzzing happy-hour scene (3pm to 6pm).

☆ Entertainment

The free weekly *Reno News & Review* (www.newsreview.com) is your best source for listings.

❶ Information

Reno-Sparks Convention & Visitors Authority Visitor Center (☑775-682-3800; www.visitrenotahoe.com; 135 N Sierra St; ⊙9am-6pm)

❶ Getting There & Around

About 5 miles southeast of downtown, **Reno-Tahoe International Airport** (RNO; www.renoairport.com; ☎) is served by most major airlines, with connections throughout the US to international routes.

The **North Lake Tahoe Express** (☑866-216-5222; www.northlaketahoeexpress.com; one way $49) operates a shuttle (six to eight daily, 3:30am to midnight) to and from the airport to multiple North Shore Lake Tahoe locations. The **South Tahoe Airporter** (☑866-898-2463; www.southtahoeairporter.com; adult/child one way $33/20) operates several daily shuttle buses from the airport to Stateline casinos.

Greyhound (☑800-231-2222; www.greyhound.com) offers several direct buses a day to Reno from San Francisco (from $18, from five hours): book in advance for lowest fares.

The **Amtrak** (☑800-872-7245; www.amtrak.com) *California Zephyr* train makes one daily departure from Emeryville/San Francisco ($55, 7½) to Reno.

The local **RTC Washoe** (☑775-348-0400; www.rtcwashoe.com) operates six wi-fi-equipped RTC Intercity buses each weekday to Carson City ($5, one hour), which loosely

BURNING MAN

Burning Man (https://burningman. org; $425; ⊙ Aug) For a week in August, 'Burners' from around the world descend on the Black Rock Desert to build the temporary Black Rock City, only to tear it all down again and set fire to an effigy of man. In between, there's peace, love, music, art, nakedness, drugs, sex and frivolity in a safe space where attendees uphold the principles of the festival.

connect with BlueGo buses – operated by **Tahoe Transportation District** (☑ 775-589-5500; www.tahoetransportation.org) – to the Stateline Transit Center in South Lake Tahoe (adult/child $4/2 with RTC Intercity transfer, one hour).

The Great Basin

A trip across Nevada's Great Basin is a serene, almost haunting experience. Anyone seeking the 'Great American Road Trip' will relish the fascinating historic towns and quirky diversions tucked away along lonely desert highways.

Along Highway 50

The transcontinental Hwy 50 cuts across the heart of Nevada, connecting Carson City in the west to Great Basin National Park in the east. Better known here by its nickname, 'The Loneliest Road in America,' it once formed part of the Lincoln Hwy, and follows the route of the Overland Stagecoach, the Pony Express and the first transcontinental telegraph line. Towns are few, and the only sounds are the hum of the engine or the whisper of wind.

About 25 miles southeast of Fallon, the **Sand Mountain Recreation Area** (☑ 775-885-6000; www.blm.gov/nv; 7-day permit $40, Tue & Wed free; ⊙ 24hr; ℗) is worth a stop for a look at its 600ft sand dune and the ruins of a Pony Express station. Just east, enjoy a juicy burger at an old stagecoach stop, **Middlegate Station** (☑ 775-423-7134; www.facebook.com/middlegate.station; 42500 Austin Hwy, cnr Hwys 50 & 361; mains $6-17; ⊙ 6am-2am) then toss your sneakers onto the **Shoe Tree** on the north side of Hwy 50 just ahead.

A fitting reward for surviving Hwy 50 is the awesome, uncrowded **Great Basin National Park** (☑ 775-234-7331; www.nps.gov/grba; 100 Great Basin; ⊙ 24hr) **FREE**. Near the

Nevada–Utah border, it's home to 13,063ft Wheeler Peak, which rises abruptly from the desert. Hiking trails near the summit take in superb country with glacial lakes, ancient bristlecone pines and even a permanent ice field. Admission is free; in summer, you can get oriented at the **Lehman Caves Visitor Center** (www.nps.gov/grba; 5500 W Hwy 488, Baker; ⊙ 8am-4:30pm), just north of Baker. Stargazing is fantastic from the park's campgrounds.

If you want a roof over your head, try the **Stargazer Inn** (☑ 775-234-7323; stay@stargazernevada.com; 115 S Baker Ave, Baker, Hwy 50; r from $78; ℗ ⊛ ❀ ☎ ⊛) ✐, a revamped roadside motel in Baker. The inn is also home to **Kerouac's** (☑ 775-234-7323; 115 S Baker Rd, Baker; pizzas from $12; ⊙ 7-10am & 5-8:30pm Apr-Oct; ℗ ⊛), known for its wood-fired pizzas and inventive cocktails.

Along Highways 375 & 93

Hwy 375 is dubbed the 'Extraterrestrial Hwy', both for its huge number of UFO sightings and because it intersects Hwy 93 near top secret **Area 51**, part of Nellis Air Force Base, supposedly a holding area for captured UFOs. Some people may find Hwy 375 more unnerving than the Loneliest Road; it's a desolate stretch of pavement where cars are few and far between. In the tiny town of Rachel, on Hwy 375, **Little A'Le' Inn** (☑ 775-729-2515; www.littlealeinn.com; 9631 Old Mill St, Rachel; RV sites $20, r $45-190; ⊙ restaurant 8am-10pm; ⊛ ☎ ⊛) accommodates earthlings and aliens alike, and sells extraterrestrial souvenirs. Probings not included.

ARIZONA

Arizona is made for road trips. Yes, the state has its showstoppers – Monument Valley, the Grand Canyon, Cathedral Rock – but you'll remember the long, romantic miles under endless skies for as long as you do the icons in between. Each drive reveals more of the state's soul: for a dose of mom-and-pop friendliness, follow Route 66 into Flagstaff; to understand the sheer will of Arizona's mining barons, take a twisting drive through rugged Jerome; and Native American history becomes contemporary as you drive past mesa-top Hopi villages dating back 1000 years.

History

American Indian tribes and their ancestors inhabited Arizona for millennia before

Francisco Vásquez de Coronado set out from Mexico City in 1540, leading an expedition whose members were the first Europeans to clap eyes on the Grand Canyon and Colorado River. Settlers and missionaries followed in his wake, before the US annexed Arizona following the Mexican–American War in the mid-19th century. The Indian Wars, in which the US Army battled American Indians to protect settlers and claim land for the government, officially ended in 1886 with the surrender of Apache warrior Geronimo.

Railroad and mining expansion followed and people started arriving in ever larger numbers. After President Theodore Roosevelt visited Arizona in 1903 he supported the damming of its rivers to provide year-round water for irrigation and drinking, thus paving the way to statehood: in 1912 Arizona became the last of the 48 contiguous US states to be admitted to the Union.

The state shares a 250-mile border with Mexico and has found itself at the forefront of the immigration debate on repeated occasions. Most recently, some of the state's border facilities, notably at Yuma, have become overburdened as the number of Central American migrants seeking asylum has spiked. Detention centers have run out of space, resulting in the creation of temporary tent camps to house migrants who are waiting for their cases to be heard.

ℹ️ Information

Although Arizona is on Mountain Standard Time, it's the only western state that does not observe daylight saving time from spring to early fall – except for on the Navajo Reservation. Generally speaking, lodging rates in southern Arizona (including Phoenix, Tucson and Yuma) are much higher in winter and spring, considered to be the 'high season', so great deals can be found in the hotter areas in summer.

Arizona Office of Tourism (☎602-364-3700; www.tourism.az.gov) Free state information.

Arizona State Parks (☎877-697-2757; www. azstateparks.com) Sixteen of the state's parks have campgrounds, open to online reservations.

Public Lands Interpretative Association Information about USFS, NPS, Bureau of Land Management (BLM) and state lands and parks.

Phoenix

Phoenix is Arizona's indubitable cultural and economic powerhouse, a thriving desert metropolis boasting some of the best Southwestern and Mexican food you'll find anywhere. And with more than 300 days of sunshine a year, exploring the 'Valley of the Sun' is an agreeable proposition (except in the sapping heat from June to August).

Culturally, it offers an opera, a symphony, several theaters and three of the state's finest museums – the Heard, Phoenix Art and Musical Instrument Museums – while the Desert Botanical Garden is a stunning introduction to the region's flora and fauna. For sports fans, there are professional baseball, football, basketball and ice-hockey teams, and more than 200 golf courses.

⦿ Sights

Greater Phoenix consists of several distinct cities. Phoenix, the largest, combines a business-like demeanor with top-notch museums, a burgeoning cultural scene and great sports facilities. Southeast of here, lively, student-flavored Tempe (*tem*-pee), hugs 2-mile-long Tempe Town Lake, while suburban Mesa, further east, holds a couple of interesting museums. Two ritzy enclaves lie northeast of Phoenix – Scottsdale, known for its cutesy old town, galleries and lavish resorts, and the largely residential Paradise Valley.

ARIZONA FACTS

Nickname Grand Canyon State

Population 7.17 million

Area 113,998 sq miles

Capital city Phoenix (population 1,660,272)

Other cities Tucson (population 535,677), Flagstaff (71,975), Sedona (10,336)

Sales tax 5.6%

Birthplace of Cesar Chavez (1927–93), singer Linda Ronstadt (b 1946)

Home of The OK Corral, mining towns turned art colonies

Politics Majority vote Republican

Famous for Grand Canyon, saguaro cacti

Best souvenir Pink cactus-shaped neon lamp from roadside stall

Driving distances Phoenix to Grand Canyon Village 235 miles, Tucson to Sedona 230 miles

Phoenix

★ Heard Museum   MUSEUM
(Map p838; ☑ 602-252-8848; https://heard.
org; 2301 N Central Ave; adult/senior/child
$18/13.50/7.50; ⊙ 9:30am-5pm Mon-Sat, from
11am Sun; P) This extraordinary museum
spotlights the history, life, arts and culture of
American Indian tribes in the Southwest. Visitors will find art galleries, ethnographic displays, films, a get-creative kids' exhibit and an
unrivaled collection of Hopi kachinas (elaborate spirit dolls, many gifted by Presidential
nominee Barry Goldwater). The Heard emphasizes quality over quantity and is one of
the best museums of its kind in America.

★ Musical Instrument Museum   MUSEUM
(☑ 480-478-6000; www.themim.org; 4725 E Mayo
Blvd; adult/teen/child $20/15/10; ⊙ 9am-5pm;
P) From Uganda thumb pianos to Hawaiian
ukuleles to Indonesian boat lutes, the ears
have it at this lively museum that celebrates
the world's musical instruments. More than
200 countries and territories are represented within five regional galleries, with wire-
less recordings bringing many to life as you
get within 'earshot' (headsets are provided).
You can also bang a drum in the Experiences Gallery and listen to Taylor Swift or Elvis
Presley rock out in the Artist Gallery.

★ Desert Botanical Garden   GARDENS
(Map p838; ☑ 480-941-1225; www.dbg.org; 1201
N Galvin Pkwy; adult/child $25/13; ⊙ 8am-8pm
Oct-Apr, 7am-8pm May-Sep) Blue bells and Mexican gold poppies are just two of the colorful
showstoppers blooming from March to May
along the Desert Wildflower Loop Trail at
this well-nurtured botanical garden, a lovely
place to reconnect with nature while learning
about desert plant life. Looping trails lead
past a profusion of desert denizens, arranged
by theme (including a Sonoran Desert nature
loop and an edible desert garden). It's pretty
dazzling year-round, but the flowering spring
season is the busiest and most colorful.

Phoenix Art Museum   MUSEUM
(Map p838; ☑ 602-257-1880; www.phxart.org;
1625 N Central Ave; adult/senior/child $23/20/14;
⊙ 10am-5pm Tue & Thu-Sat, 10am-9pm Wed, noon-
5pm Sun; P⛟) Arizona's premier repository
of fine art includes works by Claude Monet,
Diego Rivera and Georgia O'Keeffe. Make a
beeline for the Western Gallery, to see how
the astonishing Arizona landscape has inspired everyone from the early pioneers to

modernists. Got kids? Pick up a Kidpack at
Visitor Services, examine the ingeniously
crafted miniature period Thorne Rooms or
visit the PhxArtKids Gallery.

Scottsdale

For a list of permanent and temporary public art displays, visit www.scottsdalepublic
art.org.

Old Town Scottsdale   AREA
(Map p838; www.oldtownscottsdaleaz.com) Tucked
among Scottsdale's malls and bistros is its
Old Town, a Wild West–themed enclave filled
with cutesy buildings, covered sidewalks
and stores hawking mass-produced 'Indian'
artifacts. There's also a museum, sculptures,
saloons, a few galleries with genuine American Indian art, and horse-drawn buggies and
singing cowboys in the cooler months.

Taliesin West   ARCHITECTURE
(☑ 888-516-0811; www.franklloydwright.org; 12621
N Frank Lloyd Wright Blvd; tours $35-75; ⊙ 8:30am-
6pm Oct-May, shorter hours Jun-Sep, closed Tue
& Wed Jun-Aug) Taliesin West was the desert
home and studio of Frank Lloyd Wright, one
of America's greatest 20th-century architects. A prime example of organic architecture, with buildings incorporating elements
and structures found in surrounding nature,
it was built between 1938 and 1940, and
is still home to an architecture school. It's
now a National Historical Monument, open
to the public for informative guided tours –
reservations are essential.

Tempe

Founded in 1885 and home to around
50,000 students, **Arizona State University** (ASU; Map p838; ☑ 480-965-2100; www.asu.
edu) is the heart and soul of Tempe. The
Gammage Auditorium (Map p838; ☑ box
office 480-965-3434, tours 480-965-6912; www.
asugammage.com; 1200 S Forest Ave, cnr Mill Ave
& Apache Blvd; entry free, performances from $50;
⊙ box office 10am-5pm Mon-Thu summer, 10am-
6pm Mon-Fri rest of year) was Frank Lloyd
Wright's last major building. Easily accessible by light-rail from downtown Phoenix,
Mill Avenue, Tempe's main drag, is packed
with restaurants, themed bars and other
collegiate hangouts. You could also check
out **Tempe Town Lake** (Map p838; www.tem
pe.gov/lake), an artificial lake with boat rides
and hiking paths.

Mesa

★ Arizona Museum of Natural History MUSEUM

(☑ 480-644-2230; www.arizonamuseumofnatural history.org; 53 N MacDonald St, Mesa; adult/senior/child $12/10/7; ◷ 10am-5pm Tue-Fri, from 11am Sat, from 1pm Sun) Even if you're not staying in Mesa, this museum is worth a trip, especially if your kids are into dinosaurs (and aren't they all?). In addition to the multilevel Dinosaur Mountain, there are loads of life-sized casts of the giant beasts plus a touchable apatosaurus thighbone. Other exhibits highlight the Southwest's pre-conquest past, and that of the Americas more broadly, from a prehistoric Hohokam village to an entire hall on ancient Mesoamerican cultures.

⚡ Activities

★ Camelback Mountain HIKING

(Map p838; ☑ 602-261-8318; www.phoenix.gov; ◷ sunrise-sunset) This 2704ft twin-humped mountain sits smack in the center of the Phoenix action. The two trails, the Cholla Trail (6131 E Cholla Lane) and the Echo Canyon Trail (4925 E McDonald Dr), are short but steep, with 1264ft of elevation gain over a mere 1.2 miles and lots of hands-on scrambling over boulders. A great workout followed by stellar views.Get here early – the Echo Canyon Trail in particular is extremely popular.

Salt River Recreation WATER SPORTS

(☑ 480-984-3305; www.saltrivertubing.com; 9200 N Bush Hwy; tubes & shuttle $17; ◷ 9am-6:30pm May-late Sep) With Salt River Recreation you can float in an inner tube on the Lower Salt River through the stark Tonto National Forest. The launch is in northeast Mesa, about 15 miles north of Hwy 60 on Power Rd.

Floats are two, three or five hours long, including the shuttle-bus ride back. Cash only.

Cactus Adventures MOUNTAIN BIKING

(☑ 480-688-4743; www.cactusadventures.com; half-day rental from $45; ◷ 8am-8pm) Cactus Adventures rents hardtails and full-suspension bikes for use at South Mountain and offers guided hiking and biking tours at various parks (from $250). For rentals, staff will meet you at the trailhead. There is no shop; reserve ahead.

Ponderosa Stables HORSEBACK RIDING

(☑ 602-268-1261; www.arizona-horses.com; 10215 S Central Ave; 1/2/3hr rides $40/60/80; ◷ 9am-8pm) This outfitter leads breakfast, lunch, dinner and sunset rides through the lovely and vast South Mountain Park. Reservations are required. The stables are around 7 miles south of downtown Phoenix, directly down Central Ave. Minimum of two riders for three-hour rides.

★★ Festivals & Events

First Fridays ART

(www.artlinkphoenix.com; ◷ 6-10pm 1st & 3rd Fri of month) Up to 20,000 people hit the streets of downtown Phoenix on the first and third Fridays of every month for this self-guided art walk, incorporating more than 70 galleries and performance spaces. Three trolleys ferry the cognoscenti from venue to venue.

Arizona State Fair FAIR

(☑ 602-252-6771; www.azstatefair.com; 1826 W McDowell Rd, Phoenix; ◷ Oct) This fair lures more than a million folks to the Arizona State Fairgrounds every October, with a rodeo, rides and amusements, livestock displays, a pie-eating contest and plenty of live performances.

SOUTHWEST PHOENIX

PHOENIX FOR KIDS

Wet 'n' Wild Phoenix (☑ 623-201-2000; www.wetnwildphoenix.com; 4243 W Pinnacle Peak Rd, Glendale; over/under 42in tall $44/34, senior $34; ◷ 10:30am-8pm Sun-Thu, to 10pm Fri & Sat Jun & Jul, reduced hours Mar-May & Aug-Oct) This water park has pools, tube slides, wave pools, waterfalls and floating rivers. It's in Glendale, 2 miles west of I-17 at exit 217.

Children's Museum of Phoenix (Map p838; ☑ 602-253-0501; www.childrensmuseumof phoenix.org; 215 N 7th St; $15; ◷ 9am-4pm Tue-Sun; ⊕) A tactile, climbable, paintable wonderland of interactive (and surreptitiously educational) exhibits.

Arizona Science Center (Map p838; ☑ 602-716-2000; www.azscience.org; 600 E Washington St; adult/child $18/13; ◷ 10am-5pm) A high-tech temple of discovery; there are more than 300 hands-on exhibits and a planetarium.

Phoenix

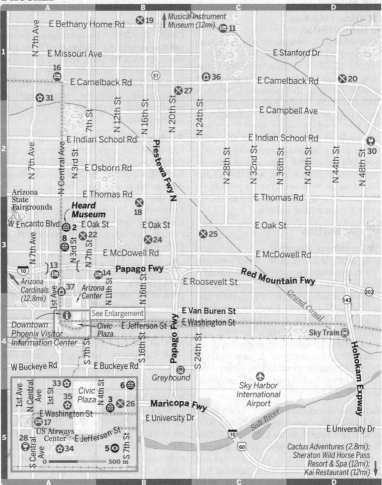

SOUTHWEST PHOENIX

🛏 Sleeping

🛏 Phoenix

HI Phoenix Hostel HOSTEL **$**
(Map p838; ☎ 602-254-9803; www.phxhostel.org;
1026 N 9th St; dm/s/d $30/45/65; ❄ @ 🛜) Fall
in love with backpacking all over again at
this small hostel with fun owners who know
Phoenix and want to enjoy it with you. The
22-bed hostel is located in a residential area
and has relaxing garden nooks. The 'talking
table' – at which laptops and other devices
are banned from 8am to 10am and 5pm to
10pm each day – is a very sociable innovation.

Maricopa Manor B&B **$$**
(Map p838; ☎ 800-292-6403, 602-264-9200;
www.maricopamanor.com; 15 W Pasadena Ave;
ste $190-240; 🅿 🛜 🌀) This small, Spanish
ranch-style place right near busy Central
Ave has six individually appointed suites,
many with French doors onto a deck over-
looking the pool, garden and fountain are-
as. Although Maricopa Manor is central, it's
well supplied with shady garden nooks, and
privacy is easily achieved.

Palomar Phoenix

HOTEL **$$$**

(Map p838; ☑ 602-253-6633, reservations 877-488-1908; www.hotelpalomar-phoenix.com; 2 E Jefferson St; r/ste from $350/360; **P ❋ ☎ ☳ ☳**) Shaggy pillows, antler-shaped lamps and portraits of blue cows. Yep, the 242 rooms of the Palomar are whimsical, and we like it. Larger than average and popping with fresh, modern style, the rooms come with yoga mats, animal-print robes and Italian Frette linens. There's a nightly wine reception, and Phoenix's major baseball and basketball stadiums are just around the corner.

Found:Re

DESIGN HOTEL **$$$**

(Map p838; ☑ 602-875-8000; www.foundre hotels.com; 1100 N Central Ave; r $280-360; **P ❋ ☎ ☳ ☳**) An art-driven hotel that exudes urban cool and a certain amount of cheekiness (you may want to avert your eyes from the Burt Reynolds nude upon entering), Found:Re's 104 rooms are plenty comfortable, with walk-in showers, quality linens, floor-to-ceiling windows and polished concrete floors. Pets stay free.

Scottsdale

Hotel Adeline

MOTEL **$$**

(Map p838; ☑ 480-284-7700; www.hoteladeline. com; 5101 N Scottsdale Rd; d from $213; **❋ ☎ ☳ ☳**) Mid-century modern furnishings grace this renovated motel, a trendy alternative to Scottsdale's more sober upscale retreats. The palm-fringed pool is the center of the action for the younger crowd.

★Bespoke Inn, Cafe & Bicycles

BOUTIQUE HOTEL **$$$**

(Map p838; ☑ 844-861-6715; www.bespokeinn.com; 3701 N Marshall Way; d from $450; **P ❋ ☎ ☳ ☳**) A small slice of 'European' hospitality in downtown Scottsdale, this breezy eight-room hotel has chocolate scones to nibble in the chic cafe, an infinity pool to loll in and Pashley city bikes to roam the neighborhood on. Rooms are plush, with handsome touches such as handcrafted furniture and nickel bath fixtures. Gourmet meals are served at the on-site restaurant Virtu. Book early.

Tempe

Sheraton Wild Horse Pass Resort & Spa

RESORT **$$$**

(☑ 602-225-0100; www.marriott.com; 5594 W Wild Horse Pass Blvd, Chandler; r from $360; **P ❋ ☎ ☳**) At sunset, scan the lonely horizon for the eponymous wild horses silhouetted against the South Mountains. Owned by the Gila

★**Arizona Biltmore Resort & Spa**

RESORT **$$$**

(Map p838; ☑ 800-950-0086, 602-955-6600; www.arizonabiltmore.com; 2400 E Missouri Ave; d from $400; **P ❋ @ ☎ ☳ ☳**) With architecture inspired by Frank Lloyd Wright and past guests including Irving Berlin, Marilyn Monroe and every president from Hoover to Bush the younger, the Biltmore is perfect for connecting to the magic of yesterday. A landmark, lending its name to much in the surrounding area, it boasts more than 700 beautifully appointed units, two golf courses, several pools and endless luxe touches.

Phoenix

River tribe and nestled on their sweeping reservation south of Tempe, this 500-room resort is a stunning alchemy of modern luxury and American Indian tradition. The domed lobby is a mural-festooned roundhouse, and rooms reflect the traditions of local tribes.

✗ Eating

✗ Phoenix

La Santisima Gourmet Tacos MEXICAN $
(Map p838; ☏602-254-6330; www.lasantisima gourmet.com; 1919 N 16th St; tacos $2.50-10; ⊙11am-10pm Mon-Sat, to 9pm Sun) Despite having 'gourmet' in the name, La Santisima keeps it real with plastic cutlery and rock music blaring in the background. Mexico City-style tacos are the headliners, but the real star may be the salsa bar, where you can choose from an array of fantastic creations ranging from pecan and peanut to jicama and Aztec chipotle. Great horchata too.

★**Pizzeria Bianco** PIZZA $$
(Map p838; ☏602-258-8300; www.pizzeria bianco.com; 623 E Adams St; Heritage Sq; pizza $14-19; ⊙11am-9pm Mon-Wed, 11am-10pm Thu-

Sat, noon-8pm Sun) James Beard–winner Chris Bianco has returned to the wood-fired oven and his thin-crust gourmet pies are as popular as ever. The tiny restaurant – a convenient stop for travelers exploring Heritage Sq – has **another location** (Map p838; ☏602-368-3273; www.pizzeriabianco.com; 4743 N 20th St; pizza $14-19; ⊙11am-9pm Sun-Thu, to 10pm Fri & Sat; ☏) in the Town & Country Shopping Center, near Biltmore Fashion Park.

Flower Child AMERICAN $
(Map p838; ☏602-429-6222; www.iamaflower child.com; 5013 N 44th St; mains $8.25-12; ⊙11am-9pm) It may be a chain, but it's healthy, inexpensive and so, so good – veg out on salads, ancient grain bowls, pho and delectable small plates, plus kombucha and cold brew on tap. This location is just around the corner from Camelback Mountain.

Green New American Vegetarian VEGAN $
(Map p838; ☏602-258-1870; www.greenveg etarian.com; 2022 N 7th St; mains $7.25-9.75; ⊙11am-9pm Mon-Sat; ☏) Your expectations of vegan food will be forever raised after dining at this hip cafe, where chef Damon Brasch stirs up savory vegan and vegetarian

dishes. Made with mock meats, the burgers, po'boys and Asian-style bowls taste as good, if not better, than their carnivorous counterparts. Order at the counter then take a seat in the garage-style digs.

★**Barrio Café** MEXICAN $$
(Map p838; ✆602-636-0240; www.barriocafe. com; 2814 N 16th St; mains $14-34; ⊙11am-10pm Tue-Sat, to 9pm Sun; ✍) Barrio's staff wear T-shirts emblazoned with *comida chingona*, which translates as 'fucking good food,' and they don't lie. This is Mexican food at its most creative: how many menus have you seen featuring guacamole spiked with pomegranate seeds, buttered corn with chipotle, aged cheese, cilantro and lime, or goat's-milk-caramel-filled churros? Drinks are half-price from 2pm to 5pm daily. No reservations.

★**Pa'la** MEDITERRANEAN $$
(Map p838; ✆602-795-9500; www.palakitchen. com; 2107 N 24th St; mains $12-22; ⊙11am-9pm Wed-Sat, to 3pm Tue) It's small, simple and you order at the counter, but don't let the casual, eco-minded ambience fool you into thinking Pa'La is anything but extraordinary. Chef Claudio Urciuoli focuses on seasonal vegetables and sustainably sourced seafood hot off the grill to deliver culinary thrills at a reasonable price.

★**Dick's Hideaway** NEW MEXICAN $$
(Map p838; ✆602-241-1881; www.richardsons nm.com; 6008 N 16th St; brunch $14-21, mains $16-32; ⊙8am-11pm Sun-Wed, to midnight Thu-Sat) At this pocket-sized ode to New Mexican cuisine, grab a small table beside the bar or settle in at the communal table in the side room and prepare for hearty servings of savory, chile-slathered New Mexican fare, from enchiladas to tamales to rellenos. We especially like the Hideaway for breakfast, when the Bloody Marys arrive with a shot of beer.

House of Tricks AMERICAN $$$
(Map p838; ✆480-968-1114; www.houseoftricks. com; 114 E 7th St; lunch $13-15, dinner $25-33; ⊙11am-10pm Mon-Sat) No, they don't do magic, but Robin and Robert Trick will still wow you with their eclectic, contemporary American menu with influences from the Southwest, the Med and Asia. The trellised garden patio usually buzzes with regulars and drop-ins, but the tables inside the vintage cottages are equally charming.

✗ **Scottsdale**

Andreoli ITALIAN $$
(✆480-614-1980; www.andreoli-grocer.com; 8880 E Vía Linda; sandwiches from $9.25, mains $20-34; ⊙10am-9pm Mon-Sat) Opened by Calabria-born Giovanni Scorzo, this Italian deli has a perpetual line out the door, and for good reason. Whether you grab a panino to go or one of the daily housemade pasta specials to enjoy in the bric-a-brac interior, the ingredients are always top-of-the-line. No reservations.

★**FnB** GASTRONOMY $$$
(Map p838; ✆480-284-4777; www.fnbrestaurant. com; 7125 E 5th Ave; mains $26-36; ⊙5-10pm Tue-Sat, to 9pm Sun) Romantic ambience and culinary wizardry join forces to provide a dinner to remember in Scottsdale. Charleen Badman, named the Southwest's best chef in 2019, highlights local produce and wine in her modern creations – sample small veggie-driven plates such as grilled asparagus with polenta, egg and chiltepin, or roasted broccoli with yogurt, grapefruit and dakka. It's all quite divine. Reserve.

✗ **Tempe**

★**Kai Restaurant** AMERICAN INDIAN $$$
(✆602-225-0100; 5594 W Wild Horse Pass Blvd, Chandler; mains $46-62, tasting menus $145-$245; ⊙5:30-9pm Tue-Sat) American Indian cuisine – based on traditional crops grown along the Gila River – soars to new heights at Kai ('seed'). Expect creations such as grilled buffalo tenderloin with smoked corn puree and cholla buds, or wild scallops with mesquite-smoked caviar and tepary-bean crackling. The unobtrusive service is flawless, the wine list expertly curated and the room decorated with American Indian art.

Kai is at the Sheraton Wild Horse Pass Resort & Spa on the Gila River Indian Reservation. Book ahead and dress nicely (no shorts or hats).

◉ **Drinking & Nightlife**

★**Wren House Brewing** BREWERY
(Map p838; ✆602-244-9184; www.wrenhouse brewing.com; 2125 N 24th St; hnoon-10pm Sun-Thu, 11am-midnight Fri & Sat; W) Snag a stool in this reconverted house for some of Phoenix's best small-batch beer. The sin cuidados – a sour farmhouse ale with hints of apricot – is heavenly; for something that packs more punch, there are two triple IPAs to choose from.

vBitter & Twisted
COCKTAIL BAR

(Map p838; ☑ 602-340-1924; www.bitterandtwistedaz.com; 1 W Jefferson St; ☺ 4pm-2am Tue-Sat) Housed in the former Arizona Prohibition Headquarters, this stylish seating-only cocktail bar shakes up some serious mixes and slings some delicious food to keep drinkers upright. Particularly lip-smacking is the dragon dumpling burger – pork and beef with Sichuan pickle and dumpling sauce.

Four Peaks Brewing Company
BREWERY

(Map p838; ☑ 480-303-9967; www.fourpeaks.com; 1340 E 8th St; ☺ 11am-midnight Mon-Wed, 11am-2am Fri & Sat, 9am-midnight Sun; 🛜) Hipsters, families, craft-beer obsessives and the plain thirsty congregate happily in this 1890s brick brewhouse, filling growlers of Kilt Lifter or Pitchfork Pale from the tap, or just chatting over a pint or two. There's also toothsome pub grub, tasting tours (Saturday, reserve online), a gift shop, and further locations in Tempe, Scottsdale and Phoenix Sky Harbor.

☆ Entertainment

Check *Arizona Republic Calendar* (www.azcentral.com/thingstodo/events) and *Phoenix New Times* (www.phoenixnewtimes.com) for listings.

Symphony Hall (Map p838; ☑ 602-262-6225; www.phoenixconventioncenter.com; 75 N 2nd St) hosts the **Arizona Opera** (Map p838; ☑ 602-266-7464; www.azopera.com) and the **Phoenix Symphony** (Map p838; ☑ box office 602-495-1999; www.phoenixsymphony.org). The latter also performs at other regional venues. The **Arizona Diamondbacks** (Map p838; ☑ 602-462-6500; http://arizona.diamondbacks.mlb.com) play baseball at downtown's air-conditioned **Chase Field** (Map p838; ☑ tours 602-462-6799; www.mlb.com/dbacks; 401 E Jefferson St; adult/senior/child $7/5/3; ☺ tours 9:30am, 11am, 12:30pm Mon-Sat, additional tours on game days), while the men's basketball team, the **Phoenix Suns** (Map p838; ☑ 602-379-7867; www.nba.com/suns), and the women's team, the **Phoenix Mercury** (Map p838; ☑ 602-252-9622; www.wnba.com/mercury), are also downtown, at **Talking Stick Resort Arena** (201 E Jefferson St). The **Arizona Cardinals** (☑ 623-433-7101; www.azcardinals.com; 1 Cardinals Dr, Glendale) play football in Glendale at **State Farm Stadium**, formerly the University of Phoenix Stadium, which hosted the Super Bowl in 2015.

Herberger Theater Center
THEATER

(Map p838; ☑ 602-252-8497; www.herbergertheater.org; 222 E Monroe St; ☺ box office 10am-5pm Mon-Fri, from noon Sat & Sun & 1hr before performances) Housing several theater companies and three stages, the Herberger also plays host to visiting troupes and productions. The predominant fare is drama and musicals, but you can also catch dance, opera and exhibitions of local art here.

Char's Has the Blues
BLUES

(Map p838; ☑ 602-230-0205; www.charshastheblues.com; 4631 N 7th Ave; ☺ 8pm-1am) Dark, intimate and very welcoming, this shabby-fronted blues and R&B shack packs 'em in with solid acts most nights of the week, but somehow still manages to feel like a well-kept secret. The cover ranges from free to $7.

🛍 Shopping

Phoenix Public Market
MARKET

(Map p838; ☑ 602-625-6736; www.phxpublicmarket.com; 721 N Central Ave; ☺ 8am-1pm Sat Oct-Apr, 8am-noon Sat May-Sep) The largest farmers market in Arizona brings the state's best produce to one open-air jamboree of good tastes. Alongside fresh fruit and vegetables, you can find indigenous foods, wonderful bread, spices, pastes and salsas, organic meat, BBQ trucks and plenty more to eat on the spot. Jewelry, textiles and body products also make appearances.

Heard Museum Shop & Bookstore
ARTS & CRAFTS

(Map p838; ☑ 602-346-8190; www.heardmuseumshop.com; 2301 N Central Ave; ☺ 9:30am-5pm Mon-Sat, from 11am Sun; 🛜) This museum store has a top-notch collection of American Indian original arts and crafts; the variety and quality of kachina dolls alone is impressive. Jewelry, pottery, American Indian books and a broad selection of fine arts can also be found, while the bookstore sells a wide array of books about the American Indian cultures of the Southwest.

Biltmore Fashion Park
MALL

(Map p838; ☑ 602-955-8400; www.shopbiltmore.com; 2502 E Camelback Rd; ☺ 10am-8pm Mon-Sat, noon-6pm Sun) Packed with high-end fashion retailers, this exclusive mall preens from its perch on Camelback just south of the Arizona Biltmore Resort.

ℹ Information

EMERGENCY & MEDICAL SERVICES

Police (emergency ✆911, non-emergency 602-262-6151; www.phoenix.gov/police; 620 W Washington St)

Both **Banner – University Medical Center Phoenix** (✆602-839-2000; www.bannerhealth.com; 1111 E McDowell Rd) and **St Joseph's Hospital & Medical Center** (✆602-406-3000; www.dignityhealth.org; 350 W Thomas Rd) have 24-hour emergency rooms.

TOURIST INFORMATION

Downtown Phoenix Visitor Information Center (Map p838; ✆877-225-5749; www.visitphoenix.com; 125 N 2nd St, Suite 120; ⊙8am-5pm Mon-Fri) The Valley's most complete source of tourist information. Located across from the Hyatt Regency.

Experience Scottsdale (Map p838; ✆800-782-1117, 480-421-1004; www.experiencescottsdale.com; 7014 E Camelback Rd; ⊙9am-6pm Mon-Sat, 10am-5pm Sun) In the Food Court of Scottsdale Fashion Square.

Mesa Convention & Visitors Bureau (✆800-283-6372, 480-827-4700; www.visitmesa.com; 120 N Center St; ⊙8am-5pm Mon-Fri)

Tempe Tourism Office (Map p838; ✆866-914-1052; www.tempetourism.com; 222 S Mill Ave, Suite 120; ⊙8:30am-5pm Mon-Fri)

ℹ Getting There & Away

Sky Harbor International Airport (PHX; Map p838; ✆602-273-3300; www.skyharbor.com; 3400 E Sky Harbor Blvd; 🛜) is 3 miles southeast of downtown Phoenix and served by airlines including United, American, Delta and British Airways. Its three terminals (Terminals 2, 3 and 4; Terminal 1 was demolished in 1990) and the parking lots are linked by free shuttles and the **Phoenix Sky Train** (www.skyharbor.com/phxskytrain; ⊙24hr).

Greyhound (Map p838; ✆602-389-4200; www.greyhound.com; 2115 E Buckeye Rd) runs buses to Tucson ($14, two hours, nine daily), Flagstaff ($25, three hours, six daily), Albuquerque (from $68, 9½ hours, three daily) and Los Angeles (from $31, 7½ hours, 10 daily). Valley Metro's No 13 bus links the airport and the Greyhound station; tell the driver your destination is the Greyhound station.

For shared rides from the airport, the citywide door-to-door shuttle service provided by **Super Shuttle** (✆800-258-3826; www.supershuttle.com) costs about $14 to downtown Phoenix and Tempe, $19 to Old Town Scottsdale and Mesa. Alternatively, expect to pay $16 to $20 to downtown for a cab or rideshare.

The Phoenix Sky Train (p843) runs through Terminals 3 and 4 to the Metro light-rail station at 44th St and E Washington St, via the airport's east economy parking area. Bus 13 also connects the airport to town ($2 per ride).

Valley Metro (✆602-253-5000; www.valleymetro.org) operates buses all over the Valley and a 20-mile light-rail line linking north Phoenix with downtown Phoenix, Tempe/ASU and downtown Mesa. Fares for both light-rail and bus are $2 per ride (no transfers) or $4 for a day pass. Buses run daily at intermittent times.

Central Arizona

North of Phoenix, the wooded, mountainous and much cooler Colorado Plateau is draped with scenic sites and attractions. You can channel your inner goddess at a vortex, hike through ponderosa-perfumed canyons, admire ancient Native American dwellings and delve into Old West history.

The main hub, Flagstaff, is a lively and delightful college town that's the gateway to the Grand Canyon South Rim. Summer, spring and fall are the best times to visit. On I-17, you can drive the 145 miles between Phoenix and Flagstaff in just over two hours. Opt for the more leisurely Hwy 89 and you'll be rewarded with beautiful landscapes and intriguing diversions.

Prescott

With its historic Victorian-era downtown and colorful Wild West heritage, Prescott feels like the Midwest-meets-cowboy country. Boasting more than 500 buildings on the National Register of Historic Places, it's the home of the world's oldest rodeo, while the infamous strip of old saloons known as Whiskey Row still plies its patrons with booze. For an engaging roundup of local history, spend an hour at the **Sharlot Hall Museum** (✆928-445-3122; www.sharlot.org; 415 W Gurley St; adult/senior/child $9/8/5; ⊙10am-5pm Mon-Sat, noon-4pm Sun May-Sep, to 4pm Oct-Apr) downtown.

Just south of downtown, the winningly retro **Motor Lodge** (✆928-717-0157; www.themotorlodge.com; 503 S Montezuma St; r/ste from $140/160; ❄🛜) welcomes guests with 12 snazzy bungalows arranged around a central driveway – it's indie lodging at its best. For breakfast, mosey into the friendly **Local** (✆928-237-4724; 520 W Sheldon St; mains $9.50-16; ⊙7am-2:30pm; 🛜), where home baking and a classic Southwestern breakfast can be counted on. Cajun and Southwest specialties spice up the menu at delightful **Iron Springs Cafe** (✆928-443-8848; www.ironspringscafe.com; 1501 Iron Springs Rd; brunch & lunch $9-12.50,

ARIZONA'S BEST SCENIC DRIVES

Oak Creek Canyon A thrilling plunge past swimming holes, rockslides and crimson canyon walls on Hwy 89A between Flagstaff and Sedona.

Hwy 89/89A Wickenburg to Sedona The Old West meets the New Weston on this lazy drive past dude ranches, mining towns, art galleries and stylish wineries.

Patagonia–Sonoita Scenic Road This one's for the birds, and those who like to track them, in Arizona's southern wine country on Hwys 82 and 83.

Kayenta–Monument Valley Star in your own Western on an iconic loop past cinematic red rocks in Navajo country.

Vermilion Cliffs Scenic Road A solitary drive on Hwy 89A through the Arizona Strip linking condor country, the North Rim and Mormon hideaways.

dinner $9-25.50; ⊙11am-8pm Wed-Sat, 9am-2pm Sun), which sits inside an old train station 3 miles northwest of downtown.

On Whiskey Row, the **Palace** (☑928-541-1996; www.historicpalace.com; 120 S Montezuma St; ⊙11am-10pm Sun-Thu, to 11pm Fri & Sat) is an atmospheric place to drink; you enter through swinging saloon doors into a big room anchored by a Brunswick bar. The **visitor center** (☑928-445-2000; www.prescott. org; 117 W Goodwin St; ⊙9am-5pm Mon-Fri, 10am-2pm Sat & Sun) has tourist information.

Jerome

This resurrected ghost town was known as the 'Wickedest Town in the West' during its late-1800s mining heyday, but its buildings have now been restored to hold galleries, restaurants, B&Bs and wine-tasting rooms.

Feeling brave? Stand on the glass platform covering the 1910ft mining shaft at **Audrey Headframe Park** (Map p848; www. jeromehistoricalsociety.com; 55 Douglas Rd; ⊙8am-5pm) FREE – it's deeper than the Empire State Building by 650ft! Just ahead, the excellent **Jerome State Historic Park** (Map p848; ☑928-634-5381; www.azstateparks.com/je-rome; 100 Douglas Rd; adult/child $7/4; ⊙8:30am-5pm) preserves the 1916 mansion of mining mogul Jimmy 'Rawhide' Douglas.

A hospital in the mining era, the **Jerome Grand Hotel** (Map p848; ☑928-634-8200; www. jeromegrandhotel.com; 200 Hill St; r$165-300, ste $400-525; ❋☐) plays up its past with medical relics in the hallways and an entertaining ghost tour kids will enjoy. The adjoining **Asylum Restaurant** (Map p848; ☑928-639-3197; www.asylumrestaurant.com; 200 Hill St; lunch $14-23.50, dinner $23.50-40; ⊙11am-3:30pm & 5-9pm; ☐), with its sweeping views, is a breathtaking spot for a fine meal and glass of wine.

Downtown, the **Spirit Room Bar** (Map p848; ☑928-634-8809; www.spiritroom.com; 166 Main St; ⊙11am-midnight) is a lively watering hole. Step into the **Flatiron Café** (Map p848; ☑928-634-2733; www.theflatironjerome.com; 416 Main St; mains $8-13.50; ⊙8:30am-3:30pm Thu-Mon) at the Y intersection for a gourmet breakfast or lunch; the specialty coffees are delicious. For information, call in at the **chamber of commerce** (Map p848; ☑928-634-2900; www.jeromechamber.com; 310 Hull Ave; ⊙11am-3pm most days).

Sedona

Nestled amid striking red sandstone formations at the south end of the 16-mile Oak Creek Canyon, Sedona attracts spiritual seekers, artists and healers, as well as day-trippers from Phoenix trying to escape the oppressive heat. Many New Age types believe that this area is the center of vortexes (not 'vortices' here in Sedona) that radiate the earth's power, and you'll find all sorts of alternative medicines and practices on display. More tangibly, the surrounding canyons offer outstanding hiking, biking, swimming and camping.

⊙ Sights & Activities

New Agers believe Sedona's rocks, cliffs and rivers radiate Mother Earth's mojo. The four best-known vortexes are **Bell Rock** (Map p848; Hwy 179) near the Village of Oak Creek east of Hwy 179; **Cathedral Rock** (Map p848; Back O Beyond Rd) near Red Rock Crossing; **Airport Mesa** (Map p848; Airport Rd); and **Boynton Canyon** (Map p848; Dry Creek Rd, Coconino NF). Airport Rd is also a great location for watching the Technicolor sunsets.

Red Rock State Park PARK
(Map p848; ☑928-282-6907; www.azstateparks. com/red-rock; 4050 Red Rock Loop Rd; adult/child $7/4; ⊙8am-5pm) Not to be confused with Slide Rock State Park (p845), this 286-acre park includes an environmental education center, picnic areas and 5 miles of well-marked, interconnecting trails in gorgeous red-rock country. Trails range from flat

creekside saunters to moderate climbs to scenic ridges. Ranger-led activities include nature and bird walks. Swimming in the creek is prohibited. It's 9 miles west of downtown Sedona off Hwy 89A, on the eastern edge of the 15-mile Lime Kiln Trail.

Slide Rock State Park
SWIMMING

(Map p848; ☎928-282-3034; www.azstateparks. com/slide-rock; 6871 N Hwy 89A; per car Mon-Thu $20, Fri-Sun $30 Mar-Sep, $10 Oct-Feb; ⊗8am-7pm May-Aug, shorter hours rest of year) One of Sedona's most popular and most crowded destinations, this state park 7 miles north of town features an 80ft sandstone chute that whisks swimmers through Oak Creek. Short trails ramble past an old homestead, farming equipment and an apple orchard, but the park's biggest draw is the set of wonderful natural rock slides.

West Fork Trail
HIKING

(Map p848; Hwy 89A; day use per vehicle/bicycle $10/2; ⊗8am-7pm) This deservedly popular trail crosses Oak Creek a dozen times as it winds through the canyon, where walls soar more than 200ft in some places. The trail is marked for the first 3 miles, but you can scramble along the stream bed as far as 14 miles upstream. Parking is limited: arrive before 8:30am.

Pink Jeep Tours
DRIVING

(Map p848; ☎800-873-3662; www.pinkadven turetours.com; 204 N Hwy 89A; ⊗6am-10pm) This veteran of Sedona's tour industry seems to have 4WDs everywhere. Once you join a tour, laughing and bumping around, you'll see why they're so popular. Pink runs 15 thrilling, bone-rattling off-road and adventure tours, most lasting from two hours (adult from $65, child from $60) to four hours (adult from $155, child from $140).

🛏 Sleeping

Sedona and nearby Oak Creek Canyon host many beautiful B&Bs, creekside cabins, motels and full-service resorts. Dispersed camping is not permitted in Red Rock Canyon. The Forest Service runs three campgrounds, without hookups, in the woods of Oak Creek Canyon, just off Hwy Alt 89. It costs $22 to camp, and you don't need a Red Rock Pass. Reservations are accepted for some sites at all three. Six miles north of town, Manzanita has 18 sites, showers and is open year-round; 11.5 miles north, Cave Springs has 84 sites, and showers; Pine Flat, 12.5 miles north, has 56 sites.

Cozy Cactus
B&B $$$

(Map p848; ☎928-284-0082; www.cozycactus. com; 80 Canyon Circle Dr, Village of Oak Creek; d

---

VERDE VALLEY WINE TRAIL

Vineyards, wineries and tasting rooms are increasingly thick on the ground in the well-watered valley of the Verde River. Bringing star power is Maynard James Keenan, lead singer of the band Tool and owner of Caduceus Cellars and Merkin Vineyards. His 2010 documentary *Blood into Vine* takes a no-holds-barred look at the wine industry.

In Cottonwood, drive or float to **Alcantara Vineyards** (Map p848; ☎928-649-8463; www. alcantaravineyard.com; 3445 S Grapevine Way; wine tasting $10-15; ⊗11am-5pm) on the Verde River, then stroll through Old Town where **Arizona Stronghold** (Map p848; ☎928-639-2789; www.azstronghold.com; 1023 N Main St; wine tasting $9; ⊗noon-7pm Sun-Thu, to 9pm Fri & Sat), **Merkin Vineyards Osteria** (Map p848; ☎928-639-1001; www.merkinvineyardsosteria.com; 1001 N Main St; ⊗11am-9pm; 🛜) and **Pillsbury Wine Company** (Map p848; ☎928-639-0646; www.pillsburywine.com; 1012 N Main St; wine tasting $8-12; ⊗11am-6pm Sun-Thu, to 9pm Fri & Sat) are three of the best wine-tasting rooms on oenophile-friendly Main St.

In Jerome, start at **Cellar 433** (Map p848; ☎928-634-7033; www.cellar433.com; 240 Hull Ave; wine tastings $10-12; ⊗11am-6pm Mon-Wed, to 7pm Thu-Sun) near the visitor center. From there, stroll up to Keenan's **Caduceus Cellars** (Map p848; ☎928-639-9463; www.caduceus.org; 158 Main St; wine tastings $15; ⊗11am-6pm Sun-Thu, to 8pm Fri & Sat), near the Connor Hotel.

Three wineries with tasting rooms hug a stretch of Page Springs Rd east of Cornville: bistro-housing **Page Springs Cellars** (Map p848; ☎928-639-3004; www.pagespringscellars. com; 1500 Page Springs Rd, Cornville; wine tasting $11; ⊗11am-7pm Sun-Wed, to 9pm Thu-Sat), the welcoming **Oak Creek Vineyards** (Map p848; ☎928-649-0290; www.oakcreekvineyards.net; 1555 N Page Springs Rd, Cornville; wine tasting $10; ⊗10am-6pm Sun-Thu, to 8pm Fri & Sat) and the mellow-rock-playing **Javelina Leap Vineyard** (Map p848; ☎928-649-2681; www.javelina leapwinery.com; 1565 Page Springs Rd, Cornville; wine tasting $12; ⊗11am-6pm).

RED ROCK PASS

To park on National Forest land around Sedona and Oak Creek Canyon, you'll need to buy a Red Rock Pass, which is available at ranger stations, visitor centers and vending machines at most trailheads and picnic areas. Passes cost $5 per day or $15 per week and must be displayed under the windshield of your car. You don't need a pass if you're just stopping briefly for a photograph or to enjoy a viewpoint, or if you have one of the Federal Interagency Passes.

$275-345; ❄️🛜) This seven-room B&B, run by Carrie and Mark, works well for outdoorsy types – the Southwest-style house bumps up against Agave Trail, and is just around the bend from cyclist-friendly Bell Rock Pathway. Post-adventuring, get comfy beside the firepit on the back patio, perfect for wildlife-watching and stargazing, and enjoy the three-course breakfast that awaits you the next morning.

★ El Portal   INN $$$

(Map p848; ☑928-203-9405; www.elportalse dona.com; 95 Portal Lane; r $300-500; ❄️🛜🐾) 🐾 This discreet little inn is a beautiful blend of Southwestern and Craftsman style. It's a pocket of relaxed luxury tucked away in a corner across from the galleries and restaurants of Tlaquepaque, and marvelously removed from the chaos of Sedona's tourist-heavy downtown. The look is rustic but sophisticated, incorporating reclaimed wood, Navajo rugs, river rock and thick adobe walls.

✕ Eating & Drinking

Sedona Memories   DELI $

(Map p848; ☑928-282-0032; 321 Jordan Rd; sandwiches $8.50; ⏰10am-2pm Mon-Fri) This tiny local spot assembles gigantic sandwiches on slabs of homemade bread. A great choice for a picnic, as they pack 'em tight to-go, so there's less mess. You can also nosh on their quiet porch. If you call in your order, they'll toss in a free cookie.

Black Cow Café   ICE CREAM $

(Map p848; ☑928-203-9868; 229 N Hwy 89A; medium ice cream $5; ⏰10:30am-9pm) Many claim the Black Cow's homemade ice cream is the best in town. Try the prickly pear.

★ Elote Cafe   MEXICAN $$$

(Map p848; ☑928-203-0105; www.elotecafe.com; Arabella Hotel, 771 Hwy 179; mains $23-29; ⏰5-10pm Tue-Sat) Come here for some of the best, most authentic Mexican food in the region. Elote Cafe serves unusual traditional dishes you won't find elsewhere, like the namesake *elote* (fire-roasted corn with spicy mayo, lime and cotija cheese) or smoked chicken in guajillo chilies. Reservations are not accepted: come early, order a margarita and get ready to make some new friends.

Hudson   AMERICAN $$$

(Map p848; ☑928-862-4099; www.thehudson sedona.com; Hillside Shopping Center, 671 Hwy 179; mains $15-43; ⏰11:30am-9pm) Prickly-pear ribs, butternut-squash ravioli, fireball chicken wings and a variety of salads bring an element of urban cool to Sedona. But it's not just the food that makes you want to linger past happy hour – those great big views from the half-moon banquettes and outdoor patio are equally enticing. Great bar too.

ℹ️ Information

Many places signed 'Tourist Information' really just want to sell you a timeshare. Stick to the following, which sell the Red Rock Pass and provide free hiking guides and maps.

Red Rock Country Visitor Center (Map p848; ☑928-203-2900; www.fs.usda.gov/coconino; 8375 Hwy 179; ⏰9am-4:30pm) Just south of the Village of Oak Creek.

Sedona Chamber of Commerce Visitor Center (Map p848; ☑928-282-7722; www. visitsedona.com; 331 Forest Rd; ⏰8:30am-5pm) Located in the pedestrian center of Uptown Sedona.

ℹ️ Getting There & Around

Ace Xpress (☑928-649-2720; www.acexshut tle.com; one way/round trip adult $68/109, child $35/55) and **Groome Transportation** (☑928-350-8466; www.groometransportation. com; one way adult/child $55/28) run shuttle services between Sedona and Phoenix's Sky Harbor International Airport.

Amtrak and Greyhound both stop in nearby Flagstaff.

Barlow Jeep Rentals (☑928-282-8700; www. barlows.us; 3009 W Hwy 89A; half-/1-/3-day Jeep rental $295/395/585; ⏰8am-6pm) is great for exploring 4WD roads. Free maps and trail information are provided. **Bob's Taxi** (☑982-282-1234) is a good local operator, while rental cars are available at **Enterprise** (☑928-282-2052; www. enterprise.com; 2090 W Hwy 89A; per day from $50; ⏰8am-5:30pm Mon-Fri, 9am-2pm Sat).

Flagstaff

Flagstaff's laid-back charms are many, from a pedestrian-friendly historic downtown crammed with eclectic vernacular architecture to hiking and skiing in the country's largest ponderosa pine forest. And the locals are a happy, athletic bunch, skewing more toward granola than gunslinger: buskers play bluegrass on street corners, while cycling culture flourishes. Northern Arizona University (NAU) gives Flag its college-town flavor, while its railroad history still figures firmly in the town's identity. Throw in a healthy appreciation for craft beer, freshly roasted coffee beans and an all-around good time, and you have the makings of the perfect northern Arizonan escape.

⊙ Sights

★Lowell Observatory OBSERVATORY
(Map p848; ☑928-774-3358; www.lowell.edu; 1400 W Mars Hill Rd; adult/senior/child $17/16/10; ☺10am-10pm Mon-Sat, to 5pm Sun) Astronomers, get ready to geek out! Sitting atop a hill just west of downtown, this national historic landmark – famous for the first sighting of Pluto in 1930 – was built by Percival Lowell in 1894. Check out the solar telescope or go on a tour during the day. Once evening falls, visitors can stargaze through on-site telescopes (weather permitting). A new exhibit, the Giovale Open Deck Observatory (GODO), which houses six telescopes alongside interactive displays, opened in October 2019.

★Museum of Northern Arizona MUSEUM
(Map p848; ☑928-774-5213; www.musnaz.org; 3101 N Fort Valley Rd; adult/senior/child $12/10/8; ☺10am-5pm Mon-Sat, noon-5pm Sun) Housed in an attractive Craftsman-style stone building amid a pine grove, this small but excellent museum spotlights local American Indian archaeology, history and culture, as well as geology, biology and the arts. Intriguing permanent collections are augmented by exhibitions on subjects such as John James Audubon's paintings of North American mammals. On the way to the Grand Canyon, it makes a wonderful introduction to the human and natural history of the region.

**Riordan Mansion
State Historic Park** HISTORIC SITE
(Map p848; ☑928-779-4395; www.azstateparks.com/riordan-mansion; 409 W Riordan Rd; tour adult/child $10/5; ☺9:30am-5pm May-Oct, 10:30am-5pm Thu-Mon Nov-Apr) Having made a fortune from their Arizona Lumber Company, brothers Michael and Timothy Riordan built this sprawling duplex in 1904. The Craftsman-style design was the brainchild of architect Charles Whittlesey, who also designed El Tovar in Grand Canyon Village. The exterior features hand-split wooden shingles, log-slab siding and rustic stone. Filled with Edison, Stickley, Tiffany and Steinway furniture, the interior is a shrine to arts and crafts.

🏃 Activities

Flagstaff Bicycle Revolution MOUNTAIN BIKING
(Map p848; ☑928-774-3042; www.flagbikerev.com; 3 S Mikes Pike; per 24hr hardtail/full suspension $45/70; ☺8am-6pm Mon-Fri, 9am-5pm Sat & Sun) Flagstaff's best mountain-biking shop, with both hardtail (no rear suspension) and full-suspension bikes available to rent. You can ride directly to the trails from the shop, and it's sandwiched between great pizza and beer for postride celebrations.

Arizona Snowbowl SKIING
(Map p854; ☑928-779-1951; www.snowbowl.ski; 9300 N Snowbowl Rd; ski pass adult/child $89/59; ☺9am-4pm Nov-Apr) About 14 miles north of downtown Flagstaff, Arizona Snowbowl is small but lofty, with eight lifts that service 55 ski runs between 9200ft and 11,500ft.

From June through mid-October, ride the chairlift to 11,500ft, where you can hike, hear ranger talks, go on a mini ropes course and take in the desert and mountain views.

🛏 Sleeping

Unlike in southern Arizona, summer is high season here.

★Motel DuBeau MOTEL $
(Map p848; ☑928-774-6731; www.modubeau.com; 19 W Phoenix Ave; dm/r from $29/87; 🅿@⚗) Built in 1929 as Flagstaff's first motel, the DuBeau has clean, well-run accommodations. In addition to private rooms, which all have refrigerators and cable TV, there is one seven-bed dorm room. There is also a kitchen and laundry facilities. Note there is no air-con in summer.

On-site Nomads serves beer, wine and meals.

★Inn at 410 B&B $$
(Map p848; ☑928-774-0088; www.inn410.com; 410 N Leroux St; r $210-325; 🅿❄⚗) This fully renovated 1894 house offers 10 spacious, beautifully decorated and themed

Flagstaff to Sedona

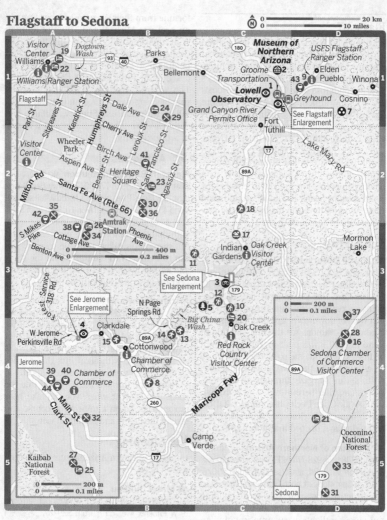

See Flagstaff Enlargement

See Sedona Enlargement

See Jerome Enlargement

SOUTHWEST CENTRAL ARIZONA

bedrooms, each with a fridge and bathroom, and many with four-poster beds and delightful views. A short stroll from downtown, the inn has a shady orchard garden and a cozy dining room, where a full gourmet breakfast and afternoon snacks are served.

Hotel Monte Vista HISTORIC HOTEL $$
(Map p848; ☎928-779-6971; www.hotelmonte vista.com; 100 N San Francisco St; r $130-190; ❇🛜) A huge, old-fashioned neon sign towers over this 1926 landmark hotel, hinting at what's inside: an array of feather lampshades, vintage furniture, bold colors and eclectic decor. Rooms are named for the movie stars who stayed here, and resident ghosts supposedly make regular appearances. Now for the downsides: it's noisy, wi-fi doesn't work in many rooms and street parking can be a headache.

✗ Eating

Flagstaff's college population and general dedication to living well translates into one of the best dining scenes in northern Arizona. There are a number of grocery stores in town – this is the best place to stock up before heading to the Grand Canyon.

Flagstaff to Sedona

★**Macy's** CAFE $
(Map p848; ☑928-774-2243; www.macyscoffee. net; 14 S Beaver St; mains $6-9.50; ⊙6am-6pm; 🛜🌱) The delicious coffee – house-roasted in the original, handsome, fire-engine-red roaster in the corner – at this Flagstaff institution has kept local students and caffeine devotees buzzing and sated since the 1980s. The all-vegetarian menu includes many vegan choices, along with traditional cafe grub including pastries, steamed eggs, waffles, yogurt and granola, salads and sandwiches.

Pizzicletta PIZZA $
(Map p848; ☑928-774-3242; www.pizzicletta.com; 203 W Phoenix Ave; pizzas $12-16; ⊙5-9pm Sun-Thu, to 10pm Fri & Sat) Tiny Pizzicletta, where the excellent thin-crusted wood-fired pizzas are loaded with gourmet toppings such as arugula and aged prosciutto, is housed in a sliver of a white-brick building. Inside there's an open kitchen, one long table with iron chairs, Edison bulbs and industrial surrounds. You can order in while you enjoy

some suds at **Mother Road Brewing Company** (Map p848; ☑928-774-9139; www.mother roadbeer.com; 7 S Mikes Pike; ⊙2-9pm Tue & Wed, 2-10pm Thu, noon-10pm Fri & Sat, noon-9pm Sun; 🛜) next door.

★**Criollo Latin Kitchen** FUSION $$
(Map p848; ☑928-774-0541; www.criollolatin kitchen.com; 16 N San Francisco St; lunch $12-16, dinner $19-23; ⊙11am-9pm Mon-Fri, from 9am Sat & Sun) 🌱 Sister to Brix Restaurant & Wine Bar (p850) and **Proper Meats + Provisions** (Map p848; ☑928-774-9001; www.proper meats.com; 110 E Rte 66; sandwiches $12-14; ⊙10am-9pm) 🌱, this on-trend Latin-fusion restaurant gives similar encouragement to local producers, sourcing ingredients from Arizona wherever possible. Set up your day with the Haitian brunch of slow-roasted pork with over-easy eggs, pinto beans and Ti-Malice hot sauce, or come back at happy hour (3pm to 6pm Monday to Friday) for fish tacos and $3.50 margaritas.

★**Coppa Cafe** CAFE **$$$**
(Map p848; ☏928-637-6813; www.facebook.
com/coppacafeaz; 1300 S Milton Rd; lunch $11-
15, mains $15-32; ⊙3-9pm Wed-Fri, 11am-3pm &
5-9pm Sat, 10am-3pm Sun; 🐾) Brian Konefal
and Paola Fioravanti, who met at an Italian
culinary school, are the husband-and-wife
team behind this friendly, art-strewn bis-
tro with egg-yolk-yellow walls. Expect in-
gredients foraged from nearby woods (and
further afield in Arizona) in dishes such as
slow-roasted top loin with wildflower butter,
or clay-baked duck's egg with a 'risotto' of
Sonoran wheat and wild herbs.

Brix Restaurant &
Wine Bar INTERNATIONAL **$$$**
(Map p848; ☏928-213-1021; www.brixflagstaff.com;
413 N San Francisco St; mains $23-40; ⊙5-9pm
Tue-Sun) Brix offers seasonal, locally sourced
and generally top-notch fare in a handsome
room with exposed brick walls and an intimate copper bar. Sister business Proper
Meats + Provisions (p849) supplies charcuterie, free-range pork and other fundamentals
of delectable dishes, such as cavatelli with
Calabrese sausage, kale and preserved lemon. The wine list is well curated, and reservations are recommended.

🍷 **Drinking & Entertainment**

For details about festivals and music programs, call the **Visitor Center** (Map p848;
☏928-213-2951; www.flagstaffarizona.org; 1 E
Rte 66; ⊙8am-5pm Mon-Sat, 9am-4pm Sun) or
check www.flagstaff365.com. On Friday and
Saturday nights in summer, people gather
on blankets for free music and family movies at Heritage Sq. The fun starts at 5pm.

On Thursday pick up a free copy of *Flagstaff Live!* (www.azdailysun.com/flaglive_
new) for current shows and happenings
around town.

★**Hops on Birch** PUB
(Map p848; ☏928-440-5380; www.hopsonbirch.
com; 22 E Birch Ave; ⊙noon-1:30am; 🐾) Sim-

CAMPING AROUND
FLAGSTAFF
••••••••••••••••••••••••••••••••••

Free dispersed camping is permitted in the Coconino National Forest
surrounding Flagstaff. There are also
campgrounds in Oak Creek Canyon to
the south of town and Sunset Crater to
the north.

---

ple and handsome, Hops on Birch has 34
rotating beers on tap, live music five nights
a week and a friendly local-crowd vibe. In
classic Flagstaff style, dogs are as welcome
as humans.

Museum Club BAR
(Map p848; ☏928-440-5214; www.museumclub.
net; 3404 E Rte 66; ⊙11am-2am) This country-music roadhouse on Route 66 has been
kicking up its heels since 1936. Inside what
looks like a huge log cabin you'll find a large
wooden dance floor, animal mounts and a
sumptuous elixir-filled mahogany bar. The
origins of the name? In 1931 it housed a taxidermy museum.

ℹ️ **Information**

USFS Flagstaff Ranger Station (Map p848;
☏928-526-0866; www.fs.usda.gov/coconino;
5075 N Hwy 89; ⊙8am-4pm Mon-Fri) Provides
camping and hiking information on the Mt
Elden, Humphreys Peak and O'Leary Peak areas
north of Flagstaff.

Visitor Center (p850) Located inside the
Amtrak station, the visitor center has a great
Flagstaff Discovery map and tons of informa-
tion on things to do.

ℹ️ **Getting There & Away**

Greyhound (Map p848; ☏928-774-4573; www.
greyhound.com; 880 E Butler Ave; ⊙10am-
5:30am) stops in Flagstaff en route to/from
Albuquerque, Las Vegas, Los Angeles and
Phoenix. **Groome Transportation** (Map p848;
☏928-350-8466; www.groometransportation.
com) has shuttles that run between Flagstaff,
Grand Canyon National Park, Williams, Sedona
and Phoenix's Sky Harbor International Airport.

Operated by **Amtrak** (☏928-774-8679; www.
amtrak.com; 1 E Rte 66; ⊙24hr), the *Southwest
Chief* stops at Flagstaff on its daily run between
Chicago and Los Angeles.

Mountain Line Transit (☏928-779-6624;
www.mountainline.az.gov; one way adult/child
$1.25/0.60) has several fixed bus routes daily;
pick up a user-friendly map at the visitor center.
Buses are equipped with ramps for passengers
in wheelchairs.

If you need a taxi, call **Action Cab** (☏928-
774-4427; www.facebook.com/actioncabtax-
iandtours). Several major car-rental agencies
operate from the airport and downtown.

Williams

Affable Williams, 60 miles south of Grand
Canyon Village and 35 miles west of Flagstaff, is a gateway town with character. Classic motels and diners line Route 66, and the

old-school homes and train station give a nod to simpler times.

Most tourists visit to ride the turn-of-the-20th-century **Grand Canyon Railway** (Map p848; 800-843-8724; www.thetrain.com; 233 N Grand Canyon Bvd, Railway Depot; return adult/child from $67/32; departs 9:30am) to the Canyon's South Rim, which departs Williams 9:30am and returns at 5:45pm. Even if you're not a train buff, a trip is a scenic stress-free way to visit the Grand Canyon. Characters in period costumes provide historical and regional narration, and banjo folk music sets the tone.

The **Red Garter Inn** (Map p848; 800-328-1484; www.redgarter.com; 137 W Railroad Ave; d $175-200;) is an 1897 bordello turned B&B where the ladies used to hang out the windows to flag down customers. The four rooms have nice period touches and the downstairs bakery has good coffee. The funky little **Grand Canyon Hotel** (Map p848; 928-635-1419; www.thegrandcanyonhotel. com; 145 W Route 66; dm $37, r $80-150; Apr-Nov;) has small themed rooms, a hostel-style dorm, a separate carriage house and no TVs. You can also sleep inside a 1929 Santa Fe caboose or a Pullman railcar at the **Canyon Motel & RV Park** (Map p848; 928-635-9371; www.thecanyonmotel.com; 1900 E Rodeo Rd; tent/RV sites from $30/42, railway car/ cabooses from $110/205;), just east of downtown.

Grand Canyon National Park

No matter how much you read about the **Grand Canyon** (Map p854; 928-638-7888; www.nps.gov/grca; 20 South Entrance Rd; 7-day entry per car/person $35/20), or how many photographs you've seen, nothing really prepares you for the sight of it. The sheer immensity of the canyon grabs you first, followed by the dramatic layers of rock, which pull you in for a closer look. Next up are the artistic details – rugged plateaus, crumbly spires, maroon ridges – that flirt and catch your eye as shadows flicker across the rock.

Snaking along its floor are 277 miles of the Colorado River, which has carved the canyon over the past six million years and exposed rocks up to two billion years old – half the age of the earth. The two rims of the Grand Canyon offer quite different experiences; they lie more than 200 miles apart by road and are rarely visited on the same trip. Most

WALNUT CANYON

The Sinagua cliff dwellings at **Walnut Canyon** (Map p848; 928-526-3367; www.nps.gov/waca; I-40 exit 204; adult/child $15/free; 8am-5pm Jun-Oct, from 9am Nov-May, trails close 1hr earlier) are set in the nearly vertical walls of a small limestone butte amid this stunning forested canyon. The mile-long Island Trail steeply descends 185ft (more than 200 stairs), passing 25 rooms built under the natural overhangs of the curvaceous butte. The shorter, wheelchair-accessible Rim Trail affords several views of the cliff dwellings from across the canyon.

visitors choose the South Rim with its easy access, wealth of services and vistas that don't disappoint. The quieter North Rim has its own charms; at 8200ft elevation (1000ft higher than the South Rim), its cooler temperatures support wildflower meadows and tall, thick stands of aspen and spruce.

June is the driest month, July and August the wettest. January has average overnight lows of 13°F (-11°C) to 20°F (-7°C) and daytime highs around 40°F (4°C). Summer temperatures inside the canyon regularly soar above 100°F (38°C). While the South Rim is open year-round, most visitors come between late May and early September. The North Rim is open from mid-May to mid-October.

Information

The most developed area in the Grand Canyon National Park is **Grand Canyon Village**, 6 miles north of the South Rim Entrance Station. The North Rim has one entrance, which is 30 miles south of Jacob Lake on Hwy 67; continue another 14 miles south to the actual rim. The North and South Rims are 215 miles apart by car, 21 miles on foot through the canyon, or 10 miles as the condor flies.

The park entrance ticket is valid for seven days and can be used at both rims. All overnight hikes and backcountry camping in the park require a permit. The **Backcountry Information Center** (Map p854; 928-638-7875; www. nps.gov/grca/planyourvisit/backcountry-permit.htm; Grand Canyon Village; 8am-noon & 1-5pm, phone staffed 8am-5pm Mon-Fri; Village) accepts applications for backpacking permits ($10, plus $8 per person per night) starting four months before the proposed month. Your chances are decent if you apply early and provide alternative hiking itineraries.

SUNSET CRATER VOLCANO NATIONAL MONUMENT

Around AD 1064 a cinder cone erupted on this **spot** (Map p854; ☏928-526-0502; www.nps.gov/sucr; Park Loop Rd 545; car/motorcycle/bicycle & pedestrian $25/20/15; ☉visitor center 9am-5pm, park 24hr), spewing ash across 800 sq miles, spawning the Kana-A lava flow. Now the 8029ft Sunset Crater is quiet, and short trails wind through the Bonito lava flow (formed c 1180) and up Lenox Crater (7024ft). More ambitious hikers and bikers can ascend O'Leary Peak (8965ft; 8-mile round trip), or there's a gentle, 0.3-mile, wheelchair-accessible loop overlooking the petrified flow.

Sunset Crater is 19 miles northeast of Flagstaff. Access fees include entry to nearby **Wupatki National Monument** (Map p854; ☏928-679-2365; www.nps.gov/wupa; Park Loop Rd 545; car/motorcycle/bicycle/pedestrian $25/20/15/15; ☉visitor center 9am-5pm, trails sunrise-sunset), and are valid for seven days.

Reservations are accepted in person or by mail or fax, not by phone or email. For more information see www.nps.gov/grca/planyourvisit/backcountry-permit.htm.

If you arrive at the South Rim without a permit, head to the backcountry office, by **Maswik Lodge** (Map p854; ☏928-638-2631, advanced reservations 888-297-2757; www.grandcanyonlodges.com; 202 South Village Loop Dr, Grand Canyon Village; r South/North $215/304; P✳@☎; ☐Village), to join the waiting list. As a conservation measure, the park no longer sells bottled water. Fill your flask at water filling stations along the rim or at **Canyon Village Market** (Map p854; ☏928-638-2262; www.visitgrandcanyon.com; Market Plaza, Grand Canyon Village; sandwiches & pizzas $6-11; ☉6:30am-9pm late May-Sep, deli to 8pm, shorter hours rest of year; ☐Village).

SOUTH RIM VISITOR CENTERS

Grand Canyon Visitor Center (Map p854; ☏park headquarters 928-638-7888; www.nps.gov/grca/planyourvisit/visitorcenters.htm; Grand Canyon Visitor Center Plaza, Grand Canyon Village; ☉9am-5pm; ☐Village, ☐Kaibab/Rim, ☐Tusayan (Mar 1-Sep 30)) Three hundred yards behind Mather Point, a large plaza holds the visitor center and the **Visitor Center Plaza Park Store** (Map p854; ☏Grand Canyon Association 800-858-2808; www.grandcanyon.

org; ☉8am-8pm Jun-Aug, shorter hours rest of year). Outdoor bulletin boards display information about trails, tours, ranger programs and the weather.

National Geographic Visitor Center (Map p854; ☏928-638-2468; www.explorethecanyon.com; 450 Hwy 64; IMAX adult/child $14/10; ☉visitor center 8am-10pm Mar-Oct, 9am-8pm Nov-Feb, theater 8:30am-8:30pm Mar-Oct, 9:30am-6:30pm Nov-Feb; ☐Tusayan) In Tusayan, 7 miles south of Grand Canyon Village; pay your $30 vehicle entrance fee here to spare yourself a potentially long wait at the park entrance. The IMAX theater screens the terrific film *Grand Canyon – The Hidden Secrets*. In addition to the visitor centers already mentioned, information is available inside the park:

Desert View Watchtower (Map p854; ☏928-638-8960; www.nps.gov/grca/learn/photos-multimedia/mary-colter---indian-watchtower.htm; Desert View, Desert View Dr; ☉8am-7pm Apr-Sep, to 6pm Oct-Mar; stairs close 30min before closing; P☞)

Kolb Studio (Map p854; ☏928-638-2771; www.nps.gov/grca/planyourvisit/art-exhibits.htm; Rim Trail, Grand Canyon Village Historic District; ☉8am-7pm Mar-May & Sep-Nov, to 6pm Dec-Feb, to 8pm Jun-Aug; ☐Village (Hermits Rest Route Transfer stop), ☐Hermits Rest (Mar 1-Nov 30; Village Route Transfer))

Tusayan Museum & Ruins (Map p854; ☏928-638-7888; www.nps.gov/grca; Desert View Dr; ☉9am-5pm; P☞)

Verkamp's Visitor Center (Map p854; ☏928-638-7888; www.nps.gov/grca/planyourvisit/verkamps.htm; Rim Trail, Grand Canyon Village Historic District; ☉8am-7pm Mar-late May & Sep-Nov, to 6pm Dec-Feb, to 8pm late May-Aug; ☐Village (Train Depot or Village East stop))

Yavapai Geology Museum (Map p854; ☏928-638-7888; www.nps.gov/grca/planyourvisit/yavapai-geo.htm; Rim Trail, Grand Canyon Village Historic District; ☉8am-7pm Mar-late May & Sep-Nov, to 6pm Dec-Feb, to 8pm late May-Aug; P☞; ☐Kaibab/Rim)

South Rim

If you don't mind bumping elbows with other travelers, you'll be fine on the South Rim, where you'll find an entire village worth of lodging, restaurants, bookstores, libraries, a supermarket and a deli. Museums and historic stone buildings illuminate the park's human history, and rangers lead daily programs on subjects from geology to resurgent condors. In summer, when day-trippers converge en masse, escaping the crowds can be as easy as taking a day hike below the rim or merely tramping a hundred yards away from a scenic overlook.

🏃 Activities

Driving & Hiking

A **scenic route** follows the rim on the west side of Grand Canyon Village along Hermit Rd. Closed to private vehicles March through November, the 7-mile road is serviced by free park shuttle buses; cycling is encouraged because of the relatively light traffic. Stops along the route offer spectacular views, and interpretive signs explain canyon features.

Desert View Drive starts east of Grand Canyon Village and follows the canyon rim for 26 miles to Desert View, the east entrance of the park. Pullouts offer tremendous views.

Hiking trails along the South Rim include options for every skill level. The **Rim Trail** is the most popular, and easiest, walk in the park. It dips in and out of the scrubby pines of Kaibab National Forest to connect scenic points and historical sights over 13 miles. Portions are paved, and every viewpoint is accessed by one of the three shuttle routes. Along the **Trail of Time**, bordering the Rim Trail just west of Yavapai Geology Museum, every meter represents one million years of geologic history.

Hiking down into the canyon itself is a serious undertaking; most visitors are content with short day hikes. Bear in mind that the climb back out of the canyon is much harder than the descent into it, and do not attempt to hike all the way to the Colorado River and back in a single day. On the most popular route, the beautiful **Bright Angel Trail**, the scenic 8-mile drop to the river is punctuated with four logical turnaround spots. Summer heat can be crippling; day hikers should either turn around at one of the two resthouses (a 3- or 6-mile round trip) or hit the trail at dawn to safely make the longer hikes to **Indian Garden** and **Plateau Point** (9.2- and 12.2-mile round trips, respectively).

The steeper and much more exposed **South Kaibab Trail** is one of the park's prettiest routes, combining stunning scenery and unobstructed 360-degree views with every step. Hikers overnighting at **Phantom Ranch** generally descend this way, and return the next day via the Bright Angel. Summer ascents can be dangerous, and during this season rangers advise day hikers to turn around at **Cedar Ridge** (about 3 miles round trip) for the park's finest short day hike.

Cycling

Bright Angel Bicycles & Cafe at Mather Point   CYCLING

(Map p854; ☑ bike shop 928-638-3055, reservations 928-679-0992; www.bikegrandcanyon. com; Grand Canyon Visitor Center Complex; 24hr rental adult/child 16yr & under $47/31.50, 5hr rental $31.50/20, wheelchair $10.50, single/double stroller up to 8hr $18/31; ⏱ 8am-6pm May–mid-Sep, 9am-5pm mid-Sep–Oct, 8am-5pm Mar & Apr; 🚼; 🚌 Village, 🚌 Kaibab/Rim) Bicycle rental and tours. Reserve in advance online or by phone; with the exception of the peak stretch from June through mid-August, however, walk-ins can usually be accommodated. Helmets included; add-on pull-along trailer options available. The recommended seasonal two-hour **Hermit Shuttle Package** (adult/child $36/26) shuttles riders from the shop to **Hopi Point** (Map p854; www. nps.gov/grca; Rim Trail, Hermit Rd; 🅿; 🚌 Hermits Rest west-bound (Mar 1-Nov 30)), and picks them up at **Hermits Rest** (Map p854; ☑ 928-638-2351; www.nps.gov/grca/learn/photosmultimedia/colter_hermits_photos.htm; Hermit Rd; ⏱ 8am-8pm May-Sep, 9am-5pm Oct-Mar, 9am-6:30pm Apr; 🚼; 🚌 Hermits Rest (Mar 1-Nov 30)).

👣 Tours

★ Grand Canyon Mule Rides   TOURS

(Map p854; ☑ 888-297-2757, next-day reservations 928-638-2631; www.grandcanyonlodges.com/plan/mule-rides; Bright Angel Lodge, Grand Canyon Village Historic District; 2hr mule ride $143, 1-/2-night mule ride incl meals & accommodations $606/875; per 2 people $1057/1440; ⏱ rides available year-round, hours vary; 🚼) If you want to descend into the canyon, the only option is an overnight to Phantom Ranch (p855). These 10-mule trains follow the **Bright Angel Trail** (Map p854; www.nps.gov/grca; Rim Trail, Grand Canyon Village Historic District; 🚼; 🚌 Village, 🚌 Hermits Rest (Mar 1-Nov 30)) 10.5 miles (5½ hours) down, spend one or two nights at Phantom Ranch, and return 7.8 miles (five hours) along the **South Kaibab Trail** (Map p854; www.nps.gov/grca; South Kaibab Trailhead, off Desert View Dr; 🚌 Kaibab/Rim). Alternatively, the 4-mile Canyon Vistas ride stays on the rim.

🛏 Sleeping

The South Rim's six lodges are operated by **Xanterra** (Grand Canyon Lodges; ☑ advanced reservations 888-297-2757, international 303-297-2757, reservations within 48hrs 928-638-2631; www.xanterra.com; 10 Albright St, Grand Canyon).

Grand Canyon National Park

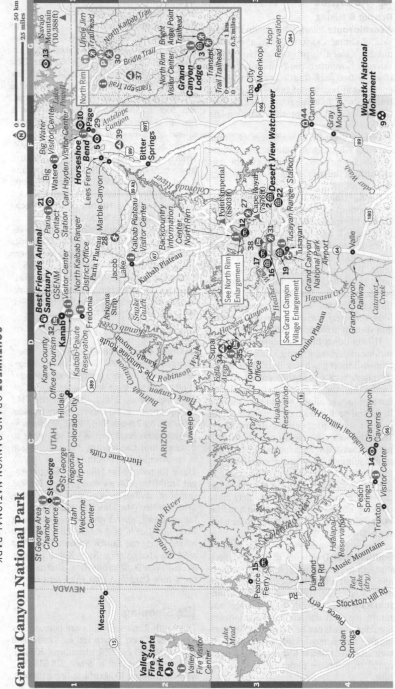

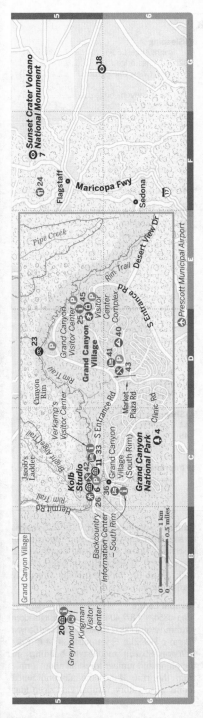

Contact them to make advance reservations (essential in summer), although it's best to call Phantom Ranch, down beside the Colorado River, directly. For same-day reservations or to reach a guest, call the South Rim **switchboard** (☎928-638-2631). If you can't find accommodations in the national park, try Tusayan (at South Rim Entrance Station), Valle (31 miles south), Cameron (53 miles east), Williams (about 60 miles south) or Flagstaff (80 miles southeast). All campgrounds and lodges are open year-round except Desert View.

★**Desert View Campground** CAMPGROUND $
(Map p854; www.nps.gov/grca/planyourvisit/cg-sr. htm; Desert View, Desert View Dr; campsites $12; ☺mid-Apr–mid-Oct; P🐾) 🍃 In the piñon-juniper 25 miles from the tourist hub of Grand Canyon Village and close to the rim, this first-come, first-served 50-site NPS campground is relatively quiet, with a spread-out design that ensures a bit of privacy. The best time to secure a spot is mid-morning, when people are breaking camp, and it usually fills by noon.

Facilities include toilets and drinking water, but no showers or hookups; there's a general store with basic supplies next door.

★**Bright Angel Lodge** LODGE $
(Map p854; ☎advanced reservations 888-297-2757, reservations within 48hr 928-638-2631; www. grandcanyonlodges.com; Rim Trail, Grand Canyon Village Historic District; r/cabins from $140/243; P🐾; 🚌Village) This 1935 log-and-stone **historic lodge** (Map p854; ☎928-638-2631; www.nps.gov/grca/learn/photosmultimedia/col ter_ba_photos.htm; Rim Trail, Grand Canyon Village Historic District; P👣; 🚌Village) on the canyon ledge delivers simple charm and the small public spaces bustle with activity. Buckey and Powell Lodge rooms, an excellent choice for budget accommodations, offer bright, handsome and simple rooms (refrigerator, but no TV) only steps from the rim, while rustic Rim Cabins and suites are some of the South Rim's best accommodations.

Phantom Ranch CABIN, DORMITORY $
(Map p854; ☎888-297-2757; www.grandcanyon lodges.com; bottom of canyon, 9.9 miles below South Rim on Bright Angel, 7.4 miles below South Rim on South Kaibab, 13.6 miles below North Rim on North Kaibab; dm $65, cabin d $169, available by lottery; 🐾) Bunks at this camp-like complex on the canyon floor are in private cabins sleeping two to 10 people and four hiker-only single-sex dorms, each with five bunks. Rates include bedding, soap and towels, but meals

Grand Canyon National Park

are extra and must be reserved when booking your accommodations. Phantom is accessible by mule trip, on foot or via raft on the Colorado River.

Trailer Village RV Park CARAVAN PARK $
(Map p854; ☏877-404-4611; www.visitgrand canyon.com; Market Plaza, Grand Canyon Village; RV sites with full hookups $49-59; ☉year-round; P☎🐾; 🚌Village east-bound) A trailer park with RVs lined up tightly at paved pull-through sites on a rather barren patch of ground. You'll find picnic tables, barbecue grills and full hookups, but coin-operated showers and laundry are a half-mile walk to

Camper Services (☏928-638-6350; www.vis itgrandcanyon.com/trailer-village-rv-park/rv-camp er-services; Market Plaza, Grand Canyon Village; ☉hours vary; 🚌Village). It's about a 1-mile walk along the bicycle-friendly Greenway Trail to the canyon rim.

Yavapai Lodge MOTEL $$
(Map p854; ☏877-404-4611; www.visitgrandcan yon.com/yavapai-lodge; Market Plaza, Grand Canyon Village; r $168-212; ☉year-round; P☀@☎🐾; 🚌Village) Sixteen motel-style buildings in the piñon and juniper forest sit about a mile from the rim. Handsome air-conditioned rooms at two-story Yavapai East sleep four

to six; family rooms include bunk beds. Pet-friendly drive-up rooms in single-story Yavapai West sleep up to four, but do not have air-conditioning and are more dated.

⭐**El Tovar**   LODGE $$$
(Map p854; ☑ advanced reservations 888-297-2757, reservations within 48hr 928-638-2631; www. grandcanyonlodges.com; Rim Trail, Grand Canyon Village Historic District; r $263-354; ⊙ year-round; 🅿 ❄ 🛜; 🚍 Village west-bound (Train Depot stop)) Perched on the Rim Trail at the canyon edge, the public spaces of this 1905 wooden lodge ooze old-world national-park glamour and charm. Unfortunately, the 78 rooms and suites do not consistently share the historic aesthetic; some are lovely, with four-poster beds or a spectacular balcony, but standard rooms rival roadside motels. Stay here for the service and location.

🍴 Eating & Drinking

Grand Canyon Village has all the eating options you need, but nobody comes to Grand Canyon for the food! Arizona Room, El Tovar and **Harvey House Cafe** (Map p854; ☑ 928-638-2631; www.grandcanyonlodges. com/dine/harvey-house-cafe; Bright Angel Lodge, Grand Canyon Village Historic District; mains $13-21; ⊙ 6:30am-10pm; 🛗; 🚍 Village west-bound) are the only table-service restaurants on the South Rim, though several bars serve small plates and snacks. The other restaurants are cafeteria-style or fast food. You can make advanced reservations (dinner only) at Arizona Room and El Tovar.

    Phantom Ranch Canteen (Map p854; ☑ US 888-297-2757, outside US 303-297-2757; www. grandcanyonlodges.com/dine/phantom-ranch-cafe; Phantom Ranch, (bottom of the canyon); breakfast $23.65, dinner vegetarian stew/steak $24/48; ⊙ breakfast 5am & 6:30am, Apr-Oct, 5:30am & 7am Nov-Mar, dinner 5pm & 6:30pm, canteen 8am-4pm & 8-10pm, from 8:30am Nov-Mar), below the rim near the Colorado River, offers family-style breakfasts and dinners by advanced reservation only.

Yavapai Lodge Restaurant   CAFETERIA $
(Map p854; www.visitgrandcanyon.com; Yavapai Lodge, Grand Canyon Village; breakfast $7-9, lunch & dinner $10-16; ⊙ 7am-9pm; 🅿 🛗; 🚍 Village)) Breakfast buffet ($15) or à la carte; lunch and dinner are barbecue, hot and cold sandwiches and pizza, as well as beer and wine. Place your order on a touchscreen, pick up your drinks, and your number will be called when the food is ready. Efficient

and convenient, but not much better than what you'd expect at a school cafeteria.

⭐**El Tovar Dining Room**   AMERICAN $$$
(Map p854; ☑ 928-638-2631; www.grandcanyon lodges.com/dine/el-tovar-dining-room-and-lounge; El Tovar, Grand Canyon Village Historic District; mains $20-30; ⊙ restaurant 6:30-10:30am, 11:15am-2pm & 4:30-9:30pm, lounge 11:30am-11pm; 🅿 🛗; 🚍 Village) Classic national park dining at its best. Dark-wood tables are set with china and white linen, eye-catching murals spotlight American Indian tribes and huge windows frame views of the Rim Trail and canyon beyond. Breakfast options include El Tovar's pancake trio (buttermilk, blue cornmeal and buckwheat pancakes with pine-nut butter and prickly-pear syrup), and blackened trout with two eggs.

Arizona Room   AMERICAN $$$
(Map p854; ☑ ex 6432 928-638-2631; www.grand-canyonlodges.com/dine/arizona-room; Bright Angel Lodge, Grand Canyon Village Historic District; lunch $13-26, dinner $27-40; ⊙ 11:30am-3pm & 4:30-9:30pm Feb-Oct, dinner only Nov-Jan; 🛗; 🚍 Village) Antler chandeliers hang from the ceiling, picture windows overlook the Rim Trail and canyon beyond, and the seasonal menu gives a Western vibe. Reservations (dinner only) are accepted online or by phone 30 days in advance, but are usually available within the week.

ℹ️ Getting There & Around

Most people arrive at the canyon in private vehicles or on a tour. Parking can be a chore in Grand Canyon Village. Once inside the park, free park shuttles operate along three routes: around Grand Canyon Village, west along Hermits Rest Route and east along Kaibab Trail Route. Buses typically run every 15 minutes, from one hour before sunset to one hour afterward. In summer a free shuttle from Bright Angel Lodge, the Hiker's Express, has early-morning pickups at the Backcountry Information Center and Grand Canyon Visitor Center, and then heads to the South Kaibab trailhead.

North Rim

Solitude reigns supreme on the North Rim. There are no shuttles or bus tours, no museums, shopping centers, schools or garages. In fact, there isn't much of anything here beyond a classic rimside national park lodge, a campground, a motel, a general store and miles of trails carving through sunny meadows thick with wildflowers, willowy aspen and towering ponderosa pines

The entrance to the North Rim is 24 miles south of **Jacob Lake** on Hwy 67; Grand Canyon Lodge (p858) lies another 20 miles beyond. At 8000ft, it's about 10°F (6°C) cooler here than the South Rim – even on summer evenings you'll need a sweater. All facilities on the North Rim are closed from mid-October to mid-May, although you can drive into the park and stay at the campground until snow closes the road from Jacob Lake.

🏃 Activities

The short and easy, half-mile paved trail to **Bright Angel Point** (Map p854; www.nps.gov/grca) is a canyon must. Beginning from the back porch of Grand Canyon Lodge, it goes to a narrow finger of an overlook with fabulous views.

The **North Kaibab Trail** (Map p854; www.nps.gov/grca; Inner Canyon), the North Rim's only maintained rim-to-river trail, connects with trails to the South Rim in the Phantom Ranch (p855) area. The first 4.7 miles are the steepest, dropping 3050ft to **Roaring Springs** – a popular all-day hike. If you prefer a shorter day hike below the rim, walk just 0.75 miles down to **Coconino Overlook**, or 2 miles to the **Supai Tunnel** to get a taste of steep inner-canyon hiking. The 28-mile round trip to the Colorado River is a multiday affair.

For a short hike up on the rim, which works well for families, try the 4-mile round-trip **Cape Final Trail** (Map p854; www.nps.gov/grca; Cape Royal Rd), on the **Walhalla Plateau** east of Grand Canyon Lodge, which leads through ponderosa pines to sweeping views of the eastern Grand Canyon area.

Canyon Trail Rides   TOURS
(Map p854; ☏435-679-8665; www.canyon rides.com; North Rim; 1/3hr mule ride $45/90; ⊗7:30am, 8:30am, 12:30pm, 1:30pm, 2:30pm mid-May–mid-Oct) You can make reservations anytime for the upcoming year, but, unlike mule trips on the South Rim, you can usually book a trip upon your arrival at the park; just duck inside the Grand Canyon Lodge to the Mule Desk. Rides don't reach the Colorado River, but the North Kaibab Trail trip gives a taste of life below the rim.

Each of the three rides has specific age and weight restrictions, but if you're under 7 years old or weigh over 220lbs, you're out of luck.

Book in advance online or by calling ☏928-638-9875 within a week of your ride.

🛏 Sleeping & Eating

North Rim Campground   CAMPGROUND $
(Map p854; ☏877-444-6777; www.recreation.gov; tent sites $18, RV sites $18-25; ⊗by reservation May 15-Oct 15, first-come, first-served Oct 16-31; 🐾) Operated by the NPS, this campground, 1.5 miles north of the Grand Canyon Lodge, offers shaded sites on level ground among the ponderosas. Sites 11, 14, 15, 16 and 18 have canyon views...and cost $25 – but site 10 is pretty sweet too. You can – and should – make reservations online up to six months in advance.

Walk-up sites are available for hikers and bikers only. There's water, a store, a snack bar, coin-operated showers and laundry facilities, but no hookups.

Grand Canyon Lodge   HISTORIC HOTEL $$
(Map p854; ☏advance reservations 877-386-4383, same-day reservations 928-638-2611; www.grand canyonforever.com; r/cabins from $146/161; ⊗May 15-Oct 15) 🐾 Guest rooms are not in the **lodge** (Map p854) itself; most are in log cabins nearby. Four of the Western Cabins have the only canyon views to speak of, and that's where you want to be if you can justify the $22 surcharge. Book them at least a year in advance.

Grand Canyon
Lodge Dining Room   AMERICAN $$
(Map p854; ☏May-Oct 928-638-8560; www.grandcanyonforever.com/dining; breakfast $8-11, lunch $10-15, dinner $18-35; ⊗6:30-10am, 11:30am-2:30pm & 4:30-9:30pm May 15-Oct 15; 🐾🍴) While the solid dinner menu includes buffalo steak, western trout and several vegetarian options, don't expect great culinary memories – the view is the thing. Lunch is just OK, and the breakfast buffet is entirely forgettable; order something prepared. Although seats beside the window are wonderful, views from the dining room are so huge it really doesn't matter where you sit.

If you didn't make reservations in advance for dinner, you can still take advantage of the buffet across the lobby ($33; 4:30pm to 6:15pm) which has disappointing cafeteria sides to go with the delicious hand-cut steaks.

ℹ Information

Backcountry Information Center – North Rim (Map p854; ☏928-638-7875; www.nps.gov/grca; Administrative Bldg; ⊗8am-5pm May 15-Oct 15) Backcountry permits for overnight camping on and below the rim, at Tuweep Campground, or camping anytime between November 1 and May 14.

RAFTING THE COLORADO

A boat trip down the Colorado is an epic, adrenaline-pumping adventure, which will take you beyond contact with civilization for several nights. The biggest single drop at Lava Falls plummets 37ft in just 300yd. But the true highlight is experiencing the Grand Canyon by looking up, not down from the rim. Its human history comes alive in ruins, wrecks and rock art. Commercial trips run from three days to three weeks and vary in the type of watercraft used.

Arizona Raft Adventures (Map p848; ☑ 800-786-7238, 928-526-8200; www.azraft.com; 4050 East Huntington Dr, Flagstaff, AZ 86004; 6-16-day raft trips $2305-4675, 8-/10-day motor trips $2945/3455) This multi-generational family-run outfit offers motor, oar and paddle (with opportunities for both paddling and floating) trips. Look online for details on photography, music, yoga and kayak 'specialty adventure' trips.

Arizona River Runners (☑ 800-477-7238, 602-867-4866; www.raftarizona.com; 15211 North Cave Creek Rd, Suite A, Phoenix AZ, 85032; 3-day combined ranch visit & motor trips from $1475, 13-day full-canyon oar trips from $4145) At its game since 1970, this outfit offers oar-powered and motorized trips. In addition to regular trips it has 'Hiker's Special' trips that take place over five to 15 days in the cooler temperatures of April. The company also caters to travelers with special needs, offering departures for people with disabilities.

Kaibab National Forest Visitor Center (Jacob Lake) Go here for the skinny on dispersed camping and viewpoints outside the park.

North Rim Visitor Center (Map p854; ☑ 928-638-7888; www.nps.gov/grca; ⊙ 8am-6pm May 15-Oct 15) Beside Grand Canyon Lodge, this is the place to get information on the park, and the starting point for ranger-led nature walks.

❶ Getting There & Away

The only access road to the Grand Canyon North Rim is Hwy 67, which closes with the first snowfall and reopens in spring after the snowmelt (exact dates vary).

Although only 11 miles from the South Rim as the crow flies, it's a grueling 215-mile, four- to five-hour drive on winding desert roads between here and Grand Canyon Village. You can drive yourself or take the **Trans-Canyon Shuttle** (☑ 928-638-2820; www.trans-canyonshuttle.com; one way $90). Reserve at least two weeks in advance.

Although trails do connect the two rims, the three-day route should not be attempted by anyone except experienced canyon hikers in excellent physical condition.

Around the Grand Canyon

Havasupai Canyon

In a hidden side canyon off the Colorado River, complete with stunning, spring-fed waterfalls and azure swimming holes, this beautiful spot is hard to reach, but the hike down and back up makes the trip unique – and an amazing adventure.

Located on the Havasupai Indian Reservation, Havasu Canyon is just 35 miles directly west of the South Rim, but it's more like 195 miles by road. The four falls lie 10 miles below the rim, accessed via a moderately challenging hiking trail that starts from Hualapai Hilltop, and is reached by following a 62-mile road that leaves Route 66 7 miles east of Peach Springs.

All trips require an overnight stay, which must be reserved in advance.

The village of Supai, 8 miles along the trail, is home to **Supai Lodge** (Map p854; ☑ 928-448-2111, 928-448-2201; www.theofficialhavasupaitribe.com; Supai; r for up to 4 people $440, plus entrance fee per person $110; ⊙ Feb-Nov; ❄), where basic motel-style rooms have nothing to recommend them bar the location. Reservations must be made a year in advance. The **Supai Cafe** (Map p854; Supai; mains $5.50-13; ⊙ hours vary) serves hamburgers, bean burritos and a frybread taco.

The **Havasu Campground** (Map p854; ☑ 928-448-2180; www.havasupaireservations.com; Havasu Canyon; per person 3 nights $300-375; ⊙ Feb-Nov), 2 miles beyond, has primitive campsites along a creek. There are several composting toilets, and drinking water is available. Although the campground accommodates 350 people per night, not all campsites are designated – expect a somewhat crowded experience. Getting a permit to camp is a maddeningly near-impossible thing – begin planning more than a year before your trip.

Continue deeper into Havasu Canyon to reach the waterfalls and blue-green swimming holes.

For detailed information about traveling into Havasu Canyon, see www.theofficialhavasupaitribe.com.

Hualapai Reservation

Run by the Hualapai Nation, around 215 driving miles west of the South Rim or 70 miles northeast of Kingman, the remote site known as Grand Canyon West is NOT part of Grand Canyon National Park.

If you're coming from Peach Springs, note that it's a two-hour drive, even though it looks closer. Check the directions on the website before you head out as there's no cell service here. Don't miss the Joshua Tree Forest on the way in.

Grand Canyon West VIEWPOINT
(Map p854; ☑928-769-2636, 888-868-9378; www.grandcanyonwest.com; Hualapai Reservation; per person $47-77; ☑7am-7pm Apr-Sep, 8am-5pm Oct-Mar) The only way to visit Grand Canyon West, the section of the Grand Canyon overseen by the Hualapai Nation, is to purchase a package tour. These are based on a hop-on, hop-off shuttle ride, which loops to three stops along the rim. Tours include two viewpoints, cowboy activities at an ersatz Western town and informal American Indian performances. The **Skywalk**, a glass platform perched 4000ft above the canyon floor, is the primary draw, vertigo permitting.

Northern & Eastern Arizona

Between the brooding buttes of Monument Valley, the blue waters of Lake Powell and the fossilized logs of the Petrified Forest National Park are photogenic lands locked in ancient history. Inhabited by Native Americans for centuries, this region is dominated by the Navajo reservation – widely known as the Navajo Nation – which spills into surrounding states. The Hopi reservation is here as well, completely surrounded by Navajo land.

Lake Powell

The country's second-largest artificial reservoir, Lake Powell, stretches north from Arizona into Utah. Set amid striking redrock formations, sharply cut canyons and dramatic desert scenery, and part of the **Glen Canyon National Recreation Area**

(☑928-608-6200; www.nps.gov/glca; 7-day pass per vehicle $30, per pedestrian or cyclist $15), it's water-sports heaven. For stand-up paddleboard and kayak rentals, try **Lake Powell Paddleboards** (Map p854; ☑928-645-4017; www.lakepowellpaddleboards.com; 836 Vista Ave; per day SUP/kayak/bike $40/30/35; ☑8am-6pm Apr-Sep, 9am-5pm Oct-Mar).

The lake was created by the construction of Glen Canyon Dam, 2.5 miles north of what's now the region's central town, Page. The Carl Hayden Visitor Center is located beside the dam.

To visit otherworldly **Antelope Canyon**, a stunning sandstone slot canyon, you must join a Navajo-led tour. Several tour companies offer trips into **Upper Antelope Canyon**, which is easier to navigate. Expect a bumpy ride and a bit of a cattle call; try **Roger Ekis' Antelope Canyon Tours** (Map p854; ☑928-645-9102; www.antelopecanyon.com; 22 S Lake Powell Blvd; adult/child from $60/50; ☑tours 7am-4:30pm). The more strenuous **Lower Antelope Canyon** sees much smaller crowds.

A deservedly popular hike is the 1.2 mile round trip to **Horseshoe Bend** (Map p854; Hwy 89; parking $10; ☑sunrise-sunset), where the Colorado wraps around a stone outcrop to form a perfect U on a jaw-dropping scale. The trailhead is south of Page off Hwy 89, across from mile marker 541.

Chain hotels line Page's main strip, Hwy 89, but there are independent alternatives along 8th Ave. Experience the beauty of the Navajo land from up close at **Shash Diné EcoRetreat** (Map p854; ☑928-640-3701; www.shashdine.com; off Hwy 89; r $150-200), a family ranch where visitors can stay in a traditional hogan, covered sheepherder wagon, canvas tent or cabin. Breakfast is included; at night bring your own food to enjoy around the campfire.

For breakfast in Page, the **Ranch House Grille** (Map p854; ☑928-645-1420; www.ranchhousegrille.com/page; 819 N Navajo Dr; mains $9-15; ☑6am-3pm) has good food, huge portions and fast service. Later in the day, settle in at **State 48 Tavern** (Map p854; ☑928-645-1912; www.state48tavern.com; 614 N Navajo Dr; sandwiches $12-14, mains $18-27; ☑5-10pm Wed-Fri & Mon, from 11am Sat & Sun), where dishes include pear-and-gorgonzola burgers and coconut shrimp tacos, and the beer selection is good.

Navajo Nation

The Navajo Nation is vast: at 27,000 sq miles it's bigger than some US states, and spreads across the junction of Arizona, New Mexico,

Colorado and Utah. It also contains natural beauty of staggering richness, and, of course, the living culture, language, institutions, farms and homes of the Diné (Navajo), the country's largest American Indian nation.

Unlike the rest of Arizona, the Navajo Nation observes mountain daylight saving time. During summer, the reservation is one hour ahead of Arizona. For details about hiking and camping, and required permits, visit www.navajonationparks.org.

CAMERON

This historic settlement serves as the gateway to the east entrance of the Grand Canyon's South Rim, which is 32 miles away. The tiny, windswept community is one of the few worthwhile stops on Hwy 89 between Flagstaff and Page. The **Cameron Trading Post** (Map p854; ☑ 928-679-2231; www.camerontradingpost.com; Hwy 89; ☺ 6am-10pm Mar-Oct, shorter hours Nov-Feb), just north of the Hwy 64 turnoff to the Grand Canyon, offers food, lodging, a gift shop and a post office.

NAVAJO NATIONAL MONUMENT

The sublimely well-preserved Ancestral Puebloan cliff dwellings of Betatakin and Keet Seel are protected within the **Navajo National Monument** (☑ 928-672-2700; nps.gov/nava; Hwy 564; ☺ visitor center 8am-5:30pm Jun-early Sep, 9am-5pm rest of year) **FREE** and can only be reached on foot. This walk in the park is no walk in the park, but there's truly something magical about approaching these ancient stone villages in relative solitude, among the piñon and juniper. The National Park Service controls access to the site and maintains the visitor center, which is informative and has excellent staff.

During summer months, the park observes daylight saving time.

CANYON DE CHELLY NATIONAL MONUMENT

The many-fingered Canyon De Chelly (duh-*shay*) contains several beautiful Ancestral Puebloan sites, including ancient cliff dwellings. For centuries, though, it has been home to Navajo farmers, who winter on the rims then move to hogans (traditional roundhouses) on the canyon floor in spring and summer. The canyon is private Navajo property administered by the NPS. Enter hogans only with a guide and don't photograph people without their permission.

The only lodging in the park is **Thunderbird Lodge** (☑ 928-674-5842, 800-679-2473; www.thunderbirdlodge.com; Rural Rte 7; r $100-130; ✳ ☎ ☀ ☀), just outside the canyon itself. It has comfortable rooms and an inexpensive cafeteria serving Navajo and American meals. The nearby Navajo-run campground has about 90 sites on a first-come, first-served basis ($14), with water but no showers. Cash only. The peaceful, Navajo-run **Spider Rock Campground** (☑ 928-781-2016, 928-781-2014; www.spiderrockcampground.com; Navajo Hwy 7; tent/RV sites $11/16, hogans $31-47; ☎ ☀) on the South Rim Drive is surrounded by piñon and juniper trees

The Canyon de Chelly **visitor center** (☑ 928-674-5500; www.nps.gov/cach; Rte 7; ☺ 8am-5pm) is 3 miles off Rte 191, beyond the small village of Chinle, near the mouth of the canyon. Two scenic drives follow the canyon's rim, but you can only explore the canyon floor on a guided tour. Stop by the visitor center, or check the park website, for a list of tour companies. The only unguided hiking trail you can follow in the park is a short but very

SOUTHWEST NORTHERN & EASTERN ARIZONA

HOPI RESERVATION

Direct descendants of the Ancestral Puebloans, the Hopi have arguably changed less in the last five centuries than any other Native American group. Their village of Old Oraibi may be the oldest continuously inhabited settlement in North America. Hopi land is surrounded on all sides by the Navajo Nation. Hwy 264 runs past the three mesas (First, Second and Third Mesa) that form the heart of the reservation.

On Second Mesa, 8 miles west of First Mesa, the **Hopi Cultural Center Restaurant & Inn** (☑ 928-734-2401; www.hopiculturalcenter.com; Mile 379, Hwy 264; r from $100; ☺ restaurant 7am-9pm; ✳ ☎ ☀) is as visitor-oriented as things get on the Hopi reservation. It provides food and lodging, and holds the small **Hopi Museum** (☑ 928-734-6650; Mile 379, Hwy 264; adult/child $3/1; ☺ 8:30am-5pm Mon-Fri, 9am-3pm Sat), filled with historic photographs and cultural exhibits.

Photographs, sketching and recording are not allowed anywhere on the reservation. Alcohol and drug use are also prohibited.

spectacular round-trip route that descends to the amazing **White House Ruin**.

MONUMENT VALLEY NAVAJO TRIBAL PARK

When Monument Valley rises into sight from the desert floor, it is surprisingly familiar. Its brick-red spindles, sheer-walled mesas and grand buttes, stars of countless films, TV commercials and magazine ads, are part of the modern consciousness. And Monument Valley's epic beauty is only heightened by the barren landscape surrounding it.

For up-close views of the towering formations, visit the **Monument Valley Navajo Tribal Park** (☑435-727-5870; www.navajonation parks.org; per 4-person vehicle $20; ☺drive 6am-7pm Apr-Sep, 8am-4:30pm Oct-Mar, visitor center 6am-8pm Apr-Sep, 8am-5pm Oct-Mar), where a rough and unpaved scenic driving loop covers 15 miles of stunning valley views. You can drive it yourself, or arrange a tour through one of the kiosks in the parking lot, which will take you to areas where private vehicles can't go (1½ hours $65; two-hour trail ride $150).

Inside the tribal park, the sandstone-colored **View Hotel** (☑435-727-5555; www.monumentvalleyview.com; Indian Rte 42, Monument Valley Navajo Tribal Park; r/ste from $210/349; ❋@☎) blends naturally with its surroundings, and most of the 95 rooms have private balconies facing the monuments. The Navajo-accented food at the adjoining restaurant (mains $11 to $15, no alcohol) aren't life-changing, but the vista makes up for all.

The peerlessly-situated **View Campground** (☑435-727-5802; www.monumentval leyview.com/campground; Indian Rte 42, Monument Valley Navajo Tribal Park; tent & RV sites $30; ☺Mar-Oct) is a cheaper option, while historic **Goulding's Lodge** (☑435-727-3231; www.gouldings.com; Monument Valley, Utah; d from $245, apt $310-330; ❋☎❋❋), just over the road in Utah, offers basic rooms, camping and small cabins. Book early for summer. Kayenta, 20 miles south, has a handful of acceptable motels and borderline-acceptable restaurants; try the **Wetherill Inn** (☑928-697-3231; www.wetherill-inn.com; 1000 Main St/Hwy 163; r $155; ❋@☎❋) if everything in Monument Valley is booked.

Petrified Forest National Park

Home not only to an extraordinary array of fossilized logs that predate the dinosaurs but also the multicolored sandscape of the Painted Desert, this **national park** (☑928-524-6228; www.nps.gov/pefo; vehicle/cyclist $20/10; ☺7am-7pm mid-Apr–Aug, shorter hours rest of year) is a compulsory spectacle. The park straddles I-40 at exit 311, 25 miles east of **Holbrook**. Its **visitor center** (☑928-524-6228; 1 Park Rd, Petrified Forest National Park; ☺8am-6pm mid-Apr–mid-Oct, to 5pm rest of year), just half a mile north of I-40, holds maps and information on guided tours, while the 28-mile paved park road beyond offers a splendid scenic drive. There are no campsites, but a number of short trails, ranging from less than a mile to 2 miles, pass through the stands of petrified trees and ancient Native American dwellings. Those prepared for rugged backcountry camping need to pick up a free permit at the visitor center.

Western Arizona

Sun worshippers flock to the Colorado River in and around Lake Havasu City, while road-trippers cruise Route 66, which offers well-preserved stretches of classic highway near Kingman. Much further south, beyond I-10 towards Mexico, the wild, empty landscape is among the most barren in the West. If you're already here, there are some worthwhile sites, but there's nothing worth planning an itinerary around unless you're a Route 66 or boating fanatic.

Kingman & Around

Among Route 66 aficionados, Kingman is known as the main hub of the longest uninterrupted stretch of the historic highway, running from Topock to Seligman. Among its early-20th-century buildings is the former Methodist church at 5th and Spring Sts where Clark Gable and Carole Lombard eloped in 1939. Hometown hero Andy Devine had his Hollywood breakthrough as the perpetually befuddled driver of the eponymous *Stagecoach* in John Ford's Oscar-winning 1939 movie.

Pick up maps and brochures at the historic **Kingman Visitor Center** (Map p854; ☑928-753-6106, 866-427-7866; www.goking man.com; 120 W Andy Devine Ave; ☺8am-5pm), housed in an old powerhouse and entailing a small but engaging Route 66 museum and a display of electric cars.

Wednesday through Sunday, drive up to the **Hualapai Mountain Resort** (☑928-757-3545; www.hmresort.net; 4525 Hualapai Mountain Rd; r/ste from $79/159; ☺Wed-Sun; ☎) and its restaurant, set amid towering pines, There's tasty pit-smoked meats at **Floyd & Co Real Pit BBQ** (Map p854; 928-757-8227; www.floyd andcompany.com; 420 E Beale St; mains $8.50-13; 11am-8pm Tue-Thu, to 9pm Fri & Sat) and commendable coffee at **Beale Street Brews** (Map p854; 928-753-1404; www.bealestreet brews.net; 510 E Beale St; 6am-6pm;).

Southern Arizona

This is a land of Stetsons and spurs, where cowboy ballads are sung around the campfire under starry, black-velvet skies and thick steaks sizzle on the grill. Anchored by the bustling college town of Tucson, it's a vast region, where long, dusty highways slide past rolling vistas and steep, pointy mountain ranges. Majestic saguaro cacti, the symbol of the region, stretch out as far as the eye can see.

Tucson

Fun-loving, outdoorsy and one of the most culturally invigorating places in the Southwest, Tucson (*too*-sawn) is an unexpected treasure. Set in a flat valley hemmed in by snaggletoothed mountains and swathes of saguaro, Arizona's second-largest city smoothly blends Native American, Spanish, Mexican and Anglo traditions. Distinct neighborhoods and 19th-century buildings give a rich sense of community and history not found in the more modern, sprawling Phoenix. The eclectic shops toting

vintage garb, scores of funky restaurants and dive bars don't let you forget Tucson is a college town at heart, home turf to the 45,000-strong University of Arizona (UA).

◉ Sights & Activities

Downtown Tucson and the historic district lie east of I-10 exit 258. The University of Arizona campus is a mile northeast of downtown; 4th Ave, the main drag here, is packed with cafes, bars and interesting shops. Many of Tucson's most fabulous treasures lie on the periphery, or even beyond town.

★**Arizona-Sonora Desert Museum** MUSEUM
(520-883-2702; www.desertmuseum.org; 2021 N Kinney Rd; adult/senior/child $22/20/9; 8:30am-5pm Oct-Feb, 7:30am-5pm Mar-Sep, to 10pm Sat Jun-Aug) Home to cacti, coyotes and palm-sized hummingbirds, this 98-acre ode to the Sonoran Desert is part zoo, part botanical garden and part museum – a trifecta that'll entertain young and old for half a day easily. Desert denizens, from precocious coatis to playful prairie dogs, inhabit natural enclosures, the grounds are thick with desert plants, and docents give demonstrations. Strollers and wheelchairs are available, and there's a gift shop, an art gallery, a restaurant and a cafe.

Arizona State Museum MUSEUM
(520-621-6302; www.statemuseum.arizona.edu; 1013 E University Blvd; adult/senior/child $8/6/

SOUTHWEST SOUTHERN ARIZONA

ROADSIDE ATTRACTIONS ON ROUTE 66

Four hundred miles of America's Highway stretches across Arizona, with plenty of kitschy sights, listed here from west to east, along the way.

Wild burros of Oatman Feral mules, the progeny of mining days, beg for treats in the middle of the road.

Grand Canyon Caverns & Inn (Map p854; 928-422-3223; www.gccaverns.com; Mile 115, Rte 66; tour adult/child from $16/11; 9am-5pm May-Sep, 9:30am-4pm Oct-Apr) A guided tour 21 stories underground loops past mummified bobcats, civil-defense supplies and a $900 motel room (or cave).

Burma Shave signs Red-and-white ads from a bygone era between Grand Canyon Caverns and Seligman.

Snow Cap Drive-In (928-422-3291; www.delgadillossnowcap.t2-food.com; 301 East Chino; mains $5-6.50; 10am-6pm Mar-Nov) Prankish burger and ice-cream joint open in Seligman since 1953.

Meteor Crater (Map p854; 800-289-5898; www.meteorcrater.com; Meteor Crater Rd; adult/senior/child $18/16/9; 7am-7pm Jun–mid-Sep, 8am-5pm mid-Sep–May) A 550ft-deep pockmark that's nearly 1 mile across, 38 miles east of Flagstaff.

Wigwam Motel (928-524-3048; www.galerie-kokopelli.com/wigwam; 811 W Hopi Dr; r $70-76;) Concrete wigwams with hickory logpole furniture in Holbrook.

free; ⊙10am-5pm Mon-Sat) To learn more about the history and culture of the region's American Indian tribes, visit the Arizona State Museum, the oldest and largest anthropology museum in the Southwest. The exhibit covering the tribes' cultural histories is extensive but easy to navigate, and should appeal to newbies and history buffs alike. These galleries are complemented by much-envied collections of minerals and Navajo textiles.

Old Tucson Studios FILM LOCATION

(☑520-883-0100; www.oldtucson.com; 201 S Kinney Rd; adult/senior/child $20/18/11; ⊙generally 10am-5pm Fri-Sun, closed Sep; 🅿) Nicknamed 'Hollywood in the Desert,' this old movie set of Tucson in the 1860s was built in 1939 for the filming of *Arizona*. Hundreds of flicks followed, bringing in movie stars from Clint Eastwood to Leonardo DiCaprio. Now a Wild West theme park, it's all about shoot-outs, stagecoach rides, stunt shows and dancing saloon girls. Hours vary by month – check online before you go.

Tucson Museum of Art MUSEUM

(☑520-624-2333; www.tucsonmuseumofart.org; 140 N Main Ave; adult/senior/child $12/10/7; ⊙10am-5pm Tue-Sun) For a small city, Tucson boasts an impressive art museum. There's a respectable collection of American, Latin American and modern art, and the permanent exhibition of pre-Columbian artifacts will awaken your inner Indiana Jones. The special exhibits are varied and interesting, there's a superb gift shop, and the block surrounding the building holds a number of notable historic homes. The museum stays open to 8pm on the first Thursday of the month, when admission is free from 5pm.

Pima Air & Space Museum MUSEUM

(☑520-574-0462; www.pimaair.org; 6000 E Valencia Rd; adult/senior/child $16.50/13.75/10; ⊙9am-5pm, last entry 3pm) An SR-71 Blackbird spy plane and a massive B-52 bomber are among the stars of this extraordinary private aircraft museum. Allow at least two hours to wander through hangars and across the airfield where more than 300 'birds' trace the evolution of civilian and military aviation. Take a self-guided tour using the museum's GPS-guided app, or pay an extra $6 for the one-hour tram tour departing at 10am, 11:30am, 1:30pm and 3pm from November to May.

★**Pedego** BIKE RENTALS

(☑520-441-9782; www.pedegoelectricbikes.com; 4340 N Campbell Ave, Suite 107B; half-/full-day cruisers from $45/65, mountain bikes $80/125; ⊙7am-3pm Wed-Sun) If you've never had the pleasure of riding an electric bike – which use pedal-assist technology, so you still get some exercise – this is your chance. Conveniently located steps from the Loop, you'll have plenty to explore. Even better, rent a mountain bike. You'll never feel the same about those grueling uphills again.

★☆ Festivals & Events

Tucson Gem & Mineral Show CULTURAL

(☑520-332-5773; www.tgms.org; ⊙Feb) The most famous event on the city's calendar, held on the second full weekend in February, this is the largest gem and mineral show in the world. An estimated 250 retail dealers who trade in minerals, crafts and fossils take over the Tucson Convention Center and other venues around town.

🛏 Sleeping

Lodging prices vary considerably, with lower rates in summer and fall. To sleep under the stars and saguaros, try **Gilbert Ray Campground** (☑520-883-4200; www.webcms. pima.gov; 8451 W McCain Loop Rd; tent/RV sites $10/20; 🅿) near the western district of Saguaro National Park.

★**Hotel Congress** HISTORIC HOTEL $

(☑520-622-8848; www.hotelcongress.com; 311 E Congress St; d from $120; 🅿🅰🛜🐾) Perhaps Tucson's most famous hotel, this is where infamous bank robber John Dillinger and his gang were captured during their 1934 stay, when a fire broke out. Built in 1919 and beautifully restored, this charismatic place feels very modern, despite period furnishings such as rotary phones and wooden radios (no TVs). There are a popular cafe, bar and club on-site.

★**Catalina Park Inn** B&B $$

(☑520-792-4541; www.catalinaparkinn.com; 309 E 1st St; r $125-195; ⊙late Sep–May; 🅿@🛜🐾) Style, hospitality and comfort merge seamlessly at this inviting B&B just west of the University of Arizona. Hosts Mark and Paul have poured their hearts into restoring this 1927 Mediterranean-style villa, and their efforts are on display in the six rooms, which vary in style. Don't miss the delicious breakfast – burritos, croissant French toast and more await in the mornings.

Under Canvas
GLAMPING **$$**

(📞520-303-9412; www.undercanvas.com; 14301 E Speedway; tents from $149; ⊗Sep-May; 🛜🏊) Dreaming of spending the night in the Sonoran Desert but unsure about mixing sleeping bags with snakes? This high-end camp, just a 10-minute drive from the Saguaro National Park, could be for you. Unwind in one of three tent styles (Deluxe, Stargazer and Safari), all of which come with king-sized beds, bathrooms and showers.

★Hacienda del Sol
RANCH **$$$**

(📞520-299-1501; www.haciendadelsol.com; 5501 N Hacienda del Sol Rd; r from $300; ❄@🛜🏊) An elite hilltop girls' school built in the 1920s, this relaxing refuge has artist-designed Southwest-style rooms and teems with unique touches such carved ceiling beams and louvered exterior doors to catch the courtyard breeze. The Hacienda del Sol has sheltered Spencer Tracy, Katharine Hepburn, John Wayne and other legends, so you'll be sleeping with history. Its restaurant, the Grill, is fabulous too.

✖ Eating

★Tumerico
VEGETARIAN **$**

(📞520-240-6947; www.tumerico.com; 2526 E 6th St; meals $14; ⊗8am-8pm Wed-Sat, 10am-7pm Sun, 10am-3pm Tue; 🍴) How do we love thee? Let us count the ways: ranchero tacos stuffed with veggies and jackfruit, Frida Kahlo tostadas and cilantro pesto *sopes* (topped tortillas), coconut curry bowls, kombucha on tap and CBD lattes. The mysterious 'all powers' that accompanies each order includes soup, salsa, rice, beans, veggies and coffee. The bright orange turmeric shots, however, are extra.

Prep & Pastry
BREAKFAST **$**

(📞520-326-7737; www.prepandpastry.com; 3073 N Campbell Ave; mains $9.50-14; ⊗7am-3pm) Tucson's to-die-for breakfast spot takes no reservations, so you'll have to join Yelp's waitlist to get in line. Indulgences range from duck confit to croissant sammies and French toast (stuffed with nutella, or with green chilies), plus more health-oriented options like the quinoa bowl and chickpea scramble. Mimosas, Bloody Marys and champagne turn breakfast into brunch.

★Cafe Poca Cosa
MEXICAN **$$**

(📞520-622-6400; www.cafepocacosatucson.com; 110 E Pennington St; lunch $16-20, dinner $22-30; ⊗11am-9pm Tue-Thu, to 10pm Fri & Sat) Chef Suzana Davila's award-winning nuevo-Mexican bistro is a must for fans of Mexican food in Tucson. A Spanish-English blackboard menu circulates between tables because dishes change twice daily – it's all freshly prepared, innovative and beautifully presented. The undecided can't go wrong by ordering the 'Plato Poca Cosa' and letting Suzana decide what's best. Great margaritas too.

El Charro Café
MEXICAN **$$**

(📞520-622-1922; www.elcharrocafe.com; 311 N Court Ave; lunch $10-15, dinner $13-20; ⊗10am-9pm; 🍴) This rambling, buzzing hacienda has been making great Mexican food on this site since 1922. It's particularly famous for the *carne seca*, sundried lean beef that's been reconstituted, shredded and grilled with green chile and onions. The fabulous margaritas pack a burro-stunning punch, and help while away the time as you wait for your table. Vegan options too.

🍷 Drinking & Entertainment

Congress St in downtown and 4th Ave near the University of Arizona are both busy party strips.

★Che's Lounge
BAR

(📞520-623-2088; www.cheslounge.com; 350 N 4th Ave; ⊗noon-2am) This slightly grungy but hugely popular watering hole does cheap beer and features a huge wraparound bar and the Geronimo's Revenge food truck (Thursday to Sunday). A popular college hangout, Che's rocks with live music most Saturday nights and on the patio on Sunday afternoons (4pm to 7pm) in summer.

Tap & Bottle
BAR

(📞520-344-8999; www.thetapandbottle.com; 403 N 6th Ave; ⊗noon-11pm Sun-Wed, to midnight Thu-Sat) Come to this brick-walled hangout for a fantabulous selection of draft beers, plus Belgians and sours in the back store, as well as wines by the glass.

Monsoon Chocolate
CAFE

(📞520-396-3189; www.monsoonchocolate.com; 234 E 22nd St; ⊗10am-6pm Mon-Fri, 8am-6pm Sat, 10am-4pm Sun; 🍴) Delightful single-origin chocolatier in southern Tucson, where, depending on the weather, you can sample a tongue-tingling Mexican hot chocolate or, more likely, a Frocho (chocolate granita with coconut cream), along with decadent mezcal chocolates, choco tacos and even s'mores. Simple cafe fare and excellent coffee is also served. Vegan and gluten-free options too.

Club Congress LIVE MUSIC

(☑520-622-8848; www.hotelcongress.com; 311
E Congress St; ☺live music from 7pm, club nights
from 10pm) Skinny jeansters, tousled hipsters,
aging folkies, dressed-up hotties – the crowd
at Tucson's most happening club inside the
grandly aging Hotel Congress defines the
word eclectic. And so does the musical lineup, which usually features the finest local
and regional talent, and DJs some nights.
And for a no-fuss drink, there's the Lobby
Bar for cocktails, or the Tap Room, open
since 1919.

❶ Information

General information on Tucson is available
from the **Arizona University Visitor Center**
(☑ 520-624-1817; www.visittucson.org; 811 N
Euclid Ave; ☺ 9am-5pm Mon-Fri, to 4pm Sat
& Sun), while specific information on access
and camping in the Coronado National Forest
can be found at the downtown **Coronado
National Forest Supervisor's Office** (☑ 520-
388-8300; www.fs.usda.gov/coronado; 300
W Congress St, Federal Bldg; ☺ 8am-4:30pm
Mon-Fri).

❶ Getting There & Around

Tucson International Airport (☑ 520-573-
8100; www.flytucson.com; 7250 S Tucson Blvd;
☎) is 8 miles south of downtown and served
by six airlines, with nonstop flights to Chicago,
Houston, Los Angeles and Seattle.

Greyhound (☑ 520-792-3475; www.greyhound.
com; 801 E 12th St) runs 10 buses daily to Phoenix
(from $12, two hours), among other destinations.
Flixbus (www.flixbus.com; 1119 E 6th St, University of Arizona, 6th St Garage) gets slightly better
reviews for the Phoenix trip ($10).

The *Sunset Limited*, operated by **Amtrak**
(☑ 520-623-4442; www.amtrak.com; 400 N
Toole Ave), comes through on its way west to
Los Angeles (10 hours, three weekly) and east to
New Orleans (36 hours, three weekly).

The **Ronstadt Transit Center** (215 E Congress
St, at 6th Ave) is the main hub for the public
buses with **Sun Tran** (☑ 520-792-9222; www.
suntran.com) that serve the entire metro area.
Single/day fares are $1.75/4 if paying cash or
using a ticket machine. The same fares apply
on the **SunLink** (☺ 7am-10pm Mon-Wed, 7am-
2am Thu & Fri, 8am-2am Sat, 8am-8pm Sun)
streetcar line.

Around Tucson

All the places listed here are less than 1½
hours' drive from Tucson, and make great
day trips.

Saguaro National Park

Saguaros (sah-*wah*-ros) are icons of the
American Southwest, and an entire cactus
army of these majestic, ribbed sentinels are
protected in this desert **playground** (☑ Rincon 520-733-5153, Tucson 520-733-5158, park information 520-733-5100; www.nps.gov/sagu; 7-day
pass per vehicle/motorcycle/bicycle $20/15/10;
☺ sunrise-sunset). Or, more precisely, playgrounds: the park is divided into east and
west units, separated by 30 miles and Tucson itself. Both sections – the Rincon Mountain District in the east and Tucson Mountain District in the west – are filled with
trails and desert flora; if you only visit one,
make it the spectacular western half.

The larger section is the **Rincon Mountain District**, about 15 miles east of downtown. The **Red Hills Visitor Center** (☑ 520-
733-5158; www.nps.gov/sagu; 2700 N Kinney
Rd; ☺ 9am-5pm) has information about day
hikes, horseback riding and backcountry
camping. The camping requires a permit
($8 per site per day) and must be obtained
by noon on the day of your hike. The meandering 8-mile **Cactus Forest Scenic Loop
Drive**, a paved road open to cars and bicycles, provides access to picnic areas, trailheads and viewpoints.

Hikers pressed for time should follow the
1-mile round-trip **Freeman Homestead
Trail** to a grove of massive saguaro. For a
full-fledged desert adventure, head out on
the steep and rocky Tanque Verde Ridge
Trail, which climbs to the summit of Mica
Mountain (8666ft) and back in 20 miles
(backcountry camping permit required
for overnight use). If you'd rather someone (or something) else did the hard work,
family-run **Houston's Horseback Riding**
(☑ 520-298-7450; www.tucsonhorsebackriding.
com; 12801 E Speedway Bvd; per person 2hr tour
$80) offers trail rides in the eastern section
of the Park.

West of town, the **Tucson Mountain District** has its own branch of the Red Hills Visitor Center. The **Scenic Bajada Loop Drive**
is a 6-mile graded dirt road through cactus
forest that begins 1.5 miles north of the visitor center. Two quick, easy and rewarding
hikes are the 0.8-mile **Valley View Overlook** (awesome at sunset) and the half-mile
Signal Hill Trail to scores of ancient petroglyphs. For a more strenuous trek we recommend the 7-mile **King Canyon Trail**, which
starts 2 miles south of the visitor center,

near the Arizona-Sonora Desert Museum. The half-mile informative **Desert Discovery Trail**, which is one mile northwest of the visitor center, is wheelchair accessible. Distances for all four hikes are round-trip.

As for the park's namesake cactus, don't refer to the limbs of the saguaro as branches. As park docents will quickly tell you, the mighty saguaro grows arms, not lowly branches – a distinction that makes sense when you consider their human-like features.

Saguaros grow slowly, taking about 15 years to reach a foot in height, 50 years to reach 7ft and almost a century before they begin to take on their typical many-armed appearance. The best time to visit is April, when the cacti begin blossoming with lovely white blooms – Arizona's state flower. By June and July, the flowers give way to ripe red fruit that local Native Americans eat. Their foot soldiers are the spidery ocotillo, the fluffy teddy bear cactus, the green-bean-like pencil cholla and hundreds of other plant species. It is illegal to damage or remove saguaros.

Trailers longer than 35ft and vehicles wider than 8ft are not permitted on the park's narrow scenic loop drives.

West of Tuscon

You want wide solitude? Follow Hwy 86 west from Tuscon into some of the emptiest parts of the Sonoran Desert – except for the ubiquitous green-and-white border-patrol trucks. The lofty **Kitt Peak National Observatory** (520-318-8726; www.noao.edu/kpno; Hwy 86; tours adult/child $11/7; 9am-3:45pm), about a 75-minute drive from Tucson, features the largest collection of optical telescopes in the world. Guided tours last about an hour. Book two to four weeks in advance for the worthwhile nightly observing program (adult $50; no programs from mid-July through August).

Clear, dry skies equal an awe-inspiring glimpse of the cosmos. Dress warmly, buy gas in Tucson (the nearest gas station is 30 miles from the observatory) and note that children under eight years of age are not allowed at the evening program. The picnic area draws amateur astronomers at night

To truly want to get away from it all, you can't get much further off the grid than the huge and exotic **Organ Pipe Cactus National Monument** (520-387-6849; www.nps.gov/orpi; Hwy 85; per vehicle $25) along the Mexican border. It's a gorgeous, forbidding

DON'T MISS

MINI TIME MACHINE OF MUSEUM OF MINIATURES

Divided into the Enchanted Realm, Exploring the World and the History Gallery, this delightful **museum of miniatures** (520-881-0606; www.theminitimemachine.org; 4455 E Camp Lowell Dr, Tucson; adult/senior/child $10.50/8.50/7; 9am-4pm Tue-Sat, from 10am Sun) presents dioramas that are fantastical, historical and plain intriguing. You can also walk over a snow-globey Christmas village, peer into tiny homes constructed in the 1700s and 1800s, and search for the little inhabitants of a magical tree. The museum grew from a personal collection in the 1930s. Parents may find themselves having more fun than the kids.

land that supports an astonishing number of animals and plants, including 28 species of cacti, first and foremost its namesake organ-pipe. A giant columnar cactus, it differs from the more prevalent saguaro in that its branches radiate from the base.

The 21-mile **Ajo Mountain Drive** takes you through a spectacular landscape of steep jagged cliffs and rock tinged a faintly hellish red. There are 208 first-come, first-served sites at **Twin Peaks Campground** (877-444-6777; www.recreation.gov; 10 Organ Pipe Dr; tent & RV sites $20) by the visitor center.

South of Tuscon

The magnificent **Mission San Xavier del Bac** (520-294-2624; www.patronatosanxavier.org; 1950 W San Xavier Rd; donations appreciated; museum 8:30am-4:30pm, church 7am-5pm), on the San Xavier reservation 8 miles south of Tucson, is Arizona's oldest Hispanic-era building still in use. Completed in 1797, it's a graceful blend of Moorish, Byzantine and late–Mexican Renaissance architecture, with an unexpectedly ornate interior.

At exit 69, 16 miles south of the mission, the **Titan Missile Museum** (520-625-7736; www.titanmissilemuseum.org; 1580 Duval Mine Rd, Sahuarita; adult/senior/child $10.50/9.50/7; 9:45am-5pm Sun-Fri, from 8:45am Sat, last tour 3:45pm Nov-Apr, shorter hrs May-Oct) features an underground launch site for Cold War–era intercontinental ballistic missiles. Tours are chilling, informative and should be booked ahead.

HOT DIGGITY DOG

El Guero Canelo (☑520-295-9005; www.elguerocanelo.com; 5201 S 12th Ave; hot dogs $3.50-4, mains $7.75-10.50; ⏰10am-10pm Sun-Thu, 8:30am-midnight Fri & Sat) serves Tucson's signature dish, the Sonoran hot dog, a tasty example of what happens when Mexico's cuisine meets America's penchant for excess. It's a bacon-wrapped hot dog layered with tomatillo salsa, pinto beans, shredded cheese, mayo, ketchup, mustard, chopped tomatoes and onions. A specialty so popular it's spawned three more locations in Tucson; El Guero Canelo is the place to try them.

If history or shopping for crafts interest you, head 48 miles south of Tucson to the small village of Tubac (www.tubacaz.com), with more than 100 galleries, studios and shops clustered around a Spanish Colonial–era Presidio.

Patagonia & the Mountain Empire

This lovely riparian region, sandwiched between the Mexican border and the Santa Rita and Patagonia Mountains, is one of the shiniest gems in Arizona's jewel box. It's a tranquil destination for bird-watching and wine tasting. Bird-watchers and nature-lovers wander the gentle trails at the **Patagonia-Sonoita Creek Preserve** (☑520-394-2400; www.nature.org/arizona; 150 Blue Heaven Rd, Patagonia; $8; ⏰6:30am-4pm Wed-Sun Apr-Sep, 7:30am-4pm Wed-Sun Oct-Mar), an enchanting creekside willow and cottonwood forest managed by the Nature Conservancy. The peak migratory seasons are April through May, and late August through September.

For a leisurely afternoon of wine tasting, head to the villages and surrounding wineries of **Sonoita** and **Elgin**, north of Patagonia. If you're in Patagonia for dinner, try the satisfying gourmet pizzas at **Velvet Elvis** (☑520-394-0069; www.facebook.com/velvetelvispizza; 292 Naugle Ave, Patagonia; pizzas $12-26; ⏰11:30am-8:30pm Thu-Sun; 🛜). Then get comfortable in the spacious rooms and inviting gardens at the **Duquesne House** (☑520-394-2732; www.theduquesnehouse.com; 357 Duquesne Ave, Patagonia; r $140; ✴@🛜), a former boarding house for miners.

A small **visitor center** (☑520-394-7750; www.patagoniaaz.com; 299 McKeown Ave, Patagonia; ⏰10am-4pm daily Oct-May, Fri-Sun Jun-Sep) provides information.

Southeastern Arizona

Chockablock with places that loom large in Wild West folklore, southeastern Arizona is home to the wonderfully preserved mining town of Bisbee, the OK Corral in Tombstone, and a wonderland of stone spires at Chiricahua National Monument.

Kartchner Caverns State Park

This wonderland of spires, shields, pipes, columns, soda straws and other ethereal formations has been five million years in the making, but miraculously wasn't discovered until 1974. In fact, its very location was kept secret for another 25 years in order to prepare for its opening as **Kartchner Caverns State Park** (☑information 520-586-4100, reservations 877-697-2757; www.azstateparks.com/kartchner; 2980 Hwy 90; per vehicle $7, tours adult/child $23/13; ⏰park 7am-6pm, visitor center 8am-6pm late Dec–mid-May, shorter hrs rest of year). Two tours are available, both about 90 minutes long and equally impressive.

The Big Room tour closes to the public around mid-April, when a colony of migrating female cave myotis bats starts arriving from Mexico to roost and give birth to pups in late June. Mom and baby bats hang out until mid-September before flying off to their wintering spot. While a bat nursery, the cave is closed to the public.

There's a campground (with cabins) and the entrance is 9 miles south of I-10, off Hwy 90, exit 302.

Tombstone

Dubbing itself 'The Town too Tough to Die,' Tombstone was a booming mining town during its 19th-century heyday, when the whiskey flowed and six-shooters blazed over disputes large and small, most famously at the OK Corral. Now a National Historic Landmark, it attracts hordes of tourists to its old Western buildings, stagecoach rides and gunfight reenactments.

And yes, you must visit the **OK Corral** (☑520-457-3456; www.ok-corral.com; Allen St, btwn 3rd & 4th Sts; with/without gunfight $10/6; ⏰10am-4pm), site of the legendary gunfight where the Earps and Doc Holliday took on the McLaurys and Billy Clanton on October

26, 1881. The McClaurys, Clanton and many other casualties of those violent days now rest at the **Boothill Graveyard** ([J]520-457-3300; www.tombstoneboothillgiftshop.com; 408 Hwy 80; adult/child $3/free; [O]8am-6pm) on Hwy 80 north of town.

Also make time for the dusty **Bird Cage Theater** ([J]520-457-3421; www.tombstonebird cage.com; 517 E Allen St; adult $14, senior & child $12; [O]9am-6pm), a one-time dance hall, saloon and bordello crammed with historic odds and ends. And a merman. The **Visitor Center** ([J]888-457-3929; www.tombstonecham ber.com; 395 E Allen St, at 4th St; [O]9am-4pm Mon-Thu, to 5pm Fri-Sun) has walking maps.

Bisbee

Oozing untidy, unforced old-world charm, Bisbee is a former copper-mining town that's now a delightful mix of aging bohemians, elegant buildings, sumptuous restaurants and charming hotels. Most businesses are in the Historic District (Old Bisbee), along Subway and Main Sts.

To burrow under the earth in a tour led by the retirees who once mined here, take the **Queen Mine Tour** ([J]520-432-2071; www. queenminetour.com; 478 Dart Rd, off Hwy 80; adult/child $13/5.50; [O]9am-5pm). The Queen Mine Building, just south of downtown, also holds the local **visitor center** ([J]520-432-3554; www.discoverbisbee.com; 478 Dart Rd; [O]8am-5pm Mon-Fri, 10am-4pm Sat & Sun), and is the obvious place to start exploring. Right outside of town, check out the **Lavender Pit**, an ugly yet impressive testament to strip mining.

Rest your head at **Shady Dell RV Park** ([J]520-432-3567; www.theshadydell.com; 1 Douglas Rd, Lowell; trailers $105-145; [O]closed summer & winter; [*]), a retro trailer park where meticulously restored Airstream trailers are neatly fenced off and kitted out with fun furnishings. Swamp coolers provide cold air. You can sleep in a covered wagon at the quirky but fun **Bisbee Grand Hotel** ([J]520-432-5900; www.bisbeegrandhotel.com; 61 Main St; d/ste from $94/135; [*][@]), which brings the Old West to life with Victorian-era decor and a kick-up-your spurs saloon.

For good food, stroll up Main St and pick a restaurant – you can't go wrong. For fine American food, try stylish **Cafe Roka** ([J]520-432-5153; www.caferoka.com; 35 Main St; mains $18.50-31.50; [O]5-9pm Wed-Sat, 4-8pm Sun), where four-course dinners include salad, soup, sorbet and a rotating choice of crowd-pleasing mains. Continue up Main St

for wood-fired pizzas and punk-rock style at **Screaming Banshee** ([J]520-432-1300; www. screamingbansheepizza.net; 200 Tombstone Canyon Rd; pizzas $14-19; [O]4-9pm Wed, 11am-10pm Thu-Sun). Bars cluster in the aptly named Brewery Gulch, at the south end of Main St.

Chiricahua National Monument

The towering rock spires at remote but mesmerizing **Chiricahua National Monument** ([J]520-824-3560; www.nps.gov/chir; 12856 E Rhyolite Creek Rd; [O]visitor center 8:30am-4:30pm; [*]) [FREE] in the Chiricahua Mountains sometimes rise hundreds of feet high and often look like they're on the verge of tipping over. The **Bonita Canyon Scenic Drive** takes you 8 miles to Massai Point (6870ft) where you'll see thousands of spires positioned on the slopes like some petrified army. There are numerous hiking trails, but if you're short on time, hike the **Echo Canyon Trail** at least half a mile to the Grottoes, an amazing 'cathedral' of giant boulders where you can lie still and enjoy the wind-caressed silence. The monument is 36 miles southeast of Willcox off Hwy 186/181.

UTAH

Welcome to nature's perfect playground. From red-rock mesas to skinny slot canyons, powder-bound slopes and slickrock trails, Utah's diverse terrain will stun you. The biking, hiking and skiing are world-class. And with more than 65% of the state lands public, including 14 national parks and monuments, the access is simply superb.

Southern Utah is defined by red-rock cliffs, sorbet-colored spindles and seemingly endless sandstone desert. The pine-forested and snow-covered peaks of the Wasatch Mountains dominate northern Utah. Interspersed are old pioneer remnants, ancient rock art and ruins, and traces of dinosaurs.

Mormon-influenced rural towns can be quiet and conservative, but the rugged beauty has attracted outdoorsy progressives as well. Salt Lake City (SLC) and Park City, especially, have vibrant nightlife and progressive dining scenes. So pull on your boots and stock up on water: Utah's wild and scenic hinterlands await.

History

Traces of the Ancestral Puebloan and Fremont peoples, this land's earliest human inhabitants, remain in the rock art and ruins they left behind. But the modern Ute, Paiute and Navajo tribes were living here when settlers of European heritage arrived in large numbers. Led by Brigham Young (second president of the Mormon church), Mormons fled to this territory to escape religious persecution starting in the late 1840s. They set out to settle every inch of their new land, no matter how inhospitable, which resulted in skirmishes with Native Americans – and more than one abandoned ghost town.

For nearly 50 years after the United States acquired the Utah Territory from Mexico, petitions for statehood were rejected due to the Mormon practice of polygamy (taking multiple wives). Tension and prosecutions grew until 1890, when Mormon leader Wilford Woodruff had a divine revelation and the church officially discontinued the practice. Utah became the 45th state in 1896. The modern Mormon church, now called the Church of Jesus Christ of Latter-Day Saints (LDS), continues to exert a strong influence.

ℹ Information

Utah Office of Tourism (☑ 800-200-1160; www.utah.com) Publishes the free *Utah Travel Guide* and runs several visitor centers statewide. The website has links in six languages.
Utah State Parks & Recreation Department (☑ 801-538-7220; www.stateparks.utah.gov) Produces a guide to the 40-plus state parks; available online and at visitor centers.

UTAH FACTS

Nickname Beehive State

Population 3.16 million

Area 84,900 sq miles

Capital city Salt Lake City (population 200,591), metro area (1,152,633)

Other cities St George (population 84,400)

Sales tax 4.85%

Birthplace of Entertainers Donny (b 1957) and Marie (b 1959) Osmond, beloved bandit Butch Cassidy (1866–1908)

Home of 2002 Winter Olympic Games

Politics Mostly conservative

Famous for Mormons, red-rock canyons, polygamy

Best souvenir Wasatch Brew Pub T-shirt: 'Polygamy Porter – Why Have Just One?'

ℹ Getting There & Around

International flights from Mexico, Canada, England, France and Holland land in Salt Lake City's airport (p875), as do domestic flights. Larger cities and tourist hubs have car-rental offices. An Amtrak train (www.amtrak.com) stops daily in Salt Lake City en route between Oakland, CA (19 hours) and Chicago (34 hours). Greyhound (www.greyound.com) runs long-distance service from Salt Lake City to Las Vegas, NV (eight hours), and Denver, CO (10½ hours).

Utah is not a large state, but it is a largely rural one – so unless you're staying in Salt Lake City or Park City, you'll need a car. If you're headed to the parks in southern Utah, your cheapest bet may be to fly into Las Vegas, and rent a ride there.

Salt Lake City

Sparkling Salt Lake City (SLC), with its bluebird skies and powder-dusted mountains, is Utah's capital city. The only Utah city with an international airport, it still manages to emanate a small-town feel. Downtown is easy to get around and fairly quiet come evening. It's hard to grasp that some 1.2 million people live in the metro area. While it's the Mormon equivalent of Vatican City, and the Church of Jesus Christ of Latter-Day Saints (LDS) owns a lot of land, less than half the population are church members. The university and excellent outdoor access have attracted a wide range of residents. A liberal spirit permeates the coffeehouses and yoga classes, where elaborate tattoos are the norm. Foodies find much to love among the multitude of international and organic dining options. And when the trail beckons, it's a scant 45 minutes from the Wasatch Mountains' brilliant hiking and skiing. Friendly people, great food and outdoor adventure – what could be better?

⊙ Sights & Activities

Mormon Church–related sights cluster mostly near the town center point for SLC addresses: the intersection of Main and South Temple Sts. (Streets are so wide – 132ft – because they were originally built so that four oxen pulling a wagon could turn around.) The downtown hub underwent a renaissance with the development of City Creek. To the east, the University-Foothills District has most of the museums and kid-friendly attractions.

Temple Square Area

Temple Square PLAZA
(www.visittemplesquare.com; cnr S Temple & N State Sts; ⊙ grounds 24hr, visitor center 9am-9pm) FREE The city's most famous sight occupies a 10-acre block surrounded by 15ft-high walls. LDS docents give free, 30-minute tours continually, leaving from the visitor center at the entrance on North Temple St. Sisters, brothers and elders are stationed every 20ft or so to answer questions. (Don't worry, no one is going to try to convert you – unless you express interest.) The temple is closed for renovation from 2020 to 2024 but Temple Square's other sights remain open.

Church History Museum MUSEUM
(☑ 801-240-3310; https://history.lds.org/section/museum; 45 N West Temple St; ⊙ 9am-9pm Mon-Fri, 10am-6pm Sat) FREE Adjoining Temple Sq (p871), this interactive museum has impressive exhibits of pioneer history and fine art.

Salt Lake Temple RELIGIOUS SITE
(☑ 801-240-2640; https://churchofjesuschristtemples.org/salt-lake-temple; 50 W North Temple St, Temple Sq) Lording over Temple Sq (p871) is the impressive 210ft-tall Salt Lake Temple. Atop the tallest spire stands a statue of the angel Moroni, who appeared to LDS founder Joseph Smith. Rumor has it that when the place was renovated, cleaners found old bullet marks in one of the gold-plated surfaces. The temple and ceremonies are private, open only to LDS members in good standing. The temple is closed for renovation from 2020 to 2024 to make it more earthquake-resistant.

Tabernacle CHRISTIAN SITE
(www.mormontabernaclechoir.org; Temple Sq; ⊙ 9am-9pm) FREE The domed, 1867 auditorium – with a massive 11,000-pipe organ – has incredible acoustics. A pin dropped in the front can be heard in the back, almost 200ft away. Free daily organ recitals are held at noon Monday through Saturday, and at 2pm Sunday.

Beehive House HISTORIC SITE
(☑ 801-240-2681; www.lds.org/visitbeehivehouse; 67 E South Temple St; ⊙ 10am-6pm Mon-Sat) FREE Brigham Young lived with one of his wives and families in the Beehive House during much of his tenure as governor and church president in Utah. The required tours vary; some offer historic house details over religious education, depending on the LDS docent.

Greater Downtown

Utah State Capitol HISTORIC BUILDING
(☑ 801-538-1800; www.utahstatecapitol.utah.gov; 350 N State St; ⊙ 7am-8pm Mon-Thu, to 6pm Fri, 8am-6pm Sat & Sun, visitor center 9am-5pm Mon-Fri) FREE The grand, 1916 State Capitol is set among 500 cherry trees on a hill north of Temple Sq. Inside, colorful Works Progress Administration (WPA) murals of pioneers, trappers and missionaries adorn part of the building's dome. Free guided tours (hourly, 9am to 4pm, Monday to Friday) start at the 1st-floor visitor center; self-guided tours are available from the visitor center.

Clark Planetarium MUSEUM
(☑ 385-468-7827; www.clarkplanetarium.org; 110 S 400 W; adult/child $9/7; ⊙ 10:30am-7pm Sun-Wed, to 11pm Thu-Sat) You'll be seeing stars at Clark Planetarium, home to the latest and greatest 3-D sky shows. There are free science exhibits and an IMAX theater, too. The planetarium is on the edge of the **Gateway** (☑ 801-456-0000; www.shopthegateway.com; 400 W 100 S; ⊙ 10am-9pm Mon-Sat, noon-6pm Sun), a combination indoor-outdoor shopping complex anchored by the old railway depot.

University-Foothill District & Beyond

★**Natural History Museum of Utah** MUSEUM
(☑ 801-581-6927; www.nhmu.utah.edu; 301 Wakara Way, Rio Tinto Center; adult/child 3-12yr $15/10; ⊙ 10am-5pm Thu-Tue, to 9pm Wed; ℗) Rio Tinto Center's stunning architecture forms a multistory indoor 'canyon' that showcases exhibits to great effect. Walk up through the layers as you explore both indigenous peoples' cultures and natural history. Past Worlds paleontological displays are the most impressive – an incredible perspective from beneath, next to and above a vast collection of dinosaur fossils offers the full breadth of prehistory.

This is the Place Heritage Park HISTORIC SITE
(☑ 801-582-1847; www.thisistheplace.org; 2601 E Sunnyside Ave; adult/child $14/10; ⊙ 10am-5pm; ℗ 🖬) Dedicated to the 1847 arrival of the Mormons, this heritage park covers 450 acres. The centerpiece is a living-history village where, June through August, costumed docents depict mid-19th-century life. Admission includes a tourist-train ride and activities. The rest of the year, access is limited to varying degrees at varyingly reduced prices; you'll at least be able to wander around the

exterior of some 50 historic homes. Some are replicas, but some are originals, such as Brigham Young's farmhouse.

Red Butte Garden
GARDENS

(www.redbuttegarden.org; 300 Wakara Way; adult/child $14/7; ⏱9am-5pm Oct-Mar, to 7:30pm Apr & Sep, to 9pm May-Aug; 🅿) Both landscaped and natural gardens cover a lovely 100 acres, with access to 5 miles of trails in the Wasatch foothills. Check online to see who's playing at the popular, outdoor summer concert series also held here. Daylight hours in low season and on concert days.

🛏 Sleeping

Downtown chain properties cluster around S 200 W near 500 S and 600 S; there are more in Mid-Valley (off I-215) and near the airport. At high-end hotels, rates are lowest on weekends. Parking downtown is often not included. Look for camping and alternative lodging in the Wasatch Mountains.

Kimball Condominiums
CONDO $

(☎801-363-4000; www.thekimball.com; 150 N Main St; apt from $95; 🅿❄📶) Just a half block from Temple Sq, these fully furnished condos range from older studio suites with wall beds to larger remodeled two-bedroom units that sleep up to six guests. All have kitchens and the location couldn't be better. Rates vary.

★ Engen Hus
B&B $$

(☎801-450-6703; www.engenhusutah.com; 2275 E 6200 S; r $139-179; 📶) Ideally positioned for mountain jaunts, this lovely home features four rooms with handmade quilts on log beds and flat-screen TVs. Hosts are knowledgeable about local hiking. The cozy quotient is high, with board games, a hot-tub deck and DIY laundry. Dig the buffet breakfast with the likes of caramel French toast. Has a room that's accessible to travelers in wheelchairs.

★ Inn on the Hill
INN $$

(☎801-328-1466; www.inn-on-the-hill.com; 225 N State St; r $150-260; 🅿❄@📶) Exquisite woodwork and Maxfield Parrish Tiffany glass adorn this sprawling, 1906 Renaissance Revival mansion-turned-inn. Guest rooms are classically comfortable, not stuffy, with jetted tubs and some fireplaces and balconies. Great shared spaces include patios, a billiard room, a library and a dining room where chef-cooked breakfasts are served.

DeSoto Tudor
HOMESTAY $$

(☎801-503-9810, 801-835-4009; www.desototudoroncapitolhill.com; 545 DeSoto St E; ste $159; ❄📶) Your on-site hosts Vince and Ken don't miss a beat during your stay in this homey one-bedroom suite on Capitol Hill. Expect an excellent breakfast, a generous supply of drinks and snacks stocked in the kitchen, a private outdoor hot tub overlooking the city and highly amusing conversation.

Hotel RL
HOTEL $$

(☎801-521-7373; www.redlion.com/salt-lake; 161 W 600 S; r from $135; 🅿❄@📶🏊) Sleek comfort

---

SALT LAKE CITY FOR KIDS

Salt Lake is very child-friendly city. The wonderful hands-on exhibits at the **Discovery Gateway** (☎801-456-5437; www.discoverygateway.org; 444 W 100 S; $12.50; ⏱10am-6pm Mon-Thu, to 7pm Fri & Sat, noon-6pm Sun; 👶) stimulate imaginations and senses.

Kids can help farmhands milk cows at **Wheeler Historic Farm** (☎385-468-1755; www.wheelerfarm.com; 6351 S 900 E; wagon ride $3, house tour adult/child $4/2; ⏱dawn-dusk; 👶) FREE, which dates from 1898. There's also tractor-drawn wagon rides in summer.

More than 800 animals inhabit zones such as the Asian Highlands on the landscaped 42-acre grounds at **Hogle Zoo** (☎801-584-1700; www.hoglezoo.org; 2600 Sunnyside Ave; adult/child $17/13; ⏱9am-6pm Mar-Oct, 10am-5pm Nov-Feb; 🅿👶). Daily animal encounter programs help kids learn more about their favorite species.

Tracy Aviary (☎801-596-8500; www.tracyaviary.org; 589 E 1300 S; adult/child $12/8; ⏱9am-5pm; 👶) lets little ones toss fish to the pelicans as one of its interactive programs and performances. Winged creatures from around the world call this bird park home.

With 55 acres of gardens, a full-scale working and petting farm, golf course, giant movie theater, museum, dining, shopping and a **Butterfly Biosphere** (☎801-768-2300; adult/child $20/15; ⏱10am-8pm Mon-Sat; 🅿👶), what doesn't Thanksgiving Point, located in Lehi, have? The on-site Museum of Ancient Life (p873) is one of the highest-tech and most hands-on dinosaur museums in the state. Lehi is 28 miles south of downtown SLC; to get there take exit 287 off I-15.

in a remodeled Red Lion hotel with almost 400 rooms, which feature black-and-white wall murals and flat-screen TVs. There's a classic diner attached, a modern-woodsy design lounge, 24-hour gym and outdoor pool and Jacuzzi. As big box hotels go, this one delivers.

✕ Eating

Tosh's Ramen RAMEN $
(☑ 801-466-7000; www.toshsramen.com; 1465 S State St; mains $9-15; ⊗ 11:30am-3pm & 5-9pm Mon-Sat; ℗) Ecstasy by the steaming oversized bowl, Tosh's ramen comes with silken broth and crunchy sprouts, topped with a poached egg if you like it that way. It couldn't get more authentic. Try to carve out some room for an order of sweet and spicy wings. Everyone is drawn to this happy place in a nondescript strip mall, so go early.

Oh Mai VIETNAMESE $
(☑ 801-467-6882; www.ohmaisandwich.com; 3425 State St; sandwiches $5-7; ⊗ 10am-9pm Mon-Sat; ℗ ⋰) This Vietnamese sandwich kitchen prepares crunchy banh mi baguettes with sweet and spicy fillings such as braised pork belly and jalapeño (that would be the 'sinner' sandwich), or opt for one of their vegan or vegetarian sammies. Oh Mai has other branches in town but many prefer the authenticity of the original South Salt Lake location.

Over the Counter Cafe BREAKFAST $
(☑ 801-487-8725; www.overthecountercafe.weebly. com; 2343 E 3300 S; mains $5-10; ⊗ 6:30am-2pm; ℗) Hugely popular greasy spoon with booth seating and a convivial counter around an open grill. Regulars love the ancient-grains pancakes, blueberry-lemon French toast with fresh berries and the Flintstones-size ham steaks.

★ Red Iguana MEXICAN $$
(☑ 801-322-1489; www.rediguana.com; 736 W North Temple St; mains $10-18; ⊗ 11am-10pm Mon-Thu, to 11pm Fri & Sat, 9am-9pm Sun) Mexico at its most authentic, aromatic and delicious – no wonder the line is usually snaking out the door at this family-run restaurant. Ask for samples of the mole to decide on one of six chili- and chocolate-based sauces. The incredibly tender *cochinita pibil* (shredded roast pork) tastes like it's been roasting for days.

Del Mar al Lago PERUVIAN $$
(☑ 801-467-2890; www.facebook.com/delmar.al.lago; 310 W Bugatti Dr; mains $16-25; ⊗ 11am-4pm &

MUSEUM OF ANCIENT LIFE

This family-friendly **museum** (☑ 801-768-2300; www.thanksgivingpoint.org; 3003 N Thanksgiving Way, Lehi; museum only adult/child $20/15; ⊗ 10am-8pm Mon-Sat; ℗ ⋰) houses one of the world's largest displays of mounted dinosaurs. The exhibits, many of which are hands-on, are arranged chronologically and teach about fossils found all over the world. Little ones can dig for their own bones, search for hidden gnomes within the exhibits and practice paleontology in a Saturday lab (for an additional cost).

6-9pm Mon-Thu, 11am-10pm Fri & Sat; ℗ ⋈) Get ready for a treat. Chef Wilmer from Trujillo cooks up Peru's best dishes, including ceviche (fish marinated in lime), yucca fries and *causas* (seasoned mashed potatoes) with jalapeño aioli, and the Peruvian patrons say it's authentic.

White Horse AMERICAN $$
(☑ 801-363-0137; www.whitehorseslc.com; 325 Main St; mains $10-28; ⊗ 11am-1am; ⋈) Shelves stacked high with top-notch spirits invite you to belly up to the counter and try one of the innovative cocktails mixed here. The trendy downtown spot serves excellent food as well, such as the Wagyu cheeseburger with smoked pork-belly bacon.

◖ Drinking & Nightlife

Brewpubs and bars that also serve food are mainstays of SLC's nightlife, and no one minds if you mainly drink and nibble. A complete schedule of local bar music is available in the *City Weekly* (www.cityweekly.net).

★ Fisher Brewing Company BREWERY
(☑ 801-487-2337; www.fisherbeer.com; 320 W 800 S; ⊗ 11am-10pm Sun-Thu, to 1am Fri & Sat) A former auto shop in the Granary District has been converted into an employee-owned, small-batch brewery that produces the freshest beer around. Following in the footsteps of his great-great-grandfather Albert Fisher, a German immigrant who ran A. Fisher Brewing Company from 1884 to 1967, Tony Fisher and partners have revived a family tradition but on a smaller, more intimate scale.

SOUTHWEST SALT LAKE CITY

Beer Bar
PUB

(☑ 801-355-2287; www.beerbarslc.com; 161 E 200 S; ☺ 11am-1am) With shared wooden tables and more than 140 beers and 13 sausage styles, Beer Bar is a hip little slice of Bavaria in Salt Lake City. The crowd is diverse and far more casual than at Bar X (p874) next door (a linked venue). A great place to meet friends and make friends, but it gets pretty loud.

Bar X
COCKTAIL BAR

(☑ 801-355-2287; www.beerbarslc.com; 155 E 200 S; ☺ 4pm-1am Mon-Sat, 7pm-1am Sun) So low-lit and funky, it's hard to believe you're down the street from Temple Sq (p871). Cozy up to the crowded bar with a Moscow Mule and listen to Motown or funk (or the guy at the next table saying to his date, 'Your voice is pretty').

Jack Mormon Coffee Co
COFFEE

(☑ 801-359-2979; www.jackmormoncoffee.com; 82 E St; ☺ 8am-6pm Mon-Sat; ☎) Utah's finest roaster also serves mean espresso drinks. When the temps rise, locals binge on a Jack Frost.

☆ Entertainment

Salt Lake City is as good as it gets in Utah when it comes to dance-club and live-music offerings. See the *City Weekly* (www.cityweekly.net) for listings. You'll also find a fair share of sporting events throughout the year. Classical entertainment options, especially around Temple Sq (p871), are plentiful.

THE BOOK OF MORMON, THE MUSICAL

Singing and dancing Mormon missionaries? You betcha...at least on Broadway. In the spring of 2011, *The Book of Mormon* musical opened to critical acclaim at the Eugene O'Neill Theatre in New York. The light-hearted satire about LDS missionaries in Uganda came out of the comic minds that also created the musical *Avenue Q* and the animated TV series *South Park*. No wonder people laughed them all the way to nine Tony Awards.

The LDS church's official response? Actually quite measured, avoiding any direct criticism – though it was made clear that their belief is that while 'the Book, the musical' can entertain you, the scriptures of the actual Book of Mormon can change your life.

Music

★ Mormon Tabernacle Choir
LIVE MUSIC

(☑ 801-570-0080, 801-240-4150; www.tabernaclechoir.org) Hearing the world-renowned Mormon Tabernacle Choir is a must-do on any SLC bucket list. A live choir broadcast goes out every Sunday at 9:30am. September through November, and January through May, attend in person at the Tabernacle (p871). Free public rehearsals are held here from 7:30pm to 8:30pm Thursday.

Garage on Beck
LIVE MUSIC

(☑ 801-521-3904; www.garageonbeck.com; 1199 Beck St; ☺ 11am-1am) A former auto repair garage where you can catch live music performances on weekends in the rear patio. Note that this roadhouse bar and grill has limited parking.

Theater

There are concerts on Temple Sq (p871), at the **Library** (☑ 891-524-8200; www.slcpl.org; 210 E 400 S; ☺ 9am-9pm Mon-Thu, 9am-6pm Fri & Sat, 1-5pm Sun; ☒) and in Red Butte Garden (p872) in the summertime. The Salt Lake City Arts Council provides a complete cultural events calendar on its website (www.slcgov.com/calendars). Most tickets can be reserved through **ArtTix** (☑ 801-355-2787, 385-468-1010; www.artsaltlake.org).

Eccles Theatre
THEATER

(☑ 385-468-1010; www.artsaltlake.org; 131 S Main St) Opened in 2016, this gorgeous building has two theaters (one seating 2500 people), showing Broadway shows, concerts and other entertainment.

Sports

Utah Jazz
BASKETBALL

(☑ 801-325-2500; www.nba.com/jazz; 301 S Temple St) Utah Jazz, the men's professional basketball team, plays at the **Vivint Smart Home Arena** (☑ 801-325-2000; www.vivintarena.com; 301 S Temple St), where concerts are also held.

Real Salt Lake
SOCCER

(☑ 844-732-5849; www.rsl.com; 9256 State St, Rio Tinto Stadium; ☺ Mar-Oct) Salt Lake's winning Major League Soccer team (*ree*-al) has a loyal local following and matches are fun to take in at the **Rio Tinto Stadium** (☑ 801-727-2700; www.riotintostadium.com; 9256 State St, Sandy).

🛍 Shopping

An interesting array of boutiques, antiques and cafes line up along Broadway Ave (300

South), between 100 and 300 East. Drawing on Utah pioneer heritage, SLC has quite a few crafty shops and galleries scattered around; a few can be found on the 300 block of W Pierpont Ave. Many participate in the one-day **Craft Lake City Festival** (www.craftlakecity.com) in August.

ℹ Information

EMERGENCY & MEDICAL SERVICES

Local Police (☑ 801-799-3000; www.slcpd.com; 475 S 300 E; ⊗ office 8am-5pm Mon-Fri)

Salt Lake Regional Medical Center (☑ 801-350-4111; www.saltlakeregional.org; 1050 E South Temple St; ⊗ 24hr emergency)

University of Utah Hospital (☑ 801-581-2121; www.healthcare.utah.edu; 50 N Medical Dr)

TOURIST INFORMATION

Public Lands Information Center Recreation information for nearby public lands (state parks, BLM, USFS), including the Wasatch-Cache National Forest.

Visit Salt Lake (☑ 801-534-4900; www.visitsaltlake.com; 90 S West Temple St, Salt Palace Convention Center; ⊗ 9am-5pm) Publishes a free visitor-guide booklet; large gift shop on-site at the visitor center.

ℹ Getting There & Around

Five miles northwest of downtown, **Salt Lake City International Airport** (SLC; ☑ 801-575-2400; www.slcairport.com; 776 N Terminal Dr; 🛜) has mostly domestic flights, though you can fly direct to Canada, Mexico, England, France and Holland. **Express Shuttle** (☑ 801-596-1600; www.expressshuttleutah.com; shared van to downtown $13-20) runs shared van services to the airport.

 Greyhound (☑ 800-231-2222; www.greyhound.com; 300 S 600 W; 🛜) has buses to nationwide destinations. The **Union Pacific Rail Depot** (www.amtrak.com; 340 S 600 W) is serviced daily by **Amtrak** (☑ 800-231-2222; www.amtrak.com; 340 S 600 W) trains heading to Denver and California.

Utah Transit Authority (UTA; ☑ 801-743-3882; www.rideuta.com; 🛜) runs light-rail services to the international airport and downtown area. Bus 550 travels downtown from the parking structure between Terminals 1 and 2.

Park City & Wasatch Mountains

Utah offers some of North America's most awesome skiing, with fabulous low-density, low-moisture snow – between 300in and 500in annually – and thousands of acres of high-altitude terrain. The Wasatch Mountain Range, which towers over SLC, holds numerous ski resorts, abundant hiking, camping and mountain biking – not to mention chichi Park City, with its upscale amenities and famous film festival.

Salt Lake City Resorts

Because of Great Salt Lake–affected snow patterns, these resorts receive almost twice as much snow as Park City. The four resorts east of Salt Lake City sit 30 to 45 miles from the downtown core at the end of two canyons. In summer, access the numerous hiking and biking trails that lead off from both canyons.

🏃 Activities

★**Alta** SNOW SPORTS
(☑ 801-359-1078; www.alta.com; Little Cottonwood Canyon; day lift ticket adult/child $116/60) Dyed-in-the-wool skiers make a pilgrimage to Alta, at the top of the valley. No snowboarders are allowed here, which keeps the snow cover from deteriorating, especially on groomers. Wide-open powder fields, gullies, chutes and glades, such as **East Greeley**, **Devil's Castle** and **High Rustler**, have helped make Alta famous. Warning: you may never want to ski anywhere else.

★**Snowbird** SNOW SPORTS
(☑ 800-232-9542; www.snowbird.com; Hwy 210, Little Cottonwood Canyon; day lift ticket adult/child $125/60) The biggest and busiest of all the Salt Lake City resorts, with all-round great snow riding – think steep and deep. Numerous lift-assist summer hiking trails; aerial tramway runs year-round.

Solitude SNOW SPORTS
(☑ 801-534-1400; www.skisolitude.com; 12000 Big Cottonwood Canyon Rd; day lift ticket adult/child $109/75) Exclusive, European-style village surrounded by excellent terrain. The **Nordic Center** (☑ 801-536-5774; www.solitudemountain.com/winter-activities/nordic-skiing-nordic-center; day pass adult/child $20/15; ⊗ 8:30am-4:30pm Dec–mid-Apr) has cross-country skiing in winter and nature trails in summer.

Brighton SNOW SPORTS
(☑ 801-532-4731; www.brightonresort.com; 8302 S Brighton Loop Rd; day lift-ticket adult $94, child under 11yr free; 🎿) Slackers, truants and boarders rule at Brighton. But don't be intimidated: the low-key resort where many Salt Lake residents first learned to ski remains a good

first-timers' spot, especially if you want to snowboard. Thick stands of pines line sweeping groomed trails and wide boulevards, and from the top, the views are gorgeous.

Park City

With a dusting of snow, the century-old buildings on main street create a snow-globe scene come to life. A one-time silver boom-and-bust town, pretty Park City is now lined with condos and mansions in the valleys. Utah's premier ski village boasts fabulous restaurants and cultural offerings. It recently annexed the adjacent Canyons Resort to become the largest ski resort in North America.

Park City first shot to international fame when it hosted the downhill, jumping and sledding events at the 2002 Winter Olympics. Today it's the permanent home base for the US Ski Team. There's usually snow through mid-April.

Come summer, more residents than visitors gear up for hiking and mountain biking among the nearby peaks. June to August, temperatures average in the 70s (Fahrenheit; 20s Celsius); nights are chilly. Spring and fall can be wet and boring; resort services, limited in summer compared with winter, shut down entirely between seasons.

◉ Sights

★ **Utah Olympic Park**　　　AMUSEMENT PARK
(☏435-658-4200; www.utaholympiclegacy.org; 3419 Olympic Pkwy; museum free, activity day-pass adult/child $80/55; ☉9am-6pm, tours 11am-4pm) Visit the site of the 2002 Olympic ski

jumping, bobsledding, skeleton, Nordic combined and luge events, which continues to host national competitions. There are 10m, 20m, 40m, 64m, 90m and 120m Nordic ski-jumping hills as well as a bobsled-luge run. The US Ski Team practices here year-round – in summer, the freestyle jumpers land in a bubble-filled jetted pool, and the Nordic jumpers on a hillside covered in plastic. Call for a schedule; it's free to observe.

★ **Park City Museum**　　　MUSEUM
(☏435-649-7457; www.parkcityhistory.org; 528 Main St; adult/child $12/5; ☉10am-7pm Mon-Sat, noon-6pm Sun) A well-staged interactive museum touches on the highlights of the town's history as a mining boomtown, hippie hangout and premier ski resort. There are fascinating exhibits on the world's first underground ski lift, a real dungeon in the basement and a 3-D map of mining tunnels under the mountain.

🏃 Activities

Skiing is the big area attraction, but there are enough activities to keep you more than busy in both summer and winter. Most are based out of the three resort areas: Canyons (p877), Park City Mountain (p877) and Deer Valley.

Deer Valley　　SNOW SPORTS, ADVENTURE SPORTS
(☏435-649-1000, snowmobiling 435-645-7669; www.deervalley.com; 2250 Deer Valley Dr; day lift ticket adult/child $169/105, round-trip chairlift ride $22; ☉snowmobiling 9am-5pm) Want to be pampered? Deer Valley, a resort of superlatives, has thought of everything – from tissue boxes at the base of slopes to ski valets.

CAN I GET A DRINK IN UTAH?

Yes, you can absolutely get a drink in Utah. Although a few unusual liquor laws remain, in recent years they've been relaxed and private-club membership bars are no more. Some rules to remember:

➡ Few restaurants have full liquor licenses: most serve beer and wine only. You have to order food to drink.

➡ Minors aren't allowed in bars.

➡ Mixed drinks and wine are available only after midday; 4% alcohol beer can be served from 10am. Full-strength bottled beer is sold in some bars and restaurants, and in most breweries.

➡ Mixed drinks cannot contain more than 1.5oz of a primary liquor, or 2.5oz total including secondary alcohol. Sorry, no Long Island iced teas or double shots.

➡ Packaged liquor can only be sold at state-run liquor stores; grocery and convenience stores can sell 4% alcohol beer and malt beverages. Sales in state-run stores are made from Monday through Saturday only.

Slalom, mogul and freestyle-aerial competitions in the 2002 Olympics were held here, but the resort is also famous for its superb dining, white-glove service and uncrowded slopes, as meticulously groomed as the gardens of Versailles.

Park City
Mountain Resort SNOW SPORTS, ADVENTURE SPORTS
(☑ 435-649-8111; www.parkcitymountain.com; 1345 Lowell Ave; lift ticket adult/child $156/100; ◨) From boarder dudes to parents with tots, everyone skis Park City Mountain Resort, host of the Olympic snowboarding and giant slalom events. The awesome terrain couldn't be more family-friendly – or more accessible, rising as it does right over downtown.

Canyons Village
at Park City SNOW SPORTS, ADVENTURE SPORTS
(☑ 435-649-5400; www.parkcitymountain.com; 4000 Canyons Resort Dr; lift ticket adult/child $156/100) Bolstered by tens of millions of dollars in improvements, and now merged with Park City Mountain Resort (p877), Canyons seeks novelty with the first North American 'bubble' lift (an enclosed, climate-controlled lift), expanded services, 300 new acres of advanced trails and an increased snowmaking capability. The resort currently sprawls across nine aspen-covered peaks 4 miles outside of town, near the freeway.

🎉 Festivals & Events

Sundance Film Festival FILM
(☑ 888-285-7790; www.sundance.org/festival; ⊙ late Jan) Independent films and their makers, and movie stars and their fans, fill the town to bursting for 10 days in late January. Passes, ticket packages and the few individual tickets sell out well in advance – plan ahead.

🛏 Sleeping

Mid-December through mid-April is winter high season, with minimum stays required; rates rise during Christmas, New Year's and the Sundance Film Festival. Off-season rates drop 50% or more. For better nightlife, stay in the old town. A complete list of condos, hotels and resorts in Park City is at www.visitparkcity.com.

Park City Hostel HOSTEL $
(☑ 435-731-8811; www.parkcityhostel.com; 1781 Sidewinder Dr; dm/r with shared bath from $45/90; ◘ ❄ ❖) A welcome addition to a city seriously lacking in budget accommodations. Guests hang in a paneled lounge area downstairs and gather on the rooftop for weekly

cookouts. Stay in a six-bed dorm (mixed or female-only) or private rooms with shared bathrooms. Organized outings include group bike rides and bar crawls.

Newpark Resort HOTEL $$
(☑ 435-649-3600; www.newparkresort.com; 1476 Newpark Blvd; r from $175; ◘ ❄ ❖ ❖ ❖) A stylish hotel tucked into the shopping plaza. Extra points for heated floors and elevated beds with down duvets. Rooms have wood detail, flat-screen TV and coffeemaker; some include kitchen. There's a pool and hot tub, but breakfast isn't part of the package.

Peaks Hotel HOTEL $$
(☑ 435-649-5000; www.parkcitypeaks.com; 2346 Park Ave; d/ste $219/319; ◘ ❄ @ ❖ ❖) Comfortable, contemporary rooms include access to a heated outdoor pool, hot tub, restaurant and bar. Great deals off-season. December through April, breakfast is included.

★ **Washington**
School House BOUTIQUE HOTEL $$$
(☑ 435-649-3800; www.washingtonschoolhouse.com; 543 Park Ave; r $1000; ❄ ❖ ❖) Architect Trip Bennett oversaw the restoration that turned an 1898 limestone schoolhouse on a hill into a luxurious boutique hotel with 12 suites. How did the children ever concentrate when they could gaze out at the mountains through 9ft-tall windows instead? Rates drop to $405 from May to November.

🍴 Eating

Park City is well known for exceptional upscale eating – a reasonably priced meal is harder to find. The ski resorts have numerous eating options in season. Dinner reservations are required at all top-tier places in winter. From April through November restaurants reduce opening hours variably, and may take extended breaks, especially in May.

Five5eeds BREAKFAST $
(☑ 435-901-8242; www.five5eeds.com; 1600 Snow Creek Dr; mains $10-16; ⊙ 7:30am-3pm; ◘ ❖ ◪) An Australian-owned cafe that whips out some of the finest breakfast fare in town, such as eggs Benedict topped with spicy pulled pork, Moroccan-style baked eggs and many great vegetarian options. It also pours a nice strong cuppa.

Vessel Kitchen CAFE $
(☑ 435-200-8864; www.vesselkitchen.com; 1784 Uinta Way; mains $9-15; ⊙ 11am-9pm; ◘ ◪ ◨) Folks in the know head to this gourmet cafeteria in the shopping plaza for fast-value

eats. With kombucha on tap, avocado toast and lovely winter salads and stews, there's something for everyone, even kids. Other menu standouts include braised beef with sweet-potato hash and miso steelhead trout with spaghetti squash.

Cortona Italian Cafe ITALIAN $$
(☑435-608-1373; www.cortonaparkcity.com; 1612 Ute Blvd; mains $19-32; ◷5-8:30pm Tue-Sat) The fresh Tuscan-inspired pasta dishes you get at this small atmospheric Italian restaurant put the Main St competition to shame. Cortona's signature lasagna, which must be reserved ahead, is a menu highlight, as is the signature meatball-and-fettuccini dish. Everything is made to order and can take up to 30 minutes, but it's worth the wait. Reservations required.

Good Karma INDIAN, FUSION $$
(www.goodkarmarestaurants.com; 1782 Prospector Ave; breakfast $8-13, mains $15-25; ◷8am-9pm; P☑) ✐ Whenever possible, local and organic ingredients are used in the Indo-Persian meals at Good Karma. Start the day with Punjabi eggs and dine on curries and grilled meats. You'll recognize the place by the Tibetan prayer flags flapping out front.

★**Riverhorse on Main** AMERICAN $$$
(☑435-649-3536; www.riverhorseparkcity.com; 540 Main St; mains $42-92; ◷5-9pm; ☑) A fine mix of the earthy and exotic, with crab cake, stuffed acorn squash and macadamia-crusted halibut. There's a separate menu for vegetarians. A wall-sized window and the sleek modern design create a stylish atmosphere. Reserve ahead: this is a longtime, award-winning restaurant.

🍸 Drinking & Nightlife

Main St is where it's at. In winter there's action nightly; weekends are most lively off-season. Several restaurants, such as **Squatters** (☑435-649-9868; www.squatters.com; 1900 Park Ave; burgers $10-16, mains $11-24; ◷8am-10pm Sun-Thu, to 11pm Fri & Sat; P☎☑) and **Wasatch Brew Pub** (☑435-649-0900; www.wasatchbeers.com; 250 Main St; mains $10-25; ◷11am-10pm Mon-Fri, from 10am Sat & Sun; ☎), also have good bars. For better nightlife, stay in the old town.

★**High West Distillery** BAR
(☑435-649-8300; www.highwest.com; 703 Park Ave; ◷11am-9pm, tours 1pm & 2:30pm Mon-Thu & 11:30am, 1pm & 2:30pm Fri-Sun) This former livery and Model A–era garage is now home to Park City's most happenin' nightspot. The ski-in distillery was founded by a biochemist, and his bourbon and rye whiskeys have become legendary. Book a free tour to learn more about the process.

Spur BAR
(☑435-615-1618; www.thespurbarandgrill.com; 352 Main St; ◷10am-1am) Hosts live music every night with an eclectic offering of rock, folk, blues and electronica. Grab a drink and chill upstairs on a terrace overlooking the main drag, then head back downstairs and catch a band playing in the bar's back room.

ⓘ Information

Visitor Information Center (☑435-658-9616; www.visitparkcity.com; 1794 Olympic Pkwy; ◷9am-6pm; ☎) Vast visitor center with a coffee bar, a terrace and incredible views of the mountains at Olympic Park (p876). Visitor guides available online.

ⓘ Getting There & Around

Downtown Park City is 5 miles south of I-80 exit 145, 32 miles east of Salt Lake City and 40 miles from Salt Lake City International Airport (p875). Hwy 190 (closed October through March) crosses over Guardsman Pass between Big Cottonwood Canyon and Park City.

Bus 902 (☑801-743-3882; www.rideuta.com; one way $4.50) goes between Salt Lake City and Park City several times daily in the ski season. There's also private shared van service **Canyon Transportation** (☑801-255-1841; www.canyontransport.com; shared van to Park City adult/child $41/28) which offers shared vans from mountain locations to the airport and also has point-to-point transfers and jeep rentals delivered to your location.

The excellent free **public transit system** (☑435-615-5350; www.parkcity.org/departments/transit-bus; 558 Swede Alley; ◷7am-midnight) covers most of Park City, including the three ski resorts, and makes it easy not to need a car.

Northeastern Utah

Northeastern Utah is high-wilderness terrain, much of which is more than a mile above sea level. Most travelers come to see Dinosaur National Monument, but you'll also find other dino dig sites and museums, as well as Fremont Indian rock art and ruins in the area. Up near the Wyoming border, the Uinta Mountains and Flaming Gorge attract trout fishers and wildlife-lovers alike.

Vernal

As the closest town to Dinosaur National Monument, it's not surprising that Vernal welcomes you with a large pink allosaurus. The informative film, interactive exhibits, video clips and giant fossils at the **Utah Field House of Natural History State Park Museum** (☑ 435-789-3799; www.stateparks.utah.gov/parks/utah-field-house; 496 E Main St; adult/child $7/3.50; ⊙ 9am-7pm Jun-Aug, to 5pm Sep-May;) make a great all-round introduction to Utah's dinosaurs.

Now partnered with OARS, **Don Hatch River Expeditions** (☑ 435-789-4316, 800-342-8243; www.donhatchrivertrips.com; 221 N 400 E; 1-day tour adult/child $119/99; ⊙ May-Sep) runs a variety of one- to five-day trips locally and regionally.

The locally owned **Dinosaur Inn** (☑ 435-315-0123; www.dinoinn.com; 251 E Main St; r from $80;) provides the kind of down-home hospitality you'll rarely get at chain motels, which are numerous along Main St.

Holiday Inn Express & Suites (☑ 435-789-4654; www.ihg.com; 1515 W Hwy 40; r $121-162;) offers a few upscale touches. For dinner, try the excellent pub food at **Vernal Brewing Company** (☑ 435-781-2337; www.vernalbrewingcompany.com; 55 S 500 E; mains $12-28; ⊙ 11:30am-8pm Mon-Thu, to 9pm Fri & Sat;), or go Mexican at **Don Pedro's** (☑ 435-789-3402; www.facebook.com/donpedrosofvernal; 3340 N Vernal Ave; mains $11-20; ⊙ 11am-8:30pm Mon-Thu, to 9:30pm Fri & Sat, to 8pm Sun;).

Dinosaur National Monument

Straddling the Utah-Colorado state line, **Dinosaur National Monument** (☑ 435-781-7700; www.nps.gov/dino; 11625 E 1500 S, Jensen; 7-day pass per vehicle/motorcycle/person only $25/20/15; ⊙ 24hr) protects a huge dinosaur fossil bed, discovered in 1909. Both states' sections are beautiful, but Utah has the bones. Don't miss the **Quarry Exhibit** (www.nps.gov/dino; per vehicle $20; ⊙ 8am-7pm Memorial Day–Labor Day, to 4:30pm rest of year), an enclosed, partially excavated wall of rock

---

BEARS EARS NATIONAL MONUMENT

When President Barack Obama designated **Bears Ears** (www.fs.fed.us/visit/bears-ears-national-monument) as a national monument in December 2016, his proclamation provided protection for 1.35 million acres of land filled with ancient cliff dwellings, ponderosa forests, 4000-year-old petroglyphs, mesas, canyons and glorious red-rock formations. But it didn't last long.

In December 2017, President Donald Trump countered Obama with a proclamation of his own, reducing the monument's size by a whopping 85% to 201,876 acres. He also issued a declaration that shrank Grand Staircase-Escalante National Monument (p886) nearly in half, cutting it from 1,880,461 acres to 1,003,863 acres.

Conservationists fear Trump's action could do serious ecological harm as his administration rallies to increase jobs in the fossil-fuel sector and it eases environmental protections on public lands to facilitate mining and development projects. Federal lawsuits have been filed to challenge the latest proclamation and both sides have dug in for a highly contentious years-long court battle.

Bears Ears was created as a national monument at the request of five Native American tribes. The Navajo, Hopi, Zuni, Ute Mountain and Ute Indian tribes unified in hopes that its protected status would safeguard archaeological sites dating back 8500 years; sadly, some of these ancient grounds continue to get vandalized and destroyed.

Some notable landmarks within the monument include the **Bears Ears Buttes**, **Cedar Mesa**, **White Canyon**, **San Juan River**, **Indian Creek**, **Comb Ridge**, **Goosenecks State Park** (☑ 435-678-2238; www.stateparks.utah.gov; Rd 316; vehicles $5, camp sites $10; ⊙ 24hr) and **Valley of the Gods** (www.blm.gov). Their treasures, described by David Roberts' *In Search of the Old Ones*, are nothing short of exquisite.

In Bluff, the **Bears Ears Education Center** (☑ 435-672-2402; www.friendsofcedarmesa.org/bears-ears-center; 567 W Main St; ⊙ 9am-5pm Thu-Mon Mar-Nov) , an initiative of the conservation nonprofit Friends of Cedar Mesa, was created as a grassroots effort to teach visitors about the importance of visiting Bears Ears with respect for nature and Native American culture. For more info visit www.friendsofcedarmesa.org and www.bearsearscoalition.org.

with more than 1600 bones protruding. In summer, shuttles run to the Quarry itself, 15 miles northeast of Vernal's **Quarry Visitor Center** (📞435-781-7700; www.nps.gov/dino/planyourvisit/quarry-exhibit-hall.htm; 11625 E 1500 S, Jensen; per vehicle $25; ☉8am-5:30pm late May–mid-Sep, 9am-5pm mid-Sep–mid-May) on Hwy 149; out of season you drive there in a ranger-led caravan. Follow the Fossil Discovery Trail from below the parking lot (2.2 miles round trip) to see a few more giant femurs sticking out of the rock. The rangers' interpretive hikes are highly recommended.

In Colorado, the **Canyon Area** – 30 miles further east, outside Dinosaur, CO, and home to the monument's main **visitor center** (📞970-374-3000; 4545 E Hwy 40; ☉8am-5pm May-Sep, 9am-5pm Sep-May) – holds some stunning overlooks, but thanks to its higher elevation is closed by snow until late spring. Both sections have numerous hiking trails, interpretive driving tours, Green or Yampa river access and campgrounds ($8 to 15 per campsite).

Flaming Gorge National Recreation Area

Named for its fiery red sandstone formations, this gorge-ous park has 375 miles of reservoir shoreline, part of the Green River system. Resort activities at **Red Canyon Lodge** (📞435-889-3759; www.redcanyonlodge.com; 2450 W Red Canyon Lodge, Dutch John; 2-/4-person cabin from $169/179; 🛜🐾) include fly-fishing, rowing, rafting and horseback riding; its pleasantly rustic cabins have no TVs but there's wi-fi in the restaurant. **Nine Mile Bunk & Breakfast** (📞435-637-2572; www.9mileranch.com; 9 Mile Canyon Rd; r without/with bath from $80/90, cabins with shared bath $60-95, campsites $15; ☉Apr-Nov) offers themed rooms, a log cabin and campgrounds, and can organise canyon tours.

Contact the **USFS Flaming Gorge Headquarters** (📞435-784-3445; www.fs.usda.gov/ashley; 25 W Hwy 43, Manila; park day use $5; ☉8am-5pm Mon-Fri) for the public camping lowdown. The area's 6040ft elevation ensures pleasant summers.

Moab & Southeastern Utah

Experience the earth's beauty at its most elemental in this rocky-and-rugged desert corner of the Colorado Plateau. Beyond the few pine-clad mountains, there's little vegetation to hide the impressive handiwork

of time, water and wind: the thousands of red-rock spans in Arches National Park, the sheer-walled river gorges from Canyonlands to Lake Powell, and the stunning buttes and mesas of Monument Valley. The town of Moab is the best base for adventure, with as much four-wheeling, white-knuckle rafting, outfitter-guided fun as you can handle. Or you can lose the crowd while looking for Ancestral Puebloan rock art and dwellings in miles of isolated and undeveloped lands.

Green River

The 'World's Watermelon Capital,' the town of Green River offers a good base for river running on the Green and Colorado Rivers. The legendary one-armed Civil War veteran, geologist and ethnologist John Wesley Powell first explored these rivers in 1869 and 1871. Learn about his amazing travels at the **John Wesley Powell River History Museum** (📞435-564-3427; www.johnwesleypowell.com; 1765 E Main St; adult/child $6/2; ☉9am-7pm Mon-Sat, noon-5pm Sun Apr-Oct, 9am-5pm Nov-Mar), which doubles as the local visitor center.

Holiday River Expeditions (📞435-564-3273, 800-624-6323; www.bikeraft.com; 10 Holiday River St; day trip $210; ☉8am-5pm May-Sep) runs one-day rafting trips in Westwater Canyon, as well as multiday excursions. Hikers should try the beginner-friendly and serpentine **Little Wild Horse canyon** (www.utah.com/little-wild-horse-canyon). At the Skyfall Guestrooms you'll find three colorful riverfront rooms, each themed after a unique geological formation in the area. Family-owned **Robbers Roost Motel** (📞435-564-3452; www.rrmotel.com; 325 W Main St; r from $53; 🅿❄🛜🐾) is a motorcourt budget-motel gem. Otherwise, there's the **Green River State Park campground** (📞800-322-3770; www.reserveamerica.com; Green River Blvd; tent & RV sites $35, cabins $75), or numerous chain motels where W Main St (Business 70) connects with I-70.

Residents and rafters alike flock to **Ray's Tavern** (📞435-564-3511; www.facebook.com/raystavern; 25 S Broadway; dishes $9-28; ☉11am-9:30pm; 🛜), the local beer joint, for hamburgers and fresh-cut french fries. Green River is 182 miles southeast of Salt Lake City and 52 miles northwest of Moab, and is a stop on the daily *California Zephyr* train, run by **Amtrak** (📞800-872-7245; www.amtrak.com; 250 S Broadway) to Denver, CO (from $62, 10¾ hours).

Moab

Doling out hot tubs and pub grub after a dusty day on the trail, Moab is southern Utah's adventure base camp. Mobs arrive to play in Utah's recreation capital. From the hiker to the four-wheeler, the cult of recreation borders on fetishism.

The town becomes overrun from March through October. The impact of all those feet, bikes and 4WDs on the fragile desert is a serious concern. People here love the land, even if they don't always agree about how to protect it. If the traffic irritates you, just remember – you can disappear into the vast desert in no time.

🏃 Activities

★**Canyonlands Field Institute** TOURS
(☎435-259-7750; www.cfimoab.org; 1320 S Hwy 191; ⊗8:30am-4:30pm Mon-Fri) 🌿 This non-profit operation uses proceeds from guided tours to create youth outdoor-education programs and train local guides. It offers occasional workshops and seminars throughout the summer. Top tours include Colorado River trips and a geology- and archaeology-focused three-day outing.

Corona Arch Trail HIKING
(www.utah.com/hiking/arches-national-park/bowtie-corona-arches) To take in petroglyphs and two spectacular, rarely visited rock arches, hike the moderately easy Corona Arch Trail, the trailhead for which lies 10 miles up Potash Rd (Hwy 279). Follow cairns along the slickrock to **Bowtie** and **Corona Arches**. You may recognize Corona from a well-known photograph in which an airplane is flying through it – this is one big arch! The 3-mile walk takes two hours.

Sheri Griffith River Expeditions RAFTING
(☎435-259-8229; www.griffithexp.com; 2231 S Hwy 191; river trips from $95; ⊗8am-6pm) Operating since 1971, this rafting specialist has a great selection of river trips on the Colorado, Green and Yampa Rivers – from family floats to Cataract Canyon rapids, and from a full day to a couple of weeks.

★**Rim Cyclery** MOUNTAIN BIKING
(☎435-259-5333; www.rimcyclery.com; 94 W 100 N; bike rentals per day from $40; ⊗8am-6pm) Moab's longest-running family-owned bike shop not only does rentals and repairs, it also has a museum of mountain-bike technology, and rents cross-country skis in the winter.

WORTH A TRIP

ANTELOPE ISLAND STATE PARK

White-sand beaches, birds and buffalo are what attract people to the pretty, 15-mile-long **Antelope Island State Park** (☎801-725-9263; https://stateparks.utah.gov/parks/antelope-island; Antelope Dr; day use per vehicle $10, tent & RV sites without hookups $20; ⊗6am-10pm, visitor center 9am-6pm). That's right, the largest island in the Great Salt Lake is home to a 600-strong herd of American bison (buffalo). The October roundup, for veterinary examination, is a thrilling wildlife spectacle. Hundreds of thousands of migratory birds stop to feast on tiny brine shrimp along the Great Salt Lake's shore en route to distant lands during fall and spring migrations.

🛏 Sleeping

Prices drop by as much as 50% outside March to October; some smaller places close November through March. Most lodgings have hot tubs and mini-refrigerators, and motels have laundries. Cyclists should ask whether a property provides *secure* bike storage, not just an unlocked closet.

Though there's a huge number of motels, they are often booked out. Reserve as far ahead as possible. For an extensive lodging list, see www.discovermoab.com.

Individual **BLM campsites** (☎435-259-2100; www.discovermoab.com/blm-campgrounds; Hwy 128; tent sites $20; ⊗year-round) along the Colorado River on Hwy 128 are first-come, first-served. In peak season, check with the Moab Information Center (p882) to see which sites are full.

Kokopelli Lodge MOTEL $
(☎435-259-7615; www.kokopellilodge.com; 72 S 100 E; r from $98; ❄🛜🐾) Retro styling meets desert chic at this great-value budget motel. Amenities include a hot tub, BBQ grill and secure bike storage.

Moab Rustic Inn MOTEL $
(☎435-259-6177; www.moabrusticinn.com; 120 E 100 S; r from $119; P❄🛜🐾) Spacious rooms with full-size fridges, a heated swimming pool, friendly staff, central location and on-site laundry make this one of the best budget values in town.

DON'T MISS

ROBERT REDFORD'S SUNDANCE RESORT

Robert Redford's **ski resort** (☎801-223-4849; 8841 N Alpine Loop Rd; day lift ticket adult/child $85/58, ski & snowboard rentals from $35) could not be more idyllic. There are four chairlifts and a beginner area. Most terrain is intermediate and advanced, climbing 2150ft up the northeast slope of Mt Timpanogos. It hosts the Sundance Film Festival (p877) and the nonprofit Sundance Institute.

Pack Creek Ranch
RANCH $$

(☎435-259-5091, 888-879-6622; www.packcreekranch.com; Abbey Rd, off La Sal Mountain Loop; cabins $175-265; [P][🛜][♨]) This hidden Shangri-la's log cabins are tucked beneath mature cottonwoods and willow trees in the La Sal Mountains, 2000ft above Moab. Most feature fireplaces; all have kitchens and gas grills (bring groceries). No TV or phones. Edward Abbey is among the artists and writers who came here for inspiration. Amenities include an indoor hot tub and sauna.

★ Sunflower Hill Inn
INN $$$

(☎435-259-2974; www.sunflowerhill.com; 185 N 300 E; r $246-328; [P][❄][🛜][♨]) Wow! This is one of the best bets in town. A top-shelf B&B, Sunflower Hill offers 12 rooms in a quaint country setting. Grab a room in the cozier cedar-sided, early-20th-century home over the annex rooms. All rooms come with quilt-piled beds and antiques – some even have jetted tubs. Children under 10 not allowed.

Sorrel River Ranch
LUXURY HOTEL $$$

(☎435-259-4642; www.sorrelriver.com; Mile 17, Hwy 128; r from $629; [P][❄][@][♨]) Southeast Utah's only full-service luxury resort and gourmet restaurant was originally a 1903 homestead. The lodge and log cabins sit on 240 lush acres, with riding areas and alfalfa fields along the Colorado River. Details strive for rustic perfection, with bedroom fireplaces, handmade log beds, copper-top tables and Jacuzzi tubs. There is a two-night minimum stay during busy periods.

✖ Eating

There's no shortage of places to fuel up in Moab, from backpacker coffeehouses to gourmet dining rooms. Pick up the *Moab Menu Guide* (www.moabmenuguide.com) at area lodgings. Some restaurants close or reduce their days from December through March.

Milt's Stop & Eat
BURGERS $

(☎435-259-7424; www.miltsstopandeat.com; 356 Mill Creek Dr; mains $4-10; ⊗11am-8pm Tue-Sun) Meet greasy goodness. A triathlete couple bought this classic 1954 burger stand and smartly changed nothing. Milt's is known for it's grass-fed beef-burgers, buffalo burgers, fresh-cut fries and brain freeze-inducing shakes. Be patient: the wait can be painfully long. It's a popular gathering spot after visiting the **Slickrock Trail** (☎435-259-2444; www.utah.com/mountain-biking/slickrock; Sand Flats Recreation Area, Sand Flats Rd; car/cyclist $5/2).

Thai Bella
THAI $$

(☎435-355-0555; www.facebook.com/thaibella2019; 218 N 110 W; mains $15-30; ⊗1-9:30pm Mon-Fri, from 3pm Sat & Sun; 🌱) Of the growing number of Thai restaurants in Moab this place reigns supreme. Popular menu items include spicy stir-fried drunken noodles, New Zealand sweet basil mussels, tom yum soup and an ample selection of vegetarian dishes. Meals are served in a two-story 1896 historic building with a shady garden area.

Sabaku Sushi
SUSHI $$

(☎435-259-4455; www.sabakusushi.com; 90 E Center St; rolls $8-16, mains $17-19; ⊗5-9pm Tue-Sun; 🛜) The ocean is about a million miles away, but with overnight delivery from Hawaii, you still get a creative selection of fresh rolls, catches of the day and a few Utah originals at this small hole-in-the-wall sushi joint. Go for happy hour (5pm to 6pm Tuesday through Thursday) for discounts on rolls.

★ Desert Bistro
SOUTHERN US $$$

(☎435-259-0756; www.desertbistro.com; 36 S 100 W; mains $28-45; ⊗5-9pm) Stylized preparations of game and fresh, flown-in seafood are the specialty at this welcoming white-tablecloth restaurant inside an old house. Think bison filet mignon, seared scallops with lemon adobo and wedge salad with house-cured duck-breast bacon. Everything is made on-site, from freshly baked bread to delicious pastries. Great wine list, too. Reserve ahead.

❶ Information

Moab Information Center (☎435-259-8825; www.discovermoab.com/visitor-center; 38 E Center St; ⊗8am-7pm Mon-Sat, 9am-6pm Sun; 🛜) Excellent source of information on area parks, trails, activities, camping and weather. Extensive bookstore and helpful staff.

ℹ️ Getting There & Around

Moab is 235 miles southeast of Salt Lake City, 150 miles northeast of Capitol Reef National Park, and 115 miles southwest of Grand Junction, CO.

Canyonlands Field Airport (CNY; ☑ 435-259-0408; www.moabairport.com; 110 W Aviation Way, off Hwy 191), 16 miles north of town, receives flights from Denver. Major car-rental agencies, such as **Enterprise** (☑ 435-259-8505; www.enterprise.com; 1197 S Hwy 191; ⊙ 8am-5pm Mon-Fri), have representatives at the airport.

SkyWest operates daily **United Airlines** (☑ 800-864-8331; www.united.com) flights to Denver.

There are also on-demand bus and shuttle van services, including **Porcupine Shuttle** (☑ 435-260-0896; www.porcupineshuttle.com), **Roadrunner Shuttle** (☑ 435-259-9402; www.roadrunnershuttle.com) and **Canyonlands Shuttle** (☑ 435-210-4757; www.canyonlandsshuttle.com), to get you to Grand Junction, CO, the airport and Salt Lake City.

A private vehicle is pretty much a requirement to get around Moab and the parks. Hwy 191 becomes Main St as it passes through town.

Vehicle traffic is heavy in high season. There are a number of bike paths in and around town; the Moab Information Center (p882) can offer a map guide.

Coyote Shuttle (☑ 435-260-2097; www.coyoteshuttle.com) and Porcupine Shuttle travel on request to Canyonlands Field Airport and do hiker-biker and river shuttles.

Arches National Park

Giant sweeping arcs of sandstone frame snowy peaks and desert landscapes at **Arches National Park** (☑ 435-719-2299; www.nps.gov/arch; Hwy 191; 7-day pass per vehicle/motorcycle/person only $30/25/15; ⊙ 24hr, visitor center 7:30am-5pm Apr-Sep, 9am-4pm Oct-Mar). Explore the highest density of rock arches anywhere on earth: more than 2000 in a 119-sq-mile area. Nearly 1.5 million visitors make the pilgrimage here each year; it's just 5 miles north of Moab, and small enough for you to see most of it within a day. Many noteworthy arches are easily reached by paved roads and relatively short hiking trails. To avoid crowds, consider a moonlight exploration, when it's cooler and the rocks feel ghostly.

Highlights along the park's main scenic drive include **Balanced Rock**, perched beside the main park road, and, for hikers, the moderate-to-strenuous, 3-mile round-trip

trail that ascends the slickrock to reach the unofficial state symbol, **Delicate Arch** (best photographed in the late afternoon).

Further along the road, the spectacularly narrow canyons and maze-like fins of the **Fiery Furnace** must be visited on three-hour, ranger-led hikes, for which advance reservation is usually necessary. It's not easy: be prepared to scramble up and over boulders, shimmy down between rocks and navigate narrow ledges.

The scenic drive ends 19 miles from the visitor center at **Devils Garden**. The trailhead marks the start of a 2- to 7.7-mile round-trip hike that passes at least eight arches, though most hikers only go the relatively easy 1.3 miles to Landscape Arch, a gravity-defying, 290ft-long behemoth. For stays between March and October, advance reservations are a must for the **Devils Garden Campground** (☑ 877-444-6777; www.recreation.gov; tent & RV sites $25). No showers, no hookups.

Because of water scarcity and heat, few visitors backpack, though it is allowed with free permits (available from the visitor center).

Canyonlands National Park

Red-rock fins, bridges, needles, spires, craters, mesas, buttes – **Canyonlands National Park** (☑ 435-719-2313; www.nps.gov/cany/index.htm; 7-day pass per vehicle/motorcycle/person $30/25/15, tent & RV sites without hookups $15-20; ⊙ 24hr) is a crumbling beauty, a vision of ancient earth. Roads and rivers make inroads into this high-desert wilderness stretching 527 sq miles, but much of it is still untamed. You can hike, raft and 4WD here but be sure that you have plenty of gas, food and water.

The canyons of the Colorado and Green Rivers divide the park into four entirely separate areas. The appropriately named **Island in the Sky** district, just over 30 miles northwest of Moab, consists of a 6000ft-high flat-topped mesa that provides astonishing long-range vistas. Starting from the **visitor center** (☑ 435-259-4712; www.nps.gov/cany; Hwy 313; ⊙ 8am-6pm Mar-Dec, 8am-5pm Fri-Tue Jan & Feb), a scenic drive leads past numerous overlooks and trailheads, ending after 12 miles at **Grand View Point**, where a sinuous trail runs for a mile along the very lip of the mesa. Our favorite short hike en route is the half-mile loop to oft-photographed **Mesa Arch**, a slender, cliff-hugging span that frames a magnficent view of Washer Woman Arch. Seven miles from the visitor center, the first-come, first served, 12-site **Island in** the Sky Campground (Willow Flat; ☑ 435-719-2313; www.nps.gov/cany/planyourvisit/camping.htm; tent & RV sites $15; ⊗ year-round) has vault toilets but no water, and no hookups. Determined mountain bikers can tackle primitive **White Rim Road** (Island in the Sky), a 70-mile route encircling the Island in the Sky.

Named for the spires of orange-and-white sandstone jutting skyward from the desert floor, the wild and remote **Needles** district is ideal for backpacking and off-roading. To reach the **visitor center** (☑ 435-259-4711; www.nps.gov/cany; Hwy 211; ⊗ 8am-4:30pm), follow Hwy 191 south for 40 miles from Moab, then take Hwy 211 west. This area is much more about long, challenging hikes than roadside overlooks. The awesome **Chesler Park/Joint Trail Loop** is an 11-mile route across desert grasslands, past towering red-and-white-striped pinnacles, and through deep, narrow slot canyons, at times just 2ft across. Elevation changes are moderate, but the distance makes it an advanced day hike. The first-come, first-served, 27-site **Needles Campground** (Squaw Flat; ☑ 435-719-2313; www.nps.gov/cany/planyourvisit/camping.htm; tent & RV sites $20; ⊗ year-round), 3 miles west of the visitor center, fills up every day, spring to fall. It has flush toilets and running water, but no showers or hookups.

In addition to normal entrance fees, advance-reservation permits are required for overnight backpacking, mountain biking, 4WD trips and river trips. Permits are valid for 14 days and are issued at the **Island in the Sky Visitor Center** (☑ 435-259-4712; www.nps.gov/cany; Hwy 313; ⊗ 8am-6pm Mar-Dec, 8am-5pm Fri-Tue Jan & Feb), **Needles Visitor**

① LOCAL PASSES

Southeast Utah Parks Pass Southeastern Utah national parks sell a Southeast Utah Parks Pass (per vehicle $55) that's good for a year's entry to Arches (p883) and Canyonlands (p883) National Parks (where a seven-day vehicle pass is $30) and Natural Bridges National Monument (p885).

National Park Service Passes (www.nps.gov/findapark/passes.htm, per vehicle adult/senior $80/20) Available online and at parks, allow year-long access to all federal recreation lands in Utah and beyond – and are a great way to support the Southwest's amazing parks.

Center (☑ 435-259-4711; www.nps.gov/cany; Hwy 211; ⊗ 8am-4:30pm) and **Hans Flat Ranger Station** (☑ 435-259-2652; www.nps.gov/cany; Recreation Rd 777, Hans Flat; ⊗ 8am-4:30pm). Reservations are available online (https://canypermits.nps.gov/index.cfm) and through the **Arches & Canyonlands National Park Headquarters** (☑ 435-719-2100; www.nps.gov/cany; 2282 SW Resource Blvd; ⊗ 8am-4:30pm Mon-Fri) in Moab. Remoter areas west of the rivers, only accessible southwest of the town of Green River, include **Horseshoe Canyon**, where determined hikers are rewarded with extraordinary ancient rock art, and the **Maze**, the park's remotest frontier.

Dead Horse Point State Park

Tiny but stunning **Dead Horse Point State Park** (☑ 435-259-2614; www.stateparks.utah.gov/parks/dead-horse; Hwy 313; park day-use per vehicle $20, tent/RV sites $35/40, yurts $140; ⊗ park 6am-10pm, visitor center 9am-5pm) has been the setting for numerous movies, including the climactic scenes of *Thelma & Louise*. It's not a hiking destination, but mesmerizing views merit the short detour off Hwy 313 en route to the Island in the Sky in Canyonlands National Park: look out at red-rock canyons rimmed with white cliffs, the Colorado River, Canyonlands and the distant La Sal Mountains. The excellent **visitor center** (☑ 435-259-2614; www.stateparks.utah.gov/parks/dead-horse; ⊗ 9am-5pm) has exhibits, on-demand videos, books and maps, along with ranger-led walks and talks in summer. To the south, the 21-site **campground** (☑ 800-322-3770; www.reserveamerica.com; campsites/yurts $40/140) has water; no showers, no hookups. Reserve ahead.

Bluff

One hundred miles south of Moab, this little community (population 320) makes a comfortable, laid-back base for exploring Utah's desolately beautiful southeastern corner. Founded by Mormon pioneers in 1880, Bluff sits surrounded by red rock and public lands near the junction of Hwys 191 and 162, along the San Juan River. Other than a trading post and a couple of places to eat or sleep, there's not much town.

For backcountry tours that access rock art and ruins, join **Far Out Expeditions** (☑ 435-672-2294; www.faroutexpeditions.com; 690 E Mulberry Ave; half-/full-day tours $200/325) on a day or multiday hike into the remote region. A rafting trip along the San Juan with **Wild Rivers**

Expeditions (☏ 435-672-2244; www.riversand ruins.com; 2625 S Hwy 191, Bluff; half-day trip adult/ child $200/140), a history and geology-minded outfitter, also includes ancient site visits. The hospitable **Recapture Lodge** (☏ 435-672-2281; www.recapturelodge.com; 250 Main St; d $98; P ⊖ ❄ @ 🐾 ⛵) is a rustic, cozy place to stay. Owners know the region inside and out and can help with trip planning. You might also get off-grid at **Valley of the Gods B&B** (☏ 970-749-1164; www.valleyofthegodsbandb.com; off Hwy 261; s $145, d $175-195; P) 🐾, one of the original ranches in the area.

Artsy **Comb Ridge Eat & Drink** (☏ 435-485-5555; www.combridgeeatanddrink.com; 680 Main St; breakfast mains $5-7, dinner mains $10-17; ⊙ 11:30am-3pm & 5-9pm Wed-Sat, 9:30am-2pm & 5-9pm Sun; 🐾🖊) serves standout single-pour coffee and blue-corn pancakes inside a timber and adobe cafe, while the Western-themed **Cottonwood Steakhouse** (☏ 435-672-2282; www.cottonwoodsteakhouse. com; 409 W Main St; mains $17-29; ⊙ 5:30-9:30pm Mar-Nov; 🐾) serves substantial portions of barbecued steak and beans.

Hovenweep National Monument

Beautiful, little-visited **Hovenweep** (☏ 970-562-4282; www.nps.gov/hove; McElmo Rte, off Hwy 262; tent & RV sites $15; ⊙ park dusk-dawn, visitor center 8am-6pm Jun-Sep, 9am-5pm Oct-May) **FREE**, meaning 'deserted valley' in the Ute language, showcases several neighboring Ancestral Puebloan sites, where impressive towers and granaries stand in shallow desert canyons. The Square Tower Group is accessed near the ranger station; other sites require long hikes. The **campground** (☏ 970-562-4282; www.nps.gov/hove; McElmo Rte, Hovenweep National Monument; tent & RV sites $10-15) has 31 basic, first-come, first-served sites (no showers, no hookups). The main access is east of Hwy 191 on Hwy 262 via Hatch Trading Post, more than 40 miles northeast of Bluff.

Natural Bridges National Monument

Fifty-five miles northwest of Bluff, the ultra-remote **Natural Bridges National Monument** (www.nps.gov/nabr; Hwy 275; 7-day pass per vehicle $20, camp sites $15; ⊙ 24hr, visitor center 9am-5pm Apr–mid-Oct, 9am-5pm Thu-Mon mid-Oct–Mar) protects a white sandstone canyon (it's not red!) containing three impressive and easily accessible natural bridges. The oldest, **Owachomo Bridge**, spans

180ft but is only 9ft thick. The flat 9-mile Scenic Drive loop is ideal for overlooking. The campground offers 12 basic sites on a first-come, first served basis; no showers, no hookups. There is some primitive overflow camping space, but be aware that the nearest services are in Blanding, 40 miles east.

Zion & Southwestern Utah

Wonder at the deep-crimson canyons of Zion National Park; hike among the delicate pink-and-orange minarets at Bryce Canyon; drive past the swirling grey-white-and-purple mounds of Capitol Reef. Southwestern Utah is so spectacular that the vast majority of the territory has been preserved as national park or forest, state park or BLM wilderness. The whole area is ripe for outdoor exploration, with narrow slot canyons to shoulder through, pink sand dunes to scale and wavelike sandstone formations to seek out.

Capitol Reef National Park

Not as crowded as its fellow parks but equally scenic, **Capitol Reef** (☏ 435-425-3791; www. nps.gov/care/index.htm; cnr Hwy 24 & Scenic Dr; scenic drive per vehicle/pedestrian $20/10, tent & RV sites $20; ⊙ 24hr, visitor center 8am-4:30pm) contains much of the 100-mile Waterpocket Fold, created 65 million years ago when the earth's surface buckled up and folded, exposing a cross-section of geologic history that is painterly in its colorful intensity.

Hwy 24 cuts grandly through the park, but make sure you head south on the **Capitol Reef Scenic Drive** (www.nps.gov/care/ planyourvisit/scenicdrive.htm; 7-day pass per vehicle/person $20/10), a paved, dead-end 7.9-mile road that passes through orchards – a legacy of Mormon settlement. In season you can freely pick cherries, peaches and apples, and stop by the historic **Gifford Homestead** (☏ 435-425-3791; www.nps.gov/ care/learn/historyculture/giffordhomestead.htm; Scenic Dr; ⊙ 8am-5pm Mar-Oct) to see an old homestead museum and buy fruit-filled mini-pies. Great walks en route include the **Grand Wash** and **Capitol Gorge** trails, each following the level floor of a separate slender canyon. This terrific shady and green **campground** (☏ 435-425-3791; www. recreation.gov; Campground Rd, Fruita; sites $20) has no showers, no hookups and is first-come, first served; it fills early spring through fall.

Torrey

Just 15 miles west of Capitol Reef, the small pioneer town of Torrey serves as the base for most national-park visitors. In addition to a few Old West–era buildings, there are a dozen or so restaurants and motels.

Flirting with cowboy style, **Capitol Reef Resort** (☑435-425-3761; www.capitolreefresort. com; 2600 E Hwy 24; r $169-209, cabins & tipis from $269; P✳︎@🐾) is one of the closest to the national park of the same name. Dressed with country elegance, each airy room at the 1914 **Torrey Schoolhouse B&B** (☑435-491-0230; www.torreyschoolhouse.com; 150 N Center St; r $125-165; ☉Apr-Oct; ✳︎@) has a story to tell. (Butch Cassidy may have attended a town dance here.) After consuming the gourmet breakfast, laze in the garden or the huge 1st-floor lounge.

Located behind an RV park, **Torrey Grill & BBQ** (☑435-609-6997; www.torreygrilland bbq.com; 1110 W Hwy 24; mains $18-24; ☉5-9pm Mon-Sat Apr-Oct; P) serves praiseworthy dry-rubbed spare ribs, smoked beef tri-tip and home-style apple cobbler and ice cream in a rustic setting.

Boulder

Though the tiny outpost of Boulder (www. boulderutah.com; population 240) is just 32 miles south of Torrey on Hwy 12, you have to cross Boulder Mountain to reach it. From here, the attractive **Burr Trail Rd** heads east across the northeastern corner of the Grand Staircase–Escalante National Monument, eventually winding up on a gravel road that leads either up to Capitol Reef or down to Bullfrog Marina on Lake Powell.

The small **Anasazi State Park Museum** (☑435-335-7308; www.stateparks.utah.gov/parks/anasazi; 460 N Hwy 12; $5; ☉8am-6pm Apr-Oct, to 4pm Nov-Mar) curates artifacts and a Native American site inhabited from AD 1130 to 1175. Rooms at **Boulder Mountain Lodge** (☑435-335-7460; www.boulder-utah. com; 20 N Hwy 12; r/apt/ste from $140/230/325; P✳︎@🐾) are plush, but it's the 15-acre wildlife sanctuary setting that's unsurpassed. An outdoor hot tub with mountain views is a soothing spot to bird-watch. The lodge's destination restaurant, **Hell's Backbone Grill** (☑435-335-7464; www.hellsbackbonegrill.com; 20 N Hwy 12, Boulder Mountain Lodge; breakfast $9-14, lunch $12-18, dinner $23-37; ☉7am-2pm & 5-9pm Mar-Nov; 🍴) 🌿 serves soulful, earthy preparations of regionally inspired and sourced

cuisine – book ahead – while the nearby **Burr Trail Outpost** (☑435-335-7565; www. burrtrailoutpost.com; 14 N Hwy 12; ☉7:30am-7pm Apr-Sep, 8am-5pm Oct-Mar; @) offers organic coffee and scrumptious homemade desserts.

Grand Staircase–Escalante National Monument

The 2656-sq-mile **Grand Staircase–Escalante National Monument** (GSENM; ☑435-644-1300; www.blm.gov/visit/kanab-visitor-center; 745 Hwy 89, Kanab; ☉24hr) FREE, a waterless region so inhospitable that it was the last to be mapped in the continental US, covers more territory than Delaware and Rhode Island combined. The nearest services, and GSENM visitor centers, are in Boulder and Escalante on Hwy 12 in the north, and Kanab on US 89 in the south. Otherwise, infrastructure is minimal, leaving a vast, uninhabited canyonland full of 4WD roads that call to adventurous travelers who have the time, equipment and knowledge to explore.

The most accessible and most used trail in the monument is the 6-mile round-trip hike to the magnificent multicolored waterfall on **Lower Calf Creek** (Hwy 12, Mile 75; day use $5; ☉dawn-dusk), between Boulder and Escalante. The 14 sought-after creekside sites at **Calf Creek Campground** (☑435-826-5499; www. blm.gov/visit/calf-creek-recreation-area-campground; Hwy 12; tent & RV sites $15), just off Hwy 12, fill fast; no showers, no hookups, and no reservations taken.

Escalante

This national-monument gateway town of 800 souls is the closest thing to a metropolis for many a lonely desert mile. Thirty slow and winding miles from Boulder, and 65 from Torrey, it's a good place to base yourself before venturing into the adjacent Grand Staircase–Escalante National Monument. The **Escalante Interagency Visitor Center** (☑435-826-5499; www.blm.gov/visit/escalante-interacgency-visitor-center; 775 W Main St; ☉8am-4:30pm) is a superb resource center with complete information on nearby monument and forest-service lands.

Escalante Outfitters (☑435-826-4266; www.escalanteoutfitters.com; 310 W Main St; natural history tours $45, fly-fishing from $225; ☉7am-9pm) is a traveler's oasis: the bookstore sells maps, guides, camping supplies – and liquor(!) – while the pleasant cafe serves homemade breakfast, pizzas and salads. It also rents out tiny, rustic cabins (from $55). Longtime area outfitter **Excursions of Escalante** ([phone]800-839-7567; www.excursionsofescalante.com; 125 E Main St; all-day canyoneering $185; 8am-5pm Mon-Fri, to noon Sat mid-Mar–Oct) leads canyoneering, climbing and photo hikes.

Other fine lodgings in town include **Canyons B&B** ([phone]435-826-4747; www.canyonsbnb.com; 120 E Main St; d $160; Mar-Nov;) with upscale cabin rooms that surround a shady courtyard. Sleep in an upscale yurt on a tranquil 20-acre property with **Escalante Yurts** ([phone]435-826-4222; www.escalanteyurts.com; 1605 N Pine Creek Rd; yurts $235-345;). Savor exquisite pastries and great sandwiches at French-inspired **Mimi's Bakery & Deli** ([phone]435-826-4036; www.facebook.com/mimisbakeryescalante; 190 W Main St; pastries & sandwiches $3-7; 7am-4pm Tue-Sat;).

Bryce Canyon National Park

The Grand Staircase, a series of uplifted rock layers that climb in clearly defined 'steps' north from the Grand Canyon, culminates in the Pink Cliffs formation at this deservedly popular **national park** ([phone]435-834-5322; www.nps.gov/brca; Hwy 63, Bryce; 7-day pass per vehicle/motorcycle/person only $35/30/20; 24hr, visitor center 8am-8pm May-Sep, to 6pm Oct, to 4:30pm Nov-Mar, to 6pm Apr). Not actually a 'canyon', but an amphitheater eroded from the cliffs, it's filled with wondrous sorbet-colored pinnacles and points, steeples and spires, and totem-pole-shaped 'hoodoos'. The park is 50 miles southwest of Escalante; from Hwy 12, turn south on Hwy 63.

Rim Road Scenic Drive (8000ft) travels 18 miles, roughly following the canyon rim past the **visitor center** ([phone]435-834-5322; www.nps.gov/brca; Hwy 63; 8am-8pm May-Sep, to 6pm Oct & Apr, to 4:30pm Nov-Mar;), the lodge, incredible overlooks – don't miss **Inspiration Point** – and trailheads, ending at **Rainbow Point** (9115ft). From early May through early October, a free shuttle bus runs (8am until at least 5:30pm) from a staging area just north of the park to as far south as **Bryce Amphitheater**.

The park has two camping areas, both of which accept reservations through the park website. **Sunset Campground** ([phone]877-444-6777; www.recreation.gov; Bryce Canyon Rd; tent/RV site $20/30; Apr-Sep) is bit more wooded, but is not open year-round. Coin-op laundry and showers are available at the general store near **North Campground** ([phone]877-444-6777; www.recreation.gov; Bryce Canyon Rd; tent/

NEWSPAPER ROCK STATE HISTORIC MONUMENT

This tiny recreation area showcases a single large sandstone rock **panel** (Hwy 211, Monticello) packed with more than 300 petroglyphs attributed to Ute and Ancestral Puebloan groups during a 2000-year period. The many red-rock figures etched out of a black 'desert varnish' surface make for great photos. It's located 50 miles south of Moab, east of Canyonlands National Park on Hwy 211.

RV sites $20/30). During summer, remaining first-come, first-served sites fill before noon.

The 1920s **Bryce Canyon Lodge** ([phone]435-834-8700, 877-386-4383; www.brycecanyonforever.com; Hwy 63; r & cabins $223-270; Apr-Oct;) exudes rustic mountain charm. Rooms are in modern hotel-style units, with up-to-date furnishings, and thin-walled duplex cabins with gasfire places and front porches. No TVs. The lodge **restaurant** ([phone]435-834-5361; www.brycecanyonforever.com/dining; Bryce Canyon Rd; breakfast & lunch $10-20, dinner $10-35; 7am-10pm Apr-Oct) is excellent, if expensive, while **Bryce Canyon Pines Restaurant** ([phone]435-834-5441; www.brycecanyonrestaurant.com; Hwy 12; breakfast & lunch $9.50-14, dinner mains $12-24; 7am-8pm) is a diner classic.

Just north of the park boundaries, **Ruby's Inn** (www.rubysinn.com; 1000 S Hwy 63) is a resort complex with multiple motel lodging options, plus a campground. You can also dine at several restaurants, admire Western art, wash laundry, shop for groceries, fill up with gas, and take a helicopter ride.

Eleven miles east on Hwy 12, the small-town of **Tropic** (www.brycecanyoncountry.com) has additional food and lodging.

Kanab

At the southern edge of Grand Staircase–Escalante National Monument, vast expanses of rugged desert surround remote Kanab (population 4687). Western filmmakers made dozens of movies here from the 1920s to the 1970s, and the town retains an Old West feel.

Animal-lovers can tour **Best Friends Animal Sanctuary** (Map p854; [phone]435-644-2001; www.bestfriends.org; 5001 Angel Canyon Rd, Hwy 89; 8am-5pm;) FREE, the largest no-kill animal rescue center in the country.

John Wayne and Gregory Peck are among Hollywood notables who slumbered at the somewhat dated **Parry Lodge** (Map p854; 435-644-2601; www.parrylodge.com; 89 E Center St; r from $139-159; Mar-Nov;). The renovated **Canyons Lodge** (Map p854; 435-644-3069; www.canyonslodge.com; 236 N 300 W; r from $109-199;) motel has an art-house Western feel; rooms feature original artwork. Stay there, then eat downtown at French- and Italian-inspired **Vermillion 45** (Map p854; 435-644-3300; www.vermillion45.com; 210 S 110 E; mains $14-25; 11am-11pm Wed-Sun) bistro or the classy **Sego** (Map p854; 435-644-5680; www.segokanab.com; 190 N 300 W; mains $13-30; 6-10pm Mon-Sat Apr-Oct, 5-9pm Mon-Sat Nov-Mar;), where you can expect gorgeous eats such as foraged mushrooms with goat's cheese and noodles with red-crab curry.

The **GSENM Visitor Center** (Map p854; 435-644-1300; www.blm.gov/visit/kanab-visitor-center; 745 E Hwy 89; 8am-4:30pm) provides monument information; **Kane County Office of Tourism** (Map p854; 435-644-5033; www.visitsouthernutah.com; 78 S 100 E; 8am-7pm) focuses on town and movie sites.

Zion National Park

Get ready for an overdose of awesome. **Zion National Park** (435-772-3256; www.nps.gov/zion; Hwy 9; 7-day pass per vehicle/motorcycle/person only $35/30/20; 24hr, visitor center 8am-5pm Sep-May, to 7pm Jun-Aug) abounds in amazing experiences: gazing up at the red-and-white cliffs of **Zion Canyon**, soaring high over the **Virgin River**; peering beyond **Angels Landing** after a 1400ft ascent; or hiking downriver through the notorious **Narrows**. But it also holds more delicate beauties: weeping rocks, tiny grottoes, hanging gardens and meadows of mesa-top wildflowers. Lush

SCENIC DRIVE: HIGHWAY 12

Arguably Utah's most diverse and stunning route, **Hwy 12 Scenic Byway** (www.scenicbyway12.com; Hwy 12) winds through rugged canyonland on a 124-mile journey west of Bryce Canyon to near Capitol Reef. The section between Escalante and Torrey traverses a moonscape of sculpted slickrock, crosses narrow ridge backs and climbs over 11,000ft Boulder Mountain. Pretty much everything between Torrey and Panguitch is on or near Hwy 12.

vegetation and low elevation give the magnificent rock formations a far lusher feel than the barren parks in the east.

Most visitors enter the park along Zion Canyon floor; even the most challenging hikes become congested May through September (shuttle required). If you've time for only one activity, the 6-mile **Scenic Drive**, which pierces the heart of Zion Canyon, is the one. From mid-March through early-November, you have to take a free shuttle from the **visitor center** (435-772-3256; www.nps.gov/zion; Kolob Canyons Rd; 8am-5pm late May-Sep, to 4:30pm rest of year), but you can hop off and on at any of the scenic stops and trailheads along the way.

Of the easy to moderate trails, the paved, mile-long **Riverside Walk** at the end of the road is a good place to start. The **Angels Landing Trail** is a much more strenuous, 5.4-mile vertigo-inducer (1400ft elevation gain, with sheer drop-offs), but the canyon views are phenomenal. Allow four hours round trip.

The most famous backcountry route is the unforgettable **Narrows**, a 16-mile journey into skinny canyons along the Virgin River's north fork (June through October). Plan on getting wet: at least 50% of the 12-hour hike is in the river. Split the hike into two days, reserving an overnight camping spot in advance, or finish it in time to catch the last park shuttle. A trailhead shuttle is necessary for this one-way trip.

Heading eastwards, Hwy 9 climbs out of Zion Canyon in a series of six tight switchbacks to reach the 1.1-mile Zion–Mt Carmel Tunnel, a 1920s engineering marvel. It then leads quickly into dramatically different terrain – a landscape of etched multicolor slickrock, culminating at the mountainous **Checkerboard Mesa**.

Reserve far ahead and request a riverside site in the canyon's cottonwood-shaded **Watchman Campground** (877-444-6777; www.recreation.gov; Hwy 9; tent sites $20, RV sites with hookups $30;); adjacent **South Campground** (877-444-6777; www.recreation.gov; Hwy 9; tent & RV sites $20;) is first-come, first-served only. Smack in the middle of the scenic drive, rustic **Zion Lodge** (888-297-2757, same day reservations 435-772-7700; www.zionlodge.com; Zion Canyon Scenic Dr; r/cabins $227/260;) has basic motel rooms and cabins with gas fireplaces. All have wooden porches with stellar red-rock cliff views, but no TVs. The lodge's full-service dining room, **Red Rock Grill** (435-772-7760; Zion Canyon

Scenic Dr, Zion Lodge; breakfast & sandwiches $6-17, dinner $16.50-30; 6:30-10am & 11:30am-10pm Mar-Oct, hours vary Nov-Feb), has similarly amazing views. Just outside the park, the town of Springdale offers many more services.

Note that you must pay the park entrance fee to drive on public Hwy 9 in the park, even if you are just passing through.

Springdale

Positioned at the main, south entrance to Zion National Park, Springdale is a perfect little park town – though its main drag can get bottlenecked with traffic. Stunning red cliffs form the backdrop to eclectic cafes, restaurants are big on organic ingredients, and galleries are interspersed with indie motels and B&Bs.

In addition to hiking trails in the national park, you can take outfitter-led climbing, canyoneering, mountain biking and 4WD trips on adjacent BLM lands. **Zion Adventure Company** (435-772-1001; www.zionadventures.com; 36 Lion Blvd; canyoneering day from $189; 7am-8pm late May-late Sep, shorter hours rest of the year) offers excellent excursions, Narrows outfitting and hiker-biker shuttles, while **Zion Cycles** (435-772-0400; www.zioncycles.com; 868 Zion Park Blvd; half-/full-day rentals from $30/40, car racks from $15; 9am-6pm Feb-Nov) is the most helpful bike shop in town.

Desert Pearl Inn (888-828-0898, 435-772-8888; www.desertpearl.com; 707 Zion Park Blvd; r $269-299; 🅿@🐾🖵) offers the most stylish digs in town, while **Red Rock Inn** (435-772-3139; www.redrockinn.com; 998 Zion Park Blvd; r $105-309; 🖵🖵) has eight romantic country-contemporary cottages

Zion Canyon B&B (435-772-9466; www.zioncanyonbnb.com; 101 Kokopelli Circle; r $149-215; 🖵🖵) is the most traditional local B&B, with full gourmet breakfasts and mini-spa. The owners' creative collections of art and artifacts enliven the 1930s bungalow that is **Under the Eaves Inn** (435-772-9466; www.undertheeaves.com; 980 Zion Park Blvd; r $99-189; 🅿🖵🖵); the morning meal is a coupon for a local restaurant.

For a coffee and *trés bonnes crepes* – both sweet and savory – make **MeMe's Cafe** (435-772-0114; www.memescafezion.com; 975 Zion Park Blvd; mains $11-18; 7am-9pm) your first stop of the day. It also serves paninis and waffles, and for dinner, beef brisket and pulled pork. In the evening, the Mexican-tiled patio with twinkly lights at **Oscar's Cafe** (435-772-3232; www.cafeoscars.com; 948 Zion

Park Blvd; mains $12-20, breakfast $6-13; 7am-9pm) and the rustic **Bit & Spur Restaurant & Saloon** (435-772-3498; www.bitandspur.com; 1212 Zion Park Blvd; mains $14-30; 5-11pm Mar-Oct, 5-11pm Fri-Sun Nov-Feb;) are local-favored places to hang out, eat and drink. Reserve ahead for the excellent hotel-restaurant **King's Landing** (435-772-7422; www.klbzion.com; 1515 Zion Park Blvd, Driftwood Lodge; mains $18-38; 5-9pm;).

NEW MEXICO

The Land of Enchantment casts a bewitching spell. Whether it's sunlight and shadow playing out across juniper-speckled hills, the electric glow of gypsum dunes at sunset or the Rio Grande Gorge cracking across the Taos Plateau, the landscape is undeniably mesmerizing. And it's all easily explored by hiking, cycling or paddling. The history is fascinating too, evidenced in the ancient pueblos, the homes and holding cells of trappers and outlaws, and the mud-brick churches filled with sacred art. And we haven't even mentioned the chile-smothered enchiladas, the thriving microbreweries or *Better Call Saul*. As for Meow Wolf, you'll want get in line right now.

Perhaps New Mexico's charm is best expressed in the simple but iconic paintings of Georgia O'Keeffe. The artist herself exclaimed, on her very first visit: 'Well! Well! Well!... This is wonderful! No one told me it was like this.'

But seriously, how could they?

History

Ancestral Puebloan civilization first began to flourish in the 8th century AD, and the impressive structures at Chaco Canyon were begun not long after. By the time Francisco Vasquez de Coronado got here in the 16th century, many Pueblo Indians had migrated to the Rio Grande Valley and were the dominant presence. After Santa Fe was established as the Spanish colonial capital in around 1610, Spanish colonists fanned out across northern New Mexico and Catholic missionaries began their often violent efforts to convert the Puebloans. Following the Pueblo Revolt of 1680, Native Americans occupied Santa Fe until 1692, when Don Diego de Vargas recaptured the city.

The US took control of New Mexico in 1846 during the Mexican-American War, and it became a US Territory in 1850. Native American wars with the Navajo, Apache and

SOUTHWEST NEW MEXICO

Comanche further transformed the region, and the arrival of the railroad in the 1870s prompted an economic boom.

Painters and writers set up art colonies in Santa Fe and Taos in the early 20th century, and New Mexico became the 47th state in 1912. A top-secret scientific community descended on Los Alamos in 1943 and developed the atomic bomb. Some say that four years later, aliens crashed outside of Roswell...

ℹ Information

For information on the New Mexico stretch of Route 66, visit www.rt66nm.org.

New Mexico State Parks (www.emnrd.state. nm.us) Info about state parks, with a link to campsite reservations.

New Mexico Tourism (www.newmexico.org) Information about destination planning, activities and events.

Recreation.gov (www.recreation.gov) Reservations for national park and forest campsites and tours.

Albuquerque

A bustling desert crossroads, Albuquerque is just the right mix of urban and wild: the pink hues of the Sandia Mountains at sunset, the Rio Grande's cottonwood bosque, Route 66 diners and the hometown of Walter White and Saul Goodman. It's the largest city in the state, yet you can still hear the howls of coyotes when the sun goes down.

Good hiking and mountain-biking trails abound just outside of town, while the city's modern museums explore Pueblo culture, New Mexican art and space. Take the time to let your engine cool as you take a walk among the desert petroglyphs or order up a plate of red-chile enchiladas and a local beer – and with so many great breweries here it could take a while.

◉ Sights

◉ Old Town

From its foundation in 1706 until the arrival of the railroad in 1880, the plaza, centering on the diminutive 1793 **San Felipe de Neri Church** (www.sanfelipedeneri.org; 2005 N Plaza NW, Old Town Plaza; ⊙7am-5:30pm daily, museum 9:30am-4:30pm Mon-Fri, to 5pm Sat), was the hub of Albuquerque. Today Old Town is the city's most popular tourist area.

★**Albuquerque Museum**　　　　MUSEUM
(🖉505-243-7255; www.cabq.gov/museum; 2000 Mountain Rd NW; adult/teen 13-18yr/child 4-12yr $6/6/3; ⊙9am-5pm Tue-Sun; P) Formerly known as the Albuquerque Museum of Art & History, this showpiece museum shouldn't be missed. With an engaging Albuquerque history gallery that's imaginative, interactive and easy to digest and a permanent New Mexico art collection that extends to 20th-century masterpieces from Taos, it's a great place to explore as part of any visit to Old Town. There's free admission on Sunday mornings, and free guided walking tours of Old Town on Sunday, Tuesday, Thursday and Friday at 11am (April through November).

★**American International Rattlesnake Museum**　　　MUSEUM
(🖉505-242-6569; www.rattlesnakes.com; 202 San Felipe St NW; adult/child $6/4; ⊙10am-6pm Mon-Sat, 1-5pm Sun Jun-Aug, 11:30am-5:30pm Mon-Fri, 10am-6pm Sat, 1-5pm Sun Sep-May) Anyone charmed by snakes and all things slithery will find this museum fascinating; for ophidiophobes, it's a complete nightmare, filled with the world's largest collection of different rattlesnake species. You'll also find snake-themed beer bottles and postmarks from every town named 'Rattlesnake' in the US.

◉ Around Town

★**Indian Pueblo Cultural Center**　　MUSEUM
(IPCC; 🖉505-843-7270; www.indianpueblo.org; 2401 12th St NW; adult/child 5-17yr $8.40/5.40; ⊙9am-5pm; P) Collectively run by New Mexico's 19 Pueblos, this cultural center is an essential stop-off during even the shortest Albuquerque visit. Revamped in 2016, the museum today holds fascinating displays sharing the stories of the Pueblos' collective history and individual artistic traditions, while the galleries offer changing temporary exhibitions. They're arrayed in a crescent around a plaza that's regularly used for dances and crafts demonstrations. **Pueblo Harvest Cafe** (🖉505-724-3510; www. puebloharvestcafe.com; 2401 12th St NW; lunch $13-20, dinner $12-40; ⊙7am-9pm Mon-Sat, to 4pm Sun; 🖉🌇) is recommended and there's also a large gift shop and retail gallery.

Petroglyph National Monument　　ARCHAEOLOGICAL SITE
(🖉505-899-0205; www.nps.gov/petr; 6001 Unser Blvd NW; ⊙visitor center 8am-4:30pm; P) FREE The lava fields preserved in this large desert park, west of the Rio Grande, are adorned

with more than 23,000 ancient petroglyphs (1000 BC–AD 1700). Several trails are scattered far and wide: **Boca Negra Canyon** is the busiest and most accessible (open 8:30am to 4:30pm; parking $1/2 weekday/weekend); **Piedras Marcadas** holds around 300 petroglyphs (sunrise to sunset); while **Rinconada Canyon** is a lovely desert walk (sunrise to sunset; 2.2 miles round trip), but with fewer visible petroglyphs.

Sandia Peak Tramway CABLE CAR
(☑505-856-7325; www.sandiapeak.com; 30 Tramway Rd NE; adult/youth 13-20yr/child $25/20/15, parking $2; ⊙9am-9pm Jun-Aug, 9am-8pm Wed-Mon, from 5pm Tue Sep-May; ℗) The United States' longest aerial tram climbs 2.7 miles from the desert floor in the northeast corner of the city to the summit of 10,378ft Sandia Crest. Views are spectacular at any time, though sunsets are particularly brilliant. The summit complex holds gift shops, and a new fine dining restaurant and sky bar were adding the final touches during our research period. Hiking trails lead through the woods. If you plan on hiking down (or up), a one-way ticket costs $15.

🏃 Activities

The omnipresent Sandia Mountains and the less-crowded Manzano Mountains offer outdoor activities, including hiking, skiing (downhill and cross-country), mountain biking, rock climbing and camping.

Cycling is the ideal way to explore Albuquerque under your own steam. In addition to cycling lanes throughout the city, mountain bikers will dig the foothills trails east of town and the scenic **Paseo del Bosque** (www.cabq.gov; ⊙dawn-dusk), alongside the Rio Grande. For details of the excellent network of cycling lanes, see www.bikeabq.org.

The setting for the hit AMC dramas *Breaking Bad* and *Better Call Saul,* Albuquerque is a fun destination for fans, who can check out locations seen in both shows. Cyclists can tour with **Routes Rentals** (☑505-933-5667; www.routesrentals.com; 404 San Felipe St NW; 4/24hr rental from $20/35; ⊙8am-6pm Mar-Nov, to 5:30pm Dec-Feb) or hop on an RV with **Breaking Bad RV Tours** (1919 Old Town Rd; 3hr tour per person $75).

**Elena Gallegos
Open Space** HIKING, MOUNTAIN BIKING
(☑505-452-5200; www.cabq.gov; Simms Park Rd; weekday/weekend parking $1/2; ⊙7am-9pm Apr-Oct, closes 7pm Nov-Mar) The western foothills

of the Sandias are Albuquerque's outdoor playground, and the high desert landscape here is sublime. As well as several picnic areas, this section holds trailheads for hiking, running and mountain biking; some routes are wheelchair-accessible. Come early, before the sun gets too hot, or late, to enjoy the panoramic views at sunset amid the lonesome howls of coyotes. Basic trail maps are available on your way in.

🎉 Festivals & Events

Friday's *Albuquerque Journal* (www.abqjournal.com) includes exhaustive listings of festivals and activities.

Gathering of Nations Powwow CULTURAL
(www.gatheringofnations.com; ⊙late Apr) Dance competitions, displays of Native American arts and crafts, and the 'Miss Indian World' contest. Held in late April.

★**International Balloon Fiesta** BALLOON
(www.balloonfiesta.com; $10; ⊙early Oct) The largest balloon festival in the world. You simply haven't lived until you've seen a three-story-tall Tony the Tiger land in your

SOUTHWEST ALBUQUERQUE

NEW MEXICO FACTS

Nickname Land of Enchantment

Population 2.1 million

Area 121,298 sq miles

Capital city Santa Fe (population 80,880)

Other cities Albuquerque (population 560,200), Las Cruces (102,296)

Sales tax 5.1% to 9.25%

Birthplace of John Denver (1943–97), Smokey Bear (1950–76)

Home of International UFO Museum & Research Center (Roswell)

Politics A 'purple' state, with a more liberal north and conservative south

Famous for Ancient pueblos, the first atomic bomb (1945), where Bugs Bunny should have turned left

State question 'Red or green?' (chili sauce, that is)

Highest/Lowest points Wheeler Peak (13,161ft) / Red Bluff Reservoir (2842ft)

Driving distances Albuquerque to Santa Fe 50 miles, Santa Fe to Taos 70 miles

hotel courtyard, and that's exactly the sort of thing that happens during the festival, which features mass dawn take-offs on each of its nine days, overlapping the first and second weekends in October.

Sleeping

★ El Vado
MOTEL $

(☎ 510-361-1667; www.elvadoabq.com; 2500 Central Ave SW; r $137-150, ste $150-180) The white adobe walls of this revamped Route 66 motor court darn near glow as the sun rises, when you might just catch hot-air balloons rising almost overhead. Anchored by a central pool and flanked by a taproom and a handful of small eateries, this place – built in 1937 – exudes a hip-but-welcoming vibe. Mid-century modern decor.

Andaluz
BOUTIQUE HOTEL $$

(☎ 505-388-0088; www.hotelandaluz.com; 125 2nd St NW; r/ste from $191/206; P ❋ @ ⊛ ▦) Albuquerque's finest historic hotel, built in the heart of downtown in 1939, has been modernized while retaining period details such as its stunning central atrium, where cozy arched nooks hold tables and couches. Rooms feature hypoallergenic bedding and carpets, the Más Tapas Y Vino (☎ 505-923-9080; tapas $8-22, mains $26-38; ⊙ 7am-2pm & 5-9:30pm) restaurant is notable, and there's a rooftop bar Ibiza Bar & Patio.

Böttger Mansion
B&B $$

(☎ 505-243-3639; www.bottger.com; 110 San Felipe St NW; r $120-169; P ❋ @ ⊛) The friendly proprietor gives this well-appointed B&B, built in 1912 and one minute's walk from the plaza, an edge over tough competition. Three of its seven themed, antique-furnished rooms have pressed-tin ceilings, one has a Jacuzzi, and sumptuous breakfasts are served in a honeysuckle-lined courtyard loved by bird-watchers. Past guests include Elvis, Janis Joplin and Machine Gun Kelly.

★ Los Poblanos
B&B $$$

(☎ 505-344-9297; www.lospoblanos.com; 4803 Rio Grande Blvd NW; r/ste from $255/340; P ❋ @ ⊛ ▦) This amazing 20-room inn, on a 1930s rural ranch that's a National Historic Place, is five minutes' drive north of Old Town. Near the Rio Grande, it's set amid 25 acres of gardens, lavender fields and an organic farm. Gorgeous rooms feature kiva fireplaces, while produce from the farm is served at Campo, the on-site restaurant earning national acclaim for its wood-fired fare.

Breakfast is not included in the room price, but you can dine at Campo or pick up something quick at the Farm Store. For cocktails, it's hard to beat the rustically chic Bar Campo. The lavender blooms mid-June through July.

Eating

★ Pop Fizz
MEXICAN $

(☎ 505-508-1082; www.pop-fizz.net; 1701 4th St SW, National Hispanic Cultural Center; popsicles from $2.50, snacks $6-9; ⊙ 11am-6pm Mon, to 7pm Tue-Thu & Sun, to 8pm Fri & Sat; ⊛ ▦) These all-natural paletas (popsicles) straight-up rock: cool off with flavors such as cucumber chile lime, mango or pineapple habanero – or perhaps you'd rather splurge on a cinnamon-churro ice-cream taco? The kitchen also whips up all sorts of messy goodness, including carne asada fries, Sonoran dogs and Frito pies. The mango red chile is deliciously kicky.

★ Golden Crown Panaderia
BAKERY $

(☎ 505-243-2424; www.goldencrown.biz; 1103 Mountain Rd NW; pastries $1-3, mains $10-25; ⊙ 7am-8pm Tue-Sat, from 10am Sun) Who doesn't love a friendly neighborhood cafe-bakery? Especially one in a cozy old adobe, with gracious staff, oven-fresh bread and pizza (with green chile or blue-corn crusts), fruity empanadas, smooth espresso coffees and cookies all round? Call ahead to reserve a loaf of quick-selling green-chile bread – then eat it hot, out on the patio.

Frontier
NEW MEXICAN $

(☎ 505-266-0550; www.frontierrestaurant.com; 2400 Central Ave SE; mains $4-14; ⊙ 5am-1am; ▦) This giant cantina that sprawls across several rooms has to be seen to be believed: get in line for enormous buttery cinnamon rolls, smothered enchiladas and some of the best huevos rancheros in town. It may be fast-foody, but the atmosphere and prices are unbeatable.

Level 5
AMERICAN $$

(☎ 505-246-9989; www.hotelchaco.com; 2000 Bellemah Ave; $14-54; ⊙ 7am-2pm daily, 4:30-10pm Sun-Wed, to 11pm Thu-Sat) Whoa, that view. A breathtaking panorama of Albuquerque, flanked by the Sandia Mountains, accompanies your meal, whether dining inside or out at this sleek spot atop the Hotel Chaco. Service is upbeat but a little flighty, but the fancy fare on the short and seasonal menu delivers. Much of the produce is sourced from the hotel garden below.

★ **Artichoke Cafe** MODERN AMERICAN **$$$**
(☑505-243-0200; www.artichokecafe.com; 424 Central Ave SE; lunch mains $12-19, dinner mains $24-39; ◷11am-2:30pm & 5-9pm Mon-Fri, 5-10pm Sat, 5-9pm Sun) Elegant and unpretentious, this popular bistro prepares creative gourmet cuisine with panache and is always high on foodies' lists of Albuquerque's best. The Scottish Salmon at dinner is good. It's on the eastern edge of downtown, between the bus station and I-40.

🍷 Drinking & Entertainment

Popejoy Hall (☑505-277-3824; www.popejoypresents.com; 203 Cornell Dr NE) is the primary venue for big-name national acts, local opera, symphony and theater. **Launch Pad** (☑505-764-8887; www.launchpadrocks.com; 618 Central Ave SW) is best for local acts. To find out what's happening in town, pick up the free weekly *Alibi* (www.alibi.com).

★ **Marble Brewery** MICROBREWERY
(☑505-243-2739; www.marblebrewery.com; 111 Marble Ave NW; ◷noon-midnight Mon-Sat, to 10:30pm Sun) Convivial downtown brewpub, attached to its namesake brewery, with a snug interior for winter nights and a beer garden where local bands play early-evening gigs in summer. If it's nice out, snag a spot on the rooftop deck. Be sure to try its Red Ale. There's usually a food truck or two parked outside.

Java Joe's CAFE
(☑505-765-1514; www.downtownjavajoes.com; 906 Park Ave SW; ◷6:30am-3:30pm; 🚼🐾) Best known these days for its explosive cameo role in *Breaking Bad*, this comfy coffee shop still makes a great stop-off for a java jolt or a bowl of the hottest chile in town.

Anodyne BAR
(☑505-244-1820; 409 Central Ave NW; ◷4pm-2am Mon-Sat, 7pm-midnight Sun) An excellent spot for a game of pool, Anodyne is a huge space with book-lined walls, wood ceilings, plenty of overstuffed chairs, more than 100 bottled beers and great people-watching on Central Ave.

ℹ Information

EMERGENCY & MEDICAL SERVICES
Police (☑505-768-2200; www.cabq.gov/police; 400 Roma Ave NW)
Presbyterian Hospital (☑505-841-1234; www.phs.org; 1100 Central Ave SE; ◷emergency 24hr)
UNM Hospital (☑505-272-2111; 2211 Lomas Blvd NE; ◷emergency 24hr) Holds a level 1 trauma center.

TOURIST INFORMATION
Old Town Information Center (☑505-243-3215; www.visitalbuquerque.org; 303 Romero Ave NW; ◷10am-5pm Nov-Apr, to 6pm May-Oct) Come here to get the scoop. In Plaza Don Luis.

ℹ Getting There & Around

AIR
New Mexico's largest airport, **Albuquerque International Sunport** (ABQ; ☑505-244-7700; www.abqsunport.com; 2200 Sunport Blvd SE; 🛜), is 5 miles southeast of downtown and served by multiple airlines. Free shuttles connect the terminal building with the Sunport Car Rental Center at 3400 University Blvd SE, home to all the airport's car-rental facilities.

The **Sandia Shuttle** (☑888-775-5696; www.sandiashuttle.com; Santa Fe one way $33; ◷8:45am-11:45pm) runs from the airport to Santa Fe 19 times per day.

BUS
The **Alvarado Transportation Center** (☑505-423-7433; www.cabq.gov/transit; 100 1st St SW,

---

ALBUQUERQUE FOR KIDS

Albuquerque has lots on offer for kids, from hands-on museums to cool hikes.

¡Explora! (☑505-224-8300; www.explora.us; 1701 Mountain Rd NW; adult/child 1-11yr $10/6; ◷10am-6pm Mon-Sat, from noon Sun; 🅿🚼) From the lofty high-wire bike to the mind-boggling Light, Shadow, Color area, this gung-ho museum offers a hands-on exhibit for every type of child (don't miss the elevator).

New Mexico Museum of Natural History & Science (☑505-841-2800; www.nmnaturalhistory.org; 1801 Mountain Rd NW; adult/child 3-12yr $8/5; ◷9am-5pm; 🅿🚼) Dinosaur-mad kids are certain to love this huge modern museum, on the northeastern fringes of Old Town. From the T. rex in the main atrium onwards, it's crammed with ferocious ancient beasts.

cnr Central Ave) is home to **Greyhound** (☑ 505-243-4435, 800-231-2222; www.greyhound.com; 320 1st St SW), which serves destinations throughout the state and beyond, though not Santa Fe or Taos.

ABQ Ride (☑ 505-243-7433; www.cabq.gov/transit; 100 1st St SW; adult/child $1/35¢, day pass $2) is a public bus system covering most of Albuquerque on weekdays and major tourist spots daily.

TRAIN

Amtrak's *Southwest Chief* stops at Albuquerque's **Amtrak Station** (☑ 800-872-7245; www.amtrak.com; 320 1st St SW), which is part of the Alvarado Transportation Center. Trains head east to Chicago (from $149, 26 hours) or west to Los Angeles (from $67, 16¾ hours), once daily in each direction.

A commuter light-rail line, the **New Mexico Rail Runner Express** (www.riometro.org; adult/child $10/5), shares the station. It makes several stops in the Albuquerque metropolitan area, but more importantly for visitors it runs all the way north to Santa Fe (one way $10, 1¾ hours), with eight departures on weekdays, four on Saturdays and three on Sundays.

Along I-40

Although you can zip between Albuquerque and Flagstaff, AZ, in less than five hours, the national monuments and pueblos along the way are well worth a visit. For a scenic loop, take Hwy 53 southwest from Grants, which leads to all the following sights except Acoma. Hwy 602 brings you north to Gallup.

Acoma Pueblo

The dramatic mesa-top 'Sky City' sits 7000ft above sea level and 367ft above the surrounding plateau. One of the oldest continuously inhabited settlements in North America, this place has been home to pottery-making Pueblo peoples since the 11th century. Guided tours leave from the **cultural center** (☑ 800-747-0181; www.acomaskycity.org; Rte 38; tours adult/child $25/17; ⊙ tours 9-30am-3:30pm mid-Mar–Oct, to 2:30pm Nov–mid-Mar; ℗) at the foot of the mesa and take 90 minutes. For the most dramatic drive to Sky City, take exit 102 from I-40, which is about 60 miles west of Albuquerque. Check the cultural center website before your visit for detailed directions. Also confirm it's not closed for ceremonial or other reasons.

El Morro National Monument

The 200ft sandstone outcropping at **El Morro National Monument** (☑ 505-783-4226; www.nps.gov/elmo; Hwy 53; ⊙ visitor center 9am-6pm Jun-Aug, to 5pm Sep-May, trails close 1hr earlier; ℗) **FREE**, also known as 'Inscription Rock,' has been a travelers' oasis for millennia. Thousands of carvings – from petroglyphs in the pueblo at the top (c 1275) to elaborate inscriptions by Spanish conquistadors and Anglo pioneers – offer a unique historical record. Make time for the **Mesa Top Trail** and its sweeping views in addition to the shorter **Inscription Rock Trail**. It's about 38 miles southwest of Grants via Hwy 53.

Zuni Pueblo

The Zuni are known for their delicately inlaid silverwork, which is sold in stores lining Hwy 53. Check in at the **Zuni Tourism Visitor Center** (☑ 505-782-7238; www.zunitourism.com; 1239 Hwy 53; ⊙ 9am-5:30pm Mon-Fri, plus 9am-4pm Sat Jul-Sep) for information, photo permits and tours of the pueblo, which lead you among stone houses and beehive-shaped adobe ovens to the massive **Our Lady of Guadalupe Mission**, featuring impressive kachina (spirit) murals. The **A:shiwi A:wan Museum & Heritage Center** (☑ 505-782-4403; www.ashiwi-museum.org; Ojo Caliente Rd; ⊙ 8am-5pm Mon-Fri) **FREE** displays early photos and other tribal artifacts.

The friendly, eight-room **Inn at Halona** (☑ 505-782-4547; www.halona.com; 23b Pia Mesa Rd; r from $85; ℗ ☎), decorated with local Zuni arts and crafts, is the only place to stay on the pueblo.

Santa Fe

Missions, museums and Meow Wolf. All are players in the story of 'the city different,' a place that makes its own rules without forgetting its long and storied past. Walking through its adobe neighborhoods, or around the busy plaza that remains its core, there's no denying that Santa Fe has a timeless, earthy soul. Indeed, its artistic inclinations are a principal attraction – there are more quality museums and galleries here than you could see in just one visit.

At more than 7000ft above sea level, Santa Fe is also the nation's highest state capital. Sitting at the foot of the Sangre de Cristo range, it makes a fantastic base for hiking, mountain biking and skiing. Après adventure, you can indulge in chile-smothered local cuisine, buy turquoise and silver directly from Native American jewelers in the Plaza, visit remarkable churches, or simply wander centuries-old, cottonwood-shaded lanes, daydreaming about one day moving here.

Sights

★ The Plaza
PLAZA

(Map p896) For more than 400 years, the Plaza has stood at the heart of Santa Fe. Originally it marked the far northern end of the Camino Real from Mexico; later, it was the goal for wagons heading west along the Santa Fe Trail. Today, this grassy square is peopled by tourists wandering from museum to margarita, food vendors, skateboarding kids and street musicians. Beneath the portico of the Palace of the Governors, along its northern side, Native Americans sell jewelry and pottery.

★ Georgia O'Keeffe Museum
MUSEUM

(Map p896; 505-946-1000; www.okeeffe museum.org; 217 Johnson St; adult/child $13/free; ⊙10am-5pm Sat-Thu, to 7pm Fri) With 10 beautifully lit galleries in a rambling 20th-century adobe, this museum boasts the world's largest collection of O'Keeffe's work. She's best known for her luminous New Mexican landscapes, but the changing exhibitions here range through her entire career, from her early years through to her time at Ghost Ranch. Major museums worldwide own her most famous canvases, so you may not see familiar paintings, but you're sure to be bowled over by the thick brushwork and transcendent colors on show.

Meow Wolf
MUSEUM

(505-395-6369; www.meowwolf.com; 1352 Rufina Circle; adult/child $29/21; ⊙10am-8pm Sun, Mon, Wed & Thu, to 10pm Fri & Sat, from 9am mid-Jun–mid-Aug; P🞀) If you've been hankering for a trip to another dimension but have yet to find a portal, the House of Eternal Return by Meow Wolf could be the place for you. The premise here is quite ingenious: visitors get to explore a recreated Victorian house for clues related to the disappearance of a Californian family, following a narrative that leads deeper into fragmented bits of a multiverse (often via secret passages), all of which are unique, interactive art installations.

Activities

The Pecos Wilderness and Santa Fe National Forest, east of town, have more than 1000 miles of hiking and biking trails, several of which lead to 12,000ft peaks. Contact the Public Lands Information Center for maps and details, and check weather reports for advance warnings of frequent summer storms.

Mellow Velo (Map p896; 505-995-8356; www.mellowvelo.com; 132 E Marcy St; mountain bikes per day from $40; ⊙9:30am-6pm Mon-Fri, to 5pm Sat & Sun mid-May–Oct, shorter hours Nov–mid-May) rents mountain bikes and provides trail information. Operators including New Wave Rafting Co (800-984-1444; www.newwave rafting.com; adult/child 6-11yr from $60/49; ⊙mid-Apr–Aug) offer white-water rafting adventures through the Rio Grande Gorge, the wild Taos Box and the Rio Chama Wilderness.

Dale Ball Trails
MOUNTAIN BIKING, HIKING

(www.santafenm.gov/trails_1; Cerro Gordo Rd, off Upper Canyon Rd) More than 20 miles of mountain-biking and hiking trails, with fabulous desert and mountain views a quick drive from downtown. The 9.7-mile Outer Limits trail is a classic ride, combining fast singletrack in the north with the more technical central section. Hikers should check out the 4-mile round-trip trail to Picacho Peak, with a steep but accessible 1250ft elevation gain.

Ski Santa Fe
SKIING

(505-982-4429; www.skisantafe.com; Hwy 475; lift ticket adult/13-23yr/child $80/62/54; ⊙9am-4pm Dec-Mar) Often overlooked for its more famous cousin outside Taos, the smaller Santa Fe ski area boasts the same dry powder (though not quite as much), with a higher base elevation (10,350ft). It caters to families and expert skiers, who come for the glades, steep bump runs and long groomers a mere 16 miles from town.

Santa Fe School of Cooking
COOKING

(Map p896; 505-983-4511; www.santafe schoolofcooking.com; 125 N Guadalupe St; 2hr classes $80, 3hr classes from $82; ⊙9:30am-5:30pm Mon-Fri, to 5pm Sat, 10:30am-3:30pm Sun) Sign up for green- or red-chile workshops to master the basics of Southwestern cuisine, or try your hand at *chile rellenos* (stuffed chile peppers), tamales or more sophisticated flavors such as mustard mango habanero sauce. It also offers several popular restaurant walking tours.

Festivals & Events

★ International Folk Art Market
CULTURAL

(505-992-7600; www.folkartalliance.org; ⊙mid-Jul) The world's largest folk-art market

Santa Fe

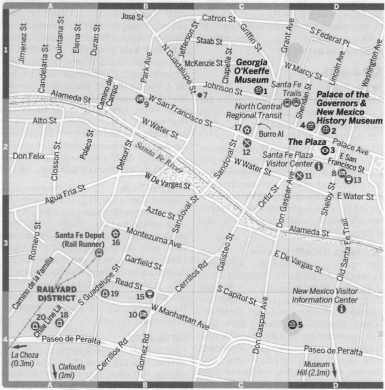

draws around 150 artists from 50 countries to the Museum of International Folk Art for a festive weekend of craft shopping and cultural events in July.

Santa Fe Indian Market
CULTURAL
(☎505-983-5220; www.swaia.org; ☉Aug) Around a thousand artists from about 220 tribes and pueblos show work at this world-famous juried show, held the weekend after the third Thursday in August. More than 100,000 visitors converge on the Plaza, at open studios, gallery shows and the Native Cinema Showcase. Come Friday or Saturday to see pieces competing for the top prizes; wait until Sunday before trying to bargain.

★ Santa Fe Fiesta & Burning of Zozobra
CULTURAL
(☎505-913-1517; www.santafefiesta.org; ☉early Sep) This 10-day celebration of the 1692 re-settlement of Santa Fe following the 1680 Pueblo Revolt includes concerts, a candle-lit procession and a Pet Parade. Everything kicks off with the Friday-night torching of **Zozobra** (www.burnzozobra.com) – a 50ft-tall effigy of 'Old Man Gloom' – before some 60,000 people in Fort Marcy Park.

🛏 Sleeping

Silver Saddle Motel
MOTEL $
(☎505-471-7663; www.santafesilversaddlemotel. com; 2810 Cerrillos Rd; r $68-85; P❄@🗑🐾) This old-fashioned, slightly kitschy Route 66 motel compound offers the best budget value in town. Some rooms have pleasant tiled kitchenettes, while all have shady wooden arcades outside and cowboy-inspired decor inside – get the Kenny Rogers or Wyatt Earp rooms if you can. It's located 3 miles southwest of the Plaza on busy Cerrillos Rd. Pet fee is $10 per night.

Black Canyon Campground
CAMPGROUND $
(☎877-444-6777; www.recreation.gov; Hwy 475; tent & RV sites $10; ☉May–mid-Oct) A mere 8

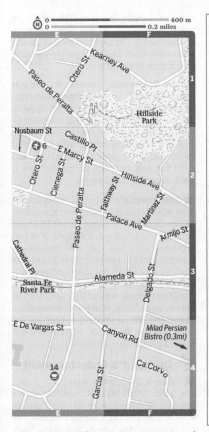

SOUTHWEST SANTA FE

miles from the Plaza is this gorgeous and secluded national forest service spot, complete with 36 sites and hiking and biking trails nearby. Water is available, but there are no hookups. If it's full, Hyde Memorial State Park is up the road, while the Big Tesuque and Aspen Basin campgrounds (free, but no potable water) are closer to the ski area.

★ **Santa Fe Motel & Inn**   HOTEL **$$**
(Map p896; ☎505-982-1039; www.santafemotel.
com; 510 Cerrillos Rd; r from $159, casitas from
$239; P✴@🛜🐾) Even the motel rooms in this downtown option, close to the Railyard and a real bargain in low season, have the flavor of a Southwestern B&B, with colorful tiles, clay sunbursts and tin mirrors. The courtyard casitas cost a little more and come with kiva fireplaces and little patios. Rates include a full hot breakfast, served outdoors in summer.

Las Palomas   BOUTIQUE HOTEL **$$**
(Map p896; ☎505-982-5560; www.laspalomas.
com; 460 W San Francisco St; r from $169;
P✴🛜🐾) Rustically modern rooms fill several low-slung buildings clustered near the intersection of W San Francisco St and Park Ave a half-mile from the plaza. A few quirks here and there – do these window shades shut all the way? – keep the pretension at bay at this glossy self-described compound. Rooms have gas or wood-fired fireplaces.

★ **La Fonda**   HISTORIC HOTEL **$$$**
(Map p896; ☎505-982-5511; www.lafondasantafe.
com; 100 E San Francisco St; r from $419; P✴@
🛜🐾🐾) Long renowned as the 'Inn at the end of the Santa Fe Trail,' Santa Fe's loveliest historic hotel sprawls through an old adobe just off the Plaza. Retaining its beautiful folk-art windows and murals, it's both classy and cozy, with some wonderful top-floor luxury suites, and superb sunset views from the

rooftop **Bell Tower Bar** (Map p896; 100 E San Francisco St; ⏱3pm-sunset Mon-Fri, noon-sunset Sat & Sun May-Nov, closed Dec-Apr).

Eating

★La Choza
NEW MEXICAN $

(☎505-982-0909; www.lachozasf.com; 905 Alarid St; lunch $10-18 dinner $12-25; ⏱11:30am-2:30pm & 5-9pm Mon-Sat; P🐾) Blue-corn burritos, a festive interior and an extensive margarita list make La Choza a perennial (and colorful) favorite among Santa Fe's discerning diners. Of the many New Mexican restaurants in Santa Fe, this one always seems to be reliably excellent. As with the Shed, its sister restaurant, arrive early or reserve.

Tia Sophia's
NEW MEXICAN $

(Map p896; ☎505-983-9880; www.tiasophias.com; 210 W San Francisco St; breakfast $8-11, lunch $9-12; ⏱7am-2pm Mon-Sat, 8am-1pm Sun; 🖊🐾) Local artists and visiting celebrities outnumber tourists at this long-standing and always packed Santa Fe favorite. Breakfast is the meal of choice, with fantastic burritos and other Southwestern dishes, but lunch is pretty damn tasty too; try the perfectly prepared *chile rellenos* (stuffed chile peppers), or the rota of daily specials. The shelf of books helps entertain the little ones.

Clafoutis
FRENCH $

(☎505-988-1809; 333 Cordova Rd; pastries $2-6, mains $5-13; ⏱7am-4pm Mon-Sat) As Oscar Wilde once quipped, the only way to get rid of temptation is to give in, and that sums up the approach you should take at this *super bon* French patisserie. Drop by for delectable pastries (*beignets* on Saturday!) or sit down for breakfast or lunch, with a tantalizing selection of crepes, omelets, quiches and brie sandwiches.

★Jambo Cafe
AFRICAN $$

(☎505-473-1269; www.jambocafe.net; 2010 Cerrillos Rd; mains $10-17; ⏱11am-9pm Mon-Sat) Hidden within a shopping center, this African-flavored cafe is hard to spot from the road; once inside, though, it's a lovely spot, always busy with locals who love its distinctive goat, chicken and lentil curries, veggie sandwiches and roti flatbreads, not to mention the reggae soundtrack.

Milad Persian Bistro
MIDDLE EASTERN $$

(☎505-303-3581; www.miladbistro.com; 802 Canyon Rd; small plates $3-16, mains $14-22; ⏱5-10pm Tue-Thu, from 11am Fri-Sun) The delicately

seasoned kabobs and bountiful salads are made for lingering at this pleasant bistro on Canyon Rd. The cozy patio is particularly well suited for chatting and people-watching over a glass of wine. Or two.

Harry's Roadhouse
AMERICAN, NEW MEXICAN $$

(☎505-989-4629; www.harrysroadhousesantafe.com; 96 Old Las Vegas Hwy; lunch $10-16, dinner $10-30; ⏱7am-9:30pm; 🐾) This casual long-time favorite on the southern edge of town feels like a rambling cottage with its various rooms and patio garden – and there's also a full bar. And, seriously, *everything* here is good. Especially the desserts.

★Cafe Pasqual's
NEW MEXICAN $$$

(Map p896; ☎505-983-9340; www.pasquals.com; 121 Don Gaspar Ave; breakfast & lunch $11-18, dinner $18-39; ⏱8am-3pm & 5:30-10pm; 🖊🐾) 🌿 Whatever time you visit this exuberantly colorful, utterly unpretentious place, the food, most of which has a definite south-of-the-border flavor, is worth every penny. The breakfast menu is famous for dishes such as *huevos motuleños,* made with sautéed bananas, feta cheese and more; later on, the meat and fish mains are superb. Reservations taken for dinner only.

Drinking & Entertainment

★Kakawa Chocolate House
CAFE

(Map p896; ☎505-982-0388; www.kakawachocolates.com; 1050 Paseo de Peralta; ⏱9:30am-6pm Mon-Sat, from noon Sun) Chocolate addicts simply can't miss this ode to the sacred bean. This isn't your mom's marshmallow-laden hot chocolate, though – these rich elixirs are based on historic recipes and divided into two categories: European (eg 17th-century France) and Meso-American (Mayan and Aztec). Bonus: it also sells sublime chocolates (prickly-pear mescal) and spicy chile caramels.

★Santa Fe Spirits
DISTILLERY

(Map p896; ☎505-780-5906; www.santafespirits.com; 308 Read St; ⏱3-8pm Sun, to 9pm Mon, to 9:30pm Tue-Thu, to 10pm Fri & Sat) The local distillery's tasting flight includes an impressive amount of liquor, including shots of Colkegan single malt, Wheeler's gin and Expedition vodka. Leather chairs and exposed rafters make the in-town tasting room an intimate spot for an aperitif; fans can reserve a spot on the hourly tours of the distillery.

★Santa Fe Opera
OPERA

(☎505-986-5900; www.santafeopera.org; Hwy 84/285, Tesuque; tours adult/child $10/free; ⏱Jul

THE MUSEUM OF NEW MEXICO

The Museum of New Mexico administers four excellent museums in Santa Fe. Two are at the Plaza; two are on Museum Hill, 2 miles southwest.

Palace of the Governors & New Mexico History Museum (Map p896; ☑505-476-5100; www.palaceofthegovernors.org; 105 W Palace Ave; adult/child $12/free; ⊙10am-5pm, closed Mon Nov-Apr) The oldest public building in the US, this low-slung adobe complex began as home to New Mexico's first Spanish governor in 1610. It was occupied by Pueblo Indians following their revolt in 1680, and after 1846 became the seat of the US Territory's earliest governors. During research the Palace was undergoing renovations; expect a new look after its scheduled 2020 reopening. The adjoining New Mexico History Museum engagingly tells the story of the state, beginning with the Spanish arrival in the 1500s. The Palace entrance is located in the History Museum.

New Mexico Museum of Art (Map p896; ☑505-476-5072; www.nmartmuseum.org; 107 W Palace Ave; adult/child $12/free; ⊙10am-5pm Tue-Sun) Built in 1917 and a prime early example of Santa Fe's Pueblo Revival architecture, the New Mexico Museum of Art has spent a century collecting and displaying works by regional artists. A treasure trove of works by the great names who put New Mexico on the cultural map, from the Taos Society of Artists to Georgia O'Keeffe, it's also a lovely building in which to stroll around, with a cool garden courtyard. Constantly changing temporary exhibitions ensure its continuing relevance.

Museum of International Folk Art (☑505-476-1200; www.internationalfolkart.org; 706 Camino Lejo; adult/child $12/free; ⊙10am-5pm, closed Mon Nov-Apr; ℙ) Santa Fe's most unusual and exhilarating museum centers on the world's largest collection of folk art. Its huge main gallery displays whimsical and mind-blowing objects from more than 100 different countries. Tiny human figures go about their business in fully realized village and city scenes, while dolls, masks, toys and garments spill across the walls. Changing exhibitions in other wings explore vernacular art and culture worldwide.

Museum of Indian Arts & Culture (☑505-476-1269; www.indianartsandculture.org; 710 Camino Lejo; adult/child $12/free; ⊙10am-5pm, closed Mon Sep-May; ℙ) This top-quality museum sets out to trace the origins and history of the various Native American peoples of the entire Southwest, and explain and illuminate their widely differing cultural traditions. Pueblo, Navajo and Apache interviewees describe the contemporary realities each group now faces, while a truly superb collection of ceramics, modern and ancient, is complemented by stimulating temporary displays.

& Aug, tours 9am Mon-Fri Jun-Aug) Many visitors flock to Santa Fe for the opera alone: the theater is a marvel, with 360-degree views of sandstone wilderness crowned with sunsets and moonrises, while at center stage the world's finest talent performs magnificent masterworks. It's still the Wild West, though; you can even wear jeans. Shuttles run to and from Santa Fe ($25) and Albuquerque ($40); reserve online.

Lensic
Performing Arts Center   PERFORMING ARTS
(Map p896; ☑505-988-7050; www.lensic.org; 211 W San Francisco St) A beautifully renovated 1930 movie house, the theater hosts touring productions and classic films as well as seven different performance groups, including the Aspen Santa Fe Ballet and the Santa Fe Symphony Orchestra & Chorus.

Jean Cocteau Cinema   CINEMA
(Map p896; ☑505-466-5528; www.jeancocteau cinema.com; 418 Montezuma Ave) Revived by George RR Martin in 2013, this is the top cinema in town for indie flicks; also has book signings, occasional live concerts and an in-theater bar.

🛍 Shopping

⭐**Santa Fe Farmers Market**   MARKET
(Map p896; ☑505-983-4098; www.santafefarm ersmarket.com; 1607 Paseo de Peralta, at Guadalupe St; ⊙7am-1pm Sat Jun-Sep, 8am-1pm Sat Oct-May, also open Tue & Wed seasonally; 👪) Local produce, much of it heirloom and organic, is on sale at this spacious indoor-outdoor market, alongside homemade goodies, inexpensive food, natural body products and arts and crafts.

Blue Rain
ART

(Map p896; ☑505-954-9902; www.blueraingal
lery.com; 544 S Guadalupe St; ◎10am-6pm Mon-
Fri, to 5pm Sat) This large space in the Railyard district is the top gallery in town representing contemporary Native American and
regional artists. There are generally several
shows on at once, encompassing everything
from modern pottery and sculpture to powerful landscapes and portraits.

Kowboyz
CLOTHING

(Map p896; ☑505-984-1256; www.kowboyz.com;
345 W Manhattan Ave; ◎10am-5:30pm) Secondhand shop selling everything you need to
cowboy up. Shirts are a great deal; the amazing selection of boots, however, demands
top dollar. Movie costumers in search of authentic Western wear often come here.

ⓘ Information

EMERGENCY & MEDICAL SERVICES
Christus St Vincent Hospital (☑505-983-
3361; www.stvin.org; 455 St Michaels Dr;
◎24hr emergency)
Police (☑505-428-3710; 2515 Camino Entrada)

TOURIST INFORMATION
New Mexico Visitor Information Center (Map
p896; ☑505-827-7336; www.newmexico.org;
491 Old Santa Fe Trail; ◎10am-5pm Mon-Fri)
Housed in the 1878 Lamy Building, this friendly
place offers helpful advice and free coffee.
Public Lands Information Center (☑505-
954-2002; www.publiclands.org; 301 Dinosaur
Trail; ◎8am-4:30pm Mon-Fri) Staff at this
hugely helpful office have maps and information on public lands throughout New Mexico,
and can talk you through all the hiking options.
Santa Fe Plaza Visitor Center (Map p896;
☑800-777-2489; www.santafe.org; 66 E San
Francisco St, Suite 3, Plaza Galeria; ◎10am-
6pm) Pop into the Plaza Galeria center for
maps and brochures. There is another visitor
center at the Railyard (410 S Guadalupe St).

ⓘ Getting There & Around

Daily flights to/from Denver, Dallas and Phoenix
serve the small **Santa Fe Municipal Airport** (SAF;
☑505-955-2900; www.santafenm.gov/airport;
121 Aviation Dr), 10 miles southwest of downtown.

The **Sandia Shuttle Express** (☑888-775-
5696; www.sandiashuttle.com; $33) connects
Santa Fe with the Albuquerque Sunport.

North Central Regional Transit (Map p896;
☑505-629-4725; www.ncrtd.org) provides free
shuttle bus service from downtown Santa Fe to
Española on weekdays, where you can transfer
to shuttles to Taos, Los Alamos, Ojo Caliente and
other northern destinations. Pickup/drop-off is

by the Santa Fe Trails bus stop at the Sheridan
Transit Center on Sheridan St, a block northwest
of the Plaza.

On weekends, the **Taos Express** (☑866-206-
0754; www.taosexpress.com; $5; ◎Sat & Sun)
runs north to Taos from the corner of Guadalupe
and Montezuma Sts, by the Railyard.

The Rail Runner (p894) commuter train offers
eight daily connections (seven on weekends)
with Albuquerque from its terminus in the Railyard and the South Capitol Station, a mile southwest. The trip takes about 1¾ hours. Arriving
passengers can make use of the free Santa Fe
Trails bus network.

Amtrak (800-872-7245; www.amtrak.com)
serves Lamy station, 17 miles southeast, with
30-minute bus connections to Santa Fe.

If driving between Santa Fe and Albuquerque,
try to take Hwy 14 (the Turquoise Trail), which
passes through the old mining town (now arts
colony) of Madrid, 28 miles south of Santa Fe.

The free **Santa Fe Pick-Up** meets arriving Rail
Runner trains and loops around downtown until
5:30pm; it also heads out to Museum Hill. Runs
past stops about every 15 minutes.

Santa Fe Trails (Map p896; ☑505-955-2001;
www.santafenm.gov/transit; adult/child $1/
free, day pass $2) operates buses from the
Downtown Transit Center, with routes M, to
Museum Hill, and 2, along Cerrillos Rd, being the
most useful for visitors.

Around Santa Fe

Las Vegas

Not to be confused with Nevada's glittery
gambling megalopolis, this Las Vegas is one
of the loveliest towns in New Mexico, and
the largest and oldest community east of the
Sangre de Cristo Mountains. Its eminently
strollable downtown has a pretty Old Town
Plaza and holds some 900 Southwestern and
Victorian buildings listed in the National
Register of Historic Places.

Built in 1882 and carefully remodeled a
century later, the elegant **Plaza Hotel** (☑505-
425-3591; http://plazahotellvnm.com; 230 Plaza
St; r $89-149; ▣@◉◉◉) is Las Vegas' most
celebrated lodging, as seen in the movie *No
Country For Old Men*. Its sister property, the
restored **Castañeda Hotel** (☑505-425-3591;
www.castanedahotel.org; 524 Railroad Ave; r $89-149,
ste $169; ▣◉◉◉), was the first in a chain of
trackside hotels from legendary hotelier Fred
Harvey. It reopened its doors in 2019.

You can get sandwiches and coffee at
Traveler's Cafe (☑505-426-8638; www.face
book.com/travelerscafenm; 1814 Plaza St; pastries

$1-4, salads & sandwiches $6-9; ⊘ 7am-7pm Mon-Sat; 🐾), right on the plaza.

Los Alamos

When the top-secret Manhattan Project sprang to life in 1943, it turned the sleepy mesa-top village of Los Alamos into a busy laboratory of secluded brainiacs. Here, in the 'town that didn't exist,' the first atomic bomb was developed in almost total secrecy. Today you'll encounter a dynamic in which souvenir T-shirts emblazoned with atomic explosions and 'La Bomba' wine are sold next to books on pueblo history and wilderness hiking.

While you can't visit the Los Alamos National Laboratory, where classified cutting-edge research still takes place, the interactive Bradbury Science Museum (📋 505-667-4444; www.lanl.gov/museum; 1350 Central Ave; ⊘ 10am-5pm Tue-Sat, from 1pm Sun & Mon; 🅿️) FREE covers atomic history in fascinating detail. At the visitor center at the Manhattan Project National Historic Park you can learn more about the secret city and pick up a map pinpointing key sites downtown and across the mesa. The small but interesting Los Alamos Historical Museum (📋 505-662-6272; www.losalamoshistory.org; 1050 Bathtub Row; $5; ⊘ 9am-5pm Mon-Fri, 10am-4pm Sat & Sun) is on the nearby grounds of the former Los Alamos Ranch School – an outdoorsy school for boys that closed when the scientists arrived.

Grab a burger or enchiladas at the Blue Window Bistro (📋 505-662-6305; www.la bluewindowbistro.com; 1789 Central Ave; lunch $9-13, dinner $9-32; ⊘ 11am-2:30pm Mon-Fri, 5-8:30pm Mon-Sat) followed by a beer at community-owned Bathtub Row Brewing (📋 505-500-8381; www.bathtubrowbrewing.coop; 163 Central Park Sq; ⊘ 2-10pm Sun-Thu, to 11pm Fri & Sat; 🐾).

Bandelier National Monument

Ancestral Puebloans dwelt in the cliffsides of beautiful Frijoles Canyon, now preserved within Bandelier (📋 505-672-3861; www.nps.gov/band; Hwy 4; 1 week entry per vehicle $25; ⊘ dawn-dusk; 🅿️🐾). The adventurous can climb ladders to reach ancient caves and kivas (chambers) used until the mid-1500s. Backcountry camping (restricted to mesa tops from July to mid-September because of flood danger) requires a free permit, or there are around 100 sites at Juniper Campground, set among the pines near the monument entrance.

Note that from 9am to 3pm from mid-May 14 to mid-October, you have to take a shuttle bus to Bandelier from the White Rock Visitor Center (📋 505-672-3193; www.nps.gov/band; 115 Hwy 4, White Rock; ⊘ 8am-6pm mid-May–mid-Oct, 10am-2pm rest of year) 8.5 miles north on Hwy 4.

Abiquiu

The Hispanic village of Abiquiu (sounds like 'barbecue'), on Hwy 84 about 45 minutes' drive northwest of Santa Fe, is famous because artist Georgia O'Keeffe lived and painted here from 1949 until her death in 1986. With the Chama River flowing through farmland and spectacular rock landscape, this ethereal setting continues to attract artists.

Your first stop should be the new Georgia O'Keeffe Welcome Center (📋 505-946-1000; www.okeeffemuseum.org; 21220 Hwy 84; ⊘ 8:30am-5pm; 🅿️), which provides an overview of the O'Keeffe sights in the area. It's also the place to check-in for one-hour tours (📋 505-685-4539; www.okeeffemuseum.org; standard tour $40; ⊘ Tue-Sat early Mar–mid-Nov) of O'Keeffe's adobe house. Tours are often booked months in advance.

Set amid 21,000 Technicolor acres 15 miles northwest, Ghost Ranch (📋 505-685-1000; www.ghostranch.org; Hwy 84; day pass adult/child $5/3; ⊘ welcome center 8am-9pm; 🅿️🐾) is a retreat center where O'Keeffe stayed many times. Besides fabulous hiking trails, it holds a dinosaur museum and offers basic lodging (📋 505-685-1000; www.ghostranch.org; tent & RV sites $35-45, dm $99, r with/without bath from $169/159; ❄️🐾) plus horseback rides ($95) and various tours. To maximize your time here, review the website before your visit.

The lovely Abiquiú Inn (📋 505-685-4378; www.abiquiuinn.com; 21120 Hwy 84; r from $170, casitas $250; 🅿️🐾) is a sprawling collection of shaded fau -adobes. Its spacious casitas have kitchenettes, and the menu at the on-site restaurant, Cafe Abiquiú (📋 505-685-4378; www.abiquiuinn.com; Abiquiú Inn; breakfast $6-12, lunch & dinner $10-29; ⊘ 7am-9pm; 🐾), includes the usual array of New Mexican specialties.

Ojo Caliente

More than 150 years old, Ojo Caliente Mineral Springs Resort & Spa (📋 505-583-2233; www.ojospa.com; 50 Los Baños Dr; r $209, cottages $249, ste from $319, tent & RV sites $40;

CANYON ROAD GALLERIES

Originally a Pueblo Indian footpath and later the main street through a Spanish farming community, Santa Fe's most famous art avenue embarked on its current incarnation in the 1920s, when artists led by Los Cinco Pintores (five painters who fell in love with New Mexico's landscape) moved in to take advantage of the cheap rent.

Today Canyon Rd is a top attraction, holding more than a hundred of Santa Fe's 300-plus galleries. The epicenter of the city's vibrant art scene, it offers everything from rare Native American antiquities to Santa Fe School masterpieces and in-your-face modern work. If gallery-hopping seems a bit overwhelming, don't worry, just wander.

Friday nights from May through October are particularly fun: that's when the galleries put on glittering openings, starting around 5pm and lasting until 7pm. Not only are these great social events, but you can also browse while nibbling on cheese, sipping Chardonnay or sparkling cider, and chatting with the artists.

P ✷ ⌘) is one of the country's oldest health resorts – and Pueblo Indians have used the springs for centuries! Fifty miles north of Santa Fe on Hwy 285, it offers 11 soaking pools with several combinations of minerals. In addition to the pleasant, if nothing special, historic hotel rooms, the resort has several plush, boldly colored suites with kiva fireplaces and private soaking tubs, and New Mexican–style cottages. Its **Artesian Restaurant** (www.ojospa.com; 50 Los Baños Dr; lunch $11-16, dinner $16-38; ☺ 7:30-11am, 11:30am-2:30pm & 5-9pm daily, to 9:30pm Fri & Sat summer; ⌘🍴) 🍴 prepares organic and local ingredients with aplomb.

Taos

A magical spot even by the standards of this Land of Enchantment, Taos remains forever under the spell of the powerful landscape that surrounds it: 12,300ft snow-capped peaks rise behind town, while a sage-speckled plateau unrolls to the west before plunging 800ft straight down into the Rio Grande Gorge. The sky can be a searing sapphire blue or an ominous parade of rumbling thunderheads so big they dwarf the mountains. And then there are the sunsets...

Taos Pueblo, a marvel of adobe architecture, ranks among the oldest continuously inhabited communities in the US, and stands at the root of a long history that also extends from conquistadors to mountain men to artists. The town itself is a relaxed and eccentric place, with classic mud-brick buildings, fabulous museums, quirky cafes and excellent restaurants. Its 5000 residents include bohemians and hippies, alternative-energy aficionados and old-time Hispanic families. It's both rural and worldly, and a bit otherworldly.

⊙ Sights

★ **Millicent Rogers Museum**　　　MUSEUM
(☑ 575-758-2462; www.millicentrogers.org; 1504 Millicent Rogers Rd; adult/child 6-16yr $10/2; ☺ 10am-5pm; P) Rooted in the private collection of model and oil heiress Millicent Rogers, who moved to Taos in 1947, this superb museum, 4 miles northwest of the Plaza, ranges from Hispanic folk art to Navajo weaving, and even modernist jewelry designed by Rogers herself. The principal focus, however, is on Native American ceramics, and especially the beautiful black-on-black pottery created during the 20th century by Maria Martínez from San Ildefonso Pueblo.

Rio Grande Gorge Bridge　　BRIDGE, CANYON
(P) Constructed in 1965, this vertigo-inducing steel bridge carries Hwy 64 across the Rio Grande about 12 miles northwest of Taos. It's the seventh-highest bridge in the US (depending on your source), rising 565ft above the river and measuring 600ft long. The views from the pedestrian walkway, west over the empty Taos Plateau and down the jagged walls of the gorge, will surely make you gulp. Vendors selling jewelry, sage sticks and other souvenirs congregate on the eastern side.

The **West Rim Trail** rolls south for 9 miles from the rest area on the western side, with views of the plateau and the Sangre de Cristo Mountains.

Martínez Hacienda　　　　　MUSEUM
(☑ 575-758-1000; www.taoshistoricmuseums.org; 708 Hacienda Way, off Lower Ranchitos Rd; adult/child $8/4; ☺ 11am-4pm Mon, Tue, Fri & Sat, from noon Sun; P) Set amid the fields 2 miles southwest of the Plaza, this fortified adobe homestead was built in 1804. It served as a trading post, first for merchants venturing

north from Mexico City along the Camino Real, and then west along the Santa Fe Trail. Its 21 rooms, arranged around a double courtyard, are furnished with the few possessions that even a wealthy family of the era would have been able to afford. Cultural events are held here regularly.

Harwood Museum of Art MUSEUM
(☑ 575-758-9826; www.harwoodmuseum.org; 238 Ledoux St; adult/child $10/free; ⊙ 10am-5pm Tue-Fri, from noon Sat & Sun; ℗) Attractively displayed in a gorgeous and very spacious mid-19th-century adobe compound, the paintings, drawings, prints, sculpture and photographs here are predominantly the work of northern New Mexican artists, both historical and contemporary. Founded in 1923, the Harwood is the second-oldest museum in New Mexico, and is as strong on local Hispanic traditions as it is on Taos' 20th-century school.

San Francisco de Asís Church CHURCH
(☑ 575-751-0518; St Francis Plaza, Ranchos de Taos; ⊙ 9am-4pm, hours vary in winter; ℗) Just off Hwy 68 in Ranchos de Taos, 4 miles south of Taos Plaza, this iconic church was completed in 1815. Famed for the rounded curves and stark angles of its sturdy adobe walls, it was repeatedly memorialized by Georgia O'Keeffe in paint, and Ansel Adams with his camera. On weekends, Mass is celebrated at 5pm on Saturday and 8am (in Spanish) and 10am Sunday.

Earthships ARCHITECTURE
(☑ 575-613-4409; www.earthship.com; Hwy 64; self-guided tours $8; ⊙ 9am-5pm Jun-Aug, 10am-4pm Sep-May; ℗) ⏏ Numbering 70 Earthships, with capacity for 60 more, Taos' pioneering community was the brainchild of architect Michael Reynolds. Built with recycled materials such as used automobile tires and cans, and buried on three sides, Earthships heat and cool themselves, make their own electricity and catch their own water; dwellers grow their own food. Stay overnight (☑ 575-751-0462; www.earthship.com; Hwy 64; earthships $169-410; ℗ 🌐 🐾) ⏏ if possible; the self-guided 'tour' is disappointing. The visitor center is 1.5 miles west of the Rio Grande Gorge Bridge on Hwy 64.

🏃 Activities

During summer, white-water rafting is popular in the Taos Box, the steep-sided cliffs that frame the Rio Grande. There are also plenty of excellent hiking and mountain-biking trails. With a peak elevation of 11,819ft and a 3274ft vertical drop, **Taos Ski Valley** (☑ 866-968-7386; www.skitaos.org; lift ticket adult/teen/child $98/81/61; ⊙ 9am-4pm) offers some of the most challenging skiing and boarding in the US and yet remains low-key and relaxed.

Los Rios River Runners RAFTING
(☑ 575-776-8854; www.losriosriverrunners.com; adult/child half-day $54/44; ⊙ late Apr-Sep) Half-day trips on the Racecourse – in one- and two-person kayaks, as you prefer – full-day trips on the Box (minimum age 12), and multinight expeditions on the scenic Chama. On its 'Native Cultures Feast and Float' you're accompanied by a Native American guide and have lunch homemade by a local Pueblo family. Its open season fluctuates based on water levels.

🛌 Sleeping

Hotel Luna Mystica CARAVAN PARK $
(☑ 505-977-2424; www.hotellunamystica.com; 25 ABC Mesa Rd; RVs $95-195, bunkhouse $25; ℗ 🌐 🐾) Vintage Airstreams and RVs come with a view – a really big view – at this new trailer park that's perched between the Sangre de Cristos mountains and the Rio Grand Gorge on the Taos mesa about 8 miles northwest of downtown. Each snazzy trailer has its own

---

CHIMAYÓ

The so-called 'Lourdes of America' – the extraordinarily beautiful two-towered adobe chapel of **El Santuario de Chimayó** (☑ 505-351-4360; www.elsantuariodechimayo.us; 15 Santuario Dr; ⊙ 9am-6pm May-Sep, to 5pm Oct-Apr; ℗) FREE – nestles amid the hills of the 'High Road' east of Hwy 84, 28 miles north of Santa Fe. It was built in 1826, on a site where the earth was said to have miraculous healing properties. Even today, the faithful come to rub the *tierra bendita* (holy dirt) from a small pit inside the church on whatever hurts. During Holy Week, about 30,000 pilgrims walk to Chimayó from Santa Fe, Albuquerque and beyond, in the largest Catholic pilgrimage in the USA. The artwork in the santuario is worth a trip on its own. Stop at **Rancho de Chimayó** (☑ 505-351-4444; www.ranchodechimayo.com; County Rd 98; lunch $9-11, dinner $12-27; ⊙ 11:30am-8:30pm Tue-Fri, from 8:30am Sat & Sun) afterward for lunch or dinner.

bathroom and kitchen, plus a firepit. All but the hostel-style bunkhouse include showers.

⭐ **Doña Luz Inn** B&B $$

(☑575-758-9000; www.stayintaos.com; 114 Kit Carson Rd; r $119-209; P ❋ @ 🛜 🐾) Vibrant and fun, this central B&B is a labor of love by owner Paul Castillo. Rooms are decorated in colorful themes from Spanish colonial to Native American, with abundant art, murals and artifacts plus adobe fireplaces, and kitchenettes. If you don't mind stairs, the sumptuous Rainbow Room has a private rooftop deck and hot tub, offering fantastic views over the city.

⭐ **Historic Taos Inn** HISTORIC HOTEL $$

(☑575-758-2233; www.taosinn.com; 125 Paseo del Pueblo Norte; r from $179; P ❋ 🛜) Lovely and lively old inn, where the 45 characterful rooms have Southwest trimmings such as heavy-duty wooden furnishings and adobe fireplaces (some functioning, some for show). The famed Adobe Bar spills into the cozy central atrium, and features live music every night – for a quieter stay, opt for one of the detached separate wings – and there's also a good **restaurant** (☑575-758-1977; www.taosinn. com; 125 Paseo del Pueblo Norte, Historic Taos Inn; breakfast & lunch $9-17, dinner $17-28; ⊙11am-3pm & 5-9pm Mon-Fri, 7:30am-2:30pm & 5-9pm Sat & Sun).

✗ Eating

Taos Diner DINER $

(☑575-758-2374; 908 Paseo del Pueblo Norte; mains $4-14; ⊙7am-3pm; 🐾) Diner grub at its finest, prepared with a Southwestern, organic spin. Mountain men, scruffy jocks, solo diners and happy tourists – everyone's welcome here. The breakfast burritos rock. There's another branch south of the plaza (216B Paseo del Pueblo Sur).

Love Apple NEW MEXICAN $$

(☑575-751-0050; www.theloveapple.net; 803 Paseo del Pueblo Norte; mains $16-18; ⊙5-9pm Tue-Sun) A real 'only in New Mexico' find, from the rustic setting in the converted 19th-century adobe Placitas Chapel, to the delicious, locally sourced and largely organic food. Everything – the local beefburger with red chile and blue cheese, the tamales with mole sauce, the wild boar tenderloin – is imbued with regional flavor. Cash only, with no ATM on-site.

⭐ **Lambert's** MODERN AMERICAN $$$

(☑575-758-1009; www.lambertsoftaos.com; 123 Bent St; lunch $10-15, dinner $23-38; ⊙11:30am-9pm; 🅿 🐾) Consistently hailed as the 'Best of Taos,' this charming old adobe north of the Plaza remains what it's always been: a cozy, romantic local hangout where patrons relax over sumptuous contemporary cuisine, with mains ranging from lunchtime's barbecue pork sliders to dinner dishes such as chicken mango enchiladas or Colorado rack of lamb.

The famed fresh-squeezed margaritas are $6 during happy hour (2:30pm to 6:30pm).

🍷 Drinking & Entertainment

Adobe Bar BAR

(☑575-758-2233; 125 Paseo del Pueblo Norte, Historic Taos Inn; ⊙11am-10pm, music from 6:30pm) There's something about the Adobe Bar. Everyone in Taos seems to turn up at some point each evening, to kick back in the comfy covered atrium, enjoying no-cover live music from bluegrass to jazz, and drinking the famed Cowboy Buddha margaritas. If you decide to stick around, you can always order food from the well-priced bar menu.

Taos Mesa Brewery BREWERY

(☑575-753-1900; www.taosmesabrewing.com; 20 ABC Mesa Rd; ⊙noon-11pm) This hangar-like space out by the airport has great beers, live music and à la carte tacos, making it a can't-miss après-ski/hike hangout. Indoor seating is limited – but that's to ensure there's space for the funk on Fridays, bluegrass on Saturdays and two-step on Sundays – or however it decides to mix it up. There's a **taproom** (☑575-758-1900; www.taosmesabrewing.com; 201 Paseo del Pueblo Sur; ⊙noon-11pm) in town.

🔒 Shopping

Taos has historically been a mecca for artists, demonstrated by the huge number of galleries and studios in and around town. Indie stores and galleries line the **John Dunn Shops** (www.johndunnshops.com) pedestrian walkway linking Bent St to Taos Plaza.

Just east of the Plaza, pop into **El Rincón Trading Post** (☑575-758-9188; 114 Kit Carson Rd; ⊙9am-5pm Mon-Fri, from 10am Sat, from 11am Sun) for classic Western memorabilia.

ℹ Information

Taos Visitor Center (☑575-758-3873; http://taos.org; 1139 Paseo del Pueblo Sur; ⊙9am-5pm; 🛜) This excellent visitor center stocks information of all kinds on northern New Mexico and doles out free coffee; everything, including the comprehensive *Taos Vacation Guide*, is also available online.

TAOS PUEBLO

Taos Pueblo (☑575-758-1028; www.taospueblo.com; Taos Pueblo Rd; adult/child under 11yr $16/free; ⊗8am-4:30pm Mon-Sat, from 8:30am Sun, closed mid-Feb–mid-Apr) is centered on twin five-story adobe complexes, set either side of the Río Pueblo de Taos, against the stunning backdrop of the Sangre de Cristos mountains. The quintessential example of ancient Pueblo architecture, they're thought to have been completed by around 1450 AD. Modern visitors are thus confronted by the same staggering spectacle as New Mexico's earliest Spanish explorers, though a small and very picturesque Catholic mission church now stands nearby.

Residents lead short guided walking tours of the pueblo (by donation), which are recommended for a better understanding of the history and surroundings. You'll also have the chance to buy fine jewelry, pottery and other arts and crafts, and possibly sample flatbread baked in traditional beehive-shaped adobe ovens. Note that the pueblo closes for 10 weeks around February through April, and at other times for ceremonies and events; call ahead or check the website for dates.

❶ Getting There & Away

From Santa Fe, take either the scenic 'High Road' along Hwys 76 and 518, with galleries, villages and sites worth exploring, or follow the lovely unfolding Rio Grande landscape on Hwy 68.

North Central Regional Transit (www.www.ncrtd.org) operates bus services through northern central New Mexico, including to Santa Fe; pickup/drop-off is at the Taos County offices off Paseo del Pueblo Sur, a mile south of the Plaza.

Taos Express (p900) has shuttle service to Santa Fe on Saturday and Sunday (one way adult/child $5/free), connecting with Rail Runner trains to and from Albuquerque.

Northwestern New Mexico

New Mexico's wild northwest is home to wide-open, empty spaces. It's still dubbed Indian country, and for good reason: huge swaths of land fall under the aegis of the Navajo, Zuni, Acoma, Apache and Laguna. This portion of New Mexico showcases remarkable ancient sites alongside modern, solitary Native American settlements. And when you've had your fill of culture, you can ride a historic narrow-gauge railroad through the mountains, hike around some trippy badlands or cast for huge trout.

Farmington & Around

The largest town in northwest New Mexico, Farmington makes a convenient base from which to explore the Four Corners area. The **visitors bureau** (☑505-326-7602; www.farmingtonnm.org; 3041 E Main St; ⊗8am-5pm Mon-Sat) has more information. **Shiprock**, a 1700ft-high volcanic plug that rises over the landscape to the west, was a landmark for the Anglo pioneers and is a sacred site to the Navajo.

Fourteen miles northeast of Farmington, the 27-acre **Aztec Ruins National Monument** (☑505-334-6174; www.nps.gov/azru; 725 Ruins Rd; ⊗8am-6pm mid-May–Aug, to 4pm Sep & Oct, 9am-4pm Nov–mid-May; Ⓟ) **FREE** features the largest reconstructed kiva in the country, with an internal diameter of almost 50ft. A few steps away, let your imagination wander as you stoop through low doorways and dark rooms inside the West Ruin.

About 35 miles south of Farmington along Hwy 371, the undeveloped **Bisti/De-Na-Zin Wilderness Area** (www.blm.gov/visit/bisti-de-na-zin-wilderness) is a trippy, surreal landscape of strange, colorful rock formations, especially spectacular in the hours before sunset; desert enthusiasts shouldn't miss it. The Farmington **BLM office** (☑505-564-7600; www.blm.gov/new-mexico; 6251 College Blvd; ⊗7:45am-4:30pm Mon-Fri) has information.

The lovely, three-room **Silver River Adobe Inn B&B** (☑505-325-8219; www.silveradobe.com; 3151 W Main St; r $115-205; ❄️🐾🛜) offers a peaceful respite among the trees along the San Juan River. Managing to be both trendy and kid-friendly, the hipish **Three Rivers Eatery & Brewhouse** (☑505-324-2187; www.threeriversbrewery.com; 101 E Main St; mains $10-27, pizza $8-22; ⊗11am-10pm; 🛜🐾) has good steaks, pub grub and its own microbrews. It's the best restaurant in town by a mile.

Chaco Culture National Historical Park

Featuring massive Ancestral Puebloan buildings set in an isolated high-desert environment, intriguing **Chaco** (🗹 505-786-7014; www.nps.gov/chcu; 7-day pass per vehicle $25; ☉ 7am-sunset; 🅿) contains evidence of 5000 years of human occupation.

In its prime, the community at Chaco Canyon was a major trading and ceremonial hub for the region – and the city the Puebloan people created here was masterly in its layout and design. **Pueblo Bonito** is four stories tall and may have had 600 to 800 rooms and kivas. As well as driving the self-guided loop tour, you can hike various backcountry trails. The 2-mile round-trip **hike** (Canyon Loop Rd) to the Pueblo Bonito Overlook ends with a bird's-eye view of its namesake pueblo and the canyon. For stargazers, there are evening astronomy presentations in summer. The park is in a remote area approximately 80 miles south of Farmington, far beyond the reach of any public transport. And the drive, much of it on an unpaved road, is extremely bumpy. **Gallo Campground** (🗹 877-444-6777; www.recreation.gov; tent & RV sites $15) is 1 mile east of the visitor center. No RV hookups.

Northeastern New Mexico

East of Santa Fe, the lush Sangre de Cristo Mountains give way to high and vast rolling plains. Dusty grasslands stretch to infinity and beyond – or at least to Texas. Cattle and dinosaur prints dot a landscape punctuated by volcanic cones. Ranching is an economic mainstay, and on many stretches of road you'll see more cattle than cars – and quite possibly herds of bison too. Boy Scouts congregate at Philmont Ranch in Cimarron in summer, but the opening of the new National Scouting Museum threatens to keep the town lively, or near lively, year-round.

The Santa Fe Trail, along which early traders rolled in wagon trains, ran from Missouri to New Mexico. You can still see the wagon ruts in some places off I-25 between Santa Fe and Raton. For a bit of the Old West without a patina of consumer hype, this is the place.

Cimarron

Cimarron once ranked among the rowdiest of Wild West towns; its name even means 'wild' in Spanish. According to local lore, murder was such an everyday occurrence in the 1870s that peace and quiet was newsworthy, one paper going so far as to report: 'Everything is quiet in Cimarron. Nobody has been killed in three days.'

Today, the town is more low-key, luring nature-minded travelers who want to enjoy the great outdoors. Driving to or from Taos, you'll pass through gorgeous **Cimarron Canyon State Park**, a steep-walled canyon with hiking trails, excellent trout fishing and camping. Also here is **Philmont Scout Ranch** (🗹 575-376-1136; www.philmontscoutranch.org; 17 Deer Run Rd; ☉ 8am-5:30pm Jun-Aug, shorter hours rest of year; 🅿) 𝗙𝗥𝗘𝗘, a 214-sq-mile adventure camp for the Boy Scouts of America. The ranch is the new home of the small-but-engaging **National Scouting Museum** (🗹 575-376-1136; www.philmontscoutranch.org; Hwy 21; ☉ 8am-5pm; 🅿) 𝗙𝗥𝗘𝗘, plus a few other themed museums.

You can stay or dine at what's reputed to be one of the most haunted hotels in the USA, the 1872 **St James** (🗹 575-376-2664; www.exstjames.com; 617 Collison St; r $85-135; ❋❄🛜) – one room is so spook-filled that it's never been rented out! Many legends of the West stayed here, including Buffalo Bill, Annie Oakley, Wyatt Earp and Jesse James, and the front desk has a long list of who shot whom in the hotel bar. Another option is **Blu Dragonfly Brewing** (🗹 575-376-1110; www.bludragonflybrewing.com; 301 E 9th St; ☉ 11am-9pm Mon-Thu, to 10pm Fri & Sat) down the road, which serves beer and barbecue.

Capulin Volcano National Monument

Rising 1300ft above the surrounding plains, **Capulin** (🗹 575-278-2201; www.nps.gov/cavo; 7-day pass per vehicle $20; ☉ 8am-4:30pm; 🅿) is the most accessible of several volcanoes in the area. A 2-mile road spirals up the mountain to a parking lot at the rim (8182ft), where trails lead around and into the crater. The entrance is 3 miles north of Capulin village, 30 miles east of Raton on Hwy 87.

Southwestern New Mexico

The Rio Grande Valley unfurls from Albuquerque down to the bubbling hot springs of funky Truth or Consequences and on toward Mexico and Texas. En route, it feeds one of New Mexico's agricultural treasures: Hatch, the so-called chile capital of the world. East of the river, the desert is so dry it's been known since Spanish times as the Jornada del Muerto. Loosely translated as the 'journey of the dead man', it was a much-feared section of the El Camino Real de Tierra Adentro, a Spanish trade route established in 1598. Pretty appropriate that the area was chosen for the detonation of the first atomic bomb, at what's now the Trinity Site.

Away from Las Cruces, the state's second-largest city, residents in these parts are few and scattered. To the west, the rugged Gila National Forest is wild with backcountry adventure, while the Mimbres Valley is rich with archaeological treasures.

Truth or Consequences & Around

An offbeat joie de vivre permeates the funky little town of Truth or Consequences ('T or C'), which was built on the site of natural hot springs in the 1880s. Originally, called, sensibly enough, Hot Springs, it changed its name in 1950, after a then-popular radio game show called, you guessed it, Truth or Consequences. Publicity these days comes courtesy of Virgin Galactic CEO Richard Branson and other space-travel visionaries driving the development of nearby **Spaceport America** (✆ 844-727-7223; www.space portamerica.com; County Rd A021; adult/child $45/30), where wealthy tourists are expected to launch into orbit sometime soon. Less wealthy tourists can take a fascinating guided trip through the facility, hopping into a wild G-force machine along the way.

About 60 miles north, sandhill cranes and Arctic geese winter in the 90 sq miles of fields and marshes at **Bosque del Apache National Wildlife Refuge** (✆ 575-835-1828; www.fws.gov/refuge/bosque_del_apache; Hwy 1; per vehicle $5; ☉ dawn-dusk; 🅿).

🛏 Sleeping

★ Riverbend Hot Springs   BOUTIQUE HOTEL $$
(✆ 575-894-7625; www.riverbendhotsprings.com; 100 Austin St; r $99-259, RV sites $75; 🅿 ❋ 🤝 🐾) This delightful place, occupying a fantastic perch beside the Rio Grande, is the only T or C hotel to feature outdoor, riverside hot tubs – tiled, decked and totally irresistible. Accommodation, colorfully decorated by local artists, ranges from motel-style rooms to a three-bedroom suite. Guests can use the public pools for free, and private tubs for $10. No children under 12 years.

Blackstone Hotsprings   BOUTIQUE HOTEL $$
(✆ 575-894-0894; www.blackstonehotsprings.com; 410 Austin St; r $90-175; 🅿 ❋ 🤝 🐾) Blackstone

embraces the T or C spirit with an upscale wink, decorating each of its 12 rooms in the style of a classic TV show, from *The Jetsons* to *The Golden Girls* to *I Love Lucy*. Best part? Each of the 10 rooms on the main property comes with its own oversized tub or waterfall fed from the hot springs.

🍷 Drinking & Nightlife

Passion Pie Cafe   CAFE $
(✆ 575-894-0008; www.facebook.com/passionpie cafe; 406 Main St; breakfast & lunch mains $6-10; ☉ 7am-3pm; 🤝) Watch T or C get its morning groove on through the windows of this espresso cafe, and set yourself up with a breakfast waffle; the Elvis (with peanut butter) or the Fat Elvis (with bacon too) should do the job. Later on there are plenty of healthy salads and sandwiches.

Truth or Consequences
Brewing Co   MICROBREWERY
(✆ 575-297-0289; www.torcbeer.com; 410 N Broadway; ☉ 3-9:30pm Mon-Wed, noon-10pm Thu, to 11pm Fri & Sat, to 9:30pm Sun) Opening its doors in 2017, this spacious and welcoming watering hole already feels like a longtime neighborhood bar. The festive patio is the place to be while sipping the smooth ales and lagers – the specialties here. We liked the Cosmic Blonde. Solo travelers will feel welcome.

Las Cruces & Around

Las Cruces and its older and smaller sister city, Mesilla, sit at the edge of a broad basin beneath the fluted Organ Mountains, at the crossroads of two major highways, I-10 and I-25. An eclectic mix of old and young, Las Cruces is home to New Mexico State University (NMSU), whose 14,000 students infuse it with a healthy dose of youthful liveliness, while at the same time its 350 days of sunshine and numerous golf courses are turning it into a popular retirement destination.

◉ Sights

For many, a visit to neighboring **Mesilla** (aka Old Mesilla) is the highlight of their time in Las Cruces. Wander a few blocks off Old Mesilla's plaza to gather the essence of a mid-19th-century Southwestern town of Hispanic heritage.

★ New Mexico Farm &
Ranch Heritage Museum   MUSEUM
(✆ 575-522-4100; www.nmfarmandranchmuseum. org; 4100 Dripping Springs Rd; adult/child 4-17yr $5/3; ☉ 9am-5pm Mon-Sat, from noon Sun; 🅿 🚶)

PEERING INTO THE COSMIC UNKNOWN

Beyond the town of Magdalena on Hwy 60, 130 miles southwest of Albuquerque, the amazing **Very Large Array** (VLA; ☑505-835-7410; https://public.nrao.edu/visit/very-large-array; junction US 60 & Hwy 52, Magdalena; adult/child under 17yr $6/free; ⊙8:30am-sunset; P) radio telescope consists of 27 huge antenna dishes sprouting like giant mushrooms in the high plains. Watch a short film at the visitor center, then take a self-guided walking tour with a window peek into the control building.

This terrific museum doesn't just display engaging exhibits on the state's agricultural history – it's got livestock too. Enclosures on the working farm alongside hold assorted breeds of cattle, along with horses, donkeys, sheep and goats. The taciturn cowboys who tend the animals proffer little extra information, but they add color, and you can even buy a pony if you have $450 to spare. There are daily milking demonstrations, plus weekly displays of blacksmithing, spinning and weaving, and heritage cooking.

White Sands Missile Test Center Museum MUSEUM (☑575-678-3358; www.wsmr.army.mil/PAO/Pages/RangeMuseum.aspx; off Hwy 70; ⊙museum 8am-4:30pm Mon-Fri, 10am-3pm Sat & Sun, missile park sunrise-sunset; P) **FREE** Explore New Mexico's military technology history with a visit to this museum, 25 miles east of Las Cruces along Hwy 70. It represents the heart of the White Sands Missile Range, a major testing site since 1945. There's a missile garden, a real V-2 rocket and a museum with lots of defense-related artifacts. Visitors have to park outside the Test Center gate and check-in with identification at the office before walking in.

🛏 Sleeping

Best Western Mission Inn MOTEL $ (☑575-524-8591; www.bwmissioninn.com; 1765 S Main St; r from $85; P❀🛜🐾🏊) An optimal accommodation option: yes it's a roadside chain motel, but the rooms are beautifully kitted out with attractive tiling, stonework and colorful stenciled designs; they're sizable and comfortable; and the rates are great.

Microwave and fridge in each room. Breakfast is included too.

Hotel Encanto de Las Cruces HOTEL $$ (☑505-522-4300; www.hotelencanto.com; 705 S Telshor Blvd; r/ste from $149/209; P❀@🛜🐾🏊) The pick of the city's larger hotels, this Spanish Colonial resort property holds 200 spacious rooms, decorated in warm Southwestern tones, plus a palm-fringed outdoor pool, an exercise room, a restaurant and a lounge with patio. Pet fee is $25 per day.

🍴 Eating & Drinking

Chala's Wood-Fired Grill NEW MEXICAN $ (☑575-652-4143; 2790 Ave de Mesilla, Mesilla; mains $4-12; ⊙8am-9pm Mon-Thu, to 10pm Fri & Sat, to 8pm Sun) With house-smoked carnitas and turkey, housemade bacon and chilepork sausage, plus *calabacitas* (squash and corn), quinoa salad and organic greens, this place rises well above the standard New Mexican diner fare. Located at the southern end of Mesilla, it's kick-back casual and the price is right.

Double Eagle BAR (☑575-523-6700; www.double-eagle-mesilla.com; 308 Calle de Guadalupe, Mesilla; ⊙11am-10pm Mon-Sat, to 9pm Sun) A glorious melange of Wild West opulence, all dark wood and velvet hangings, this fabulous old bar on the Plaza is an atmospheric spot for a cocktail. The adjoining main dining room offers continental and Southwestern cuisine, especially steaks. The whole shebang is on the National Register of Historic Places and, of course, is haunted.

More than 40 specialty margaritas are on the menu.

ℹ Information

Las Cruces Visitors Center (☑575-541-2444; www.lascrucescvb.org; 336 S Main St; ⊙8am-5pm Mon-Fri; 🛜)

Mesilla Visitor Center (☑575-524-3262; www.oldmesilla.org; 2231 Ave de Mesilla, Mesilla; ⊙8am-5pm Mon-Fri)

ℹ Getting There & Away

Greyhound (☑575-523-1824; www.greyhound.com; 800 E Thorpe Rd, Chucky's Convenience Store) Buses run to all major destinations in the area, including El Paso, Albuquerque and Tucson. The bus stop is about 7 miles north of town.

Las Cruces Shuttle Service (☑575-525-1784; www.lascrucesshuttle.com) Runs eight to 10 vans daily to the El Paso International Airport ($50 one way, $35 each additional person), and to Deming, Silver City and other destinations on request.

Silver City & Around

The spirit of the Wild West still hangs in the air in Silver City, 113 miles northwest of Las Cruces, as if Billy the Kid himself – who grew up here – might amble past at any moment. But things are changing, as the mountain-man/cowboy vibe succumbs to the charms of art galleries and coffeehouses.

Silver City is also the gateway to outdoor activities in the Gila National Forest, which is rugged country suitable for remote cross-country skiing, backpacking, camping and fishing. Two hours north of town, up a winding 42-mile road, is Gila Cliff Dwellings National Monument (575-536-9461; www.nps.gov/gicl; Hwy 15; adult/child under 16yr $10/free; trail 9am-4pm, visitor center 8am-4:30pm; P), occupied in the 13th century by the Mogollon people. Mysterious and relatively isolated, these remarkable cliff dwellings are easily accessed from a 1-mile loop trail and look very much as they would have at the turn of the first millennium. For pictographs, stop by the Lower Scorpion Campground and walk a short distance along the marked trail.

Weird rounded monoliths make the City of Rocks State Park an intriguing playground, with great camping (575-536-2800; www.emnrd.state.nm.us/SPD; 327 Hwy 61; tent/RV sites $10/14) among the formations; there are tables and firepits. For a rock-lined gem of a spot, check out campsite 43, the Lynx. Head 33 miles southeast of Silver City along Hwy 180 and Hwy 61.

For a smattering of Silver City's architectural history, overnight in the 22-room Palace Hotel (575-388-1811; www.silvercitypalacehotel.com; 106 W Broadway; r/ste from $62/98;). Exuding a low-key, turn-of-the-19th-century charm (no elevator, older fixtures), the Palace is a great choice for those tired of cookie-cutter chains.

Downtown eating options range from the comfy, come-as-you-are Javalina (575-388-1350; www.javalinacoffeehouse.com; 117 W Market St; 6am-6pm;) coffee shop to the gastronomically adventurous – and highly recommended – Revel (575-388-4920; www.eatdrinkrevel.com; 304 N Bullard St; mains lunch $10-23, dinner $17-40; 11am-9pm Mon & Tue, Thu & Fri, from 9am Sat & Sun). For a taste of local culture, head 7 miles north to Pinos Altos and the atmospheric Buckhorn Saloon (575-538-9911; www.buckhornsaloonandoperahouse.com; 32 Main St, Pinos Altos; mains $11-56; 4-10pm Mon-Sat), where the specialty is steak and there's live music most nights. Call for reservations.

Information

Gila National Forest Ranger Station (575-388-8201; www.fs.fed.us/r3/gila; 3005 E Camino del Bosque; 8am-4:30pm Mon-Fri)

Visitor Center (575-538-5555; www.silvercitytourism.org; 201 N Hudson St; 9am-5pm Mon-Sat, 10am-2pm Sun) This super-helpful office can provide everything you need to make the most of Silver City.

Southeastern New Mexico

Two extraordinary natural wonders are tucked away in New Mexico's arid southeast: the mesmerizing White Sands National Monument and the magnificent Carlsbad Caverns National Park. Also impressive, if less well known, are the thousands of petroglyphs at the Three Rivers Petroglyph Site and the sprawling lava flow at Valley of Fires Recreation Area. This region also swirls with some of the state's most enduring legends: aliens in Roswell, Billy the Kid in Lincoln, and Smokey Bear in Capitan. Most of the lowlands are covered by hot, rugged Chihuahuan Desert – once submerged under the ocean – but you can always escape to the cooler climes around the popular forest resorts of Cloudcroft or Ruidoso.

White Sands National Monument

Slide, roll and slither through brilliant towerings and hills. Sixteen miles southwest of Alamogordo (15 miles southwest of Hwy82/70), gypsum covers 275 sq miles to create a dazzling white landscape at this stark monument (575-479-6124; www.nps.gov/whsa; per vehicle/motorcycle $20/10 or adult/child under 16yr $10/free, whichever is less; 7am-9pm Jun-Aug, to sunset Sep-May; P). These captivating windswept dunes, which doubled as David Bowie's space-alien home planet in *The Man Who Fell to Earth*, are a highlight of any trip to New Mexico. Don't forget your sunglasses – the sand is as bright as snow!

Spring for a $19 plastic saucer at the visitor center gift store then sled one of the backdunes. It's fun, and you can sell the disc back for $5 at day's end. Check the park calendar for sunset strolls. Backcountry campsites, with no water or toilet facilities, are a mile from the scenic drive. Pick up a permit ($3, issued first-come, first-served) in person at the visitor center at least one hour before sunset.

Alamogordo & Around

In Alamogordo, a desert outpost famous for its space- and atomic-research programs, the four-story **New Mexico Museum of Space History** (575-437-2840; www.nmspacemuseum.org; 3198 Hwy 2001; adult/child 4-12yr $8/6; 10am-5pm Wed-Sat & Mon, from noon Sun; P) has excellent exhibits on space research and flight, and shows outstanding science-themed films in its adjoining **New Horizons Dome Theater** (adult/child $8/6).

Motels stretch along White Sands Blvd, including a decent branch of **Super 8** (575-434-4205; www.wyndhamhotels.com; 3204 N White Sands Blvd; r from $73; P). If you'd rather camp, hit **Oliver Lee State Park** (575-437-8284; www.nmparks.com; 409 Dog Canyon Rd; tent/RV sites $10/14), 12 miles south of Alamogordo. Grab good Mexican grub at the brisk **Rizo's** (575-434-2607; www.facebook.com/rizosmexican restaurant; 1480 N White Sands Blvd; mains $6-17; 9am-9pm Tue-Sat, to 6pm Sun;).

Cloudcroft

Situated high in the mountains, little Cloudcroft provides welcome relief from the lowlands heat. With turn-of-the-19th-century buildings, it offers lots of outdoor recreation, is a good base for exploration and has a low-key feel. **High Altitude** (575-682-1229; www.highaltitudenm.com; 310 Burro Ave; rentals per day from $35; 10am-5:30pm Mon-Thu, to 6pm Fri & Sat, to 5pm Sun) rents mountain bikes and will point you in the right direction for a ride.

The **Lodge Resort & Spa** (800-395-6343; www.thelodgeresort.com; 601 Corona Pl; r/ste from $135/195; P) is one of the Southwest's finest historic hotels. Rooms in the main Bavarian-style hotel are furnished with period and Victorian pieces, while the great-value **Cloudcroft Mountain Park Hostel** (575-682-0555; www.cloudcrofthostel.com; 1049 Hwy 82; dm $19, r without bathroom $37-64; P) sits on 28 wooded acres west of town. **Rebecca's** (575-682-3131; www.thelodgeresort.com; Lodge Resort, 601 Corona Pl; mains lunch $9-20, dinner $24-40; 11:30am-3pm & 5:30-8pm Mon-Thu, 11:30am-3pm & 5:30-9pm Fri & Sat, 7-10:30am & 11am-2pm Sun) offers the best food in town. Grab a beer at **Cloudcroft Brewing Co** (575-682-2337; www.facebook.com/cloudcroft brewingcompany; 1301 Burro Ave; 11am-9pm Sun & Mon, Wed & Thu, to 10pm Fri & Sat).

Ruidoso

Perched on the eastern slopes of Sierra Blanca Peak (11,981ft), Ruidoso is a year-round resort town that's downright bustling in summer, attracts skiers in winter, has a lively arts scene and is home to a renowned racetrack. The lovely Rio Ruidoso, a small creek with good fishing, runs through town.

Sights & Activities

Stretch your legs on the easily accessible forest trails on Cedar Creek Rd just west of Smokey Bear Ranger Station. Choose from the USFS Fitness Trail or the meandering paths at the Cedar Creek Picnic Area. Longer day hikes and backpacking routes abound in the White Mountain Wilderness, north of town. Always check fire restrictions around here – the forest closes during dry spells.

Hubbard Museum of the American West   MUSEUM
(575-378-4142; www.hubbardmuseum.org; 26301 Hwy 70; adult/child 6-16yr $7/2; 9am-5pm Thu-Mon; P) This town-run museum focuses on local history, with a wonderful gallery of old photos, and also displays Native American kachinas, war bonnets, weapons and pottery. Traces of its original incarnation as the Museum of the Horse linger in various horse-related exhibits – and be sure to check out the fascinating, if completely irrelevant, history of toilets in the restrooms.

Ski Apache   SKIING
(575-464-3600; www.skiapache.com; 1286 Ski Run Rd, Alto; lift ticket adult/teen/child $74/65/54; 9am-4pm) Located 18 miles northwest of Ruidoso on the slopes of Sierra Blanca Peak, Ski Apache really is owned by the Apache. Potentially it's the finest ski area south of Albuquerque, a good choice for affordability and fun. Snowfall down here can be sporadic, though – check conditions ahead. In summer, ride the gondola (adult/child $35/25), hike, mountain bike and zipline (from $95).

Sleeping & Eating

Rental cabins are popular in Ruidoso. Most have kitchens and grills, and often fireplaces and decks. Some cabins in town are cramped, while newer ones are concentrated in the Upper Canyon. There's also free primitive camping along the forest roads on the way to the ski area; for campsite specifics, ask at the **ranger station** (575-257-

4095; www.fs.usda.gov/lincoln; 901 Mechem Dr; ☺8am-4pm Mon-Fri, plus Sat late May-early Sep).

Sitzmark Chalet
HOTEL $

(☏575-257-4140; www.sitzmark-chalet.com; 627 Sudderth Dr; r from $83; P❄🐾📶) This ski-themed chalet offers 17 simple but nice rooms. Picnic tables, grills and an eight-person hot tub are welcome perks.

Upper Canyon Inn
LODGE $$

(☏575-214-7170; www.uppercanyoninn.com; 215 Main Rd; r/cabin $149/169; P❄📶🐾) Rooms and cabins here range from simple good values to rustic-chic luxury. Bigger doesn't necessarily mean more expensive, so look at a few options. The pricier cabins have some fine interior woodwork and Jacuzzis. Check-in is at 2959 Sudderth Dr.

★ Cornerstone Bakery
CAFE $

(☏575-257-1842; www.cornerstonebakerycafe.com; 1712 Sudderth Dr; mains $7-12; ☺7am-3pm Mon & Tue, Thu & Fri, to 4pm Sat & Sun; 🐾) Totally irresistible, hugely popular local bakery and cafe, where everything, from the breads, pastries and espresso to the omelets and croissant sandwiches, is just the way it should be. Stick around long enough and the Cornerstone may become your morning touchstone.

☆ Entertainment

Ruidoso Downs Racetrack
SPORTS GROUND

(☏575-378-4431; www.raceruidoso.com; 26225 Hwy 70; grandstand seats free; ☺Fri-Mon mid-May–early Sep; P) FREE National attention focuses on the Ruidoso Downs racetrack on Labor Day for the world's richest quarter-horse race, the All American Futurity, which has a purse of $3 million. The course is also home to the Racehorse Hall of Fame, and the small Billy the Kid Casino.

Flying J Ranch
LIVE MUSIC

(☏575-336-4330; www.flyingjranch.com; 1028 Hwy 48N, Alto; adult/child $28/16; ☺from 5:30pm Mon-Sat late May-early Sep, Sat only through mid-Sep; 👶) Families with little ones will love this 'Western village,' 1.5 miles north of Alto, as it delivers a full night of entertainment, with gunfights, pony rides and Western music, to go with its cowboy-style chuckwagon dinner.

❶ Information

Visitor Center (☏575-257-7395; www.ruidoso now.com; 720 Sudderth Dr; ☺8am-5pm Mon-Fri, 9am-3pm Sat) Stop by for information about things to do in the Ruidoso valley and Lincoln County.

ORGAN MOUNTAINS-DESERT PEAKS NATIONAL MONUMENT

New Mexico's newest **national monument** (☏575-522-1219; www.blm.gov/visit/omp; per vehicle $5; ☺8am-5pm; P) consists of several components, totaling almost 500,000 acres and lying within a 50-mile radius of Las Cruces. While much of it is not developed for visitors, the Organ Mountains, which rise to 9000ft east of the city, are definitely worth exploring. Several trails leave from the **Dripping Springs Visitor Center**, including the lovely Dripping Springs trail itself, a 3-mile round trip that passes the century-old remains of a sanatorium and a hotel.

Lincoln & Capitan

Fans of Western history won't want to miss little Lincoln. Twelve miles east of Capitan along the **Billy the Kid National Scenic Byway** (www.billybyway.com), this is where the gun battles known as the Lincoln County War turned Billy the Kid into a legend. The whole town is beautifully preserved in close to original form, with its unspoiled main street designated as the **Lincoln Historic Site** (☏575-653-4082; www.nmmonuments.org/lincoln; US 380; adult/child $5/free; ☺Visitor Center & Courthouse 9am-5pm, other Bldgs to 4:30pm; P).

Buy tickets to the historic town buildings at the **Anderson-Freeman Visitors Center** (http://oldlincolntown.org; US 380; ☺9am-5pm), where you'll also find exhibits on Buffalo soldiers, Apaches and the Lincoln County War. Make the fascinating **Courthouse Museum**, the well-marked site of Billy's most daring – and violent – escape, your last stop. For overnighters, the **Wortley Hotel** (☏575-653-4300; www.wortleyhotel.com; 585 Calle La Placita/US 380; r from $125; ☺Mar-Nov) has been a fixture since 1874. Enjoy a beer at **Bonito Valley Brewing Co** (☏575-653-4810; www.facebook.com/bonitovalleybrewing; 692 Calle La Placita; ☺noon-9pm Thu-Mon), which recently opened right on the main drag.

Like Lincoln, cozy Capitan is surrounded by the beautiful mountains of Lincoln National Forest. The main reason to come is so the kids can visit **Smokey Bear Historical Park** (☏575-354-2748; www.emnrd.state.nm.us; 118 W Smokey Bear Blvd, Capitan; adult/child 7-12yr $2/1; ☺9am-4:30pm), where the original Smokey is buried.

SOUTHWEST SOUTHEASTERN NEW MEXICO

CARLSBAD CAVERNS NATIONAL PARK

While a cave might not sound quite as sexy as redwoods, geysers or the Grand Canyon, there's no question that the one at **Carlsbad Caverns National Park** (☎575-785-2232, bat info 575-236-1374; www.nps.gov/cave; 727 Carlsbad Cavern Hwy; 3-day pass adult/child under 16yr $15/free; ⊙caves 8:30am-5pm late May-early Sep, to 3:30pm early Sep-late May; 🅿♿) measures up on the national parks' jaw-droppingly ginormous scale: to simply reach the main chamber, you have to either take an elevator that drops the height of the Empire State Building or, more enjoyably, take a spooky 1.25-mile subterranean walk that goes down and down (and down) from the cave mouth into the yawning darkness.

Roswell

A mysterious object crashed at a ranch near Roswell in 1947. No one would have skipped any sleep over it, but the military made a big to-do of hushing it up, and for a lot of folks, that sealed it: the aliens had landed! International curiosity and local ingenuity have transformed the city into a quirky alien-wannabe zone. Bulbous white heads glow atop the downtown streetlamps and busloads of tourists come to find souvenirs.

Believers and kitsch-seekers must check out the **International UFO Museum & Research Center** (☎575-625-9495; www.roswellufomuseum.com; 114 N Main St; adult/child 5-15yr $5/2; ⊙9am-5pm), while the annual **Roswell UFO Festival** (www.roswellufofestival.com) beams down in early July.

Ho-hum chain motels line N Main St. About 36 miles south of Roswell, the **Heritage Inn** (☎575-748-2552; www.artesiaheritageinn.com; 209 W Main St, Artesia; r/ste $109/119; 🅿🐾@🛜) in Artesia is the nicest lodging in the area.

For simple, good Mexican fare, try **Los Cerritos** (☎575-622-4919; www.loscerritosmk.com; 2103 N main St; mains $7-15; ⊙7am-9pm Mon-Sat, to 5pm Sun); for American eats, **Big D's Downtown Dive** (☎575-627-0776; www.facebook.com/bigdsdowntowndive; 505 N Main St; mains $7-13; ⊙11am-9pm Mon-Sat) has the best salads, sandwiches and burgers in town. The tasty New Mexican dishes and fine margaritas at the **Adobe Rose** (☎575-476-6157; www.adoberoserestaurant.com; 1614 N 13th St, Artesia; mains lunch $10-23, dinner $12-32; ⊙11am-9pm Mon & Wed, from 10:30am Thu, 11am-11pm Fri, 5-11pm Sat, 9am-3pm Sun) in Artesia earn their regional accolades.

Pick up local information at the **visitors bureau** (☎575-623-3442; http://roswell-nm.gov/749/Visitors-Center; 426 N Main St; ⊙10am-3pm Sun & Mon, 9am-5pm Tue-Fri, 9am-4pm Sat; 🛜); **Greyhound** (☎575-622-2510; www.greyhound.com; 515 N Main St, Pecos Trails Transit) has buses to Las Cruces.

Carlsbad

Carlsbad is the closest town to Carlsbad Caverns National Park and the Guadalupe Mountains. To the northwest **Living Desert State Park** (☎575-887-5516; www.emnrd.state.nm.us; 1504 Miehls Dr N, off Hwy 285; adult/child 7-12yr $5/3; ⊙8am-5pm Jun-Aug, from 9am Sep-May, last zoo entry 3:30pm) is a great place to see and learn about desert plants and wildlife. There's a good 1.3-mile trail that showcases different habitats of the Chihuahuan Desert, with live antelopes, wolves, roadrunners and more.

However, a recent boom in the oil industry means that even the most ordinary motel room in Carlsbad costs way more than it would elsewhere in the state – so it makes more sense to visit on a long day-trip from Roswell or Alamogordo. One unique, if perhaps overrated, boutique option is the **Trinity Hotel** (☎575-234-9891; www.thetrinityhotel.com; 201 S Canal St; r $239-269; ❄🛜), originally the First National Bank. The sitting room of one suite is inside the old vault, and the restaurant is Carlsbad's classiest.

The perky **Blue House Bakery & Cafe** (☎575-628-0555; www.facebook.com/BlueHouseBakeryAndCafe; 609 N Canyon St; pastries $3-6, mains $4-6; ⊙6am-noon Mon-Sat) brews the best coffee in these parts. For a post-hike beer and pizza, try welcoming **Guadalupe Mountain Brewing Co** (☎575-887-8747; www.gmbrewingco.com; 3324 National Parks Hwy; ⊙11am-2pm Tue-Fri, 5-9pm Tue-Thu, to 10pm Fri, 4-10pm Sat), between the national park and downtown Carlsbad.

Greyhound (☎575-628-3088; www.greyhound.com; 106 W Greene St/US 180) buses depart from Road Runner Express, 0.3 miles south of downtown. Destinations include El Paso, TX, and Las Cruces.

California

Best Places to Eat

➡ Chez Panisse (p1003)

➡ Grand Central Market (p932)

➡ June Bug Cafe (p1019)

➡ Puesto at the Headquarters (p953)

Best Places to Sleep

➡ Arrive Hotel (p971)

➡ Auberge du Soleil (p971)

➡ Chateau Marmont (p930)

➡ McCloud River Mercantile Hote (p1016)

➡ USA Hostels San Diego (p951)

Why Go?

From misty Northern California redwood forests to sun-kissed Southern California beaches, the enchanted Golden State makes Disneyland seem normal. Combining bohemian spirit and high-tech savvy, California embraces contrast and contradictions. It is home to both vibrant metropolises and rugged wilderness, snowy mountains and desert expanses, and miles and miles of spectacular coastline.

It was here that the hurly-burly gold rush kicked off in the mid-19th century, where poet-naturalist John Muir rhapsodized about the Sierra Nevada's 'range of light,' where Jack Kerouac and the Beat Generation defined what it meant to hit the road, and where the twin dream factories of tech and entertainment flourished.

Above all, this is a state that celebrates the good life – whether that means cracking open a bottle of old-vine zinfandel, climbing a 14,000ft peak or surfing the Pacific.

When to Go
Los Angeles

Jun–Aug Mostly sunny weather, occasional coastal fog; summer-vacation crowds.

Apr–May & Sep–Oct Cooler nights, many cloudless days; travel bargains galore.

Nov–Mar Peak tourism at ski resorts and in SoCal's warm deserts.

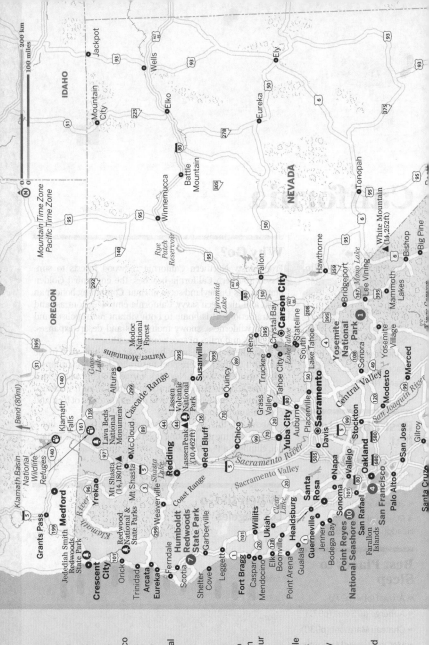

California Highlights

1 Yosemite National Park

(p1017) Chasing waterfalls and climbing granite domes in this Unesco World Heritage site.

2 Los Angeles

(p916) Making the most of multicultural neighborhoods, Hollywood studios and red-carpet nightlife.

3 Big Sur (p970)

Cruising Hwy 1 atop sculpted seacliffs on the bohemian Big Sur coast.

4 San Francisco

(p976) Riding a cable car up dizzying hills in the often foggy, always fabulous city by the bay.

5 Disneyland Resort (p941) (Re)

living your childhood dreams at the 'Happiest Place on Earth'.

Mountain Time Zone
Pacific Time Zone

200 km
100 miles

IDAHO

NEVADA

OREGON

CALIFORNIA

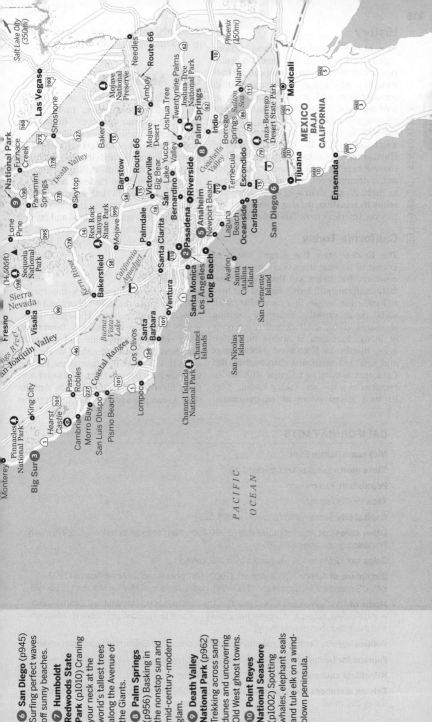

6 San Diego (p945)
Surfing perfect waves off sunny beaches.

7 Humboldt Redwoods State Park (p1010) Craning your neck at the world's tallest trees along the Avenue of the Giants.

8 Palm Springs (p956) Basking in the nonstop sun and mid-century-modern glam.

9 Death Valley National Park (p962) Trekking across sand dunes and uncovering Old West ghost towns.

10 Point Reyes National Seashore (p1002) Spotting whales, elephant seals and tule elk on a wind-blown peninsula.

History

Five hundred Native American nations called this land home for some 150 centuries before 16th-century European arrivals gave it a new name: California. Spanish conquistadors and priests came here for gold and God, but soon relinquished their flea-plagued missions and ill-equipped presidios (forts) to Mexico. The unruly territory was handed off to the US in the Treaty of Hidalgo mere months before gold was discovered here in 1848. Generations of California dreamers continue to make the trek to these Pacific shores for gold, glory and self-determination, making homes and history on America's most fabled frontier.

California Today

The Golden State has surged ahead of France to become the world's sixth-largest economy. But like a kid that's grown too fast, California still hasn't figured out how to handle the hassles that come along with such rapid growth, including housing shortages, traffic gridlock and rising costs of living. Escapism is always an option here, thanks to Hollywood blockbusters and legalized marijuana dispensaries. But California is coming to grips with its international status and taking leading roles in such global issues as environmental standards, online privacy, marriage equality and immigrant rights.

LOS ANGELES

If you think you've already got LA figured out – celebutantes, smog, traffic, bikini babes and pop-star wannabes – think again. LA is best defined by simple life-affirming moments: a cracked-ice, jazz-age cocktail after midnight, a hike high into the sagebrush of Griffith Park, a pink-washed sunset over a Venice Beach drum circle, or a search for the perfect taco. With Hollywood and Downtown LA both undergoing an urban renaissance, the city's art, music, food and fashion scenes are all in high gear. Chances are, the more you explore, the more you'll love 'La-La Land.'

⊙ Sights

A dozen miles inland from the Pacific, Downtown LA combines history and highbrow arts and culture. Hip-again Hollywood awaits northwest of Downtown, while urban-designer chic and gay pride rule West Hollywood. South of WeHo, Museum Row is Mid-City's main draw. Further west are ritzy Beverly Hills, Westwood near the University of California, Los Angeles (UCLA) campus and West LA. Beach towns

---

CALIFORNIA FACTS

Nickname Golden State

State motto Eureka ('I Have Found It')

Population 39.5 million

Area 155,780 sq miles

Capital city Sacramento (population 508,529)

Other cities Los Angeles (population 3,990,456), San Diego (population 1,425,976), San Francisco (population 883,305)

Sales tax 7.25% to 10.25% (varies by municipality)

Birthplace of Author John Steinbeck (1902–68), photographer Ansel Adams (1902–84), US president Richard Nixon (1913–94), pop-culture icon Marilyn Monroe (1926–62)

Home of The highest and lowest points in the contiguous US (Mt Whitney, Death Valley), world's oldest, tallest and biggest living trees (ancient bristlecone pines, coast redwoods and giant sequoias, respectively)

Politics Majority Democrat, minority Republican, one in four Californians vote independent

Famous for Disneyland, earthquakes, Hollywood, hippies, Silicon Valley, surfing

Kitschiest souvenir 'Mystery Spot' bumper sticker

Driving distances Los Angeles to San Francisco 380 miles, San Francisco to Yosemite Valley 190 miles

CALIFORNIA IN...

One Week

California in a nutshell: start in beachy **Los Angeles**, detouring to **Disneyland**. Head up the breezy **Central Coast**, stopping in **Santa Barbara** and **Big Sur**, before getting a dose of big-city culture in **San Francisco**. Head inland to nature's temple, **Yosemite National Park**, then zip back to LA.

Two Weeks

Follow the one-week itinerary above, but at a saner pace. Add jaunts to NorCal's **Wine Country**; **Lake Tahoe**, perched high in the Sierra Nevada; the bodacious beaches of Orange County and laid-back **San Diego**; or **Joshua Tree National Park**, near the chic desert resort of **Palm Springs**.

One Month

Do everything described in the itineraries above, and more. From San Francisco, head up the foggy **North Coast**, starting in Marin County at **Point Reyes National Seashore**. Stroll Victorian-era **Mendocino** and **Eureka**, find yourself on the **Lost Coast** and ramble through fern-filled **Redwood National & State Parks**. Inland, snap a postcard-perfect photo of **Mt Shasta**, drive through **Lassen Volcanic National Park** and ramble in California's historic **Gold Country**. Trace the backbone of the **Eastern Sierra** before winding down into otherworldly **Death Valley National Park**.

include kid-friendly Santa Monica, boho Venice, star-powered Malibu and busy Long Beach. Leafy Pasadena lies northeast of Downtown.

◉ Downtown

Though still sketchy in patches, Downtown (DTLA) continues the upward swing that began a decade or more ago. Within the large area that is Downtown, you'll find distinct neighbourhoods, each with their own unique identities and attractions.

Compact, colorful and car free, **El Pueblo de Los Angeles** historic district immerses you in LA's Spanish-Mexican roots. Its spine is festive **Olvera St** (Map p924; www.calleolvera.com; 🚻; Ⓜ Union Station, Ⓡ Union Station), where you can snap up handmade folkloric trinkets, then chomp on tacos and sugar-sprinkled churros.

Union Station (Map p924; www.amtrak.com; 800 N Alameda St; Ⓟ), built on the site of LA's original Chinatown, opened in 1939 as America's last grand rail station. It's a glamorous exercise in Mission Revival style with art deco and American Indian accents. 'New' **Chinatown** (Map p924; www.chinatownla.com) is about a half mile north along Broadway and Hill St, crammed with dim-sum parlors, herbal apothecaries, curio shops, hipster-friendly restaurants and edgy art galleries.

Southwest of Union Station, **Little Tokyo** swirls with shopping arcades, Buddhist temples, traditional gardens, authentic sushi bars and noodle shops. Just east, a burgeoning **Arts District** is one of the city's creative centers, with restaurants and shops to match.

Despite the name, South Park isn't actually a park but an emerging neighborhood around the Convention Center and **LA Live** (Map p924; 🕿 213-763-5483; www.lalive.com; 800 W Olympic Blvd; Ⓟ 🚻; Ⓜ Blue/Expo Lines to Pico Station), a dining and entertainment hub.

★**Broad**   MUSEUM
(Map p924; 🕿 213-232-6200; www.thebroad.org; 221 S Grand Ave; ⊘ 11am-5pm Tue & Wed, to 8pm Thu & Fri, 10am-8pm Sat, to 6pm Sun; Ⓟ 🚻; Ⓜ Red/Purple Lines to Civic Center/Grand Park) **FREE** From the instant it opened in September 2015, the Broad (rhymes with 'road') became a must-visit for contemporary-art fans. It houses the world-class collection of local philanthropist and billionaire real-estate honcho Eli Broad and his wife Edythe, with more than 2000 postwar pieces by dozens of heavy hitters, including Cindy Sherman, Jeff Koons, Andy Warhol, Roy Lichtenstein, Robert Rauschenberg, Keith Haring and Kara Walker.

Greater Los Angeles

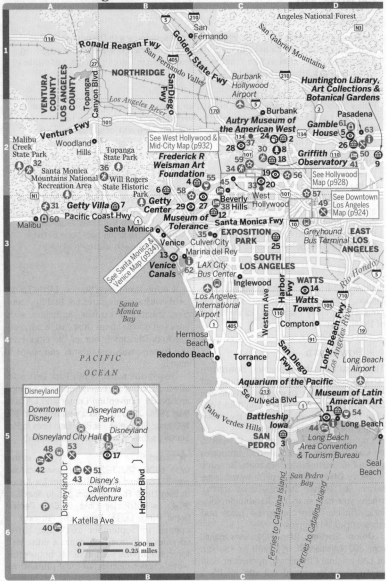

★ **Walt Disney Concert Hall** NOTABLE BUILDING (Map p924; 📞 323-850-2000; www.laphil.org; 111 S Grand Ave; 🅿; Ⓜ Red/Purple Lines to Civic Center/ Grand Park) FREE A molten blend of steel, music and psychedelic architecture, this iconic concert venue is the home base of the Los Angeles Philharmonic, but has also hosted contemporary bands such as Phoenix, and classic jazz musicians such as Sonny Rollins. The 2003 concert hall's visionary architect, Frank Gehry, pulled out all the stops for this building, a gravity-defying sculpture of heaving and billowing stainless steel.

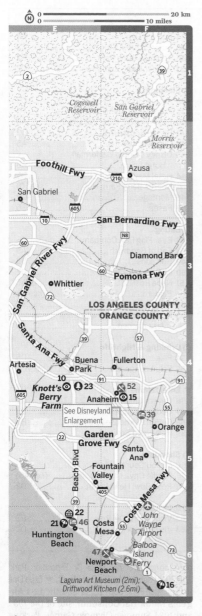

See Disneyland
Enlargement

Laguna Art Museum (2mi);
Driftwood Kitchen (2.6mi)

★ **MOCA Grand** MUSEUM

(Museum of Contemporary Art; Map p924; ☎213-626-6222; www.moca.org; 250 S Grand Ave; adult/child $15/free, 5-8pm Thu free; ⊙11am-6pm Mon, Wed & Fri, to 5pm Thu, to 5pm Sat & Sun; Ⓜ Red/Purple Lines to Civic Center/Grand Park) MOCA's superlative art collection focuses mainly on

works created from the 1940s to the present. There's no shortage of luminaries, among them Mark Rothko, Dan Flavin, Willem de Kooning, Joseph Cornell and David Hockney, in regular and special exhibits. Their creations are housed in a 1986 building by 2019 Pritzker Prize–winning Japanese architect Arata Isozaki. Galleries are below ground, yet sky-lit bright.

**Japanese American
National Museum** MUSEUM

(Map p924; ☎213-625-0414; www.janm.org; 100 N Central Ave; adult/senior & child $12/6, 5-8pm Thu & all day 3rd Thu of month free; ⊙11am-5pm Tue, Wed & Fri-Sun, noon-8pm Thu; ⊕; Ⓜ Gold Line to Little Tokyo/Arts District) A great first stop in Little Tokyo, this is the country's first museum dedicated to the Japanese immigrant experience. The 2nd floor is home to the permanent 'Common Ground' exhibition, which explores the evolution of Japanese-American culture since the late 19th century and offers moving insight into the painful chapter of America's WWII internment camps. Afterwards, relax in the tranquil garden and browse the well-stocked gift shop.

★ **Grammy Museum** MUSEUM

(Map p924; ☎213-765-6800; www.grammymuseum.org; 800 W Olympic Blvd; adult/child, senior & student $15/13; ⊙10:30am-6:30pm Sun, Mon, Wed & Thu, 10am-8pm Fri & Sat; Ⓟ⊕; Ⓜ Blue/Expo Lines to Pico Station) The highlight of LA Live (p917), this museum's interactive exhibits define, differentiate and link musical genres. Spanning three levels, the rotating exhibitions might include threads worn by the likes of Michael Jackson, Whitney Houston and Beyoncé, scribbled words from the hands of Count Basie and Taylor Swift, and instruments once used by world-renowned rock deities. Inspired? Interactive sound chambers allow you to try your own hand at singing, mixing and remixing.

LA Plaza MUSEUM

(La Plaza de Cultura y Artes; Map p924; ☎213-542-6259; www.lapca.org; 501 N Main St; ⊙noon-5pm Mon, Wed & Thu, to 6pm Fri-Sun; ⊕; Ⓜ Union Station) FREE This museum offers snapshots of the Mexican–American experience in Los Angeles, from Spanish colonization in the late 18th century and the Mexican–American War (when the border crossed the original pueblo), to the Zoot Suit Riots, activist César Chávez and the Chicana movement. Exhibitions include a re-creation of

Greater Los Angeles

1920s Main St as well as rotating showcases of modern and contemporary art by LA-based Latinx artists.

◉ Exposition Park & Around

Just south of the University of Southern California (USC) campus, this park has a full day's worth of kid-friendly museums. Outdoor landmarks include the **Rose Garden** (Map p918; ☏213-763-0114; www.laparks. org/expo/garden; 701 State Dr, Exposition Park; ☺8:30am-sunset Mar 16–Dec 31; Ⓟ; Ⓜ Expo Line to Exposition Park/USC) **FREE** and the **Los Angeles Memorial Coliseum**, site of the 1932 and 1984 Summer Olympic Games. Parking costs around $10. From Downtown, take the Metro Expo Line or DASH minibus F.

★Watts Towers   LANDMARK
(Map p918; ☏213-847-4646; www.wattstowers.org; 1761-1765 E 107th St, Watts; ☺tours 11am-3pm Thu & Fri, 10:30am-3pm Sat, noon-3pm Sun; Ⓟ; Ⓜ Blue

Line to 103rd St) The three 'Gothic' spires of the fabulous Watts Towers rank among the world's greatest monuments of folk art. In 1921 Italian immigrant Simon Rodia set out 'to make something big' and then spent 33 years cobbling together this whimsical free-form sculpture from concrete, steel and a motley assortment of found objects: green 7Up bottles to sea shells, tiles, rocks and pottery.

California Science Center MUSEUM
(Map p918; film schedule 213-744-2019, info 323-724-3623; www.californiasciencecenter.org; 700 Exposition Park Dr, Exposition Park; IMAX movie adult/student & senior/child $8.95/7.95/6.75; 10am-5pm;) FREE Top billing at the Science Center goes to the Space Shuttle *Endeavour*, one of only four space shuttles nationwide, but there's plenty else to see at this large, multistory, multimedia museum filled with buttons to push, lights to switch on and knobs to pull. A simulated earthquake and a giant techno-doll named Tess bring out the kid in everyone. Admission is free, but special exhibits, experiences and IMAX movies cost extra.

Natural History Museum of Los Angeles MUSEUM
(Map p918; 213-763-3466; www.nhm.org; 900 Exposition Blvd, Exposition Park; adult/student & senior/child $15/12/7, LA County residents 3pm-5pm Mon-Fri free; 9:30am-5pm; ; Expo Line to Expo/Vermont) Dinos to diamonds, bears to beetles, hissing roaches to African elephants –

this museum will take you around the world and back, through millions of years in time. It's all housed in a beautiful 1913 Spanish Renaissance–style building that stood in for Columbia University in the first Toby McGuire *Spider-Man* movie – yup, this was where Peter Parker was bitten by the radioactive arachnid. There's enough to see here to fill several hours.

◉ Hollywood

Just as aging movie stars get the occasional face-lift, so has Hollywood. While it still hasn't recaptured its mid-20th-century 'Golden Age' glamour, its late-20th-century seediness is receding (albeit slowly). The **Hollywood Walk of Fame** (Map p928; www.walkoffame.com; Hollywood Blvd; Red Line to Hollywood/Highland) honors more than 2600 celebrities with brass stars embedded in the sidewalk.

The Metro Red Line stops beneath **Hollywood & Highland** (Map p928; www.hollywoodandhighland.com; 6801 Hollywood Blvd; 10am-10pm Mon-Sat, to 7pm Sun; ; Red Line to Hollywood/Highland), a multistory mall with nicely framed views of the hillside **Hollywood sign** (erected in 1923 as an advertisement for a land development called Hollywoodland). Two-hour validated mall parking costs $3 (daily maximum $17).

★**TCL Chinese Theatre** LANDMARK
(Grauman's Chinese Theatre; Map p928; 323-461-3331; www.tclchinesetheatres.com; 6925

LOS ANGELES IN ...

Distances are ginormous in LA, so allow extra time for traffic and don't try to pack too much into a day.

One Day
Fuel up for the day at the **Original Farmers Market**, then go star-searching on the **Hollywood Walk of Fame** along Hollywood Blvd. Up your chances of spotting actual celebs by hitting the fashion-forward boutiques on paparazzi-infested **Robertson Boulevard**, or get a dose of nature at **Griffith Park**. Then drive west to the lofty **Getty Center** or head out to the **Venice Boardwalk** to see the seaside sideshow. Catch a Pacific sunset in **Santa Monica**.

Two Days
Explore rapidly evolving **Downtown LA**. Dig up the city's roots at **El Pueblo de Los Angeles**, then catapult to the future at dramatic **Walt Disney Concert Hall** and **Broad museum** topping Grand Ave's Cultural Corridor. Stop for a bite at **Grand Central Market**, then walk off lunch ambling between Downtown's historic buildings, **Arts District galleries** and **Little Tokyo**. At South Park's glitzy **LA Live** entertainment center, romp through the multimedia **Grammy Museum**. After dark, hit the dance floor at clubs in **Hollywood**.

Hollywood Blvd; 🚻; Ⓜ Red Line to Hollywood/Highland) FREE Ever wondered what it's like to be in George Clooney's shoes? Find his foot- and handprints alongside dozens of other stars', forever set in the concrete forecourt of this world-famous movie palace, opened in 1927 and styled after an exotic pagoda complete with temple bells and stone heaven dogs from China. Join the throngs to find out how big Arnold's feet really are, or search for Betty Grable's legs, Whoopi Goldberg's braids, Daniel Radcliffe's wand or R2-D2's wheels.

★ **Hollywood Museum**   MUSEUM
(Map p928; ☎ 323-464-7776; www.thehollywood museum.com; 1660 N Highland Ave; adult/senior & student/child $15/12/5; ⓢ 10am-5pm Wed-Sun; Ⓜ Red Line to Hollywood/Highland) For a taste of Old Hollywood, do not miss this musty temple to the stars, its four floors crammed with movie and TV costumes and props. The museum is housed inside the Max Factor Building, built in 1914 and relaunched as a glamorous beauty salon in 1935. At the helm was Polish-Jewish businessman Max Factor, Hollywood's leading authority on cosmetics. And it was right here that he worked his magic on Hollywood's most famous screen queens.

Hollywood Forever Cemetery   CEMETERY
(Map p918; ☎ 323-469-1181; www.hollywoodfor ever.com; 6000 Santa Monica Blvd; guided tours $20; ⓢ 8:30am-5pm, guided tours 10am most Saturdays; ℗) FREE Paradisiacal landscaping, vainglorious tombstones and epic mausoleums set an appropriate resting place for some of Hollywood's most iconic dearly departed. Residents include Cecil B DeMille, Mickey Rooney, Jayne Mansfield, punk rockers Johnny and Dee Dee Ramone and *Golden Girls* star Estelle Getty. Rudolph Valentino lies in the Cathedral Mausoleum (open 10am to 2pm), while Judy Garland rests in the Abbey of the Psalms.

⊙ Griffith Park

America's largest urban **park** (Map p918; ☎ 323-644-2050; www.laparks.org/griffithpark; 4730 Crystal Springs Dr; ⓢ 5am-10:30pm, trails sunrise-sunset; ℗🚻) FREE is five times the size of New York's Central Park, with an outdoor theater, **zoo** (Map p918; ☎ 323-644-4200; www.lazoo.org; 5333 Zoo Dr, Griffith Park; adult/senior/child $21/18/16; ⓢ 10am-5pm, closed Christmas Day; ℗🚻), observatory, museum, merry-go-round, antique and miniature

trains, children's playgrounds, golf, tennis and over 50 miles of hiking paths, including to the original *Batman* TV series cave.

★ **Griffith Observatory**   MUSEUM
(Map p918; ☎ 213-473-0890; www.griffithobser vatory.org; 2800 E Observatory Rd; admission free, planetarium shows adult/student & senior/child $7/5/3; ⓢ noon-10pm Tue-Fri, from 10am Sat & Sun; ℗🚻; 🚌 DASH Observatory) FREE LA's landmark 1935 observatory opens a window onto the universe from its perch on the southern slopes of Mt Hollywood. Its planetarium claims the world's most advanced star projector, while its astronomical touch displays explore some mind-bending topics, from the evolution of the telescope and the ultraviolet x-rays used to map our solar system to the cosmos itself. Then, of course, there are the views, which (on clear days) take in the entire LA Basin, surrounding mountains and Pacific Ocean.

★ **Autry Museum of the American West**   MUSEUM
(Map p918; ☎ 323-667-2000; http://theautry.org; 4700 Western Heritage Way, Griffith Park; adult/senior & student/child $14/10/6, 2nd Tue each month free; ⓢ 10am-4pm Tue-Fri, to 5pm Sat & Sun; ℗🚻) Established by singing cowboy Gene Autry, this expansive, underrated museum offers contemporary perspectives on the history and people of the American West, as well as their links to today's culture. Permanent exhibitions span Native American traditions to 19th-century cattle drives, daily frontier life (look for the beautifully carved vintage saloon bar) to costumes and artifacts from Hollywood westerns. Blockbuster temporary exhibits cover themes including Route 66, the 1960s and '70s Chicano newspaper *La Raza* and Native American artist Harry Fonseca.

⊙ West Hollywood & Mid-City

In WeHo, rainbow flags fly proudly over Santa Monica Boulevard, while celebs keep gossip rags happy by misbehaving at clubs on the fabled Sunset Strip. Boutiques along **Robertson Boulevard** and **Melrose Avenue** purvey sassy and ultrachic fashions for Hollywood royalty and celebutantes. WeHo's also a hotbed of cutting-edge interior design, fashion and art, particularly in the **West Hollywood Design District** (http://westhollywooddesigndistrict.com). Further south, some of LA's best museums line Mid-City's Museum Row along Wilshire Blvd east of Fairfax Ave.

★**Los Angeles County**
Museum of Art   MUSEUM
(LACMA; Map p932; ☑323-857-6000; www.lac
ma.org; 5905 Wilshire Blvd, Mid-City; adult/senior
& student/child $25/21/free, 2nd Tue each month
free, some holidays free; ⊙11am-5pm Mon, Tue &
Thu, to 8pm Fri, 10am-7pm Sat & Sun; Ⓟ; ⬚Metro
lines 20, 217, 720, 780 to Wilshire & Fairfax) The
depth and wealth of the collection at the
largest museum in the western US is stunning. LACMA holds all the major players –
Rembrandt, Cézanne, Magritte, Mary Cassatt, Ansel Adams – plus millennia's worth
of Chinese, Japanese, pre-Columbian and
ancient Greek, Roman and Egyptian sculpture. Recent acquisitions include massive
outdoor installations such as Chris Burden's *Urban Light* (a surreal selfie backdrop of hundreds of vintage LA streetlamps) and Michael Heizer's *Levitated
Mass,* a surprisingly inspirational 340-ton
boulder perched over a walkway.

La Brea Tar Pits & Museum   MUSEUM
(Map p932; www.tarpits.org; 5801 Wilshire Blvd,
Mid-City; adult/student & senior/child $15/12/7, 1st
Tue of month Sep-Jun free; ⊙9:30am-5pm; Ⓟ🚼)
Mammoths, saber-toothed cats and dire
wolves roamed LA's savanna in prehistoric
times. We know this because of an archaeological trove of skulls and bones unearthed
here at the La Brea Tar Pits, one of the
world's most fecund and famous fossil sites.
A museum has been built here, where generations of young dino hunters have come
to seek out fossils and learn about paleontology from docents and demonstrations in
on-site labs.

◉ **Beverly Hills & the Westside**

Westwood is home to the well-tended UCLA
campus, while Beverly Hills claims **Rodeo
Drive** (Map p918), a prime people-watching
spot – no trip to LA would be complete without a saunter along it. Guided tours of celebrity homes depart from Hollywood.

★**Getty Center**   MUSEUM
(Map p918; ☑310-440-7300; www.getty.edu; 1200
Getty Center Dr, off I-405 Fwy; ⊙10am-5:30pm Tue-
Fri & Sun, to 9pm Sat; Ⓟ🚼; ⬚734, 234) 🆓 In
its billion-dollar, in-the-clouds perch, high
above the city grit and grime, the Getty Center
presents triple delights: a stellar art collection (everything from medieval triptychs to

baroque sculpture and impressionist brushstrokes), Richard Meier's cutting-edge architecture, and the visual splendor of seasonally changing gardens. Admission is free, but
parking is $20 ($15 after 3pm).

★**Museum of Tolerance**   MUSEUM
(Map p918; ☑reservations 310-772-2505; www.
museumoftolerance.com; 9786 W Pico Blvd; adult/
senior/student $15.50/12.50/11.50, Anne Frank Exhibit $15.50/13.50/12.50; ⊙10am-5pm Sun-Wed &
Fri, to 9:30pm Thu, to 3:30pm Fri Nov-Mar; Ⓟ) Run
by the Simon Wiesenthal Center, this powerful, deeply moving museum uses interactive
technology to engage visitors in discussion
and contemplation around racism and bigotry. Particular focus is given to the Holocaust, with a major basement exhibition
that examines the social, political and economic conditions that led to the Holocaust
as well as the experience of the millions persecuted. On the museum's 2nd floor, another
major exhibition offers an intimate look into
the life and impact of Anne Frank.

★**Frederick R Weisman**
Art Foundation   MUSEUM
(Map p918; ☑310-277-5321; www.weismanfoun
dation.org; 265 N Carolwood Dr; ⊙90min guided
tours 10:30am & 2pm Mon-Fri, by appointment
only) 🆓 The late entrepreneur and philanthropist Frederick R Weisman had an
insatiable passion for art, a fact confirmed
when touring his former Holmby Hills home.
From floor to ceiling, the mansion (and its
manicured grounds) bursts with extraordinary works from visionaries such as Picasso,
Kandinsky, Miró, Magritte, Rothko, Warhol,
Rauschenberg and Ruscha. There's even a
motorcycle painted by Keith Haring. Tours
should be reserved at least a few days ahead.

Westwood Village
Memorial Park Cemetery   CEMETERY
(Map p918; ☑310-474-1579; 1218 Glendon Ave,
Westwood; ⊙8am-6pm; Ⓟ) You'll be spending
quiet time with entertainment heavyweights
at this compact cemetery, hidden behind
Wilshire Blvd's wall of high-rise towers. The
northeast mausoleum houses Marilyn Monroe's simple crypt, while just south of it, the
Sanctuary of Love harbors Dean Martin's
crypt. Beneath the central lawn lie a number of iconic names, including actress Natalie Wood, pin-up Bettie Page, and crooner
Roy Orbison (the latter lies in an unmarked
grave to the left of a marker labeled 'Grandma Martha Monroe').

Downtown Los Angeles

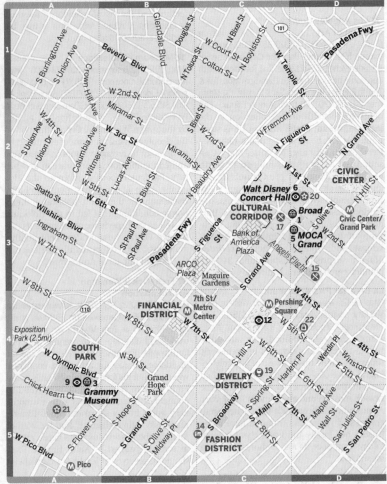

Malibu

The beach is king, of course, and whether you find a sliver of sand among the sandstone rock towers and topless sunbathers at **El Matador** (📞818-880-0363; 32215 Pacific Coast Hwy; 🅿️) or enjoy the wide loamy blonde beaches of Zuma and Westward, you'll have a special afternoon. Many A-listers have homes here and can sometimes be spotted shopping at the village-like **Malibu Country Mart** (Map p918; 📞310-456-7300; www.malibucountrymart. com; 3835 Cross Creek Rd; ⏰10am-midnight Mon-Sat, to 10pm Sun; 🚼; 🚍MTA line 534) shopping center.

One of Malibu's natural treasures is canyon-riddled **Malibu Creek State Park** (Map p918; 📞818-880-0367; www.malibucreek statepark.org; 1925 Las Virgenes Rd, Cornell; parking $12; ⏰dawn-dusk), a popular movie and TV filming location with hiking trails galore (parking $12). A string of famous Malibu beaches include aptly named Surfrider near Malibu Pier, secretive El Matador, family fave Zuma Beach and wilder Point Dume (beach parking $3 to $12.50).

⭐ **Getty Villa**   MUSEUM
(Map p918; 📞310-430-7300; www.getty.edu; 17985 Pacific Coast Hwy, Pacific Palisades; ⏰10am-

5pm Wed-Mon; **P**; **line** 534 to Coastline Dr) **FREE** Stunningly perched on an ocean-view hillside, this museum in a replica 1st-century Roman villa is an exquisite, 64-acre showcase for Greek, Roman and Etruscan antiquities. Dating back 7000 years, they were amassed by oil tycoon J Paul Getty. Galleries, peristiles, courtyards and lushly landscaped gardens ensconce all manner of friezes, busts and mosaics, along with millennia-old cut, blown and colored glass and brain-bending geometric configurations in the Hall of Colored Marbles. Other highlights include the Pompeii fountain and Temple of Herakles.

◎ Santa Monica

The belle by the beach mixes urban cool with a laid-back vibe. Tourists, teens and street performers throng car-free, chain-store-lined Third Street Promenade. For more local flavor, shop posh Montana Ave or eclectic Main St, backbone of the neighborhood once nicknamed 'Dogtown,' – the birthplace of skateboard culture. There's free 90-minute parking in most public garages downtown.

★ **Santa Monica Pier**   LANDMARK
(Map p934; ☎310-458-8901; www.santamonica pier.org;) Once the very end of the legendary Route 66 and still the object of a tourist love affair, this much-photographed pier dates back to 1908 and is the city's

most compelling landmark. It's dominated by **Pacific Park** (Map p934; ☎ 310-260-8744; www.pacpark.com; 380 Santa Monica Pier; per ride $5-10, all-day pass adult/child under 8yr $35/19; ⊙ daily, seasonal hrs vary; ☝; Ⓜ Expo Line to Downtown Santa Monica) amusement park with arcades, carnival games, a Ferris wheel and roller coaster. Nearby is a vintage **carousel** (Map p934; ☎ 310-394-8042; adult/child $2/1; ⊙ hrs vary; ☝) and an **aquarium** (Map p934; ☎ 310-393-6149; www.healthebay.org; 1600 Ocean Front Walk; adult/child $5/free; ⊙ 2-6pm Mon-Thu, 12:30-6pm Fri-Sun; ☝; Ⓜ Expo Line to Downtown Santa Monica) ✿. The pier is most photogenic when framed by California sunsets and when it comes alive with free concerts and outdoor movies in the summertime.

⊙ Venice

Prepare for sensory overload on Venice's **Boardwalk** (Ocean Front Walk; Map p934; Venice Pier to Rose Ave), a one-of-a-kind experience. Buff bodybuilders brush elbows with street performers and sellers of sunglasses, string bikinis, Mexican ponchos and cannabis, while cyclists and rollerbladers whiz by on the bike path, and skateboarders and graffiti artists get their own domains. A few blocks away, **Abbot Kinney Blvd** (Map p934; ☐ Big Blue Bus line 18) is the epicenter of 'new Venice', chockablock with trendy boutiques, restaurants and cafes. The **Venice Canals** (Map p918) offer a genteel escape among funky to modernist homes around the waterways that lent the neighborhood its name.

⊙ Long Beach

Stretching along LA County's southern flank, Long Beach forms half of America's busiest container-ship port along with the port of LA, across a channel. Yet there's little clue of the industrial edge in Long Beach's busy downtown – Pine Ave is crowded with restaurants and bars – and in the restyled waterfront. The Metro Blue Line connects Downtown LA with Long Beach in under an hour. Passport (www.lbtransit.com) minibuses shuttle around major tourist sights for free.

★**Battleship Iowa**   MUSEUM, MEMORIAL
(Map p918; ☎ 877-446-9261; www.pacific battleship.com; 250 S Harbor Blvd, San Pedro; adult/senior/child $20/17/12; ⊙ 10am-5pm, last entry 4pm; Ⓟ ☝; ☐ Metro Silver Line) This WWII to Cold War–era battleship is now permanently moored in San Pedro Bay and open to visitors as a museum. It's massive – 887ft long (that's 5ft longer than *Titanic*) and about as tall as an 18-story building. Step onto the gangway and download the free app to take a self-guided audio tour of everything from the stateroom, where FDR stayed, to missile turrets and the enlisted men's galley, which churned out 8000 hot meals a day during WWII.

★**Aquarium of the Pacific**   AQUARIUM
(Map p918; ☎ tickets 562-590-3100; www.aquar iumofpacific.org; 100 Aquarium Way, Long Beach; adult/senior/child $30/27/19; ⊙ 9am-6pm; Ⓟ ☝) Long Beach's most mesmerizing experience, the Aquarium of the Pacific is a vast, high-tech indoor ocean where sharks dart, jellyfish dance and sea lions frolic. More than 11,000 creatures inhabit four re-created habitats: the bays and lagoons of Baja California, the frigid northern Pacific, tropical coral reefs and local kelp forests. The stunning new 29,000-sq-ft Pacific Visions pavilion uses sound, touch, visual art, cutting-edge video technology and natural exhibits to show humanity's relationship with the ocean and sustainability.

★**Museum of Latin American Art**   MUSEUM
(Map p918; ☎ 562-437-1689; www.molaa.org; 628 Alamitos Ave, Long Beach; adult/senior & student/ child Wed-Sat $10/7/free, Sun free; ⊙ 11am-5pm Wed & Fri-Sun, to 9pm Thu; Ⓟ) This gem of a museum is the only one in the US to present art created since 1945 in Latin America and in Latino communities in the US through important temporary and traveling exhibits. Recent thought-provoking shows included Caribbean art, tattoo art and the works of LA's own Frank Romero.

⊙ Pasadena

Below the lofty San Gabriel Mountains, this city drips with wealth and gentility, feeling a world apart from urban LA. It's known for its early 20th-century arts-and-crafts architecture and the Tournament of Roses Parade on New Year's Day. Amble on foot around the shops, cafes, bars and restaurants of Old Town Pasadena, along Colorado Blvd east of Pasadena Ave. Metro Gold Line trains connect Pasadena and Downtown LA in 20 minutes.

★**Huntington Library, Art Collections & Botanical Gardens**   MUSEUM, GARDEN
(Map p918; ☑ 626-405-2100; www.huntington.org; 1151 Oxford Rd, San Marino; adult weekday/weekend & holidays $25/29, child $13, 1st Thu each month free; ⊙ 10am-5pm Wed-Mon; ℙ) One of the most delightful, inspirational spots in LA, the Huntington is rightly a highlight of any trip to California thanks to a world-class mix of art, literary history and over 120 acres of themed gardens (any one of which would be worth a visit on its own), all set amid stately grounds. There's so much to see and do that it's hard to know where to begin; allow three to four hours for even a basic visit.

★**Gamble House**   ARCHITECTURE
(Map p918; ☑ bookstore 626-449-4178, info 626-793-3334, tickets 844-325-0812; https:// gamblehouse.org; 4 Westmoreland Pl, Pasadena; tours adult/student & senior/child $15/12.50/free; ⊙ tours 10:30am, 11:30am & 1:30pm Tue, 11:30am-3pm Thu & Fri, noon-3pm Sat & Sun; ℙ) This mansion in northwest central Pasadena has been called one of the 10 most architecturally significant homes in America. The 1908 masterpiece of California arts-and-crafts architecture was built by Charles and Henry Greene for Procter & Gamble heir David Gamble. Incorporating 17 woods, art glass and subdued light, the entire home is a work of art, with its foundation, furniture and fixtures all united by a common design and theme inspired by its Southern California environs and Japanese and Chinese architecture.

Norton Simon Museum   MUSEUM
(Map p918; ☑ 626-449-6840; www.nortonsimon. org; 411 W Colorado Blvd, Pasadena; adult/senior/ student & child $15/12/free; ⊙ noon-5pm Mon, Wed & Thu, 11am-8pm Fri & Sat, 11am-5pm Sun; ℙ) Rodin's *The Burghers of Calais* standing guard by the entrance is only a mind-teasing overture to the full symphony of art in store at this exquisite museum. Norton Simon (1907–93) was an entrepreneur with a Midas touch and a passion for art who parlayed his millions into an admirable collection of Western art and Asian sculpture. Meaty captions really help tell each piece's story.

🏃 Activities

Despite spending a lot of time jammed on freeways, Angelenos love to get physical. Theirs is a city made for pace-quickening

---

STUDIO TOURS

Did you know it takes a week to shoot a half-hour sitcom? Or that you rarely see ceilings on shows because the space is filled with lights and lamps? You'll learn these and other nuggets of information about the make-believe world of film and TV while touring a working studio. Star-sighting potential is better than average, except during 'hiatus' (May to August) when studios are deserted. Reservations are required and so is photo ID.

Paramount (Map p918; ☑ 323-956-1777; www.paramountstudiotour.com; 5555 Melrose Ave; regular/VIP tours $60/189, After Dark tours $99; ⊙ tours 9:30am-5pm, last tour 3pm) *Star Trek, Indiana Jones* and *Shrek* are among the blockbusters that originated at Paramount, the longest-operating movie studio and the only one still in Hollywood proper. Two-hour tours through the back lots and sound stages are available daily year-round and are led by passionate, knowledgeable guides.

Sony (Map p918; ☑ 310-244-8687; www.sonypicturesstudiostours.com; 10202 W Washington Blvd; tour $50; ⊙ tours usually 9:30am, 10:30am, 1:30pm & 2:30pm Mon-Fri; Ⓜ Expo Line to Culver City) Running on weekdays only, this two-hour tour includes visits to the sound stages where *Men in Black, Spider-Man,* and *Charlie's Angels* were filmed. Munchkins hopped along the Yellow Brick Road in *The Wizard of Oz,* filmed when this was still the venerable MGM studio.

Warner Bros (Map p918; ☑ 877-492-8687, 818-972-8687; www.wbstudiotour.com; 3400 Warner Blvd, Burbank; tours adult/child 8-12yr from $72/62; ⊙ 8:30am-3:30pm, extended hrs Jun-Aug; 🚌 155, 222, 501 stop about 400yd from tour center) This tour offers the most fun and authentic look behind the scenes of a major movie studio. Consisting of a two-hour guided tour and a self-guided tour of Studio 48, the adventure kicks off with a video of WB's greatest film hits – among them *Rebel Without a Cause* and *La La Land* – before a tram whisks you to sound stages, back-lot sets and technical departments, including props, costumes and the paint shop. Tours run daily, usually every half-hour.

Hollywood

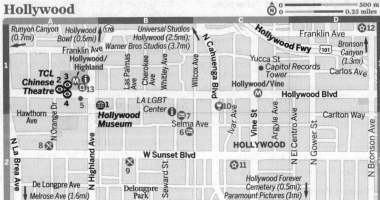

Hollywood

◎ Top Sights

1 Hollywood Museum	B1
2 TCL Chinese Theatre	A1

◎ Sights

3 Dolby Theatre	A1
4 Hollywood Walk of Fame	A1

◆ Activities, Courses & Tours

5 TMZ Celebrity Tour	A1

⊜ Sleeping

6 Mama Shelter	B2
7 USA Hostels Hollywood	B2

⊗ Eating

8 In & Out Burger	A2
9 Luv2eat	B2

⊖ Drinking & Nightlife

Rooftop Bar at Mama Shelter	(see 6)
10 Tramp Stamp Granny's	C1

✪ Entertainment

11 ArcLight Cinemas	C2
12 Upright Citizens Brigade Theatre	D1

⊜ Shopping

13 Hollywood & Highland	A1

thrills, with spectacular mountain hikes, one of the country's largest urban nature reserves and surf-pounded beach. Add to this almost 300 days of sunshine and you'll forgive the locals for looking so, so good.

Hiking

If hiking doesn't feel like an indigenous LA activity to you, you need to reassess. This town is hemmed in and defined by two mountain ranges and countless canyons. In the San Gabriel Mountains, trails wind from Mt Wilson into granite peak wilderness, once the domain of the Gabrielino people and the setting for California's last grizzly-bear sighting. The Chumash roamed the Santa Monica Mountains (www.nps.gov/samo/index.htm), which are smaller, but still offer spectacular views of chaparral-draped peaks with stark drops into the Pacific. The Backbone Trail spans the range, but our favorite hike is to Sandstone Peak. Day hikes

in Topanga Canyon State Park (Map p918; ☎ 310-455-2465; www.parks.ca.gov; 20828 Entrada Rd, Topanga; per vehicle $10; ⊙ 8am-dusk), Malibu Canyon (Map p918; Malibu Canyon Rd, Malibu), Point Mugu and Leo Carrillo (☎ 310-457-8143; www.parks.ca.gov; 35000 W Pacific Coast Hwy, Malibu; per car $12; ⊙ 8am-10pm; ⓟ🐾) state parks are also recommended. If you only have an hour or two, check out Runyon (Map p918; www.runyoncanyonhike.com; 2000 N Fuller Ave; ⊙ dawn-dusk) or Bronson (Map p918; ☎ 818-243-1145; www.laparks.org; 3200 Canyon Dr; ⊙ 5am-10:30pm) canyons in Hollywood. For more advice about trails in and around Southern California check out www.trails.com and www.modernhiker.com.

Yoga

The most popular style in town is Hatha yoga. Of course, it just wouldn't be LA without some unexpected offerings in the mix. Among the best are Vinyasa yoga classes to hip-hop and R&B beats at WeHo studio Y7 (www.y7-studio.com) and beer-and-yoga Sunday sessions at nearby Angel City Brewery (p936).

Cycling & In-line Skating

Get scenic exercise pedaling or skating along the paved **South Bay Bicycle Trail** (Map p934; ⊘ sunrise-sunset; 🚲), which parallels the beach for most of the 22 miles between Santa Monica and Pacific Palisades. Rental shops are plentiful in busy beach towns. Warning: it's crowded on weekends.

Surfing & Swimming

Top beaches for swimming are Malibu's **Leo Carrillo State Park**, **Santa Monica State Beach** and the South Bay's **Hermosa Beach**. Malibu's **Surfrider Beach** is a legendary surfing spot. Parking rates vary seasonally, as does water quality – check the 'Beach Report Card' at http://brc.healthebay.org.

☞ Tours

★ **Los Angeles Conservancy** WALKING
(☎ 213-623-2489; www.laconservancy.org; adult/child $15/10) Downtown LA's intriguing historical and architectural gems – from an art deco penthouse to a beaux arts ballroom and a dazzling silent-movie theater – are revealed on this nonprofit group's 2½-hour walking tours. To see some of LA's grand historic movie theaters from the inside, the conservancy also offers the Last Remaining Seats film series, screening classic movies in gilded theaters.

★ **Esotouric** BUS
(☎ 213-915-8687; www.esotouric.com; tours $64) Discover LA's lurid and fascinating underbelly on these offbeat, insightful and entertaining walking and bus tours themed around famous crime sites (Black Dahlia anyone?), literary lions (Chandler to Bukowski) and more.

TMZ Celebrity Tour BUS
(Map p928; ☎ 844-869-8687; www.tmz.com/tour; 6822 Hollywood Blvd; adult/child $52/32; ⊘ tours depart 10am-5pm most days, check website for additional hours; Ⓜ Red Line to Hollywood/Highland) Cut the shame; we know you want to spot celebrities, glimpse their homes and laugh at their dirt. Super-fun tours by open-sided bus run for two hours, and you'll likely meet some of the TMZ stars...and perhaps even celebrity guests on the bus.

Dearly Departed BUS
(☎ 855-600-3323; www.dearlydepartedtours.com; tours $25-85) This long-running, occasionally creepy, frequently hilarious tour will clue you in on where celebs kicked the bucket, George Michael dropped his trousers, Hugh Grant received certain services and the Charles Manson gang murdered Sharon Tate. Some of the tours are not for kids, so choose carefully.

★ Festivals & Events

First Friday STREET CARNIVAL
(www.abbotkinneyfirstfridays.com; ⊘ 5-11pm 1st Fri each month) Businesses along Abbot Kinney Blvd stay open late and the street is filled with food trucks at this monthly street fair.

Academy Awards FILM
(www.oscars.org; ⊘ late Feb) On Tinseltown's biggest night, visitors can ogle their favorite film stars from the red-carpet-adjacent bleachers of the **Dolby Theatre** (Map p928; ☎ 323-308-6300; www.dolbytheatre.com; 6801 Hollywood Blvd; tours adult/child, senior & student $25/19; ⊘ 10:30am-4pm; Ⓟ; Ⓜ Red Line to Hollywood/Highland). Apply in November or December for one of around 700 lucky spots, or watch it on TV.

Día de los Muertos CULTURAL
(Day of the Dead; ⊘ early Nov) LA's Mexican community honors its deceased relatives on and around November 2 with costumed parades, sugar skulls, graveyard picnics, candlelight processions and fabulous altars. Events are held across the city, including on Olvera St and at the Hollywood Forever Cemetery.

🛏 Sleeping

From rock-and-roll Downtown digs to fabled Hollywood hideaways and beachside escapes, LA serves up a dizzying array of slumber options. The key is to plan well ahead. Do your research and find out which neighborhood is most convenient for your plans and best appeals to your style and interests. Trawl the internet for deals, and consider visiting between January and April, when room rates and occupancy are usually at their lowest (Oscars week aside).

🛏 Downtown

Ace Hotel HOTEL $$$
(Map p924; ☎ 213-623-3233; www.acehotel.com/losangeles; 929 S Broadway; r/lofts from $300/450;

LOCAL KNOWLEDGE

LA INSIDER MOVES

Classic Movies in Special Spaces It's always a scene (and surprisingly not creepy) when Cinespia (http://cinespia.org) screens films on the side of a giant mausoleum at Hollywood Forever Cemetery (p922), during summer. For a different experience, check the site for occasional screenings in historic Downtown theaters usually not open to the public.

Exploring Architecture Downtown LA's intriguing historical and architectural gems – from an art-deco penthouse to a beaux-arts ballroom and a dazzling silent-movie theater – are revealed on 2½-hour walking tours by the LA Conservancy (www.laconservancy.org). Each June, the conservancy also runs its own Last Remaining Seats film series in some of the same theaters as Cinespia.

Shop with the Chefs Farmers markets throughout the county serve up California's bounty with a heaping helping of local culture. Santa Monica's famous Wednesday and Saturday farmers markets (p935) tend to draw top chefs, and the Thursday market on the south lawn of **LA City Hall** (Map p924; ☎213-485-2121; www.lacity.org; 200 N Spring St; 🕘9am-5pm Mon-Fri) [FREE] donates 10% of its proceeds to Los Angeles River Artists and Business Association (LARABA).

Scenic Drives For awesome eyefuls, a couple of beautiful routes hide in plain sight. Twisty-turny Mulholland Dr forms the border between the LA Basin and San Fernando Valley, with breathtaking views on either side. Or head west from San Pedro along Palos Verdes Dr for 14 miles of stunning coastal views that may make you forget that you're in America's second-largest metropolis.

[P][❄][wifi][pool]) The ever-hip, buzzy, 182-room Ace is big on quirky details: Haas Brothers murals in the lobby and restaurant, whimsically themed cocktails at the rooftop bar and retro-inspired rooms with boxer-style robes, blank music sheets and, in many cases, record players or guitars. Small rooms can feel tight, so consider opting for a medium. Valet parking is $40 a night.

Hollywood

USA Hostels Hollywood HOSTEL **$**
(Map p928; ☎323-462-3777; www.usahostels.com; 1624 Schrader Blvd; dm $41-46, r with bath from $129; [❄][@][wifi]; [M]Red Line to Hollywood/Vine) This sociable hostel puts you within steps of the Hollywood party circuit. Private rooms are a bit cramped, but making new friends is easy during staff-organized barbecues, comedy nights, hikes and various walking tours. Freebies include wi-fi, linens and continental breakfast with cook-your-own-pancakes. It has cushy lounge seating on the front porch and free beach shuttles.

★**Mama Shelter** BOUTIQUE HOTEL **$$**
(Map p928; ☎323-785-6666; www.mamashelter.com; 6500 Selma Ave; r from $189; [❄][@][wifi]; [M]Red Line to Hollywood/Vine) Hip, affordable Mama Shelter keeps things playful with its lobby gumball machines, foosball table and live streaming of guests' selfies and videos. Standard rooms are small but cool, with quality beds and linen and subway-tiled bathrooms with decent-sized showers. Quirky in-room touches include movie scripts, masks and Apple TVs with free Netflix. The rooftop bar (p936) is one of LA's best.

West Hollywood & Mid-City

Palihotel BOUTIQUE HOTEL **$$**
(Map p932; ☎323-272-4588; www.pali-hotel.com; 7950 Melrose Ave, Mid-City; r from $175; [P][@][wifi]) We love the rustic wood-paneled exterior, the polished-concrete floor in the lobby, the elemental Thai massage spa, and the 32 contemporary rooms with two-tone paint jobs, a wall-mounted flat-screen TV, and enough room for a sofa. Some have terraces. Terrific all-around value.

Chateau Marmont HOTEL **$$$**
(Map p932; ☎323-656-1010; www.chateaumarmont.com; 8221 W Sunset Blvd, Hollywood; r $465, ste from $845; [P][⊖][❄][wifi][pool]) The French-flavored indulgence may look dated, but this faux castle has long lured A-listers with its hilltop perch, five-star mystique and legendary discretion. Howard Hughes used to spy on bikini beauties from the same balcony suite that became the favorite of U2's Bono. If nothing else, it's worth stopping by for a

cocktail at **Bar Marmont** (Map p932; ☑ 323-650-0575; www.chateaumarmont.com; 8171 Sunset Blvd, Hollywood; ◷ 6pm-2am).

★ **Mondrian**   HOTEL $$$
(Map p932; ☑ 323-650-8999, reservations 800-606-6090; www.mondrianhotel.com; 8440 Sunset Blvd, West Hollywood; r/ste from $329/369; P@❄❂) This chic, sleek tower has been an LA showplace since the 1990s. Giant doors facing the Sunset Strip frame the entrance, opening to a lobby of minimalist elegance: white walls, blond woods, billowy curtains and model-good-looking staff. Upstairs, mood-lit hallways with tiny light boxes (by famed light artist James Turrell) lead to recently renovated rooms with chandeliers, rain showers and down duvets.

🛏 Beverly Hills

Montage   HOTEL $$$
(Map p918; ☑ 310-860-7800; www.montagebeverlyhills.com; 225 N Canon Dr, Beverly Hills; r/ste from $695/1175; P@❄❂) Drawing on-point eye candy and serious wealth, the 201-room Montage balances elegance with warmth and affability. Models and moguls lunch by the gorgeous rooftop pool, while the property's sprawling five-star spa is a Moroccan-inspired marvel, with both single-sex and unisex plunge pools. Rooms are classically styled, with custom Sealy mattresses, dual marble basins, spacious showers and deep-soaking tubs.

Avalon Hotel   HOTEL $$$
(Map p918; ☑ 310-277-5221; www.avalon-hotel.com/beverly-hills; 9400 W Olympic Blvd, Beverly Hills; r from $309; P◷❄@❄❂❂) Mid-century modern gets a 21st-century spin at this fashion-crowd fave, which was Marilyn Monroe's old pad in its days as an apartment building. Funky retro rooms are all unique, but most have arched walls, marble slab desks and night stands, as well as playful art and sculpture. Perks include a sexy hourglass-shaped pool. Call it affordable glamour.

🛏 Santa Monica

HI Los Angeles – Santa Monica   HOSTEL $
(Map p934; ☑ 310-393-9913; www.hilosangeles.org; 1436 2nd St; dm $38-70, r with shared bath $130-150, with private bath $180-220; ◷❄@❄; Ⓜ Expo Line to Downtown Santa Monica) Near the beach and Promenade, this hostel has an enviable location and modernized facilities

that rival properties charging much more. Its approximately 275 beds in single-sex dorms are clean and safe, private rooms are decorated with hipster chic and public spaces (courtyard, library, TV room, dining room, communal kitchen) let you lounge and surf.

Sea Shore Motel   MOTEL $$
(Map p934; ☑ 310-392-2787; www.seashoremotel.com; 2637 Main St; r $140-195, ste $240-300; P❄❂) The friendly, family-run lodgings at this comfy 25-unit motel put you just a Frisbee toss from the beach on happening Main St (quadruple-pane windows help cut street noise). The tiled, rattan-decorated rooms are basic, but 2nd-floor rooms have high ceilings and, a few doors down, families can stretch out in suites (basically full apartments) with kitchen and balcony.

Palihouse   BOUTIQUE HOTEL $$$
(Map p934; ☑ 310-394-1279; www.palihousesantamonica.com; 1001 3rd St; r from $295; P❄@❄❂) LA's grooviest hotel brand (not named Ace) occupies the 38 rooms, studios and one-bedroom apartments of the 1927 Spanish Colonial Embassy Hotel, with antique-meets-hipster-chic style. Each comfy room is slightly different, but look for picnic-table-style desks and wallpaper with intricate sketches of animals. Most rooms have full kitchens (and we love the coffee mugs with lifelike drawings of fish).

🛏 Long Beach

Hotel Maya   BOUTIQUE HOTEL $$
(Map p918; ☑ 562-435-7676; https://hotelmayalongbeach.com; 700 Queensway Dr, Long Beach; r from $179; P❄@❄❂❂) West of the *Queen Mary*, this boutique, waterside property hits you with hip immediately upon entering the rusted-steel, glass and magenta-paneled lobby. The feel continues in the 199 rooms (coral tile, river-rock headboards, Mayan-icon accents), set on 11 palmy acres in four 1970s-era hexagonal buildings with views of downtown Long Beach that are worth the upcharge.

🛏 Pasadena

Bissell House B&B   B&B $$
(Map p918; ☑ 626-441-3535; www.bissellhouse.com; 201 S Orange Grove Ave, South Pasadena; r from $159; P❄❂) Antiques, hardwood floors and a crackling fireplace make this secluded Victorian (1887) B&B on 'Millionaire's Row'

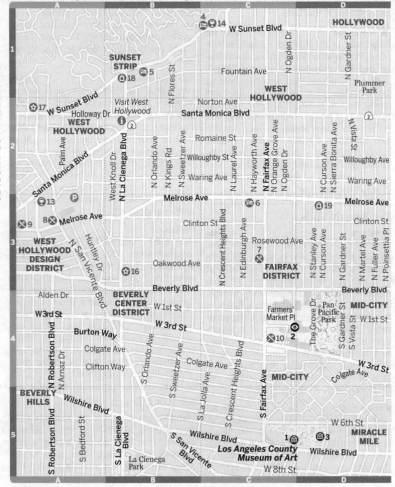

a bastion of warmth and romance. The hedge-framed garden feels like a sanctuary, and there's a pool for cooling off on hot summer days. The Prince Albert room has gorgeous wallpaper and a claw-foot tub. All seven rooms have private bathrooms.

✕ Eating

Bring an appetite. A big one. LA's cross-cultural makeup is reflected at its table, which is an epic global feast. And while there's no shortage of just-like-the-motherland dishes – from Cantonese *xiao long bao* to Ligurian *farinata* – it's the takes on

tradition that really thrill. Ever tried Korean-Mexican tacos? Or a vegan cream-cheese donut with jam, basil and balsamic reduction? LA may be many things, but a culinary bore isn't one of them.

✕ Downtown

★ Grand Central Market   MARKET
(Map p924; www.grandcentralmarket.com; 317 S Broadway; ⊙ 8am-10pm; ☎; Ⓜ Red/Purple Lines to Pershing Sq) Designed by prolific architect John Parkinson and once home to an office occupied by Frank Lloyd Wright, LA's beaux arts market hall has been satisfying

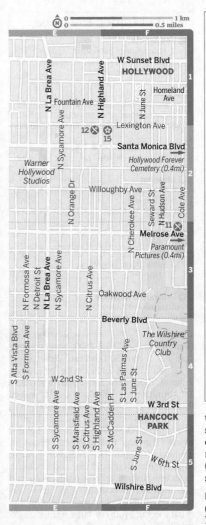

to order and topped with sultry, smoky, slow-cooked stews. Do yourself a favor and order the sampler plate ($7.25), a democratic mix of six mini tacos. The *chiles torreados* (blistered, charred chili) taco is a must for serious spice-lovers.

Howlin' Ray's CHICKEN, SOUTHERN $
(Map p924; ☎213-935-8399; www.howlinrays.com; 727 N Broadway, Suite 128, Far East Plaza, Chinatown; mains $9-16; ☺11am-7pm Tue-Fri, 10am-7pm Sat & Sun; P; M Gold Line to Chinatown) It's hard to overstate the phenomenon that is Howlin' Ray's. Customers gladly queue for two hours or more – check Twitter for current wait times – at this noisy takeout counter with a smattering of seats and many picnic tables. The reward: Nashville-style fried chicken, spiced from country (mild) to howlin' ('can't touch this!').

Manuela MODERN AMERICAN $$
(Map p924; ☎323-849-0480; www.manuela-la.com; 907 E 3rd St; mains lunch $16-21, dinner $22-48; ☺11:30am-3:30pm & 5:30-10pm Wed &

appetites since 1917 and today is DTLA's gourmet mecca. Lose yourself in its bustle of neon signs, stalls and counters, peddling everything from fresh produce and nuts, to sizzling Thai street food, hipster breakfasts, modern deli classics, artisanal pasta and specialty coffee.

Guisados TACOS $
(Map p918; ☎323-264-7201; www.guisados.co; 2100 E Cesar Chavez Ave, Boyle Heights; tacos from $2.95; ☺9am-8pm Mon-Fri, to 9pm Sat, to 5pm Sun; M Gold Line to Mariachi Plaza) Guisados' citywide fame is founded on its *tacos de guisados:* warm, thick, nixtamal tortillas made

Santa Monica & Venice

Otium MODERN AMERICAN $$$
(Map p924; ☑213-935-8500; http://otiumla.com; 222 S Hope St, Downtown; dishes $8-60; ⏱11:30am-2:30pm & 5:30-10pm Tue-Thu, 11:30am-2:30pm & 5:30-11pm Fri, 11am-2:30pm & 5:30-11pm Sat, 11am-2:30pm & 5:30-10pm Sun; 🛜; Ⓜ Red/Purple Lines to Civic Center/Grand Park) In a modernist pavilion beside the Broad (p917) is this fun, of-the-moment hot spot helmed by chef Timothy Hollingsworth. Prime ingredients conspire in unexpected ways, from the crunch of wild rice and amaranth in an eye-candy salad of avocado, beets and pomegranate, to octopus with green garlic, black trumpet mushroom and *tom kha* (Thai coconut broth) to 'large-format' steaks (to $185).

Hollywood

In & Out Burger BURGERS $
(Map p928; ☑800-786-1000; www.in-n-out.com; 7009 Sunset Blvd; burgers from $2.10; ⏱10:30am-1am Sun-Thu, to 1:30am Fri & Sat; ♿; Ⓜ Red Line to Hollywood/Highland) This LA burger chain is a point of pilgrimage for locals and visitors alike. Yes, this is fast food, but In & Out has been hand-crafting burgers since 1948: fresh (not frozen) beef, hand-cut French fries etc. The basic burger comes piled with lettuce, tomato, secret

Thu, 11:30am-3:30pm & 5:30-11pm Fri, 10am-4pm & 5:30-11pm Sat, 10am-4pm & 5:30-10pm Sun; 🛜) This it-kid inside the **Hauser & Wirth** (Map p924; ☑213-943-1620; www.hauserwirth-losangeles.com; 901 E 3rd St; ⏱11am-6pm Wed & Fri-Sun, to 8pm Thu) FREE arts complex boasts a woody warm, loftlike space and an oft-tweaked menu that beautifully fuses California meats, produce and seafood with smoky Southern accents. Pique the appetite with cream biscuits, barbecued oysters or yellow peach salad with whipped feta and honey vinegar, then lose yourself in mains with herbs from the on-site garden.

spread (like Thousand Island dressing) and raw or sautéed onion.

Luv2eat
THAI $

(Map p928; ☑323-498-5835; www.luv2eatthai. com; 6660 W Sunset Blvd, Hollywood; mains $9-16; ⊙11am-3:30pm & 4:30-11:30pm; ℗) Don't let the odd name and strip-mall location put you off; Luv2eat is something of a temple for LA's Thai foodies. Cordon Bleu–trained, Polo Lounge (p937) alumna Chef Fern and Thailand-bred Chef Pla offer generous serves of authentic chefs' specials, dishes you don't normally see even in this town loaded with Thai restaurants. They nail the standards, as well.

Salt's Cure
MODERN AMERICAN $$

(Map p932; ☑323-465-7258; http://saltscure. com; 1155 N Highland Ave; mains lunch $12-24, dinner $18-36; ⊙11am-3pm Mon, to 10pm Tue-Fri, 10am-10pm Sat, 10am-3pm Sun) Wood-paneled, concrete-floored Salt's Cure is an out, proud locavore. From the in-season vegetables to the house-butchered and cured meats, the menu celebrates all things Californian. Expect sophisticated takes on rustic comfort grub, whether it's capocollo with chili paste or tender duck breast paired with impressively light oatmeal griddle cakes and blackberry compote.

★ Providence
MODERN AMERICAN $$$

(Map p932; ☑323-460-4170; www.providencela. com; 5955 Melrose Ave; lunch mains $38-48, dinner tasting menus $120-240; ⊙noon-2pm & 6-10pm Mon-Fri, 5:30-10pm Sat, 5:30-9pm Sun; ℗) Consistently near the top of every list of great LA restaurants, chef Michael Cimarusti's James Beard–winning, two-Michelin-starred darling turns superlative seafood into arresting, nuanced dishes that might see abalone paired with eggplant, turnip and nori, or spiny lobster conspire decadently with macadamia nut and earthy black truffle. À la carte options are available at lunch only.

✕ West Hollywood & Mid-City

Original Farmers Market
MARKET $

(Map p932; ☑323-933-9211; www.farmersmarket la.com; 6333 W 3rd St; ⊙9am-9pm Mon-Fri, to 8pm Sat, 10am-7pm Sun; ℗⛐) The Farmers Market is a great spot for a casual meal any time of day, especially if the rug rats are tagging along. Its narrow walkways are lined with choices: gumbo and diner classics to French bistro, Singapore-style noodles and tacos, sitdown or takeout. Before or afterwards, check

out the **Grove** (Map p932; www.thegrovela.com; 189 The Grove Dr; ℗⛐; ⛐MTA lines 16, 17, 780 to Wilshire & Fairfax) mall, next door.

Gracias Madre
VEGAN, MEXICAN $$

(Map p932; ☑323-978-2170; www.graciasmadre weho.com; 8905 Melrose Ave, West Hollywood; mains lunch $12-17, dinner $12-18; ⊙11am-11pm Mon-Fri, from 10am Sat & Sun; ☑) Gracias Madre shows just how tasty – and chichi – organic, plant-based Mexican cooking can be. Sit on the gracious patio or in the cozy interior and feel good as you eat healthily: sweet-potato flautas, coconut 'bacon,' plantain 'quesadillas,' plus salads and bowls. We're consistently surprised at innovations like cashew 'cheese,' mushroom 'chorizo' and heart-of-palm 'crab cakes.'

Canter's
DELI $$

(Map p932; ☑323-651-2030; www.cantersdeli. com; 419 N Fairfax Ave, Mid-City; mains $8-29; ⊙24hr; ℗) As old-school delis go, Canter's is hard to beat. A fixture in the traditionally Jewish Fairfax district since 1931, seen-it-all waitresses serve up the requisite pastrami, corned beef and matzo-ball soup, plus all-day breakfast, in a rangy room with deli and bakery counters up front.

Catch LA
FUSION $$$

(Map p932; ☑323-347-6060; http://catch restaurants.com/catchla; 8715 Melrose Ave, West Hollywood; shared dishes $8-39, dinner mains $34-79; ⊙11am-3pm Sat & Sun, 5pm-2am daily; ℗) An LA-scene extraordinaire. You may well find sidewalk paparazzi stalking celebrity guests and a doorman to check your reservation, but all that's forgotten once you're in this 3rd-floor rooftop restaurant/bar above WeHo. The Pacific Rim–inspired menu features supercreative cocktails and shared dishes such as truffle sashimi, blackcod lettuce wraps, and scallop and cauliflower with tamarind brown butter.

✕ Santa Monica

Santa Monica Farmers Markets
MARKET $

(Map p934; www.smgov.net/portals/farmers-market; Arizona Ave, btwn 2nd & 3rd Sts; ⊙Arizona Ave 8:30am-1:30pm Wed, 8am-1pm Sat; ⛐) ✑ You haven't really experienced Santa Monica until you've explored one of its outdoor farmers markets stocked with organic fruits, vegetables, flowers, baked goods and freshly shucked oysters. The mack daddy is the Wednesday market, around the intersection of 3rd and Arizona – it's the biggest and arguably the best for fresh produce, and is often patrolled by local chefs.

Cassia   SOUTHEAST ASIAN **$$$**
(Map p934; ☑310-393-6699; www.cassiala.com; 1314 7th St; appetizers $12-18, mains $19-76; ◐5-10pm Sun-Thu, to 11pm Fri & Sat; ℗) Ever since it opened in 2015, open, airy Cassia has made about every local and national 'best' list of LA restaurants. Chef Bryant Ng draws on his Chinese-Singaporean heritage in dishes such as *kaya* toast (with coconut jam, butter and a slow-cooked egg), 'sunbathing' prawns, and the encompassing Vietnamese pot-au-feu: short-rib stew, veggies, bone marrow and delectable accompaniments.

✖ Venice

Gjelina   AMERICAN **$$$**
(Map p934; ☑310-450-1429; www.gjelina.com; 1429 Abbot Kinney Blvd, Venice; veggies, salads & pizzas $10-18, large plates $15-45; ◐8am-midnight; ♨; ☐ Big Blue Bus line 18) If one restaurant defines the new Venice, it's this. Carve out a spot on the communal table between the hipsters and yuppies, or get your own slab of wood on the elegant stone terrace, and dine on imaginative small plates (raw yellowtail spiced with chili and mint and drenched in olive oil and blood orange) and sensational thin-crust, wood-fired pizza.

✖ Long Beach

Pigburd   AMERICAN **$$**
(Map p918; ☑562-269-0731; http://pigburd.com; 743 E 4th St, East Village, Long Beach; mains $15-29; ◐3-10pm Mon & Tue, 9am-10pm Wed, Thu & Sun, 9am-11pm Fri & Sat) There's much to love about this bistro near downtown Long Beach: small-family-farm–raised meats, eggs and produce, an evolving menu of comfort foods fashioned from the same, and low-key service, all under a high-rafter roof with generous windows to watch the world go by. *And* many of its staff are disabled veterans, so you're doing good while eating well.

✖ Pasadena

La Grande Orange   CALIFORNIAN **$$**
(Map p918; ☑626-356-4444; www.lgostation cafe.com; 260 S Raymond Ave, Pasadena; pizzas $15-17, mains $15-47; ◐11am-10pm Mon-Thu, to 11pm Fri, 10am-11pm Sat, 9am-9pm Sun; ℗; Ⓜ Gold Line to Del Mar) Pasadena's original train station (c 1911) has been handsomely renovated into

this cheery, popular dining room beneath lovingly aged wooden beams. The kitchen in the former ticket booth serves a menu of New American cooking: mesquite-grilled burgers and seafood, salads and pricier Midwestern aged steaks. Watch today's Gold Line trains go by from the generous bar.

🍷 Drinking & Nightlife

Whether you're after an organic CBD espresso, a craft cocktail made with peanut-butter-washed Campari, or a saison brewed with Chinatown-sourced oolong tea, LA pours on cue. From postindustrial coffee roasters and breweries to mid-century lounges, classic Hollywood martini bars and cocktail-pouring bowling alleys, LA serves its drinks with a generous splash of wow. So do the right thing and raise your glass to America's finest town.

🍸 Downtown

Clifton's Republic   COCKTAIL BAR
(Map p924; ☑213-627-1673; www.cliftonsla.com; 648 S Broadway; ◐11am-midnight Tue-Thu, to 2am Fri, 10am-2:30am Sat, 10am-midnight Sun; 🛜; Ⓜ Red/Purple Lines to Pershing Sq) Opened in 1935 and back after a $10-million renovation, multilevel, mixed-crowd Clifton's defies description. Order drinks from a Gothic church altar amid taxidermied forest animals, watch burlesque performers shimmy in the shadow of a 40ft faux redwood, or slip through a glass-paneled door to a luxe tiki paradise where DJs spin in a repurposed speedboat.

Angel City Brewery   MICROBREWERY
(Map p924; ☑213-622-1261; www.angelcitybrew ery.com; 216 S Alameda St; ◐4pm-1am Mon-Thu, to 2am Fri, noon-2am Sat, noon-1am Sun) Where suspension cables were once manufactured, craft brews are now made and poured. Located on the edge of the Arts District, this is a popular spot to knock back an India pale ale or chai-spiced Imperial stout, listen to some tunes and chow down some food-truck tacos.

🍷 Hollywood

Rooftop Bar at Mama Shelter   BAR
(Map p928; ☑323-785-6600; www.mamashelter. com/en/los-angeles/restaurants/rooftop; 6500 Selma Ave; ◐noon-1am Mon-Thu, 11am-2pm Fri & Sat, 11am-1am Sun; Ⓜ Red Line to Hollywood/ Vine) Less a hotel rooftop bar and more lush, tropical-like oasis with killer views of the

Hollywood sign and LA skyline, multicolored daybeds and tongue-in-cheek bar bites like 'boujee fries' and outré tacos. Pulling everyone from hotel guests to locals from the nearby Buzzfeed offices, it's a winner for languid cocktail sessions, landmark spotting and a game of giant Jenga.

Tramp Stamp Granny's BAR
(Map p928; ☑ 323-498-5626; www.trampstamp grannys.com; 1638 N Cahuenga Blvd; ⊗8pm-1am Tue & Wed, 6pm-1am Thu & Fri, 8pm-2am Sat; Ⓜ Red Line to Hollywood/Vine) In the heart of Hollywood, this piano bar owned by Darren Criss (star of *Glee* and *The Assassination of Gianni Versace*) is a little bit classy, a little bit trashy and a whole lot of fun. Talented pianists tickle the ivories as guests sing along to favorite tunes – look for theme nights (Disney, anyone?). Drinks are creative and strong.

⚲ West Hollywood

Abbey GAY & LESBIAN
(Map p932; ☑ 310-289-8410; www.theabbey weho.com; 692 N Robertson Blvd, West Hollywood; ⊗11am-2am Mon-Thu, from 10am Fri, from 9am Sat & Sun) It's been called the best gay bar in the world, and who are we to argue? Once a humble coffeehouse, the Abbey has expanded into the bar/club/restaurant of record in WeHo. It has so many different-flavored martinis and mojitos that you'd think they were invented here, plus a menu of upscale pub food (mains $14 to $21).

⚲ Beverly Hills

Polo Lounge COCKTAIL BAR
(Map p918; ☑ 310-887-2777; www.dorchestercol lection.com/en/los-angeles/the-beverly-hills-hotel; Beverly Hills Hotel, 9641 Sunset Blvd, Beverly Hills; ⊗7am-1:30am) For a classic LA experience, dress up and swill martinis in the Beverly Hills Hotel's legendary bar. Charlie Chaplin had a standing lunch reservation at booth 1 and it was here that HR Haldeman and John Ehrlichman learned of the Watergate break-in in 1972. There's a popular Sunday jazz brunch (adult/child $95/20).

⚲ Santa Monica

Basement Tavern BAR
(Map p934; www.basementtavern.com; 2640 Main St; ⊗5pm-2am) A creative speakeasy, housed in the basement of the Victorian, and our favorite well in Santa Monica. We love it for its craft cocktails, cozy booths,

---

LGBTIQ LA

LA is one of the country's gayest cities and has made many contributions to gay culture. Your gaydar may well be pinging throughout the county, but the rainbow flag flies especially proudly in Boystown, along Santa Monica Blvd in West Hollywood, which is flanked by dozens of high-energy bars, cafes, restaurants, gyms and clubs. Most cater to gay men, although there's plenty for lesbians, trans and mixed audiences. Thursday through Sunday nights are prime time.

If nightlife isn't your bag, there are plenty of other ways to meet, greet and engage. Outdoor options include the **Frontrunners** (www.lafrontrunners.com) running club and the **Great Outdoors** (www.greatoutdoorsla.org) hiking club. The latter runs day and night hikes, as well as neighborhood walks. For insight into LA's fascinating queer history, book a walking tour with **Out & About Tours** (www.thelavendereffect.org/tours; tours from $30).

There's gay theater all over town, but the **Celebration Theatre** (Map p932; ☑ 323-957-1884; www.celebrationtheatre.com; 6760 Lexington Ave, Hollywood) ranks among the nation's leading stages for LGBT plays. The **Cavern Club Theater** (Map p918; www.cavernclubtheater.com; 1920 Hyperion Ave, Silver Lake) pushes the envelope, particularly with uproarious drag performers; it's downstairs from Casita del Campo restaurant. If you're lucky enough to be in town when the **Gay Men's Chorus of Los Angeles** (www.gmcla.org) is performing, don't miss out: this amazing group has been doing it since 1979.

The festival season kicks off in mid- to late May with the **Long Beach Pride Celebration** (☑ 562-987-9191; www.longbeachpride.com; 450 E Shoreline Dr, Long Beach; parade free, festival admission adult/child & senior $25/free; ⊗mid-May) and continues with the three-day **LA Pride** (www.lapride.org) in mid-June with a parade down Santa Monica Blvd. On Halloween (October 31), the same street brings out 500,000 outrageously costumed revelers of all persuasions.

island bar and nightly live-music calendar that features blues, jazz, bluegrass and rock bands. It gets way too busy on weekends for our taste, but weeknights can be special.

🍷 Long Beach

Pike
BAR

(Map p918; ☑562-437-4453; www.pikelong beach.com; 1836 E 4th St, Long Beach; ⊙11am-2am Mon-Fri, from 9am Sat & Sun; 🚊line 22) Adjacent to Retro Row, this nautical-themed dive bar, owned by Chris Reece of the band Social Distortion, brings in the cool kids for live-music acts every night – with no cover, thank you – and serves beer by the pitcher or bottle, and cocktails such as the Mezcarita and Greenchelada (a *michelada* with cucumber, jalapeño and lime).

☆ Entertainment

Hollywood Bowl
CONCERT VENUE

(Map p918; ☑323-850-2000; www.hollywood bowl.com; 2301 N Highland Ave; rehearsals free, performance costs vary; ⊙Jun-Sep) Summers in LA just wouldn't be the same without alfresco melodies under the stars at the Bowl, a huge natural amphitheater in the Hollywood Hills. Its annual season – which usually runs from June to September – includes symphonies, jazz bands and iconic acts such as Blondie, Bryan Ferry and Angélique Kidjo. Bring a sweater or blanket as it gets cool at night.

Upright Citizens Brigade Theatre
COMEDY

(Map p928; ☑323-908-8702; http://franklin. ucbtheatre.com; 5919 Franklin Ave; tickets $5-12) Founded in New York by *Saturday Night Live* alums Amy Poehler and Ian Roberts along with Matt Besser and Matt Walsh, this sketch-comedy group cloned itself in Hollywood in 2005. With numerous nightly shows spanning anything from stand-up comedy to improv and sketch, it's arguably the best comedy hub in town. Valet parking costs $7.

There's a second location southeast at 5419 W Sunset Blvd, near Thai Town and off Western Ave.

Geffen Playhouse
THEATER

(Map p918; ☑310-208-5454; www.geffen playhouse.com; 10886 Le Conte Ave, Westwood) Entertainment megamogul David Geffen forked over $17 million to get his Mediterranean-style playhouse back into shape. The center's season includes both American classics and freshly minted works, and it's not unusual to see well-known film and TV actors treading the boards.

Los Angeles Philharmonic
CLASSICAL MUSIC

(Map p924; ☑323-850-2000; www.laphil.org; 111 S Grand Ave) The world-class LA Phil performs classics and cutting-edge works at the Walt Disney Concert Hall (p918), under the baton of Venezuelan phenom Gustavo Dudamel.

Dodger Stadium
BASEBALL

(Map p918; ☑866-363-4377; www.dodgers.com; 1000 Vin Scully Ave) Few clubs can match the Dodgers' history (Jackie Robinson, Sandy Koufax, Kirk Gibson and sportscaster Vin Scully), success and fan loyalty, and this 1950s-era stadium is still considered one of baseball's most beautiful, framed by views of palm trees and the San Gabriel Mountains. Best views are from behind home plate, or gorge in the all-you-can-eat pavilion in right field.

Largo at the Coronet
LIVE MUSIC, PERFORMING ARTS

(Map p932; ☑310-855-0530; www.largo-la.com; 366 N La Cienega Blvd, Mid-City) Ever since its early days on Fairfax Ave, Largo has been progenitor of high-minded pop culture (it nurtured Zach Galifianakis to stardom). Now part of the Coronet Theatre complex, it features edgy comedy, such as Sarah Silverman and Nick Offerman, and nourishing night music such as the Preservation Hall Jazz Band.

ArcLight Cinemas
CINEMA

(Map p928; ☑323-464-1478; www.arclightcinemas. com; 6360 W Sunset Blvd; Ⓜ Red Line to Hollywood/Vine) Assigned seats, exceptional celeb-sighting potential and a varied program that covers mainstream and art-house movies make this 14-screen multiplex the best around. If your taste dovetails with its schedule, the awesome 1963 geodesic Cinerama Dome is a must. Bonuses: age-21-plus screenings where you can booze it up, and Q&As with directors, writers and actors. Parking is $3 for four hours.

LA Lakers
BASKETBALL

(Map p924; ☑888-929-7849; www.nba.com/lak ers; tickets from $65) One of two NBA basketball teams in Los Angeles (the other is the **Clippers** (Map p924; ☑213-204-2900; www. nba.com/clippers; tickets from $20)), the Lakers are based at Downtown's **Staples Center**

LA FOR CHILDREN

Keeping kids happy is child's play in LA. The sprawling Los Angeles Zoo (p922) in family-friendly Griffith Park (p922) is a sure bet. Dino fans will dig the La Brea Tar Pits (p923) and the Natural History Museum (p921), while budding scientists crowd the Griffith Observatory (p922) and California Science Center (p921). For under-the-sea creatures, head to the Aquarium of the Pacific (p926) in Long Beach. The amusement park at Santa Monica Pier (p925) is fun for all ages. Activities for younger kids are more limited at tween/teen-oriented **Universal Studios Hollywood** (Map p918; ☑ 800-864-8377; www.universalstudioshollywood.com; 100 Universal City Plaza, Universal City; 1-/2-day regular admission from $109/149, child under 3yr free; ⊙ daily, hours vary; ℗ 🚼; Ⓜ Red Line to Universal City). In neighboring Orange County, Disneyland (p941) and Knott's Berry Farm (p943) are the first and last word in theme parks.

(Map p924; ☑ 213-742-7100; www.staplescenter.com; 1111 S Figueroa St). Although few teams can match the Lakers' legacy – many players are so legendary they go by one name: Kareem, Magic, Shaq, Kobe, LeBron – results on the court have been disappointing these last several seasons.

🛍 Shopping

Consider yourself a disciplined shopper? Get back to us after your trip. LA is a pro at luring cards out of wallets. After all, how can you *not* bag that supercute vintage-fabric frock? Or that tongue-in-cheek tote? And what about that mid-century-modern lamp, the one that perfectly illuminates that rare, signed Hollywood film script you scored? Creativity and whimsy drive this town, right down to its racks and shelves.

🏠 Downtown

Raggedy Threads VINTAGE
(Map p924; ☑ 213-620-1188; www.raggedythreads.com; 330 E 2nd St; ⊙ noon-7pm Mon-Sat, to 6pm Sun; Ⓜ Gold Line to Little Tokyo/Arts District) A tremendous vintage Americana store just off the main Little Tokyo strip. There's plenty of beautifully ragged denim, with a notable collection of pre-1950s workwear from the US, Japan and France. You'll also find a good number of Victorian dresses, soft T-shirts and a wonderful turquoise collection at decent prices.

Last Bookstore in Los Angeles BOOKS
(Map p924; ☑ 213-488-0599; www.lastbookstorela.com; 453 S Spring St; ⊙ 10am-10pm Mon-Thu, to 11pm Fri & Sat, to 9pm Sun) What started as a one-man storefront is now California's largest new-and-used bookstore, and a sight to behold spanning two levels of an old bank building. Eye up the cabinets of rare books

before heading upstairs, home to a horror-and-crime book den, a book tunnel and a few art galleries to boot. The store also houses a terrific vinyl collection.

🏠 West Hollywood

Melrose Avenue FASHION & ACCESSORIES
(Map p932) This legendary, rock-and-roll shopping strip is as famous for its epic people-watching as for its consumer fruits. You'll see hair (and people) of all shades and styles, and everything from Gothic jewels to awesome vintage wear, custom sneakers to weed and stuffed porcupines, albeit sometimes for a price. The strip is located between Fairfax and La Brea Aves.

Fred Segal FASHION & ACCESSORIES
(Map p932; ☑ 323-432-0560; www.fredsegal.com; 8500 Sunset Blvd, West Hollywood; ⊙ 10am-9pm Mon-Sat, 11am-6pm Sun) No LA shopping trip is complete without a stop at Fred's. Recently relocated from its long-standing Melrose Ave location, this 13,000-sq-ft warren of high-end boutiques draws celebs and beautiful people for the very latest in Cal-casual couture under one impossibly chic, slightly snooty roof. The only time you'll see bargains (sort of) is during sales in summer and January.

🏠 Pasadena

Rose Bowl Flea Market MARKET
(Map p918; www.rgcshows.com; 1001 Rose Bowl Dr, Pasadena; admission from $9; ⊙ 9am-4:30pm 2nd Sun each month, last entry 3pm, early admission from 5am) Every month, rain or shine, since the 1960s, the Rose Bowl football field has hosted the 'Flea Market of the Stars,' with rummaging hordes seeking the next great treasure. Over 2500 vendors and some

NAVIGATING THE FASHION DISTRICT

Bargain hunters love the frantic, 100-block warren of fashion in southwestern Downtown that is the Fashion District. Deals can be amazing, but first-timers are often bewildered by the district's size and immense selection. For orientation, check out www.fashiondistrict.org.

20,000 buyers converge here. It's always a great time, and you can enjoy street-fairstyle refreshments such as burgers, dogs, fries, sausages, sushi (this is LA), lemonade, cocktails etc.

❶ Information

DANGERS & ANNOYANCES

Despite the apocalyptic panoply of dangers doled out by the entertainment industry – guns, violent crime, earthquakes – Los Angeles is generally a safe place to visit. Probably the greatest danger is posed by car accidents (buckle up and do not hold a phone while driving – it's the law), and the greatest everyday annoyance is traffic, which can mysteriously materialize – or inexplicably clear – when you least expect it.

MEDIA

Eater LA (http://la.eater.com) Up-to-the-minute news and reviews covering the city's ever-evolving food scene.

KCRW 89.9 FM (www.kcrw.com) LA's cultural pulse, the best radio station in the city beams National Public Radio (NPR), eclectic and indie music, intelligent talk, and hosts shows and events throughout Southern California.

LA Weekly (www.laweekly.com) Free alternative news, live music and entertainment listings.

LAist (http://laist.com) Arts, entertainment, food and pop-culture gossip.

Los Angeles Magazine (www.lamag.com) Monthly lifestyle magazine with a useful restaurant guide and some tremendous feature stories.

Los Angeles Times (www.latimes.com) Major, center-left daily newspaper.

MEDICAL SERVICES

Cedars-Sinai Medical Center (☑ 310-423-3277; http://cedars-sinai.edu; 8700 Beverly Blvd, West Hollywood; ⊗24hr) 24-hour emergency room skirting West Hollywood.

Keck Medicine of USC (☑ 323-226-2622; www.keckmedicine.org; 1500 San Pablo St, Downtown; ⊗24hr emergency room) 24-hour emergency department just east of Downtown.

Ronald Reagan UCLA Medical Center (☑ 310-825-9111; www.uclahealth.org; 757 Westwood Plaza, Westwood; ⊗24hr emergency room) 24-hour emergency room on the UCLA campus.

TOURIST INFORMATION

Downtown LA Visitor Center (Map p924; www.discoverlosangeles.com; Union Station, 800 N Alameda St; ⊗9am-5pm; Ⓜ Red/Purple/Gold Lines to Union Station) Maps and general tourist information in the lobby of Union Station.

Los Angeles Visitor Information Center (Map p928; ☑ 323-467-6412; www.discoverlosangeles.com; Hollywood & Highland, 6801 Hollywood Blvd; ⊗9am-10pm Mon-Sat, 10am-7pm Sun; Ⓜ Red Line to Hollywood/Highland) The main tourist office for Los Angeles, located in Hollywood. Maps, brochures and lodging information, plus tickets to theme parks and attractions.

Santa Monica Visitor Information Center (Map p934; ☑ 800-544-5319; www.santamonica.com; 2427 Main St) The main tourist information center in Santa Monica, with free guides, maps and helpful staff.

❶ Getting There & Away

AIR

The main LA gateway is **Los Angeles International Airport** (LAX; Map p918; www.lawa.org/welcomeLAX.aspx; 1 World Way). Its nine terminals are linked by the free LAX Shuttle A, leaving from the lower (arrival) level of each terminal. Cabs and hotel and car-rental shuttles stop here as well. Ticketing and check-in are on the upper (departure) level.

The hub for most international airlines is the Tom Bradley International Terminal.

Some domestic flights also arrive at **Burbank Hollywood Airport** (BUR, Bob Hope Airport; Map p918; www.burbankairport.com; 2627 N Hollywood Way, Burbank), which is handy if you're headed for Hollywood, Downtown or Pasadena. To the south, on the border with Orange County, the small **Long Beach Airport** (Map p918; www.lgb.org; 4100 Donald Douglas Dr, Long Beach) is convenient for Disneyland and is served by Alaska, JetBlue and Southwest.

BUS

The main bus terminal for **Greyhound** (Map p918; ☑ 213-629-8401; www.greyhound.com; 1716 E 7th St) is in an industrial part of Downtown, so try not to arrive after dark. Some Greyhound buses go directly to the terminal in **North Hollywood** (11239 Magnolia Blvd) and a few also pass through **Long Beach** (1498 Long Beach Blvd).

CAR

From San Francisco and Northern California, the fastest route to LA is on I-5 through the San Joaquin Valley. Hwy 101 is slower but more picturesque, while the most scenic – and slowest – route is via Hwy 1 (Pacific Coast Hwy, or PCH).

From San Diego and other points south, I-5 is the obvious route. From Las Vegas or the Grand Canyon, take I-15 south to I-10 then head west into LA.

TRAIN

Amtrak (www.amtrak.com) trains roll into Downtown's historic **Union Station** (📞 800-872-7245; www.amtrak.com; 800 N Alameda St). Interstate trains stopping in LA are the daily *Coast Starlight* to Seattle, the daily *Southwest Chief* to Chicago and the thrice-weekly *Sunset Limited* to New Orleans. The *Pacific Surfliner* travels numerous times daily between San Diego, Santa Barbara and San Luis Obispo via LA.

🛈 Getting Around

TO/FROM THE AIRPORT

LAX FlyAway (📞 866-435-9529; www.lawa. org/FlyAway) buses travel nonstop for $9.75 to Downtown's Patsaouras Transit Plaza at Union Station (45 minutes), Hollywood ($8, one to 1½ hours), Van Nuys ($9, 50 minutes) and Long Beach ($9, 50 minutes).

For scheduled bus services, catch the free shuttle bus from the airport toward parking lot C. It stops by the LAX City Bus Center hub for buses serving all of LA County.

Taxis are readily available outside the terminals. The flat rate to Downtown LA is $46.50, plus $4 LAX airport surcharge and the customary 15% to 20% tip.

Fares for ride-hailing companies Uber and Lyft can cost 30% to 40% less than taxis. These companies both drop off and pick up passengers on the departure level (upstairs); board by the signs lettered A through G outside terminals.

CAR & MOTORCYCLE

The usual international car-rental agencies have branches near LAX and throughout LA. Offices and lots are outside the airport, but each company has free shuttles leaving from the lower level. LA's traffic is some of the worst traffic in the country. Avoid rush hour (7am to 9am and 3:30pm to 6:30pm).

PUBLIC TRANSPORTATION

Most public transportation is handled by **Metro** (📞 323-466-3876; www.metro.net), which offers maps, schedules and trip-planning help through its website.

To ride Metro trains and buses, buy a reusable TAP card. Available from TAP vending machines at Metro stations with a $1 surcharge, the cards allow you to add a preset cash value or day passes. The regular base fare is $1.75 per boarding, or $7/25 for a day/week pass with unlimited rides.

TAP cards are accepted on DASH and municipal bus services and can be reloaded at vending machines or online on the TAP website (www. taptogo.net).

TAXI

With their (generally) cheaper fares and more convenient services, ride-hailing apps Uber and Lyft have drastically reduced demand for taxis in the region.

Beverly Hills Cab (📞 800-273-6611; www. beverlyhillscabco.com) A solid, dependable company, with good rates to the airport and a wide service area.

Taxi Taxi (📞 310-444-4444; www.santamonicataxi.com) Easily the best and most professional fleet available. It'll drive you anywhere, but can only pick up in Santa Monica.

SOUTHERN CALIFORNIAN COAST

Disneyland & Anaheim

Mickey is one lucky guy. Created by animator Walt Disney in 1928, this irrepressible mouse caught a ride on a multimedia juggernaut that rocketed him into a global stratosphere of recognition, money and influence. Plus, he lives in Disneyland, the 'Happiest Place on Earth,' an 'imagineered' hyper-reality where the streets are always clean, employees – called 'cast members' – are always upbeat and there are parades every day.

Today, **Disneyland Resort®** (Map p918; 📞 714-781-4636; www.disneyland.com; 1313 Harbor Blvd; 1-day pass adult $104-149, child 3-9yr $96-141, 2-day pass adult/child 3-9yr $225/210; ⊙ open daily, seasonal hr vary), which comprises the original Disneyland Park and newer Disney California Adventure theme park, remains a magical experience for the more than 14 million kids, grandparents, honeymooners and international tourists who visit every year.

Anaheim, the workaday city that grew up around the park, has itself developed some surprising pockets of cool that have nothing to do with the Mouse House.

◉ Sights & Activities

Spotless, wholesome **Disneyland Park®** is still laid out according to Walt's original plans. It's here you'll find plenty of rides and some of the attractions most associated with the Disney name – Main Street USA, Sleeping Beauty Castle and Tomorrowland, plus the newest blockbuster, Star Wars: Galaxy's Edge.

Disneyland Resort's larger but less crowded park, **Disney California Adventure®**, celebrates the natural and cultural glories of the Golden State but lacks the original's density of attractions and depth of imagination. The best rides are on the old-fashioned California pleasure pier, Soarin' Around the World (a virtual hang glide), and Guardians of the Galaxy – Mission: BREAKOUT!, which drops you 183ft down an elevator chute.

Going on all the rides at both theme parks requires at least two days, as queues for top attractions can be an hour or more. To minimize wait times, arrive midweek (especially during summer) before the gates open, buy print-at-home tickets online and take advantage of the parks' Fastpass system, which pre-assigns boarding times at select rides and attractions. For seasonal park hours and schedules of parades, shows and fireworks, check the official website.

While of course Disneyland Resort dominates Anaheim tourism, it's worth visiting the redeveloped neighborhoods around city hall, the **Anaheim Packing District** (Map p918; www.anaheimpackingdistrict.com; S Anaheim Bl) and **Center Street** (Map p918; www.centerstreetanaheim.com; W Center St). By the latter is the Frank Gehry–designed **hockey rink** where the Anaheim Ducks practice; it's open to the public.

Sleeping

For the full-on Disney experience, there are three different hotels within Disneyland Resort, though there are less-expensive options just beyond the Disney gates in Anaheim. If you want a theme-park hotel for less money, try **Knott's Berry Farm** (Map p918; 714-995-1111; www.knotts.com/stay/knotts-berry-farm-hotel; 7675 Crescent Ave, Buena Park; r $79-169; P@🛜🏊).

Disneyland Resort

★**Disney's Grand Californian Hotel & Spa** RESORT $$$
(Map p918; info 714-635-2300, reservations 714-956-6425; https://disneyland.disney.go.com/grand-californian-hotel; 1600 S Disneyland Dr; r from $507; P🅿️❄️@🛜🏊) Soaring timber beams rise above the cathedral-like lobby of the six-story Grand Californian, Disney's homage to the arts-and-crafts architectural movement. Cushy, recently renovated rooms have triple-sheeted beds, down pillows, bathrobes and all-custom furnishings. Outside there's a faux-redwood waterslide into the pool. At night, kids wind down with bedtime stories by the lobby's giant stone hearth.

Disneyland Hotel HOTEL $$$
(Map p918; 714-778-6600; www.disneyland.com; 1150 Magic Way, Anaheim; r from $409; P@🛜🏊) Though built in 1955, the year Disneyland opened, the park's original hotel has been rejuvenated with a dash of bibbidi-bobbidi-boo. There are three towers with themed lobbies (adventure, fantasy and frontier), and the 972 good-sized rooms now boast Mickey-hand wall sconces in bathrooms and headboards lit like the fireworks over Sleeping Beauty Castle.

Anaheim

Best Western Plus Stovall's Inn MOTEL $$
(Map p918; 714-778-1880; www.bestwestern.com; 1110 W Katella Ave; r $99-175; P➡️❄️@🛜🏊) Generations of guests have been coming to this 289-room motel about 15 minutes' walk to Disneyland. Around the side are two pools, two Jacuzzis, a fitness center, kiddie pool and a garden of topiaries (for real). The remodeled sleek and modern-design rooms sparkle; all have air-con, a microwave and minifridge. Rates include a hot breakfast and there's a guest laundry.

Ayres Hotel Anaheim HOTEL $$
(Map p918; 714-634-2106; www.ayreshotels.com/anaheim; 2550 E Katella Ave; r $139-259; P➡️❄️@🛜🏊; ARTIC, Amtrak to ARTIC) This well-run minichain of business hotels delivers solid-gold value. The 133 recently renovated rooms have microwaves, minifridges, safes, wet bar, pillow-top mattresses and contemporary European-inspired design. Fourth-floor rooms have extra-high ceilings. Rates include a full breakfast buffet and evening social hours Monday to Thursday with craft beer, wine and snacks.

Eating & Drinking

From stroll-and-eat Mickey-shaped pretzels ($4) and jumbo turkey legs ($10) to deluxe, gourmet dinners (sky's the limit), there's no

KNOTT'S BERRY FARM

What, Disney's not enough for you? Find even more thrill rides and cotton candy at **Knott's Berry Farm** (Map p918; ☎714-220-5200; www.knotts.com; 8039 Beach Blvd, Buena Park; adult/child 3-11yr $84/54; ☺from 10am, closing hours vary 5-11pm; P ⚑). This Old West–themed amusement park teems with packs of speed-crazed adolescents testing their mettle on a lineup of rides. Gut-wrenchers include the Boomerang 'scream machine,' wooden GhostRider and 1950s-themed Xcelerator. Younger kids will enjoy tamer action at Camp Snoopy. From late September through October, the park transforms at night into Halloween-themed 'Knott's Scary Farm.'

When summer heat waves hit, jump next door to **Knott's Soak City** (Map p918; ☎714-220-5200; www.knotts.com/play/soak-city; 8039 Beach Blvd, Buena Park; adult/child 3-11yr $53/43; ☺10am-5pm, 6pm or 7pm mid-May–mid-Sep; P ⚑) water park. Save time and money by buying print-at-home tickets for either park online.

shortage of eating options, though most are pretty expensive and targeted to mainstream tastes. Phone **Disney Dining** (☎714-781-3463; http://disneyland.disney.go.com/dining) to make reservations up to 60 days in advance. Restaurant hours vary seasonally, sometimes daily. Check the Disneyland app or Disney Dining website for same-day hours.

If you want to steer clear of Mickey Mouse food, drive to the Anaheim Packing District (3 miles northeast), Old Towne Orange (7 miles southeast), Little Arabia (3 miles west) or Little Saigon (8 miles southwest).

✕ Disneyland Resort

Earl of Sandwich   SANDWICHES $

(Map p918; ☎714-817-7476; www.earlofsandwichusa.com; Downtown Disney; mains $6.50-9; ☺8am-11pm Sun-Thu, to midnight Fri & Sat; ⚑) This counter-service chain near the Disneyland Hotel (p942) serves grilled sandwiches that are both kid- and adult-friendly. The 'original 1762' is roast beef, cheddar and horseradish, or look for chipotle chicken with avocado or holiday turkey. There are also pizza, salad and breakfast options.

Ralph Brennan's
New Orleans Jazz Kitchen   CAJUN $$

(Map p918; ☎714-776-5200; http://rbjazzkitchen.com; Downtown Disney; mains lunch $15.50-25, dinner $26.50-39.50; ☺8am-10pm Sun-Thu, to 11pm Fri & Sat; ⚑) Hear live jazz combos on the weekends and piano on weeknights at this resto-bar with NOLA-style Cajun and Creole dishes: gumbo, po-boy sandwiches, jambalaya, plus a (less adventurous) kids menu and specialty cocktails. There's breakfast and lunch express service if you don't have time to linger.

★ Napa Rose   CALIFORNIAN $$$

(Map p918; ☎714-300-7170; https://disneyland.disney.go.com/dining; Grand Californian Hotel & Spa; mains $38-48; ☺5:30-10pm; ⚑) High-back arts-and-crafts-style chairs, leaded-glass windows and towering ceilings befit Disneyland Resort's top-drawer restaurant. On the plate, seasonal 'California Wine Country' (read: NorCal) cuisine is as impeccably crafted as the Sleeping Beauty Castle. Kids menu available. Reservations essential. Enter the hotel from Disney California Adventure or Downtown Disney.

✕ Anaheim

★ Pour Vida   MEXICAN $

(Map p918; ☎657-208-3889; www.pourvidalatinflavor.com; 185 W Center St Promenade; tacos $2-8; ☺10am-7pm Mon, to 9pm Tue-Thu, to 10pm Fri, 9am-10pm Sat, 9am-8:30pm Sun) Chef Jimmy, who has worked in some of LA's top kitchens, returned to his Mexican roots to make some of the most gourmet tacos we've ever seen: pineapple skirt steak, tempura oyster, heirloom cauliflower...*caramba*! Even the tortillas are special, made with squid ink, spinach and a secret recipe. It's deliberately informal, all brick and concrete with chalkboard walls.

❶ Information

For information or help inside the parks, just ask any cast member or visit Disneyland's **City Hall** (Map p918; ☎714-781-4565; Main Street USA) or Disney California Adventure's guest relations lobby.

Both can also help out with foreign-currency exchange. Multiple ATMs are found in both theme parks and at Downtown Disney.

MISSION SAN JUAN CAPISTRANO

Detour inland from the Orange County beaches to **Mission San Juan Capistrano** (☑ 949-234-1300; www.missionsjc.com; 26801 Ortega Hwy; adult/child $10/7; ⏱ 9am-5pm; 🅿), one of California's most beautifully restored Spanish Colonial missions. Plan on spending at least an hour poking around the sprawling mission's tiled roofs, covered arches, lush gardens, fountains and courtyards – including the padre's quarters, soldiers' barracks and the cemetery.

The Serra Chapel – whitewashed outside with restored frescoes inside – is believed to be the oldest existing building in California (1782). It's certainly the only one still standing in which Junípero Serra (the founder of the mission) gave Mass. Serra founded the mission on November 1, 1776, and tended it personally for many years.

Admission includes a worthwhile free audio tour with interesting stories narrated by locals.

Travelex (☑ 714-687-7977; 100 West Lincoln Ave, inside US Bank, Anaheim; ⏱ 9am-5pm Mon-Fri, to 1pm Sat) Also exchanges foreign currency near Anaheim City Hall.

ℹ️ Getting There & Around

Disneyland and Anaheim can be reached by car (off the I-5 Fwy) or Amtrak or Metrolink trains at Anaheim's **ARTIC** (Anaheim Regional Transportation Intermodal Center; 2150 E Katella Ave, Anaheim) transit center. From here to Disneyland proper it's a short taxi, ride share or **Anaheim Resort Transportation** (ART; ☑ 888-364-2787; www.rideart.org; adult/child fare $3/1, day pass $6/2.50, multiple-day passes available) shuttle. The closest airport is Orange County's **John Wayne Airport** (SNA; Map p918; www.ocair.com; 18601 Airport Way, Santa Ana).

The miniature biodiesel Disneyland Railroad chugs in a clockwise circle around Disneyland, stopping at Main Street USA, New Orleans Square, Mickey's Toon Town and Tomorrowland, taking about 20 minutes to make a full loop. Between the Tomorrowland and Main Street USA stations, look out for dioramas of the Grand Canyon and a Jurassic-style 'Primeval World.' From Tomorrowland, you can catch the zero-emissions monorail directly to Downtown Disney.

Orange County Beaches

If you've seen *The OC* or *The Real Housewives*, you might imagine you already know what to expect from this giant quilt of suburbia connecting LA and San Diego, lolling beside 42 miles of glorious coastline. In reality, Hummer-driving hunks and Botoxed beauties mix it up with hang-loose surfers and beatnik beach artists to give each of Orange County's beach towns a distinct vibe of its own.

Seal Beach & Huntington Beach

Just across the LA–OC county line, old-fashioned **Seal Beach** is refreshingly noncommercial, with a quaint walkable downtown. Less than 10 miles further south along the Pacific Coast Hwy (Hwy 1), Huntington Beach – aka 'Surf City, USA' – epitomizes SoCal's surfing lifestyle. Fish tacos and happy-hour specials abound at bars and cafes along downtown HB's Main St, not far from a shortboard-sized **surfing museum** (Map p918; ☑ 714-960-3483; www.surfingmuseum.org; 411 Olive Ave; admission $3; ⏱ noon-5pm Tue-Sun).

Here you'll find slick and serene **Paséa** (Map p918; ☑ 855-622-2472; http://meritagecollection.com/paseahotel; 21080 Pacific Coast Hwy; r May-Aug from $359, rest of year from $280; 🅿 ➕ ❄ @ 🛜 ♨) hotel. Floors are themed for shades of blue, from denim to sky, and each of its 250 shimmery, minimalist, high-ceilinged rooms has an ocean-view balcony. As if the stunning pool, gym and Balinese-inspired spa weren't enough, it also connects to **Pacific City** (Map p918; www.gopacificcity.com; 21010 Pacific Coast Hwy; ⏱ hours vary), with its unique and fun food court. Head here for pressed sandwiches (Burnt Crumbs – the spaghetti grilled cheese is so Instagrammable), Aussie meat pies (Pie Not), coffee (Portola) and ice cream (Han's). For the best views, take your meal to the deck.

Newport Beach & Balboa Peninsula

Next up is the ritziest of the OC's beach communities: yacht-filled Newport Beach. Families and teens steer toward Balboa Peninsula for its beaches, vintage wooden pier and quaint amusement center. From near the 1906 Balboa Pavilion, **Balboa Island**

Ferry (Map p918; www.balboaislandferry.com; 410 S Bay Front; adult/child $1/50¢, car incl driver $2; ⊙6:30am-midnight Sun-Thu, to 2am Fri & Sat) shuttles across the bay to Balboa Island for strolls past historic beach cottages and boutiques along Marine Ave.

Bear Flag Fish Company (Map p918; ☑949-673-3474; www.bearflagfishco.com; 3421 Via Lido; mains $10-16; ⊙11am-9pm Tue-Sat, to 8pm Sun & Mon; ⊕) is *the* place for generously sized, grilled and *panko*-breaded fish tacos, ahi burritos, spankin' fresh ceviche and oysters. Pick out what you want from the ice-cold display cases, then grab a picnic-table seat. About the only way this seafood could be any fresher is if you caught and hauled it off the boat yourself!

Laguna Beach

Continuing south, Hwy 1 zooms past the wild beaches of **Crystal Cove State Park** (Map p918; ☑949-494-3539; www.parks.ca.gov; 8471 N Coast Hwy; per car $15; ⊙6am-sunset; Ⓟ⊕) ☞ before winding downhill into Laguna Beach, the OC's most cultured seaside community. Secluded beaches, glassy waves and eucalyptus-covered hillsides create a Riviera-like feel. Art galleries dot the narrow streets of the 'village' and the coastal highway, where the **Laguna Art Museum** (☑949-494-8971; www.lagunaartmuseum.org; 307 Cliff Dr; adult/student & senior/child under 13yr $7/5/free, 5-9pm 1st Thu of month free; ⊙11am-5pm Fri-Tue, to 9pm Thu) exhibits modern and contemporary Californian works. Soak up the natural beauty right in the center of town at Main Beach.

Ocean views and ridiculous sunsets alone ought to be enough to bring folks in, but gourmet **Driftwood** (☑949-715-7700; www.driftwoodkitchen.com; 619 Sleepy Hollow Lane; mains lunch $15-37, dinner $25-44; ⊙9-10:30am & 11am-2:30pm Mon-Fri, 5-9:30pm Sun-Thu, to 10:30pm Fri & Sat, 9am-2:30pm Sat & Sun) steps up the food with seasonal menus centered around fresh, sustainable seafood, plus options for landlubbers.

If you're in town over summer, don't miss the **Festival of Arts** (www.foapom.com; 650 Laguna Canyon Rd; admission $7-10; ⊙noon-11:30pm Mon-Fri, 10am-11:30pm Sat & Sun Jul & Aug; ⊕), a two-month celebration of original artwork in almost all its forms. About 140 exhibitors display works ranging from paintings and hand-crafted furniture to scrimshaw. Plus there are kid-friendly art workshops and live music and entertainment daily.

San Diego

San Diego calls itself 'America's Finest City', and its breezy confidence and sunny countenance filter down to folks you encounter every day on the street. It feels like a collection of villages each with their own personality, but it's the nation's eighth-largest city and we're hard-pressed to think of a more laid-back place.

What's not to love? San Diego bursts with world-famous attractions for the entire family, including the zoo, the museums of Balboa Park, plus a bubbling Downtown, beautiful hikes for all, more than 60 beaches and America's most perfect weather.

⊙ Sights

⊙ Downtown & Embarcadero

San Diego's Downtown is the region's main business, financial and convention district. Whatever intense urban energy Downtown generally lacks, it makes up for in fun shopping, dining and nightlife in the historic **Gaslamp Quarter** (formerly a notorious strip of saloons, gambling joints and bordellos known as Stingaree), and the hipster havens of **East Village** and **North Park**. The waterfront **Embarcadero** is great for a stroll. In the northwestern corner of Downtown, vibrant **Little Italy** brims with progressive eats.

★**Maritime Museum** MUSEUM
(Map p948; ☑619-234-9153; www.sdmaritime.org; 1492 N Harbor Dr; adult/child $18/8; ⊙9am-9pm late May-early Sep, to 8pm early Sep-late May; ⊕) Next to the new Waterfront Park, this collection of 11 historic sailing ships, steam boats and submarines is easy to spot: just look for the 100ft-high masts of the iron-hulled square-rigger *Star of India*, a tall ship launched in 1863 to ply the England–India trade route. Also moored here is a replica of the *San Salvador* that brought explorer Juan Rodriguez Cabrillo to San Diego's shore in 1542. It's easy to spend hours looking at the exhibits and clambering around the vessels.

USS Midway Museum MUSEUM
(Map p948; ☑619-544-9600; www.midway.org; 910 N Harbor Dr; adult/child $22/9; ⊙10am-5pm, last admission 4pm; Ⓟ⊕) The hulking aircraft carrier USS *Midway* was one of the navy's flagships from 1945 to 1991, last playing a

Greater San Diego

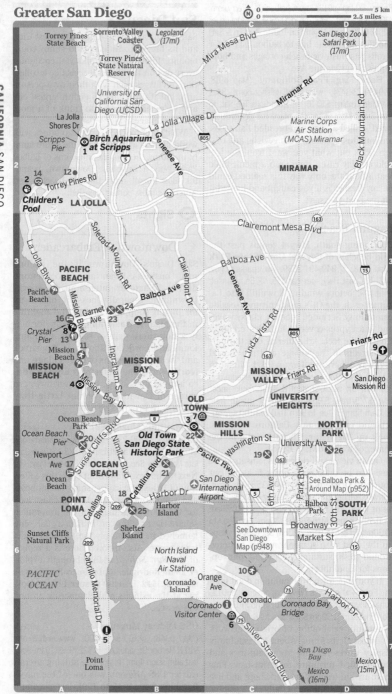

Torrey Pines State Beach

Sorrento Valley Coaster

Legoland (17mi)

Mira Mesa Blvd

San Diego Zoo Safari Park (17mi)

Torrey Pines State Natural Reserve

Miramar Rd

University of California San Diego (UCSD)

Marine Corps Air Station (MCAS) Miramar

La Jolla Village Dr

La Jolla Shores Dr

Scripps Pier

Birch Aquarium at Scripps
1

Genesee Ave

805

MIRAMAR

Black Mountain Rd

2 14
12
Torrey Pines Rd

Children's Pool

LA JOLLA

52

Clairemont Mesa Blvd

163

15

La Jolla Blvd

PACIFIC BEACH

Soledad Mountain Rd

Balboa Ave

Clairemont Dr

Balboa Ave

Genesee Ave

Pacific Beach

Garnet Ave 24
16 23

Mission Blvd

15

Linda Vista Rd

805

Crystal Pier
8
13

Ingraham St

MISSION BAY

163

Friars Rd
9

Mission Beach 11

MISSION BEACH

Mission Bay Dr
4

5

MISSION VALLEY

Friars Rd

UNIVERSITY HEIGHTS

8 San Diego Mission Rd

OLD TOWN

8
3 7

22

MISSION HILLS

Washington Street

NORTH PARK

University Ave 26

Ocean Beach Park

Ocean Beach Pier

Old Town San Diego State Historic Park

19

163

Sunset Cliffs Blvd

Nimitz Blvd

Catalina Blvd

Newport Ave 17
20

OCEAN BEACH

21

San Diego International Airport

Pacific Hwy

6th Ave

Park Blvd

See Balboa Park & Around Map (p952)

Ocean Beach

POINT LOMA

Catalina Blvd

18
25

Harbor Dr

Shelter Island

Harbor Island

See Downtown San Diego Map (p948)

Balboa Park

SOUTH PARK

30th St

Broadway

Market St

94

Sunset Cliffs Natural Park

209

Cabrillo Memorial Dr

PACIFIC OCEAN

North Island Naval Air Station

Coronado Island

Orange Ave

10

Coronado

75

Coronado Bay Bridge

Harbor Dr

5

15

Coronado Visitor Center
6
75

Silver Strand Blvd

San Diego Bay

Mexico (15mi)

5

Point Loma

Mexico (16mi)

Greater San Diego

combat role in the First Gulf War. On the flight deck, walk right up to some two dozen restored aircraft, including an F-14 Tomcat and F-4 Phantom jet fighter. Admission includes an audio tour along the narrow confines of the upper decks to the bridge, the admiral's war room, the brig and the 'pri-fly' (primary flight control; the carrier's equivalent of a control tower).

Museum of Contemporary Art   MUSEUM
(MCASD Downtown; Map p948; ☑ 858-454-3541; www.mcasd.org; 1001 Kettner Blvd; adult/under 25yr $10/free; ⊙ 11am-5pm Thu-Tue) In an upcycled Santa Fe Depot baggage building, this well-respected museum presents changing exhibits drawn from a collection spanning the arc of artistic expression from the 1950s to the present. Genres where it's especially strong are minimalism, pop art, conceptual art and art from Southern California. The museum opens late and has free entry from 5pm to 8pm on the third Thursday of each month.

◉ Coronado

Technically a peninsula, Coronado Island is joined to the mainland by a 2.2-mile-long bridge. The peninsula's main draw is the **Hotel del Coronado** (Map p946; ☑ tours 619-522-8100, 619-435-6611; www.hoteldel.com; 1500 Orange Ave; tours $40; ⊙ tours 10am daily, 2pm Sat & Sun; ☑) FREE, known for its seaside Victorian architecture and illustrious guestbook, which includes Thomas Edison, Babe Ruth and Marilyn Monroe.

At the entrance to the bay, **Point Loma** has sweeping views across sea and city from the Cabrillo National Monument (p950). **Mission Bay**, northwest of Downtown, has lagoons, parks and recreation, from water skiing to camping and SeaWorld. The nearby coastal neighborhoods – Ocean Beach, Mission Beach and Pacific Beach – epitomize the SoCal beach scene.

The hourly **Coronado Ferry** (Map p948; ☑ 800-442-7847; www.flagshipsd.com; 990 N Harbor Dr; one-way tickets $5; ⊙ 9am-9:30pm Sun-Thu, to 10:30pm Fri & Sat) departs from the Embarcadero's **Broadway Pier** (1050 N Harbor Dr) and from Downtown's convention center. All ferries arrive on Coronado at the foot of 1st St, where **Bikes & Beyond** (Map p946; ☑ 619-435-7180; www.bikes-and-beyond.com; 1201 1st St; per hr/day from $8/30; ⊙ 9am-sunset) rents cruisers and tandems, perfect for pedalling past Coronado's white-sand beaches that sprawl south along the Silver Strand.

◉ Balboa Park

Balboa Park is an urban oasis brimming with more than a dozen museums, gorgeous gardens and architecture, performance spaces and a zoo. Early 20th-century beaux-arts and Spanish Colonial Revival–style buildings (the legacy of world's fairs) are grouped around plazas along east–west El Prado promenade.

The free Balboa Park Tram bus makes a continuous loop around the park; however, it's most enjoyable to walk, heading past

Downtown San Diego

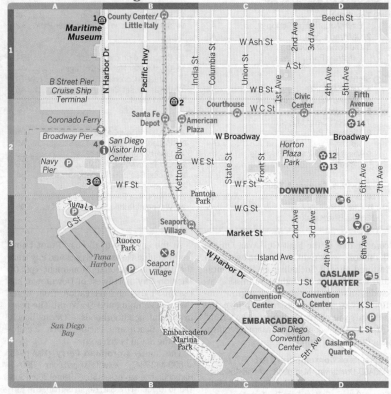

the 1915 **Spreckels Organ Pavilion** (Map p952; ☑ 619-702-8138; http://spreckelsorgan.org) FREE, the shops and galleries of the **Spanish Village Art Center** (Map p952; ☑ 619-233-9050; http://spanishvillageart.com; 1770 Village Pl; ☉ 11am-4pm) FREE and the international-themed exhibition cottages by the **United Nations Building**.

San Diego Zoo ZOO
(Map p952; ☑ 619-231-1515; https://zoo.sandiego zoo.org; 2920 Zoo Dr; day pass adult/child from $56/46; 2-visit pass zoo &/or safari park adult/child $90/80; ☉ 9am-9pm mid-Jun–early Sep, to 5pm or 6pm early Sep–mid-Jun; ☑ ☻) ✐ This justifiably famous zoo is one of SoCal's biggest attractions, showing more than 3000 animals representing more than 650 species in a beautifully landscaped setting, typically in enclosures that replicate their natural habitats. Its sister park is **San Diego Zoo Safari Park** (☑ 760-747-8702; www.sdzsafaripark.org; 15500 San Pasqual Valley Rd, Escondido; day pass adult/child from $56/46, 2-visit pass safari park &/or zoo adult/child $90/80; ☉ 9am-6pm; ☑ ☻) in northern San Diego County.

Arrive early, as many of the animals are most active in the morning – though many perk up again in the afternoon. Pick up a map at the zoo entrance to find your favorite exhibits.

Fleet Science Center MUSEUM
(Map p952; ☑ 619-238-1233; www.rhfleet.org; 1875 El Prado; adult/child 3-12yr incl IMAX film $22/19; ☉ 10am-5pm Mon-Thu, to 6pm Fri-Sun; ☻) A top pick in Balboa Park, this hands-on science museum features interactive displays, including a room geared to the milk-tooth set. Look out for opportunities to build gigantic structures or to become a human battery, and ask about demonstrations of the mysterious Tesla Coil. The biggest draw, though, is the **Giant Dome Theater**, which presents several different films and planetarium shows daily.

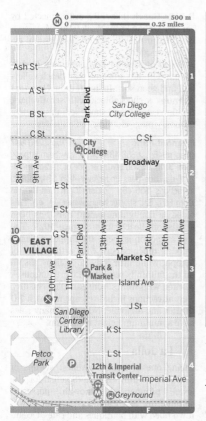

to Rivera. American landscape paintings are another focus, and the Asian galleries have some eye-catchers. On Fridays, admission is just $5 from 5pm to 8pm.

San Diego Air & Space Museum MUSEUM
(Map p952; ☑ 619-234-8291; www.sandiego airandspace.org; 2001 Pan American Plaza; adult/youth/child under 2yr $20/$11/free; ☺ 10am-4:30pm; ⊞) An ode to flight, the circular museum houses an extensive display of historical aircraft and spacecraft (originals, replicas and models), including a hot-air balloon from 1783, an Apollo command module and a Vietnam-era Cobra helicopter. Also look for memorabilia from legendary aviators such as Charles Lindbergh and astronaut John Glenn or catch films in the 3-D/4-D theater.

◉ Old Town & Mission Valley

★Old Town San Diego
State Historic Park HISTORIC SITE
(Map p946; ☑ 619-220-5422; www.parks.ca.gov; 4002 Wallace St; ☺ visitor center & museums 10am-5pm May-Sep, 10am-4pm Mon-Thu, to 5pm Fri-Sun Oct-Apr; ℗ ⊞) **FREE** On the site of San Diego's first European settlement, Old Town consists of a cluster of restored or rebuilt historic 19th-century buildings filled with

San Diego Natural History Museum MUSEUM
(The Nat; Map p952; ☑ 877-946-7797; www.sdnhm. org; 1788 El Prado; adult/child 3-17yr/under 2yr $29/12/free; ☺ 10am-5pm; ⊞) The 'Nat' houses 7.5 million specimens, including rocks, minerals, fossils and taxidermied animals, as well as an impressive dinosaur skeleton and an eye-opening exhibit on how climate change affects California's water supply, all in beautiful spaces. Kids love the 2-D and 3-D movies about the natural world in the giant-screen cinema and the fun and educational programs held most weekends.

San Diego Museum of Art MUSEUM
(SDMA; Map p952; ☑ 619-232-7931; www.sdmart. org; 1450 El Prado; adult/student/child under 17yr $15/8/free; ☺ 10am-5pm Mon, Tue, Thu & Sat, to 8pm Fri, noon-5pm Sun) Pride of place in SDMA's permanent collection goes to its Spanish old masters (El Greco, Goya) and a respectable selection of works by other international heavy hitters from Matisse to Magritte, Cassatt

quaint exhibits, souvenir stores and cafes. A good place to start is at the visitor center in 1853 **Robinson-Rose House**; see the neat model of the pueblo in 1872 and pick up a self-guided tour pamphlet ($3). Staff also run free guided tours daily at 11am and 2pm.

Mission Basilica
San Diego de Alcalá   CHURCH
(Map p946; ☑619-281-8449; www.missionsan diego.org; 10818 San Diego Mission Rd; adult/child/under 5yr $5/2/free; ◷9am-4:30pm; P) Padre Junípero Serra founded the first of California's 21 missions in 1769 on Presidio Hill near present-day Old Town but, five years later, it was moved about 6 miles upriver to be closer to water and more arable land. Destroyed, rebuilt and expanded multiple times, today's mission is the fifth on the site and an active parish. It's a lovely place to visit, not only for its historical significance but also to relax amid birdsong and bougainvillea in the serene garden.

Junípero Serra Museum   MUSEUM
(Map p946; ☑619-232-6203; www.sandiegohis tory.org/serra_museum; 2727 Presidio Dr; entry by donation; ◷10am-4pm Fri-Sun early Jun-early Sep, to 5pm Sat & Sun early Sep-early Jun; P) This museum stands atop Presidio Hill, the original site of Mission San Diego de Alcalá. Inside the Spanish Revival building, a small collection of artifacts and pictures offers insight into the earliest days of European settlement.

◉ Point Loma

On a map, Point Loma looks like an elephant's trunk guarding the entrance to San Diego Bay. Highlights are the **Cabrillo National Monument** (Map p946; ☑619-557-5450; www.nps.gov/cabr; 1800 Cabrillo Memorial Dr; per car/walk-ins $20/10; ◷9am-5pm, tide pools to 4:30pm; P) – at the end of the trunk; shopping and dining at **Liberty Public Market** (Map p946; ☑619-487-9346; http://libertypublicmarket.com; 2820 Historic Decatur Rd; dishes $5-20; ◷11am-7pm; P) – at its base; and seafood meals around **Shelter Island**.

◉ Mission Bay & Beaches

San Diego's big three beach towns are ribbons of hedonism where armies of tanned, taut bodies frolic in the sand. West of amoeba-shaped Mission Bay, surf-friendly **Mission Beach** and its northern neighbor,

Pacific Beach (aka 'PB'), are connected by car-free **Ocean Front Walk** (Map p946) FREE, which swarms with skaters, joggers and cyclists year-round.

South of Mission Bay, bohemian **Ocean Beach** (OB) has a fishing pier, beach volleyball and good surf. Its main drag, **Newport Avenue**, is chockablock with scruffy bars, flip-flop eateries and shops selling surf gear, tattoos, vintage clothing and antiques.

Belmont Park   AMUSEMENT PARK
(Map p946; ☑858-488-1549; www.belmontpark. com; 3146 Mission Blvd; per ride or attraction $4-7, all-day ride pass under/over 48in $34/24, incl attractions $56/46; ◷11am-10pm Sun-Thu, to 11pm Fri & Sat, shorter hours winter; P) This old-style family amusement park has been a Mission Beach fixture since 1925. The star attraction is the Giant Dipper, a classic wooden roller coaster with a top speed of 50mph, while little kids love taking a spin on the faithfully recreated Liberty Carousel, painted with scenes from San Diego history. New attractions include escape rooms, a 7-D theater and a zipline. Note that many rides have a minimum height restriction.

◉ La Jolla

Facing one of SoCal's loveliest sweeps of coastline, wealthy La Jolla (Spanish for 'the jewel,' pronounced la-hoy-ah) possesses shimmering beaches and an upscale downtown filled with boutiques and cafes. Oceanfront diversions include the **Children's Pool** (Map p946; 850 Coast Blvd; ◷24hr;) FREE – no longer for swimming, it's now home to barking sea lions; kayaking; exploring sea caves at **La Jolla Cove**; and snorkeling at **San Diego-La Jolla Underwater Park** (Map p946).

Torrey Pines
State Natural Reserve   STATE PARK
(☑858-755-2063; www.torreypine.org; 12600 N Torrey Pines Rd; ◷7:15am-sunset, visitor center 9am-4pm Oct-Apr, to 6pm May-Sep; P) FREE This reserve preserves the last mainland stands of the Torrey pine (*Pinus torreyana*), a species adapted to sparse rainfall and sandy, stony soils. Steep sandstone gullies have eroded into wonderfully textured surfaces, and the views over the ocean and north, including whale-watching, are superb. Volunteers lead nature walks at 10am and 2pm on weekends and holidays. Several trails wind through the reserve and down to the beach.

SURFING IN SAN DIEGO

A good number of residents moved to San Diego just for the surfing, and gee, is it good. Even beginners will understand why surfing is so popular here.

Fall brings strong swells and offshore Santa Ana winds. In summer swells come from the south and southwest, and in winter from the west and northwest. Spring brings more frequent onshore winds, but the surfing can still be good. For the latest beach, weather and surf reports, call **San Diego County Lifeguard Services** (☑ 619-221-8824; www.sandiego.gov/lifeguards).

Beginners should head to Mission or Pacific Beach (p950) for beach breaks (soft-sand bottomed). About a mile north of Crystal Pier, **Tourmaline Surfing Park** is a crowded but good improvers' spot for those comfortable surfing reef.

Rental rates vary depending on the quality of the equipment, but figure on soft boards from around $7/20 per hour/day or $13/32 including wetsuit. Packages are available from **Cheap Rentals** (Map p946; ☑ 858-488-9070; https://cheap-rentals.com; 3689 Mission Blvd, Pacific Beach; bicycles per day from $15; ☺ 10am-6pm) and **Pacific Beach Surf Shop** (Map p946; ☑ 858-373-1138; www.pbsurfshop.com; 4208 Oliver Ct; 90min private lessons $80-100; ☺ 8am-6:30pm).

★ **Birch Aquarium at Scripps** AQUARIUM (Map p946; ☑ 858-534-3474; www.aquarium. ucsd.edu; 2300 Expedition Way; adult/child $19/15; ☺ 9am-5pm; P 🎡) ✐ This state-of-the-art aquarium is a wonderous underwater world where you can watch sea horses dance, sharks dart, kelp forests sway, and even meet a rescued loggerhead turtle. The Hall of Fishes has more than 60 fish tanks, simulating marine habitats from the Pacific Northwest to tropical seas. The Tide Pool Plaza, with its fabulous ocean views, is the place to get touchy-feely with sea stars, hermit crabs, sea cucumbers, lobsters and tidal-zone critters.

🏃 Activities

There are plenty of hikes in and around San Diego, but most outdoor activities involve the ocean, which is a dream playground for surfers, paddleboarders, kayakers and boaters.

Flagship Cruises BOATING (Map p948; ☑ 619-234-4111; www.flagshipsd. com; 990 N Harbor Dr; 2hr harbour tours adult/child $32/16) In business since 1915, this outfit runs harbor tours, dinner cruises and seasonal whale-watching cruises from its launchpad at the Embarcadero.

Hike Bike Kayak ADVENTURE SPORTS (Map p946; ☑ 858-551-9510; www.hikebikekayak. com; 2222 Avenida de la Playa; kayak rentals from $35, tours $49-79; ☺ 9am-sunset) HBK runs a variety of tours including the popular kayak exploration of La Jolla's cove and caves, and a bike tour down Mt Soledad and along the coast. Also rents kayaks, snorkeling gear

and stand up paddleboards, bodyboards and surfboards.

🛏 Sleeping

The San Diego Tourism Authority runs a room **reservation line** (☑ 800-350-6205; www.sandiego.org).

For camping try **Campland on the Bay** (Map p946; ☑ 858-581-4260; www.campland.com; 2211 Pacific Beach Dr, Mission Bay; RV & tent sites $100-456 Jun-Aug, $55-364 Sep-May; P ☎ 🎡 🐾) in Mission Bay, or **KOA** (☑ 619-427-3601; www. sandiegokoa.com; 111 N 2nd Ave, Chula Vista; tent/RV with hookup sites from $60/90, std/deluxe cabins from $120/200; P @ ☎ 🎡 🐾), about 8 miles south; both are full-service resorts geared toward families and groups.

🛏 Downtown & Around

★ **USA Hostels San Diego** HOSTEL $ (Map p948; ☑ 619-232-3100; www.usahostels.com; 726 5th Ave, Downtown; dm/r with shared bath from $32/80; ❄ @ ☎) There's lots of color, comforts and character at this convivial hostel in a former Victorian-era hotel. Dorms have upscale features such as air-conditioning, proper mattresses, reading lights and privacy screens. A full kitchen and a communal lounge invite chilling. Rates include linens, lockers and bagels for breakfast.

★ **Kimpton Solamar** HOTEL $$ (Map p948; ☑ 619-819-9500; www.hotelsolamar. com; 435 6th Ave; r $150-300; P ❄ @ ☎ 🎡 🐾) The 235-room Solamar delivers hip style without breaking the bank. Rooms sport hodge-podge decor with eccentric lamps,

Balboa Park & Around

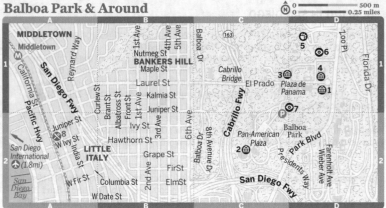

Balboa Park & Around

◎ Sights
1 Fleet Science Center D1
2 San Diego Air & Space
  Museum...C2
3 San Diego Museum of Art C1
4 San Diego Natural History
  Museum...D1
5 San Diego Zoo.....................................D1
6 Spanish Village Art Center D1
7 Spreckels Organ Pavilion D1

⊗ Eating
8 Juniper & Ivy...A2

patterned carpets, yoga mats and wallpapered bathrooms. Relax around the heated pool where there are cabanas and firepits or in the bar during the social hour with free drinks and snacks. Parking costs $47.

🛏 Beaches

Inn at Sunset Cliffs HOTEL **$$**
(Map p946; ☎619-222-7901; www.innatsunsetcliffs.com; 1370 Sunset Cliffs Blvd; r/ste from $200/315; P❋❄@🐾🛜) Wake up to the sound of surf crashing onto the rocky shore at this privately owned 1950s charmer wrapped around a flower-bedecked courtyard with a heated pool. Spiffed up in 2018, the 24 rooms and suites (some with full kitchens) now sparkle in shiny white and blue hues and sport laminate flooring, blond furniture and attractive bathrooms.

Pearl Hotel BOUTIQUE HOTEL **$$**
(Map p946; ☎619-226-6100; www.thepearlsd.com; 1410 Rosecrans St, Point Loma; r $120-290; P❋🛜❄) This 1959 gem is showing its age,

which is why new owners are giving it a bigbucks face-lift while preserving its mid-century-modern bone structure. The 23 rooms wrap around a peanut-sized swimming pool where guests and locals mingle during 'dive-in movies' on Wednesday nights.

Crystal Pier Hotel & Cottages COTTAGE **$$$**
(Map p946; ☎858-483-6983; www.crystalpier.com; 4500 Ocean Blvd, Pacific Beach; units Jun-Sep $225-450, Oct-Mar $185-350; P❄🛜) Charming Crystal Pier consists of 29 breezy cottages from the 1930s built right on a wooden pier and flaunting dreamy ocean views from spacious decks. All but one have small kitchens, and newer, larger cottages sleep up to six. Book eight to 11 months in advance for summer reservations. Minimum-stay requirements vary by season. Rates include parking.

Hotel del Coronado LUXURY HOTEL **$$$**
(Map p946; ☎619-435-6611; www.hoteldel.com; 1500 Orange Ave; r from $319; P❄❋@🛜❄🏊) Now managed by Hilton, San Diego's iconic hotel provides the essential Coronado experience: over a century of history, a pool, full-service spa, well-equipped gym, shops, restaurants, manicured grounds and a white-sand beach. Even the basic rooms have luxurious marbled bathrooms. Make sure to book a room in the main Victorian-era hotel, not in the adjacent seven-story 1970s tower.

🍴 Eating

San Diego has a thriving dining culture, with an emphasis on Mexican and Californian cuisine and seafood. San Diegans eat dinner early, usually around 6pm or 7pm, and most restaurants are ready to close by 10pm. Breakfast is a big affair. There's a burgeoning farm-to-table and gourmet scene, especially in Little Italy and, to some extent, North Park.

✕ Downtown & Around

★ Old Town Mexican Café   MEXICAN $
(Map p946; ☏ 619-297-4330; www.oldtownmex cafe.com; 2489 San Diego Ave; mains $5-17; ⊙ 7-11pm Sun-Thu, to midnight Fri & Sat; ⛟) In business since the 1970s, this vibrant Mexican joint delivers authentic south-of-the-border fare despite the clichéd folkloric look. Marvel at staff churning out fresh tortillas at lightning speed while you sip a margarita and anticipate the arrival of menu stars such as crispy carnitas and succulent ribs.

★ Puesto at the Headquarters   MEXICAN $$
(Map p948; ☏ 610-233-8880; www.eatpuesto. com; 789 W Harbor Dr; 3 tacos $17; ⊙ 11am-10pm) In the old San Diego Police Headquarters, this vibrant eatery serves modern Mexican street food that knocked our *zapatos* off. Start with some creamy guacamole before moving on to innovative tacos: chicken in hibiscus-chipotle sauce with avocado and pineapple-habanero salsa in a blue-corn tortilla. Sit on the spacious patio or inside amid murals and floating potted plants.

Basic   PIZZA $$
(Map p948; ☏ 619-531-8869; www.barbasic.com; 410 10th Ave; small/large pizzas from $15/33; ⊙ 11:30am-2am; ⛟) East Village hipsters feast on fragrant thin-crust brick-oven-baked pizzas under Basic's high ceiling (it's in a former warehouse). Toppings span the usual to the newfangled, such as the mashed pie with mozzarella, mashed potatoes and bacon. Wash them down with a craft beer or cocktail.

★ Juniper & Ivy   CALIFORNIAN $$$
(Map p952; ☏ 619-269-9036; www.juniperandivy. com; 2228 Kettner Blvd; small plates $13-28, mains $19-48; ⊙ 5-10pm Sun-Thu, to 11pm Fri & Sat) Spearheading the new crop of Little Italy's fine-dining restaurants, J&I is the creation of star chef Richard Blais, who performs culinary sorcery with whatever is fresh, in season and locally available. While the menu is in constant flux, the sharing concept and the irresistible buttermilk biscuits are constant. It's all beautifully presented in the spacious setting of an open-beamed warehouse.

✕ Balboa Park & Around

Waypoint Public   GASTROPUB $
(Map p946; ☏ 619-255-8778; www.waypointpub lic.com; 3794 30th St, North Park; mains $10-17; ⊙ 11am-10pm Mon-Wed, to 11pm Thu, to 1am Fri, 8am-1am Sat, to 10pm Sun; ⛟) Waypoint's comfort-food menu is designed to pair with craft beer. The focus is squarely on burgers and sandwiches, including a wicked tri-tip with whiskey peppercorn sauce and blue cheese. For desert, beeramisu and lavender crème brûlée beckon. Walls are attractively done up in reclaimed wood, and glass garage doors roll up to the outside, all the better for hipster-watching in busy North Park.

★ Hash House a Go Go   AMERICAN $$
(Map p946; ☏ 619-298-4646; www.hashhousea gogo.com; 3628 5th Ave, Hillcrest; mains breakfast $12-22, dinner $15-29; ⊙ 7:30am-2:30pm daily, 5:30-9pm Tue-Sun) This buzzing bungalow with its old-school dining room, busy bar and breezy patio dishes up rib-sticking 'twisted farm food' straight from the American Midwest. Towering Benedicts, large-as-your-head pancakes and – wait for it – hash seven different ways will keep you going for the better part of the day.

✕ Beaches

★ Pacific Beach Fish Shop   SEAFOOD $
(Map p946; ☏ 858-483-1008; www.thefishshop pb.com; 1775 Garnet Ave; tacos/fish plates from $5/16; ⊙ 11am-10pm) You can't miss this fishy-themed joint with its enormous swordfish hanging outside. Inside, it's a casual, communal bench affair. Choose from more than 10 types of fresh fish at the counter, from ahi to yellowtail, then pick your marinade (garlic butter to chipotle glaze) and your style – fish plate with rice and salad, taco or sandwich, perhaps?

★ Hodad's   BURGERS $
(Map p946; ☏ 619-224-4623; www.hodadies.com; 5010 Newport Ave, Ocean Beach; burgers $5-15; ⊙ 11am-10pm) Since the flower-power days of 1969, OB's legendary burger joint has served great shakes, massive baskets of onion rings and succulent hamburgers wrapped in paper. The walls are covered in license plates; grunge/surf-rock plays (loud!); and your bearded, tattooed server might sidle into your booth to take your order. No shirt, no shoes, no problem, dude.

★ **Point Loma Seafoods** SEAFOOD $

(Map p946; ☑619-223-1109; www.pointlomasea foods.com; 2805 Emerson St, Point Loma; mains $8-17; ⊙9am-7pm Mon-Sat, 10am-7pm Sun) From California spiny lobster to harpoon-caught swordfish, the seafood at this been-there-for-ever fish market is off-the-boat-fresh and finds its destiny in sandwiches, salads, fried dishes and sushi. Order at the counter, then devour at a picnic table on the upstairs marina-view deck. Superb value for money.

Patio on Lamont AMERICAN $$

(Map p946; ☑858-412-4648; www.thepatioon lamont.com; 4445 Lamont St; mains lunch $8-17, dinner $16-38; ⊙11am-11pm Mon-Thu, to midnight Fri, 9am-midnight Sat, to 11pm Sun; 🐾) Although the wicker-chair look is getting a bit dated, this popular neighborhood restaurant is like a fine bottle of wine that gets better with age. Loyalists love the New American fare and the dog-friendly enclosed patio with wood-burning fireplace.

🍷 Drinking & Nightlife

As befits a cosmopolitan city, San Diego's bar scene is diverse, ranging from craft-beer bars, live-music pubs and classic American pool bars, to beach bars with tiki cocktails, gay clubs offering drag shows, and even a few speakeasies. You can also venture out to one of the 100-plus craft breweries or the vineyards in the Temecula area.

★ **Bang Bang** CLUB

(Map p948; ☑619-677-2264; www.bangbangsd. com; 526 Market St; cover $20-30; ⊙5pm-midnight Wed, Thu & Sun, to 2am Fri & Sat) This Gaslamp hot spot serves sushi and Asian bites five nights a week and turns into a steamy dance club (EDM, minimal, deep house) on Fridays and Saturdays. Enter via a tiled Tokyo subway-style staircase to mingle with shiny happy people below a giant disco ball or share a giant punch bowl with your posse. Cocktails $15.

Noble Experiment BAR

(Map p948; ☑619-888-4713; http://nobleexperi mentsd.com; 777 G St; ⊙6pm-2am Tue-Sun) A stack of kegs masquerading as a door inside the Neighborhood restaurant is your key to this 'speakeasy' that is so well known you need to make advance reservations. Once inside the 30-seat lair, order a Dealer's Choice and study the brass skulls and oil paintings while the bartender whips up a bespoke potion according to your tastes.

Prohibition Lounge COCKTAIL BAR

(Map p948; http://prohibitionsd.com; 548 5th Ave; ⊙8pm-1:30am Tue-Sun) Find the unassuming doorway on 5th Ave with 'Eddie O'Hare's Law Office' on it, then flip the light switch on to alert the door staff, who'll guide you into a sensuously lit basement exuding a 1920s Prohibition vibe. If your date doesn't make you swoon, the innovative craft cocktails will. Dress nicely and keep that cell phone off.

☆ Entertainment

Check out the San Diego *CityBeat* or *San Diego Union Tribune* for the latest movies, theater, galleries and music gigs around town. **Arts Tix** (Map p948; ☑858-437-9850; www.sdartstix.com; Horton Plaza Park, South Pavilion; ⊙10am-4pm Tue-Thu, to 6pm Fri & Sat, to 2pm Sun), in a kiosk on Horton Plaza, has discounted tickets (up to half-price) for same-day evening or next-day matinee performances; it also offers regular and discounted tickets to other events. Ticketmaster (www.ticketmaster.com) also sells tickets to gigs around the city.

Balboa Theatre PERFORMING ARTS

(Map p948; ☑619-570-1100; http://sandiego theatres.org; 868 4th Ave) This elegant 1924 building began life as a vaudeville and movie theater, then presented Mexican films to a growing Latino audience in the 1930s before becoming a residence for US Navy bachelors during WWII. It now presents everything from Broadway shows to comedy and opera.

House of Blues LIVE MUSIC

(Map p948; ☑619-299-2583; www.houseof blues.com/sandiego; 1055 5th Ave; ⊙concerts usually 7pm) This Gaslamp venue presents an eclectic lineup of concerts (some free), a good-mood-inducing Sunday Gospel brunch, raucous party nights and other events. Come early for the daily happy hour (4pm to 6pm).

ℹ Information

MEDIA

Free listings magazines *San Diego Citybeat* (http://sdcitybeat.com) and *San Diego Reader* (www.sdreader.com) cover the active music, art and theater scenes. Find them in shops and cafes.

KPBS 89.5 FM (www.kpbs.org) National public radio station.

San Diego Magazine (www.sandiegomagazine. com) Glossy monthly.

San Diego Union Tribune (www.sandiegounion tribune.com) The city's major daily.

MEDICAL SERVICES

Scripps Mercy Hospital (☑ 619-294-8111; www.scripps.org; 4077 5th Ave; ⊙ 24hr) has a 24-hour emergency room. There are also 24-hour drugstores around the city, including CVS stores on Garnet Ave in Pacific Beach, on University Ave in North Park and on Market St in the Gaslamp Quarter.

TOURIST INFORMATION

Coronado Visitor Center (Map p946; ☑ 619-437-8788; www.coronadovisitorcenter.com; 1100 Orange Ave; ⊙ 9am-5pm Mon-Fri, 10am-5pm Sat & Sun)

San Diego Visitor Info Center (Map p948; ☑ 619-236-1242; www.sandiegovisit.org; 996 N Harbor Dr; ⊙ 9am-5pm) Across from the B St Cruise Ship Terminal; helpful staff offer very detailed neighborhood maps, sell discounted tickets to attractions and maintain a hotel-reservation hotline.

USEFUL WEBSITES

Gaslamp Quarter Association (http://gas lamp.org) Everything you need to know about the bustling Gaslamp Quarter, including parking secrets.

San Diego Tourism Authority (www.sandiego. org) Search hotels, sights, dining, rental cars and more, and make reservations.

❶ Getting There & Away

AIR

Most flights arriving into **San Diego International Airport** (SAN; Map p946; ☑ 619-400-2400; www.san.org; 3325 N Harbor Dr; ☎), just 3 miles west of Downtown, are domestic. All major US airlines serve San Diego, as do Air Canada, British Airways, Lufthansa, Japan Airlines and WestJet.

BUS

Greyhound (Map p948; ☑ 619-515-1100; www. greyhound.com; 1313 National Ave; ⊙ 5am-11:45pm; ☎) buses depart frequently for Los Angeles (from $12, three to 3½ hours) and there are several daily departures to Anaheim (from $14, 2½ hours). Buses to San Francisco (from $49, 11 to 13 hours, about seven daily) require a transfer in LA.

Several Flixbus (www.flixbus.com) buses daily make the trip to LA, where you can transfer to destinations including Las Vegas, Palm Springs and San Francisco. Fares fluctuate with demand but are generally very competitive.

CAR & MOTORCYCLE

Allow at least two hours to drive the 125 miles between San Diego and LA Downtowns in off-peak traffic. With peak traffic, it's anybody's guess. If your car has two or more passengers, you can use the high-occupancy vehicle lanes, which shave off a fair amount of time in heavy traffic.

TRAIN

Amtrak runs the *Pacific Surfliner* several times daily to Anaheim (two hours), LA (three hours) and Santa Barbara (5¾ hours) from the historic **Santa Fe Depot** (Amtrak Station; ☑ 800-872-7245; www.amtrak.com; 1050 Kettner Blvd). Some trains continue north to San Luis Obispo (8½ hours). Within San Diego County, trains stop in Solana Beach, Oceanside, San Clemente and San Juan Capistrano. Fares start from around $35 and the coastal views are enjoyable.

❶ Getting Around

While most people get around San Diego by car, it's possible to have an entire vacation here using your own two feet along with municipal buses and trolleys run by the Metropolitan Transit System (www.sdmts.com). Most buses/trolleys cost $2.25/2.50 per ride. Transfers are not available, so purchase a day pass (one-/two-/three-/four-day passes $5/9/12/15) if you're going to be taking more than two rides in a day. You will need a rechargeable Compass Card ($2 one-time purchase) available from ticket vending machines at trolley stations and the **MTS Transit Store** (☑ 619-234-1060; www.sdmts. com; 1255 Imperial Ave; ⊙ 8am-5pm Mon-Fri), which also has route maps. On buses, day passes may be purchased without a Compass Card ($7; exact fare required).

PALM SPRINGS & THE DESERTS

From swanky Palm Springs to desolate Death Valley, Southern California's desert region swallows up 25% of the entire state. What at first may seem harrowingly barren will eventually transform in your mind's eye to perfect beauty: weathered volcanic peaks, booming sand dunes, purple-tinged mountains, cactus gardens, tiny spring wildflowers pushing up from hard-baked soil, lizards scurrying beside colossal boulders and, in the night sky, uncountable stars. California's deserts are serenely spiritual, surprisingly chic and ultimately irresistible, whether you're a bohemian artist, movie star, rock climber or 4WD adventurer.

Palm Springs

The Rat Pack is back, baby, or at least its hangout is. In the 1950s and '60s, Palm Springs, some 100 miles east of LA, was the swinging getaway of Frank Sinatra, Elvis Presley and other Hollywood stars. Once the Rat Pack packed it in, Palm Springs surrendered to golfing retirees. However, in the mid-1990s, new generations discovered the city's retro-chic vibe and elegant mid-century-modern structures built by famous architects. Today, retirees and snowbirds mix comfortably with hipsters, hikers and a sizable LGBTQI+ community on getaways from LA and from across the globe.

◉ Sights & Activities

Driving along the I-10, about 20 miles west of Palm Springs, keep an eye out for the **World's Biggest Dinosaurs** (📞951-922-8700; www.cabazondinosaurs.com; 50770 Seminole Dr, Cabazon; adult/child $13/11; ⊙9am-6pm Mon-Fri, to 7pm Sat & Sun; 🅿🐾) on the north side of the freeway.

★ **Palm Springs Aerial Tramway** CABLE CAR
(📞760-325-1391; www.pstramway.com; 1 Tram Way, Palm Springs; adult/child $26/17, parking $8; ⊙1st tram up 10am Mon-Fri, 8am Sat & Sun, last tram up 8pm, last tram down 9:45pm daily, varies seasonally; 🅿🐾) This rotating cable car climbs nearly 6000ft vertically and covers five different vegetation zones, from the Sonoran desert floor to pine-scented Mt San Jacinto State Park, in 10 minutes during its 2.5-mile journey. From the mountain station (8561ft), which is 30°F to 40°F (up to 22°C) cooler than the desert floor, you can enjoy stupendous views, dine in two restaurants (ask about ride 'n' dine passes), explore more than 50 miles of trails or visit the natural-history museum.

★ **Sunnylands** HISTORIC BUILDING, GARDENS
(📞760-202-2222; www.sunnylands.org; 37977 Bob Hope Dr, Rancho Mirage; visitor center & gardens free, house tours $48; ⊙house tours Wed-Sun, visitor center & gardens 8:30am-4pm Thu-Sun mid-Sep–early Jun; 🅿) One of America's 'first families' of the 20th century, industrialist/diplomat/philanthropist couple Walter (1908–2002) and Leonore (1918–2009) Annenberg entertained seven US presidents, royalty, Hollywood celebrities and heads of state at their 200-acre winter retreat. The estate's art-filled main home, a 1966 mid-century-modern masterpiece by A Quincy Jones, is accessible only by

90-minute guided tour; book online far in advance. No reservations are required for the exhibits at the visitor center (built 2012) or magnificent desert gardens, inspired by impressionist paintings.

★ **Palm Springs Art Museum** MUSEUM
(📞760-322-4800; www.psmuseum.org; 101 Museum Dr, Palm Springs; adult/student $14/6; ⊙10am-5pm Fri-Tue, noon-8pm Thu; 🅿) Art fans should not miss this museum and its changing exhibitions drawn from a stellar collection of international modern and contemporary painting, sculpture, photography and glass art. The permanent collection includes works by Henry Moore, Ed Ruscha, Mark di Suvero, Frederic Remington and many more heavy hitters. Other highlights are glass art by Dale Chihuly and William Morris and a collection of pre-Colombian figurines. Free entry from 4pm to 8pm Thursdays.

Living Desert Zoo & Gardens ZOO
(📞760-346-5694; www.livingdesert.org; 47900 Portola Ave, Palm Desert; adult/child $20/10; ⊙9am-5pm Oct-May, 8am-1:30pm Jun-Sep; 🅿🐾) 🍃 This amazing animal park showcases desert plants and animals alongside exhibits on regional geology and Native American culture. Highlights include a walk-through wildlife hospital and an African-themed village with a fair-trade market and storytelling grove. Camel rides, giraffe feeding, a spin on the endangered species carousel, and a hop-on, hop-off shuttle cost extra. It's educational, fun and worth the 15-mile drive down-valley. Allow for a visit of two to three hours.

Indian Canyons HIKING
(📞760-323-6018; www.indian-canyons.com; 38520 S Palm Canyon Dr, Palm Springs; adult/child $9/5; ⊙8am-5pm daily Oct-Jun, Fri-Sun Jul-Sep) Streams flowing from the San Jacinto Mountains sustain rich plant varieties in oases around Palm Springs. Home to Native American communities for centuries, these canyons are a hiker's delight. Follow the Palm Canyon trail to the world's largest oasis of fan-palm trees, the Murray Canyon trail to a seasonal waterfall, or the Andreas Canyon trail to rock formations along a year-round creek.

🛏 Sleeping

Palm Springs and the desert towns of the Coachella Valley offer an astonishing variety of lodging, including fine vintage-flair boutique hotels, full-on luxury resorts and chain motels. Some places don't allow children.

★**Arrive Hotel** HOTEL **$$**

(☑760-227-7037; www.arrivehotels.com; 1551 N Palm Canyon Dr, Palm Springs; studios $190-390; P🐕❄🛜⛱🐾) 🅿 Rusted steel, wood and concrete are the main design ingredients of this stylish lair where the bar doubles as reception. The 32 spacious, phone-less rooms, some with enclosed patio, tick hipster boxes such as rain shower, Apple TV and fancy bath products. At weekends the pool, bar and restaurant turn into a lively party zone for both guests and locals.

★**El Morocco Inn & Spa** BOUTIQUE HOTEL **$$**

(☑760-288-2527; http://elmoroccoinn.com; 66810 4th St, Desert Hot Springs; r $150-230; ⊙check-in 8:30am-7pm or by arrangement; P🐕❄🛜⛱) Heed the call of the casbah at this drop-dead gorgeous hideaway where the scene is set for romance. Twelve exotically furnished rooms wrap around a pool deck where your enthusiastic hosts serve free 'Morocco-tinis' during happy hour. The on-site spa offers tempting treatments; the Moroccan Mystical Ritual includes a 'Moroccan Rain' massage that uses seven detoxifying essential oils. Breakfast included.

Caliente Tropics MOTEL **$$**

(☑760-327-1391; www.calientetropics.com; 411 E Palm Canyon Dr, Palm Springs; r from $170; P❄🛜⛱🐾) Frank Sinatra and the Rat Pack once frolicked poolside at this newly spruced 1964 tiki-style motor lodge. Wrap up the day with a tropical potion in the dimly lit Reef Bar before drifting off to dreamland on quality mattresses in spacious rooms decorated with Polynesian posters.

★**L'Horizon** BOUTIQUE HOTEL **$$$**

(☑760-323-1858; http://lhorizonpalmsprings. com; 1050 E Palm Canyon Dr, Palm Springs; r from $340; P❄🛜⛱🐾) The intimate William F Cody–designed retreat that saw celebs such as Marilyn Monroe and Ronald Reagan lounging poolside has been rebooted as a sleek and chic adults-only desert resort, with 25 bungalows scattered across generous grounds for maximum privacy. Treat yourself to alfresco showers, a chemical-free swimming pool and a private patio.

✖ Eating

A lineup of zeitgeist-capturing restaurants has seriously elevated the level of dining in Palm Springs. The most exciting, including several with eye-catching design, flank N Palm Canyon Dr in the Uptown design district.

★**Cheeky's** CALIFORNIAN **$**

(☑760-327-7595; www.cheekysps.com; 622 N Palm Canyon Dr; mains $9-15; ⊙8am-2pm; ❄) Waits can be long and service only so-so at this breakfast and lunch spot, but the farm-to-table menu dazzles with witty inventiveness. The kitchen tinkers with the offerings on a weekly basis but perennial faves such as custardy scrambled eggs and grass-fed burger with pesto fries never rotate off the list.

Trio CALIFORNIAN **$$**

(☑760-864-8746; www.triopalmsprings.com; 707 N Palm Canyon Dr; mains lunch $10-22, dinner $15-32; ⊙11am-10pm Mon-Thu, to 11pm Fri, 10am-11pm Sat, 10am-10pm Sun; 🐾) The winning formula in this '60s modernist space: updated American comfort food (awesome Yankee pot roast) enjoyed surrounded by eye-catching artwork and picture windows. The $23 prix-fixe three-course dinner (served until 6pm) is a steal, and the all-day daily happy hour lures a rocking after-work crowd with bar bites and cheap drinks.

★**Workshop Kitchen + Bar** AMERICAN **$$$**

(☑760-459-3451; www.workshoppalmsprings. com; 800 N Palm Canyon Dr; small plates $16-21, mains $28-38; ⊙5-10pm Mon-Thu, to 11pm Fri & Sat, 10am-2pm Sun; ❄) Hidden away in the back of the ornate 1920s El Paseo building, a large patio with olive trees leads to this starkly beautiful space. At its center is a long, communal table flanked by mood-lit booths. The kitchen crafts market-driven American classics reinterpreted for the 21st century and the bar is among the most happening in town.

🍷 Drinking & Nightlife

Drinking has always been in style in Palm Springs and many bars and restaurants have hugely popular happy hours that sometimes run all day. A handful of speakeasy bars spice up the cocktail scene and craft beer continues to be a draw. Friday is the big night out for the gay crowd.

Arenas Rd, east of Indian Canyon Dr, is nightlife central for the LGBTQI+ community.

★**Bootlegger Tiki** COCKTAIL BAR

(☑760-318-4154; www.bootlegkertiki.com; 1101 N Palm Canyon Dr; ⊙4pm-2am) Crimson light bathes even pasty-faced hipsters with a healthy glow, as do the pretty crafted cocktails at this teensy tiki bar with blowfish lamps and rattan walls.

Birba BAR

(☑760-327-5678; www.birbaps.com; 622 N Palm Canyon Dr; ☺5-11pm Tue-Sun Nov-May, 6-10pm Wed, Thu & Sun, to 11pm Fri & Sat Jun-Oct; ☏) On a balmy night, Birba's hedge-fringed patio with twinkle lights and a sunken firepit brings a dolce vita vibe to the desert. Unwind with a glass of frizzante or smooth cocktails such as the tequila-based Heated Snake, and stave off the blur with pizza or a plate of cheese and prosciutto.

🛍 Shopping

For art galleries, design and fashion boutiques – including the fabulous **Trina Turk** (☑760-416-2856; www.trinaturk.com; 891 N Palm Canyon Dr; ☺10am-6pm Mon-Sat, 11am-5pm Sun) – head 'Uptown' to North Palm Canyon Dr. Thrift, vintage and consignment shops are scattered around downtown Palm Springs and down-valley along Hwy 111. For luxe labels, poke around Palm Desert's El Paseo, while bargain bunnies should steer 20 miles west on I-10 to the Desert Hills Premium Outlets mall.

ⓘ Information

Palm Springs Historical Society (☑760-323-8297; www.pshistoricalsociety.org; 221 S Palm Canyon Dr; ☺10am-4pm) Volunteer-staffed nonprofit organization. Maintains two museums and offers guided tours focusing on local history, architecture and celebrities.

Palm Springs Modern App Free app for iPhone and Android covering more than 80 iconic mid-century modern private homes and public buildings on three tours enhanced with videos, audio and photographs.

Palm Springs Visitors Center (☑760-778-8418; www.visitpalmsprings.com; 2901 N Palm Canyon Dr; ☺9am-5pm) Well-stocked and well-staffed official visitor center in a 1965 Albert Frey–designed gas station at the Palm Springs Aerial Tram turnoff, 3 miles north of downtown.

ⓘ Getting There & Around

Palm Springs International Airport (PSP; ☑760-318-3800; www.palmspringsairport.com; 3400 E Tahquitz Canyon Way) is a regional airport served year-round by 10 airlines, including United, American, Virgin, Delta and Alaska, and has flights throughout North America.

Palm Springs and the Coachella Valley are pancake-flat, and more bike lanes are being built all the time. Many hotels have loaner bicycles, or try **Bike Palm Springs** (☑760-832-8912; www.bikepsrentals.com; 194 S Indian Canyon Dr; std/kids/electric/tandem bikes half-day from $25/15/45/40, full day $35/20/60/50;

☺8am-5pm Oct-May, to 10am Jun-Sep) or Palm Desert–based **Funseekers** (☑760-647-6042, 760-340-3861; www.palmdesertbikerentals.com; 73-865 Hwy 111, Palm Desert; bicycle per 24hr/3 days/week from $25/60/95; ☺8:30am-5pm Mon-Fri, to 4pm Sat & Sun).

SunLine (☑760-343-3451; www.sunline.org; tickets $1) Alternative-fuel-powered public buses travel around the valley, albeit slowly. Bus 111 links Palm Springs with Palm Desert (one hour) and Indio (1½ hours) via Hwy 111. Buses have air-conditioning, wheelchair lifts and a bicycle rack. Cash only (bring exact change).

Buzz Trolley (www.sunline.org; ☺noon-10pm Thu-Sat) This free shuttle operates from noon to 10pm Thursday through Sunday at more or less 20-minute intervals on a loop covering N Palm Canyon Dr from Via Escuela as far as Smoketree on E Palm Canyon and then back up Indian Canyon Dr.

Joshua Tree National Park

Looking like something from Dr Seuss, the whimsical Joshua trees (actually tree-sized yuccas) welcome visitors to this 794,000-acre **park** (☑760-367-5500; www.nps.gov/jotr; 7-day pass per car $30; 🅿🚽) 🏕 at the transition zone of two deserts: the low and dry Colorado and the higher, moister and slightly cooler Mojave.

Rock climbers know 'JT' as the best place to climb in California; hikers seek out hidden, shady, desert-fan-palm oases fed by natural springs and small streams; and mountain bikers are hypnotized by the desert vistas.

In springtime the Joshua trees send up a huge single cream-colored flower. Mormon settlers named the trees for their branches stretching up toward heaven, which reminded them of the biblical prophet Joshua pointing the way to the promised land. The mystical quality of this stark, boulder-strewn landscape has inspired many artists, most famously the band U2, who titled their hit 1987 album *The Joshua Tree*.

⊙ Sights & Activities

If your time is limited, focus your exploration on the park's northern end where clumps of Joshua trees and otherworldly rock formations create a dramatic landscape. A drive from the west entrance in Joshua Tree to the Oasis Visitor Center in Twentynine Palms (or vice versa) takes about two hours and is a great introduction. Lots of roadside pullouts invite closer inspection as do numerous trails.

Barker Dam and **Hidden Valley** loop trails, both about 1 mile long, offer a quick

WORTH A TRIP

PIONEERTOWN

Looking like an 1870s frontier town, **Pioneertown** (Pioneertown Rd; ⊗24hr; P 🐾) FREE, about 5 miles north of 29 Palms Hwy/Hwy 62, was actually built in 1946 as a Hollywood Western movie set. Gene Autry and Roy Rogers were among the original investors, and more than 50 movies and several TV shows were filmed here in the 1940s and '50s. These days, it's fun to stroll around the old buildings and drop into the local honky-tonk for refreshments. Mock gunfights take place on 'Mane St' at 2:30pm every second and fourth Saturday, September to June.

Make a night of it and bed down at the **Pioneertown Motel** (☑760-365-7001; www. pioneertown-motel.com; 5040 Curtis Rd, Pioneertown; d from $185; P ❋ 🐾 ☎), where yesteryear's silver-screen stars slept while filming. New owners have upgraded the elegant-rustic rooms with wooden A-frame ceilings, Native American rugs, decorative Western paraphernalia and the essential creature comforts.

immersion into JT's lunar landscape. For sunset-worthy views of the park and the entire Coachella Valley, drive up to **Keys View**.

If you're interested in pioneer history, book ahead for a tour of **Keys Ranch** (☑ reservations 760-367-5522; www.nps.gov/jotr; tours adult/child 6-11yr $10/5, plus park admission; ⊗tours Oct-May; P 🐾).

The southern end of the park is a stark and windy desert landscape. A highlight here is the **Cholla Cactus Garden** (0.25-mile loop). For a scenic 4WD route, tackle bumpy 18-mile **Geology Tour Road**, also open to mountain bikers.

🛏 Sleeping

Of the park's eight campgrounds, only **Cottonwood** (☑760-367-5500, reservations 877-444-6777; www.nps.gov/jotr; Pinto Basin Rd; tent & RV sites $20; P) and **Black Rock** (☑760-367-5500, reservations 877-444-6777; www.nps.gov/jotr; Joshua Lane; tent & RV sites $20; P) have potable water, flush toilets and dump stations. The two also accept reservations, as do **Indian Cove** (☑760-362-4367, reservations 877-444-6777; www.nps.gov/jotr; Indian Cove Rd, Twentynine Palms; tent & RV sites $20; P) and Jumbo Rocks. The others are first-come, first-served and have pit toilets, picnic tables and fire grates. None have showers, but there are some at **Coyote Corner** (☑760-366-9683; www.jtcoyotecorner.com; 6535 Park Blvd, Joshua Tree; ⊗9am-6pm) in Joshua Tree. Details are available at www.nps.gov/jotr or by calling ☑760-367-5500.

Between October and May, campsites fill by Thursday noon, especially during the springtime bloom. If you arrive too late, there's overflow camping on Bureau of Land Management (BLM) land north and south of the park as well as in private campgrounds.

For details, see www.nps.gov/jotr/planyour visit/camping-outside-of-the-park.htm.

Budget and midrange motels line Hwy 62. Twentynine Palms and Yucca Valley have mostly national chain motels, while pads in Joshua Tree as well as in Pioneertown and Landers north of Hwy 62 come with plenty of charm and character.

Harmony Motel MOTEL **$**
(☑760-401-1309, 760-367-3351; www.harmony motel.com; 71161 29 Palms Hwy/Hwy 62, Twentynine Palms; r $90-95; P ➰ ❋ 🛜 ☎) This immaculately kept 1950s motel, run by the charming Ash, was where U2 stayed while working on the *Joshua Tree* album. It has a small pool and seven large, cheerfully painted and handsomely decorated rooms (some with kitchenette) set around a tidy desert garden with serenely dramatic views. Free coffee and tea are available in the communal guest kitchen.

★**Kate's Lazy Desert** CABIN **$$**
(☑845-688-7200; www.lazymeadow.com; 58380 Botkin Rd, Landers; Airstreams Mon-Thu $175, Fri & Sat $200; P ➰ ❋ 🛜 ☎) Owned by Kate Pierson of the band B-52s, this desert camp has a coin-sized pool (May to October) and half-a-dozen artist-designed Airstream trailers to sleep inside. Sporting names such as 'Tinkerbell,' 'Planet Air' and ' Hot Lava,' each is kitted out with matching fantasia-pop design, a double bed and a kitchenette.

★**Sacred Sands** GUESTHOUSE **$$$**
(☑760-974-2353, 760-424-6407; www.sacred sands.com; 63155 Quail Springs Rd, Joshua Tree; studios/ste $339/369; P ➰ ❋ 🛜) 🌱 In an isolated, pin-drop-quiet spot, these two desert-chic suites are the ultimate romantic retreat. Each has a kitchenette and a private patio with outdoor shower, hot tub and

hanging bed for sleeping under the stars. There are astounding views across the desert hills and into Joshua Tree National Park. Rates include a fridge stocked with breakfast supplies. Two-night minimum.

✗ Eating

There's no food available inside the park, but there are supermarkets and convenience stores in the communities along Hwy 62 (especially Yucca Valley). Restaurants range from mom-and-pop-run greasy spoons to organic delis, funky diners and ethnic eats. On Saturday mornings, locals gather for gossip and groceries at the **farmers market** (www.joshuatreefarmersmarket.com; 61705 29 Palms Hwy/Hwy 62, Joshua Tree; ⊗8am-1pm Sat) in Joshua Tree. Before hitting the trail, rocks or road, fuel up at **Crossroads Cafe** (☑760-366-5414; www.crossroadscafejtree.com; 61715 29 Palms Hwy/Hwy 62, Joshua Tree; mains $9-17; ⊗7am-9pm; 🛜🖐), a JT institution.

★ **La Copine**　　　　INTERNATIONAL $$
(☑760-289-8537; www.lacopinekitchen.com; 848 Old Woman Springs Rd, Flamingo Heights; dishes $8-24; ⊗2-7pm Thu-Sun; 🖐) It's a long road from Philadelphia to the high desert, but that's where Nikki and Claire decided to take their farm-to-table cuisine from pop-up to bricks and mortar. Their roadside bistro serves zeitgeist-capturing dishes such as the signature salad with smoked salmon and poached egg, rock shrimp ceviche or banh mi sandwich. No reservations.

❶ Information

Entry permits ($30 per vehicle) are valid for seven days and are available at the three park entrances as well as National Park Service (NPS) visitor centers at **Joshua Tree** (www.nps.gov/jotr; 6554 Park Blvd, Joshua Tree; ⊗8am-5pm; 🛜), **Oasis** (☑760-367-5522; www.nps.gov/jotr; 74485 National Park Dr, Twentynine Palms; ⊗8:30am-5pm) and **Cottonwood** (www.nps.gov/jotr; Cottonwood Springs; ⊗8:30am-4pm; 🖐). On weekends (Friday to Sunday) from November to February and daily in March and April, free shuttle buses loop around key stops in the northern park hourly from the Twentynine Palms Transit Center and the Oasis Visitor Center. No park pass is required.

There are no park facilities aside from restrooms, so bring all the drinking water and food you'll need. Get gas and stock up in the communities on 29 Palms Hwy (aka Hwy 62) along the park's northern boundary: Yucca Valley, Joshua Tree or Twentynine Palms. Coming from the south (via I-10), Indio is the nearest larger town.

Anza-Borrego Desert State Park

Shaped by an ancient sea and tectonic forces, enormous and little-developed **Anza-Borrego** (☑760-767-4205; www.parks.ca.gov; day use $10; 🅿) 🖉 covers 640,000 acres, making it the largest state park in California. Human history here goes back more than 10,000 years, as recorded by Native American pictographs and petroglyphs. The park is named for Spanish explorer Juan Bautista de Anza, who arrived in 1774 while pioneering a colonial trail from Mexico and no doubt running into countless *borregos,* the wild bighorn sheep that once ranged as far south as Baja California. (Today only a few hundred of these animals survive due to drought, disease, poaching and off-highway driving.) In the 1850s Anza-Borrego became a stop along the Butterfield Stagecoach line, which delivered mail between St Louis and San Francisco.

◉ Sights & Activities

Two miles west of central Borrego Springs, the park **visitor center** (☑760-767-4205; www.parks.ca.gov; 200 Palm Canyon Dr, Borrego Springs; ⊗9am-5pm daily Oct-May, Sat, Sun & holidays only Jun-Sep) has natural-history exhibits, information handouts and updates on road conditions. Driving through the park is free, but if you camp, hike or picnic, a day-use parking fee ($10 per car) applies. You'll need a 4WD to tackle most of the 500 miles of backcountry dirt roads. If you're hiking, always bring plenty of water.

Park highlights accessible without 4WD include the popular (and busy) 3-mile round-trip **Borrego Palm Canyon Nature Trail**, the easy 2-mile round-trip **Pictograph Trail** in Blair Valley, which has Native American pictographs and pioneer traces, and the fairly strenuous 6-mile round-trip **Maidenhair Falls Trail** into Hellhole Canyon. Check road and trail conditions at the visitor center before setting out.

Further south, you can soak in concreted hot-spring pools at **Agua Caliente Regional Park** (☑760-765-1188; www.sdparks.org; 39555 Great Southern Overland Stage Route of 1849/County Rte S2; per car $3, pools per person $3; ⊗9:30am-sunset Sep-May).

More than 500 miles of the park's dirt and paved roads (but never hiking trails) are open to mountain bikes. Popular routes are Grapevine Canyon off Hwy 78 and Canyon

Sin Nombre in the Carrizo Badlands. Flatter areas include Blair Valley and Split Mountain. Get details at the visitor center.

🛏 Sleeping

A handful of motels and hotels cluster in and around Borrego Springs, but not all are open year-round. Otherwise, camping is the only way to spend the night in the park. In addition to developed campgrounds, free backcountry camping is permitted anywhere. Note that vehicles must be parked no more than one vehicle length off the road and that all campfires must be in metal containers. Gathering vegetation (dead or alive) is strictly prohibited.

Borrego Palm Canyon Campground   CAMPGROUND $
(☎ 800-444-7275; www.reservecalifornia.com; 200 Palm Canyon Dr, Borrego Springs; tent/RV sites $25/35; ⓟ🐾) Near the Anza-Borrego Desert State Park Visitor Center (p960), this campground is a great base from which to explore the park. Despite its size, it fills up quickly on weekends, thanks in part to its modern amenities, including drinking water, flush toilets and hot, coin-operated showers.

★ **La Casa del Zorro**   RESORT $$$
(☎ 760-767-0100; www.lacasadelzorro.com; 3845 Yaqui Pass Rd; r from $240 mid-Oct–Apr, $90-160 May–mid-Oct; ⓟ❄🛜🏊🐾) Completely updated, this venerable 1937 resort is again the region's grandest stay. The ambience exudes desert romance in 67 elegantly rustic poolside rooms and family-sized casitas sporting vaulted ceilings and marble bathtubs. A staggering 28 pools and Jacuzzis are scattered across the 42 landscaped acres, and there's a spa, five tennis courts, a fun bar and a gourmet restaurant.

🍴 Eating

Borrego Springs has a few restaurants, from spit-and-sawdust Mexican joints to fine dining. The best supermarket is **Center Market** (☎ 760-767-3311; www.centermarket-borrego.com; 590 Palm Canyon Dr, Borrego Springs; ⊗8:30am-6:30pm Mon-Sat, to 5pm Sun; ⓟ), also in Borrego Springs. In summer many places keep shorter hours or have closing days.

★ **Red Ocotillo**   INTERNATIONAL $$
(☎ 760-767-7400; http://redocotillo.com; 721 Avenida Sureste, Borrego Springs; mains $11-20; ⊗7am-8:30pm; 🛜🐾🏊) Empty tables are as rare as puddles in the desert at this artily painted charmer in a central Borrego Springs bungalow. Carb-load for a day on the trail with the breakfast burrito; tuck into bulging sandwiches at lunch; or wrap up the day with short ribs and serves of linguine with homemade pesto sauce. Lovely desert views from the patios.

ℹ Information

Borrego Springs has an ATM, two gas stations, a supermarket and a post office, all on Palm Canyon Dr. There's free public wi-fi around Christmas Circle.

Call the wildflower hotline (760-767-4684) for information on seasonal blooms.

Mojave National Preserve

If you're on a quest for the 'middle of nowhere,' you'll find it in the wilderness of the **Mojave National Preserve** (☎760-252-6100; www.nps.gov/moja; btwn I-15 & I-40; ⓟ) 🆓FREE, a 1.6-million-acre jumble of sand dunes, Joshua trees, volcanic cinder cones and habitats for bighorn sheep, jackrabbit and desert tortoise. Warning: no gas is available here.

Southeast of Baker and the I-15 freeway, Kelbaker Rd crosses a ghostly landscape of cinder cones before arriving at **Kelso Depot**, a 1920s Mission-style railroad station. It now houses the park's main **visitor center** (☎760-252-6100; www.nps.gov/moja; Kelbaker Rd, Kelso; ⊗9am-5pm), which has excellent natural and cultural history exhibits.

It's another 12 miles south on Kelbaker Rd to the **Kelso Dunes**. Under the right conditions they emanate low humming sounds caused by shifting sands – running downhill sometimes jump-starts the effect. From Kelso Depot, Kelso–Cima Rd takes off northeast.

Some 27 miles northeast of Kelso Depot, via Kelso–Cima Rd, **Cima Dome** is a 1500ft hunk of granite spiked with volcanic cinder cones and crusty lava outcrops. Its slopes are smothered in the world's largest **Joshua tree forest**. For close-ups, tackle the 3-mile round-trip **Teutonia Peak**; the trailhead is on Cima Rd, 5 miles northwest of Cima Junction.

There is no food inside the preserve, so stock up in Baker, on the northwestern edge along I-15, before heading out. Here, you'll also find plenty of cheap but charmless motels. Coming from the northeast, the casino hotels in Primm on the Nevada border offer slightly better options. If you're traveling on the I-40, Needles is the closest town to spend the night. Once you're in the preserve, camping is the only option.

SALTON SEA & SALVATION MOUNTAIN

East of Anza-Borrego and south of Joshua Tree awaits a most unexpected sight: the **Salton Sea** (☑760-393-3810; www.parks.ca.gov; 100-225 State Park Rd, North Shore; day use per car $7; ⊙park 24hr, visitor center 10am-4pm; P), California's largest lake in the middle of its largest desert. It was created accidentally in 1905 after high spring flooding breached irrigation canals built to bring Colorado River water to farmland in the Imperial Valley. To this day, it provides habitat for around 400 species of migratory birds, but their survival is threatened by rising salinity from decades of phosphor and nitrogen in agricultural runoff that's yet to be cleaned up.

Perhaps even more bizarre is **Salvation Mountain** (☑760-624-8754; www.salvation mountaininc.org; 603 E Beal Rd, Niland; donations accepted; ⊙dawn-dusk; P), a 100ft-high hill of hand-mixed adobe and straw slathered in paint and decorated with flowers, found objects and Christian messages. It's the life's work of folk artist Leonard Knight (1931–2014).

Death Valley National Park

The very name evokes all that is harsh, hot and hellish – a punishing, barren and lifeless place of Old Testament severity. Yet closer inspection reveals that in **Death Valley** (☑760-786-3200; www.nps.gov/deva; 7-day-pass per car $30; P ⯑) ⯑ nature is putting on a truly spectacular show: singing sand dunes, water-sculpted canyons, boulders moving across the desert floor, extinct volcanic craters, palm-shaded oases, stark mountains rising to 11,000ft and plenty of endemic wildlife. This is a land of superlatives, holding the US records for hottest temperature (134°F/57°C), lowest point (Badwater, 282ft below sea level) and largest national park outside Alaska (more than 5000 sq miles).

Furnace Creek is Death Valley's commercial hub, home to the park's main visitor center, a general store, gas station, post office, ATM, wi-fi, golf course, lodging and restaurants.

Park entry permits ($30 per vehicle) are valid for seven days and available from self-service pay stations at the park's access roads and at the visitor center.

◎ Sights & Activities

In summer, stick to paved roads, limit your exertions outdoors to early morning hours and night, and visit higher-elevation areas of the park. From **Furnace Creek**, drive 5 miles southeast up to **Zabriskie Point** for spectacular views across the valley and golden badlands eroded into waves, pleats and gullies. Keep going for another 20 miles to **Dante's View** where, on clear days, you can simultaneously see the highest (Mt Whitney,

14,505ft) and lowest (Badwater) points in the contiguous USA.

Badwater is an eerily beautiful landscape of crinkly salt flats 15 miles south of Furnace Creek. Along the way, **Golden Canyon** is easily explored on a short hike. A 9-mile detour along **Artists Drive** through a narrow canyon is best in late afternoon when the exposed minerals and volcanic ash erupt in colorful fireworks.

Some 23 miles northwest of Furnace Creek, near Stovepipe Wells Village, you can trek across Sahara-like **Mesquite Flat** sand dunes – magical at sunrise and under a full moon – and scramble past the multihued rock walls of **Mosaic Canyon**.

About 55 miles northwest of Furnace Creek, whimsical **Scotty's Castle** (☑760-786-3200; www.nps.gov/deva; ⊙closed) was the desert home of Walter E Scott, alias 'Death Valley Scotty,' a quintessential teller of tall tales who captivated people with his stories of gold. The castle is closed due to flood damage until at least 2020.

⯑ Sleeping & Eating

Camping is plentiful but if you're looking for a place with a solid roof, in-park options are limited, pricey and often fully booked in springtime. Alternative bases are the gateway towns of Beatty (40 miles from Furnace Creek), Lone Pine (40 miles), Death Valley Junction (30 miles) and Tecopa (70 miles). Options a bit further afield include Ridgecrest (120 miles) and Las Vegas (140 miles).

If you're camping, bring in supplies from outside the park or else pay top dollar at stores in Stopepipe Wells, Furnace Creek and Panamint Springs. Generally speaking, restaurants here are expensive and mediocre.

Mesquite Spring Campground CAMPGROUND $
(☑760-786-3200; www.nps.gov/deva; Hwy 190; tent & RV sites $14) In the northern reaches of the park, this first-come, first-served campground has only 30 spaces and is a handy base for Ubehebe Crater and Racetrack Rd. At an elevation of 1800ft, it's also a lot cooler than the desert floor. Sites come with firepits and tables, and there's water and flush toilets. No RV hookups.

Ranch at Death Valley RESORT $$
(☑760-786-2345; www.oasisatdeathvalley.com; Hwy 190, Furnace Creek; d from $190; P◯❄️🛜🏊) Tailor-made for families, this rambling resort consists of 224 rooms with patios or balconies in one- and two-story buildings that flank lawns and lanes. Recent upgrades have resulted in a welcoming Spanish Colonial town square and an upgraded general store and saloon bar. The grounds also encompass a playground, a spring-fed swimming pool, tennis courts, a golf course and the **Borax Museum** (☑760-786-2345; www.furnacecreekresort.com; off Hwy 190, Furnace Creek; ◯9am-9pm Oct-May, hours vary in summer; P👟) **FREE**.

★**Inn at Death Valley** HOTEL $$$
(☑760-786-2345, reservations 800-236-7916; www.oasisatdeathvalley.com; Furnace Creek, Hwy 190; d from $390; P◯❄️@🛜🏊) Roll out of bed, pull back the curtains and count the colors of the desert at this 1927 Spanish Mission–style hotel that emerged from a major rejuvenation in 2018. After a day of sweaty touring, languid valley views await as you relax by the spring-fed swimming pool with a spa and pool bar, in the warmly furnished lounge or in the library. A class act throughout.

ℹ️ Information

Furnace Creek Visitor Center (☑760-786-3200; www.nps.gov/deva; Furnace Creek; ◯8am-5pm; 🛜) Modern visitor center with engaging exhibits on the park's ecosystem and indigenous tribes as well as a gift shop, clean toilets, (slow) wi-fi and friendly rangers to answer questions and help plan your day. First-time visitors should watch the gorgeously shot 20-minute movie. Check the schedule for ranger-led activities.

CENTRAL COAST

Too often forgotten or dismissed as 'flyover' country between San Francisco and LA, this fairy-tale stretch of California coast is packed with wild beaches, misty redwood forests where hot springs hide, and rolling golden hills of fertile vineyards and farm fields.

Coastal Hwy 1 pulls out all the stops, scenery-wise. Flower-power Santa Cruz and the historic port town of Monterey are gateways to the rugged wilderness of the bohemian Big Sur coast. It's an epic journey snaking down to vainglorious Hearst Castle, past lighthouses and edgy cliffs atop which endangered condors soar.

Get acquainted with California's agricultural heartland along inland Hwy 101, named El Camino Real (the King's Highway) by Spanish conquistadors and Franciscan friars. Colonial missions still line the route, which passes through Paso Robles' flourishing wine and craft-beer country. Then soothe your nature-loving soul in collegiate San Luis Obispo, ringed by sunny beach towns and volcanic peaks.

Santa Barbara

Perfect weather, beautiful buildings, excellent bars and restaurants, and activities for all tastes and budgets make Santa Barbara a great place to live (as the locals will proudly tell you) and a must-see place for visitors to Southern California. Check out the Spanish Mission church first, then just see where the day takes you.

👁️ Sights

Overlooking busy municipal beaches, 1872 **Stearns Wharf** (www.stearnswharf.org; ◯daily; P👟) **FREE** is the West's oldest continuously operating wooden pier; it's strung with touristy shops and restaurants. Outside town off Hwy 101, bigger palm-fringed **state beaches** await at Carpinteria, 12 miles east, and El Capitan and Refugio, more than 20 miles west.

★**Old Mission Santa Barbara** CHURCH
(☑805-682-4713; www.santabarbaramission.org; 2201 Laguna St; adult/child 5-17yr $12/7; ◯9am-4:15pm Sep-Jun, to 5:15pm Jul & Aug; P) California's 'Queen of the Missions' reigns above the city on a hilltop perch more than a mile north of downtown. Its imposing Ionic facade, an architectural homage to an ancient Roman chapel, is topped by an unusual twin-bell tower. Inside the mission's 1820 stone church, notice the striking Chumash artwork. In the cemetery the elaborate mausoleums of early California settlers stand out, while the graves of thousands of Chumash lie largely forgotten.

RHYOLITE

Just outside the Death Valley eastern park boundary (about 35 miles from Furnace Creek), the ghost town of **Rhyolite** (off Hwy 374; ☺24hr; P) FREE epitomizes the hurly-burly, boom-and-bust story of Western gold-rush mining towns in the early 1900s; it had 8000 residents during its peak years between 1904 and 1916. Among the skeletal remains of houses, highlights are the Spanish Mission–style train station, a three-story bank building and a house made of 50,000 beer bottles.

Near Rhyolite, just east of Death Valley National Park, **Goldwell Open Air Museum** (☎702-870-9946; www.goldwellmuseum.org; off Hwy 374; ☺park 24hr, visitor center 10am-4pm Mon-Sat, to 2pm summer; P) FREE was begun in 1984 by the late Belgian artist Albert Szukalski with his haunting version of Da Vinci's *Last Supper*. Other Belgian friends soon joined him and added further, often bizarre, sculptures. Today there are seven sculptures as well as a visitor center and a small store.

★**MOXI** MUSEUM
(Wolf Museum of Exploration & Innovation; ☎805-770-5000; www.moxi.org; 125 State St; adult/child $15/10; ☺10am-5pm; ⚑) This next-gen science museum is an interactive treasure trove of exhibits and experiences related to sound, technology, speed, light and color that are sure to delight and enlighten little ones. On three floors they can learn about music (by stepping inside a giant guitar), building a race car, or re-creating sound effects from famous movie scenes. Don't miss the views from the Sky Garden roof terrace and a nerve-challenging walk across a glass ceiling.

★**Santa Barbara County Courthouse** HISTORIC BUILDING
(☎805-962-6464; http://sbcourthouse.org; 1100 Anacapa St; ☺8am-5pm Mon-Fri, 10am-5pm Sat & Sun) FREE Built in Spanish-Moorish Revival style in 1929, the courthouse features hand-painted ceilings, wrought-iron chandeliers and tiles from Tunisia and Spain. On the 2nd floor, step inside the hushed mural room depicting Spanish-colonial history, then head up to El Mirador, the 85ft clock tower, for arch-framed panoramas of the city, ocean and mountains. Explore on your own or join a free hour-long tour offered at 2pm daily and 10:30am Monday to Friday, starting in the Mural Room on the 2nd floor.

🏃 Activities

Santa Barbara Sailing Center CRUISE
(☎805-962-2826; www.sbsail.com; Marina 4, off Harbor Way; ☺9am-6pm, to 5pm winter; ⚑) Climb aboard the *Double Dolphin,* a 50ft sailing catamaran, for a two-hour coastal or sunset cruise ($40); join a whale-watching trip ($50), offered from mid-February to mid-May; or hop on for a one-hour spin around the harbor

to view marine life ($25). The outfit also offers kayak and SUP rentals and tours.

Condor Express CRUISE
(☎805-882-0088; https://condorexpress.com; 301 W Cabrillo Blvd; 150/270min cruises adult from $50/99, child 5-12yr from $30/50; ⚑) Take a whale-watching excursion aboard the high-speed catamaran *Condor Express.* Whale sightings are guaranteed, so if you miss out the first time, you'll get a free voucher for another cruise.

🛌 Sleeping

Prepare for sticker shock: even basic motel rooms by the beach command more than $200 in summer. Don't arrive without reservations and expect to find something reasonably priced, especially not on weekends. A good selection of renovated motels are tucked between the harbor and the 101 freeway, just about walking distance to everything. Cheaper motels cluster along upper State St and Hwy 101 northbound to Goleta and southbound to Carpinteria, Ventura and Camarillo.

★**Santa Barbara Auto Camp** CAMPGROUND $$
(☎888-405-7553; http://autocamp.com/sb; 2717 De La Vina St; d $180-390; P❄☎☺) 🌿 Ramp up the retro chic and bed down with vintage style in one of six shiny silver Airstream trailers parked next to a historic RV park near upper State St, north of downtown. Sporting crisp mid-century-modern looks, all come with TV, fancy bedding and bath products, as well as a basic kitchen, patio with electric barbecue, and two cruiser bikes.

Harbor House Inn INN $$
(☎805-962-9745; www.harborhouseinn.com; 104 Bath St; r from $190; P☺❄☎) Two blocks

from the beach, this meticulously run inn offers bright sandy-hued studios with hardwood floors, small kitchens and mod cons such as SmartTVs with free Netflix and Hulu. If you're staying two nights or more, rates include a welcome basket of breakfast goodies. Make use of free loaner beach towels, chairs, umbrellas and three-speed bicycles.

★ **Hotel Californian**   BOUTIQUE HOTEL **$$$**
(www.thehotelcalifornian.com; 36 State St; r from $400; P🅿❄🛜🏊) Hotel Californian is the new kid on the once-run-down block that is the lower end of State St. Spearheading the area's rehabilitation, it would be worth staying here just for the prime location (next to the beach, Stearns Wharf and the Funk Zone) but its appeal goes way beyond geography. A winning architectural mix of Spanish Colonial and North African Moorish styles set a glamorous tone.

✕ Eating

Restaurants abound along downtown's State St, and even the wharf and pier have a few gems among the touristy claptrap. More creative kitchens are found in the Funk Zone, while east of downtown, Milpas St has great taco shops. Book a week or two ahead for popular places or somewhere you're particularly keen to eat, especially on summer weekends..

La Super-Rica Taqueria   MEXICAN **$**
(☑805-963-4940; 622 N Milpas St; tacos $2.50; ⏱11am-9pm Thu-Tue; 🚻) Although there's plenty of good Mexican food in town, La Super-Rica is deluged daily by locals and visitors keen on tasting the dishes once so loved by the late culinary queen Julia Child. Join the line outside the airy casita to tuck into tacos, tamales and other Mexican staples, and see for yourself what the fuss is about.

★ **Mesa Verde**   VEGAN **$$**
(☑805-963-4474; http://mesaverderestaurant. com; 1919 Cliff Dr; shared plates $10-18; ⏱11am-9pm Mon-Fri, 11am-3:30pm & 5-9pm Sat & Sun; 🅿) 🍴 A top pick for plant-based dining, Mesa Verde has so many delicious, innovative all-vegan sharing plates on the menu that meat-avoiding procrastinators will be in torment. If in doubt, pick a selection and brace yourself for flavor-packed delights. Meat-eaters welcome (and possibly will be converted). Cash only.

★ **Lark**   CALIFORNIAN **$$$**
(☑805-284-0370; www.thelarksb.com; 131 Anacapa St; shared plates $12-32, mains $19-48; ⏱5-10pm Tue-Sun, bar to midnight; 🅿) 🍴 A top spot to savor SoCal's bountiful farm and fishing goodness, chef-run Lark was named after an antique Pullman railway car and is based at a former fish market transformed into a buzzy casual restaurant in the Funk Zone. The menu morphs with the seasons, presenting inspiring flavor combinations such as crispy Brussels sprouts with dates or juniper-smoked duck breast. Make reservations.

🍷 Drinking & Nightlife

On lower State St, most of the boisterous watering holes have happy hours, tiny dance floors and rowdy college nights. The Funk Zone's eclectic mix of bars and wine-tasting rooms provides a trendier, more sophisticated alternative.

★ **Figueroa Mountain Brewing Co**   CRAFT BEER
(☑805-694-2252; www.figmtnbrew.com; 137 Anacapa St; ⏱11am-11pm) Father and son brewers have brought their gold-medal-winning hoppy IPA, Danish red lager and potent stout from Santa Barbara's Wine Country to the Funk Zone. Knowledgeable staff will help you choose. Clink glasses below vintage-style posters in the 'surf-meets-Old-West' taproom or on the open-air patio while acoustic acts play.

ℹ Information

Outdoors Santa Barbara Visitors Center
(☑805-456-8752; http://outdoorsb.sbmm.org; 4th fl, 113 Harbor Way; ⏱11am-5pm Sun-Fri, to 3pm Sat) In the same building as the maritime museum, this volunteer-staffed visitor center offers info on Channel Islands National Park and has a harbor-view deck.

Santa Barbara Visitors Center (☑805-965-3021, 805-568-1811; www.santabarbaraca.com; 1 Garden St; ⏱9am-5pm Mon-Sat, 10am-5pm Sun Feb-Oct, to 4pm Nov-Jan) Drop by for maps and brochures and consult the helpful staff about how to get the most out of your stay. The website has handy downloadable DIY maps and itineraries, from food-and-drink routes to wine trails, art galleries and outdoors fun.

ℹ Getting There & Around

If you're driving on Hwy 101, take the Garden St or Carrillo St exits for downtown.

Greyhound (☑805-965-7551; www.grey hound.com; 224 Chapala St; 🛜) operates a few direct buses daily to LA (from $14, three hours), Santa Cruz (from $42, six hours) and San Francisco (from $42, nine hours). **Amtrak** (☑800-872-7245; www.amtrak.com; 209 State St) trains run south to LA (from $31, 2¾ hours) via Carpinteria, Ventura and Burbank's airport, and north to San Luis Obispo (from $34, three hours) and Oakland (from $54, 8¾ hours), with stops in Paso Robles, Salinas and San Jose.

Local buses operated by the **Metropolitan Transit District** (MTD; ☑805-963-3366; www.sbmtd.gov) cost $1.75 per ride (exact change, cash only). Equipped with front-loading bike racks, these buses travel all over town and to adjacent communities; ask for a free transfer upon boarding. For bicycle rentals, **Wheel Fun Rentals** (☑805-966-2282; http://wheelfunrentalssb.com; 24 E Mason St; ◷8am-8pm Apr–mid-Oct, to 6pm mid-Oct–Mar; ▥) has a handy location in the Funk Zone near Stearns Wharf.

Santa Barbara to San Luis Obispo

You can speed up to San Luis Obispo in less than two hours along Hwy 101, or take all day detouring to wineries, historical missions and hidden beaches.

Santa Ynez & Santa Maria Valleys

A scenic backcountry drive north of Santa Barbara follows Hwy 154, through the wine country (www.sbcountywines.com) of the Santa Ynez and Santa Maria Valleys. Ride along with **Sustainable Vine Wine Tours** (☑805-698-3911; www.sustainablevinewinetours.com; tours from $150) ☑, or follow the pastoral **Foxen Canyon Wine Trail** (www.foxencanyonwinetrail.com) north to discover cult winemakers' vineyards. In the town of **Los Olivos**, where two dozen rare wine-tasting rooms await, **Los Olivos Wine Merchant & Café** (☑805-688-7265; www.winemerchantcafe.com; 2879 Grand Ave; mains $15-28; ◷11:30am-8pm Mon-Thu, to 8:30pm Fri, 11am-8:30pm Sat, 11am-8pm Sun) is a charming Cal-Mediterranean bistro with a wine bar.

Solvang

Point the compass south to the Danish-immigrant village of Solvang (www.solvangusa.com), which abounds with windmills and fairy-tale bakeries. Fuel up on bourbon vanilla French toast, charcuterie or bacon-wrapped tenderloin at **Succulent Café** (☑805-691-9444; www.succulentcafe.com; 1555 Mission Dr; mains breakfast & lunch $5-15, dinner $16-37; ◷10am-3pm Mon & Wed-Fri, 8:30am-3pm Sat & Sun, 5-9pm Sun & Mon; ☑▨) ☑. For a picnic lunch or BBQ takeout, swing into **El Rancho Marketplace** (☑805-688-4300; http://elranchomarket.com; 2886 Mission Dr; ◷6am-11pm), east of Solvang's 19th-century Spanish Colonial **mission** (☑805-688-4815; www.missionsantaines.org; 1760 Mission Dr; adult/child under 12yr $5/free; ◷9am-5pm; ℗).

Lompoc & Around

From Solvang, follow Hwy 246 about 15 miles west of Hwy 101 to **La Purísima Mission State Historic Park** (☑805-733-3713; www.lapurisimamission.org; 2295 Purísima Rd, Lompoc; per car $6; ◷park 9am-5pm, visitor center 10am-4pm Tue-Sun year-round, also 11am-3pm Mon Jul & Aug; ℗▥) ☑. Exquisitely restored, it's one of California's most evocative Spanish Colonial missions, with flowering gardens, livestock pens and adobe buildings. South of Lompoc off Hwy 1, Jalama Rd travels 20 twisting miles to windswept **Jalama Beach County Park** (☑805-568-2461; www.countyofsb.org/parks/jalama; Jalama Beach Rd, Lompoc; per car $10). Book ahead for its extremely popular **campground** (☑805-568-2460; www.countyofsb.org/parks/jalama.sbc; 9999 Jalama Rd, Lompoc; tent/RV sites/cabins from $35/50/190; ℗▨), which also has simple cabins with kitchenettes.

Pismo Beach & Around

Where Hwy 1 rejoins Hwy 101, **Pismo Beach** is a long, lazy stretch of sand with a **butterfly grove** (☑805-773-5301; www.monarchbutterfly.org; Hwy 1; ◷10am-4pm late Oct-Feb; ▥) ☑ **FREE**, where migratory monarchs rest in eucalyptus trees from late October until February. Adjacent **North Beach Campground** (☑805-473-7220, reservations 800-444-7275; www.reservecalifornia.com; 399 S Dolliver St; tent & RV sites $35; ▨) offers beach access and hot showers. Dozens of motels and hotels stand by the ocean and along Hwy 101, but rooms fill quickly, especially on weekends. **Pismo Lighthouse Suites** (☑805-773-2411; www.pismolighthousesuites.com; 2411 Price St; ste $190-500; ℗☺@⊛▨▨) has everything vacationing families need, including a giant outdoor chessboard. In downtown Pismo, **Old West Cinnamon Rolls** (☑805-773-1428; www.oldwestcinnamonrolls.com; 861 Dolliver St; rolls $3-4; ◷6:30am-5:30pm; ▥) offers gooey goodness. Uphill at the **Cracked Crab** (☑805-773-2722; www.crackedcrab.com; 751 Price St; mains $16-61; ◷11am-9pm Sun-Thu, to 10pm Fri & Sat; ▥), make sure you don a plastic bib

CHANNEL ISLANDS NATIONAL PARK

Channel Islands National Park (☑805-658-5730; www.nps.gov/chis; 1901 Spinnaker Dr, Ventura; ☺visitor center 8:30am-5pm) 🖉 FREE comprises five uninhabited islands off the coast of Ventura that are home to more than 150 endemic plant and animal species. It's a paradise for diving, hiking, kayaking, camping and other outdoor activities.

Boats leave from Ventura Harbor, 32 miles south of Santa Barbara on Hwy 101, where the park's **visitor center** (Robert J Lagomarsino Visitor Center; ☑805-658-5730; www.nps. gov/chis; 1901 Spinnaker Dr, Ventura; ☺8:30am-5pm; 🛗) has info and maps. The main tour-boat operator is **Island Packers Cruises** (☑805-642-1393; http://islandpackers.com; 1691 Spinnaker Dr, Ventura; Channel Island day trips from $59, wildlife cruises from $38); book ahead. If you want to camp, secure transportation first, then make a reservation on www. recreation.gov and bring food and water.

before a fresh bucket o' seafood gets dumped on your butcher-paper-covered table.

The nearby town of **Avila Beach** has a sunny waterfront promenade, an atmospherically creaky wooden fishing pier and a historical **lighthouse** (☑805-773-2411; www. pismolighthousesuites.com; 2411 Price St; ste $190-500; 🅿😊@🛜🏊🐕). Back toward Hwy 101, pick juicy fruit and feed the goats at **Avila Valley Barn** (☑805-595-2816; www.avilavalley barn.com; 560 Avila Beach Dr; ☺9am-6pm May-Sep, 9am-5pm Apr, Oct & Nov, 9am-5pm Thu-Mon Dec-Mar; 🛗), then do some stargazing from a private redwood hot tub at **Sycamore Mineral Springs** (☑805-595-7302; www.syca moresprings.com; 1215 Avila Beach Dr; 1hr per person $17.50-22.50; ☺8am-midnight, last reservation 10:30pm).

San Luis Obispo

Almost midway between LA and San Francisco, at the junction of Hwys 101 and 1, San Luis Obispo is a popular overnight stop for road-trippers. It also makes a handy base from which to explore coastal towns Pismo Beach, Avila Beach and Morro Bay, as well as Hearst Castle. SLO may not have any big-ticket sights, unless you count the Spanish-Colonial **mission** (☑805-543-6850; www.missionsanluisobispo. org; 751 Palm St; suggested donation $5; ☺9am-5pm late Mar-Oct, to 4pm Nov–mid-Mar; 🛗) and, perhaps, the kooky Madonna Inn. But this refreshingly low-key city does have an enviably high quality of life, helped along by CalPoly university students who inject a healthy dose of hubbub into the streets, bars and cafes. Thursdays are great time to be in SLO – the farmers market turns downtown's Higuera St into a party with live music and sidewalk BBQs.

🛏 Sleeping

Motels cluster off Hwy 101, especially off Monterey St northeast of downtown and around Santa Rosa St (Hwy 1). A slew of openings in recent times has increased the range of accommodations in town.

HI Hostel Obispo HOSTEL $
(☑805-544-4678; www.hostelobispo.com; 1617 Santa Rosa St; dm $33-45, r with shared bath from $65; ☺closed 11am-4:30pm; 🅿😊@🛜) On a tree-lined street near SLO's train station, this avocado-colored hostel inhabits a converted Victorian, giving it a bit of a B&B feel. Meet fellow travelers in the communal kitchen, fireplace lounge or garden, or rent a bike (from $10 per day) to explore the town. Complimentary sourdough pancakes and coffee for breakfast. BYOT (bring your own towel). Check in from 4:30pm to 10pm.

Madonna Inn HOTEL $$
(☑805-543-3000; www.madonnainn.com; 100 Madonna Rd; r $209-329, plus resort fee per night $15; 🅿❄@🛜🏊) The fantastically campy Madonna Inn is a garish confection visible from Hwy 101. Curious global tourists and irony-loving hipsters adore the 110 themed rooms – Yosemite Rock, Caveman and hot-pink Floral Fantasy (check out photos online) are sure to fulfil any fantasy. Even if you're not staying, it's worth a mind-bending spin around the main building. Wi-fi works in common areas only.

🍴 Eating & Drinking

Downtown SLO has several excellent restaurants, befitting the area's farm-to-fork focus and wine-country heritage.

Higuera St is littered with college-student-jammed bars. Craft-beer fans have plenty to look forward to, while grape-lovers will have no trouble finding places to sample regional wines.

Luna Red
FUSION $$

(☑805-540-5243; www.lunaredslo.com; 1023 Chorro St; small plates $4-17, mains $23-27; ☻11:30am-10pm Mon-Thu, to 1am Fri, 10am-1am Sat, to 10pm Sun; ☎☑) ✐ Local bounty from the land and sea pervades Luna's globally inspired small-plates menu meant for sharing, as is the big paella served straight from the pan. Cocktails and glowing lanterns create a sophisticated vibe indoors, although in fine weather the mission-view garden patio is the place to linger over weekend brunch or late-night drinks. Reservations recommended.

Guiseppe's Cucina Rustica
ITALIAN $$

(☑805-541-9922; www.giuseppesrestaurant.com; 849 Monterey St; pizzas from $15, mains $15-39; ☻11:30am-3pm daily, 4:30-9:30pm Sun-Thu, to 10:30pm Fri & Sat; ☎) ✐ Visit garlic-perfumed Guiseppe's for a leisurely lunch of toothsome salads, pizza and antipasti starring produce harvested on the owner's farm. Out the back, the facade of the heritage Sinsheimer Brothers building overlooks a shaded courtyard that's perfectly suited to languid dinners of chicken parmigiana and a glass of hearty SLO County red.

Luis Wine Bar
WINE BAR

(☑805-762-4747; www.luiswinebar.com; 1021 Higuera St; ☻3-11pm Sun-Thu, to midnight Fri & Sat) This downtown wine bar is an urbane but unpretentious alternative to SLO's more raucous student-heavy drinking dens. About half of the roughly 60 wines on the list are available by the glass, and there's also a solid craft-beer selection, along with cheese and charcuterie platters.

❶ Information

San Luis Obispo Visitor Center (☑805-781-2777; www.visitslo.com; 895 Monterey St; ☻9:30am-5pm Sun-Wed, to 6pm Thu-Sat)

❶ Getting There & Away

Amtrak (☑800-872-7245; www.amtrak.com; 1011 Railroad Ave) runs daily Seattle–LA *Coast Starlight* and twice-daily SLO–San Diego *Pacific Surfliner* trains. Both routes head south to Santa Barbara (from $28, 2½ hours) and Los Angeles (from $43, 5½ hours). The *Coast Starlight* connects north via Paso Robles to Salinas (from $29, three hours) and Oakland (from $42, six hours). Several daily Thruway buses link to more regional trains.

❶ Getting Around

SLO Transit (☑805-541-2877; www.slocity.org; single rides $1.50, day pass $3.25) provides daily bus service on eight fixed routes within city limits. It also runs the **Old SLO Trolley** (tickets 50¢; ☻5-9pm Thu year-round, 5-9pm Fri Jun-early Sep & 5-9pm Sat Apr-Oct), which loops between downtown and upper Monterey St every 20 minutes between 5pm and 9pm on Thursdays year-round, on Fridays from June to early September and on Saturdays from April through October.

SLO Regional Transit Authority (RTA; ☑805-541-2228; www.slorta.org; single-ride fares $1.75-3.25) operates countywide bus routes, including to the Hearst Castle Visitor Center (weekends only), Pismo Beach and Morro Bay. All routes converge on downtown's **transit center** (cnr Palm & Osos Sts).

Morro Bay to Hearst Castle

On this epic journey Hwy 1 snakes through wine country, along the coast and past lighthouses before arriving at the vainglorious Hearst Castle.

Morro Bay & Around

A dozen miles northwest of San Luis Obispo via Hwy 1, Morro Bay is a sea-sprayed fishing town where **Morro Rock**, a volcanic peak jutting up from the ocean floor, is your first hint of the coast's upcoming drama. (Never mind those distracting power-plant smokestacks.) Hop aboard boat cruises or rent kayaks along the Embarcadero, which is packed with touristy shops. Midrange motels cluster uphill off Harbor and Main Sts and along Hwy 1. A classic seafood shack, **Giovanni's Fish Market & Galley** (☑805-772-2123; www.giovannisfishmarket.com; 1001 Front St; mains $5-15; ☻market 9am-6pm, restaurant 11am-6pm; ☻) cooks killer fish and chips and garlic fries.

South of Morro Bay there are state parks for coastal hikes and **camping** (☑reservations 800-444-7275; www.reservecalifornia.com; campsites/RV sites $35/50; ☻). First up is **Morro Bay State Park** (☑museum 805-772-2694, park 805-772-6101; www.parks.ca.gov; 60 State Park Rd; park entry free, museum adult/child under 17yr $3/free; ☻park 6am-10pm, museum 10am-5pm; ☻☻), which also has a child-oriented natural history museum. Further south, even wilder **Montaña de Oro State Park** (☑805-772-6101; www.parks.ca.gov; 3550 Pecho Valley Rd, Los Osos; ☻6am-10pm; ☻☻) ✐ FREE features coastal bluffs, tide pools, sand dunes, peak hiking and mountain-biking trails. Its Spanish name (which means 'mountain of gold') comes from native California poppies that blanket the hillsides in spring.

Cayucos

Heading north of downtown Morro Bay along Hwy 1, giant platters of delicious Cal-Mexican grub await at unassuming **Taco Temple** (☑805-772-4965; www.tacotemple.com; 2680 Main St; mains $8-17; ☻11am-9pm; ❸), a cash-only joint in a supermarket parking lot. Further north in laid-back Cayucos, **Ruddell's Smokehouse** (☑805-995–5028; www.smokerjim.com; 101 D St; dishes $5.50-13; ☻11am-6pm; ❸) does a roaring trade in smoked-fish tacos by the beach. Vintage motels on Cayucos' Ocean Ave include the cute family-run **Seaside Motel** (☑805-995-3809; www.seasidemotel.com; 42 S Ocean Ave; d $110-180; ❸❸❸). For more comfort, fall asleep to the sound of the surf at the **Shoreline Inn on the Beach** (☑805-995-3681; www.cayucosshorelineinn.com; 1 N Ocean Ave; r $200-250; ❸❸❸❸).

Paso Robles Wine Country

North of Harmony (population: just 18 souls), Hwy 46 leads east into the vineyards of Paso Robles wine country (www.pasowine.com). For a hoppy antidote, swing by **Firestone Walker Brewing Company** (☑805-225-5913; www.firestonebeer.com; 1400 Ramada Dr; tours from $10; ☻visitor center 10am-5pm Mon-Thu, to 6pm Fri-Sun; ❸) off Hwy 101 in Paso Robles. It runs daily brewery tours (from $10; reservations recommended), or just stop by the visitor center for samples or into the restaurant for a meal.

Cambria & Hearst Castle

North of Harmony along Hwy 1, quaint Cambria has lodgings along unearthly pretty Moonstone Beach, where the **Blue Dolphin Inn** (☑805-927-3300; www.cambriainns.com; 6470 Moonstone Beach Dr; r $189-429; ❸❸❸❸) has modern rooms with romantic fireplaces. Inland, **Bridge Street Inn** (☑805-215-0724; www.bsicambria.com; 4314 Bridge St; r $50-100, vans $30; ❸❸❸) sleeps like a hostel but feels like a grandmotherly B&B, while the **Cambria Palms Motel** (☑805-927-4485; www.cambriapalmsmotel.com; 2662 Main St; r $100-125; ☻check-in 3-9pm; ❸❸❸) lulls

guests to sleep with its 1950s retro vibe. An artisan cheese and wine shop turned breezy bistro, **Indigo Moon** (☑805-927-2911; www.indigomooncafe.com; 1980 Main St; mains lunch $10-22, dinner $18-38; ☻11am-3pm & 5-9pm; ❸) ❷ dishes up market-fresh salads and sandwiches at lunch and more complex Cali fare at night. With a sunny patio and a takeout counter, **Linn's Easy as Pie Cafe** (☑805-924-3050; www.linnsfruitbin.com; 4251 Bridge St; dishes $8-12; ☻10am-7pm Mon-Thu, to 8pm Fri & Sat; ❸) is famous for its olallieberry pie.

About 10 miles north of Cambria, hilltop **Hearst Castle** (☑reservations 800-444-4445; www.hearstcastle.org; 750 Hearst Castle Rd; tours adult/child 5-12yr from $25/12; ☻from 9am; ❸❸) is California's most famous monument to wealth and ambition. Newspaper magnate William Randolph Hearst entertained Hollywood stars and royalty at this fantasy estate that drips with European antiques, accented by shimmering pools and surrounded by flowering gardens. It can only be seen on tours – book ahead online or show up early in the day and hope for the best.

Across Hwy 1, overlooking a historic whaling pier, **Sebastian's** (☑805-927-3307; www.facebook.com/SebastiansSanSimeon; 442 SLO-San Simeon Rd; mains $9-14; ☻11am-4pm Tue-Sun) sells Hearst Ranch beef burgers and giant sandwiches for impromptu beach picnics. Five miles back south along Hwy 1, past a forgettable row of budget and mid-range motels in San Simeon, **Hearst San Simeon State Park** (☑805-772-6101; www.reservecalifornia.com; Hwy 1; tent/RV sites $20/35) offers both primitive and developed creekside campsites.

Point Piedras Blancas is home to an **enormous elephant seal colony** that breeds, molts, sleeps, frolics and, occasionally, goes aggro on the beach. Keep your distance from these wild animals who move faster on the sand than you can. The signposted vista point, about 4.5 miles north of Hearst Castle, has interpretive panels. Seals haul out year-round, but the frenzied birthing and mating season runs from January through March. Nearby, the 1875 **Piedras Blancas Light Station** (☑805-927-7361; www.piedrasblancas.gov; Hwy 1, San Simeon; tours adult/child 6-17yr $10/5; ☻tours 9:45am Mon, Tue & Thu-Sat mid-Jun–Aug, 9:45am Tue, Thu & Sat Sep–mid-Jun) is an outstandingly scenic spot; access is only via guided tours that can be booked online.

WORTH A TRIP

PINNACLES NATIONAL PARK

A study in geological drama, **Pinnacles National Park's** (☑831-389-4486; www.nps.gov/pinn; 5000 Hwy 146, Paicines; per car $15; ⊙park 24hr, east visitor center 9:30am-5pm, west visitor center 9am-4:30pm; P⊞) ♪ craggy monoliths, sheer-walled canyons and twisting caves are the result of millions of years of erosion. In addition to hiking and rock climbing, the park's biggest attractions are its two talus caves. **Balconies Cave** is always open for exploration, while **Bear Gulch Cove** is generally closed from mid-May to mid-July when the resident colony of Townsend's big-eared bats raises their offspring. While in the park, keep an eye out for endangered California condors circling above.

Pinnacles is best visited during spring or fall; summer's heat is too extreme.

Big Sur

Much ink has been spilled extolling the raw beauty and energy of this 100-mile stretch of craggy coastline sprawling south of Monterey Bay. More a state of mind than a place you can pinpoint on a map, Big Sur has no traffic lights, banks or strip malls. When the sun goes down, the moon and stars are the only illumination – if summer fog hasn't extinguished them, that is.

Lodging, food and gas are pricey in Big Sur. Demand for rooms is high year-round, especially on weekends, so book ahead. The free *Big Sur Guide* (www.bigsurcalifornia.org), an info-packed newspaper, is available at roadside businesses. The day use parking fee (per car $10) charged at Big Sur's state parks is valid for same-day entry to all parks.

Gorda & Around

Coming from Hearst Castle, it's about 25 miles to blink-and-you-miss-it Gorda, home of **Treebones Resort** (☑805-927-2390; www.treebonesresort.com; 71895 Hwy 1; campsites $95, yurt with shared bath from $320; P⊖⊜⊛) ♪, which offers back-to nature clifftop yurts. Basic United States Forest Service (USFS) campgrounds are just off Hwy 1 at shady **Plaskett Creek** (☑reservations 877-477-6777; www.recreation.gov; Hwy 1; tent & RV sites $35) and oceanside **Kirk Creek** (☑805-434-1996, reservations 877-444-6777; www.recreation.gov; Hwy 1; tent & RV sites $35).

Twenty miles north of Gorda is new-agey **Esalen Institute Hot Springs** (☑831-667-3000; www.esalen.org; 55000 Hwy 1; per person $35; ⊙1am-3am), famous for its esoteric workshops and hot-tubbing from 1am to 3am. Same-day reservations can only be made online starting at 9am and usually sell out within minutes. It's surreal.

Another 3 miles north, partly closed **Julia Pfeiffer Burns State Park** (☑831-667-2315; www.parks.ca.gov; Hwy 1; day use per car $10; ⊙30min before sunrise-30min after sunset; P⊞) ♪ hides 80ft-high **McWay Falls**, one of California's only coastal waterfalls. From the viewpoint, you can photograph the water tumbling over granite cliffs into the ocean – or onto the beach, depending on the tide.

Henry Miller Memorial Library & Around

Head north from Julia Pfeiffer Burns State Park for another 8 miles to reach the beatnik **Henry Miller Memorial Library** (☑831-667-2574; www.henrymiller.org; 48603 Hwy 1; ⊙11am-5pm Wed-Mon) **FREE**, the art and soul of Big Sur bohemia. It has a jam-packed bookstore, hosts concerts and other cultural events, and features eccentric outdoor sculptures. Just up the road, eating takes a backseat to dramatic panoramic views at clifftop **Nepenthe** (☑831-667-2345; www.nepenthebigsur.com; 48510 Hwy 1; mains lunch $18-24, dinner $18-52; ⊙11:30am-10pm; ⊛⊘⊞), meaning 'island of no sorrow.'

Most of Big Sur's commercial activity is concentrated just north along Hwy 1, including private campgrounds with rustic cabins, motels, restaurants, gas stations and shops. Right by the post office, you can put together a picnic at the **Big Sur Deli & General Store** (☑831-667-2225; www.bigsurdeli.com; Big Sur Village; sandwiches $4-9; ⊙7am-8pm; ⊛), attached to the laid-back **Big Sur Taphouse** (☑831-667-2197; www.bigsurtaphouse.com; Big Sur Village; ⊙noon-10pm; ⊛), with craft beer, Mexican pub grub and board games.

Just north, look left for the turnoff onto Sycamore Canyon Rd, which drops two narrow, twisting miles to crescent-shaped **Pfeiffer Beach** (☑805-434-1996; www.campone.com; Sycamore Canyon Rd; day use per car $10; ⊙9am-8pm; P⊞⊛), where there's a towering offshore sea arch. Strong currents make it too dangerous for swimming. Dig down into the sand – it's purple!

Pfeiffer Big Sur State Park

Back on Hwy 1, drop by **Big Sur Station** (☎831-667-2315; 47555 Hwy 1; ⊙9am-4pm; 🛜) for information on camping or hiking (or if you just need a bathroom and decent cell-phone coverage). Behind the station, **Pfeiffer Big Sur State Park** (☎831-667-2315; www.parks.ca.gov; 47225 Hwy 1; per car $10; ⊙30min before sunrise-30min after sunset; 🅿♿) 🏊 is crisscrossed by sun-dappled trails through redwood forests. Make reservations for the **campground** (☎reservations 800-444-7275; www.reservecalifornia.com; 47225 Hwy 1; tent & RV sites $35-50; 🅿♿) or ramp up the luxury and watch the surf break far below from your private deck at the impossibly romantic **Post Ranch Inn** (☎831-667-2200; www.postranchinn. com; 47900 Hwy 1; d from $995; 🅿♿❄@🛜🏊).

Another gem is **Glen Oaks** (☎831-667-2105; www.glenoaksbigsur.com; 47080 Hwy 1; d $300-650; 🅿♿🛜) 🏊, a 1950s redwood-and-adobe motor lodge turned luxe hideaway with woodsy cabins and cottages. Rooms at the nearby **Big Sur River Inn** (☎831-667-2700; www.bigsurriverinn.com; 46840 Hwy 1; mains breakfast & lunch $12-27, dinner $12-40; ⊙8am-9pm; 🅿🛜) are a bit more ho-hum but the creekside restaurant serves solid American fare and a mean apple pie.

Andrew Molera State Park

Some 5 miles on from the Big Sur River Inn, don't skip **Andrew Molera State Park** (☎831-667-2315; www.parks.ca.gov; Hwy 1; day use per car $10; ⊙30min before sunrise-30min after sunset; 🅿♿) 🏊, a gorgeous trail-laced pastiche of grassy meadows, waterfalls, ocean bluffs and rugged beaches. Learn all about endangered California condors at the park's **Discovery Center** (☎831-620-0702; www. ventanaws.org/discovery_center; Andrew Molera State Park; ⊙10am-4pm Sat & Sun late May-early Sep; 🅿♿) 🏊 FREE. From the dirt parking lot, a 0.3-mile trail leads to a primitive no-reservations **campground** (Trail Camp; www.parks.ca.gov; Hwy 1; tent sites $25).

Point Sur State Historic Park

Six miles before the landmark **Bixby Creek Bridge**, you can take a tour (including a seasonal moonlight walk) of the 1889 lighthouse at **Point Sur State Historic Park** (☎831-625-4419; www.pointsur.org; off Hwy 1; adult/child 6-17yr from $15/5; ⊙tours 10am & 2pm Wed & Sat, 10am Sun Apr-Sep, 1pm Wed, 10am Sat & Sun Oct-Mar) FREE. Check online or call for tour schedules and directions to the meeting point. Arrive early since space is limited (no reservations).

Carmel-by-the-Sea

With borderline fanatical devotion to its canine citizens, quaint Carmel has the well-manicured feel of a country club. Watch behatted locals toting fancy-label shopping bags to lunch and dapper folk driving top-down convertibles along Ocean Ave, the village's slow-mo main drag.

👁 Sights & Activities

Escape downtown Carmel's harried shopping streets and stroll tree-lined neighborhoods on the lookout for domiciles both charming and peculiar. The *Hansel and Gretel* houses on Torres St, between 5th and 6th Aves, are just how you'd imagine them. Another eye-catching house on Guadalupe St near 6th Ave is shaped like a ship and made from local river rocks and salvaged ship parts.

⭐ **Point Lobos State Natural Reserve** STATE PARK
(☎831-624-4909; www.pointlobos.org; Hwy 1; per car $10; ⊙8am-7pm, last entry 6:30pm mid-Mar-early Nov, to 5pm early Nov-mid-Mar; 🅿♿) 🏊 They bark, they laze and bathe and they're fun to watch – sea lions are the stars in this state park some 4 miles south of Carmel, along with the dramatically rocky coastline and its excellent tide-pooling. Even a short hike through this spectacular scenery is rewarding. Note that parking inside the reserve is limited to 150 cars, and spaces fill quickly in summer. Arrive before 9:30am or after 3pm to avoid the crowds. Alternatively, park on Hwy 1 and walk in.

ℹ DRIVING HIGHWAY 1

Driving this narrow two-lane highway through Big Sur and beyond is very slow going. Allow at least three hours to cover the 140 miles between the Monterey Peninsula and San Luis Obispo, and much more if you want to stop and explore the coast. Don't travel Hwy 1 at night as it's too risky and, more to the point, it's futile, because you'll miss out on the terrific views. Watch out for cyclists and make use of signposted roadside pullouts to let faster-moving traffic pass.

★ **Mission San Carlos Borromeo de Carmelo** CHURCH
(☑ 831-624-1271; www.carmelmission.org; 3080 Rio Rd; adult/child 7-17yr $9.50/5; ⊙9:30am-5pm) Carmel's strikingly beautiful mission is an oasis of solemnity with flowering gardens and a thick-walled basilica filled with Spanish Colonial art and artifacts. The mission was originally established by Franciscan friar Junípero Serra in 1770 in nearby Monterrey, but poor soil and the corrupting influence of Spanish soldiers forced the move to Carmel two years later. The mission became Serra's home base and he died here in 1784.

🛏 Sleeping

In summer and on weekends, shockingly overpriced boutique hotels, inns and B&Bs fill up quickly in Carmel-by-the-Sea. Ask the **Carmel Visitor Center** (☑ 831-624-2522; www.carmelcalifornia.org; Ocean Ave btwn Junipero & Mission, 2nd fl, Carmel Plaza; ⊙10am-5pm) about last-minute deals. For better-value lodgings, head north to Monterey.

🍴 Eating & Drinking

Low lighting and conversation-friendly sound levels characterize Carmel's old-world dining scene, although a few eateries are trying for a more modern, lively vibe. The best option for late-night drinks is the cool, energetic scene at **Barmel** (☑831-626-2095; www.facebook.com/BarmelByTheSea; San Carlos St btwn Ocean & 7th Aves; ⊙3pm-2am Mon-Sat, to midnight Sun).

★ **Cultura Comida y Bebida** MEXICAN $$
(☑831-250-7005; www.culturacarmel.com; Dolores St btwn 5th & 6th Aves; mains $19-32; ⊙5:30pm-midnight daily, 10:30am-3:30pm Sat & Sun; ☑) In a brick-lined courtyard, this vivaciously elegant restaurant pairs art and candlelight with food inspired by Oaxacan flavors and an entire library's worth of mezcal. The ambience is upscale but relaxed and suitable both for a date night or an outing with your posse. The Cultura mole with smoked pork and saffron tortillas is a signature dish.

La Bicyclette FRENCH $$
(☑831-622-9899; www.labicycletterestaurant.com; cnr Dolores St & 7th Ave; mains lunch $19-29, dinner $20-44; ⊙11am-3:30pm & 4:45-10pm) Rustic French comfort food using seasonal local ingredients and an open kitchen baking wood-fired-oven pizzas packs couples into this bistro. Excellent local wines by the glass. It's also a top spot for a leisurely lunch.

Monterey

Life in still delightfully rough-around-the-edges Monterey revolves around the sea. The city's biggest draw is a world-class aquarium overlooking Monterey Bay National Marine Sanctuary, which protects dense kelp forests and a sublime variety of marine life, including seals and sea lions, dolphins and whales.

⊙ Sights

The aquarium sits on the edge of **Cannery Row** (☒), which made Monterey the sardine capital of the world in the 1930s. Today it's an unabashedly touristic strip lined with souvenir shops and standard eateries in faux retro buildings. For more authenticity, take a stroll past downtown's cluster of restored buildings from the Spanish and Mexican periods.

★ **Monterey Bay Aquarium** AQUARIUM
(☑ info 831-648-4800, tickets 866-963-9645; www.montereybayaquarium.org; 886 Cannery Row; adult/child 3-12yr/13-17yr $50/30/40, tours $15; ⊙9:30am-6pm May-Aug, 10am-5pm Sep-Apr; ☒) 🔋 Monterey's most mesmerizing experience, this enormous aquarium occupies the site of a humongous sardine cannery. All kinds of aquatic creatures inhabit its halls and outside areas, from sea stars and slimy sea slugs to animated sea otters and surprisingly nimble 800lb tuna. The aquarium is much more than an impressive collection of glass tanks; thoughtful placards underscore the bay's cultural and historical contexts.

Monterey State Historic Park HISTORIC SITE
(☑831-649-2907, 831-649-7118; www.parks.ca.gov/mshp; 20 Custom House Plaza; ⊙Pacific House 10am-4pm Tue-Sun) FREE Old Monterey is home to an extraordinary assemblage of 19th-century brick and adobe buildings administered as a state park and linked by a 2-mile self-guided walking tour called the 'Path of History.' Pick up a copy at Pacific House Museum, which also doubles as the park HQ. Route highlights are the nearby Custom House and the Old Whaling Station. Note that buildings are open according to a capricious schedule dictated by state funding.

🏃 Activities

You can spot whales off the coast of Monterey Bay year-round. The season for blue and humpback whales runs from April to early December, while gray whales pass by from mid-December through March. **Sanctuary**

Cruises (☑ info 831-917-1042, tickets 831-350-4090; www.sanctuarycruises.com; 7881 Sandholdt Rd; tours $45-55; ☑) ✐ tour boats depart from Fisherman's Wharf and Moss Landing. Reserve trips at least a day in advance; be prepared for a bumpy, cold ride.

Monterey Bay Whale Watch   BOATING
(☑ 831-375-4658; www.gowhales.com; Fisherman's Wharf; 3hr tours adult/child 4-12yr $49/39; ☑ ☑) Right on Fisherman's Wharf, this is one of the oldest whale-watch tour operators in Monterey. Morning and afternoon boat rides are led by knowledgeable marine biologists for extra insight into the animals and their habitat. Sightings are guaranteed or you get another trip on them.

Adventures by the Sea   CYCLING, KAYAKING
(☑ 831-372-1807; www.adventuresbythesea.com; 299 Cannery Row; per day bicycle $35, SUP set $50, 1-/2-seater kayak $35/60, kayak tours from $60; ☺ 9am-sunset; ☑) No matter if you fancy kayaking with sea otters, joining a kayak tour across the kelp-forest canopy, learning to paddleboard or exploring the area on a hybrid or e-bike, these folks can set you up. They have six locations in all, with Cannery Row being the largest and most central.

Aquarius Dive Shop   DIVING
(☑ 831-375-1933; www.aquariusdivers.com; 2040 Del Monte Ave; snorkel-/scuba-gear rental $35/65, dive tours from $65; ☺ 9am-6pm Mon-Thu, to 7pm Fri, 7am-7pm Sat, 7am-6pm Sun) Talk to this five-star PADI-certified operation for gear rentals, classes and guided dives into Monterey Bay.

🛏 Sleeping

Book ahead for special events, on weekends and in summer. To avoid the tourist congestion and jacked-up prices of Cannery Row, look to Pacific Grove. Cheaper motels line Munras Ave, south of downtown, and N Fremont St, east of Hwy 1.

HI Monterey Hostel   HOSTEL $
(☑ 831-649-0375; www.montereyhostel.org; 778 Hawthorne St; dm $49-60, tr/q with shared bathroom $129/149; ℗☺@☎) Four blocks from Cannery Row and the aquarium, this simple, clean hostel houses single-sex and mixed dorms, as well as private rooms for three to five people. Days start with free make-your-own-pancake breakfasts and might conclude with barbecue parties or story-swapping in the lounge with piano. Check in from 2pm to 10pm

Monterey Hotel   HOTEL $$
(☑ 831-375-3184; www.montereyhotel.com; 407 Calle Principal; r $210-450; ℗☺☎☎) Steps from Fisherman's Wharf, this 1904 Victorian is honeycombed with 69 rooms that channel historic character, with antique furniture, ceiling fans, plantation shutters and fireplaces (in some). 'Historic' rooms are a tad twee; opt for the 'deluxe' categories if you need more elbow room. Breakfast included.

⭐ **Jabberwock**   B&B $$$
(☑ 831-372-4777; www.jabberwockinn.com; 598 Laine St; r $240-400; @☎) Barely visible behind a shroud of foliage, this 1911 khaki-shingled Craftsman-style house hums a playful *Alice in Wonderland* tune through seven immaculate rooms, a few with fireplaces and Jacuzzis for two. Over afternoon wine and hors d'oeuvres, ask the genial hosts about the house's many salvaged architectural elements. Weekends have a two-night minimum. Breakfast included.

🍴 Eating

Away from the tourist zones, there's dining gold to be unearthed in Monterey. For casual indie eateries, head uphill from Cannery Row to Lighthouse Ave to feast on everything from Hawaiian barbecue and Thai flavors to sushi and kebabs. For more contemporary and upscale plates, head downtown around Alvarado St.

LouLou's Griddle in the Middle   AMERICAN $
(☑ 831-372-0568; www.loulousgriddle.com; Municipal Wharf 2; mains $9-15; ☺ 7:30am-3pm Wed-Mon; ☑☑) Stroll down the municipal wharf to this zany diner, best for breakfasts of hubcap-sized pancakes and omelets served with fresh salsa and awesome fried potatoes. At lunchtime, you can fill the tummy with seafood and burgers.

Zab Zab   NORTHERN THAI $
(☑ 831-747-2225; www.zabzabmonterey.com; 401 Lighthouse Ave; mains $11-19; ☺ 11am-2:30pm & 5-9pm Tue-Fri, noon-9pm Sat & Sun; ☑) Our pick of Lighthouse Avenue's lineup of low-key global eateries, Zab Zab channels the robust flavors of northeast Thailand. The bijou cottage is perfect in cooler weather, but during summer the best spot is on the deck surrounded by a pleasantly overgrown garden.

⭐ **Montrio Bistro**   CALIFORNIAN $$$
(☑ 831-648-8880; www.montrio.com; 414 Calle Principal; shared plates $6.50-20, mains $20-46; ☺ 4:30-10pm Sun-Thu, to 11pm Fri & Sat; ☎) ✐ With

'clouds' hanging from the ceiling and tube sculptures wriggling towards them, it's apparent that much thought has gone into the design of this dining-scene stalwart set inside a 1910 firehouse, Fortunately, the New American fare, prepared with ingredients hunted and gathered locally, measures up nicely. Drink and snack prices during happy hour (daily until 6:30pm) are practically a steal.

ℹ Information

Monterey Visitors Center (☑ 831-657-6400; www.seemonterey.com; 401 Camino el Estero; ⊙ 10am-6pm May-Aug, to 5pm Sep-Apr) Free tourist brochures and accommodations booking service for all of Monterey County.

ℹ Getting There & Away

Monterey-Salinas Transit (MST; ☑ 888-678-2871; www.mst.org; Jules Simoneau Plaza; single rides $1.50-3.50, day pass $10) operates local and countywide buses, including routes to Pacific Grove, Carmel, Big Sur (weekends only, daily in summer) and Salinas. Routes converge on downtown's **Transit Plaza** (cnr Pearl & Alvarado Sts).

From late May until early September, MST's free trolley loops around downtown, Fisherman's Wharf and Cannery Row between 10am and 7pm or 8pm daily (weekends only September to April).

Santa Cruz

Santa Cruz is counterculture central, a touchy-feely, new-agey city famous for its leftie-liberal politics and easygoing ideology – except when it comes to dogs (rarely allowed off-leash) and parking (meters run seven days a week).

Santa Cruz has a vibrant but chaotic downtown. On the waterfront is the famous beach boardwalk, and in the hills redwood groves embrace the University of California, Santa Cruz (UCSC) campus. Plan at least half a day here, but to appreciate the aesthetic of jangly skirts, crystal pendants and Rastafarian dreadlocks, stay longer and plunge headlong into the rich local brew of surfers, students, punks and eccentric characters.

◉ Sights & Activities

One of the best things to do in Santa Cruz is simply stroll, shop and watch the sideshow along **Pacific Avenue** downtown. A 15-minute walk from there is the beach and the **Santa Cruz Wharf** (www.santacruzwharf. com), where seafood restaurants, gift shops and barking sea lions compete for attention.

Ocean-view **West Cliff Drive** follows the waterfront southwest of the wharf, paralleled by a paved recreational path. Great for sunsets, sandy **Natural Bridges State Beach** (☑ 831-423-4609; www.parks.ca.gov; 2531 W Cliff Dr; day use per car $10; ⊙ beach 8am-sunset, visitor center 10am-4pm; 🅿 ♿), fronted by a natural sandstone bridge, is a family favorite and tops for wildlife-viewing.

Award-winning **Richard Schmidt Surf School** (☑ 831-423-0928; www.richardschmidt. com; 849 Almar Ave; lessons 2hr group/1hr private $100/130; ♿) offers small group lessons either at Cowell Beach or at Pleasure Point in Capitola. Experienced surfers can hire or buy boards and other gear at **O'Neill Surf Shop** (☑ 831-475-4151; www.oneill.com; 1115 41st Ave, Capitola; wetsuit/surfboard rental from $20/30; ⊙ 9am-8pm Mon-Fri, from 8am Sat & Sun).

★ **Santa Cruz**
Beach Boardwalk   AMUSEMENT PARK
(☑ 831-423-5590; www.beachboardwalk.com; 400 Beach St; boardwalk free, per ride $4-7, all-day pass $40; ⊙ daily late May-Aug, most weekends Sep-Apr, weather permitting; 🅿 ♿) The West Coast's oldest beachfront amusement park, this 1907 boardwalk has a glorious old-school Americana vibe. The smell of cotton candy mixes with the salt air, which is punctuated by the squeals of kids hanging upside down on carnival rides. Famous thrills include the **Giant Dipper**, a 1924 wooden roller coaster, and the 1911 **Looff carousel**, both National Historic Landmarks. During summer, catch free movies on Wednesdays, and Friday-night concerts by rock veterans you may have thought already dead.

★ **Seymour Marine**
Discovery Center   MUSEUM
(☑ 831-459-3800; http://seymourcenter.ucsc.edu; 100 McAllister Way; adult/child 3-16yr $9/7; ⊙ 10am-5pm Tue-Sun Sep-Jun, daily Jul & Aug; 🅿 ♿) ✿ This educational center is part of UCSC's Long Marine Laboratory. Interactive natural-science exhibits include tidal touch pools and aquariums, while outside you can gawk at the world's largest blue-whale skeleton.

Santa Cruz Surfing Museum   MUSEUM
(☑ 831-420-6289; 701 W Cliff Dr; entry by donation; ⊙ 10am-5pm Thu-Tue Jul 4-early Sep, noon-4pm Thu-Mon early Sep-Jul 3; ♿) A mile southwest of the wharf along the coast, this tiny museum inside an old lighthouse is packed with memorabilia, including vintage redwood surfboards. Fittingly, its location on Lighthouse Point overlooks two popular surf breaks.

★**Santa Cruz Food Tour** FOOD
(☑866-736-6343; www.santacruzfoodtour.com; per person $69; ⊙2:30-6pm Fri & Sun Apr-Oct) These congenial walking tours are the perfect way to plug into Santa Cruz's progressive, global and sophisticated food scene. Guides also deliver a healthy serving of local knowledge and interesting insights into Santa Cruz history, culture and architecture. You'll be walking for about 2 miles and will eat enough for most people not to need dinner afterwards.

🛏 Sleeping

Despite a couple of hotel openings, Santa Cruz does not have enough beds to satisfy demand: expect high prices at peak times for nothing-special rooms. Places near the beach boardwalk (p974) range from friendly to frightening. For a decent motel, cruise Ocean St inland or Mission St (Hwy 1). More hotels are in the pipeline, which should improve the city's accommodations options in the short- to mid-term.

Book well ahead to **camp** (☑800-444-7275; www.reservecalifornia.com; tent/RV sites $35/65) at state beaches off Hwy 1 south of Santa Cruz or up in the foggy Santa Cruz Mountains off Hwy 9. Family-friendly campgrounds include Henry Cowell Redwoods State Park in Felton and New Brighton State Beach in Capitola.

HI Santa Cruz Hostel HOSTEL $
(☑831-423-8304; www.hi-santacruz.org; 321 Main St; dm $28-42, r with shared bath $85-160; ⊙office 8-11am & 3-9pm; @🛜) Budget overnighters dig this cute hostel set inside five rambling Victorian cottages and surrounded by flowering gardens, just two blocks from the beach. Whip up meals in the communal kitchen or watch a DVD (free rentals) in the funky furnished lounge with fireplace. Main con: the midnight curfew.

Dream Inn HOTEL $$$
(☑831-740-8069; www.dreaminnsantacruz.com; 175 W Cliff Dr; r $270-560; P🐾❄@🛜🏊) Proud of being Santa Cruz's only oceanfront hotel, the Dream Inn has good-sized rooms brimming with retro-chic charm and turquoise color accents. Catch hypnotic bay views from private balconies. The sleek swimming pool, fronted by sandy Cowell Beach, is just steps away.

Babbling Brook Inn B&B $$$
(☑831-427-2437; www.babblingbrookinn.com; 1025 Laurel St; r $280-370; 🐾🛜) Built around a running creek amid meandering gardens and old pine and redwood trees, this wood-shingled inn has 13 cozy rooms named after impressionist painters and decorated in French-provincial style. Most have gas fireplaces, some have Jacuzzis and all have feather beds. There's afternoon wine and hors d'oeuvres, plus a full breakfast included.

🍴 Eating

There's some delicious dining to be done in Santa Cruz, which has seriously upped the kitchen ante in recent years. Seafood features prominently on menus, many of which are also driven by the regional-seasonal-organic trifecta. Pacific Ave in downtown has some excellent mid- to upscale options, while Mission St, near UCSC, and 41st Ave in Capitola offer cheaper eats.

★**Soif** CALIFORNIAN $$
(☑831-423-2020; www.soifwine.com; 105 Walnut Ave; mains $18-34; ⊙5-9pm Sun-Tue, noon-9pm Wed & Thu, noon-10pm Fri & Sat; 🍴) 🌿 A perennial local foodie fave, this chic and cosmopolitan lair harnesses mostly native products and turns them into triumphs of flavor pairings: Manila clams might cuddle with chorizo and fennel, or duck breast befriend roasted figs. There's a perfect wine match for each dish and, if you like it, you can pick up a bottle in the affiliated wine shop.

Akira Santa Cruz JAPANESE $$
(☑831-600-7093; www.akirasantacruz.com; 1222 Soquel Ave; nigiri $4-10, maki $7-17; ⊙11am-11pm; 🍴) Complemented by sake, craft brews and a buzzy surf-town ambience, Akira's menu harnesses briny-fresh tuna, salmon, eel and shellfish for a huge variety of sushi and new-gen spins on Japanese cuisine. Bento boxes for lunch ($11.50 to $16) are good value, and there's an entire page of classic and innovative vegetarian rolls.

🍷 Drinking & Nightlife

Santa Cruz's downtown overflows with bars, lounges and coffee shops. Heading west on Mission St (Hwy 1), craft breweries and wine-tasting rooms fill the raffish industrial ambience of the Swift and Ingalls St Courtyards.

★**515** COCKTAIL BAR
(☑831-425-5051; www.515santacruz.com; 515 Cedar St; ⊙5pm-midnight Sun-Tue, to 1:30am Wed-Sat) This locally beloved cocktail parlor is the perfect place for a night of dapper drinking. Settle into a huge armchair amid the

vintage-chic decor to celebrate classic and masterfully concocted libations. Le Pample-mousse, a delicious blend of vodka, Aperol and citrus, is a perennial favorite.

Verve Coffee Roasters
CAFE

(☏831-600-7784; www.vervecoffee.com; 1540 Pacific Ave; ⊙6:30am-9pm; ☏) To sip finely roasted artisan espresso or a cup of rich pour-over coffee, join the surfers and hip-sters at this high-ceilinged industrial-zen cafe. Single-origin brews and house blends rule. The mod design is a study of how to get creative with wood.

Lupulo Craft Beer House
CRAFT BEER

(☏831-454-8306; www.lupulosc.com; 233 Cath-cart St; ⊙11:30am-10pm Mon-Thu, to 11:30pm Fri, 10am-11:30pm Sat, 11am-10pm Sun) Named with the Spanish word for hops, Lupulo Craft Beer House is an essential downtown desti-nation for traveling beer fans. Modern decor combines with an ever-changing tap list – often including hard-to-get seasonal brews from local breweries – and good bar snacks ($4 to $15) such as empanadas, tacos and charcuterie plates. Almost 400 bottled and canned beers create delicious panic for the indecisive drinker.

❶ Information

Santa Cruz Visitor Center (☏831-425-1234; www.santacruz.org; 303 Water St, Suite 100; ⊙9am-noon & 1-4pm Mon-Fri, 11am-3pm Sat & Sun)

❶ Getting There & Around

Santa Cruz is 75 miles south of San Francisco via coastal Hwy 1 or Hwy 17, a nail-bitingly narrow, winding mountain road. Monterey is about 45 miles further south via Hwy 1.

Santa Cruz Shuttles (☏831-421-9883; www.santacruzshuttles.com) runs shared shuttles to/from airports at San Jose ($55), San Francis-co ($85) and Oakland ($85).

Greyhound (☏831-423-4082; www.greyhound.com; 920 Pacific Ave; ☏) has a few daily buses to San Francisco (from $16, 3½ hours), Salinas (from $12, one hour), Santa Barbara (from $39, 5½ hours) and Los Angeles (from $22, nine hours).

Santa Cruz Metro (☏831-425-8600; www.scmtd.com; 920 Pacific Ave; single rides/day pass $2/6) operates local and countywide bus routes that converge on downtown's **Metro Center** (☏831-425-8600; www.scmtd.com; 920 Pacific Ave; single rides/day pass $2/6). The Highway 17 Express bus links Santa Cruz with San Jose's Amtrak/CalTrain station ($7, 50 minutes, once or twice hourly).

From late May through early September, the ze-ro-emission **Santa Cruz Electric Shuttle** (www.santacruztrolley.com; per ride 25¢; ⊙noon-8pm late May-early Sep) connects downtown and the beach from noon to 8pm daily.

SAN FRANCISCO & THE BAY AREA

San Francisco

Grab your coat and a handful of glitter, and enter a wonderland of fog and fabulousness. So long, inhibitions; hello, San Francisco!

⊙ Sights

Most major museums are downtown, though Golden Gate Park is home to the de Young Museum and the California Academy of Sciences. The city's most historic districts are the Mission, Chinatown, North Beach and the Haight. Galleries are clustered downtown and in North Beach, the Mission, Potrero Flats and Dogpatch. You'll find hilltop parks citywide, but Russian, Nob and Telegraph Hills are the highest and most panoramic.

⊙ Downtown, Civic Center & SoMa

Downtown has all the amenities: art galleries, swanky hotels, first-run theaters, malls and entertainment megaplexes. High-end stores ring **Union Sq** (Map p982; btwn Geary, Powell, Post & Stockton Sts; ☐ Powell-Mason, Powell-Hyde, Ⓜ Powell, Ⓑ Powell) now, but this people-watch-ing plaza has been a hotbed of protest, from pro-Union Civil War rallies to AIDS vigils.

Civic Center is a zoning conundrum, with great performances and Asian art treasures on one side of City Hall and dive bars and soup kitchens on the other. Some head to South of Market (SoMa) for high-tech deals, others for high art, but everyone gets down and dirty on the dance floor.

★ San Francisco
Museum of Modern Art
MUSEUM

(SFMOMA; Map p982; ☏415-357-4000; www.sfmoma.org; 151 3rd St; adult/ages 19-24yr/under 18yr $25/19/free; ⊙10am-5pm Fri-Tue, to 9pm Thu, atrium 8am Mon-Fri; ☝; ☐5, 6, 7, 14, 19, 21, 31, 38, Ⓜ Montgomery, Ⓑ Montgomery) The expanded San Francisco Museum of Modern Art is a mind-boggling feat, nearly tripling in size to accommodate a sprawling collection of modern and contemporary masterworks over seven floors of galleries – but then, SFMOMA has defied limits ever since its 1935 founding. The museum was a visionary early investor in then-emerging art forms including photography, installations, video, performance art, digital art and industrial design. Even during the Depression, SFMOMA envisioned a world of vivid possibilities, starting in San Francisco.

Asian Art Museum MUSEUM
(Map p982; ☑ 415-581-3500; www.asianart.org; 200 Larkin St; adult/student/child $15/10/free, 1st Sun of month free; ☺ 10am-5pm Tue, Wed & Fri-Sun, to 9pm Thu; ☜ ; M Civic Center, B Civic Center) Imaginations race from subtle Chinese ink paintings to seductive Hindu temple carvings and from elegant Islamic calligraphy to cutting-edge Japanese minimalism across three floors spanning 6000 years of Asian art. Besides the largest collection of Asian art outside Asia – 18,000 works – the museum offers excellent programs for all ages, from shadow-puppet shows and tea tastings with star chefs to mixers with cross-cultural DJ mash-ups.

Contemporary Jewish Museum MUSEUM
(Map p982; ☑ 415-655-7856; www.thecjm.org; 736 Mission St; adult/student/child $14/12/free, after 5pm Thu $8; ☺ 11am-5pm Mon, Tue & Fri-Sun, to 8pm Thu; ☜ ; ☐ 14, 30, 45, B Montgomery, M Montgomery) That upended blue-steel box miraculously balancing on one corner atop the Contemporary Jewish Museum is appropriate for an institution that upends conventional ideas about art and religion. Architect Daniel Libeskind designed this museum to be rational, mystical and powerful: building onto a 1907 brick power station, he added blue-steel elements to form the Hebrew word *l'chaim* (life). But it's the contemporary-art commissions that truly bring the building to life.

Museum of the African Diaspora MUSEUM
(MoAD; Map p982; ☑ 415-358-7200; www.moadsf.org; 685 Mission St; adult/student/child $10/5/free; ☺ 11am-6pm Wed-Sat, noon-5pm Sun; P ☜ ; ☐ 14, 30, 45, M Montgomery, B Montgomery) MoAD assembles an international cast of characters to tell the epic story of diaspora, including a moving video of slave narratives told by Maya Angelou. Standouts among quarterly changing exhibits have included homages to '80s New Wave icon Grace Jones, architect David Adjaye's photographs of contemporary African landmarks and Alison Saar's sculptures of figures marked by history. Public events include poetry slams, Yoruba spiritual music celebrations and lectures examining the legacy of the Black Panthers' free-school-breakfast program.

Glide Memorial United Methodist Church CHURCH
(Map p982; ☑ 415-674-6090; www.glide.org; 330 Ellis St; ☺ celebrations 9am & 11am Sun; ☜ ; ☐ 38, M Powell, B Powell) When the rainbow-robed Glide gospel choir enters singing their hearts out, the 2000-plus congregation erupts in cheers, hugs and dance moves. Raucous Sunday Glide celebrations capture San Francisco at its most welcoming and uplifting, embracing the rainbow spectrum of culture, gender, orientation, ability and socioeconomics. After the celebration ends, the congregation keeps the inspiration coming, serving 2000 meals a day and connecting homeless individuals and families with shelter and emotional support. Yes, Glide welcomes volunteers.

Powell St Cable Car Turnaround LANDMARK
(Map p982; www.sfmta.com; cnr Powell & Market Sts; ☐ Powell-Mason, Mason-Hyde, M Powell, B Powell) Peek through the passenger queue at Powell and Market Sts to spot cable-car operators leaping out, gripping the chassis of each trolley and slooowly turning the car atop a revolving wooden platform. Cable cars can't go in reverse, so they need to be turned around by hand here at the terminus of the Powell St lines. Riders queue up midmorning to early evening to secure a seat, with raucous street performers and doomsday preachers on the sidelines as entertainment.

◉ Embarcadero

★ Ferry Building LANDMARK
(Map p982; ☑ 415-983-8000; www.ferrybuildingmarketplace.com; cnr Market St & the Embarcadero; ☺ 10am-7pm Mon-Fri, 8am-6pm Sat, 11am-5pm Sun; ☜ ; ☐ 2, 6, 9, 14, 21, 31, M Embarcadero, B Embarcadero) Hedonism is alive and well at this transit hub turned gourmet emporium, where foodies happily miss their ferries over Sonoma oysters and bubbly, SF craft beer and Marin-raised beef burgers, and locally roasted coffee and just-baked cupcakes. Star chefs are frequently spotted at the farmers market (p993) that wraps around the building all year.

★ Exploratorium MUSEUM
(Map p982; ☑ 415-528-4444; www.exploratorium.edu; Pier 15/17; adult/child $29.95/19.95,

6-10pm Thu $19.95; ⊙10am-5pm Tue-Sun, over 18yr only 6-10pm Thu; P⊕; ME, F) ✎ Is there a science to skateboarding? Do toilets really flush counterclockwise in Australia? At San Francisco's hands-on science museum, you'll find out things you wish you learned in school. Combining science with art and investigating human perception, the Exploratorium nudges you to question how you perceive the world around you. The setting is thrilling: a 9-acre, glass-walled pier jutting straight into San Francisco Bay, with large outdoor portions you can explore free of charge, 24 hours a day.

Transamerica Pyramid & Redwood Park
NOTABLE BUILDING

(Map p982; www.thepyramidcenter.com; 600 Montgomery St; ⊙10am-3pm Mon-Fri; ⊕Embarcadero, ⊞Embarcadero) The defining feature of San Francisco's skyline is this 1972 pyramid, built atop a whaling ship abandoned in the gold rush. A half-acre redwood grove sprouted out front, on the site of Mark Twain's favorite saloon and the newspaper office where Sun Yat-sen drafted his Proclamation of the Republic of China. Although these transplanted redwoods have shallow roots, their intertwined structure helps them reach dizzying heights – Twain himself couldn't have penned a more perfect metaphor for San Francisco.

◉ Chinatown & North Beach

Grant Ave is Chinatown's economic heart, but its soul is **Waverly Place** (Map p982; ⊟1, 30, ⊟California, Powell-Mason, MT), lined with historic clinker-brick buildings and flag-festooned temple balconies. Chinatown's 41 historic **alleyways** (Map p982; btwn Grant Ave, Stockton St, California St & Broadway; ⊟1, 30, 45, ⊟Powell-Hyde, Powell-Mason, California) have seen it all since 1849: gold rushes and revolution, incense and opium, fire and icy receptions. **Chinatown Alleyway Tours** (Map p982; ☎415-984-1478; www.chinatownalleywaytours.org; Portsmouth Sq; adult/student $26/16; ⊙tours 11am Sat; ⊕; ⊟1, 8, 10, 12, 30, 41, 45, ⊟California, Powell-Mason, Powell-Hyde) and **Chinatown Heritage Walking Tours** (Map p982; ☎415-986-1822; https://tour.cccsf.us; Chinese Culture Center, Hilton Hotel, 3rd fl, 750 Kearny St; adult $30-40, student $20-30; ⊕; ⊟1, 8, 10, 12, 30, 41, 45, ⊟California, Powell-Mason, Powell-Hyde) offer community-supporting, time-traveling strolls through defining moments in American history.

Wild parrots circle over the Italian cafes and bohemian bars of North Beach, serving enough espresso to fuel your own Beat poetry revival.

★Coit Tower
PUBLIC ART

(Map p982; ☎415-249-0995; www.sfrecpark.org; Telegraph Hill Blvd; nonresident elevator fee adult/child $9/6, mural tour full/2nd fl only $9/6; ⊙10am-6pm Apr-Oct, to 5pm Nov-Mar; ⊟39) The exclamation mark on San Francisco's skyline is Coit Tower, with 360-degree views of downtown and wraparound 1930s Works Progress Administration (WPA) murals celebrating SF workers. Initially denounced as communist, the murals are now a national landmark. For a parrot's-eye panoramic view of San Francisco 210ft above the city, take the elevator to the tower's open-air platform. Book your docent-led, 30- to 40-minute mural tour online – tour all murals ($9),

---

SAN FRANCISCO IN...

One Day

Grab a leather strap on the Powell-Mason cable car and hold on: you're in for hills and thrills. Hop off at Washington Square Park, where parrots squawk encouragement for your hike up to **Coit Tower** for 1930s murals celebrating SF workers and 360-degree panoramas. Next, catch your prebooked ferry to **Alcatraz**, where D-Block solitary raises goose bumps. Hop the Powell-Mason cable car to North Beach, to take in free-speech landmark **City Lights Books**. Sample North Beach's best pasta at **Cotogna** then toast the wildest night in the west with potent Pisco sours at **Comstock Saloon**.

Two Days

Start your day in the Mission amid mural-covered garage doors lining **Balmy Alley**, then step inside meditative **Mission Dolores**. Break for burritos before hoofing it to the Haight for flashbacks at vintage boutiques and the Summer of Love site: **Golden Gate Park**. Glimpse bay views atop the **de Young Museum**, take a walk on the empirical side at the **California Academy of Sciences** and brave winds on the **Golden Gate Bridge**.

San Francisco & the Bay Area

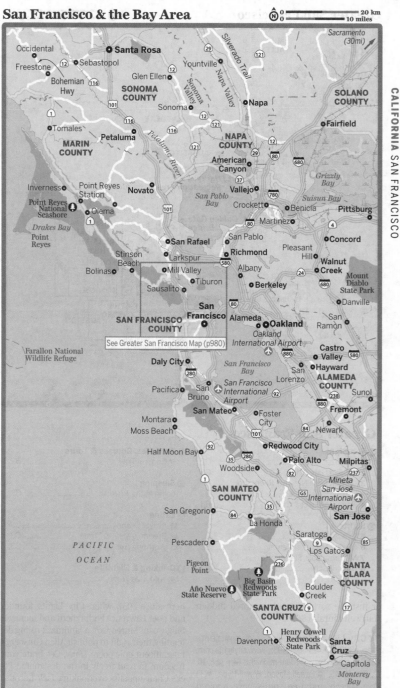

Greater San Francisco

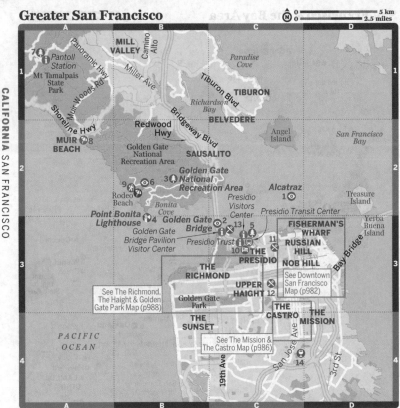

Greater San Francisco

or just the seven recently restored hidden stairwell murals ($6).

★ **City Lights Books**   CULTURAL CENTER
(Map p982; ☏ 415-362-8193; www.citylights.com; 261 Columbus Ave; ⊙ 10am-midnight; ⊞; ▣ 8, 10, 12, 30, 41, 45, ▣ Powell-Mason, Powell-Hyde, Ⓜ T) Free speech and free spirits have rejoiced

here since 1957, when City Lights founder and poet Lawrence Ferlinghetti and manager Shigeyoshi Murao won a landmark ruling defending their right to publish Allen Ginsberg's magnificent epic poem *Howl*. Celebrate your freedom to read freely in the designated Poet's Chair upstairs overlooking Jack Kerouac Alley, load up on zines on the mezzanine and entertain radical ideas downstairs in the new Pedagogies of Resistance section.

Beat Museum   MUSEUM
(Map p982; ☎ 800-537-6822; www.kerouac.com; 540 Broadway; adult/student $8/5, walking tours $30; ⏱ museum 10am-7pm, walking tours 2-4pm Sat; 🚌 8,10,12,30,41,45, 🚋 Powell-Mason, Ⓜ T) The closest you can get to the complete Beat experience without breaking a law. The 1000-plus artifacts in this museum's literary-ephemera collection include the sublime (the banned edition of Ginsberg's *Howl*, with the author's own annotations) and the ridiculous (those Kerouac bobblehead dolls are definite head-shakers). Downstairs, watch Beat-era films in ramshackle theater seats redolent with the odors of literary giants, pets and pot. Upstairs, pay your respects at shrines to individual Beat writers. A seismic retrofit may mean closures; call ahead.

⊙ Russian Hill & Nob Hill

You've seen the switchbacks of the 900 block of **Lombard Street** (Map p982; 🚋 Powell-Hyde) in a thousand photographs. Incorrectly dubbed 'the world's crookedest street,' it is undeniably scenic, with its red-brick pavement and lovingly tended flowerbeds. While you're here, explore San Francisco's twin downtown hills – hop off a cable car, head to tiki-bar happy hour, hear a cathedral organ recital, or just watch the Bay Bridge lights twinkle.

★**Cable Car Museum**   HISTORIC SITE
(Map p982; ☎ 415-474-1887; www.cablecarmuseum.org; 1201 Mason St; donations appreciated; ⏱ 10am-6pm Apr-Sep, to 5pm Oct-Mar; ♿; 🚋 Powell-Mason, Powell-Hyde) **FREE** That clamor you hear riding cable cars is the sound of San Francisco's peak technology at work. Gears click and wire-hemp ropes whir as these vintage contraptions are hoisted up and over hills too steep for horses or buses – and you can inspect those cables close-up here, in the city's still-functioning cable-car barn. See three original 1870s cable cars stored here and browse a bonanza of SF memorabilia (actual cable-car bells!) in the museum shop.

★**Diego Rivera Gallery**   GALLERY
(Map p982; ☎ 415-771-7020; www.sfai.edu; 800 Chestnut St; ⏱ 9am-7pm; 🚌 30, 🚋 Powell-Mason) **FREE** Diego Rivera's 1931 *The Making of a Fresco Showing the Building of a City* is a *trompe l'oeil* fresco within a fresco, showing the artist himself pausing to admire his own work and the efforts of workers around him,

as they build the modern city of San Francisco. The fresco covers an entire wall of the Diego Rivera Gallery in the **San Francisco Art Institute** (SFAI; Map p982; ☎ 415-771-7020; www.sfai.edu; 800 Chestnut St; ⏱ Walter & McBean Galleries 11am-7pm Tue, to 6pm Wed-Sat, Diego Rivera Gallery 9am-7pm; 🚌 30, 🚋 Powell-Mason) **FREE**. For sweeping views of the city Diego admired, head to the terrace cafe for espresso and panoramic bay vistas.

★**Grace Cathedral**   CHURCH
(Map p982; ☎ 415-749-6300; www.gracecathedral.org; 1100 California St; suggested donation adult/child $3/2; ⏱ 8am-6pm Mon-Sat, to 7pm Sun, services 8:30am, 11am & 6pm Sun; 🚌 1, 🚋 California) San Francisco's Episcopal cathedral has been rebuilt three times since the gold rush and the current reinforced-concrete Gothic cathedral took 40 years to complete. Spectacular stained-glass windows include a 'Human Endeavor' series dedicated to science, depicting Albert Einstein uplifted in swirling nuclear particles. San Francisco history unfolds on murals covering the 1906 earthquake to the 1945 UN charter signing. People of all faiths wander indoor and outdoor inlaid-stone labyrinths, meant to guide restless souls through three spiritual stages: releasing, receiving and returning.

⊙ The Marina, Fisherman's Wharf & Presidio

Since the gold rush, this waterfront has been the point of entry for new arrivals – and it remains a major attraction for sea-lion antics and getaways to and from Alcatraz. To the west, the Marina has chic boutiques in a former cow pasture and organic dining along the waterfront. At the adjoining Presidio, you'll encounter Shakespeare on the loose and public nudity on a former army base.

★**Golden Gate Bridge**   BRIDGE
(Map p980; ☎ toll information 877-229-8655; www.goldengatebridge.org/visitors; Hwy 101; northbound free, southbound $7-8; 🚌 28, all Golden Gate Transit buses) San Franciscans have passionate perspectives on every subject, especially their signature landmark, though everyone agrees that it's a good thing that the Navy didn't get its way over the bridge's design – naval officials preferred a hulking concrete span, painted with caution-yellow stripes, over the soaring art-deco design of architects Gertrude and Irving Murrow and engineer Joseph B Strauss, which, luckily, won the day.

Downtown San Francisco

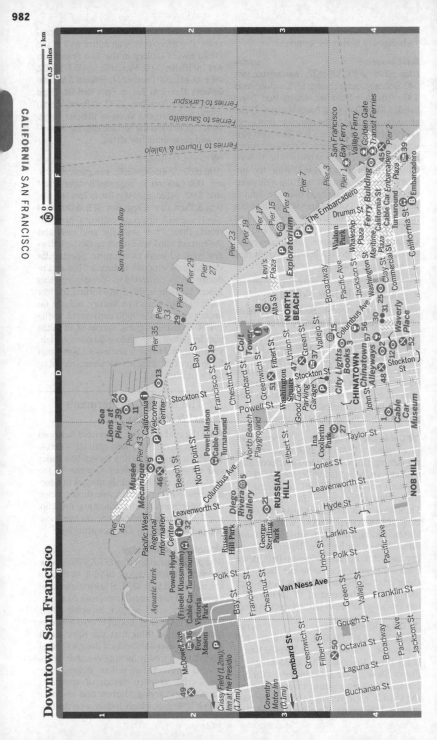

San Francisco Bay

Aquatic Park

Sea Lions at Pier 39

Musée Mécanique

Pacific West Regional Information Center

Powell-Hyde Cable Car Turnaround (Friedel Klussmann)

Fort Mason

McDowell Ave

Crissy Field (1.2mi); Inn at the Presidio (1.7mi)

Coventry Motor Inn (0.1mi)

Russian Hill Park

George Sterling Park

Lombard St

Diego Rivera Gallery

RUSSIAN HILL

Columbus Ave

North Beach Playground

North Beach

Cable Car Turnaround

Powell-Mason

California St Welcome Center

Ferries to Larkspur

Ferries to Sausalito

Ferries to Tiburon & Vallejo

Pier 45

Pier 43

Pier 41

Pier 39

Pier 35

Pier 33

Pier 31

Pier 29

Pier 27

Pier 23

Pier 19

Pier 17

Pier 15

Pier 9

Pier 7

Pier 3

Pier 1

Pier 2

San Francisco Bay Ferry

Vallejo Ferry

Golden Gate Transit Ferries

Ferry Building

Cable Car Embarcadero Turnaround

The Embarcadero

Maritime Plaza

Whaleship Plaza

Walton Park

Exploratorium

Levi's Plaza

Drumm St

Broadway

Pacific Ave

Jackson St

Washington St

Clay St

California St

Commercial St

NORTH BEACH

Alta St

Union St

Green St

Vallejo St

Coit Tower

Filbert St

Greenwich St

Lombard St

Washington Square

Good Luck Parking Garage

Stockton St

City Lights Books

Columbus Ave

CHINATOWN

Waverly Place

Chinatown Alleyways

John St

Stockton St

Cable Car Museum

NOB HILL

Ina Coolbrith Park

Taylor St

Jones St

Leavenworth St

Hyde St

Larkin St

Polk St

Van Ness Ave

Franklin St

Gough St

Octavia St

Laguna St

Buchanan St

Union St

Green St

Vallejo St

Broadway

Pacific Ave

Jackson St

Greenwich St

Filbert St

Chestnut St

Bay St

Francisco St

North Point St

Beach St

Stockton St

Leavenworth St

Victoria Park

Polk St

Francisco St

Chestnut St

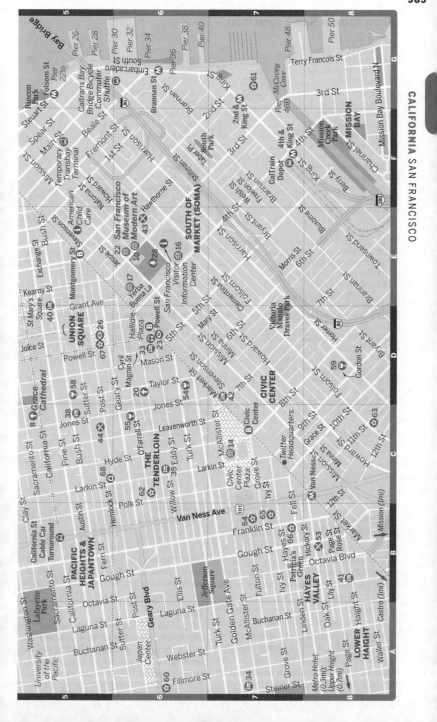

Bay Bridge

Pier 22½
Pier 26
Pier 28
Pier 30
Pier 32
Pier 34
Pier 36
Pier 38
Pier 40
Pier 48
Pier 50

Rincon Park
Folsom St
Pier 7
Steuart St
Spear St
Main St
Beale St
Temporary Transbay Terminal
American Terminal
Fremont St
Natoma St
Howard St

Caltrans Bay Bridge Bicycle Commuter Shuttle
Embarcadero
South St

Brannan St
King St
Berry St
2nd St
3rd St

Terry Francois St
McCovey Cove
3rd St

Pier 46B

MISSION BAY

Mission Bay Boulevard N

1st St
Stevenson St
Jessie St

San Francisco Museum of Modern Art

SOUTH OF MARKET (SOMA)

Stillman St
Taber Pl
South Park
Welsh St
Freelon St
Brannan St

4th & King St
King St
Channel St

Mission Creek Park

Mission St

CalTrain Depot

Bush St
Exchange St
Kearny St
Grant Ave
Powell St

Yerba Buena La

San Francisco Visitor Information Center

5th St
4th St
Clementina St
Folsom St
Harrison St
Bryant St

Morris St
Buxome St

6th St
7th St

Townsend St
Brannan St

St Mary's Square
UNION SQUARE
Joice St
Powell St

Hallidie Plaza

Cyril Magnin St
Mason St
Market St
Stevenson St

Mary St
Minna St
Mission St
Howard St

Victoria Manalo Draves Park

Homer St

Gordon St
Bryant St

Grace Cathedral

Sutter St
Post St
Geary St
Taylor St
Jones St

O'Farrell St
Leavenworth St

THE TENDERLOIN

Turk St
Eddy St
Larkin St

7th St
8th St

CIVIC CENTER

Twitter Headquarters

Grace St
9th St
10th St
11th St
12th St

Howard St
Minna St
Mission St

Sacramento St
California St
Pine St
Bush St
Hyde St

California St Cable Car Turnaround

PACIFIC HEIGHTS & JAPANTOWN

Austin St
Hemlock St
Larkin St
Polk St

Willow St
McAllister St
Civic Center

Civic Center Plaza

Ivy St
Grove St

Van Ness Ave

12th St
Mission St

Clay St
Washington St

University of the Pacific

Lafayette Park

Clay St
Sacramento St
California St
Fern St
Gough St

Franklin St
Gough St

Hayes St
Patricia's Green

Octavia Blvd
Page St
Rose St

HAYES VALLEY

Hickory St

Sacramento St
Octavia St
Laguna St
Buchanan St

Japan Center

Geary Blvd

Jefferson Square

Fulton St
Ivy St
Linden St
Oak St
Lily St
Haight St

LOWER HAIGHT

Washington St
Webster St
Fillmore St
Steiner St

Post St
Sutter St
Geary Blvd
Turk St
Golden Gate Ave
McAllister St
Grove St
Page St
Waller St
Haight St

Laguna St
Buchanan St

Metro Hotel (0.3mi);
Upper Haight (0.7mi)

Mission (1mi)
Castro (1mi)

Downtown San Francisco

★ **Sea Lions at Pier 39**   SEA LIONS
(Map p982; ☎415-623-4734; www.pier39.com; Pier 39, cnr Beach St & the Embarcadero; ⊙24hr; ⍟; ⍟47, ⍟Powell-Mason, ⍟E, F) Sea lions took over San Francisco's most coveted waterfront real estate in 1989 and have been making a public display of themselves ever since. Naturally these unkempt squatters have become San Francisco's favorite mascots, and since California law requires boats to make way for marine mammals, yacht owners have to relinquish valuable slips to accommodate as many as 1000 sea lions. These giant mammals 'haul out' onto the docks between January and July, and whenever else they feel like sunbathing.

Crissy Field   PARK
(Map p980; ☎415-561-4700; www.nps.gov; 1199 East Beach; ⍟⍟; ⍟30, PresidiGo Shuttle) War is for the birds at Crissy Field, a military airstrip turned waterfront nature preserve with knockout Golden Gate views. Where military aircraft once zoomed in for landings, bird-watchers now huddle in the silent

rushes of a reclaimed tidal marsh. Joggers pound beachside trails and the only security alerts are raised by puppies suspiciously sniffing surfers. On foggy days, stop by the certified-green **Warming Hut** (Map p980; ☑ 415-561-3042; www.parksconservancy.org/visit/eat/warming-hut.html; 983 Marine Dr; items $4-9; ☺ 9am-5pm; 🅿 ♿; 🚇 PresidiGo shuttle) 🍃 to browse regional-nature books and warm up with fair-trade coffee.

◉ The Mission & the Castro

The best way to enjoy the Mission is with a book in one hand and a burrito in the other, amid murals, sunshine and the usual crowd of filmmakers, techies, grocers, skaters and novelists. Calle 24 (24th St) is SF's designated Latino Cultural District, and the Mission is also a magnet for Southeast Asian Americans, lesbians and dandies. In the Castro, rainbow flags wave their welcome to all in the world's premier LGBTQ+ culture destination.

★Clarion Alley   PUBLIC ART
(Map p986; https://clarionalleymuralproject.org; btwn 17th & 18th Sts; 🚌 14, 22, 33, 🅱 16th St Mission, Ⓜ 16th St Mission) In this open-air street-art showcase, you'll spot artists touching up pieces and making new ones, with the full consent of neighbors and Clarion Alley Collective's curators. Only a few pieces survive for years, such as Megan Wilson's daisy-covered *Tax the Rich* or Jet Martinez' glimpse of Clarion Alley inside a forest spirit. Incontinent art critics often take over the alley's eastern end – pee-eew! – so topical murals usually go up on the western end.

★Women's Building   NOTABLE BUILDING
(Map p986; ☑ 415-431-1180; www.womensbuilding.org; 3543 18th St; 🚌 14, 22, 33, 49, 🅱 16th St Mission, Ⓜ J) A renowned and beloved Mission landmark since 1979, the nation's first women-owned-and-operated community center is festooned with one of the neighborhood's most awe-inspiring murals. The *Maestrapeace* mural was painted in 1994 and depicts hugely influential women, including Nobel Prize–winner Rigoberta Menchú, poet Audre Lorde, artist Georgia O'Keeffe and former US Surgeon General Dr Joycelyn Elders.

★Balmy Alley   PUBLIC ART
(Map p986; ☑ 415-285-2287; www.precitaeyes.org; btwn 24th & 25th Sts; 🚌 10, 12, 14, 27, 48, 🅱 24th St Mission) Inspired by Diego Rivera's 1930s San Francisco murals and provoked by US foreign policy in Latin America, 1970s Mission

muralistas (muralists) led by Mia Gonzalez set out to transform the political landscape one mural at a time. The earliest works by Mujeres Muralistas ('Women Muralists') and Placa ('Mark-making') created a united artistic front. Today, murals span three decades, from a memorial for El Salvador activist Archbishop Óscar Romero to a homage to female artists, including Frida Kahlo and Georgia O'Keeffe.

Mission Dolores   CHURCH
(Misión San Francisco de Asís; Map p986; ☑ 415-621-8203; www.missiondolores.org; 3321 16th St; adult/child $7/5; ☺ 9am-4:30pm May-Oct, to 4pm Nov-Apr; 🚌 22, 33, 🅱 16th St Mission, Ⓜ J) The city's oldest building and its namesake, whitewashed adobe Misión San Francisco de Asís was founded in 1776 and rebuilt from 1782. Today the modest adobe structure is overshadowed by the ornate adjoining 1913 **basilica**, built after the 1876 brick Gothic cathedral collapsed in the 1906 earthquake. It now features stained-glass windows depicting California's 21 missions and, true to Mission Dolores' name, seven panels depict the Seven Sorrows of Mary.

◉ The Haight

Hippie idealism lives in the Haight, with street musicians, anarchist comic books and psychedelic murals galore. Browse local designs and go gourmet in Hayes Valley, where Zen monks and jazz legends drift down the sidewalks.

★Haight Street   STREET
(Map p988; btwn Central & Stanyan Sts; 🚌 7, 22, 33, 43, Ⓜ N) Was it the fall of 1966 or the winter of '67? As the Haight saying goes, if you can remember the Summer of Love, you probably weren't here. The fog was laced with pot, sandalwood incense and burning military draft cards, entire days were spent contemplating trippy Grateful Dead posters, and the corner of **Haight and Ashbury Streets** (Map p988; 🚌 6, 7, 33, 37, 43) became the turning point for an entire generation. The Haight's counterculture kids called themselves freaks and flower children; *San Francisco Chronicle* columnist Herb Caen dubbed them 'hippies.'

◉ Golden Gate & Around

Hard-core surfers and gourmet adventurers meet in the foggy Avenues around Golden Gate Park. This is one totally chill global

The Mission & The Castro

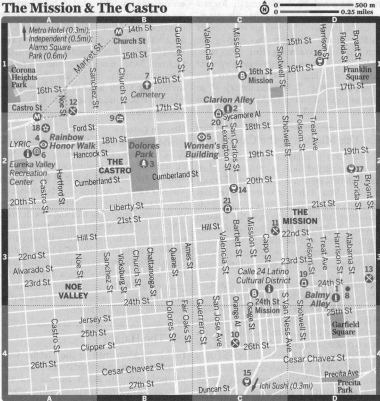

village, featuring bluegrass and Korean BBQ, disc golf and tiki cocktails, French pastries and cult-movie matinees. Beyond the park, time seems to slow down, with the tranquil, mostly residential avenues stretching out toward Ocean Beach.

★ **Golden Gate Park** PARK
(Map p988; https://goldengatepark.com; btwn Stanyan St & Great Hwy; P⊞; ⬛5, 7, 18, 21, 28, 29, 33, 44, Ⓜ N) 🆓 From bonsai and buffalo to redwoods and protests, and from flowers, Frisbees and free music to free spirits, Golden Gate Park seems to contain just about everything San Franciscans love about their city. You could wander it for a week and still not see it all, with attractions including the **de Young Museum** (Map p988; ☎415-750-3600; http://deyoung.famsf.org; 50 Hagiwara Tea Garden Dr; adult/child $15/free, 1st Tue of month free; ⊙9:30am-5:15pm Tue-Sun; ⬛5, 7, 44, Ⓜ N), **California Academy of Sciences** (Map p988; ☎415-379-8000; www.calacademy. org; 55 Music Concourse Dr; adult/student/child $35.95/30.95/25.95; ⊙9:30am-5pm Mon-Sat, from 11am Sun; P⊞; ⬛5, 6, 7, 21, 31, 33, 44, Ⓜ N)

🌳, **San Francisco Botanical Garden** (Strybing Arboretum; Map p988; ☎415-661-1316; www. sfbg.org; 1199 9th Ave; adult/child $9/2, before 9am daily & 2nd Tue of month free; ⊙7:30am-5pm, extended hours in summer & spring, last entry 1hr before closing, bookstore 10am-4pm; ⬛6, 7, 44, Ⓜ N), 🌳, **Japanese Tea Garden** (Map p988; ☎415-752-1171; www.japaneseteagardensf.com; 75 Hagiwara Tea Garden Dr; adult/child $8/2, before 10am Mon, Wed & Fri free; ⊙9am-6pm Mar-Oct, to 4:45pm Nov-Feb; P; ⬛5, 7, 44, Ⓜ N), **Conservatory of Flowers** (Map p988; ☎415-831-2090; www.conservatoryofflowers.org; 100 John F Kennedy Dr; adult/student/child $9/6/3, 1st Tue of month free; ⊙10am-6pm Tue-Sun; ⬛5, 7, 21, 33, Ⓜ N) and **Stow Lake** (Map p988; www.sfrecpark.org; ⊙5am-midnight; ⬛7, 44, Ⓜ N).

The Mission & The Castro

☞ Tours

★ Precita Eyes
Mission Mural Tours   WALKING
(Map p986; ☎ 415-285-2287; www.precitaeyes.
org; 2981 24th St; adult/child $20/3; 🚌 12, 14, 48,
49, Ⓑ 24th St Mission) Muralists lead weekend
walking tours covering 60 to 70 Mission murals within a six- to 10-block radius of mu-
ral-bedecked Balmy Alley (p985). Tours last
from one hour to two hours and 15 minutes
(for the more in-depth, private Classic Mural Walk). Proceeds fund mural upkeep and
overheads at this community arts nonprofit.

Public Library City Guides   TOURS
(☎ 415-557-4266; www.sfcityguides.org) **FREE**
Volunteer local historians lead nonprof-
it tours organized by neighborhood and
theme: Victorian San Francisco, Castro
Tales, Alfred Hitchcock's San Francisco,
Gold Rush City, Deco Downtown, Secrets of
Fisherman's Wharf, Russian Hill Stairways
and more. Book ahead for the popular Diego
Rivera Mural tour inside the Stock Exchange
Luncheon Club. Tips are welcome.

Emperor Norton's
Fantastic Time Machine   WALKING
(Map p982; ☎ 415-548-1710; www.sftimemachine.
com; $30; ⊙ 11am Thu & Sat, waterfront tour 11am
Sun; 🚌 30, 38, Ⓑ Powell St, Ⓜ Powell St, 🚋 Powell-Mason, Powell-Hyde) Huzzah, San Francisco
invented time-travel contraptions! They're
called shoes, and you wear them to follow
the self-appointed Emperor Norton (aka historian Joseph Amster) across 2 miles of the
most dastardly, scheming, uplifting and ur-
ban-legendary terrain on Earth...or at least

west of Berkeley. Sunday waterfront tours
depart from the Ferry Building; all others
depart from Union Sq's Dewey Monument.

🛏 Sleeping

San Francisco hotel rates are among the
world's highest. Plan ahead – well ahead – and
grab bargains when you see them. If you have
the choice, San Francisco's boutique properties beat chains for a sense of place – but take
what you can get at a price you can afford.

🛏 Downtown, Civic Center & SoMa

★ HI San Francisco City Center   HOSTEL $
(Map p982; ☎ 415-474-5721; www.sfhostels.org;
685 Ellis St; dm $33-70, r $90-165; @ 🛜; 🚌 19,
38, 47, 49) 🍃 The seven-story, 1920s Ather-
ton Hotel was remodeled in 2001 into a
much-better-than-average hostel, with private baths in all rooms, including dorms.
And it scores bonus points for ecofriendli-
ness: the place is powered mainly by solar
panels, and shower heads change color
based on the length of a shower.

★ Yotel San Francisco   HOTEL $
(Map p982; ☎ 415-829-0000; www.yotel.com/
en/hotels/yotel-san-francisco; 1095 Market St;
d $149-209; ❄ 🛜; 🚌 6, 7, 9, 21, Ⓑ Civic Center,
Ⓜ Civic Center) Newly situated within the
long-standing Grant building, this chic
downtown hotel is a West Coast first for parent company Yotel, a chain of compact, tech-
nology-forward luxury stays. Design choices
conserve time and space at every turn, from

The Richmond, The Haight & Golden Gate Park

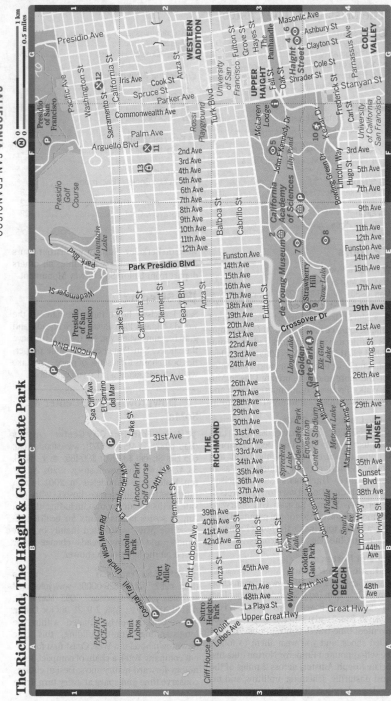

The Richmond, The Haight & Golden Gate Park

the self-check-in kiosks to the adjustable 'smartbeds' (which morph into couches) to the playful 'sky cabins,' cozy lofted sleeping quarters with extralong mattresses and large flat-screen TVs.

★**Axiom** BOUTIQUE HOTEL **$$**
(Map p982; ☎415-392-9466; www.axiomhotel. com; 28 Cyril Magnin St; d $189-342; @🞲🞲; 🚃Powell-Mason, Powell-Hyde, Ⓑ Powell, ⓂPowell) Of all the downtown SF hotels aiming for high-tech appeal, this one gets it right. The lobby is razzle-dazzle LED, marble and riveted steel, but the games room looks like a start-up HQ, with arcade games and foosball tables. Guest rooms have low-slung, gray-flannel couches, king platform beds, dedicated routers for high-speed wireless streaming to Apple/Google/Samsung devices, and Bluetooth-enabled everything.

Hotel Vitale BOUTIQUE HOTEL **$$$**
(Map p982; ☎415-278-3700; www.hotelvitale.com; 8 Mission St; r $385-675; 🞲@🞲🞲; ⓂEmbarcadero, Ⓑ Embarcadero) When your love interest or executive recruiter books you into the waterfront Vitale, you know it's serious. The office-tower exterior disguises a snazzy hotel with sleek, up-to-the-minute luxuries. Beds are dressed with silky-soft 450-thread-count sheets, and there's an excellent on-site spa with two rooftop hot tubs. Rooms facing the bay offer spectacular Bay Bridge views, and Ferry Building dining awaits across the street.

Hotel Mayflower HISTORIC HOTEL **$**
(Map p982; ☎415-673-7010; www.sfmayflower hotel.com; 975 Bush St; d $130-190; Ⓟ🞲🞲🞲; 🚃2, 3, 27) Location, comfort and character at half the cost of places down the block. Built in 1926, Hotel Mayflower has a Spanish Mission–style cloister lobby and vintage cage elevator straight out of a Hitchcock movie. Guest rooms are snug and simple but ship-shape, with sepia-toned San Francisco murals and

wrought iron bed frames. Rates include muffin breakfasts; parking is a bargain at $20.

North Beach & Chinatown

★**Hotel Bohème** BOUTIQUE HOTEL **$$**
(Map p982; ☎415-433-9111; www.hotelboheme. com; 444 Columbus Ave; r $195-295; 🞲@🞲; 🚃10, 12, 30, 41, 45, Ⓜ T) Eclectic, historic and unabashedly romantic, this quintessential North Beach boutique hotel has jazz-era color schemes, wrought-iron beds, paper-umbrella lamps, Beat poetry and artwork on the walls. The vintage rooms are smallish, some face noisy Columbus Ave (quieter rooms are in back) and bathrooms are teensy, but novels beg to be written here – especially after bar crawls. No elevator or parking lot.

Orchard Garden Hotel BOUTIQUE HOTEL **$$$**
(Map p982; ☎415-393-9917; www.theorchard gardenhotel.com; 466 Bush St; r $278-332; Ⓟ🞲🞲@🞲; 🚃2, 3, 30, 45, Ⓑ Montgomery) San Francisco's original LEED-certified, all-green-practices hotel uses sustainably grown wood, chemical-free cleaning products and recycled fabrics in its soothingly quiet rooms. Don't think you'll be trading comfort for conscience: rooms have unexpectedly luxe touches, like high-end down pillows, Egyptian-cotton sheets and organic bath products. Toast sunsets with a cocktail on the rooftop terrace. Book directly for deals, free breakfast and parking.

The Marina, Fisherman's Wharf & Presidio

★**HI San Francisco Fisherman's Wharf** HOSTEL **$**
(Map p982; ☎415-771-7277; www.hiusa.org; Fort Mason, Bldg 240; dm $40-64, r $116-160; Ⓟ@🞲; 🚃28, 30, 47, 49) Trading downtown convenience for a parklike setting with

Alcatraz

A HALF-DAY TOUR

Book a ferry from Pier 33 and ride 1.5 miles across the bay to explore America's most notorious former prison. The trip itself is worth the money, providing stunning views of the city skyline. Once you've landed at the ❶ **Ferry Dock & Pier**, you begin the 580yd walk to the top of the island and prison; if you need assistance to reach the top, there's a twice-hourly tram.

As you climb toward the ❷ **Guardhouse**, notice the island's steep slope; before it was a prison, Alcatraz was a fort. In the 1850s, the military quarried the rocky shores into near-vertical cliffs. Ships could then only dock at a single port, separated from the main buildings by a sally port (a drawbridge and moat in what became the guardhouse). Inside, peer through floor grates to see Alcatraz's original prison.

Volunteers tend the brilliant ❸ **Officers' Row Gardens**, an orderly counterpoint to the overgrown rose bushes surrounding the burned-out shell of the ❹ **Warden's House**. At the top of the hill, by the front door of the ❺ **Main Cellhouse**, beautiful shots unfurl all around, including a view of the ❻ **Golden Gate Bridge**. Above the main door of the administration building, notice the ❼ **historic signs & graffiti**, before you step inside the dank, cold prison to find the ❽ **Frank Morris cell**, former home to Alcatraz's most notorious jail-breaker.

TOP TIPS

➡ Book at least one month prior for self-guided daytime visits, longer for ranger-led night tours. For info on garden tours, see www.alcatraz gardens.org.

➡ Be prepared to hike; a steep path ascends from the ferry landing to the cell block. Most people spend two to three hours on the island. You need only reserve for the outbound ferry; take any ferry back.

➡ There's no food (just water) but you can bring your own; picnicking is allowed at the ferry dock only. Dress in layers as weather changes fast and it's usually windy.

ADRIEN_G/SHUTTERSTOCK ©

Historic Signs & Graffiti
During their 1969–71 occupation, Native Americans graffitied the water tower: 'Home of the Free Indian Land.' Above the cellhouse door, examine the eagle-and-flag crest to see how the red-and-white stripes were changed to spell 'Free.'

DOPTIS/SHUTTERSTOCK ©

Warden's House
Fires destroyed the warden's house and other structures during the Indian Occupation. The government blamed the Native Americans; the Native Americans blamed agents provocateurs acting on behalf of the Nixon administration to undermine public sympathy.

Parade Grounds

Officers' Row Gardens
In the 19th century soldiers imported topsoil to beautify the island with gardens. Well-trusted prisoners later gardened – Elliott Michener said it kept him sane. Historians, ornithologists and archaeologists choose today's plants.

Main Cellhouse

During the mid-20th century, the maximum-security prison housed the day's most notorious troublemakers, including Al Capone and Robert Stroud, the 'Birdman of Alcatraz' (who actually conducted his ornithology studies at Leavenworth).

FRANCKREPORTER/GETTY IMAGES ©

View of the Golden Gate Bridge

The Golden Gate Bridge stretches wide on the horizon. Best views are from atop the island at Eagle Plaza, near the cellhouse entrance, and at water level along the Agave Trail (September to January only).

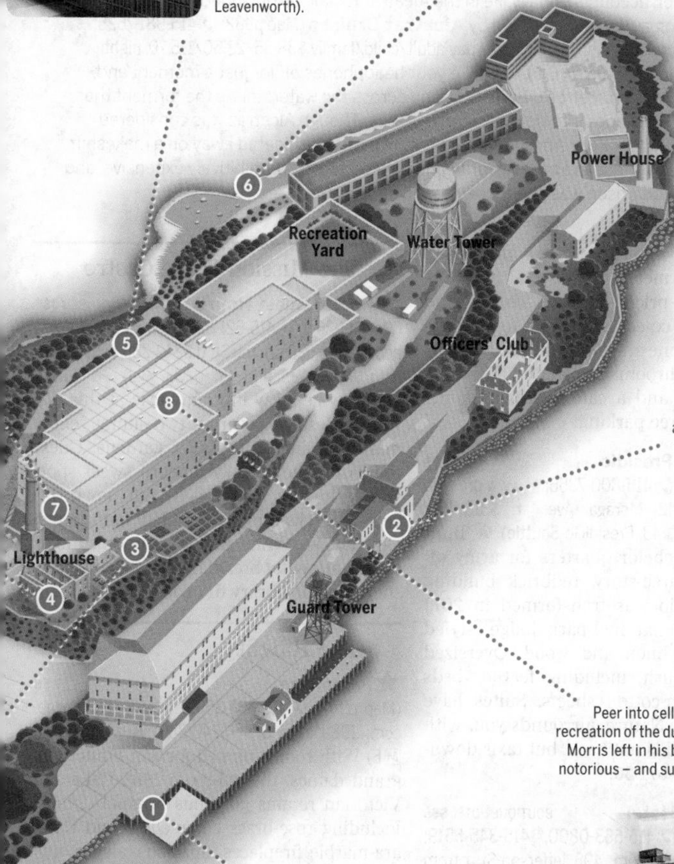

6
Power House
Recreation Yard
Water Tower
5
Officers' Club
8
7
2
3
Lighthouse
4
Guard Tower
1

Guardhouse

Alcatraz's oldest building dates to 1857 and retains remnants of the original drawbridge and moat. During the Civil War the basement was transformed into a military dungeon – the genesis of Alcatraz as a prison.

Frank Morris Cell

Peer into cell 138 on B-Block to see a recreation of the dummy's head that Frank Morris left in his bed as a decoy to aid his notorious – and successful – 1962 escape from Alcatraz.

OSCITY/SHUTTERSTOCK ©

Ferry Dock & Pier

A giant wall map helps you get your bearings. Inside nearby Building 64, short films and exhibits provide historical perspective on the prison and details about the Native American Occupation.

DON'T MISS

ALCATRAZ

For over 150 years, the name **Alcatraz** (Map p980; ☑ Alcatraz Cruises 415-981-7625; www. alcatrazcruises.com; tours adult/child 5-11yr day $38.35/23.50, night $45.50/27.05; ☺ call center 8am-7pm, ferries depart Pier 33 half-hourly 8:45am-3:50pm, night tours 5:55pm & 6:30pm; 🚹) has given the innocent chills and the guilty cold sweats. Over the decades, it's been a military prison, a forbidding maximum-security penitentiary and disputed territory between Native American activists and the FBI. No wonder that first step you take onto 'the Rock' seems to cue ominous music: dunh-dunh-dunnnnh!

First-person accounts of daily life in the Alcatraz lockup are included on the award-winning audio tour provided by **Alcatraz Cruises** (Map p982; ☑ 415-981-7625; www.alcatrazcruises.com; Pier 33; tours day adult/child/family $38.35/23.50/115.70, night adult/child $45.50/27.05; Ⓜ E, F). But take your headphones off for just a moment and notice the sound of carefree city life traveling across the water: this is the torment that made perilous escapes into riptides worth the risk. Though Alcatraz was considered escape-proof, in 1962 the Anglin brothers and Frank Morris floated away on a makeshift raft and were never seen again. Security and upkeep proved prohibitively expensive, and finally the island prison was abandoned to the birds in 1963.

million-dollar waterfront views, this hostel occupies a former army-hospital building, with bargain-priced private rooms and dorms (some co-ed) with four to 22 beds (avoid bunks one and two – they're by doorways). All bathrooms are shared. There's a huge kitchen and a cafe overlooking the bay. Limited free parking.

★ **Inn at the Presidio** HOTEL $$
(Map p980; ☑ 415-800-7356; www.presidio lodging.com; 42 Moraga Ave; r $310-495; P☺@☎☀; ☐43, PresidiGo Shuttle) ✎ Built in 1903 as bachelor quarters for army officers, this three-story, redbrick building in the Presidio was transformed in 2012 into a smart national-park lodge, styled with leather, linen and wood. Oversized rooms are plush, including feather beds with Egyptian-cotton sheets. Suites have gas fireplaces. Nature surrounds you, with hiking trailheads out back, but taxis downtown cost $25 to $30.

★ **Argonaut Hotel** BOUTIQUE HOTEL $$$
(Map p982; ☑ 415-563-0800, 415-345-5519; www.argonauthotel.com; 495 Jefferson St; r from $389; P☺☀☎☀; ☐19, 47, 49, ☐Powell-Hyde) ✎ Fisherman's Wharf's top hotel was built as a cannery in 1908 and has century-old wooden beams and exposed-brick walls. Rooms sport an over-the-top nautical theme, with porthole-shaped mirrors and plush, deep-blue carpets. Though all rooms have the amenities of an upper-end hotel – ultracomfy beds, iPod docks – some are tiny with limited sunlight. Parking starts at $65.

🛏 The Mission & the Castro

★ **Parker Guest House** B&B $$$
(Map p986; ☑ 415-621-3222; www.parkerguest house.com; 520 Church St; d $249-289, with shared bath $209-249; P@☺☎; ☐33, ☐J) ✎ Make your gay getaway in grand style at this Edwardian estate, covering two sunny yellow mansions linked by secret gardens. Guest rooms hit the swanky modern sweet spot: stately, inviting beds piled with down duvets and gleaming retro-tiled bathrooms. Unwind over wine in the sunroom, linger over continental breakfasts, or get cozy with sherry by the library fireplace.

🛏 The Haight

★ **Parsonage** B&B $$
(Map p982; ☑ 415-863-3699; www.theparsonage. com; 198 Haight St; r $240-280; @☎; ☐6, 71, ☐F) With rooms named for San Francisco's grand dames, this 23-room 1883 Italianate Victorian retains gorgeous original details, including rose-brass chandeliers and Carrara-marble fireplaces. Spacious, airy rooms offer antique beds with cushy SF-made McRoskey mattresses; some rooms have wood-burning fireplaces. Take breakfast in the formal dining room, and brandy and chocolates before bed. Two-night minimum.

Chateau Tivoli B&B $$
(Map p982; ☑ 415-776-5462; www.chateautivoli. com; 1057 Steiner St; d $205-215, with shared bath $160-185, q $220-325; ☎; ☐5, 22) The source of neighborhood gossip since 1892, this gilded

and turreted mansion graciously hosted Isadora Duncan, Mark Twain and (rumor has it) the ghost of a Victorian opera diva – and now you too can be Chateau Tivoli's guest. Nine antique-filled rooms and suites set the scene for romance; most have claw-foot bathtubs, though two share a bathroom. No elevator or TVs.

✖ Eating

Downtown, Civic Center & SoMa

Ferry Plaza Farmers Market   MARKET $
(Map p982; ☎415-291-3276; www.cuesa.org; cnr Market St & the Embarcadero; street food $3-12; �10am-2pm Tue & Thu, from 8am Sat; ✐🖈; 🚊2, 6, 9, 14, 21, 31, Ⓜ Embarcadero, Ⓑ Embarcadero) ✦
The pride and joy of SF foodies, the Ferry Building market showcases more than 100 prime purveyors of California-grown organic produce, pasture-raised meats and gourmet prepared foods at accessible prices. On Saturdays, join top chefs early for prime browsing, and stay for eclectic bayside picnics of Namu Korean tacos, RoliRoti porchetta, Dirty Girl tomatoes, Nicasio cheese samples and Frog Hollow fruit turnovers.

farm:table   AMERICAN $
(Map p982; ☎415-300-5652; www.farmtablesf.com; 754 Post St; dishes $6-9; �7:15am-1pm Tue-Fri, 8am-2pm Sat & Sun; ✐; 🚊2, 3, 27, 38) ✦ A ray of sunshine in the concrete heart of the city, this plucky little storefront showcases seasonal California organics in just-baked breakfasts and farmstead-fresh lunches. Daily specials include a rotation of homemade cereals, savory tarts and game-changing toast – mmmm, ginger peach and mascarpone on whole-wheat sourdough! Tiny space, but immaculate kitchen and great coffee.

★In Situ   CALIFORNIAN, INTERNATIONAL $$
(Map p982; http://insitu.sfmoma.org; 151 3rd St, SFMOMA; mains $20-50; �11am-3:30pm Mon, 5-9pm Thu-Sat, 11am-3:30pm & 5-8pm Sun; 🚊5, 6, 7, 14, 19, 21, 31, 38, Ⓑ Montgomery, Ⓜ Montgomery) The landmark gallery of modern cuisine attached to SFMOMA also showcases avant-garde masterpieces – but these ones you'll lick clean. Chef Corey Lee collaborates with more than 100 star chefs worldwide, scrupulously re-creating their signature dishes with California-grown ingredients so that you can enjoy Nathan Myhrvold's caramelized carrot soup, Tim Raue's wasabi

lobster and Albert Adrià's Jasper Hill Farm cheesecake in one unforgettable sitting.

★Benu   CALIFORNIAN, FUSION $$$
(Map p982; ☎415-685-4860; www.benusf.com; 22 Hawthorne St; tasting menu $310; �5:30-8:30pm Tue-Thu, to 9pm Fri & Sat; 🚊10, 12, 14, 30, 45) SF has pioneered Asian fusion cuisine for 150 years, but the pan-Pacific innovation chef-owner Corey Lee brings to the plate is gasp-inducing: foie-gras soup dumplings – what?! Dungeness crab and truffle custard pack such outsize flavor into Lee's faux-shark's-fin soup, you'll swear Jaws is in there. A Benu dinner is an investment, but don't miss star sommelier Yoon Ha's ingenious pairings ($210). There's a 20% service charge.

✖ North Beach & Chinatown

★Liguria Bakery   BAKERY $
(Map p982; ☎415-421-3786; 1700 Stockton St; focaccia $4-6; �8am-2pm Tue-Fri, 7am-2pm Sat, 7am-noon Sun; ✐🖈; 🚊8, 30, 39, 41, 45, 🚋Powell-Mason, Ⓜ T) Bleary-eyed art students and Italian grandmothers line up by 8am for cinnamon-raisin focaccia hot out of the 100-year-old oven, leaving 9am dawdlers a choice of tomato or classic rosemary and garlic. Latecomers, beware: when they run out, they close. Take yours in waxed paper or boxed for picnics – just don't kid yourself that you're going to save some for later. Cash only.

★Golden Boy   PIZZA $
(Map p982; ☎415-982-9738; www.goldenboypizza.com; 542 Green St; slices $3.25-4.25; �11:30am-midnight Sun-Thu, to 2am Fri & Sat; 🚊8, 30, 39, 41, 45, 🚋Powell-Mason) 'If you don't see it don't ask 4 it' reads the menu – Golden Boy has kept punks in line since 1978, serving Genovese focaccia-crust pizza that's chewy, crunchy and hot from the oven. You'll have whatever second-generation Sodini family *pizzaioli* (pizza-makers) are making and like it – especially pesto and clam-and-garlic. Grab square slices and draft beer at the bomb-shelter counter.

★Mister Jiu's   CHINESE, CALIFORNIAN $$
(Map p982; ☎415-857-9688; http://misterjius.com; 28 Waverly Pl; mains $14-45; �5:30-10:30pm Tue-Sat; 🚊30, 🚋California, Ⓜ T) Success has been celebrated in this historic Chinatown banquet hall since the 1880s – but today, scoring a table at Mister Jiu's is reason enough for celebration. Build memorable banquets from chef Brandon Jew's ingenious Chinese/Californian signatures: quail

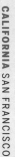

CALIFORNIA SAN FRANCISCO

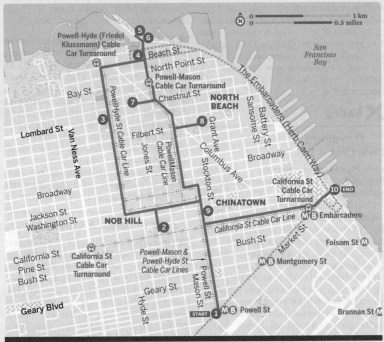

Map labels:
Powell-Hyde (Friedel Klussmann) Cable Car Turnaround
Beach St
North Point St
Powell-Mason Cable Car Turnaround
Chestnut St
NORTH BEACH
Bay St
The Embarcadero (Herb Caen Way)
San Francisco Bay
1 km
0.5 miles
Lombard St
Van Ness Ave
Filbert St
Jones St
Powell-Hyde St Cable Car Line
Powell-Mason Cable Car Line
Grant Ave
Columbus Ave
Stockton St
Battery St
Sansome St
Broadway
Broadway
Jackson St
Washington St
NOB HILL
CHINATOWN
California St Cable Car Turnaround
10 END
California St Cable Car Line
Embarcadero
California St
Pine St
Bush St
California St Cable Car Turnaround
Powell-Mason & Powell-Hyde St Cable Car Lines
Bush St
Market St
Folsom St
Geary St
Hyde St
Geary St
Powell St
Mason St
Montgomery St
Geary Blvd
START 1 Powell St
Brannan St

City Walk
SF by Cable Car

START POWELL ST CABLE CAR TURNAROUND
END FERRY BUILDING
LENGTH 2 MILES; TWO HOURS

The ultimate SF joyride is in a cable car. At the **1 Powell St Cable Car Turnaround** (p977), you'll see operators turn the car atop a revolving wooden platform, and a vintage kiosk where you can buy an all-day Muni Passport for $23. Board the red-signed Powell-Hyde cable car and begin your 338ft ascent of Nob Hill.

Nineteenth-century city planners were sceptical of inventor Andrew Hallidie's 'wire-rope railway' – but after more than a century of near-continuous operation, his wire-and-hemp cables have seldom broken. Hallidie's cable cars even survived the 1906 earthquake and fire that destroyed 'Snob Hill' mansions, returning the faithful to the rebuilt **2 Grace Cathedral** (p981) – hop off to say hello to SF's gentle patron St Francis.

Back on the Powell-Hyde car, enjoy Bay views as you careen past crooked, flow-er-lined **3 Lombard Street** (p981) toward **4 Fisherman's Wharf**. The waterfront terminus is named for 'Cable Car Lady' Friedel Klussmann, who saved cable cars from mayoral modernization plans in 1947.

At the wharf, emerge from the submarine **5 USS Pampanito** to glimpse SF with the joyous relief of a WWII sailor on shore leave. Witness Western saloon brawls in vintage arcade games at the **6 Musée Mécanique** (p999) before hitching the Powell-Mason cable car to North Beach.

Hop off to see Diego Rivera's 1934 city-scape at the **7 San Francisco Art Institute** (p981), or follow your rumbling stomach directly to **8 Liguria Bakery** (p993). Stroll through North Beach and Chinatown alleyways, or take the Powell-Mason line to time-travel through the **9 Chinese Historical Society of America**. Nearby, catch a ride on the city's oldest line: the California St cable car. The terminus is near the **10 Ferry Building** (p977), where champagne-and-oyster happy hour awaits.

and Mission-fig sticky rice, hot and sour Dungeness crab soup, Wagyu sirloin and tuna heart fried rice. Don't skip dessert – pastry chef Melissa Chou's salted plum sesame balls are flavor bombs.

★ Good Mong Kok
DIM SUM $

(Map p982; ☑ 415-397-2688; 1039 Stockton St; dumpling orders $2-5; ⊙ 7am-6pm; ☐ 30, 45, ☐ Powell-Mason, California, Ⓜ T) Ask Chinatown neighbors about their go-to dim sum and the answer is either grandma's or Good Mong Kok. Lines snake out the door of this counter bakery for dumplings whisked from vast steamers into takeout containers to enjoy in Portsmouth Sq. The menu changes by the minute/hour, but expect classic pork *siu mai*, shrimp *har gow* and BBQ pork buns; BYO chili sauce and black vinegar.

⊠ The Marina, Fisherman's Wharf & Presidio

Fisherman's Wharf Crab Stands
SEAFOOD $

(Map p982; Taylor St; mains $5-22; Ⓜ F) Men and women in rolled-up sleeves stir steaming cauldrons of Dungeness crab at several side-by-side takeout crab stands at the foot of Taylor St, the epicenter of Fisherman's Wharf. Crab season typically runs winter through spring, but you'll find shrimp and other seafood year-round.

★ Kaiyo
FUSION $$

(Map p982; ☑ 415-525-4804; https://kaiyosf.com; 1838 Union St; small plates $12-28, share plates $19-28; ⊙ 5-10pm Tue, Wed & Sun, to 11pm Thu & Sat, 10:30am-3pm Sat & Sun; ☐ 41, 45) For a deliciously deep dive into the cuisine of the Japanese-Peruvian diaspora, head to Cow Hollow's most playful and inventive new restaurant, where the Pisco and whiskey cocktails are named for anime characters and a neon-green moss wall runs the length of the *izakaya*-style dining room. But the real adventure is the food.

Greens
VEGETARIAN, CALIFORNIAN $$

(Map p982; ☑ 415-771-6222; www.greensrestaurant.com; 2 Marina Blvd, Bldg A, Fort Mason Center; mains $18-28; ⊙ 5:30-9pm Mon, 11:30am-2:30pm & 5:30-9pm Tue-Thu, 11:30am-2:30pm & 5-9pm Fri, 10:30am-2:30pm & 5-9pm Sat & Sun; ☑ ♿; ☐ 22, 28, 30, 43, 47, 49) 🍴 Career carnivores won't realize there's zero meat in the hearty blackbean chili, or in Greens' other flavor-packed vegetarian dishes, made using ingredients from a Zen farm in Marin. And, oh, what views! The Golden Gate rises just outside

the window-lined dining room. The on-site cafe serves to-go lunches, but for sit-down meals, including Saturday and Sunday brunch, reservations are recommended.

★ Atelier Crenn
FRENCH $$$

(Map p980; ☑ 415-440-0460; www.ateliercrenn. com; 3127 Fillmore St; tasting menu $335; ⊙ 5-9pm Tue-Sat; ☐ 22, 28, 30, 43) The menu arrives in the form of a poem and then come the signature white chocolate spheres filled with a burst of apple cider. If this seems an unlikely start to a meal, just wait for the geoduck rice tart in a glass dome frosted by liquid nitrogen, and about a dozen more plates inspired by the childhood of chef Dominique Crenn in Brittany, France.

⊠ The Mission & the Castro

★ La Palma Mexicatessen
MEXICAN $

(Map p986; ☑ 415-647-1500; www.lapalmasf.com; 2884 24th St; tamales, tacos & huaraches $3-10; ⊙ 8am-6pm Mon-Sat, to 5pm Sun; ☑; ☐ 12, 14, 27, 48, ☐ 24th St Mission) 🍴 Follow the applause: that's the sound of organic tortilla-making in progress. You've found the Mission mother lode of handmade tamales, and *pupusas* (tortilla pockets) with potato and *chicharones* (pork crackling), *carnitas* (slow-roasted pork), *cotija* (Oaxacan cheese) and La Palma's own tangy tomatillo sauce. Get takeout or bring a small army to finish the meal at sunny sidewalk tables.

★ Al's Place
CALIFORNIAN $$

(Map p986; ☑ 415-416-6136; www.alsplacesf.com; 1499 Valencia St; share plates $15-21; ⊙ 5:30-10pm Wed-Sun; ☑; ☐ 12, 14, 49, Ⓜ J, ☐ 24th St Mission) 🍴 The Golden State dazzles on Al's plates, featuring homegrown heirloom ingredients, pristine Pacific seafood and grass-fed meat. Painstaking preparation yields sundrenched flavors and exquisite textures: crispy-skin cod with frothy preserved-lime dip, and grilled peach melting into velvety foie gras. Dishes are half the size but thrice the flavor of mains elsewhere – get two or three and you'll be California dreaming.

Frances
CALIFORNIAN $$$

(Map p986; ☑ 415-621-3870; www.frances-sf.com; 3870 17th St; mains $26-34; ⊙ 5-10pm Sun & Tue-Thu, to 10:30pm Fri & Sat; ☐ 24, 33, Ⓜ F, K, L, M) 🍴 Rebel chef-owner Melissa Perello earned a Michelin star for fine dining, then ditched downtown to start this market-inspired neighborhood bistro. Daily menus showcase rustic flavors and luxurious textures with impeccable technique – handmade ricotta *malfatti* pasta with buttery squash and crunchy pepitas, juicy pork chops with blood orange and earthy Japanese sweet potatoes – plus cult wine served by the ounce, directly from Wine Country.

The Haight

★ Brenda's Meat & Three   SOUTHERN US $$

(Map p980; ☎415-926-8657; http://brendas meatandthree.com; 919 Divisadero St; mains $9-20; ☺8am-10pm Wed-Mon; ☒5, 21, 24, 38) The name means one meaty main course plus three sides – though only superheroes finish ham steak with Creole red-eye gravy and grits, let alone cream biscuits and eggs. Chef Brenda Buenviaje's portions are defiantly Southern, which explains brunch lines of marathoners and partiers who forgot to eat last night. Arrive early, share sweet-potato pancakes, and pray for crawfish specials.

Rich Table   CALIFORNIAN $$

(Map p982; ☎415-355-9085; http://richtablesf. com; 199 Gough St; mains $17-37; ☺5:30-10pm Sun-Thu, to 10:30pm Fri & Sat; ☒5, 6, 7, 21, 47, 49, Ⓜ Van Ness) 🍴 Impossible cravings begin at Rich Table, where mind-bending dishes like porcini doughnuts, sardine chips, and *burrata* (mozzarella and cream) funnel cake blow up Instagram feeds nightly. Married co-chefs and owners Sarah and Evan Rich riff on seasonal San Francisco cuisine with the soul of SFJAZZ stars and the ingenuity of Silicon Valley regulars.

Golden Gate Park & Around

★ Arsicault Bakery   BAKERY $

(Map p988; ☎415-750-9460; 397 Arguello Blvd; pastries $3-7; ☺7am-2:30pm Mon-Fri, to 3:30pm Sat & Sun; ☒1, 2, 33, 38, 44) Armando Lacayo left his job in finance because he, like his Parisian grandparents before him, was obsessed with making croissants. After perfecting his technique, Lacayo opened a modest bakery in the Inner Richmond in 2015. Within a year, *Bon Appétit* magazine had declared it the best new bakery in America and the golden, flaky, buttery croissants regularly sell out.

★ Spruce   CALIFORNIAN $$$

(Map p988; ☎415-931-5100; www.sprucesf.com; 3640 Sacramento St; mains $19-44; ☺11:30am-2pm & 5-10pm Mon-Thu, 11:30am-2pm & 5-11pm Fri, 10am-2pm & 5-11pm Sat, 10am-2pm & 5-9pm Sun; ☒1, 2, 33, 43) 🍴 VIP all the way: Baccarat crystal chandeliers, tawny leather chairs, rotating art collections and 2500 wines. Ladies who lunch dispense with polite conversation, tearing into grass-fed burgers on house-baked English muffins loaded with pickled onions and heirloom tomatoes grown on the restaurant's own organic farm. Want fries with that? Oh, yes, you do: Spruce's are cooked in duck fat.

🍷 Drinking & Nightlife

San Francisco set the gold standard for Wild West saloons, until drinking was driven underground in the 1920s with Prohibition. Today San Francisco celebrates its historic saloons and speakeasies – and with Wine Country and local distillers providing a steady supply of America's finest hooch, the West still gets wild nightly.

★ Bourbon & Branch   BAR

(Map p982; ☎415-346-1735; www.bourbonand branch.com; 501 Jones St; ☺6pm-2am; ☒27, 38) 'Don't even think of asking for a cosmo' reads the House Rules at this Prohibition-era speakeasy, recognizable by its deliciously misleading Anti-Saloon League sign. For award-winning cocktails in the liquored-up library, whisper the password ('books') at the O'Farrell entrance. Reservations required for front-room booths and Wilson & Wilson Detective Agency, the noir-themed speakeasy-within-a-speakeasy (password supplied with reservations).

★ Comstock Saloon   BAR

(Map p982; ☎415-617-0071; www.comstock saloon.com; 155 Columbus Ave; ☺4pm-midnight Mon, to 2am Tue-Thu, noon-2am Fri, 11:30am-2am Sat, 11:30am-4pm Sun; ☒8, 10, 12, 30, 45, ☒Powell-Mason, Ⓜ T) During this 1907 saloon's heyday, patrons relieved themselves in the marble trough below the bar – now you'll have to tear yourself away from Comstock's authentic pisco punch and martini-precursor Martinez (gin, vermouth, bitters, maraschino liqueur). Arrive to toast Emperor Norton's statue at happy hour (4pm to 6pm) and stay for the family meal (whatever kitchen staff's eating). Reserve booths to hear when ragtime-jazz bands play.

★ Li Po   BAR

(Map p982; ☎415-982-0072; www.lipolounge.com; 916 Grant Ave; ☺2pm-2am; ☒8, 30, 45, ☒Powell-Mason, Powell-Hyde, Ⓜ T) Beat a hasty retreat to red-vinyl booths where Allen Ginsberg and Jack Kerouac debated the meaning of life under a golden Buddha. Enter the 1937

LGBTIQ+ SF

It doesn't matter where you're from, who you love or who's your daddy: if you're here and queer, welcome home. The Castro is the heart of the gay cruising scene, but raging dance clubs and leather bars can be found in SoMa. Head to the Tenderloin for trans venues and queer cabaret, or the Mission for women's bars, arts venues and community spaces.

SF Pride (⊙ Jun) month is undoubtedly the biggest event on the calendar, with over 1.5 million people hitting parades and parties. While you're in town, check out America's first gay-history museum, **GLBT History Museum** (Map p986; ☏ 415-621-1107; www.glbthistory. org/museum; 4127 18th St; $5, 1st Wed of month free; ⊙ 11am-6pm Mon-Sat, noon-5pm Sun, closed Tue fall-spring; Ⓜ Castro St), which showcases a century of San Francisco LGBTQ+ ephemera, or get to know LGBT icons as you walk through the Castro following the **Rainbow Honor Walk** (Map p986; http://rainbowhonorwalk.org; Castro St & Market St; Ⓜ Castro St).

The *Bay Area Reporter* (www.ebar.com) is released every Wednesday and has community news and events, or grab a copy of the *San Francisco Bay Times* (http://sfbay times.com). The free *Gloss Magazine* (www.glossmagazine.net) locks down nightlife and parties. Or head to the following:

Aunt Charlie's Lounge (Map p982; ☏ 415-441-2922; www.auntcharlieslounge.com; 133 Turk St; cover free-$5; ⊙ noon-midnight Mon & Wed, to 2am Tue & Thu, to 12:30am Fri, 10am-12:30am Sat, 10am-midnight Sun; 🚌 27, 31, Ⓜ Powell, Ⓑ Powell) Knock-down, drag-out winner for gender-bending shows and dance-floor freakiness in a tiny space.

El Rio (Map p986; ☏ 415-282-3325; www.elriosf.com; 3158 Mission St; cover free-$10; ⊙ 1pm-2am Mon-Sat, to midnight Sun; 🚌 12, 14, 27, 49, Ⓑ 24th St Mission) Mix it up with world music, salsa, house, live bands and SF's flirtiest patio.

Stud (Map p982; ☏ 415-863-6623; www.studsf.com; 399 9th St; cover $5-8; ⊙ 5pm-2am Tue-Thu, to 4am Fri, 7pm-4am Sat, 7pm-2am Sun; 🚌 12, 19, 27, 47) Shows and DJs nightly, plus the tantalizing aroma of bourbon, cologne and testosterone.

Oasis (Map p982; ☏ 415-795-3180; www.sfoasis.com; 298 11th St; tickets $15-35; 🚌 9, 12, 14, 47, Ⓜ Van Ness) SF's dedicated drag venue, hostessed by SF drag icons Heklinka and D'Arcy Drollinger.

Jolene's (Map p986; ☏ 415-913-7948; http://jolenessf.com; 2700 16th St; ⊙ 4pm-2am Thu-Fri, from 11am Sat & Sun; 🚌 12, 22, 55, Ⓑ 16th Mission St) Women on the dance floor, at the bar, all over the wallpaper, right at home.

Wild Side West (Map p980; ☏ 415-647-3099; www.wildsidewest.com; 424 Cortland Ave; ⊙ 2pm-2am; 🚌 24) Cheers to queers and beers in the herstory-making sculpture garden.

---

faux-grotto doorway and dodge red lanterns to place your order: Tsingtao beer or a sweet, sneaky-strong Chinese mai tai made with *baijiu* (rice liquor). Brusque bartenders, basement bathrooms, cash only – a world-class dive bar.

Stookey's Club Moderne   LOUNGE
(Map p982; www.stookeysclubmoderne.com; 895 Bush St; ⊙ 4:30pm-2am Mon-Sat, to midnight Sun; 🚌 1, 🚋 Powell-Hyde, Powell-Mason, California) Dangerous dames lure unsuspecting sailors into late-night schemes over potent hooch at this art-deco bar straight out of a Dashiell Hammett thriller. Chrome-lined 1930s Streamline Moderne decor sets the scene for intrigue, and wisecracking white-jacketed bartenders shake the stiffest Corpse Reviver cocktails in town. Arrive early to find room

on the hat rack for your fedora, especially on live jazz nights.

Trick Dog   BAR
(Map p986; ☏ 415-471-2999; www.trickdog bar.com; 3010 20th St; ⊙ 3pm-2am; 🚌 12, 14, 49) Drink adventurously with ingenious cocktails inspired by local obsessions: San Francisco muralists, Chinese diners or conspiracy theories. Every six months, Trick Dog adopts a new theme and the menu changes – proof you can teach an old dog new tricks and improve on classics like the Manhattan. Arrive early for bar stools or hit the mood-lit loft for high-concept bar bites.

20 Spot   WINE BAR
(Map p986; ☏ 415-624-3140; www.20spot.com; 3565 20th St; ⊙ 5-11pm Mon-Thu, to 12:30am Fri

& Sat; 🚇 14, 22, 33, Ⓑ 16th St Mission) Find your California mellow at this neighborhood wine lounge in an 1885 Victorian building. After decades as Force of Habit punk-record shop – note the vintage sign – this corner joint has earned the right to unwind with a glass of Berkeley's Donkey and Goat sparkling wine and not get any guff. Caution: oysters with pickled persimmon could become a habit.

⭐ Entertainment

Sign up at Gold Star Events (www.goldstarevents.com) for discounts on comedy, theater, concerts and opera, or stop by the **TIX Bay Area** (Map p982; ☑ 415-433-7827; http://tixbayarea.org; 350 Powell St; 🚇 Powell-Mason, Powell-Hyde, Ⓑ Powell, Ⓜ Powell) Union Sq ticket booth for cheap tickets for same-day or next-day shows.

⭐ **San Francisco Symphony** CLASSICAL MUSIC
(Map p982; ☑ box office 415-864-6000, rush-ticket hotline 415-503-5577; www.sfsymphony.org; Grove St, btwn Franklin St & Van Ness Ave; tickets $20-150; 🚇 21, 45, 47, Ⓜ Van Ness, Ⓑ Civic Center) From the moment conductor Michael Tilson Thomas bounces up on his toes and raises his baton, the audience is on the edge of their seats for another thunderous performance by the Grammy-winning SF Symphony. Don't miss signature concerts of Beethoven and Mahler, live symphony performances with such films as *Star Trek,* and creative collaborations with artists from Elvis Costello to Metallica.

⭐ **SFJAZZ Center** JAZZ
(Map p982; ☑ 866-920-5299; www.sfjazz.org; 201 Franklin St; tickets $25-120; 🚹; 🚇 5, 6, 7, 21, 47, 49, Ⓜ Van Ness) 🎷 Jazz legends and singular talents from Argentina to Yemen are showcased at North America's newest, largest jazz center. Hear fresh takes on classic jazz albums and poets riffing with jazz combos in the downstairs Joe Henderson Lab, and witness extraordinary main-stage collaborations by legendary Afro-Cuban All Stars, raucous all-women mariachis Flor de Toluache, and Balkan barnstormers Goran Bregović and his Wedding and Funeral Orchestra.

⭐ **Fillmore Auditorium** LIVE MUSIC
(Map p982; ☑ 415-346-6000; http://thefillmore. com; 1805 Geary Blvd; tickets from $20; ☺ box office 10am-3pm Sun, plus 30min before doors open to 10pm show nights; 🚇 22, 38) Jimi Hen-drix, Janis Joplin, the Grateful Dead – they all played the Fillmore and the upstairs bar is lined with vintage psychedelic posters to prove it. Bands that sell out stadiums keep rocking this historic, 1250-capacity dance hall, and for major shows, free posters are still handed out. To squeeze up to the stage, be polite and lead with the hip.

⭐ **Castro Theatre** CINEMA
(Map p986; ☑ 415-621-6120; www.castrotheatre. com; 429 Castro St; adult/child, senior & matinee $13/10; Ⓜ Castro St) Every night at the Castro, crowds roar as the mighty organ rises – and no, that's not a euphemism. Showtime at this 1922 art deco movie palace is heralded with Wurlitzer organ show tunes, culminating in sing-alongs to the Judy Garland anthem 'San Francisco.' Architect Timothy Pflueger's OTT Spanish-Moorish-Asian style inspired the *Wizard of Oz* sets, but earthquake-shy San Franciscans avoid sitting under his pointy metal chandelier.

⭐ **Giants Stadium** BASEBALL
(AT&T Park; Map p982; ☑ 415-972-2000, tours 415-972-2400; http://sanfrancisco.giants.mlb.com; 24 Willie Mays Plaza; tickets $14-349, stadium tour adult/senior/child $22/17/12; ☺ tour times vary; 🚹; Ⓜ N, T) Baseball fans roar April to October at the Giants' 81 home games. As any orange-blooded San Franciscan will remind you, the Giants have won three World Series since 2010 – and you'll know the Giants are on another winning streak when superstitious locals wear team colors (orange and black) and bushy beards (the Giants' rallying cry is 'Fear the Beard!').

Great American Music Hall LIVE MUSIC
(Map p982; ☑ 415-885-0750; www.gamh.com; 859 O'Farrell St; shows $20-45; ☺ box office noon-6pm Mon-Fri, 5pm-close on show nights; 🚹; 🚇 19, 38, 47, 49) Everyone busts out their best sets at this opulent 1907 bordello turned all-ages venue – indie rockers like the Band Perry throw down, international legends such as Salif Keita grace the stage, and John Waters hosts Christmas extravaganzas. Pay $25 extra for dinner with prime balcony seating to watch shows comfortably, or rock out with the standing-room scrum downstairs.

San Francisco Ballet DANCE
(Map p982; ☑ tickets 415-865-2000; www.sfballet.org; 301 Van Ness Ave, War Memorial Opera House; tickets $22-150; ☺ ticket sales over the phone 10am-4pm Mon-Fri; 🚇 5, 21, 47, 49, Ⓜ Van Ness, Ⓑ Civic Center) The USA's oldest ballet

SAN FRANCISCO FOR CHILDREN

San Francisco has the fewest kids per capita of any US city, yet many locals make a living entertaining kids – from Pixar animators to video-game designers – and this town is full of attractions for young people.

Hit the award-winning, hands-on exhibits at the Exploratorium (p977) to investigate the science of skateboarding and glow-in-the-dark animals, then free the world from Space Invaders at **Musée Mécanique** (Map p982; ☑415-346-2000; www.museemecanique.com; Pier 45, Shed A; ☺10am-8pm; 🖈; 🚊47, 🚋Powell-Mason, Powell-Hyde, Ⓜ E, F). Don't be shy: bark back at the sea lions at Pier 39 (p984), and ride a unicorn on the pier's vintage **San Francisco carousel** (Map p982; www.pier39.com; Pier 39; 1 ride $5, 3 rides $10; ☺10am-9pm Sun-Thu, to 10pm Fri & Sat; 🖈; 🚊47, 🚋Powell-Mason, Ⓜ E, F).

Chase butterflies through the rainforest dome, pet starfish in the petting zoo and squeal in the Eel Forest at the California Academy of Sciences (p986), or brave the shark tunnel at **Aquarium of the Bay** (Map p982; ☑415-623-5300; www.aquariumofthebay.org; Pier 39; adult/child/family $28/18/75; ☺10am-8pm late May-early Sep, shorter hours rest of year; 🖈; 🚊47, 🚋Powell-Mason, Ⓜ E, F). The **Children's Creativity Museum** (Map p982; ☑415-820-3320; http://creativity.org/; 221 4th St; $12.95; ☺10am-4pm Tue-Sun summer, Wed-Sun rest of year; 🖈; 🚊14, Ⓜ Powell, Ⓑ Powell) allows future tech moguls to design their own video games and animations, then let off some steam at the playgrounds in **Golden Gate Park** (Koret Children's Quarter; Map p988; ☑415-831-2700; www.golden-gate-park.com/childrens-play ground.html; carousel per ride adult/child $2/1; ☺sunrise-sunset, carousel 10am-4:15pm; 🖈; 🚊7, 33, Ⓜ N), **Dolores Park** (Map p986; http://sfrecpark.org/destination/mission-dolores-park; Dolores St, btwn 18th & 20th Sts; ☺6am-10pm; 🖈🖈; 🚊14, 33, 49, Ⓑ16th St Mission, Ⓜ J) or **Yerba Buena Gardens** (Map p982; ☑415-820-3550; www.yerbabuenagardens.com; cnr 3rd & Mission Sts; ☺6am-10pm; 🖈; Ⓜ Montgomery, Ⓑ Montgomery).

company is looking sharp in more than 100 shows annually, from *The Nutcracker* (the US premiere was here) to modern originals. Performances are at the War Memorial Opera House from January to May, and you can score $15 to $20 same-day standing-room tickets at the box office (open four hours before curtain on performance days only).

🔒 Shopping

★**Park Life**   GIFTS & SOUVENIRS
(Map p988; ☑415-386-7275; www.parklifestore. com; 220 Clement St; ☺10am-7pm Mon-Sat, to 6pm Sun; 🚊1, 2, 33, 38, 44) The Swiss Army knife of hip SF emporiums, Park Life is design store, indie publisher and art gallery rolled into one. Browse among presents too clever to give away, including toy soldiers in yoga poses, Park Life catalogs of Shaun O'Dell paintings of natural disorder, sinister Todd Hido photos of shaggy cats on shag rugs, and a Picasso bong.

★**Community Thrift**   CLOTHING
(Map p986; ☑415-861-4910; www.community thriftsf.org; 623 Valencia St; ☺10am-6:30pm; 🚊14, 22, 33, 49, Ⓑ16th St Mission) 🍐 When local collectors and retailers have too much of a good thing, they donate it to nonprofit Community

Thrift, where proceeds go to 200-plus local charities – all the more reason to gloat over your $5 totem-pole teacup, $10 vintage windbreaker and $14 disco-era glitter romper. Donate your cast-offs (until 5pm daily) and show some love to the Community.

Adobe Books & Backroom Gallery   BOOKS
(Map p986; ☑415-864-3936; www.adobe books.com; 3130 24th St; ☺noon-8pm Mon-Fri, from 11am Sat & Sun; 🚊12, 14, 48, 49, Ⓑ24th St Mission) Wall-to-wall inspiration – including just-released fiction, limited-edition art books, rare cookbooks, well-thumbed poetry – plus zine-launch parties, comedy nights and art openings. Mingle with Mission characters debating all-time-greatest pulp-fiction covers and SF history (founder Andrew is a whiz) and see SF artists at the Backroom Gallery (well worth the walk to the back of the store) before they hit Whitney Biennials.

Gravel & Gold   HOMEWARES
(Map p986; ☑415-552-0112; www.gravelandgold. com; 3266 21st St; ☺noon-7pm Mon-Sat, to 5pm Sun; 🚊12, 14, 49, Ⓑ24th St Mission) 🍐 Get back to the land and in touch with California's roots without leaving sight of a Mission sidewalk. Gravel & Gold celebrates

SAN FRANCISCO'S BEST SHOPPING AREAS

All those tricked-out dens, well-stocked spice racks and fabulous ensembles don't just pull themselves together – San Franciscans scour their city for them. Here's where to find what:

Polk Street Vintage looks, local art, indie designers and smart gifts.

Valencia Street Made-in-SF gifts, West Coast style and scents, pirate supplies.

Haight Street Vintage, drag glam, steampunk gear and hats galore, plus anarchist comics, vinyl LPs and skateboards for total SF makeovers.

Hayes Valley Local designers, gourmet treats, home decor.

Union Square Ringed by department stores and megabrands, including Neiman Marcus, Macy's, Saks and Apple.

California's hippie homesteader movement with hand-printed smock-dresses, signature boob-print totes and wiggly stoner-striped throw pillows. It's homestead California-style with hand-thrown stoneware mugs, Risograph posters and rare books on '70s beach-shack architecture – plus DIY maker workshops (see website).

Hero Shop   FASHION & ACCESSORIES
(Map p982; 415-829-3129; http://heroshopsf.com; 982 Post St; 11am-7pm Mon-Sat; 2, 3, 19, 27, 38, 47, 49) On the cutting edge of the Tenderloin, Hero transforms casual browsers into SF fashionistas with statement pieces by rising-star local designers: Stevie Howell's boho silk tunics, Future Glory's handmade marbled-leather handbags, Culk's souvenir sweatshirts. It's no accident Hero's selection seems unusually well edited – owner Emily Holt left her job as *Vogue*'s fashion-trend editor to open this boutique.

ℹ Information

DANGERS & ANNOYANCES

Keep your city smarts and wits about you, especially at night in the Tenderloin, South of Market (SoMa), the Upper Haight and the Mission. If you're alone in these areas at night, consider ride-share or a taxi instead of waiting for a bus.

MEDICAL SERVICES

San Francisco City Clinic (415-487-5500; www.sfcityclinic.org; 356 7th St; 8am-4pm Mon, Wed & Fri, 1-6pm Tue, 1-4pm Thu) Low-cost services.

San Francisco General Hospital (Zuckerberg San Franciso General Hospital and Trauma Center; emergency 415-206-8111, main hospital 415-206-8000; https://zuckerberg sanfranciscogeneral.org; 1001 Potrero Ave; 24hr; 9, 10, 33, 48) Best ER for serious trauma.

University of California San Francisco Medical Center (415-476-1000; www.ucsfhealth.org; 505 Parnassus Ave; 24hr; 6, 7, 43, N) ER at leading university hospital.

TOURIST INFORMATION

SF Visitor Information Center (www.sanfran cisco.travel/visitor-information-center) Muni Passports, activities deals, and event calendars.

ℹ Getting There & Away

AIR

One of America's busiest, **San Francisco International Airport** (www.flysfo.com; S McDonnell Rd) is 14 miles south of downtown off Hwy 101 and accessible by BART (30 minutes). Travelers arriving at **Oakland International Airport** (OAK; 510-563-3000; www.oaklandairport.com; 1 Airport Dr; ; B Oakland International Airport), 15 miles east of downtown, have a longer trip to reach San Francisco – but OAK has fewer weather-related flight delays than SFO.

BUS

From the **Temporary Transbay Terminal** (Map p982; cnr Howard & Main Sts; 5, 38, 41, 71), you can catch the following buses:

AC Transit (510-891-4777; www.ac-transit.org; single ride East Bay/trans-Bay $2.35/5.50) Buses to the East Bay.

Greyhound (800-231-2222; www.greyhound.com) Buses leave daily for Los Angeles ($21 to $33, eight to 12 hours), Truckee ($32 to $40, 5½ hours) near Lake Tahoe and other major destinations.

Megabus (877-462-6342; https://us.megabus.com) Low-cost bus service to San Francisco from Los Angeles, Sacramento and Anaheim.

SamTrans (800-660-4287; www.samtrans.com) Southbound buses to Palo Alto and the Pacific coast.

TRAIN

Caltrain (www.caltrain.com; cnr 4th & King Sts) connects San Francisco with Silicon Valley hubs and San Jose.

Amtrak (800-872-7245; www.amtrak.com) serves San Francisco via stations in Oakland and Emeryville (near Oakland), with free shuttle-bus connections to San Francisco's Ferry Building and Caltrain station, and Oakland's Jack London Sq.

ℹ️ Getting Around

San Franciscans mostly walk, bike, ride Muni or ride-share instead of taking a car or cab. Traffic is notoriously bad and parking is next to impossible. Avoid driving until it's time to leave town. For Bay Area transit options, departures and arrivals, call 511 or check www.511.org. A *Muni Street & Transit Map* is available online.

Cable cars Frequent, slow and scenic, from 6am to 12:30am daily. Single rides cost $7; for frequent use, get a Muni Passport ($23 per day).

Muni streetcar and bus Reasonably fast, but schedules vary by line; infrequent after 9pm. Fares are $2.75 cash, or $2.50 with a reloadable Clipper card.

BART High-speed transit to East Bay, Mission St, SF airport and Millbrae, where it connects with Caltrain.

Taxi Fares are about $3 per mile; meters start at $3.50.

Marin County

Just across the Golden Gate Bridge from San Francisco, Marin County is a collection of wealthy, wooded hamlets that tenuously hang by haute hippie roots as a more conservative tech-era population moves in. Its southern peninsula nearly touches the north-pointing tip of the city, and is surrounded by ocean and bay. But Marin is wilder and more mountainous. Redwoods grow on the coastside hills, surf crashes against cliffs, and hiking and cycling trails crisscross blessedly scenic Point Reyes, Muir Woods and Mt Tamalpais. Nature is what makes Marin County such an excellent day trip or weekend escape from San Francisco.

Marin Headlands

The headland cliffs and hillsides rise majestically at the north end of the Golden Gate Bridge, their rugged beauty all the more striking given the fact that they're only a few miles from San Francisco's urban core. A few forts and bunkers are left over from a century of US military occupation – which is, ironically, the reason the headlands are today protected **parklands** (Map p980; ☑415-561-4700; www.nps.gov/goga; **P**) **FREE**, free of development. It's no mystery why this is one of the Bay Area's most popular hiking and cycling destinations: as the trails wind through the headlands, they afford stunning views of the sea, the Golden Gate Bridge and

San Francisco and lead to isolated beaches and secluded picnic spots.

Historical **Point Bonita Lighthouse** (Map p980; ☑415-331-1540; www.nps.gov/goga/pobo. htm; ☉12:30-3:30pm Sat-Mon; **P**) **FREE** is a breathtaking half-mile walk from Field Rd parking area. From the tip of Point Bonita, you can see the Golden Gate Bridge and the San Francisco skyline. Harbor seals haul out seasonally on nearby rocks. For a longer walk, the **Coastal Trail** (Map p980; www.nps. gov/goga/planyourvisit/coastal-trail.htm) meanders 3.5 miles from **Rodeo Beach** (Map p980; www. parksconservancy.org/visit/park-sites/rodeo-beach. html; off Bunker Rd; **P**🚻) inland, past abandoned military bunkers, to intersect the Tennessee Valley Trail. It then continues almost 3 miles along the headlands all the way to **Muir Beach** (Map p980; www.nps.gov/goga/planyourvis it/muirbeach.htm; off Pacific Way; **P**🚻) 🏄.

Above Rodeo Lagoon, the **Marine Mammal Center** (Map p980; ☑415-289-7325; www.marine-mammalcenter.org; 2000 Bunker Rd; by donation, audio tour adult/child $9/5; ☉10am-4pm; **P**🚻) 🏄 rehabilitates injured, sick and orphaned sea mammals before returning them to the wild, and has educational exhibits about these animals and the dangers they face.

Mt Tamalpais State Park

Standing guard over Marin County, majestic Mt Tamalpais (Mt Tam) holds more than 200 miles of hiking and biking trails, lakes, streams, waterfalls and an impressive array of wildlife – from plentiful newts and hawks to rare foxes and mountain lions. Wind your way through meadows, oaks and madrone trees to breathtaking vistas over the San Francisco Bay, Pacific Ocean, towns, cities and forested hills rolling into the distance.

This serene 2572ft mountain, comprising **Mt Tamalpais State Park** (Map p980; ☑415-388-2070; www.parks.ca.gov/mttamalpais; per car $8; ☉7am-sunset; **P**) 🏄, the Marin Municipal Water District, **Muir Woods National Monument**, several Marin County open-space areas and part of the Golden Gate Recreation Area, is a hiking paradise. You can download a map of the mountain's trails and get lots of hiking ideas at OneTam (www.onetam.org).

One of the best hikes on the mountain is the **Steep Ravine Trail**. From the park headquarters at **Pantoll Station** (Map p980; ☑415-388-2070; www.parks.ca.gov; 801 Panoramic Hwy; ☉hours vary; 🐾), it follows a wooded creek to the coast (about 2.1 miles each way).

Point Reyes National Seashore

Windswept Point Reyes peninsula is a rough-hewn beauty that has always lured marine mammals and migratory birds; it's also home to scores of shipwrecks. **Point Reyes National Seashore** (☑415-654-5100; www.nps.gov/pore; P ♿) ✏FREE protects 110 sq miles of pristine ocean beaches and coastal wilderness and has excellent hiking and camping opportunities. Be sure to bring warm clothing, as even the sunniest days can quickly turn cold and foggy.

Crowning the peninsula's westernmost tip, with wild terrain and ferocious winds, **Point Reyes Lighthouse** (☑415-669-1534; www.nps.gov/pore; end of Sir Francis Drake Blvd; ⊙10am-4:30pm Fri-Mon, lens room 2:30-4pm Fri-Mon; P) FREE feels like the end of the earth and offers the best whale-watching along the coast. The lighthouse sits below the headlands; to reach it you need to descend more than 300 stairs. Numerous beaches grace the peninsula, providing ample opportunities for swimming and animal-spotting: **Drakes** and **Heart's Desire** are both popular with families.

Pop into the **Bear Valley Visitor Center** (☑415-464-5100; www.nps.gov/pore; 1 Bear Valley Rd, Point Reyes Station; ⊙10am-5pm Mon-Fri, 9am-5pm Sat & Sun), a mile west of Olema, at Point Reyes National Seashore's headquarters, for maps, information and worthwhile exhibits.

Berkeley

Berkeley is synonymous with protest, activism and left-wing politics. Beyond those tropes is a busy, attractive city, a blend of yuppie and hippie and student, all existing side by side with great Asia-Pacific regional restaurants, twee toy stores, Latin American groceries, high-end organic food halls and the misty green campus of the University of California, Berkeley (aka 'Cal').

⊙ Sights

Telegraph Ave has traditionally been the throbbing heart of studentville in Berkeley, the sidewalks crowded with undergrads, postdocs and youthful shoppers squeezing their way past throngs of vendors, buskers and panhandlers.

★**Tilden Regional Park**   PARK
(☑510-544-2747; www.ebparks.org/parks/tilden; ⊙5am-10pm; P ♿ 🐾; 🚌AC Transit 67) ✏FREE This 2079-acre park, in the hills east of town, is Berkeley's best. It has nearly 40 miles of hiking and multiuse trails of varying difficulty, from paved paths to hilly scrambles, including part of the magnificent Bay Area Ridge Trail. There's also a miniature steam train ($3), a children's farm and environmental education center, a wonderfully wild-looking botanical garden and an 18-hole golf course. Lake Anza is good for picnics and from spring through fall you can swim ($3.50).

University of California, Berkeley UNIVERSITY (☑510-642-6000; www.berkeley.edu; ⊙hours vary; P; 🚌Downtown Berkeley) 'Cal' is one of the country's top universities, California's oldest university (1866), and home to 40,000 diverse, politically conscious students. Next to **California Memorial Stadium** (☑510-642-2730; www.californiamemorialstadium.com; 2227 Piedmont Ave; ⊙hours vary; ♿; 🚌AC Transit 52), the **Koret Visitor Center** (☑510-642-5215; http://visit.berkeley.edu; 2227 Piedmont Ave; ⊙8:30am-4:30pm Mon-Fri, 9am-1pm Sat & Sun; 🚌AC Transit 36) has information and maps, and leads free campus walking tours (reservations required). Cal's landmark is the 1914 **Campanile** (Sather Tower; ☑510-642-6000; http://campanile.berkeley.edu; adult/child $4/3; ⊙10am-3:45pm Mon-Fri, 10am-4:45pm Sat, to 1:30pm & 3-4:45pm Sun; ♿; 🚌Downtown Berkeley), with elevator rides ($4) to the top and carillon concerts. The **Bancroft Library** (☑510-642-3781; www.lib.berkeley.edu/libraries/bancroft-library; University Dr; ⊙archives 10am-4pm or 5pm Mon-Fri; 🚌Downtown Berkeley) FREE displays the small gold nugget that started the California gold rush in 1848.

🛏 Sleeping

Graduate Berkeley   BOUTIQUE HOTEL $$
(☑510-845-8981; www.graduatehotels.com/berkeley; 2600 Durant Ave; d $180-240; P ♥ @ 🐾 🛜; 🚌AC Transit 51B) Located a block from campus, this classic 1928 hotel has been cheekily renovated to highlight the connection to the university. The lobby is adorned with embarrassing yearbook photos and a ceiling mobile of exam books, and smallish rooms have dictionary-covered shower curtains and bongs repurposed into bedside lamps.

★**Claremont Resort & Spa**   RESORT $$$
(☑510-843-3000; www.fairmont.com/claremont-berkeley; 41 Tunnel Rd; d from $300; P ♥ @ 🛜 🏊 🐾) The East Bay's classy crème de la crème, this Fairmont-owned historic hotel is a glamorous white 1915 building with elegant restaurants, a fitness center, swimming

pools, tennis courts and a full-service spa. The bay-view rooms are superb. It's located at the foot of the Berkeley Hills, off Hwy 13 (Tunnel Rd) near the Oakland border. Parking is $30.

✖ Eating & Drinking

★**Cheese Board Collective**   PIZZA $
(☑510-549-3183; www.cheeseboardcollective.coop; 1504 & 1512 Shattuck Ave; slices/half-pizzas/whole pizzas $2.75/12/24; ⊙11:30am-3pm & 4:30-8pm Tue-Sat; ☑🖲; ☑AC Transit 7) Worker owned since 1971, this co-op boasts (surprise) a great collection of cheese, a bakery with a changing selection of fresh bread, and a new vegetarian pizza and salad every day; options may include asparagus and onion or crushed tomato and goat cheese. Live music is often playing at this delicious Berkeley institution. Expect lines!

★**Great China Restaurant**   CHINESE $$
(☑510-843-7996; www.greatchinaberkeley.com; 2190 Bancroft Way; mains $13-21; ⊙11:30am-2:30pm Wed-Mon, 5:30-9pm Mon, Wed & Thu, to 9:30pm Fri, 5-9:30pm Sat & Sun; ⓑDowntown Berkeley) Berkeley does not lack for good Chinese food, but this enormous, upscale restaurant elevates the genre with Northern Chinese specialties like duck-bone soup, cumin-in-braised lamb, steamed fish with ginger and scallions, and thrice-cooked pork belly. Come with friends and order as much as you can – your taste buds will not forget this.

Gather   CALIFORNIAN $$
(☑510-809-0400; www.gatherrestaurant.com; 2200 Oxford St; dinner mains $18-30; ⊙11:30am-2pm & 5-9pm Mon-Thu, 11:30am-2pm & 5-10pm Fri, 10am-2pm & 5-10pm Sat, 10am-2pm & 5-9pm Sun; ☑; ⓑDowntown Berkeley) 🍃 When vegan foodies and passionate farm-to-table types dine out together, they often end up here. Inside a salvaged-wood interior punctuated by green vines streaking down over an open kitchen, dishes are created from locally sourced ingredients and sustainably raised meats. Reservations recommended.

★**Chez Panisse**   CALIFORNIAN $$$
(☑cafe 510-548-5049, restaurant 510-548-5525; www.chezpanisse.com; 1517 Shattuck Ave; cafe dinner mains $21-35, restaurant prix-fixe dinner $75-125; ⊙cafe 11:30am-2:45pm & 5-10:30pm Mon-Thu, 11:30am-3pm & 5-11pm Fri & Sat, restaurant seatings 5:30pm & 8pm Mon-Sat; ☑; ☑AC Transit 7) 🍃 Foodies come to worship here at the church of Alice Waters, inventor of California cuisine.

Panisse is located in a lovely arts-and-crafts house in Berkeley's 'Gourmet Ghetto,' and you can choose to pull out all the stops with a prix-fixe meal downstairs or go less expensive and a tad less formal in the upstairs cafe. Reservations accepted one month ahead.

Fieldwork Brewing Company   BREWERY
(☑510-898-1203; www.fieldworkbrewing.com; 1160 6th St; ⊙11am-10pm Sun-Thu, to 11pm Fri & Sat; ☑AC Transit 12) At this industrial brewery taproom you can sit down on the outdoor patio with a tasting flight of IPAs or a glass of rich Mexican hot-chocolate stout. It's dog-friendly, and there are racks for hanging up your bicycle inside the front door. There's a short menu of Mexican-Californian food too.

❶ Getting There & Around

To get to Berkeley, catch a Richmond-bound train to one of three BART stations: Ashby, Downtown Berkeley or North Berkeley. Or drive over the Bay Bridge from San Francisco, then follow either I-80 (for University Ave, Berkeley Marina, downtown Berkeley and the university campus) or Hwy 24 (for College Ave and the Berkeley Hills).

Local buses, cycling and walking are the best ways to get around Berkeley.

NORTHERN CALIFORNIA

The Golden State goes wild in Northern California, with coast redwoods swirled in fog, Wine Country vineyards and hidden hot springs. Befitting this dramatic meeting of land and water is an unlikely mélange of local residents: timber barons and hippie tree huggers, dreadlocked Rastafarians and biodynamic ranchers, pot farmers and political radicals of every stripe. Come for the scenery, but stay for the top-notch wine and farm-to-fork restaurants, misty hikes among the world's tallest trees and rambling conversations that begin with 'Hey, dude!' and end hours later.

Wine Country

Surprising, lyrical, elegant and sophisticated, Northern California's Wine Country spans the diverse landscapes, people and flavors of Napa and Sonoma Counties.

With its rolling hills of grass, verdant valleys, evergreen-capped mountainsides and lulling rivers, the landscape here delivers surprises at every corner. But it's really the food and wine that draws people here. This is the epicurean capital of the United States, and the restaurants, wineries and tasting rooms rival anything Europe has to offer.

On the western side of the region, you have Sonoma County, where people still drive pickups and cold fingers of fog run all the way up the valleys from the sea to create amazing cold-weather wine varietals.

Head east of Eden for the world-class wineries of Napa County, which offers up truly out-of-this-world fine dining and plenty of open spaces for an afternoon picnic or hike.

Both valleys are a 90-minute drive from San Francisco and Oakland. Napa, further inland, has about 500 wineries and attracts the most visitors (expect heavy traffic on summer weekends). Sonoma County has more than 425 wineries and around 40 in Sonoma Valley, which is less commercial and less congested than Napa. If you have time to visit only one, for ease go with Sonoma.

Napa Valley

Napa Valley is exactly what you expect when you think of Wine Country: hillside chateau wineries, bold cabernets, vast expanses of perfectly ordered grape vines, grassy slopes speckled by the tungsten sun, restaurant dinners that go on for hours, and some of the finest and most luxurious small-scale boutique hotels anywhere in California.

Most journeys here start and end in the city of Napa proper. In the town center there are tasting rooms, live jazz and plenty of fine-dining options, plus the option to party late into the night at down-home pubs and eateries that draw a young local crowd.

◉ Sights & Activities

★ Hess Collection   WINERY, GALLERY

(☑ 707-255-1144; www.hesscollection.com; 4411 Redwood Rd, Napa; museum & tours free, tasting $25-35; ⊙10am-5pm, last tasting 5pm) ✎ Art-lovers: don't miss Hess Collection, whose galleries display mixed-media and large-canvas works, including pieces by Francis Bacon and Robert Motherwell. In the elegant stone-walled tasting room, find well-known cabernet sauvignon and chardonnay, but also try the Viognier. There's garden service in the warmer months, which is lovely, as Hess overlooks the valley. Make reservations and be prepared to drive a winding road. Bottles are $30 to $100. A public tour runs at 10:30am.

★ Robert Sinskey Vineyards   WINERY

(☑ 707-944-9090; www.robertsinskey.com; 6320 Silverado Trail, Napa; bar tasting $40, seated food

& wine pairings $70-175; ⊙10am-4:30pm; ℗) ✎ The fabulous hillside tasting room, constructed of stone, redwood and teak, resembles a small cathedral – fitting, given the sacred status here bestowed upon food and wine. It specializes in bright-acid organic pinot noir, plus exceptional aromatic white varietals, dry rosé and Bordeaux varietals such as merlot and cab franc, all crafted for the dinner table. Small bites accompany bar tastings, and seated food and wine experiences are curated by chef Maria Sinskey herself. Reserve ahead for sit-down tastings and culinary tours.

★ Frog's Leap   WINERY

(☑ 707-963-4704; www.frogsleap.com; 8815 Conn Creek Rd, Rutherford; tasting incl tour $25-35; ⊙10am-4pm by appointment only; ℗♿🐾) ✎ Meandering paths wind through magical gardens and fruit-bearing orchards surrounding an 1884 barn and farmstead with cats and chickens. The vibe is casual and down-to-earth, with a major emphasis on *fun*. Sauvignon blanc is its best-known wine but the merlot merits attention. There's also a dry, restrained cabernet, atypical of Napa.

★ Tres Sabores   WINERY

(☑ 707-967-8027; www.tressabores.com; 1620 Sth Whitehall Lane, St Helena; tour & tasting $40; ⊙10:30am-3pm, by appointment; 🐾) ✎ At the valley's westernmost edge, where sloping vineyards meet wooded hillsides, Tres Sabores is a portal to old Napa – no fancy tasting room, no snobbery, just great wine in a spectacular setting. Bucking the cabernet custom, Tres Sabores crafts elegantly structured, Burgundian-style zinfandel and spritely sauvignon blanc, which the *New York Times* dubbed a top 10 of its kind in California. Reservations are essential.

⌂ Sleeping

Pricey and fabulous hotels are scattered throughout Napa Valley, with the most opulent stays perched in and around St Helena and Yountville. Calistoga is a bit more relaxed and affordable, and the best budget option, without question, is a yurt (or campsite) in **Bothe-Napa Valley State Park** (☑ 800-444-7275; www.parks.ca.gov; 3801 Hwy 128; camping & RV sites $35, yurts $55-70, cabins $150-225; ♿🐾).

Napa Winery Inn   HOTEL $

(☑ 707-257-7220; www.napawineryinn.com; 1998 Trower Ave, Napa; r from $125; ℗♿❄@🛜🏊🐾) Request a remodeled room at this good-value hotel, north of downtown, decorated with generic Colonial-style furniture. It has a hot tub and good service. There are complimentary wine receptions each night: weekdays 5:30pm to 6:30pm, to 7pm weekends.

★ **Auberge du Soleil** LUXURY HOTEL $$$
(☑707-963-1211; www.aubergedusoleil.com; 180 Rutherford Hill Rd, Rutherford; r $1325-4025; ⊖❄🛜🏊) The top splurge for a no-holds-barred romantic weekend, Auberge's hillside cottages are second to none. The view will very much define your lodging choice, but opting for a valley view room with panoramic windows is well worth the splurge. Most of the rooms come with a fireplace.

★ **Carneros Resort & Spa** RESORT $$$
(☑707-299-4900; www.carnerosresort.com; 4048 Sonoma Hwy, Napa; r from $500; P⊖❄🛜🏊🐾) Carneros Resort & Spa's contemporary aesthetic and retro small-town agricultural theme shatter the predictable Wine Country mold. The semidetached, corrugated-metal cottages look like itinerant housing, but inside they're snappy and chic, with cherry-wood floors, ultrasuede headboards, wood-burning fireplaces, heated-tile bathroom floors, giant tubs and indoor-outdoor showers.

✖ Eating

★ **Oxbow Public Market** MARKET
(☑707-226-6529; www.oxbowpublicmarket.com; 610 & 644 1st St, Napa; ⊙7:30am-9:30pm; P🚻) ● Showcasing all things culinary (produce stalls, kitchen shops and everywhere something to taste), Oxbow is foodie central with an emphasis on seasonal eating and sustainability. Some vendors and restaurants open early or close late. Come hungry.

Farmstead MODERN AMERICAN $$
(☑707-963-4555; www.longmeadowranch.com; 738 Main St, St Helena; mains $19-33; ⊙11:30am-9:30pm Mon-Thu, to 10pm Fri & Sat, 11am-9:30pm Sun; 🅿) ● An enormous open-truss barn with big leather booths and rocking-chair porch, Farmstead draws an all-ages crowd and farms many of its own ingredients – including grass-fed beef and lamb – for an earthy menu highlighting wood-fired cooking.

★ **French Laundry** CALIFORNIAN $$$
(☑707-944-2380; www.thomaskeller.com/tfl; 6640 Washington St, Yountville; prix-fixe dinner from $325; ⊙seatings 11am-12:30pm Fri-Sun, 5-9pm daily) The pinnacle of California dining, Thomas Keller's three-Michelin-star rated French Laundry is epic, a high-wattage culinary experience on par with the world's best. Book

one month ahead on the online app Tock, where tickets are released in groupings. This is the meal you can brag about the rest of your life.

★ **Restaurant at Meadowood** CALIFORNIAN $$$
(☑707-967-1205; www.meadowood.com; 900 Meadowood Lane, St Helena; 12-course menu $275; ⊙5:30-9:30pm Tue-Sat) If you couldn't score reservations at French Laundry, fear not: Meadowood – the valley's only other three-Michelin-star restaurant – has a slightly more sensibly priced menu, elegantly unfussy dining room and lavish haute cuisine that's not too esoteric. The restaurant at Auberge (p1005) has better views, but Meadowood's food and service far surpass it.

Sonoma Valley

Here in the delightfully laid-back, unapologetic and fun-loving Sonoma Valley, winemakers ply their craft, foodies flock to amazing restaurants, and there are plenty of adventures to be had in the 13,000 acres of parkland.

Heading up valley, you pass through the tiny village of Glen Ellen, which has a handful of small eateries and access to the valley's best natural area at **Jack London State Historic Park** (☑707-938-5216; www.jacklondonpark.com; 2400 London Ranch Rd, Glen Ellen; per car $10, admission to cottage $3; ⊙9:30am-5pm; P🚻) ● and then on to the gorgeous wineries and roadside attractions of the Kenwood area.

⊙ Sights & Activities

★ **Gundlach-Bundschu Winery** WINERY
(☑707-938-5277; www.gunbun.com; 2000 Denmark St, Sonoma; tasting $20-30, incl tour $30-60; ⊙11am-5:30pm Sun-Fri, to 7pm Sat Apr-Oct, to 4:30pm Nov-Mar; P) ● California's oldest family-run winery looks like a castle but has a down-to-earth vibe. Founded in 1858 by a Bavarian immigrant, its signatures are gewürztraminer and pinot noir, but 'GunBun' was the first American winery to produce 100% merlot. Down a winding lane, it's a terrific bike-to winery with picnicking, hiking, a lake and frequent concerts, including a two-day folk-music festival in June. Tour the 1800-barrel cave by reservation only. Bottles are $20 to $50.

Benziger WINERY
(☑707-935-3000; www.benziger.com; 1883 London Ranch Rd, Glen Ellen; tasting $20-50, tours $25-50;

ⓘ BOOKING TASTINGS

Because of strict county zoning laws, many Napa wineries cannot legally receive drop-in visitors; unless you've come strictly to buy, you'll have to call ahead. This is *not* the case with all wineries. We recommend booking one tasting, plus a lunch or dinner reservation, and planning your day around those appointments.

🕑 11am-5pm Mon-Fri, 10am-5pm Sat & Sun; P 🎫

🍷 If you're new to wine, make Benziger your first stop for Sonoma's best crash course in winemaking. The worthwhile tour (reservations recommended) includes an open-air tram ride (weather permitting) through biodynamic vineyards and a five-wine tasting. Great picnicking, excellent for families. The large-production wine is OK (head for the reserves); the tour's the thing. Bottles are $20 to $80.

Bartholomew Estate Winery　　　WINERY
(🖉 707-509-0450; www.bartholomewestate.com; 1000 Vineyard Lane, Sonoma; tasting $15; 🕑 11am-4:30pm; P) 🍷 Formerly Bartholomew Park Winery has transformed into Bartholomew Estate, ushering in a change of ownership and winemaker to the historic vineyards, which have been cultivated since 1857. You could easily while away an afternoon tasting the sauvignon blanc, rosé and zinfandel vintages, hiking the 3-mile trail through the grounds and admiring the plein-air artworks in the gallery adjacent to the tasting room.

🛏 Sleeping

The most sensible bases for exploring this valley are historic downtown Sonoma and lush, romantic Glen Ellen. To save some duckets, give Petaluma down south a second look or consider camping in the **Sugarloaf Ridge State Park** (🖉 707-833-6084; www.reservecalifornia.com/CaliforniaWebHome/; 2605 Adobe Canyon Rd, Kenwood; tent & RV sites $35, online reservation fee $7.99; 🖨 🎫).

Beltane Ranch　　　B&B $$
(🖉 707-833-4233; www.beltaneranch.com; 11,775 Hwy 12, Glen Ellen; d $185-375; P 🖨 🛜) 🍷 Surrounded by horse pastures and vineyards, Beltane is a throwback to 19th-century Sonoma. The cheerful 1890s ranch house has double porches lined with swinging chairs and white wicker. Though it's technically a B&B, each country-Americana-style room and the

cottage has a private entrance – nobody will make you pet the cat. No phone or TV means zero distraction from pastoral bliss.

Olea Hotel　　　BOUTIQUE HOTEL $$$
(🖉 707-996-5131; www.oleahotel.com; 5131 Warm Springs Rd, Glen Ellen; r from $340; P 🖨 ❄ 🛜 ☕) This lovely property extends up a hillside off a Glen Ellen back road. Impeccably redeveloped following a brush with the 2017 fires, each room feels a little different, but comes with modern prints, and bright and shiny appointments. Some even have private balconies and fireplaces. Rooms 14, 15 and 16 have vaulted ceilings and the best views. There's a lovely pool and hot-tub area.

🍴 Eating

There are some very good restaurants in downtown Sonoma and Glen Ellen's Jack London Village. Also, don't miss the indulgent and fabulous food-and-wine pairing at **St Francis Winery** (🖉 707-538-9463; www.stfranciswinery.com; 100 Pythian Rd at Hwy 12, Santa Rosa; tasting $15, wine & cheese pairing $25, wine & food pairing $68; 🕑 10am-5pm).

★**Cafe La Haye**　　　CALIFORNIAN $$
(🖉 707-935-5994; www.cafelahaye.com; 140 E Napa St, Sonoma; mains $19-25; 🕑 5:30-9pm Tue-Sat) 🍷 One of Sonoma's top tables for earthy New American cooking, La Haye only uses produce sourced from within 60 miles. Its dining room gets packed cheek-by-jowl and service can border on perfunctory, but the clean simplicity and flavor-packed cooking make it many foodies' first choice. Reserve well ahead.

Glen Ellen Star　　　CALIFORNIAN, ITALIAN $$$
(🖉 707-343-1384; www.glenellenstar.com; 13648 Arnold Dr, Glen Ellen; pizzas $15-20, mains $24-50; 🕑 5:30-9pm Sun-Thu, to 9:30pm Fri & Sat; 🖉) 🍷 Helmed by chef Ari Weiswasser, who once worked at Thomas Keller's French Laundry (p1005), this petite Glen Ellen bistro shines a light on the best of Sonoma farms and ranches. Local, organic and seasonal ingredients star in dishes such as spring-lamb ragù, whole roasted fish with broccoli Di Cicco or golden beets with harissa crumble. Reservations recommended.

Healdsburg & Russian River Valley

'The River,' as locals call it, has long been a summer-weekend destination for Northern Californians who come to canoe, wander country lanes, taste wine, hike redwood forests and live at a lazy pace. In winter the river floods, and nobody's here.

The towns of this area are as diverse as the landscape. Without a doubt, the hippest and most sophisticated town, the once-sleepy farming village of Healdsburg has come to life with amazing restaurants, wonderful shops and tasting rooms, and plenty of glitz and glamour. Young, hip and growing, the county seat of Santa Rosa offers urban chic, while out-west towns like Sebastopol retain much of their downhome appeal.

◉ Sights & Activities

★ Macrostie
WINERY
(☑ 707-473-9303; www.macrostiewinery.com; 4605 Westside Rd, Healdsburg; tasting $25-35, with tour $55; ⏱ 11am-5pm Mon-Thu, 10am-5pm Fri-Sun) For its creamy and crisp chardonnays and earthy pinots, along with top-notch service and an elegant tasting room, Macrostie is the talk of Wine Country. The sit-down tastings are relaxed and highly personal, with gorgeous views of the vineyard. Visionary winemaker Heidi Bridenhagen holds the distinction of being the youngest female on the job in Sonoma Valley. Pair your tasting with a delicious charcuterie plate that includes three local cheeses, prosciutto, olives, almonds and dried fruit.

Francis Ford Coppola Winery   WINERY, MUSEUM
(☑ 707-857-1471; www.francisfordcoppolawinery.com; 300 Via Archimedes, Geyserville; tasting $15-30; ⏱ 11am-6pm; P ♿) ✦ The famous movie director's vineyard estate is a self-described 'wine wonderland.' Taking over historic Chateau Souverain, this hillside winery has a bit of everything: wine-tasting flights, a free museum of moviemaking memorabilia, a shameless gift shop and two modern Italian-American restaurants. The most satisfying tasting is the reserve flight ($25 to $30) upstairs. Bottles are $12 to $90. Outside you'll find boccie courts by two **swimming pools** (day pass adult/child $35/15; ⏱ 11am-6pm daily Jun-Sep, Fri-Sun Apr, May & Oct; ♿).

Bella
WINERY
(☑ 707-395-6136; www.bellawinery.com; 9711 W Dry Creek Rd, Healdsburg; tasting $20; ⏱ 11am-4:30pm; P) Atop the valley's north end, always-fun Bella has cool caves built into the hillside. The estate-grown grapes include 112-year-old vines from Alexander Valley. The focus is on big reds – zinfandel and syrah – but there's terrific rosé (good for barbecues) and late-harvest zinfandel (great with brownies).

The wonderful vibe and dynamic staff make Bella special. Bottles are $25 to $55.

🛏 Sleeping

Russian River offers excellent resorts, inns and cottages, particularly in upscale Healdsburg and in and around Guerneville. Lodgings are harder to come by in small towns such as Duncan Mills, but wherever you find yourself, there's probably a campground nearby. Santa Rosa has plenty of options, and some cheaper spots for people on a budget.

★ Shanti Permaculture Farm   FARMSTAY $
(☑ 707-874-2001; www.shantioccidental.com; 16,715 Coleman Valley Rd, Occidental; tent & RV sites $55-80, cottages & yurts $99-225; ⊖ 🛜) Tucked back in the redwoods on scenic Coleman Valley Rd, this is the ultimate NorCal farmstay. The knowledgeable Oregonian owner educates guests about ecofriendly agricultural concepts such as biochar and *hugelkultur,* and shows off her chickens, ducks, goats and enormous llama. While the operation feels somewhat rustic, it is impressively MacGyvered and the one-bedroom cottage is surprisingly posh.

Astro
BOUTIQUE HOTEL $$
(☑ 707-200-4655; www.theastro.com; 323 Santa Rosa Ave; r from $170; ⊖ 🌐 🛜) A designer's dream, this throwback motel has wonderful and unique touches in each room. Most of the furnishings go back to the 1960s. Like what you see? No problem, all the furniture is for sale. Out back, a lounge and bar gives an easy central spot to gather, drink martinis or simply revel in the kitsch of 1960s Californiana.

★ Hotel Healdsburg
HOTEL $$$
(☑ 707-431-2800; www.hotelhealdsburg.com; 25 Matheson St, Healdsburg; r from $314; ⊖ 🌐 @ 🛜 ⛲) Smack on the plaza, the fashion-forward HH has a coolly minimalist style of concrete and velvet, with requisite top-end amenities, including sumptuous beds and extradeep tubs. There's a full-service spa. The restaurant, **Dry Creek Kitchen** (☑ 707-431-0330; www.drycreekkitchen.com; 317 Healdsburg Ave; mains $32-44, tasting menu $29, wine pairing $48; ⏱ 5:30-9:30pm Sun-Thu, to 10pm Fri & Sat), is run by celeb-chef Charlie Palmer.

★ Applewood Inn
INN $$$
(☑ 707-869-9093; www.applewoodinn.com; 13,555 Hwy 116, Guerneville; r $275-500; ⊖ 🌐 @ 🛜 ⛲) A hideaway estate on a wooded hilltop south of town, cushy Applewood has marvelous 1920s-era detail, with dark wood and heavy

furniture that echo the forest. Some rooms have Jacuzzi and couples' shower; some have fireplace. Amenities include a small spa and two heated pools, but the best perk is the coupon for complimentary tastings at more than 100 wineries.

✗ Eating

Healdsburg is the area's culinary capital and its **Tuesday** (☑707-824-8717; www.healdsburg-farmersmarket.org; Plaza & Center Sts; ◷9am to 1pm May 29-Aug 28) and **Saturday** (www.healdsburgfarmersmarket.org; North & Vine Sts; ◷8:30am-noon Sat May-Nov) markets feature plenty of vendors and small tastings, but Santa Rosa, Sebastopol and Occidental are nothing to sneeze at, either. In general, this region is a foodie's dream, with prices far more reasonable than over in Napa Valley.

Chalkboard   CALIFORNIAN $$
(☑707-473-8030; www.chalkboardhealdsburg.com; 29 North St, Healdsburg; mains $20-27; ◷4:30-9pm Mon-Fri, 11:30am-10pm Sat & Sun) With its tony grotto setting, sunny back patio and changing daily menu, this top restaurant focuses on pulling the freshest ingredients from local farms. The small-plate menu is ideal for sharing. Don't miss out on a housemade pasta or fresh melon soup to start, followed by locally caught scallops, crispy fried chicken and steak.

★ Backyard   CALIFORNIAN $$$
(☑707-820-8445; www.backyardforestville.com; 6566 Front St, Forestville; mains lunch & brunch $14-30, dinner mains $22-30; ◷11:30am-9pm Mon & Fri, 9am-9pm Sat, to 8pm Sun) This relaxing, alfresco spot gets every fruit, vegetable and animal from local farmers or fishers and the chef knows just what to do with all of it. California-inspired dishes are simple and delicious; the steak, piquillo-pepper and duck-egg hash was perhaps the world's most perfect brunch. The coffee and artisanal doughnut holes are winners.

★ SingleThread
Farm-Restaurant-Inn   JAPANESE $$$
(☑707-723-4646; www.singlethreadfarms.com; 131 North St, Healdsburg; tasting menu per person $293; ◷dinner daily from 5:30pm, lunch Sat & Sun from 11:30am) The most ambitious project in Northern California is SingleThread, a world-class restaurant and, secondarily, an inn, where *omotenashi* (warm hospitality in Japanese) reigns and dishes from an 11-course tasting menu are prepared in handmade Japanese

donabe (earthenware pots). The cuisine is California-Japanese and guests book tickets in advance, offering up their preferences and dietary restrictions, and the chef abides.

North Coast

This is not the legendary California of the Beach Boys' song – there are no palm-flanked beaches and very few surfboards. The jagged edge of the continent is wild, scenic and even slightly foreboding, where spectral fog and an outsider spirit have fostered the world's tallest trees, most potent weed and a string of idiosyncratic two-stoplight towns. Explore hidden coves with a blanket and a bottle of local wine, scan the horizon for migrating whales and retreat at night to fire-warmed Victorians. As you travel further north, find valleys of redwood, wide rivers and mossy, overgrown forests. Expect cooler, damper weather too.

Coastal Highway 1 to Mendocino

Often winding precariously atop ocean cliffs, this serpentine slice of Hwy 1 passes salty fishing harbors and hidden beaches. Use roadside pullouts to scan the Pacific horizon for migrating whales or to amble coves bounded by startling rock formations and relentlessly pounded by the surf. The 110-mile stretch from Bodega Bay to Fort Bragg takes at least three hours of nonstop driving; at night or in the fog it takes steely nerves and much, much longer.

BODEGA BAY

Bodega Bay, the first pearl in a string of sleepy fishing villages, was the setting for Hitchcock's terrifying 1963 psycho-horror flick *The Birds*. Today the skies are free from blood-thirsty gulls, but you'd best keep an eye on that picnic basket as you explore the arched rocks, blustery coves and wildflower-covered bluffs of **Sonoma Coast State Park** (www.parks.ca.gov; per car $8), with beaches rolling beyond Jenner, 10 miles north. **Bodega Bay Sportfishing Center** (☑707-875-3495; www.bodegabaysportfishing.com; 1410b Bay Flat Rd; fishing trips from $130, whale-watching $60; ◓) runs winter whale-watching trips. Landlubbers hike Bodega Head or saddle up at **Chanslor Ranch** (☑707-589-5040; https://chanslorstables.com; 2660 N Hwy 1; rides from $40; ◷9am-5pm).

Stop by classic dockside crab shack **Spud Point** (☑707-875-9472; www.spudpointcrab.com; 1910 Westshore Rd; mains $6.75-12; ◷9am-5pm;

P)) for salty-sweet crab sandwiches and real clam chowder (that consistently wins local culinary prizes).

JENNER & AROUND

Where the wide, lazy Russian River meets the Pacific, you'll find Jenner, a cluster of shops and restaurants dotting coastal hills. Informative volunteers protect the resident colony of harbor seals at the river's mouth during pupping season, between March and August. **Water Treks Ecotours** (707-865-2249; www.watertreks.com; 2hr kayak rental from $50, 4hr guided tours from $120; hours vary) rents kayaks on Hwy 1; reservations recommended.

Twelve miles north of Jenner, the salt-weathered structures of **Fort Ross State Historic Park** (707-847-3437; www.fortross.org; 19005 Hwy 1; per car $8; park sunrise-sunset, visitor center 10am-4:30pm) preserve an 1812 trading post and Russian Orthodox church. It's a quiet place, but the history is riveting: this was once the southernmost reach of Tsarist Russia's North American trading expeditions. The small, wood-scented museum offers historical exhibits and respite from the windswept cliffs.

SALT POINT STATE PARK

Several miles further north, **Salt Point State Park** (707-847-3221; www.saltpoint.org; 25050 Hwy 1; per car $8; park sunrise-sunset, visitor center 10am-3pm Sat & Sun Apr-Oct; P) abounds with hiking trails and tide pools and has two **campgrounds** (800-444-7275; www.reserveamerica.com; Salt Point State Park; tent & RV sites $35; P). At neighboring **Kruse Rhododendron State Natural Reserve**, pink blooms spot the misty greenwoods between April and June. Cows graze the fields on the bluffs heading north to **Sea Ranch** (www.tsra.org), where public-access hiking trails lead downhill from roadside parking lots (per car $7) to pocket beaches.

There are two good places to stay enroute to Point Arena: campers should head to **Gualala Point Regional Park** (707-785-2377; http://parks.sonomacounty.ca.gov; 42401 Hwy 1, Gualala; parking $7, tent & RV sites $35; 6am-sunset summer, 8am-sunset winter; P) for the best drive-in camping on this stretch of the coast; in Anchor Bay, don't miss **Mar Vista Cottages** (707-884-3522; www.marvistamendocino.com; 35101 Hwy 1, Anchor Bay; cottages $195-310; P🐾). These elegantly renovated 1930s fishing cabins offer a simple, stylish seaside escape with a vanguard commitment to sustainability.

POINT ARENA & AROUND

Stop on Main St for the cutest patisserie on this stretch of coast, run by Franny and her mother, Barbara. The fresh berry tarts and creative housemade chocolates at **Franny's Cup & Saucer** (707-882-2500; www.frannyscupandsaucer.com; 213 Main St; cakes from $2; 8am-4pm Wed-Sat) seem too beautiful to eat, until you take the first bite and immediately want to order another.

Two miles north of Point Arena town, detour to wind-battered **Point Arena Lighthouse** (707-882-2809; www.pointarenalighthouse.com; 45500 Lighthouse Rd; adult/child $8/1; 10am-3:30pm mid-Sep–mid-May, to 4:30pm mid-May–mid-Sep; P), built in 1908. View the Fresnel lens in the museum then ascend 145 steps to get jaw-dropping coastal views. Eight miles north of the Little River crossing at Hwy 128 is **Van Damme State Park** (707-937-0851; www.parks.ca.gov; 8001 N Hwy 1, Little River; per car $8; hours vary; P), where the popular 5-mile round-trip Fern Canyon Trail passes through a lush river canyon with young redwoods, continuing another mile each way to a pygmy forest.

Mendocino

In Mendocino, a historical village perched on a gorgeous headland, baby boomers stroll around New England saltbox and water-tower B&Bs, quaint shops and art galleries. Wilder paths pass berry brambles, wildflowers and cypress trees standing guard over rocky cliffs and raging surf at Mendocino Headlands State Park (www.parks.ca.gov). The **Ford House Museum & Visitor Center** (707-937-5397; www.mendoparks.org; 45035 Main St; 11am-4pm) is nearby.

Just south of town, paddle your way up the Big River with **Catch a Canoe & Bicycles, Too** (707-937-0273; www.catchacanoe.com; 10051 S Big River Rd, The Stanford Inn By The Sea; 3hr kayak, canoe or bicycle rental adult/child $35/15; 9am-5pm). North of town, 1909 **Point Cabrillo Light Station** (707-937-6123; www.pointcabrillo.org; 45300 Lighthouse Rd; park sunrise-sunset, lighthouse 11am-4pm) FREE is a perfect winter whale-watching perch.

Accommodations standards are high in stylish Mendocino and so are prices; two-day minimums often crop up on weekends. For a range of cottages and B&Bs, contact **Mendocino Coast Reservations** (707-937-5033; www.mendocinovacations.com; 45084 Little Lake St; 9am-4pm).

Alegria (☑707-937-5150; www.oceanfront magic.com; 44781 Main St; r $239-309; ❄🐾) is the perfect romantic hideaway: beds have views over the coast, decks have ocean views and all rooms have wood-burning fireplaces; outside, a gorgeous path leads to a big, amber-gray beach. The cluster of 1950s roadside cottages that make up **Andiron Seaside Inn & Cabins** (☑707-937-1543; http://theandiron.com; 6051 N Hwy 1, Little River; d $134-284; P❄🐾❄) 🐾 is another good choice. With hip vintage decor, it's a refreshingly playful option amid the cabbage-rose and lace aesthetic of Mendocino.

For refined, inspired cooking, you can't do better than **Café Beaujolais** (☑707-937-5614; www.cafebeaujolais.com; 961 Ukiah St; lunch mains $11-20, dinner mains $24-42; ⏱11:30am-2:30pm Wed & Thu, to 3pm Fri-Sun, 5:30-9pm daily; P) 🐾, Mendocino's iconic, beloved country-Cal-French restaurant occupying an 1893 farmhouse. The locally sourced menu changes with the seasons, but the dry-aged duck breast is a gourmand's delight. Follow the boardwalk lit with fairy lights to cozy, casual **Luna Trattoria** (☑707-962-3093; www.lunatrattoria.com; 955 Ukiah St; mains $12-29; ⏱5-9pm Tue-Thu & Sun, to 10pm Fri & Sat), serving up generous portions of Northern Italian fare. The bread and pastas are homemade, and there's a lovely garden out back.

Along Highway 101 to Avenue of the Giants

To get into the most remote and wild parts of the North Coast behind the 'Redwood Curtain' quickly, eschew winding Hwy 1 for inland Hwy 101, which occasionally pauses under the traffic lights of small towns. Diversions along the way include bountiful redwood forests past Leggett and the abandoned wilds of the Lost Coast.

A short detour off Hwy 101 just before Ukiah leads you to **Boonville**, home to Bavarian-style **Anderson Valley Brewing Company** (☑707-895-2337; www.avbc.com; 17700 Hwy 253, Boonville; tasting from $10, tours & disc-golf course free; ⏱11am-6pm Sat-Thu, to 7pm Fri; P🐾) 🐾 and the impressive **Boonville Hotel** (☑707-895-2210; www.boonvillehotel.com; 14050 Hwy 128, Boonville; d $215-395; P❄❄🐾); the in-house **restaurant** (lunch mains $10-15, dinner tasting menu from $48; ⏱6-8pm Thu-Sat, from 5:30pm Sun Apr-Nov, 6-8pm Fri & Sat, 1-2:30pm Sun Dec-Mar; P🐾), under the helm of renowned chef Perry Hoffman, features distinctive haute cuisine made up of seasonal produce, local seafood and meat, along with foraged greens and mushrooms.

UKIAH

Although Ukiah is mostly a place to gas up, it's worth stopping for an arty pizza at **Cultivo** (☑707-462-7007; www.cultivorestaurant.com; 108 W Standley St; pizzas $14-19, mains $19-24; ⏱11:30am-9pm Mon-Thu, to 10pm Fri & Sat) or a vegetarian Asian-influenced meal at **Jyun Kang Vegetarian Restaurant** (☑707-468-7966; www.cttbusa.org; City of Ten Thousand Buddhas; mains $6-12; ⏱11:30am-3pm Wed-Mon; 🐾).

LEGGETT

North of tiny Leggett on Hwy 101, take a dip in the Eel River at **Standish-Hickey State Recreation Area** (☑707-925-6482; www.parks.ca.gov; 69350 Hwy 101; day use per car $8, camping incl 1 car $35, extra car $8; ❄), where hiking trails traipse through virgin and second-growth redwoods. South of Garberville on Hwy 101, **Richardson Grove State Park** (☑707-247-3318, 707-247-3378; www.parks.ca.gov; 1600 Hwy 101, Garberville; per car $8) also protects old-growth redwood forest beside the river. Both parks have developed **campgrounds** (☑reservations 800-444-7275; www.reservecalifornia.com; 1600 Hwy 101; tent & RV sites $35, cabins $80; P).

LOST COAST

The Lost Coast tempts hikers with the most rugged coastal backpacking in California. It became 'lost' when the state's highway bypassed the mountains of the King Range, which rises over 4000ft within a few miles of the ocean. From Garberville, it's 23 steep, twisting miles along a paved road to **Shelter Cove**, the main supply point but little more than a seaside subdivision with a general store, cafes and none-too-cheap ocean-view lodgings.

HUMBOLDT REDWOODS STATE PARK

Along Hwy 101, 82-sq-mile **Humboldt Redwoods State Park** (☑707-946-2409; www.parks.ca.gov; Hwy 101; P) 🐾 **FREE** protects some of California's oldest redwoods, including more than half of the world's tallest 100 trees. Magnificent groves rival those in Redwood National Park, a long drive further north. If you don't have time to hike, at least drive the awe-inspiring **Avenue of the Giants**, a 32-mile, two-lane road parallel to Hwy 101. Book ahead for **campsites** (☑information 707-946-1811, reservations 800-444-7275; www.reservecalifornia.com; tent & RV sites $20-35; P❄).

Highway 101 from Eureka to Crescent City

There is a solid choice of accommodations throughout the southern redwood coast, including in Eureka, Arcata and Crescent City. Enthusiastic campers can choose between the wilderness options on the Lost Coast or more developed camping in the state parks.

You'll find a plethora of natural-food stores and markets along this stretch of the highway. Eureka and Arcata have a particularly fine choice of dining venues.

EUREKA

Past the strip malls sprawling around its edges, the heart of Eureka is Old Town, abounding with fine Victorian buildings, antique shops and restaurants. Cruise the harbor aboard the blue-and-white 1910 **Madaket** (Madaket Cruises; ☑707-445-1910; www.humboldt-baymaritimemuseum.com; 1st St; narrated cruises adult/child $22/18; ⊘1pm, 2:30pm & 4pm Tue-Sun, 1pm & 2:30pm Mon mid-May–mid-Oct) – 75-minute cruises cost adults $22 and depart from the foot of C St, while sunset cocktail cruises ($10) serve from the state's smallest licensed bar. The **visitor center** (☑707-733-5406; www.fws.gov/refuge/Humboldt_Bay/visit/VisitorCenter.html; Loleta; ⊘8am-5pm) is on Hwy 101, south of downtown.

Constructed in period style, the aesthetically remodeled rooms of the **Carter House Inns** (☑707-444-8062; www.carterhouse.com; 301 L St; r $184-395; P⊖⊛⊛⊛) have modern amenities and top-quality linens; suites have in-room Jacuzzis and marble fireplaces. It's also home to the sophisticated **Restaurant 301** (☑707-444-8062; www.carterhouse.com; 301 L St; mains $22-38; ⊘5-9pm) ✔, serving up contemporary Californian fare using produce sourced from its organic gardens.

Exuding a cozy bistro-style ambience with red-and-white checkered tablecloths and jaunty murals, perennially popular **Cafe Nooner** (☑707-443-4663; www.cafenooner.com; 409 Opera Alley; mains $10-17; ⊘11am-4pm; 🖫) serves organic and Med-inspired cuisine with choices that include a Greek-style meze platter, plus kebabs, salads and soups. For thin-crust pizza, head to perennially busy **Brick & Fire** (☑707-268-8959; www.brickandfirebistro.com; 1630 F St; dinner mains $17-24; ⊘11:30am-9pm Mon & Wed-Fri, 5-9pm Sat & Sun; 🖳).

ARCATA

On the north side of Humboldt Bay, Arcata is a patchouli-dipped haven of radical politics. Biodiesel-fueled trucks drive in for the Saturday **farmers market** (www.humfarm.org; 9am to 2pm April to November, from 10am December to March) on the central plaza, surrounded by art galleries, shops, cafes and bars. Make reservations to soak at **Finnish Country Sauna & Tubs** (☑707-822-2228; http://cafemokkaarcata.com; 495 J St; per 30min adult/child $10.25/2; ⊘noon-11pm Sun-Thu, to midnight Fri & Sat; 🖳). Northeast of downtown stands eco-conscious, socially responsible **Humboldt State University** (HSU; ☑707-826-3011; www.humboldt.edu; 1 Harpst St; P) ✔.

Pop by Arcata's best grocery store, **Wildberries Marketplace** (☑707-822-0095; www.wildberries.com; 747 13th St, Arcata; sandwiches $5-8; ⊘6am-midnight; P✔), to stock up on supplies, or linger over a 'brew with a view' at **Six Rivers Brewery** (☑707-839-7580; www.sixriversbrewery.com; 1300 Central Ave, McKinleyville; ⊘11:30am-11:30pm Sun-Wed, to 12:30am Thu-Sat), one of the first female-owned breweries in California.

TRINIDAD

Sixteen miles north of Arcata, Trinidad sits on a bluff overlooking a breathtakingly beautiful fishing harbor. Stroll sandy beaches or take short hikes around Trinidad Head after meeting tide-pool critters at the **HSU Telonicher Marine Laboratory** (☑707-826-3671; www.humboldt.edu/marinelab; 570 Ewing St; $1; ⊘9am-4:30pm Mon-Fri year-round, plus 10am-5pm Sat & Sun Aug-May; P🖳) ✔. Heading north of town, Patrick's Point Dr is dotted with forested campgrounds, cabins and lodges. **Patrick's Point State Park** (☑707-677-3570; www.parks.ca.gov; 4150 Patrick's Point Dr; per car $8; ⊘sunrise-sunset; P🖳) ✔ has stunning rocky headlands, beachcombing, an authentic reproduction of a Yurok village and a **campground** (☑information 707-677-3570, reservations 800-444-7275; www.reservecalifornia.com; 4150 Patrick's Point Dr; tent & RV sites $35 plus $8 for any additional vehicle; P⊛) with coin-operated hot showers.

REDWOOD NATIONAL PARK

Heading north, Hwy 101 passes Redwood National Park's **Thomas H Kuchel Visitor Center** (☑707-465-7765; www.nps.gov/redw; Hwy 101, Orick; ⊘9am-5pm Apr-Oct, to 4pm Nov-Mar; 🖳). Together, the national park and three state parks – Prairie Creek, Del Norte and Jedediah Smith – are a World Heritage site containing more than 40% of the world's

WORTH A TRIP

ORR HOT SPRINGS

A soak in the thermal waters of the rustic **Orr Hot Springs** (☎707-462-6277; www.orrhotsprings.org; 13201 Orr Springs Rd; day use adult/child $30/25; ⊗by appointment 10am-10pm) is heavenly. While it's not for the bashful, the clothing-optional resort is beloved by locals, back-to-the-land hipsters, backpackers and liberal-minded tourists. Enjoy the private tubs, a sauna, a spring-fed, rock-bottomed swimming pool, steam room, massage and magical gardens. Make reservations.

There are also six yurts as well as **rooms** (☎707-462-6277; www.orrhotsprings.org; 13201 Orr Springs Rd; tent sites per adult/child $70/35, r & yurt $220, cottages $297.60; ℗⊗☀) on-site, should you wish to linger.

remaining old-growth redwood forests. The national park is free, while state parks have an $8 day-use parking fee and developed campgrounds (p1010). This patchwork of state- and federally managed land stretches all the way north to the Oregon border, interspersed with several towns. Furthest south, you'll encounter **Redwood National Park** (☎707-464-6101, 707-465-7335; www.nps.gov/redw; Hwy 101, Orick; ℗♿) 🍃**FREE**, where a 1½-mile nature trail winds through **Lady Bird Johnson Grove**.

PRAIRIE CREEK REDWOODS STATE PARK

Six miles north of Orick, the 10-mile Newton B Drury Scenic Parkway runs parallel to Hwy 101 through **Prairie Creek Redwoods State Park** (☎707-465-7335; www.parks.ca.gov; Newton B Drury Scenic Pkwy; day-use parking fee $8; ℗♿) 🍃. Roosevelt elk graze in the meadow outside the **visitor center** (☎707-488-2039; www.parks.ca.gov; Newton B Drury Scenic Pkwy; ⊗9am-5pm May-Sep, to 4pm Oct-Apr), where sunlight-dappled hiking trails begin. Three miles back south, mostly unpaved Davison Rd heads northwest to Gold Bluffs Beach, dead-ending at the trailhead for unbelievably lush **Fern Canyon**.

North of tiny Klamath, Hwy 101 passes the **Trees of Mystery** (☎707-482-2251; www.treesofmystery.net; 15500 Hwy 101; museum free, gondola adult/child $18/9; ⊗9am-4:30pm; ℗♿), a kitschy roadside attraction.

DEL NORTE COAST REDWOODS STATE PARK

Next up, Del Norte Coast Redwoods State Park preserves virgin redwood groves and unspoiled coastline. The 4.5-mile round-trip **Damnation Creek Trail** careens over 1000ft downhill past redwoods to a hidden rocky beach, best visited at low tide. Find the trailhead at a parking turnout near mile marker 16 on Hwy 101.

CRESCENT CITY & AROUND

Backed by a fishing harbor and bay, Crescent City is drab because, after more than half the town was destroyed by a tidal wave in 1964, it was rebuilt with utilitarian architecture. When the tide's out, you can walk across to the 1856 **Battery Point Lighthouse** (☎707-464-3089; https://delnortehistory.org; South A St; adult/child $5/1; ⊗10am-4pm Apr-Sep, 10am-4pm Sat & Sun Oct-Mar) from the south end of A St.

Beyond Crescent City, **Jedediah Smith Redwoods State Park** (☎707-465-7335; www.parks.ca.gov; Hwy 199, Hiouchi; day-use parking fee $8; ⊗sunrise-sunset; ℗) 🍃 is the northernmost park in the system. The redwood stands here are so dense that there are few trails, but a couple of easy hikes start near riverside swimming holes along Hwy 199 and rough, unpaved Howland Hill Rd, a 10-mile scenic drive. The Redwood National & State Parks' **Crescent City Information Center** (☎707-465-7306; www.nps.gov/redw; 1111 2nd St; ⊗9am-5pm Apr-Oct, to 4pm Nov-Mar) has maps and info.

Sacramento

California's capital is a city of contrasts. Home to the **California State Capitol** (☎916-324-0333; http://capitolmuseum.ca.gov; 1315 10th St; ⊗8am-5pm Mon-Fri, from 9am Sat & Sun; ♿) 🍃**FREE**, here legislators' SUVs go bumper-to-bumper with farmers' muddy, half-ton pickups at rush hour. The people of 'Sac' are a resourceful lot that have fostered small but thriving food, art and nightlife scenes. They rightfully crow about **Second Saturday**, the monthly Midtown gallery hop that is the symbol of the city's cultural awakening. Their ubiquitous farmers markets, farm-to-fork fare and craft beers are another point of pride.

⊙ Sights

★ **Golden 1 Center**   STADIUM
(☎box office 916-840-5700; www.golden1center.com; 500 David J Stern Walk) 🍃 Welcome to the

arena of the future. This gleaming home to the Sacramento Kings is one of the most advanced sports facilities in the country. Made with the highest sustainability standard, it's built from local materials, powered by solar and cooled by five-story airplane hangar doors that swing open to capture the pleasant Delta breeze.

★ **California Museum**   MUSEUM
(☎ 916-653-0650;   www.californiamuseum.org; 1020 O St; adult/child $9/6.50; ⊙ 10am-5pm Tue-Sat, from noon Sun; ♠) This modern museum is home to the California Hall of Fame and so the only place to simultaneously encounter César Chávez, Mark Zuckerberg and Amelia Earhart. The California Indians exhibit is a highlight, with artifacts and oral histories of more than 10 tribes.

🛏 Sleeping

The capital is a magnet for business travelers, so Sacramento doesn't lack hotels. Many have good deals during legislative recesses. Unless you're in town for something at Cal Expo, stay Downtown or Midtown, where there's plenty to do within walking distance. If you're into kitschy motor lodges from the 1950s, cross the river into West Sac for the last-standing members of Motel Row on Rte 40.

Greens Hotel   BOUTIQUE HOTEL $
(☎ 916-921-1736; www.thegreenshotel.com; 1700 Del Paso Blvd; r from $109; 🅿😊❄@🛜🏊) This stylishly updated mid-century motel is one of Sacramento's hippest places to stay. The area is charming, with a cute coffee shop and an art gallery next door, and Greens' secure parking, pool and spacious grounds make this an ideal place for families to stop en route to or from Tahoe. The chic rooms are also classy enough for a romantic getaway.

★ **Citizen Hotel**   BOUTIQUE HOTEL $$
(☎ 916-442-2700; www.thecitizenhotel.com; 926 J St; r from $180; 🅿❄@🛜🏊) After an elegant, ultrahip upgrade, this long-vacant 1927 beaux-arts tower became Downtown's coolest place to stay. The details are spot-on: luxe linens, wide-striped wallpaper and a rooftop patio with a great view of the city. There's an upscale farm-to-fork **restaurant** (☎ 916-492-4450; 926 J St; mains $29-55; ⊙ 6:30-10:30am, 11:30am-2:30pm & 5:30-10pm Mon-Thu, to 11pm Fri, 8am-2pm & 5:30-11pm Sat, to 9pm Sun; 🛜) on the ground floor.

🍴 Eating & Drinking

Skip the overpriced fare in Old Sacramento or by the capitol and head Midtown or to the Tower District. A cruise up J St or Broadway passes a number of hip, affordable restaurants where tables spill onto the sidewalks in the summer. Many source farm-fresh ingredients.

La Bonne Soupe Cafe   DELI $
(☎ 916-492-9506; 980 9th St; items $5-8; ⊙ 11am-3pm Mon-Fri) In a new space as of 2018, this beloved French cafe continues to serve divine soup and sandwiches, assembled with such care that the line of downtowners snakes out the door. In a hurry? Skip it. This humble lunch counter is focused on quality that predates drive-through haste.

Be sure not to confuse it with the similarly named spot next door, La Bou Bakery & Cafe.

★ **Empress Tavern**   NEW AMERICAN $$$
(☎ 916-662-7694; www.empresstavern.com; 1013 K St; mains $24-41; ⊙ 3-10pm Mon-Thu, to 11pm Fri, 5-11pm Sat) In the catacombs under the historic Crest Theater, this gorgeous restaurant hosts a menu of creative, meat-focused dishes (including family-style options like beef-cheek stroganoff and grilled-pork porterhouse). The space itself is just as impressive as the food; the arched brick ceilings and glittering bar feel like a speakeasy supper club from a bygone era.

★ **Fieldwork Brewing Company**   BREWERY
(☎ 916-329-8367;   www.fieldworkbrewing.com; 1805 Capitol Ave; ⊙ 11am-10pm Sun-Thu, to 11pm Fri & Sat) Bustling with activity, this ultrahip brewpub has 22 rotating taps of excellent draft beer. Playful variations of hoppy IPAs are the specialty (the Pulp IPA is a recurring favorite), but it does lighter seasonal brews like the Salted Watermelon Gose. It also has a small food menu and board games – making it an easy place to linger when the weather is sweltering.

ℹ Getting There & Around

Sacramento is at the intersection of major highways, and you'll likely pass through en route to other California destinations. The **Sacramento International Airport** (SMF; ☎ 916-929-5411; www.sacramento.aero/smf; 6900 Airport Blvd) is one of the nearest options for those traveling to Yosemite National Park.

The regional **Yolobus** (☎ 530-666-2877; www.yolobus.com) route 42B costs $2 and runs hourly between Sacramento International Airport and Downtown, and also goes to West Sacramento, Woodland and Davis. Local **Sacramento**

Regional Transit (RT; ☎ 916-321-2877; www.sacrt.com; fare $2.50) buses run around town and RT also runs a trolley between Old Sacramento and Downtown, as well as Sacramento's light-rail system, which is best for commuting from outlying communities.

Sacramento is also a fantastic city to cruise around by bike; rent them from **Trek Bicycles Sacramento** (☎ 916-447-2453; www.facebook.com/TrekBicycleSacramento; 2419 K St; per day $40-100; ☉10am-7pm Mon-Fri, to 6pm Sat, 11am-5pm Sun).

Gold Country

Hollywood draws the dreamers and Silicon Valley lures fortune-hunters, but this isn't the first time droves of aspiring young folk have streamed into the Golden State. After a sparkle in the American River caught James Marshall's eye in 1848, more than 300,000 prospectors from America and abroad started digging for gold in the Sierra foothills. Soon California entered statehood with the official motto 'Eureka' solidifying its place as the land of opportunity.

The miner forty-niners are gone, but a ride along Hwy 49 through sleepy hill towns, past clapboard saloons and oak-lined byways is a journey back to the wild ride that was modern California's founding: umpteen historical markers tell tales of gold-rush violence and banditry.

Hwy 50 divides the Northern and Southern Mines. Winding Hwy 49, which connects everything, provides plenty of vistas of the famous hills. The Gold Country Visitors Association (https://visitgoldcountry.com) has many more touring ideas.

❶ Getting There & Around

You can reach the region by train on the transcontinental line that links Sacramento and Truckee/Reno and has a stop in Auburn. Auburn is the main entry point of the area, a short hop on the I-80 from Sacramento. From Auburn pick up Hwy 49, the classic route through the Gold Country.

Northern Mines

Known as the 'Queen of the Northern Mines,' the narrow streets of Nevada City gleam with lovingly restored buildings, tiny theaters, art galleries, cafes and shops. The **visitor center** (☎ 530-265-2692; www.nevadacitychamber.com; 132 Main St; ☉9am-5pm Mon-Fri, 11am-4pm Sat, noon-3pm Sun) dispenses information and self-guided walking-tour maps. On Hwy 49, the **Tahoe National**

Forest Headquarters (☎ 530-265-4531; www.fs.usda.gov/tahoe; 631 Coyote St; ☉8am-4:30pm Mon-Fri) provides camping and hiking information.

The six-room **Broad Street Inn** (☎ 530-265-2239; www.broadstreetinn.com; 517 W Broad St; r $119-134; ❋☎) 🅿 in the heart of town is a favorite for its good-value modern rooms: brightly but soothingly furnished and elegant. Unusually friendly and fun, **Outside Inn** (☎ 530-265-2233; http://outsideinn.com; 575 E Broad St; d $94-230; 🅿☻❋☎☒☒) is the best option for active explorers, while Peter Selaya's organic- and local-ingredient menu at elegant **New Moon Cafe** (☎ 530-265-6399; www.thenewmooncafe.com; 203 York St; dinner mains $25-44; ☉11:30am-2pm Tue-Fri, 5-8pm Tue-Sun) 🅿 changes with the seasons.

Moving on, just over a mile east of utilitarian **Grass Valley** and Hwy 49, **Empire Mine State Historic Park** (☎ 530-273-8522; www.empiremine.org; 10791 Empire St; adult/youth 6-16yr $7/3; ☉10am-5pm; 🅿👪) marks the site of one of the richest mines in California. From 1850 to 1956 it produced about 5.8 million troy ounces of gold – over $8 billion in today's market.

If it's hot, one of the best swimming holes in the area is at **Auburn State Recreation Area** (☎ 530-885-4527; www.parks.ca.gov; 501 El Dorado St; per car $10; ☉7am-sunset). It's just east of Auburn, an I-80 pit stop about 25 miles south of Grass Valley.

Coloma is where California's gold rush started. Riverside **Marshall Gold Discovery State Historic Park** (☎ 530-622-3470; www.parks.ca.gov; Hwy 49, Coloma; per car $8; ☉8am-8pm late May-early Sep, to 5pm early Sep-late May; 🅿👪☒) pays tribute to James Marshall's riot-inducing discovery, with restored buildings and gold-panning opportunities. The park is also home to **Argonaut Farm to Fork Cafe** (☎ 530-626-7345; www.argonautcafe.com; 331 Hwy 49, Coloma; items $8-12; ☉8am-4pm; ☎☒👪), serving up truly delicious soups, sandwiches, baked goods and coffee.

Southern Mines

The towns of the Southern Mines – from Placerville to Sonora – receive less traffic and their dusty streets retain a whiff of Wild West, today evident in the motley crew of Harley riders and gold prospectors (still!) who populate them.

Some, like **Plymouth** (ol' Pokerville), **Volcano** and **Mokelumne Hill**, are virtual ghost towns, slowly crumbling into photogenic oblivion. Others, like **Sutter Creek**, **Murphys** and **Angels Camp**, are gussied-up showpieces of Victorian Americana. Get off the beaten path at family-run vineyards and subterranean caverns, where geological wonders reward those who first navigate the touristy gift shops above ground.

Lacy B&Bs, cafes and ice-cream parlors are found in nearly every town. For something different, try the **Imperial Hotel** (☎209-267-9172; www.imperialamador.com; 14202 Old Hwy 49, Amador City; r $110-155, ste $125-195; ❋☎) in Plymouth. Built in 1879, it's one of the area's most inventive updates, with sleek art-deco touches accenting the warm red brick, a genteel bar and a very good, seasonally minded restaurant (dinner mains $16 to $38).

A short detour off Hwy 49, **Columbia State Historic Park** (☎209-588-9128; www.parks.ca.gov; 11255 Jackson St; ⊙most businesses 10am-5pm; ℗) FREE preserves blocks of authentic 1850s buildings complete with shopkeepers and street musicians in period costumes. Near Sonora, **Railtown 1897 State Historic Park** (☎209-984-3953; www.railtown1897.org; 10501 Reservoir Rd, Jamestown; adult/child $5/3, incl train ride $15/10; ⊙9:30am-4:30pm Apr-Oct, 10am-3pm Nov-Mar, train rides 10:30am-3pm Sat & Sun Apr-Oct; ℗🚃) offers excursion trains through the surrounding hills where Hollywood Westerns including *High Noon* have been filmed.

California's Northern Mountains

Remote, empty and eerily beautiful, these are some of California's least visited wild lands, an endless show of geological wonders, clear lakes, rushing rivers and high desert. The major peaks – Lassen, Shasta and the Trinity Alps – have few geological features in common, but all offer backcountry camping under starry skies.

Redding to Mt Shasta

Much of the drive north of Redding is dominated by Mt Shasta, a 14,180ft snowcapped goliath at the southern end of the volcanic Cascades Range. It arises dramatically, fueling the anticipation felt by mountaineers who seek to climb its slopes.

Roadside motels are abundant, including in Mt Shasta city. Redding has the most chain lodgings, clustered near major highways. Campgrounds are abundant, especially on public lands.

Greyhound (www.greyhound.com) buses heading north and south on I-5 stop at the depot (628 S Weed Blvd) in Weed, 8 miles north of Mt Shasta city on I-5. Services include Redding (from $22, one hour and 20 minutes, four daily), Sacramento (from $40, 5½ hours, four daily) and San Francisco (from $55, 7½ hours, two or three times daily).

REDDING & AROUND

Don't believe the tourist brochures: Redding, the region's largest city, is a snooze. The best reason to detour off I-5 is the **Sundial Bridge**, a glass-bottomed pedestrian marvel designed by Spanish neofuturist architect Santiago Calatrava. It spans the Sacramento River at **Turtle Bay Exploration Park** (☎530-243-8850; www.turtlebay.org; 844 Sundial Bridge Dr; adult/child $16/12, after 2:30pm $11/7; ⊙9am-5pm Mon-Sat, from 10am Sun late Mar-Oct, 9am-4:30pm Wed-Fri, from 10am Sat & Sun Nov–mid-Mar; 🚼), a kid-friendly science and nature center with botanical gardens.

Six miles west of Redding along Hwy 299, explore a genuine gold-rush town at **Shasta State Historic Park** (☎520-243-8194; www.parks.ca.gov; 15312 CA 299; museum entry adult/child $3/2; ⊙10am-5pm Thu-Sun). Although the devastating Carr Fire ripped through this park in 2018, the main attractions were all salvaged. Three miles west, **Whiskeytown National Recreation Area** (☎530-246-1225; www.nps.gov/whis; 14412 Kennedy Memorial Dr, Whiskeytown; ⊙10am-4pm) was the starting point of the fire, which burned 93% of the park's 42,000 acres before destroying 1604 nearby structures. The park's visitor center is back up and running, and people are again showing up at **Whiskeytown Lake** for its sandy beaches, water sports and camping opportunities. But the park's interior remains in rough shape, with several roads and all of the trails (including waterfall hikes and mountain-biking routes) still closed. In sleepy **Weaverville**, another 35 miles further west, **Joss House State Historic Park** (☎530-623-5284; www.parks.ca.gov; 630 Main St; tour adult/child $4/2; ⊙tours hourly 10am-4pm Thu-Sun; ℗) preserves an ornate 1874 Chinese immigrant temple.

SHASTA LAKE

North of Redding, I-5 crosses deep-blue Shasta Lake, California's biggest reservoir, formed by colossal **Shasta Dam** (☎530-247-8555; www.usbr.gov/mp/ncao/shasta-dam.html; 16349 Shasta Dam Blvd; ⊙visitor center

8am-5pm, tours 9am, 11am, 1pm & 3pm Sep-May, 9am, 10:15am, 11:30am, 1pm, 2:15pm, 3:30pm Jun-Aug; P ⊕) FREE and ringed by houseboat marinas and RV campgrounds. High in the limestone megaliths on the lake's northern side are prehistoric **Lake Shasta Caverns** (☑ 530-238-2341; www.lakeshastacaverns.com; 20359 Shasta Caverns Rd, Lakehead; 2hr tour adult/child 3-15yr $30/18; ⊙ tours every 30min 9am-4pm late May-early Sep, hourly 9am-3pm Apr-late May & early-late Sep, 10am, noon & 2pm Oct-Mar; P ⊕), where tours include a catamaran ride or a dinner cruise on the lake.

DUNSMUIR

Another 35 miles north on I-5, Dunsmuir is a teeny historic railroad town with vibrant art galleries inhabiting a quaint downtown district. Simple and elegant, **Café Maddalena** (☑ 530-235-2725; www.cafemaddalena.com; 5801 Sacramento Ave; mains $21-28; ⊙ 5-9pm Thu-Sun Feb-Dec) put Dunsmuir on the foodie map. The menu was designed by chef Brett LaMott (of Trinity Cafe fame) and changes seasonally to feature dishes from southern Europe and northern Africa. Head over to **Dunsmuir Brewery Works** (☑ 530-235-1900; www.dunsmuirbreweryworks.com; 5701 Dunsmuir Ave; mains $8-14; ⊙ 11am-8pm Sun, to 8:30pm Tue-Thu, to 9pm Fri & Sat Oct-Mar, extended hours Apr-Sep; ⊛) afterwards, for a crisp ale or perfectly balanced porter.

At the **Railroad Park Resort** (☑ 530-235-4440; www.rrpark.com; 100 Railroad Park Rd; tent/RV sites from $29/37, d $135-200; ✳⊛⊛⊛), 2 miles south of town, visitors can spend the night inside refitted vintage railroad cars and cabooses. The grounds are fun for kids, who can run around the engines and plunge in a centrally situated pool and hot tub.

Six miles south off I-5, **Castle Crags State Park** (☑ 530-235-2684; www.parks.ca.gov; 20022 Castle Creek Rd; per car $8; ⊙ sunrise-sunset) shelters forested **campsites** (☑ reservations 800-444-7275; www.reservecalifornia.com; tent & RV sites $25). Be awed by stunning views of Mt Shasta from the top of the park's hardy 5.6-mile round-trip **Crags Trail**.

Just north of Dunsmuir, a detour to the town of McCloud rewards with the **Mc-Cloud River Mercantile Hotel** (☑ 530-964-2330; www.mccloudmercantile.com; 241 Main St; r $139-275; P ⊕⊛), built in 1897. This former lumber company store has been exquisitely restored, and features an old-fashioned candy counter and a 1930s-era soda fountain on the 1st floor. Oh, and the former butcher shop is now a delicious new restaurant, **Mc-Cloud Meat Market and Tavern**.

MT SHASTA CITY

Nine miles north of Dunsmuir, Mt Shasta City lures climbers, new-age hippies and back-to-nature types, all of whom revere the majestic mountain looming overhead. Usually open and snow-free beyond Bunny Flat from June until October, **Everitt Memorial Hwy** ascends the mountain to a perfect sunset-watching perch at almost 8000ft – simply head east from town on Lake St and keep going. For experienced mountaineers, climbing the peak above 10,000ft requires a Summit Pass ($25), available from **Mt Shasta Ranger Station** (☑ 530-926-4511; www.fs.usda.gov/stnf; 204 W Alma St; ⊙ 8am-4:30pm Mon-Fri), which has weather reports and sells topographic maps. Stop by downtown's **Fifth Season** (☑ 530-926-3606; http://thefifthseason.com; 300 N Mt Shasta Blvd; ⊙ 9am-6pm Mon-Fri, from 8am Sat, 10am-5pm Sun Apr-Nov, 8am-6pm Dec-Mar) outdoor-gear shop for equipment rentals. **Shasta Mountain Guides** (☑ 530-926-3117; http://shastaguides.com; 230 N Mt Shasta Blvd; 2-day climbs per person from $795) offers multiday mountaineering trips.

Only antique on the outside, bright Victorian 1904 **Shasta MountInn** (☑ 530-261-1926; www.shastamountinn.com; 203 Birch St; r $150-175; P ⊖⊛) farmhouse is all relaxed minimalism, bold colors and graceful decor on the inside. Each airy room has a great bed and exquisite views of the luminous mountain. Pick up an organic, locally roasted coffee at **Seven Suns Coffee & Cafe** (☑ 530-926-9701; 1011 S Mt Shasta Blvd; ⊙ 6am-4pm; ⊛) and stock up on groceries and organic produce at **Berryvale Grocery** (☑ 530-926-1576; www.berryvale.com; 305 S Mt Shasta Blvd; cafe items from $3; ⊙ store 8am-8pm, cafe to 7pm; ♠⊕) ✦.

Northeast Corner
LAVA BEDS NATIONAL MONUMENT

Lava Beds National Monument (☑ 530-667-8113; www.nps.gov/labe; 1 Indian Well HQ, Tulelake; 7-day entry per car $25; P ⊕) ✦ is a monument to centuries of turmoil. This park's got it all: lava flows, cinder and spatter cones, volcanic craters and amazing lava tubes. It was the site of the Modoc War, and ancient Native American petroglyphs are etched into rocks and pictographs painted on cave walls. Pick up info, flashlights and maps at the **visitor center** (☑ 530-667-8113; www.nps.gov/labe; Tulelake; ⊙ 10am-4pm with extended but varying hours in summer, spring & fall), where hard hats and kneepads are available for purchase. Nearby is the park's basic **campground** (www.nps.gov/labe/planyourvisit/campgrounds.htm; tent & RV sites $10; ☒), where drinking water is available.

KLAMATH BASIN NATIONAL WILDLIFE REFUGE COMPLEX

Over 20 miles northeast of the park, the dusty town of **Tulelake** off Hwy 139 has basic motels, roadside diners and gas. Comprising six separate refuges in California and Oregon, **Klamath Basin National Wildlife Refuge Complex** is a prime stopover on the Pacific Flyway and an important wintering site for bald eagles. When the spring and fall migrations peak, more than a million birds can fill the sky. The **visitor center** (☎ 530-667-2231; www.klamathbasinrefuges.fws.gov; 4009 Hill Rd, Tulelake; ☺ 9am-4pm) is off Hwy 161, about 4 miles south of the Oregon border. Self-guided 10-mile auto tours of the Lower Klamath and Tule Lake refuges provide excellent birding opportunities. Paddle the Upper Klamath refuge's 9.5-mile canoe trail by launching from **Rocky Point Resort** (☎ 541-356-2287; 28121 Rocky Point Rd, Klamath Falls, OR; canoe & kayak rental per hour/half-day/day $20/45/60; ☺ Apr-Oct; ☒☒). For gas, food and lodging, drive into Klamath Falls, OR, off Hwy 97.

LASSEN VOLCANIC NATIONAL PARK

Quietly impressive **Lassen Volcanic National Park** (☎ 530-595-4480; www.nps.gov/lavo; 38050 Hwy 36 E, Mineral; 7-day entry per car mid-Apr–Nov $30, Dec–mid-Apr $10; ☒) ✎ has hydrothermal sulfur pools, boiling mud pots and steaming pools, as glimpsed from the **Bumpass Hell** boardwalk. Tackle **Lassen Peak** (10,457ft), the world's largest known plug-dome volcano, on a strenuous, but non-technical 5-mile round-trip trail. The park has two entrances: an hour's drive east of Redding off Hwy 44, near popular **Manzanita Lake Campground** (☎ reservations 877-444-6777; www.recreation.gov; tent & RV sites $15-26; ☒); and a 40-minute drive northwest of Lake Almanor off Hwy 89, by the **Kom Yah-mah-nee Visitor Facility** (☎ 530-595-4480; www.nps.gov/lavo; 21820 Lassen National Park Hwy, Mineral; ☺ 9am-5pm, closed Mon & Tue Nov-Mar; ☒) ✎. Hwy 89 through the park is typically snow-free and open to car from June though October.

Sierra Nevada

The mighty Sierra Nevada – baptized the 'Range of Light' by poet-naturalist John Muir – is California's backbone. This 400-mile phalanx of craggy peaks, chiseled and gouged by glaciers and erosion, both welcomes and challenges outdoor-sports enthusiasts. Cradling three national parks (Yosemite, Sequoia and Kings Canyon), the Sierra is a spellbinding wonderland of superlative wilderness, boasting the contiguous USA's highest peak (Mt Whitney), North America's tallest waterfall (Yosemite Falls) and the world's oldest and biggest trees (ancient bristlecone pines and giant sequoias, respectively).

Yosemite National Park

The jaw-dropping head-turner of America's national parks, and a Unesco World Heritage site, **Yosemite** (☎ 209-372-0200; www.nps.gov/yose/index.htm; per vehicle $35) (yo-*sem*-it-ee) garners the devotion of all who enter. From the waterfall-striped granite walls buttressing emerald-green Yosemite Valley to the sky-scraping giant sequoias catapulting into the air at Mariposa Grove, the place inspires a sense of awe and reverence – over four million visitors wend their way to the country's third-oldest national park annually. But lift your eyes above the crowds and you'll feel your heart instantly moved by unrivaled splendors: the haughty profile of Half Dome, the hulking presence of El Capitan, the drenching mists of Yosemite Falls, the gemstone lakes of the high country's subalpine wilderness and Hetch Hetchy's pristine pathways.

Sights

There are four main entrances to the park ($30 per vehicle): South Entrance (Hwy 41), Arch Rock (Hwy 140), Big Oak Flat (Hwy 120 W) and Tioga Pass (Hwy 120 E). Hwy 120 traverses the park as Tioga Rd, connecting Yosemite Valley with the Eastern Sierra.

Yosemite Valley

From the ground up, this dramatic valley cut by the meandering Merced River is so inspiring: rippling-green meadow grass, stately pines, cool, impassive pools reflecting looming granite monoliths, and cascading ribbons of glacially cold white water. Often overrun and traffic-choked, **Yosemite Village** is home to the park's main **visitor center** (☎ 209-372-0200; www.nps.gov/yose; 9035 Village Dr, Yosemite Village; ☺ 9am-5pm), **museum** (www.nps.gov/yose; 9037 Village Dr, Yosemite Village; ☺ 9am-5pm summer, 10am-4pm rest of year, often closed noon-1pm) ✎ **FREE**, photography gallery, movie theater, general store and many more services. Half Dome Village (also known as Curry Village) is another valley hub, offering public showers and outdoor-equipment rental and sales, including camping gear.

Spring snowmelt turns the valley's famous waterfalls into thunderous cataracts; most are reduced to a mere trickle by late summer. **Yosemite Falls** is North America's tallest waterfall, dropping 2425ft in three tiers. A wheelchair-accessible trail leads to the bottom of this cascade or, for solitude and different perspectives, you can trek the grueling trail to the top (6.8 miles round trip). No less impressive are other waterfalls around the valley. A strenuous granite staircase beside **Vernal Fall** leads you, gasping, right to the waterfall's edge for a vertical view – look for rainbows in the clouds of mist.

You can't ignore the valley's monumental **El Capitan** (7569ft), an El Dorado for rock climbers. Toothed **Half Dome** (8842ft) soars above the valley as Yosemite's spiritual centerpiece. The classic photo op is at **Tunnel View** on Hwy 41 as you drive into the valley.

Glacier Point

Rising over 3000ft above the valley floor, dramatic Glacier Point (7214ft) practically puts you at eye level with Half Dome. It's at least an hour's drive from Yosemite Valley up Glacier Point Rd (usually open from May into November) off Hwy 41, or a strenuous hike along the **Four Mile Trail** (around 5 miles one way) or the less-crowded, waterfall-strewn **Panorama Trail** (8.5 miles one way). To hike one-way downhill from Glacier Point, reserve a seat on the **Glacier Point Hikers' Bus** (☑888-413-8869; one-way/return $26/52; ☉mid-May–Oct).

Wawona

At Wawona, an hour's drive south of Yosemite Valley, drop by the **Pioneer Yosemite History Center** (www.nps.gov/yose/planyourvisit/upload/pyhc.pdf; Wawona; rides adult/child $5/4; ☉24hr, rides 10am-2pm Wed-Sun May-Sep; [P][🚲]) FREE, with its covered bridge, historic buildings and horse-drawn stagecoach rides. Further south stands towering **Mariposa Grove**, home to more than 500 giant sequoias including the Grizzly Giant. Free shuttle buses usually run to the grove from spring through fall.

Tuolumne Meadows

A 90-minute drive from Yosemite Valley, high-altitude Tuolumne Meadows (*twol*-uh-mee) draws hikers, backpackers and climbers to the park's northern wilderness. The Sierra Nevada's largest subalpine meadow (8600ft) is a vivid contrast to the valley, with wildflower fields, azure lakes, granite peaks, polished domes and cooler temperatures. Hikers and climbers have a paradise of options, and lake swimming and picnicking are also popular. Access is via scenic Tioga Rd (Hwy 120), which is only open seasonally. West of Tuolumne Meadows and **Tenaya Lake**, stop at **Olmsted Point** for epic vistas of Half Dome.

Hetch Hetchy

A 40-mile drive northwest of Yosemite Valley, Hetch Hetchy is the site of perhaps the most controversial dam in US history. Despite not existing in its natural state, Hetch Hetchy Valley remains pretty and mostly crowd-free. A 5.4-mile round-trip hike across the dam and through a tunnel to the base of **Wapama Falls** lets you get thrillingly close to an avalanche of water crashing down into the sparkling reservoir.

🏃 Activities

With more than 800 miles of hiking trails, you're spoiled for choice. Easy valley-floor routes can get jammed – escape the teeming masses by heading up. Other diversions include rock climbing, cycling, trail rides, swimming, rafting and cross-country skiing.

For overnight backpacking trips, wilderness permits (from $10) are required year-round. A quota system limits the number of hikers leaving daily from each trailhead. Make reservations up to 26 weeks in advance, or try your luck at the Yosemite Valley Wilderness Center (p1019) or another permit-issuing station, starting at 11am on the day before you aim to hike.

🛏 Sleeping

Camping, even if it's car camping in a campground near busy Yosemite Village, enhances the being-out-in-nature feeling. Backcountry wilderness camping is for the prepared and adventurous. All lodging reservations within the park, including for facilities at Housekeeping Camp and Half Dome Village, are handled by **Aramark/Yosemite Hospitality** (☑888-413-8869; www.travelyosemite.com) and can be made up to 366 days in advance; reservations are critical from April to October. Rates – and demand – drop from December to March. Other park visitors overnight in nearby gateway towns like Fish Camp, Midpines, El Portal, Mariposa and Groveland; however, commute times into the park can be long.

★ **Majestic Yosemite Hotel** HISTORIC HOTEL **$$$**
(☑ reservations 888-413-8869; www.travelyosem ite.com; 1 Ahwahnee Dr; r/ste from $580/1400; P ➔ @ ☎ ✖) The crème de la crème of Yosemite's lodging, this sumptuous historic property (formerly called the Ahwahnee) dazzles with soaring ceilings and atmospheric lounges featuring mammoth stone fireplaces. Classic rooms have inspiring views of Glacier Point, Half Dome and Yosemite Falls. Cottages are scattered on the immaculately trimmed lawn next to the hotel. For high season and holidays, book a year in advance.

May Lake High Sierra Camp CABIN **$$$**
(www.travelyosemite.com/lodging/high-sierra-camps; tent & RV sites per person $155) Because it's the easiest of the High Sierra camps to access, May Lake is also the best for children – at least those who'll be untroubled by the mile-plus hike to get here. Views of Mt Hoffman are quite stunning. Breakfast and dinner included in rates, and showers available.

Yosemite Valley Lodge MOTEL **$$$**
(☑ 209-372-1001, reservations 888-413-8869; www. travelyosemite.com; 9006 Yosemite Lodge Dr; r from $260; P ➔ @ ☎ ✖) ◢ A short walk from Yosemite Falls, this low-slung complex contains a wide range of eateries, a lively bar, a big pool and other amenities. The rooms, spread out over 15 buildings, feel like they're a cross between a motel and a lodge, with rustic wooden furniture and nature photography. Rooms have cable TV, a fridge and coffeemaker, and small patios or balcony panoramas.

Outside Yosemite

Gateway towns that have a mixed bag of motels, hotels, lodges and B&Bs include Fish Camp, Oakhurst, El Portal, Midpines, Mariposa, Groveland and, in the Eastern Sierra, Lee Vining.

★ **Yosemite Bug**
Rustic Mountain Resort HOSTEL **$**
(☑ 209-966-6666; www.yosemitebug.com; 6979 Hwy 140, Midpines; tent sites/dm/tent cabins from $25/38/65, r from $175, with shared bath from $139; P ➔ @ ☎) This folksy place feels like a secret oasis tucked away on a forested hillside about 25 miles from Yosemite. A wide range of accommodations lines its narrow ridges (cabins, dorms, private rooms and permanent tents). The **June Bug Cafe** (☑ 206-966-6666; www.yo

semitebug.com/cafe; Yosemite Bug Rustic Mountain Resort, 6979 Hwy 140, Midpines; mains $8-24; ☉ 7-10am, 11am-2pm & 6-9pm; P ☎ ◢) ◢ is highly recommended and worth the trip alone, as are the massages and spa with hot tub and yoga studio ($12 per day).

★ **Evergreen Lodge** CABIN **$$$**
(☑ 209-379-2606; www.evergreenlodge.com; 33160 Evergreen Rd, Groveland; tents $110-145, cabins $230-495; ☉ usually closed Jan–mid-Feb; P ➔ ✱ @ ☎ ✖) ◢ Outside Yosemite National Park near the entrance to Hetch Hetchy, this classic, nearly century-old resort consists of lovingly decorated and comfy cabins (each with its own cache of board games) spread among the trees. Accommodations run from rustic to deluxe, and all cabins have private porches without a distracting phone or TV. Roughing-it guests can cheat with comfy, prefurnished tents.

✖ Eating

You can find food options for all budgets and palates within the park, from greasy slabs of fast food to swanky cuts of top-notch steak. All places carry good vegetarian options. The **Village Store** (Yosemite Village; ☉ 8am-8pm, to 10pm summer) has the best selection (including health-food items and some organic produce), while stores at Half Dome Village, Wawona, Tuolumne Meadows and the Yosemite Valley Lodge are more limited.

❶ Information

Yosemite's entrance fee is $35 per vehicle, $30 per motorcycle or $20 for those on a bicycle or on foot and is valid for seven consecutive days. Passes are sold (you can use cash, checks, traveler's checks or credit/debit cards) at the various entrance stations. From late May to early October, passes are also sold at visitor centers in Oakhurst, Groveland, Mariposa and Lee Vining. You can also pay online (https://your-passnow.com/ParkPass/park/yose).

Upon entering the park, you'll receive a National Park Service (NPS) map and a copy of the seasonal *Yosemite Guide* newspaper, which includes an activity schedule and current opening hours of all facilities. The official NPS website (www. nps.gov/yose) has the most comprehensive and current information.

For recorded park information, campground availability, and road and weather conditions, call 209-372-0200.

Yosemite Valley Visitor Center (p1017) Park's busiest information desk. Shares space with bookstore run by Yosemite Conservancy and part of the museum complex in the center of Yosemite Village.

Yosemite Valley Wilderness Center (📞 20 9-372-0308; Yosemite Village; ⏱ 8am-5pm May-Oct) Wilderness permits, maps and back-country advice.

Yosemite Medical Clinic (📞 209-372-4637, emergency 911; 9000 Ahwahnee Dr, Yosemite Village; ⏱ 9am-7pm Mon-Fri early Jun-early Jul, 9am-7pm Mon-Sat late Jul–mid-Sep, to 5pm Mon-Fri late Sep-late May) A 24-hour emergency service is available.

❶ Getting There & Around

Yosemite is accessible by car year-round from the west (via Hwys 120 W and 140) and south (Hwy 41), and in summer also from the east (via Hwy 120 E). Roads are plowed in winter, but snow chains may be required. Gas up year-round at Wawona or Crane Flat inside the park (you'll pay dearly), at El Portal on Hwy 140 just outside its western boundary, or at Lee Vining at the junction of Hwys 120 and 395 outside the park in the east.

Roadside signs with red bears mark the many spots where bears have been hit by motorists (many hundreds have been injured and more than 100 killed since 1995), so think before you hit the accelerator, and follow the pokey posted speed limits – they are strictly enforced. Valley visitors are advised to park and take advantage of the **Yosemite Valley Shuttle Bus** (www.nps. gov/yose/planyourvisit/publictransportation. htm; ⏱ 7am-10pm). Even so, traffic in the valley can feel like rush hour in LA.

Yosemite is one of the few national parks that can easily be reached by public transportation. Greyhound buses and Amtrak trains serve Merced, west of the park, where they are met by buses operated by the **Yosemite Area Regional Transportation System** (YARTS; 📞 877-989-2787; www.yarts.com), and you can buy Amtrak tickets that include the YARTS segment all the

way into the park. Buses travel to Yosemite Valley along Hwy 140 several times daily year-round, with a variety of stops in Mariposa, Midpines and El Portal along the way. One-way tickets to Yosemite Valley are $16 ($9 child and senior, three hours) from Merced.

Cycling is an ideal way to take in Yosemite Valley. You can rent a wide-handled cruiser (per hour/day $12/34) or a bike with an attached child trailer (per hour/day $20.25/61) at the **Yosemite Valley Lodge** (per hour/day $12/34; ⏱ 8am-6pm summer only, weather dependent) or **Half Dome Village** (per hour/day $12/34; ⏱ 10am-4pm Mar-Oct). Strollers and wheelchairs are also rented here.

Sequoia & Kings Canyon National Parks

Joined by a high-altitude roadway bisecting a national forest and contiguous with a number of wilderness areas, these two parks combined offer vast stretches of alpine bliss. Groves of giant sequoias, wildflower-strewn meadows, gushing waterfalls, dramatic gorges and spectacular vistas reveal themselves at nearly every turn. General Grant Grove (p1021) and the **Giant Forest** (off Generals Hwy), in Kings Canyon and Sequoia respectively, are obvious highlights.

Throw in opportunities for caving, rock climbing and backcountry hiking through granite-carved Sierra landscapes as well as backdoor access to 14,505ft Mt Whitney – the tallest peak in the lower 48 states – and you have all the ingredients for two of the best parks in the country.

The two **parks** (📞 559-565-3341; www. nps.gov/seki; 7-day entry per car $35; 🅿 ♿) 🚲 though distinct, are operated as one unit with a single admission fee; for 24-hour

---

CAMPING IN YOSEMITE

Competition for sites at one of the park's 13 campgrounds is fierce from May to September, and there are no first-come, first-served campgrounds in Yosemite Valley. Those outside the valley tend to fill by noon, especially on weekends and around holidays.

All campgrounds have flush toilets, except for Tamarack Flat, Yosemite Creek and Porcupine Flat, which have vault toilets and no potable water. Those at higher elevations get chilly at night, even in summer, so pack accordingly. The **Yosemite Mountaineering School** (📞 209-372-8344; www.travelyosemite.com; Half Dome Village; ⏱ 8:30am-5pm Apr-Oct) rents camping gear.

If you hold a wilderness permit, you may spend the nights before and after your trip in the backpacker campgrounds at Tuolumne Meadows, Hetch Hetchy, White Wolf and behind North Pines in Yosemite Valley.

Opening dates for seasonal campgrounds vary according to the weather. For the most accurate camping information, contact Yosemite National Park directly or visit www.nps. gov/yose/planyourvisit/campgrounds.htm.

recorded information, including road conditions, call the number listed or visit the parks' comprehensive website.

◉ Sights

Sequoia National Park

For a primer on the ecology and history of giant sequoias, the pint-sized **Giant Forest Museum** (☑ 559-565-3341; www.nps.gov/seki; 47050 Generals Hwy, cnr Crescent Meadow Rd; ⊙ 9am-4:30pm winter, to 6pm summer; ℙ) 🅿 FREE will entertain both kids and adults. Hands-on exhibits teach about the life stages of these big trees, which can live for more than 3000 years, and the fire cycle that releases their seeds and allows them to sprout on bare soil.

Discovered in 1918 by two parks employees who were going fishing, unique **Crystal Cave** (www.recreation.gov; Crystal Cave Rd, off Generals Hwy; tours adult/child/youth from $16/5/8; ⊙ late May–late Sep; ℙ) was carved by an underground river and has marble formations estimated to be up to 100,000 years old. Tickets for the 50-minute introductory tour are only sold online in advance or at the Giant Forest Museum and Foothills Visitor Center, not at the cave. Bring a jacket.

Worth a detour is **Mineral King Valley** (Mineral King Rd), a late-19th-century mining and logging camp ringed by craggy peaks and alpine lakes. The 25-mile one-way scenic drive – navigating almost 700 white-knuckle hairpin turns – is usually open from late May until late October.

Kings Canyon National Park & Scenic Byway

Just north of Grant Grove Village, **General Grant Grove** (N Grove Trail, off Hwy 180; ℙ🚻) brims with majestic giants. Beyond, Hwy 180 begins its 30-mile drive down into Kings Canyon, serpentining past chiseled rock walls laced with waterfalls. The road meets the **Kings River**, its roar ricocheting off granite cliffs soaring over 8000ft high, making this one of North America's deepest canyons.

At the bottom of the canyon, **Cedar Grove** (off Hwy 180) is the last outpost before the rugged grandeur of the Sierra Nevada backcountry begins. A popular day hike climbs 8.2 miles round trip to gushing **Mist Falls** (Road's End, Hwy 180) from Roads End. A favorite of birders, an easy 1.5-mile nature trail loops around **Zumwalt Meadow** (off Hwy 108; 🚻), just west of Roads End. Watch for lumbering black bears and springy mule deer.

ⓘ TIOGA PASS

Hwy 120 is the only road connecting Yosemite National Park with the Eastern Sierra, climbing through Tioga Pass (9945ft). Most maps mark this road 'closed in winter' which, while literally true, is also misleading. Tioga Rd is usually closed from the first heavy snowfall in October or November, not reopening until May or June. Call 209-372-0200 or check www.nps.gov/yose/planyourvisit/conditions.htm for current road conditions.

The scenic byway past Hume Lake to Cedar Grove Village is usually closed from mid-November to late April.

🏃 Activities

With more than 866 miles of marked trails, the parks are a backpacker's dream. Trails are officially open year-round to experienced hikers (you may need snow gear, snow shoes, navigation tools, crampons and ice picks in winter). Most come mid-May to October, when trails are far more accessible.

In Kings Canyon, Cedar Grove offers the best backcountry trail access, while in Sequoia head to Mineral King and Lodgepole. Jennie Lakes Wilderness in the Sequoia National Forest boasts pristine meadows and lakes at lower elevations.

Park-approved, bear-proof food canisters, which are always recommended, are mandatory in some places, especially for wilderness trips (eg Rae Lakes Loop). Rent bear canisters at park visitor centers and trailhead ranger stations or at the Lodgepole, Grant Grove and Cedar Grove Village markets (from around $5 per three-day trip). To prevent wildfires, campfires are usually only allowed in existing campfire rings in some backcountry areas.

🛏 Sleeping

Camping is the most affordable way to experience the parks, though sites fill up fast in high season (May to October). It's advisable to camp early, rather than wait until evening to secure your spot. Wilderness camping is free (permits required in quota season). Sequoia has one official in-park lodging option. The town of Three Rivers, just outside **Ash Mountain Entrance** (Generals Hwy, via

Sierra Dr; car/walk-in/motorcycle $35/20/30), offers the most accommodations.

DNC Parks & Resorts (☎801-559-4930; www.visitsequoia.com) offers lodging in Sequoia and Kings Canyon National Parks.

NPS & USFS Campgrounds (☎877-444-6777; www.recreation.gov) provides a reservation service for many of the campgrounds in the parks, while some Sequoia National Forest lodgings can be organised through **Sequoia-Kings Canyon Park Services Company** (☎559-565-3388; www.sequoia-kingscanyon.com).

Cedar Grove Lodge LODGE $
(☎559-565-3096; www.visitsequoia.com; 108260 West Side Dr, Cedar Grove Village; r from $151; ⏲mid-May–mid-Oct; P) The only indoor sleeping option in Kings Canyon, this riverside lodge offers 21 motel-style rooms. Three ground-floor rooms with shady furnished patios have spiffy river views and kitchenettes. All rooms have phones.

★**Sequoia High Sierra Camp** CABIN $$$
(☎866-654-2877; www.sequoiahighsierracamp.com; off Forest Rte 13S12; tent cabins with shared bath incl all meals $500; ⏲early Jun–mid-Sep) A mile's hike deep into the Sequoia National Forest, this off-the-grid, all-inclusive resort is nirvana for those who don't think luxury camping is an oxymoron. Canvas bungalows are spiffed up with pillow-top mattresses, feather pillows and cozy wool rugs. Restrooms and a shower house are shared. Reservations are required and there's usually a two-night minimum stay. Prices are based on 2 people per tent.

Eating

Eating options are limited. Most visitors bring supplies, then enjoy campground cookouts and restock basic grocery items at the small markets in Lodgepole, Grant Grove and Cedar Grove villages (not open year-round). Simple eating options are at Wuksachi, John Muir and Cedar Grove, Lodgepole, Stoney Creek and Hume Lake, which have seasonal restaurants and snack bars. Three Rivers, just south of Sequoia, is the place to fill up.

The few park lodges – **Wuksachi** (☎information 866-807-3598, reservations 888-252-5757; www.visitsequoia.com; 64740 Wuksachi Way; r $123-340; P), **John Muir** (☎877-436-9617; www.visitsequoiakingscanyon.com; 86728 Hwy 180, Grant Grove Village; r from $210; P) and Cedar Grove – have restaurants, as do a couple of spots in the adjoining Sequoia National Forest. Three Rivers, just south of Sequoia, is a good place to fill up.

Information

Lodgepole Village and Grant Grove Village are the parks' main hubs. Both have visitor centers, post offices, markets and ATMs. Lodgepole has a coin-operated laundry and public showers (summer only). Expensive gas is available at Hume Lake (year-round) and Stony Creek (closed in winter) outside the parks on national-forest land.

Kings Canyon Visitor Center (☎559-565-4307; www.nps.gov/seki; Hwy 180, Grant Grove Village; ⏲8am-5pm in summer, hours vary off-season) In the Grant Grove Village of Kings Canyon.

Lodgepole Visitor Center (☎559-565-4436; 63100 Lodgepole Rd, Lodgepole Village; ⏲7am-5pm late May–mid-Oct) Located in the heart of Sequoia.

USFS Hume Lake District Office (☎559-338-2251; www.fs.fed.us/r5/sequoia; 35860 E Kings Canyon Rd/Hwy 180, Dunlap; ⏲8am-4:30pm Mon-Fri) Stop here for recreation information, maps and campfire and wilderness permits for the Sequoia National Forest. The office is more than 20 miles west of the Big Stump Entrance.

Getting There & Around

Sequoia and Kings Canyon are both accessible by car only from the west, via Hwy 99 from Fresno or Visalia. It's 38 miles east on Hwy 198 from Visalia into Sequoia National Park – you pass through the gateway town of Three Rivers before entering the park. From Fresno, it's 47 miles east on Hwy 180 to Kings Canyon. The two roads are connected by the Generals Hwy, inside Sequoia. There is no access to either park from the east.

Car, motorcycle, shuttle bus, bike and foot are ways to get around the parks. The shuttles are only available in Sequoia National Park in the summer.

Eastern Sierra

Vast, empty and majestic, here jagged peaks plummet down into the desert, a dramatic juxtaposition that creates a potent scenery cocktail. Hwy 395 runs the entire length of the eastern side of the Sierra Nevada, with turnoffs leading to pine forests, wildflower-strewn meadows, placid lakes, hot springs and glacier-gouged canyons. Hikers, backpackers, mountain bikers, fishers and skiers all find escapes here.

Bishop, Lone Pine and Bridgeport have the most motels. Mammoth Lakes has a few motels and hotels and dozens of inns, B&Bs,

condos and vacation rentals. Reservations are essential everywhere in summer.

Backcountry camping requires a wilderness permit, available at ranger stations.

BODIE STATE HISTORIC PARK

At **Bodie State Historic Park** (☑760-616-5040; www.parks.ca.gov/bodie; Hwy 270; adult/child $8/5; ☉9am-6pm Apr-Oct, to 4pm Nov-Mar; road often closed in winter; ℗☀), the weathered buildings of a gold-rush boomtown sit frozen in time on a dusty, windswept plain. To get here, head east for 13 miles (the last three unpaved) on Hwy 270, about 7 miles south of Bridgeport. Snow usually closes the access road in winter and early spring.

MONO LAKE

Further south at **Mono Lake** (www.monolake.org; off Hwy 395), unearthly tufa towers rise from the alkaline water like drip sand castles. Off Hwy 395, **Mono Basin Scenic Area Visitor Center** (☑760-647-3044; www.fs.usda.gov/inyo; 1 Visitor Center Dr; ☉8am-5pm May-Sep, hours vary Oct-Dec, closed Jan-Apr; ♿) has excellent views and educational exhibits, but the best photo ops are from the mile-long nature trail at the **South Tufa Area** (Test Station Rd, near Hwy 120; adult/child $3/free; ℗♿). From the nearby town of Lee Vining, Hwy 120 heads west into Yosemite National Park via seasonal Tioga Pass.

A top regional draw, the open tasting room at **June Lake Brewing** (☑858-668-6340; www.junelakebrewing.com; 131 S Crawford Ave; ☉noon-8pm Mon, Wed, Thu, Sun, to 9pm Fri & Sat) serves around 10 drafts, including Deer Beer Brown Ale and some awesome IPAs. Brewers swear the June Lake water makes all the difference. Flights are around $8.

MAMMOTH LAKES & AROUND

Continuing south on Hwy 395, detour along the scenic 16-mile **June Lake Loop** or push on to **Mammoth Lakes**, a popular four-seasons resort guarded by 11,053ft **Mammoth Mountain** (☑760-934-2571, 760-934-2571, 24hr snow report 888-766-9778; www.mammothmountain.com; access via Minaret Rd; adult/13-17yr/5-12yr/under 5yr from $79/65/32/free), a top-notch skiing area. The slopes morph into a mountain-bike park in summer, when scenic gondola rides run.

Warm and cozy, oozing traditional ski-lodge appeal, and only steps from the base of the Panorama Gondola, the location of **Mammoth Mountain Inn** (☑760-934-2581; www.themammothmountaininn.com; 10400 Min-

SUPERSIZED FORESTS

When it's time to pay your respects to the most massive trees on the planet, there's nowhere better to go than Sequoia National Park. Giant sequoias (*Sequoiadendron giganteum*) can live for almost 3000 years, and some of the ancient standing in the Giant Forest have been around since the fall of the Roman Empire. There the world's largest living specimen, the **General Sherman Tree**, is taller than a 27-story building and measures over 100ft around its massive trunk – crane your neck as you stare in awe at its leafy crown.

aret Rd; r from $129-239, condos from $259-1199; ☀@☎☀) is spectacular no matter the time of year. In business since 1924, the charming year-round **Tamarack Lodge** (☑760-934-2442; www.tamaracklodge.com; 163 Twin Lakes Rd; r from $129, without bathroom from $99, cabins $255-425; ℗☺@☎☀) ✔ on Lower Twin Lake has a cozy fireplace lodge, a bar and an excellent restaurant, 11 rustic rooms and 35 cabins.

There's also camping and day hiking around Mammoth Lakes Basin and Reds Meadow, the latter near the 60ft-high basalt columns of **Devils Postpile National Monument** (☑760-934-2289; www.nps.gov/depo; access off Minaret Summit Rd/Reds Meadow Rd; shuttle day pass adult/child $8/4; ☉Jun-Oct, weather depending), formed by volcanic activity.

The in-town **Mammoth Lakes Welcome Center & Ranger Station** (☑760-924-5500; www.visitmammoth.com; 2510 Hwy 203; ☉8am-5pm, 8:30am-4:30pm winter) has helpful maps and information, and you can grab comfort food such as shepherd's pie, fondue and pork tenderloin at **Mammoth Tavern** (☑760-934-3902; www.mammothtavern.com; 587 Old Mammoth Rd; mains $14-35; ☉4-9:30pm Tue-Thu & Sun, 5-10pm Fri & Sat). Alternatively, treat yourself to innovative, Norwegian-inspired creations, such as Canadian duck breast with arctic lingonberries and pan-seared day-boat scallops, at chef Ian Algerøen's **Skadi** (☑760-914-0962; www.skadirestaurant.com; 94 Berner St; mains $32-40; ☉5pm-close Wed-Mon). Reservations required.

Hot-springs fans can soak in primitive pools off Benton Crossing Rd or view the geysering water at Hot Creek Geological Site, both off Hwy 395 southeast of town. Or detour to Benton to soak in your own hot-springs tub and snooze beneath the moonlight at **Benton Hot Springs** (☑760-933-2287; www.bentonhotsprings. org; Hwy 120, Benton; tent & RV sites per 2 people $60-70, B&B r from $119; P ✳ 🛜 🐾), a small, historic resort in a 150-year-old former silver-mining town nestled in the White Mountains. Choose from 11 well-spaced campsites with private tubs or a room in the themed, antique-filled B&B, with semiprivate tubs.

BISHOP & AROUND

Further south, Hwy 395 descends into the Owens Valley. In frontier-flavored Bishop, the historical **Laws Railroad Museum** (☑760-873-5950; www.lawsmuseum.org; Silver Canyon Rd; suggested donation $10; ☺10am-4pm Sep-May, from 9.30am Jun-Aug; 👶) is a kid-friendly attraction with rides on vintage trains. A gateway for packhorse trips, Bishop accesses the Eastern Sierra's best fishing and rock climbing. Budget a half-day for the thrilling drive up to the **Ancient Bristlecone Pine Forest**. These gnarled, otherworldly looking trees – the world's oldest – are found above 10,000ft on the slopes of the White Mountains. The road (closed by snow in winter and early spring) is paved to the **Schulman Grove Visitor Center** (☑760-873-2500; www.fs.usda. gov/inyo; White Mountain Rd; per person/car $3/6; ☺10am-5pm Jun-Aug, to 4pm Fri-Sun May-Jun), where hiking trails await. From Hwy 395 in Big Pine, take Hwy 168 east for 12 miles, then follow White Mountain Rd uphill for 10 miles.

LONE PINE & AROUND

Hwy 395 barrels south to **Manzanar National Historic Site** (☑760-878-2194; www. nps.gov/manz; 5001 Hwy 395; ☺9am-4:30pm; P) 🌿**FREE**, which memorializes the camp where some 10,000 Japanese Americans were unjustly interned during WWII. Further south in Lone Pine, you'll finally glimpse Mt Whitney (14,505ft), the highest mountain in the lower 48 states. The heart-stopping, 12-mile scenic drive up **Whitney Portal Road** (closed in winter and early spring) is spectacular. Climbing the peak is hugely popular, but requires a permit (per person $21) that must be obtained on www.recreation.gov. Just south of town, the **Eastern Sierra Interagency Visitor Center** (☑760-876-6222; www.fs.fed.us/r5/inyo; cnr Hwys 395 & 136; ☺8am-5pm, 8:30am-4:30pm winter) issues wilderness permits, dispenses outdoor-recreation info and sells books and maps.

A popular launchpad for Mt Whitney trips and a locus of posthike washups (public showers are available), the **Whitney Portal Hostel & Hotel** (☑760-876-0030; www.whitneyportalstore.com; 238 S Main St; dm/d from $32/92; ✳ 🛜 🐾) has the cheapest beds in town – reserve dorms months ahead for July and August. Just off the main streets, at **Alabama Hills Cafe** (☑760-876-4675; www.alabamahillscafe.com; 111 W Post St; breakfast items $9.50-$14; ☺6am-3pm Fri-Sun, to 2pm Mon-Thu; 🛜 🍴), everyone's favorite breakfast joint, the portions are big, the bread is freshly baked and the soups hearty. Sandwiches and fruit pies make lunch an attractive option too.

West of Lone Pine, the bizarrely shaped boulders of the Alabama Hills have enchanted filmmakers of Hollywood Westerns. Peruse memorabilia and movie posters back in town at the **Museum of Western Film History** (☑760-876-9909; www.museumofwesternfilmhistory.org; 701 S Main St; adult/under 12yr $5/free; ☺10am-5pm Mon-Sat, to 4pm Sun; P 👶 🐾).

Lake Tahoe

Shimmering in myriad shades of blue and green, Lake Tahoe is the USA's second-deepest lake and, at 6245ft high, it is also one of the highest-elevation lakes in the country. Driving around the spellbinding 72-mile scenic shoreline will give you quite a workout behind the wheel. Generally, the north shore is quiet and upscale; the west shore, rugged and old-timey; the east shore, undeveloped; the south shore, busy and tacky, with aging motels and flashy casinos.

❶ Information

Lake Tahoe Visitors Authority (☑775-588-5900; www.tahoesouth.com; 169 Hwy 50, Stateline, NV; ☺9am-5pm Mon-Fri) Tourist information, maps, brochures and money-saving coupons, with a second center in Stateline

Lake Tahoe Bicycle Coalition (www.tahoebike. org) publishes a bike map that's a great resource for pedaling around the area.

Desolation Wilderness Permits (☑877-444-6777; www.recreation.gov; per adult $5-10)

❶ Getting There & Around

Greyhound buses from Reno, Sacramento and San Francisco run to Truckee, and you can also get the daily **Zephyr** (☑800-872-7245; www. amtrak.com) train here from the same destinations. From Truckee, take the **Truckee Transit** (☑530-550-1212; www.laketahoetransit.com) to Donner Lake, or **Tahoe Area Rapid Transit** (TART; ☑530-550-1212; https://tahoetruckee transit.com; 10183 Truckee Airport Rd; single/day pass $1.75/3.50) buses to the north and west shores of the lake.

Tahoe Ski Trips (☑ 925-680-4386; www. tahoeskitrips.net; bus $89) offers shuttles connecting San Francisco and other Bay Area pickup locations with Tahoe's slopes.

From late fall through early spring, drivers should always pack snow chains in case a storm rolls in, and stash some emergency supplies (eg blankets, water, flashlights) in the trunk. Before hopping in the car, check road closures and conditions:

California Department of Transportation (Caltrans; ☑ 800-427-7623; www.dot.ca.gov)

Nevada Department of Transportation (NDOT; ☑ 877-687-6237, within Nevada 511; www.nevadadot.com)

With a saucy acronym and reliable service, bike-rack-equipped Tahoe Area Rapid Transit runs buses year-round along the north shore as far as Incline Village, down the western shore to **Ed Z'berg Sugar Pine Point State Park** (☑ 530-525-7982; www.parks.ca.gov; per car $10) and north to Squaw Valley and Truckee via Hwy 89. The main routes typically depart hourly from about 6am until 6pm daily.

SOUTH LAKE TAHOE & WEST SHORE

With retro motels and eateries lining busy Hwy 50, South Lake Tahoe gets crowded. Gambling at Stateline's casino hotels, just across the Nevada border, attracts thousands, as does the world-class ski resort **Heavenly** (☑ 775-586-7000; www.skiheavenly.com; 3860 Saddle Rd; adult/child 5-12yr/youth 13-18yr $154/85/126; ☉ 9am-4pm Mon-Fri, from 8:30am Sat, Sun & holidays; ⋆). In summer a trip up Heavenly's gondola guarantees fabulous views of the lake and the **Desolation Wilderness**, with its raw granite peaks, glacier-carved valleys and alpine lakes favored by hikers. Get maps, information and overnight wilderness permits (per adult or dog $5; day permits are free) from the **USFS Taylor Creek Visitor Center** (☑ 530-543-2674; www.fs.usda.gov/ltbmu; Visitor Center Rd, off Hwy 89; ☉ 8am-4:30pm late May-Oct). It's 3 miles north of the 'Y' intersection of Hwys 50/89, at **Tallac Historic Site** (☑ 530-544-7383; www.tahoeheritage.org; Tallac Rd; optional tour adult/child $10/5; ☉ 10am-4pm daily late May-Sep; ⋆) FREE, preserving swish early-20th-century vacation estates.

From sandy, swimmable **Zephyr Cove** (☑ 775-589-4901; www.zephyrcove.com; 760 Hwy 50; per car $10; ☉ sunrise-sunset) across the Nevada border or the in-town Ski Run Marina, **Lake Tahoe Cruises** (☑ 775-586-4906; www.zephyrcove.com; 760 Hwy 50; adult/child from $65/33) plies the 'Big Blue' year-round. Paddle under your own power with **Kayak Tahoe** (☑ 530-544-2011; www.kayaktahoe.com; 3411 Lake Tahoe Blvd; kayak single/double 1hr $25/35, 1 day

$65/85, lessons & tours from $50; ☉ 9am-5pm Jun-Sep). Back on shore, chic motels include the **Alder Inn** (☑ 530-544-4485; www.alderinn.com; 1072 Ski Run Blvd; r $89-149; ⓟ ⊜ ⊚ ⊛ ⊠) and the hip **Basecamp Hotel** (☑ 530-208-0180; www. basecamphotels.com; 4143 Cedar Ave; d $109-229, 8-person bunk room $209-299, pet fee $40; ⊚ ⊛) ✎, which has a rooftop hot tub, or pitch a tent at lakeside **Fallen Leaf Campground** (☑ info 530-544-0426, reservations 877-444-6777; www.recreation.gov; 2165 Fallen Leaf Lake Rd; tent & RV sites $33-35, yurts $86; ☉ mid-May–mid-Oct; ⊛). Fuel up at vegetarian-friendly **Sprouts** (☑ 530-541-6969; www.sproutscafetahoe.com; 3123 Harrison Ave; mains $7-10; ☉ 8am-8pm; ⊘⋆) natural-foods cafe, or with a peanut-butter-topped burger and garlic fries at the **Burger Lounge** (☑ 530-542-2010; 717 Emerald Bay Rd; dishes $6-10; ☉ 11am-8pm Jun-Sep, to 7pm Thu-Mon Oct-May; ⋆).

Hwy 89 threads northwest along the thickly forested west shore to **Emerald Bay State Park** (☑ 530-541-6498; www.parks. ca.gov; ☉ sunrise-sunset), where granite cliffs and pine trees frame a sparkling fjord-like inlet. A 1-mile trail leads steeply downhill to **Vikingsholm Castle** (☑ 530-525-7232; http:// vikingsholm.com; tour adult/child 7-17yr $10/8; ☉ 10:30am-3:30pm or 4pm late May-Sep; ⓟ), a 1920s Scandinavian-style mansion. From there, the **Rubicon Trail** ribbons 4.5 miles north along the lakeshore past petite coves to **DL Bliss State Park** (☑ 530-525-7277; www. parks.ca.gov; per car $10; ☉ late May-Sep; ⓟ) ✎, offering sandy beaches. Further north, **Tahoma Meadows B&B Cottages** (☑ 530-525-1553; www.tahomameadows.com; 6821 W Lake Blvd; cottages $169-339, pet fee $20; ⓟ ⊜ ⊚ ⊛) rents darling country cabins.

NORTH & EAST SHORES

A busy commercial hub, **Tahoe City** is great for grabbing food and supplies and renting outdoor-sports gear. It's not far from **Squaw Valley Alpine Meadows** (☑ 800-403-0206; www.squawalpine.com; 1960 Squaw Valley Rd, off Hwy 89, Olympic Valley; adult/child 5-12yr/youth 13-22yr $169/109/139; ☉ 9am-4pm Mon-Fri, from 8:30am Sat, Sun & holidays; ⋆), a mega-sized ski resort that hosted the 1960 Winter Olympics. Après-ski crowds gather at woodsy **Bridgetender Tavern & Grill** (☑ 530-583-3342; www. tahoebridgetender.com; 65 W Lake Blvd; ☉ 11am-11pm Mon-Thu, to midnight Fri, 9am-midnight Sat, to 11pm Sun) back in town. In the morning, gobble eggs Benedict with house-smoked salmon at down-home **Fire Sign Cafe** (www. firesigncafe.com; 1785 W Lake Blvd; mains $10-15; ☉ 7am-3pm; ⊘⋆), 2 miles further south.

CALIFORNIA SIERRA NEVADA

In summer, swim or kayak at **Tahoe Vista** or **Kings Beach**. Overnight at **Cedar Glen Lodge** (☑530-546-4281; www.tahoecedarglen. com; 6589 N Lake Blvd; r, ste & cottages $219-579, pet fee $30; @☎☏❄), where rustic-themed cottages and rooms have kitchenettes, or well-kept, compact **Hostel Tahoe** (☑530-546-3266; www.hosteltahoe.com; 8931 N Lake Blvd; dm/d/q from $35/85/100; @☎). East of Kings Beach's lakeside eateries, Hwy 28 barrels into Nevada. Catch a live-music show at a just-over-the-border casino, or for more happening bars and bistros, drive further to Incline Village.

With pristine beaches, lakes and miles of multiuse trails, **Lake Tahoe-Nevada State Park** (☑775-831-0494; www.parks.nv.gov; per car/bicycle $10/2; ☺8am-1hr after sunset; ℗) is the east shore's biggest draw. Summer crowds splash in the turquoise waters of **Sand Harbor**. The 13-mile **Flume Trail**, a mountain biker's holy grail, ends further south at **Spooner Lake**. Back in Incline Village, **Flume Trail Bikes** (☑775-298-2501; http://flumetrailtahoe.com; 1115 Tunnel Creek Rd; mountain-bike rental per day $35-67, shuttle $16, state park entrance $2; ☺8am-6pm, closed winter) offers bicycle rentals and shuttles.

TRUCKEE & AROUND

North of Lake Tahoe off I-80, Truckee is not in fact a truck stop but a thriving mountain town, with coffee shops, trendy boutiques and dining in downtown's historical district. Ski bums have several resorts to pick from, including glam **Northstar**

California (☑530-562-1010; www.northstarcalifornia.com; 5001 Northstar Dr, off Hwy 267; adult/child 5-12yr/youth 13-18yr $160/94/131; ☺8am-5pm); kid-friendly **Sugar Bowl** (☑530-426-9000; www.sugarbowl.com; 629 Sugar Bowl Rd, off Donner Pass Rd, Norden; adult/child 6-12yr/youth 13-22yr $118/69/97; ☺9am-4pm); and **Royal Gorge** (☑530-426-3871; www.royalgorge.com; 9411 Pahatsi Rd, off I-80 exit Soda Springs/Norden, Soda Springs; adult/youth 13-22yr $35/20; ☺8:30am-4pm; ♿☏), paradise for cross-country skiers.

West of Hwy 89, **Donner Summit** is where the infamous Donner Party became trapped during the fierce winter of 1846–47. About half survived – some by cannibalizing their dead friends. The grisly tale is chronicled at the museum inside **Donner Memorial State Park** (☑530-582-7892; www.parks.ca.gov; Donner Pass Rd; per car $5-10, varies seasonally; ☺visitor center 10am-5pm; ℗♿), which offers **camping** (☑530-582-7894, reservations 800-444-7275; www.reservecalifornia.com; tent & RV sites $35; ☺late May-late Sep). Nearby **Donner Lake** is popular with swimmers and paddlers.

On the outskirts of Truckee, green-certified **Cedar House Sport Hotel** (☑530-582-5655; www.cedarhousesporthotel.com; 10918 Brockway Rd; r $180-345, pet fee $50-100; ℗☺@☎☏) ⌀ offers stylish boutique rooms and an outstanding restaurant. Down pints of Donner Party Porter at **Fifty Fifty Brewing Co** (www.fiftyfiftybrewing.com; 11197 Brockway Rd; ☺11:30am-9pm Sun-Thu, to 9:30pm Fri & Sat).

Pacific Northwest

Best Places to Eat

➡ Ned Ludd (p1066)
➡ Chow (p1075)
➡ Ox (p1066)
➡ Sitka & Spruce (p1040)

Best Places to Sleep

➡ Timberline Lodge (p1073)
➡ Crater Lake Lodge (p1076)
➡ Hotel Monaco (p1039)
➡ Olympic Lights B&B (p1051)
➡ Historic Davenport Hotel (p1055)

Why Go?

As much a state of mind as a geographical region, the northwest corner of the US is a land of subcultures and new trends, where evergreen trees frame snow-dusted volcanoes, and inspired ideas scribbled on the back of napkins become tomorrow's start-ups. You can't peel off the history in layers here, but you *can* gaze wistfully into the future in fast-moving, innovative cities such as Seattle and Portland, which are sprinkled with food carts, streetcars, microbreweries, green belts, coffee connoisseurs and weird urban sculpture.

Ever since the days of the Oregon Trail, the Northwest has had a hypnotic lure for risk-takers and dreamers; the metaphoric carrot still dangles. There's the air, so clean they ought to bottle it; the trees, older than many of Rome's Renaissance palaces; and the end-of-the-continent coastline, holding back the force of the world's largest ocean. Cowboys take note: it doesn't get much more 'wild' or 'west' than this.

When to Go
Seattle

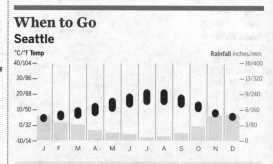

Jan–Mar Most reliable snow cover for skiing in the Cascades and beyond.

May Festival season: Portland Rose, International Film Festival and Oregon Shakespeare Festival.

Jul–Sep The best hiking months, between the spring snowmelt and the first fall flurries.

Pacific Northwest Highlights

1 San Juan Islands (p1050) Cycling and kayaking around the quieter corners.

2 Oregon Coast (p1076) Exploring this gorgeous region, from scenic Astoria to balmy Port Orford.

3 Olympic National Park (p1046) Admiring trees older than Europe's Renaissance castles.

4 Pike Place Market (p1032) Watching the greatest outdoor show in the Pacific Northwest.

5 Portland (p1059) Walking the green and serene neighborhoods, energized by beer, coffee and food-cart treats.

6 Crater Lake National Park (p1076) Witnessing the impossibly deep-blue waters and scenic panoramas.

7 Bend (p1074) Mountain biking, rock climbing or skiing in this outdoor mecca.

8 Walla Walla (p1057) Tasting sumptuous reds and whites in the surrounding wine regions.

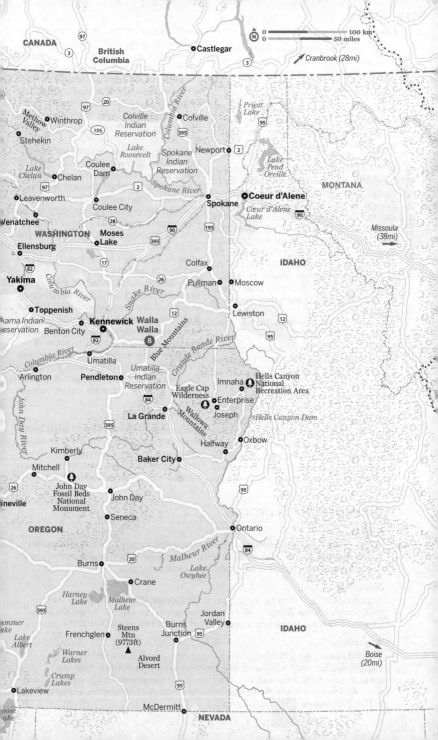

History

Native American societies, including the Chinook and the Salish, had long-established coastal communities by the time Europeans arrived in the Pacific Northwest in the 18th century. Inland, on the arid plateaus between the Cascades and the Rocky Mountains, the Spokane, Nez Percé and other tribes thrived on seasonal migration between river valleys and temperate uplands.

Three hundred years after Columbus landed in the New World, Spanish and British explorers began probing the northern Pacific coast, seeking the fabled Northwest Passage. In 1792 Captain George Vancouver was the first explorer to sail the waters of Puget Sound, claiming British sovereignty over the entire region. At the same time, an American, Captain Robert Gray, found the mouth of the Columbia River. In 1805 the explorers Lewis and Clark crossed the Rockies and made their way down the Columbia to the Pacific Ocean, extending the US claim on the territory.

In 1824 the British Hudson's Bay Company established Fort Vancouver in Washington as headquarters for the Columbia region. This opened the door to waves of settlers, but had a devastating impact on the indigenous cultures, which were assailed by European diseases and alcohol.

In 1843 settlers at Champoeg, on the Willamette River south of Portland, voted to organize a provisional government independent of the Hudson's Bay Company, thereby casting their lot with the US, which formally acquired the territory from the British by treaty in 1846. Over the next decade, some 53,000 settlers came to the Northwest via the 2000-mile Oregon Trail.

Arrival of the railroads set the region's future. Agriculture and lumber became the pillars of the economy until 1914, when WWI and the opening of the Panama Canal brought increased trade to Pacific ports. Shipyards opened along Puget Sound, and the Boeing aircraft company set up shop near Seattle.

Big dam projects in the 1930s and '40s provided cheap hydroelectricity and irrigation. WWII offered another boost for aircraft manufacturing and shipbuilding, and agriculture continued to thrive. In the postwar period, Washington's population, especially around Puget Sound, grew to twice that of Oregon.

In the 1980s and '90s, the economic emphasis shifted with the rise of the high-tech industry, embodied by Microsoft in Seattle and Intel in Portland.

Hydroelectricity production and massive irrigation projects along the Columbia have threatened the river's ecosystem in the past few decades, and logging has also left its scars. But the region has reinvigorated its eco-credentials by attracting some of the country's most environmentally conscious companies, and its major cities are among the greenest in the US. It stands at the forefront of US efforts to tackle climate issues.

Local Culture

The stereotypical image of a Pacific Northwesterner is a casually dressed, latte-sipping urbanite who drives a Prius, votes Democrat and walks around with an unwavering musical diet of Nirvana-derived indie rock

THE PACIFIC NORTHWEST IN...

Four Days
Hit the ground running in **Seattle** to see the main sights, including **Pike Place Market** and the **Seattle Center**. After a couple of days, head down to **Portland**, where you can do as the locals do and cycle to bars, cafes, food carts and shops.

One Week
Add a couple of outdoorsy highlights such as **Mt Rainier**, **Olympic National Park**, the **Columbia River Gorge** or **Mt Hood**. Or explore the spectacular Oregon Coast (try **Cannon Beach**) or the historic seaport of **Port Townsend** on the Olympic Peninsula.

Two Weeks
Crater Lake is unforgettable, and can be combined with a trip to **Ashland** and its Shakespeare Festival. Equally rewarding are the ethereal **San Juan Islands** up near the watery border with Canada, and **Bend**, the region's capital of outdoor activities. Like wine? Washington's **Walla Walla** is packed with attractive tasting rooms, and Oregon's **Willamette Valley** is a Pinot Noir paradise.

blaring from their headphones. But, as with most fleeting regional generalizations, the reality is far more complex.

Noted for their sophisticated cafe culture and copious microbrew pubs, the urban hubs of Seattle and Portland are the Northwest's most emblematic cities. But head east into the region's drier and less verdant interior, and the cultural affiliations become increasingly more traditional. Here, strung along the Columbia River Valley or nestled amid the arid steppes of southeastern Washington, small towns host raucous rodeos, tourist centers promote cowboy culture, and a cup of coffee is exactly that – no lattes, no matcha tea.

In contrast to the USA's hardworking eastern seaboard, life out west is more casual and less frenetic. Ideally, Westerners would rather work to live than live to work. Indeed, with so much winter rain, the citizens of the Pacific Northwest will dredge up any excuse to shun the nine-to-five treadmill and hit the great outdoors a couple of hours (or even days) early. Witness the scene in late May and early June, when the first bright days of summer prompt a mass exodus of hikers and cyclists to make enthusiastically for the national parks and wilderness areas for which the region is justly famous.

✪ Getting There & Around

AIR
Seattle-Tacoma International Airport, aka 'Sea-Tac,' and Portland International Airport are the main airports for the region, serving many North American and several international destinations.

BOAT
Washington State Ferries (www.wsdot.wa.gov/ferries) links Seattle with Bainbridge and Vashon Islands. Other WSF routes cross from Whidbey Island to Port Townsend on the Olympic Peninsula, and from Anacortes through the San Juan Islands to Sidney, BC. Victoria Clipper (www.clippervacations.com) operates services from Seattle to Victoria, BC; ferries to Victoria also operate from Port Angeles. Alaska Marine Highway ferries (www.dot.state.ak.us/amhs) go from Bellingham, WA, to Alaska.

BUS
Greyhound (www.greyhound.com) provides service along the I-5 corridor from Bellingham in northern Washington down to Medford in southern Oregon, with connecting services across the US and Canada. East–west routes fan out toward Spokane, Yakima, the Tri-Cities (Kennewick, Pasco and Richland in Washington), Walla Walla and Pullman in Washington, and Hood River and Pendleton in Oregon. Private bus companies service most of the smaller towns and cities across the region, often connecting to Greyhound or Amtrak.

CAR
Driving your own vehicle is by far the most convenient way of touring the Pacific Northwest. Major and minor rental agencies are commonplace throughout the region. I-5 is the major north–south artery. In Washington I-90 heads east from Seattle to Spokane and into Idaho. In Oregon I-84 branches east from Portland along the Columbia River Gorge to link up with Boise in Idaho.

TRAIN
Amtrak (www.amtrak.com) runs train services north (to Vancouver, Canada) and south (to California), linking Seattle, Portland and other major urban centers with the *Cascades* and *Coast Starlight* routes. The famous *Empire Builder* heads east to Chicago from Seattle and Portland (joining up in Spokane).

WASHINGTON

Washington state is the heart of the Pacific Northwest. With that title comes everything you'd hope for, from the lush, green Olympic Peninsula to the wild white peaks of the Cascade Mountains and the relaxed, kayaker-friendly San Juan Islands. Head east and you'll see another side of the state: aridly beautiful, with upscale wineries and cowboy-style breakfasts in equal measure, plus orchards, wheat fields and pioneer history.

The biggest urban jolt is Seattle, but each of the state's main population centers – Spokane, Bellingham, Olympia – has its own charm. Still, to get the most out of visiting Washington, you'll want to leave the cities behind and lose yourself in the mountains and the woods, along the coast or on the islands. The best experiences here are mostly unmediated.

Seattle

Combine the brains of Portland, OR, with the beauty of Vancouver, Canada, and you'll get something approximating Seattle. It's hard to believe that the Pacific Northwest's largest metropolis was considered a 'secondary' US city until the 1980s, when a combination of bold innovation and unabashed individualism turned it into one of the dotcom era's biggest trendsetters, spearheaded by an unlikely alliance of coffee-sipping computer geeks and navel-gazing musicians.

WASHINGTON FACTS

Nickname Evergreen State

Population 7.3 million

Area 71,362 sq miles

Capital city Olympia (population 51,609)

Other cities Seattle (population 744,955), Spokane (population 217,108), Bellingham (population 89,045)

Sales tax 6.5%

Birthplace of Singer and actor Bing Crosby (1903–77), guitarist Jimi Hendrix (1942–70), computer geek Bill Gates (b 1955), political commentator Glen Beck (b 1964), musical icon Kurt Cobain (1967–94)

Home of Mt St Helens, Microsoft, Starbucks, Amazon.com, Evergreen State College

Politics Democrat governors since 1985

Famous for Grunge rock, coffee, Grey's Anatomy, *Twilight*, volcanoes, apples, wine, precipitation

State vegetable Walla Walla sweet onion

Driving distances Seattle to Portland174 miles, Spokane to Port Angeles 365 miles

Surprisingly elegant in places and coolly edgy in others, Seattle is notable for its strong neighborhoods, top-rated university, monstrous traffic jams and proactive city mayors who harbor green credentials. Although it has fermented its own pop culture in recent times, it has yet to create an urban mythology befitting Paris or New York, but it does have 'the Mountain.' Better known as Rainier, Seattle's unifying symbol is a 14,411ft mass of rock and ice, which acts as a perennial reminder to the city's huddled masses that raw wilderness, and potential volcanic catastrophe, are never far away.

◉ Sights

◎ Downtown

★ Pike Place Market   MARKET
(Map p1034; ☑206-682-7453; www.pikeplacemarket.org; 85 Pike St, Pike Place; ☉9am-6pm Mon-Sat, to 5pm Sun; ☑Westlake) ☑ A cavalcade of noise, smells, personalities, banter and urban theater sprinkled liberally around a spatially challenged waterside strip, Pike Place Market is Seattle in a bottle. In operation since 1907 and still as soulful today as it was on day one, this wonderfully local experience highlights the city for what it really is: all-embracing, eclectic and proudly unique. A 2017 expansion of the market infrastructure added vendor space, weather-protected common areas, extra parking, and housing for low-income seniors.

★ Seattle Art Museum   MUSEUM
(SAM; Map p1034; ☑206-654-3210; www.seattleartmuseum.org; 1300 1st Ave, Downtown; adult/student $25/15; ☉10am-5pm Wed & Fri-Mon, to 9pm Thu; ☑University St) While not comparable with the big guns in New York and Chicago, Seattle Art Museum is no slouch. Always re-curating its art collection with new acquisitions and imported temporary exhibitions, it's known for its extensive Native American artifacts and work from the local Northwest school, in particular by Mark Tobey (1890–1976). Modern American art is also well represented, and the museum gets some exciting traveling exhibitions (including Yayoi Kusama's infinity mirrors).

★ Olympic Sculpture Park   PARK
(Map p1034; ☑206-654-3100; 2901 Western Ave, Belltown; ☉sunrise-sunset; ☑33) **FREE** This ingenuous feat of urban planning is an official offshoot of the Seattle Art Museum and bears the same strong eye toward design and curation. There are more than 20 sculptures to stop at and admire in this green space that sprawls out over reclaimed urban decay. You can also enjoy them in passing while traversing the park's winding trails. Views of the Puget Sound and Olympic Peninsula in the background will delight anyone looking for some great pictures for social media.

◉ Pioneer Square & the International District

Seattle's birthplace retains the grit of its 'Skid Row' roots with redbrick architecture and a rambunctious street life that's tempered by art galleries and locavore restaurants. The International District's legacy as home to many of the city's southeast Asian immigrant communities makes for unique shopping and exquisite dining, while SoDo (south of downtown) is an austere warehouse district that's steadily attracting new distilleries and dispensaries.

★ **Klondike Gold Rush National Historical Park**   MUSEUM
(Map p1034; ☑ 206-553-3000; www.nps.gov/klse; 319 2nd Ave S, Pioneer Sq; ⊗ 9am-5pm daily Jun-Aug, 10am-5pm Tue-Sun Sep-Feb, 10am-5pm daily Mar-May; ⬛ First Hill Streetcar) FREE Eloquently run by the US National Park Service, this wonderful museum has exhibits, photos and news clippings from the 1897 Klondike gold rush, when a Seattle-on-steroids acted as a fueling depot for prospectors bound for the Yukon in Canada. Entry would cost $20 anywhere else; in Seattle it's free!

Wing Luke Museum of the Asian Pacific American Experience   MUSEUM
(Map p1034; ☑ 206-623-5124; www.wingluke. org; 719 S King St, International District; adult/child $17/12; ⊗ 10am-5pm Tue-Sun; ⬛ First Hill Streetcar) The beautiful Wing Luke museum examines Asia Pacific American culture, focusing on prickly issues such as Chinese settlement in the 1880s and Japanese internment camps during WWII. Recent temporary exhibits include 'A Day in the Life of Bruce Lee.' There are also art exhibits and a preserved immigrant apartment. Guided tours are available; the first Thursday of the month is free (with extended hours until 8pm).

◉ **Seattle Center**

★ **Space Needle**   LANDMARK
(Map p1034; ☑ 206-905-2100; www.spaceneedle. com; 400 Broad St, Seattle Center; adult/child $37.50/32.50, incl Chihuly Garden & Glass $49/39; ⊗ 9:30am-11pm Mon-Thu, 9:30am-11:30pm Fri & Sat, 9am-11pm Sun; ⬛ Seattle Center) This streamlined, modern-before-its-time tower built for the 1962 World's Fair has been the city's defining symbol for more than 50 years. The needle anchors the complex now called the **Seattle Center** (Map p1034; ☑ 206-684-8582; www.seattlecenter.com; 400 Broad St, Seattle Center; ⬛ Seattle Center) and draws more than one million annual visitors to its flying saucer–like observation deck and pricey rotating restaurant.

★ **Museum of Pop Culture**   MUSEUM
(Map p1034; ☑ 206-770-2700; www.mopop.org; 325 5th Ave N, Seattle Center; adult/child $28/19; ⊗ 10am-5pm Jan-late May & Sep-Dec, 10am-7pm late May-Aug; ⬛ Seattle Center) The Museum of Pop Culture (formerly EMP, the 'Experience

Music Project') is an inspired marriage between super-modern architecture and legendary rock-and-roll history that sprang from the imagination (and pocket) of Microsoft co-creator Paul Allen (1953–2018). Inside its avant-garde frame, designed by Canadian architect Frank Gehry, you can tune into the famous sounds of Seattle (with an obvious bias toward Jimi Hendrix and grunge) or attempt to imitate the masters in the Interactive Sound Lab.

★ **Chihuly Garden & Glass**   MUSEUM
(Map p1034; ☑ 206-753-4940; www.chihulygarden andglass.com; 305 Harrison St, Seattle Center; adult/child $26/17, incl Space Needle $49/39; ⊗ 10am-8pm Sun-Thu, to 9pm Fri & Sat; ⬛ Seattle Center) Opened in 2012 and reinforcing Seattle's position as a leading city of the arts, this exquisite exposition of the life and work of dynamic local sculptor Dale Chihuly is possibly the finest collection of curated glass art you'll ever see. It shows off Chihuly's creative designs in a suite of interconnected dark and light rooms before depositing you in an airy glass atrium and – finally – a landscaped garden in the shadow of the Space Needle. Glassblowing demonstrations are a highlight.

◉ **Capitol Hill**

Capitol Hill is Seattle's most unashamedly hip neighborhood, where the exceptionally rich mix with the exceptionally eccentric. While gentrification has let some of the air out of its tires, this is still Seattle's best crash pad for dive-bar rock and roll, LGBTIQ+ mirth and on-trend dining. More straitlaced First Hill is home to an art museum and multiple hospitals.

◉ **Green Lake & Fremont**

Fremont pitches young hipsters among old hippies in an unlikely urban alliance, and vies with Capitol Hill as Seattle's most irreverent neighborhood, with junk shops, urban sculpture and a healthy sense of its own ludicrousness. To the north, family-friendly Green Lake is a more affluent suburb centered on a park favored by fitness devotees.

Fremont Troll   SCULPTURE
(N 36th St & Troll Ave, Fremont; ⬛ 62) The Fremont Troll is an outlandish sculpture that lurks beneath the north end of the Aurora Bridge at N 36th St. The troll's creators – artists Steve Badanes, Will Martin, Donna Walter and

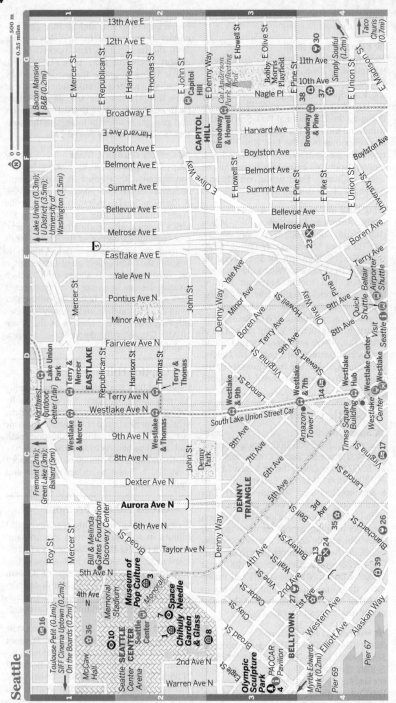

Seattle

PACIFIC NORTHWEST SEATTLE

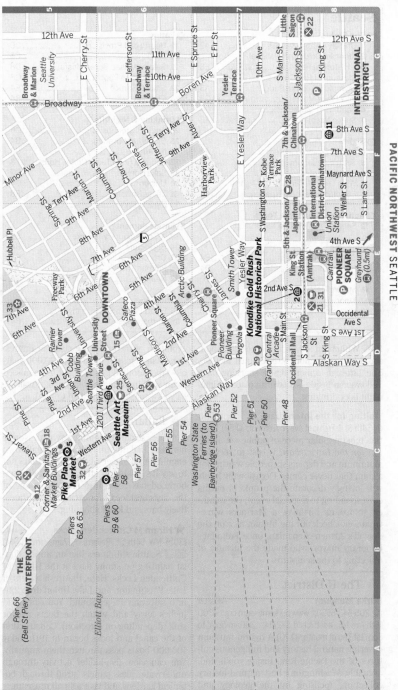

Seattle

Ross Whitehead – won a competition sponsored by the Fremont Arts Council in 1990. The 18ft-high cement figure snacking on a Volkswagen Beetle is a favorite place for late-night beer drinking.

Waiting for the Interurban MONUMENT
(N 34th St & Fremont Ave N, Fremont; 🚍 62) Seattle's most popular piece of public art, *Waiting for the Interurban,* is cast in recycled aluminum and depicts six people waiting for a train that never comes. Occasionally locals will lovingly decorate the people in outfits corresponding to a special event, the weather, someone's birthday, a Mariners win – whatever. Check out the human face on the dog; it's Armen Stepanian, once Fremont's honorary mayor, who made the mistake of objecting to the sculpture.

◉ The U District

Burke Museum MUSEUM
(📞 206-543-5590; www.burkemuseum.org; 4300 15th Ave NE; adult/child $22/14; ⊙10am-5pm, to 8pm 1st Thu of month; 🚍70) A hybrid museum covering natural history and indigenous cultures of the Pacific Rim. Inside you'll find, arguably, Washington's best natural-history collection, focusing on the geology and

evolution of the state. It guards an impressive stash of fossils, including a 20,000-year-old saber-toothed cat. Also not to be missed is an awe-inspiring collection of Kwakwaka'wakw masks from British Columbia.

◉ Ballard

A former seafaring community with Nordic heritage, Ballard still feels like a small town engulfed by a bigger city. However, that's not to say it's lacking in attractions. The neighborhood has come into its own as one of the city's best locals for exciting restaurants, lively bars and killer shopping.

★Hiram M Chittenden Locks CANAL
(3015 NW 54th St, Ballard; ⊙7am-9pm; 🚍44) FREE Seattle shimmers like an impressionist painting on sunny days at the Hiram M Chittenden Locks. Here, the fresh waters of Lake Washington and Lake Union drop 22ft into saltwater Puget Sound. You can stand inches away and watch the boats rise or sink (depending on direction). Construction of the canal and locks began in 1911; today 100,000 boats pass through them annually. You can view fish-ladder activity through underwater glass panels, stroll through botanical gardens and visit a small museum.

✖ Activities

Cycling

Despite frequent rain and hilly terrain, cycling is still a major form of both transportation and recreation in the Seattle area. In 2014 the city finally inaugurated a public bike-sharing scheme, which closed in March 2017 due to lack of ridership. In 2018 several private companies, including Lyft and Lime, began the practice again.

In the city, commuter bike lanes are painted green on many streets, city trails are well maintained, and the friendly and enthusiastic cycling community is happy to share the road. The wildly popular 20-mile Burke-Gilman Trail winds from Ballard to Log Boom Park in Kenmore on Seattle's Eastside. There, it connects with the 11-mile long **Sammamish River Trail**, which winds past the Chateau Ste Michelle winery in Woodinville before terminating at Redmond's Marymoor Park.

Other good places to cycle are around **Green Lake** (☑ 206-684-4075; 7201 E Green Lake Dr N, Green Lake; ⊙ 24hr; 🚍 62), which is congested but pretty, at sublime **Alki Beach** (☑ 206-684-4075; 1702 Alki Ave SW, West Seattle; ⊙ 4am-11:30pm; 🚍 37) or, closer to downtown, through scenic **Myrtle Edwards Park** (☑ 20 6-684-4075; 3130 Alaskan Way, Belltown; ⊙ 24hr; 🚍 33). The latter trail continues through Interbay to Ballard, where it links with the Burke-Gilman.

Anyone planning on cycling in Seattle should pick up a copy of the *Seattle Bicycling Guide Map,* published by the City of Seattle's Transportation Bicycle & Pedestrian Program and available online (www.cityofseattle.net/transportation/bikemaps.htm) and at bike shops.

Water Sports

Seattle is striated with kayak-friendly marine trails. The **Lakes to Locks Water Trail** links Lake Sammamish with Lake Washington, Lake Union and – via the Hiram M Chittenden Locks – Puget Sound. For launching sites and maps, check the website of the Washington Water Trails Association (www.wwta.org).

Northwest Outdoor Center   KAYAKING
(☑ 206-281-9694; www.nwoc.com; 2100 Westlake Ave N, Lake Union; rental per hr kayak/SUP $18/20; ⊙ 10am-8pm Mon-Fri, 9am-6pm Sat & Sun Apr-Sep, closed Mon & Tue Oct-Mar; 🚍 62) Located on the west side of Lake Union, this place rents kayaks and stand up paddleboards (SUPs)

and offers tours and instruction in sea and white-water kayaking.

☞ Tours

★ **Seattle Free Walking Tours**   WALKING
(Map p1034; www.seattlefreewalkingtours.org; 2001 Western Ave, Pike Place) **FREE** A nonprofit tour company that does an intimate two-hour walk taking in Pike Place, the waterfront and Pioneer Square, among other tours. Each tour is 'pay what you can,' and the company notes that comparable walking tours run around $20. Reserve online.

✖ Festivals & Events

Seafair   FAIR
(www.seafair.com; ⊙ Jun-Aug) This waterfront festival is hugely popular and runs in one capacity or another from June through August. Come for music, pirate ships, food stalls and an excuse to be out in the nice weather.

Bumbershoot   PERFORMING ARTS
(www.bumbershoot.com; Seattle Center; 3-day pass from $434; ⊙ Sep) A fair few people – Seattleites or otherwise – would say that this is Seattle's finest festival, with major arts and cultural events at the Seattle Center on the Labor Day weekend in September. Bank on live music, comedy, theater, visual arts and dance, but also bank on crowds and hotels stuffed to capacity. Book well in advance!

🛏 Sleeping

Reserve ahead in summer, when hotels book up and prices tend to skyrocket.

ℹ SEATTLE CITYPASS

If you're going to be in Seattle for a while and plan on seeing its premier attractions, consider buying a Seattle **CityPASS** (www.citypass.com/seattle; per adult/child 5-12yr $99/79). Good for nine days, the pass gets you entry into five sights: the Space Needle, Seattle Aquarium, Argosy Cruises Seattle Harbor Tour, Museum of Pop Culture *or* Woodland Park Zoo and Pacific Science Center *or* Chihuly Garden & Glass. You wind up saving about 49% on admission costs and you never have to stand in line. You can buy one at any of the venues or online.

City Hostel Seattle HOSTEL **$**
(Map p1034; ☎206-706-3255; www.hostelseattle.com; 2327 2nd Ave, Belltown; dm/d from $36/125; 🚭[@]📶; 🚊Westlake) This well-located, boutique 'art hostel' has colorful murals painted by local artists splashed on the walls of every room. There's also a common room, hot tub, in-house movie theater and all-you-can-eat breakfast. Dorms have four or six beds and some are women-only. There are also several private rooms, some with shared bathroom. Guests consistently praise the friendly staff.

Moore Hotel HOTEL **$**
(Map p1034; ☎206-448-4851; www.moorehotel.com; 1926 2nd Ave, Belltown; d with/without bath from $165/117; 📶; 🚌13) Old-world and allegedly haunted, the hip and whimsical Moore is undoubtedly central Seattle's most reliable bargain, offering fixed annual prices for its large stash of simple but cool rooms. Bonuses – aside from the dynamite location – are the cute ground-floor cafe, and zebra- and leopard-skin-patterned carpets.

Hotel Hotel Hostel HOTEL, HOSTEL **$**
(☎206-257-4543; www.hotelhotel.co; 3515 Fremont Ave N, Fremont; dm $34-36, d with/without bath $140/120; 📶; 🚌5) Fremont's only real hotel is a good one, encased in a venerable old building replete with exposed brick and chunky radiators. In true Fremont fashion, Hotel Hotel is technically more of a hostel (with dorms), but it also passes itself off as an economical hotel on account of its private rooms with an assortment of shared and en-suite bathrooms.

The industrial-chic decor means it's comfortable without being fancy. A buffet breakfast is included in the price, and there is a common room and a kitchen.

★**University Inn** BOUTIQUE HOTEL **$$**
(☎206-632-5055; www.universityinnseattle.com; 4140 Roosevelt Way NE; r from $226; [P]❄[@]📶🏊; 🚌74) This spotless, modern, well-located place is good – especially when you factor in the waffles served with the complimentary breakfast. The hotel is four blocks from campus and just three from the bustle of 'the Ave.' The 102 rooms come in three levels of plushness. All of them offer such basics as a coffee maker, hair dryer and wi-fi; some have balconies, sofas and Bluetooth docking stations.

★**Bacon Mansion B&B** B&B **$$**
(☎206-329-1864; www.baconmansion.com; 959 Broadway E, Capitol Hill; r with/without bath $244/189, ste from $269; [P][@]📶; 🚌49) A 1909 Tudor-style mansion whose imposing exterior belies the quirky charm of its friendly hosts, this four-level B&B on a quiet residential street just past the Capitol Hill action is one of the best in the area. Among its charming amenities are a pleasant garden and a grand piano in the main room that guests are invited to play.

Graduate Seattle HOTEL **$$**
(☎206-634-2000; www.graduatehotels.com; 4507 Brooklyn Ave NE; r from $237; [P]❄📶🐾) This new kid on the block brings hip sophistication to the U District's hotel scene. Eclectic furniture and walls full of framed photographs almost make this place feel more like a passed-down vacation home than a new hotel, but then amenities such as the 24-hour gym and incredible rooftop bar bring it all back into focus.

★**Palihotel** BOUTIQUE HOTEL **$$$**
(Map p1034; ☎206-596-0600; www.palisociety.com; 107 Pine St, Downtown; r from $298; ❄📶)

SEATTLE FOR CHILDREN

Make a beeline for the Seattle Center, preferably on the monorail, where food carts, street entertainers, fountains and green spaces will make the day fly by. One essential stop is the **Pacific Science Center** (Map p1034; ☎206-443-2001; www.pacificsciencecenter.org; 200 2nd Ave N, Seattle Center; adult/child $26/18; 🕒10am-5pm Mon-Fri, to 6pm Sat & Sun; 👪; [S]Seattle Center), which entertains and educates with virtual-reality exhibits, laser shows, holograms, an IMAX theater and a planetarium. Parents won't be bored either.

Downtown on Pier 59, **Seattle Aquarium** (Map p1034; ☎206-386-4300; www.seattleaquarium.org; 1483 Alaskan Way, Waterfront; adult/child $35/25; 🕒9:30am-5pm; 👪; 🚊University St) is a fun way to learn about the natural world of the Pacific Northwest. Even better is **Woodland Park Zoo** (☎206-548-2500; www.zoo.org; 5500 Phinney Ave N, Green Lake; adult/child May-Sep $22.95/13.95, Oct-Apr $15.50/10.50; 🕒9:30am-6pm May-Sep, to 4pm Oct-Apr; 👪; 🚌5) in the Green Lake neighborhood, one of Seattle's greatest tourist attractions and consistently rated as one of the top 10 zoos in the country.

The rare new hotel that isn't a utilitarian business tower, Palihotel is an understated boutique (part of a small, but expanding, chain) whose early-20th-century 'forest green walls and overstuffed leather chairs' aesthetic is as chic as it is cozy. Although the theme is antique, the building's remodel ensures 21st-century luxuries like air-conditioning and rain showers.

★ Hotel Monaco
BOUTIQUE HOTEL **$$$**

(Map p1034; ☑206-621-1770; www.monaco-seattle.com; 1101 4th Ave, Downtown; d/ste $293/406; P@🛜🐾; ☑University St) 🌊 Whimsical and with dashes of European elegance, the downtown Monaco is a classic Kimpton hotel whose rooms live up to the hints given off in the illustrious lobby. Bed down amid the bold, graphic decor and reap the perks (complimentary bikes, fitness center, free wine tasting, in-room yoga mats).

Maxwell Hotel
BOUTIQUE HOTEL **$$$**

(Map p1034; ☑206-286-0629; 300 Roy St, Queen Anne; r/ste from $311/371; P✳@🛜🐾; ☑RapidRide D Line) Located in Lower Queen Anne, the Maxwell has a huge designer-chic lobby with a floor mosaic and colorful furnishings that welcomes you with aplomb. Upstairs the slickness continues in 139 gorgeously modern rooms with hardwood floors and Scandinavian bedding. There's a small pool, a gym, free bike rentals and complimentary cupcakes.

Hotel Max
BOUTIQUE HOTEL **$$$**

(Map p1034; ☑206-441-4200; www.hotelmax seattle.com; 620 Stewart St, Belltown; r from $263; P✳@🛜🐾; ☑South Lake Union Streetcar) It's tough to get any hipper than a hotel that has a whole floor dedicated to Seattle's indie Sub Pop record label (that unleashed Nirvana on an unsuspecting world). The 5th floor pays homage to the music with giant grunge-era photos and record players with vinyls in every room. The art theme continues throughout the hotel (there's a Warhol in the lobby).

✖ Eating

The best budget meals are to be found in Pike Place Market (p1032). Take your pick from fresh produce, baked goods, deli items and takeout ethnic foods.

★ Taco Chukis
TACOS **$**

(www.facebook.com/TacosChukis; 2215 E Union St, CD; tacos $2.20-2.75; ☺11am-9pm; ☑2) At the moment in Seattle there are few bites of

food better than the signature taco at Taco Chukis. It's a simple design (juicy pork, guacamole, melted cheese and brilliantly tangy grilled pineapple) that's executed so well you're likely to get into line immediately after finishing to order a couple more.

★ Salumi Artisan Cured Meats
SANDWICHES **$**

(Map p1034; ☑206-621-8772; www.salumicured meats.com; 404 Occidental Ave S, Pioneer Sq; sandwiches $10.50-12.50; ☺11am-3pm Mon-Sat; ☑International District/Chinatown) This well-loved deli used to be known for the long lines at its tiny storefront, and although it has moved to a bigger spot, you can still expect a wait for taste of the legendary Italian-quality salami and cured-meat sandwiches (grilled lamb, pork shoulder, meatballs). You can expect a regular sandwich menu, as well as daily sandwich, soup and pasta specials.

Un Bien
CUBAN **$**

(☑206-588-2040; www.unbienseattle.com; 7302 ½ 15th Ave NW, Ballard; mains $11-16; ☺11am-9pm Wed-Sat, to 8pm Sun; ☑RapidRide D Line) Lines can get long at this Cuban take-out spot far from Ballard's commercial center, but the wait is worth it to finally sink your teeth into a perfectly juicy and tangy pork sandwich. The restaurant is owned by brothers working from family recipes and you can taste the affection in every bite.

★ Bitterroot
BARBECUE **$$**

(☑206-588-1577; www.bitterrootbbq.com; 5239 Ballard Ave NW, Ballard; mains $11-19; ☺11am-2am; ☑40) People come to Bitterroot for two things: smoked meat and whiskey. Thankfully this restaurant with a pleasing modern roadhouse vibe does both exceptionally well. You can get your meat in sandwich form, or by itself with sides like cast-iron cornbread and roasted cauliflower. Likewise, the extensive whiskey menu comes neat or as an expertly mixed craft cocktail.

★ Ma'Ono
HAWAIIAN **$$**

(☑206-935-1075; www.maonoseattle.com; 4437 California Ave SW, West Seattle; mains $12-17; ☺5-10pm Wed & Thu, 5-11pm Fri, 9am-3pm & 5-11pm Sat, 5-10pm Sun; ☑55) The fried chicken sandwich – served on a King's Hawaiian roll with cabbage and a perfectly spicy sauce – at this West Seattle spot is one of the best things between two slices of bread currently available in Seattle. Treat yourself to one during the always-packed brunch with a guava mimosa and side of roasted sweet potato with caramelized lime.

★ Seven Stars Pepper
SICHUAN $$

(Map p1034; ☎206-568-6446; www.sevenstarspepper.com; 1207 S Jackson St, International District; mains $9-20; ⊗11am-3pm & 5-9:30pm Mon-Wed, 11am-9:30pm Thu, to 10pm Fri & Sat, to 9pm Sun; ☐First Hill Streetcar) Don't be put off by Seven Stars Pepper's uninspiring location on the 2nd floor of a run-down strip mall: this Szechuan restaurant is one of the best in the city. Everything on the menu is exceptional, but the hand-cut *dan dan* noodles are a must-order. They are thick and flavorful with just the right amount of chewiness.

Le Pichet
FRENCH $$

(Map p1034; ☎206-256-1499; www.lepichetseattle.com; 1933 1st Ave, Pike Place; dinner mains $22-25; ⊗8am-midnight; ☐Westlake) Say *bonjour* to Le Pichet, just up from Pike Place Market, a cute and very French bistro with pâtés, cheeses, wine, *chocolat* and a refined Parisian feel. Dinner features delicacies such as Niçoise chickpea crepes and Basque seafood stew. The specialty is a roast chicken (for two $45) – just know that there's an hour's wait when you order one.

★ Sitka & Spruce
MODERN AMERICAN $$$

(Map p1034; ☎206-324-0662; www.sitkaandspruce.com; 1531 Melrose Ave, Capitol Hill; plates $16-35; ⊗11:30am-2pm & 5-10pm Tue-Thu, to 9pm Mon, to 11pm Fri, 10am-2pm & 5-11pm Sat, to 9pm Sun; ☐; ☐10) The king of all locavore restaurants, Sitka & Spruce was the pilot project of celebrated Seattle chef Matt Dillon. It has since become something of an institution and a trendsetter, with its country-kitchen decor and a constantly changing menu concocted with ingredients from Dillon's own Vashon Island farm. Sample items include housemade charcuterie and roasted-asparagus-and-liver parfait. Great choice for vegetarians too.

★ Heartwood Provisions
FUSION $$$

(Map p1034; ☎206-582-3505; www.heartwoodsea.com; 1103 1st Ave, Downtown; mains $24-37; ⊗4:30-10pm Sun-Thu, to 11pm Fri & Sat, also 9:30am-2pm Sat & Sun; ☐University St) Cocktails are having a moment as the alcoholic libation du jour in Seattle and nowhere is that more clear than at Heartwood, a handsome restaurant and bar with a menu of mixed drinks that is unmatched. Come for dinner,

where each dish is infused with Southeast Asian flavors and has its own cocktail pairing (optional for an additional $7).

★ Tavolàta
ITALIAN $$$

(Map p1034; ☎206-838-8008; 2323 2nd Ave, Belltown; mains $18-32; ⊗5-11pm; ☐13) Owned by top Seattle chef Ethan Stowell, Tavolàta is a dinner-only, Italian-inspired eatery emphasizing homemade pasta dishes and hearty mains such as a rack of wild boar with fig *mostarda* (a sweet and spicy mustard and fruit sauce). Many consider it among the best Italian spots in the city.

🍷 Drinking & Nightlife

★ Unicorn
BAR

(Map p1034; ☎206-325-6492; www.unicornseattle.com; 1118 E Pike St, Capitol Hill; ⊗2pm-1:45am Mon-Fri, from 11am Sat & Sun; ☐11) Even if Unicorn's circus theme doesn't exactly tickle your fancy, its commitment to the spectacle makes it worth a visit. Cocktails like the Cereal Killer (made with Fruit Loop–flavored vodka) hark back to the joys of giant lollipops and cotton candy, while the colorful explosion of decoration and pinball machine collection are likely to make even hardened cynics smile.

★ Ancient Grounds
CAFE

(Map p1034; ☎206-7749-0747; 1220 1st Ave, Downtown; ⊗7:30am-4:30pm Mon-Fri, noon-6pm Sat; ☐University St) If it's not enough that this cozy coffee nook serves some of the best espresso shots in the city, Ancient Grounds also doubles as a showroom for a well-curated selection of antiques. While waiting for your latte you can pick through a rack of vintage kimonos or peruse a display of wooden masks from indigenous communities of the Pacific Northwest.

★ Saké Nomi
SAKE

(Map p1034; ☎206-467-7253; www.sakenomi.us; 76 S Washington St, Pioneer Sq; flight of 3 $22; ⊗2-10pm Tue, Wed, Fri & Sat, from 5pm Thu, 2-6pm Sun; ☐First Hill Streetcar) Regardless if you're a sake (Japanese rice wine) connoisseur or casual enjoyer, you're likely to expand your palate and your cultural horizons at this cozy retailer and tasting room in Pioneer Sq. The Japanese and American wife-husband duo who run the place have a clear love for what they do, which shows in their wonderfully educational tasting menu.

★Fremont Brewing Company BREWERY

(📞206-420-2407; www.fremontbrewing.com; 1050 N 34th St, Fremont; ⊙11am-9pm; 🚼🐾; 🚌62) 🍃 This microbrewery, in keeping with current trends, sells its wares via an attached tasting room rather than a full-blown pub. Not only is the beer divine (try the seasonal bourbon barrel-aged Abominable), but the industrial-chic tasting room and 'urban beer garden' are highly inclusive spaces, where pretty much everyone in the 'hood comes to hang out at communal tables.

★Zeitgeist Coffee CAFE

(Map p1034; 📞206-583-0497; www.zeitgeistcoffee. com; 171 S Jackson St, Pioneer Sq; ⊙6am-7pm Mon-Fri, from 7am Sat, 8am-6pm Sun; 🐾; 🚋First Hill Streetcar) Possibly Seattle's best (if also busiest) indie coffee bar, Zeitgeist brews smooth *doppio macchiatos* to go with its sweet almond croissants and other luscious baked goods. The atmosphere is trendy industrial, with brick walls and large windows for people-watching. Soups, salads and sandwiches are also on offer.

★Blue Moon BAR

(📞206-675-9116; www.bluemoonseattle.wordpress. com; 712 NE 45th St; ⊙4pm-2am Mon-Fri, from 2pm Sat & Sun; 🚌74) A legendary counter-culture dive that first opened in 1934 to celebrate the repeal of Prohibition, Blue Moon makes much of its former literary patrons – including Dylan Thomas and Allen Ginsberg. The place is agreeably gritty and unpredictable, with graffiti carved into the seats and punk poets likely to stand up and start pontificating at any moment. Frequent live music.

Zig Zag Café COCKTAIL BAR

(Map p1034; 📞206-625-1146; www.zigzagseattle. com; 1501 Western Ave, Pike Place; ⊙5pm-2am; 🚇University St) If you're writing a research project on Seattle's culinary history, you'll need to reserve a chapter for the Zig Zag Café. This is the bar that repopularized the gin-based Jazz Age cocktail 'The Last Word' in the early 2000s. The drink went viral and the Zig Zag's nattily attired mixers were rightly hailed as the city's finest alchemists.

Cloudburst Brewing MICROBREWERY

(Map p1034; 📞206-602-6061; www.cloudburst brew.com; 2116 Western Ave, Belltown; ⊙2-10pm Wed-Fri, noon-10pm Sat & Sun; 🚌13) The brain-child of former experimental brewer at Elysian Brewing, Steve Luke, Cloudburst Brewing became an instant Seattle favorite.

BALLARD'S BARS & BEER CULTURE

Ballard's bars, breweries and pubs are almost a neighborhood in their own right. If you want the local gossip and unique libations of every stripe this is where you should gravitate. Look out for historic, century-old bars, modern cocktail lounges, inventive brewpubs – massive to nano – and gastropubs with carefully configured retro decor.

Replicating the success of Luke's past brewing creations, Cloudburst Brewing features hoppy beers with sassy names, and the bare-bones tasting room is always packed to the gills with beer fans who want to support craft beer in Seattle.

Panama Hotel Tea & Coffee House CAFE

(Map p1034; 📞206-515-4000; www.panamahotel. net; 607 S Main St, International District; tea $3-6; ⊙8am-9pm; 🐾; 🚋First Hill Streetcar) The intensely atmospheric teahouse inside the Panama Hotel has such a thoroughly back-in-time feel that you'll be reluctant to pull out your laptop (although there is wi-fi). It's in a National Treasure–designated 1910 building containing the only remaining Japanese bathhouse in the US, and doubles as a memorial to the neighborhood's Japanese residents forced into internment camps during WWII.

No Anchor BAR

(Map p1034; 📞206-448-2610; www.noanchorbar. com; 2505 2nd Ave, Belltown; ⊙noon-11pm Mon-Thu, noon-midnight Fri, 11am-midnight Sat, 11am-11pm Sun; 🚌13) Most things on the menu at No Anchor feel like a big risk, and they often pay off. The cocktails feature ingredients such as maple syrup and toasted coconut, while the menu of bar bites has eccentric offerings such as pickled mussels. Beer novices will feel welcomed by the large draft menu featuring a 'what to pick' guide.

☆ Entertainment

Consult *The Stranger*, *Seattle Weekly* or the daily papers for listings. Tickets for big events are available at TicketMaster (www. ticketmaster.com).

★Crocodile LIVE MUSIC

(Map p1034; 📞206-441-4618; www.thecrocodile. com; 2200 2nd Ave, Belltown; 🚌13) Nearly old

GRUNGE: PUNK'S WEST COAST NIRVANA

Synthesizing Generation X angst with a questionable approach to personal hygiene, the music popularly categorized as 'grunge' first stage dived onto Seattle's scene in the early 1990s. The anger had been fermenting for years – not purely in Seattle but also in its sprawling satellite towns and suburbs. Some said it was inspired by the weather, others cited the Northwest's geographic isolation. It didn't matter which. Armed with dissonant chords and dark, sometimes ironic lyrics, a disparate collection of bands stepped sneeringly up to the microphone to preach a new message from a city that all of the touring big-name rock acts serially chose to ignore. There were Screaming Trees from collegiate Ellensburg, the Melvins from rainy Montesano and Nirvana from the timber town of Aberdeen, while Hole frontwoman Courtney Love had ties to Olympia and the converging members of Pearl Jam came from across the nation.

Historically, grunge's roots lay in West Coast punk, a musical subgenre that first found a voice in Portland, OR, in the late 1970s, led by the Wipers, whose leather-clad followers congregated in legendary dive bars such as Satyricon. Another musical blossoming occurred in Olympia, WA, in the early 1980s, where DIY musicians Beat Happening invented 'lo-fi' and coyly mocked the corporate establishment. Mixing in elements of heavy metal and scooping up the fallout of an itchy youth culture, Seattle quickly became alternative music's pulpit, spawning small, clamorous venues where boisterous young bands more interested in playing rock music than 'performing' could lose themselves in a melee of excitement and noise. It was a raucous, energetic scene characterized by stage diving, crowd-surfing and barely tuned guitars, but driven by raw talent and some surprisingly catchy tunes, the music filled a vacuum.

A crucial element in grunge's elevation to superstardom was Sub Pop Records, an independent Seattle label whose guerrilla marketing tactics created a flurry of hype to promote its ragged stable of cacophonous bands. In August 1988, Sub Pop released the seminal single 'Touch Me I'm Sick' by Mudhoney, a watershed moment. The noise got noticed, most importantly by the British music press, whose punk-savvy journalists quickly reported the birth of a 'Seattle sound,' later christened grunge by the brand-hungry media. Suitably inspired, the Seattle scene began to prosper, spawning literally hundreds of new bands, all cemented in the same DIY, anti-fashion, audience-embracing tradition. Of note were sludgy Soundgarden, who later went on to win two Grammys; metal-esque Alice in Chains; and the soon-to-be-mega Nirvana and Pearl Jam. By the dawn of the 1990s, every rebellious slacker with the gas money was coming to Seattle to hit the clubs. It was more than exciting.

What should have been grunge's high point came in October 1992, when Nirvana's second album, the hugely accomplished *Nevermind,* knocked Michael Jackson off the number-one spot, but the kudos ultimately killed it. After several years of railing against the mainstream, Nirvana and grunge had been incorporated into it. The media blitzed in, grunge fashion spreads appeared in *Vanity Fair* and half-baked singers from Seattle only had to cough to land a record contract. Many recoiled, most notably Nirvana vocalist and songwriter Kurt Cobain, whose drug abuse ended in suicide in his new Madison Park home in 1994. Other bands soldiered on, but the spark – which had burnt so brightly while it lasted – was gone. By the mid-1990s, grunge was officially dead.

---

enough to be called a Seattle institution, the Crocodile is a clamorous 560-capacity venue that first opened in 1991, just in time to grab the coattails of the grunge explosion. Everyone who's anyone in Seattle's alt-music scene has since played here, including a famous occasion in 1992 when Nirvana appeared unannounced, supporting Mudhoney.

★ **A Contemporary Theatre**　THEATER
(ACT; Map p1034; ☎206-292-7676; www.act theatre.org; 700 Union St, Downtown; ☒University

St) One of the three big theater companies in the city, the ACT fills its $30 million home at Kreielsheimer Pl with performances by Seattle's best thespians and occasional big-name actors. Terraced seating surrounds a central stage and the interior has gorgeous architectural embellishments.

Big Picture　CINEMA
(Map p1034; ☎206-256-0566; www.thebigpic ture.net; 2505 1st Ave, Belltown; tickets $14.50) It's easy to miss Big Picture when exploring

Seattle's Belltown neighborhood. For those in the know, it's an 'underground' cinema experience with affordable tickets of first-run screenings in an intimate setting. Order a cocktail from the bar (where you can linger before your showtime), and then another to be delivered mid-screening.

Neumos LIVE MUSIC
(Map p1034; ☑ 206-709-9442; www.neumos.com; 925 E Pike St, Capitol Hill; ☒ First Hill Streetcar) This punk, hip-hop and alternative-music joint is, along with the Crocodile (p1041) in Belltown, one of Seattle's most revered small music venues. Its storied list of former performers is too long to include, but if they're cool and passing through Seattle, they've probably played here. The audience space can get hot and sweaty, and even smelly, but that's rock and roll.

Tractor Tavern LIVE MUSIC
(☑ 206-789-3599; www.tractortavern.com; 5213 Ballard Ave NW, Ballard; tickets $8-20; ☒ 8pm-2am; ☒ 40) One of Seattle's premier venues for folk and acoustic music, the Tractor books local songwriters and regional bands, plus quality touring acts. Music tends to run toward country, rockabilly, folk, bluegrass and old-time. It's an intimate place with a small stage and great sound; occasional square dancing is frosting on the cake.

Intiman Theatre THEATER
(Map p1034; ☑ 206-441-7178; www.intiman.org; 201 Mercer St, Seattle Center; tickets from $25; ☒; ☒ Seattle Center) A beloved theater company based at the Cornish Playhouse in the Seattle Center. Artistic director Jennifer Zeyl curates magnificent stagings of Shakespeare and Ibsen as well as work by emerging artists.

🛍 Shopping

★ Elliott Bay Book Company BOOKS
(Map p1034; ☑ 206-624-6600; www.elliottbay book.com; 1521 10th Ave, Capitol Hill; ☒ 10am-10pm Mon-Thu, to 11pm Fri & Sat, to 9pm Sun; ☒ First Hill Streetcar) Seattle's most beloved bookstore offers more than 150,000 titles in a large, airy, wood-beamed space with cozy nooks that can inspire hours of serendipitous browsing. In addition to the size, the staff recommendations and displays of books by local authors make this place extra special. Bibliophiles will be further satisfied with regular book readings and signings.

★ Herban Legends DISPENSARY
(Map p1034; ☑ 206-849-5596; www.herbanlegends. com; 55 Bell St, Belltown; ☒ 8am-11:45pm; ☒ 13) Herban Legends is both a brilliantly silly pun and one of Seattle's best dispensaries. It manages to feel very professionally run while maintaining a breezy vibe missing from other weed shops in town. The staff are always ready with a great recommendation and there is even a merch shop at the front should you want a coffee mug.

Lucca Great Finds GIFTS & SOUVENIRS
(☑ 206-782-7337; www.luccagreatfinds.com; 5332 Ballard Ave NW, Ballard; ☒ 11am-6pm Mon-Fri, to 7pm Sat, 10am-5pm Sun) One of the best things about this Ballard boutique is that it offers two shopping experiences: in the front is a chic PNW-themed homewares store that will have you redesigning your apartment in your head while you browse, and in the back is a stationery shop with reams of enviably stylish wrapping paper and rows of charming greeting cards.

ℹ Information

EMERGENCY & MEDICAL SERVICES

Harborview Medical Center (☑ 206-744-3000; www.uwmedicine.org/harborview; 325 9th Ave, First Hill; ☒ Broadway & Terrace) Full medical care, with emergency room.

Seattle Police (☑ 206-625-5011; www.seattle. gov/police)

MEDIA

KEXP 90.3 FM (stream at http://kexp.org) Legendary independent music and community station.

Seattle Magazine (www.seattlemag.com) A slick monthly lifestyle magazine.

Seattle Times (www.seattletimes.com) The state's largest daily paper.

TOURIST INFORMATION

Visit Seattle (Map p1034; ☑ 206-461-5800; www.visitseattle.org; 701 Pike St, Downtown; ☒ 9am-5pm daily Jun-Sep, Mon-Fri Oct-May; ☒ Westlake) Information desk inside the Washington State Convention Center's 1st-floor lobby. You can pick up leaflets even when the desk is closed.

ℹ Getting There & Away

AIR

Sea-Tac International Airport (SEA; ☑ 206-787-5388; www.portseattle.org/Sea-Tac; 17801 International Blvd; ☒) Located 13 miles south of downtown Seattle, Sea-Tac has flights all over the US and to some international destinations. Amenities include restaurants, money changers, baggage storage, car-rental agencies, a cell (mobile) phone waiting area (for drivers waiting to pick up arriving passengers) and free wi-fi.

BOAT

The **Victoria Clipper** (206-448-5000; www. clippervacations.com; 2701 Alaskan Way, Belltown) ferry from Victoria, BC, docks at Pier 69 just south of the Olympic Sculpture Park in Belltown. **Washington State Ferries** (Map p1034; www.bainbridgeisland.com; 801 Alaskan Way, Pier 52, Waterfront; foot passenger/bike/car $8.50/9.50/19.15) services from Bremerton and Bainbridge Island use Pier 52.

BUS

Various intercity coaches serve Seattle and there is more than one drop-off point – it all depends on which company you are using.

Bellair Airporter Shuttle (Map p1034; 866-235-5247; www.airporter.com; 705 Pike St, Downtown) Runs buses to Yakima, Bellingham and Anacortes, and stops at King Street Station (for Yakima) and the Washington State Convention Center (for Bellingham and Anacortes).

Cantrail (Map p1034; www.cantrail.com; adult/child $45/23) Amtrak's bus connector runs four daily services to Vancouver (one way from $42) and picks up and drops off at King Street Station.

Greyhound (206-628-5526; www.greyhound.com; 503 S Royal Brougham Way, SoDo; Stadium) Connects Seattle with cities all over the country, including Chicago (from $157 one way, two days, three daily), San Francisco ($91, 20 hours, two daily) and Vancouver (Canada; $18, four hours, three daily). The company has its own terminal just south of King Street Station in SoDo, accessible on the Central Link light rail (Stadium Station).

Quick Shuttle (Map p1034; 800-665-2122; www.quickcoach.com; tickets $29-59;) Fast and efficient, with five to six daily buses to Vancouver ($43). Picks up at the Best Western Executive Inn in Taylor Ave N near the Seattle Center. Grab the monorail or walk to downtown.

TRAIN

King Street Station (206-296-0100; www. amtrak.com; 303 S Jackson St, International District) Amtrak serves Seattle's King Street Station. Three main routes run through town: the Amtrak Cascades (connecting to Vancouver, Canada; and Portland and Eugene, OR); the very scenic Coast Starlight (connecting Seattle to Oakland and Los Angeles, CA) and the Empire Builder (a cross-continental to Chicago, IL).

❶ Getting Around

TO/FROM THE AIRPORT

There are a number of options for making the 13-mile trek from the airport to downtown Seattle. The most efficient is the light-rail service run by **Sound Transit** (www.soundtransit. org). It runs every 10 to 15 minutes between 5am and midnight; the ride between Sea-Tac Airport and downtown (Westlake Center) takes 36 minutes. There are additional stops in Pioneer Sq and the International District; the service was extended to Capitol Hill and the U District in 2016.

Shuttle Express (425-981-7000; www. shuttleexpress.com) has a help desk, and pickup and drop-off point on the 3rd floor of the airport garage. It offers rideshare services that are more comfortable than public transit, but less expensive than a cab.

Taxis are available at the parking garage on the 3rd floor. Fares to downtown start at around $55.

PUBLIC TRANSPORTATION

Buses are operated by **King County Metro Transit** (206-553-3000; http://kingcounty.gov/depts/transportation/metro.aspx), part of the King County Department of Transportation. The website has schedules, maps and a trip planner.

Pay as you enter the bus; there's a flat fee of $2.75/1.50 per adult/child; you'll receive a slip that entitles you to a transfer until the time noted.

Monorail (206-905-2620; www.seattlemonorail.com; adult/youth $2.25/1.25; 7:30am-11pm Mon-Fri, 8:30am-11pm Sat & Sun) This cool futuristic tram, built for the 1962 World's Fair, travels only between two stops: Seattle Center and Westlake Center. Fares are $2.25/1.25 per adult/child. Hours change slightly throughout the year, check the website for up-to-date info.

Seattle Streetcar (www.seattlestreetcar.org; $2.25) Two lines. One runs from downtown Seattle (Westlake) to South Lake Union; the other goes from Pioneer Sq via the International District, the Central District and First Hill to Capitol Hill. Stops allow connections with numerous bus routes. Trams run approximately every 15 minutes throughout the day.

TAXI

All Seattle taxi cabs operate at the same rate, set by King County: $2.60 at meter drop, then $2.50 per mile.

Seattle Orange Cab (206-522-8800; www. orangecab.net)

Seattle Yellow Cab (206-622-6500; www. seattleyellowcab.com)

STITA Taxi (206-246-9999; www.stitataxi. com)

Olympia

Small in size but big in clout, Washington state capital Olympia is a political, musical and outdoor powerhouse. Look no further than the street-side buskers on 4th Ave, the smartly attired bureaucrats marching across the lawns of the resplendent state legislature and the Gore-Tex-clad outdoor fiends overnighting before rugged sorties into the Olympic Mountains. Progressive Evergreen State College has long lent the place an artsy turn (creator of *The Simpsons* Matt Groening studied here), while the dive bars and pawn shops of downtown provided an original pulpit for riot-grrrl music and grunge.

Olympia's economy has struggled in the wake of the timber industry's collapse, with increasing homelessness among the knock-on effects. But while it may have a few rough edges, it's still a fun little city.

⊙ Sights

Washington State Capitol LANDMARK
(☏360-902-8880; www.olympiawa.gov/community/visiting-the-capitol.aspx; 416 Sid Snyder Ave SW; ⊙7am-5:30pm Mon-Fri, 11am-4pm Sat & Sun) **FREE** Olympia's capitol complex is set in a 30-acre park overlooking Capitol Lake with the Olympic Mountains glistening in the background. The campus' crowning glory is the magnificent **Legislative Building**. Completed in 1927, it's a dazzling display of craning columns and polished marble, topped by a 287ft dome that is only slightly smaller than its namesake in Washington, DC. Free, 50-minute tours are available on the hour 10am to 3pm weekdays, 11am Saturday and Sunday, starting just inside the main doors.

Olympia Farmers Market MARKET
(☏360-352-9096; www.olympiafarmersmarket.com; 700 N Capitol Way; ⊙10am-3pm Thu-Sun Apr-Oct, Sat & Sun Nov & Dec, Sat Jan-Mar) Second only to Seattle's Pike Place in size and character, Olympia's local market is a great place to shop for organic herbs, vegetables, flowers, baked goods and the famous specialty: oysters.

⊨ Sleeping & Eating

Most of Olympia's cool, budget-friendly options have been transformed into much-needed affordable housing, but there are a lot of private-room options (Airbnb etc), plus the usual chain hotels (not a great bargain here) and some nice B&Bs.

Swantown Inn B&B $$
(☏360-753-9123; www.swantowninn.com; 1431 11th Ave; r from $159; ❋ 🅟) In the tradition of Washington state B&Bs, the Swantown Inn features great personal service and meticulous attention to detail in an 1887 Queen Anne–style mansion that's listed on the state historical register. Within sight of the imposing capitol dome, there are four elegantly furnished rooms, and a formidable homemade breakfast.

★**Traditions Cafe &
World Folk Art** HEALTH FOOD $
(☏360-705-2819; www.traditionsfairtrade.com; 300 5th Ave SW; mains $6-12; ⊙9am-6pm Mon-Sat, 11am-5pm Sun; 🅟) 🍴 This comfortable hippie enclave at the edge of Heritage Park offers fresh salads and tasty, healthy sandwiches (smoked salmon with lemon-tahini dressing is a winner), coffee drinks, herbal teas, local ice cream, beer and wine. Posters advertise community-action events, and in the corner is a 'Peace and Social Justice Lending Library.' It's attached to an eclectic folk-art store.

❶ Information

The **State Capitol Visitor Center** (☏360-902-8880; www.olympiawa.gov/community/visiting-the-capitol.aspx; 103 Sid Snyder Ave SW; ⊙9am-5pm Mon-Fri), run by the Olympia-Lacey-Tumwater Visitor & Convention Bureau, offers information on the capitol campus, the Olympia area and Washington state. There's another visitor information office inside the main doors of the Legislative Building.

Olympic Peninsula

Surrounded on three sides by sea and exhibiting many of the characteristics of a full-blown island, the remote Olympic Peninsula is about as 'wild' and 'west' as America gets. What it lacks in cowboys it makes up for in rare, endangered wildlife and dense primeval forest. The peninsula's roadless interior is largely given over to the notoriously wet Olympic National Park, while the margins are the preserve of loggers, Native American reservations and a smattering of small but interesting settlements, most notably Port Townsend. Equally untamed is the western coastline, America's isolated end point, where tempestuous ocean and misty old-growth Pacific rainforest meet in aqueous harmony.

Olympic National Park

Declared a national monument in 1909 and a national park in 1938, the 1406-sq-mile **Olympic National Park** (www.nps.gov/olym; 7-day access per vehicle $30, pedestrian/cyclist $15, 1yr unlimited entry $55) shelters a unique rainforest, copious glaciated mountain peaks and a 57-mile strip of Pacific coastal wilderness that was added to the park in 1953. One of North America's great wilderness areas, most of it remains relatively untouched by human habitation. Opportunities for independent exploration in this huge backcountry region abound, be they for hiking, fishing, kayaking or skiing.

EASTERN ENTRANCES

The graveled Dosewallips River Rd follows the river from Hwy 101 (turnoff approximately 1km north of Dosewallips State Park); due to a washout, the gravel Dosewallips River Rd now ends just 8.5 miles in from Hwy 101, where hiking and bicycle trails begin. Even hiking smaller portions of the two long-distance paths, including the 14.9 mile Dosewallips River Trail, with views of glaciated **Mt Anderson**, is reason enough to visit the valley. Another eastern entry for hikers is the **Staircase Ranger Station** (☏ 360-877-5569; ⊙ May-Oct), just inside the national-park boundary, 15 miles from Hoodsport on Hwy 101. Two campgrounds along the eastern edge of the national park are popular: **Dosewallips State Park** (☏ 888-226-7688; www.parks.state. wa.us/499/dosewallips; 306996 Hwy 101; primitive tent sites $12, standard tent sites $27-37, RV sites $30-45) and **Skokomish Park Lake Cushman** (☏ 360-877-5760; www.skokomishpark.com; 7211 N Lake Cushman Rd, Hoodsport; tent/RV sites from $33/52; ⊙ late May-early Sep). Both have running water, flush toilets and some RV hookups. Reservations are accepted.

NORTHERN ENTRANCES

The park's easiest – and hence most popular – entry point is at **Hurricane Ridge**, 18 miles south of Port Angeles. At the road's end, an interpretive center gives a stupendous view of Mt Olympus (7965ft) and dozens of other peaks. The 5200ft altitude can mean you'll hit inclement weather, and the winds here (as the name suggests) can be ferocious. Aside from various summer trekking opportunities, the area maintains the small, family-friendly **Hurricane Ridge Ski & Snowboard Area** (www.hurricaneridge.com;

all-lift day pass $30-40; ⊙ 10am-4pm Sat & Sun mid-Dec–Mar).

Popular for boating and fishing is **Lake Crescent**, the site of the park's oldest and most reasonably priced **lodge** (☏ 888-896-3818; www.olympicnationalparks.com; 416 Lake Crescent Rd; lodge r from $139, cottage from $245; ⊙ May-Nov, limited availability winter; P ♿ 🐾 🍴). Sumptuous Northwestern-style food is served in the lodge's ecofriendly restaurant. From **Storm King Ranger Station** (☏ 360-928-3380; 343 Barnes Point Rd; ⊙ May-Sep) on the lake's south shore, a 1-mile hike climbs through old-growth forest to Marymere Falls.

Along the Sol Duc River, the **Sol Duc Hot Springs Resort** (☏ 360-327-3583; www.olym picnationalparks.com; 12076 Sol Duc Hot Springs Rd, Port Angeles; cabins from $200; ⊙ Mar-Oct; ♿ 🐾) ✎ has lodging, dining, massage and, of course, hot-spring pools, as well as great day hikes.

WESTERN ENTRANCES

Isolated by distance and home of one of the country's rainiest microclimates, the Pacific side of the Olympics remains the wildest. Only US 101 offers access to its noted temperate rainforests and untamed coastline. The **Hoh River Rainforest**, at the end of the 19-mile Hoh River Rd, is a Tolkienesque maze of dripping ferns and moss-draped trees. The **Hoh Rain Forest Visitor Center** (☏ 360-374-6925; ⊙ 9am-4:30pm Sep-Jun, to 6pm Jul & Aug) has information on guided walks and longer backcountry hikes. The attached **campground** (☏ 360-374-6925; www.nps.gov/olym/planyourvisit/camping.htm; campsites $20; ⊙ year-round) has no hookups or showers, and it's first-come, first-served.

A little to the south lies **Lake Quinault**, a beautiful glacial lake surrounded by forested peaks. It's popular for fishing, boating and swimming, and is surrounded by some of the nation's oldest trees. **Lake Quinault Lodge** (☏ 360-288-2900; www.olympicnational parks.com; 345 S Shore Rd; r $250-450; ♿ 🐾 🍴), a luxury classic of 1920s 'parkitecture,' has a massive fireplace, a manicured cricket-pitch-quality lawn and a dignified lakeview restaurant serving upscale American cuisine. For a cheaper sleep nearby, try the ultrafriendly **Quinault River Inn** (☏ 360-288-2237; www.quinaultriverinn.com; 8 River Dr; r $175, RV site $50; ⊖ ♿ 🐾 🍴) in Amanda Park, a favorite with anglers.

A number of short hikes begin just outside the Lake Quinault Lodge, or you cantry the longer **Enchanted Valley Trail**, a medium-grade 13-miler that begins from the Graves Creek Ranger Station at the end of South Shore Rd and climbs up to a large meadow resplendent with wildflowers and copses of alder trees.

ℹ Information

The park entry fee is $10/25 per person/vehicle, valid for one week and payable at park entrances. Many park visitor centers double as United States Forestry Service (USFS) ranger stations, where you can pick up permits for wilderness camping ($8).

Forks Chamber of Commerce (☏ 360-374-2531; www.forkswa.com; 1411 S Forks Ave; ⊘ 10am-5pm Mon-Sat, 11am-4pm Sun, to 4pm Mon-Sat, 11am-4pm Sun winter; ☏)

Olympic National Park Visitor Center (☏ 360-565-3130; www.nps.gov/olym; 3002 Mt Angeles Rd; ⊘ 9am-6pm Jul & Aug, to 4pm Sep-Jun)

USFS Headquarters (☏ 360-956-2402; www.fs.fed.us/r6/olympic; 1835 Black Lake Blvd SW; ⊘ 8am-4:30pm Mon-Fri)

Port Townsend

Inventive eateries, elegant *fin de siècle* hotels and an unusual stash of year-round festivals make Port Townsend an Olympic Peninsula rarity: a weekend vacation that doesn't require hiking boots. Cut off from the rest of the area by eight bucolic miles of two-lane highway, this is not the spot to base yourself for national-park exploration unless you don't mind driving a lot. Instead, settle in and enjoy one of the prettiest towns in the state.

◉ Sights

Fort Worden State Park   STATE PARK
(☏ 360-344-4412; www.parks.state.wa.us/511/fort-worden; 200 Battery Way; ⊘ 6:30am-dusk Apr-Oct, 8am-dusk Nov-Mar) FREE This attractive park located within Port Townsend's city limits is the remains of a large fortification system constructed in the 1890s to protect the strategically important Puget Sound area from outside attack – supposedly from the Spanish during the 1898 war. Sharp-eyed film buffs might recognize the area as the backdrop for the movie *An Officer and a Gentleman.*

Visitors can arrange tours of the **Commanding Officer's Quarters** (☏ 360-385-1003; Fort Worden State Park, 200 Battery Way; adult/child $6/1; ⊘ tours by appointment), a 12-bedroom mansion. You will also find the **Puget Sound Coast Artillery Museum** (www.coastartillery museum.org; adult/child $4/2; ⊘ 11am-4pm),

which tells the story of early Pacific coastal fortifications. And there are cultural and musical programs year-round at the **Centrum** (www.centrum.org; Fort Worden State Park).

Hikes lead along the headland to **Point Wilson Lighthouse Station** and some wonderful windswept beaches. On the park's fishing pier is the **Port Townsend Marine Science Center** (☏ 360-385-5582; www.ptmsc.org; 532 Battery Way; adult/child $5/3; ⊘ noon-5pm Fri-Sun Apr-Oct; ⚐), featuring four touch tanks and kid-friendly interpretive programs. There are also several camping and lodging possibilities.

🛏 Sleeping & Eating

Manresa Castle   HISTORIC HOTEL $
(☏ 360-385-5750; www.manresacastle.com; cnr 7th & Sheridan Sts; d from $75, ste $149-229; ☏) One of Port Townsend's signature buildings has been turned into a historic hotel-restaurant that's light on fancy gimmicks but heavy on period authenticity. This 40-room mansion, built by the town's first mayor, sits high on a bluff above the port and is one of the first buildings to catch your eye as you arrive by ferry.

★ **Palace Hotel**   HISTORIC HOTEL $$
(☏ 360-385-0773; www.palacehotelpt.com; 1004 Water St; r from $150; ☏☏) Built in 1889, this beautiful Victorian building was once a brothel run by the locally notorious Madame Marie, who did business out of the 2nd-floor corner suite. It's been reincarnated as an attractive, character-filled period hotel with antique furnishings (plus all the modern amenities). Pleasant common spaces; kitchenettes available. The cheapest rooms share a bathroom. Rates are higher on festival weekends.

Doc's Marina Grill   AMERICAN $$
(☏ 360-344-3627; www.docsgrill.com; 141 Hudson St; mains $13-28; ⊘ 11am-11pm) With a great location by Port Townsend's marina, Doc's offers something for everyone. There are burgers, sandwiches, fish-and-chips, various salads, pastas, steaks, seafood and a few vegetarian options. It's housed in a historic building that was a nurses' barracks back in the 1940s.

★ **Finistere**   FRENCH $$$
(☏ 360-344-8127; www.restaurantfinistere.com; 1025 Lawrence St; dinner mains $24-34, tasting menu $50; ⊘ 3-9pm Wed-Fri, 10am-2pm & 3-9pm Sat & Sun) When Sweet Laurette (formerly in this location) closed, local foodies despaired, but Finistere is a worthy replacement. With

PACIFIC NORTHWEST OLYMPIC PENINSULA

a staff whose experience includes Per Se, Canlis, Tilth and other swoon-inducing restaurant names, you expect (and get) a high level of food and service: think saffron risotto with seafood, rabbit lasagna, steak tartare, multiple cheese-plate options, and smoked-salmon tartine for brunch.

❶ Information

Visitor Center (☏360-385-2722; www. ptchamber.org; 2409 Jefferson St; ⏱9am-5pm Mon-Fri, 10am-4pm Sat & Sun) Pick up a useful walking-tour map and guide to the downtown historic district here.

❶ Getting There & Away

Washington State Ferries (☏206-464-6400; www.wsdot.wa.gov/ferries/; car & driver/passenger $11.90/3.45) operates daily trips about every 90 minutes (more in high season) to Coupeville on Whidbey Island from the downtown terminal (35 minutes).

Port Angeles

One might wonder if Port Angeles suffers from abandonment issues. People come here mainly to leave: whether by ferry to Victoria, Canada, or on excursions into the northern parts of Olympic National Park. Most of the town – propped up by the lumber industry and backed by the steep-sided Olympic Mountains – is strictly utilitarian, but the downtown core near the ferry dock has plenty of charm.

🏃 Activities

The **Olympic Discovery Trail** (www.olympic discoverytrail.com) is a 30-mile off-road hiking and cycling trail between Port Angeles and Sequim, starting at the end of Ediz Hook, the sand spit that loops around the bay. Bikes can be rented at **Sound Bikes & Kayaks** (☏360-457-1240; www.soundbikeskayaks. com; 120 E Front St; bike rental per hr/day $10/40; ⏱10am-6pm Mon-Sat, 11am-4pm Sun).

🛏 Sleeping & Eating

Downtown Hotel HOTEL $
(☏360-565-1125; www.portangelesdowntown hotel.com; 101 E Front St; d with/without bath $80/60; ❋🐾) Nothing special on the outside but surprisingly spacious and tidy within, this no-frills, family-run place down by the ferry launch is Port Angeles' secret bargain. The dated but comfy rooms are decked out in wicker and wood, and several have water views. The cheapest rooms share

a bathroom in the hallway. The soundproofing isn't great, but the location is tops.

Olympic Lodge HOTEL $$
(☏360-452-2993; www.olympiclodge.com; 140 Del Guzzi Dr; d from $140; ❋@☎☒) This is the most comfortable place in town, offering gorgeous rooms, an on-site bistro, a swimming pool with hot tub, and complimentary cookies and soup in the afternoon. Prices vary widely depending on day and month.

★ **Next Door Gastropub** AMERICAN $$
(☏360-504-2613; www.nextdoorgastropub. com; 113 W First St; burgers $13-16, mains $11-24; ⏱11am-midnight Mon-Thu, 11am-1am Fri & Sat, 10am-midnight Sun) Arguably the best place to eat on the peninsula and definitely serving the best burger (go for the Mrs Newton with bacon, fig jam and Brie), this small, lively pub is like a little slice of Portland someone dropped here. It's no secret, so expect to wait a *looong* time for a table. Great beer list and a Sunday brunch.

❶ Information

Port Angeles Visitor Center (☏360-452-2363; www.portangeles.org; 121 E Railroad Ave; ⏱9:30am-5:30pm Mon-Fri, 10am-5:30pm Sat, noon-3pm Sun May-Sep, 10am-5pm Mon-Sat, noon-3pm Sun Oct-Apr) Adjacent to the ferry terminal, this small office is loaded with brochures and staffed by enthusiastic volunteers.

❶ Getting There & Away

Clallam Transit (☏360-452-4511; www. clallamtransit.com; fares per person $1-10, day pass from $3) Buses go to Forks and Sequim, where they link up with other transit buses that circumnavigate the Olympic Peninsula.

Coho Vehicle Ferry (☏888-993-3779; www. cohoferry.com; car & driver one way $66, foot passenger $19) Runs to/from Victoria, Canada (1½ hours, twice daily, four times daily in summer).

Dungeness Line (☏360-417-0700; www. dungeness-line.com; Gateway Transit Center, 123 E Front St; one way to Seattle from $39) Runs buses twice a day between Port Angeles, Sequim, Port Townsend, downtown Seattle and Seattle-Tacoma International Airport.

Northwest Peninsula

Several Native American reservations cling to the extreme northwest corner of the continent and are welcoming to visitors. The small weather-beaten settlement of **Neah Bay** on Hwy 112 is home to the Makah Indian Reservation, whose **Makah Museum**

(☑360-645-2711; www.makahmuseum.com; 1880 Bayview Ave; adult/child 5yr & under $6/free; ⊙10am-5pm) displays artifacts from one of North America's most significant archaeological finds, the 500-year-old Makah village of Ozette. Several miles beyond the museum, a short boardwalk trail leads to stunning **Cape Flattery**, a 300ft promontory that marks the most northwesterly point in the lower 48 states.

Convenient to the Hoh River Rainforest and the Olympic coastline is **Forks**, a one-horse lumber town that's now more famous for its *Twilight* paraphernalia. It's a central town for exploring Olympic National Park; a good accommodation choice is the **Miller Tree Inn** (☑360-374-6806; www.millertreeinn. com; 654 E Division St; r from $175; 🐾🐕).

Northwest Washington

Wedged between Seattle, the Cascades and Canada, northwest Washington draws influences from three sides. Its urban hub is collegiate Bellingham, while its outdoor highlight is the pastoral San Juan Islands, an extensive archipelago that glimmers like a sepia-toned snapshot from another era. Anacortes is the main hub for ferries to the San Juan Islands and Victoria, Canada.

Whidbey Island

While not as detached (there's a bridge connecting it to adjacent Fidalgo Island at its northernmost point) or nonconformist as the San Juans, Whidbey Island is almost as quiet and pastoral. Having six state parks is a bonus, along with a plethora of B&Bs, two historic fishing villages (Langley and Coupeville), famously good clams and a thriving artist's community.

Deception Pass State Park (☑360-675-2417; www.parks.state.wa.us/497/deception-pass; 41229 N State Hwy 20; day pass $10; ⊙dawn-dusk) straddles the eponymous steep-sided strait that flows between Whidbey and Fidalgo Islands, and incorporates lakes, islands, campsites and 38 miles of hiking trails.

Ebey's Landing National Historical Reserve (☑360-678-6084; www.nps.gov/ebla; 162 Cemetery Rd, Coupeville) `FREE` comprises 17,400 acres encompassing working farms, sheltered beaches, two state parks and the town of **Coupeville**. This small settlement is one of Washington's oldest towns and has an attractive seafront, antique stores and a number of old inns, including the **Captain**

Whidbey Inn (☑360-678-4097; www.captain whidbey.com; 2072 W Captain Whidbey Inn Rd; r/cabins from $205/420; 🐾), a newly updated log-built inn dating to 1907. For the famous fresh local clams, head to **Christopher's** (☑360-678-5480; www.christopheronwhidbey. com; 103 NW Coveland St; lunch mains $12-16, dinner mains $16-26; ⊙11:30am-2pm & 5-8pm Sun, Mon, Wed & Thu, to 8:30pm Fri & Sat).

🛈 Getting There & Around

Regular **Washington State Ferries** (WSF; ☑888-808-7977; www.wsdot.wa.gov/ferries) link Clinton to Mukilteo and Coupeville to Port Townsend. Free **Island Transit** (☑360-678-7771; www.islandtransit.org) buses run the length of Whidbey every hour daily, except Sundays, from the Clinton ferry dock.

Bellingham

Welcome to a green, liberal and famously livable settlement with a distinctively libertine, nothing-is-too-weird ethos. Mild in both manners and weather, the city is an unlikely alliance of espresso-sipping students, venerable retirees and all-weather triathletes, with brewpubs on every corner. Bellingham's downtown has been revitalized in recent years with intra-urban trails, stylishly refurbished warehouses, independent food co-ops, tasty brunch spots and – in genteel Fairhaven – a rejuvenated historic district.

◎ Sights & Activities

Bellingham offers outdoor sights and activities by the truckload. **Whatcom Falls Park** is a natural wild region that bisects Bellingham's eastern suburbs. The change in elevation is marked by four sets of waterfalls, including **Whirlpool Falls**, a popular summer swimming hole.

Fairhaven Bicycles   CYCLING
(☑360-733-4433; www.fairhavenbicycles.com; 1108 11th St; bike rental per day from $50; ⊙10am-6pm Mon & Wed-Sat, 11am-5pm Sun) Bellingham is one of the most bike-friendly cities in the Northwest, with a well-maintained intra-urban trail going as far south as **Larrabee State Park** (www.parks.state.wa.us/536/larrabee; Chuckanut Dr; ⊙dawn-dusk). This outfit rents bikes and has maps on local routes.

Moondance
Sea Kayak Adventures   KAYAKING
(www.moondancekayak.com; 348 Cove Rd; half-day tours adult/child $70/60; ⊙Apr-Sep) If you're interested in getting out on the water, try

this outfit, which runs family-friendly guided trips in Chuckanut Bay, launching from Larrabee State Park (p1049).

Sleeping & Eating

Larrabee State Park CAMPGROUND $
(☑ 888-226-7688, 360-676-2093; www.parks.state.wa.us/536/larrabee; Chuckanut Dr; primitive sites $12, tent/RV sites from $27/35) Seven miles south of Bellingham, along scenic Chuckanut Dr, these campsites sit among Douglas firs and cedars with access to Chuckanut Bay and its 20-plus miles of hiking and biking trails. Light sleepers should note that trains pass by the campground frequently throughout the night; bring earplugs.

Heliotrope Hotel MOTEL $
(☑ 360-201-2914; www.heliotropehotel.com; 2419 Elm St; r with shared bath $99, r/ste from $109/130; ☎❄) A 1950s motor inn that's been given a stylish makeover, this fun motel has 17 ground-floor rooms in various configurations, plus a secluded grassy yard with a firepit and a central lobby area designed to encourage hanging out. There's no breakfast but staff have lots of suggestions for restaurants (and nightlife) within walking distance.

★ Hotel Bellwether BOUTIQUE HOTEL $$$
(☑ 360-392-3100; www.hotelbellwether.com; 1 Bellwether Way; r from $250; ❄✳@☎❄) Bellingham's finest and most charismatic hotel lies on the waterfront and offers views of Lummi Island. Standard rooms (some with water views) come with Italian furnishings and Hungarian-down duvets, but the finest pick is the 900-sq-ft lighthouse suite (from $599), a converted three-story lighthouse with a wonderful private lookout. There's a spa and a restaurant on the premises.

★ Pepper Sisters MODERN AMERICAN $$
(☑ 360-671-3414; www.peppersisters.com; 1055 N State St; mains $11-17; ⊗4:30-9pm Tue-Thu & Sun, to 9:30pm Fri & Sat; ❄) This cheerful, colorful restaurant serves innovative food that is hard to categorize – let's call it New Mexican cuisine with a Northwestern twist. Try the grilled eggplant tostada, chipotle-and-pink-peppercorn enchilada or Southwest pizza (with green chilies, jack cheese and tomatillo sauce); there's even a chicken-strip-free kids' menu.

Colophon Cafe CAFE $
(1208 11th St, Fairhaven; sandwiches $8-16, soups $8-10; ⊗9am-8pm Mon-Thu, 9am-9pm Fri & Sat, 10am-7pm Sun) Linked with Fairhaven's famous literary haven, **Village Books** (www.villagebooks.com; 1210 11th St; ⊗9am-9pm Mon-Sat, 10am-7pm Sun), the Colophon is a multi-ethnic eatery for people who like to follow their panini with Proust. Renowned for its African peanut soup and chocolate brandy cream pies, the cafe has indoor seating along with an outside wine garden and is ever popular with the local literati.

❶ Information

Downtown Info Center (☑ 360-671-3990; www.bellingham.org; 1306 Commercial St; ⊗11am-3pm Tue-Sat, to 5pm summer) A downtown location of Bellingham's visitor info center.

❶ Getting There & Away

Bellingham is the terminal for **Alaska Marine Highway** (AMHS; ☑ 800-642-0066; www.dot.state.ak.us/amhs; 355 Harris Ave; per person one way from $460) ferries, which travel once a week up the Inside Passage to Juneau, Skagway and other southeast Alaskan ports.

The **Bellair Airporter Shuttle** (www.airporter.com) runs around the clock to Sea-Tac Airport (round trip $74) and Anacortes (round trip $35).

San Juan Islands

There are 172 landfalls in this expansive archipelago, but unless you're rich enough to charter your own yacht or seaplane, you'll be restricted to seeing the big four – San Juan, Orcas, Shaw and Lopez Islands – all served daily by Washington State Ferries. Communally, the islands are famous for their tranquility, whale-watching opportunities, sea kayaking and general non-conformity.

A great way to explore the San Juans is by sea kayak or bicycle. Cycling-wise, Lopez is flat and pastoral and San Juan is worthy of an easy day loop, while Orcas offers the challenge of undulating terrain and a steep 5-mile ride to the top of Mt Constitution.

❶ Getting There & Around

Two airlines have scheduled flights from the mainland to the San Juans. **Kenmore Air** (☑ 866-435-9524; www.kenmoreair.com) flies from Lake Union and Lake Washington to Lopez, Orcas and San Juan Islands daily on three- to 10-person seaplanes. Fares start at around $150 one way. **San Juan Airlines** (☑ 800-874-4434; www.sanjuanairlines.com) flies from Anacortes and Bellingham to the three main islands.

Washington State Ferries (p1049) leave Anacortes for the San Juans; some continue to Sidney, Canada, near Victoria. Ferries run to Lopez Island (45 minutes), Orcas Landing (60 minutes) and Friday Harbor on San Juan Island (75 minutes). Fares vary by season; the cost of the entire round trip is collected on westbound journeys only (except those returning from Sidney).

Shuttle buses ply Orcas and San Juan Island between May and October.

San Juan Island

San Juan Island is the archipelago's unofficial capital, a harmonious mix of low forested hills and small rural farms that resonates with a dramatic and unusual 19th-century history. The only real settlement is Friday Harbor, home to the visitor center and **Chamber of Commerce** (☑360-378-5240; www.sanjuanisland.org; 165 1st St S, Friday Harbor; ☺10am-5pm).

◉ Sights

San Juan Island
National Historical Park   HISTORIC SITE
(☑360-378-2240; www.nps.gov/sajh; ☺visitor center 8:30am-5pm Jun-Aug, to 4:30pm Sep-May) FREE Known more for their scenery than their history, the San Juans nonetheless hide one of the 19th century's oddest political confrontations, the so-called 'Pig War' between the USA and Britain. This curious standoff is showcased in two separate historical parks at either end of the island, which once housed opposing **American** (☑360-378-2240; www.nps.gov/sajh; 4668 Cattle Point Rd, Friday Harbor; ☺grounds 8:30am-11pm) FREE and **English** (☑360-378-2240; www.nps.gov/sajh; ☺8:30am-11pm) FREE military encampments.

Lime Kiln Point State Park   STATE PARK
(☑360-902-8844; www.parks.state.wa.us/540/lime-kiln-point; 1567 Westside Rd; ☺8am-dusk) Clinging to the island's rocky west coast, this beautiful park overlooks the deep Haro Strait and has a reputation as one of the best places in the world to view whales from the shoreline. The word is out, however, so the view areas are often packed with hopeful picnickers. There's a small **interpretive center** (☑360-378-2044; ☺11am-4pm Jun–mid-Sep) FREE in the park, along with trails, a restored lime kiln and the landmark **Lime Kiln Lighthouse**, built in 1919.

🛏 Sleeping & Eating

San Juan County Park
Campground   CAMPGROUND $
(☑360-378-1842;   https://secure.itinio.com/sanjuan/island/campsites; 380 West Side Rd; hiker & cyclist sites per person $10, campsites from $35) San Juan's best campground is beautifully located in a county park on the scenic western shoreline. The site includes a beach and boat launch, along with 20 tent pitches, flush toilets and picnic tables. At night the lights of Victoria, Canada, flicker theatrically from across the Haro Strait. Reservations are mandatory during peak season.

★**Olympic Lights B&B**   B&B $$
(☑888-211-6195, 360-378-3186; www.olympiclights.com; 146 Starlight Way; r $165-185; ☺Jun-Sep; ☎) Once the centerpiece of a 320-acre estate, this splendidly restored 1895 farmhouse now hosts an equally formidable four-room B&B that stands on an open bluff facing the snow-coated Olympic Mountains. Sunflowers adorn the garden and the hearty breakfasts include homemade buttermilk biscuits. Two-night minimum.

Market Chef   DELI $
(☑360-378-4546; 225 A St, Friday Harbor; sandwiches from $9; ☺10am-4pm Mon-Fri) ◢ Super-popular and famous for its delicious sandwiches, including its signature curried-egg salad with roasted peanuts and chutney, or roast beef and rocket. Salads are also available; local ingredients are used. If you're in town on a Saturday in summer, visit Market Chef at the San Juan Island Farmers Market (10am to 1pm).

★**Duck Soup Inn**   FUSION $$$
(☑360-378-4878; www.ducksoupsanjuans.com; 50 Duck Soup Lane; mains $21-39; ☺5-10pm Wed-Sun Apr-Oct) It ain't cheap, but it's really good. Situated 4 miles northwest of Friday Harbor amid woods and water, Duck Soup offers the best island fine dining using the fruits of its own herb garden to enhance menu items such as oysters, scallops and Ethiopian lentil stew. The extensive wine list includes island-produced chardonnay.

Orcas Island

More rugged than Lopez yet less crowded than San Juan, Orcas has struck a delicate balance between friendliness and frostiness, development and preservation, tourist dollars and priceless privacy – for the time being, at least. The ferry terminal is at Orcas Landing, 8 miles south of the main village, Eastsound.

On the island's eastern lobe is **Moran State Park** (☑360-376-6173; 3572 Olga Rd; Discover Pass required at some parking lots per day/year $10/35; ◷6:30am-dusk Apr-Sep, 8am-dusk Oct-Mar), dominated by Mt Constitution (2409ft), with 40 miles of trails and an amazing 360-degree mountaintop view. **Camping** (☑360-376-2326; www.moranstatepark.com; campsites from $25) is a great option here.

🛏 Sleeping

★ Golden Tree Hostel   HOSTEL $
(☑360-317-8693; www.goldentreehostel.com; 1159 North Beach Rd, Eastsound; dm/d with shared bath $47/110; ◷Apr-Oct; @🛜🚲) Located in an 1890s-era heritage house, this hip hostel offers cozy rooms and pleasant common spaces, along with a hot tub and sauna in the grassy garden. Options include a tipi, a bus and a geodesic dome. There's even a separate recreation building with pool, Foosball, shuffleboard and darts. Bicycle rentals are $20. Friday pizza nights. Reserve in summer.

Doe Bay Village Resort & Retreat   HOSTEL $
(☑360-376-2291; www.doebay.com; 107 Doe Bay Rd, Olga; campsites from $60, cabins from $100, yurts from $80; 🛜🚲) 🌿 One of the least expensive resorts in the San Juans, Doe Bay has the atmosphere of an artists' commune combined with a hippie retreat. Accommodations include sea-view campsites and various cabins and yurts, some with views of the water.

Outlook Inn   HOTEL $$
(☑360-376-2200; www.outlookinn.com; 171 Main St, Eastsound; r/ste from $109/250; @🛜🚲) Eastsound's oldest and most eye-catching building, the Outlook Inn (1888) is an island institution. Budget rooms are cozy and neat (try for room 30), while the luxurious suites have fireplaces, Jacuzzis and stunning water views from their balconies. Excellent attached cafe.

🍴 Eating & Drinking

★ Brown Bear Baking   BAKERY $
(cnr Main St & North Beach Rd, Eastsound; pastries $7; ◷8am-4pm Thu-Mon) No one wants to pay $7 for a pastry, but the trouble is that once you start eating the baked goods here, nothing else will do. Options include croissants *aux amandes*, quiche using fresh Orcas Island eggs and roast veggies, caramel sticky

buns and fruit pie. Balance the nutritional ledger with one of the hearty soups or sandwiches.

★ Inn at Ship Bay   SEAFOOD $$$
(☑877-276-7296; www.innatshipbay.com; 326 Olga Rd; mains $27-36; ◷5-10pm Tue-Sat) 🌿 Locals unanimously rate this place as the best fine-dining experience on the island. The chefs work overtime preparing everything from scratch using the freshest local ingredients. Seafood is the specialty and it's served in an attractive 1860s orchard house a couple of miles south of Eastsound. There's also an on-site 11-room hotel (doubles from $195). Reservations recommended.

Island Hoppin' Brewery   BREWERY
(www.islandhoppinbrewery.com; 33 Hope Lane, Eastsound; ◷11am-9pm) The location just off Mt Baker Rd near the airport makes this tiny brewery hard to find, but the locals sure know it's there – this is *the* place to go to enjoy local brews on tap. Don't come hungry – only snacks are served, but you're welcome to bring your own food. A ping-pong table adds some action.

Lopez Island

If you're going to Lopez – or 'Slow-pez,' as locals prefer to call it – take a bike. With its undulating terrain and salutation-offering residents (who are famous for their three-fingered 'Lopezian wave'), this is the ideal cycling isle. A leisurely pastoral spin can be tackled in a day, with good overnight digs available next to the marina in the **Lopez Islander Resort** (☑360-468-2233; www.lopezfun.com; 2864 Fisherman Bay Rd; r from $159; 🛜🚲). For something more upscale, try the **Edenwild Inn** (☑360-468-3238; www.edenwildinn.com; Lopez Rd, Lopez Village; ste from $218; 🛜), a Victorian mansion set in lovely formal gardens.

If you arrive cycleless, call up **Village Cycles** (☑360-468-4013; www.villagecycles.net; 214 Lopez Rd; rental per hr $7-13), which can deliver a bicycle to the ferry terminal for you.

North Cascades

Dominated by Mt Baker and – to a lesser extent – the more remote Glacier Peak, the North Cascades region is made up of a huge swath of protected forests, parks and wilderness areas that dwarf even the expansive Rainier and St Helens parks to the south. The crème de la crème is the North

Cascades National Park, a primeval stash of old-growth rainforest, groaning glaciers and untainted ecosystems whose savage beauty goes unexplored by all but 2500 or so annual visitors who penetrate its rainy interior. Dotting this rugged landscape are a tiny handful of small towns, many of which are not much more than a gas station, a cafe and a general store.

Mt Baker

Rising like a ghostly sentinel above the sparkling waters of upper Puget Sound, Mt Baker has been mesmerizing visitors to the Northwest for centuries. A dormant volcano that last belched smoke in the 1850s, this haunting 10,781ft peak shelters 12 glaciers, and in 1999 registered a record-breaking 95ft of snow in one season.

Well-paved Hwy 542, known as the Mt Baker Scenic Byway, climbs 5100ft to **Artist Point**, 56 miles from Bellingham. Near here you'll find the **Heather Meadows Visitor Center** (Mt Baker Hwy, Mile 56; ⊙10am-4pm mid-Jul–late Sep) and a plethora of varied hikes, including the 7.5-mile **Chain Lakes Loop** that leads you around a half-dozen lakes surrounded by huckleberry meadows.

Receiving more annual snow than any ski area in North America, the **Mt Baker Ski Area** (☑360-734-6771; www.mtbaker.us; lift tickets adult/child $61/38) has 38 runs, eight lifts and a vertical rise of 1500ft. The resort has gained something of a cult status among snowboarders, who have been coming here for the Legendary Baker Banked Slalom every January since 1985.

On your way up the mountain, stop for a bite at authentic honky-tonk bar and restaurant **Graham's** (☑360-599-9883; 9989 Mt Baker Hwy, Glacier; mains $9-14; ⊙noon-9pm Mon-Fri, 8am-9pm Sat & Sun) and grab munchies at **Wake & Bakery** (☑360-599-1658; www.getsconed.com; 6903 Bourne St, Glacier; snacks from $4; ⊙7:30am-5pm), both in the town of **Glacier**.

Leavenworth

Blink hard and rub your eyes. This isn't some strange Germanic hallucination. Leavenworth is a former lumber town that underwent a Bavarian makeover back in the 1960s after the re-routing of the cross-continental railway threatened to put it permanently out of business. Swapping wood for tourists, Leavenworth today has successfully reinvented itself as a traditional *Romantische Strasse* village, right down to the beer, sausages and lederhosen-loving locals (25% of whom are of German descent). The classic *Sound of Music* mountain setting helps, as does the fact that Leavenworth serves as the main activity center for sorties into the nearby Alpine Lakes Wilderness.

The **Leavenworth Chamber of Commerce** (☑509-548-5807; https://leavenworth.org; 940 US 2; ⊙8am-5pm Mon-Thu, 8am-6pm Fri & Sat, 10am-4pm Sun) can advise on the local outdoor activities. Highlights include the best climbing in the state at **Castle Rock** in Tumwater Canyon, about 3 miles northwest of town off US 2.

The **Devil's Gulch** is a popular off-road mountain-bike trail (25 miles, four to six hours). Local outfitters **Der Sportsmann** (☑509-548-5623; www.dersportsmann.com; 837 Front St; cross-country ski/snowshoe rental $18/16; ⊙10am-6pm Mon-Thu, to 7pm Fri, 9am-7pm Sat, 9am-6pm Sun) rents mountain bikes.

🍴 Sleeping & Eating

Hotel Pension Anna · · · · · · · · · · · · HOTEL **$$**
(☑509-548-6273; www.pensionanna.com; 926 Commercial St; r from $240; ☏) The most authentic Bavarian hotel in town is also spotless and incredibly friendly. Each room is kitted out in imported Austrian decor, and the European-inspired breakfasts (included) may induce joyful yodels. A recommended room is the double with hand-painted furniture, but the spacious suite in the adjacent St Joseph's chapel is perfect for families.

Enzian Inn · HOTEL **$$**
(☑509-548-5269; www.enzianinn.com; 590 US 2; d from $240; ☏☀) At this Leavenworth classic the day starts with a blast on an alpenhorn before breakfast. If that doesn't send you running for your lederhosen, consider the free putting green (with resident grass-trimming goats), the indoor and outdoor swimming pools, and the nightly pianist pounding out requests in the Bavarian lobby.

München Haus · · · · · · · · · · · · · · · · GERMAN **$**
(☑509-548-1158; www.munchenhaus.com; 709 Front St; brats $4-7; ⊙11am-8pm, to 10pm Fri & Sat) The Haus is 100% alfresco, meaning that the hot German sausages and pretzels are essential stomach warmers in winter, while the Bavarian brews will cool you down in summer. The casual beer-garden atmosphere is complemented by an aggressively jaunty accordion soundtrack, laid-back staff, a kettle of cider relish and an epic mustard bar. Hours vary outside summer.

Lake Chelan

Long, slender Lake Chelan is central Washington's watery playground. The town of Chelan, at the lake's southeastern tip, is the primary base for accommodations and services, and has a **USFS Ranger Station** (☑509-682-4900; www.fs.usda.gov/detail/okawen/about-forest/offices; 428 W Woodin Ave; ⊙7:45am-4:30pm Mon-Fri).

Lake Chelan State Park (☑509-687-3710; https://parks.state.wa.us/531/Lake-Chelan; 7544 S Lakeshore Rd; primitive/standard sites from $12/27) has 144 campsites; a number of lakeshore campgrounds are accessible only by boat. If you'd rather sleep in a real bed, try the great-value **Midtowner Motel** (☑800-572-0943; www.midtowner.com; 721 E Woodin Ave; r from $125; ❄@☎☂) or the delightful **Riverwalk Inn** (☑509-682-2627; www.riverwalkinnchelan.com; 205 E Wapato Ave; d $69-199; ☎☂), both in town.

Several wineries have also opened in the area and many have excellent restaurants. Try **Tsillan Cellars** (☑509-682-9463; www.tsillancellars.com; 3875 US 97A; ⊙noon-6pm) or the swanky Italian **Sorrento's Ristorante** (☑509-682-9463; https://tsillancellars.com/dining; 3875 US 97A; mains $20-38; ⊙5pm-late daily, plus noon-3pm Sat, 11am-3pm Sun).

Link Transit (☑509-662-1155; www.linktransit.com) buses connect Chelan with Wenatchee and Leavenworth ($2.50 one way).

Beautiful **Stehekin**, on the northern tip of Lake Chelan, is accessible only by **boat** (☑509-682-4584; www.ladyofthelake.com; 1418 W Woodin Ave; one way $22-37, round trip to Stehekin $61), or a long hike across Cascade Pass, 28 miles from the lake. You'll find lots of information about hiking, campgrounds and cabin rentals at www.stehekin.com. Most facilities are open from mid-June to mid-September.

Methow Valley

The Methow's combination of powdery winter snow and abundant summer sunshine has transformed this valley into one of Washington's primary recreation areas. You can bike, hike and fish in summer, and cross-country ski on the second-biggest snow trail network in the US in winter.

The 200km of trails are maintained by the nonprofit **Methow Valley Sport Trails Association** (MVSTA; ☑509-996-3287; www.methowtrails.org; 309 Riverside Ave, Winthrop; ⊙8:30am-3:30pm Mon-Fri) ⚐, which in winter provides the most comprehensive network of hut-to-hut (and hotel-to-hotel) skiing in North America. An extra blessing is that few people seem to know about it. For classic accommodations and easy access to the skiing, hiking and cycling trails, decamp at the exquisite **Sun Mountain Lodge** (☑509-996-2211; www.sunmountainlodge.com; 604 Patterson Lake Rd; r from $285, cabins from $415; ❄☎☂), 10 miles west of the town of Winthrop. Winthrop is also the locus of the area's best eating: try the fine-dining **Arrowleaf Bistro** (☑509-996-3920; www.arrowleafbistro.com; 253 Riverside Ave; mains $22-28; ⊙4-10pm Wed-Sun).

North Cascades National Park

Even the names of the lightly trodden, dramatic mountains in **North Cascades National Park** (www.nps.gov/noca) sound wild and untamed: Desolation Peak, Jagged Ridge, Mt Despair and Mt Terror. Not surprisingly, the region offers some of the best backcountry adventures outside of Alaska.

The **North Cascades Visitor Center** (☑206-386-4495, ext 11; 502 Newhalem St, Newhalem; ⊙9am-5pm mid-May–Sep) ⚐, in the small settlement of Newhalem on Hwy 20, is the best orientation point for visitors and is staffed by expert rangers who can enlighten you on the park's highlights.

Built in the 1930s for loggers working in the valley (which was soon to be flooded by Ross Dam), the floating cabins at the **Ross Lake Resort** (☑206-486-3751; www.rosslakeresort.com; 503 Diablo St, Rockport; cabins $205-385; ⊙mid-Jun–late Oct; ☻) on the eponymous lake's west side are the state's most unique accommodations. There's no road in – guests can either hike the 2-mile trail from Hwy 20 or take the resort's tugboat-taxi-and-truck shuttle from the parking area near Diablo Dam.

Northeastern Washington

Spokane

Washington's second-biggest population center is situated at the nexus of the Pacific Northwest's 'Inland Empire', on the banks of the Spokane River. It's home to the impressive Northwest Museum of Arts & Culture, Gonzaga University, the 1974 World's Fair site, and a dramatic waterfall right in the middle of a well-preserved historic downtown core. There are plenty of rough edges left, but a patient visitor can find a lot of surprising beauty and charm in this oft-maligned city.

⊙ Sights

★ Northwest Museum of
Arts & Culture
MUSEUM

(MAC; ☎509-456-3931; www.northwestmuseum.org; 2316 W 1st Ave; adult/child $10/5; ⊙10am-5pm Tue-Sun, to 8pm 3rd Thu of month; ⚿) In a striking state-of-the-art building in the beautiful Browne's Addition neighborhood, this museum is well worth a visit. It has one of the finest collections of Native American artifacts in the Northwest, and stages ambitious temporary exhibits several times a year that illuminate key regional artists (such as glass master Dale Chihuly) and cultural phenomena (pioneer quilts, indigenous beadwork etc).

Riverfront Park
PARK

(www.spokaneriverfrontpark.com; ⚿) The site of the 1974 World's Fair and Exposition, this downtown park has numerous highlights, including a 17-point Sculpture Walk and the scenic Spokane Falls. A short gondola ride, the Spokane Falls SkyRide (adult/child $7.75/5.75; ⊙11am-7pm) takes you directly across the falls, or get an equally spectacular view from the Monroe Street Bridge, built in 1911 and still one of the largest concrete arches in the USA. An ongoing renovation project means that a few areas of the park are closed due to construction.

⎙ Sleeping & Eating

Hotel Ruby
MOTEL $

(☎509-747-1041; www.hotelrubyspokane.com; 901 W 1st Ave; r from $81; ⓟ❄🐾📶) An arty redesign of a formerly basic motel, the Ruby has a '70s feel, with cool original art on the walls and a sleek cocktail lounge adjoining the lobby. Rooms have mini fridge and microwave, and you can use the gym at the nearby sister hotel, Ruby 2, cool in its own right (rooms from $78). The downtown location rules.

★ Historic Davenport Hotel
HISTORIC HOTEL $$

(☎800-899-1482; www.thedavenporthotel.com; 10 S Post St; r from $200; ❄📶🏊) This historic landmark (opened in 1914) is considered one of the best hotels in the country. Even if you're not staying here, linger in the exquisite lobby or have a drink in the Peacock Lounge. The adjacent, modern Davenport Tower sports a safari-themed lobby and bar.

★ Ruins
AMERICAN, FUSION $$

(☎509-443-5606; 825 N Monroe St; small plates $6-17; ⊙11am-3pm & 5-10pm Tue-Fri, 9:30am-2pm & 5-11pm Sat, 9:30am-2pm & 5-9pm Sun, 5-10pm Mon) This stylish little place has a constantly changing menu of mostly small plates and snacks to pair with perfectly crafted cocktails. Expect fresh twists on anything from pad Thai to street tacos, banh mi to burgers, plus some heartier fare (recently a carne asada plate) for sharing – or not. Slip in late and grab a seat at the bar.

★ Wild Sage
American Bistro
NORTHWESTERN US $$$

(www.wildsagebistro.com; 916 W 2nd Ave; mains $18-42; ⊙4-9pm Mon-Thu, to 10pm Fri-Sun) 🌱 The intimate yet simple decor and fresh local ingredients, creatively and elegantly prepared, see Wild Sage consistently rated as one of Spokane's top dining spots. The Alaskan halibut, honey-Dijon chicken and coconut-cream layer cake come highly recommended, and there's a gluten-free menu and an excellent selection of wines and craft cocktails.

⛾ Drinking & Entertainment

Atticus Coffee
COFFEE

(222 N Howard St; tea/espresso from $2/3; ⊙7:30am-6pm Mon-Sat, 9am-5pm Sun) As much a well-curated gift shop as a coffeehouse, this bookish, bright and convivial cafe serves an amazing selection of loose teas and perfect coffee. Good luck resisting the urge to pick up a handmade mug, artisan soap or kitty-faced pot holder while you're here. Wi-fi is available Monday to Friday.

No-Li Brewhouse
BREWERY

(☎509-242-2739; www.nolibrewhouse.com; 1003 E Trent Ave; mains $12-18; ⊙11:30am-10pm Sun-Thu, 11am-11pm Fri & Sat) A massively popular hangout near Gonzaga University, Spokane's best microbrewery serves some weird and wonderful flavors, including a tart cherry ale and an imperial stout with coffee, chocolate and brown-sugar tones. Food-wise, check out the cod and chips cooked in batter made with the brewery's own pale ale.

❶ Information

Visitor Information Center (☎888-776-5263, 509-744-3341; www.visitspokane.com; 620 W Spokane Falls Blvd; ⊙10am-7pm Jun-Sep, to 6pm rest of year) Near the riverfront, this office has plenty of information on the city and region.

❶ Getting There & Away

Spokane International Airport (www.spokaneairports.net) Alaska, American, Delta, Frontier, Southwest and United airlines all offer nonstop services to 16 destinations including Seattle, Portland OR; San Francisco, CA; Denver, CO;

PACIFIC NORTHWEST NORTHEASTERN WASHINGTON

WORTH A TRIP

GRAND COULEE DAM

While the more famous Hoover Dam (conveniently located between Las Vegas and the Grand Canyon) gets around 1.6 million visitors per year, the four-times-larger and arguably more significant **Grand Coulee Dam** (inconveniently located far from everything) gets only a trickle of tourism. If you're in the area, don't miss it – it's one of the country's most spectacular displays of engineering and you'll get to enjoy it crowd-free.

The **Grand Coulee Dam Visitor Center** (☑509-633-9265; www.usbr.gov/pn/grand coulee/visit; ☉9am-11pm mid-May–Jul, to 10:30pm Aug, to 9:30pm Sep, to 5pm Oct–mid-May) details the history of the dam and surrounding area with movies, photos and interactive exhibits. Free guided tours of the facility run daily at 10am, noon, 2pm and 3:30pm and involve taking a glass-walled elevator 465ft down into the Third Power Plant, where you can view the generators from an observation deck.

Minneapolis, MN; Salt Lake City, UT; and Phoenix, AZ.

Spokane Intermodal Center (221 W 1st Ave) Buses and trains depart from this station.

South Cascades

More rounded and less hemmed in than their saw-toothed cousins to the north, the South Cascades are nonetheless higher. Their pinnacle in more ways than one is 14,411ft Mt Rainier, the fifth-highest mountain in the lower 48 states and arguably one of the most dramatic stand-alone mountains in the world. Further south, fiery Mt St Helens needs zero introduction, while unsung Adams glowers way off to the east like a sulking middle child.

Mt Rainier National Park

The USA's fifth-highest peak outside Alaska, majestic Mt Rainier is also one of its most beguiling. Encased in a 368-sq-mile national park, the mountain's snowcapped summit and forest-covered foothills boast numerous hiking trails, huge swaths of flower-carpeted meadows, and an alluring conical peak that presents a formidable challenge for aspiring climbers.

Mt Rainier National Park (www.nps.gov/mora; car $30, pedestrian & cyclist $15, 1yr pass $55) has four entrances. Call 800-695-7623 for road conditions. The National Park Service (NPS) website includes downloadable maps and descriptions of dozens of park trails. The most famous is the hard-core, 93-mile-long Wonderland Trail, which completely circumnavigates Mt Rainier and takes 10 to 12 days to tackle.

Campgrounds in the park have running water and toilets, but no showers or RV hookups. Reservations at park **campsites** (☑800-365-2267; www.nps.gov/mora; campsites $20) are strongly advised during summer and can be made up to two months in advance by phone or online. For overnight backcountry trips, you'll need a wilderness permit – check the NPS website for details.

NISQUALLY ENTRANCE

The busiest and most convenient gate to Mt Rainier National Park, Nisqually lies on Hwy 706 via Ashford, near the park's southwest corner. It's open year-round. Longmire, 7 miles inside the Nisqually entrance, has a **museum and information center** (☑360-569-6575; Hwy 706, Longmire; ☉museum 9am-4:30pm year-round, info center May-Oct) **FREE**, a number of important trailheads, and the rustic **National Park Inn** (☑360-569-2275; Hwy 706, Longmire; r with/without bath from $203/138; ❄), complete with an excellent restaurant.

More hikes and interpretive walks can be found 12 miles further east at loftier **Paradise**, which is served by the informative **Henry M Jackson Visitor Center** (☑360-569-6571; Paradise; ☉10am-5pm daily May-Oct, Sat & Sun Nov-Apr), and the vintage **Paradise Inn** (☑360-569-2275; Paradise; r with/without bath from $182/123; ☉mid-May–Oct; ☺), a historical 'parkitecture' inn constructed in 1916. Climbs to the top of Rainier leave from the inn; excellent four-day guided ascents are led by **Rainier Mountaineering Inc** (☑888-892-5462; www.rmiguides.com; 30027 Hwy 706 E, Ashford; 4-day climb $1163).

OTHER ENTRANCES

The three other entrances to Mt Rainier National Park are **Ohanapecosh**, accessed via Hwy 123 and the town of Packwood, where lodging is available; **White River**, off Hwy 410, literally the highroad (6400ft) to the beautiful viewpoint at the **Sunrise Lodge**

Cafeteria (Sunrise Park Rd, Sunrise; mains $6-12; ☺10am-7pm Jul & Aug, 11am-3pm Sat & Sun Sep); and remote **Carbon River** in the northwest corner, which gives access to the park's inland rainforest.

Mt St Helens National Volcanic Monument

What it lacks in height, Mt St Helens makes up for in fiery infamy – 57 people perished on the mountain when it erupted with a force of 1500 atomic bombs on May 18, 1980. The cataclysm began with an earthquake measuring 5.1 on the Richter scale, which sparked the biggest landslide in recorded history and buried 230 sq miles of forest under millions of tons of volcanic rock and ash. Today it's a fascinating landscape of recovering forests, new river valleys and ash-covered slopes. There's an $8 per adult fee to enter the National Monument.

NORTHEASTERN ENTRANCE

From the main northeast entrance on Hwy 504, your first stop should be the **Silver Lake Visitor Center** (☑360-274-0962; https://parks.state.wa.us/245/Mount-St-Helens; 3029 Spirit Lake Hwy; adult/child $5/free; ☺9am-4pm Mar–mid-May & mid-Sep–Oct, to 5pm mid-May–mid-Sep, 9am-4pm Thu-Mon Nov-Feb; ⊕) ⯑, which has films, exhibits and free information about the mountain (including trail maps). For a closer view of the destructive power of nature, venture to the **Johnston Ridge Observatory** (☑360-274-2140; www.fs.usda.gov; 24000 Spirit Lake Hwy; day use $8; ☺10am-6pm mid-May–Oct), situated at the end of Hwy 504, which looks directly into the mouth of the crater. A welcome stop in an accommodations-light area, the **Eco Park Resort** (☑360-274-7007; www.ecoparkresort.com; 14000 Spirit Lake Hwy, Toutle; campsites $25, 6-person yurts $95, cabins $150; ⯑) offers campsites and RV hookups, and basic two- or four-person cabins.

SOUTHEASTERN & EASTSIDE ENTRANCES

The southeastern entrance via the town of **Cougar** on Hwy 503 holds some serious lava terrain, including the 2-mile-long Ape Cave lava tube, which you can explore year-round; be prepared for the chill as it remains a constant 41°F (5°C). Bring two light sources per adult or rent lanterns at **Apes' Headquarters** (☑360-449-7800; Forest Rd 8303; ☺10am-5pm mid-Jun–early Sep) for $5 each.

The eastside entrance is the most remote, but the harder-to-reach **Windy Ridge** viewpoint on this side gives you a palpable, if eerie, sense of the destruction from the blast. It's often closed until June. A few miles down the road you can descend 600ft on the mile-long Harmony Trail (hike 224) to **Spirit Lake**.

Central & Southeastern Washington

The sunny, dry, near-California-looking central and southeastern parts of Washington harbor one not-so-secret weapon: wine. The fertile land that borders the Nile-like Yakima and Columbia River Valleys is awash with enterprising new wineries producing quality grapes that now vie with the Napa and Sonoma Valleys for recognition. Yakima and its more attractive cousin Ellensburg once held the edge, but nowadays the real star is Walla Walla.

Yakima & Ellensburg

The main reason to stop in Yakima is to visit one of the numerous wineries that lie between here and Benton City; pick up a map at the **visitor center** (☑800-221-0751; www.visityakima.com; 101 N 8th St; ☺8:30am-5pm Mon-Fri).

A better layover is Ellensburg, a diminutive settlement 36 miles to the northwest that juxtaposes the state's largest rodeo (each Labor Day) with a town center that has some well-preserved historic buildings. Grab your latte at local roaster **D&M Coffee** (☑509-925-5313; www.dmcoffee.com; 323 N Pearl St; ☺7am-8pm; ☎) ⯑ and eat at the unconventional **Yellow Church Cafe** (☑509-933-2233; www.theyellowchurchcafe.com; 111 S Pearl St; lunch mains $12-17, dinner mains $14-27; ☺11am-9pm Mon-Thu, 8am-9pm Fri-Sun; ⯑) or fantastic upstart the **Red Pickle** (☑509-367-0003; 301 N Pine St; mains from $10, cocktails $8; ☺11am-9pm Wed-Sun, 4-9pm Tue).

Greyhound services both cities, with buses to Seattle, Spokane and points in between.

Walla Walla

Walla Walla has converted itself into the hottest wine-growing region outside of California. While venerable Marcus Whitman College is the town's most obvious cultural attribute, you'll also find zany coffee bars, cool wine-tasting rooms, fine Queen Anne architecture, and one of the state's freshest and most vibrant farmers markets.

◉ Sights & Activities

You don't need to be sloshed on wine to appreciate Walla Walla's historical and cultural heritage. Its Main St has won countless historical awards, and to bring the settlement to life, the local **chamber of commerce** (☏509-525-0850; www.wwvchamber.com; 29 E Sumach St; ⊘8:30am-5pm Mon-Fri) has concocted some interesting walking tours, complete with leaflets and maps. Main St and environs are also crammed with tasting rooms. Expect tasting fees of $5 to $10.

Fort Walla Walla Museum MUSEUM
(☏509-525-7703; www.fwwm.org; 755 Myra Rd; adult/child $9/4; ⊘10am-5pm Mar-Oct, to 4pm Nov-Feb; ⊕) This museum occupies the fort's old cavalry stables, with a recreated pioneer village outside. The main exhibit hall contains displays on the Lewis and Clark expedition, local agriculture and military history, and the four large stable buildings hold collections of farm implements, a jail cell and a plastic replica of a 33-mule team used for harvesting wheat in the 1920s.

Waterbrook Wine WINE
(☏509-522-1262; www.waterbrook.com; 10518 W US 12; tasting $5-15; ⊘11am-5pm Sun-Thu, to 6pm Fri & Sat) About 10 miles west of town, this large, extremely manicured modern winery feels a bit slick and commercial, but it has attentive staff and the pond-side patio is a great place to sample from the long selection of wines on a sunny day. Full menu served Thursday to Sunday.

Amavi Cellars WINE
(☏509-525-3541; www.amavicellars.com; 3796 Peppers Bridge Rd; tasting $10; ⊘10am-4pm) South of Walla Walla, amid a scenic spread of grape and apple orchards, you can sample some of the most talked-about wines in the valley (try the syrah and cabernet sauvignon). The classy yet comfortable patio has views of the Blue Mountains.

⌑ Sleeping & Eating

Walla Walla Garden Motel MOTEL $
(☏509-529-1220; www.wallawallagardenmotel.com; 2279 Isaacs Ave; s/d from $72/94; ❸❄☎) A simple family-run motel halfway to the airport, the Garden Motel is welcoming and bike-friendly, with safe bike storage and plenty of local maps.

Marcus Whitman Hotel HOTEL $$
(☏509-525-2200; www.marcuswhitmanhotel.com; 6 W Rose St; r from $159; ℗❄☎❈) Walla Walla's best-known landmark is also the town's only tall building, impossible to miss with its distinctive rooftop turret. In keeping with the settlement's well-preserved image, the redbrick 1928 beauty has been elegantly renovated and decorated, with ample rooms and suites in rusts and browns, embellished with Italian-crafted furniture, huge beds and great views over the nearby Blue Mountains.

Graze CAFE $
(☏509-522-9991; www.grazeplaces.com; 5 S Colville St; sandwiches $8-12; ⊘10am-7:30pm Mon-Sat, to 3:30pm Sun; ✐) Amazing sandwiches are packed for your picnic or (if you can get a table) eaten in at this simple cafe. Try the turkey-and-pear panini with provolone and blue cheese or the flank-steak torta with pickled jalapeños, avocado, tomato, cilantro and chipotle dressing. There are plenty of vegetarian options.

★**Saffron Mediterranean Kitchen** MEDITERRANEAN $$$
(☏509-525-2112; www.saffronmediterraneankitchen.com; 125 W Alder St; flatbreads $14-16, mains $25-45; ⊘2-9pm Mon-Fri, noon-9pm Sat & Sun) This place isn't about cooking, it's about alchemy: Saffron takes seasonal, local ingredients and turns them into pure gold. The Med-inspired menu lists dishes such as asparagus-fontina flatbread, wood-grilled quail with dates and olives, and eggplant, lamb and pork-belly lasagna. Then there are the intelligently paired wines – and gorgeous atmosphere. Reserve.

❶ Getting There & Away

Alaska Airlines has two daily flights to Seattle-Tacoma International Airport from **Walla Walla Regional Airport** (www.wallawallaairport.com; 45 Terminal Loop), northeast of town off US 12.

Greyhound buses run once daily to Seattle ($47, six hours) via Pasco, Yakima and Ellensburg; change buses in Pasco for Spokane.

OREGON

It's hard to slap a single characterization onto Oregon's geography and people. Its landscape ranges from rugged coastline and thick evergreen forests to barren, fossil-strewn deserts, volcanoes and glaciers. As for its denizens, you name it – Oregonians run the gamut from pro-logging conservatives to tree-hugging liberals. What they have in common is an independent spirit, a love of the outdoors and a fierce devotion to where they live.

It doesn't usually take long for visitors to feel a similar devotion. Who wouldn't fall in love with the spectacle of glittering Crater Lake, the breathtaking colors of the Painted Hills in John Day or the hiking trails through deep forests and over stunning mountain passes? And then there are the towns: you can eat like royalty in hip Portland, see top-notch dramatic productions in Ashland or sample an astounding number of brewpubs in Bend.

Portland

Best coffee. Most food carts. Top craft breweries. Number-one hipster haven. Portland is a city of indie-spirited superlatives and humble, off-beat charms.

⊙ Sights

⊙ Downtown

⭐**Tom McCall Waterfront Park**   PARK
(Map p1060; Naito Pkwy) This popular riverside park, which lines the west bank of the Willamette River, was finished in 1978 after four years of construction. It replaced a freeway with 1.5 miles of paved sidewalks and grassy spaces, and now attracts joggers, in-line skaters, strollers and cyclists. During summer the park is perfect for hosting large outdoor events such as the **Oregon Brewers Festival** (www.oregonbrewfest.com; Tom McCall Waterfront Park; admission free, 10-token tasting package $20, additional tokens $1; ☉late Jul). Walk over the Steel and Hawthorne bridges to the **Eastbank Esplanade**, making a 2.6-mile loop.

⭐**Pioneer Courthouse Square**   LANDMARK
(Map p1060; www.thesquarepdx.org; 🚇Red, Blue, Green) The heart of downtown Portland, this brick plaza is nicknamed Portland's 'living room' and is the most-visited public space in the city. When it isn't full of sunbathers or office workers lunching, the square hosts concerts, festivals, rallies, farmers markets, and even summer Friday-night movies – aka **Flicks on the Bricks** (Map p1060; https://thesquarepdx.org/events; ☉7pm Fri Jul & Aug).

Oregon Historical Society   MUSEUM
(Map p1060; ☎503-222-1741; www.ohs.org; 1200 SW Park Ave; adult/child $10/5; ☉10am-5pm Mon-Sat, noon-5pm Sun; 🚇Red, Blue) Along the tree-shaded **South Park Blocks** (Map p1060) sits the state's primary history museum, which in 2019 unveiled a permanent 7000-sq-ft interactive exhibit that delves into Oregon's history, peoples and landscape. Stations include a canoe-building exercise, a walk-through covered-wagon replica and historical role-playing games. There are interesting sections on various immigrant groups, Native American tribes and the travails of the Oregon Trail. Temporary exhibits furnish the downstairs space. Check the website for free admission days.

Portland Art Museum   MUSEUM
(Map p1060; ☎503-226-2811; www.portlandartmuseum.org; 1219 SW Park Ave; adult/child $20/free; ☉10am-5pm Tue, Wed, Sat & Sun, to 8pm Thu & Fri; 🚌6, 38, 45, 55, 58, 68, 92, 96, 🚇NS Line, A-Loop) Alongside the South Park Blocks, Portland Art Museum's excellent exhibits include Native American carvings, Asian and American art, photography and English silver. The museum also houses the Whitsell Auditorium, a first-rate theater

OREGON FACTS

Nickname Beaver State

Population 4.25 million

Area 98,466 sq miles

Capital city Salem (population 169,800)

Other cities Portland (population 647,800), Eugene (population 169,000), Bend (population 94,520)

Sales tax None

Birthplace of Former US president Herbert Hoover (1874–1964), actor and dancer Ginger Rogers (1911–95), writer and merry prankster Ken Kesey (1935–2001), filmmaker Gus Van Sant (b 1952), The Simpsons creator Matt Groening (b 1954)

Home of Oregon Shakespeare Festival, Nike, Crater Lake

Politics Democrat governors since 1987

Famous for Forests, rain, microbrews, coffee, anti-fascism demonstrators

State beverage Milk (dairy's big here)

Driving You can't pump your own gas in most of Oregon. Portland to Eugene 110 miles, Portland to Astoria 96 miles

Portland

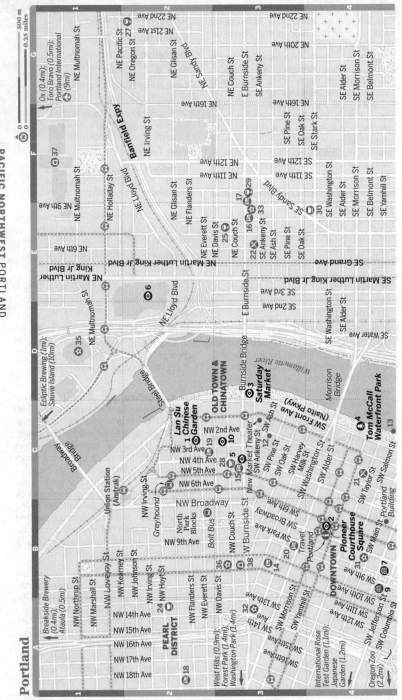

500 m
0.25 miles

Ox (0.4mi);
Toro Bravo (0.5mi);
Portland International
(9mi)

Breakside Brewery
(0.4mi);
Ataula (0.5mi)

PEARL
DISTRICT

Ecliptic Brewing (1mi);
Sauvie Island (10mi)

Banfield EXPY

NE 22nd Ave
NE 21st Ave
NE Pacific St
NE Oregon St
NE Multnomah St
NE Multnomah St
NE Holladay St
NE Lloyd Blvd
NE 9th Ave
NE 6th Ave
NE Multnomah St
NE Irving St

NE Sandy Blvd
NE Glisan St
NE Flanders St
NE Everett St
NE Davis St
NE Couch St

NE 16th Ave
NE 11th Ave
NE 12th Ave

NE Martin Luther King Jr Blvd
NE Lloyd Blvd
NE Multnomah St

SE Martin Luther King Jr Blvd
SE Grand Ave
E Burnside St
SE 2nd Ave
SE 3rd Ave
SE Water Ave

NE 22nd Ave
NE 20th Ave
NE Couch St
NE Burnside St
NE Ankeny St
E Burnside St
SE Pine St
SE Oak St
SE Stark St

SE 16th Ave
SE 12th Ave
SE 11th Ave

SE Washington St
SE Alder St
SE Morrison St
SE Belmont St

SE Alder St
SE Morrison St
SE Belmont St
SE Yamhill St

SE Sandy Blvd
SE Ankeny St
SE Ash St
SE Pine St
SE Oak St

SE Washington St
SE Alder St

SE Stark St

Willamette River
Burnside Bridge
Morrison Bridge

Steel Bridge
Broadway Bridge

Union Station
(Amtrak)

Greyhound
Bolt Bus

North
Park
Blocks

NW Broadway
NW Park Ave
SW Park Ave
SW Broadway
SW 6th Ave

NW Irving St
NW Hoyt St
NW Flanders St
NW Everett St
NW Davis St
NW Couch St
W Burnside St

NW Marshall St
NW Lovejoy St
NW Kearney St
NW Johnson St
NW Irving St

NW Northrup St
NW Marshall St

NW 9th Ave
NW Broadway

NW 14th Ave
NW 15th Ave
NW 16th Ave
NW 17th Ave
NW 18th Ave

SW 13th Ave
SW 14th Ave
SW 15th Ave
SW 16th Ave

SW Morrison St
SW Yamhill St
SW Taylor St
SW Salmon St
SW Main St
SW Jefferson St
SW Columbia St

SW 9th Ave
SW 10th Ave
SW 11th Ave
SW 12th Ave

DOWNTOWN

Pioneer
Courthouse
Square

Portland
Building

Tom McCall
Waterfront Park

SW Front Ave
(Naito Pkwy)

SW Ankeny St
SW Pine St
SW Oak St
SW Harvey
Milk St
SW Washington St
SW Alder St

New Market Theater
NW 2nd Ave
NW 3rd Ave
NW 4th Ave
NW 5th Ave
NW 6th Ave

OLD TOWN &
CHINATOWN

Saturday
Market

Lan Su
Chinese
Garden

Travel
Portland

West Hills (0.9mi);
Forest Park (1.4mi);
Washington Park (1.4mi)

International Rose
Test Garden (1.1mi);
Japanese
Garden (1.2mi);
Oregon Zoo
(2.2mi)

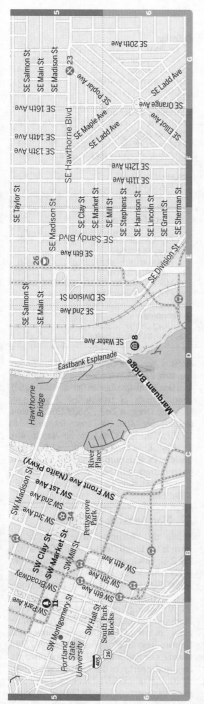

that frequently screens rare or international films and that is part of the Northwest Film Center and school.

◉ Old Town & Chinatown

The core of rambunctious 1890s Portland, once-seedy **Old Town** had a well-earned reputation as the lurking ground of unsavory characters. Now it's home to some lovely historic buildings, plus Waterfront Park, Saturday Market and a few good pockets of nightlife.

Old Town is generally lumped together with the city's historic **Chinatown** – no longer the heart of the Chinese community (that's moved to outer Southeast) but still home to the ornate **Chinatown Gateway** (Map p1060; cnr W Burnside St & NW 4th Ave; 📵20), tranquil **Lan Su Chinese Garden** (Map p1060; 📞503-228-8131; www.lansugarden. org; 239 NW Everett St; adult/student \$11/8; ⏱10am-7pm mid-May–mid-Oct, to 5pm mid-Oct–mid-Mar, to 6pm mid-Mar–mid-May; 📵8, 77, 📵Blue, Red) and the so-called **Shanghai Tunnels** (Map p1060; 📞503-622-4798; 120 NW 3rd Ave; adult/child \$13/8; 📵12, 19, 20, 📵Blue, Red), some of which can be toured.

★**Saturday Market**   MARKET
(Map p1060; 📞503-222-6072; www.portlandsat urdaymarket.com; 2 SW Naito Pkwy; ⏱10am-5pm Sat, 11am-4:30pm Sun Mar-Dec; ♿; 📵12, 16, 19, 20, 📵Red, Blue) The best time to walk along the Portland Waterfront is on a weekend, when you can catch this famous market showcasing arts and crafts, street entertainers and food carts.

◉ The Pearl District & Northwest

Encompassing three distinctive districts, Northwest Portland is home to some of the city's top art galleries, trendy restaurants and plentiful shopping options – all connected by wonderfully walkable streets. Nob Hill's craftsman-style storefronts house neighborhood-feel restaurants and retail shops amid century-old Victorian homes. In the face of Portland's rapid development, industrial Slabtown is up and coming with new high-rise residences and more. Characterized by its cobblestone streets and old loading docks, the once-industrial Pearl District is now one of the state's chicest neighborhoods, boasting a wealth of galleries, eateries and boutiques.

PACIFIC NORTHWEST PORTLAND

Portland

⊙ Top Sights

⊙ Sights

✪ Activities, Courses & Tours

⊜ Sleeping

✖ Eating

⊙ Drinking & Nightlife

✪ Entertainment

⊜ Shopping

⊙ West Hills

★ Forest Park   PARK

(☎503-223-5449; www.forestparkconservancy.
org) Abutting the more manicured Washington Park to the south (to which it is linked by various trails) is the far wilder 5100-acre Forest Park, an urban Northwest forest that harbors plants and animals and hosts an avid hiking fraternity. The **Portland Audubon Society** (☎503-292-6855; www.audubonportland.org; 5151 NW Cornell Rd; ⊙9am-5pm, nature store 10am-6pm Mon-Sat, to 5pm Sun; ☒20) FREE maintains a bookstore, wildlife rehabilitation center and 4.5 miles of trails within its Forest Park sanctuary.

Washington Park   PARK

(www.washingtonparkpdx.org; ✪; ☒63, ☒Blue, Red) Tame and well-tended Washington Park contains several key attractions within its 410 acres of greenery. The **International Rose Test Garden** (www.waparkrosefriends. org; 400 SW Kingston Ave; ⊙7:30am-9pm; ☒63) FREE is the centerpiece of Portland's famous rose blooms; there are more than 700 varieties on show here, plus great city views. Further uphill is the **Japanese Garden** (☎503-223-1321; www.japanesegarden.org; 611 SW

Kingston Ave; adult/child $16.95/11.50; ⊙noon-7pm Mon, 10am-7pm Tue-Sun mid-Mar–Sep, noon-4pm Mon, 10am-4pm Tue-Sun Oct–mid-Mar; ☒63), another oasis of tranquility. If you have kids, the **Oregon Zoo** (☎503-226-1561; www.oregonzoo.org; 4001 SW Canyon Rd; adult/child $17.95/12.95; ⊙9:30am-6pm Jun-Aug, to 4pm Sep-May; ✪; ☒63, ☒Blue, Red) and **Portland Children's Museum** (☎503-233-6500; www.portlandcm.org; 4015 SW Canyon Rd; $11, 2nd Sun of month 9am-noon $3; ⊙9am-5pm; ✪; ☒63, ☒Red, Blue) should be on your docket.

⊙ Northeast & Southeast

Across the Willamette River from downtown is the **Lloyd Center** (Map p1060; ☎503-282-2511; www.lloydcenter.com; 2201 Lloyd Center; ⊙10am-7pm Mon, to 8pm Tue-Sat, 11am-6pm Sun; ☒Red, Blue, Green), Oregon's largest shopping mall and where notorious ice-queen Tonya Harding first learned to skate. A few blocks to the southwest are the unmissable glass towers of the **Oregon Convention Center** (Map p1060; www.oregoncc.org; 777 NE Martin Luther King Jr Blvd; ☒Red, Blue, Green, Yellow), and nearby is the **Moda Center** (Map p1060; ☎503-235-8771; www.rosequarter.com/venue/moda-center; 1 N Center Court St; ☒Yellow), home of professional basketball team the Trailblazers.

Further up the Willamette, **N Mississippi Ave** used to be full of run-down buildings, but is now a hot spot of trendy shops and eateries. Northeast is artsy **NE Alberta St**, a long ribbon of art galleries, boutiques and cafes (don't miss the **Last Thursday** (☑ 503-823-1052; www.lastthurspdx.com; ☺ 6-9pm last Thu of month) street-art event here). **SE Hawthorne Blvd** (near SE 39th Ave) is affluent hippy territory, with gift stores, cafes, coffee shops and two branches of Powell's bookstores. One leafy mile to the south, **SE Division St** has become a foodie destination, with plenty of excellent restaurants, bars and pubs. The same is true of **E Burnside at NE 28th Ave**, though it has a more concentrated and upscale feel.

🏃 Activities

Hiking

Portland boasts the 5100-acre Forest Park (p1062) within city limits, which will keep avid hikers busy for a while. There's also a network of trails in **Hoyt Arboretum** (☑ 503-865-8733; www.hoytarboretum.org; 4000 Fairview Blvd; ☺ trails 5am-10pm, visitor center 9am-4pm Mon-Fri, from 10am Sat & Sun; ☒ Washington Park) **FREE**, easily reached by light rail, and more to explore at **Tryon Creek State Natural Area** (☑ 503-636-9886; www.oregonstateparks.org; 11321 SW Terwilliger Blvd).

If that's not enough, the hiking wonderlands of Mt Hood (p1072) and the Columbia River Gorge (p1071) are each less than an hour's drive away.

Cycling

Portland often tops lists of the USA's most bike-friendly cities.

Look for pleasant paths along the **Willamette River** downtown, or try the 21-mile **Springwater Corridor**, which heads out to the suburb of Boring.

Mountain bikers can head to **Leif Erikson Dr**, or for singletrack and technical trails, **Hood River** and **Mt Hood** (both about an hour's drive away) have great options.

For scenic farm country, head to **Sauvie Island** (www.sauvieisland.org; Hwy 30; daily parking pass $10), 10 miles northwest of downtown Portland.

Everybody's Bike Rentals & Tours   CYCLING
(☑ 503-358-0152; www.pdxbikerentals.com; 305 NE Wygant St; rentals per hr $8-25, tours per person from $39; ☺ 10am-5pm; ☒ 6) It's true that Portland is best seen by bicycle, and this company offers low-key, fun tours of the city and its surroundings – whether you're into food and farms or beer and parks. Try the 'Beyond Portlandia' tour for an off-the-beaten-path glimpse of the city. Bicycle rentals, from commuters to mountain bikes, are also available.

Kayaking

Situated close to the confluence of the Columbia and Willamette Rivers, Portland has miles of navigable waterways.

Portland Kayak Company   KAYAKING
(☑ 503-459-4050; www.portlandkayak.com; 6600 SW Macadam Ave; rental per hr from $14; ☺ 10am-6pm Mon-Fri, from 9am Sat, to 5pm Sun; ☒ 43) Kayaking rentals (minimum two hours), instruction and tours – notably a three-hour circumnavigation of Ross Island on the Willamette River ($49), available at 10am and 2pm daily and at sunset (starts 6pm) May through September.

PACIFIC NORTHWEST PORTLAND

PORTLAND FOR CHILDREN

Washington Park has the most to offer families with young kids. Here you'll find the world-class Oregon Zoo (p1062), which is set in a beautiful natural environment parents will also enjoy. Next door is the Portland Children's Museum (p1062) and **World Forestry Center** (☑ 503-228-1367; www.worldforestry.org; 4033 SW Canyon Rd; adult/child $8/5; ☺ 10am-5pm, closed Tue & Wed Labor Day-Memorial Day; 🚻; ☒ 63, ☒ Blue, Red), both offering fun learning activities and exhibits.

On the other side of the **Willamette River**, the **Oregon Museum of Science and Industry** (OMSI; Map p1060; ☑ 503-797-4000; www.omsi.edu; 1945 SE Water Ave; adult/child $14.50/9.75; ☺ 9:30am-7pm Jun-Aug, to 5:30pm Tue-Sun Sep-May; 🚻; ☒ 9, 17, ☒ A Loop, B Loop, ☒ Orange) is a top-notch destination with a theater, planetarium and even a submarine to explore. Further south is **Oaks Amusement Park** (☑ 503-233-5777; www.oakspark.com; 7805 SE Oaks Park Way; ride bracelets $19-41, individual rides $4.95, skating $7-7.50; ☺ hours vary; 🚻; ☒ 35, 99), home to pint-size roller coasters, miniature golf and carnival games.

☞ Tours

Pedal Bike Tours CYCLING
(Map p1060; ☎503-243-2453; www.pedalbike
tours.com; 133 SW 2nd Ave; tours from $49;
⏰10am-6pm; 🚌15, 16, 51, 🚊Blue, Red) Offers
all sorts of themes – history, doughnuts,
beer – plus day trips to the Columbia Gorge.
The three-hour 'bike and boat' package includes a historic bike tour of downtown and
a sightseeing cruise with **Portland Spirit**
(Map p1060; ☎503-224-3900; www.portlandspir
it.com; cnr SW Salmon St & Waterfront; sightseeing/
dinner cruise from $32/78; 🚌4, 10, 14, 15, 30).

Portland Walking Tours WALKING
(☎503-774-4522; www.portlandwalkingtours.com;
per person $23-79) Food, chocolate, under-
ground and even ghost-hunting tours are
available daily. A tour of 'makers and their
spaces' offers a glimpse behind the scenes
of Portland's indie-creative side, from crafts
and woodworking to leather goods and a
brewery. Each tour meets at a different location; reservations recommended.

✵ Festivals & Events

Pickathon MUSIC
(www.pickathon.com; 16581 SE Hagen Rd, Happy
Valley; weekend pass $325; ⏰Aug) This fam-
ily-friendly music festival has been going
strong for more than 20 years, thanks to outstanding music lineups and a fun, stress-free
atmosphere. Camping is free with a weekend pass, and kids under 12 get in free with
a parent. Bicycling to the festival is strongly
encouraged. It's in Happy Valley, 10 miles
southeast of downtown.

Feast Portland FOOD & DRINK
(www.feastportland.com; tickets from $25; ⏰mid-
Sep) Taste the food and drink that's at the
forefront of Oregon cuisine at this festival,
with more than 30 events of varying sizes
and levels of involvement. Proceeds benefit
an organization that fights hunger. Book
early as some events sell out months ahead.

🛏 Sleeping

Tariffs listed are for the summer season,
when reservations are a good idea. Prices at
top-end hotels are highly variable depending on occupancy and day of the week.

Hawthorne Portland Hostel HOSTEL $
(☎503-236-3380; www.portlandhostel.org; 3031
SE Hawthorne Blvd; dm $35-39, d with shared bath
$77; ❀@🛜; 🚌14) 🍃 This ecofriendly hostel
with two private rooms and spacious dorms

has a great Hawthorne location. There are
summertime open-mike nights in the grassy
backyard, and bicycle rentals (and a fix-it
station) are available. The hostel composts
and recycles, harvests rainwater for toilets,
and has a nice eco-roof. Discounts are offered to those who are bicycle touring.

Northwest Portland Hostel HOSTEL $
(Map p1060; ☎503-241-2783; www.nwportland
hostel.com; 425 NW 18th Ave; dm $36-42, d with
shared bath from $100; ❀@🛜; 🚌77) Perfectly
located between the Pearl District and NW
21st and 23rd Aves, this friendly, clean hostel takes up four old buildings and features
plenty of common areas, including a small
deck and garden patio. Dorms are spacious
and private rooms can be as nice as those in
hotels, though all share outside bathrooms.
Non-HI members pay $3 extra.

★Kennedy School HOTEL $$
(☎503-249-3983; www.mcmenamins.com/kenne
dyschool; 5736 NE 33rd Ave; r $135-235; 🛜; 🚌70)
This former elementary school is now home
to a hotel (sleep in old classrooms!), a restau-
rant with a great garden courtyard, several
bars, a microbrewery and a movie theater.
Guests can use the soaking pool for free. The
whole school is decorated in the McMenam-
ins' distinctive art style – mosaics, fantasy
paintings and historical photographs.

★Ace Hotel BOUTIQUE HOTEL $$
(Map p1060; ☎503-228-2277; www.acehotel.com;
1022 Harvey Milk St; s with shared bath from $200,
d from $285; 🅿❀❀@🛜❀) A well-estab-
lished brand, the Ace fuses industrial, minimalist and retro styles to great effect. From
the photo booth in its lobby to the recycled
fabrics and salvaged-wood furniture in its
rooms, the hotel feels very chic and very
Portland. There's a Stumptown coffee shop
and underground bar on-site, and **Clyde
Common** bistro (Map p1060; ☎503-228-
3333; www.clydecommon.com; 1014 Harvey Milk
St; mains $25-40; ⏰6-11pm Sun-Wed, to midnight
Thu-Sat, brunch 10am-3pm Sat & Sun) adjoins the
lobby. The location can't be beat.

★Society Hotel HOTEL $$
(Map p1060; ☎503-445-0444; www.thesociety
hotel.com; 203 NW 3rd Ave; dm $55, d from $130;
🛜; 🚌8, 77, 🚊Red, Blue, Green, Orange) This pret-
ty hotel in the historic 1881 Mariners Build-
ing – originally a lodging house for sailors
– has impeccable fashion sense. Options
include dorms as well as private rooms.
There's a lively bar and rooftop deck, plus

Wednesday wine tastings and drag bingo on Thursday. Some corner rooms have huge windows designed to catch sunlight.

Jupiter Next BOUTIQUE HOTEL **$$**
(Map p1060; ☑503-230-9200; https://jupiter hotel.com; 900 E Burnside St; d from $180) Jupiter Next, the upmarket big sister of the adjacent '60s-retro **Jupiter Hotel** (Map p1060; ☑503-230-9200; www.jupiterhotel.com; 800 E Burnside St; d from $149; ❄️🛜🐾; 🚊20), brings a modern boutique offering to Portland's central eastside district. The six-floor geometric structure is completely bedecked in roofing shingles and its 67 rooms have oversized windows that offer postcard-perfect views of the city. Extra touches include digital concierges and bedside CBD chocolates.

Hey Love (Map p1060; ☑503-206-6223; www. heylovepdx.com; 920 E Burnside St, Jupiter Next; ⏱7am-2am), the hotel's tropical tippling den, serves tasty international fare daily for lunch and dinner, in addition to weekend brunch.

★**Hoxton** BOUTIQUE HOTEL **$$$**
(Map p1060; ☑503-770-0500; https://thehoxton. com/oregon/portland/hotels; 15 NW 4th Ave; d from $275; ❄️🛜) From London-based Hoxton hoteliers comes this US outpost, right inside the Chinatown Gateway. An airy, Northwestern modernist aesthetic – clean lines, natural materials and mid-century accents – features throughout expansive communal areas and the 119 rooms, ranging in usual Hoxton sizes (Shoebox, Snug, Cozy and Roomy). Standards include breakfast bag delivery, books curated by locals and rip-off-free munchies for purchase at reception.

★**Woodlark** BOUTIQUE HOTEL **$$$**
(Map p1060; ☑503-548-2559; https://woodlark hotel.com; 813 SW Alder St; d from $275; ❄️🛜🐾) Stitching together two revived National Historic Register buildings, this new boutique hotel delivers sumptuous design with swanky amenities. Mid-century modern furnishings, tropical plants and elemental accents make up the opulent lobby, while forest-green-upholstered headboards and foliage-themed wallpaper feature throughout the 150 rooms. Luxury plant-based toiletries, in-room streaming fitness programs, and menus for pillows and spiritual texts come standard.

✖ Eating

Portland has become nationally recognized for its food scene, with dozens of young, top-notch chefs pushing the boundaries of ethnic and regional cuisines and making the most of locally sourced, sustainably raised ingredients.

★**Luc Lac** VIETNAMESE **$**
(Map p1060; ☑503-222-0047; www.luclackitchen. com; 835 SW 2nd Ave; mains $9-13; ⏱11am-2:30pm & 4pm-midnight Sun-Thu, 11am-2:30pm & 4pm-4am Fri & Sat) This bustling Vietnamese kitchen draws downtown lunch crowds and late-night bar-hoppers with superbly executed classics such as *pho*, vermicelli bowls and banh mi. Count on queuing any time of day to score a seat in the swanky dining room, where pink paper parasols hang from the ceiling. Happy hour (4pm to 7pm) has a more relaxed vibe and small plates run just $3.

★**Yonder** SOUTHERN US **$**
(☑503-444-7947; www.yonderpdx.com; 4636 NE 42nd Ave; mains $8-17; ⏱11am-9pm Wed-Sun) Yonder's excellent fried chicken is available 'dusted' (adorned with dry spice), 'dipped' (tossed in a zesty sauce) or 'hot' (just spicy enough to be memorable, without injury), served with cornbread or a biscuit with sweet sorghum butter. Add a side of pimento mac 'n' cheese or bacon-braised collard greens, then wash it down with a craft cocktail. Down-home good!

Nong's Khao Man Gai THAI **$**
(Map p1060; ☑503-740-2907; www.khaomangai. com; 609 SE Ankeny St; mains $11-16; ⏱10:50am-9pm; 🚊20) The widely adored food cart where it all started has closed, but Nong's brick-and-mortar locations still dish out her signature menu item: tender poached chicken with rice in a magical sauce. A handful of other options (including vegetarian) and add-ons are available, as well as occasional specials.

There's another branch located at 417 SW 13th Ave.

★**Stammtisch** GERMAN **$$**
(☑503-206-7983; www.stammtischpdx.com; 401 NE 28th Ave; small plates $5-9, mains $14-24; ⏱3pm-1:30am Mon-Fri, 11am-1:30am Sat & Sun; 🦽; 🚊19) Dig into serious German food – with a beer list to match – at this dark and cozy neighborhood pub. Don't miss the *Maultaschen* (a gorgeous pasta pocket filled with leek fondue in a bright, lemony wine sauce), the clams with *Landjäger* sausage in white wine broth, or the paprika-spiced roast chicken.

PORTLAND'S FOOD CARTS

Some of Portland's most amazing food comes from humble little kitchens-on-wheels. Found all over town clumped together in parking lots or otherwise unoccupied spaces, food carts offer hungry wanderers a chance to try unusual dishes at low prices, and they often have covered seating areas if you don't like to walk while you eat. Many of Portland's beloved eateries got their start as food carts, with specialties that were such hits that brick-and-mortar locations were established to serve increasing demands.

★**Bullard**   SOUTHERN US $$
(Map p1060; ☑503-222-1670; www.bullardpdx.com; 813 SW Alder St; dinner mains $16-32; ⊙11am-3pm & 5-10pm Mon-Thu, 11am-3pm & 5-11pm Fri, 10am-11pm Sat, 10am-10pm Sun) Inside the Woodlark hotel (p1065) is this nod to chef Doug Adams' roots and chosen home, where the meat-centric menu is decidedly Tex-as-meets-Oregon. 'Supper' plates showcase the likes of 12-hour smoked Painted Hills beef ribs served with fresh flour tortillas, grilled rainbow trout with a black-eyed pea and celery salad, and a pork chop with heirloom hominy and local collard greens.

★**Tasty n Daughters**   AMERICAN $$
(☑503-621-1400; www.tastyndaughters.com; 4537 SE Division St; small plates $3-14, mains $12-19; ⊙9am-2:30pm & 5-10pm) After a nine-year run, chef John Gorham, of **Toro Bravo** (☑503-281-4464; www.torobravopdx.com; 120 NE Russell St; tapas $3-17, mains $13-24; ⊙5-10pm Mon-Thu, to 11pm Fri & Sat) fame, took brunch favorite Tasty n Sons, formerly on N Williams, to southeast Portland. The reboot – renamed to accurately reflect his offspring – retained favorites like *shakshuka* and patatas bravas, but added fresh pasta and seafood to the menu. Most notable is a new Turkish influence – the pide breakfast pizza is a must.

OK Omens   AMERICAN $$
(Map p1060; ☑503-231-9959; www.okomens.com; 1758 SE Hawthorne Blvd; dishes $8-18; ⊙5pm-midnight; ☐14) OK Omens is a hit, not least for its epic wine list and menu of adventurous shareable dishes. Crowd favorites include a spicy Caesar-style salad with buttermilk fried chicken, hoisin-roasted carrots, adorable cheddar-filled beignets, crab pasta

topped with thinly sliced jalapeños, and burgers. On Sunday, happy hour lasts all day.

★**Ava Gene's**   ITALIAN $$$
(☑971-229-0571; www.avagenes.com; 3377 SE Division St; mains $25-35; ⊙5-10pm Mon-Thu, to 11pm Fri, 4:30-11pm Sat, 4:30-10pm Sun; ☐4) This renowned trattoria-inspired eatery – owned by Duane Sorenson, who founded Stumptown Coffee (p1067) – serves rustic Italian cuisine, with exquisite pasta and vegetable dishes as highlights. Exceptional ingredients, a great wine list and cocktails, and outstanding service make it a swoon-worthy dining experience worth seeking out. Reserve ahead.

★**Ox**   STEAK $$$
(☑503-284-3366; www.oxpdx.com; 2225 NE Martin Luther King Jr Blvd; mains $14-56; ⊙5-10pm Sun-Thu, to 11pm Fri & Sat; ☐6) One of Portland's most popular restaurants is this upscale, Argentine-inspired steakhouse. Start with the smoked bone-marrow clam chowder, then go for the gusto: the grass-fed beef rib eye. If there's two of you, the *asado* (barbecue grill; $94) is a good choice, allowing you to try several different cuts. Reserve ahead.

★**Ataula**   SPANISH $$$
(☑503-894-8904; www.ataulapdx.com; 1818 NW 23rd Pl; tapas $9-17, paella dishes $35-40; ⊙4:30-10pm Tue-Sat; ☐15, 77) This critically acclaimed Spanish tapas restaurant offers outstanding cuisine. If these are on the menu, try the *nuestras bravas* (sliced, fried potatoes in milk aioli), *croquetas* (salt-cod fritters), *xupa xup* (chorizo 'lollipop') and *ataula montadito* (salmon with mascarpone yogurt and black-truffle honey). Great cocktails, too. Be sure to reserve.

Ned Ludd   AMERICAN $$$
(☑503-288-6900; www.nedluddpdx.com; 3925 NE Martin Luther King Jr Blvd; small plates $3-18, mains $25-28; ⊙5-9pm Sun-Thu, to 10pm Fri & Sat; ☐6) ⋒ Quintessentially Portland, this offbeat, upscale joint exudes thick artisan vibes, from its rustic-peasant decor to the prominent brick wood-fired oven where all dishes are cooked. The beautifully presented small plates are rotated daily. This is not a place to simply fill your tummy but one in which to sample eclectic 'American craft' delicacies.

🍷 Drinking & Nightlife

Drinking, whether it's coffee or a craft brew, cider or kombucha, is practically a sport in Portland. In winter it's a reason to hunker down and escape the rain; in summer, an excuse to sit on a patio or deck and soak up the long-awaited sunshine. Whatever your poison, there's bound to be a handcrafted, artisan version of it here.

★**Push x Pull** COFFEE
(Map p1060; https://pushxpullcoffee.com; 821 SE Stark St; ☯7am-5pm Mon-Fri, 8am-4pm Sat & Sun) A labor of love by a group of java-obsessed pals, this roastery and cafe specializes in natural-process coffees and offers a rotating selection of single-origins, plus local baked goods. Bright wood paneling and turquoise-painted walls that perfectly match the industrial schoolhouse furniture and espresso machines make for a cheery space – not to mention the delightfully friendly owners and staff.

★**Barista** COFFEE
(Map p1060; ☏503-274-1211; www.baristapdx.com; 539 NW 13th Ave; ☯6am-7pm Mon-Fri, from 7am Sat & Sun; ☷77) One of Portland's best coffee shops, this tiny, stylish shop is owned by award-winning barista Billy Wilson. Beans are sourced from specialty roasters. Three other locations in town.

Coava Coffee COFFEE
(Map p1060; ☏503-894-8134; www.coavacoffee. com; 1300 SE Grand Ave; ☯6am-6pm Mon-Fri, 7am-6pm Sat & Sun; ☏; ☷6, 15, ☷B Loop) The decor takes the concept of 'neo-industrial' to extremes, but it works – Coava delivers where it matters. The pour-over makes for a fantastic cup of java, and the espressos are exceptional, too. Also at 2631 SE Hawthorne Blvd.

★**Proud Mary** CAFE
(☏503-208-3475; https://proudmarycoffee.com; 2012 NE Alberta St; ☯7am-4pm Mon-Fri, from 8am Sat & Sun) From the land of flat whites and avocado toast comes Proud Mary, the notable Melbourne-based coffee roaster that aptly chose Portland for their first US outpost. In addition to superb coffee, they sling delicious, Insta-worthy breakfast, brunch and lunch plates such as vanilla and ricotta hotcakes, a smoked pork-belly satay sandwich and Aussie meat pies. Smoothies and fresh juices, too.

Deadstock Coffee COFFEE
(Map p1060; ☏971-220-8727; www.deadstock coffee.com; 408 NW Couch St; ☯7:30am-5pm Mon-Fri, 9am-6pm Sat, 10am-4pm Sun) Deadstock's ethos that 'coffee should be dope' comes through in its signature concoctions and blends, such as the LeBronald Palmer (a mix of iced coffee, sweet tea and lemonade)

and 'Fresh Prince' (Ethiopian light-roast beans). Owner Ian Williams once worked his way from janitor to shoe designer at Nike HQ, and it's the world's only coffee shop dedicated to sneaker culture.

Stumptown Coffee Roasters COFFEE
(☏503-230-7702; www.stumptowncoffee.com; 4525 SE Division St; ☯6am-7pm Mon-Fri, from 7am Sat & Sun; ☏; ☷4) Stumptown was the first micro roaster to put Portland on the coffee map, and this small, narrow space is where it all started.

★**Breakside Brewery** BREWERY
(☏503-444-7597; www.breakside.com; 1570 NW 22nd Ave; ☯11am-10pm Sun-Thu, to 11pm Fri & Sat; ☷8) Known for experimental brews laced with fruits, vegetables and spices, plus a nationally lauded IPA, Breakside expanded beyond its original location at 820 NE Dekum St in northeast Portland and opened a bigger venue in Slabtown in 2017. Sixteen taps, great grub and two levels of seating (plus a large patio) in a cheery industrial space make it one of Portland's finest brewpubs.

★**Culmination Brewing** MICROBREWERY
(Map p1060; ☏971-254-9114; www.culmination brewing.com; 2117 NE Oregon St; plates $5-16; ☯noon-9pm Sun-Thu, to 10pm Fri & Sat; ☷12) At this comfortable tasting room in a refurbished old warehouse, you'll find some of the city's best beers (including the top-notch Phaedrus IPA plus a whole array of limited-edition seasonals) and a brief but unusually ambitious food menu. If the *pêche* is available, try it – even if you don't normally like 'fruit' beers.

Ecliptic Brewing BREWERY
(☏503-265-8002; www.eclipticbrewing.com; 825 N Cook St; ☯11am-10pm Sun-Thu, to 11pm Fri & Sat; ☷4) It's in kind of a chilly industrial space, but the beer speaks for itself – Ecliptic was founded by John Harris, who previously brewed for McMenamins, Deschutes and Full Sail. The brewery's astronomically named creations (such as the Craft Beer medal–winning Spica Pilsner) are ambitious and wildly successful. Food includes lamb picatta, tempura asparagus and a goat's cheese and beet melt sandwich.

Cider Riot BREWERY
(Map p1060; ☏503-662-8275; www.ciderriot.com; 807 NE Couch St; ☯4-11pm Mon-Fri, noon-11pm Sat, noon-9pm Sun; ☷12, 19, 20) Portland's best cider company now has its very own pub and tasting room, so you can sample Everybody

DON'T MISS

POWELL'S CITY OF BOOKS

Powell's City of Books (Map p1060; ☑800-878-7323; www.powells.com; 1005 W Burnside St; ⊙9am-11pm; 🚇20) is one of the USA's largest independent bookstores, with a whole city block of new and used titles, and a well-attended series of readings.

There's another branch at 3723 SE Hawthorne Blvd (with a Home and Garden bookstore next door), and one at the airport.

Pogo, Never Give an Inch or Plastic Paddy at the source. Ciders here are dry and complex, made with regional apples and hyper-regional attitude.

☆ Entertainment

Music, particularly of the indie rock persuasion, is one of Portland's primary exports – but jazz, punk, electronic, blues, metal, hiphop and other genres also have a place in the scene, with acts playing both renowned local venues and unassuming neighborhood bars. Other entertainment runs the gamut from theater and ballet to burlesque and drag, and there's plenty of cinema and sports, too.

Live Music

Doug Fir Lounge   LIVE MUSIC
(Map p1060; ☑503-231-9663; www.dougfirlounge. com; 830 E Burnside St; ⊙7am-2:30am; 🚇20) Combining futuristic elements with a rustic log-cabin aesthetic, this venue has helped transform the LoBu (lower Burnside) neighborhood from seedy to slick. Doug Fir books great bands and the sound quality is usually tops. The attached restaurant offers a killer breakfast and weekend brunch, and a bar menu ($8 to $13) until close.

Crystal Ballroom   LIVE MUSIC
(Map p1060; ☑503-225-0047; www.crystalball roompdx.com; 1332 W Burnside St; 🚇20) This large, historic ballroom has hosted some major acts, including James Brown and Marvin Gaye in the early '60s, and Devendra Banhart and Two Door Cinema Club today. The bouncy, 'floating' dance floor makes dancing almost effortless.

Mississippi Studios   LIVE MUSIC
(☑503-288-3895; www.mississippistudios.com; 3939 N Mississippi Ave; 🚇4) This intimate bar is good for checking out budding acoustic talent along with more-established musical acts. Excellent sound system, and good restaurant-bar with patio (and awesome burgers) next door.

Performing Arts

Portland Center Stage   THEATER
(Map p1060; ☑503-445-3700; www.pcs.org; 128 NW 11th Ave; tickets from $25; 🚇4, 8, 44, 77) The city's main theater company performs in the Portland Armory – a renovated Pearl District landmark with state-of-the-art features.

Arlene Schnitzer Concert Hall   CLASSICAL MUSIC
(Map p1060; ☑503-248-4335; www.portland5. com; 1037 SW Broadway; 🚇10, 14, 15, 35, 36, 44, 54, 56) This beautiful, if not acoustically brilliant, downtown venue, built in 1928, hosts a wide range of shows, lectures, concerts and other performances.

Keller Auditorium   PERFORMING ARTS
(Map p1060; ☑503-248-4335; www.portland5. com; 222 SW Clay St; 🚇38, 45, 55, 92, 96) Built in 1917 and formerly known as the Civic Auditorium, Keller hosts a wide range of performers, from big-name musicians (Sturgill Simpson) to the Portland Opera (www. portlandopera.org) and the Oregon Ballet Theatre (www.obt.org), along with some Broadway productions.

🔒 Shopping

Portland's downtown shopping district extends in a two-block radius from Pioneer Courthouse Sq and hosts all of the usual suspects. The Pearl District is dotted with highend galleries, boutiques and home-decor shops. On weekends, you can visit the quintessential Saturday Market by the Skidmore Fountain. For a pleasant, upscale shopping street, head to NW 23rd Ave.

Eastside has lots of trendy shopping streets that also host restaurants and cafes. SE Hawthorne Blvd is the biggest, N Mississippi Ave is the newest and NE Alberta St is the most artsy and funkiest.

ⓘ Information

EMERGENCY & MEDICAL SERVICES

Legacy Good Samaritan Medical Center (☑503-413-7711; www.legacyhealth.org; 1015 NW 22nd Ave) Convenient to downtown.

Portland Police Bureau (☑503-823-0000; www.portlandoregon.gov/police; 1111 SW 2nd Ave) Police and emergency services.

MEDIA

KBOO 90.7 FM (www.kboo.fm) Progressive local station run by volunteers; alternative news and views.

Portland Mercury (www.portlandmercury. com) Free local sibling of Seattle's *The Stranger*.

Willamette Week (www.wweek.com) Free weekly covering local news and culture.

TOURIST INFORMATION

Travel Portland (Map p1060; 503-275-8355; www.travelportland.com; 701 SW 6th Ave, Pioneer Courthouse Sq; ⊗8:30am-5:30pm Mon-Fri, 10am-4pm Sat Nov-Apr, plus 10am-2pm Sun May-Oct; ☒Red, Blue, Green, Yellow) Super-friendly volunteers staff this office in Pioneer Courthouse Sq. There's a small theater with a 12-minute film about the city, and TriMet bus and light-rail offices inside.

ⓘ Getting There & Away

AIR

Portland International Airport (503-460-4234; www.flypdx.com; 7000 NE Airport Way; ☒; ☒Red) Award-winning Portland International Airport has daily flights all over the US, as well as to several international destinations. It's situated just east of I-5 on the banks of the Columbia River (a 20-minute drive from downtown).

BUS

Bolt Bus (Map p1060; 877-265-8287; www. boltbus.com) Connects Portland with Seattle (from $25), Bellingham ($40), Eugene ($15) and Vancouver ($50), among other cities. Buses leave from the corner of NW 8th Ave and NW Everett St.

Greyhound (Map p1060; 503-243-2361; www.greyhound.com; 550 NW 6th Ave; ☒Green, Orange, Yellow) Greyhound connects Portland with cities along I-5 and I-84. Destinations beyond Oregon include Chicago, Denver, San Francisco, Seattle and Vancouver.

TRAIN

Union Station (800-872-7245; www.amtrak. com; 800 NW 6th Ave; ☒17, ☒Green, Yellow) Amtrak services depart from here for Chicago, Oakland, Seattle and Vancouver.

ⓘ Getting Around

TO/FROM THE AIRPORT

Tri-Met's light-rail MAX red line takes about 40 minutes to get from downtown to the airport (adult/child $2.50/1.25). If you prefer a bus, **Blue Star** (503-249-1837; www.bluestarbus. com; per person one way from $14) offers shuttle services between PDX and several downtown stops.

Taxis charge around $35 to $40 (not including tip) from the airport to downtown.

BICYCLE

Clever Cycles (503-334-1560; www.clever cycles.com; 900 SE Hawthorne Blvd; rentals per day $30, cargo bikes $60; ⊗11am-6pm Mon-Fri, to 5pm Sat & Sun; ☒10, 14) Rents folding, family and cargo bikes.

CAR

Parking on the east side of the city is generally easy to find; downtown, SmartPark garages, some with electric-vehicle charging stations, offer affordable parking (see www.portlandoregon. gov/transportation/35272). Downtown, Northwest and the Pearl District often have metered parking; finding a spot here can be harder. Carshare programs are also popular.

It only became legal to pump your own gasoline in Oregon in 2019. Most stations have free full-serve attendants on-site, who will do everything from start to finish.

CHARTER SERVICE

For custom bus or van charters and tours, try **EcoShuttle** (503-548-4480; www.ecoshuttle.net; per 3hr from $500). Its vehicles run on 100% biodiesel.

PUBLIC TRANSPORTATION

The MAX light rail connects to most of the major metro areas (and suburbs) and is easily navigable. Buses connect with many stops.

TAXI

Cabs are available 24 hours by phone. Downtown, you can sometimes flag them down, and some bartenders will call you a cab on request. **Broadway Cab** (503-333-3333; www.broadwaycab.com) and **Radio Cab** (503-227-1212; www.radiocab.net) are two reliable operators. Rideshare services are usually abundant in Portland.

Willamette Valley

The Willamette Valley, a fertile 60-mile-wide agricultural basin, was the Holy Grail for Oregon Trail pioneers who headed west more than 170 years ago. Today it's the state's breadbasket, producing more than 100 kinds of crops – including renowned pinot noir grapes. Salem, Oregon's capital, is about an hour's drive from Portland at the northern end of the valley, and most of the other attractions in the area make easy day trips as well. Toward the south is Eugene, a dynamic college town worth a day or two of exploration.

Salem

Oregon's legislative center is renowned for its cherry trees, art-deco capitol building and Willamette University.

The university's **Hallie Ford Museum of Art** (☑ 503-370-6855; www.willamette.edu/arts/hfma; 700 State St; adult/child $6/free, Tue free; ⊙ 10am-5pm Tue-Sat, 1-5pm Sun) showcases the state's best collection of Pacific Northwest art, including an impressive Native American gallery.

The **Oregon State Capitol** (☑ 503-986-1388; www.oregonlegislature.gov; 900 Court St NE; ⊙ 8am-5pm Mon-Fri) FREE, built in 1938, looks like a background from a lavish Cecil B De-Mille movie; free tours are offered. Rambling 19th-century **Bush House** (☑ 503-363-4714; www.salemart.org; 600 Mission St SE; adult/child $6/3; ⊙ tours 1-4pm Thu-Sun Apr-Sep, Fri-Sun Oct-Mar) is an Italianate mansion now preserved as a museum with historical accents, including original wallpapers and marble fireplaces.

You can get oriented at the **Visitors Information Center** (☑ 503-581-4325; www.travelsalem.com; 388 State St; ⊙ 9am-5pm Mon-Fri, 10am-4pm Sat; 🐾). Salem is served daily by **Greyhound** (www.greyhound.com; 500 13th St SE) buses and **Amtrak** (☑ 503-588-1551; www.amtrak.com; 500 13th St SE) trains.

Eugene

'Track Town' offers a great art scene, fine restaurants, boisterous festivals, miles of riverside paths and several lovely parks. Its location at the confluence of the Willamette and McKenzie Rivers, just west of the Cascades, means there's plenty of outdoor recreation on offer – especially around the McKenzie River region, the Three Sisters Wilderness and Willamette Pass.

◎ Sights

Saturday Market   MARKET
(☑ 541-686-8885; www.eugenesaturdaymarket.org; 8th Ave & Oak St; ⊙ 10am-5pm Sat Apr–mid-Nov) For great fun and a quintessential introduction to Eugene's peculiar vitality, don't miss the Saturday Market, held each Saturday from April through November. Local artisans sell handcrafted works, and there's live music throughout the day on the stage in the food court. Between Thanksgiving and Christmas it's renamed the **Holiday Market** (☑ 541-686-8885; www.holidaymarket.org; 796 W 13th Ave, Lane Events Center; ⊙ 10am-6pm mid-Nov–Dec) and moves indoors to the Lane Events Center.

Alton Baker Park   PARK
(100 Day Island Rd) This popular 400-acre riverside park, which provides access to the **Ruth Bascom Riverbank Trail System**, a 12-mile bikeway that flanks both sides of the Willamette, is heaven for cyclists and joggers. There's good downtown access via the De-Fazio Bike Bridge.

University of Oregon   UNIVERSITY
(☑ 541-346-1000; www.uoregon.edu; 1585 E 13th Ave) Established in 1872, the University of Oregon is the state's foremost institution of higher learning, with a focus on the arts, sciences and law. The campus is filled with historic ivy-covered buildings and includes a **Pioneer Cemetery**, with tombstones that give a vivid insight into life and death in the early settlement. Campus tours are held in summer.

🛌 Sleeping

Eugene has a handful of budget chain motels and hotels, plus a couple of lovely inns and a hostel. Prices can rise sharply during key football games (September to November) and at graduation (mid-June).

**Eugene Whiteaker
International Hostel**   HOSTEL $
(☑ 541-343-3335; www.eugenehostel.org; 970 W 3rd Ave; dm/r from $35/50; ⊛ @ 🐾) This casual hostel in an old, rambling house has an artsy vibe, nice front and back patios to hang out on, and a free simple breakfast. Towels and bedding are included in the price.

★**C'est La Vie Inn**   B&B $$
(☑ 541-302-3014; www.cestlavieinn.com; 1006 Taylor St; r from $180; ⊛ ✳ @ 🐾) This gorgeous Victorian house, run by a friendly French woman and her American husband, is a neighborhood showstopper. Beautiful antique furniture fills the living and dining areas, while the four tastefully appointed rooms (each named for a French artist) offer comfort and luxury. Hosts provide a full breakfast, as well as afternoon port and other nice touches.

✗ Eating & Drinking

Krob Krua Thai Kitchen   THAI $
(☑ 541-636-6267; www.krobkrua.com; 254 Lincoln St; mains $7-9; ⊙ 11am-9pm Tue-Sun) Superb Thai curries, noodles, salads, soups and wok-fired dishes are served at this joint in the same

space as **WildCraft Cider Works** (☑ 541-735-3506; https://wildcraftciderworks.com; 232 Lincoln St; ⊙ 11:30am-9pm Tue-Thu, to 11pm Fri & Sat, to 8pm Sun), where you can enjoy your food in the tasting room and wash it down with a cider. Spring for the Dungeness crab and shrimp dumplings, the namesake *krob krua* noodles with beef, or the green-curry fried rice.

★ **Izakaya Meiji Company**   IZAKAYA $$
(☑ 541-505-8804; www.izakayameiji.com; 345 Van Buren St; small plates $3-13; ⊙ 5pm-1am) This hip *izakaya* (Japanese pub serving small plates) in the heart of the Whiteaker district draws nightly crowds with handcrafted libations, sake, shochu and over 100 different whiskeys, plus a seasonal menu of shareable dishes. Feeling adventurous? Try the *shiokara*, an acquired delicacy of salted, fermented squid viscera. Or just stick with the curry udon. You can't go wrong here.

Beppe & Gianni's Trattoria   ITALIAN $$
(☑ 541-683-6661; www.beppeandgiannis.net; 1646 E 19th Ave; mains $15-26; ⊙ 5-9pm Sun-Thu, to 10pm Fri & Sat) One of Eugene's most beloved restaurants, Beppe & Gianni's serves up homemade pastas and excellent desserts. Expect a wait, especially on weekends.

★ **Ninkasi Brewing Company**   BREWERY
(☑ 541-344-2739; www.ninkasibrewing.com; 272 Van Buren St; ⊙ noon-9pm Sun-Wed, to 10pm Thu-Sat) If you like hops, head to this tasting room to sample some of Oregon's most distinctive and innovative microbrews at the source. There's a sweet patio with occasional food trucks, or you can bring in your own food. Brewery tours are at 11am on Monday, Wednesday and Friday, and at 4pm Tuesday, Thursday and Saturday.

ℹ Information

Visitor Center (☑ 541-484-5307; www.eugenecascadescoast.org; 754 Olive St; ⊙ 8am-5pm Tue-Fri, from 9am Mon) This center is open weekdays. On weekends, stop by the visitor center (☑ 541-484-5307; www.eugenecascadescoast.org; 3312 Gateway St, Springfield; ⊙ 9am-6pm) in Springfield for information.

ℹ Getting There & Around

Located about 7 miles northwest of the center, **Eugene Airport** (☑ 541-682-5544; www.flyeug.com; 28801 Douglas Dr) offers domestic flight services.

Greyhound (☑ 541-344-6265; www.greyhound.com; 987 Pearl St) provides long-distance

services to Salem, Corvallis, Portland, Medford, Grants Pass, Hood River, Newport and Bend.

Trains leave from the **Amtrak station** (☑ 541-687-1383; www.amtrak.com; 433 Willamette St) for Portland's Union Station ($28, three hours, nine daily); Seattle, WA; and Vancouver, Canada, among other places.

Local bus service is provided by **Lane Transit District** (☑ 541-687-5555; www.ltd.org). For bike rentals, head to **Paul's Bicycle Way of Life** (☑ 541-344-4105; www.bicycleway.com; 556 Charnelton St; rentals per day $24-48; ⊙ 10am-6pm Mon-Fri, to 5pm Sat & Sun).

Columbia River Gorge

The fourth-largest river in the US by volume, the mighty Columbia runs 1243 miles from Alberta, Canada, into the Pacific Ocean just west of Astoria. For the final 309 miles of its course, the heavily dammed waterway delineates the border between Washington and Oregon and cuts though the Cascade Mountains via the spectacular Columbia River Gorge. Sheltering numerous ecosystems, waterfalls and magnificent vistas, the land bordering the river is protected as a National Scenic Area and is a popular sporting nexus for windsurfers, cyclists, anglers and hikers.

Not far from Portland, **Multnomah Falls** is a huge tourist draw, while **Vista House** offers stupendous gorge views. And if you want to stretch your legs, the Gorge is riddled with hiking trails.

Hood River & Around

Famous for its surrounding fruit orchards and wineries, the town of Hood River – 63 miles east of Portland on I-84 – is also a huge mecca for windsurfing and kiteboarding. Premier wineries have taken hold in the region, providing good wine-tasting opportunities as well.

◉ Sights & Activities

Mt Hood Railroad   RAIL
(☑ 800-872-4661; www.mthoodrr.com; 110 Railroad Ave; adult/child from $35/30; 🖢) Built in 1906, the railroad once transported fruit and lumber from the upper Hood River Valley to the main railhead in Hood River. The vintage trains now transport tourists beneath Mt Hood's snowy peak and past fragrant orchards. The line is about 21 miles long and ends in pretty Parkdale. See the website for schedules and fares. Reserve in advance.

Cathedral Ridge Winery
WINE

(☑ 800-516-8710; www.cathedralridgewinery.com; 4200 Post Canyon Dr; tastings from $15; ⊙ 11am-5pm) This attractive winery in pretty farm country at the edge of town has signature red blends and a slew of awards on display. In nice weather, sit outdoors and take in the awesome view of Mt Hood. Various tours and tastings are available.

Hood River Waterplay
WATER SPORTS

(☑ 541-386-9463; www.hoodriverwaterplay.com; I-84 exit 64; 2hr windsurfing course $99, SUP lessons per hr from $48; ⊙ May-Oct) Interested in windsurfing, kayaking, SUP, catamaran sailing and so on? Contact this company, with rentals and classes at its waterfront location.

Discover Bicycles
CYCLING

(☑ 541-386-4820; www.discoverbicycles.com; 210 State St; rentals per day $40-100; ⊙ 10am-6pm Mon-Sat, to 5pm Sun) This shop rents road bikes, hybrids, mountain bikes, e-bikes and mountain e-bikes and can give advice on area trails.

🛏 Sleeping & Eating

Hood River Hotel
HISTORIC HOTEL $$

(☑ 541-386-1900; www.hoodriverhotel.com; 102 Oak St; d/ste from $110/152; ❄❀🏠🐾) Located right in the heart of downtown, this lovingly restored 1913 hotel offers comfortable, hip yet vintage rooms. Beds are comfy but some bathrooms are minuscule. The suites have the best amenities and views. Kitchenettes are also available, and there's an excellent restaurant and a relaxing sauna on the premises. Heat in the winter is via ancient steam radiator plus space heaters.

Columbia Gorge Hotel
HOTEL $$$

(☑ 800-345-1921; www.columbiagorgehotel.com; 4000 Westcliff Dr; r $149-439; ❄❀@🏠🐾) Hood River's most famous place to stay is this historic Spanish-style hotel, set high on a cliff above the Columbia. The atmosphere is classy and the grounds are lovely, and there's a fine restaurant on the premises. Rooms have antique beds and furnishings. River-view rooms cost more but are worth it.

★ pFriem Tasting Room
GASTROPUB $$

(☑ 541-321-0490; www.pfriembeer.com; 707 Portway Ave; mains $13-18; ⊙ 11:30am-9pm) The highly regarded beers at this brewery are matched by a hearty menu that is definitely not run-of-the-mill: think mussels and *frites*, beef tongue, pork terrine, and a stew made with braised lamb and duck confit. It's located near the waterfront along a stretch of industrial-chic development and tables are cozied right up to the brewing vats.

ⓘ Information

Chamber of Commerce (☑ 541-386-2000; www.hoodriver.org; 720 E Port Marina Dr; ⊙ 9am-5pm Mon-Fri, 10am-4pm Sat & Sun Apr-Oct, 9am-5pm Mon-Fri Nov-Mar) Visitor information for Hood River and the surrounding area.

ⓘ Getting There & Away

Greyhound (☑ 541-386-1212; www.greyhound.com; 110 Railroad Ave) Hood River is connected to Portland by daily Greyhound buses (from $21, one hour, three daily).

Oregon Cascades

The Oregon Cascades offer plenty of dramatic volcanoes that dominate the skyline for miles around. Mt Hood, overlooking the Columbia River Gorge, is the state's highest peak, and has year-round skiing plus a relatively straightforward summit ascent. Tracking south you'll pass Mt Jefferson and the Three Sisters before reaching Crater Lake, the ghost of erstwhile Mt Mazama that collapsed in on itself after blowing its top approximately 7000 years ago.

Mt Hood

The state's highest peak, 11,240ft Mt Hood pops into view over much of northern Oregon whenever there's a sunny day, exerting an almost magnetic tug on skiers, hikers and sightseers. In summer, wildflowers bloom on the mountainsides and hidden ponds shimmer in blue, making for some unforgettable hikes; in winter, downhill and cross-country skiing dominates people's minds and bodies.

Mt Hood is accessible year-round on Hwy 26 from Portland (56 miles), and from Hood River (44 miles) on Hwy 35. Together with the Columbia River Hwy, these routes comprise the Mt Hood Loop, a popular scenic drive. **Government Camp**, the center of business on the mountain, is at the pass over Mt Hood.

🏃 Activities

Skiing

Hood is rightly revered for its skiing. There are six ski areas on the mountain, including **Timberline** (☑ 503-272-3158; www.timberlinelodge.com; Government Camp; lift tickets adult/child $73/63), which lures snow-lovers with the longest ski season in the US (nearly year-round). Closer to Portland, **Mt Hood**

SkiBowl (☑503-272-3206; www.skibowl.com; Hwy 26; lift tickets $59, night skiing $43) is no slacker either. It's the nation's largest night-ski area and popular with city slickers who ride up for an evening of powder play. The largest ski area on the mountain is **Mt Hood Meadows** (☑503-337-2222; www.skihood.com; lift tickets adult/child up to $89/44), where the best conditions usually prevail.

Hiking

The Mt Hood National Forest protects an astounding 1200 miles of trails. A Northwest Forest Pass ($5 per day) is required to park at most trailheads.

One popular trail loops 7 miles from near the village of Zigzag to beautiful **Ramona Falls**, which tumbles down mossy columnar basalt. Another heads 1.5 miles up from US 26 to **Mirror Lake**, continues half a mile around the lake, then tracks 2 miles beyond to a ridge.

The 41-mile **Timberline Trail** circumnavigates Mt Hood through scenic wilderness. Noteworthy portions include the hike to McNeil Point and the short climb to Bald Mountain. From Timberline Lodge, Zigzag Canyon Overlook is a 4.5-mile round trip.

Climbing Mt Hood should be taken seriously, as deaths do occur, though dogs have made it to the summit and the climb can be done in a long day. Contact **Timberline Mountain Guides** (☑541-312-9242; www.timberlinemtguides.com; 2-day summit per person $780) for guided climbs.

🛌 Sleeping & Eating

Most area **campsites** (☑877-444-6777; www.recreation.gov; tent & RV sites $16-39) have drinking water and vault toilets. Reserve on busy weekends, though some walk-in sites are usually set aside. For more information, contact a nearby ranger station.

★Timberline Lodge　　　LODGE $$
(☑800-547-1406; www.timberlinelodge.com; 27500 Timberline Rd; bunk r $165-221, d from $180; ❄🐕🌐) As much a community treasure as a hotel, this gorgeous historic lodge offers a variety of rooms, from dorms that sleep up to 10 to deluxe fireplace rooms. There's a year-round heated outdoor pool, and the ski lifts are close by. Enjoy awesome views of Mt Hood, nearby hiking trails, two bars and a good dining room. Rates vary widely.

Huckleberry Inn　　　INN $$
(☑503-272-3325; www.huckleberry-inn.com; 88611 E Government Camp Loop; r $95-165, 10-bed dm $160; ❄🌐) Simple and comfortably rustic rooms are available here, along with bunk rooms that sleep up to 10. It's in a great central location in Government Camp. The casual restaurant (which doubles as the hotel's reception) serves good breakfasts. Peak holiday rates are higher.

Rendezvous Grill & Tap Room　AMERICAN $$
(☑503-622-6837; www.thevousgrill.com; 67149 E Hwy 26, Welches; mains $12-29; ⊙11:30am-8pm Tue-Sun, to 9pm Fri & Sat) This excellent restaurant offers outstanding dishes such as wild salmon with caramelized shallots and artichoke hash or chargrilled pork chop with rhubarb chutney. Lunch means gourmet sandwiches, burgers and salads on the patio. Bonus: excellent cocktails.

Mt Hood Brewing Co　　　PUB FOOD $$
(☑503-272-3172; www.mthoodbrewing.com; 87304 E Government Camp Loop, Government Camp; mains $12-24; ⊙11am-9pm) Government Camp's only brewery-restaurant offers a friendly, family-style atmosphere and pub fare including hand-tossed pizzas, sandwiches and short ribs.

ⓘ Information

For maps, permits and information, contact regional ranger stations. If you're approaching from Hood River, visit the **Hood River Ranger Station** (☑541-352-6002; 6780 OR 35, Parkdale; ⊙8am-4:30pm Mon-Fri). The **Zigzag Ranger Station** (☑503-622-3191; 70220 E Hwy 26; ⊙7:45am-4:30pm Mon-Sat) is more handy for Portland arrivals. Mt Hood **Information Center** (☑503-272-3301; 88900 E Hwy 26; ⊙9am-5pm) is in Government Camp. The weather changes quickly here; carry chains in winter.

ⓘ Getting There & Away

From Portland, Mt Hood is one hour (56 miles) by car along Hwy 26. Alternatively, you can take the prettier and longer approach via Hwy 84 to Hood River, then Hwy 35 south (1¾ hours, 95 miles).

The **Central Oregon Breeze** (☑800-847-0157; www.cobreeze.com; Government Camp Rest Area, Government Camp Loop) shuttle between Bend and Portland stops briefly at Government Camp, 6 miles from the Timberline Lodge. **Sea to Summit** (☑503-286-9333; www.seatosummit. net; round trip from $59) runs regular shuttles from Portland to the ski areas during the winter.

Sisters

Once a stagecoach stop and trade town for loggers and ranchers, today Sisters is a bustling tourist destination whose main street is lined with boutiques, art galleries and eateries housed in Western-facade buildings. Visitors come for the mountain scenery, spectacular hiking, fine cultural events and awesome climate – there's plenty of sun and little precipitation here.

At the southern end of Sisters, the **city park** (City Park Camping; ☑541-323-5220; www.ci.sisters.or.us/creekside-campground; S Locust St; tent/RV sites $20/40; ☻ Apr-Nov) has campsites, but no showers. For ultra comfort, bag a room in the luxurious **Five Pine Lodge** (☑866-974-5900; www.fivepinelodge.com; 1021 Desperado Trail; d from $242, cabins from $265; ☻❉@☎☒☻).

For refined French food you might not expect out here, head to **Cottonwood Cafe** (☑541-549-2699; www.cottonwoodinsisters.com; 403 E Hood Ave; breakfast $9-13, lunch mains $11-13; ☻8am-3pm), while **Three Creeks Brewing** (☑541-549-1963; www.threecreeksbrewing.com; 721 Desperado Ct; mains $12-26, pizzas $10-14; ☻11:30am-9pm Sun-Thu, to 10pm Fri & Sat) is the place for home brew and pub grub.

❶ Information

Chamber of Commerce (☑541-549-0251; www.sisterscountry.com; 291 E Main Ave; ☻10am-3pm Mon-Fri)

❶ Getting There & Away

Cascades East Transit (☑541-385-8680; https://cascadeseasttransit.com; one-way fare $1.50) connects Sisters with Bend (30 minutes, three daily) and Redmond (25 minutes, three daily).

Bend

Bend is where all lovers of the outdoors should live – it's an absolute paradise. You can ski fine powder in the morning, paddle a kayak in the afternoon and play golf into the evening. Or would you rather go mountain biking, hiking, mountaineering, stand up paddleboarding, fly-fishing or rock climbing? It's all close by and top drawer. Plus, you'll probably be enjoying it all in great weather, as the area gets nearly 300 days of sunshine each year.

◉ Sights

⭐**High Desert Museum** MUSEUM
(☑541-382-4754; www.highdesertmuseum.org; 59800 Hwy 97; adult/child $12/7; ☻9am-5pm May-Oct, 10am-4pm Nov-Apr; ☻) This excellent museum, about 3 miles south of Bend, charts the exploration and settlement of the West, using reenactments of a Native American camp, a hard-rock mine and an old Western town. The region's natural history is also explored; kids love the live snake, tortoise and trout exhibits, and watching the birds of prey and otters is always fun.

Guided walks and other programs are well worth attending – don't miss the raptor presentation.

⊀ Activities

Bend is a mountain-biking paradise, with hundreds of miles of awesome trails to explore. The good Bend Area Trail Map ($12.99; www.adventuremaps.net/shop/product/product/bend-area-trail-map) is available at the Visit Bend tourist office and elsewhere.

The king of Bend's mountain-biking trails is **Phil's Trail** (www.bendtrails.org/trail/phils-trail-complex) network, which offers a variety of excellent fast singletrack forest trails just minutes from town. If you want to catch air, don't miss the Whoops Trail. You can rent a bike from adventure-oriented **Cog Wild** (☑541-385-7002; www.cogwild.com; 255 SW Century Dr, Suite 201; half-day tours from $60, rentals $35-80; ☻9am-6pm).

Bend is also the gateway to some of Oregon's best skiing, 22 miles southwest of town at **Mt Bachelor Ski Resort** (☑800-829-2442; www.mtbachelor.com; lift tickets adult/child $99/56, cross-country day pass $21/14; ☻Nov-May; ☻).

🛏 Sleeping

There's an endless supply of cheap motels, hotels and services on 3rd St (US 97). Because of festivals and events, Bend's lodging rates head north most weekends, and booking ahead is recommended.

Bunk + Brew Hostel HOSTEL $
(☑458-202-1090; www.bunkandbrew.com; 42 NW Hawthorne Ave; dm $45, d $109-139; ❉@☎) This super-cosy, central and social hostel lets you bunk in the oldest brick building in Bend. Everything is small but feels like home, plus a sauna and new bathhouse were under construction when we passed. Make friends in the kitchen or movie/video-game room or take off on a walking or biking beer tour of town literally right out the door.

⭐**McMenamins Old St Francis School** HOTEL $$
(☑541-382-5174; www.mcmenamins.com; 700 NW Bond St; r from $189; ❉❉☎) Surely one of

SMITH ROCK STATE PARK

Smith Rock State Park (☎800-551-6949; www.oregonstateparks.org; 9241 NE Crooked River Dr; day use $5) Best known for its glorious rock climbing, Smith Rock State Park boasts rust-colored 800ft cliffs that tower over the pretty Crooked River. Nonclimbers have several miles of fine hiking trails, some of which involve a little simple rock scrambling. Nearby Terrebonne has a climbing store, along with some restaurants and grocery stores. The formations in the park are simply spectacular.

There's camping right next to the park, or at Skull Hollow (no water; campsites $5), 8 miles east. The nearest motels are a few miles south in Redmond.

Smith Rock Climbing Guides Inc (☎541-788-6225; www.smithrockclimbingguides. com; Smith Rock State Park, Terrebonne; half-day per person from $65) This company offers a variety of climbing instruction (basic, lead, trad, multipitch, aid and self-rescue), along with guided climbs to famous routes at Smith Rock State Park. Gear is included. Prices depend on the number in your group. Open by appointment.

McMenamins' best venues, this old schoolhouse has been remodeled into a hotel – two rooms even have side-by-side claw-foot tubs. The fabulous tiled saltwater Turkish bath alone is worth the stay; nonguests can soak for $5. A restaurant-pub, three bars, a movie theater and artwork complete the picture.

★ **Oxford Hotel**   BOUTIQUE HOTEL $$$
(☎541-382-8436; www.oxfordhotelbend.com; 10 NW Minnesota Ave; r from $319; ❄✿🐾📶) 🐾
Bend's premier boutique hotel is deservedly popular. The smallest rooms are still huge (470 sq ft) and are decked out with ecofriendly features such as soy-foam mattresses and cork flooring. High-tech aficionados will love the iPod docks and smart-panel desks. Suites (with kitchen and steam shower) are available, and the basement restaurant is slick.

The modern design and chic, cool-tone muted color scheme would fit in fine in a major city, so it simply sparkles in the more town-sized Bend.

✖ Eating

The Bite   FOOD TRUCK $
(☎541-610-6457; www.thebitetumalo.com; 19860 7th St, Tumalo; mains $8-16; ☉11am-9pm) Great setting in Tumalo, between Bend and Sisters. Get your beer on tap at the Bite bar then purchase food from one of the handful of food trucks to eat at outdoor picnic tables or indoors by the bar. People regularly drive out here just to order the delectable, sustainable and wild-caught sushi at the Ronin Sushi cart.

★ **El Sancho**   MEXICAN $
(☎458-206-5973; www.elsanchobend.com; 335 NE Dekalb Ave; tacos $2.75-3.25; ☉11am-10pm)

Fantastic, great-value Mexican served in a cool atrium-like setting that opens up in summer or is heated in winter. Every taco, from the chipotle chicken to Oaxacan cheese and green chile, is as good as you'll find anywhere. Extras include fried plantains, tamales, chicken tortilla soup and kick-ass margaritas and pisco sours.

★ **Chow**   AMERICAN $
(☎541-728-0256; www.chowbend.com; 1110 NW Newport Ave; mains $10-17; ☉7am-2pm) 🐾 The signature poached-egg dishes here are spectacular and involve layers of delicious things like polenta cakes, roasted vegetables, Mexican cheeses and cornmeal-crusted tomatoes (don't miss the housemade hot sauces). Gourmet sandwiches including crab patty or braised corned beef are served for lunch. Much of the produce is grown in the garden, and there are good cocktails, too.

★ **Sunriver Brewing Co**   GASTROPUB $$
(☎541-408-9377; www.sunriverbrewingcompany.com; 1005 NW Galveston Ave; mains $12-15; ☉11am-10pm Sun-Thu, to 11pm Fri & Sat) In a town of many, many breweries, Sunriver stands out, not only for its delicious, award-winning beers (try the flagship Vicious Mosquito IPA), but also for its great food – from bratwurst sausages with fried brussels sprouts to a creamy mac 'n' cheese topped with sockeye salmon. The pub front opens up to let the outside in on sunny days.

★ **Bos Taurus**   STEAK $$$
(☎541-241-2735; www.bostaurussteak.com; 163 NW Minnesota Ave; mains $20-79; ☉5-10pm) Like a museum of the finest beef, Bos Taurus is a must-splurge for meat lovers. The chefs here picked their cattle ranches via blind taste

test and everything beyond has also been refined to the smallest detail. There's always a fish dish and coq au vin on the menu for nonbeef eaters. Service is impeccable. Reserve ahead.

Zydeco AMERICAN $$$
(☑541-312-2899; www.zydecokitchen.com; 919 NW Bond St; dinner mains $17-38; ⏰11:30am-2:30pm & 5-9pm Mon-Fri, 5-9pm Sat & Sun) Zydeco is one of Bend's most acclaimed restaurants, and with good reason. Start with the duck fries (french fries fried in duck fat) or beet salad with goat cheese, then move on to your main course: seared ahi tuna, crawfish jambalaya or roasted duck with mushroom gravy. Reserve.

❶ Information

Visit Bend (☑541-382-8048; www.visitbend. com; 750 NW Lava Rd; ⏰9am-5pm Mon-Fri, 10am-4pm Sat & Sun) Great information, plus maps, books and recreation passes available for purchase.

❶ Getting There & Around

Central Oregon Breeze (☑541-389-7469; www.cobreeze.com; 3405 N Hwy 97, Circle K) offers transport to Portland two or more times daily ($52 one way, reserve ahead).

High Desert Point (☑541-382-4193; www.or egon-point.com/highdesert-point; Hawthorne Station) buses link Bend with Chemult, where the nearest train station is located (65 miles south). It also has bus services to Eugene, Ontario and Burns.

Cascades East Transit (☑541-385-8680; www.cascadeseasttransit.com) is the regional bus company in Bend, covering La Pine, Mt Bachelor, Sisters, Prineville and Madras. It also provides bus transport within Bend.

Newberry National Volcanic Monument

Newberry National Volcanic Monument (☑541-593-2421; www.fs.usda.gov/recarea/des chutes/recarea/?recid=66159; Hwy 97; day use $5; ⏰May-Sep) showcases 400,000 years of dramatic seismic activity. Start your visit at the **Lava Lands Visitor Center** (☑541-593-2421; www.fs.usda.gov; 58201 S Hwy 97; ⏰9am-5pm late May-Oct), 13 miles south of Bend. Nearby attractions include **Lava Butte**, a perfect cone rising 500ft, and **Lava River Cave**, Oregon's longest lava tube. Four miles west of the visitor center is **Benham Falls**, a good picnic spot on the Deschutes River.

Newberry Crater was once one of the most active volcanoes in North America, but after a large eruption a caldera was born. Close by are **Paulina Lake** and **East Lake**, deep bodies of water rich with trout, while looming above is 7985ft **Paulina Peak**.

Crater Lake National Park

It's no exaggeration: Crater Lake is so blue, you'll catch your breath. And if you get to see it on a calm day, the surrounding cliffs are reflected in those deep waters like a mirror. It's a stunningly beautiful sight. **Crater Lake** (☑541-594-3000; www.nps.gov/crla; 7-day vehicle pass winter/summer $15/25) is Oregon's only national park.

The classic tour is the 33-mile rim drive (open from approximately June to mid-October), but there are also exceptional hiking and cross-country-skiing opportunities. Note that because the area receives some of the highest snowfalls in North America, the rim drive and north entrance are sometimes closed up until early July.

You can stay at the **Cabins at Mazama Village** (☑888-774-2728; www.craterlakelodges. com; d $160; ⏰late May-Sep; ⊕) or the majestic **Crater Lake Lodge** (☑888-774-2728; www.craterlakelodges.com; r from $197; ⏰late May–mid-Oct; ⊕📶), opened in 1915. Campers head to **Mazama Campground** (☑888-774-2728; www.craterlakelodges.com; Mazama Village; tent/RV sites $22/32; ⏰Jun–mid-Oct; 📶🐾). For more information, head to **Steel Visitor Center** (☑541-594-3000; www.nps.gov/crla/planyourvisit/visitorcenters.htm; Park Headquarters; ⏰9am-5pm May-Oct, 10am-4pm Nov-Apr).

Oregon Coast

This magnificent littoral zone is paralleled by Hwy 101, a scenic highway that winds its way through towns, resorts, state parks (more than 70 of them) and wilderness areas. Everyone from campers to gourmets will find a plethora of ways to enjoy this exceptional region, which is especially popular in summer (reserve accommodations in advance).

Astoria

Named after America's first millionaire, John Jacob Astor, Astoria sits at the 5-mile-wide mouth of the Columbia River and was the first US settlement west of the Mississippi. The city has a long seafaring history and has seen its old harbor, once home to poor artists and writers, attract fancy hotels and restaurants in recent years. Inland are many historical houses, including lovingly restored Victorians – a few converted into romantic B&Bs. It's nonbeach-y vibe gives it a special ambience on the coast.

⊙ Sights

Adding to the city's scenery is the 4.1-mile **Astoria-Megler Bridge**, the longest continuous truss bridge in North America, which crosses the Columbia River into Washington state. See it from the **Astoria Riverwalk**, which follows the trolley route. **Pier 39** is an interesting covered wharf with an informal cannery museum and a couple of places to eat.

Columbia River Maritime Museum MUSEUM
(☑503-325-2323; www.crmm.org; 1792 Marine Dr; adult/child $14/5; ⊙9:30am-5pm; ⊡) Astoria's seafaring heritage is well interpreted at this wave-shaped museum. It's hard to miss the retired Coast Guard boat, frozen mid-rescue, through a huge outside window. Other exhibits highlight the salmon-packing industry and the Chinese immigrants who made up the bulk of its workforce; the river's commercial history; and the crucial job of the bar pilot.

You get a keen sense of the treacherous conditions that define this area, known for good reason as the 'Graveyard of the Pacific.'

Fort Stevens State Park PARK
(☑ext 21 503-861-3170; www.oregonstateparks. org; 100 Peter Iredale Rd, Hammond; day use $5) Ten miles west of Astoria, this park holds the historic military installation that once guarded the mouth of the Columbia River. Near the **Military Museum** (☑503-861-2000; http://visitftstevens.com; day-use fee $5; ⊙10am-6pm May-Sep, to 4pm Oct-Apr) are gun batteries dug into sand dunes – interesting remnants of the fort's mostly demolished military stations (truck and walking tours available).

There's a popular beach at the small *Peter Iredale* 1906 shipwreck, and good ocean views from parking lot C. There's also camping and 12 miles of paved bike trails.

🛏 Sleeping & Eating

Fort Stevens State Park CAMPGROUND $
(☑503-861-1671; https://oregonstateparks.org; 100 Peter Iredale Rd, Hammond; tent/RV sites $22/32, yurts/cabins $46/90) About 560 sites (most for RVs) are available at this popular campground 10 miles west of Astoria. Great

for families; reserve in summer. Entry off Pacific Dr.

Commodore Hotel BOUTIQUE HOTEL $$
(☑503-325-4747; www.commodoreastoria.com; 258 14th St; d with/without bath from $164/89; ☒⊛⊜) Hip travelers should make a beeline for this stylish hotel, which offers attractive but small, minimalist rooms. Choose a room with bathroom or go Euro style (sink in room, bathroom down the hall; 'deluxe' rooms have better views). There's a lounge-style lobby with cafe, free samples of local microbrews from 5pm to 7pm, an impressive movie library and record players to borrow.

Bowpicker SEAFOOD $
(☑503-791-2942; www.bowpicker.com; cnr 17th & Duane Sts; dishes $8-12; ⊙11am-6pm Wed-Sun) On just about every list of great seafood shacks is this adorable place in a converted 1932 gillnet fishing boat, serving beer-battered chunks of albacore and steak fries and that's it. Some say it's the best fish-and-chips in the US.

Fort George Brewery PUB FOOD $
(☑503-325-7468; www.fortgeorgebrewery.com; 1483 Duane St; mains $7-17, pizzas $14-26; ⊙11am-11pm, from noon Sun) Fort George has established itself as one of the state's best and

LEWIS & CLARK: JOURNEY'S END

In November 1805 William Clark and his fellow explorer Meriwether Lewis of the Corps of Discovery staggered, with three dozen others, into a sheltered cove on the Columbia River, 2 miles west of the present-day Astoria-Megler Bridge, completing what was indisputably the greatest overland trek in American history.

After the first truly democratic ballot in US history (in which a woman and a black slave both voted), the party elected to make their bivouac 5 miles south of Astoria at Fort Clatsop, where the Corps spent a miserable winter in 1805–06. Today this site is called the **Lewis and Clark National Historical Park** (☑503-861-2471; www.nps. gov/lewi; 92343 Fort Clatsop Rd; adult/child $5/free; ⊙9am-6pm mid-Jun–Aug, to 5pm Sep–mid-Jun). Here you'll find a reconstructed Fort Clatsop, along with a visitor center and historical reenactments in summer.

most reliable craft brewers. Its atmospheric brewery-restaurant is in a historic building that was the original settlement site of Astoria. Apart from the excellent beer, you can get gourmet burgers, housemade sausages, salads and, upstairs, wood-fired pizza. Head to the Lovell Taproom for views over the production line.

Astoria Coffeehouse & Bistro   AMERICAN $$
(☑ 503-325-1787; www.astoriacoffeehouse.com; 243 11th St; breakfast & lunch mains $6-18, dinner mains $15-32; ☺ 7am-9pm Sun, to 10pm Mon-Thu, to 11pm Fri & Sat) ✐ Small, popular cafe with attached bistro offering an eclectic menu – things like coconut chicken red curry, chili-relleno burger, fish tacos and build-your-own mac 'n' cheese. Everything is made in-house, even the ketchup. There's sidewalk seating and excellent cocktails. Expect a wait at dinner and Sunday brunch. Excellent and changing $5 breakfast and lunch specials available daily.

🛈 Getting There & Away

Northwest Point (☑ 503-484-4100; http://oregon-point.com/northwest-point) Daily buses head to Seaside, Cannon Beach and Portland; check the website for schedules.
Pacific Transit (☑ 360-642-9418; www.pacifictransit.org) Buses go over the border to Washington.

Cannon Beach

Charming Cannon Beach is one of the most popular beach towns on the Oregon coast. Several premier hotels here cater to a fancier clientele, as do the town's many boutiques and art galleries. In summer the streets are ablaze with flowers. Lodging is expensive, and the streets are jammed: on a warm, sunny Saturday, you'll spend a good chunk of time just finding a parking spot.

⊙ Sights & Activities

Photogenic **Haystack Rock**, a 295ft seastack, is the most spectacular landmark on the Oregon coast and is accessible from the beach at low tide. Birds cling to its ballast cliffs and tide pools ring its base.

The coast to the north, protected inside **Ecola State Park** (☑ 503-436-2844; https://oregonstateparks.org; day use $5), is the Oregon you may have already visited in your dreams: sea stacks, crashing surf, hidden beaches and gorgeous pristine forest. The park is 1.5 miles from town and is crisscrossed by

paths, including part of the **Oregon Coast Trail**, which leads over Tillamook Head to the town of Seaside.

The Cannon Beach area is good for surfing, though not the beach itself. The best spots are **Indian Beach** in Ecola State Park, 3 miles to the north, and **Oswald West State Park**, 10 miles south. **Cleanline Surf Shop** (☑ 503-738-2061; www.cleanlinesurf.com; 171 Sunset Blvd; board/wetsuit rentals from $20/15; ☺ 10am-6pm Sun-Fri, 9am-6pm Sat) is a friendly local shop that rents out boards and wetsuits.

🛏 Sleeping

Cannon Beach is pretty exclusive; for budget choices head 7 miles north to Seaside.

★**Ocean Lodge**   HOTEL $$$
(☑ 503-436-2241, 888-777-4047; www.the-oceanlodge.com; 2864 S Pacific St; d $219-369; ☺ ❋ 🐾 🛏) This gorgeous place has some of Cannon Beach's most luxurious rooms, most with ocean view and all with fireplace and kitchenette. A complimentary continental breakfast, an 800-DVD library and pleasant sitting areas are available to guests. Located on the beach at the southern end of town.

🍴 Eating & Drinking

Here you'll find everything from coffee shops to one that doubles as a fine restaurant. If you're just after a warm cup of buttery clam chowder with a view, stop in at **Mo's** (☑ 503-436-1111; www.moschowder.com; 195 W Warren Way; chowder $4.25-10; ☺ 11am-9pm; 🐾).

★**Irish Table**   IRISH $$$
(☑ 503-436-0708; www.theirishtable.com; 1235 S Hemlock St; mains $26-30; ☺ 5:30-9pm Fri-Tue) ✐ Excellent restaurant hidden at the back of Sleepy Monk Coffee, serving a fusion of Irish and Pacific Northwest cuisine made with local and seasonal ingredients. The menu is small and simple, but the choices are tasty; try the vegetarian shepherd's pie, lamb-loin chops or seared Piedmontese flat-iron steak. If the curried mussels are on the menu, don't hesitate.

Sleepy Monk Coffee   COFFEE
(☑ 503-436-2796; www.sleepymonkcoffee.com; 1235 S Hemlock St; drinks & snacks $2-7; ☺ 8am-3pm Mon, Tue & Thu, to 4pm Fri-Sun) ✐ For organic, certified-fair-trade coffee, try this little coffee shop on the main street. Sit on an Adirondack chair in the tiny front yard and

enjoy the rich brews, all tasty and roasted on the premises. Good homemade pastries, too.

ℹ Information

Chamber of Commerce (☏ 503-436-2623; www.cannonbeach.org; 207 N Spruce St; ⏰ 10am-5pm) Has good local information, including tide tables.

ℹ Getting There & Around

Northwest Point (☏ 541-484-4100; www.oregon-point.com/northwest-point) Buses run from Astoria to Portland (and vice versa) every morning (one way $18, three hours), stopping at Cannon Beach (two hours). Buy tickets online or at the Beach Store, next to Cannon Beach Surf.

Sunset Empire Transit (☏ 503-861-7433; www.ridethebus.org; 900 Marine Dr; one-way fare $3) Buses go to Seaside ($1, 13 minutes) or Astoria ($1, 30 minutes) plus other coastal stops. The Cannon Beach bus runs the length of Hemlock St to the end of Tolovana Beach; the schedule varies depending on day and season.

Tillamook County Transportation (The Wave; ☏ 503-815-8283; www.tillamookbus.com) Buses go south toward Manzanita ($3, 30 minutes) and Lincoln City ($9, two hours) several times daily.

Newport

Tied with Astoria as home to Oregon's largest commercial fishing fleet, Newport is a lively tourist city with several fine beaches and a world-class aquarium. In 2011 it became the Pacific Fleet Headquarters of NOAA (National Oceanic and Atmospheric Administration). Good restaurants – along with some tacky attractions, gift shops and barking sea lions – abound in the historic bayfront area, while bohemian Nye Beach offers art galleries and a friendly village atmosphere. The area was first explored in the 1860s by fishing crews who found oyster beds at the upper end of Yaquina Bay.

◉ Sights

The world-class **Oregon Coast Aquarium** (☏ 541-867-3474; www.aquarium.org; 2820 SE Ferry Slip Rd; adult/3-12yr/13-17yr $25/15/20; ⏰ 10am-6pm Jun-Aug, to 5pm Sep-May; 🅿) is an unmissable attraction, featuring a sea-otter pool, surreal jellyfish tanks and Plexiglas tunnels through a shark tank. Nearby, the **Hatfield Marine Science Center** (☏ 541-867-0100; www.hmsc.oregonstate.edu; 2030 SE Marine Science Dr; ⏰ 10am-5pm Jun-Aug, to 4pm

Thu-Mon Sep-May; 🅿) FREE is much smaller, but still worthwhile.

For awesome tide-pooling and views, don't miss the **Yaquina Head Outstanding Natural Area** (☏ 541-574-3100; www.blm.gov/learn/interpretive-centers/yaquina; 750 NW Lighthouse Dr; vehicle fee $7; ⏰ 8am-sunset, interpretive center 10am-6pm) FREE, site of the coast's tallest lighthouse and an interesting interpretive center.

🛏 Sleeping & Eating

Campers can head to large and popular **South Beach State Park** (☏ 541-867-4715; https://oregonstateparks.org; tent/RV sites $21/31, yurts $47; 🐾), 2 miles south on Hwy 101. Book-lovers can stay at the **Sylvia Beach Hotel** (☏ 541-265-5428; www.sylviabeachhotel.com; 267 NW Cliff St; d $150-260; 🐾) and nautical and romantic types at the shipshape **Newport Belle** (☏ 541-867-6290; http://newportbelle.com; 2126 SE Marine Science Dr, South Beach Marina, H Dock; d $165-175; ⏰ Feb-Oct; 🐾 🐾).

For crab po'boys, pan-fried oysters and other tasty seafood, head to **Local Ocean Seafoods** (☏ 541-574-7959; www.localocean.net; 213 SE Bay Blvd; mains $17-35; ⏰ 11am-9pm, to 8pm winter) – it's especially great on warm days, when the glass walls open to the port area.

ℹ Information

Visitor Center (☏ 541-265-8801; www.newportchamber.org; 555 SW Coast Hwy; ⏰ 8:30am-5pm Mon-Fri)

Yachats & Around

One of the Oregon coast's best-kept secrets is the neat and friendly little town of Yachats (ya-*hots*). Lying at the base of massive Cape Perpetua, Yachats offers the memorable scenery of a rugged and windswept land. People come here to get away from it all, which isn't hard to do along this relatively undeveloped stretch of coast.

Lining the town is the 804 Coast Trail, providing a lovely walk and access to tide pools and fabulous ocean vistas. It hooks up with the Amanda trail to the south, eventually arriving at Cape Perpetua Scenic Area.

◉ Sights

⭐ **Cape Perpetua Scenic Area** PARK (www.fs.usda.gov; Hwy 101; day use $5) Located 3 miles south of Yachats, this volcanic remnant was sighted and named by England's

Captain James Cook in 1778. Famous for dramatic rock formations and crashing surf, the area contains numerous trails that explore ancient shell middens, tide pools and old-growth forests. Views from the cape are incredible, taking in coastal promontories from Cape Foulweather to Cape Arago.

For spectacular ocean views, head up Overlook Rd to the **Cape Perpetua** day-use area.

Deep fractures in the old volcano allow waves to erode narrow channels into the headland, creating effects such as **Devil's Churn**, about a half-mile north of the visitor center. Waves race up this chasm, shooting up the 30ft inlet to explode against the narrowing sides of the channel. For an easy hike, take the paved **Captain Cook Trail** (1.2 miles round trip) down to tide pools near **Cooks Chasm**, where at high tide the geyser-like spouting horn blasts water out of a sea cave. (There's also parking along Hwy 101 at Cooks Chasm.)

The **Giant Spruce Trail** (2 miles round trip) leads up Cape Creek to a 500-year-old Sitka spruce with a 15ft diameter. The **Cook's Ridge–Gwynn Creek Loop Trail** (6.5 miles round trip) heads into deep old-growth forests along Gwynn Creek; follow the Oregon Coast Trail south and turn up the Gwynn Creek Trail, which returns via Cook's Ridge.

The **visitor center** (☎541-547-3289; www.fs.usda.gov/siuslaw; 2400 Hwy 101; vehicle fee $5; ⊙9:30am-4:30pm Jun-Aug, 10am-4pm Sep-May) details human and natural histories, and has displays on the Alsi tribe.

Heceta Head Lighthouse   LIGHTHOUSE

(☎541-547-3416; www.hecetalighthouse.com; day use $5; ⊙11am-3pm, to 2pm winter) Built in 1894 and towering precipitously above the churning ocean, this lighthouse, 13 miles south of Yachats on Hwy 101, is supremely photogenic and still functioning. Tours are available; hours may be erratic, especially in winter, so call ahead. Park at Heceta Head State Park for views.

Sea Lion Caves   CAVE

(☎541-547-3111; www.sealioncaves.com; 91560 Hwy 101, Florence; adult/child $14/8; ⊙9am-5pm; 🚗) Fifteen miles south of Yachats is an enormous sea grotto that's home to hundreds of Steller sea lions. An elevator descends 208ft to a dark interpretive center, and a caged-off observation area lets you watch (and smell) the sea lions jockeying for the best seat on the rocks. From late September to November there are no sea lions in the cave.

Kids in particular will love this stop. There are lots of interesting coastal birds to look for here as well.

🛏 Sleeping & Eating

Ya'Tel Motel   MOTEL $

(☎541-547-3225; www.yatelmotel.com; cnr Hwy 101 & 6th St; d $69-119; ❄@🛜🐾) This eight-room motel has personality, along with large, clean rooms, some with kitchenette. A large room that sleeps six is also available ($119). Look for the (changeable) sign out front, which might say something like, 'Always clean, usually friendly.'

Green Salmon Coffee House   CAFE $

(☎541-547-3077; www.thegreensalmon.com; 220 Hwy 101; coffee drinks $2-7; ⊙7:30am-2:30pm; 🌿) 🍃 Organic and fair trade are big words at this eclectic cafe, where locals meet for tasty breakfast items (pastries, lox bagels, homemade oatmeal). The inventive list of hot beverages ranges from regular drip coffee to lavender rosemary cocoa to CBD infused. Vegan menu available, plus a used-book exchange.

Oregon Dunes National Recreation Area

Stretching for 50 miles between Florence and Coos Bay, the Oregon Dunes form the largest expanse of coastal dunes in the USA. They tower up to 500ft and undulate inland as far as 3 miles to meet coastal forests, harboring curious ecosystems that sustain an abundance of wildlife, especially birds. The area inspired Frank Herbert to pen his epic sci-fi *Dune* novels. Hiking trails, bridle paths, and boating and swimming areas are available, but avoid the stretch south of Reedsport as noisy dune buggies dominate. Find out more at the **Oregon Dunes National Recreation Area Visitor Center** (☎541-271-6000; www.fs.usda.gov/siuslaw; 855 Hwy 101; ⊙8am-4:30pm Mon-Sat Jun-Aug, Mon-Fri Sep-May) in Reedsport.

State parks with camping include popular **Jessie M Honeyman** (☎800-452-5687, 541-997-3641; https://oregonstateparks.org; 84505 Hwy 101 S; tent/RV sites $21/31, yurts $46; 🐾), 3 miles south of Florence, and pleasant, wooded **Umpqua Lighthouse** (☎541-271-4118; https://oregonstateparks.org; 460 Lighthouse Rd; tent/RV sites $19/29, yurts/deluxe yurts $43/92;

🏕), 4 miles south of Reedsport. There's plenty of other camping in the area, too.

Port Orford

Occupying a rare natural harbor and guarding plenty of spectacular views, the scenic hamlet of Port Orford sits on a headland wedged between two magnificent state parks. **Cape Blanco State Park** (🗷541-332-2973; https://oregonstateparks.org; Cape Blanco Rd) FREE, 9 miles to the north, is the second-most-westerly point in the continental US, and the promontory is often lashed by fierce 100mph winds. As well as hiking, visitors can tour the **Cape Blanco Lighthouse** (🗷541-332-2207; https://oregonstateparks.org; 91814 Cape Blanco Rd; admission by donation; ⊙10am-3:15pm Wed-Mon Apr-Oct) – built in 1870, it's the oldest and highest operational lighthouse in Oregon.

Six miles south of Port Orford, in **Humbug Mountain State Park** (🗷541-332-6774; https://oregonstateparks.org; Hwy 101), mountains and sea meet in aqueous disharmony, generating plenty of angry surf. You can climb the 1750ft peak on a 3-mile trail through old-growth cedar groves.

For an affordable stay try **Castaway-by-the-Sea Motel** (🗷541-332-4502; www.castawaybythesea.com; 545 W 5th St; d $110-140, ste $140-185; 🐾@🖤🏕); for a more luxurious cabin, **Wildspring Guest Habitat** (🗷866-333-9453; www.wildspring.com; 92978 Cemetery Loop Rd; d $298-328; 🐾@🏕). Eating well in this fishing village means a visit to slick **Redfish** (🗷541-366-2200; www.redfishportorford.com; Hawthorne Gallery, 517 Jefferson St; mains $10-32; ⊙11am-9pm Mon-Fri, 10am-9pm Sat & Sun) 🐾 for the freshest seafood in town.

Southern Oregon

With a warm, sunny and dry climate that belongs in nearby California, Southern Oregon, the state's 'banana belt,' is an exciting place to visit. Rugged and remote landscapes are entwined with a number of designated 'wild and scenic' rivers, which are famous for their challenging white-water rafting, world-class fly-fishing and excellent hiking.

Ashland

This pretty city is the cultural center of Southern Oregon thanks to its internationally renowned Oregon Shakespeare Festival (OSF), which runs for nine months of the year and attracts hundreds of thousands of theatergoers from all over the world. The festival is so popular that it's Ashland's main attraction, packing it out in summer and bringing in steady cash flows for the town's many fancy hotels, upscale B&Bs and fine restaurants.

Even without the OSF, however, Ashland is still a pleasant place whose trendy downtown streets buzz with well-heeled shoppers and youthful bohemians. In late fall and early winter – those few months when the festival doesn't run – folks come to ski at nearby Mt Ashland. And wine-lovers, take note: the area has several good wineries worth seeking out.

👁 Sights & Activities

Lithia Park   PARK
(59 Winburn Way) Adjacent to Ashland's three splendid theaters lies what is arguably the loveliest city park in Oregon, the 93 acres of which wind along Ashland Creek above the center of town. Unusually, the park is in the National Register of Historic Places. It is embellished with fountains, flowers, gazebos and an ice-skating rink (winter only), plus a playground and woodsy trails.

Schneider Museum of Art   MUSEUM
(🗷541-552-6245; http://sma.sou.edu; 1250 Siskiyou Blvd; suggested donation $5; ⊙10am-4pm Mon-Sat) If you like contemporary art, check out this Southern Oregon University museum, where new exhibitions go up every month or so. The university also puts on theater and opera performances, along with classical concerts.

Momentum River Expeditions   RAFTING
(🗷541-488-2525; www.momentumriverexpeditions.com; 3195 East Main St 2; 1-day rafting trips $185; ⊙Apr-Sep) This outfit runs one- to three-day rafting trips on the Upper Klamath River. Unlike many Oregon rivers that get low into summer, the Upper Klamath has strong flowing rapids deep into the season. It also offers multi-sport trips that combine rafting with mountain biking, running and backcountry camping.

🛏 Sleeping

From May to October, try to arrive with reservations. Rooms are cheaper in Medford, 12 miles north of Ashland.

Ashland Hostel   HOSTEL $
(🗷541-482-9217; www.theashlandhostel.com; 150 N Main St; dm $30, r $50-139; 🐾❄@🏕)

DON'T MISS

OREGON SHAKESPEARE FESTIVAL

As a young town, Ashland was included in the Methodist Church's cultural education program, called the Chautauqua Series. By the 1930s, one of the venues, Chautauqua Hall, had deteriorated to a dilapidated wooden shell. Angus Bowmer, a drama professor at the local college, noted the resemblance of the roofless structure to drawings of Shakespeare's Globe Theatre. He convinced the town to sponsor two performances of Shakespeare's plays and a boxing match (the Bard would have approved) as part of its 1935 July 4 celebration. The plays proved a great success, and the **OSF** (OSF; ☑541-482-4331; www.osfashland.org; cnr Main & Pioneer Sts; tickets $30-136; ⊙ Tue-Sun Feb-Oct) was off and running.

Though it's rooted in Shakespearean and Elizabethan drama, the OSF does an equal amount of revivals and international contemporary theater. Eleven productions run in three theaters: the outdoor **Elizabethan Theatre** (June to October), the **Angus Bowmer Theatre** and the intimate **Thomas Theatre**. No children under six. Performances sell out quickly, but the box office sometimes has (usually discounted) rush tickets an hour before showtime.

Check with the **OSF Welcome Center** (☑541-482-2111; 76 N Main St; ⊙11am-5pm Tue-Sun) for other events, including scholarly lectures, play readings, concerts and pre-show talks. There are backstage tours (adult/child $20/14), which should be booked a week or so in advance.

This is a central and somewhat upscale hostel (shoes off inside!) in a bungalow on the National Register. Most private rooms share bathrooms; some can be connected to dorms. Hangout spaces include the cozy basement living room and the shady front porch. No pets, and no alcohol or smoking on the premises; call ahead, as reception times are limited. All ages are welcome.

Palm BOUTIQUE HOTEL **$$**
(☑541-482-2636; www.palmcottages.com; 1065 Siskiyou Blvd; d $141-289; ❄✲☎✲☎) Fabulous small motel remodeled into 16 charming garden-cottage rooms and suites (some with kitchens). It's an oasis of green on a busy avenue, complete with grassy lawns and a saltwater pool. A house nearby harbors three large suites (from $249). Lots of ecopractices from zero gasoline use to free charging stations for electric vehicles.

✗ Eating & Drinking

Morning Glory CAFE **$**
(☑541-488-8636; 1149 Siskiyou Blvd; mains $10-17; ⊙8am-1:15pm) This colorful, casual cafe is one of Ashland's best breakfast joints. Creative dishes include the Alaskan-crab omelet, vegetarian hash with roasted chilies, and shrimp cakes with poached eggs. For lunch there's gourmet salad and sandwiches. Go early or late to avoid a long wait.

Agave MEXICAN **$**
(☑541-488-1770; www.agavetaco.net; 5 Granite St; tacos $3.75-6; ⊙11:30am-8pm Tue-Sun, later hours summer) Tasty and creative tacos are cooked up at this popular restaurant. There's the regular stuff such as *carnitas* (little meats) and grilled chicken, but for something more exotic go for the shredded duck or sautéed lobster. There's ceviche, salads and tamales, too.

Caldera Brewery & Restaurant BREWPUB **$$**
(☑541-482-4677; www.calderabrewing.com; 590 Clover Lane; mains $10-23; ⊙11am-10pm; ♿) This bright, airy brewery-restaurant just off I-5 has pleasant outdoor seating and views of the countryside. It's kid-friendly until 10pm and serves pizza, fancy pasta, burgers and good salads. Wash it all down with one of the 40 beers on tap. Also located at 31 Water St, on the river in downtown Ashland, with more of a cozy pub atmosphere.

Greenleaf DINER **$$**
(☑541-482-2808; www.greenleafrestaurant.com; 49 N Main St; mains $10-16; ⊙8am-8pm; ✐) This casual diner, with booths as well as counter seating, focuses on sustainable ingredients in innovative combinations. There are lots of vegetarian options, and the specials board is well worth checking out, although the regular menu is so massive that you might not ever need to venture that far. There's a whole gluten-free menu, too.

ℹ Information

Jacksonville

This small but endearing former-gold-prospecting town is the oldest settlement in southern Oregon and a National Historic Landmark. The town's main drag is lined with well-preserved buildings dating from the 1880s, now converted into boutiques and galleries. Music-lovers shouldn't miss the September **Britt Festival** (☎ 541-773-6077; www.brittfest.org; cnr 1st & Fir Sts; tickets around $42; ⊙ Jun-Sep), a world-class musical experience that brings in top-name performers. Seek more enlightenment at the **Chamber of Commerce** (☎ 541-899-8118; www.jacksonvilleoregon.org; 185 N Oregon St; ⊙ 10am-3pm daily May-Oct, to 2pm Mon-Sat Nov-Apr).

Jacksonville is full of fancy B&Bs; for budget motels head 6 miles east to Medford. The **Jacksonville Inn** (☎ 541-899-1900; www.jacksonvilleinn.com; 175 E California St; r $159-325; ☻✳☎☎) is the most pleasant abode, shoehorned downtown in an 1863 building with regal antique-stuffed rooms. There's a fine restaurant on-site.

Oregon Caves National Monument & Preserve

This very popular cave (singular) lies 19 miles east of Cave Junction on Hwy 46. Three miles of passages are explored via 90-minute cave tours that include 520 rocky steps and dripping chambers running along the River Styx. Dress warmly, wear shoes with good traction and be prepared to get dripped on.

Cave Junction, 28 miles south of Grants Pass on US 199 (Redwood Hwy), provides the region's services – though one of the best accommodations in the area is **Out 'n' About Treesort** (☎ 541-592-2208; www.treehouses.com; 300 Page Creek Rd, Takilma; tree houses $150-330; ☻) – super-fun tree houses in Katilma, 12 miles south. For fancy lodgings right at the cave there's the impressive **Oregon Caves Chateau** (☎ 541-592-3400; www.oregoncaveschateau.com; 20000 Caves Hwy; r $117-212; ⊙ May-Oct; ☻) – be sure to grab a milkshake at the old-fashioned soda fountain here.

Eastern Oregon

Oregon east of the Cascades bears little resemblance to its wetter western cohort, either physically or culturally. Few people live here – the biggest town, Pendleton, numbers only 17,000 – and the region holds high plateaus, painted hills, alkali lake-beds and the country's deepest river gorge.

John Day Fossil Beds National Monument

Within the soft rocks and crumbly soils of John Day country lies one of the world's greatest fossil collections, laid down between six and 50 million years ago. The national monument includes 22 sq miles at three different units: Sheep Rock Unit, Painted Hills Unit and Clarno Unit. Each has hiking trails and interpretive displays.

Visit the excellent **Thomas Condon Paleontology Center** (☎ 541-987-2333; www.nps.gov/joda; 32651 Hwy 19, Kimberly; ⊙ 10am-5pm daily Mar-May, Sep & Oct, 10am-5pm Tue-Sat Nov-Feb) FREE, 2 miles north of US 26 at the **Sheep Rock Unit**. Displays include a three-toed horse and petrified dung-beetle balls, along with many other fossils and geologic history exhibits. If you feel like walking, take the short hike up the Blue Basin Trail.

The **Painted Hills Unit**, near the town of Mitchell, consists of low-slung, colorfully banded hills formed about 30 million years ago. Ten million years older is the **Clarno Unit**, which exposes mud flows that washed over an Eocene-era forest and eroded into distinctive, sheer white cliffs topped with spires and turrets of stone.

Rafting is popular on the John Day River, the longest free-flowing river in the state. **Oregon River Experiences** (☎ 800-827-1358; www.oregonriver.com; 4-/5-/9-day trips per person $675/795/1365; ⊙ May-Jun) offers trips of up to nine days. There's also good fishing for smallmouth bass and rainbow trout; find out more at the Oregon Department of Fish & Wildlife (www.dfw.state.or.us).

Most towns in the area have at least one hotel; these include the atmospheric **Historic Oregon Hotel** (☎ 541-462-3027; www.theoregonhotel.net; 104 E Main St, Mitchell; d with/without bath from $65/55; ☎) in Mitchell. The town of John Day has most of the district's services and there are several public campgrounds in the area (sites $5), including Lone Pine and Big Bend, both on Hwy 402.

Wallowa Mountains Area

The Wallowa Mountains, with their glacier-hewn peaks and crystalline lakes, are among the most beautiful natural areas in Oregon. The only drawback is the large number of visitors who flock here in summer, especially to the pretty Wallowa Lake area.

Escape them all on one of several long hikes into the nearby **Eagle Cap Wilderness**, such as the 6-mile one-way jaunt to **Aneroid Lake** or the 8-mile trek on the **Ice Lake Trail**.

Just north of the mountains, in the Wallowa Valley, **Enterprise** is a homely backcountry town with several motels – try the **Ponderosa** (☑ 541-426-3186; www.theponderosamotel.com; 102 E Greenwood St; r from $90; ❈ 🛜 ❈). If you like beer and good food, don't miss the town's microbrewery, **Terminal Gravity Brewing** (☑ 541-426-3000; www.terminalgravitybrewing.com; 803 SE School St; mains $9-17; ⊙ 11am-9pm, to 8pm Sun & Mon). Just 6 miles south is Enterprise's fancy cousin, the upscale town of **Joseph**. Expensive bronze galleries and artsy boutiques line the main strip, along with some good eateries.

Hells Canyon

The mighty Snake River has taken 13 million years to carve its path through the high plateaus of eastern Oregon to its present depth of 8000ft, creating America's deepest gorge.

For perspective, drive 30 miles northeast from Joseph to Imnaha, where a slow-going 24-mile gravel road leads up to **Hat Point**. From here you can see the Wallowa Mountains, Idaho's Seven Devils, the Imnaha River and the wilds of the canyon itself. This road is open from late May until snowfall; give yourself two hours each way for the drive.

For white-water action and spectacular scenery, head down to **Hells Canyon Dam**, 25 miles north of the small community of Oxbow. A few miles past the dam, the road ends at the **Hells Canyon Visitors Center** (www.fs.usda.gov; Hells Canyon Rd, Hells Canyon Dam; ⊙ 8am-4pm May-Oct), which has good advice on the area's campgrounds and hiking trails. Beyond here, the Snake River drops 1300ft through wild rapids accessible only by jet boat or raft. **Hells Canyon Adventures**

(☑ 800-422-3568; www.hellscanyonadventures.com; 4200 Hells Canyon Dam Rd; jet-boat tours adult/child from $100/70; ⊙ May-Sep) is the main operator running raft trips and jet-boat tours (reservations required).

The area has many campgrounds and more solid lodgings. Just outside Imnaha is the beautiful **Imnaha River Inn** (☑ 541-577-6002; www.imnahariverinn.com; 73946 Rimrock Rd; s/d without bath from $75/135), a B&B replete with Hemingway-esque animal trophies. For more services, head to the towns of Enterprise, Joseph and Halfway.

Steens Mountain & Alvord Desert

The highest peak in southeastern Oregon, Steens Mountain (9773ft) is part of a massive, 30-mile-long fault-block range that was formed about 15 million years ago.

Beginning in Frenchglen, the gravel 59-mile **Steens Mountain Loop Rd** is Oregon's highest road, offers the range's best sights, and has access to camping and hiking trails. You'll see sagebrush, bands of juniper and aspen forests, and finally fragile rocky tundra at the top. **Kiger Gorge Viewpoint**, 25 miles up from Frenchglen, is especially stunning. It takes about three hours all the way around if you're just driving through, but you'll want to see the sights, so give yourself much more time. You can also see the eastern side of the Steens via the **Fields-Denio Rd**, which goes through the Alvord Desert between Hwys 205 and 78. Take a full tank of gas and plenty of water, and be prepared for weather changes at any time of year.

Frenchglen, with a population of roughly 12, nonetheless supports the historic **Frenchglen Hotel** (☑ 541-493-2825; www.frenchglenhotel.com; 39184 Hwy 205; d/tr without bath $79/87, Drovers' Inn d/q $125/145; ⊙ mid-Mar–early Nov; ⊖ ❈ 🛜 ❈), with eight small rooms, huge meals (reserve for dinners), a small store with a seasonal gas pump and not much else. There are camping options on the Steens Mountain Loop Rd, such as the BLM's pretty **Page Springs** ($8 per vehicle, open year-round). A few other campgrounds further into the loop are very pleasant, but accessible in summer only. Water is available at all of these campgrounds. Free backcountry camping is also allowed in the Steens.

Alaska

Best Places to Eat

➡ Snow City Café (p1089)

➡ Pel'Meni (p1096)

➡ Rustic Goat (p1089)

➡ Bar Harbor Restaurant (p1102)

➡ Ludvig's Bistro (p1094)

Best Places to Stay

➡ Gustavus Inn (p1100)

➡ Copper Whale Inn (p1089)

➡ Ultima Thule Lodge (p1092)

➡ Inn at Creek Street (p1101)

➡ Mendenhall Lake Campground (p1095)

Why Go?

Pure, raw, unforgiving and humongous in scale, Alaska is a place that arouses basic instincts and ignites what Jack London termed the 'call of the wild.' Yet, unlike London and his gutsy, gold-rush companions, visitors today will have a far easier time penetrating the region's vast, feral wilderness. Indeed, one of the beauties of the 49th state is its accessibility. Nowhere else in North America is it realistically possible to climb an unclimbed mountain, walk where – quite conceivably – no human foot has trodden before, or sally forth into a national park that gets fewer annual visitors than the International Space Station.

With scant phone coverage and a dearth of hipster-friendly coffee bars to plug in your iPad, Alaska is a region for 'doing' rather than observing. Whether you go it alone with bear spray and a backpack, or place yourself in the hands of an experienced 'sourdough' (Alaskan old-timer), the rewards are immeasurable.

When to Go
Anchorage

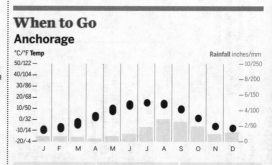

Jun & Jul Summer solstice festivals and 20-hour days; salmon runs hit their peaks.

Late Sep The mystical northern lights begin to appear in the night skies.

Feb Longer days and warmer temps make late February the best time for winter sports.

Alaska Highlights

1 Denali National Park & Preserve (p1103) Gawking at the hulking, icy mass of Mt Denali.

2 Anchorage (p1087) Exploring the world-class Anchorage Museum, before heading out for some summer nightlife.

3 Glacier Bay (p1099) Seeing (and hearing!) chunks of ice fall dramatically from the face of Margerie Glacier.

4 Sitka (p1093) Getting a compelling glimpse into the history of Russian Alaska.

5 Mendenhall Glacier (p1095) Hiking alongsid Alaska's most popular river of ice.

6 Chilkoot Trail (p1099) Following in the footsteps of the Klondike stampeders of 1898, near Skegway.

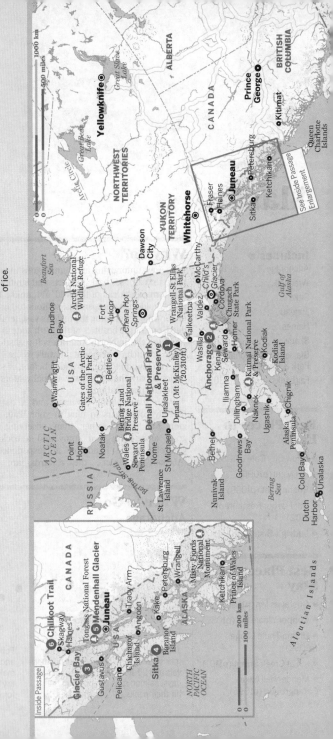

History

Indigenous Alaskans – Athabascans, Aleuts and Inuit, and the coastal tribes Tlingits and Haidas – migrated over the Bering Strait land bridge 20,000 years ago. In the 18th century, waves of Europeans arrived: first British and French explorers, then Russian whalers and fur traders, naming land formations, taking otter pelts and leaving the cultures of the Alaska Native peoples in disarray.

With the Russians' finances badly over extended by the Napoleonic Wars, US Secretary of State William H Seward was able to purchase the territory from them for $7.2 million – less than 2¢ an acre – in 1867. There was uproar over 'Seward's Folly,' but the land's riches soon revealed themselves: whales initially, then salmon, gold and finally oil. After Japan bombed and occupied the Aleutian Islands in WWII, the military built the famous Alcan (Alaska–Canada) Hwy, which connected the territory with the rest of the USA. The 1520-mile Alcan contributed greatly to postwar Alaska becoming a state in 1959.

The Good Friday earthquake in 1964 left Alaska in a shambles, but recovery was boosted when oil was discovered under Prudhoe Bay, resulting in the construction of a 789-mile pipeline to Valdez. For most Alaskans, the abundant oil made it hard to see beyond the gleam of the oil dollar.

In 1989 the *Exxon Valdez*, a 987ft Exxon oil supertanker, rammed Bligh Reef a few hours out of the port of Valdez, spilling almost 11 million gallons of crude oil into Prince William Sound. The spill eventually contaminated 1567 miles of shoreline and killed an estimated 100,000 to 250,000 birds and 2800 sea otters and decimated fish populations. The fisheries are just now recovering from the spill, as are animal populations, though you can still find oil just below the sand on many beaches.

In 2006 Sarah Palin, a former mayor of Wasilla, stunned the political world by beating the incumbent governor to become Alaska's first female governor as well as its youngest at 42. Two years later presidential candidate John McCain named her as his running mate on the Republican ticket. Commanding a little less international attention was Republican Senator Ted Stevens who, when he left office in 2009, had served the state for a record 41 years.

In 2015, Alaska legalized the possession of recreational marijuana, making the state the third in the union to green-light cannabis. Other political issues have not been resolved with such finality; drilling of the Arctic National Wildlife Refuge remains an environmental flash point, as does the potential creation of the Pebble Mine, which would be adjacent to Bristol Bay, the largest sockeye salmon fishery in the world.

Land & Climate

It's one thing to be told Denali is the tallest mountain in North America; it's another to see it crowning the sky in Denali National Park. It's a mountain so tall, so massive and so overwhelming it has visitors stumbling off the park buses. As a state, Alaska is the same, a place so huge, so wild and so unpopulated it's incomprehensible to most people until they arrive.

❶ Getting There & Away

Whether you're from the US or overseas, traveling to Alaska is like traveling to a foreign country. By sea it takes almost a week on the Alaska Marine Highway ferry to reach Whittier in Prince William Sound from the lower 48. By land a motorist in the Midwest needs 10 days to drive straight to Fairbanks.

If you're coming from the US mainland, the quickest and least expensive way to reach Alaska is to fly nonstop from a number of cities. If you're coming from Asia or Europe, it's almost impossible to fly directly to Alaska as few international airlines maintain a direct service to Anchorage, except for seasonal flights from Frankfurt on **Condor Airlines** (☑ 866-960-7915; www.condor.com). Most international travelers come through the gateway cities of Seattle, Portland, Minneapolis or Denver.

Flights, cars and tours can be booked online at lonelyplanet.com/bookings.

ANCHORAGE

Locals like to say that Anchorage is only 30 minutes from Alaska: wedged between 5000ft peaks and an inlet filled with salmon and whales, the Big Apple of the north is unlike any other city.

At first glance the traffic, strip malls and suburban sprawl can feel off-putting. But inside those strip malls are top-notch restaurants serving fresh seafood and locally grown produce, and the two roads that lead in and out of town spool right into some of the most majestic wilderness in the world. This is a city where bears are seen wandering bike paths, moose munch on neighborhood gardens, and locals pull salmon from a creek within blocks of hotels and office buildings.

Dive into this city of parks, museums and restaurants and you'll see why almost half the state's population calls it home.

⊙ Sights

★ Anchorage Museum   MUSEUM
(www.anchoragemuseum.org; 625 C St; adult/child $18/9; ⊙10am-6pm Tue-Sat, from noon Sun; ⊞) This world-class facility is Anchorage's cultural jewel. The West Wing, a four-story, shimmering, mirrored facade, adds 80,000 sq ft to what was already the largest museum in the state, while the Rasmuson Wing adds art from across the international North. The museum's flagship exhibit is the **Smithsonian Arctic Studies Center** (with more than 600 Alaska Native objects, such as art, tools, masks and household implements), which was previously housed in Washington, DC.

★ Alaska Native
Heritage Center   CULTURAL CENTER
(☑907-330-8000; www.alaskanative.net; 8800 Heritage Center Dr; adult/child $25/17; ⊙9am-5pm mid-May–mid-Sep) If you can't travel to the Bush region to experience Native Alaska culture firsthand, visit this 26-acre center and see how humans survived – and thrived – before central heating. This is much more than just a museum: it represents a knowledge bank of language, art and culture that will survive no matter how many sitcoms are crackling through the Alaskan stratosphere. It's a labor of love, and of incalculable value.

Alaska Zoo   ZOO
(www.alaskazoo.org; 4731 O'Malley Rd; adult/child $15/7; ⊙9am-9pm; ⊞) The unique wildlife of the Arctic is on display at this zoo, the only one in North America that specializes in northern animals, including snow leopards, Amur tigers and Tibetan yaks. Alaskan native species, from wolverines and moose to caribou and Dall sheep, are abundant. What kids will love watching, however, are the bears. The zoo has all Alaskan species, but the polar bears are clearly the star attraction.

Alaska Native Medical Center   GALLERY
(www.anmc.org; 4315 Diplomacy Dr; ⊙24hr) FREE This hospital has a fantastic collection of Alaska Native art and artifacts: take the elevator to the top floor and wind down the staircase past dolls, basketry and tools from all over Alaska. It's an informal presentation but a worthy visit.

Ship Creek Viewing Platform   VIEWPOINT
FREE From mid- to late summer, king, coho and pink salmon spawn up Ship Creek, the historical site of Tanaina Indian fish camps. At the overlook you can cheer on those love-starved fish humping their way toward destiny, and during high tide see the banks lined with anglers trying to hook them in what has to be one of the greatest urban fisheries anywhere in the USA. Take C St north, cross Ship Creek Bridge and turn right on Whitney Rd.

Alaska Aviation Heritage Museum   MUSEUM
(☑907-248-5325; www.alaskaairmuseum.org; 4721 Aircraft Dr; adult/child $17/10; ⊙10am-6pm) On the south shore of Lake Hood (the world's busiest floatplane lake), this museum is a tribute to Alaska's colorful Bush pilots and their faithful planes. Housed within are 25 planes along with historic photos and displays of pilots' achievements, from the first flight to Fairbanks (1913) to the early history of Alaska Airlines.

⟑ Tours

★ Alaska Railroad   RAIL
(☑customer service 907-265-2494, reservations 800-544-0552; www.akrr.com; 411 W 1st Ave) Has many one-day tours from Anchorage that begin with a train ride. Its nine-hour Spencer Glacier Float Tour (per person $242) trundles to Spencer Lake and includes a gentle raft trip among icebergs. The Glacier Quest Cruise ($223) rumbles to Whittier and includes a four-hour boat cruise in Prince William Sound; watch glaciers calve while feasting on king crab cakes.

Ghost Tours of Anchorage   HISTORY
(☑907-274-4678; www.ghosttoursofanchorage.com; per person $15; ⊙7:30pm Tue-Sun) This excellent and quirky 90-minute downtown walk takes place nightly (rain or shine) in summer. To join, just show up in front of Snow City Café at 4th Ave and L St – site of perhaps the most notorious murder in Anchorage's history.

⊨ Sleeping

Bent Prop Inn Midtown   HOSTEL $
(☑907-222-5220; www.bentpropinn.com; 3104 Eide St; dm $30-35; ⊛) The microdorms here are the best deal in town: in converted

LGBT ALASKA

The gay community in Alaska tends to be less open than in major US cities, and Alaskans in general are not as tolerant of diversity. In 1998 Alaska passed a constitutional amendment banning same-sex marriages. That said, since Obergefell v. Hodges (2015) legalized same-sex marriage in the USA, public opinion polls in Alaska have generally swung toward greater acceptance of that concept.

In Anchorage, the only city in Alaska of any real size, there is **Identity Inc** (☎907-929-4528; www.identityinc.org), which has a gay and lesbian helpline, a handful of openly gay clubs and bars, and a weeklong PrideFest (http://alaskapride.org) in mid-June. The Southeast Alaska Gay & Lesbian Alliance (www.seagla.org) is based in Juneau and offers links and travel lists geared to gay visitors.

Alaskans affect a live and let live attitude, but don't always exhibit these values as regards LGBT visitors. If in doubt, same-sex couples may want to err on the side of discretion.

one-bedroom apartments, these come with four beds, a private kitchen and a living room – it's like dorms meet the suite life. Regular dorms are co-ed and have six beds. There are two kitchens, coin-operated laundry and big-screen TV. The one private apartment goes for $149.

★ **Copper Whale Inn** INN $$
(☎907-258-7999; www.copperwhale.com; cnr W 5th Ave & L St; r $200-240, ste $290; @☎) An ideal downtown location and a bright and elegant interior make this inn one of the best midrange places in Anchorage. The suite has a full kitchen. Two relaxing waterfall courtyards make it easy to consume that novel, while many rooms and the breakfast lounge give way to views of Cook Inlet. Are those beluga whales out there?

Anchorage Grand Hotel LUXURY HOTEL $$
(☎907-929-8888; www.anchoragegrand.com; 505 W 2nd Ave; r $199; @☎) This converted apartment building rests on a quiet street with 31 spacious suites that include full kitchens and separate living and bedroom areas. Many overlook Ship Creek and Cook Inlet, and its downtown location is convenient to everything.

Hotel Captain Cook HOTEL $$$
(☎907-276-6000; www.captaincook.com; 939 W 5th Ave; r $295-370; @☎☒) The grand dame of Anchorage accommodations still has an air of an Alaskan aristocrat, right down to the finely dressed door staff. There are plenty of plush services and upscale shops on offer: hot tubs, a fitness club, beauty salon, jewelry store and four restaurants, including the famed Crow's Nest bar on the top floor.

✖ Eating

★ **Snow City Café** CAFE $
(☎907-272-2489; www.snowcitycafe.com; 1034 W 4th Ave; breakfast $8-15, lunch $10-15; ☺6:30am-3pm Mon-Fri, to 4pm Sat & Sun; ☎) Consistently voted best breakfast by *Anchorage Press* readers, this busy cafe serves healthy grub to a clientele that ranges from the tattooed to the up-and-coming. For breakfast, skip the usual eggs and toast and try a 'crabby' omelet or a sockeye smoked-salmon Benedict.

Red Chair Cafe BREAKFAST $
(www.theredchaircafe.com; 337 E 4th Ave; breakfast $12-16; ☺7am-3pm) The best and worst thing about eating in this steampunk-decorated cafe is choosing which brunch dish. The hollandaise sauce is made fresh daily, as are the muffins. Or should you go for the stuffed poblano pepper, the lemon poppy-seed pancakes or the kale baked skillet? Better have another strawberry and lime mimosa while you decide.

Fromagio's Artisan Cheese SANDWICHES $
(www.fromagioscheese.com; 3555 Arctic Blvd; sandwiches $11; ☺11am-6pm Tue-Sat, closed Sun & Mon) A cheesemonger that serves gourmet sandwiches. Stop in for lunch, sample some exotic cheeses and then grab some for a picnic while on your hike.

Rustic Goat BISTRO $$
(☎907-334-8100; www.rusticgoatak.com; 2800 Turnagain St; pizzas $14-16, mains $18-32; ☺6am-10pm Mon-Thu, to 11pm Fri, 7am-11pm Sat, to 10pm Sun) This sweet little bistro is in the suburban Turnagain neighborhood, but it feels like a city loft. Old-growth timbers support two stories of windows that look out to the Chugach Mountains. The assorted menu includes wood-fired pizzas, steaks

and salads. In the morning it's a casual coffee shop.

🍷 Drinking & Nightlife

Williwaw   BAR
(www.williwawsocial.com; 609 F St; ⏰11am-late Mon-Fri, from 10am Sat, closed Sun) It almost feels like you're in the big city when you spend a sunny evening at the rooftop bar surrounded by Anchorage's downtown buildings. A hidden speakeasy mixes upscale drinks (entry requires a password – note the payphone in the lobby), and there are live musical acts every weekend on the 1st floor. By day, a coffee shop serves up espressos.

Bernie's Bungalow Lounge   LOUNGE
(www.bernieslounge.com; 626 D St; ⏰11am-midnight Mon-Thu, to 2:30am Fri, 2pm-3:30am Sat) Pretty people, pretty drinks: this is the place to see and be seen. Its outdoor patio, complete with a water-spewing serpent, is the best in Anchorage, and on summer weekends it rocks late into the night with DJs up in the VIP room.

☆ Entertainment

★ Cyrano's Theatre Company   THEATER
(⏰907-274-2599; www.cyranos.org; 3800 Debarr Rd) This small off-center playhouse is the best live theater in town, staging everything from *Hamlet* to *Archy and Mehitabel* (featuring comical cockroach and a cat characters), Mel Brooks' jazz musical based on the poetry of Don Marquis, and an ever-changing lineup of original shows. Shows typically run Thursday to Sunday.

Alaska Center for the Performing Arts   PERFORMING ARTS
(⏰tickets 907-263-2787; www.myalaskacenter.com; 621 W 6th Ave) Impresses tourists with the 40-minute film *Aurora: Alaska's Great Northern Lights* (adult/child $15/7), screened on the hour from 9am to 9pm during summer in its Sydney Laurence Theatre. It's also home to the **Anchorage Opera** (⏰907-279-2557; www.anchorageopera.org), **Anchorage Symphony Orchestra** (⏰907-274-8668; www.anchoragesymphony.org), **Anchorage Concert Association** (⏰907-272-1471; www.anchorageconcerts.org) and **Alaska Dance Theatre** (⏰907-277-9591; www.alaskadancetheatre.org).

Chilkoot Charlie's   LIVE MUSIC
(⏰907-272-1010; www.koots.com; 2435 Spenard Rd; ⏰11:45am-2:30am Mon-Thu, 10:30am-3am Fri & Sat, to 2:30am Sun) More than just Anchorage's favorite meat market, 'Koots,' as the locals call it, is a landmark. The sprawling, wooden edifice has 10 bars, four dance floors and a sawdust-strewn floor. Many live acts perform here and there's at least one fun thing happening every night of the week.

ℹ Information

Alaska Public Lands Information Center
(⏰907-644-3680; www.alaskacenters.gov; 605 W 4th Ave, Suite 105; ⏰9am-5pm) In the Federal Building (you'll need photo ID). The center has handouts for hikers, mountain bikers, kayakers, fossil hunters and just about everyone else, on almost every wilderness area in the state. There are also excellent wildlife displays, free movies, fun dioramas, and ranger-led walks (11am and 3:15pm).

WORTH A TRIP

THE WILDS OF KODIAK ISLAND

Kodiak is the island of plenty. Consider its famous brown bears, the second-largest ursine creatures in the world (after the polar bear). Thanks to an unblemished ecosystem and an unlimited diet of rich salmon that spawn in Kodiak's lakes and rivers, adult male bears can weigh up to 1400lb.

Part of the wider Kodiak Archipelago and the second-largest island in the US after Hawaii's Big Island, Kodiak acts as a kind of ecological halfway house between the forested Alaskan Panhandle and the treeless Aleutian Islands. Its velvety green mountains and sheltered, ice-free bays were the site of the earliest Russian settlement in Alaska and are still home to one of the US's most important fishing fleets.

The island's main attraction – beyond its bears – is its quiet Alaskan authenticity. Only a small northeastern section of Kodiak is populated. The rest is roadless wilderness protected in the Kodiak National Wildlife Refuge.

Most travelers arriving on Kodiak Island come via plane or boat through Kodiak town.

Anchorage Convention & Visitors Bureau
(☑ 907-276-4118; www.anchorage.net) Has a useful website. Ring before your trip and ask to be provided a guide.

Log Cabin & Downtown Information Center
(☑ 907-257-2363; www.anchorage.net; 524 W 4th Ave; ⊙ 8am-7pm) Has pamphlets, maps, bus schedules, city guides in several languages and a lawn growing on its roof.

Visitors Center (☑ Domestic Terminal 907-266-2437, International Terminal 907-266-2657; Anchorage International Airport; ⊙ 9am-4pm) Two visitor-center kiosks are located in the baggage-claim areas of both airport terminals.

❶ Getting There & Away

AIR

Ted Stevens Anchorage International Airport
(ANC; www.dot.state.ak.us/anc; ☎; ☐7) The vast majority of visitors to Alaska, and almost all international flights, land here, at Alaska's biggest airport.

BUS

Anchorage is a hub for various small passenger and freight lines that make daily runs between specific cities. Always call first; Alaska's volatile bus industry is as unstable as an Alaska Peninsula volcano.

Alaska Park Connection (☑ 800-266-8625; www.alaskacoach.com) Offers daily service from Anchorage north to Talkeetna ($65, 2½ hours) and Denali National Park ($90, six hours), and south to Seward ($65, three hours).

Alaska/Yukon Trails (☑ 907-888-5659; www.alaskashuttle.com) Runs a bus up the George Parks Hwy to Denali ($75, six hours) and Fairbanks ($99, nine hours).

Homer Stage Lines (☑ 907-868-3914; http://stagelineinhomer.com) Will take you to Homer ($90, 4½ hours) and points in between.

Interior Alaska Bus Line (☑ 800-770-6652; www.interioralaskabusline.com) Has regular services between Anchorage and Glennallen ($70, three hours), Tok ($120, eight hours) and Fairbanks ($160, 17 hours), and points in between.

Seward Bus Line (☑ 907-563-0800; www.sewardbuslines.net) Runs between Anchorage and Seward ($50, three hours). For an extra $5, you can arrange an airport pickup/drop-off.

CAR

Avoid renting a car at the Anchorage airport if possible, as you will be hit with an extra 11.11% airport rental tax. Rental agencies within Anchorage generally have cheaper rates, and while they can't pick you up at the airport, if you drop the car off during business hours some rental places will provide you with a ride to the airport.

Also keep in mind that if you can rent a vehicle in May or September as opposed to June, July or August, you will usually save an additional 30%.

TRAIN

Alaska Railroad (☑ 800-544-0552; www.akrr.com) From its downtown depot, the Alaska Railroad sends its *Denali Star* north daily to Talkeetna (adult/child $106/53), Denali National Park ($174/87) and Fairbanks ($249/125). The *Coastal Classic* stops in Girdwood ($84/42) and Seward ($110/55), while the *Glacial Discovery* connects to Whittier ($89/45). Discounted rates are available in May and September.

SOUTHEAST ALASKA

Southeast Alaska is so *un-Alaska*. While much of the state is a treeless expanse of land with a layer of permafrost, the Panhandle is a slender, long rainforest that stretches 540 miles from Icy Bay, near Yakutat, south to Portland Canal and is filled with ice-blue glaciers, rugged snowcapped mountains, towering Sitka spruce and 1000 islands known as the Alexander Archipelago.

Before WWII, the Southeast was Alaska's heart and soul, and Juneau was not only the capital but the state's largest city. Today the region is characterized by big trees and small towns. Each community here has its own history and character: from Norwegian-influenced Petersburg to Russian-tinted Sitka. You can feel the gold fever in Skagway and see a dozen glaciers near Juneau. Each town is unique and none of them is connected to another by road. Jump on the state ferry or book a cruise and discover the idiosyncrasies.

Wrangell

Wrangell is Southeast Alaska's rough, gruff coastal outpost, a small boom-bust fishing community colored by centuries of native Tlingit settlement and more recent incursions by the Russians and British. Posh it isn't. Lacking the fishing affluence of Petersburg or the cruise-ship-oriented economy of Ketchikan, the town nurtures a tough outback spirit more familiar to Alaska's frigid north than its drizzly Panhandle. A collapse in the lumber industry in the 1990s hit the town hard, a blow from which it has only recently recovered.

If people stop in Wrangell at all, it's normally as a launchpad for excursions to the

ALASKA WRANGELL

Anan bear-watching observatory and the incredible Stikine River delta nearby. However, the countryside around town, a mishmash of boggy muskeg and tree-covered mountains, offers fine hiking, a fact not lost on Scottish American naturalist John Muir, who decamped here in 1879 on the first of four Alaska visits.

⊙ Sights & Activities

★**Wrangell Museum** MUSEUM
(☏907-874-3770; www.wrangell.com/museum; 296 Campbell Dr; adult/child/family $5/2/12; ⊙10am-5pm Mon-Sat Apr-Sep, 1-5pm Fri & Sat Oct-Mar) This impressive museum is what the colorful history and characters of Wrangell deserve. As you stroll through the many rooms, an audio narration automatically comes on and explains each chapter of Wrangell's history, from Tlingit culture and the gold-rush era to the time Hollywood arrived in 1972 to film the movie *Timber Tramps*. You can marvel at a collection of Alaskan art that includes a Sidney Laurence painting or be amused that this rugged little town has had two presidential visits.

During the winter the museum is technically only open two days a week; that said, you can usually arrange to visit from 9am to 5pm weekdays as long as you call ahead.

Petroglyph Beach ARCHAEOLOGICAL SITE
(Evergreen Ave; ♿) **FREE** Thought Alaska's history started with the Klondike gold rush? Not so. Historians and anthropologists should home in on this state historic park on Wrangell's north side, where you can see primitive rock carvings believed to be at least 1000 years old, plus a viewing deck

with interpretive displays and replicas. Turn right and walk north on the beach about 50yd. Before you reach the wrecked fishing vessels, look for faint carvings on the large rocks, many of them resembling spirals and faces.

★**Anan Creek Wildlife Observatory** WILDLIFE WATCHING
(☏907-225-3101; www.fs.usda.gov/detail/r10/specialplaces; permits $10; ⊙8am-6pm Jul & Aug) Thirty miles southeast of Wrangell on the mainland, Anan Creek is the site of one of the largest pink-salmon runs in Southeast Alaska. Here you can watch eagles, harbor seals, black bears and brown bears chowing down on the spawning humpies. This is one of the few places in Alaska where black and brown bears coexist – or at least put up with each other – at the same run. Permits are required from early July through August.

🛏 Sleeping & Eating

Wrangell Hostel HOSTEL $
(☏907-874-3534; 220 Church St; dm $20; ⊙Jun-Sep) The First Presbyterian Church doubles up as a basic hostel, with single-sex dorm rooms with inflatable mattresses, showers and a large kitchen and dining room. It has no curfew and will graciously let you hang out here during an all-day rain. There's no sign, just knock or push on the church door.

★**Ultima Thule Lodge** LUXURY HOTEL $$$
(☏907-854-4500; www.ultimathulelodge.com; 4-night 4-day package per person $7950) ✈ Located in the lonely backcountry of Wrangell-St Elias National Park on the Chitina River, over 100 miles from the nearest road, this

---

ALASKA FOR KIDS

The best that Alaska has to offer cannot be found in stuffy museums or amusement parks filled with heart-pounding rides. It's outdoor adventure, wildlife and scenery on a grand scale, attractions and activities that will intrigue the entire family – whether you're a kid or a parent.

Pioneer Park (☏907-459-1087; Airport Way; ⊙stores & museums noon-8pm late May-early Sep, park 5am-midnight; ℗♿) Train rides, salmon bakes and genuine pioneer history entertain the offspring in Fairbanks.

Mendenhall Glacier (p1095) Fascinating and easily accessible natural feature that's capable of dropping the jaws of any age group.

Sitka Sound (☏907-752-0660; www.kayaksitka.com) Sheltered waters, plenty of wooded islands and a good local guiding company make this one of Alaska's best family sea-kayaking spots.

Petroglyph Beach Search for ancient rock carvings and sea life at low tide in Wrangell.

fabulously luxurious lodge is the last thing you expect in such an inhospitable environment. But far from being just another expensive resort, Ultima Thule is elegant, tasteful, unpretentious and as beautiful as the land that envelops it.

★ **Stikine Inn Restaurant**   AMERICAN **$$**
(☑ 907-874-3388; www.stikineinn.com/dining; 107 Stikine Ave; mains lunch $14-18, dinner $16-30; ⊙ 11am-8pm) It's not hard being the best restaurant in Wrangell, but the Stikine goes above and beyond the call of duty with dishes like rockfish tacos, and a lobster po'boy that manages to be decadent without a decadent price. Everything's made a little more hunky dory by the view (water and fishing boats) and service (small-town Alaska friendly).

❶ Information

USFS Office (☑ 907-874-2323; www.fs.usda.gov; 525 Bennet St; ⊙ 8am-4:30pm Mon-Fri) Located 0.75 miles north of town; has information on regional USFS cabins, trails and campgrounds.

Wrangell Visitor Center (☑ 800-367-9745, 907-874-2829; www.wrangell.com; 293 Campbell Dr; ⊙ 10am-5pm Mon-Sat) In the plush Nolan Center, it stocks the free *Wrangell Guide* and shows a 10-minute film on the area in a small theater.

❶ Getting There & Away

Daily northbound and southbound flights are available with Alaska Airlines (p1104) on the so-called 'Milk Run' serving Seattle, Ketchikan, Petersburg, Juneau and Anchorage. Many claim the flight north to Petersburg is the world's shortest jet flight – around nine minutes on a good day with fabulous views to boot.

The **airport** (☑ 907-874-3309, 907-874-3107; Airport Rd) is just over a mile from the town center; an easy walk with light luggage.

Sitka

It's not always easy to uncover reminders of Alaska's 135-year-long dalliance with the Russian Empire – until you dock in Sitka. This sparkling gem of a city, which kisses the Pacific Ocean on Baranof Island's west shore, is one of the oldest non-native settlements in the state and the former capital of Russian Alaska (when it was known as New Archangel).

The bonus for visitors is that Sitka mixes wonderfully preserved history with outstanding natural beauty. Looming on the horizon, across Sitka Sound, is impressive Mt Edgecumbe, an extinct volcano with a graceful cone similar to Japan's Mt Fuji. Closer in, myriad small, forested islands turn into beautiful ragged silhouettes at sunset, competing for attention with the snowcapped mountains and sharp granite peaks flanking Sitka to the east. And in town picturesque remnants of Sitka's Russian heritage are tucked around every corner. It's like Skagway but with less tourists.

◉ Sights & Activities

★ **Sitka National Historical Park**   HISTORIC SITE
(☑ 907-747-0110; www.nps.gov/sitk; Lincoln St; ⊙ trails 6am-10pm, visitor center 8am-4:30pm May-Sep) 🆓 This mystical juxtaposition of tall trees and totems is Alaska's smallest national park and the site where the Tlingits were finally defeated by the Russians in 1804.

The mile-long **Totem Trail** winds its way past 18 totems first displayed at the 1904 Louisiana Exposition in St Louis and then moved to the park. These intriguing totems, standing in a thick rainforest setting by the sea and often enveloped in mist, have become synonymous with the national park and, by extension, the city itself.

★ **Russian Bishop's House**   HISTORIC BUILDING
(☑ 907-747-0110; Lincoln St; ⊙ 8am-4:30pm May-Sep) 🆓 East of downtown along Lincoln St, the Russian Bishop's House is the oldest intact Russian building in Sitka. Built in 1843 by Finnish carpenters out of Sitka spruce, the two-story log house is one of only four surviving examples of Russian colonial architecture in North America. The National Park Service (NPS) has restored the building to its 1853 condition, when it served as a school and residence for the Russian bishop, Innocent (Ivan Veniaminov).

Sitka Sound Science Center   AQUARIUM
(☑ 907-747-8878; www.sitkascience.org; 834 Lincoln St; $5; ⊙ 9am-4pm; 👶) Sitka's best children's attraction is this hatchery and science center. Outside, the facade is being restored to its original appearance. Inside the science center are five aquariums, including the impressive 800-gallon 'Wall of Water' and three touch tanks where kids can get their hands wet handling anemones, sea cucumbers and starfish.

Whale Park PARK

(Sawmill Creek Rd) If you can't afford a wild-life cruise, try Whale Park, 4 miles south of downtown, which has a boardwalk and free spotting scopes overlooking the ocean. Best of all is listening to whale songs over the 'hydrophone.' Fall is the best time to sight cetaceans; as many as 80 whales – mostly humpbacks – can gather between mid-September and year's end.

Alaska Raptor Center WILDLIFE RESERVE

(☎907-747-8662; www.alaskaraptor.org; 1000 Raptor Way; adult/child $13/6; ☉8am-4pm May-Sep; P☷) ✒ This is no zoo, or bird show for gawping kids. Rather, think of it more as a raptor hospital and rehab center – and a good one at that. The 17-acre center treats 200 injured birds a year, with its most impressive facility being a 20,000-sq-ft flight-training center that helps injured eagles, owls, falcons and hawks regain their ability to fly.

🛏 Sleeping

Sitka International Hostel HOSTEL $

(☎907-747-8661; www.sitkahostel.org; 109 Jeff Davis St; dm/d $24/65; ☏) Sitka's typically bohemian hostel is downtown in the historic Tillie Paul Manor, which once served as the town's hospital. The charismatic building crammed with all sorts of information and mementos features a men's room with its own kitchen and several women's rooms, along with a family room, another small kitchen and a lovely sun porch with a mountain view.

Cascade Creek Inn INN $$

(☎907-747-6804; www.cascadecreekinnandcharters.com; 2035 Halibut Point Rd; r $170-210; ☏) Perched right above the shoreline, all 10 rooms in this handsome wooden inn face the ocean and have a private balcony overlooking it. There are four top-floor rooms with kitchenettes. Sure, you're 2.5 miles north of town, but the inn's oceanfront deck is worth the ride on the downtown bus.

Aspen Suites Hotel HOTEL $$$

(☎907-747-3477; www.aspenhotelsak.com/sitka; 210 Lake St; ste $289-300; P@☏) This new chain has infiltrated several Alaskan cities in the last couple of years, Juneau and Haines among them. The new Sitka offering opened in the summer of 2017 with Aspen's characteristic selection of businesslike suites complete with kitchenettes, sofas and large bathrooms. There's also an on-site gym and a surgical level of cleanliness (and newness) throughout.

🍴 Eating & Drinking

★**Grandma Tillie's Bakery** BAKERY $

(☎907-738-5768; www.facebook.com/grandma tilliesbakery; 1318 Sawmill Creek Rd; baked goods $3-8; ☉6:30am-2pm Wed-Sat) Pink drive-through bakery located 1 mile east of the town center that is – frankly – worth the walk, let alone the drive, courtesy of its sponge-y fresh savory rolls and rich chewy cookies. We'll stick our neck out and announce that these are, possibly, the best baked goods in Southeast Alaska.

★**Ludvig's Bistro** MEDITERRANEAN $$$

(☎907-966-3663; www.ludvigsbistro.com; 256 Katlian St; mains $28-40; ☉4:30-9pm) Sophistication in the wilderness! Sitka's boldest restaurant has only seven tables, and a few stools at its brass-and-blue-tile bar. Described as 'rustic Mediterranean fare,' almost every dish is local, even the sea salt. If seafood paella is on the menu, order it. The traditional Spanish rice dish comes loaded with whatever fresh seafood the local boats have netted that day.

★**Baranof Island Brewing Co** BREWERY

(☎907-747-2739; www.baranofislandbrewing.com; 1209 Sawmill Creek Rd; ☉2-8pm; ☷) Encased in a handsome new taproom since July 2017, the Baranof is a local legend providing microbrews for every pub and bar in town. For the real deal, however, the taproom's the place. Line up four to six tasters and make sure you include a Halibut Point Hefeweisen and a Redoubt Red Ale.

ℹ Information

Sitka Information Center (☎907-747-8604; www.sitka.org; 104 Lake St; ☉9am-4:30pm Mon-Fri) Ultra-helpful office opposite the Westmark hotel downtown. Also staffs a desk at the **Harigan Centennial Hall** (☎907-747-3225; 330 Harbor Dr; ☉9am-5pm) when there's a cruise ship in town.

USFS Sitka Ranger District Office (☎907-747-6671, recorded information 907-747-6685; 2108 Halibut Point Rd; ☉8am-4:30pm Mon-Fri) Has information about local trails, camping and USFS cabins. It's 2 miles north of town. More central is the visitor center at Sitka National Historical Park (p1093).

ⓘ Getting There & Away

Sitka Airport (SIT; ☑ 907-966-2960; Airport Rd) On Japonski Island, 1.5 miles, or a 20-minute walk, west of downtown. The Ride Sitka green line bus runs to the island but stops short of the airport.

Alaska Airlines (p1104) Flights to/from Juneau (45 minutes) and Ketchikan (one hour).

Harris Aircraft Services (☑ 907-966-3050; www.harrisair.com; Airport Rd) Floatplane air-taxi service to small communities and USFS cabins as well as larger Southeast towns such as Juneau.

Juneau

Juneau is a capital of contrasts and conflicts. It borders a waterway that never freezes but lies beneath an ice field that never melts. It was the first community in the Southeast to slap a head tax on cruise-ship passengers but still draws more than a million a year. It's the state capital but since the 1980s Alaskans have been trying to move it. It doesn't have any roads that go anywhere, but half its residents and its mayor opposed a plan to build one that would.

Welcome to America's strangest state capital. In the winter it's a beehive of legislators, their loyal aides and lobbyists locked in political struggles. In summer it's a launchpad for copious outdoor adventures. Superb hiking starts barely 10 minutes from downtown, a massive glacier calves into a lake 12 miles up the road, and boats and seaplanes take off from the waterfront bound for nearby bear-viewing, ziplining and whale-watching.

◉ Sights & Activities

★**Mendenhall Glacier**   GLACIER
Going to Juneau and not seeing the Mendenhall is like visiting Rome and skipping the Colosseum. The most famous of Juneau's ice floes, and the city's most popular attraction, flows 13 miles from its source, the Juneau Icefield, and has a half-mile-wide face. It ends at Mendenhall Lake, the reason for all the icebergs.

Alaska State Museum   MUSEUM
(☑ 907-465-2901; www.museums.state.ak.us; 395 Whittier St; adult/child $12/free; ☺ 9am-5pm May-Aug, 10am-4pm Sep-Apr; ⓐ) Demolished and rebuilt in a snazzy new $140-million complex in 2016, the result is impressive. Sometimes called SLAM (State Library, Archives and Museum), the museum shares digs with the state archives along with a gift store, the Raven Cafe, an auditorium, a research room and a historical library. The beautifully curated displays catalog the full historical and geographic breadth of the state, from native canoes to the oil industry.

Mt Roberts Tramway   CABLE CAR
(☑ 888-461-8726; www.mountrobertstramway.com; 490 S Franklin St; adult/child $35/18; ☺ 11am-9pm Mon, from 8am Tue-Sun; ⓐ) As far as cable cars go, this tramway is rather expensive for a five-minute ride. But from a marketing point of view its location couldn't be better. It whisks you right from the cruise-ship dock up 1750ft to the timberline of Mt Roberts, where you'll find a restaurant, gift shops, a small raptor center and a theater with a film on Tlingit culture.

★**Kawanti Adventures**   ADVENTURE SPORTS
(☑ 907-225-8400; www.kawanti.com; adult/child $169/119) Possibly Alaska's most adrenaline-laced zip, these five lines are located at beautiful Eaglecrest Ski Area on Douglas Island. On your adventure, you'll have time to stop and take a breath in fully enclosed tree houses, before finishing with a bout of axe throwing.

✬ Festivals & Events

★**Celebration**   CULTURAL
(www.sealaskaheritage.org/institute/celebration; ☺ Jun) In June of even-numbered years, Southeast Alaska's three main tribal groups, the Tlingit, Haida and Tsimshian, gather for the aptly named 'Celebration,' the largest native cultural event in Alaska. The festival's sentiment is as simple as its name: to celebrate and revitalize ancient traditions in native dance, music and art which, by the early 20th century, were in danger of extinction.

⌂ Sleeping

★**Mendenhall Lake Campground**   CAMPGROUND $
(☑ reservations 877-444-6777; www.recreation.gov; Montana Creek Rd; tent/RV sites $10/28) One of Alaska's most beautiful USFS campgrounds. The 69-site area (17 sites with hookups) is on Montana Creek Rd, off Mendenhall Loop Rd, and has a separate seven-site walk-in area. The campsites are alongside Mendenhall Lake, and many have spectacular views of the icebergs or even the glacier that discharges them.

BEARS OF ADMIRALTY ISLAND & PACK CREEK

Just 15 miles south of Juneau is Admiralty Island National Monument, a 1493-sq-mile preserve, of which 90% is designated wilderness. The monument has a wide variety of wildlife – from Sitka black-tailed deer and nesting bald eagles to harbor seals, sea lions and humpback whales – but more than anything else, Admiralty Island is known for bears. The 96-mile-long island has one of the highest populations of bears in Alaska, with an estimated 1500 brown bears, more than all the lower 48 states combined. It's the reason the Tlingit called Admiralty Kootznoowoo, 'the Fortress of Bears.'

Pack Creek (permits adult $20-50, child $10-25) The monument's main attraction for visitors is Pack Creek, which flows from 4000ft mountains before spilling into Seymour Canal on the island's east side. The extensive tide flats at the mouth of the creek draw a large number of bears in July and August to feed on salmon. This, and its proximity to Juneau, make it a favorite spot for observing and photographing the animals.

Alaska Seaplanes (☑907-789-3331; www.flyalaskaseaplanes.com) has daily flights from Juneau to Angoon ($154, 40 minutes), the only community on Admiralty Island. Also conducts a Pack Creek flightseeing bear tour ($849).

All the sites are well spread out in the woods, and 20 can be reserved in advance.

Alaskan Hotel HOTEL $
(☑800-327-9347, 907-586-1000; www.thealaskanhotel.com; 167 S Franklin St; r with/without bathroom $110/90; ☎) Welcome to a quintessential gold-boom hotel, with heavily patterned wallpaper clashing with the heavily patterned carpet, lots of wood paneling and walls that would probably relate some lewd erstwhile antics could they talk (it's the oldest operating hotel in Alaska, dating from 1913).

★ **Silverbow Inn** BOUTIQUE HOTEL $$$
(☑907-586-4146; www.silverbowinn.com; 120 2nd St; r $109-289; @☎) A swanky (for Alaska) boutique inn with 11 rooms. The 100-year-old building emanates a retro-versus-modern feel with antiques and rooms with private baths, king and queen beds and flat-screen TVs. A 2nd-floor deck features a hot tub with a view of Douglas Island's mountains. Breakfast is served in the morning and there's a cocoa and cookies 'happy hour' in the afternoon.

✖ **Eating**

★ **Pel'Meni** DUMPLINGS $
(2 Marine Way; dumplings $7; ⊙11:30am-1:30am Sun-Thu, to 3:30am Fri & Sat) Juneau was never part of Russia's Alaskan empire, but that hasn't stopped the city succumbing to a silent invasion of *pelmeni* (homemade Russian dumplings), filled with either potato or beef, spiced with hot sauce, curry and cilantro, and

tempered with a little optional sour cream and rye bread on the side.

★ **Saffron** INDIAN $$
(☑907-586-1036; www.facebook.com/saffronindiancomfortcuisine; 112 N Franklin St; mains $8-19; ⊙11am-3pm & 5-9pm Mon-Fri, 5-9pm only Sat; ☝) Juneau flirts with *nuevo* Indian food at Saffron and the results are commendable. There are plenty of delicate breads to go with the aromatic curries with a strong bias toward vegetarian dishes (including a good spinach paneer). For lunch it offers *thalis* (small taster-sized plates). Everything is made from scratch and the exotic cooking smells lure you in from the street.

Tracy's King Crab Shack SEAFOOD $$
(☑907-723-1811; www.kingcrabshack.com; 432 S Franklin St; crab $13-45; ⊙10:30am-9pm) The best of the food shacks along the cruise-ship berths is Tracy's. On a boardwalk surrounded by a beer shack and a gift shop, she serves up outstanding crab bisque, mini crab cakes and 3lb buckets of king-crab pieces ($110). Grab a friend or six and share.

🍷 **Drinking & Nightlife**

Alaskan Brewing Company BREWERY
(☑907-780-5866; www.alaskanbeer.com; 5364 Commercial Blvd; ⊙11am-7pm daily May-Sep, noon-7pm Mon-Sat, to 6pm Sun Oct-Apr) Established in 1986 (ancient history in craft-brewing years), Alaska's largest brewery has always been a pioneer. Its amber ale (along with many other concoctions) is ubiquitous across the state and rightly so. Note: this is not a brewpub but a tasting room with tours. It isn't located

downtown either, but 5 miles to the north-west in Lemon Creek.

ⓘ Information

Alaska Division of Parks (☑907-465-4563; www.dnr.state.ak.us/parks; 400 Willoughby Ave; ☺8am-4:30pm Mon-Fri) Head to the 5th floor of the Natural Resources Building for state-park information, including cabin rentals.

Juneau Visitor Center (☑907-586-2201; www.traveljuneau.com; 800 Glacier Ave; ☺8am-5pm) The visitor center is in the cruise-ship terminal right next to the Mt Roberts Tramway and has all the information you need to explore Juneau, find a trail or book a room. The center also maintains smaller booths at the airport, at the marine ferry terminal and **downtown** (Marine Way; ☺hours vary) near the library.

USFS Juneau Ranger District Office (☑907-586-8800; www.fs.usda.gov/detail/tongass/about-forest/offices; 8510 Mendenhall Loop Rd; ☺8am-4:30pm Mon-Fri) This impressive office is in Mendenhall Valley and is the place for questions about cabins, trails, kayaking and Pack Creek bear-watching permits. It also serves as the USFS office for Admiralty Island National Monument.

ⓘ Getting There & Away

Juneau International Airport (JNU; ☑907-789-7821; 1873 Shell Simmons Dr) is located 9 miles northwest of downtown. There is a bus link.

Alaska Airlines (p1104) offers scheduled jet service to Seattle (two hours), all major Southeast cities, Glacier Bay (30 minutes), Anchorage (two hours) and Cordova (2½ hours) daily in summer.

Alaska Seaplanes (☑907-789-3331; www.flyalaskaseaplanes.com) flies daily floatplanes from Juneau to Angoon ($154), Gustavus ($119), Pelican ($189) and Tenakee Springs ($154).

Haines

The first thing you notice about Haines is that it *isn't* Skagway, the tourist showpiece situated 33 nautical miles to the north. Instead, this is a quiet, independent, un-prepossessing town of native artists, outdoor-adventure lovers and 100% Alaskans hooked on the tranquil life. People come here to see bald eagles in the wild, dissect one thousand years of Chilkat-Tlingit culture, ponder the remains of an old military barracks and enjoy the best drinking scene in an American town of this size.

After logging fell on hard times in the 1970s, Haines swung its economy toward tourism; not so much cruise ships (Haines receives a mere 40,000 cruisers per season), but more independent travelers. Haines is particularly popular with RVers in summer and heli-skiers in winter. As a result, the businesses here are uniquely Hainesian, and most likely the person behind the counter is the one who owns the store.

◎ Sights & Activities

★**Jilkaat Kwaan Cultural Heritage & Bald Eagle Preserve Visitor Center** CULTURAL CENTRE (☑907-767-5485; www.jilkaatkwaanheritagecenter.org; 9 Chilkat Ave; adult/child $15/7.50; ☺10am-4pm Mon-Fri, from noon Sat, closed Oct-Apr) Part of a welcome renaissance in Tlingit art and culture in Alaska, this heritage center is located in the ancient native village of Kluk-wan, 22 miles north of Haines. The center includes some of the most prized heirlooms of Alaska Native culture, namely four elaborate house posts and a rain screen (the legendary 'whale house collection') carved by a Tlingit Michelangelo over 200 years ago and only recently made available for public viewing.

Fort Seward HISTORIC SITE (www.nps.gov/places/fort-william-h-seward.htm; Ft Seward Dr) Alaska's first permanent military post is reached by heading uphill (east) at the Front St–Haines Hwy junction. Built in 1903 and decommissioned after WWII, the fort is now a National Historic Landmark, with a handful of restaurants, lodges and art galleries in the original buildings. A walking-tour map of the fort is available at the visitor center, or you can just wander around and read the historical panels that have been erected there.

Fjord Express BOATING (☑907-766 3395, 800-320-0146; www.alaskafjordlines.com; Small-Boat Harbor; adult/child $179/149) Don't have time to make it to Juneau? The Fjord Express zips you down Lynn Canal in a catamaran (will stop for whales, sea lions and other marine wildlife), and then rumbles around Juneau's top sights in a bus before dropping you back in Haines. A light breakfast and dinner are included. It departs Haines at 8:30am and returns at 7:30pm.

The trip is $135 one way.

🛌 Sleeping

Bear Creek Cabins & Hostel   HOSTEL $

(☑907-766-2259; www.bearcreekcabinsalaska.com; Small Tract Rd; dm/cabins $20/68; 🌐) A rare Southeastern Alaska hostel of sorts, this place is a 20-minute walk outside town – follow Mud Bay Rd and when it veers right, continue straight onto Small Tract Rd for 1.5 miles. The complex consists of eights cabins (most sleep four) clustered around a grassy common area.

Aspen Suites Hotel   HOTEL $$

(☑907-766-2211; www.aspenhotelsak.com/haines; 409 Main St; r $159-169; P🌐@🌐) One of six Aspen hotels in Alaska, this slick building offers rooms more akin to studio apartments, all equipped with kitchenettes and comfortable sofas. There's coffee on tap at reception, a small fitness room and a clean, polished sheen to the whole operation.

✖ Eating & Drinking

★ Fireweed Restaurant   BISTRO $$

(☑907-766-3838; 37 Blacksmith Rd; salads $10-19, pizzas $14-30; ⏱4:30-9pm Tue-Sat; 🌐) This clean, bright and laid-back bistro is in an old Fort Seward building and its copious salads are an ideal antidote to the Southeast's penchant for grease. A quick scroll down the menu will reveal words like 'organic,' 'veggie' and 'grilled' as opposed to 'deep fried' and 'captain's special.'

★ Haines Brewing Company   BREWERY

(☑907-766-3823; www.hainesbrewing.com; Main St, cnr 4th Ave; ⏱noon-7pm Mon-Sat) Surely one of the finest small breweries in America, this Haines operation, founded in 1999, has recently opened a lovely new tasting room in what passes for downtown Haines. The beautiful wood and glass structure serves all of the locally brewed favorites, including Spruce Tip Ale, Elder Rock Red and the potent Black Fang stout (8.2% alcohol content).

ℹ Information

Alaska Division of Parks (⏱8am-5pm Mon-Fri) Call for information on state parks and hiking.

Haines Convention & Visitors Bureau (☑907-766-6418; www.visithaines.com; 122 2nd Ave; ⏱8am-5pm Mon-Fri, 9am-4pm Sat & Sun) Has restrooms, free coffee and racks of free information for tourists. There is also a lot of information on Canada's Yukon for those heading up the Alcan.

ℹ Getting There & Away

There is no jet service to Haines, but **Alaska Seaplanes** (☑907-789-3331; www.flyalaskaseaplanes.com) will take you to Juneau seven times a day ($134). The **airport** (HNS; off Haines Hwy) is 3 miles northwest of town just off the Haines Hwy.

Skagway

At first sight, Skagway appears to be solely an amusement park for cruise-ship day-trippers, a million of whom disgorge onto its sunny boardwalks every summer. But, haunted by Klondike ghosts and beautified by a tight grid of handsome false-fronted buildings, this is no northern Vegas. Skagway's history is very real.

⊙ Sights & Activities

★ Klondike Gold Rush National Historical Park Museum & Visitor Center   MUSEUM

(☑907-983-9200; www.nps.gov/klgo; Broadway St, at 2nd Ave; ⏱8:30am-5:30pm May-Sep) FREE The recently improved NPS center is in the original 1898 White Pass & Yukon Route depot. The center is spread over two interconnecting buildings. One contains a small museum explaining some of the Klondike background with an emphasis on the two routes out of Skagway: Chilkoot Pass and White Pass. The other space is a visitor center staffed by park rangers.

Skagway Museum   MUSEUM

(☑907-983-2420; cnr 7th Ave & Spring St; adult/child $2/free; ⏱9am-5pm Mon-Fri, 10am-5pm Sat, 10am-4pm Sun) Skagway Museum is not only one of the finest in a town filled with museums, but it's one of the finest in the Southeast. It occupies the entire 1st floor of the venerable century-old McCabe Building, a former college, and is devoted to various aspects of local history, including Alaska Native baskets, beadwork and carvings, and, of course, the Klondike gold rush.

★ White Pass & Yukon Route Railroad   RAIL

(☑800-343-7373; www.wpyr.com; 231 2nd Ave; ⏱May-Sep) This epic gold-rush-era railroad has departures from Skagway, AK; Fraser, British Columbia; and Carcross and Whitehorse, Yukon. The line was built across White Pass between 1898 and 1900 just in time to catch the coattails of the gold rush.

In WWII it was used to transport troops to Whitehorse in Canada.

Skagway Float Tours RAFTING
(☑907-983-3688; www.skagwayfloat.com; 3rd & Broadway St; ☺9am-6:30pm Mon-Sat, to 4pm Sun) Fancy spot of bliss on the river? Try the three-hour tour of the ghost town of Dyea that includes a 45-minute float down the placid Taiya River (adult/child $85/65); there are two per day at 9am and 1:30pm. The Hike & Float Tour ($110/90) is a four-hour outing that includes hiking 2 miles of the Chilkoot Trail then some floating back; there are four per day (fewer on weekends).

🛏 Sleeping

Morning Wood Hotel HOTEL $
(☑907-983-3200; www.skagwayhotelandrestaurant.com/morning-wood-hotel; 444 4th Ave; r with/without bath $175/99; 🛜) A buoyant hotel with a handsome, if typical, false-fronted wooden exterior. Inside, the rooms (located at the rear) aren't fancy, but at least they come with deluxe bathroom accessories and sharp color accents. There's an affiliated restaurant and bar.

Skagway Inn INN $$
(☑907-983-2289; www.skagwayinn.com; Broadway St, at 7th Ave; r $159-264; @🛜) In a restored 1897 Victorian building that was originally one of the town's brothels (what building still standing in Skagway wasn't?) this beautiful downtown inn features 10 rooms, four with shared baths. All are small but filled with antique dressers, iron beds and chests, and named after the 'ladies' who worked here. Breakfast is included, as are ferry/airport/train transfers.

🍴 Eating & Drinking

Woadie's South East Seafood SEAFOOD $$
(☑907-983-3133; State St & 4th Ave; mains $14-19; ☺11:30am-7pm Mon-Thu, noon-6pm Fri & Sat) A food cart with its own deck and awning, equipped with picnic tables, delivers the town's best fish at a lightning pace. Report to the window and place your order for fresh oysters, crab or halibut. BYO booze is allowed.

Skagway Fish Company SEAFOOD $$$
(☑907-983-3474; Congress Way; mains $18-52; ☺11am-9pm) Overlooking the harbor, with crab traps on the ceiling, this is a culinary homage to fish. You can feast heartily on halibut stuffed with king crab, shrimp and

CHILKOOT TRAIL

The **Chilkoot Trail** (☑907-983-9234; www.nps.gov/klgo; Broadway St at 2nd Ave, Skagway) , the epic trek undertaken by over 30,000 gold-rush stampeders in 1897–8, is sometimes known as the 'Last Great Adventure' or the 'Meanest 33 Miles in America.' Its appeal is legendary and, consequently, more than 3000 people spend three to five days following the historic route between Dyea (Alaska) and Bennett (British Columbia, Canada) every summer.

veggies, or king-crab bisque, but surprisingly, what many locals rave about are its baby back ribs. Its bar has the best view in town.

ℹ Information

Klondike Gold Rush National Historical Park Museum & Visitor Center (p1098) For general info on Skagway's historical sites, museums and free walking tours. Run by the National Park Service.

Skagway Convention & Visitors Bureau (☑907-983-2854; www.skagway.com; cnr Broadway St & 2nd Ave; ☺8am-6pm Mon-Fri, to 5pm Sat & Sun) For information on lodging, tours, restaurant menus and what's new, visit this bureau housed in the can't-miss **Arctic Brotherhood Hall** (Broadway St, at 2nd Ave).

Trail Center (☑907-983-9234; www.nps.gov/klgo; Broadway St, btwn 5th & 6th Aves; ☺8am-5pm Jun-Sep) If you're stampeding to the Chilkoot Trail, you'll need to stop off here the day before to pick up trail passes, get the latest trail and weather conditions, and watch a mandatory bear-awareness video. Expert rangers from both the US NPS and Parks Canada are there to answer any questions.

ℹ Getting There & Away

Yukon-Alaska Tourist Tours (☑866-626-7383, Whitehorse 867-668-5944; www.yukonalaskatouristtours.com) offers a bus service to Whitehorse (one way $72), departing the train depot in Skagway at 2:30pm daily.

Glacier Bay National Park & Preserve

Glacier Bay is the crowning jewel of the cruise-ship industry and a dreamy destination for anybody who has ever paddled a kayak. Seven tidewater glaciers spill out of the mountains and fill the sea with icebergs of all shapes, sizes and shades of blue, making Glacier Bay National Park and Preserve an icy wilderness renowned worldwide.

Apart from its high concentration of tidewater glaciers, Glacier Bay is a dynamic habitat for humpback whales. Other wildlife seen at Glacier Bay includes porpoises, sea otters, brown and black bears, wolves, moose and mountain goats.

The park is an expensive side trip, even by Alaskan standards. Plan on spending at least $400 for a trip from Juneau. Of the 500,000 annual visitors, more than 95% arrive aboard a ship and never leave it. The rest are a mixture of tour-group members, who head straight for the lodge, and backpackers, who gravitate toward the free campground.

◉ Sights & Activities

Gustavus   TOWN
(☎907-500-5143; www.gustavusak.com) About 9 miles from Bartlett Cove is the small settlement of Gustavus, an interesting backcountry community. The town's 400 citizens include a mix of professional people – doctors, lawyers, former government workers and artists – who decided to drop out of the rat race and live on their own in the middle of the woods. Electricity only arrived in the early 1980s and in some homes you must pump water at the sink or build a fire before you can have a hot shower.

Spirit Walker Expeditions   KAYAKING
(☎800-529-2537; www.seakayakalaska.com; 1 Grandpa's Farm Rd) Kayaking specialist Spirit Walker runs paddling trips to Point Adolphus where humpback whales congregate during the summer. Trips begin with a short boat ride pulling the kayaks across Icy Strait to Point Adolphus and run $489 for a day paddle ($399 per person for four or more) and $1239 for a three-day paddle.

🛏 Sleeping & Eating

Bartlett Cove Campground   CAMPGROUND $
(www.nps.gov/glba; free) This NPS facility a quarter-mile south of Glacier Bay Lodge is set in a lush forest just off the shoreline, and camping is free. There's no need for reservations; there always seems to be space. It's a walk-in campground, so no RVs.

Glacier Bay Lodge   LODGE $$
(☎888-229-8687; www.visitglacierbay.com; 199 Bartlett Cove Rd; r $219-249; ◎May-Sep) This is essentially a national-park lodge and the only accommodations in the park itself. Located at Bartlett Cove, 8 miles northwest of Gustavus, the self-contained lodge has 55 rooms, a crackling fire in a huge stone fireplace and a dining room that usually hums in the evening with an interesting mixture of park employees, backpackers and locals from Gustavus.

★Gustavus Inn   INN $$$
(☎907-697-2254; www.gustavusinn.com; Mile 1, Gustavus Rd; r per person all-inclusive $250; P�far🏠) 🍽 This longtime Gustavus favorite is a charming family homestead lodge mentioned in every travel book on Alaska, with good reason. It's thoroughly modern and comfortable, without being sterile or losing its folksy touch. The all-inclusive inn is well known for its gourmet dinners, which feature homegrown vegetables and fresh local seafood served family-style.

Sunnyside Market   CAFE $
(☎907-697-3060; www.facebook.com/Sunnyside MarketGustavus; 3 State Dock Rd; sandwiches $7-10; ◎8am-7pm; 🚗) 🍽 This bright market and cafe is your one-stop choice for organic sundries, deli sandwiches and breakfast burritos. There are two tables inside and plenty outside under a sunny overhang. On Saturday there's an artsy market.

ℹ Information

Glacier Bay National Park Visitor Center
(☎907-697-2661; www.nps.gov/glba; ◎11am-8pm) On the 2nd floor of Glacier Bay Lodge, this center has exhibits, a bookstore and an information desk. There are also daily guided walks from the lodge, park films and slide presentations.

Gustavus Visitors Association (☎907-500-5143; www.gustavusak.com) Has loads of information on its website.

Visitor Information Station (☎907-697-2627; www.nps.gov/glba; ◎7am-7pm Jun-Aug, 8am-5pm May & Sep) Campers, kayakers and boaters can stop at the park's Visitor Information Station at the foot of the public dock in Bartlett Cove for backcountry and boating permits, logistical information and a 20-minute orientation video.

ℹ Getting There & Away

Alaska Airlines (p1104) Offers the only jet service, with a daily 25-minute trip from Juneau to Gustavus.

Alaska Seaplanes (☎907-789-3331; www.flyalaskaseaplanes.com) Has up to five flights

per day between Gustavus and Juneau for $119 one way.

The cheapest way to reach Gustavus is via the **Alaska Marine Highway** (☑ 800-642-0066; www.ferryalaska.com). Several times a week the MV *LeConte* makes the round-trip run from Juneau to Gustavus (one way $44, 4½ hours) along a route that often features whale sightings. **TLC Taxi** (☑ 907-697-2239) meets most ferry arrivals and also charges $15 per person for a trip to Bartlett Cove.

Ketchikan

Close to Alaska's southern tip, where the Panhandle plunges deep into British Columbia, lies rainy Ketchikan, the state's fourth-largest city, squeezed onto a narrow strip of coast on Revillagigedo Island abutting the Tongass Narrows. Ketchikan is known for its commercial salmon fishing and indigenous Haida and Tlingit heritage – there is no better place in the US to see totem poles in all their craning, colorful glory. Every year between May and September, Ketchikan kowtows to around one million cruise-ship passengers, a deluge that turns the town into something of a tourist circus. Some cruisers stay in town, ferrying between souvenir shops and Ketchikan's emblematic totems. Others jump on boats or seaplanes bound for the Gothic majesty of Misty Fiords National Monument, a nearby wilderness area.

Despite the seasonal frenzy, Ketchikan retains a notable heritage exemplified by the jumbled clapboard facades of **Creek Street**, perched on stilts above a river.

◉ Sights

★Saxman Native
Village & Totem Park   HISTORIC SITE
(☑ 907-225-4421; www.capefoxtours.com; $5; ⊙ 8am-5pm) On South Tongass Hwy, 2.5 miles south of Ketchikan, is this incorporated Tlingit village of 475 residents. It's best known for Saxman Totem Park, which holds 24 totem poles from abandoned villages around the Southeast, restored or recarved in the 1930s. Among them is a replica of the Lincoln Pole (the original is in the Alaska State Museum in Juneau), which was carved in 1883, using a picture of Abraham Lincoln as a reference, to commemorate the first sighting of white people.

Southeast Alaska Discovery Center   MUSEUM
(www.alaskacenters.gov; 50 Main St; adult/child $5/free; ⊙ 8am-4pm; 🖈) Three large totems greet you in the lobby of this center run by the National Park Service (NPS), while a school of silver salmon suspended from the ceiling leads you toward a slice of re-created temperate rainforest. Upstairs, the exhibit hall features sections on Southeast Alaska's ecosystems and Alaska Native traditions.

🛏 Sleeping

Last Chance Campground   CAMPGROUND $
(www.recreation.gov; Ward Lake Rd; tent & RV sites $10) In a beautiful area north of Ketchikan, a couple of miles beyond Ward Lake, with four scenic lakes, 19 drive-in sites and three trails that run through the lush rainforest.

Ketchikan Hostel   HOSTEL $
(☑ 907-225-3319; www.ketchikanhostel.com; 400 Main St; dm $20; ⊙ May-Sep) In common with several other Alaskan towns, Ketchikan's 'hostel' is located inside a church (a Methodist one) with no street signage. The facility includes a large kitchen, three small common areas and single-sex dorm rooms. It's clean, but no-frills, and doors are locked after curfew (11pm). Reservations are recommended in July.

★Inn at Creek Street –
New York Hotel   BOUTIQUE HOTEL $$
(☑ 907-225-0246; www.thenewyorkhotel.com; 207 Stedman St; r $89-149; 🖈) A historic boutique hotel that strikes a delicate balance between old-world ambience and modern comfort. The eight rooms have a 1920s period feel without seeming 'olde,' with soft quilts, flat-screen TVs, refrigerators and private baths.

🍴 Eating

Burger Queen   BURGERS $
(☑ 907-225-6060; 518 Water St; burgers $7-10; ⊙ 11am-7pm Tue-Sat, to 3pm Sun & Mon) Ketchikan's favorite burger joint is definitely not a chain. Ten varieties, including one with a Polish sausage *and* a hamburger patty, plus 30 flavors of milkshake are served out of a small space just north of the road tunnel. It's something of a local legend.

Alaska Fish House   FISH & CHIPS $$
(☑ 907-225-4055; 3 Salmon Landing; mains $13-24; ⊙ 10am-9pm) Take your pick of fish – cod, salmon or halibut – and then your coating – in batter or a bun. The chips are default. And all this before the menu gets down to the crab: whole or just the legs. For those lacking seafood taste buds there are burgers.

★ Bar Harbor
Restaurant
MODERN AMERICAN $$$

(☑907-225-2813; 55 Schoenbar Ct, Berth 4; mains $22-42; ☺10am-3pm & 5-8pm Mon-Sat, 10am-3pm Sun) This slightly pricey seafood restaurant, usually touted among locals as the best in town, recently reopened in a new cruise-dock location on Berth 4. Expect larger than normal crowds descending on its modern ocean-themed interior to feast on creative seafood and chowder renditions.

ℹ Information

Ketchikan Visitor Information & Tour Center
(☑907-225-6166; www.visit-ketchikan.com; 131 Front St, City Dock; ☺7am-6pm) Vast modern building on the cruise-ship dock with brochures, free maps, courtesy phones and toilets. Adjoining it is a huge tour center complete with up to 20 booths where various activity companies set up desks in the summer to catch the cruise-ship trade. Reservations for most activities can be made here.

Southeast Alaska Discovery Center
(☑907-228-6220; www.alaskacenters.gov/visitors-centers/ketchikan; 50 Main St; ☺8am-4pm daily May-Sep) You don't need to pay the admission fee to get recreation information at this Alaska Public Lands Information Center. Park passes are also sold here.

ℹ Getting There & Away

Ketchikan's **Alaska Marine Highway Ferry Terminal** (☑907-228-7255, reservations 800-642-0066; www.dot.state.ak.us/amhs; 3501 Tongass Ave) is 2 miles north of the city center.

Northbound ferries leave almost daily in summer, heading for Wrangell ($68, six hours), Petersburg ($79, 9½ hours), Sitka ($135, 25 hours), Juneau ($138, 24 hours) and Haines ($167, 26 hours). Heading south, there's at least one departure a week for Bellingham, WA ($342, 40 hours) and also Prince Rupert in Canada ($69, 7½ hours).

Inter-Island Ferry Authority (☑907-225-4838; www.interislandferry.com) vessels are capable of holding vehicles and depart Ketchikan's ferry terminal at 3:30pm daily, bound for Hollis on Prince of Wales Island (one way adult/child $49/22.50, three hours). Rates for the ferry vary and are based on your vehicle's length; a subcompact one way costs $50.

FAIRBANKS

Fairbanks is the only 'city' in the interior, and the largest settlement for hundreds of miles, but it has many characteristics of a small town. Everyone seems to know everyone, and 'everyone' includes some truly fascinating characters – sled-dog breeders, crusading environmentalists, college students, gun nuts, military personnel, outdoor enthusiasts, bush pilots, and the rest of the usual Alaska cast of oddities. Because the city sits at the nexus of some truly epic routes – north to the Arctic, east to Canada and south to Denali – you'll almost inevitably end up spending time here, and that time is rarely boring.

This is a spread-out burg that's admittedly heavy on ugly strip malls, but the residential streets of compact downtown are pretty as a picture, and during winter, this is ground zero for viewing the aurora borealis.

◉ Sights & Activities

★ University of Alaska
Museum of the North
MUSEUM

(☑907-474-7505; www.uaf.edu/museum; 907 Yukon Dr; adult/child $14/8; ☺9am-7pm daily Jun-Aug, to 5pm Mon-Sat Sep-May) In an architecturally abstract, igloo- and aurora-inspired edifice sits one of Alaska's finest museums, with artifact-rich exhibits on the geology, history, culture and trivia of each region of the state. You are greeted by an 8ft 9in, 1250lb stuffed bear and signposted around very well laid-out exhibits, which examine the state's regions as geographic *and* cultural units.

**Morris Thompson Cultural &
Visitors Center** CULTURAL CENTER
(☑907-459-3700; www.morristhompsoncenter.org; 101 Dunkel St; ☺8am-9pm mid-May–mid-Sep, to 5pm mid-Sep–mid-May; 🅿) There are a few contenders for 'best visitor center in Alaska' but this one, an ingenious mix of museum, info point and cultural center, has to be in the running. Inside are exhibits on Alaskan history and Alaska Native culture, as well as daily movies and cultural performances. Outside, on the grounds, don't miss the historic cabin and moose-antler arch.

Ꮯᖴ Tours

Northern Alaska Tour Co SCENIC FLIGHTS
(☑907-474-8600; www.northernalaska.com) The Arctic Circle may be an imaginary line, but it's become one of Fairbanks' biggest draws, with small air-charter companies doing booming business flying travelers on sightseeing excursions across it. This company offers day flights to Barrow ($990) and van

DENALI NATIONAL PARK & PRESERVE

In our collective consciousness, Alaska represents the concept of the raw wilderness. But that untamed perception can be as much a deterrent as a draw. For many travelers, in-depth exploration of this American frontier is a daunting task.

Enter **Denali National Park & Preserve** (☎907-683-9532; www.nps.gov/dena; George Parks Hwy; $15; ℗🏛) 🖉: a parcel of land both primeval and easily accessible. Here, you can peer at a grizzly bear, moose, caribou, or even wolves, all from the comfort of a bus. On the other hand, if independent exploration is your thing, you can trek into 6 million acres of tundra, boreal forest and ice-capped mountains – a space larger than Massachusetts. This all lies in the shadow of Denali, once known as Mt McKinley and to native Athabascans as the Great One. Denali, at 20,308ft (6190m) is North America's highest peak, rightly celebrated as an icon of all that is awesome and wild in a state where those adjectives are ubiquitous.

Consider making reservations at least six months in advance for a park campsite during the height of summer, and at least three months ahead for accommodations outside the park. The park entrance fee is $15 per person, good for seven days.

There's only one road through the park: the 92-mile unpaved Park Rd, which is closed to private vehicles after Mile 15 in summer. Shuttle buses run from the middle of May until September past Mile 15. Sometimes, if the snow melts early in April, visitors will be allowed to proceed as far as Mile 30 until the shuttle buses begin operation. The park entrance area, where most visitors congregate, extends a scant 4 miles up Park Rd. It's here you'll find the park headquarters, visitor center and main campground, as well as the **Wilderness Access Center** (Wilderness Access Center (WAC); ☎907-683-9532; Mile 0.5, Park Rd; ⊙5am-7pm late May–mid-Sep), where you pay your park entrance fee and arrange campsites and shuttle-bus bookings to take you further into the park. Across the lot from the WAC sits the **Backcountry Information Center** (BIC; ☑backcountry office mid-May–mid-Sep 907-683-9590, general info year round 907-683-9532; Mile 0.5, Park Rd; ⊙9am-6pm late May–mid-Sep), where backpackers get backcountry permits and bear-proof food containers.

There are few places to stay within the park, excluding campgrounds, and only one restaurant. The majority of visitors base themselves in the nearby communities of Canyon, McKinley Village, Carlo Creek and Healy.

From May 15 to June 1, park services are just starting up and access to the backcountry is limited. Visitor numbers are low but shuttle buses only run as far as **Toklat River** (Mile 53, Park Rd; ⊙9am-7pm late May–mid-Sep) 🖉 FREE. From June 1 to 8, access increases and the shuttle buses run as far as **Eielson Visitor Center** (☎907-683-9532; www.nps.gov/dena/planyourvisit/the-eielson-visitor-center.htm; Mile 66, Park Rd; ⊙9am-5:30pm early Jun–mid-Sep) FREE. After June 8, the park is in full swing till late August.

Shuttle buses stop running after the second Thursday after Labor Day in September. Following a few days in which lottery winners are allowed to take their private vehicles as far along Park Rd as weather allows, the road closes to all traffic until the following May.

While most area lodges close, **Riley Creek Campground** (www.nps.gov/dena; Mile 0.25, Park Rd; tent sites $15, RV sites $24-30) 🖉 stays open in winter and camping is free, though the water and sewage facilities don't operate. If you have the equipment, you can use the unplowed Park Rd and the rest of the park for cross-country skiing, snowshoeing or dogsledding.

tours across the Arctic Circle ($180 to $220), among many other options.

🛏 Sleeping

Sven's
Basecamp Hostel   HOSTEL, CAMPGROUND **$**
(☎907-456-7836; www.svenshostel.com; 3505 Davis Rd; tent sites $9, tents/cabins/tree houses $35/85/135; ℗🛜) Sven, from Switzerland, welcomes all kinds of travelers and vagabonds to this fine, multifarious hostel. This is where you'll meet some of Alaska's most intrepid, sweatiest explorers and hear plenty of travel tales. Accommodations are in cabins, shared tents, a plush tree house or your own tent. Showers are coin-operated and

there's table football, books, a movie room and kitchen.

Springhill Suites
HOTEL $$$

(☑907-451-6552; www.marriott.com; 575 1st Ave; r $320; P @ 🛜 🐾) A northerly branch of the Marriott empire, Springhill Suites is renovated and offers clean, bland rooms spiced up with local artwork. You can't beat the location on the Chena River smack downtown for convenience. Amenities include an indoor pool and fitness center.

🍴 Eating & Drinking

Big Daddy's
BBQ & Banquet Hall
BARBECUE $$

(☑907-452-2501; www.bigdaddysbarb-q.com; 107 Wickersham St; mains $9-19; ⊙11am-10pm Mon-Sat, noon-9pm Sun) This must be, as the owners claim, the northernmost Southern barbecue in the USA, and if you like slow-smoked ribs, juicy brisket, bowls of baked beans and creamy mac 'n' cheese, it does not disappoint. Wash it all down with one of the cold beers on tap, and roll yourself out the door when you finish.

Pike's Landing
AMERICAN $$$

(☑907-479-6500; www.pikes-landing.com; 4438 Airport Way; mains $18-43; ⊙11am-11pm) For fine dining riverfront style, head to this restaurant, which has a cozy-cabin main dining room, a huge deck that looks out over the water and solid American-Alaskan mains: prime-rib sandwiches, roasted salmon, coconut shrimp and the like. Reservations for dinner are a good idea.

The Big I
BAR

(☑907-456-6437; 122 Turner St; ⊙10am-2am Sun-Thu, to 3:30am Fri, 9am-2am Sat; 🛜) This excellent dive has a large outdoor drinking area, sassy bartenders, grizzled locals and lots of bush kitsch lining the walls, which look like they haven't been scrubbed since the time of the Bering land bridge. Live music acts liven up the scene on some nights.

ℹ Information

Alaska Public Lands Information Center (☑907-459-3730; www.alaskacenters.gov/visitors-centers/fairbanks; 101 Dunkel St, Fairbanks; ⊙8am-6pm) Located in the Morris Thompson Cultural & Visitors Center, this is the place to head if you're planning on visiting any state or national parks and reserves in the region. Pick up one of its detailed free brochures on the Steese, Elliot, Taylor and Denali Hwys.

Department of Fish & Game Office (☑907-459-7206; www.adfg.alaska.gov; 1300 College Rd)

Fairbanks Convention & Visitors Bureau (☑907-456-5774; www.explorefairbanks.com; 101 Dunkel St; ⊙8am-9pm mid-May–mid-Sep, to 5pm mid-Sep–mid-May)

ℹ Getting There & Around

Alaska Airlines (☑800-252-7522; www.alaskaair.com) offers direct services to Anchorage, where there are connections to the rest of Alaska, the lower 48 and overseas, on a daily basis. There are also handy direct flights to Seattle with Delta and Alaska. For travel into the bush, try **Ravn Alaska** (☑907-266-8394; www.flyravn.com), **Warbelow's Air Ventures** (☑907-474-0518; www.warbelows.com; 3758 University Ave S) or **Wright Air Service** (☑907-474-0502; www.wrightairservice.com; 3842 University Ave).

Alaska Railroad (☑800-544-0552, 907-265-2494; www.alaskarailroad.com) leaves Fairbanks daily at 8:15am from mid-May to mid-September. The train gets to Denali National Park & Preserve (adult/child $77/39) at noon, Talkeetna (adult/child $147/74) at 4:40pm, Wasila (adult/child $249/125) at 6:15pm and Anchorage (adult/child $249/125) at 8pm. The **station** (☑800-544-0552; www.alaskarailroad.com; 1031 Alaska Railroad Depot Road; ⊙6:30am-2:30pm) is at the southern end of Danby St. **MACS** (Metropolitan Area Commuter Service; ☑907-459-1010; http://fnsb.us/transportation/Pages/MACS.aspx) Red Line buses run to and from the station.

Hawaii

Best Places to Eat

➜ Alan Wong's (p1109)

➜ Hy's Steakhouse (p1112)

➜ Umekes Fishmarket Bar & Grill (p1115)

➜ Frida's Mexican Beach House (p1121)

Best Places to Sleep

➜ Halekulani (p1111)

➜ Four Seasons Resort Hualalai (p1116)

➜ Royal Grove Hotel (p1111)

➜ Hanalei Dolphin Cottages (p1124)

Why Go?

Snapshots of these islands scattered in the cobalt blue Pacific Ocean are heavenly, without the need for any embellishment by tourist brochures. They show off nature's diversity at its most divine, from fiery volcanoes to lacy rainforest waterfalls to crystal-clear aquamarine bays. Whether it's surfing, swimming, fishing or picnicking with the *'ohana* (extended family and friends), encounters with nature are infused with *aloha 'aina* – love and respect for the land.

Past the postcard images, Hawaii proudly maintains its own distinct, multicultural identity apart from the US mainland. Spam, shave ice, surfing, ukulele and slack key guitar music, hula, pidgin, aloha shirts, 'rubbah slippah' (flip-flops) – these are just some of the touchstones of everyday life, island style. Pretty much everything here feels easygoing, low-key and casual, bursting with genuine aloha and fun. You'll be equally welcome whether you're a globe-trotting surf bum, a beaming couple of fresh-faced honeymooners or a big, multigenerational family with rambunctious kids.

When to Go
Honolulu

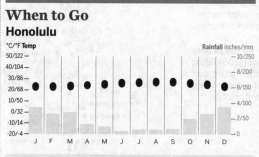

Dec–Apr & Jun–Aug	May & Sep	Oct & Nov
Prices peak; high season for tourism, surfing and whale-watching.	Shoulder months; mostly sunny, cloudless days.	Dry, hot weather; fewer visitors mean cheaper accommodations.

Hawaii Highlights

1 Kaua'i (p1122) Trekking the dramatic Na Pali Coast, then lazing in glorious Hanalei Bay.

2 Maui (p1120) Driving the twisting seaside Hana Hwy past black-sand beaches and jungle waterfalls.

3 Haleakalā National Park (p1122) Catching dawn over the 'house of the rising sun.'

4 Pearl Harbor (p1112) Visiting the sunken USS *Arizona*, for a dramatic reminder of the islands' strategic importance in the Pacific.

5 Waimea Canyon (p1124) Taking challenging hikes to waterfalls framed by volcanic rock formations.

6 Mauna Kea (p1116) Stargazing atop Hawaii's highest mountain on the Big Island.

7 Wailua River (p1123) Kayaking this sacred river to waterfall swimming holes.

8 Kohala Mountain Road (p1119) Taking a little road trip over vast sweeps of Big Island beauty.

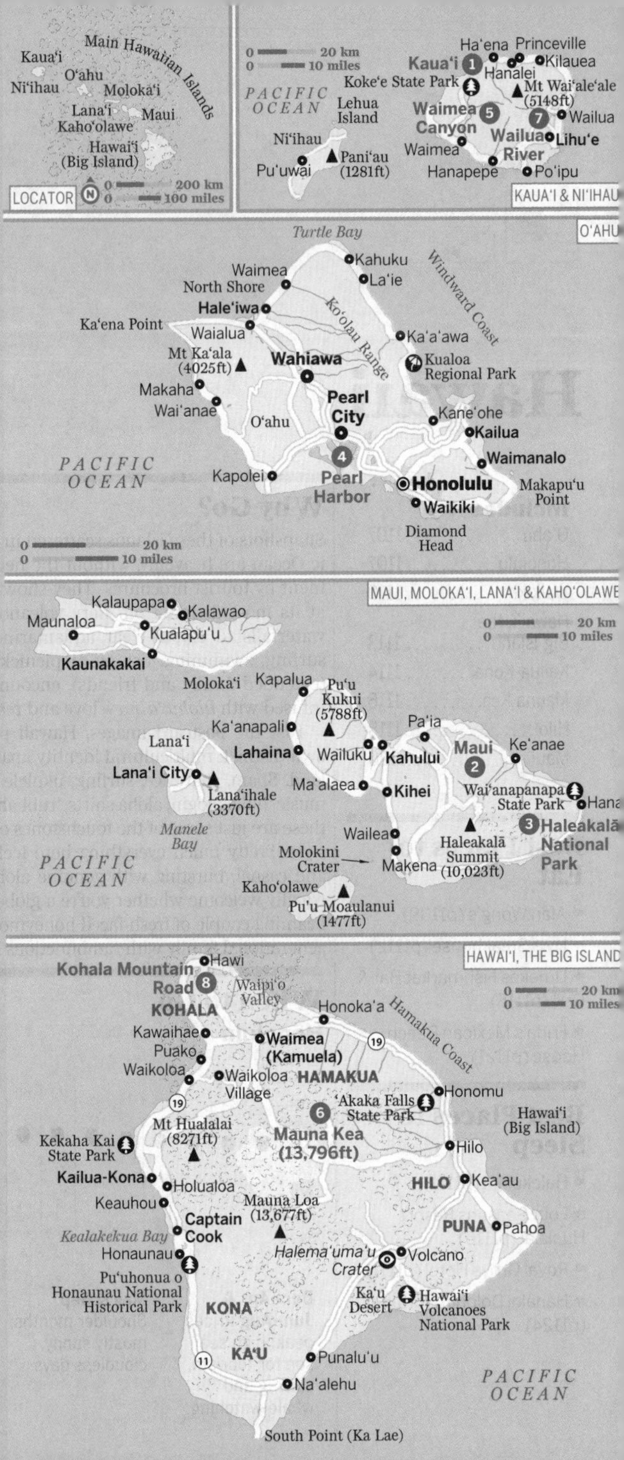

LOCATOR
Main Hawaiian Islands
Kaua'i
O'ahu
Ni'ihau
Moloka'i
Lana'i
Maui
Kaho'olawe
Hawai'i (Big Island)
0 200 km
0 100 miles
KAUA'I & NI'IHAU
0 20 km
0 10 miles
PACIFIC OCEAN
Ha'ena
Princeville
Kilauea
Kaua'i 1
Hanalei
Koke'e State Park
Mt Wai'ale'ale (5148ft)
Lehua Island
Waimea Canyon 5
Wailua River 7
Wailua
Lihu'e
Ni'ihau
Waimea
Pu'uwai
Pani'au (1281ft)
Hanapepe
Po'ipu
O'AHU
Turtle Bay
Kahuku
La'ie
Waimea
North Shore
Windward Coast
Hale'iwa
Ko'olau Range
Ka'ena Point
Waialua
Ka'a'awa
Mt Ka'ala (4025ft)
Wahiawa
Kualoa Regional Park
Makaha
Pearl City
Wai'anae
O'ahu
Kane'ohe
Kailua
4 Pearl Harbor
Waimanalo
PACIFIC OCEAN
Kapolei
Honolulu
Makapu'u Point
Waikiki
Diamond Head
0 20 km
0 10 miles
MAUI, MOLOKA'I, LANA'I & KAHO'OLAWE
0 20 km
0 10 miles
Kalaupapa
Kalawao
Maunaloa
Kualapu'u
Kaunakakai
Moloka'i
Kapalua
Pu'u Kukui (5788ft)
Ka'anapali
Pa'ia
Lana'i
Lahaina
Wailuku
Kahului
Maui 2
Ke'anae
Lana'i City
Lana'ihale (3370ft)
Ma'alaea
Kihei
Wai'anapanapa State Park
Hana
3 Haleakalā National Park
Manele Bay
Wailea
Haleakalā Summit (10,023ft)
PACIFIC OCEAN
Molokini Crater
Makena
Kaho'olawe
Pu'u Moaulanui (1477ft)
HAWAI'I, THE BIG ISLAND
0 20 km
0 10 miles
Hawi
Kohala Mountain Road 8
Waipi'o Valley
KOHALA
Honoka'a
Hamakua Coast
Kawaihae
Waimea (Kamuela)
19
Puako
Waikoloa
Waikoloa Village
HAMAKUA
Honomu
19
'Akaka Falls State Park
Mt Hualalai (8271ft)
6 Mauna Kea (13,796ft)
Hawai'i (Big Island)
Kekaha Kai State Park
Hilo
Kailua-Kona
Holualoa
HILO
Kea'au
Keauhou
Mauna Loa (13,677ft)
Captain Cook
PUNA
Pahoa
Kealakekua Bay
Honaunau
Halema'uma'u Crater
Volcano
Pu'uhonua o Honaunau National Historical Park
KONA
Ka'u Desert
Hawai'i Volcanoes National Park
11
KA'U
Punalu'u
Na'alehu
PACIFIC OCEAN
South Point (Ka Lae)

History

Hawaii's discovery and colonization is one of humanity's epic tales, starting with ancient Polynesians who found their way to these tiny islands – the world's most isolated – in the midst of Earth's largest ocean. Almost a millennium passed before Western explorers, whalers, missionaries and entrepreneurs arrived on ships. During the tumultuous 19th century, global immigrants came to work on Hawaii's plantations. In 1893 the kingdom founded by Kamehameha the Great was overthrown, making way for US annexation.

Language

Hawaii has two official languages: English and Hawaiian. While Hawaiian's multisyllabic, vowel-heavy words may look daunting, the pronunciation is actually quite straightforward and with a little practice, you'll soon get the hang of it. There's also an unofficial vernacular, pidgin (formerly referred to as Hawai'i Creole English), which has a laid-back, lilting accent and a colorful vocabulary that permeates everyday speech.

The *'okina* punctuation mark (') is the Hawaiian language's glottal stop, which determines the pronunciation and meaning of words. In this guide, Hawai'i (with the *'okina*) refers to the island of Hawai'i (the Big Island), to ancient Hawai'i and to the Kingdom of Hawai'i pre-statehood. Hawaii (without the *'okina*) refers to the US territory that became a state in 1959.

Note that in Hawaii, however, organizations decide for themselves whether to include the *'okina* or not – eg University of Hawai'i at Manoa.

O'AHU

O'ahu attacks your senses. Tropical aromas and temperatures, turquoise waters, a kaleidoscope of colorful fish, verdant rainforest and sensuous scenery, plus so much to do.

On O'ahu, an island out in the middle of the Pacific Ocean, people are easygoing, low-key and casual, bursting with genuine aloha and fun. Everyone knows how lucky they are to be living in this tropical paradise and O'ahu proudly maintains its own identity apart from the US mainland.

Honolulu

Here in Honolulu, away from the crowded haunts of Waikiki, you get to shake hands with the real Hawaii. A boisterous Polynesian capital, Honolulu delivers an island-style mixed plate of experiences.

Eat your way through the pan-Asian alleys of Chinatown, where 19th-century whalers once brawled and immigrant traders thrived. Gaze out to sea atop the landmark Aloha Tower, then sashay past Victorian-era brick buildings, including the USA's only royal palace. Browse at the world's largest open-air shopping center at Ala Moana, then poke your nose into the city's impressive art museums.

HAWAII HONOLULU

HAWAII IN...

Four Days
Anyone on a trans-Pacific stopover will land at Honolulu, so spend the few days you have on O'ahu. In between surfing and sunning on Waikiki beach (p1110), check out Honolulu's museums and wander Chinatown (p1108), summit Diamond Head (p1112) and snorkel Hanauma Bay (p1113).

One Week
With a week, fit in another island – say, Hawai'i, the Big Island (p1113). Lounge on golden beaches in North Kona (p1116) and South Kohala (p1116); visit coffee farms in South Kona (p1115); summit Hawaii's highest peak, Mauna Kea (p1116); and say aloha to the goddess Pele at Hawai'i Volcanoes National Park (p1119).

Two Weeks
With two weeks, tack on a third island. On Kaua'i (p1122), kayak the Wailua River (p1123) to take a dip in a jungle waterfall, hike in spectacular Waimea Canyon (p1124), hang 10 at Hanalei Bay (p1123), and trek or paddle past towering sea cliffs on the Na Pali Coast (p1123). If you choose Maui (p1120), explore the old whaling town of Lahaina (p1120), head to Haleakalā National Park (p1122) to see sunrise at the volcano's summit, take a whale-watching cruise, and snorkel or dive.

Ocean breezes rustle palm trees along the harborfront, while in the cool, mist-shrouded Koʻolau Range, forested hiking trails offer postcard city views. At sunset, cool off with an amble around Magic Island or splash in the ocean at Ala Moana Beach. After dark, migrate to Chinatown's edgy art and nightlife scene.

◉ Sights & Activities

Honolulu's compact downtown is just a lei's throw from the harborfront. Nearby, the buzzing streets of Chinatown are packed with food markets, antiques shops, art galleries and hip bars. Between downtown and Waikiki, Ala Moana has Hawaii's biggest mall and the city's best beach. The University of Hawaiʻi campus is a gateway to the Manoa Valley. A few outlying sights, including the Bishop Museum, are worth putting into your schedule.

★ Bishop Museum   MUSEUM
(☎808-847-3511; www.bishopmuseum.org; 1525 Bernice St; adult/child $25/17; ◷9am-5pm; ⓟ♿)
🚶 Like Hawaii's version of the Smithsonian Institute in Washington, DC, the Bishop Museum showcases a remarkable array of cultural and natural history exhibits. It is often ranked as the finest Polynesian anthropological museum in the world. Founded in 1889 in honor of Princess Bernice Pauahi Bishop, a descendant of the Kamehameha dynasty, it originally housed only Hawaiian and royal artifacts. These days it honors all of Polynesia. Book online for reduced admission rates.

★ Chinatown Markets   MARKET
(www.chinatownnow.com; ◷8am-6pm) The commercial heart of Chinatown revolves around markets and food shops. Noodle factories, pastry shops and produce stalls line the narrow sidewalks, always crowded with cart-pushing grandmothers and errand-running families. An institution since 1904, the O'ahu Market sells everything a Chinese cook needs: ginger root, fresh octopus, quail eggs, jasmine rice, slabs of tuna, long beans and salted jellyfish. You owe yourself a bubble tea if you spot a pig's head among the stalls.

★ ʻIolani Palace   PALACE
(☎808-522-0832; www.iolanipalace.org; 364 S King St; grounds free, basement galleries adult/child $5/3, self-guided audio tour $20/6, guided tour $27/6; ◷9am-4pm Mon-Sat) No other place evokes a more poignant sense of Hawaii's history. The palace was built under King David Kalakaua in 1882. At that time, the Hawaiian monarchy observed many of the diplomatic protocols of the Victorian world. The king traveled abroad meeting with leaders around the globe and received foreign emissaries here. Although the palace was modern and opulent for its time, it did little to assert Hawaii's sovereignty over powerful US-influenced business interests, who overthrew the kingdom in 1893.

Blue Hawaiian Helicopters   SCENIC FLIGHTS
(☎800-745-2583, 808-871-8844; www.bluehawaiian.com; 99 Kaulele Pl; tours $230-570) This may well be the most exciting thing you do on

LGBT HAWAII

The state of Hawaii has strong minority protections and a constitutional guarantee of privacy that extends to sexual behavior between consenting adults.

Locals tend to be private about their personal lives, so you will not see much public hand-holding or open displays of affection, either same-sex or opposite-sex. Everyday LGBTQ life is low-key – it's more about picnics and potlucks, not nightclubs. Even in Waikiki, the laid-back gay scene comprises just a half dozen or so bars, clubs and restaurants.

That said, Hawaii is a popular destination for LGBTQ travelers, who are served by a small network of gay-owned and gay-friendly B&Bs, guesthouses and hotels. For more information on recommended places to stay, beaches, events and more, check out the following resources:

Out Traveler (www.outtraveler.com/hawaii) LGBTQ-oriented Hawaii travel articles free online.

Pride Guide Hawaii (www.gogayhawaii.com) Free island visitor guides for gay-friendly activities, accommodations, dining, nightlife, shopping, festivals, weddings and more.

Hawai'i LGBT Legacy Foundation (http://hawaiilgbtlegacyfoundation.com) News, resources and a community calendar of LGBTQ events, mostly on Oʻahu.

Purple Roofs (www.purpleroofs.com) Online directory of gay-owned and gay-friendly B&Bs, vacation rentals, guesthouses and hotels.

O'ahu. The 45-minute Blue Skies of O'ahu flight takes in Honolulu, Waikiki, Diamond Head, Hanauma Bay and the whole of the Windward Coast, then the North Shore, central O'ahu and Pearl Harbor. Everything you need to know, including video clips, is on the website. Book well ahead.

🛏 Sleeping

Hostelling International (HI) Honolulu
HOSTEL $

(☑ 808-946-0591; www.hostelsaloha.com; 2323a Seaview Ave, University Area; dm/r $28/66; ☺ reception 8am-noon & 4pm-midnight; P @ 🛜) Along a quiet residential side street near the UH Manoa campus, this tidy, low-slung house just a short bus ride from Waikiki has same-sex dorms and basic private rooms kept cool by the tradewinds. Some students crash here while looking for apartments, so it's often full. It has a kitchen, a laundry room, lockers and two free parking spaces.

Aston at the Executive Centre Hotel
HOTEL $$

(☑ 855-945-4090; www.astonexecutivecentre.com; 1088 Bishop St, Downtown; rooms from $239; ☺ @ 🛜 ⛱) Honolulu's only downtown hotel is geared for business travelers and extended stays. Large, modern suites get kitchenettes, while one-bedroom condos add a full kitchen and washer/dryer. A fitness center, heated lap pool and complimentary continental breakfast round out the executive-class amenities. Convenient to the restaurants of Downtown and Chinatown.

🍴 Eating

★ Tamura's Poke
SEAFOOD $

(☑ 808-735-7100; www.tamurasupermarket.com/daily-poke-menu; 3496 Wai'alae Ave, Kaimuki; poke $9-12; ☺ 9:30am-9pm Mon-Sat, to 8pm Sun; P) Arguably the best *poke* on the island is up on Wai'alae Rd in undistinguished-looking Tamura's Fine Wines & Liquors. Head inside, turn right, wander down to *poke* corner and feast your eyes. The 'spicy ahi' and the smoked marlin are to die for. Ask for tasters before you buy and take away.

Sadie's BBQ Inn
KOREAN $$

(☑ 808-454-4488; http://sadiesbbqinn.com; 850 Kamehameha Hwy, Pearl City; mains $14-19; ☺ 10am-9pm) A charming locally owned hole-in-the-wall in Pearl City Shopping Center, Sadie's specializes in authentic Korean eats. Mouthwatering choices include loco moco, chicken katsu (both $13.95) and

steamed kalbi ($24.95), all served in generous portions. Cheery red booths line the dining space and a takeout window obliges patrons on-the-go. Peruse the handwritten daily specials board or choose from an array of *banchan* (small dishes).

★ Alan Wong's
HAWAII REGIONAL $$$

(☑ 808-949-2526; www.alanwongs.com; 1857 S King St, Ala Moana & Around; mains $35-43; ☺ 5-10pm) 🍷 One of O'ahu's big-gun chefs, Alan Wong offers his creative interpretations of Hawaii Regional Cuisine (HRC; Hawaii's homegrown cuisine) with a menu inspired by the state's diverse ethnic cultures. Emphasis is on fresh seafood and local produce. Order Wong's time-tested signature dishes such as ginger-crusted *onaga* (red snapper), steamed shellfish bowl, and twice-cooked *kalbi* (short ribs). Make reservations weeks in advance.

🍷 Drinking & Nightlife

★ La Mariana Sailing Club
BAR

(☑ 808-848-2800; www.lamarianasailingclub.com; 50 Sand Island Access Rd, Greater Honolulu; ☺ 11am-9pm) Time warp! Who says all the great tiki bars have gone to the dogs? Irreverent and kitschy this 1950s joint by the lagoon is filled with yachties and long-suffering locals. Classic mai tais are as killer as the other tropical potions, complete with tiki-head swizzle sticks and tiny umbrellas. Grab a waterfront table and dream of sailing to Tahiti.

★ Tea at 1024
TEAHOUSE

(☑ 808-521-9596; www.teaat1024.net; 1024 Nu'uanu Ave, Chinatown; ☺ 11am-1pm Wed-Fri, seatings at 11am, 1pm & 3pm Sat & Sun) Tea at 1024 takes you back in time to another era. Cutesy sandwiches, scones and cakes accompany your choice of tea as you relax and watch the Chinatown crowd rush by the window. It even has bonnets for you to don to add to the ambience. Set menus run from $24.95 per person and reservations are recommended.

ℹ Information

There are staffed tourist-information desks in the airport arrivals areas. While you're waiting for your bags to appear on the carousel, you can peruse racks of free tourist brochures and magazines, which contain discount coupons for activities, tours, restaurants etc.

For pre-trip planning in several languages, browse the information-packed website of the **Hawaii Visitors & Convention Bureau** (☑ 800-464-2924; www.gohawaii.com).

ⓘ Getting There & Around

Most visitors to Oʻahu arrive via Honolulu International Airport.

Honolulu is the gateway to Hawaii. It has flights from major North American cities as well as Asia and Australia. It is also a hub of interisland service for flights serving the neighboring islands.

Honolulu International Airport (HNL; ☑ 808-836-6411; www.airports.hawaii.gov/hnl; 300 Rodgers Blvd; ☎), Oʻahu's main commercial airport, is about 6 miles northwest of Downtown Honolulu and 9 miles northwest of Waikiki. The airport is run by the local government, which gives it a certain throwback character: shopping is limited and food concessions are paltry but gate areas have large and restful seat areas that haven't been replaced by commerce. It even has a beautiful and mostly secret outdoor tropical garden near gate 49. Wait for your flight sniffing plumeria rather than fast food.

The public transit system is comprehensive and convenient. You can get a bus to most parts of Oʻahu, but to explore thoroughly and reach off-the-beaten-path sights, you'll need your own wheels.

Waikiki

Once a Hawaiian royal retreat, Waikiki revels in its role as a retreat for the masses. This famous strand of sand moves to a rhythm of Hawaiian music at beachfront high-rises and resorts. In this jungle of modern hotels and malls, you can, surprisingly, still hear whispers of Hawaii's past, from the chanting of hula troupes at Kuhio Beach to the legacy of Olympic gold medalist Duke Kahanamoku.

Take a surfing lesson from a bronzed instructor, then spend a lazy afternoon lying on Waikiki's golden sands. Before the sun sinks below the horizon, hop aboard a catamaran and sail off toward Diamond Head. Sip a sunset mai tai and be hypnotized by the lilting harmonies of slack key guitar, then mingle with the colorful locals, many of whom have made this their lifetime playground, who come here to party after dark too.

⊙ Sights

Yes, the beach is the main sight, but Waikiki also has historic hotels, evocative public art, amazing artifacts of Hawaiian history, and even a zoo and aquarium.

★ **Royal Hawaiian Hotel**   HISTORIC BUILDING
(☑ 808-923-7311; www.royal-hawaiian.com; 2259 Kalakaua Ave; ☺ tours 1pm Tue & Thu) FREE With its Moorish-style turrets and archways, this gorgeously restored 1927 art-deco landmark, dubbed the 'Pink Palace,' is a throwback to the era when Rudolph Valentino was *the* romantic idol and travel to Hawaii was by Matson Navigation luxury liner. Its guest list reads like a who's-who of A-list celebrities, from royalty to Rockefellers, along with luminaries such as Charlie Chaplin and Babe Ruth. Today, historic tours explore the architecture and lore of this grande dame.

Kuhio Beach Park   BEACH
(off Kalakaua Ave; ☝) If you're the kind of person who wants it all, this beach offers everything from protected swimming to outrigger-canoe rides, and even a free sunset-hula and Hawaiian-music show. You'll find restrooms, outdoor showers, a snack bar and beach-gear-rental stands at **Waikiki Beach Center** (off Kalakaua Ave), near the police substation. Also here is the **Kuhio Beach Surfboard Lockers** (off Kalakaua Ave, Kuhio Beach Park), an iconic storage area for local surfers. World-famous **Canoes** (Pops) surf break is right offshore – you can spend hours watching surfers of all types riding the curls.

★ **Queen's Surf Beach**   BEACH
(Wall's; off Kalakaua Ave, Kapiʻiolani Beach Park; ☝) Just south of Kuhio Beach, the namesake beach for the famous surf break is a great place for families as the waves are rarely large when they reach shore but they are still large enough for bodyboarding, which means older kids can frolic for hours. At the south end of the beach, the area in front of the pavilion is popular with the local gay community.

★ **Wizard Stones of Kapaemahu**   STATUE
(off Kalakaua Ave, Kuhio Beach Park) Near the police substation at Waikiki Beach Center, four ordinary-looking boulders are actually the legendary Wizard Stones of Kapaemahu, said to contain the mana (spiritual essence) of four wizards who came to Oʻahu from Tahiti around AD 400. According to ancient legend, the wizards helped the island residents by relieving their aches and pains, and their fame became widespread. As a tribute when the wizards left, the islanders placed the four boulders where the wizards had lived.

🏃 Activities

★ **Oʻahu Diving**   DIVING
(☑ 808-721-4210; www.oahudiving.com; 2-dive trips for beginners $145) Specializes in first-time experiences for beginner divers without certification, as well as deep-water boat dives offshore and PADI refresher classes if you're already certified and have some experience under

your diving belt. Trips depart from various locations near Waikiki.

Snorkel Bob's
SNORKELING

(☑808-735-7944; www.snorkelbob.com; 700 Kapahulu Ave; snorkel set rental per week from $9; ☺8am-5pm) A top spot to get your gear. Rates vary depending on the quality of the snorkeling gear and accessories packages, but excellent weekly discounts are available and online reservations taken. You can even rent gear on O'ahu, then return it to a Snorkel Bob's location on another island.

🛏 Sleeping

Waikiki's main beachfront strip, along Kalakaua Ave, is lined with hotels and sprawling resorts. Some of them are true beauties with either historic or boutique atmosphere. Most are aimed at the masses, however.

Further from the sand, look for inviting small hotels on Waikiki's backstreets. Many are quite affordable year-round. And don't forget the hundreds of condos, time-shares and apartments on offer on Airbnb (www.airbnb.com) and he like.

★ Royal Grove Hotel
HOTEL $

(☑808-923-7691; www.royalgrovehotel.com; 161 Uluniu Ave; r/ste per night from $115/550; ✻@✻) No frills but plenty of aloha characterize this kitschy, candy-pink, six-story hotel that attracts so many returning snowbirds it's nearly impossible to get a room in winter without reservations. Retro motel-style rooms in the main wing are basic but do have balconies. All rooms have kitchenettes. Inquire about discounted weekly off-season rates. Great budget option.

Waikiki Central Hotel
HOTEL $$

(☑808-922-1544; www.waikikicentral.com; 2431 Prince Edward St; r $139-169; P✻🛜) Don't judge this six-story, 1970s-era apartment complex based off of its innocuous cover. Inside this standout budget option are compact yet cheery rooms with kitchenettes that feel fresh and modern.

★ Halekulani
RESORT $$$

(☑844-873-9424; www.halekulani.com; 2199 Kalia Rd; r $530-960, ste $1160-1860; P✻@🛜✻) Evincing modern sophistication, this family-owned resort lives up to its name, which means 'House Befitting Heaven.' It's an all-encompassing experience of gracious living, not merely a place to crash. Meditative calm washes over you immediately as you step onto the lobby's cool stone tiles. The design focuses

on the blue Pacific, and the hubbub of Waikiki is walled away. There's no resort fee.

Surfjack Hotel & Swim Club
BOUTIQUE HOTEL $$$

(☑808-923-8882, reservations 855-945-4082; www.surfjack.com; 412 Lewers St; r $275-570; ✻🛜✻) If the Don Draper fantasy still sizzles years after *Mad Men*, then you'll love this retro-chic 10-story hotel that recreates a posh early 1960s world that may not have existed but which would have been cool if it had. Rooms in this vintage building encircle a courtyard pool. All have balconies and reimagined mid-century furniture your parents would have thrown out.

✕ Eating

★ Rainbow Drive-In
HAWAIIAN $

(☑808-737-0177; www.rainbowdrivein.com; 3308 Kanaina Ave; meals $4-10; ☺7am-9pm; 🖶) If you only hit one classic Hawaiian plate-lunch joint, make it this one. Wrapped in rainbow-colored neon, this famous drive-in is a throwback to another era. Construction workers, surfers and gangly teens order all their down-home favorites such as burgers, mixed-plate lunches, *loco moco* and Portuguese sweet-bread French toast from the takeout counter. Many love the hamburger steak.

Tonkatsu Ginza Bairin
JAPANESE $$

(☑808-926-8082; www.pj-partners.com/bairin; 255 Beach Walk; mains $15-36; ☺11am-9:30pm Sun-Thu, to 10:30pm Fri & Sat) Why go to Tokyo for perfect pork *tonkatsu* when you can enjoy the lightly breaded bits of deep-fried pork goodness right here in Waikiki? Since 1927 the family behind this restaurant has been serving *tonkatsu* at a Ginza restaurant. At this far-flung expansion, nothing has been lost. Besides the namesake there is great sushi, rice bowls and more.

MAC 24/7
AMERICAN $$

(☑808-921-5564; www.mac247waikiki.com; 2500 Kuhio Ave, Hilton Waikiki Beach; mains $9-315;

(⌚24hr; 👪) If it's 3am and you're famished, skip the temptation for a cold $25 burger from room service (*if* you have room service) and drop by Waikiki's best all-night diner. The dining room has a bold style palette (the better to perk you up for the menu) and by day has a lovely garden view. Food (and prices) are a cut above.

Hy's Steakhouse STEAK **$$$**

(☎808-922-5555; www.hyswaikiki.com; 2440 Kuhio Ave; mains $40-95; ⌚5-10pm) Hy's is so old-school that you expect to find inkwells on the tables. This traditional steakhouse has a timeless old leather and wood interior. But ultimately, it's not whether you expect to see Frank and Dean at a back table; rather, it's the steak at Hy's that is superb.

Drinking & Entertainment

Beach Bar BAR

(☎808-922-3111; www.moana-surfrider.com; 2365 Kalakaua Ave, Moana Surfrider; ⌚10:30am-10:30pm) Waikiki's best beach bar is right on a lovely stretch of beach. The atmosphere comes from the historic **Moana Surfrider** (☎808-922-3111; www.moana-surfrider.com; 2365 Kalakaua Ave; ⌚tours 11am Mon, Wed & Fri) FREE hotel and its vast banyan tree. The people-watching of passersby, sunbathers and surfers is captivating day and night. On an island of mediocre mai tais, the version here is one of O'ahu's best. Although it's always busy, turnover is quick so you won't wait long for a table. There's live **entertainment** (☎808-922-3111; www.moana-surfrider.com; 2365 Kalakaua Ave, Moana Surfrider; ⌚10:30am-10:30pm) much of the day.

Hula's Bar & Lei Stand GAY

(☎808-923-0669; www.hulas.com; 134 Kapahulu Ave, 2nd fl, Waikiki Grand Hotel; ⌚10am-2am; 📶) This friendly, open-air bar is Waikiki's legendary gay venue and a great place to make new friends, boogie and have a few drinks. Hunker down at the pool table, or gaze at the spectacular vista of Diamond Head. The breezy balcony-bar also has views of Queen's Surf Beach, a prime destination for a sun-worshipping LGBTQ crowd.

Getting There & Around

Waikiki is a district of the city of Honolulu, so much of the transport information applies to both.

A bus in a crude disguise, the **Waikiki Trolley** (☎808-593-2822; www.waikikitrolley.com; 1-day passes $25-45, 4 days from $62) runs five color-coded lines designed for tourists that shuttle around Waikiki and serve major shopping areas and tourist sights in Diamond Head, Honolulu and Pearl Harbor. The passes, good for unlimited use, aren't cheap but can be purchased from any hotel activity desk or at a discounted rate online.

Pearl Harbor

The WWII-era rallying cry 'Remember Pearl Harbor!' that once mobilized an entire nation dramatically resonates on O'ahu. It was here that the surprise Japanese attack on December 7, 1941, hurtled the US into war in the Pacific. Every year about 1.6 million tourists visit Pearl Harbor's unique collection of war memorials and museums, all clustered around a quiet bay where oysters were once farmed.

The iconic offshore shrine at the sunken USS *Arizona* doesn't tell the only story. Nearby are two other floating historical sites: the USS *Bowfin* submarine, aka the 'Pearl Harbor Avenger,' and the battleship USS *Missouri*, where General Douglas MacArthur accepted the Japanese surrender at the end of WWII. Together, for the US, these military sites represent the beginning, middle and end of the war. To visit all three, as well as the Pacific Aviation Museum, dedicate at least a day.

Getting There & Away

The entrance to the Valor in the Pacific Monument and the other Pearl Harbor historic sites is off the Kamehameha Hwy (Hwy 99), southwest of Aloha Stadium. From Honolulu or Waikiki, take H-1 west to exit 15A (Arizona Memorial/Stadium), then follow the highway signs for the monument, not the signs for Pearl Harbor (which lead onto the US Navy base). There's plenty of free parking.

From Waikiki, bus 42 ('Ewa Beach) is the most direct, running twice hourly between 6am and 3pm, taking just over an hour each way. The 'Arizona Memorial' stop is right outside the main entrance to the National Park site.

Diamond Head

A dramatic backdrop for Waikiki Beach, Diamond Head is one of the best-known landmarks in Hawaii. Ancient Hawaiians called it Le'ahi, and at its summit they built a *luakini* heiau, a temple dedicated to the war god Ku and used for human sacrifices. Ever since 1825, when British sailors found calcite crystals sparkling in the sun and mistakenly thought they'd struck it rich, the sacred peak has been called Diamond Head.

The coast is an easy walk from Waikiki and there are some good beaches below the cliffside road and viewpoints.

★**Diamond Head**
State Monument   STATE PARK
(☏ 800-464-2924; www.hawaiistateparks.org; off
Diamond Head Rd btwn Makapu'u & 18th Aves; per
pedestrian/car $1/5; ⊙ 6am-6pm, last trail entry
4:30pm; ⊞) The extinct crater of Diamond
Head is now a state monument, with picnic
tables and a spectacular hiking trail up to the
761ft-high summit. The trail was built in 1908
to service military observation stations located along the crater rim.

Diamond Head Lookout   VIEWPOINT
(3483 Diamond Head Rd) From this small park-
ing area, there are fine views over **Kuilei
Cliffs Beach Park** (3450 Diamond Head Rd) and
up the coast toward Kahala. On the east side
of the parking area, look for the Amelia Earhart Marker, which recalls her 1935 solo flight
from Hawaii to California. It's an enjoyable
1.4-mile walk beyond **Kaimana Beach** (Sans
Souci Beach) in Waikiki.

Hanauma Bay

This wide, curved bay of turquoise waters
protected by a coral reef and backed by palm
trees is a gem, especially for snorkelers. You
come here for the scenery, you come here for
the beach, but above all you come here to
snorkel – and if you've never been snorkeling
before, it's a perfect place to start.

The bay is a park and a nature preserve. It
is hugely popular; to beat the crowds, arrive
as soon as the park opens.

★**Hanauma Bay Nature Preserve**   PARK
(☏ 808-396-4229; www.honolulu.gov/parks-hbay/
home; 100 Hanauma Bay Road; adult/child under 13yr
$7.50/free, parking $1; ⊙ 6am-6pm Wed-Mon Nov-
Mar, to 7pm Wed-Mon Apr-Oct; ⊞) From an overlook, you can peer into the translucent waters
and see the outline of the 7000-year-old coral reef that stretches across the width of the
bay. You're bound to see schools of glittering
silver fish, the bright-blue flash of parrotfish
and perhaps sea turtles so used to snorkelers
they're ready to go eyeball-to-mask with you.
Feeding the fish is strictly prohibited.

Marine Educational Center   MUSEUM
(☏ 808-397-5840;   http://hbep.seagrant.soest.
hawaii.edu; 100 Hanauma Bay Rd; ⊙ 8am-4pm Wed-
Mon; ⊞) ⊘ Past the park's entrance ticket
windows is an excellent educational center
run by the University of Hawai'i. Interactive, family-friendly displays teach visitors
about the unique geology and ecology of the
bay. Everyone should watch the informative

12-minute video about environmental precautions before snorkeling. Visit the website for
links to a great app that covers snorkeling in
the bay.

Bus 22 runs between Waikiki and Hanauma Bay (50 minutes, every 30 to 60 minutes).
Buses leave Waikiki between 8am and 4pm
(4:45pm on weekends and holidays). Buses
back to Waikiki pick up at Hanauma Bay from
10:50am until 5:20pm (5:50pm on weekends
and holidays).

Kailua & Windward Coast

Welcome to O'ahu's lushest, most verdant
coast, where turquoise waters and light-
sand beaches share the dramatic backdrop
of misty cliffs in the Ko'olau Range. Cruise
over the *pali* (mountains) from Honolulu
(only 20 minutes) and you first reach Kailua, a pleasant place with an extraordinary
beach.

Many repeat visitors make this laid-back
community their island base, whether they
intend to kayak, stand-up paddle (SUP), snorkel, dive, drive around the island or just laze
on the sand. To the south, more beautiful
beaches (and good food) await in Waimanalo. North up the coast, Kamehameha Hwy
narrows into a winding two-lane road with
a dramatic oceanfront on one side and small
rural farms, towns and frequent sheer cliffs on
the other.

The coast is the main part of the
round-island drive that also circles through
the North Shore. Don't be surprised if you
want to hit the brakes and stay a while.

HAWAI'I, THE BIG ISLAND

Indulge your spirit of adventure on the biggest Hawaiian island. It's still a vast frontier,
full of unexpected wonders.

Less than a million years old, Hawai'i is a
baby in geological terms. Here you'll find the
Hawaiian Islands' tallest, largest and only active volcanic mountains. Kilauea, on the eastern side, is the world's most active volcano,
spewing molten lava continuously since 1983.
If you see glowing, red-hot lava, you are witnessing Earth in the making, a thrilling and
humbling experience. At 33,000ft tall when
measured from the ocean floor, Mauna Kea
is the world's tallest mountain, and its significance cannot be overstated – as a sacred place
to Hawaiians and a top astronomical site to
scientists.

❶ Getting There & Around

Virtually all visitors arrive on the Big Island by air, mostly from Honolulu International Airport on O'ahu. Travelers must then catch an interisland flight to one of the Big Island's two primary airports: Kona International Airport at Keahole or Hilo International Airport.

Car Rental Having your own set of wheels is the best way to see all of the Big Island. If you're planning off-the-beaten-track adventures then consider a 4WD vehicle, but for basic sightseeing it's unnecessary.

Bike Although getting around the island by bicycle is possible for very fit, enthusiastic cyclists, riding between towns is no casual cruise. Weather conditions can be challenging, and roads with no shoulder for bicycles can be risky. In towns, however, bikes can be an efficient, green option.

Bus Public transit by bus is available, but service is limited and you'll probably find it way too time-consuming.

Resort Shuttle Some hotels and resorts run complimentary shuttles to major sights.

Taxi Most cab companies serve only a limited area, and won't drive island-wide.

Kailua-Kona

Kailua-Kona, also known as 'Kailua,' 'Kona Town' and sometimes just 'Town,' is a love-it-or-leave-it kind of place. On the main drag of Ali'i Dr, along the shoreline, Kailua works hard to evoke the nonchalance of a sun-drenched tropical getaway, but in an injection-molded, bargain-priced way.

But we like it. Spend enough time here and you'll scratch past the souvenirs to an oddball identity built from a collision of two seemingly at-odds forces: mainlanders who want to wind down to Hawaiian time, and ambitious Big Islanders who want to make it in one of the few local towns worthy of the title. Somehow, this marriage works. Kailua-Kona can be tacky, but it's got character.

◉ Sights & Activities

★ **Magic Sands Beach**   BEACH
(La'aloa Beach Park; Ali'i Dr; ☉ sunrise-sunset; P 🚻) This small but gorgeous beach (also called White Sands and, officially, La'aloa Beach) has turquoise water, great sunsets, little shade and possibly the best bodysurfing and bodyboarding on the Big Island. Waves are consistent and just powerful enough to shoot you across the water into a sandy bay (beware: the north side of the bay has more rocks). During high winter surf the beach can vanish literally overnight, earning the nickname 'Magic Sands.' The park is about 4 miles south of central Kailua-Kona.

**Three Ring Ranch
Exotic Animal Sanctuary**   WILDLIFE RESERVE
(☎ 808-331-8778; www.threeringranch.org; 75-809 Keaolani Sbd, Kailua-Kona; minimum donation per person $50; ☉ tours by reservation) 🌿 Dr Ann Goody runs this animal sanctuary on five lovely acres in upland Kona. This isn't a zoo, or even a conventional sanctuary; instead, Dr Goody cares for and genuinely communicates with her charges, which include flamingos, zebras, tortoises and more. Guests are invited to wander the grounds on guided tours, but at all times, you are aware this is a place dedicated to education and animal healing, as opposed to viewing. You must call or email for reservations.

Jack's Diving Locker   DIVING
(☎ 808-329-7585; www.jacksdivinglocker.com; 75-5813 Ali'i Dr, Coconut Grove Marketplace, Bldg H; manta snorkel/dive from $125/175; ☉ 8am-6pm; 🚻) 🌿 With top-notch introductory dives and courses, plus extensive programs for kids, this eco-conscious dive outfitter has a 5000-sq-ft facility with a store, classrooms, tank room and Hawaii's only 12ft-deep indoor dive pool. Sign up for a boat or shore dive, as well as a night manta-ray dive. Snorkelers are welcome on many dive-boat trips.

🛏 Sleeping

My Hawaii Hostel   HOSTEL $
(☎ 808-374-2131; www.myhawaiihostel.com; 76-6241 Ali'i Drive; dm/r $40/80; P ❋ 🛜) This simple, clean, well-renovated hostel is a welcome addition to the slim pickings that are the Kailua-Kona budget accommodations scene. While $40 is a bit steep for the dorm rooms, the private chambers are about as good value for money as you'll find. Note that it's located about 2 miles south of downtown Kailua-Kona.

Kona Tiki Hotel   HOTEL $$
(☎ 808-329-1425; www.konatikihotel.com; 75-5968 Ali'i Dr; r $99-199; P 🛜 ≋) You can find affordable oceanfront views at this retro three-story hotel, a quirky, well-kept complex south of downtown Kailua-Kona with very friendly owners. The motel-style rooms are basic, but all have a fridge and enchanting lanai. Book well ahead, because the hotel regularly fills with nostalgic repeat guests.

🍴 Eating & Drinking

⭐ **Umekes Fishmarket Bar & Grill**　　　HAWAII REGIONAL **$**

(☑ 808-238-0571; www.umekesrestaurants.com; 74-5563 Kaiwi St; mains $8-18; ⏰ 11am-9pm Mon-Sat, to 8pm Sun; 🅿 ♿) Umekes takes island-style food to the next level. Local ingredients such as ahi tuna, crab salad and salted Waimea beef are served plate-lunch style with excellent, innovative sides such as seasoned seaweed and cucumber kimchi (along with heaping scoops of rice). It's some of the best-value grinds on the island. There's another location downtown at 75-143 Hualalai Road, in Ali'i Plaza.

Jackie Rey's Ohana Grill　　HAWAII REGIONAL **$$**

(☑ 808-327-0209; www.jackiereys.com; 75-5995 Kuakini Hwy; mains lunch $13-19, dinner $17-39; ⏰ 11am-9pm Mon-Fri, from 5pm Sat & Sun; 🅿 ♿) Jackie Rey's is a casual grill with a delightfully retro-kitsch Hawaii vibe. Haute versions of local *grinds* include guava-glazed ribs, wasabi-seared ahi and *mochiko* (rice flour-battered) fish with Moloka'i purple sweet potatoes.

Kona Brewing Company　　　AMERICAN **$$**

(☑ 808-334-2739; www.konabrewingco.com; 74-5612 Pawai Place; mains $14-25; ⏰ 11am-10pm; ♿) 🌿 Expect a madhouse crowd at this sprawling, eco-sustainable brewpub, with tiki torch-lit outdoor seating and laid-back waitstaff. Pizza toppings verge on gourmet, but crusts can be soggy; BBQ sandwiches and fish tacos are better bets. Enter the parking lot off Kaiwi St.

❶ Getting There & Around

Both the public Hele-On Bus and privately operated Keauhou and Kona Trolley make stops within Kailua-Kona.

The drive from Kailua-Kona to Hilo is 75 miles and takes at least 1¾ hours via Saddle Rd, 95 miles (two hours) via Waimea and 125 miles (three hours) via Ka'u and Volcano.

To avoid snarly commuter traffic on Hwy 11 leading into and away from Kailua-Kona, try the Mamalahoa Hwy Bypass Rd. It connects Ali'i Dr in Keauhou with Haleki'i St in Kealakekua, between Miles 111 and 112 on Hwy 11.

South Kona Coast

South Kona, more than any other district of Hawai'i, embodies the many strands that make up the geo-cultural tapestry of Hawai'i, the Big Island. There is both the dry lava desert of the Kohala Coast and the wet, misty

KONA COFFEE FARMS

Many coffee-farm tours are perfunctory 15-minute affairs. The tour at **Kona Coffee Living History Farm** (☑ 808-323-3222; www.konahistorical.org; 82-6199 Mamalahoa Hwy; 1hr tour adult/child 7-17yr $15/5; ⏰ 10am-2pm Mon-Fri; 🅿), run by the Kona Historical Society, an affiliate of the Smithsonian Institute, is different and deep. More than an exploration of how coffee is produced, it's an evocative look at rural Japanese immigrant life in South Kona throughout decades of the 20th century. Restored to Hawai'i's pre-statehood era, this 5.5-acre working coffee farm once belonged to the Uchida family, who lived here until 1994.

jungles of Puna and Hilo; fishing villages inhabited by country-living locals next to hippie art galleries established by counter-culture exiles from the US mainland, next to condos plunked down by millionaire land developers.

In addition, the dozen or so miles heading south from Kailua-Kona to Kealakekua Bay are among Hawai'i's most action-packed, historically speaking. It's here that ancient Hawaiian *ali'i* (royalty) secretly buried the bones of their ancestors, *kapu* (taboo) breakers braved shark-infested waters to reach the *pu'uhonua* (place of refuge), and British explorer Captain Cook and his crew fatally first stepped ashore in Hawaii.

❶ Getting There & Away

The Belt Rd that rings the island becomes Hwy 11 in South Kona, and it's a twisty, sometimes treacherous route – while there aren't many hairpin turns, folks who are used to flatland driving will need to acclimate themselves to driving in the mountains.

In some places the highway is quite narrow; while cycling is relatively common, make sure to wear reflective gear and sport good lighting on your rig. Note that mile markers decrease as you head further south; this may seem weird given that mile markers decrease going *north* in North Kona, but you're technically on Hwy 11, as opposed to Hwy 19, down here.

The **Hele-On Bus** (www.heleonbus.org) passes through the area sporadically, mainly in the morning and early evening, taking commuters to and from resorts; it can also drop travelers off along the way.

North Kona Coast

If you thought the Big Island was all jungle mountains and white-sand beaches, the severe North Kona Coast, its beige deserts and black-and-rust lava fields will come as a shock. Yet always, at the edge of your eyesight, is the bright blue Pacific, while bits of green are sprinkled like jade flecks amid the dry. Turn off the Queen Ka'ahumanu Hwy and make your way across the eerie lava fields to snorkel with sea turtles, bask on almost deserted black-sand beaches and catch an iconic Kona sunset. On clear days, gaze *mauka* (inland) at panoramas of Mauna Kea and Mauna Loa volcanoes, both often snow-dusted in winter, and in the foreground between the two, Mt Hualalai.

North Kona technically runs 33 miles along Queen Ka'ahumanu Hwy (Hwy 19) from Kailua-Kona up the Kona Coast to Kawaihae. Honokohau Harbor is an easy 2-mile drive from downtown Kailua.

🛌 Sleeping

This sparsely populated area is light on accommodations options; it's far easier to find resorts further north (South Kohala) or guesthouses, rentals and the like further south (Kailua-Kona and South Kona). Either way, you won't be more than a 30-minute drive from North Kona's best sights.

★ **Four Seasons Resort Hualalai** RESORT $$$
(☑ 808-325-8000, 888-340-5662; www.foursea sons.com/hualalai; 72-100 Ka'upulehu Dr; r/ste from $1065/1790; 🅿 ❄ @ 🛜 🏊) This luxury resort earns its accolades with top-flight service and lavish attention to detail like fresh orchids in every room, embracing lush gardens and an oceanview infinity pool. Some poolside rooms have rejuvenating lava-rock garden outdoor showers. The golf course and spa are both outstanding, or snorkel with 75 species of tropical fish in the King's Pond.

ℹ Getting There & Away

The **Hele-On Bus** (www.heleonbus.org) runs at least one daily line out to the resorts at Kohala that pass through North Kona. Otherwise, North Kona is an easy drive north of Kailua-Kona; just be aware of heavy traffic conditions around the airport during rush hour (7am to 9am and 3:30pm to 6pm). You can also cycle out here (bring water); this is one of the few areas of the Belt Rd with a wide shoulder. Note that mile markers *decrease* as you head north.

South Kohala Coast

The Queen Ka'ahumanu Hwy (Hwy 19) cuts through stark fields of lava, but as you head toward the ocean, rolling emerald golf course slopes edge onto condo complexes and electric teal pools. This is the Gold Coast of the Big Island, and whatever your feelings are on resorts, this is where you'll find some of the area's best beaches.

Oddly enough, South Kohala also contains numerous ancient Hawaiian sights. This coast was more populated at the time of their creation than it is now, and the region is packed with village sites, heiau (temples), fishponds, petroglyphs and historic trails – areas that are often preserved for visitors.

The waters off the coast in South Kohala are pristine and teeming with marine life – and they're relatively uncrowded. The reef drops off more gradually here than along the Kona Coast, so you might see sharks, dolphins, turtles and manta rays.

This is resort country, and the accommodations options are pricey. Modern amenities and plush digs are the norm. Note that many units within resorts are owner-occupied condos, which are often rented to short-term visitors via the usual rental website booking engines.

Whole house rentals are the norm in Puako, and there are some camping options on Kohala beaches. Check out www.waikolo ahawaiivacations.com, www.2papayas.com and www.hawaiis4me.com for rentals in the area.

ℹ Getting There & Away

The resorts and sights of South Kohala are located north of Kailua-Kona off Hwy 19 – depending on which resort you're going to, they're located about 25 to 35 miles away from town.

The Pahala–South Kohala Hele-On Bus plies this route twice a day Monday to Saturday, and once a day on Sundays.

Traffic jams around KOA airport during rush hours can eat up your travel time.

Mauna Kea

Mauna Kea (White Mountain) is called Mauna O Wakea (Mountain of Wakea) by Hawaiian cultural practitioners. While all of the Big Island is considered the first-born child of Wakea (Sky Father) and Papahānaumoku (Earth Mother), Mauna Kea has always been the sacred *piko* (navel) connecting the land to the heavens.

BEACHES OF NORTH KONA

Makalawena Beach If what you're after is an almost deserted, postcard-perfect scoop of soft, white-sand beach cupping brilliant blue-green waters (got your attention?), head to 'Maks.' Although popular, this string of idyllic coves absorbs crowds so well you'll still feel like you've found paradise. The northernmost cove is sandier and gentler, while the southernmost cove is (illegally) a naked sunbathing spot. Swimming is splendid, but beware of rough surf and rocks in the water. Bodyboarding and snorkeling are other possibilities.

Kua Bay (Manini'owali Beach; www.hawaiistateparks.org; ⊙8am-7pm; P ♿) This crescent-shaped white-sand beach is fronted by sparkling turquoise waters that offer first-rate swimming and bodyboarding, and good snorkeling on the north side of the bay (by the large rock outcroppings) when waters are calm. A paved road leads right up to it, and thus the beach, also known as Manini'owali, draws major crowds, especially on weekends. Arrive late and cars will be parked half a mile up the road. The parking area has bathrooms and showers.

Honokohau Beach (⊙daylight hours; ♿) At this beautiful hook-shaped beach with a mix of black lava, white coral and wave-tossed shells, the water is usually too cloudy for snorkeling, but just standing on shore you'll see *honu* (green sea turtles). You may spot more *honu* munching on *limu* (seaweed) around the ancient **'Ai'opio fishtrap**, bordered by a Hawaiian **heiau** at the beach's southern end. Inland are **anchialine ponds** – pools of brackish water that make unique habitats for marine and plant life.

For the scientific world, it all began in 1968 when the University of Hawai'i (UH) began observing the universe from atop the mountain. The summit is so high, dry, dark and pollution-free that it allows investigation of the furthest reaches of the observable universe.

Many Hawaiians are opposed to the summit 'golf balls' – the white observatories now dotting the skyline. While not antiscience, they believe unchecked growth threatens the mountain's *wahi pana* (sacred places), including heiau (temples) and burial sites. Litter, vandalism and pollution (including toxic mercury spills) have been a problem. Visit with respect, and pack out your trash.

★**Mauna Kea Visitor
Information Station** TOURIST INFORMATION
(MKVIS; ☎808-961-2180; www.ifa.hawaii.edu/info/vis; ⊙8am-3pm) FREE Modestly sized MKVIS packs a punch with astronomy and space-exploration videos and posters galore, and information about the mountain's history, ecology and geology. Budding scientists of all ages revel in the gift shop, while knowledgeable staff help you pass the time acclimatizing to the 9200ft altitude. Check the website for upcoming special events, such as lectures about science and Hawaiian culture.

❶ Getting There & Away

Coming from Waimea or Kona take Saddle Road (Hwy 200) or the new Daniel K Inouye reroute. From Hilo, drive *mauka* (inland) on Kaumana Dr

(Hwy 200) or Puainako Extension (Hwy 2000), both of which become Saddle Road. Start with a full tank of gas – there are no service stations out here.

The Visitor Information Station (MKVIS) and the summit beyond are on Mauna Kea Access Rd, near Mile 28 on Saddle Road. MKVIS is 6 miles uphill from Saddle Road; the summit is another 8 miles beyond that. Call 808-935-6268 for current road conditions.

Hamakua Coast

Stretching from Waipi'o Valley to Hilo, the Hamakua Coast combines rugged beauty and bursting fertility. Here you'll find rocky shores and pounding surf, tropical rainforests and thunderous waterfalls. The color green takes on new meaning, especially in Waipi'o Valley, which you can explore on horseback or by a steep, exhilarating hike.

On the slopes of Mauna Kea, farmers grow vanilla, tea, mushrooms and other boutique crops, modernizing and diversifying island agriculture. Visit these small-scale farms for a close-up look at island life (and to sample its delicious bounty). Sugarcane once ruled the Hamakua Coast, with acres of plantations and massive trains chugging along the coast and across towering bridges spanning the tremendous gulches. Stop at old-time museums and delve into the rich history here. Pause to imagine the 'old plantation days.' Go slow, explore the back roads and step back in time.

A car is essential to navigate the Hamakua Coast along Hwy 19. Honoka'a, the biggest town along the Hamakua Coast, is approximately 50 miles from Kailua-Kona and 40 miles from Hilo. Expect the drive to take 75 minutes from Kona and an hour from Hilo.

The **Hele-On Bus** (☑808-961-8744; www.heleonbus.org; per trip adult/senior & student $2/1) route between Kona and Hilo stops at various towns along the coast, including Honoka'a, Pa'auilo, Laupahoehoe, Hakalau, Honomu and Papaikou. Buses run between Kona and Hilo three times daily. Service between Hilo and Honoka'a is more frequent. Check the website for schedules.

Hilo

Kailua-Kona may host more visitors, but Hilo is the beating heart of Hawai'i Island. Hidden beneath its daily drizzle lies deep soil and soul, from which sprouts a genuine community and aloha spirit. Hilo's demographics still mirror its sugar-town roots, with a diverse mix of Native Hawaiians, Japanese, Filipinos, Portuguese, Puerto Ricans, Chinese and Caucasians.

People might seem low-key, but they're a resilient lot. Knocked down by two tsunamis, threatened with extinction by Mauna Loa lava flows, deluged with the highest annual rainfall in the USA and always battling for its share of tourist dollars, Hilo knows how to survive and to thrive.

Hilo had a life before tourism, and it remains refreshingly untouristy. Yet it offers many attractions: compelling museums, a walkable downtown, two thriving farmers markets and dozens of indie restaurants. Hilo is an ideal base for exploring Hawai'i Volcanoes National Park, Mauna Kea, Puna and the Hamakua Coast.

◉ Sights

★ **Lili'uokalani Park** PARK
(189 Lihiwai St; 👫) Savor Hilo's simple pleasures with a picnic lunch in scenic Japanese gardens overlooking the bay. Named for Hawaii's last queen (r 1891–93), the 30-acre county park features soaring trees, sprawling lawns and quaint footbridges over shallow ponds. At sunrise or sunset, join the locals jogging or power walking the perimeter, or simply admire the Mauna Kea view.

★ **Pacific Tsunami Museum** MUSEUM
(☑808-935-0926; www.tsunami.org; 130 Kamehameha Ave; adult/child $8/4; ⏰10am-4pm Tue-Sat)

You cannot understand Hilo without knowing its history as a two-time tsunami survivor (1946 and 1960). This seemingly modest museum is chock-full of riveting information, including a section on the Japanese tsunami of 2011, which damaged Kona. Allow enough time to experience the multimedia exhibits, including chilling computer simulations and heart-wrenching first-person accounts.

'Imiloa Astronomy Center of Hawai'i MUSEUM
(☑808-969-9700; www.imiloahawaii.org; 600 'Imiloa Pl; adult/child 5-12yr $19/12; ⏰9am-5pm Tue-Sun; 🅿👫) 'Imiloa, which means 'exploring new knowledge,' is a $28 million museum and planetarium complex with a twist: it juxtaposes modern astronomy on Mauna Kea with ancient Polynesian ocean voyaging. It's a great family attraction and the natural complement to a summit tour. One planetarium show is included with admission.

🛏 Sleeping

★ **Arnott's Lodge** HOSTEL, CAMPGROUND $
(☑808-339-0921; www.arnottslodge.com; 98 Apapane Rd; camping per person $18, dm $35-65, r with/without bath $92/80, ste $110; 🅿😊❄🐾📶) Hilo's longest-running hostel remains solid value, with a dizzying variety of lodging options close to Onekahakaha Beach. All rooms and dorms are clean, safe and comfortably furnished. The Deluxe Suite ($110) is especially pleasant, with an airy high ceiling and private kitchenette. Camping is also available. Ask about its **adventure tours** (☑808-339-0921; www.arnottslodge.com; 98 Apapane Rd, Hilo; tours $180; ⏰tours Wed-Mon) to Mauna Kea.

★ **Dolphin Bay Hotel** HOTEL $$
(☑877-935-1466, 808-935-1466; www.dolphinbayhotel.com; 333 Iliahi St; studio $109-199; 🅿😊📶) This family-owned hotel attracts countless loyal, repeat guests – which is no surprise. Its 18 apartment-style units are spotless and reasonably priced and all include full kitchen. Welcoming staffers are generous with island advice and provide free coffee, fruit and banana bread for breakfast. The property, bursting with tropical flora, is conveniently located within a five-minute walk of downtown Hilo.

🍴 Eating & Drinking

★ **Suisan Fish Market** SEAFOOD $
(☑808-935-9349; www.suisan.com/our-services/fish-market; 93 Lihiwai St; takeout poke $10-18, poke per lb $18; ⏰8am-5pm Mon-Fri, to 4pm Sat) For a fantastic variety of freshly made *poke* (sold

by the pound), Suisan is a must. Buy a bowl of takeout *poke* and rice and eat outside the shop or across the street at Lili'uokalani Park. Could life be any better?

Restaurant Kenichi
JAPANESE $

(☑ 808-969-1776; www.restaurantkenichi.com; 684 Kilauea Ave; mains $9-19; ⏱ 10am-2pm & 5-9pm Mon-Sat; ⛋) For delicious, untouristy dining, Kenichi has it all: Japanese comfort food, high-volume flavor, cheerful staff and a simple dining room crowded with locals. Favorites include steaming ramen bowls made with house *dashi* (broth), succulent grilled *saba* (mackerel), boneless Korean chicken and rib-eye steak, rushed to your table, aromatic and sizzling. Save room for nostalgic desserts like banana cream pie.

Bayfront Kava Bar
BAR

(☑ 808-345-1698; http://bayfrontkava.com; 277 Keawe St; cup of kava $5; ⏱ 5-10pm Mon-Sat) If you're curious about kava ('awa in Hawaiian), try a cup at this minimalist bar. Friendly staff serve freshly brewed, locally grown kava root in coconut shells. Get ready for tingling taste buds and a calm buzz. Live music and art exhibitions kick off on a regular basis.

❶ Getting There & Away

The drive from Hilo to Kailua-Kona (via Waimea) along Hwy 19 is 95 miles and takes about 2½ hours. Driving along Saddle Road can cut travel time by about 15 minutes.

Hawai'i Volcanoes National Park

From the often-snowy summit of Mauna Loa, the world's most massive volcano, to the boiling coast where lava pours into the sea, Hawai'i Volcanoes National Park (car/bicycle or pedestrian 7-day pass $25/12) is a microcontinent of rainforests, volcano-induced deserts, high-mountain meadows, coastal plains and plenty of geological marvels in between.

At the heart of it all is Kilauea – the earth's youngest and most active shield volcano. Since 1983 Kilauea's East Rift Zone has been erupting almost nonstop, and while an active volcano tends to draw visitors, it can also be a geologic liability. From May to August of 2018, sustained eruptions yielded seismic activity and lava flows that quite literally reshaped Hawai'i Volcanoes National Park (and resulted in the destruction of 700 homes). Some attractions have been indefinitely closed, but other activities, including the stunning Chain

WORTH A TRIP

KOHALA MOUNTAIN ROAD

Arguably the Big Island's best scenic drive, Kohala Mountain Rd (Hwy 250) affords stupendous views of the Kohala–Kona coastline and three majestic volcanic mountains: Mauna Kea, Mauna Loa and Hualalai. Start from Waimea, climb past an overlook, and then follow the spine of the peninsula through green pastures until you finally descend to the sea at Hawi. The name changes to Hawi Rd close to that town.

of Craters Road and most of the park's backcountry, remain open to visitors.

In any case, local national park staff excel at managing this chaotic landscape. Their education programs deftly blend modern science with ancient beliefs and customs, and their outreach feels boundless. Ample interpretive signs, unusually informative trail guides, a slew of well-thought-out ranger-led hikes, living history programs and a weekly lecture series all provide visitors with a solid connection to the park and the people of Hawai'i.

Of all the national parks in the USA, this is the one where you *really* want to check conditions before visiting; check out www. nps.gov/havo/planyourvisit for up to date information.

The park's two vehicle-accessible campgrounds are relatively uncrowded outside of summer months. Nights can be crisp, cool and wet. Campsites are first-come, first-served (with a seven-night limit). Nearby Volcano Village has the most variety for those who prefer a roof over their heads.

★ Kilauea Visitor
Center & Museum
MUSEUM

(☑ 808-985-6101; www.nps.gov/havo; Crater Rim Dr; ⏱ 9am-5pm; ⛋) 🖉 Stop here first. Extraordinarily helpful (and remarkably patient) rangers and volunteers can advise you about volcanic activity, air quality, road closures, hiking-trail conditions and how best to spend however much time you have. Interactive museum exhibits are small but family friendly, and will teach even science-savvy adults about the park's delicate ecosystem and Hawaiian heritage. All of the rotating movies are excellent. Pick up fun junior ranger program activity books for your kids before leaving.

ℹ Information

Air Quality (www.hawaiiso2network.com) Air-quality updates from nine monitoring stations throughout the park.

Hawai'i County Civil Defense (www.hawaii county.gov/civil-defense) Information on lava flows and volcanic activity.

Trail & Road Closures (www.nps.gov/havo/ closed_areas.htm) Updated information on trail and road closings.

USGS Hawaiian Volcano Observatory (http:// hvo.wr.usgs.gov) Kilauea Volcano eruption updates, current earthquake and atmospheric conditions, and webcams.

ℹ Getting There & Around

The park is 30 miles (45 minutes) from Hilo and 95 miles (2¾ hours) from Kailua-Kona via Hwy 11. The turnoffs for Volcano village are a couple of miles east of the main park entrance. Hwy 11 is prone to flooding, washouts and closures during rainstorms. Periods of drought may close Mauna Loa Rd and Hilina Pali Rd due to wildfire hazards.

The public **Hele-On Bus** (☑ 808-961-8744; www.heleonbus.org; adult one-way $2) departs five times a day Monday through Saturday (no service Sunday) from Hilo, arriving at the park visitor center about 1¼ hours later. One bus continues to Ka'u. There is no public transportation once you get inside the park, and hitchhiking is illegal in all national parks.

Cyclists are permitted on paved roads, and a handful of dirt ones, including the Escape Rd but not on any trails – pavement or no.

MAUI

According to some, you can't have it all. Perhaps those folks haven't been to Maui, which consistently lands atop travel-magazine reader polls as one of the world's most romantic islands. And why not? With its sandy beaches, deluxe resorts, gourmet cuisine, fantastic luau feasts, whale-watching, surfing, snorkeling and hiking, it leaves most people more in love than when they arrived.

ℹ Getting There & Away

Maui has a large number of nonstop flights to/ from cities on the mainland, including Los Angeles, San Diego, San Francisco, Seattle, Dallas, Chicago and Vancouver, BC. Otherwise it's common to connect through Honolulu.

Kahului International Airport (OGG; ☑ 808-872-3830; www.airports.hawaii.gov/ogg; 1 Kahului Airport Rd) All trans-Pacific flights to Maui arrive in Kahului, the island's main airport. There's a staffed **Visitor Information Desk** in the baggage claim area that's open 7:45am to 10pm daily. There are racks of local travel brochures beside the desk.

Kapalua Airport (JHM; ☑ 808-665-6108; www. airports.hawaii.gov/jhm; 4050 Honoapiilani Hwy) Off Hwy 30, south of Kapalua in West Maui, this regional airport has flights with **Mokulele Airlines** (☑ 866-260-7070; www.mokuleleairlines. com) to Moloka'i and Honolulu.

Lahaina

With its weathered storefronts, narrow streets and bustling harbor, plus a few chattering mynahs, Hawaii's most historic town looks like a port-of-call for Captain Ahab. Is this the 21st century, or an 1850s whaling village? In truth, it offers a mix of both.

Tucked between the West Maui Mountains and the sea, Lahaina has long been a convergence point. Ancient Hawaiian royals were the first to gather here, followed by missionaries, whalers and sugar plantation workers. Today it's a base for creative chefs, passionate artists and dedicated surf instructors.

Near the harbor, storefronts that once housed saloons, dance halls and brothels now teem with art galleries, souvenir shops and, well, still plenty of watering holes. As for the whalers, they've been replaced by a new kind of leviathan hunter: whale-watchers as dedicated as Ahab in their hunt. Between January and March, they don't have to look hard.

◎ Sights & Activities

★ **Banyan Tree Square**   PARK
(cnr Front & Hotel Sts) A leafy landmark (the largest tree in Hawaii) stands in the center of Lahaina. Remarkably, it sprawls across the entire square. Planted as a seedling on April 24, 1873, to commemorate the 50th anniversary of missionaries in Lahaina, the tree has become a virtual forest unto itself, with 16 major trunks and scores of horizontal branches reaching across the better part of an acre. The square was recently given a major restoration, which fixed the paving tiles and teak benches.

★ **Wo Hing Museum**   MUSEUM
(www.lahainarestoration.org/wo-hing-museum; 858 Front St; adult/child incl admission to Baldwin House $7/free; ⊙9am-5pm) This three-story temple, built in 1912 as a meeting hall for the benevolent society Chee Kung Tong, provided Chinese immigrants with a place to preserve their cultural identity, celebrate festivities and socialize in their native tongue. After WWII, Lahaina's ethnic Chinese population spread far and wide and the temple fell into decline.

Now restored and turned into a museum, it houses ceremonial instruments, a teak medicine cabinet c 1900, jade pieces dating back thousands of years and a Taoist shrine.

Trilogy Excursions BOATING
(☑ 888-225-6284, 808-874-5649; www.sailtrilogy.com; 207 Kupuohi St; 4hr snorkel trip adult/child from $125/70) Offering snorkeling tours in Maui for more than 40 years, this family-run operation specializes in catamaran tours. There's a variety of trips, including ones to the reef at Olowalu and the much-loved islet of Molokini. In season there are whale-watching trips as well as dinner and sunset cruises. Day trips to Lana'i are popular.

🍴 Eating & Drinking

Frida's Mexican Beach House MEXICAN $$$
(☑ 808-661-1287; www.fridasmaui.com; 1287 Front St; mains $20-40; ⊙ 11am-9:30pm) Not your cheap taco joint, Frida's (with plenty of imagery from its namesake Frida Kahlo) has a superb waterfront location, with a large open dining area on a terrace that will have your blood pressure falling minutes after arriving. Steaks and seafood with a Latin flair feature on the upscale menu. Cocktails are creative; yes, there are margaritas!

★ Fleetwood's on Front St BAR
(☑ 808-669-6425; www.fleetwoodsonfrontst.com; 744 Front St; ⊙ 11am-10pm Sun-Thu, to 11pm Fri & Sat) With its comfy pillows, cushy lounges and ornate accents, this rooftop oasis – owned by Fleetwood Mac drummer Mick Fleetwood – evokes Morocco. But views of the Pacific and the West Maui Mountains keep you firmly rooted in Hawaii. At sunset, a conch-shell blast announces a tiki-lighting ceremony that's followed by a bagpipe serenade – from a kilt-wearing Scot.

❶ Getting There & Away

It takes about one hour to drive between Lahaina and the airport in Kahului.

Hawaii Executive Transportation (☑ 877-242-5777; www.hawaiiexecutivetransportation.com; 1/2/3/4 passengers $51/59/64/66; ⊙ dispatch 7am-10pm) provides van service between the airport and Lahaina, and serves most addresses in town. A taxi between Lahaina and the airport costs about $80.

The **Maui Bus** (☑ 808-871-4838; www.mauicounty.gov/bus; single ride $2, day/month pass $4/45) runs the Lahaina Islander route 20 between Kahului bus hub and Lahaina (one hour), stopping at Ma'alaea Harbor, where a connection can be made to Kihei via the Kihei Villager bus

DON'T MISS

BIG BEACH

The glory of Makena State Park, this untouched **beach** (Oneloa Beach; www.dlnr.hawaii.gov/dsp/parks/maui; Makena Rd; ⊙ 6am-6pm; P) is arguably the finest on Maui. In Hawaiian it's called Oneloa, literally 'Long Sand.' And indeed the golden sands stretch for the better part of a mile and are as broad as they come. The waters are a beautiful turquoise. When they're calm you'll find kids boogieboarding, but at other times the shorebreaks can be dangerous, suitable for experienced bodysurfers only, who get tossed in the transparent waves.

service. Another route, the Ka'anapali Islander, connects Lahaina and Ka'anapali (30 minutes). Both Islander routes depart from the Wharf Cinema Center hourly from 6:30am to 8:30pm.

The **Expeditions Ferry** (☑ 808-661-3756; www.go-lanai.com; Lahaina Harbor; adult/child one way $30/20) to Lana'i uses the **Ferry Dock** (off Wharf St) in Lahaina Harbor.

Kihei

Two reasons to visit Kihei? The beaches and your budget. Yes, it's overrun with strip malls and traffic, but with 6 miles of easy-to-access beaches, loads of affordable accommodations and a variety of dining options, it offers everything you need for an enjoyable beach vacation. An energetic seaside town, Kihei also works well for short-trip vacationers seeking reliable sunshine – on average Kihei is sunny 276 days per year. It's also home to the island's busiest bar scene.

To zip from one end of Kihei to the other, take the Pi'ilani Hwy (Hwy 31). It runs parallel to and bypasses the stop-start traffic of S Kihei Rd. Well-marked crossroads connect these two routes.

◉ Sights

★ Keawakapu Beach BEACH
(☑ 808-879-4364; www.mauicounty.gov/facilities; P) From break of day to twilight, this stretch of sand is a showstopper. Extending from south Kihei to Wailea's Mokapu Beach, Keawakapu is set back from the road and is less visible than Kihei's main roadside beaches just north. It's also less crowded, and is a great place to settle in and watch the sunset.

DON'T MISS

HALEAKALĀ NATIONAL PARK

Haleakalā National Park (☎808-572-4400; www.nps.gov/hale; Summit District: Haleakalā Hwy, Kipahulu District: Hana Hwy; 3-day pass car $25, motorcycle $20, individual on foot or bicycle $12; P) has two distinct sections, and if you have just one day to visit, head to the summit. Whether you make a pre-dawn haul up the mountain to watch the sunrise, or mosey up after breakfast, begin your explorations here. Not only is the **visitor center** (www.nps.gov/hale; Haleakalā Hwy; ⊙sunrise-noon; P) the ideal perch for crater views, it's also a fine starting point for jaunts into the crater.

Next, burn off the morning chill with an invigorating hike on the sun-warmed cinders of the unearthly **Keonehe'ehe'e (Sliding Sands) Trail** (www.nps.gov/hale).

Once you've completed your lunar-like crater hike, continue your road trip to Maui's highest point, **Pu'u'ula'ula (Red Hill) Overlook** (www.nps.gov/hale; Haleakalā Hwy; P). Admire the *'ahinahina* (silversword) garden and take in a ranger talk.

It's time to head back down the mountain. Make your way to the **Kalahaku Overlook** (www.nps.gov/hale; Haleakalā Hwy; P) lookout, a crater rim-hugger with an eye-popping, wide-angle view of the cinder cones dotting the crater floor.

You've seen the starkly barren side of Haleakalā. Now make acquaintance with its lush green face by taking a half-mile walk along the **Hosmer Grove Trail** (www.nps.gov/hale; off Haleakalā Hwy), in forest brimming with birdsong. Like many animals in the park, some of these birds are found nowhere else.

This leg covers 17 miles.

Sleeping

★**Pineapple Inn Maui** INN $$
(☎877-212-6284, 808-298-4403; www.pineappleinnmaui.com; 3170 Akala Dr; r $179-219, cottage $235-295; P) The Pineapple Inn may be the best deal going in South Maui. This inviting boutique property offers style and functionality with a personal touch, and it's less than a mile from the beach. The four rooms, which have ocean-view lanai and private entrances, are as attractive as those at the exclusive resorts, but at a fraction of the cost. Rooms have kitchenettes, and the two-bedroom cottage comes with a full kitchen.

Eating & Drinking

★**Café O'Lei** HAWAIIAN $$
(☎808-891-1368; www.cafeoleirestaurants.com; 2439 S Kihei Rd, Rainbow Mall; lunch $9-19, dinner $19-32; ⊙10:30am-3:30pm & 4:30-9:30pm) This strip-mall bistro looks ho-hum at first blush. But step inside: the sophisticated atmosphere, innovative Hawaii Regional Cuisine, honest prices and excellent service knock Café O'Lei into the fine-dining big league. For a tangy treat, order the blackened mahimahi with fresh papaya salsa. Look for unbeatable lunch mains, with salads, for under $10, and a sushi chef after 4:30pm (Tuesday to Saturday).

★**5 Palms** COCKTAIL BAR
(☎808-879-2607; www.5palmsrestaurant.com; 2960 S Kihei Rd, Mana Kai Maui; ⊙8am-11pm) For sunset cocktails beside the beach, this is the place. Arrive an hour before the sun goes down because the patio bar, just steps from stunning Keawakapu Beach, fills quickly. During happy hour, sushi and an array of delicious appetizers are half price, with a one drink minimum, while mai tais and margaritas are $5.75. Popular with tourists and locals.

Getting There & Away

The **Maui Bus** (☎808-871-4838; www.mauicounty.gov/bus; single ride $2, day pass $4) serves Kihei with two routes. One route, the Kihei Islander, connects Kihei with Wailea and Kahalui; stops include Kama'ole Beach Park III, Pi'ilani Village shopping center, and Uwapo at South Kihei Rd. The other route, the Kihei Villager, primarily serves the northern half of Kihei, with a half-dozen stops along South Kihei Rd and at Pi'ilani Village shopping center and Ma'alaea. Both routes operate hourly from around 6am to 8pm and cost $2.

KAUA'I

Emerald mountains, weeping waterfalls, red-rock canyons, jaw-dropping beaches, clear seas and big waves. Kaua'i's natural gifts are unparalleled in Hawaii, the USA, the world.

Tourist information kiosks aren't really a thing on Kaua'i, but the local tourist board, **Kaua'i Visitors Bureau** (☎808-245-3971; www.gohawaii.com/kauai; 4334 Rice St, Suite 101; ⊙8am-4:30pm Mon-Fri), does have a useful website.

ⓘ Getting There & Around

Getting here is easy, especially from the mainland USA and Canada, with numerous flights daily. Often, flights will get here with layovers in Honolulu. There are no ferry services here.

Renting a car is highly recommended unless you're on a very tight budget.

Lihu'e

The island's commercial center is strip-mall plain, but there's an abundance of economical eateries and shops along with a down-to-earth, workaday atmosphere that's missing in resort areas. While Kalapaki Beach is a charmer, Lihu'e is more a place to stock up on supplies after arrival at the airport before heading out on your island adventure.

Lihu'e arose as a plantation town in 1849 when sugar was king, and its sugar mill (still standing south of town along Kaumuali'i Hwy) was Kaua'i's largest. The mill closed in 2000, ending more than a century of operations. It left behind an ethnic melting pot of Asian, European and Hawaiian traditions that make the town what it is today.

Activities center on Kalapaki Beach with a few top golf courses and cool beaches nearby. This is the kickoff point for helicopter tours and a few fun excursions to waterfalls.

Wailua

To ancient Hawaiians, the Wailua River was among the most sacred places across the islands. The river basin, near its mouth, was one of the island's two royal centers (the other was Waimea) and home to the high chiefs. Here, you can find the remains of many important heiau (ancient stone temples); together they now form a national historic landmark.

Long and narrow **Hikina'akala Heiau** (Rising of the Sun Temple) sits south of the Wailua River mouth, which is today the north end of Lydgate Beach Park. In its heyday, the temple (built around AD 1300) was aligned directly north to south, but only a few remaining boulders outline its original massive shape. Neighboring **Hauola Pu'uhonua** (meaning 'the place of refuge of the dew of life') is marked by a bronze plaque. Ancient Hawaiian *kapu* (taboo) breakers were assured safety from persecution if they made it inside.

Believed to be the oldest *luakini* (temple dedicated to the war god Ku, often a place for human sacrifice) on the island, **Holoholoku Heiau** is a quarter-mile up Kuamo'o Rd on the left. It's believed to be Kaua'i's oldest heiau.

Toward the west, against the flat-backed birthstone marked by a plaque reading **Pohaku Ho'ohanau** (Royal Birthstone), queens gave birth to future royals. Only a male child born here could become king of Kaua'i.

Perched high on a hill overlooking the meandering Wailua River, well-preserved **Poli'ahu Heiau**, another *luakini,* is named after the snow goddess Poli'ahu, one of the sisters of the volcano goddess Pele. The heiau is immediately before **'Opaeka'a Falls Lookout**, on the opposite side of the road.

Although Hawaiian heiau were originally imposing stone structures, most now lie in ruins, covered with scrub. They are still considered powerful vortices of mana (spiritual essence) and should be treated with respect.

ⓘ Getting There & Around

Don't look for a town center. Most attractions are scattered along coastal Kuhio Hwy (Hwy 56) or Kuamo'o Rd (Hwy 580) heading *mauka* (inland). Driving north, Kapa'a Bypass runs from just north of the Wailua River to beyond Kapa'a, usually skipping the Waipouli and Kapa'a gridlock.

Hanalei Bay & the North Shore

There are few towns with the majestic natural beauty and barefoot soul of Hanalei. The bay is the thing, of course. Its half-dozen surf breaks are legendary, partly because local surf gods such as the late Andy Irons cut their teeth here. Even if you aren't here for the waves, the beach will demand your attention with its wide sweep of cream-colored sand and magnificent jade mountain views.

So will the pint-sized town where you may take a yoga class, snack on sushi, shop for chic beach gear, vintage treasures and stunning art, or duck into a world-class dive bar. Sure, Hanalei has more than its share of adults with Peter Pan syndrome, and you'll see as many men in their sixties waxing their surfboards as you will groms with 'guns' (big-wave surfboards). Which begs the query: why grow up at all when you can grow old in Hanalei?

⊙ Sights & Activities

Na Pali Coast Wilderness State Park   PARK
(www.dlnr.hawaii.gov/dsp/parks/kauai/napali-coast-state-wilderness-park; end of Hwy 560) FREE
Roadless, pristine and hauntingly beautiful, this 16-mile-long stretch of cliffs, white-sand beaches, turquoise coves and waterfalls links the island's northern and western shores.

WAIMEA CANYON STATE PARK

Of all Kaua'i's unique wonders, none can touch Waimea Canyon for grandeur. Few would expect to find a gargantuan chasm of ancient lava rock, 10 miles long and over 3500ft deep. Flowing through the canyon is Waimea River, Kaua'i's longest, fed by tributaries that bring reddish-brown waters from Alaka'i Swamp's mountaintop.

The southern boundary of Waimea Canyon State Park is about 6 miles uphill from Waimea. You can reach the park by two roads: more scenic Waimea Canyon Dr (Hwy 550), which starts in Waimea just past Mile 23, or Koke'e Rd (Hwy 552), starting in Kekaha off Mana Rd. The two routes merge between Miles 6 and 7.

★ **Black Pot Beach Park (Hanalei Pier)**   BEACH

This small section of Hanalei Bay near the Hanalei River mouth usually offers the calmest surf among the wild North Shore swells. Also known as Hanalei Pier for its unmistakable landmark, the sand is shaded by ironwood trees and is popular mainly with novice surfers. In summer, swimming and snorkeling are decent, as is kayaking and SUP.

★ **Ho'opulapula Haraguchi Rice Mill & Taro Farm Tours**   TOURS

(☑808-651-3399; www.haraguchiricemill.org; tours incl lunch adult/child 5-12yr $70/50; ⊙tours usually 9:45am Wed, by reservation only) 🖋 Learn about cultivating taro on Kaua'i at this sixth-generation family-run nonprofit farm. On farmer-guided tours, which take you out into the *lo'i kalo* (Hawaiian wet taro fields), you'll get a glimpse of the otherwise inaccessible Hanalei National Wildlife Refuge and learn about Hawaii's immigrant history.

🛏 Sleeping & Eating

★ **Hanalei Dolphin Cottages**   COTTAGE $$$

(☑877-465-2824; www.hanaleicottages.com; 5-5016 Kuhio Hwy; 2-bedroom cottages $329; ﹇P﹈﹇🐾﹈﹇🛜﹈) Launch a canoe, kayak or SUP board right from your backyard on the Hanalei River. A lazy walk from the heart of Hanalei town, each of the four cottages is styled similarly, with bamboo furniture, a full kitchen, BBQ grill and private outdoor (and indoor) showers. Cleaning fee $130.

Chicken in a Barrel   BARBECUE $

(☑808-826-1999; www.chickeninabarrel.com; Ching Young Village, 5-5190 Kuhio Hwy; meals $10-17; ⊙11am-8:30pm Mon-Sat, to 7pm Sun; ♿) Using a custom-made 50-gallon barrel drum smoker, this island BBQ joint is all about the bird. Grab a heaping plate of chicken or a hoagie sandwich with chili-cheese fries. It does ribs and pulled pork too. Whichever you choose, you won't have to eat again all day. There are other locations around Kaua'i.

❶ Getting There & Away

There's one road into and out of Hanalei. During heavy rains (common in winter), the Hanalei Bridge occasionally closes due to flooding and those on either side are stuck until it reopens.

If you opted not to rent a car, the **North Shore Shuttle** (☑888-409-2702; https://kauains shuttle.com; $11) links Princeville to Haena State Park, about half a mile from Ke'e Beach and the edge of Na Pali Coast Wilderness State Park.

Po'ipu & South Shore

Po'ipu is the nexus of South Shore tourism... and with good reason. This is one of the sunniest spots on the island – with notably less rain (and less green) than other spots to the north. There are amazing sun-kissed beaches, plenty of top-end resorts and vacation rental condos, plus some of Kaua'i's best restaurants.

While most vacations here center on the beaches and waterborne activities such as surfing, diving, snorkeling, paddle boarding or just beach bumming, the South Shore also has two world-renowned botanical gardens that showcase beautiful collections of endemic species. The undeveloped Maha'ulepu Coast has lithified sand-dune cliffs and pounding surf that make for an unforgettable walk. And in between, you have the lasting remnants of the sugar-plantation area, with friendly art galleries, intimate restaurants and interesting historic perspectives in the cozy centers of Koloa and Kalaheo.

❶ Getting There & Around

Navigating is easy, with just two main roads: Po'ipu Rd (along eastern Po'ipu) and Lawa'i Rd (along western Po'ipu). You'll need a car, scooter or bike to go anywhere here besides the beach. It's possible to walk along the roads, but the vibe is more suburbia than surf town.

The **Kaua'i Bus** (☑808-246-8110; www.kauai. gov/Bus; 3220 Ho'olako St, Lihu'e; one-way fare adult/senior & child 7-18yr $2/1) runs through Koloa into Po'ipu, stopping along Po'ipu Rd at the turnoff to Po'ipu Beach Park and also by the Hyatt.

Understand USA

History

From the arrival of the first people up to 40,000 years ago, to the rise of the United States to number one on the world stage in the 20th century, American life has been anything but dull. War against the British, westward expansion, slavery and its abolishment, Civil War and Reconstruction, the Great Depression, the post-war boom, and more recent conflicts in the 21st century – they've all played a part in shaping the nation's complicated identity.

Turtle Island & Indigenous Peoples

According to oral traditions and sacred myths, indigenous peoples have always lived on the North American continent, which some called Turtle Island. When Europeans arrived, approximately two to 18 million Native American people occupied the turtle's back, north of present-day Mexico, and spoke more than 300 languages.

Among North America's most significant prehistoric cultures were the Mound Builders, who inhabited the Ohio and Mississippi River valleys from around 3500 BC to AD 1400. In Illinois, Cahokia was once a metropolis of 20,000 people, the largest in pre-Columbian North America. Burial or ceremonial mounds from this era rise up throughout the Eastern USA, including several along the Natchez Trace in Mississippi.

In 1502 Italian navigator Amerigo Vespucci used the term Mundus Novus (New World) to describe his discoveries. His reward? In 1507 new maps labeled the western hemisphere 'America.'

In the Southwest, Ancestral Puebloans occupied the Colorado Plateau from around AD 100 to 1300, until warfare, drought and scarcity of resources likely drove them out. You can still see their cliff dwellings at Colorado's Mesa Verde National Park and desert adobe pueblos at New Mexico's Chaco Culture National Historical Park.

The diverse population in the USA also included groups like the Wampanoag in New England, the Hopi and Apache in the Southwest, the Calusa in southern Florida and the Shawnee in Illinois. By the early 19th century, most of these populations were decimated. European colonists introduced diseases to which indigenous peoples had no immunity. More than any other factor – war, slavery or famine – epidemics devastated Native American populations by anywhere from 50% to 90%.

TIMELINE	20,000–40,000 BC	8000 BC	7000 BC–AD 100
	The first peoples to the Americas arrive from Central Asia by migrating over a wide land bridge between Siberia and Alaska (when sea levels were lower than today).	Widespread extinction of ice-age mammals including the woolly mammoth, due to cooperative hunting by humans and a warming climate. Indigenous peoples begin hunting smaller game and gathering native plants.	'Archaic period' marked by nomadic hunter-gatherer lifestyle. By the end of this period, corn, beans and squash (the agricultural 'three sisters') and permanent settlements are well established.

It was the Great Plains cultures – including Crow, Blackfeet, Cheyenne, Comanche and Arapaho – that came to epitomize 'Indians' in the popular American imagination, in part because they put up the longest fight against the USA's westward expansion. Oklahoma is rich in sites that interpret Native American life before Europeans arrived, including the National Hall of Fame for Famous American Indians in Anadarko and Washita Battlefield National Historic Site, where infamous Lt Col George Custer attacked a Cheyenne village.

Oklahoma is also home to Cherokee Heritage Center near Tahlequah. Thousands of Cherokee were forced to march to Oklahoma from their native lands in the Southern USA, after the Indian Removal Act of 1830. More than 4000 are estimated to have died during the long journey, which came to be called the Trail of Tears.

The People: Indians of the American Southwest (1993), by Stephen Trimble, is a diverse account of indigenous history and contemporary culture as related by Native Americans themselves.

Enter the Europeans

In 1492, Christopher Columbus, backed by Spain, voyaged west looking for the East Indies. He found the Bahamas. With visions of gold, Spanish conquistadors quickly followed: Alonso Álvarez de Piñeda mapped what is now the Texas Gulf Coast, Hernando de Soto became the first European to cross the Mississippi and Ponce de León wandered through Florida looking for the fountain of youth. Not to be left out, the French landed in Canada and New England, while the Dutch and English cruised North America's eastern seaboard.

By the 17th century, indigenous North Americans numbered only about a million, and many of the continent's once-thriving societies were in turmoil and transition. In 1607 English noblemen established North America's first permanent European settlement in Jamestown. Earlier settlements had ended badly, and Jamestown almost did, too: the English chose a swamp, planted their crops late and died from disease and starvation. Some despairing colonists ran off to live with the local tribes, who provided the settlement with enough aid to survive.

For Jamestown and America, 1619 proved a pivotal year: the colony established the House of Burgesses, a representative assembly of citizens to decide local laws, and it received its first boatload of 20 African slaves.

The next year was equally momentous, as a group of radically religious Puritans pulled ashore at what would become Plymouth, MA. The Pilgrims were escaping religious persecution under the 'corrupt' Church of England, and in the New World they saw a divine opportunity to create a new society that would be a religious and moral beacon. The Pilgrims signed a 'Mayflower Compact,' one of the seminal texts of American democracy, to govern themselves by consensus.

HISTORY ENTER THE EUROPEANS

1492	1607	1620	1675
Christopher Columbus travels to America, making three voyages throughout the Caribbean. He calls the indigenous people 'Indians,' mistakenly thinking he has reached the Indies.	The English found the first English colony, the Jamestown settlement, on marshland in present-day Virginia. The first few years are hard, with many dying from sickness and starvation.	The *Mayflower* lands at Plymouth with 102 English Pilgrims, who have come to the New World to escape religious persecution. The Wampanoag tribe saves them from starvation.	For decades, the Pilgrims and local tribes live fairly cooperatively, but deadly conflict erupts in 1675. King Philip's War lasts 14 months and kills more than 5000 people (mostly Native Americans).

Capitalism & Colonialism

For the next two centuries, European powers competed for position and territory in the New World, extending European politics into the Americas. As Britain's Royal Navy came to rule Atlantic seas, England increasingly profited from its colonies and eagerly consumed the fruits of their labors – sweet tobacco from Virginia, sugar and coffee from the Caribbean.

Over the 17th and 18th centuries, slavery in America was slowly legalized into a formal institution to support this plantation economy. By 1800, one out of every five persons was a slave.

Meanwhile, Britain mostly left the American colonists to govern themselves. Town meetings and representative assemblies, in which local citizens (that is, white men with property) debated community problems and voted on laws and taxes, became common.

However, by the end of the Seven Years' War in 1763, Britain was feeling the strains of running an empire: it had been fighting France for a century and had colonies scattered all over the world. It was time to clean up bureaucracies and share financial burdens.

The colonies, however, resented English taxes and policies. Public outrage soon culminated in the 1776 Declaration of Independence. With this document, the American colonists took many of the Enlightenment ideas then circulating worldwide – of individualism, equality and freedom; of John Locke's 'natural rights' of life, liberty and property – and fashioned a new type of government to put them into practice.

Frustrations came to a head with the Boston Tea Party in 1773, after which Britain clamped down hard, shutting Boston's harbor and increasing its military presence. In 1774 representatives from 12 colonies convened the First Continental Congress in Philadelphia's Independence Hall to air complaints and prepare for the inevitable war ahead.

Revolution & The Republic

In April 1775 British troops skirmished with armed colonists in Massachusetts, and the Revolutionary War began. George Washington, a wealthy Virginia farmer, was chosen to lead the American army. Trouble was, Washington lacked gunpowder and money (the colonists resisted taxes even for their own military), and his troops were a motley collection of poorly armed farmers, hunters and merchants, who regularly quit and returned to their communities due to lack of pay. On the other side, the British 'Redcoats' represented the world's most powerful military. The inexperienced General Washington had to improvise constantly, sometimes wisely retreating, sometimes engaging in 'ungentlemanly' sneak attacks. During the winter of 1777–78, the American army nearly starved at Valley Forge.

Native American Sights

Serpent Mound (OH)

National Museum of the American Indian (Washington, DC)

Trail of Tears (Southeastern USA)

Mashpee Wampanoag Indian Museum (MA)

Emerald Mound (MI)

Museum of the Cherokee Indian (NC)

Cahokia Mounds (IL)

1756–63	1773	1775	1776
In the Seven Years' War (or the 'French and Indian War'), France loses to England and withdraws from Canada. Britain now controls most territory east of the Mississippi River.	To protest a British tax on tea, Bostonians dress as Mohawks, board East India Company ships and toss their tea overboard during what would be named the Boston Tea Party.	Paul Revere rides from Boston to warn colonial 'Minutemen' that the British are coming. The next day, 'the shot heard round the world' is fired at Lexington, starting the Revolutionary War.	On July 4, the colonies sign the Declaration of Independence. Famous figures who helped create this document include John Hancock, Samuel Adams, John Adams, Benjamin Franklin and Thomas Jefferson.

Meanwhile, the Second Continental Congress tried to articulate what exactly they were fighting for. In January 1776 Thomas Paine published the wildly popular *Common Sense,* which passionately argued for independence from England. Soon, independence seemed not just logical, but noble and necessary, and on July 4, 1776, the Declaration of Independence was finalized and signed. Largely written by Thomas Jefferson, it elevated the 13 colonies' particular gripes against the monarchy into a universal declaration of individual rights and republican government.

However, to succeed on the battlefield, General Washington needed help, not just patriotic sentiment. In 1778 Benjamin Franklin persuaded France (always eager to trouble England) to ally with the revolutionaries, and they provided the troops, material and sea power that helped win the war. The British surrendered at Yorktown, VA, in 1781, and two years later the Treaty of Paris formally recognized the 'United States of America.'

At first, the nation's loose confederation of fractious, squabbling states was hardly 'united.' So the founders gathered again in Philadelphia, and in 1787 drafted a new-and-improved Constitution: the US government was given a stronger federal center, with checks and balances between its three major branches; and to guard against the abuse of centralized power, a citizen's Bill of Rights was approved in 1791.

With the Constitution, the scope of the American Revolution solidified to a radical change in government, and the preservation of the economic and social status quo. Rich landholders kept their property, which included their slaves; Native Americans were excluded from the nation; and women were excluded from politics. These blatant discrepancies and injustices, which were widely noted, were the results of both pragmatic compromise (eg to get slave-dependent Southern states to agree) and also widespread belief in the essential rightness of things as they were.

Westward, Ho!

As the 19th century dawned on the young nation, optimism was the mood of the day. With the invention of the cotton gin in 1793 – followed by threshers, reapers, mowers and later combines – agriculture was industrialized, and US commerce surged. The 1803 Louisiana Purchase doubled US territory, and expansion west of the Appalachian Mountains began in earnest.

Relations between the US and Britain – despite lively trade – remained tense, and in 1812 the US declared war on England again. The two-year conflict ended without much gain by either side, although the British abandoned their forts, and the US vowed to avoid Europe's 'entangling alliances.'

For 100-plus years, Tecumseh's Curse loomed over presidents elected in a year ending in zero (every 20 years). Tecumseh was a Shawnee warrior whom president-to-be William Henry Harrison battled in 1811. Tecumseh hexed him as revenge. Harrison became president in 1840, but died a month later. Lincoln and Kennedy were also purported to be victims.

1787	1791	1803	1804–06
The Constitutional Convention in Philadelphia draws up the US Constitution. Power is balanced between the presidency, Congress and judiciary.	Bill of Rights adopted as constitutional amendments outlining citizens' rights, including free speech, assembly, religion and the press; the right to bear arms; and prohibition of 'cruel and unusual punishments.'	France's Napoleon sells the Louisiana Territory to the US for just $15 million, thereby extending the boundaries of the new nation from the Mississippi River to the Rocky Mountains.	President Thomas Jefferson sends Meriwether Lewis and William Clark west. Guided by the Shoshone tribeswoman Sacagawea, they trailblaze from St Louis, MO, to the Pacific Ocean and back.

In the 1830s and 1840s, with growing nationalist fervor and dreams of continental expansion, many Americans came to believe it was 'Manifest Destiny' that all the land should be theirs. The 1830 Indian Removal Act aimed to clear one obstacle, while the building of the railroads cleared another hurdle, linking Midwestern farmers with East Coast markets.

In 1836 a group of Texans fomented a revolution against Mexico. (Remember the Alamo?) Ten years later, the US annexed the Texas Republic, and when Mexico resisted, the US waged war for it – and while they were at it, took California, too. In 1848 Mexico was soundly defeated and ceded this territory to the US. This completed the USA's continental expansion.

By a remarkable coincidence, only days after the 1848 treaty with Mexico was signed, gold was discovered in California. By 1849 surging rivers of wagon trains were creaking west filled with miners, pioneers, entrepreneurs, immigrants, outlaws and prostitutes, all seeking their fortunes. This made for exciting, legendary times, but throughout loomed a troubling question: as new states joined the USA, would they be slave states or free states? The nation's future depended on the answer.

The Civil War

The US Constitution hadn't ended slavery, but it had given Congress the power to approve (or not) slavery in new states. Public debates raged constantly over the expansion of slavery, particularly since this shaped the balance of power between the industrial North and the agrarian South.

Since the founding, Southern politicians had dominated government and defended slavery as 'natural and normal,' which an 1856 *New York Times* editorial called 'insanity.' The Southern proslavery lobby enraged Northern abolitionists. But even many Northern politicians feared that ending slavery would be ruinous. Limit slavery, they reasoned, and in the competition with industry and free labor, slavery would wither without inciting a violent slave revolt – a constantly feared possibility. Indeed, in 1859 radical abolitionist John Brown tried unsuccessfully to spark just that at Harpers Ferry.

The economics of slavery were undeniable. In 1860 there were more than four million slaves in the US, most held by Southern planters – who grew 75% of the world's cotton, accounting for more than half of US exports. Thus, the Southern economy supported the nation's economy, and it required slaves. The 1860 presidential election became a referendum on this issue, and the election was won by a young politician who favored limiting slavery: Abraham Lincoln.

In the South, even the threat of federal limits was too onerous to abide, and as President Lincoln took office, 11 states eventually seceded from the union and formed the Confederate States of America. Lincoln faced the nation's greatest moment of crisis. He had two choices: let the

In 1835, Andrew Jackson became the first US president on whom an assassination attempt was made. Fortunately for Jackson, Richard Lawrence's two pistols both misfired. Jackson beat Lawrence with his cane in retaliation, until the would-be assassin was wrestled away by aides (including Davy Crockett).

James McPherson is a preeminent Civil War historian, and his Pulitzer Prize–winning *Battle Cry of Freedom* (1988) somehow gets the whole heartbreaking saga between two covers.

Southern states secede and dissolve the union or wage war to keep the union intact. He chose the latter, and war soon erupted.

It began in April 1861, when the Confederacy attacked Fort Sumter in Charleston, SC, and raged on for the next four years – in the most gruesome combat the world had ever known until that time. By the end, as many as 750,000 soldiers, nearly an entire generation of young men, were dead; Southern plantations and cities (most notably Atlanta) lay sacked and burned. The North's industrial might provided an advantage, but its victory was not preordained; it unfolded battle by bloody battle.

As fighting progressed, Lincoln recognized that if the war didn't end slavery outright, victory would be pointless. In 1863 his Emancipation Proclamation expanded the war's aims and freed all slaves in the seceded states. In April 1865, Confederate General Robert E Lee surrendered to Union General Ulysses S Grant in Appomattox, VA. The Union had been preserved, but at a staggering cost. The Thirteenth Amendment to the constitution was ratified in December 1865, abolishing slavery nationwide.

Great Depression, the New Deal & World War II

In October 1929 investors, worried about a gloomy global economy, started selling stocks, and seeing the selling, everyone panicked until they had sold everything. The stock market crashed, and the US economy collapsed like a house of cards.

Thus began the Great Depression. Frightened banks called in their dodgy loans, people couldn't pay, and the banks folded. Millions lost their homes, farms, businesses and savings, and as much as 25% of the American workforce became unemployed. The droughts of the Dust Bowl further exacerbated problems, prompting the largest migration in American history as three million people moved out of the Great Plains states toward California in search of work.

In 1932 Democrat Franklin D Roosevelt was elected president on the promise of a 'New Deal' to rescue the US from its crisis, which he did with resounding success. When war once again broke out in Europe in 1939, the isolationist mood in America was as strong as ever. However, the extremely popular President Roosevelt, elected to an unprecedented third term in 1940, understood that the US couldn't sit by and allow victory for fascist, totalitarian regimes. Roosevelt sent aid to Britain and persuaded a skittish Congress to go along with it.

Then, on December 7, 1941, Japan launched a surprise attack on Hawaii's Pearl Harbor, killing more than 2000 Americans and sinking several battleships. As US isolationism transformed overnight into outrage, Roosevelt suddenly had the support he needed. Germany also declared war on the US, and America joined the Allied fight against Hitler and the

Authoritative and sobering, *Bury My Heart at Wounded Knee* (1970), by Dee Brown, tells the story of the late 19th-century Indian Wars from the perspective of Native Americans.

1870	1880–1920	1882	1896
Freed black men are given the right to vote, but the South's segregationist 'Jim Crow' laws (which remain until the 1960s) effectively disenfranchise black people from every meaningful sphere of daily life.	Millions of immigrants flood in from Europe and Asia, fueling the age of cities. New York, Chicago and Philadelphia swell in size, becoming global centers of industry and commerce.	Racist sentiment, particularly in California (where more than 50,000 Chinese immigrants have arrived since 1848) leads to the Chinese Exclusion Act, the only US immigration law to exclude a specific race.	In *Plessy v Ferguson*, the US Supreme Court rules that 'separate but equal' public facilities for blacks and whites are legal, arguing that the Constitution addresses only political, not social, equality.

Axis powers. From that moment, the country put almost its entire will and industrial prowess into the war effort.

Initially, neither the Pacific nor European theaters went well for the US. In the Pacific, fighting didn't turn around until the US unexpectedly routed the Japanese navy at Midway Island in June 1942. Afterwards, the US drove Japan back with a series of brutal battles recapturing Pacific islands.

In Europe, the US dealt the fatal blow to Germany with its massive D-Day invasion of France on June 6, 1944: unable to sustain a two-front war (the Soviet Union was savagely fighting on the eastern front), Germany surrendered in May 1945.

Nevertheless, Japan continued fighting. Newly elected President Harry Truman – ostensibly worried that a US invasion of Japan would lead to unprecedented carnage – chose to drop experimental atomic bombs on Hiroshima and Nagasaki in August 1945. Created by the government's top-secret Manhattan Project, the bombs devastated both cities, killing more than 200,000 people. Japan surrendered days later. The nuclear age was born.

You can follow the Lewis and Clark expedition on its extraordinary journey west to the Pacific and back again online at www.pbs.org/lewisandclark, which features historical maps, photo albums and journal excerpts.

The Red Scare, Civil Rights & the Wars in Asia

The US enjoyed unprecedented prosperity in the decades after WWII, but little peace.

Formerly wartime allies, the communist Soviet Union and the capitalist USA soon engaged in a running competition to dominate the globe. The superpowers engaged in proxy wars – notably the Korean War (1950–53) and Vietnam War (1954–75) – with only the mutual threat of nuclear annihilation preventing direct war. Founded in 1945, the UN couldn't overcome this worldwide ideological split and was largely ineffectual in preventing Cold War conflicts.

Meanwhile, with its continent unscarred and its industry bulked up by WWII, the American homeland entered an era of growing affluence. In the 1950s, a mass migration left the inner cities for the suburbs, where affordable single-family homes sprang up. Americans drove cheap cars using cheap gas over brand-new interstate highways. They relaxed with the comforts of modern technology, secured low-interest housing loans and free education through programs like the GI Bill, and got busy, giving birth to a 'baby boom.'

Middle-class whites did, anyway. Structural racism nationwide and Jim Crow laws in the South prevented African Americans from having the same opportunities. Echoing 19th-century abolitionist Frederick Douglass, the Southern Christian Leadership Coalition (SCLC), led by African American preacher Martin Luther King Jr, aimed to end segregation and

1898	1906	1908	1914
Victory in the Spanish-American War gives US control of the Philippines, Puerto Rico and Guam, and indirect control of Cuba. But the Philippines' bloody war for independence deters future US colonialism.	Upton Sinclair publishes *The Jungle*, an exposé of Chicago's unsavory meatpacking industry. Many workers suffer through poverty and dangerous, even deadly, conditions in choking factories and sweatshops.	The first Model T (aka 'Tin Lizzie') car is built in Detroit, MI. Assembly-line innovator Henry Ford is soon selling one million automobiles annually.	US wins the right to build and run the Panama Canal, linking the Atlantic and Pacific Oceans, by inciting a Panamanian revolt over independence from Colombia.

THE AFRICAN AMERICAN EXPERIENCE: THE STRUGGLE FOR EQUALITY

It's impossible to properly grasp American history without taking into account the great struggles and hard-won victories of African Americans who come from all spheres of life.

Slavery

From the early 17th century until the 19th century, an estimated 600,000 enslaved people were brought from Africa to the US. Those who survived the horrific transport on crowded ships (which sometimes had 50% mortality rates) were sold in slave markets (African men cost $27 in 1638). The majority ended up on Southern plantations where whipping, branding and family separation were commonplace.

Free at Last

While some revisionist historians describe the Civil War as being about states' rights, the war was really over slavery. Following the Union victory at Antietam, Lincoln drafted the Emancipation Proclamation, which freed all enslaved people in Confederate territories. African Americans joined the Union effort, with more than 180,000 serving by war's end.

Jim Crow Laws

During Reconstruction (1865–77) federal laws provided civil rights protection for newly freed blacks. Southern bitterness, however, coupled with centuries of prejudice, fueled a backlash. By the 1890s, Jim Crow laws (named after a derogatory character in a minstrel show) appeared. African Americans were effectively disenfranchised, and America continued to practice racial violence against blacks.

Civil Rights Movement

Beginning in the 1950s, a movement grew in African American communities to fight for equality. Rosa Parks, who refused to give up her seat to a white passenger, inspired the Montgomery bus boycott. There were sit-ins at segregated lunch counters; massive demonstrations led by Martin Luther King Jr in Washington, DC; and harrowing journeys by 'freedom riders' that aimed to end bus segregation. The work of millions paid off: in 1964 President Johnson signed the Civil Rights Act, which banned discrimination and racial segregation, followed by the 1965 Voting Rights Act.

Black Lives Matter

In the 21st century, a new black rights movement was born. Spurred by the 2013 acquittal of George Zimmerman after he shot and killed 17-year-old Trayvon Martin, activists Patrisse Cullors, Opal Tometi and Alicia Garza started a hashtag, #blacklivesmatter, to draw attention to the many ways in which racism harms the black community. The movement grew as the women encouraged social-media users to share their own stories, piecing together incidents across the country to create a convincing, devastating portrait of structural racism.

1917	1920s	1941–45	1948–51
President Woodrow Wilson enters US into WWI. The US mobilizes 4.7 million troops, and suffers around 116,000 of the war's 11 million military deaths.	Spurred by African American migration to northern cities, the Harlem Renaissance inspires an intellectual flowering of literature, art and music. Important figures include WEB Du Bois and Langston Hughes.	WWII: America deploys 16 million troops and suffers 400,000 deaths. Overall, civilian deaths outpace military deaths two to one, and total 50 to 70 million people from over 50 countries.	The US-led Marshall Plan funnels $12 billion in material and financial aid to help Europe recover from WWII. The plan also aims to contain Soviet influence and reignite America's economy.

'save America's soul': to realize colorblind justice, racial equality and economic opportunity for all.

Beginning in the 1950s, King preached and organized nonviolent resistance in the form of bus boycotts, marches and sit-ins, mainly in the South. White authorities often met these protests with water hoses and batons, and demonstrations sometimes dissolved into riots, but with the 1964 Civil Rights Act, African Americans spurred a wave of legislation that swept away racist laws and laid the groundwork for a more just and equal society.

Meanwhile, the 1960s saw further social upheavals: rock and roll spawned a youth rebellion, and the 1967 Summer of Love in San Francisco's Haight-Ashbury neighborhood catapulted hippie culture into mainstream America.

President John F Kennedy was assassinated in Dallas in 1963, followed by the assassinations in 1968 of his brother, Senator Robert Kennedy, and of Martin Luther King Jr. Americans' faith in their leaders and government was further shocked by the bombings and brutalities of the Vietnam War, as seen on TV, which led to widespread student protests.

Yet President Richard Nixon, elected in 1968 partly for promising an 'honorable end to the war,' instead escalated US involvement and secretly bombed Laos and Cambodia. Then, in 1972, the Watergate scandal broke: a burglary at Democratic Party offices was, through dogged journalism, tied to 'Tricky Dick,' who, in 1974, became the first US president to resign from office.

The tumultuous 1960s and '70s also witnessed the sexual revolution, women's liberation, struggles for gay rights, energy crises over the supply of crude oil from the Middle East and, with the 1962 publication of Rachel Carson's *Silent Spring,* the realization that the USA's industries had created a polluted, diseased environmental mess.

> *Hidden Figures,* a biopic about three real-life mathematicians – Katherine Johnson, Dorothy Vaughn and Mary Jackson – whose talents were integral to the NASA space launch despite the limitations placed on them as black women in the 1960s, was Fox's second-highest-grossing movie of 2016 and earned three Oscar nominations.

Reagan, Clinton & Bush

In 1980 Republican California governor and former actor Ronald Reagan campaigned for president by promising to make Americans feel good about America again. The affable Reagan won easily, and his election marked a pronounced shift to the right in US politics.

Reagan wanted to defeat communism, restore the economy, deregulate business and cut taxes. To tackle the first two, he launched the biggest peacetime military buildup in history, and dared the Soviets to keep up. They went broke trying, and the USSR collapsed.

Military spending and tax cuts created enormous federal deficits, which hampered the presidency of Reagan's successor, George HW Bush. Despite winning the Gulf War – liberating Kuwait in 1991 after an Iraqi invasion – Bush was soundly defeated in the 1992 presidential election by Southern Democrat Bill Clinton. Clinton had the good fortune to

1963	1964	1965–75	1969
On November 22, President John F Kennedy is publicly assassinated by Lee Harvey Oswald while riding in a motorcade in Dallas, TX.	Congress passes the Civil Rights Act, outlawing discrimination on basis of race, color, religion, sex or national origin. First proposed by Kennedy, it was one of President Johnson's crowning achievements.	US involvement in the Vietnam War tears the nation apart as 58,000 Americans die, along with four million Vietnamese and 1.5 million Laotians and Cambodians.	American astronauts land on the moon, fulfilling President Kennedy's unlikely 1961 promise to accomplish this feat within a decade and culminating in the 'space race' between the US and USSR.

catch the Silicon Valley–led high-tech internet boom of the 1990s, which seemed to augur a 'new economy' based on white-collar telecommunications. The US economy erased its deficits and ran a surplus, and Clinton presided over one of America's longest economic booms.

In 2000 and 2004, George W Bush, the eldest son of George HW Bush, won the presidential elections so narrowly that the divided results seemed to epitomize an increasingly divided nation. 'Dubya' had the misfortune of being president when the high-tech bubble burst in 2000, but he nevertheless enacted tax cuts that returned federal deficits even greater than before. He also championed the right-wing conservative 'backlash' that had been building since Reagan.

On September 11, 2001, Islamic terrorists flew hijacked planes into New York's World Trade Center and the Pentagon in Washington, DC. This catastrophic attack united Americans behind their president as he vowed revenge and declared a 'war on terror.' Bush soon attacked Afghanistan in an unsuccessful hunt for Al-Qaeda terrorist cells, then he attacked Iraq in 2003 and toppled its anti-US dictator, Saddam Hussein. Meanwhile, Iraq descended into civil war.

Following scandals and failures – torture photos from Abu Ghraib, the federal response in the aftermath of Hurricane Katrina and the inability to bring the Iraq War to a close – Bush's approval ratings reached historic lows in the second half of his presidency.

> In *The Souls of Black Folk* (1903), WEB Du Bois, who helped found the National Association for the Advancement of Colored People (NAACP), eloquently describes the racial dilemmas of politics and culture facing early 20th-century America.

The Obama Presidency

In 2008, hungry for change, Americans elected political newcomer Barack Obama, America's first African American president. He had his work cut out for him. These were, after all, unprecedented times economically, with the US in the largest financial crisis since the Great Depression. What started as a collapse of the US housing bubble in 2007 spread to the banking sector, with the meltdown of major financial institutions. The shock wave quickly spread across the globe, and by 2008 many industrialized nations were experiencing a recession.

Wars in Afghanistan and Iraq, launched a decade prior, continued to simmer on the back burner of the ever-changing news cycle until 2011, when, in a subterfuge operation vetted by President Obama, Navy Seals raided Osama bin Laden's Pakistan hideout and killed the Al-Qaeda leader, bringing an end to the search for America's greatest public enemy.

The economy remained in bad shape, however, and the ambitious $800-billion stimulus package passed by Congress in 2009 hadn't borne much fruit in the eyes of many Americans – even though economists estimated that the stimulus did soften the blow of the recession.

With lost jobs, overvalued mortgages and little relief in sight, millions of Americans found themselves adrift. High federal spending and government

> If history is a partisan affair, Howard Zinn makes his allegiance clear in *A People's History of the United States* (1980 and 2005), which tells the often-overlooked stories of laborers, minorities, immigrants, women and radicals.

1969	1973	1989	1990s
When NYC police raid a gay bar, the Stonewall Inn, patrons fight back. Three days of resulting riots spark the gay rights movement.	In *Roe v Wade*, the Supreme Court legalizes abortion. Today this decision remains controversial and divisive, pitting 'right to choose' advocates against the 'right to life' anti-abortion lobby.	The 1960s-era Berlin Wall is torn down, marking the end of the Cold War between the US and the USSR (now Russia). The USA becomes the world's last remaining superpower.	The World Wide Web debuts in 1991. Silicon Valley, CA, leads a high-tech internet revolution, remaking communications and media, and overvalued tech stocks drive the massive boom (and subsequent bust).

bailouts (of the banking and auto industries) to combat the recession were controversial efforts, and flat wages contributed to the problem. People were upset and gathered in large numbers to voice their anger. On the left, this expressed itself as the Occupy Wall Street movement, which called out banks and corporations as having too much influence over the democratic process. On the right, it manifested as the Tea Party, a wing of politically conservative Republicans who believed that government handouts would destroy the economy and, thus, America. Republicans also doubted Obama's landmark 2010 health-care reform (derisively named 'Obamacare').

Obamacare was a major victory for the president. It brought health-care coverage to more Americans, lowered costs and closed loopholes that allowed insurance companies to deny coverage to individuals based

FIGHTING FOR CHANGE: FIVE WHO SHAPED HISTORY

American history is littered with larger-than-life figures who brought dramatic change through bold deeds, sometimes at great personal cost. While presidents tend to garner all the attention, there are countless lesser-known visionaries who have made enormous contributions to civic life.

Rachel Carson (1907–64) An eloquent writer with a keen scientific mind, Carson helped spawn the environmental movement. Her pioneering work *Silent Spring* illustrated the ecological catastrophe unleashed by pesticides and unregulated industry. The ensuing grassroots movement spurred the creation of the Environmental Protection Agency.

Cesar Chavez (1927–93) A second-generation Mexican American who grew up in farm labor camps (where entire families labored for $1 a day), Chavez was a charismatic and inspiring figure – Gandhi and Martin Luther King Jr were among his role models. He gave hope, dignity and a brighter future to thousands of poor migrants by creating the United Farm Workers.

Harvey Milk (1930–78) California's first openly gay public servant was a tireless advocate in the fight against discrimination, encouraging gays and lesbians to 'come out, stand up and let the world know… Only that way will we start to achieve our rights.' Milk, along with San Francisco mayor George Moscone, was assassinated in 1978.

Betty Friedan (1921–2006) Founder of the National Organization for Women (NOW), Friedan was instrumental in leading the feminist movement of the 1960s. Friedan's groundbreaking book *The Feminine Mystique* inspired millions of women to envision a life beyond being a mere 'homemaker.'

Ralph Nader (b 1934) The frequent presidential contender (in 2008, Nader received 738,000 votes) is one of America's staunchest consumer watchdogs. The Harvard-trained lawyer has played a major role in ensuring Americans have safer cars, cheaper medicines and cleaner air and water.

2001	2003	2005	2008–09
On September 11, Al-Qaeda terrorists hijack four commercial airplanes, flying two into NYC's twin towers, and one into the Pentagon (the fourth crashes in Pennsylvania); nearly 3000 people are killed.	After citing evidence that Iraq possesses weapons of mass destruction, President George W Bush launches a preemptive war that will cost more than 4000 American lives and some $3 trillion.	On August 29, Hurricane Katrina hits the Mississippi and Louisiana coasts, rupturing poorly maintained levees and flooding New Orleans. More than 1800 people die, and cost estimates exceed $110 billion.	Barack Obama becomes the first African American president. The stock market crashes due to mismanagement by major American financial institutions. The crisis spreads worldwide.

on preexisting conditions. Yet, when Obama returned to the White House in 2013 for his second term, he did so without the same hope and optimism that once surrounded him. Times had changed, and America, like much of the world, had struggled through tough years since the global economic crisis erupted in 2007.

Obama did manage to get unemployment rates back under 5% by 2016, but he had mixed success spurring the sluggish economy. As his presidency came to a close, he turned his focus to liberal and globally minded causes that stoked resentment on the populist right, including climate change, environmental protections, LGBT+ rights and the negotiation of rapprochements with Iran and Cuba. By the time Obama left office, America was a starkly divided nation of those who believed strongly in his progressive ideals, and others who felt increasingly left behind by the global economy.

The 2016 Election & the Trump Presidency

When Donald J Trump, real-estate magnate and former host of TV reality game show *The Apprentice*, announced he was running for president in June 2015, many around the world thought it was a publicity stunt. What ensued could be described as a media circus: coverage of the campaign, which pitted Trump, with no prior political experience, against Hillary Clinton, former Secretary of State (2009–13) and First Lady, was relentless.

In his victory speech, Trump declared 'I will be president for all Americans,' though many are unsure that they are included in his definition of what an American is. Uncertainty, in fact, seems to be the defining quality of the Trump presidency. Scandal and controversy have surrounded the administration in its first term, during which the nation's democratic integrity has been challenged by conflicts of interest between public office and private enterprise. Public protest has become a key feature of the sociopolitical landscape, starting with the Women's March the day after the inauguration, the largest single-day demonstration in recorded US history with an estimated four million participants in some 653 cities around the country. The release of the Mueller Report in 2019, which summarized the findings of a two-year investigation of Trump's connections to Russia, only muddied the waters; lacking a firm conclusion and heavily redacted, the ambiguity of the report allowed both the left and the right to argue that it supports their case. Also in 2019, the New York Times released 10 years of Trump's tax documents, showing that his businesses lost nearly $1 billion between 1985 and 1994.

Despite Trump's controversies and low approval ratings, the outcome of the 2020 election is far from certain; as of this writing, a crowded field of Democrats, including former vice president Joe Biden and senators Bernie Sanders and Elizabeth Warren, are vying for the nomination.

Suspicious of political factoids? Factcheck.org is a nonpartisan, self-described 'consumer advocate' that monitors the accuracy of statements made by US politicians during debates, speeches, interviews and in campaign ads. It's a great resource for separating truth from bombast and is particularly handy during election cycles.

2013	2015	2018	2019
Scandal erupts when former National Security Agency contractor Edward Snowden leaks classified information about an intelligence program that monitors communication between American citizens and its allies.	In a historic decision, the US Supreme Court legalizes same-sex marriage, giving gay couples in all 50 states the right to marry.	A former student kills 17 and wounds 17 others with a semi-automatic rifle at a high school in Parkland, Florida. Many survivors become gun control advocates, launching an influential youth movement.	Several states – including Alabama, Ohio, Georgia and Arkansas – pass extremely restrictive abortion laws, challenging *Roe v Wade* in the hope that the conservative-led Supreme Court will overturn it.

The Way of Life

One of the world's great melting pots, America boasts an astonishing variety of cultures and creeds. The country's diversity was shaped by its rich history of immigration, though today regional differences (East Coast, South, West Coast and Great Lakes) play an equally prominent role in defining American identity. Religion, sport, politics and, of course, socio-economic backgrounds are also pivotal in creating the complicated American portrait.

Multiculturalism

America has long been called a 'melting pot,' which presumes that new-comers came and blended into the existing American fabric. The country hasn't let go of that sentiment completely. On one hand, diversity is celebrated (Cinco de Mayo, Martin Luther King Jr Day and Chinese New Year all get their due), but on the other hand, many Americans are comfortable with the status quo.

Immigration is at the crux of the matter. Immigrants currently make up around 14% of the population. Nearly 1.4 million foreign-born individuals move to the US legally each year, with the majority from India, China and Mexico. Another 10.7 million or so are in the country illegally. This is the issue that makes Americans edgy, especially as it gets politicized.

'Immigration reform' has been a Washington buzzword for nearly two decades. Some people believe the nation's current system deals with illegal immigrants too leniently – that higher walls should be built on the border, immigrants who are in the country unlawfully should be deported and employers who hire them should be fined. Other Americans think those rules are too harsh – that immigrants who have been here for years working, contributing to society and abiding by the law deserve amnesty. Perhaps they could pay a fine and fill out the paperwork to become citizens while continuing to live here with their families. Despite several attempts, Congress has not been able to pass a comprehensive package addressing illegal immigration, though it has put through various measures to beef up enforcement. The issue of immigration, legal or otherwise, has become a recurring battleground during the presidency of Donald Trump.

> The US holds the world's second-largest Spanish-speaking population, behind Mexico and just ahead of Spain. Latinx people are also the fastest-growing minority group in the nation.

Politics has a lot to do with Americans' multicultural tolerance. When asked if immigration strengthens the nation, most Americans (62%) said yes, according to a 2019 survey by the Pew Research Center. But when these responses were parsed by political party, there was a divide. While more than 80% of Democrats and Democratic-leaning independents responded that immigration strengthened the nation, only 49% of Republicans did.

Many people point to the election of President Barack Obama as proof of America's multicultural achievements. It's not just his personal story that stands out (white mother, black father, Muslim name, time spent living among the diverse cultures of Hawaii, Indonesia and Chicago, among others), or that he was the first African American to hold the nation's highest office (in a country where as recently as the 1960s African Americans couldn't even vote in certain regions). It's that Americans of all races and creeds voted overwhelmingly to elect the self-described 'mutt' and embrace his message of diversity and change.

Religion

When the Pilgrims (early settlers to the US who fled their European homeland to escape religious persecution) came ashore, they were adamant that their new country would be one of religious tolerance. They valued the freedom to practice religion so highly they refused to make their Protestant faith official state policy. What's more, they forbade the government from doing anything that might sanction one religion or belief over another. Separation of church and state became the law of the land.

Today Protestants are on the verge of becoming a minority in the country they founded. According to a 2014 study by the Pew Research Center, Protestant numbers have declined steadily to under 50%. Meanwhile, other faiths have held their own or seen their numbers increase.

The country is also in a period of exceptional religious fluidity. Forty-four percent of American adults have left the denomination of their childhood for another denomination, another faith or no faith at all, according to Pew. A unique era of 'religion shopping' has been ushered in. As for the geographic breakdown: the USA's most Catholic region is shifting from the Northeast to the Southwest; the South is the most evangelical; and the West is the most unaffiliated.

All that said, America's biggest schism isn't between religions or even between faith and skepticism. It's between fundamentalist and progressive interpretations within each faith. Most Americans don't care much if you're Catholic, Episcopalian, Buddhist or atheist. What they do care about are your views on abortion, contraception, LGBT+ rights, stem-cell research, teaching of evolution, school prayer and government displays of religious icons. The country's Religious Right (the oft-used term for evangelical Christians) has pushed these issues onto center stage, and the group has been effective at using politics to codify its conservative beliefs into law. This effort has prompted a slew of court cases, testing the nation's principles on separation of church and state. The split remains one of America's biggest culture wars, and it almost always plays a role in politics, especially during elections.

> Americans are increasingly defining their spiritual beliefs outside of organized religion. The proportion of those who say they have 'no religion' is now around 23%. Some in this catch-all category disavow religion altogether (around 7%), but the majority sustain spiritual beliefs that simply fall outside the box.

THE WAY OF LIFE RELIGION

Lifestyle

The USA has one of the world's highest standards of living. The median household income in 2018 was around $62,000, though it varies by region (with higher earnings in the Mid-Atlantic, Northeast and West and lower earnings in the South). Wages also vary by ethnicity, with African Americans and Latinxs earning less than whites and Asians ($40,232 and $50,486 respectively, versus $65,273 and $81,331 as of 2017). Likewise the

KNOW YOUR GENERATIONS

American culture is often stratified by age groups. Here's a quick rundown to help you tell Generation X from Z, and then some.

Baby Boomers Those born from 1946 to 1964. After American soldiers came home from WWII, the birthrate exploded (hence the term 'baby boom'). Youthful experimentation, self-expression and social activism was often followed by midlife affluence.

Generation X Those born between 1965 and the early 1980s. Characterized by their rejection of Baby Boomer values, skepticism and alienation.

Millennials Those born from the early 1980s to the late 1990s. Weaned on iPods, instant messaging and social networking, they are the largest living generation in the US.

Generation Z Those born in the 2000s. These kids and young adults have never known a world without the internet and often interact more on social media than face to face.

wage gap between men and women continues to persist, with women earning roughly 80% of what men earn.

About 90% of Americans are high-school graduates, while some 35% go on to graduate from college with a four-year bachelor's degree.

More often than not there are two married parents in an American household, and both of them work. Single parents head 25% of households. According to the Bureau of Labor Statistics, the average adult works 42 hours per week. Divorce is common – some 40% of first marriages go kaput – but both divorce and marriage rates have declined over the last three decades. Despite the high divorce rate, Americans spend more than $55 billion annually on weddings. The average number of children in an American family is two.

While many Americans hit the gym or walk, bike or jog regularly, 47% don't get the amount of daily activity recommended by the Centers for Disease Control and Prevention (CDC). Health researchers speculate this lack of exercise and Americans' fondness for sugary and fatty foods have led to rising obesity and diabetes rates. More than two-thirds of Americans are overweight, with one-third considered obese, the CDC says.

About 25% of Americans volunteer their time to help others or help a cause. This is truer in the Great Lakes states, followed by the West, South and Northeast, according to the Corporation for National and Community Service. Eco-consciousness has entered the mainstream: most big chain grocery stores – including Walmart – now sell organic foods, and many cities are pushing to go 'zero waste.' Still, only 34% of waste generated in the US is recycled, according to the Environmental Protection Agency.

Americans tend to travel close to home. As of 2018, 42% of Americans have passports, so most people take vacations within the 50 states, and America's reputation as the 'no-vacation nation,' with many workers having only five to 10 paid annual vacation days, contributes to this stay-at-home scenario. That said, 41.7 million US citizens traveled outside of North America in 2018, a 9% increase over 2017. According to the US Department of Commerce's Office of Travel and Tourism Industries, Mexico and Canada are the top countries for international getaways, followed by the UK, Dominican Republic, France, Italy and Germany.

Sports

What really draws Americans together, sometimes slathered in blue body paint or with foam-rubber cheese wedges on their heads, is sports. It provides a social glue, so whether a person is conservative or liberal, married or single, Mormon or pagan, chances are come Monday at the office they'll be chatting about the weekend performance of their favorite team.

The fun and games go on all year long. In spring and summer there's baseball nearly every day. In fall and winter a weekend or Monday night

NPR radio host Terry Gross interviews Americans from all walks of life, from rock stars to environmental activists to nuclear scientists. Listen online at www.npr.org/freshair.

STATES & TRAITS

Some regional US stereotypes have solid data behind them, thanks to a 2008 study titled *The Geography of Personality*. Researchers processed more than a half-million personality assessments collected from individual US citizens, then looked at where certain traits stacked up on the map. Turns out 'Minnesota nice' is for real – the most 'agreeable' states cluster in the Great Lakes, Great Plains and South. The most neurotic states? They line up in the Northeast. But New York didn't place number one, as you might expect; that honor goes to West Virginia. Many of the most 'open' states lie out West. California, Nevada, Oregon and Washington all rate high for being receptive to new ideas, although they lag behind Washington, DC, and New York. The most dutiful and self-disciplined states sit in the Great Plains and Southwest, led by New Mexico. Go figure.

doesn't feel right without a football game on, and through the long days and nights of winter there's plenty of basketball to keep the adrenaline going. Those are the big three sports. Auto racing has revved up interest in recent years. Major League Soccer (MLS) is attracting an ever-increasing following. And ice hockey, once favored only in northern climes, is popular nationwide – the LA Kings are two-time Stanley Cup winners while teams from sun-soaked Nashville, Tampa Bay and Vegas have made it to the finals.

Baseball

Baseball may not command the same TV viewership (and subsequent advertising dollars) as football, but with 162 games over a season versus 16 for football, its ubiquity allows it to maintain its status as America's pastime.

Besides, baseball isn't about seeing it on TV, it's all about the live version: being at the ballpark on a sunny day, sitting in the bleachers with a beer and hot dog, and indulging in the seventh-inning stretch, when the entire park erupts in a communal singalong of 'Take Me Out to the Ballgame.' The playoffs, held every October, still deliver excitement and unexpected champions. The New York Yankees, Boston Red Sox and Chicago Cubs continue to be America's favorite teams, even when they're abysmal.

Tickets are relatively inexpensive – the cheap seats average about $25 at most stadiums – and are easy to get for most games. Minor-league baseball games cost half as much, and can be even more fun, with lots of audience participation, stray chickens and dogs running across the field, and wild throws from the pitcher's mound. For info, click to www.milb.com.

Football

Football is big, physical and rolling in dough. With the shortest season and least number of games of any major sport, every match takes on the emotion of an epic battle, where the results matter and an unfortunate injury can deal a lethal blow to a team's play-off chances.

Football is also the toughest because it's played in fall and winter in all manner of rain, sleet and snow. Some of history's most memorable matches have occurred at below-freezing temperatures. Green Bay Packers fans are in a class by themselves when it comes to severe weather. Their stadium in Wisconsin, known as Lambeau Field, was the site of the infamous Ice Bowl, a 1967 championship game against the Dallas Cowboys where the temperature plummeted to –13°F – mind you, that was with a wind-chill factor of –48°F.

The rabidly popular Super Bowl is pro football's championship match, held in late January or early February. The bowl games (such as Rose Bowl and Orange Bowl) are college football's title matches, held on and around New Year's Day.

In recent years the National Football League has come under fire for failing to adjust the rules of the sport in reaction to overwhelming proof that repeated concussions (a byproduct of tackles) have a permanent effect on players. A 2017 study by Boston University of the brains of 111 NFL players showed that 110 had a degenerative brain disease, chronic traumatic encephalopathy (CTE). Though TV ratings for NFL games have taken a slight hit, the sport remains popular: 1.06 million children and teens played tackle football in 2017, according to a study by JAMA Pediatrics.

Basketball

The men's teams bringing in the most fans these days include the Chicago Bulls, the Los Angeles Lakers, the Cleveland Cavaliers, the San Antonio Spurs and, last but not least, the Golden State Warriors, which won three championships (and made it to every NBA final) between 2015 and

Despite the gains made in women's sports since the 1970s, playing fields, pay and facilities for female professional athletes continue to lag far behind those for men. Perhaps the most notable example of this inequity is the men's and women's US soccer teams. Despite winning four World Cups and four Olympic medals, the USWNT is paid far less than the men's team, and they have filed a gender discrimination lawsuit against the US Soccer Federation.

THE WAY OF LIFE SPORTS

Key Sports Sites

Baseball (www.mlb.com)

Football (www.nfl.com)

Basketball (www.nba.com, www.wnba.com)

Auto Racing (www.nascar.com, www.indycar.com)

2019. Small-market teams such as Oklahoma City and Milwaukee have true-blue fans and star players like Russell Westbrook and Giannis Antetokounmpo, and such cities can be great places to take in a game.

Though not as celebrated, the women's professional basketball teams (known as the WNBA) put on thrilling performances as well. The Washington Mystics, Los Angeles Sparks and Minnesota Lynx are a few teams to watch, and standouts include Breanna Stewart (Seattle Storm), Brittney Griner (Phoenix Mercury), A'ja Wilson (Las Vegas Aces) and Candace Parker (LA Sparks).

College-level basketball also draws millions of fans, especially every spring when March Madness rolls around. This series of men's college play-off games culminates in the Final Four, when the four remaining teams compete for a spot in the championship game. The Cinderella stories and unexpected outcomes rival the pro league for excitement.

Politics

There's nothing quite like a good old-fashioned discussion of politics to throw a bucket of cold water onto a conversation. Many Americans have fairly fixed ideas when it comes to political parties and ideologies, and bridging the Republican–Democratic divide can often seem as insurmountable as leaping over the Grand Canyon. Here's a quick cheat sheet on the American two-party system.

Republicans

Known as the GOP (Grand Old Party), Republicans believe in a limited role of federal government. They also prescribe fiscal conservatism: lower taxes, privatization and reduced government spending constitute the path toward prosperity. Historically, Republicans were strong supporters of the environment: Theodore Roosevelt was a notable conservationist who helped create the National Parks system, and Nixon established the Environmental Protection Agency in 1970. More recently, however, Republicans have sided with business over environmental regulation, particularly under the Trump administration. Climate change remains a hot topic: as of 2019, 150 Republican members of Congress deny its basic tenets. This includes James Inhofe, a veteran lawmaker from Oklahoma and senior member of the Environment and Public Works Committee – he is the author of the book *The Greatest Hoax: How the Global Warming Conspiracy Threatens Your Future*. Republicans are typically socially conservative, and are often opposed to same-sex marriage, abortion and transgender rights. A fundamentalist wing of the party believes in creationism and a literal interpretation of the Bible. The Republican Party is most successful in rural regions, and has more support in the South and Great Plains.

Democrats

The Democratic Party is liberal and progressive. The role model for most Democrats is Franklin Roosevelt, whose New Deal policies (namely creating government jobs for the unemployed and regulating Wall Street) are credited with partially ending the Great Depression. Democrats believe government should take an active role in regulating the economy to help keep inflation and unemployment low, and in a progressive tax structure to reduce economic inequality. They also have a strong social agenda, endorsing the government to take an active role in providing poverty relief, maintaining a social safety net, creating a health-care system for all and ensuring civil and political rights. By and large, Democrats support abortion rights and same-sex marriage, and believe in subsidizing alternative energy sources to help combat climate change, which most party members accept as indisputable. The Democratic Party is strongest in big cities and in the Northeast.

Even college and high-school football games enjoy an intense amount of pomp and circumstance, with cheerleaders, marching bands, mascots, songs and mandatory pre- and post-game rituals, especially the tailgate – a full-blown beer-and-barbecue feast that takes place over portable grills in stadium parking lots.

Just before Trump's inauguration in 2017, four former aides to President Obama launched a podcast network, Crooked Media. Its flagship show, *Pod Save America*, quickly climbed the podcast charts thanks to its likable hosts and their snarky, smart take on politics and the media – each episode draws about 1.5 million listeners.

Native Americans

North America's indigenous people are extremely diverse, with unique customs and beliefs, molded in part by the landscapes where they live – from the Inuit in the tundra of Alaska, to the many tribes of the arid Southwest. Although the population is a fraction of its pre-Columbian size (about 2% of the US population), there are more than six million Native Americans from 573 tribes, speaking some 175 languages and residing in every region of the United States.

The Tribes

Today, the Cherokee, Navajo, Chippewa and Sioux are the largest tribal groupings in the lower 48 (ie excluding Alaska and Hawaii). Other well-known tribes include the Choctaw (descendants of a great mound-building society originally based in the Mississippi Valley), the Iroquois (who invented the game of lacrosse) the Apache (a nomadic hunter-gatherer tribe that fiercely resisted forced relocation) and the Hopi (a Pueblo people with Southwest roots dating back 2000 years).

Culturally speaking, America's modern tribal nations grapple with questions about how to prosper in contemporary America while protecting their traditions from erosion and their lands from further exploitation.

Cherokee

The Cherokee (www.cherokee.org) were a dominant presence on the continent prior to European contact. They lived in fertile river valleys, in small villages set with sturdy wooden-frame houses surrounded by cornfields. There was also a central square and a council house for religious ceremonies and meetings that could hold all of the villagers. Cherokee society was originally matrilineal, with bloodlines traced through the mother. Like some other native tribes, the Cherokee recognize seven cardinal directions: north, south, east and west along with up, down and center (or within).

Through warfare and alliances, the Cherokee soon amassed a territory that covered a huge swath of the present-day South, including Tennessee, the Carolinas, Virginia and Kentucky. By 1821, the Cherokee had established a writing system consisting of 86 characters, and literacy spread quickly. The syllabary was created by Sequoyah, who believed that by claiming the written

900
Ancestral Pueblo peoples living near Chaco Canyon develop massive adobe 'great houses.'

1100
North America's largest city outside Mesoamerica, Cahokia, boasts a population larger than medieval London.

1680
The Pueblo successfully rise up against the Spanish in the Pueblo Revolt. They maintain their independence until 1692.

1831–1836
Southeastern tribes are forcibly relocated west of the Mississippi by the US government. Thousands die along what is known as the Trail of Tears.

1876
Lakota chief Sitting Bull defeats Custer at the Battle of Little Big Horn, one of the last military victories by Native Americans.

1934
The Indian Reorganization Act transfers land and mineral rights back to tribes and encourages preservation of their cultures.

1968
The American Indian Movement (AIM) is founded to support Native American rights.

2011
FNX, the first Native American television network, launches.

2019
Joy Harjo, of the Muscogee Creek Nation, becomes the first Native American US poet laureate.

word for themselves, the Cherokee could be on a more equal footing with white men. The first person he taught to read was his six-year-old daughter, Ayoka.

However, after the Indian Removal Act passed in 1830, the Cherokee were forcibly relocated east of the Mississippi alongside other southeastern tribes in a forced march known as the Trail of Tears. Ever since, the majority of the Cherokee population (some 200,000 plus) reside in Oklahoma. Tahlequah, OK, has been the Cherokee capital since 1839; the Annual Cherokee National Holiday has been celebrated there since 1953 with a weekend of festivities.

Today the Trail of Tears routes make up a National Historic Trail (www.nps.gov/trte) that goes through nine states. Significant stops include the Museum of the Cherokee Indian in Cherokee, North Carolina, and New Echota Historic Site near Calhoun, Georgia.

Navajo

The Navajo Reservation (www.discovernavajo.com) is by far the largest and most populous in the US. Also called the Navajo Nation and Navajoland, it covers 17.5 million acres (over 27,000 sq miles) in Arizona and parts of New Mexico and Utah, and more than 300,000 people call Navajo Nation home.

The Navajo (Diné) were nomads and warriors who both traded with and raided the neighboring Pueblos and Apaches. They borrowed generously from other traditions: they acquired sheep and horses from the Spanish, learned pottery and weaving from the Pueblos, and picked up silversmithing from Mexico.

By the 1860s, settlers and the US military were encroaching onto Navajo territory. Violent clashes were common as Navajo defended the land they had held for centuries. Beginning in 1863, the US military decided to solve their 'Navajo problem' by rounding up more than 10,000 Navajos and marching them at gunpoint toward a desolate corner of New Mexico and a camp called Bosque Redondo, some 400 miles away. Hundreds died on the 'Long Walk,' and more died of disease and poor treatment during the four years they were held at the camp before being released and allowed to return to their lands.

In the 1940s, the Navajo became vital to the US's World War II efforts, thanks to the 'Navajo code-talkers.' A group of 29 men created a code based on the Navajo language to communicate with US Marines in the Pacific. Thanks to the complexity of the Navajo language, their efforts foiled Japanese code-breakers for the duration of the war and was pivotal to the success of the Battle of Iwo Jima.

Today, the Navajo are renowned for their woven rugs, pottery and inlaid silver jewelry, as well as for their intricate sandpainting, which is used in healing ceremonies. Many Navajo rely on the tourist economy, and there's a robust collection of museums, monuments and cultural experiences – including traditional village visits – in Arizona and Utah.

Chippewa

The Chippewa are based in Minnesota, Wisconsin and Michigan – in fact, the state name 'Michigan' comes from the Ojibwe language. Although Chippewa, or Ojibwe, is the commonly used term for this tribe, they are part of the Anishinaabe group of indigenous peoples and often refer to themselves as Anishinaabe.

According to legend, the Chippewa once lived on the Atlantic coast and gradually migrated west over 500 years. They established communities, surviving by fishing, hunting, and farming corn and squash. They also harvested (by canoe) wild rice, which remains an essential Chippewa tradition. Poet Henry Wadsworth Longfellow pulled from Chippewa culture for his 1855 poem 'The Song of Hiawatha.'

The mounds built by the prehistoric peoples of North America as recently as the 16th century are impressive feats of engineering. Platform mounds, basically four-sided earthen pyramids, were sites of temples, dances or ceremonies, while effigy mounds, like Serpent Mound in what is now Ohio, took the shape of culturally significant animals.

In the early 1920s, dozens of wealthy Osage Indians were murdered in Oklahoma over their mineral land rights. Most of the crimes remain unsolved. The story is told in David Grann's *Killers of the Flower Moon* (2017).

NATIVE AMERICAN ART & CRAFTS

It would take an encyclopedia to cover the myriad artistic traditions of America's tribal peoples, from pre-Columbian rock art to the contemporary multimedia scene.

What ties such diverse traditions together is that Native American art and crafts are not just functional for everyday life, but can also serve ceremonial purposes and have social and religious significance. The patterns and symbols are woven with meanings that provide a window into the heart of Native American peoples. This is as true of Zuni fetish carvings as it is of patterned Navajo rugs, Southwestern pueblo pottery, Sioux beadwork, Inuit sculptures and Cherokee and Hawaiian wood carvings, to name just a few examples.

In addition to preserving their culture, contemporary Native American artists have used sculpture, painting, textiles, film, literature and performance art to reflect and critique modernity since the mid-20th century, especially after the civil rights activism of the 1960s and cultural renaissance of the '70s. *Native North American Art* by Berlo and Phillips offers an introduction to North America's varied indigenous art.

Many tribes run craft outlets and galleries, usually in the main towns of reservations. The Indian Arts & Crafts Board (www.doi.gov/iacb) lists Native American–owned galleries and shops state-by-state (click on 'Source Directory').

The modern 'dreamcatcher,' popularized by the New Age movement, was inspired by the Chippewa 'spider-web charm.' Sinew was wrapped around a willow frame to create a protective charm related to the guardian spirit Spider Woman (Asibikaashi). Chippewa would hang the spider-web charms over a cradle to allow her protection to reach them.

Today about 175,000 Chippewa live in North America, mainly on reservations.

Sioux

The Sioux (www.lakotadakotanakotanation.org) is not one tribe, but a consortium of three major tribes – Eastern Dakota, Western Dakota and Lakota – speaking different dialects but sharing a common culture. Each tribe also has various sub-branches.

Prior to European arrival they lived in the southeast, but were first encountered by Europeans in modern-day Minnesota, Iowa and Wisconsin. The Sioux slowly expanded west to what is now the Dakotas, Nebraska and Montana by 1800.

The Sioux were fierce defenders of their lands, and fought many battles to preserve them, including the Black Hills war and the infamous Wounded Knee Massacre, though the slaughter of the buffalo (on which they had survived) did as much to remove them from their lands as anything else. That spirit of protest endures today: The Sioux were among the founders of the American Indian Movement in 1968, launched a fight against the South Dakota foster system to prevent the state from seizing Native American children, and led the movement to block the Dakota Access Pipeline in 2016.

Today, the approximately 130,000 Sioux live in Minnesota, Nebraska, Montana, North Dakota and South Dakota – the latter contains the 2-million-acre Pine Ridge Reservation, the nation's second largest.

Arts & Architecture

The American people's love of entertainment is evident to anyone who's ever been to a touring Broadway musical or lavish Hollywood film. From its biggest entertainers to its eccentric artists, reclusive novelists, postmodern dancers and rule-breaking architects, Americans have had an outsized influence on arts scenes the world over. Geography and race are the key elements that join together to inspire the varied regionalism at the core of each discipline.

Film

Hollywood and American film are virtually inseparable. No less an American icon than the White House itself, Hollywood is increasingly the product of an internationalized cinema and film culture. This evolution is partly pure business: Hollywood studios are the showpieces of multinational corporations, and funding flows to talent that brings the biggest grosses, regardless of nationality.

But this shift is also creative. It's Hollywood's recognition that if the studios don't incorporate the immense filmmaking talent emerging worldwide, they will be made irrelevant by it. Co-option is an old Hollywood strategy, used most recently to subvert the challenge posed by the independent film movement of the 1990s that kicked off with daring homegrown films like *Sex, Lies, and Videotape* and *Reservoir Dogs,* and innovative European imports. That said, for the most part, mainstream American audiences remain steadfastly indifferent to foreign films.

Television

It could be argued that TV was the defining medium of the 20th century. In its brief history, TV has proved to be one of the most passionately contested cultural battlegrounds in American society, blamed for a whole host of societal ills, from skyrocketing obesity to plummeting attention spans and school test scores. The average American still watches loads of TV a week (35.5 hours if you believe the commonly touted figure), but they are watching differently, often streaming their favorite shows via providers such as Netflix and Amazon Prime.

For many decades, critics sneered that TV was lowbrow, and movie stars wouldn't be caught dead on it. But well-written, thought-provoking shows have existed almost since the beginning. In the 1950s, the original

WOMEN ON SCREEN

After years of being dominated by men, the TV and film industries are finally making space for female-led projects. Creative talents such as Issa Rae, Mindy Kaling, Gina Rodriguez and Rachel Bloom have starred in or produced stellar TV projects, while the all-female (and African American) stars of *Hidden Figures* drew flocks of eager moviegoers and the complicated moms of *Big Little Lies* lit up HBO. Perhaps the ultimate expression of this change is the emergence of the female superhero, from TV's Supergirl and Jessica Jones to top-grossing films like *Wonder Woman* and *Captain Marvel*.

I Love Lucy show was groundbreaking: shot on film before a live audience and edited before airing, it pioneered syndication. It established the sitcom ('situation comedy') formula, and showcased a dynamic female comedian, Lucille Ball, in an interethnic marriage.

Indeed, 'good' American TV has been around for a long time, whether through artistic merit or cultural and political importance. The 1970s comedy *All in the Family* aired an unflinching examination of prejudice, as embodied by bigoted patriarch Archie Bunker, played by Carroll O'Connor. Similarly, the sketch-comedy show *Saturday Night Live*, which debuted in 1975, pushed social hot buttons with its subversive, politically charged humor.

In the 1980s, videotapes brought movies into American homes, blurring the distinction between big and small screens, and the stigma Hollywood attached to TV slowly faded. The decade also saw the rise of shows such as *The Golden Girls*, a humorous sitcom that explored themes like aging and mortality (as well as more taboo topics such as sexuality among the elderly). It starred four retired women living in Miami and was both critically acclaimed and a commercial success.

In the 1990s, TV audiences embraced the unformulaic, no-holds-barred-weird cult show *Twin Peaks,* leading to a slew of provocative idiosyncratic series such as *The X-Files.*

These days, the most popular shows are a mix of edgier, long-narrative serial dramas, as well as cheap-to-produce, 'unscripted' reality TV: what *Survivor* started in 2000, the contestants and 'actors' of *The Voice, Dancing with the Stars, Project Runway* and *Keeping up with the Kardashians* keep alive today, for better or for worse.

As cable TV has emerged as the frontier for daring and innovative programming, some of the TV shows of the past decade have proved as riveting and memorable as anything American viewers (and the scores of people around the world who watch American TV) have ever seen. Streaming services such as Netflix, Amazon and Hulu, and niche networks such as AMC and HBO, have created numerous lauded series, including *Mad Men* (which followed the antics of 1960s advertising execs in NYC), *Portlandia* (a satire of Oregonian subcultures) and *Breaking Bad* (about a terminally ill high-school teacher who starts cooking meth to safeguard his family's financial future). More recent favorites include *The Marvelous Mrs Maisel* (about a Jewish female comic trying to make it in 1950s NYC), *Atlanta* (a comedy-drama starring Donald Glover), *Stranger Things* (a supernatural saga set in the 1980s that recalls *The Goonies*) and *The Handmaid's Tale* (a near-future dystopia based on Margaret Atwood's 1985 novel). A number of previously canceled series have also returned from the dead with mixed results in the last few years, including *The Twilight Zone, Veronica Mars, The X-Files* and *90210* (for the third time).

Literature

America first articulated a vision of itself through its literature. Until the American Revolution, many of the continent's colonial citizens identified with England, but after independence, an immediate call went out to develop an American national voice. Not until the 1820s, however, did writers take up the two aspects of American life that had no counterpart in Europe: the untamed wilderness and the frontier experience.

James Fenimore Cooper is credited with creating the first truly American literature with *The Pioneers* (1823). In Cooper's 'everyman' humor and individualism, Americans first recognized themselves.

In his essay *Nature* (1836), Ralph Waldo Emerson articulated similar ideas, but in more philosophical and spiritual terms. Emerson claimed

Books Once Banned in America

Are You There, God? It's Me, Margaret (Judy Blume)

Lord of the Flies (William Golding)

1984 (George Orwell)

The Catcher in the Rye (JD Salinger)

Adventures of Huckleberry Finn (Mark Twain)

The Color Purple (Alice Walker)

that nature reflected God's instructions for humankind as plainly as the Bible did, and that individuals could understand these through rational thought and self-reliance. Emerson's writings became the core of the transcendentalist movement, which Henry David Thoreau championed in *Walden; or, Life in the Woods* (1854).

Literary highlights of this era include Herman Melville's ambitious *Moby Dick* (1851) and Nathaniel Hawthorne's examination of the dark side of conservative New England in *The Scarlet Letter* (1850). Canonical poet Emily Dickinson wrote haunting, tightly structured poems, which were first published in 1890, four years after her death.

Civil War & Beyond

The celebration of common humanity and nature reached its apotheosis in Walt Whitman, whose poetry collection *Leaves of Grass* (1855) signaled the arrival of an American literary visionary. In Whitman's informal, intimate, rebellious free verse were songs of individualism, democracy, earthy spirituality, taboo-breaking sexuality and joyous optimism that encapsulated the heart of a throbbing new nation.

But not everything was coming up roses. Abolitionist Harriet Beecher Stowe's controversial novel *Uncle Tom's Cabin* (1852) depicted African American life under slavery with Christian romanticism, but also enough realism to inflame passions on both sides of the 'great debate' over slavery, which would shortly plunge the nation into civil war.

After the Civil War (1861–65), two enduring literary trends emerged: realism and regionalism. Regionalism was especially spurred by the rapid late 19th-century settlement of the West (think novelist Jack London), but it was also popular in the South (Kate Chopin's stories about the Louisiana Bayou) and the Great Plains (Willa Cather's *My Ántonia*).

However, it was Samuel Clemens (aka Mark Twain) who came to define this era of American letters. In *Adventures of Huckleberry Finn* (1884), Twain made explicit the quintessential American narrative of an individual journey of self-discovery. The image of Huck and Jim – a poor white teenager and a runaway black slave – standing outside society's norms and floating together toward an uncertain future down the Mississippi River challenges American society still. Twain wrote in the vernacular, loved 'tall tales' and reveled in satirical humor and absurdity, while his folksy, 'anti-intellectual' stance endeared him to everyday readers.

Disillusionment & Diversity

With the dramas of world wars and a newly industrialized society for artistic fodder, American literature came into its own in the 20th century.

Dubbed the 'Lost Generation,' many US writers, most famously Ernest Hemingway, became expats in Europe. Hemingway's novels exemplified the era, and his spare, stylized realism has often been imitated, yet never bettered. Other notable American figures at Parisian literary salons included modernist writers Gertrude Stein and Ezra Pound, and iconoclast Henry Miller, whose semiautobiographical novels were published in Paris, only to be banned for obscenity and pornography in the USA until the 1960s.

F Scott Fitzgerald eviscerated East Coast society life with his fiction, while John Steinbeck became the great voice of rural working poor in the West, especially during the Great Depression. William Faulkner examined the South's social rifts in dense prose riddled with bullets of black humor.

Between the world wars, the Harlem Renaissance also flourished, as African American intellectuals and artists took pride in their culture and undermined racist stereotypes. Among the most well-known writers were poet Langston Hughes and novelist Zora Neale Hurston.

After WWII, American writers delineated ever-sharper regional and ethnic divides, pursued stylistic experimentation and often caustically repudiated conservative middle-class American values. Writers of the 1950s Beat Generation, such as Jack Kerouac, Allen Ginsburg and Lawrence Ferlinghetti, threw themselves like Molotov cocktails onto the profusion of smug suburban lawns. Meanwhile, novelists JD Salinger and Ken Kesey, Russian immigrant Vladimir Nabokov and poet Sylvia Plath darkly chronicled descents into madness by characters who struggled against stifling social norms.

The South, always ripe with paradox, inspired masterful short-story writers and novelists Flannery O'Connor and Eudora Welty and novelist Dorothy Allison. The mythical romance and modern tragedies of the West have found their champions in Chicano writer Rudolfo Anaya, Larry McMurtry and Cormac McCarthy, whose characters poignantly tackle the rugged realities of Western life.

As the 20th century ended, American literature became ever more personalized, starting with the 'me' decade of the 1980s. Narcissistic, nihilistic narratives by writers such as Jay McInerney and Bret Easton Ellis catapulted the 'Brat Pack' into pop culture.

Since the 1990s, an increasingly diverse, multiethnic panoply of voices reflects the society Americans live in. Ethnic identity (especially that of immigrant cultures), regionalism and narratives of self-discovery remain at the forefront of American literature, no matter how experimental. The quarterly journal *McSweeney's,* founded by Dave Eggers, publishes titans of contemporary literature such as Joyce Carol Oates and Michael Chabon, as well as inventive humor pieces from new voices.

For a sweeping, almost panoramic look at American society, read Jonathan Franzen's *The Corrections* (2001). More recent literary hits include Angela Flournoy's 2015 National Book Award–winning debut, *The Turner House*, which traces the history of a Detroit family through three generations. Paul Beatty's electric satire about race in America, *The Sellout* (2015) made him the first US author to win Britain's Man Booker Prize. And Tommy Orange's piercing debut, *There There* (2018) follows 12 contemporary Native Americans who come together at a powwow in Oakland, California. Watch out for emerging writers such as Lisa Halliday, Brit Bennett, Ling Ma and Yaa Gyasi.

Painting & Sculpture

New York is the red-hot center of the art world, and its make-or-break influence shapes tastes across the nation and around the globe. But the USA's modern art scene is diverse, and pops up in some unusual and out-of-the-way places. Today's visual art and sculpture often engages with the political and social issues of the day in surprising ways.

Shaping a National Identity

Artists played a pivotal role in the USA's 19th-century expansion, disseminating images of far-flung territories and reinforcing the call to Manifest Destiny. Thomas Cole and his colleagues in the Hudson River School translated European romanticism to the luminous wild landscapes of upstate New York, while Frederic Remington offered idealized, often stereotypical portraits of the Western frontier.

After the Civil War and the advent of industrialization, realism increasingly became prominent. Eastman Johnson painted nostalgic scenes of rural life, as did Winslow Homer, who later became renowned for watercolor seascapes.

Art in Out-of-the-Way Places

Marfa (Texas)

Santa Fe (New Mexico)

Bentonville (Arkansas)

Traverse City (Michigan)

Lucas (Kansas)

Bellingham (Washington)

Beacon (New York)

Provincetown (Massachusetts)

An American Avant-Garde

New York's Armory Show of 1913 introduced the nation to European modernism and changed the face of American art. It showcased impressionism, fauvism and cubism, including the notorious 1912 *Nude Descending a Staircase, No. 2* by Marcel Duchamp, a French artist who later became an American citizen. The show was merely the first in a series of exhibitions evangelizing the radical aesthetic shifts of European modernism, and it was inevitable that American artists would begin to grapple with what they had seen. Alexander Calder, Joseph Cornell and Isamu Noguchi produced sculptures inspired by surrealism and constructivism, while the precisionist paintings of Charles Demuth, Georgia O'Keeffe and Charles Sheeler combined realism with a touch of cubist geometry.

In the 1930s, the Federal Art Project of the Works Progress Administration (WPA), part of Franklin D Roosevelt's New Deal, commissioned murals, paintings and sculptures for public buildings nationwide. WPA artists borrowed from Soviet social realism and Mexican muralists to forge a socially engaged figurative style with regional flavor.

Abstract Expressionism

You know Pollack, de Kooning and Rothko – but what about the women who shaped 20th-century abstract painting? In *Ninth Street Women* (2018), Mary Gabriel reveals how five female artists, including Lee Krasner and Grace Hartigan, worked their way to the top of the NYC art world.

In the wake of WWII, American art underwent a sea change at the hands of New York School painters such as Franz Kline, Jackson Pollock, Elaine de Kooning and Mark Rothko. Moved by surrealism's celebration of spontaneity and the unconscious, these artists explored abstraction and its psychological potency through imposing scale and the gestural handling of paint. The movement's 'action painter' camp went extreme; Pollock, for example, made his drip paintings by pouring and splattering pigments over large canvases.

Having stood the test of time, abstract expressionism is widely considered to be the first truly original school of American art.

Art + Commodity = Pop

Once established in America, abstract expressionism reigned supreme. However, stylistic revolts had begun much earlier, in the 1950s. Most notably, Jasper Johns came to prominence with thickly painted renditions of ubiquitous symbols, including targets and the American flag, while Robert Rauschenberg assembled artworks from comics, ads and even – à la Duchamp – found objects (a mattress, a tire, a stuffed goat). Both artists helped break down traditional boundaries between painting and sculpture, opening the field for pop art in the 1960s.

America's postwar economic boom also influenced pop. Not only did artists embrace representation, they drew inspiration from consumer images such as billboards, product packaging and media icons. Employing mundane mass-production techniques to silkscreen paintings of movie stars and Coke bottles, Andy Warhol helped topple the myth of the solitary artist laboring heroically in the studio. Roy Lichtenstein combined newsprint's humble Benday dots with the representational conventions of comics. Suddenly, so-called 'serious' art could be political, bizarre, ironic and fun – and all at once.

Minimalism

What became known as minimalism shared pop's interest in mass production, but all similarities ended there. Like the abstract expressionists, artists such as Donald Judd, Agnes Martin and Robert Ryman eschewed representational subject matter; their cool, reductive works of the 1960s and '70s were often arranged in gridded compositions and fabricated from industrial materials.

The '80s & Beyond

By the 1980s, civil rights, feminism and AIDS activism had made inroads in visual culture; artists not only voiced political dissent through their work, but embraced a range of once-marginalized media, from textiles and graffiti to video, sound and performance. The decade also ushered in the so-called Culture Wars, which commenced with tumult over photographs by Robert Mapplethorpe and Andres Serrano. Break-out artists Futura 2000, Keith Haring and Jean-Michel Basquiat moved from the subways and the streets to the galleries, and soon to the worlds of fashion and advertising.

In February 2018, the presidential portraits of Michelle and Barack Obama were unveiled in the Smithsonian. Artists Amy Sherald and Kehinde Wiley, who painted the first lady and the president, were the first black artists to be commissioned for official presidential portraits.

To get the pulse of contemporary art in the US, check out works by artists such as Cindy Sherman, Kara Walker, Diamond Stingily, Chuck Close, Max Hooper Schneider, Kerry James Marshall, Eddie Martinez and Josh Smith.

Top US Photographers
- Ansel Adams
- Walker Evans
- Man Ray
- Alfred Stieglitz
- Richard Avedon
- Robert Frank
- Dorothea Lange
- Cindy Sherman
- Edward Weston
- Diane Arbus
- Lee Friedlander

ARTS & ARCHITECTURE THEATER

Theater

American theater is a three-act play of sentimental entertainment, classic revivals and urgent social commentary. From the beginning, Broadway musicals (www.livebroadway.com) have aspired to be 'don't-miss-this-show!' tourist attractions. And today, they continue to be one of NYC's biggest draws. Broadway shows earn over a billion dollars in revenue from ticket sales each year, with top shows pulling in a cool $1 million a week. The most successful Broadway shows, including the hip-hop hit *Hamilton* (which re-imagines the life of Founding Father Alexander Hamilton), often go on to even greater earnings worldwide. (Gross worldwide earnings of *The Phantom of the Opera* has now topped an astounding $6 billion.) Meanwhile, long-running classics such as *The Lion King* and *Wicked* continue to play before sold-out houses.

Independent theater arrived in the 1920s and '30s, with the Little Theatre Movement, which emulated progressive European theater and developed into today's 'off-Broadway' scene. Always struggling and scraping, and mostly surviving, the country's 2000 nonprofit regional theaters are breeding grounds for new plays and fostering new playwrights. Some also develop Broadway-bound productions, while others sponsor festivals dedicated to the Bard himself, William Shakespeare.

Eugene O'Neill – the first major US playwright, and still widely considered the best – put American drama on the map. After WWII, American playwrights joined the nationwide artistic renaissance. Two of the most famous were Arthur Miller, who famously married Marilyn Monroe and wrote about everything from middle-class male disillusionment to the dark psychology of the mob mentality of the Salem witch trials, and the prolific Southerner Tennessee Williams.

As in Europe, absurdism and the avant-garde marked American theater in the 1960s. Few were more scathing than Edward Albee, who started provoking bourgeois sensibilities. Neil Simon arrived at around the same time; his ever-popular comedies kept Broadway humming for 40 years.

Other prominent, active American dramatists emerging in the 1970s include David Mamet, Sam Shepard and innovative 'concept musical' composer Stephen Sondheim. August Wilson created a monumental 10-play 'Pittsburgh Cycle' dissecting 20th-century African American life.

Today, American theater is evolving in its effort to remain a relevant communal experience in an age of ever-isolating media. Shows including *Breakfast with Mugabe* explore the trauma of the past, while *Avenue Q,*

AMERICA DANCES

America fully embraced dance in the 20th century. New York City has always been the epicenter for dance innovation and the home of many premier dance companies, but every major city supports resident and touring troupes, both ballet and modern.

Modern ballet is said to have begun with Russian-born choreographer George Balanchine's *Apollo* (1928) and *Prodigal Son* (1929). With these, Balanchine invented the 'plotless ballet' – in which he choreographed the inner structure of music, not a pantomimed story – and thereby created a new, modern vocabulary of ballet movement. In 1934, Balanchine founded the School of American Ballet; in 1948 he founded the New York City Ballet, turning it into one of the world's foremost ballet companies. Jerome Robbins took over that company in 1983, after achieving fame choreographing huge Broadway musicals such as *West Side Story* (1957). Broadway remains an important venue for dance today. National companies elsewhere, such as San Francisco's Lines Ballet, keep evolving contemporary ballet.

The pioneer of modern dance, Isadora Duncan, didn't find success until she began performing in Europe at the turn of the 20th century. Basing her ideas on ancient Greek myths and concepts of beauty, she challenged the strictures of classical ballet and sought to make dance an intense form of self-expression.

Martha Graham founded the Martha Graham School for Contemporary Dance in 1926 after moving to New York, and many of today's major American choreographers developed under her tutelage. In her long career she choreographed more than 140 works and developed a new dance technique, now taught worldwide, aimed at expressing inner emotion and dramatic narrative. Her most famous work was *Appalachian Spring* (1944).

Merce Cunningham, Paul Taylor and Twyla Tharp succeeded Graham as leading exponents of modern dance; they all have companies that are active today. In the 1960s and '70s, Cunningham explored abstract expressionism in movement, collaborating famously with musician John Cage. Taylor experimented with everyday movements and expressions, while Tharp is known for incorporating pop music, jazz and ballet.

Another student of Martha Graham, Alvin Ailey, was part of the post-WWII flowering of African American culture. He made his name with *Revelations* (1960), two years after he founded the still-lauded Alvin Ailey American Dance Theater in New York City.

Other celebrated postmodern choreographers include Mark Morris and Bill T Jones. Beyond New York, San Francisco, Los Angeles, Chicago, Minneapolis and Philadelphia are noteworthy for modern dance.

with its trash-talking, love-making puppets, presents a hilarious send-up of life on *Sesame Street*. More immersive experiences such as *Sleep No More* put theater-goers inside the play to wander freely among wildly decorated rooms – including a graveyard, stables, a psychiatric ward and a ballroom – as the drama (loosely based on *Macbeth*) unfolds around them.

Architecture

In the 21st century, computer technology and innovations in materials and manufacturing allow for curving, asymmetrical buildings once considered impossible, if not inconceivable. Architects are being challenged to 'go green,' and the creativity unleashed is riveting, transforming skylines and changing the way Americans think about their built environments. The public's architectural taste remains conservative, but never mind: avant-garde 'starchitects' are revising urban landscapes with radical visions that the nation will catch up with – one day.

The Colonial Period

Perhaps the largest indigenous influence on American architecture are the adobe dwellings of the Southwest. In the 17th and 18th centuries, Spanish colonists incorporated elements of what they called the Native

American *pueblo* (village). It reappeared in late-19th- and early-20th-century architecture in both the Southwest's Pueblo Revival style and Southern California's Mission Revival style.

Elsewhere until the 20th century, immigrant Americans mainly adopted English and continental European styles and followed their trends. For most early colonists in the eastern US, architecture served necessity rather than taste, while the would-be gentry aped grander English homes, a period well preserved in Williamsburg, VA.

After the Revolutionary War, the nation's leaders wanted a style befitting the new republic and adopted neoclassicism. Virginia's capitol, designed by Thomas Jefferson, was modeled on an ancient Roman temple, and Jefferson's own private estate, Monticello, sports a Romanesque rotunda.

Professional architect Charles Bulfinch helped develop the more monumental federal style, which paralleled the English Georgian style. The grandest example is the US Capitol in Washington, DC, which became a model for state legislatures nationwide. As they moved into the 19th century, Americans, mirroring English fashions, gravitated toward the Greek and Gothic Revival styles, still seen today in many churches and college campuses.

Building the Nation

In the 19th century, small-scale architecture was revolutionized by 'balloon-frame' construction: a light frame of standard-milled timber joined with cheap nails. Easy and economical, balloon-frame stores and houses made possible swift settlement of the expanding west and, later, the surreal proliferation of the suburbs. Home-ownership was suddenly within reach of average middle-class families, making real the enduring American Dream.

After the Civil War, influential American architects studied at Paris' École des Beaux-Arts, and American buildings began to show increasing refinement and confidence. Major examples of the beaux-arts style include Richard Morris Hunt's Biltmore Estate in North Carolina and New York's Public Library.

In San Francisco and other cities across America, Victorian architecture appeared as the 19th century progressed. Among well-to-do classes, larger and fancier private houses added ever more adornments: balconies, turrets, towers, ornately painted trim and intricate 'gingerbread' wooden millwork.

In a reaction against Victorian opulence, the Arts and Crafts movement arose after 1900 and remained popular until the 1930s. Its modest bungalows, such as the Gamble House in Pasadena, CA, featured locally handcrafted wood and glasswork, ceramic tiles and other artisan details.

Reaching for the Sky

By the 1850s, internal iron-framed buildings had appeared in Manhattan, and this freed up urban architectural designs, especially after the advent of Otis hydraulic elevators in the 1880s. The Chicago School of architecture transitioned beyond beaux-arts style to produce the skyscraper – considered the first truly 'modern' architecture, and America's most prominent architectural contribution to the world at that time.

In the 1930s, the influence of art deco – which became instantly popular in the US after the Paris Exposition of 1925 – meant that urban high-rises soared, becoming fitting symbols of America's technical achievements, grand aspirations, commerce and affinity for modernism.

Modernism & Beyond

When the Bauhaus school fled the rise of Nazism in Germany, architects such as Walter Gropius and Ludwig Mies van der Rohe brought their pioneering modern designs to American shores. Van der Rohe landed in Chicago, where Louis Sullivan, considered to be the inventor of the modern skyscraper, was already working on a simplified style of architecture in which 'form ever follows function.' This evolved into the International style, which favored glass 'curtain walls' over a steel frame. IM Pei, who designed Cleveland's Rock and Roll Hall of Fame, is considered the last living high-modernist architect in America.

In the mid-20th century, modernism transitioned into America's suburbs, especially in Southern California. Mid-century modern architecture was influenced not only by the organic nature of Frank Lloyd Wright's homes, but also the spare, geometric, clean-lined designs of Scandinavia. Post-and-beam construction allowed for walls of sheer glass that gave the illusion of merging indoor and outdoor living spaces. Today, a striking collection of mid-century modern homes and public buildings by Albert Frey, Richard Neutra and other luminaries can be found in Palm Springs, CA.

Rejecting modernism's 'ugly boxes' later in the 20th century, postmodernism reintroduced decoration, color, historical references and whimsy. In this, architects such as Michael Graves and Philip Johnson took the lead. Another expression of postmodernism is the brash, mimetic architecture of the Las Vegas Strip, which Pritzker Prize–winning architect Robert Venturi held up as the triumphant antithesis of modernism (he sardonically described the latter as 'less is a bore').

Today, aided and abetted by digital tools, architectural design favors the bold and the unique. Leading this plunge into futurama has been Frank Gehry; his Walt Disney Concert Hall in Los Angeles is but one example. Other notable contemporary architects include Richard Meier (Los Angeles' Getty Center), Thom Mayne (San Francisco's Federal Building) and Daniel Libeskind (San Francisco's Contemporary Jewish Museum and the Denver Art Museum's Hamilton Building).

Even as the recession crippled the American economy in 2008 and stalled new construction, several phenomenal new examples of visionary architecture have burst upon the scene in American cities. Notable examples include Jeanne Gang's Aqua Building in Chicago, Santiago Calatrava's soaring World Trade Center transportation hub in New York City, Renzo Piano's California Academy of Sciences in San Francisco, David Adjaye's shimmering National Museum of African American History and Culture in Washington, DC, and Norman Foster's spaceship-like Apple Park in Cupertino, CA.

Art-deco architecture simultaneously appeared nationwide in the design of movie houses, train stations and office buildings across the country, and in neighborhoods such as downtown Detroit and Miami's South Beach. Remarkable examples of art-deco skyscrapers include NYC's Chrysler Building and Empire State Building.

The Music Scene

American popular music is the nation's heartbeat and its unbreakable soul. It's John Lee Hooker's deep growls and John Coltrane's passionate cascades. It's Hank Williams' yodel and Elvis' pout. It's Beyoncé and Bob Dylan, Duke Ellington and Patti Smith. It's a feeling as much as a form – always a foot-stomping, defiant good time, whether folks are boot scooting to bluegrass, sweating to zydeco, jumping to hip-hop or stage-diving to punk rock.

Blues

The South is the mother of American music, most of which has roots in the frisson and interplay of black-white racial relations. The blues developed after the Civil War, out of the work songs, or 'shouts,' of enslaved people and out of the 'call and response' pattern of black spiritual songs, both of which were adaptations of African music.

Improvisational and intensely personal, the blues remain at heart an immediate expression of individual pain, suffering, hope, desire and pride. Nearly all subsequent American music has tapped this deep well.

At the turn of the 20th century, traveling blues musicians, and particularly female blues singers, gained fame and employment across the South. Early pioneers included Robert Johnson, WC Handy, Ma Rainey, Huddie Ledbetter (aka Lead Belly) and Bessie Smith, who some consider the best blues singer who ever lived. At the same time, African American Christian choral music evolved into gospel, the greatest singer of which, Mahalia Jackson, came to prominence in the 1920s.

After WWII, blues from Memphis and the Mississippi Delta dispersed northward, particularly to Chicago, in the hands of a new generation of musicians such as Muddy Waters, Buddy Guy, BB King, John Lee Hooker and Etta James. In the 1960s and 1970s, the blues influenced a wave of rock bands like Cream and the Allman Brothers.

Today's generation of blues players include the likes of Bonamassa, Warren Haynes (a longtime player for the Allman Brothers), Tedeschi Trucks Band, Alabama Shakes, the Marcus King Band, Shemekia Copeland and the sometimes-blues players the Black Keys.

Jazz

Down in New Orleans, Congo Sq – where enslaved people gathered to sing and dance from the late 18th century onward – is considered the birthplace of jazz. There, ex-slaves adapted the reed, horn and string instruments used by the city's often French-speaking, multiracial Creoles – who preferred formal European music – to play their own African-influenced music. This cross-pollination produced a steady stream of innovative sounds.

The first variation was ragtime, so-called because of its 'ragged,' syncopated African rhythms. Beginning in the 1890s, ragtime was popularized by musicians such as Scott Joplin, and was made widely accessible through sheet music and player-piano rolls.

Dixieland jazz, centered on New Orleans' infamous Storyville red-light district, soon followed. In 1917 Storyville shut down and New Orleans' jazz musicians dispersed. In 1919 bandleader King Oliver moved to Chicago,

One of rock music's most phenomenal success stories, Prince (1958–2016), was born Prince Rogers Nelson in Minneapolis. He originally tried out for the high-school basketball team, but being too short at 5ft 2in, he was cut. His back-up hobby? He took up the guitar.

and his star trumpet player, Louis Armstrong, soon followed. Armstrong's distinctive vocals and talented improvisations led to the solo becoming an integral part of jazz throughout much of the 20th century.

The 1920s and '30s are known as the Jazz Age, but music was just part of the flowering of African American culture during New York's Harlem Renaissance. Swing – an urbane, big-band jazz style – swept the country, led by bandleaders Duke Ellington and Count Basie. Jazz singers Ella Fitzgerald and Billie Holiday combined jazz with its Southern sibling, the blues.

After WWII, bebop (aka bop) arose, reacting against the smooth melodies and confining rhythms of big-band swing. A new crop of musicians came of age, including Charlie Parker, Dizzy Gillespie and Thelonious Monk. Critics at first derided such 1950s and '60s permutations as cool jazz, hard-bop, free or avant-garde jazz, and fusion (which combined jazz and Latin or rock music) – but there was no stopping the postmodernist tide deconstructing jazz. Pioneers of this era include Miles Davis, Dave Brubeck, Chet Baker, Charles Mingus, John Coltrane, Melba Liston and Ornette Coleman.

Country

Early Scottish, Irish and English immigrants brought their own instruments and folk music to America, and what emerged over time in the secluded Appalachian Mountains was fiddle-and-banjo hillbilly, or 'country,' music. In the Southwest, steel guitars and larger bands distinguished 'western' music. In the 1920s, these styles merged into 'country and western' music and became centered on Nashville, TN, especially once the Grand Ole Opry began its radio broadcasts in 1925. Classic country artists include Hank Williams, Johnny Cash, Willie Nelson, Patsy Cline, Loretta Lynn and Dolly Parton.

Country music influenced rock and roll in the 1950s, while rock-flavored country was dubbed 'rockabilly.' In the 1980s, country and western achieved new levels of popularity with stars like Garth Brooks, George Strait, Alan Jackson and Randy Travis, and introduced elements of pop, with artists like Shania Twain and Faith Hill dominating the charts.

On today's country scene, male artists like Eric Church, Luke Bryan and Blake Shelton often dominate the Billboard charts, due to the conservative gatekeepers of country radio. Still, innovative female artists like Margo Price and Kacey Musgraves are earning critical acclaim, as well as alt-country artists like Chris Stapleton and Jason Isbell.

Folk

The tradition of American folk music was crystallized by Woody Guthrie, who traveled the country during the Depression singing politically conscious songs. In the 1940s, Pete Seeger emerged as a tireless preserver of America's folk heritage. Folk music experienced a revival during 1960s protest movements, but then-folkie Bob Dylan ended it almost single-handedly when he plugged in an electric guitar to shouts of 'traitor!'

Folk has seen a resurgence in the 21st century, particularly in the Pacific Northwest. Iron and Wine's mournful tunes channel pop, blues and rock, while Joanna Newsom, with her extraordinary voice and unusual instrumentation (she plays the harp), adds a new level of complexity to folk. Indie folk singers making waves in recent years (and expanding the boundaries of the genre) include Edward Sharpe and the Magnetic Zeros, Laura Gibson, Lord Huron, Father John Misty and Angel Olsen.

Rock & Roll

Most say rock and roll was born in 1954 the day Elvis Presley walked into Sam Phillips' Sun Studio and recorded 'That's All Right.' Initially, radio stations weren't sure why a white country boy was singing 'black music,' or whether they should play it. Two years later Presley scored his first big breakthrough with 'Heartbreak Hotel.'

The US Soundtrack

'Respect,' Aretha Franklin (1967)

'America,' Simon & Garfunkel (1968)

'Summertime,' Ella Fitzgerald (1968)

'Carolina in My Mind,' James Taylor (1968)

'City of New Orleans,' Arlo Guthrie (1972)

'Jolene,' Dolly Parton (1973)

'Born to Run,' Bruce Springsteen (1975)

'Vacation,' the Go-Gos (1982)

'Holiday,' Madonna (1983)

'Fast Car,' Tracy Chapman (1988)

'California Love,' 2Pac (1995)

'I've Been Everywhere,' Johnny Cash (1996)

'West Coast,' Coconut Records (2007)

'Empire State of Mind,' Jay-Z (2009)

'Old Town Road,' Lil Nas X (2019)

Musically, rock and roll was a hybrid of guitar-driven blues, black rhythm and blues (R&B), and white country-and-western music. R&B evolved in the 1940s out of swing and the blues and was then known as 'race music.' With rock and roll, white performers and some African American musicians transformed 'race music' into something that white youths could embrace freely – and oh, did they.

Rock and roll instantly abetted a social revolution even more significant than its musical one: openly sexual, as it celebrated youth and dancing freely across color lines, rock scared the nation. Authorities worked diligently to control 'juvenile delinquents' and to sanitize and suppress rock and roll, which might have withered if not for the early 1960s 'British invasion,' in which the Beatles and the Rolling Stones, emulating Chuck Berry, Little Richard and others, shocked rock and roll back to life.

The 1960s witnessed a full-blown youth rebellion, epitomized by the drug-inspired psychedelic sounds of the Grateful Dead and Jefferson Airplane, and the electric wails of Janis Joplin and Jimi Hendrix. Ever since, rock has been about music *and* lifestyle, alternately torn between hedonism and seriousness, commercialism and authenticity.

Punk arrived in the late 1970s, led by the Ramones and the Dead Kennedys, as did the working-class rock of Bruce Springsteen and Tom Petty. As the counterculture became the culture in the 1980s, critics prematurely pronounced 'rock is dead.' Rock was saved (by the Talking Heads, REM, Nirvana, Sonic Youth, Pavement and Pearl Jam among others) as it always has been: by splintering and evolving, whether it's called new wave, heavy metal, grunge, indie rock, skate punk, hardcore, goth, emo or electronica.

In the early 2000s guitar groups the Killers, the Strokes, the Yeah Yeah Yeahs and the White Stripes were dubbed the saviors of rock for their stripped-back sound that saw the genre established as the commercial mainstream. While American rock music may be waiting for its next big revival, it's not going anywhere soon.

Rap & Hip-Hop

From the ocean of sounds coming out of the early 1970s – funk, soul, Latin, reggae, and rock and roll – young DJs from the Bronx in NYC began to spin a groundbreaking mixture of records together in an effort to drive dance floors wild. And so hip-hop was born. Groups such as Grandmaster Flash and the Furious Five were soon taking the party from the streets to the trendy clubs of Manhattan and mingling with punk and new wave bands including the Clash and Blondie.

As groups like Run-DMC, Public Enemy and the Beastie Boys sold millions, the sounds and styles of the growing hip-hop culture rapidly diversified. The confrontational 'gangsta rap' of Niggaz With Attitude (aka NWA) came out of Los Angeles, and the group got both accolades and bad press for its daring sounds and social commentary – which critics called battle cries for violence – on racism, drugs, sex and urban poverty.

Come the turn of the millennium, what started as some kids playing their parents' funk records at illegal block parties had evolved into a multibillion-dollar business and the second-most popular music genre in the USA. Russell Simmons and P Diddy stood atop media empires, and stars Queen Latifah and Will Smith were Hollywood royalty. A white rapper from Detroit, Eminem, sold millions of records.

Hip-hop is sometimes seen as a wasteland of commercial excess – glorifying consumerism, misogyny, homophobia, drug use and a host of other social ills. But just as the hedonistic days of arena rock and roll gave birth to the rebel child of punk, the evolving offspring of hip-hop and DJ culture are constantly breaking the rules. Today, rap/hip-hop is the most popular music in the USA, and major players include Drake, Kendrick Lamar and Cardi B. Drawing critical acclaim are rising stars such as Danny Brown, Anderson .Paak and Kamaiyah.

Music retailers usually combine hip-hop and rap into one category. What's the difference? Most would say that rap is a type of music, and hip-hop is a culture that includes rap as well as breakdancing, DJing and graffiti art. Rap must always contain a vocal element (its signature rhythmic rhymes) but hip-hop can be strictly instrumental.

The Land & Wildlife

The USA is home to creatures both great and small, from the ferocious grizzly to the industrious beaver, with colossal bison, snowy owls, soaring eagles, howling coyotes and doe-eyed manatees all part of the great American menagerie. The nation's varied geography — coastlines along two oceans, mountains, deserts, rainforests, and massive bay and river systems — harbor ecosystems where an extraordinary array of plant and animal life can flourish.

Geography

The USA is big, no question. Covering nearly 3.8 million sq miles, it's the world's third-largest country, trailing only Russia and Canada, its friendly neighbor to the north. The continental USA is made up of 48 contiguous states ('the lower 48'), while Alaska, its largest state, is northwest of Canada, and the volcanic islands of Hawaii, the 50th state, are 2300 miles southwest of the mainland in the Pacific Ocean.

High in the White Mountains (east of California's Sierra Nevada) stand the oldest single living plant species on earth. Known as bristlecone pines (Pinus longaeva), these bare and dramatically twisted trees date back more than 4000 years and have long mystified scientists with their extraordinary longevity.

It's more than just size, though. America feels big because of its incredibly diverse topography, which began to take shape around 50 to 60 million years ago.

In the contiguous USA, the east is a land of temperate, deciduous forests and contains the ancient Appalachian Mountains, a low range that parallels the Atlantic Ocean. Between the Appalachians and the coast lies the country's most populated, urbanized region, particularly in the corridor between Washington, DC, and Boston, MA.

To the north are the Great Lakes, which the USA shares with Canada. These five lakes are the greatest expanse of fresh water on the planet, constituting nearly 20% of the world's supply.

Going south along the East Coast, things get wetter and warmer till you reach the swamps of southern Florida and make the turn into the Gulf of Mexico, which provides the USA with its southern coastline.

West of the Appalachians are the vast interior plains, which lie flat all the way to the Rocky Mountains. The eastern plains are the nation's breadbasket, roughly divided into the northern 'corn belt' and the southern 'cotton belt.' The plains, an ancient sea bottom, are drained by the mighty Mississippi River, which together with the Missouri River forms the world's fourth-longest river system, surpassed only by the Nile, Amazon and Yangtze Rivers. Going west, farmland slowly gives way to cowboys and ranches in the semiarid, big-sky Great Plains.

The young, jagged Rocky Mountains are a complex set of tall ranges that run all the way from Mexico to Canada, providing excellent skiing. West of these mountains are the Southwestern deserts, an arid region of extremes that has been cut to dramatic effect by the Colorado River system. This land of eroded canyons leads to the unforgiving Great Basin as you go across Nevada. Also an ancient sea bottom, the Great Basin is used as a training ground and a test range by the US military. It's also where the USA plans to bury its nuclear waste.

Then you reach America's third major mountain system: the southern, granite Sierra Nevada and the northern, volcanic Cascades, which both parallel the Pacific Coast. California's Central Valley is one of the most fertile places on earth, while the coastline from San Diego to Seattle is celebrated in folk songs and Native American legends – a stretch of sandy beaches and old-growth forests, including coast redwoods.

But wait, there's more. Northwest of Canada, Alaska reaches the Arctic Ocean and contains tundra, glaciers, an interior rainforest and the lion's share of federally protected wilderness. Hawaii, in the Pacific Ocean, is a string of tropical island idylls.

Land Mammals

Nineteenth-century Americans did not willingly suffer competing predators, and federal eradication programs nearly wiped out every single wolf and big cat and many of the bears in the continental US. Almost all share the same story of abundance, precipitous loss and, today, partial recovery.

The grizzly bear, a subspecies of brown bear, is one of North America's largest land mammals. Male grizzlies can stand 7ft tall, weigh up to 850lb and consider 500 sq miles home. At one time, as many as 100,000 grizzlies roamed the West, but by 1975 fewer than 1000 remained. Conservation efforts, particularly in the Greater Yellowstone Region, have increased the population in the lower 48 states to about 1500 today. By contrast, Alaska remains chock-full of grizzlies, with upwards of 30,000. Despite a decline in numbers, black bears survive nearly everywhere. Smaller than grizzlies, these opportunistic, adaptable and curious animals can survive on very small home ranges.

Another extremely adaptable creature is the coyote, which looks similar to a wolf but is about half the size, ranging from 15lb to 45lb. An icon of the Southwest, coyotes are found all over, even in cities. The USA has one primary big-cat species, which goes by several names: mountain lion, cougar, puma and panther. In the east, a remnant population of panthers is found within Everglades National Park. In the West, mountain lions

Wilderness Films

Wild (Jean-Marc Vallée, 2014)

Winged Migration (Jacques Perrin, 2001)

Grizzly Man (Werner Herzog, 2005)

Into the Wild (Sean Penn, 2007)

Beasts of the Southern Wild (Benh Zeitlin, 2012)

The Revenant (Alejandro González Iñárritu, 2015)

RETURN OF THE WOLF

The wolf is a potent symbol of America's wilderness. This smart, social predator is the largest species of canine – averaging more than 100lb and reaching nearly 3ft at the shoulder. An estimated 400,000 once roamed the continent from coast to coast, from Alaska to Mexico.

Wolves were not regarded warmly by European settlers. The first wildlife legislation in the British colonies was a wolf bounty. As 19th-century Americans tamed the West, they slaughtered the once-uncountable herds of bison, elk, deer and moose, replacing them with domestic cattle and sheep, which wolves found equally tasty.

To stop wolves from devouring the livestock, the wolf's extermination soon became official government policy. Up until 1965, for $20 to $50 an animal, wolves were shot, poisoned, trapped and dragged from dens until in the lower 48 states only a few hundred gray wolves remained in northern Minnesota and Michigan.

In 1944 naturalist Aldo Leopold called for the return of the wolf. His argument was ecology, not nostalgia. His studies showed that wild ecosystems need their top predators to maintain a healthy biodiversity; in complex interdependence, all animals and plants suffered with the wolf gone.

Despite dire predictions from ranchers and hunters, gray wolves were reintroduced to the Greater Yellowstone region in 1995–96 and Mexican wolves to Arizona in 1998.

Protected and encouraged, wolf populations have made a remarkable recovery, with more than 6000 now counted in the continental US, and around 8000 in Alaska. In 2019, the US Fish & Wildlife Service proposed removing the gray wolf from the endangered species list; a decision is pending.

AMERICA'S WORST NATURAL DISASTERS

Earthquakes, wildfires, tornadoes, hurricanes and blizzards – the US certainly has its share of natural disasters. Just a few of the more infamous events that have shaped the national consciousness:

Johnstown Flood In 1889 torrential rains overwhelmed the South Fork dam that stood high on the Little Conemaugh River in Central Pennsylvania. When the dam broke, some 20 million tons of water and debris quickly inundated nearby Johnstown, killing over 2200 people and destroying 1600 homes.

Galveston Hurricane In 1900 Galveston – then known as 'the jewel of Texas' – was practically obliterated by a category-4 hurricane. Fifteen-foot waves destroyed buildings and at one point the entire island was submerged. More than 8000 perished, making it America's deadliest natural disaster.

1906 San Francisco Earthquake A powerful earthquake (estimated to be around an 8 on the Richter scale) leveled the city, followed by even more devastating fires. The quake was felt as far away as Oregon and Central Nevada. An estimated 3000-plus died, while more than 200,000 people (of a population of 410,000) were left homeless.

Dust Bowl During a prolonged drought of the 1930s, the overworked topsoil of the Great Plains dried up, turned to dust and billowed eastward in massive windstorm-fueled 'black blizzards,' reaching all the way to NYC and Washington, DC. Millions of acres of crops were destroyed and more than 500,000 people were left homeless. The great exodus westward by stricken farmers and migrants was immortalized in John Steinbeck's *The Grapes of Wrath*.

Hurricane Katrina August 29, 2005, is not a day easily forgotten in New Orleans. A massive category-5 hurricane swept across the Gulf of Mexico and slammed into Louisiana. As levees failed, floods inundated more than 80% of the city. The death toll reached 1836, with more than $100 billion in estimated damages.

Hurricane Sandy In 2012 this hurricane affected some 24 states, with New Jersey and New York among the hardest hit. More than 100 died in the USA, and estimated damages amounted to more than $65 billion. It was also the largest Atlantic hurricane ever recorded, with storm winds spanning over 1100 miles.

Hurricane Irma On September 10, 2017, one of the largest hurricanes ever recorded barreled over Florida, causing flooding and destruction. Hurricane Irma made landfall in the Florida Keys as a category 4 storm the width of Texas. Homes and businesses in Everglades City were left battered and mud-soaked after an 8ft storm surge; in the Keys, a Federal Emergency Management Agency survey reported that 25% of buildings had been destroyed, with another 65% damaged.

are common enough for human encounters to be on the increase. These powerful cats are about 150lb of pure muscle, with short, tawny fur and long tails.

The story of the great American buffalo (or bison) is a tragic one. These massive herbivores numbered as many as 65 million in 1800 – in herds so thick they 'darkened the whole plains,' as explorers Lewis and Clark wrote. They were killed for food, hides, sport and to impoverish Native Americans, who depended on them for survival. By the 20th century, only a few hundred bison remained. Overcoming near extinction, new herds arose from these last survivors, so that one of America's noblest animals can again be admired in its gruff majesty – among other places, in Yellowstone, Grand Teton and Badlands National Parks.

Marine Mammals & Fish

Perhaps no native fish gets more attention than salmon, whose spawning runs up Pacific Coast rivers provide famous spectacles. However, both

Pacific and Atlantic salmon are considered endangered; hatcheries release millions of young every year, but there is debate about whether this practice hurts or helps wild populations.

As for marine life, gray, humpback and blue whales migrate annually along the Pacific Coast, making whale-watching very popular. Alaska and Hawaii are important breeding grounds for whales and marine mammals, and Washington's San Juan Islands are visited by orcas. The Pacific Coast is also home to ponderous elephant seals, playful sea lions and endangered sea otters.

In California, Channel Islands National Park and Monterey Bay preserve unique, highly diverse marine worlds. For coral reefs and tropical fish, Hawaii and the Florida Keys are the prime destinations. The coast of Florida is also home to the unusual, gentle manatee, which moves between freshwater rivers and the ocean. Around 10ft long and weighing on average 1000lb, these agile, expressive creatures number around 6500 today, and may once have been mistaken for mermaids.

The Gulf of Mexico is another vital marine habitat, perhaps most famously for endangered sea turtles, which nest on coastal beaches.

Birds

Birding is the most popular wildlife-watching activity in the US, and little wonder – all the hemisphere's migratory songbirds and shorebirds rest here at some point, and the USA consequently claims some 800 native avian species.

The bald eagle was adopted as the nation's symbol in 1782. It's the only eagle unique to North America, and perhaps half a million once ruled the continent's skies. By 1963, habitat destruction and, in particular, poisoning from DDT had caused the population to plummet to 487 breeding pairs in the lower 48 states. By 2007, however, bald eagles had recovered so well, increasing to almost 9800 breeding pairs across the continent (plus 30,000 in Alaska), that they were removed from the endangered species list.

Another impressive bird is the endangered California condor, a prehistoric, carrion-eating bird that weighs about 20lb and has a wingspan of over 9ft. Condors were virtually extinct by the 1980s (reduced to just 22 birds), but they have been successfully bred and reintroduced in California and northern Arizona, where they can sometimes be spotted soaring above the Grand Canyon.

The Environmental Movement

The USA is well known for its political and social revolutions, but it also birthed modern environmentalism. The USA was the first nation to make significant efforts to preserve its wilderness, and US environmentalists often spearhead preservation efforts worldwide.

America's Protestant settlers believed that civilization's Christian mandate was to bend nature to its will. Not only was wilderness deadly and difficult, it was also a potent symbol of humanity's godless impulses, and the Pilgrims set about subduing both with gusto.

Then, in the mid-19th century, taking their cue from European Romantics, the USA's transcendentalists claimed that nature was not fallen, but holy. In *Walden; or, Life in the Woods* (1854), iconoclast Henry David Thoreau described living for two years in the woods, blissfully free of civilization's comforts. He persuasively argued that human society was harmfully distant from nature's essential truths. This view marked a profound shift toward believing that nature, the soul and God were one.

Unusual Wildlife Reads

Rats (Robert Sullivan)

Pigeons (Andrew Blechman)

Secret Life of Lobsters (Trevor Corson)

American Buffalo (Steven Rinella)

The Beast in the Garden (David Baron)

THE LAND & WILDLIFE BIRDS

John Muir & National Parks

The continent's natural wonders – vividly captured by America's 19th-century landscape painters – had a way of selling themselves, and rampant nationalism led to a desire to promote them. In the late 1800s, US presidents began setting aside land for state and national parks.

Scottish naturalist John Muir soon emerged to champion wilderness for its own sake. Muir considered nature superior to civilization, and he spent much of his life wandering the Sierra Nevada mountain range and passionately advocating on its behalf. Muir was the driving force behind the USA's emerging conservation movement, which had its first big victory in 1890 when Yosemite National Park was established. Muir founded the Sierra Club in 1892 and slowly gained national attention.

Environmental Laws & Climate Change

In the late 19th and early 20th centuries, the USA passed a series of landmark environmental and wildlife laws that resulted in significant improvements in the nation's water and air quality, and the partial recovery of many near-extinct plants and animals. The movement's focus steadily broadened – to preserving entire ecosystems, not just establishing parks – as it confronted devastation wrought by pollution, overkill of species, habitat destruction through human impact and the introduction of nonnative species.

Today environmentalism is a worldwide movement, one that understands that each nation's local problems also contribute to a global threat: climate change. In the USA, the dangers of global warming are inspiring an environmental awareness as widespread as at any time in US history. Whether or not average Americans believe God speaks through nature, they're increasingly disturbed by the messages they are hearing.

Survival Guide

Directory A–Z

Accessible Travel

If you have a physical disability, the USA can be an accommodating place. The Americans with Disabilities Act (ADA) requires that all public buildings, private buildings built after 1993 (including hotels, restaurants, theaters and museums) and public transit be wheelchair accessible. However, call ahead to confirm what is available. Some local tourist offices publish detailed accessibility guides. For tips on travel and thoughtful insight on traveling with a disability, check out online posts by Martin Heng, Lonely Planet's Accessible Travel Manager: twitter.com/martin_heng, or download Lonely Planet's free Accessible Travel guide from http://lptravel.to/AccessibleTravel.

Phone companies offer relay operators, available via teletypewriter (TTY) numbers, for the hearing impaired. Most banks provide ATM instructions in Braille and via earphone jacks for hearing-impaired customers. Major airlines, Greyhound buses and Amtrak trains will assist travelers with disabilities; just describe your needs when making reservations at least 48 hours in advance. Service animals are allowed to accompany passengers, but bring documentation.

Some car-rental agencies, such as Budget and Hertz, offer hand-controlled vehicles and vans with wheelchair lifts at no extra charge, but you must reserve them well in advance. Wheelchair Getaways (www.wheelchairgetaways.com) rents accessible vans throughout the USA. In many cities and towns, public buses are accessible to wheelchair riders and will 'kneel' if you are unable to use the steps; just let the driver know that you need the lift or ramp.

Most cities have taxi companies with at least one accessible van, though you'll have to call ahead. Cities with underground transport have varying levels of facilities such as elevators for passengers needing assistance – DC has the best network (every station has an elevator), while NYC has elevators in about a quarter of its stations.

Many national and some state parks and recreation areas have wheelchair-accessible paved, graded-dirt or boardwalk trails. US citizens and permanent residents with permanent disabilities are entitled to a free 'America the Beautiful' Access Pass. Go online (www.nps.gov/findapark/passes.htm) for details.

Some helpful resources for travelers with disabilities:

Disabled Sports USA (www.disabledsportsusa.org) Offers sport, adventure and recreation programs for those with disabilities. Also publishes *Challenge* magazine.

Flying Wheels Travel (www.flyingwheelstravel.com) A full-service travel agency, highly recommended for those with mobility issues or chronic illness.

Mobility International USA (www.miusa.org) Advises USA-bound disabled travelers on mobility issues, and promotes the global participation of people with disabilities in international exchange and travel programs.

Customs Regulations

For a complete list of US customs regulations, visit the official portal for US Customs and Border Protection (www.cbp.gov).

Duty-free allowance per person is as follows:

➡ 1L of liquor (provided you are at least 21 years old)

➡ 100 cigars and 200 cigarettes (if you are at least 18 years old)

➡ $200 worth of gifts and purchases ($800 if you're a returning US citizen)

➡ If you arrive with $10,000 or more in US or foreign currency, it must be declared. There are heavy penalties for attempting to import illegal drugs. Forbidden items include drug paraphernalia, lottery tickets, items with fake brand names, and most goods made in North Korea, Cuba, Iran, Syria and Sudan. Fruit, vegetables and other food or plant material must be declared or left in the arrival-area bins.

Discount Cards

The following passes can net you savings on museums, accommodations and some transport:

American Association of Retired Persons (AARP; www. aarp.org) Paid membership ($16 per year) earns discounts on hotels, car rentals and more for US travelers from any country, aged 50 and older.

International Student Identity Card (ISIC: www.isic.org) Discount card for full-time students of any nationality who are 12 years old and over; similar cards available for full-time teachers and for youth 30 years and under.

Student Advantage Card (www. studentadvantage.com) For US and foreign students.

Membership in the **American Automobile Association** (AAA; www.aaa.com) and reciprocal clubs in the UK, Australia and elsewhere can also earn discounts.

Electricity

AC 120V is standard; buy adapters to run most non-US electronics.

Type A
120V/60Hz

Type B
120V/60Hz

Embassies & Consulates

In addition to the following foreign embassies in Washington, DC (see www. embassy.org for a complete list), most countries have an embassy for the UN in New York City. Some countries have consulates in other large cities – check online, look under 'Consulates' in the *Yellow Pages,* or call local directory assistance.

Australian (☎202-797-3000; www.usa.embassy.gov.au; 1601 Massachusetts Ave NW; ◷8:30am-5pm Mon-Fri; Ⓜ Red Line to Farragut North)

Canadian (☎202-682-1740; www.can-am.gc.ca; 501 Pennsylvania Ave NW, Penn Quarter; ◷9am-noon Mon-Fri; Ⓜ Green, Yellow Line to Archives)

French (☎202-944-6000; www.franceintheus.org; 4101 Reservoir Rd NW; ◷8:45am-12:30pm & 2:30-3:30pm Mon-Fri; Ⓜ Red Line to Dupont Circle, then bus D6)

German (☎202-298-4000; www.germany.info; 4645 Reservoir Rd NW; ◷8-11:45am & 1-2:30pm Mon-Thu, 8am-noon Fri; ▯D6)

Irish (☎202-462-3939; www. embassyofireland.org; 2234 Massachusetts Ave NW; ◷9am-1pm & 2-4pm Mon-Fri; Ⓜ Red Line to Dupont Circle)

Mexican (☎202-728-1600; https://embamex.sre.gob.mx/eua; 1911 Pennsylvania Ave NW; ◷9am-6pm Mon-Fri; Ⓜ Orange, Silver, Blue Lines to Farragut West)

Netherlands (☎202-244-5300; www.netherlandsworldwide.nl/countries/united-states; 4200 Linnean Ave NW, Forest Hills; ◷8:30am-4:30pm Mon-Fri; Ⓜ Red Line to Van Ness-UDC)

New Zealand (☎202-328-4800; www.mfat.govt.nz/usa; 37 Observatory Circle NW, Embassy Row; ◷9am-4pm Mon-Fri; Ⓜ Red Line to Dupont Circle, then bus N2 or N4)

UK (☎202-588-6500; www. gov.uk/government/world/usa; 3100 Massachusetts Ave NW, Embassy Row; ◷9am-4pm Mon-Fri; Ⓜ Red Line to Dupont Circle, then bus N2 or N4)

Food & Drink

In a country of such size and regional variation, you could spend a lifetime eating your way across America and barely scratch the surface. Owing to such scope, dining American-style could mean many things: from munching on pulled-pork sandwiches at an old roadhouse to feasting on sustainably sourced seafood in a waterfront dining room.

Health

The USA offers excellent health care. The problem is that, unless you have good insurance, it can be prohibitively expensive. It's essential to purchase travel health insurance if your regular policy doesn't cover you when you're abroad.

Bring any medications you may need in their original containers, clearly labeled. A signed, dated letter from your physician that describes all medical conditions and medications, including generic names, is also a good idea.

Insurance

Health-care costs in the USA are extremely high. All travelers are advised to carry a valid health-insurance policy. Without insurance you may be billed the full cost of any care you receive. Costs can easily rise into the thousands of dollars, especially for emergency-room visits. If your health insurance doesn't cover you for medical expenses abroad, consider supplemental insurance. Find out in advance if your insurance plan will make payments directly to providers or reimburse you later for overseas health expenditures.

Medical Checklist

Recommended items for a medical kit:

➡ acetaminophen (Tylenol) or aspirin

➡ antibacterial ointment (eg Bactroban) for cuts and abrasions

➡ antihistamines (for hay fever and allergic reactions)

➡ anti-inflammatory drugs (eg ibuprofen)

➡ bandages, gauze, gauze rolls

➡ sunblock

➡ insect repellent for the skin

Resources

The World Health Organization publishes regular international health advisories for travelers, along with the book *International Travel and*

Health, available free online at www.who.int/ith/en.

It's usually a good idea to consult your government's travel-health website before departure:

Australia (www.smartraveller. gov.au)

Canada (www.hc-sc.gc.ca, www. travel.gc.ca)

UK (www.travelhealthpro.org.uk)

Vaccinations

No vaccinations are currently recommended or required for temporary visitors to the USA. For the most up-to-date information, see the Centers for Disease Control website (www.cdc.gov).

Availability & Cost of Health Care

In general, if you have a medical emergency your best bet is to find the nearest hospital and go to its emergency room. If the problem isn't urgent, you can call a nearby hospital and ask for a referral to a local physician, which is usually much cheaper than a trip to the emergency room. Stand-alone, for-profit, urgent-care centers can be convenient, but may perform large numbers of expensive tests, even for minor illnesses.

Pharmacies are abundantly supplied, but you may find that some medications that are available over the counter in your home country (such as Ventolin, for asthma) require a prescription in the USA and, as always, if you don't have insurance to cover the cost of prescriptions, they can be shockingly expensive.

Tap Water

Tap water is drinkable virtually everywhere in the USA.

Insurance

No matter how long or short your trip, make sure you have adequate travel insurance, purchased before departure. At a minimum, you need coverage for medical emergencies and treatment, including hospital stays and an emergency flight home if necessary. Medical treatment in the USA is of the highest caliber, but the expense could bankrupt you.

You should also consider getting coverage for luggage theft or loss and trip cancellation. If you already have a homeowner's or renter's policy, see what it will cover and consider getting supplemental insurance to cover the rest. If you have prepaid a large portion of your trip, cancellation insurance is a worthwhile expense. A comprehensive travel-insurance policy that covers all these things can cost up to 10% of the total outlay of your trip.

If you will be driving, it's essential that you have liability insurance. Car-rental agencies offer insurance that covers damage to the rental vehicle and separate liability insurance, which covers damage to people and other vehicles.

Worldwide travel insurance is available at www.lonely planet.com/travel-insurance. You can buy, extend and claim online anytime – even if you're already on the road.

Internet Access

Travelers will have few problems staying connected in the tech-savvy USA. Most hotels, guesthouses, hostels and motels have wi-fi (usually free, though luxury hotels are more likely to charge for access); ask when reserving.

Across the US, most cafes offer free wi-fi. Some cities

have wi-fi-connected parks and plazas. If you're not packing a laptop or other web-accessible device, try the public library – most have public terminals (though they have time limits) in addition to wi-fi. Occasionally out-of-state residents are charged a small fee.

If you're not from the US, remember that you will need an AC adapter for your laptop, plus a plug adapter for US sockets; both are available at larger electronics shops, such as Best Buy.

Legal Matters

If you are stopped by the police, bear in mind that there is no system of paying traffic or other fines on the spot. Attempting to pay a fine to an officer is frowned upon at best and may result in a charge of bribery. For traffic offenses, the police officer or highway patrol will explain the options to you. There is usually a 30-day period to pay a fine. Most matters can be handled by mail.

If you are arrested, you have a legal right to an attorney, and you are allowed to remain silent. There is no legal reason to speak to a police officer if you don't wish to, but never walk away from an officer until given permission to do so. Anyone who is arrested is legally allowed to make one phone call. If you can't afford a lawyer, a public defender will be appointed to you free of charge. Foreign visitors who don't have a lawyer, friend or family member to help them should call their embassy; the police will provide the number upon request.

As a matter of principle, the US legal system presumes a person innocent until proven guilty. Each state has its own civil and criminal laws, and what is legal in one state may be illegal in others.

Drinking

Bars and stores often ask for photo ID to prove you're of legal drinking age (21 years or over). Being 'carded' is standard practice; don't take it personally. The sale of liquor is subject to local government regulations – some counties prohibit liquor sales on Sunday, after midnight or before breakfast. In 'dry' counties, alcohol sales are banned altogether.

Driving

In all states, driving under the influence of alcohol or drugs is a serious offense, subject to stiff fines and even imprisonment. A blood alcohol level of 0.08% or higher is illegal in all jurisdictions.

Marijuana & Other Substances

The states have quite different laws regarding the use of marijuana, and what's legal in one state may be illegal in others. As of mid-2019, recreational use of small amounts of marijuana (generally up to 1oz/28g) was legal in Alaska, California, Colorado, Maine, Massachusetts, Michigan, Nevada, Oregon, Vermont, Washington and the District of Columbia. Another 15 states have decriminalized marijuana (treating recreational use as a civil violation similar to a minor traffic infraction), while others continue to criminalize nonmedical use, punishing possession of small amounts as a misdemeanor and larger amounts as a felony. Thus, it's essential to know the local laws before lighting up – see http://norml.org/laws for a state-by-state breakdown.

Aside from marijuana, recreational drugs are prohibited by federal and state laws. Possession of any illicit drug, including cocaine, ecstasy, LSD, heroin and hashish, is a felony potentially punishable by a lengthy jail sentence. For foreigners, conviction of any

drug offense is grounds for deportation.

LGBTIQ+ Travelers

There has never been a better time to be gay in the USA. LGBT+ travelers will find lots of places where they can be themselves without thinking twice. Beaches and big cities typically are the most gay-friendly destinations.

Hot Spots

Manhattan has loads of great gay bars and clubs, especially in Hells Kitchen, Chelsea and the West Village. A few hours away (by train and ferry) is Fire Island, the sandy gay mecca on Long Island. Other East Coast cities that flaunt it are Boston, Philadelphia, Washington, DC, Massachusetts' Provincetown on Cape Cod and Delaware's Rehoboth Beach. Even Maine brags a gay beach destination: Ogunquit.

In the South, there's always steamy 'Hotlanta,' and Texas gets darn-right gay-friendly in Austin and parts of Houston and Dallas. Florida, Miami and the 'Conch Republic' of Key West support thriving gay communities, though Fort Lauderdale attracts bronzed boys and girls, too. New Orleans has a lively gay scene.

In the Great Lakes region, seek out Chicago and Minneapolis. Further west, you'll find San Francisco, probably the happiest gay city in America. There's also Los Angeles and Las Vegas, where pretty much anything goes. When LA or Vegas gets to be too much, flee to the desert resorts of Palm Springs.

Lastly, for an island idyll, Hawaii is generally gay-friendly, especially in Waikiki.

Attitudes

Most major US cities have a visible and open LGBT+

community that is easy to connect with. Same-sex marriage was legalized nationwide by the US Supreme Court in 2015, and a 2019 Pew Research survey showed a majority of Americans (61%) support same-sex marriage.

The level of acceptance varies nationwide. In some places, there is absolutely no tolerance whatsoever, and in others acceptance is predicated on LGBT+ people not 'flaunting' their sexual preference or identity. Bigotry still exists. In rural areas and conservative enclaves, it's unwise to be openly out, as violence and verbal abuse can sometimes occur. When in doubt, assume locals follow a 'don't ask, don't tell' policy.

Resources

The Queerest Places: A Guide to Gay and Lesbian Historic Sites by Paula Martinac is full of juicy details and history, and covers the country. Visit her blog at www.queerestplaces.com.

Advocate (www.advocate.com) Gay-oriented news website reports on business, politics, arts, entertainment and travel.

Damron (www.damron.com) Publishes the classic gay travel guides, but they're advertiser-driven and sometimes outdated.

Gay & Lesbian National Help Center (www.glnh.org) Counseling, information and referrals.

Gay Travel (www.gaytravel.com) Online guides to dozens of US destinations.

National LGBTQ Task Force (www.thetaskforce.org) National activist group's website covers news, politics and current issues.

Out Traveler (www.outtraveler. com) Gay-oriented travel articles.

Purple Roofs (www.purpleroofs. com) Lists gay-owned and gay-friendly B&Bs and hotels.

Money

ATMs

ATMs are available 24/7 at most banks, and in shopping centers, airports, grocery stores and convenience shops. Most ATMs charge a service fee of $2.50 or more per transaction and your home bank may impose additional charges. Withdrawing cash from an ATM using a credit card usually incurs a hefty fee.

For foreign visitors, ask your bank or credit-card company for exact information about using its cards in stateside ATMs. If you will be relying on ATMs (not a bad strategy), bring more than one card and carry them separately. The exchange rate on ATM transactions is usually as good as you'll get anywhere. Before leaving home, notify your bank and credit-card providers of your travel plans, to avoid triggering fraud alerts.

Credit Cards

Major credit cards are almost universally accepted. In fact, it's almost impossible to rent a car or make hotel reservations without one. It's highly recommended that you carry at least one credit card, if only for emergencies. Visa and MasterCard are the most widely accepted.

Foreign visitors may have to go inside to pre-pay at gas stations, since most pay-at-the-pump options require a card with a US zip code. Some airlines also require a US billing address – a hassle if you're booking domestic flights once in the country. Note, too, that you may be asked to 'sign' for credit card purchases, or face a confused clerk or waiter when your card does not require a signature, as US credit card companies have yet to embrace the chip + PIN method available elsewhere in the world. It's normal for restaurant servers to take your card to a pay station to

process instead of allowing you to pay at the table. Mobile pay options (Apple Pay, Google Pay) are becoming increasingly common and are a good way to bridge the technology gap.

Money Changers

Banks are usually the best places to exchange foreign currencies. Most large city banks offer currency exchange, but banks in rural areas may not. Currency-exchange counters at the airport and in tourist centers typically have the worst rates; ask about fees and surcharges first. Travelex (www. travelex.com) is a major currency-exchange company, but American Express (www. americanexpress.com) travel offices may offer better rates.

Taxes

Five states (Alaska, Delaware, Montana, New Hampshire and Oregon) do not impose a statewide sales tax. Elsewhere, sales tax varies by state and county, and ranges from 5% to 10%. Most prices you see advertised will exclude tax, which is calculated upon purchase.

Hotel taxes are charged in addition to sales tax and vary by city and state from around 10% to 18.75% (New York City).

Tipping

Tipping is *not* optional; only withhold tips in cases of outrageously bad service.

Airport & hotel porters $2 per bag, minimum per cart $5

Bartenders 15% to 20% per round, minimum per drink $1

Hotel housekeepers $2 to $5 per night, left under the card provided

Restaurant servers 15% to 20%, unless a gratuity is already charged on the bill

Taxi drivers 10% to 15%, rounded up to the next dollar

Valet parking attendants At least $2 on return of the keys

Opening Hours

Typical opening times are as follows:

Banks 8:30am–4:30pm Monday to Thursday, to 5:30pm Friday (and possibly 9am–noon Saturday)

Bars 5pm–midnight Sunday to Thursday, to 2am Friday and Saturday

Nightclubs 10pm–4am Thursday to Saturday

Post offices 9am–5pm Monday to Friday

Shopping malls 9am–9pm

Stores 9am–6pm Monday to Saturday, noon–5pm Sunday

Supermarkets 8am–8pm, some open 24 hours

Post

For postal information, including post-office locations and hours, contact the US Postal Service (www.usps.com), which is reliable and inexpensive.

The postal rates for first-class mail within the USA are 55¢ for letters weighing up to 1oz (15¢ for each additional ounce) and 35¢ for postcards.

International airmail rates are $1.15 for a 1oz letter or postcard.

For sending urgent or important letters and packages either domestically or internationally, FedEx (www.fedex.com) and UPS (www.ups.com) offer more expensive door-to-door delivery services.

Public Holidays

On the following national public holidays, banks, schools and government offices (including post offices) are closed, and transportation, museums and other services operate on a Sunday schedule. Holidays falling on a weekend are usually observed the following Monday.

New Year's Day January 1

Martin Luther King Jr Day Third Monday in January

Presidents' Day Third Monday in February

Memorial Day Last Monday in May

Independence Day July 4

Labor Day First Monday in September

Columbus Day Second Monday in October

Veterans' Day November 11

Thanksgiving Fourth Thursday in November

Christmas Day December 25

During spring break, high school and college students get a week off from school so they can overrun beach towns and resorts. This occurs throughout March and April. For students of all ages, summer vacation runs from June to August.

Safe Travel

Despite its seemingly apocalyptic list of dangers – violent crime, riots, earthquakes, tornadoes – the USA is actually a pretty safe country to visit. The greatest danger for travelers is posed by car accidents (buckle up – it's the law).

Crime

For the traveler it's not violent crime but petty theft that is the biggest concern. When possible, withdraw money from ATMs during the day, or in well-lit, busy areas at night. When driving, don't pick up hitchhikers, and lock valuables in the trunk of your car. In hotels, you can secure valuables in your room or hotel safes.

Scams

Pack your street smarts. In big cities, don't forget that three-card-monte card games are always rigged, and that expensive electronics, watches and designer items sold on the cheap from sidewalk tables are either fakes or stolen.

Natural Disasters

Most areas with predictable natural disturbances – tornadoes on the Great Plains and the South, tsunamis in Hawaii, hurricanes in the Gulf and Atlantic Coasts, earthquakes in California – have an emergency-siren system to alert communities to imminent danger. These sirens are tested periodically at noon, but if you hear one and suspect trouble, turn on a local TV or radio station, which will be broadcasting safety warnings and advice. Incidentally, hurricane season runs from June to November.

The US Department of Health and Human Services (www.phe.gov) has preparedness advice, news and information on all the ways your vacation could go horribly, horribly wrong. But relax: it probably won't.

Telephone

The US phone system comprises regional service providers, competing long-distance carriers and several cell-phone and payphone companies. Overall, the system is very efficient, but it can be expensive. Avoid making long-distance calls on a hotel phone or on a pay phone. It's usually cheaper to use a regular landline or cell phone. Most hotels allow guests to make free local calls.

Telephone books can be handy resources: some list community services, public transportation and things to see and do as well as phone and business listings. Online phone directories include www.411.com and www.yellowpages.com.

Cell/Mobile Phones

Tri- or quad-band phones brought from overseas will generally work in the USA. However, you should check with your service provider to see if roaming charges apply, as these will turn even local US calls into pricey international calls.

It's often cheaper to buy a compatible prepaid SIM card for the USA, such as those sold by AT&T, which you can insert into your international cell phone to get a local phone number and voicemail. Telestial (www.telestial.com) offers these services.

If you don't have a compatible phone, you can buy inexpensive, no-contract (prepaid) phones with a local number and a set number of minutes, which can be topped up at will. Virgin Mobile, T-Mobile, AT&T and other providers offer phones starting around $20, with a package of minutes starting around $20 for 400 minutes, or $30 monthly for unlimited minutes. Elec-

tronics stores such as Radio Shack and Best Buy sell these phones.

Huge swaths of rural America, including many national parks and recreation areas, don't pick up a signal. Check your provider's coverage map.

Dialing Codes

All phone numbers within the USA consist of a three-digit area code followed by a seven-digit local number.

Typically, if you are calling a number within the same area code, you only have to dial the seven-digit number (though if it doesn't work, try adding 1 + the area code at the beginning). If you're calling long distance, dial 🖉1 plus the area code plus the phone number. More information on dialing:

US country code 🖉1

Making international calls Dial 🖉011 + country code + area code + local number

Calling other US area codes or Canada Dial 🖉1 + area code + seven-digit local number

Directory assistance nationwide 🖉411

Toll-free prefix 🖉1-800 (or 888, 877, 866). Some toll-free numbers only work within the US

Pay-per-call prefix 🖉1-900. These calls are charged at a premium per-minute rate – phone sex, horoscopes, jokes etc

Phonecards

If you're traveling without a cell phone or in a region with limited cell service, a prepaid phonecard is an alternative solution. Phonecards typically come precharged with a fixed number of minutes that can be used

on any phone, including landlines. You'll generally need to dial an 800 number and enter a PIN (personal identification number) before placing each call. Phonecards are available from online retailers such as amazon.com and at some convenience stores. Be sure to read the fine print, as many cards contain hidden charges such as 'activation fees' or per-call 'connection fees' in addition to the per-minute rates.

Time

The USA uses daylight saving time (DST). At 2am on the second Sunday in March, clocks are set one hour ahead ('spring forward'). Then on the first Sunday of November, clocks are turned back one hour ('fall back'). Just to keep you on your toes, Arizona (except the Navajo Nation) and Hawaii don't follow DST.

The US date system is written as month/day/year. Thus, 8 June 2020 becomes 6/8/20.

Toilets

Toilets in the USA are universally of the sit-down variety and generally of high standard. Most states have rest areas with free toilets along major highways; alternatively, you can seek out toilets at gas stations, coffee shops and chain restaurants – technically these are for the use of paying customers, but you may be able to use them free of charge by asking or discreetly entering. Public buildings such as airports, train and bus stations, libraries and museums usually have free toilet facilities for public use. Some towns and cities also provide public toilets, though these are not widespread.

Tourist Information

For links to the official tourism websites of every US state and most major cities, see www.visit-usa.com. The similarly named www.visit theusa.com is jam-packed with itinerary planning ideas and other useful info.

Any tourist office worth contacting has a website, where you can download free travel e-guides. Some local offices maintain daily lists of hotel-room availability, but few offer reservation services. All tourist offices have self-service racks of brochures and discount coupons; some also sell maps and books.

State-run 'welcome centers,' usually placed along interstate highways, tend to have free state road maps, brochures and other travel planning materials. These offices are usually open longer hours, including weekends and holidays.

Many cities have an official convention and visitors bureau (CVB). These sometimes double as tourist bureaus, but since their main focus is drawing the business trade, CVBs can be less useful for independent travelers. These entities tend to list only the businesses that are bureau/chamber members, so not all of the town's hotels and restaurants receive coverage – keep in mind that good, independent options may be missing.

Similarly in prime tourist destinations, some private 'tourist bureaus' are really agents that book hotel rooms and tours on commission. They may offer excellent service and deals, but you'll get what they're selling and nothing else.

Visas

Visitors from the UK, Australia, New Zealand, Japan and many EU countries don't need visas for stays of less than 90 days, though they must get approval from the Electronic System for Travel Authorization (ESTA). Visitors from Canada need neither a visa nor ESTA approval for stays of less than 90 days. Citizens of other nations should check http://travel.state.gov.

Be warned that all visa information is highly subject to change. US entry requirements keep evolving as national security regulations change. All travelers should double-check current visa and passport regulations *before* coming to the USA.

The US State Department (www.travel.state.gov) maintains the most comprehensive visa information, providing downloadable forms, lists of US consulates abroad and even visa wait times calculated by country.

Visa Applications

Apart from most Canadian citizens and those entering under the Visa Waiver Program (p1173), all foreign visitors will need to obtain a visa from a US consulate or embassy abroad. Most applicants must schedule a personal interview, to which you must bring all your documentation and proof of fee payment. Wait times for interviews vary, but afterwards, barring problems, visa issuance takes from a few days to a few weeks.

➡ Your passport must be valid for the entirety of your intended stay in the USA, and sometimes six months longer, depending on your country of citizenship. You'll need a recent photo (2in by 2in) and you must pay a nonrefundable $160 processing fee, plus in a few cases an additional visa-issuance reciprocity fee. You'll also need to fill out the online DS-160 nonimmigrant visa electronic application.

➡ Visa applicants are required to show documents of financial stability (or evidence that a US resident will provide financial support), a round-trip or onward ticket and 'binding obligations' that will ensure their return home, such as family ties, a home or a job. Because of these requirements, those planning to travel through other countries before arriving in the USA are generally better off applying for a US visa while they're still in their home country, rather than while on the road.

➡ The most common visa is a nonimmigrant visitor's visa: type B-1 for business purposes, B-2 for tourism or visiting friends and relatives. A visitor's visa is good for multiple entries over one or five years, and specifically prohibits the visitor from taking paid employment in the USA. The validity period depends on what country you are from. The actual length of time you'll be allowed to stay in the USA is determined by US immigration at the port of entry.

➡ If you're coming to the USA to work or study, you will need a different type of visa, and the company or institution to which you are going should make the arrangements.

Grounds for Exclusion & Deportation

If on your visa application form you admit to being a subversive, smuggler, prostitute, drug addict, terrorist or an ex-Nazi, you may be excluded. You can also be refused a visa or entry to the USA if you have a 'communicable disease of public health significance' or a criminal record, or if you've ever made a false statement in connection with a US visa application. However, if any of these last three apply, you're still able to request an exemption; many people are granted them and then given visas.

Communicable diseases include tuberculosis, the Ebola virus, gonorrhea, syphilis, infectious leprosy and any disease deemed subject to quarantine by Presidential Executive Order. US immigration doesn't test people for disease, but officials at the point of entry may question anyone about his or her health. They can exclude anyone whom they believe has a communicable disease, perhaps because they are carrying medical documents, prescriptions or medicine. Being an IV drug user is also grounds for exclusion. Visitors may be deported if US immigration finds out they have HIV but did not declare it. Being HIV-positive is no longer grounds for deportation, but failing to provide accurate information on the visa application is.

The US immigration department has a very broad definition of a criminal record. If you've ever been arrested or charged with an offense, that's a criminal record, even if you were acquitted or discharged without conviction. Don't attempt to enter through the VWP if you have a criminal record of any kind; assume US authorities will find out about it.

Often United States Citizenship and Immigration Services (USCIS) will grant an exemption (a 'waiver of ineligibility') to a person who would normally be subject to exclusion, but this requires referral to a regional immigration office and can take some time (allow at least two months). If you're tempted to conceal something, remember that US immigration is strictest of all about false statements. It will often view favorably an applicant who admits to an old criminal charge or a communicable disease, but it is extremely harsh on anyone who has ever attempted to mislead it, even on minor points. After you're admitted to the USA, any evidence of a false statement to US immigration is grounds for deportation.

Prospective visitors to whom grounds of exclusion may apply should consider their options *before* applying for a visa.

Entering the USA

➡ Everyone arriving in the US needs to fill out the US customs declaration. US and Canadian citizens, along with eligible foreign nationals participating in the Visa Waiver Program, can complete this procedure electronically at an APC (Automated Passport Control) kiosk upon disembarking. All others must fill out a paper customs declaration, which is usually handed out on the plane. Have it completed before you approach the immigration desk. For the question, 'US Street Address,' give the address where you will spend the first night (a hotel address is fine).

➡ No matter what your visa says, US immigration officers have absolute authority to refuse admission to the country, or to impose conditions on admission. They may ask about your plans and whether you have sufficient funds; it's a good idea to list an itinerary, produce an onward or round-trip ticket and have at least one major credit card.

➡ The Department of Homeland Security's registration program, called Office of Biometric Identity Management, includes every port of entry and nearly every foreign visitor to the USA. For most visitors (excluding, for now, most Canadian and some Mexican citizens), registration consists of having a digital photo and electronic (inkless) fingerprints taken; the process takes less than a minute.

Visa Extensions

To stay in the USA longer than the date stamped on your passport, go to a local USCIS (www.uscis.gov) office to apply for an extension well before the stamped date. If the date has passed, your best chance will be to bring a US citizen with you to vouch for your character, and to produce lots of other verification that you are not trying to work illegally and have enough money to support yourself. However, if you've overstayed, the most likely scenario is that you will be deported. Travelers who enter the USA under the VWP are ineligible for visa extensions.

PRACTICALITIES

Newspapers & Magazines The *New York Times*, *Wall Street Journal* and *USA Today* are the national newspapers; *Time* and *Newsweek* are the mainstream news magazines.

Radio & TV National Public Radio (NPR) can be found at the lower end of the FM dial. The main TV broadcasting channels are ABC, CBS, NBC, FOX and PBS (public broadcasting); the major cable channels are CNN (news), ESPN (sports), HBO (movies), Weather Channel.

DVDs DVDs are coded for Region 1 (US and Canada only).

Weights & Measures Weights are measured in ounces (oz), pounds (lb) and tons; liquids in fluid ounces (fl oz), pints, quarts and gallons; and distance in feet (ft), yards (yd) and miles.

Short-Term Departures & Re-entry

➡ It's temptingly easy to make trips across the border to Canada or Mexico, but on return to the USA, non-Americans will be subject to the full immigration procedure.

➡ Always take your passport when you cross the border.

➡ If your immigration card still has plenty of time on it, you will probably be able to re-enter using the same one, but if it has nearly expired, you will have to apply for a new card, and border control may want to see your onward air ticket, sufficient funds and so on.

➡ Traditionally, a quick trip across the border has been a way to extend your stay in the USA without applying for an extension at a USCIS office. Don't assume this still works. First, make sure you hand in your old immigration card to the immigration authorities when you leave the USA, and when you return make sure you have all the necessary application documentation from when you first entered the country. US immigration will be very suspicious of anyone who leaves for a few days and returns immediately hoping for a new six-month stay; expect to be questioned closely.

➡ Citizens of most Western countries will not need a visa to visit Canada, so it's really not a problem at all to cross to the Canadian side of Niagara Falls, detour up to Québec, or pass through on the way to Alaska.

➡ Travelers entering the USA by bus from Canada may be closely scrutinized. A round-trip ticket that takes you back to Canada will most likely make US immigration feel less suspicious.

➡ Mexico has a visa-free zone along most of its border with the USA, including the

VISA WAIVER PROGRAM

Currently under the Visa Waiver Program (VWP), citizens of 38 countries (including most EU countries, Japan, the UK, Australia and New Zealand) may enter the USA without a visa for stays of 90 days or less.

If you are a citizen of a VWP country, you do not need a visa *only if* you have a passport that meets current US standards *and* you have received approval from the Electronic System for Travel Authorization (ESTA) in advance. Register online with the Department of Homeland Security at https://esta.cbp.dhs.gov/esta at least 72 hours before arrival; once travel authorization is approved, your registration is valid for two years. The fee, payable online, is $14.

In essence, ESTA requires that you register specific information online (name, address, passport info etc). You will receive one of three responses: 'Authorization Approved' (this usually comes within minutes; most applicants can expect to receive this response); 'Authorization Pending' (you'll need to check the status within the next 72 hours); or 'Travel not Authorized.' The latter option means you will need to apply for a visa.

Visitors from VWP countries must still produce at the port of entry all the same evidence as for a nonimmigrant visa application. They must demonstrate that their trip is for 90 days or less, and that they have a round-trip or onward ticket, adequate funds to cover the trip and binding obligations abroad.

In addition, the same 'grounds for exclusion and deportation' apply, except that you will have no opportunity to appeal or apply for an exemption. If you are denied entry under the VWP at a US point of entry, you will have to use your onward or return ticket on the next available flight.

Baja Peninsula and border towns such as Tijuana and Ciudad Juárez. As of 2019, residents of the US, Canada, the UK, Japan, and Schengen countries (Europe) no longer need a tourist visa anywhere in Mexico. Others may need a Mexican visa or tourist card to travel beyond the border zone.

Volunteering

Volunteer opportunities abound in the USA, and they can be a great way to break up a long trip. They can also provide truly memorable experiences: you'll get to interact with people, society and the land in ways you never would by just passing through.

Casual, drop-in volunteer opportunities are plentiful in big cities, where you can socialize with locals while helping out nonprofit organizations. Check weekly alternative newspapers for calendar listings, or browse the free classified ads online at Craigslist (www.craigslist.org). The public website Serve.gov and private websites Idealist.org and VolunteerMatch (www.volunteermatch.org) offer free searchable databases of short- and long-term volunteer opportunities nationwide.

More formal volunteer programs, especially those designed for international travelers, typically charge a hefty fee of $250 to $1000, depending on the length of the program and what amenities are included (eg housing, meals). None cover the costs of travel to the USA.

Recommended volunteer organizations:

Habitat for Humanity (www. habitat.org) Focuses on building affordable housing for those in need.

Sierra Club (www.sierraclub. org) 'Volunteer vacations' restore wilderness areas and maintain trails, including in national parks and nature preserves.

Volunteers for Peace (www. vfp.org) Grassroots, multiweek volunteer projects emphasize manual labor and international exchange.

Wilderness Volunteers (www. wildernessvolunteers.org) Weeklong trips helping maintain national-park lands and outdoor recreation areas.

World Wide Opportunities on Organic Farms USA (www. wwoofusa.org) Represents more than 2000 organic farms in all 50 states that host volunteer workers in exchange for meals and accommodations, with opportunities for both short- and long-term stays.

Women Travelers

Women traveling alone or in groups should not expect to encounter any particular problems in the USA. The community website www. journeywoman.com facilitates women exchanging travel tips, and has links to other helpful resources. The booklet *Her Own Way*, published by the Canadian government, is filled with general travel advice, useful for any woman; click to travel. gc.ca/travelling/publications/

her-own-way to download the PDF or read it online.

Some women carry a whistle, mace or cayenne-pepper spray in case of assault. If you purchase a spray, contact a police station to find out about local regulations. Laws regarding sprays vary from state to state, and federal law prohibits them being carried on planes.

If you're assaulted, consider calling a rape crisis hotline before calling the police, unless you are in immediate danger, in which case you should call ☑911. But be aware that not all police have much sensitivity training or experience assisting sexual-assault survivors, whereas staff at rape crisis centers will tirelessly advocate on your behalf and act as a link to other community services, including hospitals and the police. Telephone books have listings of local rape-crisis centers, or contact the 24-hour National Sexual Assault Hotline on ☑800-656-4673. Alternatively, go straight to a hospital emergency room.

Work

If you are a foreigner in the USA with a standard non-immigrant visitor's visa, you are expressly forbidden to partake in paid work and will be deported if you're caught working illegally. Employers are required to establish the bona fides of their employees or face fines, making it much tougher than it once was for a foreigner to get work.

To work legally, foreigners need to apply for a work visa before leaving home. A J-1 visa, for exchange visitors, is issued to young people (age limits vary) for study,

student vacation employment, work in summer camps and short-term traineeships with a specific employer. One organization that can help arrange international student exchanges, work placements and J-1 visas is International Exchange Programs (IEP), which operates in Australia (www.iep.com.au) and New Zealand (www.iep.co.nz).

For nonstudent jobs, temporary or permanent, you need to be sponsored by a US employer, who will have to arrange an H-category visa. These are not easy to obtain, since the employer has to prove that no US citizen or permanent resident is available to do the job.

Seasonal work is possible in national parks and at tourist attractions and ski resorts. Contact park concessionaire businesses, local chambers of commerce and ski-resort management. Lonely Planet's *The Big Trip: Your Ultimate Guide to Gap Years and Overseas Adventures* has more ideas on how best to combine work and travel.

Au Pair in America (www. aupairinamerica.com) Find a job as an au pair in the USA.

Camp America (www.camp america.co.uk) Offers opportunities to work in a youth summer camp.

Council on International Educational Exchange (www. ciee.org) CIEE helps international visitors find USA-based jobs through its four work-exchange programs (Work & Travel USA, Internship USA, Professional Career Training USA and Camp Exchange USA).

InterExchange (www.inter exchange.org) Camp, au pair and other work-exchange programs.

Transportation

GETTING THERE & AWAY

Flights, cars and tours can be booked online at lonelyplanet.com/bookings.

Entering the Country

If you're flying to the US, the first airport that you land in is where you must go through immigration and customs, even if you're flying to another destination. Upon arrival, all international visitors must register with the Department of Homeland Security's Office of Biometric Identity Management program, which entails having your fingerprints scanned and a digital photo taken.

Once you go through immigration, you collect your baggage and pass through customs. If you have nothing to declare, you'll probably clear customs without a baggage search, but don't assume this. If you're continuing on the same plane or connecting to another flight, your checked baggage must be rechecked. There are usually airline representatives just outside the customs area who can help you.

If you're a single parent, grandparent or guardian traveling with anyone under 18 years of age, carry proof of legal custody or a notarized letter from the non-accompanying parent(s) authorizing the trip. This isn't required, but the USA is concerned with thwarting child abduction, and not having authorizing papers could cause delays or even result in being denied admittance to the country.

Passports

Every visitor entering the USA from abroad needs a passport. Visitors from most countries only require a passport valid for their intended period of stay in the USA. However, nationals of certain countries require a passport valid for at least six months longer than their intended stay. For a country-by-country list, see the latest 'Six-Month Club Update' from US Customs and Border Protection (www.cbp.gov). If your passport does not meet current US standards, you'll be turned back at the border. All visitors wishing to enter the USA under the Visa Waiver Program must have an e-Passport with a digital photo and an integrated RFID chip containing biometric data.

Air

Airports

The USA has more airports than any other country, but only a baker's dozen form the main international gateways. Even travel to an international gateway sometimes requires a connection in another gateway city (eg London–Los Angeles flights

---

CLIMATE CHANGE & TRAVEL

Every form of transport that relies on carbon-based fuel generates CO_2, the main cause of human-induced climate change. Modern travel is dependent on airplanes, which might use less fuel per mile per person than most cars but travel much greater distances. The altitude at which aircraft emit gases (including CO_2) and particles also contributes to their climate change impact. Many websites offer 'carbon calculators' that allow people to estimate the carbon emissions generated by their journey and, for those who wish to do so, to offset the impact of the greenhouse gases emitted with contributions to portfolios of climate-friendly initiatives throughout the world. Lonely Planet offsets the carbon footprint of all staff and author travel.

may involve transferring in Houston). That said, in recent years many mid-size airports in cities like Austin, Charleston, Indianapolis and Nashville have begun offering at least one nonstop flight to hub cities in Europe.

The USA does not have a national air carrier. The largest USA-based airlines are American, Delta, United and Southwest.

International gateway airports in the USA:

Atlanta Hartsfield-Jackson Atlanta International Airport (ATL, Atlanta; ☏800-897-1910; www.atl.com)

Boston Logan International Airport (BOS; ☏800-235-6426; www.massport.com/logan-airport)

Chicago O'Hare International Airport (ORD; ☏800-832-6352; www.flychicago.com/ohare; 10000 W O'Hare Ave)

Dallas DFW International Airport (DFW; ☏972-973-3112; www.dfwairport.com; 2400 Aviation Dr)

Fort Lauderdale Fort Lauderdale-Hollywood International Airport (FLL; ☏866-435-9355; www.broward.org/airport; 100 Terminal Dr)

Honolulu Honolulu International Airport (HNL; ☏808-836-6411; www.airports.hawaii.gov/hnl; 300 Rodgers Blvd; ☏)

Houston George Bush Intercontinental Airport (IAH; ☏281-230-3100; www.fly2houston.com/iah; 2800 N Terminal Rd, off I-59, Beltway 8 or I-45; ☏)

Los Angeles Los Angeles International Airport (LAX; www.lawa.org/welcomeLAX.aspx; 1 World Way)

Miami Miami International Airport (MIA; ☏305-876-7000; www.miami-airport.com; 2100 NW 42nd Ave)

New York JFK International Airport (JFK; ☏718-244-4444; www.jfkairport.com; Ⓢ A to Howard Beach, E, J/Z to

Sutphin Blvd-Archer Ave then Airtrain)

Newark Newark Liberty International Airport (EWR; ☏973-961-6000; www.newarkairport.com)

San Francisco San Francisco International Airport (SFO; www.flysfo.com; S McDonnell Rd)

Seattle Sea-Tac International Airport (SEA; ☏206-787-5388; www.portseattle.org/Sea-Tac; 17801 International Blvd; ☏)

Washington Dulles International Airport (IAD; ☏703-572-2700, 703-572-8296; www.flydulles.com)

Land

Canada

BUS

Greyhound has direct connections between main cities in Canada and the northern USA, but you may have to transfer to a different bus at the border. Book through Greyhound USA (www.greyhound.com) or Greyhound Canada (www.greyhound.ca).

CAR & MOTORCYCLE

If you're driving into the USA from Canada, bring the vehicle's registration papers, proof of liability insurance and your home driver's license. Canadian driver's licenses and auto insurance are typically valid in the USA, and vice versa.

If your papers are in order, taking your own car across the US–Canadian border is usually fast and easy, but occasionally the authorities of either country decide to search a car *thoroughly*. On weekends and holidays, especially in summer, traffic at the main border crossings can be heavy and waits long.

TRAIN

Amtrak (www.amtrak.com) and VIA Rail Canada (www.viarail.ca) operate daily services between Montreal

and New York, Toronto and New York (via Niagara Falls), and Vancouver and Seattle. Customs inspections occur at the border.

Mexico

BUS

Greyhound USA (www.greyhound.com) and Greyhound México (www.greyhound.com.mx) operate direct bus routes between main towns in Mexico and the USA.

For connections to smaller destinations south of the border, there are numerous domestic Mexican bus companies.

CAR & MOTORCYCLE

If you're driving into the USA from Mexico, bring the vehicle's registration papers, proof of liability insurance and your driver's license from your home country. Mexican driver's licenses are valid, but it's worth having an International Driving Permit (IDP).

Very few car-rental companies will let you take a car from the US into Mexico. US auto insurance is not valid in Mexico, so even a short trip into Mexico's border region requires you to buy Mexican car insurance, available for around $25 per day at most border crossings, as well as from AAA (www.aaa.com).

For a longer driving trip into Mexico (25km or more beyond the border), you'll need a Mexican *permiso de importación temporal de vehículos* (temporary vehicle import permit), available at the border for $60 or online from Banjercito (www.banjercito.com.mx/registroVehiculos) for $53.

Sea

If you're interested in taking a cruise ship to America, as well as to other interesting ports of call, a good specialized travel agency is Cruise Web (www.cruiseweb.com).

You can also travel to and from the USA on a freighter,

though it will be much slower and less cushy than a cruise. Nevertheless, freighters aren't spartan (some advertise cruise-ship-level amenities), and they are much cheaper (sometimes by half). Trips range from a week to two months; stops at interim ports are usually brief.

For more information, try Cruise and Freighter Travel Association (www.travltips. com), which has listings for freighter cruises and other boat travel.

Tours

Group travel can be an enjoyable way to get to and tour around the USA.

Reputable tour companies:

American Holidays (www.amer icanholidays.com) Ireland-based company specializes in tours to North America.

Contiki (www.contiki.com) Party-hardy sightseeing tour-bus vacations for 18- to 35-year-olds.

North America Travel Service (www.northamericatravelservice. co.uk) UK-based tour operator arranges luxury US trips.

Trek America (www.trekamerica. com) Active outdoor adventures for 18- to 38-year-olds.

GETTING AROUND

Air

When time is tight, book a flight. The domestic air system is extensive and reliable, with dozens of competing airlines, hundreds of airports and thousands of flights daily. Flying is usually more expensive than traveling by bus, train or car, but it's the way to go when you're in a hurry.

Main 'hub' airports in the USA include all international gateways plus many other large cities. Most cities and towns have a local or county airport, but you usually have to travel via a hub airport to reach them.

Airlines in the USA

Overall, air travel in the USA is very safe (much safer than driving out on the nation's highways); for comprehensive details by carrier, check out airsafe.com.

The main domestic carriers:

Alaska Airlines (www.alaskaair. com) Has direct flights to Anchorage from Seattle, Chicago, Los Angeles and Denver. It also flies between many towns within Alaska.

American Airlines (www. aa.com) Nationwide service.

Delta Air Lines (www.delta.com) Nationwide service.

Frontier Airlines (www.flyfron tier.com) Denver-based airline with service across the continental USA.

Hawaiian Airlines (www. hawaiianairlines.com) Nonstop flights between the Hawaiian islands and various spots on the mainland.

JetBlue Airways (www.jetblue. com) New York City–based airline serving many East Coast cities, plus other destinations across the USA.

Southwest Airlines (www.south west.com) Dallas-based budget airline with service across the continental USA and Hawaii.

Spirit Airlines (www.spirit.com) Florida-based budget airline; serves many US gateway cities.

United Airlines (www.united. com) Nationwide service.

Virgin America (www.virgin america.com) California-based airline serving over two dozen cities, from Honolulu to Boston.

Air Passes

International travelers who plan on doing a lot of flying might consider buying a North American air pass. Passes are normally available only to non–North American citizens, and they must be purchased in conjunction with an international ticket. Conditions and cost structures can be complicated, but all passes include a certain number of domestic flights (from as few as two to as many as 16, depending on airline network) that typically must be used within a 60-day period. Often you must plan your itinerary in advance, but sometimes dates (and even destinations) can be left open. Talk with a travel agent to determine if an air pass will save you money. Networks offering air passes include Star Alliance (www.staralliance.com), One World (www.oneworld.com) and Skyteam (www.skyteam. com).

Bicycle

Regional bicycle touring is popular. It means coasting along winding backroads (because bicycles are often not permitted on freeways) and calculating progress in miles per day, not miles per hour. Cyclists must follow the same rules of the road as automobiles, but don't expect drivers to respect your right of way. Better World Club (www.betterworldclub.com) offers a bicycle roadside-assistance program.

For epic cross-country journeys, get the support of a tour operator; it's about two months of dedicated pedaling coast to coast.

For advice, route maps, guided tours and lists of local bike clubs and repair shops, browse the websites of Adventure Cycling (www. adventurecycling.org) and the League of American Bicyclists (www.bikeleague.org). If you're bringing your own bike to the USA, be sure to call around to check oversize luggage prices and restrictions. Amtrak trains and Greyhound buses will transport bikes within the USA, sometimes charging extra.

It's not hard to buy a bike once you're here and resell it before you leave. Every city and town has bike shops; if you prefer a cheaper, used bicycle, try garage sales, bulletin boards at hostels and colleges, or the free classified ads on Craigslist (craigslist. org). These are also the best places to sell your bike, though stores selling used bikes may also buy from you.

Long-term bike rentals are also easy to find. Rates run from $100 per week and up, and a credit-card authorization for several hundred dollars is usually necessary as a security deposit.

Some cities are more amenable to bicycles than others, but most have at least a few dedicated bike lanes and paths, and bikes can usually be carried on public transportation.

Bike Shares

Many US cities offer bike-share programs, which give access to a network of bicycles for a nominal fee (usually about $5 per day). These programs are designed for commuter and transportation use, not recreation, so you'll have to pay extra if you keep the bike for more than 30 minutes. New York City, Washington, DC, Chicago and Los Angeles all have bike-share programs, as do smaller cities such as Birmingham, AL, and Milwaukee, WI.

Boat

There is no river or canal public-transportation system in the USA, but there are many smaller, often state-run, coastal ferry services. These provide efficient, scenic links to the many islands off both coasts. Most larger ferries will transport private cars, motorcycles and bicycles.

The most spectacular coastal ferry runs are on the southeastern coast of Alaska and along the Inside Passage. The Great Lakes have several islands that can be visited only by boat, such as Mackinac Island, MI; the Apostle Islands, off Wisconsin; and remote Isle Royale National Park, MI. Off the Pacific coast, ferries serve the scenic San Juan Islands in Washington and Catalina Island in California.

Bus

To save money, travel by bus, particularly between major towns and cities. Middle-class Americans prefer to fly or drive, but buses let you see the countryside and meet folks along the way. As a rule, buses are reliable, cleanish and comfortable, with air-conditioning, barely

reclining seats, lavatories and no smoking.

Greyhound (www.greyhound.com) is the major long-distance bus company, with routes throughout the USA and Canada. Routes generally trace major highways and stop at larger population centers. To reach country towns on rural roads, you may need to transfer to local or county bus systems; Greyhound can usually provide their contact information.

Competing with Greyhound is the extensive Trailways network (www.trailways.com). The 70-plus bus companies that make up Trailways operate on an interlining basis with Greyhound and New England–based Peter Pan (https://peterpanbus.com), and the Trailways website searches both Greyhound and Trailways fares. Other long-distance bus lines that offer decent fares and free wi-fi (though it doesn't always work) include Megabus (www.megabus.com) and BoltBus (www.boltbus.com).

Most baggage has to be checked in; label it loudly and clearly to avoid it getting lost. Larger items, including skis, surfboards and bicycles, can be transported, but there may be an extra charge. Call to check.

The frequency of bus services varies widely, depending on the route. Despite the elimination of many tiny destinations, non-express Greyhound buses still stop every 50 to 100 miles to pick up passengers, and long-distance buses will stop for meal breaks and driver changes.

Many bus stations are clean and safe, but some are in dodgy areas. If you arrive in the evening, it's worth spending the money on a taxi. Some towns have just a flag stop. If you are boarding at one of these, pay the driver with exact change.

Most cities and larger towns have dependable local

BUS FARES

Sample standard one-way adult fares and trip times on Greyhound.

ROUTE	FARE ($)	DURATION (HR)
Boston–Philadelphia	25	7
Chicago–New Orleans	130	20-30
Los Angeles–San Francisco	25	7½-13
New York–Chicago	65	18-23
New York–San Francisco	175	72
Washington, DC–Miami	150	25-30

bus systems, though they are often designed for commuters and provide limited service in the evening and on weekends. Costs range from free to between $1 and $4 per ride.

Costs

For lower fares on Greyhound, purchase tickets ahead of time (purchasing 14 or more days in advance usually nets the best bargains). Special promotional fares are regularly offered on Greyhound's website, especially for online bookings (see www.greyhound.com/promos for details).

As for other Greyhound discounts: tickets for children aged two to 16 are discounted 20% during non-peak periods; seniors over 62 years get a whopping 5% off; and students get 10% off if they have purchased the $23 Student Advantage Discount Card (www.studentadvantage.com).

Reservations

Tickets for most trips on Greyhound, Trailways, Megabus and BoltBus can be bought online. You can print all tickets at home or, in the case of Megabus or BoltBus, simply show ticket receipts through an email on a smartphone. Greyhound also allows customers to pick up tickets at the terminal using 'Will Call' service.

Seating is normally first-come, first-served. Greyhound recommends arriving an hour before departure to get a seat.

Car & Motorcycle

For information on car travel see Driving in the USA (p1182).

Local Transportation

Except in large US cities, public transportation is rarely the most convenient

TRAIN FARES

Sample standard, one-way, adult coach-class fares and trip times on Amtrak.

ROUTE	FARE ($)	DURATION (HR)
Chicago–New Orleans	130	20
Los Angeles–San Antonio	125	29
New York–Chicago	130	19
New York–Los Angeles	250	72
Seattle–Oakland	100	23
Washington, DC–Miami	140	23

option for travelers, and coverage can be sparse to outlying towns and suburbs. However, it is usually cheap, safe and reliable.

More than two-thirds of the states in the nation have adopted 511 as an all-purpose local-transportation help line.

Subway

The largest subway systems are in New York City, Chicago, Boston, Washington, DC, the San Francisco Bay Area, Philadelphia, Los Angeles and Atlanta. Other cities have small, one- or two-line rail systems that mainly serve downtown areas.

Light rail systems (trams and trollies) are becoming increasingly popular in the US. Denver, Seattle, San Diego, Minneapolis and Portland are among the many places with light rail systems, as are most cities with subways (the networks usually connect, and rides are transferable).

Taxis & Ride-Sharing Services

Taxis are metered, with flagfall charges of around $3 to start, plus $2 to $3 per mile. They charge extra for waiting and handling baggage, and drivers expect a 10% to 15% tip. Taxis cruise the busiest areas in large cities; elsewhere, it's easiest to phone and order one.

Ridesharing companies such as Uber (www.uber.com) and Lyft (www.lyft.com) have seen a surge in popularity as an alternative to taxis.

Train

Amtrak (www.amtrak.com) has an extensive rail system throughout the USA, with Amtrak's Thruway buses providing connections to and from the rail network to some smaller centers and national parks. Compared with other modes of travel, trains are rarely the quickest, cheapest, timeliest or most convenient option, but they turn the journey into a relaxing, social and scenic all-American experience, especially on western routes, where double-decker Superliner trains boast spacious lounge cars with panoramic windows.

Amtrak has several long-distance lines traversing the nation east to west, and even more running north to south. These connect all of America's biggest cities and many of its smaller ones. Long-distance services (on named trains) mostly operate daily on these routes, but some run only three to five days per week. See Amtrak's website for detailed route maps.

Commuter trains provide faster, more frequent

ALL ABOARD!

Who doesn't enjoy the steamy puff and whistle of a mighty locomotive as glorious scenery streams by? Dozens of historic narrow-gauge railroads still operate today as attractions, rather than as transportation. Most trains only run in the warmer months, and they can be extremely popular – so book ahead.

1880 Train (p677) Classic steam train running through rugged Black Hills country in South Dakota.

Cass Scenic Railroad (304-456-4300; www.wvstateparks.com; 242 Main St, Cass; adult/child 4-11yr $66/56; P) Nestled in the Appalachian Mountains in West Virginia.

Cumbres & Toltec Scenic Railroad Depot (888-286-2737; www.cumbrestoltec.com; 5234B Hwy 285; trips from adult/child $99/49) Living, moving museum from Chama, NM, into Colorado's Rocky Mountains.

Durango & Silverton Narrow Gauge Railroad (p783) Ends at historic mining town Silverton in Colorado's Rocky Mountains.

Great Smoky Mountains Railroad (800-872-4681; www.gsmr.com; 226 Everett St; Nantahala Gorge trip adult/child 2-12yr from $51/29) Rides from Bryson City, NC, through the Great Smoky Mountains.

Mt Hood Railroad (p1071) Winds through the scenic Columbia River Gorge outside Portland, OR.

Skunk Train (707-964-6371; www.skunktrain.com; 100 W Laurel St; adult/child $84/42; 9am-3pm) Runs between Fort Bragg, CA, on the coast and Willits further inland, passing through redwoods.

Also worth riding are the vintage steam and diesel locomotives of Arizona's Grand Canyon Railway (p851), Georgia's **Blue Ridge Scenic Railway** (877-413-8724; www.brscenic.com; 241 Depot St; adult $44-79, child $29; mid-Mar–Dec) and New York State's Delaware & Ulster Railroad (p147).

services on shorter routes, especially the northeast corridor from Boston, MA, to Washington, DC. Amtrak's high-speed Acela Express trains are the most expensive, and rail passes are not valid on these trains. Other commuter rail lines include those serving the Lake Michigan shoreline near Chicago, IL, major cities on the West Coast and the Miami, FL, area.

Classes & Costs

Amtrak fares vary according to the type of train and seating. On long-distance lines, you can travel in coach seats (reserved or unreserved), business class, or 1st class, which includes all sleeping compartments. Sleeping cars include simple bunks (called 'roomettes'), bedrooms with en-suite facilities and suites sleeping four with two bathrooms. Sleeping-car rates include meals in the dining car, which offers everyone sit-down meal service (pricey if not included). Food service on commuter lines, when it exists, consists of sandwich and snack bars. Bringing your own food and drink is recommended on all trains.

Various one-way, round-trip and touring fares are available from Amtrak, with discounts of 15% for students with a valid ID and seniors aged 62 and over, and 50% for children aged two to 12 when accompanied by a paying adult. AAA members get 10% off. Web-only 'SmartFares' offer 30% discounts on certain undersold routes (destinations change weekly; see www.aaa.com for details).

Generally the earlier you book, the lower the price. To get many of the standard discounts, you need to reserve at least three days in advance. If you want to take an Acela Express or Metroliner train, avoid peak commute times and aim for weekends.

Amtrak Vacations (www.amtrakvacations.com) offers vacation packages that include car rental, hotels, tours and attractions. Air-Rail packages let you travel by train in one direction, then return by plane the other way.

Reservations

Reservations can be made any time from 11 months in advance up to the day of departure. Space on most trains is limited, and certain routes can be crowded, especially during summer and holiday periods, so it's a good idea to book as far in advance as you can. This also gives you the best chance of fare discounts.

Rail Passes

Amtrak's USA Rail Pass offers coach-class travel for 15 ($459), 30 ($689) or 45 ($899) days, with travel limited to eight, 12 or 18 one-way 'segments,' respectively. A segment is *not* the same as a one-way trip. If reaching your destination requires riding more than one train (for example, getting from New York to Miami with a transfer in Washington, DC), that one-way trip will actually use two segments of your pass.

Present your pass at an Amtrak office to pick up your ticket(s) for each trip. Reservations should be made by phone (call 800-872-7245, or 215-856-7953 from outside the USA). Book desired dates as far in advance as possible, as seats allocated for USA Rail Pass holders are limited. At some rural stations, trains will only stop if there's a reservation. Tickets are not for specific seats, but a conductor on board may allocate you a seat. Business-class,

first-class and sleeper accommodations cost extra and must be reserved separately.

All travel must be completed within 330 days of purchasing your pass. Passes are not valid on the Acela Express, Auto Train, Thruway motorcoach connections, or the Canadian portion of Amtrak routes operated jointly with Via Rail Canada.

Driving in the USA

For maximum flexibility and convenience, and to explore rural America and its wide-open spaces, a car is essential. Fuel prices average around $2.90/gallon, and you can often score fairly inexpensive rentals (NYC excluded), with rates as low as $25 per day.

Automobile Associations

The American Automobile Association (AAA; www.aaa.com) has reciprocal membership agreements with several international auto clubs (check with AAA and bring your membership card from home). For its members, AAA offers travel insurance, tour books, diagnostic centers for used-car buyers and a wide-ranging network of regional offices. AAA advocates politically for the auto industry.

A more ecofriendly alternative, the Better World Club (www.betterworldclub.com), donates 1% of revenue to assist environmental cleanup, offers ecologically sensitive choices for every service it provides and advocates politically for environmental causes.

With these organizations, the primary member benefit is 24-hour emergency roadside assistance anywhere in the USA. Both also offer trip planning, free travel maps, travel-agency services, car insurance and a range of travel discounts (eg on hotels, car rentals, attractions).

Bring Your Own Vehicle

It's possible to drive your own car over the border from Canada (p1176) or Mexico (p1176). Unless you're moving to the USA, don't even think about freighting your car from overseas.

Driver's License

Foreign visitors can legally drive a car in the USA for up to 12 months using their home driver's license. However, an International Driving Permit (IDP) will have more credibility with US traffic police, especially if your home license doesn't have a photo or isn't in English. Your automobile association at home can issue an IDP, valid for one year, for a small fee. Always carry your home license together with the IDP.

To ride a motorcycle in the USA, you will need either a valid US state motorcycle license or an IDP specially endorsed for motorcycles.

Insurance

Don't put the key into the ignition if you don't have insurance, which is legally required. You risk financial ruin and legal consequences if there's an accident. If you already have auto insurance, or if you buy travel insurance that covers car rentals, make sure your policy has adequate liability coverage for where you will be driving, as different states specify different minimum levels of coverage.

Car-rental companies will provide liability insurance, but most charge extra. Rental companies almost never include collision-damage insurance for the vehicle. Instead, they offer an optional Collision Damage Waiver (CDW) or Loss Damage Waiver (LDW), usually with an initial deductible cost of between $100 and $500. For an extra premium, you can usually get this deductible covered as well. Paying for some or all of this insurance increases the cost of a rental car by as much as $30 a day.

Many credit cards offer free collision damage coverage for rental cars if you rent for 15 days or less and charge the total rental to your card. This is a good way to avoid paying extra fees to the rental company, but note that if there's an accident, sometimes you must pay the car-rental company first and then seek reimbursement from the credit-card company. There may be exceptions that are not covered, too, such as 'exotic' rentals (eg

4WD Jeeps or convertibles). Check your credit-card policy.

Purchase

Buying a car is much more hassle than it's worth, particularly for foreign visitors and for trips of less than four months. Foreigners will have the easiest time arranging this if they have stateside friends or relatives who can provide a fixed address for registration, licensing and insurance.

Once purchased, the car's transfer of ownership papers must be registered with the state's Department of Motor Vehicles (DMV) within 10 days – you'll need the bill of sale, the title (or 'pink slip') and proof of insurance. Some states also require a 'smog certificate.' This is the seller's responsibility, so don't buy a car without a current certificate. A dealer will submit all necessary paperwork to the DMV for you.

For foreigners, independent liability insurance is difficult to virtually impossible to arrange without a US driver's license. A car dealer or AAA may be able to suggest an insurer who will do this. Even with a local license, insurance can be expensive and difficult to obtain if you don't have evidence of a good driving record. Bring copies of your home auto-insurance policy if it helps establish that you are a good risk. All drivers under 25 years old will have problems getting insurance.

Finally, selling a car can become a desperate business. Selling to dealers gets you the worst price, but involves a minimum of paperwork. Otherwise, fellow travelers and college students are the best bets – but be sure the DMV is properly notified about the sale, or you may be on the hook for someone else's traffic tickets later on.

Rental

Car

Car rental is a competitive business in the USA. Most rental companies require that you have a major credit card, be at least 25 years old and have a valid driver's license. Some major national companies may rent to drivers between the ages of 21 and 24 for an additional charge of around $25 per day. Except in Michigan and New York, those under age 21 are not permitted to rent at all.

Car-rental prices vary wildly, so shop around. The average daily rate for a small car ranges from around $25 to $75, or $125 to $500 per week. If you belong to an auto club or frequent-flier program, you may get a discount (or earn rewards points or miles).

Some other things to keep in mind: most national agencies make 'unlimited mileage' standard on all cars, but independents might charge extra for this. Tax on car rental varies by state and agency location; always ask for the total cost *including* all taxes and fees. Most agencies charge more if you pick the car up in one place and drop it off in another, and usually only national agencies offer this option. Be careful about adding extra days or turning in a car early – extra days may be charged at a premium rate, or an early return may jeopardize any

weekly or monthly discounts you originally arranged.

Some major national companies, including Avis, Budget and Hertz, offer 'green' fleets of hybrid or electric rental cars (eg Toyota Prius or Nissan Leafs), though you'll usually have to pay quite a bit more. Some independent local agencies, especially on the West Coast, also offer hybrid-vehicle rentals. Try Hawaii's Bio-Beetle (www.bio-beetle.com) or Green Motion USA (www.greenmotionusa.com) in Florida or California.

Motorcycle & RV

If you dream of cruising across America on a Harley, EagleRider (www.eaglerider.com) rents motorcycles in major cities nationwide. If a recreational vehicle (RV) is more your style, places such as www.usarvrentals.com and www.cruiseamerica.com can help. Beware: rental and insurance fees for these vehicles are expensive.

Road Conditions & Hazards

America's highways are thought of as legendary ribbons of unblemished asphalt, but that's not always the case. Road hazards include potholes, city commuter traffic, wandering wildlife and cell-phone-wielding, kid-distracted or enraged drivers. Caution, foresight, courtesy and luck usually gets you past them. For nationwide traffic and

FUELING UP

Many gas stations in the USA have fuel pumps with automated credit-card pay screens. Some machines ask for your ZIP code after you swipe your card. For foreign travelers, or those with cards issued outside the US, you'll have to pay inside before fueling up. Just indicate how much you'd like to put on the card. If there's still credit left over after you fuel up, pop back inside and the attendant will put the difference back on your card.

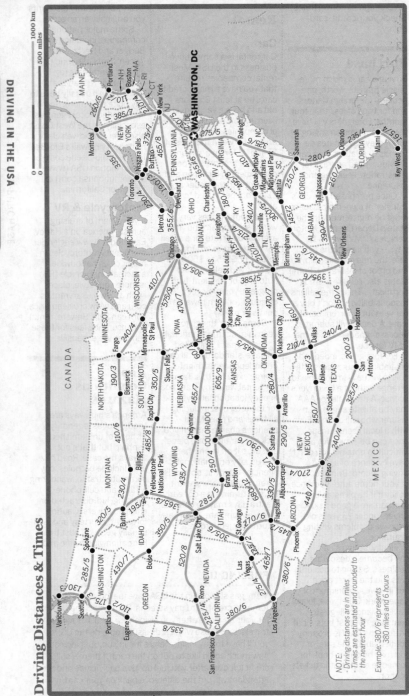

Driving Distances & Times

1000 km
500 miles
0

WASHINGTON, DC

NOTE:
- Driving distances are in miles
- Times are estimated and rounded to the nearest hour

Example: 380/6 represents 380 miles and 6 hours

road-closure information, check www.fhwa.dot.gov/trafficinfo.

➡ In places where winter driving is an issue, many cars are fitted with steel-studded snow tires, while snow chains can sometimes be required in mountain areas.

➡ Driving off-road, or on dirt roads, is often forbidden by car-rental companies, and it can be very dangerous in wet weather.

➡ In deserts and range country, livestock sometimes graze next to unfenced roads. These areas are signed as 'Open Range' or with the silhouette of a steer.

➡ Where deer and other wild animals frequently appear roadside, you'll see signs with the silhouette of a leaping deer. Take these signs seriously, particularly at dusk and dawn.

Road Rules

➡ In the USA, cars drive on the right-hand side of the road.

➡ The use of seat belts is required in every state except New Hampshire, and child safety seats or seat belts for children under 18 are required in every state. Most car-rental agencies rent child safety seats for $10 to $14 per day, but you must reserve them when booking.

➡ In some states, motorcyclists are required to wear helmets.

➡ On interstate highways, the speed limit is usually 70mph. Unless otherwise posted, the speed limit is generally 55mph or 65mph on highways, 25mph to 35mph in cities and towns, and as low as 15mph in school zones (strictly enforced during school hours). It's forbidden to pass a school bus when its lights are flashing.

➡ Unless signs prohibit it, you may turn right at a red light after first coming to a full stop – note that turning right on red is illegal in NYC.

➡ At four-way stop signs, cars should proceed in order of arrival; when two cars arrive simultaneously, the one on the right has the right of way. When in doubt, just politely wave the other driver ahead.

➡ When emergency vehicles (ie police, fire or ambulance) approach from either direction, pull over safely and get out of the way.

➡ In many states, it's illegal to talk on a handheld cell phone while driving; use a hands-free device instead.

➡ The maximum legal blood-alcohol concentration for drivers is 0.08%. Penalties are very severe for 'DUI' – driving under the influence of alcohol and/or drugs. Police can give roadside sobriety checks to assess if you've been drinking or using drugs. If you fail, they'll require you to take a breath test, urine test or blood test to determine the level of alcohol or drugs in your body. Refusing to be tested is treated the same as if you'd taken the test and failed.

➡ In some states it's illegal to carry 'open containers' of alcohol in a vehicle, even if they're empty.

➡ If you are pulled over by the police, do not get out of your car. Wait for the officer to approach your window – in the meantime, collect your license, proof of insurance and registration or rental agreement, and have them ready for the officer to inspect.

Behind the Scenes

SEND US YOUR FEEDBACK

We love to hear from travelers – your comments keep us on our toes and help make our books better. Our well-traveled team reads every word on what you loved or loathed about this book. Although we cannot reply individually to your submissions, we always guarantee that your feedback goes straight to the appropriate authors, in time for the next edition. Each person who sends us information is thanked in the next edition – the most useful submissions are rewarded with a selection of digital PDF chapters.

Visit **lonelyplanet.com/contact** to submit your updates and suggestions or to ask for help. Our award-winning website also features inspirational travel stories, news and discussions.

Note: We may edit, reproduce and incorporate your comments in Lonely Planet products such as guidebooks, websites and digital products, so let us know if you don't want your comments reproduced or your name acknowledged. For a copy of our privacy policy visit lonelyplanet.com/privacy.

WRITER THANKS

Isabel Albiston

Thanks to everyone in Massachusetts who answered my questions so patiently and treated me so kindly, especially to all the museum guides who showed me around along the way. Thanks also to Leah, Julie and Andrea for your warm hospitality and to Trisha for commissioning me for such a great project. Lastly, huge thanks to Ellie, Alan and Liz for traveling out to join me at the end of my trip.

Mark Baker

So many people came out of the woodwork to help me carry out research in Minnesota and Wisconsin. A partial list would include, in Minnesota: Monte Hanson, Alex Friedrich, Leif Pettersen, Liz Puhl, Zach Peterson, Stacey Mae McGowan Olson and Robert Olson. In Wisconsin, I'd like to thank Sarah Lewison, Richard Ryan and Joan Menefee, among many others. I'd also like to thank Trisha Ping, the Lonely Planet Destination Editor who first invited me to pitch for this project.

Amy C Balfour

For Mississippi insights, thank you Jim Foley, Eone Moore, Lake Andrews, Sarah Nobles, Kevin Webb and Erik Arnold. Team Tennessee includes Jeff and Heather Kelsey, Lauren Batte, Jim Hester, Frank Watson, Chad Graddy and David Wells. Melissa and Michael Peeler, thank you for letting me crash at your place and for escorting me to all the good restaurants, watering holes and Memphis hot-

spots. With a shout-out to Mary, Anna and Margie for their recommendations. And yes, Michael, I'll include Celtic Crossing!

Thank you Brandon Dekema and Christy Germscheid for your Enchanted Circle tips and Angel Fire hospitality! Thanks also to Todd Norman, Matt Redington, John White, Marty Robertson, Elizabeth Edgren, Charise May and Ellen McBee. Much obliged for the meet-up and the Central New Mexico suggestions, Michael Benanav – all right on!

Robert Balkovich

Thank you to my family – my mother, father and sister – and friends for their love and support. Special thanks to Michael, Raghnild, Elizabeth and Ming for their hospitality and wealth of tips, and to Matthew for your friendship on the road. Special thanks to Karin, for sharing your love of Seattle with me and setting me off on the right foot, and to Lynae for the wonderful home away from home where I made many great memories.

Ray Bartlett

Huge thanks to Trisha and Evan, the rest of the Lonely Planet staff, and my family and friends. You rock. Met such great folks along the way, thanks for making the trip what it was: Charissa and Bret; Tara, Amber, and Shannon; Palma and Karyn; May Lee; Theresa and Jessenia; Rebeckah and Ashley; 'Cousin' Steve; Ericha and Bria; Austin (Habari!); Yimee Nguyen; Sabrina V; Michael Milgate; Kelley Luikey; birder Sara; Swanee;

Jason and Sam; and, of course, Kiko the Mermaid. Can't wait to be back again soon.

Greg Benchwick

This book wouldn't be possible without my family. Dad, Mom, Cara, Bry and little baby Violeta. Love you guys. Thanks to the beautiful editors, cartographers and whole team at Lonely Planet for making an amazing book. And to the on-the-ground people that helped along the way, like Chris at Pine Needles in Durango and the lovely Sara.

Celeste Brash

Thanks to my husband Josh and my kids who have come with me on so many Oregon trips over the years. And to many friends old and new that helped out this time around, including Ticari, Chris & Ashley, Nathan, Dana, Jon & Kara, Ron & Nisa, Elizabeth, Pattye, Rachel Cabakoff, Amanda Castleman, Dave Nevins, Amy Hunter, all my LP co-authors and Ben Buckner for seeing this through.

Jade Bremner

Thanks to knowledgeable Destination Editor Trisha Ping for all her wisdom on the Southern States. Plus, the hardworking Georgia and North Carolina barbecue chefs for cooking all that mind-blowingly good smoky meat and sauce that fueled my entire trip around the South. Thanks to North Carolina locals Norm and Skye for their top tips and local advice. Last, but definitely not least, thanks to everyone working hard behind the scenes – Cheree Broughton, Dianne and Jane, Helen Elfer and Neill Coen.

Gregor Clark

Thanks to the many fellow Vermonters who shared their favorite spots in the Green Mountain State with me this edition – especially Shawn O'Neil, Margo Whitcomb, Victoria St John, Jim Lockridge and Joy Cohen – and to Gaen, Meigan and Chloe for a lifetime of companionship on our family adventures in this gorgeous place we call home.

Stephanie d'Arc Taylor

As always, I don't do anything without support and inspiration from Queen Xtine. My home team: Maya G, A&E, Daniel and Danielle. Carlo, grazie. The friendly park rangers at Great Basin and staff at Kerouac's (I'm not stalking you, promise). That guy at Napa Auto Parts in Lone Pine. At LP: Ben Buckner, Lauren Keith, Alicia Johnson, Martine Power and Sasha Drew for your attention. Thanks to my late father for showing me the calm beauty of the Basin & Range.

Michael Grosberg

Many thanks to all those who shared their experiences, knowledge and deep passion for Glacier, Whitefish and Waterton including Brian Schott, Greg Fortin, Riley Polumbus,

Rhonda Fitzgerald, Chris Schustrom, Cricket Butler, BJ Elzinga, Marc Ducharme, Michelle Gaudet, Kimmy Walt, Angel Esperanueva and Monica Jungster. And to Carly, Rosie, Willa and Boone for keeping in touch while in the wilderness.

Ashley Harrell

Thanks to Erin Morris for welcoming me to your state; Kourtnay King and Paul Haynes for taking me in and enabling me; Chandler Routman for getting me out of the house; Jason, Elizabeth, Iris and Loulou Ryan for being a great family; Patty Pascal for your unbridled enthusiasm; Halsey Perrin, Kim Jamieson and Ruta Fox for your help and expertise; and Chris Dorsel for still being amazing.

Thanks to Freda Moon for the advice on Mendocino; Amy Benziger for putting up with my research detours in Tahoe (and in general); the nice Norwegian couple who stopped in Sequoia to pick up two dirty hitchhikers, and Steven Sparapani and Osa Peligrosa, for joining me on an epic road trip across 3,000 awe-inspiring miles of Northern California.

John Hecht

Many thanks to all the kind folks in Utah who offered their help, be that in the brewpubs, on the trails or wherever else our paths may have crossed. I also want to thank destination editor Ben Buckner, the book's co-writers and my lovely wife Lau for all their support.

Adam Karlin

Thank you to the staff, students and faculty of the University of New Orleans CWW for helping me find my voice when it comes to writing about the South. Thank you mom and dad for all you do, and thank you my favorite traveling companions: Rachel, Sanda and Isaac.

Brian Kluepfel

To my wife and North Star, Paula Zorrilla. To Trisha at Lonely Planet, and Robert and Adam, my writing cohorts. To Marc in Atlantic City, Brooke in Montauk, and Tom K in Hoboken for local knowledge. To Joe Dawson, Laura Tafuri and Karen Ramos for cool beach recommendations. And to all the lovely toll-takers on the Garden State Parkway, some of whom I now know on a first-name basis.

Ali Lemer

Many thanks to Will Coley, Nicole Marsella, Adam Michaels, Regis St Louis and Trisha Ping, and to Professor Kenneth Jackson, who taught me more about NYC history than anyone. My work is dedicated to the memory of my father, Albert Lemer, a first-generation New Yorker who inspired my enthusiasm for international travel as much as he kindled my love of our shared hometown – the greatest city in the world.

Vesna Maric

Thanks to Trisha Ping and Evan Godt for commissioning me; to Alicia Estefania and Susana Felices; and a huge thanks to Marta Vila for her generosity. Thank you to Atena Sherry for fun times.

Virginia Maxwell

Thanks to DC locals Barbara Balman and Bob Bresnahan for their convivial company and insider tips; to Trisha Ping for giving me the gig and supplying interesting leads; to DC expert Karla Zimmerman; and to traveling companions Eveline Zoutendijk, George Grundy and Ryan Ver Berkmoes. At home in Australia, thanks and much love to Peter Handsaker, who coped with apartment-renovation chaos and didn't blame me for my absence (well, not too much).

MaSovaida Morgan

Thank you to the lovely souls in Savannah and beyond who provided tips, guidance and feedback for this project. In particular, many thanks to Chad Faries and Emily Jones, Robert Firth, and Trisha Ping for bringing me on. Special thanks and love to Ny, Ty and Haj.

Barbara Noe Kennedy

I can't thank enough the endless line of Washingtonians who always point me in the right direction, keeping me up to date with the latest and greatest happenings. But no one can surpass the tireless devotion of Kate Gibbs at Destination DC, who's always there to answer my next question or let me know about the next exhibition – thanks! I also would like to thank my husband, David Kennedy, who is always game to experience all that DC has to offer – so much fun!

Becky Ohlsen

I would like to thank editor Ben Buckner for the gig, Celeste Brash for her work on the previous edition, Paul Smith for being a great travel companion, and all the dedicated volunteers at the many wonderful tiny museums, state parks, national parks and campgrounds visited along the way.

Lorna Parkes

Thank you to the residents of New York for your friendliness, as well as your endearing day-to-day sidewalk and subway rage; the latter I expected, but the former not so much. Thanks to Kat and Heather who at various points joined me to rate the best cocktail mixologists and live-music dives. Thanks most of all to Austin and Lily who waited patiently for me to return home, and to Rob and my in-laws for holding family life together in my absence.

Christopher Pitts

Thanks to the inordinately kind people of Arizona, in particular my Mom, Michael and Maddie in Scottsdale, and Ellen and Norman for their great tips. In Cochise Stronghold, thanks to Tolin for leading the way on the Sheephead. At home, bises as always to my dearest partners in crime, Perrine, Elliot and Celeste.

Trisha Ping

Thanks to Alicia Johnson for the sports intel, Bailey Freeman for the local edit and Martine and Sasha for signing me on!

Kevin Raub

Thanks to Trisha Ping and all my fellow partners in crime at Lonely Planet. On the road, Jordan Mazzoni, Erika Dahl, Ali Lechlitner, Anita and Kevin Welch, Jana and Bill Swigart, Tom and Alice Erlandson, Erika Dahl, Marla Cichowski, Gina Speckman, Jessica Waytenick, Jeff Berg, Luanne Mattson, Sarah Prasil, Erin Hawkins, Erin White, Tyra Miller and Morgan Snyder.

Simon Richmond

Many thanks to the following people who generously shared their time and knowledge about Philadelphia: Jerry Silverman, Lindsay Ryan, Tish Byrne, Mason Wray and Rajeev Shankar.

Regis St Louis

I am grateful to countless innkeepers, park rangers, baristas, shop owners and folks 'from away' who shared Maine insight. Special thanks to Brother Arnold for a fabulous meal at Sabbathday Shaker Village, Scott Cowger for the tips and barn tour in Hallowell, Jack Burke and Julie Van De Graaf for their kindness in Castine, and Gregor Clark and Diane Plauche for general Maine suggestions. Special thanks to my family, who make coming home the best part of travel.

Ryan Ver Berkmoes

Thanks to my dear cousin Brian Sebelski and his family for a warm KC welcome. Thanks to Judy Tuwaletstiwa (and Phillip) for an artful welcome and for the Soya introduction. In Omaha, big thanks to Aram and Jill. We'll always have Johnny's. And to the Plum beyond the setting sun in the west beckoning me home.

Mara Vorhees

To the server at a Gloucester restaurant, who recommended that I spend my afternoon at a certain delightful beach (which is not in this book). Thanks for sharing your secret spot. I won't tell.

Benedict Walker

A special thanks to Cheryl Cowie and Keri Berthelot for their guidance, support and Reiki II's on the road. As always, to Trish Walker for countless hours in the prayer chair, and a big shout-out to family; Andy, Sally and P for making sure I didn't overdo the lobster! In memory of Kevin Hennessy, Ainsley Crabbe and Ben Carey, my fellow adventurers who passed away in other lands while I was researching this title. A little part of you remains in Rhode Island for me, always. You'll like it there!

Greg Ward

Thanks to the many wonderful people who helped me on the road, especially at Historic Stagville Plantation, Price's Chicken Coop, Bryson City Bicycles and the Orange County Visitor Center. Thanks too to my editor Trisha Ping for giving me this opportunity, and to my dear wife Sam for everything else.

Karla Zimmerman

Many thanks to Paula Andruss, Lisa Beran, Lisa DiChiera, Ruggero Fatica, Chuck Palmer, Keith Pandolfi and Bob Sanders for taking the time to share their favorite local spots. Thanks most to Eric Markowitz, the world's best partner-for-life and road trip companion. You top my Best List every time.

ACKNOWLEDGEMENTS

Climate map data adapted from Peel MC, Finlayson BL & McMahon TA (2007) 'Updated World Map of the Köppen-Geiger Climate Classification', *Hydrology and Earth System Sciences*, 11, 1633–44.

Cover photograph: Statue of Liberty, New York City; Michele Falzone/AWL Images ©

Illustrations pp98–9, pp274–5 by Javier Zarracina; pp990–1 by Michael Weldon.

BEHIND THE SCENES

THIS BOOK

This 11th edition of Lonely Planet's *USA* guidebook researched, written and curated by Trisha Ping, Isabel Albiston, Mark Baker, Amy C Balfour, Robert Balkovich, Ray Bartlett, Greg Benchwick, Andrew Bender, Alison Bing, Celeste Brash, Jade Bremner, Gregor Clark, Stephanie d'Arc Taylor, Michael Grosberg, Anthony Ham, Ashley Harrell, John Hecht, Adam Karlin, Brian Kluepfel, Ali Lemer, Vesna Maric, Virginia Maxwell, Hugh McNaughtan, MaSovaida Morgan, Becky Ohlsen, Lorna Parkes, Christopher Pitts, Kevin Raub, Charles Rawlings-Way, Simon Richmond, Andrea Schulte- Peevers, Regis St Louis, Ryan Ver Berkmoes, Mara Vorhees, Greg Ward and Karla Zimmerman. This guidebook was produced by the following:

Destination Editors Ben Buckner, Evan Godt, Trisha Ping, Sarah Stocking

Senior Product Editors Martine Power, Vicky Smith

Regional Senior Cartographer Alison Lyall

Product Editor Joel Cotterell

Book Designer Katherine Marsh

Assisting Editors Sarah Bailey, James Bainbridge, Judith Bamber, Imogen Bannister, Michelle Bennett, Nigel Chin, Katie Connolly, Samantha Cook, Lucy Cowie, Michelle Coxall, Melanie Dankel, Barbara Delissen, Andrea Dobbin, Bailey Freeman, Emma Gibbs, Carly Hall, Victoria Harrison, Jennifer Hattam, Gabrielle Innes, Helen Koehne, Kellie Langdon, Jodie Martire, Lou McGregor, Rosie Nicholson, Lauren O'Connell, Kristin Odijk, Susan Paterson, Monique Perrin, Mani Ramaswamy, Sarah Reid, Fionnuala Twomey, Sam Wheeler, Monica Woods

Cartographers Rachel Imeson, Valentina Kremenchutskaya

Cover Researcher Meri Blazevski

Thanks to Sain Alizada, Will Allen, Aron Blesch, Carolyn Boicos, Sasha Drew, Bruce Evans, Virginie Guegan, Robert Layton, Charlotte Orr, Rachel Rawling, Carol Sweetenham

Index

NOTES

Map Legend

Sights

- Beach
- Bird Sanctuary
- Buddhist
- Castle/Palace
- Christian
- Confucian
- Hindu
- Islamic
- Jain
- Jewish
- Monument
- Museum/Gallery/Historic Building
- Ruin
- Shinto
- Sikh
- Taoist
- Winery/Vineyard
- Zoo/Wildlife Sanctuary
- Other Sight

Activities, Courses & Tours

- Bodysurfing
- Diving
- Canoeing/Kayaking
- Course/Tour
- Sento Hot Baths/Onsen
- Skiing
- Snorkeling
- Surfing
- Swimming/Pool
- Walking
- Windsurfing
- Other Activity

Sleeping

- Sleeping
- Camping
- Hut/Shelter

Eating

- Eating

Drinking & Nightlife

- Drinking & Nightlife
- Cafe

Entertainment

- Entertainment

Shopping

- Shopping

Information

- Bank
- Embassy/Consulate
- Hospital/Medical
- Internet
- Police
- Post Office
- Telephone
- Toilet
- Tourist Information
- Other Information

Geographic

- Beach
- Gate
- Hut/Shelter
- Lighthouse
- Lookout
- Mountain/Volcano
- Oasis
- Park
- Pass
- Picnic Area
- Waterfall

Population

- Capital (National)
- Capital (State/Province)
- City/Large Town
- Town/Village

Transport

- Airport
- BART station
- Border crossing
- Boston T station
- Bus
- Cable car/Funicular
- Cycling
- Ferry
- Metro/Muni station
- Monorail
- Parking
- Petrol station
- Subway/SkyTrain station
- Taxi
- Train station/Railway
- Tram
- Underground station
- Other Transport

Routes

- Tollway
- Freeway
- Primary
- Secondary
- Tertiary
- Lane
- Unsealed road
- Road under construction
- Plaza/Mall
- Steps
- Tunnel
- Pedestrian overpass
- Walking Tour
- Walking Tour detour
- Path/Walking Trail

Boundaries

- International
- State/Province
- Disputed
- Regional/Suburb
- Marine Park
- Cliff
- Wall

Hydrography

- River, Creek
- Intermittent River
- Canal
- Water
- Dry/Salt/Intermittent Lake
- Reef

Areas

- Airport/Runway
- Beach/Desert
- Cemetery (Christian)
- Cemetery (Other)
- Glacier
- Mudflat
- Park/Forest
- Sight (Building)
- Sportsground
- Swamp/Mangrove

Note: Not all symbols displayed above appear on the maps in this book

Greg Ward
Texas, The South Since whetting his appetite for travel by following the hippie trail to India, and later living in northern Spain, Greg has written guides to destinations all over the world. As well as covering the USA from the Southwest to Hawaii, he has ranged on recent assignments from Corsica to the Cotswolds, and Japan to Corfu. See his website, www.gregward.info, for his favorite photos and memories.

Karla Zimmerman
Great Lakes, The South, Washington, DC Karla lives in Chicago, where she eats doughnuts and yells at the Cubs, and writes stuff for books, magazines and websites when she's not doing the first two things. She has contributed to 70-plus guidebooks and travel anthologies covering destinations in Europe, Asia, Africa, North America and the Caribbean. To learn more, follow her @karlazimmerman on Instagram and Twitter.

Other contributors
Barbara Noe Kennedy contributed to the Washington, DC section. Lonely Planet Tennessee staff Ben Buckner, Evan Godt, Alicia Johnson, Alexander Howard, Bailey Freeman and Sarah Stocking contributed to the Nashville section. Charles Rawlings-Way curated the Great Lakes, Great Plains and Texas chapters, and Martine Power curated the Florida chapter.

Christopher Pitts

Arizona Chris's first expedition in life ended in failure when he tried to dig from Pennsylvania to China at the age of six. He went on to study Chinese in university, living for several years in China. After more than a decade in Paris, the lure of Colorado's sunny skies and outdoor adventure proved too great to resist.

Kevin Raub

Great Lakes, The South Atlanta native Kevin started his career as a music journalist in New York, working for *Men's Journal* and *Rolling Stone* magazines. He ditched the rock 'n' roll lifestyle for travel writing and has written nearly 50 Lonely Planet guides, focused mainly on Brazil, Chile, Colombia, USA, India, the Caribbean and Portugal. Along the way, the confessed hophead is in constant search of wildly high IBUs in local beers. Follow him on Twitter and Instagram (@Raub OnTheRoad).

Simon Richmond

Pennsylvania Journalist and photographer Simon has specialised as a travel writer since the early 1990s, covering countries including Australia, China, India, Iran, Japan, Korea, Malaysia, Mongolia, Myanmar (Burma), Russia, Singapore, South Africa and Turkey. He has lived in the UK, Japan and Australia, and is now based back in the UK in Folkestone on the east Kent coast. His travel features have been published in newspapers and magazines around the world, including in the UK's *Independent, Guardian, Times, Daily Telegraph* and *Royal Geographical Society Magazine,* and in Australia's *Sydney Morning Herald* and *Australian* newspapers and *Australian Financial Review* magazine.

Andrea Schulte-Peevers

California Born and raised in Germany and educated in London and at UCLA, Andrea has traveled the distance to the moon and back in her visits to some 75 countries. She has earned her living as a professional travel writer for more than two decades and authored or contributed to nearly 100 Lonely Planet titles.

Regis St Louis

New England, The South Regis grew up in a small town in the American Midwest – the kind of place that fuels big dreams of travel – and he developed an early fascination with foreign dialects and world cultures. He spent his formative years learning Russian and a handful of Romance languages, which served him well on journeys across much of the globe. Regis has contributed to more than 50 Lonely Planet titles, covering destinations across six continents. His travels have taken him from the mountains of Kamchatka to remote island villages in Melanesia, and to many grand urban landscapes. When not on the road, he lives in New Orleans.

Ryan Ver Berkmoes

Great Plains Ryan has written more than 110 guidebooks for Lonely Planet. He grew up in Santa Cruz, California, which he left at age 17 for college in the Midwest, where he first discovered snow. All joy of this novelty soon wore off. Since then he has been traveling the world, both for pleasure and for work – which are often indistinguishable. He has covered everything from wars to bars, and definitely prefers the latter. Ryan calls New York City home. Read more at ryanverberk moes.com and at @ryanvb.

Mara Vorhees

New England, Washington, DC & the Capital Region Mara writes about food, travel and family fun around the world. Her work has been published by *BBC Travel, Boston Globe, Delta Sky,* the *Vancouver Sun* and more. For Lonely Planet, she regularly writes about destinations in Central America and Eastern Europe, as well as New England, where she lives. She often travels with her twin boys in tow, earning her expertise in family travel. Follow their adventures at www.havetwinswilltravel.com.

Benedict Walker

New England Born in Newcastle, Australia, Ben holds notions of the beach core to his idea of self, though he's traveled thousands of miles from the sandy shores of home to live in Leipzig, Germany. Ben was given his first Lonely Planet guide when he was 12. Two decades later, he'd write chapters for the same publication: a dream come true. A communications graduate and travel agent by trade, Ben whittled away his twenties gallivanting around the globe. He thinks the best thing about travel isn't as much where you go as who you meet: living vicariously through the stories of kind strangers enriches one's own experience. Come along for the ride on Instagram @wordsandjourneys.

apartment to a vast California ranch to a jungle cabin in Costa Rica, where she started writing for Lonely Planet.

John Hecht
Utah Los Angeles native John has contributed to more than a dozen Lonely Planet guidebooks and trade publications, mostly focused on Latin America and the US. He headed down south to Mexico more than two decades ago and is still livin' the Mexican dream in his adopted country.

Adam Karlin
Alaska; Hawaii; New England; Pennsylvania; The South; Yellowstone, Grand Teton, Zion, Bryce Canyon and Grand Canyon National Parks Adam has contributed to dozens of Lonely Planet guidebooks, covering an alphabetical spread that ranges from the Andaman Islands to the Zimbabwe border. As a journalist, he has written on travel, crime, politics, archeology and the Sri Lankan Civil War, among other topics. He has sent dispatches from every continent barring Antarctica (one day!) and his essays and articles have featured on the BBC and NPR, and in multiple non-fiction anthologies. Adam is based out of New Orleans. Learn more at http://walkonfine.com, or follow @adamwalkonfine on Instagram.

Brian Kluepfel
New England, New Jersey Brian had lived in three states and seven different residences by the time he was nine, and just kept moving, making stops in Berkeley, Bolivia, the Bronx and the 'burbs further down the line. His journalistic work across the Americas has ranged from the Copa America soccer tournament in Paraguay to an accordion festival in Québec. His titles for Lonely Planet include *Costa Rica, Bolivia* and *Ecuador*. He writes a blog about Venezuelan baseball players and another regarding birds of many nations called www.brianbirdwatching.blogspot.com.

Ali Lemer
New York, New Jersey & Pennsylvania Ali has been a Lonely Planet writer and editor since 2007, and has authored guidebooks and travel articles on Russia, NYC, Los Angeles, Melbourne, Bali, Hawaii, Japan and Scotland. A native New Yorker and naturalized Melburnian, Ali has also lived in Chicago, Prague and the UK, and has traveled extensively around Europe and North America.

Vesna Maric
Florida Vesna has been a Lonely Planet author for nearly two decades, covering places as far and wide as Bolivia, Algeria, Sicily, Cyprus, Barcelona, London and Croatia, among others. Her latest work has been updating Florida, Greece and North Macedonia.

Virginia Maxwell
Washington, DC, Virginia Although based in Australia, Virginia spends at least half of her year updating Lonely Planet destination coverage across the globe. The Mediterranean is her major area of interest – she has covered Spain, Italy, Turkey, Syria, Lebanon, Israel, Egypt, Morocco and Tunisia for Lonely Planet – but she also covers Finland, Bali, Armenia, the Netherlands, the USA and Australia. Follow her @maxwellvirginia on Instagram and Twitter.

Hugh McNaughtan
New York, New Jersey & Pennsylvania A former English lecturer, Hugh swapped grant applications for visa applications, and turned his love of travel into a full-time thing. Having done a bit of restaurant-reviewing in his home town (Melbourne) he's now eaten his way across four continents. He's never happier than when on the road with his two daughters. Except perhaps on the cricket field...

MaSovaida Morgan
Oregon, The South MaSovaida is a Lonely Planet writer and multimedia storyteller whose wanderlust has taken her to more than 35 countries across six continents. Prior to freelancing, she was Lonely Planet's Destination Editor for South America for four years and worked as an editor for newspapers and NGOs in the Middle East and United Kingdom. Follow her on Instagram @MaSovaida.

Becky Ohlsen
Washington Becky is a freelance writer, editor and critic based in Portland, Oregon. She writes guidebooks and travel stories about Scandinavia, Portland and elsewhere for Lonely Planet.

Lorna Parkes
New York City Londoner by birth, Melburnian by palate and former Lonely Planet staffer in both cities, Lorna has contributed to numerous Lonely Planet books and magazines. She's discovered she writes best on planes, and is most content when researching food and booze. Wineries and the tropics (not at the same time!) are her go-to happy places, but Yorkshire will always be special to her. Follow her @Lorna_Explorer.

Ray Bartlett

Florida Ray has been travel writing for nearly two decades, bringing Japan, Korea, Mexico, Tanzania, Guatemala, Indonesia, and many parts of the USA to life in rich detail for publishers, newspapers and magazines. Among other pursuits, he surfs regularly and is an accomplished Argentine tango dancer. Follow him on Instagram and Twitter @kaisoradotcom.

Greg Benchwick

Colorado A longtime Lonely Planet travel writer, Greg has rumbled in the jungles of Bolivia, trekked across Spain on the Camino de Santiago, interviewed presidents and Grammy Award winners, dodged flying salmon in Alaska and climbed mountains (big and small) in between.

Andrew Bender

California Award-winning travel and food writer Andrew has written three dozen Lonely Planet guidebooks (from *Amsterdam* to *Los Angeles*, *Germany* to *Taiwan* and over a dozen titles about Japan), plus numerous articles for lonelyplanet.com.

Alison Bing

California Over many guidebooks and 20 years in San Francisco, author Alison has spent more time on Alcatraz than some inmates, become an aficionado of drag and burritos, and willfully ignored Muni signs warning that safety requires avoiding unnecessary conversation.

Celeste Brash

Oregon Celeste has been writing guidebooks for Lonely Planet since 2005 and her travel articles have appeared in publications from *BBC Travel* to *National Geographic*. She's currently writing a book about her five years on a remote pearl farm in the Tuamotu Atolls.

Jade Bremner

The South Jade has been a journalist for more than a decade. Wherever she goes she finds action sports to try, and it's no coincidence many of her favorite places have some of the best waves in the world. Jade has edited travel magazines and sections for *Time Out* and *Radio Times* and has contributed to the *Times*, CNN and the *Independent*. She feels privileged to share tales from this wonderful planet we call home and is always looking for the next adventure.

Gregor Clark

New England Gregor is a US-based writer whose love of foreign languages and curiosity about what's around the next bend have taken him to dozens of countries on five continents. Chronic wanderlust has also led him to visit all 50 states and most Canadian provinces on countless road trips through his native North America. Since 2000, Gregor has regularly contributed to Lonely Planet guides, with a focus on Europe and the Americas.

Stephanie d'Arc Taylor

Nevada A native Angeleno, Stephanie has published work with the *New York Times*, the *Guardian*, *Roads & Kingdoms* and *Kinfolk Magazine* (among others), and co-founded Jaleesa, a venture-capital-funded social impact business in Beirut.

Michael Grosberg

Glacier National Park Michael has worked on more than 50 Lonely Planet guidebooks. Other international work included development on Rota in the western Pacific; in South Africa, where he investigated and wrote about political violence and trained newly elected government representatives; and teaching in Quito, Ecuador.

Anthony Ham

Idaho, Montana, Wyoming Anthony is a freelance writer who travels the world in search of stories. His particular passions are the wildlife, wild places and wide open spaces of the planet, from the Great Plains of the US to the Amazon, East and Southern Africa, and the Arctic. He writes for magazines and newspapers around the world, and his narrative nonfiction book on Africa's lions will be published in 2020.

Ashley Harrell

California, The South After a brief stint selling day spa coupons door-to-door in South Florida, Ashley decided she'd rather be a writer. She went to journalism grad school, convinced a newspaper to hire her, and started covering wildlife, crime and tourism, sometimes all in the same story. Fueling her zest for storytelling and the unknown, she traveled widely and moved often, from a tiny NYC

OUR STORY

A beat-up old car, a few dollars in the pocket and a sense of adventure. In 1972 that's all Tony and Maureen Wheeler needed for the trip of a lifetime – across Europe and Asia overland to Australia. It took several months, and at the end – broke but inspired – they sat at their kitchen table writing and stapling together their first travel guide, *Across Asia on the Cheap.* Within a week they'd sold 1500 copies. Lonely Planet was born.

Today, Lonely Planet has offices in Franklin, London, Melbourne, Oakland, Dublin, Beijing and Delhi, with more than 600 staff and writers. We share Tony's belief that 'a great guidebook should do three things: inform, educate and amuse'.

OUR WRITERS

Trisha Ping

A year working abroad in Mulhouse, France, and a fascination with languages turned Trisha into a lifelong traveler. Over her 15-year career as a writer and editor, she spent two years as a Destination Editor at Lonely Planet and is now the publisher of BookPage. She lives in Nashville, Tennessee. Trisha researched and curated the Plan Your Trip, Understand USA and Survival Guide chapters.

Isabel Albiston

New England After six years working for the *Daily Telegraph* in London, Isabel left to spend more time on the road. A job as a writer for a magazine in Sydney, Australia, was followed by a four-month overland trip across Asia and five years living and working in Buenos Aires, Argentina. Isabel started writing for Lonely Planet in 2014 and has contributed to more than a dozen guidebooks. She's currently based in Ireland.

Mark Baker

Great Lakes Mark is a freelance travel writer with a penchant for offbeat stories and forgotten places. He's originally from the United States, but now makes his home in the Czech capital, Prague. He writes mainly on Eastern and Central Europe for Lonely Planet as well as other leading travel publishers, but finds real satisfaction in digging up stories in places that are too remote or quirky for the guides. Prior to becoming an author, he worked as a journalist for the *Economist*, Bloomberg News and Radio Free Europe, among other organisations. Find him on Instagram and Twitter @markbakerprague, and his blog at www.markbakerprague.com.

Amy C Balfour

Capital Region, New England, New Mexico, The South Amy practiced law in Virginia before moving to Los Angeles to try to break in as a screenwriter. After a stint as a writer's assistant on *Law & Order*, she jumped into freelance writing, focusing on travel, food and the outdoors. She has hiked, biked and paddled across Southern California and the Southwest, and recently criss-crossed the Great Plains in search of the region's best burgers and barbecue. She has written many books for Lonely Planet and her essays have appeared in the *Los Angeles Times* and *Southern Living,* and the travel anthologies *Go Your Own Way* and *The Thong Also Rises*.

Robert Balkovich

New England, New York State, Washington Robert was born and raised in Oregon, but has called New York City home for almost a decade. When he was a child and other families were going to theme parks and grandma's house, he went to Mexico City and toured Eastern Europe by train. He's now a writer and travel enthusiast seeking experiences that are ever so slightly out of the ordinary to report back on. Follow on Instagram @oh_balky.

 OVER PAGE MORE WRITERS

Published by Lonely Planet Global Limited
CRN 554153
11th edition – Apr 2020
ISBN 978 1 78701 787 0
© Lonely Planet 2020   Photographs © as indicated 2020
10 9 8 7 6 5 4 3 2 1
Printed in Singapore